The Dictionary of Art · volume nine

The Dictionary of Art

9

Diploma work
TO
Egypt, ancient,
§x: Painting and
drawing

GROVE

WITHDRAWAL

The Dictionary of Art

edited by JANE TURNER, in thirty-four volumes, 1996

Reprinted with minor corrections, 1998

This edition is distributed within the United Kingdom and Europe
by Macmillan Publishers Limited, London, and within the United States and Canada by
Grove's Dictionaries Inc., New York.

Text keyboarded by Wearset Limited, Sunderland, England
Database management by Pindar plc, York, England
Imagesetting by William Clowes Limited, Suffolk, England
Printed and bound by China Translation and Printing Services Ltd, Hong Kong

British Library Cataloguing in Publication Data

The dictionary of art
 1. Art - Dictionaries 2. Art - History -
  Dictionaries
 I. Turner, Jane
 703

ISBN 1-884446-00-0

Library of Congress Cataloging in Publication Data

The dictionary of art / editor, Jane Turner.
 p. cm.
 Includes bibliographical references and index.
 Contents: 1. A to Anckerman
 ISBN 1-884446-00-0 (alk. paper)
 1. Art—Encyclopedias.
 I. Turner, Jane, 1956–
 N31.D5 1996   96–13628
 703—dc20   CIP

Contents

List of Colour Illustrations

PLATE I. **Drawing**

1. Michelangelo: *Studies for the Libyan Sibyl*, red chalk, 289×214 mm, 1508–12 (New York, Metropolitan Museum of Art/Photo: Metropolitan Museum of Art, Purchase, 1924, Joseph Pulitzer Bequest; no. 24.197.2)

2. Antoine Watteau: *Six Studies of Heads, and Hands Holding a Flute*, red, black and white chalk (*aux trois crayons*), 205×264 mm, *c.* 1715 (Rouen, Musée des Beaux-Arts/Photo: Lauros-Giraudon, Paris)

PLATE II. **Drawing**

1. Pablo Picasso: *Embrace of the Minotaur*, pen and black ink, grey wash, on blue wove paper, 480×628 mm, 1933 (Chicago, IL, Art Institute of Chicago/Photo: Art Institute of Chicago, Gift of Tiffany and Margaret Blake; no. 1967.516/© Succession Picasso/DACS, 1996)

2. Henry Moore: *Seated and Reclining Figures*, wax crayon, black chalk, pencil, watercolour, pen and black ink, 354×225 mm, 1942 (New York, Museum of Modern Art/Photo: © Museum of Modern Art, James Thrall Soby Bequest)

PLATE III. **Dye**

1. Warp ikat cotton cloth, from Sumba, Indonesia, 20th century (London, British Museum/Photo: Trustees of the British Museum)

2. Tie-dyed (*adire*) cotton cloth, from Nigeria, 20th century (Manchester, University of Manchester, Whitworth Art Gallery/Photo: Whitworth Art Gallery, University of Manchester)

PLATE IV. **Dye**

1. Batik cotton cloth, from central Java, Indonesia, late 19th century (London, Victoria and Albert Museum/Photo: Bridgeman Art Library, London)

2. *Strawberry Thief* by William Morris, cotton cloth dyed using the discharge process, manufactured by Morris and Co., London, 1883 (Manchester, University of Manchester, Whitworth Art Gallery/ Photo: Whitworth Art Gallery, University of Manchester)

General Abbreviations

The abbreviations employed throughout this dictionary, most of which are listed below, do not vary, except for capitalization, regardless of the context in which they are used, including bibliographical citations and for locations of works of art. The principle used to arrive at these abbreviations is that their full form should be easily deducible, and for this reason acronyms have generally been avoided (e.g. Los Angeles Co. Mus. A. instead of LACMA). The same abbreviation is adopted for cognate forms in foreign languages and in most cases for plural and adjectival forms (e.g. A.= Art, Arts, Arte, Arti etc). Not all related forms are listed below. Occasionally, if a name, for instance of an artists' group or exhibiting society, is repeated within the text of one article, it is cited in an abbreviated form after its first mention in full (e.g. The Pre-Raphaelite Brotherhood (PRB) was founded...); the same is true of archaeological periods and eras, which are abbreviated to initial letters in small capitals (e.g. In the Early Minoan (EM) period...). Such abbreviations do not appear in this list. For the reader's convenience, separate full lists of abbreviations for locations, periodical titles and standard reference books and series are included as Appendices A–C in vol. 33.

A.	Art, Arts	Anthropol.	Anthropology	Azerbaij.	Azerbaijani
A.C.	Arts Council	Antiqua.	Antiquarian, Antiquaries	B.	Bartsch [catalogue of Old Master prints]
Acad.	Academy	app.	appendix		
AD	Anno Domini	approx.	approximately	*b*	born
Add.	Additional, Addendum	AR	Arkansas (USA)	BA	Bachelor of Arts
addn	addition	ARA	Associate of the Royal Academy	Balt.	Baltic
Admin.	Administration			*bapt*	baptized
Adv.	Advances, Advanced	Arab.	Arabic	BArch	Bachelor of Architecture
Aesth.	Aesthetic(s)	Archaeol.	Archaeology	Bart	Baronet
Afr.	African	Archit.	Architecture, Architectural	Bask.	Basketry
Afrik.	Afrikaans, Afrikaner	Archv, Archvs	Archive(s)	BBC	British Broadcasting Corporation
A.G.	Art Gallery	Arg.	Argentine	BC	Before Christ
Agrar.	Agrarian	ARHA	Associate of the Royal Hibernian Academy	BC	British Columbia (Canada)
Agric.	Agriculture			BE	Buddhist era
Agron.	Agronomy	ARIBA	Associate of the Royal Institute of British Architects	Beds	Bedfordshire (GB)
Agy	Agency			Behav.	Behavioural
AH	Anno Hegirae	Armen.	Armenian	Belarus.	Belarusian
A. Inst.	Art Institute	ARSA	Associate of the Royal Scottish Academy	Belg.	Belgian
AK	Alaska (USA)			Berks	Berkshire (GB)
AL	Alabama (USA)	Asiat.	Asiatic	Berwicks	Berwickshire (GB; old)
Alb.	Albanian	Assist.	Assistance	BFA	Bachelor of Fine Arts
Alg.	Algerian	Assoc.	Association	Bibl.	Bible, Biblical
Alta	Alberta (Canada)	Astron.	Astronomy	Bibliog.	Bibliography, Bibliographical
Altern.	Alternative	AT&T	American Telephone & Telegraph Company	Biblioph.	Bibliophile
a.m.	ante meridiem [before noon]			Biog.	Biography, Biographical
Amat.	Amateur	attrib.	attribution, attributed to	Biol.	Biology, Biological
Amer.	American	Aug	August	bk, bks	book(s)
An.	Annals	Aust.	Austrian	Bkbinder	Bookbinder
Anatol.	Anatolian	Austral.	Australian	Bklore	Booklore
Anc.	Ancient	Auth.	Author(s)	Bkshop	Bookshop
Annu.	Annual	Auton.	Autonomous	BL	British Library
Anon.	Anonymous(ly)	Aux.	Auxiliary	Bld	Build
Ant.	Antique	Ave.	Avenue	Bldg	Building
Anthol.	Anthology	AZ	Arizona (USA)		

Bldr	Builder	Chin.	Chinese	Cur.	Curator, Curatorial, Curatorship
BLitt	Bachelor of Letters/Literature	Christ.	Christian, Christianity	Curr.	Current(s)
BM	British Museum	Chron.	Chronicle	CVO	Commander of the [Royal] Victorian Order
Boh.	Bohemian	Cie	Compagnie [French]		
Boliv.	Bolivian	Cinema.	Cinematography	Cyclad.	Cycladic
Botan.	Botany, Botanical	Circ.	Circle	Cyp.	Cypriot
BP	Before present (1950)	Civ.	Civil, Civic	Czech.	Czechoslovak
Braz.	Brazilian	Civiliz.	Civilization(s)	$	dollars
BRD	Bundesrepublik Deutschland [Federal Republic of Germany (West Germany)]	Class.	Classic, Classical	*d*	died
		Clin.	Clinical	d.	denarius, denarii [penny, pence]
Brecons	Breconshire (GB; old)	CO	Colorado (USA)		
Brez.	Brezonek [lang. of Brittany]	Co.	Company; County	Dalmat.	Dalmatian
Brit.	British	Cod.	Codex, Codices	Dan.	Danish
Bros	Brothers	Col., Cols	Collection(s); Column(s)	DBE	Dame Commander of the Order of the British Empire
BSc	Bachelor of Science	Coll.	College		
Bucks	Buckinghamshire (GB)	collab.	in collaboration with, collaborated, collaborative	DC	District of Columbia (USA)
Bulg.	Bulgarian			DDR	Deutsche Demokratische Republik [German Democratic Republic (East Germany)]
Bull.	Bulletin	Collct.	Collecting		
bur	buried	Colloq.	Colloquies		
Burm.	Burmese	Colomb.	Colombian	DE	Delaware (USA)
Byz.	Byzantine	Colon.	Colonies, Colonial	Dec	December
C	Celsius	Colr	Collector	Dec.	Decorative
C.	Century	Comm.	Commission; Community	ded.	dedication, dedicated to
c.	*circa* [about]	Commerc.	Commercial	Democ.	Democracy, Democratic
CA	California	Communic.	Communications	Demog.	Demography, Demographic
Cab.	Cabinet	Comp.	Comparative; compiled by, compiler	Denbs	Denbighshire (GB; old)
Caerns	Caernarvonshire (GB; old)			dep.	deposited at
C.A.G.	City Art Gallery	Concent.	Concentration	Dept	Department
Cal.	Calendar	Concr.	Concrete	Dept.	Departmental, Departments
Callig.	Calligraphy	Confed.	Confederation	Derbys	Derbyshire (GB)
Cam.	Camera	Confer.	Conference	Des.	Design
Cambs	Cambridgeshire (GB)	Congol.	Congolese	destr.	destroyed
can	canonized	Congr.	Congress	Dev.	Development
Can.	Canadian	Conserv.	Conservation; Conservatory	Devon	Devonshire (GB)
Cant.	Canton(s), Cantonal	Constr.	Construction(al)	Dial.	Dialogue
Capt.	Captain	cont.	continued	diam.	diameter
Cards	Cardiganshire (GB; old)	Contemp.	Contemporary	Diff.	Diffusion
Carib.	Caribbean	Contrib.	Contributions, Contributor(s)	Dig.	Digest
Carms	Carmarthenshire (GB; old)	Convalesc.	Convalescence	Dip. Eng.	Diploma in Engineering
Cartog.	Cartography	Convent.	Convention	Dir.	Direction, Directed
Cat.	Catalan	Coop.	Cooperation	Directrt	Directorate
cat.	catalogue	Coord.	Coordination	Disc.	Discussion
Cath.	Catholic	Copt.	Coptic	diss.	dissertation
CBE	Commander of the Order of the British Empire	Corp.	Corporation, Corpus	Distr.	District
		Corr.	Correspondence	Div.	Division
Celeb.	Celebration	Cors.	Corsican	DLitt	Doctor of Letters/Literature
Celt.	Celtic	Cost.	Costume	DM	Deutsche Mark
Cent.	Centre, Central	Cret.	Cretan	Doc.	Document(s)
Centen.	Centennial	Crim.	Criminal	Doss.	Dossier
Cer.	Ceramic	Crit.	Critical, Criticism	DPhil	Doctor of Philosophy
cf.	confer [compare]	Croat.	Croatian	Dr	Doctor
Chap., Chaps	Chapter(s)	CT	Connecticut (USA)	Drg, Drgs	Drawing(s)
		Cttee	Committee	DSc	Doctor of Science/Historical Sciences
Chem.	Chemistry	Cub.	Cuban		
Ches	Cheshire (GB)	Cult.	Cultural, Culture	Dut.	Dutch
Chil.	Chilean	Cumb.	Cumberland (GB; old)	Dwell.	Dwelling
				E.	East(ern)

EC	European (Economic) Community
Eccles.	Ecclesiastical
Econ.	Economic, Economies
Ecuad.	Ecuadorean
ed.	editor, edited (by)
edn	edition
eds	editors
Educ.	Education
e.g.	*exempli gratia* [for example]
Egyp.	Egyptian
Elem.	Element(s), Elementary
Emp.	Empirical
Emul.	Emulation
Enc.	Encyclopedia
Encour.	Encouragement
Eng.	English
Engin.	Engineer, Engineering
Engr., Engrs	Engraving(s)
Envmt	Environment
Epig.	Epigraphy
Episc.	Episcopal
Esp.	Especially
Ess.	Essays
est.	established
etc	*etcetera* [and so on]
Ethnog.	Ethnography
Ethnol.	Ethnology
Etrus.	Etruscan
Eur.	European
Evangel.	Evangelical
Exam.	Examination
Excav.	Excavation, Excavated
Exch.	Exchange
Excurs.	Excursion
exh.	exhibition
Exp.	Exposition
Expermntl	Experimental
Explor.	Exploration
Expn	Expansion
Ext.	External
Extn	Extension
f, ff	following page, following pages
F.A.	Fine Art(s)
Fac.	Faculty
facs.	facsimile
Fam.	Family
fasc.	fascicle
fd	feastday (of a saint)
Feb	February
Fed.	Federation, Federal
Fem.	Feminist
Fest.	Festival
fig.	figure (illustration)
Fig.	Figurative
figs	figures
Filip.	Filipina(s), Filipino(s)
Fin.	Finnish
FL	Florida (USA)
fl	*floruit* [he/she flourished]
Flem.	Flemish
Flints	Flintshire (GB; old)
Flk	Folk
Flklore	Folklore
fol., fols	folio(s)
Found.	Foundation
Fr.	French
frag.	fragment
Fri.	Friday
FRIBA	Fellow of the Royal Institute of British Architects
FRS	Fellow of the Royal Society, London
ft	foot, feet
Furn.	Furniture
Futur.	Futurist, Futurism
g	gram(s)
GA	Georgia (USA)
Gael.	Gaelic
Gal., Gals	Gallery, Galleries
Gaz.	Gazette
GB	Great Britain
Gdn, Gdns	Garden(s)
Gdnr(s)	Gardener(s)
Gen.	General
Geneal.	Genealogy, Genealogist
Gent.	Gentleman, Gentlemen
Geog.	Geography
Geol.	Geology
Geom.	Geometry
Georg.	Georgian
Geosci.	Geoscience
Ger.	German, Germanic
G.I.	Government/General Issue (USA)
Glams	Glamorganshire (GB; old)
Glos	Gloucestershire (GB)
Govt	Government
Gr.	Greek
Grad.	Graduate
Graph.	Graphic
Green.	Greenlandic
Gr.-Roman	Greco-Roman
Gt	Great
Gtr	Greater
Guat.	Guatemalan
Gym.	Gymnasium
h.	height
ha	hectare
Hait.	Haitian
Hants	Hampshire (GB)
Hb.	Handbook
Heb.	Hebrew
Hell.	Hellenic
Her.	Heritage
Herald.	Heraldry, Heraldic
Hereford & Worcs	Hereford & Worcester (GB)
Herts	Hertfordshire (GB)
HI	Hawaii (USA)
Hib.	Hibernia
Hisp.	Hispanic
Hist.	History, Historical
HMS	His/Her Majesty's Ship
Hon.	Honorary, Honourable
Horiz.	Horizon
Hort.	Horticulture
Hosp.	Hospital(s)
HRH	His/Her Royal Highness
Human.	Humanities, Humanism
Hung.	Hungarian
Hunts	Huntingdonshire (GB; old)
IA	Iowa
ibid.	*ibidem* [in the same place]
ICA	Institute of Contemporary Arts
Ice.	Icelandic
Iconog.	Iconography
Iconol.	Iconology
ID	Idaho (USA)
i.e.	*id est* [that is]
IL	Illinois (USA)
Illum.	Illumination
illus.	illustrated, illustration
Imp.	Imperial
IN	Indiana (USA)
in., ins	inch(es)
Inc.	Incorporated
inc.	incomplete
incl.	includes, including, inclusive
Incorp.	Incorporation
Ind.	Indian
Indep.	Independent
Indig.	Indigenous
Indol.	Indology
Indon.	Indonesian
Indust.	Industrial
Inf.	Information
Inq.	Inquiry
Inscr.	Inscribed, Inscription
Inst.	Institute(s)
Inst. A.	Institute of Art
Instr.	Instrument, Instrumental
Int.	International
Intell.	Intelligence
Inter.	Interior(s), Internal
Interdiscip.	Interdisciplinary
intro.	introduced by, introduction
inv.	inventory

Inven.	Invention	m	metre(s)	Moldov.	Moldovan
Invest.	Investigation(s)	m.	married	MOMA	Museum of Modern Art
Iran.	Iranian	M.	Monsieur	Mon.	Monday
irreg.	irregular(ly)	MA	Master of Arts; Massachusetts (USA)	Mongol.	Mongolian
Islam.	Islamic			Mons	Monmouthshire (GB; old)
Isr.	Israeli	Mag.	Magazine	Montgoms	Montgomeryshire (GB; old)
It.	Italian	Maint.	Maintenance	Mor.	Moral
J.	Journal	Malay.	Malaysian	Morav.	Moravian
Jam.	Jamaican	Man.	Manitoba (Canada); Manual	Moroc.	Moroccan
Jan	January	Manuf.	Manufactures	Movt	Movement
Jap.	Japanese	Mar.	Marine, Maritime	MP	Member of Parliament
Jav.	Javanese	Mason.	Masonic	MPhil	Master of Philosophy
Jew.	Jewish	Mat.	Material(s)	MS	Mississippi (USA)
Jewel.	Jewellery	Math.	Mathematic	MS., MSS	manuscript(s)
Jord.	Jordanian	MBE	Member of the Order of the British Empire	MSc	Master of Science
jr	junior			MT	Montana (USA)
Juris.	Jurisdiction	MD	Doctor of Medicine; Maryland (USA)	Mt	Mount
KBE	Knight Commander of the Order of the British Empire			Mthly	Monthly
		ME	Maine (USA)	Mun.	Municipal
KCVO	Knight Commander of the Royal Victorian Order	Mech.	Mechanical	Mus.	Museum(s)
		Med.	Medieval; Medium, Media	Mus. A.	Museum of Art
kg	kilogram(s)	Medic.	Medical, Medicine	Mus. F.A.	Museum of Fine Art(s)
kHz	kilohertz	Medit.	Mediterranean	Music.	Musicology
km	kilometre(s)	Mem.	Memorial(s); Memoir(s)	N.	North(ern); National
Knowl.	Knowledge	Merions	Merionethshire (GB; old)	n	refractive index of a medium
Kor.	Korean	Meso- Amer.	Meso-American	n.	note
KS	Kansas (USA)	Mesop.	Mesopotamian	N.A.G.	National Art Gallery
KY	Kentucky (USA)	Met.	Metropolitan	Nat.	Natural, Nature
Kyrgyz.	Kyrgyzstani	Metal.	Metallurgy	Naut.	Nautical
£	libra, librae [pound, pounds sterling]	Mex.	Mexican	NB	New Brunswick (Canada)
		MFA	Master of Fine Arts	NC	North Carolina (USA)
l.	length	mg	milligram(s)	ND	North Dakota (USA)
LA	Louisiana (USA)	Mgmt	Management	n.d.	no date
Lab.	Laboratory	Mgr	Monsignor	NE	Nebraska; Northeast(ern)
Lancs	Lancashire (GB)	MI	Michigan	Neth.	Netherlandish
Lang.	Language(s)	Micrones.	Micronesian	Newslett.	Newsletter
Lat.	Latin	Mid. Amer.	Middle American	Nfld	Newfoundland (Canada)
Latv.	Latvian	Middx	Middlesex (GB; old)	N.G.	National Gallery
lb, lbs	pound(s) weight	Mid. E.	Middle Eastern	N.G.A.	National Gallery of Art
Leb.	Lebanese	Mid. Eng.	Middle English	NH	New Hampshire (USA)
Lect.	Lecture	Mid Glam.	Mid Glamorgan (GB)	Niger.	Nigerian
Legis.	Legislative	Mil.	Military	NJ	New Jersey (USA)
Leics	Leicestershire (GB)	Mill.	Millennium	NM	New Mexico (USA)
Lex.	Lexicon	Min.	Ministry; Minutes	nm	nanometre (10^{-9} metre)
Lg.	Large	Misc.	Miscellaneous	nn.	notes
Lib., Libs	Library, Libraries	Miss.	Mission(s)	no., nos	number(s)
Liber.	Liberian	Mlle	Mademoiselle	Nord.	Nordic
Libsp	Librarianship	mm	millimetre(s)	Norm.	Normal
Lincs	Lincolnshire (GB)	Mme	Madame	Northants	Northamptonshire (GB)
Lit.	Literature	MN	Minnesota	Northumb.	Northumberland (GB)
Lith.	Lithuanian	Mnmt, Mnmts	Monument(s)	Norw.	Norwegian
Liturg.	Liturgical			Notts	Nottinghamshire (GB)
LLB	Bachelor of Laws	Mnmtl	Monumental	Nov	November
LLD	Doctor of Laws	MO	Missouri (USA)	n.p.	no place (of publication)
Lt	Lieutenant	Mod.	Modern, Modernist	N.P.G.	National Portrait Gallery
Lt-Col.	Lieutenant-Colonel	Moldav.	Moldavian	nr	near
Ltd	Limited				

Nr E.	Near Eastern	Per.	Period	Ptg(s)	Painting(s)
NS	New Style; Nova Scotia (Canada)	Percep.	Perceptions	Pub.	Public
		Perf.	Performance, Performing, Performed	pubd	published
n. s.	new series			Publ.	Publicity
NSW	New South Wales (Australia)	Period.	Periodical(s)	pubn(s)	publication(s)
NT	National Trust	Pers.	Persian	PVA	Polyvinyl acetate
Ntbk	Notebook	Persp.	Perspectives	PVC	polyvinyl chloride
Numi.	Numismatic(s)	Peru.	Peruvian	Q.	quarterly
NV	Nevada (USA)	PhD	Doctor of Philosophy	4to	quarto
NW	Northwest(ern)	Philol.	Philology	Qué.	Québec (Canada)
NWT	Northwest Territories (Canada)	Philos.	Philosophy	*R*	reprint
		Phoen.	Phoenician	*r*	*recto*
NY	New York (USA)	Phot.	Photograph, Photography, Photographic	RA	Royal Academician
NZ	New Zealand			Radnors	Radnorshire (GB; old)
OBE	Officer of the Order of the British Empire	Phys.	Physician(s), Physics, Physique, Physical	RAF	Royal Air Force
				Rec.	Record(s)
Obj.	Object(s), Objective	Physiog.	Physiognomy	red.	reduction, reduced for
Occas.	Occasional	Physiol.	Physiology	Ref.	Reference
Occident.	Occidental	Pict.	Picture(s), Pictorial	Refurb.	Refurbishment
Ocean.	Oceania	pl.	plate; plural	*reg*	*regit* [ruled]
Oct	October	Plan.	Planning	Reg.	Regional
8vo	octavo	Planet.	Planetarium	Relig.	Religion, Religious
OFM	Order of Friars Minor	Plast.	Plastic	remod.	remodelled
OH	Ohio (USA)	pls	plates	Ren.	Renaissance
OK	Oklahoma (USA)	p.m.	post meridiem [after noon]	Rep.	Report(s)
Olymp.	Olympic	Polit.	Political	repr.	reprint(ed); reproduced, reproduction
OM	Order of Merit	Poly.	Polytechnic		
Ont.	Ontario (Canada)	Polynes.	Polynesian	Represent.	Representation, Representative
op.	opus	Pop.	Popular	Res.	Research
opp.	opposite; opera [pl. of opus]	Port.	Portuguese	rest.	restored, restoration
OR	Oregon (USA)	Port.	Portfolio	Retro.	Retrospective
Org.	Organization	Posth.	Posthumous(ly)	rev.	revision, revised (by/for)
Orient.	Oriental	Pott.	Pottery	Rev.	Reverend; Review
Orthdx	Orthodox	POW	prisoner of war	RHA	Royal Hibernian Academician
OSB	Order of St Benedict	PRA	President of the Royal Academy	RI	Rhode Island (USA)
Ott.	Ottoman			RIBA	Royal Institute of British Architects
Oxon	Oxfordshire (GB)	Pract.	Practical		
oz.	ounce(s)	Prefect.	Prefecture, Prefectural	RJ	Rio de Janeiro State
p	pence	Preserv.	Preservation	Rlwy	Railway
p., pp.	page(s)	prev.	previous(ly)	RSA	Royal Scottish Academy
PA	Pennsylvania (USA)	priv.	private	RSFSR	Russian Soviet Federated Socialist Republic
p.a.	per annum	PRO	Public Record Office		
Pak.	Pakistani	Prob.	Problem(s)	Rt Hon.	Right Honourable
Palaeontol.	Palaeontology, Palaeontological	Proc.	Proceedings	Rur.	Rural
		Prod.	Production	Rus.	Russian
Palest.	Palestinian	Prog.	Progress	S	San, Santa, Santo, Sant', São [Saint]
Pap.	Paper(s)	Proj.	Project(s)		
para.	paragraph	Promot.	Promotion	S.	South(ern)
Parag.	Paraguayan	Prop.	Property, Properties	s.	solidus, solidi [shilling(s)]
Parl.	Parliament	Prov.	Province(s), Provincial	Sask.	Saskatchewan (Canada)
Paroch.	Parochial	Proven.	Provenance	Sat.	Saturday
Patriarch.	Patriarchate	Prt, Prts	Print(s)	SC	South Carolina (USA)
Patriot.	Patriotic	Prtg	Printing	Scand.	Scandinavian
Patrm.	Patrimony	pseud.	pseudonym	Sch.	School
Pav.	Pavilion	Psych.	Psychiatry, Psychiatric	Sci.	Science(s), Scientific
PEI	Prince Edward Island (Canada)	Psychol.	Psychology, Psychological	Scot.	Scottish
Pembs	Pembrokeshire (GB; old)	pt	part	Sculp.	Sculpture

SD	South Dakota (USA)	suppl., suppls	supplement(s), supplementary	Urb.	Urban
SE	Southeast(ern)			Urug.	Uruguayan
Sect.	Section	Surv.	Survey	US	United States
Sel.	Selected	SW	Southwest(ern)	USA	United States of America
Semin.	Seminar(s), Seminary	Swed.	Swedish	USSR	Union of Soviet Socialist Republics
Semiot.	Semiotic	Swi.	Swiss		
Semit.	Semitic	Symp.	Symposium	UT	Utah
Sept	September	Syr.	Syrian	*v*	*verso*
Ser.	Series	Tap.	Tapestry	VA	Virginia (USA)
Serb.	Serbian	Tas.	Tasmanian	V&A	Victoria and Albert Museum
Serv.	Service(s)	Tech.	Technical, Technique	Var.	Various
Sess.	Session, Sessional	Technol.	Technology	Venez.	Venezuelan
Settmt(s)	Settlement(s)	Territ.	Territory	Vern.	Vernacular
S. Glam.	South Glamorgan (GB)	Theat.	Theatre	Vict.	Victorian
Siber.	Siberian	Theol.	Theology, Theological	Vid.	Video
Sig.	Signature	Theor.	Theory, Theoretical	Viet.	Vietnamese
Sil.	Silesian	Thurs.	Thursday	viz.	*videlicet* [namely]
Sin.	Singhala	Tib.	Tibetan	vol., vols	volume(s)
sing.	singular	TN	Tennessee (USA)	vs.	versus
SJ	Societas Jesu [Society of Jesus]	Top.	Topography	VT	Vermont (USA)
Skt	Sanskrit	Trad.	Tradition(s), Traditional	Vulg.	Vulgarisation
Slav.	Slavic, Slavonic	trans.	translation, translated by; transactions	W.	West(ern)
Slov.	Slovene, Slovenian			w.	width
Soc.	Society	Transafr.	Transafrican	WA	Washington (USA)
Social.	Socialism, Socialist	Transatlant.	Transatlantic	Warwicks	Warwickshire (GB)
Sociol.	Sociology	Transcarpath.	Transcarpathian	Wed.	Wednesday
Sov.	Soviet	transcr.	transcribed by/for	W. Glam.	West Glamorgan (GB)
SP	São Paulo State	Triq.	Triquarterly	WI	Wisconsin (USA)
Sp.	Spanish	Tropic.	Tropical	Wilts	Wiltshire (GB)
sq.	square	Tues.	Tuesday	Wkly	Weekly
sr	senior	Turk.	Turkish	W. Midlands	West Midlands (GB)
Sri L.	Sri Lankan	Turkmen.	Turkmenistani		
SS	Saints, Santi, Santissima, Santissimo, Santissimi; Steam ship	TV	Television	Worcs	Worcestershire (GB; old)
		TX	Texas (USA)	Wtrcol.	Watercolour
		U.	University	WV	West Virginia (USA)
SSR	Soviet Socialist Republic	UK	United Kingdom of Great Britain and Northern Ireland	WY	Wyoming (USA)
St	Saint, Sankt, Sint, Szent			Yb., Y.-b.	Yearbook, Year-book
Staffs	Staffordshire (GB)	Ukrain.	Ukrainian	Yem.	Yemeni
Ste	Sainte	Un.	Union	Yorks	Yorkshire (GB; old)
Stud.	Study, Studies	Underwtr	Underwater	Yug.	Yugoslavian
Subalp.	Subalpine	UNESCO	United Nations Educational, Scientific and Cultural Organization	Zamb.	Zambian
Sum.	Sumerian			Zimb.	Zimbabwean
Sun.	Sunday	Univl	Universal		
Sup.	Superior	unpubd	unpublished		

A Note on the Use of the Dictionary

This note is intended as a short guide to the basic editorial conventions adopted in this dictionary. For a fuller explanation, please refer to the Introduction, vol. 1, pp. xiii–xx.

Abbreviations in general use in the dictionary are listed on pp. vii–xii; those used in bibliographies and for locations of works of art or exhibition venues are listed in the Appendices in vol. 33.

Alphabetization of headings, which are distinguished in bold typeface, is letter by letter up to the first comma (ignoring spaces, hyphens, accents and any parenthesized or bracketed matter); the same principle applies thereafter. Abbreviations of 'Saint' and its foreign equivalents are alphabetized as if spelt out, and headings with the prefix 'Mc' appear under 'Mac'.

Authors' signatures appear at the end of the article or sequence of articles that the authors have contributed; in multipartite articles, any section that is unsigned is by the author of the next signed section. Where the article was compiled by the editors or in the few cases where an author has wished to remain anonymous, this is indicated by a square box (☐) instead of a signature.

Bibliographies are arranged chronologically (within section, where divided) by order of year of first publication and, within years, alphabetically by authors' names. Abbreviations have been used for some standard reference books; these are cited in full in Appendix C in vol. 33, as are abbreviations of periodical titles (Appendix B). Abbreviated references to alphabetically arranged dictionaries and encyclopedias appear at the beginning of the bibliography (or section).

Biographical dates when cited in parentheses in running text at the first mention of a personal name indicate that the individual does not have an entry in the dictionary. The presence of parenthesized regnal dates for rulers and popes, however, does not necessarily indicate the lack of a biography of that person. Where no dates are provided for an artist or patron, the reader may assume that there is a biography of that individual in the dictionary (or, more rarely, that the person is so obscure that dates are not readily available).

Cross-references are distinguished by the use of small capital letters, with a large capital to indicate the initial letter of the entry to which the reader is directed; for example, 'He commissioned LEONARDO DA VINCI . . .' means that the entry is alphabetized under 'L'.

D

[continued]

Diploma work. A representative work of art presented to and retained by the Royal Academy of Arts (*see* LONDON, §VI) by each Academician on his or her election. Clause 3 of the Academy's Instrument of Foundation, signed by George III in December 1768, specified that each newly elected Academician 'shall not receive his letter of Admission, till he hath deposited in the Royal Academy, to remain there, a Picture, Bas-relief, or other specimen of his abilities, approved of by the then sitting Council of the Academy'. The practice of submitting a Diploma work, or Diploma piece, went back at least to the Accademia di S Luca, Rome, founded in 1593, although a less remote connection is to be found in the system organized by the Académie Royale de Peinture et de Sculpture in Paris, where every *agréé* had to submit a sample of work—a *morceau de réception*—prior to receiving formal admission into the Académie. (In France the admission of the *agréé* into the Académie was dependent on acceptance of the work; it was not, as in England, a mere precondition.) On the whole, procedures were less strictly observed in England than in France. Academicians were, for example, permitted to submit 'temporary' works, which in theory would later be replaced by a more representative example of the artist's work. Temporary works often remained in the collection, however, hence the mediocrity of a number of Diploma works. Associate Academicians were not required to submit Diploma works, nor were the Royal Academy's 36 founder-members. Although in 1771 the Academy's Council decided it was 'proper' for members to present 'some or other specimen of their abilities', few bothered. The only Academician to have his Diploma work returned to him was James Barry who, having presented it in 1773, had it returned to him on his expulsion in 1799.

Aside from the exceptions referred to above, not all past and present Academicians are represented by Diploma works: Nathaniel Marchant's *Gem and Cast*, presented in 1809, is missing; William Calder Marshall's sculpture in sugar, *An Infant Satyr*, presented in 1852, slowly disintegrated; and John Hoppner's Diploma work of 1795 was subsequently borrowed by the artist and never returned (although in 1810 his widow offered a self-portrait of the artist as a substitute). As a result of this incident, J. M. W. Turner, then serving on the Council, put

forward a resolution to prevent works from removal under any pretext.

From 1791 Diploma works were hung in the Council Room of the Academy. In 1810 the Council Room was opened to the public during the annual exhibition, following which Richard Cosway's *Venus and Cupid* was promptly stolen (it was returned in 1818). The first catalogue of the Diploma works, containing 68 items, was published in 1819. Significant works then included John Singleton Copley's *Tribute Money* (1779), Henry Fuseli's *Thor Battering the Midguard Serpent* (1790) and J. M. W. Turner's *Dolbadarn Castle, North Wales*, presented in 1802. Works continued to hang in the Council Room until 1836, by which time many were in a poor condition. In 1857, when works were cleaned for the first time for the Manchester Art Treasures Exhibition, according to the Keeper, John Prescott-Knight, they were 'caked with filth'. In 1869 the Royal Academy moved to its present location at Burlington House in Piccadilly. Sydney Smirke RA was commissioned to design a third storey for the existing building; completed by 1885, it comprised four galleries, three of which housed the collection of over 160 Diploma works. Among the most noteworthy were John Constable's *Boat Passing a Lock* (1829), Charles West Cope's *Night Alarm* (1848), William Powell Frith's *Sleeping Model* (1853) and Augustus Egg's *Night before Naseby* (1860). Apart from closure during World War I, these galleries remained open to the public, free of charge, until 1939.

After World War II the Diploma galleries did not reopen, and in 1951 the Council decided to use space hitherto reserved for Diploma works for special exhibitions. By the 1990s a number of works were displayed in various rooms and corridors of the Academy. Although no longer displayed en masse, Diploma works have been the subject for a number of touring exhibitions, including those in Nottingham (1959 and 1973); Birmingham, Sheffield, Bolton, Swansea and Plymouth (1961–2); Bournemouth (1965); Leicester (1982); Bath (1983); and Swansea (1985). In 1982 and 1988 there were touring exhibitions in the USA.

By the 1990s, the number of Diploma works stood at over 430. They included oil paintings, sculptures, architectural drawings and (included from 1855) engravings. In

Diploma work by William Orpen: *Le Chef de l'Hôtel Chatham, Paris*, oil on canvas, 1.27×1.14 m, 1921 (London, Royal Academy)

1936, due to lack of space, it was requested that Academicians should, if possible, limit the size of their Diploma works. The collection continues to grow, although most other academies in Europe abandoned the practice in the 19th century. Among the significant works added since the 1890s are Hubert von Herkomer's *On Strike* (1890), Stanley Spencer's *Farm Gate* (1950), Frederick Gibberd's plans for the Metropolitan Cathedral of Christ the King, Liverpool (1970), Eduardo Paolozzi's *Naked Head* (1979) and possibly the best-known Diploma work of all (due to the controversy surrounding its initial purchase through the Chantrey Bequest), William Orpen's *Le Chef de l'Hôtel Chatham, Paris* (see fig.), presented to the Royal Academy in 1921.

BIBLIOGRAPHY
W. Sandby: *The History of the Royal Academy of Arts*, 2 vols (London, 1862)
Paintings and Sculpture in the Diploma and Gibson Galleries, Royal Academy of Arts (London, 1931)
W. R. M. Lamb: *The Royal Academy* (London, 1935)
S. C. Hutchison: *The History of the Royal Academy, 1768–1986* (London, 1968, 2/1986)
R. Ormond: 'The Diploma Paintings from 1840 Onwards', *Apollo*, lxxxix (1969), pp. 56–63
                                        MARTIN POSTLE

Dipoinos. *See under* DAIDALOS, §2.

Dipper. Small cup that clips to a palette and is used to hold various liquids.   □

Dipre [d'Amiens; d'Ypres], **Nicolas** (*b* Paris; *fl* 1495; *d* by ?14 March 1532). French painter. Documents describe him as *parisianus*, and he appears to have belonged to a family of painters from Ypres or Amiens. His father, Nicolas Dipre the elder (*fl* 1464, *d* before 1508), known as Colin d'Amiens, worked as a painter in Paris and was sufficiently well known in 1481 to be commissioned to produce a design for the tomb of Louis XI; his grandfather was probably the André d'Ypres documented in Amiens from 1435 to 1444. Nicolas Dipre is first referred to in 1495 in Avignon, where he worked for the rest of his life, gaining a widespread reputation. In May 1508 he married Honorée, the daughter of the joiner Jean Bigle, with whom he often collaborated.

From 1495 to 1514 Dipre appears to have been regularly employed by the city of Avignon, supplying decorations, heraldry, processional banners and other items. He received commissions for altarpieces from Rodrigue Boutin (1498), from the Confrérie de la Conception de la Vierge for St Siffrein in Carpentras (11 March 1499), from Brisson Novet of Saint-Rémy-de-Provence (Oct 1499), from Baptiste de Ponte (1508) and for the chapel of the City Hall in Avignon (1511). A contract for a *Pietà with SS Lazarus and Claude* for the Chapelle St Lazare in Avignon (14 March 1532) may refer to Nicolas's son Antoine (1509-62), also a painter, for Nicolas was probably dead by then.

According to the contract for the St Siffrein altarpiece, it was to have a large panel of the *Virgin* in azure and gold flanked by the *Expulsion of Joachim* and *Joachim and the Shepherds* and by the *Meeting of Joachim and Anna at the Golden Gate* and the *Birth of the Virgin*; above was a *Coronation of the Virgin* and *Two Prophets*. The predella comprised five scenes relating to the *Conception of the Virgin*, the subjects of which were unspecified. The work, for which Dipre was paid 115 florins, was to be finished by 20 April 1500. A fragmentary panel of the *Meeting of Joachim and Anna at the Golden Gate* (390×440 mm; Carpentras, Mus. Duplessis) has been associated with this altarpiece (Sterling, 1941) and has formed the basis for a reconstruction of a corpus of works for Dipre. It is characterized by a summary but effective narrative treatment, clearly defined construction, intense colouring, stocky figures with large heads and awkward gestures; this somewhat rustic style is nevertheless accompanied by a certain skill in the evocation of space, an occasional solemnity of tone and the presence of poetic and moving passages.

Five predella panels in this style, of similar dimensions and all topped with four-centred arches, were long associated with the Carpentras altarpiece: a *Presentation of the Virgin* (Paris, Louvre), a *Marriage of the Virgin* (Denver, CO, A. Mus.), a *Calvary* (Detroit, MI, Inst. A.), an *Adoration of the Shepherds* (San Francisco, CA, de Young Mem. Mus.) and an *Adoration of the Magi* (Pont-Saint-Esprit, Mus. Paul Raymond). However, the appearance in 1986 of two comparable panels representing the *Meeting of Joachim and Anna at the Golden Gate* and the *Birth of the Virgin* (Paris, Louvre), scenes already depicted in the principal register of the altarpiece according to the text of the contract, called this identification into question. Other panels, in particular an imposing altarpiece wing, now divided in two, representing *Gideon's Fleece* and *Jacob's*

Ladder (Avignon, Mus. Petit Pal.), have also been attributed to Dipre.

BIBLIOGRAPHY

M. Achard: 'Notes sur quelques anciens artistes d'Avignon', *Rev. Bib. Paroiss. & Faits Relig. Prov. Ecclés. Avignon* (1856), p. 374

L. H. Labande: *Les Primitifs français: Peintres et peintres-verriers de la Provence occidentale* (Marseille, 1932), pp. 108–10, 174–5

H. Chobaut: 'Documents inédits sur les peintres et peintres-verriers d'Avignon, du Comtat et de la Provence occidentale de la fin du XIVe et du premier tiers du XVIe siècle', *Mém. Acad. Vaucluse*, iv (1939), pp. 83–145

C. Sterling: *La Peinture française: Les Peintres du Moyen Age* (Paris, 1941), pp. 49–50; XVe siècle, suppl. A, pp. 27–8, 40

——: 'Two XV Century Provençal Painters Revived (1): Nicolas Dipre', *Gaz. B.-A.*, xxii (1942), pp. 9–16

M. Laclotte and D. Thiébaut: *L'Ecole d'Avignon* (Paris, 1983), pp. 113–14, 266–9

D. Thiébaut: 'Dipre', *Musée du Louvre: Nouvelles acquisitions du département des peintures (1983–1986)* (Paris, 1987), pp. 106–8

M. C. Léonelli: 'Dipre', *La Peinture en Provence au XVIe siècle* (exh. cat., Marseille, Cent. Vieille Charité, 1987–8), pp. 42–5, 195

D. Thiébaut: 'Nicolas Dipre: Deux nouveaux éléments de prédelle au Louvre', *Rev. Louvre*, iv (1989), pp. 215-24

DOMINIQUE THIÉBAUT

Dipteral. Term applied to a building, usually a temple, with two rows of columns flanking the long walls of the cella externally (*see* GREECE, ANCIENT, fig. 8f).

Diptych. Two wood, ivory or metal panels of equal size, usually hinged together so that they can be folded, and closed with some form of clasp. There are usually images on the inside surfaces of the panels and sometimes also on the outer sides. The panels are most commonly vertical rectangles; Gothic examples often have gables, while those from the 15th century may be round-headed.

The diptych as a work of art seems to have originated in Late Antique ivory-carving as a luxury form of writing tablet. These ivories have carved images on the exterior faces, while a sunken field inside could be filled with wax for writing on with a stylus. Such objects commonly functioned as gifts from the imperial consuls at the beginning of their term of office (*see* EARLY CHRISTIAN AND BYZANTINE ART, fig. 81). They were carved with an image of either the consul or the ruling emperor, seated or standing in an attitude of authority and sometimes presiding over such activities as wild beast fights. These consular diptychs, of which most survive from the 4th and 5th centuries AD, continued to be produced up to the 6th century. Similar ivory diptych writing tablets also served as marriage gifts and were decorated with mythological or cult subjects. A good example of such a diptych, the function of which is debated, is the late 4th-century AD pair of plaques inscribed with the names of the Roman families of the Nicomachi and the Symmachi, which has representations of pagan priestesses making offerings at altars (London, V&A; Paris, Mus. Cluny).

The ivory diptych as a private devotional object with representations of religious subjects was used in the Early Christian period; the earliest examples date from the end of the 4th century. In some cases a single seated or standing figure occupied each panel, while others were decorated with a series of narrative scenes from the Life of Christ. Examples include a diptych (*c.* 550; Berlin, Bodemus., Inv. 564/5) with *Christ* and the *Virgin* shown seated and accompanied by saints and angels. In the 8th and 9th centuries Carolingian artists often reused such Early Christian ivory diptychs or used them as models for front and back covers of books (*see* CAROLINGIAN ART, fig. 15); the format then became rare, until the diptych was revived by French Gothic ivory-carvers in the late 13th century and the 14th. Many examples survive, almost all produced in Paris. The most popular type seems to have incorporated numerous narrative scenes from the *Life of Christ*, but some have only a single figure or a single narrative subject on each panel.

Goldsmiths and enamellers occasionally used the diptych format. There are a few Byzantine examples, notably the Georgian 13th-century diptych of the Empress Tamara (Tbilisi, Mus. A. Georg.), in which a reliquary of the True Cross belonging to the Empress was, after her death, enclosed in a diptych with enamels and panel paintings; a small number of Gothic examples also survive, including the reliquary diptych of Thilo von Lorich, a commander of the Teutonic Order (see fig. 1).

With the rise of the cult of icons it seems that the painted diptych was adopted as a convenient format. Only one example survives from the Early Christian period, showing half-length images of *SS Peter and Paul* (Rome, Vatican, Mus. Sacro Crist.); it was probably produced in Rome in the 7th century. In the Byzantine empire examples of diptych icons (both painted and mosaic panels) occur from the 11th century on; the earlist to survive is in the monastery of St Catherine on Mt Sinai. These diptychs follow iconographic programmes similar to those found on Early Christian examples, with scenes from the Life of Christ and half- or full-length figures of standing saints. Certain very influential devotional subjects were formulated in these Byzantine examples and were followed by Italian artists in the 14th century. The most famous is the pairing of a half-length image of the *Virgin and Child* with that of the *Man of Sorrows*, a popular *Andachtsbild* of the late medieval West.

1. Reliquary diptych of Thilo von Lorich, silver, 178×105 mm (closed), 1388 (Warsaw, Museum of the Polish Army)

Painted diptychs were very popular from the second half of the 13th century until the early 16th in Italy, Germany and the Netherlands. A few examples also exist from England (e.g. the Wilton Diptych, London, N.G.; see fig. 2), France and Spain. Such works fulfilled the function of small-scale devotional paintings intended for private rooms or small altars in side chapels or oratories. Their size varies from very small examples for personal use to large diptychs suitable for a chapel altar. The early examples in the second half of the 13th century are all Italian, mainly from Tuscany and Venice. The dependence of Italian painters on Byzantine models suggests that icons from the Byzantine empire influenced this development. Some of these may have been produced in the Crusader kingdoms in the eastern Mediterranean; several 13th-century Crusader diptych icons still survive in the monastery of St Catherine on Mt Sinai.

Painted diptychs achieved the height of their popularity in the 14th century. In Italy various artists, including Simone Martini, Lippo Memmi and particularly Bernardo Daddi and his workshop, favoured this form. Several German examples of the first half of the 14th century survive from the school of Cologne, but contemporary French works are mostly known from their representation as altarpieces in illuminated manuscripts, particularly those of the period of Charles V. From this evidence it is clear that in France the diptych was popular by the third quarter of the 14th century, but hardly any have survived. Similarly,

the format was taken up in the Netherlands, and many 15th-century examples were produced by leading artists. In some instances the donor is represented in prayer facing the figure of the Virgin or Christ on the opposite panel (e.g. Memling's *Martin van Nieuwenhove* with the *Virgin and Child*, 1487; Bruges, Memlingmus.). This iconographic arrangement may have been developed by Jan van Eyck, who also produced diptychs with such elaborate narrative subjects as the *Crucifixion* and *Last Judgement* diptych (?*c.* 1428; New York, Met.). Rogier van der Weyden, Hugo van der Goes and Memling preferred to focus on an emotive group within a narrative scene (e.g. Memling's *Deposition* and *Lamentation*, Granada, Mus. Capilla Real; Hugo van der Goes's *Fall of Man* and *Lamentation* diptych, *c.* 1475–80; Vienna, Ksthist. Mus.; see GOES, HUGO VAN DER, fig. 3). In the second half of the 15th century, half-length portraits of husband and wife occasionally occur in diptych form. The French painter Nicolas Froment made such a work (the Matheron Diptych, *c.* 1479; Paris, Louvre) for King René I of Anjou and his second wife, Joanna of Laval. Netherlandish works of this type usually place both portraits in the same panel and are not in the form of a hinged diptych (e.g. Memling's *Old Man and Woman*, now divided into two panels: Berlin, Tiergarten; Paris, Louvre; for further illustration see MOSTAERT, JAN).

These 14th- and 15th-century painted diptychs have both narrative scenes and single figures of Christ, the

2. Wilton Diptych, tempera on panel, 475×292 mm (closed), *c.* 1400 (London, National Gallery)

Virgin and saints. The concentration on single figures or groups, often as busts or even just heads, is a very frequent formula; focusing the viewer's attention on the figure was better achieved by presenting a close-up of the image, thus emphasizing more strongly the illusion of its physical presence. Diptychs declined in popularity from the 16th century, and the format became rare though not obsolete.

BIBLIOGRAPHY

LM: 'Diptychon'; *RDK*: 'Diptychon'

R. Delbrueck: *Die Consulardiptychen und verwandter Denkmäler* (Berlin, 1929)

O. Pächt: 'The Avignon Diptych and its Eastern Ancestry', *De artibus opuscula: Essays for E. Panofsky* (Princeton, 1961), pp. 402–21

W. Kermer: *Studien zum Diptychon in der sakralen Malerei* (Neunkirchen-Saar, 1967)

R. Koechlin: *Les Ivoires gothiques français* (Paris, 1968)

K. J. Shelton: 'The Diptych of the Young Office Holder', *Jb. Ant. & Christ.*, xxv (1982), pp. 132–71

B. Kiilerich and H. Torp: 'Hic est: Hic Stilicho: The Date and Interpretation of a Notable Diptych', *Jb. Dt. Archäol. Inst.*, civ (1989), pp. 319–71

H. Belting: *The Image and its Public in the Middle Ages: Form and Function of Early Paintings of the Passion* (New Rochelle, 1990)

NIGEL J. MORGAN

Dipylon Master. *See* VASE PAINTERS, §II.

Directoire style. Style fashionable in France, especially in Paris, named after the short-lived Directoire period (Oct 1795–Nov 1799). It was marked at first by the collapse of the French economy and then by the rapidly growing wealth of financial speculators, although Ride Felice wrote: 'Many styles are misnamed, none more so than this one; even if it exists . . . was ever a style established in such a short time?' (Felice, n.d.). The style itself displayed elements of the classicism that had prevailed in the later part of the 18th century and had been known in the ARABESQUE STYLE, GROTESQUE and ETRUSCAN STYLE. A new austerity was introduced after the Revolution, and reflecting the taste of the new class of military officials, politicans and financial speculators, it became rapidly more opulent. Under the influence of Charles Percier and Pierre François Leonard Fontaine it was developed into the flourishing EMPIRE STYLE.

The Directoire style is exhibited mainly in interior decoration (see Krafft and Ransonette) and in the applied arts. Distinguishing characteristics are the use of colour that is light in tone and of grotesque motifs shown in outline. The classical forms of the lightly built furniture, by such cabinetmakers as Georges Jacob the younger (*see* JACOB (ii)), show restrained use of materials (e.g. chair, ebony; 1796–7, Paris, Mus. A. Dec.). Decorative motifs also included such Revolutionary symbols as the Phrysian bonnet or cap of Liberty, clasped hands as an emblem of Fraternity, fasces and oak leaves, applied to furniture, ceramics and textiles. In Germany the style was promoted in F. Bertuche's journal *Journal des Luxus und der Moden*, which published interior decorative schemes and fashion designs (Weimar, 1793–1810).

BIBLIOGRAPHY

R. Felice: *Le Meuble français sous Louis XVI et l'empire* (Paris, n.d.)

J. C. Krafft and N. Ransonette: *Plans, coupes et élévations des plus belles maisons et hôtels construits à Paris et dans les environs, au IX–X* (Paris, 1771–1802)

F. Coutet: *Intérieurs Directoire et Empire* (Paris, 1932)

G. Janneau: *Le Style Directoire* (Paris, 1938)

HANS OTTOMEYER

Diricksen [Diriksen], **Felipe** (*b* El Escorial, Madrid, 1590; *d* Madrid, 1679). Spanish painter and collector of Flemish descent. He was the grandson of Anton van Wingaerde and was trained in Madrid in the family tradition. After the death of Bartolomé González in *c.* 1627–8, he aspired to occupy the vacant post of Pintor del Rey, having served as Arquero de Corps since 1611. In spite of his lengthy career as a painter, his work is scarce. In 1620 a portrait of *Philip III* (untraced) is documented. Among his other works are *SS Isidore, Teresa, Philip Neri, Ignatius and Francis Xavier* (untraced) and a series of six canvases (e.g. *St Mark*, 1627) in the chapel of Mosén Rubí de Bracamonte, Ávila. A portrait of *Doña María Gasca de la Vega* (Pastrana, Colegiata), depicting the sitter kneeling, was also painted in the 1620s; its horizontal format is similar to the *Mater Dolorosa with St John and the Magdalene* (1645; Madrid, Convento de la Encarnación). Two dated portraits survive of male members of the Ibarra family (both 1628; Eibar, Ayuntamiento) as well as a *Portrait of a Woman* (1630; Madrid, Fluxa Col.). There is little documentation about his activities in the 1630s. A painting of *St James* (Toledo, Carmelitas Descalzos) is dated 1643. The following year he received payment for 12 canvases for the church of S Juan de Letrán in Pedroso (La Rioja), of which two survive: a *Calvary* and *St John on Patmos* (both Pedroso, parish church). In 1648 he purchased at auction drawings and papers from the collection of the painter Antonio Puga (*c.* 1610–48). In May 1678 he took Jusepe Ramírez as an apprentice for a seven-year period. On his death a year later, Juan Carreño de Miranda evaluated his paintings. Diricksen's style is clearly within the tradition of painting in Madrid at the beginning of the 17th century. His compositions are simple, often representing isolated figures in a monumental manner. Especially in works before 1640, figures are accentuated by the use of chiaroscuro and drapery is rendered in broad folds. From 1640 his paintings retain their monumentality while evolving towards clearer tones and looser brushwork, as in the *Apostle St Peter* (*c.* 1642; Pedroso, parish church). His portraits are executed in the tradition of the court style learnt from González, although at times the influence of Velázquez is apparent.

BIBLIOGRAPHY

J. Moreno Villa: 'Documentes sobre pintores recogidos en el Archivo de Palacio', *Archv Esp. A. & Arqueol.*, xii (1936)

D. Angulo Iñiguez and A. E. Pérez Sánchez: *Historia de la pintura española: Pintura madrileña del primer tercio del siglo XVII* (Madrid, 1969), pp. 339–48

D. Angulo Iñiguez: 'Pintura del siglo XVII', *Ars Hispaniae*, xv (Madrid, 1971), pp. 53, 240

ISMAEL GUTIÉRREZ PASTOR

Dirk van Staren. *See* VELLERT, DIRK.

Dirr [Dürr]. German family of sculptors and stuccoists. Johann Georg Dirr (*b* Weilheim, Ober-Bayern, 2 April 1723; *d* Mimmenhausen, nr Konstanz, 9 Oct 1779) and his brother Franz Anton Dirr (*b* Weilheim, 8 June 1724; *d* Überlingen, nr Konstanz, 15 June 1801) were sons of the sculptor Martin Dirr (1674–1733). They were taught in Weilheim by their stepfather, Franz Xaver Schmädl, whose training left its mark on their style, especially on that of Johann Georg Dirr, whose work is very sensitively executed. There is evidence that the brothers worked in Mimmenhausen as journeymen in the workshop of JOSEPH ANTON FEUCHTMAYER from 1749 and 1752 respectively. In 1753 Johann Georg Dirr moved to Stockach, but in 1756 he went back to the workshop in Mimmenhausen and in 1759 was mentioned as being in joint charge there together with Feuchtmayer. The two men collaborated on commissions in the pilgrimage church at Neubirnau (1749–53, 1756; portions *in situ*), on the figures on the high altar (partly destr.) and side altar in the former Augustinian (now Benedictine) abbey church, Beuron (1759–61), on the high altar in the former Franziskanerkirche at Überlingen (1761; *in situ*) and on the choir-stalls in the Klosterkirche in St Gall (from 1764; *in situ*). Dirr's independent stuccowork, which was considerably influenced by Johann Michael Feuchtmayer, included work (1758; destr.) at the Schloss at Rimpach, the Schloss at Tettnang (1758–60; *in situ*) and the Prälatur in Salem, redecorated in 1764, which was a high point in his career. Altars in the former Zisterzienserinnenklosterkirche SS Marien und Johann Baptista in Baindt (1763; *in situ*), in Herdwangen (1765; *in situ*) and in the Schlosskapelle in Heiligenberg (1765; partly destr. 1878) were influenced by Joseph Anton Feuchtmayer. Johann Georg Dirr's late work is inclined to melancholy expressiveness, the most important example being the groups of putti in the Klosterkirche, Salem (1773–5; *in situ*). From 1773 he worked on a new high altar and new side altars for the Klosterkirche, which was to be the most important Neo-classical ensemble in southern Germany; it was completed by JOHANN WIELAND according to his own designs. For his classical designs Dirr used engraving plates by François de Neufforge as sources.

From 1761 Franz Anton Dirr worked independently in Überlingen, showing only a tentative move towards classicism. His altars clearly reveal the influence of Feuchtmayer, with whom he worked on the decoration of the Wallfahrtskirche St Marien in Birnau. Many of the numerous surviving drawings (e.g. elevation of the high altar for the Franziskanerkirche, Überlingen; Konstanz, Städt. Wessenberg-Gemäldegal.) come from a collection of patterns derived from drawings by Joseph Anton Feuchtmayer and an engraving by Jakob Schmuzer and were put together between 1752 and 1760. Franz Anton Dirr had two sons: Alois Dirr (1763–1823), a sculptor; and Johann Sebastian Dirr (*b* 1766), a painter who achieved local recognition for his miniature *vedute* depicting the area near Lake Constance.

BIBLIOGRAPHY

Thieme–Becker

L. Schnorr von Carolsfeld: *Der plastische Schmuck im Inneren des Münsters zu Salem aus den Jahren 1774–84 von Johann Georg Dürr und Johann Georg Wieland* (Berlin, 1906)

H. Sauer: *Zeichnungen der Mimmenhausener Bildner und ihres Kreises*, Studien zur deutschen Kunstgeschichte, cccvii (Strasbourg, 1936), pp. 66–79

W. Boeck: 'Altarfiguren der sechziger von Feuchtmayer und Dirr', *Joseph Anton Feuchtmayer* (Tübingen, 1948), pp. 279–90

G. P. Woeckel: 'Zwei Gruppen musizierender Engel von Johann Georg Dirr', *Berlin. Mus.*, 8 (1958), pp. 45–50

E. Fründt: 'Zur Neuaufstellung einer Sandsteinplastik des 18. Jahrhunderts in der Skulpturensammlung: Ein Bericht über den Stand der Forschung zur Frage Joseph Anton Feuchtmayer und seine Gehilfen', *Forsch. & Ber.: Staatl. Mus. Berlin*, 5 (1962), pp. 67–72

J. Grünenfelder: 'Beiträge zum Bau der St. Gallener Landkirchen unter Offizial P. Iso Walser, 1759–1785', *Z. Ver. Gesch. Bodensees*, lxxxv (1967), pp. 1–334

E. Dillmann, C. Zoege von Manteuffel and H.-J. Schulz: *Johann Georg Dirr* (Friedrichshafen, 1980)

C. Häussler-Stockhammer: *Die Stukkaturen Johann Georg Dirrs in Schloss Salem: Formvariation und Ornamentästhetik in einem Dekorationsprogramm des späten Rokoko* (Sigmaringen, 1986)

U. Knapp: 'Kontinuität und Wandel in einer Künstlerfamilie: Die Dirr in Mimmenhausen und Überlingen', *Johann Sebastian Dirr: Ansichten vom Bodensee*, ed. S. Tann and B. Wiedmann (Friedrichshafen, 1987), pp. 71–81

——: *Die Wallfahrtskirche Birnau: Planungs- und Baugeschichte* (Friedrichshafen, 1989), pp. 17ff, 118, 126, 128, 146ff, 161, 167, 181ff, 188, 192

——: 'Entwurf und Kopie: Zeichnungen Joseph Anton Feuchtmayer und seiner Werkstatt zum Hochaltar in der Meersburger Schlosskapelle', *Z. Dt. Ver. Kstwiss.*, xliii (1989), pp. 37–71

ULRICH KNAPP

Discalced Carmelites. *See* CARMELITE ORDER.

Discher, (Carl) Marcus. *See* TUSCHER, MARCUS.

Disdéri, André-Adolphe-Eugène (*b* Paris, 28 March 1819; *d* Paris, 4 Oct 1889). French photographer. He managed a series of commercial studios in Paris from 1854 to 1875 and is best known for the patent he took out in November 1854, for the *carte-de-visite* (*see* PHOTOGRAPHY, §I). The *carte*, so named because of its resemblance to the size of a French visiting-card, was a small-format photograph that was produced by dividing a full-plate, collodion-on-glass negative into eight parts that were exposed in a four-lens camera. By allowing eight tiny prints with several poses to be generated on one plate, Disdéri's patent significantly lowered the cost of photographic portraits. His first successful studio on the Boulevard des Italiens produced hundreds of thousands of such portraits of aristocratic and bourgeois sitters and also published series on the Palace of Versailles, the Exposition Universelle in Paris (both in 1855) and the Paris Commune (1871). The convenience and cheapness of the photographic *carte* assured its success, and it became the most popular type of photographic portraiture, supplanting the daguerreotype. It was easy to imitate, however, and despite initial financial success Disdéri died penniless.

BIBLIOGRAPHY

E. A. McCauley: *A. A. E. Disdéri and the Carte de Visite Portrait Photograph* (New Haven, 1985)

ELIZABETH ANNE MCCAULEY

Disegno e colore. Controversy that developed in Italy in the 16th century over the relative merits of design or drawing (It. *disegno*) and colour (*colore*). It was fundamentally a debate over whether the value of a painting lay in the idea originating in the artist's mind (the invention), which was explored through drawings made prior to the painting's execution, or in the more lifelike imitation of nature, achieved through colour and the process of painting itself.

1. 16th-century Italy: origins of the controversy. 2. 17th-century Italy. 3. 17th to 19th-century England and France.

1. 16TH-CENTURY ITALY: ORIGINS OF THE CONTROVERSY. The *disegno e colore* debate focused on the rivalry between the two dominant traditions of 16th-century Italian painting, central Italian and Venetian. Central Italian, especially Florentine, painting depended on drawing and on the use of preparatory studies and cartoons, and the depiction of the human figure was the supreme test of an artist's skill; Venetian painters built up their pictures directly on the canvas, creating a more spontaneous and expressive art. The difference between the two approaches was formulated in the writings of Giorgio Vasari (*see* VASARI, (1)) and LODOVICO DOLCE. The first edition of Vasari's *Vite* (1550), while showing some enthusiasm for Venetian art and paying tribute to Titian at the end of the life of Giorgione, was nonetheless written to proclaim the superiority of the Florentine school and of Michelangelo. The Venetian Dolce's *Dialogo della pittura* (1557) rejected this view, defending the Venetian tradition and exalting Titian above both Raphael and Michelangelo. Dolce's definition of the three parts of painting—*disegno, invenzione* and *colorire*—was the traditional one and had been expressed slightly earlier by the Venetian PAOLO PINO, in his *Dialogo della pittura* (Venice, 1548). Dolce defined *disegno* as 'the form with which the painter presents his material', while *colorito* was equated with nature's diversity and variety. He praised Titian's closeness to nature and the vitality of his forms, which depended on his use of colour. In this power to suggest life lay colouring's claim to supremacy; 'And certainly colouring is so important and compelling that, when the painter produces a good imitation of the tones and softness of flesh, and the rightful characteristics of any object there may be, he makes his paintings seem alive.' In the 1568 edition of the *Vite*, Vasari was more critical of Venetian art than previously. He gave an expanded theoretical definition of *disegno*, which he called the 'father of the three arts', and defined *disegno*, which derives from the intellect, as an idea of the forms of nature. This idea found objective expression through the artist's hands, or drawing; thus *disegno* is a 'manifest expression and embodiment of the concept which he has in his mind'. Titian is censured for his lack of *disegno*. Vasari described a visit he had made with Michelangelo to Titian's studio, where Michelangelo is reported as lamenting that 'in Venice they did not learn to draw well from the beginning, and that those painters did not pursue their studies with more method. . . . if Titian had been assisted by art and design as much as he was by nature . . . then no one could achieve more or work better'. Vasari's severest criticism was reserved for Tintoretto, whose freedom of touch seemed to him both extravagant and capricious.

Proponents of *disegno* were concerned to stress its intellectual aspects, underlining its theoretical rather than its manual or practical character and proposing that painting should be elevated to the status of a liberal art, on a level with poetry. These intellectual aspects are stressed in the works of the late Mannerist writers Paolo Lomazzo and Federico Zuccaro. In his *Trattato dell'arte della pittura* (Milan, 1584) and *Idea del tempio della pittura* (Milan, 1590), Lomazzo imbued *disegno* with an almost spiritual quality, equating it with *eurythmia* or proportion, providing a fundamental framework for the work of art. Yet he was also concerned to reconcile it with *colore* and so urged artists to learn from the different perfections of great artists. In 1584 he wrote of the dangers of limiting oneself to a single artist's example and claimed that the best procedure was for the painter to form his own style by selecting and combining the most beautiful aspects of the great masters. In the *Idea* (p. 60) he gave a concrete example of this precept by describing his idea of a perfect pair of pictures: Adam drawn by Michelangelo and coloured by Titian, and Eve drawn by Raphael and coloured by Correggio. In the writings of Zuccaro, Neo-Platonic elements dominate; he envisaged *disegno* as equivalent to the 'idea' in the artist's mind, derived from God, and distinguished between *disegno interno* (the ordering faculty of the artist) and *disegno esterno* (the actual linear outline; see Blunt, 1940, p. 141, n. 1).

From the early 1590s the debate focused on the art of the Carracci family. At this time Annibale and Agostino Carracci were partisans of *colore*; around 1592–3 they made marginal notes in a 1568 edition of Vasari's *Vite* (untraced), which are an indignant response to Vasari's attacks on Tintoretto and Veronese. On his arrival in Rome in 1595, however, Annibale responded to the power of Roman *disegno* and produced works that were admired by his contemporaries for bridging the schism between *disegno e colore*. Giovanni Battista Agucchi (see Mahon, 1947) wrote that Annibale and Agostino set out to unite Roman *disegno* with the beauty of Lombard colouring; Giulio Mancini, in his *Considerazione sulla pittura*, later characterized Annibale's art as uniting 'the manner of Raphael with that of Lombardy'. Their art was seen as following Lomazzo's recommendation that the artist should select the best aspects of the greatest masters. This was the generally accepted view in the mid-17th century; Pietro Testa, for example, in his ideal Parnassus, describes the greatness of the Carracci in terms of the way they mastered the union of *disegno* and *colore*.

2. 17TH-CENTURY ITALY. The debate between Venetian colour and Tuscan design continued in the 17th century. Cesare Ripa's personification of *Disegno* in his *Iconologia* (Padua, 1630; see fig. 1) parallels Vasari's earlier abstract definition. Ripa's image is a young man 'of noble aspect, in rich and sumptuous clothing, holding in his right hand a pair of compasses, in his left a mirror'. Ripa explained that the youth has a noble aspect because *disegno* is '*il nervo*' of all created things; handsome, because 'all artistic creations may be called more or less beautiful, according to whether they have more or less *disegno*.' The compasses show that *disegno* is the theoretical part of painting, while the mirror suggests that through *disegno* art reflects ideas born in the imagination.

Marco Boschini, the most passionate exponent of the Venetian aesthetic, wrote in the preface to *Le ricche miniere della pittura veneziana* (Venice, 2/1674) that 'without colouring *il disegno* may be called a body without a soul.' He acknowledged the tenet that *disegno* was the basis of art but asserted that without colour it remained imperfect. In opposition, the Florentine Filippo Baldinucci, in his

D I S S E G N O.

1. *Disegno*, illustration from *Iconologia* by Cesare Ripa (Padua, 1630), p. 193 (Cambridge, University Library)

Vocabolario toscano del disegno (1680), stressed the importance of the artist's initial conception as the essence of *disegno*, an idea made manifest through long practice in drawing. Baldinucci also asserted that the concept of a work of art should include 'not only paintings, but also drawings . . . including the most spontaneous sketches and studies.'

Classical artists in the 17th century adopted an aesthetic position that stressed the supremacy of drawing. Domenichino, Poussin and Carlo Maratti believed that through drawing the artist gave expression to an idea conceived in the intellect. Poussin, whose art was later idolized by supporters of *disegno*, insisted on the artist's intellectual and rational control over his material. He wrote of colour: 'Colours in painting are a snare to persuade the eyes, like the charm of the verse in poetry' (Blunt, 1964). (For an illustration of Poussin's *SS Peter and John Healing the Lame Mary see* PERSPECTIVE, colour pl. VII, fig. 2.)

3. 17TH TO 19TH-CENTURY ENGLAND AND FRANCE. In England, Richard Haydocke's translation of Lomazzo's *Trattato dell'arte della pittura* familiarized English readers with the Italian debate. Edward Norgate's *Miniatura* (*c.* 1646; ed. M. Hardie, Oxford, 1919), while denigrating drawing as an activity that 'conduceth to make profitable things but is none itself', nonetheless extols 'the profound and exquisite study of Designe'. Franciscus Junius, in *The Painting of the Ancients*, described colour as greater than drawing, because of the lifelikeness that it can bestow. In a chapter on colour he stated: 'Colour moves us more in pictures than a simple delineation,' since 'coloured pictures . . . shew a more lively spirit . . . they most commonly ravish our sight with the bewitching pleasure of delightsome and stately ornaments'. In the emotional language there is a censorious note; colour is seen as a tempting snare and associated with notions of deceit attached to other forms of 'painting', such as painting the face, or the 'false colours' of rhetoric. Even

the supporters of colour sometimes adopted this attitude; thus even Junius advised a 'discreet and warie moderation' in its use.

The moralizing note sounded strongly in the debate in France in the later 17th century, when the adherents of each party associated the virtues that they admired with the work of Poussin and Rubens respectively (*see also* POUSSINISME, RUBÉNISME). The members of the Académie Royale de Peinture, led by Le Brun, believed in the superiority of drawing over colour, holding that its appeal was to reason rather than to the senses, and that it was therefore intrinsically more noble. The use of contour and the emphasis on form of Raphael and of Poussin were held to embody an aesthetic purity, in contrast to the siren-like charm of Venetian and Rubensian colouring. Colour was portrayed as a mechanical part of painting, without the intellectual dignity of drawing. André Félibien, who wrote primarily as a man of taste and was not an Academician, expressed varying and flexible views. In his fifth *Entretien* he discussed Venetian colour and expressed admiration for the intellectual subtlety of that of Titian; he praised the mastery of it as being even more important to art than skill in drawing. The supreme master of colour for Félibien, however, was not Titian but Poussin, since *coloris* implies the handling of colours, not their brightness or intensity. In the seventh and eighth *Entretiens* Félibien focused on Rubens and Poussin and finally espoused the cause of *disegno*. Rubens is praised for the beauty of his colour yet criticized for his lack of an ideal of beauty and for his neglect of drawing. For Félibien, Poussin represented the virtues of *disegno* in the highest sense; his artistic achievement was unsurpassed, as master not only of drawing but also of colour. Poussin's first *Self-portrait* (1649; Berlin, Bodemus.; engraved by Jean Pesne, *d* 1700; see fig. 2) shows the artist holding a volume entitled *De lumine et colore* (this inscription was possibly a later addition), indicating that the supreme master of *disegno* was also interested in light and colour. Far from opposing *disegno* to *colore*, Poussin understood them to be inseparable.

The first theoretical defence of colour and of the Venetian tradition was made in Charles-Alfonse du Fresnoy's didactic poem *De arte graphica*, translated in 1668 by ROGER DE PILES as *L'Art de peinture*, where colour is described as the 'soul' or 'perfection' of the art. In his notes to the poem, de Piles defended colour more vigorously; for him colour usurped some of the intellectual functions that his opponents ascribed to drawing. De Piles, who was not a member of the Académie and wrote as an amateur, published his *Dialogue sur le coloris* in 1673 and his *Cours de peinture* in 1708, among other works, and became established as the chief spokesman for colour. In his *Dialogue sur le coloris*, he acknowledged that both drawing and colour are essential parts of painting yet claimed that it was colour that gave perfection and life to drawing and colour that, above all, characterized the art of painting. For de Piles it was Rubens, whose art united the colour and chiaroscuro of Flanders with an Italianate sense of form and composition, who was supreme. This victory of the Rubénistes opened the way to a freer, more painterly approach in the early 18th century, when such artists as Antoine Coypel, Jean-Charles Delafosse and François de Troy (ii) were influenced by the writings of de Piles. Yet in the 19th century, in the opposition of Ingres and Delacroix, the quarrel of drawing versus colour was reborn. Where Ingres believed in drawing as the idealistic element in art, Delacroix sought to reconcile drawing and painting and believed that Titian, the greatest of the colourists, was also 'the first of draughtsmen (if by drawing we understand drawing from nature and not that in which the artist's imagination plays a greater part than imitation)' (Delacroix, *Journal*, 25 Jan 1857). The freedom and colour of Delacroix was admired by the Impressionists, whose spontaneous art of colour and atmosphere challenged the classical tradition of Ingres.

BIBLIOGRAPHY

GENERAL
M. Kemp: *The Science of Art* (London, 1990), pp. 274ff
F. Gage: *Colour and Culture* (London, 1993), pp. 117ff

ITALY
G. Vasari: *Vite* (1550; rev. 2/1568); ed. G. Milanesi (1878–85)
L. Dolce: *Dialogo della pittura* (Venice, 1557); ed. M. Roskill (New York, 1968)
G. Mancini: *Considerazioni sulla pittura* (MS., 1617–21); ed. A. Marucchi (Rome, 1956)
A. F. Blunt: *Artistic Theory in Italy, 1450–1600* (Oxford, 1940)
D. Mahon: *Studies in Seicento Art and Theory* (London, 1947)
——: 'Eclecticism and the Carracci', *J. Warb. & Court. Inst.*, xvi (1953), pp. 303–41
D. Rosand: 'The Crisis of the Venetian Renaissance Tradition', *L'Arte*, 11–12 (1970), pp. 6–12
D. Posner: *Annibale Carracci* (London, 1971)
E. Cropper: *The Ideal of Painting: Pietro Testa's Düsseldorf Notebook* (Princeton, 1984) [esp. pp. 57ff]

ENGLAND
P. Lomazzo: *Trattato dell'arte della pittura* (Milan, 1584); Eng. trans. by R. Haydocke as *A Tracte Containing the Artes of Curious Painting, Carvinge & Buildinge* (Oxford, 1598)
F. Junius: *De pictura veterum* (Amsterdam, 1634); Eng. trans. as *The Painting of the Ancients* (London, 1638)

FRANCE
A. Félibien: *Entretiens sur les vies et sur les ouvrages de plus excellens peintres anciens et modernes* (Paris, 1666–85/*R* Trévoux, 1725)
C.-A. du Fresnoy: *De arte graphica* (Paris, 1667); Fr. trans. by R. de Piles (Paris, 1668); Eng. trans. by J. Dryden (London, 1695)
A. Félibien: *Conférences de l'Académie royale de peinture et de sculpture* (Paris, 1669)
R. de Piles: *Dialogue sur le coloris* (Paris, 1673)
——: *Conversations sur la connoissance de la peinture* (Paris, 1674)
——: *Abrégé de la vie des peintres* (Paris, 1699)
——: *Cours de peinture par principes* (Paris, 1708; Eng. trans., London, 1743)
B. Teyssèdre: *Roger de Piles et les débats sur le coloris au siècle de Louis XIV* (Paris, 1957)
A. F. Blunt, ed.: *Nicolas Poussin: Lettres et propos sur l'art* (Paris, 1964)
T. Puttfarken: *Roger de Piles' Theory of Art* (London and New Haven, 1985)

CLAIRE PACE

Disieult [Disieux], **Jean** [Jehan]. *See* DIZIEULT, JEAN.

Dismorr, Jessica (*b* Gravesend, Kent, 1885; *d* London, 29 Aug 1939). English painter and illustrator. She studied at the Slade School, London, in 1902–3, then trained under Max Bohm at Etaples and in 1910–13 at La Palette, Paris, under Jean Metzinger, John Duncan Fergusson and Dunoyer de Segonzac. As a result she developed a Fauvist style using rich impastos. She contributed several brusquely simplified illustrations to *Rhythm* magazine during 1911 and exhibited Fauvist canvases at the Allied Artists' Association in 1912 and 1913. She exhibited with S. J. Peploe and Fergusson at the Stafford Gallery in 1912,

2. Nicolas Poussin: *Self-portrait*, 1649; engraving by Jean Pesne (London, British Museum)

but an encounter with Wyndham Lewis the following year led to a dramatic change in her work. By spring 1914 she had become an enthusiastic member of the Rebel Art Centre, and her name appeared on the list of signatures at the end of the Vorticist manifesto in the first issue of *Blast* magazine (1914).

Little survives of Dismorr's Vorticist work, but her illustrations in *Blast* show that she shared the Vorticist's involvement with the dynamism of the machine-age city. *Abstract Composition* (1914–15; London, Tate) employs sturdy, girder-like forms to animate a vision that she described in the poem *Monologue*, published in the second issue of *Blast* (1915). Here she admired 'the new machinery that wields the chain of muscles fitted beneath/my close coat of skin', outlining the amalgam of human and mechanical imagery that lay at the centre of Vorticism.

After participating in the Vorticist Exhibition of June 1915, Dismorr did voluntary war work in France. She was included in the Vorticist Exhibition of January 1917, held in New York and in 1926 became a member of the London Group and the Seven and Five Society. In later life her work became completely abstract, in tune with avant-garde developments of the 1930s. She contributed to *Axis* magazine in 1937.

WRITINGS

'Poems and Notes', *Blast*, 2 (1915), pp. 65–9
'Critical Suggestions', *Little Rev.*, vi/5 (1919), pp. 31–5
'Some Russian Artists', *The Tyro*, 2 (1922), pp. 19–20

BIBLIOGRAPHY

Jessica Dismorr and her Circle (exh. cat., foreword Q. Stevenson; London, Archer Gal., 1972)
Jessica Dismorr, 1885–1934 (exh. cat., intro. Q. Stevenson; London, Mercury Gal., 1974)

RICHARD CORK

Disney, Walt(er Elias) (*b* Chicago, IL, 5 Dec 1901; *d* Burbank, CA, 15 Dec 1966). American film maker, animator and entrepreneur. Much of his childhood was spent in rural Missouri, but during his adolescence the family moved to Kansas City, where he formed an interest in drawing and in Vaudeville theatre. He received little formal training, but by the age of 18 he was earning his living as a cartoonist, first in print and then in the fledgling field of animation. While still in Kansas City, Disney began, with his most important early associate Ubbe ('Ub') Iwerks, to produce animated shorts including *Alice's Wonderland* (1923), in which a young girl, filmed in live action, cavorted with cartoon characters. In 1923 Disney moved to Los Angeles, where Iwerks and other members of the Kansas City team joined him. They continued to produce similar comedies until 1927, when these were superseded by a fully animated series starring Oswald the Lucky Rabbit. By this time Disney himself had given up animation to concentrate on a supervisory role, but his ability to provide cartoon stories with dramatic structures and his flair for squeezing humour from visual jokes helped make Oswald a success. Disney lost the rights to the character to an unscrupulous distributor, however, precipitating the crisis that led to his greatest triumph. Urgently needing a new character, Disney created a mouse named Mickey (reputedly the name was chosen by Disney's wife after many others, such as Mortimer, had been considered). The prototype Mickey, based on circles for ease of animation, was drawn by Iwerks, and the first group of short films featuring the character was produced just as the public was responding enthusiastically to the first sound feature, *The Jazz Singer*, produced in 1927 by Warner Brothers. Recognizing that the future of the motion picture lay with sound, Disney devised a way of wedding sound to animated action, using sound effects and musical accents to underline visual jokes and to propel the film forward. *Steamboat Willie* (1928), the first film to employ this technique, was an immediate success, and soon Mickey Mouse was an international folk hero. At first the Mickey Mouse cartoons used boisterous, unsophisticated humour, but eventually Mickey was domesticated and transformed into an emblem of suburban, middle-class America and an essential part of the iconography of 20th-century American culture. The wilder humour was assigned to such new characters as Pluto, Goofy and especially Donald Duck. In 1929 Disney produced *Skeleton Dance*, the first of a series called *Silly Symphonies*, in which Donald Duck first appeared in 1934. These were cartoons whose basic structure was provided by the musical score, the finest examples being *Music Land* and *Who Killed Cock Robin?* (both 1935). Disney used the series to introduce many technical advances, from full Technicolor to the multiplane camera, but its chief importance lay in helping the studio prepare for the production of full-length feature films.

Snow White and the Seven Dwarfs (1937), the first full-length animated fiction film ever made, was anticipated with scepticism by many experts. Disney had assembled a gifted team of artists, however, and had even inaugurated a studio school to train new talent. More important to the film's success, however, was Disney's imagination, which gave the film its overall shape. A commercial and critical success, *Snow White* was quickly followed by four more ambitious animated features: *Pinocchio* (1940), *Fantasia* (1940), *Dumbo* (1941) and *Bambi* (1942). These gave great opportunities to some of the younger artists trained at the studio, and display a level of sustained technical excellence, but they also demonstrate the limitations of Disney's vision. *Fantasia*, an attempt to wed animation to Classical music, was seen by some as a particular disappointment, showing that Disney was on unsure ground when he strayed from his populist roots.

After World War II Disney resumed feature animation with *Cinderella* (1950), but such films as *Peter Pan* (1953) and *The Lady and the Tramp* (1955) lacked the intensity and overwhelming narrative drive of *Snow White*. This was partly due to Disney's increasing involvement in live action films, television and particularly theme parks.

The first of these was Disneyland, which opened in July 1955 in Anaheim, CA. Based on projecting adults and children into the fantasy world of Disney's films, using architectural re-creations of scenes and life-size impersonations of the characters, it was a huge commercial success, despite Disney's original difficulty in finding financial backing. It was less popular with most architects, however, although some, such as Charles Eames, were enthralled by it. In 1971 it was followed by Disney World, a much larger project covering 27,000 acres in Florida. This was intended to be a complete holiday centre, with several amusement parks based on different themes but also containing hotels, campsites and golf courses and an industrial park as a showcase for American business. It also incorporated many innovations in what was effectively urban design, such as a monorail system, non-polluting vehicles, pedestrian malls, a conservation area and an airport for STOL (short take-off and landing) aircraft. The use of prefabricated units for the hotel suites was also innovative. Disney also intended Disney World to be the home of perhaps his most ambitious project, the Experimental Prototype Community of Tomorrow (EPCOT), which was planned as a testing ground for new building materials and design systems and opened in 1982.

Disney was the most important figure in the evolution of the animated film, taking the crude cartoons of the silent era and, with his key associates, forging a medium that was capable of sustaining elaborate story lines and exhilarating flights of visual invention. He was sometimes chided for a lack of cultural sophistication, but it was precisely his roots in popular culture and his feeling for its iconography that gave his best films their underlying strength and that were responsible for his significant influence on such Pop artists as Andy Warhol, Roy Lichtenstein and Claes Oldenburg, and on later artists such as Keith Haring (1958–90).

BIBLIOGRAPHY
R. D. Field: *The Art of Walt Disney* (London, 1944)
B. Thomas: *The Art of Animation: The Story of the Disney Studio Contribution to a New Art* (New York, 1966)
C. Finch: *The Art of Walt Disney: From Mickey Mouse to the Magic Kingdoms* (New York, 1973)
F. Thomas and O. Johnston: *Disney Animation: The Illusion of Life* (New York, 1981)
R. R. Beard: *Walt Disney's EPCOT: Creating the New World of Tomorrow* (New York, 1982)
B. D. Kurtz: *Keith Haring, Andy Warhol and Walt Disney* (London and Munich, 1992)

CHRISTOPHER FINCH

D'Isola, Aimaro. *See under* NEO-LIBERTY.

di sotto in sù [It.: 'from below upwards']. Term applied to extreme foreshortening and perspective in a ceiling or fresco painting. It creates the illusion that figures and objects are suspended above the viewer in space and not confined to the picture plane (*see* ILLUSIONISM, fig. 1). Andrea Mantegna first made sophisticated use of this convention, which was later used by many artists of the 16th–18th centuries.

RUPERT FEATHERSTONE

Display of art. With the rise of COLLECTING in antiquity and with the appreciation of objects for their own sake rather than for their religious or other connotations came the issue of how to display works of art. Their arrangement was usually symmetrical within a carefully considered decorative scheme. Collectors adapted religious traditions of display and were inspired by Classical precedent. The medieval domestic use of a few portable paintings led, by the 16th century, to their display *en masse* in galleries. The culmination of this tendency was to 'carpet' walls with symmetrically arranged paintings. By the second half of the 19th century, organization by school and chronology was accompanied by a belief that paintings should be sparsely hung so that each could be properly appreciated. With sculpture, there was more information available about ancient methods of display, and Classical principles proved extremely long-lived, both indoors and outdoors. Factors of size, rarity and fragility did much to determine the forms of display used for other media: drawings were, for example, often put into albums, and when still scarce, porcelain was displayed in places where silver and gold objects might have been expected, but its increased availability led, as with paintings, to massed displays on shelves and in display cases. With their proliferation, MUSEUMS have increasingly become the most important generators of alternative modes of display. This article deals with the display of art in Western cultures, calling on European examples to illustrate the predominant trends that have developed.

I. Lighting. II. Paintings. III. Sculpture. IV. Drawings, prints and watercolours. V. Miniatures, medals, coins and gems. VI. Ceramics. VII. Plate. VIII. Tapestries and carpets. IX. Arms and armour.

I. Lighting.

1. TOP- AND SIDELIGHTING. Until the invention of gas and electric lighting in the 19th century, illumination depended on daylight, firelight, lamplight (fed by oil) and candlelight. For interior lighting, the Romans, like the Greeks and their predecessors, relied on oil lamps. Daylight was admitted laterally and from above. Vitruvius (*On Architecture*, VI.iv) recommended a north light for picture galleries. Roman development of toplighting via a dome or lunette was particularly suited to the display of sculpture and pictures, which could be placed freely against the wall without glare from side windows. The most significant examples of Roman toplighting, both in Rome, were a group of rooms in Nero's Domus Aurea (after AD 64; largely destr. AD 104) and the Pantheon (AD 118–25), both lit by an oculus. The Pantheon in particular inspired many subsequent display spaces, although toplighting was not generally adopted for picture and sculpture galleries until the second half of the 18th century. In domestic interiors lighting was usually from the side, and this applied to rooms specifically constructed for the display of art: the *studiolo* in Italy, the closet or cabinet in England and the *cabinet* (*see* CABINET (i)) in France. The first larger galleries were also sidelit: the Galerie François I (*c.* 1533–40) at Fontainebleau; the Galleria degli Stucchi (1559) in the Palazzo Capodiferro-Spada, Rome; and the Galleria delle Statue of the Uffizi (*c.* 1574–81), Florence. This became the traditional design, despite the disadvantages of glare. The gallery of the Palazzo Colonna (1654–1703), Rome, for example, is sidelit (see fig. 1); chandeliers are hung in front of both registers of windows, and there are sconces placed either side of the windows so that at night the windows continued to be 'read' as the source of light. This also allowed a clear view of pictures and sculpture placed on the piers. Early- to mid-18th-century galleries were also sidelit (e.g. the Elector's gallery at Düsseldorf). The gallery at Kassel, built (1749–51) by William VIII, Landgrave of Hesse-Kassel, has an upper register of triforium windows to augment the sidelighting.

1. Gallery of the Palazzo Colonna, Rome, by Antonio del Grande and Girolamo Fontana II, 1654–1703

Toplighting was employed primarily in churches in post-Roman, European architecture. The Tribuna (designed *c.* 1580) of the Uffizi is lit by windows above the cornice. Three picture rooms in the Duc d'Orléans's Palais-Royal, Paris, were lit by skylights in the early 18th century. Toplighting was recommended for the display of art by the architect Jacques-François Blondel in 1752. The use of toplighting in the Museo Pio-Clementino (1771–93) in Rome, built by Alessandro Dori (*d* 1772), Michelangelo Simonetti, Pietro Camporese the elder and Giuseppe Camporese and combining a central rotunda modelled on the Pantheon (see fig. 2) with high sidelighting in the adjoining galleries, set an important precedent. Its design was anticipated by the sculpture gallery (1767–*c.* 1780) at Newby Hall, N. Yorks, by Robert Adam, which was also inspired by the Pantheon.

By 1800 toplighting was *de rigueur*. The combination of large toplit galleries (for large history pictures) with smaller sidelit spaces (for smaller works) was adopted by Leo von Klenze for the Alte Pinakothek (1825–36), Munich, by Gottfried Semper for the Gemäldegalerie (begun 1847), Dresden, and by Karl Hasenauer for the Kunsthistorisches Museum (*c.* 1885), Vienna. Toplight was admitted by skylights or thermal windows, as in the Royal Academy's Great Room (1780) in Somerset House, London, by William Chambers (an important model in England); John Soane's gallery at Fonthill Abbey (1787; destr.), Wilts; the first conversion of the Grande Galerie of the Louvre, Paris, by Charles Percier and Pierre-François-Léonard Fontaine (1805–10; the skylights were extended in 1856); Soane's Dulwich Picture Gallery (1811–14); and the North Gallery (extended 1824–7) at Petworth House, W. Sussex.

2. Sala Rotonda (1772–81) by Michelangelo Simonetti, Museo Pio-Clementino, Vatican, Rome; engraving by V. Feoli after F. Costa

Apart from reducing glare, toplighting significantly increased wall space for display, such galleries relying on height to direct light on to the walls and away from the floor. The upper register of pictures was often canted forward to reduce glare and increase visibility, as seen in the engraving after Johann Heinrich Ramberg of the Royal Academy Exhibition of 1787 (*see* EXHIBITION, fig. 3). The floor was often a light colour to augment the illumination of the lowest register of pictures (the light decreases in intensity towards the base of the wall). A darkish wall (usually red) reduced reflection and concentrated the eye on the pictures.

Theoreticians and architects gave much thought to the problem of lighting works of art. Sebastiano Serlio and Vincenzo Scamozzi (1615) both recommended the Pantheon's toplighting as a model for the display of antiquities. Sir Henry Wotton declared (1624) that galleries and 'Repositories for works of rarity in Picture or other Arts' should face north as they 'require a steadie and unvariable light'. Maximilian I, Elector of Bavaria, had a north-lit gallery (completed 1612) built in accordance with the latest Italian ideas. Artists' studios usually admit a north light (e.g. Rubens's studio, 1610–17, in Antwerp). The Green Closet (1610; remodelled 1637–9) at Ham House, Richmond, Surrey (see fig. 8 below), designed for the display of miniatures and cabinet pictures, also faces north.

2. CURTAINS AND BLINDS. An orientation to the north reduced the potential for the damage of works of art by light (*see* CONSERVATION AND RESTORATION, §II, 1). The Green Closet at Ham House was provided (by 1677) with curtains that could be drawn across the walls to protect the pictures from light and dirt—similar curtains can be seen in the engraving in Thomas Hope's *Household Furniture and Interior Decoration* (1807) of his picture gallery in London. Curtains were hung from rails attached to picture frames, as seen in the *Gallery of Archduke Leopold William* (1651; Petworth House, W. Sussex, NT) and were also used to screen pictures of a horrifying or erotic nature. Silk curtains 'all for pictures' were listed at Wimbledon House, London, in 1649. In 1687 the pictures in the Dauphin's closet at Versailles were fitted with spring roller blinds of painted satin. The gilt frames of J. M. W. Turner's watercolours in the Turner bequest (London, Tate) were originally provided with green roller blinds. Shutters could also be used to regulate the light. In the 17th century, windows in the Netherlands and France had up to four tiers of shutters that could be manipulated to create different light effects.

3. MIRRORS. Mirror-glass serves to increase the amount of light. It was used to line rooms—the earliest being Catherine de' Medici's Cabinet de Miroirs—and the Galerie des Glaces (begun 1678) at Versailles was astonishing because of the number and size of its mirror plates (by 1700 the French achieved dimensions of 2.03×1.14 m for a single plate). In 1684 Louis XIV planned to display his gemstone vessels on a ground of mirrors in the Petite Galerie at Versailles, where in the Chambre du Roi the garniture of the chimney-piece was reflected in nine panes of mirror-glass. The use of mirrors continued to fascinate designers: John Soane made extensive use of circular

convex mirrors in his house (1792–1824) in London, where he also experimented with toplighting via a variety of differently shaped skylights, the light being filtered through both plain and coloured glass. The windows of the picture galleries at Apsley House (1828), London, and Somerley (*c.* 1850–51), Hants, were covered by panels of mirror-glass at night.

4. ARTIFICIAL LIGHTING. Until the invention of gas and then electric lighting, galleries were designed for daylight use. Only on special occasions were they lit at night, as this was extremely expensive. Wall-sconces (sometimes backed with reflective metal) were placed at intervals, and when hung on either side or above pictures, they assumed the function of a picture light (as seen in Abraham Bosse's engraving of the Chambre du Roi at Fontainebleau, 1645; Paris, Bib. N.), as did candles before a sacred image. Robert Adam designed a picture frame incorporating candles as picture lights (drawing, 1771; London, Soane Mus.). Chandeliers of crystal or glass (produced in France after *c.* 1670) were expensive status symbols, as were those of gold and silver. Brass chandeliers were common in the Netherlands in the 17th century. Before the development of improved oil lamps (e.g. the Argand lamp, patented in 1783), numerous candles were used to create dazzling effects. The high cost of candles was considered in choosing the colour of a room: white rooms were cheapest in this respect, whereas darker rooms (usually decorated in red or green for pictures) required more candles. In the dining-room of Charles Townley's London house (acquired *c.* 1774) at 7 Park Street, Westminster (now 14 Queen Anne's Gate), 'lamps hung so as to form the happiest contrast of light and shadow, and the improved effect of the marble by these means, almost reached animation' (J. Dalloway: *Of Statuary and Sculpture among the Ancients with Some Account of Specimens Preserved in England* (London, 1816), p. 330). Both Benvenuto Cellini and Canova used candlelight to achieve similar nocturnal effects. Oil lamps could be hired for special occasions—John Soane lit up his house in London for three nights in March 1825. On Napoleon's nocturnal visits to the Louvre, square lamps on long handles were carried before him and directed on the principal works of art, as shown in a drawing (*c.* 1810; Paris, Louvre) by Benjamin Zix (1772–1811). Improved oil chandeliers or gasoliers were hung in several major picture galleries (e.g. the candelabrum of 30 oil lamps donated to the Royal Academy by the Prince Regent (later George IV) in 1812 and converted to gas in 1817).

The use of electricity for display lighting was pioneered by the South Kensington Museum (1878–81; now the V&A) in London to allow for evening openings and by William Armstrong (1810–1900) for the picture gallery (1880–81) at Cragside, Northumb. The Royal Academy in London had installed electric lighting by 1893, and the British Museum, London, was fully lit by 1890, though other public museums did not introduce full artificial lighting systems until the 1930s. The first electric picture lights (i.e. attached above, below or on the frame of a painting) supplanted gas or oil equivalents in the 1890s (e.g. at Knole, Kent) and were given decorative metal covers (usually helmet shaped). Their inability to throw light beyond the top or bottom of a picture remains a problem although improved versions are being developed. In museums, electric light was initially introduced in the form of pendant fittings (as with oil and gas), as in the case of the hanging lanterns installed at the National Gallery in London in 1935. Daylight was largely excluded from 19th-century toplit public galleries when their height was reduced (1945–80) by false ceilings (with hidden electric lighting) to facilitate a single tier hang and to minimize light damage to pictures. Even at the end of the 20th century, when several 19th-century public galleries had been restored to their original form, the banks of spotlights in front of the skylights were an unfortunate visual encumbrance and usually precluded the appreciation of pictures and sculpture by daylight alone.

See also LIGHTING.

II. Paintings.

1. Before *c.* 1500. 2. *c.* 1500–*c.* 1700. 3. *c.* 1700–*c.* 1870. 4. After *c.* 1870.

1. BEFORE *c.* 1500. Greek easel paintings were displayed in public buildings; the Propylaia, the gateway to the Acropolis in Athens, incorporated a picture gallery (*pinacotheca*). Although none survive, Greek Old Masters were as highly valued as statues by Roman collectors. At first hung as trophies of conquest in religious and public buildings, they were avidly collected by the 1st century BC. Pliny complained of the inaccessibility of paintings and statues in private collections, and Agrippa argued that they should be publicly exhibited (Pliny: *Natural History*, XXXV.ix). The emperors Augustus and Tiberius hung pictures both in public (*Natural History*, XXXV.x) and in private; Tiberius reserved a particularly valuable painting by Parrhasios of Ephesos for his bedroom (*Natural History*, XXXV.xxxvi). The wall paintings of Pompeii give some idea of how pictures were displayed in private settings. The Ixion Room (1st century AD) in the House of the Vettii shows large mythological paintings 'hung' (in *trompe l'oeil*) in the centre of each wall. The decoration is arranged symmetrically around them, much as smaller pictures might have been hung in the picture gallery described in Petronius' *Satyricon* (LXXXIII). Pliny described the fashion for tapestrying the walls of galleries with old pictures (*Natural History*, XXXV.ii). With the rise of Christianity, paintings were designed for church or domestic use. Portable icons were held to possess miraculous powers and were carried in church services, and small images were venerated in private houses. The Venerable Bede recorded that paintings from Rome were hung in the abbeys of Jarrow and Monkwearmouth, founded by Bishop Benedict in AD 674 and 682 respectively.

By the 15th century Books of Hours (e.g. the Très Riches Heures (*c.* 1411/13–16 and *c.* 1485–6; Chantilly, Mus. Condé, MS. 65) of Jean, Duc de Berry) included scenes from the lives of their courtly owners, which suggest that medieval interiors were rich in textiles but poor in paintings. The life of a medieval aristocrat was peripatetic, hence the utility of a Book of Hours, which could be easily carried. Paintings were less portable and more prone to damage, but panel paintings with shutters that formed a box when closed overcame these problems.

Diptychs, triptychs and polyptychs could either be hung on the wall or placed on a table to form an altarpiece. Inventories reveal that they were usually hung in bedrooms, as was the 'painting of Our Lady in a tabernacle with two painted shutters' listed in the inventory of a Medici palace in Florence in 1418.

By the mid-15th century the tabernacle form was gradually replaced by the framed picture. At first the frame and panel tended to be carved from a single piece of wood, and such pictures were sometimes still kept in boxes. Towards the end of the 15th century in Florence, the tondo became popular. Usually provided with a heavy gilt annular frame, tondi, like other devotional images, tended to be listed in bedchambers in early inventories; an illustration in Girolamo Savonarola's *Predica dell'arte del bene morire* (Florence, 1496) depicts a bedroom with a large tondo of the *Virgin and Child*, with a bracket beneath for candles. Paintings (which have often subsequently been detached and framed separately) also formed part of the decoration of cassoni (marriage chests), a standard item of bedroom furniture in Italy in the 15th and 16th centuries; those painted with decorative panels were unusually expensive and luxurious and were sometimes protected by an outer box in transit. Grand beds were also decorated with panel paintings. The bedroom was recommended by Alberti (1485) and later theorists (e.g. Giulio Mancini) as a suitably private and therefore secure place for the display and contemplation of the householder's most valuable possessions, which would have included paintings and painted furniture.

2. *c.* 1500–*c.* 1700. Before the mid-16th century paintings were far from common in domestic interiors. The increasing popularity of portraits (previously kept, like religious or other subject pictures, in private rooms) was the principal factor that led to a wider distribution of paintings throughout the house. In Italy, as well as the bedroom, the study or STUDIOLO was a repository for paintings. Despite their small size, such rooms were designed with great care, so that both thematically and in terms of their arrangement, paintings were in harmony with their setting. The *studiolo* of Francesco I, Grand Duke of Tuscany, in the Palazzo Vecchio, Florence, designed (1570–75) by Vasari, with its two tiers of paintings, a barrel vault inset with more paintings, niches for sculpture and an allegorical scheme devised by Vincenzo Borghini, is a particularly rich survivor of the genre. It has, however, lost its original profusion of smaller portable works of art, which were displayed in the room itself and in cupboards concealed by Vasari's paintings. This Italian concept of a small, richly decorated room for the display of art spread northwards, where it spawned the *Kunstkammern* (*see* KUNSTKAMMER), *Schatzkammern* and *Wunderkammern* of Vienna, Augsburg, Munich, Prague and other cities. The Green Closet at Ham House is a surviving English example (see fig. 8 below).

Another room specifically designed for the display of paintings, sculpture and other works of art was the gallery, which derived from the colonnaded loggia, a space that had been used since antiquity for display. The word 'gallery' to describe a long enclosed room (i.e. a filled-in loggia) and eventually any large display space seems to have been coined in France, where one of the earliest examples is the Galerie François I at Fontainebleau, decorated (*c.* 1533–40) by Rosso Fiorentino, Francesco Primaticcio and other Italians. It was emulated in Italy: the Galleria degli Stucchi of the Palazzo Capodiferro-Spada in Rome, designed by Giulio Mazzoni in 1559 may be the earliest. In galleries symmetry was considered the essence of good display. In the Palazzo Capodiferro-Spada, as at Fontainebleau, the pictures are set in fixed positions at regular intervals in elaborate plasterwork and are, in effect, part of the architecture. In the Sala del Anticollegio (after 1574) in the Doge's Palace, Venice, the plasterwork frames paintings by Veronese, Tintoretto and Jacopo Bassano arranged symmetrically above the dado; lesser paintings by Montemezzano (*d* after 1602) are set in the upper frieze. This style of gallery decoration persisted in France (e.g. the gallery of the Hôtel Lambert (*c.* 1650), Paris, designed by Louis Le Vau and decorated by Charles Le Brun).

One of the most influential of galleries was the octagonal Tribuna of the Uffizi in Florence, designed (*c.* 1580) by Bernardo Buontalenti as a showcase for part of the Medici collection of paintings, sculpture and antiquities. Its octagonal shape enhanced the even illumination of the pictures and avoided the cramped corners of a square room. Although the extant drawn and painted views of the room date from the early 18th century onwards, the numerous pictures listed in the inventory of 1589 suggest that they were arranged similarly from the outset. Johan Zoffany's idealized view of 1771–8 (Windsor Castle, Berks, Royal Col.; see fig. 3) shows the richness of the gallery, with its pictures in gilt frames hung on scarlet velvet, a scheme admired by English Grand Tourists eager to emulate its grandeur in their own houses. Giuseppe Magni's wall-by-wall drawings (1748–after 1764; Florence, Uffizi) of the arrangement of the paintings and sculpture are more literal (Zoffany improved on the picture hang by incorporating masterpieces from the Palazzo Pitti, Florence), but the works of both artists reveal the careful attention to symmetry and balance in the size and subject of the pictures as well as their frames. Each wall was treated as a separate entity with a symmetrical hang, similar but not identical to that of the neighbouring walls. The paintings and other works were arranged for aesthetic effect rather than in chronological order, by subject or by school; portraits and subject paintings were mingled, but landscapes and flower paintings appear to have been excluded. Zoffany showed that the pictures were suspended from a rail fixed beneath the cornice. This adaptable method of picture hanging was employed by William III for his private apartments at Hampton Court in 1700 but was not generally adopted in galleries until the early 19th century. Pictures were usually hung from nails (with decorative heads, where visible) and sometimes with silken or woollen cords often with decorative tassels (as depicted in the engravings of Abraham Bosse and Daniel Marot I) rather than the more usual brass chain or wire. At Ham House in 1679 pictures were 'hung with silk strings' (Buckminster Park, Grantham, Lincs, Tollemache MS.; in P. Thornton and M. Tomlin: 'The Furnishing and Decoration of Ham House', *Furn. Hist.*, xvi (1980), p. 70).

With the increase in the number of pictures in individual collections in the second half of the 16th century, more

3. *Tribuna of the Uffizi* by Johan Zoffany, oil on canvas, 1.24×1.55 m, 1771–8 (Windsor Castle, Berks, Royal Collection)

wall space was required, and greater flexibility was sought. Pictures were hung freely between cornice and dado. Indeed, in some cases they were hung from floor to ceiling, the dado having been dispensed with. Symmetry remained the norm, smaller pictures being grouped in tiers and rows around larger pictures. The architecture and contents of the room dictated the arrangement—doors, chimney-pieces, windows, sculpture and furniture introducing a rhythm to the picture hang. Pictures were either hung sparsely, to enhance the colour or ornament of the wall, or thickly, in some cases frame to frame, so that the impression was of a wall carpeted with pictures. Artists and architects advised on picture hanging: Rubens and Antonio Maria Viani made designs in 1604 for the arrangement of Duke Vincenzo I Gonzaga's Mantuan picture gallery (1594–1611/12). In Italy the preferred background colours for pictures were red (scarlet, crimson or maroon), as in the scarlet Tribuna of the Uffizi, or green. Walls were either painted or hung with material or paper (plain, striped or damask). The division of collections by subject-matter existed alongside the system of variety found at the Tribuna. Thus in the Uffizi a separate gallery was allocated to the important Medici collection of self-portraits, but the majority of the private rooms in the Palazzo Pitti contained mixed collections of pictures arranged symmetrically (see the drawings (Florence, Uffizi) by Giacinto Maria Marmi (*b c.* 1600), a 17th-century Medici curator). The landscape paintings in the Palazzo Colonna (1654–1703; see fig. 1 above) and the Palazzo Doria-Pamphili (*c.* 1650; remodelled 1731–5), both in Rome, were intermingled with other pictures in the main galleries as well as being accorded separate rooms.

North of the Alps and in Spain picture galleries were arranged on Italian principles by collectors who had either visited Italy in person or whose advisers had done so. In the Netherlands paintings of pictures and sculpture galleries were produced from the late 16th century (*see* CABINET PICTURE). Such representations, whether literal, imaginary or a mixture of both, show how pictures were hung in palatial northern European interiors. Willem van Haecht II's *Alexander the Great Visiting the Studio of Apelles* (1628; The Hague, Mauritshuis; see fig. 4) incorporates a view of what is probably Rubens's sculpture rotunda at the far end of a huge picture gallery. Although fanciful, van Haecht's representation undoubtedly records the general appearance of several galleries in contemporary Antwerp, showing, for example, that walls were divided in two by a cornice with a pronounced shelf, on which the upper register of paintings rested. The picture gallery in Brussels of Archduke Leopold William, Governor of the south

4. *Alexander the Great Visiting the Studio of Apelles* by Willem van Haecht II, oil on canvas, 1.05×1.50 m, 1628 (The Hague, Mauritshuis)

Netherlands, is depicted in a series of paintings by David Teniers (ii) (for an example *see* TENIERS, (2), fig. 3). Teniers was also the curator of the collection and in 1660 published details of it in *Theatrum pictorium*, the first catalogue of a picture collection to be printed and illustrated (*see* CATALOGUE, §2). The Archduke owned 517 Italian Old Master pictures, which were hung frame to frame from cornice to floor, in the manner revealed by other picture gallery views of this date. Such paintings show that the colour of the walls (where visible) was usually a neutral grey, brown or umber. Even the greatest masterpieces were often hung high on the wall and were taken down to be viewed on an easel or simply propped up against a chair. Leopold William and other collectors of High Renaissance pictures tended to group them together, though usually not exclusively. Charles I hung his finest Italian pictures in the Privy Lodging Rooms at Whitehall Palace, London. Van Mander (1602) recorded that Emperor Rudolf II had separate galleries for Italian and Northern paintings. Queen Christina of Sweden, having acquired Rudolf's collection by the conquest of Prague in 1648, hung the Italians in the Palazzo Riario, Rome, where she even planned a gallery devoted to Raphael.

In Philip IV's Buen Retiro Palace, Madrid (completed 1633; furnished 1633–40) there were 'more pictures than walls' according to an astonished French visitor in 1667. Some attempt was made to group paintings by subject (there were galleries of portraits and of identically sized landscapes), but the scale of the palace demanded the usual miscellany, hung thickly and symmetrically in 'rich uniform frames'. At least one gallery was painted red, the grandly furnished rooms being linked together *en enfilade*.

3. *c.* 1700–*c.* 1870.

(i) Symmetrical arrangement and wall colour. (ii) Framing and uniformity. (iii) Arrangement by school.

(i) Symmetrical arrangement and wall colour. Fashions in picture hanging came and went from the late 16th century onwards, the tide ebbing and flowing between fullness and sparseness. The 16th- and 17th-century French and Italian fashion for placing pictures in fixed positions within an architectural framework of plaster ornament was revived by Robert Adam in late 18th-century England (e.g. at Kedleston Hall, Derbys, NT, begun 1760) and re-emerged in the late 19th century. The 17th-century northern European preference for carpeting the wall persisted in auction houses and academy exhibitions. This method was taken up at the Royal Academy, London, and by the Académie Royale de Peinture et de Sculpture, Paris, to fulfil the requirement for the easy distribution of large numbers of pictures (*see* LONDON, fig. 20, and EXHIBITION, fig. 3). The shelf dividing the wall in two was the 'line' immediately below which it was desirable to have one's pictures hung and above which they tended to be 'skied' (rendered less visible). This style of hanging also continued in public and private galleries, especially in

5. *Sir John Murray's Art Gallery* by Pieter Christoffel Wonder, oil on canvas, 1.68×2.20 m, 1830 (England, private collection)

northern Europe, but after *c.* 1750 pictures were usually hung less thickly, though still in profusion. A many-tiered symmetrical arrangement, derived from Italian galleries such as the Uffizi and Pitti in Florence, was the norm in Europe until the mid-19th century. Pieter Christoffel Wonder's painting *Sir John Murray's Art Gallery* (1830; priv. col.; see fig. 5) shows a group of English collectors in an imaginary gallery and illustrates the lasting influence of the Italian tradition of picture hanging and gallery decoration. By contrast, the Prince Regent, later King George IV, hung Dutch pictures singly, one to a panel, in the Blue Velvet Room (1811) at Carlton House, London.

In the 18th and 19th centuries red became the standard colour for picture rooms and galleries in northern Europe, a tradition derived from Italy. Gustav Friedrich Waagen, the chronicler of English collections, repeatedly (1838, 1854, 1857) praised the use of red rooms for pictures; notable examples include the staterooms at Holkham Hall (begun 1734), Norfolk, in silk and velvet damask, Uppark, W. Sussex (damask flock wallpaper *c.* 1750, renewed in 1851 or 1859) and Felbrigg Hall, Norfolk ('flower'd red paper' in the Great Parlour and red silk damask in the adjoining cabinet; both supplied in 1751). Toplit 19th-century private galleries were almost invariably painted red (e.g. Grosvenor House (1807–8), London, by William Porden and Attingham Park (1807–10), Salop, by John Nash (i)), as were public galleries (e.g. Dulwich Picture

Gallery). Red was the usual colour in 19th-century continental picture galleries, as in Leo von Klenze's Alte Pinakothek (1825–36), Munich. In 1826 Karl Friedrich Schinkel, impressed by the red silk hangings of the Palazzo Pitti in Florence, rejected 'grey half-tones, which injure the depth of paintings' and hung the picture galleries of the Altes Museum (1823–30), Berlin, with dark-red wall-paper. Green was an early alternative to red, for example in the Green Closet, Ham House, London, the Green Gallery of the Munich Residenz (1733), and in the picture galleries at Osterley Park House (1767) and Dudley House (1850), both in London. Blue was also popular: in 1769 Mrs Parker of Saltram House, Devon, was seeking Genoese 'patterns of blue damask' and wished 'to fix upon the best blue for setting off the pictures'. Johan Zoffany's portrait (1769; Aske Hall, N. Yorks) depicts Sir Lawrence Dundas in his blue-painted London drawing-room hung with Dutch pictures. At Chiswick House (*c.* 1725–9), London, the picture rooms were hung with both red and green velvet. Arthur Wellesley, 1st Duke of Wellington, chose yellow silk damask for the gallery at Apsley House (1828–9), London, ignoring advice that it would not prove a good foil to either pictures or gilding.

(ii) Framing and uniformity. The symmetry that was demanded in picture hanging gave rise in the 16th and 17th centuries not only to a preference for similar frames (usually ebony, ebony with a gold insert or gilt; see fig. 4

above) but also to a requirement for consistency of size (*see* FRAME, §I). The standardization of frames became a commonplace of gallery design. In 1746, for example, Frederick-Augustus II, Elector of Saxony (*reg* 1733–63), placed all his pictures in uniform Rococo frames (which survive in the Gemäldegalerie Alte Meister in Dresden). Paintings were reduced or increased in size or were converted to ovals (which gave a pleasing variety of shape) so that they fitted exactly into a hanging scheme. In the early 18th century about 40% of the pictures in the imperial collections at Vienna and at least a third of the Wittelsbach collection then in the palace of Schleissheim, near Munich, were treated in this way. The view (1714; Nuremberg, Ger. Nmus.) of the Habsburg picture gallery in Prague by Johann Bretschneider (*fl* 1678–1723) shows about 150 pictures hung in perfect symmetry on one wall—a feat that would have been impossible without altering the original sizes of the paintings. Not all collectors subscribed to this fashion. The Elector-Archbishop of Mainz and Prince-Bishop of Bamberg Lothar Franz von Schönborn wrote (after 1715): 'As to taking off much from the good pieces or for the sake of uniformity adding something to them—nobody shall move me to do this, as it is very prejudicial to the pictures and to their painters.' Nonetheless, the Elector's gallery at Pommersfelden, near Bamberg, which he hung personally in August 1715, bore the characteristics of the age, with the pictures hung frame to frame in symmetrical patterns. The engraving (*c.* 1730; Munich, Staatl. Graph. Samml.) by Salomon Kleiner of the gallery shows that each frame was provided with a tablet on the bottom edge. Such tablets (of varied design) became standard in large collections. Usually gilt with black lettering, they record some or all of the following information: the inventory number, the artist's name and the subject of the picture. In the Uffizi, Florence, a public museum since 1737, the dates of birth and death of each painter were added in 1795, and French public collections gradually standardized their labels between 1795 and *c* 1840. However, inventory numbers and other information continued to be painted directly on to the picture surface or frame (e.g. *View of Archduke Leopold William's Gallery* by David Teniers (ii), 1653; Vienna, Ksthist. Mus., no. 9008).

(iii) Arrangement by school. In the course of the 18th century, although pictures continued to be hung symmetrically in tiers, more of the wall was revealed. An exception, harking back to 17th-century Brussels, Antwerp, Vienna and Prague, may be seen in Russian palaces. In the Picture Hall of the Catherine Palace, Pushkin, and in the picture gallery in the palace of Oranienbaum, both interiors of the mid-18th century, the pictures are tightly packed together in the 17th-century manner. However, Russian practice usually corresponded to the less crowded but nonetheless lavish style of hanging depicted in the engravings of the Electoral Gallery of Düsseldorf, established by the Elector John William (*reg* 1690–1716) in the early 18th century. The catalogue (1778) shows that the pictures were hung symmetrically in tiers but not frame to frame, in fine, purpose-built rooms with sidelighting. A new development was their arrangement according to school: Italian, Dutch and Flemish pictures were hung separately, rather than

intermingled. Arrangement by school and according to date (a commonplace of museums since the mid-19th century) became increasingly fashionable. In Madrid in 1775 Anton Raphael Mengs regretted that the Spanish royal collections were not arranged in this way and that they were scattered about the various palaces rather than united in a single gallery. By 1796 the English patron and collector Frederick Augustus Hervey, Bishop of Derry and 4th Earl of Bristol, intended to arrange his pictures at Ickworth, Suffolk, to show the historical progress of painting.

In Florence, Naples and the states of Germany a more systematic approach to display was joined with a feeling that works of art should be more easily available to the public. Between 1776 and 1778 in Vienna the imperial Habsburg collections were moved from the Stallburg and hung in the Upper Belvedere according to school and with a catalogue (1783) by Christian von Mechel, who intended the pictures to be educational. The dismantling of the Stallburg gallery in the Vienna Residenz, arranged on 17th-century lines by Emperor Charles VI between 1720 and 1728, led to criticism. This was possibly the most elaborate of uniform displays, with identically framed pictures fitted into a decorative scheme (see 3 vol. illus. inv. by A. Storffer, 1720, pp. 30, 33; Vienna, Ksthist. Mus.). Those who preferred the old style of rigidly symmetrical hanging spoke of the 'murder of the gallery'. With the increasing public reverence paid to works of art and the wider establishment of museums, the principles behind the changes in Vienna gained a broader currency. The Louvre, greatly enriched by Napoleon's conquests, was hung according to chronology and school by its Director, Vivant Denon. This classification was not rigidly adhered to, however, when grandeur could be achieved by mingling the schools. Thus the Grande Galerie (toplit after 1808 to provide more hanging space for looted masterpieces) was hung with altarpieces and portraits by the great Italians and by Rubens. The pictures were provided with matching plain 'gallery' frames. The smaller altarpieces were double-hung, and the top edges of all the frames covered the cornice of the gallery, as seen in Benjamin Zix's drawing of the *Marriage Procession of Napoleon, 2 April 1810* (Sèvres, Mus. N. Cér.).

Schinkel's Altes Museum (1823–30) in Berlin was one of the first buildings specifically designed for the public display of works of art to be arranged according to medium, period and place of origin (*see* SCHINKEL, KARL FRIEDRICH). In most private houses with large collections of pictures, the schools were not segregated. At Petworth House, W. Sussex, for example, the 700 paintings were hung thickly even in the bedrooms, and the effect was of an 'immensity of pictures' throughout the house. Most of the modern English pictures of George Wyndham, the 3rd Earl of Egremont, were, however, grouped together in the North Gallery (enlarged 1824–7), where they were displayed with antique and modern sculpture. Sir Richard Colt-Hoare (1758–1838) arranged his collection at Stourhead, Wilts, more rigorously, separating (to a great extent) portraits, landscapes, Old Masters, British pictures and works on paper. This was also the practice of the 1st Earl of Leicester at Holkham Hall, Norfolk, in the mid-18th century.

The National Gallery in London (founded 1824) was at first too small for the pictures to be arranged systematically. Consequently, they were crowded together, frames touching, as shown in the watercolour *The National Gallery* (London, V&A) by Frederick Mackenzie (1787–1854). It was not until 1853 that the National Gallery determined to classify its pictures according to schools. This went in tandem with the rising conception of the gallery's educational purpose and its duty to put together a comprehensive collection. By 1857 the early Italian pictures had a room of their own, and the gradual extension of the gallery in the 1860s and 1870s allowed the finer pictures to be seen at eye level, 'generally with a small margin of wall between them'. This was in accordance with the views of Gustav Friedrich Waagen, who stressed in his paper *Thoughts on the New Building for the National Gallery* (1853) the need for space between pictures so that their effect was 'heightened, and these intervals must be wider or narrower according to the artistic value and requirement of the pictures'. He also insisted that large paintings should be no more than 4.5 m from the ground and small ones no more than 1.8 m: 'If pictures are hung higher than this, they have a merely decorative value.' The Director of the gallery, Sir Charles Lock Eastlake, wished the pictures to allow individual study rather than being melded together in a crowded hang. Nonetheless, the 20th-century norm of single rows of widely spaced pictures was intended by neither Waagen nor Eastlake. In 1856 the Syndics of the Fitzwilliam Museum, Cambridge, stated that the symmetrical and decorative arrangement hitherto traditional in Europe 'was absolutely essential in a large collection in order that its general aspect may give that pleasure to the eye which the pictures are capable of affording'.

4. AFTER *c.* 1870. By 1887, however, pictures were hung in a single line in many rooms in the National Gallery (and in the galleries in Vienna and elsewhere on the Continent), and a spare hang was thereafter considered desirable. The idea that paintings should be appreciated as individual works of art derived from the Aesthetic Movement, which by the 1870s was thinning out the clutter of Victorian drawing-rooms. Whistler's influential one-man exhibitions (from 1874) encouraged this view. The traditional multi-tiered hang (pejoratively christened 'the usual patchwork quilt' by Coutts Lindsay, founder of the Grosvenor Gallery in London) was soon discarded altogether. The great size and height of earlier galleries became an embarrassment. By 1900 at the Bowes Museum in Barnard Castle and at the City of Birmingham Art Gallery (both founded 1867), the upper parts of the walls were painted a lighter colour than the lower parts in an attempt to reduce the apparent height of the ceilings. Between 1945 and 1980 false ceilings and walls were installed in numerous museums to create smaller spaces suitable for a single row of pictures and to obliterate the architecture designed for more spacious display.

In the 20th century the traditional background colours for the display of pictures—red and green, particularly the former—were supplanted by more neutral whites, umbers and greys. Damask was replaced by hessian or paper. This change of heart again derived from the Aesthetic Movement. Edward Burne-Jones, for example, objected to the red silk damask of the Grosvenor Gallery (opened 1877), declaring that 'both red and green are far too strong', sucking 'all the colour out of pictures'. After World War I green and red were painted over in the National Gallery and the Fitzwilliam Museum. Light coloured backgrounds became the norm.

The idea that picture galleries should be 'palaces of art' and decorated accordingly returned to favour in the latter part of the 20th century. The rehanging and redecoration on traditional lines of the National Galleries of Scotland and the Dulwich Picture Gallery in the 1980s began the trend. Even the National Gallery in London, one of the galleries most badly served by mid-20th-century alterations, was redecorated and rehung in the early 1990s. This rediscovery of traditional values of display was the result of an increasing scholarly interest in the history of the presentation of pictures. In England it derived to a great extent from the Victoria and Albert Museum's and the National Trust's research into, and presentation of, country and town-house interiors. The partial re-creation in 1980 by the Victoria and Albert Museum of the arrangement of pictures of Arthur Wellesley, the 1st Duke of Wellington, in the gallery at Apsley House, London, was an important precedent. The survival of traditional arrangements of pictures in country houses and elsewhere, for example in the Colonna and Doria-Pamphili galleries in Rome and in the Corsini and Pitti palaces in Florence, has been significant.

The display of old pictures in a modern setting presents specific problems. For example, the Clore Gallery extension (1980–85) to the Tate Gallery, designed by James Stirling to house the Turner bequest, would have been more suitable for the Tate's modern collection, which is still ill at ease in the Victorian galleries. Whereas the Turner galleries of 1910 were hung in 'rich patterned silk crimson damask' with *verde antico* skirting and white-and-gold ceilings, the pictures were at first hung in the new extension on a neutral oatmeal hessian, a choice that seemed curious when Turner himself favoured a red background for his paintings (as in his own picture gallery, *c.* 1816–22). The Sainsbury Wing (1987–91) of the National Gallery, London, by Venturi, Rauch and Scott Brown is more securely founded on the tradition of toplit gallery and church architecture.

Museums such as the Solomon R. Guggenheim Museum (1957–60), New York, by Frank Lloyd Wright were designed to display modern art in an innovative manner. Certain kinds of 20th-century works were painted expressly for museums, being too large for domestic use. The settings designed for them are intentionally neutral, eschewing ornament and strong colours; white is the usual background. Such galleries as the Saatchi Gallery (1984), London, are strongly lit warehouse spaces, inspired by the modernist aesthetic of the Bauhaus. Despite the emphasis on the autonomy of the work of art and thus its implied independence of setting, many 20th-century painters took a keen interest in the way their pictures were displayed. Mondrian wished his Neo-Plasticist paintings to be hung in rooms designed according to De Stijl precepts. He also rejected the use of frames, as this would prevent the visual expansion of pictures beyond their physical limits into the wall space, an expansion that he saw as infinite. The association perceived between painting and music by such artists as Kandinsky led to the idea of looking at a painting while listening to appropriate music (*see also* SOUND AND ART). Duncan Grant's *Abstract Kinetic Collage Painting* (1914; London, Tate), for example, was intended to be viewed in motion while music by J. S. Bach was played. Mark Rothko was greatly concerned about the hanging of his works, fearing that an insensitive display would make them appear merely decorative. Ideally, he wished his paintings to fill an entire room and to be illuminated by indirect light. He therefore refused to allow the series (London, Tate) commissioned in 1958 for the Four Seasons Restaurant of the Seagram Building in New York to be displayed in its intended location, as he deemed the surroundings to be inappropriate. The fact that some 20th-century painters have made the mode of execution almost as important as the finished product led to the act of painting itself becoming an object of display (*see* PROCESS ART). Yves Klein, for example, invited spectators to witness the 'painting' of his *Anthropometries* (1960), which involved paint-smeared, naked women pressing their bodies against paper while his 'Symphonie Monoton' was played by an orchestra.

III. Sculpture.

1. Before *c.* 1500. 2. *c.* 1500–*c.* 1700. 3. After *c.* 1700.

1. BEFORE *c.* 1500. Temples, public buildings and monuments in Greece and Rome contained free-standing or relief sculpture. The Greek temple was designed as a showcase for the image of the god within it. Once there was an art market (as in ancient Rome), earlier religious and public works of art became artefacts admired for their beauty and acquired for private settings. Religious architecture was subsequently adapted for the secular display of sculpture. Thus the sculpture gallery imitated the characteristics of Greek and Roman temples—the porticos and atria adorned with sculpted ornament, the halls of columns and niches within which sculpture was set on plinths.

In Greece public and religious sculpture was designed to be clearly seen: Praxiteles' *Aphrodite of Knidos* (369–364 BC; copy, Rome, Vatican, Mus. Pio-Clementino; for illustration *see* KNIDOS) was placed in a little temple open on all sides 'so that the beauties of the statue may be seen from every point of view' (Pliny's *Natural History*, XXXVI.iv). The cella of the Parthenon (*see* ATHENS, §II, 1(i)(b)) had an interior two-storey colonnade designed for viewing Pheidias' chryselephantine *Athena Parthenos* (446–438 BC; destr.) from every angle. By the end of the 4th century BC there is evidence of the collecting of earlier sculpture, and by *c.* 170 BC Eumenes II of Pergamon (*reg* 197–160 BC) had created a museum.

Roman collectors eagerly sought Greek statues, and their opportunities increased when Greece became part of the Empire in 146 BC. Pliny wrote of the 'vast multitude' of Greek statues in Rome (*Natural History*, XXXVI.iv). According to Pausanius (*Guide to Greece*, X) Nero looted 500 bronze statues from Delphi; his collection was arranged in the reception rooms of the Domus Aurea in Rome (Pliny's *Natural History*, XXXIV.xix). The emperor

Titus set up the *Laokoon* (Rome, Vatican, Mus. Pio-Clementino; *see* ROME, ANCIENT, fig. 59) in a niche within his palace in Rome. According to Samuel Rogers (1814), the niche and its surroundings were painted vermilion; this may have set a precedent, given the enduring use of red as a foil for both pictures and sculpture. Pliny recorded that the ancient Romans placed sculpted portraits of their ancestors in the atria and on the façades of their houses (*Natural History*, XXXV.ii). Asinius Pollio (76 BC–AD 4) was the first to adapt the custom (*c.* 39–28 BC) for the decoration of libraries with images of famous authors and philosophers (Pliny's *Natural History*, XXXV.ii)—a tradition that was particularly long-lasting, being a standard feature of 18th-century interior decoration, for example. The choice of appropriate subject-matter was important. Cicero used the figures of Mercury and Minerva, symbolizing eloquence and wisdom, in the decoration of the library, study and meeting hall at his villa in Tusculum. Greek and Roman sculpture was sometimes designed in pairs, revealing a taste for complementary if not entirely identical statues that could be placed symmetrically, as in the *Furietti Centaurs* (Rome, Mus. Capitolino) and, on a monumental scale, the *Dioscuri* in the Piazza del Quirinale, Rome.

The gardens of the emperor Hadrian's vast residence near Tivoli (AD 118–25) were filled with temples in the Greek and Egyptian styles designed as settings for the Imperial collection of ancient and contemporary sculpture. Pools were surrounded by open colonnades within which statues were placed so that they were reflected in the water. Marble with a high crystalline content, which reflected the light from the sky and water, was favoured for garden statuary. At the Pantheon (AD 118–28) in Rome, also constructed by Hadrian, statues of gods were displayed in marbled niches. Its original design—a rotunda toplit by an oculus—and its survival made it the most influential of Roman interiors designed for the display of sculpture.

2. *c.* 1500–*c.* 1700.

(i) Revival of antique concepts and the *studiolo*. (ii) The sculpture gallery. (iii) The restoration of antique sculpture and the Roman villa. (iv) The spread of Italian ideas of display in Europe.

(i) Revival of antique concepts and the studiolo. The ancient Roman practice of placing sculpture in atria and outdoors was revived in 15th-century Italy (*see* ROME, §VII, 2). Just as the ancient Romans had displayed ancestral portraits to emphasize their lineage, so the Florentine Poggio Bracciolini argued that humanists could demonstrate their nobility of spirit by acquiring ancient sculpture. The courtyard, being the public entrance to the house, was the ideal place for its display. The most significant event for the future display of sculpture was the construction (completed 1506) by Bramante of niches in the Cortile del Belvedere of the Vatican for Julius II. From his garden of antiquities near S Pietro in Vincoli the Pope brought the *Apollo Belvedere* (Rome, Vatican, Mus. Pio-Clementino), and other statues, for example the *Laokoon*, were gradually housed in adjacent niches. As recorded in a drawing (Madrid, Escorial, Bib. Monasterio S Lorenzo) by Francisco de Holanda, the niches were round-headed with *trompe l'oeil* trellis decoration in the arches. In the centre

of the courtyard were the huge *Tiber* (Paris, Louvre) and *Nile* (Rome, Vatican, Braccio Nuo.) statues as centrepieces of fountains that watered orange trees set in rows.

In Rome during the first half of the 16th century there were about 30 other collections of Greco-Roman statues. Maarten van Heemskerck's sketchbook (Berlin, Kupferstichkab.) records that they were usually displayed (sometimes in a fragmentary state) in courtyards and loggias. Works by contemporary sculptors were sometimes included in such collections, just as Donatello's *Judith* (Florence, Pal. Vecchio) was displayed (*c.* 1456–94) with the antique sculpture in the garden of the Palazzo Medici, Florence (now Palazzo Medici–Riccardi). Michelangelo's *Bacchus* (Florence, Bargello) is shown among Greek, Roman and Egyptian antiquities in the garden in Rome of the banker Jacopo Galli in a drawing (1532–5; Berlin, Kupferstichkab.) by Maarten van Heemskerck. It was often assumed to be antique.

Whereas most medieval sculpture had been devotional, Renaissance statuettes were intended to be handled, looked at from every angle and displayed in *studioli*. In 1504 the *studiolo* of Isabella d'Este, Marchesa of Mantua, in Mantua contained statuettes as well as other *cose antiche*. Classical antiquities—statuettes, marble busts, coins, vases, spearheads—became obligatory for such small rooms, where they were displayed in a coherent manner alongside similar objects of more recent manufacture—maiolica, glass, porcelain and statuary, as well as paintings. For the *studiolo* (1570–75) of Francesco I, Grand Duke of Tuscany, in the Palazzo Vecchio, Florence, its designer, Vasari, recommended that the statuettes be displayed on a shelf supported by pilasters at cornice height, but they were actually placed in niches between paintings. Giambologna's *Apollo* (1572–5; Florence, Pal. Vecchio) was provided with a mechanism so that it could be revolved within its niche and seen in the round.

The use of shelves at shoulder height for the display of sculpture and antiquities was characteristic of both small and large rooms in the 16th and 17th centuries. A sculpture shelf, punctuated by separate consoles supporting statues by Giambologna, encompassed the octagonal Tribuna (designed *c.* 1580) of the Uffizi, Florence. Statuettes of Classical design were also used as overdoors, as seen in Vittore Carpaccio's *Dream of St Ursula* (*c.* 1490; Venice, Accad.) and Girolamo da Santacroce's *Birth of the Virgin* (Padua, Scu. Carmine). Portrait busts were similarly displayed. Vasari recorded the custom 'of doing inexpensive casts of those who died; and so one can see in every house in Florence, over the chimney-pieces, doors, windows and cornices, endless examples of such portraits'. It was probably not until after *c.* 1500 that special pedestals, in imitation of ancient Roman practice, were made to support busts at eye-level.

(ii) The sculpture gallery. The sculpture gallery appears to have been a French invention, albeit derived from the ancient Roman and Italian concept of a loggia or arcade with one side open to the elements; an example at the château of Gallon was recorded in 1510. According to Benvenuto Cellini, the Galerie François I (*c.* 1533–40) at Fontainebleau contained sculpture, including bronzes after the Antique displayed on pedestals. In *c.* 1574 Francesco

I determined to create two separate galleries for sculpture and pictures in the Uffizi. The sculpture gallery, shown in an early 18th-century view (Florence, Uffizi) by Benedetto de Greyss (*b* 1714), was situated in the glazed loggia running around the top storey of the courtyard. Although portraits were hung in a long line between the windows and beneath the cornice, and the ceiling was decorated with grotesques, the effect was of serried ranks of statues interspersed with pairs of busts, all on shoulder-high plinths. This rich and ordered symmetrical arrangement became typical of the display of sculpture in the 17th and 18th centuries.

Symmetry could not be achieved quite so precisely with sculpture as with paintings, which could be reduced or increased in size and given identical frames. Nevertheless, as in the Tribuna or the galleries of the Uffizi, sculpture was placed according to size and subject-matter, thereby forming an essential element of the architecture of display. The symmetrical placing of busts or full-length statues in niches was an early characteristic of sculpture galleries. The Galleria degli Stucchi (1559) of the Palazzo Capodiferro–Spada, possibly the earliest gallery in a Roman palace, contains antique busts in round niches framed (as at Fontainebleau) by stucco figures. The Galleria Arco Farnese (1597–1604), Rome, has two registers of sculpture niches.

(iii) The restoration of antique sculpture and the Roman villa. The symmetrical display of antique sculpture dictated a preference for figures standing upright and a prejudice against bending or crouching subjects, which would interrupt the horizontal line of a row of statues. This desire for harmony led to the restoration of antique sculpture: torsos, limbs and heads were made or put together to create complete figures out of antique fragments. Such restoration was first carried out in the mid-15th century and became common practice in the course of the 16th century. Some famous fragments (e.g. Rome, Musei Vaticani) were never restored, and the sculpture galleries of Charles I were full of fragmentary figures, but by *c.* 1750 English collectors 'had no value for statues without heads' and Francis Russell, Marquess of Tavistock (1739–67) declared that he would not give a guinea 'for the finest torso ever discovered'. The acquisition of original antique sculpture was usually the prerogative of the great Italian collectors, at least until the 18th century. It was mainly in Italy, for example, that often important antique pieces were used to embellish façades. The niches of the garden façade of the Palazzo Medici, Florence (now Palazzo Medici–Riccardi), contained full-length statues (*c.* 1460–94). In Rome the garden façade of the Villa Medici was inlaid with ancient bas-reliefs (after 1584), an arrangement emulated at the Borghese (see fig. 6), Pamphili and Giustiniani villas. The Villa Medici was designed as a setting for ancient sculpture, which was displayed indoors in the sculpture gallery (completed 1584) and in garden pavilions and parterres. In such gardens, niches, balustrades, orangeries, temples, fountains and grottoes were ornamented with a profusion of antique and contemporary works. The layout was symmetrical, clipped shrubs and trees were placed in pots and tubs to enhance the sense of order, and hedges were cut to form niches for statuary (as at the Villa Borghese,

6. Villa Borghese, Rome; etching from Giovanni Battista Piranesi: *Varie vedute di Roma* (Rome, 1748)

1617–19). A sloping site was often chosen to enhance the effect of a villa rising above terraces of statuary, as at the Villa Aldobrandini (*c.* 1600) and other villas at Frascati.

(iv) The spread of Italian ideas of display in Europe. The Italian style of formal gardening was adopted in Spain, France and the Netherlands, whence it spread to England, Russia and other northern countries. Most of the statuary displayed in palatial gardens was contemporary (e.g. the fountain groups at Versailles, Het Loo and Aranjuez), but the sheer number of statues required to punctuate the vistas dictated the widespread use of copies after the Antique. Italian principles were also adopted for the display of sculpture in palatial and domestic interiors throughout Europe. The most complete late 16th-century Italianate sculpture gallery in northern Europe is Albert V's Antiquarium (1568–*c.* 1571) in the Residenz in Munich. Three tiers of busts interspersed with full-length statues in niches flank a long, groin-vaulted gallery painted in the antiquarian style of Raphael's Vatican loggias.

There are numerous Flemish paintings from the late 16th century onwards that illustrate the display of sculpture. The cabinet of Nicolaas Rockox, painted by Frans Francken (ii) (*c.* 1635; Munich, Alte Pin.; *see* FRANCKEN, (5), fig. 1), indicates Italian influence in the Roman Imperial bust over the door and statuettes on the mantelpiece and on a table strewn with curiosities. A shelf at head height supports Classical busts between two rows of pictures. Rubens's buff-coloured apsidal sculpture gallery (*c.* 1618) may be depicted in van Haecht's *Alexander the Great Visiting the Studio of Apelles* (see fig. 4 above). Here,

the sculpture was placed in niches; pictures had a separate gallery, and the remaining pictures and statues were dispersed elsewhere within Rubens's house in Antwerp. The engraving (1659; for illustration *see* MAZARIN, (1)) of Cardinal Jules Mazarin's upper gallery in the Palais Mazarin, Paris (now Hôtel de Chevry-Tubeuf), by Robert Nanteuil and François Chauveau reveals Italian influence both in the decoration (ceiling paintings (1646–8) by Giovanni Francesco Romanelli) and in the symmetrical arrangement of the statues on pedestals and in niches (decorated with landscapes (1644–50) by Giovanni Francesco Grimaldi). Although the emphasis was on sculpture, the gallery also contained pictures and cabinets for small works of art. At Versailles the Galerie des Glaces by Jules Hardouin Mansart and Charles Le Brun (begun 1678) contained statues in niches and busts on silver tables. The mirrors (in several rooms) multiplied the viewpoint of sculpture, and a variety of different marbles in panels in the walls provided the richest of settings. Here the most obvious influence was the gallery of the Palazzo Colonna (1654–1703), Rome. The engravings (1709; Oxford, Bodleian Lib.) by Charpentier and Chevallier of an ideal arrangement of the bronze statuettes belonging to François Girardon show that symmetrical profusion was a fundamental aim of French display.

Thomas Howard, 2nd Earl of Arundel, was portrayed by Daniel Mijtens I (*c.* 1618; *see* LONDON, fig. 16) in a grey gallery with two ranks of full-length antique statues placed at regular intervals on grey pedestals against the walls. The pair to this portrait (both London, N.P.G., on loan to Arundel Castle, W. Sussex) shows Arundel's wife seated in a brown picture gallery. According to Henry Peacham (1634), Arundel's collection of antiquities was the first in England, the statuary being divided in Italian fashion between the garden and galleries of Arundel House. George Villiers, 1st Duke of Buckingham, acquired a collection of antique statuary from Rubens in 1627 and placed it in 'galleries and rooms' in his house in London where the garden contained Giambologna's *Samson and the Philistine* (*c*. 1566; London, V&A). This statue was a gift from Charles I, whose large collection of antique and modern statuary was similarly displayed in galleries, cabinets and gardens, often among a profusion of pictures, as in the cabinets at Whitehall Palace, London, where, in 1639, bronze statuettes and reliefs were placed on ebony plinths or in black frames. Until the demise of the great London house in the 20th century, the finest statues and pictures were often displayed in the capital to augment a family's prestige rather than in a less accessible country seat.

3. After *c*. 1700.

(i) Development of traditional ideas. (ii) Other developments.

(i) Development of traditional ideas.

(a) Italy. In the 18th century the increasing availability of casts and restored originals, the publication of engravings and above all the popularity of the Grand Tour brought the appreciation of statuary to a wider audience and further disseminated Italian concepts of display. In Rome, concern about the illegal export of antique statues led to Pope Clement XII's purchase (1733–4) of the second collection of Cardinal Alessandro Albani and its installation in a new museum on the Capitol. Successive popes bought regularly for the Museo Capitolino (completed 1740), and the style of display established there, at the Museo Pio-Clementino (1771–93) in the Vatican and in such private collections as the Albani and Borghese set a standard for the rest of Europe.

As well as being placed on plinths, Classical statuary was also displayed in symmetrical patterns on the wall. As in picture hanging, smaller pieces were grouped around a large centrepiece. Though this style of display is most familiar from the publications of Piranesi, whose own museum of antiquities was arranged symmetrically, it has a longer pedigree, as is shown by a set of drawings (*c*. 1700–20; Florence, Uffizi) of the sculpture rooms of the Uffizi. Here, as in a Roman triumphal arch, reliefs were set into the walls, flanked by busts and statuettes on brackets. At the base a line of antique sarcophagi supported funerary urns and monuments. This *horror vacui* remained a characteristic of 18th-century museum displays and was reinterpreted by John Soane in his house (*see* §(c) below) in the early 19th century.

In the Museo Capitolino the statues are deployed according to size and subject-matter, the portrait busts being placed in rows in the Sala degli Imperatori on two tiers of shelves (the lower set forward). The walls above were inset with reliefs arranged symmetrically. The architecture is Neo-classical, with the aim of creating rooms redolent of Roman antiquity. The Museo Pio-Clementino (1771–93) was designed along similar lines to incorporate

the Cortile del Belvedere of Julius II. Rooms of busts, animals, muses, vases and candelabra were arranged by category. A rotunda, modelled on the Pantheon and paved with mosaic, displayed full-length statues in niches, originally painted grey, but repainted Pompeian red *c*. 1860 (see fig. 2 above and *see* Museum, fig. 4). In the Galleria delle Statue (1772–80) the statues were placed on plinths in long rows against grey walls inset with reliefs and allegorical paintings, certain statues being placed in niches decorated with landscapes. Antonio Asprucci's sculpture galleries at the Villa Borghese (after 1782, for Prince Marcantonio IV Borghese) were even richer (especially as the Baroque ceiling paintings were left intact). Busts and statues of colossal size were placed on great plinths (set with reliefs) at the same height as the dado rail, thus connecting the statuary with the architecture. Busts were placed in niches over the doors, and the walls were covered with decorative grotesques. In the Gran Salone of the Villa Albani (1755–62), Rome, built for Cardinal Alessandro Albani by Carlo Marchionni, the sculpture niches were lined with mirror-glass to reveal the backs of the statues.

(b) Sweden, France and Spain. The influence of these Italian rooms was felt throughout Europe. In Stockholm, Gustav III built a museum of antiquities (1792–4) inspired directly by the Museo Pio-Clementino (see fig. 7). The grand gallery (painted grey as a foil to the white marble) housed full-length statues; the small gallery (also grey with a yellow marble dado) contained a shelf of busts with reliefs above and a line of statues in the centre of the room. A little tomblike antechamber contained Egyptian antiquities, and there were separate rooms for vases, medals and prints. Neo-classical Swedish statuary was later placed alongside the antiques, and ivy was planted in the galleries as a reminder of the link between art and nature. At the Louvre in Paris between 1800 and 1815 the great collection of Classical statuary (much of it looted by Napoleon from Italy) was displayed on the ground-floor on high pedestals—the *Laokoon* was placed in a niche as it had been in Rome. French and Italian Neo-classicism inspired the exquisite small sculpture gallery in the Casita del Labrador, Aranjuez. Built 1803–6 by Isidro González Velásquez to house the collection given to Charles IV by José Nicolás de Azara, the plinths and walls are decorated in coloured marbles, the sculpture niches are painted blue, and the ceiling paintings (1806) are by Zacarías González Velázquez. The façade of the Casita is adorned with antique and Neo-classical busts and statues in the Italian villa tradition.

(c) England and elsewhere. In England before the mid-18th century, sculpture for interiors or gardens was usually modern and was placed in an architectural context (on a bracket over a chimney-piece, in an entrance hall or to punctuate a garden layout). A few collections made in Italy in the 18th century remain in sculpture galleries designed on Italian lines. At Holkham Hall (begun 1734), Norfolk, and Petworth House, W. Sussex, NT, sidelit sculpture galleries were built by Matthew Brettingham (i) in the 1750s. Full-length statues were displayed in niches (and, at Petworth, on green plinths), with busts on brackets set high on the walls, which were painted grey at Holkham

7. *Small Gallery of King Gustav III's Museum of Antiquities, Stockholm* by Pehr Hilleström, oil on canvas, 1796 (Stockholm, Nationalmuseum)

and grey-blue at Petworth. An inventory (1764) and Turner's watercolours (*c.* 1827; London, Tate) reveal that at Petworth sculpture was also distributed throughout the staterooms: on pedestals in the corners of rooms (as in such continental palaces as the Palacio Real, Madrid) and on pier tables. The Petworth Gallery was extended (1824–7) to accommodate Neo-classical statues and pictures (by Flaxman, Turner and their contemporaries) alongside the antique sculpture. It was then painted white but was red by *c.* 1865.

The collections of CHARLES TOWNLEY, Thomas Hope and JOHN SOANE were most influential in terms of their display. Townley transformed his house in London into a setting for his collection of antique sculpture, which was acquired by the British Museum, London. An idealized view of its arrangement (1781–3; Burnley, Towneley Hall A.G. & Mus.; *see* ZOFFANY, JOHAN, fig. 2) shows a symmetrical disposition of reliefs and free-standing sculpture on a blue ground in a toplit drawing-room. In reality the sculpture was set against Pompeian red and blue marbling.

In Hope's rectangular toplit sculpture gallery at his house in Duchess Street (1799–1804), London, the statues were arranged in rows on either side, the yellow walls being left plain to concentrate attention 'on the contours of more important works of art'. This Neo-classical purity, with every detail of the room suggestive of an ancient

setting, was applied also to the rooms of antiquities, which were given Roman names: lararium (for statuettes; originally of *lares*, household gods), columbarium (for urns ranged 'in recesses' as in Roman tombs). Egyptian statuary was placed in a 'canopus' in the Egyptian style. In the new wing at the Deepdene (1823; destr.), Surrey, Hope had four sculpture galleries, two for ancient and two for Neo-classical sculpture, although their segregation was less exclusive than at Duchess Street. The main gallery was painted buff, and the pedestals of the statues incorporated round-headed niches containing Greek vases or antique fragments. In the Theatre of the Arts at the Deepdene, based on the semicircular plan of a Roman theatre, busts and cinerary urns were set in two tiers beneath five niches, the floor being set with mosaic from Hadrian's villa, Rome. A watercolour (1826; London, Lambeth Archvs Dept, Minet Lib.), one of a set by Penry Williams (1798–1885), shows the room open to the garden, indicative of Hope's interest in the juxtaposition of art and nature. In the Orangery and Sculpture Gallery a marble copy of the colossal *Jason* (Copenhagen, Thorvaldsens Mus.) by Thorvaldsen was placed with other statues among orange trees. A conservatory filled with exotic plants linked the different sculpture galleries.

Unlike the buildings of Hope, Soane's house (1792–1824; *see* SOANE, JOHN, fig. 3) in London has survived intact (open as a museum since 1833). Soane was closely influenced by Hope's ideas and those of Charles-Louis Clérisseau, Piranesi and others, but he produced a profoundly individual synthesis of antiquities, casts, curiosities and pictures set in distinctive architectural spaces. However crowded his arrangements, they were designed to balance one another. His grouping of reliefs and fragments recalls the early 18th-century drawings of the Uffizi, with numerous objects being arranged symmetrically in tiers. However, unlike Hope's, the groupings were crowded and eclectic. While Soane suffered from a *horror vacui* and freely mixed works of art and curiosities in the European tradition of the *Kunstkammer*, Hope placed his full-length statues against bare walls as in a Greek temple and aimed to show his collection in rooms decorated to match the individual media or civilizations on display. Soane's collection was more a romantic vision of the past in the manner of Clérisseau's Ruin Room (*c.* 1766) at the Villa Medici in Rome and was pervaded by the spirit of Piranesi's *Invenzioni capric di carceri* (Rome, *c.* 1745–60).

Soane's appreciation of fragmentary antique sculpture became more widespread from the early 19th century onwards. Canova dissuaded Thomas Bruce, 7th Earl of Elgin, from restoring the marble sculptures (London, BM) from the Parthenon in Athens, which he first exhibited in London in 1806, and this view was upheld by British sculptors in 1816. In the presentation of sculpture, Neoclassicism remained the norm in the 19th century. Leo von Klenze's Glyptothek in Munich, built (1816–30) in Greek style for Ludwig I of Bavaria, was intended to convey a sense of reverence for antique sculpture. This was also the aim of Schinkel's Altes Museum (1823–30) in Berlin, where in the Pantheon-like central 'rotunda' the antique statues were placed on high pedestals; people were meant to look up to them. The walls gave the impression of pale grey marble. Klenze's statue galleries (1842–51) in the Hermitage, St Petersburg, and Raffaele Stern's Braccio Nuovo del Vaticano (1817–22), continued this temple-like approach to display based on rigorous symmetry, with reliefs set into the walls, toplighting, coffered ceilings and a unified scheme of decoration. At the Hermitage the pedestals of the statues were painted to match the skirting-board and dado. The sculpture galleries of the British Museum in London, the Fitzwilliam Museum (founded 1816) in Cambridge and the Ashmolean Museum (founded 1839) in Oxford were all designed in the same spirit. The British Museum archives record changing attitudes to colour: the galleries of the new museum (1823–47) by Robert Smirke were at first painted grey. The rediscovery of ancient polychromy, the dirtying of the sculptures by the London smog and a feeling that a darker colour would enhance sculptural contours led to the Elgin Room being painted red by 1839. Most of the other galleries had followed suit by 1850, with polychrome ceilings. This richer style of decoration was approved of by Klenze (on a visit to London in 1853), who had devised polychrome schemes with marble walls for the Glyptothek, Munich, and the Hermitage, St Petersburg. The red survived until *c.* 1930, being replaced by greys, blues, mauves and greens. Private house statue galleries also conformed to the Neo-classical style, even when their contents were somewhat less rigorous in concept. Prince Albert's polychrome gallery by Ludwig Grüner at Osborne House (1845–51), Isle of Wight, and the marbled sculpture hall at Brodsworth, Yorks (*c.* 1866), are examples of the continuing preference to separate sculpture from other works of art in a Neo-classical setting. A 20th-century interpretation of this tradition is the British Museum Duveen Gallery (*c.* 1933–62) by John Russell Pope for the display of the Parthenon sculptures.

(ii) Other developments. Hope's re-creation of ancient interiors as settings for sculpture anticipated the modern museum practice of placing works of art in 'period rooms', as, for example, in the furniture galleries of the Victoria and Albert Museum in London. This approach to display was also anticipated by Alexandre Lenoir (*see* LENOIR, (1)), whose Musée des Monuments Français (opened in 1793) was devoted to the preservation of France's monuments. This was the first museum to display medieval art and to attempt a visual history of a nation chronologically in a series of period interiors. The effect was similar to the architecture and cast courts of the Victoria and Albert Museum. The arrangement of the rooms and the garden recalled Clérisseau's drawings of the Roman catacombs but also looked forward to the medievalizing displays of such museums as the Cloisters, New York, which contains some of Lenoir's material. With the restoration of the Bourbon monarchy, the museum was dispersed and the monuments returned to their original settings. It was felt that religious monuments should not be regarded as works of art but as articles of faith. Thus Quatremère de Quincy, the philosopher of the anti-Lenoir group, declared that the display of medieval sculpture (and particularly sepulchral art) in a museum amounted to 'lack of taste' and 'impiety'. Interest in the Middle Ages increased in the course of the 19th century, and examples of medieval art were again removed from their places of origin to be put on public display. Thus ALEXANDRE DU SOMMERARD, whom Balzac ridiculed as the 'prince du bric-à-brac', created what is now the Musée de Cluny, Paris, opened in 1844. Similar collections were made in Italy (Venice, Correr; Rome, Lateran Pal.), Germany (Munich, Schloss Nymphenburg) and England (London, BM and V&A).

In the 20th century the SCULPTURE GARDEN continued the long tradition of displaying sculpture outdoors. These outdoor sites are sometimes selected for their association with a particular sculptor, as in the sculpture garden near the former studio of Henry Moore at Much Hadham, Herts. Many museums of modern art have also created sculpture gardens.

Much 20th-century sculpture was designed to dominate its surroundings, making a separation of the work and its mode of display difficult. For example, Kurt Schwitters's *Merzbau* (1923–36; destr. 1943; *see* SCHWITTERS, KURT, fig. 2) in Hannover was a proliferating arrangement of Dadaist assemblages and sculptures that gradually took over the interior of the artist's house. Edward Kienholz's tableaux (e.g. *The Beanery*, 1965; Amsterdam, Stedel. Mus.) have a similarly invasive effect, each work consisting of a whole interior constructed by the artist from sculptures and assemblages. This move away from a neat separation of sculpture from its setting was partly the result of a dissatisfaction with the idea of the discrete art object that can be bought and sold easily and that can be found only in the context of a museum or gallery. Greater extremes were reached with the LAND ART of the 1960s onwards, most of which was only accessible through the photographs and documents created by the artist (e.g. Robert Smithson's *Spiral Jetty*, 1970). The INSTALLATION is also, by definition, intended for a single location, unless reconstructed elsewhere by the artist. Inevitably the artist is intimately involved its display.

IV. Drawings, prints and watercolours.

Because of their fugitive nature, drawings were traditionally mounted on the pages of albums (*see also* DRAWING, §V) rather than being on permanent display. Vasari's practice of setting drawings within decorative mounts and arranging them according to artist and school set a standard for subsequent connoisseurs. His *Libro de' disegni* was mounted in at least five volumes, the dimensions of which were recorded by Pierre-Jean Mariette as 610×460 mm. Conceived as a supplement to illustrate his *Vite*, it incorporated engraved portraits of draughtsmen whose drawings were pasted several to a page and arranged decoratively. For example, the engraved portrait of *Filippino Lippi* was placed in the centre of an arrangement of five of his drawings (Oxford, Christ Church). A similar undertaking is represented by the 16 leatherbound volumes of drawings compiled in the 17th century by Sebastiano Resta. In the 17th century, albums and portfolios of drawings were often kept in cabinets or on tables in picture galleries and cabinet rooms, and this tradition was continued by such later collectors as Thomas Hope and William Young Ottley.

Vasari gave his drawings individual mounts with often elaborate architectural designs varying from page to page. More commonly, collectors selected a limited range of patterns and sometimes confined themselves to a single mount design. Drawings were pasted on to heavy paper and bordered with parallel lines of ink or watercolour, usually with coloured washes in between. The junction between drawing and mounting sheet was often marked by a thick gold line. The effect was similar to that of a picture frame. The so-called *Casa Gennari* mounts of drawings by Guercino were applied in the early 18th century, but their distinctive ruled lines have a modern appearance (see Turner 1994, figs 20 and 24); in this case, the mounts were probably made in Italy for the English collector John Bouverie, who acquired the Guercino drawings in the 1740s. Mounts may often be associated with a particular collection and, where they have survived, form an element of a drawing's provenance; unfortunately, many old mounts were removed in the 20th century in the belief that they were extraneous, irrelevant later accretions. Mounts named after collectors include the so-called 'Mariette' and 'Lawrence' mounts.

Prints and drawings were also, of course, framed and hung on the walls, sometimes covered with curtains to protect them from the light. Framed and glazed drawings were listed at Whitehall Palace, London, in 1639. George Vertue published (1758) the arrangement of Holbein drawings by Caroline of Ansbach (1682–1737), George II's queen, in a small, densely hung cabinet room. Prints in particular (being usually less rare) were often hung thickly (*see also* PRINTS, §VII, 1). In the 18th century the fashion for dispensing with wooden frames and mounting prints directly on to the wall or on to a support stretched on battens was catered for by engravers (such as Francis Vivares in England), who supplied borders, masks and ribbons for the decoration of print rooms (a collection of such material is in London, V&A). This practice may have originated in England; certainly there are numerous survivals dating from the 18th century, for example Uppark, W. Sussex (*c.* 1770), Woodhall Park, Herts (1782), Petworth House, W. Sussex (before 1764; destr. *c.* 1800) and elsewhere. The practice then spread throughout Europe as at the Green Cabinet at Rosersborg, Sweden, hung in 1799 with the collection of prints owned by Prince Karl (later Karl XIII, *reg* 1809–18). The effect was of a picture gallery in miniature, the prints being hung symmetrically in tiers. Print rooms were also designed to contain drawings and engravings in matching frames. According to Matthew Brettingham (ii), the Blue Satin Dressing-room at Holkham Hall, Norfolk, was hung with 55 Old Master drawings in 'frames and glasses' together with the Raphael cartoon for *La Belle Jardinière* (Holkham Hall, Norfolk) and a grisaille copy of Michelangelo's *Battle of Cascina*. Princess Elizabeth (daughter of George III) arranged her own drawn copies of Old Master and English engravings in gilt frames and *verre églomisé* mounts in a small room at Frogmore House, Berks, *c.* 1790.

Watercolours were usually displayed like paintings. Watercolours (some by Turner), framed in gold and hung on a red ground, are shown in a painting (1835; London,

8. The Green Closet, Ham House, Richmond, Surrey, 1610; remodelled 1637–9

BM) by John Scarlett Davis of the library of B. G. Windus in London. In the exhibitions of the New Society of Painters in Watercolours, London, watercolours were hung in gold frames on red hangings in a crowded arrangement reminiscent of the Royal Academy, as depicted in a painting (London, V&A) of the exhibition of 1834 by George Scharf (1788–1860).

V. Miniatures, medals, coins and gems.

Miniatures were often worn as sentimental pieces of jewellery mounted as a ring, necklace or brooch. They were also either kept in boxes in cupboards or hung on the wall, usually as the bottom tier of a picture hang, often above and to the sides of a fireplace. This is how miniatures were exhibited at the Royal Academy, London (*see* EXHIBITION, fig. 3). They were usually framed individually in metal, enamel or wood with a ring at top centre for a single pin whose head could be hidden by a decorative bow. Sometimes a group would be mounted together within a larger frame as in 1639 at Whitehall Palace, London (one of two frames survives; Duke of Buccleuch priv. col.). In 1783, in Queen Charlotte's dressing-room at Buckingham House, London, Horace Walpole noted that six large glazed frames, divided into hexagonal compartments, contained 'a vast quantity of enamelled pictures, miniatures and Cameos' on a background of red damask matching the wall hangings (P. Toynbee, ed.: 'Horace Walpole's Journals of Visits to Country Seats, etc', *Walpole Soc.*, xvi (1928), p. 79). When the size of the collection warranted it, miniatures were grouped together in a small cabinet room as at Whitehall Palace in 1639. The collection

of the Dutch stadholders and royal family was displayed in a separate room in successive palaces and was still shown in this way *c.* 1900 at the palace of Kneuterdijk, The Hague. The miniatures of Cardinal Leopoldo de' Medici were kept in a special room in his apartment in the Palazzo Pitti in Florence. Miniatures were often displayed with small oil paintings, statues and other artefacts in such rooms, which were hung on the same principles as picture galleries. Indeed, they were usually sited adjacent to galleries, providing by contrast an intimate and densely hung cabinet. The Green Closet at Ham House, Richmond, Surrey (see fig. 8), with an Italianate painted ceiling, was provided with curtains that ran the length of the wall as a protection against light and dust. The miniatures and small paintings were arranged in decorative patterns on green silk damask so thickly that even the cheeks of the fireplace were used to hang columns of paintings; there were 57 in 1677 and 95 by 1844. Another miniatures cabinet adjacent to a long gallery was at Syon House, Middx, designed (1760–69) by Robert Adam. In Horace Walpole, the 4th Earl of Orford's 'Tribune' at Strawberry Hill, Middx., a pedimented cabinet (1743; London, V&A) in the Palladian style hung above a Gothick chest (like a diptych over an altar) in the apse of the room. An engraving shows that the cabinet was densely packed with miniatures, which were also hung on the backs of the doors.

From at least the early 16th century, when the term 'cabinet' first appeared in France, cabinets were also designed to display medals, coins, jewels and other *objets d'art* and antiquities. Elaborate Florentine ones stood in

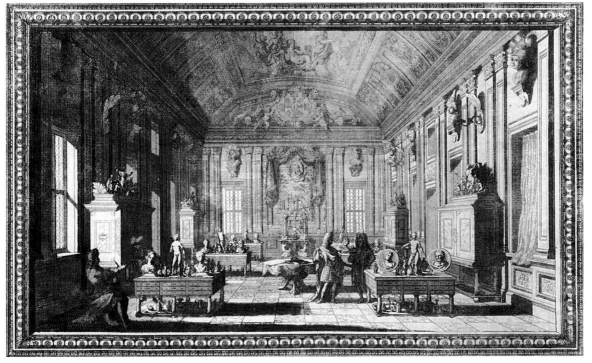

9. *Ideal View of the Cabinet of Antiquities in the Berlin Stadtschloss* by Samuel Blesendorf; engraving from Lorenz Beger: *Thesaurus Brandenburgicus,* i (Cologne, 1696)

the Uffizi Tribuna (1583–6), at Versailles (1683) and in English houses such as Badminton House (1728), Glos, and Stourhead (1742), Wilts, while the Augsburg dealer and designer Philipp Hainhofer supplied versions complete with contents. Cabinets are generally fitted with numerous shallow drawers or trays lined with fabric, for example in the case of the medal cabinet in the form of a temple (*c.* 1765; Blair Castle, Tayside), or black velvet as in the jewel cabinet made by Vile & Cobb for Queen Charlotte, wife of George III (1761; Windsor Castle, Berks, Royal Col.). Medals and gems could also be hung within a cabinet or on open display. Consul Joseph Smith's gems (acquired 1762 by George III; Royal Col.) have uniform gold mounts with a suspension ring. A particularly grand arrangement of cabinets within an elaborate room dedicated to the display of coins, medals, gems, statuettes and antiquities is shown in Samuel Blesendorf's engraving (1696) of the collection of Frederick III, Elector of Brandenburg (see fig. 9).

VI. Ceramics.

It was not until the late 15th century that porcelain came into Europe in any quantity, and until at least the late 16th century it was regarded as sufficiently rare and valuable to be kept in a private place—a study or cabinet of curiosities—often mounted in gold or silver. A 14th-century silver-mounted celadon bowl given to New College, Oxford University, in 1532 by Archbishop William Warham (?1450–1532) was presumably exhibited with the college

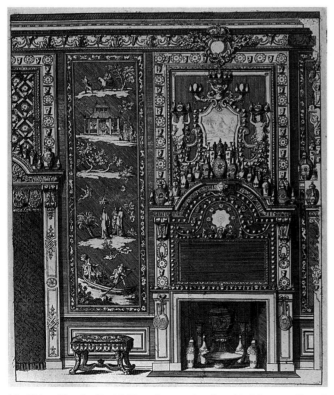

10. *China Closet* by Daniel Marot I; engraving from his *Nouveaux livres de partements*, before 1702 (London, Victoria and Albert Museum)

silver on special occasions. In the 1550s Cosimo I de' Medici kept most of his collection in cupboards in his Guardaroba Secreta in the Palazzo Vecchio, Florence, as did Alvise Odoni (*d* 1555) of Venice. Ferdinand, Count of Tyrol (*reg* 1564–95), owned 233 pieces of porcelain, which were kept in cabinets as part of the great cabinet of curiosities at Schloss Ambras (near Innsbruck). In paintings of domestic interiors (as opposed to galleries), porcelain is shown where one would equally expect to see silver, gold or sculpture: on a buffet or sideboard (Bartholomeus van Bassen: *Interior, c.* 1620; Darmstadt, Hess. Landesmus.), on a chimney-piece (Emanuel de Witte: *Family Group*, 1673; Lewis S. Fry priv. col., see Praz, pl. 98) or along the cornice of a room (Gonzales Coques: *The Visit, c.* 1630; Geneva, Mus. A. & Hist.; *see* NETHERLANDS, THE, fig. 34). In the bedroom of Christian IV (*reg* 1588–1648) at Rosenborg Castle, Copenhagen, were *blanc de chine* figures over the doors, and in his study Arita blue-and-white bottles were displayed over the chimney-piece. Jean Le Pautre's engravings of designs for chimney-pieces (after 1665) depict decorative sets of porcelain (garnitures). Pottery of European manufacture could also be accorded special status; maiolica plates, for example, were designed to make an impact when exhibited upright on a sideboard, and their bold colours and often pictorial compositions were intended to be legible from a distance.

The increasing availability of Chinese and Japanese porcelain in northern Europe in the course of the 17th century led to its display *en masse*, often in conjunction with agates, crystals, bronzes and other richly mounted curiosities, such as in the cabinet at Versailles of the Grand Dauphin, son of Louis XIV, in 1689 (*see* CERAMICS, §II). Already by 1632 porcelain was displayed on shelves in the Oude Hof, Noordeinde, The Hague, the palace of the Dutch stadholder whose widow, Amalia von Solms, owned numerous pieces. The 65 pieces in Charles I's collection at Somerset House, London, in 1649 were probably displayed on hanging shelves of turned gilt-wood. Similar shelves survive in the collection at Drayton House, Northants, and are depicted in such paintings as Jan Josef Horemans the elder's *Interior in Antwerp* (1716; Amsterdam, Ksthand. Schlichte Bergen).

The plan in 1684 to display Louis XIV's collection of hardstone vessels at Versailles on brackets in symmetrical, multi-tiered patterns with mirror-glass behind seems to have inspired the main characteristics of the style of porcelain display (see fig. 10) associated with Daniel Marot I. He was almost certainly the designer in 1686 of the china closet owned by Queen Mary (later Mary II, Queen of England and Scotland) at Honselaarsdijk, in which the lacquer panelling, mirrored ceiling and massed porcelain clearly corresponded with his engravings of similar rooms. Queen Mary's inventory (1696–7) from Hampton Court, London, lists the arrangement of all sizes of porcelain and Delftware on shelves, overdoors, above the chimney (Marot called a corner fireplace with stepped shelves for porcelain a *cheminée à l'anglaise*), on pedestals (sets of carved walnut pedestals for large porcelain jars survive at Hampton Court and at Petworth House, W. Sussex, NT) and in symmetrical garnitures above and below cabinets and tables. Engravings by Salomon Kleiner and Paul Decker I also disseminated this style of display.

The extravagance of Queen Mary's collection was eclipsed by the splendour of late 17th- and early 18th-century displays of porcelain on the Continent. At Oranienburg, north of Berlin, a room (1688–95) by Christof Pitzler was literally covered in porcelain stacked on the cornice and hung in tiers on the walls. Seven huge giltwood pyramidal *étagères* bore about 100 jars and vases, which were reflected in mirrors behind (see Broebes). At Charlottenburg, Berlin, Johann Friedrich Eosander created *c.* 1705 another extraordinary concoction, again with mirrored walls, with tier upon tier of small bottles on individual brackets flanking larger vases and Chinese figures. Large covered vases stood on pedestals in the corners of the room and in the fireplace. The shapes and colours were gradated to increase the effect of rich and harmonious symmetry (see Merian); it was restored after World War II.

This taste continued into the Rococo and beyond. The Spiegelkabinett at Schloss Weissenstein, Pommersfelden, built in 1719 for the Elector-Archbishop of Mainz and Prince-Bishop of Bamberg, Lothar Franz von Schönborn, has all the characteristics of massed display, with porcelain placed on brackets between mirrors and on the dado and with the woodwork in an airy Rococo style by Ferdinand Plitzner. The taste for profusion was shared by Frederick-Augustus II, King of Poland and Elector of Saxony, whose vast collections of Oriental and Meissen porcelain (*c.* 57,000 pieces) were distributed according to country of origin, subject and colour in the Japanese Palace at Dresden (begun *c.* 1720), built by Matthäus Daniel Pöppelmann and Zacharias Longuelune. Drawings (Dresden, Kupferstichkab.) show the porcelain arranged in tiers. The logical conclusion of this crowded display was to make the walls themselves of porcelain (*see* CABINET (i), §4(i)). Such a room was constructed (1757–9) by Giuseppe Gricci in the royal villa of Portici for Charles VII, King of Naples. Made of 3000 interlocking pieces by the Capodimonte Porcelain Factory in Naples, a similar room (1760–65; *in situ*) was constructed at Aranjuez after Charles succeeded, as Charles III, to the throne of Spain in 1759 and set up the Fábrica del Buen Retiro, near Madrid.

Sèvres, Meissen, Chelsea, Bow and Wedgwood produced sets of ornamental porcelain in colours corresponding to the palette of fashionable decoration (e.g. deep red and blue or basalt in the Neo-classical period). Figurines were also made for the mantelpiece or dining-table (e.g. Meissen's *commedia dell'arte* subjects), and these were displayed as part of a table setting for dessert or on wall brackets—'single figures for brackets' were advertised in 1759. Wedgwood's basalt figures after the Antique, produced from 1769, were displayed on mantelpieces like small bronzes. From the mid-18th century, cabinets (*see* CABINET (ii)) for the display of ceramics were made. Designed for bedrooms and closets, they were often in the Chinese taste (e.g. by Adam at Nostell Priory, W. Yorks, and Osterley Park House, London). Aside from cabinets, Chippendale also engraved 'Stands for China Jarrs'—a Rococo version of the 17th-century stands for large pieces of porcelain.

Ancient Greek and Etruscan pottery was traditionally shown on shelves, bookcases or cabinets (e.g. in the Galleria Clementina, the Museo Pio-Cristiano and the Museo Gregoriano Etrusco of the Vatican). The Roman practice of placing funerary urns in niches in a columbarium appealed to late 18th- and early 19th-century antiquarians. Thomas Hope constructed three columbaria for the display of antique pottery in his house (1799–1804) at Duchess Street, London, and placed Greek vases in niches within the bases of antique statues at the Deepdene (1824–31), Surrey. The display of porcelain formed an important element in the decoration of the interiors created by the Prince Regent (later George IV). His Oriental porcelain was despatched to Brighton Pavilion by 1819, when the last trace of chinoiserie was expunged from Carlton House (1783–1827), London, and with the porcelain went such furniture as the lacquer and gold, mirror-backed display cabinets (1787–90) by Adam Weisweiller. In London, China gave way to Sèvres. The inventories and illustrations of Carlton House show that grand garnitures of Sèvres porcelain elaborately mounted in gold were part of the fixed decoration—unlike smaller items, which were moved round at will—and linked the piece of furniture that supported them with the pictures hanging above. Their colour was adjusted according to the decoration of the room (e.g. blue in the Blue Velvet Room). Sèvres was designed primarily for display: stands and ormolu mounts together with protective glass domes were supplied by the Sèvres factory or by dealers. Even the useful wares—cups and saucers, broth basins etc—were purchased by the nobility at the annual sales in Louis XVI's private apartments at Versailles for display on tables, cabinets and chimney-pieces in Parisian hôtels.

Ceramics were a significant element of mid-19th-century Romantic decoration. At Cotehele House, Cornwall, Tudor sideboards were used once again to display English delftware, maiolica and German stoneware. Oriental porcelains were grouped *en masse* in a manner reminiscent of the late 17th century. Again, the predominant preference was for blue-and-white wares. Rooms were designed by Aesthetic Movement architects (e.g. E. W. Godwin and R. Norman Shaw) or artists and decorators (e.g. Whistler and William Morris) with considerable potential for the display of porcelain. Shelves over fireplaces and doors or above the wainscot were fashionable (e.g. at Wightwick Manor, W. Midlands, NT). In the case of the Peacock Room at 49 Prince's Gate, London, designed by Thomas Jeckyll for F. R. Leyland, the porcelain was housed in shelves that covered the walls, space being left only for Whistler's painting *La Princesse du pays de porcelaine* (1863–4; Washington, DC, Freer) over the chimney. The late 19th- and 20th-century tendency to display collections of porcelain in glazed bookcases or secrétaires rather than in specially designed cases would have appeared unusual to an 18th- or early 19th-century eye used to a more rigid decorum of display.

VII. Plate.

The display of plate was an important element of dining-room decoration. Its intrinsic value, quite apart from its often elaborate design, established the status of its owner. Large pieces were primarily for display, such as the nef placed prominently on the dining-table of Charles, Duc de Berry ('January' from the Très Riches Heures, *c.* 1411/13–16 and *c.* 1485–6; Chantilly, Mus. Condé, MS. 65). On important occasions flamboyant pieces of plate, sometimes in conjunction with other treasures, were piled high on a table set apart from the dining-table itself. A similar effect might be achieved with pewter or pottery. In Italy this table or sideboard was called a *credenza* (Credence table, on which evidence of a family's 'credentials' could be placed), and objects in precious metals were specially made for it. It was often provided with shelves rising from front to back so that the whole array could be clearly seen. The number of shelves could be indicative of rank, and certainly a greater number produced a richer effect. In 15th-century Italy one or two shelves were usual, so the nine tiers set up by the Florentines at a state banquet in 1476 were an exceptional sight. This may have been in allusion to the ancient Roman triumph; Pompey paraded 'enough gold vessels inlaid with gems to fill nine display stands' (Pliny's *Natural History*, XXXVII. vi). Credence tables were usually provided with a rich cloth to set off the metalwork and a *spalliera* or board behind, also elaborately draped (seen, for example, in a drawing by Maso Finaguerra, *Susanna and the Elders, c.* 1460; London, BM). At the court of Louis XIV such buffets attained a particular richness, silver being combined with porcelain and hardstone vessels, as shown in a painting (*c.* 1700; New York, Met.) by François Desportes. This extravagance was emulated in Italy, leading to such creations as the huge sideboard and centrepiece displays of silver shown in two engravings (Bologna, Archv Stato) of banquets in Bologna in 1693 and 1701 by Giacomo Maria Giovannini (1667–1717) and Francesco Antonio Meloni (1676–1713) respectively.

The symmetrical disposition of silver on a sideboard was a feature of Neo-classical dining-rooms. A coloured drawing (*c.* 1762; Kedleston Hall, Derbys) by Robert Adam, for example, shows an arrangement of silver and silver-gilt urns, cisterns, knifeboxes and plates flanking a tripod designed by James Stuart. The Prince Regent (later George IV) laid emphasis on pieces large enough to make an impact. His plate was not only for display on the sideboard or dining-table provided, as in 1814, with a mirrored plateau in the centre to reflect 'exquisite groups in silver-gilt' but was on permanent show in several rooms at Carlton House, London (velvet-covered stands for silver were provided in 1817 for the Gothic Dining-room). The Carlton House Plate Closet was conceived as a museum with plate glass showcases (completed by James Wyatt, *c.* 1812) and was lit by an Argand oil lamp. In 1813 green baize was abandoned in favour of red cloth, which gave a richer effect. The Plate Closet was a veritable *Schatzkammer* containing not only gold and silver but also all kinds of *objets de luxe*, curiosities such as the turban ornament of Tipu Sultan, Sultan of Mysore (*reg* 1782–99), and a multi-purpose pocket-knife (1821) under a glass dome.

Furniture of gold or silver was also made; little has survived, as most was subsequently melted down in times of financial distress. The silver side-tables, pier glasses and stands (1676–81) at Knole, Kent, are rare examples of such royal furniture. At Versailles, the Galerie des Glaces was furnished with silver pier-tables and silver tubs for orange trees. Such furniture would have shimmered in candlelight. In Russia, by contrast, it was considered vulgar and harmful to polish silver furniture or display-plate, which was always left tarnished as in the Kremlin, Moscow, and the Hermitage, St Petersburg.

VIII. Tapestries and carpets.

The nomadic life of the medieval aristocrat conditioned his choice of furnishings. Tapestries, which were easily portable, were displayed as expensive status symbols (*see also* TAPESTRY, §III). They were hung on hooks or rods, sometimes leaving a passage for servants behind, and despite their absorption of cooking smells were hung in dining halls. Sets of tapestries provided consistency in the decoration of a room and provided insulation. In the 17th century, pictures were sometimes replaced by tapestries in the winter: this was done at the Pitti Palace, Florence, and the Buen Retiro Palace, Madrid. They could be commissioned in exact sizes to suit a specific room, or they could be bought and cut to fit. Panelled rooms were designed to display tapestries (e.g. the Tapestry Bedroom at Uppark, W. Sussex, NT, *c.* 1690; destr. 1989).

Tapestries could also be used as wall hangings on which pictures and mirrors were hung. The Long Gallery at Hardwick Hall (1592–7), Derbys, is hung with portraits suspended by nails driven through tapestries (purchased 1592) for which the room was designed. The practice can also be seen in Abraham Bosse's engravings of Parisian interiors of the 1630s and 1640s and in an engraving (1699) of the Académie de Peinture's exhibition in the Grande Galerie of the Louvre (*see* EXHIBITION, fig. 1). Hanging pictures on tapestries became unfashionable by the mid-18th century but the practice continued in some houses and royal palaces.

Tapestries continued to be woven in bordered panels, which made up a unified system of decoration for a particular room (e.g. the Beauvais tapestries in Adam's tapestry drawing-rooms at Newby Hall (*c.* 1770–75), N. Yorks, and London, Osterley Park House, NT (*c.* 1772–5)). Tapestry *en suite* was used for seat furniture. In other schemes tapestries were nailed to battens and bordered by gilt fillets, as in the Neo-classical rooms, *c.* 1800, hung with Spanish tapestries after Goya in the Escorial, Madrid. This practice was introduced in the 17th century and may have derived from 16th-century Italy. At Uppark and Petworth House (both W. Sussex) the tapestries in several bedrooms were nailed to the wall with decorative upholstery pins and framed with wallpaper. This seems to have been a brief fashion of the 1850s.

Until the 18th century (and still in the Netherlands) carpets were often placed on tables and other furniture as well as on the floor. Placing an Oriental carpet on the floor was an act of conspicuous consumption given its rarity and cost. Once carpets had become relatively common in Italy, after *c.* 1500, their use on the floor became more widespread. Nonetheless, fine carpets continued to be placed on furniture as a matter of course, and this is documented in numerous illustrations. The Ushak carpets bought before 1601 for Hardwick Hall, Derbys, still lie on contemporary tables. Carpets designed for floors were sometimes an intrinsic element of a decorative scheme. The 93 Savonnerie carpets woven in 1660–70 for the

Grande Galerie of the Louvre, for example, were linked stylistically with the wall decoration. In the 18th century (e.g. in the decorative schemes of Robert Adam) carpets were designed to reflect the pattern of the ceiling plaster-work, as in the carpets at Osterley Park House (1765–80), London, and Saltram House (1768–9), Devon. The fact that at this date the furniture would have been placed against the walls (and dining-tables kept in a passage until required) meant that the design of the carpet would have been clearly visible.

IX. Arms and armour.

Carved reliefs of trophies of arms on ancient Roman buildings indicate an appreciation of the decorative pos-sibilities of arms and armour. In 1560 Fra Sabba da Castiglione declared that they were one of the prime ornaments of a house. Inventories that list a rack of arms in a bedroom (Siena, Fece Inv., 1450) or entrance hall (Venice, Ram Inv., 1592) indicate a decorative display. The substantial Medici collection was displayed (from c. 1590) next to the Tribuna of the Uffizi, Florence, and was dispersed in the late 18th century when an armoury within an art gallery seemed inappropriate. The concept was revived in the 19th century: arms and armour were exhibited in the Art Treasures Exhibition in 1857 in Manchester, and there is still an armoury in the Wallace Collection in London. At Dresden, the armoury (of medieval origin) is still displayed as part of the Electoral art collections, and was divided in the 16th century between the Kunstkammer, the Harnischkammer (for armour) and the Rüstkammer (for weapons and equipment). The engravings (1688) of the cabinet of curiosities in the monastery of Sainte-Geneviève, Paris, show arms hung in showcases.

The life-size armoured figures of the Habsburg collec-tion were displayed in niches by Ferdinand, Count of Tyrol (reg 1564–95), at Schloss Ambras (near Innsbruck). The armoury in the Palacio Real, Madrid, with a central row of caparisoned equestrian figures, maintains the tradition, though the similar 17th-century Line of Kings has long gone from the Royal Armouries at the Tower of London. The practice was revived by the scholar and collector Samuel Rush Meyrick, who, inspired by Schloss Ambras, had Goodrich Court (1828–31; destr. 1950), Hereford & Worcs, built by Edward Blore as a setting for his extensive collection. The Hastilude Chamber contained a tableau of a tournament, while the niches of the Grand Armoury contained equestrian figures with naturalistically painted faces (see the engravings (1830) by Joseph Skelton (c. 1785–after 1850)). Some visitors found this revival of a Renaissance style of display 'puerile' and felt that it detracted from the nobility of the collection; the debate still continues.

More usual in England was the display of arms and armour in halls. At Chirk Castle in Wales, arms from the English Civil War (1642–8) were listed as being in the hall in 1680. In 1699 Christopher Wren deployed 3000 weap-ons in patterns on the staircase at Hampton Court in London. The Boughton House, Northants, armoury was founded in the 16th century and was decoratively displayed by Louis Barbar in 1718. In 1788 trophies of arms were hung on either side of Benjamin West's huge painting *Clive Receiving the Diwani of Bengal* in the ballroom at Powis Castle, Powys, which also contained an Elephant Room for elephant armour captured from Tipu Sultan in 1799. In George IV's armoury at Carlton House in London were ten paintings (c. 1790–92) by Philippe Jacques de Louterbourg illustrative of warfare. Mahogany cases, racks and plinths were supplied by such leading cabinet-makers as Thomas Tatham and Benjamin Lewis Vulliamy. Horace Walpole's armoury on the staircase at Strawberry Hill, Twickenham, was a heterogeneous collection redolent of the romantic past, like Sir Walter Scott's collection at Abbotsford House (1812–32), Borders, or William Beck-ford's at Fonthill Abbey, Wilts.

See also EXHIBITION.

BIBLIOGRAPHY

GENERAL
Early sources

L. B. Alberti: *De re aedificatoria* (1485; Eng. trans., London, 1726)
S. da Castiglione: *Ricordi* (Venice, 1554)
R. Borghini: *Il riposo in cui della pittura e della scultura si favella* (Florence, 1584)
G. P. Lomazzo: *Trattato dell'arte de la pittura* (Milan, 1584, rev. Rome, 1844)
V. Scamozzi: *L'idea dell'architettura universale* (Venice, 1615)
H. Wotton: *Elements of Architecture* (London, 1624)
H. Peacham: *The Compleat Gentleman* (London, 1634)
W. Salmon: *Polygraphice* (London, 1672)
J. van Sandrart: *Teutsche Academie* (1675–9); ed. H. R. Peltzer (1925)
B. Cellini: *Vita* (Naples, 1728; Eng. trans., London, 1956)

Specific buildings

M. Brettingham: *The Plans, Elevations and Sections of Holkham in Norfolk . . .* (London, 1773)
J. Britton: *Graphical and Literary Illustrations of Fonthill Abbey* (London, 1823)
W. G. S. Cavendish: *Handbook of Chatsworth and Hardwick* (London, 1845)
Comte de Laborde: *Le Palais Mazarin* (Paris, 1846)
J. R. Rorimer: *The Cloisters* (New York, 1946)
F. J. Sánchez Cantón: *The Prado* (London, 1959)
P. Descargues: *The Hermitage* (London, 1961)
P. Verlet: *Versailles* (Paris, 1961)
F. Rossi: *The Uffizi and Pitti* (London, 1966)
L. Neppi: *Palazzo Spada* (Rome, 1975)
F. J. B. Watson: 'Mentmore and its Art Collections', *Mentmore* (sale cats, London, Sotheby's, 18–27 May 1977)
P. Thornton and M. Tomlin: *The Furnishing and Decoration of Ham House* (London, 1980)
E. A. Safarik and G. Torselli: *La Galleria Doria-Pamphili a Roma* (Rome, 1982)
S. F. Millensen: *Sir John Soane's Museum* (Ann Arbor, 1987)
Carlton House: The Past Glories of George IV's Palace (exh. cat., London, Queen's Gal., 1991)
C. Rowell: 'The North Gallery at Petworth: An Historical Re-appraisal', *Apollo*, cxxxviii/377 (July 1993), pp. 29–36

Interior design

T. Hope: *Household Furniture and Interior Decoration* (London, 1807)
C. Percier and P. F. L. Fontaine: *Recueil de décorations intérieures* (Paris, 1812)
M. Praz: *An Illustrated History of Interior Decoration* (London, 1964)
J. Fowler and J. Cornforth: *English Decoration in the 18th Century* (London, 1974)
J. Cornforth: *English Interiors, 1790–1848: The Quest for Comfort* (London, 1978)
P. Thornton: *17th Century Interior Decoration in England, France and Holland* (New Haven and London, 1978)
C. McCorquodale: *The History of Interior Decoration* (Oxford, 1983)
P. Thornton: *Authentic Decor: The Domestic Interior; 1620–1920* (London, 1984)
D. Watkin: *The Royal Interiors of Regency England* (London, 1984)

The Fashionable Fireplace (exh. cat. by C. Gilbert and A. Wells-Cole, Leeds, Temple Newsam House, 1985)

C. Gere: *Nineteenth-century Decoration* (London, 1989)

C. Wainwright: *The Romantic Interior: The British Collector at Home, 1750–1850* (New Haven and London, 1989)

H. Groth: *Neoclassicism in the North: Swedish Furniture and Interiors, 1770–1850* (London, 1990)

P. Thornton: *The Italian Renaissance Interior, 1400–1600* (London, 1991)

Artists and patrons

O. Millar: *Zoffany and his Tribuna* (London, 1967)

D. Watkin: *Thomas Hope and the Neo-classical Idea* (London, 1968)

J. Summerson, D. Watkin and G. Tilman Mellinghoff, eds: *John Soane* (London, 1983)

G. Jackson-Stops, ed.: *Robert Adam and Kedleston: The Making of a Neo-classical Masterpiece* (London, 1987)

Christian IV and Europe (exh. cat., ed. S. Heiberg; Hillerød, Fredriksborg Slot; Kronberg; Rosenberg; and elsewhere; 1988)

M. Butlin, M. Luther and I. Warrell: *Turner at Petworth: Painter and Patron* (London, 1989)

A. MacGregor, ed.: *The Late King's Goods: Collections, Possessions and Patronage of Charles I in the Light of the Commonwealth Sales Inventories* (London and Oxford, 1989)

J. M. Muller: *Rubens: The Artist as Collector* (Princeton, 1989)

Karl Friedrich Schinkel: A Universal Man (exh. cat., ed. M. Snodin; London, V&A, 1991)

Treasures of a Polish King: Stanislaus Augustus as Patron and Collector (exh. cat., ed. A. Rottermund; London, Dulwich Pict. Gal., 1992)

Countries

C. Westmacott: *British Galleries of Painting and Sculpture* (London, 1824)

G. F. Waagen: *Works of Art and Artists in England*, 3 vols (London, 1838)

——: *Treasures of Art in Great Britain*, 3 vols (London, 1854)

——: *Galleries and Cabinets of Art in Great Britain* (London, 1857)

W. Prinz: *Die Entstehung der Galerie in Frankreich und Italien* (Berlin, 1970)

Herinneringen aan Italië: Kunst en toerisme in de 18de eeuw (exh. cat., ed. R. de Leeuw; The Hague, Rijksdienst Beeld. Kst, 1984)

The Treasure Houses of Britain (exh. cat., ed. G. Jackson-Stops; Washington, DC, N.G.A., 1985)

De wereld binnen handbereik: Nederlandse kunst- en rariteitenverzamelingen, 1585–1735 [The world within reach: Dutch rare art collections, 1585–1735] (exh. cat., Amsterdam, Hist. Mus., 1992)

La Jeunesse des musées: Les Musées de France au XIXe siècle (exh. cat., ed. C. Georgel; Paris, Mus. d'Orsay, 1994)

Cities

A. Jameson: *A Handbook to the Public Galleries of Art in and near London* (London, 1842)

——: *Companion to the Most Celebrated Private Galleries of Art in London* (London, 1844)

I. Càllari: *I palazzi di Roma* (Rome, 3/1944)

V. Kennett and A. Kennett: *The Palaces of Leningrad* (London, 1973)

A. Blunt: *Guide to Baroque Rome* (London, 1982)

C. S. Sykes: *Private Palaces: Life in the Great London Houses* (London, 1989)

G. Heres: *Dresdener Kunstsammlungen im 18. Jahrhundert* (Leipzig, 1991)

Metropole London: Macht und Glanz einer Weltstadt, 1800–1840 (exh. cat., ed. C. Fox; Essen, Kultstift. Ruhr, 1992)

Other

J. Britton: *The Union of Architecture, Sculpture and Painting . . .* (London, 1827)

C. L. Eastlake: *Hints on Household Taste* (London, 1868, 4/1878)

C. Murray: *Museums: Their History and their Use*, 3 vols (Glasgow, 1904)

J. von Schlosser: *Die Kunst und Wunderkammern der Spätrenaissance* (Leipzig, 1908)

F. H. Taylor: *The Taste of Angels: A History of Art Collecting from Rameses to Napoleon* (Boston and London, 1948)

H. Tietze: *Treasures of the Great National Galleries* (London, 1955)

N. von Holst: *Creators, Collectors and Connoisseurs* (London, 1967)

H. Murray-Baillie: *Etiquette and the Planning of State Apartments in Baroque Palaces* (Oxford, 1967)

The Age of Neo-classicism (exh. cat., London, RA and V&A, 1972)

W. Liebenwein: *Studiolo* (Berlin, 1977)

J. Alsop: *The Rare Art Traditions: The History of Art Collecting and its Linked Phenomena* (London, 1982)

M. Henig, ed.: *A Handbook of Roman Art* (London, 1983)

D. Stillman: *English Neo-classical Architecture*, 2 vols (London, 1988)

B. Mundt and P. Krutisch, eds: *Schatzkästchen und Kabinettschrank: Möbel für Sammler* (Berlin, 1989)

LIGHTING

C. A. Guillaumot: *Mémoire sur la manière d'éclairer la galerie du Louvre* (Paris, 1796)

G. Thomson: *The Museum Environment* (London, 1978)

R. S. Taylor: 'Swan's Electric Light at Cragside', *NT Stud.* (1981), pp. 27–35

A. Laing: *Lighting* (London, 1982)

H. Lank: 'The Function of Natural Light in Picture Galleries', *Burl. Mag.*, cxxvi (1984), pp. 4–6

Lighting: A Conference on Lighting in Museums, Galleries and Historic Houses: Bristol, 1987

M. Compton: 'The Architecture of Daylight', *Palaces of Art: Art Galleries in Britain, 1790–1800* (exh. cat., ed. G. Waterfield; London, Dulwich Pict. Gal., 1991–2)

J. Bourne and V. Brett: *Lighting in the Domestic Interior* (London, 1992)

H. Lank: 'The Display of Paintings in Public Galleries', *Burl. Mag.*, cxxxvi (1992), pp. 165–71

Country House Lighting, 1660–1890 (exh. cat., Leeds, Temple Newsam House, 1992)

PAINTINGS

K. van Mander: *Schilder-boek* ([1603]–1604)

G. Mancini: *Considerazioni sulla pittura* (*c.* 1621); ed. A. Marucchi, 2 vols (Rome, 1956–7)

W. Sanderson: *Graphice: The Use of the Pen and Pensil* (London, 1658)

D. Teniers the younger: *Theatrum pictorium* (Brussels, 1660)

R. de Piles: *Conversations sur la connaissance de la peinture* (Paris, 1677/R Geneva, 1970)

——: *Dissertation sur les ouvrages des plus fameux peintres* (Paris, 1681)

——: *Cours de peinture par principes* (Paris, 1718)

S. Kleiner: *Représentation au naturel des châteaux de Weissenstein au dessus de Pommersfeld, et à celui de Geubach . . .* (Augsburg, 1728)

N. de Pigage: *La Galerie électorale de Dusseldorff*, 2 vols (Basle, 1778)

L. Lanzi: *La Real Galleria di Firenze* (Florence, 1782)

C. H. Tatham: *The Gallery at Castle Howard* (London, 1811)

W. Y. Ottley: *Stafford Gallery* (London, 1818)

W. Buchanan: *Memoirs of Painting*, 2 vols (London, 1824)

C. Eastlake: *The National Gallery: Observations on the Unfitness of the Present Building for its Purpose* (London, 1845)

'The New Turner Gallery', *Connoisseur*, xxviii (1910), pp. 63–4

A. Luzio: *La galleria dei Gonzaga venduta all'Inghilterra* (Milan, 1913)

C. Holmes and C. Collins-Baker: *The Making of the National Gallery, 1824–1924* (London, 1924)

G. Gluck: *The Picture Gallery of the Vienna Art Museum* (Vienna, 1925)

J. Denucé: *The Antwerp Art Galleries: Inventories of the Art-collections in Antwerp in the 16th and 17th Centuries* (Antwerp, 1932)

L. H. Wüthrich: *Christian von Mechel* (Basle, 1956)

S. Speth-Holterhoff: *Les Peintres flamands des cabinets d'amateurs au XVIIe siècle* (Brussels, 1957)

A. Blunt: 'Petworth Rehung: The Restoration and Rehanging of the Petworth Collection, 1952–53', *NT Stud.* (1980), pp. 119–33

J. Cornforth: 'Patterns of Picture Hanging', *Country Life*, clxix (4 June 1981), pp. 1592–6; clxix (11 June 1981), pp. 1698–9

S. Jervis: 'Picture Frames and Picture Hanging at Apsley House', *Catalogue of Paintings in the Wellington Museum*, ed. C. M. Kauffmann (London, 1982), pp. 17–21

La Galleria Palatina: Storia della quadreria granducale di Palazzo Pitti (exh. cat., ed. M. Mosco; Florence, Pitti, 1982)

G. Jackson-Stops and others, eds: *The Fashioning and Functioning of the British Country House*, Studies in the History of Art, xxv (Washington, DC, 1989), pp. 133–53, 155–74

David Teniers the Younger (exh. cat. by M. Klinge, Antwerp, Kon. Mus. S. Kst., 1991)

Palaces of Art: Art Galleries in Britain, 1790–1800 (exh. cat., ed. G. Waterfield; London, Dulwich Pict. Gal., 1991–2)

A. Scarpa-Sonino: *Cabinet d'amateur: Le grandi collezioni d'arte nei dipinti dal XVII al XIX secolo* (Milan, 1992)

SCULPTURE

G. B. Falda: *Li giardini di Roma* (Rome, *c.* 1680)

J. Kennedy: *A Description of the Antiquities and Curiosities at Wilton House* (Salisbury, 1769)

R. Westmacott: *Account of the Arrangement of the Collection of Antique Sculpture Lately Placed in the British Museum* (London, 1808)

J. Dallaway: *Of Statuary and Sculpture among the Ancients with Some Account of Specimens Preserved in England* (London, 1816)

J. E. Biet and J. P. Bres: *Souvenirs du Musée des monuments français* (Paris, 1821)

L. Courajod: *Alexandre Lenoir*, 3 vols (Paris, 1878–87)

C. Pietrangeli: *Guida dei musei capitolini* (Rome, 1961)

D. Coffin: *The Villa in the Life of Renaissance Rome* (Princeton, 1979)

F. Haskell and N. Penny: *Taste and the Antique* (New Haven and London, 1981)

B. Cook: *The Townley Marbles* (London, 1985)

C. Pietrangeli: *I musei vaticani: Cinque secoli di storia* (Rome, 1985)

P. Bober and R. Rubenstein: *Renaissance Artists and Antique Sculpture* (London, 1986)

G. B. Waywell: *The Lever and Hope Sculptures* (Berlin, 1986)

G. Hoyer, ed.: *Das Antiquarium der Münchner Residenz*, 2 vols (Munich, 1987)

E. Southworth: 'The Ince Blundell Collection: Collecting Behaviour in the 18th Century', *J. Hist. Col.*, iii/2 (1991), pp. 219–34

I. Jenkins: *Archaeologists and Aesthetes: The Sculpture Collections of the British Museum in the 19th Century* (London, 1992)

G. Vaughan: 'The Restoration of Classical Sculpture in the 18th Century and the Problem of Authenticity', *Why Fakes Matter: Essays on Problems of Authenticity*, ed. M. Jones (London, 1992), pp. 41–51

S. Walker: 'The Sculpture Gallery of Prince Livio Odescalchi', *J. Hist. Col.*, vi/2 (1994), pp. 189–219

OTHER MEDIA
Drawings

A. E. Popham: 'Sebastian Resta and his Collections', *Old Master Drgs*, xi (June 1936), pp. 1–19

Le Cabinet d'un grand amateur: P.-J. Mariette, 1694–1774 (exh. cat. by R. Bacou, Paris, Louvre, 1967)

J. Byam Shaw: *Drawings by Old Masters at Christ Church, Oxford*, 2 vols (Oxford, 1976)

Old Master Drawings from Holkham (exh. cat. by C. Whitfield and G. Naughton, London, Agnew's, 1977)

Drawings by Guercino from British Collections (exh. cat. by N. Turner and C. Plazzotta, London, BM, 1991)

N. Turner: 'John Bouverie as a Collector of Drawings', *Burl. Mag.*, cxxxvi (1994), pp. 90–99

Miniatures, medals, coins and gems

L. Beger: *Thesaurus Brandenburgicus Selectus*, 3 vols (Cologne, 1696–1701)

G. Reynolds: *Wallace Collection Catalogue of Miniatures* (London, 1980)

Die brandenburgisch-preussische Kunstkammer (exh. cat. by P. Bloch, F. Dreier and others, Berlin, Staatl. Museen, 1981)

S. Jervis: 'Cabinets and Curiosities', *Country Life*, clxxviii (24 Oct 1985), pp. 1278–9

Splendori di pietre dure: L'arte di corte nella Firenze dei Granduchi (exh. cat., ed. A. Giusti; Florence, Pitti, 1988–9), pp. 53–61

Portretten in miniatur (exh. cat. by M. Tiethoff and K. Schaffers, The Hague, Mauritshuis, 1991)

M. McCrory: 'Coins at the Courts of Innsbruck and Florence: The Numismatic Cabinets of Archduke Ferdinand II of Tyrol and Grand Duke Francesco I de' Medici', *J. Hist. Col.*, vi/2 (1994), pp. 153–73

Ceramics

M. Merian: *Theatrum Europaei*, xvi and xvii (Frankfurt am Main, 1717–18) [contains prints by Eosander von Göthe]

J. B. Broebes: *Vue des palais de plaisance de sa Majesté le Roi de Prusse* (Augsburg, 1773)

G. Jackson-Stops and others, eds: *The Fashioning and Functioning of the British Country House*, Studies in the History of Art, xxv (Washington, DC, 1989), pp. 177–92, 195–215

Porcelain for Palaces: The Fashion for Japan in Europe, 1650–1750 (exh. cat. by O. Impey and others, London, BM, 1990)

F. J. B. Watson and J. Whitehead: 'An Inventory Dated 1689 of the Chinese Porcelain in the Collection of the Grand Dauphin, Son of Louis XIV, at Versailles', *J. Hist. Col.*, iii/1 (1991), pp. 13–52

M. Chilton: 'Rooms of Porcelain', *The International Ceramics Fair: London, 1992*, pp. 24–33

C. Lyons: 'The Museo Mastrilli and the Culture of Collecting in Naples, 1700–1755', *J. Hist. Col.*, iv/1 (1992), pp. 1–26

Tapestries and carpets

P. Verlet: *The Savonnerie, its History: The Waddesdon Collection* (London, 1982)

P. Clabburn: *The National Trust Book of Furnishing Textiles* (London, 1988)

M. Girouard: *Hardwick Hall* (London, 1989)

Arms and armour

C. du Molinet: *Le Cabinet de la bibliothèque de Sainte Geneviève* (Paris, 1692)

J. Skelton: *Engraved Illustrations of Antient Arms and Armour... at Goodrich Court, Herefordshire* (London, 1830)

S. Bevan, C. Blair and A. Norman: 'The Armoury', *Boughton House: The English Versailles*, ed. T. Murdoch (London, 1992), pp. 158–69

CHRISTOPHER ROWELL

Dissemination. Term for the processes by which aspects of artistic production are communicated from certain regions and cultures to others. The topic has received relatively little theoretical consideration.

1. Examples and problems. 2. Formulations.

1. EXAMPLES AND PROBLEMS.

(i) The issues. (ii) Models from the social sciences.

(i) The issues. Anthropologists and geographers have often sought to explain how and why certain techniques, forms, practices or modes of behaviour appeared at different times in different places. Some have argued that spontaneous and unrelated inventions occurred, while others have claimed that certain widespread phenomena are easier to explain through the impact of a single localized discovery. Or, to put it another way, certain types of commonalities have universally appeared independently of each other, while others required a common source. The making and transformation of the several alloys of tin and copper known as bronze is an example of the first type, with independently evolved Bronze Ages existing in Western Asia, China, Africa and the Americas. The alphabet is an example of the latter: the original version, invented on the Phoenician coast in the 8th century BC, spread eastward and westward to spawn every other known alphabet on earth. Matters are more complicated in less well-documented matters, such as the invention of the wheel, the domestication of horses or camels, or any number of cultural traits or modes of behaviour that, at one point or another, became characteristic of several discrete cultural entities. In such instances enough variations exist in the appearance of traits or activities to make diffusion from a single centre unprovable. To assert it probably would be irrelevant or ideologically charged with regional, national or cultural vainglories, leading to unproductive debates about who discovered what and where. On the other hand, a purely topical and discretely independent explanation of every phenomenon, while perhaps satisfactory to local pride, is rarely correct and perhaps trivializes human creativity by rejecting qualitative differences between comparable features and distributing medals equally to all.

The issue of diffusion or dissemination is obviously a major, if neglected, one in the history of art. Generally sublimated under the vague term 'influence', it is an issue that strikes at the heart of the ethics of art, as it ultimately concerns itself with the far more invidious question of 'originality'. These questions may be approached first by looking at differing examples of what can be meant by diffusion or dissemination in the visual arts.

(a) Classical sculpture. The expansion of Hellenistic and Roman civilization (and military force) out of the Mediterranean basin was more or less concomitant with the mastering of the naturalistic representation of man in three

1. Dissemination of Classical motifs on a stone relief from Gandhara, north-west Pakistan, *c.* 360 mm, 2nd–3rd century AD (London, British Museum)

dimensions. (With this came two-dimensional pictorial representation giving the illusion of space, but the evidence for this is less well preserved.) One consequence was the development in Gaul, Egypt, Syria, Mesopotamia and Anatolia of a sculptural art that cannot, most of the time, be confused with either Classical Greek or Hellenistic sculpture but that would not have developed certain characteristics of modelling or of body structure without the existence of the Greek exploration of ways to show the human body, nude or dressed, alone or in a group. Another consequence in Bactria (Afghanistan), Central Asia, and Gandhara (north-west Pakistan) was the creation of a local art that shows distinct Mediterranean influence, including decorative effects such as Corinthian-style pillars and bead-and-reel motifs in some reliefs from Gandhara (see fig. 1; *see also* INDIAN SUBCONTINENT, §IV, 5(ii)(a)). In the case of early Buddhist sculpture, examples exist, in narrative reliefs of the lives of the Buddha, for instance (see fig. 2), of direct relations between Mediterranean and Central Asian forms. Specific Mediterranean examples were probably available to Gandharan artisans, but the true impulse probably came through an awareness of the general qualities of the newly received sculpture rather than through individual combinations of forms.

(b) Chinese ceramics. Within the long and complicated history of ceramic art, Chinese ceramics played a singular part. For reasons that are often impossible to reconstruct, as they deal with issues of taste and snobbery in poorly documented times, on several occasions non-Chinese cultures sought to acquire and eventually to copy or imitate Chinese wares. One of the most spectacular instances occurred in the regions of Iraq and Iran in the 8th–10th centuries AD, when a society of immense luxury consumption acquired large quantities of ceramic wares and, despite having its own ceramic traditions, expected its potters to approximate expensive imported Chinese wares and thereby make them cheaper. The response of local technology was remarkable. Some types of wares were made that actually were imitations of Chinese types; but more spectacularly, the type of research and experimentation needed for these imitations spawned the richest array of new techniques for surface treatment ever invented in an equivalent period of time (*see* ISLAMIC ART, §V, 2(ii) and (iii)). Several centuries later, beginning in the 14th century, blue-and-white wares, whether or not initially manufactured in China, were transmitted to the Muslim world and Western Europe, and something of the same phenomenon took place, with perhaps more emphasis on surface designs than on techniques of manufacture (see fig. 3). Originals from China were used at the highest levels of society, more or less clever imitations were made for lower ranks, or else Chinese models were acknowledged to be behind a decoration that could no longer be considered Chinese, as with several types of Ottoman designs known as *čini* (*see* BLUE-AND-WHITE CERAMIC; CHINA, §VII, 4(iii) and (v); and ORNAMENT AND PATTERN, §III).

(c) Palladianism. This architectural style, taken up by 18th-century English architects from Palladio's 16th-century modification of Classical Roman features, flourished in England and spread internationally. A certain type of

2. Dissemination of Classical forms on an early Buddhist Shibi *jātaka* relief from Gandhara, north-west Pakistan, *c.* 245 mm, 2nd–3rd century AD (London, British Museum)

symmetrical conception for a formal building with a central cupola, a colonnaded porch topped by a triangular pediment, and a variable number of extensions on the other façades came to affect the architecture of banks, state houses or gentrified Virginia estates in the United States, provincial Russian churches and palaces or imperial transformations in 18th-century Berlin or St Petersburg, the expression of Chinese communist power in Central Asian cities such as Kashgar, and even Lutyens' grandiose British imperial vision for New Delhi (*see* PALLADIANISM and NEO-CLASSICISM). The transmission of the type took place through travelling and visits to major examples of the originals in Italy and elsewhere, as well as through books whose drawings were often, until the advent of photography, do-it-yourself manuals of architectural construction. Yet the more important issue here concerns neither the type nor its transmission, but the reason why different times, different areas, different functions and even different cultures understood one particular model of a building or monument as uniquely significant.

(d) 19th-century landscape painting. This is a particularly complicated example of dissemination. Landscape painting flourished profusely in the later 19th century in nearly every European country, in North America and, towards the very end of the century, in Ottoman Turkey. Received wisdom customarily gives pre-eminence to a Paris-centred or Paris-based production of landscapes beginning with Corot and leading to Matisse, while other 20th-century artists involved with the representation of nature are avoided or consigned to footnotes. All other landscape painting is measured against what happened in France and is seen as influenced by an alleged dominating centre; it is thought of as being more or less—usually less—successful in following Parisian trends (for instance in Ottoman Turkey), as being independent and different (much German landscape) or as independent and similar but, therefore, of lesser quality (as in Russian, Swiss or Danish landscape painting). The point here is that for a period when communications had become relatively easy and contacts or influences difficult to prove or disprove, it might seem reasonable to assume a connection between artists, patrons or localities leading to comparable results, and yet these connections either did not exist or are very difficult to establish. The contrast could not be greater with the second half of the 20th century, when every movement from Surrealism to *Neo-realisme* became available through colour reproduction in slick magazines all over the world at reasonably low prices. As a result, wherever there is a group of artists, the manner or style of a given group in New York, London or Paris can be

3. Dissemination of Chinese design on a Persian dish, diam. 273 mm, 17th or 18th century, derived from exported late Ming ceramics (London, Victoria and Albert Museum)

imitated, just as Chinese ceramics were imitated in Baghdad during the 9th century. In such an era dissemination is total—or could be so, as only political and ideological barriers prevent the near-complete domination of the planet by the commercialized art of the West. In return, tastes for the 'quaint' and 'exotic' are catered for by shops importing artefacts from Peru, Tanzania or Tibet to the centres of Western art. At no time has art been more like cuisine in its patterns of diffusion and dissemination. As international chains create the same coffee shops in similar hotels all over the world, the food of others becomes the 'exotic' food of snobbish Western cities.

(ii) Models from the social sciences. These examples illustrate the difficulties of handling the issue of dissemination in respect of the arts. One way of approaching it is simply to transfer to the study of the arts concepts, categories and premises developed in the social sciences. For instance, the opposition or contrast between diffusionism and evolutionism, as argued in anthropology, could be considered for the history of European painting in the 19th century, so that non-Parisian artistic movements might be explained as examples of discrete histories with an 'organic' tendency toward certain kinds of changes or as results of movements, spontaneous or not, inspired by a hierarchy of creative centres. Something of the same sort of reasoning could be made for Italian painting from the 14th until the 17th centuries, for Gothic architecture or for Hellenistic and Roman sculptures. Modern history of art began after Darwin and, wittingly or not, most historians of art have been affected by the obligation to rank undated artefacts chronologically. They sought salvation in a more or less expressed evolutionism that requires the concept of an avant-garde and assumes that the simplification or the exaggeration of any one form is later than a mimetic image of the same topic. Diffusionism, on the other hand, prevails among those (A. Kinglsey Porter, K. Weitzmann, among medievalists) who see a single source (northern Italian architecture, manuscript illumination) behind major developments such as Romanesque architecture or the representation of biblical subjects in medieval art.

One difficulty with a direct transfer of concepts from the social sciences is that for periods before the 19th century, there is not, nor will there ever be, the quantity and type of data that would make reasonable conclusions possible. Another difficulty derives from the degree of abstraction reached by definitions in the social sciences. For example, Fritz Graebner, the main theoretician of diffusionism, wrote: 'The more complex a cultural trait is, the more secondary traits it contains that are not essential to its function (*criterion of form*), and the more similar the traits (*criterion of quantity*) shared by two areas, the more likely it is that the presence of these traits is due to diffusion.' To translate this statement into an operational procedure so as to identify what is Italian in a Dürer or Persian in a Mughal miniature would require the breakdown of every work of art into a complete collection of objectively verifiable formal, iconographic and expressive features. Such an objective, while theoretically possible in the computer age, seems incompatible with the actual procedures of art historians. Purely theoretical and abstract statements dealing with very general ideas thus shatter when pitted against concrete works of art. Very specific points like the tracing of the origins of a common iconographic motif (with very successful examples in Janson's study of apes or in Settis-Frugoni's *Historia Alexandri*) or stylistic device (as in a great deal of J. Baltrusaitis' work on Romanesque ornament and on the fantastic in art) can easily become learned or subjective trivia, at best exciting jolts through unexpected associations.

Yet it is difficult to deny that since time immemorial, techniques, designs, patterns, styles and subjects travelled from place to place, probably from centres to peripheries but possibly according to some other model. Existing systems from the social sciences, such as the 'central place' model dear to some geographers, have been used with some success in the study of Ancient Near Eastern art. One reason is, no doubt, that the issues of Ancient Near Eastern art are so often tied to the information system provided by archaeology, very much of a social science in its assumptions, if not always in its practice. It is difficult, however, to imagine what would be gained in transforming the dissemination of Florentine-trained artists and methods in the 15th century into circles of varying sizes related to each other by arrows, the type of diagram that fills the pages of geographical and anthropological studies.

2. FORMULATIONS. In other words, the true and undeniable fact of dissemination in the arts does not easily enter into existing models and requires its own definition of what it is. Three chief questions require answering: What is disseminated? How is it disseminated? What are the epistemological consequences and implications of dissemination?

(i) What is disseminated. The most obvious subject for dissemination consists in what can broadly be called techniques. These can be defined at two levels. One is the very practical, almost mechanical, way of doing something, or else the awareness and utilization of some material. Prussian blue is an early 18th-century invention that spread rapidly because it was simple to make and replaced earlier, more expensive blues. The two firings, with the second in a reducing atmosphere, that made lustreware possible were first used on pottery *c.* 800 AD, almost certainly in Iraq. From there it spread to regions such as Egypt and Iran, and later to Spain, Italy and France, though other intermediate or culturally connected areas such as Central Asia or Anatolia more or less escaped its appearance within their ceramic technology. From the proverbial silkworms carried in their walking sticks by two monks from China that created a Mediterranean silk industry, all the way to contemporary acrylics, there have been always and everywhere materials wilfully or accidentally transferred from one area to the other which modified or revolutionized local artistic production.

Such examples, however interesting they may be for the history of techniques and materials, are of relatively little importance for the history of art, as their intellectual usefulness rarely extends beyond means to date an object. They may, however, be considered at a different and more complex level. Nearly all the examples of dissemination given so far, and probably many others as well, imply that whatever is disseminated is very rarely a specific form, a stylistic trait or a subject of representation. Dissemination must be distinguished from copying. Even if repeated many times, the act of copying is an end in itself; it leads to and ends with an object, as happened in so many examples of Roman sculpture repeating Greek ones and Renaissance sculptors continuing the same process. Dissemination differs from influence or casual impact, because the object that is the stimulus alters something in the art of a receiving cultural setting without being itself cloned within that culture. It was not concrete Greek forms so much as a considered awareness of Greek sculpture that transformed Central Asian and Indian sculpture. Similarly, Near Eastern ceramics were modified by the general visual effect of Chinese ceramics, not by a specific example. When French Renaissance painting or architecture copied Italian models less obviously than before, Italian art truly disseminated itself in French art. In other words, what is transmitted at this level is an intangible and invisible attitude in the process of making which alters the finished product and its by-products. It implies intelligence and a consciousness of one's actions, the awareness of what one seeks as a patron or as an artist–artisan and a competence in finding the means to express whatever it is that one wishes. For instance, Chinese ceramics did not have a significant impact in Byzantium, Africa or Western Europe (not, at least, until the 17th century), in large part because the need and taste for these novelties was not in evidence, and had the need been present, the competence may not have existed. For while it is not the competence itself that is transmitted, no dissemination is possible without a modification of a hitherto existing competence.

Dissemination, then, is the transformation of an existing creative or manufacturing energy by consumption (taste) or production (competence) through the acknowledged or subsumed effect of an idea or of a body of forms from the outside.

(ii) The means of dissemination. At the most abstract level, dissemination requires first of all the matching of two human capacities, individual or social. One is taste, the actual or potential ways to use and to enjoy a manufactured object. Taste could be that of an individual patron and of a class of patrons, but it could also be that of users and buyers. The other capacity is the competence to meet the requirements of taste or to propose something different to a prevailing taste. This matching is a necessary but not a sufficient condition for dissemination. The latter also requires that something hitherto alien to or absent from the setting of a given culture had been brought into a taste–competence equation. Social scientists dealing with diffusion refer to this equation as the communication network. What were the means through which this network operated?

Since the subject has never been properly studied, a few examples only can be proposed. A most common explanation for dissemination is the movement of craftsmen and artists. The appearance of paper in the West Asian world is usually attributed to a few Chinese papermakers taken prisoner in AD 751 at the Battle of Talas in Central Asia (*see* PAPER, §III, 3). Leonardo is a particularly celebrated example of an Italian artist brought to France, and it is to an Italian architect who thought he was following local practices that the Russians owe the extraordinary Uspensky Cathedral (*see* MOSCOW, §IV, 1(ii)). Later on, French and Italian artists participated in the making of 18th-century St Petersburg, and in the 20th century, architects (far more than painters, whose works move more easily than their authors) fly from one studio to the other in a worldwide dissemination of Bauhaus, modernism and Post-modernism. There are probably several typologies of the means of dissemination to be worked out from an eventual roster of artists, craftsmen, architects and artisans moving or being forcibly moved from one region to the other and changing or, on the contrary, failing to change the art of some other culture. Chinese artists brought to Iran under the Mongol dynasty of the Ilkhanids (1256–1353) revolutionized the methods of Persian painting, but Guillaume Boucher (*fl* 13th century), a French jeweller who built wonderful automata for Mongol princes in Mongolia, seems to have left no posterity.

A second means of dissemination is through manuals, models and images. Here too various distinctions can be imagined and deserve further investigation. For certain techniques of painting, for the organization of a church's decoration, for lustreware, for the formulation of systems of proportion, there were manuals designed to help artisans and designers meet whatever standard of form was expected of them. Most of these were, however, internal documents within a given cultural continuity. They were not for export, and except for the special cases of Classical texts such as Vitruvius, picked up anew by the Italian Renaissance, it would not have been written texts as such that would have modified someone else's art. Images, on the other hand, were certainly major means of transmitting artistic ideas. Heavily illustrated books were essential to the spread of Italianate Baroque architectural values all over Europe and the Americas. Western prints led to a dead-end in their effect on Persian miniatures of the mid- to late 17th century, but they were successfully translated by Indian masters into frequently stunning landscapes or representations of people and animals. The 20th-century Japanese architect Kenzō Tange was inspired by photographs of Le Corbusier's works to develop his own contemporary style. In a more general way, the art or architecture magazine with beautiful reproductions has become the ubiquitous agent of transmission of visual forms and, to some degree, of ideas throughout the world.

It is easy to see how contemporary media and distribution of practices disseminate creative ideas and techniques, but the phenomenon itself found one of its most telling examples in the transmission of images in the Middle Ages through illuminated manuscripts. While some scholars may have exaggerated the rigidity and immutability of the process, there is no doubt that church-affiliated scriptoria diffused representations by copying manuscripts that were, in turn, distributed all over the Christian world, sometimes even beyond, where these books became models for local traditions. The study of these disseminated features is central to the scholarship on Carolingian, Ottoman and Byzantine book illumination. In many instances, the means of dissemination have become the end of investigation, and, because the underlying theoretical assumptions of the explanation have not been worked out, the implications of perfectly justified observations have not received appropriate attention. In particular, the distinction between copying and assimilating has rarely been introduced. But the inadequacies of the conclusions drawn from this research do not belie the fact that manuscripts, illustrated or not, provide one of the rare examples of dissemination before the Renaissance, with a large number of examples in different cultural settings.

A third means of dissemination is through apprenticeship. Pupils, students or even professionals travel in order to profit from a master or to learn from a place. Established in the West through the many schools and institutes in Rome, the notion of a centre and/or a master underlies all sorts of formal or informal, short- or long-term organizations, ateliers, studios or other establishments that, at least since Roman times, sprang up in obvious places such as Paris or in most unexpected ones (Cranbrook, MI; Taliesin, AZ; Ahmadabad, India) to promote contemporary architecture and design, collecting followers from many remote areas and lands who then returned to practise in the way of a master or of a place.

Movement of craftsmen or artists to where jobs are, transmission of books or images, operation of centres—such are the main means of dissemination. They are nearly all related to the functioning of economies and the location of jobs and money. This is particularly true of late 20th-century Western culture when corporate taste, fellowships and grants, and investments in publishing affect what is being transmitted, who goes where and who studies what. The extent to which these means are manipulated for a variety of ideological purposes is difficult to determine, but it is reasonable to assume that more complex uses of the processes of dissemination occur today than can be imagined for the past. And yet even in the past, the dissemination of mosaic techniques in Islamic art (with key examples in the great mosques of Damascus and Córdoba), which has been interpreted in ideological terms (the power of the Muslim ruler compelling the Byzantine one to yield his technicians), could just as easily be explained in economic ones (artisans go where there is a market). Both the economics of art and its ideological manipulation clearly created a ready-made climate for dissemination.

(iii) Implications. However little studied as a singular phenomenon of the arts, dissemination is one of the components of the process of artistic creativity. Often significant only at the level of technical detail or technological transfer, dissemination may well become a useful overall concept in dealing with issues of relationship between schools, artists, countries, regions or media. It does lead into the devious ways of artistic economies and of the operation of the market on the making of art. It also affects our understanding of the ideological forces behind much of the created world. The study of dissemination concentrates on the process of making rather than the manner of interpretation, and such a study may well help in evaluating the balance between individuality and tradition that characterizes most works of art. Thus it strikes at the core of a central issue of the arts, the relationship between the originality that is so praised by critics and the absence of it in the reality of any one work of art. In wondering about originality, the study of dissemination leads to wondering about art itself.

BIBLIOGRAPHY
F. Graebner: 'Diffusion', *International Encyclopedia of the Social Sciences*, iv (New York, 1930; rev. 1968), p. 171
H. Buchtal: 'The Western Aspects of Gandhara Sculpture', *Proc. Brit. Acad.*, 31 (1945), pp. 150–76
L. Olschki: *Guillaume Boucher* (Baltimore, 1946)
H. W. Janson: *Ape and Ape-lore* (London, 1952)
K. Weitzmann: *Roll and Codex* (Princeton, 1970)
C. Settis-Frugoni: *Historia Alexandri* (Rome, 1976)
O. Kurz: *The Decorative Arts of Europe and the Islamic East* (London, 1977)
J. Baltrusaitis: *Le Moyen-âge fantastique* (Paris, 1981)
J. Carswell: *Blue and White* (Chicago, 1985)
A. Craiger-Smith: *Lustre Pottery* (London, 1985)
J. Soustiel: *La Céramique islamique* (Paris, 1985)
J. Baltrusaitis: *Formations, transformations* (Paris, 1986)
J. C. Harle: *The Art and Architecture of the Indian Subcontinent* (London, 1986) [esp. pp. 71–85]
M. Vickers, ed.: *Pots and Pans* (Oxford, 1986)

OLEG GRABAR

Distéfano, Juan Carlos (*b* Buenos Aires, 1933). Argentine painter and sculptor. He studied at the Escuelas Nacionales de Bellas Artes, Buenos Aires, and in 1960 was awarded the Beca de Italia scholarship. He lived in Barcelona from 1977 to 1979, when he returned to Buenos Aires. After some noteworthy work as a graphic designer, Distéfano began to investigate new materials for use in making his sculptures. As a draughtsman he had an accurate, almost Renaissance line, which he extended to his explorations of sculpture. This was made possible by his use of polyester, glass fibre, resins and acrylic colours, together with moulds and bleaches, in a complex process.

By distancing himself from traditional materials and through his use of vibrant colour, Distéfano achieved unforeseen surface qualities and textures. His works, with their strong plastic content, became visibly dramatic and tensely expressive. His subjects were always tortured human figures who sought to express a monologue in their committed silence. His pictorial sense was always pre-eminent in his skilful conjunction of volume and space.

OSVALDO SVANASCINI

Distelbarth, Friedrich (*b* Ludwigsburg, 1768; *d* Stuttgart, 1836). German sculptor. He was educated in Stuttgart, where in 1782 he entered the Hohe Karlsschule, founded by Charles-Eugene, Duke of Württemberg for children of the deserving poor. His principal master there was the sculptor Johann Heinrich von Dannecker, himself a product of the same education, which aimed to train those studying the visual arts as artist-craftsmen, who could be employed on embellishing the ducal palaces. In 1795 Distelbarth went to Rome, where he remained until 1799; among his early works executed there was a marble bust of *Bacchus* (signed and dated, *Rome 1795*; ex-Shepherd Gal., New York; untraced), which revealed his successful study of both antiquity and the sculpture of contemporary Neo-classicists such as Antonio Canova. In 1796 Distelbarth married an Italian woman; he may have hoped to remain in Rome and follow Canova's example by attracting patronage for ideal statues from the international tourists. However, the European wars that broke out at the close of the century disturbed the flow of visitors to Rome, and he instead found employment in Paris. For most of the period from 1799 to 1808 he worked as a member of the huge team of foreign artists and artisans that was attracted to Paris by the major projects of Napoleon's empire. Distelbarth was principally employed as one of the sculptors working on the lengthy restoration of the Louvre. In 1808 Dannecker called him back to Stuttgart, where he spent the rest of his life, first assisting Dannecker and later taking over teaching duties at the Karlsschule. His own artistic production was largely limited to decorative reliefs and garden groups, mostly after others' designs. One such work was a group of *Nymphs* (sandstone, 1808–10; ex-Schlossgarten, Stuttgart; untraced), after a model by Dannecker.

BIBLIOGRAPHY
Thieme–Becker

PETER WALCH

Disteli, Martin (*b* Olten, 28 May 1802; *d* Solothurn, 18 March 1844). Swiss draughtsman, etcher and illustrator. He trained first in Switzerland and then in Germany. Returning to Olten in 1823 he decided on an artistic career. In 1825 he visited Munich; German art, particularly the works of Peter Cornelius and Moritz Retzsch, was an important influence on the extremely linear style of his graphic work, which is also reminiscent of John Flaxman. In 1829 he published his first series of etchings, *Umrisse zu A. E. Fröhlichs Fabeln,* based on the animal characters of the French caricaturist J.-J. Grandville. From this time on his works satirized the power of the aristocracy and the clergy, in particular the Jesuits. The liberal movement, which infiltrated numerous Swiss cantons immediately

after the July Revolution of 1830 in France, pushed Disteli towards a military career. At the same time he supplied drawings—animal caricatures and also scenes from Swiss history, both ancient and modern—to various Swiss republican almanacs and journals (e.g. *Alpenrosen: Ein Taschenbuch,* 1830–39; *Züricher Kalender von David Bürkli,* 1833–7). His illustrations for the *Abenteuer des Freyherrn von Münchhausen* (Solothurn, 1841) and the *Wahrhaftige Geschichte des deutschen Michels und seiner Schwestern* (Zurich, 1843) were anti-aristocratic and republican in tone. From 1839 he dedicated himself almost exclusively to the publication of an illustrated almanac, of which 30,000 copies were printed. The *Schweizerischer Bilderkalender,* commonly known as the *Disteli Kalender,* gave his radical and nationalist opinions full scope. Shortly before his death, he illustrated the first published poem of Gottfried Keller, entitled *Sie kommen die Jesuiten,* which appeared in a supplement to *Die freie Schweiz* in 1844.

PRINTS
Umrisse zu A. E. Fröhlichs Fabeln (Aarau, 1829)

BIBLIOGRAPHY
G. Wälchli: *Martin Disteli, 1802–1844: Zeit–Leben–Werk* (Zurich, 1943)
Martin Disteli . . . und fluchend steht das Volk vor seinen Bildern (exh. cat. by L. Leitess, I. Noseda and B. Wiebel, Olten, Kstmus., 1978)
J. Coulin: *Der Anti-Philister: Martin Distelis Kalender* (Basle, 1990)

PHILIPPE KAENEL

Distemper [Fr. *peinture à la colle*]. Aqueous paint composed of pigments held together by animal glue or casein. It has been used since ancient Egyptian times for wall painting, house decoration and the painting of theatrical scenery. It has been employed only occasionally for easel painting.

RUPERT FEATHERSTONE

Distyle. Term applied to a building with a portico of two columns. When the pair of columns is between antae, the configuration is described as distyle *in antis* (*see* GREECE, ANCIENT, fig. 7).   □

Di Suvero, Mark (*b* Shanghai, China, 18 Sept 1933). American sculptor of Italian and French parentage. He spent his early childhood in the Far East, before his family moved to San Francisco, CA, in 1941. He entered San Francisco City College in 1953 and attended the University of California at Santa Barbara from 1954 to 1955, completing his BA in Philosophy at Berkeley in 1956. It was during these years that he first took seriously his interest in art, and studied sculpture primarily. Moving to New York in 1957, he became aware of the work of the Abstract Expressionists and the associated sculpture of David Smith. A work-related accident in 1960 left his legs and spine permanently impaired and confined him to a wheelchair for nearly two years. Subsequently, the scale of his work shifted dramatically from smaller, ruggedly Expressionistic pieces in cast bronze and unhewn wood to monumental constructions in steel. The resultant sculpture necessarily exceeded the limits of museum and gallery walls, as did his aspiration for its exhibition. His favourite materials became synonymous with those of the modern construction industry: I-Beams, steel cables, wooden ties and scrap metal were used in di Suvero's work of the mid-1960s.

Di Suvero created several pieces condemning the US government's participation in the Vietnam War. *Tower of Peace* (1966; dismantled shortly thereafter) was erected in a site between La Cienega and Sunset Boulevards, Los Angeles (see Antin). In 1971 in protest at the war he began a self-imposed exile in Europe lasting four years. The Whitney Museum of American Art held a retrospective exhibition in 1975, and increasingly his sculpture was selected for public installation, for example *Isis* (1978; Washington, DC, Hirshhorn). Di Suvero's heroic monumentalism and striking use of impersonal materials to figurative ends recommend that his oeuvre be treated separately from the historically parallel yet aesthetically distinct project of Minimalist sculpture in America.

BIBLIOGRAPHY

D. Antin: 'Los Angeles: Tower of Peace', *ARTnews*, lxii/2 (1966), pp. 25, 71

Mark di Suvero (exh. cat. by J. K. Monte, New York, Whitney, 1975)

Mark di Suvero (exh. cat. by B. Rose, Houston, TX, Contemp. A. Mus., 1978)

J. R. Klein: 'Idealism Realized: Two Public Commissions by Mark di Suvero', *A. Mag.*, lvi/4 (1981), pp. 80–90

W. Saunders: 'Risk and Balance: Mark di Suvero', *A. America*, lxxi/2 (1983), pp. 128–35

Mark di Suvero (exh. cat. by T. Osterwold, Stuttgart, Württemberg. Kstver., 1988)

DERRICK R. CARTWRIGHT

Dittborn, Eugenio (*b* Santiago, 1943). Chilean painter, printmaker, draughtsman and video artist. He studied at the Escuela de Bellas Artes of the Universidad de Chile in Santiago (1961–5), at the Escuela de Fotomecánica in Madrid (1966), the Hochschule für Bildende Kunst in West Berlin (1967–9) and at the Ecole des Beaux-Arts in Paris.

Dittborn, together with other theorists and artists working in Chile in the 1970s, based his work on critical examination of the marginal position of Chilean art in relation to international developments, adopting to this end practices at odds with Chilean traditions. Rejecting conventional forms of painting as well as the usual methods of producing and presenting prints, he instead favoured photography as a source both of imagery and technique by means of screenprinting. He found his imagery ready-made in the portraits featured in old Chilean criminology magazines; he combined mechanical techniques such as offset lithography and screenprinting with traditional handcrafting methods of embroidery and drawn-threadwork; and in the mid-1980s he even went so far as to produce works on brown wrapping paper, which he folded and then distributed through the ordinary post, calling them his own variant of correspondence art. Dittborn used such contrasts within his work to reflect disparate realities, mirroring the social interaction of different levels in society and underlining the racially mixed origins of Latin American practices by exaggerating the clash between domestic crafts and advanced modern technology.

BIBLIOGRAPHY

Eugenio Dittborn (exh. cat., Buenos Aires, Cent. A. & Comunic., 1979)

R. Kay: *Del espacio de acá: La obra de E. Dittborn* (Santiago, 1980)

Pinturas postales (exh. cat. by E. Dittborn and others, Santiago, 1985)

M. Ivelić and G. Galaz: *Chile: Arte actual* (Santiago, 1988)

MILAN IVELIĆ

Diu. Island and fortified port off the southern tip of the Kathiawar Peninsula in Gujarat, India. Diu rose to prosperity under the Sultans of Gujarat, especially Mahmud Bigara (*reg* 1458–1511), whose slave-governor Malik Ayaz fortified the harbour, but the island is best known for its Portuguese monuments. In 1535 Sultan Bahadur Shah (*reg* c. 1526–37) bartered the Diu fort for Portuguese help against Mughal attacks. Subsequent sieges by Gujarati and Ottoman forces in 1538 and 1546 failed to retake it, and in 1544 the Portuguese viceroy Dom João de Castro occupied the whole island. Diu remained under Portuguese control until 1961.

The first Portuguese fort, which had 6 m-high walls, massive towers and a deep ditch, was largely destroyed in the siege of 1538. It was rebuilt by Governor Nuno da Cunha, who also constructed a strongly bastioned wall with a single gate across the island. After the second siege, de Castro excavated a further moat and built new defences with triangular bastions designed by Francisco Pires. The subsequent prosperity of Diu can be seen in the tall, stone, Indian merchants' houses with carved wooden doors, verandahs and balconies; a number of temples and mosques also survive. This prosperity also enabled Franciscans, Dominicans, Jesuits and other Christian orders to build lavishly. Among the most splendid of their churches is the Sé Matriz Cathedral, originally the Jesuit church of St Paul, founded in 1601 and restored in 1807, when it was rededicated to Our Lady of the Immaculate Conception; it is notable for its classical façade and elaborate surface decoration.

BIBLIOGRAPHY

A. B. de Bragança Pereira: *Os Portugueses em Diu* (Bastora, 1935)

M. S. Commissariat: *A History of Gujarat*, i (Bombay, 1938)

C. de Azevedo: *Arte cristã na Índia Portuguesa: Arte de Goa, Damão e Diu* (Lisbon, 1959)

M. N. Pearson: *Merchants and Rulers in Gujarat: The Response to the Portuguese in the Sixteenth Century* (London, 1976)

J. B. HARRISON

Divino, el. *See* MORALES, LUIS DE.

Divisionism. Term invented by Paul Signac to describe the Neo-Impressionist separation of colour into dots or patches applied directly to the canvas. Following the rules of colour-contrasts laid out by Ogden Rood and Michel-Eugène Chevreul, this method was intended to produce maximum brilliance scientifically and to avoid the muddiness caused by physically mixing colours before applying them to the canvas. Seen close to, a Divisionist canvas is a mass of contrasting dots: at a distance, the colours enhance each other to produce an effect of shimmering luminosity. Divisionism refers to the general principle of the separation of colour, unlike the term POINTILLISM, which refers specifically to the use of dots. Employed in France by members of the Neo-Impressionist group, Divisionism was also popular in Belgium among Les XX and in the Netherlands. In Italy the use of Divisionism, stimulated by Vitorio Grubicy, characterizes the advanced experiments of such painters as Angelo Morbelli, Giovanni Segantini, Giuseppe Pellizza da Volpedo, Gaetano Previati and Plino Nomelli; a Divisionist phase also marked the early works of the Futurist artists Umberto Boccioni, Giacomo Balla, Carlo Carrà and Gino Severini, among others.

See also NEO-IMPRESSIONISM.

AURORA SCOTTI TOSINI

Divriği. Small town in central Anatolia (Turkey), *c.* 100 km south-east of Sivas. Founded in the mid-9th century AD and known as Tephrikè to the Byzantines, the town was taken by the Saljuqs of Rum after the Battle of Manzikert in 1071. In the 12th century it came into the possession of the Mangujak (Mengücek) Turkomans, under whom several remarkable buildings and fortifications were erected. The Kale ('citadel') Mosque, constructed for the Mangujak sovereign Shahinshah ibn Sulayman ibn Amir Ishak by the builder Hasan ibn Piruz of Maragha in 1180–81, is a simple structure of three aisles perpendicular to the qibla wall. The wider central aisle has a barrel vault, while the side aisles are each covered by four cupolas. A small kiosk once stood against the north-west corner of the building, but only its lower part remains. The masonry portal was once decorated with glazed brick. The sovereign's mausoleum (?1196), erroneously known as that of Sitte Melik, is a two-storey octagonal prism on a cubic plinth containing the crypt. The side of the octagon that contains the entrance is richly decorated with geometric bands inscribed in a rectangular frame. The mausolea of Kamereddin (1196) and Kemankeş (1240–41) are rather plain.

The most important building in the town comprises the congregational mosque founded by Ahmad Shah ibn Sulayman Shah in 1228–9 and the adjacent hospital, ordered in the same year by Turan Malik, his wife. The prayer-hall has five aisles perpendicular to the qibla wall, which are covered with a variety of vaults (rest.) supported on pillars. The central aisle is wider, and the bay in front of the mihrab is covered with a ribbed cupola resting on a dodecagonal drum. The building is notable for the north portal, where the deep mouldings of the pointed arch are embellished with exuberant arabesque and vegetal motifs projecting from the wall in high and even undercut relief, and the magnificent ebony minbar (1240–41) signed by Ahmad ibn Ibrahim of Tbilisi (*see* ISLAMIC ART, §VII, 2(iii)). The hospital, standing behind the qibla wall, has four iwans facing a small court with an open oculus in the centre. Along the sides and in the corners are cells for the patients. An anonymous mausoleum, presumed to be for Ahmad Shah, stands in the north-east corner. The hospital also has remarkable vaulting and exuberant decoration on its portal; the same foreman, Khurremshah ibn Mughith of Ahlat, supervised both buildings (*see* ISLAMIC ART, §II, 5(iii)).

BIBLIOGRAPHY

M. van Berchem and H. Edhem: *Matériaux pour un Corpus Inscriptionum Arabicarum, 3ème partie: Asie Mineure* (Cairo, 1917), pp. 55–99
A. Gabriel: *Monuments turcs d'Anatolie* (Paris, 1934), ii, pp. 169–89
Y. Crowe: 'Divriği: Problems of Geography, History and Geometry', *The Art of Iran and Anatolia from the 11th to the 13th Century AD*, ed. W. Watson (London, 1975), pp. 28–39
Y. Önge, İ. Ateş and S. Bayram, eds: *Divriği Ulu Camii ve Darüşşifası* [The congregational mosque and hospital of Divriği] (Ankara, 1978)
T. A. Sinclair: *Eastern Turkey: An Architectural and Archaeological Survey*, 3 vols (London, 1987–9), ii, pp. 394–406

RAHMI HÜSEYIN ÜNAL

Dix, (Wilhelm Heinrich) Otto (*b* Untermhaus, nr Gera, 2 Dec 1891; *d* Singen, 25 July 1969). German painter, printmaker and watercolourist. His initial training (1905–14) in Gera and Dresden was as a painter of wall decorations, but he taught himself the techniques of easel painting from 1909 and began concentrating on portraits and landscapes in a veristic style derived from northern Renaissance prototypes. After seeing exhibitions of paintings by Vincent van Gogh (Dresden, 1912) and by the Futurists (1913), he quickly fused these influences into a randomly coloured Expressionism. Volunteering as a machine-gunner during World War I, he served in the German army (1914–18), making innumerable sketches of war scenes, using alternately a realistic and a Cubo-Futurist style. The experience of war, moreover, became a dominant motif of his work until the 1930s. He later commented: 'War is something so animal-like: hunger, lice, slime, these crazy sounds . . . War was something horrible, but nonetheless something powerful . . . Under no circumstances could I miss it! It is necessary to see people in this unchained condition in order to know something about man' (Kinkel, 1961; repr. in 1985 exh. cat., p. 280).

After the war (1919) Dix became a student at the Dresden Akademie der Bildenden Künste (now Hochschule für Bildende Künste) and became a founder-member of the Dresdner Sezession Gruppe 1919, a group of radical Expressionist and Dada artists and writers. In erotic allegories, gruesome scenes of war and revolution, and depictions of legless, drastically disfigured war cripples—works exhibited in Berlin at the *1. Internationalen Dada-Messe* in 1920—he employed a mixed-media technique that fused painting and collage using found objects. In his printmaking he echoed the motifs of his paintings, resulting in five portfolios of engravings and one of woodcuts by 1922.

In 1920 Dix resumed working in a highly veristic fashion, drawing nudes at the Akademie and painting portraits of friends and working-class models. These realist works also included socially critical motifs; a large portrait of *Parents I* (1921; Basle, Ksthalle); scenes of brothels; and a massive depiction of *The Trench* (1921–3; destr., see Löffler, 1982, pls. 62–3), filled with distended and deformed corpses. 'I told myself', he later commented, 'that life is not colourful at all. It is much darker, quieter in its tonality, much simpler. I wanted to depict things as they really are' (Wetzel, 1965; repr. in 1985 exh. cat., pp.288–9). Critical and commercial success followed Dix's shift to a revised form of realism. In 1923 he had his first solo exhibition at the Galerie I. B. Neumann in Berlin. At the exhibition of 1925 in Mannheim that first identified the objective art of NEUE SACHLICHKEIT as a new movement, Dix was presented as one of its leading painters, although his work was also coming under increasing attack as it gained wider recognition.

The Trench, purchased in 1923 for the Wallraf-Richartz-Museum, Cologne, became a focus of nationalist attack for its perceived anti-military stance, with the result that the museum returned the painting. Controversy also ensued when Dix was accused of pornography after exhibiting *Girl before Mirror* (1922; destr., see Löffler, 1981, pls. 1922–38), of an aged prostitute wearing a corset that left her genitalia exposed as she gazed into a mirror. Dix was acquitted, but attacks from right-wing political organizations continued to link him and other Neue Sachlichkeit artists with an alleged widespread left-wing plot to undermine German morality and mores. Dix's membership in the 1920s of such radical artists' organizations as Junge Rheinland and Berlin's Rote Gruppe, and his association with other left-wing groups and causes, continued to encourage the politicization of his work's reception. For example, *The Trench* travelled throughout Germany under sponsorship of the pacifist 'Nie wieder Krieg!' organization, which also patronized his portfolio of 50 engravings and etchings, *War* (1924; e.g. London, BM), based on his wartime sketches and strongly reminiscent of Goya.

After losing his rights to a studio at the Dresden Akademie in 1922, Dix moved to Düsseldorf, married Martha Koch, established links with the innovative Galerie Ey and changed the subject-matter of his work to less overtly political themes. War ceased to be a constant concern, and an extensive series of watercolours explored frequently violent or morbid erotic motifs. In paintings in which he used a technique of mixed oil and tempera—believed to be of northern Renaissance origin—portraits were dominant since Dix became favoured as a portrait painter of Germany's literary and theatrical bohemia and its notable patrons. Supported by the Galerie Nierendorf, Dix moved to Berlin in 1925 to participate more directly in the city's art scene, and to organize a series of collective exhibitions in Berlin, Munich and Dresden.

In late 1926 Dix was appointed to a professorship at the Dresden Akademie: it marked the high point of his success. Soon after he began one of his most ambitious works, his first triptych, *Metropolis* (1927–8; Stuttgart, Gal. Stadt; see fig.): in this, the motif, favoured earlier, of begging war cripples is contrasted with sexual display,

decadent sensual abandon and the apathy of the wealthy. With *Metropolis* Dix resumed a tactic of overt social criticism in his large public paintings. The theme of war also returned in a monumental commentary on the tenth anniversary of the end of World War I, again using the medieval triptych format with its religious associations, in *War* (1928–32; Dresden, Gemäldegal. Neue Meister); its central panel is an extended reprise of *The Trench*, flanked by wings depicting German soldiers marching in anonymous unity into battle, then emerging wounded, individualized and demoralized from it; on the predella are three corpses in tattered uniforms. Intending that it be displayed in a modern city in a bunker-like crypt, Dix identified *War* as 'the altarpiece as a site of silence and peace, surrounded by the bustle of human life outside, as site of meditation and as unidealized memorial of the nameless martyr–soldier' (interview, 1964; cited by Schmidt, 1981, p. 262).

While continuing to paint portraits and nudes, Dix injected an increasingly pessimistic and allegorical content into his work during the early 1930s. Nudes emerged as witches or personifications of melancholy. Named as a member of the Preussische Akademie der Künste in 1931, Dix was relieved of all honours and his teaching position immediately after the Nazi election victories of 1933, on the grounds that his paintings included morally offensive works that were 'likely to adversely affect the military will of the German people'. In allegorical paintings using traditional Christian motifs (e.g. the *Triumph of Death*, 1934; Stuttgart, Gal. Stadt; and the *Temptation of St Anthony*, 1936–7; Friedrichshafen, Städt. Bodensee-Mus.), Dix continued to provide a critical commentary on the character and consequences of Nazism. The large painting *Flanders* (2.0×2.5 m, 1934–6; Berlin, Alte N.G.) and *Lot and his Daughters* (1939; priv. col., on loan to Aachen, Suermondt-Ludwig-Mus.), with a bombed, burning Dresden in the background, once more reiterated the slaughter of World War I as a pessimistic warning for the future. Meanwhile he was forbidden to exhibit, and his work was confiscated from German museums to feature in various

Otto Dix: *Metropolis*, triptych, oil and tempera on wood, central panel 1.81×2.01 m, side panels each 1.81×1.01 m, 1927–8 (Stuttgart, Galerie der Stadt Stuttgart)

exhibitions of *entartete Kunst* (including the most infamous one in Munich, 1937). He moved from Dresden to seek seclusion, first in 1934 at Schloss Randegg near Singen, then in 1936 in the small town of Hemmenhofen on Lake Constance. Participating in the 'inner emigration' of numerous German artists and intellectuals, supported by a small number of patrons, Dix employed a polemically significant Old Master technique, such as was also often advocated for Nazi art, emulating German Renaissance painters. He also changed his art's most frequent content to the relatively neutral one of landscape, but landscape markedly bereft of human presence and in rejection of contemporary events.

Christian and biblical themes also became increasingly prevalent as Dix changed his mode of painting once more during the first years of World War II, returning to a heavily impastoed *alla prima* manner, but in dull colours, without the sensuality of his early oils. Drafted into the German territorial army in 1945, Dix was captured by French troops, served as prisoner of war at Colmar and then was allowed to return to Hemmenhofen. Continuing to evolve his new technique, he maintained an interest in portraits and self-portraits, Christian motifs, especially the Passion, and landscapes, and resumed printmaking. In politically divided Germany, he was unusual in his ability to negotiate between the West and East German regimes, making annual visits to Dresden, appointed to the academies of both West and East Berlin, and the recipient of major awards in both the Federal Republic of Germany and the German Democratic Republic.

BIBLIOGRAPHY

O. Conzelmann: *Otto Dix* (Hannover, 1959)
F. Löffler: *Otto Dix: Leben und Werk* (Dresden, 1960; Eng. trans., New York, 1982)
H. Kinkel: 'Der Unerbittliche: Zum siebzigsten Geburtstag des Malers Otto Dix', *Stuttgart. Ztg* (1 Dec 1961)
'Otto Dix im Gespräch mit Karl Heinz Hagen', *Neues Deutschland* (Dec 1964)
M. Wetzel: 'Professor Otto Dix: Ein harter Mann, dieser Maler', *Diplomat. Kurier* (1965)
F. Karsch: *Otto Dix: Das graphische Werk* (Hannover, 1970)
D. Schubert: *Otto Dix in Selbstzeugnissen und Dokumenten* (Hamburg, 1980)
L. Fischer: *Otto Dix: Ein Malerleben in Deutschland* (Berlin, 1981)
F. Löffler: *Otto Dix: Werkverzeichnis der Gemälde* (Recklinghausen, 1981)
D. Schmidt: *Otto Dix im Selbstbildnis* (E. Berlin, 1981)
F. Löffler: *Otto Dix* (New York, 1982)
O. Gunter and H. Dickel: *Otto Dix: Bildnis der Eltern—Klassenschicksal und Bildformel* (Frankfurt am Main, 1984)
Otto Dix, 1891–1969 (exh. cat., Munich, Villa Stuck, 1985)
F. Löffler: *Otto Dix: Bilder zur Bibel* (E. Berlin, 1986)
E. Karcher: *Otto Dix, 1891–1969: Leben und Werk* (Cologne, 1988; Eng. trans., Cologne, 1988)
B. Reinhardt, E. Keuerleber and D. Scholz: *Otto Dix: Bestandskatalog/Inventory Catalogue, Galerie der Stadt* (Stuttgart, 1989) [in Ger. and Eng.]
Otto Dix: Die Zeichnungen im Dresdner Kupferstich-Kabinett (exh. cat. by H.-U. Lehmann, Dresden, Kupferstichkab., 1991)
Otto Dix, 1891–1969 (exh. cat., ed. K. Hartley; London, Tate, 1992)
                                                                REINHOLD HELLER

Dixnard, Pierre-Michel. *See* IXNARD, PIERRE-MICHEL D'.

Dixon, Jeremy (*b* Bishop's Stortford, 31 May 1939). English architect. He trained at the Architectural Association, London (1958–63). From 1972 he worked in partnership with his wife Fenella Mary Anne Dixon (née Clemens) and from 1984 with Edward Jones. Dixon first came to international prominence in 1972 when he was selected with Fenella Dixon to design the new County Hall at Northampton, although his well-publicized proposal of a ten-storey Modernist pyramid was rejected due to spending cuts. A subsequent tour of Britain's towns and cities triggered ideas of 'contextual architecture' and its relation to art and history. A proponent of Post-modern architecture, Dixon completed a number of public commissions awarded in open competition, including the Housing Association project, St Mark's Road, west London (1979–80); the new coffee shop at the Tate Gallery, London (1981); and the redesign of the interior offices at—and the extension to—the Royal Opera House, Covent Garden, London (1987). Dixon's gifts lay particularly in his ability to interpret a development with an imaginative boldness of vision. The new gallery of the Henry Moore Institute, Leeds (1992), was designed as a massive Minimalist sculpture, faced with black polished granite, the interior completed in oak and stone. On the other hand, the housing projects in west London, perhaps his most successful projects, are modest in scale. These low-budget constructions, with their open-plan layout, make a succinct model for inexpensive housing and its place in a progressive society. At Lanark Road, Maida Vale, London, Dixon built a group of five villa-style houses (1984), each of which was subdivided into seven flats, which were offered to tenants on a housing list at a modest fixed price.

BIBLIOGRAPHY

C. Amery: 'Domestic Design', *Financial Times* (20 Feb 1984)
K. Powell: 'Streetwise Postmodernist', *The Telegraph* (8 Aug 1988)
D. Sudjic: 'Bringing Clad Tidings', *The Guardian* (5 April 1993)

Dixon, John (*b* Dublin, *c.* 1740; *d* London, Dec 1811). Irish engraver, active in England. After training in the Dublin Society's schools, he worked in line and mezzotint before moving to London *c.* 1765. By 1770 he had engraved four fine mezzotints after Reynolds; these and other portraits and humorous prints were published by William Wynne Ryland. From 1771 Dixon himself published some of his prints, most of them after Reynolds. His major prints include Rembrandt's *Framemaker* (1769; see Charrington, no. 44) and the highly praised *Tygress* after George Stubbs (see Lennox Boyd, no. 33). He was a man of some social as well as professional presence, becoming director of the Society of Artists in 1772. His final exhibit, *Fitzgerald James, 1st Duke of Leinster* (see Chaloner Smith, no. 22) after Reynolds, was described by Horace Walpole as 'a masterpiece of Art which has never been excelled'; it appeared in 1775, the year in which Dixon married a rich widow of some social standing and had to agree to give up his profession.

BIBLIOGRAPHY

DNB; Strickland [with a list including subject prints]; Thieme–Becker
J. Chaloner Smith: *British Mezzotinto Portraits*, i (London, 1878), pp. 203–18
A. Graves: *The Society of Artists of Great Britain (1760–1791): The Free Society of Artists (1761–1783)* (London, 1907), p. 78
J. Charrington: *A Catalogue of the Mezzotints after, or said to be after, Rembrandt* (Cambridge, 1923)

C. E. Russell: *English Mezzotint Portraits and their States: Catalogue of Corrections of and Additions to Chaloner Smith's 'British Mezzotinto Portraits'*, ii (London, 1926), pp. 53–5

C. Lennox Boyd, R. Dixon and T. Clayton: *George Stubbs: The Complete Engraved Work* (Abingdon, 1989), pp. 132–3

DAVID ALEXANDER

Dixon, Nicholas (*fl c.* 1660–65; *d* after 1707). English painter. His first signed portrait miniatures date from the early 1660s, but there is no documentary record before 1673, when he succeeded Samuel Cooper as Limner to Charles II. His oval miniature of *Catharine of Braganza* (Windsor Castle, Berks, Royal Col.) is a well-drawn and colourful example of his reticent approach to the interpretation of character. He also held the post of Keeper of the King's Picture Closet, which appears to have stimulated his ambition to enlarge his scope. He had, in 1668, painted a rectangular miniature of *Lady Anne Cavendish, William Cavendish, 1st Duke of Devonshire, and their Page* (Burghley House, Cambs), a composition of three half-lengths in a landscape that derives from van Dyck and Lely. He went on to make a number of limned copies of Old Master paintings. Having held a lottery of miniatures in 1685, he staged another lottery in 1698 called 'The Hopeful Adventure', in which there were money prizes and a large collection of miniatures to be won. This venture was not a success, and in 1708 he sold 70 of the limnings to John Holles, 1st Duke of Newcastle; 30 of these are now in the Portland Collection, Welbeck Abbey, Notts. He is believed to have died in poor circumstances soon after this transaction.

Dixon derived from Lely the mannerism of drawing his sitters' eyes with a languorous half-closed look and, with Peter Cross, carried the 17th-century method of stippling on vellum, derived from the example of John Hoskins, into the first years of the 18th century.

BIBLIOGRAPHY

J. Murdoch and others: *The English Miniature* (New Haven, 1981), pp. 135–9

GRAHAM REYNOLDS

Diyala region [Arab. Diyālá]. Region of ancient Mesopotamia, south of modern Ba'quba and north-east of Baghdad, Iraq. The area incorporates five major cities that flourished first during the Jemdet Nasr and Early Dynastic periods (*c.* 3100–*c.* 2340 BC) and has provided numerous examples of Sumerian architecture and sculpture. The region was also important during the Isin–Larsa period (*c.* 2000–*c.* 1760 BC).

Until the middle of the 1st millennium BC, the main stream of the Tigris River below Samarra' followed a line some distance to the east of its present course. In Abbasid times this ancient bed formed part of the Nahrawan canal, which, together with the tributary waters of the River Diyala, created a wide basin of cultivatable land. Later, with the Nahrawan fallen into disrepair and the Diyala deflected by a weir, the whole province became a wilderness strewn with abandoned city-mounds.

There has been much excavation since 1930: of the five major cities Tell Asmar, Khafajeh, Tell Agrab and Ischali were investigated by the Chicago Oriental Institute (under the direction of Henri Frankfort) and Tell Harmal by Iraqi archaeologists. The Americans also conducted a general survey of the Diyala region. Finds are in the Oriental Institute Museum of the University of Chicago, IL, and in the Iraq Museum in Baghdad. These investigations fully clarified the political history of the enclave. From initial settlements in the final centuries of the 3rd millennium BC there emerged a group of Sumerian city-states. The evidence from Early Dynastic (ED) strata at these sites enabled contemporary finds elsewhere in southern Mesopotamia to be divided chronologically into three phases, dated respectively *c.* 2900–*c.* 2750 (ED I), *c.* 2750–*c.* 2600 (ED II) and *c.* 2600–*c.* 2350 BC (ED III). An important discovery concerned the dichotomy in temple design between ground-level sanctuaries and platform-shrines foreshadowing the ziggurat. Sculpture was plentiful, particularly in the form of votive statuary, allowing the stylistic disparity between stone and metal to be studied. Fine relief-carving on cylinder seals (*see* ANCIENT NEAR EAST, §II, 1(ii)) revealed the fabric of Sumerian legend, animated occasionally by cuneiform writing.

The imperial regime of the Akkadian monarchy is not well represented in these Diyala cities, but everywhere traces are found of the Isin–Larsa interlude preceding Hammurabi's conquests in the 18th century BC. The region had by then become a political entity with a partly documented history and a known name: Eshnunna. Its governors had a temple at Asmar that was rivalled in splendour by a magnificent cult-centre at Ischali. Their genealogy is recorded on stamped bricks, and there are small archives of tablets. A much richer harvest of contemporary literature was recovered from Harmal.

1. TELL ASMAR [anc. Eshnunna]. This city was excavated in 1930–36 and became known as the type site for the Diyala region as a whole. During the 19th and 18th centuries BC, Eshnunna attained the dignity of a state capital. The administrative buildings and temples of the Eshnunna governors were conspicuous, with the earliest shrine dedicated to a deified king of Ur. Elsewhere on the site, house ruins of an earlier, Akkadian, date lay beneath the surface, and an elaborately planned building, with much attention given to drainage, was identified as a palace or guild-centre. A small temple formed part of the same complex, and its antecedents revealed the archaeological anatomy of the Early Dynastic period. Stray remnants of painted pottery dated the first phase (ED I), during which a small, shapeless shrine stood among private houses. In Early Dynastic II this was replaced by the more sophisticated Square Temple with three sanctuaries, one of which produced the now famous hoard of discarded Sumerian statues (Baghdad, Iraq Mus. and U. Chicago, IL, Orient. Inst. Mus.; see fig. 1). In the next phase (ED III) the Square Temple was replaced by a single-shrine building that survived, with frequent rebuilding, until Akkadian times. It was a simple rectangular affair with an altar at one end and a side-entrance, and it was the prototype of subsequent ground-level temples. In this period the shrine produced few objects except for a pottery sequence that now forms the chronological basis for the whole Early Dynastic period. Nearby was found a seal providing a link with the Indus civilization.

The Sumerian (ED II) statues from the Square Temple, differing considerably in style from statues found in Early

1. Diyala region, Tell Asmar, group of Sumerian statues from the Square Temple, gypsum, limestone and alabaster, h. of the largest 720 mm, Early Dynastic period, *c.* 2700 BC (Baghdad, Iraq Museum; Chicago, IL, University of Chicago, Oriental Institute Museum)

Dynastic III levels at Khafajeh, aroused much interest. The geometrical simplification of forms in the Asmar statues was distinctive, but it is now regarded as a regional peculiarity rather than a reliable dating criterion. Similar statues have, however, also been found at TELL CHUERA in Syria. The identities of the two largest statues from the Square Temple have also remained controversial. Symbolic carving on the base of the male statue (height 720 mm) tempted the excavators to identify the pair as a god and goddess. Since, like the remaining statues, they were depicted in an attitude of prayer, wide-eyed with hands clasped, their distinctive features could equally be attributed to civic status. A rich deposit of copper vessels and implements found in the neighbouring 'palace' was related by an inscription to Abu, god of vegetation, who may therefore have been patron of the Square Temple. The excavators failed to reveal any building dedicated to the god Tishpak, evidently patron of the city in later times.

2. KHAFAJEH [anc. Tutub]. The site of this city, excavated mainly by Pinhas Delougaz in 1930–38, lies on the east bank of the River Diyala, some 20 km above its present confluence with the Tigris. Its occupation started in the Jemdet Nasr period and spanned all three Early Dynastic phases. Damaged Sumerian sculpture (dated to ED II) was looted from Khafajeh and reached Baghdad dealers in 1929. Subsequent careful clearance in the vicinity of the looters' holes revealed the fragmentary plan of a ground-level temple, somewhat larger than that at Asmar and dedicated in this case to the moon god, Sin. Lateral chambers had been added to the basic element of a rectangular sanctuary, while further dependencies, dating from successive rebuildings, surrounded a small courtyard that was entered by a towered gateway; the asymmetrical plan was clearly adapted to the site available. Ritual vessels and small objects were found undisturbed in the deeper levels and in three smaller single-shrine temples among the neighbouring houses.

Elsewhere in the city, a platform-temple was surrounded by an oval enclosure, but the whole complex was denuded almost down to pavement level. This Oval Temple (dating to ED II and III) had a double enceinte with space between the walls for a capacious annexe, presumably quarters for priests. The inner enclosure was surrounded by outbuildings arranged to form a rectangular courtyard. Half filling this space was the outline of the buttressed platform and its stepped approach. Buried beneath pavement level was a group of three copper supports (U. Chicago, IL, Orient. Inst. Mus.; Baghdad, Iraq Mus.) in the form of nude male figures (h. 400–550 mm).

3. TELL AGRAB. This site, some 20 km south-east of
Asmar, was excavated by Seton Lloyd. The mound is
about 500 m across and is surrounded by a defensive wall,
which is 5 m thick with semicircular buttresses. Surface
pottery testifies to its occupation throughout the first half
of the 3rd millennium BC. The Shara Temple (dating to
ED II) was located on the surface in a low-lying area
adjoining the city wall. This temple was an enlarged version
of the Square Temple at Asmar, measuring 60 m across.
Two subsidiary shrine chambers and living quarters for
the priests were well preserved, as was the impressive
sanctuary, where thousands of beads and small amulets
lay partly trodden into the pavement. Along the sanctuary
wall was a row of small pedestals for offerings. The high
altar was built in two stages, with the upper one reached
by a miniature stairway. Fragments of statues and other
objects lay scattered around it, while others were actually
built into its structure or deposited in a small sacristy near
by. There were hundreds of ceremonial mace heads carved
from a wide variety of coloured stones. Among larger
objects was a damaged stand, ornamented in deep relief
with mythical scenes, and a carved chlorite vase imported
from further east. There were miniature copper statues
with inlaid eyes and a tiny quadriga group (a standing
figure driving four onagers) cast in copper by the lost-wax
process (Baghdad, Iraq Mus.). The number and variety of
cylinder seals were remarkable, and the combined corpus
from the three main Diyala sites forms the basis for the
division of the Early Dynastic into three phases.

4. ISCHALI [anc. Neribtum]. Thorkild Jacobsen conducted excavations at this site, a few km south of Khafajeh,

2. Diyala region, Ischali, Ishtar–Kititum Temple, Isin–Larsa period, *c.* 1800 BC;
reconstruction drawing by H. D. Hill (Chicago, IL, University of Chicago,
Oriental Institute Museum)

on the east bank of the Diyala. The temple (100×60 m),
built by a late governor of Eshnunna (*c.* 1800 BC), has
been described as 'perhaps the finest monument of the
Isin–Larsa period' (see fig. 2; for plan *see* TEMPLE, fig. 1).
It was dedicated to Ishtar–Kititum, a local aspect of the
great goddess, and was raised on a 3 m platform (Akkad.
kisu) of kiln-baked bricks. The plan incorporates three
separate shrines approached through an outer and an inner
courtyard, with a monumental stairway between. Two of
the shrines adhere to the Babylonian formula with entrance, sanctuary and altar all on a single axis (*Breitraum*
type). The third consists of a long room with a side
approach, more common in Assyria (*Langraum* type).

5. TELL HARMAL [anc. Shaduppum]. The site is a
small mound on the eastern outskirts of modern Baghdad.
The inscribed tablets found there show it to have been an
outlying administrative centre for the Eshnunna government. Though modest in size, it was heavily fortified, and
the buildings within its walls included no fewer than three
temples, the largest of which had inner and outer gateways
flanked by finely modelled, almost life-size, terracotta
lions.

BIBLIOGRAPHY
H. Frankfort: *Illus. London News* (21 Sept 1935 and 5 Sept 1936)
[preliminary reports on excavations at Ischali]
——: *Sculpture of the Third Millennium BC from Tell Asmar and Khafajah*,
Orient. Inst. Pub., xliv (Chicago, 1939)
H. Frankfort, S. Lloyd and T. Jacobsen: *The Gimilsin Temple and the
Palace of the Rulers at Tell Asmar*, Orient. Inst. Pub., xliii (Chicago,
1940)
P. Delougaz: *The Temple Oval at Khafajah*, Orient. Inst. Pub., liii (Chicago,
1940)
P. Delougaz and S. Lloyd: *Pre-Sargonid Temples in the Diyala Region*,
Orient. Inst. Pub., lviii (Chicago, 1942)
H. Frankfort: *More Sculpture from the Diyala Region*, Orient. Inst. Pub., lx
(Chicago, 1943)
T. Baqir: 'Tell Harmal', *Sumer*, ii (1946), pp. 22–30; iv (1948), pp. 52–3
P. Delougaz: *Pottery from the Diyala Region*, Orient. Inst. Pub., lxiii
(Chicago, 1952)
H. Frankfort: *Stratified Cylinder Seals from the Diyala Region*, Orient. Inst.
Pub., lxxii (Chicago, 1955)
S. A. al-Alusi: 'Excavations at Tell Harmal', *Sumer*, xv (1959), pp. 47–8
N. al-Asil: 'The Seventh Season at Tell Harmal', *Sumer*, xvii (1961), pp.
201–8 [in Arabic]
R. M. Adams: *Land Behind Baghdad: A History of Settlements in the Diyala
Plains* (Chicago, 1965)
P. Delougaz, H. D. Hill and S. Lloyd: *Private Houses and Graves in the
Diyala Region*, Orient. Inst. Pub., lxxxviii (Chicago, 1967)

SETON LLOYD

Diyarbakır [Diyarbekır, Diyār Bakr; Arab. Diyārbakr,
Āmīd; anc. Amida]. Turkish city in south-east Anatolia.
Located on the upper reaches of the Tigris River, the city
of Amida was already an important political and commercial centre in Roman times; it served as the provincial
capital of northern Jazira (Upper Mesopotamia) under the
Muslims, who conquered the region of the Diyar Bakr
('abode of the [tribe of] Bakr') in AD 640. It was often
called Kara ('Black') Amid on account of its ramparts and
houses, which were built of black basalt frequently laid in
alternating courses with white limestone. The city plan,
dating from Roman times, comprises intersecting arteries
and a regular grid of streets. The arteries lead to gates at
the four cardinal points of the city wall (h. 8–12 m; w. 3–
5 m), which has a roughly elliptical trace (1700×1300 m)
and stretches for 5.5 km, supposedly the longest medieval

city wall in existence. Built of masonry rubble between basalt ashlar facings and reinforced with square, round and polygonal towers, the wall is decorated with figural representations and inscription plaques recording repeated repairs from the 10th century to the 19th. Carved by local masons, the inscribed bands attest to a continuous tradition of fine ornamental epigraphy in the region.

The Great Mosque (Ulu Cami), located to the northwest of the central intersection on a site successively occupied by a temple and a church, was founded in the 7th century but rebuilt in the 12th (*see* ISLAMIC ART, fig. 40). Its spacious court (62×31 m) has double-storey façades employing classical spolia flanking the prayer-hall on the south; the hall has three aisles parallel to the qibla intersected by a raised aisle leading to the mihrab, a plan undoubtedly inspired by that of the Great Mosque of Damascus in Syria. Under the patronage of the Artuqid dynasty (*reg* 1098–1232), the Zinciriye Madrasa (1198) and the Mesudiye Madrasa (1198–1223), incorporated within the congregational mosque, were built. Both have open courts, great iwans and elaborately decorated masonry. Remains of the Artuqid palace (1201–22) include a court with a central pool and four iwans.

After the capture of the city by the Ottomans in 1514, it became an important commercial centre, as attested by several large caravanserais, such as the Deliller Han (1527) and the Hasan Pasha Han (1573–5). In addition to many mosques in which a simple portico precedes a domed prayer-hall, there are several grander structures. The Büyük Mehmed or Fatih Pasha Mosque (1518–20) is the first Ottoman mosque to have a central dome surrounded by four semi-domes. The mosque of Behram Pasha (1572) is notable for its harmonious proportions, striped masonry and exquisite tile decoration (*see* ISLAMIC ART, §II, 7(i)). Diyarbakır tiles of the 16th century imitate contemporary Iznik wares but are distinguished by a bluish glaze subject to crackle.

BIBLIOGRAPHY
Enc. Islam/2: 'Diyār Bakr'
M. van Berchem, J. Strzygowski and G. Bell: *Amida* (Heidelberg, 1910)
S. Flury: *Islamische Schriftbänder Amida-Diarbekr* (Basle and Paris, 1920) (also pubd as 'Bandeaux ornementés à inscriptions arabes', *Syria*, i (1920), pp. 235–49, 318–28 and ii (1921), pp. 54–62)
A. Gabriel: *Voyages archéologiques dans la Turquie orientale* (Paris, 1940)
O. Aslanapa: 'Erster Bericht über die Ausgrabungen des Palastes von Diyarbakir', *Istanbul. Mitt.*, xii (1962), pp. 115–28
G. Godwin: *A History of Ottoman Architecture* (Baltimore, 1971), pp. 178 and 309–10
J. Raby: 'Diyarbekir: A Rival to Iznik. A Sixteenth-century Tile Industry in Eastern Anatolia', *Istanbul. Mitt.*, xxvii (1977–8), pp. 429–59
A. Kuran: 'Anatolian-Seljuk Architecture', *The Art and Architecture of Turkey*, ed. E. Akurgal (Oxford, 1980), pp. 80–84, 91
T. Allen: *A Classical Revival in Islamic Architecture* (Wiesbaden, 1986), pp. 37–41
T. A. Sinclair: *Eastern Turkey: An Architectural and Archaeological Survey*, 3 vols (London, 1987–9), iii, pp. 164–95

ÇIĞDEM KAFESÇIOĞLU

Diziani, Gaspare (*b* Belluno, 1689; *d* Venice, 17 Aug 1767). Italian painter and draughtsman. His earliest training was in Belluno with Antonio Lazzarini (1672–1732), the last exponent in the Veneto of Baroque tenebrism. Having moved to Venice, he joined the workshop of Gregorio Lazzarini and later that of Sebastiano Ricci, who was in Venice until 1715 and exerted the strongest

influence on his development; presumably Diziani was familiar with Ricci's many paintings in Belluno before becoming his pupil. Between 1710 and 1720 he painted a group of eight pictures that included the *Mary Magdalene* for S Stefano, Belluno, and the *Entry into Jerusalem* for S Teodoro, Venice. His speed of production and technical assurance are demonstrated especially in his preparatory oil sketches, with colour applied in rapid and spirited penlike strokes. He was also working as a scenery painter in many Venetian theatres, an employment that led to commissions first in Munich (1717) and later in Dresden, where he was highly acclaimed. According to Canal, Diziani was invited to Rome by Cardinal Pietro Ottoboni in 1726, to paint a 'magnificent decoration for the church of S Lorenzo in Damaso'; Longhi, however, placed this visit earlier than the journeys to Munich and Dresden. The decoration is now known only through an engraving by Claude Vasconi (see Pavanello, fig. 3).

Diziani's first known signed and dated painting is the *Ecstasy of St Francis* (1727; Belluno, S Rocco), clearly influenced by Ricci. His works reveal two contrasting tendencies that remain evident throughout his oeuvre and make it difficult to establish a chronology: a refined and geometric style, inspired by Ricci; and a style inspired by the more rounded forms of Classical sculpture. The *St Augustine Triumphing over Heresy* (Venice, Accad. Pitt. & Scul.), the *Beheading of St Eurosia* (priv. col.; ex-Villa Rinaldi-Barberini, Asolo) and the *Virgin of the Carmelites*, painted on the ceiling of the parish church in Mira, were all executed before 1732. In 1733 he painted such frescoes as the *Adoration of the Magi*, the *Flight into Egypt* and the *Massacre of the Innocents* in the sacristy of S Stefano, Venice; these adopt pictorial motifs from Ricci and reveal an impetuous, almost violent style. Probably dating from the same period are the *Martyrdom of SS Felix and Fortunatus* (Chioggia Cathedral), two paintings of Carmelite subjects (Venice, S Maria del Carmelo) and the grandiose and theatrical *Conversion of St Paul* (Padua, S Giustina).

In 1746 Diziani painted frescoes of mythological and allegorical subjects in the Palazzo Riccati, Castelfranco Veneto, and the following year, with some help from assistants, in the Palazzo Spineda in Treviso (all *in situ*). The small but elaborate and light-filled *Annunciation* (Belluno, Mus. Civ.) also dates from 1747. In 1751 he accepted commissions to paint the fresco of the *Trinity in Glory with Dominican Saints* for S Bartolomeo, Bergamo, and the canvas of *God the Father with SS Francis and Antony* for the baldacchino of the Basilica di S Antonio (il Santo) in Padua (Padua, Mus. Antoniano). Both these large-scale works exhibit an extraordinary passion and liveliness of expression, possibly influenced by the work of Carlo Carlone (ii), active in Bergamo a few years earlier. The *Blessed Virgin and Saints* (1753; Condino Cathedral; see fig.) marks an important change of direction towards a more Rococo style, as was being adopted by Giambattista Tiepolo and Giovanni Battista Pittoni. This is equally apparent in such altarpieces as the *Adoration of the Shepherds* (Clusone, S Maria Assunta), the *Assumption of the Virgin with Saints* (Belluno, S Gervasio) and those sent to the Friuli, to Tolmezzo Cathedral, S Pietro ai Volti in Cividale and S Vito al Tagliamento Cathedral. These works,

Gaspare Diziani: *Blessed Virgin and Saints*, oil on canvas, 1753 (Condino Cathedral)

nevertheless document an unremitting activity. The drawings are occasionally more lively than the finished paintings, some of which appear suppressed by academic compositional requirements. Among his drawings engraved as book illustrations are those for an edition of Dante's *Divine Comedy* published by Zatta (Venice, 1757). With Francesco Fontebasso, his collaborator at this time on decorations in the palazzi Belloni and Contarini, he also provided illustrations for an edition of Palladio's *Quattro libri dell'architettura* (Venice 1740–60), notably the frontispiece representing an *Allegory of Architecture* (1740) and *Architecture with Sculpture and Painting* at the start of Book IV. He is also documented as an official restorer of public paintings. In 1760 he succeeded Tiepolo and Pittoni as president of the Accademia di Pittura Veneziana, of which he had been a founder in 1755. He was re-elected to this post for a two-year term in 1766 but died the following year, in a café in the Piazza S Marco in Venice. He was married in 1731 and had ten children. Two of his sons became painters and frequently worked with him: Giuseppe Diziani (1732–1803), a history painter, and Antonio Diziani (1737–97), a landscape painter.

BIBLIOGRAPHY

Thieme–Becker

V. da Canal: *Vita di Gregorio Lazzarini* (1732); ed. G. A. Moschini (Venice, 1809)

A. Longhi: *Compendio delle vite de' pittori veneziani* (Venice, 1762), p. 25

G. B. Baldissone: 'Gaspare Diziani e la sua famiglia', *Archv Stor. Belluno, Feltre & Cadore*, 77 (1941), pp. 1310–11

F. Valcanover: *Pitture del settecento nel Bellunese* (Venice, 1954)

R. Pallucchini: *La pittura veneziana nel settecento* (Venice, 1960)

A. P. Zugni Tauro: *Gaspare Diziani* (Venice, 1971)

B. Aikema: 'Per Gaspare Diziani', *Boll. Mus. Civ. Ven.*, xxv/1 (1980), pp. 7–18

A. Dorigato: 'Disegni di Gaspare Diziani e della sua cerchia', *Disegni antichi del Museo Correr di Venezia*, ed. T. Pignatti (Venice, 1981), pp. 15–149

G. P. Pavanello: 'Per Gaspare Diziani decoratore', *A. Ven.*, xxxv (1981), pp. 126–36

F. Valcanover: 'Per il catalogo di Gaspare Diziani', *Stud. Trentini Sci. & Stor.*, lx/2 (1981), p. 277

R. Bossaglia and others: *Il cielo domenicano di Gaspare Diziani: Studi e ricerche in occasione del restauro* (Bergamo, 1983)

S. Claut: 'Quesiti dizianeschi', *Archv Stor. Belluno, Feltre & Cadore*, lvii/254 (1986), pp. 31–5

——: 'Gaspare Diziani', *Ornamenta Ecclesiae* (Asolo, 1988), pp. 13–26

——: 'Per Gaspare Diziani: Questioni cronologiche e qualche inedito', *A. Ven.*, xlii (1988), pp. 146–51

R. Tomić: 'Slike talijanskih slikara 17. i 18. stoljeca u Dalmacij i Istri' [Paintings by Italian painters of the 17th and 18th centuries in Dalmatia and Istria], *Prilozi Povijesti Umjetnosti Dalmac.*, xxx (1990), pp. 281–6

SERGIO CLAUT

all from 1755, are characterized by a transparent luminosity, an absence of chiaroscuro contrast and, in some cases, a brighter palette. Their rhetoric is softened by a nervous handling of the curving folds of drapery. The altarpiece of 1757 in S Floriano, Storo, and the *Saints of the Counter-Reformation* (Belluno Cathedral) are close in style and probably also in date. The *Madonna of the Rosary* (1757; parish church of Završje, Croatia), with its vivacious small scenes of the 15 mysteries of the rosary around the border, underpins the chronology of Diziani's work in the 1760s and 1770s. In 1760, with the assistance of his sons, Diziani decorated the mezzanine of the Villa Rinaldi-Barberini. An enthusiasm for narrative led him to paint decorative cycles on both sacred and secular themes, among the latter the *Stories of Alexander* (Paris, de Balkany priv. col.), *Amphitrite, Pan and Syrinx* (Como, priv. col.), *Thetis and Vulcan* (Vienna, priv. col.), *Moses Trampling on Pharaoh's Crown* (Warsaw, N. Mus.)—works in which his early experience of painting for the theatre found a mature and somewhat rhetorical expression. His last works, such as the ceiling (1760–62) of the Scuola di S Giovanni Evangelista, Venice, look forward to Neo-classicism.

Drawings form a significant part of Diziani's oeuvre. A large collection of them, possibly the largest by an individual Venetian 18th-century artist, is held at the Museo Correr, Venice. Their uneven quality and varied techniques may encourage doubts over their attribution, but they

Dizieult [Dizieulz; Disieult; Disieux], **Jean** [Jehan] (*fl* 1530; *d* Senlis, 1553). French architect. The accounts of the cathedral chapter of Senlis name Jean Dizieult and Pierre Chambiges (*see* CHAMBIGES, (2)) as master masons of their church in 1530. Jean is also referred to as lieutenant to the master of the King's Works for the bailly of Senlis; Pierre de Chambiges served as master. The two were responsible for the reconstruction of the cathedral transepts, which had been burnt in 1504. The ornate, plastic style of the two façades places them among the major monuments of late Flamboyant architecture in France. The south transept was probably designed by Pierre. Construction was clearly under way by July 1530, when the masters received an advance to complete the portal, including sculptures, and to obtain materials for the next winter's work. The transept was complete in April 1534, when workers began glazing the rose window and leading the roof. Since Pierre was working at Chantilly during this time, it is thought that Jean supervised the construction. The north transept was begun soon thereafter but remained unfinished in 1560. Jean Dizieult was the sole master responsible for the construction of its less ornate and slightly more linear façade. The chapter complained in 1538 of his slow progress, which they attributed to his responsibility for the upkeep of royal buildings. No specific royal buildings have been attributed to him.

Jean Dizieult was apparently held in high esteem as a citizen of Senlis. In the crossbowmen's games of 1538, he was described as a member who exhibited as much skill in shooting as in his work on the cathedral portals. In 1553 his widow's declaration records the death of 'Jean Dizieult, lieutenant master of the King's Works. . .one of the great glories of Senlis'.

BIBLIOGRAPHY

E. Müller: 'Essai d'une monographie des rues, places, et monuments de Senlis', *Com. Archéol. Senlis: C. R. & Mém.*, 2nd ser., v (1879), pp. 249–440; vi (1880), pp. 1–160; vii (1881), pp. 121–330; viii (1882/3), p. 229
E. Lefèvre-Pontalis: 'Senlis', *Congr. Archéol. France*, lxxii/1 (1905), pp. 89–108
M. Vachon: *Les Chambiges: Une Famille parisienne de maistres-maçons, 1490–1643* (Paris, 1907), pp. 77–86
M. Aubert: *Monographie de la Cathédrale de Senlis* (Senlis, 1910)
E. Pilon: *Senlis et Chantilly* (Grenoble, 1937)
R. Nelson: *Martin Chambiges and the Development of French Flamboyant Architecture* (diss., Baltimore, MD, Johns Hopkins U., 1973), pp. 282–305

ELLEN M. SHORTELL

Djakarta. *See* JAKARTA.

Djane. *See* TANIS.

Djanira (da Motta e Silva) (*b* Avaré, 1914; *d* Rio de Janeiro, 31 May 1979). Brazilian painter. She spent her childhood and youth in the country in the south of Brazil. On moving to Rio de Janeiro *c.* 1939, she taught herself to paint and in 1940 had five months of informal teaching under Emeric Marcier (*b* 1916) in Rio de Janeiro, always retaining in her work a non-academic spontaneity and freshness. Her development was not, however, that of a naive painter. Her precise, poetic vision of the landscape, ethnic character and working life of Brazil often concentrated on workers such as coffee-pickers, miners, woodcutters, fishermen, cowherds, weavers and workers in car factories. The Museu Nacional de Belas Artes, Rio de Janeiro, has many of her works: paintings, drawings and engravings from various periods, among them the canvases *The Circus* (1944) and *Mestizo Children* (1952).

BIBLIOGRAPHY

M. Barata and others: *Djanira no acervo do Museu Nacional de Belas Artes* [Djanira in the collection of the National Museum of Fine Art] (Rio de Janeiro, 1985)
R. Sampaio: 'Interiores, figuras e paisagens' [Interiors, figures and landscapes], *Seis décadas de arte moderna na Coleção Roberto Marinho* (Rio de Janeiro, 1985), pp. 260–67

ROBERTO PONTUAL

Djeba. *See* EDFU.

Djeitun. *See* DZHEYTUN.

Djemila [anc. Cuicul]. Roman town in Algeria, founded *c.* AD 97 as a colony for army veterans. It was given a local, non-Roman name (Cuicul), but its modern name Djemila (Arab.: 'beautiful') is a fitting description for one of the most picturesque sites in North Africa. It lies 60 km from the Mediterranean Sea in rugged, mountainous but fertile countryside, its well-defended position enhanced by the construction of defences enclosing an area of some 200×400 m. The uneven topography necessitated a polygonal arrangement of walls, but within them the streets were laid out in orderly, parallel lines. Systematic excavation since 1909 has revealed many of the internal squares and buildings.

The gate into the colony is still standing; from here the *cardo maximus* leads to the forum, a great square with elegant porticos on two sides. Here also was the capitolium, the *curia*, the judicial basilica and a *macellum* (market building). The basilica (built after AD 169) was paid for by a priest, C. Julius Crescens, while the *macellum* was donated by L. Cosinius Primus, a magistrate from Carthage, and his brother. This underlines the fact that many public buildings in Roman towns were financed by rich individuals seeking social advancement.

The town developed rapidly, so that by the middle of the 2nd century AD the area within the walls was largely filled. There were public baths, temples and houses, the more elegant with peristyle courts. So fast an expansion soon resulted in construction outside the walls of the original colony, in common with most other North African towns. On the higher ground to the south, a huge bath complex was built (AD 183–5), and a theatre was set into the side of the ridge at about the same time. It held only about 3000 spectators, a reminder of the town's relatively modest size. Soon afterwards, in the period of the first African dynasty, the Severans (*reg* AD 193–235), a square (erroneously called a forum) was constructed outside the main gate. There were porticos on two sides, as well as a great Corinthian temple, still largely standing, dedicated to the family of the Severans (AD 229; *see* ROME, ANCIENT, fig. 6). In addition, there was a striking arch (AD 216) at the start of the road to Setif (anc. Sitifis) and elegant fountains. Private houses, some of them quite grand, began to spread over the area around the square and on the hill to the south.

Further public building took place towards the end of the 3rd century AD, including the renovation of the water supply system, but it was during the 4th century that there was a major investment in building. Many private houses were provided with attractive figured mosaics (many in Djemila, Mus. Archéol.), while a judicial basilica (AD 364–7) and a cloth market were added to the Severan Square. Christianity, the official religion of the Empire from AD 313, also brought changes to the town. Most of the known Christian buildings date to the early 5th century AD, forming a huge complex with two basilican churches, a round baptistery decorated with mosaics and a bishop's palace in the south-east part of the 'new town', but there was also a large church within the old centre. Whether Djemila was taken by the Vandals is unknown, but there are traces of what may be a small Byzantine fort (5th century AD), and in AD 553 Bishop Cresconius is known to have attended a synod in Istanbul. Thereafter the town slipped into obscurity and was almost deserted when the French occupied it in 1839.

BIBLIOGRAPHY

P.-A. Février: *Djemila* (Algiers, 1968)
Y. Allais: 'Le Quartier occidental de Djemila (Cuicul)', *Ant. Afr.*, v (1971), pp. 95–120
P.-A. Février: *Djemila: Guide* (Algiers, 1971, 2/1978)
H. Blanchard-Lemée: *Maisons à mosaïque du quartier central de Djemila (Cuicul)* (Aix-en-Provence, 1976)

T. W. POTTER

Djibuti, Republic of [Jibuti; Arab. Jumhūriyya al-Jibuti; formerly French Somaliland (1896–1967), French Territory of the Afars and the Issas (1967–77)]. Country on the north-east coast of Africa, bordered by Eritrea to the north, by Ethiopia to the west and south-west, and by Somalia to the south. Djibuti gained independence in 1977. The official languages are French and Arabic. About 89% of the total land area of *c.* 22,000 sq. km is desert. Most of the population live in the capital and port of Djibuti city with the remainder following a nomadic way of life. This entry covers the art produced in Djibuti since colonial times. (For art of the region in earlier periods *see* AFRICA, §VII, 2.)

Djibuti city was founded in 1888 and doubled in size between 1896 and 1899. During this period there was much building in the colonial style: streets were also laid out. The port, which handles about half of Ethiopia's trade, is the basis of the country's economy. The population (395,000; UN estimate, 1989) comprises the Afars, concentrated largely in the north and west, and the Issas (the Somali people in Djibuti) in the south. Both adhere to Islam. The Afars are descendants of settlers from Arabia, who arrived around the 3rd century BC. Later the Issas from Somalia settled in the south and along the coastal region. Trade brought Arab and Portuguese influences in the 16th century. In the 1880s the French influences marked out French Somaliland, which became an overseas territory in 1946.

The culture of the Afars and Issas was, traditionally, orally based, with little painting and few artefacts. Although French administration made some attempt to protect the cultural past, its achievements in this area were limited. Those traditional crafts that are still practised include the engraving of daggers and knives, the production of copperwork and silverwork, wood-carving and jewellery-making, especially necklaces of amber or malachite. Ethnic links across national borders, the Afars with Ethiopia and the Issas with Somalia, remain culturally important in present-day Djibuti: a factor enhanced by nomadic migration. Djibuti has no museum, although one was planned in 1947, for which a collection was begun and housed in the General Secretariat. In the 1960s some of this material still decorated the antechamber of the Ministry of Affairs. A craft school was established at Tadjoura in 1956 with the encouragement of the Roman Catholic mission.

BIBLIOGRAPHY

Enc. Islam/1
M. Chailley: *Notes sur les 'Afar de la région de Tadjoura: Tadjoura, Sismo, Djibouti, novembre 1935–septembre 1937* (Paris, 1960)
J. Jouve: 'Le Musée de Djibouti', *Pount* (Oct 1966), pp. 5–6
J. Trampont: *Djibouti hier: De 1887 à 1939* (Paris, 1990)

Djiwal, Jack. *See* WUNUWUN, JACK.

Djogdjakarta [Djokjakarta]. *See* YOGYAKARTA.

Djuric, Miodrag. *See* DADO.

Dlabač, Jan Bohumír [Gottfried] (*b* Cerhenice, nr Plaňany, 17 July 1758; *d* Prague, 4 Feb 1820). Czech writer and art historian. While studying in Prague he was influenced by Stanislav Vydra (1741–1804), a professor who encouraged him to contribute to the incipient Czech national revival. In 1778 he entered the Premonstratensian monastery in Strahov, and from 1802 he was in charge of its enormous library. In 1796 he became a member of the Royal Czech Society of Sciences and later (1813–18) its Director.

Dlabač started writing poetry in 1782. A history of Strahov appeared in 1805–7. In 1815, after 28 years of work, he published in Prague three volumes of *Allgemeines historisches Künstler Lexikon für Böhmen*. This dictionary provided unprecedentedly exhaustive records of artists and musicians, including biographical data and complete lists of their works. It also contained entries on individual objects, evaluations, criticisms and sources. Dlabač personally visited churches, monasteries and palaces to compile it, copying inscriptions from tombstones, bells and other sources. Many dozens of manuscripts on the topics of history, arts and science were preserved in Strahov in his legacy. In 1818 he published a guide in Czech to Bohemia.

WRITINGS

Historische Darstellung des Ursprunges und der Schicksale des königlich Stiftes Strahow (1805–7)
Allgemeines historisches Künstler Lexikon für Böhmen zum Theile auch für Mähren und Schlesien, 3 vols (Prague, 1815)
Krátké vypsání království českého s mapou Čech [A brief description of the kingdom of Bohemia with a map of Bohemia] (1818)

BIBLIOGRAPHY

Ottův slovník naučný [Otta encyclopaedia], vii (Prague, 1893), pp. 675–6
B. Ryba: *Soupis rukopisů Strahovské knihovny* [List of Strahov Library manuscripts] (Prague, 1970–79), iii–v, index, vi/2
Kapitoly z českého dějepisu umění [Chapters from the Czech history of arts], i (Prague, 1986), p. 53

IVO KOŘÁN

Dłubak, Zbigniew (*b* Radomsko, nr Częstochowa, 24 April 1921). Polish photographer, writer and painter. He was self-taught as an artist. Just after World War II he founded and became one of the most active members of the avant-garde Club of Young Artists and Scientists (Klub Młodych Artystow i Naukowcow), Warsaw. Club activities, as well as his own ideas concerning possible union between the new, radical left-wing art and the political and social situation in the country, reached an impasse with the rise of Socialist Realism in 1949. He was the editor of the magazine *Fotografia* from 1953 to 1972 and a lecturer at the Film School, Łódź, from 1966 to 1975. From 1982 he lived in Paris.

In the 1940s Dłubak produced extreme close-up photographs with metaphoric titles. His 'cool medium' (deliberately banal) documentary works of the 1950s (e.g. the series *Existences*, 1955–66) clashed with official, optimistic, propaganda images. Later his work and his numerous theoretical writings were stimulated by studies in semiotics. They are concerned with the emergence and intelligibility of signs dependent on an ever-changing cultural context (hence the term 'contextual art', coined in the 1970s), in which objects of which the artist is solely a producer become works of art only through participation in an exchange of meanings. Dłubak maintained that since there is no system of signs able to form any universal set of rules, the artistic process must be 'reversed' into a gradual distortion and destruction of common symbols and images (e.g. the photo-environments *Iconospheres I–II*, 1967–8, and the series *Tautologies*, 1970, and *Desymbolizations*, 1977–80). He also produced series of abstract, Minimalist paintings (e.g. *Ammonites*, 1957–63; *Anthropolites*, 1963–5; *Systems*, 1974–8).

WRITINGS
Wybrane teksty o sztuce 1948–1977 [Selected essays on art 1948–1977] (Warsaw, 1977)

BIBLIOGRAPHY
'Zbigniew Dłubak interviewed by Szymon Bojko', *Projekt* (1975), no. 4 [in Eng.]
Zbigniew Dłubak: Desymbolizacje [Zbigniew Dłubak: desymbolizations] (exh. cat., ed. J. Ładnowska; Łódź, Mus. A., 1978)

EWA MIKINA

Dmitriyev, Maksim (Petrovich) (*b* Povalishino, Tambov province, 6 Aug 1853; *d* 1948). Russian photographer. He was born into a peasant family and at the age of 14 went to Moscow, where he worked in the photographic studio of Nastyukov. In 1874 he did some work for Andrey Karelin in Nizhny Novgorod and went to work for him in 1879. In 1886 Dmitriyev opened his own portrait studio in Nizhny Novgorod, where he worked until the 1920s.

Dmitriyev's early portraits are strongly influenced by Karelin; he produced a number of group portraits and particularly tasteful prints, and he was also attracted to landscape prints in the style of the Peredvizhniki (WANDERERS). He first exhibited in 1889, the year in which he embarked on a unique and massive documentation of the Volga. This series of more than 1200 photographs of the Volga and the regions around it from Rybinsk to Astrakhan took him nine years and demonstrates the extraordinary breadth of his interest. It encompasses landscape, historic sites, local and national types and the daily life, habits and occupations of ordinary people, all taken on large glass plates (500×600 mm), from which he made contact prints. He also made use of anastigmatic lenses to achieve sharper focus. The result is a remarkably detailed portrait of a vast region and its inhabitants, concentrating in particular on Nizhny Novgorod. Dmitriyev published a number of albums from this series, and the prints show his aesthetic competence, particularly his compositional skills (e.g. *Unloading the Barge*, 1890; see Morozov, 1977, fig. 16), his fondness for the device of the path or river edge leading into the distance and reflections in the water. The photographs were also conceived as serious documents; they were published in scientific journals, and Dmitriyev was elected a member of the Russian Geographical Society.

Dmitriyev's documentation of daily life attests to his strong social awareness. This is also evident in his portraiture, in the way in which he situated the character and photographed his wide range of sitters with a characteristic expression, as in his portraits of the *Peasant from the Nizhny Novgorod Region* (1890s; see Morozov, 1986, p. 106), sitting at the roadside in his felt boots and fur coat, and of the *Merchant* (1880s; see Morozov, 1986, p. 106), standing in a rich domestic interior leaning his arm on a gilt-embossed tome. This social awareness and a concern for the poorer sections of society, already seen, for instance, in his documentary series on the *Burgov Night Shelter* (1890s; see Morozov, 1986, p. 105), came to the fore in the series that he published as *Neurozhaynyy 1891–92 god v nizhegorodskoy gubernii* ('The bad harvest of 1891–2 in the Nizhny Novgorod region'; Nizhny Novgorod, 1893). Here he brought his compositional skills and his ability to capture subjects in simple, natural poses to the service of a political campaign for funds to combat the famine and cholera that he witnessed. Highly praised in progressive circles, his series laid the foundations of photoreportage. Newspapers, in the control of the rich, rarely published his photographs, and as a result he issued a great quantity as *cartes*. This latter series was greatly admired by the writer Maksim Gor'ky, who later became a friend. Gor'ky's novels, stories and plays are thought to have gained inspiration from Dmitriyev's photographs and in 1902 Gor'ky commissioned him to photograph some local people to help with the characterization for his play *Detstvo* (*My Childhood*) for a production by the Moscow Arts Theatre.

BIBLIOGRAPHY
G. Boltyansky: *Ocherki po istorii fotografii v SSSR* [Studies in the history of photography in the USSR] (Moscow, 1939), pp. 64–8
S. Morozov: *Pervye russkiye fotografy-khudozhniki* [The first Russian photographer-artists] (Moscow, 1952)
——: *Fotograf-khudozhnik Maksim Dmitriyev* [The photographer-artist Maksim Dmitriyev] (Moscow, 1960)
——: 'Early Photography in Eastern Europe: Russia', *Hist. Phot.*, i/4 (1977), pp. 327–47
——: *Tvorcheskaya fotografiya* [Creative photography] (Moscow, 1986)

KEVIN HALLIWELL

Dmitrov. Town on the River Yakhroma, *c.* 65 km north of Moscow, Russia. It was founded in 1154 by Yury Dolgoruky, Prince of Vladimir (*reg* 1149–57), on Russia's main north–south trade route along the Volga basin. By the 13th century it was the centre of a small independent principality, which became part of the principality of Moscow in 1364.

Although the 12th- or 13th-century wooden kremlin was destroyed during the Polish-Lithuanian invasions of the early 17th century, its earthen ramparts (l. over 1000 m, h. *c.* 15 m) survive. The well-proportioned central cross-domed cathedral of the Dormition, built of brick in 1509–33, was paid for by Yury Ivanovich, Prince of Dmitrov. Its façades resemble the cathedral of the Archangel Michael in Moscow's Kremlin (*see* MOSCOW, §IV, 1(iii)) with their recessed wall panels, multi-profiled horizontal cornices separating the *zakomary* (semicircular gables) from the bays below, and arched windows in the tympana. Unique to the cathedral of the Dormition are three large glazed, multi-coloured ceramic reliefs of the 15th to 16th century: a tondo (diam. *c.* 3 m) with *St George the Victor* near the south portal and two scenes of the *Crucifixion* inserted in the tympana of the central *zakomary* of the north and south façades. Inside the cathedral is an iconostasis from the late 17th century, decorated with delicate floral carving and icons from the 16th to the 18th century.

The second-oldest building in the town is the church (*c.* 1537) of the monastery of SS Boris and Gleb, situated near the kremlin. It is built of brick and has a Greek-cross plan with a central dome resting on four piers. In 1562 a carved stone cross was mounted on the wall, and in 1656 the small, single-cell chapel of St Aleksey was added on its south-west corner. The vaults and drum of the church's dome were apparently reconstructed *c.* 1680. The monastic complex also comprises a building of monks' cells (1672), the gate-church of St Nicholas with the refectory (1672–7) and a quadrangular brick-walled enclosure with round corner towers (1685–9).

Dmitrov's other major buildings include the Rococo church of the Kazan' Mother of God (1735), the church of the Presentation of the Virgin, with a notable carved iconostasis (1768), and the Trinity Church of the Tikhvin Mother of God (1794–1801).

BIBLIOGRAPHY

N. Bylov: *Dmitrovsky Borisoglebsky Monastyr'* [The monastery of SS Boris and Gleb in Dmitrov] (Moscow, 1888)

I. Tokmakov: *Istoriko-statisticheskoye arkheologicheskoye opisaniye goroda Dmitrova s uyezdom i svyatnyami* [The historic, statistical and archaeological records of the town of Dmitrov with its district and its sacred objects] (Moscow, 1893)

M. Tikhomirov: *Gorod Dmitrov* [The town of Dmitrov] (Moscow, 1925)

Dmitrovskiy istoriko-khudozhestvennyy muzey: putevoditel' [A guide to the Dmitrov Museum of History and Art] (Dmitrov, 1986)

M. I. ANDREYEV

do. For Portuguese proper names consisting of a given name or names followed by this prefix and another part or parts, *see under* the part of the name following the prefix; for tripartite surnames, *see under* the first part of the surname.

Do, Giovanni (*b* Valencia, before 1617; *d* Naples, ?1656). Spanish painter, active in Italy. An *Adoration of the Shepherds* (*c.* 1623; Naples, Capodimonte) was attributed to Do by de Dominici in 1742 and remains the only work the attribution of which is widely accepted. Yet modern scholars (Causa; Bologna: see 1991 exh. cat.) who have reconstructed his career believe him to have made a major contribution to Neapolitan painting in the first half of the 17th century. Little documentary information survives. He is first mentioned in 1617 in Valencia, among the followers of Jerónimo Rodriguez de Espinosa (father of Jerónimo Jacinto Espinosa), and was enrolled in the Colegio de Pintores of Valencia. His style was formed in Valencia and Toledo in the circle of Pedro Orrente, Jerónimo Jacinto Espinosa and Juan van der Hamen y León, artists who were moving away from the Tuscan tradition of Counter-Reformation devotional painting towards the new realism of Caravaggio. By 1626 Do was in Naples, and that year he married Grazia, sister of Paceco de Rosa; the marriage contract describes him as Spanish and gives Giovanni Battista Caracciolo and Jusepe de Ribera as witnesses.

Most scholars date the *Adoration of the Shepherds* early in Do's career, around 1623; Pérez Sánchez (1985 exh. cat.) has proposed a slightly later date. The picture's refined simplicity and gravity remain close to the Counter-Reformation style of Valencian artists, while some details,

such as the still-life in the foreground or the old woman's headdress, suggest an affinity with the realism of Francisco Ribalta. Between 1620 and 1630 Do moved towards the style of Ribera, who at this time was the dominant practitioner of naturalistic painting in Naples. Whether or not he was, as de Dominici describes him, a pupil and imitator of Ribera (in which connection de Dominici instances especially his half-length figures of philosophers and portraits of St Jerome), it is likely that Do was the closest of his followers and that his work furthered the influence of Spanish elements in Neapolitan painting. Ribera's influence is evident in the *Adoration of the Shepherds* (*c.* 1630; Madrid, Real Acad. S Fernando, Mus.), which is now attributed to Do after previous attributions to Ribera and, later, to Luca Giordano. According to de Dominici, Do's independent works were distinguishable from Ribera's by the beauty of his flesh tints, achieved through the use of a little charcoal black and lake.

Neapolitan 18th- and 19th-century sources, following de Dominici, mention an *Adoration of the Shepherds* (ex-Gesù e Maria, Naples). Works attributed to Do, not yet identified, are cited for the first time in two 18th-century inventories: that of the van den Einden collection lists a *Martyrdom of St Lawrence*, while the Duca di Limatola possessed four pictures of the *Doctors of the Church* and one of *St Augustine*. Three paintings of the *Adoration of the Shepherds* have been attributed to Do on the basis of the Capodimonte picture: one in Valencia Cathedral (destr.), another, formerly attributed to Ribera, in Madrid (Escorial, Bib. Monasterio S Lorenzo) and a third in the Suermondt-Ludwig-Museum, Aachen. Most scholars reject the identification of Do with the Master of the Annunciation to the Shepherds (Marini).

BIBLIOGRAPHY

Thieme–Becker

B. de Dominici: *Vite* (1742–5), i, pp. 22–3

R. Causa: *La pittura del seicento a Napoli dal naturalismo al barocco* (1972), ii of *Storia di Napoli* (Cava dei Tirreni and Naples, 1967–78), pp. 929, 973, n. 49

M. Marini: *Pittori a Napoli, 1610–1656: Contributi e schede* (Naples, 1974), pp. 103–7

Painting in Naples from Caravaggio to Giordano (exh. cat., ed. F. Ferrante; London, RA, 1982), pp. 171–2

Civiltà del seicento a Napoli (exh. cat., ed. S. Cassani; Naples, Capodimonte, 1984), i, pp. 134–5, 259–60

Pintura napoletana de Caravaggio a Giordano (exh. cat., ed. A. E. Pérez Sánchez; Madrid, Prado, 1985), p. 120

Battistello Caracciolo e il primo naturalismo a Napoli (exh. cat, ed. F. Bologna; Naples, Mus. N. S Martino, 1991), pp. 128–34, 286–7

ANNACHIARA ALABISO

Dobbermann, Jacob (*b* Danzig [now Gdańsk], 1682; *d* Kassel, *bur* 14 May 1745). Polish amber- and ivory-carver, active in Germany. He almost certainly came from a family of amber-carvers in Danzig; he was probably in London in 1711, but from 1716 until his death he worked at the court of Kassel with the title Bernstein- und Helffenbein-arbeiter, producing small-scale pieces for Charles Landgrave of Hesse-Kassel and later for his son William VIII. By the time of his death he had been appointed Hof-künstler in Bernstein. Two of his surviving ambers are in the Hessisches Landesmuseum in Kassel: a figure of *Cleopatra* and a group of *Time and Opportunity* (both *c.* 1725). His known works in ivory include a relief, *Homage to Venus*, and two statuettes representing *Frederick Wil-*

liam, Elector of Brandenburg, and *Henry IV of France* (all London, V&A), a figure of the *Virgin* (*c.* 1720–30; Kassel, Hess. Landesmus.) and one probably representing *Jean-François Paul de Gondi, Cardinal of Retz* (before *c.* 1740; Germany, Reiner Winkler priv. col.). Many of his works are based on engraved sources by Jan Muller and Simon Thomassin, and his style seems to have been inspired primarily by Netherlandish prototypes.

BIBLIOGRAPHY

O. Pelka: *Die Meister der Bernsteinkunst* (Nuremberg, 1916), pp. 32–3
A. Rohde: *Bernstein: Ein deutscher Werkstoff* (Berlin, 1937), pp. 58–60
C. Theuerkauff: 'Unrecognized Ivory Carvings by Jacob Dobbermann', *Burl. Mag.*, cviii (1966), pp. 72–8
Barockplastik in Norddeutschland (exh. cat., ed. J. Rasmussen; Hamburg, Mus. Kst & Gew., 1977), pp. 505–14
C. Theuerkauff: *Elfenbein: Sammlung Reiner Winkler* (Munich, 1984), pp. 33–7

MARJORIE TRUSTED

Döbel [Däbeler; Döbeler], **Michael** (*b* Schweidnitz [now Świdnica, Poland], 25 Dec 1635; *d* Berlin, 8 Aug 1702). German sculptor, architect and ivory-carver. After receiving early training from his father, Johann Michael Döbel, he was granted a scholarship by Frederick William, Elector of Brandenburg, which allowed him to travel extensively in Europe and to visit Egypt (1655–8). In 1663–4 he and his brother Johann Christoph Döbel (1640–1713) assisted their father in the execution of the marble monument to *Chancellor Johann von Kospoth* for Königsberg [now Kaliningrad] Cathedral (*in situ*). Having moved to Berlin in 1665, he married the daughter of the Court Sculptor, Johann Arnold Villars. His appointment as state architect of Prussia in 1667 took him back to Königsberg, but when he was appointed Court Sculptor and Architect in 1702 he returned to Berlin, leaving his brother in charge of his Königsberg office. Among Döbel's major works were the sculptural decoration (1676–7) for the Elector of Brandenburg's summer palace at Bornim (destr. 1945) and the wooden pulpit (1690; destr. 1945) for Berlin Cathedral. He also supervised building programmes in Potsdam and was responsible for ceiling decoration (1690; destr. 1945) at Königliches Schloss, Berlin. Among his few surviving works is an ivory-carving depicting *Michael Wisniowecki, King of Poland* (1669–73), which is a small, oblong relief portrait. Two life-size busts in sandstone of *Frederick William, Elector of Brandenburg*, and his wife *Dorothea of Holstein-Glücksburg* (Berlin, Jagdschloss Grunewald) and some ivory carved heads (untraced) for walking sticks have also been attributed to Döbel.

BIBLIOGRAPHY

Thieme–Becker

H. Straube: *Die Bildhauerfamilie Döbel* (diss.)
Barockplastik in Norddeutschland (exh. cat. by J. Rasmussen, Hamburg, Mus. Kst & Gew., 1977)
C. Theuerkauff: *Nachmittelalterliche Elfenbeine: Die Bildwerke in Elfenbein des 16.–19. Jahrhunderts* (Berlin, 1986)

HANNELORE HÄGELE

Dobell, Sir **William** (*b* Newcastle, NSW, 24 Sept 1899; *d* Wangi Wangi, NSW, 13 May 1970). Australian painter. After an apprenticeship with an architect in Newcastle, he went to Sydney to attend evening classes at Julian Rossi Ashton's art school, while employed at an architectural metalwork company. His talent gained him early recognition in the Society of Artists. In 1929 his first prize in the Australian Art Quest and the Society of Arts Travelling Scholarship enabled him to travel overseas. He studied at the Slade School of Fine Art in London for 15 months under Henry Tonks and Philip Wilson Steer, as well as receiving private tuition from William Orpen. In 1929–30 he was awarded prizes for life painting and figure drawing.

Dobell's study of major Dutch artists in 1930 and visits to Paris and Belgium in 1931 gave him, as a provincial artist, essential grounding in the European portrait tradition. His style, a blend of realism and expressionism, was an assimilation of a wide range of influences, from Rembrandt to Chaïm Soutine. *Boy at the Basin* (1932; Sydney, A.G. NSW), a finely composed, Dutch-inspired interior with precise brushwork, even texture and soft light, summarizes the achievement of this early period.

On his return to London, the street life of the 1930s became Dobell's subject-matter, from powerful satirical works (e.g. *Mrs South Kensington*, 1937; Sydney, A.G. NSW) to quickly captured glimpses of London low life (e.g. *Street Singer*, 1938; Perth, A.G. W. Australia). This series of paintings, which included the vivid, incisive and detached depiction of the *Dead Landlord* (gouache, 1936; Melbourne, Joseph Brown Gal.), remains the strongest area of social commentary in Dobell's oeuvre. His London portraits, for example the *Sleeping Greek* (1936; Sydney, A.G. NSW), reveal his penetrating insight into the character of his sitters and his extraordinary skill in varying his painting style to suit the subject. His ability to paint the anonymous individual as a significant type established him as an unusual portrait painter.

In 1939 Dobell returned to Sydney, teaching for a short period at East Sydney Technical College. With the outbreak of World War II he worked as a camouflager for the Civil Construction Corps. In 1944 he won the Archibald Prize Competition for his portrait of *Joshua Smith* (destr.; see Gleeson, p. 117). Its vivid expressive colours, linear distortion and almost mannerist attenuation of form represented a shocking contrast to the traditional English academic mode that had previously dominated Australian portraiture. The award provoked widespread controversy, and two unsuccessful artists took Dobell to court, claiming that the picture was a caricature, not a portrait, and therefore breached Archibald's original intentions. The conservative press attacked Dobell as the personification of 'bizarre' modern art, despite his own opinion of his work as part of a conservative European tradition. Although the award was upheld, the intense public scrutiny distressed Dobell, who temporarily abandoned portraiture and experimented with other genres such as landscape. He was vindicated in 1948, when he won the Archibald Prize with the portrait of *Margaret Olley* (Sydney, A.G. NSW), a looser, more baroque treatment of form.

By the 1950s Dobell had achieved great recognition. The large demand for portrait commissions, however, led to uneven quality and irregular output. In 1950 an extended visit to New Guinea encouraged him to seek new subject-matter and treatments. In the early 1960s he tried to reconcile the restrictive conventions of portraiture with the divergent demands of modern art. He first experimented with abstraction, then with the dissolution of form in portraiture in his white drawings, such as the *Kindly Man* (1968; Canberra, N.G.). In 1966 he was knighted. A new discipline appeared in his last major work, *Thelma Clune* (1970; see 1985 exh. cat., p. 30). The legacy from Dobell's estate allowed the establishment of the Dobell Foundation to promote and benefit art in New South Wales.

WRITINGS
V. Freeman, ed.: *Dobell on Dobell* (Sydney, 1970)

BIBLIOGRAPHY
S. Ure Smith, ed.: *The Art of William Dobell* (Sydney, 1946)
J. Gleeson: *William Dobell: A Biographical and Critical Study* (London, 1964, 2/1969, Sydney, 1981)
B. Adams: *Portrait of an Artist: A Biography of William Dobell* (Melbourne, 1983)
William Dobell: The Painting of a Portrait (exh. cat. by S. Hunt, Sydney, Macquarie Gals, 1985)

SUSAN HUNT

Dobie, James (*b* Edinburgh, 11 April 1849; *d* London, *c*. 1911). British etcher. He was a prolific copyist of popular subjects by contemporary painters and exhibited regularly at the Royal Academy from 1885. His earliest exhibited works were the sombre *Fata Morgana* after G. F. Watts, and *Cassandra* after Solomon J. Solomon (1860–1927). Although he continued to copy the work of such Victorian artists as Edward John Poynter and John William Waterhouse, he is better known for his etchings after the genre painter Walter Dendy Sadler (1854–1923). Dobie produced over 100 plates after this minor but popular artist between 1894 and 1911. He was employed frequently by the *Art Journal* from 1890 to 1894. His original etching *Fishing Boats at Hastings* was published by *The Portfolio* in 1882.

BIBLIOGRAPHY
Engen
H. Beck: *Victorian Engravings* (London, 1973)

Dobrović, Nikola (*b* Pečuj, 12 Feb 1897; *d* Belgrade, 11 Jan 1967). Serbian architect, teacher and urban planner. He graduated in architecture (1923) at Prague University and settled in Dubrovnik in 1934. After World War II, he became Director of the Institute for Urbanism and, in 1948, a professor at the Architectural Faculty at the University of Belgrade. His main works include the Masaryk Centre (1928) near Prague; the Yugoslav Students' Centre (1932) in Prague; the Grand Hotel (1936) on the island of Lopud; and several villas in Dubrovnik. He was also successful in numerous architectural competitions: Complex Terazije (1930; unexecuted), Belgrade; a beach resort and a hospital (both 1932; unexecuted), in Split; and, in Belgrade, the headquarters (1946; unexecuted) of the Communist Party of Yugoslavia, the Tašmajdan Museum complex (1948), and the Ministry of Defence (1953). Dobrović also led a team that developed an urban plan for Belgrade (1947–8; unexecuted). He was mainly preoccupied with architectural compositions that display very dynamic forms, and with their relationship to larger urban complexes.

WRITINGS
'Osnovne postavke idejnog uređenja budućeg grada Štipa' [Basic assumptions in the preliminary urbanistic scheme for the organization of the future town of Štip], *Arhitektura* [Zagreb], 4 (1952), pp. 36–8

BIBLIOGRAPHY
'Nikola Dobrović, 1897–1967', *Arhit. Urb.*, xxiv (1984), pp. 31–3

PAUL TVRTKOVIĆ

Dobrovol's'ky, Anatoli (Volodymyrovych) [Anatoly Vladimirovich] (*b* Buki, nr Zhytomyr, 19 May 1910; *d* 1988). Ukrainian architect and urban planner. He graduated from the architectural faculty of the Engineering Construction Institute, Kiev, in 1934. In the late 1930s he built a clubhouse with a 400-seat hall in the village of Leski, near Chernihiv, in Ukrainian SSR (now Ukraine). After submitting competition designs (1944–6) for the reconstruction of the centre of Kiev, he worked on the plan (1947–9) for the redevelopment of the Khreshchatyk, Kiev's main street, with Aleksandr Vlasov, A. I. Zavarov (*b* 1917), Viktor Yelizarov and Boris Priymak (*b* 1909). The street was treated as a linear chain of squares with gaps between the buildings opening up perspectives across the city. The colour scheme is dominated by the use of ceramic facings, and the buildings, essentially Neo-classical in structure, are heavily decorated with Ukrainian motifs. Dobrovol's'ky's buildings on the Khreshchatyk include a multistorey tower block (1954; with others), with a semicircular pediment and belvedere with spires, and the Moskva Hotel (1954–61), where he worked with V. A. Sozansky, Boris Priymak, A. M. Miletsky (*b* 1918) and A. Y. Kosenko (*b* 1915). His modest residential buildings (1949–51) in the Darnytsya district of Kiev are sparsely decorated, with a complex version of Ukrainian Baroque restricted to the pediments.

From 1950 to 1955 Dobrovol's'ky was Chief Architect of Kiev. For the new underground railway system he designed the Khreshchatyk metro station (1960; with others) in which the Neo-classical pylon structure of the lower hall is decorated with Ukrainian motifs executed in glazed tiles; he also designed the Voksal'na metro station and adjoining suburban railway station (1960; with I. L. Maslenkov), where the ground-level Neo-classical hall includes echoes of Ukrainian Baroque. In the 1960s, while continuing to work in Kiev, he turned from historicism towards Rationalist reinforced-concrete constructions. At Boryspol' Airport (1960–65; with A. I. Malinovsky, D. I. Popenko and Y. N. Yevreinov) the asymmetrical composition, unified by the 50 m concrete vault spanning the departure lounge, is somewhat lifeless. The opposing directions of his later architecture are illustrated on the one hand by the functional Moskovs'ky Bridge (1971), in which the supporting shrouds are secured in a tall, triangular pier, and on the other by the dramatic and extravagant Kureni Restaurant (1972).

BIBLIOGRAPHY
'Mastera sovremennogo Sovetskogo zodchestva' [Masters of contemporary Soviet building], *Arkhit. SSSR*, 11 (1978), pp. 46–51
N. P. Bilinkina and A. V. Ryabushina: *Istoriya Sovetskoy arkhitektury* [History of Soviet architecture] (Moscow, 1985), pp. 121, 182, 195, 201
——: *Sovremenaya Sovetskaya arkhitektura* [Contemporary Soviet architecture] (Moscow, 1985), pp. 148, 151

A. V. IKONNIKOV

Dobson, Frank (Owen) (*b* London, 18 Nov 1886; *d* London, 22 July 1963). English sculptor, painter and designer. The son of a commercial artist, from 1902 to 1904 he worked in the studio of the academic sculptor William Reynolds-Stephens. The few surviving paintings from before 1914 show the influence of such French painters as Paul Cézanne and Paul Gauguin. By the time Dobson enlisted in the Artists' Rifles in October 1914 he had begun to carve. In 1920 he was selected by Wyndham Lewis as the only sculptor in the 'Group X' exhibition. His first post-war carvings such as *Man Child* (1921; London, Tate) exhibit an aggressive angularity, which suggests a conscious intention to adopt the Vorticist style of Henri Gaudier-Brzeska and Jacob Epstein (*see* ENGLAND, fig. 33). This was a short-lived phase, and from the mid-1920s Dobson was to concentrate on the naked female figure treated in a calm, simplified monumental fashion. The most obvious affinity was with the work of Aristide Maillol: *Reclining Figure* (1924–5; U. London, Courtauld Inst. Gals) has the same combination of a broad-hipped female with a formalized block-like treatment; *Cornucopia* (1925–7; U. Hull, A. Col.) is closer to Indian sculpture in its curvilinear form. Unlike some contemporaries Dobson had an undogmatic view of the relative values of carving and modelling. In this respect his attitude was close to that of Roger Fry who praised his work as 'true and pure sculpture' because of its lack of literary or illustrative elements. The limitation of the emotional range of Dobson's work (he regarded any violent action as unsuitable subject-matter) was viewed as positive.

His concentration on the human figure as a vital source of inspiration distanced him from modernist practice in the 1930s. Subsequently the apparent lack of development in his work, his professorship at the Royal College of Art (1946) and his membership of the Royal Academy led to his identification as part of the artistic establishment.

WRITINGS
'Sculpture', *RIBA J.*, xliii/9 (1936), pp. 457–66
'The Quest', *The Anatomy of Design: A Series of Inaugural Lectures*, ed. R. Moynihan (London, 1951) [lecture given at the Royal College of Art]

BIBLIOGRAPHY
R. Mortimer: *Frank Dobson* (London, 1926)
Frank Dobson (exh. cat., ed. F. Watson; ACGB, 1966)
M. Easton: 'Frank Dobson's *Cornucopia*', *Burl. Mag.*, cxi (1969), pp. 382–6
True and Pure Sculpture: Frank Dobson (exh. cat., ed. R. Hopper; U. Cambridge, Kettle's Yard, 1981)

JOHN GLAVES-SMITH

Dobson, John (*b* Chirton, North Shields, Northumb., 1787; *d* Newcastle upon Tyne, 8 Jan 1865). English architect. Dobson was the son of a farmer who recognized Dobson's talent and encouraged his remarkable ability for drawing. He became a pupil of David Stephenson (1757–1819), the leading architect in Newcastle upon Tyne, and also studied perspective drawing under Boniface Moss [Musso], an Italian refugee. He took drawing lessons from John Varley in London and returned to Newcastle in 1811.

The rapid economic development of Newcastle and its hinterland made it possible for Dobson to build up an extensive and lucrative architectural practice that was confined almost entirely to north-east England. He built nearly a hundred country houses for industrialists turned gentry or old landowners enriched by coal, and erected many churches and public buildings, including prisons, hospitals, schools and toll-houses in the rapidly expanding towns. His name is associated above all with the rebuilding of the centre of Newcastle, and until recently the whole of Grey Street and most of the early 19th-century buildings in the city centre were attributed to him. This, however, is

an exaggeration: Dobson did produce plans for a new layout for central Newcastle in the 1820s but they were not adopted, and the arrangement of streets finally built in the 1830s differed significantly. It seems certain that the planning of central Newcastle as executed was the work of the developer Richard Grainger, and that Dobson designed only a few of the main buildings, though his rich classical style, here more Roman than Greek, set the tone for the overall development and uniform magnificence of the city centre. Those buildings in Newcastle that are known to have been designed by him include Eldon Square (1825–31; part destr.), the New Markets (1835–6), part of Grey Street (1836–9) and the magnificent Central Railway Station (1847–50) with its noble stone portico and cast-iron framed interior. Its construction contained several innovations of Dobson's own devising, for which he won a medal at the Paris Exposition Universelle of 1858. His engineering skills were also displayed in the various warehouses he designed at Newcastle and in such projects as the underpinning (1832–3) of the foundations of the medieval tower of the cathedral of St Nicholas.

Dobson's finest works were his country houses built in both classical and Tudor Gothic styles. A good Tudor Gothic example is Holme Eden Hall, near Carlisle, Cumbria, designed in 1833 for Peter Dixon, a cotton manufacturer; it presents a cheerful display of turrets, chimneys and gables inspired by East Barsham Manor (early 16th century), Norfolk. Dobson also restored several old castles, including Chipchase Castle for John Reed in 1819, and Craster Tower for Thomas Wood-Craster in 1839 (both Northumb.). His classical houses are especially impressive with their lucid, rational plans, their well-proportioned rooms arranged round spacious staircases and severe Grecian exteriors constructed of superb stonework. One of Dobson's earliest commissions, in 1811, was to assist Sir Charles Monck Middleton with full-scale detail drawings of Greek capitals for the internal and external columns for his new house at Belsay, Northumb. Nunnykirk Hall, Northumb., designed in 1825, is the best of Dobson's large Greek Revival houses, with a huge Ionic *porte-cochère*, neatly channelled rustication and beautiful biscuit-coloured ashlar stonework.

Dobson had hoped that his architectural practice would be continued by his younger son Alexander, who had trained under Sydney Smirke (1798–1877), but Alexander was killed in 1854.

BIBLIOGRAPHY
Colvin
Obituary, *Builder*, xxiii (1865), p. 27
M. J. Dobson: *A Memoir of John Dobson* (London, 1885)
L. Wilkes and G. Dodds: *Tyneside Classical: The Newcastle of Grainger, Dobson and Clayton* (London, 1964)
M. Girouard: 'Dobson's Northumbrian Houses', *Country Life*, cxxxix (17 Feb 1966), pp. 352–6; cxxxix (24 Feb 1966), pp. 406–9
L. Wilkes: *John Dobson: Architect and Landscape Gardener* (Stocksfield, 1980)

JOHN MARTIN ROBINSON

Dobson, William (*b* London, *bapt* 4 March 1611; *d* London, *bur* 28 Oct 1646). English painter. His father, William Dobson, was a gentleman of St Albans employed by Francis Bacon, Viscount Verulam, on the building and decoration at Verulam House and Gorhambury; he was also probably Master of the Alienation Office and a member of the Painter-Stainers' Company, but according to John Aubrey, 'he spending his estate luxuriously upon women, necessity forced his son William Dobson to be the most excellent painter that England has yet bred'.

Dobson was apprenticed to William Peake (*c.* 1580–1639) and later seems to have joined the studio of Francis Cleyn, who introduced him to his personal vocabulary of International Mannerism and could have provided access to Charles I's collection, where Dobson would have seen works by Titian and other Venetians and more recent paintings by Rubens and van Dyck, all of which influenced his style. It is unlikely that he worked directly with van Dyck, since their techniques are so different. Dobson was also aware of the Utrecht followers of Caravaggio, and his *Executioner with the Baptist's Head* (Liverpool, Walker A.G.) was copied with slight variations from an early work by Matthias Stomer. This tenebrist influence is apparent in later works and also the early *Self-portrait* (priv. col.), if less so in the companion portrait of his second wife, *Judith Dobson* (after 1637; same priv. col.): he had married Judith Sander on 18 December 1637 at St Bride's, Fleet Street, London. In both works the approach is vigorous, truthful and free of conventions derived from van Dyck.

Dobson apparently inherited his father's instability, and Symonds stated that 'one Mr Vaughan of the Exchequer office did relieve him out of prison and thereupon he made his picture which Dobson would use to say twas his master piece'—an incident that could have occurred before the Civil War, when Dobson followed the embattled Charles I to Oxford. Only the *Self-portrait* and its pendant can be certainly assigned to the years before he set up practice in Oxford, however. He probably arrived there late in 1642, and, according to Walpole, he set up his studio in the High Street, near St Mary's Church. His business seems to have been brisk from the start, as he was employing a Mr Hesketh as his assistant by April 1643, and there are signs of the intervention of a drapery painter in the *Officer with a Page* (1642; Knole, Kent, NT), his earliest securely dated work.

The extent of Dobson's royal patronage is unknown, but it is possible that he was indeed appointed Serjeant-Painter and a Groom of the Bedchamber, as suggested by Oldys to Vertue. The King seems to have sat only for a full-face head (Brit. Royal Col.), presumably to be used for the production of repetitions, but Dobson painted *Charles, Prince of Wales* (*c.* 1643; Edinburgh, N.P.G.), and *James, Duke of York*, as well as the Palatine princes *Rupert* and *Maurice. Charles, Prince of Wales* is arguably his most important work and his most successful and individual essay in the Baroque style. The similar *John, 1st Lord Byron* (U. Manchester, Whitworth A.G.), which draws on motifs from both Cleyn and van Dyck, is probably contemporary.

In spite of the short duration of Dobson's career, his style developed and finally deteriorated so that it is possible to gauge an approximate chronology for most of his works. His lack of sound training and his technical weaknesses were offset by his evident pleasure in the use of paint and his natural instinct for colour, enhanced by his powers of observation. His earlier works were painted with thick pigment and lush impasto. His compositions were carefully contrived to indicate the special interests of his sitters, but this often led to overcrowding, which sometimes dictated unusual formats and required additions of the coarse canvas that Dobson favoured. Around 1645 he altered his technique radically, painting thinly and tightly with a meagre palette, causing the grain of the support to obtrude. He painted more head-and-shoulder portraits at that time and used conventional poses. While it must have become increasingly difficult to obtain materials in wartime Oxford, the failure of the royalist cause and personal disillusionment must have contributed to this clear deterioration of technique. Dobson's powers of observation and characterization remained unimpaired, however, and the fragility of the later paintings adds to their air of melancholy.

Although he produced a large number of bust portraits, Dobson is more often associated with an individual type of half- or three-quarter-length portrait with symbolic accessories. *Endymion Porter* (London, Tate; see fig.), a relatively early work, was a prototype, and similar schemes were followed in the *Naval Commander* (*c.* 1643–4; London, N. Mar. Mus.), *Colonel Richard Neville* (*c.* 1643–4; London, N.P.G.), *3rd Earl of Northampton* (*c.* 1644–5; Castle Ashby, Northants) and *Sir Edward Walker* (*c.* 1645; Stratford-on-Avon, Royal Shakespeare Mus.). His two full-lengths, probably close in date to each other, are totally different from one another in mood. The *Earl of Peterborough* (1644; Drayton House, Northants) is an essay in the 'mock-heroick' genre, painted with a superbly refined colour scheme and wry humour, while *Sir William Compton* (*c.* 1643; Castle Ashby, Northants) is perhaps the most noble of all his portraits of young cavaliers, with the solitary figure set against a virtually monochrome setting.

William Dobson: *Endymion Porter*, oil on canvas, 1.50×1.27 m, *c.* 1643 (London, Tate Gallery)

Without suitable earlier models, Dobson experienced problems with the compositions of his group portraits, and that possibly depicting the *Streatfield Family* (New Haven, CT, Yale Cent. Brit. A.) shows clear signs of alterations and additions. The *Prince Rupert, Colonel Murray and Colonel Russell* (Ombersley Courts, Hereford & Worcs) is remarkable for its vigorous and inelegant attempt at a realistic portrayal of an actual, if unexplained, incident. The enigmatic *Self-portrait with ?Nicholas Lanier and Sir Charles Cotterell* (*c.* 1645; London, Syon House) is closely related to his 'allegorical' half-lengths and emphasizes the equality of status that Dobson enjoyed with his sitters. Cotterell was clearly a close friend and probably provided the artist with some respite from his anxieties. A group of portraits all in the artist's later style still survives at Rousham, Cotterell's house in Oxfordshire, and there is the curious allegorical subject picture, the *Civil Wars of France*, for which Cotterell devised the programme and Dobson drew on Cleyn's quirky Mannerism. The pair of head-and-shoulder portraits in conventional poses within oval surrounds of *Lord and Lady Rockingham* (Rockingham Castle, Northants) exemplifies Dobson's later style, but *The Girl* (1645; Birmingham, Mus. & A.G.) is a sad echo of the artist's former powers.

Oxford capitulated to the Parliamentary forces in June 1646, and Dobson was back in London by August, when he was nominated (but not elected) Steward of the Painter-Stainers' Company. He died in poverty at his house in St Martin's Lane in the following October. He left no followers of any significance, and his influence on his contemporaries was negligible.

Two major exhibitions have confirmed Dobson's status as the most important native-born English painter between Hilliard and Hogarth. His vitality and insight make his portraits unmistakable, and his talents were perfectly suited to recording the main protagonists of the royalist cause.

BIBLIOGRAPHY
R. Symonds: *Note Book, 1651–3* (London, BM, MS. Egerton. 1636, fols 180, 206); fully transcribed in M. Beal: *A Study of Richard Symonds* (New York, 1984), pp. 299, 311
J. Aubrey: *Brief Lives* (1669–96; London, BM, MS.); ed. A. Clark, i (London, 1898), p. 78
R. Graham: 'A Short Account of the Most Eminent Painters, both Ancient and Modern', *The Art of Painting*, ed. Du Fresnoy (Eng. trans., London, 1695)
B. Buckeridge: 'An Essay towards an English School of Painters', *The Art of Painting*, ed. R. de Piles (London, ?1706), pp. 368–70
H. Walpole: *Anecdotes of Painting in England* (1762–71); ed. R. N. Wornum, ii (1849), pp. 351–4
C. H. Collins Baker: *Lely and the Stuart Portrait Painters*, i (London, 1862), pp. 99–101
'The Note Books of G. Vertue', *Walpole Soc.*, i (1911); ii (1912); iii (1913); iv (1914); v (1915); index p. 64; vi (1916), pp. 9, 72, 175
William Dobson, 1611–1646 (exh. cat. by O. Millar, London, Tate, 1951)
E. K. Waterhouse: *Painting in England, 1530 to 1790* (London, 1953, rev. 4/1978), pp. 80–85
M. Whinney and O. Millar: *English Art, 1625–1714* (Oxford, 1957), pp. 84–8
O. Millar: *The Tudor, Stuart and Early Georgian Pictures in the Collection of Her Majesty The Queen* (London, 1963), pp. 113–14
W. Vaughan: *Endymion Porter and William Dobson* (London, 1970)
The Age of Charles I (exh. cat. by O. Millar, London, Tate, 1972), pp. 99–102
William Dobson, 1611–1646 (exh. cat. by M. Rogers, London, N.P.G., 1983) [most comprehensive study of Dobson and his work to date; most known works illustr.]

RICHARD JEFFREE

Dobuzhinsky, Mstislav (Valerianovich) (*b* Novgorod, 14 Aug 1875; *d* New York, 20 Nov 1957). Russian graphic artist, painter and stage designer. He first studied art from 1885 to 1887 at the School of the Society for the Encouragement of the Arts, St Petersburg, and then enrolled in St Petersburg University from where he graduated in Law in 1898. Unwilling to give up his early interest in art, in 1899 he went to Munich to study under Anton Ažbé and Simon Hollósy and met there the large colony of Russian artists, including Igor' Grabar'. He also saw the work of German Jugendstil artists.

Dobuzhinsky returned to St Petersburg in 1901, and in 1902 he was invited by Grabar' to join the World of Art (Mir Iskusstva) group in 1902. His first works were historical landscapes in the manner of Alexandre Benois, but he soon began to portray the specific traits of the contemporary industrialized city and its suburbs, in both paintings and prints. In *Man in Glasses* (1905–6; Moscow, Tret'yakov Gal.), a portrait of the poet and art critic Konstantin A. Syunnerberg (1871–1942), who wrote under the pseudonym Konst. Erberg, factory chimneys seen through the windows contrast sharply with the figure of the poet and his books. One of Dobuzhinsky's most telling images, *October Idyll*, an illustration in the satirical journal *Zhupel*, i (1905), shows a blood-spattered wall, a doll, a single shoe and a pair of glasses to commemorate the brutal response to the political uprisings of 1905. From 1907 he was active as stage designer, teacher and book illustrator. He left Russia in 1924 for Lithuania, and he subsequently lived in Europe and the USA, where he continued to work on stage designs and painted street scenes, which often focused on the new industrialized suburbs. He produced a series of drawings called *City Dreams* (1906–*c.* 1913; see Gusarova, pls 43–6), which include fantastic and sometimes menacing elements. Even after he left Russia, his stage designs were often for works by Russian composers, including the opera *Khovanshchina* by Modest Musorgsky, produced at the Metropolitan Opera, New York, in 1950 (see Gusarova, pl. 143).

BIBLIOGRAPHY
A. Gusarova: *Mstislav Dobuzhinsky* (Moscow, 1982) [Eng. summary; colour illus.]
G. Chugunov: *M. V. Dobuzhinsky* (Leningrad, 1984)
M. Rosci: 'Dobuzinskij e Boccioni', *Mir iskusstva* [World of art] (Turin, 1984)

MARIAN BURLEIGH-MOTLEY

Doccia. Italian centre of porcelain production. In 1737 a factory producing hard-paste porcelain works was founded at Doccia by the Marchese Carlo Ginori (1702–57), assisted by the painter Karl Wendelin Anreiter von Zirnfeld (1702–57) and the technician Giorgio delle Torri (*fl* 1737–43), both from Vienna (see ITALY, fig. 88). The early paste was rather grey, with a dull glaze. Between *c.* 1770 and 1790, however, a tin glaze was used to whiten the body, and after 1803 clays from Limoges were used for this purpose. Several formulae were in use throughout the 19th century. Until 1757 factory production was highly experimental; some early pieces are similar to wares from the factory of Claudius Innocentius Du Paquier (*d* 1751) in Vienna, where Anreiter is thought to have worked. Underglaze-blue, stencilled decoration was common between *c.* 1737 and 1745 (e.g. teapot, *c.* 1742–5; London,

V&A). Useful wares were modelled with an emphasis on sculptural, relief and pierced decoration. Painted decoration included armorials, genre scenes and East Asian flowers in intense tones of puce, iron-red, acid yellow and green. Large-scale figures and groups were copied from bronze casts, moulds and wax models in the Marchese's collection by such sculptors as Massimiliano Soldani (e.g. *Deposition*, *c.* 1770; London, BM) and Giuseppe Piamontini (e.g. *Massacre of the Innocents*, *c.* 1700; Boston, MA, Mus. F.A.). The factory's chief modeller during this period was Gasparo Bruschi (*c.* 1701–80). After 1757 sculpture was smaller in scale, the figures were painted with pronounced stippled flesh tones and features picked out in brown-black and iron-red. Production during the 19th century was influenced by French wares. After *c.* 1850 the factory was modernized, but due to economic difficulties it was merged in 1896 with the Società Ceramica of Milan.

BIBLIOGRAPHY

L. Ginori Lisci: *La porcellana di Doccia* (Milan, 1963)
G. Liverani: *Il museo delle porcellane di Doccia* (Florence, 1967)
K. Lankheit: *Die Modellsammlung der Porzellanmanufaktur Doccia* (Munich, 1982)
A. d'Agliano: *Le porcellane italiane a Palazzo Pitti* (Florence, 1986)
C. Hess: ' "Primo Esperimento in Grande": A Pair of Vases from the Factory of Geminiano Cozzi', *Getty Mus. J.*, 18 (1990), pp. 141–56

CLARE LE CORBEILLER

Doceno, il. *See* GHERARDI, CRISTOFANO.

Docimium. *See* DOKIMEION.

Dock [wharf]. Artificial basin for the loading, unloading and repair of ships. It is often accompanied by such ancillary structures as warehouses, transit sheds and offices, and the use of the word is therefore sometimes extended to the whole harbour complex. The earliest examples date from Classical times: in the 6th and 5th centuries BC, for instance, large ship sheds were constructed along the harbour at Peiraeus, Athens, which served as the base for the Athenian navy. The Romans also built large docks at Mediterranean ports such as Gadir (Cádiz) in the 1st century BC. Vitruvius even set down guidelines for dock construction, suggesting that they should be built of stone, with towers on both sides, from which chains for unloading cargo could be drawn across by machinery. The period of greatest activity in dock construction, however, came between the late 17th century and the early 20th, a period of dramatic growth in maritime trade.

There are two basic forms of modern dock. The dry dock is mainly for shipbuilding and repair, and it developed from the individual slipway, the upper part of which was eventually enclosed with wooden or stone walls and fitted with a wooden lock-gate to shut out high tides. The origin of the lock is unclear; Portsmouth, Hants, had a permanent dry dock constructed of timber and masonry, but without a lock-gate, in 1496. It was only with the advent of the steam engine in the 18th century that dry docks could be pumped dry irrespective of the tide. In some Mediterranean ports with a very low tidal range (e.g. Marseille), dry docks with mechanical pumping installations existed in the mid-18th century. The wet, or impounded, dock attempts to overcome high tidal ranges by creating an artificial basin controlled by a lock that keeps the level of water within constant. Wet dock construction originated in late 17th-century France and Britain, both of which had high tidal ranges at their channel ports and were in the vanguard of the development of civil engineering. Le Havre allegedly had a lock-gate and basin as early as the late 16th century.

Britain's first wet dock was at Blackwall (*c.* 1660), London, built for large ships bound for the East Indies. Le Havre followed this example in 1667. As the volume of trade and the size of ships increased, congestion of ports became a serious problem. The first wet dock built to ease congestion on the River Thames was Howland Great Wet Dock (1697–1700), Rotherhithe, its walls still of timber. The most important 18th-century dock builders in Britain were found in Liverpool and Hull (*see* HULL, §1). The Liverpool Corporation built the first commercial wet dock there in 1715 and engaged in the construction of new docks along the waterfront throughout the century. They were built mainly of brick and lime mortar backed by rubble. The first private dock company, the Hull Dock Company, opened its dock in 1774, and three interconnecting wet docks were built in 1829. In engineering terms, dock construction depended on two factors, waterproof mortar and the construction of the walls. The mortar problem was largely solved by John Smeaton's 'Roman cement' in the mid-18th century, while in 1797–1800 John Rennie introduced lighter stone and brick walls with arched recesses (so-called 'hollow walls') at Grimsby.

There were two waves of intense dock building in the 19th century, one at the beginning, due to an increase in trade, and one in the latter part, the result of new transport and communication systems. Increased world trade at the turn of the century led to an enormous increase in the number of ships carrying freight. Political instability in mainland Europe and Napoleon's occupation of such major ports as Hamburg and Amsterdam gave Britain the opportunity to monopolize trade (*see* LONDON, §II, 4). Ports such as London became increasingly congested, and cargo handling grew slow and inefficient. There was no adequate space for the proper handling and storing of goods before they were sold, and the shipping companies had a serious problem with theft and looting. The West India merchants were the first to take action, petitioning Parliament for an extension to the legal quays. Granted in 1799, the West India Dock (1802) was built by William Jessop (1745–1841); it consisted of two parallel docks for import and export, divided by an avenue of brick warehouses. The whole complex was guarded by a high perimeter wall and guardhouses.

London Dock (1802–05), Wapping, by John Rennie, was the first to use steam engines for excavating and driving piles, and Rennie's East India Docks (begun 1805) introduced cast iron for the warehouse roofs. Dock warehouses were usually austere brick structures built in the style of contemporary industrial architecture. Architecturally, one of the most impressive docks was St Katharine's Dock (completed by 1828; rest. 20th century), London, by Thomas Telford and Philip Hardwick (*see* HARDWICK, (2)). Two irregular basins were enclosed by brick warehouses, standing on Greek Doric columns of granite and cast iron. The façades were recessed at intervals

Albert Dock, Liverpool, by Jesse Hartley, 1839–45 (restored)

for cranes, which hauled cargo straight from the ships. This system was followed by Jesse Hartley (1780–1860) at Albert Dock, Liverpool (see fig.; *see also* LIVERPOOL, §1). This type was commercially unsuccessful, however, and already outdated at completion.

The advent of the steamship and the railway fundamentally changed the requirements of docks; many large steamships could not use locks designed for sailing ships. The dock basin was often too small, accommodating only a few steamers at a time. The railway made immediate countrywide distribution possible, but most city-centre docks had no space to build railway connections and often lacked sufficient quay space to handle and sort goods. The second generation of docks were either long and narrow or were subdivided by jetties to increase quay space. The development of mechanical dredgers for excavation facilitated deeper docks for ever-increasing ship sizes. Dock-side warehouses were abandoned in favour of one- or two-storey transit sheds, often with integral cranes. The introduction of hydraulic systems from the 1850s, mainly developed by William Armstrong (1810–1900), facilitated the handling of such heavy and bulky cargo as minerals and machinery. Railway connections became imperative, and docks were often moved to cheaper land outside the main port.

The inter-war years of the 20th century saw an international economic depression, particularly in the coal trade, and this began the descent of many ports into economic decline. Some docks continued to be built, for example Southampton, London and Liverpool, but as ship sizes continued to increase, many older docks became redundant. Much of the cargo carried by smaller vessels was taken over by air freight, and large container shipping again changed the system and requirements of cargo handling and storage. In the late 20th century more and more ports declined, and their docks became redundant and derelict, in some cases being redeveloped for residential, recreational or other commercial uses. Notable examples include the London Docklands (*see* LONDON, §II, 6), Liverpool's Albert Dock, Rowe's Wharf in Boston, MA, and Darling Harbour in Sydney.

BIBLIOGRAPHY
H. Straub: *A History of Civil Engineering* (London, 1952)
J. Richards: *The Functional Tradition in Early Industrial Architecture* (London, 1958)
G. Jackson: *The History and Archaeology of Ports* (Tadworth, 1983)
N. Ritchie-Noakes: *Old Docks* (London, 1987)
L. M. Akveld and J. R. Bruijn, eds: 'Shipping Companies and Authorities in the 19th and 20th Century: Their Common Interest in the Development of Port Facilities', *Proceedings of the Congress to Commemorate the 25th Anniversary of the Netherlands Association for Maritime History: The Hague, 1989*   □

Döcker, Richard (*b* Weilheim an der Teck, 13 June 1894; *d* Stuttgart, 9 Nov 1968). German architect, teacher and writer. He studied architecture at the Technische Hochschule, Stuttgart, with an interruption for military service in World War I, and completed a doctorate there (1923) under Paul Bonatz. He first attracted notice in 1921 with some Expressionist designs (unexecuted) for high-rise towers for central sites in Stuttgart, but after 1922 he became involved with Modernism. He was a member of Der Ring, the Deutscher Werkbund and CIAM, and he was a leading proponent of Neues Bauen in southern Germany. He achieved professional recognition in 1927 through his work as site architect in charge of construction at the Weissenhofsiedlung, Stuttgart, the Deutscher Werkbund's exhibition housing estate for which he himself designed two houses (destr. 1939–45). Döcker's commissions ranged from large private houses to standardized low-cost housing and commercial buildings. All his work is concerned with the need for human scale, good lighting, access to air and sunlight and the integration of new buildings into the existing environment. These requirements were particularly well satisfied by a low-roofed, terraced layout that became a feature of his work and found its definitive formulation in the Vetter House (1927) on a steeply sloping site in Birkenwaldstrasse, Stuttgart. He also employed the terraced theme in hospital design, for example the Krankenhaus (1927) at Waibling, and hospitals with sun terraces became something of a Döcker speciality. He also developed various types of school design, including a version with pavilions and open-air classrooms. After 1933, when Hitler took power, Döcker's career as a Modernist was interrupted and he was forbidden to practise. He was subsequently involved in petitions for Modernist solutions to the reconstruction of German cities and in 1946 was appointed to direct rebuilding in Stuttgart. In 1947 he was appointed to a chair of architecture at the Technische Hochschule, Stuttgart, for which he also produced a master development plan. Later work included his design (1955–9) for the campus of the University of Sind, Hyderabad, which won him international recognition and where his approach has been compared to Le Corbusier's at Chandigarh.

WRITINGS
Kleinwohnungstypen (diss., Stuttgart, Tech. Hochsch., 1923)
Terrassentyp (Stuttgart, 1929)

BIBLIOGRAPHY
F. Mehlau-Wiebking: *Richard Döcker: Ein Architekt im Aufbruch zur Moderne* (Brunswick and Wiesbaden, 1988)
K. Kirsch: *The Weissenhofsiedlung: Experimental Housing Built for the Deutscher Werkbund, Stuttgart, 1927* (New York, 1989)
FRIEDERIKE MEHLAU-WIEBKING

Dodd, Robert (*b* 1748; *d* London, Feb 1815). English painter and engraver. He exhibited at the Society of Arts from 1780 and at the Royal Academy, London, from 1782 to 1809. He had gained some reputation as a landscape artist by 1771 but soon concentrated on marine scenes. He became a ship portraitist and above all a prolific recorder of naval actions in the American and French Revolutionary wars such as the *Sinking of the 'Vengeur de Peuple' at the Battle of the Glorious First of June, 1794* (1795; London, N. Mar. Mus.). He was also praised for his handling of storm scenes, notably a series depicting the loss of the *Ramillies* in the West Indies hurricane of September 1782 (1783–5; London, N. Mar. Mus.). His work was engraved by others but he also executed over 100 plates himself, mostly in aquatint, including views of the naval dockyards at Chatham, Woolwich and Deptford and also of the Thames at Blackwall and Greenwich, the last-named based on his oil painting of 1792 (London, N. Mar. Mus.). His works form a valuable historical record but his essentially modest abilities were surpassed by similar commercial contemporaries. His brother Ralph Dodd (*c.* 1756–1817) also painted some marine pictures.

BIBLIOGRAPHY
Archibald; *DNB*
G. W. Younger: 'Robert and Ralph Dodd: Marine Painters', *Mariner's Mirror*, x/3 (1924), pp. 247–351
PIETER VAN DER MERWE

Dodeigne, Eugène (*b* Rouvreux, nr Liège, Belgium, 27 July 1923). French sculptor. In 1935 he was apprenticed to his father as a mason. From 1936 to 1943 he studied drawing and modelling at the Ecole des Beaux-Arts in Tourcoing under the French sculptor Robert Coin (*b* 1901). In 1942 he was awarded a medal for a nude exhibited at the Salon des Artistes Français, and in 1943 he entered the Ecole des Beaux-Arts in Paris. While in Paris he studied sculpture from all periods, especially primitive sculpture at the Musée de l'Homme. During World War II he was a pupil of the French sculptor Marcel Gimond (*b* 1894). In 1948 he moved to Vézelay, and in 1950 to Bondues, near Lille. His early stone works up to 1950, such as *Sandstone* (1946; priv. col., see 1976 exh. cat., pl. 1), show the influence of primitive art. From 1950 to 1955 he worked mainly in wood, producing tall, elegant works reminiscent of the sculpture of Arp and Brancusi, such as *Upright* (1952; priv. col., see 1976 exh. cat., pl. 2b). In 1953 he had his first one-man exhibition at the Galerie Marcel Evrard in Lille.

From 1955 to 1960 Dodeigne worked in stone, producing smoothly finished, abstract sculptures such as *Stone* (1957; Lille, Mus. B.-A.). After *c.* 1960 he created sculptures of tormented human figures in roughly finished stone, such as *Untitled* (1965; Otterlo, Kröller–Müller), which were influenced by Auguste Rodin. In 1970 he made a large group of figures, *The Ten* (Bondues, Fond. Septentrion). He invariably used Belgian granite when working in stone, but after 1963 he also worked in bronze, producing flowing, dynamic sculptures of human forms similar to those executed in stone.

BIBLIOGRAPHY
Eugène Dodeigne: Sculptures and Drawings (exh. cat., London, Buckingham Gal., 1971)
Dodeigne: Sculptures et dessins (exh. cat. by M. Vilet, Lille, Mus. B.-A., 1976)
A. M. Hammacher: *Dodeigne* (Lannoo, 1981)

Dodgson, Campbell (*b* Crayford, Kent, 13 Aug 1867; *d* London, 11 July 1948). English museum official and collector. He read theology and classics at Oxford, then abandoned the idea of ordination and in 1893 was appointed to the Department of Prints and Drawings at the British Museum. In 1912 he succeeded Sir Sidney Colvin (1845–1927) as Keeper of the Department, a post he held until his retirement in 1932. Dodgson quickly established an international reputation as an authority on early German prints, his numerous contributions in this field including the *Catalogue of Early German and Flemish Woodcuts in the British Museum* and a catalogue raisonné of Dürer's intaglio prints. Among his publications on other prints are *Old French Colour Prints*, the Roxburghe Club catalogue of the proof states of Goya's *Desastres de la guerra* and catalogues of the oeuvre of seven contemporary British ctchers, including Muirhead Bone and Augustus John. Dodgson was co-editor of the Dürer Society publications (1898–1908), on the advisory council of the *Burlington Magazine* from its inception in 1903, editor of the invaluable *Print Collector's Quarterly* (1921–36) and one of the founders of *Old Master Drawings* (1927–39). A man of considerable private means, he assembled a personal collection of prints, drawings and books, 5000 of which were bequeathed to the British Museum. The collection focused almost entirely on the work of contemporary artists, both British and foreign, since these were not previously represented in the national collection. His desire to support living graphic artists was also reflected in the separate prints and drawings fund that he set up in 1919 for the Contemporary Art Society. He received honorary degrees from Oxford and Cambridge and the Goethe medal from the German government for his services to the history of German art. He was elected FBA in 1939.

WRITINGS
Grotesque Alphabet of 1464 (London, 1899)
Catalogue of Early German and Flemish Woodcuts in the British Museum, 2 vols (London, 1903 and 1911)
Muirhead Bone's Etchings and Drypoints (London, 1909)
ed.: *Woodcuts of the XV Century in the John Rylands Library, Manchester* (London, 1915)
A Catalogue of Etchings by Augustus John, 1901–1914 (London, 1920)
Old French Colour Prints (London, 1924)
Albrecht Dürer: Numbered Catalogue of Engravings, Drypoints and Etchings with Technical Details (London, 1926)
ed.: *Woodcuts of the XV Century in the Ashmolean Museum, Oxford* (London, 1929)
ed.: *Woodcuts of the XV Century in the . . . British Museum*, 2 vols (London, 1934–5)
ed.: *Prints in the Dotted Manner in the . . . British Museum* (London, 1937)
Regular contributions to *Burl. Mag.* [105 articles and notes, 1903–19], *Prt Colr Q.*, *Old Master Drgs* and various Ger. periodicals

BIBLIOGRAPHY
DNB
The Times (14 and 22 July 1932)
Obituary, *Burl. Mag.*, xc (1948), p. 293
A. E. Popham: Obituary, *Proc. Brit. Acad.*, xxxvi (1950), pp. 291–7
J. Byam Shaw: 'Reminiscences of Campbell Dodgson', *JBS—Selected Writings* (privately printed, 1968)
P. Roth: 'Campbell Dodgson, 1867–1948', *Prt Rev.*, iv (1975), pp. 34–7
'Note on Campbell Dodgson, 1867–1948', *From Manet to Toulouse-Lautrec: French Lithographs, 1860–1900* (exh. cat. by F. Carey and A. Giffiths, London, BM, 1978), pp. 7–9 [almost all items in exh. from Dodgson Bequest]
F. Carey: 'Campbell Dodgson', *Landmarks in the History of Print Collecting* (exh. cat., ed. A. V. Griffiths; Houston, TX, Mus. F.A. and elsewhere; 1996)

LAURA SUFFIELD

Dodgson, Charles L(utwidge). *See* CARROLL, LEWIS.

Dodona. Site of ancient sanctuary in Epiros, north-west Greece. It is in many ways the remotest of Greek sanctuaries: Epiros was largely uninfluenced by the main developments of the Archaic and Classical periods, retaining its tribal organization at a time when more progressive regions were forming city states. The sanctuary was dedicated to Zeus, probably because the high mountains surrounding it attract spectacular thunderstorms. Despite the site's remoteness, the Greeks were aware of Zeus of Dodona from early times; for example he is invoked in the *Iliad* (XIV.233) as Achilles prepares to allow Patroklos to lead his Myrmidons once more into battle. The cult was oracular, and the oracles were associated with a sacred oak tree in the sanctuary, whose prophecies (the whispering of its leaves) were interpreted by a hereditary family of priests, the Selloi. The sanctuary offers a good example of an important cult that flourished without the need for a temple. For a long time it had no architectural embellishment, consisting simply of the precinct containing the sacred oak tree surrounded by tripods, though a simple shrine was added at the beginning of the 4th century BC. Architectural development came only after the formation of the unified kingdom of Epiros, which flourished under Pyrrhos (*reg* 297–272 BC). The sacred precinct was enclosed on three sides by a stoa, the shrine itself was eventually given a prostyle porch, and a propylon was built opposite it (all still small in scale). The most prominent structure is the theatre, which dates from Pyrrhos' time and is one of the largest in Greece, with three zones of seating. Its *orchestra* was converted into an arena in Roman times.

BIBLIOGRAPHY
S. I. Dakaris: 'To ieron tis Dodones' [The sanctuary at Dodona], *Archaiol. Deltion*, xvi (1960), pp. 4–40
——: 'Das Taubenorakel von Dodona und das Totenorakel bei Ephyra', *Ant. Kst*, suppl. 1 (1963), pp. 35–55
H. W. Parke: *The Oracles of Zeus* (Oxford, 1967)
S. I. Dakaris: *Archaeological Guide to Dodona* (Dodona, 1971)

R. A. TOMLINSON

Dods, Robin [Smith, Robert]. (*b* Dunedin, New Zealand, 9 June 1868; *d* Sydney, 23 July 1920). Australian architect. Educated in Brisbane, Australia, he served his articles with the architects Hay & Henderson in Edinburgh (1886–90) while also studying at the Edinburgh Architectural Association where he formed a lasting friendship with architect Robert Lorimer. From 1890 to 1894 Dods worked in several prominent London offices, including the fortifications branch of the Imperial War Office, Dunn & Watson, and in the office of Aston Webb. He was admitted to the RIBA in 1891 and in the same year travelled to Italy. He was awarded a special prize in the Tite Prize competition (1893) and a medal of merit in the Soane Medallion (1894). Dods returned to Brisbane in 1896 having won a competition for a nurses' home at the Brisbane Hospital, and entered partnership with architect Francis Hall (1862–1939) as Hall & Dods (1896–1916). The practice enjoyed a variety of commissions from domestic work (where Dods adapted the Queensland timber vernacular in a radically new way) to commercial buildings, hospital and ecclesiastical work. Significant work by Dods in Brisbane includes the New Zealand Insurance Building (1908–9; destr., see Tanner, pp. 92, 93), Mater Misericordiae Hospital (1908–11; extended), AML&F Building (1912; destr., see Tanner, p. 91) and St Brigid's Roman Catholic Church (1913), Red Hill.

In 1904 Dods was appointed the Brisbane Diocesan Architect for the Church of England. In this capacity he supervised the building of the first stage (1906–10) of J. L. Pearson's five-aisled fully stone-vaulted St John's Cathedral, as well as designing St John's Institute (1904) and the Diocesan Offices (1909), which form part of the cathedral precinct. With the prospect of larger projects Dods moved to Sydney in 1913 and with his new partners created the firm of Spain, Cosh & Dods (1913–20). However, World War I severely curtailed building at this time, although two large projects (South British Insurance

Building, Hunter Street, Sydney, 1918; destr., see Riddel, pl. 229; and the Newcastle Club, 1918–24; altered) were completed posthumously. In 1919 Dods collaborated with such prominent architects as W. Hardy Wilson and Leslie Wilkinson to produce 'Domestic Architecture in Australia' (1919), in which he confirmed a national debt to Francis Greenaway and looked hopefully towards the USA, not to Frank Lloyd Wright or Walter Burley Griffin, but to a more conservative movement based on the European tradition. Influenced by C. F. A. Voysey and the philosophy of the Arts and Crafts Movement, Dods exhibited a confident exploitation and adaptation of Australian regional traditions in his buildings. His rigorous pursuit of an appropriated Australian architecture (in both his buildings and his writings) make him one of Australia's most significant architects.

WRITINGS

with W. H. Wilson: 'The Architect and the Future', *Art in Australia* (1919) [special issue: 'Domestic Architecture in Australia', eds S. U. Smith and B. Stevens]

BIBLIOGRAPHY

J. Egan: *The Work of Robin Dods ARIBA* (diss., U. Sydney, 1931)
R. J. Riddel: *Some Influences and their Origins in the Architecture of Robin Dods (1868–1920)* (diss., London, Archit. Assoc., 1976)
N. Lund: 'Robin Dods, 1868–1920', *Architects of Australia*, ed. H. Tanner (Melbourne, 1981)

R. J. RIDDEL

Doesburg, Theo van (*b* Utrecht, 30 Aug 1883; *d* Davos, Switzerland, 7 March 1931). Dutch painter, architect, designer and writer. He was officially registered as the son of Wilhelm Küpper and Henrietta Catharina Margadant, but he was so convinced that his mother's second husband, Theodorus Doesburg, was his father that he took his name. Little is known of his early life, but he began painting naturalistic subjects *c.* 1899. In 1903 he began his military service, and around the same time he met his first wife, Agnita Feis, a Theosophist and poet. Between about 1908 and 1910, much influenced by the work of Honoré Daumier, he produced caricatures, some of which were later published in his first book *De maskers af!* (1916). Also during this period he painted some Impressionist-inspired landscapes and portraits in the manner of George Hendrik Breitner. Between 1914 and 1915 the influence of Kandinsky became clear in such drawings as *Streetmusic I* and *Streetmusic II* (The Hague, Rijksdienst Beeld. Kst) and other abstract works.

With the mobilization of the Dutch forces following the outbreak of World War I, van Doesburg was sent to Tilburg near the Belgian front. His first marriage was already in difficulty, and in Tilburg he met Lena Milius, who became his second wife (1917). In 1915 he met the painter Janus de Winter, who became the subject of a second pamphlet by van Doesburg. De Winter was a mystic and Theosophist who worked mainly in watercolours and pastels. His influence can be seen in van Doesburg's expressive and highly charged pastels and self-portraits of this period including *Despair* (1915; The Hague, Rijksdienst Beeld. Kst). Also in 1915 he discovered the work of PIET MONDRIAN, whose 'spirituality' was of an entirely different order from that of De Winter. Almost immediately he began to contemplate and organize a new periodical, *De stijl: Maandblad voor nieuwe kunst, wetenschap en kultuur*, not to be fully realized for another two years. In the meantime he wrote a considerable amount, including a good deal of criticism.

In 1916 van Doesburg participated in the foundation of the artists' associations De Anderen and De Sphinx. Although his enthusiasm for these was short-lived, he met other like-minded artists, including Bart van der Leck, and even such architects as J. J. P. Oud, all of whom became actively engaged in *De stijl*. In August 1916 Oud commissioned him to design a stained-glass window for a house he was building in Broek-in-Waterland. This commission was followed by numerous others in stained glass, a medium that provided an opening into architectural design and a fruitful area for the further exploration of important themes. These included reduction of natural appearances into simplified geometric forms and the development of an art based on mathematical principles, ideas that van Doesburg thought the Cubists had been attempting. He produced series of drawings from a single subject where the heavy, emphatic outline was progressively 'essentialized' to a minimum of horizontal and vertical lines bounding coloured planes. This technique of painterly composition lent itself admirably to the creation of stained-glass windows. The windows were usually designed for specific buildings for which van Doesburg would also produce colour-schemes and even tiled floors, in which he would continue to elaborate his compositional principles (e.g. his collaborative work in 1917 with Oud at the Vakantiehuis De Vonk, Noordwijkerhout, illustrated in *De stijl*, Nov 1918; and with Gerrit Rietveld in a room for Bart de Ligt, 1919, illustrated in *De stijl*, 1920). He acted as colour consultant for the De Lange House (1917), Alkmaar, by Jan Wils, and the Hotel De Dubbele Sleutel (1918; destr. 1975), Woerden.

From as early as 1912 van Doesburg had published an impressive number of articles. He signed his work under various names, including I. K. Bonset (in his role as a Dadaist poet) and Aldo Camini (in his role as a Futurist), as well as his own. In his writings on art he revealed himself to be a very self-conscious artist, who engaged in a constant dialogue between theory and practice, and between his work in painting and in architecture, also exploring the relationship of his work to that of others. During 1917 discussion continued concerning the naming of official collaborators of *De stijl*. The first issue was dated October and appeared in November 1917 (*see* STIJL, DE).

In 1920 and 1921 van Doesburg undertook work in Drachten for the architect Cornelis de Boer. Van Doesburg's colour-schemes (produced for a block of middle-class housing and for an agricultural school across the street) linked interior with exterior, and the primary colours on the housing had their counterpoint in the secondary colours of the agricultural school.

While working on these colour-schemes he also became increasingly involved in Dada activities, including the publication of four issues of *Mécano* (1922–3), attending a Constructivist/Dadaist Congress in Weimar in September 1922 (with Tristan Tzara, Hans Arp, Kurt Schwitters, Hans Richter, Hannah Höch and others), and participating in performances in Hannover and Weimar and a Dada

Theo van Doesburg: *Counter-composition XVI*, oil on canvas, 1.0×1.8 m, 1925 (The Hague, Haags Gemeentemuseum)

tour of the Netherlands to commemorate his final departure from his native land.

Through these activities and through his editorship of *De stijl*, van Doesburg gradually developed international contacts. At the end of 1920 he visited the Bauhaus; there has been some speculation that he was to have been appointed to the staff. On a second extended visit in May 1922, he gave his controversial De Stijl course to Bauhaus students at his studio in Weimar. There he met the young Dutch architect Cornelis van Eesteren, whose interest in De Stijl ideas resulted in collaborative projects that formed the centrepiece for the great exhibition *Les Architectures du Stijl* at Léonce Rosenberg's Galerie de l'Effort Moderne in Paris in 1923. Rosenberg had commissioned van Doesburg and other members of De Stijl to design an 'ideal house' for him as early as December 1920. In response to this earlier request van Eesteren designed a house for Rosenberg in late 1922. The designs were sent in early 1923 to Gerrit Rietveld who built the model. A second model for a '*maison particulière*' was designed by van Eesteren with a colour-scheme by van Doesburg, and a third model for a '*maison d'artiste*' was designed principally by van Doesburg. This third model and Rietveld's Schröder House (1924) are two of the prime examples of Elementarist architecture (*see* ELEMENTARISM). There has long been a dispute over the precise contributions of van Doesburg and van Eesteren to the second and third models, and the dispute over attribution caused the split in their partnership at the end of 1924.

Despite van Doesburg's efforts, De Stijl was not given its own pavilion at the Exposition des Arts Décoratifs et Industriels Modernes (1925) in Paris. Although disappointed, he made a considerable breakthrough in his painting and architecture *c*. the end of 1924. Having previously concentrated on a format that included only horizontal and vertical elements he reintroduced the diagonal into his paintings, subsequently giving them the titles 'counter-compositions'; these form an interesting comparison with Mondrian's lozenge paintings of the following year, although it was the emphasis that van Doesburg gave to the diagonal that caused a split between the two. In producing a 'Flower Room' for Charles, Vicomte de Noailles, van Doesburg used the 'counter-compositional' technique to create a dynamic tension between the upright architectural structure and the diagonal emphasis of the colour-scheme. This theme was continued in works of the next few years, most notably between 1926 and 1928 when he collaborated with Hans Arp and Sophie Taeuber-Arp on the renovation of the Café de l'Aubette, an entertainment complex in Strasbourg. Van Doesburg himself designed the major rooms, including the Café-Brasserie, the Petite Salle-Dancing and the Ciné-Dancing. These last two rooms were designed in contrast to one another: the former with horizontal–vertical compositions in primary colours; the latter with diagonal compositions closely resembling his painting *Counter-composition XVI* (1925; The Hague, Gemeentemus.; see fig.). In his article 'Schilderkunst: Van compositie tot contra-compositie' he explained the theory behind these works.

From 1925 van Doesburg intended to build a studio-house for himself and his third wife, Nelly van Moorsel. It was to have been a double house to accommodate themselves and the Arps, but after a number of designs were explored, the Arps withdrew, and van Doesburg produced his first architectural work free from collaboration with other architects. It marked his transition from painter to architect. Unfortunately, before the house was finished, he died of a heart attack following a bout of asthma. Shortly before his death he published his first and only issue of *Art concret* (*see* CONCRETE ART) and was involved in planning a new group of artists, the emergent Abstraction–Création, which was to have been based at van Doesburg's Studio-House in Meudon.

UNPUBLISHED SOURCES

Drachten, Streekmus. Smallingerland Bleekerhûs [drgs for Drachten proj.]
The Hague, Rijksdienst Beeld. Kst [sketches and architectural drgs]
Paris, Pompidou [drgs for Café de l'Aubette]

WRITINGS

De nieuwe beweging in de schilderkunst [The new movement in painting] (Delft, 1917/*R* Amsterdam, 1983)
Drie voordrachten over de nieuwe beeldende kunst [Three lectures on the new plastic art] (Amsterdam, 1919)
Mécano, 1–4/5 (1922–3; *R* Cologne, 1979)
Grundbegriffe der neuen gestaltenden Kunst, Bauhausbücher 6 (Munich, 1925) [originally pubd as a ser. of articles, 1919]

BIBLIOGRAPHY

H. L. C. Jaffé: *De Stijl, 1917–1931: The Dutch Contribution to Modern Art* (London, 1956)
J. Leering and others: *Theo van Doesburg, 1883–1931* (Eindhoven, 1968)
J. Baljeu: *Theo van Doesburg* (London, 1974)
K. Schippers, ed.: *I. K. Bonset, Nieuwe Woordbeeldingen; De gedichten van Theo van Doesburg* (Amsterdam, 1975)
R. P. Welsh: 'Theo van Doesburg and Geometric Abstraction', *Nijhoff, van Ostayen and De Stijl* (The Hague, 1976)
P. Georgel and E. de Lillers: *Théo van Doesburg: Projets pour l'Aubette* (Paris, 1977)
S. Polano, ed.: *Theo van Doesburg: Scritti di arte e di architettura* (Rome, 1979)
C. Weyergraf: *Piet Mondrian und Theo van Doesburg: Deutung von Werk und Theorie* (Munich, 1979)
H. Hedrick: *Theo van Doesburg: Propagandist and Practitioner of the Avant-Garde, 1909–1923* (Ann Arbor, 1980)
C. Boekraad, ed.: *Theo van Doesburg: Naar een beeldende architectuur* (Nijmegen, 1983)
H. L. C. Jaffé: *Theo van Doesburg* (Amsterdam, 1983)
E. van Straaten, ed.: *Theo van Doesburg 1883–1931* (The Hague, 1983)
L. Vancrevel, ed.: *Theo van Doesburg: Het andere gezicht van I. K. Bonset* (Amsterdam, 1983)
Y. -A. Bois and others: *De Stijl à Paris et l'architecture en France* (Liège and Paris, 1985)
C. Boekraad, ed.: *Theo van Doesburg: De Stijl en de europese architectuur* (Nijmegen, 1986)
A. Doig: *Theo van Doesburg: Painting into Architecture, Theory into Practice* (Cambridge, 1986)
E. van Straaten: *Theo van Doesburg: Painter and Architect* (The Hague, 1988)
S. Lemoine, ed.: *Theo van Doesburg: Peinture, architecture, théorie* (Paris, 1990)

For further writings and bibliography *see* STIJL, DE and ELEMENTARISM.

ALLAN DOIG

Doetechum [Duetecum], van. Dutch family of etchers. The brothers Jan [Johannes] van Doetechum (i) (*b* Deventer, *fl* 1554–*c.* 1600) and Lucas van Doetechum (*b* Deventer, *fl* 1554; *d* before March 1584) worked extensively for Antwerp print publishers, first Hieronymus Cock and later Gerard de Jode (i). They may have learnt etching from Cock, but their style is distinct from his; they combined firmly drawn, and frequently ruled, shading lines, the weight of which was controlled by variable biting, with the occasional use of an engraver's burin. Their earliest signed work is the *Funeral Procession of Charles V* (1559), designed by Cock and published by Christoph Plantin. They appear to have worked entirely from the designs of other artists. They produced a few large figure compositions (e.g. the *Resurrection*, 1557, after Frans Floris) but specialized in landscape (after Pieter Bruegel, I and Hans Bol, among others), architectural and ornamental designs (especially after Cornelis Floris and Hans

Vredeman de Vries) and topographical views and maps. During the 1570s and 1580s they devoted themselves increasingly to the etching of maps, contributing to the *Theatrum orbis terrarum* (1570) of Abraham Ortelius, Gerard de Jode's *Speculum orbis terrarum* (1578) and Lucas Jansz. Waghenaer's *Spieghel der zeevaerdt* (1584–5). In 1584 Jan had a shop in Deventer (Lucas was evidently dead by this time). In 1587, when Deventer fell to the Spanish, he fled to Haarlem and remained there until his death. His sons, Jan van Doetechum (ii) (*d* 1630) and Baptist van Doetechum (*fl c.* 1589–1606), were also etchers. The van Doetechums were famous in their own time for having invented a mode of etching that closely resembled engraving and for the volume of work they produced; their use of the medium foreshadows Jacques Callot and particularly Abraham Bosse.

See also ETCHING, §II, 1.

PRINTS

G. de Jode: *Speculum orbis terrarum* (Antwerp, 1578); facs. with intro. by R. Skelton (Amsterdam, 1965)
L. J. Waghenaer: *Spieghel der zeevaerdt* (Leiden, 1584–5); facs. with intro. by R. Skelton (Amsterdam, 1964)

BIBLIOGRAPHY

Hollstein: *Dut. & Flem.* [very incomplete list of works]
M. Quad von Kinkelbach: *Teutscher Nation Herligkeit* (Cologne, 1609), pp. 431–2 [mention of their technical invention in etching]
J. Denucé: *Oud-Nederlandsche kaartmakers in betrekking met Plantijn*, i (Amsterdam, 1912/*R* 1964), pp. 201–6
Zwischen Renaissance und Barock: Das Zeitalter von Bruegel und Bellange (exh. cat., ed. K. Oberhuber; Vienna, Albertina, 1967), pp. 39–45, 114–22
T. Riggs: *Hieronymus Cock: Printmaker and Publisher* (New York, 1977), pp. 140–47, 153–5
R. V. Tooley: *Tooley's Dictionary of Mapmakers* (New York, 1979), p. 167
L. Voet: *The Plantin Press (1555–1589): A Bibliography*, 6 vols (Amsterdam, 1980–83), nos 939, 2480, 2487
G. Schilder: *Monumenta Cartographica Neerlandica*, i (Alphen aan den Rijn, 1986), pp. 3–37

TIMOTHY RIGGS

Dogon. Gur-speaking people numbering *c.* 250,000 who live in *c.* 700 villages in Mali, east of the confluence of the Niger and Bani rivers. They are particularly renowned for their figure sculpture, masking traditions and architecture. Major collections of Dogon art include that made by the French ethnologist Marcel Griaule in the 1930s (now in Paris, Mus. Homme; see also 1985 exh. cat., nos 12–28). Other important collections were made by Leo Frobenius and can be found at the Museen für Völkerkunde in Berlin and Hamburg. Many private collections resulted from the interest in the Dogon and their geographical predecessors, the Tellem, that began in the 1950s. One of the finest private collections, that of Lester Wunderman, is now divided between the Metropolitan Museum of Art, New York, and the Musée Dapper, Paris.

1. Introduction. 2. Geography and cultural history. 3. Dogon artists. 4. Figure sculpture. 5. Masks and masquerades. 6. Architecture. 7. Domestic arts. 8. Metalwork.

1. INTRODUCTION. There were a number of early studies of the Dogon (Desplagnes, Frobenius and Arnaud), but much of the scholarly knowledge of Dogon art and culture is the result of research by a group of French scholars led by Marcel Griaule. Griaule first visited Dogon country in 1931, as leader of the 'Mission Dakar–Djibouti'

research and collecting expedition organized by the Musée de l'Homme, Paris (Griaule, 1933). This generated an enormous body of literature, focusing first on Dogon social organization, material culture and religious beliefs, but ultimately concentrating on cosmology. In 1947 Ogotemmêli, an old hunter, was chosen by the elders to instruct Griaule in deeper levels of Dogon culture (Griaule, 1948). He revealed a vast body of myths, which Griaule saw as underpinning all aspects of Dogon life. Subsequently, the interpretations of Dogon culture became increasingly removed from observable events and activities.

Although Griaule and his followers contributed hugely to the study of African culture, their approach has not proved entirely satisfactory. Criticisms of the Griaule school have focused on its methodology, its idealized and ahistorical view of Dogon culture, its lack of attention to daily life, and the internal contradictions and inconsistencies of the mythological system. Nevertheless, most studies of Dogon art have depended on the work of the Griaule school. Many have accepted Griaule's mythological interpretations unquestioningly and used them as the point of departure for their own analysis of Dogon art (e.g. Laude, 1964; 1973 exh. cat.), which thus becomes further removed from any direct observation of the function and meaning of the objects. Attempts to redress this imbalance involve both new fieldwork (van Beek, 1988; 1991 exh. cat.) and a return to existing literature for additional data (1988 exh. cat.).

2. GEOGRAPHY AND CULTURAL HISTORY. Dogon territory is dominated by the Bandiagara Escarpment. This row of cliffs, c. 200 km long and up to c. 600 m high, makes access to Dogon villages difficult and in the past provided a natural defence against attacks. Neighbouring groups include the Mossi, Kurumba, Samo and Bwa to the south, the Songhai and Tuareg to the north, and the Bamana and Fulani to the west. The population is densest along the rocky scree at the base of the cliffs, although some Dogon live on the plateau above, and others have settled on the vast Séno Plain, which stretches to the border of Burkina Faso. Most Dogon are farmers who use techniques developed to suit their difficult environment to produce subsistence crops of millet, rice, fonio and manioc as well as cash crops of onions, tobacco and cotton. The Dogon have no centralized political institutions, and they are further divided by their great variety of dialects. Each village comprises several extended families, governed by an assembly of male elders. In each region political authority resides with the patriarch of the oldest family (hogon), who is also a priest.

Although Dogon early history is complex and has not been thoroughly studied, it is known that Soninke peoples from the kingdom of Ghana and Mande peoples from the kingdom of Mali settled the region. Some came via Djenne and the Inland Niger Delta region, others from Yatenga (now in Burkina Faso). In the late 15th century the Songhai conquest of Djenne and the expansion of the Mossi in Yatenga encouraged the Dogon to seek refuge on the Bandiagara cliffs. Such substyles of Dogon art as masks similar to those of the Mossi (1983 exh. cat., p. 6) and wood sculptures resembling terracotta figures of the

Inland Niger Delta region (de Grunne, 1983–6, 1988; Leloup, 1988) may reflect the peoples' varied origins and history.

According to oral traditions, when the Dogon arrived on the Bandiagara cliffs they encountered a group of people whom they called Tellem. Archaeological investigations have discovered granaries and areas where communal burials and funerary rituals were performed, confirming that the Tellem inhabited the cliffs from the 11th to the 16th century, when the Dogon arrived and replaced them (1977 exh. cat.; Bedaux, 1988, 1991). Although no Tellem living-quarters have been located, objects found in the burial caves give an excellent idea of Tellem material culture. Despite being of such organic materials as wood, leather, bark fibre and cotton, the finds were preserved in the dry environment of the caves and represent the earliest-known examples of their type from Sub-Saharan Africa. They include male corpses dressed in woven, tailored cotton garments and female corpses in short bark fibre aprons; they were then wrapped in woven cotton and woollen blankets. Objects buried with the bodies include leather sandals, aprons, bags, knife sheaths, such personal ornaments as rings, bracelets, hairpins and lip plugs as well as pendants of iron, bronze, wood, stone and beads. Many of the grave goods are either tools or utensils (e.g. hoe handles, quivers, bows and arrows, clay pots, wooden bowls and spoons). A few of the caves contained wooden neckrests.

Archaeologists also found two examples of wooden figurative sculpture in the Tellem caves (Bedaux, 1991, pls 1.23, 1.24). These small figures (c. 180 mm high) feature rudimentary limbs and minimal, geometric forms for their heads and torsos. Facial features and other details are obscured by a thick crust of sacrificial materials. (For the significance of these and their relationship to later Dogon art, see §3 below.) Pottery bowls with three or four feet were also found in the caves. Similar bowls have been found elsewhere in West Africa, particularly in areas closely associated with the Mali empire. These and other Tellem objects indicate contacts that occurred in West Africa at an early date and over vast distances, and show that the peoples of the Bandiagara cliffs participated in the broader cultural developments of the Niger valley.

3. DOGON ARTISTS. Although masks may be carved by their wearers, most wood and iron objects are made by blacksmiths. There are two groups of Dogon smiths: the jemo, who live on the plain, and their former slaves and pupils, the iru, who live on the plateau. The blacksmiths' mastery of earth, air and fire, and their ability to make vital tools accords them a privileged place in Dogon society (Dieterlen, 1965). Respect may also derive from their role in the myth of creation, in which the first blacksmith descended from heaven bringing fire, iron and seeds for cultivation. Both jemo and iru serve as peacemakers and as intermediaries between the living and the ancestors, and between humankind and God (Amma). Little attention has yet been paid to their training, technique, styles, patronage and aesthetics, or to the contributions of individual smiths to the development of Dogon art.

4. FIGURE SCULPTURE. Dogon sculpture is character-ized by such geometric stylization of facial features and body parts as pointed oval eyes, lozenge-shaped mouths, arrow-shaped noses and cylindrical torsos and limbs.

1. Dogon figure sculpture, wood, h. 730 mm, 19th or 20th century (New York, Metropolitan Museum of Art)

Substyles range from sculptures with thin, elongated limbs and body parts, and geometricized features, as in the figure of the seated couple (New York, Met.; see fig. 1), to those that are full-volumed, relatively naturalistic and with pre-cise depictions of hairstyles and ornaments as in the figure of the woman with mortar and pestle (New York, Met.; see fig. 2). Others are extremely simple, with only minimal references to human anatomy and resemble the figures found in the Tellem caves (e.g. 1988 exh. cat., nos 16–19). Some substyles may be the work of individual carvers or workshops: for example c. 12 works, characterized by tightly structured vertical and horizontal elements have been attributed to the 'Master of Ogol' (e.g. 1988 exh. cat., no. 14; Leloup, 1988). Information about the place of origin of these sculptures or the context in which they were used is seldom available, making a regional or functional classification of styles very difficult. Lack of reliable information also affects dating of the styles, although some may be among the oldest types of African wood sculpture. The simplified, surviving geometric sculp-tures found in great numbers in the caves above Dogon villages in the 1950s and two similar sculptures retrieved in archaeological investigations of the Tellem caves (Lang-lois, 1954; 1959 exh. cat.; Bedaux, 1991) are believed to be the work of Tellem artists and are often dated to before the 16th century. Figures with similar stylistic features, whether or not found in the Tellem caves, are often assumed to date from this period.

There are many difficulties with this way of distinguish-ing Tellem from Dogon styles of sculpture. Sculptures in Tellem style have been found in use on Dogon altars in the 20th century, and there is more continuity than disparity between the two styles. The Dogon themselves identify as 'Tellem' any works whose origins are unfamiliar to them, regardless of their age, style or actual origin in the Tellem caves. Thus, while this group constitutes a distinct, recognizable style, it is not certain that they were all made by the Tellem, or even that they date from the period of Tellem presence.

Dogon sculptural forms include figures standing, kneel-ing, sitting or riding; raising one or both arms in a variety of poses; and holding or wearing articles related to their gender, age, occupation or social status. Interpretation of these gestures has been complicated by the mythological slant followed by many scholars. For example, after Griaule's conversations with Ogotemmêli in 1947, he and Germaine Dieterlen identified almost all human images as Nommo, the key figure in later versions of the Dogon creation myth. While this may reflect a deeper level of knowledge, it also lacks the richness apparent in more context-specific interpretations.

A common sculptural form is a standing male raising its arms above its head in a gesture that may be one of prayer. Such figures range from over 2 m tall (1969 exh. cat., fig. 228) to under 0.5 m tall (1988 exh. cat., nos 16–20). Male figures are sometimes seated on relatively elaborate stools that, along with their beards and orna-ments, identify them as men of authority (e.g. 1986 exh. cat., no. 6). Other male figures play such musical instru-ments as drums, balafons, harps and clappers, some of which identify them as priests of various cults (Klobe, 1977). Male figures riding horses have been identified as

2. Dogon figure sculpture, wood, h. 565 mm, 19th or 20th century (New York, Metropolitan Museum of Art)

images of the *hogon* (*see* §2 above), both because horses are a luxury and because of the relationships in myth between the *hogon* and horses (de Grunne, 1983–6).

Figures of women abound and often incorporate children, reflecting their importance in Dogon society. Some women stand with the mortar and pestle used for pounding millet and other grains, the staples of the Dogon diet (see fig. 2). These may reflect the constant need for rain and healthy crops as well as being a way of thanking an ancestor for the work she did during her lifetime. Kneeling female

figures may refer to the position women assume at funerals to express grief (1988 exh. cat., nos 8, 10–12). A similar meaning is possible for figures holding their hands over their faces, a gesture not found elsewhere in African art but adopted by grieving Dogon women at funerals (1988 exh. cat., nos 21–2). For some, these represent a mythical character who committed incest with his mother, the earth, and hid his face in shame (1973 exh. cat., nos 1–3). This interpretation has little basis in Dogon myths, nor is there any evidence that, in Dogon terms, covering one's face expresses shame. Figures expressing grief, such as those kneeling or covering their faces, may be commissioned to depict mourning family members and to accompany their prayers to the gods to intercede when death plagues the family.

Another frequent form presents a seated man and woman, with the man's arm around the woman's shoulders (see fig. 1 above). Although sometimes identified as the 'primordial couple' (DeMott, 1982)—a vague term considering the complexity of Dogon cosmogony—it is more useful to view them as the 'ideal' couple, in which the balance between male and female roles is indicated by their gestures and attributes (1988 exh. cat., no. 23).

Information about the functions of Dogon figurative sculpture can be found in early studies by the Griaule school, who concluded that the figures housed the souls of deceased family members (Dieterlen, 1941). Members of the Griaule school also found sculptures in other contexts, including shrines commemorating women who died during pregnancy or childbirth, sanctuaries dedicated to the mythical ancestors who lived in the era before the appearance of death among mankind, altars made to augment a living individual's personal force, altars for blacksmiths and hunters and rain-making altars. Subsequent fieldwork suggests a different function. Rather than representing ancestors, sculptures intercede between humans and the gods (van Beek, 1988), being commissioned to help solve particular problems. The owner prays to the god and makes sacrifices on the figure, which represents the supplicant and acts as a record of the prayers. The figure's pose, therefore, may be a position of prayer (e.g. kneeling or standing with arms raised), or may portray what the owner would like to achieve through prayer (e.g. a mother with a child (*see* AFRICA, fig. 71), or a man with the trappings of wealth and power). After the owner's death, the figure may be preserved as an image of that person. These more recent findings do not necessarily contradict those of Griaule and his followers: meanings may have changed over four or five decades, or there may be regional variations in the functions of figure sculpture.

5. MASKS AND MASQUERADES. Dogon masks are seen in great numbers at publicly performed rituals and have been studied in great detail (Griaule, 1938; DeMott, 1982; Dieterlen, 1989; 1991 exh. cat.). Dogon masks are generically called *imina*, a term embracing the head covering, the costume, the accoutrements and the person wearing them. It also refers to the fibres (from the bark of *hibiscus canabinus*) used in manufacture, and considered the key component of the ensemble.

There are two types of mask: one is made primarily of fibres, and the other incorporates a wooden headpiece

3. Dogon maskers, Sanga region, Mali; from a photograph by Eliot Elisofon, 1959

(see fig. 3). Fibre masks are caplike, made of knotted fibre and cover the head and face. Cowrie shells are sewn around the eye-holes, and a crest of fibres, either loose or plaited to resemble a woman's coiffure, is attached to the top of the head. Most represent such human characters as blacksmiths, leatherworkers, priests, the *hogon* and their wives, or men and women of other ethnic groups (DeMott, 1982, figs 16–30). Dogon wooden masks are rectangular, boxlike forms of two basic types. In one, the face has three raised vertical rectangular bars that define the sides of the face and the nose, and two rectangular channels into which the rectangular eye-holes are cut (1988 exh. cat., nos 25–7; DeMott, 1982, figs 32, 41–2). Above the face rises a superstructure that varies according to the identity of the mask. Common examples of this type of wooden mask are animal masks (e.g. antelopes and rabbits); the Kanaga, surmounted by a double-barred cross with short vertical elements projecting from each arm of the cross (see fig. 3); the tall narrow 'multi-storey house' (Sirige) mask; and the Satimbe mask topped by a female figure. The second type of wooden mask, also rectangular, but with a bulging brow and an exaggerated mouth, may depict warriors, predatory animals or hyenas (1988 exh. cat., no. 28; DeMott, 1982, figs 37–9).

The making and use of Dogon masks are overseen by the men's society (Awa), which is responsible for performing rituals pertaining to death. One such ritual is Sigi, which commemorates the arrival of death among humankind. In the Sigi ceremony the 'Great Mask', or 'Mother of Masks' (Imina na), is used. Imina na have rectangular boxlike faces, and they are surmounted by a tall planklike superstructure pierced with triangular or rectangular holes (Griaule, 1938, figs 29–36). They are never worn, being displayed in a stationary position or while carried on the shoulder. Participation in the ceremony confers status, and a T-shaped wooden staff (*dolaba*), the principal accessory that the men hold in their hands and use as a seat (1988 exh. cat., figs 9, 10, no. 47), becomes an emblem of their involvement. Sigi is held every 60 years and is

passed from one village to another in a cycle that takes several years to complete, a new Imina na being made in each village.

Masks are also made for commemorative rituals (Dama) that take place several years after burial. A Dama requires lengthy and costly preparations, which enhance the prestige of the deceased and his descendants. When the necessary food has been produced and collected, new wooden masks are carved, and fibres are prepared and dyed for their costumes and for fibre hood-masks. The Dama ritual lasts six days, during which the mask society performs in the village, on the terrace of the deceased's house and in the *hogon*'s sacred fields. The soul of the deceased is led out of the village and sent on his way to the afterlife. For women, the Dama does not include masked dancing, unless the sole female member of the men's mask society is being remembered. For the Dama of an important elder, hundreds of masked dancers perform, creating a spectacle of sculpture, costume, song and dance.

During the 1930s Griaule documented more than 70 mask types. He considered these to be a visual summary of the Dogon world and of the return of order following the disruption caused by death. He also saw the Dama ceremony as an embodiment of the links between Dogon society and the mythical time when masks were first used to counteract the effects of death. Even at this time, however, Griaule was noticing changes in masking traditions. Since then, as contacts with the outside world increased, even more changes have occurred. By the 1990s masked dances were no longer restricted to funerals and Dama, but were also performed for tourists and visiting dignitaries. In reflecting economic, religious and social changes, masked rituals have continued to be an important part of Dogon cultural identity (Imperato, 1971; 1991 exh. cat.).

6. ARCHITECTURE. Although many studies of Dogon architecture consider its symbolic and mythological references (Calame-Griaule, 1955; Brasseur, 1968; N'Diaye, 1972), it can also be described in terms of its relationship to the environment. The Bandiagara cliffs provide excellent defensive sites but lack flat land and permanent sources of water. The Dogon have adapted to these conditions, building tightly packed dwellings, many with an upper storey that provides additional storage and work space as well as a sheltered terrace. Dogon homes are generally rectangular and flat roofed. Made of mud brick and stone, their blocky, faceted shapes resemble the craggy cliffs. The dwelling occupied by the head of a household is distinguished by a decorative façade (1988 exh. cat., figs 3, 4, 7).

Every Dogon compound includes several free-standing granaries, used to store not only millet and other foodstuffs but also personal valuables and even family altars. Narrow, with mud-brick walls and thatched roofs, they are raised on stones and logs as protection against moisture. Windows, midway up the walls, provide access and have relief-carved shutters depicting dense rows of human figures, animals and geometric motifs (see fig. 4 and 1988 exh. cat., nos 43–4).

One of the most distinctive structures in a Dogon village is the *togu na*, an open-sided shelter where men rest and converse (1988 exh. cat., fig. 1). In villages on the cliffs, *togu na* roofs, made of thick stacks of millet stalks, are supported by pillars of stone or mud-bricks, while on the Séno Plain, they are made of carved wood. The latter are massive, rectangular, forked posts, carved with figures of women with enormous conical breasts, male figures, animals, masks and other objects (1988 exh. cat., nos 41–2). Painted and relief designs reflecting the objects and people that characterize late 20th-century Mali have also been recorded (Spini and Spini, 1976; Huet, 1988).

7. DOMESTIC ARTS. Objects used in daily life are plain or have only minimal incised geometric decoration. Some utilitarian objects, used in rituals or by persons of elevated rank, are more elaborate in form. This category includes stools with curved, relief-carved supports depicting figures with raised arms (1988 exh. cat., no. 48). Such stools feature in sculptures of seated male elders or 'ideal' couples. Wooden vessels include a distinctive, footed vessel with a lid surmounted by a figure of a horse and rider (Paulme, 1940, p. 208; 1969 exh. cat., fig. 242) and from which the *hogon* is said to be served. Large wooden containers, sometimes over 2 m long, as well as smaller versions, are used for sacrificial food served at the yearly celebration of the millet harvest. These rectangular, troughlike vessels are carved with a horse's head at one end and lizards, abstract geometric motifs and figures with raised arms on their sides. They have been interpreted as representations of the ark that descended from heaven bringing humankind's ancestors (1988 exh. cat., nos 50–51; 1969 exh. cat., no. 238).

8. METALWORK. The Dogon use iron for bracelets and anklets. These are usually twisted or incised with geometric patterns (1988 exh. cat., nos 55–9). Small bronze figures with simplified features and sinuous limbs are worn as pendants or attached to the iron bracelets (1988 exh. cat., nos 59–61). Such ornaments are worn by the *hogon*, other priests and women, and are placed on ancestral altars as a link to the spirit of the wearer after death. Other iron objects include small, simplified animals and staffs surmounted by human figures (1988 exh. cat., nos 29–38). Placed in shrines and around the house of the *hogon*, these are believed to attract and secure spiritual forces of benefit to the community.

4. Dogon granary shutter, wood and iron, 781×527 mm (New York, Metropolitan Museum of Art)

BIBLIOGRAPHY

GENERAL WORKS

L. Desplagnes: *Le Plateau central nigérien* (Paris, 1907)

L. Frobenius: *Auf dem Wege nach Atlantis* (Berlin, 1911)

R. Arnaud: 'Notes sur les montagnards Habé des cercles de Bandiagara et de Hombori (Soudan français)', *Rev. Ethnog. & Trad. Pop.*, ii (1921), pp. 241–314

M. Griaule: 'Introduction méthodologique', *Minotaure*, 2 (1933), pp. 7–12

D. Paulme: *Organisation sociale des Dogon (Soudan français)* (Paris, 1940)

G. Dieterlen: *Les Ames des Dogon*, Travaux et mémoires de l'Institut d'Ethnologie, xl (Paris, 1941)

M. Griaule: *Dieu d'eau: Entretiens avec Ogotemmêli* (Paris, 1948); Eng. trans. as *Conversations with Ogotemmêli: An Introduction to Dogon Religious Ideas* (London, 1965)

G. Calame-Griaule: 'Notes sur l'habitation du plateau central nigérien (région de Bandiagara)', *Bull. Inst. Fr. Afrique Noire*, ser. B, xvii (1955), pp. 477–99

G. Dieterlen: 'Contribution à l'étude des forgerons en Afrique occidentale', *Annu.: Ecole Pratique Hautes Etud.*, lxxiii (1965–6), pp. 1–28

J. Gallais: 'Le Paysan dogon (République du Mali)', *Cah. Outre-mer*, xviii (1965), pp. 123–43

M. Griaule and G. Dieterlen: *Le Renard pâle*, Travaux et mémoires de l'Institut d'Ethnologie, xxii (Paris, 1965; Eng. trans., 1986)

M. Douglas: 'If the Dogon . . .', *Cah. Etud. Afr.*, 28 (1967), pp. 659–72

G. Brasseur: *Les Etablissements humains au Mali*, Mémoires de l'Institut Fondamental d'Afrique Noire, lxxxiii (Dakar, 1968)

G. Dieterlen: 'Les Cérémonies soixantenaires du Sigui chez les Dogon', *Africa*, xli/1 (1971), pp. 1–11

D. Paulme: 'Sanga 1935', *Cah. Etud. Afr.*, 65 (1977), pp. 7–12

J. Clifford: 'Power and Dialogue in Ethnography: Marcel Griaule's Initiation', in *Observers Observed: Essays on Ethnographic Fieldwork*, ed. G. W. Stocking jr, History of Anthropology, i (Madison, 1983), pp. 121–56

W. van Beek: 'Dogon Restudied: A Field Evaluation of the Work of Marcel Griaule', *Current Anthropol.*, xxxii/2 (1991), pp. 139–67

ART-HISTORICAL WORKS

M. Griaule: *Masques dogons*, Travaux et mémoires de l'Institut d'Ethnologie, xxxiii (Paris, 1938, rev. 1963)

P. Langlois: *Arts soudanais: Tribus dogons* (Brussels, 1954)

Sculpture of the Tellem and the Dogon (exh. cat. by M. Leiris and J. Damase, London, Hanover Gal., 1959)

J. Laude: 'La Statuaire du pays dogon', *Rev. Esthét.*, xvii (1964), pp. 46–68

Art of Oceania, Africa, and the Americas from the Museum of Primitive Art (exh. cat., New York, Met., 1969)

P. Imperato: 'Contemporary Adapted Dances of the Dogon', *Afr. A.*, v/1 (1971), pp. 28–33

F. N'Diaye: 'Contribution à l'étude de l'architecture du pays dogon', *Obj. & Mondes*, xii (1972), pp. 269–86

African Art of the Dogon: The Myths of the Cliff Dwellers (exh. cat. by J. Laude, New York, Brooklyn Mus., 1973)

T. Spini and S. Spini: *Togu Na: The African 'House of Men, House of Words'* (New York, 1976)

M. Klobe: 'A Dogon Figure of a Koro Player', *Afr. A.*, x/4 (1977), pp. 32–5

Tellem: Een bijdrage tot de geschiedenis van de Republiek Mali (exh. cat. by R. M. A. Bedaux, Berg en Dal, Afrika Mus., 1977)

B. DeMott: *Dogon Masks: A Structural Study of Form and Meaning* (Ann Arbor, 1982)

S. Pern: *Masked Dancers of West Africa: The Dogon* (Amsterdam, 1982)

B. de Grunne: 'Heroic Riders and Divine Horses: An Analysis of Ancient Soninké and Dogon Equestrian Figures from the Inland Niger Delta Region in Mali', *Minneapolis Inst. A. Bull.*, lxvi (1983–6), pp. 79–86

The Dogon of Mali and Upper Volta (exh. cat. by C. Roy, Munich, Fred Jahn, 1983)

African Masterpieces from the Musée de l'Homme (exh. cat. by S. M. Vogel and F. N'Diaye, New York, Cent. Afr. A., 1985)

African Aesthetics: The Carlo Monzino Collection (exh. cat. by S. M. Vogel, New York, Cent. Afr. A., 1986)

R. M. A. Bedaux: 'Tellem and Dogon Material Culture', *Afr. A.*, xxi/4 (1988), pp. 38–45, 91

B. de Grunne: 'Ancient Sculpture of the Inland Niger Delta and its Influence on Dogon Art', *Afr. A.*, xxi/4 (1988), pp. 50–55, 92

J.-C. Huet: 'The Togu Na of Tenyu Ireli', *Afr. A.*, xxi/4 (1988), pp. 34–7, 91

H. Leloup: 'Dogon Figure Styles', *Afr. A.*, xxii/1 (1988), pp. 44–51, 98–9

W. E. A. van Beek: 'Functions of Sculpture in Dogon Religion', *Afr. A.*, xxi/4 (1988), pp. 58–65, 91

Art of the Dogon: Selections from the Lester Wunderman Collection (exh. cat. by K. Ezra, New York, Met., 1988)

G. Dieterlen: 'Masks and Mythology among the Dogon', *Afr. A.*, xxii/3 (1989), pp. 34–43

R. M. A. Bedaux: 'The Tellem Research Project: The Archaeological Context', *Tellem Textiles*, ed. R. Bolland, Meded. Rijksmus. Vlkenknd., xxvii (Leiden, 1991), pp. 14–36

W. E. A. van Beek: 'Enter the Bush: A Dogon Mask Festival', *Africa Explores: 20th Century African Art* (exh. cat. by S. Vogel, New York, Cent. Afr. A., 1991), pp. 56–73

KATE EZRA

Dogtooth [tooth]. Pointed motif, most frequently associated with English architecture of the late 12th century and the early 13th, formed in relief by four leaves radiating from a central raised point with openings carved between them. The treatment of the leaves is sometimes quite plain, resulting in a form that resembles a pyramid. At other times they are richly foliated. The pointed profile of the ornament undoubtedly explains its association with canine incisors, although John Britton described this label, which seems to have come into use in the 1820s, as difficult to explain owing to the frequently foliated appearance of dogtooth, and like A. W. N. Pugin, he believed a more appropriate term should be found. Francis Bond suggested that dogtooth ornament had developed by undercutting the earlier nailhead form, with the result resembling a decayed tooth.

Dogtooth was used most extensively in conjunction with hollow mouldings on arches and vault ribs, as seen in William of Sens's work in Canterbury Cathedral (1174–8). Earlier examples occur on the Water Tower of *c.* 1155 built under Prior Wibert at Canterbury, as well as on the contemporary north doorway of the west front of Lincoln Cathedral. From Canterbury and Lincoln the dogtooth motif has been traced back to northern France, where it was employed from the 1130s until the end of the 12th century, for example at Thérouanne Cathedral (ruined).

BIBLIOGRAPHY

A. Pugin and E. Wilson: *Specimens of Gothic Architecture*, 2 vols (London, 1825)

J. Britton: *Dictionary of the Architecture of the Middle Ages* (London, 1838)

F. Bond: *English Church Architecture* (London, 1913), ii, p. 709

P. Johnson: 'Romanesque Ornament in Britain: Its Sources and Evolution', *J. Brit. Archaeol. Assoc.*, xxx (1924), pp. 91–104

J. Bony: 'French Influences on English Gothic Architecture', *J. Warb. & Court. Inst.*, xii (1949), pp. 1–15

G. Zarnecki: *Romanesque Lincoln: The Sculpture of the Cathedral* (Lincoln, 1988)

D. Kahn: *Canterbury Cathedral and its Romanesque Sculpture* (London, 1991)

LISA A. REILLY

Dōhachi. *See* TAKAHASHI DŌHACHI.

Dohan. *See* KAIGETSUDŌ, (3).

Doicescu, Octav (*b* Brăila, 8 Jan 1902; *d* Bucharest, 10 May 1981). Romanian architect, urban planner, theorist and teacher. He trained (1925–32) at the High School of Architecture and at the Academy of Fine Arts, Bucharest. In 1936–9 he was responsible for extensive development projects in Bucharest, including those for the integration into the city of such new areas as the Herastrau residential quarter, Baneasa housing estate and Cotroceni Avenue. He also contributed to the design of important buildings, such as the Village Museum (1936), and designed Mioritza Fountain, Mioritza Fountain Square (1936), all in Bucharest. In the late 1930s he travelled in Italy, particularly Tuscany, where he found affinities with his own approach to architecture in the restrained use of decoration to achieve natural light effects on surfaces, in the flat roofs and in the subtle handling of materials. Doicescu developed an architectural style characterized by simple volumes adapted to environmental and functional requirements, revealing a sensitivity in his use of materials and rejecting any artificial assimilation of the International Style or the highly decorative Byzantine Revival tradition in Romanian architecture. In 1939 he designed the Romanian House for the World's Fair, New York, where he also met Frank Lloyd Wright, whose architectural views he shared. The Romanian House embodied Doicescu's conception of proportion, rhythm and balance, ideas that were presented in the review *Simetria*, which he edited (1939–47) with the philosopher, mathematician and aesthetician Mathyla Ghyka (1881–1965) and G. M. Cantacuzino [Cantacuzène]. Doicescu's search for a 'lyrical architecture', based on economy of detail and rhythmic balance, also reflected his friendship with the sculptor CONSTANTIN BRANCUSI, with whom he collaborated on a project (1938–41; unexecuted) for a temple at Indore, India (see Varia). At the end of World War II he became a professor at the Institute of Architecture, Bucharest, and a member of the Romanian Academy. He contributed to the reconstruction of towns destroyed during the war, designed domestic and industrial buildings, and built the Bucharest Opera House (1953). His last project, the Polytechnic Institute (1970), Bucharest, expressed his continued reservations about extreme functionalism and his preference for spatially integrated architecture.

BIBLIOGRAPHY

G. Cantacuzène: 'Tendances dans l'architecture roumaine', *Archit. Aujourd'hui*, v/5 (1934), pp. 57–62

R. Moitry-Bizary: 'Architecture en Roumanie: Bucarest', *Archit. Aujourd'hui*, v/5 (1934), pp. 55–6

P. Derer, ed.: *Octav Doicescu: Despre arhitectura: Scrieri, cuvintari* [Octav Doicescu: on architecture: writings, speeches] (Bucharest, 1983) [with extensive bibliog.]

R. Varia: *Brancusi* (New York, 1986), pp. 292–4

ANDREI DOICESCU

Doirat, Etienne (*b* Paris, *c.* 1670; *d* 25 June 1732). French cabinetmaker. He became a *maître-ébéniste* in Paris *c.* 1700 and was one of the first Parisian cabinetmakers to stamp his work. He operated a large-scale business from two workshops, one in the Faubourg Saint-Antoine, which he managed himself, and one in the Rue Saint-Honoré, which he placed under the direction of his son-in-law Louis-Simon Painsun (1700–*c.* 1748), who used the mark L.S.P. Doirat's period of activity coincided with the evolution of the Louis XV style, and most of his works are a combination of this and other earlier styles. Although some of his furniture (e.g. pier-table, Bamberg, Neue Residenz, Staatsgal.) derives its form from furniture by André Charles Boulle, in general it reflects the influence of Gilles-Marie Oppendord, A. Vassé (1681–1736) and Nicolas Pineau. In particular, Pineau's influence can be seen in the composition of the central cartouche on some commodes (e.g. of 1725–30; Malibu, CA, Getty Mus.) or the indentation used in place of the apron (ex-Lady Dudley col., London). Doirat was one of the first cabinetmakers to divide the commode (e.g. Fulda, Schloss Fasanerie) into three rows of drawers of unequal size, with the first reduced to a frieze and fitted side doors.

BIBLIOGRAPHY

J. Viaux: *Bibliographie du meuble (Mobilier civil français)*, 2 vols (Paris, 1966–88)

J. D. Augarde: 'Signaturen französischer Möbel', *Kst & Ant.*, 84 (1984), pp. 53–9

——: 'Etienne Doirat, menuisier en ébène', *Getty Mus. J.*, xiii (1985), pp. 33–52

JEAN-DOMINIQUE AUGARDE

Doisneau, Robert (*b* Gentilly, Val-de-Marne, 14 April 1912; *d* Paris, 1 April 1994). French photographer. He attended the Ecole Estienne in Paris (1926–9), where he studied engraving, and after leaving the school he had various jobs designing engraved labels and other items. He found his training of little use, however, and soon began to experiment with photography, teaching himself the techniques. In 1931 he worked as an assistant to the photographer André Vigneau. The following year Doisneau's series of photographs of a flea market in Paris was published in the periodical *Excelsior*. His early photographs have many of the features of his mature works: for example the seeming unawareness of the camera shown by the people in *Sunday Painter* (1932; see *Trois secondes d'éternité*, pl. 61) and the comic subject both add to the photograph's charm, a quality Doisneau valued greatly. In 1934 he obtained a job as an industrial photographer at the Renault factory in Billancourt, Paris, where he was required to take photographs of the factory interior and its machines as well as advertising shots of the finished cars. In the summer of 1939 he was dismissed for being repeatedly late and then worked briefly for the Rapho photographic agency in Paris, producing more photographs of the capital.

During World War II, Doisneau served in the light infantry and in 1945 joined the Alliance Photo agency, whose members included Henri Cartier-Bresson. He also started work on a series of reportages for the literary magazine *Le Point*. In 1946 he resumed work for the Rapho agency, also working on features for the weekly *Action*. The same year he met the poets Blaise Cendrars and Jacques Prévert (*b* 1900). His photos of the 1940s included such works as *Waltzing on Bastille Day* (1949; see *Trois secondes d'éternité*, pl. 130) showing a couple dancing in an empty street at night. In 1947 Doisneau won the Prix Kodak, and from 1948 to 1952 he worked for *Vogue*. From 1948 he started working with the cellist Maurice Baquet, which occupied him intermittently until the publication of *Ballade pour violoncelle et chambre noire* (1981). Unlike Doisneau's other photographs the works that comprise this series are deliberately contrived, often with surrealistic results. In 1951 Doisneau had his first one-man show at La Fontaine des Quatre Saisons in Paris.

Beginning with *La Banlieue de Paris* (1948), which had a text by Cendrars, Doisneau published a series of photographic books expressing his attachment to Paris: *Sortilège de Paris* (1952), *Les Parisiens tels qu'ils sont* (1954), *Instantanés de Paris* (1955) and *Gosses de Paris* (1956). Although occasionally he set up images to provide a certain effect or went to people's houses to photograph them in their own environment, his usual technique merely involved waiting in a certain spot for the right scene to materialize. It is these characteristics of chance and naturalness that lend his images their affecting humanity, and he repeatedly captured the slightly unusual but basically everyday events of the city. This reflected his aversion to the extremes of human life loved by so many photojournalists and also to the superficial exoticism sought by some photographers during brief visits abroad. As well as his photographs of Paris he took several portrait works, including the famous image of *Picasso and the Loaves* (1952; see *Trois secondes d'éternité*, pl. 47), showing Picasso seated before a table on which were two large bread 'hands'.

Doisneau travelled to the USA in 1960 and to the USSR in 1968, and during the 1960s he continued to produce photographs of Paris. *Trois secondes d'éternité* (1979) is a selection of photographs of various subjects from the 1930s up to the 1970s. His later works remained unchanged in subject and style, although his output decreased. In 1983 he was awarded the Grand Prix National de la Photographie. Doisneau gave an account of his work as well as of his meetings with such artists as Braque, Brancusi, Léger and Picasso in *A l'imparfait de l'objectif* (1989).

WRITINGS

A l'imparfait de l'objectif: Souvenirs et portraits (Paris, 1989)

PHOTOGRAPHIC PUBLICATIONS

La Banlieue de Paris, text by B. Cendrars (Paris, 1948, *R* 1983)

Sortilège de Paris, text by F. Cali (Paris, 1952)

Les Parisiens tels qu'ils sont, text by R. Giraud and M. Ragon (Paris, 1954)

Instantanés de Paris, text by H. Plécy (Lausanne, 1955)

My Paris, text by M. Chevalier (London and New York, 1972)

Le Paris de Robert Doisneau et Max-Pol Fouchet, text by M.-P. Fouchet (Paris, 1974)

Trois secondes d'éternité (Paris, 1979); Eng. trans. as *Robert Doisneau: Photographs* (New York and London, 1980)

Ballade pour violoncelle et chambre noire (Paris, 1981)
Les Doigts pleins d'encre, text by Cavanna (Paris, 1990)

BIBLIOGRAPHY
J.-F. Chevrier: *Robert Doisneau* (Paris, 1982)
S. Roumette: *Robert Doisneau* (Paris, 1983; Eng. trans., London, 1991)

PHILIP COOPER

Dōjin. *See* FŪGAI EKUN.

Dokathismata. *See under* AMORGOS.

Dokimeion [Docimium; now Iscehisar]. Roman and Byzantine town on the southern edge of the Phrygian plateau in central Turkey, about 40 km north-east of Synada (now Şuhut). CHARLES TEXIER discovered the site in the early 19th century. The town was founded, like many others, in the aftermath of the campaigns of Alexander the Great in 336–323 BC and the subsequent creation of the Hellenistic kingdoms in the eastern Mediterranean. Little remains of the diocesan town apart from the fortification wall around its acropolis.

Phrygia was renowned throughout antiquity for its marble quarries, the most famous of which were those situated to the south-east of ancient Dokimeion. As is attested by inscriptions, they formed part of the imperial assets from at least the middle of the 1st century AD. The price of the greatly valued marble was regulated by officials of the imperial administration. (Prices for marble from Dokimeion are specified in the Diocletian Edict on Prices (AD 301) and in the edict of Arcadius and Honorius (AD 414).) Dokimean marble, also called Synnadean (after Synada) or Phrygian marble, is known for its rich diversity of colours, ranging from white (used in sculpture) to yellow, reddish and even purple. According to Strabo (*Geography* XII.viii.14), Dokimean marble mainly served architectural purposes: it was exported already cut into columns, monoliths and veneer. In Rome, the precious pavonazetto—white marble with veining of purple or red—was first used extensively in the Forum Augustum (officially opened in 2 BC). In late antiquity, Dokimean marble was conveyed to Ravenna for the construction of S Vitale (*see* RAVENNA, §2(vii)) and to Constantinople for use in Ayia Sophia (AD 532–7) and the church of the Holy Apostles (AD 536–50) and in the parts of the Great Palace erected under Theophilos (*reg* 829–42).

One of the most important workshops of Roman sarcophagi during the first three centuries AD has been located in Dokimeion. It also produced gravestones for regional use. From the early 2nd century, two main types of sarcophagi, one decorated with cupids holding up garlands and the other with friezes showing Amazonomachies or hunting scenes, were exported not only to the surrounding areas but also to Pamphylia and to Rome. From about AD 160 onwards, most of these types were replaced by large sarcophagi with an architectural frame and projecting columns, between which figures were set. The production of sarcophagi ended *c.* AD 260, although stone was still extracted from the quarries until the 11th century. Most Roman and early Byzantine portraits from Phrygia are made of a fine-grained white marble of the quality also found in Dokimeion. Two busts from Kandilli (Istanbul, Archaeol. Mus., 5129 and 5130), one representing the emperor Marcus Aurelius (*reg* AD 161–80), the

other his wife, the empress Faustina the younger, were most likely made of Dokimean marble. However, it is still not proven whether there were Phrygian centres of high-quality portrait sculpture other than Antioch.

BIBLIOGRAPHY
C. Texier: *Description de l'Asie Mineure*, i (Paris, 1838)
J. Inan and E. Rosenbaum: *Roman and Early Byzantine Portrait Sculpture in Asia Minor* (London, 1966), pp. 77, 79
J. Röder: 'Marmor Phrygium: Die antiken Marmorbrüche von İscehisar in Westanatolien', *Jb. Dt. Archäol. Inst.*, lxxxvi (1971), pp. 253–312
M. Waelkens: *Dokimeion: Die Werkstatt der repräsentativen kleinasiatischen Sarkophage: Chronologie und Typologie ihrer Produktion*, Archäologische Forschungen, ii (Berlin, 1982)
J. C. Fant: 'Four Unfinished Sarcophagus Lids at Docimium and the Roman Imperial Quarry System in Phrygia', *Amer. J. Archaeol.*, lxxxix (1985), pp. 655–62
K. Belke and N. Mersich: *Phrygien und Pisidien*, Tabula Imperii Byzantini, vii (Vienna, 1990)

KALINKA HUBER

Dokoupil, Jiří Georg (*b* Bruntál, Czechoslovakia, 3 June 1954). German painter, printmaker and sculptor, of Czech birth. In 1968, when the Russian invasion took place, he fled with his parents from Czechoslovakia to Germany. From 1976 to 1978 he studied painting at the Fachhochschule für Kunst und Design in Cologne, and also in Frankfurt am Main, and in New York at the Cooper Union under Hans Haacke and Joseph Kosuth. In 1980 Dokoupil founded a loosely-connected group, Mülheimer Freiheit, with his colleagues Hans-Peter Adamski (*b* 1947), Peter Bömmels (*b* 1951), Walter Dahn (*b* 1954), Gerhard Kever (*b* 1956) and Gerhard Naschberger (*b* 1955) from the Cologne studio community. They shared an expressive, spontaneous contact with heterogeneous styles and themes, the unacademic use of quotations from art history, and an interest in community art. After the group's dissolution in 1982 Dokoupil retained his eclectic approach, aiming to be provocative by his stylistic pluralism and virtuoso quotation of well-known symbols from art history and from everyday merchandise aesthetics, and by his use of multifarious painting media and forms of expression. His subjective pictorial imaginings were intended as contemporary answers to the growing flood of pictures and news produced by the mass media. By rearranging well-known emblems and commercial names or objects, his sculptures and paintings became ciphers, often with ironical or self-critical purposes, as in the series *Corporation & Products* (1985; see 1985 exh. cat.), which included 43 painted fired clay sculptures and 13 paintings (e.g. *KRUPP*, acrylic and pigment on jute; Cologne, P. Maenz priv. col., see 1989 exh. cat., p. 87). After a period of residence in Tenerife (1988–9), Dokoupil's group paintings became more extensive and peaceful, as in his *Fruit-Paintings* of 1990 (e.g. *171 Apples*; see 1990 exh. cat.), in which real fruit was attached to the canvas, and his *Candle-Paintings* (e.g. *Chinese Acrobat*, 1990; see 1991 exh. cat.), which consist of photographic images made on the canvas with soot. His exhibition of paintings of the *Neue Kölner Schule* (1982) at the Paul Maenz Galerie in Cologne greatly increased his reputation. In 1983–4 he was a guest professor at the Kunstakademie in Düsseldorf and in 1989 at the Circulo de bellas Artes, Madrid.

BIBLIOGRAPHY
Jiří Georg Dokoupil: Neue Kölner Schule (exh. cat., Cologne, Paul Maenz Gal., 1982)

Jiří Georg Dokoupil Corporations & Products: The Sculptures—Die Skulpturen (exh. cat., Cologne, Paul Maenz Gal.; San Francisco, CA, Gal. Paule Anglim; Los Angeles, CA, Asher-Faure; 1985)
Dokoupil (exh. cat. by F. Rivas, Madrid, Fund. Caja Pensiones, 1989)
Dokoupil: Fruit-Paintings, 1990 (exh. cat., Vienna, Gal. Krinzinger, 1990)
Dokoupil: Candle-Paintings, 1990–1991 (exh. cat., Vienna, Gal. Krinzinger, 1991)

ULRIKE LEHMANN

Dokuchayev, Nikolay (Vasil'yevich) (*b* Moscow, 29 April 1891; *d* 2 June 1944). Russian architect, urban planner, theorist and teacher. He graduated from the College of Painting, Sculpture and Architecture, Moscow, in 1916, and took a further year's course at the Academy of Arts in Petrograd (now St Petersburg). Returning to Moscow after the Revolution, he worked from 1918 to 1924 in the Mossoviet architectural studio, headed by Aleksey Shchusev, on the first plan for reconstructing Moscow as the Soviet capital. In the same period he began teaching at his former school, which was formed initially into the State Free Art Studios (Rus. *Svomas*) and, from 1920, the VKHUTEMAS. During 1921 he became involved in the formal and spatial researches of the six-man Working Group of Architects of INKHUK (Rus.: Institute of artistic culture), Moscow. With two of his colleagues in the group, Nikolay Ladovsky and Vladimir Krinsky, who were fellow teachers, he devised curricula for the Vkhutemas, firstly that of the school's General Studio, set up in opposition to historicists, and then of the Basic Course through which all new students of the institute passed.

In 1923 Dokuchayev, Ladovsky and Krinsky formed the Soviet Union's first avant-garde architectural society, ASNOVA (Rus.: Association of new architects), in opposition to the old-guard Moscow Architectural Society (MAO), which still dominated professional life. Seeking to lay new foundations for architecture through research into its formal and expressive elements, ASNOVA were also opposed to the Constructivists. Dokuchayev made frequent use of the professional press to make sharp attacks on this rival design ideology, defending ASNOVA's view of architecture as an expressive synthesis of 'form, construction and space' against all threats of 'Functionalism' and any reduction of its creative processes to a 'method' (see 'Arkhitektura i tekhnika'). He became a member of the Union of Soviet Architects when the separate independent architectural groups were officially disbanded in 1932 and subsequently worked on various planning projects, treating urban form, in the typical manner of ASNOVA, as a relationship between perceptual aspects of volume and the dynamics of transportation movements through its spaces. His own designs, however, made less impact than his extensive teaching and writing, in which he covered a range of issues, such as planning, international Modernism and housing.

WRITINGS
'Vyssheye arkhitekturnoye obrazovaniye' [Higher education in architecture], *Stroitel'stvo Moskvy*, iv (1935), pp. 5–7
'Ploshchad' i transportnaya magistral' [The urban square and transport artery], *Arkhit. SSSR*, iv (1939), pp. 42–3
'Nikolay Vasil'yevich Dokuchayev', *Mastera sovetskoy arkhitektury ob arkhitekture* [Masters of Soviet architecture on architecture], ed. M. G. Barkhin (Moscow, 1975), pp. 186–210

BIBLIOGRAPHY
'Arkhitektura i tekhnika' [Architecture and technology], *Sov. Isk.* [Soviet art], viii–ix (1926), pp. 3–9
C. Lodder: *Russian Constructivism* (New Haven and London, 1983)
A. Senkevitch: 'Aspects of Spatial Form and Perceptual Psychology in the Doctrine of the Rationalist Movement in Soviet Architecture in the 1920s', *VIA*, vi (1983), pp. 78–115
S. O. Chan-Magomedov: *Pioniere der sowjetischen Architektur* (Dresden, 1983); Eng. trans. as S. O. Khan-Magemedov: *Pioneers of Soviet Architecture* (London, 1987)
——: *Vhutemas, Moscou, 1920–1930*, 2 vols (Paris, 1990)

CATHERINE COOKE

Dokuryū Shōeki [Duli Xingyi; Dai Mangong; Tianwai yi xianren] (*b* Hangzhou Prefect., Zhejiang Prov., 1596; *d* Nagasaki, 1672). Chinese Ōbaku Zen monk, calligrapher, poet, seal-carver and medical expert, active in Japan. Dokuryū was one of many learned men from south-east China to emigrate to Japan during the political turmoil following the collapse of the Ming dynasty in 1644. He arrived in Nagasaki in 1653 accomplished in several disciplines and quickly became a major force in the development of these arts and skills in Japan. Together with TŌKŌ SHIN'ETSU, Dokuryū is revered for having introduced techniques and practices of late Ming literati seal-carving to Japan. On his arrival there, Dokuryū became an itinerant scholar and medical specialist, establishing ties with émigré Chinese abbots and Japanese political figures. When the distinguished Chinese prelate Yinyuan Longqi (known in Japan as INGEN RYŪKI) arrived in 1654, Dokuryū was ordained as his disciple and received the Buddhist names Dokuryū and Shōeki.

He was Ingen's scribe from 1655 until 1658, when he took up residence at the Rinzai Zen monastery Heirinji (Saitama Prefect.) under the patronage of the shogunal minister Matsudaira Nobutsuna (1596–1662). A year later he retired to Nagasaki. Coming out of seclusion in 1664, he made the first of four trips to the Kikkawa domain in Iwakuni (now in Yamaguchi Prefect.), where he served as a physician and taught the literary arts. He was then invited to become scribe at the monastery Fukujuji (now in Fukuoka Prefect.), founded in 1665 by SOKUHI NYOITSU, one of Ingen's chief disciples. In 1669 Dokuryū again retired to Nagasaki, where he remained in ill-health until his death. His cremated remains were taken to Manpukuji. His most distinguished Japanese pupils were the calligraphers KŌ TEN'I and Kitajima Setsuzan (1636–97). The former established a memorial chapel to his teacher, the Taikeidō at Heirinji, in 1716. On the 100th anniversary of Dokuryū's death, Ten'i's son erected a monument to him (now in Tama Cemetery, Tokyo Prefect.).

Dokuryū's accomplishments in cursive (Jap. *sōsho*; Chin. *cao shu*), seal (Jap. *tensho*; Chin. *zhuan shu*) and clerical (Jap. *reisho*; Chin. *li shu*) scripts are noted in Chinese sources. He also mastered regular (Jap. *kaisho*; Chin. *kai shu*) and running (Jap. *gyōsho*; Chin. *xing shu*) scripts. His cursive script has been compared to that of the celebrated late Ming master painter–calligrapher ZHANG RUITU. Revered among Dokuryū's works in cursive script are the *Bai fa qian shu shi* ('Poem on combing my white hair one thousand times'; hanging scroll, ink on paper; n.d.; Kyoto, N. Mus.); *Jiu qiu ye yu shi juan* ('Poetry handscroll of evening rains in autumn'; ink on paper; 1666; priv. col., see *Shodō zenshū*, xxii, pls 74–5); and his last verses, a sickbed poem (Jap. *byōjūge*) and a death poem (Jap. *yuige*) (both handscrolls, ink on paper; 1672; Uji,

Manpukuji). In 1671 he inscribed a portrait of himself by Kita Genki (*fl c*. 1664–1709; Cleveland, OH, Mus. A.). Dokuryū was a stern critic of contemporary Japanese calligraphers, finding them lacking both in scholarship and in technique (*see* JAPAN, §VII, 2(vi)). In addition to numerous examples of his calligraphy, five collections of literary works and three treatises on smallpox, the treatment of which he is credited with bringing to Japan, survive.

BIBLIOGRAPHY
G. Toyama: 'Minmatsu no kikasō to nihon bunka' [Late Ming period naturalized monks and Japanese culture], *Shodō zenshū*, ed. K. Shimonaka, xxii (Tokyo, 1959), pp. 26–31, pls 73–5
S. Yoshinaga: *Tenkan rōjin dokuryū eki kō kinen* [A chronological history of Tianjian Laoren Duli [Xing]yi] (Fukuoka, 1961)
Obaku: Zen Painting and Calligraphy (exh. cat. by S. Addiss; Lawrence, U. KS, Spencer Mus. A.; New Orleans, LA, Mus. A., 1978)
M. Ōtsuki, S. Katō and Y. Hayashi, eds: *Ōbaku bunka jinmei jiten* [Biographical dictionary of Ōbaku cultural figures] (Kyoto, 1988)
ELIZABETH HORTON SHARF

Dolabella, Tommaso [Tomasz] (*b* Belluno, *c*. 1570; *d* Kraków, 17 Jan 1650). Italian painter, active in Poland. In Venice *c*. 1585–90 he assisted Antonio Vassilacchi, a pupil of Veronese. Of his many paintings there the ceiling (1592) of the Sala del Senato in the Doge's Palace is outstanding; he also painted a cycle of ten scenes of the *Life of Christ* (1592–4) for S Pietro, Perugia. In 1598 King Sigismund III Vasa brought him to Kraków, then the capital of Poland, naming him *pictor regius*. Wawel Castle in Kraków needed decoration following a fire in 1595: the King looked to the renowned Venetian style, already represented in Kraków by works by Titian and Veronese. Dolabella worked for Sigismund uninterruptedly until *c*. 1609, producing many military and historical pieces celebrating his rule, besides portraits of the royal family. Of these, only the portrait of *Sigismund III on Horseback* (*c*. 1611; Kraków, Wawel Castle) survives.

When Sigismund transferred his court to Warsaw in 1609, Dolabella remained in Kraków, producing paintings for wealthy monasteries such as that of the Dominicans. Of his paintings for them between 1618 and 1638, the best surviving are two huge canvases from the refectory, the *Marriage Feast at Cana* and the *Last Supper*, painted in the manner of Veronese. Outside Kraków, Dolabella created his historical masterpiece, the *Battle of Lepanto* (*c*. 1632), for the Dominicans in Poznań. He also completed, in 1626, a well-known cycle of religious paintings in Kraśnik, the *Mystical Judgement*, the *Rosary Procession* and the *Thanksgiving Mass* (Kráśnik Monastery, Parish Church of the former Canons Regular).

Dolabella was again connected with the court during the reign of Vladislav IV (*reg* 1632–48), for whom he painted scenes of the *Life of St Vladislav* (1632–3; four *in situ*) for the royal chapel in the Camaldolite church in Kraków's Bielany district. His later paintings are increasingly marred by contributions from his large Kraków workshop. He also occasionally made engravings. Stylistically, Dolabella's work until *c*. 1620 betrayed strong Venetian influences—warmth, saturation of colour, *sfumato* and multi-figure compositions. Afterwards, his palette changed and adapted to the local traditions of Polish painting. Dolabella brought to Poland the finest aspects of Venetian

painting: he was the creator of the country's school of Baroque painting.

(*see also* POLAND, §III, 3).

BIBLIOGRAPHY
Thieme–Becker
W. Tomkiewicz: *Dolabella* (Warsaw, 1959)
M. Walicki, W. Tomkiewicz and A. Ryszkiewicz: *Malarstwo Polskie: Manieryzm, Barok* [Polish painting: Mannerism, Baroque] (Warsaw, 1971), pp. 15, 335
M. Karpowicz: *Sztuka polska XVII wieku* [Polish art of the XVIIth century] (Warsaw, 1975), pp. 21–5
ANDREW STOGA

Dolce, Ludovico (*b* Venice, 1508; *d* Venice, 1568). Italian writer, critic and dramatist. He belonged to a noble but impoverished Venetian family. Dolce studied in Padua and became a versatile writer, typical of his times, who took his material from the works of others, with adaptations and quotations often bordering on plagiarism. He became an 'editorial consultant', working mainly for the Venetian publisher Giolito de' Ferrari, for whom he edited many contemporary works as well as translations of the classics by Virgil, Horace and Cicero. He wrote five comedies, a few tragedies, poems and treatises and a few biographies of illustrious persons, such as the Emperor Charles V. Most of these were superficial works, written to gain fame and money; but they demonstrate a response to a new interest in public cultural debate.

Thus it was natural for Dolce to take an interest in the problems of the fine arts. From about 1540 the two most celebrated artistic capitals of Italy, Florence and Venice, debated the merits of their rival traditions, of DISEGNO E COLORE. Many Venetian artists travelled to Rome, and Giorgio Vasari visited Venice in 1541, with other Tuscan artists. The Tuscan writer Pietro Aretino lived in Venice from 1527, and became a supporter of the Venetian school, admiring Titian even more than Michelangelo. Dolce was in close contact with Aretino, especially between 1535 and 1545; they exchanged letters, and Dolce dedicated writings to him and published his works. Dolce's interest in painting is first mentioned in a letter he wrote to Paolo Crivelli (Pino, 1574) on 10 March 1545: when Aretino was condemning the immorality of Michelangelo's *Last Judgement* in the Sistine Chapel, Dolce expressed admiration for the Tuscan master and some reservations about Venetian painting, except for Titian. Nevertheless in a letter to Gasparo Ballini (post-1550, as it shows a knowledge of Vasari's *Vite*, first published in that year; *Lettere*, 1559), he vigorously repeated Aretino's unfavourable opinion of Michelangelo, expressing a preference for Raphael and again for Titian. Around 1554 in his last artistic letter, to the collector Alessandro Contarini, he wrote a long eulogy of Titian's painting *Venus and Adonis* (1551–4; Madrid, Prado), which he praised for its naturalism and sweetness of feeling.

Dolce's masterpiece of art criticism (and perhaps his only published work on that subject) is the *Dialogo della pittura* (1557), titled in memory of Aretino, who had died the previous year. This work is polemical advocacy, inspired by Aretino, of the Venetian school, which was also supported in Paolo Pino's *Dialogo di pittura* (1548), against the superiority of the Florentine tradition set out in Vasari's *Vite* (1550). In it Dolce also defended the rights of the educated layman against the specialized technical knowledge of professional painters. The structure of this dialogue has some elements in common with that of Pino: the defence of the Venetian school, based on colour and naturalism; the recognition of the antiquity of painting and the view that it was superior to sculpture; and the importance of drawing. There are, however, considerable differences, and the historical significance of Dolce's work is different, because of the moment when it was written. It is certainly a celebration of Titian, the incomparable master of colour and leader of the Venetian school of art (and Vasari drew on it in the 1568 edition of the *Vite*), but it follows a complex line which also includes an enthusiastic discussion of Raphael, as a learned painter and the upholder of the classical doctrine of *ut pictura poësis*. To the professional painter, Vasari, Dolce opposed a criterion of value for painting which is closer to rhetoric: and the three parts of painting, *invention*, *drawing* and *colour*, correspond exactly to the *inventio*, *dispositio* and *elocutio* of rhetorical theory.

Vasari was also the champion of Florentine Mannerism. Dolce contrasted the balance and harmony of Raphael, close to the naturalism of Venetian art, with the Mannerist excesses of Michelangelo. He condemned Michelangelo not only for his overriding interest in the drawing of the nude but also for the excessive virtuoso display of his skill in foreshortening. Dolce was selective in his arguments, though, and even in the case of Titian concentrated on his mature work; he could not accept the Mannerist paintings of Titian's late years.

WRITINGS
La poetica d'Horatio (Venice, 1536)
Dialogo della pittura intitolato l'Aretino (Venice, 1557); ed. P. Barocchi as *Trattati d'arte del cinquecento tra manierismo e controriforma* (Bari, 1960), i, p. 34 [critical bibliog. on Dolce], pp. 143, 206 [commentary]
Lettere di diversi eccellentissimi huomini, ed. Dolce (Venice, 1559/R in Bottari-Ticozzi: *Raccolta* (1822–5), v, p. 166
Dialogo nel quale si ragiona della qualità, diversità e proprietà dei colori (Venice, 1564)

BIBLIOGRAPHY
B. Pino: *Della nuova scielta di lettere* (Venice, 1574), ii, pp. 194, 196, 200, 323
E. Cicogna: 'Memoria intorno la vita e gli scritti di M. L. D. letterato veneziano del secolo XVI', *Memorie dell'I. R. Istituto veneto di scienze, lettere ed arti*, xi (Venice, 1862), pp. 93–207
M. L. Gengaro: *Orientamenti della critica d'arte nel rinascimento cinquecentesco* (Milan/Messina, 1941), pp. 110–52
M. W. Roskill: *Dolce's Aretino and Venetian Art Theory of the Cinquecento* (New York, 1968) [text and trans. of *Dialogo della pittura* and letters to Ballini and Contarini]
F. Bernabei: 'Tiziano e Ludovico Dolce', *Tiziano e il manierismo europeo: Atti del convegno alla Fondazione Cini di Venezia, Civiltà veneziana saggi n. 24: Firenze, 1978*, pp. 307–37

FRANCO BERNABEI

Dolcebuono, Giovanni [Gian] **Giacomo** (*fl* Milan, 1465; *d* Aug 1504). Italian sculptor and architect. In 1465 he witnessed a document at the offices of the Fabbrica of Milan Cathedral together with Francesco Solari and Giovanni Antonio Amadeo, Dolcebuono's lifelong associate. All three were living in the parish of S Martini in Compedo, the neighbourhood of the Solari family of sculptors and architects, which suggests that Amadeo and Dolcebuono may have been trained by them. Dolcebuono's association with the Solari is confirmed by a document of 1467, in which Guiniforte Solari, then architect to the Fabbrica, and Giovanni Solari, Guiniforte's father and formerly an architect to the Fabbrica, hired Dolcebuono as a journeyman labourer for two years. By 1479 he was a member of the Scuola dei Quattro Coronati, the society of stonecutters at the Fabbrica. In 1472 he was paid for measuring for and designing the altar of St Joseph at the respectable rate of ten *soldi* per day. Documents of 1473 refer to his working on a *maestà* for the church of S Celso.

Another document from 1473 shows Dolcebuono entering an agreement with Amadeo, Lazzaro Palazzi (*fl* 1464–1508), Giovanni Antonio Piatti (*d* 1479), and Angelo da Lecco (*fl* 1458–1505) to collaborate on the façade of the Certosa di Pavia (*see* PAVIA, §2(i)), should any of them receive the commission (which Amadeo subsequently did), and also to work together on other projects in Milan and elsewhere. A 17th-century manuscript attributed to Matteo Valerio says that starting in 1491 Amadeo undertook to execute the façade of the Certosa, and that the design of the façade was the work of Dolcebuono and the painter Ambrogio Bergognone. This agreement, together with many other documents demonstrating Dolcebuono's prolonged association with Amadeo, makes it difficult to distinguish his work from that of Amadeo. That Dolcebuono was a master sculptor is proved by an apprenticeship document of 1474 in which he promises to teach his apprentice 'arte lapicide et a talio et a figuris. . .'. Dolcebuono continued to work for the Fabbrica throughout the 1470s, and from 1489 he also worked at the church of the Incoronata in Lodi. Between 1490, when he and Amadeo were chosen by the Fabbrica of Milan Cathedral as engineers to finish the lantern, and his death, surviving documents usually mention the two as collaborators. In 1490 they were associated with Francesco di Giorgio Martini as architects of the lantern.

It is probable that Dolcebuono and Amadeo collaborated with Bramante on the construction of the lantern of S Maria delle Grazie, Milan, in the 1490s. Between 1491 and 1494 Dolcebuono was architect to S Maria presso S Celso, Milan, providing columns and terracottas for the sanctuary. In 1493 it was decided to replace Dolcebuono at S Maria presso S Celso with Cristoforo Solari, but in 1494 he was replaced instead by Amadeo. In 1497 and 1498, however, Dolcebuono and Amadeo worked together as engineers on the lantern of S Maria presso S Celso, on Pavia Cathedral and on the lantern of Milan Cathedral. In 1501 Dolcebuono was still active as an architect at S Maria presso S Celso. In 1503 he and Amadeo made a wooden model for the Porta verso Compedo of Milan Cathedral. On 12 August 1504 Dolcebuono and Amadeo, as architects to the Fabbrica, evaluated stone for the doorway, but Dolcebuono was dead by September. No sculpture has been attributed to Dolcebuono, and his association with Amadeo makes it difficult to define his individual architectural style. Nevertheless, the general style in which he worked is defined by the projects with which he was involved, which form the major architectural monuments of the Lombard Renaissance.

BIBLIOGRAPHY
Thieme–Becker
G. L. Calvi: *Notizie sulla vita e sulle opere dei principali architetti scultori e pittori che fiorirono in Milano durante il governo dei Visconti e degli Sforza*, ii (Milan, 1865), pp. 175–90

C. Baroni: *Documenti per la storia dell'architettura a Milano nel rinascimento e nel barocco*, i (Florence, 1940)

G. Borlini: 'Gian Giacomo Dolcebuono', *Rendi. Reale Ist. Lombard. Sci. & Lett.*, lxxvii (1954), pp. 53–71

M. L. Rizzardi: 'La Chiesa di San Maurizio in Milano non è opera del Dolcebuono', *Ist. Lombard. Sci. & Lett., Cl. Lett., Sci. Mor. & Polit.: Rendi.*, lxxxix–xc (1956), pp. 582–6

G. Borlini: 'The Façade of the Certosa di Pavia', *A. Bull.*, xlv/4 (1963), pp. 323–36

R. V. Schofield: 'Bramante and Amadeo at Santa Maria delle Grazie in Milan', *A. Lombarda*, 78 (1987), pp. 41–58

R. V. Schofield, J. Shell and G. Sironi: *Giovanni Antonio Amadeo: Documents/I documenti* (Como, 1989)

CHARLES R. MORSCHECK JR

Dolci, Carlo (*b* Florence, 25 May 1616; *d* Florence, 1687). Italian painter. The major Florentine painter of the 17th century, he enjoyed an international reputation in his own lifetime. He was a gifted portrait painter and painted a number of large altarpieces, but his reputation is largely based on his half-length, single-figure paintings, characterized by their intense religiosity and meticulous technique. His mature style was complex and sophisticated. Intended for cultivated and aristocratic circles, his was never a popular art in any sense. Baldinucci described the painter's 'tormented fantasy' and 'dark fantasms', and his disturbed personality is evident throughout his work after the later 1640s.

1. Carlo Dolci: *St Andrew Praying before Martyrdom*, oil on canvas, 1120×920 mm, 1643 (Birmingham, City of Birmingham Museum and Art Gallery)

1. Life and work. 2. Posthumous reputation.

1. LIFE AND WORK.

(i) To 1650. His first pictures appear to have been painted in the mid-1620s, but no dated works from this phase have come to light. *St Francis Contemplating the Crucifix* (untraced, see McCorquodale, 1979, p. 146, fig. 9) may be among his earliest works and reveals the impact of his studies with Jacopo Vignali, whose studio he entered in 1625. Dolci's natural inclination to paint intense and subjective religious work was nurtured by contact with Vignali's visceral and emotive approach during the later 1620s. He was also aware of the strong contemporary tendency to favour simple, direct narrative, as seen in the work of Matteo Rosselli, Francesco Curradi and others. His love of detail in lavish textiles, jewellery and the human face and hands rendered with obsessive (but never finicking) attention to texture set him apart from contemporary Florentine painters.

In 1631 Dolci painted a bust-length portrait of *Steffano della Bella* (Florence, Pitti). It is likely that he knew and copied Early Netherlandish painting in addition to more recent Flemish work, and the portrait of *Fra Ainofo de' Bardi* (1632; Florence, Pitti) shows that he had studied Flemish art as much for style as technique. This picture already reveals Dolci's genius for portraiture, and his precocity, which ensured his immediate success in discriminating Florentine circles. The census of Florence of 1632 reveals that in that year he was described as 'painter'; he was probably supporting the household in which he was the only male, his father having died in 1620.

Baldinucci named his first patrons as Piero de' Medici, the Duc de Guise, the musician Antonio Landini and Cardinal Leopoldo de' Medici. Dolci maintained this level of success throughout his life. His small *Adoration of the Magi* (Blenheim Pal., Oxon) may be the version painted for Cardinal Leopoldo and reveals Dolci's synthesis of elements from contemporary figure compositions and his youthful passion for brilliant colour.

The major works almost certainly of the 1630s are the three known pictures of evangelists (Los Angeles, CA, priv. col.; Italy, priv. col.; Malibu, CA, Getty Mus.) possibly from the set that Dolci painted for Giovanbattista Galli. The work in Malibu, *St Matthew*, features a child model identical with that in another early picture, the *Guardian Angel* (Budapest, Mus. F.A.). In these works Dolci combines a perfection of surface finish, probably influenced by Bronzino's, with quasi-Caravaggesque chiaroscuro and modelling and, in *St Matthew*, the softness of Correggio. The paintings' refined sensibility, tactile surfaces and obviously portrait heads are features of his subsequent work.

Baldinucci listed few pictures of the earliest period, passing rapidly to the 1640s. It seems reasonable to assume that the *Virgin of the Lilies* (1642; Montpellier, Mus. Fabre) is at the core of a group that includes the Budapest *Guardian Angel*, the *Marriage of the Virgin* (priv. col., see del Bravo, pl. 456) and possibly the intensely moving portrait of *Serafina Pezzuoli* (Florence, S Gaetano). These would thus be datable between the later 1630s and about 1643, the date of *St Andrew Praying before Martyrdom* (Birmingham, Mus. & A.G.; see fig. 1), which shows a greater degree of realism and less sweetness than its predecessors. The last of the type personified by the Montpellier picture is the *Allegory of Poetry* (Florence, Gal. Corsini) from the end of the decade, which is also the best example of the blurred dividing line for Dolci between portraiture, religious and allegorical themes.

During the 1640s Dolci increasingly absorbed Florentine art of the 15th and 16th centuries, and probably worked more intensively as a copyist. Archival evidence shows that he copied the work of Correggio, among others; the latter's *Virgin Adoring the Infant Christ* (Florence, Uffizi) arrived in Florence in 1617 and was of fundamental importance for the evolution of Dolci's style. His *St Andrew Praying before Martyrdom* is filled with quotations from works by other masters, including Titian's *Youth with a Fur Collar* (New York, Frick), after which Dolci appears to have made a drawing. In 1645 he produced a homage to Michelangelo in the form of copies (Florence, Uffizi; Paris, Louvre) made of the latter's portrait of *Andrea Quaretisi* (London, BM). Dolci's ability as a sophisticated pasticheur of 15th-century art is best seen in his small tondo of *St Ursula* (Kedleston Hall, Derbys) of *c.* 1640. He may also have repainted the head

of Christ in Domenico Ghirlandaio's *Last Supper* (Florence, Ognissanti). This tendency belongs to a contemporary revival of 15th-century style in much Florentine painting. In 1648 Dolci selected Fra Angelico as the subject of his presentation painting for the Accademia del Disegno.

Dolci was never adept at evolving complex figure compositions, for which he depended on other artists, and in 1647 he painted the *Penitent St Jerome* (1647; New York, R. Feigen priv. col., see 1979 exh. cat., p. 52, no. 18), based on a larger painting by Lodovico Cigoli (1603; priv. col.). The *Penitent St Jerome, Flight into Egypt* (Burghley House, Cambs) and the *Guardian Angel* (Corsham Court, Wilts) are among a group of small-scale, small-figure pictures, mainly of the 1640s, which all show loose brushwork and a childlike simplicity of expression and gesture. Baldinucci noted Dolci's genius for painting 'little figures . . . in which he displayed a unique manner . . . mainly on copper and canvas'. Dolci's talent as a portrait miniaturist is best seen in his tiny likeness of Baldinucci (1645; Florence, Uffizi) and in his many exceptionally refined chalk portraits.

Christ in the House of the Pharisee (1649; Corsham Court, Wilts; see fig. 2) forms a fitting culmination to the

2. Carlo Dolci: *Christ in the House of the Pharisee*, oil on canvas, 1.75×2.16 m, 1649 (Corsham Court, Wilts)

decade and achieves a grandeur unusual for Dolci. Here again the composition is based on a work by Cigoli (1596; Rome, Gal. Doria-Pamphili), which was known to Dolci through a print by Cornelis Galle (i). The modello (Stockholm, Nmus.) for this work survives, as do those for others. However, the *Vision of St John on Patmos* (Florence, Pitti), although connected with a lost canvas painted for the Rinuccini family, does not appear to be a modello.

(ii) 1650 and after. In the 1650s and early 1660s Dolci created a series of aggressively didactic works, exemplifying his 'firm intention to paint only works which would inspire the fruits of Christian piety in those who saw them' (Baldinucci) and establishing a style that was to prevail throughout his career. This is the official Dolci, and the contrast with the smaller, more private works of the 1640s could not be greater. The half-length, single-figure paintings, an *Allegory of Sincerity* (Vienna, Ksthist. Mus.) and *Charity* (1657; Prato, Cassa di Risparmio), and the *Infant Christ with a Garland of Flowers* (Lugano, Col. Thyssen-Bornemisza) reveal a certain tendency towards simplification of the picture format. A new Baroque fullness first appears in the study (Paris, Louvre) for the *Penitent Mary Magdalene* (Parma, Accad. B.A.) and is developed in the amply draped figures of the *Allegory of Sincerity* and *Charity*, and, with increasing refinement, in the *St Margaret* (begun 1664; Florence, Pitti).

These half-length single figures are remarkably different from his rare, larger compositions. In 1656 he painted the *Presentation of the Miraculous Image at Soriano* for S Andrea a Cennano at Montevarchi, the deliberate destruction of which has been a great loss for the study of his work, as it provided, together with the *Vision of St Louis of Toulouse* (1676–81; Florence, Pitti), the only means of assessing his own, large-scale compositional inventions. The lost composition is known from photographs (see McCorquodale, 1976, p. 316, fig. 3) and fragments, notably the particularly beautiful crowned head of the Virgin. Other figures in the *Presentation* reflect his interest in the use of rich drapery, which is especially evident in works of this period.

In 1662 Dolci painted a *Vase of Flowers* (Florence, Uffizi) for Giovanni Carlo de' Medici, under the influence of contemporary Dutch painting. Baldinucci noted that he excelled as a still-life painter, but no other examples of this kind are known. He painted a pair of portraits, *Sir Thomas Baines* and *Sir John Finch* (both Cambridge, Fitzwilliam), between 1665 and 1670, when Finch (1626–82) was English Resident at the court of Grand Duke Ferdinand II. *Sir Thomas Baines* is the more impressive of the two and presents the scholarly sitter, surrounded by the works of Classical writers, with a sober objectivity. In 1672 Dolci travelled to Innsbruck to paint Claudia de' Medici. The result, *Claudia Felice as Galla Placidia* (1675; Florence, Pitti), is the most remarkable of his likenesses, apart from the precocious *Fra Ainolofo de' Bardi*. Perfectly sidestepping the problem of the state portrait with a didactic intent, he successfully combined the cerebral and the sensuous (a unique achievement in 17th-century Florence). It is also the best example of his ability to render every surface texture arrestingly tangible, a quality also particularly evident in the head of the Virgin from the dismembered Montevarchi altarpiece. In more intimate portraiture, notably the many chalk studies of his wife and children, the degree of informality and incisiveness is startling; the best example is the drawing of Dolci's wife in the Institut Néerlandais, Paris (other examples: London, BM; Florence, Uffizi; Paris, Louvre; Chatsworth, Derbys). This unvarnished naturalism is rarely apparent in the painted portraits, with one striking exception, an *Allegory of Caterina degli Scolari as Peace* (ex-Cowper priv. col.; known through photographs). Exactly how subtle Dolci's portraiture was in comparison with that of his Florentine contemporaries is most evident in his *Self-portrait* (1674; Florence, Uffizi). Here Dolci is shown melancholy and elegantly clad, and the painting also includes a self-portrait drawing that shows him bespectacled and in working clothes, obsessively drawing, thus creating a unique play on the contemplative versus the creative process.

In the mid-1670s Dolci became severely depressed (Baldinucci), although little stylistic change is apparent during the following years and several of his principal pictures date from this final decade. The *Guardian Angel* (Prato, Mus. Opera Duomo), installed in Prato Cathedral in 1675, continues his revivalist experiments, though it recalls Mannerist more than 15th-century art, and includes a superb still-life of flowers. The *Vision of St Louis of Toulouse* (1676–81; Florence, Pitti) contains some of Dolci's most beautiful painted passages, in spite of a certain compositional awkwardness. His *Allegory of Patience* (signed and dated 1677; ex-Hanbury priv. col., see Gregori, p. 226, fig. 24) is one of his most seductive images, with a suaveness redolent of French 18th-century art. In 1680 he created his celebrated *Salome* (untraced), the culmination of his richly clad three-quarter-length figures. It is now known only through fine versions, for example one in the Glasgow Art Gallery and Museum, probably by Onorio Marinari (1627–1716). Baldinucci stated that it was painted for the Marchese Pier Francesco Rinuccini, and that 'it had as great a success at Florence as almost any of his works'. The picture was last seen at the Demidov sale of 1870. The picture's pendant, also for the Rinuccini family, is *David with the Head of Goliath* (1680; ex-Matthiesen F.A., London; see 1979 exh. cat., p. 63). The *Christ Consecrating the Elements of the Mass* (1680; Corsham Court, Wilts; Dresden, Gemäldegal. Alte Meister), a strikingly simple presentation of a single figure, emphasizes the consistency of Dolci's handling of this theme since the late 1650s.

Baldinucci dated the artist's final psychological decline to Luca Giordano's arrival in Florence in 1682, and the ill-fated encounter between the two diametrically opposed talents. Dolci dated two versions of *Ecce homo* in 1681 (Florence, Gal. Corsini; ex-Wellington priv. col.). In addition to bearing the pious inscriptions frequently found on the backs of his paintings, these are apparently his latest dated works. Baldinucci listed 'many pictures entirely finished by his hand, and others not completed. . .'. Their completion and the question of studio participation in the production of countless copies and versions occasioned by the immense popularity of his work remain largely unstudied. Francesco Saverio Baldinucci in his *Vite*, writing on the painter Onorio Marinari, declares that Marinari was 'also a very able imitator, above all of the delicate manner of Carlo Dolci', while Bartolomeo Bimbi spent much time making copies after Dolci on commission. Of Dolci's daughter, Agnese Dolci (*d* 1689), no securely autographed painting is yet known, although a supposedly signed *Self-portrait* is known from photographs (Florence, Fond. Longhi). A *Christ and the Samaritan Woman with St Teresa* was auctioned in Florence in 1984; Dolci's autograph study for the figure of Christ is in the Louvre, Paris, but the finished painting clearly includes the work of other hands. In S Agostino at Anghiari is a further important document for the study of Dolci's studio, a large altarpiece of the *Finding of the True Cross*, full of Dolci's stylistic mannerisms but not from his hand.

Dolci's style is full of conflict, but this is often not immediately evident on account of the immaculate finish of his best work. His obsessiveness derives from the anguish inherent in what Matteo Marangoni called 'his nostalgic vision of a world of perfection'. His figures, in spite of their ostensibly arresting tangibility, have an other-worldliness often emphasized by their airless, undefined settings and (where these survive) the infinite glazes of which he was master. His ideal of beauty was also intensely personal; it is as remote from Bolognese classicism as from Caravaggesque realism. A delicate melancholy pervades much of his work, whether religious paintings, such as the celebrated *St Cecilia* (*c*. 1671; Dresden, Gemäldegal. Alte Meister) or portraits, such as *Claudia Felice as Galla Placidia* or *Sir Thomas Baines*. Baldinucci listed among Dolci's pupils Alessandro Lomi, or Loni (1655–1702), whose superb signed *Virgin at the Sepulchre* (Florence, priv. col.) reveals him as the only painter capable of perpetuating Dolci's pietistic imagery without mere plagiarism and in keeping with the trends of the Late Baroque and even the dawn of the Rococo style.

2. POSTHUMOUS REPUTATION. Dolci's works were highly prized by the English aristocracy as early as the 17th century, when many of his finest pictures were already in British collections. Sir John Finch created the first important collection of Dolci's works in Britain, which was dispersed in 1947. In 1836 Johann David Passavant called Dolci 'that favourite of the English' but, ironically, it was English writers, such as Robert Browning and John Ruskin, who first snidely attacked his reputation, which remained low until the 1960s. Throughout this period of unpopularity critics despised his piety and obsessive finish, the very qualities for which he had earlier been admired. His reputation was also damaged by the many copies of his work, the first of which emerged during his own career, and the comparative rarity of original works. Since the 1960s, as 17th-century Italian art has been restored to favour, both the complexity and the quality of Dolci's art have been revalued.

BIBLIOGRAPHY
F. Baldinucci: *Notizie* (1681–1728); ed. F. Ranalli (1845–7), v, pp. 335–64
F. S. Baldinucci: *Vite* (1725–30); ed. A. Matteoli (1975)
G. Heinz: 'Carlo Dolci: Studien zur religiösen Malerei im 17. Jahrhundert', *Jb. Ksthist. Samml. Wien*, lvi (1960), pp. 197–234
C. del Bravo: 'Carlo Dolci, devoto del naturale', *Paragone*, xiv/163 (1963), pp. 32–41
C. McCorquodale: 'A Fresh Look at Carlo Dolci', *Apollo*, xcvii/135 (1973), pp. 477–88
M. Gregori: 'A Cross-section of Florentine Baroque Painting: The Piero Bigongiari Collection', *Apollo*, c/151 (1974), pp. 198–209
C. McCorquodale: 'Some Paintings and Drawings by Carlo Dolci in British Collections', *Kunst des Barock in der Toskana* (Florence and Munich, 1976), pp. 313–20
——: 'Carlo Dolci's *David with the Head of Goliath*', *Connoisseur*, 787 (1977), pp. 54–9
Painting in Florence, 1600–1700 (exh. cat. by C. McCorquodale, London, RA, 1979), nos 15–25
C. McCorquodale: 'Some Unpublished Works by Carlo Dolci', *Burl. Mag.*, cxxi/912 (1979), pp. 142–50
Il seicento fiorentino: Arte a Firenze da Ferdinando I a Cosimo III, 3 vols (exh. cat., ed. A. Parronchi and A. Brook; Florence, Pal. Strozzi, 1986–7), i (*Pittura*), pp. 434–56; ii (*Disegno*), pp. 355–60; iii (*Biografia*), pp. 81–3
M. Gregori and E. Schleier, eds: *La pittura in Italia: Il seicento*, ii (Milan, 1988, rev. 1989), pp. 726–7 [with bibliog.]

CHARLES MCCORQUODALE

Dolendo. Dutch family of artists. Zacharias Dolendo (*b* Leiden, between 1561 and 1573; *d* Leiden, before 1604) was an engraver. Only dated prints document the activity of this artist, whose early death was attributed by van Mander to drinking and wild behaviour. He was nevertheless a more accomplished engraver than his brother, Bartholomeus [Bartholomäus] (Willemsz.) Dolendo (*b* ?Leiden, *c*. 1571; *d* Leiden, *c*. 1629): Zacharias worked for many years with Jacques de Gheyn II and was one of Gerrit Dou's first teachers. A series of prints after designs by Hendrick Goltzius, for example the *Blind Leading the Blind* (1586; Hollstein, no. 86), suggests early contact with this master. However, the strongest influence on Zacharias Dolendo's work was de Gheyn, who often provided designs for and published his engravings. Zacharias's manner of engraving is most characteristically a miniaturized version of the Goltzius manner as seen in de Gheyn prints, with finer, tighter, but nonetheless graceful, linear hatching and silvery modulations of tone. He could alter his burin technique with skill, for example in the series of *Christ and the Apostles* (Hollstein, nos 30–43), which conveys the bold and eccentric linearity of de Gheyn drawings, and in the series of the *Passion* after Karel van Mander (Hollstein, nos 9–22), which he and de Gheyn engraved in the fine, delicate manner of Lucas van Leyden.

Bartholomeus Dolendo was also an engraver, as well as a goldsmith. He is recorded in documents of 1589, 1613 and 1621 as being in Leiden. He may have worked in Hendrick Goltzius's workshop, although it is equally likely that he learnt engraving from his brother. His small oeuvre includes reproductive engravings after Leonardo, Lucas van Leyden, Michiel Coxcie and the late Mannerists Goltzius and Bartholomeus Spranger. His prints of the *Four Evangelists* and *St Paul Shipwrecked* (Hollstein, nos 13, 14) record two rare compositions by the painter Aertgen van Leyden. His engravings show experimentation with a number of burin techniques, varying from the hard metallic manner of such mid-16th-century Antwerp engravers as Pieter van der Heyden to the bold, tapered, burin line popularized by Goltzius. Evidence of Bartholomeus's activity as a goldsmith is found in one of his signatures and in a record of his having made a shield for the Leiden Chamber of Rhetoric.

BIBLIOGRAPHY
Hollstein: *Dut. & Flem.*; Thieme–Becker
K. van Mander: *Schilder-boeck* ([1603]–1604), fol. 295

A. Bredius: 'Een rederijkers-blazoen, door Bartholomeus Dolendo ge-
sneden' [A rhetorician's coat of arms, cut by Bartholomeus Dolendo],
Oud-Holland, iv (1886), pp. 130–31
*Graphik der Niederlände, 1508–1617: Kupferstiche und Radierungen von
Lucas van Leyden bis Hendrik Goltzius* (exh. cat. by K. Renger and
C. Syre, Munich, Staatl. Graph. Samml., 1979), p. 62
J. Q. van Regteren-Altena: *Jacques de Gheyn: Three Generations*, i (The
Hague, 1983)
DOROTHY LIMOUZE

Dollmann, Georg von (*b* Ansbach, 21 Oct 1830; *d*
Munich, 3 March 1895). German architect. He studied
from 1846 in Munich at the Technische Hochschule and
the Kunstakademie as a pupil of Leo von Klenze. He later
became von Klenze's artistic assistant on the construction
of the Befreiungshalle (1842–64) at Kelheim and on Count
Stourdza's Chapel (1864–6) in Baden-Baden, both completed after von Klenze's death. His first independent
work was the Gothic Revival parish church (1865–8) at
Giesing, near Munich. In 1868 he entered the service of
Ludwig II, King of Bavaria (*see* WITTELSBACH, §III(4)),
and in 1875 he took over responsibility for all royal
building. In this capacity he had to convert Ludwig's
romantic, often highly detailed, ideas into architecture,
which limited Dollmann's own creative work. His designs
were in an effusive, colourful, 'fairytale', historicist style,
in keeping with the King's preferences, derived not only
from the medieval and Baroque, but also from Oriental
and Byzantine models (evident, for example, in his Byzantine castle project (1869–70) for Linderhof). His first
building was the continuation (1872–86) of Schloss
Neuschwanstein, begun in 1868 to designs by his predecessor Eduard Riedel (1813–85). Here, his creative contribution was limited to a few decorative alterations. His first
complete design for Ludwig, produced in a late Baroque
style, was the royal palace of Linderhof (1874–8) in the
Bavarian Alps. His designs for Schloss Herrenchiemsee, a
copy of the château de Versailles, were produced over five
years before building work began in 1878 (work suspended
1885; *see* PALACE, fig. 4). Disagreements arose in 1884 in
connection with another projected palace for Ludwig II,
Schloss Falkenstein, which caused Dollmann to leave the
royal service and retire.

BIBLIOGRAPHY
G. Baumgartner: *Königliche Träume* (Munich, 1981)
H. G. Evers: *Ludwig II von Bayern: Theaterfürst, König, Bauherr*, ed.
J. A. Schmoll gen. Eisenwerth (Munich, 1986)
G. Schickel: *Neugotischer Kirchenbau in München* (Munich, 1987)
DIETRICH NEUMANN

Dolls and dolls' houses. *See under* TOYS AND GAMES.

Dolmen. Type of prehistoric tomb. The term has been
applied at different times and in different contexts to
various types of tomb. The word dolmen comes from
Celtic linguistic roots: *men* means stone and *dol* is usually
derived from *tol* or table (some derive it from *doll* meaning
hole); thus 'stone table'. During the early development of
prehistoric studies in western and central Europe and
Scandinavia, the word was used as a general classification
for Megalithic tombs (*see* MEGALITHIC ARCHITECTURE,
§1). In some countries, for example France, it was used to
describe a wide range of tomb types; in Germany and
eastern Europe it has tended to be used for monuments
with a circular or polygonal chamber and with both the
supporting stones (orthostats) and capstones dressed on
the inside only. In most of Europe it is not now used as a
general term, being considered outdated and antiquarian;
however, it has continued to be associated with particular
tomb types, such as the *dolmens à couloir* of Brittany and
portal dolmens in Ireland.

See also PREHISTORIC EUROPE, §§IV, 2(v)(b) and V, 3(iii), and
RUSSIA, fig. 5.

SARA CHAMPION

Dolní Věstonice. Sites near Břeclav, Moravia [now Czech
Republic], on the southern slopes of the Pavlov Mountains, 30–70 m above the River Dyje. It was an important
centre of the Gravettian culture (*c.* 30,000–*c.* 18,000 BP) of
the Upper Palaeolithic period (*see also* PREHISTORIC
EUROPE, §II). Excavations at Dolní Věstonice I began in
1924 under the direction of Karl Absolon and were
continued from 1947 to 1979 by Bohuslav Klima, who
later investigated Dolní Věstonice II between 1985 and
1987. Dolní Věstonice II, situated upslope from locality I,
was also excavated from 1985 to 1988 by Jiří Svoboda. It
contains more human remains but few art objects. The
archaeological level is found deep in layers of stratified
loess (loamy material deposited by the wind), dated to
c. 26,000 BP. The material excavated from the sites is held
by the Moravian Museum, Brno. Klima has argued that
the unique nature of the art and artefacts found at Dolní
Věstonice supports the case for the existence of the
Pavlovian culture (*see also* PAVLOV). The local economy
was based on the intensive hunting of mammoth, and
many mammoth bones were accumulated in a huge heap;
other animal remains included the bones of foxes, hares,
wolves, horses, reindeer and birds.

Although the art of Dolní Věstonice is rather diverse,
most of the objects found at the site are ceramic: among
the several dwellings found, one isolated example contained a kiln with over 2300 fired pieces. These had been
produced from wetted loess modelled with fingers and
stone tools to form the bodies of animals and humans;
the heads and feet were formed separately and added to
the figures before being fired at a low temperature.
Mammoth ivory and bone were also used to produce
engravings and figurines. A nearly complete example of a
unique style of ceramic female figurine was discovered by
Absolon in 1925. The figure has an exaggerated hip line,
narrow shoulders and enormous breasts; characteristic
features also found on other female statuettes from Dolní
Věstonice include a horizontal line dividing the thighs and
buttocks and incised slanting eyes. Some highly stylized
ivory female figures can only be recognized as such by the
breasts; model breasts also occur in isolation as pendants.
Model animals of widely differing quality were formed
from loess. Only 77 of these animal figurines are sufficiently complete to be identified: of these, 21 are bears, 9
lions, 8 mammoths, 6 horses, 5 wolves, 4 rhinoceroses, 6
owls and 3 foxes. Only the bears and lions were marked
with the incisions sometimes interpreted as symbolic
killings. Such figurines have generally been assumed to
represent charms, but whereas Absolon and Klima saw
their burning as secondary and accidental, Pamela Vandiver considers that exposure to the fire was part of the
ritual. The masterpiece of Dolní Věstonice art is a small

human face, probably female, sculpted in ivory: the hair, eyes, nose, mouth and a small chin are all well rendered. Klima has associated this slightly disproportionate face with the body of a woman, who also suffered from a facial distortion, suggesting that the piece may have been a portrait.

BIBLIOGRAPHY

K. Absolon: *Die Erforschung der diluvialen Mammutjägerstation von Unter-Wisternitz an den Pollauer Bergen in Mähren: Arbeitsbericht über das zweite Jahr 1925* (Brno, 1938)
B. Klima: 'Upper Palaeolithic Art in Moravia', *Antiquity*, xxxii (1958), pp. 8–14
——: *Dolní Věstonice: Výzkum tábořiště lovcu mamutu v letech 1947–1952* [Research into the campsite of the mammoth hunters in the years 1947–52], Monumenta Archaeologia (Prague, 1963)
——: 'Les Représentations animales du Paléolithique supérieur de Dolní Věstonice (Tchécoslovaquie)', *La Contribution de la zoologie et de l'éthnologie à l'interprétation de l'art des peuples chasseurs préhistoriques*, ed. H.-G. Bandi and others (Fribourg, 1984), pp. 323–32
P. B. Vandiver and others: 'The Origins of Ceramic Technology: Evidence from Dolní Věstonice, Czechoslovakia, *c.* 26,000 BP' (in preparation)

JOACHIM HAHN

Domanovszky, Endre (*b* Budapest, 23 Jan 1907; *d* Budapest, 15 May 1974). Hungarian painter and tapestry designer. He studied under Oszkár Glatz (1872–1958) at the School of Fine Arts, Budapest, and held his first exhibition there in 1929. His refined drawing style was influenced by 19th-century Neo-classicism, but he soon superseded this with the lyric sensibility of his colours. In the 1930s his main interest was in tapestry, and he exhibited internationally, although some of his tapestries were lost at the outbreak of World War II. His works are often influenced in their presentation by the narrative technique of folk tales, although folklore is not an exclusive topic in his oeuvre, which also comprises such monumental commissions as the tapestry *Saint Stephen* (1938; Pécs, Pannonius Mus.).

In the 1940s Domanovszky returned to painting. The still-lifes and interiors of this period are Constructivist compositions with a colour scheme full of explosive tension. His *Putters* (1948; Budapest, N.G.) is a formal summary of this period and it signals a new thematic strand. He developed his mural-painting skills during the execution of the 4×21 m *Agricultural Tableau* (Budapest, Min. Agric.), painted in seven parts between 1952 and 1955. His greatest commission (completed 1955), the fresco on the façade of the entry to the steel works at Dunaújváros, symbolizes the friendship between workers and peasants and is divided into three interrelated dynamic groups, the division into columns also reflecting the architectural environment. A friezelike mural painted on aluminium for the Hungarian pavilion at the Exposition Universelle of 1958 in Brussels signalled the formal renewal of his oeuvre and the successful alliance of decorative and functional. In *Wedding* and *Market*, two monumental sgraffiti painted in 1960 and 1961 in the railway station at Debrecen, the dynamic scenes are held together in disciplined planes, even while using a colour scheme more complex than that normally required by sgraffito.

From 1958 Domanovszky returned to tapestry. In *Dispute* (1968), which covers the length of the vice-chancellor's office in the University of Heavy Industry at Miskolc, the blue and black figures emerge rhythmically against a background of yellows. In his *Monuments of County Vas* (1969; Szombathely, County Building) the flashlike thematic references are linked horizontally and vertically as if in montage. Domanovszky's paintings and drawings received a new impetus at this time, reflecting in their colour scheme and composition the dynamism of the great murals, and they in turn affected the murals' livelier coloration. From 1948 to 1974 he was professor (and rector, 1972–4) at the School of Fine Arts, Budapest.

BIBLIOGRAPHY

B. Ujváry: *Domanovszky Endre* (Budapest, 1938)
Domanovszky Endre (exh. cat., foreword N. Arady; Budapest, A. Hall, 1959)
Z. D. Fehér: *Domanovszky Endre* (Budapest, 1962)
B. Ujváry: *Domanovszky Endre* (Budapest, 1976)

NÓRA ARADI

Domány, Ferenc. *See under* HOFSTÄTTER & DOMÁNY.

Dombet [Dombay], **Guillaume** (*b* Cuisery, nr Chalon-sur-Saône; *fl* 1414; *d* before 19 Aug 1461). Burgundian painter. He is first mentioned in Avignon in 1414. His three sons, Aubry, Jacques and Jean (who returned to Cuisery in 1452 or 1453), were also painters. His daughter Peyronnette married a painter from Tournai, Arnolet de Catz (*fl* 1430–34), who became Guillaume's associate in 1430. When suffering from a serious illness, Guillaume made his will on 4 December 1458 and requested to be buried in Notre-Dame-la-Principale, Avignon.

Guillaume Dombet appears to have had a flourishing career as a master glazier. He supplied stained-glass windows for the Papal Palace in Avignon (1414), for Aix Cathedral (1415; 1444; 1449), for the synagogue in Aix (1418), for the Franciscan church in Marseille (1425), for Ste Marthe in Tarascon (1432) and for the St Pierre-de-Luxembourg Chapel near the Celestine church in Avignon (1448). At the same time he worked on many altarpieces, often in collaboration with his sons. He received commissions for Aix Cathedral (1415), for the Franciscan church in Aix (1420), for Notre-Dame-du-Salut (1423), for the Cordeliers of Tarascon (1429), from the Prior of Estezargues (1447) and for the church of Caderousse (1452). Guillaume was also employed on more modest tasks, including the painting of coats of arms and the provision of scaffolding for the Corpus Christi procession in Avignon.

With the exception of the stained-glass windows of the chapel of St Mitre in Aix Cathedral (commissioned in 1444; *in situ*); and a small fragment representing a lion rampant (Avignon, Pal. Papes & Mus.) from the four stained-glass windows for the St Pierre-de-Luxembourg Chapel, Avignon (commissioned in 1448), none of these works survives. The latter is, however, too modest to give a clear indication of Guillaume Dombet's style. The style of the surviving windows in the St Mitre Chapel shows echoes of south Netherlandish paintings of the 1430s by Jan van Eyck and the Master of Flémalle and a close dependence on the altarpiece of the *Annunciation* (Aix-en-Provence, Ste Marie-Madeleine; Brussels, Pal. B.-A.; Rotterdam, Mus. Boymans–van Beuningen). It has been argued that Guillaume Dombet would have been too old in 1444 to assimilate this new style and that the windows are probably the work of his son Aubry, who is documented in Provence from 1439 to 1461 (Sterling, 1966). The tomb slab of *Bishop Avignon Nicolaï*, a fairly mediocre work for which Guillaume Dombet received payment in the same year, may perhaps also be by Aubry.

Boyer suggested that Guillaume Dombet was responsible for the Aix *Annunciation*, with the collaboration of Jean Chapus, but this theory has not been accepted. Sterling proposed, however, that his son Aubry Dombet may have executed the reverses of two of its wings (Brussels, Pal. B.-A.; Rotterdam, Mus. Boymans–van Beuningen). He attributed the *Pietà of Tarascon* (Paris, Mus. Cluny), probably the 'new' panel described in an inventory of 1457 in Tarascon Castle, to another of Guillaume's sons, Jacques, who is documented in Provence from 1451 to 1461.

BIBLIOGRAPHY

Abbé H. Requin: 'Documents inédits sur les peintres, peintres-verriers et enlumineurs d'Avignon au XVe siècle', *Réun. Soc. B.-A. Dépt.* (1889), pp. 118–217

L. H. Labande: *Les Primitifs français: Peintres et peintres-verriers de la Provence occidentale* (Marseille, 1932), pp. 79–81

P. Pansier: *Les Peintres d'Avignon aux XIVe et XVe siècles: Biographies et documents* (Avignon, 1934), pp. 91–116

J. Boyer: 'Le Maître d'Aix enfin identifié', *Conn. A.*, lxxii (1958), pp. 39–43

C. Sterling: 'La Pietà de Tarascon et les peintres Dombet', *Rev. Louvre*, xvi/1 (1966), pp. 13–26

M. Laclotte and D. Thiébaut: *L'Ecole d'Avignon* (Paris, 1983), pp. 74, 223–4, 233–4

DOMINIQUE THIÉBAUT

Dome [Lat. *domus*: 'house']. Rounded vault covering an interior space. A very small domed roof, for example a lantern mounted on the eye of a dome proper (e.g. St Paul's Cathedral, London), is known as a cupola. In Italian *cupola* is used for a monumental dome.

1. Structure. 2. Types. 3. History.

1. STRUCTURE. A dome can either be composed of curved segments or be a shell of revolution. Filippo Brunelleschi's dome at Florence Cathedral (*see* FLORENCE, fig. 12 and BRUNELLESCHI, FILIPPO, fig. 1) is segmental, octangular at every section. A shell of revolution is generated by rotating an arch about a vertical central axis. To produce a hemispherical surface the arch will be semicircular, but any shape of arch, similarly rotated, will give rise to a shell of revolution; and every horizontal cross-section is still circular. The simplest form of dome is that of such a shell of revolution: for example, the inner masonry dome of St Paul's Cathedral is roughly hemispherical, and has an open eye, while the main dome is conical; but both are shells of revolution, as is the surface of the timber outer dome. A dome can have either a single or a double shell.

As tensile forces cannot be developed within the construction of a masonry or concrete dome (*see* MASONRY, §III, 2(i)), the dome will thrust both downwards and sideways at its supports, unless either the dome is very small (so that the stones can interlock) or encircling ties are provided. Thus in normal construction the lines of thrust in a full hemisphere embracing 180° are not vertical at the periphery, and a masonry dome embracing more than 180° would have to be very small and thick. Onion domes (*see* §2 below) can be realized in timber, which is capable of resisting tension. The shallower the dome, the greater the thrust. The first central dome of Hagia Sophia, Istanbul, survived only about 20 years, collapsing in an earthquake in AD 557. The dome was rebuilt to its present higher rise embracing about 140°, with a corresponding reduction of thrust, and later major earthquakes (in 986 and 1346) caused only partial damage. The dome is of brick, and the main portion is *c.* 750 mm thick. There are traces of iron and timber ties round the periphery, but the main horizontal thrusts are taken on the north and south sides by wide arches capable of resisting lateral loading, and on the east and west sides by buttressing semidomes.

The thrusts from a dome are directly proportional to the weight of the material, and the supporting structure is relieved by lightening the dome itself. Since the stresses in the dome are very small, voids can be introduced by the use, for example, of empty clay pots, without leading to any danger of local failure due to overstressing of the construction. The mass of the main dome of Hagia Sophia is more than 1000 tonnes. The mass of the dome of Florence Cathedral, including the weight of the lantern (itself over 500 tonnes) is more than 30,000 tonnes, and the dome has a mean span of 42 m (a figure comparable with the spans of the Pantheon and St Peter's, Rome). The total thickness of the dome is *c.* 4.2 m, so that the span to thickness ratio is 10:1 (comparable figures are about 40:1 for Hagia Sophia, 100:1 for the shell of a hen's egg, and 1000:1 for a modern reinforced concrete shell roof). With such large masses there are clear advantages to be gained from a saving in material, not only to reduce thrusts but also to save on costs.

Michelangelo's dome of St Peter's, Rome (built posthumously by the engineers Carlo Fontana and Giacomo della Porta; *see* ROME, fig. 36), is of double shell construction, with interconnected skins, as at Florence Cathedral, but unlike the latter it is a shell of revolution, so that although the 16 ribs define visually the surface of the dome, they are not structurally effective. As at Florence, the dome of St Peter's is subject to the pathology of all masonry structures, in which buttressing yields slightly under lateral thrust: meridional cracks rise from the base almost to the summit of the dome (*see* MASONRY, §III, 3(iv) for discussion of this and other matters concerning the structure of domes).

Whether single or double shell, a masonry dome can be built almost without CENTERING. (Brunelleschi was not believed at the Florence Expertise of 1407 when he stated that he could construct a dome without falsework. He was still not believed in 1418 but was nevertheless entrusted with the work.) A dome is built as a succession of horizontal rings. During construction there is a tendency for each ring to fall inwards, but when the ring is complete the unfinished dome is entirely stable, and can be left with an open eye. Some small support may be needed as each ring is built, but none is needed for the work as a whole. This is in marked contrast to the building of an arch; until the keystone is placed, the entire weight of the masonry must be supported from falsework.

JACQUES HEYMAN

Dome, types: (a) bulbous; (b) cut-off; (c) diaphanous; (d) fluted; (e) melon; (f) onion; (g) pumpkin; (h) ribbed; (i) segmental

2. TYPES.

Bulbous. A dome with a profile greater than a hemisphere, the lower part oversailing the base (see fig. (a)). Unlike onion domes (see below), bulbous domes are usually of masonry or brick, the oversailing section providing additional dead-weight, resisting any tendency to spread. They are found in Islamic architecture, especially in the Middle East and India, most famously at the Taj Mahal (1631–47; *see* AGRA, §II, 1 and fig. 1).

Calotte [Fr.: 'skull-cap']. A low, flattish dome formed from the upper section of a hemisphere. They are often exposed externally and may be wooden (see *False* below), masonry (requiring heavy buttressing or tension rings to prevent spreading) or corbelled. Examples include the Four Courts (1786–1802) in Dublin (for illustration *see* GANDON, JAMES) and above the Congresso Nacional complex (1958–60) in Brasília (*see* NIEMEYER, OSCAR, fig. 2). See also *Saucer* below.

Cut-off. A masonry, concrete or corbelled dome, where the apex is omitted for interior lighting (see fig. (b)). Domes built with compressed rings or wedge-shaped radial voussoirs, or indeed in concrete, may be cut off at almost any point without injury. The Pantheon (AD 118–24; *see* ROME, §V, 8) is a famous example, although the idea first appeared earlier in Nero's Domus Aurea (after AD 64; *see* ROME, §V, 5). In Islamic buildings the type was used either for lighting or to collect rain-water, for example at the Yeşil Cami (1378–92), Iznik, and above the sadirvan (washing tank) of the Ulu Cami (1396–1400) at Bursa. The term may also be applied to a dome that is more than semicircular in plan, but less than a full circle, such as at the 'Temple of Venus' (3rd century AD), Baalbek.

Diaphanous. An openwork structure, in brick or with stone ribs, allowing patterns of daylight through the structure of the dome (see fig. (c)), for example over the octagonal crossing (14th century) of the bazaar at Isfahan (Iran) and at S Lorenzo (1668–87) in Turin (*see* GUARINI, GUARINO, fig. 1).

False. A wooden dome-shaped roof, sometimes built over a masonry dome for visual effect or alone where earthquakes are frequent, for example at the Great Mosque (706–15), Damascus (*see* ISLAMIC ART, fig. 18). The dome of the Dome of the Rock (691–2) in Jerusalem was originally wooden (*see* ISLAMIC ART, fig. 17), as are the 14th-century outer domes of S Marco, Venice, the outer profile of St Paul's Cathedral (1675–1710; *see* MASONRY, fig. 5), London, and the outer dome (19th century) of Aachen Cathedral.

Fluted. A dome with exterior vertical channels or ridges from base to apex (see fig. (d)). It was very common in Egypt in the Mamluk period, for example at the Sultan Barquq Mosque (1382–99) in Cairo, and was used widely in Islamic brick structures, such as the fluted melon dome of the Gur-i Mir (1404–5) in Samarkand (*see* ISLAMIC ART, fig. 15) and the Şehzade Mehmed Türbe (*c.* 1550), Istanbul. The type may have originated in the Tao-Klardjeti region of Georgia, for example at the monastery (9th–10th centuries; dome collapsed) of Opiza, Turkey.

Geodesic. Dome-shaped structure based on octahedrons or tetrahedrons (*see* GEODESIC DOME).

Melon. A pointed masonry or brick dome, slightly greater than a hemisphere (see fig. (e)). They first occur in Georgia, for example at Oshki Church (958–73; now Ösk, Turkey; *see* TAO-KLARDJETI, fig. 2). From there the motif was assimilated into Islamic building, for example at Samarkand (see *Fluted* above) and for the mausoleum complex (1472–4) of Qa'itbay (*reg* 1468–96) in Cairo (*see* ISLAMIC ART, fig. 58).

Onion. A common form, greater than a hemisphere and considerably pointed at the apex with an ogee profile (see fig. (f)). Commonly wooden, they may be found in many European styles, for example at the five-domed Kazan' Church (1640–50) at Kolomenskoye, in Austrian and south German Baroque and at the Brighton Pavilion (1815–21), designed by John Nash (for illustration *see* BRIGHTON). Masonry examples occur in late Mughal architecture, for example at the Malika Jahan Mosque (17th century) and contemporary mausolea at Bijapur.

Pumpkin. A dome with a scalloped interior surface, revealing the creased brick shells from which they are made (see fig. (g)). The type is probably of Roman origin. The Bodrum Cami, Istanbul, preserves the dome of the Myrelaion Monastery (begun 919), while the early Islamic adoption of the form appeared from 786 at the Great Mosque, Córdoba. Some masonry domes, such as that of Aachen Cathedral (1664), have outer false pumpkins in wood.

Ribbed. A constructional technique based on intersecting arches around a circular plan, or connecting curved ribs to an apex ring, and infilling the resulting panels to form a dome (see fig. (h)). The Romans used brick ribs and concrete fill, for example for the 'Temple of Minerva Medica' (early 4th century AD; collapsed 1828; *see* ROME, ANCIENT, fig. 36) in the Licinian Gardens, Rome, while medieval examples, such as that of Zamora Cathedral (1151–74) and the treasury (1153–67) of Canterbury Cathedral, were entirely stone-built. The dome of Florence Cathedral (1420–36; *see* FLORENCE, fig. 12) employs a complex ribbed system, of which only those of the angles remain visible. Ribs were used as a decorative feature in later styles, such as in Paris at the church of Val-de-Grâce (begun 1645), designed by François Mansart, and the Naksidil Sultan Türbe (1817–18), Istanbul.

Saucer. Shallow domes in masonry or concrete set either upon angle groins, as in the Piazza d'Oro vestibule of Hadrian's Villa (AD 118–34), Tivoli, and at St Lazare (consecrated 1106), Avallon, or upon pendentives, for example in Rome at the Villa Madama (*c.* 1516), designed by Giulio Romano. The type is sometimes referred to as a sail vault (*see* VAULT). Unlike calottes (see above), saucer domes are not expressed externally but do require similar buttressing to resist bursting. The reading-room (1860–67) of the Bibliothèque Nationale, Paris, has glazed cast-iron saucer domes (*see* LABROUSTE, (2)).

Segmental. A dome expressing the distinct sides of a polygonal ground-plan in masonry or concrete panels, sometimes between ribs (see fig. (i)). In Rome a concrete octagonal dome in the Domus Aurea (after AD 64) starts in this manner, while a similar dome in Domitian's Domus Augustana (AD 92) maintains the segmental character to the open apex. SS Sergios and Bakchos (527–36), Istanbul, is a Byzantine brick adaptation (*see* ISTANBUL, §III, 8). Segmental brick domes were popular in medieval Italy, for example for S Michele (early 12th century), Pavia, and Parma Cathedral (consecrated 1106; *see* PARMA, fig. 1). Florence Cathedral has a ribbed segmental dome. Borromini's design for S Ivo della Sapienza (1642–50), Rome, provides a Baroque example (for illustration *see* UNIVERSITY PALACE; *see also* BORROMINI, FRANCESCO, fig. 5).

Semi-dome. Half a dome, usually an apse, and part of the basic vocabulary of Roman and Renaissance architecture. Symbolically, semi-domes cover Roman cult images, Imperial balconies, Christian altars and Islamic mihrabs. Perhaps the earliest occur in the *frigidarium* of the Stabian Baths (2nd century BC) at Pompeii, with four semi-domes surrounding a major cut-off dome. Later examples exist throughout the Roman world, for example at the Markets of Trajan (AD 112), Rome, and at Hagia Sophia (532–7), Istanbul. The apsidal semi-dome became the established setting for the Christian altar in Byzantine, Carolingian, Ottonian and Romanesque architecture and is echoed in the rib-vaulted Gothic apse. Ottoman Turkey exploited the form, achieving a perfect harmony of dome and semi-domes at the Sokullu Mehmet Pasha Mosque (1571–2) in Istanbul. During the Renaissance and Classical revivals semi-domes were used again as the principal setting for the altar, while countless others exist in a variety of buildings, for example for the vestibule (1734) of Holkham Hall, Norfolk, designed by William Kent, above the royal box in the opera house (1748, 1768–70) by Anges-Jacques Gabriel at Versailles, and for the Boston Public Library (1887–95), Boston, MA (*see* MCKIM, MEAD & WHITE, fig. 2).

3. HISTORY. The dome is one of the most important and potent motifs in architecture. Near Eastern in origin,

domes were first exploited by the Romans, for whom they became an Imperial symbol, while for the Byzantines they were the focal point of major church interiors. After a lapse in Western architecture, the dome was revived in Romanesque architecture in southern Europe, but its use declined during the Gothic period. Renaissance architects seized upon the dome as a centre-piece compatible both with antiquity and Christianity and, after the success of Brunelleschi's masterpiece, the dome (1420–36) of Florence Cathedral, it became a prerequisite for Italian Renaissance churches. Its popularity spread across Catholic and Protestant Europe, and was especially favoured in the Baroque, when domes were built on churches and major public buildings. In the 18th century and the early 19th, the dome became a composite European symbol, linking Christianity with a lingering notion of the *Pax Romana*. Modern domes, constructed in various non-traditional materials, may be found covering such diverse structures as sports arenas, department stores and futuristic video–hologram entertainment centres.

(i) Origins, to c. *1000.* The early history of the dome is obscure, although Vitruvius mentioned houses with domes in Colchis (western Georgia), perhaps similar to excavated remains (5th–4th millennia BC) at Imiris-gora, Georgia. The Assyrians built domes in baked brick or clay and, while none survives, semicircular and pointed domes are depicted on reliefs (London, BM) from the South-west Palace at Nineveh, built by Sennacherib (*reg* 704–681 BC). Both the Egyptians and Greeks avoided the dome, despite the occurrence of sizeable, well-constructed, corbelled domes in the Bronze Age. The so-called Treasury of Atreus (*c.* 1350–*c.* 1250 BC) at Mycenae is one of a group of tholos tombs, originally covered by corbelled 'beehive' domes *c.* 15 m in diameter and almost as high. Thirty-four rings of corbels are capped by a single stone, the interior faces shaped into the domed profile and the whole structure buried for stability (for illustration *see* THOLOS TOMB).

Masonry vaults hardly developed in the architecture of ancient Greece, perhaps owing to the high risk of earthquakes. The tiny choregic monument of Lysikrates (335/4 BC; *see* GREEK REVIVAL, fig. 1) in Athens is a rare exception, being covered with a shallow dome shaped from a single block.

The Romans exploited their new concrete technology (*see* ROME, ANCIENT, §II, 1(ii)(c)) to construct domes 'monolithically' like lids over a box, reducing the problem of earthquake damage. Roman architectural planning was more sophisticated than Greek and the internal volumes and spatial interplay of rooms and shifting axes encouraged greater utilization of various polygonal and curving shapes. These were best covered by domes or semi-domes (*see* §2 above). The semi-dome possibly developed to terminate and buttress barrel vaults, or a sequence of cross or groin vaults, both favourite forms of the Republican era. The Domus Augustana, built by Domitian from AD 92, established the apsidal semi-dome as a symbol of Imperial authority. Both Roman and Byzantine emperors were commonly depicted beneath domes or semi-domes, and many Imperial palaces featured domical audience halls. The apsidal semi-dome soon became a standard motif in

many public buildings, including markets, such as Trajan's (AD 112) in Rome, civic basilicas, where it was the setting for Imperial magistrates, and in temples, as in the exedra (mid-3rd century AD) at the Temple of Jupiter, Baalbek.

The largest and most famous of all domes, that over the Pantheon (AD 118–25; diam. 43.2 m; *see* ROME, §V, 8, and fig. 26) was built in concrete, brick and tufa by Hadrian as 'a temple dedicated to many gods' (Dio Cassius: LIII.xxvii.2). The elevations include three exedrae to house the gods or cult images, alternating with rectangular bays, all recessed within the thickness of the supporting rotunda wall. Masonry domes were less common in the provinces owing to problems of abutment, although the 'Temple of Venus' (3rd century AD) at Baalbek was covered by a cut-stone dome (diam. 10 m). Domes were also extremely common over polygonal garden pavilions and above the plunge-pools of Roman bathhouses, such as those at Hadrian's Villa (AD 118–34) in Tivoli. Domes were not popular in the lightweight brick architecture adopted by the early Christians, although the semi-dome remained the chosen setting for the cult-altar, for example in S Maria Maggiore (begun *c.* 432), Rome. A number of small domes were built, for example in Rome at S Costanza (*c.* 350) and over the baptistery (?432–40) of S Giovanni in Laterano (*see* ROME, §VI, 15(iii)), and at Ravenna above the mausoleum of Galla Placidia (*c.* 425–*c.* 450) and the Arian baptistery (late 5th century; *see* RAVENNA, fig.1). With the return to a monumental masonry style that occurred in both Ravenna and Constantinople during the 6th century the dome was revived as a central feature of ecclesiastical architecture. The best-known examples, S Vitale (consecrated 547) at Ravenna and Hagia Sophia (532–7; destr. 558; rebuilt 562; *see* ISTANBUL, §III, 1(ii)(a)), have much in common, although they are vastly different in scale. S Vitale has a lightweight dome (diam. 18 m) constructed from interlocking earthen pots, a north Italian, late Roman technique. This enabled the dome to be raised above a drum with clerestory windows. The brick dome of Hagia Sophia, with windows cut into the base of the hemisphere, is flanked by giant semi-domes, which themselves have supporting exedrae. The interior represents the highest development of the dome's exploitation of spatial potential, structural ingenuity and monumental symbolism, the great central dome representing not only the vault of Heaven, but a giant ciborium providing a suitable cover for the Emperor as Christ's representative (*see* CIBORIUM (ii)). The domed interior of Hagia Sophia became the model for much Byzantine church planning, although all followers were severely impoverished in both scale and construction. Domes raised upon pendentives were standard until *c.* 600, when squinches were adopted by Byzantine and, later, Islamic architects.

(ii) Western architecture, after c. *1000.* The 11th-century rebuilding of S Marco, Venice, reintroduced the large-scale dome into Western architecture and inspired numerous masonry domes in southern Europe. Many have corbelled construction, such as the domed churches of south-west France (*see* ROMANESQUE, §II, 5 and fig. 15), while others are ribbed, for example at S María la Mayor (1160–1240), Toro, and Zamora Cathedral (12th century;

for illustration *see* ZAMORA). Domes over the crossing are a feature of many German Imperial cathedrals, including those at Speyer, Worms and Mainz. Brick segmental domes (*see* §2 above) are found in north Italy in the early 12th century, for example at S Michele, Pavia, and S Ambrogio, Milan. The fashion declined with the advent of Gothic: the few examples include the dome (1259–64) of Siena Cathedral.

The dome of Florence Cathedral marked a new era for the dome in Western architecture (*see* BRUNELLESCHI, FILIPPO, §I, 1(i), and fig. 1). The great double-shell dome, with its marked external ribbing, rises to a height of 112 m and covers a 42-m octagonal drum with immense power and grace, quite dwarfing the architecture of the choir. Elsewhere in Florence at S Lorenzo (1421–8; *see* BRUNEL-LESCHI, FILIPPO, fig. 2) and the Pazzi Chapel (1442–*c.* 1465), Brunelleschi established the dome as a central feature of the new Renaissance style. Wherever the style spread, domes were built, for example at Pietro Lombardo's S Maria dei Miracoli (1485–9), Venice (for illustration *see* LOMBARDO, §II(1)), and Bramante's S Maria delle Grazie (1492–7), Milan, and it was the dominant theme for all the designs of the new St Peter's, Rome, from Serlio to Michelangelo (*see* ROME, §V, 14(ii)(c), and fig. 38). The eventual form, erected from 1588 to 1593 by Giacomo della Porta and Carlo Fontana, confirmed the dome as the supreme architectural motif for monumental ecclesiastical and public buildings. Domes soon crowned the major works of Europe, including Wren's triple-shell dome of St Paul's Cathedral (1675–1710), London, with its central brick cone (*see* MASONRY, fig. 5), at the Hôtel des Invalides (1676–91; *see* MANSART, (2) and fig. 1) and the Panthéon (begun 1755; *see* SOUFFLOT, JACQUES-GERMAIN, §3 and fig. 3), in Paris, the Karlskirche (1715–37) in Vienna (*see* VIENNA, §V, 2, and AUSTRIA, fig. 6) and James Gibbs's Radcliffe Library (1737–48), Oxford. The cast-iron dome (1855–63; diam. 30 m) of the Capitol in Washington, DC, was designed by Thomas Ustick Walter (*see* WASHINGTON, DC, fig. 5). Cast-iron domes were particularly popular in France, as in the reading-room (1860–67) of the Bibliothèque Nationale, Paris (*see* LABROUSTE, (2)). Modern domes in steel or concrete achieved spectacular dimensions, for example the Centennial Hall (1912–13; diam. 70 m) by Max Berg in Wrocław (for illustration *see* BERG, MAX) and the Leipzig Market Hall (1928) by Deschinger and Ritter, 1928, with twin 82-m domes.

(iii) Islamic architecture and Asia. The dome held a particular fascination for Islamic architects, who for centuries strove to exceed Hagia Sophia, introducing the dome to Iran, western Central Asia and India. Domes appear on some of their earliest monuments, such as the Dome of the Rock (691–2), Jerusalem (*see* ISLAMIC ART, fig. 17), the Great Mosque (begun 785) at Córdoba (*see* CÓRDOBA (i), fig. 2) and the Great Mosque (836) at Kairouan (*see* ISLAMIC ART, §II, 4(iii) and fig. 25). In Seljuk architecture the dome was closely associated with tombs (türbe), such as those of Melik Gazi (last quarter of the 13th century), Kırşehir (Turkey), and continued under the Ottomans, for example in the complex (1390–95) of Bayezid I Yıldırım (*reg* 1389–1402) at Bursa. After the fall of Constantinople in 1453, domes dominated mosque

design, paralleling their contemporary revival in Italy. Development of the Islamic brick-built dome culminated in the major works of SINAN (ii), including the double-shell dome of the Selimiye Mosque (1569–75; for illustration *see* EDIRNE), which finally surpassed the dome of Hagia Sophia.

Solid masonry or earth domes (stupas) were a common feature of Buddhist architecture from the 3rd century BC, but the form never developed further (*see* STUPA, §1). Jaina temples, such as that begun in 1022 at Dilwara (*see* MT ABU, §2), have 'flat' domes constructed from gigantic marble corbels, elaborately carved and undercut. Corbelled domes can also be found in Sri Lanka, Malaysia and Indonesia.

BIBLIOGRAPHY
K. Lehman: 'The Dome of Heaven', *A. Bull.*, xxvii (1945), pp. 1–27
A. Grabar: *Martyrium: Recherches sur les cultes des reliques et l'art chrétien antique*, 2 vols (Paris, 1946)
R. Wittkower: *Architectural Principles in the Age of Humanism* (London, 1949, rev. 2/1962)
E. B. Smith: *The Dome* (Princeton, NJ, 1950)
J. G. Davies: *The Architectural Setting of Baptism* (London, 1962)
H. Colvin: *Architecture of the After-life* (New Haven and London, 1991)

For further bibliography see under the headings of the subjects given above.

FRANCIS WOODMAN

Domela(-Nieuwenhuis), César (*b* Amsterdam, 15 Jan 1900). Dutch painter. His father was Ferdinand Domela-Nieuwenhuis, an anarchist spokesman. After his father's death he travelled to the freethinker's colony in Ascona, Switzerland, where he began his artistic career in 1920. A self-taught artist, he first painted landscapes and still-lifes that were related to Synthetic Cubism in their abstraction, for example *Landscape* (1922; artist's col., see Clairet, p. 63). Through travelling to Jena, Berne and Berlin, he met Constructivist artists and became friends with Arthur Segal and others. He exhibited with the Novembergruppe in 1923. Having moved to Paris, by 1924 he met Theo van Doesburg and Piet Mondrian and joined De Stijl. *10 Constructive Studies* (linocuts, 1923; artist's col., see 1987 exh. cat., pp. 50–51) were reproduced in *De Stijl* in 1924 (vi/8). Having painted his first Neo-plastic work, in the following year he introduced the diagonal in his work, showing his desire for a dynamic composition, seen in *Neo-plastic Composition No. 5C* (1925; Utrecht, Cent. Mus.). In Amsterdam he exhibited with well-known abstract artists.

Domela settled in Berlin in 1927 and concentrated his attention on advertising commissions, using typography and photomontage in work for clients such as AEG and Ruths-Speicher. At the same time he did some posters and printing work for anarchist publications, often as a sympathetic gesture. His dynamic experiments with typography and photomontage led Domela away from the two-dimensional surface of easel painting. He executed some interior designs in which the architecture is emphasized by colour areas and the shapes in the interior (furniture or paintings) acquire an autonomous status (e.g. his studio, Kantstrasse, Berlin, 1927). Also at this time he made reliefs in which three-dimensional elements (of metal and glass) are added to the painted compositions (e.g. *Neo-plastic Relief No. 10*, 1930; The Hague, Gemeentemus.). He contributed to a variety of avant-garde magazines, including *Internationale revue i 10* and *Cercle et carré*. In 1931 he organized the first large international exhibition of *Fotomontage* in the Staatliche Kunstbibliothek. However, he and his wife Ruth were forced to flee Berlin in 1933.

In Paris, Domela initially tried to find advertising work; with Frederick Kahn he set up a silkscreen studio (1934), but the artistic climate in Paris had different requirements from that of Berlin. He continued to experiment with reliefs. He adopted curved lines as a contrast to the severe horizontal–vertical principles of the De Stijl period. Having used hard materials like shark-skin, crocodile leather and rosewood, whose tactile qualities were plastic elements within the composition, from 1934 he also used synthetic materials. Thereafter the relief became a particularly characteristic form of expression for Domela. Over the years he developed the art form to a high level, seen for example in *Relief: Small Monument in Memory of my Friends Piet and Does, No. 113, 1967* (priv. col., see Clairet, p. 181). With Sophie Taeuber-Arp and Hans Arp he launched the magazine *Plastique* in 1937. Following World War II Domela organized three exhibitions of abstract art at the Centre des Recherches on the Rue Cujas. He also co-founded the Salon des Realités Nouvelles, where he exhibited until 1968. He designed a number of large reliefs for architectural settings, including four (1955) for the offices of the insurance company Utrecht in Rotterdam, and one (1974) for a private house in Cormillon, Drôme. Over the years he formulated his ideas about art in lectures and publications. He greatly influenced a number of artists, including A. E. Gallatin, Charles Biederman, the artists belonging to the Latin-American group Made, Nicolas de Staël and Jean Deyrolle.

BIBLIOGRAPHY
César Domela: Werke, 1922–1972 (exh. cat., Düsseldorf, Städt. Ksthalle, 1972)
A. Clairet: *Domela: Catalogue raisonné de l'oeuvre en relief* (Paris, 1978)
H. L. C. Jaffé: *Domela* (Paris, 1980)
Domela: Schilderijen, reliefs, beelden, grafiek, typografie, fotos (exh. cat., The Hague, Gemeentemus., 1980)
Domela: 65 ans d'abstraction (exh. cat., Paris, Mus. A. Mod. Ville Paris; Grenoble, Mus. Peint. & Sculp.; 1987)

EVELINE VERMEULEN

Domenchin de Chavannes, Pierre-Salomon (*b* Paris, 1672 or 1673; *d* Paris, 1744). French painter. In 1701 he was approved (*agréé*) by the Académie Royale de Peinture et de Sculpture and in 1709 was received (*reçu*) as a landscape painter with a *Landscape with Shepherds* (Paris, Ecole N. Sup. B.-A.). The inventory of Louis XIV's pictures, taken in 1709–10, shows that already at that time there were three of Domenchin's works in the royal collections; commissions throughout the artist's career eventually brought this number to around 20. His landscapes adorned the royal residences of Marly, the Tuileries, the Luxembourg, Versailles (Cabinets du Roi, Petits Appartements de la Reine) and Fontainebleau, where he painted a *Landscape with Antique Ruins* and a *Landscape with Castle in the Roman Style* for the Petits Appartements du Roi, as well as two pictures for the Cabinet de la Reine, where he collaborated with Francisque Millet. The works that Domenchin painted for the king, as well as those he exhibited at the Salon of 1737 (*Harvest*; *Country Pastime*)

and that of 1738 (*Landscape at Sunrise*; *Landscape at Sunset*; *Shepherds with their Flocks*), indicate his taste for picturesque and bucolic landscapes enlivened by human and animal figures, as also seen in his *Pastoral Landscape* (Paris, Louvre) and *Mountainous Landscape with a Tower* (Grenoble, Mus. Grenoble). Domenchin was very occasionally attracted by mythological subjects, as in *Apollo Guarding King Admetus's Flocks*, which he painted for the Tuileries.

BIBLIOGRAPHY
Bellier de La Chavignerie–Auvray
H. Herluison: *Actes d'état-civil d'artistes français, peintres, graveurs, architectes, etc . . . extraits des registres de l'Hôtel de Ville de Paris détruits dans l'incendie du 24 mai 1871* (Paris, 1873)
A. de Corde de Montaiglon: *Procès-verbaux de l'Académie royale de peinture et de sculpture (1648–1793)*, 10 vols, iii–v (Paris, 1875)
J. Guiffrey, ed.: *Comptes des bâtiments du roi sous le règne de Louis XIV (1664–1715)* (Paris, 1881–1901)
Livrets des Salons de l'Académie des arts de Lille, 1773–1788 (Lille, 1882)
N. Bailly: *Inventaire des tableaux du roi* (Paris, 1899)
F. Engerand: *Inventaire des tableaux commandés et achetés par la direction des bâtiments du roi (1709–1792)* (Paris, 1900)

HÉLÈNE GUICHARNAUD

Domènech i Montaner, Lluís (*b* Barcelona, 27 Dec 1849; *d* Barcelona, 27 Dec 1923). Spanish Catalan architect, professor, historian and politician. He is considered one of the protagonists of Catalan architectural Modernism, which is characterized by rationalism, and which contrasted with the more expressionist Modernism headed by Gaudí. His essay 'En busca de una arquitectura nacional' in the magazine *La Renaixença* (Feb 1878) proposed the renewal of tradition and upheld the authenticity of architecture from a rational point of view. One of his first works was a building for the Editorial Montaner y Simón (1880) in Barcelona. For the Exposición International (1888), Barcelona, he built the Hotel Internacional (destr.) and the Café-Restaurante del Parque de la Ciudadela (now the Museo de Zoologia), a building that demonstrates his rationalist concern and his predilection for brick. It was here, after the exhibition, that he and some other artists set up a workshop for architecture-related arts, in line with the Modernist ideal of artistic integration. Such integration is evident in the Instituto Pere Mata (1897–1919), Reus; the Casa Thomas (1889), Barcelona; the Casa Navàs (1901), Reus; the Casa Lleó Morera (1905), Barcelona; and the Casa Fuster (1908), Barcelona—all mature works executed in his decorative so-called 'floral' style.

The Palau de la Música (1908), Barcelona, with its polychromy and ornamentation and its appropriate structural solutions achieved on a difficult site, is his most outstanding work. The double façade with an inner glass wall independent of the outer structure—also used for the Casa Fuster—is a characteristic Domènech element. The Hospital de Sant Pau complex (1910), Barcelona, demonstrates his skill in combining brick and stone, and in employing ceramic decoration. As well as his practical work as an architect, Domènech i Montaner was a professor and was appointed director of the Escuela de Arquitectura, Barcelona. He was also a politician and was president of the nationalist group, Unió Catalanista, and a representative in Madrid for the Lliga Regionalista party. As an art historian he published a *Història general del arte* (Barcelona, 1886–1901) and several monographs including *Monestir de Sant Cugat del Vallés* (Barcelona, 1918) and

Històrià i arquitectura del monestir de Poblet (Barcelona, 1925).

BIBLIOGRAPHY

O. Bohigas: 'Lluís Domènech i Montaner', *Archit. Rev.* [London], cxlii/850 (1967), pp. 426–36
M. L. Borràs: *Lluís Domènech i Montaner* (Barcelona, 1970)
O. Bohigas: *Lluís Domènech i Montaner: Arquitecte Modernista* (Barcelona, 1973)
L. L. Domènech-Girbau and L. Figueras: *Lluís Domènech i Montaner i el director d'orquestra* (Barcelona, 1989)

JORDI OLIVERAS

Domenichino [Zampieri, Domenico] (*b* Bologna, Oct 1581; *d* Naples, 6 April 1641). Italian painter and draughtsman. On the basis of his frescoes and altarpieces he became established as the most influential exponent of the 17th-century classical style. Through his critical analysis of the art of Raphael and Annibale Carracci he was influential in the creation of a modern canon of the ancients; and he was perhaps the most complete example of a 17th-century artist struggling to reconcile tradition with the demand for spectacle.

1. Life and work. 2. Working methods and technique. 3. Character and personality. 4. Critical reception and posthumous reputation.

1. LIFE AND WORK.

(i) Bologna and Rome, 1581–1612. (ii) Bologna and Rome: the mature works, 1612–17. (iii) Bologna and Fano, 1617–21. (iv) Rome, 1621–31. (v) Naples, 1631–41.

(i) Bologna and Rome, 1581–1612. Known as Domenichino by his contemporaries from at least 1614, he was the son of a well-to-do shoemaker. After attending grammar school in Bologna he entered the studio of the Fleming Denis Calvaert, before joining the Carracci's Accademia degli Incamminati *c.* 1595. There he excelled in the invention of historical and poetic subjects and became close friends with Francesco Albani. He probably collaborated with other Carracci pupils on the frescoes in the oratory of S Colombano in Bologna (*c.* 1598–1600) before following Albani and Guido Reni to Rome in 1602. There Domenichino set himself to master the Roman style of Annibale Carracci, who had left Bologna at the same time as Domenichino entered the Carracci academy (Accademia degli Incamminati), and its sources in Raphael. He often copied Annibale's compositions, as in the *Pietà* (1603; Brocklesby Park, Lincs, see Spear, pl. 10); *Susanna and the Elders* (1603; Rome, Gal. Doria-Pamphili); and the *Adoration of the Shepherds* (*c.* 1607–8; Edinburgh, N.G.). In turn Annibale supported the young artist as a rival to the rising talent of Reni by allotting to him three ceiling frescoes of mythological landscapes with scenes from Ovid's *Metamorphoses* in the Palazzetto Farnese, a casino in the garden of Palazzo Farnese (*c.* 1602–4), and entrusting to him the execution of the greater part of the frescoes on the walls of the Galleria in the Palazzo itself. Domenichino was also favoured by the Bolognese Giovanni Battista Agucchi and his brother, Cardinal Girolamo (*d* 1605), to whom he was introduced by Francesco Poli, Maestro di Cerimonie of Cardinal Pietro Aldobrandini. Agucchi was an influential theorist who stimulated Domenichino's intellectual interests and remained a loyal supporter. Around 1604 Domenichino moved into the Agucchi household after impressing the Cardinal with the

Liberation of St Peter from Prison (1604; untraced, ex-Potsdam, Schloss Sanssouci), a canvas that Giovanni Battista had urged him to paint. There he produced his first landscapes as well as other small works. For Cardinal Girolamo's titular church, S Onofrio, he frescoed three exterior lunettes, now much damaged, with scenes from the *Life of St Jerome* (1604–5).

Annibale Carracci also persuaded Cardinal Odoardo Farnese to give Domenichino the commission to fresco the newly rebuilt Cappella dei SS Fondatori at the abbey of Grottaferrata. Annibale himself provided drawings for two pendentives, but Domenichino was probably responsible for the entire design of the elaborate decorative scheme, including both fictive and true marble revetments and stucco work, as well as for the narrative scenes on the walls. Execution of this commission, on which work began in 1608, was interrupted by other projects. Domenichino was in Rome in January 1609 and before Annibale died completed the fresco of the *Flagellation of St Andrew* directly opposite Reni's *St Andrew Led in Martyrdom* (1609) in the oratory of S Andrea at S Gregorio Magno. Here too Annibale persuaded the patron, Cardinal Scipione Borghese, to give Domenichino a larger share of the commission than the architectural and other ornament for which he was becoming known. Domenichino rewarded Annibale with a clearly articulated narrative. The figures are set on a strictly organized perspectival stage framed by architecture. The bodily and facial movements of the flagellators to the right, and of the female onlookers to the left, express both the violence of the action and the shocked response to it. All this established Domenichino's defence of Annibale's Roman Raphaelesque style, directly opposing Reni's more graceful interpretation, where expressive tension is relaxed, and the scene is shown as a procession in a landscape setting also derived from Annibale.

In July and August 1609, under Albani's supervision, Domenichino completed (with assistants) ceiling frescoes of scenes from the *Life of Diana* in the Sala di Diana in Vincenzo Giustiniani's palace at Bassano di Sutri (Bassano Romano, Pal. Odescalchi). Domenichino's combination of architectural perspective and particular scenes in *quadri riportati* followed and paid homage to Annibale's precedent in the Galleria Farnese, if now on a smaller scale in accordance with the size of the room. The larger scenes completed subsequently in the chapel at Grottaferrata (*c.* 1609–10) of the *Meeting of St Nilus and Emperor Otto III* and the *Building of the Abbey Church* reveal a growing independence from the later works of Annibale, which Spear has associated with the confrontation with Reni in Rome. The two scenes, one a procession and the other a centralized composition against the architectural background of the building of the abbey, offered Domenichino the opportunity to combine the qualities of both his and Reni's frescoes at S Gregorio. Though accepting aspects of Reni's naturalism and looser brushwork, Domenichino retained his interest in narrative anecdote, legible expression and even caricature.

(ii) Bologna and Rome: the mature works, 1612–17. In 1612 Domenichino made a short visit to Bologna. In 1614 his *Last Communion of St Jerome* (Rome, Pin. Vaticana; see

fig. 1) was unveiled; it seems that while he was in Bologna he had already hoped to win the commission through the agency of Poli and Aldobrandini, and he took the opportunity to study Agostino Carracci's *Last Communion of St Jerome* (1590s; Bologna, Pin. N.), a picture of the same unusual theme then in the Certosa di Bologna. In a radical criticism of Agostino's masterpiece, Domenichino declared his independence by reversing the image and by giving greater emphasis to the act of confession and the administering priest. In contrast to Agostino's warm golden browns, Domenichino's rich palette and emphasis on finely wrought surfaces indicate his reconsideration of Raphael's *St Cecilia* (not completed before 1516; Bologna, Pin. N.) in Bologna and of Correggio's works in Parma. In 1615 Domenichino received final payment for a cycle of frescoes in the Polet Chapel of S Luigi dei Francesi, Rome; he had made preliminary designs for the two main scenes before his visit to Bologna in 1612. The St Cecilia frescoes also testify to Domenichino's recent re-acquaintance with Emilian art (the connection between *St Cecilia Distributing Alms to the Poor* and Annibale's *Almsgiving of St Roch* (1594–5; Dresden, Gemäldegal., then in Reggio Emilia, S Prospero) being noted especially by Malvasia); but here again it is the work of Raphael, especially the *Fire in the Borgo* (Rome, Vatican, Stanza dell'Incendio), that was Domenichino's point of departure. The scenes are crowded with narrative incident revelatory of human passions.

Up to his departure from Rome for Bologna again in 1617 Domenichino enjoyed Aldobrandini patronage, designing the carved wooden ceiling for S Maria in Trastevere (1616–17), into which he inserted an *Assumption of the Virgin*, and inventing and partially executing the ten landscape frescoes with scenes from the *Life of Apollo* for the Villa Aldobrandini at Frascati (payments between 1616 and 1618; completed by assistants; 2½ panels *in situ*; 7½, London, N.G). Also originally intended for Aldobrandini was the *Diana with Nymphs at Play* (1618; Rome, Gal. Borghese), in which Domenichino produced a modern, Roman version of a Venetian mythology through reference to his study of Raphael and Correggio. This was, however, commandeered by Scipione Borghese, for whom Domenichino also produced the '*Cumaean' Sibyl* (1616–17; Rome, Gal. Borghese), the first of several similar subjects in which a new graceful female type, ultimately deriving from Raphael's *St Cecilia* and already employed in the St Cecilia frescoes, was developed as a subject in its own right.

(iii) Bologna and Fano, 1617–21. In 1617 Domenichino agreed to complete in the first six months of 1618 a series of frescoes with scenes from the *Life of the Virgin* for Guido Nolfi's family chapel in Fano (for which Gerolamo Rainaldi provided the decorative scheme). Domenichino left Rome for Bologna and thence went to Fano with his new wife for what he considered the happiest period in his life. The grave simplicity of these narrative frescoes is in strong contrast to the ambitious altarpieces begun during this period in Bologna. These were the *Madonna of the Rosary* (1617–c. 1625; ex-S Giovanni in Monte; Bologna, Pin. N.); the *Martyrdom of St Agnes* (c. 1619–22; ex-Bologna, S Agnese; Bologna, Pin. N.; see fig. 2); and the *Martyrdom of St Peter Martyr* (c. 1619–25; Bologna, Pin. N.). All three reveal the importance of Domenichino's re-examination of the traditions of north Italy in these years. In the *Madonna of the Rosary* he contrasted an iconic image, presented by St Dominic, of the Virgin and Child surrounded by figures of the joys, sorrows and glories of the Virgin in the upper half, with a dramatic scene below in which young and old, male and female, lay and clergy meet their violent deaths. In the even larger *Martyrdom of St Agnes* there is a similar division across the height of the canvas. Below, the martyrdom provides a more brilliantly hued and more moving version of the combination of violence and pathos that had characterized his earlier *Flagellation of St Andrew* and *Martyrdom of St Cecilia*. The apse of clouds above supporting musical angels points to Bolognese adaptations by Guido, Annibale and others of designs by Correggio. Such a division into earthly action and heavenly perpetuity had already proved especially attractive to Guido (the *Assumption of the Virgin*, 1616–17; Genoa, S Ambrogio) and to Ludovico Carracci (*Martyrdom of SS Ursula and Leonard*, 1592; Bologna, Pin. N.).

The *Martyrdom of St Peter Martyr* is another milestone in Domenichino's marriage of north Italian models with the relief style and the mastery of exaggerated facial

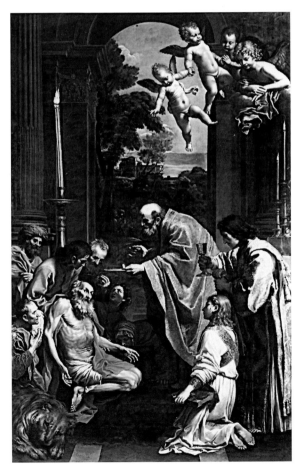

1. Domenichino: *Last Communion of St Jerome*, oil on canvas, 4.19×2.56 m, 1614 (Rome, Pinacoteca Vaticana)

2. Domenichino: *Martyrdom of St Agnes*, oil on canvas, 5.33×3.42 m, *c.* 1619–22 (Bologna, Pinacoteca Nazionale)

expression that he had acquired in Rome. For the *Last Communion of St Jerome* he had taken a masterpiece by Agostino as his starting-point; now he chose to remake one of Titian's most famous altarpieces of the same subject (destr.), once more reversing the image and analytically distancing emotional content through the economy and isolation of gesture, even as he preserved Titian's intensity of colour.

(iv) Rome, 1621–31. On the election of Gregory XV in 1621, Domenichino returned to Rome. He was made Papal Architect and awarded a pension. Though the Bolognese Pope was to die too soon for the appointment to be productive, there are signs that the post was intended to be more than honorific, and that Domenichino's interest in decorative schemes extended to architecture. Among other projects he was entrusted with the entire design for the Cappella della Strada Cupa in S Maria in Trastevere (1628–30). Fictive architecture plays a major role in the *quadratura* framing of Domenichino's most important secular fresco of the decade, the ceiling of *Truth Disclosed by Time* in Palazzo Costaguti (*c.* 1622), although this was executed by Agostino Tassi, who was especially expert in this genre. In 1621–2 Domenichino and Giovanni Battista Viola, with Paul Bril and Guercino, painted landscape frescoes in the Camerino dei Paesi in the Villa Ludovisi,

Rome; these landscapes are tranquil pastoral scenes, conveying a vision of nature inherited from Classical poets. Spear has re-attributed several of Domenichino's landscapes to Viola, and problems of attribution remain; these frescoes provide the firmest point of comparison. Domenichino's landscapes were inspired by the classic ideal provided by Annibale, and later landscapes, such as the *Landscape with Hercules and Achelous* (see fig. 3)and *Landscape with Hercules and Cacus* (both *c.* 1622–3; Paris, Louvre), attained a new heroic grandeur. Among the surviving portraits by Domenichino, the austere formality of the double portrait of *Pope Gregory XV and Cardinal Ludovico Ludovisi* (1621–3; Béziers, Mus. B.-A.) contrasts with the vivid immediacy of his earlier portrait of *G. B. Agucchi* (York, C.A.G.), the attribution of which has been questioned.

Domenichino's most important project as a designer and painter in the 1620s, if not in his entire career, was the decoration of the apse and pendentives of S Andrea della Valle, Rome. He designed the complex stucco divisions for the choir and semi-dome that were executed by Jacques Sarazin. In designing the frescoes Domenichino competed with Giovanni Lanfranco, who decorated the dome (completed by the summer of 1627) and who may have hoped for the entire commission. At this time Lanfranco levelled the novel charge of plagiarism against Domenichino's *Last Communion of St Jerome*. Their competition has been seen as confrontation between the 'classical Baroque' and 'full Baroque' styles, but both artists were developing the north Italian traditions of Correggio's illusionism. In the pendentives depicting the *Evangelists* (1624–5) Domenichino united these traditions with the grandeur of Michelangelo's *ignudi* on the Sistine Chapel ceiling and the witty effects of Annibale's interpretation of Raphael in the Galleria Farnese. In the history of *trompe l'oeil* effects these are as important as Lanfranco's dome, for the monumental figures move in space as if in the open sky, and the clouds physically overlay the egg-and-dart moulding of the arches. The scale, legibility and artistic boldness of the figures rely on the precedent of Caravaggio's altarpieces of the first decade of the century, but Domenichino carried the advances of the earlier generation to a new level of grandeur.

In the irregularly shaped narrative scenes of the semi-dome Domenichino faced an even more difficult task. He treated the areas as *quadri riportati* but also exploited the curvature of the surface to set up movements across real space. The *Flagellation of St Andrew* (see fig. 4), vivid with pictorial witticisms, and *St Andrew Adoring the Cross*, richly composed, with a crowd of spectators, contrast sharply with the sober simplicity of the central scene, the *Calling of Peter and Andrew*. Here there are no spectators and the whole is built around a series of dynamic and subtle movements by the boatman and the Apostles that cross in space, both real and imaginary, as if to denote the cross of St Andrew, who rises up to heaven in the scene above. Though Domenichino may have begun work on the choir by mid-1623, the real campaign occupied him from 1625 to 1628.

In the 1620s Domenichino also received commissions for important altarpieces: the *Martyrdom of St Sebastian* for St Peter's (1625–31; Rome, S Maria degli Angeli) and

3. Domenichino: *Landscape with Hercules and Achelous*, oil on canvas, 1.21×1.49 m, *c.* 1622–3 (Paris, Musée du Louvre)

the *Virgin and Child with SS John the Evangelist and Petronius* for the Bolognese church in Rome (1626–9; Milan, Brera). He also worked after 1626 on S Ignazio, a project supervised by Orazio Grassi, for which Domenichino made drawings for the nave. In the pendentives in SS Biagio e Carlo ai Catinari, left incomplete on his departure from Rome for Naples, he developed the *trompe l'oeil* effects seen in S Andrea so that the figures, clouds and shadows extend even more boldly across the frame. The result is the more remarkable given that the figures are more restrained and, as allegorical personifications, less natural in appearance.

(v) Naples, 1631–41. Despite success in Rome, Domenichino was lured to Naples in 1631 to decorate the Cappella del Tesoro di S Gennaro in the Cathedral, a project that had defeated the Cavaliere d'Arpino, Reni and Fabrizio Santafede. The jealousy of the Neapolitan painters and the demands of the Spanish Viceroy were so great that in the summer of 1634 Domenichino fled to the Aldobrandini Villa at Frascati. There, and in Rome, he was protected by Francesco Angeloni, nephew of Cardinal Pietro Aldobrandini, and made the acquaintance of Giovanni Battista Passeri. His visit was important for the younger generation of artists, such as Nicolas Poussin, Pietro Testa and the

critic Giovanni Pietro Bellori, all of whom shared his views on the rational order of painting.

Domenichino had returned to Naples by June 1635. He continued to fear for his life, passing any time he had in writing letters to his friends and the study and reconstruction of ancient musical instruments. The luminous pendentives he completed in the Cappella del Tesoro (*c.* 1631–40) are painted in an ideal, restrained style that has been compared to the upper part of the *Madonna del Rosario*. The three lunettes, which show scenes from the *Life of St Gennaro* (1631–7), are characterized by the more dramatic approach to narrative that Domenichino had learnt from Raphael's *Repulse of Attila* in the Stanza d'Eliodoro and *Battle of Ostia* in the Stanza dell'Incendio (both Rome, Vatican) many years before. Of the six altarpieces to be painted on copper, only four were completed. The artist died over the fifth, also leaving the dome unfinished. It is not clear whether he was poisoned, as some contemporaries believed, or whether he died of natural causes or of the strain of working among enemies.

2. WORKING METHODS AND TECHNIQUE. In the Carracci Accademia, Domenichino learnt to follow the practice of the masters of the High Renaissance by combining sketches, life drawings and cartoons in the

4. Domenichino: *Flagellation of St Andrew* (*c.* 1622–7), fresco, S Andrea della Valle, Rome

development of his invention. His skill as a caricaturist, with which he was said to have entertained members of the Court at Frascati in 1634, had a similar origin and contributed to his success as a portraitist. The inventory of drawings owned by his pupil Francesco Raspantino (*fl* 1637–64) suggests that Domenichino owned over 900 drawings by the Carracci, a treasure-house of models. Most of his drawings are detailed studies in chalk or in pen and wash; his first thoughts he claimed to fix in his mind in an extended period of meditation. Most interesting in this respect is the large group of drawings for the *Last Communion of St Jerome* in which his entire pictorial imagination was focused on the revision of an existing composition through constant analysis.

Domenichino's practice was concentrated and economical, and he constantly reworked his own ideas. Despite changes in materials and techniques in both drawing and painting, his approach to drawing never changed, and his style was extraordinarily consistent. His dedication to Raphael and to the mature style of Annibale was not limited to the area of drawing but also led him to explore the qualities of colour and texture they had mastered. He studied the surface effects of Correggio and Veronese, which had earlier inspired Annibale, and also Reni's translation of these into a more translucent and loose manner. Yet even in as voluptuous a work as the '*Persian*' *Sibyl* (*c.* 1623–5; London, Wallace), in which the bright flesh of the dark-eyed woman is set off by a primary triad

of red, yellow and blue, Domenichino did not emulate the *bravura* of Venetian brushwork. It was his rational approach to colour, in which saturated hues were applied in accordance with a Raphaelesque ideal (even in the S Andrea della Valle frescoes, where rich pigments were applied *a secco*) that Poussin found so compelling. The principles of analysis he learnt from Domenichino guided his own response to the sensuous luminosity of Titian's *Bacchanals* then in the Ludovisi collection in Rome (London, N.G., and Madrid, Prado).

Domenichino already employed assistants in his frescoes at Bassano di Sutri, and he continued to do so when the scale and pressure of commissions demanded. At Frascati, for example, Giovanni Battista Viola appears to have helped execute the landscapes, Alessandro Fortuna (1596–1623) the figures. As a formal teacher and *capomaestro* he appears to have been intolerant and nervous. Giovanni Battista Ruggieri, who assisted him in S Andrea della Valle and elsewhere in the late 1620s, was reputedly expelled from the studio because Domenichino found his facility of execution threatening. Pietro da Cortona charged that Domenichino held back promising students, and both Alessandro Algardi (whom he had promoted) and Andrea Camassei quarrelled with him. Clearly Domenichino did not attempt to re-create the Accademia in which he had been trained, but nevertheless a group of younger students and associates were inspired by his intellectual presence and his dedication to drawing. Among these were Giovanni

Pietro Bellori and Giovanni Francesco Romanelli; most deeply devoted to Domenichino was Pietro Testa. Poussin was not his student but drew in the studio on his arrival in Rome. Testa and he became friends there and were devoted to Domenichino's analysis of expression, landscape, poetic invention and the text of Vitruvius.

3. CHARACTER AND PERSONALITY. Domenichino combined a meditative, painstaking approach to painting with a reclusive, even anti-social personality. From the moment when he hid from his parents because he feared punishment after leaving Calvaert's studio, to his last days in Naples, when he hid from the world in fear of his life, his timidity and anxiety appear to have been excessive. According to his wife, Marsibilia, he doted on her, representing her features frequently; but his domestic life must have been strange. The couple's nutritional theories led to the starvation of their two male children. Marsibilia, according to Malvasia, was not allowed to keep a dog, for the artist claimed that high-pitched yaps pierced his skull. Domenichino insisted on working in secrecy and isolation, and the house was said to be like a dormitory for friars. Although he had considerable connections with the aristocracy, he did not seem to prefer such company to any other. Annibale probably found his character as attractive as his talent, and in many ways Domenichino was the heir of the neuroses of Annibale's final years. He also inherited Annibale's drawings, ideas and friends. Agucchi began to write his *Trattato della pittura* through conversations with Annibale, but he also held substantial discussions with Domenichino when he was living in the Agucchi household. Years later Domenichino referred to his attempt to differentiate between the Roman, Venetian, Lombard and Tuscan schools, a differentiation that found its way into Agucchi's treatise.

Domenichino was especially interested in the theory of ancient music and both made and commissioned instruments capable of playing ancient harmonies. His interest involved a wider study of ancient theories of harmony that had as much to do with architecture, colour theory and cosmology as with the practice of music itself.

4. CRITICAL RECEPTION AND POSTHUMOUS REPUTATION. Domenichino was a highly influential painter. Artists who understood Raphael through Domenichino's eyes admired his narrative clarity, which had inspired Annibale's famous anecdote about the *vecchiarella*, an old woman, who had vividly explained each detail of the story of the martyrdom of St Andrew to her child as she looked at Domenichino's fresco. Poussin believed that the much-attacked *Last Communion of St Jerome* was equalled only by Raphael's *Transfiguration*. For Francesco Albani and Andrea Sacchi it was the St Cecilia frescoes that competed with Raphael's work as models of perfection.

Even in the 17th century, however, Domenichino's process of imitation (what Pope-Hennessy called mastication), in which he made deliberate references to the traditions of art and appealed to the reason of the spectator, had to be defended against charges that the artist's work was both laboured and unoriginal. On the other hand his realistic expression of the *affetti* was criticized, especially in France, for impropriety.

Domenichino's legacy of drawings, paintings and ideas immediately encouraged a turn to more classical ideals in landscape and in history painting in Rome in the 1640s; his landscapes provided an important example for the heroic landscapes of Nicolas Poussin and Claude Lorrain. John Constable found Domenichino's landscapes to be of the highest order: of that in the *Last Communion* he wrote that it resembled a 'requiem to soothe the departing spirit . . . its effect like that of solemn music heard from an adjoining apartment'. Domenichino's reputation was especially linked with that of Raphael and his works highly prized by artists from Jean-Auguste-Dominique Ingres to Edgar Degas, who espoused the classical tradition. On the other hand Lanfranco's attack on the *Last Communion of St Jerome* and stories of the circumstances of the artist's death fuelled the paradoxical portrayal of Domenichino as a sincere genius persecuted by enemies. As a result he was defended by Romantics from Eugène Delacroix to Robert and Elizabeth Barrett Browning. Yet in the later 19th century his critical fortunes declined in parallel with those of the Bolognese school.

BIBLIOGRAPHY

Thieme-Becker

G. Mancini: *Considerazioni sulla pittura* (1610–20s); ed. A. Marucchi and L. Salerno (Rome, 1956–7), i, pp. 243–4

G. Baglione: *Vite* (1642); ed. V. Mariani (1935), pp. 381–8

G. P. Belloni: *Vite* (1672); ed. E. Borea (1976), pp. 307–73

C. C. Malvasia: *Felsina pittrice* (Bologna, 1678); ed. G. Zanotti (1841), 2 vols, ii, pp. 219–44

G. B. Passeri: *Vite* (1679); ed. J. Hess (1934), pp. 19–71

C. P. Landon: *Vie et oeuvre complète de Dominique Zampieri, dit le Dominiquin (Vie et oeuvres des peintres les plus célèbres de toutes les écoles)* (Paris, 1803–5)

L. Serra: *Domenico Zampieri detto il Domenichino* (Rome, 1909)

D. Mahon: *Studies in Seicento Art and Theory* (London, 1947) [first pubn and study of the treatise Agucchi wrote with Domenichino]

J. Pope-Hennessy: *The Drawings of Domenichino in the Collection of His Majesty the King at Windsor Castle* (London, 1948) [first serious study of Domenichino as a draughtsman, and still indispensable as a lively and penetrating view of the artist's character]

E. Borea: *Domenichino* (Milan, 1965)

D. Posner: 'Domenichino and Lanfranco: The Early Development of Baroque Painting in Rome', *Essays in Honor of Walter Friedländer* (New York, 1965), pp. 135–46 [the standard interpretation of the relationship between the two artists' works in S Andrea della Valle as one of stylistic confrontation, now superseded by Spear's reassessment of the chronology of the comm. on the basis of docs]

R. E. Spear: *Domenichino*, 2 vols (New Haven and London, 1982) [the most thorough, reliable and richly illus. monograph; full bibliog.]

E. Cropper: 'New Documents Concerning Domenichino's *Last Communion of St Jerome*', *Burl. Mag.*, cxxvi (1984), pp. 149–51

C. Whitfield: 'Les Paysages du Dominiquin et de Viola', *Mnmt Piot*, lxix (1987), pp. 61–127

R. Spear: 'Domenichino Addenda', *Burl. Mag.*, cxxi (1989), pp. 5–16

C. Dempsey: 'The Most Difficult Iconographical Problem in the World: Domenichino's *Madonna of the Rosary*, Il luogo ed il ruolo della città di Bologna tra Europa continentale e mediterranea, ed. G. Perini (Bologna, 1992), pp. 341–54

S. Ginzburg: 'The Portrait of Agucchi at York Reconsdidered', *Burl. Mag.*, cxxxvi (1994), pp. 4–14 [reattributes ptg to Annibale Carracci]

ELIZABETH CROPPER

Domenico Battaggio, Giovanni di. See BATTAGGIO, GIOVANNI DI DOMENICO.

Domenico da Cortona [Bernabei, Domenico; Boccador; Dominique de Cortone] (*b* Cortona, ?1470; *d* Paris, ?1549). Italian woodworker and architect. He was apparently the son of a goldsmith from Cortona nicknamed Beccaloro, a nickname he inherited and which was changed in France to Boccador. In 1495 he was among the 22 artists and artisans brought from Naples by Charles VIII, King of France, which suggests that he was one of the Tuscans who had settled in Naples in the service of the house of Aragon, although he is not mentioned in the accounts of the Aragonese treasury. A tradition preserved in Cortona in the 18th century maintained that he was trained by Giuliano da Sangallo (P. Le Sueur); this too could indicate a stay in Naples, since Sangallo provided a palace design there for the Duke of Calabria (the future Alfonso II, King of Naples).

On arrival in France, Domenico was paid as *menuisier et faiseur de châteaux*, which probably means that he specialized in the construction of wooden architectural models, a practice then current in Tuscany. In the following years he was paid as a joiner and was in the service of Queen Anne of Brittany. He became a naturalized Frenchman in 1510. In 1514 he erected a triumphal arch in wood for festivities celebrated in Paris; at that time he was referred to as *maître des oeuvres de maçonnerie du roi*. In 1519 he executed a model of the château of CHAMBORD, which is assumed to be the first design for the château and is known through drawings by André Félibien (priv. col.). The following year Domenico erected in Ardres the temporary wooden pavilions employed for the court at the meeting of Francis I with Henry VIII, King of England, at the Field of the Cloth of Gold. Yet it was only in 1532 that Domenico was paid under the title of architect, the King having commissioned from him a design for a new Hôtel de Ville in Paris (destr. 1871). Work was only finished in 1628, and Domenico's design was not adhered to in the first floor of the main façade. The regular plan, however, and the Italianate detailing and elevation of the courtyard made this the first building in Paris in the true Renaissance style. The ground floor of the main façade, with its columns and its bays screened by arches, probably influenced Pierre Lescot's design for the Louvre (1546).

BIBLIOGRAPHY

A. Félibien: *Histoire des maisons royales et bastimens de France* (1674–; Paris, Bib. N.); as *Mémoires pour servir à l'histoire des maisons royalles et bastimens de France* (Paris, 1874)
P. Le Sueur: *Dominique Cortone dit le Boccador* (Paris, 1928)
——: 'Nouveau document sur Dominique de Cortone', *Bull. Soc. Hist. A. Fr.* (1935), pp. 30–35
J. Guillaume: 'Léonard de Vinci, Dominique de Cortone et l'escalier du modèle en bois de Chambord', *Gaz. B.-A.*, lxxi (1968), pp. 93–108
F. and P. Le Sueur: 'Vues des châteaux du Blésois au XVIIe siècle par André Félibien...', *Mém. Soc. Sci. & Lett. Loir-et-Cher*, xxi (1911), pls XII–XV

BERTRAND JESTAZ

Domenico di Bartolo (Ghezzi) (*b* Asciano, Siena, *c.* 1400; *d* Siena, before 1445). Italian painter. His few surviving works show that he played a pivotal role in the movement from Gothic painting to the Renaissance style in Siena during the 15th century. He is first documented in 1420, as an apprentice on an unidentified project for Siena Cathedral, and his name appears near the end of the *Ruolo dei pittori*, the list of the painters' guild compiled from 1428. Inferences about his artistic education are suggested by the first work securely assignable to him, a small panel of the *Virgin and Child Enthroned with SS Peter and Paul* (Washington, DC, N.G.A.). This shows an early awareness of Florentine art of the 1420s and complete

familiarity with the new artistic language of the Renaissance. The architectural setting, in classical style, is apparently inspired by the new conception of the altarpiece as a *sacra conversazione*, favoured by Fra Angelico at the beginning of the 1420s. The Virgin, housed in a shell niche, is crowned with a garland held by putti reminiscent of Donatello. She sits firmly and solemnly on a marble throne, holding the muscular child. The composition is a free variation on a model by Masaccio, whose early work, like Domenico's, shares many features with the sculpture of Luca della Robbia. Another Florentine element, apparently derived from Paolo Uccello, is the halo with star points, also used by Domenico in later works. The strongly Florentine orientation of this early work refutes the theory that he was trained by Taddeo di Bartolo, who Vasari believed was his uncle. According to Vasari, Domenico worked in Florence, executing two important paintings (untraced): an *Annunciation* for Santa Trìnita and the main altarpiece of S Maria del Carmine, both *c.* 1436. This corroborates the stylistic evidence of the panel in Washington and confirms his familiarity with Masaccio's frescoes in the Carmine.

It is possible that in the early 1420s Domenico painted within the Sienese Gothic tradition, although no such work is known. The panel fragment of the *Virgin and Child Enthroned* (Princeton U., NJ, A. Mus.), which has been connected with the Carmine commission (Strehlke, see 1988 exh. cat.), cannot be dated before the early 1430s, shortly before his first signed and dated painting, the *Madonna of Humility* (1433; Siena, Pin. N.; see fig.). This is Domenico's masterpiece and one of the highpoints of 15th-century Sienese painting, a beautifully balanced composition combining refined expression and broad cultural references. Probably commissioned by Cardinal Antonio Casini or Bishop Carlo Bartoli, it represents a synthesis of Domenico's Florentine influences, including those of Uccello, Masaccio and Donatello. Its dynamic sculptural quality and simulated low-relief effects make it one of the earliest translations of Donatello's sculptural style into painting, contemporary with those of Florentine artists. Fra Filippo Lippi indicated a similar interest in his early *Madonna of Humility* (Milan, Castello Sforzesco). Domenico's study of Luca Della Robbia is evident in the background angels in his *Madonna of Humility*: they recall the earliest parts of Luca's *cantoria* (singing-gallery) made for Florence Cathedral (1432–8, probably completed *c.* 1434). The extraordinary range of greens, pinks and blues shows a Sienese sense of colour, heightened by a clear light that recalls Domenico Veneziano. The date of the work, in fact, suggests that it preceded Veneziano, who began painting around the mid-1430s and whose training seems to have been Florentine. A link between the two artists is also suggested by a comparison between Domenico's *Virgin and Child* (1437; Philadelphia, PA, Mus. A.) and Veneziano's *Virgin and Child* (Bucharest, N. Mus. A.), both of which have as a background a rose garden seen in perspective. The elegant inscription on the Siena panel is one of the first examples of the humanist revival of Roman majuscule script; its precedent, in Siena, was probably the inscription on Donatello's tomb of *Bishop Giovanni Pecci* (*d* 1426) in Siena Cathedral.

Domenico di Bartolo: *Madonna of Humility*, panel, 930×595 mm, 1433 (Siena, Pinacoteca Nazionale)

Giuliana, Perugia, which reflects traditional Gothic solutions. From 1440 to 1444 he executed one of his most significant works, a series of frescoes in the pilgrims' hostel in the Hospital of S Maria della Scala, Siena, commissioned by its rector Giovanni Buzzichelli. The cycle, painted according to a secular humanistic programme, illustrates the daily life and history of the Hospital. Three of the scenes were commissioned from another artist familiar with the new Renaissance taste, il Vecchietta, but only one scene survives. Domenico was assigned five scenes: three with episodes of everyday life and two with events from the history of the Hospital (*see* SIENA, §III, 2 and fig. 8). These scenes are filled with minutely painted details, which tend to fragment the narrative. Domenico's last commission was the fresco of the *Coronation of the Virgin* in the Cancelleria di Biccherna (now Sala della Giunta) in the Palazzo Pubblico of Siena. He painted the four angel heads at the top, but work was interrupted, probably by his death, and the fresco was completed by Sano di Pietro in 1445.

BIBLIOGRAPHY

G. Vasari: *Vite* (1550, rev. 2/1568); ed. G. Milanesi (1878–85), ii, pp. 40–42

G. Milanesi: *Documenti per la storia dell'arte senese*, 3 vols (Siena, 1854–6), i, p. 49; ii, pp. 161–2, 171–3

R. Wagner: *Domenico di Bartolo Ghezzi* (Göttingen, 1898)

C. Brandi: *Quattrocentisti senesi* (Milan, 1949), pp. 105–20, n. 70–79

R. Longhi: 'Fatti di Masolino e di Masaccio', *Opera completa*, viii/1 (Florence, 1956/*R* 1975), pp. 43–4, n. 28

E. Carli: *I pittori senesi* (Milan, 1971), pp. 28–9

C. B. Strehlke: 'La *Madonna dell'Umiltà* di Domenico di Bartolo e San Bernardino', *A. Crist.*, 705 (1984), pp. 381–90

D. Gallavotti Cavallero: *Lo spedale di Santa Maria della Scala in Siena: Vicende di una committenza artistica* (Pisa, 1986), pp. 160–72, n. 105–57

F. Zeri, ed.: *La pittura in Italia: Il quattrocento* (Milan, 1987), i, pp. 316–18; ii, pp. 618–19 [entry by C. Alessi]

Painting in Renaissance Siena, 1420–1500 (exh. cat. by K. Christiansen, L. B. Konter and C. B. Strehlke, New York, Met., 1988)

P. Tottiti: *La Pinacoteca Nazionale di Siena* (Genoa, 1990), pp. 245–7

Una scuola per Piero: Luce, colore e prospettiva nella formazione fiorentina di Piero della Francesca (exh. cat., ed. L. Bellosi; Florence, Uffizi, 1992) [entry by G. Damiani]

GIOVANNA DAMIANI

It may have been Donatello's Sienese works, produced in the late 1420s, that inspired Domenico to broaden his artistic education in Florence. He must have returned to Siena before April 1433, however, as according to documents he drew from life the Holy Roman Emperor Sigismund (*reg* 1410–37), who was in Siena until that date. The portrait was reinterpreted in the marble pavement of Siena Cathedral the following year. The Princeton panel fragment of the *Virgin and Child Enthroned*, identified by Strehlke with the Carmine panel, may also date from the first half of the 1430s. Again it shows his profound stylistic interest in Florentine art: the monumental throne, shown in perspective from below, is clearly inspired by Masaccio's painting of the subject (London, N.G.) for the Pisan Carmelites; the central group also recalls Masaccio's solutions, rather than the sculptural quality of Jacopo Della Quercia.

From 1435 to 1440 Domenico frescoed scenes from the *Lives of the Four Patron Saints of Siena* in the sacristy of the cathedral; only a small fragment survives. He seemed to turn away from Florentine interests in the altarpiece (Perugia, G.N. Umbria) painted in 1438 for S

Domenico di Michelino [Domenico di Francesco] (*b* ?1417; *d* Florence, 18 April 1491). Italian painter. He took his name from his teacher, a carver in bone and ivory named Michelino. He was elected to the Compagnia di S Luca in 1442 and joined the Arte dei Medici e degli Speziali on 26 October 1444. In 1459 he received payment from Lorenzo Pucci for a processional banner (untraced) for a confraternity based in S Francesco, Cortona. Four years later he was paid for some figures of saints (untraced) for a cupboard belonging to the Compagnia di S Maria della Purificazione e di S Zanobi, a Florentine confraternity of which he had been a member since 1445.

Domenico's only surviving documented work is the painting of *Dante Reading from the 'Divine Comedy'* (see fig.) in the north aisle of Florence Cathedral, where Lenten readings from the *Divine Comedy* had been held since at least 1432. On 30 January 1465 Domenico was charged by the *operai* of the cathedral to execute a painting of the poet within six months for the sum of 100 lire. The figure of Dante was based on a modello supplied by Alesso Baldovinetti. On 19 June 1465 Baldovinetti and Neri di Bicci appraised the work and declared that since Domenico

CVI COELVM CEGNIT MEDIVMQVE IMVMQVE TRIBVNAL·····LVSTRAVITQVE ANIMO CVNCTA POETA SVO····DOCTVS ADEST DANTES SVA QVEM FLORENTIA SAEPE···
SENSIT CONSILIIS AC PIETATE PATRE··········NIL POTVIT TANTO MORS SAEVA NOCERE POETAE····QVEM VIVVM VIRTVS CARMEN IMAGO FACIT···

Domenico di Michelino: *Dante Reading from the 'Divine Comedy'*, tempera on linen, 1465 (Florence Cathedral)

had added so many details of his own invention, he should receive the sum of 155 lire.

Ciaranfi assembled a homogeneous group of paintings close to the *Dante* in style. Additions were proposed by Offner. These works form a consistent, sometimes repetitive corpus, although Berenson assigned several of them to Giusto di Andrea. Berenson suggested that a *Last Judgement* (Berlin, Kaiser-Friedrich Mus., destr.) was begun by Giusto's father, Andrea di Giusto, and completed by Domenico di Michelino with an assistant. This work was dated 1456 and was commissioned for the Villani Chapel in S Benedetto fuori Porta Pinti, Florence. The design was heavily dependent on Fra Angelico, who according to Vasari (ii, p. 522) was Domenico's master, although this theory is unlikely. It is probable that the design of the *Last Judgement* can be attributed to Andrea di Giusto, who may have also painted the spandrels; Domenico appears to be responsible for the rest of the painting (for further attributed work *see* CASSONE, fig. 4).

Other influences are apparent in the *Virgin and Child with Six Saints* (San Giovanni Valdarno, S Maria delle Grazie) where the use of colour, the milky tonality and the drapery style of the figure of St Anthony Abbot are strongly reminiscent of Filippo Lippi, while the bright, broad-cheeked faces recall Pesellino. This work, although attributed to Giusto di Andrea by Berenson, was given to Domenico by Ciaranfi and Offner. Domenico also appears to have collaborated with Benozzo Gozzoli on the framing elements for Gozzoli's altarpiece for the Compagnia di S Maria della Purificazione (1461; London, N.G.). Each painted a pilaster enclosing three saints (Florence, Accad. B.A. & Liceo A.). A group of paintings (*c.* 1440–53) by Domenico's workshop have been ascribed by several critics to an anonymous artist dubbed the Master of the Buckingham Palace Madonna.

BIBLIOGRAPHY

G. Vasari: *Vite* (1550, rev. 2/1568); ed. G. Milanesi (1878–85)
A. M. Ciaranfi: 'Domenico di Michelino', *Dedalo*, vi (1925–6), pp. 522–38
R. Altrocchi: 'Michelino's *Dante*', *Speculum*, vi (1931), pp. 15–59
R. Offner: 'The "Mostra del Tesoro di Firenze Sacra"', *Burl. Mag.*, lxiii (1933), p. 174, n. 27
R. W. Kennedy: *Alesso Baldovinetti* (New Haven, CT, 1938), pp. 133–4
W. Cohn: 'Notizie storiche intorno ad alcune tavole fiorentine del '300 e '400', *Riv. A.*, xxxi (1956), pp. 43–5
B. Berenson: *Florentine School*, ii (1963), pp. 5, 60–61, 92–3
J. Shearman: *The Early Italian Pictures in the Collection of Her Majesty the Queen* (Cambridge, 1983), pp. 235–6

ELIOT W. ROWLANDS

Domenico di Niccolò [dei Cori; Spinelli] (*b* Siena, *c.* 1363; *d* Siena, *c.* 1453). Italian sculptor, designer and architect. He is known primarily for the large number of carved and polychromed wood statuettes of the Virgin, Virgin and Child, Christ and saints that he produced throughout his career for churches in and around Siena. The works attributed to his early career (*c.* 1395–1400) are characterized by broad, architectonic forms, suggestive of Nicola Pisano; however, such elements were superseded *c.* 1414 by an elegance of gesture and expressive drama that marked the beginnings of Domenico's mature gothicizing style. His rekindling of the Gothic spirit is strongly evident in the *Mourning Virgin* and the *Mourning St John* executed for Siena Cathedral (1414–15; Siena, S Pietro a Ovile; restored 1923). These 'Dolenti' reveal a new emotionalism and suggest a direct rapport with Sienese painting of the early 15th century. Around the same time Domenico executed intarsia choir-stalls for the new chapel in the Palazzo Pubblico, Siena (1415–*c.* 1428). His exceptional skill in this intricate and complex art form brought him high praise and the appellation 'dei cori'. The intarsie consist chiefly of decorative geometric designs and small scenes illustrating verses from the Credo, such as 'Descendit de coelis' and 'Et ascendit in coelum'. Their abstract, calligraphic quality is pronounced, and their sophisticated expressiveness is comparable to that of the 'Dolenti'. The *Risen Christ* (1442) made for the Ospedale di S Maria della Scala (Siena, Col. Chigi-Saracini) is one of his last known works and perhaps his most powerful. From at least 1394 Domenico was employed in various capacities by the Opera del Duomo in Siena; in 1402 he became a master of the cathedral's fabric and in 1413 was promoted to *capomaestro*.

BIBLIOGRAPHY

G. Previtali: 'Domenico "dei cori" e Lorenzo Vecchietta: Necessità di una revisione', *Stor. A.*, 38–40 (1980), pp. 141–4

A. Bagnoli: 'Domenico di Niccolò "dei cori"', *Scultura dipinta: Maestri di legname e pittori a Siena, 1250–1450* (exh. cat., ed. A. Bagnoli and R. Bartalini; Siena, Pin. N., 1987), pp. 104–32

Domenico di Paris (*b* Padua; *fl c.* 1443–1501). Italian sculptor, bronze-caster and wood-carver. A pupil and son-in-law of NICCOLÒ BARONCELLI, he followed his master from Padua to Ferrara. That he was called 'Domenico del Cavallo' in later documents attests to his considerable role in the making of the bronze equestrian monument to *Niccolò III d'Este, Marquis of Ferrara* (destr. 1796), which was begun by Baroncelli in 1443 and dedicated on 2 June 1451. After Baroncelli's death (1453), Domenico was head of the workshop and was paid in 1454, 1456 and 1457 for the monument to *Borso d'Este, Duke of Ferrara* (destr. 1796), begun by Baroncelli in 1451. In 1466 he completed the life-size bronze statues of *St George* and *St Maurelius* begun by Baroncelli for the high altar of Ferrara Cathedral; he also executed two marble lions for the high altar (all *in situ*). On 3 April 1467 he undertook to execute reliefs to cover the ceilings of upper rooms in the Palazzo Schifanoia, Ferrara. Although the contract makes no mention of the walls, the elaborate polychromed stucco decorations on the walls of the antechamber are universally given to him and Bongiovanni di Geminiano. Based on similarities to the putti and the figures of Virtues in the antechamber, two terracotta reliefs of the *Virgin Adoring the Christ Child* (Berlin, Bodemus.; Berlin, Gal. Goldschmidt-Wallerstein) have been attributed to him. Neither of these

works can be identified with a terracotta altarpiece with figures in relief for which he was paid in 1466.

Domenico's other documented works have been destroyed. They included two large bronze candlesticks (1461), a lead *Hercules* (1472), wood-carvings made with other artists for a sumptuous carriage in 1473, some work in 1490 in connection with a marriage chest painted for Isabella d'Este, models for vases executed in 1492 and 60 wooden roses carved in 1501 for the oratory of the Confraternità delle Morte in Ferrara. On 21 January 1492 and 24 December 1493 he was paid for a wooden model for the summit of the cathedral campanile, and in 1493 he cast various components for the third storey.

BIBLIOGRAPHY

Thieme–Becker

A. Frizzi: *Memorie per la storia di Ferrara* (Ferrara, 1791–1809), iv, pp. 8, 24

G. Antonelli: 'Appendice', *Memorie originali italiane riguardanti le belle arti* by M. Gualandi, iv (Bologna, 1843), pp. 36–41, 48

V. N. Pietrucci: *Biografia degli artisti padovani* (Padua, 1858/R Bologna, 1970), p. 215

L. N. Cittadella: *Notizie relative a Ferrara per la maggior parte inedite ricavate da documenti ed illustrate*, i (Ferrara, 1864), pp. 46, 100–02, 416, 419–22, 578, 668, 704

G. Gruyer: 'La Sculpture à Ferrare', *Gaz. B.-A.*, n. s. 3, vi (1891), pp. 177–203 (188, 191–2)

——: *L'Art ferrarais à l'époque des princes d'Este* (Paris, 1897), i, pp. 297, 316–7, 423, 516; ii, p. 489

A. Venturi: 'Miscellanea: Una scultura di Domenico di Paris padovano', *L'Arte*, vii (1904), pp. 158–9

G. Agnelli: 'I monumenti di Niccolò III e Borso d'Este in Ferrara', *Atti & Mem. Deput. Ferrar. Stor. Patria*, xxiii (1918), pp. 1–32

L. Dussler: 'An Unknown Sculpture by Domenico di Paris', *Burl. Mag.*, xlvii (1926), pp. 301–2

P. Schubring: 'Zwei Madonnenreliefs von Giovanni da Pisa und Domenico Paris', *Der Cicerone*, xviii (1926), pp. 566–8 (567)

G. Medri: *La scultura a Ferrara* (Rovigo, 1957), pp. 51–3

C. M. Rosenberg: *Art in Ferrara during the Reign of Borso d'Este (1450–1471): A Study in Court Patronage* (diss., Ann Arbor, U. MI, 1974), pp. 65, 177–82

——: 'The Iconography of the "Sala degli Stucchi" in the Palazzo Schifanoia in Ferrara', *A. Bull.*, lxi (1979), pp. 377–84 (378)

JILL E. CARRINGTON

Domenico Veneziano [Domenico di Bartolomeo da Venezia] (*fl* 1438; *d* Florence, *bur* 15 May 1461). Italian painter. Venetian by birth or descent, he was one of the founders of Renaissance painting in Florence in the first half of the 15th century and the most enigmatic. His training (north Italian or Florentine), the chronology of his few surviving works (his only documented fresco cycle has perished and there is only one major altarpiece) and his relationship to contemporary painters, sculptors and theorists (particularly Alberti) have been debated; they cannot, given the shortage of evidence, be resolved satisfactorily. Yet, despite these difficulties, Domenico's altarpiece for S Lucia de' Magnoli in Florence (the St Lucy altarpiece; main panel in Florence, Uffizi), with its ambitious architectural setting, acutely described figures and its pale colours bathed in a convincing outdoor light, would alone assure him a central place in the history of Renaissance art.

1. Life and work. 2. Working methods and technique. 3. Relationship to contemporaries and influence.

1. LIFE AND WORK.

(i) Early works, to mid-1440s. (ii) *St Lucy* altarpiece, mid-1440s. (iii) Other late works, mid-1440s and after.

(i) Early works, to mid-1440s. Although Domenico is mentioned by such contemporaries as Filarete (*Trattato dell'architettura*, c. 1461–2; see Wohl, 1980, p. 349) and Alamano Rinuccini (dedicatory epistle to the Latin translation of Philostratus' *Life of Apollonius*, 1473; see Wohl, 1980, pp. 349–50), he is, surprisingly, omitted from Cristoforo Landino's commentary of Dante of 1480 with its characterization of the work of Masaccio, Filippo Lippi, Andrea del Castagno, Paolo Uccello and Fra Angelico. Vasari's biography of Domenico is subordinate to the life of Andrea del Castagno and contains a considerable amount of bad information: Domenico is credited with having introduced the practice of oil painting into Florence and his fresco of *SS John the Baptist and Francis* (Florence, Mus. Opera Santa Croce) is ascribed to Castagno, whom Vasari erroneously claimed had murdered Domenico (*see* CASTAGNO, ANDREA DEL).

The first document relating to Domenico is a letter he wrote from Perugia in 1438 to Piero de' Medici, then in Ferrara. The letter attests to Domenico's presence in central Italy by that date and confirms his activity in Perugia (where Vasari records a cycle of frescoes of unspecified subject in the Baglioni Palace, destr. 1540). It also reveals a familiarity with events in Florence that suggests some prior activity in the city. Domenico expresses his hope to obtain the commission for a major altarpiece he understands Cosimo de' Medici is contemplating (usually identified as Fra Angelico's high altarpiece for S Marco; Florence, Mus. S Marco). He is also aware that Filippo Lippi is already engaged on an altarpiece, commissioned on 8 March 1437 for Santo Spirito (the Barbadori Altarpiece; Paris, Louvre). The letter contains orthographic peculiarities characteristic of both Venice and Florence (Wohl, 1980; Beck), further suggesting that by 1438 at the latest Domenico had assimilated Florentine habits. No special importance can be attached to Domenico's use of 'da Venezia' or 'Veneziano' until his death; this was common practice among those whose birthplace or citizenship differed from the city or region in which they worked, and it is, in consequence, idle to speculate when and under what circumstances Domenico arrived in central Italy. Although an apprenticeship to Gentile da Fabriano or to Pisanello is not impossible, his work is, from the outset, decisively Florentine, not Venetian, in its concerns.

Any interpretation of Domenico's career relies on the chronology assigned to his surviving paintings, none of which is documented. No consensus has been reached (the most thorough and convincing chronology is that of Wohl, 1980). A guiding principle is Domenico's increasing command of the use of perspective for pictorial and narrative effects and greater subtlety in physiognomic description. On this basis, one may accept Vasari's assertion that the much damaged fresco of the *Virgin and Child Enthroned* (London, N.G.) for an exterior tabernacle from the Canto de' Carnesecchi in Florence is his earliest work. Characteristically, the ovoid head of the Virgin, the tooled gold leaf of her brocade dress and the pale flesh tints, the accomplished foreshortening of God the Father and the dove and the accentuated perspective of the throne (the vanishing point is in the lap of the Virgin), have their closest parallel in the work of Masolino, not in

Gentile da Fabriano or Pisanello. It is conceivable that Domenico worked with Masolino in Rome between 1428 and 1433 (the throne recalls the work of the Cosmati workshop in Rome) or at Castiglione d'Olona, west of Milan, c. 1433–5, and this could partly explain the penchant Domenico shared with Masolino for perspective as a means both of suggesting depth and of generating abstract surface patterns. The relatively primitive perspective structure of the Carnesecchi Tabernacle, with its tunnelling effect at the expense of the figures, would accord with a date in the early 1430s.

The next reasonably datable work is a *Virgin and Child* (Bucharest, Mus. A.). The more massive proportions of the Virgin, the active pose of the Christ Child (dependent on Donatello's dancing putti on the *cantoria* of 1433–9 for Florence Cathedral; now Florence, Mus. Opera Duomo) and the use of a highly focused light find an analogy in Filippo Lippi's *Virgin and Child* known as the Tarquinia *Madonna* (1437; Rome, Pal. Barberini), while the preference for geometric clarity in the design and details such as the rhythmic disposition of the fingers of the Virgin's hands provide a precedent for Piero della Francesca's *Madonna of Mercy* (Sansepolcro, Pin.). Piero is mentioned in 1439 as Domenico's assistant in a payment for the lost fresco cycle in the choir of S Egidio, Florence, and the *Virgin and Child* in Bucharest establishes the importance of this training. Some of the same traits characterize the roughly contemporary tondo of the *Adoration of the Magi* (Berlin, Gemäldegal.; see fig. 1), the astonishing landscape of which is the basis for that in Piero's *Baptism* (London, N.G.). The origins of that landscape style (north Italian or, more probably, Flemish) have been debated (see especially Zeri), but there is general agreement that its remarkable perspective structure, with a vanishing-point separate from that of the foreground scene, depends on Donatello's stucco tondo relief of *St John on Patmos* (probably completed by 1443) in the Old Sacristy of S Lorenzo, Florence. The application of perspective to landscape painting was as innovative as the acute, descriptive technique with which the background details are represented and had a notable impact on Piero della Francesca. Domenico's tondo has sometimes been identified with an item in a Medici inventory of 1497 (Pudelko; Wohl, 1980), and it has been argued that the commission came from Piero de' Medici and involved Medici portraits and devices (Ames-Lewis), but the inventory names Pesello (i.e. Pesellino) as the artist and gives different dimensions from those of the painting in Berlin.

Part of the importance of the *Virgin and Child* in Bucharest and the *Adoration of the Magi* in Berlin derives from the fact that they were painted shortly before or contemporary with Domenico's lost frescoes on the west wall of the choir of S Egidio, which were begun in 1439 and appear to have been largely completed by 1443, although there is an additional payment in June 1445. One scene was completed by Alesso Baldovinetti in 1461; Wohl (1980) attempted to demonstrate that Domenico completed only the sinopia for this, but as he was paid more than Andrea del Castagno for three companion scenes on the opposite wall, this analysis is likely to be incorrect. Vasari recorded the subjects and general character of the scenes, of which a few fragments were salvaged in 1938.

1. Domenico Veneziano: *Adoration of the Magi*, tempera on panel, diam. 840 mm, *c.* 1439–41 (Berlin, Gemäldegalerie)

They showed, from top to bottom, the *Meeting at the Golden Gate*, the *Birth of the Virgin* and the *Marriage of the Virgin* and were conspicuous for their elaborate architectural settings and profuse details, such as a child beating the door with a hammer in the *Birth of the Virgin* and a dwarf in the *Marriage of the Virgin*. The composition for the *Marriage of the Virgin* is probably reflected in a small panel of the same subject (Florence, I Tatti; Meiss), in which the architecture of the open courtyard, with a straight entablature supported by columns, prefigures a feature of Alberti's architecture also found in the work of Piero della Francesca.

(ii) 'St Lucy' altarpiece, mid-1440s. This altarpiece (main panel, Florence, Uffizi; predella panels, Washington, DC,

N.G.; Berlin, Gemäldegal.; Cambridge, Fitzwilliam; see fig. 2), painted for the high altar of the small church of S Lucia de' Magnoli, probably dates from the mid-1440s and is roughly contemporary with Fra Angelico's S Marco Altarpiece (Florence, Mus. S Marco) and Filippo Lippi's *Coronation of the Virgin* (Florence, Uffizi) for S Ambrogio. Like those two works, it marks the climax of early Renaissance painting in Florence. No earlier 15th-century altarpiece, and few later ones, employ such an ambitious architectural setting (Verga's suggestion that Piero della Francesca was involved in the design is highly improbable). In the S Marco Altarpiece architecture serves as a screen between a projected, geometric patterned carpet and the distant landscape, and in Filippo Lippi's *Coronation of the*

2. Domenico Veneziano: *St Lucy* altarpiece, main panel, tempera on panel, 2.09×2.16 m, mid-1440s (Florence, Galleria degli Uffizi)

Virgin the complicated, stepped, box-like space compromises a profusion of decorative detail and a superabundance of figures, but in the *St Lucy* altarpiece architecture both defines the space and articulates the figural content.

The four saints (Francis, John the Baptist, Zenobius and Lucy) occupy a foreground defined by an inlaid pavement and a raised arcade beneath which sit the Virgin and Child. The arcade also divides the picture surface vertically into three parts—as in a Gothic triptych—and behind the arcade is a pentagonal exedra comprising three shell niches and two vaulted bays, above which are visible a blue sky and three orange trees (Marian symbols). The notion that this inventive scheme could have been evolved without recourse to some sort of preliminary ground-plan drawings (Wohl, 1980, argues for the use of a surface grid that should not, however, be confused with the *velo* device recommended by Alberti for studying foreshortening of

individual objects) is contradicted by the analyses of Verga, Battisti and Welliver, who have recreated the layout of the architecture. The resulting impression is of the apse of an open-roofed church viewed through a raised rood screen, or *tramezzo*. The reference to ecclesiastical architecture, with the Virgin/Ecclesia at its focus, is unquestionably intentional. It recurs, notably, in Filippo Lippi's contemporary *Annunciation* (Munich, Alte Pin.) and, significantly, receives its most complete statement in Piero della Francesca's altarpiece of the *Virgin and Child Enthroned with Saints and Federigo da Montefeltro* (Milan, Brera). The polychromatic inlaid details of the architecture relate to a well-established Tuscan tradition also used by Alberti, and the design of the exedra seems to reflect Brunelleschi's tribunes for Florence Cathedral. The pointed arches of the arcade have parallels in contemporary Florentine architecture and were necessitated by the fact that the

3. Domenico Veneziano: *Miracle of St Zenobius*, predella panel of the *St Lucy Altarpiece*, tempera on panel, 286×325 mm, mid-1440s (Cambridge, Fitzwilliam Museum)

spans of the arcade are narrower than those of the exedra (Welliver).

The unusually low viewing-point (in the lap of the Virgin) has been seen as contradicting Alberti's recommendations, but it was determined by the approximate height of a viewer standing before the altar in the church and expresses Alberti's intention that perspective be used to create a fictive extension of the viewer's space (this idea was later developed by Mantegna). Likewise, the light source coincides with the primary source of illumination in the church (the 45° angle at which it falls also enhances the geometric clarity of the composition). The inventive use of perspective as a factor of design applies also to the five narrative panels of the predella, each of which originally had a fictive moulding enhancing Alberti's concept of painting as a window. In the idyllic *Annunciation* (Cambridge, Fitzwilliam; *see* ITALY, fig. 31) the perspective structure is normative: the horizon is level with the Virgin's head and the vanishing-point is located on what was originally the vertical axis (the angle of the shadow was,

like the perspective of the pavement, determined by a visible incision). In the *Martyrdom of St Lucy* (Berlin, Gemäldegal.) the vanishing-point coincides with the focus of the action, emphasized by the orthogonals, one of which is described by the sceptre of the governor ordering the execution. In the *Miracle of St Zenobius* (Cambridge, Fitzwilliam; *see* fig. 3) the focus of the perspective is off-centre and organizes the receding buildings into two sets of converging diagonals that generate a sensation of heightened drama to the story, enacted in a shallow area across the foreground. The source for this unusually free and imaginative use of perspective as a narrative device is, again, Donatello's relief sculpture.

The iconography of the altarpiece seems, on the whole, unexceptional, although it has been the subject of an elaborate exegesis, and the inscription on the steps (an invocation to the Virgin) has been thought to camouflage a variety of erudite meanings (Wohl, 1980; Welliver). The blond tonality of the altarpiece and the innovative description of light have been commented on by numerous critics (see especially Pudelko) and mark a shift from the more saturated colour and dense shadows of Domenico's earlier work. Interestingly, the same shift is observable in Piero della Francesca's *Baptism* (London, N.G.) and *St Jerome* (1450; Berlin, Gemäldegal.); Domenico was employed in Arezzo in 1450 (Dabell) and may be responsible for this shift in Piero's work. (Vasari also records that the two artists worked together in Loreto, but this cannot be verified.)

(iii) Other late works, mid-1440s and after. Documents relating to Domenico's life after 1445 are remarkably uninformative. In 1447–8 he painted two chests (untraced) for the marriage of Marco Parenti to Caterina Strozzi; an idea of their appearance may be gleaned from the *desco da parto* (birth tray) illustrating the *Triumph of Fame* (1449; New York, Hist. Soc.) for Lorenzo de' Medici (the Magnificent), the design of which Domenico Veneziano may have been responsible for, although the execution is due to Giovanni di ser Giovanni, known as Scheggia. In 1454 Domenico was nominated, together with Filippo Lippi and Fra Angelico, to evaluate the work of Benedetto

4. Domenico Veneziano: *SS John the Baptist and Francis*, 2.00×0.80 m, tempera on panel, *c.* 1445–61 (Florence, Museo dell'Opera di Santa Croce)

Bonfigli in the Palazzo de' Priori in Perugia, and three years later, with Filippo Lippi, he evaluated Pesellino's *Trinity* (London, N.G.); these references confirm his central position in Florence.

Only three works may be connected with the last 16 years of Domenico's life. A *Virgin and Child* (Washington, DC, N.G.A.) is, perhaps, slightly later than the *St Lucy* altarpiece and marks an increased refinement of figure type and colour harmonies. Another *Virgin and Child* (Florence, I Tatti) is sometimes considered an early work, but its sophisticated design and decorative use of gold leaf are paralleled in Florentine art of the mid-15th century. In a detached fresco of *SS John the Baptist and Francis* (Florence, Mus. Opera Santa Croce; see fig. 4), originally on the *tramezzo* of Santa Croce, Domenico reached new depths of expressiveness. The fresco also reveals his continued concern with perspective to achieve an effect of immediacy and urgency (the saints are shown *di sotto in sù* and from the right, in accordance with the natural viewing point in the church).

A number of other works from these years may be presumed lost, but it is doubtful that Domenico's level of production was great; his work is the product of a slow, deliberate process; again similar to that of Piero della Francesca. In the letter of 1438 he estimated it would take Filippo Lippi five years to complete the altarpiece on which Lippi was employed, and this may be taken as indicative of his own rate of production. Moreover, allowance must be made for the possibility of an extensive career outside Florence: his name occurs in few Florentine documents; it is not known when (or if) he joined the painters' guild, though his name does occur in the records of the Compagnia di S Luca, and only in 1455 is there a record of his lease of a house in Florence.

2. WORKING METHODS AND TECHNIQUE. Vasari claimed that Domenico learnt the technique of oil painting in Venice from Antonello da Messina and introduced it to Florentine painters, most notably in his destroyed murals in S Egidio. The first half of this claim is clearly incorrect and derives from Vasari's misconception of Venetian painting in general and his classification of Domenico as a Venetian artist. There is a payment for linseed oil in 1441 for use on the murals in S Egidio, but Wohl (1980) has convincingly argued that this oil was used not as a principal medium but as a binder in adding details *a secco*, a technique recorded by Cennino Cennini. There has been no scientific analysis of the medium employed by Domenico in his panel paintings, which, however, have the appearance of being executed in tempera. Nonetheless, Piero della Francesca's use of an oil or oil-like medium in his earliest documented work, commissioned in 1445, the *Madonna of Mercy* in Sansepolcro, suggests that his master may have had some awareness of the technique.

Domenico's use of full-scale cartoons in designing his paintings is of primary importance for the subsequent history of Florentine painting. This can be demonstrated in his fresco of *SS John the Baptist and Francis* for Santa Croce and in the *Virgin and Child* in Washington, in both of which *spolveri* are visible. These are among the earliest examples of a technique also employed by Andrea del

Castagno and Piero della Francesca, who may well be indebted to Domenico for it. The use of cartoons was obviously due to Domenico's deep concern for details and his desire to plan all aspects of a composition prior to painting. Concomitant was his concern with perspective and the point from which the works would be viewed. The one surviving sinopia for the murals at S Egidio establishes that, like Uccello, Domenico began work by defining the space in which the figural action would take place. The accomplished complexity of the *St Lucy* altarpiece would have been impossible without the aid of cartoons and the mastery of perspective, both of which are central to subsequent Renaissance art in Florence.

It is clear that sculpture in general played a significant role in Domenico's art: the importance of Donatello's reliefs in the Old Sacristy of S Lorenzo has already been noted. Domenico's frescoed figure of *St John the Baptist* would scarcely be conceivable without the example of Donatello's wooden statue of the *Magdalene* for the Florence Baptistery (Florence, Mus. Opera Duomo), and the composition of the Virgin and Child in the *St Lucy* altarpiece is in many respects a painted counterpart to Luca della Robbia's terracotta tondo on Orsanmichele. This interest extended to antique sculpture as well: the pose of the young St John the Baptist in the predella panel (Washington, DC, N.G.A.) from the *St Lucy* altarpiece seems to derive from a Roman sarcophagus showing Hercules in combat with Diomedes (Wohl, 1980), and his almost Hellenic beauty—he is the most beautifully painted male nude of the first half of the 15th century—possibly reflects a familarity with antique bronze statuettes. Each of these interests, however, was subservient to Domenico's refined sensibility and his apparent conception of painting as an intellectual endeavour rather than a craft.

3. RELATIONSHIP TO CONTEMPORARIES AND INFLU-ENCE. The relationship of Domenico Veneziano's work to that of his presumed pupil, Piero della Francesca, has been discussed briefly above, but it should be emphasized that this extended from figure types and colour in Piero's early paintings to the use of perspective both as a device of pictorial composition and as a means of describing space. In the case of Piero, Alberti can be shown to have played a crucial role in these concerns, and it is probable that he had a direct impact on Domenico as well, possibly in 1434–6, when he was in Florence as part of the papal retinue and composed his treatise on painting, or between 1439 and 1443. It is even conceivable that the shift in style documented by the *St Lucy* altarpiece may owe something to Alberti. Given the sparse evidence, however, it is almost impossible to gauge the extent of Alberti's influence, though an eloquent attempt has been made by Longhi to relate Domenico's work to ideas in *De pictura* (1435).

Vasari's portrayal of Domenico as a gentleman-painter ('amiable, he sang and liked to play the lute') is probably based not on fact but on his view of Venetian painters in general (the characterization is curiously like that of Giorgione). The fact that Vasari coupled the lives of Domenico and Andrea del Castagno in a single biography seems, on the other hand, well-grounded. Domenico has been ascribed a collaborative role in Castagno's fresco cycle in S Tarasio, Venice, which is dated 1442 (Muraro),

and although this has been denied (most emphatically by Zeri), it is not impossible: the figure of St John the Evangelist is painted in a manner closely resembling that of Domenico. In 1451 Castagno was commissioned to fresco three scenes opposite Domenico's in S Egidio, and his late work reveals a refinement of colour and sensitivity to landscape and light that unquestionably derive from Domenico. (However, Hartt's erroneous attribution to Domenico of the sinopia for Castagno's *St Jerome* in the SS Annunziata is based on a misunderstanding of its function as a preliminary design done without the aid of a cartoon.) It is worth noting that in the 16th century Domenico's fresco of *SS John the Baptist and Francis* in Santa Croce passed as the work of Castagno or Antonio del Pollaiuolo. The attribution to Pollaiuolo emphasizes the importance of Domenico's unequalled powers of description among his contemporaries, as does the confusion of Pollaiuolo's *Portrait of a Lady* (Berlin, Gemäldegal.) as a work of Domenico's (the only two portraits that may reasonably be attributed to Domenico are those of *Matteo Olivieri* and *Michele Olivieri*, Washington, DC, N.G.A.; Norfolk, VA, Chrysler Mus.; both poorly preserved). The most direct influence was that exerted on Alesso Baldovinetti, whose work is in many respects an academic corruption of Domenico's.

Domenico's influence extended well beyond Florence. Zeri has convincingly argued that Domenico di Bartolo's frescoes in the Ospedale della Scala, Siena, and Benedetto Bonfigli's in the Cappella de' Priori, Perugia, derive to some extent from those of Domenico in Perugia and Florence. Zeri has also demonstrated Giovanni Boccati's dependence on Domenico's landscape style. The Master of the Barberini Panels, who, like Boccati, was from the Marches, was among Domenico's most faithful imitators and to a degree so also was the Sienese artist Vecchietta. Interestingly, it is impossible to establish any certain influence of Domenico on Venetian art, underscoring his role as a central Italian artist.

BIBLIOGRAPHY

G. Vasari: *Vite* (1550, rev. 2/1568); ed. G. Milanesi (1878–85), ii, pp. 667–89

G. Pudelko: 'Studien über Domenico Veneziano', *Mitt. Ksthist. Inst. Florenz*, iv (1932–4), pp. 145–200

M. Salmi: *Paolo Uccello, Andrea del Castagno, Domenico Veneziano* (Rome, 1936)

A. Busuioceanu: 'Una nuova Madonna di Domenico Veneziano', *L' arte*, n. s., viii (1937), pp. 3–15

R. W. Kennedy: *Alesso Baldovinetti: A Critical and Historical Study* (New Haven and London, 1938)

R. Longhi: 'Il Maestro di Pratovecchio', *Paragone*, 35 (1952), pp. 10–30

M. Muraro: 'Domenico Veneziano at San Tarasio', *A. Bull.*, xxix (1959), pp. 151–8

M. Meiss: 'Contributions to Two Elusive Masters', *Burl. Mag.*, ciii (1961), pp. 57–61

F. Zeri: *Due dipinti, la filologia e un nome* (Turin, 1961)

D. Gioseffi: 'Domenico Veneziano: L'esordio masaccesco e la tavola con i SS Girolamo e Giovanni Battista della National Gallery di Londra', *Emporium*, cxxxv (1962), pp. 51–72

C. Shell: 'Domenico Veneziano, Two Clues', *Festschrift Ulrich Middeldorf* (Berlin, 1968), pp. 150–54

F. Hartt: *The History of Italian Renaissance Art* (New York, 1969), p. 226

M. Hall: 'The *Tramezzo* in S Croce, Florence and Domenico Veneziano's Fresco', *Burl. Mag.*, cxii (1970), pp. 797–9

E. Battisti: 'Mantegna come prospettico', *A. Lombarda*, xvi (1971), pp. 104–7

H. Wohl: 'Domenico Veneziano Studies: The Sant'Egidio and Parenti Documents', *Burl. Mag.*, cxiii (1971), pp. 635–40

W. Welliver: 'The Symbolic Architecture of Domenico Veneziano and Piero della Francesca', *A. Q.*, xxxvi (1973), pp. 1–30

C. Verga: 'Un pavimento di Piero?', *Crit. A.*, xlii (1977), pp. 100–15

F. Ames-Lewis: 'Domenico Veneziano and the Medici', *Jb. Berlin. Mus.*, xxi (1979), pp. 67–90

J. Beck: 'Was Domenico Veneziano Really *Veneziano*?', *A. News*, lxxix/10 (Dec 1980), pp. 168–9

H. Wohl: *The Paintings of Domenico Veneziano, ca. 1410–1461: A Study in Florentine Art of the Early Renaissance* (New York, 1980); review by K. Christiansen in *Apollo*, cxiv/233 (1981), pp. 66–7

F. Dabell: 'Domenico Veneziano in Arezzo and the Problem of Vasari's Painter Ancestor', *Burl. Mag.*, cxxvii (1985), pp. 29–32

KEITH CHRISTIANSEN

Domingo y Marqués, Francisco (*b* Valencia, 12 March 1842; *d* Madrid, 22 July 1920). Spanish painter. He belonged to the Valencian school and received his academic training at the Escuela de S Carlos, part of the Academia de Valencia, as a scholar in Rome (1868) and as a pupil of Rafael Montesinos (a follower of the Valencian artist Vicente López y Portaña). Domingo y Marqués's paintings reflect the contemporary emphasis on the Spanish tradition, particularly as represented by the work of Ribera, Ribalta, Velázquez and Goya. In common with some of his contemporaries, he placed much emphasis on the use of light as a basic element in painting. His long periods in Paris also led to a knowledge of French art, and in some circles in France he came to be highly regarded. He was a founder-member of the short-lived Agrupación Courbet, a group of artists established in Barcelona in 1918 in a spirit of protest against official teaching and artistic methods. His skill as a draughtsman and his facility as a colourist are best seen in his portraits, which are among the finest painted in Spain at that time. His technical ability, however, was not accompanied by a strong creativity, and a great deal of his work consists of small genre paintings in which he depicted 17th- and 18th-century scenes along the lines of those by Ernest Meissonier.

BIBLIOGRAPHY
Barón de Alcahalí: *Diccionario biográfico de artistas valencianos* (Valencia, 1897)

R. Contreras [Marqués de Lozoya]: *Historia del arte hispánico* (Madrid, 1945)

S. Aldana Fernández: *Guía abreviada de artistas valencianos* (Valencia, 1970)

ANDRÉS UBEDA DE LOS COBOS

Domingues, Domingos (*fl c.* 1308–31). Portuguese architect. Only two works by him are known, both royal commissions: the cloister of Alcobaça Abbey, built in 1308 by order of King Diniz (*reg* 1279–1325), and Sta Clara-a-Velha, Coimbra, begun in 1316 under the patronage of Isabella, the wife of King Diniz. The Alcobaça cloister is a spacious construction appropriate to the grandiose proportions of the earlier church. Despite being a Cistercian foundation, the austerity prescribed by Bernard of Clairvaux was disregarded, and the capitals of the cloister have naturalistic foliage in high relief and zoomorphic elements in the Romanesque tradition. The cloister is only the second in Portugal, after that of Coimbra Old Cathedral (built in the second half of the 12th century), to have ambitiously designed proportions and complete vaulting. Sta Clara-a-Velha is remarkable in that the church is vaulted throughout, unlike most Portuguese Gothic churches, where only the chevet is vaulted. Domingues gave the nave a Romanesque barrel vault reinforced by strong arches, and only the central rib running longitudinally the length of the church reveals its Gothic date. A more original solution was adopted in the aisles: by raising them to the same height as the nave, it was possible to have two-light windows in the outer walls, admitting indirect subdued lighting to the nave. Hall churches were not common in Portugal in this period, and Domingues may have been inspired by Alcobaça Abbey.

BIBLIOGRAPHY
Viterbo
P. Dias: 'Domingos Domingues, arquitecto régio do século XIV', *Mundo A.* (Coimbra, 1982)

——: 'O gótico', *História da arte em Portugal*, iv (Lisbon, 1986), pp. 39–42

JOSÉ CUSTÓDIO VIEIRA DA SILVA

Domínguez, Oscar (*b* La Laguna, Tenerife, 7 Jan 1906; *d* Paris, 31 Dec 1957). Spanish painter and sculptor, active in France. He first lived in Paris in 1927 while working for his family's banana export business, coming into contact there with avant-garde groups and from 1929 undergoing the influence of Surrealism. Typical of the dreamlike and highly sexual early works that formed the basis of his first one-man exhibition, held in May 1933 at the Círculo de Bellas Artes in Tenerife, is *Surrealist Landscape* (1933; Tenerife, E. Westerdahl priv. col., see Westerdahl, p. 18).

The Surrealist influence became even more marked after Domínguez's meeting in 1934 with André Breton and Paul Eluard; in 1935 he became a member of the official Surrealist group, playing an active part in their activities and while still in Paris encouraging the dissemination of the movement in Spain. Domínguez had a particularly strong role in the promotion of Surrealism on the Canary Islands, not only through his contributions to the avant-garde journal *Gaceta de arte* from its inception in 1932, but also through his role as co-organizer of the *Exposición internacional del surrealismo* held in 1935 at the Ateneo in Santa Cruz de Tenerife, with the *Gaceta*'s editor, the critic Eduardo Westerdahl (1902–80). The presence on this occasion of Breton and other important figures of the Surrealist group had an enormous impact on artistic developments in Tenerife.

On settling in Paris in 1934, Domínguez continued to take part in Surrealist activities and in their exhibitions (Copenhagen and London, 1936; Tokyo, Paris and Amsterdam, 1937); his work was also included in the influential *Fantastic Art, Dada, Surrealism* exhibition held at MOMA, New York, in 1936. During this period Domínguez invented a technique that he called decalcomania, an elaboration of the automatism practised by other Surrealists, which involved the casual blotting of a gouache drawing into an ambiguously suggestive image (e.g. *Untitled*, 1936–7; New York, MOMA; see fig.). He also became one of the most prolific producers of poetic and irrational Surrealist objects such as *The Marksman (Conversion of Energy)* (painted plaster, objects and glass, h. 460 mm, 1935; Paris, Charles Ratton priv. col., see 1978 exh. cat., p. 303). Although he was in Paris during the Spanish Civil War (1936–9), the political turmoil of these events and of World War II left a profound and permanent impression on his work.

Domínguez moved to Marseille in 1940, continuing to exhibit internationally until his suicide in 1957. Both in cosmic landscapes such as *Nostalgia for Space* (1939; New York, MOMA) and in overtly sexual works such as *The Calculator* (1943; untraced, see Westerdahl, p. 8), one of a series of machine-like objects, he demonstrated an unceasing preoccupation with the subconscious, with automatism and with unfettered spontaneity, all of which made him one of the most characteristic and loyal adherents of the Surrealist movement.

BIBLIOGRAPHY
P. Waldberg: *Black Irises for Oscar Domínguez* (London, 1961)
E. Westerdahl: *Oscar Domínguez* (Barcelona, 1968)
G. Xuriguera: *Oscar Domínguez* (Paris, 1973)
F. Castro: *Oscar Domínguez y el surrealismo* (Madrid, 1978)
Dada and Surrealism Reviewed (exh. cat. by D. Ades, London, ACGB, 1978), pp. 303, 420

M. DOLORES JIMÉNEZ-BLANCO

Dominica. *See under* ANTILLES, LESSER.

Dominican Order [Order of Preachers; Blackfriars]. Religious order of mendicant friars founded by St Dominic (1170–1221) and santioned by the papacy in 1216. Like the Franciscans (*see* FRANCISCAN ORDER), the Dominicans spread very rapidly throughout Europe and beyond. With the First and Second Orders (for men and women) they included a Third or Tertiary Order for lay people who wished to dedicate themselves to a religious life. The Dominicans were above all scholars and preachers, but they exerted a significant influence on art and architecture, of which they were powerful patrons.

I. Introduction. II. Iconography. III. Patronage.

I. Introduction.

Domingo de Guzmán, St Dominic, was born at Calervega, near Burgos in Spain. Of noble birth, he received a good education, beginning at the house of his uncle, not far from his home town. He early became aware of his vocation to the priesthood, and between 1184 and 1198 he continued his education at Palencia, where he studied the liberal arts (trivium and quadrivium), philosophy and theology and where he later taught. While he was at the university there was a great famine throughout Spain, and, moved by compassion, Dominic sold his books in aid of the poor, setting an example that was followed by theologians and professors. After his ecclesiastical training Dominic was ordained and subsequently summoned by the Bishop of Osma, Diego de Acebes (*reg* 1190–1201), who made him a canon regular of his church. He was appointed subprior of the chapter, and he made an intensive study of the Latin Fathers; he began the practice of reciting the Divine Office, a privilege of canons that he later included in the liturgy of his order.

In 1203 King Alfonso VIII of Castile entrusted to Diego de Acebes diplomatic negotiations concerning the marriage of Alfonso's son Fernando to a Danish princess. The bishop appointed Dominic as his co-ambassador, and the subsequent journey is recorded in a low relief depicting two mounted clerics with a servant on the tomb (1258) of *Don Pedro de Osma* in the chapter house of Osma Cathedral. The two men got as far as Toulouse, where they changed their route owing to the death of the princess

Oscar Domínguez: *Untitled*, ink transfer (decalcomania), 154×218 mm, 1936–7 (New York, Museum of Modern Art)

and went on a pilgrimage to Rome. They visited Pope Innocent III, whom they told of their change of ministry and of their wish to undertake the conversion of the heretics, then returned to Toulouse, where Dominic had previously become aware of the Catharist (Albigensian) heresy. During his first night there Dominic converted a heretic with whom he was lodging; following this clear demonstration of his vocation he began to call himself Brother Dominic. Jordan of Saxony relates Dominic's first miracle, which took place after a debate that he held with heretics at about this time: in order to settle the dispute both his and their books were submitted to a 'judgement of God' by being thrown into the fire three times; each time those of Dominic leapt out of the flames. The miracle was also included in the Golden Legend, written a few decades later by JACOPO DA VORAGINE.

The new institution of the Friars Preachers began to take shape, and Dominic became the proclaimer of the Christian faith. Before Diego de Acebes decided to return to his diocese he founded the first convent for contemplative Dominican nuns at Prouille, near Toulouse, 'for noble women who for reasons of poverty were entrusted by their parents to heretics to be kept and brought up'. According to legend a ball of fire showed the site of the new house, of which 'Dominic was the spiritual father, the material provider, the lawgiver' (Vicaire). The acts of the General Chapter at Valence (1259) made a correction attributing the foundation of the Prouille convent to Dominic.

Dominic remained in Languedoc only about ten years (1207–17). His apostolic mission coincided with the first Albigensian crusade, proclaimed on 10 March 1208 by Innocent III, which provided the religious and social background against which Dominic continued his task of preaching. By 1214 he had a number of followers, and Pierre Seila of Toulouse gave them 'some tall and well-made houses' in Toulouse, where the new community gathered. From then on, those who followed Dominic began to conform to the religious way of life and adopted the monastic traditions by taking the vow of obedience, attending Divine Office and contributing their worldly goods to the common purse.

According to Jordan, Bishop Fulk of Toulouse gave them tithes in his diocese so that they could live and study. In 1215 Dominic accompanied Bishop Fulk to the Fourth Lateran Council in Rome and gave an account of his work to Innocent III. The Pope was initially opposed, but following a dream in which he saw Dominic supporting the crumbling Lateran Basilica (see fig. 1), he gave his approval. Dominic allowed his friars to choose one of the rules that were approved by the Church; they opted for the Augustinian Rule (*see* AUGUSTINIAN CANONS) and committed themselves to a life of strict observance, regulated by the vow of poverty. The Bishop assigned to them the church of St Romain, Toulouse, and next to it they built a cloister with cells in which they could study and sleep; by the end of 1215 there were 16 friars there. This church was soon followed by two others on the outskirts of the city.

In the summer of 1216 Innocent III was succeeded as pope by Honorius III, from whom Dominic obtained approval for the Order of Preachers as well as for its name and was granted the Bull of Approval of the Order (22 December 1216). The Order continued to grow and became more organized. Dominic remained the leader with the title of Master of the Order, and the friars made their vows of obedience to him. One of Dominic's first decisions was to disperse the friars into the world, starting with the cities of Paris, Rome, Bologna and Madrid. This may have been related to a vision that, according to his third biographer, Constantino da Orvieto, and the Golden Legend, Dominic had while praying in St Peter's during his visit to Rome. While he prayed he saw the Apostles Peter and Paul approach him; St Peter gave him a staff, St Paul a book, and they said to him, 'Go, preach, for God has chosen you for this ministry.' Then he appeared to see his sons scattered throughout the world, going in pairs to spread the divine word. This experience was included in the narrative cycle of the life of the saint by medieval artists, who probably based their interpretation on that in the Golden Legend.

In 1218 Dominic was in Paris, where he organized the convent of St Jacques, founded a university college and established the *Studium generale*. The Paris convent was the place of the earliest Dominican friars' intellectual training, and it was soon followed by foundations in other university towns, including Bologna, Rome, Madrid, Segovia, Cologne, Oxford, Orléans, Limoges, Lyons and Reims. In 1219 Dominic went to Bologna, where he settled in the convent of S Nicolò delle Vigne, and from where he organized the foundation of convents in Bergamo, Florence, Verona and Milan. He visited Honorius III in Rome to tell him of the new foundations and obtained from him the Bull of Mendicancy, which constituted the Friars Preachers as a new order within the Church. At the Pope's request, in 1221 Dominic founded a new convent of S Sisto Vecchio, Rome, to which some Dominican nuns from Prouille also came. In her *Relatio miraculorum* the Dominican nun Cecilia Cesarini related how Dominic resuscitated the young Roman Napoleone Orsini, who had fallen from his horse when riding to the ceremony of the convent's inauguration, to which he had

1. Nicola Pisano and assistants: *St Dominic Shouldering the Lateran Basilica* (centre), with the *Approval* (left) *and Confirmation* (right) *of the Dominician Order*, detail from the Arca di S Domenico (1265–7), marble relief, S Domenico, Bologna

been invited by his uncle Cardinal Stefano. A community of friars was temporarily installed at S Sisto, until Honorius granted them a house on the Aventine and the Early Christian basilica of S Sabina.

In May 1220 the Pope entrusted Dominic with converting the heretics of northern Italy. Before setting out on this campaign Dominic went to Bologna to celebrate the first General Chapter (17 May 1220), at which canon lawyers and theologians drew up the second part of the Book of Constitutions. On 30 May 1221 the second General Chapter decided that owing to the great number of friars, it should be divided into provinces (Spain, Provence, Lombardy, Rome). The government of the Order consisted of the master general, the general chapter, provincial priors and provincial chapters; it was agreed that the meetings of the general chapter would take place alternately in Bologna and Paris. Dominic did not complete his mission, dying on 6 August 1221 at S Nicolò delle Vigne, surrounded by his friars. He was initially buried in a wooden coffin in the floor at S Domenico, Bologna, but on 25 May 1233 his remains were translated to a cypresswood coffin and a plain marble tomb located above ground. The second and final translation took place on 5 June 1267 at the instigation of the general master, Fra Giovanni da Vercelli. The new tomb (*in situ*; later remodelled; see fig. 1; *see also* §II below), commissioned from Nicola Pisano, was made of white marble; classical in style, the sarcophagus was supported by caryatids, with low reliefs on each side.

The founder's death did not impede the Order's rapid expansion, which slowed down only at the beginning of the 14th century, partly owing to internal dissent. A reform movement centred in Tuscany aimed to return to the early ideals of poverty and strict adherence to the Rule; numerous observant houses were established in central Italy (e.g. S Marco, Florence) and later throughout Europe. Through their preaching, scholarly work and worldwide missionary activity, the Dominicans remained an influential order until the 20th century.

II. Iconography.

Dominican friars are recognizable by their religious dress, of which the three inner components (tunic, scapular and hood) are white, while the cloak and the hood are black. St Dominic himself is always depicted standing, his head slightly inclined and his face oval. The expression is usually concentrated in the eyes, which sometimes appear to have a fixed gaze. The stylized hands are often breast-high; the right is used more often than the left, in the act of blessing, or holding a book or simply exposed. St Dominic is always shown with the clerical tonsure (as laid down for the mendicant orders by the Constitutions of 1228), and he has been painted both with and without a beard and moustache.

1. St Dominic. 2. Other Dominican saints.

1. ST DOMINIC.

(i) Attributes. (ii) Life and miracles. (iii) Later developments.

(i) Attributes. St Dominic is usually represented with a book, and he may also have a star, a dog with a flaming torch, or a rosary as his attributes. He is sometimes also

2. Francesco Traini: *St Dominic*, tempera on panel, 1344–5 (Pisa, Museo Nazionale di S Matteo)

shown holding a lily, symbolizing chastity, as in Francesco Traini's *St Dominic* altarpiece (1344–5; Pisa, Mus. N. S Matteo; see fig. 2).

The star, symbolic of light and of the preaching of St Dominic, is an attribute supported by such literary sources as the letter from Pope Gregory IX (*reg* 1227–41) to Jordan of Saxony, Pedro Ferrando (Dominic's second biographer) and Cecilia Cesarini. According to Jordan, Dominic's mother had a vision of her son with 'the moon on his forehead', prefiguring that one day he would be a 'light unto the people'. Elsewhere Jordan wrote that the saint shone like the morning star; Pedro Ferrando recorded St Dominic's birth by saying 'there arose a new star'; other Dominican writers, including Cecilia Cesarini and Jacobus da Voragine, recorded the 'star on his forehead'. Artists have represented the attribute in different ways, although it is always a star rather than a moon. In medieval depictions it is usually on St Dominic's forehead or to the side of his halo, but in the Baroque period the star itself was omitted, while the overall radiance was accentuated.

The black and white dog with a flaming torch in its mouth also derives from literary sources and is described by Jordan of Saxony, who related that St Dominic's mother had a vision of giving birth to such a creature. Both Jordan and other authors saw the dog as the symbol of the preacher, while its bark was the sacred doctrine. Pedro Ferrando contrasted the barking of the dog with the image of the heretics disguised as wolves. In medieval representations the dog always appears in scenes of the saint's birth and childhood. With time it acquired greater prominence and independence within the picture, losing its symbolic quality, as for example in Traini's altarpiece, in an illuminated Antiphonary (Florence, S Maria Novella, MS. 1354, fol. 151), in a Passional (Rome, Vatican, Bib. Apostolica, MS. 8541) and in a panel by Pere Nicolau (Valencia, Mus. B.A.). An unusual presentation of the dog, whereby it is enveloped in flames, is to be seen in Pedro Berruguete's panel of *St Dominic* (Madrid, Prado) from a dismantled altarpiece. In Baroque art many painters fused the symbol of the dog and torch with that of a globe. The latter represented the world inhabited by men to whom St Dominic directed his preaching and whom he illuminated with his word. This is the iconography shown by Claudio Coello in his *St Dominic* (Madrid, Prado) and in his *Virgin of the Rosary and St Dominic* (Madrid, Real Acad. S Fernando), as well as by Antonio Palomino in the *Virgin Giving the Rosary to St Dominic* (Miami, FL, Dominican convent).

An extension of this iconography, whereby the friars were represented as hounds of the Lord, stemmed from the pun on the name *Dominicani*. The first artist to illustrate this theme was Andrea da Firenze (i), whose frescoes glorifying the Dominican Order decorate the chapter house, or Spanish Chapel, of S Maria Novella, Florence. On the right wall are scenes of the *Church Militant* and the *Church Triumphant*, where St Dominic is shown in five roles: as a soldier of the *militia Christi* who preaches, defends, debates and expounds the truth of the faith and reconciles men. At the lower right Andrea depicted a fierce fight between a pack of wolves and the black and white 'hounds of the Lord', shown trying to snatch back the sheep: a metaphor for the friars' struggle against heresy.

The book, an attribute shared by many saints, especially founders of religious orders, is particularly relevant to St Dominic and the Order of Preachers, as scholarship was part of their vocation. St Dominic encouraged his friars to study, and he introduced study as a means to the ministry of the salvation of souls. St Dominic is often shown holding a volume, either open or closed (e.g. see fig. 2). Sometimes it is held open in both hands. When open and with writing visible the choice of text varies, indicating that a symbolic meaning was intended, rather than a specific reference to any particular text. The clearest iconographical presentation of the attribute is that on the Arca di S Domenico, where the book is given prominence and is used by the artist as a technical and interpretative device. In the scene of the *Burning of the Heretical Books*, for example, the book is the focal point of the composition. In the relief of the *Approval and Confirmation of the Dominican Order* (see fig. 1 above), there are two clearly visible objects, the rolled official parchment and the book, which carry different meanings. The ceremony of handing over the Bull of Approval by the Pope is signified by the roll of parchment, while the act of the Confirmation of the Order is shown in the presentation of the book. In the Arca the transferring of the book from hand to hand is very significant: it is given to St Dominic both by Honorius II and (in the scene *St Dominic Receives the Commission to Preach from SS Peter and Paul*) by St Paul; it is then seen to be passed on by St Dominic to his friars. It seems that what is transferred is not the book itself but its doctrinal content (*Traditio doctrinae*). Each of the seven times the book is carved in the Arca di S Domenico reliefs it appears in exactly the same shape and size; this suggests that for the patrons and the artist the book is the same one in each case, as is the doctrine.

As the institution of the ROSARY, composed of five or fifteen sequences of ten beads corresponding to the fifteen joyful, sorrowful and glorious mysteries, was formerly ascribed to St Dominic, it is frequently depicted as his attribute, hanging from his belt or around his neck. There is, however, no mention of it in the literary sources relating to St Dominic, and its attribution to him is possibly the result of popular legend lacking historical foundation. It is particularly significant that such early artists as Nicola Pisano and Fra Angelico did not depict this attribute; it was not represented at all before the popularization of the rosary by two Dominicans, Alano de Rupe (1428–75) and Jakob Splenger (*fl* 1436; *d* 1495). Confraternities were subsequently formed to encourage the use of the rosary among the faithful, and this stimulated its representation in art. Paintings of the Virgin of the Rosary were hung in chapels used by the confraternities; the earliest known example (untraced) was commissioned *c.* 1475 by the Confraternity of the Rosary in Cologne and is known from a woodcut of 1476. While he was in Venice, Albrecht Dürer painted an ambitious version entitled the *Virgin of the Rose Garlands* (1506; Prague, N.G.) for the German community there. (For a discussion of his altarpiece for the Confraternity of the Rosary in Haarlem, *see* GEERTGEN TOT SINT JANS.) A *Virgin and Child* (1488) by the Dominican engraver Franciso Domenech shows the mother and child surrounded by a garland of roses and includes a representation of the fifteen mysteries as well as of four Dominicans; St Dominic holds in his right hand a rosary of ten beads (for later developments of the theme see §(iii) below).

(ii) Life and miracles. Among the first painted depictions of St Dominic are two panels (*c.* 1250–53; Naples, Capodimonte and S Domenico Maggiore) by unknown masters of the Roman school. One panel is iconographically

interesting because on either side of the standing figure of the saint there are small compartments with scenes from his life, in the manner of a *vita retable*, a format that was very popular at the time and often used for depictions of St Francis (for illustration *see* BERLINGHIERI, (2)). A development of this type was produced by Francesco Traini. In his altarpiece of *St Dominic* (see fig. 2) painted for S Caterina, Pisa, the saint in the central panel is flanked by eight scenes showing his birth, his shouldering of the Lateran basilica, his vision of SS Peter and Paul, the burning of the heretical books, two miracles (the resurrection of Napoleone Orsini and the saving of pilgrims from a shipwreck), his vision of ladders to Heaven and his death. In another example, an anonymous altar frontal (early 14th century; Barcelona, Mus. B.A. Catalunya) from S Miguel, Tamarit de Litera (nr Huesca), the same form was adopted, and two additional scenes from the saint's life were included. The *Resurrection of Napoleone Orsini* was a frequent subject for other types of painting, for example by Fra Angelico in the predella of the *Coronation of the Virgin* (Paris, Louvre).

The earliest iconographic model in sculpture is the Arca di S Domenico (*c.* 1264–7; Bologna, S Domenico), St Dominic's tomb (see §i above), commissioned from Nicola Pisano and produced with the help of assistants (*see* PISANO (i), (1); for the 15th-century remodelling *see* NICCOLÒ DELL'ARCA). The four reliefs on the sides of the sarcophagus form a narrative cycle of the *Life of St Dominic*, with the saint shown in a variety of attitudes and situations. The iconography is based on passages in Jordan of Saxony's *Libellus*, Constantine of Orvieto's *Narratio* and Cecilia Cesarini's *Relatio*, brought together in the Golden Legend. The present arrangement of the reliefs shows the *Resurrection of Napoleone Orsini*; the *Burning of the Heretical Books*; the *Supper of St Dominic*; *Approval of the Order by Innocent III*; *St Dominic Shouldering the Lateran Basilica* and *Approval and Confirmation of the Dominican Order* (see fig. 1 above); the *Miraculous Apparition of the Virgin*; the *Cure of the Blessed Reginald of Orleans*; *St Dominic Receives the Commission to Preach from SS Peter and Paul*; and the *Mission of the Friars Preachers in Rome and Fanjeaux*. These four relief panels constituted a basic source for later artists and are a fundamental reference for the study of Dominican iconography.

No doubt owing to their scholarly work the Dominicans commissioned and owned large numbers of manuscripts; consequently, specific iconographic types soon developed. As manuscripts were frequently and easily transported there was a vigorous exchange of iconographic models between convents, and a new artistic idiom spread rapidly. Dominican illustration for liturgical purposes drew on literary sources and involved the decoration of choir-books for the feasts of St Dominic (24 May and 5 August). Numerous examples of such works survive from Dominican convents all over Italy. Dominican manuscript illustration also reflects the oral and written tradition of St Dominic as a man of prayer. The Madrid Codex, the Carcassonne Codex and other manuscripts (e.g. Rome, Vatican, Bib. Apostolica, MS. lat. Ross. 3) are versions of a Dominican prayer treatise (*De modi orandi*) that records and illustrates the saint's *Nine Ways of Prayer*, which were accompanied by appropriate expressive gestures. This

iconography, at first widely dispersed in manuscript form, was later adopted for other purposes. Fra Angelico, for example, based his cell frescoes at S Marco, Florence, directly on the treatise illustrations.

(iii) Later developments. In the late 16th century, during the Counter-Reformation, Dominican iconography broke with traditional types and compositions, and many new themes appeared. The art of the period was influenced by the spiritual revival that resulted from the Council of Trent and especially by the provisions laid down concerning images, which amounted to a revision of religious iconography as a defence against Protestant attack. Emphasis was placed on the glorification of the Order's patron, and statues of St Dominic were included in series of founder saints, as for example at St Peter's, Rome, where a marble

3. Giambattista Tiepolo: *St Dominic Distributing the Rosary* (1739), fresco, S Maria del Rosario (I Gesuati), Venice

St Dominic (1702; *in situ*) by Pierre Legros (ii) was installed in the choir.

The new Dominican iconography was no longer based on biographical sources; its aims were for art to become theological and dogmatic, to present arguments, to persuade and to teach in order to stimulate religious feeling and devotion.

The legend of St Dominic receiving the rosary from the Virgin became a favourite theme of Baroque artists. In many renderings the Virgin is shown in the clouds in the upper zone, with St Dominic standing below. In Caravaggio's *Virgin of the Rosary* (1607; Vienna, Ksthist. Mus.) a Dominican, possibly St Dominic, is shown giving rosaries to the devout. Variations on the theme exist in such works as Murillo's *Virgin Giving the Rosary to St Dominic* (1638–40; Seville, Pal. Arzobisp.), painted for the Dominican convent of S Tomás, Seville, and in Claudio Coello's *Virgin of the Rosary and St Dominic* (1668–70; Madrid, Real Acad. S Fernando, Mus.), with St Dominic in the centre and compositionally linking the Virgin and Child holding a rosary with a group of the faithful. A later variant includes the figure of St Catherine of Siena. Sassoferrato's *Virgin of the Rosary* (1643; Rome, S Sabina) is a good example of the most common arrangement with the three figures. The Virgin is shown at the apex of a notional triangle, with St Dominic and St Catherine below, receiving a rosary from the Virgin and the Child respectively.

The exaltation of sanctity is reflected in the large representations of visions, ecstasies and apotheoses of saints that became extremely popular. St Dominic appears in spectacular scenes of rhetorical glorification on vaults, ceilings, domes and retrochoirs, for example in Guido Reni's fresco of the *Apotheosis of St Dominic* (1615; Bologna, S Domenico) and in Giovanni Battista Piazzetta's painting (1727; Venice, SS Giovanni e Paolo) of the same subject. A splendid example exists in S Maria del Rosario (I Gesuati), Venice, where Giambattista Tiepolo painted the ceiling fresco of *St Dominic Distributing the Rosary* (1739; see fig. 3), flanked by the *Appearance of the Virgin to St Dominic* and *St Dominic Carried to Heaven*.

Mannerist and Baroque artists developed other subjects that had previously often been forgotten, especially death, martyrdom, religious asceticism, suffering and penitence. El Greco originated the theme of St Dominic praying (usually kneeling) before the crucifix and painted it at least eight times between 1580 and 1605. The same subject was treated by Francisco de Zurbarán in his *St Dominic at Prayer* (Madrid, Col. Duque de Alba), a half-length frontal view, and by Luis Tristán de Escamilla, who painted a half-length *St Dominic as Penitent* (*c.* 1615–20; Toledo, Casa & Mus. El Greco), half-naked and in the act of self-flagellation.

A completely new theme, typical of Spanish religious art, is the *Passion of St Dominic*, in which the saint is shown passing through the stages of Christ's Passion. Such images were painted particularly for Dominican convents and possibly were initiated by the Dominican artist Juan Bautista Maino. Examples abound in painting and sculpture, and Juan Martínez Montañés's life-size figure of *Penitent St Dominic* (1606–7; Seville, Mus. B.A.; see fig. 4) for the Dominican convent of Porta Coeli in Seville is an interesting illustration of religious realism and asceticism.

4. Juan Martínez Montañés: *Penitent St Dominic* polychrome wood, 1606–7 (Seville, Museo de Bellas Artes)

A new iconographic theme of *St Dominic in Soriano*, totally unconnected with the Counter-Reformation, also developed in the 16th century. It stemmed from a cult in the Italian convent of Soriano that was centred on a portrait of St Dominic believed to have been painted by divine intervention. On 15 September 1530, a Dominican friar at the convent had a vision of the Virgin, St Mary Magdalene and St Catherine of Alexandria presenting him with the celestial painting. This event led to the construction of a sanctuary that became very widely celebrated, and it also became a popular subject for artists. The composition always includes St Catherine showing the image of the saint and accompanied by the Virgin and St Mary Magdalene, with the friar kneeling to receive the painting. The portrait always shows St Dominic standing, holding a lily and a book. This iconography became widely known in Spain through Juan Bautista Maino, who painted it four times. One version (destr. 1652), painted for S Tomás in Madrid, was replaced by Antonio Pereda's painting (*c.* 1656; Madrid, Mus. Cerralbo) of the same theme. Overall, the figure of St Dominic lost some of its religious intensity in Baroque painting, although spatially he was given greater prominence. The principal subject became somewhat impoverished by the addition of increasingly dominant symbolic attributes that distract attention from the main theme of the composition.

2. OTHER DOMINICAN SAINTS. A number of other Dominicans who were canonized played an important role as patrons; they were often represented alongside St Dominic or on their own as subjects of altarpieces and other works of art. St Peter Martyr (*c.* 1205–52) was a determined opponent of heresy but was murdered by Cathars and canonized only a year later. His popularity as a saint grew rapidly, and it became compulsory for Dominican churches to have a depiction of him in addition to one of St Dominic. Peter Martyr is usually shown as a Dominican with a knife or hatchet embedded in his skull. Sometimes, for example in Giovanni Bellini's *St Peter Martyr* (London, N.G.), he is shown in the scene of his martyrdom, being pursued by his assassin. St Thomas Aquinas, another very important Dominican saint, was a great theologian, renowned for his rigorous stand against heresy. He was often portrayed as a stout Dominican, sometimes with a star on his breast and holding a book and a chalice or lily. (For a monumental representation of the *Triumph of St Thomas Aquinas* (*c.* 1365; Florence, S Maria Novella) *see* ANDREA DA FIRENZE (i).)

St Catherine of Siena (*c.* 1347–80) was a Dominican Tertiary. She devoted herself to helping the poor of Siena but also did much to help bring back the papacy from Avignon to Rome. As a patron saint of Siena she was often represented in Sienese altarpieces and usually shown holding a book, a cross or a lily. In emulation of Christ and St Francis, she received the stigmata following a vision and was often represented with the marks on her body. This led to great opposition from the Franciscans and even a papal ban on images of her with the stigmata, but this was later lifted. St Catherine of Siena was also sometimes depicted in a mystic marriage, whereby she receives a ring from the infant Christ who is held by the Virgin. This scene was no doubt influenced by the existing analogous inconography involving St Catherine of Alexandria, from whom she can be distinguished by her habit and veil.

III. Patronage.

The Dominicans attracted the patronage of all social classes from early on, and the extensive body of legislation drawn up during the 13th century to govern the construction and decoration of their churches and conventual buildings reflects official attempts to resist the increasingly lavish architecture and furnishings. The policies were a development of the philosophy of St Dominic, who had claimed to love poverty and had wished 'small and lonely dwellings' for his friars. Legislation recommending small and humble buildings was passed at the first General Chapter meeting in Bologna in 1220. A much more vigorous and precise set of recommendations and bans was approved in 1228: maximum measurements (especially height) were specified, and such elements as stone vaults were permitted only in church choirs. In 1252 sculpture and painting were totally prohibited, and on several occasions it was decreed that carved tombs were to be removed from Dominican churches or moved to less important locations therein. Such stipulations were reiterated many times at general and provincial chapter meetings, and overall they were adhered to; buildings

remained simple for most of the 13th century. There were, however, difficulties in universally enforcing the regulations, and there were also various impracticalities. Consequently, the General Chapter of 1297 in Venice decreed that larger churches should be built in order to contain the large congregations, although decoration was still prohibited. By that time the Dominicans already had foundations in hundreds of European cities, especially in Italy, France and Spain as well as Germany, the Netherlands, England, Poland and Hungary. (For further discussion *see under* the relevant geographical headings in GOTHIC, §II.) Some of these buildings, for example the Jacobin church (founded 1227; rebuilt 1285–98), Toulouse, were quite impressive structures and vaulted throughout (*see* TOULOUSE, fig. 1). At the first foundation in Italy, S Domenico in Bologna, a new church, convent and cloister were built between 1228 and 1240 to replace the earlier S Nicolò delle Vigne, and various buildings were subsequently added. There were in fact two churches, linked by a covered passage: one 'internal or conventual', Gothic in style with nave, two aisles and cross-vaulting, and the other 'external or for the laity', with simple columns and a wooden ceiling. The Arca di S Domenico was initially placed in the right aisle of the larger church, so that the relics could conveniently be venerated, and it was consecrated by Innocent IV on 14 October 1251. In 1298 work began on enlarging the chancel, which was rebuilt in a Gothic style; the tower was added in 1313. A chapel with two vaulted areas was elaborated to contain the Arca, and in 1377 the Master General Elias Raymond of Toulouse blessed the first stone of a work that lasted until 1411–13. Magnificent examples of intarsia and sculpture were added in the 1530s under the patronage of LEANDRO ALBERTI. In 1587 the chapel was enlarged by Floriano Ambrosini and built on a square plan and with a semicircular apse. In addition to the existing rich decoration by leading Italian artists, Guido Reni painted a fresco of the *Apotheosis of St Dominic* (1613–15) in the apse, and at about the same time such artists as Alessandro Tiarini, Mario Roghetti (*fl* 1616), Lionello Spada and Giovanni Andrea Donducci made other significant contributions.

Growth was interrupted in the mid-14th century by signs of decadence, and the situation was worsened by the Black Death of 1348–9, which took a great toll. Communities had to be refounded, and new buildings were built at the expense of patrons. Vigorous revival followed, and the rapid expansion of the order in Italy led to the construction of conventual churches of the mendicant type in most cities, including Naples, Pisa, Ferrara, Florence (*see* FLORENCE, §IV, 6 and fig. 20) and Venice (*see* VENICE, §IV, 3 and fig. 22). S Maria Novella in Florence and SS Giovanni e Paolo in Venice were among the most important foundations in Italy, attracting lavish patronage over several centuries.

The only example of a Gothic conventual church built in Rome is S Maria sopra Minerva, which was built by Pope Zacharias (*reg* 741–52) and passed to the Dominicans in 1266–75. In 1280 it was converted for use as a preaching church to designs by Fra Ristoro de' Campi (*d* 1284) and Fra Sisto di Firenze (*d* 1290). It is a rectangular space with nave and two aisles, transepts, apsidal chancel and lateral chapels on either side. Later the wooden ceiling above the nave was completed and the walls covered with decorative woodwork, stucco and false marble. In the 17th century it was redecorated in the Baroque style, and the aisles were remodelled once more in 1848–55. The interior and chapels contain tombs and monuments of popes, cardinals, bishops and noblemen, as well as the tombs of *St Catherine of Siena* and *Fra Angelico*; through the centuries leading artists and architects were commissioned to remodel the building and to contribute to its splendid decoration.

In the 15th century two opposing movements were current in the Dominican Order: Renaissance humanism and the Observant reform. Both were centred in Florence, where two Dominican foundations reflected the social and cultural situation: S Maria Novella housed the unreformed friars, while S Marco followed the Strict Observance. The convent of S Marco, designed by Michelozzo di Bartolomeo on 15th-century architectural principles, benefited from generous Medici patronage and had several outstanding members, including the energetic preacher GIROLAMO SAVONAROLA and the artist Fra Bartolomeo, who painted a famous portrait of Savonarola (Florence, Mus. S Marco). FRA ANGELICO was undoubtedly the dominant artistic figure there. He was able to combine his professions of friar and painter extremely successfully, and he frequently depicted the iconography of St Dominic, both on a small scale—in altarpiece predellas for example, where he showed narrative scenes—and in frescoes and larger altarpieces, with images of a more contemplative kind. The fine Perugia Triptych (1437; Perugia, G.N. Umbria), for example, has an exquisite portrayal of St Dominic, who appears to be in serene contemplation, while in the cloister fresco of *Christ on the Cross Adored by St Dominic* the saint kneels to embrace the Cross with an expression of mystic devotion. Such artists as Ambrosio da Bindo (*d* 1404), Bartolomeo di Pietro Perugino (*d* 1411) and especially Guillaume de Marcillat continued Fra Angelico's artistic idiom in stained glass. Marcillat was summoned to Rome by Pope Julius II but later settled in Arezzo, where he executed a window (untraced) for the Dominican convent showing *St Dominic Founding the Dominican Order*.

In Milan, the Dominicans moved (1462) from S Eustorgio to a new foundation dedicated to St Dominic, changing its dedication in 1465 to S Maria delle Grazie. The new church, the larger cloister and the refectory were the work of Guiniforte Solari, who planned a basilica with a nave and two aisles separated by granite piers. In 1492 Bramante replaced the existing chancel and transept with a monumental dome flanked by apses and a semi-circular choir. Inside are paintings by Bernardino Butinone (*St Dominic*), Tommaso and Francesco Cazzaniga, Bonifacio and Benedetto Bembo, Paris Bordone and many others. The refectory is celebrated for Leonardo da Vinci's *Last Supper*, while on the opposite wall Giovanni Donato da Montorfano painted a large *Crucifixion* (1495) with many recognizable figures, including St Dominic.

In 15th-century Spain, Ferdinand and Isabella provided royal support for Dominican architecture and art, and the Hispano-Flemish style associated with this reign was crystallized in several royal foundations. The Convento de S Tomás (1483–94) in Ávila, a typically mendicant church and convent, was built by Martín de Solórzano. Beneath the raised altar is the tomb of *Prince John* (*d* 1497), son of Ferdinand and Isabella, carved by Domenico Fancelli. Pedro Berruguete painted the main altarpiece of *St Thomas Aquinas* (*in situ*) and two others of *St Dominic* and *St Peter Martyr* (both Madrid, Prado). At Santa Cruz, Segovia (a foundation built under St Dominic himself in 1218), the Catholic kings commissioned a new church (built 1492), designed by Rodrigo Gil de Hontañón and Juan Guas and similar to S Tomás, Avila. Other examples of this patronage include the Museo National de Escultura Religiosa, Valladolid (for illustration *see* VALLADOLID), and S Cruz la Real, Granada. There the Dominican church and convent were founded immediately after the capture of Granada by Ferdinand and Isabella in 1492. The architecture is typically mendicant, with a single nave and adjoining cloister. In the crossing, opposite the altar of St Dominic, is an altarpiece of the *Virgin of the Rosary* by Blás Moreno (1726–56). In the 16th century, foundations such as S Esteban in Salamanca, commissioned by Juan Alvarez de Toledo (son of the Duque de Alba) and begun in 1524 by Juan de Alava, attracted considerable patronage. The building was continued from 1530 by Fray Martín de Santiago (*d* 1548), who completed the nave and the side chapels, and decorated by numerous artists including José Benito de Churriguera, who made the magnificent retable (*see* RETABLE, fig. 2) commissioned in 1692 by the royal confessor, Pedro de Matilla, a Dominican. Claudio Coello's *Martyrdom of St Stephen* (*in situ*) was painted as the centrepiece of the retable. In 1705 Antonio Palomino painted the *Triumph of the Church through the Dominican Order* for the retrochoir.

The French Revolution marked the beginning of a century of crisis in the Dominican Order, two of whose members nevertheless produced distinguished work. Vincenzo Marchese (*d* 1891) published a book on Dominican painters, sculptors and architects that ran to four editions. Hyacinthe Besson (1816–61) was a French painter and a pupil of Henri Lacordaire (1802–61), with whom he worked to re-establish the Dominican Order in France. His major achievement is a series of wall paintings depicting Roman scenes in the life of St Dominic, in the chapter house of S Sisto Vecchio, Rome.

The Dominican Order was also represented in avant-garde movements in 20th-century religious art, especially in the 1940s in France and in the 1950s in Spain. Marie-Alain Couturier (*d* 1954) was a notable French Dominican painter, art critic and editor (1937–54) of the periodical *L'Art Sacré*. The revival of religious art led to his involvement with such leading artists of the time as Maurice Denis, Picasso, Léger, Bonnard, Matisse and Rouault. Several canvases by Couturier hang in the convent of S Sabina, Rome, and he contributed significantly to the construction of churches at Audincourt and Assy. Henri Matisse, who convalesced after two major operations in the Dominican convent at Vence in France, built the Chapelle du Rosaire in gratitude to the nuns who nursed him. He worked there from 1948 to 1951, designing the stained-glass windows and painting a *St Dominic*, in the form of a black line drawing on white ceramic tiles (all *in situ*).

In Spain, Fray José Manuel de Aguilar was involved in bringing about a revival of the Order. In 1950–60 he founded the Movimiento de Arte Sacro, which was joined by a number of artists and led to the creation of a periodical, *Arte Religioso Actual* (ARA), that disseminated the guiding principles, both artistic and liturgical, of religious art and had a great influence in ecclesiastical circles. During these years, the Dominicans in Spain began a series of pioneering works in avant-garde religious architecture. In 1952 Miguel Fisac Serna designed the Dominican Colegio Apostólico de Arcas Reales, Valladolid, which was awarded a gold medal at an exhibition of religious architecture in Vienna in 1952. In 1957 he designed the church and convent of S Pedro Mártir at Alcobendas, Madrid. In both these convents there are sculptures of St Dominic by Jorge Oteiza and Pablo Serrano. The architecture of the Portuguese Dominican Fray Francisco Coello (*b* 1935) also belongs to this revival. His first work was the sanctuary and college of the Virgen del Camino (1961) for the Dominicans of León, which was decorated by the sculptor Josep María Subirachs and the mosaicist and glass-painter Fray Domingo Iturgaiz (*b* 1932). To celebrate the eighth centenary of the birth of St Dominic, Subirachs executed a monolithic monument (1970) set on the mountainside at Montserrat. It is 3 m high and is composed of eight blocks of travertine, representing the eight centuries of the history of the order. It is also worth mentioning the work of such Dominican artists as the Argentinian Guillermo Butler (*d* 1961), most of whose work is on Dominican subjects; the American sculptor Matthew MacGlynn (1906–77), whose bronze statue of *St Dominic* is in the convent of Madonna dell'Arco, Naples; the Belgian A. D. Charpentier, who executed a complete series of paintings on the *Life of St Dominic* (1987); and the mosaicist and glass-painter Domingo Iturgaiz, who made a series of compositions on the theme of the *Modos de orar de Santo Domingo de Guzmán* for the crypt and chapel of the Dominicans at Caleruega.

BIBLIOGRAPHY

V. Marchese: *Memorie dei più insigni pittori, scultori e architetti domenicani* (Bologna, 1845, rev. 1878)

Jacobus da Voragine: *Legenda aurea: Vulgo historia lombardica dicta* [MS.; 1255–66]; ed. T. Graesse (Dresden, 1846); Eng. trans. and adaptation by G. Ryan and H. Ripperger, 2 vols (London, 1941/*R* 1969)

J. J. Berthier: *Le Tombeau de Saint Dominique* (Paris, 1895)

Monumenta ordinis fratrum praedicatorum historica (Leuven and Rome, 1896–1937)

P. Mandonnet and M. H. Vicaire: *Saint Dominique: L'Idée, l'homme et l'oeuvre* (Paris, 1938)

A. D'Amato: *Le reliquie di S Domenico* (Bologna, 1946)

G. Meersseman: 'L'Architecture dominicaine au XIII siècle: Législation et pratique', *Archv Fratrum Praedicatorum*, xvi (1946), pp. 136–90

G. Kaftal: *St. Dominic in Early Tuscan Painting* (Oxford, 1948)

J. Pope-Hennessy: 'The Arca of St Dominic: A Hypothesis', *Burl. Mag.*, xciii (1951), pp. 347–51

V. D. Carro: *Caleruega, cuna de Santo Domingo*, ii (Madrid, 1955)

M. H. Vicaire: *Histoire de Saint Dominique* (Paris, 1957)

A. D'Amato and V. Alce: *Bologna domenicana* (Bologna, 1961)

S. Bottari: *L'Arca di S Domenico in Bologna* (Bologna, 1964)

W. A. Hinnebusch: *History of the Dominican Order*, 2 vols (New York, 1966–73)

V. Koudelka: *Santo Domingo y Roma*, Albumes Dominicanos, iv (Madrid, 1968)

D. A. Iñiguez and A. E. Pérez Sánchez: *La pintura madrileña: Primer tercio del siglo XVII* (Madrid, 1969)

V. D. Carro: *Domingo de Guzmán: Historia documentada* (Madrid, 1973)

J. Cannon: *Dominican Patronage of the Arts in Central Italy: The Provincia Romana, c. 1220–c.1320* (diss., U. London, Courtauld Inst., 1980)

D. Iturgaiz: 'Iconografía de Santo Domingo de Guzmán en el Beato Angélico', *Cienc. Tomista*, n. 368 (1985), pp. 511–79

G. Bedouelle: *La fuerza de la palabra; Domingo de Guzmán* (Salamanca, 1987)

L. Galmes and T. Gómez Vito: *Santo Domingo de Guzmán: Fuentes para su conocimiento* (Madrid, 1987)

D. Iturgaiz and others: *Retablo de artistas* (Caleruega, 1987)

A. D'Amato: *I domenicani a Bologna: I, 1218–1600* (Bologna, 1989)

D. Hurgaiz: *Caleruega, primer lugar dominicano* (Burgos, 1989)

D. Iturgaiz: *Iconografía de Santo Domingo de Guzmán: La fuerza de la imagen* (Burgos, 1992)

W. Hood: *Fra Angelico at S Marco* (New Haven, 1993)

D. Iturgaiz: 'Iconografía miniada de Santo Domingo de Guzmán', *Archv Dominicano*, xiv (1993), pp. 325–76

DOMINGO ITURGAIZ

Dominican Republic. Country occupying the eastern two-thirds of the Caribbean island of Hispaniola; the western part is occupied by Haiti (see fig. 1). The capital is Santo Domingo, and Spanish is the official language. The population (7.3 million in 1991) is of mixed African, Indian and European descent. It has the highest mountain in the Caribbean, Pico Duarte (3075 metres), but also includes much rich agricultural land with large plantations. Cultivation of sugar-cane began in the 16th century. Its need for a large workforce led to imposition of slavery on the Amerindian population and importation of Africans for forced labour. Ratification of the abolition of slavery took place in 1844. Mining of nickel and textile manufacture are also important, although tourism is the main source of foreign exchange.

I. Introduction. II. Cultures. III. Architecture. IV. Painting, graphic arts and sculpture. V. Patronage and collecting. VI. Art institutions.

I. *Introduction.*

It is the oldest settlement of European origin in America. After its discovery by Christopher Columbus in 1492 it was named Santo Domingo and became the base from which Spain conquered the New World. It was ruled by France (1795–1808) but reverted to Spanish rule until declaring independence in 1821; it was, however, invaded and ruled by Haiti from 1822 until 1844 when it again became independent, adopting a constitution and the name Dominican Republic, but it was re-annexed by Spain in 1861. Four years later it applied unsuccessfully to join the USA, finally settling for independence. Incursions from neighbouring Haiti and economic instability continued. The USA occupied the Republic from 1916 until 1924. Rafael Trujillo became President in 1930 and established a long, ruthless dictatorship until assassination in 1961. The Dominican Republic continues to experience violence and economic hardship.

BIBLIOGRAPHY

D. Suro: *Arte dominicano* (Santo Domingo, 1969)

F. Moya Pons: *Manual de historia dominicana* (Santiago, 1974)

D. de los Santos and V. Peguero: *Visión general de la historia dominicana* (Santiago, 1977)

JANET HENSHALL MOMSEN

II. *Cultures.*

1. AMERINDIAN. The first inhabitants of the region came in three waves of emigration from the vicinity of Venezuela and Guyana. The first group, the Ciboney, were a pre-agricultural and pre-ceramic people, the second—the Arawaks—were farmers and the third—the Caribs—were able navigators and warriors. At the time of the

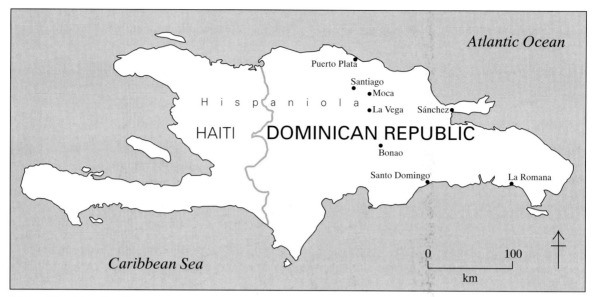

1. Map of Dominican Republic

Spaniards' arrival the island was populated by the Tainos ('good men'), an Arawak people who comprised the largest Amerindian group in the Antilles. Besides fishing and hunting, the Tainos based their collective economy on farming, yucca being their main crop. The communal organization was family-orientated. Their dwellings (*bohíos*) were built by the men, and the women undertook domestic tasks, including making pottery and basketwork. The children helped the adults, their special assignment being to scare birds from the crops; their paternal grandparents looked after their education. Taino culture was based on a polytheistic and animistic religion. Their beliefs and myths, particularly those concerning creation, reveal

2. Taino Amerindian stone trigonolite decorated with a human face, 180×230 mm, 19th century (Santo Domingo, Museo del Hombre Dominicano)

a strong bond with nature and forgetfulness of the people's South American origins. Each of the five tribal chiefs (*caciques*) had a guardian divinity, or *zemi*. Officiating priests and witch doctors, the shamans or *behiques*, were powerful intermediaries between gods and men. Two great ceremonies were an essential part of religious ritual: the *cohoba* in which, under the influence of inhaled hallucinogenic powders, chiefs and *behiques* received guiding messages from the *zemi*; and the *areyto*, a didactic but entertaining celebration that included songs, dances and the recitation of historic events. The Tainos' principal game was *batey*, an outdoor ball-game.

Indigenous arts were linked to farming conditions and domestic needs. The Tainos worked with fibres, wood, shell, bone, clay and stone. The most important stone item was the trigonolite, a three-pointed propitiatory idol (see fig. 2), but axes, pestles and animal yokes were also produced. In ceramics there was a variety of forms and decorative motifs, the Chicoid style being the most outstanding. Articles included bowls, pots, saucepans and anthropomorphic or zoomorphic vases, while decoration comprised dotted lines, incisions and modelling. Figuration alternated with geometric abstraction. Similar forms of expression appear in the rock drawings or petroglyphs found in caves, such as the Cuevas de Bonbón. The naturalistic or schematic figures represented humans (more often male than female), animals (mainly birds and fish), or a combination of animal and human features; among the abstract forms, the triangle was predominant.

In spite of the extermination of the Amerindian population through maltreatment, sickness and killing within 50 years of colonization, their cultural legacy is a valuable one. There has been a vigorous development of archaeology and ethno-anthropological research and there is a growing awareness among the Dominican people of their Amerindian heritage. The influence of Pre-Columbian art has also been significant on such late 20th-century artists as Paul Giudicelli.

BIBLIOGRAPHY

P. Henriquez Ureña: 'Palabras antillanas en el diccionario de la Academia', *Rev. Filol. Esp.*, xxii/2 (1935), pp. 175–86

D. Suro: 'Arte Taino', *Cuad. Hispamer.*, xxxv (1952), pp. 21ff

C. Colón: *Diario de Colón* (Madrid, 1968)

J. Bosch: *De Christobal Colón a Fidel Castro, colección hombres, hechos e ideas* (Madrid, 1970)

J. Arrom: *Mitología y artes prehispánicas de las Antillas* (Mexico City, 1971)

M. Veloz Maggiolo: *Arqueología prehistórica de Santo Domingo* (Singapore, 1972)

F. Maya Pons: *Historia colonial de Santo Domingo* (Santiago, 1977)

D. de los Santos and V. Peguero: *Visión general de la histórica dominicana* (Santiago, 1977)

D. Logan: *Nuevas pictografías en la Isla de Santo Domingo: Las Cuevas de Bonbón* (Santo Domingo, 1978)

C. Magnier: *Santo Domingo* (Montreuil, 1984)

C. Huggins, P. Glinton and B. Smith: *Bahamian Art, 1492–1992* (Nassau, 1992)

L'Art des sculpteurs tainos: Chefs-d'oeuvre des Grandes Antilles précolombiennes (exh. cat., Paris, Petit Pal., 1994)

2. AFRO-CARIBBEAN. It is difficult to evaluate objectively the importance of the African heritage of the Dominican Republic, and the topic remains the subject of debate between the Hispanophile and the Africanist schools of thought. When Columbus arrived in Santo Domingo, slavery was a practice already known in Spain, but the aim of a massive importation of black slaves to Hispaniola did not exist, for the first of them had already been converted to Catholicism when they were brought over from Spain. The cultivation and processing of sugarcane, however, needed a considerable workforce. The Spanish preferred the more submissive Amerindians, but their rapid extinction led to importation of slaves from West Africa, mainly Dahomey, Bantu and Yoruba, peoples brought in legally and as contraband. In the 17th century the sugar industry and slave trade declined simultaneously. The extreme poverty of the Spanish section of the island, however, mitigated the conditions of slavery: the suffering of both master and slave led to closer inter-racial relationships. By the abolition of slavery in the mid-19th century, mainly African cultural features had become mixed through assimilation with Spanish customs. Maltreatment of the black population also destroyed many of their native practices, so rendering difficult the recognition of the original cultural and ethnic groupings. This applies particularly to magical religious rites, for example the funeral ceremonies that commemorated the first anniversary of a death. Indeed, religious syncretism constitutes one of the main elements of Afro-Caribbean culture, expressed in the practice of Vodoun, a form of worship whose myths, rites and gods fuse elements of African myths and magic with Christian theology. Despite its original links with and similarities to Haitian Vodoun (*see* HAITI, §II, 2), Dominican Vodoun has a separate identity. It attributes supreme authority to God, and there are intermediate divinities, known as *loas*, who have supernatural powers but human tastes, vices and passions. These divinities are divided into four groups: the elements of water, fire, earth and air. The major *loas* include the Barón del Cementerio, Belié Belcán, Candelo, Anaísa and Metré Sillí.

Magic and witchcraft are fundamental, and myths, much less important than rites, are closely linked to the benefits or help that the believer seeks through ceremonial practice.

Dominican Vodoun lacks a hierarchical priesthood. The service is conducted by the witch-doctor, who can be male or female and acts as an intermediary between the divinities and the 'clients'. To transmit petitions he goes into a trance or state of being possessed. Aspects of Catholicism are present in Vodoun since all practitioners are baptized and claim to be churchgoers. The principal point of contact is in the devotion to saints, for the Afro-Caribbean *loas* have their counterparts in Catholic holy figures (see fig. 3). There is a domestic form of devotion, the *velaciones*, night vigils to saints, consisting of singing, praying or dancing, and their objects of worship are altars, crucifixes, candles and coloured lithographs of saints, sold in the markets.

Musical groups accompany the overall religious practices and ceremonies; their violent rhythmic body movements, shouts and shrill noises reveal their African origin. The dances, called Holandés, Danois, Fango, Bambula and Jodú, were prohibited in the mid-19th century as 'obscene' and scandalous. A fusion of African and European sources is also present in the national Dominican dance of *merengue*, variants of which exist in Puerto Rico, Cuba and Haiti. African influences also extend to the construction of rural houses, basketry and wooden tools, and even to language: words of African languages, especially Bantu, have entered into the 'creole' Spanish of the country.

3. Jorge Severino: *St Marta La Dominadora*, acrylic and oil on canvas, 1.83×1.02 m, 1978 (Santo Domingo, Museo de Arte Moderno); Afro-Caribbean representation of the saint as a *loa*

BIBLIOGRAPHY

F. Moya Pons: *Manual de historia dominicana* (Santiago, 1974)
H. Tolentino Dipp: *Raza e historia en Santo Domingo* (Santo Domingo, 1974)
C. E. Deive: *Vudu e magia en Santo Domingo* (Santo Domingo, 1979)
F. Lizardo: *Cultura africana en Santo Domingo* (Santo Domingo, 1979)
J. Bosch: *Composición social dominicana* (Santo Domingo, 1986)
F. Franco: *Los negros, los mulatos y la nación dominicana* (Santo Domingo, 1989)
C. Albert: *Mujer y esclavitud en Santo Domingo* (Santo Domingo, 1990)
W. W. Megenney: *África en Santo Domingo: Su herencia lingüística* (Santo Domingo, 1990)
C. Huggins, P. Glinton and B. Smith: *Bahamian Art, 1492–1992* (Nassau, 1992)

III. Architecture.

The characteristic, popular architecture of the Pre-Columbian region consisted of timber-framed, thatch-roofed houses or *bohíos*. This building type survives in rural areas, and the name has been retained. The arrival of the Spaniards led to the introduction of urban planning. Urban settlements on the island multiplied, and the capital, Santo Domingo, founded in 1496 by Columbus's brother, Bartolomé, was laid out on a rectilinear grid on the west bank of the Ozama River. The earliest colonial monuments in Santo Domingo include the hospital of Nicolas de Ovando (Governor, 1502–9), which was in ruins by the late 18th century and partly destroyed in 1929. Its complex plan and elevations are preserved in the Archivo de Indias, Seville. Ovando also commissioned the Torre del Hominaje (1503), built by Cristobal de Tapia, a battlemented structure resembling a medieval keep, commanding the approaches to the Ozama. Work on a new cathedral began in 1521 and was completed in 1538. In 1541 it was dedicated to S María de la Encarnación. It is a sturdy, Gothic cross-vaulted church with lateral chapels and three naves of equal height. The Plateresque-style façade has been attributed to the Spanish architect Rodrigo Gil de Liendo and to Luis de Moya, his master builder from 1531 (see fig. 4). A number of Gothic monastic churches with features of Mudéjar origin were built in the first half of the 16th century but all are partly or wholly ruined. Liendo was also largely responsible for the church of S Francisco

4. Cathedral of S María de la Encarnación, Santo Domingo, 1521–38; façade attributed to Rodrigo Gil de Liendo and Luis de Moya

(1547–69), Santo Domingo, on which the Spanish masons Antón and Alonso Gutiérrez Navarrete probably worked, and which dates from the 1520s. The most important palace was the Alcázar (1510–14) of Almirante Don Diego Colón in Santo Domingo (partly ruined, partly restored). Its unusual plan had two arcaded sides to its square, inner patio and recalls contemporary country mansions in southern Spain. Its design was copied in the Casa de Engombe, Santo Domingo, a little later in the 16th century. By the mid-1530s the Plateresque style was well established, for example the chapel of S Aña (*c.* 1535) in the cathedral.

When the seat of Spanish government in the Caribbean moved to HAVANA, in 1552, Hispaniola became depopulated, and little was built for over two centuries: two notable exceptions, both in Santo Domingo, are the Jesuit church of La Compañía (1714–40), with a forbidding façade recalling the sobriety of Cuban Baroque, and the church of S Bárbara (begun *c.* 1700), with a heavy rectangular tower that overwhelms the façade, rising to an impressive bell-tower storey. British influence began to replace that of Spain, especially in domestic architecture. These buildings mainly comprised single-storey timber-framed and weatherboarded houses with Georgian-style sash-windows, often set back from the street and incorporating a covered public walkway in the structure. Decorative bracket-inserts at the heads of timber columns were fretted, often imitating *mudéjar* arch profiles, and fretwork fascias and panels abounded; the style became eclectic as the century progressed and imported cast- and wrought-iron elements such as columns and balustrades increasingly became available. There are notable examples of such features in buildings at Puerto Plata, Santiago, La Vega, Moca and La Romana; at Sánchez, there is a Victorian Gothic Revival, timber-framed and corrugated iron-clad church (*c.* 1890) with an ogee cupola above a tiny bell-tower. Although some vernacular idioms still persist in rural areas, this style was largely superseded when the USA assumed direct rule. The Americans introduced simple rectilinear buildings in brick and reinforced concrete and brought framed multi-storey buildings to Santo Domingo before the end of the 1920s; later examples of these show touches of Art Deco.

In 1930, at the beginning of the dictatorship of Leónidas Trujillo Molina, a hurricane damaged buildings in Santo Domingo and elsewhere. In the same year Dominican architects trained in Europe and the USA returned home. The most important included Guillermo González and José Antonio Caro Alvarez. González's five-storey apartment building (1937) in the Avenida Pasteur, Santo Domingo, has distinct overtones of Le Corbusier's work and was the first building to show the influence of the European Modern Movement. A number of public buildings were constructed during the Trujillo regime, including university buildings, the Palacio Nacional, Palacio de Bellas Artes and various works for the Feria de la Paz (1955), but real growth took place upon the country's stabilization in the mid-1960s. An international pluralism developed during the 1970s, for example the Museo del Hombre Dominicano (see fig. 5), Plaza de la Cultura, by Caro Alvarez (with José A. Caro Ginebra Carbonell and Danilo Caro Ginebra) and the Banco Central by Rafael Calventi, both in Santo Domingo. The headquarters of the Asociación de Ahorros y Prestamos (1978) by William Reid Cabral is a square glass building with an external structure derivative of Oscar Niemeyer's Brasília Baroque, while the Galerias Comerciales (1979) by Eduardo Selman is a five-storey neo-Brutalist building. An active group of younger Postmodernist architects included Oscar Imbert, Gustave Moré, Marcelo Albuquerque and, most notably, Plácido Piña. Piña's Banco Hipotecaria Domenicano (1980), Santo Domingo, and Casa Salene ('El Ediculo') at San Pedro Marcoris (1983), are sophisticated examples of an appropriate cultural coding carefully related to form and function. The vast Columbus Lighthouse, completed in 1992 for the 500th anniversary of Columbus's arrival, was designed by the British architect John Lea Gleave, whose design was chosen in an international competition (1928–30) sponsored by the Pan-American Union.

BIBLIOGRAPHY

A. Kelsey: *Program and Rules for the Competition to Select an Architect for the Monumental Lighthouse in the Dominican Republic to the Memory of Christopher Columbus* (Washington, DC, 1928)

D. Angulo Iñiguez, E. Marco Dorta and M. J. Buschiazzo: *Historia del arte hispano-americano*, 3 vols (Barcelona, 1945–56), i, pp. 79–120; iii, pp. 164–5

E. W. Palm: *Arquitectura y arte colonial en Santo Domingo* (Santo Domingo, 1974)

M. Ugarte: *Monumentos coloniales: Colección Museo de las Casas Reales* (San Sebastián, 1978)

Codia, lvi (1978) [special issue marking the Evento Arquitectura]

L. Alemar: *La ciudad de Santo Domingo* (Santo Domingo, 1980)

R. Segre, ed.: *Latin America in its Architecture* (New York, 1981)

R. Calventi: *Arquitectura contemporánea dominicana/Contemporary Dominican Architecture* (Santo Domingo, 1986) [bilingual text]

E. Pérez Hontas Carimos: *Monumentos y sitas del Gran Caribe/Monuments and Sites of the Greater Caribbean* (Santo Domingo, 1989) [bilingual text]

J. F. Liernur: *America latina: Architettura, gli ultimi vent'anni* (Milan, 1990), pp. 102–7

A. Gardinier: 'Bâtiment phare', *D'architectures*, xxiv (1992), p. 36

C. Huggins, P. Glinton and B. Smith: *Bahamian Art, 1492–1992* (Nassau, 1992)

IV. Painting, graphic arts and sculpture.

Despite the existence of a sophisticated Amerindian art (*see* §II, 1 above), Dominican art did not begin to develop a national style until after Independence. This was strongly influenced by visiting European artists, such as Juan Fernández Corredor, who arrived from Madrid in 1883. From this date until 1900 all the main 19th-century European trends—Neo-classicism, Romanticism, Impressionism—mixed and fused to create a Dominican style. The first large exhibition in Santo Domingo, the Salón Artístico of 1890, comprised landscape and portrait paintings and copies of famous works.

The first Dominican painter, printmaker and caricaturist was Domingo Echavarría (*d* 1849); other pioneers included Abelardo Rodríguez Urbaneta (1870–1933), an outstanding painter, sculptor, photographer and musician. Typical subjects included portraits, landscapes, imaginary historical scenes and patriotic allegories; between 1920 and 1940 figure painting gained popularity. Realism and neo-Impressionism became the dominant trends; abstract art remained unknown. The work of the modern Dominican artists Yoryi Morel (1909–78) and Jaime Colsón (1901–75) exemplifies its two main styles. Morel's work was of a vernacular nature—rustic scenes, fiestas and rituals and tropical bucolic landscapes, orchestrated with

5. Museo del Hombre Dominicano, Plaza de la Cultura, Santo Domingo, 1972–6, by José Antonio Caro Alvarez, José A. Caro Ginebra and Danilo Caro Ginebra

impressionistic touches—while Colsón's drew its inspiration from the Ecole de Paris, drawing on Cubism or a Neo-classicism charged with a metaphysical or mythological message. The first important Dominican woman artist was Celeste Woss y Gil (1890–1985), who introduced modernist treatment of the nude to Dominican painting. Another important figure was Darío Suro (*b* 1918).

The 1940s were a decisive decade for Dominican art due to an influx of European painters and sculptors fleeing totalitarian regimes. Paradoxically, they were welcomed by the dictator Rafael Trujillo, who wished to cultivate a liberal image. Some of these artists were just passing through; others remained, including the German Georg Hausdorf (1894–1959), the Spanish painters José Vela Zanetti (*b* 1913) and Josep Gausachs (1889–1958) and the Spanish sculptor Manolo Pascual. Deeply moved by a 'new world', these artists gave free rein to their inspiration to create some of their best work. This, and their teaching, made a significant contribution to the development of Dominican art. Gilberto Hernández Ortega, Eligio Pichardo and Paul Giudicelli (see fig. 6) were among the first graduates of the Escuela Nacional de Bellas Artes (see §VI below).

The dominant style in painting during the 1950s and 1960s was Expressionism, sometimes incorporating elements of realism, magic or fantasy. Works were largely figurative, with occasional examples of abstraction; Afro-Caribbean features appeared, while European stylistic influences persisted. Colours were strong, brushstrokes forceful, texture generous and form a controlled baroque. Notable figures of the period included Guillo Pérez, Fernando Peña Defillo, Silvano Lora, Ada Balcácer, Domingo Liz and Mariano Eckert. Dominican sculpture also assumed a national character distinguished by direct carving, predominantly in precious woods, of massive scale in elongated, totemic forms. Outstanding sculptors included Antonio Prats-Véntos, Luichy Martínez-Richiez and Gaspar Mario Cruz. The 1960s were marked by struggles for the restoration of democracy. Nationalist art flourished, characterized by militant and passionate works of figurative Expressionism. Painters included Cándido Bidó, Elsa

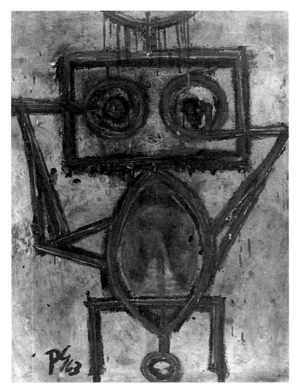

6. Paul Giudicelli: *Meditation on the Armour of a Soldier*, mixed media on canvas, 1.50×1.25 m, 1963 (Santo Domingo, Museo de Arte Moderno)

Núñez, Ramón Oviedo, José Rincón Mora, José Cestero, Asdrúbal Domínguez and Jorge Severino.

During the 1970s the diverse styles that emerged as a result of developing international contacts included Pop art, Photorealism and Surrealism; abstraction continued to lag behind. Sculpture did not make great advances; the only noteworthy sculptors were José Ramón Rotellini, Ramiro Matos and Soucy de Pellerano. Printmaking, which had been retarded by an attitude that scorned the multiple original work, was developed by Miki Vicioso, Rosa Tavárez and Carlos Sangiovanni. Although a number of artists left the country, including Vicente Pimentel, Alonso Cuevas, Manuel Montilla and Aurelio Grisanty, others, such as Iván Tovar and Martínez-Richiez, returned. Other artists active at this time included Geo Ripley, heading the avant-garde, Alberto Bass, a Social Realist, Guadalupe, who drew on the essence of Pre-Columbian art and Danicel, who attempted a symbiosis between the history of art and Afro-Caribbean research. The pursuit of form went beyond thematic commitment and individual values outweighed collective interests. On the theoretical side, art criticism developed.

In the 1980s, parallel to the general population explosion, there was a rise in the number of young artists. Those under the age of 30 favoured abstraction, often mixed with figurative art, neo-Surrealism and neo-Expressionism and were more interested in working on paper through drawings and prints. In sculpture permanent installations were encouraged. International recognition began to grow for such artists as Radhamés Mejía, Víctor Ulloa, Tony Capellán and Jesús Desangles.

BIBLIOGRAPHY
M. Valldeperes: *El arte de nuestro tiempo* (Ciudad Trujillo, 1957)
D. Suro: *Arte dominicano* (Santo Domingo, 1969)
E. Rodriguez Demorizi: *Pintura y escultura en Santo Domingo* (1972)
M. de Tolentino: 'Arte dominicano', *Listín Diario* (1972–90) [regular contributions]
D. de los Santos: *La pintura en la sociedad dominicana* (Santiago, 1978)
J. Miller: *Historia de la pintura dominicana* (Santo Domingo, 1979)
M. de Tolentino: *Pintores dominicanos jóvenes para las Américas* (Santo Domingo, 1986)
——: 'El expresionismo en la pintura dominicana', *100 años de pintura dominicana* (Santo Domingo, 1989)
C. Huggins, P. Glinton and B. Smith: *Bahamian Art, 1492–1992* (Nassau, 1992)

V. Patronage and collecting.

Commissions and money to support the arts became most significant in the second half of the 20th century. In 1942 the national Biennales, held in Santo Domingo, were established and were held regularly until 1960, then resumed in 1972. In the period after 1961 the strength of national art life depended largely on institutional and financial backing by private companies, including events organized by the official cultural sector. This was accompanied by a flourishing of exhibitions. Private enterprise favoured art that contributed to the community and educational work, including support of group and individual exhibitions, publications and publicity. The companies who offered this support included those producing rum, drinks and cigarettes (Brugal, Bermúdez, Barcelo, E. León Jiménes) and several multinationals (the Dominican Telephone Company, Falconbridge). The E. León Jiménes Art Competition was founded in 1964 as a national contest and has promoted young achievements in sculpture, painting and drawing. Banks and financial institutions also offered patronage. The State made tax reductions for patronage in the context of 'aid for institutions with non-profit making aims'.

The Museo de Arte Moderno in Santo Domingo (formerly Galería de Arte Moderno; founded 1976) has the largest collection of art due to its official character and its donations. There are, however, a considerable number of institutions and individuals that have systematically acquired paintings and sculptures. These include the Banco Central, the Universidad Autónoma de Santo Domingo and the *voluntariado* of the Museo de las Casas Reales. Financial institutions have also been noteworthy for the size of their national collections: the Banco Popular, Bancredito, Nacional de Vivienda and others. In the late 20th century the number of private collectors also increased. The bulk of collections comprised paintings and works of confirmed value, with little interest in works on paper. High, rising prices led to a shift in the social class of collectors, moving from the middle classes and 'intellectuals', who were the first collectors in Santo Domingo, to economically powerful sectors.

An art market as such was non-existent until the mid-20th century but reached its peak during the 1980s when galleries multiplied. Cultural centres and museums also sold art works during temporary exhibitions. The commercial art market was concentrated in Santo Domingo with outlets in tourist centres throughout the country.

BIBLIOGRAPHY

R. Herrera Cabral: 'Protección al arte', *Listín Diario* (25 March 1966)
——: 'Actividades culturales', *Listín Diario* (29 Oct 1966)
D. de los Santos: *La pintura en la sociedad dominicana* (Santiago, 1978)
M. de Tolentino: 'Necesidades del arte y los artistas dominicanos', *Listín Diario* (21 Aug 1978)
A. Schwartz: *Valorización del arte* (Santo Domingo, 1979)
M. de Tolentino: 'Un asunto discutido: El precio de las obras de arte', *Listín Diario* (11–12 July 1980)
Fundación Brugal: *Estatutos* (Santo Domingo, 1987)
M. de Tolentino: 'El estado y la condición del artista', *Listín Diario* (18 Aug 1989)
Reglamento, XIII Concurso E. León Jiménes (Santiago, 1989)
M. Loli de Severino: *La inversión en el arte* (Santo Domingo, 1991)
C. Huggins, P. Glinton and B. Smith: *Bahamian Art, 1492–1992* (Nassau, 1992)
D. de los Santos: *Concurso de arte Eduardo León Jiménes: 25 años de historia* (Santo Domingo, 1993)

VI. Art institutions.

The Dominican Republic has a surprising number and diversity of art institutions, which are concentrated in Santo Domingo in the cultural Plaza de la Cultura Juan Pablo Duarte complex. The first Museo Nacional was established in 1927 as the repository of objects of varying value, including objets d'art, archaeological and historical items. In 1942 the museum was completely modernized, and the collection was transferred under the supervision of the newly created Dirección General de Bellas Artes. A museum dedicated exclusively to art dates from 1943 when the Galería de Bellas Artes opened. According to the original statute it was to preserve and exhibit 'works belonging to the government which form the nucleus of the "Museum of Modern Art" which this gallery aspires to become'. It also organized individual and group national and international exhibitions. When the Palacio de Bellas Artes was built in 1956, sculptures, paintings and drawings were transferred there. In 1963 the Galería Nacional de Bellas Artes had nine sumptuous rooms, covering two storeys, containing works of Dominican and exiled European artists, for the most part oil paintings. The small collection had its source in Biennale awards and donations. The first museum guide was published in 1963 by the Director Aida Cartagena Portalatín. In 1976 the collection was transferred to the new Galería de Arte Moderno (now Museo de Arte Moderno), which opened in December in a building of three storeys and a basement designed by José Miniño. Except for one of the rooms, all spaces are open and interlinked, making it a flexible museum space. It includes an auditorium, children's workshop, library and printshop. The predominantly national collection comprises more than 700 sculptures, paintings, drawings, prints and photographs. Outside Santo Domingo there is a museum for the E. León Jiménes Art Collection in Santiago, and a single rural museum in Ríos de Neybo, created by Silvano Lora.

Although the first formal, official, professional art education was offered from 1942 when the Escuela Nacional de Bellas Artes was established in Santo Domingo, drawing and painting were taught in the capital from 1885, including classes by the Spanish painter Juan Fernández Corredor. There is also evidence of a public municipal school of drawing in 1890. In Santo Domingo in 1908 the versatile Abelardo Rodríguez Urbaneta established his Academia de Dibujo, Pintura y Escultura, of which he was director until 1933. Other painters who had their own academies include García Godoy and Yoryi Morel in the provinces and Celeste Woss y Gil in the capital. Immigrant European artists made up an important element of the initial professional body of the Escuela Nacional when it was founded. The first director was the Spanish sculptor Manolo Pascual, and subjects taught included life painting, colour, modelling, perspective, landscape, anatomy, applied arts and prints, and theory and history of fine arts. In three years of study and one postgraduate year the school prepared students for the title of Professore de Dibujo, the only degree that it awarded. The faculty, mostly graduates of the school, decided to reform the programme in 1978, but this was not realized until 1989. Three years of general study were offered, followed by two years of specialization in painting, sculpture and drawing. At university level, professional technical training was offered at the Universidad Autónoma de Santo Domingo and APEC Escuela de Arte. In 1975 the Colegio Dominicano de Artistas Plastico opened in Santo Domingo. In the 1990s the Universidad Pedro Henríquez Ureña opened an Escuela de Artes Plasticas with the ultimate aim of awarding the degree of Licentiate in Art. Under the overall direction of the Dirección General de Bellas Artes five provincial schools offered a basic education but were in financial difficulties in the late 20th century. At this time the Escuela Cándida Bidó in Bonao was created. A branch of the Parsons School, the Escuela de Arte Diseño was in operation in Altos de Chavón (La Romana) with an international orientation.

BIBLIOGRAPHY

R. Diaz Niese: 'Un lustro de esfuerzo artístico', *Cuad. Dominicanos Cult.*, xxiii/11 (1945)
A. Cartagena Portalatín: *Galería de Bellas Artes: Catálogo general* (Santo Domingo, 1963)
E. Rodriguez Demorizi: *Pintura y escultura en Santo Domingo* (Santo Domingo, 1972)
M. de Tolentino: 'La Escuela de Bellas Artes se cuestiona', *Listín Diario* (1, 5 and 7 Feb 1981)
D. Henríquez: 'Reseña de la plástica dominicana', *Arte contemporáneo dominicano*, ed. G. Nader (Santo Domingo, 1984)
S. Pérez de Ruiz: *Obras integradas a la Galería de Arte Moderno desde 1978 hasta 1984* (Santo Domingo, 1984)
M. de Tolentino: 'Lo que esperamos de la GAM', *Listín Diario* (18 Dec 1988)

MARIANNE DE TOLENTINO

Dominici, Bernardo de (*b* Naples, 13 Dec 1683; *d* Naples, 30 April 1759). Italian art historian and painter. He was the son of a Maltese painter, Raimondo de Dominici (1645–1705). His mother, Camilla Tartaglione, was from Naples. He lived for many years in the household in Naples of Niccolò Gaetani and Aurora Sanseverino, the Duca and Duchessa di Laurenzano, working for the latter, in his own words, 'in qualità di Pittor di Paesi, Marine e Bambocciate' ('as a painter of landscapes, seascapes and scenes of everyday life'). No examples of his work have yet been identified; the only record of specific paintings is in the 1741 post-mortem inventory of Niccolò Gaetani's collection, where 11 small landscapes are listed. De Dominici did not write on his own life and made only occasional written references to his painting, such as that he made landscapes in the manner of Joachim Franz Beich and learnt to paint nocturnal marine pictures from the Flemish artist Paul Ganses. Before 1721 he began to compile biographical notices on painters who had been close to his father (e.g. Mattia Preti and Luca Giordano) or were well known to himself (Francesco Solimena), in collaboration with Francesco Saverio Baldinucci (1663–1738). His first published work, a life of Giordano, appeared in the 1728 edition of Bellori's *Le vite de' pittori, scultori ed architetti moderni* and was reprinted, as a book with some additions, in Naples in 1729.

The Laurenzano household was one of the gathering places for the Neapolitan branch of the Accademia dell'Arcadia, a literary and philosophical society. Thus de Dominici met such distinguished scholars as Giovanni Battista Vico, the archaeologist Francesco Valletta (1680–1760) and the classicist Matteo Egizio (1674–1746), all of whom assisted him by giving advice and by facilitating his access to information when he was preparing his major work, the *Vite de' pittori, scultori ed architetti napoletani*. This, published in three volumes between 1742 and 1745, was to some extent a product of the Accademia; for instance de Dominici's reappraisal of high medieval art was clearly motivated by the parallel interests of Arcadian literary criticism.

The *Vite* presents the history of art in Naples, from its mythic origins in late antiquity up to the mid-18th century, as a progressive development culminating in the work of Solimena. The author's critical stance was influenced by Bellori's ideas and by the opinions of major artists such as Preti, Giordano, Paolo De Matteis and Solimena. Thus he strongly advocated decorum in the representation of sacred history and expressed a preference for idealized figures (as in the art of Annibale Carracci and Guido Reni) as opposed to the naturalistic effects achieved by Caravaggio and his followers. The material for the *Vite* was drawn from oral tradition, artists' memoirs, local guide books, histories and many non-Neapolitan sources. There was little accurate information available for the period before the 16th century, hence the book is generally unreliable with regard to ancient, medieval and early Renaissance artists. Within ten years of his death de Dominici was accused of invention and in the late 19th century condemned as wholly unreliable ('il Falsario': the falsifier). This attitude has been revised after new research on the later periods and especially on Solimena (Bologna), and the *Vite* is now regarded as indispensable for any study of 17th- and 18th-century art in Naples. Scholars are gradually exploiting the information the book provides on the history of art collecting, art restoration, theatre and music. The claim that de Dominici invented manuscript sources has also been questioned (Willette, 1986). Nevertheless, the *Vite* needs to be viewed critically. The account of the early Neapolitan school is an euhemeristic interpretation of the fragmentary history of artists and monuments that came down to de Dominici largely in the form of stories. The biographies of 16th- and 17th-century artists contain some surprising errors, such as wrong (though precisely given) birth and death dates and inexplicable affirmations, such as that Giovanni Battista Caracciolo was a solitary bachelor, whereas in fact he was married and had ten children.

WRITINGS

Notizie della vita dell'ecc.mo pittore Luca Giordano Napoletano and *Notizie della vita del cav. D. Luca Giordano* (Florence, Bib. N., cod. II.II.110,

fols 90*r*–105*v* and 112*r*–123*v* respectively); ed. B. Santi in *Zibaldone baldinucciano* (Florence, 1980–81), i, pp. 349–72, 375–90 [two other MSS, pp. 373–4, 391–2, are attributed to de Dominici in error]

'Vita del Cavaliere D. Luca Giordano pittore napoletano', in G. P. Bellori: *Le vite de' pittori, scultori ed architetti moderni* (Rome, 1672, 2/1728), pp. 304–94; rev. as book (Naples, 1729)

Vite de' pittori, scultori ed architetti napoletani, 3 vols (Naples, 1742–5/*R* Bologna, 1979, 2/1840–46) [the 1979 reprint was made from a flawed example of the 1742–5 prtg]

BIBLIOGRAPHY

DBI; Thieme–Becker

F. S. Baldinucci: *Vita del pittore Luca Giordano . . .* (MS. *c.* 1713–21); ed. B. Santi in *Zibaldone baldinucciano* (Florence, 1980–81), ii, p. 415 [on date of MS. see Willette (1986), p. 265, n. 38]

O. Giannone: *Giunte sulle 'Vite de' pittori napoletani* (MS., before 1768–73); ed. O. Morisani (Naples, 1941)

A. Comolli: *Bibliografia storico-critica dell'architettura civile ed arti subalterne* (Rome, 1788–92) ii, pp. 244–53

N. F. Faraglia: 'Le memorie degli artisti napoletani pubblicate da Bernardo De Dominici', *Archv Stor. Prov. Napoletane*, vii (1882), pp. 329–64; viii (1883), pp. 83–110, 259–86

B. Croce: 'Sommario critico della storia dell'arte nel napoletano I: Il Falsario', *Napoli Nob.*, i (1892), pp. 122–6, 140–44; also in *Aneddoti di varia letteratura* (Bari, 1942, rev. 2/1953–4), ii, pp. 323–44 [with additions]

G. Ceci: 'Il primo critico del De Dominici', *Archv Stor. Prov. Napoletane*, xxxiii (1908), pp. 618–38; also as *La storia dell'arte napoletana di Onofrio Giannone* (Naples, 1909) [illus.]

U. Prota Giurleo: 'Notizie su Massimo Stanzione e sul presunto suo manoscritto falsificato dal De Dominici', *Napoli Riv. Mun.*, lxxxi/11 (1955), pp. 17–32

F. Bologna: *Francesco Solimena* (Naples, 1958), pp. 157–61, 171, 209–10

G. Previtali: *La fortuna dei primitivi: Dal Vasari ai neoclassici* (Turin, 1964), pp. 64–9

L. Grassi: *Teorici e storia della critica d'arte: Il settecento in Italia* (Rome, 1979), pp. 56–60

T. Willette: 'Bernardo De Dominici e le *Vite de' pittori, scultori ed architetti napoletani*: Contributo alla riabilitazione di una fonte', *Ricerche sul '600 napoletano* (Milan, 1986), pp. 253–71

J. Colton: 'The Fall and Rise of Bernardo De Dominici', *A Taste for Angels: Neapolitan Painting in North America, 1650–1750* (exh. cat., New Haven, CT, Yale U. A.G., 1987), pp. 57–68

M. Pasculli Ferrara: 'Les Peintres napolitains en France au XVIIe siècle (d'après les *Vite* de De Dominici)', *Seicento: La Peinture italienne du XVIIe siècle et la France* (Paris, 1990), pp. 52–79

T. Willette: 'Bernardo De Dominici e la sua *Vita* di Stanzione', in S. Schütze and T. Willette: *Massimo Stanzione* (Naples, 1992), pp. 153–86

THOMAS WILLETTE

Dominique Florentin. *See* BARBIERE, DOMENICO DEL.

Domitian [Titus Flavius Domitianus] (*b* Rome, 24 Oct AD 51; *reg* AD 81–96; *d* Rome, 18 Sept AD 96). Roman emperor and patron, the second son of Vespasian and the brother of Titus, his predecessor. He began the Romanization of Britain and improved the organization of the border provinces. He tried to establish an absolute monarchy but was killed in a plot organized by members of his own family. A great movement for urban renewal took place in his reign. The monumental area of the Campus Martius, badly damaged by a fire in AD 80, was rebuilt and enlarged with the erection of the Porticus Divorum (a portico containing two small temples dedicated to the deified Vespasian and Titus). The odeum was built, as well as the stadium for the Ludi Capitolini, called the Circus Agonalis or Stadium Domitiani (before AD 86); it is now the Piazza Navona. The Temple of Jupiter Optimus Maximus on the Capitol was rebuilt, that of the Deified Vespasian completed (and Titus added to its dedication), and that of the Dii Consentes erected in the Forum Romanum. The Palatine was totally reconstructed, and a large part of it became the Flavian Palace (*see* ROME, §V, 2). This was to remain the official residence of the emperor until late antiquity. The Via Sacra was transformed, and at its head the Arch of Titus was erected, perhaps for use as a tomb (AD 81; *see* TRIUMPHAL ARCH, §1 and fig. 1). Near the Colosseum, which was also completed (*see* ROME, §V, 6), rose a monumental fountain, the Meta Sudans. The area between the Forum Augustum and the Templum Pacis was developed with the construction of the Forum Transitorium (ded. AD 97 by Nerva), at the end of which rose the Temple of Minerva (*see* ROME, §V, 2).

BIBLIOGRAPHY

P. H. von Blanckenhagen: *Flavische Architektur und ihre Dekoration: Untersucht am Nervaforum* (Berlin, 1940)

A. M. Colini: *Stadium Domitiani* (Rome, 1943)

H. Finsen: 'La Résidence de Domitien sur le Palatin', *Anlct. Romana Inst. Dan.*, suppl. v (Rome, 1969)

LUCA LEONCINI

Domnick. German collectors. After studying medicine, Ottomar Domnick (*b* Greifswald, 20 April 1907; *d* Tübingen, 14 June 1989) specialized in neurology and psychiatry. In 1938 he settled in Stuttgart and married Greta Gerhardt (*b* Posen, 15 Oct 1909), also a doctor, with whom he built up his collection after the war. He was mainly interested in abstract painting, committing himself to its cause in a variety of ways: in 1947 he set up a series of lectures in his consulting rooms that he published under the title *Die schöpferischen Kräfte in der abstrakten Malerei: Ein Zyklus* (1947); in 1948 he organized a travelling exhibition of modern French art in West German cities; and in 1950 came the short film for the cinema *Neue Kunst—Neues Sehen*, which was an introduction to non-objective painting.

The Domnicks' collection included a preponderance of works by Fritz Winter, Hans Hartung, Willi Baumeister (about whose work Ottomar Domnick made a documentary film for the cinema in 1954) and many early pictures by Arnulf Rainer. Ottomar Domnick's involvement in further experimental film work, for example *Jonas* (1957), which shows modern man isolated in the city, led to a lull in new picture purchases. In 1952 the Staatsgalerie in Stuttgart accepted the Domnick collection and housed it for a considerable time, but a plan for them to take it over permanently came to nothing. Instead, the Domnicks had a private museum built in 1966–7 at Nürtingen, near Stuttgart, that also served as their home, and where they staged an international cycle of 12 cello concerts (1973–80). From 1977 they added large-scale metal sculptures to the collection, again exclusively abstract, among them works by Alf Lechner, Volkmar Haase, Bernhard Luginbühl and Max Schmitz; these were displayed in a specially laid-out park. In 1984 Ottomar provided sponsorship for prizes to encourage young film directors and cellists. The museum building and collection are to be left to the federal state of Baden-Württemberg on condition that they be preserved as an entity as a document of their period.

WRITINGS

O. Domnick, M. Rousseau and J. J. Sweeney: *Hans Hartung* (Stuttgart, n.d.)

O. Domnick: *Die schöpferischen Kräfte in der abstrakten Malerei: Ein Zyklus* (Bergen, 1947)

——: *Hauptweg und Nebenwege: Psychiatrie, Kunst, Film in meinem Leben* (Hamburg, 1977) [autobiography]

O. Domnick and G. Domnick: *Die Sammlung Domnick: Eine Dokumentation* (Stuttgart, 1982)

ACHIM SOMMER

Domogatsky, Vladimir (Nikolayevich) (*b* Odessa, 2 May 1876; *d* Moscow, 30 March 1939). Russian sculptor. Before studying law at Moscow University (1897–1902), he received lessons in sculpture from Sergey Volnukhin (1859–1921); these proved decisive in his choice of career. His early work, dominated by human and animal figure studies, is impressionistic and clearly influenced by Paolo Trubetskoy, Auguste Rodin and Rembrandt Bugatti, for example *Boy in a Fur Coat* (bronze, 1904) and *Boy on a Horse* (plaster, 1904; both Moscow, Tret'yakov Gal.). Around 1913, however, after several stays in Paris and two years teaching at the Stroganov Institute, Moscow (1908–10), Domogatsky began to concentrate on working in marble and henceforth his oeuvre is dominated by portrait busts and reliefs of his contemporaries and of great cultural figures of the past (e.g. *Vladimir Solov'yov*, marble, 1915; *Michelangelo*, marble, 1917; both Moscow, Tret'yakov Gal.). In these he attempted psychological penetration with a generalized modelling of form. After the 1917 Revolution, Domogatsky participated in Lenin's Plan of Monumental Propaganda, for which he created a heroic figure of *Byron* (plaster, 1918–19; St Petersburg, Rus. Mus.). He became chairman of the sculpture section of GAKhN, the State Academy of Artistic Sciences (1922–30); head of the Tret'yakov Gallery's sculpture section (1923–5); president of the Society of Russian Sculptors (1926–8); and professor and dean of the sculpture faculty at the Moscow Institute of Fine Art (1937–9). It was in these roles that his influence was most lasting. He continued to work on portraiture, concentrating on leading Russian and Soviet figures, as well as turning his attention to nude studies and more idealized depictions of Soviet life on the collective farm or in the sports arena. He also combined his practical work with research, studying the history and theory of sculpture, restoration and the analysis of sculpture technology.

WRITINGS

Teoreticheskiye raboty, issledovaniya, stat'i, pis'ma khudozhnika [Theoretical works, research articles, letters of the artist] (Moscow, 1984)

BIBLIOGRAPHY

B. N. Ternovets: 'Tvorchestvo V. N. Domogatskogo' [The creative work of V. N. Domogatsky], *Iskusstvo* (1935), no. 1, pp. 55–83

A. V. Bakushinsky: *V. N. Domogatsky* (Moscow, 1936)

A. V. Paramonov: *Vladimir Nikolayevich Domogatsky* (Moscow, 1957)

Skul'ptura i risunki skul'ptorov kontsa XIX–nachala XX veka [The sculpture and drawings of sculptors of the end of the 19th century and beginning of the 20th] (exh. cat., ed. M. Kalpakchi; Moscow, Tret'yakov Gal., 1977), pp. 387–404

JEREMY HOWARD

Domon, Ken (*b* Sakata, 25 Oct 1909; *d* 1990). Japanese photographer. He wanted to be a painter but in 1933, feeling his talent to be limited, he became a technician in the Kōtarō Miyauchi Photography Studio in Tokyo, where he studied the techniques of portrait photography. In 1935 he joined the staff of the Nippon Kōbō ('Japan studio') agency, headed by Yōnosuke Natori, and took photographs for *Nippon*, a magazine designed to provide an introduction to Japanese culture for foreigners. In 1939 he left and began to photograph examples of traditional

Japanese culture, such as *bunraku* ('puppet theatre') and the Buddhist temple Murōji near Nara. At the same time he began to take portraits of cultural figures such as painters, writers and musicians. He received the first *ARS* photography cultural award in 1943. From 1950 he became a judge of the monthly contest in the photography magazine *Camera* (Tokyo) and his advocacy of 'realism photography' was very influential on amateur photographers. His method of documenting the contradictions of society as directly as possible was perfected in the two collections *Hiroshima* (Tokyo, 1958) and *Chikuho no kodomotachi* ('The children of Chikuho'; Tokyo, 1960). From the 1960s he concentrated on photographing temple architecture and Buddhist images; these works are collected in the series *Koji junrei* ('Old temple pilgrimage'; 5 vols, Tokyo, 1963–75). In 1983 the Domon Ken Memorial Museum was founded in Sakata to commemorate his achievements.

Contemp. Phots
BIBLIOGRAPHY
New Japanese Photography (exh. cat. by J. Szarkowski and S. Yamagishi, New York, MOMA, 1974), pp. 18–27
Japanese Photography Today and its Origins (exh. cat. by A. Colombo and I. Donisello; Bologna, Gal. A. Mod.: Milan, Pal. Reale; Brussels, Pal. B.-A.; London, ICA; 1979), pp. 63, 68

KŌHTARŌ IIZAWA

Dompé, Hernán (*b* Buenos Aires, 24 July 1946). Argentine sculptor. He studied at the Escuela Nacional de Bellas Artes "Manuel Belgrano" and the Escuela Nacional de Bellas Artes "Prilidiano Pueyrredon". Taking as his starting-point forms associated with Inca, Aztec and Maya civilization as experienced by him in journeys through Peru and Mexico—encompassing nature and architecture as well as pieces made of clay—Dompé treated his sources as catalysts in his pursuit of a regional identity, rather than as models with a supposed universal validity. Synthesizing in this way the values of a humanistic sculpture into a form of modern discourse and using mixed techniques including modelling, he transmuted objective reality into the material presence of marble or sedimentary rock elaborated with the most refined of traditional techniques. Giving preference to symbolic values (e.g. *Totem*, 197×0.51×0.24 m, 1983; wood and iron version, Buenos Aires, Mus. N. B.A.), Dompé thus stressed a contextual reading of his works that transcends the specific time and place of its production.

BIBLIOGRAPHY
J. Glusberg: *Materialización de una perspectiva regional* (in preparation)

JORGE GLUSBERG

Domus. Roman house (*see* ROME, ANCIENT, fig. 8).

Donaldson, T(homas) L(everton) (*b* London, 17 Oct 1795; *d* London, 1 Aug 1885). English architect, archaeologist and teacher. He was the son of an architect, James Donaldson (*c.* 1756–1843), and great-nephew of Thomas Leverton. Trained in his father's office and at the Royal Academy, London, Donaldson travelled in Italy, Greece and Asia Minor from 1818 to 1823 and on his return set up in practice. His first sizeable commission (won in competition) was for the church of the Holy Trinity,

Brompton Road, London (1826–9), constructed in the non-archaeological Commissioners' Gothic style, which was typical of those churches built as a result of the 1818 Act. Other works include the library (1848–9) of University College, Gower Street, London, in a classical style, and University Hall (1848–9; formerly Dr Williams's Library), Gordon Square, London, in a Tudor Gothic style.

Donaldson's principal achievements were not as an architect but in his other roles and in his wide range of publications. He was the leader of the RIBA for more than 40 years and as Honorary Secretary framed the royal charter granted to the Institute three years after its foundation in 1834. Its purpose was given as 'the general advancement of Civil Architecture and for promoting and facilitating the acquirements of the knowledge of the various Arts and Sciences connected therewith'. He also devised the RIBA's motto, 'Usui Civium, Decori Urbium' and designed the Mycenaean lions medal of the Institute. He was the first Professor of Construction and Architecture at University College and, from 1842 to 1865, helped to lay the groundwork for the system of architectural education that was to replace pupillage.

WRITINGS
Pompeii Illustrated with Picturesque Views (London, 1827)
Collection of the Most Approved Examples of Doorways from Ancient Buildings in Greece and Italy (London, 1833)
Architectural Maxims and Theorems (London, 1847)
Architectura numismatica (London, 1859) [the first book entirely devoted to architectural medals]
Handbook of Specifications (London, 1859)

BIBLIOGRAPHY
Colvin
S. Blutman: 'The Father of the Profession', *RIBA J.*, lxxiv (1867), pp. 542–4
RIBA cat.: C–F (Farnborough, 1972), pp. 82–3 [with bibliog.]

JILL LEVER

Donatello [Donato di Niccolo di Betto Bardi] (*b* Florence, 1386 or 1387; *d* Florence, 13 Dec 1466). Italian sculptor. He was the most imaginative and versatile Florentine sculptor of the early Renaissance, famous for his rendering of human character and for his dramatic narratives. He achieved these ends by studying ancient Roman sculpture and amalgamating its ideas with an acute and sympathetic observation of everyday life. Together with Alberti, Brunelleschi, Masaccio and Uccello, Donatello created the Italian Renaissance style, which he introduced to Rome, Siena and Padua at various stages of his career. He was long-lived and prolific: between 1401 and 1461 there are 400 documentary references to him, some for nearly every year. However, there is no contemporary biography, and the earliest account, in Vasari's *Vite* (1550), is confused.

I. Life and work. II. Working methods and technique. III. Character and personality. IV. Critical reception and posthumous reputation.

I. Life and work.

1. Training and early work, before 1409. 2. Florence, Pisa and Rome, 1409–42. 3. Padua, 1443–53. 4. Old age, 1454–66.

1. TRAINING AND EARLY WORK, BEFORE 1409. The earliest record of Donatello's artistic career is his apprenticeship to Lorenzo Ghiberti between 1404 and 1407, when the latter was engaged in preparing the models for the bronze reliefs on the north doors of the Baptistery in

1. Donatello: *St John the Evangelist*, marble, h. 2.10 m, completed 1415 (Florence, Museo dell'Opera del Duomo)

Florence. This would have given him a grounding in Late Gothic style design as practised by Ghiberti and in the techniques of modelling in wax and clay, in preparation for casting in bronze. However, Ghiberti was not a marble-carver and Donatello must have acquired this skill elsewhere, probably in the flourishing workshops of Florence Cathedral, where his earliest documented sculptures, two small marble statues of *Prophets* for the Porta della Mandorla (1406), are found. Two years later, in 1408, Donatello was commissioned to carve a full-size marble statue of *David* (Florence, Bargello) to crown one of the cathedral buttresses. This was his first major statue and

took several years to carve. It was never erected on the buttress but was acquired in 1416 by the City Council of Florence for display as a civic emblem in the Palazzo della Signoria—a sign of their early recognition of Donatello's talent. It was painted, gilded and set on a pedestal inlaid with mosaic and must have looked highly ornamental. This would have appealed to the then current taste for Late Gothic art. All traces of colour are now lost and the statue looks rather bland. Its most remarkable feature is the head of Goliath lying at David's feet: it is carved with great assurance and reveals the young sculptor's genuinely Renaissance interest in an ancient Roman type of mature, bearded head.

Also in 1408, Donatello was the youngest of four sculptors to receive a commission to carve an over life-size seated figure of an Evangelist for each of the four niches flanking the great western portal of Florence Cathedral (*see* FLORENCE, §IV, 1(i)(b)). His *St John the Evangelist* (Florence, Mus. Opera Duomo; see fig. 1) took until 1415 to finish, perhaps because he chose to pioneer a new style of maximum realism and psychological impact. The broad swathes of drapery in the Evangelist's toga serve as a foil for the enlarged, relaxed hands and the noble, bearded head. Donatello also deliberately distorted the proportions of the figure in order to compensate for the effects of foreshortening, when it was seen from below by passers-by, a most sophisticated device. The torso is unnaturally elongated and looks unstable when seen straight on (as in many of the standard photographs), but it has a solid pyramidal appearance when a lower viewpoint is adopted, corresponding with that of an observer when the statue was in its original niche. Giovanni Pisano had made the heads of his *Prophets* (after *c.* 1284) for the façade of Siena Cathedral jut forward pronouncedly, to make them more visible from below, but he did not adjust their proportions. Donatello was acutely conscious of the settings of all his statues, and this may be counted as a Renaissance tendency. According to Vasari, Donatello is also supposed at this early stage of his career to have carved and painted a wooden Crucifix for Santa Croce, Florence (*in situ*), but its attribution is no longer universally accepted.

2. FLORENCE, PISA AND ROME, 1409–42.

(i) Statuary and portraiture. (ii) Narrative reliefs.

(i) Statuary and portraiture. In 1411, while still at work on the *St John*, Donatello was commissioned by the Arte dei Linaioli (Linen Drapers' Guild) to carve a different Evangelist, this time standing, for their niche on the guildhall of Orsanmichele. The ponderation of the resultant statue of *St Mark* (marble, 1411–13; *in situ*), which gives him an air of authority, is derived from ancient Roman figures of senators: the weight-bearing leg is emphasized by parallel folds of drapery (like the flutes on a Classical column) and is clearly differentiated from the relaxed leg, only the knee of which can be seen through the thick wrinkles of the toga. The saint stands on a cushion, a totally unrealistic idea, but one that permitted Donatello to indicate the weight of the figure by the indentations made by the feet. The cushion may also have referred to the products of the textile guild that commissioned the statue. A radical

contrast in style may be remarked between Donatello's completely Renaissance *St Mark* and Ghiberti's contemporaneous, but still very Gothic, bronze statue of *St John the Baptist* (1412) in a niche near by.

Soon afterwards, perhaps around 1414, the Arte dei Corazzai (Guild of Armourers) ordered from Donatello a marble statue for Orsanmichele of their patron, *St George* (Florence, Bargello; *see* FLORENCE, fig. 17), a knight in armour and thus an advertisement for their wares. This has always been one of Donatello's most admired statues. The sculptor overcame a difficult problem, for the unyielding metal plates of armour did not permit him to express the potential movements of the limbs and body inside. Donatello could only use the pose to hint at them: *St George* is balanced expectantly on the balls of his feet. Otherwise Donatello could express emotion only in the face and the hands, protruding from the armour. In the clenched right-hand fist a hole indicates that the knight once held a weapon, probably a sword fashioned in gilt-metal, as it would have been impossible to carve out of marble. 'In the head', Vasari wrote, 'there may be seen the beauty of youth, courage and valour in arms, and a proud and terrible ardour; and there is a marvellous suggestion of life bursting out of the stone.'

The success of the statues of *St Mark* and *St George* encouraged the Guelph party to commission from Donatello a yet more ambitious one of their patron, *St Louis of Toulouse*. The statue (*c.* 1418–22; Florence, Mus. Opera Santa Croce) is in gilded bronze, the most glamorous—and the most expensive—sculptural material. To meet this complex technical challenge, Donatello called on the expert assistance of Michelozzo, an experienced metallurgist, who until then had been working with Ghiberti. The crinkly drapery of the voluminous cope gives vivacity to what might otherwise have been a rather bland figure of a youthful bishop: the figure was to be so large that, for technical reasons, the cope had to be modelled, and then cast and gilded, in several separate sections. This must have inspired the artist to give it a life of its own. The gloves, mitre and crozier—even the face—were also made separately and fixed together over an iron armature inside the figure. The brightly gilded masterpiece was installed in a Brunelleschian, Renaissance niche on Orsanmichele in 1422.

Late in 1415 Donatello began work on two life-size marble statues of *Prophets*—*Jeremiah* and *Habakkuk*—for some niches high on Giotto's Campanile. (The originals, grimy and weathered by centuries of exposure, are now in the Museo dell'Opera del Duomo and have been replaced with modern copies on the Campanile.) These statues were the earliest of a whole series, the execution of which lasted until the end of the mid-1430s; for the sake of speed, some were carved in collaboration with other sculptors. They were to be seen high above eye-level, so their features and drapery had to be boldly chiselled, yet their movements were constricted by the narrow lancet shapes of the pre-existing niches. Donatello met this challenge by adapting the plastic forms of drapery that he had had to model in wax or clay for his *St Louis* to the different medium of marble; gnarled hands and wizened faces—some quite hideous, but all the more moving—express the pathos of these Old Testament prophets,

2. Donatello: *Niccolò da Uzzano*, painted terracotta, h. 460 mm, ?1430s (Florence, Muzeo Nazionale del Bargello)

whose messages were rarely heeded. Their heads look like portraits. They are clearly indebted to ancient Roman ancestor busts and statues but are further enlivened by Donatello's fertile imagination and minute observation of his fellow men.

Donatello's interest in ancient Roman busts is demonstrated by a gilt-bronze reliquary for the head of the Early Christian martyr *St Rossore* (Pisa, Mus. N. S Matteo), a relic that reached the friars of Ognissanti in Florence in 1422. St Rossore (also known as St Lussorio or Lussurgiu) was a soldier who was beheaded under the Roman emperor Diocletian; thus Donatello's choice of the classic bust form used by the Romans to commemorate their ancestors was particularly appropriate. This form had survived in the Middle Ages as a container for head relics, but the faces had tended to be purely symbolic. Donatello, on the contrary, endowed his saint with lifelike, though imaginary, features and, with its knitted brow, an expression of intense anxiety appropriate to a victim of execution. This is the first datable example of a revival of the Roman type of realistic bust.

Two other undated and undocumented busts are generally associated with Donatello: one in bronze, like the *St Rossore*, shows a handsome youth in Classical guise, with a cameo (the original of which was owned by the Medici) around his neck (Florence, Bargello). It is very like the bronze statue of *David* (Florence, Bargello) that the sculptor produced later in his career for Cosimo I de' Medici and has similar, Neo-Platonic overtones (*see* §4 below). The other bust, modelled in terracotta and realistically painted (Florence, Bargello), represents the patrician *Niccolò da Uzzano* (1359–1431). Its identification and attribution, though sometimes doubted, have been affirmed by a recent cleaning, which revealed the high quality of its modelling and painting (see fig. 2). It remains uncertain whether Donatello portrayed the sitter from the life, or after his death, using a mask cast from the face and then revitalized by retouching the clay before it finally set. In either case, this is probably the earliest true portrait bust of the Renaissance, predating by a considerable number of years that of *Piero de' Medici* by Mino da Fiesole (1453; Florence, Bargello), often claimed as the first. It is more likely that the credit for such a significant re-invention should go to an artist of greater calibre than Mino and occur at a date earlier than the middle of the century, by which time the Renaissance was well under way.

Portraiture was also Donatello's major personal contribution to a commission that he undertook *c.* 1424 jointly with Michelozzo (by then his business partner): the monumental tomb of *Baldassarre Coscia, the Anti-Pope John XXIII* (*d* 1419; Florence, Baptistery). Donatello himself must have been responsible for the ennobled rendering of the fleshy, care-worn face and complex drapery of the effigy, which was cast, like the *St Louis*, in bronze and then gilded. The design of the wall monument, which was inserted between two of the Roman columns supporting the Baptistery, is an early manifestation of Renaissance architecture and is probably joint work, for Michelozzo was the more architecturally minded (though Donatello's personal involvement with architecture dates back to 1419, when he submitted an unsuccessful model to the competition for the cupola of Florence Cathedral). The carving of the marble components of the Anti-Pope's tomb was delegated to their assistants. The harmonious composition of the various elements, such as the effigy on a bier, the sarcophagus, the Virgin and Child in the lunette above and the division of the background into panels, were to inspire all the major 15th-century tomb monuments in Tuscany and Rome, which have collectively been called 'the humanist tomb' (Pope-Hennessy). Donatello was thus involved in yet another major innovation in Renaissance sculpture and architecture.

(ii) Narrative reliefs. Once he had mastered the art of modelling scenes in relief in Ghiberti's workshop, Donatello applied this knowledge to a variety of minor commissions, for example some gilded decorative friezes in the old houses of the Medici, mentioned by Vasari; and probably some renderings of the Virgin and Child, which were a prerequisite of every lady's bedroom and a staple product of sculptors' workshops. It is not until 1417, however, that there is a documentary reference to a relief in a public place, one showing *St George and the Dragon* (Florence, Bargello), which was carved in marble on the lintel at the foot of the niche for his statue of *St George* on Orsanmichele. It is the first manifestation of Donatello's interest in a form of extremely shallow relief-carving (It. *rilievo schiacciato*: 'flattened-out relief') that was more closely allied to graphic art than to sculpture (*see* §II below). Years of weathering have disguised the original subtlety of carving of the relief, but the receding hills and wind-battered trees in the background can still be made out. Straightforward linear perspective was also used to imply depth in the blind arcade at the right.

The next datable marble panel, the *Assumption of the Virgin* (Naples, S Angelo a Nilo), is on the tomb of *Cardinal Rinaldo Brancacci* (*d* 1427), which was carved by Donatello and Michelozzo at Pisa and sent to Naples. In it Donatello flattened the relief of all the figures, even the centrally enthroned Virgin, whose notionally projecting knees he had to swing sideways.

While in Pisa, Donatello was in close contact with the painter Masaccio: their work from *c.* 1426—notably several Madonnas—reflects mutual influences. Most Masaccio-esque of all Donatello's shallow reliefs is the lovely marble panel (London, V&A; see fig. 3) combining two quite distinct episodes from the New Testament, the *Ascension* and *Christ Giving the Keys to St Peter*. Though it was recorded in 1492 in an inventory of Lorenzo the Magnificent's effects in the Palazzo Medici, its earlier history is unknown. It is generally dated in the 1420s because it is composed in a way redolent of Masaccio's fresco of the *Tribute Money* in the Brancacci Chapel, with a half circle of Apostles surrounding the Saviour. Both the sculpture

3. Donatello: *Ascension* with *Christ Giving the Keys to St Peter*, marble, 410×1145 mm, 1420s (London, Victoria and Albert Museum)

and the fresco are populated by the same deeply serious figures, impressively modelled and individually character-ized. In contrast with the usual, idealized renderings of the Virgin, which portray her still youthful, untainted by sin, Donatello dared to show her as a wizened old peasant woman with coarse hands, as she might really have looked when her son was about the age of 30. The heads of the Apostles, especially of St Peter, are dexterously gouged out of the marble on a tiny scale with amazing confidence and freedom. Distant walled cities, hilltops and receding rows of trees are scratched into the rear planes so deftly that their very sketchiness helps to suggest distance, creating an effect that is termed 'aerial' perspective (as distinct from linear means).

Of several other marble reliefs in the same technique attributed to Donatello, the most interesting is the *Feast of Herod* (Lille, Mus. B.-A.). Its subject is the same as in Donatello's earliest documented bronze relief (1423–5), made for the parapet of the font in the baptistery of Siena Cathedral, but the treatment is very different. The marble relief is remarkable for its complicated architectural set-ting: Herod's vast palace is laid out correctly in perspective across the surface of the marble panel, but the principal episode is diminished in both scale and impact. The size of the figures in the foreground—one third of the height of the total field—and several other technical features correspond closely with Alberti's instructions for creating an ideal picture, and this seems to be a deliberate demon-stration on Donatello's part of how this theory could be put into practice. In the Sienese bronze panel, the drama is witnessed in close focus owing to Donatello's use of a viewpoint for his perspectival scheme that is closer and higher than normal. The principal characters are large and few in number, so that their expressions can be clearly seen. The sequence of arcades, arranged one behind another towards the background, creates an effect of great space, and it is there that the earlier episode of the actual beheading is depicted.

Donatello continued to be much involved with relief-carvings in the 1430s: a sacramental tabernacle in St Peter's, Rome, its architecture peopled by angels and framing a scene of the *Entombment* (c. 1432); an external pulpit with panels of dancing putti for Prato Cathedral (commissioned in 1428, but delayed until 1438); and a *Singing Gallery* (*Cantoria*) for Florence Cathedral (1433–9). The latter was to correspond with one already com-missioned from Luca della Robbia (1431), while Donatello and Michelozzo had been away in Rome. Luca had chosen logically to illustrate the verses of Psalm 150 with a series of closed compositions of child-musicians or dancers on panels separated by pilasters, with the relevant verses of the psalm incised above and below. In the pulpit for Prato Cathedral, Donatello had used a similar scheme of panels divided by pilasters, but by cutting off from view some of the limbs of his infant dancers, he suggested that they were dancing in a continuous row behind the architecture. For the Florence *Cantoria*, he pursued this concept further, and the putti are carved on two long slabs of marble, performing two continuous dances in a circle, physically behind the series of free-standing paired colonnettes that articulate the structure. Background and colonnettes are encrusted with mosaic *tesserae* to provide a colourful foil for the frieze of dancers in plain white marble. No such specific theme as Luca's is depicted, but Donatello was probably trying to convey an ecstatic dance of the souls of the innocent in paradise.

Similar in its architectural ornament to the *Singing Gallery*—and also ensconced in the wall of a building—is the *Tabernacle of the Annunciation* in Santa Croce, Florence. It is undocumented but formed the altarpiece of a former side chapel belonging to the Cavalcanti family. Carved in deep relief out of grey sandstone (*pietra serena*, a favourite Tuscan building stone), it shows the two participants at life size and almost in the round, as in a *tableau vivant*, on a tiny stage behind a proscenium arch. For the sake of clarity, the ornamental details of the architecture and Mary's bedchamber are picked out in gilding, and the scene is enlivened by two pairs of mischievous infants teetering on the cornice above.

Following Brunelleschi's completion of the Old Sacristy at S Lorenzo for the Medici in 1429, and probably after the return of these patrons from a brief exile in 1433, Donatello created a series of vigorously modelled and brightly painted reliefs in the eight great roundels on its walls and pendentives, as well as in two lunettes over the doorways flanking its chancel. There are no documents for them, nor for the twin pairs of bronze doors, but since from 1433 until 1443 the sculptor was living and working in an old inn owned by the Medici, for which he was asked only a nominal rent, perhaps his work on their family mausoleum in S Lorenzo was taken for granted and his expenses met out of petty cash. On the walls the four *Evangelists*, accompanied by their symbolic beasts, are seen in their studies, as though through portholes. Dona-tello typically refused to idealize these humble folk of the New Testament, showing them instead as haggard old men, deeply absorbed in the effort of penning their gospels. They are incongruously shown seated on orna-mental thrones and with desks covered with Renaissance details.

On the pendentive roundels the theme was four epi-sodes from the *Life of St John the Evangelist*. Here Donatello exploited all that he had learnt about creating the illusion of perspective, either by linear or 'aerial' means. Several of the participants are shown only in part, as though cut off by the circumference of the roundel, a bold device that implies that the scenes continue beyond the spectator's field of vision: this gives an effect of 'photo-graphic immediacy' to the miraculous dramas. The extraor-dinary freedom with which the figures are modelled bespeaks a truly great artist at the height of his creative powers. It calls to mind late 19th- or early 20th-century sculptors such as Degas, Rodin or Epstein, all of whom enjoyed the feeling of life that is conveyed by quick, spontaneous modelling, the building up of an image out of ductile materials and the refraining from any attempt at finish, which would have tended to deaden the effect.

Donatello also saw the potential for casting such rough images into bronze. The doors in the Old Sacristy are decorated with pairs of saintly figures in earnest discussion or meditation, and these are only the beginning of a crescendo of production of narrative reliefs: for the high altar in the basilica of S Antonio, Padua (*see* §3 below); for the west doors of Siena Cathedral (never cast); and for the twin pulpits in the nave of S Lorenzo, Florence, produced at the end of Donatello's life (*see* §4 below).

3. PADUA, 1443–53. In 1443 Donatello left Florence for Padua, where he stayed for a decade. His first commission was for a life-size bronze Crucifix (1441–9) for the rood screen in the basilica of S Antonio (the Santo): he modelled a strongly muscled, but idealized mature male body, departing from Gothic prototypes, which had tended to stress the physical anguish of the crucifixion. Shortly afterwards, a bequest enabled the friars to project a new high altar: regrettably Donatello's architectural and sculptural masterpiece was dismantled a century later, but the bronze statuary survives and the general scheme seems to be reflected in the composition of Mantegna's S Zeno Altarpiece (Verona, S Zeno). Beneath an open tabernacle of ornamental, classicizing form, with eight columns and a curved pediment with volutes at either end, were disposed seven life-size bronze statues. A central *Virgin and Child* (in an unusual pose recalling local, Byzantine art) was flanked in a *sacra conversazione* by six patron saints, including SS Anthony and Francis. They were modelled and cast with freedom, and not highly finished, as they would never have been visible close to or in a clear light. At the level of the predella of a normal painted altarpiece were inserted four rectangular, panoramic relief scenes of the *Miracles of St Anthony*. In front of imaginatively conceived, Roman architectural backgrounds, interior or exterior (their details picked out with gilding), Donatello mustered groups of amazed bystanders round the principal actions of the saint and those immediately involved, in a way reminiscent of a modern stage director. Between these four narratives were interspersed twelve panels with charming *Musician Angels*, and four with the *Symbols of the Evangelists* and one of the *Dead Christ*, while on the back of the structure of the altar was a great relief of the *Entombment*, carved in stone and inlaid with mosaic and glazed coloured strips. Here Donatello's dramatic powers were unleashed in figures of frenzied holy women bewailing the event. Full documentation allows this major project to be followed step by step, giving an insight into the wide delegation of tasks to which Donatello had to resort in order to push work forward to completion by 1450.

Donatello's other important Paduan commission, of a very different kind, was the creation of a bronze equestrian monument (1447–53) to Erasmo da Narni (1370–1443), known as *Gattamelata*, a deceased captain-general of the Venetian army (see fig. 4). This is the earliest surviving equestrian statue from the Renaissance. It was a revival of an ancient Roman type known at the time principally from the *Marcus Aurelius* in Rome. To support the great weight of the thickly cast bodies of horse and rider on only four legs was a great technical achievement: Donatello would have liked to have had one forehoof raised free, as in his ancient prototype (as well as in the *Horses* on S Marco, Venice, which were much nearer to Padua), but he did not dare. Instead he fell back on the device of propping it up by a cannon ball conveniently lying on the field of battle. The General is brilliantly portrayed and idealized as a heroic man of action, using a close-cropped Roman hairstyle and the classical type of light war-horse. Details on his armour also recall antiquity, though the long

4. Donatello: equestrian monument to *Gattamelata*, bronze on marble and stone base, h. 3.4 m, 1447–53 (Padua, Piazza del Santo)

broadsword and cannon ball reflect contemporary warfare. This was an image that inspired Verrocchio, challenged Leonardo da Vinci and, ultimately, in the work of Giambologna 150 years later, spread to all the great squares of Europe, as a symbol appropriate for monarchs. The end of Donatello's stay in Padua was marred by disputes with several of his patrons over completion of his work and payment. He was much in demand elsewhere, but, in order to return to his native city, he turned down invitations from the Gonzaga in Mantua, the Este in Modena and King Alfonso I of Naples.

4. OLD AGE, 1454–66. By 1454 Donatello was renting a house and shop on the Piazza del Duomo in Florence. Possibly Cosimo de' Medici had prevailed on Donatello to return, as his great new palace was nearing completion and needed some major sculptural decoration. Donatello was by then nearly 70 years old and becoming infirm, though his spirit and imagination were unbowed. He was ill in 1456, for his doctor, Giovanni Chellini (of whom there is a marble portrait bust by Antonio Rossellino, 1456; London, V&A), received in lieu of a fee an unusual bronze roundel of the *Virgin and Child with Angels* (London, V&A). Even so, the sculptor made substantial purchases of materials for casting bronze statuary, one example of which was the impassioned figure of *St John the Baptist* for a chapel in Siena Cathedral (*in situ*). The following year Donatello actually moved to Siena in order to work on a side chapel and on some bronze doors for the cathedral. From his stay there only a large marble

roundel of the *Virgin and Child* over the Porta del Perdono of the cathedral, finished by assistants, survives: panels modelled in wax on wood made in preparation for casting into bronze for the doors were abandoned, and, disheartened, their author returned to Florence.

In 1459 Donatello must have begun several major commissions for his favourite patron, Cosimo de' Medici. Most enigmatic both in treatment and in dating—for it is absolutely undocumented—is the nearly nude bronze *David* (Florence, Bargello; *see* STATUE, fig. 1), which stood on an ornamental pedestal in the centre of the newly built courtyard of the Medici palace (some scholars prefer to date the statue to before Donatello's Paduan sojourn). It was at the centre of a complex intellectual scheme comprising eight of the great marble medallions that decorate the walls of the courtyard, above the arcade. These are enlargements of important antique gems, most of which were owned by the Medici, but their meaning is obscure. It has been suggested that the nudity and sensuousness of the boy David, as well as some surprising details of his costume, none of which is derived from the biblical story, may result from a Neo-Platonic philosophical interpretation of David as an allegory of heavenly love (Ames-Lewis). (Cosimo was the founder of the Neo-Platonic Academy in Florence.) Donatello's other commission for the palace, this time for a fountain in the back garden, was a more easily explicable group, also on an Old Testament theme, *Judith Slaying Holofernes* (Florence, Pal. Vecchio). It is an allegory of Humility triumphing over Pride, as is known from a lost, but recorded, inscription.

The last work for Cosimo is a series of bronze panels depicting the *Passion of Christ* (*see* PULPIT, fig. 2) and the *Martyrdom of St Lawrence* for the twin pulpits in the nave of the Medici parish church at S Lorenzo. One is dated June 1465. They are grimly realistic, abandoning all traditional restraints and the usual tendency towards idealization, glossing over the full horror of some episodes. The original wax modelling must have been vigorous and passionate: in the dramatic bronze narratives that resulted, it seems as if Donatello was so emotionally involved that he attacked the cold metal surfaces of the scenes with a savagery resulting from his personal empathy with the sufferings of the saviour. Work does not seem to have been finished at the time of Donatello's death (1466), and several hands can be traced in the chasing. Surprisingly, in view of the artist's fame, the panels were not installed on the pulpits until the 16th century: perhaps they were too avant-garde for mid-15th-century taste, which was more attuned to the suave, but less demanding, narrative style of Ghiberti's *Gates of Paradise* doors on the Baptistery (installed in 1452).

This constitutes the work of Donatello's old age, apart from an undocumented painted wood statue of *St Mary Magdalene* (Florence, Mus. Opera Duomo; see fig. 5 below), which is usually held to be a late work because of its overwrought, emotional effect. Such reasoning is no longer entirely acceptable, for a very similar, painted wooden statue of the haggard *St John the Baptist* (Venice, S Maria Gloriosa dei Frari), produced by Donatello for a chapel of the Florentine community in Venice, has been found, after cleaning, to be dated 1438. Perhaps it was carved at the behest of the Medici, as a thank-offering for

hospitality that they had received during their brief exile there in 1433. So the sculptor was capable of such horrifically gripping imagery far earlier in his career than had previously been supposed: it was not confined to his old age.

II. Working methods and technique.

Donatello is remarkable for the sheer range of materials in which he worked: he turned his hand with equal facility, apparently, to modelling in clay, stucco or wax (nothing survives in wax, but casts from wax models in terracotta and bronze do); and to finishing bronze in the cold metal (though he did not do his own casting, but delegated it, as was normal, to specialist foundries, some of which are recorded). He carved marble and grey Tuscan sandstone (the *macigno* or so-called *pietra serena*), as well as wood, which he then painted, probably himself, to enhance its naturalistic appearance. In the *Madonna dei Cordai* (Florence, Mus. Bardini) Donatello used a curious technique of jigsawing the contours of a Virgin and Child out of wood and applying it to a flat background, then modelling the figures over it in a composition material. He filled the background with pretence *tesserae* of gilt leather to resemble mosaic (which he also used in reality on the Prato pulpit and the *Cantoria*) and painted and varnished the whole. He also designed, but did not execute, a stained-glass window for the drum of Florence Cathedral (*Coronation of the Virgin*; *in situ*) and, perhaps in collaboration with a member of the Barovier family of Murano, planned to make casts in glass from the reverse of the bronze roundel that he eventually gave to Dr Chellini (London, V&A).

Donatello's principal technical innovation was in the field of relief-carving. Apparently in the late 1410s and early 1420s he devised a method of carving—almost drawing—a scene in very shallow relief, the technique known as *rilievo schiacciato*. Within a depth of about 10 to 20 mm, the sculptor conveyed a much greater imaginary depth by means of only very slight indentations on the surface of the marble. The contours of the figures were drawn in with the corner of a chisel and crystals of marble whittled away round the edges to leave in relief the volumes of the bodily forms. The planes of the various figures were compressed in depth, unlike the standard Roman or medieval technique, where they had been left standing out, half or more in the round, in front of a flat background. Donatello's technique allowed the forms to merge into the background more fluently, so that a spatial continuum was suggested, as in a painting.

In the marble relief of the *Assumption* of 1427 Donatello invented stylized forms—almost like stratified slate—to indicate thickly massed cirrus clouds, between which angels are visible in a tumbling mass of limbs swooping through the air, as though swimming in the sea. This bold illusion may once have been heightened by touches of colour and gilding, as was normal in marble sculpture at that time. This kind of 'aerial' perspective was even more subtle than the use of architectural settings to provide linear means of suggesting recession through the newly discovered rules of geometrical perspective. In the larger fields of the roundels in the Old Sacristy at S Lorenzo,

than his predecessors. In his reliefs, after he had initially mastered the techniques of shallow-carving or modelling, stylistic development is to be noted chiefly in the increased elaboration of groups of *dramatis personae* and in the boldness of movement. As his technique became accomplished and his self-confidence grew, the modelling became freer and more 'impressionistic'—even 'expressionistic' on occasions, when the apparent roughness of execution reflects the emotional violence of the subject. In the series of *Passion* reliefs (Florence, S Lorenzo) made at the end of his life, lack of finish seems not to betray loss of control due to old age, nor yet interruption by death, but rather a supremely confident and economical use of a lifetime's repertory of forms and motifs to indicate his intensity of feeling towards his Christian subject. Donatello could also render purity and beauty with supreme ease, for instance when depicting the Virgin (e.g. in the *Annunciation* or in his several reliefs showing her with the baby Jesus) or indeed the boy *David*. Such images were in tune with the optimistic styles of Ghiberti or Luca della Robbia, which were extremely popular in the worldly, mercantile centre that was Florence.

Where Donatello excelled, however, and where he was perhaps too demanding for his contemporaries, was in his rendering of drama and pathos, nearly always in a Christian context. The gaunt, painted wood statues of *St John the Baptist* (1438; Venice, S Maria Gloriosa dei Frari) and *St Mary Magdalene* (?c. 1456–60; Florence, Mus. Opera Duomo; see fig. 5), as well as his bronze *St John* for Siena Cathedral, border on the horrific and are deliberately shocking to a casual observer. The choice of wood may reflect a wish to relate these figures to the Gothic tradition of wood-carving in Germany and the alpine regions, where it was always used expressively. The intense empathy that Donatello manifested with his chosen subjects, whether carved in wood or marble or cast in bronze (see fig. 6), is deeply moving and is still much appreciated, despite the general loss of religious belief in modern society. The very humanity of such works retains its appeal across six centuries. But even if Donatello's expressiveness is all his own, to some extent he was drawing on an earlier Tuscan Gothic tradition of fiercely dramatic narrative founded by Giovanni Pisano, who, where necessary, as in the *Massacre of the Innocents* (*c.* 1300; Pistoia, S Andrea), did not flinch from inflicting the full horror of the event on the spectator.

As was normal practice in the early 15th century, Donatello entered into working partnerships, either informally (as with Brunelleschi on occasions, and later with Nanni di Bartolo for several of the *Prophets* for the Campanile) or formally (as with Michelozzo in the mid-1420s for the co-production of tombs). He also employed assistants, though their names are not always recorded: lesser sculptors such as the bronze specialist Maso di Bartolomeo and the marble-carver Pagno di Lapo Portigiani (1408–70) moved in and out of his orbit. Vespasiano da Bisticci, in his *Vita* of Cosimo *il vecchio* de' Medici, talked of the banker making a weekly allowance to the sculptor 'enough for him and four assistants', and perhaps this was the average number of personnel in Donatello's Florentine workshop. The most informative series of archival documents about his working methods is that

5. Donatello: *St Mary Magdalene*, polychrome and gilt wood, h. 1.88 m, ?c. 1456–60 (Florence, Museo dell'Opera del Duomo)

Donatello laid out the architectural settings with ruler and set square in the damp stucco, and then cut back the material with spatulas to indicate successive, receding planes: the spaces thus suggested were then populated with figures at various scales literally added on top. They had to be modelled around projecting nail-heads to help them adhere to the perilously inward-sloping background.

It was by exploiting linear perspective that Donatello was able to achieve a still more gripping effect of realism

6. Donatello: the Medici *Crucifixion*, bronze relief with parcel gilt, 930×700 mm, 1454–6 (Florence, Museo Nazionale del Bargello)

concerning the production during the 1440s of the high altar in S Antonio, Padua, where Donatello functioned as an impresario, managing a large team engaged on various aspects or component parts of the vast sculptural undertaking. Giovanni da Pisa (i), Niccolò Pizzolo, Urbano da Cortona and, ultimately, Bartolomeo Bellano are the best known of his assistants.

III. Character and personality.

Donatello left no writings or correspondence and may have been virtually illiterate, which would have been normal in the humble background from which he came: his father was a wool-carder and had been involved in the Ciompi Revolt in 1378, even being briefly exiled for murdering someone in street violence. The sculptor seems to have taken a perverse pride in his 'working class' origins, and his affections for the Medici may have stemmed from their being non-noble and their espousal of the popular, democratic cause. Presumably Donatello acquired his knowledge of the Bible and ancient mythology by word of mouth, especially from the Neo-platonic philosophers whom Cosimo also patronized.

In 1525 Donatello's character was described by Summonte as 'rough and very straightforward' ('rozo e semplicissimo'), which seems a fair summary. He did not aspire to a more 'gentlemanly' role in society, unlike his

ex-master and rival Lorenzo Ghiberti, who associated himself with the literary side of humanism by penning his *Commentarii*. Also in contrast to Ghiberti, who vaingloriously included his self-portrait on both pairs of doors for the Florentine Baptistery (one showing him wearing the *mazzocchio*, the turban-like headgear of a Florentine gentleman), Donatello showed a complete lack of attention to his own appearance, as was remarked on twice by contemporaries. Manetti, in his biography of Brunelleschi, in which he described their joint, early visit to Rome, wrote:

> Neither of them had family problems since they had neither wife nor children, there or elsewhere. Neither of them paid much attention to what they ate and drank or how they were dressed or where they lived, as long as they were able to satisfy themselves by seeing and measuring.

This was corroborated by Vespasiano da Bisticci in his life of Cosimo:

> Since Donatello did not dress as Cosimo would have liked him to, Cosimo gave him a red cloak with a hood, and a gown under the cloak, and dressed him all afresh. One morning of a feast day he sent it all to him to make him wear it. Donatello did, once or twice, and then he put it aside and did not want to wear it any more, for it seemed too dandified for him.

Donatello was evidently a popular figure in Florence, notorious for making sarcastic, and occasionally coarse, remarks. He even featured as a speaking character in a miracle play written during his lifetime, called *Nebuchadnezzar, King of Babylon*. His delays on producing the pulpit for Prato are referred to in passing, as though they were a well-known scandal. A number of catch-phrases originating from his lips were recorded in a 16th-century anthology of more or less scurrilous tales. Some are difficult to interpret today, but the general tone is of tight-lipped, Tuscan humour, deriving from someone who was evidently renowned for his eccentricity and sharp wit. Vasari recorded various unkind remarks made to, or about, fellow artists, for example to Paolo Uccello: it is hard to tell if they were meant to be hurtful or merely sarcastically humorous. Vasari also noted the sculptor in frustration crudely swearing at his statue of *Habakkuk*: 'Favella, favella, che ti venga il caccasangue' ('Speak, speak, or may you get bloody shit!').

Donatello was frequently obstreperous with his patrons, particularly bodies of churchmen from outside Florence, for instance the unfortunate Cathedral Works of Prato, who had legitimate cause for complaint over his irresponsible attitude and dilatoriness in fulfilling his contractual obligations to them. Having tried to encourage him by some seasonal presents, ultimately they resorted to asking Cosimo de' Medici to intervene on their behalf. Duke Ludovico Gonzaga used the same expedient in 1458, when he was trying to get the sculptor to finish some work for which he had made models several years earlier: in the exchange of correspondence Ludovico called Donatello 'very tricky' ('molto intricato') and admitted that he 'had a mind made up in such a way that if he does not come, one cannot entertain any hope of it, even if one pesters him'. This is an extraordinary admission from a grand patron dealing with an artist, then normally regarded as a mere artisan. Clearly Donatello was an exception to any rule.

If Donatello's behaviour with his patrons was exceptional, so too was the perceptive generosity of Cosimo, who seems to have recognized the artist's sheer genius and been prepared to put up with his stubbornness and impertinence. Besides living nearly rent-free for a whole decade (1434–43) in an old inn that Cosimo had bought for eventual demolition to make way for his grand new palace, according to Vespasiano da Bisticci, in the sculptor's old age, when work was hard to find, Cosimo gave him commissions deliberately in order to keep him busy and paid him by banker's order on a weekly basis. This background accounts for the complete absence of documents for payment and hence firm dates for any of Donatello's work for the Medici. Cosimo also arranged in his will that the sculptor should be looked after by his heir, Piero I (the Gouty), and given accommodation and a pension in his old age, and should eventually be buried beside him in the family vault beneath S Lorenzo. This came to pass and was an extraordinary honour.

IV. Critical reception and posthumous reputation.

Donatello's reputation was made within his own lifetime and has remained high ever since, though with a mild waxing and waning of popularity according to the taste of successive centuries. He was counted as a friend by Cosimo de' Medici and by Alberti, who in his *De pictura* (1436) listed him directly after Brunelleschi as 'this our very great friend' ('quel nostro amicissimo Donato scultore') and before Ghiberti, Luca della Robbia and Masaccio. Bartolomeo Fazio included him in his *De viris illustribus* (1456) as 'excelling for his talent and no less for his technique; he is well known for his sculpture in bronze and marble, because he succeeds in giving life to the faces of his figures, and in this respect he shares the glory of the masters of antiquity'. In the same year his medical doctor Chellini noted that he was a 'singular and principal master in making figures of bronze and wood and terracotta'. A note of criticism of some of Donatello's more irrationally exaggerated figures on the bronze doors of the Old Sacristy was sounded by the architect–sculptor Filarete in his *Trattato d'architettura* (1461–4), who preferred a degree of decorum: apostles should behave like apostles and not like fencers.

In 1481 Cristoforo Landino (*Apologia*) praised the late sculptor highly:

> Donato the sculptor is to be numbered among the men of old, admirable as he is for his compositions and his variety, and his ability with great lifelikeness to arrange and place his figures, all of which appear to be in motion. He was a great copyist of antiquity and also understood about perspective.

Amid general posthumous praise, there were occasionally subjective, though partially justifiable, criticisms. For instance, the Mannerist sculptor Baccio Bandinelli wrote in 1547 that when Donatello made the bronze pulpits for S Lorenzo he was 'so old that his eyesight was not up to judging them properly, nor to giving them a beautiful finish, and even though they are a good invention, he never made an uglier work'. The apparent lack of finish was also criticized by Michelangelo (according to Condivi,

1553), who admired Donatello in other respects. Vasari (1568) was at pains to flatter his own patron, the Grand Duke Cosimo I, by stressing the enlightened patronage that Donatello had enjoyed from his collateral ancestor and namesake, Cosimo *il vecchio*. He also published an elegant literary conceit of Vincenzo Borghini's that drew a parallel between Donatello and Michelangelo: 'Either the spirit of Donatello works in Michelangelo; or Michelangelo's one worked beforehand in Donatello.' However, Vasari's *Vita* of Donatello contains more than average distortions and is confusing to a modern reader because it is based not on a chronological approach so much as on a topographical one, probably because it was derived from an earlier guidebook to Florence. Certain statues such as *St Mark* (admired by Michelangelo) and *St George* (praised by Vasari) have always remained relatively popular, while others, sometimes owing to their removal around the city, became dissociated from his name, for example the *St Louis*, which, amazingly, was recognized only in the early 20th century.

Centenaries of the sculptor's birth and death have been potent stimuli to reassessment in the past two centuries. That in 1886–7 was celebrated partly because it happened to coincide with the completion of the Gothic Revival façade of Florence Cathedral. It was permanently commemorated—as was the fashion at the time—with bronze portraits and inscriptions, one mounted on the north aisle of Santa Croce, the Pantheon of Florence; another on the façade of one of the several studios he used near the cathedral; and a third on a tomb in the Renaissance style (1896; complete with a bronze effigy) by Dario Guidotti (*fl* 1892–1900) and Raffaello Romanelli (*b* 1856) in the Martelli Chapel of S Lorenzo. A pioneering exhibition was mounted in the Museo del Bargello, Florence, and a number of grandiloquent speeches by eminent professors were published as pamphlets.

The beginning of modern art-historical literature on Donatello in Italian (Milanesi, 1887) was soon followed by major monographs in German (Semper and von Tschudi, both in 1887; Schottmuller, 1904; Schubring, 1907; Kauffmann, 1935). In England Lord Balcarres addressed the subject in 1903, to be closely followed by Maud Cruttwell in 1911, both giving very respectable 'overviews' for the educated, Anglo-Saxon general reader. In 1941 a well-illustrated Phaidon Press monograph by Goldscheider appeared. The major monograph on the artist is by H. W. Janson, incorporating the notes and photographs of Jeno Lanyi. It has gone through several editions since 1957 and consists of an exhaustive and invaluable catalogue raisonné, but without a discursive biography. The latter was supplied by a *de luxe* volume by Hartt, with new photographs by Finn (1973). Bennett and Wilkins (1984) published a volume of extended scholarly essays on various aspects of the sculptor's activity.

The quincentenary of Donatello's death, in 1966, gave rise to an international congress, the acts of which were published in 1968, and renewed interest was kindled by the rediscovery in England of the bronze roundel given in 1456 to Dr Chellini (see Radcliffe and Avery, 1976), which resulted in a number of essays addressing the question of Donatello's reliefs of the Madonna. The sixth centenary of the sculptor's birth, in 1986, occasioned a loan exhibition of sculpture at the Detroit Institute of Arts and the Forte di Belvedere in Florence, as well as one in the Bargello, drawn solely from its own collection, with accompanying catalogues (see 1985 and 1985–6 exh. cats) and conferences (see 'Donatello Studien', 1989). Also coinciding with these centenary celebrations were the publication in Italian of a volume of new photographs and catalogue entries (Pope-Hennessy, Ragioneri and Perugi, 1985) and an introductory biography (Avery, 1986). A spate of booklets and articles has since appeared, notably on some of the sculptures that were restored as a result of the sixth centenary.

BIBLIOGRAPHY

EARLY SOURCES

L. B. Alberti: *De pictura* (MS., 1436); ed. C. Grayson: *Opera volgari* (Bari, 1973), iii, p. 7
G. Chellini: *Libro debitori, creditori e ricordanze* (MS., 1456); ed. A. De Maddalena: 'Les Archives Saminiati: De l'économie à l'histoire de l'art', *An., Econ., Soc., Civilis.*, xiv (1955), pp. 738–44
B. Facio: *De viris illustribus* (MS., 1456); ed. L. Mehus (Florence, 1745); Eng. trans. in M. Baxandall: 'Bartholomaeus Facius on Painting: A Fifteenth-century Manuscript of *De viris illustribus*', *J. Warb. & Court. Inst.*, xxvii (1964), pp. 90–107 [106–7]
A. Averulino [Filarete]: *Trattato d'architettura* (MS., 1461–4); ed. A. M. Finoli and L. Grassi (Milan, 1972), pp. 658–9
A. Manetti: *Vita di Filippo Brunelleschi* (MS., *c.* 1480); ed. D. De Robertis and G. Tanturli (Milan, 1976), pp. 67–9, 109–10
C. Landino: *Apologia* (MS., 1481); repr. in *Dante con l'esposizione di Cristoforo Landino e di Alessandro Vellutello* (Venice, 1564)
Vespasiano da Bisticci: *Le vite* (MS., ?1493); ed. A. Greco (Florence, 1970), ii, pp. 193–4
P. Summonte: letter to Marcantonio Michiel (MS., 1525); ed. F. Nicolini: *L'arte napoletana del rinascimento e la lettera di Pietro Summonte a Marcantonio Michiel* (Naples, 1925)
B. Bandinelli: letter to Cosimo I de' Medici (MS., 7 Dec 1547); ed. G. Bottari and S. Ticozzi: *Raccolta di lettere sulla pittura, scultura ed architettura*, ii (Milan, 1822), p. 72
G. Vasari: *Vite* (1550, rev. 2/1568); ed. G. Milanesi (1878–85), ii, pp. 395–426
A. Condivi: *Vita di Michelangelo Buonarroti* (Rome, 1553)

GENERAL

W. Bode: *Florentine Sculptors of the Renaissance* (London, 1928)
J. Pope-Hennessy: *Italian Renaissance Sculpture* (London, 1958, rev. 3/New York, 1985)
——: *Catalogue of Italian Sculpture in the Victoria and Albert Museum* (London, 1964)
——: *Essays on Italian Sculpture* (London, 1968)
C. Avery: *Florentine Renaissance Sculpture* (London, 1970)

MONOGRAPHS

G. Milanesi: *Catalogo delle opere di Donatello* (Florence, 1887)
H. Semper: *Donatellos Leben und Werke* (Innsbruck, 1887)
H. von Tschudi: 'Donatello e la critica moderna', *Riv. Stor. It.*, iv/2 (1887), pp. 193–228
Lord Balcarres: *Donatello* (London and New York, 1903)
F. Schottmuller: *Donatello* (Munich, 1904)
P. Schubring: *Donatello*, Klass. Kst Gesamtausgaben (Stuttgart and Leipzig, 1907)
M. Cruttwell: *Donatello* (London, 1911)
H. Kauffmann: *Donatello* (Berlin, 1935)
L. Goldscheider: *Donatello: Complete Phaidon Edition* (London, 1941)
H. W. Janson: *The Sculpture of Donatello* (Princeton, 1957, rev. 2/1963)
G. Castelfranco: *Donatello* (Milan, 1963)
L. Grassi: *All the Sculpture of Donatello* (London, 1964)
F. Hartt and D. Finn: *Donatello: Prophet of Modern Vision* (New York, 1973, 2/London, 1974)
A. Parronchi: *Donatello e il potere* (Florence, 1980)
M. Greenhalgh: *Donatello and his Sources* (London, 1982)
B. A. Bennett and D. G. Wilkins: *Donatello* (Oxford, 1984)
J. Pope-Hennessy, G. Ragioneri and L. Perugi: *Donatello* (Florence, 1985)

C. Avery: *L'invenzione dell'umano: Introduzione a Donatello* (Florence, 1986)
——: *Donatello: An Introduction* (New York, 1994)

EXHIBITION CATALOGUES AND CONGRESSES

Donatello e il suo tempo: Atti dell'VIII Convegno internazionale di studi sul rinascimento: Firenze, 1966
Italian Renaissance Sculpture in the Time of Donatello (exh. cat., ed. A. P. Darr; Detroit, MI, Inst. A., 1985); It. edn as *Donatello e i suoi: Scultura fiorentina del primo rinascimento* (ed. A. P. Darr and G. Bonsanti; Florence, Forte Belvedere, 1986)
Omaggio a Donatello (exh. cat. by P. Barocchi and others, Florence, Bargello, 1985)
'Donatello Studien', *It. Forsch. Kstgesch.*, 3rd ser., xvi (1989)

SPECIALIST STUDIES

F. Ames-Lewis: 'Donatello's Bronze *David* Reconsidered', *A. Hist.*, ii/2 (1974), pp. 140–55
J. Pope-Hennessy: 'The Medici *Crucifixion* of Donatello', *Apollo*, ci (1975), pp. 82–7; repr. in J. Pope-Hennessy: *The Study and Criticism of Italian Sculpture* (Princeton, 1980), pp. 119–28
——: 'The Madonna Reliefs of Donatello', *Apollo*, ciii (1976), pp. 172–91; repr. in J. Pope-Hennessy: *The Study and Criticism of Italian Sculpture* (Princeton, 1980), pp. 71–105
A. Radcliffe and C. Avery: 'The Chellini *Madonna* by Donatello', *Burl. Mag.*, cxviii (1976), pp. 377–87
V. Herzner: 'Regesti donatelliani', *Riv. Ist. N. Archeol. & Stor. A.*, ii (1979), pp. 169–228
C. Avery: 'Donatello's Madonnas Reconsidered', *Apollo*, cxxiv (1986), pp. 174–82
C. Elam and others: 'Donatello at Close Range', *Burl. Mag.*, cxxix (1987), special suppl., pp. 1–52
L. Dolcini: *Donatello e il restauro della 'Giudita'* (Florence, 1988)

CHARLES AVERY

Donati, Enrico (*b* Milan, 19 Feb 1909). American painter and sculptor of Italian birth. He studied economics at the Università degli Studi, Pavia, and in 1934 moved to the USA, where he attended the New School for Social Research and the Art Students' League in New York. His first one-man shows were in New York in 1942, at the New School for Social Research and the Passedoit Gallery. At this stage he was clearly drawn to Surrealism. This was reinforced by meeting André Breton and coming into contact with Duchamp and the other European Surrealists in New York at the time. A typical work of this period, *St Elmo's Fire* (1944; New York, MOMA), contains strange organic formations suggestive of underwater life. Donati was one of the organizers of the *Exposition internationale du Surréalisme* held in Paris in the summer of 1947, to which he contributed a painting and two sculptures. In the late 1940s he responded to the crisis in Surrealism by going through a Constructivist phase, from which he developed a calligraphic style and drew on to melted tar, or diluted paint with turpentine. He also became associated with *Spazialismo*, founded by Lucio Fontana. Thus began his long fascination with surface and texture, including mixing paint with dust, that culminated in the 1950s in his *Moonscapes*, a series that has similarities with the work of Dubuffet. The fossil became a major theme for Donati through the 1960s, and he gave new importance to colour in his *Fossil* works, for example in *Red Yellow Fossil* (1964; Miami, Hills Col., see Selz, p. 19). In 1961 he was given a major retrospective at the Palais des Beaux-Arts in Brussels and frequently exhibited at group shows in the USA and elsewhere. He held a number of important teaching and advisory posts, including Visiting Lecturer at Yale University (1962–72).

BIBLIOGRAPHY
A. Breton: *Surrealism and Painting* (Paris, 1928, rev. Paris, 1965; Eng. trans., London and New York, 1972), pp. 195–8
P. Selz: *E. Donati* (Paris, 1965)
Enrico Donati: Surrealist Paintings and Objects from the Forties (exh. cat., New York, Zabriskie Gal., 1987)

Donato, Carlota de Santamarca y. *See under* SANTAMARCA.

Donato de' Bardi. *See* BARDI, DONATO DE'.

Donauer [Thonauer; Tonauer], **Hans, I** (*b* ?Munich, *c.* 1540; *d* Munich, before May 1596). German painter. He worked at the Munich court of Duke William V of Bavaria, and his career is known from court documents. As was customary for a court artist, his work covered several fields: he was active in fresco and oil painting and as a draughtsman; he also apparently organized festivities and painted miniatures. In his later years he was entrusted with duties relating to building maintenance. In artistic conception Donauer's work lay between his predecessor Hans Mielich, a decisive influence, and Friedrich Sustris, active at the court from 1573. Though an artist of lesser stature than either, Donauer had a certain creative power that set him apart from the purely craftsmanlike type of court artist.

In 1567 Donauer was accorded the right to practise as a master painter in Munich; that same year he entered the service of the court, and he remained on good terms with it throughout his life. Of his eight children, all the sons became painters, training in his workshop: Hans Donauer II (1569–1644) in Munich, Wilhelm Donauer in Augsburg, Georg Donauer (*b* 1571) at the court in Stuttgart. Other apprentices in his workshop included Hans Rottenhammer I and Hans Keppler (a master in 1605). Donauer's activities at court took him to Italy in 1569; in Rome he was commissioned to make purchases for the duke's Kunstkammer and to make studies of life at the Italian Renaissance courts. In 1578 he was sent as a painter to the emperor's court in Prague.

The main surviving works by Donauer are frescoes in the banqueting hall at Dachau castle (1567); two globes (1575–6; Munich, Bayer. Staatsbib.); a book of tournaments (1574; Munich, Bayer. Hauptstaatsarchv) for Pfalzgraf Philipp Ludwig of Neuburg (1547–1614); frescoes in the Rittersaal at Burg Trausnitz in Landshut (destr. 1961); and the topographical pictures (1586) in the Antiquarium at the Residenz in Munich. Recorded but untraced works are the interior painting (1567) of the chapel at Dachau Castle and the interior painting (1577) of the Neue Veste building (Munich, Residenz); pieces kept in the Kunstkammer (Munich, Mint); a painting of the *Last Supper* and one of *St Mary Magdalene* (1586–7); a picture of a deer and also other decorations made for tournaments. Two undocumented ascriptions are a death portrait of *Duke Albert V* (1579; Munich, Bayer. Staatsgemäldesammlung) and a falcon series (1578; Stockholm, Nmus.).

The overall impression made by Donauer's work is of an archaizing style of painting, bound to tradition. His dependence on models is striking. This is true even of his first work, the fresco cycle at Dachau Castle. The mythological figures are based on and rendered according to Italian models, while the ornamentation stems from Netherlandish scroll and strapwork. Other important works in his oeuvre are the globes of heaven and earth. The former in particular links astronomical and astrological data together skilfully into an exciting representation. The 22 drawings in the book devoted to tournaments show greater artistic freedom. They recount the course of the festival procession and show the fantastical costumes of the knights taking part. The sketchlike drawings of participants, as if dashed off in a hurry, are full of life. The style of the figures verges on caricature. Finally, the 102 views of towns and castles in the Antiquarium at the Residenz show Donauer breaking new ground with regard to subject-matter. Up until that time no other similar large series of true-to-life pictures had been on display. Even today the coordination between the views and the atmosphere of the room is remarkable. Yet here painting as such was secondary to a graphically linear style of representation, naturally required by the subject-matter. Donauer's work, despite its evidence of imagination and aesthetic endeavour, did not make a distinct impact on his period or those around him.

BIBLIOGRAPHY
Thieme–Becker
O. Hartig: 'Münchner Künstler und Kunstsachen', *München. Jb. Bild. Kst*, n. s. 1, viii (1931), p. 377
B. P. Baader: *Der bayerische Renaissancehof Herzog Wilhelms V* (Leipzig, 1943), pp. 59, 240, 242, 247, 287, 289, 312, 321
E. Abress: *Hans Donauer d. Ä. Bayerischer Maler und Hofkünstler am Hofe Herzog Wilhelms V* (diss., U. Munich, 1988)

ELISABETH ABRESS

Donducci, Giovanni Andrea. *See* MASTELLETTA.

Dong Duong [Dông-du'o'ng]. Important group of Cham monuments 20 km south-east of Mi Son in central Vietnam. According to two inscriptions discovered on the site, some of the monuments date from AD 875 and others from the beginning of the 10th century. Dong Duong was probably a royal Mahayana Buddhist monastery founded by King Indravarman II of Champa (*reg c.* 875–89) and formed part of his capital, Indrapura. The buildings, which are of brick and in an advanced state of ruin, are aligned precisely on an east–west axis, extending for more than 1300 m within a rectangular enclosure, which is preceded by an avenue 760 m long leading to a large rectangular basin surrounded by wide berms. They comprise several sanctuaries grouped within an inner enclosure and preceded by two successive long pillared halls, characteristic of the usual layout of Cham religious monuments but here adapted, in a manner unique in Cham art, to Buddhist practice, particularly with regard to the layout of the interior and the exterior piers supporting the stupa (*see* CHAMPA, §II, 1(iii) and fig. 3). The Buddhist sculpture of Dong Duong is of such importance and originality that the style of this period is known as the Dong Duong style (*see* CHAMPA, §III, 3 and fig. 6). However, seven other stelae found on the site demonstrate that the Mahayana Buddhist fervour that had inspired it was short-lived and was succeeded during the 10th century by a reversion to Shaivism.

BIBLIOGRAPHY
P. Stern: *L'Art du Champa (ancien Annam) et son évolution* (Toulouse, 1943), pp. 16–17, 49–50

P. Dupont: 'Les Apports chinois dans le style bouddhique de Dông-du'o'ng', *Bull. Ecole Fr. Extrême-Orient*, xliv (1947–50), pp. 267–74

J. Boisselier: *La Statuaire du Champa: Recherches sur les cultes et l'iconographie* (Paris, 1963), pp. 87–139

EMMANUEL GUILLON

Dongen, (Cornelis Theodorus Maria) Kees van (*b* Delfshaven, nr Rotterdam, 26 Jan 1877; *d* Monte Carlo, 28 May 1968). French painter and printmaker of Dutch birth. He took evening classes in geometric drawing from 1892 to 1897 at the Akademie voor Beeldende Kunsten in Rotterdam. In 1895 he began working intermittently for the newspaper *Rotterdamsche Nieuwsblad*, for which he made, among other things, a series of bright watercolour drawings of Rotterdam's red-light district and illustrations of Queen Wilhelmina's coronation. Van Dongen's first paintings used dark tones in imitation of Rembrandt, who remained the most important model for his work; his later book on Rembrandt was, in fact, a projection of his own life. By the mid-1890s he was using more vivid contrasts of black and white, for example in *Spotted Chimera* (1895; priv. col., see Chaumeil, pl. 1), his palette soon becoming brighter and his line more animated. In *Le Muet Windmill* (1896; priv. col., see Chaumeil, pl. 7), a red ochre monochrome painting, he successfully enlivened the colour by means of broad, energetic brushstrokes.

From 1897 van Dongen lived mostly in Paris, where he held his first exhibition in 1898 and met Félix Fénéon, who introduced him in 1903 to the group of painters associated with the *Revue Blanche*. He also made a name for himself by publishing popular, politically orientated drawings in a number of periodicals—for example in *L'Assiette au Beurre*, 30 (26 Oct 1901; see Chaumeil, figs 26–8), a special issue devoted to prostitution in contemporary Paris, a phenomenon thought to be symptomatic of the degeneration of the bourgeoisie—anticipating FAUVISM with the bright colours and sketchy style of these drawings in India ink and wash. His Fauve period began with the oil painting *Sideshow* (1904; Paris, Bernheim-Jeune; see Chaumeil, pl. I), which reinterpreted the Neo-Impressionist technique of divisionism in terms of loose, dynamic brushstrokes of unmixed colour and blurred boundaries between spaces and forms. Although coming into contact with the work of Die Brücke in 1908, van Dongen remained dedicated to Fauvism until 1912 in works such as *Saltimbanque with Nude Breast (The Dancer Nini at the Folies Bergères)* (*c.* 1907–8; Paris, Pompidou), developing his characteristic style of sensuous curved lines, warm tones and violent brushwork. Women were his favourite subjects, sometimes shown nude and almost invariably presented in an erotic manner in endlessly varied

Kees van Dongen: *In the Plaza: Women at a Balustrade*, oil on canvas, 0.81×1.00 m, *c.* 1911 (St Tropez, Musée de l'Annonciade)

poses, set inside a circus, theatre or music-hall as in *In the Plaza: Women at a Balustrade* (*c.* 1911; St Tropez, Mus. Annonciade; see fig.). He also painted colourful flower-pieces far removed from conventional still-lifes.

Van Dongen's travels through Spain, Morocco and Egypt in 1910 and 1913 resulted in a series of sombre but striking landscapes. His continuing attraction to the exotic led him to accept a commission to illustrate an edition of *Les Mille et Une Nuits* (Paris, 1918) by Dr Mardrus. In 1911 he participated in the first exhibition of the MODERNE KUNSTKRING, and in 1913 he exhibited paintings with rather elongated figures whose sharp contours made them resemble silhouettes, such as the *Spanish Shawl (Woman with Pigeons)* (1913; Paris, Pompidou). These led in turn to monochrome figures with decorative arabesques, which he continued to paint until well into the 1920s and which show his natural feeling for pose in its purest form.

From 1918 van Dongen concentrated on portraits of the beau monde in Paris, earning a reputation as chronicler of the period. With the portrait of *Charles Rappoport* (exh. Paris, Salon d'Automne, 1920; Rotterdam, Mus. Boymans–van Beuningen) he established a formula for the modern official portrait, painting the sitter's face and hands in detail using subtle tones, while leaving the background largely grey with the exception of some colourful accessory or a patch of bright material. In their diversity van Dongen's portraits managed to give a characteristic, in some cases deliberately stereotyped, depiction of his contemporaries that lent them also a documentary value. Portraits remained his principal genre, although in the 1950s he reduced the format. In lithography he found the graphic medium best suited to his fluent line; he developed a decorative version of the portrait by using elongated arabesques and by stylizing the face with unusually large eyes and mouth, as in *Brigitte Bardot* (*c.* 1955; see Kyriazi, 1976, p. 84). He became a French citizen in 1929.

WRITINGS
Van Dongen raconte ici la vie de Rembrandt et parle à ce propos de Rembrandt, des femmes et de l'art (Paris, 1927)

BIBLIOGRAPHY
E. des Courières: *Van Dongen* (Paris, 1925)
C. Wentinck: *Van Dongen* (Amsterdam, 1963)
L. Chaumeil: *Van Dongen: L'Homme et l'artiste—La Vie et l'oeuvre* (Geneva, 1967)
Kees van Dongen (exh. cat. by J. C. Ebbinge Wubben and B. Dorival, Paris, Mus. N. A. Mod.; Rotterdam, Mus. Boymans–van Beuningen, 1967)
G. Diehl: *Van Dongen* (Paris, 1968; Eng. trans., Milan, n.d. [*c.* 1970])
Hommage à van Dongen (exh. cat., Marseille, Mus. Cantini, 1969)
J. M. Kyriazi: *Van Dongen et le fauvisme* (Paris and Geneva, 1971)
——: *Van Dongen après le fauvisme* (Lausanne, 1976)
Kees van Dongen (exh. cat. by J. van Adrichen and others, Rotterdam, Mus. Boymans–van Beuningen, 1990)

For further bibliography *see* FAUVISM.

ANNEKE E. WIJNBEEK

Donghi, Antonio (*b* Rome, 16 March 1897; *d* Rome, 16 July 1963). Italian painter. He studied painting at the Istituto di Belle Arti in Rome (1908–16) before military service in France. In the post-World War I 'return to tradition' of the Scuola Romana he shared an interest in 17th- and 18th-century painting with Francesco Trombadori (1886–1961) and Carlo Socrate (1889–1967), with whom he exhibited at the Rome Biennale of 1923. In one-man shows a year later, at the Sala Stuard and Galleria

Bragaglia in Rome, Donghi exhibited the important *commedia dell'arte* painting *Carnival* (1923; New York, priv. col., see 1985 exh. cat., p. 104). The critic Ugo Ojetti saw his clear realism and choice of subject-matter (people, still-lifes and cityscapes) as egalitarian and related to Caravaggesque influences. The disconcerting immobility of his figures (e.g. *Woman at the Window*, 1926; Florence, Pitti) also drew comparisons with the work of Seurat and of Henri Rousseau, and it was identified as 'magic realism' by Franz Roh (*Expressionismus, magischer Realismus*, Leipzig, 1925).

Donghi won wider recognition when *Carnival* won the 1st Honourable Mention at the International Exhibition of 1927 at the Carnegie Institute, Pittsburgh. He visited Paris in the following year. His figures became more impassive, and the peculiarity of such works as *Song* (1934; priv. col., see 1985 exh. cat., p. 33) bears comparison with the contemporary work of Magritte. Despite exhibiting regularly Donghi was falling from favour by the mid-1930s; he turned to teaching, becoming professor of figure drawing at the Accademia di Belle Arti in 1936, and in 1938 professor of pictorial techniques at the Istituto Centrale per il Restauro, Rome. Although he continued to paint landscapes (e.g. *Lark Hunting*, 1942; priv. col., see 1985 exh. cat., p. 47) his work appeared anachronistic in the post-war context, and his reputation was not restored until 20 years after his death.

BIBLIOGRAPHY
Antonio Donghi (exh. cat., ed. L. Pistoi; Rome, Gal. Oca, 1983)
Donghi: Sessanta dipinti dal 1922 al 1961 (exh. cat. by A. Trombadori and M. Fagiolo dell'Arco, Rome, Pal. Braschi, 1985)

MATTHEW GALE

Dong Qichang [Tung Ch'i-ch'ang; *zi* Xuanzai; *hao* Sibo, Siweng, Xiangguang, Xiangguang jushi; Wenmin] (*b* Shanghai, 10 Feb 1555; *d* Dec 1636). Chinese painter, calligrapher, connoisseur, theoretician, collector and high official.

1. Early career, to 1599. 2. Later career, 1599–1636.

1. EARLY CAREER, TO 1599. At the age of 12 Dong Qichang, the son of a local school-teacher, passed the prefectural civil-service examination to qualify as a Government Student (*shengyuan*) and was awarded a coveted place in the prefectural school. Mortified, however, at being ranked below his younger kinsman Dong Chuanxu because of his clumsy calligraphy, from 1571 Dong resolved to study calligraphy in earnest. His initial models were rubbings of works by the Tang-period (AD 618–907) calligraphers Yan Zhenqing and Yu Shinan (558–638), but soon realizing the superior merits of the Six Dynasties (AD 222–589) calligraphers, he turned to the works of Zhong You (AD 151–230) and the great Wang Xizhi (*see* WANG (i), (1)). After three years he was confident of having grasped their style, and no longer admired works by the Ming-period (1368–1644) masters Wen Zhengming and Zhu Yunming.

Dong moved (*c.* 1567) to Huating (modern Songjiang), near Shanghai, where his talents won him a reputation. He was engaged by the retired Minister of Rites, Lu Shusheng, as a tutor to Lu's son, and was a frequent visitor at the home of the painter Gu Zhengyi (*fl* 1575–96), who granted him ready access to his collection of Yuan (1279–1368) paintings. In 1571 or thereabouts, Dong began to study calligraphy with Mo Ruzhong (1509–89), a former official and accomplished calligrapher, whose son Mo Shilong (1538–87) was considered by many to be the most promising painter of the day; Dong's admiration for Shilong was mixed with feelings of rivalry. By 1580 Dong had gained entrée to the largest and finest private collection of the period, that of XIANG YUANBIAN, who lived in nearby Jiaxing. The superb pieces of calligraphy in the collection, many from the Jin (AD 265–420) and Tang periods, together with Wang Xizhi's *Guannu tie* that Dong saw on a trip to Nanjing, convinced Dong of the superficiality of his earlier calligraphic efforts and of the overwhelming importance of basing his style and his theories on original works.

Dong executed his first painting in 1577, but none of his early works survive. They were apparently modelled on the Yuan masters, whose paintings dominated collections in the Jiangnan region (the south) and whose styles were universally favoured by its gentry. Like many of the connoisseurs and scholar-painters of his acquaintance, Dong preferred the styles of HUANG GONGWANG and NI ZAN to those of Wang Meng and Wu Zhen (collectively known as the Four Masters of the Yuan).

In 1588 Dong passed the provincial civil-service examination to gain the *juren* degree, and in 1589 he passed the national examination for the *jinshi* degree. He was then appointed to the Hanlin Academy in Beijing, membership of which was virtually a prerequisite for those, like Dong, who aspired to high political office. One of Dong's teachers in the Academy was the Vice Minister of Rites, Han Shineng, who had probably the finest private collection of paintings and calligraphy in the capital. Dong quickly became Han's favourite pupil, borrowing valuable early works to study and copy.

In Beijing, Dong began to search for works by the five great landscapists of the Five Dynasties (AD 907–960) and Northern Song (960–1127) periods: Jing Hao, Guan Tong, Dong Yuan, Juran and Li Cheng. His attention soon focused on DONG YUAN, whom he proclaimed—with the dogmatic confidence characteristic of his pronouncements—as the pivotal figure in the development of what he called the Southern school or orthodox tradition (*zhengchuan*) of landscape painting, in which, of course, he placed himself. His ideas are crystallized in two famous passages in the *bieji* section ('miscellaneous writings') of his *Rongtai ji* ('Collected writings of the Minister of Rites'). Together they define his concept of the Northern and Southern schools (*Nanbei zong*), in which the pre-eminent masters of the past are divided into two 'lineages': the NORTHERN SCHOOL, with its dependence on years of technical training, that had its beginning in the highly coloured blue-and-green (*qinglü*) style of the Tang painter Li Sixun (*see* LI, (1)); and the SOUTHERN SCHOOL, with its emphasis on inborn talent, that began with the graded ink washes of WANG WEI, reached maturity with Dong Yuan and found new expression in the works of the Four Yuan Masters. Dong never composed a methodical treatise setting forth his theories at length; his ideas on art are to be gleaned simply from the loose collection of short separate passages, many of them originally colophons,

grouped under the headings *Shupin* ('Evaluation of calligraphy') and *Huazhi* ('Aim of painting') at the end of his collected writings.

In 1591, while on a trip to Fujian Province, Dong missed the examination that marked the end of his course of study at the Hanlin Academy. He retired to Huating and for two years devoted his time to calligraphy and painting, borrowing works to copy from his old mentor, Gu Zhengyi. In 1593, he returned to Beijing to take up the post of Junior Compiler in the Hanlin Academy. In the same year he received his first invitation to inscribe a colophon on an important work, Wang Wei's *River and Mountains after Snow* (Kyoto, Ogawa priv. col.), proof of his growing reputation as a connoisseur. In 1596 he was dispatched to Changsha in Hunan Province as an imperial envoy, and the following year he went to Nanchang, Jiangxi Province, to conduct the provincial examination. He returned delighted to have seen the rolling hills and river scenery of the south that had inspired Dong Yuan, and with the satisfaction of having purchased two works that ensured his reputation as a collector: Huang Gongwang's *Dwelling in the Fuchun Mountains* and Jiang Shen's *River and Mountains for a Thousand Li* (both Taipei, N. Pal. Mus.).

One of Dong Qichang's earliest extant dated paintings is the *Wanluan Thatched Hall* (1597; Taiwan, priv. col., see *EWA*, xiv, pl. 193), showing a landscape that departs starkly from the dense, intricate, tapestry-like images perpetuated by the Wu school followers of Wen Zhengming. Banks and cliffs are stripped almost bare of vegetation to reveal deeply crevassed and folded shapes whose interest lies in their formal arrangement within the composition. The textured inner contour of each fold highlights the outer contour of the fold before, creating a surface pattern of light and dark and a recession into space, which here and there is brought abruptly to a halt by a bordering band of white. Dong delighted in ambiguities: a cliff that fades suddenly into space, a mountain without visible support, a cloud that eats through the surface of a cliff. Only a handful of paintings before 1605 survive, but in each Dong has conducted a new experiment, combining a variety of inventive shapes against blank areas of paper or silk. Although in several, Dong purported to draw inspiration from early models, the resulting landscapes show an artist unmistakably engaged in forming a radically new style.

In 1598 Dong was appointed tutor to the eldest son of the Wanli emperor (*reg* 1573–1620), whom the emperor stubbornly refused to name as heir apparent. During a tutoring session, Dong had the misfortune to elicit from the young prince a response that the court enthusiastically hailed as auguring well for a future ruler. Almost certainly this incurred the emperor's displeasure; early in 1599 Dong was relegated to the provinces, though awarded a nominal promotion. Unhappy at this prospect, Dong refused the appointment, little knowing that he was to be denied a post in the capital until after the emperor's death more than 20 years later.

2. LATER CAREER, 1599–1636. Between 1599 and 1604 Dong remained in retirement at Huating, without even the tender of official employment; eventually, perhaps fearing to lose all opportunity, he accepted the first

appointment offered him, as education intendant of Huguang (modern Hubei and Hunan provinces). Some 18 months later a student riot resulted in the destruction of his official residence, and he obtained permission to resign. In 1609 he accepted a second provincial appointment in Fujian Province but resigned after only 45 days. Although offered three more provincial appointments in the following decade, he resolved to remain in retirement at home.

Dong's self-imposed retirement left him at leisure to follow his artistic pursuits. His paintings of 1616–17 show a style that has fully matured: the heavy shading of the *Wanluan Thatched Hall*, and the thin, pencil-like strokes that impart to his other early works something of the quality of drawings, are replaced by a rich texture of tones from velvet-black to palest grey, punctuated by bands of still paler paper or silk, drawing the eye inward and upward. Dong still delighted in spatial ambiguities and occasional visual tricks such as a small upturned clifftop, left unpainted, that looks like a hole in the painting; but the appealing experimental shapes and forms of his early works are replaced by a more standardized variety of landscape elements, whose excitement lies in the vitality of their brushwork and in the pattern of their combination (see fig. 1). Clearly, the catalyst that produced this new style was a resurgent interest in the Yuan-period styles of Huang Gongwang and Ni Zan. In his *Qingbian Mountains* (1617; Cleveland, OH, Mus. A.), for example, Dong used the clumps of small boulders, or 'alum rocks', tiny trees and wavy hemp-fibre strokes (*pima cun*) of Huang Gongwang, and in his *Living in Lofty Retirement* (1617; Beijing, Pal. Mus.) he borrowed the dry brushwork, angular strokes and compositional scheme from Ni Zan. Within the cool, calculated and even monumental structures Dong erected, however, such elements assume a new character entirely of his own making.

In 1616 Dong's house in Huating was burnt to the ground by an angry mob, incensed by his ill-usage of a family named Fan. According to one version of the story, Dong accused a member of the Fan family of having composed a ballad recounting Dong's passion for the beautiful daughter of a neighbour's servant and her abduction one night by his second son, Zuchang. Fan resolutely protested his innocence, and when he died soon after, his wife arrived at the Dong compound with a group of her maids to accuse Dong of responsibility. An angry Zuchang imprisoned the women and had them beaten or raped, so enraging the townspeople that they burnt the house and its contents. Dong was, nonetheless, officially exonorated. This incident may account for the dearth of Dong's paintings from the years immediately preceding 1616 and for Dong's erstwhile unpopularity in the People's Republic of China (1949–), where he was rated as a notorious example of the landlord class.

On the death of the Wanli emperor in 1620, many officials who had withdrawn or been forced into retirement during his long reign were reappointed. The most prominent was Ye Xianggao, who became Grand Secretary in 1621, under the Tianqi emperor (1621–7). Hoping to offset the growing power of the eunuch faction, Ye reinstated those who shared his political views, a group known to history as the Donglin party, which advocated renewed morality in government. Among the friends he

1. Dong Qichang: *Landscape*, hanging scroll, ink on paper, 1676×529 mm, 1617 (Melbourne, National Gallery of Victoria)

reappointed was Dong Qichang, who returned to Beijing in 1622. Dong placed his talents as a calligrapher at the service of the Donglin group; his calligraphies and paintings, extant and recorded, testify to his friendship with prominent figures in the movement, although he was never considered a member of the Donglin camp. He was awarded a series of posts, including one placing him in charge of the Hanlin Academy in Nanjing during an 18-month assignment in the south, culminating in an appointment as Vice Minister of Rites in 1623. During this time he assisted in the complication of the *Veritable Records of the Emperor Shenzong* [Wanli] and the *Veritable Records of the Emperor Guanzong* [Taichang].

Dong's paintings of the early and mid-1620s rarely exhibit the monumental compositions so impressive in works dating from only a few years earlier. Instead, Dong formulated a new design, into which he introduced a diversity of shapes, with mountains simplified in structure and reduced in height so that foreground vies with background in size, and open areas of water and sky assume a new prominence. Many of Dong's most innovative compositions occur in several series of large album leaves, perhaps because he produced them primarily for his own amusement rather than as gifts, and because as a format new to him they constituted a fresh experiment. In these Dong evinces a new interest in colour, not on silk as occasionally in the past, but on paper. Clear tones—greens, browns, light blues, pale pink, ochre, orange and small touches of tomato red—are orchestrated in carefully constructed compositions to create some of the most strikingly beautiful colour paintings of the Ming period, an achievement with which Dong has never been properly credited. A splendid example is his *Large Album of Landscapes*, with ten leaves variously dated 1621, 1623 and 1624 (Kansas City, MO, Nelson–Atkins Mus. A.; see fig. 2).

At the end of 1624 the Donglin party succumbed to the machinations of the eunuch faction led by the ruthless eunuch Wei Zhongxian, who by now entirely dominated the young Tianqi emperor. Dong was quick to dissociate himself from his Donglin connections and attempted to foster at least a semblance of friendly ties with the opposition by complying with requests for his services as a calligrapher and painter. His manoeuvring was successful: early in 1625 he was promoted, though to a post of only nominal power, as Minister of Rites in Nanjing. In 1626 he resigned and returned to Huating.

In 1627 the Tianqi emperor died and Wei Zhongxian committed suicide to avoid arrest. Under the Chongzhen emperor (*reg* 1628–44) the fortunes of the Donglin party recovered briefly, before waning again late in 1629 in the face of new opposition. By appealing to an interest in painting and calligraphy, Dong fostered friendships with individuals in both camps; at the end of 1631 he was recalled to the capital as Minister of Rites in charge of the Household Administration of the Heir Apparent. In 1634 he was promoted to the first rank and soon afterwards he retired to Huating.

Dong's late paintings are usually smaller and more intimate than his works of the preceding decade. His album leaves are more like sketches or studies than finished works, often characterized by short, pointed, staccato strokes across rocky surfaces, resulting in a curious flattening of the design, the antithesis of the volumetric forms he had hitherto striven to achieve. Yet two of Dong's largest and most magnificent works were painted in this

2. Dong Qichang: *Landscape after a Poem by Du Fu*, ink and colour on paper, 562×356 mm, 1621; album leaf from his *Large Album of Landscapes*, 1621–4 (Kansas City, MO, Nelson–Atkins Museum of Art)

period: *In the Shade of Summer Trees* (h. 3.21 m; Taipei, N. Pal. Mus.), constructed in the monumental mode reminiscent of Dong's paintings *c.* 1617, and *Landscape after Wang Xia and Li Cheng* (h. 2.55 m; datable after 1630; Shanghai Mus.), which restricts its use of landscape forms to little more than large foreground trees and the silhouette of a single mountain in the distance, separated by a wide expanse of water. But although compositionally the two paintings are very different, there is an emphasis in both on tonal values and soft, wet brushwork; they illustrate to perfection Dong's dictum that a painted landscape should be compounded of three or four large sections easily grasped by the eye. They share an air of stability, lent by a strong reliance on the horizontal, that makes them doubly impressive.

Dong was buried outside Suzhou at the foot of a small mountain overlooking Lake Tai, Jiangsu Province. His reputation, enormous in his lifetime, became even greater after his death. In the hands of such later Chinese painters as the Four Wangs from the early Qing period (1644–1911)—Wang Shiming, Wang Jian, Wang Yuanqi and Wang Hui—his theories and style became the basis of a new orthodoxy (*see* ORTHODOX SCHOOL), exerting a powerful influence on the course of Chinese painting up to modern times. Even the great individualist painter ZHU DA drew on Dong's style for inspiration, creating a style uniquely his own, just as Dong had transformed the style of the Yuan master Huang Gongwang. It was the narrow vision of Dong's followers in the 'orthodox' manner, rather than any property inherent in Dong's style, that caused it in the end to have a stultifying effect on their works. The Qing emperors Kangxi (*reg* 1662–1722) and Qianlong (*reg* 1736–96) both admired Dong's calligraphy and frequently copied his works. The four final volumes of the *Sanxi tang fatie* ('Calligraphy from the Sanxi tang'), the great compendium of rubbings from calligraphy in the imperial collection, initiated in 1747, are entirely devoted to Dong's work, outstripping by two volumes the rest of Ming calligraphy combined. As a theorist, collector and connoisseur, recording his views and attributions on countless paintings and pieces of calligraphy that passed beneath his eye, Dong, more than any other figure, changed the course of Chinese painting and its history.

See also CHINA, §§IV, 2(vi) and V, 3(iv)(a).

WRITINGS
Rongtai ji [Collected writings of the Minister of Rites] (*c.* 1630); (rev. 3/1635/*R* in Ming dai yishujia ji huikan) (Taipei, 1968)

BIBLIOGRAPHY
EWA: 'Tung Ch'i-ch'ang'
Zhang Tingyu and others, eds: *Ming shi* [History of the Ming dynasty] (1739, rev. Beijing, 1974), *juan* 288
Qingfu Shanren, ed.: *Dong Huating shuhua lu* [Record of calligraphies and paintings by Dong Qichang] (19th century)
N. Wu: *Tung Ch'i-ch'ang: The Man, His Time, and His Landscape Painting*, 2 vols (diss., New Haven, CT, Yale U., 1954)
——: 'Tung Ch'i-ch'ang (1555–1636): Apathy in Government and Fervor in Art', *Confucian Personalities*, ed. A. Wright and D. Twitchett (Stanford, 1962), pp. 260–93
S. Bush: *The Chinese Literati on Painting: Su Shih (1037–1101) to Tung Ch'i-ch'ang (1555–1636)* (Cambridge, MA, 1971), pp. 158–79
Shodō Geijutsu [The art of calligraphy], viii (Tokyo, 1972/*R* 1976), pp. 184–6, 207–14, pls 103–54
Gugong lidai fashu quanji [Collected calligraphies from successive dynasties in the Palace Museum] (Taipei, 1976–9), viii, pp. 29–178; xix, pp. 83–109; xxi, pp. 127–57; xxiv, pp. 13–140; xxv; xxvi, pp. 3–25; xxvii, pp. 3–59; xxx, pp. 55–81
Wai-kam Ho: 'Tung Ch'i-ch'ang's New Orthodoxy and the Southern School Theory', *Artists and Traditions: Uses of the Past in Chinese Culture*, ed. C. Murck (Princeton, 1976), pp. 113–29
Jo I, Tō Kishō [Xu Wei, Dong Qichang], v of *Bunjinga suihen: Chūgoku hen* [Masterpieces of literati painting: China] (Tokyo, 1979/*R* 1986)
Rong Geng: *Congtie mu* [Catalogue of collectanea of calligraphy rubbings], 3 vols (Hong Kong, 1980–82), pp. 262–72, 1220–76
H. Kohara, ed.: *Tō Kishō no shoga* [Dong Qichang's calligraphy and painting], 2 vols (Tokyo, 1981)
J. Cahill: *The Compelling Image* (Cambridge, MA, 1982), pp. 36–69
——: *The Distant Mountains: Chinese Painting of the Late Ming Dynasty, 1570–1644* (New York and Tokyo, 1982), pp. 87–128
Xu Bangda: *Gu shuhua weie kaobian* [Detection of forgeries in pre-modern Chinese calligraphy and painting] (Jiangsu, 1984), *juan* 2, text, pp. 147–58; pls, pp. 300–28
C. Riely: 'Tung Ch'i-ch'ang's Life', *The Century of Tung Chi'i-ch'ang, 1555–1636*, ed. Wai-kan Ho (Seattle and Kansas City, MO, 1992), pp. 387–457
Wai-kam Ho, ed.: *The Century of Tung Ch'i-ch'ang, 1555–1636* (Seattle and Kansas City, MO, 1992)
C. Riely: *Tung Ch'i-ch'ang's Life (1555–1636): The Interplay of Politics and Art* (diss., Cambridge, MA, Harvard U., 1995)

CELIA CARRINGTON RIELY

Dong Son [Dongson]. Site in northern Vietnam on the south bank of the Ma River in Thanh Hoa Province. There are traces of very early settlement, but the chief importance of the site lies in the large number of bronze objects, some of them dating from *c.* 600 BC, found in burial sites on the riverbank. These burials are simple ditches in which the dead were placed in a stretched-out position, in marked contrast to the contemporary Chinese brick-vaulted tombs found in Tonkin and Thanh Hoa. Besides bronze objects, the burials contain arms and other implements made of iron, as well as jade ornaments, polished stone axes and schist tools, indicating that a pre-Bronze Age culture also existed in the region. The bronzes include arms, ploughshares and other agricultural implements, receptacles of various kinds and, most important, a number of the decorated kettledrums that are the best known and most characteristic products of the Dong Son culture, as well as objects of Chinese origin. The bronze is composed of 55% copper, 15–16% tin and 17–19% lead.

Dong Son drums and other bronze objects have been found all over South-east Asia from southern China and north-east Thailand to the eastern islands of Indonesia. The discovery of so many bronze drums at Dong Son and other sites in northern Vietnam suggests that there was an indigenous industry in the area or at least that Dong Son was its main centre of diffusion. Most of the objects show a close affinity in form, style and decoration to the art of central China in the 4th–3rd centuries BC, and it has been suggested that the Dongsonian people formed part of the last great southward migration of Indonesian peoples from the Asian mainland to the archipelago and that they acquired Chinese techniques of pottery and of working bronze and iron during that period. In AD 43 Dong Son, having resisted 300 years of Chinese expansion, was finally incorporated into the Han empire.

BIBLIOGRAPHY
F. Heger: *Alte Metalltrommeln aus Südostasien* (Leipzig, 1902)
V. Goloubew: 'L'Age du Bronze au Tonkin et dans le Nord-Annam', *Bull. Ecole Fr. Extrême-Orient*, xxix (1929), pp. 1ff
——: 'Sur l'origine et la diffusion des tambours métalliques', *Praehist. Asiae Orient.*, i (1932), pp. 137ff
B. Karlgren: 'The Date of the Early Dong-Son Culture', *Bull. Mus. Far E. Ant.*, xiv (1942), pp. 1–28
J. Janse: *The Ancient Dwelling Site of Dong S'on (Thanh-Hoa, Annam)* (1958), iii of *Archaeological Research in Indo-China* (Cambridge, MA, 1947–58)
G. Coedès *Les Peuples de la péninsule indochinoise* (Paris, 1962); Eng. trans by H. M. Wright as *The Making of South East Asia* (London, 1966)
C. Higham: *The Archaeology of Mainland Southeast Asia from 10,000 BC to the Fall of Angkor* (Cambridge, 1989/*R* 1991)

JOHN VILLIERS

Dong Yuan [Tung Yüan; *zi* Shuda; *hao* Beiyuan] (*b* Zhongling, near Jin xain, Jiangxi Province, *c.* AD 900; *d* ?Zhongling, 962). Chinese painter. He was a near contemporary of Li Cheng and was considered a foremost representative of the Northern Song (960–1127) monochrome landscape painting tradition as interpreted in southern China at the end of the 10th century. During this time landscape painting became established as the most important category of Chinese painting (*see* CHINA, §§V, 1(ii) and 3(iv)(b)). For many centuries afterwards, Dong exerted great influence on painters of landscape. Dong Qichang, the influential theorist and artist, traced the original source of the literati painting (*wen ren hua*) tradition (*see* CHINA, §V, 4(ii)) of monochrome-ink landscape painting to Wang Wei, Juran and Dong Yuan.

Little is known of Dong Yuan's life except that he lived mainly in Nanjing. It is also known that *c.* AD 937 he was ordered to paint a picture of Mt Lu, which indicates that he was by then established as a prominent painter. In 947 he was asked to collaborate with four other (now unidentifiable) noted artists in the depiction (destr.) of a snowfall that took place on New Year's Day. He was a member of the imperial court of Li Jing (*reg* AD 943–61), the second emperor of the Southern Tang dynasty (937–75), and served in the official capacity of Assistant Director of the North Park (Bei yuan), whence his *hao*. As he is also credited with having painted a fairly substantial number of scrolls, it appears that his official duties were not very demanding.

The subject-matter and titles of some of Dong's paintings suggest a rather easy-going temperament. He painted a range of different subjects, including such animals as tigers, buffalo and water dragons, as well as peaceful rustic scenes. He is best known for his landscapes, which were executed in two styles. One of these was a monochrome ink-painting style in the tradition of Wang Wei. All the attributed examples of this style are in Japanese collections; they are allegedly of dubious authenticity (Sirén, p. 211). The other style was more closely identified with the traditions of antiquity, using polychrome pigments in the manner of Li Sixun. The extant examples of this style are more reliable expressions of the original conception. It was also more frequently imitated. Guo Ruoxu (*fl* 11th century), a minor court official at the capital of the Northern Song dynasty, Bianliang (modern Kaifeng), writing *c.* 1024, characterized the two styles as a 'wet manner', which resembled Wang Wei's, and a coloured style like that of Li Sixun—a reference to Li's 'blue-and-green manner' of much-imitated brilliantly coloured works. At the beginning of the 14th century Tang Hou wrote in the *Gujin Huajian* ('Criticisms of past and present painting') that there were two kinds of landscapes by Dong Yuan; in one, the peaks were like lumps of alum, painted with diluted ink. In these pictures there were also groves and distant trees or mysterious scenery extending far into the distance. The mountains and rocks were painted with hemp-fibre texture strokes or 'wrinkles' (*pima cun*). The other type of landscape was executed in strong and archaistic colour, with few texture strokes. Coloured garments were rendered in red or blue paint, white garments in chalk. It is not clear whether Dong used both styles simultaneously, although Tang Hou claimed that the first style was associated with his youth and gave way in later years to the second.

Dong Yuan chose for his subject-matter primarily scenes from Jiangnan, the region south of the Yangzi River. He painted local hill country and depicted mists in a novel way. The compositions of his paintings generally consist of open vistas of rivers and mud-flats viewed in aerial perspective and interrupted by low ranges of rolling hills very different in character from the monumental cliffs of the north. The misty quality of southern China is depicted with an overall evenness that gives equal value to all pictorial elements, precluding any strong focal points. In the absence of documented authentic works, it is difficult to ascertain what, beyond such general qualities, constituted Dong's individual style. Indeed, although many artists claimed to work in his tradition, each appears to have found something different in it.

The fundamental quality most frequently mentioned in the numerous descriptions of Dong Yuan's style is his ability to transform the Jiangnan landscape into pictures essentially true to nature and at the same time 'stimulating to poets'. One of the earliest comments is by Shen Gua (1030–94) in the *Mengxi bitan* ('Brush talks by the stream of dreams'): in the section called *Tuhua ge* ('Song on the history of painting'), he wrote that Dong Yuan and the monk Juran, working south of the Yangzi, established their independent styles by the use of pale ink and the rendering of light mist. Dong was noted especially for his open views and autumn landscapes. Dong's pupil Juran adopted Dong's technique so completely that the style of the two is frequently referred to as the Dong–Ju manner. They initiated a tradition that was to become extremely influential during the Yuan (1279–1368) and ensuing periods. It was characterized by hemp-fibre texture strokes instead of colour washes to create tactile surfaces and was adaptable to the portrayal of lush marshy scenery and low hills. Critics claimed that such brushstrokes were best seen from a distance. Neither Dong Yuan nor Juran was widely known or appreciated during the Northern Song period, although the catalogue of the paintings in the collection of Emperor Huizong (*reg* 1101–26), the *Xuanhe huapu* ('Xuanhe collection of painting'; preface dated 1120), lists 78 works by Dong. The painter and critic Mi Fu, of the late Northern Song period, was the first to identify him as a genius, unsurpassable and divine (*shen*).

In essence, Dong Yuan provides the link between Wang Wei and the later literati. During the Yuan period critical acclaim raised him to the status of a leading master. Although no fully documented examples of paintings in either of Dong's two styles are extant, the *Festival for the Evocation of Rain* (*Longsu jiaomin tu*; see fig.) is generally accepted as typical of his interpretation of the blue-and-green style of Li Sixun (*see* LI, (1)), whether it was painted by Dong himself or after his manner. The attribution was made by Dong Qichang, who acquired the work in 1597. The painting has darkened considerably with age and may have been retouched, but the basic elements of Dong Yuan's manner are clearly evident. It is a panoramic bird's-eye view filled with broad expanses of water reaching back to the distant horizon. It differed from other contemporary paintings of the north, in which the view, seen from ground-level, was obstructed by mountains. Clustered rock forms build up the rounded crests of low mountains in 'hemp-fibre texture strokes', and vegetation is sparse. Although human forms are not dwarfed by high mountains, their place in the landscape proclaims their relative insignificance before the wonders of nature. It has been suggested (*see* Loehr, p. 115) that the title might also be translated as *Genteel Townsfolk at Leisure*: certainly the people depicted appear to be engaged in carefree activities. Another painting associated with Dong Yuan is *Clear Weather in the Valley* (horizontal scroll, ink and traces of colour on paper, 375×1508 mm; late 10th century; Boston, MA, Mus. F.A.); it has been attributed to him at least since the Ming period (1368–1644) by such authorities as Dong Qichang and Wang Shimin. However, its general style indicates that it cannot pre-date the 12th century.

Dong Yuan (attrib.): *Festival for the Evocation of Rain* (*Longsu jiaomin tu*), hanging scroll, ink and colours on ?silk, 1.56×1.60 m, 10th century (Taipei, National Palace Museum)

Early evidence of Dong's influence is to be seen in such works as *Autumn Colours on the Qiao and Hua Mountains* (*Qiao Hua giuse tu*; handscroll, ink and light colours on paper, 284×932 mm, 1296; Taipei, N. Pal. Mus.) by Zhao Mengfu (for illustration *see* ZHAO, (1)). This scroll uses aerial perspective and the open vista as well as the soft colour washes that had come to be associated with paintings from antiquity. Other masters of the Yuan period were equally influenced. Even Sheng Mao was sometimes linked to the tradition because of his use of rounded masses of mountains with small groups of humpy rocks and 'unravelled-rope' modelling strokes.

A treatise entitled *Xie shanshui jue* ('Secrets of describing landscape') by Huang Gongwang, which was published in Tao Zongyi's *Zhuogeng lu* ('Records compiled after ceasing to farm') in 1366, described Dong's general painting technique. The shoals described by Huang as part of the repertory were frequently used in Yuan painting as a device to carry the eye across junctures of water and land. Wu Zhen also followed in Dong Yuan's tradition; its ultimate refinement is to be seen in the sparse forms painted by Ni Zan, who also, according to Dong Qichang, developed his textural stroke from Dong Yuan. In addition to such literary references, there is concrete evidence that early and middle Yuan artists made copies from originals by Dong, which must have been in local collections. Artists appear to have taken full advantage of the new opportunities for travel that opened up at that time, providing greater access to collections for both viewing and study.

Yuan painters, while not always in tune with Dong Yuan's compositional conceptions, admired the unity in his work—described by Mi Fu as 'plain, insipid naturalness'—created by giving equal emphasis to all pictorial elements and painting them in a free, wet manner. The Yuan-period interpretation of Dong's work served as a conduit to the WU SCHOOL of the Ming dynasty (1368–1644), where it was significant in the development of the reinvigorated literati style. Still later, Dong Yuan was a model for adherents of Dong Qichang's SOUTHERN SCHOOL of scholar–amateur idealist painting (then called *nanzenghua*) after the latter proclaimed him as its greatest master.

BIBLIOGRAPHY

Franke: 'Tung Yüan'

Guo Ruoxu: *Tuhua jianwen zhi* [Experiences in painting] (*c.* 1024); ed. Huan Miaozi (Shanghai, 1963); Eng. trans. in *Xuanhe huapu* [Xuanhe collection of paintings] (preface dated 1120); ed. Yu Jianhua (Beijing, 1964)

A. C. Soper: *Kuo Jo-hsü's 'Experiences in Painting' (T u-hua chien-wen chih): An Eleventh Century History of Chinese Painting* (Washington, DC, 1951/R 1971)

O. Sirén: *Chinese Painting: Leading Masters and Principles*, i (London, 1956), pp. 208–12

Chinese Art Treasures: A Selected Group of Objects from the Chinese National Palace Museum and the Chinese National Central Museum, Taichung (exh. cat., preface W. Shih-chieh; Washington, DC, N.G.A.; New York, Met.; Boston, MA, Mus. F.A.; and elsewhere; 1961–2), no. 14

R. M. Barnhart: 'Marriage of the Lord of the River: A Lost Landscape by Tung Yüan', *Artibus Asiae*, suppl. xxvii (1970) [whole issue]

R. M. Barnhart, Y. Iriya and Y. Nakada: *Tō Gen, Kyonen* [Dong Yuan, Juran], ii of *Bunjinga suihen* [Selections of literati painting] (Tokyo, 1977)

M. Loehr: *The Great Painters of China* (New York, 1980), pp. 110–30

W. Ho and others: *Eight Dynasties of Chinese Painting: The Collections of the Nelson-Atkins Museum of Art, Kansas City, and the Cleveland Museum of Art* (exh. cat., Kansas City, MO, Nelson-Atkins Mus. A.; Cleveland, OH, Mus. A.; Tokyo, N. Mus.; 1980–81), no. 6

Chūgoku no bijutsu: Kaiga [Fine art of China: painting] (Kyoto, 1982); Eng. trans., ed. T. Miyagawa as: *Chinese Painting* (Tokyo, 1983), pp. 123–4, 173

MARY S. LAWTON

Doni, Agnolo (*b* Florence, 29 Aug 1474; *d* Florence, 5 Jan 1539). Italian merchant and patron. He came from a family of dyers and enrolled in the Arte della Lana (clothmakers' guild) in 1488. He made a considerable fortune from the cloth trade; the status he attained is reflected in his marriage in 1504 to the Florentine noblewoman Maddalena Strozzi. The couple took up residence in the house that Agnolo had had built. According to Vasari, Morte da Feltro decorated the wedding chests (untraced) for the furnishings for the marital bedroom, built by the del Tasso workshop. The del Tasso shop also probably made the elaborate painted and gilded frame, designed by Michelangelo, for the painting he executed for Agnolo, the Doni Tondo, *Holy Family with St John the Baptist* (1506; Florence, Uffizi).

In the same year, Agnolo commissioned portraits of himself and his wife from Raphael (Florence, Pitti). Vasari reported that Agnolo collected antique art as well as modern works; he probably bought Donatello's *Amor Atys* (Florence, Bargello), a work once thought to be antique, which remained in the possession of the Doni family until 1778. Agnolo's collection, which was visited by artists and connoisseurs, was further enriched in 1516 by the addition of the *Holy Family with St John* (Rome, Pal. Barberini) by Fra Bartolommeo.

BIBLIOGRAPHY

G. Vasari: *Vite* (1550, rev. 2/1568); ed. G. Milanesi, iv (1879), p. 325; viii (1881), pp. 158–9

A. Cecchi: 'Agnolo e Maddalena Doni committenti di Raffaello', *Studi su Raffaello. Atti del congresso internazionale di studi: Urbino and Florence, 1984*, pp. 429–39

ALESSANDRO CECCHI

Doni, Antonio [Anton] **Francesco** (*b* Florence, 16 May 1513; *d* Venice, Sept 1574). Italian writer. The son of a scissors-maker, he joined the Servite Order at an early age but was expelled from it in 1540 for sexual malpractice. He began to study law at Piacenza (1542), then set up a printing press in Florence and finally settled in Venice in 1547, where he earned his living as a hack writer for the vernacular press. His wide-ranging interest in the visual arts was reflected in a treatise on *disegno*, a discourse on *imprese*, a book on medals, several letters and dedications to such contemporary artists as Tintoretto, Vasari, Francesco Salviati and Battista Franco, a projected artistic guide to Florence, many descriptions of paintings and countless references to painters and sculptors scattered throughout his work. In the six dialogues of the *Disegno* (1549) the respective merits of painting and sculpture are discussed by personifications of art and nature and by the painter Paolo Pino and the sculptors Silvio Cosini and Baccio Bandinelli. Doni defines *disegno* as a form of cogitation of divine origin. The superiority of one art over another is dependent on the means available to reproduce the image the artist has conceived. To this end the speakers in the dialogue set forth the technical refinements of their profession. Thus, despite the arguable value of the conclusion pronounced in favour of sculpture, the *Disegno* is one of the most valuable documents on workshop practice in the 16th century.

Doni was able to combine his writing with his love of art in emblematic literature. In the early 1560s he drafted his *Nuova opinione sopra le imprese* (not published until 1858), a collection of anecdotes that also pokes fun at the fashion for *imprese*, which were devices or mottoes (*see* IMPRESA). By showing the flexibility of this genre, in which the meaning of the image is affected by the accompanying text, this short treatise reveals the kind of influence the visual arts exercised on his writing. Similarly, most of his publications of the 1550s, such as *La zucca*, *I marmi* and *I mondi* (all 1552) and *La morale filosofia* (1553), were composed around some 200 allegorical vignettes designed by Giuseppe Salviati for Francesco Marcolini's *Le sorti* (Venice, 1540). Doni developed a technique whereby these pictures became both the illustrations and bases for multiple improvised texts. Indeed, the same engravings were reprinted in many books, accompanied by entirely different interpretations. The relationship between text and image is most successful in *Le pitture* (1564), a series of allegorical figures based on Petrarch's *Trionfi* and arising from meditations on love, fortune, time, chastity, religion, disdain, reform, death, dreams, man, the republic and magnanimity. The origin of these personifications is most probably the work of Giulio Camillo; Federico Zuccaro used them for his decoration (1566–8) of the Villa d'Este,

Tivoli, and Cesare Ripa included several in his *Iconologia* (Rome, 1593).

In his book *I mondi* Doni invented utopias, and in *I cancellieri* (1562) he described imaginary villas decorated with frescoes. He also planned but never wrote an elaboration of a vast iconographic work dedicated to the memory of Petrarch and Italy. He was himself skilled at drawing and mingled with the major artists and writers of his day. His writings, which he recognized as belonging to the capricious genre of the *groteschi*, bear witness both to contacts between the worlds of literature and the studio and to the impact of the visual arts on Renaissance culture.

WRITINGS

Disegno (Venice, 1549); ed M. Pepe (Milan, 1970) [with a bibliog. of Doni's principal writings on art, extracts from which were published by P. Barocchi: *Scritti d'arte del cinquecento*, i (Milan, 1971), pp. 554–91]
I marmi (Venice, 1552)
I mondi (Venice, 1552)
La zucca (Venice, 1552)
La morale filosofia (Venice, 1553)
Il cancellieri (Venice, 1562)
Le pitture (Padua, 1564)
Le ville (Bologna, 1565); ed. U. Bellochi (Modena, 1969)
Nuova opinione sopra le imprese (Venice, 1858)

BIBLIOGRAPHY

M. Pepe: 'Di alcune lettere di Anton Francesco Doni e di una sua opera perduta', *Accad. & Bib. Italia*, xxxiv (1966), pp. 136–40
——: 'Anton Francesco Doni e la teoria dell'arte nel cinquecento', *Rass. Cult. & Vita Scolast.*, xxiii (1969)
D. Arasse: '*Ars memoriae* et symboles visuels: La critique de l'imagination à la fin de la Renaissance', *Symboles de la Renaissance* (Paris, 1976), pp. 57–73
C. Cordiè: *Opere di Pietro Aretino e di Anton Francesco Doni* (Milan, 1976), pp. 581–96 [with a critical bibliog.]
L. Bolzoni: *Il teatro della memoria: Studi su Giulio Camillo* (Padua, 1984), pp. 59–76

FRANÇOIS QUIVIGER

Donini [Luini], **Tommaso** [il Caravaggino] (*bapt* Rome, 24 Dec 1601; *d* Rome, 21 March 1637). Italian painter. His real name and the dates of his baptism and death were traced by D'Amico (1979); previously he was known as Tommaso Luini, the name given to him in Baglione's brief account of his artistic career. He is better documented as a criminal than as a painter: a court deposition of 1621 gives his age as 20; and his statement of 1635, when he was on trial for stabbing another painter in the leg, reveals that he had studied with Giovanni Lanfranco and Angelo Caroselli and had attended Andrea Sacchi's drawing academy between 1630 and 1632. Only three of the public commissions recorded by Baglione survive, all in Rome: the former high altarpiece of S Carlo al Corso, *God the Father with Angels Adoring the Holy Sacrament* (1630–32; now on the left transept altar), and the lateral paintings in the second chapel on the right in S Maria in Via, *St Philip Benizzi Healing a Lame Man* and the *Death of St Philip Benizzi* (both *c.* 1630–32). Sacchi's association with Donini is documented by two drawings (1630–32; Düsseldorf, Kstmus.) for the S Carlo altarpiece. There is also a study by Sacchi for the head of one of the monks watching St Philip Benizzi perform his miracle (Holkham Hall, Norfolk). In style the painting is clearly indebted to Sacchi, in particular to his *Vision of St Romuald* (1631; Rome, Pin. Vaticana), but the companion painting has the strong chiaroscuro and more robust naturalism associated with Caravaggio. Donini was called 'il Caravaggino', but whether because of his style of painting or his personal behaviour as a litigious outsider is not known. D'Amico attributed three more Roman altarpieces to him, but the evidence for this remains inconclusive.

BIBLIOGRAPHY

G. Baglione: *Vite* (1642); ed. V. Mariani (1935), pp. 241–2
G. B. Passeri: *Vite* (1679); ed. J. Hess (1934), p. 226, n. 4
F. Titi: *Descrizione delle pitture, sculture e architettura. . .in Roma* (Rome, 1763), pp. 341, 351, 367, 373
A. Moir: *The Italian Followers of Caravaggio* (Cambridge, 1967)
A. Sutherland Harris: *Andrea Sacchi* (Oxford, 1977)
F. D'Amico: 'Su Tommaso Donini detto il Caravaggino e sul Savonanzi', *Boll. A.*, 6th ser., lxiv/3 (1979), pp. 79–86

ANN SUTHERLAND HARRIS

Donjon [Fr.: 'keep']. Term derived from the Latin *dominium*, meaning lordship, signifying that part of a castle that was the ultimate strongpoint and refuge and contained the most prestigious residential accommodation for the lord himself. It was thus an essentially feudal concept: as the inner sanctum of lordship it was regarded as the particular symbol thereof, and for practical and symbolic reasons it was given a structural and architectural emphasis to make it the *pièce maîtresse* of the castle. In French the word retains much of its original meaning, though confined to the tower keep, which is only one form of donjon, but in English, through a very early secondary usage (1186), it has come to mean 'a dark subterranean place of confinement' (OED). The word 'keep', which has been adopted more or less as an English synonym for donjon in its original meaning, first appeared in the 16th century.

There are several types of donjon. The word was applied by contemporaries to the motte and its timber superstructure (palisade and tower) of those early castles constructed in the 'motte-and-bailey' form. Surviving mottes, even denuded of all superstructure, can still be very impressive (e.g. Thetford, Norfolk; Pleshey, Essex; La Ferté-en-Bray, Seine-Maritime) and were a formidable obstacle to attack; it is interesting and significant that on the late 11th-century BAYEUX TAPESTRY the motte is used as the symbol of a castle. It is also clear from both literary and archaeological evidence that the timber tower within the palisade upon the summit was or could contain the apartments of the lord and could be surprisingly elaborate, as in the description of the timber 'house' or *arx* that Lambert, lord of Ardres, built upon the motte at Ardres (*super dunjonem*) in 1117.

Little detail is known about the timber superstructure on the motte, though at South Mimms (Herts), one of the few such sites to be excavated, the foundations of the elaborate residential tower were on the natural ground level within the motte that had thus been added to it, and the motte itself had been revetted in timber. Much more is known from surviving structural evidence, especially in England, of mottes with later stone superstructures. Thus the so-called 'shell' keep (common in England, less so in France and elsewhere) consists of a ring wall (sometimes polygonal) about the summit of the motte, replacing the presumed original timber stockade, with the necessary seigneurial accommodation set about the inner face of the wall and thus about a courtyard. The combination of motte and stone keep was formidable; the integration of the two into one unit is emphasized at, for example,

Donjon at Tretower, Brecon, Wales, first half of the 13th century

Farnham, Surrey, and Berkeley, Glos, where the shell wall is built up from the base of the motte to revet it; towers could be added to the *enceinte*, as at Berkeley and Farnham, Lewes, E. Sussex, and Tamworth, Staffs. Further, though to raise so heavy a building upon a usually artificial mound might be difficult, great towers of stone, though seldom rectangular, are sometimes found within the shell keep, like the timber towers of old on the palisaded motte. Such a combination of motte, 'shell' keep and tower keep, as still exists at Launceston (Cornwall), Tretower (see fig.) and Gisors (Eure), is formidable, while a towering donjon complex, as developed at Alnwick ('the Seven Towers of the Percies'), Northumb., and Sandal (destr.), W. Yorks, must have been as impressive as the greatest tower keep.

The usually free-standing great tower (*magna turris*), known as the tower keep, was, nevertheless, the most favoured type of donjon, readily combining strength, self-contained accommodation and architectural dominance. Especially prevalent in the 12th century, it is found almost everywhere from the beginning (Doué-la-Fontaine, Maine-et-Loire, *c.* 950) to the end (Tattershall; Vincennes, 15th century) of the history of the medieval castle. The tall, slender tower of western Germany (and, for example, in Loudun, France) is, however, more properly a *Bergfried* or watch-tower than a seigneurial residence, and the *torre del homenaje* in Spain must have served as something other than the inner sanctum of lordship in those castles that were in reality garrison forts. The earliest tower keeps were rectangular, and that shape predominated throughout, but cylindrical great towers were built from the early 12th century and were especially fashionable in the early 13th century and in France, while in between there were various experimental shapes: polygonal (Orford, Suffolk; Gisors), quadrilobe (Etampes, Essonne; Clifford's Tower at York) and the dramatic *en bec* with solid prow (CHÂTEAU-GAILLARD; the Tour Blanche at Issoudun).

In view of the importance of the donjon in concept and function it is surprising to find castles without one, yet there are from beginning to end castles with no motte,

'shell' keep or tower keep. In many cases the explanation is a fourth type of donjon, comprising an inner enclosure as an inner sanctum of lordship, suitably strengthened and architecturally emphasized, as is or was the case at CAERNARFON CASTLE or Conwy Castle, Gwynedd. Yet there remain even major castles (e.g. Beaumaris; Harlech; both Gwynedd) with no trace even of that, and one must conclude in such cases no ultimate strongpoint was thought necessary in practice, and in concept the whole castle was a sufficient symbol of lordship.

See also CASTLE, §I; JAMES OF ST GEORGE.

R. ALLEN BROWN

Donkey's Tail [Rus. Oslinyy Khvost]. Russian group of painters active in 1911–15. It was led by Mikhail Larionov and Natal'ya Goncharova. The name was chosen by Larionov and recalled a famous artistic scandal in Paris, when a picture, painted by tying a brush to a donkey's tail, was exhibited without comment at the Salon des Indépendants of 1905. The Donkey's Tail group was the result of a difference in aesthetic ideology within the JACK OF DIAMONDS group. While most of their colleagues in Jack of Diamonds preferred to rely on the example of contemporary French and German painting, Larionov and Goncharova adopted the view that their art should evolve from the stylistic traditions of popular Russian art forms, such as the icon and *lubok* (a type of wood-engraving). A few, such as Kazimir Malevich and Alexsey Morgunov (1884–1935), shared their views and resigned in order to help found Donkey's Tail in 1911. The official launch of the group took place in early 1912 at the Jack of Diamonds conference, when Goncharova and Larionov interrupted the proceedings and, 'in a halo of scandal' (Livshits), proclaimed the formation of Donkey's Tail and their secession from Jack of Diamonds.

In March 1912 the group held its first exhibition, inviting young artists such as Kirill Zdanevich (1892–1969), Mikhail Le Dantyu (1891–1917), Aleksandr Shevchenko, Tatlin and the émigré Chagall to participate. The exhibition received a great deal of critical attention in the press, its artists being considered the most radical of the avant-garde. The artists of Donkey's Tail shared a common aesthetic ideology. As Voloshin noted, they painted scenes of everyday Russian life, pictures of soldiers, hairdressers, chiropodists and prostitutes, all executed in the popular style of the *lubok*, using bright colours, flat shapes and crudely articulated forms. Religious subjects based on the style of Russian icons were also characteristic of Donkey's Tail, as were Oriental themes, since the group had rejected the West and now looked to Eastern art for inspiration.

In April 1913 Donkey's Tail altered its name to Mishen' ('Target') and held a second exhibition in Moscow. By this time Larionov's and Goncharova's aesthetic of a return to the subjects and styles of traditional Russian art forms had crystallized under the name of NEO-PRIMITIVISM, and masterpieces of the style, such as Larionov's *Spring* (1912; Paris, Pompidou), were exhibited. To emphasize the correlation between their own work and that of naive and popular Russian art forms, the group included in the exhibition works by children, house- and signboard-painters and naive artists such as the Georgian Niko

Pirosmanashvili. Target also served as a platform for Larionov's and Goncharova's new abstract style of Rayist painting (*see* RAYISM), and so the somewhat motley aspect of the exhibition can well be imagined. Nonetheless, the works exhibited at both Donkey's Tail and Target were the most important and experimental in Russian art of the pre-war period.

In the summer of 1913 the group published an almanac entitled *Oslinyy Khvost i Mishen'* ('Donkey's Tail and Target'), in which the artists reproduced their works, and published two Rayist manifestos and two critical essays about their work. By March 1914 several members of the original group, including Malevich, Morgunov and Fonvizin, had left. The remainder held a third exhibition entitled *No. 4: Futurists, Rayists, Primitives*. Works of different tendencies were shown, including non-objective Rayist works, Neo-primitive paintings and poems by Vasily Kamensky (1864–1961). With Larionov's and Goncharova's move to the West in 1915 the group dissolved.

WRITINGS
Oslinyy Khvost [Donkey's Tail] (exh. cat., Moscow, 1912)
Oslinyy Khvost i Mishen' [Donkey's Tail and Target] (Moscow, 1913)
Vystavka Kartin Gruppy Khudozhnikov 'Mishen'' [Exhibition of paintings by the 'Target' group of artists] (exh. cat., Moscow, 1913)
Vystavka Kartin No. 4: Futuristy, Luchisty, Primitivy [Exhibition of paintings no. 4: Futurists, Rayists, Primitives] (exh. cat., Moscow, 1914)

BIBLIOGRAPHY
M. Voloshin: 'Moskva: Khudozhestvennaya Zhizn': Oslinyy Khvost' [Moscow: artistic life: Donkey's Tail], *Apollon*, 7 (1912), pp. 105–6
B. Livshits: *Polutoraglazyy strelets* [The one-and-a-half-eyed archer] (Leningrad, 1933; Eng. trans., 1977)
J. Howard: *The Union of Youth: An Artists' Society of the Russian Avant-Garde* (Manchester, 1992)
A. Parton: *Mikhail Larionov and the Russian Avant-Garde* (Princeton and London, 1993)
ANTHONY PARTON

Donndorf, (Karl) Adolf (von) (*b* Weimar, 16 Feb 1835; *d* Stuttgart, 20 Dec 1916). German sculptor. After four years at a teachers' seminary he moved to Dresden in 1853 and there studied at the art academy under Ernst Friedrich-August Rietschel, who instructed him in the tradition of Christian Daniel Rauch and the classicists of the Akademie in Berlin. On Rietschel's death in 1861 he completed the *Luther* monument (bronze and granite, 1861–8; Worms, Lutherplatz), which Rietschel had designed. During his period in Dresden he completed or began several monuments, such as the equestrian statue of the *Grand Duke Charles Auguste* (bronze, granite and marble, 1867–75; Weimar, Platz der Demokratie) and the statue of the artist *Peter Cornelius* (bronze and granite, 1873–8; Düsseldorf, Hofgtn) and sculpted numerous portraits. In 1874 he travelled to Italy, and in 1876 the Kunstschule in Stuttgart offered him a professorship, which he rather reluctantly accepted. Shortly before moving to Stuttgart, Donndorf received an important private commission for the James Fountain (1875–81) in New York (Union Square), of which he later made replicas for Zwittau (1892), Weimar (1895) and Stuttgart (1898). With his three equestrian monuments of *Emperor William I* (1888–1901, Heidelberg; 1888–1904, Saarbrücken (destr. World War II); and 1897–1902, Hohensyburg) and his monuments of *Otto von Bismarck* (1895–9, Saarbrücken; 1902–3, Eisenach) he distinguished himself by imbuing the tradition of late classical monumental art with realism. In his sculptures of historical figures he tended to idealize his subjects, as in the *Schiller* monument (marble and granite, 1905–9; Stuttgart, nr Hoftheater). Between 1889 and 1895 he created his own *Luther* monument (bronze and granite; Eisenach, Platz der Deutsch-Sowjetischen Freundschaft), in which he surpassed his earlier joint work in both inventiveness and technical skill. Donndorf was much admired for the likenesses he achieved in his portrait busts (e.g. *Bismarck*, marble, 1895–7; Heidelberg, Bismarckplatz), his funerary monuments (e.g. *Karl Gerok*, 1895–8; destr.) and his statues (e.g. of *Emperor William I*) as well as in his portraits of children. In 1907 a Donndorf Museum was opened in Weimar, where plaster casts of most of his works were kept until the museum's destruction shortly after World War II.

BIBLIOGRAPHY
L. Donndorf: *Adolf Donndorf: Unveröffentlichte Biographie*, 3 vols (Weimar, 1932)
F. Lincke: 'Der Bildhauer Adolf Donndorf: Sein Leben und Werk', *Sächs. Heimatbl.*, xxiv (1978)
U. Fuchs: *Der Bildhauer Adolf Donndorf: Leben und Werk* (Stuttgart, 1986)
HANNELORE HÄGELE

Donner. Austrian family of artists. (1) Georg Raphael Donner worked as a sculptor, architect, medallist and goldsmith, though he is best known for his lead sculptures. His brother (2) Matthäus Donner was also a successful sculptor and medallist.

(1) Georg Raphael Donner (*b* Esslingen im Marchfeld [now in Vienna], *bapt* 25 April 1693; *d* Vienna, 15 Feb 1741). Sculptor, architect, medallist and goldsmith. He was apprenticed to Johann Kaspar Prenner, the Court Jeweller, to the Venetian sculptor Giovanni Giuliani and probably also to Bengt Richter (1630–1735), the Court Medallist of Swedish origin. Before 1720 Donner travelled to Dresden to work with Balthasar Permoser and possibly also to Berlin, to study metal casting with Johann Jacobi (1661–1726). In 1724 he was appointed Court Sculptor of *objets d'art*, but nothing that he produced in this capacity has been preserved. His sole extant piece of work from that period is the signed *Pietà* (terracotta, 1721; Prague, N.G.) from Schloss Waldstein in Dux, Bohemia, based on Mannerist prototypes. His subsequent work shows his familiarity with Mannerist sculpture.

Between 1725 and 1728 Donner worked in Salzburg for Archbishop Franz Anton, Graf Harrach, probably on the recommendation of Jean Luca von Hildebrandt, designing the staircase and producing marble statues for the Schloss Mirabell (*see* SALZBURG, fig. 3). The only signed statue, the over life-size figure of *Paris*, stands in a niche; it has clear references to antiquity and differs from traditional Baroque decorative sculpture in its independent and unified construction. Donner also worked on numerous dies for the Salzburg Mint, but he could not obtain a post as medallist; he was, however, commissioned by Charles, Elector of Bavaria, to produce a medallion to commemorate his consecration in 1727.

From some time after 1728 until 1739 Donner was in the service of Prince-Archbishop Imre, Count Eszterházy, Primate of Hungary, whose residence was in Pressburg (now Bratislava). From 1730 he worked as the Archbishop's director of building work, responsible for building the Elemosynarius Chapel in Pressburg Cathedral (consecrated in 1732). On one occasion in 1733 he was employed as a goldsmith to make a golden chalice, possibly the one now in Bratislava Cathedral. However, his chief employment was as Court Sculptor. Among his most important work from this period is the decoration of the Elemosynarius Chapel. The influence of the Italian Baroque style is displayed in the over life-size marble statues of the ephebe-like angels and of the kneeling figure of the Archbishop in a niche. The gilded bronze reliefs on the altar predella with scenes from the *Passion* are reminiscent of antique reliefs in their austere, planar composition. Donner's crowning achievement as a sculptor during his time in Pressburg was the provision of new furnishings and sculpture for the cathedral, including the high altar (consecrated in 1735), two side altars and the choir-stalls. The altar, which was partially dismantled in 1865, included the monumental equestrian group of *St Martin and the Beggar* (*in situ*) and two kneeling angels (Budapest, N.G.). For the first time Donner used on large figures the technique of casting in lead, which he had already tried out on a small scale; but contrary to the usual practice, his lead castings were neither gilded nor coloured; rather, the soft transitions of the modelling were shown to advantage by the dull gleam of the lead. At the same time, the leaden colour isolated the figures from the architecture of the altar and emphasized their intrinsic merit. No attempt was made to achieve the usual Baroque illusionistic effects; instead, the group was marked by a strictly axial conception and concentrated movements. Because of his supposedly Hungarian origins, St Martin wears the costume of a hussar, but in spite of the detail in which this is reproduced, the robe was of secondary importance to the spiritual relationship of the saint and the beggar.

Donner's activity for the Prince-Archbishop did not preclude him from producing works for the imperial court. In 1734 he executed the *Apotheosis of Emperor Charles VI* (Vienna, Belvedere) for the chief ranger of the imperial forests, Gregor Wilhelm von Kirchner; this over life-size marble group of the Emperor in antique armour, with a female genius crowning him, is a brilliant piece of work. Two other works in marble are the relief portraits of *Charles VI* (1735; Vienna, Ksthist. Mus.) and of *Gundacker Ludwig Josef, Graf Althann*, the Imperial Director of building work (1738–9; Vienna, Akad. Bild. Kst.). These masterpieces of portrait sculpture by far surpass all such works in contemporary Vienna.

In 1739 Donner moved to Vienna, prompted probably by the demands of work for the imperial court and by the numerous commissions that he had undertaken from 1737 for the Vienna city council. These included lavabo reliefs representing *Christ and the Woman of Samaria* and *Hagar in the Wilderness*, for Stephansdom (1737–8). Preparatory models for these have been preserved (Vienna, Belvedere); in their final form they were carved in Carrara marble. Because of the virtuosity with which the marble was handled, never before seen in Vienna, the two reliefs were greeted with such acclaim that instead of being placed in the cathedral, they were presented by the city council to the imperial treasury. A further development of this style is seen in the plaster models (Vienna, Hauptmünzamt) of the *Baptism* and *David's Water Sacrifice*, ordered by the

Vienna city council in 1739 to replace the reliefs that had been given away. These works, however, never got beyond the model stage. Donner's *Andromeda* fountain, with figures cast in lead, made in 1740–41 for the courtyard of the Altes Rathaus, is similar in style.

Donner's masterpiece for the city council was the *Providentia* fountain (1739) in Neuer Markt (replica *in situ*; original in Vienna, Belvedere). *Providence* enthroned forms the centrepiece of the fountain (see fig.), surrounded by four putti playing with fish, which symbolize the Danube. In a supplementary contract, the city council ordered four figures representing the tributaries of the Danube, to rest on the rim of the basin. The *Providentia* fountain is unusual in the Baroque period, in that the lead sculptures are distinct, both in contour and in colour, from the architectonic framework, which is confined to the pedestal and the fountain's edge. The fountain's design recalls Mannerist models in Florence, Augsburg and Munich; the figure of *Providence* is depicted in a turning movement, reminiscent of the Mannerist *figura serpentinata*, indicating Donner's leanings towards traditions of form that contrasted with the vital extrovert character of Baroque as practised by Bernini. The river-god figures on the rim are based on antique models, varying freely as regards form but sharing the characteristic serenity of Classical sculpture.

Georg Raphael Donner: *Providence*, lead figure from the *Providentia* fountain, h. 3.37 m, 1739 (Vienna, Belvedere, Österreichisches Barockmuseum)

Donner's last large-scale work was the monumental *Pietà* (1741) for an altar in Gurk Cathedral in Carinthia. The over life-size lead statues (*in situ*) represent the Virgin holding the outstretched body of Christ on her lap, an angel enveloping and comforting her and two putti holding Christ's hands and feet; the group, which has something of the quality of a relief, is arranged in a strict triangular composition, given depth by the angel approaching from behind. The Gurk *Pietà*, with its theme of solace, is one of the few of Donner's works to portray a spiritual relationship in a more expressive manner than the generality of his work.

The theme of solace emerges several times in Donner's *Passion* reliefs, which he created as models or finished works in wax, apparently without a commission. The subjects are the *Deposition* and the *Pietà*; there are two versions of each. The wax reliefs made by Donner himself (1734–5) are in the Österreichisches Barockmuseum (Belvedere) in Vienna (workshop versions, Vienna, Ksthist. Mus., and Vienna, priv. col., see Maué, 1986, pls 10–11). Two other wax reliefs on religious subjects, *Christ before Pilate* and the *Consolation of Mary* (1736–8), are also in the Österreichisches Barockmuseum (workshop version of the *Consolation*, Vienna, Ksthist. Mus.). The *Passion* reliefs are conceived as pendants and show how Donner varied what he portrayed: for example, in one of a pair of reliefs, the main group of figures is in the centre, whereas in the other the centre is left free. Donner's reliefs on mythological subjects, the *Judgement of Paris* and *Venus in Vulcan's Forge*, illustrate the same principle. There is no version of these by Donner himself, only workshop versions in plaster (Vienna, Hauptmünzamt; workshop versions in lead, Budapest, Mus. F.A.; bronze copies dated *c.* 1780, Vienna, Belvedere).

Donner's lead statuettes, also based on mythological subjects, include the powerful *Mercury with Cupid* made in the early 1730s (Klosterneuburg, Mus. Chorherrenstiftes) and *Venus* and *Mercury*, two slim, small-headed figures conceived as a pair (late 1730s; Vienna, Belvedere). Features common to all the statuettes are the emphasis on construction, the slight contrapposto and the unity of outline.

Despite the important contracts that had brought him fame and honour, Donner died very poor. He left nine reliefs dating from the mid- or late 1730s to his brother (2) Matthäus Donner, who used them in teaching classes at the Vienna Akademie der Bildenden Künste. Two of the other professors, Jakob Christoph Schletterer, a collaborator of Donner's, and Balthasar Ferdinand Moll, a former pupil, also taught their own versions of Donner's style; consequently, the academic style has been wrongly ascribed to Donner's influence. This influence was further perpetuated by the numerous replicas of Donner's statuettes. The *Providentia* fountain, in particular, became a formula freely adapted in countless versions, both large and small. Porcelain figures made in Vienna were an important branch of this industry. It was only in the early Neo-classical period that the truly sculptural qualities of Donner's oeuvre were recognized, creating admiration for the severe early works. Thanks to him, moreover, lead became the characteristic material of Viennese sculpture.

BIBLIOGRAPHY

Thieme–Becker
A. Pigler: *Georg Raphael Donner* (Vienna, 1929)
K. Blauensteiner: *Georg Raphael Donner* (Vienna, 1944)
M. Schwarz: *Georg Raphael Donner, Kategorien der Plastik* (Munich, 1968)
G. Schikola: 'Wiener Plastik der Renaissance und des Barocks', *Geschichte der bildenden Kunst in Wien: Plastik in Wien*, Gesch. Stadt Wien, vii/1 (Vienna, 1970), pp. 85–162
M. Malikova: 'Die Schule Georg Raphael Donners in der Slowakei', *Mitt. Österreich. Gal.*, xvii/61 (1973), pp. 77–180
G. Prokopp: 'Levéltári adatok Georg Raphael Donner Poszonyi éveihez' [archival details of Georg Raphael Donner's activity in Pressburg], *A. Hung.*, vi/2 (1978), pp. 329–39 [with Ger. summary]
C. Diemer: *Georg Raphael Donner: Die Reliefs* (Nuremberg, 1979)
E. Baum: *Katalog des österreichischen Barockmuseums im Unteren Belvedere in Wien*, i (Vienna, 1980), pp. 97–141
G. Hajos and E. Vancsa: *Die Kunstdenkmäler Wiens: Die Profanbauten des III., IV. und V. Bezirkes*, Österreichisches Kunsttopographie, xliv (Vienna, 1980), pp. 190–91
I. Rusina: *Renesancná a baroková plastika v Bratislava*, Pamiatky Bratislavy, viii (Bratislava, 1983), pp. 5–6, 23, 84–100, pls 23–31
C. Maué: 'Zu den Modellen Georg Raphael Donners', *Entwurf und Ausführung in der europäische Barockplastik, Beiträge zur internationalen Kolloquium des bayerischen Nationalmuseums und des Zentralinstituts für Kunstgeschichte München* (Munich, 1986) pp. 157–76
Georg Raphael Donner (exh. cat., Vienna, Belvedere, 1993), pp. 133–41

(2) Matthäus Donner (*b* Esslingen im Marchfeld [now in Vienna], *bapt* 30 Aug 1704; *d* Vienna, 26 Aug 1756). Sculptor and medallist, brother of (1) Georg Raphael Donner. He trained with Bengt Richter and studied sculpture at the Akademie der Bildenden Künste in Vienna. In 1731 he designed the reverse of the academy's medal, showing *Minerva with Putti*; the same design also won second prize for sculpture. In 1732 he won first prize for sculpture with a terracotta group of *Samson Overcoming the Lion* (Vienna, Hauptmünzamt), which was strongly influenced by academic models. In the 1730s and early 1740s he was principally noted as a medallist, being appointed Court Medallist in 1743 and Director of the Vienna Academy of Engraving in 1745. The medals struck on the occasion of the marriage of Queen Maria Theresa (1736) and of her coronation in Hungary (1741) and Bohemia (1743) show Donner's superb technique and subtle characterization. In 1749 he became Chief Engraver at the Münzamt, producing, among other works, a commemorative medal of the *Empress Elisabeth Christine*.

Donner was at the same time working as a sculptor, receiving commissions for plaster portrait reliefs (both 1735; Vienna, Hauptmünzamt) and portrait busts (both 1737; Vienna, Akad. Bild. Kst.) of the Holy Roman Emperor *Charles VI* and the empress *Elisabeth Christine* and a plaster portrait relief of *Charles VI* (before 1740; Vienna, Hauptmünzamt). In 1750 he executed bronze busts of *Maria Theresa* and of *Emperor Francis I* (Vienna, Ksthist. Mus.; plaster models, Vienna, Hauptmünzamt) and a pewter relief of *Maria Theresa* (Vienna, Hauptmünzamt). From 1743 he was Professor of Sculpture at the Akademie der Bildenden Künste. Most of Donner's other sculptures, chiefly reliefs, are artistically inferior to his portraits; they include a pair of bronze plaques representing the *Parting of Venus and Adonis* and *Venus with a Shepherd* (both 1738; Berlin, Skulpgal.). They are chiefly notable for the way in which they perpetuate Georg Raphael Donner's repertory of forms. However, Donner's last work of sculpture, the monumental bronze relief of *Field-Marshal Leopold Josef, Graf von Daun* (1755; Wiener Neustadt, Mus. Theresian. Milakad.), is Rococo sculpture at its best and shows him as an independent artist, emerging from his brother's shadow.

BIBLIOGRAPHY

Schau- und Denkmünzen, welche unter der glorwürdigen Regierung der Kaiserin Königin Maria Theresia geprägt worden sind (Vienna, 1782/*R* Graz, 1970)

H. Kábdebo: *Matthäus Donner und die Geschichte der Wiener Graveur-Akademie in der ersten Periode ihres Bestandes* (Vienna, 1880)

E. Baum: *Katalog des österreichischen Barockmuseums im Unteren Belvedere in Wien*, i (Vienna, 1980), pp. 141–4

Maria Theresia und ihre Zeit (exh. cat., Vienna, Schloss Schönbrunn, 1980)

H. Jungwirth and K. Schulz: *Münzen und Medaillen des österreichischen Heldenzeitalters, 1683–1794* (exh. cat., Brussels, Nbank Charleroi & Brugge, 1987)

CLAUDIA MAUÉ

Donoso, José Jiménez. *See* JIMÉNEZ DONOSO, JOSÉ.

Donostia. *See* SAN SEBASTIÁN.

Donzelli, Giuseppe. *See* NUVOLO, GIUSEPPE.

Donzello [Donzelli]. Italian family of painters. (1) Pietro del Donzello and (2) Ippolito del Donzello were the sons of a messenger for the city administration (*donzello dell Signoria*) in Florence. They are both documented in a Florentine *catasto* (land registry declaration) of 1480 and were not of Neapolitan origin, as is often stated erroneously.

Thieme–Becker

BIBLIOGRAPHY

(1) Pietro del Donzello (*b* Florence, 1452; *d* Florence, 24 Feb 1509). He is first mentioned in the 1480 *catasto*. He was a pupil of Giusto di Andrea and worked mainly as a craftsman, painting standards and shields. His earliest documented work is a standard with an allegorical figure of *Lombardy* (1483; untraced) for the Sala dell'Udienza in the Palazzo della Signoria, Florence. In 1488 he may have been in Naples working on the decoration at Poggio Reale (*see* (2) below). He is also known to have painted standards and shields for the Opera del Duomo between 1503 and 1507, and benches for the refectory of the Ospedale di S Matteo in 1506. His only documented paintings were made for Florence, a *Crucifixion with Two Angels* (1506; untraced) for the Ospedale di S Matteo and an *Annunciation* (*in situ*) for one of the Frescobaldi chapels in Santo Spirito. The latter suggests that he was a modest, graceful follower of the style of Domenico Ghirlandaio and Lorenzo di Credi.

BIBLIOGRAPHY

M. Bori: 'L'annunciazione di Pietro del Donzello in una cappella Frescobaldi nella chiesa di Santo Spirito', *Riv. A.*, iv (1906), pp. 117–23

E. Fahy: *Some Followers of Domenico Ghirlandaio* (New York and London, 1976), pp. 41–2, 187, 220–21

MINA BACCI

(2) Ippolito del Donzello (*b* ?Florence, *c.* 1456; *d* Florence or Naples, 1494). Brother of (1) Pietro del Donzello. He trained with Neri di Bicci *c.* 1469–73 in Florence and is documented there in 1485. He went to Naples, probably in 1488, at the request of Guiliano da Maiano (*see* MAIANO, DA, (1)) to work on the decoration of the villa at Poggio Reale (from 1487; destr. late 18th century), which Giuliano had designed for the Duke of Calabria (later Alfonso II, King of Naples). Ippolito's frescoes there (destr.) included a battle scene and numerous portraits. Many works in Naples are assigned to him, but none is secure.

BIBLIOGRAPHY

G. Vasari: *Vite* (1550, rev. 2/1568); ed. G. Milanesi (1878–85), ii, pp. 70, 470, 474–5, 485–6

Doo, George Thomas (*b* Surrey, 6 Jan 1800; *d* Sutton, Surrey, 13 Nov 1886). English engraver. He was a pupil of Charles Heath (i). In 1824 he published his first plate, engraved after a portrait of the *Duke of York* (exh. RA 1822; untraced) by Thomas Lawrence. In 1836 he was appointed Engraver in Ordinary to William IV and in 1842 received a similar appointment to Queen Victoria. With his colleague John Henry Robinson, he petitioned the Queen and Albert, the Prince Consort, on the matter of his profession's exclusion from full membership of the Royal Academy (under whose auspices, incidentally, he exhibited 24 pieces between 1830 and 1882). As a result, a new class of Academician Engravers and Associate Engravers was instituted. Doo himself became an ARA in 1856 and a full Academician in 1857. His *tour de force* is the crisp line-engraving after William Etty's gigantic painting, *The Combat* (exh. RA 1825; Edinburgh, N.G.), published in June 1849.

BIBLIOGRAPHY

Victorian Engravings (exh. cat. by H. Beck, London, V&A, 1973)

ANTHONY DYSON

Doodle. Scribbling or form of sketching performed unconsciously or semiconsciously, when otherwise engaged or simply bored, such as while listening to someone on the telephone or during a lecture. There are examples of marginal doodles by many artists throughout the history of art, but the activity has attracted special attention in the 20th century, due to the influence of psychoanalysis (*see also* AUTOMATISM).

Doolittle, Amos (*b* Cheshire, CT, ?1754; *d* New Haven, CT, 31 Jan 1832). American engraver. Doolittle learnt to engrave in metal through his apprenticeship to a silversmith. His career as an independent craftsman was interrupted by army service during the American Revolution, during which time he met Ralph Earl, whose drawings of battle scenes, including the battles of Lexington and Concord, Doolittle was later to engrave on copper. The success of these historical scenes, for example *A View of the Town of Concord*, published in New Haven in 1775, enabled Doolittle to abandon his trade as a silversmith. Responding to patriotic demand for images of the new American leaders, Doolittle engraved likenesses of successive American presidents, including George Washington, John Adams and Thomas Jefferson. The tribute to Washington he first issued in 1788, *A Display of the United States of America* (1794; New Haven, CT, Yale U. A.G.), was reworked five times. He also engraved book illustrations, scenic views and bookplates. Although not the first engraver in America, as he was later to claim, Doolittle was the only one of his generation to attempt to expand beyond service work to original compositions on a regular basis.

BIBLIOGRAPHY
I. M. G. Quimby: 'The Doolittle Engravings of the Battle of Lexington and Concord', *Winterthur Port.*, iv (1968), pp. 83–108

DAVID M. SOKOL

Doomer, Lambert (Harmensz.) (*b* Amsterdam, *bapt* 11 Feb 1624; *d* Amsterdam, 2 July 1700). Dutch painter, draughtsman and collector. He was trained to be a joiner by his father, Harmen Doomer (1595–1650), a prosperous manufacturer of ebony picture frames and cabinets. Doomer's father supplied frames to Rembrandt, who in 1640 painted his portrait (New York, Met.) and that of his wife *Baertge Martens* (St Petersburg, Hermitage; *see* PORTRAITURE, fig. 5). Lambert probably spent some time in Rembrandt's studio *c.* 1644, where he developed his skill as a draughtsman.

In 1646 Doomer sailed via the Isle of Wight to Nantes, where his brothers Maerten and Hendrik were living. From July to September 1646, together with the Dutch landscape painter and draughtsman Willem Schellinks, Doomer travelled along the Loire to northern France, visiting and recording châteaux and towns such as Angers, Saumur, Tours, Amboise and Orléans, as well as Dieppe and Le Havre. Back in Amsterdam, Doomer led a financially secure life on the income of the factory run by one of his brothers. He made several journeys through the Netherlands (visiting Utrecht, Enkhuizen, Arnhem and Nijmegen), and in 1663 he travelled up the Rhine via Cleve, Mönchengladbach and Cologne to Bingen. A year after his marriage in 1668 to Metje Harmens, he moved to Alkmaar, where the house in which he lived still exists. From 1673 to 1681 he lived at the *mannengasthuis* (old men's home) in Alkmaar, marrying his second wife, Geesje Esdras, in 1679. In 1695 he returned to Amsterdam.

Of the more than 300 drawings by him that have survived, most are topographical views of the Netherlands, France and Germany, executed with subtle watercolour washes and some white gouache over black chalk. Doomer is one of the most important and characteristic of Dutch topographical draughtsmen, comparable to Roelant Roghman, Willem Schellinks and Herman Saftleven II. However, his drawings surpass those of his contemporaries in their special quality of atmosphere and in their pictorial and Romantic treatment of subject-matter. The topographical drawings are also interesting from a historical viewpoint, since they show the 17th-century appearance of buildings and monuments that no longer exist, for example several castles on the Rhine destroyed by French troops in 1689. In later years Doomer made numerous copies of his own topographical views. About 1671–3 he produced an extensive group of replicas on account-book paper; these second versions constitute almost a quarter of his surviving drawings. In 1665 Doomer provided 11 drawings for the important collection of topographical landscape drawings assembled by the Amsterdam lawyer

Lambert Doomer: *View of Newport on the Isle of Wight, with Carisbrooke Castle in the Background*, pen and brown ink and watercolour washes over black chalk, 411×571 mm, 1665 (Vienna, Österreichische Nationalbibliothek); copy by the artist of a travel sketch of 1646

Laurens van der Hem, now preserved in the Atlas van der Hem (Vienna, Österreich. Nbib.; see fig.). Doomer was himself a collector and purchased items from the sale of Rembrandt's art collection in 1658, including an album of drawings by Roelandt Savery (now dispersed), some of which he copied (e.g. *Alpine Landscape*; Berlin, Kupferstichkab.). He also copied drawings by Jan Hackaert (e.g. *The Glärnisch*, 1692; Bremen, Ksthalle). Although some of these landscapes depict alpine mountains, Doomer apparently never visited Switzerland.

Doomer's achievements as an amateur painter are less important than his achievements as a draughtsman. He was inspired by such contemporary Amsterdam artists as Ferdinand Bol. There are at least 25 surviving oil paintings by Doomer, dating from *c.* 1644 to *c.* 1684, and there are references to others in the artist's will, old inventories and in 18th- and 19th-century sale catalogues. Some paintings, such as *Farmhouse and Well* (Amsterdam, Rijksmus.) and *Pont Neuf in Angers* (Paris, Louvre), are presumably based on topographical drawings; others, such as *The Ford* (Strasbourg, Mus. B.-A.) and *Shepherd Couple* (Oldenburg, Landesmus.), seem to use individual motifs from his sketches. Doomer copied Rembrandt's portraits of his parents and produced group portraits, for example the *Young Couple by a Globe* (?1684; Burlington, U. VT, Fleming Mus.), the *Regentesses of the Proveniershuis at Alkmaar* and the *Regents of the Proveniershuis at Alkmaar* (completed in 1680 and 1681 respectively; both Alkmaar, Stedel. Mus.), for which a rare preliminary study survives (Amsterdam, Chr. P. van Eeghen priv. col., see Schulz, 1974, no. 43). Doomer's best work as a painter is *Hannah and Samuel before Eli* (1668; Orléans, Mus. B.-A.), with its highly individualized, portrait-like depictions of the main characters. Doomer's portraits and biblical pictures reveal his antiquarian interests, for example in the figures' old-fashioned clothing. His genre pictures and still-lifes, such as *Still-life with Thistles* (1675; Copenhagen, Stat. Mus. Kst), not only emphasize elements of still-life but, like the *Expulsion of the Prodigal Son* (1695; Oelde, Egon Rusche priv. col., see Bernt, no. 342), also contain veiled sexual allusions.

BIBLIOGRAPHY

H. van den Berg: 'Willem Schellinks en Lambert Doomer in Frankrijk', *Oudhdknd. Jb.*, xi (1942), pp. 1–31

W. Schulz: 'Zur Frage von Lambert Doomers Aufenthalt in der Schweiz', *Z. Schweiz. Archäol. & Kstgesch.*, xxvii (1970), pp. 5–20

——: 'Doomer and Savery', *Master Drgs*, ix (1971), pp. 253–9, pls 28–43

——: *Lambert Doomer, 1624–1700: Leben und Werke*, 2 vols (diss., Free U. Berlin, 1972)

——: *Lambert Doomer: Sämtliche Zeichnungen*, (Berlin, 1974); review by P. Schatborn in *Similus*, ix (1974), pp. 48–55

——: 'Zu einigen Zeichnungen des Rembrandt-Schülers Lambert Doomer in den Staatlichen Museen zu Berlin', *Forsch. & Ber. Staat. Mus. Berlin*, xvii (1976), pp. 73–95

——: 'Lambert Doomer als Maler', *Oud-Holland*, lxxxii (1978), pp. 69–105

W. Bernt: *Die niederländerischen Maler* (Munich, 1979)

WOLFGANG SCHULZ

Door. Movable closure of an entranceway to a building or room. The symbolic significance of the door has provided many opportunities for artistic decoration and attracted the attention of many major artists. This has led not only to the creation of magnificently formed, carved or decorated door panels but also to some richly decorated examples of OVERDOOR and to the creation of elaborate sculptural schemes in the tympana of Classical, Romanesque and other buildings (*see* TYMPANUM).

I. Ancient world. II. Western world. III. Islamic world. IV. Indian subcontinent. V. East Asia. VI. South-east Asia. VII. Africa. VIII. Pre-Columbian Americas.

I. Ancient world.

1. EGYPT AND THE ANCIENT NEAR EAST. The concept of the door was important in ancient Egypt, and stelae frequently depict closed doors (*see* STELE, §2). Although some actual doors have survived, none is of great artistic merit. The rectangular leaves of a miniature door on a shrine (h. 505 mm; Cairo, Egyp. Mus.) from the tomb of Tutankhamun were decorated with scenes in gold leaf in three registers on the exterior and four on the interior. Each leaf had a horizontal bolt at a different level running through hoops. It is likely that palace and temple doors would have resembled these on a larger scale. Stone doorsockets have survived (e.g. Chephren Valley Temple at Giza; *in situ*).

In the Ancient Near East gateways were places of assembly and judgement (Ruth 4:1–12). Palace and temple doorways from at least the middle of the 3rd millennium BC were protected by lions or mythical winged beasts of terracotta, copper, bronze or stone (e.g. London, BM), and terracotta figurines of dogs or protective genii were buried beneath doorways (e.g. London, BM). Fragments of bronze bands that decorated the gates of several Assyrian palaces and temples have survived. The best-preserved are the two pairs (London, BM, and Baghdad, Iraq Mus.) from a ?palace and the Temple of Mamu at Balawat in northern Iraq, decorated with hunting and battle scenes and dating to the reign of Assurnasirpal II (*reg* 883–859 BC), and an impressive set of larger gates from the palace. The latter, reconstructed in the British Museum in London, were made of cedar and probably stood more than 7 m high. They pivoted on massive cedar trunks, which turned in inscribed stone doorsockets. Vertical bronze strips, inscribed and decorated with rosettes, ran the whole height of each leaf along its edge, and a total of 16 horizontal strips *c.* 270 mm high were nailed across the leaves and round the pivots. These bronze strips were decorated in repoussé with scenes from the campaigns of the Assyrian king Shalmaneser III (*reg* 858–824 BC).

BIBLIOGRAPHY

L. W. King: *Bronze Reliefs from the Gates of Shalmaneser, King of Assyria, 860–825 BC* (London, 1915)

H. Brunner: 'Tür und Tor', *Lexikon der Ägyptologie*, iv (Wiesbaden, 1986), pp. 778–87

M. S. B. Damerji: *The Development of the Architecture of Doors and Gates in Ancient Mesopotamia* (Tokyo, 1987)

DOMINIQUE COLLON

2. GREECE AND ROME. In Classical languages there is no distinction between the opening at ground-level for entry and its mobile closure, the door panel. The doors of Greek and Roman antiquity are reasonably familiar to us through detailed descriptions in some literary, epigraphic and papyrological texts, through depictions on vases and examples in marble that closed funerary monuments (in Macedonia and Asia Minor) or important public buildings.

The doorframes found at some sites (for example, Olynthos, Delos and Pompeii) also provide useful evidence. A few wooden doors have been partially preserved, such as those found in Kassope (in Epirus) or at Dura-Europos in Syria. Finally, in rural Greece and Cyprus it is still possible to find very old doors that hardly differ from the doors of antiquity. These were usually made from vertical planks put together with horizontal traverses at the top, at the bottom and just above halfway. They had iron nails; in the richest doors these nails were numerous, in elaborate designs (discus, acanthus, flower) in gilded or silver-plated bronze. There was also a decorative ring or knocker. Occasionally finished off with marquetry work in precious wood or ivory, this decoration sometimes necessitated shutters lining the main door in order to protect it (e.g. the Doric Temple of Apollo at Delos, begun in the 5th century BC).

The doors of antiquity usually had two panels that opened inwards, pivoting on the doorstep and the lintel by a system of pins and sockets (see fig. 1), but from the 6th century BC in the Cyclades hinges were also used. While the 'Doric' door had wooden coffering or just a simple layer of stucco on the ends of the stones that formed the bay, the frame of the 'Ionic' door was in stone, which was more or less moulded (e.g. the Erechtheion, Athens, 5th century BC), with doorjambs clearly leaning inwards. Above, there might be a frieze, carried by consoles, an impost with latticework, a (false) pediment or even a triangular beam. 'Secret doors', hidden in a wall, also occurred, as did 'false double doors', where one half was painted in *trompe l'oeil* on the wall.

BIBLIOGRAPHY
H. Klenk: *Die antike Tür* (diss., U. Giessen, 1924)
A. Büsing-Kolbe: 'Frühe griechische Türen', *Jb. Dt. Archäol. Inst.*, xciii (1978), pp. 66–174
R. Ginouvès and R. Martin: 'Baies', *Dictionnaire méthodique de l'architecture grecque romaine*, ii (Rome, 1992)

MARIE-CHRISTINE HELLMANN

II. Western world.

1. Early Christian and medieval, before *c*. 1400. 2. Renaissance, *c*. 1400-*c*. 1550. 3. Mannerist Baroque and Rococo, *c*. 1550–*c*. 1750. 4. After *c*. 1750.

1. EARLY CHRISTIAN AND MEDIEVAL, BEFORE *c*. 1400.

(i) Wood. (ii) Bronze. (iii) Iron.

(i) Wood. There are relatively few surviving historiated wooden doors. The earliest surviving example from Christian times is at S Sabina, Rome, dated by inscription to *c*. 432. These cypress-wood doors originally contained 28 panels crowded with Old and New Testament scenes. Ten panels are lost, and the remainder have been rearranged at least twice. Of the 5th-century doors from S Ambrogio, Milan (Milan, Mus. Sacro S Ambrogio), only three original panels survive, showing scenes from the *Life of David* and some ornamental peacocks. The frames, mostly copies of the original, are carved with beautifully arranged foliage. The doors have been altered several times and were virtually rebuilt in 1750. These Italian wooden doors were clearly an important influence on Bishop Bernward of Hildesheim's bronze doors (*see* §(ii) below), but their direct descendants in wood are the 11th-century doors of St Maria im Kapitol, Cologne. These depict the *Life of Christ*, with traces of red, blue and green colour still surviving in the figures. Their construction, with the panels held by ornamental frames and rotating on a har post (a sturdy beam, projecting from the top and bottom of the

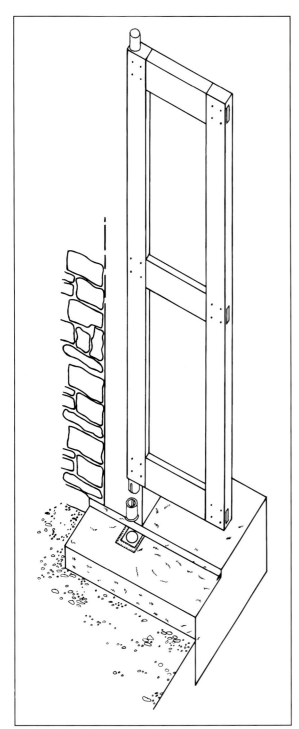

1. Hellenistic wooden door panel with pin-and-socket hinge; reconstruction drawing based on the bronze socket and pivot found at Delos (Delos, Archaeological Museum)

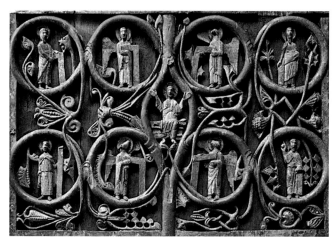

2. Wooden door, Gurk Cathedral, Austria, from the west portal, central section of the left valve, *c.* 1200–30

door, which fitted into sockets on the lintel and threshold, allowing the door to rotate), relates them to both wooden and bronze Late Antique doors. In Italy the 12th-century doors at S Pietro, Alba Fucense, and S Maria in Cellis, Carsoli, both in the Abruzzi, also continue this tradition, although in a somewhat rustic fashion. These doors are carved with the Tree of Life motif and scenes from the *Life of Christ*.

The group of doors in the Auvergne, France, at Le Puy Cathedral (larch-wood; by 1189), St Gilles, Chamalières-sur-Loire (pine-wood; 1130s), St Pierre at Blesle (pine-wood; *c.* 1200) and Ste-Croix, Lavoute-Chilhac (after 1137), are an independent development. They are carved with flat, low relief in contrast to all the previous examples, which employ rounded forms. Furthermore, they are not made with the standard classical panel-and-frame construction. Those at Le Puy are made from vertical planks hinged to open in concertina fashion. In the other three examples a veneer technique is employed with decorative components applied to the backing planks by nails and interlocking joints. Scenes from the *Infancy* and *Passion of Christ* are carved on the two pairs of doors at Le Puy. Each scene is explained by an inscription, and around the edge of the doors is pseudo-Kufic ornament as well as the name of the carver, GAUZFREDUS. The flat surfaces of the figures would have been painted. The other three doors are badly weathered, and their decoration is less coherent than that at Le Puy. Each door has a foliate or interlace border and an inlaid Greek cross at the top. Their decoration is mainly geometric with several apotropaic knots and a few single human or animal figures.

At Gurk Cathedral, Austria, an original and attractive design was used to frame the scenes on the west doors. Attached to the flat surface of the door are openwork lime-wood roundels linked to each other in a 'Tree of Jesse' design (see fig. 2). Within the roundels are scenes from the *Life of Christ*, prophets and Christ with the Apocalyptic Beasts. The complex iconography is related to that of the Klosterneuburg altar by NICHOLAS OF VERDUN. The reliefs are painted in green and red against the silvery background of the door. For stylistic and historical reasons the doors are dated to the first third of the 13th century.

Quite outside the Mediterranean Christian tradition is the door of Urnes Church, Norway (*c.* 1060; *see* URNES, §2). The doorway is carved in high relief with the figure of a great beast fighting a serpent, and the door itself continues in low relief the theme of sinuous fighting animals. Although used for a Christian church, both the style and subject derive from pagan sources, close parallels being found on the low-relief carvings of the 11th-century Scandinavian grave stones. The Urnes door is presumably the last remnant of an earlier pagan Nordic tradition.

During the later Middle Ages the decoration of wooden doors became limited to abstract tracery designs. They frequently followed patterns used in window tracery. One of the earliest traceried doors was made in 1241–8 for the Ste Chapelle, Paris, but the fashion did not develop widely for another 50 years. Particularly splendid examples can be seen at York Minster (south transept), St Nicholas, King's Lynn, and Norwich Cathedral (north gateway). A few tracery doors have carved figures, sometimes under canopies. A crucifix, pelican and dove are carved at St John's, Finchingfield, Essex, while Evangelists and saints are found at St Lawrence, Harpley, Norfolk.

BIBLIOGRAPHY
A. Goldschmidt: *Die Kirchentür des Heiligen Ambrosius in Mailand* (Strasbourg, 1902)
R. Hamann: *Die Holztür der Pfarrkirche zu St Maria im Kapitol* (Marburg, 1926)
I. Galvini: *Storia dell'architettura in Abruzzo*, i (Milan, 1927)
W. F. Volbach: *Early Christian Art* (New York, 1961), nos 102–5
R. Hauglid: *Norske Stavkirker* (Oslo, 1973)
W. Cahn: *The Romanesque Wooden Doors of the Auvergne* (New York, 1974)
F. S. L. Johnson: 'The West Portal Reliefs of Gurk Cathedral', *J. Brit. Archaeol. Assoc.*, 3rd ser., xxxvii (1974), pp. 2–20
G. Randall: *Church Furnishing in England and Wales* (London, 1980)
M. Pippal: 'Figurale Holztüren des Hochmittelalters im deutschsprachigen Raum', *Le porte di bronzo dall'antichità al secolo XIII*, ed. G. P. Carratelli (Rome, 1990)

(ii) Bronze. During the Carolingian renaissance, Classical bronze-casting was revived on a large scale after a break of some 400 years. The monumental and severe doors of ancient Rome that still survive at the Pantheon, S Giovanni in Laterano (from Diocletian's Curia) and the Temple of Romulus in the Forum served as a model and technical challenge to Charlemagne's bronze-founders. The Roman doors were cast as separate elements of panels and frames, but Charlemagne's doors were cast in one piece, a technique that continued to be employed in northern Europe. The most spectacular examples (discussed below) are those now at Hildesheim Cathedral, where each leaf (4.72×1.12 m), covered in three-dimensional relief figures and including the lion-head ring bosses, is cast in one piece (see fig. 3). In Italy the native medieval technique involved casting separate relief panels and frames and attaching them to a wooden core. Many doors in Italy were made by Byzantine craftsmen or in the Byzantine fashion: they consist either of small, flat bronze panels, incised and inlaid (damascened) with silver, enamel or niello, or of cut-out bronze motifs applied to the surface of the bronze.

The three pairs of doors at Charlemagne's palatine chapel (now the cathedral) at Aachen (*c.* 800) and those

expressive figures Man's Fall and Redemption. The doors at Augsburg Cathedral, also made in the 11th century, are more closely related to the Byzantine technique and style. They are made of panels and frames cast singly and attached to the wooden core of the door, and they illustrate single subjects such as *Samson and the Lion, King David* and centaurs. Some of the scenes are repeated from the same model. The iconography, including the secular subjects, seems to relate to the struggle between good and evil. The doors now at Novgorod Cathedral were originally made for Płock Cathedral (Poland) but were removed to Russia before the 15th century. The panels, fixed to a wooden core, include scenes from the *Life of Christ* and from the Old Testament and figures of the bronze-founders themselves with their tools, Bishop Alexander of Płock (1129–56) and Archbishop Wichmann of Magdeburg (1152–92), depicted without the pallium he received in 1154. The inscriptions identifying the figures thus date the doors to 1152–4. There was a well established bronze foundry at Magdeburg, so the doors were probably a gift from Wichmann to Alexander. The iconography of the doors at Gniezno Cathedral (Poland) shows that they were clearly made as a political statement. They depict the *Life of St Adalbert*, apostle to the Slavs and patron of the cathedral. Adalbert's relics were removed from Gniezno to Prague in 1038, but Gniezno attempted to restore its influence after the discovery of Adalbert's head in 1127, a claim matched by Prague in 1141. The doors were probably made as a consequence of the rivalry in the last quarter of the 12th century, although an earlier date has also been suggested, and were reinstated when the cathedral was rebuilt in the 14th century. The style, particularly that of the broad decorative frames, is related to sculpture and manuscript illumination from the Rhine–Meuse area.

The earliest recorded medieval bronze doors were made for the royal abbey of Saint-Denis, near Paris, begun by Charlemagne's father, Pepin, in 745 and completed by Charlemagne in 775. They depicted the *Life of St Denis* and the *Patrons of the Church*. These doors were moved from the main entrance to the north doorway of the west façade when Abbot Suger commissioned two further gilt-bronze doors for the west end of the church in 1140. Suger's central doors consisted of four pairs of framed roundels depicting the *Passion and Resurrection of Christ* and included the figure of Suger in the *Journey to Emmaus* scene. All the Saint-Denis doors were melted down in 1794. In England the doors of Bury St Edmunds Abbey have vanished without a trace. They were made by Master Hugo, possibly based on an Italian or Mosan model, at the instigation of Abbot Anselm (1121–48), who originally came from Rome. The tantalizing fragments (Dublin, N. Mus.) excavated at Donore, Co. Meath, Ireland, indicate that bronze panelled doors may also have existed there: the plaques, incised with *Kerbschnitt* (abstract chip-carving) and animal ornament, and the animal-head door ring may have come from the doors of a large shrine dating from the 8th century.

The doors of the tiny mausoleum of Bohemond I (*d* 1111) at Canosa Cathedral, Italy, also have a shrinelike quality. Situated in the Norman lands of Apulia, these earliest Italian (as opposed to Byzantine) medieval doors show a mixture of cultural influences. The left leaf, cast in

3. Leaf of the bronze west doors, Hildesheim Cathedral, Germany, 1015; originally in the church of St Michael, Hildesheim

of Mainz Cathedral (*c.* 1000) are models of classic restraint, with between four and sixteen plain panels surrounded by frames of low-relief egg-and-dart, acanthus or simple mouldings. Each has a pair of lion-head door rings. Bishop Bernward of Hildesheim had clearly seen both these and the wooden doors of Milan and Rome (*see* §(i) above), carved with biblical scenes, when he commissioned his bronze doors for St Michael's, Hildesheim (dated by inscription 1015; moved to the cathedral by Bishop Godehard, 1022–38). The panels bear eight pairs of Old and New Testament scenes, illustrating with poignant,

one, has three roundels of pseudo-Kufic inscriptions, while the right, cast in four separate panels, has two roundels of Islamic geometric ornament and two panels of incised historical figures in the Byzantine style cast, according to the inscription, by Roger of Melfi. The mausoleum itself is first recorded in 1118. The two doors at Tróia Cathedral (Apulia), though roughly contemporary, are very different in style and technique. The west doors combine the animal exuberance of northern work with the flat severity of Byzantine doors. Divided into 28 panels by frames with lush foliage bosses, they have eight openwork, lion-head door rings and two free-standing scaly, winged dragons biting the knockers. Four panels of incised figures include the bronze-founder ODERISIUS OF BENEVENTO, while the inscription dates them to 1119 (eight panels were replaced in the 16th or 17th century). The south doors, made in 1127, also by Oderisius, are subdued by comparison: they have only four lion-head door rings with twenty further panels of incised, damascened figures of saints and bishops of Tróia. Oderisius also made bronze doors with winged dragons (now lost) for S Giovanni in Capua.

The doors of the Cappella Palatina, Palermo (ded. 1140), must have had an antique prototype. They consist of eight plain panels with two lush acanthus bosses and lion-head masks surrounded by broad acanthus borders, echoing the stone acanthus frame of the doorway. Severely classicizing doors are also found in the chapel of the Lateran Baptistery, Rome. Made in 1195–6, their four panels bear incised architectural designs and one relief figure of *Ecclesia*. At S Zeno Maggiore, Verona, both the figure style and the composition of the metal indicate that the bronze panels were made at two different dates, one before the rebuilding of the church in 1138 and the other slightly later. Each of the 48 panels and their frames is cast separately, with the earlier style found mainly on the left valve. They depict Old and New Testament scenes, the *Life of St Zeno* and allegorical figures. As products of the first workshop are found on both sides of the Alps, it is debatable whether the craftsmen originally came from Verona or Magdeburg. Their openwork foliage style is found, for instance, on a candlestick at Klosterneuburg (Klosterneuburg, Mus. Chorherrenstiftes) and a casket (Hamburg, Mus. Kst & Gew.). They appear to have moved their workshop to Magdeburg for casting the Płock doors: the same style of foliage and ornament, cast solid rather than as openwork, is found on the latter doors. The figure style of the later Verona panels is more localized and is related to that of the sculpture on the west portal of S Zeno by NICHOLAUS.

The cathedral doors of Ravello, Trani and Monreale (north aisle) are all signed by BARISANUS OF TRANI. The Ravello doors, dated 1179, are the earliest and the most important because the subjects of their 54 low-relief panels form a coherent iconographic programme. The other two doors are smaller and simply reuse the same moulds in a less coherent arrangement. At Ravello the panels bear a hierarchical programme starting with *Christ in Majesty* at the top, ranging down through scenes of *Redemption* and *Judgement*, the donor with his hopes of salvation and equestrian saints protecting the church. BONANUS OF PISA made the doors at both Pisa Cathedral (*c.* 1180, east door,

south transept) and Monreale Cathedral (*c.* 1185, west door). The inscriptions on these doors contain the earliest surviving written examples of the Tuscan vernacular, mixed with Latin. The Pisan panels, surrounded by orderly rosettes applied to the frames, illustrate the *Life of Christ*, starting at the bottom with two panels of prophets and ending at the top with *Christ and the Virgin Enthroned*. At Monreale the scenes start with the Old Testament at the bottom and end with Christ and the Virgin, as at Pisa. The west doors of Benevento Cathedral with their 72 figural panels represented the most ambitious iconographic programme of all the Italian doors. They were almost totally destroyed in World War II, but earlier photographs and a few fragments survive (Benevento, Bib. Capitolare). The panels illustrated the *Life of Christ*, the Archbishop of Benevento and his 24 suffragans. The iconography is derived from Byzantine sources, while the style is related to local early 13th-century sculpture in Campania. Although many Italian churches enjoyed the prestige of bronze doors, Florence Cathedral had none until the guild responsible for the Baptistery decided in 1322 to commission a pair. Representatives were sent to Pisa to study and draw those in the cathedral, and founders were brought in from Venice. The gilt-bronze work produced by Andrea Pisano was in place by 1336. The lattice pattern of the crossbars of the framework enclose 28 square panels. Of these, 20 depict scenes from the *Life of St John the Baptist*, in Gothic quadrilobed shapes and with great elegance and economy; the two bottom rows of panels, which would be hidden whenever there were crowds pressing round the doors at baptisms, were dedicated to the theme of the *Virtues* (see also PISANO (ii), (1)).

The Byzantine group of doors in Italy was either made in Constantinople or cast in Italy by Byzantine craftsmen. Most can be dated quite closely by inscriptions, which often identify the donor and his desire for salvation. Their iconography concerns the intercession of the Virgin and saints while their foliate crosses represent the Tree of Life. Pantaleone of Amalfi gave the doors to S Paolo fuori le mura, Rome, in 1070 and to Amalfi Cathedral around the same time. The inscription at S Paolo asks the patron saint to open the doors of eternal life. Doors similar to those at Amalfi were given by Pantaleone Viarecta in 1087 to S Sebastiano, Atrani (later moved to S Salvatore). They depict on incised panels the Virgin of Intercession and Christ. Two original panels, inscribed with the dedication inscription of Maurus of Amalfi and the date 1066, are incorporated with nine later panels of silver-inlaid figures on the basilica doors at S Benedetto, Montecassino. A *domino* Pantaleone had doors made in Constantinople for S Michele Arcangelo, Monte Sant'Angelo (Puglia), in 1076. The door was dedicated to St Michael and illustrates the Archangel's intervention in the Old and New Testaments. At S Marco, Venice, there are four bronze doors in the narthex. Two on the exterior are of Classical style with panels of fish-scale designs, one made in the 6th century and the other in 1300 by Bertuccio. The door in the south portal of the nave was made in 1080 in Constantinople and depicts inlaid figures of Christ, the Virgin and saints. The central nave door, commissioned by Leo da Molino in 1112, was made locally, influenced by the south door. It shows a heavenly hierarchy starting with Christ and proceeding through the prophets, saints and martyrs, with Molino himself prostrate before St Mark.

BIBLIOGRAPHY
I. Falke and J. Lanyi: 'The Genesis of Andrea Pisano's Bronze Doors', *A. Bull.*, xxv (1943), pp. 132–53
W. Braunfels: 'Karls des Grossen Bronzewerkstatt', *Karolingische Kunst*, iii of *Karl der Grosse*, ed. W. Braunfels and H. Schnitzler (Düsseldorf, 1965), pp. 168–202
U. Gotz: *Die Bildprogramme der Kirchentüren des 11. und 12. Jahrhunderts* (diss., Tübingen U., 1971)
G. Matthiae: *La Porte bronzée byzantine in Italia* (Rome, 1971)
M. E. Frazer: 'The Gates of Paradise', *Dumbarton Oaks Pap.*, xxvii (1973), pp. 147–62
F. Grassi: *I frammenti della porta di bronzo beneventana* (Pompeii, 1977)
K. Clark and D. Finn: *The Florence Baptistery Doors* (London, 1980) [good plates]
U. Mende: *Die Bronzetüren des Mittelalters, 800–1200* (Munich, 1983) [the fullest, best-illustrated account]
H. Bloch: *Montecassino in the Middle Ages* (Cambridge, MA, 1986)
M. Ryan: 'The Donore Hoard: Early Medieval Metalwork from Moynalty near Kells, Ireland', *Antiquity*, lxi/231 (1987), pp. 57–63
G. P. Carratelli, ed.: *Le porte di bronzo dall'antichità al secolo XIII* (Rome, 1990)

(iii) Iron. In Britain, Scandinavia, Germany, Spain and France well over 1000 medieval doors have survived decorated with applied scrolls and figures of iron. The techniques for making cast iron were not widespread in Europe before the 14th century, so the metal used was always hammered or wrought iron. There is no evidence from the Classical world that iron was used for this sort of decoration on doors or even chests. One reason seems to be that important Classical doors of wood or bronze rotated round a har post (*see* §(i) above) and did not require iron reinforcement, whereas the doors of northern Europe generally hung from iron strap hinges, which naturally lend themselves to embellishment. Illustrations from manuscripts and ivories depict scrolled iron straps on doors from the 9th century onwards (e.g. St Gall, Stift.-Bib., Cod. 22, fol. 136; Lothair Crystal, London, BM; Bible of Charles the Bald, Rome, S Paolo fuori le mura, fol. 50). The earliest surviving examples are from the 11th century at Urnes in Norway and Hadstock (Essex), but the heyday for this type of decoration was from the 12th century to the early 14th.

Because the iron was produced primarily by village blacksmiths, there are distinct regional varieties in design. In England, a few doors such as those at All Saints, Staplehurst (Kent), and St Helen's, Stillingfleet (N. Yorks), are covered with enigmatic figurative designs, but the most common form of Romanesque hinge was the C shape. This was non-functional and attached to the front of the door, often with a load-bearing strap through its centre. The C and strap could be embellished with various terminals: fleurs-de-lis, barbs and lobes with tendrils. Typical examples are found at St John the Baptist, Kingston Lisle (Oxon), the Nativity of the Virgin, Madley (Hereford & Worcs), and St Nicholas, Castle Hedingham (Essex). Later in the 12th century greater interest was shown in surface decoration, foliage and geometric ornament. The hinges from the slype of St Albans Abbey, now St Albans Cathedral (1160s; London, V&A), have chiselled zigzag patterns, leaves and lively raised animal-head terminals. Also from this phase are the high-quality hinges at All Saints, Faringdon, and St Mary, Uffington (Oxon), and Durham Cathedral (nave, south-west door). In the

13th century the new technique of stamping the iron scrolls with dies enabled smiths to produce accurate repetitive motifs of leaves and flowers. This elegant technique was most widespread in the Ile-de-France and England. The smith Gilebertus stamped his name on the doors of St George's Chapel, Windsor (1247–9). They are covered in flowing spiral designs of leaves and flowers, as are the doors of York Minster chapter house (1280–85). The master blacksmith Thomas de Leghtune made the stamped iron grille around the tomb of Queen Eleanor in Westminster Abbey (1293–4), and he used stamps of the same design on doors at All Saints, Leighton Buzzard, and All Saints, Turvey (Beds). A simpler way of making the delicate foliage terminals was to cut out tiny sheets of iron, like biscuits. Although technically less sophisticated, many attractive designs were made using the cut-out method. Fine examples are found at Lichfield Cathedral (1290s), St Lawrence and All Saints, Eastwood (Essex), and Worksop Priory (Notts). After 1350 woodwork tracery eventually replaced iron decoration on doors, and the smiths responded to the change of fashion by making iron tracery. Much of this is crude punched and filed work, but iron tracery of the highest quality is found on the gates in front of the tomb of *Edward IV* in St George's Chapel, Windsor (1483). An important repository for English and

4. Iron-clad door, Rogslösa Church, Östergötland, Sweden, *c*. 1200

European ironwork is at the Victoria and Albert Museum, London.

In Sweden an exceptional number of iron-clad church doors survive from the late 12th century and the 13th. Bold figurative scenes are found, for instance, at Rogslösa and Väversunda (Östergötland), where the struggle between good and evil, the Fall and Redemption through the Crucifixion are illustrated (see fig. 4). Many doors are covered with horizontal bands of geometric designs: interlocking circles, crosses and scrolls, as at Bjälbo (Östergötland). On Gotland a distinctive form of design was used between the 12th and 14th centuries, consisting of back-to-back C shapes, separated by a horizontal strap. Delicate cut-out foliage was also used from the 13th century onwards (e.g. Högby, Östergötland; Stockholm, Stat. Hist. Mus. 4779). A large collection of Swedish medieval doors is now preserved in the Statens Historisk Museum, Stockholm. The more modest survivals in Norway include a fine series of dragon-headed lock plates from Arnafjord (U. Bergen, Hist. Mus.), Hurum and Hedal (both *in situ*). The most outstanding group of doors in Denmark is found on the island of Funen. Their entire surface is decorated with horizontal rows of iron black-letter inscriptions, which generally cite their date and patron. Fine examples from the 15th and 16th centuries are at Sondersø, Hastrup and Indslev.

Clearly a great deal of iron has been lost from the wealthy churches of the former Holy Roman Empire, where the survivals are somewhat scattered. The Romanesque C shape is found at Maulbronn Abbey and St Ägidius, Mittelheim; horizontal rows of 'trees' are seen at the Liebfrauenkirche, Wiener Neustadt (Austria), and Heiligenleiten, near Pettenbach (Austria); and figurative scenes occur at the Dorfkirche, Wahren (now in Leipzig, Mus. Gesch.), and the Dorfkirche, Eisdorf, Germany. The finest cut-out work, of delicate leaves and branches, is at St Elizabeth, Marburg (1270s), while later, more rigid cut-out designs are in the Germanisches Nationalmuseum, Nuremberg, at St Vincenz, Hattenheim, and St Trinitatis, Kaub.

French ironwork can be divided into distinct regions. In the Massif Central the designs are distinguished by the extensive use of palmette leaves, raised human and animal heads and patterns based on a lozenge shape. Examples from the 12th and 13th centuries are at Auzelles, St Léger Abbey, Ebreuil, St Etienne, Gannat (London, V&A, M396–1924), St Barthélemy, Liginiac, St Etienne, Neuvy-Saint-Sépulchre, and Saint-Leonard de Noblat (New York, Cloisters). In both the French and Spanish Pyrenees, one style predominates for most of the Middle Ages and even recurs in the 17th century. It consists of pairs of tightly curled spirals arranged in rows along hinge straps, often covering the whole door. Vigorous examples of this type are found at Ste Marie, Corneilla de Conflent, La Trinité, Prunet et Belpuig, and the Assomption de la Vierge, Serralongue, France; others are at the Museu d'Art de Catalunya, Barcelona, and carved on a cloister capital at Girona Cathedral. In Burgundy the style is less homogeneous, but it can be characterized by elegant attenuated C shapes with scrolled terminals found at Notre-Dame, Montréal, St Martin, Chablis, from the 12th century and at Pontigny Abbey (if genuinely medieval). Possibly the finest hinges made in the Middle Ages were those decorating the west doors of Notre-Dame, Paris, from the 1240s. They were made with a profusion of stamped designs, sprays and bouquets of flowers and leaves. A few fragments of the original survive in the Musée de Cluny, Paris, but the present hinges are 19th-century replicas. Stamped ironwork achieved its greatest flowering in the Ile-de-France in the 13th century, being used for doors, candlesticks, grilles and chests. The largest collection of medieval ironwork is preserved in Rouen (Mus. Le Secq des Tournelles). It is quite likely that stamped ironwork originated in the Sambre-Meuse region, inspired by similar techniques in goldsmithing. Early 13th-century examples are found at St Jacques, Liège, and Liège Cathedral sacristy, and there is a sumptuous 15th-century door with cut-out terminals at Notre-Dame, Halle.

BIBLIOGRAPHY

H. Lueer: *Geschichte der Metallkunst*, i (Stuttgart, 1904)
J. Starkie Gardner: *Ironwork*, i (London, 1927)
M. Mackeprang: 'Fyenske jaernbundne kirkedøre fra middelalderen' [Iron-bound church doors from the Middle Ages], *Aab. Nord. Oldknd. Hist.* (1943), pp. 1–30
R. Hauglid: *Norske Stavkirker* (Oslo, 1973)
M. N. Delaine: 'Les Peintures de portes médiévales dans le centre de la France', *Rev. Auvergne*, lxxxviii/2 (1974), pp. 81–8
——: 'La Ferronnerie monumentale de la Bourgogne médiévale', *An. Bourgogne*, l/198 (1978), pp. 65–84
J. Geddes: *English Decorative Ironwork, 1100–1350* (diss., U. London, 1978)
L. Karlsson: *Medieval Ironwork in Sweden*, 2 vols (Stockholm, 1988) [excellent pls, covers most of Europe]

JANE GEDDES

2. RENAISSANCE, *c.* 1400–*c.* 1550. The medieval tradition of covering doors with bronze reliefs was continued in the Renaissance only in Italy. In 1401, when Lorenzo Ghiberti won the competition to make the second set of doors for the Baptistery in Florence, he exactly followed the pattern used by Pisano 70 years earlier (*see* §1(ii) above); in contrast to Pisano's rapid progress, however, Ghiberti's doors took a quarter of a century to finish. This may have been due partly to outside factors, such as finance, but also Ghiberti's designs for the New Testament story are distinctly more complex and sophisticated, introducing as they did numerous Renaissance motifs. When Ghiberti was commissioned to make the third and last pair of doors (1425–52), he was able to persuade his patrons to abandon the cramped Gothic design in favour of ten large, square panels, which would permit a freer rendering of settings and backgrounds and a more modern and painterly approach. Conversely, it meant that each panel had to rely on the medieval tradition of 'continuous narration' to incorporate several episodes that were actually diverse in time into one great scene as though they were simultaneous: for example, the first panel gave the whole story of the Creation and Fall of Man. They were completely gilded, conspicuously advertising the affluence of the patron guild. So glamorous were they, and so suave was Ghiberti's figure style, that Michelangelo called them, aptly, the 'Gates of Paradise', a poetic name that has remained in common use (*see also* FLORENCE, §IV, 1(ii)(c)).

Probably in the 1430s, Donatello contributed two pairs of bronze doors in the Old Sacristy of S Lorenzo, Florence, with hyperactive pairs of Apostles or martyrs in square fields against neutral backgrounds. These were followed by a commission (1437) to produce two larger pairs for the two sacristies of Florence Cathedral, but Donatello failed to deliver these, and in 1446 a new contract was drawn up with his associates Michelozzo di Bartolomeo and Maso di Bartolommeo, as well as Luca della Robbia for one pair for the north sacristy. These were not completed until 1469. Luca played the major role and predictably created a series of ten panels that were blander than anything that Donatello would have designed: the four *Evangelists* and four *Fathers of the Church* were shown calmly writing or teaching, with the *Virgin and Child* next to *St John the Baptist* completing the sequence at the top. Heads project from the intersections of the frame, following the example of Ghiberti, and three are thought to be portraits of the sculptors involved.

In Rome, meanwhile, the architect–sculptor Filarete, aided by Simone Ghini, had been furnishing an enormous pair of bronze doors, with some gilding and enamelling, for the main portal of Old St Peter's (*c.* 1445). Installed in the new basilica, they are impressive for sheer size and exuberance of ornament, which includes, for example, inhabited scrolls of acanthus with medallion portraits on the frame (see FILARETE, fig. 1). The four rectangular panels with large figures of *Christ* and the *Virgin Enthroned*, *St Paul* and *St Peter* with Eugene IV, the papal donor, at his feet are, however, rather disappointing aesthetically in comparison with the contemporary doors made in Florence, for Filarete's gifts of composition and drapery were limited; if anything they seem to reflect an admiration for the hieratic figures on Early Christian ivory consular diptychs and, possibly, Byzantine bronze doors. More interesting are the two square panels at eye-level showing the *Decapitation of St Paul* and the *Crucifixion of St Peter*. Here Filarete managed lively narratives, with interesting historical references, for example to the Council of Ferrara in 1439, as well as a proud self-portrait and inscription.

In the next generation (*c.* 1475) the example of Filarete's narratives, packed with anecdote, was followed by Guglielmo Monaco, an artillery founder, in his doors for the gateway of the Castel Nuovo in Naples (now in the Palazzo Reale). He depicted the recent victories of Ferrante I of Aragon over Jean d'Anjou in minute detail in four large, square fields, with an upper pair forming a lunette when closed. The junctions of the frame are marked with medallions with heraldic devices and the artist's self-portrait and signature. What might have been a spectacular exercise in narrative relief by Donatello in his late, 'expressionist' style, challenging Ghiberti's ideal serenity, a pair of bronze doors for the western portal of Siena Cathedral, for which he made models in 1457–9, came to nought. There survives no record of the subject or design, unless they are reflected in the reliefs cast a few years later for the left-hand pulpit (*c.* 1465) in S Lorenzo, Florence. During the High Renaissance in Italy only one bronze door was made, the concave one by Jacopo Sansovino for the sacristy in S Marco, Venice (see fig. 5). With only two large, square narrative panels (*Entombment* and *Resurrection*), a frame broad enough to contain niches with statuettes of Evangelists, and portrait busts projecting from the junctions, Sansovino's reliance on the 'Gates of

5. Bronze door to the sacristy of S Marco, Venice, by Jacopo Sansovino, *c.* 2.16×1.17 m, commissioned 1546, installed 1572

Paradise' is manifest: indeed it is a tribute to that masterwork of the early Renaissance. In 1565 several sculptors contributed to the temporary doors made out of ephemeral materials for Florence Cathedral on the occasion of the nuptials of Prince Francesco de' Medici (later Francesco I, Grand Duke of Tuscany). Of these only Giambologna's *Adoration of the Shepherds* survives (gilt stucco, Fiesole, Mus. Bandini).

In northern Europe and in Spain no significant doors were cast in bronze during the whole of the Renaissance (or indeed the Baroque). Oak was in common use because of its durability for external doors, while internally walnut might be preferred, as it takes a high polish. As in the Late Gothic epoch, the panels of such doors were carved in low relief, but a new, classicizing, repertory of ornament was introduced. Aediculae, round niches with figures and portrait medallions of heroes or heroines of antiquity or of contemporary grandees were particularly popular. They were interspersed with geometric patterns of raised mouldings, pertinent coats of arms and heraldic devices, mottoes or initials/monograms, with the proper coronets where applicable. In France, such doors are to be seen in the Palais du Louvre, Paris, and the châteaux of Chenonceaux and Ecouen and elsewhere. Trophies of armour, musical instruments or agricultural implements and Michelangelesque chained prisoners were popular. The principal subject-matter was often drawn from engravings after the work of great painters, such as Rosso or Francesco Primaticcio. Series of allegories that lent themselves to symmetrical disposition, such as the *Four Elements* or the *Four Seasons*, were much favoured. Good examples from France and other countries are to be found in the great museums of decorative art, such as the Victoria and Albert Museum, London, the Metropolitan Museum, New York, the Musée des Arts Décoratifs, Paris, and the Musée de la Renaissance in the château of Ecouen.

3. MANNERIST, BAROQUE AND ROCOCO, *c.* 1550–*c.* 1750. The next three noteworthy commissions for bronze doors span the Mannerist and early Baroque periods, around the turn of the 16th century. The earliest were cast for the four relatively modest doorways of the Santa Casa, within the basilica of S Maria di Loreto, by Girolamo Lombardo and Ludovico Lombardo between 1568 and 1576. Their design was uniform, a simplified variant of Sansovino's sacristy door in Venice, which the Lombardi must have known well. More important by virtue of their size and location were the three pairs of bronze doors for the basilica itself in Loreto commissioned a decade later (1590), the central pair from Guglielmo Lombardo and Antonio Lombardo the younger, the northern pair from TIBURZIO VERGELLI and Giovanni Battista Vitali (*d* 1640) and the southern one from Antonio Calcagni, Sebastiano Sebastiani (*d c.* 1626) and Tarquinio Jacometti. Their general design was deliberately homogenous, although the larger central pair varies slightly. On the central doors the story of Genesis from the Creation to the Punishment of Cain is recounted in large, bold figures, reminiscent of those carved round the portal of S Petronio, Bologna, by JACOPO DELLA QUERCIA. Each door has three large, squarish narrative fields recalling Ghiberti's, with scope for much background detail, and a varying number of subsidiary panels with smaller figures. The central door has the traditional heads projecting from cartouches in its framework, while the other doors have statuettes or subsidiary scenes framed in ovals by strapwork ornaments. Finished at various dates between 1596 and 1610, they are a brilliant artistic and technical achievement, all too rarely acknowledged because of the seclusion of the town of Loreto.

When a disastrous fire (1595) in Pisa Cathedral destroyed the west doors by Bonanus of Pisa, the Tuscans were prompted to meet the challenge of the doors being created for Loreto at that very moment, and so replacements were commissioned in 1600 from a team composed of Giambologna's followers, to work under his aegis: many younger sculptors or goldsmiths cut their artistic

teeth on modelling individual panels. The higher central pair of doors, dedicated to the *Life of the Virgin*, has four horizontal rectangular panels of narrative on either leaf, while the lower doors on either side have only three panels, more upright in proportions, dedicated to the *Life of Christ*. Giambologna's methods of creating the effect of perspective were adhered to by all the participants, and the effect is uniform and satisfactory. The framework is richly encrusted with foliage inhabited by charming little creatures such as squirrels, owls, birds and lizards (as in the doorjambs by Vittorio Ghiberti for the south doors of the Baptistery in Florence (*see* GHIBERTI, (2)), while other, more exotic animals, with symbolic meanings particular to the Medici, occupy some of the subsidiary panels. There are no projecting heads, let alone portraits of the artists, but the coats of arms of the Grand Dukes and of the cities of Florence and Pisa feature prominently. There are statuettes of apostles in niches at the corners of every door-leaf, with others inserted at the middle of those in the central doorway; these are cast from the same moulds as some of Giambologna's and Susini's own earlier independent statuettes.

During the high Baroque period in Rome, perhaps surprisingly, no very significantly sculptural bronze doors were manufactured. Mention may however be made of the superb grille, designed by Cosimo Fanzago, which closes the chapel of S Gennaro in Naples, a work of controlled design and abstract decoration, apart from a life-size bust of the saint that leans out in benediction from a central niche above and the cherubim that smile from the centres of the access gates. Far more disciplined, although of course their function is entirely different, are the small bronze doors of the chapel of St Philip in S Girolamo della Carità in Rome, dating from the first quarter of the 18th century. Designed by the architect Filippo Juvarra, the central grotesque handles and other ornaments were modelled by Camillo Rusconi. In Venice, openwork gates were made for the enclosure of the Loggetta by Antonio Gai in 1734; on their tops coquettish lions of St Mark with open gospels flank serious seated female allegorical figures, while below are two square frames with two more female allegories ensconced in a fantastic network of trophies of arms, putti and fluttering ribbons, all carefully cast, chased and polished to perfection. Similar in conception, but much freer and more overtly Rococo in design, are the curvaceous gates (1756) of the Scuola di S Rocco in Venice by Giuseppe Filiberti and his son: each has a *Miracle of St Roch* precariously set amid ebullient rocaille scrolls, while the tops when closed form a broken pediment of Baroque counter-curves and an urn in the middle, crowned with twin putti who play impertinently with the saint's pilgrim hat and his pet dog.

4. AFTER *c.* 1750. The tradition of making great doors in bronze re-emerged after almost two centuries of quiescence towards the close of the 19th century, as part of the general revival of interest in past historic styles. As in earlier days they represented confident statements of religious devotion and civic or national pride. Almost every city in Italy whose cathedral was not endowed with older sculpted doors sought to rectify this by commissioning some in an appropriate—usually neo-Gothic—style

from the most renowned sculptors of the day. In Florence, where the cathedral was dedicated to the Virgin Mary, a Marian theme was mandatory. Six of her 'Joys' were spread over the main panels of the three pairs of doors, with her *Assumption* and *Coronation* reserved for the central ones. These Ghibertesque reliefs are framed by ogival canopies and surrounded by appropriate statuettes and busts in niches. The central and north (left-hand) pairs of doors (1897; 1903) are by Augusto Passaglia (1838–1918), while the south (right-hand) pair, which interestingly vary in design from the corresponding pair despite being set within a symmetrical frame, were by Giuseppe Cassioli (*b* 1865). At Padua in 1895, for the basilica of S Antonio, Camillo Boito designed and Guglielmo Michieli modelled a pair with a more restrained sculptural component, showing only the four *Fathers of the Church*, standing beneath transitional, Late Gothic canopies. These are set off by a foil of square panels above and below with holy monograms and symbols in low relief, all framed with a running frieze of Madonna lilies recalling Ghiberti and Luca della Robbia.

In Milan around this time Ludovico Pogliaghi was modelling an amazing and masterly pair of bronze doors (1894–1906) for the restored façade of the cathedral. His swaying, graceful figures in the International Gothic style filtered through Ghiberti are infected with the added sinuosity of line and fluidity of surface characteristic of Art Nouveau. Nevertheless, all was held rigidly in control by a firm cruciform frame, with a great central quadrilobe on each leaf (containing the *Pietà* and the *Assumption of the Virgin*), a shape that was derived visually from the cope clasps of Gothic precious metalwork. The *Life of Christ* is disposed in rows of canopied rectangles that recall Flemish oak retables of the 15th century as well as Italian Gothic altar frontals in silver (for example at Pistoia). Above the hinged leaves is an openwork panel, set amid complex ogival tracery, which has at its centre (seemingly rising from a vertical shaft like a Tree of Jesse running up the central division) a deep relief of the *Coronation of the Virgin*. The Art Nouveau style of fluid modelling is also represented by a pair of bronze doors made by Pier Enrico Astorri (1882–1926) for the monument to Pope Pius X in St Peter's, Rome, which are centred with large female figures, allegorical of painting and music, with four subsidiary scenes on squarish panels above and below. Siena Cathedral has doors by E. Manfrini glorifying the Virgin Mary and modelled in a tame low relief of no great distinction in the mid-20th century. Far more distinguished, and one of the sculptor's acknowledged masterpieces, is the *Door of Death* (see fig. 6) at St Peter's, created by Giacomo Manzù. Here the sculptor's experiences in World War II and the chosen theme led him to create a series of visual meditations on aspects of death that are in their modern way as expressive as Donatello's last reliefs of the *Passion*.

The most effective and celebrated bronze portal of the modern period in northern Europe is Rodin's monumental *Gates of Hell* (Paris, Mus. Rodin; see RODIN, AUGUSTE, fig. 3)). These were commissioned in 1880 by the Minister of Fine Arts as an entrance for a planned new museum of decorative arts, but the sculptor's ambition to emulate the

6. *Door of Death*, basilica of St Peter, Rome, by Giacomo Manzù, bronze, 1964–7

artistry of Ghiberti's 'Gates of Paradise' and Michelangelo's fresco of the *Last Judgement* with a theme chosen from a universally famous Florentine literary source, Dante's *Inferno*, led to a lengthy period of gestation as novel ideas flooded into his mind's eye. Rodin was, after all, in the throes of pioneering an entirely new style of sculpture when he received this major commission. It proved to be a catalyst, however, stimulating his imaginative and technical powers in the effort to invent a repertory of suitably dynamic forms to render Dante's vivid verbal imagery. This took time and incurred increasing expense, a crucial factor, as the enormous cost of 40,000 francs made it impossible to cast the work, and at Rodin's death the *Gates of Hell* remained tragically and almost symbolically uncast. The first bronze cast was not made until 1925 and therefore lacks any finishing touches that the artist might have chosen to apply (although it was not his custom to intervene much once casting had been done).

Virtually every figure in Rodin's early repertory was pressed into service in the mêlée of distraught human beings that is the subject of the doors: colossal statues in bronze of *Adam* and *Eve* were to flank the door, and they are clearly indebted to Michelangelo, especially to the *Slaves* from the tomb of *Julius II*, which Rodin had seen in the Louvre. On top three casts of an identical figure, derived from Adam, stand in rotated positions to form a group of the *Three Shades*, while below them sat his best-known statue, *The Thinker*, a representation of man himself, sunk in contemplation of his destiny. A plethora of smaller figures, crouching, writhing, curled up in terror or flying in mid-air, most of them known also in separate casts, and to be seen individually, was employed to populate Rodin's deeply personal, psychological and encyclopedic vision of Hell. The huge low-relief sculpture that resulted was a phenomenal achievement by any standards and is a monument to Rodin's creative genius, technical facility and control of his chosen medium of modelling wax. In it Rodin arguably achieved his ambition to stand alongside Dante, Ghiberti and Michelangelo in terms of artistic renown.

BIBLIOGRAPHY

E. Rumler: *Portes modernes: Architecture, ferronnerie, sculpture* (Paris, *c.* 1910)
A. Pettorelli: *Il bronzo e il rame nell'arte decorativa italiana* (Milan, 1926)
A. Elsen: *Rodin's Gates of Hell* (Minneapolis, 1980)
K. Clark and D. Finn: *The Florence Baptistery Doors* (London, 1980)
F. Grimaldi and K. Sordi: *Scultori a Loreto: Fratelli Lombardi, Antonio Calcagni e Tiburzio Vergelli*
M. Scalini: 'La Porte bronzée', *L'arte italiana del bronzo* (Busto Arsizio, 1988), pp. 17–29

CHARLES AVERY

III. Islamic world.

Doors in the Islamic world were usually made of joined wood, as large planks were scarce throughout the region (*see* ISLAMIC ART, §VII). Decoration, often elaborate, was applied to the interior and exterior doors of public and private buildings and to city gates. By far the largest number of doors survive from interiors. The standard arrangement consists of a pair of valves, each with two vertical stiles connected by four or more rails and enclosing three or more panels. The middle panel was often larger than the upper or lower ones. In earlier times, particularly under the Abbasid dynasty (*reg* 750–1258), the panels of interior doors were carved in the BEVELLED STYLE (*see also* ISLAMIC ART, fig. 213), and in Egypt under the Tulunid (*reg* 868–905) and Fatimid (*reg* 979–1171) dynasties, the abstract designs were sometimes transformed into representations of animals or accompanied by inscriptions. In later times the panels were also inlaid or painted, or replaced by turned spoolwork. In Anatolia, where wood was commonly available, large planks were sometimes carved with patterns to imitate joinery. Marquetry of ivory, bone, ebony and other woods provided colour, and under the Ottoman dynasty (*reg* 1281–1924) mother-of-pearl was added to wooden doors for the finest royal foundations. A pair of doors from a pavilion in the harem at Topkapı Palace (1578–9) in Istanbul, for example, has panels of minute marquetry in mahogany, lead, tin, ebony and ivory and veneer in ivory, ebony, mother-of-pearl and tortoiseshell, this last set over gold foil to add glitter. In Iran, interior doors were often painted and sometimes heavily varnished in a technique known as 'Islamic lacquer' (*see* ISLAMIC ART, §VIII, 10). In Egypt spoolwork (Arab. *mashrabiyya*) was occasionally used, as in the doors within the mausoleum (1284–5) of the Mamluk sultan Qala'un in Cairo (*see* ISLAMIC ART, fig. 56).

Exterior doors often had fittings of metal. Several important fittings of iron or brass survive from the central Arab lands in the 12th and 13th centuries. For example, the striking door handles that once adorned the Great Mosque at Cizre (early 13th century) in eastern Turkey are of cast and incised bronze in the form of confronted

dragons (e.g. Berlin, Mus. Islam. Kst; Copenhagen, Davids Saml.; Istanbul, Mus. Turk. & Islam. A.). Many buildings erected under the Mamluk sultans of Egypt (*reg* 1250–1517) had heavy wooden doors elaborately plated with metal in complex geometric designs, often further embellished with silver and gold inlay (*see* ISLAMIC ART, §IV, 3(iii)). Some of the most famous are those made for the complex of Hasan (1356–62) in Cairo, which were so magnificent that they were illegally removed and installed by al-Mu'ayyad Shaykh (*reg* 1412–21) in his funerary complex near by (*see* fig. 7). City gates, normally of huge, sturdy planks, were also adorned with metal fittings, which are often the only part to have survived. The Khatir Gate (1040–41) at Yazd in central Iran had iron plates decorated with figures, elephants and a foundation inscription naming the amirs who funded the work; the city gate (1063) from Gandja in Azerbaijan removed to the GELATI MONASTERY in Georgia was inscribed with the names of the ruler and the qadi who supervised the work. The smiths who made these fittings were considered important craftsmen and often signed their work. City gates had symbolic and apotropaic associations, for texts report that they were often removed by conquerors and reinstalled elsewhere as signs of sovereignty.

7. Doors, wood plated with bronze, from the complex of Hasan (1356–62) in Cairo, subsequently installed (*c.* 1420) in the funerary complex of al-Mu'ayyad Shaykh (photograph shows one-half of one valve)

Doors were often the focus of elaborate surrounds of carved stucco or stone. A rich tradition of figural sculpture developed in parts of Turkey, Syria, Iraq and Iran in the 12th and 13th centuries, and door surrounds and the spandrels of gateways were decorated with real and imaginary creatures. The Talisman Gate (1221; destr. 1917) at Baghdad, for example, was decorated with a seated monarch, presumably the Abbasid caliph al-Nasir (*reg* 1180–1225), holding two dragons by their tongues (*see* ISLAMIC ART, fig. 78). The portal to the funerary madrasa of al-Nasir Muhammad (*reg* 1294–1340 with interruptions) in Cairo is a Gothic portal made of white marble that had been removed by Khalil (*reg* 1290–94) from a crusader church in Acre. Door posts, a lintel with joggled voussoirs in two colours of marble and a panel with an Arabic inscription were added for the new setting. The Egyptian historian al-Maqrizi (1364–1442) considered this portal one of the marvels of human endeavour. Many doorways were crowned by *muqarnas* semi-domes (*see* MUQARNAS, fig. 1) and framed by a flat masonry or brick structure known as a PĪSHTĀQ.

BIBLIOGRAPHY
Enc. Iran; *Enc. Islam*, ii: 'Bâb' [Door]
K. Brisch: 'Zum Bâb al-Wuzurā' (Puerta de San Esteban) der Hauptmoschee von Córdoba', *Studies in Islamic Art and Architecture in Honour of Professor K. A. C. Cresswell* (Cairo, 1965), pp. 30–48
S. S. Blair: *The Monumental Inscriptions from Early Islamic Iran and Transoxiana* (Leiden, 1992), nos 41, 49

SHEILA BLAIR

IV. Indian subcontinent.

In ancient India the entrance to a sacred space, for example a tree-shrine or stupa complex, was marked by a free-standing gate (*see* TORAṆA). In early stone temples, built from the first half of the 5th century AD, doors (Skt *dvāra*) generally had a frame of two or three jambs (*śākhā*s, literally 'branches') carved with rosettes and scroll motifs (*see* INDIAN SUBCONTINENT, fig. 28). The lintel often extended beyond the jambs to create a T-shape. Small figures of the river goddesses Ganga and Yamuna standing on mythic crocodiles (*makara*s), or tortoises, were set in the upper corners or flanking the bottom of the door. By the 9th century, doors had become more elaborate (see fig. 8), typically comprising four main parts: the lintel (*uttarāṅga*), side jambs, threshold (*uḍamabara*) and projecting stepping-stone (*maṇḍāraka*). The lintel often bore a depiction of the nine planets (*navagraha*) or flying divinities holding garlands and an image of a divinity in the keystone (*lalāṭabimba*). The jambs, made of three, five, seven or nine parallel vertical sections, were ornamented with scrolls (*patraśākhā*s), entwined serpents (*nāgaśākhā*s), amorous couples (*gandharva-* or *mithunaśākhā*s), divinities (*rūpaśākhā*s), lions (*simhaśākhā*s) or pilasters (*stambhaśākhā*s). Door-guardians (*dvārapāla*s) were positioned at the base of the jambs adjacent to the figures of Ganga and Yamuna and their attendants. The threshold could have scrolls, pots of plenty (*pūrṇaghaṭa*s), lions, elephants and celestial beings. The semicircular stepping-stone known as a half-moon (*ardhacandra*) or moonstone (*candraśīla*) was often carved with lotus petals and flanked by conches.

The texts on architecture and art (collectively termed *Śilpa śāstra*) prescribed the proportions for doors, although surviving examples show that there was considerable variation in practice. For temple doors, the height was to be twice the width, while in domestic structures a height of three times the width was allowed. The width of a temple door was to be calculated from either the side wall of the temple (one eighth of it) or the width of the sanctum (one fifth of it). The width of the jambs, lintel and threshold should be equal to a quarter of the door's height and their depth equal to a quarter of the door's width.

Entrances were usually closed by door panels (*kavāṭa*s). These could be wooden, brass or gilded and were often carved or painted with scenes from the lives of Krishna and Rama or with celestial beings (*nāyikā*s, *apsarasa*s). They could also be embossed and inlaid with brass and ivory, often in geometric or floral patterns. Hinges (*bhramaraka*s) fixed the doors at top and bottom, and bolts (*argala*s) closed and fastened the panels. Chains (*valaya*s) served as handles. Strips of copper, brass or iron (*patraka*s) cut in the form of creepers were added for additional strength. The regulations regarding doors were laid down in detail to stress the religious importance of the entrance and to ensure that doors were strong enough to protect the images and precious objects housed inside. The intimate relationship between the temple door and the divinity is seen in the fact that the idol in a sanctum is always placed exactly opposite the door so that the ornate doorframe serves as a surround for the image. Usually the height of the main idol depends on the height of the door;

8. Sandstone door to a shrine, Mahavira Temple complex, Osian, Rajasthan, late 10th century

the idol, including pedestal, should be the height of the opening minus one eighth.

Temple doors marked a symbolic transition from the 'outer' to the 'inner' world. The river goddesses, indicative of the waters, purified this passage by their presence. The opening being the most vulnerable point, door-keepers or guardians were placed beside the river goddesses, and other motifs symbolizing well-being, prosperity and fertility were employed as ornament. The entrance—specifically the threshold—had to be passed in the correct manner as indicated by the rule in the *Visnudharmottara purāna* (*c*. 7th century) that a priest or devotee had to step over the threshold, right foot first, without touching it. The importance of the door, in both a domestic and a religious context, is shown by the consecration rites and subsequent rituals stipulated in the *Agni purāna* (chap. 61). In rural India women still paint auspicious signs and diagrams around a main entrance or on the floor in front of a threshold, often with white rice-paste, which is considered propitious.

See also INDIAN SUBCONTINENT, §§III, 4(i)(a) and 5(i)(e).

BIBLIOGRAPHY

T. Bhattacharyya: *The Canons of Indian Art* (2/Calcutta, 1963)
H. U. Stietencron: *Ganga und Yamuna: Zur symbolischen Bedeutung von Flussgöttinnen an indischen Tempeln* (Wiesbaden, 1972)
P. Chandra, ed.: *Studies in Indian Temple Architecture* (New Delhi, 1975)
M. Meister, M. A. Dhaky and Krishna Deva, eds: *Foundations of North Indian Style*, iii of *Encyclopaedia of Indian Temple Architecture* (New Delhi and Philadelphia, 1988)
D. Thiagarajan: 'Doors and Woodcrafts of Chettinad', *Living Wood: Sculpture Traditions of Southern India* (exh. cat., ed. G. Michell; London, Whitechapel A.G., 1992), pp. 53–72
J. Jain-Neubauer: *Dvāra: The Entrance to the Temple in North India* (New Delhi, 1995)

JUTTA JAIN-NEUBAUER

V. East Asia.

1. CHINA. According to Chinese tradition, doors were invented in imitation of mussels and oysters. In the earliest Chinese dictionary, the *Showen jie zi* ('Dictionary of words and phrases', AD 121), the pictogram *men* denotes a door with two leaves and *hu* a door with one leaf. Modern scholarship dates the first appearance of both types of door to the Western Han period (206 BC–AD 9), but from the Han (206 BC–AD 220) to the Tang (AD 618–907) period the inward-opening double-leaf plank door (*ban men*) was the main type in use. The earliest extant example of this can be found in the east hall of Foguang Temple (Foguang si) in Shanxi Province (AD 857). Depending on the method of construction, plank doors can be divided into three kinds. The chequer-board door (*qipan men*) consists of a frame with vertical timber boarding fitted into it. The boarding is flush with the frame on the front of the door, while three to five ledges are fixed to the frame at the back with mortise-and-tenon joints. If the front was made smooth with no seams visible, the door would be called *jingmian men*, or mirror-surfaced door. The pierced plank door (*shita men*) consists of three to five timber vertical planks of the same thickness fastened at the back with ledges. In the *Yingzao fashi* ('Building standards', 1103; *see* CHINA, §II, 2(v)) the outermost planks on the left and right for this type of door are thicker than the other planks. Sometimes two-pointed nails were also used between

adjoining planks. The ledges are fixed to the planks either by iron nails or by fitting the ledges on to rebates 10–12 mm deep on the boarding; occasionally both means are employed to make a door more durable.

From the Five Dynasties period (AD 907–60), plank doors continued to be used in the gateways of palaces, temples and residences, but lattice doors—which opened inwards, admitted light into the interior and were dismountable—also became common. Generally, four door-leaves were fitted between each pair of columns on a façade, but the number varied from two to eight depending on the distance between the columns. In the Song period (960–1279), the width-to-height ratio of a door-leaf was 1:2 or a little less than 1:3; under later dynasties it was 1:3 or 1:4, with ratios of 1:5 and 1:6 in the domestic dwellings of Jiangsu and Zhejiang provinces. The major components of the lattice door are the latticework, a lower panel (*qun ban*, sometimes called a skirtboard), a number of ledges and, sometimes, one to three small panels (*taohuan ban*). In the Qing period (1644–1911) it was common to make two layers of latticework, with the inner layer dismountable and gauze or thin paper pasted on it. The latticework, constructed with small timber pieces, commonly carried geometric designs (*see* CHINA, figs 46 and 47), sometimes incorporating figures of tortoises, bats or plants. In some instances, dragons, phoenixes, flowers, plants and human figures were cut on a single solid board.

BIBLIOGRAPHY
Zhongguo gudai jianzhu jishu shi [History of ancient Chinese architectural technology] (Beijing, 1986), pp. 150–56

STANISLAUS FUNG

2. KOREA AND JAPAN. As with most structural elements in Korean architecture, doors took their form from Chinese models, most of them being made of vertical planks of wood. They might be single or double, the latter occurring most frequently in temples and palaces. In stone architecture, such as the pagoda of Punhwang Temple at Kyŏngju (*c*. early 7th century AD), guardian figures were carved on the door frames in high relief.

Lattice doors, also of Chinese inspiration, survive from as early as the mid-14th century at Pusŏk Monastery, Yŏngju, North Kyŏngsang Province, and remain a prominent traditional form. Wooden lattice patterns may be simple cross or fret designs or can exhibit a complex geometry; the interstices are often adorned with flower designs. The lattice forms are frequently placed on both sides of sheets of mulberry paper.

Chinese door types entered the Japanese architectural vocabulary by the 7th century AD. A distinctively Chinese flavour is frequently retained, particularly in Buddhist architecture, though variations also occur. At the ISE SHRINE, reconstructed every 20 years since the 7th century AD, the main buildings have hinged double doors made of single planks of cypress-wood, minimally ornamented and unpainted. This type is seen again at the HŌRYŪJI, Nara, where there also appears a more Chinese form, built of several vertical and horizontal planks. This latter type, popular from the 8th century AD, was often brightly painted and ornamented. By the 12th century additional forms included doors with lattice-networks resembling shutters on the exteriors of buildings and sliding doors for interiors. In large buildings major doorways had four divisions, so that each half could fold back upon itself.

The *fusuma*, or sliding panel, came into wide use during the 16th century. Consisting of a latticed wooden frame covered with paper or occasionally silk, it became a popular format for painting. These doors also provided great flexibility to create varied internal spaces. A variation on the *fusuma* is the *shōji*, sliding doors (or windows) fitted with translucent white paper pasted over wooden latticework. As part of the exterior walls they could function as both doors and windows, framing wide horizontal expanses of a garden or landscape. Closed *shōji* generated a soft, diffuse light to give interiors an intimate sense of enclosure (*see also* JAPAN, §III, 4(ii)(a)).

BIBLIOGRAPHY
R. T. Paine and A. Soper: *The Art and Architecture of Japan* (Harmondsworth, 1955, 3/1981)
Kim Choung Ki [Kim Chŏng-gi], Hwang Su Yong [Hwang Su-yŏng] and Chung Yong Ho [Chŏng Yŏng-ho], eds: *Architecture*, vi of *The Arts of Korea* (Seoul, 1979)
M. Bussagli: *China, Korea, Japan*, ii of *Oriental Architecture* (Milan, 1981)
Im Sŏk-che: *Ko kŏnch'uk mi* [Traditional architecture of Korea], *Hanguk-ŭi mi* [Beauties of Korea] (Seoul, 1988)
P. Mason: *History of Japanese Art* (New York, 1993)

VI. South-east Asia.

In South-east Asia the doors of temples are often extremely elaborate, and, although they are almost invariably made of wood, many different materials and techniques are employed in their decoration. Since the entrance to a Hindu or Buddhist temple marks the transition from the material world outside to the spiritual world within, the consecrated interior, the door and its frame are usually ornately decorated with Hindu or Buddhist scenes and figures of celestial guardians. For example, among the most striking features of Khmer temple architecture throughout the pre-Angkor and Angkor periods (6th–15th centuries) are the decorated sandstone lintels, frontons, colonnettes and thresholds that surround the doors of sanctuaries and other religious buildings. Many of the stone door frames are carved to replicate wooden ones, and the jambs sometimes incorporate inscriptions identifying the donor of the temple and the date of its foundation. There is usually a stone sill across the threshold. In Khmer, Javanese and Burmese temples the principal door of the sanctuary, usually on the east, is often the only real door, those on the other three sides being false. These stone or brick false doors give some idea of the appearance of the original wooden doors, of which almost no examples earlier than the 18th century have survived anywhere in South-east Asia. One of the few 18th-century buildings in the Thai city of Ayutthaya left intact after the Burmese sack in 1767 is the ordination hall (*ubosot*, *bot*) of the royal monastery of Wat Na Phra Men. At the east end of this hall is a projecting porch, which has twin pillars with lotus capitals and gilded brackets in the form of *nāga*s (mythical serpents) supporting the eaves. The porch is surmounted by a gable of carved and gilded wood, in the centre of which is a figure of Vishnu on his mount, the part-bird, part-human Garuda. Underneath is a large window flanked on either side by a door beneath a smaller version of the central porch, with identical pillars, brackets and gable.

Both doors and window shutters are sumptuously decorated with gilt and mosaic (see fig. 9).

The wood (usually ebony or teak) doors of later temples and monastic buildings in Thailand, Laos and Burma frequently have highly elaborate decoration, utilizing a variety of techniques ranging from relief carving, fretwork, inlaid mirror glass and mother-of-pearl to lacquering, gilding and painting. Common motifs include images of deities, *garuḍa*s, *nāga*s, *haṃsa*s (geese) and other beasts from Hindu mythology, as well as floral and vegetal motifs, representing harmony and natural abundance. Buddhist figures are frequently depicted on Lao temple doors (e.g. at Wat Nang, Luang Prabang), or they may be painted with scenes from the Hindu epic the *Rāmāyaṇa*. More often than Thai examples, Lao temple doors will incorporate human figures, including representations of Europeans, a famous example being the doors of Vat Pa Ke, Luang Prabang, which depict two Dutchmen. In Burma figures of the *nat* spirits are common. In Vietnam, Chinese styles have influenced the decoration of temple doors, as for example the doors of the Keo Pagoda (14th–15th century; *see* VIETNAM, §II, 1(i)(a)), Thai Binh Province, which are pierced and carved with Chinese dragons. Some panels of doors and window shutters of Thai halls of the Ratanakosin period (after 1782) are also decorated with Chinese designs in black and gold lacquer.

Palace doors in Thailand, Burma and Laos often have soaring *toraṇa*s and elaborately carved jambs and are embellished with gilding and mirrorwork. A replica of a

9. Door of *ubosot*, monastery of Wat Na Phra Men, Ayutthaya, Thailand, gilded and lacquered wood and glass inlay, 18th century (restored 20th century)

door (Rangoon, N. Mus.) from the royal palace in Mandalay, which was destroyed by fire in World War II, is decorated with foliage scrolls, and another example (London, V&A) is made up of a series of carved and gilded panels covered in glass set in lacquer. Malay and Indonesian palace doors are generally plainer, sometimes with carved panels and a pierced wooden panel above, which may incorporate foliage and flower designs, as well as Islamic-influenced geometric designs. In Malaysia the frame of the door may be decorated with finely carved foliage or cloud designs. Some of the carvings on palace doors in Terengganu and Kelantan show Chinese influence.

Among the peoples of insular South-east Asia the doors of clan houses, chiefs' houses and granaries are also frequently decorated, indicating their importance. The decorations often symbolize important beliefs and religious ideas. The cult-house doors of the Ngada people in Flores in the Lesser Sunda Islands often incorporate scrolled *nāga* or dragon carvings, as do the doors of Kayan and Kenyah chiefs' apartments in Borneo. The doors of many longhouses in Kalimantan (Indonesian Borneo) are painted with dog and *nāga* motifs. Buffalo heads are carved on the granary doors of the Toraja people in central Sulawesi, and the doors of Toraja tombs may have similar heads or a human figure carved on them. The doors of Torajan chiefs' houses may incorporate the same carved scrolls and geometric designs that cover the walls. The older granary doors of the Batak people in northern Sumatra often have a carved lizard motif representing the power of the protecting deity. The houses of the Tetum people in Timor in the Lesser Sunda Islands are traditionally carved in relief with geometric motifs and female figures with prominent breasts. Sometimes only the breasts are depicted, stressing the association of the house with motherhood. The interior doors may also be carved with geometric motifs and human heads, which may represent a warrior or a headhunter.

BIBLIOGRAPHY

M. Smithies: *Old Bangkok* (Singapore, 1986)
——: *Yogyakarta: Cultural Heart of Indonesia* (Singapore, 1986)
J. P. Barbier and D. Newton, eds: *Islands and Ancestors: Indigenous Styles of Southeast Asia* (Munich, 1988)
R. Ringis: *Thai Temples and Temple Murals* (Singapore, 1990)
R. Waterson: *The Living House: An Anthropology of Architecture in South-East Asia* (Singapore, 1990)
J. Dumarçay: *The Palaces of South-East Asia: Architecture and Customs* (Singapore, 1991)
A. Sibeth: *The Batak: Peoples of the Island of Sumatra* (London, 1991)
Naengnoi Punjabhan and Somchai na Nakhonphanom: *The Art of Thai Wood Carving* (Bangkok, 1992)

☐

VII. Africa.

Numerous African peoples decorate the entrances of their buildings, using materials and techniques as diverse as carved and sculpted wood, modelled clay, painted plaster, lashed bamboo and woven fibre. All across the continent, in the region below the Sahara Desert, earth is the principal building material used by sedentary peoples. Thus among the Hausa of northern Nigeria, for example, house entrances are moulded of earthen plaster with raised patterns of Islamic script designed to protect the space within. Mud portals may also be inlaid with stones or ceramic shards, as among the Dagomba of northern Ghana, whose decorated openings are a measure of wealth.

In the savannah and forest regions, where timber is plentiful, doors are constructed of wood, often elaborately carved with culturally specific designs. Among several West African peoples, such as the Dogon of Mali and the Senufo of the Côte d'Ivoire, designs carved on granary or shrine doors depict mythical personages and animals as well as abstract ideographs (*see* DOGON, fig. 4). Such images communicate symbolic messages that invoke the spirits or deities or render sacrosanct the area protected by the door. The Bamana of Mali are known for their delicately engraved door-locks (*see* BAMANA, fig. 1). The Igbo of south-eastern Nigeria use carved wooden panels as entrance doorways into the compounds of titled members of the prestigious men's association, Ozo. Members of sufficiently high rank are entitled to commission sculptors to carve the panels. Carved doors and panels were also apparently formerly adopted for use in the houses of wealthy families as a means of displaying wealth (see Ugwunwa, p. 122). Igbo doors are delicately carved with deeply cut abstract designs in striated and hatched patterns that catch the sunlight to produce high contrasts of light and shadow. The Nupe of Nigeria also produced elaborate chip-carved doors (*see* NUPE, §4; *see also* AFRICA, fig. 120).

In highly stratified societies decorated doors proclaim and enhance the prestige of their owners. Among the Yoruba of south-west Nigeria, for example, the carved doors of rulers' palaces depict exploits of the king's reign.

10. Yoruba door by Olowe of Ise, wood and paint, h. 2.3 m, from the palace at Ikere-Ekiti, south-western Nigeria, *c.* 1906 (London, British Museum)

A well-known early 20th-century example by the renowned carver Olowe of Ise records the visit of a British official to the Ogoga or King of Ikere (see fig. 10). The right panel shows the visitor being carried in a litter and accompanied by members of his entourage. On the left panel is shown the seated king, along with his wives, children and retainers. This door is carved in high relief, its figures sculpted almost in the round. On the East African littoral known as the Swahili Coast, the art of ornamental door-carving reached a pinnacle of development in the 18th and 19th centuries. Commissioned by wealthy men engaged in the Indian Ocean trade system, Swahili doors indicated the affluence and prestige of their owners. Lintels, side-posts and centre-posts of the double-leafed Swahili doors were embellished heavily with geometric or floral designs in styles that varied from place to place and over time (for illustration *see* SWAHILI). In some areas geometric and curvilinear patterns were blended. The door panels themselves were nearly always left uncarved, although they were sometimes studded with brass or iron bosses. In the late 19th century, during a period of unprecedented prosperity, the doors became increasingly baroque in style and massive in proportions, especially in Zanzibar. As the volume of trade diminished around the turn of the 20th century, the art of door-carving declined with it. Nevertheless, hundreds of Swahili doors remained extant in towns and cities along the East African coast in the late 20th century.

In Africa, as elsewhere, portals, doorways and doors are points of structural stress and constitute psychological as well as physical thresholds between the known and the unknown, between sanctuary and the public world and between safety and vulnerability. Doorways in Africa thus often carry symbolic messages in their decoration and sometimes function as centres of ritual activity (see Blier, p. 124).

BIBLIOGRAPHY
L. Prussin: 'The Architecture of Islam in West Africa', *Afr. A.*, i/2 (1968), pp. 32–5, 70–74
——: *Architecture in Northern Ghana* (Berkeley, 1969)
——: 'Fulani-Hausa Architecture', *Afr. A.*, x/1 (1976), pp. 8–19, 97–8
N. C. Neaher: 'An Interpetation of Igbo Carved Doors', *Afr. A.*, xv/1 (1981), pp. 49–55, 88
W. Fagg and J. Pemberton III: *Yoruba Sculpture of West Africa* (New York, 1982)
E. O. Ugwunwa: 'Igbo Carved Doors and Panels of Onitsha Area', *W. Afr. J. Archaeol.*, xiii (1983), pp. 121–9
N. I. Nooter: 'Zanzibar Doors', *Afr. A.*, xvii/4 (1984), pp. 34–9, 96
S. P. Blier: *The Anatomy of Architecture: Ontology and Metaphor in Batammaliba Architectural Expression*, Res Monographs in Anthropology and Aesthetics (Cambridge, 1987)
J. S. Aldrick: *Nineteenth-Century Carved Doors of Mombasa and the East African Coast* (diss., U. Durham, 1988)

NANCY INGRAM NOOTER

VIII. Pre-Columbian Americas.

1. NORTH AMERICA. Among some Northwest Coast cultures, the entrances to their cedar plank houses were through circular 'doors' at the bases of carved and painted poles (*see* NATIVE NORTH AMERICAN ART, §II, 1). Elsewhere, the door was primarily a functional element in the dwellings and other structures of Native North Americans. An antechamber-like, vaulted ice-block entryway preceded the main chamber of the traditional Arctic igloo and was blocked by hanging skins to create a cold air trap. In the south-west of what is now the USA, entrance to pit dwellings and to the apartment-like buildings of cliff dwellings was through holes in the roofs. Interior doorways in cliff dwellings were rectangular, trapezoidal and keyhole-shaped. The tipis of the Plains Indians were closed by an overlapping flap of buffalo hide or canvas, and the doorway was pitched facing east, away from the prevailing Plains winds. Earth lodges had tunnel-like entryways. Doorways in the longhouses, wigwams, huts and timber houses and temples of the Woodlands cultures were covered, when needed, with hanging hides or had timber doors. In 1540 Hernando de Soto described red-painted doors on the temples of the Mississippian towns he visited.

2. MESOAMERICA. Mesoamerican doorways are usually rectangular, and most are undecorated. Some Maya doorways are slightly trapezoidal (e.g. the arch at LABNÁ; the Temple of the Seven Dolls, DZIBILCHALTÚN) or are corbel-arched (e.g. the Temple of the Cross, PALENQUE). Palace-like buildings throughout the Central Highlands, Southern Highlands and Maya region have multiple doorways along their façades, and double doorways were frequently created by dividing an entrance with a column or square-sectioned pillar. In Maya structures the jambs and lintels were sometimes stepped in (e.g. at UXMAL). Lintels and jambs were made with massive dressed stone slabs, plain or carved, or of wood. Classic-period (*c.* AD 250–*c.* 900) YAXCHILÁN, for example, is especially famous for its carved stone lintels, showing scenes of conquest and ceremony, with hieroglyphic dates and texts; another example, from Kuná, shows a ruler holding a ceremonial bar of authority. Extant examples of wooden lintels from the Maya region are of *sapodilla* (*sapote* or *zapote*), both intricately carved (e.g. at TIKAL) and plain (e.g. at Playa del Carmen).

In the Classic period and the Early Post-Classic period (*c.* AD 900–*c.* 1200) the Maya Río Bec, Chenes and Puuc architectural styles (*see* MESOAMERICA, PRE-COLUMBIAN, §III, 2(ii)) featured highly stylized, intricately sculpted 'monster-mouth' or 'serpent-mouth' doorways in which the lintel, panels above it and jambs were carved to represent the teeth and jaws of mythical monsters (see fig. 11). Two classic examples are the Río Bec-style monster doorway at Chicanná (central Yucatán) and the triple doorway at Xpuhil (Campeche, Mexico), which fronts a tripartite pyramid platform. Each doorway is carved in the form of a monster or serpent mouth with stylized teeth hanging over the lintel, and each of the three steep-stepped pyramid towers supports a false (non-usable) temple with fake doorways of the same monster-mouth style. On the eastern side of the Maya region, Temple 22 (the Temple of Meditation) at COPÁN has an outer doorway carved as a giant serpent mouth and an inner doorway carved with intricately intertwined monster motifs and human figures seated on skulls. Holes near the doorways were presumably for curtains or hanging mats.

The façade sculptures at many Maya sites run right up to the jambs of many doorways and over the lintels. For example, at the principal palace at SAYIL attached columns flank the doors across the porticoed façade. At other sites Chac (rain god) and other masks in sculpted stucco surround the walls right up to the doorways.

11. 'Monster-mouth' doorway in a reconstruction of the façade of Temple II at Hochob, Campeche, Mexico, Chenes style, Late Classic period, c. AD 600–c. 900 (Mexico City, Museo Nacional de Antropología)

In the Oaxaca Valley early doorways have been found at San José Mogote, where the stone threshold is carved with a captive figure and the hieroglyph for '1 Earthquake' (c. 650 BC), and at Dienzu, where a lintel at the entrance to a tomb dated c. 300 BC is carved as a jaguar face. Later doorways elsewhere in Mesoamerica were usually plain and were often behind porticoed fronts. The supports of such porticos were frequently carved, as at the Palace of Quetzalpapálotl at Classic-period TEOTIHUACÁN, where the square-sectioned pillars have representations of quetzal birds and owls. The inner doorways at many Teotihuacán élite residences were surrounded by wall paintings (see MESOAMERICA, PRE-COLUMBIAN, §V).

In the Early Post-Classic period (c. AD 900–c. 1200) lintels over temple doorways at CHICHÉN ITZÁ, and by analogy at TULA, were supported by 'serpent columns': square-sectioned pillars of which the upright shafts were carved with stylized scales as the bodies, the forward-projecting tops carved as stylized rattle tails and the bases, also projecting forward, carved as open-mouthed serpents. In the Late Classic period (c. 1200–1521) the lintels at MITLA, in the Southern Highlands, were massive single blocks surrounded by characteristic Zapotec–Mixtec wall mosaics of small stone slabs (see MESOAMERICA, PRE-COLUMBIAN, §III, 2(i)). The doorway to the circular main temple at the Aztec site of MALINALCO is in the shape of a serpent's jaws with a slit tongue projecting from the threshold.

3. SOUTH AMERICA. Doorways in Andean cultures were mostly rectangular, functional and undecorated. One doorway, known as the 'Black and White Portal', at Early Horizon (c. 900 BC–c. 200 BC) CHAVÍN DE HUÁNTAR features flanking black and white pillars, probably representing duality. Stepped-in jambs of adobe were a feature of the Titicaca Basin, including the Early Intermediate-phase constructions (c. 200 BC–c. AD 600) at Chiripa and at TIAHUANACO. The Gateway of the Sun at Middle Horizon (c. AD 600–c. 1000) Tiahuanaco is a monolithic entrance decorated with a staff-bearing deity over the centre and repetitive winged figures across the lintel. The trapezoidal doorway was a particular feature of Inca architecture (e.g. at MACHU PICCHU) and also occurred earlier at Tiahuanaco; at PACHACAMAC and other Inca sites (e.g. Tambo Colorado) there are stepped-in trapezoidal examples.

BIBLIOGRAPHY
I. Marquina: *Arquitectura prehispanica* (Mexico City, 1950, 2/1964/*R* 1981)
G. Kubler: *The Art and Architecture of Ancient America*, Pelican Hist. A. (Harmondsworth, 1962, rev. 3/1984)
M. D. Coe: *The Maya* (London and New York, 1966, rev. 4/1987)
M. P. Weaver: *The Aztecs, Maya and their Predecessors: Archaeology of Mesoamerica* (New York, 1972, rev. 2/1981)
D. Heyden and P. Gendrop: *Pre-Columbian Architecture of Mesoamerica* (New York, 1975)
D. Snow: *The Archaeology of North America: American Indians and their Origins* (London and New York, 1976, rev. 1980)
G. Gasparini and L. Margolies: *Arquitectura inka* (Caracas, 1977; Eng. trans., Bloomington and London, 1980)
J. D. Jennings, ed.: *Ancient Native Americans* (San Francisco, 1978)

H. Stierlin: *L'Art maya des Olmèques à Toltec-Maya* (Fribourg, 1981; Eng. trans., New York, 1981)

——: *L'Art aztèque et ses origines* (Fribourg, 1982; Eng. trans., New York, 1982)

——: *L'Art inca et ses origines de Valdivia à Machu Picchu* (Fribourg, 1983; Eng. trans., New York, 1984)

L. S. Cordell: *Prehistory of the Southwest* (New York, 1984)

M. Coe, D. Snow and E. Benson: *Atlas of Ancient America* (Oxford, 1986)

R. W. Keatinge, ed.: *Peruvian Prehistory: An Overview of Pre-Inca and Inca Society* (Cambridge, 1988)

M. E. Moseley: *The Incas and their Ancestors: The Archaeology of Peru* (London, 1992)

DAVID M. JONES

Doort [Dort], **Abraham van der** (*b* ?1575–80; *d* London, before 23 June 1640). Dutch wax-modeller, drawing-master and administrator. He may have been the son of the engraver Peter van der Doort (*fl c.* 1590–1600) and the brother of the portrait painter JACOB VAN DOORT and the painter Isaak van der Doort. Having formerly been employed at the court of Rudolf II in Prague, he arrived in England *c.* 1610 to seek service with Henry, Prince of Wales, becoming Keeper of his Cabinet Room. After Henry's unexpected death in December 1612 and the subsequent dissolution of his household, van der Doort seems to have left England. Yet, on the re-establishment of the Prince of Wales's household for Henry's brother Charles (*see* STUART, House of, (6)), he successfully petitioned for reappointment to the Cabinet Room, with the aid of a letter of recommendation from Maurice, Landgraf of Hesse-Kassel. Occasionally van der Doort contributed rarities to Charles's collections, which he had acquired himself. After Charles's succession in 1625, he was also appointed Surveyor of Pictures, Provider of Patterns of Coins and Master Embosser and Maker of Medals. These several posts— which he retained until his suicide—are indicative of his versatility. His connoisseurship and experience of foreign courts contributed to the taste and sophistication of the early Stuart court. However, it is as the compiler of a barely comprehensible, yet invaluable, catalogue of Charles's collections (*c.* 1639) that van der Doort is chiefly remembered. His original wax designs have not survived; nevertheless, it was his image of Charles I, stamped on the coinage, that was to become the most widely known among his subjects of all the King's portraits.

WRITINGS

O. Millar, ed.: 'Abraham van der Doort's Catalogue of the Collections of Charles I', *Walpole Soc.*, xxxvii (1960)

BIBLIOGRAPHY

D. F. Allen: 'Abraham Vanderdort and the Coinage of Charles I', *Numi. Chron.*, n.s. 5, i, (1941), pp. 54–75

T. Wilks: *The Court Culture of Prince Henry and his Circle, 1603–1613* (diss., U. Oxford, 1987)

TIMOTHY WILKS

Doort [Doordt; Dort], **Jacob van (der)** (*b* ?Hamburg; *d* Stockholm, 1629). Dutch painter and wax-modeller. He may have been the son of the Hamburg engraver Peter van der Doort (*fl c.* 1590–1600) and the brother of the wax-modeller and drawing-master ABRAHAM VAN DER DOORT and the painter Isaak van der Doort. Jacob had his workshop in Hamburg and worked as a portrait painter at the royal and ducal courts of northern Europe, where he produced miniatures and large-scale portraits in the courtly style then generally used for royal portraits and characterized by the static pose of the sitter and the use of strong colour contrasts, mainly between red, black, white and gold. In 1610 van Doort was staying in Copenhagen, where he made miniature portraits of *King Christian IV*, his wife *Anne Catherine of Brandenburg* (*d* 1612) and their son *Christian* (all Copenhagen, Rosenborg Slot). On the eve of the war against Sweden (1611) he painted a full-length portrait of *Christian IV in Armour* (Copenhagen, Amalienborg). He also portrayed members of the Danish aristocracy (e.g. *Christian Ericksen and Sophie Krabbé*, Hillerød, Frederiksborg Slot), and such commissions frequently took him to neighbouring courts: in 1620–21 (and later in 1627–8) he was in Gottorp at the court of Schleswig-Holstein and in 1626 in Nykøbing at the court of Christian IV's mother, Sophie of Mecklenburg. In 1623–4 and 1626 he was in Copenhagen again, where he painted a number of portraits of Christian IV's second wife, Kirsten Munk, including one (1623, Hillerød, Frederiksborg Slot) signed *IvD*. After 1626 he worked mainly for the Swedish king Gustav II Adolph (*reg* 1611–32) in Stockholm, where he died.

BIBLIOGRAPHY

H. Gerson: *Ausbreitung und Nachwirkung der holländischen Malerei des 17. Jahrhunderts* (Haarlem, 1942), pp. 211, 216, 460, 461

P. Eller: 'Rosenborgtidens Malere, Jacob van Doort', *Dansk kunsthistorie 2: Billedkunst og Skulptur, Rigets maend lader sig male, 1500–1750* (Copenhagen, 1973), pp. 143–7

——: *Frederiksborg Museum: The Museum of National History at Frederiksborg Castle* (Copenhagen, 1979), pp. 45–7

S. Heiberg: 'Art and Politics: Christian IV's Dutch and Flemish Painters', *Leids Ksthist. Jb.* (1984), pp. 12–16 [entire issue devoted to art in Denmark, 1600–50]

M. J. T. M. STOMPÉ

Doppelmayr, Johann Gabriel (*b* Nuremberg, 30 Sept 1677; *bur* Nuremberg, 8 Dec 1750). German mathematician, physicist and writer. In 1696 he began his law studies at the University of Altdorf. He continued his education in 1699 at the University of Halle, where he changed his course of study from law to the natural sciences and in 1700–02 travelled in northern Germany, the Netherlands and England, studying science and languages. In 1702 he returned to Nuremberg, becoming professor of mathematics at the Gymnasium Egidianum and remaining there until his death, which probably occurred as the result of an experiment in physics. His literary works largely disseminated existing scientific knowledge and translated scientific writings. However, his *Historische Nachricht von den Nürnbergischen Mathematicis und Künstlern* ... (Nuremberg, 1730) comprises short biographies of Nuremberg artists, scientists and craftsmen from the age of Dürer to the early 18th century. He became a member of the Royal Society, London, in 1713, of the Leopoldina and the Preussische Akademie der Wissenschaften, Berlin, in 1715 and of the Imperial Academy, St Petersburg, in 1741.

WRITINGS

Historische Nachricht von den nürnbergischen Mathematicis und Künstlern ... (Nuremberg, 1730), ii of *Documenta Technica*, ed. K.-H. Manegold and W. Treue (Hildesheim and New York, 1972)

BIBLIOGRAPHY

ADB; *NDB*

J. C. Adelung: *Fortsetzung und Ergänzung zu Christian Gottlieb Jöchers allgemeinen Gelehrten-Lexicon*, ii (Leipzig, 1787)

C. von Imhoff: *Berühmte Nürnberger aus neun Jahrhunderten* (Nuremberg, 1984)

ANGELA LOHREY

Dorazio, Piero (*b* Rome, 29 June 1927). Italian painter. He began painting shortly after World War II. His first works were influenced by Cubism and show a knowledge of the work of artists in Rome who were at that time engaged in the figurative renewal of Italian art. However, the influence of Futurist works and his acquaintance with the Russian avant-garde and De Stijl led Dorazio to adopt an abstract idiom. In 1947, with Giulio Turcato, Pietro Consagra, Carla Accardi, Ugo Attardi (*b* 1923), Antonio Sanfilippo (1923–80), Mino Guerrini (*b* 1927) and Achille Perilli (*b* 1927), he founded the FORMA group, declaring himself to be a 'formalist' and to have the aim of creating 'objective abstract forms' in which 'the form is both the means and the end'. He made frequent visits to France and to the USA, where he exhibited for the first time in 1950 at the Museum of Non-objective Painting in New York. Here he came into contact with the American abstract painters and with action painting, both of which played a key role in helping him perfect his own form of abstraction. The USA became very important to him, and during the 1950s he made several prolonged visits there, returning to teach at the University of Pennsylvania, Philadelphia, in 1960 and 1963. The period from 1958 to 1963 was in some ways the high point in Dorazio's artistic development: during this time he produced his series of 'textures' and 'grids' (e.g. *Colle Maggio*, 1962; Stockholm, Mod. Mus.). During the 1960s he was frequently invited to participate in abstract exhibitions such as *Monochrome Malerei* (1960; Leverkusen, Schloss Morsbroich) and contributed to the founding of the groups Zero and Nul, while in Italy he exhibited at numerous Venice Biennali. He continued teaching in the USA until 1970, when he decided to dedicate himself solely to painting.

In the late 1960s Dorazio produced paintings with wide bands of colour; these evolved after 1974 into thread-like and rhythmical forms (e.g. *Andromeda*, 1976; Milan, Lorenzelli A.), recalling earlier experiments. Colour was his fundamental consideration: he was concerned to free himself from drawing completely in order not to be made a prisoner of its conceptual idealism. To this end, his painted surfaces have neither beginning nor end. Dorazio's attitude had little in common, however, with the Americans Jackson Pollock, Mark Rothko and Barnett Newman, whose concern with the concrete and physical problems of colour led them to develop a sort of pictorial symbolism. Interviewed in 1983, Dorazio stated that: 'For me, colour is an instrument, not a means of expression: it is a means between myself and something else; I am not colour, and I do not personify it as Pollock did.' For Dorazio, instead, it was painting as a language that was of prime importance. Allied to this was Dorazio's notion of the enduring nature of the problems of paintings. Such a notion should not of course be interpreted as simple traditionalism but rather as an attempt to examine the universal pictorial structure of art above and beyond its historical context. Individual and traditional elements were deliberately made to co-exist in Dorazio's work, although he recognized that the interpretation of tradition was a deliberate and rational activity through which the artist could become conscious of his own art. Decoration and pattern, therefore, came to be important to Dorazio as pure, timeless, impersonal elements with a potentially infinite rhythm, built from colour and without need of symbolic or narrative support.

BIBLIOGRAPHY
Piero Dorazio (exh. cat., essay E. Fry; Buffalo, NY, Albright–Knox A.G., 1979)
D. Durbe and M. Fagiolo dell'Arco: *Dorazio* (Milan, 1983)
Dorazio (exh. cat., ed. D. Durbe; Rome, G.N.A. Mod., 1983–4)
Piero Dorazio (exh. cat. by M. Meneguzzo, Milan, Lorenzelli A., 1984) [in It. and Eng.]
A. Zevi: *Dorazio* (Ravenna, 1985)
Piero Dorazio (exh. cat. by N. Vernizzi, Grenoble, Mus. Grenoble; Bologna, Gal. A. Mod.; 1990–91)

MARCO MENEGUZZO

Dorchester, 1st Viscount. *See* CARLETON, DUDLEY.

Dórdio Gomes, (Simão César) (*b* Arraiolos, Alentejo, 1890; *d* Oporto, 1976). Portuguese painter. After studying at the Escola de Belas Artes in Lisbon and spending a year in Paris (1910–11), he returned to Alentejo and painted naturalistic portraits of individuals and of groups from the region. During a second sojourn in Paris (1921–6) he was impressed by the work of Cézanne, whose influence is felt in his landscapes of the 1920s and 1930s, for example *Houses in Malakoff* (1923; Oporto, Mus. N. Soares dos Reis), and in the paintings of horses, 1927–30. He returned to a romantic regionalism in the series of large oil panels depicting agricultural activities and local festivities for the town hall in Arraiolos. In 1933 he moved to Oporto, where he was an influential teacher at the Escola Superior de Belas Artes until 1960. He continued to paint landscapes as well as executing numerous frescoes with mythological or religious themes for public places, for example the *Assumption of the Virgin* (1953; Oporto, Church of the Redemption).

BIBLIOGRAPHY
M. Mendes: *Dórdio Gomes* (Lisbon, 1958)
J.-A. França: *A arte em Portugal no século XX* [Art in Portugal in the 20th century] (Lisbon, 1974, rev. 1985)

RUTH ROSENGARTEN

Dordrecht. Town in the Netherlands. The oldest in the county of Holland, it developed from a settlement by the banks of the River Thuredrecht, which was an important link in the trade routes from England, Flanders, the Rhine Valley and the Meuse. The town was granted a charter by William I, Count of Holland, in 1220. In the 14th century the town's growth was strongly assisted by the staple rights granted by the Counts, and the town became the main centre of the county. Following the St Elisabeth's Flood of 1421, much of the surrounding land was submerged, and the town became an island. Thereafter, Dordrecht remained a prosperous trading town but had to give up its leading position to Amsterdam and Rotterdam.

Dordrecht is dominated by the 13th-century Grote Kerk, which was rebuilt after a fire in 1457. Construction of the tower began in 1339. Inside the church are Renaissance choir-stalls made between 1538 and 1542 by a group of wood-carvers from the circle of Jan Terwen. Panels on the stalls depict allegorical processions in an antique style. The same workshop also made the cowl from the Kloveniersdoelen (Dordrecht, Mus. van Gijn). The frieze from the mantelpiece shows a fight between naked combatants. The Stadhuis also dates from the town's period of expansion; it was built in 1383 as a trading hall for Flemish merchants and has been used as the town hall since 1544. The building was remodelled in a Neo-classical style in 1835–45 by the municipal architect G. N. Itz (1799–1869). The core of the Groothoofdspoort also dates from the 14th century. The harbour was improved in 1618 and 1619. Many 16th- to 18th-century small houses possess brick stepped gables with corbelled storeys, the so-called Dordrecht type, while the middle classes had their houses built in the style then prevailing in The Hague and Amsterdam.

Around 1584 the glassmaker and stained-glass window painter Gerrit Gerritsz. Cuyp (*c.* 1565–1644) settled in Dordrecht. He undertook several commissions for the town council, making stained-glass windows as civic gifts for other places. One window of 1596–7 and the associated cartoon are at the St Janskerk in Gouda. His son Jacob Gerritsz. Cuyp (*see* CUYP, (1)) was a fine painter and entered the painters' guild in 1617. At the end of his life Jacob collaborated with his son Aelbert Cuyp (*see* CUYP, (3)), who painted some of the landscape backgrounds to his group portraits.

Among Rembrandt's pupils who came from Dordrecht and worked there were Samuel van Hoogstraten, Nicolaes Maes and Aert de Gelder. De Gelder faithfully continued Rembrandt's style. Aelbert Cuyp introduced elements of Italian landscape painting, including effects of sunlight, into Dordrecht painting. Adriaen van der Burg (1693–1733) painted portraits and interior genre scenes. He taught the talented Aert Schouman, a painter and glass-engraver, who learnt the stipple technique from Frans Greenwood (1680–1763), active in Dordrecht from 1726. Schouman executed portraits and decorative painting, chiefly after 1726 in The Hague, which was, next to Amsterdam, the cultural centre of the Netherlands in the 18th century. One of his pupils was his nephew Martinus Schouman (1770–1848), who specialized in marine paintings and drawings. Johannes Christiaan Schotel and J. F. van den Blijk (1806–76) continued this tradition in Dordrecht.

As a decorative painter, Aert Schouman was followed by the brothers Abraham van Strij I and Jacob van Strij. Together they executed many wall paintings, overdoors and overmantels. They were inspired by such 17th-century masters as Gabriel Metsu, Pieter de Hooch and Aelbert Cuyp. The van Strij brothers were closely involved in establishing Pictura (1774), the society of painters and draughtsmen in Dordrecht.

BIBLIOGRAPHY

M. van Balen: *Beschrijvinge der stad Dordrecht* [Descriptions of the city of Dordrecht] (Dordrecht, 1677)
J. L. van Dalen: *Geschiedenis van Dordrecht* [History of Dordrecht], 2 vols (Dordrecht, 1931–3/*R* Schiedam, 1987)
Kunstreisboek door Nederland [Art journey through the Netherlands] (Amsterdam, 1960/*R* 1977)
Tweehonderd jaar Pictura: Een tekengenootschap in Dordrecht [Two hundred years of Pictura: a drawing society in Dordrecht] (exh. cat. by J. M. de Groot, I. Voorsteegh and G. J. Schweizer, Dordrecht, Dordrechts Mus., 1975)
Aelbert Cuyp en zijn familie: Schilders te Dordrecht [Aelbert Cuyp and his family: painters of Dordrecht] (exh. cat. by W. Veerman, J. M. de Groot and J. G. van Gelder, Dordrecht, Dordrechts Mus., 1977)
A. Molendijk and T. W. Jensma: *De Grote of Onze Lieve Vrouwekerk van Dordrecht: Koor en kapittel* [The Grote or Onze Lieve Vrouwekerk of Dordrecht: choir and capital] (Dordrecht, 1983)
M. E. Stades-Visscher: *Het stadhuis te Dordrecht* (Dordrecht, 1983)
T. W. Jensma and A. Molendijk: *De preekstoel on de Grote of Onze Lieve Vrouwekerk van Dordrecht* [The pulpit of the Grote or Onze Lieve Vrouwekerk of Dordrecht] (Dordrecht, 1984)
A. Meffert and R. Smook: *G. N. Itz: Stadsbouwmeester van Dordrecht, 1823–1867* (Delft, 1985)
Kunst voor de Beeldenstorm [Art before the iconoclasm], 2 vols (exh. cat., ed. J. P. Filedt Kok, W. Halsema and W. T. Kloek; Amsterdam, Rijksmus., 1986)
T. W. Jensma and A. Molendijk: *De Grote- of Onze Lieve Vrouwekerk van Dordrecht* (Zwolle, 1987)
F. G. A. M. Smit: *Frans Greenwood, 1680–1763; Dutch Poet and Glass Engraver* (Peterborough, 1988)

C.M. DE BRUYN

Doré, Gustave(-Paul) (*b* Strasbourg, 6 Jan 1832; *d* Paris, 23 Jan 1883). French illustrator, painter and sculptor. He was born into a cultivated and well-to-do family. By the age of five he was drawing on every piece of paper that came within his reach. He was particularly fond of caricaturing his parents, friends and teachers. In 1838 he was already capable of producing entire series of illustrations such as *Mr Fox's Meeting* (1839; priv. col.) and *Scenes from the Public and Private Life of Grandville's Animals* (1845; Strasbourg, Mus. B.-A.). By 1843, while studying at the Lycée in Bourg-en-Bresse, he was making brilliant attempts at lithography such as *La Martinoire du Bastion* (1845; Bourg-en-Bresse, Mus. Ain). In 1847 Charles Philippon, founder of *Caricature* and *Charivari*, saw drawings by Doré, who was passing through Paris. He took Doré on, published his *Labours of Hercules* and urged his parents to set him up in the capital. From then on, while still a pupil at the Lycée Charlemagne, Doré found himself contractually bound to produce a drawing a week for Philippon's *Journal pour rire* for the next three years. Largely self-taught and artistically independent by nature, Doré relied primarily on his natural creative flair. His artistic training was slight, although *c.* 1849 he made regular visits to the atelier of Henri Scheffer (1798–1862), the academy of Dupuis and the Louvre and studied engravings in the Bibliothèque Nationale. He also began to take an interest in painting, but the first picture he showed at the 1850 Salon was badly received by the critics.

Freed from his studies and supported by his mother—a very important influence on his life, with whom he shared a house in the Rue St Dominique—Doré embarked on the immense task of illustrating the masterpieces of world literature: e.g. Byron's *Complete Works* (1853), Dumas's *Les Compagnons de Jehu* (1858), Montaigne's *Essais* (1859), Dante's *Divine Comedy* (1861, 1868), Perrault's *Contes* (1862), Cervantes's *Don Quixote* (1863), Chateaubriand's *Atala* (1863), Milton's *Paradise Lost* (1866), *The Holy Bible* (1866), Hugo's *Les Travailleurs de la mer* (1867), La Fontaine's *Fables* (1867), Tennyson's *Idylls of the King* (1867), Coleridge's *The Rime of the Ancient Mariner* (1875), Ariosto's *Orlando furioso* (1879) and Poe's *The Raven* (1883).

Doré depicted the contemporary life of Paris with biting realism in his collections, *La Ménagerie parisienne* (1854) and *Le nouveau Paris* (1860), but probably his greatest achievement was his collaboration from 1868 with the English journalist Blanchard Jerrold on *London: A Pilgrimage* (published 1872). In hundreds of rough sketches he concentrated on recording the details of London social life. The finished drawings worked up from them in the studio emphasized the gulf between rich and poor, and the stark medium of wood-engraving proved particularly suited to capturing the grim life of the latter. Doré's experience of the Paris Commune, while working on the project, only deepened his pessimism, and such images as *Scripture Reader in a Night Refuge* (see fig.) and *Over London by Rail*, in which huddled figures are dwarfed by surrounding gloom and soulless architecture, have come to symbolize the horrors of 19th-century urban life. Van Gogh was particularly influenced by Doré's vision of London, reworking *Newgate—Exercise Yard* as *In the Prison Courtyard* (Moscow, Pushkin Mus. F.A.).

Thanks to his exceptional capacity for hard work, Doré also led an active career as a painter, with a pronounced taste for very large canvases. He bought the former Amiros gymnasium in the Rue Bayard, Paris, in order to have a studio measuring up to his ambitions. His first series of colossal pictures, *Paris as It Is* (1854; untraced), was in a violently social realist style and was a failure with the public. However, he fared better with the *Battle of Inkerman* (4.8×5 m; exh. Salon, 1857; Versailles, Château), which was purchased by the State. Much greater acclaim came from outside France, with the opening of the Doré Gallery in New Bond Street, London, in 1868; this received about two-and-a-half million visitors before its closure in 1892. The 20 vast religious compositions shown there, such as *Ascension* (6.09×4.11 m; 1879) and the *Vale of Tears* (4.27×6.4 m; 1883; both Paris, Petit Pal.), were often expanded from his black-and-white illustrations: Doré's dramatic exploitation of chiaroscuro effects and generally monochrome palette reflected their graphic origins. In 1892 most of these pictures were sent to the USA to be shown as a travelling exhibition until 1898, when they were dispersed.

Doré was compelled by the human figure but also responsive to nature. He loved to travel, especially in the mountains of the Pyrenees, the Alps and Scotland. He made numerous drawings, watercolours and paintings giving his somewhat fantastical vision of the world of peaks and valleys, as for example in *Scottish Lake—After*

Gustave Doré: *Scripture Reader in a Night Refuge*, wood-engraving, 190×238 mm; from *London: A Pilgrimage* (London, 1872) (London, British Museum)

the Storm (1875; Grenoble, Mus. Grenoble) and *Cirque de Gavarnie* (Lourdes, Mus. Pyrénéen).

At the Salon of 1877 Doré exhibited sculpture for the first time with *Love Triumphing over Death* (terracotta; Providence, RI Sch. Des., Mus. A.). He also showed the equally allegorical *Glory* (plaster, 1878; Maubeuge, Mus. Boez) and *Madonna* (plaster, exh. Salon 1880; bronze version, Albuquerque, U. NM, A. Mus.). His most famous sculpture was the monument to *Alexandre Dumas père* (1883; Paris, Place Malesherbes). But in general his sculpture was hardly better received by the French critics than his paintings. This lack of success affected him deeply, at a time when his health was also failing from overwork. The death of his mother in 1881 was a severe blow, and two years later he died from a heart attack.

Doré's extraordinary powers of observation were well served by his technical gifts. All his life he seemed to look at everything and note it down with an insatiable appetite. His supreme mastery of drawing and watercolour enabled him to record his impressions of city crowds, characteristic types from different professions, the horrors of war, the strangeness of animals and the splendour of landscape. He was not, however, a Realist and was criticized by Castagnary, Champfleury and others for this. He was, rather, a great visionary, who wanted to live in other worlds (those of fiction, past history, heaven and hell), and someone who agonized over the fate of mankind, visualizing it through disturbing colour contrasts, claustrophobic spaces, dense crowds in which the individual is lost, and the sorrow of women and children. Truculence and caricature only represent the superficial aspects of his art, which is essentially a restless meditation on life and death. His work constitutes an incredibly rich and complex world and provides a link between Romanticism and Symbolism.

BIBLIOGRAPHY

B. Roosevelt: *Gustave Doré* (London, 1885)
B. Jerrold: *Life of Gustave Doré* (London, 1891)
J. Valmy-Baysse: *Gustave Doré* (Paris, 1930)
H. Leblanc: *Catalogue de l'oeuvre complet de Gustave Doré* (Paris, 1931)
F. Haskell: 'Doré's London', *Archit. Des.*, xxxviii (1968), pp. 600–04; also in *Past and Present in Art and Taste* (New Haven, CT, 1987), pp. 129–40
N. Gosling: *Gustave Doré* (London, 1973)
A. Renonciat: *La Vie et l'oeuvre de Gustave Doré* (Paris, 1983)
GILLES CHAZAL

Dorer, Bartholomäus. *See* DAUCHER, (1).

Dorflinger, Christian (*b* Alsace, 16 March 1828; *d* White Mills, PA, 1915). American glass manufacturer of French birth. He was apprenticed to his uncle at the age of ten to learn glassmaking at the Compagnie des Verreries et Cristalleries de St Louis in eastern France and in 1846 moved to the USA with his family. He first worked in a small glasshouse in Philadelphia. Between 1852 and 1860 Dorflinger built three glasshouses in Brooklyn, NY, each larger than the one before, for the manufacture of lamps, of glass tubes for table lamps and later of blanks for other factories. In his third factory, the Greenpoint Glass Works, he produced blown, cut and engraved tableware of such superior quality that in 1861 it was chosen for use in the White House, Washington, DC, by Mrs Mary Todd Lincoln (1818–82).

In 1863 Dorflinger moved to a farm in White Mills, PA, where in 1865 he built a small glasshouse. Experienced glass workers from Greenpoint taught local farm boys their craft, and French glass artists from St Louis were invited to work there. In about 1870 Dorflinger rebuilt an old glassworks in Honesdale, PA. In 1881 his three sons joined him, forming C. Dorflinger & Sons, which included the two Pennsylvania glassworks and the Greenpoint factory, which had been leased to other managers since 1873. By 1903 the White Mills factory alone employed 650 workers. In addition to cutting its own glass, the company sold both colourless and cased blanks to more than 22 decorating shops in the area. Dorflinger's own wares were shipped to the company's warehouses in New York and from there were sold through fine department and jewellery stores across the USA. Dorflinger's works also made services for the presidential administrations of Ulysses S. Grant (1822–85), Benjamin Harrison (1833–1901) and Woodrow Wilson (1856–1924), as well as for dignitaries and royalty around the world. In 1915 Dorflinger's sons closed the White Mills works; potash was in short supply because of World War I, and Prohibition decreased the demand for drinking vessels. Many of the craftsmen went to Corning, NY.

BIBLIOGRAPHY

A. C. Revi: *American Cut and Engraved Glass* (New York, 1965)
J. Q. Feller: *Dorflinger: America's Finest Glass, 1852–1921* (Marietta, 1988)
ELLEN PAUL DENKER

Dorfmeister, Johann Georg (*b* Vienna, 22 Sept 1736; *d* Saska, Banat [now Caraş-Severin, Romania], 1786). Austrian sculptor. He received his basic training from his brother-in-law, Johann Georg Leuthner (1725–85). From 1757 to 1761 he studied at the Akademie der Bildenden Künste, Vienna, with Matthäus Donner and with Balthasar Ferdinand Moll, who also gave him practical instruction in metal-casting. Under the influence of the sculpture of Georg Raphael Donner (*see* DONNER, (1)) he developed a graceful variant of the classicizing Viennese late Baroque style. His figures, with supple, attenuated limbs, elaborate contrapposto poses and sensitive surface execution, could almost be described, in the Viennese context, as Rococo.

Dorfmeister hoped to gain the favour of the imperial court with an alabaster allegorical group, the so-called *Memorial* (1760–61; Vienna, Belvedere), which shows the Emperor Francis I and Maria-Theresa being petitioned by the sculptor in the form of a putto. He later received a commission from the court for a figure of *Atlas* (1775) for the Nationalbibliothek, Vienna, and further commissions for architectural sculpture (?1784) for the Theresianum, Vienna. He was successful as an ecclesiastical sculptor. In Vienna he executed altar figures for the Mariahilferkirche (1770–71); for St Paul in the Barnabite monastery (1771); and for the Gumpendorfer Parish Church (1780–82). In Lower Austria he made altar figures for the pilgrimage churches at Sonntagberg (*c.* 1767) and Maria Taferl (1777–81). Of his ephemeral sculptures, a terracotta nativity group from Celje has survived (1772; Munich, Bayer. Nmus.). In keeping with late 18th-century taste, Dorfmeister produced numerous small-scale sculptures, including *Diana and Endymion* (lead, 1765; Vienna,

Belvedere), which was his reception piece for admission to the Akademie; an allegorical relief (alabaster, after 1761; Vaduz, Samml. Liechtenstein); and a *Diana* (alabaster; Graz, Alte Gal.). In his late works, such as the funerary monument of *Prince Grassalkovich* (1781) in Besnyö, near Gödöllö, Hungary, Dorfmeister adapted to the nascent current of Neo-classicism without losing his own Baroque origins.

BIBLIOGRAPHY

Thieme–Becker

M. Poch-Kalous: 'Wiener Plastik im 19. Jahrhundert', *Geschichte der bildenden Kunst in Wien: Plastik in Wien*, Gesch. Stadt Wien, vii/1 (Vienna, 1970), p. 171
R. Schmidt: *Österreichisches Künstlerlexikon von den Anfängen bis zur Gegenwart* (Vienna, 1974), pp. 450ff
C. Diemer: *Georg Raphael Donner: Die Reliefs* (Nuremberg, 1979), p. 265
E. Baum: *Katalog des österreichischen Barockmuseums im Unteren Belvedere in Wien* (Munich, 1980) [with full bibliography]

INGEBORG SCHEMPER-SPARHOLZ

Doria. Italian family of patricians, soldiers, seamen, patrons and collectors. First documented in 1089, the family resided initially in Genoa and became prominent in its government. From the start Doria art patronage had a strong element of self-celebration, evident from the inscriptions in the family church of S Matteo (founded 1125; rebuilt 1278).

I. Dolceacqua branch. II. Genoese branch. III. Roman branch (Doria-Pamphili).

I. Dolceacqua branch.

Among the Doria family's many branches, the Doria of Dolceacqua, in the province of Imperia, counted among its members the renowned seaman-statesman (1) Andrea I Doria, who built the Palazzo Doria (now Palazzo Doria–Pamphili) in Fassolo, west of Genoa. With the advent of the Counter-Reformation, the Doria family played an active role in promoting the establishment of reformed religious orders in Genoa. In 1583 Nicolò Doria (1539–94) founded the monastery of S Anna for the Barefoot Carmelites, while (2) Giovanni Andrea I Doria and his wife Zenobia del Carretto sponsored the installation of the Trinitarians in the church of S Benedetto (1593). Their son (3) Andrea II Doria and grandson Giovanni Andrea II Doria (1607–40) are best known respectively for building the Carmelite monastery and church (1603–8) at Loano and the town's parish church of S Giovanni (1633–8). Together with Carlo Doria, Duca di Tursi (1575–1650), who gave his support for the building of the Carmelite monasteries of S Teresa (1623) and Spirito Santo (1642) in Savona, these two played a decisive role in the propagation of the Carmelite Order in Ligurian territory.

See also DORIA (ii) and DORIA-PAMPHILI.

BIBLIOGRAPHY

DBI

C. Fusero: *I Doria* (Varese, 1973)

LORENZA ROSSI

(1) Andrea I Doria (*b* Oneglia, Imperia, 30 Nov 1466; *d* Genoa, 25 Nov 1560). Admiral and patron. He was the most important political, military and economic figure in Genoa during the 16th century. At the age of 18 he left his native city and lived in some of the most important centres of the Italian Renaissance (Rome, Urbino and Naples). Once he had become an admiral, he associated with the heads of the major European powers of the time—the papacy, France and the Holy Roman Empire—and it was through these contacts that he acquired the well-informed and innovative knowledge of art that enabled him to become one of the major Italian patrons of his period. He settled in Genoa in 1527 and, shortly after his marriage to Peretta Usodimare, accomplished his longheld plan to build a noble residence in Fassolo, to the west of the city (*see* GENOA, fig. 2). The decoration and furnishings of the Palazzo Doria (now Doria-Pamphili) are proof of his advanced and cosmopolitan taste. Perino del Vaga was entrusted with supervising the entire work, from construction to decoration, which employed him from 1528 to early 1533. It is assumed that the building was completely finished when Emperor Charles V was a guest there in 1533. Perino paid particular attention to the design of the first floor and the apartments of the newlyweds. The southern façade of the palazzo, as was the custom in Genoa at the time, was frescoed—by Perino, Domenico Beccafumi and Pordenone. Plans for decorating the northern façade, however, remained as designs (Amsterdam, Rijksmus.; Chantilly, Mus. Condé). The frescoes followed Roman contemporary taste, depicting Classical subjects that referred allusively to the patron's successful career. This self-celebratory iconographic programme reached its height in the dome of the drawing-room of Doria's apartment, with a fresco depicting *Jove Hurling Thunderbolts at the Giants* (*see* GENOA, fig. 3). By identifying himself with Jupiter, an allegorical subject used by the Emperor himself, Andrea Doria clearly showed the level of his self-esteem. In line with the most up-to-date European trends, he decorated the walls of his palazzo with tapestries, woven directly in Flanders from cartoons by Perino del Vaga, their subjects relating to the frescoes in the rooms where they were to be hung.

Between 1543 and 1557 Andrea Doria entrusted two sculptors, Giovanni Angelo Montorsoli and Silvio Cosini, the latter already working in Fassolo, with the decorative restoration of S Matteo, Genoa, his family church. The presbytery and the crypt where the Admiral was to be buried were decorated in distinctly Renaissance style, again with self-glorifying images. Such iconography is less evident in the decoration of the nave by Giovanni Battista Castello (i) and Luca Cambiaso, but this work is believed to have been done for the same patron. There are two portraits of Andrea Doria in the Palazzo Doria–Pamphili, one (1526) by Sebastiano del Piombo (*see* SEBASTIANO DEL PIOMBO, fig. 4) and the other by Bronzino, which is actually a copy of the original (?*c.* 1533; Milan, Brera).

BIBLIOGRAPHY

A. Merli and L. T. Belgrano: 'Il palazzo del Principe d'Oria a Fassolo in Genova', *Atti Soc. Ligure Stor. Patria*, x (1874) [engrs; whole issue]
E. Parma Armani: 'Il palazzo del Principe Andrea Doria a Fassolo in Genova', *L'Arte*, x (1970), pp. 12–63
E. Grendi: 'Andrea Doria, uomo del rinascimento', *Atti Soc. Ligure Stor. Patria*, xciii (1979)
G. L. Gorse: *The Villa Doria in Fassolo, Genoa* (diss. Providence, RI, Brown U., 1980)
P. Boccardo: *Andrea Doria e le arti* (Rome, 1989)

MATILDE FASSIO

(2) Giovanni Andrea [Gian Andrea] **I Doria** (*b* Genoa, 6 Feb 1539/40; *d* Genoa, 2 Feb 1606). Admiral and patron, nephew and adopted son of (1) Andrea Doria I.

On Andrea I's death, he took up residence at the Palazzo Doria at Fassolo. In 1575, after a period of civil strife, he was awarded the title of Conservatore della Libertà della Patria, and subsequently pride in his civic role, and the devout spirituality of his wife, Zenobia del Carretto, determined the nature of his patronage. He was involved in extending the Palazzo Doria, and adorning it with works of art, from 1565 until his last years. After 1575 the architecture was directed by Giovanni Ponzello; Lazzaro Calvi (1502–?1607) painted frescoes celebrating the Doria family; five chapels where Mass could be celebrated were constructed within the palazzo. The garden was embellished by Marcello Sparzo (*fl* 1565–1606), a stuccoist from Urbino, whose works included a statue of *Jupiter* (1586). In 1589 Doria acquired 12 marble heads of emperors for the southern part of the garden; Taddeo (*d* 1613), Giuseppe and Battista Carlone produced the Fountain of Neptune (1599–1601) for the lower garden. Works of art for the interior included 60 portraits of famous men, bought in Rome in 1591. The stuccowork in four of the rooms in the eastern part is by Sparzo (1599). The church of S Benedetto, adjacent to the palazzo, was rebuilt by Ponzello in 1592, and an altarpiece created by Andrea Semino's sons, Giulio Cesare and Alessandro. Benedetto Brandimarte (*fl* 1588–92), who had been summoned from Lucca in 1581, painted an *Annunciation* (untraced) and organ shutters (*in situ*).

Giovanni Andrea also employed Ponzello to build the Palazzo Doria at Loano (1574–8; now Palazzo Comunale) and the church of S Agostino there (1588–96), for which Sparzo created stucco statues of the *Four Evangelists*, *Gabriel* and the *Annunciation*; Giovanni Battista Paggi painted an altarpiece, the *Martyrdom of St Andrew* (*c.* 1590); the Semino brothers painted the *Baptism* (1590), and Benedetto Brandimarte the *Nativity* and the *Assumption of the Virgin* (dated 1592). At Pegli, a suburb of Genoa, Giovanni Andrea employed (1592) Andrea Ceresola (il Vannone; *fl* 1575–1619) to supervise the aggrandisement of the Villa Doria-Centurione; Lazzaro Tavarone was commissioned to paint mythological frescoes. Ceresola also constructed the church of Nostra Signora delle Grazie at Pegli, for which Paggi and Andrea Semino created altarpieces.

Giovanni Andrea was Admiral of the Spanish fleet in the Mediterranean, and he sent paintings by Genoese and Tuscan artists to King Philip II. He also sent Luca Cambiaso (1583) and Benedetto Brandimarte to work at the Spanish court. Marcantonio Calvi, grandson of Lazzaro Calvi (1502–1607), was sent to Venice to acquire paintings by Titian, Veronese and Andrea del Sarto, which were presented to Philip II on behalf of the Admiral.

BIBLIOGRAPHY
R. Bracco: *Il principe Giannandrea Doria* (Genoa, 1960)
L. Magnani: 'Committenza e arte sacra a Genova dopo il concilio di Trento: Materiali di ricerca', *Stud. Stor. A.*, v (1983–5), pp. 133–84

(3) Andrea II Doria (*b* Genoa, 1570; *d* Genoa, 11 July 1612). Admiral and patron, son of (2) Giovanni Andrea Doria I. Like his father before him, he became Admiral to the King of Spain (1591). In addition to the religious example set by his mother, Zenobia del Carretto, his marriage (1592) to Giovanna Colonna (*d* 1620), the daughter of Fabrizio Colonna and Anna Borromeo, the sister of Carlo Borromeo, introduced him to distinguished members of the Catholic Church and deeply influenced his patronage; his wife had been instructed by Giuseppe Calasanzio, and his sister-in-law had Filippo Neri as confessor, both clerics who were sanctified. His patronage was first directed towards the building (1603–8) of a Carmelite monastery and church in the feud of Loano. The church has a Latin cross-plan and is surmounted by a cupola. Inside, the high altar and the four lateral altars are flanked by columns of Carrara marble, the bases of which carry the heraldic devices of an eagle and a crowned column. For the altarpieces Doria and his wife employed mainly Tuscan artists. Domenico Passignano painted the *Martyrdom of St Andrew*, which alludes to the patron's name, and the *St John the Baptist Preaching*. Giovanna Colonna, probably to honour her uncle, who was canonized in 1610, ordered a *St Carlo Borromeo Ministering to the Plague-stricken* from Francesco Vanni. The high altar, *St Francis Receiving the Stigmata*, was entrusted to a Genoese artist, Giovanni Battista Paggi. The patronage of Andrea II and Giovanna is recorded in an inscription, dated 1609, over the entrance on the façade of the church, which is dedicated to the Virgin of Mount Carmel. In 1607 Doria contracted Pietro Accame, Antonio Accame and Andrea Berbena to build a monastery near the church of the Soccorso at Pietra Ligure (Savona), intended for the Reformed Franciscans. He later adopted Giovanni Battista Cantone's plan for enlarging the church with two chapels and a large choir. The Doria were also involved in the construction of a church and monastery at Borghetto Santo Spirito for the followers of S Francesco of Paola. The building of the Palazzo del Commissario (Palazzo Palestro) at Loano was also due to Andrea II. On his death, Giovanna became regent and contributed to the embellishment of the monastery of S Benedetto at Fassolo.

BIBLIOGRAPHY
R. Bracco: *Il principe Giannandrea Doria* (Genoa, 1960), pp. 226–34
——: *Donna Zanobia del Carretto Doria: La prima turista di Loano* (Genoa, 1971), pp. 38–46
A. Carattino: *Il Carmelo di Loano* (Savona, 1972)
A. Arecco: *Loano* (Albenga, 1984), pp. 56–64

LORENZA ROSSI

II. Genoese branch.

In the late 16th century and the early 17th the Genoese branch of the Doria family that was descended from the celebrated Admiral Lamba Doria (*c.* 1250–1317) rose to prominence both in the politico-economic sphere and in art patronage. Agostino Doria (*c.* 1540–1607) was Doge in 1601–3, in which period Rubens must have visited Genoa and later painted members of the family, among them *Agostino Doria and his Family* (untraced) and *Brigida Spinola Doria* (1606; Washington, DC, N.G.A.), the wife of Giacomo, eldest son of Agostino. A rich art collection, housed in the family palazzo, which lay between the Piazza S Matteo and the Vico Falamonica, included family portraits by the Venetian artists Titian and Tintoretto and works by the Genoese Giovanni Battista Paggi. Two of Agostino's sons, (1) Gian Carlo Doria and (2) Marcantonio Doria, became important collectors; Gian Carlo was a patron, above all, of the Lombard school, Marcantonio of Neapolitan and Caravaggesque painters.

(1) Gian Carlo Doria (*b* Genoa, 1576; *d* Genoa, 1625). He was not involved in affairs of church or state; consequently little is known of his life. In his early years he was trained in Naples to manage the family's enormous wealth. His first artistic contacts were made in the first decade of the 17th century: in 1606 Rubens painted the equestrian portrait of *Gian Carlo Doria with the Insignia of the Spanish Order of Santiago de Compostela* (Genoa, Pal. Spinola), and in the following year Gian Carlo commissioned the large-scale *Massacre of the Innocents* (?destr.) from Giovanni Battista Paggi. In 1608 he married Veronica Spinola. In 1611 he commissioned the first works from Giulio Cesare Procaccini, of whom he became an enthusiastic patron. In 1618 he invited Procaccini to Genoa, where the artist stayed as his guest until 1620 and profoundly influenced Genoese art.

Documents show that in 1614 and 1615 Gian Carlo travelled to Milan, the second time taking Luciano Borzone as his artistic adviser. Apart from Milan, Gian Carlo's cultural interests turned towards Florence, where he was a friend of Grand Duke Cosimo II de' Medici, and Naples, where he was apprenticed by the poet Giambattista Marino, who in 1619 dedicated to him the first part of his *Galleria*. In Genoa, in the loggia of his palazzo (formerly in the Via D. Chiossone; destr. WWII), Gian Carlo opened the Accademia del Nudo, where artists drew from the live model, and this contributed to the education of a whole generation of early 17th-century Genoese painters. His last recorded commission dates from 1621, when Procaccini painted for him the series of *Twelve Apostles* (some Genoa, Pal. Rosso). In the same period (1620–21) Simon Vouet visited Genoa and was a guest of the Doria family in their villa at Sampierdarena, where he executed portraits of the family (e.g. *Gian Carlo Doria*, Paris, Louvre).

The catalogue of Gian Carlo's collection of paintings, which is known only in part, contained 463 works. Apart from those already mentioned, the artists included Luca Cambiaso, Bernardo Strozzi, Titian, Palma Giovane, Domenico Passignano, Santi di Tito and the Cavaliere d'Arpino. After Gian Carlo's death, this remarkable patrimony was soon dispersed through sales and through transfers to the family collections of his brothers (2) Marcantonio Doria and Gian Luca Doria (1585–?1626).

BIBLIOGRAPHY
F. Bologna: 'Tre note caravaggesche', *Prospettiva*, xxx–xxxvi (1983–4), pp. 202–4
G. de Vito: 'The Portraits of Giovan Carlo Doria by P. P. Rubens and S. Vouet', *Burl. Mag.*, cxxix/2 (1987), pp. 83–4
P. Boccardo: 'Gio. Carlo Doria e la serie degli Apostoli di G. C. Procaccini', *Boll. Mus. Civ. Genov.*, x/28–30 (1988) [suppl.]
——: *Materiali per una storia del collezionismo artistico a Genova nel XVII secolo* (diss., U. Milan, 1989), pp. 15–20, 33–8

PIERO BOCCARDO

(2) Marcantonio Doria (*b* 1585; *d* 1651). Brother of (1) Gian Carlo Doria. At the age of 20 he married the widow of Agostino Grimaldi, a member of a wealthy Genoese family that owned land around Salerno. He devoted himself to acquiring territory in southern Italy, and on 2 February 1636 Philip IV of Spain granted him the title of Prince of Angria. Thus the Dorias became illustrious members of the Neapolitan aristocracy. Unlike others of his family, who cultivated a general interest in the arts alongside their financial and commercial activities,

Marcantonio placed greatest emphasis on his cultural activities. Archival sources reveal him as an unusually enlightened patron, who, within the context of a style of collecting aimed exclusively at creating wealth and expressing personal prestige, was sensitive to the most advanced tendencies in contemporary art, especially painting.

Marcantonio patronized the most significant Genoese and Neapolitan painters, thus creating an artistic interchange between the two cities. His farsighted sponsorship and his personal taste are suggested by his unconditional admiration for Caravaggio, who in one letter is actually referred to as Doria's 'friend' (Pacelli, 1980) and who in 1610 painted for Marcantonio the *Martyrdom of St Ursula* (Naples, Banca Commerc. It.). Other documents reveal the existence of a close relationship with Neapolitan circles even before his contacts with Caravaggio, and they show that the Prince was involved in the acquisition of works by Giovanni Battista Caracciolo, Giovanni Bernardino Azzolino and Jusepe de Ribera, whose paintings further enriched the already considerable collection that Marcantonio's forebears had established of pictures by Italy's most famous artists. In 1605 Marcantonio offered Caravaggio 6000 scudi to fresco the loggia of his villa at Sampierdarena near Genoa, which Caravaggio rejected. Caracciolo contributed a scene from the *Life of Abraham* to this decoration, and in 1624 Orazio Gentileschi added to these frescoes (all destr.). The commissioning of this remarkable series of Caravaggesque frescoes bears witness to Marcantonio's courageous patronage of new art. His farsightedness is further illustrated by the will he made in 1651, in which Caravaggio's painting is placed on the same level as long-celebrated works. This same will provides evidence of the philanthropic and deeply religious nature of this noble and progressive patron, who requested for himself a funeral 'with no pomp at all' and who also provided for a series of donations to hospitals, convents and churches.

BIBLIOGRAPHY
V. Pacelli and F. Bologna: 'Caravaggio, 1610: La Sant' Orsola confitta dal tiranno "per Marcantonio Doria"', *Prospettiva*, xxiii (1980), pp. 24–30
V. Pacelli: 'Il testamento di Marcantonio Doria: Un avvio per la migliore conoscenza dei rapporti artistici fra Napoli e Genova', *Ricerche sul seicento napoletano* (Milan, 1985), pp. 77–88

MARIA SICA

III. Roman branch (Doria–Pamphili).

A prominent Roman noble family, the Doria–Pamphili were distinguished by their service to the Roman Curia and were the owners of the Palazzo Doria–Pamphili, in Rome. The name Doria–Pamphili [Doria–Pamphilii; Doria–Pamphilj] was formally adopted in 1763, representing the union of the Doria family of Genoa and the PAMPHILI family of Rome. (All the works mentioned are in the Galleria Doria–Pamphili, Rome.)

In 1671 Prince Giovanni Andrea IV Doria (1653–1737) married Anna Pamphili-Landi, of the patrician family that reached pre-eminence in Rome under Pope Innocent X, Giovanni Battista Pamphili (*see* PAMPHILI, (1)). As a result of this alliance, after the death of Anna's nephew Prince Girolamo Pamphili in 1760, the palazzi and possessions of the Doria family passed to the Doria heir, Anna's son Prince Giovanni Andrea V Doria (1704–65). He moved the seat of his family from Genoa to Rome, and it was his son Prince Andrea IV Doria (1747–1820) who assumed the name Doria-Pamphili.

The Palazzo Doria–Pamphili in the Via del Corso dates back to the 1440s, as an early Renaissance courtyard indicates. It passed into the Pamphili family via Olimpia Aldobrandini, Princess of Rossano (1623–81), who married in 1647 Prince Camillo Pamphili (*see* PAMPHILI, (2)), nephew of Innocent X. It was altered and extended for the Pamphili family, notably in 1659–75 by Antonio del Grande and in 1731–5 by Gabriele Valvassori. In the 19th century the Doria-Pamphili family, in particular Prince Alfonso Doria-Pamphili (1851–1914), employed the architect Andrea Busiri-Vici (1818–1902) to remodel many of the rooms.

The collection of paintings began with a nucleus that had belonged to Francesco Maria II della Rovere, Duke of Urbino. Works by Raphael, Parmigianino and Lanfranco came from the Aldobrandini family. The collection was greatly added to by Camillo Pamphili, who bought paintings from Caravaggio, the workshop of Guercino and from Claude. His son Cardinal Benedetto Pamphili (1653–1730) was a patron of foreign artists and bought still-lifes. The portrait by Velázquez of *Innocent X* (1650) and the bust by Bernini of *Innocent X* are among the chief glories of the collections, but the Doria marriage brought the fine portrait of *Andrea Doria* (1526; *see* SEBASTIANO DEL PIOMBO, fig. 4) and the portrait of *Giannettino Doria* (1546–7) by Bronzino. Among the many 18th- and 19th-century portraits of the Doria-Pamphili are those by Alessandro Capalti (1810–68) of *Filippo-Andrea Doria-Pamphili* (1813–76), his wife *Mary Talbot* and their children. Filippo-Andrea's grandson Don Alfonso Doria-Pamphili made a number of important acquisitions, including an *Annunciation* triptych by Filippo Lippi and three works by Bernardino Parenzo. The Doria–Pamphili family continues to live in the family palazzo, and the collection in the gallery is considered rare among major private collections in having survived so well the political vicissitudes of Italy in the 19th and 20th centuries.

BIBLIOGRAPHY
G. B. Di Crollanza: *Dizionario storico blasonic delle famiglie nobili e notabili italiane*, vi (Pisa, 1886), p. 163
T. Amayden and C. A. Bertini: *La storia delle famiglie romane*, i (Rome, 1910), p. 381
L. Vertova: *Tesori d'arte delle grande famiglie* (Milan, 1966)
E. A. Safařík and G. Torselli: *La Galleria Doria–Pamphilj a Roma* (Rome, 1969, rev. 2/1982)
J. Garms, ed.: *Quellen aus dem Archiv Doria Pamphilj zur Kunsttätigkeit in Rom unter Innocent X* (Vienna, 1972)
V. Rubrichi: 'Il fondo detto Archiviolo dell'Archivio Doria–Pamphili in Roma', *Misc. Soc. Romana Stor. Patria*, xxii (1972)
A. Carandente: *Il Palazzo Doria–Pamphilii* (Rome, 1975)
A. Blunt: *Guide to Baroque Rome* (London, 1982), pp. 178–9

GIUSEPPE PINNA

Doric order. *See under* ORDERS, ARCHITECTURAL.

Dorigny. French family of painters, draughtsmen and printmakers. (1) Michel Dorigny was one of the principal collaborators with Simon Vouet and probably the best engraver of his works. After Vouet's death, he became an independent painter of considerable reputation. Had he not died at a relatively young age, he might have rivalled

Charles Le Brun as an important history and decorative painter during the reign of Louis XIV. His sons (2) Louis Dorigny and (3) Nicolas Dorigny were also painters and printmakers.

(1) Michel Dorigny (*b* Saint-Quentin, 1616; *d* Paris, 20 Feb 1665). He served his apprenticeship with Georges Lallemand and from 1638 was associated with Simon Vouet, in the following decade making etchings after about 80 of his works (e.g. ceiling paintings for the chapel of the Hôtel Séguier, Paris; for a full discussion of this aspect of Dorigny's work see 1990–91 exh. cat., pp. 76–80). He was also active as a painter and was one of Vouet's principal collaborators on his altarpieces and decorative schemes (e.g. staircase of the Hôtel Hesselin, Paris) until the death of the Premier Peintre in 1649. The previous year he had married Vouet's second daughter. Dorigny also made a score of prints of his own, and a series of six *Bacchanales* (Paris, Bib. N.) indicates the style of the artist at the time of his close association with Vouet. The composition of one of these *Bacchanales* is repeated in the decoration of the arcading of a room in the Hôtel de Ville at Port-Marly, near Paris. This decorative scheme, originally in the château of Colombes, Hauts-de-Seine, has thus been attributed to Dorigny. It represents the *Four Seasons*, with a ceiling showing *Daybreak and the Dew*. Dorigny's style in these canvases was directly influenced by that of Vouet, but his figures are heavier and more rounded, his colouring livelier, contrasting with earthier flesh tones. A group of paintings

Michel Dorigny: *Crucifixion*, oil on canvas, 1.07×0.77 m (Paris, Musée du Louvre)

illustrating the *Story of Diana* (two Paris, Petit Pal.) are also probably by him. Paris guides of the 17th and 18th centuries associate Dorigny's name with the execution of a number of prestigious decorative schemes, including the hôtel of the Abbé de la Rivière, the Hôtel Hesselin and the Hôtel Amelot de Bisseuil, but no traces of these works survive.

The death of Vouet marked a change of orientation in the career of Dorigny, who thereafter became independent. One of his own prints dated 1652, representing the *Virgin and Child* (see 1990–91 exh. cat., p. 53), still bears the stamp of Vouet's art, but the decorations painted by Dorigny towards the end of the 1650s show a distinct evolution. The painter adopted a more classicizing, calmer style. His forms are more rigorously constructed, his figures more stable, as the ceilings painted for the Pavillon de la Reine at the château of Vincennes and the decorations of the Hôtel Lauzun, Paris, show. The partially documented Vincennes decorations—executed in the pavilion built by Louis Le Vau in 1659—are *Fame Holding the Portrait of Philippe d'Orléans, Zephyrus and Flora* (both *in situ*), *Parnassus* (destr. World War II) and the *Four Quarters of the World* (Paris, Louvre). Those of the Hôtel Lauzun, now attributed to Dorigny (Brejon de Lavergnée, 1982), are related to the artist's drawings in the Cholmondeley albums in the Louvre.

Dorigny's work as a draughtsman falls into two categories: studies in black chalk, very close to those of Vouet, and terser and very original studies in pen and ink. An important group of these pen and ink drawings is owned by the Société des Amis des Musées de Vincennes. An example of his religious painting is his altarpiece of the *Crucifixion* (Paris, Louvre; see fig.).

BIBLIOGRAPHY

R.-A. Weigert: *Inventaire du fonds français: Graveurs du dix-septième siècle*, Paris, Bib. N., Cab. Est., iii (Paris, 1954), pp. 474–90
B. Brejon de Lavergnée: 'New Light on Michel Dorigny', *Master Drgs*, xix (1981), pp. 445–55
——: 'Contribution à la connaissance des décors peints à Paris et en Ile-de-France au XVIIème siècle: Le Cas de Michel Dorigny', *Bull. Soc. Hist. A. Fr.* (1982), pp. 69–83
V. Théveniaud: 'Michel Dorigny (1617–1665): Approches Biographiques', *Bull. Soc. Hist. A. Fr.* (1982), pp. 63–7
Vouet (exh. cat. by J. Thuillier, B. Brejon de Lavergnée and D. Lavalle, Paris, Grand Pal., 1990–91), pp. 53–7, 76–80

BARBARA BREJON DE LAVERGNÉE

(2) Louis Dorigny (*b* Paris, 14 June 1654; *d* Verona, 29 Nov 1742). Son of (1) Michel Dorigny. He trained with his father and was a follower of Charles Le Brun. In 1671 he went to Italy, where he worked as a decorative painter and engraver for the rest of his life, with the exception of the years 1704–6, when he was in Paris, hoping to be received (*reçu*) as a member of the Académie Royale, and 1711–12, when he visited Vienna to decorate the Winter Palace of Prince Eugene of Savoy (now Austrian Ministry of Finance). He was at first active in Rome, Umbria and the Marches. In 1678 he settled in Venice, where he decorated churches and palazzi in the city and on the mainland, painting in both fresco and oils. Among his works are the ceiling of S Silvestro (1678) and decorations at the Palazzo Museli. In 1687 he moved permanently to Verona and decorated, notably, the cathedrals at Udine and Trento, as well as working at the Villa Rotonda near

Vicenza (*c.* 1700–04) and the Villa Allegri at Grezzana (1717–20). Among his works in oils are *Joseph Explaining his Dreams to Pharaoh* (Verona, S Nicolò) and *Susanna and the Elders* (Bordeaux, Mus. B.-A.). His engravings include 32 plates for the *Pensées chrétiennes* of Père Bonhours (1684) and six illustrations for Ovid's *Metamorphoses*.

BIBLIOGRAPHY

Thieme–Becker
L. Coggiola Pittoni: 'Louis Dorigny', *Gaz. B.-A.*, n. s. 5, xiii (1935), pp. 321–35
R.-A. Weigert: *Inventaire du fonds français: Graveurs du dix-septième siècle*, Paris, Bib. N., Cab. Est. cat., iii (Paris, 1954), pp. 473–4
N. Ivanoff: 'Contributi a Ludovico Dorigny', *Emporium*, cxxxii (1960), pp. 242–9
——: 'Un profilo di Ludovico Dorigny', *A. Ant. & Mod.*, vi (1963), pp. 144–51
F. d'Arcais, G. Pavanello and others: *Gli affreschi nelle ville venete dal seicento all'ottocento*, 2 vols (Venice, 1978)
B. Aikema: 'Tre oltramontani operanti nel veneto: De Coster, Dorigny e Vernansal', *Not. Pal. Albani*, xii/1–2 (1983), pp. 251–60

(3) Nicolas Dorigny (*b* Paris, *bapt* 2 June 1658; *d* Paris, 1 Dec 1746). Son of (1) Michel Dorigny. He trained with his father but abandoned painting for engraving early in his career. In 1687 he went to Rome, summoned by his brother (2) Louis Dorigny, producing there a series of reproductions of antique statues, published by Rossi in 1704. From Rome he went to London, where he worked for the British royal family. Between 1711 and 1719 he engraved Raphael's cartoons of the *Acts of the Apostles* (London, V&A), for which he was knighted by George I in 1720. He returned to France suffering from eye trouble and was received (*reçu*) as a member of the Académie Royale in 1725. He exhibited at the Salons of 1739 and 1743. He made more than 140 prints, combining etching and engraving in an expansive, vigorous style close to that of Gérard Audran. Besides portraits, his works are mostly reproductive prints after the Italian masters, particularly Raphael, Carlo Maratti, Domenichino, Guercino and Giovanni Lanfranco. The Nationalmuseum, Stockholm, has a number of his drawings commissioned by Count Tessin, including Roman sculptures, coats of arms and catafalques.

BIBLIOGRAPHY

Thieme–Becker
R.-A. Weigert: *Inventaire du fonds français: Graveurs du dix-septième siècle*, Paris, Bib. N., Cab. Est. cat., iii (Paris, 1954), pp. 490–507
P. Bjurström: *Drawings in Swedish Public Collections: French Drawings Sixteenth and Seventeenth Centuries*, Stockholm, Nmus. cat. (Stockholm, 1976), nos 357–85

VÉRONIQUE MAYER

Dorigny, Charles (*fl* 1534–51). French painter. He is recorded as a painter in 1534 at the Hôtel de Ville in Paris and in 1535–6 at Fontainebleau, where his duties included working under Rosso Fiorentino in the Galerie François I. His name continues to appear in the royal accounts between 1540 and 1550, and in 1549 he collaborated with the sculptor Jean Goujon and the painter Jean Cousin (i) on temporary decorations for the entry of Henry II into Paris. His wife, Jacqueline Bordier, was also a painter, and is recorded in 1551 as working on the decorations at the Hôtel de Ville, Paris. The only work convincingly attributed to Dorigny is the *Deposition* in Ste Marguerite, Paris; this was previously thought to be by Francesco Salviati, but Shearman (1966) connected it with a commission given to Dorigny in 1548 for an altarpiece for the Orléans Chapel in the church of the Celestines in Paris. This painting, with its evocations of the work of Rosso and of Andrea del Sarto, establishes Dorigny as one of the outstanding French painters of the mid-16th century.

BIBLIOGRAPHY
Thieme–Becker
F. Gébelin: 'Un Manifeste de l'école néo-classique en 1549: L'Entrée de Henri II à Paris', *Bull. Soc. Hist. Paris & Ile-de-France,* li (1924), pp. 35–45
J. Shearman: 'Le XVIe Siècle européen', *Burl. Mag.,* cviii (1966), pp. 60–61
L'Ecole de Fontainebleau (exh. cat., ed. S. Béguin; Paris, Grand Pal., 1972–3), pp. 78–9

PHILIPPE ROUILLARD

Dorner, Johann Jakob, I (*b* Ehrenstetten, nr Freiburg im Breisgau, 18 July 1741; *d* Munich, 22 May 1813). German painter. He became a pupil of the Freiburg painter Franz Joseph Rösch (*c.* 1724–77) in 1753. In 1759 he moved to Augsburg to learn fresco painting from Joseph Bauer, then travelled to Venice. In 1760 he worked with Joseph Mages (1728–69) in Augsburg as a façade painter and in 1761 went to Munich, where he was employed copying the Dutch paintings at Schloss Schleissheim. Following his portrait of *Elector Max III Joseph at the Lathe with Graf Salern* (*c.* 1765; Munich, Schloss Nymphenburg), he was appointed a court painter in 1765. Between 1766 and 1769 he visited Düsseldorf and the Netherlands. After nine months at the Antwerp academy he was awarded first prize in history and genre painting. He also studied etching (1769) in Paris under Jean-Georges Wille.

After his appointment as a gallery inspector in Munich in 1770, Dorner worked mainly as a restorer. He was involved in setting up the Hofgartengalerie, which opened in 1783, and instituted the first public art exhibition in Munich in 1788 with works by his pupils. His landscapes, historical pictures, portraits and genre scenes such as *The Knife-grinder* (1770; Munich, Alte Pin.), based on the so-called minor 17th-century Dutch masters and on Nicolaes Berchem, Jan Both, Caspar Netscher and Rembrandt, played an important role in the development of genre painting in 19th-century Munich. His son, Johann Jakob Dorner II (1775–1852), worked as a landscape painter and printmaker in Munich.

BIBLIOGRAPHY
U. Immel: *Die deutsche Genremalerei im 19. Jahrhundert* (diss., Heidelberg, Ruprecht-Karls-U., 1967), pp. 95–8
B. Hardtwig: *Nach-Barock und Klassizismus. Neue Pinakothek, München,* iii (Munich, 1978), pp. 27–54

JOSEF STRASSER

Dornicke, Jan van. *See* MERTENS, JAN.

Dorpat. *See* TARTU.

Dorsch. German family of gem-engravers. (Johann) Christoph Dorsch (*b* Nuremberg, 10 July 1676; *d* Nuremberg, 17 Nov 1732) was the son of Erhard Dorsch (1649–1712), who worked on glass and the cutting of armorial seals on precious stones. Christoph Dorsch studied anatomy and drawing; he turned to engraving relatively late in life yet was one of the most industrious craftsmen of his time, turning out large quantities of gems. He specialized in cutting series of dynasties and rulers from the earliest times to his own days, in cornelian, grey agate and glass,

such as 252 popes of Rome (Leiden, Rijksmus. Oudhd.), 126 emperors to Charles VI and the kings of France from the Dark Ages to Louis XV (both series engraved in Bayer; examples at Leiden, Rijksmus. Oudhd.). The portraits, mostly fanciful, are derived from prints and medals. Dorsch's daughter Susanna Maria (*b* Nuremberg, 1701; *d* 1765) was an abler artist than either her father or her brother Paul Christoph, also an artist. Among her gems are Classical subjects and portraits of such contemporary rulers as the Holy Roman Emperor *Francis I* and his consort *Maria-Theresa* (sealing-wax impressions; The Hague, Rijksmus. Meermanno–Westreenianum). Following her second marriage, in 1738, to the painter Johann Justin Preissler, she occasionally signed herself '(Mme) Preisler(n)'.

BIBLIOGRAPHY
Thieme–Becker
[J. J. Bayer]: *Gemmarum affabre sculptarum thesaurus quem suis sumptibus haud exiguis nec parvo studio collegit Io. Mart. ab, Ebermayer Norimbergensis* ([Nuremberg], 1720)

GERTRUD SEIDMANN

Dorset, Dukes of. *See* SACKVILLE.

D'Orsi, Achille (*b* Naples, 6 Aug 1845; *d* Naples, 8 Feb 1929). Italian sculptor. The son of a small landowner, in 1857 he entered the Regio Istituto di Belle Arti in Naples, where he studied under the guidance of the sculptor Tito Angelini (1806–78). He first exhibited in 1863, with the terracotta *Wounded Soldier of Garibaldi* (Naples, Capodimonte), a work inspired by Garibaldi's campaign against the Bourbon rulers of Naples. D'Orsi's main interest, however, was in subjects from everyday life, and this allied him to the contemporary artistic and literary current of *Verismo*. Among his works of this kind were his plaster statue of *A Fisherman* (1864; untraced) and the *Old Woman at the Grave* (terracotta, 1876; Naples, Accad. B.A.), which have affinities with sculptures by his principal rival, Vincenzo Gemito.

D'Orsi's first national success, at the Esposizione Artistica in Naples (1877), was the life-size group *The Parasites* (bronzed plaster, Naples, Capodimonte; bronze version, Florence, Pitti). This savage satire on the decadence of ancient Rome depicts two drunken revellers in the aftermath of a banquet, with the moralizing quotation *Corruptio optimi viri pessima* ('The corruption of a good man is a very bad thing'). D'Orsi combined archaeological precision in the accessories with a realistic analysis of the debauched features and anatomy of the protagonists. The work recalls the 'modern' treatment of the ancient world already undertaken in the genre paintings of Jean-Léon Gérôme and Lawrence Alma-Tadema. In 1878 D'Orsi was appointed honorary professor of the Istituto, where he taught until 1916, passing through all the stages of a secure academic career.

At the Esposizione Nazionale in Turin (1880) D'Orsi exhibited *At Posillipo* and *Proximus tuus* ('Thy neighbour'; Rome, G.N.A. Mod.; see fig.). The former, which is modelled on Gemito's *Little Fisherboy* (1877; Florence, Bargello; for illustration *see* GEMITO, VINCENZO), portrays a nude urchin crouching on a rock with a fish trap; it was bought by Umberto I. The latter created a scandal that had major repercussions on D'Orsi's career, so much so

Achille D'Orsi: *Proximus tuus*, bronzed plaster, h. 790 mm, 1880 (Rome, Galleria Nazionale d'Arte Moderna-Arte Contemporanea)

that he is now known almost exclusively for this work. *Proximus tuus*, a life-size statue in bronzed plaster, represents an exhausted peasant labourer seated on the ground with outstretched legs, during a pause in his work. The face is like a mask, hollow-cheeked; it stares into space, mouth half-open, like a beast of burden worn out by brutal labour. Conservative critics complained of the work's excessive realism, failing to appreciate the message of fraternity that the sculptor intended to convey in the Latin title, recalling Christ's injunction to love one's neighbour. They also ignored the formal precedents of the statue: an identical arrangement can be seen in Jean-François Millet's pastel *Le Vigneron*. *Proximus tuus* was read as a symbol of class solidarity and was widely reproduced in socialist propaganda and held up as a model to politically committed artists.

In his later work D'Orsi returned to a less controversial kind of sculpture with the bronze statue of a watercarrier, *At Frisio* (1883; Rome, G.N.A. Mod.) the bust of the painter *Filippo Palizzi* (bronze, 1895; Rome, G.N.A. Mod.) and the monuments to *Alfonso of Aragon* (marble, 1889; Naples, Pal. Reale) and *Umberto I* (bronze, 1911; Naples, Via Nazario Sauro).

BIBLIOGRAPHY
M. M. Lamberti: 'Aporie dell'arte sociale: Il caso *Proximus tuus*', *Ann. Scu. Norm. Sup. U. Pisa*, n. s. 2, xiii (1983), pp. 1077–137
M. S. De Marinis: *Il tempo, la vita e l'arte di Achille d'Orsi* (Rome, 1984)
MARIA MIMITA LAMBERTI

Dorsman [Dortsman], **Adriaen** (*b* Flushing, 1625; *d* Amsterdam, *bur* 8 Oct 1682). Dutch architect and engineer. Dorsman trained in his father's carpentry workshop and became a member of St Joseph's Guild in Flushing before studying mathematics and military engineering at the University of Leiden (from 1652). Around 1655 he settled in Amsterdam, where he designed a number of distinguished canal houses. A remarkable design (1666; Leiden, Rijksuniv., Prentenkab.), which was never executed, was for the façade of a house for Jan Six, a member of the city council and a patron of Rembrandt. The flat façade is composed of two storeys and three bays, with a square cornice at the upper level. The entrance is articulated by a classical frame, enriched with statues on pedestals. Dorsman refrained from using pilasters and a pediment, which were commonly applied at that time. He sought to express sophistication in costly materials and harmonious proportions, much as in the later work of Philips Vingboons.

Also in Amsterdam, Dorsman designed for the Lutherans the Nieuwe (or Ronde) Kerk (1668–71), a stately building with a circular core on plan; a drum, treated as an attic, carries a copper-clad timber dome surmounted by a lantern. The exposed front half of the façade presides monumentally over the Singel Canal, articulated by an order of clustered pilasters standing on a banded plinth and supporting a heavy Doric entablature. Between the pilasters huge rectangular windows light the nave. For the construction of the dome the advice was sought of Philips and Justus Vingboons, as well as of the town carpenter of Middelburg, Louis Jolijt, who had finished the dome of the Oostkerk, Middelburg, to the designs of Bartholomaeus Drijfhout and Pieter Post, in 1667. Half of the dome space incorporates two raked galleries, thus creating a substantial seating area. The pulpit, which is placed over the entrance, makes a combined unit with the organ above. To have given the pulpit of this typically Protestant church such emphasis while maintaining its proximity to the congregation was remarkable. The church was seriously damaged by fire in 1822 but was rebuilt with only a few minor alterations and decorated in the same way as before.

Dorsman's most important work is the twin house (1671; now partly occupied by the Museum van Loon); built for Jeremias van Rae, governor of the Walloon Orphanage (Walensweehuis), on the Keizersgracht, Amsterdam, the interior decoration was altered during the 18th century. The flat stone façades, two storeys and one mezzanine high, are crowned by a Doric entablature and a balustraded attic concealing a low roof. As in the design for the house of Jan Six, the centre of the composition is emphasized, in this instance by the addition of a balcony over the entrance and the inward curve of the attic. The middle bay was not treated decoratively, as became common later in the 17th century. Dorsman occasionally designed horizontally channelled stone façades. A notable example of this type of rustication is to be found on the façade of the house at Amstel 216 (1672), which he designed for Gijsbert Dommer. The narrower façade of this house exhibits many similarities to those he designed for van Rae.

In 1672 Dorsman designed the Walloon Orphanage (now the Maison Descartes), a large, brick building with hipped roofs. Although in this respect the building is closer to local tradition than are his private houses, it still exudes a calm elegance. Also in 1672 Dorsman was appointed Inspector of Fortifications at Amsterdam. As a military engineer he collaborated in 1678 on the defences of Naarden, an extremely modern system of city fortification for the period.

BIBLIOGRAPHY
W. J. Kooiman: *De Ronde Lutherse kerk te Amsterdam* (Amsterdam, 1941)
F. A. J. Vermeulen: *Handboek tot de geschiedenis der Nederlandse bouwkunst* [Guide to the history of Dutch architecture], iii (The Hague, 1941)
W. Kuyper: *Dutch Classicist Architecture* (Delft, 1980)
PAUL H. REM

Dort, Abraham van der. *See* DOORT, ABRAHAM VAN DER.

Dort, Jacob van. *See* DOORT, JACOB VAN.

dos. For Portuguese proper names consisting of a given name or names followed by this prefix and another part or parts, *see under* the part of the name following the prefix; for tripartite surnames, *see under* the first part of the surname. □

Dosekun, Olusoji (Omoshola) (*b* Ibadan, 10 Sept 1951). Nigerian architect. He was one of the 17 foundation students admitted to the two-tier architecture degree programme of the new School of Environmental Design at the University of Lagos in 1971 under John S. Myers and David Aradeon. After graduating with the BES (pre-architecture, 1974) and MED (architecture) degree in 1977, he served four years of apprenticeship in the Ilorin architectural offices of Niger Consultants. In the period 1981–5, he served as the Project Manager of the Economic and Technical Services Limited on the Agbara Estate project, the residential and industrial estate on the Badagry Expressway. Since 1985, when he opened his architectural office, the Siji Dosekun Partnership has been responsible for various projects. In Grailland, the sanctuary for the Grail followers in the Iju Hills (1985), his use of red bricks on the Gate House and fence walls, in conjunction with the green foliage and tall trees on the undulating landscape, achieves a spiritually uplifting ambience at the entry gates. Dosekun was a leading member of the generation of young Nigerians educated completely within the country in the 1970s, and his houses and residential projects continually question the basic assumptions expressed in Nigerian domestic architecture of the 1950s–1970s. By completely separating the dining- from the living-room in the four-storey apartment building constructed for the Integrated Capital Service Ltd in south-west Ikoyí (1992), Dosekun's design enshrines the privacy of the family during meals. It also restores a measure of family control over its entertainment budget in a culture noted for its open-house hospitality. With the reintroduction of the fanlight and the consequent high ceilings (an idiom of the architectural language of early 20th-century Lagos), his design allowed air to circulate through the staggered corridor into the sleeping spaces in the east and west wings.

For a general discussion of modern Nigerian architecture *see* NIGERIA, §IV.

WRITINGS
A Place to Dwell (diss., U. Lagos, 1974)

DAVID ARADEON

Dōsen. *See* ASHIKAGA YOSHIMOCHI.

Doshi, Balkrishna V(ithaldas) (*b* Pune, 26 Aug 1927). Indian architect, urban planner and teacher. He entered the J. J. College of Architecture, Bombay, in 1947 but left for London in 1951 and took courses at the North London Polytechnic. After attending the eighth meeting of CIAM (1951) in Hoddesdon, Doshi moved to Paris to work for Le Corbusier; this formative experience influenced his subsequent approach to architecture and planning. In 1955 he returned to India to help supervise Le Corbusier's work at Chandigarh and Ahmadabad, and in 1956 he set up his own practice in Ahmadabad. Early independent commissions included some relatively luxurious houses and subsequently several industrial buildings, but his first significant work was the Institute of Indology (1962), Ahmadabad. In this building a concrete frame structure combines the principle of the 'parasol' with a monumental verandah as a response to the hot climate of the region. In 1962 Doshi was instrumental in arranging for Louis Kahn to work in India, and he was greatly influenced by Kahn's use of light, geometry and structure. Another important work of the 1960s was the first phase of the Ahmadabad School of Architecture (1968), a brick building based on ideas similar to his own house there (1961).

Much of Doshi's effort was devoted to housing, for example the Gujarat State Fertilisers Township (1969), Baroda, which consisted of a number of house types arranged along a pedestrian walkway and around courtyards. Similar principles were employed in the Electronics Corporation of India Township (1971) at Hyderabad. One of Doshi's most important residential buildings, which was a breakthrough in terms of the integration of his design and planning ideas, was his own studio, Sangath (1981), to the west of Ahmadabad, consisting of a series of barrel-vaulted structures partially sunk into the ground in an enclave of landscaped terraces and water cascades (see fig.). He used the same idea for the larger Gandhi

Balkrishna V. Doshi : Sangath complex, near Ahmadabad, 1981

Labour Institute (1984) just a kilometre away. Doshi's work was facilitated by the partnership he formed in 1977 with Allan Stein and Jai Rattan Bhalla, architects based in Delhi, as it allowed him to practise more extensively throughout the country and to undertake larger projects. He also set up the Vastu-Shilpa Foundation in the early 1980s to study low-cost housing design and 'squatter' settlements. The results of his research were embodied in a number of publications and in his design for a low-cost housing scheme (1983–6) in Indore for 6500 families. In this project the only structure provided was a kitchen/sanitary service core, and he suggested a number of house design solutions that could be adapted by individual house owners. His planning ideas are summarized in his conceptual plan for Vidyahar Nagar (1984–6), the satellite town for Jaipur, which encouraged a rich mix of land uses and vehicular and pedestrian links, with controlled transitions from public to private spaces in a carefully energy-conscious scheme.

Doshi also designed a number of important public buildings, for example the Indian Institute of Management (1977–85), Bangalore, and the Maharashtra Institute of Development Administration (1991), Pune. In 1991, after winning a limited competition, he began work on the design of a new centre in Bombay for the Diamond Merchants of India. This was by far the largest architectural project in the country at the time, with a brief calling for nearly 100,000 sq. m of development, including offices, shops, housing, workshops and storage areas. In order to realize the project, Doshi expanded his office in Ahmadabad and opened another in Bombay. Doshi also taught architecture for many years, mainly in association with the Ahmadabad School of Architecture and Planning after he became its first Honorary Director in 1962, but also at universities around the world. He won a number of awards during his career, including the Indian Architects Gold Medal for architectural education and the Gold Medal of the French Académie d'Architecture, both in 1988.

For another illustration of Doshi's work *see* INDIA, fig. 1.

WRITINGS

with J. L. Sert, M. Safdie and N. Ardalan: *Habitat Bill of Rights* (Vancouver, 1976)
Bohra Houses in Gujarat (Ahmadabad, 1983)
'Le Corbusier: Acrobat of Architecture', *Archit. & Des.* [India], iii/6 (1987)

BIBLIOGRAPHY

'Balkrishna Doshi', *Archit. Forum*, cxxxviii/4 (1973), pp. 32–41
A. Pettruccioli: 'The Institutions of Man', *Spazio & Soc.*, xxi (1983), pp. 64–75
'Balkrishna V. Doshi Interviewed', *5th Col.*, v/2 (1985), pp. 32–6
W. J. Curtis: *Balkrishna Doshi: An Architecture for India* (Ahmadabad, 1988)

HASAN-UDDIN KHAN

Dosio, Giovanni Antonio [Giovannantonio] (*b* San Gimignano, 1533; *d* Naples, 1609). Italian sculptor, architect, draughtsman, antiquarian, engineer and decorator. He began his career as a goldsmith and engraver. He arrived in Rome in 1548 and the next year entered the workshop of the sculptor and architect Raffaele da Montelupo, where he worked mostly on wall decorations for mausoleums. Around this time he carved a statue of *Hope* for the tomb of *Giulio del Vecchio* in SS Apostoli, Rome. Between 1552 and 1564 he was in close contact with Michelangelo, and he may have participated with Guglielmo della Porta in the reconstruction of S Silvestro al Quirinale, Rome. Della Porta and Dosio associated with the artistic circle around the Carafa family, for whom they may have planned a chapel. In 1561 Dosio was working as a sculptor and stuccoist for the patrician Torquato de' Conti. Other sculptural work in Rome includes a funerary monument with posthumous portrait bust for the poet *Annibal Caro* (1567–70) and another to *Giovanni Pacini* (1567–8; both S Lorenzo in Damaso).

During his early years in Rome, Dosio's approach to architecture was eclectic, as can be seen from his numerous drawings, datable between 1556 and 1576 (Florence, Uffizi). These range from engineering drawings that follow Vitruvius or are clearly inspired by sources such as Francesco di Giorgio Martini, Giuliano da Sangallo and Baldassare Peruzzi to studies of Michelangelo's sculpture and architecture, for example in connection with the tomb of Pope Julius II and the Medici chapel and façade of S Lorenzo, Florence. These drawings have proved valuable sources for studying the Roman architectural works of Bramante, Raphael and Michelangelo. The drawings Dosio also made for prints dealt with various architectural themes: church façades, centrally planned churches and semi-fortified villas (*see* VILLA, §II, 1). In the latter he sought a synthesis between the closed, defensive geometry of closely spaced bastions and the open fluidity of country dwellings. Rather than the singularly defensive solutions deriving from Michelangelo, they evoke the compositional experiments of Jacopo Vignola at the Villa Farnese, Caprarola, where in his later career Dosio planned the sunken gardens (1580–83).

Dosio entered the world of antiquarian culture as an illustrator of Roman antiquities. He is remarkable among the Tuscan Mannerists for his vast philological and antiquarian study of ancient monuments, a study motivated not so much by any clear plan of semantic codification as by an inexhaustible encyclopedic curiosity. Though he did not belong to the Accademia della Virtù, founded in Rome in 1542 to promote the knowledge of Vitruvius and Roman architecture, his work accords with its principles. Many of his accurately executed reliefs are pervaded by a limpid atmospheric quality, and tonal modelling is used only to give realistic emphasis to the volumes of buildings. Dosio was one of the first artists to experiment with the genre of the VEDUTA, realizing that attractive perspectives and archaeological precision were greatly appreciated in the flourishing Roman antique market for which he worked. Bernardo Gamucci used some of Dosio's drawings in *Le antichità di Roma* (1565), and Giovanni Battista de' Cavalieri included Dosio's 50 views of Roman architectural ruins in his collection of engravings, *Urbis Romae aedificiorum illustrium* (1569). Dosio acted as an intermediary for Niccolò Gaddi in the latter's purchases of antique works of art and made drawings of funerary cippi for the Mantuan antiquarian Jacopo Strada. His correspondence with Gaddi (1574) mentions plans for a treatise on architecture, but this was never successfully realized.

From 1576 to 1590 Dosio worked mainly in Florence, where he had assisted Bartolomeo Ammannati at the Medici villa at l'Ambrogiana (1574), and in 1575–6 rebuilt the Gaddi Chapel in S Maria Novella; he received increasingly prestigious appointments in the city. He proposed a setting for Donatello's altar in Il Santo, Padua (?1579), and built a palazzo for Filippo Giacomini (now the Palazzo Giacomini–Larderel) with a façade in the classical style (1580). On the invitation of Cardinal Alessandro de' Medici, he planned the façade of the Archbishop's palace in the Piazza S Giovanni (1582, partially executed). Revisiting Rome the same year, he supervised the completion of the plans by Antonio da Sangallo (ii) for S Maria di Monserrato. In 1585 he began work on the Niccolini Chapel in Santa Croce, Florence. In 1586 he took part in a competition organized by Francesco I de' Medici, Grand Duke of Tuscany, for the façade of the cathedral (model Florence, Opera del Duomo) and another competition connected with the Medici Chapel in S Lorenzo. He was one of the main designers of the decorations for the wedding (1589) of Ferdinand I de' Medici and Christina of Lorraine, arranging the *apparati* for the Ponte alla Carraia and for the Palazzo Vecchio, where he produced an architectural pastiche reminiscent of Pirro Ligorio's bizarre scenographic imagination, freely exploiting his erudition in his design for a temporary façade for the cathedral.

After 1590 Dosio worked in Naples, where, in 1591, he was paid as an engineer of the royal court and had numerous supervisory duties. He made one return visit to Rome, remodelling the Palazzo Medici (now Palazzo Madama) with Lodovico Cigoli. Between 1601 and 1603 he supervised work in the Neapolitan church of the Girolamini. At the Certosa di S Martino from 1590 he worked on an extension, plans for side chapels and the cloister and a puteal, all of which were completed by Giovanni Giacomo di Conforto and Cosimo Fanzago (*see* NAPLES, §IV, 3). In Naples, Dosio was active in the field of church interior design, producing the tabernacles (1598) in the Brancaccio Chapel in the cathedral and supervising the works in Il Gesù Nuovo (1605). He died while he was modernizing the convent.

Dosio oscillated between classicism and Mannerism. His work shows sensitivity to the composure and equilibrium of Raphael and Peruzzi and a critical and attentive observation of Michelangelo's manner, although he could not recognize his innovative importance.

See also NAPLES, fig. 9.

BIBLIOGRAPHY

V. Daddi Giovannozzi: 'Il palazzetto Giacomini–Larderel del Dosio', *Riv. A.*, xvii (1935), pp. 209–10
L. Wachler: 'Giovannantonio Dosio', *Röm. Jb. Kstgesch.*, iv (1940), pp. 143–251
V. Daddi Giovannozzi: 'Di alcune incisioni dell'apparato per le nozze di Ferdinando de' Medici e Cristina di Lorena', *Riv. A.*, xxii (1940), pp. 85–100
E. Luporini: 'Formazione, cultura e stile di Giovannantonio Dosio', *Studi in onore di Matteo Marangoni*, ed. C. L. Ragghianti (Florence, 1957), pp. 224–37
——: 'Un libro di disegni di Giovanni Antonio Dosio', *Crit. A.*, iv/24 (1957), pp. 442–67
F. Borsi and others, eds: *Roma antica e i disegni di architettura agli Uffizi* (Rome, 1976) [with list of writings by Dosio and bibliog.]
C. Bertocci and C. Davis: 'A Leaf from the Scholz Scrapbook', *Met. Mus. J.*, xii (1977), pp. 93–100
C. Przyborowski: *Die Ausstattung der Fürstenkapelle an der Basilika von San Lorenzo in Florenz: Versuch einer Rekonstruktion* (Würzburg, 1982)
G. Tedeschi Grisanti: '*Dis manibus, pili, epitaffi et altre cose antiche*: Un codice inedito di disegni di Giovannantonio Dosio', *Boll. A.*, n. s. 5, lxviii/2 (1983), pp. 69–102
R. Pane: 'Dosio e Fanzago', *Napoli Nob.*, xxii/5–6 (1983), pp. 161–7
M. I. Catalano: 'Per Giovanni Antonio Dosio a Napoli: Il puteale del chiostro grande nella Certosa di San Martino', *Stor. A.*, 50 (1984), pp. 35–41

ANTONIO MANNO

Dossal. Term for an Italian panel painting hung in front of or behind an altar.

□

Dossena, Alceo (*b* Cremona, 8 Oct 1878; *d* Rome, 11 Oct 1937). Italian sculptor. He showed early evidence of a natural talent for drawing and sculpture and at the age of 12 he left school and worked first as a cartoon-maker for a silk-weaver, and later as assistant to a marble-carver. After his apprenticeship he began to work independently as an artisan, restoring balustrades, columns and statues for churches and palaces in Cremona and neighbouring cities. He also carved statues for cemeteries, garden fountains and fireplaces, mainly in the 15th-century Lombard style. In 1900 he moved to Parma, where he continued to work as a stone-carver, also producing imitations of 15th-century low reliefs and busts. In 1916 his talent for imitation was discovered by two Roman antiquarians, Alfredo Fasoli and Alfredo Pallesi, who persuaded him to work exclusively for them in return for a modest salary. Dossena was a versatile artist, working in various styles from the Etruscan to the Renaissance, and using such materials as terracotta, marble, wood and bronze. His works were sold without his knowledge on the art market, where they were admired by authoritative critics. They were attributed to such artists as Giovanni Pisano (i), Donatello, il Vecchietta, Mino da Fiesole and even Simone Martini, and were bought for huge sums by museums and collectors all over Europe and the USA. In 1928 the international press exposed the fraud, which was organized by Fasoli and Pallesi in collusion with other highly esteemed antiquarians. The affair ended in court, and Dossena, cheated and badly paid, was shown to be the swindle's major victim.

With the trial, Dossena became well known. His ability to capture the spirit of past masters and to use sophisticated techniques to distress materials earned him many commissions in Italy and abroad. In 1930 Hans Cürlis, Director of the Berlin Institut für Kulturforschung, filmed him in his Roman studio. The Victoria and Albert Museum in London bought from him three terracotta reliefs representing the *Virgin and Child*, executed in the 15th-century Florentine style. In the same years there were a few exhibitions of his works: in 1929 at the Galleria Corona in Naples and the Galleria Micheli in Milan, and in 1930 at the Kunsthalle in Berlin. In 1933 an auction of his sculptures was held at the Plaza Hotel in New York. Among Dossena's most typical works, executed before 1928, are the marble tomb of *Catherina de Sabello* (Boston, MA, Mus. F.A.) in the style of Mino da Fiesole, and the marble *Virgin Annunciate and Angel* (U. Pittsburgh, PA, A.G.) in the 14th-century Sienese style.

BIBLIOGRAPHY

DBI
W. Lusetti: *Alceo Dossena, scultore* (Rome, 1955)

D. Sox: *Unmasking the Forger: The Dossena Deception* (New York, 1987)

R. Ferrazza: 'Alceo Dossena e i falsi d'autore', *Palazzo Dauanzati e le collezioni di Elia Volpi* (Florence, 1993), pp. 223–54

——: 'Alceo Dossena', *Sembrare e non essere: I falsi nell'arte e nella civiltà*, eds M. Jones and M. Spagnol (Milan, 1993), pp. 237–42

ROBERTA FERRAZZA

Dossenberger [Daisenberger]. German family of masons and architects. Thomas Daisenberger (1642–81), his son Matthias Daisenberger (*d* 1712) and his nephew Joseph Dossenberger (i) (*b* Wollishausen, nr Augsburg, 17 Feb 1694; *d* Wollishausen, 22 May 1754) were masons active in the region of Augsburg. In 1732 Joseph Dossenberger worked on the parish church in Agawang, near Augsburg, to the design of Joseph Meitinger, as well as the parish church at Reinhartshausen (begun 1739), a simple hall church with a chancel narrower than the nave. Joseph's sons, Hans Adam Dossenberger (*b* Wollishausen, 25 Dec 1716; *d* Wollishausen, 5 April 1759) and Joseph Dossenberger (ii) (*b* Wollishausen, 9 March 1721; *d* Wettenhausen, nr Günzburg, 15 May 1785), also followed their father's trade.

Hans Adam Dossenberger probably received his first training from his father and is thought to have served an apprenticeship with Dominikus Zimmermann. He is first mentioned in connection with the building of the church at Reinhartshausen, where his father was in charge. He and his brother worked together on the presbytery (1746) at Dietkirch and the parish church (1747) at Wollishausen. Hans Adam's design (1748) for a parish church at Grossaitingen was never carried out, but the parish church (begun 1754) at Herbertshofen was built to his designs. Both Grossaitingen and Herbertshofen were conceived as simple hall churches, projecting slightly in the middle of the side walls and with relatively deep choirs. Hans Adam's chief work, the pilgrimage church of St Thekla (1756–8) at Welden, was built in conjunction with the hunting-lodge (destr.) of the Fugger family; the church interior originally consisted of three bays, and it has striking parallels with the pilgrimage church at Neubirnau, near Überlingen, designed by Peter Thumb and Joseph Anton Feuchtmayer; the double-skinned outer wall of the nave and the ornamental curves of the fenestration clearly reveal the influence of Dominikus Zimmermann, particularly his parish church (1736–41) at Günzburg.

Joseph Dossenberger (ii) also probably trained under his father. In 1748 he was appointed architect to the Augustinian abbey at Wettenhausen; he is later described as inspector or director of buildings for the margravate of Burgau, at the court of the Prince of Thurn and Taxis and for the monasteries of Oberelchingen, Ursberg and Roggenburg, all in Bavaria. He designed several parish churches in Bavaria, including those at Wollishausen (begun 1747), Hochwang (1751), Allerheiligen, near Scheppach (1753–5), Deisenhausen (1765–7) and Scheppach (begun 1768); all are variations on the hall church, with an emphasis on the two central bays to suggest transepts and incorporating a choir. The buildings, strikingly simple externally, are articulated internally by pilasters that accentuate the space and by projecting segments of the entablature; behind these, the wall surfaces appear to recede so that the pilasters, mouldings and ceiling stuccowork seem to span the internal space like a canopy. The ornamental window forms, influenced by Josef Schmuzer and Dominikus Zimmermann, are especially characteristic; in the central bays of the naves and on the longer sides of the choirs these are often combined with fanlights to produce extremely decorative fenestration.

In the parish church (1769–71) at Dischingen, near Heidenheim, Joseph Dossenberger (ii) departed from this type of plan and adopted early Neo-classical elements. The long walls of the hall of the church were progressively stepped, and the transverse axis was emphasized, leading to the appearance of a more centralized space. At the same time the window forms became more severe, and the decorative elements were reduced to triglyphs and coffering. In 1773 he began a Neo-classical renovation of the 12th-century abbey church at Oberelchingen. Here he combined forms characteristic of early Neo-classical buildings with Rococo-style ornamental details such as garlands and curving cornices within a strict classical architectural framework. The parish church (1784) at Breitenthal, near Krumbach, which is attributed to Dossenberger, reverts to the spatial arrangement traditional for parish churches in Bavarian Swabia, although classical articulation and decorative elements were also applied. In his secular buildings the continuation of traditional styles is evident: early buildings are articulated with discreet decorative pilasters or pilaster-strips, while those constructed in the 1770s, such as the Elchingen Amtshaus (1771; destr.) in Stoffenried, near Krumbach, feature heavily rusticated lower storeys and coffered wall surfaces above.

Joseph Dossenberger (ii) was typical of the master masons who produced architectural designs in Upper Swabia and Bavarian Swabia in the 18th century; they often rose to occupy important positions in monastic foundations and generally designed relatively traditional buildings, which could then be decorated in accordance with the taste of the day, so facilitating the adaptation of new forms of decoration.

BIBLIOGRAPHY

F. Mayer: 'Die Dossenberger und Wirth', *Schwabens Vergangenheit*, xxxvii (1936)

A. Wohlhaupter and N. Lieb: *Die Brüder Hans Adam und Joseph Dossenberger: Zwei Baumeister des schwäbischen Spätbarocks* (Munich, 1950)

N. Lieb: 'Die schwäbische Baumeisterfamilie Dossenberger', *Bl. Bayer. Landesver. Familienknd.*, xxiv/2 (1961), pp. 422–4

G. Nebinger: 'Die schwäbische Baumeisterfamilie Dossenberger: Ein Geschlecht des oberbayerischen Pfaffenwinkels', *Bl. Bayer. Landesver. Familienknd.*, xxiv/2 (1961), pp. 425–38

K. H. Koepf: 'Neues über die Baumeister Hans Adam und Joseph Dossenberger', *Das Münster*, xxi (1968), pp. 201–4

——: *Joseph Dossenberger (1721–1785): Ein schwäbischer Baumeister des Rokoko* (Weissenhorn, 1973)

——: 'Die schwäbischen Baumeister Dossenberger', *Lebensbild. Bayer. Schwaben*, xi (1976), pp. 140–62

ULRICH KNAPP

Dossi. Italian family of painters. (1) Dosso Dossi and his less talented younger brother (2) Battista Dossi were the leading painters at the court of Ferrara under Alfonso I d'Este and Ercole II d'Este. Their father was a native of the Trentino who became bursar at the court of Duke Ercole I of Ferrara and whose property, the Villa Dossi in the province of Mantua, gave the brothers their surname. Their activities were typical of Renaissance court artists: decorating palazzi and villas with frescoes and canvases, usually on mythological or poetic themes; providing designs for tapestries, theatre sets, festival decorations, banners, coins and tableware; painting portraits and small-scale devotional works; gilding their employer's furniture and decorating and varnishing carriages and barges. Most of this work, mentioned in ducal records, is now lost. They also painted altarpieces and, when permitted to do so by the Duke of Ferrara, larger decorative projects for other patrons.

(1) Dosso Dossi [Giovanni di Niccolò de Lutero] (*b* ?Ferrara, *c.* 1490; *d* Ferrara, 1541–2). Although responsive to a wide range of outside influences, the most important of which were probably those of Giorgione in Venice and Raphael in Rome, he was an artist of great originality with a strong feeling for effects of light and colour. Landscape plays a prominent and highly expressive role in his work. He was employed, as were also the poets Matteomaria Boiardo (?1441–94) and Ludovico Ariosto, at the court of Ferrara, which was internationally renowned for its culture, especially its musical life and collections of art: one of his best-known works is an illustration of a magical scene from Ariosto's poetry, *Melissa* (1520s; Rome, Gal. Borghese), a painting of opulent colour and texture.

1. EARLY WORKS, TO *c.* 1522. His earliest biographers, including Vasari, indicated a birthdate of *c.* 1475; but modern critics, guided by the style of his earliest known works, are generally agreed that he cannot have been born much before 1490. He is first recorded in Mantua in 1512, working at a Gonzaga palazzo, and his name appears in the Este accounts at Ferrara in 1514. Vasari's report that he was a pupil of Lorenzo Costa di Ottavio, court painter at Mantua from 1507, seems inherently plausible, even though it is difficult to detect any stylistic link between the two artists. Giorgione was the dominant influence on Dosso's earliest works and it seems likely that before settling in Ferrara in 1514 he had spent some time in Venice.

Longhi (1927) identified a group of mainly religious pictures datable to *c.* 1512–17 as Dosso's first works. The key work—the *Holy Family with St John and Two Donors* (Philadelphia, PA, Mus. A.)—shows in its composition and poetically suggestive use of light and landscape that the artist was familiar with developments in Venice *c.* 1510. Yet the work's naturalism and anti-classical restlessness also suggest a relationship with Lombard painting, and the attribution has remained controversial. It has received support from Volpe's (1982) identification of a large altarpiece, of the *Virgin and Child with Five Saints* (Ferrara, Pal. Arcivescovile), with that recorded by the 18th-century local historian Cittadella as an early work by Dosso. Stylistically this picture is very close to the works in Longhi's group, the Philadelphia picture in particular. Since it appears to be a direct response to Raphael's *St Cecilia* (before 1516; Bologna, Pin. N.), which reached northern Italy only in 1515, both Dosso's paintings may be dated *c.* 1516–17.

1. Dosso Dossi: *Three Ages of Man*, oil on canvas, 775×1118mm, 1518–20 (New York, Metropolitan Museum of Art)

In 1516 and 1518 Dosso is recorded as visiting Venice, and in 1517 Florence. Such pictures as the *Bacchanal* (London, N.G.) and the *Circe* (Washington, DC, N.G.A.) may date from this period. They would form a transition between his earlier work and the innovative style of a frieze depicting scenes from the *Life of Aeneas*. This was painted for the Camerino d'Alabastro, one of the ducal apartments in the Via Coperta, the passage joining the Este castle in Ferrara to the nearby palazzo, and Dosso received a series of payments for it in 1518–22. Three of its scenes have been identified as *Aeneas in the Elysian Fields* (Ottawa, N.G.), the *Sicilian Games* (U. Birmingham, Barber Inst.) and *Aeneas on the Libyan Coast* (Washington, DC, N.G.A.). In these paintings and in such works as the *Three Ages of Man* (1518–20; New York, Met.; see fig. 1) and his various representations of *St Jerome in the Wilderness* (e.g. *c.* 1520; Vienna, Ksthist. Mus.), the scene is dominated by landscape and by the most dramatic effects of nature. This interest in landscape may have been stimulated by his early experience of the art of Giorgione in Venice, and also by the work of northern European painters represented in the ducal collection, such as Joachim Patinir and Albrecht Altdorfer. Dosso tended to develop, often to the point of exaggeration, many of the revolutionary characteristics of Giorgione's *Tempest* (*c.* 1506–7; Venice, Accad.), with its vital, dynamic conception of nature, its sense of moist fecundity and its dramatic juxtaposition of flashes of light and patches of glowing colour against areas of deep shadow. In his early works certain areas of the canvas are sometimes painted with extreme sketchiness and forms often seem insubstantial. His vision of landscape was also indebted to his cultivated courtly environment; he may have been consciously seeking to re-create the works of antique painters such as Ludius, who, according to Pliny (*Natural History*, XXXV), specialized in scenes in which rustic figures were subordinate to the extensive landscape. Paolo Giovio's praise of Dosso as a practitioner of self-sufficient landscape painting, written in the late 1520s, suggests an awareness of Pliny's account.

2. MIDDLE YEARS, *c.* 1522–34. In the course of the 1520s Dosso became increasingly involved with the art of Raphael. Stylistic evidence would suggest that he visited Rome *c.* 1520. His altarpiece of the *Virgin and Child in Glory Escorted by SS Lawrence and James with SS John the Baptist, Sebastian and Jerome* (1522; Modena Cathedral), although still markedly naturalistic, reveals an ambition to emulate the heroic idealism and grandiose compositions of High Renaissance Rome. The *Virgin and Child with SS George and Michael* (*c.* 1525; Modena, Gal. & Mus. Estense) suggests a similar response to the early Roman works of Raphael. In 1524–6 Dosso was paid for further work in the rooms of the Via Coperta, including the large circular ceiling of the Camera del Pozzuolo, fragments of which— the *Man Embracing a Woman* (London, N.G.) and the *Page with a Basket of Flowers* (Florence, Longhi priv. col.; see Gibbons, fig. 25)—survive. *SS John the Evangelist and Bartholomew* (1527; Rome, Pal. Barberini), which includes portraits of the della Sale family as donors, seems to be influenced by the heavily muscular figure style of Giulio Romano, who arrived at the neighbouring court of Mantua

in 1524. The so-called *Tubal-Cain (Allegory of Music)* (Florence, Mus. Horne), which may actually show Vulcan, Venus and Cupid, may also date from the late 1520s. In the early 1530s Dosso collaborated with Garofalo on a polyptych for the high altar of S Andrea, Ferrara (now Ferrara, Pin. N.).

With his brother Battista, Dosso was employed *c.* 1530 by Francesco Maria I della Rovere, Duke of Urbino, to decorate the Villa Imperiale, near Pesaro, working alongside Agnolo Bronzino and Raffaelle dal Colle. In the Sala delle Cariatidi he painted maidens transformed into leafy caryatids who support a fictive pergola and frame an enchantingly fresh illusionistic landscape (*see* LANDSCAPE PAINTING, fig. 4). In 1531–2, with Battista and other north Italian artists, including Romanino, he decorated rooms in Trent Castle for the cardinal-bishop Bernardo Cles (1485–1539). The Trent Castle frescoes, now damaged, are mainly mythological and suggest the influence of Giulio Romano's decorations in Mantua; most original are the idyllic pastoral landscapes, illustrating Aesop's fables, in the Sala del Tribunale. On both these occasions it probably suited Duke Alfonso's diplomatic purposes to allow the painter to absent himself from court. Two altarpieces followed: the *Immaculate Conception* (1532; destr.) and the *St Michael with the Assumption* (1533–4; Parma, G.N.).

In these middle years Dosso's chronology remains highly problematic, and the varied dates suggested for a *Myth of Pan* (Malibu, CA, Getty Mus.; see fig. 2) illustrate these difficulties. The subject, not yet satisfactorily identified, is clearly mythological and is portrayed in a spirit of poetic enchantment. The stylistic sources are wide-ranging. The pose of the female nude is derived from Marcantonio Raimondi's engraving of the *Judgement of Paris* after Raphael, while two of the putti are almost quotations from Raphael's *Galatea* (Rome, Villa Farnesina). The sensuousness of the pictorial handling, however, owes more to Venetian painting than to the Roman High Renaissance; and absolutely characteristic of Dosso himself is the romantic background landscape, with its lush, even sultry pastureland, and its fantastic Gothic city shimmering between the mountains and the sea. Yet the handling is more disciplined than in the works of the early 1520s; the still-life details in the foreground are painted with a sharp precision that contrasts with the broadly executed and windswept landscapes of 1518–22. At the same time the treatment of the figures, still comparatively squat, has not yet attained the Mannerist elegance of Dosso's late works. The picture perhaps dates from the early 1530s, the era of stylistically similar works such as the *Immaculate Conception* (1532) and the Parma *St Michael* (*c.* 1534).

3. LAST WORKS, AFTER 1534. In his late works Dosso displayed a post-classical preciosity akin to that of central Italian Mannerism. In 1540 he was paid, together with Battista, for two canvases, *St George and the Dragon* and *St Michael* (both Dresden, Gemäldegal. Alte Meister). In the *St Michael* forms are described with an ornamental, spiralling play of lines that also characterizes the contemporary Ferrarese works of the younger and stylistically more up-to-date Girolamo da Carpi. The *Stregoneria* ('Sorcery', *c.* 1540; Florence, Uffizi), in which the female figures share a similar aesthetic ideal, almost certainly dates late

2. Dosso Dossi: *Myth of Pan*, oil on canvas, 1.60×1.32 m, ?early 1530s (Malibu, CA, J. Paul Getty Museum)

in Dosso's career. Yet this picture, a curious collection of figures and objects that has been variously interpreted as an allegory of Hercules (Gibbons) and as Bacchus in his votaries (Calvesi) also suggests an interest in the naturalism of such genre painters as Giulio Campi and Pieter Aertsen.

4. WORKING METHODS AND POSTHUMOUS REPU-TATION.   Dosso placed a much higher priority on rich and varied pictorial effects than on formal structure and draughtsmanship. Numerous pentiments revealed by X-ray photographs of the *Myth of Pan* show that Dosso

followed the example of Giorgione, dispensing with pre-paratory drawings and sketching his design straight on to the canvas. Only a very small number of drawings can be attributed to him, and even these attributions are contro-versial since none relates to a known painting. The single possible exception is a drawing of *St Luke Portraying the Virgin* (Paris, Louvre).

Dosso's art, with the significant exception of his land-scapes, was not greatly admired by his earliest biographer, Vasari, for whom Dosso's tendency towards the bizarre and preference for expressive colour over careful draughtsmanship meant that he lacked a true sense of style, or *maniera*. As fellow Emilians reacting against the Mannerism of which Vasari was a typical exponent, the Carracci brothers may have been more sympathetic to his robust vitality. Yet for them too Dosso must have seemed too undisciplined and idiosyncratic, and lacking in a classical sense of beauty. The ascendancy of Bologna in Emilian painting in the later 16th century, and the political degradation of Ferrara after 1598, when many of Dosso's works, above all his frescoes, were lost, prevented his art from having the impact on the 17th century that it might otherwise have had.

(2) Battista Dossi [Battista di Niccolò di Lutero] (*b* ?Ferrara, 1490–95; *d* Ferrara, 1548). Brother of (1) Dosso Dossi. He spent almost his entire career in the service of the court at Ferrara, where his name first occurs in the ducal accounts in 1517, and frequently collaborated with his brother. From 1517 he may have worked in Rome in Raphael's workshop, where he is mentioned in a letter of 1520 from the Duke's agent in Rome (Campori). In 1557 the Venetian Lodovico Dolce reported that 'one of the pair [i.e. the Dossi] stayed for a time here in Venice, so as to paint under Titian, and the other was under Raphael in Rome'. In August 1520, four months after Raphael's death, Battista is documented back in Ferrara. He collaborated with Dosso on the frescoes in the Villa Imperiale in Pesaro (*c.* 1530) and in 1531–2 again worked with his brother on the frescoes in Trent Castle. In 1533 he was commissioned to paint a *Deposition* for the Confraternity of the Cross in S Francesco Faenza (untraced), for which both brothers were paid in 1536. In the same year his name is recorded as the principal author of a *Nativity with Saints and Donors* (Modena, Gal. & Mus. Estense), commissioned by Duke Alfonso for Modena Cathedral; and in 1540 he was paid, together with Dosso, for the two canvases, *St Michael* and *St George* (both Dresden, Gemäldegal. Alte Meister). In these years the career of Battista, who evidently performed best under the guidance of Dosso, is obscured by that of his brother. It is not always easy to identify the extent and nature of his contribution even in those works in which he is known to have had a hand. Something of his early experience in Raphael's workshop may perhaps be detected in a tendency towards Romanism in his figure style and in a lack of feeling for the atmospheric qualities of Venetian painting. His *Nativity with Saints and Donors* is a key work: the composition and the clearly drawn and elaborately posed figures are influenced by the art of the Roman High Renaissance, while the extensive landscape is inspired by, though less inventive and expressive than, those by Dosso.

The works executed after Dosso's death constitute the touchstones for reconstructing Battista's independent oeuvre. They reveal him as a much weaker artist than his brother, imitating the externals of Dosso's style but lacking his flair and energy. The most important surviving works documented from these years are the *Justice* and the *Hour Leading forth the Horses of Apollo* (both 1544; Dresden, Gemäldegal. Alte Meister). The depiction of *Justice* is prosaic, the details of her costume pedantically literal and

the entire figure completely unintegrated with the background landscape. On Dosso's death Battista took over the direction of the workshop and his name thereafter appears with greater frequency in the ducal rolls in connection with the usual round of court commissions. The Ferrarese painter Camillo Filippi was his pupil.

BIBLIOGRAPHY
G. Vasari: *Vite* (1550, rev. 2/1568); ed. G. Milanesi (1878–85), v, pp. 96–101
L. Dolce: *L'Aretino ovvero dialogo della pittura* (Venice, 1557), pp. 9v–10
P. Giovio: *Fragmentum trium dialogorum Pauli Jovii espiscopi Nucevini*, in G. Tiraboschi: *Storia della letteratura italiana* (Florence, 1812), vii/4, p. 1722
G. Campori: *Notizie inedite di Raffaello d'Urbino* (Modena, 1863), p. 29
R. Longhi: 'Un problema di cinquecento ferrarese (Dosso giovine)', *Vita artistica*, ii (1927), pp. 31–5; also in *Opere complete di Roberto Longhi*, ii (Florence, 1967)
——: *Officina ferrarese* (Florence, 1934); also in *Opere complete di Roberto Longhi*, v (Florence, 1968)
E. H. Gombrich: 'Renaissance Artistic Theory and the Development of Landscape Painting', *Gaz. B.-A.*, n. s. 5, xli (1953), pp. 335–60; repr. in *Norm and Form: Studies in the Art of the Renaissance* (London, 1966)
P. Pouncey: 'Un disegno attribuibile a Dosso Dossi', *A. Ant. & Mod.*, 12 (1960), p. 385
A. Mezzetti: *Il Dosso e Battista ferraresi* (Ferrara, 1965) [cat., register of doc., bibliog. and pl., some colour]
F. Gibbons: *Dosso and Battista Dossi, Court Painters at Ferrara* (Princeton, 1968) [cat., register of doc., bibliog. and pl.]; review by M. Calvesi in *Stor. A.*, 1–2 (1969), pp. 168–74
C. Volpe: 'Dosso: Segnalazioni e proposte per il suo itinerario', *Paragone*, xxv/293 (1974), pp. 20–28
B. Wind: 'Genre as a Season: Dosso, Campi, Caravaggio', *A. Lombarda*, 42–3 (1975), pp. 70–73
S. Schaefer: 'Battista Dossi's *Venus and Cupid*', *Bull. Philadelphia Mus. A.*, 320 (1978), pp. 13–24
A. Braham and J. Dunkerton: 'Fragments of a Ceiling Decoration by Dosso Dossi', *N.G. Tech. Bull.*, v (1981), pp. 27–37
M. Calvesi: 'Dosso e il "sacramento" di Bacco', *Stor. A.*, 46 (1982), pp. 209–13
A. Corbara: 'Sulla faentina *Deposizione della Croce* dei Dossi. Un documento di ricerca nello studio del manierismo ferrarese', *Le arti a Bologna e in Emilia dal XVI al XVII secolo: Atti del XXIV Congresso Internazionale di Storia dell'Arte: Bologna, 1982*, iv, pp. 81–6
A. Mezzetti: 'Un ciclo zodiacale del Dosso a Ferrara', *Boll. A.*, lxvii/16 (1982), pp. 61–70
C. Volpe: 'Una pala d'altare del giovane Dosso', *Paragone*, xxxiii/383–5 (1982), pp. 3–14
A. de Marchi: 'Sugli esordi veneti di Dosso Dossi', *A. Veneta*, xl (1986), pp. 20–28
Bernardo Cles e l'arte del rinascimento nel Trentino (exh. cat., Trent, Castello Buonconsiglio, 1986)
The Age of Correggio and the Carracci (exh. cat., Bologna, Pin. N.; Washington, DC, N.G.A.; New York, Met.; 1986–7)
A. Buzzoni: 'La pittura a Bologna, Ferrara e Modena nel cinquecento', *La pittura in Italia: Il cinquecento*, ed. G. Briganti (Milan, 1988), pp. 255–77
P. Leone de Castris: 'Indagini sul giovane Dosso', *Ant. Viva*, xxvii/1 (1988), pp. 3–9

PETER HUMFREY

Dossi, Carlo [Pisani-Dossi, Alberto Carlo] (*b* Zenevredo, nr Pavia, 27 March 1849; *d* Dosso Pisani, nr Como, 16 Nov 1910). Italian writer and diplomat. He worked as a ministerial functionary in Rome and then as a diplomat abroad. A very precocious writer, he belonged to the Lombard movement of Gli Scapigliati, which expressed the Italian reaction to the Realism and *verismo* of the mid-19th century. He had a particular interest in the writer Giuseppe Rovani (1818–74), theorist of Gli Scapigliati, of whom he wrote an unfinished biography. Dossi was the author of short, refined stories, confessions and aesthetic reflections, generally published in expensive limited editions. His works reveal a delicate and subtle sensibility and a style that was innovative in its eccentricity. His diplomatic career did not prevent him from participating in the artistic and cultural life of Milan and then of Rome, in the course of which—and in his travels abroad—he took a lively interest in archaeology. Dossi's taste for the figurative arts was partly guided by the aesthetic principle (represented in Italy by Rovani and Gli Scapigliati) of collaboration between the different arts. It was also informed by his youthful interest in such painters as Tranquillo Cremona and such sculptors as Giuseppe Grandi, whose anti-Realist characteristics and impressionistic style were congenial to Dossi's interest in the fragmentary.

WRITINGS

L'Altrieri (Milan, 1868)
Vita di A. Pisani (Milan, 1870)
Ritratti umani (Milan, 1873)
Goccie d'inchiostro (Rome, 1880, rev. Milan, 1979) [rev. edn incl. biog. by D. Isella, pp. 259–65]
I mattoidi al primo concorso del monumento in Roma a Vittorio Emanuele II (Rome, 1884)
Fricassea critica di arte, storia e letteratura (Como, 1906)
P. Levi and G. P. Lucini, eds: *Opere*, 5 vols (Milan, 1910–27)
G. Nicodemi, ed.: *Rovaniana*, 2 vols (Milan, 1946)
D. Isella, ed.: *Note azzurre*, 2 vols (Milan, 1964)

BIBLIOGRAPHY

G. P. Lucini: *L'ora topica di Carlo Dossi* (Varese, 1911)
D. Isella: *La lingua e lo stile di Carlo Dossi* (Milan and Naples, 1958)

FRANCO BERNABEI

Dostoyevsky, Fyodor (Mikhaylovich) (*b* Moscow, 11 Nov 1821; *d* St Petersburg, 9 Feb 1881). Russian writer and critic. Of all the visual arts, he most frequently turned to painting for his analysis of artistic aims and ideas. While he used paintings in his creative writing to supplement and maximize the effect of the truths he sought to express, he most cohesively pronounced his approach to art in his reviews of Russian art exhibitions (1861 and 1873). Essentially opposed to the idea that realism could reflect nature as it is, he maintained that all art was inevitably idealized since it subjected nature to the processes of perception and emotion. For Dostoyevsky, the essence of painting was the clear expression of truth, this deriving from a sincerity in the treatment of the subject and the continual questioning of convictions. The artist has a dual nature: the poet in him gives birth to the idea while the craftsman gives it substance. Painting should aspire to the synthesis of beauty and prayer, the most effective art of such 'positive beauty' being images of the Virgin, and, in particular, Raphael's *Sistine Madonna* (*c.* 1512–14; Dresden, Gemäldegal. Alte Meister). Rationalism in art should be transformed by the infusion of spiritual feeling in order to avoid sinking to the level of melodrama. In his examination of Russian painting of the 1860s and 1870s, he was most critical of its achievements with regard to historical themes, especially berating Nikolay Ge for his false mixture of genre and history. However, he welcomed the Gogolesque truths to be found in Il'ya Repin's *Volga Barge Haulers* (1870–73; St Petersburg, Rus. Mus.) as well as the expression of Russianness in Vasily Perov and Arkhip Kuindzhi. While praising the progress of Russian genre painting, he bemoaned the fact that generally Russian art failed to prioritize fundamental issues, that it therefore could not be understood by foreigners and that its creators lacked daring and independence of ideas.

WRITINGS

'Vystavka v akademii khudozhestv za 1861 god' [The exhibition at the Academy of Arts in 1861], *Vremya*, 10 (1861), pp. 147–68; also in F. M. Dostoyevsky: *Polnoye sobraniye sochineniy* [Complete collected works], ed. V. Bazanov, xix (Leningrad, 1979), pp. 151–68
'Po povodu vystavki' [About the exhibition], *Grazhdanin*, 13 (26 March 1873), pp. 423–6; also in *Polnoye sobraniye sochineniy*, xxi (Leningrad, 1980), pp. 68–77

BIBLIOGRAPHY

N. Lapshin: *Estetika Dostoyevskogo* [Dostoyevsky's aesthetics] (Berlin, 1923)
V. Bogdanov, ed.: *F. M. Dostoyevsky ob iskusstve* [F. M. Dostoyevsky on art] (Moscow, 1973)
V. Bulkin: 'Dostoyevsky i zhivopis' [Dostoyevsky and painting], *Problemy izobrazitel'nogo iskusstva XIX stoletiya* [Questions of fine art of the 19th century] (Leningrad, 1990), pp. 143–55

☐

Döteber, Christian Julius (*b* Leipzig; *fl* Sweden, from 1630s, *d* Stockholm, in or after 1675). German sculptor and architect active in Sweden. In 1641 he was employed as a sculptor for the German (Tyska) church in Stockholm. His main work—now known as the Petersen House (1645–9) in Stockholm—is one of Sweden's chief examples of the German-Netherlandish Renaissance style. Built as the residence of Regner Leuhusen (1601–55), the vice governor of Stockholm, it is characterized by its stepped, scrolled gables, with obelisks and other ornamental details, and especially by its double portal with a very rich setting of figures and ornamentation substituting for columns carrying the heavy open segmental pediments of the crowning structure. The allegorical figures represent the Four Seasons, and the twin composition is surmounted by the figure of Minerva. Döteber left Sweden *c.* 1648, becoming an apprentice in Danzig (now Gdańsk) and later possibly working in Rostock. In the first half of the 1660s he was active in Leipzig, where he executed putti and figure sculptures for the Nikolaikirche.

BIBLIOGRAPHY

Thieme–Becker
I. Simonsson: 'Bildhuggaren Christian Julius Döteber' [Sculptor Christian Julius Döteber], *Konsthistoriska Sällskapets Publikationer* (1918), pp. 12–30
G. Axel-Nilsson: *Dekorativ stenhuggarkonst i yngre vasastil* [Ornamental sculpture in the early Vasa style] (Stockholm, 1950)
Svenskt konstnärslexikon, iii (Malmö, 1953), p. 67

TORBJÖRN FULTON

Dotremont, Christian (*b* Tervuren, 12 Dec 1922; *d* Buizingen, nr Halle, 1979). Belgian writer and painter. During World War II he contributed regularly to *La Main à plume*, the publication of the Parisian Surrealist group. Immediately after the War he published half-literary, half-theoretical texts in politically oriented Belgian periodicals. He was a fervent supporter of the alliance of Surrealism and Communism; in April 1947, in opposition to André Breton, he founded the movement Surréalisme Révolutionnaire in Brussels. In November 1948, when it became clear that further cooperation between the Belgian and French wings of this movement had become impossible, Dotremont, with Asger Jorn, Karel Appel, Constant and Corneille founded the COBRA movement (1948–51).

Dotremont became the prime spokesperson in the movement. In the *Cobra* periodical, of which he became the chief editor, he explained his ideas. He also produced numerous texts about the work of his fellow members. His most important artistic contribution to the Cobra movement was his cooperation as a poet with the artists of Cobra in, for example, the *peintures-mots* such as *Un visage suffit à nier le miroir* (1948; Silkeborg, Kstmus.), made with Asger Jorn, in which word and image were mixed together. He was to continue this type of collaboration on an intensive basis, even after the demise of the Cobra movement. From 1962 he developed a series of quasi-Oriental calligraphic signs based on his own handwriting, which he called logograms; he subsequently built up an entire painted oeuvre based on these signs. His special fascination with the Scandinavian countries is expressed most strongly in his novel *La Pierre et l'oreiller* (Paris, 1955).

PUBLISHED WRITINGS
Lettres d'amour (Paris, 1943) [with drgs by René Magritte]
'Le Grand Rendez-vous naturel' (Manifesto), *Cobra*, 4 (1949) [pubd in a special enclosure]; *Cobra*, 6 (1950), pp. 4–5, 12
Isabelle: Texts on Cobra, 1948–1978 (Brussels, 1985)

BIBLIOGRAPHY
M. Butor and M. Sicard: *Dotremont et ses écrivures* (Paris, 1978)
Christian Dotremont: 'Vois ce que je t'écris' (exh. cat., Liège, Mus. A. Mod.; Namur, Maison Cult.; Brussels, Cent. A. Contemp.; 1984)

WILLEMIJN STOKVIS

Dotremont, Philippe (*b* Boussu-les-Mons, 1898; *d* 1969). Belgian industrialist and collector. He had a successful career in the sugar and construction industries before becoming one of the foremost collectors of contemporary American art in Europe. His collection continually reflected the newest developments in art. The first painting he acquired (1937), a work by Jakob Smits, was followed by paintings by other Flemish Expressionists. He then bought canvases by Klee, Picasso, Kandinsky and Léger, but after World War II he concentrated on acquiring works by contemporary artists, especially Americans. Dotremont, who never travelled to the USA, bought mainly on the basis of colour transparencies presented to him by dealers. Selections from his collection were shown in Amsterdam (1954), New York (1958) and Basle (1961). By this time he owned approximately 150 paintings; critics responded favourably to the American paintings, also noting work by artists from Italy, Spain and the Cobra group. Among the Americans represented were Alexander Calder, Mark Tobey, Sam Francis, Willem de Kooning, Clyfford Still, Franz Kline, Robert Motherwell, Adolph Gottlieb, Philip Guston and Joan Mitchell. Dotremont also owned works by Dubuffet, Arp, Miró, Josef Albers and Georges Mathieu. Forty-three contemporary paintings, sculptures, mobiles, collages and watercolours, including works by Miró, Picasso, Jackson Pollock, Rauschenberg, Arp and Calder, were sold from the Dotremont Collection at Parke Bernet, New York, on 14 April 1965.

BIBLIOGRAPHY
Collectie Philippe Dotremont (exh. cat., Amsterdam, Stedel. Mus.; Eindhoven, Stedel. Van Abbemus.; 1954)
Twenty Contemporary Painters from the Philippe Dotremont Collection, Brussels (exh. cat., New York, Guggenheim, 1958)
Moderne Malerei seit 1945 aus der Sammlung Dotremont (exh. cat., Basle, Ksthalle, 1961)
G. Schoenberger: 'La Collection Dotremont à la Kunsthalle Bâle', *A. Int.*, v/7 (20 Sept 1961), pp. 30–33

AMY WALSH

Dotted print [Fr. *criblé*; Ger. *Schrotblatt*]. Type of print made by a process of relief-engraving on metal, used by goldsmiths in the second half of the 15th century. The plates were usually made for printing on paper but sometimes for decoration. The metal used was a malleable one, such as copper, tin, brass or lead. It was cut using a hammer to hit punches of different thicknesses; on one end of the steel stem of each punch was a motif in relief that, when punched into the metal plate, created an indented cavity. These motifs included dots, crosses, fleurons, lozenges, stars and circles. The background, which constitutes the part in relief, carries the ink and appears black when printed; the hollows of the punch marks, of varying size and proximity to each other, produce the whites that make up the subject and suggest the modelling and half-tones. The white, positive part of the image is rarely composed solely of white dots, although they predominate; white strokes and hatch marks are also used. The process of the dotted manner is similar to goldsmith's work and to the way plates are worked for tooling leather, for instance in bookbinding. Dotted prints intended to be printed on paper bear traces of the nails that pinned them down, which suggests that the plate was fixed to wood and then put through a press. Such impressions bear inscriptions that appear the right way

Hand-coloured dotted print of *St Bernardino of Siena*, 235×177 mm, 1454 (Paris, Bibliothèque Nationale)

round, while proofs with inscriptions in reverse come from plates that were probably made for goldsmith's work (enamel) or for decorating an object. In several cases plates appear to have been reused for PASTE PRINTS.

The dotted manner was restricted to regions of the Rhine, and to the Netherlands, Cologne, Basle and Lake Constance. The earliest-known dotted print with a date is of *St Bernardino of Siena* (Paris, Bib. N.; see fig.). At the foot of the plate, a five-line text is engraved, with the date 1454. The plate is highly developed technically and can perhaps be linked to a group of images in the same style, with the subject in relief, against a white background, and with borders of ribbons festooned to look like clouds in a black sky scattered with stars; the corners are occupied by medallions bearing the symbols of the Evangelists. The *St Bernardino* is coloured in several arcs with yellow-green, brownish red and bright red. The most spectacular dotted prints are those for which the engraver used virtually nothing but a punch; these are vigorously modelled, with a decorative quality far removed from ordinary prints. Dotted prints were succeeded by metalcuts, which made possible a greater variety of effects and which mixed black-and white-line engraving, relief and dotted manner printing. It is practically impossible to isolate the different techniques of relief-engraving on metal and to describe their history separately, since they were rarely used in isolation but were mixed on the same plate.

BIBLIOGRAPHY

W. L. Schreiber: *Manuel de la gravure sur bois et sur métal au XVe siècle*, 5 vols (Berlin and Leipzig, 1891–1910; 10 vols, Stuttgart, 3/1969)

H. Bouchot: *Les Deux Cents Incunables xylographiques du Département des Estampes* (Paris, 1903)

P. Gusman: *La Gravure sur bois et d'épargne sur métal du XIVe au XXe siècle* (Paris, 1916)

——: 'La Gravure en taille d'épargne sur métal', *Byblis*, III (1922), pp. 118–24

A. Blum: 'Les Débuts de la gravure sur métal', *Gaz. B.-A.*, vi (1931), pp. 65–77

A. M. Hind: *An Introduction to a History of Woodcut with a Detailed Survey of Work Done in the Fifteenth Century*, 2 vols (London, 1935; R London and New York, 1963)

Fifteenth-century Woodcuts and Metalcuts from the National Gallery of Art (exh. cat. by R. S. Field, Washington, DC, N.G.A., 1966)

GISÈLE LAMBERT

Dotti, Carlo Francesco (*b* Como, 31 Dec 1669; *d* Bologna, 3 June 1759). Italian architect. He came from a family of architects who practised in Bologna; he was the son of the architect Giovanni Paolo Dotti (*fl* 1659–70). Carlo Francesco was one of the most important architects in the first half of the 18th century in Bologna, and he developed a resolute and innovative Baroque style. His major works are the Arco del Meloncello and the sanctuary of Madonna di S Luca, which formed one of the main ecclesiastical complexes in Bologna. A competition was held in 1714 for an arch to provide a pedestrian passage across the Via Saragozza; Dotti's design, uniquely, was a two-storey structure that spanned the road. The original drawing (Bologna, Archv Stato) shows the arch straight in plan; the executed work (1718–32), however, was doubly curved in plan and is asymmetrical, with one side concealing adjacent buildings. These scenographic features may suggest the involvement of Dotti's contemporary, the stage designer Francesco Galli-Bibiena. The Arco del Meloncello gives access to a *porticus*, originally 3 km long, now of 666 arches, which leads up the Monte della Guardia to the sanctuary (1723–57), where it forms a doubly curved gallery similar in appearance to the Arco and ending in pentagonal stair pavilions that form the entrance portico of the church. The church has a Greek-cross plan with apsidal ends, probably based on SS Luca e Martina (begun 1634), Rome, by Pietro Berrettini da Cortona, although the separate sanctuary possibly links it to the first, unexecuted, design (1660–62; Archv S Maria in Campitelli) for S Maria in Campitelli, Rome, by Carlo Rainaldi; the free-standing columns articulating the spaces, however, are in the early 17th-century Bolognese manner of Giovanni Ambrogio Mazenta. The design was selfconsciously scenographic, with the single drum, rising above the more complex base, dominating the hillside.

In 1731 Dotti became architect to the Senate of Bologna, at a time of retrenchment. The church of S Domenico (1728–32), the convent of S Giovanni Battista dei Celestini (1729–54; since altered) and the library of the Istituto delle Scienze (1738) all had interiors in the early 17th-century Bolognese style, with lateral windows, plain walls and free-standing columns. Dotti's private works were also modest in scope and included the double staircase (1735) of the Palazzo Davia Bargellini, executed by Alfonso Torreggiani, renovations (1736–8) to the Palazzo Monti, and the façade (after 1740) of the Palazzo Agucchi, designed in the Bolognese manner with an arcaded ground floor. Outside Bologna, he worked on the restoration of S Giovanni (1733–7), Minerbo, and S Sebastiano (1745), Renazzo, near Ferrara. In 1743 he was invited to submit a proposal for the reinforcement of the dome of St Peter's, Rome.

Dotti prepared two unexecuted designs (Bologna, Mus. S Petronio; *see* BOLOGNA, §IV, 2) for the east façade of the basilica of S Petronio, Bologna; begun in 1390 by Antonio di Vincenzo, S Petronio was still unfinished, and there was controversy between 'classicists' and 'Goths' over the correct way to complete it. Dotti produced a design to satisfy each: his first design (1748) was a development of Francesco Terribilia's Gothic design of 1580; his second (1752) was in a mid-17th-century Roman style, with a façade articulated in depth by clusters of engaged columns.

Dotti's two sons also were architects: Giovanni Paolo (1707–55) collaborated with him and Giovanni Giacomo (1724–after 1792) published Dotti's work.

WRITINGS

Ragioni con le quali si dimostra il perche sia inviolabile il quesito famoso delle terre aggravate con inequale proporzione delle pertiche espresso in due dialoghi: E si dimostra la fallacia delle regole fino ad ora ostentate (Bologna, 1710)

Esame sopra le forze delle catene e braga con che si mostrano le bragature essere inutili per reggere l'urto degli archi e volte e come possa reggere la simplice catena horizzontale, posta nella sommita degli archi senza bragature, come anche tante fabbriche munite con dette catene a braga, che reggonsi fino al giorno d'oggi possano essere un'argomento forte, per dimonstrarle valide, come viene creduto da molti (Bologna, 1730)

Scrittura volante sul proposito del nuovo teatro pubblico in difesa del sentimento di C. F. Dotti e del Torreggiani architetto, contro le opposizioni del sig. Antonio Bibiena inventore e direttore della fabbrica del nuovo pubblico teatro (Bologna [*c.* 1756])

BIBLIOGRAPHY

DBI

R. Wittkower: *Art and Architecture in Italy, 1600–1750*, Pelican Hist. A. (Harmondsworth, 1958, rev. 1991)

C. Ricci and G. Zucchini: *Guida di Bologna* (Bologna, 1968)
A. M. Matteucci: *Carlo Francesco Dotti e l'architettura bolognese del settecento* (Bologna, 1969)
R. Wittkower: *Gothic versus Classic* (London, 1974)
J. Varriano: *Italian Baroque and Rococo* (New York, 1986)

□

Dottori, Gerardo (*b* Perugia, 11 Nov 1884; *d* Perugia, 13 June 1977). Italian painter. He was born into a family of modest economic means and received his first lessons in drawing in the workshop of a Perugian antiquarian. From 1904 to 1912 he studied at the Accademia di Belle Arti in Perugia, supporting himself by working as a mural painter. On completing his studies he aligned himself with FUTUR-ISM and stimulated the dull and provincial artistic atmosphere of Perugia by founding a group and a journal entitled *La Griffa*. Even before completing his studies he produced dynamic paintings of movement, such as *Explosion of Red on Green* (1910; London, Tate), a virtually abstract work. He participated in the first Mostra Internazionale Futurista Exhibition in Rome, alongside Balla, Fortunato Depero and Enrico Prampolini, and his first one-man show (Rome, Gal. A. Bragaglia, 1920) was opened by Filippo Tommaso Marinetti.

Dottori's style is characterized by its attention to nature and to landscape, subjects that were usually extraneous to the urban and mechanical themes of Futurism. In the works exhibited by him at the Venice Biennale in 1924 and 1926, such as the triptych *Umbrian Dawn* (1921; Milan, F. Azari priv. col., see Ballo, fig. 33), the Umbrian landscape appears dismembered and freshly appraised through the dynamic syntax of Futurism. His ideas on 'total landscape' were influential on the drafting of the *Manifesto dell'aeropittura* in 1929, the principal text of the phase of Futurism known as AEROPITTURA.

Dottori lived mostly in Rome during the 1930s, contributing to newspapers and journals such as *Giornale d'Italia*, *Oggi e domani* and *L'Impero* and taking part in various exhibitions including Futurist group shows and the first Esposizione Internazionale d'Arte Sacra, held in Rome in 1930, at which he enjoyed considerable success. He settled permanently again in Perugia in 1939, teaching at the Accademia di Belle Arti and serving as its director between 1940 and 1947.

BIBLIOGRAPHY
G. Ballo: *Dottori aeropittore futurista* (Rome, 1970)
A. C. Ponti and M. Duranti: *Intervista su Gerardo Dottori* (Perugia, 1977)
Gerardo Dottori: Nelle collezioni pubbliche e private (exh. cat. by M. Duranti, Perugia, Gal. A., 1988)

VALERIO RIVOSECCHI

Dotzinger. German family of architects. They were active in the Rhineland in the 15th century.

(1) Johann Dotzinger (*fl* 1432–48/9). He is named from 1432 as Master of Works at Basle Minster, but the gap in the Minster account books from 1449 makes it impossible to establish when he ceased to be active there. The tabernacle that was built to his plans between 1435 and 1438 (destr.) must have been a most impressive and rich structure. The east and south walks of the large cloister were designed by Johann: the east walk was built under his direction, and the south walk was at least begun by him. The walls were retained from an earlier structure, so the window mouldings and vaults may be attributed to Johann.

The vault of the east walk has a series of intersecting ribs forming stars, with four converging lozenges. The curvature of the diagonal ribs produces a dynamic sense of movement. The heraldic keystones and the roof bosses are decorated with foliage. In the vault of the south walk parallel lines of ribs cross to produce a series of lozenges of equal size along the vault surface, each ornamented with free-standing tracery. The two vaults are so different that the contrast must have been deliberately conceived by Johann to enrich the structure. The forms used by Johann in Basle are related to those developed in the circle of MADERN GERTHENER, which suggests that Dotzinger was born and trained in the middle Rhine region.

Johann was probably not a sculptor; the sculptures on the tabernacle were certainly carved by another. There is no direct evidence that Johann worked outside Basle, but he did travel on several occasions. It is possible to recognize in his few surviving works an architect with imagination and wit, who introduced new architectural forms to the upper Rhine.

(2) Jodok Dotzinger (*d* Strasbourg, 1470s). Son or nephew of (1) Johann Dotzinger. He was said to come from Worms and must therefore have been born in the middle Rhine region, where he was trained in the circle of Madern Gerthener. Later he travelled to Basle, where (1) Johann Dotzinger was working, and thence he must have established contact with Matthäus Ensingen, probably working with him in Berne. He came to Strasbourg from Weissenburg in Alsace, where he had built the Holy Sepulchre (mid-1440s) in the collegiate church; this would

Jodok Dotzinger: baptismal font, stone, 1453, Strasbourg Cathedral

have been his first commission in his own right. The Holy Sepulchre is a canopy tomb of considerable height. At the level of the canopy, between the three richly decorated front piers, are keel arches decorated with tracery.

He was employed from 1451 as foreman of the mason's lodge of Strasbourg Cathedral. His first work in Strasbourg was the baptismal font (see fig.), which bears the date 1453, presumably made at the request or on the recommendation of Matthäus Ensingen, whom he succeeded as Master of Works in 1452. The font is heptagonal in plan, an unusual feature. The basin is rotated by half a side's width in relation to the base. The entire font is decorated with rich tracery, which also fills the nodding ogees. Twisted fluting and branchwork decoration of the socle appeared here for the first time, as did decorative forms that were widely disseminated in the Gothic architecture of the second half of the 15th century, making Jodok's significance very clear. The stylistic influences apparent on the font reveal Jodok's personal connections and the development of his career.

At the cathedral Jodok was engaged in replacing the nave vaults. He introduced applied columns to the choir walls and constructed two small spiral stairs in the choir; he also added eight traceried gables to the crossing tower. Both the columns and gables were removed in later centuries. All these works, even the early ones, have been

either destroyed or, as in the case of the nave vaults, so altered as to give no impression of Jodok's style. Jodok seems also to have taken over as Master of Works at Old St Peter's, Strasbourg, at about the same time; there he built a new choir, which was vaulted in 1475 but has been completely altered. Only the spire of the small turret on the roof survives. There is stylistic but not documentary evidence for his contribution in the 1460s to the cloister at Basle Minster. His mason's mark was a large M with a cross over the centre.

BIBLIOGRAPHY

Basler Münsterbauverein: *Baugeschichte des Basler Münsters* (Basle, 1895)

J. Julier: *Studien zur spätgotischen Baukunst am Oberrhein*, Heidelberger Kunstgeschichtliche Abhandlungen, n. s. 13 (Heidelberg, 1978)

B. Schock-Werner: *Das Strassburger Münster im 15. Jahrhundert* (Cologne, 1983)

BARBARA SCHOCK-WERNER

Dou, Gerrit [Gerard] (*b* Leiden, 7 April 1613; *d* Leiden, *bur* 9 Feb 1675). Dutch painter. The first and most famous member of the group of artists referred to as the LEIDEN 'FINE' PAINTERS, he specialized in small-format paintings, the details and surfaces of which are carefully observed and meticulously rendered. He was greatly praised as a painter of artificial light by Samuel van Hoogstraten in 1678, and he was responsible for popularizing both the night scene and the 'niche' format, pictorial devices ultimately derived from the art of his famous master, Rembrandt. Dou used them in images of ordinary people ostensibly engaged in mundane activities.

1. Life and work. 2. Symbolism and meaning. 3. Working methods and technique. 4. Critical reception and posthumous reputation.

1. LIFE AND WORK. Dou was the youngest son of a glazier who probably belonged to the Dutch Reformed Church. From an early age he was trained in his father's profession, first with the engraver Bartolomäus Dolendo, then with the glazier Pieter Couwenhorn. Dou is mentioned in the records of the Leiden glaziers' guild in 1625 and 1627, the years in which he worked on a commission to repair and make new windows for the churchwardens of Oestgeest. On 14 February 1628 he was sent to Rembrandt to study painting. According to Orlers, Dou was an 'excellent master' by the time he left Rembrandt's studio three years later, and his work was widely admired. He was a founder-member of the Leiden Guild of St Luke and served as ensign (*vaendrager*) in the local militia company, a position indicative of his elevated social status and his bachelorhood. He died a wealthy man and was buried in the St Pieterskerk.

In the 1630s Dou painted three types of picture: *tronies* (uncommissioned physiognomic studies), portraits and single, full-length figures. *Tronies* were popular in Rembrandt's Leiden circle, and the same elderly models who posed for Dou, often in exotic dress, were also depicted by Rembrandt and Jan Lievens. Portraits, which comprise most of Dou's early work, were an essential source of income for many artists and may have been so for Dou, at least initially. His sitters are usually shown in half- or three-quarter length, conservatively dressed and, for the most part, lacking animation. The third type of picture featured figures absorbed in or distracted from their everyday activities. His earliest dated painting, the *Young*

1. Gerrit Dou: *Village Grocer*, oil on panel, 380×280 mm, 1647 (Paris, Musée du Louvre)

Violinist (1637; Edinburgh, N.G.), is an example of this type. The thinly and finely painted surface, the prevalence of meticulously observed and rendered still-life objects of various materials, the subtle chiaroscuro and interest in light reflections and effects and the arrested movement are characteristic of Dou's early style.

By the mid-1640s Dou was painting fewer portraits while enlarging his genre repertory. The signed and dated *Village Grocer* (1647; Paris, Louvre; see fig. 1) marks the change. The large number of figures in this painting is unusual for Dou, whereas the inclusion of accumulated still-life accessories is common in his art. He also introduced the so-called 'niche' format into his painting, a device previously reserved almost exclusively for portraiture. In this favoured format, figures and objects are placed beyond the framing arch of a *trompe-l'oeil* window, giving the artist an opportunity to display his skills of illusionism and providing a simple aid to spatial organization: the window ledge functions both to establish the foreground plane, opening up the pictorial space behind, and to support objects that seem to project forward into the viewer's space.

From the early 1650s Dou's paintings attain a certain monumentality. His figures become larger in scale, his choice and arrangement of still-life objects more judicious. In such works as *The Doctor* (1653; Vienna, Ksthist. Mus.) or the *Woman with a Basket* (1657; Waddesdon Manor, Bucks, NT) he meticulously rendered the frozen attitude of a figure in its environment, the surface qualities of varied materials and the descriptive properties of light. A painted curtain draped across the picture functions like the niche by symbolically separating the deceptively naturalistic figures and action from the real world. Dou's tendency to place equal emphasis on all the elements in his paintings is in striking contrast to the more unified narrative and integrated atmosphere presented in the contemporary genre scenes of Gerard ter Borch (ii), Pieter de Hooch and Johannes Vermeer. By the late 1650s Dou had developed his interest in light effects by translating two types of subject-matter into night scenes: artificially-lit genre scenes and, more commonly, single female figures standing at a window, peering into darkness and illuminated only by a candle or lantern. His *Woman Laying a Table* (Frankfurt am Main, Städel. Kstinst.) is an exercise in virtuosity in which a lantern, a candle and a fire are depicted together, each throwing light in its characteristic way.

Two further types of subject-matter were introduced in his paintings of the 1660s. First, he decorated the shutters designed to protect his paintings from dust and strong light with still-life paintings, only a few of which survive. They are known as *bedriegertjes* (scenes populated with illusionistically-rendered objects meant to deceive the eye). In the *Still-life* (Dresden, Gemäldegal. Alte Meister) that once protected a night scene set in a cellar, the emphatically tangible objects, some of which seem to spill out into the spectator's space, are placed in a niche. As in his genre scenes, an illusionistic curtain in front of the niche refers to the actual practice of using curtains to protect paintings and heightens the *trompe-l'oeil* effect of the image. Secondly, he explored the possibilities of depicting the nude. As the subject of an independent painting, the nude was rare in the north in the 17th century and was usually restricted to drawings, prints and a few history paintings. The four known nudes by Dou (three in St Petersburg, Hermitage; one in The Hague, Rijksdienst Beeld. Kst.) are unidealized and unclassical; there are no attributes to identify them as specific personages or personifications, nor are they engaged in a particular activity. Dou's last dated works are from 1672. In his late style, exemplified by *The Dentist* (Dresden, Gemäldegal. Alte Meister), the still-life objects are masterfully painted, but the last few paintings lack Dou's earlier microscopic detail, and the overall finish tends to be hard.

2. SYMBOLISM AND MEANING. Dou's paintings depict the everyday life of the Dutch bourgeoisie, without the obvious picturesque trappings of a rustic or theatrical nature. Many of the popular images that he created and developed, however, contain veiled symbolism, usually derived from traditional moralizing or didactic themes, allowing them to be read on more than one level. In keeping with the rhetorical character of Dutch representations of artists in the 17th century, Dou presented himself as teacher and admonisher in his *Self-portrait Aged Fifty* (1663; Kansas City, MO, Nelson–Atkins Mus. A.;

2. Gerrit Dou: *Self-portrait Aged Fifty*, oil on panel, 571×404 mm, 1663 (Kansas City, MO, Nelson–Atkins Museum of Art)

see fig. 2). The *Old Woman Peeling Apples* (Berlin, Ge-mäldegal.), surrounded by attributes of her domestic industry, can be seen as the exemplar of the pious and virtuous life. The objects in the *Still-life* in Dresden are primarily associated with *vanitas* depictions, which empha-size the transitoriness of earthly life, in keeping with the strong tradition for such themes in Leiden. Yet some of Dou's paintings are iconographically more complex: for example, his famous *Triptych* (known through a copy by William Joseph Laquy, Amsterdam, Rijkmus.), which came to be known as *The Nursery*, has been interpreted as representing Aristotle's three stages of learning—nature, teaching and practice. He also used the still-lifes on the shutters of his paintings to comment on or add to the meaning of the picture inside. The visual richness of his imagery and the possibilities of multi-layered interpretation must have played a large part in the appeal of his paintings to contemporary audiences.

3. WORKING METHODS AND TECHNIQUE. Sandrart, with Pieter van Laer, visited Dou *c.* 1639, but his descrip-tion of his studio and his working method included in the *Teutsche Academie*, written some 35 years later, is suspect. In it he claimed that Dou needed eyeglasses from the age of 30 and took days to paint the smallest detail; that he was extremely fastidious concerning his tools, materials and working conditions; and that he was a failed portrait painter because of his slow working method.

Dou worked on oak panels, usually of small dimensions and often prepared with a warm, reddish-brown ground. The palette in his earliest works consists of aqua, lilac, rose and green, with the gradual introduction of gold. These colours, applied in thin glazes, and the enveloping chiaroscuro echo those in Rembrandt's Leiden paintings. By the mid-1640s Dou had changed to saturated golds, reds and blues, although he still frequently retained the warm chiaroscuro learnt in Rembrandt's studio. His last paintings are marked by strong local colour and by a more roughly painted surface, particularly in the skin and clothing.

Only a few drawings have been attributed, somewhat controversially, to Dou, who apparently, unlike his master and many of his contemporaries, did not use them regularly as part of the preparatory process. Sumowski has identified what he believes to be a rare preliminary sketch in pencil (England, priv. col., see Sumowski, 1980, no. 531) for the painting of the *Venison Shop* (London, N.G.) and an autograph copy in red and white chalk (Paris, Louvre) after a lost picture of a *Woman Cooking Sausages*, which, according to the inscription of the drawing's *verso*, was sent to the Elector of Mainz in 1650. The few drawings surely by the artist are independent portrait studies, such as the signed and dated *Portrait of the Artist's Mother* (1638; Paris, Louvre) and the signed and dated portrait of '*Anne Spiering*' (1660; priv. col., see Sumowksi, 1980, no. 530).

The precise role played by pupils in Dou's studio practice is not known, but from as early as 1645 he attracted a large number of students, among them his nephew Domenicus van Tol, Rans van Mieris (i), Pieter van Slingeland, Godfried Schalken and possibly Gabriel Metsu.

4. CRITICAL RECEPTION AND POSTHUMOUS REPU-TATION. Dou's ability as a painter was recognized early in his career. In Angel's address to the artists of Leiden in 1641, published the following year, Dou's painting style was held up as a paradigm to his fellow painters. He was also lauded as a contemporary artist who, like the great masters of antiquity, had a patron (Pieter Spiering) willing to pay handsomely for the right of first refusal to his paintings. Spiering (*d* 1652) was the son of the most important tapestry manufacturer in Delft and was Swedish minister to The Hague from the mid-1630s to his death. He ostensibly bought Dou's paintings for Queen Christina, but the works were clearly more to Spiering's taste for the finished than to Christina's taste for the Italianate. Dou charged for his paintings at the rate of one Flemish pound per hour. According to Sandrart, his small paintings sold for the then substantial price of 600–1000 Dutch guilders.

Dou's fame was international by 1660. When the Dutch States General decided to make a gift to Charles II on his accession to the English throne, Dou was appointed an appraiser for the States and, in addition, the States acquired three paintings from him for the new monarch. When the paintings given by the Dutch were exhibited at Whitehall, London, Charles singled out Dou, Titian and Elsheimer for praise. Dou's painting skills impressed Charles so much that he invited the artist to his court; Dou, however, chose to remain in Leiden. Visits to Dou's studio by such foreign scholars and aristocrats as the Dane Ole Borch (1662), the Frenchman Balthasar de Monconys (1663) and Co-simo III de' Medici (1669) are further indications of his popularity. In addition, a painting by Dou appeared in the inventory of 1662 of the Archduke Leopold William of Austria, who had been Governor of the Netherlands from 1646 to 1656.

Dou was no less highly regarded at home. In July 1669 the Burgomasters of Leiden commissioned a painting by Dou, 'whose art was famous and held in great esteem'; the commission was later withdrawn, however. Eleven paintings by Dou appeared in the collection of François de la Boë Sylvius, professor of chemistry and medical science at Leiden University, on his death in 1672. Dou's greatest patron in the second half of his career was Johan de Bye, a prominent Leiden citizen and pious Remonstrant. De Monconys, who visited de Bye during his Leiden sojourn, saw there 'a large quantity of paintings by Dou'. On 18 September 1665 de Bye exhibited 27 of his paintings by Dou, representing all types of subject-matter from every phase of Dou's career.

Dou's students and followers varied in talent and in what they took from their master. Van Mieris, whom Dou considered the 'prince of his pupils', derived his style from Dou and even amplified Dou's polished surface finish; Pieter van Slingeland was primarily interested in Dou's subject-matter; van Tol was content merely to repeat and imitate his compositions; and Schalken single-mindedly pursued one aspect of Dou's work, the candlelight scenes. Moreover, the work of many minor Leiden artists, for example Jacob van Spreeuwen (*b* 1661) and Jan Adriaensz. van Staveren (*c.* 1625–after 1668), reveals the influence of Dou, although there is no evidence that they worked directly with him. The popularity of Dou's pictures, reflected in market prices, the demand of collectors and the influence of his style, pictorial devices and subject-matter continued to grow well into the 19th century.

BIBLIOGRAPHY

J. Orlers: *Beschrijvinge der stadt Leyden* (2/Leiden, 1641)

P. Angel: *Lof der schilder-konst* (Leiden, 1642/*R* Utrecht, 1969, facs. Amsterdam, 1972), p. 56

J. von Sandrart: *Teutsche Academie* (1675–9); ed. A. R. Peltzer (1925), pp. 195–6

S. van Hoogstraten: *Inleyding tot de hooge schoole der schilderkonst, anders de zichtbaere werelt* [Introduction to the academy of painting, or the visible world] (Rotterdam, 1678/*R* Soest, 1969, Ann Arbor, 1980), pp. 262, 268

J. Smith: *A Catalogue Raisonné of the Works of the Most Eminent Dutch, Flemish and French Painters*, i (London, 1829), and suppl. (1842)

W. Martin: *Het leven en de werken van Gerrit Dou beschouwd met het schildersleven van zijn tijd* (Leiden, 1901); abridged Eng. trans. by C. Bell (London, 1902); expanded Fr. trans. by L. Dimier (Paris, 1911)

C. Hofstede de Groot: *Hollandischen Mäler*, i (1907)

W. Martin: *Gerard Dou*, Klass. Kst Gesamtausgaben (Stuttgart and Berlin, 1913)

A. Wheelock jr: 'A Reappraisal of Gerard Dou's Reputation', *The William A. Clark Collection* (Washington, DC, 1978), pp. 60–67

W. Sumowski: *Drawings of the Rembrandt School*, iii (New York, 1980)

——: *Gemälde der Rembrandtschüler*, i (Landau, 1983)

Leidse fijnschilders: Van Gerrit Dou tot Frans van Mieris de jonge, 1630–1760 (exh. cat., ed. E. J. Sluijter and others; Leiden, Stedel. Mus. Lakenhal, 1988)

De Hollandse fijnschilders: Van Gerard Dou tot Adriaen van der Werff (exh. cat. by P. Hecht, Amsterdam, Rijksmus., 1989)

R. Baer: *The Paintings of Gerrit Dou* (diss., New York, Inst. F.A., 1990)

RONNI BAER

Douaihy, Saliba (*b* Ehden, Lebanon, 14 Sept 1912). American painter and stained-glass artist, of Lebanese birth. After an apprenticeship with the Lebanese painter Habib Srour (1860–1938) in Beirut, he studied from 1932 to 1936 at the Ecole des Beaux-Arts, Paris. In 1934 he received the top award for drawing at the school and later exhibited his work at the Salon des Artistes Français. After graduating in 1936, he returned to Lebanon, opening a studio in Beirut, and becoming well known in the early 1940s for his frescoes in the Maronite church at Diman. At the same time his paintings of Lebanese life and the countryside came to public notice when he exhibited at the gallery of the Hotel St–Georges, Beirut, though by the late 1940s he had begun to simplify the style of his work. In 1950 he moved to New York, where his paintings became increasingly abstract, consisting of flat forms of brilliant colour with hard straight edges. Although he was influenced by the artistic life around him, and by his acquaintance with Rothko, Hans Hofmann and Ad Reinhardt, he did not join any group or movement. He became an American citizen in 1963 and in 1966 confirmed his reputation with a one-man show at the Contemporaries Gallery, New York. He also continued to produce representational religious works, for example in 1955 painting 27 panels for the newly constructed church of Mar Hanna near Zgharta in Lebanon. In 1971 he worked in stained glass at the Maronite convent church at Annaya in Lebanon, where he employed for the first time his own technique in which the coloured glass was built up in overlapping layers, without lead bars. A further commission, completed in 1978, resulted in 65 stained-glass windows for the church of Our Lady of the Cedars of Lebanon, at Jamaica Plain, near Boston, MA. In 1975 he left the USA and in the 1980s worked in Paris.

BIBLIOGRAPHY

E. Lahoud: *Contemporary Art in Lebanon* (Beirut and New York, 1974), pp. 65–72

The Art of Saliba Douaihy: A Retrospective Exhibition (exh. cat. by M. M. Domit, Raleigh, NC Mus. A., 1978)

Lebanon–The Artist's View: 200 Years of Lebanese Painting (exh. cat., British Lebanese Association; London, Barbican Cent., 1989), pp. 111–14

S. J. VERNOIT

Doublure. Ornamental lining, often of leather or parchment, on the inside face of a book cover (*see* BOOKBINDING, §I). ☐

Douce, Francis (*b* London, 13 July 1757; *d* London, 30 March 1834). English collector. He abandoned the legal profession to devote himself to intellectual pursuits: in 1779 he was elected to the Society of Antiquaries, London, and at the British Library, London, studied art history and acquired a considerable knowledge of incunabula and medieval manuscripts. In 1807 he joined the Department of Manuscripts at the British Museum, London, of which he later became Keeper. In 1811 a dispute with the trustees caused him to resign his post. In 1823 Douce inherited some £50,000 from the sculptor Joseph Nollekens and started to form large collections of medieval manuscripts and incunabula and drawings and prints of the 16th to 18th centuries; in the latter field he had a predilection for scenes of sorcery, and grotesque and macabre subjects. He had a particular interest in medieval society and in Classical art, on which he collected an important body of published works, by, for example, Winckelmann (in French translation); he also owned an edition of *Antiquités étrusques, grecques et romaines* by Pierre François Hugues d'Hancarville. Although his own numerous manuscripts contain collections of unstructured notes and numerous plans for books, his only published work (1807) was a compilation of early illustrations of Shakespeare. He bequeathed his books and his collections of manuscripts, prints and drawings, and coins and medals to the Bodleian Library, Oxford. In 1863 the prints and drawings, among them Dürer's *Pleasures of the World* and Grünewald's *Elderly Woman with Clasped Hands*, were transferred to the Ashmolean Museum, Oxford.

WRITINGS

Illustrations of Shakespeare and Ancient Manners, 2 vols (London, 1807)

BIBLIOGRAPHY

[S. W. Singer]: Obituary, *Gent. Mag.*, n.s. 3, ii (1834), pp. 213–17

'Francis Douce Centenary', *Bodleian Q. Rec.*, vii/81 (1934)

A. N. L. Munby: *Connoisseurs and Medieval Miniatures, 1750–1850* (Oxford, 1972), pp. 35–56

Dürer to Cézanne: Northern Drawings from the Ashmolean Museum, Oxford (exh. cat. by C. Lloyd, New Brunswick, NJ, Rutgers U., Zimmerli A. Mus.; Cleveland, OH, A. Mus.; 1982–3), pp. vi–vii

The Douce Legacy: An Exhibition to Commemorate the 150th Anniversary of the Bequest of Francis Douce, 1757–1834 (exh. cat., Oxford, Bodleian Lib., 1984)

PASCAL GRIENER

Doucet, Jacques(-Antoine) (*b* Paris, 19 Feb 1853; *d* Paris, 17 July 1929). French couturier, patron, collector and bibliophile. He joined his family's clothing business in 1875 and played a central role in its development into one of the premier *haute couture* houses in Paris. He may initially have bought art for public relations purposes;

however, it became a central interest in his life, partly, it seems, because the superior exercise of taste allowed him to compensate for social disappointments. Following a fashion that was already quite widespread by 1880, he built up an outstanding collection of 18th-century French art and design, which he housed in a magnificent 18th-century style hôtel in the Rue Spontini: it included Jean-Honoré Fragonard's *Le Feu aux poudres* (Paris, Louvre), Jean-Siméon Chardin's *House of Cards* (Winterthur, Samml. Oskar Reinhart) and Jean-Baptiste Perronneau's portrait of *Abraham Van Robais* (Paris, Louvre). When, apparently for sentimental reasons, Doucet sold the entire collection at auction in 1912, the results were sensational. A pastel by Maurice-Quentin de La Tour, the portrait of *Duval de l'Epinoy* (Lisbon, Mus. Gulbenkian), broke the sale record held by Jean-François Millet's *The Angelus* and the total proceeds of 13 million francs far outstripped all precedents. After 1912, Doucet changed direction. He became a major patron of innovative interior design and emerged after World War I as one of the most discerning and adventurous collectors of contemporary art in Paris. He commissioned a number of young designers, including Eileen Gray, Paul Iribe (1883–1935), Joseph Csáky and Pierre-Emile Legrain, to produce furniture and fittings for his apartment in the Avenue du Bois, and repeated this exercise on a grander scale in 1925 when he constructed a studio attached to his house in Neuilly. This suite of rooms became a showpiece for his collection of modern art, which ranged from Cézanne (*Old Woman with a Rosary*; London, N.G.), Seurat and Henri Rousseau (the *Snakecharmer*, Paris, Louvre) to Max Ernst and Picabia. A place of honour was accorded to the *Demoiselles d'Avignon* (New York, MOMA), which Doucet bought directly from Picasso in 1924 for 25,000 francs. In this acquisition, as in virtually all his activities, Doucet followed specialist advice. Between 1920 and 1924 he employed André Breton to inform him on the purchase of both works of art and manuscripts; and many other writers, including Pierre Reverdy, Louis Aragon and Max Jacob, received subsidies from him for similar services. In this respect Doucet functioned selfconsciously as a traditional princely patron. As part of his grand, comprehensive approach to his first collection, he had conceived the notion of systematically documenting it. This project rapidly expanded into the creation of a scholarly library, complemented by collections of drawings and prints, which could be consulted by the public. From 1911 the library was also the base for a major scholarly initiative subsidized by Doucet, the *Répertoire d'art et d'archéologie* (Paris, 1910–). In 1917 Doucet donated his remarkable library to the University of Paris (the Bibliothèque Doucet). After his death, this gift was complemented by that of the project that had succeeded it, the Bibliothèque Littéraire. This was a collection of rare editions and manuscripts relating to the modern movement and was based on guidelines established by the writer André Suarès (1868–1948), who was Doucet's adviser and confidant from 1913 onwards. In the late 1920s Doucet also established, through the work of Léon Moussinac (1890–1964) and his wife Jeanne Moussinac, one of the first important collections of writings on the cinema. The Bibliothèque Littéraire combined literary with artistic patronage, since the items were sumptuously bound by Legrain and Rose Adler (1890–1989).

BIBLIOGRAPHY
Collection de M. J. D. (sale cat., Paris, Gal. Drouot, 16–17 May 1906)
E. Dacier: *La Collection Jacques Doucet* (Paris, 1911)
——: 'La Collection Jacques Doucet', *Rev. A. Anc. & Mod.*, xxxi (1912), pp. 321–38
Collection Jacques Doucet (sale cat., Paris, Gal. Georges Petit, 5–8 June 1912)
Clément-Janin: 'Quelques souvenirs sur Jacques Doucet', *Candide* (Paris, 2 Jan 1930)
M. Dormoy: *Jacques Doucet* (Paris, 1930)
Collection Jacques Doucet (sale cat., Paris, Gal. Drouot, 28 Nov 1930)
M. Dormoy: *Jacques Doucet* (Abbeville, 1931)
J.-F. Revel: 'Jacques Doucet: Couturier et collectionneur', *L'Oeil*, lxxxiv (1961), pp. 44–51, 81, 106
Ancienne collection Jacques Doucet (sale cat., Paris, Gal. Drouot, 28 Nov 1972)
Ancienne collection Jacques Doucet (sale cat., Paris, Galliera, 21 March 1974)
F. Chapon: *Mystère et splendeurs de Jacques Doucet* (Paris, 1984)

MALCOLM GEE

Doudelet, Charles (*b* Lille, 8 Feb 1861; *d* Ghent, 7 Jan 1938). Belgian painter, sculptor, illustrator and stage designer. He studied music at the Koninklijk Muziekconservatorium and sculpture at the Gewerbeschule, Ghent (after 1877). He visited Paris in 1887 and Italy in 1890, with a grant from the city of Ghent. He was deeply impressed by the masters of the Quattrocento, and was encouraged to take up painting after meeting Constantin Meunier (1891). He painted Symbolist scenes and was influenced by Art Nouveau. After exhibiting his work with Les XX in Brussels (1893), he made decorative panels for Oostakker Castle.

As an illustrator Doudelet worked on Pol De Mont's *Van Jezus* (Antwerp, 1897) and books by Maurice Maeterlinck, for example *Douze chansons* (Paris, 1896) and *Pelléas et Mélisande* (Brussels, 1892). He illustrated the periodicals *Réveil* (1895–6), *De Vlaamsche school*, *Mercure de France*, *Woord en beeld* and *Elseviers maandblad*. In 1912 he exhibited work in Brussels in the Internationale tentoonstelling van religieuze kunst, and in Rotterdam. In 1914 he published *La Guerre et la paix*, which was illustrated with 18 lithographs. Doudelet also designed theatrical sets for Maeterlinck, for example *L'Oiseau bleu* (first performed in Moscow, at the Art Theatre, on 30 Sept 1908 in a production by Konstantin Stanislavsky). He shared with Maeterlinck a fascination for the figure of the medieval Flemish poet Jan van Ruusbroec (1293–1381), who was the subject of five drawings (engr. by E. Pellens for *La Revue blanche*, Paris, 1896), a painting (*c.* 1896; Brussels, Ruusbroecgenootschap col.) and a sculpture (*c.* 1927; lost). After returning to Italy in 1900 to prepare a study of the history of typography for the Belgian government, he stayed in Florence until 1925. In 1989 the 'Cabinet Charles Doudelet' was opened in the Museum Arnold Vander Haeghen in Ghent.

BIBLIOGRAPHY
F. De Smet: 'Charles Doudelet', *Gand A.*, ii (1923), pp. 61–9
J. Crick: *Leven en werken onzer beeldende Kunstenaars* (Ghent, 1933), p. 178
A. Ampe: 'Karel Doudelet en zijn Ruusbroec-voorstellingen', *Jb.: Kon. Mus. S. Kst.* (1983), pp. 261–92

JEAN-PIERRE DE BRUYN

Douffet, Gérard (*bapt* Liège, 6 Aug 1594; *d* Liège, 1660). Flemish painter. He was trained in Liège by Jean Taulier (*d*?1636), probably one of the late Mannerists of the school of Lambert Lombard. It seems likely that he next went to a painter in Dinant known only as Perpète. Abry recorded that Douffet worked in Rubens's workshop from 1612 to 1614; this is doubtful, though he probably did study in Antwerp. After 1614 Douffet probably went to Italy, and in 1620 and 1622 he is recorded, with Valentin de Boulogne, in Rome. He knew such Caravaggisti as Bartolomeo Manfredi and Nicolas Tournier. No work from this period is known.

Douffet's oeuvre consists of only about 20 known paintings. The earliest is the *Finding of the True Cross* (1624; Munich, Alte Pin.). In this he appears uninfluenced by the Rubensian Baroque style of painting then current in the Spanish Netherlands, a surprising fact considering the proximity of the town of Liège to the Flemish border.

Gérard Douffet: *Visit of Pope Nicholas V to the Tomb of St Francis*, oil on canvas, 4.04×3.47 m, 1627 (Munich, Alte Pinakothek)

Instead he introduced Italian-style Caravaggism to Liège. This canvas seems closer to Simon Vouet than to Valentin and the other followers of Manfredi, which is one of the reasons for rejecting the identification of Douffet with the MASTER OF THE JUDGEMENT OF SOLOMON (*see* MASTERS, ANONYMOUS, AND MONOGRAMMISTS, §I). The *Visit of Pope Nicholas V to the Tomb of St Francis* (1627; Munich, Alte Pin.; see fig.) is Douffet's most important work. This large and enigmatic picture was the first explicit manifestation of Counter-Reformation painting in Liège. Although theatrical, the work is scholarly and is more restrained in its Caravaggesque naturalism; it clearly reflects the strong classicizing style of painting practised in Liège ever since Lambert Lombard. *Christ Appearing to St James the Greater* (1633; Schleissheim, Altes Schloss) is Douffet's last significant work. While the harsh contrasts are still reminiscent of the Caravaggisti, the monumental fullness of the forms and the imposing architectural setting seem to refer to the Bolognese school.

In 1634 Douffet was made official painter to the Prince Bishop of Liège, Ferdinand Wittelsbach of Bavaria (*d* 1650). He was then at the peak of his fame, but this soon declined as his art weakened and became repetitious. Among his late works are the *Deposition* (Kornelimünster, St Kornelius), which is very Flemish in spirit, the triptych of the *Baptism of Christ* (Verviers, St Remacle), *Vulcan's Forge* (1645) and *Judah and Tamar* (both Liège, Mus. A. Wallon). His last known work is the *Raising of the Cross* (*c.* 1655; Nantes, Mus. B.-A.); painted while Douffet was suffering from illness, this large altarpiece lacks the expressive force of his earlier paintings. In contrast to the variable quality of his subject pictures, Douffet's portraits are of a consistently high quality (e.g. *Ferdinand of Bavaria*, ?1634; Dusseldorf, Kstmus.). They are characterized by very strong modelling, another reflection of his Caravaggesque training. Douffet was a major influence on most of the 17th-century painters in Liège, including his only known pupil, Bertholet Flémal.

BIBLIOGRAPHY

L. Abry: *Les Hommes illustrés de la nation liégeoise*, ed. H. Helbig and S. Bormans (Liège, 1867)
J. Helbig: *La Peinture au pays de Liège et sur les bords de la Meuse* (Liège, 1903)
P.-Y. Kairis: *Le Peintre Gérard Douffet (1594–1660): Fondateur de l'école liégeoise du XVIIe siècle* (diss., U. Liège, 1982)
E. Larsen: *Seventeenth-century Flemish Painting* (Freren, 1985), pp. 261–4
J. Hendrick: *La Peinture au pays de Liège: XVIe, XVIIe, XVIIIe siècles* (Liège, 1987)

PIERRE-YVES KAIRIS

Dougga [anc. Thugga]. Site of one of the best-preserved Roman towns in Africa, built on a plateau overlooking the valley of Oued Khalled in north-western Tunisia. A fine collection of archaeological material has been found there. Dougga dates back to the earliest phase of Libyan antiquity and certainly belonged to the kingdom of Numidia long before the reign of Masinissa (*d* 148 BC); writing on the invasion of Agathalus at the end of the 4th century BC, Diodorus Siculus mentioned the king Ailymas, whose domain included the territory of 'Tebagga'. During the Second Punic War between Rome and Carthage (218–201 BC), Dougga was under the Carthaginians, but it was won back by Masinissa and retained by his successors until the death of Juba I in 46 BC. Of the Numidian town there remain the megalithic wall (4th century BC), the dolmens and the Mausoleum of Atban, one of the finest Libyo-Punic monuments in North Africa; the bilingual inscription from it is now in London (BM). There are also some stelai (2nd–1st century BC), which provide evidence of the worship of Ba'al Hammon, the principal god of the Carthaginians; their inscriptions are a source of valuable information for religious beliefs and the Punic and Libyan languages.

After the battle of Thapsus in 46 BC Julius Caesar annexed the kingdom of Juba I, and Dougga became part of Africa Nova. A settlement developed at the foot of the plateau where the indigenous community lived. In the 1st century AD the forum and the market were built as tangible signs of the Roman presence at Dougga. For generations the two communities lived side by side, each keeping its own administrative organization, beliefs and customs. For this reason, and because of the uneven terrain, the plan of the town did not follow the normal grid pattern: the streets of Dougga are winding and do not form any right angles. The two communities finally merged, and in AD 195 they built a temple to Saturn over a temple to the Punic Ba'al. The process of Romanization was slow but profound; in AD 205 Dougga became a *municipium*, and in AD 261 it was declared a *colonia*.

Dougga reached the height of its territorial expansion under the Antonines and Severans (AD 138–235), when it covered more than 25 ha; its population seems to have been between 5000 and 10,000. The town profited a great deal from local benefactors; for example, P. Marcius Quadratus had the theatre built between AD 168 and 169, while the capitolium was constructed between AD 166 and 167 at the expense of two brothers of the Marcii family. The former building was built into the hillside at the top of the city slope and could seat over 3000 spectators; the latter is an imposing Corinthian tetrastyle building, the frieze of its portico bearing a dedication to the Capitoline triad and supporting a pediment in which is represented the imperial apotheosis. Adjoining the capitolium is a Temple of Mercury from the time of Commodus (*reg* AD 180–92); this faces the Square of the Wind Rose, which has a 3rd-century AD compass rose engraved on its pavement. The Temple of Caelestis (Severan) is set to the west of the forum in a unique crescent-shaped enclosure (w. 50 m) with a circular portico around it. There are also two arches of Severan date, the Licinian Baths of Imperial type (AD 259–68) and some magnificent houses decorated with superb mosaics depicting mythological scenes, as well as scenes of drinking and chariot racing (mostly in Tunis, Mus. N., Bardo; *see* AFRICA, fig. 115).

Christianity has left only the remains of a modest church (late 4th or early 5th century AD). In the 4th century AD and especially after the Vandal conquest the decline of Dougga was inevitable, despite the efforts of the Byzantines from AD 539 to fortify areas of the town.

BIBLIOGRAPHY

C. Poinssot: *Les Ruines de Dougga* (Tunis, 1958)
G.-C. Picard: *La Civilisation de l'afrique romaine* (Paris, 1959)
J. G. Février: 'La Constitution municipale de Dougga à l'époque numide', *Mél. Carthage* (1964–5), pp. 85–91
W. Seston: 'Les "Portes" de Thugga à la constitution de Carthage', *Rev. Hist. T.*, ccxxxvii (April–June 1967), pp. 277–94

M'HAMED FANTAR

Doughty, Thomas (*b* Philadelphia, PA, 19 July 1793; *d* New York, 24 July 1856). American painter. Doughty belonged to the generation of American landscape painters that included Thomas Cole and Asher B. Durand and was an important precursor of the HUDSON RIVER SCHOOL. Basically self-taught, he worked as a leather currier in Philadelphia, PA, before becoming an artist. In 1816 Doughty exhibited *Landscape—Original* (untraced) at the Pennsylvania Academy of the Fine Arts. Four years later he listed himself in the Philadelphia directory as a landscape painter. Old Master landscapes (or copies) exhibited at the Pennsylvania Academy, together with contemporary European paintings and compositions by fellow Philadelphians Thomas Birch and Joshua Shaw, access to major private collections (such as those of his patron Robert Gilmor jr of Baltimore, MD, and Joseph Bonaparte of Bordentown, NJ), engravings and artists' manuals all contributed to his knowledge of the European landscape tradition. Among Doughty's earliest surviving landscapes are *View of Baltimore from Beech Hill, the Seat of Robert Gilmor jr* (1822; Baltimore, MD, Mus. A.) and *Landscape with Pool* (*c.* 1823; Philadelphia, PA Acad. F.A.), which show his mastery of atmospheric effects and command of his medium. They also reveal in their Claudean compositions the artist's familiarity with the then popular aesthetic of the Picturesque. Although Doughty occasionally depicted cityscapes (*View of the Waterworks on the Schuylkill*, 1826; priv. col., see 1973 exh. cat., no. 7), he is best known for his romantic interpretations of sublime American scenery, which were often poetic evocations rather than faithful portraits of specific places (e.g. *On the Beach*, 1827–8; Albany, NY, Inst. Hist. & A.).

A frequent exhibitor at the Pennsylvania Academy, Doughty was elected an Academician in 1824. He also showed regularly in New York and Boston. The works he created during the 1820s are considered to be among his finest. They document his travels along the Eastern seaboard in search of picturesque and sublime subjects and include sites in New York, Massachusetts and Connecticut as well as Pennsylvania and Delaware. During the 1830s Doughty lived for periods in Boston, Philadelphia and New York. In 1835 he painted *In Nature's Wonderland* (1835; Detroit, MI, Inst. A.), one of his most affecting compositions and the embodiment of the romantic aesthetic in its depiction of the solitary hunter standing in awe of nature's grandeur. In 1837 Doughty made his first trip to Europe. The so-called *Tintern Abbey* (*c.* 1838; Washington, DC, Corcoran Gal. A.), although similar in composition to *In Nature's Wonderland*, shows the impact of this English sojourn not only in the choice of subject (a Gothic ruin in a moonlit landscape) but also in its painterly style and tonal handling of colour.

Doughty travelled even more frequently in the 1840s, as he tried to make a living from his art at a time when Cole, Durand and other younger artists were in the ascendancy. After a second trip to Britain and the Continent in the mid-1840s, he settled in Manhattan, where he remained until his death, except for brief stays in upstate New York and New Jersey. The final years of Doughty's life were marred by a decline in his health, reputation and income. Although he was still capable of producing an effective work such as *Autumn on the Hudson* (*c.* 1850; Washington, DC, Corcoran Gal. A.), the paintings from late in his career generally show a deterioration in his abilities. Nevertheless, his life-time's contribution to the development of American landscape was substantial.

UNPUBLISHED SOURCES
H. N. Doughty: *Biographical Sketch of Thomas Doughty* (transcript, Washington, DC, N. Mus. Amer. A., 1969)

BIBLIOGRAPHY
F. H. Goodyear jr: *The Life and Art of Thomas Doughty* (MA thesis, Newark, U. DE, 1969)
Thomas Doughty, 1793–1856 (exh. cat. by F. H. Goodyear jr, Philadelphia, PA Acad. F.A., 1973)
Views and Visions: American Landscape before 1830 (exh. cat. by E. J. Nygren and others, Washington, DC, Corcoran Gal. A., 1986)

EDWARD J. NYGREN

Doughty, William (*b* York, 1 Aug 1757; *d* Lisbon, 1780 or 1782). English painter and engraver. His earliest known works are three etchings dated 1772–3, after portrait drawings by such painters as Thomas Barrow (*fl* 1770–1819) and Lewis Vaslet (*d* 1808). In 1775 William Mason, poet and Precentor of York Minster, wrote to Joshua Reynolds recommending Doughty as a pupil. Reynolds agreed, and Doughty was enrolled at the Royal Academy Schools, London, on 8 April 1775, remaining in Reynolds's house until 1778. During this time he sent five portraits to the Academy, including perhaps his finest work, an oval bust-length portrait of *William Mason* (exh. RA 1778; York, C.A.G.). His oval bust of *William Whitehead*, Poet Laureate (?exh. RA 1778; London, V&A), was engraved in 1787 for Mason's edition of Whitehead's *Works* (pubd 1788), and Mason's patronage can also be detected in the commission, probably of 1777, to paint a posthumous likeness of the poet Thomas Gray (untraced). In 1778 Doughty visited York and Ireland, but the only memorable result was the half-length portrait of *Miss Sisson* (Dublin, N.G.) with fashionably piled-up hair, holding an open book, a striking composition in spite of its obvious debt to Reynolds. Doughty returned to London, where, in 1779, he settled in Little Titchfield Street, Cavendish Square, and executed five powerful mezzotints after pictures by Reynolds: *Mary Palmer*, *Admiral Keppel*, *Dr Johnson*, *William Mason* and *Ariadne* (all 1779). Reynolds was particularly pleased with the plate of *Dr Johnson* and advised Doughty 'by all means to stick to mezzotint'. In 1780 Doughty married and sailed for India but died on the way.

BIBLIOGRAPHY
York Art Gallery Catalogue of Paintings, ii (York, 1963), pp. 12–14
J. Ingamells: 'William Doughty: A Little-known York Painter', *Apollo*, lxxx/29 (1964), pp. 33–7

DAVID MANNINGS

Douglas, Aaron (*b* Topeka, KS, 27 April 1899; *d* Nashville, TN, 3 Feb 1979). American painter and illustrator. He was a leading artist of the Harlem Renaissance of the 1920s and 1930s (*see* AFRICAN AMERICAN ART, §2). He studied at the University of Nebraska and then in Paris with Charles Despiau and Othon Friesz (1925–31). Douglas was the earliest Black American artist consciously to include African imagery in his work, which emphasized the creativity and continuity of African American culture, despite slavery and segregation. He was, however, criticized by his comtemporaries for his idealism. In 1934, under the sponsorship of the Public Works of Art project (*see* UNITED STATES OF AMERICA, §XII), he designed a number of murals, including four panels depicting *Aspects of Negro Life* for the Schomberg Library in Harlem (New York, Pub. Lib.); this work and such others as *Judgment Day* (1939; USA, priv. col., see exh. cat., no. 99) and *Building More Stately Mansions* (1944; Nashville, TN, Fisk U.) are executed in a strongly two-dimensional and decorative style with elongated, angular figures. His work also includes landscapes, portraits and book illustrations and jackets.

BIBLIOGRAPHY

J. A. Porter: *Modern Negro Art* (New York, 1943), pp. 105, 114–15, 118, 181

Two Centuries of Black American Art (exh. cat. by D. D. Driscoll, Los Angeles, CA, Co. Mus. A., 1976), pp. 57–8, 61–2, 68, 99, 153

M. Park and G. E. Markowitz: *New Deal for Art* (New York, 1977)

L. M. Igoe: *250 Years of Afro-American Art* (New York and London, 1981), pp. 628–35

Douglas, John (*b* Sandiway, nr Northwich, Cheshire, 11 April 1830; *d* Chester, 23 May 1911). English architect. The son of a builder, he became a pre-eminent provincial architect, receiving national and international recognition. He studied under E. G. Paley (1823–95) of Lancaster and practised in Chester from *c.* 1860 until his death, including partnership with Daniel Porter Fordham (*c.* 1846–99) from *c.* 1884 and with Charles Howard Minshull (1858–1934) from *c.* 1897. More than 500 commissions (mainly domestic and ecclesiastical) range from Scotland to Surrey, but most are in Cheshire and North Wales. Many represent consistent employment by steady clients, most notably Hugh Lupus Grosvenor, 1st Duke of Westminster. Douglas executed over 200 works for him, principally on the Eaton Estate, near Chester, including lodges in the park and model farms and cottages. Douglas's early work was robustly High Victorian Gothic; with maturity he assimilated the influence of Cheshire timber framing, late medieval Flemish and German brick architecture and the contemporary vernacular revival and Aestheticism of R. Norman Shaw and E. Nesfield. He was also inspired by the Jacobean vernacular and his churches are an important contribution to the Perpendicular Gothic Revival. Despite his eclectic sources his buildings are highly individual and usually recognizable. Consistently thorough in quality, they display sure proportions, picturesque effects of vertically emphasized outline and massing, careful detailing and a superb sense of craftsmanship. His feeling for materials, particularly for woodwork, is seen in the magnificent half-timbered range in St Werburgh Street (*c.* 1895–8), Chester, which he built at personal financial risk to prevent the view of the cathedral being spoilt.

BIBLIOGRAPHY

ed.: *The Abbey Square Sketch Book*, 3 vols (Chester, 1872–*c.* 1898) [sketches and measured drawings]

'John Douglas, Architect', *Brit. Architect*, xlix (1898), pp. 360–61

Obituary, *Brit. Architect*, lxxv (1911), pp. 362–3

C. Aslet: 'Estate Buildings at Eaton Hall, Cheshire', *Country Life*, clxxxi (5 March 1987), pp. 88–93

E. H. Hubbard: *The Work of John Douglas* (London, 1991)

EDWARD HUBBARD

Douglas, Robert Langton (*b* Lavenham, Suffolk, 1 March 1864; *d* Fiesole, 14 Aug 1951). English art historian,

dealer and museum director. His interest in art was encouraged by Walter Pater and Charles Fairfax Murray, and in 1900 he relinquished his appointment in the Church of England and became Professor of Modern History at the University of Adelaide, Victoria (1900–02). His monograph on Fra Angelico (1901) was followed by *A History of Siena* (1902). An article on Sassetta in the *Burlington Magazine* (i (1903), pp. 306–19) led to a breach with Bernard Berenson. He revised (1903–11) the first four volumes of *A New History of Painting in Italy* (1864–6) by J. A. Crowe and Giovanni Battista Cavalcaselle and was invited in 1904 by R. H. Benson to arrange an exhibition of Sienese art at the Burlington Fine Arts Club, London. He worked as an art dealer from that time, and his clients included J. Pierpont Morgan and John G. Johnson; he sold paintings, including Giotto's *Dormition of the Virgin* (Berlin, Gemäldegal.), to Wilhelm von Bode at the Kaiser-Friedrich Museum (destr.), Berlin, and was connected with the sale of Giovanni Bellini's *St Francis in Ecstasy* and Gerard David's *Deposition* to Henry Clay Frick (both New York, Frick); he sold the *Epiphany* ascribed to Giotto to the Metropolitan Museum of Art, New York, and Albrecht Altdorfer's *Christ Taking Leave of his Mother* to Julius Wernher (London, N.G.). He continued to deal during military service in World War I, and in 1916 he was appointed Director of the National Gallery of Ireland, Dublin, then a part-time job. He resigned in 1923 after a disagreement with the trustees. During the 1920s, when American collectors were especially keen to purchase Old Masters, he formed an extensive clientele that included Otto H. Kahn and Philip Lehman. In 1940 he settled in New York and assisted the Duveen Brothers firm of art dealers, writing brochures for them, and contributed articles to the *Burlington Magazine*, *Art in America*, *Art Quarterly* and the *Connoisseur*.

WRITINGS

Fra Angelico (London, 1901, 2/1902)

A History of Siena (London, 1902)

ed.: J. A. Crowe and G. B. Cavalcaselle: *A New History of Painting in Italy* (London, 1864–6), with S. A. Strong, i–ii (London, rev. 1903); iii (London, rev. 1908); with G. de Nicola, iv (London, rev. 1911)

Leonardo da Vinci: His Life and his Pictures (Chicago, 1944)

Piero di Cosimo (Chicago, 1946)

BIBLIOGRAPHY

Obituary, *Burl. Mag.*, xcii (1951), p. 330

D. Sutton: *Robert Langton Douglas: Connoisseur of Art and Life* (London, 1980)

DENYS SUTTON

Douglas-Hamilton, Alexander. *See* HAMILTON, ALEXANDER.

Doulton Ceramic Factory. English ceramic manufactory. The firm was established in 1815, when John Doulton (1793–1873) became a partner in the small Vauxhall Walk pottery in Lambeth, London, which produced such utilitarian stonewares as ink bottles and spirit flasks. In 1820 the company became Doulton & Watts. Doulton's son Henry Doulton (1820–97) joined the firm in 1835, and the business was expanded to include architectural terracotta and chemical stonewares. Influenced by the sanitary improvements of the 1840s, Henry Doulton opened a factory specializing in stoneware drainpipes and sanitary fittings, and the success of this venture assured the company's future prosperity.

The artistic side of the business developed in the 1860s, and from 1866 the pottery was closely associated with the Lambeth School of Art, the students decorating the stoneware before its salt-glaze firing. The favourable reception of their first decorative stonewares encouraged Henry Doulton to establish an art studio. George Tinworth (1843–1913), the first artist to be employed, produced vases, figures and religious plaques. He was followed by the first woman artist to be employed by Doulton, Hannah Barlow (1851–1916), who used the sgraffito technique to decorate her wares with animal studies. By the 1890s the studio employed more than 300 artists.

Henry Doulton's interest in the Potteries in Staffordshire began in 1877, when he invested in a factory in Burslem making a variety of earthenwares. By 1882 the firm was trading as Doulton & Co., and over the next few years the factory expanded to produce bone china. The art department, first under the direction of John Slater (1844–1915) and subsequently under Charles Noke (1858–1941), specialized in hand-painted ornamental wares and later figures and other sculptural pieces, which brought international recognition to the company in the 20th century. In 1901 the Royal Warrant was granted by Edward VII, and the company was renamed Royal Doulton. The production of stonewares for artistic, architectural and industrial purposes continued at Lambeth until 1956, by which time the majority of the firm's business was centred in the Burslem factory.

BIBLIOGRAPHY
D. Eyles: *Royal Doulton, 1815–1965* (London, 1965)
The Doulton Story (exh. cat. by P. Atterbury and L. Irvine, London, V&A, 1979)

LOUISE IRVINE

Dōun. *See* IKENAGA DŌUN.

Douris. *See* VASE PAINTERS, §II.

Douvanli [Duvanli; Douvanlij]. Thracian cemetery of the 6th–5th centuries BC in the Upper Maritsa Valley, Bulgaria. Most of the burials date to the later 5th century BC, and several of the mounds *(mogili)*—each of which has a different name—contained rich inventories of local and imported grave goods. The Moushovitsa Mogila is probably the earliest burial: dating to the last decade of the 6th century BC, it is notable for a sheet-gold pectoral or neckpiece decorated with punch-worked ducklike birds. The Koukouva Mogila, from *c.* 450 BC, contained a silver wine-serving vessel of the stylistically Persian *amphore-à-bec* type (Taylor, pl. 105); the magnificent gilded handles are in the form of winged lions with ibex horns. The body of the vessel has two bands of lotus and palmette decoration in low repoussé. This piece was certainly imported and must have been but one of many Persian pieces that were seen and used in Thrace in the years after Darius' expedition against the Scythians (*c.* 513 BC).

Emulation of the Persian style is evident in the sheet-gold neck pectoral from the Bashova Mogila, dating to the late 5th century BC. The object is itself typologically eastern, with a punch-worked lion emblem produced by beating

on to a carved wooden die (*patrix*); while owing something to Scythian ANIMAL STYLE pieces (*see also* SCYTHIAN AND SARMATIAN ART), its Persian features are apparent in the frontal orientation of the face, the way in which the jowls have been worked and the lozenge decoration of the mane. The border of crescent shapes was worked with a pattern punch. The flimsiness of the sheet may indicate that the piece was specially made for the funeral. A similar gold pectoral is also known from the nearby cemetery of Trebenishte, but the type is otherwise unknown in the rest of Europe.

See also THRACIAN AND DACIAN ART.

BIBLIOGRAPHY
B. Filov: *Die Grabhügelnekropole bei Duvanlij in Südbulgarien* (Sofia, 1934)
I. Venedikov and T. Gerassimov: *Thracian Art Treasures* (London, 1975)
T. Taylor: 'The Persian Empire', *Cambridge Ancient History*, iv, ed. J. Boardman (Cambridge, 1988)

TIMOTHY TAYLOR

Dova, Gianni (*b* Rome, 18 Jan 1925; *d* Pisa, 14 Oct 1991). Italian painter. He studied at the Accademia di Belle Arti di Brera in Milan under Aldo Carpi, Carlo Carra and Achille Funi. In Milan in 1946 he signed the 'Manifesto del Realismo' also called 'Oltre Guernica', which was published in the magazine *Numero*. With a group of young northern Italian artists of the post-war generation, including Giuseppe Ajmone, Ennio Morlotti and Emilio Vedova, he published this manifesto in opposition to the Novecento Italiano and the 'formalism' of avant-garde groups of the past, and to focus on the social content of the present. He made his début in 1947 with a one-man show at the Galleria Cavallino in Venice. At first his art developed around abstraction and geometry. He participated in 1949–50 in the *Mostra d'arte concreta* in Milan and in 1951 in the exhibition *Arte astratta e concreta in Italia* at the Galleria Nazionale d'Arte Moderna in Rome. He became part of the Movimento Spaziale that was conceived and propagated by Lucio Fontana, with whom he wrote the *Manifesto dell'arte spaziale* in 1951. He developed a style that encompassed elements of Surrealism and that alluded to biomorphic forms. In the 1950s he took part in the most important artistic events in Italy and abroad: his contacts in Paris grew more numerous, and he was awarded a prize in 1957 at the Biennale in São Paulo. In January 1954 he collaborated on *Phases*, a magazine of the movement of *Arte nucleare*, founded in 1952 by Enrico Baj and Sergio Dangelo (*b* 1931), and which promoted a style of painting that was fantastical and surrealistic. In the 1960s Dova became internationally famous. In such paintings as *Forest in Quimper* (1969; priv. col., see 1971 exh. cat., p. 80), Dova created a fantastical juxtaposition of suggestions and allusions. He used a very personal technique, mixing enamels with water, which allowed him to obtain surfaces of an extreme fluidity and transparency, a highly technological and at the same time organic effect. In the late 1970s the crisp forms and dark colours that had created a sense of mystery gave way to a brighter palette and more gestural brushwork. This produced greater drama as in *Waves and Rocks in Sardinia* (1986; priv. col., see 1988 exh. cat., p. 59).

WRITINGS
with L. Fontana: *Manifesto dell'arte spaziale* (Milan, 1951)

BIBLIOGRAPHY
Gianni Dova (exh. cat. by F. Russoli, Milan, Pal. Reale, 1971)
Gianni Dova. Opere recenti (exh. cat. by M. Rotta, Arezzo, Gal. Com. A. Contemp., 1987)
Dova (exh. cat. by L. Cavallo, Florence, Cent. Tornabuoni, 1988)

SILVIA LUCCHESI

Dove, Arthur (Garfield) (*b* Canandaigua, NY, 2 Aug 1880; *d* Long Island, NY, 23 Nov 1946). American painter. He worked as an illustrator in New York (1903–7). In 1907 he travelled to Paris and southern France, where under the influence of Henri Matisse and Paul Cézanne he experimented with a style characterized by bright colours, curvilinear rhythms and non-naturalistic representation. On his return to the USA in 1909, his association with Alfred Stieglitz began. In 1910 he moved to a farm in Westport, CT. At this time he created some of the first distinctively non-representational works produced by an American, for example the *Abstractions* series (all priv. cols, see Morgan, pp. 100–103). The ten pastels that he showed in his first one-man exhibition at the 291 Gallery (1912) consisted of simplified, stylized motifs, the circular and saw-tooth forms of which interpenetrated and overlapped to create an organic Futurism. In them he expressed his belief that objects are not discrete, isolated entities, but active forces whose rhythms are in constant interplay with their environments.

By repeating and interlocking shapes in a compressed space and by using overall colour and textural similarities, Dove pictorially manifested his belief that the character of life was interpenetration and movement. In 1917 he ceased painting and produced only pastels. He did not resume painting until 1921 after separating from his wife and moving to a houseboat with the painter Helen Torr (1886–1967), whom he married in 1924 after the death of his first wife. In 1922 he bought a yawl on which they lived for the next five years, cruising Long Island Sound in the summer and mooring in Halesite, Long Island, in the winter. During this period he experimented with found materials, which he organized into delicate, whimsical and, at times, almost representational assemblages and collages, for example *Grandmother* (collage, 1925; New York, MOMA).

By 1927 the strain and damp of the boat forced Dove and Torr to spend winter on land and sail only in the summer. His painting, which had been sporadic during his years on the boat, began to accelerate. In works such as *Fog Horns* (1929; Colorado Springs, CO, F.A. Cent.) he developed a characteristic imagery of irregular, circular shapes swelling outward with haloes of modulated colour. This work rhapsodically celebrates the vital, generative forces of nature, which Dove presented as neither autonomous nor finite, but as part of a larger, embracing totality. He developed this style on his return to Geneva, NY, in 1933 to settle his family's estate following the death of his remaining parent. He stayed there until 1938, when he decided after suffering a heart attack to relocate to an abandoned post office in Centerport, Long Island. His subsequent paintings, for example *Willows* (1940; New York, MOMA), continued to manifest the harmonious interdependence of objects in nature, but the vocabulary with which he expressed this harmony became more geometric and two-dimensional. The serenity and calmness of these works suggest a contemplative harmony and union between the forces of nature. From 1930 he was supported by regular payments from his patron, Duncan Phillips, in return for a first selection of works at Dove's exhibitions.

BIBLIOGRAPHY
Arthur Dove (exh. cat. by B. Haskell, San Francisco, CA, Mus. A., 1974)
Arthur Dove and Duncan Phillips: Artist and Patron (exh. cat. by S. M. Newman, Washington, DC, Phillips Col., 1981)
S. Cohn: *Arthur Dove: Nature as Symbol* (Ann Arbor, 1982/*R* 1985)
A. L. Morgan: *Arthur Dove: Life and Work, with a Catalogue Raisonné* (Newark, 1984)

BARBARA HASKELL

Dovecot. Building to house flocks of pigeons, which were popular until the 18th century because they provided fresh meat throughout the winter and required little attention. In large numbers, however, they were a menace, because they fed off any standing crop, and in England, Scotland and France ownership of dovecots was restricted by law to landowners, monasteries and parochial clergy. Nevertheless, there were 26,000 dovecots in England in the 17th century. With the introduction of root crops towards the end of the 17th century, however, animals could be fed throughout the winter, and the building of dovecots for anything other than ornamental purposes declined, particularly in England. In Scotland, however, they played a significant part in the local economy until the 19th century.

The needs of the birds dictated some internal and external features of the dovecot: nesting-boxes lined the walls; many had a potence (a revolving ladder on a stick) to allow access to the highest nesting-boxes; to deter animal predators from climbing up, the sides often had decorative brick string courses, as at the Manoir d'Ango, Varengeville, near Dieppe, France. Sometimes they were constructed on legs or above lodge gates, a style particularly favoured in the Auvergne, France, and in Scotland (e.g. at Megginch Castle, Tayside, 1809; and the spired dovecot built over the 'pend', or entrance gateway, at Rosebery House, Lothian, ?early 19th century). Often they were miniature representations of the local vernacular architecture; for example, many were half-timbered in Herefordshire, crow-stepped in Caithness and gabled in Gloucestershire. They varied in shape, size and material; they could be square, rectangular, octagonal (e.g. at Erddig, Clwyd), round, beehive-, pepperpot- (e.g. at Cliveden House, Bucks) or thimble-shaped. Often they were surmounted by an elegant cupola or lantern, or by pinnacles and crow-stepped gables.

In Scotland, where dovecots were traditionally more widespread, the architectural evolution of the type can be clearly traced. Cylindrical towers or beehive-shaped pigeon-houses were popular until the end of the 16th century; in the 17th century these were replaced by 'lectern' dovecots (square or rectangular buildings with single-pitched roofs). Their architectural variety increased as their economic importance declined, and the greatest range of styles is found in the 18th century, when they became ornaments for the country-house park. At Penicuik House, Lothian, there is a replica of a Roman temple of victory (1766), complete with potence; and at Exton, Leics, a

'Gothick' dovecot is incorporated into an arcaded cowshed.

Dovecots were built not only in Europe but elsewhere. In Iran they were built around Isfahan, where pigeon manure was used to fertilize the extensive melon plantations. These generally were circular towers, with white, often sculpted, plaster exteriors, surmounted by cupolas pierced with holes to allow access for the birds.

BIBLIOGRAPHY
A. O. Cooke: *A Book of Dovecotes* (1920)
L. Lambton: *Beastly Buildings* (London, 1985)
P. Hansell and J. Hansell: *Doves and Dovecotes* (Bath, 1988)

VICTORIA MERRILL

Dover Castle. Castle in Kent, England, overlooking the seaport at the narrowest part of the English Channel. It has been described as 'the key of England' (Matthew Paris: *Chronica majora*, Rolls Series, iii, 28; 13th century). Occupation of the site has been traced to the Iron Age. In Roman times Dover was a military settlement and later a Saxon Shore fort. The Pharos (lighthouse; probably 1st century AD; see fig. (a)) survives as the bell-tower of the church of St Mary-in-Castro ((b); *see also* ANGLO-SAXON ART, fig. 3), within the castle precinct.

Although larger in area than the norm, Dover could not be a more instructive example of an 'English' castle. Founded immediately after the battle of Hastings in 1066 by WILLIAM I, it is even more than usually a product of the Norman Conquest, the site having been sought by the Norman duke in 1051 as a surety for his succession to the English throne. The castle was raised (in eight days according to William of Poitiers, the Conqueror's biographer) within the existing Anglo-Saxon burgh on the hilltop, on the analogy of Old Sarum, Portchester, Wallingford etc. The late 10th-century or early 11th-century church of St Mary-in-Castro (restored by George Gilbert Scott the elder in 1862 and William Butterfield in 1888) survives from the Old English burgh, which itself occupies the position of a former Iron Age fortress. Thus the Conqueror's work doubly shows the essential difference in concept and scale between the feudal castle and the larger communal fortress of earlier ages. Part of the bank of the Norman castle was revealed by excavation in 1961–3, beneath the misnamed 'Harold's Earthwork' near the south transept of the church. It was probably a relatively small fortified enclosure placed centrally within the burgh, very much like the Norman castle at Old Sarum. From then, as with so many 'English' castles, the theme of Dover's architectural history is continuity and development on the same site.

The first recorded works are those of Henry II (*reg* 1154–89), who evidently began the expansion that was to take in the whole Old English and Iron Age site to produce the colossal castle visible today. He built the great rectangular keep of *c.* 1181–8, a new donjon in the prestigious form of a great tower (c). This was one of the most sophisticated in the realm, with an elaborate forebuilding, two residential floors above a basement (the upper for the king himself, rising through two storeys with a mural gallery, now marred by the brutal 'bomb proof' arches inserted in the late 1790s), two chapels and many mural chambers, excellent garderobe arrangements and even

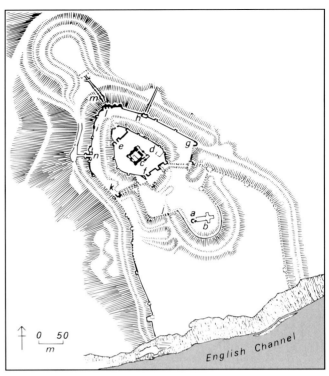

Dover Castle, plan, 1066–1256: (a) Pharos; (b) church of St Mary-in-Castro; (c) tower; (d) inner bailey; (e) King's Gate; (f) Palace Gate; (g) Avranches Tower; (h) Fitzwilliam Gate; (i) Godsfoe Tower; (j) Colton Gate; (k) Peverell's Tower and Gate; (l) Norfolk Towers; (m) St John Tower; (n) Constable's Tower and Gate

plumbing. The tower keep stands within the same king's inner bailey (d), the curtain wall of which displays one of the earliest surviving systems of scientifically disposed mural towers, 14 in all, rectangular and originally open-backed. There are two gateways (the King's Gate (e), north; the Palace Gate (f), south), each consisting of a pair of mural towers flanking the gate passage and each with a barbican in front of it. Residential buildings on the east side supplemented the grander accommodation in the keep. Henry II also began the outer curtain of the castle on the east side, perhaps from the cliff edge to the Avranches Tower ((g); a length now vanished), certainly from the polygonal Avranches Tower inclusive to the later Fitzwilliam Gate (h). It follows, therefore, that the principle of concentric fortification was practised at Dover a century before such textbook examples as Beaumaris or Caerffili.

Henry II died before the work was finished, to be continued not by his immediate successor, Richard I, but by John (*reg* 1199–1216). Between 1205 and 1214 he completed his father's outer curtain about the north end of the site, with a twin-towered gatehouse at the northern apex and a series of towers, which are D-shaped except for the Godsfoe Tower (i), along the west, and evidently brought his towered wall and defences looping back via the Colton Gate (j) round St Mary-in-Castro to join the eastern curtain near the Avranches Tower.

The final development of the castle took place between 1217 and 1256, during the long reign of Henry III. He extended the outer curtain on the west from Peverell's Tower (k) to the cliff edge (and possibly on the east from the Avranches Tower), raised the huge Harold's Earthwork about the church and Roman Pharos (which became the bell-tower) and built more sumptuous residential accommodation (now masked by mid-18th-century barrack blocks) to replace that of Henry II in the inner bailey. These works also included at an early stage the reparation of the damage done by the French siege of 1216, when the eastern of the two towers of the king's new northern gate was mined. In consequence the gate was blocked for all time by the splendid trinity of the present Norfolk Towers (l), the damaged former eastern gate rebuilt solid and joined to its western partner by another solid tower, this time *en bec* (Fr.: keel-shaped), in the place of the former entrance passage. To deny to any future enemy the high ground from which the 1216 attack had been launched, the cylindrical St John Tower (m) was built out in front of the Norfolk Towers, and a great spurwork beyond that, all reached by underground passages. The twin-towered Fitzwilliam Gate (also *en bec*) was inserted in the north-east outer curtain as a sally port. The main entrance to the new castle thus being blocked, the elaborate and formidable Constable's Gate (n) was built in the north-west outer curtain.

The remaining architectural history of Dover is of adequate maintenance, eventual decay and then, for over a century after 1745, a series of works to convert the medieval castle into a 'modern' fortress equipped for and against heavy guns. Much of the medieval fabric was destroyed, especially on the east and south of the inner bailey, walls were earthed up, and unsightly brickwork appears all over the place. The cutting down of almost all the towers for artillery robs the castle of its proper majesty.

BIBLIOGRAPHY

J. Newman: *North-east and East Kent*, Bldgs England (Harmondsworth, 1969; 2/1976), pp. 285–93
R. A. Brown: *Dover Castle* (London, 1974)

R. ALLEN BROWN

Dovizi, Bernardo da. *See* BIBBIENA, BERNARDO.

Dowdeswell, (C.) William (*b* 1832; *d* 1915). English dealer. In 1878 he opened a gallery at 133 New Bond Street, London, and later moved to new premises at 160 New Bond Street. He published prints by such late 19th-century artists as Charles Meryon, Jules Jacquemart, Félix Bracquemond, Seymour Haden and Whistler, the last being a friend of his son Walter Dowdeswell. In 1912 Walter left the gallery to work with the dealer Joseph Duveen in London. With no heir to inherit the family business, Walter's library was sold (6 Feb 1912) and the gallery was liquidated at auction (London, Christie's, 7–9 Feb). In 1920 there were two more sales of property (London, Puttick and Simpson's).

BIBLIOGRAPHY

F. Lugt: *Marques* (1921)

Downey, Juan (*b* Santiago, 11 May 1940). Chilean painter, printmaker and video artist. He studied architecture at the Universidad Católica de Chile in Santiago and printmaking at Taller 99, a workshop in Santiago run by Nemesio Antúnez, where he explored new technical methods for representing machine imagery and energy. In 1962 he travelled to Spain and then to Paris, where he studied at Stanley William Hayter's Atelier 17.

In the mid-1960s Downey settled in the USA, where he became interested in video art, which became his primary medium, and made contact with the pioneers of the genre. Proposing to work directly with energy rather than simply representing it, he presented his first audio-visual installation in 1966, conveying light, sound and energy by means of closed-circuit television. Conceiving of the artist as a cultural communicator and keen to appropriate to his own ends methods of image reproduction derived from advanced technology, he created a series entitled *Video Transamérica*, which he began in 1971 and worked on for nearly 20 years, in order to provide information on indigenous Latin American cultures and to make known their present state. The series includes *Yucatán* (1973) as well as *Yanomami Healing One* and *Yanomami Healing Two* (both 1977), the latter of which document his experiences amongst the Yanomami Indians of southern Venezuela and represent an attempt to get closer to the roots of Latin America through the study of anthropology and iconography. Subsequent series included *The Thinking Eye*, begun in 1979, a survey of Western culture from the pyramids of Egypt to the skyscrapers of Manhattan from an autobiographical point of view, and *The Looking Glass*, in which he analysed the use of mirrors in masterpieces of painting, in palaces and gardens, in mythology and in daily life. His main concern here was with culture in its sociopolitical context. Rupturing the conventional narrative form of commercial television, Downey consistently used video to achieve fresh insights.

WRITINGS

with others: *Festival Downey: Video porgue TeVe* (Santiago, 1987)

BIBLIOGRAPHY

G. Galaz and M. Ivelić: 'El video arte en Chile', *Rev. Aisthesis*, 19 (1986)

VIDEO RECORDINGS

A. Hoy: *Juan Downey: The Thinking Eye* [videotape, 1987]

MILAN IVELIĆ

Downing, A(ndrew) J(ackson) (*b* Newburgh, NY, 31 Oct 1815; *d* Hudson River, NY, 28 July 1852). American writer, horticulturist, landscape gardener and architect. From the age of seven he was trained in the family nursery garden by his elder brother Charles Downing (1802–85), an experimental horticulturist. Before he was 15, Downing came under the influence of André Parmentier (1780–1830), a Dutch-trained landscape gardener, and he studied the 280-ha estate that Parmentier had landscaped in the English manner at Hyde Park, NY. Downing was also influenced by the mineralogist Baron Alois von Lederer (1773–1842) and the landscape painter Raphael Hoyle (1804–38). In 1834 Downing's first article, 'Ornamental Trees', appeared in journals in Boston, MA, and France. His article 'The Fitness of Different Styles of Architecture for Country Residences' (1836) was the first important discussion of the topic in America. He expressed enthusiasm for a variety of styles and insisted they must be used in appropriate settings. His *Landscape Gardening* (1841) was the first such work by an American, and *Cottage Residences* (1842) was the first American book on rural architecture. Downing also contributed numerous articles on horticulture, landscape gardening and rural architecture to Hovey's *Magazine of Horticulture*, Boston, from 1835 to 1846, when he founded and edited a monthly journal of rural art, *The Horticulturist*.

Downing's first known landscape design was for a scientifically arranged, one-and-a-half ha ornamental botanical garden, added to the Downing Nursery in 1836. He also laid out his villa grounds in the natural style; these became known to numerous visitors and to others through published plans. He was subsequently asked to landscape estates from New England to Maryland, for example Matthew Vassar's estate at Poughkeepsie, NY, and a 'National Park' (1851; uncompleted) in Washington, DC. In 1839 Downing designed a villa (destr. 1918) for himself at Newburgh. He designed many of the buildings illustrated in his works, evolving an original American 'bracketed style', featuring overhanging, bracketed eaves, and a roof pitched higher than 'Italian' and lower than 'Gothic'. In *The Architecture of Country Houses* (1850) Downing included designs not only for cottages, farm houses and villas but also for interiors and furniture; in addition he promoted the latest developments in heating and ventilation. Downing's own design for 'A lake or river villa' may be the first design published in England or America to have been influenced by Ruskin's ideas. In 1850 Downing formed a partnership with Calvert Vaux and opened a practice in Newburgh, which quickly became America's largest architectural firm, the first to specialize in landscape architecture, the combined arts of landscape design, horticulture and architecture. Downing & Vaux's staff included the English architect F. C. Withers, Downing's former pupil F. J. Scott (1826–1919) and an assistant, Clarence Cook (1828–1900).

Downing lived in a time when there was a widespread desire to make real the promise of the Declaration of Independence and to create a new and more perfect civilization. Science and technology were already seen as essential ingredients, but it was Downing's prose style that overcame the nation's puritanical suspicion of art and created the awareness that the useful should be made beautiful. In uniting art with patriotism and 'Yankee ingenuity', Downing became the principal spokesman for a philosophy that replaced Romanticism with Pragmatic Idealism. In his work and writings he established a national agenda for domestic architecture and landscaping, suburban planning and urban parks. His ideas were carried forward by many followers, the most important being Calvert Vaux and F. L. Olmsted.

WRITINGS
'Ornamental Trees', *New England Farmer* (29 Jan 1834), pp. 225–6, and *An. Inst. Hort. Fromont* (June 1834), pp. 74–80
'The Fitness of Different Styles of Architecture for Country Residences', *Amer. Gdnr Mag.*, ii (1836), pp. 281–6 [afterwards *Magazine of Horticulture*]
Landscape Gardening with Remarks on Rural Architecture (New York, 1841, rev. by H. W. Sargent, 6/1859/*R* 1967)
Cottage Residences (New York, 1842, rev. by G. E. Harney, 5/1873/*R* 1981)
Fruits and Fruit Trees of America (New York, 1845, rev. 14/1853–6; new edns by C. Downing to 1900)

The Architecture of Country Houses (New York, 1850/*R* 1969)
Regular contributions to *The Horticulturalist*, 7 vols (1846–52)

BIBLIOGRAPHY
G. W. Curtis, ed.: *Downing's Rural Essays* (New York, 1853/*R* 1974) [incl. Downing's editorials]
G. B. Tatum: 'Andrew Jackson Downing, Arbiter of American Taste' (diss., Princeton U., 1950)
A. C. Downs: 'Downing's Newburgh Villa,' *Bull. Assoc. Preserv. Technol.*, iv (1972), pp. 1–113
——: *Downing and the American House* (Newtown Square, PA, 1988)

ARTHUR CHANNING DOWNS

Downman, John (*b* Ruabon, N. Wales, 1750; *d* Wrexham, 24 Dec 1824). English painter and draughtsman. He became a pupil of Benjamin West in 1768 and entered the Royal Academy Schools, London, the following year. In 1770 and 1772 he exhibited portraits at the Royal Academy and showed his first subject picture in 1773. He left for a period of study in Italy and was in Rome with Joseph Wright of Derby from 1773 to 1774. When he next exhibited at the Royal Academy (1777) he was living in Cambridge, but from 1778 to 1804 his considerable annual contribution to the Academy exhibitions was sent from various London addresses. His very popular small portraits were often shown in groups of six or nine. His occasional subject pictures were based on themes from mythology, Classical history, poetry and the theatre. They included a scene from *As You Like It* (untraced) painted for John Boydell's Shakespeare Gallery. Downman became ARA in 1795 and travelled widely in later life, marrying in Exeter in 1806 and sending works to the Royal Academy (1805–12 and 1816–19) from all over the country.

Downman's oil portraits are attractive, crisp and neat in the manner of similar work by Francis Wheatley, but his portrait drawings are much more distinctive. The technique of black chalk and stumping on very fine paper with flesh tints added in red chalk and watercolour is complemented by a light touch and a fine sense of style, as in *George John Spencer, Viscount Althorp* (1777; Cambridge, Fitzwilliam). Downman retained the studies for many of his finished drawings from the mid-1770s until his death and had them bound in over 20 albums of varying sizes (several in London, BM, and Cambridge, Fitzwilliam). The pretty elegance of the portrait drawings becomes cloyingly effeminate in many of Downman's subject pictures, although some, such as *The Sybarite* (pencil, black chalk, watercolour and gouache, 1805; London, V&A), are almost startlingly glossy.

BIBLIOGRAPHY
G. C. Williamson: 'John Downman, ARA: His Life and Works', *Connoisseur* (1907) [extra number]
E. Croft-Murray: 'John Downman's "Original First Studies of Distinguished Persons"', *BM Q.*, xiv (1939–40), pp. 60–66

GEOFFREY ASHTON

Doxaras. Greek family of painters.

(1) Panagiotes Doxaras (*b* Mani, Peloponnese, 1662; *d* Corfu, 1729). He settled in Zakynthos *c.* 1685 and studied with the post-Byzantine painter Leo Moskos. From 1694 to 1699 he fought against the Turks on the side of the Venetians, who later rewarded him with estates in Leuchada and the title of 'knight'. He studied painting in Venice between 1699 and 1704. From 1704 to 1715 he lived in Kalamata and spent his remaining years in Zak-ynthos, Leuchada and Corfu. The four pictures— *Christ, Blessed Virgin, St John the Baptist* and *St Demetrios* (*c.* 1721–2)—on the templon of St Demetrios, in Leuchada, should probably be counted among his few surviving works. Doxaras was the first painter in modern Greek art to be the subject of research (1843) and the first painter syste-matically to paint in oil rather than tempera. He reinvigo-rated post-Byzantine religious painting, orienting it decisively towards the West. The most typical example of this is his decoration of the Heavenly Vault (ceiling) of the church of St Spyridon in Corfu with scenes from the life and miracles of the saint (1727). Though preserved only in a copy by Nikolaos Aspiotes (Corfu, St Spyridon), it was directly modelled on works by Paolo Veronese in the Doge's Palace in Venice. To the almost exclusively religious post-Byzantine painting he added at least one new subject area, the portrait, and perhaps others. He thus anticipated the development of the secular themes that were later to predominate in the art of the modern Greek state. The portrait of *Johann Matthias, Graf von der Schulenburg* (1719; Athens, G. Perdios priv. col., see Char-alampidis, 1983) is the only surviving example of this aspect of his work. Doxaras also attempted to give a theoretical foundation to his work: he translated Raphaël Trichet du Fresne's *Trattato della pittura di Leonardo da Vinci* (1651) into Greek *c.* 1720 (preserved in MSS at Athens, N. Lib., and Venice, Bib. N. Marciana) and wrote *Peri zographias* (1726), in which he recommends his pupils to represent their subjects as naturally as possible.

WRITINGS

Peri zographias [On painting] (MS.; 1726); ed. S. P. Lambros (Athens, 1871)

BIBLIOGRAPHY

N. Misirli: *Helleneke zographeke: 18ou–19ou aionas* [Greek painting: 18th–19th centuries] (Athens, 1993), pp. 22–3, 200–201 [with complete bibliog.]

(2) Nikolaos Doxaras

(*b* Kalamata, 1705; *d* Zakyn-thos, 2 March 1775). Son of (1) Panagiotes Doxaras. He lived at various times in Zakynthos, Leuchada, Corfu and Kephalonia. A protégé of Johann Matthias, Graf von der Schulenburg, he studied military engineering and painting in Venice from 1729 to 1738. The Heavenly Vault (ceiling) of the Phaneromene church in Zakynthos (1754–9) and the Heavenly Vault of the church of St Menas in Leuchada (1762) represent opposing poles of his work, which was influenced by the Italian Baroque. His output was limited because of his other activities, though several of his works have been destroyed. His paintings of the *Death of the Virgin* and the *Assumption of the Virgin* (1754–9) were destroyed in the earthquakes on Zakynthos (1953), while the *Birth of the Virgin* (Zakynthos, Zakynthos Mus.), from the same group, as well as three small sketches for it (Athens, N. Lib.), survive. Another group was lost in a later fire. *The Bridegroom* (1756; Athens, Loverdos priv. col.) can also be attributed to him.

BIBLIOGRAPHY

A. Moustoxydes: 'Panagiotes Doxaras', *Ellenomnemon*, i (1843), pp. 17–40
S. Lydakes: *Lexiko ton ellenon zographon kai charakton* [Dictionary of Greek painters and engravers] (1976), pp. 108–9, iv of *Oi ellenes zographoi* [The Greek painters], ed. S. Lydakes and A. Karakatsane (Athens, 1974–6)
A. Charalampidis: *Symvole ste melete tes ephanesiotikes zographikes tou 18ou kai 19ou aiona* [Contribution to the study of painting on the Ionian Islands in the 18th and 19th centuries] (Ioannina, 1978), pp. 25–32, 36–42
——: 'Ergo tou Panagiote Doxara se xene idiotike sylloge' [A work by Panagiotes Doxaras in a private collection abroad], *Aphieroma ste mneme S. Pelekanides* [Papers in honour of S. Pelekanides] (Thessaloniki, 1983), pp. 433–44
N. Misirli: *Helleneke zographeke: 18ou–19ou aionas* [Greek painting: 18th and 19th centuries] (Athens, 1993), pp. 24–5, 199–200

ALKIS CHARALAMPIDIS

Doxiadis, Constantinos A. (*b* Stenimachos [now Asen-ovgrad, Bulgaria], 14 May 1913; *d* Athens, 28 June 1975). Greek urban and regional planner, architect, theorist and administrator. At the outbreak of World War I he and his family arrived in Athens from Bulgaria as refugees. He studied architecture (1930–35) at the National Technical University of Athens and received a doctoral degree (1935) from the Universität Berlin–Charlottenburg, having pre-sented a highly original and controversial thesis on plan-ning in ancient Greece. He was Head of the Town Planning Office of the Greater Athens area (1937–9) and of the Department of Regional and Town Planning of the Ministry of Public Works (1939–45) during the German occupation of Greece. Simultaneously he was part of the Underground Resistance movement, preparing plans for the post-war reconstruction of Greece. After the war, as Under-Secretary and Director-General of the Ministry of Housing and Reconstruction (1945–8) and as Under-Secretary and Coordinator of the Recovery Programme of the Ministry of Coordination (1948–51), he was the major figure in Greek reconstruction, but faced political oppo-sition to implementation of his plans.

From 1951 to 1953 Doxiadis lived in Australia and then returned to Greece. His firm, Doxiadis Associates, Con-sulting Engineers, was founded in Athens in 1951. He was its president (1951–72) and chairman (1973–5), and at the time of his death it had grown into one of the world's largest planning practices. His experience in handling Marshall Plan aid to Greece led to a number of commis-sions within the Point Four Program for development aid to Middle and Near Eastern countries. Among the early major planning projects of Doxiadis Associates were the national housing programmes for Iraq (1955–6) and Lebanon (1957–8) and regional plans for the Accra–Tema–Akosombo area, Ghana (1960–61). Other regional plans include those for the province of Guipúzcoa, Spain (1964–5); Benghazi (Banghāzī), Libya (1966–70); and the Rio Plata basin in South America (1968–9). Urban plans were developed for Skopje, Yugoslavia (now Macedonia; 1954–66); Khartoum and Port Sudan, Sudan (1959), Homs (now Ḥimṣ), Hama and Salemiyah, Syria (1959–61); Accra and Tema (1960–62); Saigon (now Ho Chi Minh City), Vietnam (1964–5); Playa de las Americas, Tenerife, Canary Islands, Spain (1965–6); and Lusaka, Zambia, and Riyadh, Saudi Arabia (both 1968–72). One of his most important projects was the city development plan for Islamabad, the new capital of Pakistan (1959–63).

Doxiadis's firm was involved in planning for developed countries as well: in the USA they drew up renewal plans for Detroit, MI (1964–71), Miami, FL (1965–6), and Cleveland, OH (1970–72). The Detroit plan led to the Great Lakes Megalopolis scheme of 1969–70, around the

Constantinos A. Doxiadis: Doxiadis Associates headquarters, Athens, 1955–61

core cities of Chicago, Detroit, Cleveland and Pittsburgh. The last major planning projects of the firm before Doxiadis's death included regional plans for the provinces of Barcelona, Girona and Lérida, Spain (1970–75), and for the central and northern regions of Saudi Arabia (1972–6), and urban plans for Kirkūk, Iraq (1973–6), and the University of Patras, Greece (1972–5).

Doxiadis also practised as an architect, providing for clients functional buildings in a late Modern style that exhibit a high degree of integration with the environment. The most significant ones are the headquarters of Doxiadis Associates (1955–61; see fig.); buildings for the University of the Punjab (1959–73), Lahore, Pakistan, and the University of Agriculture (1961), Lyallpur (now Faisalabad), Pakistan; the 'Aspra Spitia' housing (1962–4), Antikyra, Greece; the Abbott Pharmaceutical Plant (1966), Madrid, Spain; the 'Apollonion' vacation complex (1970–81), Porto Rafti, Attica, Greece; and the Polytechnic and Trade Training Centre (1972–5), Marka, Amman, Jordan.

Doxiadis was convinced that in the field of housing the qualitative and quantitative needs were colossal because of a new era humanity had entered, characterized by an enormous increase in population and overcongestion of human settlements. Conventional architectural practices were insufficient for meeting such demands; what was needed was a new, multidisciplinary and scientific way of creating human settlements, capable of adding a fourth dimension, that of time, to architectural design and urban planning. The term he gave *c.* 1944 to this new science or study of human settlements was 'ekistics' (from the modern Greek *oikistikē*: 'of or relating to settlement'). It was conceived as the overall study of housing, covering all aspects and all levels of planning. With this concept, he became an early pioneer in the recognition that the massive

regional planning problems of his time would require systems-thinking approaches and complex and difficult solutions. In practice, however, his finished plans tended to be growth and development orientated and to be presented in the traditional CIAM form: flat delineation of the assignment of functions to areas. Ekistics was in many respects eclectic but also included a number of novel concepts, such as 'Dynapolis', the dynamic city with a parabolic unidirectional growth that can expand in space and time, and 'Ecumenopolis', the coming city that would cover the entire earth. Perhaps Doxiadis's greatest contribution was as a publicist: in his use of such terms as 'dystopia' and 'entopia' in the optimistic context of post-war consumer society, he did much to alert the world to the problems inherent in unplanned economic and urban growth. He lectured at various universities and at the post-graduate Centre of Ekistics of the Athens Technical Organization, which he founded in 1958 and which publishes the planning journal *Ekistics*. From 1963 until 1974 he organized the Delos Symposia, conferences on human settlements, urban planning and economics, the proceedings of which were published in *Ekistics*.

WRITINGS
Raumordnung in griechischen Städtebau (Heidelberg, 1937); Eng. trans. as *Architectural Space in Ancient Greece* (Cambridge, MA, 1972)
Architecture in Transition (London, 1963, New York, 3/1968)
Between Dystopia and Utopia (Hartford, CT, 1966, Athens, 3/1974)
Ekistics: An Introduction to the Science of Human Settlements (London, 1968)
The Great Urban Crimes we Permit by Law (Athens, 1973)
Anthropopolis: City for Human Development (Athens, 1974, New York, 2/1975)
Building Entopia (Athens and New York, 1975)
BIBLIOGRAPHY
J. Tywhitt, ed.: 'C. A. Doxiadis, 1913–75: Pursuit of an Attainable Ideal', *Ekistics*, xli/247 (1976) [issue dedicated to Doxiadis]

ALEXANDER KOUTAMANIS

Doyen, Gabriel-François (*b* Paris, 20 May 1726; *d* St Petersburg, 13 March 1806). French painter. In 1748 he won second place in the Prix de Rome competition and subsequently became a pupil of Carle Vanloo at the Ecole Royale des Elèves Protégés, Paris. In 1752 he arrived to complete his artistic education at the Académie de France in Rome, where he discovered the art of Raphael and of Domenichino, as well as that of such Baroque masters as Pietro da Cortona, Luca Giordano and Francesco Solimena. He also stayed in Parma and visited Venice, Bologna and Turin. His experiences in Italy confirmed him in his lifelong vocation for large-scale history painting.

In 1756 Doyen returned to Paris and began to paint the *Death of Virginia* (exh. Salon 1759; Parma, G.N.), a huge work (*c.* 4×7 m) recalling the great Italian decorative paintings of the 16th and 17th centuries, yet innovative in its use of a subject from Livy and its combination of antique costumes and setting with rich late Baroque colouring. The picture won high praise from the critics, Denis Diderot in particular. Doyen was immediately approved (*agréé*) as an associate member by the Académie Royale and received (*reçu*) as a full member in the same year. The painting was bought by Philippe de Bourbon, Duke of Parma (*d* 1765) as the first acquisition for his newly founded gallery in Parma. Doyen then turned to Homer, a fashionable source since the publication in 1757 of the Comte de Caylus's *Tableaux tirés d'Homère et de Virgile*, and over 20 years produced a series of paintings of vast dimensions: the tumultuous and poetic *Venus Wounded by Diomedes* (exh. Salon 1761; St Petersburg, Hermitage), the systematically dramatic *Andromache Hiding Astyanax from Ulysses* (exh. Salon 1763; Arkhangel'skoye Pal.) and finally *Mars Defeated by Minerva* (exh. Salon 1781; Poitiers, Mus. B.-A.). In the last-named canvas Doyen took up a favourite theme, that of the Homeric battle. But to the public at the 1781 Salon, discovering a new and more austere type of painting in Jacques-Louis David's *Belisarius Receiving Alms* (Lille, Mus. B.-A.), the overcharged ardour, the confusion of the principal action to the detriment of the harmony of the whole and the freedom of brushwork in Doyen's picture must have seemed old-fashioned. Doyen nevertheless continued to work in this vein in the 1780s, exhibiting the clamorous *Priam Demanding the Body of Hector from Achilles* (Paris, Louvre, on dep. Algiers, Mus. N. B.-A.) at the Salon of 1787.

Doyen also worked on a number of important decorative projects. After the death of Carle Vanloo in 1765, he was given the task of completing the decoration of the Chapelle Saint-Grégoire in the church of the Invalides, Paris. Vanloo had left only bare indications for the project, but Doyen's seven scenes from the *Life of St Gregory* (completed 1772) are probably the outstanding masterpieces of large-scale decorative painting in late 18th-century France. Also in 1772 he produced a *Triumph of Amphitrite* for the dining-room of the Petit Trianon, Versailles. However, the powerful drawing and the amplitude of the forms were not in accord with fashionable Neo-classical taste, and it appears that the work was not hung.

Unlike his contemporary Jean-Baptiste-Henri Deshays, Doyen had little experience of religious painting apart from the Rubensian *Adoration of the Magi* (Mitry-Mory, Seine-et-Marne, parish church), painted in 1766 for Mme de Pompadour's château of Bellevue, and another picture of the same subject (Darmstadt, Hess. Landesmus.). It was nevertheless in this field that he produced his masterpiece, *St Geneviève and the Miracle of the Victims of Burning-sickness (Le Miracle des Ardents)* (exh. Salon 1767; Paris, St Roch; see fig.), hailed by the Salon critics as one of the most brilliant paintings of the century. Doyen prepared for the picture not only by making numerous drawings and sketches (e.g. Paris, Louvre, and Bayonne, Mus. Bonnat) but also by travelling to Flanders to study the great compositions of Rubens. In addition, he doubtless drew on his memories of the work of Guercino and Mattia Preti. The powerful composition and intense colouring of *St Geneviève* had an impact on contemporaries such as François-Guillaume Ménageot, whose *Chaste Susanna* (1779; Douai, St Pierre) was clearly inspired by Doyen's painting. The realistic studies Doyen made from dying patients in the hospices for the afflicted figures that writhe in the lowest portion of the composition anticipate the procedures of Jean-Antoine Gros and Théodore Gericault by 50 years. In its vigorous romanticism Doyen's picture was in striking contrast to the conventional classicizing

Gabriel-François Doyen: *St Geneviève and the Miracle of the Victims of Burning-sickness*, oil on canvas, 1767 (Paris, St Roch)

quality of Jean-Marie Vien's *St Denis Preaching the Faith in France*, which was also painted for St Roch (*in situ*) and was shown in the same Salon. It is, however, a measure of the stylistic uncertainties of the 1760s that neither Diderot nor the general public was able to decide between the respective merits of the two artists. A further important commission for a religious painting followed in 1773, the *Last Communion of St Louis* for the high altar of the chapel of the Ecole Militaire, Paris (*in situ*). This is a meditation on the death of a hero pervaded by memories of Poussin's *Death of Germanicus* (Minneapolis, MN, Inst. A.), the acknowledged prototype of the genre.

Doyen became a fashionable painter and was well received at court; he was appointed Premier Peintre to the Comte d'Artois (later Charles X) in 1773 and to the Comte de Provence (later Louis XVIII) in 1775. The town of Reims commissioned from him ephemeral decorations for the celebrations of the coronation of Louis XVI in 1774, and in 1775 he executed a great commemorative painting in the tradition of Nicolas de Largillierre, *Louis XVI Being Received as Grand Master of the Order of the Saint Esprit* (Versailles, Château).

In 1791 and 1792 Doyen was involved with his pupil Alexandre Lenoir (*see* LENOIR, (1)) in the formation of the famous storehouse of works of art in the recently suppressed convent of the Petits Augustins, Paris, the purpose being to save and catalogue works threatened by the unsettled events of the French Revolution. However, in 1792 he accepted an invitation from Catherine II to settle in Russia and took up an appointment as a professor at the Imperial Academy in St Petersburg. After Catherine's death, he continued to work for Paul I, executing a number of portraits and decorative works, among them a ceiling (destr.) in the Winter Palace, St Petersburg. The lyricism of his inspiration as well as the freedom of his technique and the amplitude of his forms made Doyen one of the most innovative history painters of his period.

BIBLIOGRAPHY
D. Diderot: *Salons* (1759–81); ed. J. Seznec and J. Adhémar (Oxford, 1957–67, rev. 1983)
H. Stein: *Le Peintre Doyen et l'origine du Musée des Monuments français* (Paris, 1888)
M. Hérold: 'A propos du *Miracle des Ardents* de Gabriel-François Doyen (1726–1806)', *Rev. Louvre*, 2 (1968), pp. 65–72
M. Sandoz: *Gabriel-François Doyen (1726–1806)* (Paris, 1975)
Diderot et l'art de Boucher à David: Les Salons, 1759–1781 (exh. cat., ed. M.-C. Sahut and N. Volle; Paris, Hôtel de la Monnaie, 1984–5)

NATHALIE VOLLE

Doyle. English family of artists of Irish origin.

(1) John Doyle [H. B.] (*b* Dublin, 1797; *d* London, 2 Jan 1868). Painter and printmaker. Dispossessed of his family estate, he left Ireland for London in 1821. He studied with the Italian landscape painter Gaspar Gabrielli (*fl* 1803–33) at the Royal Dublin Society's schools and with the miniature painter John Comerford (*c.* 1770–1832). He then spent nearly a decade experimenting with portraiture, first in oils and then in lithographs. The ease and economy of the latter, a relatively new medium, loosened Doyle's line, and from 1829 to 1851 he produced a series of 917 prints satirizing the public face of English politics. For these prints he adopted the cipher 'H. B.' (from two 'J. D.'s, one on top of the other). From the Catholic Relief Bill until the Ecclesiastical Title Act, H. B.'s prints caused London 'to smile in a quiet, gentlemanlike kind of way' (according to William Makepeace Thackeray) at faintly animalized depictions of Arthur, Duke of Wellington, Prime Ministers Disraeli, Palmerston and Melbourne, and the ubiquitous John Bull (or, as H. B. had it, 'The man wot is easily led by the nose').

(2) Richard [Dicky] **Doyle** (*b* London, Sept 1824; *d* London, 10 Dec 1883). Illustrator, printmaker and painter, son of (1) John Doyle. When only 16 years old he published the first of his *Comic Histories, the Eglinton Tournament: Or, the Days of Chivalry Revived*, a burlesque of medievalism, selected from among his rather more grotesque pen-and-ink juvenilia. The public success of these images assured Doyle of a ready demand for work throughout his career. In 1843 he joined the staff of *Punch*, but his graphic skills found little immediate outlet. At first Doyle contributed only peripheral elaborations—inventive headings, borders, initials and tail-pieces—possibly inspired by the Gothic Revival interest in medieval tracery and grotesquerie. Following the success of his *Punch* cover design in 1849, which was retained for over a hundred years, Doyle began the series *Manners and Customs of ye Englyshe*, in which, with a pared-down line nearly unshaded, he represented large gatherings. In *A Cydere Cellare* and *Ye Commons* the members of these masses are just differentiated, and modern life is quietly medievalized; the middle classes glance discreetly at other classes, their institutions and themselves. Although he was notoriously shy and often portrayed himself as a small, thin figure, eyes hidden under tousled hair, Doyle did not shrink from resigning from *Punch* when it opposed the papacy's plans to establish a regular diocesan hierarchy in England in 1850.

Doyle's 'etched outline manner' brought him further success with *The Foreign Tour of Messrs Brown, Jones and Robinson* (1854), a caricatured Grand Tour, and *Bird's Eye Views of Society* (1861–3), in a slightly darker mood. Among the numerous works illustrated by Doyle, which include books by John Ruskin and Leigh Hunt, Thackeray's *The Newcomes* (1854–5) represents the most sympathetic collaboration: a version of the domestic absurd that absorbed and extended Doyle's style into elegant, denser vignettes. His fantasy was redirected in his oil and watercolour landscapes of outlying areas of Wales and Scotland, where his grotesques reappear as supernatural fairies amid mundane nature in such works as *The Fairy Tree* (exh. RA 1868). By the early 1880s, with *The Triumphant Entry: A Fairy Pageant* (Dublin, N.G.), such studied naivety had disappeared; here, several hundred little people, in a wide and hierarchic panorama, recall the structure of Doyle's earlier pictures, which have influenced the forms, boundaries and stereotypes of modern caricature.

BIBLIOGRAPHY
A. R. Montalba: *The Doyle Fairy Book* (London, 1890)
D. Hambourg: *Richard Doyle: His Life and Work* (London, 1948)
G. M. Trevelyan: *The Seven Years of William IV: A Reign Cartooned by John Doyle* (London, 1952)
R. Engen: *Richard Doyle* (Stroud, 1983)
Richard Doyle and his Family (exh. cat. by R. Engen, M. Heseltine and L. Lambourne, London, V&A, 1983–4)

LEWIS JOHNSON

Dra Abu el-Naga. *See under* THEBES (i), §IX.

Dragalevtsi Monastery Church. Monastic church in Bulgaria, 10 km south of Sofia on the northern slopes of the Vitocha Mountains. The monastery, consecrated to the Virgin, was founded by King John Alexander (*reg* 1331–71) towards the middle of the 14th century, but has since been destroyed; a small church (*c.* 10×4.5 m), however, remains. Its single nave has a barrel vault, and its decorations, which were painted at a much later date, are blackened and of little interest. Work of greater interest was executed in the narthex, however, which was also vaulted. Most of its walls are still covered with original scenes paid for, according to an inscription, by a certain Radislav Mavr in 1476. The principal schemes depicted on the upper parts of the walls are the *Last Judgement* and the *Second Coming*. They are interspersed with various other images including *Christ* and the *Virgin and Child* surrounded by an aureola shown on the east wall over the door leading to the nave and the *Hospitality of Abraham* and the *Sacrifice of Isaac* shown on the west wall. The latter scenes were intended to point up parallels between the Old and New Testaments. The lower north and west walls are occupied with scenes depicting respectively a monk tempted by the devil into leaving the monastery and a family portrait of *Radoslav Mavr*. The top of the narthex's vault contains two medallions, one showing a bust of *Christ* surrounded by the symbols of the four evangelists, the other the *Virgin at Prayer*; the latter is surrounded by celestial 'thrones' having the appearance of winged wheels. Eleven prophets with unfurled scrolls are depicted flanking the medallions. The lower part of the vault is occupied by the following scenes: the *Entombment*, the *Trinity* (Christ with the Ancient of Days seated on a throne and the Dove representing the Holy Ghost), *Christ with the Good Thief in Paradise* and the *Three Marys at the Tomb*. The exterior of the western wall was also decorated and formed part of an exonarthex, but these paintings were executed on the orders of a certain Kraislav and date to the late 15th century or early 16th. They include the *Virgin and Child* surrounded by four angels shown bowing to her, three warrior saints, *Daniel in the Lions' Den* and the *Seven Youths and Daniel among the Lions in a Cave*. The frescoes in the narthex are similar in style to those at the church of St George at Kremikovtsi.

BIBLIOGRAPHY

A. Grabar: *La Peinture religieuse en Bulgarie* (Paris, 1928)

TANIA VELMANS

Dragging up. *See* Retroussage.

Dragon, Vittore Grubicy de. *See* Grubicy, Vittore.

Dragoş (Coman) (*fl* first half of 16th century). Romanian painter. He was the painter of the main mural ensemble at the church in Arbore village, Suceava district, which was founded by the nobleman Luca Arbore. The wall painting, executed in 1541, entirely covers the internal and external walls. In the interior's iconographic plan appear two votive scenes in the naos and in the arcosolium of the pronaos, showing the family of the founder in the *Cavalcade of Military Saints*. In the western arcade of the exterior Dragoş depicted the lives of *St George, St Demitrius, St Nichita* and *St Paraschiva* and on the south wall the *Acatist*

Hymn, ending with the *Siege of Constantinople* and an ample *Last Judgement*. The work shows an extraordinary compositional inventiveness, combining iconographic styles derived from the West and from the post-Byzantine tradition. It is plausible that Dragoş travelled to the southern Alps and that he was also familiar with contemporary Russian icons. His figures have much movement and grace; some of those with harmonious profiles (e.g. *Deisis*, on the south façade) have lost colour, remaining only stains with finely traced contours, yet they stand out with extreme elegance in their sophisticated draperies, on an azure background that has admirably resisted erosion.

BIBLIOGRAPHY

V. Drăgut: *Dragoş Coman: Le Maître des fresques d'Arbore* (Bucharest, 1969)

V. Drăgut and D. Grigorescu: *History of Romanian Art* (Bucharest, 1990), pp. 69–70

TEREZA-IRENE SINIGALIA

Drake, (Johann) Friedrich (*b* Bad Pyrmont, 23 June 1805; *d* Berlin, 6 April 1882). German sculptor. He came to Berlin in October 1827 and trained in the studio of Christian Daniel Rauch who influenced him greatly for many years, and at the Königliche Akademie der Künste. In early works such as the marble relief based on Goethe's *Fifth Roman Elegy* (1832; Heidelberg, priv. col., see Bloch and Grzimek, p. 141) and the marble and bronze group *Nymph Catching a Butterfly* (1837–9; Luxembourg, Pal. Grand-Ducal) he shows his preference for themes that connect him with ancient art and the German art of the 16th century. The style of these works is, to a large extent, drawn from works by Rauch, although Drake lent his portrayals a genre character and softened classical strictness with gentler modelling and an emphasis on expression. In the field of architectural sculpture he was content to stay within accepted architectonic limits, for example in the group of eight figures on the Schlossbrücke in Berlin (1842–53; *in situ*) and the tympanum on the Neues Museum (1854; largely destr., see Essers, p. 143). In the allegorical figures of the eight provinces in the White Hall of the Berlin Stadtschloss (1844; destr., see Essers, pp. 134–7), adaptation to the Baroque surrounds is restricted to the diagonal composition and a lively draping of the figures, while the figures on the Thesentür of Wittenberg Cathedral are based on Florentine sculpture of the 15th century.

These monuments are the artist's most important public commissions. Up to this point Drake had kept to the style he had learnt in Rauch's studio: the head is a portrait of its subject, gestures and stances are gentle, and the clothing is simply draped with no emphasis on the nature of the material. The volume of the body is, where necessary, altered to provide a dignified appearance. Drake's independent achievement is to be found in later works within the field of monumental sculpture. In the marble Berlin monument for *Frederick William III* (1849; Berlin, Tiergarten), Drake's portrayal of the King shows him looking much like one of his own subjects, not distinguished by any external characteristics from the figures on the statue's plinth. In the bronze equestrian statue of *William I* (1864; Cologne, Hohenzollernbrücke), Drake succeeded in combining representation and pathos without excess dramatization. With his bronze *Victory* on the Victory Column

(1869–73; now Berlin, Tiergarten), he created a landmark for Berlin. His funereal monuments extend from the classicist marble reliefs for *Gräfin von der Schulenburg* (1842; Rühstadt, Dorfkirche) to the monument in Wiesbaden with eight sandstone figures for *Duchess Pauline of Nassau* (1857–60; Wiesbaden, Alter Friedhof), in which Gothic elements are added to a classical construction.

Within the field of portrait sculpture, the statuettes from the period of his first independent works (1833–7) are particularly charming in their combination of the public and the private: for example *Wilhelm von Humboldt* in bronze (1834; destr., see Bloch and Grzimek, pl. 86). A high level of realism brings out the individuality of the characters portrayed and pushes classicism into the background. Drake's work shows the highest degree of development in his busts: starting with a strong dependence on Rauch's formal methods, he ends with a naturalism in the treatment of individual features, as in those of *Friedrich von Raumer* (1870; Berlin, Alte N.G.) and *Richard Lepsius* (1870; Berlin, Bodemus.). It is only here that he manages almost completely to overcome the classicism of Rauch and to join the neo-Baroque trend of Reinhold Begas, which dominated the second half of the 19th century.

BIBLIOGRAPHY

F. Ahlbeck: 'Künstler und Werkstätten: Friedrich Drake', *Dt. Kstbl.*, iii (1852), pp. 150–53, 161–3
W. Heinrich: *Christian Rauch und seine Schüler Ernst Rietschel und Friedrich Drake* (Basle, 1884)
P. Meyerheim: 'Friedrich Drake: Erinnerungen zu seinem 100ten Geburtstag', *Z. Bild. Kst.*, n. s., xvi (1905), p. 257
M. Kuhn: *Die Siegessäule* (W. Berlin, 1968)
V. Essers: *Johann Friedrich Drake* (Munich, 1976)
P. Bloch and W. Grzimek: *Das klassische Berlin: Die Berliner Bildhauerschule im neunzehnten Jahrhundert* (Frankfurt am Main, W. Berlin and Vienna, 1978)
P. Bloch, S. Einholz and J. von Simson: *Ethos and Pathos: Die Berliner Bildhauerschule, 1786–1914* (Berlin, 1990)

VOLKMAR ESSERS

Drake, Nathan (*b* Lincoln, *c.* 1728; *d* York, 19 Feb 1778). English painter. He was the son of the Rev. Samuel Drake, rector of St Mary's, Nottingham, and was apprenticed to his brother, a cabinetmaker in York, where he appears to have settled in 1752 and spent much of the rest of his life. He worked as a portrait, landscape, topographical and sporting painter. His hunting scenes often include a view of a country house, a fine example being *William Tufnell and his Hounds at Nun Monkton Priory, York* (signed and dated 1769; priv. col.). These tend to be somewhat conservative in character, but his purely topographical subjects, such as the *Newport Arch, Lincoln* (signed; Lincoln, Usher Gal.), include groups of figures recalling Canaletto or Samuel Scott. Drake's portraits are few, but there is a small signed oil of a *Sportsman* (London, Apsley House, Wellington Mus.). Several of his views, as well as his illustrations to James Thomson's *The Seasons*, were engraved. He exhibited (1771–6) at the Society of Arts.

BIBLIOGRAPHY

Waterhouse: *18th C.*
J. Harris: *The Artist and the Country House* (London, 1979), pp. 225, 241; pl. 265
Manners and Morals: Hogarth and British Painting, 1700–1760 (exh. cat., ed. E. Einberg; London, Tate, 1988), pp. 197, 241

RICHARD JEFFREE

Draperie mouillée [Fr.: 'wet drapery']. Term applied in painting and sculpture to the clinging drapery that looks as if it were damp and reveals the underlying form of a figure.

□

Drapery painter [draperyman]. Independent specialist in the painting of draperies, usually employed by a portrait painter with a large portrait practice; to be distinguished from assistants who were members of a workshop or studio. In the traditional Renaissance workshop an established master undertook the comprehensive training of apprentices and equipped them with all the skills necessary for an independent artist. The emergence of specialist drapery painters was a consequence of the breakdown of the apprenticeship system. An increasing dependence on technical manuals suggests that this occurred in Holland after *c.* 1660. The situation is less clear in other countries. For instance, in 18th-century France, workshops such as that of HYACINTHE RIGAUD were extensive and well-organized, with experts, including drapery painters, executing their own specialized parts of each portrait. For other 18th-century French painters, such as Nicolas de Largillierre, the present state of research is inconclusive.

Little direct evidence survives to show the structure and organization of the English workshop during the 16th century, and therefore the role of assistants remains obscure. The most important artists in England in the following century, Sir Anthony van Dyck, Sir Peter Lely and Sir Godfrey Kneller, were all foreign portrait painters and used primarily foreign assistants. This practice failed to foster native talent and increased the painters' reliance on imported skills. What training was carried out in studios was often directed towards producing specialized assistants. Everhard Jabach's account to Roger de Piles (quoted in 1991 exh. cat.) of van Dyck's methods of dealing with a large portrait practice, describes how he 'drew the figure and clothes with a great flourish and exquisite taste for about a quarter of an hour. He then gave these drawings to his skilful assistants for them to paint the sitter in the clothes which had been sent at the special request of van Dyck…he [then] passed his brush lightly and quickly over what they had done'. Lely refined these methods of working and sustained a long association with John Baptist Gaspars (*fl* 1641–92), known as Lely's Baptist, who later worked for John Riley as well as Kneller. Other members of Lely's studio, Willem Wissing and Jan van der Vaardt, later collaborated on a portrait of *Frances, Duchess of Richmond and Lennox* (1687; London, N.P.G.), a rare instance of a portrait signed by both master and drapery painter.

During the first half of the 18th century all the leading English portrait painters employed drapery painters. Both William Hogarth's and George Vertue's acerbic comments (quoted in Whitley) on the role of the Antwerp painter JOSEPH VAN AKEN show the dependence of many of the fashionable painters on his skills. Lesser figures such as John Vanderbank employed him, as well as provincial painters such as Hamlet Winstanley (1694–1756), who sent his 'masks' by coach to be completed in London. Such leading artists as Allan Ramsay, Thomas Hudson and Joseph Wright of Derby also employed him, and one highly fashionable composition, closely modelled on Rubens's portrait of his second wife, *Hélène Fourment* (Lisbon, Mus. Gulbenkian), was used by all three artists several times. It has been demonstrated that the design originated with van Aken, leaving little doubt that his services were eagerly sought after. Many of his drawings (Edinburgh, N.G.) have not been distinguished from those of Ramsay.

PETER TOMS, a pupil of Hudson while Joshua Reynolds was in his studio, worked for many important artists of the succeeding generation, although not for Gainsborough or Romney. Some indication of the scale of fees and the structure of payments is to be found in Edward Edwards's *Anecdotes of Painters* (1808, p. 54), in which he claimed that Toms, normally paid 20 guineas for painting the clothing, hands and accessories of a full-length portrait, received only 12 for the portrait of *Lady Elizabeth Keppel* (1762; Woburn Abbey, Beds), at a time when Reynolds was charging 100 guineas for a full-length. Toms also worked for Francis Cotes and Johan Zoffany.

The importance of fashionable portraiture declined in the first half of the 19th century (with the exception of that of Sir Thomas Lawrence). At the same time a new emphasis was placed on an artist's individual handling of the paint medium. Portraiture became simply one among a number of genres, and the role of the drapery painter inevitably declined.

BIBLIOGRAPHY

W. Martin: 'The Life of a Dutch Artist in the Seventeenth Century', *Burl. Mag.*, vii (1905), pp. 125–8, 416–27; viii (1906), pp. 13–24

W. T. Whitley: *Artists and their Friends in England, 1700–1799* (London, 1928)

J. Steegmann: 'A Drapery Painter of the 18th Century', *Conn.*, xcvii (1936), pp. 309–15

J. D. Stewart: *Sir Godfrey Kneller* (London, 1971)

L. Campbell: 'The Early Netherlandish Painters and their Workshops' (Leuven, n.d.)

M. Kirby Talley: *Portrait Painting in England: Studies in the Technical Literature* (London, 1981) [privately pubd, Mellon Cent.]

Largillierre and the Eighteenth-century Portrait (exh. cat. by M. N. Rosenfeld, Montreal, Mus. F.A., 1982)

The Drawings of Anthony van Dyck (exh. cat. by C. Brown, New York, Pierpont Morgan Lib., 1991)

ELIZABETH ALLEN

Drawbridge, John (*b* Wellington, NZ, 27 Dec 1930). New Zealand painter and printmaker. After training as an art teacher he was awarded the National Art Gallery travelling scholarship in 1957 and studied at the Central School of Art and Design in London. His initial interest in textile design shifted to printmaking and he gained wider experience from 1960 to 1961 in printing workshops in Paris. He was one of a number of New Zealand artists working in England at the time, including Melvin Day (*b* 1923), Patrick Hanly and Don Peebles (*b* 1922). He was commissioned to produce a large mural for New Zealand House in London, completed in 1963.

Drawbridge returned to New Zealand in 1964 to teach in the School of Design at Wellington Polytechnic. He continued to produce both paintings and prints, particularly the group *Tanya Coming and Going* (1967; Canberra, N.G.). He also completed further major official commissions. One was a kinetic work for the New Zealand pavilion at Expo '70 in Osaka, Japan: a rotating dish behind the mural caused light passing through perspex rods to ripple across the work's surface. A similar effect was achieved when this mural was reworked for installation in the National Library, Wellington (1987): the two sides of the ribbed mural were painted in different patterns, and, as the viewer passed by, the image shifted and changed. The largest was a curved sculptural mural for Parliament House in Wellington (1973–6).

BIBLIOGRAPHY

A. Kirker: 'John Drawbridge: From Print to Construction', *A. NZ*, 24 (1982), pp. 18–21

JIM BARR, MARY BARR

Drawing. Term that refers both to the act of marking lines on a surface and to the product of such manual work. Whether it is summary or complete, a drawing is defined less by its degree of finish or support than by its media and formal vocabulary. Manipulating line, form, value and texture, with an emphasis on line and value rather than colour, drawing has been employed since ancient times for both aesthetic and practical purposes. The language of drawing has been used to record, outline and document images that the draughtsman has observed, imagined, recalled from memory or copied.

I. Introduction. II. Function and purpose. III. Materials and techniques. IV. History. V. Collections. VI. Conservation.

I. Introduction.

There are several qualities unique to drawing that distinguish it from other art forms. It has always been considered among the most intimate and personal of all the arts. Since the early Renaissance, a drawn sketch was central to the process of artistic creation as thoughts and images were first rendered into graphic form. Although 'first idea' sketches represent only one aspect of the creative process (*see* §II, 1 below), idea-generating sketches possess the aura of fiery inspiration. That spirit of invention and originality has lent allure and renown to the drawings of great masters, such as Leonardo da Vinci, Rembrandt, Degas and Picasso.

Drawing has traditionally served as the foundation for all the arts. To attain sovereignty in painting, sculpture or architecture, first it was necessary to master the fundamentals of drawing, for as the great 19th-century French painter Ingres declared, 'drawing is the probity of art'. Training consisted of copying the master's own designs and drawings before progressing to the stage of drawing from the nude (the preferred method of studying the figure in art academies). Anatomy and perspective were also subjects learnt through drawing. As an exercise, drawing trained the eye and the hand, conferring judgement and teaching discipline. In the workshop, academy or drawing-room, the practice of drawing has sustained professional art education and served as the ideal pastime of the cultivated amateur and dilettante. Moreover, the infinite variety that can be achieved with the sparest of means makes drawing an ever-challenging artistic activity. Drawings can be appreciated as works of art in their own right, independent of any auxiliary function they may serve in relation to the design and execution of a project. A copy or a reworked drawing, when the corrections are executed by great masters such as Rubens or Rembrandt (see fig. 5 below), disclose fresh insights about the nature of an original and the creative process itself.

Since drawings first served as adjuncts to the working process, they were generally unsigned. Yet even though they are usually less ambitious or finished compared to works in other media, they often reveal the genius and style of their creators in a clear and characteristic way. The traditional approach to the study of drawings, particularly Old Master drawings, has consequently been to investigate problems of attribution and style. The connoisseur's primary mission has been to define an authoritative corpus of drawings for individual masters and their followers, for localized workshops or regional schools. The objective of classifying drawings according to artist and school was to provide a firm foundation for further study. Pursuing such a line of inquiry was long thought to represent the most scientific basis for the study of drawings.

Since the 1960s, however, new approaches to the study of drawings have been advanced, which focus, for instance, on the role of drawings and their function within the creative process. Furthermore, as a result of developments in scientific examination and the restoration of paintings and frescoes, an entirely new category of drawings, UNDERDRAWING, has emerged. The study of underdrawings—defined as any drawing forming the starting-point in the execution of a work of art that is completely covered during the working process—has resulted in an exciting new field of scholarship, modifying previous assumptions about the definition of the medium.

Throughout the 20th century creative drawing has served to stimulate an original approach to form. From Fauve watercolours to Cubist collages or Surrealist 'automatic drawings', the role of drawing has been continually redefined and expanded. For such artists as Picasso, Matisse, Miró, Stuart Davis and Jackson Pollock, as well as Cy Twombly, Joseph Beuys and Keith Haring, drawing has been not only a source of artistic inspiration but also a means of expression. The trend towards abstraction and non-representational art, combined with the influence of Freud's theories of the subconscious, demanded a new approach to the creative process and new attitudes about its product. In addition, the tendency of 20th-century artists to use popular culture as a source has spurred interest in a variety of non-traditional artistic media. In the same period the artistic use of mixed media has served to sever the boundaries between the traditional media. Practitioners have continually adapted and redefined the nature of the format and the support as their artistic goals have changed, thus constantly renewing and expanding the expressive potential of one of the oldest art forms.

II. Function and purpose.

1. CREATIVE DRAWINGS. The process of formulating a design is often initiated by the *première pensée*, a quick thumb-nail sketch or even a doodle. Such form-searching sketches serve to explore a range of alternatives, with many ideas sometimes jotted down on a single page. The key purpose is to generate creative energy and record the process of brainstorming on paper. Another form of creative drawing, executed either as a finished work or without explicit purpose, is the independent drawing, such as a portrait, botanical illustration or caricature, in which the creative impulse is not only materialized but also

completely articulated. Since creative drawings may appear as finished, as detailed or as free as the artist or designer wishes, they include drawings at opposite ends of the creative spectrum: both the inchoate or experimental stage of idea generation and the final or definitive statement realized within a graphic medium.

2. STUDY DRAWINGS. These are subsidiary drawings—preparatory drawings, detail drawings and process drawings—produced in relation to the execution of another work of art or design, which is usually in a different medium. Preparatory and detail drawings help an artist to work out the final form of a composition. Process drawings, on the other hand, assist in the transfer of an image to a different scale or format; they have a mechanical function and contribute to the routine replication of both unique and popular images.

Before the 15th century it was customary for artists' workshops, when commissioned to produce a new work, to reuse a rather restricted set of compositional designs, elaborating and adapting previous work as circumstances required. These exempla, mounted and bound together in a model or PATTERN BOOK, were a valuable workshop resource: serving as storehouses of available models, they helped to streamline workshop production. For artist and patron alike, tradition and custom governed decision-making rather than originality and invention. However, as a consequence of the 15th-century revival of humanism, with a renewed interest in the written and material heritage of the ancient world and a growing awareness of the natural world, both artist and patron placed a new premium on originality. To devise and fabricate customized designs, it was necessary to spend more time and effort in compositional planning and analysis. Renewed interest in anatomy, linear perspective and the representation of the illusion of the human figure moving through space inspired artists to study drapery and the human figure, in the nude and costumed, in greater detail than ever before (see colour pl. I, fig. 1). Artists copied fragments of antique statuary, dissected corpses and posed living models to perfect their understanding of the human form. The drapery study evolved to aid the artist in his examination of the structure of the body and the covering garment as well as the play of light and shadow on solids and voids (see fig. 1). The representation of gesture and the illusion of movement were enhanced by an understanding of how drapery moved, both revealing and concealing the human form, while artists also paid attention to the contribution of the ornamental pattern of drapery to the overall surface design and to the expression of human feelings. In costume studies, unlike drapery studies (which may be regarded as fabric still-lifes), drapery and the human figure were integrated in order to record the harmony between movement and expression, in which the drapery defined the body's structure, accentuated motion or underscored the spiritual content of the picture. Based on prototypes inspired by Classical sculpture, studies of draped figures were a form of routine drawing exercise, independent of a specific project, although the large number of surviving examples also reflects their use as direct preparatory studies.

1. Albrecht Dürer: *Drapery Study*, point of brush and grey wash, heightened with white, on green prepared paper, 179×245 mm, preparatory study for the Heller Altarpiece, 1508 (Vienna, Graphische Sammlung Albertina)

Drapery and costume studies were usually executed at a relatively advanced stage in the development of a design, immediately before the final preparatory compositional drawing or modello (*see* MODELLO, §I), or before beginning work on the intended support. The custom was to work out a composition in stages, beginning with a rapid notational sketch of various ideas, followed by a more definitive drawing fixing the outlines of the composition and detail studies from posed models to clarify the individual figures. The posed models were often sketched first as nudes and only at a later stage as clothed figures, with the drapery or garment delineated over the anatomical sketch. Costume studies of draped figures served a similar role to that of other detail studies drawn from the posed model, particularly *garzone* drawings, so called after the Italian word for studio assistant. Dressed in everyday clothes, the *garzone* assumed the poses of both male and female figures. In some instances, notably in the work of Raphael, successive stages of compositional development were combined on a single sheet.

Before the 15th century all stages of work, including both design and execution, were customarily executed on the support itself (e.g. wall or panel) and not as an adjunct drawn on an independent surface. Such underdrawings, including the *sinopia* design for a fresco, were usually concealed under the subsequent layers of paint (for illustrations *see* SINOPIA and UNDERDRAWING). Although not intended to be seen by the viewer, some detailed compositions are thought to have been prepared for the approval of the patron. Knowledge of this aspect of drawing practice, previously documented only in damaged or incomplete works as well as in examples partially visible to the naked eye, has been expanded by the discovery of new procedures to detach frescoes from the wall and separate layers of paint and plaster, as well as advances in scientific methods of technical examination of Netherlandish panel painting of the 15th and 16th centuries, particularly infra-red photography and reflectography (*see also* TECHNICAL EXAMINATION, §II). The discovery of *sinopie* on walls and underdrawings on panels has dramatically expanded the corpus of graphic material from a period from which relatively little independent work on paper survives. Research has yielded new information about a range of art-historical problems, including issues of attribution, chronology, studio practice and personal style, as well as drawing function, for example, the relationship between underdrawings and preliminary drawings on paper and printed graphics.

Process drawings, utilized as tools to assist in basic workshop production, were seldom thought to possess any intrinsic artistic value, and such sheets were customarily disregarded after use. The process of transferring, reducing or enlarging the approved preliminary design to the final support often distorted the image. It was an exacting job and was usually delegated to trained assistants. Even when a composition is worked up on the support itself rather than independently on paper, process drawings retain a central role in the operations of successful workshops. Commercial production of reproductive engravings and book illustrations requires that images be transferred from one medium and format to another. Designs for tapestries, stained glass, costumes, stage designs, ornaments and decorative and religious objects are conceived with their translation into different media in mind.

3. PRESENTATION AND CONTRACT DRAWINGS. A presentation drawing is a type of detailed compositional drawing prepared for the patron's approval, which explicitly outlines the agreed composition (for illustration *see* PRESENTATION DRAWING). Such designs are often coloured so that the patron can both evaluate the colour scheme and more easily envisage the final outcome. A contract drawing is a specific type of formal presentation drawing in which the artist and patron sign the agreed design, giving the drawing the force of a legal contract. For durability and because long-term projects, particularly architectural and decorative schemes, required years to complete, presentation and contract drawings were often executed on parchment. The contract drawing was required to serve as a reference for the numerous parties involved in a project (*see also* ARCHITECTURAL DRAWING).

III. Materials and techniques.

1. Supports. 2. Media and tools. 3. Techniques and processes.

1. SUPPORTS. Almost any plane surface may serve as a SUPPORT for a drawing. Stationary or fixed supports range from the walls of prehistoric caves to the tombs of ancient Egypt and Etruria. From the temples of Classical Greece and the villas of ancient Rome to the Renaissance and Baroque buildings of Italy, walls, ceilings and even floors have served as supports for drawings. The most popular portable supports for writing—papyrus, parchment, cloth and paper—have also been the most favoured for drawing. Even in prehistoric and ancient times and in the many centuries before the availability of paper, artists sketched designs and drafted plans with a stylus, brush, charcoal or pen and ink on such reusable or disposable supports as chiselled stones, painted terracotta and limestone shards (ostraca), palimpsests and prepared tablets made of clay, wax or boxwood.

PAPYRUS, grown in the Nile Delta and used by the ancient Egyptians as a writing and drawing surface, is a thick, fibrous water-plant, strips of which were beaten with a mallet until they were cemented together by the natural sap. The sap also acted as size to reduce absorbency and prevent ink from 'bleeding'. Papyrus was an ideal support for writing and drawing on scrolls because of the ease with which it could be extended by the addition of new strips. Its successor from the 5th century AD was PARCHMENT, a protein substance derived from treated animal skins, usually sheep, goat or calf. Vellum is a superior grade of parchment made from unblemished calf skins. For centuries prepared skins served as a support for writing, manuscript illumination and drawing because of their translucent ivory colour, large format, even finish, double-sided surfaces, flexibility, durability and strength. Bleached and degreased parchment formed a flawless white writing surface; rubbed with powdered pumice, chalk and resin, then burnished, it formed a smooth, opaque ground for illumination. Adding pigment produced a coloured or toned ground. Although by the mid-15th century paper was less costly and easier to prepare than parchment, which it superseded as the writing and drawing support most commonly used, parchment continued to be preferred for works intended for frequent use and multiple users, including architectural plans, pattern books and designs. Moreover, the durability of parchment made it a favoured support, especially in northern Europe, for highly finished independent drawings such as portraits, miniatures, botanical illustrations and official documents.

PAPER is a substance made in the form of thin sheets or leaves from rags, straw, hemp, wood, bamboo, mulberry bark or other vegetable fibres. According to tradition, it was invented in China in AD 105. East Asian or 'Oriental' papers may be distinguished from Western examples by their smooth but porous surface texture as well as their translucency and sheen. Through commerce and conquest, paper and papermaking gradually moved westward from Asia through the Islamic world; by the 12th and 13th centuries paper was being manufactured in Spain and Italy. Papermaking in Europe from 1300 to 1800 was a highly skilled and regulated craft, producing a pure, permanent and durable surface, which was resistant to internal deterioration. At the beginning of the 19th century the discovery that wood products could be used for making paper and that paper itself could be formed in continuous lengths changed papermaking from a skilled handicraft into a modern industry. From the end of the 20th century the computer monitor began to replace paper as the most common support for drawing (*see* COMPUTER ART).

2. MEDIA AND TOOLS. The interplay between supports and media presents the artist with an almost infinite variety of creative possibilities. Identifying media and interpreting their sequence of application is not an exact science, but cataloguers of drawings generally list media and techniques according to their order of application, from the initial line or stroke to the finishing touches or highlights and heightening accents. The subject is generally divided into two categories: either by fine or broad strokes or by dry or wet application. Fine strokes characterize metalpoint and pen and ink, while broad strokes are typical of chalk, pastel, crayon (conté, greasy or coloured), charcoal and graphite (for illustration *see* CRAYON); dry media include chalks, pastels, charcoal, crayon and graphite, while wet media include inks, washes, watercolour, gouache and tempera. Almost all the basic drawing media and tools were in use by the first half of the 16th century, their application having been thoroughly investigated by many 15th-century artists, including Hieronymus Bosch, Martin Schongauer, the Housebook Master, Jean Fouquet, Pisanello, Domenico Ghirlandaio and Leonardo da Vinci. Later, technical innovation was related to the realization of new expressive effects by combining media, highly personal experimentation (evident, for example, in the work of Giovanni Benedetto Castiglione) or finding new

applications of seemingly outmoded techniques (e.g. the 19th-century revival of metalpoint, watercolour and pastel). In the 20th century traditional definitions of drawing have been challenged as much by the choice of ephemeral materials (e.g. the use of river mud by Richard Long) as by the techniques with which they are applied.

(i) Ink and wash. The most common colouring agent is INK, which is available in a wide range of colours and can be applied with either a pen or brush. India or Chinese ink is produced from lampblack, an oily carbon substance, mixed with gum arabic hardened by baking. Its deep black colour resists fading but reacts to moisture; diluted with water, it becomes grey WASH. 'Iron-gall' ink, which was cheap and easy to produce, was traditionally the principal writing and drawing medium. Made from gall-nuts and iron rust, filings or salts mixed with gum arabic, it initially flows violet–black in colour but fades with age to tones of brown and yellow. Sometimes mixed with vitriol, iron-gall ink is highly acidic; it corrodes and eats holes through paper fibres (*see* INK, fig. 3). Bistre is a light, transparent brown pigment extracted from wood soot, preferably beechwood; sepia is a deep brown ink obtained from the secretions of the cuttlefish.

The PEN, commonly used since antiquity for writing, has also been the most important and popular instrument for drawing. Quill pens, cut from the flesh end of the wing feathers of birds or fowl, pared and slit to a blunt, medium or fine point, were a versatile instrument yielding effortlessly to the personal pressure, touch and calligraphic style of draughtsmen. More fragile and less flexible than the quill, the reed pen is cut from the stems of bamboo-like grasses and is used for short strokes, producing broad, uniform, angular effects. When employed by such masters as Rembrandt (for illustration *see* PEN) and van Gogh, the superiority of the reed pen for hatching and emphatic, expressive linework is self-evident. Metal pens, which were first produced in the 19th century, are mass-produced in many shapes and sizes; the hard, crisp, regular strokes of their steel points may be seen in the pen drawings of such artists as Picasso (see colour pl. II, fig. 1) and Henry Moore. The BRUSH, although generally used for the broad application of wash or watercolour, is also used to render fine, supple lines, evident, for example, in Dürer's many studies (Berlin, Kupferstichkab.; Vienna, Albertina; see fig. 1 above) for the Heller Altarpiece (1508; ex-Residenz Munich, destr. 1729). Made from animal hairs or bristles, the most sought-after brushes were composed of badger, squirrel or sable hair.

(ii) Friable sticks. Of the dry media, CHARCOAL, a carbon residue obtained by charring sticks of wood, preferably willow, in a fire, is probably the oldest drawing medium (*see* DÜRER, (1), fig. 4). Friable, easily rubbed and of moderate intensity, once applied it must be sprayed with a FIXATIVE. Because it is easily erased, charcoal was recommended for preliminary sketches such as underdrawings and cartoons for frescoes. The Venetians, notably Tintoretto and Jacopo Bassano, produced velvety effects with charcoal by dipping the sticks in linseed oil, which also served as a permanent fixative. This technique was later adopted by other artists, such as the 17th-century Dutch Italianate Nicolaes Berchem.

CHALK is available in both natural and synthetic form. In its natural state it is simply one of several minerals cut into sticks: calcite or calcium carbonate (white), carbon (black) or haematite (red). Black or 'Italian' chalk is a compact, clayey schist traditionally from Piedmont; it varies in tone from black to grey (*see* CELLINI, BENVENUTO, fig. 2; GRÜNEWALD, MATTHIAS, fig. 4; RAPHAEL, fig. 10; and REMBRANDT VAN RIJN, fig. 6), Red chalk, sometimes called *sanguine* (from Lat. *sanguis, sanguinis:* 'blood'), is iron oxide mixed with clay. It displays great warmth and chromatic strength (see colour pl. I, fig. 1) but has a limited value range: it varies widely from an orange–red and brown–red to a deep purplish–red colour. Although indelible, it responds to rubbing with the finger or a stump (a coil of leather or paper ending in a point, used for blending chalk lines into an area of tone; *see* STUMPING). In the form of calcite or steatite (tailor's chalk), natural white chalks have been used for heightening and highlights. For evoking the natural range of flesh tints the combination of red, black and white chalk, a three-colour technique known as *aux trois crayons*, was greatly favoured by Rubens, Watteau (see colour pl. I, fig. 2) and Paul-César Helleu (for illustration *see* HELLEU, PAUL-CÉSAR).

PASTEL is a coloured chalk fabricated from powdered, dry, natural pigments mixed with chalk and a binder, such as gum tragacanth, and pressed into a stick. Mixing powdered pigments together extends the range of available hues and tones. With each stroke, friction causes the pigment to powder and rub off as the rough texture of the paper holds the colour. Rosalba Carriera, Maurice-Quentin La Tour (*see* PASTEL, colour pls IV and V) and Jean-Etienne Liotard made pastel portraits highly fashionable in the 18th century, but Degas (*see* DEGAS, EDGAR, fig. 4; NUDE, fig. 5; and PASTEL, colour pl. III) and the Impressionists extended the expressive range of the medium to include all the genres traditionally associated with painting (*see* IMPRESSIONISM, colour pl. VI, fig. 1).

(iii) Metalpoint. A STYLUS with a point of metal (gold, silver, lead or copper) used in combination with a toned or coloured ground is one of the oldest recorded techniques; it was used by the Romans on writing tablets and by medieval scribes to lay in their lines. An inelastic medium, METALPOINT produces a delicate, even, permanent stroke, which is nevertheless responsive to disciplined individual handling (see fig. 2). Only leadpoint (graphite) yields a visible mark on unprepared paper; metalpoint strokes oxidize to a grey–brown colour. The necessary surface preparation, applied with a brush in layers and then burnished after drying, consists of whiting or gypsum, powdered bone, pigment and size. Coloured grounds in shades of pink, mauve, ochre, green and blue were popular in Italy; the tonal range of metalpoint was further expanded by the addition of white heightening with a brush, as in the cursive silverpoint sketches of Filippino Lippi and Raphael. Recommended by Leonardo for open-air sketching in pocketbooks, metalpoint was the first easily portable medium and the predecessor of the pencil. It flourished in Italy, Germany and the Netherlands in the 15th century for figure, portrait and animal studies (*see* LEONARDO DA VINCI, fig. 7) but fell into disuse after *c.* 1525, when broader and more forceful effects were sought. By the 17th century

metalpoint was, with few exceptions, used only for small-scale portrait drawings, of which one of the most touching is Rembrandt's inscribed portrait of his young wife, *Saskia van Uylenburgh* (1633; Berlin, Kupferstichkab.; *see* REM-BRANDT VAN RIJN, fig. 2).

(iv) Graphite and pencil. GRAPHITE, which was first quarried in Cumberland, England, in 1560, is a crystalline form of carbon that produces a hard, thin and supple grey line. From its metallic lustre and colour, it can be distinguished from the darker, duller finish of black chalk. It was popular in the 17th and 18th centuries for small-scale portrait drawings on parchment. Watteau used it in combination with red chalk for softer, more tonal effects. When the Napoleonic Wars led to a restricted supply of English graphite in France during the 1790s, a French chemist, Nicolas-Jacques Conté (1755–1805), formulated a mixture of refined graphite and clay to serve as a substitute (*see* CRAYON); from this developed the modern wood-encased 'lead' PENCIL. The pencil drawings of Ingres (*see* INGRES, JEAN-AUGUSTE-DOMINIQUE, fig. 2) suggest the purity of line that made pencil the favourite instrument of such draughtsmen as Burne-Jones, Degas, Adolph Menzel (see fig. 8 below), Klimt and Picasso.

(v) Pigments. WATERCOLOUR, a mixture of coloured pigments and a clear binder (gum arabic) soluble in water, produces a transparent colour layer that becomes completely integrated with the paper support (or the parchment support in the cases of botanical and scientific illuminations). GOUACHE, or bodycolour, is an opaque pigment produced by the addition of white lead and size to watercolour; when it fully coats the surface it resembles painting. Often these media were applied together: Dürer's series of panoramic alpine landscapes (1494–5; e.g. Berlin, Kupferstichkab.; Bremen, Ksthalle; Oxford, Ashmolean; Paris, Louvre) displays the luminous qualities of watercolour alternating with the depth of colour and solidity of gouache, an effect that may also be seen in a more intimate vein in the elegant compositions depicting French gardens by Louis-Gabriel Moreau (for illustration *see* MOREAU, (1)). The 18th-century revival of watercolour in England, evoking the memory of van Dyck's sketches of the English countryside (*see* WATERCOLOUR, colour pl. VII, fig. 1), was again inspired by the desire to record landscape observed directly from nature, culminating in the work of Constable, Richard Parkes Bonington and Turner (*see* WATERCOLOUR, colour pl. VIII, fig. 1), who influenced the French Romantics, such as Delacroix (*see* WATERCOLOUR, colour pl. VII, fig. 2), the Impressionists and even Cézanne.

3. TECHNIQUES AND PROCESSES. The draughtsman may employ any one or a combination of four categories of techniques, usually in the following order: preparatory, creative, corrective and transfer to another support.

(i) Preparatory. The preliminary steps of readying media and preparing the support to receive its application by the master were usually undertaken by workshop assistants as part of their training. Numerous manuals relate how to grind or select colours, make charcoal, choose inks, cut quills and buy paper. Such treatises outline how to apply,

2. Domenico Ghirlandaio: *Head of an Old Man*, silverpoint, heightened with white, on pink prepared paper, 320×295 mm, *c.* 1480 (Stockholm, Nationalmuseum)

colour and burnish a ground and how to give a paper a 'tooth' to accept pastel. The durability and lasting beauty of a drawing depend on the purity of materials and the practitioner's understanding of the rules of the craft.

(ii) Creative. The creative stage of drawing refers to its execution. A mark or line used to convey an artistic effect on a blank surface constitutes the basic element of drawing, but form may also be conceptualized in relation to light and shade as well as lines and planes. While a pen drawing by Matisse (*see* MATISSE, HENRI, fig. 5) or Klee exemplifies the purely linear approach, one of Seurat's conté crayon studies on textured paper illustrates the search for pure tone (*see* SEURAT, GEORGES, fig. 4). Through inflected lines or contours, the draughtsman suggests and circumscribes form. To model forms and evoke a sense of space or atmosphere, the artist employs additional techniques. 'Hatching' refers to shading by setting down parallel straight or curved lines at various intervals (see fig. 3); 'crosshatching' refers to shading with sets of lines in two or more directions (*see* GOLTZIUS, HENDRICK, fig. 1). 'Graining' describes the process of turning from the point to the side of the stick of chalk, crayon, pastel or pencil to create a series of broad, parallel strokes. Gradations of tone achieved by rubbing chalk, charcoal or pastel with the finger, brush or stump is called 'stumping' (see fig. 8 below). To emphasize the play of light, the artist applies accents or highlights, often referred to as 'white heightening' (see figs 1–3). In chiaroscuro drawings a toned or coloured surface preparation serves as the 'middleground' for the application of highlights and shading (see fig. 1 above).

(iii) Corrective. In terms of the corrective process, on working drawings intended to be seen only by other members of the workshop scant effort was wasted on masking changes, making it relatively easy to identify pentiments (*see* PENTIMENT). Breadcrumbs or feathers

3. Titian: *Pastoral Landscape with a Nude Woman Asleep*, pen and brown ink, heightened with white, 195×298 mm, *c.* 1565 (Malibu, CA, J. Paul Getty Museum)

were traditionally employed to rub out errors in broad media; for fine media a coat of opaque pigment was used for covering the rejected passage before redrawing the motif. Sometimes a 'silhouette' or redrawn paper patch was used, trimmed to cover exactly the area to be corrected. Sometimes a work was retouched, involving the superimposition of the work of one master on top of another. A discrepancy in technique and style between the original design and the graphic additions is often an indication of retouching, as in Rembrandt's corrections over the compositional exercises of his pupils (see fig. 5 below) or in Rubens's enthusiastic revisions with the brush on drawings in his collection.

(iv) Transfer. The transfer, reduction or enlargement of the approved preliminary design to the designated surface for the finished work was a central element of workshop routine. Traditional techniques included placing the drawing over a blank surface or sheet of paper, rubbing the *verso* with chalk and incising the contours with a stylus, but it could also be done 'blind' (for illustration of the latter technique *see* STYLUS); applying a sheet of tracing paper and copying the outlines by tracing (for illustration *see* TRACING); and pricking the contours of the design, especially a full-sized CARTOON, with a needle and pouncing coloured dust or charcoal through the holes on to a new support (for illustrations *see* POUNCING and RAPHAEL, fig. 10). Changing the scale of an image without changing the proportions could be achieved using grid lines, usually at right angles, ruled on to a drawing, a process known as squaring (for illustration *see* SQUARING

UP). An exact but reversed duplicate of an original drawing, called a counterproof, offset or squeeze, is made by placing a thin sheet of moistened paper on top of a drawing and running both sheets through a press (for illustration *see* COUNTERPROOF). For procedures involving image reversal, such as printmaking or tapestry-weaving, counterproofs allow the designer to see the composition in the same direction as the craftsman assigned to reproduce it.

BIBLIOGRAPHY

J. Meder: *Die Handzeichnung* (Vienna, 1919); Eng. trans. by W. Ames and rev. as *The Mastery of Drawing*, 2 vols (New York, 1978)

C. A. Mitchell: *Inks: Their Composition and Manufacture* (London, 1937)

C. de Tolnay: *History and Technique of Old Master Drawings: A Handbook* (1943)

J. Watrous: *The Craft of Old-Master Drawing* (Madison, 1957/R 1975)

R. W. Scheller: *A Survey of Medieval Modelbooks* (Haarlem, 1963)

D. M. Mendelowitz: *Drawing* (New York, 1967)

R. R. Johnson: *The Role of Parchment in Graeco-Roman Antiquity* (diss., microfilm, Ann Arbor, 1968)

R. D. Harley: *Artists' Pigments, 1600–1835* (London, 1970)

R. Reed: *Ancient Skins, Parchments and Leathers* (London and New York, 1972)

D. E. Greene: *Pastel* (New York and London, 1974)

N. Lewis: *Papyrus in Classical Antiquity* (Oxford, 1974)

P. Marzio: *The Art Crusade: An Analysis of American Drawing Manuals, 1820–1860*, Smithsonian Studies in History and Technology, xxxiv (Washington, DC, 1976)

Wash and Gouache: A Study of the Development of the Materials of Watercolors (exh. cat. by M. Cohn, Cambridge, MA, Fogg, 1977)

E. Andrews: *A Manual for Drawing and Painting* (London, 1978)

B. Chaet: *An Artist's Notebook: Techniques and Materials* (New York, 1979)

P. Goldman: *Looking at Drawings: A Guide to Technical Terms* (London, 1979)

T. Jirat-Wasiutynski and V. Jirat-Wasiutynski: 'Uses of Charcoal in Drawings', *A. Mag.*, lv/2 (1980), pp. 128–35

C. Ashwin: *Encyclopaedia of Drawing* (London, 1982)

M. Hambly: *Drawing Instruments: Their History, Purpose and Use for Architectural Drawings* (Cambridge, MA, 1982)

J. Bolton: *Method and Practice: Dutch and Flemish Drawing Books, 1600–1750* (Landau, 1985)

P. Bicknell: *Gilpin to Ruskin: Drawing Masters and their Manuals, 1800–1860* (London, 1987)

J. Krill: *English Artists' Paper: Renaissance to Regency* (London, 1987)

I. Simpson: *The Encyclopaedia of Drawing Techniques* (London, 1987)

J. Stephenson: *Graphic Design Materials and Equipment* (London, 1987)

M. Hambly: *Drawing Instruments, 1580–1980* (London, 1988)

Art and Computers: A National Exhibition (exh. cat., intro J. Lansdown; Middlesbrough, Cleveland Gal., 1988)

Creative Copies: Interpretive Drawings from Michelangelo to Picasso (exh. cat. by E. Haverkamp-Begemann, New York, Drg Cent., 1988)

J. Martin: *The Encyclopedia of Coloured Pencil Techniques: A Unique A–Z Directory of Coloured Pencil Drawing Techniques with a Step-by-step Guide to their Use* (London, 1992)

IV. History.

1. Ancient. 2. Medieval. 3. Renaissance. 4. 17th century. 5. 18th century. 6. 19th century. 7. 20th century.

1. ANCIENT. From the animal imagery preserved on the walls of the prehistoric caves of Lascaux, France, and Altamira, Spain (for illustrations *see* LASCAUX and ALTAMIRA), to the linear geometric designs decorating archaic Greek vases and the etched figures ornamenting Etruscan bronze mirrors, drawing is one of the oldest surviving examples of material and artistic culture. From the earliest recorded history art was placed in the service of religion and ceremony. Even after nomadic life gave way to a settled and organized social existence, surviving artefacts demonstrate that beliefs about gods and the heavens, the natural world and the afterlife were most powerfully conveyed through drawn representations, for example in such ancient Egyptian papyri as the Books of the Dead (*see* EGYPT, ANCIENT, §XI, 4 and fig. 75), the surface decoration of ancient Greek vases (*see* GREECE, ANCIENT, §V) and ancient Roman pinakes—small pictures drawn or painted on marble, which were framed and hung on the wall—of which fine examples have been excavated from the ruins of villas at Herculaneum and Pompeii.

2. MEDIEVAL. Evidence of medieval drawing practices derives principally from manuscripts, particularly illuminated manuscripts (*see* MANUSCRIPT, §III), which were produced first in the scriptoria of major monastic centres, for example Reims, St Gall, Winchester, Canterbury, and Regensburg, and later in workshops in the major urban centres, such as Paris and Bruges. The most lavishly illuminated religious and literary manuscripts were commissioned for the clergy, aristocracy or monarchy, but many practical or didactic treatises were also produced. These included diagrams, maps, architectural plans and scientific illustrations. In addition, studies of figures, motifs and narrative scenes were carefully copied into model books (for illustration *see* MANUALS, MANUSCRIPT), to be reused by artists in new commissions (*see also* PATTERN BOOK, §I,1 and fig. 1).

With the early medieval change in text format from the continuous SCROLL to the paginated codex, or book, the scribe and illuminator were faced with new formal problems for the pictorial representation of text and image (*see* BOOK, §3). In the codex marginal sketches occasionally enlivened the borders of single pages as comic or grotesque figurative imagery spilt beyond designated text columns and provided a genial commentary on the limits imposed by the codex format (*see* BORDER, MANUSCRIPT, figs 1–3). The newly Christianized regions of northern Europe possessed indigenous artistic styles, for example the 'carpet' and animal interlace, the abstract motifs of which provided new sources of visual inspiration when combined with Christian or other texts. Among the most magnificent examples are the LINDISFARNE GOSPELS (*c.* 698; London, BL) and the Book of Kells (late 8th century; Dublin, Trinity Coll.; *see* KELLS, BOOK OF; *see also* IRELAND, fig. 7). The celebrated Utrecht Psalter (9th century; Utrecht, Bib. Rijksuniv.) emulates the page layout and script of Late Antique codices. Echoing the illusionistic pictorial style derived from such 5th-century manuscripts as the Vatican Virgil (Rome, Vatican, Bib. Apostolica, MS. Lat. 3225), the sketchy, graphic outline idiom, with its insistent linear rhythms, is a touchstone of medieval religious fervour as well as draughtsmanship (for illustration *see* UTRECHT PSALTER).

The notebooks of the 13th-century French architect Villard de Honnecourt occupy a unique position within the medieval graphic tradition, combining an instructional manual with theoretical precepts. His schematic and uninflected method of constructing figures, animals and structures in outline from geometric shapes documents the medieval artist's functional but purely conceptual and unnaturalistic approach to drawing form (*see* VILLARD DE HONNECOURT, figs 1 and 2). Executed in pen and ink over leadpoint or stylus, the collection of 33 parchment leaves (*c.* 1230–40; Paris, Bib. N., MS. Fr. 19093) is noteworthy for its wide-ranging categories of subject-matter and commentary. Some have dismissed Villard's collection of drawings as too discursive and fragmentary to have served as a practical pattern book for working craftsmen, but it remains the most explicit surviving document to detail the working procedures, activities and interests of the Gothic artist.

During the later Middle Ages pattern books were routinely employed by artists or craftsmen as practical aids to streamline workshop production and to transmit standardized formal and iconographic elements. Such compendia of miscellaneous drawings of animals, birds, human figures, ornament and architectural elements were composed of copies after other works of art, not studies from nature; the finest surviving example of the naturalistic type is that associated with the workshop of the Lombard illuminator Giovannino de Grassi, whose designs consist not only of animals and birds (e.g. Bergamo, Bib. Civ. A. Mai, MS. vii. 14, fol. 4*v*) but also a decorative 'human alphabet', executed in pen and ink, heightened with wash and watercolour (*see* GRASSI, DE, (1)). CENNINO CENNINI, writing in the late 14th century and the early 15th, recognized the central role drawing held in the training of the apprentice, whose artistic formation evolved from copying the master's own drawings and other workshop models before progressing to working from nature or casts.

3. RENAISSANCE. In terms of drawing practice, one of the key signals of the transition from the height of the international phase of the Late Gothic period during the 14th century to the Early Renaissance was the transformation of the medieval model book or pattern book tradition into that of the modern sketchbook. The increase in the availability and reduction in cost of paper during the 15th century encouraged the trend towards active and incidental drawing. Painters were attracted by its ease of use, informality and the freedom to experiment that it allowed. Within 50 years the fixed imagery of the pattern book was replaced by instantaneous responses to natural phenomena, contemporary events or imaginary conceits captured on paper.

Breaking with the static formulae of the pattern book while retaining its format, the two celebrated bound albums of drawings by the Venetian artist Jacopo Bellini (Paris, Louvre; London, BM) are unique in the 15th century in size, shape and content. Handsome, oversize and intentionally sumptuous, the albums are characterized by an elegance of material (leadpoint on paper for the London volume, silverpoint or pen and ink on parchment for the Paris volume), handling and concept, prompting scholars to conclude that they must have been intentionally designed as precious and independent works of art, to be admired and treasured as symbols of the artist's originality and genius (*see* BELLINI, (1), §2 and figs 2–4). They also illustrate several major artistic trends that developed during the early Renaissance, although in general the most lasting changes in drawing practices took place in Tuscany rather than in the Veneto. At this time drawing gained a new importance as the foundation for artistic theory, training and practice. The concept of an artist possessing a recognizable drawing style was in the process of emerging as a fundamental artistic issue. In addition, drawing became the means by which a new kind of pictorial realism could be achieved. Artists were able to plan and organize multifigure narrative compositions of unprecedented complexity on paper, which was portable, yet permanent, rather than on the wall or canvas.

Sketching and sketchbooks were expressive of the Renaissance outlook, being an individual rather than a shared or communal mode of graphic expression. The transition from pattern book to a modern sheet of studies is exemplified in Pisanello's pen-and-ink *Studies of Hanging Corpses* (*c.* 1430s; London, BM; see fig. 4), obviously meticulously observed from a gallows and drawn on the same sheet as a bust of a boy and a woman in profile.

Drawings were instrumental in the effort to create new and original artistic forms within the context of the revival of theories and models based on Classical antiquity. Documenting and copying ancient architectural prototypes as in the Codex Escurialensis (compiled *c.* 1500 in the Ghirlandaio workshop; Madrid, Escorial, Bib. Monasterio S Lorenzo, MS. Vit. 17), was one method of study, as was the drawing of human anatomy through dissection of cadavers (*see* ACADEMY, fig. 1) and study of ancient statuary. The most famous 15th-century anatomical studies were those of Leonardo (Windsor Castle, Berks, Royal Lib.; *see* ANATOMICAL STUDIES, fig. 1), but the heroic nudes of Mantegna, Antonio Pollaiuolo and Signorelli were significant sources of influence for the depiction of

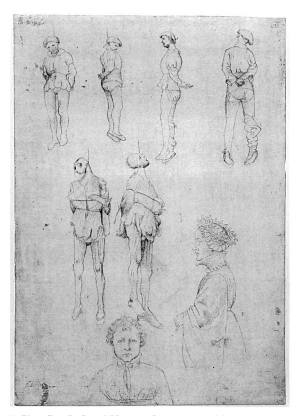

4. Pisanello: *Studies of Hanging Corpses*, pen and brown ink, over black chalk, 283×193 mm, *c.* 1430s (London, British Museum)

the human figure in full motion and the display of physical exertion. Scientific research also culminated in the rediscovery of the principles of linear and aerial perspective (*see* PERSPECTIVE, fig. 1), which enabled artists to render not only the play of light and shade on solid forms in space but also the optical effects of spatial recession within an ambient light and atmosphere.

By 1500 the type of personal, casual and exploratory drawing pioneered by Leonardo had been accepted as the first step in solving problems of artistic design: whether carried out in the exacting medium of silverpoint or the more fluid medium of pen and ink, or even chalk, ideal for those mysterious effects of shading and *sfumato* for which he remains so famous, Leonardo's drawings united conceptual power and often violent themes with unsurpassed delicacy of touch and precision of handling (*see* LEONARDO DA VINCI, figs 6–9). Sometimes executed in small, prepared-paper pocketbooks (*taccuino de viaggi*), his anatomical, drapery and nature studies, as well as his 'brainstorming' figure studies depicting rapidly jotted alternative renderings of a single motif on one sheet, laid the groundwork for the development of a new creative procedure based on a system of drawing.

Virtually all the great painters of the Renaissance in Italy were also great draughtsmen: Verrocchio, Botticelli, Fra Bartolommeo, Michelangelo (for illustration *see* PRESENTATION DRAWING), Andrea del Sarto, Pontormo and Giorgio Vasari in Florence; Perugino, Raphael and Barocci in Umbria; Correggio and Parmigianino in Parma; Titian, Veronese and Tintoretto in Venice; Giulio Romano, Polidoro da Caravaggio, Taddeo and Federico Zuccaro and Cesare d'Arpino in Rome. As the 16th century progressed, drawing was acknowledged in both theory and practice as the foundation of all the arts of design. Frequently, it is the apparently ephemeral drawings and the various preliminary studies for major commissions that have survived to document decayed or otherwise destroyed work in more monumental formats.

It was in the workshops of Raphael and Michelangelo in Rome during the second decade of the 16th century that the formal and technical experiments of the painters of the previous century came together to produce a rationalized procedure based on drawing (see RAPHAEL, figs 5 and 10, and MICHELANGELO, fig. 9), which encompassed the essential preparatory stages in the development and execution of monumental compositions, including frescoes, tapestries and paintings on canvas. Under Raphael's leadership and in his workshop these practices flourished. It was there, also, that the leading painters of the first generation of Mannerism, such as Giulio Romano (see GIULIO ROMANO, fig. 5) and Perino del Vaga, were trained, emerging to spread not only their elegant and expressive new style across Europe but also the distinctive, systematic approach to developing a composition by means of a progressive sequence of drawings (exploratory first-idea sketch; schematic composition drawing; study sheets of particular motifs, detail studies of single figures, drapery, heads and other individual compositional elements; finished composition drawing squared for transfer; cartoons; auxiliary cartoons for details; record drawing to be retained by the workshop). This procedure, which evolved gradually over several generations, enabled the master of such a large assemblage of talents to streamline the labour of completing numerous commissions on a scale scarcely undertaken before.

This example soon influenced artists in northern Europe, who returned home after visiting Italy imbued with a style and technique based on modern artistic ideals, including the cultural heritage of the Antique—the heroic and beautiful depiction of the human figure in motion and at rest and curiosity about the natural world. Albrecht Dürer was one of the first such artists to travel to Italy. His two visits to Venice, in 1494–5 and 1505–6, had a decisive impact on his style and technique as a draughtsman. His published treatises on perspective and human proportion (see DÜRER, (1), §III, and PERSPECTIVE, fig. 2) and his adaptation of prepared blue-ground drawing supports, based on Venetian dyed blue paper, suggest the strong and lasting influence of his encounters.

Northern artists working in native styles also made major contributions to the development of drawing in the 15th and 16th centuries. An original and expressive approach to the depiction of landscape and portraiture, derived from the traditions of manuscript illumination, is exemplified by such masterpieces as the Limbourg brothers' TRÈS RICHES HEURES (Chantilly, Mus. Condé, MS. 65; for illustration see VALOIS, (3) and LIMBOURG, DE, fig. 2), with its detailed and descriptive sense of local colour in the representation of the activities associated with the months of the year, and the Turin–Milan Hours (c. 1416;

Paris, Bib. N., MS. nouv. acq. lat. 3093; Paris, Louvre, R.F. 2022–5; Turin, Mus.; Civ. A. Ant., MS. 47; section in Turin, Bib. N.U., MS. K. IV.29, destr. 1904), formerly attributed to Jan van Eyck, in which a unified depiction of the land and light endows the images with unprecedented naturalism (for illustration see TURIN–MILAN HOURS). A more romantic attitude towards nature is evident in the landscapes of Wolfgang Huber and Albrecht Altdorfer (see ALTDORFER, (1), §2, and for illustration see DANUBE SCHOOL). Incisive character studies were produced by Fouquet, Dürer, Lucas van Leyden (see LUCAS VAN LEYDEN, §2(iii)), Gerard David and especially Hans Holbein (ii) (see HOLBEIN, (3), §4 and fig. 1). The attention and care lavished on the particularities of human appearance and costume reveal the intensity of the artist's desire to capture and record the unique features of each sitter. Generally bust-length and in full or three-quarter face, portraits were often heightened with coloured chalks to give a more naturalistic range of flesh tints.

In the second half of the 16th century there were few formal or technical breakthroughs in drawing, with the exception of the graphic work of the Umbrian painter Federico Barocci, who succeeded in uniting *colorito* and *disegno*. Using pastel and oil paint to heighten the naturalism of his head and figure studies, his sketches turned away from the complexity and stylish artifice of Mannerism and pointed instead to the formal innovations that defined the Baroque (see BAROCCI, FEDERICO, §2).

4. 17TH CENTURY. The triumphant spirit of the Counter-Reformation contributed to the sense of energy, power and emotion so characteristic of the Baroque, the dominant style of the 17th century, at least in southern Europe. It would be difficult to pinpoint external religious and political events that served to modify drawing styles and practices during this period, in contrast with painting, sculpture and architecture, for which the patronage, iconography and decoration were strongly influenced by religious edicts and dynastic changes. Nevertheless, social and economic developments did contribute to trends in drawing, especially after the mid-century, when artists began to gain artistic independence, new social stature and privileges once they became associated with new, royally chartered academies.

For the first time genre and landscape gained prominence as legitimate independent artistic subjects: domestic scenes, industry, trades, commerce and pastimes were regularly depicted, as were landscapes, whether idealized and classicizing or topographically accurate. In addition, artists were inspired to treat the transient phenomena of the natural world as their subject, even if the work were still couched in allegorical terms: the times of day, the seasons and the elements. In drawings, this feeling for nature was rendered in sketches *sur le motif*; these studies were later worked up into compositions in the studio. Rather than serving as subsidiary or preparatory studies, genre and landscape drawings were often conceived and executed—particularly in the northern Netherlands—as independent works of art that could be sold. Typical of this sort of decoration were Hendrick Avercamp's watercolours depicting skaters enjoying the ice on frozen rivers, Adriaen van Ostade and Cornelis Dusart's scenes of tavern life or Pieter Molyn's chalk drawings of the Dutch countryside. Other lasting contributions to drawing practices were also made in the northern Netherlands, such as '*naer het leven*' (Dut.: 'from life') figure studies and especially scientific illustration.

The greatest contributions to the graphic arts in the northern Netherlands in the 17th century, however, were made by a single artist: Rembrandt (*see* REMBRANDT VAN RIJN, §I, 2(ii), 3(iii), 4(iii) and 5(ii), and figs 2, 6 and 10). He not only recognized the unexplored possibilities within familiar techniques and media, but he also left an enormous drawn oeuvre—a poignant, sometimes humorous, yet unsparing personal artistic diary carried out with an often stunning economy of means (*see* WATERCOLOUR, fig. 1). His most original contribution to the functional history of drawings derived from the routine production of practice drawings by his workshop. Rembrandt would assign a subject, usually a life study or a biblical scene, which both he and his pupils would depict, not as the basis for a painted composition or a print, nor as a work to be sold, but as an exercise in composition, interpretation and technique. Vast numbers of Rembrandt school drawings of this type survive (see fig. 5); they continue to vex connoisseurs and defy consensus with respect to their attribution.

Robust, economical and direct are terms that apply not only to Rembrandt's draughtsmanship but also to the approach to drawing practised by Ludovico, Agostino and Annibale Carracci, founders of a teaching academy in

5. Rembrandt pupil retouched by Rembrandt: *Life Study of a Man Standing*, pen and brown ink, brown and grey wash, touches of red chalk, heightened with white, over black chalk, 252×193 mm, *c.* 1646 (London, British Museum)

Bologna. In Italy the return to study from life, to a realistic attitude to the figure coupled with a renewed appreciation of the classical values of the High Renaissance, pointed the way towards stylistic renewal. Annibale's decorations of the Gallery of the Palazzo Farnese in Rome (completed in 1599) gave monumental form to the subsequent Baroque heroic figural ideal. Many figure studies attest to the careful preparation these frescoes entailed (*see* CARRACCI, (3), fig. 6), but, as a draughtsman, his most lasting influence stems from his treatment of landscape, genre and caricature. His linear pen-and-ink landscape drawings, which combined 16th-century Venetian conventions and classicizing motifs, served as a point of reference for refinements engineered by his pupil Domenichino and, later, by Guercino and, more conventionally, Grimaldi. Poussin and Claude were imbued with the same spiritual allegiance to the Antique, but in their drawings it was expressed more pictorially with a richer technique in which the penwork was either mixed with additional media or even replaced by wash. The simplicity of their pure wash landscapes depicting the Roman campagna display an almost oriental sensibility (*see* CLAUDE LORRAIN, fig. 2).

Venetian-inspired pastoral landscapes with travellers, shepherds and flocks of animals displayed a Romantic attitude (which was to find great resonance in the 18th century). In the work of the technically innovative G. B. Castiglione (the inventor of the monotype), dilute colour pigments were bound in oil to resemble coloured washes. His drawings occupied a place at the intersection of the arts of painting, drawing and printmaking.

Caricature drawings, which first appeared in Italy in the 17th century in the studio of the Carracci, had two sources of inspiration: Leonardo, who was the first in Italy to experiment with the manipulation of physical deformity and distortion for artistic effect, and the fantastic creatures devised by Bosch, Pieter Bruegel the elder, and Jacques de Gheyn II, which reflected an enduring north European tradition of symbolic associations within a social and narrative context. As an art form, caricature found its most persuasive artistic expression in drawings and prints as a blend of genre, portraits and allegory. Combining humour and distortion, it began as an extension of the realistic portrayals of anonymous types drawn from common life combined with the comic, recognizable but unofficial pen portraits of specific and often celebrated individuals. The existence of many of these fluent, witty pen sketches by Bernini, Guercino, Mola and Testa affirm the popularity of caricature in 17th-century Rome (*see* CARICATURE, §2).

The establishment of the Académie Royale de Peinture et de Sculpture in Paris in 1648 must be regarded as the most significant French contribution to the development of drawings in the 17th century, because of its effect on codifying drawing categories and artistic procedures. The Académie's central influence in terms of the history of drawings derived from its teaching programme based around the life-drawing class (*see* PARIS, §VI, 1(ii)). (From this institution and from its product, drawings of male nudes studied from life, the term 'academy' came to refer to all drawings of nudes (*see* ACADEMY FIGURE).) Among the greatest French draughtsmen were Poussin and Claude, although they spent almost their entire careers in Italy.

6. Claude Lorrain: *Coastal Landscape with Aeneas Hunting*, pen and brown ink, with grey and grey-brown washes, 183×251 mm, from the *Liber veritatis*, 1672 (London, British Museum)

Poussin's intellectual rigour and allegiance to the Antique was countered by Claude's more romantic and pictorial sensibility. Claude placed an unprecedented value on his drawings, especially as a documentary record to authenticate his paintings. His *Liber veritatis* (London, BM; see fig. 6) is a life-long record not only of his major compositions but also of his own graphic development (*see also* CLAUDE LORRAIN, §II, 2).

5. 18TH CENTURY. By 1700 the locus of artistic, technical and thematic innovation in the graphic arts had shifted away from Rome, Antwerp and Amsterdam to Venice, Paris and London. Political developments in France and England as well as social and economic trends helped to shape the culture of the Enlightenment, a period in which the intellectual and philosophical foundations of the modern age were largely established. During this period, generations of English gentlemen travelled to the Continent on the Grand Tour to find inspiration for the design of their country seats, to collect antiquities and to commission decorations for their estates. They also demonstrated their cultivation by forming collections of drawings. In France, patronage shifted from the Crown and court at Versailles to wealthy financiers in Paris, which became the new artistic capital of Europe. The refinement of this worldly lifestyle was chronicled in drawings, which

were often arranged as part of the décor of small rooms or *cabinets*. In addition, contemporary drawings, especially designs for book illustrations, vignettes and frontispieces, popularized Parisian life and manners throughout Europe.

Among the most significant developments during the 18th century was the appreciation of drawings as an independent form of artistic expression, regardless of their original purpose. As a consequence of an increase in their popularity and value as collectibles, and the growth of public art exhibitions and auctions, drawings began to be executed as autonomous works and transformed into objects to be framed and displayed rather than to be stored and consulted on an occasional basis. As the price of original drawings increased, so did the need to supply inexpensive yet high quality substitutes: inventions in reproductive printmaking made it possible to imitate all kinds of drawing media, including pastel, chalk, wash and watercolour.

Eclipsed by Rome since the end of the 16th century, Venetian artists once again came to the forefront in the 18th century: from Giovanni Antonio Pellegrini, Sebastiano and Marco Ricci, Giovanni Battista Piazzetta and Canaletto to Giambattista and Giandomenico Tiepolo, Giovanni Antonio and Francesco Guardi to the architect and graphic artist, Piranesi, an optical and atmospheric approach to form conveyed through pen and vaporous wash on brilliant white paper served as the dominant Venetian stylistic mode throughout much of the century. The Venetians also developed new types of drawings, such as the capriccio, a type of landscape in which identifiable monuments and sites have been imaginatively rearranged according to the artist's fancy (*see* CAPRICCIO, §2). In the hands of such view painters as Giovanni Paolo Panini (*see* PANINI, GIOVANNI PAOLO, §2) or, later, HUBERT ROBERT, the poetic and atmospheric qualities so evident in the capriccios of the Venetians were replaced by a more anecdotal approach, blending architectural precision with human activities. Another drawing type to flourish in Venice in the 18th century was the *scherzi di fantasia*, inventive compositions in which the artist explored the sources of his own private dreams and demons in mysterious, personal fantasies. Also utilized as pretexts for invention and composition were traditional themes, for example the life and death of Punchinello, the Everyman drawn from the improvisational theatrical tradition of the *commedia dell' arte*, which was chronicled in Giandomenico Tiepolo's celebrated cycle of over a hundred drawings, ironically entitled *Divertimento per li regazzi* (see fig. 7). The Tiepolos' imagery did indeed border occasionally on the macabre. In fact, an undercurrent of disquiet flowed throughout the century and gained strength, with Fuseli's sense of the bizarre (*see* FÜSSLI, (3), fig. 1) and the menacing visions of Goya, which sought to define the fearful realm beyond reason. Goya's nightmarish wash drawings illustrate a world in which witchcraft flourished and where the forces of darkness have overtaken the spirit and have extinguished the light of reason.

At the other end of the spectrum is the pastel portrait, which although usually associated with 18th-century France (*see* PASTEL, §2), was actually introduced there by the Venetian artist ROSALBA CARRIERA, who visited Paris in 1718. Her light palette and impressionistic touch were highly regarded and inspired French artists to emulate her technique and French patrons to appreciate the freshness and delicacy of this new art form. The pastels of MAURICE-QUENTIN DE LA TOUR and JEAN-BAPTISTE PERRONEAU are haunting reminders of an age that wished to be remembered as carefree; in fact, pastel portraiture has become synonymous with the 18th century (*see* PASTEL, colour pls IV and V).

As practised during the 17th century, caricature was based on the humorous depiction of individual likeness, but it developed in the 18th century from the description of likeness to that of manners and situation. Moreover, it was carried out not as a pastime but as a professional activity. As society itself became increasingly complex and fluid, social commentary and political satire in the graphic

7. Giandomenico Tiepolo: *Title-page for Punchinello's 'Divertimento per li regazzi'*, pen and light brown ink, light brown wash, over black chalk, 355×470 mm, ? late 1790s (Kansas City, MO, Nelson–Atkins Museum of Art)

arts developed as one aspect of the Enlightenment attitude. The questioning of values and standards, so central to the enterprise of the Enlightenment, assumed visual form through drawings and prints intended to be interpreted as social commentary and political satire. Pier Leone Ghezzi's humorous renditions of local dignitaries and the touring English *milordi* (*see* GHEZZI, (2), §3, and CARICATURE, fig. 1), as well as the work of Hogarth and Rowlandson, suggest that the English, as subjects and authors, possessed a special genius for this form of social critique. At the end of the century, it gained a political dimension after the outbreak of the French Revolution and the Napoleonic Wars with the invention of modern political propaganda and cartoons directed towards a mass audience.

The impulse to record motifs and compositions for future reference, in the style of model book pages, is seen at its most eloquent in the 18th century in the works and working method of Antoine Watteau. Abandoning academic practices, which required the working-out of each new composition through a series of sketches and studies of individual figures, he instead favoured the earlier pattern book tradition, whereby he composed new paintings by consulting his sketchbooks for appropriate figures, a practice that attracted criticism from his biographers. Nevertheless, in Watteau's drawings many diverse stylistic and technical traditions were exquisitely united, from the legacy of Venetian 16th-century landscape to the use of *trois crayons* to give warmth to flesh tones. His *mise-en-page*, with clusters of figures and heads viewed from different angles depicted on the same sheet of studies (for illustrations see colour pl. I, fig. 2 and CHALK), exerted lasting influence throughout the 18th century and into the 19th (*see* WATTEAU, (1), §5).

6. 19TH CENTURY. Late 18th-century and early 19th-century drawing is characterized by a renewed emphasis on line, from the pure outline drawings of the Neo-classical artist John Flaxman (*see* FLAXMAN, JOHN, §2) to those of the Art Nouveau illustrator Aubrey Beardsley, a reductive linear style that extended beyond England as a result of commercial printmaking and illustration. The uninflected contours and economical graphic language of Neo-classical drawing represented a belief in the perfectibility of form through adherence to both academic and antique precepts. In Beardsley's case, the serpentine line conveys a *fin-de-siècle* unease, even menace, and serves as a carrier of emotion and symbolism (for illustration *see* BEARDSLEY, AUBREY).

Technological advances had a significant impact on the graphic arts: for example, the invention of synthetic graphite (first produced in France during the Napoleonic Wars), combined with the industrial production of machine-woven paper (later manufactured from wood pulp instead of rags), made it possible for such artists as JEAN-AUGUSTE-DOMINQUE INGRES to achieve the nuanced effects created by a fine, hard pencil line on a polished, smooth drawing surface. Printing processes, such as lithography and industrial wood-engraving, stimulated the growth of popular illustration. Most significantly, however, the invention of photography irrevocably severed the direct and heretofore necessary association between drawing and representation. Photography forced artists to

search for new reasons to draw, new artistic graphic forms and new expressive meanings.

In the early 19th century artists from the German-speaking lands attained prominence as graphic innovators for the first time since the early Renaissance. Evoking a style and technique reminiscent of Italian quattrocento drawings, the Nazarenes, a group of artists banded together in a form of monastic brotherhood centred in Rome, strove for a simplicity in art and human values, which they believed was missing from contemporary life. North of the Alps, landscape, evocative of the awesome drama and power of nature, was a favourite theme of the German Romantics, such as Caspar David Friedrich (*see* FRIEDRICH, CASPAR DAVID, §2). Among the leading 19th-century German draughtsmen was ADOLPH MENZEL, whose corpus of drawings, in size and quality (see fig. 8), is on a par with that of Degas, although his range was more restricted.

The English school also attained unprecedented prominence in the graphic arts during the 19th century. During the first half of the century English artists turned both to landscape and watercolour with a degree of originality and application that set an example for artists in the rest of Europe as well as in the USA, which was beginning to develop its own artistic vision and traditions. Although American artists, beginning with John Singleton Copley and Benjamin West, continued to travel to Europe to perfect their training, a native idiom, best expressed in the work of Winslow Homer, was also born. Other American artists, including JOHN SINGER SARGENT and James McNeill Whistler (*see* WHISTLER, JAMES MCNEILL, §2(iv)), resided and worked abroad, although they are also representative of 19th-century American art, in particular the desire to measure up to European artistic standards in form and technique.

For their attempt to observe, study and record ephemeral atmospheric effects, both Constable and Turner represent a point of intersection between science and art that is reminiscent of the drawings not only of Leonardo but also of Claude, whose work was a great source of inspiration to the English school. The drawings of J. M. W. TURNER, Ruskin and Constable (*see* CONSTABLE, JOHN, §2), among others, especially the watercolours, express a pictorial vision in which atmosphere is bathed in tone and colour (*see* WATERCOLOUR, colour pl. VIII, fig. 1). The Pre-Raphaelites, in contrast, retreated from the actuality of both the natural and manmade world and espoused idealized beliefs about the artistic and social values of the early Renaissance, which they conveyed through a delicacy of line and a poetic dreaminess of interpretation.

During the first half of the 19th century French art was again divided by the perennial argument about colour versus line, the latter exemplified by the drawings of Ingres and Delacroix. Ingres's pencil united the sensuous rhythm and feeling of a poet united with the precision and detachment of a scientist of human nature. Delacroix's watercolours of tiger hunts, *odalisques* and Arab horsemen ushered in a new chapter in Europe's romance with exoticism and the orient. The *odalisques* and female nudes be Ingres attain a degree of formal artifice and stylized elegance unmatched since the appearance of the court style of the school of Fontainebleau. In his portrait

8. Adolph Menzel: *Three Old Women in Shawls*, soft carpenter pencil with stumping, 244×324 mm, 1892 (Berlin, Kupferstichkabinett)

drawings an era and a way of life are reflected: sitters are silhouetted against a pure white background, thus heightening the graphic abstraction (*see* INGRES, JEAN-AUGUSTE-DOMINIQUE, fig. 2). Indeed, exploiting the *mise en page* as an element of formal harmony was another feature of Ingres's artistry.

Later in the 19th century, also in France, Edgar Degas, along with Cézanne, might almost be said to have invented the modern drawing. In his scenes from contemporary life, especially the ballet, the theatre and the racetrack, Degas's restless curiosity was expressed through continuous experimentation, as in his work in monotype, pastel and mixed media (*see* DEGAS, EDGAR, fig. 4). A classicist by temperament and training, he rejected academic formulae or definitions of beauty and absorbed new influences, such as Japanese prints and the invention of photography. Impressionist drawings broke with previous traditions partly in their reduced emphasis on line in favour of a more pictorial, tonal and atmospheric approach to drawing. Focused on finding new ways to represent the effects of light, the Impressionists' efforts reflected scientific experiments in optics and new developments in colour theory, as well as the influence of photography, with its dissolved outlines. Pastel and watercolour were their favoured media, exemplified above all by the work of Renoir. Cézanne, whose pioneering work influenced the

Cubist and Fauve experiments during the first decade of the 20th century, discovered that light could be employed to create space and volume as well as atmosphere. Judiciously placed strokes of chalk and touches of watercolour were intended to be constructive as the artist evoked the illusion of solid form with the sparest of means (*see* CÉZANNE, PAUL, §I, 2 and fig. 6).

7. 20TH CENTURY. The protagonists in the history of drawing in the 20th century are Picasso (see colour pl. II, fig. 1) and Matisse, whose creativity had a major influence on artistic life throughout the century. Their rejection of the status quo and continual redefinition of the terms of artistic engagement remain their most lasting legacy; each worked to find artistic renewal and entirely new forms of expression based on graphic means.

The invention of COLLAGE during the first decade of the century was the single most original feature associated with 20th-century drawing. With collage, followed by the application and redefinition of found objects, a process was initiated in which the boundaries between drawing and other art forms became increasingly blurred. Moreover, during the 20th century the broad and fine media by which drawings had traditionally been created, such as chalk, pen and wash, were supplemented or even replaced

PLATE I

Drawing

1. Michelangelo: *Studies for the Libyan Sibyl*, red chalk, 289×214 mm, 1508–12 (New York, Metropolitan Museum of Art)

2. Antoine Watteau: *Six Studies of Heads, and Hands Holding a Flute*, red, black and white chalk (*aux trois crayons*), 205×264 mm, *c.* 1715 (Rouen, Musée des Beaux-Arts)

1. Pablo Picasso: *Embrace of the Minotaur*, pen and black ink, grey wash, on blue wove paper, 480×628 mm, 1933 (Chicago, IL, Art Institute of Chicago)

2. Henry Moore: *Seated and Reclining Figures*, wax crayon, black chalk, pencil, watercolour, pen and black ink, 354×225 mm, 1942 (New York, Museum of Modern Art)

PLATE III

Dye

1. Warp ikat cotton cloth, from Sumba, Indonesia, 20th century (London, British Museum)

2. Tie-dyed (*adire*) cotton cloth, from Nigeria, 20th century (Manchester, University of Manchester, Whitworth Art Gallery)

1. Batik cotton cloth, from central Java, Indonesia, late 19th century (London, Victoria and Albert Museum)

2. *Strawberry Thief* by William Morris, cotton cloth dyed using the discharge process, manufactured by Morris & Co., London, 1883 (Manchester, University of Manchester, Whitworth Art Gallery)

with new media (e.g. felt-tipped pens and wax crayons; see colour pl. II, fig. 2), new techniques and alternative supports.

In addition to changes in the craft of drawing, the function of drawing also underwent a transformation. While Cubist precepts continued to posit the value of representation and links with the observed world, other artistic trends favoured abstraction, non-representational imagery and, in the case of the Surrealists, automatic writing (see AUTOMATISM). During the post-war period this trend intensified, although with Abstract Expressionism and even Pop art some artists reverted to a more traditional view, in which drawings often served as preparatory studies and explorations of pictorial ideas on a reduced scale. It should also be noted, however, that as drawings became increasingly complex in their technique and larger in scale, the sense that they were entirely autonomous forms of artistic expression was enhanced. Also indicative of the lack of clarity differentiating art forms, drawing and writing became increasingly indistinguishable as forms of artistic expression, such as in the work of the conceptual artists Joseph Beuys, Joseph Kosuth and Jenny Holzer. This convergence is most compellingly demonstrated in the work of graffiti artists, such as Keith Haring.

BIBLIOGRAPHY
GENERAL

L. Fagan: *Handbook to the Department of Prints and Drawings in the British Museum, with Introduction and Notices of Various Schools: Italian, German, Dutch and Flemish, Spanish, French and English* (London, 1876)

Old Master Drgs (1926–40)

H. Leporini: *Die Künstlerzeichnung: Ein Handbuch für Liebhaber und Sammler* (Berlin, 1928)

A. E. Popham: *A Handbook to the Drawings and Water-colours in the Department of Prints and Drawings, British Museum* (London, 1939)

H. Tietze: *European Master Drawings in the United States* (New York, 1947/R 1973)

Drawings by Old Masters (exh. cat., London, RA, 1953)

P. J. Sachs: *Modern Prints and Drawings: A Guide to a Better Understanding of Modern Draughtsmanship* (New York, 1954)

L. Grassi: *Storia del disegno: Svolgimento del pensiero critico e un catalogo* (Rome, 1957)

J. Rosenberg: *Great Draughtsmen from Pisanello to Picasso* (Cambridge, MA, 1959)

I. Moskowitz, ed.: *Great Drawings of All Time*, 4 vols (New York, 1962)

Master Drgs (1963–)

H. Hutter: *Drawing: History and Technique* (London, 1966)

M. Evans: *Medieval Drawings* (London, 1969)

P. Rawson: *Drawing* (London, 1969)

W. Vitzthum, ed.: *Disegni dei maestri*, 16 vols (Milan, 1970–71)

C. O. Baer: *Landscape Drawings* (New York, 1973)

Old Master Drawings from American Collections (exh. cat. by E. Feinblatt, Los Angeles, Co. Mus. A., 1976)

G. Monnier and B. Rose: *Drawing* (New York and Geneva, 1979)

Drawing (1979–)

W. Strauss and T. Felker, eds: *Drawings Defined* (London, 1987) [pap. presented to the Ian Woodner Master Drawings Symposium at Cambridge, MA, Fogg]

Le Paysage en Europe du XVIe au XVIIIe siècle (exh. cat., Paris, Louvre, 1990)

G. C. Sciolla, ed.: *Drawing*, 3 vols (Milan, 1991–3)

D. Dethloff, ed.: *Drawing: Masters and Methods, Raphael to Redon* (London, 1992) [pap. presented to the Ian Woodner Master Drawings Symposium at London, RA]

B. Schreiber Jacoby: *Drawing* (in preparation)

N. Turner: *An Introduction to the Study of Old Master Drawings* (in preparation)

REGIONAL SCHOOLS

In addition to the general surveys of specific schools and periods included in the selective list below, most of the major public collections have published permanent collection catalogues and exhibition catalogues devoted to particular aspects of their holdings of drawings.

American and British

T. Bolton: *Early American Portrait Draughtsmen in Crayon* (New York, 1923/R 1970)

P. Cummings: *American Drawings: The Twentieth Century* (New York, 1976)

American Master Drawings and Watercolours: A History of Works on Paper from Colonial Times to the Present (exh. cat. by T. E. Stebbings jr, New York, Whitney Mus. Amer. A., 1976–7)

English Portrait Drawings and Miniatures (exh. cat. by P. Noon, New Haven, CT, Yale Cent. Brit. A., 1979)

D. B. Brown: *Catalogue of the Collection of Drawings in the Ashmolean Museum, Oxford: Earlier English Drawings*, iv (Oxford, 1982)

British Portrait Drawings, 1600–1900 (exh. cat. by R. Wark, San. Marino, CA, Huntington Lib. & A.G., 1982)

British Landscape Watercolours, 1600–1860 (exh. cat. by L. Stainton, London, BM, 1985)

Drawings in England from Hilliard to Hogarth (exh. cat. by L. Stainton and C. White, London, BM, 1987)

Austrian, German and Swiss

P. Ganz: *Handzeichnungen schweizerischer Meister des XV.–XVIII. Jahrhunderts*, 3 vols (Basle, 1904–8)

T. W. Michall-Viebrook: *Deutsche Barockzeichnungen* (Munich, 1925)

K. T. Parker: *Drawings of Early German Schools* (London, 1926)

K. Garzaralli-Thurnlackh: *Die barocke Handzeichnung in Österreich* (Zurich, 1928)

W. Hugelshofer: *Schweizerische Handzeichnungen des XV. und XVI. Jahrhunderts* (Freiburg, 1928)

K. T. Parker: *Alsatian Drawings of the Fifteenth and Sixteenth Centuries* (London, 1928)

H. Mohle: *Deutsche Zeichnungen des 17. und 18. Jahrhunderts* (Berlin, 1947)

G. Aurenhammer: *Die Handzeichnungen des 17. Jahrhunderts in Österreich* (Vienna, 1958)

C. T. Eisler: *Drawings of the Masters: German Drawings from the Sixteenth Century to the Expressionists* (New York, 1963)

Swiss Drawings: Masterpieces of Five Centuries (exh. cat. by W. Hugelshofer, Smithsonian Inst. Trav. Exh. Serv., 1967)

M. Bernhard: *Deutsche Romantik: Handzeichnungen* (Munich, 1973)

Zeichnung in Deutschland: Deutsche Zeichner, 1540–1640 (exh. cat. by H. Geisler, Stuttgart, Staatsgal., 1979)

Drawings from the Holy Roman Empire, 1540–1680: A Selection from North American Collections (exh. cat. by T. DaCosta Kaufmann; Princeton U., A. Mus.; Washington, DC, N.G.A.; Pittsburg, Carnegie Inst., Mus. A.; 1982–3)

The Age of Dürer and Holbein: German Drawings, 1400–1550 (exh. cat. by J. Rowlands, London, BM, 1988)

The Romantic Spirit: German Drawings, 1780–1850, from the Nationalgalerie (Berlin) and the Kupferstichkabinett (Dresden) (exh. cat., New York, Pierpont Morgan Lib., 1988)

Central European Drawings, 1680–1800: A Selection from North American Collections (exh. cat. by T. DaCosta Kaufmann; Princeton U., A. Mus.; South Bank, U. A. Mus.; 1989–90)

French

H. Zerner: *School of Fontainebleau* (New York, [n.d.])

P. Lavallée: *Le Dessin français du XIIIième au XVIième siècle* (Paris, 1930)

French Landscape Drawings and Sketches of the Eighteenth Century (exh. cat. by P. Hulton, London, BM, 1977)

French Master Drawings from the Rouen Museum: From Caron to Delacroix (exh. cat., Washington, DC, N.G.A., and elsewhere, 1981–2)

P. Bjurström: *French Drawings, Eighteenth Century* (1982), iv of *Drawings in Swedish Public Collections* (Stockholm, 1982–)

J. Bean, with L. Turčić: *15th to 18th-century French Drawings in the Metropolitan Museum of Art* (New York, 1986)

Französische Zeichnungen im Städelschen Kunstinstitut, 1550 bis 1800 (exh. cat., Frankfurt am Main, Städel. Kstinst., 1986–7)

The Art of Drawing in France, 1400–1900: Drawings from the Nationalmuseum, Stockholm (exh. cat. by P. Bjurström, New York, N. Acad. Des., 1987)

From Fontainebleau to the Louvre: French Drawing from the Seventeenth Century (exh. cat. by H. T. Goldfarb, Cleveland, Mus. A., 1989)

Maîtres français, 1500–1800: Dessins de la Donation Mathias Polakovits à l'Ecole des beaux-arts (exh. cat. by L.-A. Prat, Paris, Ecole N. Sup. B.-A., 1989)

Masterful Studies: Three Centuries of French Drawings from the Prat Collection (New York, N. Acad. Des., 1990)

French Architectural and Ornament Drawings of the Eighteenth Century (exh. cat. by M. Myers, New York, Met., 1991)

Dessins français du XVIIe siècle dans les collections publiques françaises (exh. cat., Paris, Louvre, 1993)

French Master Drawings from the Pierpont Morgan Library (exh. cat. by C. Dufour Denison, Paris, Louvre, and New York, Pierpont Morgan Lib., 1993–4)

Italian

B. Berenson: *The Drawings of the Florentine Painters* (London, 1903, rev. 2/New York, 1938/R Westport, 1970, It. trans and rev. 3/Milan, 1961)

O. Fischel: *Die Zeichnungen der Umbrer* (Berlin, 1917)

D. von Hadeln: *Venezianische Zeichnungen der Hochrenaissance* (Berlin, 1925)

——: *Venezianische Zeichnungen des Quattrocento* (Berlin, 1925)

——: *Venezianische Zeichnungen der Spätrenaissance* (Berlin, 1926)

K. T. Parker: *Northern Italian Drawings of the Quattrocento* (London, 1927)

H. Voss: *Zeichnungen der italienischen Spätrenaissance* (Munich, 1928)

A. van Schendel: *Le Dessin en Lombardie* (Brussels, 1938)

H. Tietze and E. Tietze-Conrat: *The Drawings of the Venetian Painters in the Fifteenth and Sixteenth Centuries* (New York, 1944)

L. Grassi, ed.: *Disegno italiano* (Venice, 1959–)

B. Degenhart and A. Schmitt: *Corpus der italienischen Zeichnungen, 1300–1450* (Berlin, 1968)

M. Chiarini: *I disegni italiani di paesaggio, 1600–1750* (Treviso, 1972)

Inventaire général des dessins italiens, Paris, Louvre cats (1972–)

C. Thiem: *Florentiner Zeichner des Frühbarock* (Munich, 1977)

J. Bean, with L. Turčić: *Seventeenth-century Italian Drawings in the Metropolitan Museum of Art* (New York, 1979)

P. Ward-Jackson: *Italian Drawings in the Victoria and Albert Museum: 14th–16th Centuries* (London, 1979)

The Draftsman's Eye: Late Italian Renaissance Schools and Styles (exh. cat. by E. J. Olszewski, Cleveland, Mus. A., 1979)

H. MacAndrew: *Catalogue of the Italian Drawings in the Ashmolean Museum, Oxford: Supplement*, iii (Oxford, 1980)

N. Turner: *Italian Baroque Drawings* (London, 1980)

P. Ward-Jackson: *Italian Drawings in the Victoria and Albert Museum: 17th–18th Centuries* (London, 1980)

Italian Drawings, 1780–1890 (exh. cat. by R. J. M. Olson, Washington, DC, N.G.A., 1980)

F. Ames-Lewis: *Drawing in Early Renaissance Italy* (New Haven and London, 1981)

R. Roli and G. Sestieri: *I disegni italiani del settecento* (Treviso, 1981)

J. Bean, with L. Turčić: *Fifteenth- and Sixteenth-century Drawings in the Metropolitan Museum of Art* (New York, 1982)

Bolognese Drawings in North American Collections, 1500–1800 (exh. cat. by M. Cazort and C. Johnston, Ottawa, N.G., 1982)

J. Byam Shaw: *The Italian Drawings of the Frits Lugt Collection*, 3 vols (Paris, 1983)

Drawings in the Italian Renaissance Workshop (exh. cat. by F. Ames-Lewis and J. Wright; Nottingham, U.A.G.; London, V&A; 1983)

Correggio and his Legacy: Sixteenth-century Emilian Drawings (exh. cat. by D. DeGrazia, Washington, DC, N.G.A.,1984)

Italian Portrait Drawings, 1400–1800, from North American Collections (exh. cat. by A. Gealt, Bloomington, IN, U. A. Mus., 1984)

Drawings from Venice: Masterworks from the Museo Correr (exh. cat., New York, N. Acad. Des., 1985)

Florentine Drawings of the Sixteenth Century (exh. cat. by N. Turner, London, BM, 1986)

J. Byam Shaw and G. Knox: *Italian Eighteenth-century Drawings in the Robert Lehman Collection*, New York, Met. cat. (New York, 1987)

Drawings by Raphael and his Circle: From British and North American Collections (exh. cat. by J.A. Gere, New York, Pierpont Morgan Lib., 1987)

Sixteenth-century Tuscan Drawings from the Uffizi (exh. cat. by A. M. Petrioli Tofani and C. Smyth, Detroit, MI, Inst. A., 1988)

M. Di Giampaolo, ed.: *Disegni emiliani del rinascimento* (Milan, 1989)

Renaissance et baroque dessins italiens du Musée de Lille (exh. cat., Lille, Mus. B.-A., 1989)

J. Bean, with L. Turčić: *Eighteenth-century Italian Drawings in the Metropolitan Museum of Art* (New York, 1990)

Les Dessins vénitiens des collections de l'Ecole des beaux-arts (exh. cat. by E. Brugerolles, Paris, Ecole N. Sup. B.-A., 1990)

Prize-winning Drawings from the Roman Academy, 1682–1754 (exh. cat.; Rome, Gal. N. Stamp. Ant.; New York, N. Acad. Des.; 1990)

D. Benati, ed.: *Disegni emiliani del sei- e settecento: Come nascono i dipinti* (Milan, 1991)

From Studio to Studiolo: Florentine Draughtsmanship under the First Medici Grand Dukes (exh. cat., Oberlin, OH, Allen Mem. A. Mus., 1991)

Netherlandish

M. D. Henkel: *Le Dessin hollandais des origines au XVIIe siècle* (Brussels, 1913)

A. E. Popham: *Drawings of the Early Flemish School* (New York, 1926)

A. J. J. Delen: *Teekeningen van Vlaamsche meesters* (Antwerp, 1944)

I. Q. van Regteren Altena: *Holländische Meisterzeichnungen des siebzehnten Jahrhunderts* (Basle, 1948)

F. Winkler: *Flämische Zeichnungen* (Berlin, 1948)

W. Bernt: *Die niederländischen Zeichner des 17. Jahrhunderts*, 2 vols (Munich, 1957–8)

Dutch Drawings (exh. cat. by I. Q. van Regteren Altena, Washington, DC, N.G.A., 1958–9)

J. G. van Gelder: *Dutch Drawings and Prints* (New York, 1959)

H. G. Franz: *Niederländische Landschaftsmalerei im Zeitalter des Manierismus*, 2 vols (Graz, 1969)

Rembrandt et son temps: Dessins de collections publiques et privées conservées en France (exh. cat. by R. Bacou and others, Paris, Louvre, 1970)

Dutch Masterpieces from the Eighteenth Century (exh. cat. by E. R. Mandle; Minneapolis, Inst. A.; Toledo, OH, Mus. A.; Philadelphia, Mus. A.; 1971–2)

Flemish Drawings of the Seventeenth Century from the Lugt Collection, Fondation Custodia (exh. cat., London, V&A, 1972)

A. Zwollo: *Hollandse en Vlaamse vedutenschilders te Rome* (Assen, 1973)

Dutch Genre Drawings of the Seventeenth Century (exh. cat. by P. Schatborn; New York, Pierpont Morgan Lib.; Boston, Mus. F.A.; Chicago, A. Inst.; 1973)

The Pre-Rembrandtists (exh. cat. by A. Tümpel, Sacramento, Crocker A.G., 1974)

Opkomst en bloei van het Noordnederlandse stadsgesicht in de 17de eeuw/The Dutch Cityscape in the Seventeenth Century and its Sources (exh. cat., Amsterdam, Hist. Mus., 1977)

Seventeenth-century Dutch Drawings from American Collections (exh. cat. by F. W. Robinson; Washington, DC, N.G.A.; Denver, A. Mus.; Fort Worth, Kimbell A. Mus.; 1977)

Dutch Drawings of the Seventeenth Century from the Lugt Collection, Fondation Custodia (exh. cat., New York, Pierpont Morgan Lib., 1977–8)

K. G. Boon: *Netherlandish Drawings of the Fifteenth and Sixteenth Centuries, Amsterdam, Rijksmus. cat.*, ii, 2 vols (Amsterdam, 1978)

W. Sumowski: *Drawing of the Rembrandt School*, 9 vols (New York, 1979–85)

Dutch Figure Drawings from the Seventeenth Century (exh. cat. by P. Schatborn; Amsterdam, Rijksmus.; Washington, DC, N.G.A.; 1981–2)

K. Andrews: *Catalogue of the Netherlandish Drawings in the National Gallery of Scotland*, 2 vols (Edinburgh, 1985)

Drawings by Rembrandt, his Anonymous Pupils and Followers (exh. cat. by P. Schatborn, Amsterdam, Rijksmus., 1985)

Renaissance et maniérisme dans les écoles du nord: Dessins des collections de l'Ecole des beaux-arts (exh. cat. by E. Brugerolles, Paris, Ecole N. Sup. B.-A., Hamburg, Ksthalle, 1985–6)

The Northern Landscape: Flemish, Dutch and British Drawings from the Courtauld Collections (exh. cat. by D. Farr and W. Bradford, London, Courtauld Inst. Gals, 1986)

The Age of Bruegel: Netherlandish Drawings in the Sixteenth Century (exh. cat. by J. O. Hand and others; Washington, DC, N.G.A.; New York, Pierpont Morgan Lib.; 1986–7)

M. Schapelhouman: *Netherlandish Drawings, circa 1600*, Amsterdam, Rijksmus. cat., iii (Amsterdam, 1987)

A. Kettering: *Drawings from the ter Borch Estate*, Amsterdam, Rijksmus. cat., v (Amsterdam, 1988)

Landscape in Perspective: Drawings by Rembrandt and his Contemporaries (exh. cat. by F. J. Duparc, Cambridge, MA, Harvard U., Sackler Mus.; Montreal, Mus. F.A.; 1988)

The Drawings by Rembrandt and his School in the Museum Boymans–van Beuningen (exh. cat. by J. Gitay, Rotterdam, Mus. Boymans–van Beuningen, 1988)

F. Stampfle, with J. Shoaf Turner and R. Kraemer: *Netherlandish Drawings of the Fifteenth and Sixteenth Centuries and Flemish Drawings of the Seventeenth and Eighteenth Centuries in the Pierpont Morgan Library* (New York and Princeton, 1991)

Seventeenth-century Dutch Drawings: A Selection from the Maida and George Abrams Collection (exh. cat. by W. Robinson, New York, Pierpont Morgan Lib., 1991)

Drawings by Rembrandt and his Circle in the British Museum (exh. cat. by M. Royalton-Kisch, London, BM, 1992)

Dutch Drawings from the Age of van Gogh: From the Collection of the Haags Gemeentemuseum (exh. cat., Cincinnati, OH, Mus. A., 1992)

Flemish Drawings in the Age of Rubens (exh. cat. by A.-M. Logan, Wellesley Coll., MA, Davis Mus. & Cult. Cent., 1993–4)

Spanish

A. L. Mayer: *Handzeichnungen spanischer Meister: 150 Skizzen und Entwürfe von Künstlern des 16. bis 19. Jahrhunderts* (New York, 1915)

F. J. Sánchez Cantón: *Dibujos españoles*, 5 vols (Madrid, 1930)

Spanish Baroque Drawings in North American Collections (exh. cat. by G. McKim-Smith, Lawrence, U. KS, Mus. A., 1974)

D. Angulo Iñiguez and A. E. Pérez Sánchez: *A Corpus of Spanish Drawings* (London, 1975–)

V. Collections.

The earliest Western collectors of drawings were artists: workshop collections included working drawings produced by the master and reference collections composed of other kinds of drawings by other hands. Artists have always exchanged drawings and given drawings as gifts; an extraordinary example is the red chalk drawing by Raphael of *Two Male Nudes* (Vienna, Albertina), which was subsequently inscribed and dated by Dürer: '1515, Raphael of Urbino, who is so much admired by the Pope, made this nude study and sent it to Albrecht Dürer to illustrate his hand to him'. However, the actual practice of collecting drawings developed when drawings began to circulate freely outside of the immediate workshop circle—as gifts, modelli, commissioned portraits, designs for engraving, presentation drawings and even drawings tendered as payment in kind. Although there are references to drawings at the 15th-century court of Lorenzo de' Medici in Florence, evidence of trade in drawings emerges in the first half of the 16th century.

Artists played a prominent role as agents when trade began to flourish after the midcentury. The Florentine Mannerist painter Giorgio Vasari was the first to form a collection of drawings based on historical principles, which was compiled to illustrate his chronicle of the rebirth of art in Italy, *Le vite di più eccelenti architetti, pittori, et scultori* (Florence, 1550). Vasari was the first to posit the theoretical significance of drawing, or *disegno*, which he regarded as the mother of the three sister arts of painting, sculpture and architecture and as an authentic expression of the artist's personality. He organized his *Libro di disegni*, originally composed of five large albums measuring 610×457 mm in chronological order; the drawings were liberally mentioned in the second edition of *Le vite*, published in 1568. Vasari also recognized the importance of presentation, mounting and framing; he embellished his sheets with elaborate architectural mounts of his own devising drawn in pen and brown ink or, more freely, with the brush. Often several small sheets were mounted on a single page, linked forever through Vasari's own decorative imagination. He inscribed the name of the artist within a cartouche or other device on the mount and occasionally included proofs of the woodcut portraits heading the biographies in the *Vite* (*see* MOUNTING, fig. 4). It is by these special mounts, no two of which are exactly alike, that the contents of Vasari's collection of drawings can be identified. (Distinctive mounts, inscriptions and collector's marks (*see* MARKS, §5) also provide clues to the identity of other collectors; the most authoritative manual of collectors' marks is the two-volume *Les Marques de collections* by Frits Lugt (1921; Suppl., 1956).)

Artists have always been among the most avid and discerning collectors of drawings. Besides Vasari, there are dozens of artists for whom collecting served as a commercial sideline, a creative stimulus, a source of artistic ideas and even as an expression of the artist's social status or his gentlemanly pursuit of universal knowledge. These include Timoteo Viti, Raphael's friend and follower, whose family and heirs conserved a corpus of drawings by the master into the 18th century; the German biographer Joachim von Sandrart; Rembrandt, whose profligate spending on his collection contributed to his bankruptcy, which resulted in an auction in 1658 in Amsterdam; Peter Paul Rubens, who corrected, repaired and 'improved' his drawings through retouching and reworking with pen, brush and gouache; Jonathan Richardson sr and jr, whose writings did so much to stimulate collecting in England; Benedetto Luti in early 18th-century Rome; François Boucher, whose fame owed so much to the reproduction of his own drawings; Joshua Reynolds and his successor as President of the Royal Academy, London, Benjamin West; the French Neo-classicists whose collections have so enriched the provincial museums of France, such as François-Xavier Fabre, Pierre-Adrien Pâris and Jean-Baptiste Wicar, whose superb collection of drawings by Raphael, a portion of which were ceded to Thomas Lawrence, are among the treasures of the British Museum, London, the Ashmolean Museum, Oxford, and the Musée Wicar, Lille; Lawrence himself, whose glorious collection was amassed from the choicest gleanings following the upheavals of the French Revolution and the Napoleonic campaigns; and Charles Fairfax Murray, whose collection was purchased *en bloc* by the American industrialist J. Pierpont Morgan.

Apart from practising artists, drawing collectors include monarchs and rulers, such as Rudolf II of Prague, Charles I of England, Louis XIV of France, Queen Christina of Sweden, George III and Queen Victoria and Prince Albert of England; ambassadors and statesmen, such as Thomas Howard, 2nd Earl of Arundel, Rubens, Count Carl Gustav Tessin of Sweden, not to mention Duke Albert of Saxe-Teschen; as well as businessmen, bankers, tax-farmers and industrialists, such as the banker Everard Jabach of Cologne, Pierre Crozat and Randon de Boisset in France, Fritz Koenig of the Netherlands and Henry Oppenheimer (1859–1932). The latter group's extensive travels often allowed them to negotiate interesting private transactions, such as Koenig's purchase *en bloc* of two volumes containing over 500 studies by Fra Bartolommeo (now Rotterdam, Mus. Boymans–van Beuningen).

Drawing collectors have also come from all ranks of the ecclesiastical community. Cardinal Federico Borromeo was the founder of the Ambrosiana, Milan, deeding his drawings in 1618. Cardinal Leopoldo de' Medici in Florence was expertly advised by the biographer Filippo

Baldinucci who helped assemble the nucleus of the Uffizi's collection of drawings; Baldinucci's own collection of 1200 mainly Tuscan drawings, virtually intact, entered the Louvre in 1906. On a less exalted plane the *marchand-amateur* Padre Sebastiano Resta formed a collection of drawings for Giovanni Matteo Marchetti, Bishop of Arezzo, whose heirs sold the 16 volumes of drawings in 1710 to John, Lord Somers (1650–1716), Chancellor of England, thus introducing to England a new source especially rich in early Italian drawings. One of the earliest collectors of drawings in France was the Abbé Desneux de la Noue, active in the first half of the 17th century. A century later the Abbé de Saint-Non, drawings collector and accomplished printmaker, was one of the most notable patrons of his age, assisting Jean-Honoré Fragonard and Hubert Robert during their travels through Italy.

The ranks of the scholar-collectors, many of whom were active in the drawing trade as *marchands-amateurs*, include many of the most honoured names in the field of drawing connoisseurship. Their correspondence, dictionaries, biographies, catalogues and miscellaneous writings constitute important sources of information for students of drawings. In Italy there were Baldinucci, Bellori, Malvasia, Francesco Maria Niccolò Gabburri and Anton Maria Zanetti, the last celebrated for his chiaroscuro woodcut facsimiles after his collection of drawings by Parmigianino. French scholar-collectors included Michel de Marolles, the theorist Roger de Piles and, most importantly, Pierre-Jean Mariette, the most discriminating connoisseur in France in the 18th century. Heir to the family print dealing business, Mariette early in his career catalogued the print collection of Prince Eugene of Savoy in Vienna, which prepared him for the monumental task of cataloguing the drawings for the estate auction of Pierre Crozat in 1741, when *c.* 19,000 drawings were dispersed. Mariette's own choice collection was sold at auction after his death in 1775.

England was a showcase of drawings early in the 17th century, due to the collections of King Charles I and of the Earl of Arundel. Both of these famous collections were dispersed at auction following the English Civil War (1642–51), although eventually some works re-entered the British royal collection at Windsor Castle. The 'fashionable pastime' of collecting drawings took root and flourished in England among the nobility and gentry, as well as in artistic and intellectual circles. William Cavendish, 2nd Duke of Devonshire, was most notable; he was principally responsible for the formation of the collection at Chatsworth House, Derbys. In 1723 he purchased *en bloc* over 200 drawings from the estate of Nicolaes Anthoni Flinck, son of the Rembrandt pupil Govaert Flinck, including a group of 27 landscape drawings by Rembrandt, 25 of which came directly from the insolvent artist's studio auction in 1658. In 1729, in the French edition of the Richardsons' *Account of the Statues, Basreliefs, Drawings and Pictures in Italy*, the authors referred to England as the 'Cabinet des Dessins' of Europe, implying that the collecting of drawings was well established. Foreign artists resident in England helped to determine the taste for drawings: Peter Lely's collection was auctioned after his death to pay debts in 1688 and 1694, and Prosper Henry Lankrink's drawings were sold shortly thereafter in 1693–

4. As the 18th century progressed, England became an even more illustrious repository, thanks to Dr Richard Mead, Hugh Howard, Lord Somers, General Guise, the Earl of Pembroke, the Earl of Leicester, King George III (his librarian, Richard Dalton, snared for the Crown the collections of the Venetian consul, Joseph Smith, and the Gennari family, who had inherited the studio of Guercino), John Barnard (*d* 1784), Charles Rogers (1711–84) and William Esdaile. The English dealer-experts Arthur Pond and Samuel Woodburn, executor of the Lawrence collection, did much to promote the taste for drawings in England by publishing prints after drawings and holding public exhibitions before the formation of the national museum collections.

Trade in drawings on a large scale helps explain how the cornerstones of the great national drawing collections were laid during the 17th and 18th centuries. Collections were frequently bought and sold *en bloc*. For example in 1671 Jabach was forced because of financial distress to cede his collection of more than 5000 sheets, including works purchased at the sale in 1657 of Peter Paul Rubens's collection, to Louis XIV of France. Once Jabach's business affairs improved, he assembled a second collection, portions of which also entered the French royal collection after his death. These formed the nucleus of the Cabinet du Roi, now the Cabinet des Dessins in the Louvre, Paris.

The 18th century was a period of transition, when many of the great royal and private collections began to evolve into national institutions with an ethical mandate to uplift and educate the people, as is exemplified by the Albertina, Vienna, which was founded in 1769 by Duke Albert of Saxe-Teschen. Other important print rooms were established in the 18th century by civic-minded aesthetes or scholars, such as the Städelsches Kunstinstitut, Frankfurt am Main, and the Teylers Museum, Haarlem.

The political, social and economic upheavals occasioned by the French Revolution and the Napoleonic Wars at the end of the century and the subsequent political realignments in the early 19th meant that all types of property flooded on to the market from the 1780s until the 1830s. Thus, during the early 19th century large-scale collections could still be amassed, although by that date taste dictated a more specialized approach than had previously prevailed, when drawings were as much illustrative of encyclopedic learning as of artistic merit.

Although the British Museum was founded in 1753 and the Print Room was established as an independent department in 1808, it was only after the Richard Payne Knight bequest of 1824 was added to the Sloane, Fawkener and Cracherode collections that it became a noteworthy collection, made even more important by the purchase in 1895 of the collection of Colonel J. W. Malcolm (1805–93), the transfer in 1931 of the Turner bequest and the acquisition in 1957 of the *Liber veritatis* by Claude Lorrain from Chatsworth.

Collecting continued to be a popular pastime throughout the 19th century, and the collector emerged, especially in France, as a significant theme in visual and literary imagery from Honoré Daumier and Balzac to Baudelaire and Huysmans. Drawing sales became more frequent, auction and exhibition catalogues became more precise and items of importance began to be illustrated in sales catalogues. The historicism of the period promoted a nostalgic attitude towards collecting, and a scrupulous pursuit of facts and documents in the study of a specific school or epoch was combined with a penchant for emotional release from urban life and rapid industrialization. The brothers Edmond and Jules de Goncourt, active in Paris in the 1840s and 1850s, exemplify the literary and romantic approach to collecting made so memorable by the depictions of amateurs by Daumier. Moreover, the establishment of illustrated scholarly art journals fostered new interest in the study of drawings, as did the exhibition of drawings in museums and the publication of catalogues of museum collections. This trend continued throughout the 19th century and has done so on an ever expanding scale in the 20th.

At the same time the aesthetic appeal of the individual beautiful object has tended to define the criteria governing the formation of both private and institutional collections, which, since the late 19th century, have usually been acquired item by item rather than *en bloc*. This approach is most evident in the legacies of Grenville Winthrop (1864–1943), Charles Loeser and Paul Sachs at Harvard University's Fogg Art Museum, Cambridge, MA, and Fritz Koenig's collection at the Boymans–van Beuningen Museum at Rotterdam. More recently, that attitude has served as the guiding principle for the formation of the drawings collection at the J. Paul Getty Museum at Malibu, CA, which was established in 1980.

England continued to produce collectors of distinction in the 19th and 20th centuries, such as Dr H. Wellesley, Sir J. C. Robinson, J. P. Heseltine (1843–1929) and Henry Oppenheimer, whose estate sale in 1936 remains one of the auction high-points of the 20th century. However, as the century progressed, the locus of collecting has decisively shifted across the Atlantic. Interest in drawings has been spurred in the USA for both practical and aesthetic reasons among private, corporate and museum collections. In the early years of the century there were five American collections of note: the Metropolitan Museum, the Cooper-Hewitt Museum and the Pierpont Morgan Library in New York, the Fogg Art Museum in Cambridge, MA, and the Art Institute of Chicago. Since then, new centres of strength have emerged; besides the Getty, these include the National Gallery of Art, Washington, DC, the Huntington Library and Art Gallery in San Marino, CA, and the Mellon Center for British Art in New Haven, CT, as well as a host of university museums, such as Yale, Princeton, Williams, Vasser and Oberlin, not to mention important regional print rooms, such as the museums in Boston, Cleveland, St Louis and Los Angeles, and Ottawa and Toronto in Canada. Unlike European collections, which are supported, more or less, through government subsidies, American museums usually depend on private and corporate support as well as endowment for acquisitions. Apart from the Getty, each of these collections depends for its enrichment on a circle of friends and patrons whose support ensures the growth of the collections.

BIBLIOGRAPHY

F. Lugt: *Marques* (1921)
——: *Marques*, suppl. (1956)
Drawings from the Collection of Mr and Mrs Eugene Victor Thaw (exh. cat. by F. Stampfle and C. Dufour Denison, New York, Pierpont Morgan Lib., 1975)
J. Byam Shaw: *Drawings by Old Masters at Christ Church, Oxford*, 2 vols (Oxford, 1976)
Collections de Louis XIV (exh. cat., Paris, Louvre, 1977–8)
European Drawings, 1375–1825 (exh. cat. by C. Dufour Denison and H. Mules, with J. V. Shoaf, New York, Pierpont Morgan Lib., 1981)
Old Master Drawings from the Albertina (exh. cat. by V. Birke and F. Koreny; Washington, DC, N.G.A.; New York, Pierpont Morgan Lib.; 1984)
Leonardo to van Gogh: Master Drawings from Budapest (exh. cat. by T. Gerszi and A. Czère, Washington, DC, N.G.A., 1985)
Master Drawings from the Achenbach Foundation for Graphic Arts of the Fine Arts Museums of San Francisco (exh. cat., San Francisco, CA, Achenbach Found. Graph. A., 1985)
Master Drawings from Titian to Picasso: The Curtis O. Baer Collection (exh. cat., Atlanta, GA, High Mus. A., 1985)
Drawings from the Collection of Mr and Mrs Eugene Victor Thaw, II (exh. cat. by C. Dufour Denison, W. Robinson and S. Wiles, New York, Pierpont Morgan Lib., 1985–6)
Master Drawings in the Royal Collection: From Leonardo da Vinci to the Present Day (exh. cat. by J. Roberts, London, Queen's Gal., 1986)
Master Drawings: The Woodner Collection (exh. cat. by C. Lloyd, M. Stevenson and N. Turner, London, RA, 1987)
G. Goldner and L. Hendrix: *The J. Paul Getty Museum Catalogue of the Collections: European Drawings*, 2 vols (Los Angeles, 1988–92)
Design into Art: Drawings for Architecture and Ornament in the Lodewijk Houthakker Collection, 2 vols (exh. cat., London, Hazlitt, Gooden & Fox Gal., 1989)
From Michelangelo to Rembrandt: Master Drawings from the Teyler Museum (exh. cat., New York, Pierpont Morgan Lib., 1989)
From Pisanello to Cézanne: Master Drawings from the Museum Boymans–van Beuningen (exh. cat., New York, Pierpont Morgan Lib., 1990)
Old Master Drawings from the National Gallery of Scotland (exh. cat., Washington, DC, N.G.A., 1990)
Woodner Collection: Master Drawings (exh. cat., New York, Met., 1990)

For further bibliography *see under* the biographies of individual collectors.

BEVERLY SCHREIBER JACOBY

VI. Conservation.

The purpose of drawings conservation is both to preserve and restore chemical, physical and visual integrity by removing or correcting those conditions that have contributed to the deterioration or disfigurement of the object. Deterioration of drawings may be attributed to the inherent components of the paper (e.g. high lignin content in wood-pulp paper); residues from the manufacturing process (e.g. iron or chlorine); contact with acidic materials as a result of framing or storage; incompatible materials used by the artist or in subsequent restoration (e.g. iron-gall ink; for the damage it can cause see INK, fig. 3); or overexposure to light, air pollution, extremes or fluctuations in temperature and humidity, biodeterioration or rodent activity, and mishandling. Treatment of the resulting damage depends not only on the type and condition of the paper and medium but also on the subtle aesthetic relationship of the two, and an understanding of the artist's intentions, the original appearance of the piece and its history. In the past, many empirical methods were used solely to improve a drawing's appearance, but since the mid-20th century drawings conservation has sought to preserve the work by arresting deterioration and stabilizing its condition, ideally using a process that is reversible. Preservation entails controlling the environment and the housing of an object: mounting, storage, framing and atmospheric conditions, including light, air quality, temperature and relative humidity. Conservation entails the application of intervention techniques that will effect a change in the physical condition and/or appearance of the drawing, using chemical and mechanical procedures.

1. PRESERVATION. Because of the vulnerability of pigments, inks and paper, and the susceptibility of their organic constituents to change under adverse climatic conditions, the temperature, humidity and lighting levels of the immediate environment must be thoroughly monitored. The recommended level of illumination for drawings in the museum environment is 50 lux (5 footcandles) for a maximum continuous period of three months; in all circumstances direct illumination from windows and exposure to ultraviolet radiation should be avoided. With the exception of pastels, charcoals and gouaches with a tendency to flake, most drawings should be framed with ultraviolet-filtering acrylic plastic or laminated glass with an ultraviolet filter, which, as with glass, should be separated from the art work by a mount or spacers. To guard against buckling, staining from condensation, mould growth, insect activity and desiccation of paper and binding media, drawings must be displayed and stored in a stable, air-conditioned environment of c. 20–22°C and 50% relative humidity. All storage and mounting material in contact with a drawing should be 100% acid free. The extra depth provided by a ragboard window mount will also protect the surface of a drawing from abrasion and its edges from damage, and, being non-acidic and hygroscopic, will help to equilibrate slight variations in humidity. Older mounts are often historically relevant to their drawings or were designed by the artist and should not therefore be removed, despite their acidity; in such instances, it is particularly important that all other environmental and presentation recommendations are followed in order to minimize such adverse reactions as acid migration.

2. CONSERVATION. Because of the diversity of media and paper and their respective components, and the differences in condition that result from aging, aesthetic and material benefits of any conservation procedure must be assessed for each object before embarking on any treatment. The artist's handling, pigments, the tone and texture of the sheet, and the changes that have occurred must be understood. If chemical treatment is to be pursued each component of the composition must be tested for stability. Among the most common procedures for the conservation of drawings where appropriate is washing, with or without alkalinization, ranging from immersion to humidification, and aimed at reducing discolouration, embrittlement and the acidity in paper. The mechanical strength of the support, its chemical nature and physical properties, and the solubility and textural qualities of the medium must be evaluated to determine their reaction to contact with moisture. In many instances, a severely discoloured and stained graphite drawing, for example, which is generally stable in water, may be washed by immersion, and the sheet flattened; in other cases, however, moisture cannot be used in treating a graphite composition because the extreme embrittlement of the paper cannot withstand expansion and contraction, or the work includes a mount of historical significance, or the

heavy application of the medium is readily disrupted, or simply because the sheet bears a collector's stamp that is water-soluble. Acqueous and non-acqueous deacidification, although suitable for archival material or books that will be handled, can cause subtle colour changes to paper, inks or pigments due to the chemicals and moisture used in the process. Ragboard, housing and providing a stable climate and minimal lighting will also help to slow down acid reactions. Discolouration, staining or foxing can also be reduced by bleaching, a process that utilizes a variety of reagents, applied using a range of techniques, depending on the constituents of the paper and media and the overall condition of the object. Bleaching can be detrimental and using alternative treatments, such as alkaline water or enzymes, may have to be considered.

There is rarely any question as to the desirability of repairing tears, as left unmended they are likely to enlarge when the drawing is handled, and the exposed fibres will collect dust and dirt from the air. The extent to which a loss in a drawing support should be obscured or revealed will depend on historic and aesthetic considerations. All materials used for repairing tears or losses should be compatible with the original support and the process reversible. There are no pressure-sensitive tapes that fulfil these requirements. Moreover, the repair work should be visible from the *verso* of the sheet or in transmitted light.

Whereas in the past many drawings were laid down on to a semi-rigid mount composed of several layers of paper, or on to wood-pulp board, today these backings are usually removed. Aesthetically, the slight undulations in a sheet of paper, and the textural qualities of the primary support, can be fully appreciated only if the sheet is unrestricted in its movement, while the adhesives used to bond drawings to mounts, and the acidic components of most cardboards, provoke staining, discolouration and embrittlement. In removing a backing it is necessary to consider the sensitivity of the paper and media to moisture, pressure or solvents, the benefits of removal and the historical significance of the mount: backing removal may not always be the preferred treatment when a drawing is on an extremely thin sheet or is rendered in pastel, which would easily rub, or is in such an acidic medium as iron-gall ink, which would fracture in this process.

A drawing is generally lined to strengthen the support, consolidate a severely torn sheet, remove creases or planar distortions, or stabilize the paint layer. Because it exerts tension on the primary support, light-weight, high-quality Japanese tissue applied with starch paste or methyl cellulose is customarily used. Lining a drawing may result in changes to the textural properties of the sheet and should therefore be done only when essential for the preservation of the art work. Dry-mount tissues are not desirable for lining because the heat and pressure required for their application can flatten the paint layer and paper; some also tend to yellow on aging, and reversing the process may require toxic and damaging solvents.

Works on paper may require flattening (using moisture, pressure or tension) if, for example, they have been rolled, are creased or have become distorted from changes in humidity. Not only must the sensitivity of the design layer be considered but also the delicate balance between maintaining the textural properties of the art work and eliminating the distraction of ripples and shadows. Except for drawings in media that tend to flake, a slight amount of undulation of the support in response to fluctuations in relative humidity will generally not provoke damage.

See also CONSERVATION AND RESTORATION, §II; CHALK, §2; INK, §III; and PAPER, §VI.

BIBLIOGRAPHY
A. & Archaeol. Tech. Abstr. (1966–)
A. Clapp: *Curatorial Care of Works of Art on Paper* (New York, 1972, rev. New York, 3/1987)
Bull. Amer. Inst. Conserv. Hist. & A. Works (1973–91)
Pap. Conservator (1976–90)
G. Thompson: *The Museum Environment* (London, 1978)
Bk & Pap. Grp Annu. (1982–91)
Pap. Conserv. Cat. (1984–)
M. H. Ellis: *The Care of Prints and Drawings* (Nashville, TN, 1987)
M. Shelley: *The Care and Handling of Art Objects* (New York, 1987, rev. 2/1992)
C. James and others: *Manuale per la conservazione e il restauro di disegni e stampe antichi* (Florence, 1991)

MARJORIE SHELLEY

Drawing, architectural. *See* ARCHITECTURAL DRAW-ING.

Drawing-frame. *See under* SQUARING UP.

Dreber [Franz-Dreber], **(Karl) Heinrich** (*b* Dresden, 9 Jan 1822; *d* Anticoli di Campagna, nr Rome, 3 Aug 1875). German painter. After studies at the Akademie in Dresden (1836–41) and instruction from the landscape painter Ludwig Richter, Dreber settled permanently in Rome. His *Roman Landscape* (?1844; Hamburg, Ksthalle) was executed under the influence of Richter's late Nazarene style. Characterized by linear articulations and a mingled palette, it features rural genre painting and narrative. Subsequently, Dreber was influenced by the classicizing landscape paintings of Josef Anton Koch. He also made further studies of the idealizing landscape tradition of Nicolas Poussin and Claude Lorrain. Dreber often sketched from nature in the Roman Campagna and incorporated views recorded there into his painted landscapes, adding staffage based on episodes from Classical literature and the Bible, as well as from contemporary Italian peasant life.

Sappho (1864–70; Munich, Schack-Gal.) exemplifies Dreber's mature style. The solitary, classically draped figure of the Greek poetess is seen from behind, framed by craggy rocks and the sea, motifs that Dreber had adopted from nature studies made on Capri. Delicate colours, integrated shapes and fluid values are balanced with the symbolic expression of the painting. A solemn Nature seems to reverberate with the psychic tremors of the tragic heroine who in turn becomes the embodiment of the melancholy creation. Dreber's small oeuvre, characterized by harmonious compositional balance, pantheistic content and a lyrical mood attempted a reform of Neo-classical painting. He exerted a strong influence on German Neo-Romanticism and Symbolism and prepared the way for the *Ideen-Malerei* (intellectual painting) of his friend, the Swiss artist Arnold Böcklin.

BIBLIOGRAPHY
A. Lichtwark: 'Gemälde und Zeichnungen von H. Franz Dreber in der Kunsthalle', *Jb. Ges. Hamburg. Kstfreunde*, xviii (1912), pp. 17–20
H. Börger: *Heinrich Dreber* (Hamburg, 1925)
R. Schöne: *Heinrich Dreber* (Berlin, 1940)

RUDOLF M. BISANZ

Dreier, Katherine S(ophie) (*b* New York, 10 Sept 1877; *d* Milford, CT, 29 March 1952). American patron, painter and writer. She studied art at the Brooklyn Students League (1895–7), the Pratt Institute (1900–01) and privately with Walter Shirlaw for five years. These studies were supplemented by extensive study and travel in Germany, France and England between 1902 and 1912. Dreier was also active in several Progressive Era reforms, including women's suffrage, and in 1920 she wrote a book on social reform in Argentina. In 1914 she launched her first effort to stimulate free artistic expression with the founding of the Cooperative Mural Workshops in New York, an art school and workshop modelled on the traditions of John Ruskin and William Morris. Two years later, while active in the Society of Independent Artists, Dreier met Marcel Duchamp and in 1920, with Duchamp's assistance, founded and became president of the SOCIÉTÉ ANONYME, one of the most important promoters of international modernism in the USA during the first postwar decade. Dreier guided the organization throughout its existence and was instrumental in arranging for its impressive collection of art to be donated to Yale University, New Haven, CT, in 1941. Dreier's own art became more abstract from the 1920s; such works as *Explosion* (1940–47; New Haven, CT, Yale U. A.G.) bear a distinct debt to the mystical abstractions of Vasily Kandinsky, whom Dreier had made an honorary vice-president of the Société Anonyme in 1923.

WRITINGS
trans. and intro. (New York, 1913): E. H. du Quesne-Van Gogh: *Persönliche Erinnerungen an Vincent Van Gogh* (Munich, 1911)
Five Months in the Argentine: From a Woman's Point of View, 1918 to 1919 (New York, 1920)
Western Art and the New Era (New York, 1923)
with M. Duchamp: *Collection of the Société Anonyme: Museum of Modern Art, 1920*, ed. G. H. Hamilton (New Haven, 1950)

BIBLIOGRAPHY
A. B. Saarinen: 'Propagandist: Katherine Sophie Dreier', *The Proud Possessors* (New York, 1958), pp. 238–49
R. L. Bohan: *The Société Anonyme's Brooklyn Exhibition: Katherine Dreier and Modernism in America* (Ann Arbor, 1982)
R. L. Herbert, E. S. Apter and E. K. Kenney, eds: *The Société Anonyme and the Dreier Bequest at Yale University: A Catalogue Raisonné* (New Haven, 1984)

RUTH L. BOHAN

Drelling [Drölling]. *See* DROLLING.

Drentwett. German family of artists. From the 16th century to the 18th the Drentwett family of Augsburg produced over 30 master gold- and silversmiths who received commissions from monarchs, nobility and the wealthy bourgeoisie of all parts of Europe. Members of the family were active in many fields, including cast and repoussé gold- and silverwork, engraving, enamelling and even wax modelling. The founder of the family's reputation, Balduin Drentwett (1545–1627), worked for a number of courts, notably that of the Margraves of Baden-Baden. The work of his son Elias Drentwett I (*c.* 1588–1643) includes an exceedingly fine ewer and basin (1619; Munich, Bayer. Nmus.); the ornamentation on the ewer is part cast and part repoussé, and the reliefwork on the oval basin depicts marine motifs.

Philipp Jacob Drentwett I (*c.* 1583–1652) was one of the first goldsmiths in the 17th century to produce large articles of silver, sending silver tableware, wine-coolers, buffets and ewers to Poland, Sweden and the Viennese imperial court. His son Abraham Drentwett I (1614–66) was one of the most important exponents of cartilage ornament in Augsburg. In 1650 he was commissioned to make a silver throne (Stockholm, Kun. Slottet) for the coronation of Queen Christina of Sweden; it is one of the earliest extant pieces of silver furniture. Like all silver furniture from Augsburg, it consists of a wooden carcass covered with repoussé sheet silver and with cast figural ornament. One of the finest examples of Augsburg style, his Palatinate Sword (1653; Munich, Residenz) has a silver hilt and the ends of the cross-guard in the form of lions, the bodies of which extend from cartilage ornament, holding in their paws cartouches with the arms of the Palatinate and the house of Wittelsbach. The sheath is completely covered with cartilage ornament with pinna and mascarons.

Abraham Drentwett II (1647–1729), son of Abraham Drentwett I, was a goldsmith, wax modeller and designer of ornament, his work being published in several series of engravings (e.g. *Neue Inventiones von unterschiedlich nützlicher Silber Arbeit*; *Augspurgische Goldtschmidts Arbeit*, 2 vols; and *Ein neües Lauber- und Goldschmieds-Buch*, 2 vols; (all pubd Augsburg, n.d.)). His masterpieces include the silver gilt case of a table clock (*c.* 1680–83; Vienna, Schatzkam. Dt. Ordens), covered with profuse foliate and vine ornamentation and trimmed with turquoises and garnets; behind balustrades stand cast figures representing the Virtues; on the headplate are five clockfaces with mobile allegorical figures holding staffs as clock hands and four smaller, immobile figures. Another notable work by Abraham II is a ciborium (1677; Augsburg, SS Ulrich and Afra; on loan to Augsburg, Maximilianmus.), the bowl of which is decorated with repoussé boughs of fruit and reliefs of *Manna Descending from Heaven* and the *Last Supper*, and is held on an angel's uplifted hands; the cover of the ciborium has fruit decoration and the figure of the Christ Child.

Philipp Jacob Drentwett VI (1686–1754) is perhaps best known for a covered goblet (1751–8; Munich, Toering

priv. col., see Seling, ii, nos 1005–6) made for the millennial anniversary of Wessobrunn Abbey. Two putti bear the bowl, which is decorated with rocaille motifs, as is the cover showing the arms of the Toering family; on the sides of the goblet is a relief depicting the *Dream of Tassilo*, the legend of the foundation of the abbey. This fine piece demonstrates that, both technically and artistically, the Drentwett family were still leading gold- and silversmiths in the Rococo period.

BIBLIOGRAPHY
F. X. Bayerl and others: *Goldenes Augsburg* (Augsburg, 1952)
Augsburger Barock (exh. cat., Augsburg, Rathaus and Holbeinhaus, 1968)
C. Hernmarck: *The Art of the European Silversmith, 1430–1830*, 2 vols (London and New York, 1977)
H. Seling: *Die Kunst der Augsburger Goldschmiede, 1529–1868*, 3 vols (Munich, 1980)
CAROLA WENZEL

Dreschell, Hans. *See* TROSCHEL, (1).

Dresden. German city and capital of Saxony. It is a district capital lying in a broad river basin either side of the River Elbe. Under Frederick-Augustus I, Elector of Saxony (*reg* 1694–1733), and his son Frederick-Augustus II (*reg* 1733–63) it was transformed into a city of the greatest architectural distinction. Its art collections, formed mostly by Frederick-Augustus II, made it into a leading centre for both artists and connoisseurs. The art of porcelain manufacture was reinvented in Dresden in 1707, with a factory opening at nearby MEISSEN. The city continued to be artistically active into the 20th century, with the foundation of Die Brücke in 1905. The centre of Dresden, including nearly all its finest buildings, was almost entirely destroyed in World War II. Some buildings have been restored.

I. History and urban development. II. Art life and organization. III. Centre of production. IV. Buildings.

I. History and urban development.

1. Before 1685. 2. 1685–1763. 3. After 1763.

1. BEFORE 1685. The city, whose name is derived from the Sorbish *dreždžane* ('dwellers in the marshy forest'), evolved from a Slav village on the west bank of the River Elbe at the crossing of the trade route from Nuremberg to Kraków (Poland). The original village was centred on the church that later became the Frauenkirche, but the town that grew up to the west of this settlement had a cruciform plan typical of the German colonies in the Slavonic east: traces survive in the Schlossstrasse, the Ernst-Thälmann-Strasse and the Altmarkt (see fig. 1). The town received its first charter in 1216 and developed mainly on the west bank under the protection of a small castle built by the margraves of Meissen and first mentioned in 1216. It was walled in the 13th century, and a stone bridge is documented in 1287; with the Danube bridge at Regensburg this was one of the most famous bridges of medieval Germany.

Although the first Kreuzkirche behind the Altmarkt with its relics of the True Cross became a popular place of pilgrimage, Dresden remained insignificant throughout the Middle Ages. Its houses were timber; despite a regulation made after the devastating fire of 1491 requiring that wooden buildings in the inner city should be replaced by stuccoed brick, they survived outside the wall until the

1. Dresden, view showing the Kreuzkirche (1764–92; rest. after 1950) in the foreground and the Altmarkt behind; from a post-World War II photograph

19th century. Of the Gothic churches, only a few remnants in the Sophienkirche survived into the 20th century, but they were removed in the early 1960s.

In 1485 Dresden, which then had about 5000 inhabitants, became the capital of the Albertine line of the house of Wettin, a status it retained until 1918. The electors of Saxony then made special efforts to have their status reflected in architecture, and the city's first architectural flowering began about 1530, ending only with the Thirty Years War (1618–48). Until *c.* 1700 Dresden was a magnificent Renaissance city, which disappeared beneath the Baroque transformation. The Reformation was also significant in the development of architecture and the fine arts in Dresden, which, as the capital of the leading Protestant state, became the centre of Lutheranism in Germany. The peaceful nature of its introduction meant that there was no hostility towards imagery and the arts.

After 1520 the old village round the Frauenkirche was brought within the town wall, and the Neumarkt was laid out soon afterwards. A regulation of 1545 inaugurated the controlled expansion of the city, and in the course of the 16th century the fortifications took on the form they were to retain until their removal in 1809. All that remains is the high wall of the Brühlsche Terrace with its gun emplacements parallel to the Elbe. Altendresden (later Neustadt) on the right bank of the Elbe was not fortified until 1632.

The enlargement of the castle was begun under Duke George (*reg* 1500–39) and continued by Elector Maurice (*reg* 1547–53). A portal dated 1534 includes Lombard Renaissance elements, the earliest appearance of such motifs in Dresden. The main enlargement into a four-winged structure with corner staircase towers was done following French models by Caspar Vogt von Wierandt, and despite later additions it was his alterations that gave the castle its definitive character. The sumptuous Renaissance interior decoration was removed in the 17th and 18th centuries.

The architectural development of Dresden continued during the peaceful reign of Elector Augustus (*reg* 1553–86). The rebuilding of the Kreuzkirche with a broad west front in 1584 provided a visual landmark that survived until its tower was destroyed by Prussian artillery in 1760. Of special architectural merit was the Lusthaus (destr. 1747), a rectangular, two-storey pavilion built in 1590 at the corner of the bastion overlooking the Elbe by Giovanni Maria Nosseni, a leading exponent of Mannerism in Saxony. Other surviving (if altered) architectural features include the Stallhof (1586–91; now the Johanneum, housing the transport museum) and the Langer Gang, a covered walk with an Italian-style arcade between the castle and the Stallhof, also probably designed by Nosseni. The splendour of the court buildings was reflected in civic architecture, with prestigious municipal buildings such as the Gewandhaus am Judenhof and the Neumarkt. Nothing, however, remains of the stone houses, which often had several arcaded storeys facing into the courtyards, of a kind that survive in Leipzig.

During the Thirty Years War, Dresden remained intact behind its strong defences, and when hostilities ceased in 1648 gardens and pavilions could be established outside the city. The only surviving garden, the Grosser Garten, was laid out from 1676 east of the town, on a strictly geometrical Franco-Dutch model, to the plans of the Inspector-General of Works Johann Georg Starcke (*c.* 1640–95). In the centre, surrounded by eight very small pavilions, stands Starcke's Palais im Grossen Garten, a garden palace begun in 1678. It was the first Baroque building in Saxony: the two-and-a-half-storey structure on an H-shaped ground-plan is modelled on palatial architecture in Genoa and, more particularly, in France.

In 1684 the destruction of Altendresden north of the river by fire provided an opportunity to rebuild this part of the city to a regular design. The Inspector-General of Works, WOLF CASPAR VON KLENGEL, laid out a spacious street-plan, which still survives in essence, with the broad main street leading from the bridge to the former town gate and the Neustadt marketplace, with eight streets leading into the marketplace. This area became known as Dresden-Neustadt.

2. 1685–1763. In 1694 the unexpected accession to the throne of Elector Frederick-Augustus I inaugurated the most brilliant era in the history of Dresden. After the city became a major European capital with the choice of the Elector of Saxony as King Augustus II (the Strong) of Poland in 1697, it was transformed to match its new dignity. The conversion of the ruling house to Catholicism linked Saxony closely to those countries that, as a result of the Counter-Reformation, had attained pre-eminence in the arts. The rivalry between the Catholic court and the Protestant citizens was culturally fruitful, and despite the strong bourgeois traditions of Saxony, under Polish influence the Saxon nobility achieved a predominant position. The artistic talent and discrimination of Augustus II himself ensured the presence at his court of leading artists.

Civic building projects were subject to court approval, with regulations decreeing the number of storeys, the height of eaves and the number of chimneys for whole streets. The resulting unity of style distinguished the city until its destruction. The general façade design was simple and can still be seen in a few 18th-century houses in Neustadt; terraced houses, several storeys high, usually had an odd number of window bays, with the entrance porch, often with a shallow bay window, in the middle. The roofs had prominent eaves. Façades were stuccoed and painted in bright colours. The upper floors were articulated by pilasters and the windows surmounted by pediments or cartouches. The Frauenkirche, built between 1726 and 1734 (*see* §IV, 1 below), was a city landmark until 1945.

The outstanding building, both of Dresden and of the period, was the Zwinger (1711–28; rest. after 1945; see fig. 2; *see also* §IV, 2 below). Designed by MATTHÄUS DANIEL PÖPPELMANN and BALTHASAR PERMOSER to frame a ceremonial space planned as the courtyard of a castle that was never built, it fused architecture and sculpture more intimately than in almost any subsequent building in the history of Western art.

Opposing the Zwinger across the Elbe was the Holländisches Palais, begun in 1715 but extended by Pöppelmann, Zacharias Longuelune and Jean de Bodt from 1727 to 1730 and renamed the Japanisches Palais (rest. after 1945). Intended to contrast the King's collection of

2. Dresden, aerial view showing (centre) the Zwinger, 1711–28, by Matthäus Daniel Pöppelmann and Balthasar Permoser, and (right) the Hofkirche, 1738–56, by Galetano Chiaveri; from a pre-World War II photograph

oriental porcelain with the local Meissen product, to the advantage of the latter, the building contained deliberate oriental references in the pagoda-like roofs of the corner pavilions and the Asiatic herms supporting the balcony. The skyline of the left bank was given a distinctive feature with the late Baroque Catholic Hofkirche (1738-56; rest. after 1945; fig. 2) by Gaetano Chiaveri. With the Frauen-kirche, the building dominated the view from the Elbe, its single west tower, a Roman Baroque interpretation of a northern tradition, standing at the focal-point of many axial lines. Representing a 'Catholic statement' in opposition to the Frauenkirche, since 1980 it has been the cathedral of the diocese of Dresden-Meissen.

The great period of court building ended with Frederick-Augustus I's death in 1733. His son Frederick-Augustus II was more interested in enlarging the art collections that were to become the foundation of Dresden's later reputation. The buildings were now in the more sober manner of French classicism, represented by the aged Longuelune and de Bodt and their assistant Johann Christoph Knöffel, who became very influential. His reserved, dignified style, making much use of pilasters and Rococo ornament, was used particularly in the service of the prime minister Graf Heinrich von Brühl, for whom he built a palace and a library, and the famous gallery building on the terrace later named after Brühl. The only trace of Knöffel's building is, however, the ruined Kurländer Palais of 1729.

The bombardment of Dresden by Prussian troops in 1760 during the Seven Years War caused heavy damage and many casualties. The subsequent rebuilding was in a simpler style, both owing to lack of resources and to a new bourgeois artistic ideal in opposition to that of the court. Dresden architecture also came under the influence of Johann Joachim Winckelmann, whose essay *Gedanken über die Nachahmung der griechischen Werke in der Malerey and Bildhauerkunst* was published as a book in Dresden in 1755. His views on the 'noble simplicity and serene grandeur' of Greek art seem to have affected the interior decoration (destr.) of the Hofkirche, which was deliberately left unfinished.

3. AFTER 1763. In the period of austerity after the Seven Years War many international artists left the city, and Dresden sank into provincialism. Theories of the Enlightenment were propounded by the Kunstakademie, founded in 1764. The Landhaus, the assembly building of the Saxonian estates (now the Museum für Geschichte der Stadt Dresden) was built in 1770–76 by the teacher of architecture and theoretician of classicism, Friedrich Augustus Krubsacius. It was one of the first buildings in Saxony to use Classical orders, but the stairwell is the last of the grand Baroque staircases. Contemporary interest in literature, garden design and Romantic painting rather than architecture is reflected in park buildings based either on English Gothic Revival ruins or, at the summer residence at Pillnitz, near Dresden, on Palladian or Chinese models.

At the dissolution of the Holy Roman Empire in 1806, Saxony became a kingdom, with Dresden as its capital. Building activity revived only in the 1830s, after the division of Saxony at the Congress of Vienna in 1815 and economic developments that exerted increased pressure towards liberalization and an economic boom after the state became a constitutional monarchy in 1831. The population in 1834 was 73,500, increasing to about 400,000 by 1900. Building policies in the first decades of the 19th century had a major influence on the city's development. Building restrictions in the suburbs were lifted in 1813, and the fortifications were mostly removed between 1817 and 1829. Development was controlled by the building plans of 1824 and 1827 drawn up by Gottlob Friedrich Thormeyer. The desire of the royal building authorities to preserve the beauty of the city was an important aspect of the planning process up to the 20th century. Regulations prescribed mainly two-storey buildings with free-standing residential houses for expansion zones. Streets and squares were laid out on crown land on the former fortifications. Of these, the circular Bautzner Platz in the north of Dresden-Neustadt, begun in 1811 and planned by Johann Gottlob Hauptmann (1755–1813), is particularly notable.

At Pillnitz, the Neues Palais (1812–30), the connecting building between Pöppelmann and Longuelune's Bergpalais and the Wasserpalais (both 1720–23), was built by Christian Frederick Schuricht in a style compatible with that of its neighbours; it attests to the underlying conservative mood in architecture. It contains, in the Kuppelsaal and the Schlosskapelle, the two Neo-classical interiors preserved in the Dresden area, decorated by Carl Christian Vogel von Vogelstein after 1824 in keeping with the ideas of the NAZARENES.

With the reforms of 1831, the architectural administration of Dresden passed to the middle classes, and with the appointment of Gottfried Semper to the Kunstakademie, architecture was once more in touch with mainstream European developments. Had it been fully realized, his forum plan of 1835, redesigning the square between the Zwinger, the Elbe bank, the Hofkirche and the castle, would have produced one of the most imposing city spaces of the 19th century. In 1838–41 he built the opera house (Hoftheater; *see* SEMPER, GOTTFRIED, fig. 1), opposite the Hofkirche (it burnt down in 1869 and was replaced by a new building, also by Semper, in 1871–8; see fig. 3). The open side of the Zwinger was filled in by Semper's museum in 1847–54.

The High Renaissance style favoured by Semper and his pupils appealed to the classical and humanist ideals of the Dresden middle classes and came to dominate the historicist architecture of the city until about 1885. Villas such as the Villa Rosa (1839) and the Palais Oppenheim (1845) were imitated throughout Europe. However, some villas and churches, including the neo-Gothic Johannis-kirche (1874–8, by Ludwig Möckel (1838–1915); destr.), were based on Gothic or Romanesque style. The move away from Semper's pure High Renaissance historicism was marked by the new building for the Kunstakademie (1886–93) on the Brühlsche Terrace by Constantin Lipsius.

A significant influence on the further development of Dresden was the separation of residential and industrial zones laid down in the building plan of 1858–62, followed by an even stricter segregation between 1878 and 1905. Industry, banished from the city, established itself in the western suburbs. The diverse economic structure and strong building laws preserved the character of Dresden until its destruction. Characteristic of the somewhat con-servative nature of its architecture was the rebuilding of the castle in 1889–1901 by Dunger and Fröhlich in the style of the German Renaissance, and the building of the Standehaus (the Saxon parliament building; 1901) on the Brühlsche Terrace by Paul Wallot in the Italian High Renaissance tradition.

Art Nouveau, therefore, remained marginal in Dresden, a more moderately modern style in conjunction with the local vernacular enjoying general popularity. Many public buildings were produced between 1905 and 1916 by Hans Erlwein (1872–1916), who was influenced by the Baroque tradition of south Germany. Martin Dülfer executed the main building, in brick, of the Dresden Technische Hoch-schule (founded 1828) in 1911. The first garden city in Germany, which still exists, was laid out in HELLERAU to plans drawn in 1907–8 by Richard Riemerschmid, with, among others, Hermann Muthesius and Heinrich Tessenow.

In the 1920s the general shortage of living accommo-dation led to the building of traditional estates in 'conser-vationist' style and a number of Functionalist blocks, such as those by Hans Theo Richter in Dresden–Trachau (1928–30). The Hygiene-Museum, however, built 1928–30 by Wilhelm Kreis, lies stylistically between Functionalism and Neo-classicism. Kreis's plan to remodel the city as a Gau capital during the Third Reich was not carried out, and only his Luftgaukommando was built, from 1939.

After the almost total destruction of the inner city on 13–14 February 1945, it was decided to restore only the most important buildings. The street-plan of the Altstadt was simplified and the area of the Altmarkt doubled. The ruins of a number of significant buildings, such as the Gothic Sophienkirche and the Orangerie in the Herzogin Garten, were removed. Others were left, including the Residenzschloss, the Taschenbergerpalais (1707–63), the Palais im Grossen Garten, the Kurländer Palais, the buildings of the Akademie and the Kunstverein. The Frauenkirche was left ruined to stand as a war memorial. The restoration of the Zwinger was begun in 1945 under

3. Dresden, the opera house by Gottfried Semper, 1871–8

Hubert Ermisch (1883–1950); the museum and second opera house were restored, and the Hofkirche was rebuilt.

The rebuilding of the prestigious areas round the Altmarkt was done in an eclectic, historicist manner on the Soviet model. The Neo-Baroque buildings on the Altmarkt itself were erected between 1953 and 1956 to designs by Herbert Schneider and Johannes Rascher. The less prominent buildings are in a more reserved, local style. As the population increased to 520,000 in 1989, the housing shortage was met by the hasty building of residen-tial blocks without architectural ambition and with little reference to the city's historic building traditions. After German reunification in 1990, rebuilding and reconstruc-tion of most of the ruins gathered momentum, and work was started on the reconstruction of the Frauenkirche.

BIBLIOGRAPHY

GENERAL

C. G. Carus: *Lebenserinnerungen und Denkwürdigkeiten* (Leipzig, 1865)
Dresdner Architekturalbum (Dresden, [*c.* 1876])
R. Steche: *Die Bauten, technischen und industriellen Anlagen von Dresden* (Dresden, 1878)
M. B. Lindau: *Geschichte der königlichen Haupt- und Residenzstadt Dresden* (Dresden, 2/1884)
O. Richter: *Verwaltungsgeschichte der Stadt Dresden* (Dresden, 1891)
——: *Abriss der geschichtlichen Ortskunde von Dresden* (Dresden, 1898)
——: *Atlas zur Geschichte Dresden* (Dresden, 1898)
——: *Geschichte der Stadt Dresden*, i: *Mittelalter* (Dresden, 1900)
P. Schumann: *Führer durch die Architektur Dresdens* (Dresden, 1900)
C. Gurlitt: *Beschreibende Darstellung der älteren Bau- und Kunstdenkmäler des Königreichs Sachsen*, xxi–xxiii (Dresden, 1903)
P. Schumann: *Dresden* (Leipzig, 1909)
R. Bruck: *Dresdens alte Rathäuser* (Dresden, 1910)
A. Döring: *Die neue Königsstadt* (Dresden, 1920)
W. Rauda: *Dresden: Eine mittelalterliche Kolonialgründung* (Dresden, 1933)
O. Baer: *Die Befestigungsanlagen von Altendresden* (Dresden, 1934)
E. Haenel and E. Kalkschmidt: *Das alte Dresden* (Leipzig, 2/1934)
E. Haenel: *Dresden* (Berlin, 1935)
K. Schaarschuch: *Bilddokument Dresden, 1933–1945* (Dresden, 1946) [includes records of war damage]
W. Grohmann and E. Kesting: *Dresden* (Berlin, 1955)
F. Löffler: *Das alte Dresden: Geschichte seiner Bauten* (Dresden, 1955, rev. Leipzig, 8/1987)
H. Reuther: 'Dresden zehn Jahre nach der Zerstörung', *Dt. Kst- & Dkmlpf.*, i (1955), pp. 58–69
W. Rauda: *Städtebauliche Raumordnung* (Berlin, 1957)
B. Geyer: *Das Stadtbild Alt-Dresdens: Baurecht und Baugestaltung* (Berlin, 1964)
W. Pampel: *Die städtebauliche Entwicklung Dresdens von 1830–1905* (diss., Dresden, Tech. U., 1964)

G. Dehio: *Handbuch der deutschen Kunstdenkmäler: Bezirke Dresden, Karl-Marx-Stadt, Leipzig* (Berlin, 1965)

H. Graefe: *Dresden: Vision einer Stadt* (Frankfurt am Main, 1965)

W. Hentschel: *Denkmale sächsischer Kunst: Die Verluste im Zweiten Weltkrieg* (Berlin, 1973)

W. Volk: *Dresden: Historische Strassen und Plätze heute* (Berlin, 1975)

F. Löffler: *Schicksale deutscher Baudenkmale im Zweiten Weltkrieg in der DDR*, ii (Berlin, 1978), pp. 372–442 [380 illustrations]

I. C. A. Richter: *Dresden in der Mitte des 19. Jahrhunderts* (Leipzig, 1979) [includes 48 colour etchings]

Bibliographie der Stadt Dresden, Sächsische Landesbibliothek (Dresden, 1981) [to 1960]

A. Hahn and E. Neef: *Dresden* (Berlin, 1984)

V. Helas: *Architektur in Dresden, 1800–1900* (Brunswick, 1985)

Barock in Dresden (exh. cat., Essen, Villa Hügel, 1986)

INDIVIDUAL BUILDINGS

E. Hempel: *Die Dresdner Elbfront* (Berlin, 1949)

H. Ermisch and F. Löffler: *Der Zwinger* (Berlin, 1952) [includes detailed bibliography]

H. J. Neidhardt: *Schloss Pillnitz* (Dresden, 1974)

G. Schmidt: *Dresden und seine Kirchen* (Berlin, 1976)

H. G. Hartmann: *Pillnitz: Schloss, Park und Dorf* (Weimar, 1981)

F. Löffler: *Der Zwinger zu Dresden* (Dresden, 1981)

Das Dresdener Schloss: Monument sächsischer Geschichte und Kultur (exh. cat., Dresden, Staatl. Kstsammlungen, 1989–90)

M. Zumpe: *Die Brühlsche Terrasse in Dresden* (Berlin, 1991)

II. Art life and organization.

1. BEFORE 1697. The scant remains of late medieval sculpture in Dresden show that the city, like the rest of Saxony, was at that time under the influence of Bohemia, in particular the Parler workshop of Prague. Medieval tradition lingered in the theme—the *Dance of Death*—of the first surviving early Renaissance sculpture, now in the Alter Neustädter Friedhof, the work of Christoph Walther I, a member of the family that made a significant contribution to sculpture in Dresden (*see* WALTHER).

At the Reformation, with fewer works of art required by the church, there was a switch to the production of secular works, mainly for display at court. Italian artists became prominent and remained so until the 19th century. The sgraffito paintings (destr.) in the Rezidenzschloss and city houses were first produced by Italians, later by Germans (among the latter, Lucas Cranach I), and Italian craftsmen made stucco ceilings for the Pretiosensaal of the castle in 1550. The only sign of Netherlandish influence, although pervasive in Europe at this time, is in the central section of the altarpiece of the Schlosskapelle, which was influenced by Cornelis Floris.

Mannerism is apparent in the high altar of the Sophienkirche (1606) by G. M. Nosseni, with Sebastian Walther and Christoph Walther IV, but the Thirty Years War brought artistic production to a halt. In the second half of the 17th century city houses were decorated in relief (destr.), and the Palais in Grossen Garten was decorated with statuary and naturalistic ornament heavily influenced by Antiquity.

2. 1697–*c.*1754. The upsurge of activity after the coronation of Frederick-Augustus I as Augustus II of Poland in 1697 embraced all the arts. To enhance the splendour of his residence, the King dissolved the Kunstkammer and had its art collection rearranged. In 1723–4 the treasury of the castle was turned into a public museum, named the Grünes Gewölbe from the colour of its vaults. The interior design was the responsibility of Matthäus

Daniel Pöppelmann, and the leading artists sent works for display: the court sculptor Benjamin Thomae (1662–1751), who carved the tables and consoles; Johann Joachim Kändler, from 1731 chief modeller to the Meissen porcelain factory; two masters of Saxon lacquered furniture, Martin Schnell (*c.* 1675–1740) and Christian Reinow (1685–1749); and, above all, the goldsmith Melchior Dinglinger and the sculptor Balthasar Permoser, who provided the collection with precious pieces of supreme craftsmanship and artistry. Thanks to the collaboration of the latter two with Pöppelmann, who displayed the gilded wood, mirrors, lacquered furniture and polished marble to the best possible advantage, the rooms themselves shone like gigantic gold ornaments.

The other collections still extant today were founded soon after 1720: the Kupferstichkabinett, the scientific collections, the Porzellansammlung and the Gewehrgalerie, now part of the Historisches Museum. In 1744 the paintings were moved to the Stallhof as a separate collection. The Dresden galleries owe their position among the leading art galleries in the world in particular to the high quality of the works acquired during the reign of Frederick-Augustus II.

During the Baroque period porcelain rooms had been an indispensable feature of any princely court; and it was in Dresden in 1707 that porcelain was reinvented, the first porcelain factory in Europe being established on the Albrechtsburg in Meissen in 1710 (*see* MEISSEN, §3). An unfinished project of Frederick-Augustus I was a porcelain castle, the interior of which was to be entirely decorated with porcelain. By 1721 the Holländisches Palais housed 25,000 porcelain objects, and the conversion to the Japanisches Palais from 1724 was to provide adequate accommodation for it. Since 1962 the collection has been housed in the Zwinger. The Zwinger is particularly associated with the name of Balthasar Permoser, who, through both his sculptures there and his pupils, including Josef Winterhalder, Georg Raphael Donner and Benjamin Thomae, created a school of Dresden sculpture that remained a fertile influence throughout the 18th century.

3. AFTER *c.* 1754. The court still dominated Dresden culture, with French and Italian artists predominant, the latter, especially Venetians, particularly favoured by Frederick-Augustus II. The building of the Hofkirche from 1738 attracted many Italians. The Saxons were, however, receptive to ideas of the Enlightenment, which came in from about the middle of the 18th century. Sober rationalism was already apparent in the work of the architect Johann Christoph Knöffel and in the sculptures made for the Hofkirche by Lorenzo Mattielli. A new objectivity informs the views of Dresden painted by Bernardo Bellotto, and the presence of Winckelmann in the city in 1754–5 was also significant.

It was, however, in the theatre decorations of Servandoni in 1754 that anti-court, bourgeois ideas first left their mark. They subsequently dominated the Kunstakademie (founded 1697; reorganized 1762 by Christian Ludwig von Hagedorn), which promulgated an idealizing, academic approach to history painting. More noteworthy are the realistic bourgeois portraits by Anton Graff and the tradition of Dresden landscape painting founded by Johann Christian Klengel.

Landscape painting was central to the Romantic movement that dominated Dresden painting in the generation after 1800. Literary associations with the Romantics had been established in 1799 by the publication of *Die Gemälde* by Caroline and August Wilhelm Schlegel: these writings helped to raise the most famous picture in the Gemäldegalerie, Raphael's Sistine *Madonna*, to the status of an aesthetic cult object.

Many factors contributed to the fruitful development of Romantic painting in Dresden: the long tradition of tolerance there and the number of discriminating patrons; the realist styles of such painters as Bellotto; and the Gemäldegalerie, which, having attracted artists to the city in the first place, provided them with models of the highest quality. Its characteristics were the subjective veneration of nature and an irrational anti-classical element, developed mainly outside the Kunstakademie, which cultivated mythological subjects until well into the 19th century. Landscape painting was particularly emphasized, as Nature was the vehicle through which Romantic natural philosophy could best be expressed. Its most important representatives were Caspar David Friedrich, whose presence in Dresden from 1791 influenced a whole generation of painters, and another noteworthy figure, the royal physician and professor of medicine, Carl Gustav Carus, who worked in Dresden from 1814. He, too, was a landscape painter, and his nine *Briefe über Landschaftsmalerei* (1815–24) are among the fundamental theoretical writings on Romantic painting.

The NAZARENES played an important role in the Kunstakademie from the 1820s until after the middle of the 19th century, enjoying the favour of the royal house. From about 1830 the fashion for Romantic painting was superseded by the Düsseldorf school with the appointments of Eduard Julius Friedrich Bendemann and Julius Hübner to the Akademie. For the remainder of the century Dresden painting was dominated by history painting with Nazarene overtones. It was technically very accomplished, as can be seen in Semper's second Hoftheater (reconstr. up to 1985), which was decorated in Italian High Renaissance style with figures in the late Romantic tradition. The same stylistic approach influenced the decoration of countless villas and public buildings.

The 19th-century school of Dresden sculpture was effectively founded by Ernst Julius Hähnel and Ernst Friedrich August Rietschel. Their monumental figures and friezes adorned the second Hoftheater and the Gemäldegalerie in a style of measured realism, with strong allegorical overtones. This tradition continued in the work of Johannes Schilling, and the first signs of transition to the 20th century appeared only in 1909, in the reliefs by Robert Diez (1844–1922) on the Albertinum, which show hints of Art Nouveau.

The increasing provincialism of Dresden after the abortive revolution of 1849 was not reversed by the unification of Germany in 1871. Bourgeois culture prevailed. Only the great German and international art exhibitions organized by Gotthard Kuehl (1850–1915) between 1897 and 1912 brought the city back into the

international limelight. The first two decades of the 20th century were dominated by the Neo-Impressionists. Outside the Akademie the most significant group of artists was DIE BRÜCKE, formed in a Dresden suburb in 1905, and among the founders of German Expressionism. The group left Dresden in 1910, but Expressionism continued to be the dominant influence, taught by Oskar Kokoschka at the Akademie from 1916 to 1923. Still more influential was the veristic social criticism of the NEUE SACHLICHKEIT (New Objectivity), expounded by Otto Dix, who achieved prominence through his anti-war paintings and social criticism, before being banned from exhibiting his works in 1934. In the National Socialist period painting at the Akademie was characterized by a realism of detail approaching the photographic. Many wall paintings, often with National Socialist Volk content, were removed after 1945.

The partition of Germany after World War II did not compel the immediate adoption of Socialist Realist styles. At first painters, graphic artists and sculptors had the chance to begin from where they had left off in 1933, and up to 1950 there was vigorous activity. In 1946 Hans Grundig organized the first German art exhibition, from which grew the exhibitions that take place in Dresden every four years. From 1950, however, only Socialist Realism was permitted, and both exhibitions and buying policy were under state control. Yet beside the official artists worked a large number of others, who did not conform to the requirements of the state. The Kunsthochschule, the successor to the Akademie, was, together with those of East Berlin and Leipzig, the most important centre of the visual arts under the German Democratic Republic. Dresden painting is far less literary and has

4. Dresden, memorial chapel of the former Hofkirche, *Pietà* and altar by Friedrich Press, porcelain, h. 4.4 m (*Pietà*), 1970–73

fewer links to the tradition of Neue Sachlichkeit and Neo-Expressionism. It is calmer and more distantly recalls the work of Cézanne and the Impressionists. Landscape and still-life make up a large part of less official art. Sculpture at the Kunsthochschule cultivates a kind of conservative Modernism as practised about 1900, a continuity embodied in the work of Walter Arnold (1909–79), who taught there from 1949.

It was outside the Kunsthochschule, however, that the outstanding sculptors were to be found—notably in the contrasting styles of Friedrich Press (*b* 1904) and Peter Makolis (*b* 1936). Makolis produced taut, vigorous portrait busts in polished stone, executed with great technical accuracy, while Press, a native of Westphalia resident in Dresden from 1935, supplied churches, particularly Catholic ones, with sculptural objects composed of stone, metal, wood or porcelain. They are distinguished by a spiritual Expressionism and a form that is reduced to the most lapidary terms. He designed the altar area in the Josephskirche in Dresden–Pieschen, with its group of sculptures, *Holy Jerusalem* (1966–7), the *Pietà* and altar (1970–73) in the memorial chapel of the former Hofkirche (see fig. 4), consecrated to the victims of war and unlawful violence.

BIBLIOGRAPHY

W. von Seidlitz: *Die Kunst in Dresden vom Mittelalter bis zur Neuzeit*, 2 vols (Dresden, 1921–2)
R. von Arps-Aubert: *Sächsische Barockmöbel, 1700–1770* (Berlin, 1939)
W. Hentschel: *Bibliographie zur sächsischen Kunstgeschichte* (Berlin, 1960)
Bernardo Bellotto in Dresden und Warschau (exh. cat., Dresden, Gemäldegal. Alte Meister; Warsaw, N. Mus.; Wrocław, Sil. Mus.; 1963)
Kunst in Dresden: 18.–20. Jahrhundert (exh. cat., ed. J. C. Jensen; Heidelberg, Kurpfälz. Mus., 1964)
W. Hentschel: *Dresdner Bildhauer des 16. and 17. Jahrhunderts* (Weimar, 1966)
J. Menzhausen: *Das Grüne Gewölbe* (Leipzig, 1968)
H. J. Neidhardt: *Die Malerei der Romantik in Dresden* (Wiesbaden, 1976)
The Splendor of Dresden: Five Centuries of Art Collecting (exh. cat., Washington, DC, N.G.A.; New York, Met.; San Francisco, CA Pal. Legion of Honor; 1978–9)
G. Haase: *Dresdner Möbel des 18. Jahrhunderts* (Leipzig, 1983)
K. Hoffmann: 'Einrichtung der ersten europäischen Porzellanmanufaktur in Dresden 1708 bis 1710 und deren Förderung durch August den Starken', *Internationale wissenschaftliche Konferenz. Sachsen und die Wettiner, Chancen und Realitäten: Dresden, 1989*, ed. R. Gross, pp. 256–64
J. Winkler, ed.: *Der Verkauf an Dresden, Dresden und Modena—aus der Geschichte zweier Galerien* (Modena, 1989)
M. Alther: *Dresden: Von der Königlichen Kunstakademie zur Hochschule für Bildende Künste* (Dresden, 1990)
G. Heres: *Dresdener Kunstsammlungen im 18. Jahrhundert* (Leipzig, 1991)

VOLKER HELAS

III. Centre of production.

1. METALWORK AND OBJECTS OF VERTU. The first reference to a goldsmith working in Dresden dates from 1388, and documentary evidence of goldsmithing increases around 1500. About 1530 the goldsmiths used their own seal, and the first known regulations of the guild date from 1542. The guild benefited from the establishment of Dresden as the capital of Saxony in 1549. Goldsmiths from other places were summoned to the court of the Electors of Saxony and imported new styles. The earliest indigenous Renaissance work is the gold mount on a jasper bowl (1571; Dresden, Grünes Gewölbe) by Urban Schneeweiss (1536–1600). In the following decade the court of the Electors of Saxony became one of the most

splendid in the Holy Roman Empire, and expenditure on jewellery was among the highest household costs. In 1585 Johann Kellerthaller II (*see* KELLERTHALLER, (1)) produced a highly significant jewellery and writing cabinet (Dresden, Grünes Gewölbe) with cast and embossed silver sculpture. It is the first cupboard of this size and type in Germany.

The masterpiece that goldsmiths produced to become members of the guild remained the embossed standing-cup; a pattern from about 1600 is in the Grünes Gewölbe. Most masters produced enamelled gold as well as silver repoussé work, though there was a degree of specialization. Daniel Kellerthaller (*see* KELLERTHALLER, (2)), active in the first half of the 17th century, was the first outstanding goldsmith and worked in the early Baroque style. His work shows the influence of gold- and silverwork from Prague, Nuremberg, Augsburg and perhaps even Italy. He was one of the best portrait medallists, draughtsmen and engravers and also practised the techniques of embossing and casting, of which his rose-water ewer and basin (1629; Dresden, Grünes Gewölbe) is an outstanding example.

During the reign of Frederick-Augustus I, Elector of Saxony (Augustus the Strong), there was a great increase in the demand for the work of goldsmiths, and particularly jewellers. The work of JOHANN MELCHIOR DINGLINGER reflects Frederick-Augustus's desire for magnificence and representation, and it is an expression of cultural life in the Baroque period. Dinglinger's brother and close collaborator, the enameller Georg Friedrich Dinglinger (1666–1720), produced numerous enamel portraits for the court. Johann Heinrich Köhler (1669–1736) was another court jeweller. His work is characterized by humorous and satirical themes, and he specialized in the use of monstrous pearls, as in his figurine of a *Spanish Dancing Girl* (Dresden, Grünes Gewölbe). In the reign of Frederick-Augustus II, Elector of Saxony, there was a further refinement of taste; however, there were no outstanding goldsmiths. Porcelain became more important than silver. The diamond became the most popular gem in jewellery, as is shown by the works of Jean Jacques Pallard (1701–76)

After the early 18th century the burgher class emerged as important clients, especially for municipal silverware and ceremonial gifts, particularly standing-cups. The leading goldsmiths of the Rococo style were from the Ingermann and Schrödel families; under the influence of the latter Dresden classicism flourished. The snuff-box was another favourite prestige object among the nobility and burghers of Dresden. Johann Christian Neuber (1736–1808), who became a citizen of Dresden in 1762 and Court Jeweller probably before 1775, developed the technique of *Zellenmosaik* (*see also* GERMANY, §X, 3(i)) into an art characteristic of Dresden. In addition to snuff-boxes, scent-bottles and cane handles he produced a number of large pieces, for example a fireplace made of Meissen porcelain and Saxon hardstones (1782; Dresden, Grünes Gewölbe). Goldsmithing declined in Dresden from the mid-19th century, and the interest in Saxon hardstones subsided. Craftsmen were trained in art schools rather than by the guilds. The flowering of *Jugendstil* in silverwork at the beginning of the 20th century, as seen in works for the city council of Dresden, was to be of short duration.

BIBLIOGRAPHY
W. Holzhausen: *Goldschmiedekunst in Dresden* (Tübingen, 1966)

FABIAN STEIN

2. FAIENCE. In 1708 the Meissen arcanist Johann Friedrich Böttger established a faience factory in Dresden, run by Christoph Rühle (*d* 1742), a flagstone maker from Brandenburg, and Gerhard van Melcem. They failed to produce faience at the factory, and Böttger therefore recruited the Dutch thrower Peter Eggebrecht (*d* 1738), who had been employed at the faience factory of Cornelius Funcke (1673–1733) in Berlin as manager in 1710. In 1712 Eggebrecht took over the lease of the factory and apart from a period in Russia (1718–20) remained there for the rest of his life. In 1720 Eggebrecht was able to buy the factory from Frederick-Augustus II, Elector of Saxony. In 1731 Eggebrecht attempted to obtain an appointment as inspector of the porcelain factory at Meissen with the help of his son-in-law Johann Joachim Kändler; he was, however, turned down because his knowledge of the porcelain-making process was inadequate. After his death his widow, Anna Elisabeth, continued to run the factory until 1756, when it was handed over to her daughter Charlotte Eleonore Le Lonay, who with her husband managed to keep it going for another 11 years, despite falling output. In 1767 Kändler briefly took over the business before leasing it to Christiane Sophie von Hörisch, who with the collaboration of her son, Carl Gottlieb Hörisch, continued production until 1784.

It is difficult to identify items produced at the factory, as it was not until Christiane Sophie von Hörisch took over that wares were marked (DH) on a more regular basis. The earliest pieces possibly include three unpainted, white-glazed figures: Scaramouche and Pantaloon from the *commedia dell'arte* and a peasant leaning on his stick (all Frankfurt am Main, Mus. Ksthandwk). The moulds for these are possibly the same as those used for early Meissen red-stoneware figures. A pot with a short spout (1718; Düsseldorf, Hetjens-Mus.) can probably be assumed to be the work of Eggebrecht. A marked lidded vase (1776; Düsseldorf, Hetjens-Mus.) was made during the period when Christiane or Carl was in charge. As well as faience vases made to complete Chinese garnitures and commissioned by the elector or king, the vessels produced for the Saxon court pharmacy were a speciality.

At the end of the 18th century another faience factory was established in Dresden by Messerschmidt (e.g. tureen; Düsseldorf, Hetjens-Mus.).

BIBLIOGRAPHY
E. Zimmermann: 'Dresdener Fayencen', *Der Cicerone*, iii (1911), pp. 205–17
O. Riesebieter: 'Dresdener Fayencen', *Der Cicerone*, v (1913), pp. 584–6
H. von Trenkwald: 'Dresdener Fayencefiguren', *Der Cicerone*, vi (1914), pp. 235–6
F. Fichtner: 'Dresdner Fayencen', *Ber. Dt. Ker. Ges.*, xviii (1937)
K. Hüseler: *Deutsche Fayencen*, 3 vols (Stuttgart, 1956–8)
A. Klein: *Deutsche Fayencen im Hetjens-Museum Düsseldorf* (Düsseldorf, 1962)
F. A. Dreier: *Figürliche Keramik aus 2 Jahrtausenden* (Frankfurt am Main, 1962–3)
R. Rückert: *Biographische Daten der Meissener Manufakturisten des 18. Jhs.* (Munich, 1990)

SILVIA GLASER

3. TEXTILES. Tapestries were woven in Dresden in the first half of the 16th century. In the 18th century the city was known for its production of whitework embroidery (known as *point de Saxe* or *point de Dresde*). For further details *see* GERMANY, §XI, 1, 2, 3(iii) and 5.

□

IV. Buildings.

1. FRAUENKIRCHE. Before destruction by bombing in 1945 the Frauenkirche (for illustration *see* BÄHR, GEORGE) was one of the few monumental and grand Baroque Protestant churches in Germany and one of the most important features on Dresden's skyline. It was commissioned by the civic authorities; the architect was the municipal carpenter, GEORGE BÄHR. A church dedicated to the Virgin had stood on this site since perhaps the 11th century. The first plans to replace the Late Gothic church occurred *c.* 1716–18, when Johann Christoph Naumann (*c.* 1664–1742) designed a regular scheme for the Neumarkt; the process gathered momentum with Bähr's first design (1722); a competitive design in 1725 by the court architect Johann Christoph Knöffel inspired Bähr to revise his project, incorporating some of Knöffel's suggestions. Building started in 1726, and the church was dedicated in 1734. After Bähr's death the lantern was finished by his assistant Johann Georg Schmid (1707–74).

The free-standing church was built to a square plan with three monumental façades and four diagonally set turrets, which house the gallery stairs, the whole crowned by a high dome. Apart from the east side, which had a semicircular apse to house the choir, all sides had the same elevation; the central bays and corner turrets were treated as frontispieces with pediments (triangular in the central bays and segmental in the corner units). Each frontispiece-bay had an entrance cut into the low rusticated basement, the doors of the corner units leading directly to staircases serving the galleries. On that basement stood a continuous order of pilasters with elongated round-headed windows in between. The even system was subtly varied by width and articulation (centre bays had double pilasters supporting a pediment), and by position (straight or diagonal) of the bay. The corner turrets were surmounted by small and highly decorative spires. The dome was one of the most unusual features of the church with neither precedent nor successor: a concave, curved base swept up from the main entablature to meet the actual springing point of the dome. This had an elongated, parabolic contour, resembling that of a bell.

Inside, a circular ring of piers carried a smaller, semicircular inner cupola (h. *c.* 40 m) with a view through an opening in the apex to the interior of the steeply rising main dome; the staircases were tucked away in the corners. Galleries were arranged in five tiers of different shapes to provide the necessary seating (*c.* 3600 seats, with glazed boxes in the first gallery for the more distinguished parishioners; the building was partly financed by selling boxes and seats, as well as burial-places). In the choir the colonnaded altar, the organ case above it and the pulpit were designed by Johann Christian Feige (1689–1751); the organ (1732–6) was by Gottfried Silbermann (1683–1753), and the paintings (destr.) in the inner cupola were by Johann Baptist Grone (1682–1748).

The Frauenkirche was decidedly unlike the usual type of modest and unadorned Protestant church. Its sheer size (h. overall *c.* 95 m; dome diam. 23.5 m), the fact that it was built entirely of sandstone (the dome being clad in that material) and the strange contour and prominence of the dome all suggest that the church was meant to be a statement of the true Protestant faith in the state where the Reformation originated, but where the head of state, Elector Frederick-Augustus I, had become a Catholic in 1697. The site has been maintained as a ruin since 1945 with one fragment of the choir walls standing. Rebuilding the Frauenkirche, using 40% of the original stone, began in 1992.

BIBLIOGRAPHY

C. Freyberger: *Historie der Frauenkirche in Dresden* (Dresden, 1728)
J. Sponsel: *Die Frauenkirche in Dresden*, 2 vols (Dresden, 1893–1903)
H. Scholze: 'Baugeschichtliche Betrachtungen zur Entstehung der Frauenkirche und zur Gestaltung des Neumarktes in Dresden', *Wiss. Z. Tech. U. Dresden*, xviii (1969), pp. 21–38
H. G. Franz: 'Die Frauenkirche in Dresden und ihr Erbauer George Bähr im Kontext der kursächsischen Barockbaukunst', *Jb. Zentinst. Kstgesch.*, iv (1988), pp. 143–90
H. Magirius and U. Böhme: 'Meinungsstreit: Wiederaufbau der Dresdener Frauenkirche oder Erhaltung der Ruine als Denkmal?', *Dt. Kst- & Dkmlpf.*, xlix (1991), pp. 79–90

2. ZWINGER. The Zwinger is one of Frederick-Augustus I's grand and ambitious projects. It is a large open square (116×107 m with apses 47.5 m deep added to the shorter sides), framed by galleries and pavilions (see fig. 2 above). The architect was Matthäus Daniel Pöppelmann in close collaboration with the sculptor BALTHASAR PERMOSER. It was started as an orangery, soon enlarged to serve for court festivities, and eventually converted to a museum. Its name (*Zwinger*: 'outer ward') is derived from its position in a corner of a bastion, between the inner and outer city walls.

Its modest beginning was as a new garden laid out in 1709 to a sketch plan by the Elector himself: a series of U-shaped terraces with stairs at the apex to connect the different levels on which orange trees were displayed. The terraces were built over with arcaded galleries after 1711, and the addition of lateral pavilions gave its plan the form of an omega. The ground floor of the south pavilion was furnished as a grotto, and a nymphaeum was installed behind the north pavilion with a cascade and stairs from the bastion's upper level. Niches on two sides held over life-size figures of nymphs by Permoser and his workshop.

As part of a plan to enlarge the Schloss and give the area to its west a regular scheme, a long gallery of 31 bays was added at right angles to the south pavilion in 1714–18. The two-storey gateway at the centre, the Kronentor, was loosely derived from triumphal arches and surmounted by a bulbous dome. In 1716–18 the Wallpavillon was added over the stairs midway along the curved galleries (for illustration *see* PÖPPELMANN, MATTHÄUS DANIEL). At the same time frescoes (destr.) were painted on the ceilings of the upper rooms in the side pavilions by Heinrich Fehling (north) and Louis de Silvestre (south).

In 1718 a matching group of side pavilions and curved galleries was added at the other end of the long gallery. This created the present plan of the Zwinger, with a large space, the Zwingerhof, for receptions and court festivities. Behind the new pavilions, with frescoes (1724–5; destr.) by Giovanni Antonio Pellegrini, were built an opera house (destr. 1849) and assembly rooms (destr. 1755). The fourth side was closed with stands for spectators, which were later replaced by a wooden wall painted to resemble galleries.

The galleries are carried around the square as a continuous strip: a pilastered colonnade above a high basement with arcaded windows between the pilasters; the side pavilions have two storeys of the same colonnade. This rather strict architectural system is enlivened by varied and rich architectural sculpture: keystones with masks, garlands, scrolls and shells in the frieze and on pilasters, panels of vermiculation underneath the windows and, in front of them, fauns carrying brackets for the orange trees. The Kronentor and Wallpavillon were treated even more richly: the former has walls set at an angle, free-standing columns and niches with figures, while the latter has herm pilasters and concave–convex curved walls; both have broken pediments. The pale local sandstone, the roofs painted blue with gilded ornaments, orange trees in painted ceramic pots and water running down the wall fountains all add to the general air of festivity. This is complemented by allusions to the patron, such as the Polish crown on top of the Kronentor, imperial eagles in the frieze of the north pavilion or the figure of *Hercules* carrying the globe above the Wallpavillon, which refers both to the garden of the Hesperides and to the Elector's temporary role as Reichsvikar during the interregnum of 1711.

In 1727 the Elector decreed that the library, print room, technical instruments and *Kunstkammer* of the electoral collection should be moved to the Zwinger's galleries and pavilions to create a Palais Royal des Sciences. Pöppelmann's proposals to enlarge the Zwinger on the fourth side by building a palace that would have reached across to the Elbe were never executed. The idea was taken up in the 19th century, and GOTTFRIED SEMPER suggested a 'forum of the arts' to combine the Zwinger with a new opera house and picture gallery, of which the latter was built by Semper (1847–54) in neo-Renaissance style to close the fourth side. In style and scale it is not particularly sympathetic to the Zwinger's playful and light appearance, hardening festive architecture into permanence. Five major restorations have taken place since 1783, the last one completed in 1963.

BIBLIOGRAPHY

M. D. Pöppelmann: *Vorstellung und Beschreibung des von Seiner Königlichen Majestät in Polen und Churfürstlichen Durchlaucht zu Sachsen erbauten sogenannten Zwinger-Gartens Gebäuden* (Dresden, 1729/R Dortmund, 1980)
J. Sponsel: *Der Zwinger: Die Hoffeste und die Schlossbaupläne zu Dresden* (Dresden, 1924)
H. Ermisch and F. Löffler: *Der Zwinger* (Berlin, 1952) [detailed bibliog.]
S. Asche: *Balthasar Permoser und die Barockskulptur des Dresdener Zwingers* (Frankfurt am Main, 1966)
F. Löffler: *The Zwinger in Dresden* (Leipzig, 1976)
H. Franz: 'Matthäus Daniel Pöppelmann (1662–1736) und die Architektur des Dresdener Zwingers: Zur Genese des barocken Bauwerkes', *Ksthist. Jb. Graz*, xxii (1986), pp. 7–77
M. Kirsten: 'Der Dresdener Zwinger', *Matthäus Daniel Pöppelmann*, ed. H. Marx (Münster, 1989), pp. 148–74

G. Heres: 'Die museale Nutzung des Zwingers', *Matthäus Daniel Pöppelmann und die Architektur der Zeit August des Starken*, ed. K. Milde (Dresden, 1990), pp. 401–12
J. Man: *Zwinger Palace, Dresden* (London, 1990)

JARL KREMEIER

Dresden Sketchbook. Volume of 15 paper leaves containing 23 drawings of vaults and their projections and 2 alchemical drawings of distillation furnaces (Vienna, Österreich. Nbib., Cod. vind. min. 3). The paper, of which 29 pages measure 374×253 mm and one folio measures 490×370 mm, bears a watermark that is recorded in Dresden and Leipzig between 1544 and 1567. The drawings were executed with the help of grids incised into the paper. The vault projections were sketched in ink, and some are coloured in green, red, sepia and light brown. The alchemical drawings are coloured in blue, yellow and red. The designs give basic procedures for the calculation of lengths and curvatures of the different members of a Late Gothic vault, including complex vaults with interpenetrating ribs and doubly curved elements. Some of the vaults have been identified as north-east German and Bohemian in style.

The Dresden Sketchbook is the only surviving manuscript exclusively concerned with vault projection procedure, and it is likely that its methods were used universally in the construction of Late Gothic vaults. The methods are both extremely simple and very accurate, allowing masons to calculate the elevation of the vault and the absolute curvature and lengths of the members. The absence of any explanatory text has led scholars to suppose that the system was so well understood by the mid-16th century, when this sketchbook was compiled, that masons needed only rough figures to work from, or from which to teach apprentices.

BIBLIOGRAPHY

F. Bucher: 'The Dresden Sketchbook of Vault Projection', *Proceedings of the XXII Congress of Art History: Budapest, 1969*, i, pp. 527–37
——: *Architector: The Lodge Books and Sketchbooks of Medieval Architects*, i (New York, 1979), p. v
Les Bâtisseurs des cathédrales gothiques (exh. cat., ed. R. Recht; Strasbourg, Musées Ville, 1989), pp. 282–3

Dress. Clothing or ornament used to cover and adorn the body.

I. Introduction. II. Classical. III. Late Antiquity and early Middle Ages. IV. 11th–13th centuries. V. 14th–16th centuries. VI. 17th century–early 18th. VII. Early to late 18th century. VIII. 19th century. IX. 20th century.

I. Introduction.

Throughout history, dress and art have been linked in the sense that artists have depicted costume in their work. In addition, some artists have designed textiles and costumes, both literally and imaginatively; in the latter sense dress has often been 'invented' or 'generalized' to suit artistic notions of, for example, the romantic past. Representational art can be one of the most important sources of evidence for the historical study of dress; and dress, whether through the depiction of historical, exotic or fanciful costume, can be one of the artist's most powerful resources in the creation of meaning in his work. This article is concerned primarily with the history and development of secular dress in the Western tradition. Further information on dress is given within the relevant country surveys under the heading 'Textiles', and articles on the following civilizations and countries have separate discussions of dress: see ANCIENT NEAR EAST, §II, 7(i)–(iii) and fig. 34; BURMA, §VII, 1 and fig. 19; CAMBODIA, §V; CHINA, §XIII, 8 and figs 294–7; EARLY CHRISTIAN AND BYZANTINE ART, §VII, 3(i) and figs 75–6; EGYPT, ANCIENT, §XVII, 4 and fig. 100 and §XVII, 10 and fig. 110; ETRUSCAN, §VII, 4; ISLAMIC ART, §VI, 3(i)–(v) and figs 195–9; JAPAN, figs 186–91, 214, and §XVI, 7 and figs 222–4; MESOAMERICA, PRE-COLUMBIAN, §IX, 10 and fig. 44; NEPAL, §VI, 1; SOCIETY ISLANDS and fig. 1; SRI LANKA, §VI, 3; TIBET, §V, 4 and fig. 19.

See also BEADWORK, §2(i), (ii) and fig. 2.

1. Art and the study of the history of dress. 2. The relationship of dress and art. 3. The artist and the design process. 4. Costume in art.

1. ART AND THE STUDY OF THE HISTORY OF DRESS. The history of dress is studied in a number of ways, all of which have their uses as well as their limitations. Contemporary documents, such as inventories, accounts, wills etc, are informative about the language of clothing, although the technical vocabulary can be confusing; letters, diaries and works of fiction can be enlightening as to how people felt about their dress, but such evidence is often selective and emotional; fashion journalism is vivid, but often inexact and impressionistic. Surviving items of costume (only isolated pre-16th-century examples exist, and pre-20th-century examples tend to be of upper- and middle-class origin) give much valuable information about fabrics, cut and construction, but they cannot show how dress looked when worn, and dress needs the imprint of the human body to come to life.

Once the needs of warmth and modesty have been satisfied, one of the primary functions of dress is to make a visual communication—about tribal allegiance, rank or class, for instance. The information to be gained from a wide variety of works of art is therefore vast. It includes different types of dress (working-class costume from the *bas-de-page* of a medieval illuminated manuscript, for example), the textures of dress (the raised patterns of lace, the elaborate curls of a full-bottomed wig, for example, in sculpture) and the construction of clothing (the art of drawing captures details that may not be so clearly defined elsewhere). Perhaps the most complete and satisfactory art from this point of view is painting, particularly portraiture, although genre and, with certain reservations, subject pictures should also be included. In these the dress, although it may no longer exist, has a powerful reality: as Hollander has suggested, when a garment is represented in art it is given a kind of *gravitas* that it may not possess on its own; the vision of the artist transforms the crafts of the weaver, the tailor or the dress-maker into an art object.

Over the course of the centuries, the body, via its clothing, has assumed various, often bizarre, shapes: the tendency towards distortion has usually been more pronounced as part of the romantic individualism of northern Europe than it has in the more temperate south. Images in the history of dress, fixed ineradicably through the medium of art, might include, for example, the spiky, Gothic elongation of the 15th century (*see* §V, 2(ii) below), late Elizabethan 'starched ruffs, buckram stuffings and monstrous tuberosities' (see Carlyle) and the vast, domed crinolines of the mid-19th century—a sartorial echo of the rounded, cavernous railway stations of the period. Through painting, and in particular portraiture, the fashion process may be seen at work, as artist, costume designer and sitter combine to pursue an ideal in beauty, an ideal that changes according to both the preference of the individual and the broader currents of style.

2. THE RELATIONSHIP OF DRESS AND ART. A process of selection, emphasis and stylization occurs in depictions of dress in works of art from Classical Greek sculpture to 20th-century fashion plates. It is, however, during the Renaissance, with a new emphasis on personality and physical appearance in portraiture, that this process can be seen most clearly. As portraiture came increasingly to rely for effect on the splendour of dress and its luxury components to create both a satisfactory artistic whole and an image of the rank and status of the sitter, an artist's reputation might depend on his ability to render the elaborate designs of the brocaded silks, the tactile qualities of the cut velvets and rich furs that played such an important part in the fashionable wardrobe. Equally, dress assumed a greatly enhanced role in giving meaning to a painting: clothing and the way in which it was worn demonstrated both character and accomplishments. As well as the sumptuous clothing of the noble or wealthy, examples might include the robes of the clergy, the garb of lawyers and office-holders, military uniforms and, more obliquely, the loose, informal gowns or deliberately negligent attire in which artists and intellectuals often chose to be depicted (the narcissistic individuality of Albrecht Dürer's self-portraits (*see* DÜRER, (1), fig. 2) is an obvious illustration), the 'democratic', sober, cloth suit of the progressive man of the 18th-century Enlightenment and the unconventional coloured shirts worn by the self-consciously Bohemian intelligentsia during the 1930s.

The question of how far dress reflects other contemporary art forms is a vexed one. Sometimes dress seems to respond to prevailing artistic theories, as in 15th-century Florence where costume was in tune with the natural body shape (especially when compared to the exaggerated styles seen in northern Europe) following Leon Battista Alberti's definition of perfection in all the arts, which he based on the rational and harmonious concord of every part and on what he called the laws of nature. In late Elizabethan and Jacobean England the many exquisite embroidered garments that survive took design inspiration from illustrated herbals and the illuminated borders of manuscripts (booty from the dissolution of religious houses), and at the same time they seem to reflect the jewelled brilliance of miniatures by Nicholas Hilliard and Isaac Oliver. In a later period the Rococo style, characterized by light, curvilinear forms and a love of three-dimensional decoration, affected high fashion by the middle of the 18th century—François Boucher's portraits of *Mme de Pompadour* (e.g. 1756; Munich, Alte Pin.; see fig. 45 below) in frothy silks and

flowers are among the most spectacular examples. Reacting against this kind of hothouse femininity is the austerity of Neo-classical dress, as depicted by Jacques-Louis David and such contemporaries as Louis-Léopold Boilly (see fig. 49 below): for a variety of cultural and political reasons the art of Classical antiquity inspired fashion in France in the 1790s more profoundly than any art form before or since has influenced dress (*see* §§VII, 3 and VIII below).

Conversely, artists who painted such desirable icons of taste as Mme de Pompadour or Mme Récamier (*see* §VIII below) could not help promoting certain styles of dress and types of beauty, the latter seen not just in the face but the figure also. The images in female portraits are made up of the seen—face, figure and costume—and the unseen—underwear—that creates not just the ideal form but the posture too. It is rare to find the female nude viewed objectively, for artists tend to depict the naked female form as though invisibly clothed. A 15th-century Flemish artist, for example, might paint Eve sway-backed with small, high breasts and prominent belly—an image and stance created by the voluminous fur-lined, high-waisted gowns of the period. The broad, fleshy nudes of Peter Paul Rubens reflect the love of the horizontal in dress in the early 17th century, with wide, rounded sleeves and full skirts. Francisco de Goya painted his *Maja Desnuda* (*c.* 1798; Madrid, Prado) as though dressed in invisible stays and clinging Neo-classical gown.

3. THE ARTIST AND THE DESIGN PROCESS. The involvement of the artist in the design of textiles, clothes and accessories goes back at least to the 15th century. Studies exist, attributed to such artists as Jacopo Bellini (examples, Paris, Louvre) and Pisanello (examples, Bayonne, Mus. Bonnat; Oxford, Ashmolean; Paris, Louvre, Cab. Dessins), for designs for the beautiful, large-patterned brocaded silks used for grand costume and formal hangings during the 15th and 16th centuries. In the 16th century many painters, including Giulio Romano, Hans Holbein the younger and Nicholas Hilliard, collaborated with goldsmiths to design the elaborate jewellery that was an essential accessory to the rich, complicated costume of northern Europe; the 'Armada Jewel' (London, V&A), an enamelled gold pendant set with diamonds and rubies and enclosing a miniature portrait of *Elizabeth I*, is usually attributed to Hilliard. From the 17th century onwards, both major and minor artists were involved in the design of fashion plates (*see* FASHION PLATE AND COSTUME BOOK), as a sense of fashion increasingly became an essential part of civilized life. Wenzel Hollar was among the most accomplished of such artists in the 17th century. In the early 18th century Antoine Watteau was involved in such work, while in the 1790s David used his informed interest in the Classical past to design stylish 'Republican' costumes for citizens and officials during the French Revolution. David's designs (1794; Paris, Carnavalet) were never made up (although a few of the artist's friends wore his civilian 'classical' costume). However, a similar idea—that dramatic changes in a political system ought to be mirrored in dress—occurred after the Russian Revolution of 1917, when such Constructivist artists as Varvara Stepanova and Lyubov' Popova created 'Socialist' costumes that incorporated traditional Russian themes in

simple styles that reflected the abandonment of class distinctions (*see* §IX below).

In mid-19th-century England a revolt against the conspicuous over consumption created by the Industrial Revolution, as particularly manifested in the lives of the rich bourgeoisie, inspired many artists and dress reformers. Dante Gabriel Rossetti, among other Pre-Raphaelite painters, disliked contemporary fashions, especially the bright, harsh dyes and the vulgar and over elaborate styles worn by women. Many of the Pre-Raphaelite Brotherhood designed neo-medieval or neo-Renaissance gowns that served as props for their historical paintings (*see* §VIII below). These inspired the loosely draped, flowing dresses in muted colours that later in the century would be called 'aesthetic'. The Spanish painter Mariano Fortuny y Madrazo was also inspired by Renaissance costume, designing beautiful 'artistic' gowns using silks (velvets in particular) inspired by Renaissance fabrics. His designs, intended to be timeless, married perfectly style and fabric. His most famous dress, the 'Delphos' (e.g. *c.* 1920; London, V&A), was a pleated silk tunic inspired by the Classical Greek *chiton* as worn by the bronze statue of the Delphi *Charioteer* (Delphi, Archeol. Mus.).

More in the mainstream of fashion, many of the great professional designers—among them Charles Frederick Worth (1825–95)—claimed inspiration from art or, like Paul Poiret and Elsa Schiaparelli (1890–1973), collaborated with artists (*see* §IX below). In the 20th century in particular, the boundaries between art and dress overlapped. In the 1920s, for example, women's dress can be seen merely as a rectangle of material, like a canvas, on which could be created an abstract pattern by such artists as Sonia Delaunay (*see* §IX and fig. 57 below). Many 20th-century artists explored abstract pattern-making, and, conversely, some designers began to experiment with the more painterly qualities of printed and painted fabrics.

4. COSTUME IN ART. Throughout much of the history of art, costume—whether in the form of generalized draperies or of historical, pseudo-historical, theatrical or fanciful clothing—has been essential for creating a sense of time and place in narrative painting and sculpture. In scenes from the Bible or the lives of the saints, for example, artists resorted to a variety of costume that might encompass contemporary dress for crowds and onlookers with something more distinguished for the major personages, such as quasi-ecclesiastical garments, oriental modes or vaguely 'historical' clothing. Such arbitrary but effective combinations may be seen in works as otherwise diverse in style, time and place of production as Giotto's frescoes in the Arena Chapel, Padua, and the carved altarpieces of Veit Stoss. Rules established by Renaissance academies ordained that the costume of principal characters in religious, Classical and mythological scenes should make them appear removed from contemporary life. With the rediscovery of the Classical world during the Renaissance, the costume of antiquity, interpreted in a variety of more or less archaeologically correct ways within the prevailing aesthetic of the time, proved a useful source for allegorical and mythological themes. In addition, the first printed costume books, appearing during the second half of the 16th century, were helpful to artists seeking inspiration for

the clothing of the historic past, the exotic present (there was an immense variety of regional dress in Europe alone) and the generalized modes suitable for allegory. Artists' studios would contain such costume pattern books as well as their own sketches of dress and accessories—either preliminary studies or drawings made just for pleasure and inspiration. Rubens, for example, was clearly fascinated by dress, and alongside his working costume studies for identifiable subject pictures and portraits he produced a large collection of drawings (mainly historical, but also oriental) now known as the *Costume Book* (London, BM).

Fashionable portraiture, particularly in England during the 17th and 18th centuries, often used fanciful costume to add an extra dimension to the image. Painters such as Anthony van Dyck and Joshua Reynolds (virtuosos in the depiction of the details of dress and textiles) found it convenient to paint sitters in simplified versions of the current fashions that, with a few accessories, could represent a vaguely Arcadian *mise-en-scène*. Even more popular were historical costumes in portraits: the 18th-century drapery painter Joseph van Aken, who worked for a number of fashionable London portrait painters, made a speciality of a pose and costume for contemporary sitters derived from Rubens's portrait of his sister-in-law *Susanna Fourment* (Lisbon, Mus. Gulbenkian), then thought to be a portrait of Rubens's wife by van Dyck. Later, as part of the Romantic movement in Europe, this historicizing trend influenced fashionable dress in the early 19th century (*see* §VIII and fig. 50 below).

From that time on the blurring of boundaries between reality and fantasy that was such a part of 18th-century dress and art diminished. Fancy dress in the later 19th century became mainly the preserve of small artistic circles and dress reformers. Even in France, where there was a much greater acceptance of contemporary fashion as a serious art in its own right, many artists and critics railed against the use of modern dress in painting and sculpture. In academic circles the increasing emphasis on the use of historically accurate costume and accessories in subject paintings and sculptural representations of persons and scenes from the past that had begun in the 1770s reached a peak of literalism in the work of such painters as Ernest Meissonier and Jean-Léon Gérôme. Critics such as Charles Baudelaire and painters such as Gustave Courbet and Edouard Manet, who sought to promote an art that demonstrated what was heroic in modern life, even in the dreary monotony of 19th-century masculine dress, were in a minority. Yet ultimately these arguments for and against modern dress in art were won by those who, like Courbet, stated, 'one must be of one's time'. Time has amazing powers of transformation, and contemporary dress, in the hands of a great artist, becomes sublime.

BIBLIOGRAPHY
T. Carlyle: *Sartor Resartus* (London, 1838/*R* 1984)
Q. Bell: *On Human Finery* (London, 1947, rev. 1976)
A. Hollander: *Seeing Through Clothes* (New York, 1978)
A. Ribeiro: *Dress and Morality* (London, 1986)
F. Chenoune: *A History of Men's Fashion* (Paris, 1993)

AILEEN RIBEIRO

II. Classical.

This section summarizes the major changes in fashions in dress and hairstyles in Greece and Rome between *c.* 640 BC and *c.* AD 300, using works of art as evidence. (For a discussion of textiles *see* GREECE, ANCIENT, §X, 10 and ROME, ANCIENT, §X, 10.) Although it is difficult to be sure that many of the garments seen in the visual sources have been correctly matched to the garments named, rarely and in passing, in the literary sources, conventional terms have been used below for well-defined types of garment.

1. Introduction. 2. Greek. 3. Roman.

1. INTRODUCTION. Both the main garments worn by Greek women required a piece of cloth at least as deep as the distance between the wearer's shoulders and her feet, sometimes with enough extra depth to allow the folding-over outwards of a section at the top. In the *peplos* the material (usually wool) was little wider than the circumference of the wearer's body; it was pinned twice on the shoulders, leaving room for her head and arms to pass through. The *chiton* was formed from a wider section of finer material (usually linen), buttoned along the tops of the arms to form sleeves and gathered or pleated at the waist. Both sexes wore large rectangular woollen cloaks (*himatia*), draped in a variety of ways, as well as a number of other cloaks of different, and sometimes indeterminable, shapes.

The main garment in the Roman wardrobe was the *tunica*, a T-shaped undershirt, worn on its own by slaves and working men, and by the upper classes when relaxing. Upper-class men had vertical purple stripes on their tunics, the width of the stripe depending on their rank. Formal situations demanded that citizen males should wear togas on top of their tunics. The toga appears to have had a curved outer edge with a purple border for under-age boys and the upper classes; its shape seems to have changed considerably during the Imperial period (after 27 BC), until it became so difficult to wear with any ease or dignity that even emperors, such as the philhellene Hadrian, preferred to wear the Greek *himation* (called *pallium* by the Romans) on almost every occasion. Women tended to wear an undertunic and, in the case of unmarried women, a full-length outer tunic that was belted at the waist; matrons were entitled to replace the outer tunic with the *stola*, a sleeveless dress held together on the shoulders by brooches or straps and belted at the waist. The cloak worn out of doors by women was called the *palla*.

In Greek art, no matter how naturalistic the flesh and drapery may appear to be, there is almost certainly an element of tidying-up, if not outright stylization, of the reality of the potentially lumpy appearance of the human body swathed in cloth that could refuse to fall in suitably pleasing folds. In Greek vase painting and sculpture there appear to have been conventions, sometimes confused even by the artists, for rendering the folds of wool and linen; there seem also to have been changing fashions in textiles, in arranging their folds and in the amount of surface decoration. Because of the lack of variety in colouring in vase painting before about 375 BC and the low rate of survival of colour on marble statues, there is little real evidence of how vivid and striking Greek dress might have been, for all its apparent simplicity of construction.

In Greece, Athenian dress is by far the best recorded, but even so caution has to be exercised in looking at the visual evidence, particularly when trying to match the dress of women on later 6th-century BC vase paintings with that of contemporary carved figures, the korai. On balance it is probably more correct to accept the evidence of everyday objects, such as vases, rather than the somewhat rarified korai figures, although they share many similarities in the stylization of the drapery. Greek art of the 5th century BC has been studied thoroughly, but later Greek art far less so, and therefore the dress it depicts is more difficult to discuss with any authority. The Romans added their own problems by copying, and eventually having their portrait heads added to, second- or third-hand copies of famous Greek statues, such as the so-called *Grande Erculanèse* and *Petite Erculanèse* (originally *Demeter* and *Persephone*, named from versions found at Herculaneum; now Dresden, Skulpsamml.), popular for about 600 years from *c.* 300 BC, or by copying statues created by Greek sculptors in the early Imperial period for Roman patrons. Bieber (1977) has shown how the copyists failed to make sense of the dress of the prototypes that they were copying. Very often the only fashionable elements in such statues are the hairstyles of both sexes and the presence or absence of beards on men. The popularity of bust-length portraits, whether free-standing or in relief on tomb monuments, forces attention on those aspects of the fashionable appearance. Roman painting also often relied on earlier famous paintings for inspiration, and, apart from the mummy paintings produced in Egypt for Greek and Roman patrons, it cannot be regarded as a valuable source of information on fashion.

The importance attached to the nude male figure in Greek sculpture and painting may give an unrealistic impression of how little clothing Greek, especially Athenian, men were allowed to wear in public. It has been assumed that male nudity was probably fairly common in everyday life, even on public occasions, but Demosthenes' warning of the menace of 'flashers' in 4th-century BC Athens implies that men usually wore some kind of clothing in public, although nudity was common for sport, and family scenes on gravestones show men draped in *himatia*, even in their own homes (e.g. gravestone of Ktesilaos and Theano, *c.* 400 BC; Athens, N. Archaeol. Mus., 3472). Art, however, probably reflects life in showing women as far more elaborately dressed and adorned than men and in a far greater variety of outfits, the alteration of which over the years would accord with the modern concept of fashion. Men's clothing altered relatively little over the centuries; young men were rarely shown bearded, older men almost always.

2. GREEK. It first becomes possible to interpret dress in Greek art from *c.* 630 BC to *c.* 600 BC, when it appears that women wore tight bodices and narrow skirts, with variously disposed geometric patterns, and small capes covering the upper arms (e.g. *La Dame d'Auxerre, c.* 630 BC; Paris, Louvre, 3098). Men had started to wear the tight, hip-length garment with short sleeves that persisted into the next century, as did long hair for both sexes (e.g. Black-figure amphora by the Nettos Painter showing *Herakles Slaying Nettos, c.* 625–*c.* 600 BC; Athens,

N. Archaeol. Mus., 1002; *see* GREECE, ANCIENT, fig. 95). Athenian vase paintings from *c.* 600 BC to *c.* 540 BC show women in close-fitting *peploi* covered with patterns, both abstract and figured (e.g. dinos by Sophilos showing *Marriage of Peleus and Thetis*, *c.* 600–*c.* 560 BC; London, BM, GR 1971.11–1.1; *see* GREECE, ANCIENT, fig. 96). Both sexes wore relatively plain cloaks, and some men wore cloaks with curved outer edges (e.g. neck amphora by the Amasis Painter depicting *Dionysos and Maenads*, *c.* 540 BC; Paris, Bib. N., Cab. Médailles, 222; *see* GREECE, ANCIENT, fig. 100). In no case does the material used for the clothing hang freely; this could be the result of stylization, but is more likely to be the result of using tapestry-woven or embroidered woollen fabrics, which would inevitably fall rather stiffly (e.g. belly amphora by Exekias showing *Ajax and Achilles Playing a Board Game*, *c.* 530 BC; Rome, Vatican, Mus. Gregoriano Etrusc., 344; for illustration *see* VASE PAINTERS, §II).

A number of statues of women found in East Greece and probably datable to *c.* 575–*c.* 550 BC show the style of dress evolving in Ionia that was to be crystallized in the korai figures of the later years of the century, although the crudity of the carving makes it difficult to identify the textiles involved (e.g. Cheramyes Kore, *c.* 570 BC; Paris, Louvre, 686; *see* SAMOS, fig. 3). On some of them a small mantle, probably of lightweight wool, passes under the left arm and is joined from front and back along the right shoulder and down the right upper arm, with its free ends hanging down the right side. The legs are covered by an extremely finely pleated skirt, probably of linen, which some of the figures hold to one side. The *peplos* is still found on Athenian korai at this time, possibly over a *chiton* (e.g. Peplos Kore, *c.* 540–*c.* 530 BC; Athens, Acropolis Mus., 679). East Greek outfits did not become the norm for Athenian korai until *c.* 540 BC, but once adopted they persisted until about 490 BC. The dress is often regarded by modern writers as being made from one piece of material, but the behaviour of the cloth suggests otherwise. The skirts are usually pleated and often relatively simply decorated, with a vertical band at the centre front. The bodices are usually shown as being crimped, a feature most marked when the korai do not wear the small mantle (e.g. Athens, Acropolis Mus., 681, *c.* 530–*c.* 520 BC (Antenor's Kore); and Acropolis Mus., 675, *c.* 510 BC (possibly a Chian import); *see* KORE, fig. 2). It looks as though a length of cloth was pleated round the waist and worn over the top of a crimped *chiton*, or else a pleated skirt was attached to a crimped bodice, as implied by vase paintings from a later date (see below).

Towards 540 BC the patterning on Athenian women's dress became less aggressive, sometimes being confined to vertical bands (as in the Amasis Painter amphora cited above), and a new textile appeared, usually shown as a series of wavy black lines on an entirely white garment (e.g. hydria by the Priam Painter showing *Priam Setting out to Ransom the Body of Hektor*, *c.* 510 BC; Madrid, Mus. Arqueol. N., 10920). Such a sudden shift in practice is perhaps to be explained by the introduction into the Greek world of crimped linen woven in Egypt; this would appear to be the material of the korai bodices as well. About this time too, folds start to be shown as alternating areas of black and reddish-purple, although densely patterned garments can still be found in the same scene as garments with folds (e.g. neck amphora by Exekias showing *Achilles' Spearing of Penthesilea*, *c.* 530–*c.* 525 BC; London, BM, B210).

The Red-figure technique of painting vases, introduced *c.* 530 BC, tends to show textiles with more free-falling folds. Although the new technique allowed the depiction of more flowing lines, the dress itself seems to have been changing, and painters were quite capable of mixing the styles of depicting dress (e.g. 'bilingual' amphora by the Andokides Painter showing *Herakles and Athena*, *c.* 530 BC; Munich, Staatl. Antikensamml., 2301). The wearing of the *chiton* as an underdress below the *peplos* (e.g. the Peplos Kore) may have been responsible for the gradual loosening of the *peplos* until it resembled the *chiton* so closely that it was replaced by it, or something resembling it, as a first stage in a radical change in fashion. The korai figures should not be regarded as being as reliable a source of information on dress as the vases of this period, since the illogicality of the folds on the dress (especially on the mantles) of most of the korai suggests that their sculptors were working to a formula for a type of figure wearing a type of dress they themselves had scarcely seen worn in life; full korai-like dress is quite rare on Athenian vase paintings.

Between *c.* 520 and *c.* 510 BC women's dress began to grow looser, developing narrow sleeves; eventually there was so much material in the skirt that it could be gathered into a bunch of many folds at the centre front (e.g. the flautist on a stamnos by Smikros, *c.* 520–*c.* 510 BC; Brussels, Musées Royaux A. & Hist., A 717). This last feature may indicate a division between bodice and skirt and the end of the *peplos* as the main garment. Many Red-figure vases from *c.* 510 to *c.* 480 BC show that women's bodices and skirts were made separately, as on the korai figures; the bodices were made from a crimped material (rendered by thin red wavy lines), which did not hang well in folds but could stretch, and the skirts from a material (perhaps ordinary linen) that could be set into a variety of pleats, rendered by strong black lines (e.g. a cup by Onesimos

1. Greek cup decorated by Onesimos, *Hetaira and Client*, *c.* 500–*c.* 490 BC (London, British Museum)

2. Greek calyx krater by the Laodameia Painter, ?*Phaedra* and *Lapiths and Centaurs*, *c.* 350 BC (London, British Museum)

showing *Hetaira and Client*; see fig. 1). Men's fashions were also changing: by the end of the 6th century BC some men were beginning to loop their long hair up behind their heads, wear it in a bun, plait it and wind it round the head or even cut it short (e.g. *Theseus Carrying the Amazon Antiope* from the Temple of Apollo at Eretria, *c.* 510 BC; Chalkis, Archaeol. Mus., 4; for illustration *see* ERETRIA); the *himation* slung under the right arm and over the left shoulder tends to become their usual form of dress.

From *c.* 490 BC Athenian vases suggest that considerable variety in dress was available to women. Between *c.* 490 and *c.* 470 BC there are voluminous, finely pleated garments, sometimes with overfalls as in *peploi* and sleeves as in *chitones*; an unconvincing amalgam of both garments appears; and true *peploi* are worn over short-sleeved *chitones* (e.g. cup by the Brygos Painter showing *Sick Reveller and Hetaira*, *c.* 480 BC; U. Würzburg, Wagner-Mus., 479; *see* GREECE, ANCIENT, fig. 111). The vases also show the use of patterned textiles: centre-front stripes on less full garments occur in the 460s BC, as do dot and cross patterns. In the middle of the century the *chiton* and the *peplos*, usually belted at the waist with an overfall from the shoulders, were both acceptable (e.g. calyx krater by the Niobid Painter showing *Apollo and Artemis Slaying the Niobids*, *c.* 450 BC; Paris, Louvre, G 341; *see* GREECE, ANCIENT, fig. 113). Kilting-up of the skirt became much more marked *c.* 440 BC, when large *peploi*, hitched up at the waist with overfalls of varying depths, made women look lumpy at the hips and relatively small at the bust (e.g. Parthenon, East Frieze, Slab VII, figs 50–51, 53–6, *c.* 442–*c.* 438 BC; Paris, Louvre). This lumpy look appealed to some until the mid-4th century BC when it was replaced by belting the garments under the bust.

At the very end of the 5th century BC filmy, rather clinging fabrics are seen on vases and in sculpture in garments with and without sleeves, and crimped fabric made a brief reappearance (e.g. hydria by the Meidias Painter showing *Rape of the Leucippidae*, *c.* 410–*c.* 400 BC; London, BM, E 224; *see* GREECE, ANCIENT, fig. 114; and stele of Krito and Timarista, late 5th century BC, Rhodes, Archaeol. Mus., 13638, which shows two *chitones*, one under a *peplos*; *see* RHODES, fig. 3). Vases produced

between *c.* 400 and *c.* 350 BC in Athens and South Italy suggest the continuing use of flimsy material for women's *chitones* and *peploi*, as well as a return to pattern (e.g. calyx krater by the Laodameia Painter showing ?*Phaedra* and *Lapiths and Centaurs*; see fig. 2; in this painting, as elsewhere, the cloaks of Theseus and Peirithoos are more likely to be props to convey movement than real garments). Trendall has shown that the highly elaborate patterning on clothing on South Italian vase paintings is to be linked to theatrical costumes rather than to a depiction of characters from myth in everyday dress. Sculpture and vases suggest that from *c.* 360 BC some *chitones* and *peploi* were being belted below the bust instead of at the waist

3. Greek statue of *Themis* by Chairestratos, *c.* 300–*c.* 250 BC (Athens, National Archaeological Museum)

(e.g. pelike by the Marsyas Painter showing *Peleus Abducting Thetis*, *c.* 340–*c.* 330 BC; London, BM, E 424; *see* GREECE, ANCIENT, fig. 115). Men in Greece and South Italy continued to favour the *himation* as their main garment. During the last quarter of the 4th century BC the production of figured vase painting and elaborate grave memorials ceased in Athens, and vase painting rapidly declined in the Greek cities in Italy; the development of Greek dress therefore becomes far less easy to trace in detail. There seems to have been a fashion in South Italy at this time for wearing unbelted *chitones* drawn tightly across the bust with very tight sleeves or cords running round the tops of the arms to tighten the armholes, and it appears that by *c.* 300 BC women's *chitones* were again being made of crimped material, a fashion that lasted for at least 50 years. In the 3rd century BC *chitones* were belted below the bust and round the tops of the arms (e.g. the bronze copies of the *Tyche* of Antioch by Eutychides of Sikyon, *c.* 300 BC; and the statue of *Themis* by Chairestratos, *c.* 300–*c.* 250 BC; see fig. 3; the latter appears to depict sleeves added to the garment rather than simply being a by-product of using a lot of material to wrap around the body).

In the 2nd century BC both high waistlines and overfalls on the bodice and kilting-up of the skirt were fashionable. The copying of earlier Hellenistic types in the 1st century BC makes detection of fashions very difficult. Women's hairstyles and footwear may provide clues to dates in the Hellenistic period; Morrow has shown that the latter became more elaborate in the 2nd century BC. The dress of Greek men is almost impossible to date from the end of the 5th century BC onwards.

3. ROMAN. Clear information on the fashions among Roman women begins in the 1st century BC, although the visual information is largely confined to hairstyles. The great importance attached to fashionable hairstyles is attested to by Ovid's description of them (*Art of Love* III, after 1 BC) and by the portrait statues made to accept new hairstyles (e.g. head of a woman with removable hairstyle, *c.* AD 230; Detroit, MI, Inst. A., 38.41). It appears that in the third quarter of the 1st century BC fashionable Roman women wore their hair in a series of broad shallow waves running out from a centre parting that was covered by a loop of hair, sometimes plaited, brought from the back of the head to form a flattish puff over the forehead (e.g. statue of ?*Octavia*, *c.* 40–*c.* 30 BC; Worcester, MA, A. Mus., 1978.78). The Empress Livia is shown with such a hairstyle and one of the few representations of the dress of a Roman matron (*stola*, hung from shoulder-straps, over a *tunica*), perhaps because she is praying to the gods of Rome (*c.* 35 BC; Rome, Vatican, 637). By the end of the century this hairstyle seems to have been going out of favour with younger women, who preferred to wear their hair in a garland-like series of waves around the head (e.g. relief from the Ara Pacis depicting members of the imperial family on their way to a sacrifice; see fig. 4; here the women wear the rectangular *palla* and the men's tunics vary in length from mid-calf to above the knee).

In the second quarter of the 1st century AD the hair was worn in a series of large waves down the side of the face and over the ears. The hair at the back of the head

4. Roman relief from the Ara Pacis, Rome, depicting members of the imperial family on their way to a sacrifice, 13–9 BC

was more tightly waved and drawn into a bun or a bunch of curls. Towards AD 50 the waves became harder and small 'snail-shell' curls framed the face, setting the tone for the extremely artificial hairstyles of the rest of the century (e.g. *Agrippina the Younger*, *c.* AD 50; Rome, Vatican, Mus. Gregoriano Profano, 9952). The curls seem to have been built up higher and higher over the forehead until by about AD 90 they created an inverted U-shape around the face, looking like a pile of small snail shells, with the hair at the back dressed into a series of narrow plaits that were wound into a bun at the back of the head (e.g. sepulchral relief of Ulpia Epigone, late 1st century AD; Rome, Vatican, Mus. Gregoriano Profano, 9856).

About AD 100 the bun was loosened into a coil or even into loose strands while the front curls were arranged vertically or in parallel bands framing the face; immediately below the ringlets was a flat band of hair. The band acquired greater importance, and the ringlets themselves could be flattened, before being converted into a large semicircular puff above the forehead (e.g. woman with bust of husband on sarcophagus lid; see fig. 5; the woman is shown in the *stola* and *tunica* of the Roman matron). The puff seems to have hardened into a tight roll, gradually being replaced, by about AD 130, by plaits wound round the crown of the head to resemble a large pillbox (e.g. sarcophagus lid with reclining girl, *c.* AD 130; Malibu, CA, Getty Mus., 73.AA.11). The plaits were moved on to the top of the head and by *c.* AD 140 they had been drawn into a tight bun on top of the head (e.g. *Faustina the Elder*, Chatsworth, Derbys, A 35); by *c.* AD 150 deep waves had been added round the head (e.g. *Faustina the Younger*, Rome, Mus. Capitolino, 4411). In the AD 160s and 170s the deep waves continued to be worn, with the plaits converted into a bun at the nape of the neck (e.g. unknown Antonine woman, Malibu, CA, Getty Mus., 72.AA.117). By about AD 180 or 190 the waves were confined to the top of the head, with the face being framed by a roll of hair drawn back from a centre parting to cover the ears; the bun at the nape of the neck was round and full (e.g. woman, Istanbul, Archaeol. Mus., 28).

The hairstyle associated with Empress Julia Domna (*reg* AD 193–211) is probably a modification of this last hairstyle, achieved by increasing the amount of hair used in the side rolls and loosening them, with or without sharp

5. Roman sarcophagus lid, *c.* AD 98–*c.* 117 (London, British Museum)

waves, so that they hung down the side of the head on to the neck; the rest of the hair was then gathered into a fat plait up the back of the head (e.g. *Julia Domna as Priestess of Ceres, c.* AD 220; Ostia Antica, Mus. Ostiense, 21). By about AD 225–35 the hair over the top of the head was being worn in tightly set waves (e.g. head of woman, *c.* AD 230–*c.* 240; Boston, MA, Mus. F.A., 1970.325), although the roll remained at the nape, sometimes appearing as bunches of curls. By *c.* AD 275 the hair at the back was being brought forward to sit in a small loop on top of the head, as in late Republican times, although the tight waves remained over the rest of the head (e.g. sarcophagus of ?*Plotinus, c.* AD 270; Rome, Vatican, Mus. Gregoriano Profano, 9504).

The changes in the shape and draping of the toga are perhaps the easiest aspects of men's dress to date, although they occurred slowly by modern standards. Around 100 BC the toga was clearly a garment with a curved lower edge and was not long enough to cover a man's boots; it was draped under the right arm with the two outer points overlapping on the left shoulder (e.g. *Arringatore*, Florence, Mus. Archeol.). By the time of Augustus (*reg* 27 BC–AD 14) it still allowed the ankles to be seen, but the edge worn round the waist and across the torso had developed a small pouch, destroying the previous straight line there (fig. 4 above). In addition a large part of the toga was folded over the body at the waist, under the right arm, and could be drawn up over the head to allow a man to partake in religious observances (e.g. *Augustus, Tiberius and Livia at the Altar of the Lares*, 2 BC; Florence, Uffizi, 972). By AD 96 the dextrous handling of the toga's many folds was considered by Quintilian to be an essential aspect of the education of a public speaker. In the course of the next century the section of the toga folded over from the waist reached below the knees (e.g. *Marcus Aurelius Sacrificing to Jupiter, c.* AD 176–*c.* 180; Rome, Mus. Capitolino). In the early AD 200s the pouch seems to have been formalized into a number of folds, ridiculed by the Early Christian writer Tertullian (*fl* early 3rd century AD) because it had

to be set into shape by the application overnight of large clamplike pincers. This feature appears like a small plank running diagonally across the chest (e.g. *Emperor Pupienus*, AD 238; Rome, Vatican, Braccio Nuo., 2265) and was converted into a decorative band in the imperial dress of the Byzantine Empire.

When men are not represented in the toga, their heads can provide only modest clues to changes in fashion. Most Roman men seem to have worn their hair in short, slightly straggly curls and to have been clean-shaven until the early 2nd century AD when beards became the norm, perhaps under the influence of Emperor Hadrian (*reg* AD 117–38). Beards and short hair continued to be worn until the end of the Roman period.

BIBLIOGRAPHY
L. M. Wilson: *The Roman Toga*, Johns Hopkins University Studies in Archaeology (Baltimore, 1924)
M. Bieber: *Griechische Kleidung* (Berlin, 1928)
L. M. Wilson: *The Clothing of the Ancient Romans*, Johns Hopkins University Studies in Archaeology (Baltimore, 1938)
G. M. A. Richter: *Korai: Archaic Greek Maidens* (London, 1968)
J. Boardman: *Athenian Black Figure Vases: A Handbook* (London, 1974)
——: *Athenian Red Figure Vases: The Archaic Period* (London, 1975)
M. Scott: *Dress on Greek Vase Paintings* (MA report, U. London, 1975)
M. Bieber: *Ancient Copies: Contributions to the History of Greek and Roman Art* (New York, 1977)
J. Boardman: *Greek Sculpture: The Archaic Period* (London, 1978)
Roman Portraits in the Getty Museum (exh. cat., ed. J. Frel; Tulsa, OK, Philbrook A. Cent., 1981)
H. Granger-Taylor: 'Weaving Clothes to Shape in the Ancient World: The Tunic and Toga of the Arringatore', *Textile Hist.*, xiii (1982), pp. 3–25
K. D. Morrow: *Greek Footwear and the Dating of Sculpture* (Madison, 1985)
S. Walker: *Memorials to the Roman Dead* (London, 1985)
A. D. Trendall: *Red Figure Vases of South Italy and Sicily* (London, 1989)
P. Virgili: *Acconciature e maquillage*, Vita e Costumi dei Romani Antichi (Rome, 1989)
MARGARET SCOTT

III. Late Antiquity and early Middle Ages.

The centuries from AD 200 to 1000 in the Mediterranean region and in northern Europe were a time of considerable change. The conversion of most areas of Europe to Christianity was a unifying factor in the long term; in the shorter term, large-scale migrations led to upheaval and wars. In the early 5th century the Western Roman Empire broke up as a result of increasing incursions, mainly by Germanic tribes. In the East, the Byzantine emperors struggled against Persian attacks. Between the death of Muhammad in AD 632 and the early 8th century most of the Middle East, the whole of North Africa and parts of Spain fell under Arab rule. The Viking expansion of the 9th and 10th centuries represented the final large-scale movement of people within Europe.

1. The Mediterranean region. 2. Northern Europe.

1. The Mediterranean region.

(i) c. AD *200–c. 600.* Evidence for this period is plentiful, with a significant number of surviving garments, from Christian Egypt in particular (*see* COPTIC ART, §V, 3), in addition to rich visual and literary sources. Among the visual sources is the early 5th-century ivory 'Diptych of Stilicho' (Monza, Mus. Serpero Tesoro; see fig. 6), which depicts an important late Roman family. The man, a soldier, has weapons but not armour. He wears a rectangular military cloak pinned on the right shoulder, a sword belt, a knee-length tunic loose in the body but with tight sleeves, sandals and tight-fitting trousers with feet. His wife has a draped rectangular mantle, two very long tunics with a decorated belt (the outer tunic sleeveless and with side fringes), a hairnet, shoes and handkerchief. Their son is dressed like his father except that his cloak is a civilian one; it is semicircular and equally long in front and behind. The semicircular cloak was not common before the 3rd or 4th century AD. Although probably Italian in origin, it became associated with Byzantine officialdom under the Greek name *chlamys*. Trousers also became formal dress only in the 4th century; as their name, *bracae*, or 'breeches', suggests, they were a style borrowed from Germanic barbarians. Tunics were not normally sleeved before about 250. Other major garments of the period were the dalmatic, a wide-sleeved overtunic worn by both sexes between about 250 and 450 and after that by clergy of the Western church, and the *birrus* or *paenula* (later called a chasuble), a hooded, conical cloak worn by laymen until about the 7th century and after that by the clergy.

In Late Antiquity, clothing began to have more decoration than hitherto, when it had been confined mainly to simple contrasting stripes, typically the pair of purple-coloured shoulder *clavi* (bands) on tunics. The tunic of the soldier on the 'Diptych of Stilicho' has shoulder, wrist and hem stripes, as well as square panels at shoulders and knees. Such ornaments were decorated with geometric patterns or, increasingly, with figurative designs. Clothes could also have all-over patterning, such as rows of standing figures in niches or busts in roundels. These repeating designs indicate the use of expensive new textiles in more advanced weaves (*see* EARLY CHRISTIAN AND BYZANTINE ART, §VII, 8). The traditional fibres for clothing were wool and linen, ranging from coarse to very fine. By about AD 300 silk clothes had become relatively common, for men as well as women; the tunic of the man in the diptych was almost certainly silk. Men's tunics were

6. Late Antique 'Diptych of Stilicho', ivory, 160×320 mm, early 5th century AD (Monza, Museo F. Serpero del Tesoro)

nearly always white with purple-coloured ornaments. A bright brown naturally pigmented wool was often used for cloaks such as that of the boy. Women's clothes were in general darker and more colourful than men's.

The mosaic panels in S Vitale, Ravenna, showing the Emperor Justinian and his court, are particularly informative about 6th-century dress (*see* MOSAIC, fig. 6). The shapes shown had scarcely changed since the 4th and 5th centuries, but two aspects were new: brighter, primary colours and more dominant patterning using Persian-influenced motifs (for further discussion *see* EARLY CHRISTIAN AND BYZANTINE ART, §VII, 3(i)).

The range of clothing depicted in Late Antique and early Byzantine art shows fewer draped garments than in Classical art. The rectangular Greek man's mantle, the *himation* (Lat. *pallium*), remained common in the east at least until the 6th century, while the female mantle lasted throughout the early medieval period. In general, however, the move was towards a simpler, more vertical outline. The *chlamys* and chasuble, largely replacing the toga, hung straight from the shoulders in long folds. Tight trousers and sleeves indicate a new interest in fit, though tunics were still very loose in the body.

Related changes occurred in clothing construction. In the traditional Antique method, clothes were made of one or two pieces with simple outlines, where necessary shaped during weaving (*see* ROME, ANCIENT, §X, 10). One change was to the new textiles with repeating all-over patterns. The looms for these were less adaptable, so shaping began to move from the weaving to the making-up stage. Foreign influences were also important. Most obviously, the German-style trousers required much more cutting and sewing than had previously been usual.

(ii) c. 600–c. 1000. With time, changes in construction reached all classes of clothing. The contrasting ornaments, traditionally woven in one with the rest of the garment, were increasingly applied afterwards. A second wave of foreign influence brought 'shirt-type' construction from Asia. This used the cloth vertically, had sleeves of separate pieces and gores in the side seams. This construction first occurred in the Byzantine Empire in the early 7th century, spread westwards relatively rapidly and by the 9th century was employed in some Western church vestments. Such construction may be seen in a surviving fragment of a

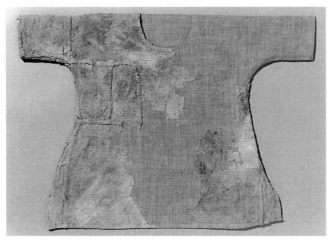

7. Fragment of a Byzantine child's tunic of shirt-type construction, from Zenobia (now Halabiyeh, Syria), *c.* AD 610 (Damascus, National Museum)

8. Fragment of a Byzantine twill-woven silk depicting paired horsemen or emperors, from Mozac, France, 730×710 mm, *c.* AD 750 (Lyon, Musée Historique des Tissus)

child's tunic (*c.* 610; Damascus, N. Mus.; see fig. 7) found at Zenobia (now Halabiyeh, Syria). Over the centuries 'shirt-type' construction became standard for European linen or cotton shirts, but initially it was used for both plain and highly decorated tunics, and its spread was due as much to taste as economics: the more fitted body further emphasized the silhouette.

The *skaramangion*, a riding tunic from Persia adopted by the Byzantine court around the 8th century, probably came to be made in this way. An early depiction of the garment appears on a fragment of compound twill-woven silk from Mozac, Puy-de-Dôme, decorated with horsemen or emperors (*c.* 750; Lyon, Mus. Hist. Tissus; see fig. 8). Judging by a later depiction of the Emperor Nikephoros III Botaneiates (*reg* 1078–81) in the *Homilies* of John Chrysostomos (1078–81; Paris, Bib. N., MS. Coislin 79, fol. 2*v*; *see* EARLY CHRISTIAN AND BYZANTINE ART, fig. 63), this long, narrow garment had vents in the lower skirt and was worn over another, still longer tunic. The fragment from Mozac also illustrates the type of silk cloth used for the best-quality clothes. The weave, one of those introduced in Late Antiquity, is very complex, and a complete roundel would measure 800 mm. The Menologion of Basil II (late 10th century; Rome, Vatican Bib. Apostolica, MS. Vat. gr. 1613; for illustration *see* MENOLOGION OF BASIL II) illustrates the flattening effect of such designs. (The Menologion is an exception to the general rule that most saints and all biblical figures in Byzantine art are shown dressed in Late Antique or even earlier styles.)

Despite the scale and rapidity of Arab expansion in the Middle East, North Africa and southern Spain from the middle of the 7th century, many conquered groups preserved their own traditions in dress. In North Africa there are surviving examples of some wool garments of pre-medieval type, in particular a man's draped mantle, a man's hooded semicircular cloak and a woman's *peplos*-type garment, the last two occurring in their oldest form in the region of the Atlas mountains.

2. NORTHERN EUROPE.

(i) c. AD 200–c. 700. Evidence for the Iron Age dress of the peoples of northern Europe (predominantly Celtic and Germanic) comes from archaeology, written descriptions, particularly by Tacitus (*Agricola* and *Germania*), and Roman reliefs, such as the column of Marcus Aurelius, Rome. Men's costume was a rectangular cloak pinned on the right shoulder and often fringed, tight trousers with feet (see §1(i) above), and, when possible, a short, fitted tunic with long sleeves. Almost all women wore a tubular garment pinned on both shoulders in the manner of the Greek *peplos* and, over this, a centrally-pinned cloak. Some also wore an undertunic. In areas under Roman rule, on the evidence of local gravestones, this dress was modified. The fringed cloak continued in the army, but civilian males took up a knee-length tunic and the 'Gallic coat', a hooded garment similar to the *paenula* (see §1(i) above) but with sleeves. Women adopted the Mediterranean long tunic and draped mantle.

From the 5th century, archaeology indicates that the Germanic invasions of previously Roman-held areas caused a revival of the older forms of dress. Many metal

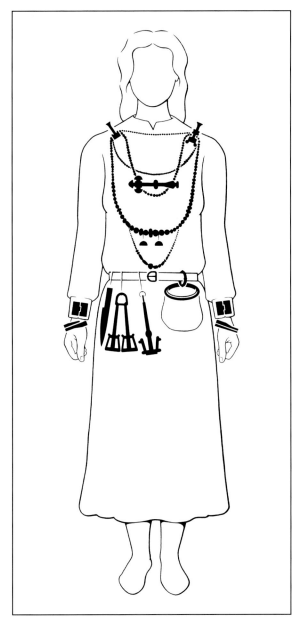

9. Anglo-Saxon metal dress fittings and jewellery, from Sleaford, Lincolnshire, 6th century AD, (London, British Museum); reconstruction drawing

similar date have been preserved in the grave of the Frankish Queen Arnegundis (d c. 570) at Saint-Denis Abbey. The garment shapes are problematic, but it seems that the Queen wore an undertunic of fine linen, a 'dress' of violet silk and an ankle-length 'coat' of red-brown silk with embroidered cuffs. A head veil, of red silk reaching to the waist, probably reflected her Christianity. In contrast, her leg wear indicated her tribal adherence. This consisted of white linen stockings, leather shoes held on by crossing straps over the instep as well as by crossing ankle straps continuing up the calves, and finally, below the knees, separate garters with tabs. Each strap had its own metal buckle and strap-end; humbler equivalents of these occur in graves throughout Frankish and Alammanic areas.

(ii) c. 700–c. 1000. Germanic styles survived in court dress until the 9th century, as is shown in a miniature of *Charles the Bald Enthroned* (fol. 5*v*) from the Codex Aureus of St Emmeram (AD 870; Munich, Bayer. Staatsbib., Clm. 14000; see fig. 10): a Carolingian emperor, probably Charles himself, wears a cloak of the old rectangular type, a knee-length tunic and shoes with crossing straps. The main decoration of the cloak and tunic, an

10. *Charles the Bald Enthroned* (detail), miniature from the Codex Aureus of St Emmeram, AD 870 (Munich, Bayerische Staatsbibliothek, Clm. 14000, fol. 5*v*)

fastenings and attachments were used, and where textiles do not survive (as is nearly always the case in England) metalwork in graves is a guide to the missing garments, as in the case of a 6th-century Anglo-Saxon grave at Sleaford, Lincs (see fig. 9): the two small long brooches on the shoulders are from the woman's *peplos*-type garment and the central cruciform brooch is from her cloak. The objects at the waist were attached to a belt, and the typically Anglian wrist-clasps indicate an undertunic with tight sleeves. The metal is mostly bronze, and the clothes were probably mainly of wool. Some clothing fragments of a

11. Birka woman's costume of pleated linen undertunic, wool *peplos* garment and wool kaftan-type jacket with silk braids, 9th century AD (Stockholm, Statens Historiska Museum); modern reproduction

poorer survival of artefacts from graves. With the spread of Christianity, the belief in the need to equip the body fully at burial declined. Additionally, the taste for metal fittings seems to have waned. Scandinavia, however, remained pagan until much later, and its climate has allowed better preservation of textiles. At Birka, a Viking trading town near modern Stockholm, all the women wore the Scandinavian version of the *peplos* garment, of wool or linen, with shoulder straps fastened by characteristic 'tortoise' brooches. Under the *peplos* they wore a linen undertunic, sometimes finely pleated, and most wore a cloak, centrally pinned. In some 9th-century burials, however, the cloak was replaced by a kaftan-type jacket of wool, cut with gores (see fig. 11), while some 10th-century graves preserve evidence of a fitted wool tunic worn between the *peplos* garment and the undertunic. Heads were covered with linen veils or caps. Some men also wore embroidered kaftans or fitted tunics with braids and with them cone- or mitre-shaped hats (an exception to the general rule that men in the early Middle Ages did not wear hats). The Oriental flavour of the Birka kaftans and tunics, though more Central Asian than Persian, is comparable to influences on contemporary Byzantine dress. It is partly explained by the Vikings' long-distance trading, which took them southwards and eastwards via Kiev.

BIBLIOGRAPHY

H. C. Broholm and M. Hald: *Costumes of the Bronze Age in Denmark* (Copenhagen, 1939)
R. Pfister: *Textiles de Halabiyeh* (Paris, 1951)
A. France-Lanord and M. Flury: 'Das Grab der Arnegundis in Saint-Denis', *Germania*, xl (1962), pp. 341–59
R. McMullen: 'Some Pictures in Ammianus Marcellinus', *A. Bull.*, xlvi (1964), pp. 435–55
E. Munksgaard: *Oldtidsdragter* [Ancient costume] (Copenhagen, 1974) [with Eng. captions and bibliog.]
Sachsen und Angelsachsen (exh. cat., ed. C. Ahrens; Hamburg, Helms-Mus., 1978)
N. B. Harte and K. G. Pointing, eds: *Cloth and Clothing in Medieval Europe: Essays in Memory of Professor E. M. Carus Wilson* (London, 1983)
B. Magnus: 'How Was He Dressed? New Light on the Garments from the Grave at Evebø/Eide in Gloppen, Norway', *Stud. Sächsforsch.*, iv (1983), pp. 293–313
J. P. Wild: 'The Clothing of Britannia, Gallia Belgica and Germania Inferior', *Aufstieg und Niedergang der römischen Welt*, ed. H. Temporini, II/xii/3 (Berlin and New York, 1985), pp. 362–422
G. R. Owen-Crocker: *Dress in Anglo-Saxon England* (Manchester, 1986)
Tissu et vêtement (exh. cat., Guiry-en-Vexin, Mus. Archéol. Dépt., 1986)
M. Nockert: 'Vid Sidenvägens ände: Textilier från Palmyra till Birka' [At the end of the Silk Road: textiles from Palmyra to Birka], *Palmyra: Öknens drottning* [Palmyra: queen of the desert] (exh. cat., ed. P. Helström, M. Nockert and S. Unge; Stockholm, Medelhavsmus., 1988), pp. 77–105

HERO GRANGER-TAYLOR

IV. 11th–13th centuries.

Changing tastes in fashion reflect the social changes taking place in Europe during this period, from the waning of the feudal system after the mid-11th century and its replacement by the 13th century with centralized monarchical governments to the increasing size of the newly enfranchised towns, the forming of guilds of craftsmen and merchants and the development of the bourgeoisie as a political force. In the 12th century, for

edging braid, is also typical of northern dress. In this instance the braid seems unusually broad and sumptuous, with sewn-on jewels, but by this date most were highly decorative, brocaded with silk or metal thread. It is said that Charlemagne, Charles the Bald's grandfather, wore Frankish dress from preference. He is portrayed in this in a bronze equestrian statue (Paris, Louvre). On his visits to Rome, however, he was persuaded by the popes to wear the long tunic and *chlamys*, in other words, a Byzantine outfit. By the end of the millennium, it seems there was some standardization of ceremonial dress at Christian courts, influenced directly or indirectly by Byzantine styles.

While the revival in the arts in this period has left enhanced visual evidence of dress, it is countered by

example, a merchant's wife, no matter how rich her husband, might be fined for dressing like a noblewoman; by 1300 she was openly flouting such distinctions and might indeed surpass the noblewoman in extravagance of dress. (This resulted, in the 14th century, in the introduction of many new sumptuary laws, in both the south and the north of Europe, curbing the growing luxury.) The new lavishness of the period can be seen in the increasing use of pieced small furs such as miniver and ermine to line garments, in the increasingly complicated cut and construction of dress and in more frequently changing fashions. High fashion in the centuries between 1000 and 1300 was fairly international in character, although some national differences did exist, particularly in styles of hair and headdresses.

1. 11th century. 2. 12th century. 3. 13th century.

1. 11TH CENTURY. The dress worn by both sexes during the 11th century was still based on types that had evolved from the intermingling of local elements with those of Late Antiquity by about the beginning of the 6th century. The cut of the basic robe or tunic was essentially the same as it had been for centuries, consisting of rectangular back and front panels sewn together down the sides, with long sleeves either of a piece with the tunic itself or attached with a straight seam. The sleeves were sometimes cut longer than the arms with the excess fabric left to form ringlike folds at the wrist, a feature occasionally mistaken for bracelets by modern commentators. A fairly wide opening at the neck allowed the garment to be pulled on over the head. The cloak was also rectangular and was kept on with a brooch or clasp, usually fastened on the shoulder to allow the arms to move freely. Clothes in general were constructed with a minimum of seams and fastened with brooches and pins.

The late Roman world bequeathed to Europe a double tradition in male dress—long, flowing robes for the upper classes and simple, short tunics for the lower—a distinction that was maintained until the end of the 10th century. By the mid-11th century, however, the short tunic had become usual dress for all classes, although enthroned kings still wore long robes, to mark their elevated status, and Christ and the saints were represented wearing them as a mark of respect. One of the primary functions of medieval dress was to denote status and thereby to act as a means of identification. On the Bayeux Tapestry (c. 1070–80; Bayeux, Mus. Tap.; see fig. 12), the scene depicting the oath taken by Harold at Bayeux, where he pledges himself to further William's interests in England, shows rank nicely defined by length of dress: William, enthroned as ruling duke in his own palace, wears long robes of state, whereas Harold, his guest and now his vassal, wears the short tunic of the ordinary fighting man. A further distinction is marked by the three-quarter-length cloaks worn by both men; their attendants are entitled to wear only shorter versions. Under the tunic men wore hose made of stuff and cut in separate sections for each leg; they were sometimes held up by decorative cross-gartering.

Although the chroniclers suggest that the wearing of long hair had not died out altogether by the 11th century, particularly in parts of northern Europe, it is evident from the visual sources that by c. 1050 men's hair was worn almost universally short and that facial hair was unusual among the young. What national differences did exist at this time tended to focus on styles of hairdressing. At the time of the Conquest, for example, the Normans were said to shave the hair from the backs of their heads, while the English wore long moustaches; both distinctions are recorded in the Bayeux Tapestry.

12. The Bayeux Tapestry (detail), linen with wool embroidery, 0.54×6.84 m, c. 1070–80 (Bayeux, Musée de la Tapisserie de la Reine Mathilde)

For most of the period from *c.* 1000 to *c.* 1300 women's dress differed only slightly from men's in its basic cut, except that it always reached to the ankles for modesty's sake. In the 11th century the female tunic was an ungirt and fairly voluminous garment, although towards 1100 it began to fit the body a little more closely, a development that had taken place in men's dress several decades before. Matrons were required to wear a large veil or kerchief that covered both the head and the shoulders, while young, unmarried women could wear their hair uncovered, either loose or plaited. The dress worn by the three women at the sepulchre in an English psalter of *c.* 1060 (London, BL, Cotton Tiberius C. VI, fol. 13*v*) illustrates well the muffling garments worn by most women during the first three-quarters of the century.

2. 12TH CENTURY. Around the beginning of the 12th century a radical transformation took place in the character of secular dress in western Europe, involving the gradual replacing of the relatively simple style of the 11th century with a new complexity and increased luxury. The Classical tradition of the long robe for men returned, although the short tunic was still worn by working men, and the sleeves of women's gowns trailed extravagantly; both men's and women's robes were elaborately pleated or smocked. The First Crusade had begun in 1096, bringing the whole of western Europe into direct contact and trade with the East, and these richer, more elaborate clothes reveal the influence of Byzantium, with its combination of Classical and oriental traditions. The Old Testament column figures on the north doorway of the Royal Portal of Chartres

13. Frontispiece, 243×185 mm, from *Moralia in Job* of St Gregory, 1111 (Dijon, Bibliothèque Municipale, MS. 168, fol. 4*v*)

Cathedral show garments in this Romanesque Byzantine style at their most elaborate (see fig. 14 below).

The characteristic features of the new style are already evident in the earliest manuscripts written and illuminated at the new abbey of Cîteaux in Burgundy, dating from the early years of the 12th century. The frontispiece to the first volume of a *Moralia in Job* of St Gregory dated 1111 (Dijon, Bib. Mun., MS. 168, fol. 4*v*; see fig. 13) shows a young man in a long, close-fitting tunic that is slit to the thigh before and behind for ease of movement, revealing legs clad in tight-fitting hose. The sleeves of the tunic widen into a bell shape at the wrist, and the shoes, cut low at the front like a slipper, are of the type called *pigaciae* in Latin, with long, pointed toes extended by several inches and stuffed with tow to make them curl up slightly. For many, the most striking—and scandalous—element of the new fashions in male dress was the growing of long hair and of facial hair. The figure here, with his shoulder-length hair and goatee beard, represents a type vilified by contemporary moralists. Ordericus Vitalis, for example, writing his *Ecclesiastical History* during the 1120s and 1130s, described how during the reign (1087–1100) of William Rufus in England 'effeminates' set the fashion in many parts of the world, parting their hair from the crown to the forehead and growing long, luxurious locks 'like women'; he also described their preference for long, over-tight shirts and tunics. His opinion was shared by other monastic historians and chroniclers of the first half of the 12th century, who castigated the new fashions as ungodly, effeminate and, it was usually implied, an incitement to lax morals. Their almost perverse delight in describing in minute detail what they found so objectionable in secular dress provides a valuable record of these changes. There are many examples of shoulder-length and longer hair for men in the other manuscripts produced at Cîteaux and elsewhere during this period, but other styles are shown as well, reflecting the sort of variety that might be expected in the dress of any society.

After 1100 women's dress also began to emerge from the comparative modesty and simplicity that had characterized it in the 11th century, although it changed more gradually than did male dress. It began to fit the body more closely, and its extremities were subject to the same process of lengthening. The veil became less voluminous and was provided with long, hanging ends that fluttered behind the wearer. Elaborate arrangements of plaits and tresses replaced the long, loose hair worn previously by young unmarried women, as shown on female figures on the Old Testament column at Chartres Cathedral (stone, *c.* 1150) and on column sculpture from other mid-12th-century churches in the Ile-de-France. The hair could also be divided into two tresses and encased in sheaths of silk stuffed at the end with artificial hair to increase their length. Women do not seem to have worn shoes with long, pointed toes, since their gowns usually covered the feet, but during the second half of the century their gowns were often designed with a long train at the back, contemptuously referred to by the moralists as *caudae*, or tails. The most distinctive feature, however, was the hanging sleeve. Found as early as the last quarter of the 11th

14. Old Testament Queen, *c*. 1150, north doorway, Royal Portal, Chartres Cathedral

underarm to the hips. Another method for making garments fit involved gathering up the fabric and stitching it on the right side in a technique resembling smocking, which gave it a slight elasticity. This may be the technique represented on the bodice of the gown worn by the Old Testament Queen on the Royal Portal of Chartres Cathedral (again, see fig. 14).

3. 13TH CENTURY. By *c*. 1180 the tight lacing and extended draperies were beginning to be abandoned in favour of simpler, more fluid shapes, while the etiolated physical ideal was replaced by one of more Classical proportions. The fabrics appear heavier and more sculptural, and there is much less surface decoration. Again, it was the sleeve that first registered change and that became, in its turn, one of the most characteristic features of 13th-century dress. The new sleeve was loose and of a piece with the tunic itself; starting often as low as the waist, it tapered to a narrow wrist. It appears in manuscript illustrations from *c*. 1180 and underwent no significant further developments until *c*. 1240.

Another important and characteristic feature of 13th-century dress was the long, sweeping, semicircular cloak, which also made its first appearance before 1200. Fastened across the chest with a cord, it was prevented from slipping off the shoulders only by the placing of a thumb under this cord. This gesture, although entirely practical in origin, had become almost an artistic convention by the mid-13th

century, in its first manifestation it took the form of a bell-shaped oversleeve covering a tight and narrow undersleeve, in which form it was also worn by men (see fig. 13). In women's dress it later became subject to all sorts of exaggeration; by the mid-12th century, as at Chartres, for example, it was frequently so long that it had to be knotted up. It could also assume more of a baglike shape or resemble a pelican's beak, while the romances, lays and *chansons de geste* of contemporary court poetry refer to objects being carried in sleeves and to sleeves so long they had to be held by a servant when washing. By the end of the century the hanging section had been reduced to little more than a long, often floor-length, cuff cut as a separate piece of fabric, draped over or attached by sewing to the sleeve proper.

The diminishing volume and lengthening draperies of 12th-century dress encouraged caricature. The mid-12th-century English psalter of Henry of Blois (London, BL, Cotton Nero C. IV, fol. 18*r*), in the scene depicting the third temptation of Christ, represents the Devil dressed in a caricature of contemporary female fashion, his tunic laced tightly at the side and his left sleeve so long that it has had to be knotted up. Great importance was attached to the proper fit of the tunic at this period, but there is no trace of buttons in the visual sources for the 11th and 12th centuries; they were not used as a means of fastening until at least a century later. The fit, therefore, was achieved by tight lacing at the back or down both sides, from the

15. Founder figure sculptures of *Hermann* and *Reglindis*, *c*. 1260, west chancel, Naumburg Cathedral

century. The mantle in this form was worn by both men and women, and from *c.* 1200 to *c.* 1260 it was often provided with a small, standing collar. The dress of the founder figures (stone, *c.* 1260; see fig. 15) in the west chancel of Naumburg Cathedral represents the culmination of the new style of upper-class dress that developed between *c.* 1180 and the mid-13th century and embodies most of its salient features. The figure of Reglindis holds her cloak (which has a rolled collar—one of the last appearances in art of this fashion) about her by supporting it with her thumb in the manner described above, while her companion figure Hermann fails to do the same with his collarless mantle, which has slipped right back off his shoulders. Beneath it he wears a sleeveless surcoat (Fr. *surcote*), the most important of a number of new garments introduced into the upper-class wardrobe during the 13th century. The surcoat, worn over the *cote*, or basic tunic, could also be provided with short, wide sleeves, which might be split along the underarm to hang loose from the shoulders.

By the mid-13th century the fashionable wardrobe was designed in several pieces, including, usually, a *cote*, surcoat and anything from one to three outer garments. These could be made of the same cloth, the whole set being referred to as a 'robe'. In addition to the ubiquitous semicircular mantle, a number of alternative outer garments are found, including one resembling a closed coat with loose, wide sleeves and a hood and another, more voluminous and also hooded, with wide sleeves laid in pleats at the shoulder, which may be the item referred to in accounts as a *garde-corps*. With the proliferation of new articles of clothing in the 13th century terminology becomes a problem, and it is not always possible to match with absolute certainty those reproduced in works of art with the references to them in contemporary literature and household accounts. All these new garments appear, however, to have been worn by both sexes. At first the new volume in dress was confined by a girdle at the waist, but increasingly, particularly in women's dress, the fabric was allowed to flow loosely down to the ankles, widening from narrow shoulders into a broad A shape, the fullness being provided by gores inserted into the skirt. Throughout the century the sleeve fitted closely over the forearm, but for a short period in mid-century attention was directed towards the armhole, where the surcoat was cut away in a wide arc to reveal a series of regular, fanlike pleats made to control the fullness in the underarm of the *cote*. This effect is clearly shown on many sculpted monuments of the mid-century, including that of *Eve* at Reims Cathedral and that of the *Rider* (*see* BAMBERG, fig. 3) in the north transept of Bamberg Cathedral (both *c.* 1240).

The main element of the female headdress in the 13th century was formed by a linen band passing once or twice around the head and chin. At the beginning of the century the ends hung down in loose folds, but gradually the band, worn around the head like a turban, reduced in size, and by 1230 it had developed into a stiffened linen band worn in conjunction with a chin-band, as found on the female figures at Naumburg Cathedral. The linen band was sometimes fluted or given a crimped edge, possibly by pressing the damp linen with a goffering iron, although Newton and Giza have suggested that linen could be woven with a 'frilled' edge.

In marked contrast to the flowing locks fashionable in the first half of the 12th century, men's hair from *c.* 1180 to *c.* 1230 was worn short, parted in the middle and tucked behind the ears. In the period 1230–*c.* 1270, however, it began to be brought over the ears in a long 'bob' framing the face and was usually worn with a deep fringe. This is the style worn by all the male figures in the west choir at Naumburg, and it became common right across Europe in the middle years of the century. Facial hair remained unfashionable throughout the 13th century, while a linen coif, once part of working-class dress, could be worn by all classes of men during this period. Towards the end of the century the length and fullness of men's hair was again pared down into a new style, which was shorter, neater and dressed with a pronounced roll curl in the neck. It is

16. Donor figure (detail) from the alterpiece of the *Virgin and Child, Two Saints and Six Scenes*, by the Magdalen Master, tempera on panel, 0.90×1.32 m, late 13th century (Paris, Musée des Arts Décoratifs)

17. Illumination from a *Book of Chess*, c. 1283 (Madrid, Escorial, Biblioteca del Monasterio de San Lorenzo, MS. J.T. 6, fol. 32)

worn in this way by the extremely elegant donor figure shown on a late 13th-century Italian altarpiece (Paris, Mus. A. Déc.; see fig. 16) by the Magdalen Master; the donor also has the front opening and sleeves of his outer garment fastened by a line of buttons. Buttons, worn from *c.* 1230 in small groups of two to three at the neck edge of garments and to fasten hoods, were initially extremely precious items and were often used as ornament as well as fasteners by the wealthy upper classes. The household accounts for the 1270s of the children of Edward I of England show buttons being bought in batches of several dozen at a time, sometimes in silver or silver gilt. On the similarly elegant figure of the *Tempter* at Strasbourg Cathedral (*see* STRASBOURG, fig. 7) a long line of buttons used in a non-functional way to decorate the side opening of his gown symbolizes worldly luxury.

The medieval artist frequently used dress in this abstract, symbolic way. Like the *Tempter* at Strasbourg, the Foolish Virgins, the Magdalene and the Damned at the Last Judgement are usually represented in the most fashionable dress of the period; those who had sinned needed to be instantly recognizable, and dress was one of the tools by which the artist could accomplish this.

High fashion in the centuries from 1000 to 1300 was fairly international in character. In Italy, which was commercially and culturally in close contact with the north of Europe, fashionable dress developed along very similar lines to that already described, although there were some minor differences in hairstyles and headdresses. The veil worn by matrons in 13th-century Italy, for example,

resembled more a striped towel wrapped turban-like around the head than the length of fine linen cloth worn in the north, while the headband with crimped edges seems not to have been an Italian fashion at all. Italy was the first country to introduce sumptuary legislation to control the growing luxury in dress; the governments of Perugia and Bologna both issued statutes in 1260–70 that attempted to restrict the use of gold, silver and pearls as ornament in dress, to limit the number of robes a person might own and to prevent the trains of women's dresses from being worn extravagantly long.

Spain, on the other hand, under Visigothic rule throughout the period, had been isolated culturally from the rest of Europe until the late 11th century, when in 1081 Alfonso VI (*reg* 1072–1109) married Constance, daughter of Robert I, Duke of Burgundy. Constance brought with her an entourage of French knights and ecclesiastics, but even after that Spanish dress retained a marked regional character. It was much more decorative than other European dress of the period, making more use of elaborately patterned fabrics, for example, as well as motley or particoloured garments. While a 13th-century 'robe' in the north of Europe tended to be composed of garments made up in the same fabric, Spanish dress made more use of the contrast between the various layers. Both sexes in the 13th century wore surcoats fastened by decorative underarm lacing, and men's short cloaks were edged with braid and had flat braid fastenings as opposed to a cord between jewelled clasps, or tassels. An illustration from a *Book of Chess* (*c.* 1283, Madrid, Escorial, MS. J.T.6; see fig. 17) shows Castilian ladies from the court of Alfonso X in high, horned headdresses at a time when women's hair in the north of Europe was being braided or netted into headdresses widening over the ears. The illustrations to this book also indicate that Spanish dress was more close-fitting than elsewhere in Europe in the 13th century; this was possibly achieved by a set-in sleeve, since embroidery on the women's gowns seems to delineate a seam around the armhole, anticipating a similar development in other parts of Europe in the early 14th century.

BIBLIOGRAPHY

P. Post: *Das Kostüm und die ritterliche Kriegstracht im deutschen Mittelalter von 1000–1500* (1939), *Deutscher Kulturatlas* (Berlin, 1928–39)
J. Evans: *Dress in Mediaeval France* (London, 1952)
C. Bernis Madrazo: *Indumentaria mediaeval española* (Madrid, 1956)
F. M. Stenton, ed.: *The Bayeux Tapestry* (London, 1957), pp. 70–75
R. Levi Pisetzky: *Storia del costume in Italia*, i (Rome, 1964)
S. M. Newton and M. Giza: 'Frilled Edges', *Textile Hist.*, xiv/2 (1983), pp. 141–52
G. Owen-Crocker: *Dress in Anglo-Saxon England* (Manchester, 1986)
J. Harris: ' "Thieves, Harlots and Stinking Goats": Fashionable Dress and Aesthetic Attitudes in Romanesque Art', *Costume*, xxi (1987), pp. 4–15

JENNIFER HARRIS

V. 14th–16th centuries.

1. Southern Europe. 2. Northern Europe.

1. SOUTHERN EUROPE. Dress in Italy and Spain between 1400 and 1600 is well recorded in the visual arts, and it is on such records that this account is based. There is also plentiful corroborative evidence in contemporary literature, diaries, letters, inventories and other documents.

(i) 14th century. (ii) 15th century. (iii) 16th century.

(i) 14th century. In Italy in the first decades of the century men wore in the house a loose, ankle-length woollen gown over a linen shirt, drawers and tailored hose, the last held up by being tied to the waistband of the drawers. Out of doors, another overgown was worn, which was more

19. *St George Tortured on the Wheel* (*c.* 1379–84) by Altichiero, fresco, oratory of S Giorgio, Padua

elaborate than the gown worn indoors, even though it was often covered by a long cloak. Headgear was a chaperon, or cowl hood, worn over a linen coif that was kept on indoors. Men were clean-shaven; their short, jaw-length hair was fringed. Good examples of male dress are found in two works by unknown artists: the *St Cecilia* altarpiece (1304–10; Florence, Uffizi) and the fresco of the *Supper of San Guido* (*c.* 1317; Pomposa, abbey refectory). Lippo Memmi's portrait of the *podestà* Nello Mino de' Tolomei in the *Maestà* (1317–18; San Gimignano, Mus. Civ.; see fig. 18) shows that striped and parti-coloured garments were common.

Women wore two gowns over underwear consisting solely of a long linen shift. The outer gown, worn outside the house, was the more decorated. Both gowns had a bodice and skirt cut separately and joined by a seam at the waist; the front was closed by buttons. The seams and openings were often embellished with reinforcing embroidery or braid. Out of doors, long cloaks gave extra covering. All married women wore their long hair in plaits wound round the head; it was always veiled, only unmarried girls being allowed loose, unveiled hair. Contemporary female dress is seen in the *St Cecilia* altarpiece, in Giotto's frescoes (*c.* 1306) in the Arena Chapel, Padua (*see* PERSPECTIVE, colour pl. VIII, fig. 1), and in Giuliano da Rimini's *Virgin and Child in Majesty* (1307; Boston, MA, Isabella Stewart Gardner Mus.).

In the 1330s young men first began to wear fitted overgowns with shorter hems. Such a gown is worn by the hawking horseman in Ambrogio Lorenzetti's *Allegory of Good Government* (1338–9; Siena, Pal. Pub.; *see* LORENZETTI, (2), fig. 2). Women also adopted wide-necked overgarments that revealed the figure, like those worn in the *Allegory* by the figures of Peace, Fortitude and Concord. These contrast with the ample gown worn by Justice,

18. *Maestà* by Lippo Memmi, fresco, 1317–18 (San Gimignano, Museo Civico)

since they have no waist seam, the bodice and skirts being cut out together. Both the old and new styles are depicted in Pietro Lorenzetti's *Birth of the Virgin* (1342; Siena, Mus. Opera Duomo; *see* LORENZETTI, (1), fig. 2). By the end of the 1340s all except elderly men, or those in high office, wore overgowns with hems well above the knees. The change was partly due to the introduction of a hip-length jacket worn under the gown and over the shirt and drawers: it buttoned from collar to hem and was tailored to fit the contours of the torso. It had eyelet holes in the hem, through which laces holding up the hose were tied. The doublet, as this practical garment came to be known, became an essential item of male clothing until the 17th century. A useful representation of the early doublet is seen in Tomaso da Modena's *Baptism of the English Prince*, an episode in his *Legend of St Ursula* (*c.* 1355–7; Treviso, Mus. Civ. Bailo). Ursula herself is shown in a tightly fitting overgown with a horizontal neckline. Tippets—long strips of fur-lined fabric a few centimetres wide—hang from her sleeve elbows. These were popular in both male and female dress until the 1370s.

Developments in style after 1360 may be observed in works such as the *Porro Family Kneeling before St Stephen* (1368; Lentate sul Seveso, S Stefano) by an unknown artist, Andrea de' Bartoli's *St Catherine before the Emperor Maxentius* (1368; Assisi, Basilica S Francesco, lower church) and Altichiero's frescoes (*c.* 1379–84; Padua, oratory of S Giorgio; see fig. 19). At this time garments were sometimes made of figured silks ornamented with birds, animals and stylized plants, as in the *Virgin and Child* (1369; Venice, Correr) by Stefano Veneziano (*fl* 1369–88). Geometric decorations around hemlines and down the outside of sleeves were also popular. Men's garments were often ornamented with dagged (jagged pendant) edges.

By the 1380s women's gowns fitted very closely over the torso, having a low horizontal neckline and full skirts; they were closed by lacing at the back. Examples of this style are illustrated in *St Ursula and her Companions*, a miniature from the *Hours of Bertrando de' Rossi* (Paris, Bib. N., MS. Lat. 757, fol. 380). Around the end of the century young married women sometimes left their hair unveiled. Their braids, worn low around the head, were decorated with ribbon or swathed in embroidered and bejewelled fabric. Older women continued to wear a linen veil, sometimes with a wimple. Out of doors men wore chaperons, pointed or cowl hoods or round hats. The linen coif that had been worn under such headgear early in the century was no longer popular. Men's hair was ear-length and parted in the centre. In the last decades of the century small, pointed beards and moustaches became usual.

In Spain, dress styles evolved in much the same direction as in Italy. Men's attire, apart from shirt and drawers, consisted of two overgarments: a long overgown or shorter gown and a calf-length sleeveless overgown, open at the sides from armhole to thigh. This was peculiar to Spain and had been worn by both sexes since the 13th

20. Altarpiece with *SS John the Baptist and John the Evangelist* (detail) by Juan de Tarragona, 2.19×2.10 m, *c.* 1365 (Barcelona, Museu d'Art de Catalunya)

century, as attested by surviving examples in Burgos (Real Monasterio de las Huelgas, Mus. Telas & Preseas). Tight-fitting garments worn over the doublet were adopted after 1350. An example of the short overtunic is worn by Henry II of Trastamara, King of Castile (*reg* 1366–7, 1369–79), who is portrayed as donor in the *Virgin of Tobed* (1369; Madrid, priv. col.) attributed to Ramón Destorrents (*fl* 1361–1410); the King, like many men of his time in Spain, is bearded. Men often wore shoulder-length hair. Many types of headcovering were worn, as was the chaperon. In the *St Mark* altarpiece (1346; Manresa Cathedral) attributed to Arnau Bassa there are examples of small round brimless hats, as well as ones with upturned brims and pointed crowns ornamented with brooches.

Women's dress varied according to region. Two garments were worn over a linen shift: the outermost might be the open-sided garment mentioned above or a long-sleeved overgown with the bodice and skirts cut out as one. As the century progressed, overgowns became more fitted. As in Italy, long tippets hanging from the sleeves at the elbow were popular in the 1360s and 1370s. The *St George* altarpiece by an unknown artist (*c.* 1480–90; Villafranca del Penedès, Mus. Civ.) shows girls wearing garments like those in contemporary Italy, combined with local styles: short sleeves that show off the triangular sleeves of the shift, or knee-length hems to reveal the skirts of the undergown. Outside the house Spanish women were enveloped in ample mantles or waist-length capes. All married women covered their hair. Close-fitting caps combined with wimples and shaped to cover the neck and shoulders are illustrated in the altarpiece of the *Virgin of the Pared Delgada* by Juan de Tarragona (1359; Tarragona Cathedral). The same style is worn by the donatrix and her daughter-in-law as depicted in the central panel of the altarpiece of *SS John the Baptist and John the Evangelist* (*c.* 1365; Barcelona, Mus. A. Catalunya; see fig. 20) by Juan de Tarragona. It was not restricted to Catalonia: the effigy of *Juana de Castro, Queen of Galicia* (*d* 1374; Santiago de Compostela Cathedral) shows her in the same type of headcovering. Spanish women were fond of jewellery. After 1350 they wore long strings of beads over their mantles and overgowns. Examples are found in the effigy of *Alamanda de Rocaberti* (*c.* 1369; Santa Coloma de Queralt, Lleida, Sta María de Belloc) and the effigy of *Juana Manuel*, wife of Henry II of Castile (*d c.* 1381; Toledo Cathedral).

(ii) 15th century. By 1400 both male and female attire in Italy was relying for impact on generous drapes rather than a close fit. Young men wore short, loose gowns over the doublet. The elderly continued to dress in the ample, more dignified full-length overgown. Both these garments and the female overgown were constructed on the same pattern, with high collars and long triangular hanging sleeves. The shape of the body was suggested by a belt, around the waist for men and under the bust for women. Examples of these styles are recorded in the frescoes of the *Cycle of the Months* (before 1407; Trento, Castello del Buonconsiglio; see fig. 21) and in a contemporary *Taccuinum sanitatis* (Vienna, Österreich. Nbib., MS. NS 2544, fol. 104*r*).

The lavishness of Italian dress in the following decades may be judged from the elaborate garments and richly patterned silks recorded by Pisanello and Gentile da Fabriano. In the *Presentation of Christ in the Temple*, a predella scene from the *Adoration of the Magi* (1423; Florence, Uffizi), Gentile depicts a woman in an overgown with trailing skirts and ground-length hanging sleeves. On her head is a large, circular headdress ornamented with embroidery, appliquéd ornaments and gems. Such clothing, worn for important festivities, contrasts with the more modest, everyday attire of her cloaked and veiled companion. By the 1430s a new cut appeared for overgarments. The bodice and skirts were made from a circle or semicircle of bias-cut fabric, so as to permit regular pleating at the back and front. Such pleats, held in place by a tape horizontally placed on the inside of the garment, remained popular until the late 1460s. Examples may be found in Piero della Francesca's *Story of the True Cross* (Arezzo, S Francesco).

By mid-century contemporary works of art show significant regional differences in dress, as may be seen by comparing the frescoes by the Zavattari brothers in the chapel of Queen Teodolinda (1441; Monza Cathedral) with those by Domenico di Bartolo (1440–44) in the Hospital of S Maria della Scala, Siena. After 1450 the hem of the man's short overgown rose above the knees, as seen in Mantegna's Camera degli Sposi (1465–74; Mantua, Pal. Ducale). The pleated overgowns worn by courtiers were

21. *January* (before 1407), fresco from the *Cycle of the Months*, Castello del Buonconsiglio, Trento

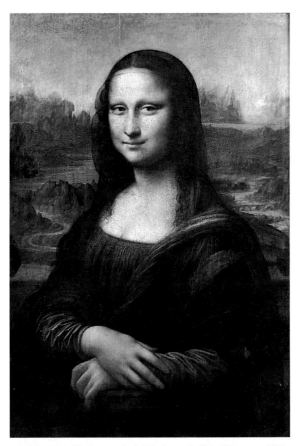

22. *'Mona Lisa'* by Leonardo da Vinci, panel, 600×470 mm, *c.* 1500–07 (Paris, Musée du Louvre)

of the head was covered with a small linen cap. Older women still wore a linen or silk veil. By the 1480s girls and young married women favoured a single plait hanging down the back, worn with a small bonnet tied under the chin and sometimes a plait-cover. This style, especially popular in Lombardy, had originated in Spain. Tuscan and Lombard versions are seen in Cosimo Rosselli's *Procession of the Bishop with the Ampule of Blood in the Piazza S Ambrogio* (1484–6; Florence, S Ambrogio; see fig. 23) and the anonymous *Pala Sforzesca* (1494; Milan, Brera).

The male overgown by the 1490s was coatlike in style. It hung from the shoulders, opened from the neck to hem and was loosely belted; the sleeves were straight. Sometimes a full-length robe of the same pattern was worn instead over the doublet and hose. Luca Signorelli's *Last Judgement* (1499–1503; Orvieto Cathedral; *see* SIGNORELLI, LUCA, fig. 4) shows young men, especially soldiers, wearing doublet and hose alone; the former was by now waist-length, the latter striped in a variety of colours. Around this time men's hair was worn shoulder-length. Small, brimless hats and skull-caps were the usual headgear, although officials in Florence and academics and lawyers elsewhere still wore the archaic chaperon. At the end of the century differences in regional dress were obvious. The Venetian styles recorded by Carpaccio in scenes from the *Life of St Ursula* (1490–98; Venice, Accad.; *see* CARPACCIO, (1), fig. 4) are clearly distinguishable from the Milanese dress worn by Ludovico Sforza and Beatrice d'Este in the *Pala Sforzesca* and also from garments worn in contemporary Florence, as painted by Ghirlandaio in scenes from the *Life of the Virgin* (*see* SPALLIERA, fig. 1)

replaced in the following decade by ones with smoothly fitting bodices and gathered skirts joined by a waist seam. From the 1460s men and women often wore detachable sleeves, sometimes made in a contrasting fabric and colour; these were tied into the armhole of the garment with laces or 'points'. Men's hose were made from cloth or silk and lined. Stocking hose (with separate legs) that laced to the doublet hem were still worn, but as the overgown hem rose, 'closed' hose with joined legs (like modern tights) became more common: these were closed in front, with a laced-on codpiece. Examples are shown in Ercole de' Roberti's scenes from the *Life of St Vincent Ferrer* (1473; Rome, Pin. Vaticana).

Between 1470 and 1500 women's overgowns had separately cut bodices and skirts with a waist seam. They laced or buttoned at the front and had either a V-shaped or a square neckline. The former showed the bodice of the undergown beneath the lacing; the latter was often covered by a silk kerchief. The sleeves were narrow and generally left unlaced along the outer arm or at the armhole, for greater comfort. Sometimes they were made in two sections and left open at the elbow, showing the sleeve of the shift or chemise beneath. The hair was left free to fall in curls framing the face, as in Leonardo's portraits of *Ginevra de' Benci* (*c.* 1473; Washington, DC, N.G.A.) and *'Mona Lisa'* (*c.* 1500–07; Paris, Louvre; see fig. 22). The plait at the back

23. *Procession of the Bishop with the Ampule of the Holy Blood in the Piazza S Ambrogio* (1484–6) by Cosimo Rosselli, fresco (detail), S Ambrogio, Florence

24. *Herod's Feast* by Pedro García de Benabarre, *c.* 1470–80 (Barcelona, Museu d'Art de Catalunya)

and scenes from the *Life of St John the Baptist* (1485–90; Florence, S Maria Novella).

Throughout the century Italian and Franco-Burgundian styles influenced men's dress in Spain, although after 1450 plain fabrics and sombre colours replaced richly patterned velvets and lavish fur trimmings. Castilian dress of the period is depicted in the initial miniature of the *Bible of the Duque d'Alba* (1430; Madrid, Pal. Liria, Fund. Casa de Alba), which shows him and other knights of the Order of Calatrava dressed in short, ample gowns, trimmed with fur around the round neck, cuffs and hem; their sword belts are worn on the hips. Their hair is cut very short above the ears, and they are clean-shaven. The regularly pleated Italian overgown, modified to Spanish taste, was worn after 1435. In the *Pubol* altarpiece by Bernat Martorell (1437; Girona, Mus. Dioc.) the donor's son wears such a gown with a dagged hem. Hanging sleeves were also worn, sometimes with a gown that opened from neck to hem, like that of the donor in the anonymous *Virgin and Child with Angel Musicians* (1439; Madrid, Mus. Lázaro Galdiano), and remained popular until the mid-16th century. The Buitrago Hospital Altarpiece (1455; Madrid, Pal. Duque del Infantado) by Jorge Inglés, portraying the

donors, the Marqués and Marquesa de Santillana, with a page and maid, illustrates a predominance of Franco-Burgundian taste in Castilian men's dress but a preference for local styles for women. Spanish headgear remained varied. The chaperon was rare after 1460, being replaced by various small caps. Brimless hats are recorded in *Herod's Feast* (*c.* 1470–80; Barcelona, Mus. A. Catalunya; see fig. 24) by Pedro García de Benabarre (*fl* 1455–80). These suited the fringed, shoulder-length hair worn by most men in the last decades of the century.

Spanish women's dress retained some distinct local features, mixed with foreign influences. The pleated overgown and hanging sleeves worn by Italian women *c.* 1430–60 do not seem to have been adopted. Overgowns had a separately cut bodice and skirt and a round or square neckline. Towards the end of the century some overgowns were front-lacing. Sleeves were often detachable, being discarded to display chemise sleeves ornamented in the Moorish style with black silk embroidery and silk ribbon. The hooped skirt or farthingale was another indigenous fashion, said to have been invented in 1468 by Queen Joanna of Castile in order to conceal her pregnancy from her husband Henry IV 'the Impotent' (*reg* 1454–74). The hoops, either osiers or wadded rolls of fabric, were attached to the outside of the skirts. These early external farthingales were worn until the mid-16th century; examples are depicted in *Herod's Feast* mentioned above and in an anonymous *Beheading of St John the Baptist* (*c.* 1500; Madrid, Prado). The single covered plait hanging down the back that Salome wears in these works with a small cap or a veil had been popular in Spain since the end of the 14th century. Other styles of headdress were the 'horned' type from France and northern Europe, worn in Navarre and northern Spain after 1410; the roll worn by the Marquesa de Santillana in the Buitrago Hospital Altarpiece of 1455; and the fabric caul. The latter is depicted by the St Quirse Master in the altarpiece of *St Clare and St Margaret* (*c.* 1460; Barcelona, Mus. A. Catalunya); like the roll, it was a Spanish style. Towards the end of the century, very conservative or older women covered their plaits at the back of the head with a small cap, over which they wore a pleated hood of silk or linen, covering the head and shoulders. Queen Isabella of Castile is wearing this in a portrait attributed to Bartolomé Bermejo (*c.* 1495; Madrid, Pal. Real).

Capes and ample cloaks remained popular throughout the century. An ankle-length sleeveless garment was sometimes worn over the outergown. Like other garments of purely Spanish origin it was still being worn in the 16th century. Jewellery was worn a great deal, generally large earrings and heavy gold necklaces; the women in the altarpiece of *St Clare and St Margaret* are depicted with earrings and necklaces, while in *Herod's Feast* Salome, Herodias, Herod and his courtiers all wear heavy necklaces of gold chains.

(iii) 16th century. Examples of early 16th-century Italian dress are found in Titian's frescoes in the Scuola di S Antonio, Padua (1511), in Louis Bréa's *Coronation of the Virgin* (1513; Genoa, S Maria del Castello) and in Andrea del Sarto's frescoes of the *Birth of the Virgin* (1514; Florence, SS Annunziata, Chiostrino dei Voti). The style was similar for both sexes. Outer garments had wide

square necks revealing the ruffled neckband of the undershirt, smooth bodices and full skirts. Women embellished their dress with pendant necklaces and with transparent silk kerchiefs draped over their shoulders. Their hair, confined in a snood, hung down the back of the neck. Men's hair was fringed and shoulder-length, becoming shorter as the century progressed. Full beards became popular at the end of the first decade.

Around 1530 the doublet and hose were established as respectable outer wear. This was due perhaps to military influences—soldiers frequently wore no overgarments—but also to the evolution of the hose. 'Closed' hose became two garments: the lower torso and thighs were covered by 'upper stocks', or breeches, decoratively slashed and slit, which closed with a codpiece and were attached by points to the doublet hem. Stocking hose, often of knitted silk, were pulled up over the knees and secured with garters. When the overgown was shortened or discarded, the breeches were embellished with panes (vertical strips of fabric attached only at the waist and leg bands) and padded for greater bulk. After *c.* 1540 the doublet and breeches were treated as a coordinated ensemble. Examples of the new style are seen in Bernardino Licinio's portrait of *Ottaviano Grimani* (1541; Vienna, Gemäldegal. Akad. Bild. Kst.) and Titian's *Ranuccio Farnese* (*c.* 1542; Washington, DC, N.G.A.). By the 1560s the breeches or trunk-hose had become shorter and rounder, with canions (extensions) from the leg bands to the knees. These can be seen in Giovanni Battista Moroni's portrait of *Gian Girolamo Grumelli* (1560; Bergamo, priv. col.). In the Veneto an alternative style was the longer knee-breeches worn by the huntsman portrayed by Veronese in a fresco (1561) at the Villa Barbaro (now Villa Volpi), Maser. Similar knee-breeches are worn by members of the *Pagello Family* (Vicenza, Mus. Civ. A. & Stor.) painted by Giovanni Antonio Fasolo at about the same date. A calf-length open robe was sometimes worn over the doublet and hose; after 1560 a short circular cape was more usual.

25. *St Bridget Taking the Veil* (1524) by Lorenzo Lotto, fresco from the *Lives of SS Bridget and Barbara*, Villa Suardi oratory, Trescore Balneario

26. *Family of Alfonso III Gonzaga, Count of Novellara*, 1581 (Rome, Galleria Colonna)

Changes in women's dress between 1520 and 1540 may be charted by comparing examples in works such as Lorenzo Lotto's *Lives of SS Bridget and Barbara* (1524; Trescore Balneario, Villa Suardi, oratory; see fig. 25), Titian's *La Bella* (*c.* 1534–6; Florence, Pitti) and Bronzino's *Eleonora of Toledo with her Son Giovanni* (*c.* 1545; Florence, Uffizi; see BRONZINO, AGNOLO, fig. 3). By the 1540s the undergown, worn over a silk or linen shift, was composed of a separate bodice and skirt. The bodice was lined with reeds or whalebone, which stiffened it, producing a smooth external appearance. It was closed back and front by laces. The skirts were full and, until the last decades of the century, unsupported; the farthingale, introduced from Spain, was briefly worn in Lombardy *c.* 1500 but never became widely popular in Italy.

In the 1540s the square neckline of the overgown was ofen filled with a decorative partlet, or small shoulder-cape, like that worn by Eleonora of Toledo. In the following decade the overgown acquired instead a high collar, as seen in Moroni's *Portrait of a Lady* (*c.* 1550; London, N.G.). In the 1570s the overgown had a close-fitting bodice with a V-shaped waist, hanging sleeves and a skirt open from waist to hem to display the underskirt.

The bodice usually had a standing collar that was open in front and supported a lace-edged ruff. In the 1580s, as seen in Lavinia Fontana's *Visit of the Queen of Sheba to Solomon* (Dublin, N.G.), women's dress was much ornamented with embroidery, brooches, lace and jewellery, as well as with pinking and slashing (*see* ITALY, §X, 6). The latter, first found in the garments of Swiss and German mercenaries in the 1480s, became usual in male and female dress from 1520, continuing throughout the century.

Metal belts were a usual accessory, especially in the 1570s. Jewellery was commonly worn. Both men and women often wore long gold chain necklaces with pendants. Pearl earrings and necklaces were worn by women from *c.* 1540 onwards, long pearl rope necklaces being worn with circular ruffs in the 1580s. The ruff was one of the most characteristic features of male and female attire after 1550: it was made from layers of starched, pleated linen, sometimes edged with lace, and was supported by a high collar and also by an underpropper when worn (from *c.* 1560) at jaw height. At the end of the century very large circular ruffs were usual, although children and some men sometimes wore only a falling band or flat linen collar. Examples of ruffs, as well as of Italian dress in the 1580s, are found in the portrait of the *Family of Alfonso III Gonzaga, Count of Novellara* by an unknown artist (1581; Rome Gal. Colonna; see fig. 26) and in Lavinia Fontana's *Gozzadini Family* (1584; Bologna, Pin. N.). An interesting example of dress *c*. 1600 is recorded in an unknown Flemish artist's *Eleonora de' Medici, Duchess of Mantua, at Prayer with her Children* (Mantua, Pal. Ducale).

As may be seen from Juan Gascos's *St Julian de Vilamirosa* (1508; Vic, Abadal priv. col.), in Spain at the beginning of the century the man's overgown had a square neckline, smooth fitting bodice and loosely gathered skirts and was belted. In subsequent decades the overgown's neckline and that of the doublet beneath became lower, revealing the linen undershirt with its ruffled neckband. The hemline grew shorter, rising in the 1540s to well above the knee. Fashions changed slowly: in some areas the doublet and hose were not adopted until after mid-century. The effigy of *Cristobal de Andino* (*c*. 1540; Burgos,

27. *Joanna of Austria* by Antonis Mor, 1.95×1.04 m, *c*. 1558–60 (Madrid, Museo del Prado)

S Lesmes) shows the deceased in a short overgown worn under a knee-length Castilian cape with a cowl hood. An equally short overtunic, with a hem 140–50 mm above the knees, is seen in the effigy of *Don Francisco de Vargas and his Wife, Doña Inés de Caruajal* (*c*. 1540–50; Madrid, S Andrés), but it is combined with an ankle-length open robe that has hanging sleeves. The attire shown in both these effigies contrasts with the doublet, hose and short circular cape worn by *Don Carlos* in the portrait by Alonso Sánchez Coello (*c*. 1555; Madrid, Prado).

Hose with vertical stripes or slashing above and around the knees were worn in Spain until *c*. 1540. The first reference to separate upper and lower hose is in 1537; knitted silk hose are documented *c*. 1528. The 'upper stocks', or breeches, became visible when the overgown was shortened or discarded *c*. 1550. They were then decorated with vertical panes and wadded for greater bulk, becoming very rotund by the 1570s. This change in shape may be seen by comparing the portrait of *Don Carlos* mentioned above with another of the same sitter painted by the same artist in 1564 (Vienna, Ksthist. Mus.).

The linen ruff was worn from *c*. 1550; Sánchez Coello's portrait of *Philip II* (*c*. 1575; Madrid, Prado) shows it edged with lace. By the 1590s the ruff was very deep and framed the head, as may be seen in El Greco's *Burial of Count Orgaz* (1586–8; Toledo, S Tomé). Men's hair, worn shoulder-length until *c*. 1520, was short from the mid-century onwards. Full beards were popular *c*. 1530 and towards the end of the century became more pointed.

The formal richness of Spanish women's dress is well recorded in contemporary portraiture, especially of royalty. At the beginning of the century the silhouette was still soft. In the altarpiece of *St Mary Magdalene* by Pedro Matàs (1526; Girona Cathedral) women's overgowns are shown with wide, square necklines and large triangular sleeves. The skirts are full but unsupported, although the farthingale was certainly worn at this date, sometimes still externally. From *c*. 1550 a separate bodice, stiffened with reeds or whalebone, and a hooped farthingale that held out the skirts in an inverted V-shape were worn beneath the overgown, which thus presented a stiffer and more tailored appearance, as in Antonis Mor's portrait of *Joanna of Austria* (*c*. 1558–60; Madrid, Prado; see fig. 27). This style was not adopted immediately; many Spanish noblewomen continued to dress like Doña Inés de Caruajal as she is portrayed in her effigy. Similar garments and headgear are seen in the effigy of the *Condesa de Castañeda* (*c*. 1550–60; Burgos Cathedral). Members of the Spanish royal family were painted on numerous occasions over a period of a few years from the 1570s, and the variety of their attire is well documented, as is its evolution. The Infanta Isabella Clara Eugenia, daughter of Philip II and Elizabeth of Valois, was painted with her sister Caterina Michaela by Sanchez Coello in 1574 and again in 1579 (both Madrid, Prado) and by Juan Pantoja de la Cruz in 1599 (Munich, Alte Pin.), when she was Archduchess of Austria. These works show that the cut of the overgown remained much the same until the end of the century; the garment was made from heavy silks, embellished with pinking, slashing and embroidery as well as brooches and gems. Between 1570 and 1600 the most significant changes in women's appearance were in the size, shape and fabric of the ruff and coordinated wrist ruffles and in the hairstyles. In the last decade of the century the ruff tended to be of delicate lace and was circular and deep, while the hair was pulled back from the face and piled up on the crown in a conical effect; it was often decorated with a small aigrette. These slight differences in style may be compared in Sanchez Coello's portrait of *Doña Ana Mendoza de la Cerda, Princesa d' Eboli* (*c.* 1579; Madrid, Pal. Duque del Infantado) and Pantoja de la Cruz's portrait of the *Infanta Isabella Clara Eugenia*.

BIBLIOGRAPHY

Il libro del sarto (Milan, 1548, 2/1579); intro. A. Mottola Molfino (Modena, 1987)

J. de Alcega: *Libro de geometria pratica, y traça* (Madrid, 1589); Eng. trans. as *A Tailor's Pattern Book* (London, 1979)

C. Vecellio: *Habiti antichi et moderni di tutto il mondo* (Venice, 1598); R as *Vecellio's Renaissance Costume Book* (New York, 1977)

J. Sempere y Guarinos: *Historia del luxo y de las leyes suntuarias de España*, 2 vols (Madrid, 1788)

P. Lanza della Scalea: *Donne e gioelli in Sicilia nel medioevo e nel rinascimento* (Palermo and Turin, 1892)

E. Polidori Calamandrei: *Le vesti delle donne fiorentine nel quattrocento* (Florence, 1924)

C. Bernis: *Indumentaria medieval española* (Madrid, 1956)

——: *Indumentaria española en tiempos de Carlo V* (Madrid, 1962)

F. Cappi Bentivegna: *Abbigliamento e costume nella pittura Italiana*, i (Rome, 1962)

R. Levi Pisetzky: *Storia del costume in Italia*, ii and iii (Milan, 1964)

E. Birbari: *Dress in Italian Painting, 1460–1500* (London, 1975)

C. Bernis: *Trajes y modas en la España de los Reyes Católicos*, 2 vols (Madrid, 1978–9)

R. M. Anderson: *Hispanic Costume, 1480–1530* (New York, 1979)

J. Herald: *Renaissance Dress in Italy, 1400–1500* (London, 1981)

J. Arnold: *Patterns of Fashion: The Cut and Construction of Clothes for Men and Women c. 1560–1620* (London, 1985, rev. New York, 1989)

D. Liscia Bemporad, ed.: *Il costume nell'età del rinascimento* (Florence, 1988)

S. M. Newton: *The Dress of the Venetians* (London, 1988)

C. Bernis: 'La moda en la España de Felipe II a través del retrato de corte', *Alonso Sánchez Coello y el retrato en la corte de Felipe II* (exh. cat., ed. S. Saavedra; Madrid, Prado, 1990), pp. 65–111

S. Tramontana: *Vestirsi e travestirsi in Sicilia: Abbigliamento, feste e spettacoli nel medioevo* (Palermo, 1993)

Moda alla corte dei Medici: Gli abiti restaurati di Cosimo, Eleonora e don Garzia (exh. cat., Florence, Pitti, 1993)

JANE BRIDGEMAN

2. NORTHERN EUROPE. Between 1300 and 1600 the types of visual source available for the study of dress vary enormously, but for a period of years in each area they tend to be concentrated in one type. The most generally useful sources for the 14th and 15th centuries are illuminated manuscripts. With their full-length views, from different angles, of people of various ages and classes, they provide a wealth of information on a wide range of types of dress. In England, for upper- or upper-middle-class persons, there are also funerary effigies or images on tomb brasses; the latter are much less satisfactory, being often mass-produced. Effigial sculpture in England continues to be useful into the 16th century for conveying the three-dimensional effect of dress, with the proviso that the date of death may not be the date of the execution of the artefact. France and the Netherlands lack the monu-

28. Illumination from the *Romance of Alexander*, c. 1340 (Oxford, Bodleian Library, MS. Bodl. 264, fol. 127*v*)

mental remains that have survived in England, but they have a variety of manuscripts that England cannot match, and the Netherlands have painters of the utmost fidelity to details of dress, from Jan van Eyck to Antonis Mor (see fig. 27 above). In the 16th century manuscript production declined sharply, but the increasing production of portraits supplies detailed depictions of (mainly) the head-and-shoulders area of the dress of the aristocracy and the wealthier middle classes.

In the countries bordering on the English Channel there seems to have been a kind of norm for male dress between 1300 and 1600. This does not mean that England was the source of this norm but rather that trade conducted in the triangle of the Netherlands, France and England helped to ensure a certain uniformity of fashion for men. The further south or east from the frontiers of the Netherlands, the notional centre of north-western Europe, the more idiosyncratic dress appears to be, particularly for women. Germany produced relatively little of use to the dress historian between the start of the 14th century and the end of the 15th; some portraits from the 16th century show the highly regionalized nature of German society reflected in the different forms of dress, particularly women's, worn in the various cities and states.

(i) 1300–1415. (ii) 1416–1500. (iii) 1501–1600.

(i) 1300–1415. At the start of the century clothing for both sexes tended to be fairly simple. It consisted of a T-shaped overgarment, called an overtunic (Fr. *surcote*), with loose straight sleeves, worn over a similarly shaped undergarment, the tunic, or *cote*, the sleeves of which fitted only on the forearm, possibly by sewing them up on the wearer. Women sometimes dispensed with the sleeves of the overtunic, displaying the tunic sleeves, tight on the forearm and bunched-up above. Women's garments were always at least ankle-length, but men had a choice of lengths from ground-length to below the knee. A cloak and sometimes a separate hood would complete the outfit to create a suit, called a 'robe'. In the 1320s and 1330s clothing was made tighter; buttons were used on the tunic sleeves, and women increasingly wore the sleeveless overtunic open down the sides of the torso, to reveal the tighter tunic and hence their figures (effigy of an unknown woman, *c.* 1330–35; Bottesford, Leics, St Mary). A three-quarter-length sleeve with a small pendent point at the back was also introduced to the overtunic. By about 1340 the outer sleeve was no more than elbow-length, but its pendent point now reached the top of the legs (effigy of an unknown man, *c.* 1340–45; Alnwick, Northumb., St Michael). As dress became tighter and more revealing of the body's outline, women in particular gradually discarded the custom of almost completely covering their heads, until by about 1340 it was more important to reveal at least part of an elaborate hairstyle. Until *c.* 1460 hoods with small shoulder-capes, closed under the chin, formed the basic head-covering for men.

Until *c.* 1340 many garments were made with one side in a fabric of a different colour from the other; sometimes one side was striped. Around 1340, however, lavish embroidery began to take the place of this feature, and clothing became even tighter round the torso. Men's garments were buttoned down the chest but flared out

29. Illumination from *Le Remède de Fortune*, 1350–55 (Paris, Bibliothèque Nationale, MS. fr. 1586, fol. 51)

from the hips in 'skirts' shortened to just above the knee, as in an illumination to the *Romance of Alexander* (see fig. 28). Some women also wore flaring skirts, but many wore their overtunics fairly tight all the way down. The tightness of their clothing seems to have caused both sexes to develop by the early 1350s a sway-back stance, and both men and women had long thin streamers hanging from the elbows of their overtunics, as depicted in an illumination to *Le Remède de Fortune* (see fig. 29).

Around 1360 documentary sources contain references to a new type of long outer garment that was worn by both sexes, so that men became indistinguishable from women when seen from behind. In the visual sources such confusion is most marked only from the start of the 15th century, when both sexes were portrayed as wearing the trailing, long-sleeved garment known as a gown or 'goun' and in French as a *houppelande*. The French word disappeared from use by *c.* 1430, when the garment it described had gone out of fashion; 'gown' survived to mean any formal outer garment with sleeves. More immediately obvious changes in the 1360s are seen in men's hip-length outer garments and the increasingly egg-shaped padding of the male torso and in the return, at least in England, of head covering for women, this time in the form of layers of veils with frills around the face, as in the effigy of *Lady Jose of Clearwell* (*c.* 1360; Newland, Glos, All Saints). French and Flemish women, and English women in court circles, seem to have preferred to wear their hair in stiffened plaits at the side of the head, pointing diagonally towards the chin, or else covered by a long-tailed hood,

30. Illumination (detail) from the Turin–Milan Hours, *c.* 1380 (Turin, Museo Civico d'Arte Antica)

31. Illumination from Chaucer's *Troilus and Criseyde*, *c.* 1400 (Cambridge, Corpus Christi College Library, MS. 61, fol. 1*v*)

open under the chin; such styles may be seen in the TURIN–MILAN HOURS (see fig. 30).

Once the *houppelande* had become more widely accepted (by about 1380), it too began to alter, first, by acquiring a standing collar, which necessitated the shortening of Englishwomen's veils and Englishmen's hair; some men, however, grew small forked beards. The *houppelande* continued to be worn unbelted, with straight sleeves, until the early 1390s, when belting (at the waist for men and below the bust for women) and wide funnel-shaped sleeves, open or closed at the cuffs, became much more common. From *c.* 1395 to *c.* 1415 it was fashionable to wear long trailing undercuffs that could completely envelop the hands, adding to the difficulties of wearing the cumbersome *houppelande*. Collars had grown so high and wide by *c.* 1410 that most men had abandoned wearing beards. Women had taken to wearing headdresses that resembled large bumps on their temples. Subsequently these turned into wide horns on which veils could be draped in a variety of ways, as seen in the Limbourg brothers' *Belles Heures de Jean de Berry* (*c.* 1408; New York, Cloisters, fol. 191). The hems of men's *houppelandes* and the sleeves of both sexes were slashed or dagged (cut into zigzags), sometimes in very intricate patterns. Smaller-scale dagging was used on men's hoods, which from about 1400 were worn on top of the head, rather like turbans, as

in the illumination to Chaucer's *Troilus and Criseyde* (see fig. 31).

(ii) *1416–1500.* From around 1415 women began to wear their collars turned down on to the shoulders (effigy of *Elizabeth Aldburgh, c.* 1426; Harewood, Yorks, All Saints), and their headdresses, particularly in England, developed a more solid, padded appearance. About 1420 the edges of dress began to lose their spikiness. The fur lining of the *houppelande* began to move towards the outside, like a rolled edge over the dagging, and a small amount of padding was used round the edge of men's hoods. The *houppelande* began to change shape during the 1420s, losing its collar and its extreme bulk in body and sleeves. The bag-shaped sleeves that came to be the norm for both sexes shrank even further in the course of the 1430s, until *c.* 1440 sleeves were either loose and straight or only slightly baggy above tight cuffs, as shown in Jan van Eyck's *Virgin and Child with Chancellor Rolin* (*c.* 1435; Paris, Louvre). Both sexes gathered their bodices into carefully set folds, held in place by belts; women still wore their belts below the bust (e.g. Rogier van der Weyden's *Magdalene Reading, c.* 1430–40; London, N.G.), but men now wore theirs on the hips. By the late 1430s any resemblance to the original *houppelande* had been lost, and the outer garment tended to be known in France as a *robe*, the meaning of this word having altered. Men began to belt their gowns or robes nearer to natural waist level.

The 1440s saw a further reduction in the amount of material used in men's and women's gowns; the folds in the skirts of men's gowns were arranged tightly down the front and back, and, to provide material for these, the sides of the gown body were flattened and the side seam split to hip level. By the end of the decade some gowns had so little material in their bodices that their wearers, male or female, could not close them above the belt. Men continued to wear hoods with a padded roll round the head. By about 1450, when the padding was reaching the proportions of a small tyre, it became fashionable to wear a small cap while carrying the hood slung over one shoulder, as in Petrus Christus's *St Eligius* (1449; New York, Met.). The horned look remained popular for women's headdresses, although the basic structure became lighter than it had been earlier. For the middle classes, starched veils were set in horn shapes, while the upper classes usually wore flowerpot-shaped caps under fine veils that were pinned into small horns or drawn up over wires to resemble pairs of flags or butterflies' wings, as seen in the illumination from the *Granting of Privileges to Ghent and Flanders* (see fig. 32). Women's sleeves were more or less tubular. In the late 1440s women's gowns continued to be narrow in the bodice, sleeves and skirt, but the hem area was extended to produce long, pointed trains (see fig. 32). Men began to wear gowns with gathered sleeve heads, giving the impression of very broad shoulders; in the case of younger men, these were set over nipped-in waists and hip-length skirts.

In many respects dress was at its most Gothic from the mid-1450s to the late 1460s. Fashionable men wore tall pointed caps, over very wide shoulders, below which the figure tapered, via nipped-in waists, hip-length gowns and long legs, to long, narrow-toed shoes, as illustrated in Jean Fouquet's *Le Lit de Justice de Vendôme* (1485–60; Munich,

Bayer. Staatsbib., Cod Gall 6, fol. 2*v*). Fashionable women wore even taller, narrow, steeple-shaped headdresses, with or without filmy veils, and gowns with very tight, skimpy bodices and sleeves above flowing skirts with long trains (e.g. Quintus Curtius's *Historia Alexandri Magni, c.* 1468; Oxford, Bodleian Lib., MS Laud Misc, fol. 127). In the late 1460s the trains were replaced by deep hems made from contrasting materials or furs, a feature that continued, along with the tall caps, into the 1470s, as in Dieric Bouts the elder's *Justice of Emperor Otto III: Ordeal by Fire* (1473; Brussels, Mus. A. Anc.).

In England the flag or butterfly type of headdress, seen frequently on brasses but not on effigies, presumably because of the difficulties of representing in the solidity of stone something so transparent, persisted into the 1480s; by then the undercap was smaller and more boxlike. By about 1480 Flemish women had also started wearing much shorter caps, with veils sometimes ironed in such a way as to produce a heart-shaped dip in the centre front (e.g. Memling's portrait of *Maria Moreel*, 1480; Bruges, Memlingmus.). About 1475 men's dress very quickly lost its width at the shoulders, and by the end of the decade it was cut even more tightly than women's; to allow it to be put on, it had to have slits in the sleeves, or incomplete armhole seams; rudimentary lapels were formed by turning back the bodice fronts (e.g. *Portrait of a Young Man* by the Master of the View of Ste Gudule, *c.* 1480; London, N.G.). This style seems to mark the start of experimentation with a new form of men's dress. The very tight look lasted only a few years, presumably because it was too constricting and uncomfortable; but by modifying it, men were able to make themselves appear much bulkier than they had done at the start of the century. Bulk was achieved not through padding but by means of several rather ill-fitting layers, consisting of gathered shirt, doublet (a tight-fitting jacket), coat (a new garment) and loose-fitting gown. In the late 1480s the hair was worn down to the shoulders and fluffed out (if a man had enough hair), and the lapels were widened to reach the point of the shoulders, providing a suitable area for displaying the newly-fashionable spotted, long-haired furs used as linings in men's gowns (e.g. Memling's portrait of *Martin van Nieuwenhove*, 1487; Bruges, Memlingmus.). The armhole seams of gowns were still sometimes left incomplete. By the early 1490s low caps with tied-up brims were in use. Together, all these features contrived to make men look more solid.

By the mid-1480s some younger women had started to wear gowns with a highish, rather square neckline, an obvious centre-front closing and a belt at natural waist level, but changes towards a squarer look took longer to develop than in men's dress. By the early 1480s women still looked very elongated in gowns with tightly fitting bodices, some with square necklines, sleeves that were beginning to develop a bell-shape at the cuffs and skirts with trains (as in Gerard David's altarpiece of the *Virgin and Child Enthroned, c.* 1490; Paris, Louvre). On their heads wealthy French and Netherlandish women wore small pieces of black velvet or satin, trimmed with gold decorations at the front edge and slit up the sides (in England called French hoods); beneath there was often another cap, with a crimped front edge that stopped below the chin. Middle-class and working-class women seem to

32. Illumination from the *Granting of Privileges to Ghent and Flanders*, after 1453 (Vienna, Österreichische Nationalbibliothek, Cod. 2583, fol. 13)

have used linen caps, some with narrow 'tails' at the sides, starched into flowerpot-like shapes or into heart-shaped frames for the face. These caps, which are presumably the origin of the starched linen caps of Dutch national dress, may be seen in the painting of the *Feast of the Antwerp Archers' Guild* (see fig. 33) by the Master of Frankfurt.

(iii) 1501–1600. Representations of the French hood are only a tiny part of the documentary evidence that by the start of the 16th century women throughout Europe were quite aware of, and interested in, foreign fashions. Deliberate attempts were often made to dress in the fashions of other countries, with a degree of accuracy that can only be guessed at. In the *Temptation of St Anthony* by Joachim Patinir and Cornelis Massys (*c.* 1516–24; Madrid, Prado), the three temptresses wear French, South German and (possibly) Italian dress. The English seem to have regarded the French as the constant inventors of new fashions that other nations adopted, while admitting that they themselves were happy to adopt any new idea, wherever it came from: Englishwomen's dress, however, generally retained a distinctive local or national air. The sources for 'foreign' outfits were perhaps the costume books, known to have been printed from 1562 onwards. Habsburg dominance of much of Europe (the Netherlands, Germany, Austria, Spain and parts of Italy) almost certainly contributed to the interchangeability of fashions in those areas, but it does not seem to have created uniformity. It is the variety of female fashions worn in the Netherlands, France, Germany and England and their reinterpretation to suit local tastes that make the 16th century far less easy to discuss in general terms than the two preceding ones.

As mentioned earlier, the outlines of male dress for the first 40 years or so of the 16th century had been established by about 1490, in the form of great physical bulk. Another, more lasting feature of male dress also made its appearance

33. *Feast of the Antwerp Archers' Guild* by the Master of Frankfurt, oil on panel, *c.* 1491–3 (Antwerp, Koninklijk Museum voor Schone Kunsten)

34. *Family of Sir Thomas More* by Hans Holbein the younger, pen and ink and brush, over black chalk, 389×524 mm, 1526 (Basle, Kupferstichkabinett)

about then: the display of men's shirts, which had slowly altered from being undergarments to being garments acceptable as outerwear on all but the most formal occasions. Because of this new importance, at the end of the 15th century they were carefully embroidered at the neck. In southern Germany the male shirt with a low neckline, exposing at least the collar bone, was a prominent feature of dress from as early as about 1480. The 'untidiness' that in north-western Europe was a necessary first step to making men's dress appear wider seems to have first been cultivated in southern Germany, with men wearing their hair in uncombed ringlets and flaunting themselves in shirts and doublets so wide at the neck that they tended to slip off the shoulders: this is most vividly seen in Albrecht Dürer's *Self-portrait* (*see* DÜRER, (1), fig. 2).

At the start of the 16th century women in Nuremberg wore tight bodices with low necklines under small shoulder-capes, long (to the knuckles) tight sleeves and skirts with a number of gathers. The headdress of married women was a large beehive-like structure (e.g. Dürer's drawings of women's costumes, 1500; Vienna, Albertina). The women of Upper Saxony were similarly dressed, with sleeves slashed at the elbows, showing puffs of undershirt,

and gloves slashed at the knuckles, as in Lucas Cranach the elder's *Martyrdom of St Catherine* (1506; Dresden, Gemäldegal.). The hair was gathered into coloured nets, sometimes under wide-brimmed hats (e.g. Cranach's *Salome*, *c.* 1530; Budapest, Mus. F.A.). By about 1515 women's dress there had acquired the form it was to keep into the 1530s; a front-laced bodice and a deeply pleated velvet skirt, with horizontal bands of cloth of gold above the hem and round the sleeves (e.g. Cranach's *Duchess Catherine of Saxony*, 1514; Dresden, Gemäldegal.). The use of contrasting bands was probably related to the fashion for slashing clothes, particularly men's clothes, to show the contrasting lining beneath; in extreme cases some men's garments appear to have had their outer surface entirely composed of strips of ribbon, held together at intervals by further strips of ribbon set at right angles, as strikingly depicted in Cranach's portrait of *Duke Henry the Pious of Saxony* (*c.* 1514; Dresden, Gemäldegal.). Slashing first appeared about 1510 and by around 1520 had become standard practice in men's dress across western Europe (anonymous portrait of *Henry VIII*, *c.* 1520; London, N.P.G.).

During the years from the 1490s to *c.* 1530 women's headdresses developed along lines that, except in the case of well-to-do French and Netherlandish women, tended to mark both the nationality and the class of the wearer. English women continued on the whole to wear a truncated version of the undercap associated with the headdresses of the 1470s and 1480s, but with the addition of a black cloth on top, slit up the sides (anonymous portrait of *Elizabeth of York*, *d* 1503; London, N.P.G.). By the mid-1520s the cap had acquired a gable shape and the front sections of the black cloth had been replaced by strips of patterned gold ribbon that were pinned up at the sides (seen, for example, in Hans Holbein the younger's drawing of the *Family of Sir Thomas More*; see fig. 34). A version of this lacked the top point of the gable and the gold ribbons. The French hood, which by 1530 closely followed the shape of the head and was decorated at the back with an inverted horseshoe-shaped piece of goldsmith's work, became more generally acceptable (e.g. portrait of *Mme de Canaples*, attributed to Jean Clouet, *c.* 1525; Edinburgh, N.G.).

The female neckline in France, England and the Netherlands had moved outwards towards the shoulders before achieving a square outline, but until *c.* 1515 it curved upwards modestly over the cleavage, as in *Virgin Enthroned with Female Saints* by Gerard David (1509; Rouen, Mus. B.-A.; *see* DAVID, GERARD, fig. 2). The trumpet-shaped sleeves grew wider and longer, until *c.* 1505 they had to be turned back on themselves at the ends; by *c.* 1510 they had been turned back to the elbow. This turning-back allowed the undersleeve to develop and become more elaborate. It gradually assumed a triangular shape when seen from the side and until the late 1520s was often pleated or stitched, perhaps quilted, in parallel straight lines. This style is seen in Holbein's portrait of *Lady Guildford* (1527; St Louis, MO, A. Mus.). After this date it was more commonly made from the same material as the centre-front panel of the underskirt, which the gown skirt was now being split to reveal (e.g. Holbein's portrait of *Queen Jane Seymour*, *c.* 1536–7; Vienna, Ksthist. Mus.). About 1515 large busts seem to have become fashionable, but by about 1530 women were trying to flatten their chests as much as possible. The gradual widening of the neckline seems to have been counteracted almost at once by the introduction of small shoulder-capes (known as partlets in England), which are common in portraits of Netherlandish women from *c.* 1520 onwards; they are not found in English portraits until about 1550 (e.g. Master A.W.'s *Portrait of a Lady*, 1536; U. London, Courtauld Inst.). Netherlandish women are also much more likely to be portrayed with smocked shirts filling in most of the square neckline, as in Joos van Cleve's triptych of the *Deposition* (*c.* 1518; Edinburgh, N.G.).

By about 1510 men's caps with laced-up brims had acquired a harder outline, eventually looking like squares when seen from the front, like that worn by *Henry VII* in the portrait by Michel Sittow (1505; London, N.P.G.). In the same decade the coat developed a square neckline, and its skirts were knee-length and set in deep folds, similar to those in women's dress in Upper Saxony. The gown and coat were gradually pushed outwards towards the shoulders, until by about 1520 much of the bodice of the doublet was on view. The outer garments were elaborately slashed, with jewelled clasps supposedly holding the slashes together. Beards also came into fashion about this time. By the late 1520s men's dress emphasized an aggressively masculine bulk of figure, with a wide gown, the sleeves of which were pushed into a leg-of-mutton shape above slits at the elbows, and with lapels that tended to protrude beyond the shoulder. Holbein's portraits of *Henry VIII* in the 1530s, such as the cartoon of 1537 (London, N.P.G.), epitomize this look. During the 1520s and 1530s the previously smocked necklines of men's shirts began to develop a tiny frill above the smocking. By the end of the 1520s the square bonnet was beginning to be replaced by a round cap, trimmed with chains and medallions under the brim with small feathers along its edge.

The bulky look persisted in men's dress until the late 1540s, after which the bulk was confined to the shoulder area, but without the leg-of-mutton sleeves. The waist was drawn in and the gown shortened to display slightly padded breeches, often slashed, which stopped above the knee. In the 1540s it became usual to close the coat right up to the neck, with the frilled shirt collar peeping over its collar (Christoph Amberger's portrait of *Christoph Fugger*, 1541; Munich, Alte Pin.). In the 1550s the gown was replaced by a short cape, and the doublet became the main garment for display, with elaborate small-scale slashing and a rising collar used to support the shirt collar in its carefully set figure-of-eight folds (e.g. Antonis Mor's portrait of the *Emperor Maximilian II*, 1550; Madrid, Prado). The shirt cuffs were set in similar, but smaller, folds. Below the waist the breeches were heavily padded, making them stand away from the body, much as women's skirts did. During the 1540s the bonnet brim was gradually turned down towards a horizontal line, and in the 1550s the crown of the bonnet began to rise.

During the 1540s a few portraits of Englishwomen show a new type of gown, with a high standing collar and puffy, full-length sleeves, which closed down the centre front. This garment was perhaps preferred by women who disliked the extremely artificial body shape that fashion was now demanding; it converted them into a series of geometric shapes, with the triangular shape of the bodice and its pointed waistline being echoed in the sleeves and skirt with its triangular centre-front opening. The conical shape of the skirt was supported by the farthingale, a Spanish invention, worn under the skirt from *c.* 1530 (*see* §1(ii) above). A square shape was provided by the neckline, which was now out to the point of the shoulders. The gowns were presumably held up by extremely tight lacing, which completely flattened the bust (e.g. portraits by Master John of *Mary Tudor*, 1544, and *Lady Jane Grey*, *c.* 1545; both London, N.P.G.). This neckline, however, was shortly to pass from fashion, as the area of the square was filled in with a high-necked shirt with a frilled collar; this fashion, sometimes with a network of jewels across the shoulders, persisted in France until the early 1570s, by which time the sleeves had shrunk inwards to fit the arms while developing a puff at the sleeve head (e.g. François Clouet's *Elizabeth of Austria, Queen of France*, ?1571; Paris, Louvre). In England the high-necked shirt was worn under a partlet with a standing collar. At first the partlet finished at the same point across the body as the old square neckline; gradually it was incorporated into the structure of the bodice of the gown itself, until by the end of the decade all-in-one bodices were worn, as in the portrait, by Antonis Mor, of *Mary Tudor* (1544; Madrid, Prado; *see* MOR, ANTONIS, fig. 1). In England in the 1550s the hood rose away from the head at the sides and developed a squared outline; in France it was reduced to little more than a curve of goldsmith's work at the back of the head, and jewels were wound into the hair, as shown in François Clouet's drawing of *Marguerite of Navarre as a Child* (*c.* 1560; Chantilly, Mus. Condé). In both countries women puffed their hair out at the temples.

During the 1550s funnel-shaped sleeves disappeared from fashion. By the end of the decade, many women in England and the Netherlands were wearing gowns (often in black) with short puffed sleeves and bands of contrasting trimming (black velvet on black satin or wool). In the Netherlands these gowns were worn open and falling loosely from the shoulders, but in England and in some areas of Germany they tended to be worn closed and almost suffocatingly tight, with high, tight collars supporting the ruffs, as in Mor's portrait of *Metgen, the Artist's Wife* (*c.* 1554; Madrid, Prado). There is some evidence that gowns of the loose type were occasionally worn in the Iberian peninsula, and it is just possible that they originated there, since they are also found in the Netherlands, on Spanish sitters (e.g. Willem Key's *Leonora Lopez de Villa Nueva, c.* 1566; Paris, Louvre). However, they are not stiff enough to fall in with Spanish taste during most of the rest of the century and were perhaps worn mainly for comfort by pregnant or older women (e.g. portrait of *Lady Dacre* by HANS EWORTH, *c.* 1555–8; Ottawa, N.G.).

Women continued to wear the short-sleeved overgown into the 1560s, but Netherlandish women preferred to wear it fastened only at the neck, a convention depicted in the *Family of Pierre de Moucheron*; see fig. 35, attributed to Cornelis de Zeeu (*fl* 1558–90). Towards the end of the decade the puff became confined to an area around the tops of the arms; sometimes the outer gown was dispensed with, to display a very tight, low-necked bodice, with croissant-like puffs as shoulder-straps and a matching

skirt. In England this allowed the display of elaborately embroidered shirts, partially opened across the upper chest (e.g. Nicholas Hilliard's *Elizabeth I*, 1572; London, N.P.G.). Frenchwomen and Netherlandish women preferred to wear gown sleeves made from rich silks, decorated with tiny slashes and puffs, and to open only the ruff (Adriaen Key's *Maria de Deckere and Daughter*, ?1575; Antwerp, Kon. Mus. S. Kst.). In the 1570s sleeves gradually grew larger, first through the addition of a gauze oversleeve and then, *c.* 1575, by making the gown sleeve run in one piece from the line of the 'croissant' to the wrist. Around 1570 women started to wear the same puffy-crowned caps as men, although the French hood still had some devotees (e.g. Master of the Countess of Warwick's portrait of an *Unknown Young Lady*, 1576; London, Tate).

In the 1560s and 1570s men also might wear a sleeveless overgarment, a jerkin, often of leather or buff, which was usually slashed and pinked over much of its surface, the pinking often extending to the sleeves of the doublet. From the 1560s men are frequently found wearing straight collars turned down over their high doublet collars (e.g. François Clouet's portrait of *Pierre Quthe*, 1562; Paris, Louvre). By 1563 men were wearing so much padding in their breeches that Charles IX of France (1560–74) tried to limit its use. Padding must also have been used in the fronts of doublets, which were beginning to acquire a keel-shaped line down the centre front, as shown in Frans Pourbus the elder's *Portrait of a Gentleman* (1574; London, Wallace). The breeches of the 1560s tended to be equally wide from hip to knee, but in the 1570s they moved further up the leg, flaring out from the waist, so that men's torsos were composed of two triangles, joined at a narrow V-shaped waistline.

In the late 1570s both men's and women's neck ruffs grew much larger, standing well out over the shoulders and much more obviously incorporating lace and cutwork. The need to provide visual balance as the ruff grew wider was presumably the reason for the puffing out of women's hair at the sides of the head, for yet another ballooning-out of the sleeves in the 1580s and for the introduction in

35. *Family of Pierre de Moucheron*, attributed to Cornelis de Zeeu (*fl* 1558–90), oil on panel, 1.08×2.46 m (Amsterdam, Rijksmuseum)

36. *Ball of the Duc de Joyeuse*, Franco-Flemish school, oil on copper, 415×650 mm, 1581 (Paris, Musée du Louvre)

France, in the early 1580s, of a drum-shaped skirt to replace the old cone-shaped one. By the end of the 1580s this new skirt, with a small self-coloured frill at the waist, was normal in England. It is seen in the Franco-Flemish school painting of the *Ball of the Duc de Joyeuse* (1581; see fig. 36). In the 1560s and 1570s women had worn men's hats and sometimes garments based on their doublets (anonymous portrait of *Elizabeth I, c.* 1575; London, N.P.G.). In the 1580s men reversed the borrowing, wore earrings and grew their hair to their shoulders. They temporarily discarded the padding from their breeches, adopting a knee-length version that fitted like a second skin; the two narrow triangles of the legs were repeated as three similar triangles above the waist—a long triangular bodice between two long triangular sleeves. By the late 1580s some breeches had shrunk to the tops of the thighs, where they were once again padded; by about 1595 it was possible to wear these shorter breeches over the longer, tighter ones. Hats developed very tall, conical crowns. The longer hair was difficult to wear with ruffs, and turned-down collars, with or without lace edges, are very common in the 1590s. By 1600 the hook at the end of the doublet's 'keel' line looked as though it were digging into the wearer's groin (*Young Man among Roses*, attributed to Hilliard, *c.* 1588; London, V&A). Fashionable women in France and England wore gowns with drum-shaped skirts beneath bodices that repeated the three triangles of men's torsos. The ruff was flattened under the chin or opened out to form a frame round the back of the head, and the hair was piled on top of the head (anonymous portrait of *Antoinette d'Orléans*, end of 16th century; Paris, Louvre).

By about 1600 the open ruff was being replaced by a standing pleated collar. Englishwomen's taste ran to mixing wildly different fabrics in the same outfit and to piling on as many jewels as possible, even though many of them are almost invisible against the patterns of the textiles of their clothes. The body's natural proportions were further obscured by 1600 by the shortening of the skirt to reveal the shoes and the lengthening of the point at the bodice's waistline; this point did not, however, turn inwards.

BIBLIOGRAPHY

J. de Alcega: *Libro de geometria pratica, y traça* (Madrid, 1589); Eng. trans. as *A Tailor's Pattern Book* (London, 1979)

C. Vecellio: *Habiti antichi et moderni di tutto il mondo* (Venice, 1598); Eng. trans. as *Vecellio's Renaissance Costume Book* (New York, 1977)

M. J. Friedländer: *Die altniederländische Malerei* (Berlin, 1924–37); Eng. trans. as *Early Netherlandish Painting*, 14 vols (Leiden, 1967–76)

R. Strong: *The English Icon: Elizabethan and Jacobean Portraiture* (London and New York, 1969)

P. Mellen: *Jean Clouet* (London, 1971) [complete edition of the drawings, miniatures and paintings]

S. M. Newton: *Fashion in the Age of the Black Prince: A Study of the Years 1340–1365* (Woodbridge, 1980)

M. Scott: *Late Gothic Europe, 1400–1500*, The History of Dress (London, 1980)

Princely Magnificence: Court Jewels of the Renaissance (exh. cat., ed. A. Somers Cocks; London, V&A, 1980)

R. M. Anderson: 'Spanish Dress Worn by a Queen of France', *Gaz. B.-A.*, cxx (1981), pp. 215–22

J. Ashelford: *The Sixteenth Century, A Visual History of Costume* (London, 1983)

A. Carter: 'Mary Tudor's Wardrobe', *Costume*, xviii (1984), pp. 9–28

J. Arnold: *Patterns of Fashion: The Cut and Construction of Clothes for Men and Women, c. 1560–1620* (London, 1985)

M. Scott: *The Fourteenth & Fifteenth Centuries*, A Visual History of Costume (London, 1986)

J. Ashelford: *Dress in the Age of Elizabeth I* (London, 1988)

MARGARET SCOTT

VI. 17th century–early 18th.

At the beginning of the 17th century Spain was still an important military, political and economic power, and Spanish dress, with its stiff geometric shapes and sombre patterned stuffs used as a foil for rich jewellery, was the dominant influence in Europe. By 1650 dramatic changes had taken place in the balance of power; Spain was in decline and most countries on the Continent had felt the effects of the Thirty Years War (1618–48). The collections of states that made up Germany and Italy were pushed to the sidelines of history—a position reflected in their somewhat static and regionalized forms of dress. By astute diplomacy, France had come to the fore: French fashions prevailed, and during the long reign of Louis XIV (1643–1715) the cultural and sartorial dictates emanating from his court at Versailles went unchallenged throughout fashionable Europe.

1. Spanish influence, *c.* 1600–25. 2. England and the Netherlands, *c.* 1625–60. 3. French dominance, *c.* 1660–1715.

1. SPANISH INFLUENCE, *c.* 1600–25. The stylized distortions of the body initiated by Spanish dress in the later 16th century often led high fashion into bizarre exaggeration: for example, at the court of James I of England. The austere and hierarchical elements of Spanish costume, on the other hand, could mingle with regional and traditional themes in certain countries, notably Italy and the Netherlands, to produce distinctive national styles. Many of the elements of Spanish dress are to be seen in

38. *Edward Sackville, 4th Earl of Dorset,* attributed to William Larkin, oil on canvas, 2.07×1.22 m, *c.* 1613 (London, Ranger's House)

the costume of the upper classes of the northern Netherlands, despite the hostility of the burgher oligarchy towards Spain. Men and women wore dark colours (the most conservative wore black) and heavily starched Spanish ruffs. In addition, the women often wore the *vlieger*, a black overgown derived from an open Spanish gown, or *ropa*, and a long pointed stomacher (*borst*), also of Spanish origin. This kind of dress, with some variations, also prevailed in the southern Netherlands: in 1609–10 Peter Paul Rubens painted himself and his new wife Isabella Brant in a Flemish interpretation of Spanish dress in *Rubens and Isabella Brant in the Honeysuckle Bower* (Munich, Alte Pin.; see fig. 37). His costume is a typical Spanish mixture of muted opulence—a black hat with jewelled hatband, a fine *reticella* lace collar, a tight-fitting embroidered doublet, patterned silk breeches and a satin cloak. Isabella Brant wears a light-hearted version of the high bourgeois 'Regent' costume (suitable for a bride) made of the richest materials: with the exception of the lace cap and ruff, the whole outfit, including the lining of the straw hat, is made of silk. The relaxed feel of Rubens's depiction of Arcadian bliss and the way in which the Baroque artist has subdued the minutiae of high fashion

37. *Rubens and Isabella Brant in the Honeysuckle Bower* by Peter Paul Rubens, oil on canvas laid down on panel, 1.78×1.36 m, 1609–10 (Munich, Alte Pinakothek)

almost conceals the fact that the costume is rich, patterned and constricting. Early 17th-century dress was highly ornamented, and its exaggerated shapes were created by padding and boning. For women high fashion demanded a tight-fitting bodice (usually boned) and on formal occasions a farthingale, a hooped under-petticoat made of cane or whalebone. While the Spanish farthingale was a relatively modest cone shape, that worn in England and France was a vast drum shape, a style particularly favoured by James I's wife Anne of Denmark, as is apparent in such portraits of her as that by Marcus Gheeraerts the younger (*c.* 1605–10; Woburn Abbey, Beds).

England in the late 16th century and the early 17th was culturally somewhat cut off from the rest of Europe and had developed a distinctive, quirky style in dress noted for an exaggeration of outline and an obsession with ornament. Vast padded sleeves, a low décolletage, a pointed boned bodice and a huge farthingale gave the fashionable woman the appearance of a doll, full of artifice and uncertain of movement. Nor were men immune to this love of exaggeration and display. On occasions of great splendour a rich and disjointed look was created by a tight doublet and vast breeches, while the head was almost cut off from the body by a large lace collar or a ruff. A portrait of *Edward Sackville, 4th Earl of Dorset* (*c.* 1613; London, Ranger's House; see fig. 38), attributed to William Larkin, shows the sitter wearing the wide, baggy breeches, aptly called 'slops', that were very much in fashion in northern Europe in the second decade of the century. The whole costume is dominated by ornament and trimming, most notably the fine floral embroidery (a long-established English taste) on doublet, breeches and cloak. Particularly striking are the luxurious shoe roses, puffball arrangements of spangled silk rivalling in delicacy the fine snowflake lace collar.

2. ENGLAND AND THE NETHERLANDS, *c.* 1625–60. During the 1620s there was a movement away from distortion, decoration and fantasy in dress towards a simplified and more fluid line allied to the contours of the body. Harsh lines, patterned silks and spiky lace gave way to a new, rounded look, plain satins and soft bobbin lace. This new mood of casual elegance, relying more on cut than on surface decoration, originated in France and was popularized in England by Henrietta Maria, the French wife of Charles I; it is exemplified in Anthony van Dyck's portrait of her (1632; Windsor Castle, Berks, Royal Col.). Although on formal occasions it was necessary to wear the stiffly boned bodice, skirt and elaborate overgown, the most popular styles were either a simple bodice and skirt or a gown made in one piece, often of satin and perhaps with large, softly billowing sleeves pinned with jewelled clasps *à l'antique*; it was fashionable to be *en déshabillé*. Such informality, however contrived, had a great appeal for artists such as van Dyck: the play of light on plain lustrous silks and the simplification of fashion essentials—sometimes it is difficult to know where the dividing line between reality and artistic invention lies—pleased the artist and his clients. It set a trend in fashionable portraiture that was taken up by Peter Lely and Godfrey Kneller in England and by Sébastien Bourdon and Pierre Mignard I in France and continued well into the 18th century.

It is difficult to see fashion in the 1630s except through van Dyck's English portraits, so perfectly did he interpret the new aesthetic of the carefully careless but aristocratic simplicity of style. By the 1630s men were wearing doublets of plain, muted colours, often slashed on the chest and sleeves with subtly contrasting silk; breeches were increasingly long and tubular. Instead of shoes many men wore boots of fine soft leather from Córdoba. A casually dishevelled look was considered modish; doublet and breeches were often partially unbuttoned, the soft boots rolled down the legs, and the cloak was slung over the shoulder. In van Dyck's portrait of *Lords John and Bernard Stuart* (*c.* 1639; London, N.G.; see fig. 39) the elegant bravado of the sitters' pose and costume is clearly displayed. The unstructured nature of the costume helped to create greater ease of movement, but it was still made of silk, albeit with far less trimming than previously. Such 'delight in disorder' was very much an aristocratic conceit, to which few could aspire with success. Alongside it was a movement towards greater sobriety in masculine dress in the later 1630s. Middle-class taste, whether in England or the Netherlands, was for sombre-coloured woollen stuffs and plain linen, as demonstrated in the portrait of *Jan Pellicorne and his Son Casper* (after 1635; London,

39. *Lords John and Bernard Stuart* by Anthony van Dyck, oil on canvas, 2.37×1.46 m, *c.* 1639 (London, National Gallery)

Wallace), previously attributed to Rembrandt. Nevertheless, most men followed the prevailing French cut in dress, which meant a short doublet and long, fairly tight breeches. An alternative style, from the mid-1640s, was an eccentric fashion originating in Germany for wide, open-ended breeches, sometimes called 'petticoat breeches', which vastly increased in size during the 1650s. With the shorter doublet of that decade, wide, square collar, short, voluminous breeches and squared-off shoes or boots, men assumed the shape of a set of squares. Such a costume, when exaggerated by the demands of high fashion and trimmed with bunches of silk ribbon, made men look like may-poles. The style may be seen in Gerard ter Borch (ii)'s *Portrait of a Man in Black* (1656; London, N.G.). Although such breeches were German in origin, the interpretation of the new style, with the constituent parts of the costume seemingly shrinking apart from each other, divided by billowing shirt and bunches of ribbon, was French in its dishevelled elegance.

3. FRENCH DOMINANCE, c. 1660–1715. By the 1660s the fashion lead of France was undisputed in tailoring, dress-making and the production of fashion accessories such as fans, gloves and hats. France even successfully challenged the long-held Italian supremacy in the production of fine silks when in the late 1660s silk-weaving was established as a state monopoly under the aegis of Louis XIV's great minister of state, Jean-Baptiste Colbert. The stipulation that silk manufacturers were to produce patterns twice a year helped to further the cause of fashion and was partly responsible for the relatively rapid changes in style that characterize the period, especially in men's dress. It is debatable how far the invention of the new style of the later 1660s—a loose-fitting, knee-length 'vest' and coat—should be attributed to France or to England.

From the early 1660s various kinds of loose, coatlike garments were experimented with. A short-sleeved vest was worn at the French court at the same time as a similar gown, possibly inspired by theatrical interpretations of the Orient, was introduced into England. Another garment was a wide-sleeved coat of military origin called a 'cassock', which could be worn over either the doublet or the 'vest'. By c. 1670 the new line had settled down, as can be seen in Gillis van Tilborgh's *The Tichborne Dole* (1671; Tichborne House, Hants; see fig. 40), in which the men wear knee-length coats and waistcoats (vests) over knee-breeches (*culottes*). The idea of the three-piece suit had been established, a concept that still remains an essential part of the male wardrobe. Both coat and waistcoat were sleeved and the same length, but the waistcoat gradually shortened as the century progressed. By the end of the 17th century the coat became the epitome of formality, fitted to the body and with fullness at the side achieved by pleats stiffened with horse-hair—the French word *justaucorps* aptly conveys the notion of tailoring close to the body. Late 17th-century fashion plates record relatively minor changes in such details as sleeves and pockets: by the 1690s the sleeve had lengthened and there was a large cuff; the flapped pockets were horizontal to begin with, became vertical in the 1680s and then went back to horizontal from the 1690s.

From the 1660s, following the relatively free and easy styles worn by women in the middle years of the century, the image conveyed in the dress of both sexes was of a ponderous, elaborate and Baroque formality. With this reversion to greater rigidity came the reintroduction of a long, pointed, boned bodice laced up the back and increasing elaboration, both in the complicated back draperies of the gown and in the three-dimensional trimming on the skirt. The type of dress worn by the

40. *The Tichborne Dole* (detail) by Gillis van Tilborgh, oil on canvas, 1.17×2.07 m, 1671 (Tichborne House, Hants)

fashionable women to the right in *The Tichborne Dole*—a boned bodice, short sleeves trimmed with layers of lace and an overskirt with a train—became fossilized as French court dress at Versailles. This costume, the *grand habit*, can be seen worn by the Duchesse de Ventadour in the group attributed to François de Troy of *Louis XIV and his Heirs* (*c.* 1710; London, Wallace; see fig. 41). The governess, who holds the leading reins of the infant Duc de Bretagne, wears formal court dress in black silk, the stiff bodice and short sleeves decorated with jewelled clasps similar to those that hold back the train at the sides. This kind of dress, with minor changes in understructure, remained the rule for formal occasions at court until the French Revolution.

It is not surprising, considering the heavy, ornate and cumbersome costume demanded on formal occasions, that on more private occasions both men and women preferred to relax in loose gowns that could be worn over shirt and breeches or over shift and stays. For men a release from the formality of the suit could be obtained by wearing one of the many popular 'oriental' morning gowns that wrapped at the front and were kept in place with a sash, and a soft cap worn over the shaved head in place of the wig. This comfortable and exotic outfit appears frequently in informal portraits of artists and men of letters. The fondness for loose draperies was reflected both in the reality of the loose morning gown for men and in the more fanciful unreality of the informal image of many fashionable female portrait sitters. Prevailing artistic notions with regard to dress—the search for a 'timeless' costume, or a fondness for the allegorical or classicizing—sometimes led to the invention of imaginary dress, albeit loosely based on the informal gown worn by women as a morning undress. Such is the case in the portrait by Willem Wissing and Jan van der Vaardt of *Frances Theresa Stuart, Duchess of Richmond and Lennox* (1687; London, N.P.G.; see fig. 42), where it is impossible to state how far the loose gown, with jewelled front fastenings, is a real garment. The ermine-lined robe draped asymmetrically in a manner deriving from Baroque portraiture is a tactful reference to the sitter's rank and to her presence at the coronation of James II in 1686. The agreeable, if contrived, negligence in attire displayed by 'La Belle Stuart' is typical of the English attitude to clothing in portraiture. It demonstrates a preference for informality compared to the rich formality seen in France, imprisoned by the stifling etiquette established by the Sun King at Versailles. The group portrait of *Louis XIV and his Heirs* (fig. 41) sums up the sartorial achievements of his reign. The seated King and the Dauphin behind his chair wear suits of rich velvet

41. *Louis XIV and his Heirs*, attributed to François de Troy, oil on canvas, 1.29×1.62 m, *c.* 1710 (London, Wallace Collection)

taste come under attack, and with it the assumption, hitherto almost undisputed, that French taste in all the arts was superior. The reign of Louis XVI (1774–93) brought a new emphasis on informality in dress, with the adoption of simpler, more functional styles from England. This was further encouraged by the political pressures of the French Revolution, when the silken splendour and cumbersome absurdities of court dress lost favour, along with the aristocratic caste, and an equation was made between democracy and simpler styles in plain fabrics such as woollen stuffs, linen and cotton. By the end of the century there was a growing divide between the costume of the sexes. Men's dress was sober, plain and work-orientated, but women continued to be conspicuous consumers of luxury in dress and accessories; denied political power or careers that would make use of their talents, they turned their energies to the creation of themselves as works of art in the field of high fashion.

1. Régence and Rococo styles, *c.* 1715–65. 2. French formality and English informality, *c.* 1765–89. 3. The influence of the French Revolution, *c.* 1789–1800.

1. RÉGENCE AND ROCOCO STYLES, *c.* 1715–65. The 18th century in France may be said to have begun in 1715, with the regency of the art-loving Philippe II, Duc d'Orléans. The RÉGENCE STYLE was characterized by a new mood of lightness that was partly the result of a feeling of relief after the strain of the last gloomy years of Louis XIV at Versailles. This lightness was reflected in all the arts, including dress. On formal occasions women

42. *Frances Theresa Stuart, Duchess of Richmond and Lennox* by Willem Wissing and Jan van der Vaardt, oil on canvas, 2.16×1.30 m, 1687 (London, National Portrait Gallery)

and great full-bottomed wigs that help to create an impressive dignity of demeanour. On the right stands Louis, Duc de Bourgogne, whose bright-coloured suit and lower wig indicate the more relaxed luxury of the early 18th century.

BIBLIOGRAPHY
F. van Thienen: *Costume of the Western World: The Great Age of Holland, 1600–1660* (London, 1951)
C. W. Cunnington and P. Cunnington: *Handbook of English Costume in the Seventeenth Century* (London, 1955, 3/1972)
De mode in Rubens' tijd [Fashion in the Time of Rubens] (exh. cat., ed. J. Walgrave; Deurne, Prov. Mus. Sterckshof, 1977)
V. Cumming: *The Seventeenth Century*, A Visual History of Costume (London, 1984)
D. de Marly: *Costume and Civilization: Louis XIV and Versailles* (London, 1987)

VII. Early to late 18th century.

Louis XIV was so successful in establishing his court as a culture in which dress and etiquette played a major part that after his death (1715) and throughout the 18th century French fashion remained dominant in Europe and its colonies. Only in the last quarter of the century, under the influence of the ideas of the Enlightenment, did court

43. *L'Enseigne de Gersaint* (detail) by Antoine Watteau, oil on canvas, 1.66×3.06 m, 1720 (Berlin, Schloss Charlottenburg)

wore an elaborately trimmed gown with stylized back drapery, the *mantua*, which was designed to reveal a decorated skirt. The most popular informal dress was a loose, floating robe known as a *sacque*, which had started as a dressing-gown or morning gown in the later 17th century, gradually gaining acceptance as day-wear in the 18th. In the early part of the century the *sacque* formed a graceful bell shape over the conical hoops that were in fashion from around 1710. The loose pleats that fell from the top of the dress at the back are sometimes called 'Watteau' pleats, after Antoine Watteau, who seems, in such paintings as *L'Enseigne de Gersaint* (1720; Berlin, Schloss Charlottenburg; see fig. 43), particularly to have appreciated the graceful fall of these unbroken pyramids of silk.

By the 1730s the *sacque* had become more formal, with a fitted waist at the sides and more regulated sewn-down pleats at the back. Usually the *sacque* was worn with a matching skirt. By the mid-18th century it was worn on formal occasions, except at court where the *grand habit* (*see* §VI, 3 above) was necessary for most ceremonial functions, and it was so identified with French taste all over Europe that it became known as a *robe à la française*. An alternative to both the *sacque* and the *mantua* was a

tight-bodied open gown in the English style, which could be worn with whalebone stays on the kind of formal occasion depicted by Charles Philips in his *Tea Party at Lord Harrington's House* (1730; New Haven, CT, Yale Cent. Brit. A.; see fig. 44). The English in the early 18th century had a somewhat ambivalent attitude—at once envious and censorious—to French dress, and the *robe à la française* was little worn there until the 1740s, when it was more tight-fitting and formal.

Few changes in men's dress are worth recording in the early 18th century. The basic outfit was still the three-piece suit, usually of silk but often in muted colours for everyday wear. On gala occasions it was trimmed with gold or silver lace, and the waistcoat, often of contrasting colour to the coat and breeches, was highly decorated with embroidery, metal lace and bullion fringe. By the 1720s full-bottomed periwigs were restricted to professional men, officially conservative in their dress. Shorter periwigs became popular, and some styles had tied locks, which derived from the military campaigns of the War of the Spanish Succession (1700–14), when there had to be practical attempts to reduce the size of the huge wigs then in vogue. In the 1730s the young man of fashion began to wear a very short wig, the back hair tied with black silk

44. *Tea Party at Lord Harrington's House* by Charles Philips, oil on canvas, 1.02×1.26 m, 1730 (New Haven, CT, Yale Center for British Art)

45. *Madame de Pompadour* by François Boucher, oil on canvas, 2.01×1.57 m, 1756 (Munich, Alte Pinakothek)

ribbon or enclosed in a black silk bag and the side hair curled, echoing the neat, curled *tête de mouton* hairstyles of the chic, seductive women painted by François Boucher.

These pretty coiffures, sometimes decorated with flowers, lace, jewels or feathers, formed the apex of the triangular silhouette of the fashionable mid-18th-century woman with her large hooped petticoat, a shape emphasized by a riot of pattern and trimming on the dress. The Rococo style in costume, which was in vogue throughout the 1740s and 1750s, demonstrated the possibilities of three-dimensional decoration on dress: frills, flounces, ruffles and flowers were explorations of the art of the serpentine curve, the shell and the scallop shapes that were also to be seen in lace patterns and fashionable accessories such as the fan. The main inspiration for the Rococo style was the Marquise de Pompadour, *maîtresse en titre* to Louis XV from 1745 and an important arbiter of taste and patron of the arts until her death in 1764 (*see* PASTEL, colour pl. V). In Boucher's portrait of her, dated 1756 (Munich, Alte Pin.; see fig. 45), she seems to embody a refinement of Rococo taste that in less expert hands could seem a fussy over-indulgence. Her dress is a sea-green taffeta open robe with matching skirt trimmed with pink roses. The stomacher of her bodice is decorated with pink and silver ribbon bows. Her hair is lightly powdered, and her mules are of striped pink and silver silk, trimmed with silver braid. The final touch is supplied by the bunch of flowers pinned to her bodice, which was undoubtedly kept fresh with the aid of a tiny water-filled 'bosom-bottle', covered with silk to match the dress.

In England the Rococo spirit in female dress was more muted, with fewer frills and with textiles in restrained floral designs, often fine, botanically inspired silks woven by Huguenot craftsmen in Spitalfields, London. More in the English spirit was an Arcadian interpretation of the Rococo, with modest ribbonry and *bergère* hats, suitable for walking out of doors. English ladies dressed in this way are shown in landscape settings in such paintings as Arthur Devis's *Sir George and Lady Strickland in Boynton Hall Park* (1751; Hull, Ferens A.G.) and Thomas Gainsborough's *Mary, Countess Howe* (1763–4; London, Kenwood House) and *Mr and Mrs Andrews* (*c.* 1748–50; London, N.G.; *see* GAINSBOROUGH, THOMAS, fig. 1).

2. FRENCH FORMALITY AND ENGLISH INFORMALITY, *c.* 1765–89. Another result of the Rococo influence was an increased lightness and elegance in the dress of men and women in the second half of the 18th century. By the 1770s the masculine suit was a triumph of elegant tailoring, the coat cut narrow across the shoulders and the fronts curving away to reveal a much shorter waistcoat. The heavy stiffened side pleats and large cuffs had disappeared; fabrics were light silks with delicate embroidery or gold or silver lace. The exception to this rule of sophisticated simplicity were the high, powdered bag wigs worn by men at this time, the formal outfit being completed by a sword and a *chapeau bras*, a flattened version of the tricorn or bicorn hat designed to be carried under the arm rather than worn on the head. This is the kind of costume depicted so well by Jean-Michel Moreau in his plates for the second and third series (1777, 1783) of the famous *Monument de costume physique et moral de la fin du dix-huitième siècle* (*see* FASHION PLATE AND COSTUME BOOK,

46. *La Sortie de l'Opéra*, engraving by G. Malbeste after Jean-Michel Moreau, 266×220 mm, *c.* 1777 (London, British Museum)

fig. 1), a work that records the manners and morals of the last years of the *ancien régime* in France. In *La Sortie de l'Opéra* (*c.* 1777; London, BM; see fig. 46) the main figure descending the stairs accompanied by attentive gentlemen is a grand lady in a formal gown (probably a *sacque*), which is worn over a large hoop and elaborately trimmed; the high headdress on top of her piled-up, pomaded and powdered hair adds a further touch of exaggerated yet stately elegance to her appearance. Her rich but awkward dress is in contrast to the stylish costume worn by the woman right of centre, whose tight-fitting *robe à l'anglaise* has the overgown fastened up in swags at the back, in a style called *à la polonaise*. Even the attendant on the right, with a basket of posies, has the back drapery of her *sacque* caught up in imitation of the popular fashion for kilting up the overskirt of the gown.

The rage for novelty that is the essence of fashion was fuelled from the 1770s onwards by the production of fashion plates, which largely replaced the dressed dolls that had previously been one of the main sources of information on styles in vogue (*see* FASHION PLATE AND COSTUME BOOK). Fashion magazines, published in England and France, coincided with a new taste for the informal in dress and in France led to the promotion of English fashions, particularly during the 1780s, the decade of Anglomania. This is most obvious in men's dress. While the French had cultivated the refinements of formal dress, with sumptuous luxury fabrics and trimmings, the English had favoured plainer, more practical and less formal garments cut with increasing professionalism. Among

47. *Morning Walk* by Thomas Gainsborough, oil on canvas, 2.36×1.79 m, *c.* 1785 (London, National Gallery)

these was the frock-coat, originally an informal hunting coat in which the large, cumbersome cuffs and side pleats of the formal coat were replaced with slit cuffs and the minimum of stiffened fabric in the skirts. It was often worn untrimmed, and its most characteristic feature was a small turned-down collar. Made of humbler materials than the formal coat, it became by mid-century the basic everyday coat for the middle-class Englishman. By the 1770s it was worn everywhere in England, except at court, and increasingly on the Continent, even in France. It is to be seen in numerous portraits of the period, perhaps most notably in Joseph Wright of Derby's portrait of *Brooke Boothby* (1781; London, Tate), reclining in relaxed comfort in a landscape setting. With the frock-coat, which was usually dark in colour, a plain waistcoat and light, often buff-coloured, breeches would be worn. Spotless plain white linen would take the place of lace, and real hair that of the formal wig. Another functional garment was the caped greatcoat, worn by coachmen and taken into the wardrobe of the man of fashion. It was a style well suited to the life of the nobility and gentry, which increasingly, in the last quarter of the century, revolved around outdoor activities; it was also, however, suited to the ethos of a growing class of businessmen and industrial entrepreneurs.

By the late 18th century the stylish Englishman was to be seen in what amounted to a uniform mode of attire. In the country he wore the appropriate costume of frock-coat and buff breeches, unpowdered hair and hunting boots. In the city or on more formal occasions he was to be seen, like William Hallett in Gainsborough's *Morning Walk* (*c.* 1785; London, N.G.; see fig. 47), with hair lightly powdered, dressed in a black suit, the frock-coat cut sharply away at the sides. A very similar costume can be seen in Jacques-Louis David's nearly contemporary portrait of the chemist *Antoine-Laurent de Lavoisier and his Wife* (1788; New York, Met.). In both paintings the women wear clothes of a carefully contrived simplicity, combining plain fabrics such as silk, gauze and starched muslin. Mme Lavoisier's hair is loosely curled on her head and trails down her back, while Mrs Hallett wears a wide-brimmed hat with a *panache* of white ostrich feathers.

The dresses of Mrs Hallett and Mme Lavoisier illustrate the love of plain fabrics that characterized women's dress in the decade before the French Revolution. Where patterns existed they were small and quite subdued, an exception being the dramatic floral designs of the printed cottons and linens increasingly worn as a fashionable *déshabillé*: by the last quarter of the 18th century the silk industries in France and England—the two leading countries of fashion—were in some danger from the modish preference for these cottons and linens. A further loss of income to those engaged in the silk industry came about as a result of the great popularity among women during the 1780s of English woollen riding habits and greatcoats, so appropriate for their more open-air existence as they came to identify with the supposed simplicities of nature and country life, as extolled by urban philosophers. Joshua Reynolds's portrait of *Lady Worsley* (1780; Harewood House, W. Yorks) shows such a riding habit.

3. THE INFLUENCE OF THE FRENCH REVOLUTION, *c.* 1789–1800. No abrupt change in styles of clothing marked the year 1789, although the turbulence of the

48. *Simon Chénard as a Sans-culotte* by Louis-Léopold Boilly, oil on canvas, 1792 (Paris, Musée Carnavalet)

French Revolution undoubtedly quickened the pace of altering fashion. It also provided a clear example of how clothes can be linked to politics. Expensive silks may have come to be associated with aristocracy, and cheaper, plainer fabrics with democracy, but it was the French court itself, in the 1780s, that had paved the way for the popularization of English sporting styles and informal cottons and linens. As early as 1774 Johann Wolfgang von Goethe dressed the hero of his novel *Die Leiden des jungen Werthers* in a romanticized version of the Englishman's sporting costume—dark-blue coat with buff waistcoat and breeches, and boots—in contrast to the aristocrats' old-fashioned, rich, 'gothic' dress. To those in France with revolutionary sympathies this kind of 'natural' dress, evoking the relative political and legal freedoms of English society, was the obvious choice. It also demonstrated kinship with the dispossessed, the *sans-culottes* (literally 'without breeches'), in their often deliberately slovenly costume of short jacket and baggy trousers—the clothing of the working man as seen, for example, in Louis-Léopold Boilly's portrait of the actor *Simon Chenard as a Sans-culotte* (1792; Paris, Carnavalet; see fig. 48).

The portraits of David and his contemporaries amply illustrate the stylish versions of English country clothing worn by upper- and middle-class Revolutionaries. Most notable, perhaps, is David's portrait of his brother-in-law *Pierre Sériziat* (exh. Salon 1795; Paris, Louvre), in which the sitter wears a dark coat, buff breeches and top-boots and sits on a caped greatcoat; the tall, tapering round hat

replaces the formal three-cornered type, too much identified with stuffy etiquette. So all-pervading did this kind of dress become in France, on both sides of the political divide, that even the *Incroyables*—ultra-fashionable young men with anti-Jacobin sentiments—wore exaggerated versions of it. In Boilly's *Point de convention* (*c*. 1795–9) a fashionable young man shows off his elegant attire, a double-breasted coat with huge lapels, skin-tight breeches, boots and a round hat. His hair is carefully dishevelled and lightly powdered, and his chin is hidden by a vast, starched cravat. In this particular case his political affiliations are to be seen in the royalist green of his cravat and in his use of hair powder. Those men who supported the Revolution tended to wear their hair cut short *à l'antique*, in a tribute to the heroic days of Classical antiquity, from which much of the political and artistic rhetoric of the period was drawn.

Late in the 1790s some men began to wear tight-fitting pantaloons, aiming at an impression of Classical semi-nudity, but these did not become widely popular until the early 19th century (*see* §VIII, 1 below). More overtly Classical to modern eyes is the style of dress worn by the woman in *Point de convention*, which consists of a sleeveless, transparent shift worn over a brief undergarment, and sandals. This is the kind of extreme Neo-classical look described by contemporaries as *à la sauvage*. The costume had its origins in the simple chemise gown—a tube of white muslin with a drawstring at the neck and a sash at the waist—popularized by Queen Marie-Antoinette and her ladies in the 1780s and illustrated in a number of portraits by Elisabeth Vigée Le Brun and in the portrait of *Lady Elizabeth Foster* (1786; Ickworth, Suffolk, NT) by Angelica Kauffman. During the 1790s it proved protean in its uses, simultaneously comfortable, fashionable and flattering. It could be made of inexpensive cotton or the finest Indian muslin, so long as it was not of silk and therefore 'undemocratic'. By *c*. 1800 most women in Europe had adopted some less extreme version of the Neo-classical dress developed in the salons of *Directoire* France. With regard to male dress, in spite of nods in the direction of *ancien régime* splendour in the uniforms of soldiers, courtiers, diplomats and civil servants in France, under the Consulate and the Empire sombre, well-tailored English styles became the fashionable ideal.

BIBLIOGRAPHY

C. W. Cunnington and P. Cunnington: *Handbook of English Costume in the Eighteenth Century* (London, 1957, rev. 1972)
A. Buck: *Dress in Eighteenth-century England* (London, 1979)
A. Ribeiro: *The Eighteenth Century*, A Visual History of Costume (London, 1983)
——: *Dress in Eighteenth-century Europe, 1715–1789* (London, 1984)
——: *Dress in the French Revolution* (London, 1988)

AILEEN RIBEIRO

VIII. 19th century.

1. Developments in mainstream fashion. 2. The revolt against fashion.

1. DEVELOPMENTS IN MAINSTREAM FASHION. The 18th-century excavations at Pompeii generated an interest in Classical antiquity that, from the 1790s, was reflected in fashionable dress. The natural body became the ideal; stays and petticoats were discarded, while men wore skin-coloured or snuff-coloured garments that gave an impression of nudity. Breeches, often in buckskin, were tight and reached below the knee. Waistcoats were short, reaching

only to the waist, and were worn with frilled shirts and muslin cravats. The English frock-coat with a high collar, which in the 18th century had been a form of rural undress, now became urban high fashion. In London society there was competition between the sporting look and a deliberately unkempt or scruffy appearance. Both fashions were simpler than the continental equivalents, and English country style made a strong impact on French fashion before the Revolution (*see* §VII, 2 above). The man who reformed the situation and applied some disciplined restraint to the sporting look was George 'Beau' Brummell (1778–1840). He demanded excellent cut, eschewed show and insisted on starch to produce a sharper line than the crumpled styles of his contemporaries. Under his influence menswear became smarter. He took the country look and disciplined it into town attire, not by introducing new garments but by improving what existed already. He showed that simple black or blue coats were appropriate for evening receptions, and by 1810 the black English evening suit was the result. British simplicity had triumphed over continental swagger, reflecting the British military triumph over the French emperor.

Trousers gradually replaced breeches from the late 18th century. There were two main reasons: around 1775 parents had dressed their sons in simple peasant trousers rather than breeches, a preference these boys retained as adults; and during the French Revolution the Revolutionary guards had worn trousers, the garb of the *sans-culottes*. Around 1800 trousers were calf length, but by 1810 shoe length became common. Trousers were mostly made in doeskin and stockinette and therefore could crease. Beau Brummell added a strap at the instep and so sported the most unwrinkled trousers in London. In contrast to Brummell there was the Romantic look as sported by George, Lord Byron (1788–1824), with windswept locks, open shirt collar and loose cravat. This style was only adopted in Bohemian circles, however, and most men took their lead from Brummell.

There was no female equivalent of Brummell to discipline women's dress, and it was climate that modified the skimpy, shiftlike dresses of 1800. The chemise-type, high-waisted gowns of the most Classical style depicted in the portraits of Josephine Bonaparte and Juliette Récamier by David (e.g. *Mme Récamier*, begun 1800, unfinished; Paris, Louvre), François Gérard (e.g. *Mme Bonaparte in her Drawing-room at Malmaison, c.* 1800; Malmaison, Château N.; for illustration *see* BONAPARTE, (2); and *Mme Récamier*, 1805; Paris, Carnavalet) and Pierre-Paul Prud'hon (e.g. *The Empress Josephine*, 1805; Paris, Louvre) had to be worn with warm shawls. The spencer jacket—a short, waist-length jacket with long sleeves—became part of the fashionable wardrobe for additional warmth, as did the overcoat or pelisse. Thus a more covered-up look soon returned after the extremes of Neo-classical semi-nudity. In the *Print Amateurs* by Louis-Léopold Boilly (1810; Paris, Louvre; see fig. 49) the young woman is wearing a more tailored type of classical dress, with the bodice cut in sections and built-up cap sleeves. The hairstyles—a braided coronet for the woman and the Titus crop for the men—are based on Classical busts. By 1810 more petticoats had been added to round out the silhouette a little; the bodice was tailored in sections to achieve the high

49. *Print Amateurs* by Louis-Léopold Boilly, oil on canvas, 325×245 mm, 1810 (Paris, Musée du Louvre)

waist and to produce a more 'dressed' style, and hems were raised to the ankle. This version of the Classical look lasted until 1820, when the first attempts to lower the waistline appeared.

The rise of Romanticism overlapped with Neo-classicism, and the first signs of the Romantic love of historical revivals in dress became apparent when Napoleon I crowned himself emperor in 1804. His court dress for males revived ruffs, and by 1805 ruffs were appearing on women's walking costumes. Full ruffs, falling ruffs, half ruffs and standing ruffs were all revived, and historical revival dominated women's fashion for the remainder of the century, with mixed dresses that combined a Classical waistline and slashed sleeves, lacing, van Dyck points and ruffs. The Tudor and Stuart periods in particular were plundered for ideas. Such artists as Richard Parkes Bonington and William Powell Frith painted scenes from history, and women's fashion followed suit, borrowing from distant and more recent history, with styles associated with Mary, Queen of Scots, and Marie-Antoinette being copied repeatedly. The novels of Sir Walter Scott added to the historical trend, which, by the 1820s, had become a major vogue. The 19th century was the first to look backwards so completely in its female wardrobe; history was fashionable, possibly because industrial changes and massive urban development made people seek security in the past.

Colour and decoration made a gradual comeback. The plain white dresses of 1800 had gained decorative edges by 1805, and by 1815 most dresses had frills, appliquéd flowers and padded bands around the hems. By 1825 the decoration was some 300 mm deep. A few coloured dresses appeared in 1805, many more by 1815, and after 1820 all dresses were coloured, with pinks, yellows, greens and reds being favoured. The Classical high waist lasted until 1822, but during 1823–4 a new waistline became established at the bottom of the ribcage. Skirts grew gradually wider, held out by horse-hair petticoats. Sleeves were modelled on the Elizabethan leg-of-mutton sleeve and expanded until they had achieved a similar size by 1827, when the look for the 1830s was established. The sleeve reached its limit in 1835, when it was as wide as the skirt. The initial imitation of the Elizabethan model involved building up the sleeve head, but during the 1830s the bulk was taken down to the elbow, and a sloping shoulderline dominated the remainder of the decade. Hats became larger, and hairstyles were built out at the sides by sausage curls. Enormous berets were worn with off-the-shoulder necklines as fashionable evening wear. In Benjamin Read's *Summer Fashions in the Colosseum, Regent's Park* (*c.* 1830; London, Marylebone Lib.; see fig. 50) the historicizing Romantic influence can be seen in the dress worn by the central lady; it combines Elizabethan leg-of-mutton sleeves, a sloping neckline in the style of the 1660s and 15th-century dagging.

In 1837 Queen Victoria came to the throne; after her marriage in 1840 the domestic mother suddenly became the feminine ideal. Fashion reflected the trend: wide hats were replaced by bonnets, sleeves became smaller, skirts lengthened to conceal the feet, and the waistline returned to its natural place. By 1840 bonnets had lace frills to conceal the neck and increasingly restricted the wearer's vision. Women's clothing became more cluttered, with shawls, burnouses and carriage cloaks, as can be seen in such paintings as William Powell Frith's *Derby Day* (exh. RA 1858; London, Tate) and the *Railway Station* (1862; Egham, U. London, Royal Holloway & Bedford New Coll.).

Men's clothing became increasingly sober. The built-up sleeve heads and wider coat skirts of the 1830s were disregarded during the 1840s. In the 1820s and 1830s Alfred, Comte d'Orsay, had tried to keep colour and jewellery in the masculine wardrobe, but by 1839 he admitted defeat and started wearing black and brown in the British manner. Such sober tones dated back to the Reformation and had been worn by merchants, doctors, priests and lawyers ever since. The rising power of the middle classes in the 19th century made their Protestant clothing ethic the dominant ideal for high society as well; the aristocracy gave up the last vestiges of splendour and started to dress like bank managers. The suit of coat, waistcoat and knee-breeches had been created by Charles II in 1666; in the 19th century its professional version, with waistcoat, frock-coat and trousers, became the uniform for males. Fantastic attire for men was now restricted to masquerade parties and ceremonial uniforms. Puritan sobriety reigned supreme. Rules over clothing became much stricter as high society tried to exclude the challenging middle classes. Black must be worn in town by gentlemen, with a top hat, which had been light-toned around 1800 but became black from the 1830s. Grey suits

50. *Summer Fashions in the Colosseum, Regent's Park* by Benjamin Read, coloured aquatint with etching, 399×572 mm, *c.* 1830 (London, St Marylebone Library)

and brown suits could only be worn in the country and at the races. The Regency cream or skin-coloured trousers could only be worn at weddings or garden parties, with the black frock-coat (see fig. 53 below). The lounge suit appeared in the 1850s and was strictly a country outfit, but by the 1880s unconventional characters were daring to wear it in town. In 1853 the turn-down shirt collar was introduced; the standing starched collar and cravat were retained with the frock-suit and with evening dress. Turn-down collars were worn in the country with increasingly narrow cravats that evolved into the tie.

By the middle of the century fashion was undergoing a revolution. Although mail coaches had delivered fashion magazines to town centres, the spread of railways from the 1830s to the 1850s meant that far more copies could be delivered at increasing speeds. The growing middle class expanded the market for information about fashion. The Singer sewing-machine sped up the rate of dress-making, and magazines began printing paper patterns, so the rate at which fashion could be copied accelerated dramatically. Women's skirts became increasingly voluminous, supported by six petticoats and a crinoline (horse-hair) petticoat. Buckram—a coarse linen stiffened with paste—was also used to widen skirts. Between 1845 and 1850 day dresses were usually plain or in a check and evening gowns had tiers of frills. During the 1850s the amount of decoration increased, and day dresses became as ornate as evening wear. The sensation of the period was the invention in 1855 of the cage, the sprung steel frame that really could increase the size of skirts. The French accused the English of having concocted it, and the English blamed the French, but both Empress Eugénie and Queen Victoria adopted it, and dresses expanded as far as the cage could allow. In 1860 the Empress Eugénie appointed a man—Charles Frederick Worth (1825–95)—as her dressmaker. Although Worth did not have a total monopoly over the Empress's clothes, he controlled the most important part—the ball gowns, the state gowns—and dictated fashion. In 1863 he introduced the shorter, ankle-length walking skirt; in 1864 he introduced the flat-fronted cage, which is shown in Monet's painting *Women*

51. *Women in the Garden* by Claude Monet, oil on canvas, 2.55×2.05 m, 1867 (Paris, Musée du Louvre)

and bustle; and diagonal decoration of lace van Dyck points across the skirt. In 1890 Worth experimented with bias-cut dresses constructed entirely from one piece of material. From 1883 he tried building up the sleeve head and subsequently revived the leg-of-mutton sleeve, which reached its apogee in 1895.

The strict rules over correct dress established by Prince Albert and upheld by Albert Edward, Prince of Wales, subsequently Edward VII (*b* 1841; *reg* 1901–10), were gradually undermined by the upper class's fondness for sport and sportswear. Hunting, shooting, archery and fishing were already established pastimes, but in the 19th century rowing, roller-skating, bicycling, yachting, tennis and golf were added. All activities required appropriate costume. The Norfolk jacket, which had more material in pleats to allow men to swing the gun better, was worn with knickerbockers and was created for the Prince of Wales. Women's shooting costumes consisted of a jacket and a short skirt ending below the knee. White tennis dresses worn with a man's straw boater became an absolute uniform for country weekends, as shown in Sir John Lavery's painting of the *Tennis Party* (1885; Aberdeen, A.G.). In Germany a Bloomer type of costume with a short dress and trousers for women and tunics and knee-breeches for men was worn for gymnastics. The jacket of the lounge suit became a weekend uniform for cricket,

in the Garden (1867; Paris, Louvre; see fig. 51) worn with light-coloured summer dresses decorated with spots or stripes; in 1860 he introduced the antique overtunic; in 1868 he abolished crinolines and cages completely, a daring innovation recorded in Monet's portrait of *Mme Gaudibert* (1868; Paris, Mus. D'Orsay; see fig. 52); and in 1869 he revived the bustle. Worth survived the downfall of the Second Empire, and, although he had to close his salon during the siege of Paris in 1870, he reopened it in 1871 with a new range of American customers and was able to carry on as the first *grand couturier* who was not dependent on the court.

He combined tunic tops with the bustle to create the principal style for women from 1869 to 1875, with the apron front as a variation on the same idea. Renoir's portrait of Alfred Sisley and his fiancée—the *Engaged Couple* (Cologne, Wallraf-Richartz-Mus.; see fig. 53)—was almost certainly completed in 1869, as it shows the bustle combined with a tunic top. Alfred Sisley is dressed for a garden party in a black frock-coat and light trousers. Between 1874 and 1877 Worth began to slim down the silhouette and created his cuirass line, which restored the body to its natural size. By 1881 he revived the bustle again, this time in a squarer shape, and applied tailoring techniques to the women's wardrobe to produce a sharper silhouette. He had invented the princess line to construct a dress without a waist seam and devised gored skirts, made from panels, to further improve fit. In John Singer Sargent's portrait of *Mme Paul Poirson* (1885; Detroit, MI, Inst. A.; see fig. 54), the sitter's gown shows all the hallmarks of Worth's designs in the 1880s: a sculptured bodice with whalebones curving from the hips and decoration restricted to van Dyck points at the neckline; a train

52. *Mme Gaudibert* by Claude Monet, oil on canvas, 2.17×1.39 m, 1868 (Paris, Musée d'Orsay)

53. *Engaged Couple* by Auguste Renoir (Cologne, Wallraf-Richartz-Museum)

rugby, football and rowing when worn as a blazer with flannel trousers; it was also turned into the dinner jacket for evening but could only be worn at private parties; full evening dress remained the dress coat. On the Isle of Wight, John Redfern, a linen draper's (*fl* 1850–1920), rapidly expanded and became a sportswear specialist in the late 1870s and early 1880s, providing yachting suits, tennis suits and boating suits, when the Prince of Wales made Cowes a fashionable venue. The Prince favoured a dark blue blazer with white duck trousers, while women were dressed in white with blue trimmings or dark blue suits with naval touches. Regular attendance by the Prince of Wales turned horse races into a fashion parade, with top hats, frock-coats and light trousers for men and garden-party dresses in white muslin or lace with large, flower-bedecked hats for women. The Prince even wore the lounge suit in tweed for country weekends, with a Homburg hat. By 1897 tweed lounge suits were being worn in town, in Hyde Park and as morning wear; women followed suit by wearing their tweeds in town. A casual dress revolution was slowly gaining ground as, from the 1860s, the aristocracy increasingly wore sportswear as part of the regular wardrobe.

2. THE REVOLT AGAINST FASHION. This began as two movements, the ideals of which eventually merged. Members of the Pre-Raphaelite Brotherhood, formed in 1848, disliked the conspicuous overconsumption of contemporary fashionable female dress. Instead they reconstructed medieval-style garments and depicted them in their paintings, for example *Mariana* by John Everett Millais (1851; Aberdeen, A.G., Makin Col.). The wives and models of members of the Brotherhood began to wear simpler clothes. For example, in 1854 Dante Gabriel Rossetti drew *Elizabeth Siddal* (Cambridge, Fitzwilliam) in a simple, wrapover dress, without crinoline petticoats, and by 1857 such unfashionable attire was beginning to be worn by women who were not artists' models. After 1860 Rossetti's interest widened to Titian-like garments with huge Renaissance sleeves, as designed by William Holman Hunt and worn by the actress Ellen Terry when she married G. F. Watts in 1864. Similar sleeves can be seen in Watts's contemporaneous portrait of Ellen Terry, *Choosing* (*c.* 1864; London, N.P.G.), and in 1867 Watts portrayed *May Prinsep* (also known as *Prayer*; Manchester, C.A.G.) in a similar Titian-type dress. Gradually an elegant alternative to the extremes of fashion emerged.

Meanwhile in the USA, Mrs Elizabeth Stanton and Mrs Amelia Bloomer started to campaign for reformed dress for women. In 1851 they proposed a Turkish model—a short skirt to the knee with trousers underneath. This

54. *Mme Paul Poirson* by John Singer Sargent, oil on canvas, 1499×851 mm, 1885 (Detroit, Institute of Arts)

proved unwise, as the male-dominated press on both sides of the Atlantic proclaimed that female dress reformers wanted to wear men's trousers and seize power. By the end of the decade Mrs Bloomer gave up her reformed costume as the fuss was detracting from her concerns for women's rights and temperance. In Britain an alternative to fashion's dictates already existed: artistic dress. Women who wanted to wear easier clothes could copy Pre-Raphaelite dress without appearing to usurp the masculine role. James McNeill Whistler adopted this dress for his sitters because of the beautiful flow of the waistless gowns (e.g. *Symphony in Flesh Colour and Pink: Mrs F. R. Leyland*, 1873; New York, Frick). Thus the movement became international. There was also support for the reform of women's dress, in particular the use of corsets, from the medical profession, and in 1881 the Rational Dress Society was founded in London and collaborated with the National Health Society to devise improved stays. In 1884 both organizations participated in the International Health Exhibition at the Royal Albert Hall, where many of the clothes on show—bloomers, knickerbockers and short skirts—were designed for the new range of sporting activities that women had begun to adopt: walking, climbing, cycling, tennis, roller-skating, cricket and yachting.

The first artistic dress had used medieval and Renaissance features, but by 1869 Thomas Armstrong was painting Grecian-type dresses (e.g. *Haytime*; London, V&A) and Albert Joseph Moore followed this ideal from the 1870s onwards. By 1883 G. F. Watts stated that Greek dress was perfect. Oscar Wilde of the Rational Dress Society agreed, and aesthetic gowns in the 1880s became more classical. In 1890 the artistic and healthy clothing movements merged in the Healthy and Artistic Dress Union, with G. F. Watts as a vice-president, and it too supported classical dress for women. For men, Oscar Wilde and Dr Gustave Jaeger agreed that knee-breeches constituted the best reformed costume, although George Bernard Shaw favoured an all-in-one combination suit, which he wore in London in the 1890s. The aesthetic gown became part of the Art Nouveau movement.

The debate had made an impact on mainstream fashion. In 1879 Worth had begun designing artistic dresses and tea gowns, the latter being confections in lace and muslin to wear at women's tea parties, when corsets might be eased. Although Worth did not approve of the abandonment of corsets, he considered himself an artist and took many historical elements, combining Renaissance sleeves with Empire waistline to produce sumptuous, waistless creations for those sufficiently brave or unconventional to wear them. By the 1890s, in mainstream women's fashion, the waist was still controlled by whalebones in the corset, and Romantic historicizing detail continued to predominate. In the portrait of *Mrs Fitzroy Bell* by Sir John Lavery (1894; Glasgow, A.G. & Mus.; see fig. 55) the dress has padded sleeves that look back to the 1830s, 1630s and 1580s, while the pendent chiffon sleeves are based on medieval styles. By 1908 fashion became classical again, and tight waists were at last abolished, although a long corset was introduced to achieve the required classical proportions. Artistic and healthy dress reformers were now busy with the question of socialist dress. World War

55. *Mrs Fitzroy Bell* by John Lavery, oil on canvas, 1.83×0.92 m, 1894 (Glasgow, Art Gallery and Museum)

I buried all such concerns ruthlessly. Reformed dress came to an abrupt halt, but in the munition factories women wore trousers, an event that speeded up a change that could have taken generations.

BIBLIOGRAPHY
M. P. Merrifield: *Dress as a Fine Art* (London, 1854)
N. Waugh: *Corsets and Crinolines* (London, 1954/*R* 1987)
——: *The Cut of Men's Clothes, 1600–1900* (London, 1964)
S. Blum, ed.: *Victorian Fashions and Clothing from Harper's Bazaar* (London and New York, 1974)
S. M. Newton: *Health, Art and Reason: Dress Reformers of the 19th Century* (London, 1974)
D. de Marly: 'The Establishment of Roman Dress in Seventeenth-century Portraits', *Burl. Mag.*, cxvii (1975), pp. 443–51
200 Jahre Mode in Wien (exh. cat., Vienna, Hermesvilla, 1976)
D. de Marly: 'Dress in Baroque Portraiture: The Flight from Fashion', *Antiqua. J.*, lx/2 (1980), pp. 268–84
——: *The History of Haute Couture, 1850–1950* (London, 1980/*R* 1986)

——: *Worth: Father of Haute Couture* (London, 1980/*R* London and New York, 1990)

C. Walkley: *The Ghost in the Looking Glass: The Victorian Seamstress* (London, 1981)

V. Foster: *The 19th Century*, A Visual History of Costume (London, 1984)

D. de Marly: *Fashion for Men: An Illustrated History* (London, 1985)

C. Walkley: *The Way to Wear'em: 150 Years of Punch on Fashion* (London, 1985)

V. Foster and C. Walkley: *Crinolines and Crimping Irons* (London, 1986)

D. de Marly: *Working Dress: A History of Occupational Clothing* (London, 1986)

——: *Dress in North America*, 2 vols (New York, 1990–93)

DIANA DE MARLY

IX. 20th century.

In the 20th century many fashion designers were stimulated by artistic developments and adapted to commercial design forms initiated by movements in avant-garde art. Modernist artists and designers who sought a totally new aesthetic as a rational response to 'modern' needs identified art as an object that should be more closely linked to its immediate environment. This meant that fashion designers often collaborated with fine artists or worked in a number of branches of the decorative arts. Similarly, many fine artists increasingly worked in the decorative arts field. As in other centuries, taste, patronage, patterns of consumption, economic factors, wars, fashion consciousness and communications were among socio-cultural determinants that also affected dress.

Following the establishment of the *haute couture* industry in Paris, led by Charles Frederick Worth (1825–95) in 1858 (*see* §VIII above), the major tendency in 20th-century dress was the rise in status of the couturier. From the beginning of the century, a number of new couture houses were established, and couturiers no longer simply executed orders but created new styles in women's dress and came to be respected as artists, their personalities becoming as influential as their designs. Around 1900 female dress imitated the sweeping lines of the fashionable Art Nouveau style and was imbued with femininity through the use of decorated, draped fabrics and curvaceous contours. Male dress was characterized by plain, narrow suits in sombre colours. Fashionable dress was still the privilege of the rich, and the leading French couturiers, such as Mme Paquin (*d* 1936), who had opened a couture house in 1891, and Redfern (*fl* 1850–1920; *see* §VIII above), a salon in Paris founded by John Redfern in 1881 and run by Charles Poynter as a branch of the London House of Redfern, were patronized by socialites, royalty and actresses.

From the late 19th century, the performing arts were influential in encouraging change in fashionable dress, in particular the productions from 1909 of Serge Diaghilev's Ballets Russes, in which, for the first time, music, stage scenery and costumes were conceived as a total visual unit. The first performance of Diaghilev's ballet *Cléopâtre* in Paris in 1909 featured costume and décor designed by Léon Bakst, but the most influential in terms of fashion was the ballet *Schéhérazade* (also designed by Bakst) in Paris in 1910. Inspired by the Orient, the fabrics and designs of the costumes (*see* THEATRE, §III, 4(ii)(a), and fig. 029623.001) and the use of new bright colours such as cerise, jade and tango strongly influenced all European fashion, in particular the dress designs of Lucile (Lady Lucy Duff Gordon, 1862–1935), Jacques Doucet, Callot Soeurs (a couture house founded in 1895 and closed in 1937) and PAUL POIRET. Poiret was further influenced by the intense colours used by the Fauves, principally Matisse, and employed the Fauvist painter Raoul Dufy to design and print bold fabrics. He popularized such garments as Turkish trousers, turbans, kimonos and 'minaret' dresses (e.g. 'Sorbet' dress, 1913; London, V&A; see fig. 56). The influence of Oriental styles in dress meant that by 1914 women's fashionable attire featured a straighter silhouette partly through adaptations of the corset.

56. 'Sorbet' tunic dress designed by Paul Poiret, 1913 (London, Victoria and Albert Museum)

The significance of Italian Futurism and Russian Constructivism in the second decade of the 20th century lay in their abilities to extend visual ideas already explored in painting and sculpture into the field of dress, in an effort to relate art to society. Futurism rejected tradition. Its celebration of dynamism, progress and technology meant that new forms and expressions were found to symbolize the modern age. The Futurist painter Giacomo Balla designed clothes and furniture from 1914. He advocated comfortable, practical and expendable clothes of brilliant colours and dynamic, asymmetric designs. Similarly, after the Russian Revolution (1917), the so-called Constructivists were keen to apply their skills to practical needs and develop new designs in conjunction with new materials. Many fine artists began to work in other fields, and in 1923/4 Varvara Stepanova and Lyubov' Popova turned to textile and clothes design for industrial production. They were interested in the problem of uniting the fabric design with the style of dress, and their designs for workers' clothes and unisex wear were simply assembled and featured combinations of one or two geometric patterns in an economic colour range. Alexandra Exter also produced designs for simple, mass-produced clothing, although in general her designs were more decorative and individualistic.

From 1906, the Cubists' reappraisal of pictorial representation and abstract use of space, light and colour, evident in the work of Picasso and Georges Braque, influenced some aspects of design and is usually associated with the popular styles shown at the Exposition Internationale des Arts Décoratifs et Industriels Modernes in Paris in 1925. On a superficial level, the surface patterns of dress and accessories of the 1920s imitated the fashionable angular style, as depicted in *Metropolis* by Otto Dix (for illustration *see* DIX, OTTO). As well as fabric design, the influence of Cubism contributed to dress in the cutting of cloth on abstract lines. This was pioneered by the French couturier Madeleine Vionnet (1876–1975), who used the bias cut and diagonal seaming in her dress designs of the 1930s. Partly through Cubism an interest in 'primitivism' stimulated the trend towards simplification, abstraction and stylization of form, the use of bold cosmetics and sculptured and cropped hairstyles as worn by *Mme Jasmy Alvin* in the portrait by Kees van Dongen (1928; Paris, Mus. A. Mod. Ville Paris).

The dress and textile designs of the Russian-born artist Sonia Delaunay reflected her interest in the expression of colour rhythms and curved forms. She adapted her bold, abstract paintings featuring curves, triangles and squares or simultaneous patterns to textile design, as shown in the scarves worn by the subjects of Robert Delaunay's portraits of *Tristan Tzara* (1922; Paris, C. Delaunay priv. col.; see fig. 57) and *Mme Heim* (1926–7; Lisbon, Mus. Gulbenkian), and to the decorative arts. Her first 'simultaneous' dress (1914) featured vibrant zigzags and pattern to remove any sense of shape; a later version is shown in Robert Delaunay's portrait of *Mme Mandel* (1923). Her later dress designs involved a patchwork of mixed fabrics of contrasting textures and embroidery.

Political and socio-economic factors that had a major impact on dress design included World War I, which led to changes in the attitude towards female dress; skirts

57. 'Simultaneous' scarf, designed by Sonia Delaunay, depicted in *Tristan Tzara* by Robert Delaunay, oil on canvas, 1922 (Paris, C. Delaunay private collection)

were shortened and clothes were made less restricting to cope with the practicalities of this period. By 1920 women's increasing social emancipation and sporting activity also encouraged the trend towards a straighter silhouette (*see* BEADWORK, colour pl. II). The French couturier Gabrielle 'Coco' Chanel (1883–1971) was particularly influential in reducing the shape of women's clothes to geometric simplicity, echoing the modernist concern with forms that were functional and sympathizing with the modern needs for practicality and comfort. As the use of casual and informal dress increased, particularly in men's apparel, Chanel introduced trousers, beach pyjamas and shorter skirts for women in the early 1920s.

Another aspect of the visual arts to influence dress from the late 1920s was the American film industry. Through fantasy and illusion, films reflected polished and romantic images and helped to disseminate glamorous and extreme styles in dress, as well as establishing guidelines for feminine and masculine beauty. From 1920 costumes for films were designed by leading French couturiers, and later there emerged such specialist costume designers as Adrian (1903–59), the chief designer at Metro-Goldwyn-Mayer in the 1930s, and Howard Greer (1886–1974), who designed costumes for Paramount films in the 1920s. During the 1930s dress designs were often based on romantic and revivalist styles, partly influenced by Surrealism. The Italian fashion designer Elsa Schiaparelli (1890–1973) was particularly innovative in incorporating certain Surrealist motifs and visual puns in her dress designs. Having opened a salon in Paris in 1929, Schiaparelli collaborated with the Surrealist artists Salvador Dalí and Jean Cocteau (see exh. cat., p. 32) in designing fabric and accessories that featured elements of surprise and humour, such as the Tear dress and Dalí's hat in the shape of a shoe horn (1937). Associated with the dream imagery of Surrealism (see fig. 58) was a new spirit of romanticism and nostalgia during the 1930s. The fashionable female dress style, often referred to as Neo-Victorianism, featured, for example, hour-glass shapes, puffed sleeves, bustles and modified crinolines, as seen in the dress designs of the American couturier Mainbocher (1891–1976), who had opened a salon in Paris in 1930. The emergence of stylized classicism in the arts, which was evident for example in the work of Picasso in the 1920s, also affected fashionable dress. Many fashion designers, such as Schiaparelli, launched 'Neo-classical' collections in the late 1930s, and the fashionable female figure became more sleek and curvaceous with flared lines following the body's contours, as shown in *Portrait of a Young Woman* by Meredith Frampton (1935; London, Tate). Mme Grès (*b* 1899), who was known as 'Alix' in the 1930s and who had trained as a sculptor, opened a salon in Paris in 1933 and was particularly influential in the use of jersey to produce classical dresses inspired by Classical drapery, as shown in one (1937; see exh. cat., p. 19) of Man Ray's many fashion photographs for *Harper's Bazaar* (New York, 1867–1970).

59. Evening-dress of silk paper taffeta designed by Jacques Fath and photographed by Cecil Beaton; from *American Vogue*, March 1951

World War II had a profound effect on male and female civilian dress, and restrictions on fabric and cut of clothes inspired the design of functional clothes that had a military look. With the restriction of imported fashion news and original designs from Paris during World War II, talent in such countries as Great Britain, the USA, Italy and Spain was exploited, and the role of France as fashion leader was severely diminished. The interdependence of the fine and applied arts persisted after the war, however, and the practice of commissioning fine artists to design fabrics was particularly influential on couture designs from the late 1940s. Lida and Zika Ascher (*b* 1910) established a textile company in London in 1939 and from 1944 contracted leading French and British painters, sculptors and graphic artists, such as Henry Moore, André Derain and Graham Sutherland, to design printed fabrics for headscarves and dresses. The fabrics were supplied regularly to leading couturiers, the abstract and pictorial patterns influencing the trend for long, pleated dresses. For example, an all-over flower design by Cecil Beaton was made up into a silk afternoon dress by the French couturier Pierre Balmain (1914–82) in 1946.

After the war, fashionable dress returned to the romantic styles that had been established in the 1930s. The trend towards femininity and a softening in female dress is usually seen as a direct response to the austerity of the war years. In 1947 Christian Dior's (1905–57) first collection, originally called the Corelle Line and dubbed the 'New Look', epitomized the trend towards extravagance and

58. Salvador Dalí: *I Dream about an Evening-dress*; from *American Vogue*, March 1937

was characterized by stiffened bodices and huge gathered skirts. The mood of nostalgia was also evident in men's apparel in the New Edwardian styles from 1950, later adapted by gangs of young men known as 'Teddy' Boys, in the form of long, draped jackets with velvet lapels, tapered trousers and longer, slicked-back hair with 'sideburns'—the modern equivalent of side whiskers. Other couturiers working in the 1950s whose designs were influenced by Dior's New Look included the Spaniard Cristóbal Balenciaga (1895–1972) and Jacques Fath (1912–54; see fig. 59). World War II also encouraged the growth of the ready-to-wear industry, made possible by new techniques of mass production and mass distribution. With a move away from formal dress, many designers began to cater for the ready-to-wear market rather than design exclusively for couture. For example the British royal couturiers Norman Hartnell (1901–79) and Hardy Amies (b 1909) began ready-to-wear lines in 1942 and 1945 respectively.

By the end of the 1950s, inspiration for fashionable dress came from popular music and pop culture as well as avant-garde art. Such exponents of Pop art as Andy Warhol, Roy Lichtenstein and Richard Hamilton celebrated mass culture, influenced the move towards gimmicky and expendable clothes for the young and popularized the use of bright colours in clothing. Op art also had considerable impact on fashion design from the mid-1960s, with its use of optical effects and patterns made up of spirals, circles and squares, as shown in the paintings by Bridget Riley (for illustration see OP ART) and Victor Vasarely. Designing essentially for the ready-to-wear and younger market were such French couturiers as Pierre Cardin (b 1922), Paco Rabanne (b 1934), André Courrèges (b 1923) and Yves Saint Laurent (b 1936), as well as the new generation of young British designers such as Mary Quant (b 1934; see fig. 60) and Ossie Clark (b 1942); some used fabric designs inspired by Op art. The use of new synthetic materials such as vinyl and PVC and the practice of channel seaming gave a geometric and strong shape to the clothes. Other dress designs resembled metal sculptures—Paco Rabanne, for example, used plastic discs and chain mail. The trend towards unisex wear and informality in dress was epitomized by the popularity of denim jeans from the late 1950s and the broadened use of utilitarian fabrics. Among the American and Italian designers who were particularly renowned for their sportswear and leisure wear were Emilio Pucci (b 1914), who produced capri trousers and resort dresses, Claire McCardell (1905–58) and Tom Brigance (b 1913), who was known as a specialist beachwear designer.

During the 1970s and 1980s wider cultural factors such as mass marketing and the emergence of various youth sub-cultures encouraged frequent changes in fashionable dress. The New Wave in popular music and the influence of street-led fashion produced innovative ready-to-wear designs. Particular designers who took inspiration from the London street-scene included the French designer Jean-Paul Gaultier (b 1952) and the English designers Vivienne Westwood (b 1941) and Katherine Hamnett (b 1948). Some of their designs were used as political expressions, others evolved as a post-punk style. The

influence of punk subculture was reflected in the 'Conceptual Chic' Collection of 1977 by Zandra Rhodes (b 1940), which consisted of evening-dresses in ripped black jersey and decorated with chains, ball bearings and diamanté safety-pins. Ethnic sources from Africa and the East also influenced fashionable dress from the late 1960s, seen in the popularity of such garments as kaftans and zouave trousers. Several Japanese designers established themselves in the West, producing layered and wrapped styles and styles with overscaled proportions as seen in the knitwear designs of ISSEY MIYAKE and Kenzo Takada. By the late 1970s such designers as Yohji Yamamoto (b 1943) and REI KAWAKUBO, who had formed the Comme des Garçons Co. in 1969, introduced adaptations of traditional Japanese dress into Western dress. During the 1980s the Pop style persisted in the designs of the Italian designer Elio Fiorucci (b 1935), particularly in his use of fluorescent accessories. From the late 1980s retrogressive styles were revived. These relied on pastiche and novelty and were

60. Mini-dress designed by Mary Quant, bonded wool and jersey, 1967 (London, Victoria and Albert Museum)

fanned by nostalgic films and television serials, further encouraging the trend for second-hand clothes.

BIBLIOGRAPHY

Q. Bell: *On Human Finery* (London, 1954)
E. W. Chase and I. Chase: *Always in Vogue* (London, 1954)
A. Latour: *Kings of Fashion* (London, 1958)
M. Garland: *Fashion* (Harmondsworth, 1962)
——: *The Indecisive Decade: The World of Fashion and Entertainment in the 30s* (London, 1968)
R. Lynam, ed.: *Paris Fashion: The Great Designers and their Creations* (London, 1972)
J. Arnold: *A Handbook of Costume* (London, 1973)
E. Ewing: *A History of 20th Century Fashion* (London, 1974)
G. Squire: *Dress, Art and Society: 1560–1970* (London, 1974)
G. Howell: *In Vogue* (London, 1975)
I. Davies: 'Corresponding Styles in Costume and the Arts', *Fashion 1900–1939* (exh. cat., London, Scottish Arts Council and V&A, 1975), pp. 50–54
P. Glynn: *In Fashion: Dress in the Twentieth Century* (London, 1978)
A. Hollander: *Seeing through Clothes* (New York, 1978)
A. J. Coulson: *A Bibliography of Design in Britain, 1851–1970* (London, 1979)
D. de Marly: *The History of Haute Couture, 1850–1950* (London, 1980/R London and New York, 1990)
I. Anscombe: *A Woman's Touch: Women in Design from 1860 to the Present Day* (London, 1984)
C. McDowell: *McDowell's Directory of Twentieth Century Fashion* (London, 1984)
C. R. Milbank: *Couture: The Great Fashion Designers* (London, 1985)
E. Wilson: *Adorned in Dreams: Fashion and Modernity* (London, 1985)
P. Byrde: *The Twentieth Century*, A Visual History of Costume (London, 1986)
G. O'Hara: *The Encyclopaedia of Fashion* (London, 1986/R 1989)
J. Miller: 'The Study of Dress and Textiles', *Design History: A Student's Handbook*, ed. H. Conway (London, 1987), pp. 15–37
J. Mulvagh: *Vogue History of 20th Century Fashion* (London, 1988)
Street Styles (exh. cat., London, V&A, 1994)

ELEANOR GAWNE

Dresser, Christopher (*b* Glasgow, 4 July 1834; *d* Mulhouse, Alsace, 24 Nov 1904). Scottish designer, botanist and writer. He trained at the Government School of Design, Somerset House, London, between 1847 and 1854, during which time he was strongly influenced by the design reform efforts of Henry Cole, Richard Redgrave and Owen Jones. In 1854 he began to lecture at the school on botany and in 1856 supplied a plate illustrating the 'geometrical arrangement of flowers' for Jones's *Grammar of Ornament*. In 1857 he presented a series of lectures at the Royal Institution entitled 'On the Relationship of Science to Ornamental Art', which he followed up in a series of 11 articles in the *Art Journal* (1857–8) on the similar subject of 'Botany as Adapted to the Arts and Art-Manufacture'. His first three books were on botanical subjects, and in 1860 he was awarded a doctorate by the University of Jena for his research in this area.

Following the International Exhibition of 1862 in London, where he was particularly interested in the Japanese collections of Sir Rutherford Alcock, Dresser visited and wrote about most of the major international exhibitions. In his first design book, *The Art of Decorative Design* (1862), Dresser stressed that plant forms should be 'conventionalized' rather than naturalistically imitated. According to the preface, he was already supplying designs to a number of well-known manufacturers, and during the 1860s he established himself as a major commercial designer, with a studio of 'Ornamental Art' in Fulham, London. The only known sketchbook by Dresser (Ipswich Mus.) dates from this period and contains annotated designs for metalwork and ceramics, and sketches of geometric and floral ornament.

In 1874 Dresser lectured on Owen Jones at the latter's memorial exhibition, and two years later he purchased a large number of Jones's drawings and sketches. The influence of Jones's colour schemes can be seen in Dresser's *Principles of Decorative Design* (1873), which was based on a series of articles in the *Technical Educator*, and in *Studies in Design* (1874–6). Dresser designed for a wide range of media: cast iron for Coalbrookdale; textiles for at least eight firms, including Warners and Crossley & Sons; wallpaper for Jeffrey & Co.; silver and plate for Elkington & Co. from 1875, for Hukin & Heath from 1878, and for James Dixon & Sons from 1879. Some of his best-known designs are for such small-scale metal objects as toast racks and claret jugs (*see* ENGLAND, fig. 81). An advocate of machine production, Dresser was an innovative designer; his works, generally austere and undecorated and usually with exposed rivets, show a primary concern for function. In 1876 Dresser visited the Philadelphia Exhibition, and from there went to Japan, where he travelled extensively in 1877, representing the British Government and also collecting Japanese objects for Tiffany & Co. of New York. Much of Dresser's subsequent work was informed by his appreciation of Japanese design. From 1879 to 1882 he was art director of the newly formed Linthorpe Art Pottery, near Middlesbrough, Cleveland, which mass-produced vases and tableware of Oriental and Pre-Columbian inspiration. He also designed ceramics for Minton & Co., the Old Hall Earthenware Co. and the Ault Pottery.

From 1879 to 1882 Dresser was in partnership with Charles Holme (1848–1923) as Dresser & Holme, wholesale importers of Oriental goods, with a warehouse in Farringdon Road, London. In 1880 Dresser was appointed art editor of the *Furniture Gazette*, a position he held for one year, during which time he frequently reproduced his own angular furniture designs. The same year he founded the Art Furnishers' Alliance in Bond Street, London, with financial backing from Arthur L. Liberty and George Chubb, a safe manufacturer whose firm also made 'artistic furniture' designed by Dresser. The business was not a commercial success and was liquidated in 1883. Dresser also designed furniture for the Bath cabinetmakers Thomas Knight. In 1882 he published a major work on the art and architecture of Japan, and in 1886 his final design book, *Modern Ornamentation*. From the mid-1880s Dresser designed Clutha glass, patented by James Couper & Sons of Glasgow. In 1889 he moved to Barnes, London, where he ran a design studio with ten assistants, including J. Moyr Smith and Archibald Knox.

WRITINGS

'Botany as Adapted to the Arts and Art-Manufacture', *A. J.* [London], n.s., iii and iv (1857–8) [series of 11 articles]
Principles of Decorative Design (London, 1873)
Japan, its Architecture, Arts and Art-Manufacture (London, 1882)

BIBLIOGRAPHY

Christopher Dresser (exh. cat. by R. Dennis and J. Jesse, London, F.A. Soc., 1972)
Christopher Dresser (exh. cat. by M. Collins, S. Durant and P. Atterbury, London, Camden A. Cent., 1979)

ROSAMOND ALLWOOD

Drevet. French family of engravers. Pierre Drevet (*b* Loire-sur-Rhône, 20 July 1663; *d* Paris, 9 Aug 1738) studied engraving with Germain Audran (1631–1710) in Lyon and then with Girard Audran in Paris. He undertook the engraving of portraits by his friend Hyacinthe Rigaud and in this type of work was able to display his technical virtuosity. In 1692 he set up as an engraver and publisher, and in 1696 he was appointed Graveur du Roi. Although he was accepted (*agréé*) by the Académie Royale in 1703 and admitted (*reçu*) in 1707, he did not complete his *morceau de réception* until 1722, with an engraving (Roux, no. 36) after Rigaud's portrait of *Robert de Cotte* (Paris, Louvre). Drevet's engraving (1712; R 81) after Rigaud's full-length portrait of *Louis XIV* (1701; Paris, Louvre) was executed by royal command. In 1726 Drevet was granted lodgings in the Palais du Louvre. He engraved 125 plates after Nicolas de Largillierre, François de Troy and, above all, Rigaud. Among his pupils were Michel Dossier (1684–1750), Simon de La Vallée (1680–after 1730) and François Chéreau, as well as his son Pierre-Imbert Drevet (*b* Paris, 22 June 1697; *d* Paris, 27 April 1739), who showed a precocious talent and a virtuosity surpassing that of his father. Pierre-Imbert's masterpiece is the engraving of *Jacques-Bénigne Bossuet* (1723; R 9) after Rigaud's portrait (Paris, Louvre). He was accepted (*agréé*) by the Académie Royale in 1724 and appointed Graveur du Roi in 1729; unfortunately he became insane. Some of his plates were made in collaboration with his father. Pierre Drevet also taught his nephew Claude Drevet (*b* Loire-sur-Rhône, 23 April 1697; *d* Paris, 23 Dec 1781), who engraved a few good portraits but mostly exploited commercially the family stock of plates. The three Drevets brought reproductive engraving to a peak in 18th-century France.

Portalis–Beraldi

BIBLIOGRAPHY
A. Firmin-Didot: *Les Drevet (Pierre, Pierre-Imbert et Claude): Catalogue raisonné de leur oeuvre* (Paris, 1876)
R. A. Weigert: 'Les Drevet, graveurs du Roy: Documents inédits', *Bull. Soc. Hist. A. Fr.* (1938), pp. 217–46
M. Roux: *Inventaire du fonds français: Graveurs du dix-huitième siècle*, Paris, Bib. N., Cab. Est. cat., vii (Paris, 1951), pp. 307–42 [R]

MADELEINE BARBIN

Drevin, Aleksandr (Davidovich) [Drévinš, Aleksandrs; Drevinishch, Rudolph Aleksandr] (*b* Venden [now Cēsis], Latvia, 3 July 1889; *d* Altay Region, 1938). Latvian painter, active in Russia. His father was Latvian and his mother German. In 1904 he enrolled at the Art School in Riga where he studied under Vil'gel'm-Karl Purvit until 1913. The following year the family moved to Moscow where he involved himself in avant-garde artistic movements as well as revolutionary political activity, for which he had already been arrested in Riga. In 1918 he exhibited several abstract works and his cycle *Refugees*. Between 1919 and 1921 he worked at Svomas, Vkhutemas and other experimental studios. In 1922 his paintings were shown in the *Erste russische Kunstausstellung* in Berlin and Amsterdam. He exhibited with former members of the Jack of Diamonds group in 1923 and with DMKh, the Society of Moscow Artists (1927–32). He was married to NADEZHDA UDAL'TSOVA and together they held exhibitions at the Russian Museum, Leningrad (1928) and the State Cultural and Historical Museum, Erevan (1934). Drevin had made enemies among his fellow artists, and his early political activities and membership of the Red Latvian Kremlin Riflemen who formed part of Lenin's personal bodyguard told against him. He was arrested and sent into enforced exile in the Altay region, where he died in 1938.

Drevin was unusual in the rapidity with which he discovered and absorbed the most recent developments in French painting without surrendering his own painterly interests, at the same time developing a style of his own. His reduction of human form into geometric units, characteristic of his *Refugees* cycle, perhaps emphasizing the plight of these anonymous victims of war and revolution, demonstrates not only his pictorial originality but also the uncompromising nature of his artistic personality. Towards the end of the 1920s Kazimir Malevich was to pursue an analogous path with his peasants and sports people. If initially Drevin saw his task as a struggle against the Constructivists led by Aleksandr Rodchenko, who proclaimed the death of easel painting, his work rapidly became a fervent affirmation of its value as personal and emotional self-expression in an increasingly mechanistic and utilitarian world. His attitude was in no sense unreasoned or complacently traditional. It had two vital aspects: first, an investigation into the act of painting, which led him to an experimental use of pigment, a form of creative research as rigorous as any undertaken by the Constructivists and, second, the creation on canvas of impulses derived from the contemplation of nature. He and Udal'tsova travelled widely in the Urals and the Altay region: in contrast to the Constructivists and most other painters of the time who were determinedly urban, he admired both wild life and the natural landscape, as can be seen in *Deer* (1932; Moscow, Tret'yakov Gal.) and *Steppe Landscape with a Horse* (1933; St Petersburg, Rus. Mus.). Animals, human figures, trees and buildings standing lonely and isolated in a mass of pigment, sometimes static, sometimes engulfing, are typical of his final creative period.

BIBLIOGRAPHY
M. B. Miasin, ed.: *Stareyshiye sovetskiye khudozhniki o Sredney Azii i Kavkaze* [Elder Soviet artists on Central Asia and the Caucasus] (Moscow, 1973)
Aleksandr Davidovich Drevin (exh. cat., ed. E. B. Rakitina; Moscow, Un. Artists, 1979)
Aleksandrs Drēvinš (exh. cat., ed. M. Markevich; Riga, City A. Mus., 1981)
Aleksandr Drevin (exh. cat., Tallin, Un. Artists, 1982)
Seven Moscow Artists, 1910–1930 (exh. cat., Cologne, Gal. Gmurzynska, 1984)

ALAN BIRD

Drew, Jane B(everley) (*b* Thornton Heath, Surrey, 24 March 1911). British architect, teacher and writer, wife of E. MAXWELL FRY. She studied at the Architectural Association, London, in 1929–34 and as a student worked for Grey Wornum on the construction of the RIBA headquarters in London. After graduating, she set up a practice with James Alliston, her first husband, building some houses and other small-scale works. From 1940 to 1945 she practised independently, and in 1941–3 she was a consultant to the British Commercial Gas Corporation, undertaking specialist studies on the design of kitchens, which culminated in the *Kitchen Planning Exhibition* (London, 1945). In 1942 Drew married Fry, and in 1944–6 they both worked as planning advisers to the resident minister for the West African Colonies, subsequently publishing *Village Housing in the Tropics* (1947), which was largely Drew's work. She also founded the *Architects Yearbook* (1946), acting as joint editor with Trevor Dannatt until 1962. In 1946 Drew and Fry set up a partnership in London and began the first of a large number of projects in Africa, mostly schools and colleges, notably University College (1953–9), Ibadan (*see* FRY, E. MAXWELL; *see also* NIGERIA, §IV, 2). In this work they pioneered the introduction of Modernism, adapting it to local materials and conditions; they also introduced a scientific approach to climatic design, and their later books on tropical architecture became standard texts. In 1951 Drew was appointed with Fry as Senior Architect on the construction of Chandigarh, the new capital city of the Punjab designed by Le Corbusier, where she worked mainly on government and private housing and associated amenities (*see* CHANDIGARH, §1). She also designed buildings in Kuwait, Iran and Ceylon (now Sri Lanka), while notable late works in Britain include housing schemes at Hatfield and Welwyn (both Herts; 1964) and at Harlow, Essex (1964); School for the Deaf (1968), Herne Hill, London; Open University (1969–77), Milton Keynes, Bucks; and Torbay Hospital (1973), Devon. Her commitment to modern art and architecture was reflected in her friendships with many contemporary artists, and in 1970 she designed premises at Carlton House Terrace, London, for the Institute of Contemporary Arts, with which she had been involved since its inception. Drew was a visiting professor at several architectural schools in the USA (1961–76) and was President of the Architectural Association (1969); she was also the first woman to be elected to the Council of the RIBA, serving in 1964–70 and again in 1971–4.

WRITINGS
with E. M. Fry: *Architecture for Children* (London, 1944/R as *Architecture and the Environment*, 1976)
Kitchen Planning (London, 1945)
with E. M. Fry and H. L. Ford: *Village Housing in the Tropics* (London, 1947)
with E. M. Fry: *Tropical Architecture in the Humid Zone* (London, 1956)
——: *Tropical Architecture in the Dry and Humid Zones* (London, 1964)

BIBLIOGRAPHY
U. Kultermann: *New Directions in African Architecture* (London, 1969)
S. Hitchens, ed.: *Fry, Drew, Knight, Creamer: Architecture* (London, 1978)
S. Flower, J. Macfarlane and R. Plant, eds: *Jane B. Drew, Architect: A Tribute from Colleagues and Friends for her 75th Birthday* (Bristol, 1986)

VALERIE A. CLACK

Drew, Sir **Thomas** (*b* Belfast, 8 Sept 1838; *d* 13 Mar 1910). Irish architect. He was articled to Charles Lanyon in 1854 and was associated with Thomas Turner (1820–91) in Belfast (1861) and William George Murray (*d* 1871) in Dublin (1862). Drew's work was essentially ecclesiastical, for the Church of Ireland and other Protestant denominations in Dublin, Belfast and north-east Ireland. He emphasized quality stonework and frequently used Celtic motifs, such as the round tower beside the entrance porch of St Jude's, Belfast (1869–73). An early work, St Philip's, Miltown Road (1864–7), forms the centrepiece of Palmerston Park, Dublin. The Mariners' Church, Kingstown (1884; now Dun Laoghaire), incorporates an impressive 12 m chancel arch with corbelled shafts of grey marble on the responds and richly carved, clustered capitals. His most notable work was St Ann's Anglican Cathedral, Belfast, begun 1898–1904 to his plans but continued in a range of styles, widely divergent from Drew's scheme. Drew envisaged an enormous Gothic Revival building on a traditional Latin cross plan. This was altered to a Romanesque Revival style, inspired by buildings in south and west France, which was felt to reflect the traditions of the early Irish Church. The coffered ceiling of red Australian sequoia wood complements the interior lining of red Dumfries stone. The exterior and much of the interior is faced with Somerset stone. Drew was also architect to St Patrick's Anglican Cathedral, Armagh, and to both Christ Church Cathedral and St Patrick's Cathedral, Dublin. He worked on the restoration of Christ Church Cathedral, Waterford (1891).

Drew's few secular projects, mainly in the classical style, include the Dublin headquarters of the Ulster Bank, College Green (1891), in granite and grey limestone, conveying the full flavour of Edwardian Baroque at its best, with a rusticated base and above, giant three-storey-high Corinthian columns supporting the pediment. His Graduates' Memorial Building (1902) in Trinity College, Dublin, although less exuberant, appears heavy and sombre. This is in an English 16th-century style, as is his Irish Highland Hotel, Bundoran (1895), and the Town Hall, Rathmines (1894–1900). He completed the dome of Thomas Ivory's Blue Coat School (King's Hospital), Blackhall Place, between 1901 and 1904 (now the Incorporated Law Society). Drew was involved with many professional bodies. He was made a fellow of the RIBA in 1889, was an original member of the Architectural Association of Ireland and in 1902 became the first president of the Ulster Society of Architects. He was knighted in 1900, in which year he was also made president of the Royal Hibernian Academy. He was the only Irish architect asked to submit a design for the Queen Victoria Memorial, London; his scheme included a reconstruction of the park façade of Buckingham Palace.

WRITINGS
Contributions (from 1863, also as ed.) to *Dublin Bldr*
'The Founding of a Cathedral in Belfast', *Irish Bldr & Engin.*, xlvi (18 June 1904), pp. 368–70

BIBLIOGRAPHY
DNB
Interview, *Irish Bldr* (30 Jan 1901), p. 617
Obituary, *Irish Bldr & Engin.*, lii (19 March 1910), p. 168
P. Larmour: *The Buildings of Belfast* (Belfast, 1987)

HUGH MAGUIRE

Dreyer, Dankvart (Christian Magnus) (*b* Assens, Fyn, 13 June 1816; *d* Barløse, Fyn, 4 Nov 1852). Danish painter. From 1831 to 1837 he studied at the Kunstakademi in Copenhagen under J. L. Lund (1777–1867) and C. W. Eckersberg. He concentrated on history, mythological and figure painting and won the Great Silver Medal in 1837. However, encouraged by his friend J. T. Lundbye, his chief preoccupation was landscape painting, to which he devoted himself during summers at home in Assens. His poetic approach to painting, based on the use of a delicate palette, glorified landscape subjects, which previously had been considered banal and unworthy of depiction. In *View from Assens* (1834; Odense, Fyn. Stiftsmus.), Dreyer depicts a scene from his native town, a cluster of houses on the shore, opposite the coast of North Slesvig, which, for all its simplicity, seems to allude to a more complex reality. He often relied on studies of details to complete his finished paintings. In one such study, a *Footbridge over a Brook in Assens, Fünen* (1842; Copenhagen, Stat. Mus. Kst), depicting a footbridge leading to the Assens churchyard, Dreyer describes the fall of light on the wood and leaves with an intensity and precision akin to Christian Købke.

In 1838 Dreyer journeyed to Jutland, where he was impressed by the windswept coasts and heathlands that subsequently provided him with a plethora of motifs. For example *Landscape at Tørring* (c. 1841; Copenhagen, Stat. Mus. Kst) demonstrates his considerable ability to record meteorological conditions; in this sense his painting shares a close affinity with that of John Constable, though Dreyer could not have known any of the latter's work. In perhaps his most renowned painting from Jutland, a *Low Beach with Dunes: The West Coast of Jutland* (1843; Copenhagen, Stat. Mus. Kst), Dreyer meticulously painted the texture of the rocky beach and the subtle nuances of light and colour created by the cloudy sky that dominates this coastal view. Historically, this work can be seen as the first of the emotionally expressive depictions of the west coast of Jutland, which culminated in the pictures of the coast at Bovbjerg by the Expressionist landscape painter Jens Søndergaard.

Like many of his contemporaries, Dreyer had an avid desire to travel, but poverty and his failure to win any academic stipends prevented him from doing so, despite some support from Bertel Thorvaldsen; he was obliged to focus exclusively on the landscapes of his native Denmark. Dreyer also produced a number of portraits and religious paintings; the most striking of these is his *Self-portrait* (1838; Odense, Fyn. Kstmus.), which captures his sensitive, retiring personality. Impoverished and forgotten, he largely gave up painting in his final years, retreating to live with his mother and sister in a farmhouse, Barløse, on Fyn. His work was only rediscovered at the beginning of the 20th century.

BIBLIOGRAPHY

Dankvart Dreyer, 1816–1852 (exh. cat. by L. Swane, Copenhagen, Kstforen., 1921)
C. W. Eckersberg og hans elever [C. W. Eckersberg and his pupils] (exh. cat., ed. H. Jönsson; Copenhagen, Stat. Mus. Kst, 1983)
Danish Painting: The Golden Age (exh. cat. by K. Monrad, London, N.G., 1984), pp. 248–55
N. Kent: *The Triumph of Light and Nature: Nordic Art* (London, 1987)
O. Feldbaek, ed.: *Dansk Identitetshistorie*, 4 vols (Copenhagen, 1992)
H. Frederiksen and I.-L. Kostrup, eds: *Ny Dansk Kunsthistorie*, 10 vols (Copenhagen, 1993)

NEIL KENT

Dreyfus, Gustave (*b* Paris, 21 March 1837; *d* Paris, 29 Sept 1914). French connoisseur and collector. In 1862–4 he served as secretary to his uncle, who was working on the construction of the Suez Canal, and in Cairo made notable acquisitions of Islamic art, which he later donated to the Louvre, Paris. On 29 November 1872 he purchased from the painter Charles Timbal (1821–80) 155 important early Renaissance sculptures, reliefs, small bronzes and paintings, collected by Timbal over the previous 20 years in Florence. To this nucleus Dreyfus occasionally made additions, in particular of bronzes: two sculptures that his heirs gave to the Louvre, the marble bust of *Diotisalvi Neroni* (c. 1465) by Mino da Fiesole and the bronze group of *St Jerome with the Lion* (1490s) by Bartolomeo Bellano,

epitomize the principal strengths of his collection. Dreyfus's reputation, however, rests on his achievement as a connoisseur and collector of Renaissance medals and plaquettes. Although barely two dozen bronze reliefs, and only a dozen medals, had been included in the purchase from Timbal, Dreyfus left two incomparable collections: one of almost 700 medals (one of the richest cabinets in public or private hands), and one of some 450 plaquettes—by far the finest assemblage of these miniature works in the world. Both collections were sold in 1930 to Joseph Duveen and were acquired in 1945 by the Kress Foundation, by which they were donated in 1957 to the National Gallery of Art, Washington, DC. There they were rejoined by the principal works from Timbal's and Dreyfus's original collection of larger sculptures, which had been sold by Duveen to Andrew W. Mellon. To Dreyfus's discrimination is thus due the pre-eminence of the sculpture collection in Washington: the most extensive—and, in its specialized areas, the finest—in the Western Hemisphere.

UNPUBLISHED SOURCES
Paris, François Goldschmidt priv. col. [MS. of C. Timbal: *Liste des objets appartenant à M. Gustave Dreyfus* (1872); and other docs]

BIBLIOGRAPHY
G. Migeon: 'Gustave Dreyfus', *Notice lue à l'assemblée générale de la société des amis du Louvre* (Paris, 1929), pp. 3–16

DOUGLAS LEWIS

Drielst, Egbert van (*b* Groningen, *bapt* 12 March 1745; *d* Amsterdam, 1818). Dutch painter, restorer and art appraiser. He began work at an early age in Steven Numan's factory of lacquered objects in Groningen. With Numan's son Hermanus he decided to improve his skills in the wallpaper factory of Jan and Johannes Luberti Augustini in Haarlem. When Numan left for Paris to continue his studies, van Drielst moved to Amsterdam, where he worked again for a short period in a wallpaper factory before he began to work independently. He became a member of the Guild of St Luke in 1768, the year he attended the Amsterdam city drawing academy to practise life drawing. He also carried out restorations and appraisals and became a friend of Adriaan de Lelie and other artists.

Van Drielst became increasingly interested in landscape, and working from nature studies he made watercolours and paintings that sold easily to such collectors as Bernardus de Bosch and Jan Gildemeester. These landscapes, which appealed to the renewed interest in nature in the 18th century, were based on the work of 17th-century Dutch painters such as Meindert Hobbema and Jacob van Ruisdael. Van Drielst was nicknamed the 'Drentse Hobbema', as he increasingly frequented the province of Drenthe to supplement his series of sketches from nature, for example the *Landscape with Peasants by a Pond and a Cottage Beyond* (1794; ex-Sotheby's, London, 1 July 1971, lot 101), which is drawn in black chalk with watercolour and inscribed *Te, Emmen in het landschap, Drenthe*.

Renowned for his reliability, informed criticism and modest behaviour, Van Drielst showed scarcely any stylistic development. He was a member of various art societies, and towards the end of his life he joined the Fourth Class of the Royal Holland Institute. He taught his stepson, the painter Jan Vuuring van Drielst (1789–1813).

BIBLIOGRAPHY
Egbert van Drielst, 'de Drentse Hobbema', 1745–1818 (exh. cat. by J. W. Niemeijer, Assen, Prov. Mus. Drenthe, 1968)

J. W. Niemeijer: 'De betekenis van Drenthe voor de vernieuwing in de landschapsschilderkunst omstreeks 1800' [The significance of Drenthe in the revival of landscape painting *c.* 1800], *Nieuwe Drentse Volksalm.* (1977), pp. 69–97

P. KNOLLE

Drijfhout [Drijffhout; Dryffhout], **Bartholomeus (Fransz.)** (*b* Dordrecht, June 1605; *d* 1649). Dutch architect, mason and sculptor. He practised as a mason and sculptor in Dordrecht until 1636, when he moved to The Hague and worked as a master mason on building schemes for the stadholder, Frederick Henry; there he met architects of the court circle such as Jacob van Campen, Pieter Post and Arent Arentsz. van 's Gravesande. In February 1645 he succeeded Post as architect to the stadholder and was made responsible for the alterations to the Oude Hof (now Paleis Noordeinde) of the stadholder's town palace, to the plans of van Campen. He also executed some of the cut stonework for the Cloth Hall (1639; now the Stedelijk Museum De Lakenhal), Leiden, by Arentsz. The only commission for which he used his own designs was the modest town hall (1648) at Vlaardingen, a low building with a projecting central range crowned by a pediment. His name, together with that of Post, is also associated with the construction of the Protestant Oostkerk (1647–67) in Middelburg. It is a variant on the Mare Kerk (begun 1631), Leiden, by Arent Arentsz. van 's Gravesande, which has an octagonal domed space with an ambulatory behind the columns that support the drum. In the Oostkerk, the columns supporting the dome stand so close to the wall that the ambulatory is all but eliminated. Externally, the octagonal dome rises straight from an attic and is surmounted by a massive lantern. There is an additional smaller octagon for the vestry and belfry. After Drijfhout's death, sculpture was added to the church, which was completed by others. The Gasthuis (Old People's Hospice) in Breda, rebuilt in 1643 (now an art centre), is thought to be the work of his brother Laureys Drijfhout. Unusually, this has a pilastered façade built entirely of bricks.

BIBLIOGRAPHY
M. D. Ozinga: *De Protestantse kerkenbouw in Nederland* [Protestant church building in the Netherlands] (Amsterdam, 1929)

F. A. J. Vermeulen: *Handboek tot de geschiedenis der Nederlandse bouwkunst* [Guide to the history of Dutch architecture], iii (The Hague, 1941)

J. Rosenberg, S. Slive and E. H. ter Kuile: *Dutch Art and Architecture, 1600 to 1800*, Pelican Hist. A. (Harmondsworth, 1966, rev. 1977)

PAUL H. REM

Droeshout, Martin (*b* Brussels, 1560s; *d* ?London, *c.* 1642). Flemish engraver, active in England. He was the second son of John and Mary Droeshout, who arrived in London from Brussels as Protestant refugees. The eldest son, Michael Droeshout, studied engraving on the Continent before rejoining the family *c.* 1590. John, presumably also an engraver, is described in manuscripts as a 'painter', indicating that he became a freeman of the Painter–Stainers' Company, London, which admitted men who worked with wood, metal and stone, as well as pigments. Martin certainly became a freeman of the Company, probably by patrimony; the Company's minutes, which survive from 1623, show that he was a leading member.

About 1605 he settled in the parish of St Olave Hart Street, near the Tower of London, and had seven children by a second wife. The engraving of *William Shakespeare* signed *Martin Droeshout*, which is on the title-page of the first collected edition of Shakespeare's plays, the 'First Folio' (1623), can be confidently attributed to Droeshout. A few other works of his survive, including a signed portrait of *James Hamilton, 2nd Marquess of Hamilton* (1589–1625), also dated 1623. Martin had two nephews, sons of his brother Michael Droeshout: the elder, John Droeshout (1599–1652), was also an engraver. The only positive fact known about the younger, Martin Droeshout the younger, is that he was born in 1601. The common attribution to him of the Shakespeare engraving cannot be sustained: the editors of the First Folio would not have entrusted such an important commission to someone who was only 15 when Shakespeare died and was still in his very early twenties when the First Folio appeared.

BIBLIOGRAPHY
A. M. Hind: *Engraving in England in the 16th and 17th Centuries*, ii (Cambridge, 1952), pp. 341–66

M. Edmond: 'It Was for Gentle Shakespeare Cut', *Shakespeare Q.*, xlii (Autumn 1991), pp. 339–44

MARY EDMOND

Drollery [Fr. *drôlerie*]. Grotesque or comic figure or any humorous design. Drolleries were frequently used to decorate the borders or margins of medieval manuscripts (*see* GRISAILLE, fig. 1) or some inconspicuous carved area in a church.

☐

Drolling [Drelling; Drölling]. French family of painters. Both (1) Martin Drolling and his son (2) Michel-Martin Drolling were portrait painters; whereas the father expanded his range by concentrating on bourgeois domestic interiors, the son produced a number of history paintings on mythological and religious subjects. Another of Martin Drolling's three children by his second wife, Louise-Elisabeth (née Belot), was Louise-Adéone Drolling (*b* Paris, 29 May 1797; *d* before 1831), otherwise known as Mme Joubert; she also practised as a painter.

(1) Martin Drolling (*b* Oberbergheim, nr Colmar, *bapt* 19 Sept 1752; *d* Paris, 16 April 1817). After receiving initial training from an unknown painter in Sélestat, Drolling moved to Paris, where he attended courses at the Académie Royale. He supplemented his education there by studying Flemish and Dutch Old Masters in the collection at the Luxembourg Palace. From the Flemish school he derived his own rich impasto, while the Dutch was to influence him in his meticulous, supremely descriptive and unsentimental style of painting as well as his choice of subject-matter: unfussy bourgeois interiors and frank portraits. Drolling first exhibited at the Salon de la Correspondance in 1781 and again in 1782 and 1789. After the French Revolution he was able to participate in the Salon at the Louvre, despite the fact that he had never become a member of the Académie Royale. He exhibited from 1793 to 1817, although the majority of his works extant today were shown after 1800. From 1802 to 1813 he was employed by the Sèvres porcelain manufactory, and many of his designs were engraved.

Drolling's works are often compared with those of his contemporary Louis-Léopold Boilly on account of their high finish and depiction of a solidly bourgeois world, though Drolling's compositions are less anecdotal and his choice of themes often more banal. He has much in common with the German and Scandinavian minor masters of the period (e.g. Carl Gustav Carus, Johannes Jelgerhuis and Georg Friedrich Kersting), but his productions lack the emblematic content of works by Caspar David Friedrich, which they resemble in style. Drolling's tendency to reduce his subject-matter to a mundane domestic level is seen in *A Young Lady (Queen Hortense) Brings Relief to a Family that has Experienced Misfortune* (Caen, Mus. B.-A.) and in the more successful *Interior of a Dining-room* (1816; Paris, priv. col.) and *Interior of a Kitchen* (1815; Paris, Louvre). A preparatory drawing for the latter work also exists (Paris, Louvre). No symbolic meanings are invested in *Interior of a Kitchen*, although occasionally Drolling did choose to illustrate a particular theme or moral.

A good collection of Drolling's portraits survives, the best examples of which testify to his great skill in this area. That of *Michel Belot* (1791) and the *Self-portrait* (c. 1791; both Orléans, Mus. B.-A.) are particularly fine.

BIBLIOGRAPHY

French Painting, 1774–1830: The Age of Revolution (exh. cat., ed. F. Cummings, R. Rosenblum and P. Rosenberg; Detroit, MI, Inst. A.; New York, Met.; Paris, Grand Pal.; 1974–5), pp. 398–9

M. O'Neill: *Orléans, Musée des Beaux-arts, catalogue critique: Les Peintures de l'école française des XVIIe et XVIIIe siècles*, cat. (Orléans, 1977), pp. 49–54

Au temps de Watteau, Fragonard et Chardin: Les Pays-Bas et les peintres français du XVIIIe siècle (exh. cat., ed. C. Lauboutin and A. Scottez; Lille, Mus. B.-A., 1985)

JOSHUA DRAPKIN

(2) Michel-Martin Drolling (*b* Paris, 7 March 1786; *d* Paris, 9 Jan 1851). Son of (1) Martin Drolling. The pupil of his father, he also studied in David's studio in 1806. He obtained the Prix de Rome in 1810 with the *Anger of Achilles* (Paris, Ecole N. Sup. B.-A.). After his stay in Rome he exhibited the *Death of Abel* (Leipzig, Mus. Bild. Kst.) in the Salon of 1817. He decorated two ceilings in the Musée Charles X in the Louvre and obtained two commissions from the Musée d'Histoire at Versailles: the *Tours States-General* (1836) and the *Alexandria Convention* (1837). His genre scenes show that while his style was generally colder, he inherited his father's love of Dutch art and use of thinly applied, porcelain-like paint, contrasting effects of light and meticulous detail. His figures were either half-length with a landscape background in the English manner (*Portrait of Manuel*, 1819; Brest, Mus. Mun.) or full-length and set in countryside, with the charming naivety of Pierre Duval Le Camus.

Drolling also attempted history painting (the *Separation of Hecuba and Polyxenas*, 1824; Le Puy, Mus. Crozatier) and allegory (*Strength*, 1818, Amiens, Mus. Picardie; *Prudence*, 1819, Bordeaux, Mus. B.-A.). These are works of a rigid, ponderous and ossified Neo-classicism. He was also involved in the decoration of Notre-Dame-de-Lorette (1823–36) in Paris, producing *Christ among the Doctors* (*in situ*), which is old-fashioned in comparison to the work of Victor Orsel in the same church and reveals Drolling as a frigid and enfeebled follower of David. The many students

at his studio in the Ecole des Beaux-Arts included Paul Baudry, Jules Breton and Jean-Jacques Henner.

BIBLIOGRAPHY

C. Gabet: *Dictionnaire des artistes français au XIXe siècle* (Paris, 1831), p. 224

P. Grunchez: *Les Concours des Prix de Rome: Catalogue* (Paris, 1986), pp. 94–5

MARIE-CLAUDE CHAUDONNERET

Drop ornament. *See* PENDANT (i).

Dröschel, Hans. *See* TROSCHEL, (1).

Drost, Willem (*b* ?Germany, *c.* 1630; *d* ?Amsterdam, after 1680). Dutch painter, draughtsman and printmaker, possibly of German origin. According to Houbraken, he was a pupil of Rembrandt, possibly in or shortly before 1650. An early etching signed *w drost 1652* is probably a self-portrait, in which Drost portrayed himself as a young man drawing. His earliest dated paintings are two pendants of 1653: the *Portrait of a Man* (New York, Met.) and the *Portrait of a Woman* (The Hague, Mus. Bredius). The man's portrait is signed *Wilhelmus Drost F./ Amsterdam 1653*; the form of the first name implies that he was of German descent.

The painting of *Bathsheba with Daniel's Letter* (Paris, Louvre; see fig.), signed and dated *Drost F. 1654*, is considered to be his masterpiece, with its subtle palette of soft flesh tones harmonizing with the varying shades of white and grey in which the cloth and the fur are splendidly rendered. Dating from the same period is his *Portrait of a Young Woman* (London, Wallace), which bears the false signature *Rembrandt ft.* Two works of contrasting styles are also dated 1654: the *Portrait of a Woman with a Fan* (Zurich, E. Haab-Escher priv. col.) and the *Woman with*

Willem Drost: *Bathsheba with Daniel's Letter*, oil on canvas, 1.03×0.87 m, 1654 (Paris, Musée du Louvre)

a Knife in a Window (ex-Brod Gal., London). The former is polished and detailed; the second is executed in a much looser manner with broad brushstrokes. These paintings show not only Drost's ability to paint in these two different traditional ways but also his participation in the stylistic debate topical around 1650: many of Rembrandt's pupils were faced with the choice of continuing to paint in the broad virtuoso manner of their master or adopting a smoother, more up-to-date style. For commissioned works such as portraits the smoother style was usually chosen, as Drost did in the *Portrait of a Woman* of 1654, whereas the *Woman with a Knife* of the same year is a more freely painted genre scene. After 1660 Drost changed definitely to the elegant, polished style of, for example, Nicolaes Maes, evident from his only dated work of this period, the portrait of *Hillegonda van Beuningen* (1663; The Netherlands, priv. col.). Around 1662 Drost must have been in Italy, where, according to Houbraken, he became friends with Jan van der Meer of Utrecht (*c.* 1640–after 1691) and Johann Carl Loth; Drost's *Self-portrait* (*c.* 1662; Florence, Uffizi) is in the manner of Loth, with heavy shadows and warm brown and red tones.

Apart from portraits and a few half-length figures in historical costume, such as the *Man in a Cuirass* (Kassel, Schloss Wilhelmshöhe), Drost painted mainly biblical scenes with full-length figures: a *Noli me tangere* (Kassel, Schloss Wilhelmshöhe); the *Young Daniel* (Copenhagen, Stat. Mus. Kst); the *Virgin Annunciate* (Prague, N.G., Šternberk Pal.); and *Ruth and Naomi* (Oxford, Ashmolean), the only painting for which there is a directly connected preparatory drawing (Bremen, Ksthalle). On stylistic grounds another 45 or so pen and ink drawings have been attributed to Drost, all characterized by profuse and remarkably even hatching.

The reconstruction of Drost's painted and drawn oeuvre by Sumowski (1980 and 1983) does not yet seem complete. A number of history paintings with large figures depicting biblical subjects, previously ascribed to Rembrandt, are apparently (or may yet prove to be) by Drost. If the attribution to Drost of *Manoah's Sacrifice* (Dresden, Gemäldegal. Alte Meister), which bears the false signature of *Rembrandt f. 1641*, is accepted, then the basis for the attribution of similar works may be formed.

BIBLIOGRAPHY
A. Houbraken: *De groote schouburgh* (1718–21), iii, p. 61
D. Pont: 'De composities "Ruth en Naomi" te Bremen en te Oxford: Toeschrijving aan Willem Drost', *Oud-Holland*, lxxv (1960), pp. 205–21
W. Sumowski: *Drawings of the Rembrandt School*, iii (New York, 1980), nos 546–69
——: *Gemälde der Rembrandtschüler*, i (Landau, 1983), pp. 608–51; review by J. Bruyn in *Oud-Holland*, xcviii (1984), pp. 153–8

B. P. J. BROOS

Drouais. French family of painters. (1) Hubert Drouais was a successful portrait painter and miniaturist whose fame was, however, eclipsed by that of his son (2) François-Hubert Drouais, one of the most fashionable court portraitists in mid-18th-century France. François-Hubert's son (3) Jean-Germain Drouais was the most promising Neo-classical history painter in the first generation of Jacques-Louis David's pupils, but he died young.

BIBLIOGRAPHY
C. Gabillot: 'Les Trois Drouais', *Gaz. B.-A.*, n. s. 2, xxxiv (1905), pp. 177–94, 288–98, 384–400; xxxv (1906), pp. 155–74, 246–58

(1) Hubert Drouais [Drouais *le père*] (*b* Saint-Samson-de-la-Roque, Eure, 5 May 1699; *d* Paris, 9 Feb 1767). He began his artistic training in Rouen and moved to Paris in 1717, where he entered the studio of the portrait painter François de Troy, who employed him principally as a copyist. Besides painting portraits in oil and pastel, Drouais also took up miniature painting. For his acceptance into the Académie Royale in 1730, however, he presented two large-scale portraits, of the painter *Joseph Christophe* (Versailles, Château) and the sculptor *Robert Le Lorrain* (Paris, Louvre). Whereas the painter is shown in front of his easel, dressed informally, the sculptor is depicted in more official garb and pose, with a model of his statue of *Hebe* for the château of Marly. At this same period Hubert Drouais was also successful with his portraits of ladies. His painting of the singer *Mlle Marie Pélissier as Flora* (before 1736; Paris, Louvre) is characteristic, with its fashionable, light-hearted mythologizing. At the Salon, where he exhibited regularly between 1741 and 1757, Drouais achieved particular renown with his miniatures. A representative example, combining portraiture with chic eroticism, is his *Portrait of a Lady in the Guise of Venus* (Paris, Louvre). His work in oil, in which the colouring often imitates the nuances of pastel, was equally popular, and he achieved success at court from 1749.

BIBLIOGRAPHY
Thieme–Becker
P. Lespinasse: *La Miniature en France au XVIIIe siècle* (Paris, 1929)
P. Rosenberg, N. Reynaud and I. Compin: *Ecole française: XVIIe et XVIIIe siècles*, 2 vols (1974), i of *Catalogue illustré des peintures*, Paris, Louvre cat. (Paris, 1974–), i, nos 239–40

CATHRIN KLINGSÖHR-LE ROY

(2) François-Hubert Drouais [Drouais *le fils*] (*b* Paris, 14 Dec 1727; *d* Paris, 21 Oct 1775). Son of (1) Hubert Drouais. He trained with his father and then with Donat Nonotte, Carle Vanloo, Charles-Joseph Natoire and François Boucher. He was made an associate member (*agréé*) of the Académie Royale in 1755, on presentation of a *Portrait of a Lady* (untraced), and quickly built up a practice at court. Towards the end of 1756 he was summoned to Versailles to paint the two infant sons of the Dauphin, the *Duc de Berry and the Comte de Provence* (São Paulo, Mus. A. Assis Châteaubriand), a painting whose success assured him of royal patronage for the rest of his life. This charming portrait of two future kings (Louis XVI and Louis XVIII) playing with a dog was exhibited at the Salon of 1757, along with seven other portraits, and the critical reaction was very favourable. These paintings illustrate themes that Drouais was to use frequently: a pastoral setting, a relaxed intimacy of pose and fancy dress: often his sitters are shown as gardeners, Savoyards, harvesters or 'montagnards'. In addition, his technique was astonishingly secure, careful, fluent and calculated to please.

Drouais was received (*reçu*) as a full member of the Académie on 25 November 1758 with portraits of *Guillaume Coustou (i)* (Versailles, Château) and *Edme Bouchardon* (Paris, Louvre; see fig.), both sculptors to the king and professors at the Académie. Henceforth, he

François-Hubert Drouais: *Edme Bouchardon*, oil on canvas, 1.29×0.97 m, 1758 (Paris, Musée du Louvre)

produced a steady succession of portraits of notable personages, including the royal favourites *Mme de Pompadour* (1763–4; London, NG), and Mme Du Barry (e.g. *Mme Du Barry as Flora*, exh. Salon 1769; New York, priv. col., see 1968 exh. cat., no. 206). Louis XV himself sat to Drouais in 1772 (exh. Salon 1773; Versailles, Château). Distinguished foreign visitors in Paris were also eager to secure his services: the Marquess of Lorne (later the 5th Duke of Argyll) and his wife sat to him in 1763 (Inveraray Castle, Strathclyde, see 1968 exh. cat., nos 209–10). The artist continued to show at the Salon and accumulated official honours: he was appointed painter to the Comte de Provence in 1772 and named counsellor to the Académie on 2 July 1774.

Drouais introduced a note of informality into the court portrait, generally avoiding both the Baroque grandeur of Nicolas de Largillierre and the mythological allegories of Jean-Marc Nattier. In the mid-18th century perhaps only Alexandre Roslin could rival Drouais in depicting feminine grace and beauty, and as a painter of children he was unequalled. He was careful to flatter his sitters shamelessly, and even in his small, bust-length portraits with the subject shown against a plain, dark background, e.g. *Girl with a Cat* (exh. Salon 1763; untraced, see 1984–5 exh. cat., p. 192), he took no interest in psychological insight. Denis Diderot, who demanded that a portrait should be expressive rather than merely charming, complained several times of Drouais's 'falseness' and compared his creamy flesh tones to chalk, but the few dissenting critics could not tarnish the artist's social and artistic celebrity.

BIBLIOGRAPHY
France in the Eighteenth Century (exh. cat. by D. Sutton, London, RA, 1968), p. 67
Diderot et l'art de Boucher à David: Les Salons, 1759–1781 (exh. cat., ed. M.-C. Sahut and N. Volle; Paris, Hôtel de la Monnaie, 1984–5), pp. 191–4

COLIN HARRISON

(3) Jean-Germain [Germain-Jean] **Drouais** (*b* Paris, 24 Nov 1763; *d* Rome, 13 Feb 1788). Son of (2) François-Hubert Drouais. He trained first with his father and in 1778 enrolled at the Académie Royale, becoming a pupil of Nicolas-Guy Brenet. Around 1781 he entered Jacques-Louis David's studio as one of his first pupils. The following year, though not officially entered for the competition, he painted that year's Prix de Rome subject, the *Return of the Prodigal Son* (Paris, St Roch), presumably as a trial for his own edification. The picture has a friezelike composition and reveals both the influence of Jean-François Peyron and David as well as debts to Poussin and Italian 17th-century sources. In 1783 Drouais reached the Prix de Rome final with the *Resurrection of the Son of the Widow of Nain* (Le Mans, Mus. Tessé) but was eliminated from the competition in extraordinary circumstances: impatient to know his master's opinion, Drouais cut a section off the canvas and smuggled it out of the competition rooms. David acknowledged it to be the best thing his favourite pupil had yet done, but by his hasty action Drouais had disqualified himself. However, the following year he won the prize, and great acclaim, with the *Woman of Canaan at the Feet of Christ* (Paris, Louvre), an extremely accomplished piece influenced by Poussin's work and David's *Belisarius* (Lille, Mus. B.-A.).

Drouais left almost immediately for Rome and there joined David, already in the city to renew his study of the Antique in preparation for his next official commission, the *Oath of the Horatii* (Paris, Louvre). Drouais was reluctant to follow the standard course of work for students at the Académie de France in Rome and spent much of his time with David, whom he almost certainly assisted with some small sections of the *Oath of the Horatii*. David left Rome in August 1785, and after his departure the insecure Drouais, who was on bad terms with the Académie's Director Louis Lagrenée, became even more isolated. He was of a difficult and volatile nature, and after a fight with a local youth he was obliged to carry a pair of pistols for protection. In 1786 he executed an extremely large painting to send to the Académie Royale in Paris, *Marius at Minturnae* (Paris, Louvre), the first truly authoritative Neo-classical work by a pupil of David. Using many of David's pictorial devices, such as a shallow, stagelike setting, a limited number of figures with clear and expressive gestures, and muted colours combined with dramatic lighting, Drouais created a taut and stark image. After seeing this picture, Jean-Baptiste-Marie Pierre, the Premier Peintre du Roi, confidently predicted that Drouais would surpass David.

Drouais's last picture was *Philoctetes* (Chartres, Mus. B.-A.), begun in 1787. The subject-matter and the brooding lighting indicate that Drouais was moving away from strictly Davidian ideals, becoming interested in a greater intensity of inward emotion. The picture was unfinished at the time of Drouais's death from smallpox, exacerbated by overwork. David himself was greatly shaken by the loss of his greatest potential rival, and said, 'In losing him, I lose my emulation. He alone could trouble my sleep.' Jean-Germain Drouais's early promise and premature death made him something of a legend in the studios of Paris.

BIBLIOGRAPHY

'Eloge historique de M. Drouais', *Mercure France* (June 1788), p. 37

P. Chaussard: 'Notice historique sur M. Drouais, élève de l'Académie Royale', *Le Pausanias français* (Paris, 1806), pp. 337–53

J. Herissay: 'Artistes normands: L'Education d'un peintre à la fin du XVIII siècle: Germain-Jean Drouais (1763–1788)', *Bull. Soc. Amis A. Dépt. Eure*, xix, xx (1903–4)

D. Wildenstein and G. Wildenstein: *Documents complémentaires au catalogue complet de l'oeuvre de Louis David* (Paris, 1973), p. 155

Jean-Germain Drouais (exh. cat., ed. P. Ramade; Rennes, Mus. B.-A. & Archéol., 1985)

S. Lee: 'Jean-Germain Drouais and the 1784 Prix de Rome', *BM Q.*, cxxx (May 1988), no. 1022, pp. 361–5

T. Crow: *Emulation: Making Artists for Revolutionary France* (New Haven and London, 1995)

SIMON LEE

Droz, Jean-Pierre (*b* La Chaux-de-Fonds, Neuchâtel, 17 April 1746; *d* Paris, 2 March 1823). Swiss medallist, active in France and England. He trained in France; in 1786 he struck a pattern écu of *Louis XVI* with an edge inscription produced by a new type of collar. This attracted the attention of Matthew Boulton, who persuaded Droz to visit England in 1787 and to work for him at the Soho Mint in 1788. There Droz effected mechanical improvements to Boulton's coining machinery and cut dies for some patterns for the English coinage. After his return to France, Droz was appointed Keeper of the Mint Museum and in 1810 won a competition to provide designs for a new coinage. He contributed a large number of medals to the Napoleonic series produced under the direction of Dominique-Vivant Denon, and several to Mudie's National Series, as well as medals celebrating *General Elliot's Defence of Gibraltar* (1787) and *King George III's Restoration to Health* (both London, BM).

BIBLIOGRAPHY

Forrer

G. Gallet: *Quelques notes sur la vie et l'oeuvre du médailleur J.-P. Droz* (Neuchâtel, 1902)

G. Pollard: 'Matthew Boulton and J.-P. Droz', *Numi. Chron.*, viii (1968), pp. 241–65

MARK JONES

Drtikol, František (*b* Příbram, 3 March 1883; *d* Prague, 13 Jan 1961). Bohemian photographer and painter. He wanted to become a painter, but his father insisted on a more secure future and made him train as a photographer at the studio of Antonín Matas in Příbram. In 1901 he took a two-year course at the Lehr- und Versuchsanstalt für Photographie in Munich. At that time the city was an important centre of *Jugendstil*. He was successful in his studies, and upon finishing he won the first prize. He then worked in the professional studios of T. Schumann in Karlsruhe, Albert Böse in Chur, Switzerland, and Josef Faix in Prague. In 1907, after three years of military service, he founded his own studio in Příbram. It was not, however, a commercial success, and in 1910 he moved to Prague and established a studio in Vodičkova Street, specializing in portrait photography. He made excellent portraits of prominent politicians and cultural figures. In 1911 he published a portfolio of oleo (oil pigment) prints, *Z dvorků a dvorečků staré Prahy*. Drtikol's own creative work in his Prague studio, with which he came to prominence, was devoted to the female nude. At first, these were influenced by *Jugendstil*, but later he adopted a style more related to Art Deco, the former voluptuousness of the female body's curves giving way to almost geometrical compositions in which the same curves formed a part of geometrical patterns, more simplified and even distorted, in a variety of artistic experiments that even approached Constructivism. As he grew more and more interested in the mystical, his photographs became more stylized, and in the 1930s he finally substituted plywood figures in order to achieve the forms, shapes and positions required. He referred to this work as 'Photopurism—a sort of abstract photography'. In 1935 Drtikol abandoned photography and took up painting and the study of Oriental philosophy, occultism and theosophy. His symbolic and mystical oil paintings reveal this inclination towards the occult, though they also contain traces of his earlier formal experiments. In 1945–6 he lectured at the State School of Graphic Arts in Prague. Afterwards, he retired into an almost complete seclusion and dedicated the last years of his life to philosophical thoughts and meditations.

Drtikol was an accomplished photographer, a master of techniques such as oleo print or gum bichromate print and the inventor of a half-tone photolithographic process (*see* PHOTOGRAPHY, §I), which he patented in 1925. His method of lighting his objects was highly inventive, and light and shade played a role in his photographs as important as that of the depicted objects. In his most famous photographs he often used large geometrical objects to point out or to contrast the subtle curves of the female body. After his arrival in Prague in 1910 he contributed to a great number of reviews and periodicals, and in 1929 a book of his nudes was published in Paris. From 1903 to 1936 he participated in some 15 major international salons and exhibitions. After he gave up photography in 1935, however, his work was virtually forgotten for almost three decades. It was only in the 1970s when, due to the growing interest in *Jugendstil*, Drtikol was rediscovered. He was then recognized, together with Josef Sudek and Jaromír Funke, as one of the major personalities of modern Czech photography and as an artist who greatly contributed to the development of modern photography in the first half of the 20th century. The Museum of Decorative Arts in Prague has a collection of *c.* 20,000 prints and all his unpublished documents.

PHOTOGRAPHIC PUBLICATIONS

Doly příbramské [Mines of Příbram] (Prague, ?1910)

Z dvorků a dvorečků staré Prahy [From the courtyards, small and big, of old Prague] (Prague, 1911; repr. as postcards, 1924)

Dorostenky: Rytmický tělocvik ve volné přírodě [Senior girls: open-air physical training] (Prague, 1914)

Pět portrétů T. G. Masaryka [Five portraits of T. G. Masaryk] (Prague, 1923)

A. Calavas, ed.: *Les Nus de Drtikol*, intro. C. de Santeul (Paris, 1929)

Žena ve světle [Woman in light] (Prague, 1938)

BIBLIOGRAPHY

Fototgraf František Drtikol: Tvorba z let 1903–1935 [The photographer František Drtikol: works from 1903 to 1935] (exh. cat., text A. Fárová; Prague, Mus. Dec. A., 1972)

Fotografie, 1922–1982, 'Frauen im Licht/Women in Light': František Drtikol, Paul Outerbridge, Helmut Newton (exh. cat., Cologne, Photokina, 1982)

Photographes tchèques (exh. cat., intro. A. Sayag, texts Z. Kirschner and A. Dufek; Paris, Pompidou, 1983)

A. Fárová: *František Drtikol: Photographe des Arts Déco* (Munich, 1986)
V. Birgus and A. Brarý: *František Drtikol* (Prague, 1988)
K. Klaricová: *František Drtikol* (Prague, 1989)

JIŘÍ BUREŠ

Drudus de Trivio (*fl c*. 1230–40). Italian marble-worker and sculptor. He was called 'de Trivio' from his place of residence in Rome, where he belonged to the group of highly productive marble workers known as the COSMATI. As a sculptor he is to be compared with Vassallettus, with whom he collaborated, although he had another workshop and was occasionally assisted by his son Angelus. All the works definitely attributable to Drudus are liturgical furniture, and he seems not to have laid pavements. Nothing substantial remains of the earliest work attributable to Drudus on the grounds of a signed inscription (destr.) in S Francesca Romana (S Maria Nuova), Rome.

With Lucas of the Laurentius family, Drudus signed the presbytery screens of Cività Castellana Cathedral (Mus. Dioc.) *c*. 1230; they described themselves as citizens of Rome and MAG[IST]RI DOCTISSIMI. Drudus, the first signatory on the inscription, probably made the flanking lions and sphinxes, which are similar both to the lions' heads on the capitals of the altar ciborium signed by him in Ferentino Cathedral and to the sphinx there. The ciborium also bears a donor inscription indicating a date of 1240. In form, in the costly materials employed and in the fine craftsmanship, the ciborium surpasses all others surviving in the region of Rome. The capitals are some of the finest examples of the classicizing work of the Cosmati. Other fragments, a lion and a sphinx from a presbytery screen, a paschal candlestick and a pair of lions from a throne are certainly from the same workshop.

The reliefs on a water basin (Rome, Pal. Venezia), also signed by Magister Drudus, show familiarity with antique decorative motifs. The basin is unique and its original function unclear. The only secure dates for the works of Drudus, in the collegiate church of Lanuvio (formerly Cività Lavinia), are known only from descriptions and a few remains. The inscription on the altar ciborium gives the date of the donation (1240) and names the donor, the artist and his son Angelus, but it is difficult to determine whether Drudus was involved in the remaining furnishings with their lions and sphinxes, because the presbytery screens bear the signature of Vassallettus, which indicates the collaboration of this important atelier.

Drudus's son, Angelus de Trivio, signed a ciborium (destr.) in S Maria in Cambiatoribus, Rome, in 1236. It is not known whether Drudus and his son were related to any of the great marble-working families. That Drudus worked not only with the principal members of the Laurentius family but also with Vassallettus suggests his independence and high standing. Too little remains of his work for a clear evaluation of his artistic achievements to be made, but he was evidently very familiar with antique decorative forms. Figural sculpture played only a very small role, however, in the tradition of the Roman marble workers, and Drudus's lions and sphinxes lack the plasticity and vigour of those from the workshop of Vassallettus.

BIBLIOGRAPHY
G. Giovannoni: 'Drudus de Trivio marmorario romano', *Miscellanea per nozze Hermanin-Hausmann* (Rome, 1904), pp 1–11
——: 'Note sui marmorari romani', *Archv Soc. Romana Stor. Patria*, xxvii (1904), pp. 3–26
——: 'Opere dei Vassalletti', *L'Arte*, xi (1908), pp. 262–83 (277, 282)
A. Galieti: 'Memorie della chiesa medievale di Cività Lavinia', *L'Arte*, xii (1909), pp. 349–58
G. Mercati: 'Sopra tre iscrizioni medievali di chiese romane ed un'opera scomparsa del marmorario Angelo de Trivio', *Atti Pont. Accad. Romana Archeol.*, xi/3–4 (1936), pp. 159ff
D. F. Glass: *Studies on Cosmatesque Pavements*, Brit. Archaeol. Rep. (Oxford, 1980)
A. M. Romanini, ed.: *Storia dell'arte e territorio: Ferentino*, Stor. Città, xv-xvi (Rome, 1980)
P. C. Claussen: *Magistri doctissimi Romani: Die römischen Marmorkünstler des Mittelalters*, Forsch. Kstgesch. & Christ. Archäol., xiv (Stuttgart, 1987)

P. C. CLAUSSEN

Drukyul, Kingdom of. *See* BHUTAN.

Drum [tambour]. Term for any generally cylinder-shaped architectural member, for example one of the stones that form a column; a cylindrical or polygonal wall below a dome, often set with windows; or the core of a capital, Corinthian or Composite, from which the ornamentation springs.   □

Drummond, Andrew (*b* Nelson, 8 Dec 1951). New Zealand sculptor and performance artist. He studied at the University of Waterloo, Ontario (1974–6), and at the University of Edinburgh (1975). Between 1976 and 1981 he worked primarily as a performance artist. Using gallery spaces and other locations outside the institutional framework, he undertook a variety of ritual activities involving a carefully selected range of materials—bones, skin, willow, copper and wax—which he used to explore the connections between human and animal, natural and cultural, in an attempt to restore a psychic and physical balance between the two. *Earth Vein* (1980) is a performance and photodocumentation piece in which Drummond inserted 500 m of copper pipe into a disused water-race in a remote region of Central Otago. By sealing each segment of pipe with muslin and beeswax, he metaphorically alluded to the healing of the body, a gesture that clearly articulated his attitude to the land.

From 1981 Drummond moved away from performance to concentrate on sculpture and installation. Objects that were previously invested with ritual meaning as part of his performance activity increasingly became self-contained vehicles for his ideas. As well as copper, wood and wax, he began to use slate, graphite and goldleaf. He remained deeply involved with his metaphorical explorations of landscape and its historical and mythical investments. He has responded in particular to the changing contexts in which he found himself through residencies that he has held in Dunedin (1980), the Orkney Islands (1984), Wanganui (1987) and Queensland, Australia (1990).

BIBLIOGRAPHY
L. Barrie: 'Andrew Drummond: Towards an Allegorical Use of the Body', *A. NZ*, 44 (1987), pp. 64–7
Andrew Drummond: Images from Another Archaeology (exh. cat., Auckland, C.A.G., 1989)
Andrew Drummond (exh. cat., essay L. Barrie; Christchurch, NZ, Jonathan Jensen Gal., 1994)

C. BARTON

Drummond, Sir **George A(lexander)** (*b* Edinburgh, 11 Oct 1827; *d* Montreal, 2 Feb 1910). Canadian businessman and collector. In 1854 he arrived in Montreal from Scotland and began his career as manager of John Redpath & Sons Sugar Refinery. He became President of the Canada Sugar Refining Co. in 1879, and the following year was appointed Senator by the Canadian government. In 1905 he became President of the Bank of Montreal. His collection, which consisted of approximately 200 paintings, was displayed in his Montreal home. Many works were acquired in the 1880s and 1890s, and there were paintings by both earlier and contemporary French, British and Dutch artists. He followed the prevailing tastes of Scottish, American and other Canadian collectors for paintings by Corot (e.g. *Happy Island, c.* 1865–8; Montreal, Mus. F.A.), the Barbizon school (e.g. Charles-François Daubigny's *Moonrise at Auvers: The Return of the Flock*, 1877; Montreal, Mus. F.A.) and the Hague school (e.g. Matthijs Maris's *Girl with Goat and Kid*, 1872; priv. col.). Academic painting was represented by three works of Benjamin Constant, including *Evening on the Terrace: A Souvenir of Morocco* (1879; Montreal, Mus. F.A.). In 1892, probably following the example set by Sir William Van Horne's purchases of French Impressionist paintings from the dealer Paul Durand-Ruel earlier in the year, he acquired Degas's *In the Studio* (or portrait of *Henri Michel-Levy*, 1878; Lisbon, Mus. Gulbenkian) and Monet's *Lucerne and Poppies* (1887; priv. col., see D. Wildenstein: *Claude Monet: Biographie et catalogue raisonné*, iii, 1979, no. 1146). His collection of British paintings included such conventional acquisitions as Reynolds's *Mrs Carnac*, as well as more innovative works (e.g. Turner's *Port Ruysdael*, 1827; New Haven, CT, Yale Cent. Brit. A.). Among his Old Master paintings was Pieter de Hooch's *Woman Cutting Bread* (Malibu, CA, Getty Mus.), purchased in 1893. In 1896–7 he served as President of the Art Association of Montreal; he was its Vice-President from 1897 to 1901. He was knighted in 1904. His collection was sold in 1919 (London, Christie's, 26–7 June) and several lots were purchased for the Art Association of Montreal. His son Huntly Redpath Drummond (1864–1957) was also a collector.

UNPUBLISHED SOURCES
Montreal, Mus. F.A. Lib. [Drummond papers]

BIBLIOGRAPHY
A Catalogue of Paintings from the Collection of the late Sir George A. Drummond (exh. cat., Montreal, A. Assoc. Montreal, 1918)
Canada Collects, 1860–1960: European Paintings (exh. cat. by E. H. Turner, Montreal, Mus. F.A., 1960)
Discerning Tastes: Montreal Collectors, 1880–1920 (exh. cat. by J. Brooke, Montreal, Mus. F.A., 1989)

JANET M. BROOKE

Drummond, William E(ugene) (*b* Newark, NJ, 28 March 1876; *d* River Forest, IL, 13 Sept 1948). American architect. He studied architecture at the University of Illinois, Urbana (1897–8). By 1899, after several months in the office of Louis Sullivan, he was working as a draughtsman in the studio of Frank Lloyd Wright in Oak Park, IL. Remaining in Wright's employ for ten years, in 1904 Drummond designed his most important work, the First Congregational Church, Austin, IL (built 1908). Although dependent on Wright's Prairie idiom, its interior spaces are boldly expressed through simple, geometric

form. In 1910 Drummond moved into a house in River Forest, IL, of his own design, which was a novel variation on Wright's open plans. Among the architects of the PRAIRIE SCHOOL, Drummond established one of the most successful practices. In 1912 he formed a partnership with Louis Guenzel (1860–1956) that lasted until 1915. During this time their firm steadily produced buildings designed in an original manner derived from Wright's work in Oak Park.

WRITINGS
'On Things of Common Concern', *W. Architect*, xxi (1915), pp. 11–15 [with important pls]

BIBLIOGRAPHY
S. Ganschinietz: 'William Drummond', *Prairie Sch. Rev.*, vi/1 (1969), pp. 5–19; no. 2, pp. 5–19
H. A. Brooks: *The Prairie School* (Toronto, 1972)

PAUL KRUTY

Drury, Alfred (*b* London, 11 Nov 1856; *d* Wimbledon, Surrey, 24 Dec 1944). English sculptor. He was first inspired to take up sculpture after seeing the collection of Francis Chantrey as a boy. He trained initially at the Oxford School of Art and then went to the National Art Training School in South Kensington, London, in the late 1870s. There he worked under Jules Dalou and developed a great admiration for the work of Alfred Stevens. Having been forced to flee after the Paris Commune of 1871, Dalou returned to France in 1880 after the political amnesty, accompanied by Drury who worked as his assistant from 1881 to 1885. While in France Drury helped Dalou with a number of projects, including his monumental *Triumph of the Third Republic* (1879–99; Paris, Place de la Nation). After his return to England in 1885 he became an assistant to Joseph Edgar Boehm and in the same year first exhibited at the Royal Academy in London, showing the terracotta *Triumph of Silenus* (1884; see Spielmann, p. 109), which like most of his early work was dominated by the influence of Dalou. The same influence is evident in later works such as *First Lesson* (1885–6; Birmingham Mus. & A.G.), executed with a mixture of realism and sentimentality. Over the next few years he continued to exhibit allegorical works and ideal figures as well as portrait busts.

In 1893 Drury exhibited a plaster model of *Circe* that was later cast in bronze (1894; Leeds C.A.G.) and this marked a transition in his work. Though still reminiscent of Dalou's works, such as *Triumph of the Third Republic*, and of French sculpture generally, Drury's work has a sexual charge uncharacteristic of these. Setting the figure of Circe on an altar-like pedestal, surrounded by boars at the base, he expressed the Symbolist idea of woman as the destructive temptress of man. From this point onwards he was influenced more by George Frampton and Alfred Gilbert, which led to a greater restraint in his work. This was evident in his portrait bust of the heroine of Giovanni Boccaccio's *Decameron*, *Griselda* (1896; London, Tate).

In 1897 Drury worked with the architect F. Inigo Thomas during his large-scale reconstruction of the Jacobean mansion Barrow Court, near Bristol. Drury decorated the 12 piers of the balustrade and those of the gateway. For the former he designed busts, which, though they were each named after a month of the year, in fact represented the cycle from infancy to old age of one person. In 1898 he was one of the sculptors commissioned to decorate City Square in Leeds and produced eight electric lamp standards and a statue of Dr Joseph Priestly, one of the city's famous past residents. The lamp standards were all designed around nude female figures, four representing Morning and four Evening.

In 1904 Drury received the important commission to decorate the War Office in Whitehall, London, the construction of which had begun in 1898. He produced eight groups of two seated figures, with two groups each representing *Peace*, *War*, *Truth and Justice* and *Victory and Fame*. The work was completed by 1905 and constitutes his greatest achievement, showing his complete absorption of the influences of Stevens, Dalou and Frampton. Immediately after finishing this project Drury was one of several sculptors commissioned to decorate the Victoria and Albert Museum in London. By 1907 he had produced several relief panels and a portrait figure of Prince Albert.

Among Drury's later works were the sculptures representing Canada, South Africa and West Africa for the Victoria Memorial (1901–24) in the Mall in London. He also won the commission to provide a statue of Reynolds for the forecourt of Burlington House in London. This was not finished and erected until 1931; the following year he received a silver medal from the Royal Society of British Sculptors for the work. Drury was made an ARA in 1900 and an RA in 1913.

BIBLIOGRAPHY

A. L. Baldry: 'The Art Movement: Decorative Sculpture by Mr Alfred Drury', *Mag. A.* (1898), pp. 442–5
——: 'Our Rising Artists: Alfred Drury, Sculptor', *Mag. A.* (1900), pp. 211–17
M. H. Spielmann: *British Sculpture and Sculptors of To-day* (London, 1901), pp. 109–14
B. Read: *Victorian Sculpture* (London, 1982)
S. Beattie: *The New Sculpture* (London, 1983), pp. 107–21, 167–74

Drury Lowe (Holden), William (*b* Darley Abbey, Derbys, 5 Oct 1802; *d* Locko Park, Derbys, 26 Feb 1877). English collector. Born William Drury Holden, he succeeded in 1849 to the estates of Locko and Denby and assumed the surname of Lowe, styling himself William Drury Lowe. In 1827 he married Caroline Curzon (1808–86). Inspired by a lifelong passion for Old Master paintings, Drury Lowe made his extensive purchases (*c.* 250 in total) largely on visits to France (where he first travelled in his twenties) and especially Italy. In 1839–40 he was in Pisa, and from 1840 to 1843 he resided in Florence. He undertook further visits to France between 1855 and 1857 and to Italy from 1862 to 1864, when he evidently bought the majority of his outstanding 14th- and 15th-century Italian paintings. After his move in 1849 to Locko Park, Derbys, from his previous home at Kimbolton (now Cambs), he considerably enlarged the mansion and added a picture gallery.

Drury Lowe bought paintings from all the main European schools, but historically his taste is of particular interest in its pioneering appreciation of the Florentine and Sienese masters of the Trecento. For example, there remain at Locko such important panels as Bernardo Daddi's *St Catherine of Alexandria*, Segna di Bonaventura's *Virgin and Child* and a *Virgin and Child* by Niccolò di

Segna (*fl* 1331–45). Among 15th-century works dispersed in 1912–13 by his grandson and namesake William Drury-Lowe (1877–1916) are Sandro Botticelli's *Virgin and Child* (Bristol, Mus. & A.G.), Andrea del Castagno's *David with the Head of Goliath* (Washington, DC, N.G.A.), Cosimo Tura's *Ercole de Ferrara* (New York, Met.) and Domenico Ghirlandaio's *A Lady* and *A Youth* (both San Marino, CA, Huntington A.G.).

BIBLIOGRAPHY

G. Waagen: *Galleries and Cabinets of Art in Great Britain* (London, 1857)
J. P. Richter: *Catalogue of Pictures at Locko Park* (London, 1901)
A. Smart: 'The Locko Park Collection', *Apollo*, lxxxvii (1968), pp. 204–7
L. Vertova: 'La raccolta di Locko Park', *Ant. Viva*, vii/3 (1968), pp. 23–30
Pictures from Locko Park, Derbyshire (exh. cat., U. Nottingham, A.G., 1968)
R. Calvocoressi: 'Locko Park: An Important Family Collection', *Connoisseur*, cxcii/772 (1976), pp. 141–5
Locko Park and the Drury-Lowes: A Derbyshire Family and its Art Treasures (exh. cat., U. Nottingham, A.G., 1982)

ALASTAIR SMART

Dryden, John (*b* Aldwincle, Northants, 9 Aug 1631; *d* London, 1 May 1700). English writer. After graduating from Trinity College, Cambridge, he settled in London for life in 1654 and never travelled beyond England. In 1668 he was appointed Poet Laureate, and Historiographer Royal two years later, but he lost both posts on the overthrow of James II in 1688. He wrote, adapted or collaborated on nearly thirty plays, as well as publishing numerous critical essays and poems, notably the two-part political satire *Absalom and Achitophel* (1681–2). His translations into English include Virgil's *Works* (1697). Throughout his career Dryden was interested in debates on the respective values of particular forms of art. In several poems, including the ode *To the Pious Memory . . . of Mrs Ann Killigrew* (1686) and his verses *To Sir Godfrey Kneller* (1694), he explored the various parallels to be made between the arts, regarding painting as the 'dumb sister' of poetry. Kneller, who painted several portraits of Dryden (e.g. 1693; London, N.P.G.), was probably one of the artists who persuaded the poet to translate into English prose the *De arte graphica* of CHARLES-ALPHONSE DU FRESNOY. In 'A Parallel betwixt Painting and Poetry', his preface to *De arte graphica*, Dryden set out an evaluation of the strengths and weaknesses of the visual arts before introducing his summary of Du Fresnoy's argument, stating that history painting could be morally instructive, if depicting heroic exploits, and that what he earlier saw as a disadvantage—painting's portrayal of many actions and feelings in one place—could be deemed an advantage. Dryden's version of Du Fresnoy's widely admired academic exegesis of UT PICTURA POESIS had a profound effect on 18th-century thought and art: as well as spawning several other translations, it occasioned 415 entries in Samuel Johnson's *Dictionary* (1755) and influenced Joshua Reynolds's aesthetic development.

WRITINGS

'A Parallel betwixt Painting and Poetry', preface to *De arte graphica* (1668; Eng. trans., London, 1695)
E. N. Hooker, H. T. Swedenberg and others, eds: *The Works* (Berkeley, 1956–)
J. Kinsley, ed.: *The Poems*, 4 vols (Oxford, 1958)

BIBLIOGRAPHY
W. K. Wimsatt: 'Samuel Johnson and Dryden's Du Fresnoy', *Stud. Philol.*, xlviii (1951), pp. 26–39
J. H. Hagstrum: *The Sister Arts: The Tradition of Literary Pictorialism and English Poetry from Dryden to Gray* (Chicago, 1958), pp. 173–209
A. D. Hope: 'Anne Killigrew, or the Art of Modulating', *Dryden's Mind and Art*, ed. B. King (Edinburgh, 1969), pp. 99–113
D. T. Mace: 'Ut pictura poesis: Dryden, Poussin and the Parallel of Poetry and Painting in the Seventeenth Century', *Encounters: Essays on Literature and the Visual Arts*, ed. J. D. Hunt (London, 1971), pp. 58–81
W. Myers: *Dryden* (London, 1973)
J. A. Winn: *John Dryden and his World* (London, 1987)

EDWINA BURNESS

Dryffhout, Bartholomeus (Fransz.). *See* DRIJFHOUT, BARTHOLOMEUS.

Drypoint [Fr. *pointe sèche*; Ger. *Kaltnadel*; It. *punta secca*; Dut. *droognaald*; Sp. *punta seca*]. Type of intaglio print. The process involves scratching lines or tones into the surface of a bare metal plate with a sharp point or other abrasive tool. The term may also refer to the process or to the tool used. It differs from etching in that acid is not used to bite the design into the plate (hence no protective ground is necessary) and from engraving in that the incising point is not pushed through the surface but rather used as a drawing tool. Drypoint may be used alone or in combination with other intaglio techniques. It may also be employed to retouch or reinforce designs on etching plates that have been worn out or blurred by use. Its earliest use dates to the 15th century.

1. Materials and techniques. 2. History.

1. MATERIALS AND TECHNIQUES. The most basic drypoint technique involves using a sharp metal point, held in the hand like a pen or pencil, to scratch lines in the surface of a metal printing plate. The traditional drypoint tool is a round steel needle (*see* ENGRAVING, fig. 1) sharpened to a point, although diamond or ruby points are often used. Artists have also used such unconventional tools as steel brushes, emery pencils or carbon rods to scratch marks of varying tonal and linear qualities into the plate. The action of drawing the tool through the plate pushes a ridge of metal called a burr on one or both sides of the furrow. The configuration and height of the burr depend on both the angle at which the tool is held and the force employed. In addition to the line itself, this upturned burr will also retain ink, and the resulting impression will reveal a soft, broad area of ink in certain areas on the print (also called burr), giving drypoint its unique character. It can also be used for thin, delicate accent lines without printed burr, in which case the metal burr is removed with a scraper.

Copper is the material most often used for the printing surface, although pewter, aluminium, zinc, steel, iron and even gelatin have been employed. The raised burr of the printing surface is quite fragile and is quickly worn down by the pressure employed in printing intaglio plates. Very few impressions are therefore able to retain the characteristic printed burr of drypoint, unless the plate is electrolytically steel-faced for reinforcement. Usually only 20 or 30 fine impressions are possible on an unfaced plate, but 100 or more can be achieved from a reinforced surface.

The most characteristic appearance of drypoint in a print is the soft texture of a printed line that has been created by a drypoint burr. Another feature (most readily seen under magnification) is the visibly sharp impression made in the paper by the metallic burr itself; this is

1. Drypoint by Rembrandt: *Clump of Trees*, 124×210 mm, 1652 (London, British Museum)

2. Rembrandt: *Clump of Trees*; macrophotographic enlargement of the tree trunk on left

sometimes seen as a single white line (where the ridge of burr has been wiped clean) amid a thicker black line (see figs 1 and 2) and sometimes as a double white line if there is burr on both sides of the scratched line. In addition, because of the force and degree of control necessary to wield the point itself, a drypoint line will have a taut, almost excited quality, which is not as fluid as an etched line nor as smoothly controlled as an engraved line. Drypoint created by broad tools, such as metal brushes or emery pencils, appears as a tonal area that under magnification reveals many fine, hairlike scratches. However, drypoint can be very difficult to recognize, especially when used in combination with other intaglio techniques. In many cases where the burr has been removed from an area of lighter drypoint detail, it can be virtually impossible to distinguish.

Drypoint has never been a major primary intaglio technique, partially because of the small number of good impressions possible and also as a result of its deceptive simplicity. Artists' manuals stress the freedom inherent in the ability to sketch directly on the plate but warn of the skill needed to control the point as it is guided through the resistant metal.

2. HISTORY. The first artist to work entirely with drypoint was the HOUSEBOOK MASTER (also known as the Master of the Amsterdam Cabinet; *see* MASTERS, ANONYMOUS, AND MONOGRAMMISTS, §I), active from *c.* 1470 to 1500. The Master executed at least 89 plates, entirely in a lively, sketchy drypoint technique, worked in a soft metal such as pewter. Albrecht Dürer executed three drypoints in 1512; *St Jerome by the Pollard Willow* (Boston, Mus. F.A.; B. 59) shows the technique's potential for suggesting atmospheric effects, particularly in the earliest impressions from the plate.

Several northern Italian printmakers experimented during the early 16th century with techniques resembling drypoint. These included Andrea Mantegna, Giovanni Antonio da Brescia, the Master of 1515, Jacopo de' Barbari, Domenico Campagnola, Pellegrino da San Daniele and Marcello Fogolino. In addition the Venetian painter and printmaker ANDREA SCHIAVONE used drypoint during the 1540s and 1550s quite extensively to supplement etched lines in a tonal fashion.

During the 17th century drypoint used alone remained rare, although landscape and genre etchers, especially in the Netherlands and Italy, frequently used it without burr to add fine accents to their prints. A unique experiment was Hercules Segers's use of closely worked, tonal patches of parallel drypoint lines with burr (*see* SEGERS, HERCULES, fig. 3). The Dutch printmaker Pieter de Grebber executed pure drypoints. In the Netherlands it was REMBRANDT VAN RIJN who made the most extensive use, until that time, of drypoint (*see* REMBRANDT VAN RIJN, §I, 4(ii)). He began adding it to his etchings in the early 1640s. He exploited drypoint burr to produce a soft yet strong effect of depth, often combining etching, engraving and drypoint to achieve a rich tonality of shadows. In more lightly worked etchings he added drypoint accents to establish depth and volume. Rembrandt's only pure drypoints were *Landscape with a Road beside a Canal* (*c.* 1652; B. 221) and *Clump of Trees* (1652; B. 222; see figs 1 and 2), the portrait of *Thomas Haaringh* (1655; B. 274) and his two large masterpieces, *Ecce homo* (or *Christ Presented to the People*, 1655; B. 76) and the *Three Crosses* (1653; B. 78). He often experimented with unusual printing papers to bring out the softness of the drypoint burr, including warm-toned Japanese papers and vellum.

Rembrandt's influence was paramount in the subsequent diffusion and development of the original drypoint style. Indeed, the next significant group of drypoint artists were 18th-century British enthusiasts for his prints, often amateurs, who even copied Rembrandt's drypoints in the same medium. These included Arthur Pond, Benjamin Wilson, Thomas Worlidge (known as the 'English Rembrandt'), James Bretherton and the Rev. Richard Byron (1724–1811). Outside Great Britain, drypoint appeared occasionally in the work of more isolated European printmakers such as Jean-Jacques de Boissieu, Jan Piotr Norblin de la Gourdaine (also influenced by Rembrandt), Daniel Nikolaus Chodowiecki and Jean Baptiste Bernard Coclers. However, in an age dominated by the reproductive engraving, drypoint was used primarily only in the finest details in combination with other intaglio techniques, as specified by contemporary manuals and encyclopedias.

During the early decades of the 19th century another group of English and Scottish artists employed drypoint, including David Wilkie, Andrew Geddes, the Rev. Edward Thomas Daniell and David Charles Read (1790–1851). From mid-century, however, two developments assured a broad resurgence of interest in drypoint as an independent medium. These were the Etching Revival in France and the steel-facing of printing plates, the latter assuring larger editions than was previously possible. In both England and France the increased emphasis on free draughtsmanship in printmaking also fostered many drypoint efforts, as did the advantage of sketching directly on the plate outside the confines of the studio.

In England the drypoint renaissance was spurred in the late 1850s by SEYMOUR HADEN and JAMES McNEILL WHISTLER. Influenced by his personal print collection (which included works by Rembrandt) and the French Etching Revival, Haden used drypoint accents more and more strongly in his landscape etchings. Whistler executed several bold drypoint portraits in 1859–60 and continued to exploit the technique in both landscape and portraiture into the early 1870s.

Whistler's subsequent influence was very strong in Europe and the USA, especially on the drypoints of such later British printmakers as Mortimer Menpes, Elizabeth Armstrong, Muirhead Bone, David Young Cameron, Frank Short and Walter Sickert. American followers included Joseph Pennell, John Henry Twachtman and Julian Alden Weir. The American Etching Revival of the 1880s included such artists as Thomas Moran and Mary Nimmo Moran and James Smillie (1833–1909) experimenting with drypoint technique.

In France drypoint was used extensively after mid-century by many, varied artists, including Charles Jacque, Alphonse Legros, Auguste Lepère, Auguste Rodin, Paul Helleu, Marcellin Desboutin, Adolphe Appian, Félix Buhot, James Tissot, Félix Bracquemond, Adolphe Hervier, Auguste Renoir, Berthe Morisot, Théodore Roussel, Eugène Delâtre, Camille Pissarro, Edgar Degas and the expatriate American Mary Cassatt. Pissarro, Degas and Cassatt experimented freely with such non-conventional tools as steel brushes and carbon rods to create tonal drypoint areas. Buhot and Rodolphe Bresdin experimented with using gelatin plates, and at this time unique works were created by scratching lines in thin gelatin sheets, inking them and framing them against a light-coloured background. Other late 19th-century European printmakers who used drypoint were James Ensor, Félicien Rops,

3. Drypoint by Max Beckmann: *Self-portrait in Bowler Hat* (detail), 2nd state, 323×247 mm, 1921 (Cambridge, MA, Fogg Art Museum)

Giovanni Boldini, Lovis Corinth, Max Liebermann and Edvard Munch.

In the 20th century in France, Picasso's earliest *Saltimbanque* prints (1905–6) included several drypoints, and he experimented with the technique until the very end of his career. Important Cubist prints of 1911 by Picasso and Georges Braque were wholly or largely made in drypoint. Other French artists who used drypoint extensively were Jacques Villon, Edouard Vuillard and André Dunoyer de Segonzac. The Surrealist André Masson worked in drypoint, as did the later abstractionist Wols.

In Germany such Expressionists as Erich Heckel, Ernst Ludwig Kirchner, Karl Schmidt-Rottluff, Max Pechstein, Emil Nolde, Max Beckmann (see fig. 3), Wilhelm Lehmbruck and, later, Rolf Nesch began to exploit drypoint's directness of approach as early as 1907, finding the tension of its lines well suited to their aesthetic. Vasily Kandinsky and Marc Chagall also executed innovative drypoints in Germany during the 1910s and 1920s.

In the USA there was an active period of printmaking between the World Wars when drypoint was used by such artists as Elie Nadelman, Peggy Bacon, George 'Pop' Hart (*b* 1868), Armin Landeck (*b* 1905) and Milton Avery. After 1945 innovations were originally stimulated by S. W. Hayter's work at Atelier 17, with Jackson Pollock and Mauricio Lasansky using the freedom of drypoint.

In the late 20th century, innovations in drypoint have included the use of 'accidental' drypoint texture, found, for example, on plates by Jim Dine and Michael Heizer, and Richard Artschwager's use of plastic printing plates. Dine also pioneered the use of abrasive electric tools to achieve tone and burr in his drypoints. Other artists working with drypoint in the late 20th century have included the German Georg Baselitz and Austrian Arnulf Rainer. Perhaps the largest drypoints ever executed were the 1.82 m high abstract works by Rolf Iseli. The Italian Mimmo Paladino adapted drypoint to his expressive draughtsmanship.

BIBLIOGRAPHY

E. Chambers: 'Engraving', *Cyclopaedia*, 5 vols (London, 1779–86), ii, no. 114 [ff 4E2*v*–4F*v*: the folios are not paginated]
——: 'Engraving', *Encyclopaedia Britannica*, 18 vols (Edinburgh, 3/1797), iv, pp. 667–72
A. von Bartsch: *Le Peintre-graveur* (1803–21) [B.]
M. Lalanne: *Traité de la gravure à l'eau forte* (Paris, 1866, 2/1878; Eng. trans., London, 1880, 2/1926/*R* 1981), pp. 48–50, 79–80
P. G. Hamerton: *Etching and Etchers* (London, 1876), pp. 140–41
S. R. Koehler: *Etching: An Outline of its Technical Processes and its History, with Some Remarks on Collections and Collecting* (New York, 1885)
A. Delâtre: *Eau-forte, pointe sèche et vernis mou* (Paris, 1887)
A. M. Hind: *A History of Engraving and Etching from the 15th Century to the Year 1914* (London, 1908, rev. 1923/*R* New York, 1963)
P. Smith: 'Some Notes on Drypoint', *On Making and Collecting Etchings*, ed. E. H. Hubbard (London, 1920), pp. 57–64
E. S. Lumsden: *The Art of Etching* (London, 1925), pp. 45–7, 127–34
S. W. Hayter: *New Ways of Gravure* (London and New York, 1949, 2/1966, rev. New York, 1981), pp. 16–24
A. H. Mayor: *Prints and People* (New York, 1971) [esp. pls 124–9]
A. Griffiths: *Prints and Printmaking* (London, 1980), pp. 74–8
B. Gascoigne: *How to Identify Prints* (New York, 1986), see II
K. Brown: *Ink, Paper, Metal, Wood—How to Recognize Contemporary Artists' Prints* (San Francisco, 1992), pp. 18–19

DAVID P. BECKER

Drysdale, Sir Russell (*b* Bognor Regis, 7 Feb 1912; *d* Sydney, 29 June 1981). Australian painter and photographer of English birth. His family settled in Melbourne in 1923, but Drysdale visited Europe twice in the early 1930s; on his second visit in 1932–3 he was particularly excited by the work of Paul Cézanne, Vincent van Gogh, Paul Gauguin, Henri Matisse and Pablo Picasso. The experience confirmed his desire to be an artist.

After returning to Melbourne, Drysdale studied for two years with George Bell, who ran the only school devoted to the teaching of modern art. In May 1938 Drysdale returned to Europe to continue his studies with Iain McNab (1890–1967) at the Grosvenor School of Art in London and then with Othon Friesz at the Académie de la Grande Chaumière in Paris. Such works as the *Rabbiter and his Family* (1938; R. G. Casey priv. col., see Dutton, p. 23) demonstrate his early interest in Australian rural life.

Drysdale returned to Australia in April 1939. He was not, however, at home in the artistic debates in Melbourne during the years of World War II and moved to Sydney in 1940. He began to exhibit paintings of rural New South Wales regularly at the Macquarie Galleries, for example *Sunday Evening* (1941; Sydney, A.G. NSW). By 1944 Drysdale's reputation was well established, and he was commissioned by the *Sydney Morning Herald* to record the effects of the drought, which by the end of 1944 was considered to be the worst in Australia's history. He accompanied a reporter to western New South Wales, and the experience had a profound effect on his work from this period; it also encouraged other Australian artists to take a new look at the Australian landscape. The *Herald* used his drawings to illustrate its reports, but Drysdale was keen to make the works into paintings, for example *Deserted Out Station* (1945; John Fairfax Ltd, see Klepac, p. 252). His work showed an awareness of both the Ecole de Paris and such contemporary English artists as Graham Sutherland and Henry Moore.

Kenneth Clark visited Australia in 1949, and through him Drysdale was invited to exhibit at the Leicester Galleries in London in 1950. During the 1950s his reputation continued to flourish at home and abroad. From the early 1950s he became increasingly interested in the Aborigines, both in their traditional lives and customs and as a partly assimilated people, producing such paintings as *Mullaloonah Tank* (1953; Adelaide, A.G. S. Australia). His sympathy for their plight was profound, but his paintings of Aboriginal subjects rarely matched the elegance of his paintings of the 1940s. During the 1950s and 1960s he undertook extended journeys into inland Australia in the company of scientists and writers, for example the zoologist A. S. Marshall (1958). Many of his most characteristic drawings emerged from these trips, although he rarely sketched directly from the subject, preferring to let the experience settle in his memory. Drysdale also illustrated Marshall's *Journey Among Men* (1962).

The most impressive aspect of Drysdale's later work was colour photography, which he first turned to on a journey in 1955, continuing the practice until 1967. During this time he recorded the journeys in a systematic as well as expressive manner. The photographs, exhibited for the first time posthumously in 1987 at the National Gallery of

Victoria, Melbourne, provided an interesting parallel to his achievement and themes in painting, confirming that his distinctive vision had its basis in a known and experienced reality.

Drysdale's health, particularly his eyesight, was severely impaired during the 1960s, and he underwent major surgery for a cataract in 1969, the year in which he was knighted. He was restricted by his health in his final years, but in 1980 he did make his first etching, *Long Ago* (see Klepac, p. 187).

BIBLIOGRAPHY
G. Dutton: *Russell Drysdale* (London, 1964)
C. Osborne: *Masterpieces of Drysdale* (London, 1975)
L. Klepac: *The Life and Work of Russell Drysdale* (Sydney, 1980)
J. Boddington: *Russell Drysdale, Photographer* (Melbourne, 1987)
PATRICK MCCAUGHEY

Duanfang [Tuan-fang; *zi* Wugiao; *hao* Taozhai] (*b* Fengrun, Hebei Province, 20 April 1861; *d* Zizhou [modern Zizhong], Sichuan Province, 27 Nov 1911). Chinese collector and high official. His Chinese ancestors, named Tao, moved to Manchuria in the Ming period (1368–1644), intermarried with the indigenous Manchu, accepted the clan name Tohoro and became part of the Manchu Plain White Banner, one of the four original military and administrative units of Manchuria. Duanfang's family returned to China after the Manchu conquest of China and the establishment of the Qing dynasty (1644–1911). He received his *juren* degree in 1882 and served in many high posts, including terms as governor and acting governor-general of various provinces. He was interested in education and modernization and was a patron to promising young men. He was killed by his own men in the 1911 uprising while attempting to return to Wuchang, Sichuan, to take up his post as acting governor-general.

Duanfang had a large and excellent collection of calligraphy and painting, as well as ancient objects of bronze and stone. He relied on expert connoisseurs for advice in obtaining and cataloguing his objects. Among these was the respected calligrapher Yang Shoujing. Duanfang's collection was dispersed in museums worldwide; noteworthy is a complete altar set of bronzes (New York, Met.). With the help of his advisers and protégés, Duanfang issued catalogues of his collection over a period of 13 years, for example on jades (published in 1896), stele rubbings (1903 and 1909), bronzes (1908 and 1909) and seals (1909).

BIBLIOGRAPHY
Hummel: 'Tuan-fang'
Yu Jianhua, ed.: *Zhongguo huajia da zidian* [Dictionary of Chinese painters] (Shanghai, 1981), p. 1258
ELIZABETH F. BENNETT

Duany, Andres. *See under* ARQUITECTONICA.

Duan Yucai [Tuan Yü-tsai; *zi* Ruoying; *hao* Maotang, Yanbei Jushi] (*b* Jintan, Jiangsu Province, 1735; *d* Suzhou, 1815). Chinese etymologist and phonetician. He took the imperial civil-service examinations in 1760 to gain his *juren* degree but twice (1761 and 1769) failed the final examinations. He was appointed a magistrate in Guizhou *c.* 1769 and from 1772 to 1778 held several such offices in Sichuan Province. In 1778 he retired from official service, pleading ill health. From 1763 onwards he was a devoted disciple

of the scholar and philosopher Dai Zhen (1723–77), whom he met in Beijing. He later compiled a chronological biography of Dai Zhen and in 1793 re-edited his literary works.

In 1775 Duan published a book on ancient phonology, the *Liushu yinyun biao* ('Classified phonology of old Chinese characters'), based on two of his own short studies. His interest in problems of phonetics led him to analyse the form and meaning of difficult characters in the ancient text *Shang shu* ('History of the Shang'), a section of the *Shujing* ('Book of documents'; probably Zhou period, *c.* 1050–256 BC). With his accumulated specialist knowledge he completed his major work on classics and etymology, the *Shuowen jiezi shu* ('Annotations on the *Shuowen jiezi*'), published 1813–15. The *Shuowen jiezi* ('Dictionary of words and phrases'), compiled by Xu Shen *c.* AD 120, is the earliest extant dictionary on the origin, formation and meaning of Chinese characters, knowledge of which is essential for understanding classical Chinese culture, as expressed in written form, and the interplay between literature and art. Duan wrote a critical edition of the dictionary and added his own annotations, using as source material all relevant known works.

BIBLIOGRAPHY
Hummel: 'Tuan Yü-ts'ai'
Q. Lin: 'Duan Yucai nianbiao', *Kong Meng Xuebao*, xl (1980), pp. 227–60
Zhou Zumou: 'Duan Yucai', *Zhongguo da baike quanshu. Yuyan, wenzi*, ed. Mei Yi (Beijing, 1988), pp. 59–60
BENT L. PEDERSEN

Duarte, King of Portugal. *See* AVIZ, (2).

Duarte, Diego [Jacques], the younger (*b* ?Antwerp, before 1616; *d* Antwerp, 15 Aug 1691). Diamond dealer, jeweller, art collector and dealer. He belonged to a Portuguese family of crypto-Jewish extraction, who established themselves in Antwerp during the 16th century. His father, Gaspar Duarte the elder (1584–1653), was a wealthy diamond dealer, jeweller in ordinary to Charles I of England, an amateur musician and a friend of the Dutch poets Constantijn Huygens and Anna Roemer Visscher. Diego the younger, named after his grandfather, continued the family business. From the correspondence of Constantijn Huygens it is clear that Duarte was a good musician and composer as well as a collector. In 1682 Duarte compiled an inventory of his collection (MS., Brussels, Bib. Royale Albert 1er), which contained more than 200 paintings, most of the highest quality, including works by such artists as Hans Holbein (ii), Adam Elsheimer, Raphael, Titian and Tintoretto. However, the core of the collection was Flemish. He owned works by Quinten Metsys, Pieter Bruegel I, Rubens, van Dyck and Jan Breughel I, among others. Duarte died a bachelor and left the greater part of his property to his niece Constancia Duarte and her husband Manuel Levy, a jeweller in Amsterdam. They moved to Antwerp in 1690 and during the next six years Levy sold most of the collection.

BIBLIOGRAPHY
G. Dogaer: 'De inventaris van de schilderijen van Diego Duarte', *Jb.: Kon. Mus. S. Kst.* (1971), pp. 195–221
E. R. Samuel: 'The Disposal of Diego Duarte's Stock of Paintings', *Jb.: Kon. Mus. S. Kst.* (1976), pp. 305–24

F. Baudouin: 'De herkomst van twee olieverfschetsen van Rubens in het Osterriethhuis te Antwerpen', *Liber Amicorum Herman Liebaers* (Brussels, 1984), pp. 373–91

FRANS BAUDOUIN

Dubai. *See under* UNITED ARAB EMIRATES.

Duban, (Jacques-)Félix (*b* Paris, 14 Oct 1797; *d* Bordeaux, 12 Oct 1870). French architect. He was the oldest of a celebrated generation of French designers who were credited with revolutionizing the government architectural services under the banner of 'Romanticism' around 1830. Unlike his friend Henri Labrouste, however, Duban had actually built little by the end of his career and remains today a somewhat nebulous personality, a symbol of potential more significant to his contemporaries than to modern observers.

Duban was the son of an ironmonger. His training began in 1813 in the studio of his older sister's husband, the successful government architect François Debret. In 1823 he won the competition for the Prix de Rome with a brilliant design for a custom-house, comprising broad square utilitarian masses boldly juxtaposed. During his subsequent five-year *pension* at the Académie de France in Rome he worked with his immediate predecessors Guillaume Abel Blouet and Emile Gilbert, and especially his successors Labrouste, Louis Duc and Léon Vaudoyer, to formulate an archaeologically precise but aesthetically unexpected vision of ancient Classical design that marked the beginning of the 'Romantic' revolution in French official architecture. His fourth-year project reconstructed the stern Roman Portico of Octavia, built by the Emperor Augustus. His fifth-year project, intended to be an original design for modern France, was overtly hostile to the classicism and ecclesiology of the dying Restoration regime: a model Protestant church based on contemporary Swiss and German examples, without roots in the Greco-Roman culture and Catholicism that the five-year stay in Rome had been intended to nurture.

On his return to Paris in the spring of 1829, Duban was hailed as the leader of an *avant-garde* movement by the younger architects. He was invited by the students to replace Blouet as *maître d'atelier* during the latter's absence in Greece. On Blouet's return, Duban joined Debret in conducting his studio, but, their views having proved divergent, in January 1832 Duban established a studio of his own. César Daly, Joseph Nicolle (1810–87), Charles-Auguste Questel and Alexandre-Dominique Denuelle (1818–79) were among his students.

In May 1829 Duban had been named assistant, or inspecteur, to Debret for the completion of the new buildings of the Ecole des Beaux-Arts, Paris. In a reorganization of 1832, Duban was named architecte-en-chef and

Félix Duban: first courtyard of the Ecole des Beaux-Arts, Paris, begun 1833; from a 19th-century photograph, with the frontispiece of the château of Anet on the right

asked to redesign the establishment, presenting a controversial project in the summer of 1833. The ornamental details of his new façades were archaicizing and intriguingly unconventional, but the real issue seems to have been Duban's creation of a series of scenographic courtyards through the middle of the complex (see fig.), filled with the fragments of French medieval and early Renaissance architecture that had been brought to the site in the 1790s, when it had served as Alexandre Lenoir's Musée des Monuments Français; since the 1970s some of these fragments have been returned to their original sites. In essence Duban transformed the institution from a school for the teaching of abstract conventions into a museum of historical variations reflecting national inflections and chronological evolution.

Besides the Ecole des Beaux-Arts, Duban obtained a number of lucrative private commissions during the July Monarchy (1830–48), notably the Hôtel Pourtalès (1835–39) on the Rue Tronchet, alterations to the château at Dampierre (1839–41), and extensions to the château at Chantilly (1846–8). He also worked for the newly founded Commission des Monuments Historiques as advisory member (from 1837) and as restoration architect of the Sainte-Chapelle, Paris (1837–48), and the château at Blois (1844–70; unexecuted). In 1833 he had also designed a particularly impressive set of temporary pavilions on the Place de la Concorde for the celebration of the anniversary of the Revolution of 1830.

The Revolution of 1848 brought Duban his greatest opportunity when he was named architect of the Palais du Louvre, now transformed into a national museum. In this capacity he restored the Galerie d'Apollon and executed elaborate Néo-Grec decorations in the Salle des Sept Cheminées and the Salon Carré. After the coup d'état of Prince Louis Napoleon, later Napoleon III (1851), Duban was asked to present a project for the union of the Louvre and Tuileries palaces, but to his bitter chagrin he was passed over in favour of the more accommodating Louis-Tullius-Joachim Visconti.

Duban soon retired (1854) from his post at the Louvre and concentrated his efforts on the buildings of the Ecole des Beaux-Arts, erecting an impressive new wing (1858–63; see PARIS, fig. 45) on the Quai Malaquais. This contained the cavernous Salle de Melpomène behind a wide vestibule and an upper studio space across the façade. His design avoided the applied decorative coating of the new Louvre visible across the Seine, having instead a thin decorative layer cut into the depth of its solid, buttressed surface. In 1867 Duban also roofed the courtyard of the Palais des Etudes wing with painted iron and glass. Otherwise he occupied himself with modifying the policies of the Académie des Beaux-Arts, to which he had been the first of the 'Romantic' generation to be elected (1854). He also served on the Conseil des Bâtiments Civils (from 1854) and executed several private commissions, notably the restoration of the Hotel Matignon for the banker the Duc de Galliera (1860). Fleeing the Prussian advance on Paris in September 1870, Duban died in Bordeaux in October of that year.

Eulogizing Duban before the Académie in November 1872, his friend the archaeologist Charles-Ernest Beulé lamented that Duban had completed no great design like Vaudoyer's Marseille Cathedral and added that, since his failure at the Louvre, he had become withdrawn and misanthropic. Beulé added that during the 1830s Duban had amused himself with exquisite architectural fantasies in watercolour, and that during the last two decades of his life he had returned to these, producing a series of nostalgic visions of Greek and Pompeian architecture. They perhaps summarized his contribution, Beulé concluded, which was more to enrich Classical conventions and suggest the richness of historical architecture than to lay down a mature new style, like those of Labrouste or Eugène-Emmanuel Viollet-le-Duc.

BIBLIOGRAPHY
V. Baltard: *Hommage à Félix Duban* (Paris, 1871)
L. Vaudoyer: *Discours prononcé aux funérailles de M. Duban* (Paris, 1871)
C.-E. Beulé: *Eloge de Duban* (Paris, 1872)
C. Blanc: *Les Artistes de mon temps* (Paris, 1876)
D. Van Zanten: 'Félix Duban and the Buildings of the Ecole des Beaux-Arts', *J. Soc. Archit. Historians* (1978), pp. 161–74
C. Marmoz: 'The Buildings of the Ecole des Beaux-Arts', *The Beaux-Arts*, ed. R. Middleton (London, 1982)
D. Van Zanten: 'The Beginnings of French Romantic Architecture and Duban's Temple Protestant', *In Search of Modern Architecture*, ed. H. Searing (Cambridge, MA, 1983)
——: *Designing Paris: The Architecture of Duban, Labrouste, Duc and Vaudoyer* (Cambridge, MA, 1987)
——: *Building Paris: Architectural Institutions and the Transformation of the French Capital, 1830–1870* (New York, 1994)
DAVID VAN ZANTEN

Du Barry, Comtesse [Bécu, Marie-Jeanne] (*b* Vaucouleurs, Lorraine, 19 Aug 1746; *d* Paris, 8 Dec 1793). French royal favourite, patron and collector. She was the daughter of Anne Bécu, a dressmaker, who took her to Paris at eight years old. She was educated at the convent of the Daughters of St Aure and in 1760 became an assistant in the shop in Paris of the celebrated dressmaker Labille. She came to the attention of Comte Jean du Barry, who installed her in his house in the Rue de la Jussienne, where she presided over a celebrated literary salon. In 1768 she married her protector's brother, Comte Guillaume du Barry, as was required for her presentation at court in 1769; by that time she had already become the mistress of Louis XV. Beautiful, graceful and intelligent, she became the last enduring liaison of the King's life.

Like the Marquise de Pompadour, her predecessor, Mme du Barry came to dominate French fashion and was a great patron of the arts. In 1769 the King presented her with the 17th-century château of Louveciennes, which she commissioned Anges-Jacques Gabriel to restore. In 1770 she commissioned Claude-Nicolas Ledoux to build for her the Pavillon du Barry in the grounds of the château; it was intended for pleasure and entertainments, much like the Petit Trianon at Versailles. It was decorated with Gobelins tapestries; most of the furniture was bought from the *marchand-mercier* Simon-Philippe Poirier (?1720–85) and made by Louis Delanois (*fl c.* 1761); the paintings were by such artists as François-Hubert Drouais, Jean-Baptiste Greuze and Jean-Honoré Fragonard. The Pavillon was a landmark in the history of French Neo-classical taste. For the Salon en cul-de-four, Fragonard was commissioned to paint a series on the theme of the *Progress of Love* (New York, Frick), which was, however, rejected, possibly because the Rococo style had become outmoded.

Joseph-Marie Vien produced another series on the same subject in the Neo-classical manner for the Pavillon (Paris, Louvre; Chambéry, Préfecture). Mme du Barry's apartments at the château of Versailles were designed by Gabriel in 1770. As a leader of fashion, she promoted exquisite furniture decorated with Sèvres porcelain plaques (*see* CERAMICS, colour pl. I, fig. 3). After the death of Louis XV in 1774, Mme du Barry spent two years in retirement in a convent; from 1776 she lived quietly at the Pavillon du Barry. A powerful symbol of the court, she was arrested and guillotined during the French Revolution.

BIBLIOGRAPHY

C. Vatel: *Histoire de Madame du Barry d'après ses papiers personnels et les documents des archives publiques*, 3 vols (Paris, 1883)
E. de Goncourt and J. de Goncourt: *La Du Barry* (Paris, 1891)
F.-M. Biebel: 'Fragonard et Mme du Barry', *Gaz. B.-A.*, lvi (1960), pp. 207–26
G. Wildenstein: 'Simon-Philippe Poirier: Fournisseur de Madame du Barry', *Gaz. B.-A.*, n. s. 5, lx (1962), pp. 365–77
B. Scott: 'Mme du Barry: A Royal Favourite with Taste', *Apollo*, xcvii (1973), pp. 60–71
S. Eriksen: *Early Neo-classicism in France* (London, 1974), pp. 150–53

ALICE MACKRELL

Dubbels, Hendrik (Jakobsz.) (*bapt* Amsterdam, 2 May 1621; *d* Amsterdam, 20 Oct 1707). Dutch painter. He worked in Amsterdam as a painter of seascapes and winter landscapes from *c.* 1641 until his death. He also did chalk and ink drawings of the same subjects. His earliest paintings were seascapes executed in the style of Jan Porcellis and using the restricted palette associated with the 'tonal' phase of Dutch painting. From *c.* 1650 to 1653 Dubbels was employed in the studio of Simon de Vlieger, where he developed close artistic contacts with Jan van de Cappelle and Willem van de Velde II, and de Vlieger's influence can be seen in the scenes of Amsterdam and its environs that Dubbels painted independently until *c.* 1658–60. He worked mainly for other Amsterdam marine painters: he was in the studio of Willem van de Velde I until 1672–3, when van de Velde and his son emigrated to England. After that Dubbels worked with his former pupil, Ludolf Bakhuizen.

Dubbels produced a relatively small body of independent work, his best pictures being painted during the 1650s, when he ranked alongside Jan van de Cappelle and Willem van de Velde II as one of Amsterdam's leading marine painters. Dubbels's works are careful, richly detailed harbour views (Kassel, Schloss Wilhelmshöhe), intimate, atmospheric 'calm seas' (London, N.G.), landscapes of beaches and rivers, winter and moonlit scenes. After 1670 he created pictures that were influenced by the younger, more tempestuous Ludolf Bakhuizen: sporting sailing manoeuvres and ships in a stiff breeze with stormy clouds (London, N. Mar. Mus.). In the 1680s and 1690s Dubbels became less ambitious artistically. He painted insipid replicas and variations of his own earlier works as well as some based on Bakhuizen's paintings.

BIBLIOGRAPHY

L. J. Bol: *Die holländische Marinemalerei des 17. Jahrhunderts* (Brunswick, 1973)
U. Middendorf: *Hendrik J. Dubbels (1621–1707)* (Freren, 1989)

ULRIKE MIDDENDORF

Dublin. Capital city of the Republic of Ireland, situated on the east coast at the mouth of the River Liffey; it has a population of *c.* 526,000. Traditionally, Dublin has two Gaelic names: *Baile Átha Cliath* (the town of the Ford of the Hurdles), derived from an agricultural and fishing community probably sited south of the Liffey, near a ford forming part of the road system of Ireland; and *Dubh Linn* (the Black Pool), from a group of monastic enclosures beside a deep pool in the River Poddle, sited to the south-east, between the present castle garden and the Steine, which flowed west of the present St Stephen's Green.

I. History and urban development. II. Art life and organization. III. Centre of production. IV. Buildings.

I. History and urban development.

1. Before 1660. 2. 1660–1800. 3. After 1800.

1. BEFORE 1660. In AD 841 Scandinavians arrived and established a permanent trading and piratical base that could be used throughout the year. Routed by the Celts in 902, they returned in 917 to establish a more permanent defended town (Irish 'dún') immediately south of the River Liffey on the present Wood Quay site. Excavated artefacts indicate that this was an important Viking trading centre. Walls enclosed the land, which was divided into plots that were trapezoidal in shape near the river and more rectangular on the higher ground. The plots were separated by post-and-wattle fences. The lines of these fences seem to have remained unchanged throughout the 10th, 11th and early 12th centuries. Houses were built to a common plan, with some exceptions and some variations. They were rectangular, consisting of low walls of post-and-wattle construction with steeply-pitched oversailing thatched roofs independently supported by internal posts. They had neither chimney nor windows.

In 1170 the Normans captured the town and banished the Vikings to Ostmantown (later Oxmantown), north of the Liffey. Between 1205 and 1220 Dublin Castle was

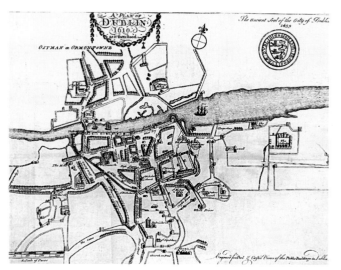

1. Map of Dublin, engraved by Jodocus Hondius I, 146×173 mm, 1610; from John Speed: *Theatre of the Empire of Great Britain* (London, 1611)

erected (little of this structure remains). Around 1300 the Viking enclosure was replaced by a stone wall incorporating the castle into its south-east corner and completely surrounding the town, which by then had grown westwards and southwards. Many churches were erected, often on sites surviving from the Gaelic monastic settlement. Most important were Christ Church and St Patrick's Cathedral (*see* §IV, 1 and 2 below), founded by Anglo-Normans who mistrusted the Danish foundation of Christ Church. Although traditional post-and-wattle construction methods continued to be used, the Normans introduced heavier timber-framed buildings and increasingly used stone.

Successive wars, plague and internecine strife limited the urban development of Dublin between the 14th and 17th centuries. John Speed's map of 1610 (see fig. 1) shows clearly the extent of the late medieval town. On the south side, stone walls enclosed a series of irregular streets surrounding Christ Church. The town extended beyond the walls stretching in linear formation along James Street to the west, Francis Street and Sheep Street (Ship Street) to the south and Dame Street to the east towards Trinity College. Houses were dotted here and there amid the churches. Ostmantown included St Michan's church, the King's Inns and St Mary's Abbey.

2. 1660–1800. The Restoration of the English monarchy in 1660 led to more settled political conditions, and the development of Dublin was encouraged by the interest of the Viceroy, James Butler, 1st Duke of Ormonde, an important patron. By 1685 a number of major projects

that contributed greatly to the quality and layout of the modern city had been accomplished. Four new bridges were thrown across the river, and Oxmantown was considerably expanded. The south bank of the river, eastwards from the castle, was reclaimed. In 1665 the City Corporation laid out St Stephen's Green on 10 ha of waste ground and divided 12 ha of the surrounding land into 89 lots to be let on long-term leases. In the absence of regulating building acts, the Corporation stipulated in the leases that the houses should be of brick, stone and wood with tiled or slate roofs and should be at least two storeys high. Wealthy families who took leases on large tracts of land and re-let smaller plots to individuals continued this practice of writing guidelines into the leases, which ensured that buildings along streets and squares were both suitable and compatible, at the same time allowing a certain degree of individuality in the detail. The old style timber-frame houses gave way to a newer type, built in brick and presenting a characteristic Dutch gable to the street. The immense Phoenix Park (940 ha) was laid out in the 1660s by the Viceroy.

In 1680, 100 ha south of the river were reclaimed for the Royal Hospital, Kilmainham, built by Sir William Robinson, architect and Surveyor General of Ireland. The hospital initiated a long tradition of classical building in Dublin. Based on the Hôtel des Invalides in Paris, it is distinguished by its enclosed classical portico, its symmetricality, decorative wood carvings and above all by the Baroque plasterwork in the chapel ceiling (replaced by a papier mâché replica in 1902). The office of Surveyor

2. Dublin, Sackville Street, by Luke Gardiner, the mall marked out by a low stone wall decorated by obelisks, 1749; from a print, early 1760s (London, British Library)

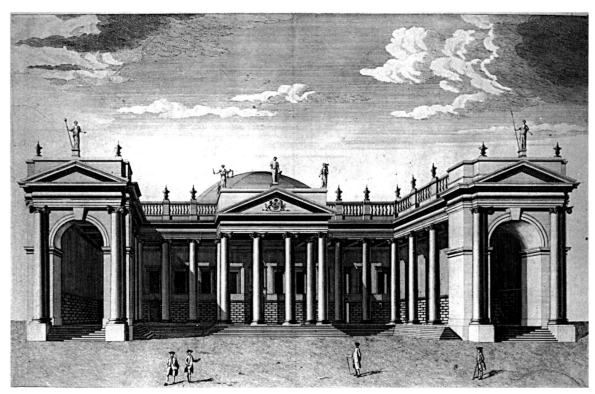

3. Dublin, Parliament House, by Edward Lovett Pearce, 1729; engraving from Bernard Scalé: *Five Plates of the Houses of Parliament* (Dublin, 1767)

General continued to provide architects for the major buildings in Dublin after Robinson's death. His immediate successor was THOMAS BURGH, most of whose buildings survive; an important exception is the Custom House (1704–8; destr. 1815) located on the east side of Essex Bridge. The plan, arcades and entrance gate of Dr Steevens's Hospital, designed by Burgh in 1721, clearly show his debt to Robinson. Burgh's best works, the Treasury at Dublin Castle (*c.* 1712) and the library at Trinity College (1712–32), are characterized by a severe form of astylar classicism, relying on eaves cornices, on the regular rhythm of the fenestration and on subtle projection and recession along the façades. Burgh was also responsible for the Royal (now Collins's) Barracks (1701–4).

A sense of optimism, coupled with a determination to make a city worthy of their new-found power, pervaded the thinking of the ruling classes in 18th-century Dublin. Monumental public and private buildings were commissioned in rapid succession. Patrons were distinguished by their awareness of architectural trends and by their grand conceptions. One such was Luke Gardiner, who was responsible for the spacious layout of Henrietta Street and Dorset Street and whose greatest achievement was the creation of Sackville Street (now O'Connell Street) from 1749. He widened Drogheda Street to 45 m, re-let the land in building leases and laid out an ornamental mall in the centre, thus creating a new fashionable residential area on a grand scale to the east of the old town (see fig. 2). This provided the basis for the late 18th-century provision of a second axis, which continued the line of Sackville Street across the river, pulling the city eastwards, away from the castle. In time Sackville Street became the new city centre north of the river. Almost without exception, architects were sought who could produce the most up-to-date designs, and the search often took patrons abroad. This constant importation of new ideas contributed greatly to the architectural excitement of the 18th century. Foreign architects were assisted and emulated by a large group of native architect-craftsmen, trained in the School of Architecture established by the Dublin Society in 1765.

English Palladianism was introduced by Sir Edward Lovett Pearce, successor to Burgh, whose Parliament House (now the Bank of Ireland), designed in 1729 (see fig. 3), uniquely combines the influences of Sir John Vanbrugh and the circle of Lord Burlington. An Ionic colonnaded screen defines three sides of a shallow atrium and is brought forward in the centre, in Vanburghian style, to create a pedimented frontispiece. The wings are terminated at each end by arches in colonnaded aedicules. Internally, the House of Commons was accommodated in an octagonal room surmounted by a dome (destr.), stepped like the Pantheon, and surrounded by a corridor comprising a series of domed squares; the House of Lords with its apse and its Diocletian window is based on the Roman baths. After Pearce's death, his protégé Richard Castle was awarded all the major projects in Dublin, which he carried out in a strict Palladian style, his free-standing buildings such as Leinster House (1745) and the Rotunda Hospital

(1749) being Palladian country villas translated into the suburbs. His other Dublin buildings include the Printing House (1734) at Trinity College, 86 St Stephen's Green (Clanwilliam House, 1738) and Tyrone House (1740; façade altered 19th century).

No great architect emerged immediately after Castle's death in 1751, and building was carried on by craftsmen–architects. These included the Darley family, the Semples—George Semple (1700–81/2) was responsible for Essex Bridge (1753) and St Patrick's Hospital (1749)—and the Ensors. John Ensor took over at the Rotunda Hospital after Castle's death, designing the round assembly room (1764) for which the hospital is named. He was employed by the 6th Lord Fitzwilliam (d 1776) to plan Merrion Square (1762). The last great exercises in Palladianism were the rebuilding of the west front of Trinity College and the Provost's House (see §IV, 3 below).

In the 18th century the external severity of the Palladian houses was belied by the luxuriant plasterwork of the interiors. The arrival in the 1730s of the Italian brothers Philip and Paul Lafranchini hastened a change that had already begun, from the heavy compartmented plasterwork of the 17th-century interiors to a lighter style incorporating flowers and foliage, shells, festoons, cherubs and scenes from classical mythology. The main source of ideas was the French Rococo movement. The works of Jean Bérain I and Nicolas Pineau were as influential in Ireland as elsewhere. Classical scenes were often based on the work of such artists as Nicolas Poussin and Antoine Watteau, whose ceiling design of *Venus Wounded by Love* was the model for the La Touche Bank ceiling, by an unknown stuccoist (now in the Bank of Ireland, College Green). Cesare Ripa's *Iconologia* (edition of 1603) was a commonly used source. Initially the designs were formally restrained within a framework but gradually they achieved full Rococo spontaneity and asymmetricality. By 1750 realistic natural detail began to play a prominent part, as in the ceilings at Mesoil House (now in the President's residence). In the Rotunda Hospital Chapel (1755–8), Bartholomew Cramillion combined magnificent figures with realistic detail in a formal framework to produce one of Dublin's most unusual ceilings. Robert West, who worked with Cramillion, went on to become the leading figure in a distinctive Irish school in which figures played a minor role, and the principal motifs were musical instruments, birds, fruit, and a flickering Rococo foliage. His finest work can be seen in his own house, 20 Lower Dominick Street (c. 1755). By 1775, with Neo-classical architecture, came a new style of plasterwork based on the flat geometric designs of Robert Adam. Michael Stapleton (d 1801) was the most prominent stuccoist of this time.

In 1757 the Wide Streets Commission was established; among the Commissioners' most notable achievements were the widening of many streets to 30 m or more and the removal of the Custom House down-river of its position east of Essex Bridge. This latter was particularly significant, for it allowed the building of Carlisle Bridge (1790; now O'Connell Bridge) connecting Sackville Street (already connected by North Frederick Street to Dorset Street in 1782 and extended towards the river in 1784) with the south side. In 1800 the line from Dorset Street was continued when Westmoreland Street and D'Olier

Street (both of which led away at an angle from the bridge) were laid out. The Commissioners exercised tight control over new building under their jurisdiction. One of their innovations was to introduce the street-side shop-front with residential quarters overhead (an idea originating from Paris) in Westmoreland Street, D'Olier Street and Cavendish Row.

Neo-classicism became the dominant style in the second half of the century, making its first major appearance in the Royal Exchange (1769, by Thomas Cooley). Square in plan, the Exchange has two main façades each with a giant Corinthian portico, one pedimented. A great circular hall (altered 1852) occupies the centre of the building. Cooley's example was quickly followed by Thomas Ivory who incorporated Neo-classical detail in his essentially Palladian Blue Coat School (1773). Ivory's later Newcomen's Bank (1781) is a much more radical building, executed with great refinement of detail.

The major architect in the Neo-classical style, the man who provides a fitting climax to the great building programme of the 18th century, is JAMES GANDON, brought to Dublin to erect the new Custom House (1781) to replace Burgh's building. Before he died he had provided the city with four major landmarks—the Custom House, an addition to Parliament House (1782), the Four Courts (1786; gutted 1922; rest.) and the King's Inns (c. 1800). The powerful design of the Four Courts (for illustration see GANDON, JAMES) dominates the riverfront site with its giant Corinthian portico, from which stretch arcaded screen walls broken by triumphal arch entrances.

3. AFTER 1800. The Act of Union of 1800 had a drastic effect on the architectural development of the city. Peers and Members of Parliament retreated to their country mansions or adjourned to London. It was difficult to sell land, and many properties lay idle. Houses built along Baggot Street, Leeson Street, Upper and Lower Mount Streets, Fitzwilliam Street, Fitzwilliam Square and Mountjoy Square were much less luxurious than their predecessors. Building activity in the 19th century led to a rise in a strong native architectural profession; the Royal Institute of Architects of Ireland was established in 1839. In the wake of Catholic Emancipation (1829) many churches were built, such as James Boulger's St Andrew's (1832–7), Pearse Street, with its Doric portico, and the Jesuit church of St Francis Xavier (1832) by Joseph Keene, which has a tetrastyle Ionic portico. Three great terminus stations were built for the new railway. From an international point of view, the most significant firm of architects during the century was that of Sir Thomas Deane and Benjamin Woodward (see DEANE & WOODWARD), whose Venetian palazzo-style Museum Building at Trinity College (1852) was hailed by John Ruskin as the first truly to incorporate his Gothic principles. Until the 1940s, building styles in Dublin were as eclectic as they were in England, although for such major public works as the Museum and Library in Kildare Street (1884–90) by Sir Thomas Manly Deane (1851–1933) and the Government Buildings in Merrion Street (1904) by Sir Aston Webb, various forms of classicism were employed. The public was introduced to modern architecture in 1941, when Desmond Fitzgerald built the Airport Terminal. The first fully-fledged Modern

Movement building in the city proper was Michael Scott's Irish Transport Board Bus Station (1950–53). In later years some striking buildings were built outside the city centre, for example the Belfield campus of University College (from the 1960s) and the cylindrical American Embassy (1964) in Ballsbridge, south Dublin.

BIBLIOGRAPHY

J. Malton: *A Picturesque & Descriptive View of the City of Dublin* (London, 1799/*R* Dublin, 1978)

J. T. Gilbert, ed.: *Calendar of Ancient Records of Dublin*, 19 vols (Dublin and London, 1889)

B. C. A. Windle: *Dublin, a Historical and Topographical Account of the City* (London, 1907)

P. J. Walsh: *Dublin c. 840 to c. 1540: The Years of Medieval Growth* (Dublin, 1922)

J. Maher: 'Francis Place in Dublin', *J. Royal Soc. Antiqua. Ireland*, lxii (1932), pp. 1–14 [incl. Francis Place's drgs of Dublin buildings (1698–9)]

C. Maxwell: *Dublin under the Georges: 1714–1850* (London, 1936)

M. Craig: *Dublin 1660–1860* (Dublin 1952/*R* 1969, 1980) [with extensive bibliog.]

C. P. Curran: *Dublin Decorative Plasterwork of the 17th and 18th Centuries* (London, 1967)

E. McParland: 'The Wide Streets Commissioners: Their Importance for Dublin Architecture in the Late 18th and Early 19th Century', *Irish Georg. Soc. Bull.*, xv (1972), pp. 1–29

H. B. Clarke: 'The Topographical Development of Early Medieval Dublin', *J. Royal Soc. Antiqua. Ireland*, cvii (1977), pp. 29–51

——: *Dublin c. 840 to c. 1540: the Medieval Town in the Modern City* (Dublin, 1978) [map with pamphlet]

R. Loeber: *A Biographical Dictionary of Architects in Ireland: 1600–1720* (London, 1981)

P. F. Wallace: 'Anglo-Norman Dublin: Continuity and Change', *Irish Antiquity*, ed. D. ó Corráin (Cork, 1981), pp. 109–18

E. Blau: *Ruskinian Gothic: The Architecture of Deane and Woodward, 1845–1861* (Princeton, 1982)

D. Cruickshank: *A Guide to Georgian Buildings of Britain & Ireland* (London, 1985)

P. F. Wallace: 'The Archaeology of Viking Dublin', *The Comparative History of Urban Origins in Non-Roman Europe: Ireland, Wales, Denmark, Germany, Poland, and Russia from the Ninth to the Thirteenth Century* (repr. from British Archaeological Reports, International Series 255, 1985, parts 1 & 2), pp. 103–45 [with extensive bibliog.]

——: 'The Archaeology of Anglo-Norman Dublin', *The Comparative History of Urban Origins in Non-Roman Europe: Ireland, Wales, Denmark, Germany, Poland, and Russia from the Ninth to the Thirteenth Century* (repr. from British Archaeological Reports, International Series 255, 1985, parts 1 & 2), pp. 379–410 [with extensive bibliog.]

NOREEN CASEY

II. Art life and organization.

Organized artistic activity began in Dublin only with the Restoration in 1660 and the return of the Viceroy. The Guild of Cutlers, Painter-Steyners and Stationers, also known as the Guild of St Luke, founded in 1670 by a charter of Charles II, was the first organization to include painters, although most of its members were not easel painters.

In Dublin craftwork was as strong as fine art, and the main impetus behind its renewed strength was the influx of refugee Huguenot craftsmen in the late 17th century (*see* HUGUENOTS). Craft guilds existed for plasterers, weavers, masons and goldsmiths among others, but these were Protestant corporations; Catholics were excluded from full membership and forbidden to open retail shops until a combination of changes in business practice and nationalist pressure forced the dissolution of all the guilds except the goldsmiths and silversmiths (kept for assaying functions) in 1840.

The Dublin Society, founded in 1731, aimed to promote such Irish industries as woven damask, printed linens and cottons, carpets, lace, cut and stained glass, pottery, engraving, medals and straw plait. It did so by means of premiums, cash grants or letters of endorsement, and its main efforts were directed towards printed linens and woven silk-poplin—industries that provided the greatest employment. The Society supported schools where figure, ornamental and architectural drawing were taught. Like plasterwork, the crafts of bookbinding, silversmithing and furniture-making (*see* §III below) all reached international standards of excellence. Maintaining this achievement, however, depended on the patronage of the wealthy Anglo-Irish landlords, and after many of them ceased to live regularly in Dublin after the Act of Union in 1800, there was a decline in the quality of luxury crafts, the rise of the professional middle class only partly compensating for this loss of patronage. In addition, the Industrial Revolution in Britain led to forms of mass production with which Dublin's industries could not compete in the free-trade area of the United Kingdom.

In the first half of the 19th century the Royal Dublin Society (R.D.S.) continued to encourage Irish industry, which, apart from Belfast linen, was still craft-based. The main initiative was the series of R.D.S. trade exhibitions held in Dublin from 1834, which culminated in the Dublin International Exhibition of 1853; the Spring Show and Industries Fair was begun by the R.D.S. in 1881.

The Irish Arts and Crafts Society, inspired by the movement led by William Morris in Britain, was founded in 1894, holding its first exhibition the following year. After 1900 the Dublin Metropolitan School of Art incorporated such crafts as metalwork, enamelling and stained glass in its curriculum. In 1902 the Dun Emer Guild was set up under Evelyn Gleeson and Lily and Elizabeth Yeats to foster weaving and bookbinding; and the Irish artistic and literary revival was the inspiration behind the establishment in 1903 of An Túr Gloine (the TOWER OF GLASS) stained-glass studios, by Sarah Purser. Interest in crafts has continued to the present, encouraged by such official bodies as the Crafts Council of Ireland, set up in 1971 (for further discussion of Irish decorative arts, *see* IRELAND, §§V–XI).

Art exhibitions began in Dublin in 1764, with the foundation of the Society of Artists in Ireland. Its first exhibition, in 1765, led to the opening of a permanent exhibition room (now the Civic Museum). After a 20-year interval, when no exhibitions were held owing to schisms among the membership, a new Society was inaugurated in 1800, exhibiting mostly in the rooms of the Dublin Society until 1819. The Royal Irish Institution was founded in 1813 to establish an art academy, and in 1823, after much insistence, the Royal Hibernian Academy (R.H.A.) was finally set up, holding its first exhibition three years later. The R.H.A. remained the most important organization for artists until after World War II, since when annual exhibitions by rival groups have become common; among its post-war Presidents (1962–78) was Maurice Mac-Gonigal (1900–79; see fig. 4).

A movement towards the creation of a permanent collection of Old Master paintings began with temporary exhibitions organized by the Royal Irish Institution, and

4. Maurice MacGonigal: *A Dublin Studio*, oil on canvas, 1.02×1.27 m, *c.* 1935 (Limerick, City Gallery of Art)

with public interest further stimulated by the International Exhibition of 1853 the National Gallery of Ireland was founded in 1854, and its premises, by Francis Fowke, were built by 1864. In the 1870s a National Portrait Collection was assembled by Henry E. Doyle, the Gallery's Director. During the 19th century, the Royal Irish Academy and the R.D.S. pioneered the collecting of ancient Irish metalwork and other antiquarian objects. These collections, which included decorative art, formed the nucleus of the National Museum of Science and Art, established in 1877 and installed in the new building by Sir Thomas Manly Deane in 1890. A subsequent movement, aimed at establishing a gallery of modern art, was led by Sir HUGH LANE, who organized exhibitions in the opening years of the 20th century. Lane donated pictures to form the nucleus of the Municipal Gallery of Modern Art, which opened in 1908, and to this he added a later gift of French paintings. In 1933 the Dublin Corporation installed its own modern art collection in Charlemont House, a building specially extended and adapted for the purpose.

In the later 19th century, as the Anglo-Irish gentry became impoverished, there was a serious decline in sales at the R.H.A., but amateur societies flourished: the Watercolour Society of Ireland was founded in 1870 and the Dublin Sketching Club two years later; many other groups

such as the Dublin Arts Club, founded in 1907, were subsequently formed. As part of the Irish cultural revival, the Oireachtas Festival held occasional exhibitions of contemporary art before World War I, and during the 1920s and 1930s the Dublin Painters group showed the most progressive art.

In 1943 the Modernists, in disagreement with the policies of the R.H.A., set up the Irish Exhibition of Living Art. This became an important rallying point for modern art in the years after World War II. Several other annual shows, by groups such as the revived Oireachtas and the Independent Painters, began to provide outlets for differing currents of contemporary art. In 1951 the Irish Arts Council was set up; 15 years later the Project Arts Centre was established as a venue for exhibiting experimental art, which, with the periodic Rosc ('Poetry of vision') exhibitions of international contemporary art (from 1967), have had an important effect on public awareness of modern art.

BIBLIOGRAPHY

W. Strickland: *A Dictionary of Irish Artists* (Dublin, 1913), ii, pp. 579–664

T. Bodkin: *Hugh Lane and his Pictures* (Dublin, 1956)

A. Crookshank and the Knight of Glin: *The Painters of Ireland* (London, 1978)

P. Harbison, H. Potterton and J. Sheehy: *The Celtic Revival: The Rediscovery of Ireland's Past* (London, 1980)

M. Gahan: 'The Development of Crafts', *The Royal Dublin Society, 1731–1981*, ed. J. Meenan and D. Clarke (Dublin, 1981)

C. de Courcy: *The Foundation of the National Gallery of Ireland* (Dublin, 1985)

J. Turpin: 'The Public Exhibitions of Art in 19th-century Dublin', *Akten des XXV. internationalen Kongresses für Kunstgeschichte*, iv, ed. E. Liskar (Vienna, 1986)

A. M. Stewart: *Royal Hibernian Academy of Arts, Exhibitors and their Works* (Dublin, 1986)

N. Gordon-Bowe: 'Women and the Arts and Crafts Revival in Ireland, c. 1886–1930', *Irish Women Artists from the Eighteenth Century to the Present Day* (exh. cat., Dublin, N. G. and Douglas Hyde Gal., 1987)

JOHN TURPIN

III. Centre of production.

1. GOLD AND SILVER. The earliest record of a named guild in Dublin is a list of craftsmen, including a goldsmith, Oliver de Nichol (*fl* 1226–61), admitted in 1226–7 to a body known as the Dublin guild merchants. The Dublin Roll of Names, which probably dates from the latter part of the 12th century, mentions craftsmen who practised gold- and silversmithing. According to extant records, goldsmiths played a prominent part in the Corpus Christi pageant of 1498, possibly suggesting that they had a guild of their own by that date, and at least five goldsmiths were given the freedom of the city in the 15th century. The Guild of All Saints, which encompassed silver- and goldsmithing, was recognized as a guild in 1557, although there is no extant record of the enrolment. There appears, however, to have been no proper control over silver- and goldsmiths, as goods below the required standard were often sold. In 1605 a complaint was raised in Dublin City Council regarding the dealings of craftsmen who manufactured plate of base or corrupt silver, and consequently the mayor of Dublin and his constables were appointed assayers of precious metal, with all silver bearing the marks of a lion, a harp and a castle. No articles with these marks, however, have been discovered. Little domestic plate has survived from this period; the majority of extant pieces dating before 1660 are chalices, for example George Gallant's Russell-Taafe Chalice (1641; Dublin, N. Mus.).

In 1637 the goldsmiths petitioned Charles I, requesting that the Guild of All Saints be incorporated by royal charter; this was granted and the guild renamed the Company of Goldsmiths of Dublin. It was given the power to supervise the assaying and marking of all gold and silver throughout Ireland. Dublin hallmarks originally consisted of a maker's mark and a crowned harp, referred to in the charter of 1637 as the 'King's majesty stamp', which were used for 22 carat gold and sterling silver. In 1638 a date letter system was introduced and used in conjunction with the above marks. A mark in the form of 'Hibernia' was introduced on 25 March 1730 to indicate that a duty had been paid; it continues to be used. In 1807 a new duty mark—the king's (or queen's) head—was introduced. It was was used until the 1890s when the duty was abolished.

The gold- and silversmiths' trade in Dublin prospered particularly during the 18th century (*see* IRELAND, §IX). The leading silversmiths included Joseph Walker (*fl* 1683–1717), Thomas Bolton (*fl* 1676; *d* 1736), Philip Kinnersley (*fl* 1702–27/8), Robert Calderwood (*fl* 1740; *d* 1766; e.g. Rococo candlesticks, 1746; priv. col.; *see* IRELAND, fig. 22) and, in the early 19th century, JAMES LE BAS. The Industrial Revolution and the imports of factory-made wares produced in England, when coupled with the Act of Union of 1800, resulted in a decline in the production of gold and silver in Dublin from which the trade never fully recovered.

BIBLIOGRAPHY

J. P. Mahaffy and D. S. M. Westropp: *The Plate of Trinity College Dublin* (London, 1918)

K. Ticher, I. Delamer and W. O'Sullivan: *Hallmarks on Dublin Silver* (Dublin, 1968)

D. Bennett: *The Company of Goldsmiths of Dublin, 1637–1987* (Dublin, 1987)

DOUGLAS BENNETT

2. GLASS. Factories producing lead glass were established in Dublin and its suburbs in the late 17th century. Their products had to compete directly with imported wares, including those by George Ravenscroft, and hence early wares are of a similar style. By 1729 the Round Glass House, which was established c. 1690 by Philip Roche (*d* 1713), had developed to the extent that it was able to advertise 'all sorts of fine, flint drinking glasses, salvers, baskets with handles and feet for desserts, fine salts ground and polished, all sorts of decanters, lamps'. This range was later extended to include more sophisticated wares for the table, lighting and functional items for apothecaries, taverns and shopkeepers. Decorated pieces included wine and beer glasses with vine borders or toasts, and in 1735 Joseph Martin, who was employed at the Glass Ware House, offered 'arms, crests, words, letters or figures carved on glass-ware'.

Due to the Glass Excise Acts and the restrictions on exports, glass manufacture in Dublin developed slowly and closely followed the fashions set by London. In the late 18th century, when conditions changed in favour of the Irish lead-glass industry, the principal developments took place in such other Irish cities as WATERFORD, Belfast and Cork (*see* CORK, §1). The manufacture of fine glass in Dublin was then undertaken also by merchants who sold imported wares alongside their own, or those made for them and marked with their names. All were similar in style. The range produced by these merchants was wide: the firm of Charles Mulvany & Co. (1785–1846) advertised in 1788 lustres, girandoles, globe lanterns, glasses, decanters, goblets, épergnes, bowls, fruit dishes and butter coolers. Situated in a major market area, the industry survived in Dublin, changing its style according to the demands of fashion. At the Potter's Alley Glass House (1863–98), which was owned by the Pugh family, production included fashionable ornamental, table and commercial lead glass in a variety of colours, as well as cut and engraved designs. The Bohemians Franz Tieze (1842–c. 1916) and Joseph Eisert (1842–71) were employed as master engravers at the works, and in order to satisfy demand, they engraved pieces in their own Bohemian patterns as well as in the Celtic Revival style as souvenirs for national celebrations and for family occasions.

BIBLIOGRAPHY

M. S. D. Westropp: *Irish Glass: An Account of Glass-making in Ireland from the XVIth Century to the Present Day* (London, 1920, rev. Dublin, 1978)

P. Warren: *Irish Glass: The Age of Exuberance* (London, 1970, rev. 1981)

MAIREAD DUNLEVY

3. STAINED GLASS. Although written evidence indicates that there were glazed windows, sometimes with stained glass, in Ireland long before the 18th century, neither the medieval glass excavated nor the few pieces *in situ* have been proved to be indigenous. The 17th-century small, heraldic, narrative or genre panels were imported after Oliver Cromwell's departure. George M'Allister (1786–1812) worked successfully but in a conventional style in Dublin and England, as did Michael O'Connor (1801–67), whose studio in Dublin was one of the most notable among about 100 studios for stained glass in the city during the 19th century. A. W. N. Pugin, who collaborated with O'Connor, employed Thomas Earley (1819–93), born in Birmingham of Irish parents, before Earley set up a branch of John Hardman & Co. in Dublin in 1864 with Henry Powell. By the end of the 19th century only the windows produced by Earley & Powell, Joshua Clarke (*c.* 1856–1921) and J. & D. Casey in Dublin were distinguishable from the increasingly eclectic style of window and the numerous imported windows. Between 1903 and 1955 three notable studios were established in Dublin: An Túr Gloine (the TOWER OF GLASS) and those of Harry Clarke (*see* CLARKE, (2); *see also* STAINED GLASS, colour pl. VII) and Evie Hone (*see* HONE, (4)).

BIBLIOGRAPHY
R. M. Butler: 'Modern Stained Glass', *Archit. Rev. [London]*, lix (1926), pp. 200–02
M. Wynne: *Stained Glass in Ireland, Principally Irish Stained Glass, 1760–1963* (PhD diss., Dublin, Trinity Coll., 1975)
N. Gordon Bowe: *Twentieth Century Irish Stained Glass* (Dublin, 1983)
N. Gordon Bowe, M. Wynne and D. Caron: *Gazetteer of Irish Stained Glass* (Dublin, 1988)
                                              NICOLA GORDON BOWE

IV. Buildings.

1. Christ Church Cathedral. 2. St Patrick's Cathedral. 3. Trinity College.

1. CHRIST CHURCH CATHEDRAL. With the neighbouring Cathedral of St Patrick, Christ Church, also known as Holy Trinity, contains some of the most distinguished Gothic architecture in Ireland. Both cathedrals were erected in the century after the English conquest (1169–70), and they are the only medieval buildings in the country designed in a sophisticated manner with three-storey elevations and high vaults. Both suffered structural failure in the 16th century and underwent major restoration in the 19th. Although modest in scale, Christ Church has the more varied architectural history, and its 13th-century nave elevation is a particularly subtle and well-balanced composition.

The cathedral was founded soon after 1028, but the existing fabric was not started until *c.* 1186–90. This was probably on the initiative of John Comyn, the first Anglo-Norman to occupy the see of Dublin (*reg* 1181–1212), which would explain the English character of the design. Construction lasted approximately fifty years over two campaigns, with a break at the start of the nave. The cathedral's short length (the 12th-century choir had only one bay before the apse) is explained by a restricted urban site. The groin-vaulted crypt, extending under all but one bay of the building, may have been intended to compensate for this lack of space. The choir terminated in a three-sided apse, with an ambulatory and three chapels beyond.

Although awkward in its layout, the plan was of a complexity unprecedented in 12th-century Ireland. The surviving medieval transepts were designed in a cumbersome Late Romanesque style. Even the passageways at triforium and clerestory level provide scant relief for the bareness of the rubble walls, built of local grey calp; for the dressings a yellow oolitic limestone was imported from Dundry near Bristol, a quarry that served many Irish workshops between 1170 and 1300. The main interest of this part of the building is a group of historiated capitals, carved with scenes of fruitpickers, musical entertainers, shepherds, grotesque animals etc. The style of these and other ornamental details is paralleled in the Severn Valley in England.

The six-bay nave (*c.* 1216–40) was badly damaged when the vaults collapsed in 1562; only the north elevation, which still leans about 0.61 m from the vertical, is authentically medieval (see fig. 5). The design is in general a typical product of the Early English style. It is low in proportion (the vaults were only 14.78 m high), there are two sets of wall passages, the mouldings are exceptionally complex, and there are abundant stiff-leaf capitals and polished limestone shafts. The elevation is, however, more disciplined and unified than is usual in English architecture of the time. The division between bays is accentuated by a filleted shaft rising unbroken from floor to vault, and a simple set of proportions—1:2, 1:3, 2:3—underlies the whole scheme.

More remarkable is the neat integration of triforium and clerestory through the use of mullions linking the two storeys together, a contrast to the more usual system

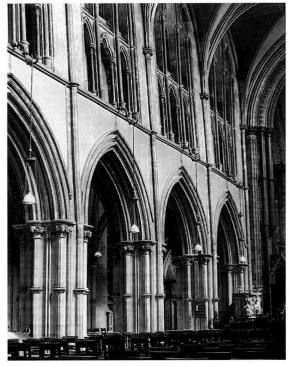

5. Dublin, Christ Church Cathedral, north elevation of nave, *c.* 1220–40

employed at St Patrick's Cathedral. Although related experiments were taking place in western England (Lichfield Cathedral, Worcester Cathedral, Pershore Abbey), the Dublin arrangement may reflect knowledge of linked elevations in French Gothic architecture (St Remi at Reims and Notre-Dame-en-Vaux at Châlons-sur-Marne). The workshop responsible for the nave has been traced to Worcestershire, where capitals in Overbury and Droitwich parish churches are carved by the same hand as those at Christ Church. Despite its qualities, the influence of the design was negligible: it was too remote to become familiar to future English masons and too grandiose to serve as a model for subsequent Irish building.

Christ Church was served by a community of Augustinian canons, and a cloister (destr.) was laid out to the south of the cathedral. Not long after the nave was completed, an elaborate chapter house was erected, the foundations of which survive. Employing Bath rather than Dundry stone, it was rectangular in plan and rib-vaulted in four bays.

The reconstruction of Christ Church by G. E. STREET is a classic example of Victorian restoration: an attempt to reinstate the building as it might have been c. 1240. Christ Church was more suited to this thorough treatment than most, for by 1869 it had become 'a worn and dingy building', a patchwork of repairs and unsightly alterations. The massive works involved included some audacious engineering, all paid for by the Dublin whiskey distiller Henry Roe. Although he had many critics, Street's restoration was generally regarded as a triumph and in 1882 the cathedral authorities published a lavish volume to celebrate what had been achieved. Particularly controversial was the demolition of the 'long choir', a 'long crooked barn-like building' added in the late 13th or 14th century, which Street replaced with a design of his own, erected on the foundations of the old crypt. The southern half of the nave was rebuilt to match the surviving northern elevation and stone vaults were restored throughout. Street took care to preserve or reproduce ancient details wherever he could, and his record of moulding profiles still survives. But the restoration was not without its sacrifices: inconsistencies in the old building were ironed out in the interests of homogeneity. Flying buttresses were added to the nave, ostensibly to stabilize the vaults but with the bonus of adding a more dramatic Gothic touch. Street also designed an array of new furnishings and fittings as well as a number of ancillary buildings, most spectacular of which is the Gothic former synod hall, ingeniously linked to the cathedral by a covered bridge.

BIBLIOGRAPHY

W. Butler: *Christ Church Cathedral: Measured Drawings of the Building Prior to Restoration* (Dublin, 1878)
R. B. McVittie: *Details of the Restoration of Christ Church Cathedral, Dublin* (Dublin, 1878)
G. E. Street and E. Seymour: *The Cathedral of the Holy Trinity Commonly Called Christ Church Cathedral* (London, 1882)
T. Drew: 'Street as a Restorer', *Dublin U. Rev.*, ii/6 (1886), pp. 518–31
W. Butler: *The Cathedral Church of the Holy Trinity Dublin* (London, 1901)
H. G. Leask: *Irish Churches and Ecclesiastical Buildings*, ii (Dundalk, 1958)
R. A. Stalley: 'Three Irish Buildings with West Country Origins', *British Archaeological Association Conference Transactions: Medieval Art and Architecture at Wells and Glastonbury: Wells, 1978*, pp. 71–6
——: 'The Medieval Sculpture of Christ Church Cathedral, Dublin', *Archaeologia*, cvi (1979), pp. 107–22

ROGER STALLEY

2. ST PATRICK'S CATHEDRAL. Now the Cathedral of the Protestant Church of Ireland, it was founded in 1190, achieving cathedral status under Bishop Henry de Londres (*reg* 1212–28). Heavily restored by Thomas Drew (1866–9), it was built between 1220 and 1254 to a cruciform plan, with an eastern Lady Chapel added by Archbishop Fulk de Saundford (*d* 1271). Like Christ Church Cathedral (*see* §1 above), it has a three-storey elevation. The arcade, triforium and three-light clerestory windows have sharply pointed arches. The west end and west tower were rebuilt after a fire in 1381, and in 1544 the quadripartite vault of the nave collapsed; the clustered piers were replaced by granite shafts.

St Patrick's is noted for its collection of memorials, the earliest example of which is the effigy of *Fulk de Saundford*. The Jacobean Renaissance style is represented in the gigantic, four-level, multi-figured, polychrome tomb of *Richard Boyle, 1st Earl of Cork* (1632), designed by Roger Leverett and carved by Edmond Tingham (*fl* 1630s). The cathedral contains works by most of the sculptors active in Ireland since the 18th century. Edward Lovett Pearce designed the monument to *Rev. William Worth* (1732) in the form of a classical aedicule. Simon Vierpyl (*c*. 1725–1810) carved the monument to *Elizabeth, Viscountess Doneraile* (1762), a mourning figure with putti, based on the tomb of the 1st Viscount (*d* 1727) by Henry Cheere in Doneraile church. John van Nost II carved the tomb to *Archbishop Smyth* (completed 1776 by Henry Darley); van Nost's pupil Patrick Cunningham (*d* 1774), the first significant native Irish sculptor, carved the lively, realistic bust of *Jonathan Swift* (1766). The north aisle contains five free-standing, full-length figures, of which the monuments to *George Nugent-Temple-Grenville, 1st Marquess of Buckingham* (1788) by Edward Smyth and *George Ogle MP* by Edward's son, John Smyth (*c*. 1773–1840), have a late Baroque animation of pose and realistically detailed costume. The Neo-classical style is evident in the memorial to *Thomas Ball* (1827) with allegorical figures, by Thomas Kirk (1781–1845), the austere sarcophagus and bust of *John Philpot Curran* (1842) by Christopher Moore (1790–1863) and Edward Hodges Baily's seated *Dean Richard Dawson* (1843). Terence Farrell (1798–1876) carved two large war memorials to the 18th Royal Irish Regiment; his son, Sir Thomas Farrell, carved the spirited naval memorial to *Captain John Boyd* (1864). Late 19th-century bronze memorials include the bust of *E. H. Lecky* (1890) by Joseph Edgar Boehm and a profile portrait relief of *John Cooksey Culwick* (1908) by Oliver Sheppard.

BIBLIOGRAPHY

H. G. Leask: *Irish Churches and Monastic Buildings*, ii (Dundalk, 1960/*R* 1966)
H. Potterton: *Irish Church Monuments* (Belfast, 1975)
V. Jackson: *St Patrick's Cathedral, Dublin* (Dublin, 1984)
——: *The Monuments in St Patrick's Cathedral, Dublin* (Dublin, 1987)

JOHN TURPIN

3. TRINITY COLLEGE. Trinity College, University of Dublin, was founded by Elizabeth I and, although freed from religious restrictions in 1873, was identified with the

6. Dublin, Trinity College, west front by Theodore Jacobsen, 1750s

Protestant Church until the 1940s. The foundation stone was laid on 13 March 1592 on the site of the suppressed monastery of All Hallows, to the east of the old city. Nothing survives of the college buildings from before the 18th century except the general layout of interlinked quadrangles. In the early 17th century, four ranges of red-brick buildings enclosed a courtyard. The west façade, with symmetrically disposed gables, was pierced by an arched entrance enriched by an order of caryatids. In front lay an enclosed lawn with a classical gateway. Later a series of subsidiary quadrangles developed eastward, setting the pattern for subsequent planning.

Library Square was begun in 1700 to the east of the original Parliament Square, with three red-brick residential ranges (of which one survives) in a shortened form and with 19th-century Dutch gables replacing the original dormer windows. Closing the square is the library (1711) by Thomas Burgh. A severe classical building, it originally had two upper storeys of white sandstone (replaced by granite in the early 19th century by Sir Richard Morrison) with contrasting granite arcades at ground level (glazed in the 1890s). Inside, a magnificent long room with a gallery accommodated the library. The classical woodwork, including two fine staircases, remains, but Deane & Woodward altered the gallery and replaced the flat compartmented ceiling by a wooden barrel vault in 1860. Richard Castle began work in the college in 1734, when he designed the Printing House with a Doric temple-front. Later, Castle built a great bell-tower (1740), which was replaced by Charles Lanyon's Campanile (1852), and a dining hall (1741) that collapsed and was rebuilt by Hugh Darley in 1758; this was badly damaged by fire in 1984 but has since been fully restored. The distinguished Palladian west front (1750s; see fig. 6), reminiscent of Colen Campbell's Wanstead, Essex (1713–22; destr. 1822), was the work of Theodore Jacobsen (*fl* 1726;

d 1772), an English amateur architect. The Provost's House (1759), probably by John Smyth (*fl* 1758–69), is a copy of Colonel Wade's House in London by Lord Burlington, with a very fine interior probably by Henry Keene. Parliament Square, the first cobbled quadrangle, is dominated by the twin Neo-classical temple fronts of the theatre (1780s) and the chapel (1790s), which face each other across the square. Designed by Sir William Chambers, they were executed by Christopher Myers and his son Graham. The interior of the chapel, with an Ionic order taken from James Stuart's *Antiquities of Athens* (1762–1816), is more severe than the theatre. The plasterwork in both buildings was executed by Michael Stapleton (*d* 1801).

New Square, laid out to the north-east of Library Square in the 1830s by Frederick Darley, was closed off from College Park in 1853 by Deane & Woodward's Venetian palazzo-style Museum Building (*see* IRELAND, fig. 5), praised by John Ruskin for the free expression of its sculptural detail. Modern architecture is well represented in the Berkeley Library (1967) by Paul Koralek, adjacent to the Old Library, and in the Arts Building (1974) by Ahrends, Burton & Koralek, built to the east, on the far side of College Park.

BIBLIOGRAPHY
C. Maxwell: *A History of Trinity College Dublin, 1591 to 1892* (Dublin, 1946)
E. McParland: 'Trinity College, Dublin', *Country Life*, clix (1976), pp. 1166, 1242, 1310
R. B. McDowell and D. A. Webb: *Trinity College Dublin 1592 to 1952: An Academic History* (Cambridge, 1982)
A. Reihill: 'The Restoration of the Dining Hall, Trinity College, Dublin', *Irish A. Rev.*, iii (1986), pp. 26–37

NOREEN CASEY

Dubois[-Pillet], **(Louis-Auguste-)Albert** (*b* Paris, 28 Oct 1846; *d* Le Puy, 18 Aug 1890). French painter and army officer. He pursued a military career at the Ecole

Impériale Militaire at Saint-Cyr, from which he graduated in 1867. He fought in the Franco-Prussian War (1870–71) and was held prisoner in Westphalia by the Germans; upon release he joined the Versailles army and participated in the suppression of the Commune. Following various assignments in the provinces, in late 1879 he was appointed to the Légion de la Garde Républicaine in Paris.

Dubois was not formally trained in art. However, by the late 1870s he must already have been a fairly accomplished painter, for his still-lifes were accepted at the Salons of 1877 and 1879. After his arrival in Paris in 1880, when he probably began to produce more experimental paintings, his works were rejected by the Salons from 1880 to 1883. Among the few extant works of this time is one of his most famous, the *Dead Child* (1881; Le Puy, Mus. Crozatier), shown at the Groupe des Indépendants in 1884. Its fame derives partly from the fact that it inspired a macabre episode in Zola's novel *L'Oeuvre* (1886), in which the artist Claude Lantier depicts dispassionately the changing hues on the face of his recently deceased infant son.

Dubois played a crucial role in founding and administering the Société des Artistes Indépendants. In 1884 he helped to write the group's statutes, and in subsequent years he seems to have exploited his freemasonic connections to gain favours from the city authorities for group exhibitions. To avoid overt connection between his artistic activities and his military career, he began around 1884 to sign his works with the scarcely disguised pseudonym 'Dubois-Pillet'. (Pillet was his mother's maiden name.) Although in the autumn of 1886 the army forbade him to participate in art exhibitions and belong to the Indépendants, he nonetheless remained a principal organizer of the group until 1888, and until his death continued to participate in their shows annually as well as in other exhibitions occasionally. In 1886 he showed in Nantes; in 1888 and 1889 with Les XX in Brussels. His first one-man show took place in September 1888 at the offices of the Symbolist journal, *Revue indépendante.*

Dubois-Pillet's involvement with the Neo-Impressionist movement stemmed from his acquaintance with Signac and Seurat in 1884. By May 1885 in the *Bread Carrier* (Le Puy, Mus. Crozatier) he was already employing small dashes of colour to create contrasts in a fairly systematic manner. His first fully Neo-Impressionist works, however, date from 1886. Although he continued to paint portraits and still-lifes, he also expanded the range of his subjects to include scenes of urban monuments and river traffic.

Dubois-Pillet experimented restlessly with the theory and practice of Neo-Impressionism. In the autumn of 1886, for example, he and Signac executed pen-and-ink drawings in dots, translating the small-scale colour gradations of Neo-Impressionist painting into a new graphic system of tonal values. Some of these drawings were published in 1887 in the Paris magazine, *Vie moderne*, including Dubois-Pillet's *Arrivals for a Ball at the Paris Hôtel de Ville* (untraced; see Rewald 1978, p. 453). At the 1888 Indépendants show, where Seurat first displayed his painted frames, Dubois-Pillet exhibited a pointillist frame around his circular painting, *Table Lamp* (New York, priv. col.; see Rewald 1978, p. 110). In this picture he also sought to record the changes in colour perception that occur in artificial light, a problem that occupied Seurat and Charles Angrand as well.

In 1889 and 1890 Dubois-Pillet adapted the Neo-Impressionist technique to accord with what he called *passage.* He wanted to accommodate the early 19th-century ideas of the English scientist Thomas Young (1773–1829) concerning the excitation and fatigue of the retinal nerves by colours. In its simplest form Dubois-Pillet's theory called for a triad of red, green and violet (or derivatives thereof) to appear in proximity and in proportion to one another. His application of *passage* in painting has not been fully analysed; the primary source of information about it remains the 1890 account by Christophe.

Perhaps in response to his repeated defiance of the order prohibiting his artistic activities, the army transferred Dubois-Pillet to Le Puy in November 1889. His last works, including *Saint-Michel d'Aiguilhe in the Snow* (1890; Le Puy, Mus. Crozatier), depict the unusual landscape and churches of the Auvergne. Dubois-Pillet died in a smallpox epidemic in 1890, and the following year the Indépendants brought together 64 paintings for a memorial show. It has sometimes been suggested that a fire subsequently destroyed a number of his works; in any event, his extant oeuvre, as catalogued by Gounot (1969), is relatively small.

BIBLIOGRAPHY

F. Fénéon: 'Treize toiles et quatre dessins de M. Albert Dubois-Pillet', *Rev. Indép.*, ix (1888), pp. 134–7; reprinted in J. Halperin, ed.: *Félix Fénéon: Oeuvres plus que complètes* (Geneva, 1970)
J. Antoine: 'Dubois-Pillet', *La Plume*, iii (1890), p. 299
J. Christophe: 'Dubois-Pillet', *Hommes Aujourd'hui*, viii/370 (1890); partly trans. in Rewald (1978), pp. 109–10
J. Rewald: *Post-Impressionism* (New York, 1956, rev. 3/1978)
R. Gounot: 'Le Peintre Dubois-Pillet', *Cah. Haute-Loire* (1969), pp. 99–131 [cat. rais.]
L. Bazalgette: *Albert Dubois-Pillet: Sa Vie et son oeuvre* (Paris, 1976)

MARTHA WARD

Dubois, Jacques (*b* Pontoise, 8 April 1694; *d* Paris, 23 Oct 1763). French cabinetmaker. He was an independent workman before becoming a *maître-ébéniste* on 5 September 1742 and a juror of his guild from 1752 to 1754. He was an exacting and talented cabinetmaker with a cosmopolitan clientele, specializing in luxury items decorated with Japanese lacquer and marquetry (for illustration *see* VERNIS MARTIN). His pieces were often sober, and this complemented the power, beauty and quality of his vigorous and exuberant bronzes with their opposing Rococo curves in the Louis XV style. His stamped works include a corner-cupboard (*c.* 1745; Malibu, CA, Getty Mus.) for Count Jan Klemens, based on a design by Nicolas Pineau, a lacquered bureau for Louis-Philippe, Duc d'Orléans (1725–85), and the 'de Vergennes' marquetry bureau (both Paris, Louvre), a commode (Genoa, Pal. Reale) for Louis XV's daughter Louise-Elizabeth (1727–59) and a large lean-to secrétaire with doors and windows (1770; Waddesdon Manor, Bucks, NT). After Dubois's death, his son René Dubois (1737–99) continued the workshop, using his father's mark but producing rigorously Neo-classical furniture.

BIBLIOGRAPHY

F. de Salverte: *Les Ebénistes du XVIIIème siècle, leurs oeuvres et leurs marques* (Paris, 1923, rev. 5/1962)

J. Viaux: *Bibliographie du meuble (Mobilier civil français)*, 2 vols (Paris, 1966–88)

A. Boutemy: *Meubles français anonymes du XVIIIème siècle* (Brussels, 1973)

JEAN-DOMINIQUE AUGARDE, JEAN NÉRÉE RONFORT

Dubois, Jean (*b* Dijon, *bapt* 20 Oct 1625; *d* Dijon, *bur* 30 Nov 1694). French sculptor and designer. He was trained by his father, a master joiner, and the influence of Bernini and Italian Baroque sculpture on his work suggests that he may have spent time in Rome. With the exception of a visit to the court of Louis XIV at Versailles in 1688, his working career was spent in Dijon, and his busy workshop produced much of the surviving late 17th-century statuary in Burgundy.

Dubois worked principally for private clients and the Church, but among his commissions were an obelisk at Plombières-les-Dijon, supported by four bronze dolphins (1674; destr.) and decorated with a marble portrait medallion of the *Dauphin* (Dijon, Mus. B.-A.), and three monumental allegorical chimney-pieces to designs by Jules Hardouin Mansart for the Palais des Etats, Dijon, depicting *Louis XIV as a Roman Emperor*, *Jason and the Dragon* and *France Triumphant* (stone, 1690–94; *in situ*; terracotta models, Dijon, Mus. B.-A.). He also executed a number of portrait busts, including that of *C. F. Jehannin* (marble, 1693; Dijon, Mus. B.-A.), and designed several schemes for interior decorations, including that (destr.) for Jean Gauthier at Plombières-les-Dijon and chimney-pieces decorated with portrait medallions (1666; Dijon, Mus. B.-A.) for the Hôtel de Berbis and the Hôtel de Vogüé, both in Dijon. He further designed numerous elaborate Baroque tombs, and kneeling figures from those of *Georges Joly de Blaisy* (*d* 1679) and *Claude Bouchu* (*d* 1683) survive (Dijon, Mus. B.-A.). Among his funerary effigies are several recumbent female figures influenced by the work of François Anguiers, such as that of *Marguerite de Valon* (*d* 1674; stone, Paris, Louvre; terracotta maquette, Dijon, Mus. B.-A.) and of *Elisabeth de la Mare* (1679; Dijon, Mus. Archéol.).

Of Dubois's many ecclesiastical decorative schemes, such as the choir of the Cistercian church of La Ferté-sur-Grosne (wooden maquettes, Dijon, Mus. B.-A.), only the ambitious Chapelle des Oeuvres at Notre Dame, Dijon (stone, 1684–90), survives intact, with its high altar adorned with cherubim, huge reliefs of the *Visitation*, the *Annunciation* and *St Helen* and its group of the *Assumption of the Virgin*. However, others are known from drawings (Paris, Louvre and Ecole N. B.-A.; Dijon, Mus. B.-A.), fragments and maquettes (Dijon, Mus. B.-A.; Paris, Louvre). Among his other surviving religious sculptures are stone statues of the *Virgin and Child*, *St Médard*, and *St Stephen* and busts of the 12 Apostles at Saint-Bénigne, Dijon, and stone statues of *St Augustine*, *St Ambrose* and *St Yves* at Saint-Michel, Dijon. The workshop continued its activity after his death under the direction of his son Guillaume Dubois (1654–1740).

BIBLIOGRAPHY

Lami

E. Fyot: *Le Sculpteur dijonnais Jean Dubois* (Dijon, 1907)

E. Garnier: 'Deux statues de Jean Dubois dans l'église de Villey-sur-Tille', *Mémoires de la commission des antiquités du département de la Côte d'Or*, xxi (1936–7), pp. 116–19

P. Querré: 'Les Dessins du sculpteur dijonnais Jean Dubois', *Archv A. Fr.*, n.s., xxii (1950–57), pp. 91–9

——: 'La Sculpture funéraire à Dijon dans la seconde moitié du XVIIe siècle', *Art baroque à Lyon: Colloque Lyon 1972*, pp. 163–75

Y. Beauvallot: 'La Construction du Palais des Etats de Bourgogne et de la Place Royale à Dijon (1674–1725)', *Mémoires de la commission des antiquités du département de la Côte d'Or* (1981) [suppl. issue], pp. 177–82, figs 90–106

GENEVIÈVE BRESC-BAUTIER

Dubois, Louis (Jean-Baptiste) (*b* Brussels, 13 Dec 1830; *d* Brussels, 27 April 1880). Belgian painter and writer. He showed an instinctive aptitude for painting while still very young. Rather than go to an academy, he worked in Thomas Couture's studio in Paris before enrolling at the Atelier Saint-Luc in Brussels (1853–63), where his contemporaries included Félicien Rops and Constantin Meunier. At the Salon of 1851 in Paris he met Gustave Courbet, whose paintings struck a chord with his own artistic aspirations. He adopted Realist theories and became their champion in Brussels. Like Courbet, he extolled a free and personal interpretation of nature and reality, under the motto 'freedom and sincerity'.

At the Salon of 1860 in Brussels, Dubois exhibited two important canvases: *Storks* (1858) and *Roulette* (1860; both Brussels, Mus. A. Anc.). These struck the critics by their boldness of composition, treatment of light and the broad and sensual handling that recalled the Belgian painterly tradition that had been dormant since the time of Rubens.

In Holland in 1869 Dubois copied Rembrandt's *Night Watch* (1642; Amsterdam, Rijksmus.) at the request of the Belgian government, and he also made copies after works by Frans Hals. In 1872 he travelled with Alfred Jacques Verwée to Italy and Normandy.

In 1868 Dubois was a founder-member of the Société Libre des Beaux-Arts, which sought to liberate art from the constraints of academic painting. In order to fight against the conservatism of contemporary art—which he felt disdained nature, life and humanity—in 1871 he founded the review *L'Art libre* and became its most important and combative editor. Under the pseudonym 'Hout' (the Flemish translation of Dubois), he criticized the Romantics, history painting, official portraiture and traditional working methods in a series of lively articles. Other texts signed 'Karl Stur' published in *La Chronique* and in *L'Art libre* have been attributed to him.

Dubois produced relatively little during a period of depression that lasted from 1863 to 1875, and his total output was small. However, his natural curiosity and need to consider reality in all its aspects encouraged him to attempt every genre: figurative paintings, still-lifes, interiors (especially kitchens), landscapes and animal scenes. His male portraits are sturdy, spare and expressive, and some were compared to those of his 17th-century predecessors, especially Jacob Jordaens; for example, *Portrait of the Artist's Father* (1854; Brussels, Mus. A. Anc.). His landscapes celebrate the desolation of the Kempen region and the life of the Ardennes. They are vast and totally devoid of human presence and were painted directly from nature at dawn or dusk with considerable subtlety (e.g. *Marsh in Kempen*, 1863; Ghent, Mus. S. Kst.). Like Courbet, Dubois attached great importance to his technique, throughout his work seeking one dominant note that would harmonize all the others. A painter before all else, he believed that art should not concern itself with expressing abstract ideas.

WRITINGS
Regular contributions to *A. Libre* from 1871

BNB
BIBLIOGRAPHY
M.-O. Maus: *Trente Années de lutte pour l'art, 1884–1914* (Brussels, 1926)
Maître de la Société Libre des Beaux-Arts (exh. cat., Brussels, 1932)
Louis Dubois (exh. cat., Brussels, Maison A., 1956)

BERNADETTE THOMAS

Dubois, Paul (i) (*b* Nogent-sur-Seine, Aube, 18 July 1829; *d* Paris, 23 May 1905). French sculptor, painter and administrator. His wealthy family allowed him to study law, which he abandoned in order to enter the sculpture workshop of Armand Toussaint (1806–62). In becoming a sculptor, he was seeking to follow his great-great uncle Jean-Baptiste Pigalle; when he first exhibited at the Paris Salon (1857), he did so under the name Dubois-Pigalle. In 1858 Paul entered the Ecole des Beaux-Arts in Paris. At his own expense, he undertook a lengthy visit to Italy (1859–62), where he lived like other students, visiting Rome, Naples and, particularly, Florence. His works began to be bought by the French state from the time of his third exhibition at the Paris Salon; among them were *St John the Baptist* (1861) and *Narcissus* (1863–5; plaster models of both, Troyes, Mus. B.-A. & Archéol.) and also the *Florentine Singer* (1865; silvered bronze version, Paris, Mus. d'Orsay), which won the Salon's medal of honour. The Comte de Nieuwerkerke and Princess Mathilde Bonaparte competed for the ownership of the main version of the latter. Dubois's talent is epitomized by these three statues, which portray elegant and refined young men; their feminine equivalents, of a similar neo-Renaissance character, are *Song*, for the façade of the Paris Opéra, designed by Charles Garnier, and the *Birth of Eve* (1873; Paris, Petit. Pal.).

Dubois's delicacy of touch was displayed even in his rare public monuments. The tomb of *General Louis Juchault de Lamoricière* (marble and bronze, unveiled 1879; Nantes Cathedral) recalls the tombs (1499) by Michel Colombe, in the same cathedral, of *Francis II* of Brittany and *Marguerite de Foix*, parents of Anne of Brittany (1477–1514). The bronze *Virtues* stationed on the tomb also reveal the influence of Michelangelo's tomb sculptures in S Lorenzo, Florence. Two of the *Virtues* were exhibited at the 1876 Salon and earned Dubois his second medal of honour. Several of his equestrian statues remained in rough-hewn versions (wax models, Troyes, Mus. B.-A. & Archéol.), though two were completed: the *Connétable Anne de Montmorency* (bronze, 1886; Chantilly, Château) and *Joan of Arc* (model, exh. Salon 1889; bronze version erected 1896; Reims, Parvis de la Cathédrale). Dubois's funerary statue of *Henri d'Orléans, Duc d'Aumale* continued the series of recumbent figures in the royal chapel at Dreux. Towards the end of his life, Dubois attempted a large composition, the monument to *French Genius*, of which the only completed fragment is *Alsace-Lorraine* or *Memory*.

Dubois was also a painter, and his portraits, whether sculpted or painted, were much in demand. His numerous busts of children are mostly in private collections and known only from their Salon listings and old photographs; however, his busts of the famous, including that of the painter *Paul Baudry* (bronze, 1878; Paris, Ecole N. Sup. B.-A.), the composer *Georges Bizet* (bronze, 1886; Paris, Père Lachaise Cemetery) and the scientist *Louis Pasteur* (bronze, 1890; Paris, Inst. France), are often found in public collections. Dubois derived a substantial income from reduced-scale editions of his works: in bronze by the firm of Barbedienne and in biscuit by the porcelain factory of Sèvres. Among his painted portraits are those of *Mme Casimir Perier* (Vizille, Château) and the *Argenti Family* (Chios, Adamantios Korais Lib.).

From 1873 Dubois was curator of the Musée de Luxembourg, and in the same year he succeeded Eugène Guillaume as director of the Ecole des Beaux-Arts. Because of his administrative duties, he produced little full-scale, finished work. However, his detailed working methods can be studied from the contents of his studio, which were generously bequeathed to French museums by his heirs. From this, it can be seen that he studied each subject minutely, making numerous drawings and wax models, which he dressed in paper or cloth.

BIBLIOGRAPHY
F. du Castel: *Paul Dubois: Peintre et sculpteur, 1829–1905* (Paris, 1964)
J.-M. Delahaye: *Paul Dubois, 1829–1905* (diss., Paris, Ecole du Louvre, 1973)
The Romantics to Rodin: French Nineteenth-century Sculpture from North American Collections (exh. cat., ed. P. Fusco and H. W. Janson; Los Angeles, CA, Co. Mus. A.; Minneapolis, MN, Inst. A.; Detroit, MI, Inst. A.; Indianapolis, IN, Mus. A.; 1980–81), pp. 242–6
G. Bresc-Bautier and A. Pingeot: *Sculptures des Jardins du Louvre, du Carrousel et des Tuileries*, ii (Paris, 1986), pp. 172–5
La Sculpture française au XIXème siècle (exh. cat., ed. A. Pingeot; Paris, Grand Pal., 1986), pp. 60–69
Sculptures en cire de l'ancienne Egypte à l'art abstrait, Notes & Doc. Mus. France, xviii (Paris, 1987), pp. 237–51
A. Le Normand-Romain: 'Le Monument du *Général de Lamoricière* à Nantes', *Rev. Pays Loire*, 303 (1988), pp. 76–88

ANNE PINGEOT

Dubois, Paul(-Maurice) (ii) (*b* Aywaille, 23 Sept 1859; *d* Uccle, 1938). Belgian sculptor and medallist. He was a pupil of J. B. Jacquet (1822–88) and Eugène Simonis at the Académie des Beaux-Arts in Brussels and in the studio of Charles Van der Stappen. In 1884 he won the Godecharle prize, using the money to visit the most important museums in Europe. He was an active participant with Les XX, exhibiting at all its salons from 1884 to 1893, and he joined its successor, La Libre Esthétique, in 1894. In 1900 he was appointed professor of sculpture at the Académie des Beaux-Arts in Mons and in 1902 at the Académie Royale in Brussels.

Dubois's natural gift for grace and elegance found expression in his portraits. He created bas-reliefs and numerous monuments and ornamental sculptures, for example the four figures in gilded bronze that decorate the façade of the Maison du Roi and the figures on the Maison des Boulangers, both in the Grand Place in Brussels. Dubois's most notable work as a medallist is the medal for the Exposition Universelle of 1905 in Liège.

Dubois was admired for his classicism at a time when the avant-garde was reacting against that style. He was at once an innovator and a traditionalist, respecting the fundamental principles of sculpture. His taste was for simple and sober forms that are not descriptive. He loved concision, and his work is characterized by its realism, never falling into excess. Sculpture of movement and dynamism did not inspire him, and he always preferred the expression of a meditative attitude to the depiction of effort or struggle. Such intimist works as *Seated Woman: Portrait of Mme Paul Dubois* (marble, 1893; Brussels, Mus. A. Mod.) show his ability to marry sensuality with ideal purity and his desire to transform and ennoble his material within a contemporary context, expressed in this work by the choice of a simple kitchen chair as seat; the pensive expression of the woman addresses itself directly to the spectator's emotions. Dubois worked mainly in bronze and marble, but he also produced jewellery, and household utensils in tin and copper.

BIBLIOGRAPHY
C. Concrardy: *La Sculpture belge au XIXe siècle* (Brussels, 1947)
La Fondation Godecharle, 1871–1971 (Brussels, 1971)

BERNADETTE THOMAS

Du Bois [Dubois], **Simon** (*b* Antwerp, *bapt* 26 July 1632; *d* London, *bur* 26 May 1708). Flemish painter, active in England. He was the youngest son of the painter Hendrik Du Bois (*c.* 1589–1646) and studied with Philips Wouwerman in 1652–3 before spending some years in Italy with his brother Edward Du Bois (1619–96). He had returned to Haarlem by 1661. The brothers settled in London *c.* 1680. Du Bois's earlier portraits are busts set within a plain oval surround. They are in the Dutch bourgeois tradition and make no concessions to prevailing English taste. *Sir William Jones* and *Elizabeth, Lady Jones*, both signed and dated 1682 (both London, Dulwich Pict. Gal.), are typical examples of his vivid style. He produced similar works on a smaller scale and oil miniatures on copper. He also painted an unusual portrait of his friend *Adrian Beverland*, a licentious poet, as a 'vertuoso deseigning' among pyramids and ruins; the work is known from a mezzotint (London, BM) by Isaac Beckett. Du Bois's patron and friend Lord Somers commissioned a full-length portrait in Lord Chancellor's robes (*c.* 1698; Wrest Park, Beds), and the artist also painted *Archbishop Tenison* (1695; London, Lambeth Pal.), but official portraiture was really beyond his range. He painted landscapes and battle scenes, usually involving Turks on horseback, as well as pastiches of Italian Old Masters. These were apparently sold as originals, and subsequent authentication has proved very difficult.

Granted denization in 1697, Du Bois also dealt in works of art, and he assembled a collection of paintings, prints and antiquities in association with Willem van de Velde the younger, whose widowed daughter, Sarah Atkins, many years his junior, he married in 1706. The collection, including works by David Teniers (i), Jan Griffier I, Simon Verelst and a dozen sea pieces by Willem van de Velde the younger, passed to Adrian Beverland.

BIBLIOGRAPHY
H. Walpole: *Anecdotes of Painting in England (1762–71)*; ed. R. N. Wornum (1849), ii, pp. 601–2
G. Vertue: 'Note Books', *Walpole Soc.*, i–v (1911–15)
C. H. Collins Baker: *Lely and the Stuart Portrait Painters*, ii (London, 1912), pp. 66–9

E. Croft-Murray and P. Hulton: *XVI and XVII centuries*, i of *British Museum Catalogue of British Drawings* (London, 1960), pp. 299–301

RICHARD JEFFREE

Dubos [Du Bos], **Jean-Baptiste**, Abbé (*b* Beauvais, 21 Dec 1670; *d* Paris, 23 March 1742). French historian, critic and diplomat. He served as a diplomat under Louis XIV and the Régence; having been rewarded with an ecclesiastical benefice, he devoted himself to writing. His principal work, *Réflexions critiques sur la poésie et sur la peinture* (1719), was important for aesthetics in France and remained in use as a popular textbook until the 19th century. It owed much of its success to the way in which it echoed some of the conflicts in the QUARREL OF THE ANCIENTS AND MODERNS, in which Dubos largely took the side of the Ancients. He did not, however, put forward a unified theory of imitation of antiquity but offered a collection of discussions of the diverse manifestations of artistic genius. He considered a work of art as an object of instinctive judgement by perceptive individuals, whose response is based not on a reasoned knowledge of the rules of art but on a 'sixth sense' possessed by everyone.

Dubos examined the means of expression used in the different arts and their ability to express discursive, narrative or descriptive contents. Having chosen for his epigraph Horace's 'Ut pictura, poesis erit' ('As is painting, so is poetry'; *see also* UT PICTURA POESIS), he did not restrict his analysis to poetry and painting but extended it to mime and music. From this emerged a primary understanding of the differences between the media of expression and the particular effects proper to each. Painting was given pride of place: 'Sight holds greater sway over the soul than the other senses'. Dubos concluded by propounding his famous theory that suggested that, during the course of history, environmental factors, climatic or human, had transformed the fine arts by influencing the nature of the works produced and the response to them.

WRITINGS
Réflexions critiques sur la poésie et sur la peinture (Paris, 1719)

BIBLIOGRAPHY
A. Lombard: *La Querelle des anciens et des modernes: L'Abbé Du Bos* (Neuchâtel, 1908)
——: *L'Abbé Du Bos: Un initiateur de la pensée moderne (1670–1742)* (Paris, 1913), pp. 181–256, 313–88
A. H. Koller: *The Abbé Dubos: His Advocacy of the Theory of Climate* (Champain, 1937)
B. Munteano: 'Survivances antiques: L'Abbé Du Bos, esthéticien de la persuasion passionnelle', *Rev. Litt. Comp.*, xxx (1956), pp. 318–50
——: 'Les Prémisses rhétoriques du système de l'abbé Dubos', *Riv. Lett. Mod. Comp.*, x (1957), pp. 5–30
E. Caramaschi: 'Du Bos et Voltaire', *Stud. Voltaire & 18th C.*, x (1959), pp. 113–236
——: 'Arte e critica nella concezione dell'abate Du Bos', *Riv. Lett. Mod. Comp.*, xii (1959), pp. 101–18; xiii (1960), pp. 248–70
E. Migliorini: 'Note alle "Réflexions critiques" di Jean-Baptiste Du Bos', *Atti Accad. Toscana Sci & Lett. 'La Colombaria'*, xxvii (1962–3), pp. 281–352
R. Démoris: 'Original absent et création de valeur: Dubos et quelques autres', *Rev. Sci. Humaines*, xl (1975), pp. 65–81
H. Vigneau: *Dubos, les lettres et les arts au début du XVIIIème siècle* (diss., U. Toulouse, 1976)
C. Paisant: *L'Esthétique de Dubos* (diss., U. Nantes, 1981)
L. Tavernier: 'Apropos Illusion: Jean-Baptiste Dubos' Einführung eines Begriffs in die französische Kunstkritik des 18. Jahrhunderts', *Pantheon*, xlii/2 (1984), pp. 158–60 [excellent bibliog.]

PASCAL GRIENER

Dubourg, Victoria. *See* FANTIN-LATOUR, (2).

Dubovskoy, Nikolay (Nikanorovich) (*b* Novocherkassk, 17 Dec 1859; *d* Petrograd [now St Petersburg], 28 Feb 1918). Russian painter. He studied (1877–82) at the Academy of Arts in St Petersburg, where he was taught by the landscape painter Mikhail Konstantinovich Klodt (1832–1902). In 1882 Dubovskoy began to participate in exhibitions as an independent landscape painter, first with the Society for the Encouragement of the Arts in St Petersburg and, from 1884, with the Wanderers (Peredvizhniki), of which he became a member in 1886. From 1899 Dubovskoy was a permanent member of the board of the Wanderers and one of its most distinguished figures, but he also became an Academician (1898), and from 1900 he was a full member of the Academy of Arts. He lived mainly in St Petersburg, but in the 1890s and 1900s he travelled extensively in European countries.

Dubovskoy's predominant interest in landscape painting was apparent while he was still a student at the Academy of Arts. His work from the 1880s is distinguished by an intimate, lyrical treatment of landscape motifs, as in *Winter* (1884; Moscow, Tret'yakov Gal.), *Spring* (1885) and *Approaching Rain* (1888; both St Petersburg, Rus. Mus.). In the 1890s Dubovskoy was attracted by the idea of the creation of generalized and monumentalized images of the Russian countryside. In later years these tendencies combined. From the end of the 1890s Dubovskoy adopted an impressionistic technique especially in the treatment of certain effects of light.

Dubovskoy's most popular work was the picture *Calm before the Storm*, which is known in several versions and copies by the artist (e.g. two versions, 1890; St Petersburg, Rus. Mus., and Moscow, Tret'yakov Gal.; the Moscow version was executed for a commission from Pavel Tret'yakov). Here, with the sun still shining brightly, a swollen, threatening storm cloud hangs like a cap over the land, the river and the village. The sense of space established by the painting's composition gives it a majestic quality, and the sharp chiaroscuro and colour contrasts add a dramatic and romantic tone. In many respects, Dubovskoy was close to the St Petersburg group of landscape artists who belonged to the Wanderers, such as Arkhip Kuindzhi and Ivan Shishkin.

BIBLIOGRAPHY
Nikolay Nikanorovich Dubovskoy (1859–1918), Novocherkassk, Mus. Hist. Don Cossaks cat. (Leiningrad, 1961)
A. A. Prokhorov: *Nikolay Nikanorovich Dubovskoy* (Leningrad, 1967)

L. I. IOVLEVA

Dubreuil, Gabriel Jouveau. *See* JOUVEAU-DUBREUIL, GABRIEL.

Dubreuil, Toussaint (*b* Paris, 1561; *d* Paris, 22 Nov 1602). French painter and draughtsman. He was a pupil at Fontainebleau of Ruggiero de Ruggieri (*d* after 1597) and was also trained by Martin Fréminet's father Médéric Fréminet, a rather mediocre painter in Paris. Dubreuil became Premier Peintre to Henry IV and is usually identified as a member of the so-called second Fontainebleau school (*see* FONTAINEBLEAU SCHOOL), together with Ambroise Dubois and Martin Fréminet. These artists were employed by the king to decorate the royal palaces, their functions being similar to those of Rosso Fiorentino and Primaticcio earlier at Fontainebleau under Francis I. Dubreuil's death meant that many of the projects in which he was involved had to be completed by assistants. Despite this and the fact that the majority of his finished work has since been lost, he is considered an important link between the Mannerism of Primaticcio and the classicism of Nicolas Poussin and his contemporaries in the following century.

At Fontainebleau both Dubreuil and Dubois worked on a methodical renewal of the decorative galleries, the allegorical portraits and the mythological tapestries. Here Dubreuil painted the *Labours of Hercules* (destr. 1703) in the Pavillon des Poêles and worked on the Galerie des Cerfs. In 1597 he began working Henry IV in a house in the Jesuit monastery on the Rue Saint-Antoine, Paris, along with the tapestry works of Girard Laurent. It was about this time that Dubreuil designed cartoons for the tapestry series of the *Legend of Psyche* and the famous *Legend of Diana*, the latter series destined for Fontainebleau, where it was installed by 1606. Only one sketch attributed to Dubreuil survives for the *Legend of Diana* series, *Diana Beseeching Jupiter* (Paris, Louvre). There were originally supposed to be eight tapestry panels, but the Parisian workshops later added two more. The series proved highly successful and was also woven by the specialized Louvre tapestry workshop (surviving sets, Paris, Mobilier N.; Madrid, Prado; Vienna, Ksthist. Mus.).

About 1600 Dubreuil was commissioned to provide 78 pictures for the Château Neuf, Saint-Germain-en-Laye, now known to have illustrated Pierre de Ronsard's epic poem *La Franciade*, first published in 1572 (see Cordellier, 1985, *Rev. Louvre* essay). This series of mythological

Toussaint Dubreuil: *Hyante and Climène Offering a Sacrifice to Venus*, oil on canvas, 1.90×1.40 m, *c.* 1600 (Paris, Musée du Louvre)

compositions was designed by Dubreuil and executed by him and his assistants, including Guillaume Dumée and Flemish masters. Most of the paintings vanished when the Château Neuf was demolished in 1777, but several survive, such as the *Toilet of Hyante and Climène* ('*Lady at her Toilet*', *c*. 1600; Paris, Louvre, on dep. Fontainebleau, Château; *see* FRANCE, fig. 19) and the scene of an ancient sacrifice, now identified as *Hyante and Climène Offering a Sacrifice to Venus* (*c*. 1600; Paris, Louvre; see fig.). The latter shows Dubreuil's use of certain Italian Mannerist devices, such as the cut-off half figures emerging in the lower foreground. However, the style is restrained and lacks the extremes of elongation typical of earlier Fontainebleau artists such as Primaticcio and especially Antoine Caron. Other compositions from the series are known from descriptions, copies and drawings. Dubreuil's own surviving drawings for the series (*c*. 20; mostly Paris, Louvre) are likewise strongly influenced by the Mannerism of his Italian predecessors but are generally more classically balanced.

Dubreuil also executed frescoes for the Tuileries Palace, Paris, and for the Petite Galerie (now the Galerie d'Apollon) of the Louvre. He painted the vaulted ceiling with a gigantomachy of scenes from Ovid's *Metamorphoses* and the Old Testament, and the walls with a series of portraits of the kings and queens of France (the latter completed by Jacob Bunel). All of Dubreuil's mural paintings in the Louvre were destroyed in the fire of 1661.

Thieme–Becker   BIBLIOGRAPHY

F. Engerand: *Inventaire des tableaux du roy rédigé en 1709 et 1710 par Nicolas Bailly* (Paris, 1899), pp. 287–95
L. Dimier: 'L'Oeuvre de Toussaint Dubreuil au Château de Saint-Germain', *Bull. Soc. N. Antiqua. France* (1905), pp. 119–24
——: 'Un Nouveau Tableau de Toussaint Dubreuil à Fontainebleau', *Bull. Mus. France*, vi (1910), pp. 85–8
J. Guiffrey and P. Marcel: *Inventaire général des dessins du Musée du Louvre et du Musée de Versailles: Ecole française*, v (Paris, 1910), pp. 31–40
M. Fenaille: *Etat général des tapisseries de la manufacture des Gobelins depuis son origine jusqu'à nos jours, 1600–1900* (Paris, 1923)
L. Dimier: *La Peinture française au XVIe siècle* (Marseille, 1942)
A. Blunt: *Art and Architecture in France, 1500–1700*, Pelican Hist. A. (Harmondsworth, 1953), p. 179
J. Adhémar: *Le Dessin français au XVIe siècle* (Lausanne, 1954)
G. Wildenstein: 'L'Activité de Toussaint Dubreuil en 1596', *Gaz. B.-A.*, lvi (1960), pp. 333–40
S. Béguin: 'Toussaint Dubreuil, premier peintre de Henri IV', *A. France*, iv (1964), pp. 86–107
L'Ecole de Fontainebleau (exh. cat. by S. Béguin and others, Paris, Grand Pal., 1972); rev. as *Fontainebleau: Art in France, 1528–1610*, 2 vols (exh. cat. by S. Béguin and others, Ottawa, N.G., 1973)
S. Béguin: 'Nouvelles attributions à Toussaint Dubreuil', *Etudes d'art français offertes à Charles Sterling* (Paris, 1975), pp. 86–107
D. Cordellier: 'Dubreuil: Peintre de *La Franciade* de Ronsard au Château Neuf de Saint-Germain-en-Laye', *Rev. Louvre*, xxxv/5–6 (1985), pp. 357–78
——: 'Toussaint Dubreuil: "Singulier en son art"', *Bull. Soc. Hist. A. Fr.* (1985), pp. 7–33

S. J. TURNER

Du Broeucq [Dubroeucq], **Jacques** (*b* ?Mons, *c*. 1505; *d* Mons, 30 Sept 1584). Flemish sculptor and architect. He is believed to have returned from a visit to Italy *c*. 1535 in order to draw up plans for the rood screen and stalls in the collegiate church of St Waudru in Mons, although the surviving design for the screen and the contract with the stone-cutter (1535) do not mention Du Broeucq's name. He worked on the funerary monument of *Bishop Eustache*

de Croy (*d* 1538; Saint-Omer, Notre-Dame); only the alabaster recumbent and praying figures of the deceased remain, but they suffice to indicate Du Broeucq's nervous sensibility and his taste for tactile values and mobile forms. The lectern in front of the praying effigy bears his signature and reveals his lifelong attraction to the grotesque ornamentation of the Renaissance. The monument is similar to that of *Louis de Brézé* (*d* 1531), which was then being built in Rouen Cathedral, with designs attributed to Jean Goujon.

In 1539 Du Broeucq rented as his studio part of a school for poor children in Mons: from then on he pursued parallel careers as sculptor and architect (none of his buildings survives). Around 1539–40 he drew up plans for the new Château de Boussu, Hainaut, for Count Jean de Hennin-Liétard. His sculptures for the rood screen were delivered in instalments throughout the 1540s. He was at his most prolific between 1545 and 1549, especially in his capacity as architect to Queen Mary of Hungary, for whom he drew up the plans and supervised the construction of the châteaux of Binche and Mariemont in Hainaut and the fortress of Mariembourg in Namur. In 1549 he produced a plan (not executed) for an imperial château in Ghent.

As a sculptor Du Broeucq is principally noted for the rood screen of St Waudru. The drawing of 1535 and those sculptures (all alabaster) that survived the ravages of the French Revolution show that within the traditional tripartite structure he introduced wholly innovative decoration and largely original themes. Between the plan and its execution there were some changes in the programme. The most novel iconographic elements were the *Theological Virtues* (whose attribution to Du Broeucq is sometimes disputed), the *Cardinal Virtues* and the *Holy Trinity*, represented in individual tondi beneath the coffered arches of the lower tier. The cycle of the *Passion* and the *Resurrection* was developed in an unusual way, being divided between 13 great reliefs and a frieze containing more than 10 small, oblong tableaux. Both in the statuary and in the reliefs of the screen, Du Broeucq's figures are of elongated proportions and command their space through movements that are often slow and balanced and through arrested gestures that give them their characteristic air of instability. The thin draperies fall in crisp, elegant folds. In the reliefs—except for those of the tondi—the use of space is oppressive and often makes a linear reading of the image necessary.

Du Broeucq's sculptural oeuvre can also be keenly appreciated in St Waudru in the relief thought to portray *Mary of Hungary*, in the numerous elements of the altar of *St Mary Magdalene* (1550) and in the statue of *St Bartholomew*, executed after Du Broeucq had been forced in 1572 to abjure his Protestant faith. Du Broeucq's last sculptures, also of alabaster, are said to have been formerly part of the tomb of *Philippe de Sainte-Aldegonde* in the church of Notre-Dame, Saint-Omer; they consist of a remarkable signed *Virgin and Child* (*in situ*) and two fragmentary angels in high relief (Saint-Omer, Mus. Hôtel Sandelin), which show a new fullness. Several sculptures in the funerary chapel of the Seigneurs de Boussu (Boussu-lez-Mons, St Géry) have recently been attributed to Du

Broeucq (Didier, addenda to 1985 exh. cat.; Gossez). Du Broeucq's later architectural work included supplying Charles V with plans for a château in Brussels (1553). These, together with the plans for Ghent, secured him in 1555 the title of Maître-artiste de l'Empereur. He was also involved in repairs to châteaux that had been burnt down in 1554 by the troops of Henry II of France; between 1560 and 1570 he submitted plans for the Stadhuis in Antwerp and executed various projects in Ath and Mons. His buildings, all either demolished or never built, are now known only in plans, pictures or descriptions. The châteaux of Boussu and of Binche were evidently sumptuous; the latter was considered modern both in its structure and in its decoration. Du Broeucq was as celebrated an architect as he was a sculptor: now the sculptures alone reveal a deeply original Mannerist sensibility. They invite comparison with the works of Goujon and even more strongly with those of Germain Pilon, which they often prefigure.

BIBLIOGRAPHY

R. Hedicke: *Jacques Dubroeucq von Mons: Ein niederländischer Meister aus der Frühzeit des italienischen Einflusses* (Strasbourg, 1904); Fr. trans. by E. Dony (Brussels, 1911)

R. Wellens: *Jacques Du Broeucq: Sculpteur et architecte de la Renaissance (1505–1584)* (Brussels, 1962)

C. Loriaux: *Jacques Du Broeucq (±1505–1584)* (Gembloux, 1971)

Jacques Du Broeucq, sculpteur et architecte de la Renaissance: Recueil d'études publié en commémoration du quatrième centenaire du décès de l'artiste (exh. cat., Mons, 1985) [4-page addenda by R. Didier distributed at exhibition]

V. Gossez: *Le Monument de Jean de Hénin-Liétard et d'Anne de Bourgogne dans l'oeuvre monumentale de la chapelle funéraire de Boussu* (diss., Brussels, U. Libre, 1988–9)

LYDIE HADERMANN-MISGUICH

Dubrovnik [Lat. Ragusium; It. Ragusa]. Croatian city and former capital (1420–1809) of the Republic of Ragusa. It is in the extreme south of the country on the east coast of the Adriatic and occupies a peninsula at the foot of Mt Srdj. The modern name of the city is derived from *dubrava* (Croat.: 'glade') and was first given to the area on the north side of the Stradum (a former canal) in the 13th century, the south side being called Ragusium Byzantines. The settlement was founded after *c.* 615 by refugees from Epidaurum (now Cavtat), who settled on the small island of Lava (later 'Lausa' and corrupted to 'Ragusa'). Despite attacks by the Saracens (866), the Bulgarians (988) and the Normans in alliance with the Byzantines (1184), the city, which became a see in 990, remained under the suzerainty of the Byzantine Empire until 1125, when it fell to Venice. The Byzantine suzerainty resumed in 1165, but the city was again under Venetian rule in 1171–2 and from 1205 to 1358. The constitution granted in 1272 established the enlightened, democratic rule of the Croatian aristocracy. Profits from trade were invested in architecture, works of art and the creation of a prototypical welfare system that provided a medical service (1301), the oldest surviving pharmacy in Europe (1317) and a home for the elderly (1347) and which abolished the slave trade (1418). The first drainage system was laid in 1296, and piped water was supplied from 1436.

The republic was under the suzerainty of Hungary-Croatia from 1359 and became a considerable maritime power. It preserved its independence by skilful diplomacy and bribery, while the rest of the Croats were dominated by a series of foreign rulers. Manufacturing and trade reached their peak in the 15th century but gradually declined after the discovery of new trade routes to the east. An earthquake in 1667 devastated the city, destroying many of its Romanesque and Gothic buildings, but there was extensive rebuilding. The republic surrendered to French forces in 1808 and was ceded to the Austro-Hungarian Empire (1815–1918), the kingdom of Yugoslavia (1918–41), the Independent State of Croatia (1941–5) and the Federative Socialist Republic of Yugoslavia. Since 1991 Dubrovnik has been part of the Republic of Croatia.

The Old Town is one of the best-preserved medieval centres in Europe, its layout following plans drawn up in 1272 and 1296. It is encircled by massive fortifications with sixteen bastions, dating in their present form from 1647–63, and only four gates. The landward defences were strengthened in height (22 m) and thickness (4.5 m) after Bosnia fell to the Turks in 1463. The northernmost bastion, Minčeta, was rebuilt (1464–5) by Michelozzo di Bartolomeo and GIORGIO DA SEBENICO as a circular tower with two platforms. In the 16th century the sea defences against Venetian invasion were raised, including Mrtvo Zvono ('Dead Bell'; 1509), St John's Fortress (1552) and St Margaret's Bastion. St Lawrence's Fortress (Lovrijenac; 1301; rebuilt 1571–6) stands on a promontory west of the walled town, and the east flank was protected by the Revelin (1538–49).

The Rector's Palace (Knežev Dvor; after 1435; see fig.) was built by Onofrio di Giordano della Cava (*fl* 1438–55) in a Neapolitan Gothic style. After a gunpowder explosion in 1463, Michelozzo's new design for the first floor remained unexecuted, but the portico was rebuilt (1468) in the Renaissance style by the Florentine architect Salvi di Michiele and local masters. The combination of Renaissance arcades and Gothic windows in the *piano nobile* became so fashionable that it was adopted for other residences, including the Sponza Palace, which has arcades (1519) by Nikola Andrijić (*fl* 1512–53) and Josip Andrijić (*fl* 1503–50). Other important secular structures include

Dubrovnik, the Rector's Palace (Knežev Dvor), portico (1468) rebuilt by Salvi di Michiele

the Old Arsenal (1272; partly destr.), two fountains (1438) designed by Onofrio and the city bell-tower (h. 31 m; 1444) built by P. Radončić, R. Grubačević and D. Utišenović. The Column of Roland (1417) by Antun Dubrovčanin (*fl* 1417–24) was modelled on those erected in the other merchant republics of the Mediterranean.

The oldest surviving churches are St Stephen (7th century), the original cathedral of St Peter (7th–8th century; damaged 1991–; both rest. 19th century), St Nicholas (façade 1607), St Luke (rest. 1786; damaged 1991) and the church of the Transfiguration (Sigurata; rebuilt). The Romanesque second cathedral (begun 1199; destr. 1667) was replaced by the present Roman Baroque structure (1672–1713) designed by Andrea Buffalini (*fl* 1656–73). The church of the city's patron, St Blaise (begun 1348; destr. 1706), was rebuilt in the Baroque style by the Venetian Marino Gropelli (*c.* 1664–*c.* 1723; damaged 1991–). Two large mendicant complexes dominate the Old Town. The Franciscan convent (begun 1317; damaged 1991–) has a fine cloister (1317–48) by Miho Brajkov of Bar, combining Romanesque and Gothic elements, and a Late Gothic south portal (1499) by Leonard Petrović and Peter Petrović. Work on the Dominican convent continued from the 13th century to the 15th; its cloister is a fine example of the transition from Gothic to Renaissance. The small church of St Saviour (1520; damaged 1991–) was built by Petar Andrijić (*fl* 1492–1553) in a mixture of Gothic and Renaissance elements derived from Lombardy.

There are several outstanding Renaissance palaces, including the Skočibuha Palace (1549–53), the Bunić Palace, which has a Baroque façade, and, outside the walls to the west, the Pucić and Crijević Palaces and the Skočibuha-Bonda Palace (1576–88; rest. 1938). After 1667 six large, cube-shaped, residential and commercial buildings by the Roman architect Cerutti (*fl* 1660–98) were erected on either side of the central section of Placa (Stradun), the city's main east–west thoroughfare, which is paved with polished grey marble (damaged 1991–). Many of Dubrovnik's streets consist of flights of steps, of which the most monumental was built in 1738 by Padalacqua (*fl* 1725–40) from Gundulić Square to the Collegium Ragusinum (1735), and Andrea Pozzo's Jesuit church of St Ignatius (1725; damaged 1991–).

As an important free merchant republic, Dubrovnik was a centre for applied arts and crafts, including objects made from pearl and ivory. The activities of goldsmiths, especially between the 14th century and the 16th, may be traced back to the city's origins under the Byzantine empire. Intricate embroidery known as 'point de Ragusa' was well-known in France during the second half of the 17th century.

From 1991 the centre of Dubrovnik suffered substantial damage from shelling by Serbian forces. It was reported that the buildings affected, in addition to those mentioned in the text above, included the Dominican church and convent, the Minčeta, the synagogue (14th century), the churches of St Anne, St George (14th–15th centuries), St John (15th century), St Joseph, St Mary and St Roko, the Rector's Palace, the granary (1542–90), the Sponza-Divona Palace, the Sorkočević Palace (1521), the Bizzaro Palace (17th century), the Bozdari Palace (1706, by Gropelli), the Bošković Manor, the chapel of the Djordjić-Maineri Palace, the convent of St Clare, the Pila Bridge and the Gučetić Mansion and Arboretum, which had a collection of 15th-century trees.

BIBLIOGRAPHY

L. Beritić: *Utvrdjenja grada Dubrovnika* [Fortifications of the city of Dubrovnik] (Zagreb, 1955) [Fr. summary]

——: *Urbanistički razvitak Dubrovnika* [Urban development of Dubrovnik] (Zagreb, [1958])

Enciklopedija likovnih umjetnosti [Encyclopaedia of art] (Zagreb, 1959–66), ii, pp. 115–21

Cultural Monuments, Historical Sites and Cities Damaged and Destroyed during the War in Croatia: A Selection, Republic of Croatia, Ministry of Education and Culture, Institute for the Protection of Cultural Monuments (Zagreb, 1991) [Eng. text]

PAUL TVRTKOVIĆ

Dubufe. French family of painters. Both (1) Claude-Marie Dubufe and his son (2) Edouard Dubufe were best known as portrait painters, though they worked in other genres as well. Edouard's wife and son were also artists, specializing in portrait busts and decorative painting respectively.

(1) Claude-Marie Dubufe (*b* Paris, 1790; *d* La Celle-Saint-Cloud, 24 April 1864). His father, a *chef d'institution*, educated him for a career in the diplomatic service. At the age of 19 he was nominated vice-consul and was on the point of leaving for America when David (who had given Dubufe some instruction) persuaded his father to allow him to train as a painter. Dubufe received no further support from his father and paid for his lessons with David by playing the violin in an orchestra. He made his Salon début in 1810 with *A Roman Allowing his Family to Die of Hunger rather than Touch a Sum of Money Entrusted to his Keeping*; like *Achilles Protecting Iphigenia* (Salon of 1812) and *Christ Calming the Tempest* (Salon of 1819), this picture has disappeared. His earliest surviving composition, *Apollo and Cyparissus* (1821; Avignon, Mus. Calvet), exhibited in 1822, is elegantly mannered in a style inspired by Girodet but did not appeal much to the critics. He then painted the first of a number of sentimental genre pictures in the manner of *The Surprise* (exh. RA 1828; London, N.G.), of which the most famous, *Souvenirs* and *Regrets* (Pasadena, CA, Norton Simon Mus.), were widely known through many engraved versions.

In 1828, following the example of Gericault and other French painters at the time, Dubufe sent two pictures, the *Temptation in the Garden of Eden* and the *Expulsion from Paradise*, to Britain and to America on a touring exhibition; this was a financial success. He continued to send more pictures to the Salon into the early 1830s when he began to devote himself entirely to portraits. His early portraits, like *Mme Dubufe* (1820; Paris, Louvre), are painted in the thin, careful, straightforward manner of David. His later work is softer and more idealized and recalls the bland mannerism of *Apollo and Cyparissus* without the freshness of his early work. He had, however, a huge fashionable appeal. He exhibited over 150 portraits at the Salon, mostly during the July Monarchy. After 1848 he attempted to extend his range by exhibiting an allegorical figure of the Republic (surely an unrecorded entry for the competition of 1848) and appears to have limited his practice as a portrait painter. In his later years he also painted the peasant girls and picturesque views of Normandy. In 1859, when the revival of mythology begun by a younger generation of Prix de Rome winners was well established, Dubufe returned to the inspiration of his youth by exhibiting a *Greek Woman Leaving her Bath* and a *Birth of Venus* (both untraced). None of these late works matched the popularity of his portraits.

BIBLIOGRAPHY
De David à Delacroix (exh. cat., Paris, Grand Pal., 1974), pp. 401–2

(2) (Louis-)Edouard Dubufe (*b* Paris, 31 March 1820; *d* Versailles, 11 Aug 1883). Son of (1) Claude-Marie Dubufe. He was trained by his father and then by Paul Delaroche. He first appeared at the Salon in 1839 with the *Annunciation*, a *Huntress* and a portrait, winning a third class medal. He followed this in 1840 with an episode in the life of St Elisabeth of Hungary, which won him a second class medal; in 1844 he won a first class medal with *Bathsheba* and a genre scene set in the 15th century (all untraced).

By the mid-1840s Dubufe seemed firmly established in the sentimental Romanticism associated with Cibot and Ary Scheffer. Baudelaire noted in 1845 that he appeared to have chosen a different path from his father's lucrative profession; in fact, he closely followed the pattern of his father's career, from a relatively unprofitable beginning in history painting into the rich world of fashionable portraits, inheriting the aristocratic sitters relinquished by his father in the early 1850s. Edouard's portraits before 1850 (e.g. *Unknown Woman*; Autun, Mus. Rolin) have a sharp, bright quality that recalls Delaroche. His later work is softer and more idealized. As with his father, it is difficult to assess Dubufe's range as a portrait painter, but there is an interesting group of works in Versailles (Château), including a memorable portrait of *Rosa Bonheur* with one arm round a bull's head, exhibited in 1857, and a darker, more intense portrait of *Harpignies* sketching *en plein air*, exhibited in 1877; these are striking images of fellow artists but perhaps not as typical as the glittering, featureless portraits of the *Empress Eugénie* in Versailles and Compiègne. As a portrait painter, he shared fashionable Paris in the Second Empire with F. X. Winterhalter.

In 1866 Dubufe attempted to break new ground by exhibiting an immense composition, 12 m long, on the theme of *The Prodigal Son*, which did not please the critics. It was bought by A. T. Stewart, the American delegate at the Exposition Universelle of 1867, who sent it to an exhibition tour of America. It was shown for the last time at the Columbian Exposition in Chicago in 1893 and then disappeared.

In 1842 Dubufe married Juliette Zimmermann, daughter of the pianist, Pierre Zimmermann. She was a sculptor specializing in portrait busts, and she exhibited at the Salon between 1842 and 1853. Their son, (Edouard Marie) Guillaume Dubufe (1853–1909), broke with family tradition by becoming a successful decorative painter, inspired by the contemporary fashion for the art of the Rococo. His work can be seen in Paris at the Hôtel de Ville, the Sorbonne, the Palais de l'Elysée and the Comédie-Française.

BIBLIOGRAPHY
Thieme–Becker

JON WHITELEY

Dubuffet, Jean(-Philippe-Arthur) (*b* Le Havre, 31 July 1901; *d* Paris, 12 May 1985). French painter, sculptor, printmaker, collector and writer. He was temperamentally opposed to authority and any suggestion of discipline and devised for himself a coherent, if rebellious, attitude towards the arts and culture. For all his maverick challenges to the values of the art world, Dubuffet's career exemplified the way in which an avant-garde rebel could encounter notoriety, then fame and eventual reverence. His revolt against beauty and conformity has come to be seen as a symptomatic and appreciable influence in 20th-century culture.

1. LIFE AND WORK. The son of a prosperous and authoritarian wine-merchant in Le Havre, Dubuffet left home for Paris at 17 to pursue irregular studies in the arts. But, growing sceptical of the artist's privileged status and savouring an affinity with 'the common man', he abandoned painting in 1924 and went to Argentina to work in a factory. A year later he returned to Le Havre and went into his father's business. In 1927 he married Paulette Brett, the daughter of one of his father's associates, and in 1929 he had established his own wholesale wine business at Bercy, near Paris. Yet commerce was not his vocation, and within a few years he had divorced and resumed painting. He was to produce many portraits of his second wife, Emilie (Lili) Carlu, whom he married in 1937, for example *Lili in Metallic Black* (1946; New York, Mr and Mrs Irving Richards col.), though he was obliged to interrupt his art when his business skirted bankruptcy. Drafted into the army in 1939, Dubuffet was briefly imprisoned for failing to salute an officer. After demobilization, he found his wine trade flourishing but elected to lease it out and devote himself to art full-time. For the third and last time, and aged 41, he again took up painting.

Dubuffet did not waste time during the next four decades: 'For the first time I allowed myself *carte blanche* to paint in perfect liberty, and at top speed, without troubling to cast a critical gaze upon my work, and experimenting in all directions.' He soon began to exhibit in Paris and attracted the attention of such intellectuals as the poets Paul Eluard and Henri Michaux and the critic Jean Paulhan (1884–1968). In 1945, soon after the Armistice, he and Paulhan journeyed to Switzerland to seek out examples of ART BRUT, a type of work more or less synonymous at the time with that of asylum inmates. In 1947 Dubuffet sold his business and over the next few years went on three long visits to the Sahara, somewhat selfconsciously (and not altogether successfully) immersing himself in what he saw as the vital culture of a non-Western, pre-literate society.

The lively succession of provocative exhibitions in Paris from the mid-1940s had established Dubuffet as an important creative force in post-war art. The *Corps de dames* series of 1950 (e.g. *Le Métafisyx*; Paris, Pompidou) confirmed his international reputation as an iconoclast, and an exhibition at the Arts Club, Chicago, in 1951 was the occasion of his notorious lecture 'Anticultural Positions'. Dubuffet had evolved a steady rhythm of productivity by this time, working from a permanent base in Paris and spending long sojourns at Vence in the south of France. His work, hitherto resolutely figurative, came close to abstraction in the 1950s as he invested more and more interest in the elaboration of textures; this was the fertile period of his series of paintings *Texturologies* (e.g. *Vie exemplaire du sol: Texturologie LXIII*, 1958; London, Tate) and of the lithographs *Phénomènes* (1958–9). In 1961, encouraged by the painter Asger Jorn, Dubuffet experimented with musical instruments and non-musical sounds, producing several eccentric records from his own tapes.

The penultimate and longest phase of Dubuffet's career began in 1962 when he invented the *Hourloupe* style. At first an idiom suited to graphics (and even the production of a rather chic deck of cards), the style speedily developed into a proliferating discourse of creative activity demanding to be realized in three dimensions. The 1970s became for Dubuffet a time of even more ambitious sculptural and environmental projects, including important public commissions such as the *Group of Four Trees* (1970–72), in Chase Manhattan Plaza, New York. Following the establishment of the Dubuffet Foundation at Périgny-sur-Yerres in 1974 and the inauguration of the Collection de l'Art Brut at Lausanne in 1976, Dubuffet returned during his last and progressively less healthy years to drawing and painting, with the assemblage pictures of *Théâtres de mémoire* (1975–8; see 1978 exh. cat.) and the airy abstract series *Non-lieux* (1984). As compulsively productive in his 80s as ever, Dubuffet kept on working until his death.

2. ANTICULTURAL POSITIONS.

Dubuffet's broad thesis, pursued in his personal manifesto of 1951 and in such texts as the anarchistic treatise *Asphyxiante culture* (1968) and countless letters, was that Western culture (and, in his view, especially French culture) constitutes a colossal enterprise of brainwashing that seeks to suppress individualism and to impose a specious conformity regulated by reverence for enshrined masterpieces from the past and the tame orthodoxy of a 20th-century art market based on commercialism and kitsch.

In common with such other artists working in Paris after the German occupation as Jean Fautrier and Alberto Giacometti, Dubuffet was drawn to a style of penury and rawness, admiring such instances of unsophisticated creativity as child art and the graffiti that adorned post-war Paris. Stimulated by studies of psychotic art by the psychiatrists Hans Prinzhorn and Walter Morgenthaler, Dubuffet collected spontaneous drawings made by the inmates of institutions, along with work inspired by spiritualism and the more outlandish forms of unschooled creativity. His conception of *art brut* was that it offers a telling alternative to the effete modes of the cultural mainstream; creative authenticity becomes synonymous with self-reliance and uninhibited expressivity.

Dubuffet's meditations on the 'outsider artists' he had collected, which were published in the series *L'Art brut* from 1964, and in other pieces about such marginals as Gaston Chaissac and Alfonso Ossorio (*b* 1916), reveal an unusually empathetic critical sensibility engaging with what some would see as altogether wayward material. In extolling the 'savage values' of the non-fashionable, the non-naturalistic, the non-beautiful, Dubuffet formulated his own negative aesthetic whereby no single scale of excellence obtains, but there are only 'interesting cases' of varying intensity. A teeming pluralism, as opposed to a

frozen hierarchy, is the controlling thought of *Asphyxiante culture*, with its cry for schools of 'deconditioning' and a return to some form of primal innocence.

Such primitivist values, in which may be discerned echoes of Dadaism and Expressionism (and even Romanticism), were largely stimulated by a relentless scorn for what he saw as the outdated doctrines of a snobbish élite. For over 40 years Dubuffet's art was a personal crusade against taste and decorum, a championing of the supposed instincts of the ordinary man, and a propagandistic display of the capricious and the clumsy, the illiterate scrawl and the jarring note.

3. THEMES AND TECHNIQUES.

There is something paradoxical about Dubuffet in that, as the champion of disorder and discovery, he should have so carefully monitored his own production. Working deliberately in series, he repeatedly followed the pattern of absorbing himself for a while in a single experiment and then releasing its products in a well-coordinated exhibition, often with an accompanying catalogue text by himself and always with meticulous dating and titling of each item. The 37 volumes of the *catalogue raisonné* (Paris, 1964–84) owe much to the artist's own conscientiousness.

In his quest for novelty Dubuffet passed through two dozen or so different styles or periods. In the period 1942–50 the emphasis in his work was on finding a technique appropriate to the model of clumsy inventiveness of which Dubuffet was enamoured. The ironically titled *Portraits 'plus beaux qu'ils croient'* (1946–7) are crude likenesses of Parisian intellectuals scratched like graffiti into an earthy impasto, for example *Joë Bousquet in Bed* (1947; New York, Guggenheim). The *Corps de dames* of 1950 represent a violation of the classical motif of the nude, with obese female figures presented in thickly smarmed oils with a vehemently slashed finish, as in *Gaudy Bunch of Flowers* (New York, Sidney Janis Gal.). In the *Paysages du mental* of 1950–52 Dubuffet indulged a growing passion for texture, generating heavy encrustations in oil paint and other unguents, sometimes also incorporating such materials as sand, glass and tar (*hautes pâtes*); these paintings reveal dense cellular shapes wherein float one or two lost figures, vestiges of the more figurative concern, for example *Rocks and Underbrush* (1952; New York, Cordier-Warren Gal.). By the late 1950s Dubuffet's style changed completely to that of undifferentiated textures; the large canvases of the cycle *Célébration du sol* (1957–9) being built up of a myriad of tiny paint splashes in a mode reminiscent of Action painting, with the intention of rendering a 'texturological' account of the earth's surface, as in *Ground's Exemplary Life* (1958; see 1966 exh. cat., pl. III). The frenzied lithographs known as the *Phénomènes* (1958–9) were marked by the admixture of a host of unseemly substances such as leaves, sand and gravel to the inking, in an investigation of arbitrary imprints and their often stunning capacity to yield images of great visual appeal. Here Dubuffet's scorn of good taste may be said to have led full-circle, to the production of a special sort of beauty.

While never conceding that any of his work had been strictly abstract, Dubuffet reasserted the figurative bias in the early 1960s in the droll urban scenes of *Paris Circus*

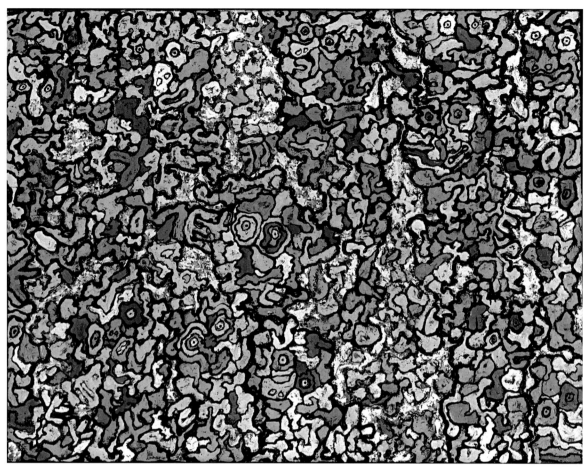

1. Jean Dubuffet: *Irish Jig*, oil on canvas, 1.14×1.46 m, 1961 (Paris, Pompidou, Musée National d'Art Moderne)

(1961–2), albeit veering towards a jazzy, jigsaw style of vivid colour and complexity, as, for example, in *Spinning Round* (1961; London, Tate). A painting such as the *Irish Jig* (1961; Paris, Pompidou; see fig. 1) seems perfectly poised between the two poles of Dubuffet's endeavour, combining the figurative depiction of dancing people with the abstractive presentation of a multiform surface.

In July 1962 Dubuffet, while doodling at the telephone, discovered the cool, anonymous idiom he called *L'Hour-loupe*, in which firm black lines framing cells of unmixed vinyl paint (red and blue in particular) were to dominate, for example *Nunc stans* (1965; Lund U., Kstmus.). His concern became to show objects not as they might appear in the world, but as properties of the mind, flat and non-assertive. A secondary wave of creativity in this vein came with Dubuffet's use, from the late 1960s, of new chemical substances in his work, polystyrene, polyester and epoxy (see fig. 2). In reaction to the tacky graininess of his earlier textural predilections, these materials were prized for their ethereal and artificial properties. They were processed into the ungainly grotesques of the *Coucou bazar* series (1971–3), sculptures in painted resins that also functioned as costumes for dancers, and exploited on a grand scale in such quasi-architectural projects as the *Jardin d'hiver*

(1969–70) at the Centre Pompidou, Paris, or the *Villa Falbala* (1970–73), a massive structure in white polyester bearing a tracery of black lines and incorporated within the moulded walls of the *Closerie Falbala* (1970) that blot out the surrounding countryside by his studios at Périgny-sur-Yerres, near Paris. In such pieces Dubuffet reached the acme of his career as a maker of forms resistant not only to cultural but also to natural precedent, allegories celebrating an individual's entire dissociation from the norm.

UNPUBLISHED SOURCES
Paris [MS. by J. Dubuffet, *Biographie au pas de course* (1985)]

WRITINGS
Prospectus aux amateurs de tout genre (Paris, 1946)
Ler dla canpane (Paris, 1948)
Labonfam abeber par inbo nom (Paris, 1950)
Peintures initiatiques d'Alfonso Ossorio (Paris, 1951)
L'Hourloupe (Paris, 1963)
'Prospectus' et tous écrits suivants, 2 vols (Paris, 1967)
Asphyxiante culture (Paris, 1968)
La Botte à nique (Geneva, 1973)
L'Homme du commun à l'ouvrage (Paris, 1973)
Bâtons rompus (Paris, 1986)

BIBLIOGRAPHY
M. Ragon: *Dubuffet* (Paris, 1958; Eng. trans., 1959)
D. Cordier: *The Drawings of Jean Dubuffet* (New York, 1960)
R. Barilli: *Dubuffet materiologo* (Bologna, 1962)

2. Jean Dubuffet: *The Inventor II*, epoxy paint with polyurethane, 1.14×0.85 m, 1967–70 (Paris, Fondation Jean Dubuffet)

P. Selz: *The Work of Jean Dubuffet* (New York, 1962)
The Lithographs of Jean Dubuffet (exh. cat., Philadelphia, PA, Mus. A., 1964–5)
M. Loreau, ed.: *Catalogue des travaux de Jean Dubuffet*, 37 vols (Paris, 1964–84)
L. Trucchi: *L'occhio di Dubuffet* (Rome, 1965)
Jean Dubuffet: Paintings (exh. cat., ed. A. Bowness; ACGB, 1966)
M. Loreau: *Jean Dubuffet: Délits, déportements, lieux de haut jeu* (Paris, 1971)
J. Berne, ed.: *Dubuffet* (Paris, 1973)
M. Loreau: *Jean Dubuffet: Stratégie de la création* (Paris, 1973)
G. Picon: *Le Travail de Jean Dubuffet* (Geneva, 1973)
M. Rowell: *Jean Dubuffet: A Retrospective* (New York, 1973)
Dubuffet: 'Théâtres de mémoire' (exh. cat., Paris, Gal. Claude Bernard, 1978)
B. Rose: 'Jean Dubuffet: The Outsider as Insider', *A. Mag.*, liii (April 1979), pp. 146–55
Brefs exercices d'école journalière (exh. cat., New York, Pace Gal., 1980)
A. Franzke: *Dubuffet* (New York, 1981)
M. Thévoz: *Dubuffet* (Geneva, 1986)
M. Glimcher: *Jean Dubuffet: Towards an Alternative Reality* (New York, 1987)
S. Webel: *L'Oeuvre gravé et les livres illustrés par Jean Dubuffet*, 2 vols (Paris, 1991)

ROGER CARDINAL

Dubugras, Victor (*b* La Flèche, Sarthe, France, 1868; *d* Rio de Janeiro, 1933). French architect, active in Brazil. He emigrated to Argentina as a child and studied architecture in Buenos Aires; he also trained with the Italian architect Francisco Tamburini (*d* 1892) who created many of the neo-Renaissance buildings in Buenos Aires. He emigrated to Brazil in 1891 and began to practise in São Paulo, assisting Francisco de Paula Ramos de Azevedo and also designing some public buildings, such as law courts and schools, in several towns in the interior of Brazil. In 1894 he was appointed professor of architectural drawing in the newly founded Escola Politécnica, São Paulo.

At this time, São Paulo was one of the fastest-growing cities in the world due to its coffee production and immigration; this industrial growth resulted in the development of a wealthy middle class who were eager to build European-style luxury homes, and it was a very important time for Dubugras. His first designs were influenced by the eclecticism then prevailing in São Paulo, but he moved away from classicism towards more medieval forms, then towards the Art Nouveau style that gave him more freedom of expression; he began to produce highly individual and imaginative solutions that were among the first to treat space as the foremost element in architecture, for example the Villa Uchôa (1903), São Paulo, which was a large splendid house, featuring heraldic ornament although it was modern in its spatial volumes, containing double-height rooms. In 1907 he designed the Mairinque Railway Station, Sorocambo, São Paulo, which can be considered as one of the first examples of modern building in Brazil; of particular interest is the way he used reinforced concrete, with ribs expressing the lines of stress in a way that anticipated future developments. In this project he adopted the geometric restraint characteristic of German and Austrian work, although in other projects, such as the Horácio Sabino house (1903; destr. 1952), Avenida Paulista, São Paulo, he continued to use the curving forms of Art Nouveau.

After 1915 Dubugras adopted the neo-colonial style that had recently been introduced in an attempt to express a national cultural identity. Seeking to avoid the grammar and vocabulary of European styles, it drew its inspiration from 18th-century colonial architecture in Brazil, adopting the Baroque ornament in new and modern architectural applications. The main proponent of the new style was Ricardo Severo (1869–1940), a partner of Francisco de Paula Ramos de Azevedo, but Dubugras was celebrated for his richly imaginative solutions, enthusiastically supported by his client, the Prefect of São Paulo, Washington Luiz. His best-known works in the style are found in the complex of buildings along the road linking São Paulo to Santos, the Caminho do Mar, including Pouso Paranapiacaba, Rancho da Maioridade, Padrão do Loreno, Cruzeiro Quinhentista and a small belvedere. After 1925 Dubugras moved to Rio de Janeiro where he abandoned the neo-colonial style and returned to the approach he had used in the Mairinque project as a point of departure in search of formal purism and rationalism combined, inevitably, with his own personal fantasy.

BIBLIOGRAPHY
C. A. C. Lemos: *Alvenaria burguesa* (São Paulo, 1985)
B. Lima de Toledo: *Victor Dubugras e as atitudes de renovação em seu tempo* (diss., São Paulo, 1985)
A. Fabris, ed.: *Ecletismo na arquitetura brasileira* (São Paulo, 1987) [chap. 4]
Y. Bruand: *Arquitetura contemporânea no Brasil*, i (São Paulo, 1981), p. 33ff

CARLOS A. C. LEMOS

Dubut, Charles-Claude (*b* Paris, *c.* 1657–87; *d* Munich, *bur* 23 May 1742). French sculptor and stuccoist, active in Germany. After training in Paris he worked in Berlin and possibly also Dresden. In 1716 Maximilian II Emanuel, Elector of Bavaria, appointed him court sculptor, and he became a member of the French artists' colony in Munich. In 1716–17 he worked at Schloss Nymphenburg; his stuccowork on the main façade has, however, been much altered by later renovation. He also made numerous stucco reliefs for the decoration of the interior. In 1719 Maximilian Emanuel had put in hand an extension of the Neues Schloss in Schleissheim: there Dubut's work is most notably represented by the Viktoriensaal, one of the finest extant Baroque interiors (*c.* 1723), in which 12 herms of *Hercules* support the ceiling above the main cornice, with putti below. Dubut's ornamental stuccowork on the corbels in the Hofkapelle (Maximilianskapelle) at Schleissheim is also noteworthy. In 1721 Dubut worked on the Badesaal, the great hall of the Badenburg in the park of Schloss Nymphenburg, where he made the consoles for the busts below the gallery.

Dubut's art was formed by the French decorative style of the Louis XV period, with its isolated and emphatic single motifs; it is very different from the flowing, animated and individual line of Johann Baptist Zimmermann, who was also working at that time at Schloss Nymphenburg and Schleissheim, where he set the tone of the decorative style. Dubut's special quality lies in his preservation of the French style of decoration at the Bavarian court, even though this involved some stereotyped repetition of certain decorative forms and figures, such as nymphs and recumbent river-gods.

After Maximilian Emanuel's death in 1726 Dubut was dismissed from court service; one reason for this was probably his dogged attachment to an outmoded style and his inability to adapt to new trends. No work that he carried out after that time is extant. In spite of his many talents—he was also a lead-caster, wax-modeller and creator of exquisite medallion portraits (examples in Cologne, Kstgewmus., B 340–41, I 291; Munich, Bayer. Nmus., R 3982)—he died in penury.

BIBLIOGRAPHY

M. Hauttmann: *Der kurbayerische Hofbaumeister Joseph Effner* (Strasbourg, 1913)

L. Hager: 'Instandgesetzte Stuckdecken im Schloss Nymphenburg und ihre Meister', *Dt. Kst- & Dkmlpf.*, xi (1953), pp. 58–62

P. Volk: 'Drei Porträtmedaillons von Charles Claude Dubut im Kunstgewerbemuseum Köln', *Wallraf-Richartz-Jb.*, xxviii (1966), pp. 279–82

——: *Guillielmus de Grof (1676–1742): Studien zur Plastik am kurbayerischen Hof im 18. Jahrhundert* (diss., U. Frankfurt am Main, 1966)

CAROLA WENZEL

Dubut, Louis-Ambroise (*b* 1769; *d* Paris, 8 Sept 1845). French architect and writer. He was one of the few pupils of Claude-Nicolas Ledoux and studied at the Ecole des Beaux-Arts, Paris. He was unsuccessful in the competition for the Prix de Rome in 1791, 1792 and 1794 but won in 1797 with a design for public granaries, which perfectly illustrated the contemporary tendency towards rationalism. While in Rome he designed an imperial library disguised as a restoration of the Temple de la Pudicité, drawings for which he exhibited at the Salons of 1802 and 1804. He

was best known for his *Architecture civile* (1803), a collection of designs for simple houses of all sizes and a work that met the approval of Jean-Nicolas-Louis Durand. This work was doubtless intended to assure its author a career in France, but his only known works under the Empire were the baths in Bourbonne (begun 1811) and the Préfecture in Aix-la-Chapelle (Aachen). After 1814 he moved to Russia, where he executed several buildings in Moscow and directed the building of a military camp for the government of Novgorod, which won him a nomination (1821) to the Academy of Arts in St Petersburg. Returning to France about 1830, he was involved (1836) in laying out the Paris–Versailles railway and worked on utilitarian buildings in Paris, such as the Marché de Beauvau (1843) and the Marché de Blancs-Manteaux (1845–6). He also worked in Caen and built the workhouse at Saint-Dizier, was involved in the restoration of Rouen Cathedral and built the prison in Einsisheim.

WRITINGS

Architecture civile: Maisons de ville et de campagne de toutes formes et de tous genres, projetées pour être construits sur des terreins de différents grandeurs (Paris, 1803, rev. 1837)

BIBLIOGRAPHY

Thieme–Becker

Nouveau mémoire sur le projet de chemin de fer de Paris à Versailles (Paris, 1836)

Restaurations de monuments antiques . . . depuis 1788 (Paris, 1879)

E. Kaufmann: *Architecture in the Age of Reason* (New York, 1955/*R* 1968), pp. 208–10

A. Drexler: *The Architecture of the Ecole des Beaux-Arts* (New York, 1977), pp. 126–7

L. Grenier: *Villes d'eaux en France* (Paris, 1985), pp. 294–5

W. Szambien: *Les Projets de l'an II* (Paris, 1986)

WERNER SZAMBIEN

Duc, (Joseph-)Louis (*b* Paris, 15 Oct 1802; *d* Paris, 22 Jan 1879). French architect. Together with Henri Labrouste, Félix-Jacques Duban and Léon Vaudoyer, he led the Romantic critique of Neo-classical architecture in Paris. His symbolically eclectic Colonne de Juillet (1840) was praised by the critic César Daly as the movement's finest manifesto to date. But the climax of Duc's career came much later (1869), when he won Napoleon III's prize for the greatest work of art of the last five years in recognition of his new west façade and vestibule for the Palais de Justice. Praised by contemporaries as incompatible as Charles Garnier and Viollet-le-Duc, his work represented and guided the transition from the tersely flat, astylar, rationally expressive architecture established by his own generation to the more figurative, sculptural architecture of the Second Empire, embodied in Garnier's Paris Opéra; it suggested to a younger generation how classical illusion might be meaningful again in contemporary architecture. In this sense Duc was at once the most conservative and the most progressive architect of his circle.

Duc was introduced to art by his father, a ceremonial swordmaker, whose shop on the Rue St Honoré gained royal patronage after the restoration of the Bourbon monarchy in 1815. He entered the Ecole des Beaux-Arts in 1821, advancing rapidly to win the Prix de Rome in 1825 with a project for an hôtel de ville for Paris. Nominally a student of André-Marie Chatillon (1782–1859), he probably owed his success to supplementary study with Jean-Nicolas Huyot and Charles Percier. In Rome he rejoined his school-friends Duban, Labrouste and Vaudoyer. Together the four abandoned the tradition by which *pensionnaires* studied acknowledged Roman masterpieces to confirm the existence of an ideal canon of proportions and ornament applicable to France. Instead they sought to prove that the ancients had programmatically varied the forms of their buildings in order to express logically their specific purpose, circumstances and system of construction. Duc's fourth-year *envoi* (1830–31), a meticulous study of the Colosseum, was highly praised in Paris, but it was submitted jointly with his disturbing final *envoi* (1831), a single sketch for an idiosyncratic column to the victims of the July Revolution, signifying that antique forms could not be transferred literally to France. Duc's project anticipated the July Monarchy's decision to erect such a monument on the Place de la Bastille. In 1832 the government tolerantly appointed him inspector for the project; they later promoted him to succeed the chief architect, Jean-Antoine Alavoine, who died in 1834. Duc redesigned Alavoine's sombre metal Doric column along the lines of his sketch, inventing a 'Corinthian' column that fused the Egyptian, Etruscan, Classical and French heritages to symbolize the revolution's triumphant outcome. Duc also designed the décor for the inauguration (1840), for which his friend Hector Berlioz composed the *Symphonie funèbre et triomphale.*

Almost immediately Duc was rewarded with the prestigious commission that became his life work: the restoration and expansion of the Palais de Justice. His former schoolmate Théodore Dommey (1801–72), who was appointed co-architect, assumed a supporting role. This was a magnificent challenge for an architect concerned with French traditions. Ever since the reign of Saint Louis (1226–70) the law courts had occupied the former palace on the Ile de la Cité, encompassing the Sainte-Chapelle and the Conciergerie. Between 1835 and 1840 Huyot designed a master-plan to restore, renovate and expand the dilapidated complex of Gothic and classical buildings, launching a 90-year programme of work. Huyot's project provided the guidelines for the work, executed chiefly by Duc but completed by his successors Honoré Daumet and Albert Tournaire (1862–1957). Duc expanded the complex to the south and west, filling out the island site, and he provided a second entrance at the west, a pendant to the traditional entrance at the east. The entrances are linked by a pair of monumental corridors, around which are ranged self-contained quarters for individual jurisdictions.

Duc first addressed the needs of the departmental tribunal at the east end. He rebuilt the civil courts between the northern riverbank and the 17th-century Salle des Pas Perdus of Salomon de Brosse, restoring and connecting the 14th-century towers of the Conciergerie and the Tour de l'Horloge with neo-Gothic façades (1842–56). Duc also reconstructed (1842–52) Germain Pilon's clockface, devastated by the Revolution of 1789, restored the Salle des Pas Perdus and rebuilt its façades (1847–78) and restored the three important 14th-century halls of the Conciergerie on the basement-level in the process of redesigning the associated prison quarters (1847–80). After the fire set by the Communards in 1871, Duc also reconstructed the Grand' Chambre, the 14th-century courtroom of the Paris Parlement, with the early 16th-century décor effaced in 1791. A new building was constructed for the misdemeanours courts (1845–54), which forms the west side of the Sainte-Chapelle courtyard. Heated disputes with the nascent historic preservation movement over its effect on the

Louis Duc: west façade of the Palais de Justice, Paris, 1857–68

Sainte-Chapelle dictated the tall, narrow proportions of the building, with two levels of courtrooms stacked above a holding prison. Duc dramatized those constraints in the lobbies, where the building is expressed as an open trabeated cage with metal beams, in which an imperial masonry staircase is suspended.

Far more sculptural was Duc's west façade and vestibule for the Palais (see fig.), executed between 1857 and 1868 as part of a new wing for the criminal assize courts and the central holding prison for the Paris prefecture of police, whose offices were being built by Emile Gilbert at the south-west angle of the complex. To represent the modern law courts, Duc used a colossal engaged order, an uncanonical Hellenistic Corinthian colonnade of primitive force and majestic character, which buttresses an immense, muscularly vaulted Salle des Pas Perdus. In his building, and in letters and notes, Duc contrasted the symbolic orders, which he called the poetic essence of architecture, to the heroic but utilitarian arch and vault, justifying their frank disjunction by arguing that they functioned at different levels. Awarded the Emperor's prize of 100,000 francs, he endowed the Institut de France (to which he was elected in 1866) with an innovative prize to encourage higher studies in architecture: the development of style or symbolic detailing.

In 1862 Duc succeeded Louis Lenormand (1801–62) as architect of the Cour de Cassation, located in the north-west angle of the complex, and revised and executed Lenormand's project for its new wings. By the time of his death Duc had completed all but the decoration of the chief courtroom. Its predominantly French Renaissance and classical character not only expresses the conservative purpose of the French supreme court but also justifies the claim Duc made to continue the French classical tradition in the 19th century. Duc also undertook a number of smaller projects throughout his career. With Duban he renovated the Ministère des Travaux Publics (1841–2) on the Boulevard St Germain. His competition entries for Napoleon's tomb at the Invalides (1841) and the Paris Opéra (1861) won a medal and fourth place respectively, and he designed a church (1851; unexecuted) in Birmingham for Cardinal Newman. Placed in charge of the Paris lycées by Georges-Eugène Haussmann in 1860, he built the Lycée Michelet at Vanves (c. 1860–66), largely modelled on an existing château by Jules Hardouin-Mansart, and executed a new wing on the Rue du Havre for the Lycée Condorcet (1861–6). He designed the tombs of the sculptor Henri Cahieux (1855) and of Duban (1871–3), both in the Montparnasse cemetery. The picturesque villa that he built for his family in the western suburb of Croissy (1864) is now gone, but the sumptuous Château Boulart (c. 1875–83), designed and executed with Louis-François Roux (b 1838), still stands on the Avenue du Maréchal Foch in Biarritz.

BIBLIOGRAPHY

C. Daly: 'Monument de juillet élevé sur la place de la Bastille', *Rev. Gén. Archit.*, i (1840), col. 406–19, 665–92, 746–59, pls 22–3, 26–8
Documents relatifs aux travaux du Palais de Justice et à la reconstruction de la Préfecture de Police, Préfecture de la Seine (Paris, 1858) [vol. of text and atlas of pls]
'Lycée de Vanves, près Paris', *Enc. Archit.*, n. s. 2, ii (1873), pp. 96, 164–6, pls 91, 99, 107, 149, 154
C. Daly: 'Villa à Croissy (Seine et Oise) par M. Duc', *Rev. Gén. Archit.*, xxxii (1875), col. 269–74, pls 54–61; xxxiii (1876), pls 53–5
P. Sédille: 'Joseph-Louis Duc, architecte (1802–1879)', *Enc. Archit.*, n. s. 2, viii (1879), pp. 65–74
L. Cernesson: 'Joseph-Louis Duc, membre de l'Institut', *Rev. Gén. Archit.*, xxxvii (1880), pp. 75–9, 156–60; xxxix (1882), pp. 124–7, 263–4
F. Narjoux: *Paris: Monuments élevés par la ville, 1850–1880*, i (Paris, 1880), pp. 1–44 [extensive engrs]
'Notices of Deceased Members: Joseph Louis Duc, Hon. and Corr. Member (Paris)', *Trans. RIBA*, xii–xiii (1880), pp. 210–17
F. Roux: 'Villa à Biarritz', *Enc. Archit.*, n. s. 2, ix (1880), pp. 171–2; pls 631–2, 640, 645–7, 670
The Architecture of the Ecole des Beaux-Arts (exh. cat., ed. A. Drexler; New York, MOMA, 1977), pp. 150–51, 166–9, 428–9 [pls of Grand Prix and Colosseum proj., Palais de Justice]
R. O'Donnell: 'Louis-Joseph Duc in Birmingham: A "Style Latin" Church for Cardinal Newman, 1851', *Gaz. B.-A.*, xcviii (1981), pp. 37–44
Roma antiqua: Forum, colisée, palatin (exh. cat., Rome, Acad. France and Ecole Fr.; Paris, Ecole B.-A.; 1985), pp. 259–91 [Colosseum proj.]
D. Van Zanter: *Designing Paris: The Architecture of Duban, Labrouste, Duc and Vaudoyer* (Cambridge, MA, 1987)
K. F. Taylor: 'Le Code et l'équité: La Transformation du Palais de Justice de Paris au XIXe siècle', *La Justice en ses temples: Regards sur l'architecture judiciaire en France* (Poitiers, 1992)
——: *In the Theater of Criminal Justice: The Palais de Justice in Second Empire Paris* (Princeton, 1993)

KATHERINE FISCHER TAYLOR

Duca. Italian family of artists. Of Sicilian origin, they were active in central Italy, mainly in Rome, in the second half of the 16th century.

(1) Giacomo [Jacopo] **del Duca** (*b* Cefalù, *c.* 1520; *d* Cefalù, 9 July 1604). Sculptor, architect, bronze-caster and garden designer. He trained in Sicily with Antonello Gaggini and then in Rome with Michelangelo, whom he met through his uncle, Antonio del Duca, Capellano of S Maria di Loreto. He became one of Michelangelo's principal assistants and continued to work for him until Michelangelo's death in 1564. He also worked independently before that date; his marble relief for the abbey of S Bartolomeo di Campagna (now Trisulti; *in situ*) was begun before 1561.

In 1562–3 Giacomo assisted Michelangelo on a new gate to Rome, the Porta Pia, commissioned by Pope Pius IV, for which he executed the winged figures above the main arch, as well as the mask on the keystone. Also in this period he worked with Michelangelo on S Maria degli Angeli, Rome, commissioned by Pius IV and built on the remains of the ancient Baths of Diocletian. The project was promoted by Antonio del Duca, who had first petitioned the papacy about it in 1541. Preliminary proposals were made by Antonio da Sangallo (ii), but in 1559 the commission was given to Michelangelo. Work began in 1562 and continued under Giacomo's supervision after Michelangelo's death. Giacomo completed the cupola over the entrance vestibule and the marble flooring, but the exact extent of his contribution is difficult to determine. (The church was remodelled in the mid-18th century by Luigi Vanvitelli.) Giacomo executed a large bronze tabernacle (begun 1565; now Naples, Capodimonte) for the church from Michelangelo's design. His work in the late 1560s probably included the monastic buildings adjacent to S Maria degli Angeli. The design of the colonnades in the large cloister, with Doric columns supporting simple semicircular arches, is particularly refined. One of his most significant works of the 1570s is the monument to *Elena Savelli* in S Giovanni in Laterano, Rome (moved but *in situ*), in which the legacy of Michelangelo is revealed in the interpenetration of architectural elements. The bronze sculpture, set in marble, includes circular reliefs and the bust of Savelli. In 1574 Giacomo was commissioned by Pope Gregory XIII to design the Porta S Giovanni, Rome. In the form of an antique triumphal arch, perhaps based on a sketch by Michelangelo, it shows Giacomo's assured use of his mentor's vocabulary. Particularly notable are the great rusticated blocks radiating from the arch, giving the whole an effect of depth and power.

Two important ecclesiastical commissions for Giacomo date from the mid-1570s. S Maria di Loreto, Rome, had been begun by Donato Bramante *c.* 1507 and continued by Sangallo. Built on a restricted site, to a centralized plan, it has a square base and an octagonal drum with a prominent cupola; the small chancel projects at the rear. The lower parts of the church and the principal façade to the south were complete when work re-started under Giacomo, after 1573. The detailing of the body of the church is restrained, but Giacomo's cupola is a powerful work, with strongly moulded ribs and circular windows in bold, simple frames; it displays his inheritance from Michelangelo in a context too refined for the strength of its forms. The complex lantern, with its pinnacles and colonettes, is too elaborate for the bold expression of the dome (see fig.). His designs for the flanking façades broadly respect Sangallo's principal elevation. From *c.* 1573 Giacomo remodelled S Maria in Trivio, Rome, a small, aisleless, rectangular church on an extremely restricted site. The façade (1575) is attractive and well-proportioned, although some of the Mannerist details are over-contrived

Giacomo del Duca: cupola and lantern of S Maria di Loreto, Rome, after 1573

and awkward. The small entrance portal is particularly complex, with a curved, broken pediment inserted in a triangular one. The doors are flanked by curious narrow modillions.

Other work by Giacomo in the 1570s includes a large tabernacle commissioned by Philip II for S Lorenzo at the Escorial in Spain (not completed) and the wall surrounding the gardens on the Palatine Hill, the Horti Farnesiani, Rome. Around 1572 he entered the service of Paolo Giordano Orsini (*d* 1585), for whom he designed a garden at Bracciano and possibly worked at the Villa Orsini, Bomarzo, as well as remodelling the presbytery of S Giovanni Battista, Campagnano. In 1582 Giacomo travelled to Innsbruck at the invitation of Archduke Ferdinand, Count of the Tyrol (1529–95), who wanted him to cast the bronze statue for the tomb of *Maximilian I* in the Hofkirche. Giacomo refused, and the work was later undertaken by his brother (2) Lodovico del Duca.

The most significant work designed by Giacomo in the 1580s was the upper gardens and *palazzina* of the Villa Farnese at Caprarola. The complex, including terraces, fountains and sculpture, is remarkable for its synthesis of natural and manmade elements. In 1585 he remodelled SS Quirico and Giulitta, Rome, and parts of the Villa Rivaldi (Rome; partially destr.) for Cardinal Alessandro Farnese. The following year he completed the remodelling of Villa Mattei (altered) on Monte Celio, Rome, for Ciriaco Mattei. His details can be identified on the lower façade, and there is a strongly moulded cornice, characteristic of his style, on the first floor. Also in 1586 he executed the Mattei Chapel in S Maria in Aracoeli (altered), Rome, notable for its stuccowork and coffered ceiling.

By 1592 Giacomo had returned to Sicily as chief architect of Messina, where his work included the tribune of S Giovanni di Malta and the Cappella del SS Sacramento in the cathedral. Despite later alterations, the chapel shows his characteristic inventiveness in the rich interrelationship of architecture and sculpture, one that anticipates the Baroque. According to Baglione, Giacomo was also a poet.

BIBLIOGRAPHY

DBI; Thieme–Becker

G. Vasari: *Vite* (1550, rev. 2/1568); ed. G. Milanesi (1878–85), vii, p. 261

G. Baglione: *Vite* (1642); ed. V. Mariani (1935), p. 54

A. Bertolotti: 'Alcuni artisti siciliani a Roma nei secolo XVI e XVII', *Archv Stor. Sicil.*, 2nd ser., iv (1879), pp. 6–10, 14

E. Lavagnino: 'Jacopo del Duca, architettore del popolo romano', *Capitolium*, x (1931), pp. 203–8

F. Basile: *Studi sull'architettura di Sicilia: La corrente michelangiolesca* (Rome, 1942), pp. 81–109

S. Benedetti: *S Maria in Loreto* (Rome, 1968)

——: 'Sul giardino grande di Caprarola', *Quad. Ist. Stor. Archit.*, 91–6 (1969), pp. 3–46

H. Geiss: 'Studien zur Farnese Villa am Palatin', *Röm. Jb. Kstgesch.*, xiii (1971), pp. 215–20

S. Benedetti: *Giacomo Del Duca e l'architettura del cinquecento* (Rome, 1973)

A. Schiavo: 'Il michelangiolesco tabernacolo di Jacopo del Duca', *Stud. Romani*, xxi/2 (1973), pp. 215–20

S. Benedetti: 'Addizioni a Giacomo Del Duca', *Quad. Ist. Stor. Archit.*, 1–10 (1987), pp. 245–60

(2) Lodovico del Duca (*b* ?Cefalù; *fl* 1551–1601). Bronze-caster, brother of (1) Giacomo del Duca. The earliest record of his activity, a letter from Giorgio Vasari of June 1551 referring to bronze heads cast by Lodovico

Lodovico del Duca: bronze copy of *Marcus Aurelius*, h. 380 mm, 1580–82 (Florence, Museo Nazionale del Bargello)

for the Palazzo Ridolfi, Florence, suggests his career was established by that date. In the early 1570s he participated in casting the bronze sculpture for the monument to *Elena Savelli* (Rome, S Giovanni in Laterano) designed by his brother Giacomo. Also in collaboration with his brother he cast the bronze rays surrounding an emblem designed by Bartolomeo Ammanati for the main façade of Il Gesù, Rome. In 1583 Lodovico was invited by Archduke Ferdinand, Count of the Tyrol, to Innsbruck to undertake the project refused by Giacomo, the casting from the model by Alexander Colin of the statue of *Maximilian I* (*d* 1519) for his tomb in the Hofkirche. The statue, for which Lodovico was paid in 1584, was his first large-scale work. During his stay in Innsbruck he also worked for the ducal court of Bavaria.

After his return to Rome, Lodovico received many commissions during the papacy of Sixtus V. From 1586 to 1590 he worked with Bastiano Torrigiani, head of the papal foundry, on a bronze-gilt tabernacle for the presbytery chapel in S Maria Maggiore, probably from a model by Andrea Riccio and Andrea Soncino. The tabernacle, in the form of a temple and decorated with figures reminiscent of Michelangelo, was cast by Lodovico, the four supporting angels by Torrigiani. In 1586 Lodovico was among many bronze-casters who worked under Domenico

Fontana on the erection of the obelisk in the piazza of St Peter's, Rome. With Torrigiani he cast the four lions supporting the obelisk from models by Prospero Antichi and Francesco da Pietrasanta (*fl* late 16th century). He cast another group of four lions by the same artists and Gregorio de Rossi (1570–1637/43) for the obelisk at S Giovanni in Laterano. For a member of the Savelli family he executed a bronze-gilt crucifix (1592) for the altar then dedicated to S Ignazio in Il Gesù, Rome. He was paid for other work in S Giovanni in Laterano in 1598, probably relating to the decoration of the Cappella del SS Sacramento.

Lodovico was also employed to evaluate works by others. In 1600 he was cited by Orazio Censore as an assessor of works in S Giovanni in Laterano; also in that year he went to Loreto to assess the work of Antonio Calcagni in the Cappella della Pietà. In addition to large commissions, Lodovico also cast small bronzes from antique models, including the copy (Florence, Bargello; see fig.) of the equestrian statue of *Marcus Aurelius* (Rome, Capitoline Hill). A small bronze plaque, a *Pietà* (Messina, Mus. Reg.), has been attributed to him (Accascina). He is last recorded in 1601, receiving four plaster models from S Maria di Loreto in Rome.

BIBLIOGRAPHY

DBI; Thieme–Becker
G. Vasari: *Vite* (1550, rev. 2/1568); ed. G. Milanesi (1878–85), viii, p. 297
G. Baglione: *Vite* (1642); ed. V. Mariani (1935), p. 51
A. Bertolotti: *Artisti bolognesi, ferraresi. . .in Roma nei secolo XV, XVI e XVII* (Bologna, 1884), pp. 78, 81, 185–6
J. Hirn: *Erzherzog Ferdinand II. von Tirol: Geschichte seiner Regierung und seiner Länder*, i (Innsbruck, 1885), pp. 375, 390
W. von Bode: *Die italienischen Bildwerke der Renaissance und des Barock*, ii (Berlin and Leipzig, 1930), p. 43
S. Benedetti: *Giacomo Del Duca e l'architettura del cinquecento* (Rome, 1973), pp. 75, 362
M. Accascina: *Oreficeria di Sicilia dal XII al XIX secolo* (Palermo, 1974), p. 230
E. Egg: *Die Hofkirche in Innsbruck* (Innsbruck, 1974), p. 40
F. Grimaldi and K. Sordi: *Scultori a Loreto* (Ancona, 1987), pp. 125, 181

Du Camp, Maxime (*b* Paris, 8 Feb 1822; *d* Baden-Baden, 9 Feb 1894). French photographer and writer. He was from a wealthy background, and he learnt calotype photography from Gustave Le Gray and Alexis de Lagrange. In 1849 he was sent by the Ministère de l'Instruction Publique on a mission to the Middle East to record the monuments and inscriptions. He undertook the trip (1849–51) with his friend the writer Gustave Flaubert, and during his travels he used a modified calotype process imparted to him by Alexis de Lagrange. He brought back *c.* 200 pictures from Egypt and some from Jerusalem and Baalbek. The album *Egypte, Nubie, Palestine et Syrie: Dessins photographiques recueillis pendant les années 1849, 1850, 1851, accompagnés d'un texte explicatif et précédés d'une introduction* was published by Gide and Baudry in 1852–4 (copy in Paris, Bib. Inst.; prints in Paris, Mus. d'Orsay; Paris, Bib. N.; Paris, Inst. Géog. N.). It contains 125 calotypes printed by Louis-Désiré Blanquart-Evrard, and it was the first printed work in France to be illustrated with photographs. It thus ushered in a new type of book and was a great success.

The photographs are of various subjects: landscapes and ancient monuments, for example the *Temple of Philae*, details of inscriptions and modern cities, for example *Houses in Cairo with Flaubert in the Foreground*. Sometimes figures are included to give an indication of scale, as in *Colossus of Abu Simbel* (*see* PHOTOGRAPHY, fig. 11), and introduce an element of the picturesque. With the clarity of his images and his direct approach to the monuments, Du Camp achieved the mission's objectives: exact reconstruction of sites and buildings. Du Camp was therefore confirmed as a pioneer of archaeological reporting, followed in the 1850s by Félix Teynard, Auguste Salzmann and John B. Greene, among others. Although he retained an interest in photography, Du Camp subsequently dedicated himself to writing. In 1853 he published an unillustrated account of the journey.

BIBLIOGRAPHY

F. Wey: 'Voyages héliographiques: Album d'Egypte de M. Maxime Du Camp', *La Lumière* (14 Sept 1851)

L. de Cormenin: 'Egypte, Nubie, Palestine et Syrie: Dessins photographiques par Maxime Du Camp', *La Lumière* (12 & 19 June 1852)

G. Flaubert: *Voyage d'Egypte, 1849–1851: Notes inédites* (Tours, 1912)

En Egypte au temps de Flaubert (exh. cat., text M. T. Jammes and A. Jammes; Paris, Grand Pal., 1976)

D. Oster and M. Dewachter, eds: *Un Voyageur en Egypte vers 1850* (Paris, 1987)

HÉLÈNE BOCARD

Ducart, Davis [Daviso de Arcort] (*fl c.* 1760; will proved 29 March 1786). Irish architect. He may have been born in Piedmont. He is first heard of in Ireland in the early 1760s and was living in Cork by 1764. He described himself as having been 'bred. . .as an Engineer', and like other 18th-century Irish architects he worked as a canal engineer as well as an architect. He has been described as the last Palladian in Ireland.

From 1767 Ducart worked on the canal between Coalisland, Co. Tyrone, and the Drumglass collieries, which involved constructing a large and handsome aqueduct near Newmills and the earliest use in either Britain or Ireland of inclined planes instead of the more usual system of locks. His earliest building was the Custom House (begun 1765) in Limerick, which announced some decorative mannerisms seen in his later works and a more exotic Palladianism than had hitherto emerged from the school of Edward Lovett Pearce and Richard Castle.

Ducart's practice remained provincial. He designed the Cork Mayoralty House (1765–73). His two most distinguished country houses, both villas with wings, are Kilshanning (*c.* 1766), Co. Cork, and Castletown Cox, Co. Kilkenny (*c.* 1767). Despite their conservative character these are individual and highly sophisticated buildings. A number of houses in Co. Cork—Castle Hyde, Tivoli, Dunkettle and The Island—have, on stylistic grounds, been associated with Ducart or perhaps reflect his influence.

BIBLIOGRAPHY

Knight of Glin: 'A Baroque Palladian in Ireland', *Country Life*, cxlii (28 Sept 1967), pp. 735–9

——: 'The Last Palladian in Ireland', *Country Life*, cxlii (5 Oct 1967), pp. 798–801

W. McCutcheon: *The Industrial Archaeology of Northern Ireland* (Belfast, 1980)

EDWARD MCPARLAND

Duccio (di Buoninsegna) (*fl* 1278; *d* Siena, before 3 Aug 1319). Italian painter. He was one of the most important painters of the 14th century and like his slightly younger contemporary, Giotto, was a major influence on the course of Italian painting. An innovator, he introduced into Sienese painting new altarpiece designs, a dramatic use of landscape, expressive emotional relationships, extremely complex spatial structures and a subtle interplay of colour. His most important and revolutionary work, the *Maestà* for Siena Cathedral, was never matched during the 14th century, if at all, and his influence lasted well into the 15th century.

Most of the surviving works attributed to Duccio are from Siena and the surrounding area, where he seems to have spent most of his working life and is mentioned in numerous documents concerning fines, property, taxation, loans and debts. Gaps in the Sienese documentation have led scholars to suggest journeys to France, Assisi and Rome. His oeuvre is by no means clear, and scholars are divided on the attribution and chronology of many of the major works that have been associated with him and his workshop.

I. Life and work. II. Working methods and technique. III. Posthumous reputation.

I. Life and work.

1. Training and early works, before 1285. 2. Documented works, 1285–1311. 3. Attributed works, 1285–*c.* 1314.

1. TRAINING AND EARLY WORKS, BEFORE 1285. It is not known with whom Duccio trained, although GUIDO DA SIENA is a likely possibility. It has also been suggested that Duccio may have been a pupil of CIMABUE and may have worked with him in the Upper Church of S Francesco, Assisi: Bologna has made comparisons between the two winged genii in the vault showing the *Four Latin Doctors of the Church* at Assisi, the Christ Child in the Castelfiorentino *Madonna* (Castelfiorentino, S Verdiana), which he viewed as a collaborative panel by Cimabue and Duccio, and the Crevole *Madonna*, which he attributed solely to Duccio.

Duccio's first recorded beginnings were modest: in 1278 he was paid for painting 12 coffers for the Commune of Siena. In the following year he was paid for painting *biccherne* (book covers) for the treasury of Siena, a type of commission he carried out frequently. A panel that is thought to date from this period because of its stylistic similarities to the documented Rucellai *Madonna* (see §2(i) below) is the Crevole *Madonna* (Siena, Mus. Opera Duomo) from S Cecilia in Crevole, near Siena. The panel had been taken here from the Eremo di Montespecchio, although it is not known if this was always its location. Its attribution to Duccio is generally accepted by critics, with the exception of Stubblebine (1979), and it has been dated to around 1280. Belting has argued that the Crevole *Madonna* shows that Duccio probably had first-hand knowledge of contemporary Byzantine painting being produced in Tuscany *c.* 1280, such as the Kahn *Madonna*, and of Byzantine art being imitated in Tuscany *c.* 1280, for example the Mellon *Madonna* (both Washington, DC, N.G.A.).

As a result of a gap between 1280 and 1285 in the documents recording Duccio's presence in Siena, Stubblebine (1979) suggested a journey to France. Others have proposed a sojourn in Assisi: Volpe's suggestion that Duccio might have painted in the Upper Church of S Francesco on the *Road to Calvary* and *Crucifixion* is less convincing than Bologna's concerning the painting of the vaults.

2. DOCUMENTED WORKS, 1285–1311.

(i) The Rucellai *Madonna*. (ii) The lost *Maestà*. (iii) The *Maestà*.

(i) The Rucellai 'Madonna'. Duccio's first documented work is the *Maestà* known as the Rucellai *Madonna* (see fig. 1), commissioned by the Società di S Maria Virginis, a company of Laudesi devoted to singing lauds to the Virgin and attached to the Dominican church of S Maria Novella, Florence. In the contract dated 15 April 1285, Duccio agreed to paint a large panel that had already been made. Some critics, for example Van Os, believe that he agreed to paint an altarpiece, the carpentry of which had already been executed according to the wishes of the patron; others, for example Cämmerer, believe that Duccio was responsible for the whole design. The altarpiece was to be painted with the Virgin and Child and 'other figures', according to the wishes of the commissioners, and payment to be 150 lire in small florins. If the final result failed to please, it was to remain in the possession of the artist,

1. Duccio: Rucellai *Madonna*, tempera on panel, 4.5×2.9 m, begun 1285 (Florence, Galleria degli Uffizi)

who would receive no payment nor any form of compensation. The contract does not specify the pictorial programme in any detail, nor does it mention a completion date. It is not certain that Duccio painted the Rucellai *Madonna* in Florence, although this is likely given the size of the panel. Stubblebine (1979) noted that in 1774 Baldinucci saw a document, now lost, in which a painter named Duccio was recorded as a resident in the parish of S Maria Novella, Florence.

The Rucellai *Madonna* is one of the largest altarpieces of its time (4.5×2.9 m). It is painted on five vertical planks of poplar, glued together and further held by an exceptionally deep frame nailed to the front, with vertical and horizontal battens nailed to the back. The whole altarpiece, including the frame, was designed using the Florentine braccio (584 mm) as a base measurement, ensuring total harmony between frame and main panel. The frame is decorated with a patterned band interspersed with 30 roundels containing busts of patriarchs, prophets, Apostles and post-Biblical saints.

Cannon (1982) pointed out that the roundels were innovative in forming a coherent iconographic programme rather than being merely decorative: at the apex is God the Father, on the right, figures from the Old Testament and, on the left, the 12 Apostles, arranged to suggest the succession of the New Testament after the Old. The stepped mouldings of the frame lead into the central composition of the Virgin and Child seated on an elaborately carved wooden throne, painted and gilded, with ball-and-reel columns, hung with a patterned textile and furnished with a gilded red cushion. The throne is held by six kneeling angels. De Wald suggested that this composition was derived from the *Belle Verrière* window in Chartres Cathedral. It has been argued that the angels are in the act of raising the throne and that the position of the angels' hands at top and bottom left, in particular, indicates that this is in fact an *Assumption of the Virgin*, reflecting the dedication of the church of S Maria Novella to the assumptive Virgin.

Hueck (1990) has challenged the previous identification of the figure in the central roundel of the lower frame as St Augustine (whose Rule was adopted by the friars) and suggested instead St Jerome, whose description of the Assumption of the Virgin is cited by the Dominican writer Jacopo da Voragine in the *Golden Legend* (completed *c.* 1273). On either side of this central roundel are St Dominic, founder of the Dominican Order, and St Augustine, and to the right is St Peter Martyr, founder of the Laudesi confraternity.

By 1681 the altarpiece had been moved into the Rucellai Chapel from which it takes its name, but its original location remains in question. Some authors (e.g. Van Os, 1984) have argued that it was commissioned by the Laudesi for the high altar. Others have argued that the Laudesi chapel was originally the chapel of St Gregory furthest to the right of the choir and that the altarpiece was part of a decorative programme that included frescoes of *Christ Enthroned* and *St Gregory ?the Great Enthroned* and, in particular, a fresco of a fictive fabric hanging resembling that on the throne. These have been attributed to Cimabue and the chapel decoration as a whole seen as a collaboration between the two painters.

The chapel was acquired by the Bardi di Vernio family in 1336. The altarpiece was seen by Vasari in the transept between the Bardi and Rucellai chapels, and Hueck (1990) has argued on the following grounds that this may always have been its intended site: it would have obscured the window in the transept chapel, the Child's orientation is emphatically to the left, thereby inappropriately focused on a corner of the chapel, there are no surviving payments for moving the heavy altarpiece out of the chapel, and the nine rings attached to the back seem to have been for securing it on a wall, inclined slightly forward to make it more prominent.

Until the association was made in 1899 between the altarpiece and the contract (discovered in 1790), the panel had been attributed to Cimabue. Even in the 20th century some scholars continued to think it was by the 'Master of the Rucellai Madonna', a pupil or follower of Cimabue. The chronological relationship of the Rucellai *Madonna* and Cimabue's three versions of the *Maestà* from Santa Trìnita (Florence, Uffizi), S Francesco, Pisa (Paris, Louvre) and the fresco in the right transept of the Lower Church, S Francesco, Assisi, is problematic since none of these works is dated, and Duccio may in any case have been Cimabue's pupil or collaborator.

Cleaning of the Rucellai *Madonna* in 1989 revealed the astonishingly high quality of the execution. Particularly fine is the three-dimensional modelling of the Virgin's robe, painted in azurite, recorded in an engraving of 1791 by Cerboni and Lasinio and subsequently concealed by overpainting. The mastery of technique and handling shows this to be the work of a mature painter. The Rucellai *Madonna* is remarkable at this date for the complexity of the three-dimensional space, evident for example in the glimpses of the back supports of the throne, the assured placing of the angels, each kneeling in its own gilded space beside the throne, and in the confident placing of the Child seated naturalistically on the Virgin's knee. This is combined with a fluent linearity, best seen in the rippling gilded border of the Virgin's robe. The composition is held together by a subtle tonal modelling and interplay of colours, particularly evident in the angels' robes, where varying shades of lilac, pink, blue and green are balanced in symmetry or counterpoint. The surface is highly decorative, especially in the mordant gilding of the throne and the Child's red robe, and the entire gilded background as well as the haloes have been patterned with a burin or composite rosette punches.

(ii) The lost 'Maestà'. On 4 December 1302 Duccio was paid 48 lire for a *Maestà* with a predella (untraced) for the chapel of the Nove in the Palazzo Pubblico, Siena; this is close in date to the first recorded PREDELLA for another lost altarpiece painted by Cimabue in 1301 for S Chiara, Pisa. Brandi (1959) and Stubblebine (1972) gathered together a number of versions of a *Maestà* that they thought reflected the documented *Maestà* of 1302, for example the small panel in the abbey church at Monte Oliveto by the eponymous master. Stubblebine also proposed a reconstruction of the predella with scenes from the Passion, as reflected in such works as Simone Martini's Orsini panels (Antwerp, Kon. Mus. S. Kst.; Berlin, Staatl.

Ksthalle; Paris, Louvre). Both critics identified the *Maestà* of 1302 as the altarpiece recorded as damaged in 1319 and restored by Segna di Bonaventura.

(iii) The 'Maestà'.

(a) Documentation. (b) Description and reconstruction. (c) Execution. (d) Sources and influence.

(a) Documentation. It is not known when Duccio began his only other surviving documented work, the *Maestà*. The date traditionally given to it was called into doubt by Pope-Hennessy (1980), who drew attention to the fact that a document dated 9 October 1308, hitherto presumed to be part of the initial commissioning process, was in fact more likely to be an interim agreement. In this document Duccio promised to make the altarpiece to the best of his ability, to work continuously on it, to accept no other commissions until the altarpiece was completed and to work on it with his own hands. In return he was to receive payment for his labour: 16 soldi for each day he worked on the altarpiece and a proportionate sum to be deducted from his monthly salary of 10 lire for the time he did not work on it himself. The agreement may indeed suggest that Duccio had been neglecting the altarpiece for other commissions. All the necessary materials were to be provided by the Opera.

Another document, transcribed by Milanesi in the 19th century and thought to date from *c.* 1308–9, records an agreement for making the rear face of the altarpiece. This was to consist of 34 *storie* (histories) with little angels above and any other painting necessary, to amount to 38 stories altogether. The payment was to be two and a half gold florins per story, of which 50 gold florins were to be paid immediately and the rest on completion of each story. The Opera was to provide the colours and anything else necessary. On 20 December 1308, Duccio received a loan from the Opera of 50 gold florins; it seems likely that the 50 gold florins paid out of the total 95 eventually due were to repay this loan, giving the document recorded by Milanesi a *terminus post quem* of 20 December 1308. White (1979), however, has argued that the loan was made in anticipation of the payment. How much, if any, of the back had been painted at this date is a problem: two years and just over five months remained before the completion date.

The signed *Maestà* was placed on the high altar of Siena Cathedral on 9 June 1311. It probably replaced the *Madonna del voto* (Siena, Mus. Opera Duomo) attributed to Guido da Siena, which itself had replaced the *Madonna degli occhi grossi* (Siena, Mus. Opera Duomo). The triumphal procession was recorded by an anonymous Sienese chronicler in the mid-14th century (L. A. Muratori, *Rerum italiarum scriptores* (Bologna, 1931–9), xv/6, p. 90):

> On the day on which it was carried to the Duomo, the shops were locked up and the Bishop ordered a great and devout company of priests and brothers with a solemn procession, accompanied by the Signori of the Nine and all the officials of the Commune, and all the populace and all the most worthy were in order next to the said panel with lights lit in their hands, and then behind were women and children with much devotion; and they accompanied it right to the Duomo making procession around the Campo, as was the custom, sounding all the bells in glory out of devotion for such a noble panel as was this.

In 1506 the altarpiece was removed from the high altar to make way for a new altar placed further towards the apse and bearing a bronze ciborium (destr.) by il Vecchietta, made originally for S Maria della Scala. In 1771 the two faces of the altarpiece were sawn apart and since then the panels have led a somewhat peripatetic existence. The dismemberment damaged the altarpiece considerably, in particular the Virgin's face.

(b) Description and reconstruction. The gigantic altarpiece (originally *c.* 5.00×4.68 m) was painted on both sides. The front was composed of eleven vertical planks and the back of five horizontal planks, with front and back nailed directly together. The two predellas, the first surviving narrative predellas, were each painted on a single horizontal plank. The pinnacles were probably painted on two horizontal planks, nailed together, as suggested by the fact that the *Incredulity of Thomas* and the *Bearing of the Body of the Virgin to the Tomb*, which were back-to-back, have not been truncated like the rest of the scenes.

The main front panel (Siena, Mus. Opera Duomo) shows the *Virgin and Child* seated on a marble throne inlaid with cosmati, surrounded by 20 angels and SS Catherine, Paul, John the Baptist, Peter and Agnes. Kneeling before them are the patron saints of Siena—SS Ansanus, Sabinus, Crescentius and Victor. The strong civic theme, typical of commissions in Siena, which was dedicated to the Virgin, is further emphasized in the inscription around the base of the throne: MATER SCA DEI SIS CAUSA SENIS REQUIE SIS DUCIO VITA TE QUIA PIXIT ITA (Holy Mother of God, be thou the cause of peace for Siena and life to Duccio because he painted thee thus). In the arcade above were ten Apostles.

The front predella was devoted to scenes from the *Infancy of Christ* based on the Gospels of SS Matthew and Luke, interspersed with standing prophets, each one carrying an inscription relevant to the preceding scene: the *Annunciation* (London, N.G.; see fig. 2), *Isaiah*, the *Nativity*, *Ezekiel* (all Washington, DC, N.G.A.), the *Adoration of the Magi*, *David*, the *Presentation in the Temple*, *Malachi*, the *Massacre of the Innocents*, *Jeremiah*, the *Flight into or Return from Egypt*, *Hosea* and *Christ among the Doctors* (all Siena, Mus. Opera Duomo). The pinnacle panels above showed scenes from the *Life and Death of the Virgin*: the *Annunciation of the Death of the Virgin*, the *Arrival of St John*, the *Gathering of the Apostles*, the *Death of the Virgin*, the *Bearing of the Body of the Virgin to the Tomb* and the *Entombment of the Virgin* (all Siena, Mus. Opera Duomo). This compendium of scenes from the Virgin's life was situated below a stained-glass window

2. Duccio: *Annunciation*, tempera on panel, 430×440 mm (London, National Gallery), predella panel from the *Maestà* altarpiece, completed 1311 (Siena, Museo dell'Opera del Duomo)

also devoted to the Virgin, the design of which was commissioned in 1287–8 and is sometimes attributed to Duccio or Cimabue (*see* GOTHIC, fig. 112).

The back was devoted entirely to the *Life of Christ*, divided into small-scale scenes. The main section (Siena, Mus. Opera Duomo) shows 26 scenes from the *Passion*, beginning with the *Entry into Jerusalem* (see fig. 3) in the bottom left-hand corner. Both this scene and the *Crucifixion* (*see* GOTHIC, fig. 63) at the centre occupy double the height allotted to the others in order to pinpoint the beginning and climax of the cycle, which finishes at the top right-hand corner. The main tier scenes are the *Entry into Jerusalem*, the *Last Supper* with *Christ Washing the Feet of the Disciples*, *Judas Taking the Bribe* with *Christ Taking Leave of the Apostles*, the *Betrayal of Christ* with the *Agony in the Garden*, *Christ brought before Annas* with the *First Denial of Peter*, the *Second Denial* with the *Third Denial*, *Christ Accused by the Pharisees* with *Christ before Pilate*, *Christ before Herod* with *Christ in the Robe before Pilate*, the *Flagellation* with the *Crowning with Thorns*, *Pilate Washing his Hands* with the *Road to Calvary*, the *Crucifixion*, the *Deposition* with the *Entombment* (*see* ICONOGRAPHY AND ICONOLOGY, fig. 7), the *Three Marys at the Tomb* with the *Descent into Limbo* and *Noli me tangere* with the *Journey to Emmaus*.

The back predella had scenes from the *Ministry of Christ*: the *Temptation at the Temple* (Siena, Mus. Opera Duomo), the *Temptation on the Mountain* (New York, Frick), the *Calling of Peter and Andrew* (Washington, DC, N.G.A.), the *Marriage at Cana* (Siena, Mus. Opera Duomo), *Christ and the Woman of Samaria* (Madrid, Mus. Thyssen-Bornemisza), *Christ Healing the Blind Man*, the *Transfiguration* (both London, N.G.; *see* CONSERVATION AND RESTORATION, colour pl. X) and the *Raising of Lazarus* (Fort Worth, TX, Kimbell A. Mus.). The back pinnacles showed *Post-Resurrection* scenes: the *Apparition behind Closed Doors*, the *Incredulity of Thomas*, the *Apparition on the Sea of Tiberius*, the *Apparition in Galilee*, the *Supper at Emmaus* and *Pentecost* (all Siena, Mus. Opera Duomo).

While the overall appearance of the altarpiece is not in question, scholars have differed in their reconstruction of the details. White's version (1979), which is based on a meticulous examination of all physical aspects of the altarpiece, has found general acceptance. The differences in the reconstructions largely concern the subject-matter and position of missing scenes. Most critics agree that the front predella originally consisted of the seven surviving panels; but there is discussion over which scenes completed the back predella—whether *John the Baptist Bearing Witness*, the *Baptism* or the *Temptation in the Wilderness* are missing from the beginning of the predella at the left-hand side, and whether the *Anointing in Bethany* is missing from the close of the predella at the right-hand side. Boskovits (1982) suggested that a fragment of the *Baptism* (Budapest, Mus. F.A.) could be one of the missing scenes. There is also discussion over whether the scenes were confined to the front face of the predella or extended to the sides to form a box predella. White noted the mention in an inventory of 1423 of a separate hanging to cover the predella, indicating that it was an independent structure. Both White and Gardner von Teuffel argued that the lost

3. Duccio: *Entry into Jerusalem*, tempera on panel, detail from the *Maestà* altarpiece, *c.* 5.00×4.68 m (originally), completed 1311 (Siena, Museo dell'Opera del Duomo)

central pinnacle panels had an *Assumption of the Virgin* surmounting a *Coronation of the Virgin* on the front, reflecting the dedication of the cathedral, matched according to Gardner von Teuffel by a *Resurrection* and *Ascension* on the back instead of an *Ascension* and *Christ in Majesty* as argued by White (1979). There is also the problem regarding the method used to support the altarpiece: Gardner von Teuffel has proposed lateral supporting buttresses.

(c) *Execution*. The design of this complex altarpiece was revolutionary and to some extent demanded *ad hoc* solutions. White (1979) has analysed how the basic design was drawn up on a system of proportion based on the square root of two, codified by Matheus Roriczer in 1486, although Maginnis noted that these calculations are missing the crucial measurement of the width, including the frame, which has been removed. The sequence of execution has not yet been established, although top to bottom is logical; it has been argued that the scenes on the back predella, for example, are spatially the most sophisticated.

The *Maestà* is innovative not only in its overall design but also in the treatment of individual scenes. Double episodes are imaginatively combined, for instance a *Flight into or Return from Egypt*, where the figure of the sleeping Joseph is repeated following the donkey in the next episode. Scenes are woven together, not only by using unity of place but also by linking emotionally connected events: the often-cited staircase, for example, which is emphasized by the serving maid's lifted arm, leads from the scene of the *First Denial of Peter* to the scene above of *Christ brought before Annas*; or the linking of *Christ Healing the Blind Man* and the adjacent *Transfiguration*. Light is used to dramatic effect, for instance in the *Three Marys at the Tomb*, where the same mountain-side as in the adjacent *Deposition* is brilliantly lit to indicate dawn. The narratives are full of finely observed detail: the Apostles removing their sandals or warming their hands before a fire, the view into the Temple with its tiled floor resembling that of the Duomo, and maiolica vessels at scenes of repasts.

The attribution of the altarpiece is problematic. The clause 'suis manibus' in the agreement does not exclude the participation of assistants. On the contrary, it implies the opposite, with a constraint on the master to put brush to panel himself. It is impossible that Duccio could have completed so large and complex an altarpiece without the help of assistants. Neither the composition of his workshop, however, nor the names of his assistants and the status or capabilities of collaborators are known. It seems quite possible that he had the collaboration of peers as well as assistants, and technical analysis of *Christ Healing the Blind Man* seems to indicate the involvement of an accomplished painter with a meticulous and purist preoccupation with architecture, possibly Pietro Lorenzetti (Stubblebine, 1979). Stubblebine considered the main front panel and the front predella to be by Duccio himself and all the other narratives by assistants, apportioning individual scenes to Segna di Bonaventura, Ugolino di Nerio, Ambrogio and Pietro Lorenzetti and Simone Martini. White (1979) rightly warned against the attribution of specific parts of the altarpiece to individual painters, a view supported by the evident complexities of medieval workshop practice.

(d) Sources and influence. The idea of painting an altarpiece on both sides may have come from Umbria, where *c.* 1272 the Master of St Francis had painted a double-sided altarpiece (dismantled; for locations *see* MASTERS, ANONYMOUS, AND MONOGRAMMISTS, §I: MASTER OF ST FRANCIS) for the church of S Francesco al Prato, Perugia. Van Os (1984) pointed out that the double-sided Stefaneschi altarpiece (Rome, Pin. Vaticana) is not relevant because it differs so considerably from the *Maestà*. The visual and literary sources of the iconography have been much explored, in particular by Stubblebine (1975), who has suggested various influences, including a Byzantine manuscript, the *Golden Legend* and trips to Rome (S Maria in Domnica, S Maria Maggiore and S Maria in Trastevere) and to France. Deuchler (1979) has argued that the depiction of the city in the *Entry into Jerusalem* is drawn from Flavius Josephus' *Bellum judaicum*.

Duccio was also evidently influenced by other artists, for example Guido da Siena and his circle, especially the *Lenten Hanging* (Siena, Pin. N., no. 8) and the dossal with *St Peter Enthroned* (Siena, Pin. N., no. 15), and the sculptures of Nicola and Giovanni Pisano, particularly the pulpits and Giovanni's full-length figures on the façade of Siena Cathedral. It is also possible that Duccio had seen the Arena Chapel (completed before 1306) in Padua and there obtained the idea of using unity of place to draw together a narrative cycle. The way in which Duccio used landscape as a dramatic tool, for instance in the *Agony in the Garden*, where a tree acts as an emphatic division between the betrayed Christ and the fleeing Apostles, is found elsewhere only in the Arena Chapel.

Given its size and complexity, it is not surprising that the direct influence of the *Maestà* was somewhat limited. On 8 January 1316 the Nove of Massa Marittima commissioned for the cathedral a version of the *Maestà* (Siena, Mus. Opera Duomo), also painted on both sides, which has been cut down and is severely damaged. On the back are scenes from the *Passion* that closely follow the *Maestà*, and on the front a *Virgin and Child Enthroned*. The altarpiece has been attributed to Duccio, although most scholars have expressed doubts. Versions deriving from the *Maestà* were also painted by Ambrogio Lorenzetti (Massa Marittima, Pin. Com.) and Simone Martini (Siena, Pal. Pub.). Individual parts of the *Maestà* had considerable influence: for example, the predella of the Santa Croce altarpiece by Ugolino di Nerio is derived from the *Passion* scenes on the *Maestà*; the organization of the *St Louis of Toulouse* altarpiece by Simone Martini also depends on the front predella of the *Maestà*. The *Maestà* was probably seen by JEAN PUCELLE, as is evident from the Belleville Breviary (Paris, Bib. N., MSS lat. 10483–4) and Hours of Jeanne d'Evreux (New York, Cloisters, MS. 54.1.2). Altarpieces with double sides remained a rarity, with the exception of the simple dossals found in Umbria in the workshop of Meo da Siena, although Sassetta's S Sepolcro altarpiece (dismantled; for locations *see* SASSETTA) was evidently derived from the *Maestà*.

3. ATTRIBUTED WORKS, 1285–*c.* 1314.

(i) Before the 'Maestà'. The exact completion date of the Rucellai *Madonna* is not known, but by 8 October 1285 Duccio was back in Siena painting a *biccherna*. Several similar commissions (all untraced) are documented during the period 1286 to 1295. In 1295 Duccio was the only painter among the six advisers, including Giovanni Pisano, who deliberated on the site for the Fonte Nuova near the Porta Ovile. Another gap in the records between 1295 and 1302 prompted Stubblebine (1979) to suggest a journey to Rome, also proposing that Duccio might be identifiable with the 'Duche de Sienne' and 'Duch le Lombart' documented as living in the Rue des Précheurs in Paris in 1296 and 1297.

A number of works attributed to Duccio have been dated to before the *Maestà*, but their exact dates remain controversial. These include the tiny panel, the *Madonna of the Franciscans* (240×171 mm; Siena, Pin. N.), of which the attribution to Duccio is generally accepted. It shows the Virgin and Child enthroned with three kneeling

Franciscan friars protected by the Virgin's cloak. The pattern of the cloth of honour held up by four angels behind the Virgin and Child has been compared to French illuminated manuscripts, and the iconography is thought to have a French prototype and to be linked with a fresco of *c*. 1300 by a western, possibly French, artist in Panagia Phorbiotissa at Asinou, Cyprus. There is little agreement over the dating of the *Madonna of the Franciscans*: Stubblebine (1979) considered it to be Duccio's earliest work, datable to the 1270s, but White (1979) dated it to the mid-1290s and Deuchler (1984) to *c*. 1300.

Another early work is the polyptych of the *Virgin and Child with Saints* (*c*. 1.39×2.41 m; Siena, Pin. N., no. 28), generally accepted to be by Duccio, although Stubblebine (1979) believed it to have been painted by Segna di Bonaventura working in Duccio's shop *c*. 1310. In the centre are the *Virgin and Child* with *St Peter* and *St Paul* on either side, and *St Augustine* (whose Rule the Dominican Order adopted) and *St Dominic* (the founder of the Order) on the outside panels, with angels in the side gables and the Redeemer blessing in the central gable. Although it has sometimes been identified with an altarpiece of the *Virgin and Child with Four Saints* seen in S Donato, Siena, by Chigi in 1625, signed by Duccio and dated 1310,

Cannon has pointed out that it is most unlikely to have been painted for that church, since S Donato was a Vallombrosan foundation, and the polyptych shows no Benedictine or Vallombrosan saint. Instead, the programme suggests that it was painted for S Domenico, Siena, since St Dominic, rarely represented outside a Dominican context, is included. The polyptych is one of the earliest altarpieces to give particular status to individual saints by showing them on separate panels. Cannon suggested that the polyptych could have been in place by 1306, when the provincial chapter meeting of the *Provincia Romana* was held in Siena. This accords with its dating by most scholars to *c*. 1300–05 on stylistic grounds.

Close to this date is a panel with the *Virgin and Child* (985×635 mm; Perugia, G. N. Umbria), originally from S Domenico, Perugia, and attributed to Duccio by all scholars. This is the only surviving panel of what was probably originally a pentaptych: traces of batten marks on the back show that it once had flanking panels. It has been suggested by Cannon that this was commissioned in response to the chapter meeting of the Order held in Siena in 1306. The building of the present church was begun in 1304, a possible *terminus post quem* for the commission. Cannon suggested that it may have been in place by 1308,

4. Duccio: triptych with *Virgin and Child with SS Dominic and Aurea*, tempera on panel, 615×775 mm (maximum), *c*. 1315 (London, National Gallery)

when the provincial chapter meeting was held in Perugia. It has also been dated to *c.* 1302 by Stubblebine (1979), *c.* 1300–05 by White (1979) and *c.* 1300 by Deuchler (1984). Only Gardner von Teuffel has judged it a 'late' work. The angels in the spandrels were taken up by Ugolino di Nerio in his Santa Croce altarpiece (dismantled; spandrel angels in Los Angeles, CA, Co. Mus. A.), and the polyptych also influenced works by the Sienese painter Meo da Siena, who settled in Perugia.

(ii) Associated with the 'Maestà'. One of the works attributed to Duccio that has been placed just before or just after the *Maestà* is the polyptych of the *Virgin and Child with Saints* (185×257 cm; Siena, Pin. N., no. 47), which is in extremely poor condition. It came originally from the hospital church of S Maria della Scala, Siena, situated at the base of the cathedral steps and administered by the cathedral canons. The hospital church was dedicated to S Maria Annunziata, and the iconographic programme of the altarpiece has been shown by Van Os (1984) to reflect this dedication. The main tier shows the Virgin and Child with SS Agnes, John the Evangelist, John the Baptist and Catherine. In the crowning central gable is the Redeemer blessing, flanked by pinnacles with angels. The intervening arcade has Old Testament prophets—Moses and David in the centre, Abraham, Isaac, Jacob and Jeremiah on the left and Isaiah, Elijah, Daniel and Malachi on the right, all carrying texts relating to the Annunciation, the Incarnation and to Mary as the Mother of God.

Another work that has been dated both before and after the *Maestà* is the triptych showing the *Virgin and Child with SS Dominic and Aurea* (see fig. 4). The attribution to Duccio was first made by Weigelt and has been accepted by Carli (1981) and by White (1979), who dates it to *c.* 1300. The attribution has been doubted by Stubblebine, who thought it to be by Simone Martini working in Duccio's shop. Deuchler (1984) agreed with the attribution to Simone and dated it *c.* 1315. In the gable are seven of the Old Testament prophets who occur in polyptych no. 47—David at the centre with Daniel, Moses and Isaiah on the left and Abraham, Jacob and Jeremiah on the right—and, with the exception of Jeremiah, they carry the same texts. Below them in the main panel are the Virgin and Child with censing angels. In the left wing is *St Dominic,* identified by an inscription. In the right wing is a female saint holding a slender blue double cross. She is almost certainly *St Aurea* of Ostia (although she has been identified by some as St Agnes), since the damaged inscription behind her begins S. AU (not, as often erroneously stated, S. AG). The identification is crucial, since it has led Cannon to suggest that it could have been commissioned by the Dominican Cardinal Niccolò da Prato (*d* 1321), who became Cardinal Bishop of Ostia in 1298.

Technical examination has revealed the distinctive scratchy underdrawing made with a quill pen found in the predella panels from the *Maestà* (*see* §II below) and confirms that Duccio was involved at the very least in the design. The measurements and design of the triptych have been shown by White (1973) to be identical with another triptych (Boston, MA, Mus. F.A.) attributed to Duccio (although more controversially), showing the *Crucifixion*

with *SS Nicholas and Gregory.* Both triptychs were evidently carpentered, gessoed and tooled in the same workshop. Moreover, both have an identical geometric design painted on the exterior, whose function is apparently to indicate which shutter is to be opened first.

(iii) Others. Numerous works have been attributed to Duccio by some scholars, though without universal agreement. These include the Stoclet *Madonna* (untraced), accepted by Stubblebine and White (both 1979); the small panels of the *Maestà* in London (N.G., no. 6386), accepted by Stubblebine (1979), and in Berne (Kstmus.), accepted by Brandi (1951) and Deuchler (1984); the triptych showing the *Flagellation, Crucifixion* and *Deposition* belonging to the Società di Esecutori di Pie Disposizioni, Siena (*in situ*); and the triptych showing the *Crucifixion* at the centre with the *Virgin and Child Enthroned* and *Annunciation* in one wing, and the *Stigmatization of St Francis* and *Christ Enthroned with the Virgin* in the other (London, Hampton Court, Royal Col.).

The seven years between the completion of the *Maestà* and Duccio's death between 1318 and 3 August 1319 have never been fully accounted for. Frescoes dating from around 1314 and probably showing the *Castello of Giuncarico,* discovered in 1979–80 beneath that of *Guidoriccio da Fogliano* in the Sala del Mappamondo in the Palazzo Pubblico, Siena, have been attributed to Duccio, as well as to Simone Martini and the Lorenzetti.

II. *Working methods and technique.*

Although there is no documentary evidence for the component members of Duccio's workshop, the sheer size of the *Maestà,* together with disparities in style and approach, implies that Duccio had the help of assistants and peer collaborators as well as workshop assistants; the coordination of this huge enterprise to produce a coherent and unified work of outstanding aesthetic quality is among Duccio's greatest achievements.

Scientific investigation of the few panels from the *Maestà* that have been examined provides some evidence of Duccio's materials and working methods. He evidently took control of the overall design. Infra-red reflectography has revealed two types of underdrawing in the *Annunciation,* which, as the opening panel of the predella, may confidently be ascribed to him: the broad, emphatic and curiously scratchy lines of a quill pen and the more fluent strokes of a brush. The distinctive quill pen strokes (found also in triptych no. 566) are found in other panels in the *Maestà,* but most revealing of workshop collaboration and of the division of labour is the nature of their presence in *Christ Healing the Blind Man.* The procedure followed in this particular scene indicates a collaboration of equals. First, the composition of the figures seems to have been designed by Duccio, with a thick, dark stroke level with the hips of the blind man at the fountain to mark where the base of the architecture was to be. A second painter seems to have been responsible for the extremely complex architecture. He incised an elaborate grid of vertical and horizontal lines for the main outlines of the buildings. One of the horizontal lines running almost the entire width of the panel was only used for one small roof. It was probably Duccio who added decorative details to the architecture with the thick strokes of a quill pen, embellishments that were ignored by the painter of the architecture, who meticulously painted the buildings in clear blocks of colour, abutting but not overlapping them, and then reinforced the vertical and horizontal lines with a metal stylus before the paint had quite dried. It has been suggested that the painter of this purist architecture was Pietro Lorenzetti. The complex procedure in executing this panel confirms the inaccuracy of assigning single panels to a single painter and suggests that the painting of the *Maestà* involved an intermeshing of collaboration, with several painters working relatively piecemeal on a single composition.

Infra-red reflectography has shown that several panels underwent changes of plan. For example, the blind man at the fountain in *Christ Healing the Blind Man* was originally bending over the fountain, presumably rinsing his eyes, but this was changed to an upright position, possibly after the adjacent *Transfiguration* had been drawn and Duccio saw the possibilities of an emotional link between the two scenes, with the healed man raising his eyes to the transfigured Christ (White, 1979). The decision to show the blind man's arm raised was made at quite a late stage, possibly to disguise with the rounded elbow a blemish in the surface.

In the *Raising of Lazarus*, the tomb was altered from a horizontal sarcophagus to a vertical one inserted in the rock, probably for greater compositional effect to punctuate the end of the predella. Thus the design and painting of the *Maestà* appear to have proceeded in an essentially empirical way, controlled, altered and refined by Duccio with *ad hoc* decisions made as work progressed.

Duccio's palette is interesting. The Virgin's robe in the Rucellai *Madonna* is painted with azurite rather than with the more expensive ultramarine, and as this is also the pigment used for the Virgin's robe in Giotto's Ognissanti *Madonna* (Florence, Uffizi), as well as in the Santa Croce Altarpiece by Ugolino di Nerio, this suggests a predilection on the part of Florentine patrons rather than the choice of the artists. In the Sienese *Maestà*, on the other hand, where the materials were supplied by the patron, the purest ultramarine was used, as well as many earth pigments. Another distinctive feature of Duccio's technique is the thickness of the mordant gilding, resulting in a raised effect, for example in the stars on the Virgin's robe in the National Gallery Triptych.

It is impossible to distinguish Duccio's assistants, pupils and followers. Much debate has focused on the relationship between Duccio and Cimabue, and several paintings, such as the *Flagellation* (New York, Frick), have been attributed to both painters interchangeably. Those Sienese contemporaries most strongly influenced by Duccio were the Master of Badia a Isola, the Master of Città di Castello, the Monte Oliveto Master, Goodhart Master and Vertine Master, and the painter of triptych no. 35, whose royal donor has never been identified. Whether they collaborated with him or not has been a matter of debate. Almost certainly among his pupils were Segna di Bonaventura, Ugolino di Nerio and Simone Martini, and the Lorenzetti brothers almost certainly trained with him.

III. Posthumous reputation.

Duccio's influence on the development of 13th- and 14th-century Italian painting cannot be overstated. Until the 19th century this contribution was considerably underestimated, partly perhaps the result of his Byzantinizing style, partly the Florentine bias of early art historians, who were themselves Florentine. He was mentioned only briefly and almost as an afterthought by Ghiberti, who, after eulogizing Ambrogio Lorenzetti and Simone Martini, inaccurately described the *Maestà*:

> There was in Siena also Duccio, who was most noble and held to the Greek manner; he was outstanding, and the large painting in Siena Cathedral is his work. On the front is shown the *Coronation of Our Lady* and on the back New Testament scenes. This picture was excellently and sapiently made: it is a magnificent work, and he was a most noble painter.

In the first edition of his *Vite*, Vasari included in the life of Duccio many misattributions, including part of the Siena Cathedral floor, and described him as still having been active in 1349 (perhaps confusing him with Ugolino di Nerio).

In the 1568 edition Vasari expanded the life: he identified a panel in Santa Trinita, which he attributed to Duccio, as an *Annunciation* and tried to find the whereabouts of the *Maestà* and failed, possibly because he was looking for a *Coronation of the Virgin* as apparently described by Ghiberti, although he knew that the altarpiece was painted on the back with small-scale biblical scenes. Vasari also attributed the Rucellai *Madonna* to Cimabue. Duccio's reputation was restored by the 16th-century Sienese writer Sigismondo Tizio (*d* 1528): 'Duccio of Siena who was at that time the foremost amongst the artists of that school ... from whose studio as from the Trojan horse there issued distinguished painters'; he was also appreciated by local Sienese writers. It was not until the late 19th century, however, with Berenson's praise (*Central Italian Painters*, 1897, pp. 16–42, 34–5), that Duccio's greatness was fully appreciated, while monographs by Stubblebine and White (both 1979) have established his place among the leading painters of the 14th century.

BIBLIOGRAPHY
EARLY SOURCES
L. Ghiberti: *I commentarii* (MS.; begun *c.* 1447); Ger. trans., ed. J. von Schlosser, as *Lorenzo Ghibertis Denkwürdigkeiten*, 2 vols (Berlin, 1912)
G. Vasari: *Vite* (1550, rev. 2/1568); ed. G. Milanesi (1878–85)
F. Baldinucci: *Notizie de' professori del disegno* (Florence, 1681–1728); ed. F. Ranelli (Florence, 1845–7/R 1974)
G. Milanesi: *Documenti per la storia dell'arte senese*, i (Siena, 1854), pp. 166, 178

GENERAL
M. Davies: *The Early Italian Schools before 1400*, London, N.G. cat. (London, 1951, rev. 1988 by D. Gordon)
H. Van Os: *Marias Demut und Verherrlichung in der sienesischen Malerei, 1300–1450* (The Hague, 1969)
H. B. Maginnis: 'The Literature of Sienese Trecento Painting, 1945–1975', *Z. Kstgesch.*, xl (1977), pp. 277–81, 304
D. Wilkins: 'Early Florentine Frescoes in Santa Maria Novella', *A. Q.* [Detroit], i (1978), pp. 141–74
C. Gardner von Teuffel: 'The Buttressed Altarpiece: A Forgotten Aspect of Tuscan Fourteenth-century Altarpiece Design', *Jb. Berlin. Mus.*, 21 (1979), pp. 21–65
E. Carli: *La pittura senese del trecento* (Milan, 1981), pp. 25–70
J. Cannon: 'Simone Martini, the Dominicans and the Early Sienese Polyptych', *J. Warb. & Court. Inst.*, xlv (1982), pp. 69–93

J. Shearman: *The Early Italian Pictures in the Collection of Her Majesty the Queen* (Cambridge, 1983), pp. 93–6
H. Van Os: *Sienese Altarpieces, 1215–1460*, i (Groningen, 1984)
Italian Painting before 1400: Art in the Making (exh. cat. by D. Bomford, J. Dunkerton, D. Gordon and A. Roy, London, N.G., 1989–90)

MONOGRAPHS

C. H. Weigelt: *Duccio di Buoninsegna* (Leipzig, 1911)
C. Brandi: *Duccio* (Florence, 1951)
J. H. Stubblebine: *Duccio di Buoninsegna and his School*, 2 vols (Princeton, 1979); reviews by M. Boskovits in *A. Bull.*, lxiv/2 (1982), pp. 496–502 and J. Pope-Hennessy in *NY Rev. Bks* (20 Nov 1980), pp. 45–7
J. White: *Duccio: Tuscan Art and the Medieval Workshop* (London, 1979); reviews by M. Boskovits in *A. Bull.*, lxiv/2 (1982), pp. 496–502 and J. Pope-Hennessy in *NY Rev. Bks* (20 Nov 1980), pp. 45–7
F. Deuchler: *Duccio: L'opera completa* (Milan, 1984) [useful catalogue and bibliog.)
G. Ragionera: *Duccio: Catalogo completo dei dipinti* (Florence, 1989)

MAESTÀ

E. T. De Wald: 'Observations on Duccio's *Maestà*, *Late Classical and Medieval Studies in Honour of Albert Matthias Friend, Jr.* (Princeton, 1955), pp. 363–86
C. Brandi: *Il restauro della 'Maestà' di Duccio* (Rome, 1959)
J. White: 'Measurement, Design and Carpentry in Duccio's *Maestà*', *A. Bull.*, lv (1973), pp. 334–66, 547–69
J. H. Stubblebine: 'Byzantine Sources for the Iconography of Duccio's *Maestà*', *A. Bull.*, lvii (1975), pp. 176–85
F. Deuchler: 'Duccio *Doctus*: New Readings for the *Maestà*', *A. Bull.*, lxi (1979), pp. 541–9
R. W. Sullivan: 'The Anointing in Bethany and other Affirmations of Christ's Divinity on Duccio's Back Predella', *A. Bull.*, lxvii (1985), pp. 32–50
——: 'Some Old Testament Themes on the Front Predella of Duccio's *Maestà*', *A. Bull.*, lxviii (1986), pp. 597–609

SPECIALIST STUDIES

E. Carli: *Vetrata duccesca* (Florence, 1946)
C. Volpe: 'Prehistoria di Duccio', *Paragone*, v/49 (1954), pp. 4–22
J. H. Stubblebine: 'Duccio's *Maestà* of 1302 for the Chapel of the Nove', *A. Q.* [Detroit], xxxv/3 (1972), pp. 239–68
——: 'Cimabue and Duccio in Santa Maria Novella', *Pantheon*, xxxi (1973), pp. 15–21
J. White: 'Carpentry and Design in Duccio's Workshop: The London and Boston Triptychs', *J. Warb. & Court. Inst.*, xxxvi (1973), pp. 92–105
F. Deuchler: 'Duccio et son cercle', *Rev. A.* [Paris], 51 (1981), pp. 17–22
H. Belting: 'The "Byzantine" Madonnas: New Facts about their Italian Origin and some Observations on Duccio', *Stud. Hist. A.*, xii (1982), pp. 7–22
M. Seidel: ' "Castrum pingatur in palatio": Ricerche storiche e iconografiche sui castelli dipinti nel Palazzo pubblico di Siena', *Prospettiva* [Florence], 28 (1982), pp. 17–35
F. Bologna: 'The Crowning Disc of a Trecento *Crucifixion* and other Points Relevant to Duccio's Relationship to Cimabue', *BM Q.*, cxxv (1983), pp. 330–40
L. Berti, ed.: *La Maestà di Duccio restaurata*, Studi e Ricerche, 6 (Florence, 1990) [essays by B. Santi, I. Hueck, M. Cämmerer, A. del Serra, O. Casazza]

DILLIAN GORDON

Duccio, Agostino di. *See* AGOSTINO DI DUCCIO.

Du Cerceau. French family of artists. The fame of the most eminent member of the family, (1) Jacques Androuet Du Cerceau (i), rests on a large body of printed works. His eldest son, (2) Baptiste Androuet Du Cerceau, and his second son, (3) Jacques Androuet Du Cerceau (ii), were both architects to Henry IV, King of France (*reg* 1589–1610), while his third son, Charles Androuet Du Cerceau (*d* 1600), has been cited as an 'architect of the King' and engineer. Baptiste Androuet's son (4) Jean Androuet Du Cerceau designed town houses and fortifications in Paris in the first half of the 17th century. The last designers of the family were the grandson of Jacques Androuet Du Cerceau (ii), Paul Androuet Du Cerceau (1623–1710), who was active in Paris as an engraver in 1660, and his son Gabriel-Guillaume Du Cerceau (*fl* 1697–1743), recorded as an architect, designer and painter.

(1) Jacques Androuet Du Cerceau (i) (*b* ?Paris, *c*. 1515; *d* ?Annecy, 1585). Engraver, ornamentalist, writer and architect.

1. Life and illustrative work. 2. Architecture. 3. Posthumous reputation.

1. LIFE AND ILLUSTRATIVE WORK. Du Cerceau's surname probably derives from the sign of the circle that marked his house and shop in Orléans. There is some confusion regarding his early years, particularly about a trip he is supposed to have made to Italy in the 1530s, which was perhaps followed by another in the train of Cardinal Georges d'Armagnac, Ambassador to Rome from 1539 to 1544. Drawings in the Staatsbibliothek, Munich, once considered as proof of the first Italian voyage, have since been reattributed to Philibert de L'Orme (Blunt, 1958), but it still seems probable that Du Cerceau made the journey at some point. Even if he did not, he would have known about both contemporary developments in Italy and Classical architecture from the wide circulation of prints, from the work of architects who studied in Italy and from Italians working in France, most notably Sebastiano Serlio.

Du Cerceau's primary aim was to disseminate the heritage of Classical art and propagate the style of the Italian Renaissance by making works accessible without foreign travel and by providing practical handbooks for architects, painters, sculptors, designers, craftsmen, cabinetmakers, goldsmiths and jewellers. What was probably his first book, *Exempla arcuum*, a series of 25 imaginary triumphal arches based on antique prototypes, appeared in Orléans in 1549. In the early 1550s he published works in Orléans on antique monuments (*Fragments antiques*, *Moyens Temples*), domestic buildings (*Petits Habitations ou logis domestiques*) and capricious ornaments (*Petites Grotesques*, *Les Vues d'optiques*, *Compositions d'architecture*); there is then a gap in his printed oeuvre until 1559, when, having established himself in Paris, he published books on Classical architecture and ornament.

He created a new mode, however, with his *Premier Livre d'architecture contenant les plans et dessaigns [sic] de cinquante bastiments tous differens* (1559), dedicated to Henry II, King of France (*reg* 1547–59). In this, the first of three pattern books, Du Cerceau set forth a series of plans and façade elevations for 50 different town houses, initiated a system of measurement and presented a variety of geometric options. The work is intended as a practical guide and is thus influenced more by economic than aesthetic considerations; however, considerable attention is paid to convenience, to the layout of apartments and to the design of houses with shops and offices at ground level. In his *Second Livre d'architecture* (1561), dedicated to Charles IX (*reg* 1560–74), Du Cerceau provided a compendium of beautiful inventions to enrich the interiors of houses as well as the surrounding courts and gardens. It includes designs for mantelpieces, dormers, portals, fountains, wells and pavilions. Not only did Du Cerceau present details, such as expenses, for builders and patrons, but he also

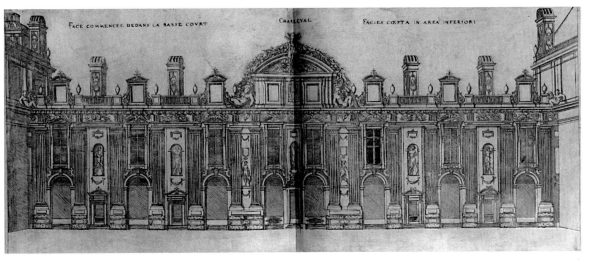

FACE COMMENCEE DEDANS LA BASSE COVRT   CHARLEVAL   FACIES COEPTA IN AREA INFERIORI

1. Jacques Androuet Du Cerceau (i): courtyard elevation of the château of Charleval, begun 1570; from his *Les Plus Excellents Bastiments de France* (Paris, 1576–9) (London, British Library)

attempted to delight his countrymen by portraying excellent works erected by and for Frenchmen; national pride is implicit in his remark that recourse to foreigners is no longer necessary. The *Troisième Livre d'architecture* (1572) is devoted to the design of country houses and their surroundings, including gardens and orchards. Behind these three books there breathes the spirit of Serlio's works on domestic architecture, known through two manuscripts (New York, Columbia U., Avery Archit. & F.A. Lib.; Munich, Bayer. Staatsbib.). The purpose of these manuscripts was similar to that of Du Cerceau's books, and Du Cerceau's debt to the Bolognese architect is apparent in his emphasis on geometry and his use of similar terms—Ichnography, Orthography and Scenography—to indicate the plan, elevation and perspective views. Du Cerceau did not publicly acknowledge Serlio's influence, though a hint of appreciation may be detected in his description of Serlio's château of Ancy-le-Franc: 'I find this house very pleasing (*mignard*).'

Du Cerceau's dedications and notes to the readers illuminate not only his intentions but also his difficulties and preoccupations. Like many artists and men of letters, he was attracted by the Calvinist Reformation. He expressed gratitude for his refuge under the beneficence of Renée of Ferrara (1510–75), who in 1560 established a Huguenot retreat at the château of Montargis (Loiret). Du Cerceau dedicated his *Livre des grotesques* (1566) to her with a hope that the inventions therein would provide delight and serve all manner of artisans in their work.

The two volumes of Du Cerceau's *Les Plus Excellents Bastiments de France* (1576–9) form the most comprehensive existing record of the architecture of the French Renaissance. Du Cerceau stated that their purpose was 'to contemplate here a part of the most beautiful and excellent buildings with which France today is still enriched'. He gave thanks for the much desired peace but regretted the 'long and arduous task' made more difficult by political conditions and the problems attendant on infirmity and advancing age. Henry II was probably the driving force

behind this unique legacy. Du Cerceau first mentioned his project in his Latin preface to the *Livre du temples* (1550), where he stated his intention to create typological studies of buildings and ornament, including a book devoted 'to châteaux, palaces, royal residences'. In 1561 he wrote in his *Second Livre d'architecture* that he was already drawing the buildings for his great work.

Neither chronological nor geographical order prevails in the presentation of the buildings, but a hierarchy is manifest. The royal palace of the Louvre (Paris) opens the first volume and Blois (Loir-et-Cher) the second. Volume I contains ten *maisons royales* and five *maisons particulières*; volume II has eight royal houses and seven private residences, dominated by more recent and even incomplete buildings, such as the Tuileries (Paris) and Charleval (nr Rouen; see fig. 1). The length of the text and the number of plates devoted to each building are not commensurate with the building's importance, but each brief description does adhere to a certain logical sequence. Du Cerceau usually began with the building's principal function, followed closely by a short account of its orientation, topographical features and surroundings. He then gave a summary of its building history and details of materials, embellishments, symbolic value, unique architectural features and its state of preservation. The patron is always cited but the architect rarely; only the Seigneur de Clagny (Pierre Lescot) is named in the passage on the Louvre and de L'Orme in the introduction to La Muette (in Paris); the latter architect is not named in the description of Anet (nr Dreux; mostly destr.; for illustration *see* ANET). Rubrics on each plate are given in Latin and French. The plates themselves are plans, illustrations in perspective, elevations and drawings of architectural details. The archaeological significance of *Les . . . Bastiments* is enormous, for many of the buildings represented have been destroyed or altered. Du Cerceau referred to models and to sketches made *in situ* in executing these designs, and he probably had access to architectural working drawings. A third volume was planned on the monuments of Paris, but

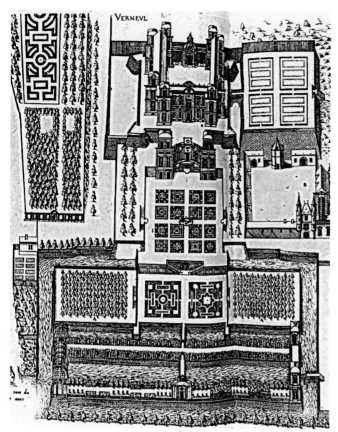

2. Jacques Androuet Du Cerceau (i): perspective view of the château of Verneuil (detail), from *c.* 1565; from his *Les Plus Excellents Bastiments de France* (Paris, 1576–9) (London, British Library)

only five designs were completed; these are bound into later editions of the two volumes.

In his last decade Du Cerceau's production was marked by the recurrence of plates used in earlier works. His *Leçons de perspective positive* (1576) was derived from the *De artificiali perspectiva* (Toulouse, 1505) of Jean Pelérin (alias Viator) and from the *Livre de perspective* (Paris, 1560) of Jean Cousin (i). Du Cerceau's last known work, the *Livre des édifices antiques romains* (1584), constitutes an enlargement of selected buildings of the ancient city that appeared in miniature on his 1578 map of Rome (one of five city maps he drew, including the plan of Paris in 1560), based in turn on Pirro Ligorio's grand map of 1561.

Relatively little attention has been given to the collections of drawings ascribed to Du Cerceau and his studio. Most significant are the magnificent preparatory drawings for *Les . . . Bastiments* in the British Museum, London (for an example *see* FONTAINEBLEAU, fig. 1) and the more modest ones in the Bibliothèque Nationale, Paris. In general, they are richer in detail than the engravings, and the draughtsmanship is more refined. Du Cerceau's usual descriptive mode is the above eye-level or bird's-eye view, which permits a clear vista of the building, its contents and surroundings. One is particularly struck by his rendering of gardens, parks and orchards, neighbouring cities

and villages. Figures drawn with style and verve animate the buildings and the landscapes.

Some volumes containing a wide spectrum of buildings and ornamental designs executed in fine vellum must have served as workshop showpieces or as objects for presentation. Among the notable manuscripts is one (Rome, Vatican, Bib. Apostolica, MS. Barb. Lat. 4398) containing 50 drawings, including designs of Madrid, Charleval, Verneuil and Saint Léger, as well as a series of imaginary triumphal arches and plans for ideal châteaux. Another (New York, Pierpont Morgan Lib.) contains plans after Andrea Palladio, thus demonstrating Du Cerceau's knowledge of the former's *Quattro libri*, published in 1570 but perhaps in limited circulation earlier. A 'sketchbook' of 97 ink drawings (Paris, Ecole B.-A.) includes a repertory of architectural motifs and perspectives. For further examples of Du Cerceau's illustrative work *see* PHILIBERT DE L'ORME, fig. 1; CHÂTEAU, fig. 1; and ECOUEN.

2. ARCHITECTURE. Du Cerceau's career as an architect is problematic. He was involved in restoration work in Montargis, home of his patroness Renée of Ferrara, and in the château of Verneuil near Senlis. His account of the latter and the ten plates illustrating the building in *Les . . . Bastiments* (see fig. 2) reveal a first-hand knowledge of the original project of 1568 and the proposed alteration in 1576 by Jacques de Savoie, who was Renée's son-in-law and the patron of Du Cerceau's later years. Family ties confirm Du Cerceau's involvement with the château, as the supervising architect, Jehan de Brosse, was married to Du Cerceau's daughter Julienne. Their son Salomon de Brosse later designed the Palais du Luxembourg, the plan and rusticated surfaces of which echo those of Verneuil. Because of its fanciful décor and manifestations of anti-classicism, the Maison Blanche (1566; destr.) at GAILLON has also been attributed to Du Cerceau. However, the most remarkable building with which his name is associated is the project for Charleval, sited in a valley near Rouen. Once more, *Les . . . Bastiments* is our fundamental source for information on the château, begun in 1570 for Charles IX. Work ceased with his death in 1574 but was resumed under Catherine de' Medici in 1577. In its monumentality and bi-axial symmetry the plan is related to other examples of late 16th-century planning, such as de L'Orme's scheme for the Tuileries, Jean Bullant's plan for Chenonceau and especially the design for the enlargement of the Louvre in Serlio's Book VI (1541–6) and in the anonymous Destailleur plan (1549–51). This is the type of plan that culminated in the grand classical châteaux of 17th-century France.

3. POSTHUMOUS REPUTATION. Critical opinion of Du Cerceau's work has, of course, been subject to change. His contemporaries Guillaume Morin and Vredeman de Vries and 17th- and 18th-century writers on architecture such as André Félibien, Henri Sauval and A. N. Dézallier d'Argenville considered *Les . . . Bastiments* a primary reference work. Although the two volumes of *Les . . . Bastiments* are fundamental sources for studies in French architecture, knowledge of the Du Cerceaus is still based largely on Geymüller's *Les Du Cerceau*. The author of this monograph considered Jacques Androuet (i) one

of the greatest architects of his time in France, an embodiment of the Renaissance. Blomfield viewed him as an ornamentalist, a virtuoso surveyor and architectural draughtsman and engraver, but one in whom 'the architectural sense is conspicuously absent', while he found the entire family typical of the architectural decline in the late 16th century, an opinion seconded by Gebelin. While assigning Verneuil and Charleval to Du Cerceau, Blunt (1953) deems his mannerism 'almost barbarous', adding that he 'was above all a decorator, and not an architect'.

Recently, a growing preoccupation with vernacular architecture has shifted the focus of studies of Du Cerceau to his pattern books on domestic architecture. It has become increasingly apparent that Du Cerceau was interested in the total patrimony of architecture, the medieval heritage as well as contemporary buildings, the ordinary town house as well as the country château, and the detailed symbolic content of the architecture as well as the environment in which it was set. Future research on the Du Cerceau family will undoubtedly focus on the production of the entire workshop and not just on the masters.

WRITINGS

Temples et habitations fortifiées (Orléans, before ?1549)
Exempla arcuum (Orléans, 1549, repr. Paris, 1559)
Fragments antiques (Orléans, 1550; n.p., 1565)
Grotesques (Orléans, 1550, repr. Paris, 1884)
Livre des temples (Orléans, 1550)
Moyens Temples (Orléans, 1550)
Petites Grotesques (Orléans, 1550, repr. 1562)
Petites Habitations ou logis domestiques (Orléans, 1550)
Compositions d'architecture (Orléans, 1551)
Les Vues d'optique (Orléans, 1551)
Premier Livre d'architecture contenant les plans et dessaigns [sic] de cinquante bastiments tous differens (Paris, 1559, repr. 1611)
Second Livre d'architecture (Paris, 1561)
Livres des grotesques (?Paris, 1566)
Livre I des instruments mathématiques et mécaniques, etc. inventés par Jacques Besson, dauphinois (Orléans, 1569)
Troisième Livre d'architecture, or *Livre d'architecture pour les champs* (Paris, 1572, 4/1648)
Leçons de perspective positive (Paris, 1576/R 1978)
Les Plus Excellents Bastiments de France, 2 vols (Paris, 1576–9, 2/1607, 3/1648); intro. D. Thomson (Paris, 1988)
Grandes Arabesques (?Paris, 1582, repr. Paris, [c. 1880])
Petites Arabesques (?Paris, n.d., repr. Paris, [c. 1880])
Petit Traité des cinq ordres de colonnes (Paris, 1583)
Livre des édifices antiques romains (n.p., 1584)

(2) Baptiste Androuet Du Cerceau (*b* Paris, *c.* 1545; *d* Paris, 1590). Architect, son of (1) Jacques Androuet Du Cerceau (i). Baptiste is first mentioned in the *Memoirs du Duc de Nevers* (1589), where he is named as a Huguenot and an architect taken into the service of Henry III in 1575 (*see* VALOIS, (17)). He is cited in a 1577 pension list of Henry III, which notes that he was working at Charleval together with his father, though receiving a larger stipend. In 1578 he succeeded Pierre Lescot as the architect of the King's buildings. In that capacity, he was responsible for the prolongation of the Grande Galerie of the Louvre, for supervising works on the château of Saint-Germain-en-Laye and for completing the Chapelle des Valois in St Denis (though Blunt, 1953, has stated that 'nothing in the chapel suggests the intervention of Baptiste'). Baptiste is also recorded as directing the King's works at St Denis and as being in charge of repairs at Fontainebleau. He also may have been involved with the Hôtel de Nevers (1582),

a town house reflecting the style of architecture in Fontainebleau and the Ile de France under Francis I and Henry II.

A number of contracts exist for the town houses that Baptiste built in Paris, including his own on the Pré aux Clercs and the Hôtel d'Angoulême (later, the Hôtel de Lamoignon), both dated 1584. The colossal pilasters and the interruption of the entablature by dormers in the latter show a style close to that of Jean Bullant. (The Hôtel d'Angoulême is attributed by some authors to Louis Metezeau.) Supposedly, Baptiste also worked on the châteaux of Verneuil and d'Ormesson and made many drawings for monasteries and designs of such religious structures as altars and chapels. Baptiste was appointed chief architect and adviser to Henry III in 1584 and supervisor of the King's buildings in 1585 (though he is also recorded as having fled Paris in that year because of his Huguenot beliefs). Under Henry IV he was put in charge of schemes for the improvement of Paris, and it is in this realm that he created his only surviving work, the Pont Neuf in Paris. This was begun in 1578, completed posthumously in 1604 and altered in 1843–53. (Unedited documents on the building of the Pont Neuf were published by R. de Lasteyrie, 1882.)

(3) Jacques Androuet Du Cerceau (ii) (*b* Paris, 1550; *d* Paris, 16 Sept 1614). Architect, son of (1) Jacques Androuet Du Cerceau (i). He is first recorded working at Charleval in the 1570s. In the late 1570s and 1580s he was architect in charge of fortifications in Tours and worked on the châteaux of Verneuil, Montceaux (nr Meaux; destr. 1798) and Nérac (Lot-et-Garonne). From 1594, as Henry IV's architect, he superintended works at the Louvre and other royal buildings and completed the west half of the Grande Galerie (1602–8), uniting the Louvre and the Tuileries, a work harshly criticized in Jacques-François Blondel's *L'Architecture française* (1753): 'here are to be found all that is most licentious in architecture: piers of unequal width, quoins of different sizes, a solid where there ought to be a void... entablatures interrupted by windows... extravagant proportions'. Jacques's later years were devoted to designing Parisian town houses, most notably the Hôtel de Mayenne (1605), modelled after the Hôtel Carnavalet, and the Hôtel de Bellegarde (1611–14), with its remarkable grand staircase.

(4) Jean Androuet Du Cerceau (*b* Paris, *c.* 1585; *d* Paris, 1649). Architect and engineer, son of (2) Baptiste Androuet Du Cerceau. In 1614 collaborated with his cousin Salomon de Brosse on the Palais du Luxembourg. His town houses in Paris are well known, especially that owned by the Duc de Sully, the minister of Henry IV and Jean's earlier patron in Poitou. Solid documentary evidence is lacking, but the Hôtel Sully (1624–9) on the Rue Saint Antoine shows stylistic affinities, especially in its richly ornamented façade, with the work of (3) Jacques Androuet Du Cerceau (ii). Jean also worked on the Hôtel Bellegarde (or Séguier; 1633–6) and the sumptuous Hôtel de Bretonvillers on the Ile Notre Dame (1635–8); at the latter he was probably responsible only for the left wing of the court, which has an elaborately sculpted façade. (The building was completed by Louis Le Vau in 1638–43 and destroyed in 1873.) In the 1630s, together with his cousin

Paul de Brosse (*fl* 1619–44) and Charles du Rhys, Jean worked on fortifications in Paris. The intricate staircase of the Cour du Cheval Blanc in Fontainebleau designed in 1632 is his replacement for the monumental horseshoe staircase by de L'Orme (*see* STAIRCASE, fig. 4). Jean's much esteemed design for the Pont au Change in Paris (1639–45; destr. 1858) is marked by a complex grouping of vaulted galleries. One of the most gifted architects of his generation, Jean expanded the ideas of Jacques (ii) and Salomon de Brosse by giving them a more modern tone.

BIBLIOGRAPHY

R. de Lasteyrie: *Mémoires de la Société de l'histoire de Paris*, iv (Paris, 1882), pp. 1–94
H. von Geymüller: *Les Du Cerceau: Leur Vie et leur oeuvre* (Paris, 1887)
R. Blomfield: *History of French Architecture, 1494–1661* (London, 1911)
F. Gebelin: *Les Châteaux de la Renaissance* (Paris, 1927)
M. Beaulieu: 'Jacques I Androuet Du Cerceau', *Pro A. & Libris*, vi (1948–9), pp. 166–82
A. Blunt: *Art and Architecture in France, 1500–1700*, Pelican Hist. A. (Harmondsworth, 1953/R 1977)
E. Cornell: 'Notes sur Du Cerceau', *Göteborgs Kstmus.*, ii (1956), pp. 69–86
I. Toesca: 'Drawings by Jacques Androuet Du Cerceau the Elder in the Vatican Library', *Burl. Mag.*, xcviii (1956), pp. 153–7
A. Blunt: *Philibert De L'Orme* (London, 1958)
J. Adhémar: 'Sur le château de Charleval', *Gaz. B.-A.*, n. s. 5, lviii (1961), pp. 241–4
R. Coope: 'History and Architecture of the Château of Verneuil-sur-Oise', *Gaz. B.-A.*, n. s. 5, lix (1962), pp. 291–318
N. Miller: 'A Volume of Architectural Drawings Ascribed to Jacques Androuet Du Cerceau the Elder in the Morgan Library, New York', *Marsyas*, xi (1962–4), pp. 33–41
E. J. Cirput: 'Notes sur un grand architecte parisien: Jean Androuet Ducerceau', *Bull. Soc. Hist. Protestantisme Fr.*, cxiii (1967), pp. 149–201
M. Tafuri: 'Alle origini del Palladianesimo: Alessandro Farnese, Jacques Androuet Du Cerceau, Inigo Jones', *Stor. A.*, xi (1971), pp. 149–61
D. A. Chevalley: *Der grosse Tuilerienentwurf in der Überlieferung Du Cerceaus* (Frankfurt, 1973)
F. Boudon and H. Couzy: 'Les Plus Excellents Bâtiments de France: Une Anthologie de châteaux à la fin du XVIe siècle', *Inf. Hist. A.*, xix (1974), pp. 8–12, 103–14
G. Rousset-Charny: 'Le Relevé d'architecture chez Jacques 1er Androuet du Cerceau: Les Plus Excellents Bâtiments de France (1576–1579)', *Inf. Hist. A.*, xix (1974), pp. 114–24
F. Paolo Fiore: 'Palazzo e tipologia trionfale: Disegni inediti del Du Cerceau', *Psicon: Riv. Int. Archit.*, iii/9 (1976), pp. 113–20
J. S. Byrne: 'Du Cerceau's Drawings', *Master Drgs*, xv (1977), pp. 147–61
——: 'Some Sixteenth-century Designs for Tombs and Fountains in the Metropolitan Museum', *Master Drgs*, xxi (1983), pp. 263–70
D. Thompson: *Renaissance Paris* (Berkeley and Los Angeles, 1984)
J.-P. Babelon: *Châteaux de France au siècle de la Renaissance* (Paris, 1989)
N. Miller: 'Blow up: A French Sixteenth-century Homage to Rome', *The Building and the Town: Essays for E. F. Sekler*, ed. W. Böhm (Vienna and Cologne, 1994), pp. 188–202

NAOMI MILLER

Ducete, Sebastián (*b* Toro, 1568; *d* Toro, 1619). Spanish sculptor. He was the son of the sculptor Pedro Ducete Díez and trained in Palencia, moving to Valladolid and later back to Toro, where he had a workshop. He collaborated with ESTEBAN DE RUEDA in a partnership whose abundant production justifies the description of the Toro workshop. In 1592 Ducete carved a *Crucifixion* and a statue of the *Virgin* for S Martin, Pinilla de Toro. He executed large *retablos* (1602) in S Sepulcro, Toro, where the poignancy in his work is apparent in the *St Andrew* and derives from the influence of Juan de Juni; in S Sofía, Toro; and in S Pedro, Villalpando, with the fine relief of the *Granting of the Chasuble to St Ildefonso* (1607),

also influenced by Juni. The ample folds in the garments of all these figures were executed by Rueda and show the influence of Gregorio Fernández. In 1618 Ducete and Rueda designed the main retable in the church at Peñaranda de Bracamonte; but Ducete died before it was begun, and Rueda was responsible for the carving, which makes it possible to identify his individual style. Rueda also completed the retable in the Carmelite convent at Medina del Campo (Valladolid, Sanctuario N.). In 1615 Ducete made a *paso* processional figure of *Christ* (untraced) with articulated arms for the Cofradía del S Entierro, to be used in the Easter Week ceremonies. A *Crucifixion* (Barcelona, Mus. Marés) is attributed to Ducete.

BIBLIOGRAPHY

J. J. Martín González: *Escultura barroca castellana*, ii (Madrid, 1971)
J. R. Nieto y Antonio Casaseca: 'Aportaciones al estudio de Sebastián de Ucete y Esteban de Rueda', *Bol. Semin. Estud. A. & Arqueol.*, xlii (1976), pp. 325–32
J. Navarro Talegon: *Catálogo monumental de Toro y su alfoz* (Zamora, 1980)
J. Urrea: 'Los maestros de Toro: Nuevos datos y obras', *Bol. Semin. Estud. A. & Arqueol.*, xlviii (1982), pp. 243–52
J. J. Martín González: *Escultura barroca en España* (Madrid, 1983), pp. 83–5

J. J. MARTÍN GONZÁLEZ

Duchamp, Gaston. *See* VILLON, JACQUES.

Duchamp, (Henri-Robert-)Marcel (*b* Blainville, Normandy, 28 July 1887; *d* Neuilly-sur-Seine, 2 Oct 1968). French painter, sculptor and writer. The art and ideas of Duchamp, perhaps more than those of any other 20th-century artist, have served to exemplify the range of possibilities inherent in a more conceptual approach to the art-making process. Not only is his work of historical importance—from his early experiments with Cubism to his association with Dada and Surrealism—but his conception of the ready-made decisively altered our understanding of what constitutes an object of art. Duchamp refused to accept the standards and practices of an established art system, conventions that were considered essential to attain fame and financial success: he refused to repeat himself, to develop a recognizable style or to show his work regularly. It is the more theoretical aspects implicit to both his art and life that have had the most profound impact on artists later in the century, allowing us to identify Duchamp as one of the most influential artists of the modern era.

1. Life and work. 2. Influence.

1. LIFE AND WORK.

(i) Early artistic experiments, to January 1912. (ii) Sexual themes, chance and the invention of the ready-made, 1912–14. (iii) New York and the 'Large Glass', 1915–23. (iv) France, 1923–42. (v) Final years in the USA, 1942–68.

(i) Early artistic experiments, to January 1912. Duchamp was born into a family of artists. His maternal grandfather, Emile-Frédéric Nicolle (1830–94), was a painter of still-lifes and an engraver of local village scenes. His older brothers Jacques Villon and Raymond Duchamp-Villon began their careers as illustrators but went on to make notable contributions to Cubism, while his younger sister Suzanne Duchamp (1889–1963) became a painter and with her husband, Jean Crotti, co-founded Tabu, an offshoot of Dada.

At the age of 15 Duchamp tried his hand at painting, beginning a series of landscapes executed in an Impressionist style, such as *Church at Blainville* (1902; Philadelphia, PA, Mus. A.); as he later acknowledged, they were inspired by reproductions he had seen of paintings by Claude Monet. On completing his schooling in Rouen he joined his older brothers in Paris, with the idea of pursuing his career as an artist. From October 1904 to July 1905 he was enrolled in painting classes at the Académie Julian, but by his own admission he preferred playing billiards. In these years he made quick sketchbook drawings of his family and casual renderings of people he had seen on the streets of Paris, including a policeman, knife-grinder, gasman, vegetable vendor, peasant and funeral coachman; these provided a repertory of images he recalled in his later work. Through contacts provided by his brothers, Duchamp supplemented his income by producing cartoons for publication in a number of Parisian journals, such as *Le Rire* and the *Courrier français*; some of these drawings were exhibited at the first Salon des Artistes Humoristes in Paris in 1907. His paintings were exhibited publicly for the first time in 1909, at the Salon des Indépendants and the Salon d'Automne, as well as in the first exhibition of the Société Normande de Peinture Moderne in Rouen.

From 1910 Duchamp emulated the structured compositions and modulated brushstrokes of Paul Cézanne, although in most instances he used intense colour in an almost Fauvist manner. These qualities are particularly evident in his *Portrait of the Artist's Father* and in the *Chess Game* (both 1910; Philadelphia, PA, Mus. A.); the latter is a relatively large composition depicting his brothers and their wives relaxing in the garden of their home and studio at 7, Rue Lemaître in Puteaux, a suburb of Paris. It was there that Duchamp joined his brothers for Sunday afternoon gatherings, encountering a host of artists and writers associated with the avant-garde, notably Guillaume Apollinaire, Henri-Martin Barzun, Albert Gleizes, Henri Le Fauconnier, Roger de La Fresnaye, František Kupka, Fernand Léger, Jean Metzinger and Georges Ribemont-Dessaignes (*see* PUTEAUX GROUP). Through his contact with the painters and sculptors in this group, Duchamp's own work began to incorporate the indeterminate spatial structure and planar fragmentation common to most Cubist painting, as in *Portrait (Dulcinea)* (1911; Philadelphia, PA, Mus. A.).

Cubism, together with his knowledge of the chrono-photography of Etienne-Jules Marey and the photographic sequences of Eadweard Muybridge, directly affected Duchamp's conception of *Nude Descending a Staircase No. 2* (Jan 1912; see fig. 1), based on a preliminary study painted in oil on cardboard, *Nude Descending a Staircase No. 1* (Dec 1911; both Philadelphia, PA, Mus. A.). This work, which later became his most famous painting, has often been described as a stylistic fusion of Cubism and Futurism, but Duchamp later maintained that at the time he had not yet seen any Futurist paintings at first hand; the first major Futurist exhibition in Paris opened at Bernheim-Jeune in February 1912.

A few months after it was painted, Duchamp submitted *Nude Descending a Staircase No. 2* to the Salon des

1. Marcel Duchamp: *Nude Descending a Staircase No. 2*, oil on canvas, 1473×889 mm, 1912 (Philadelphia, PA, Museum of Art)

Indépendants in Paris, but the hanging committee, dominated by Cubists, including his brothers and a number of friends, objected to it and particularly to its title, inscribed directly on the canvas, which they thought too provocative and not in keeping with the more traditional subjects they determined appropriate for serious Cubist painting. Duchamp withdrew his submission, an event that became the turning-point in his artistic career. Before the end of the year, however, the painting was given two public showings: first in May at an exhibition of Cubism at the Galeries Dalmau in Barcelona and in October at the Salon de la Section d'Or at the Galerie de la Boétie in Paris (*see* SECTION D'OR (ii)). It was only when it was shown in New York, however, at the ARMORY SHOW in February 1913, where it became the *cause célèbre* of the exhibition, that Duchamp's name and reputation became forever linked to the notoriety of this picture.

(ii) Sexual themes, chance and the invention of the ready-made, 1912–14. During spring 1912 Duchamp continued to experiment with the imagery of Cubist forms in motion in a brilliant series of drawings and paintings that conflated human forms with mechanistic imagery. Rather than focus on the movement of a single figure, as in *Nude Descending*

a Staircase, these works presented subjects of opposing sexual identity: the *King and Queen Surrounded by Swift Nudes* (May 1912; Philadelphia, PA, Mus. A.), inspired by the pieces and movement of a chess game; *Virgin* (two versions, July 1912; both Philadelphia, PA, Mus. A.), showing a virgin and bride, followed by the *Passage from Virgin to Bride* (July–Aug 1912; New York, MOMA); and, finally, *The Bride Stripped Bare by the Bachelors* (July–Aug 1912; Paris, Pompidou), a drawing that consists of a mechanomorphic depiction of a bride who appears to be spun around and stripped of her clothing by two men by her side. This drawing, one of a group produced during the course of an intensely productive two-month sojourn in Munich in summer 1912, was the first work by Duchamp that explicitly identified a thematic preoccupation to which he returned repeatedly over the next ten years.

It may have been in Munich that Duchamp discovered the writings of Max Stirner (1806–56), an obscure German philosopher who believed that the right of an individual was to be held supreme, considered above and beyond the needs of society. As Duchamp later revealed, it was Stirner's writings that motivated the conception of his *Three Standard Stoppages* (1913–14; New York, MOMA), conceived as measuring devices to be used exclusively in his own work in defiance of the authority of the standard metre. This work consists of three wooden slats whose

2. Marcel Duchamp: *Bicycle Wheel*, editioned replica, bicycle wheel on wooden stool, h. 1.26 m, 1964 (Cologne, Museum Ludwig)

lengths and curving profiles were determined by chance methods, allowing threads 1 m long to drop freely from a height of 1 m; the threads themselves, mounted on glass panels, also form part of the work. Duchamp similarly relied on chance operations to determine the sequence of notes in a number of musical scores that he composed in 1913, such as *Erratum musical* (priv. col.; see 1973 New York exh. cat., pp. 264–5).

In 1913 Duchamp abandoned the traditional tools and techniques of painting, prompted by his desire to elevate art and the art-making process beyond the purely visual or 'retinal', as he later called it; his adoption of an overtly intellectual approach was in conscious opposition to the French expression '*être bête comme un peintre*', which presumed that painting was a mindless activity. Concerns such as these led Duchamp to investigate complex theories of geometry (*see* FOURTH DIMENSION) and to adopt techniques of mechanical drawing generally reserved for more scientific disciplines such as physics and engineering. Such preoccupations led Duchamp to ask himself in 1913 whether it was possible for an artist to make works that were not works of art in the sense of being motivated by aesthetic considerations. He answered this question before the end of the year with his creation of the *Bicycle Wheel* (lost or destr.; editioned replica, 1964; Cologne, Mus. Ludwig; see fig. 2), a relatively simple assemblage consisting of nothing more than the inverted fork and wheel of a bicycle mounted on the seat of an ordinary household stool. Although he did not identify it as such when it was made, this was the first READY-MADE, an existing manufactured object deemed to be a work of art simply through its selection by an artist.

(iii) New York and the 'Large Glass', 1915–23. Duchamp was exempted from military conscription because of a minor heart ailment. When World War I broke out in 1914, he was persuaded by Walter Pach, who had earlier helped organize the Armory Show, to travel to the USA. On 15 June 1915 he arrived in New York, where, because of the scandalous reception given to his *Nude Descending a Staircase* in 1913, he was immediately accorded celebrity status. Pach took Duchamp directly to the home of Walter and Louise ARENSBERG, who became the artist's most enthusiastic and dedicated patrons. Duchamp was soon the centre of attention at evening gatherings held at the Arensbergs' large and impressive studio on the Upper West Side in Manhattan. These soirées constituted an unofficial salon, comparable to the open house held by Gertrude Stein in Paris, at which avant-garde writers and artists sought artistic camaraderie. He renewed his acquaintance with other French exiles, such as Gleizes and Picabia, and also met Americans who became lifelong friends, notably KATHERINE S. DREIER, Charles Demuth, Man Ray and Charles Sheeler.

In 1915 Duchamp began the construction of his most complex and intricate work, *The Bride Stripped Bare by her Bachelors, Even* (1915–23; Philadelphia, PA, Mus. A.; see fig. 3), better known as the *Large Glass*. Most of its details, however, had been determined in sketches and preparatory studies completed in Paris in 1913–14, such as *Cemetery of Uniforms and Liveries No. 2* (1914; New Haven, CT, Yale

3. Marcel Duchamp: *The Bride Stripped Bare by her Bachelors, Even* (the *Large Glass*), oil and lead wire on glass, 2.77×1.75 m, 1915–23 (Philadelphia, PA, Museum of Art)

U. A.G.) and *Glider Containing a Water Mill in Neighbouring Metals* (1913–15; Philadelphia, PA, Mus. A.). Mechanomorphic imagery, themes of sexual opposition, references to geometry and physics and a reliance on chance operations and existing objects were all factors in its conception and design. It consists of two glass panels, with the bride's domain confined to the upper section and the bachelors below. Duchamp later explained that the idea for the subject had been suggested by the games he had seen in country fairs, where, in order to win a prize, contestants throw balls at the figure of a bride and her surrounding retinue; others, however, have chosen to interpret the *Large Glass* as a more personal and self-referential statement, pointing out, for example, that the conjunction of bride and bachelors in the French title contains an amalgam of Duchamp's first name: *MAR*(iée) and *CÉL*(ibataires).

From the time of the conception and throughout the physical construction of the *Large Glass*, Duchamp kept a series of elaborate and detailed notes referring to every facet of its iconography and production. Initially he wanted these notes to be compiled and made available to viewers in the form of a catalogue attached to the *Large Glass* itself, a sort of literary guide that was to be consulted in

order to follow the workings of its individual elements in a step-by-step fashion. This catalogue never materialized, but Duchamp eventually published his notes in two limited, facsimile editions: *La Mariée mise à nu par ses célibataires, même* (*The Green Box*) (Paris, 1934) and *A l'infinitif* (New York, 1966). Both serve as important sources of information on the preparation and theoretical framework of the *Large Glass*. With Duchamp's approval and assistance, these notes were subsequently ordered and translated by a number of scholars.

Even when Duchamp's notes are consulted, however, it is unclear whether or not the stripping bride, whose biomorphic forms are derived from an earlier picture, ever attains union with the sexually aroused bachelors represented by the nine mouldlike figures below. What is evident, however, is that the pseudo-machinery of this elaborate construction is designed with one primary function in mind: to exercise the rites of courtship and lovemaking. According to the notes, it is the bride's desire that stimulates the bachelors and in turn causes the flow of 'illuminating gas' into their mouldlike bodies. In response they seem to receive a constant source of energy from an 'imaginary waterfall' that descends upon the blades of a 'glider' or 'sleigh' attached to the base of the 'chocolate grinder' positioned in the immediate central foreground. The fact that none of the elements in this fanciful construction appears to function either literally or figuratively, contributing to a sense of the ultimate lack of fulfilment, is just one more intentionally frustrating or futile aspect of its design. Appropriately to its theme, Duchamp left the *Large Glass* in a state of permanent incompletion when he signed the unfinished work in 1923. After an exhibition at the Brooklyn Museum in New York in 1926, the glass was shattered in transit. Duchamp accepted the accident as yet one more aspect of its design determined by chance; in 1936 he spent weeks painstakingly reassembling the pieces.

In December 1916 the Arensbergs and their coterie were the principal founders of the SOCIETY OF INDEPENDENT ARTISTS, a group devoted to staging annual, jury-free exhibitions in New York. For their first exhibition, held at the Grand Central Palace in April 1917, Duchamp submitted an ordinary urinal, to which he gave the simple but suggestive title *Fountain* (lost; editioned replica, 1964; Ottawa, N.G.; for illustration *see* READY-MADE) and inscribed 'R. Mutt/1917'. A majority of the Society's directors declared that this object was by no definition a work of art, and they consequently refused to exhibit it. Duchamp and Arensberg immediately resigned from the organization, but *Fountain* was not quickly forgotten. Positioned on its back, it was recorded in a photograph by Alfred Stieglitz that appeared in the second and final issue of *Blind Man* in May 1917, accompanied by editorials devoted to its defence by the American ceramicist Beatrice Wood (*b* 1893) and Louise Norton (1891–1989). Shortly after the exhibition opened, the controversial sculpture mysteriously disappeared.

During his first two years in America, Duchamp was a passive though influential participant in the New York avant-garde: he showed his work in a number of small group exhibitions, continued the construction of the *Large Glass* and occasionally issued ready-mades. These included both straightforward objects, such as a snow shovel to which he gave the title *In Advance of the Broken Arm* (1915; second version, 1945; New Haven, CT, Yale U. A.G.), and 'assisted' ready-mades such as *5cc of Paris Air* (Dec 1919; second version, 1949; Philadelphia, PA, Mus. A.), a broken and mended glass ampoule. To earn some extra pocket money, he gave French lessons; his pupils included the Stettheimer sisters—Carrie (*d* 1944), Ettie (*d* 1955) and Florine (1871–1944)—wealthy socialites and artists in their own right, who were to become exceptionally close friends. Although Duchamp generally resisted accepting specific commissions, at Dreier's request he painted *Tu m'* (1918; New Haven, CT, Yale U. A.G.), designed in a long rectangular format to fit into a space above a bookshelf. It includes a number of visual puns and ironic references to painting, including a row of superimposed diamond-shaped colour samples viewed in perspective, and allusions to earlier works, including various ready-mades and his *Three Standard Stoppages*. Its title was probably derived from the French *tu m'emmerdes*, a vulgar expression loosely translated as 'you bore me', which is precisely what the activity of painting seems to have done to Duchamp. This was his last oil painting.

In August 1918 Duchamp left for Buenos Aires, Argentina, remaining there for a little less than a year. He spent most of his time there playing chess but also managed to complete a study for the lower section of the *Large Glass*, a construction on glass bearing the elaborate title *To Be Looked at with One Eye, Close to, for Almost an Hour* (1918; New York, MOMA). He returned to Paris in June 1919, staying with Picabia for about six months. There he came into contact with many of the members of the French DADA group, including André Breton, Tristan Tzara, Louis Aragon, Paul Eluard and the French writer Philippe Soupault (1897–1990). During this visit he inscribed a reproduction of Leonardo da Vinci's *Mona Lisa* with the letters *L.H.O.O.Q.* (1919; Paris, priv. col., see 1973 New York exh. cat., opposite p. 128); when read aloud in French, the result, loosely translated as 'she has a hot arse', produces a ribald commentary on a widely acknowledged masterpiece.

On his return to New York in January 1920, Duchamp resumed contact with a number of his American friends, particularly Man Ray, whose aesthetic sensibilities were so much in keeping with Duchamp's that, over the course of the ensuing year and a half, he was to become Duchamp's closest artistic confidant and collaborator. Together they tried to produce an anaglyphic film, which was supposed to give the illusion of three dimensions, but the film was destroyed in the developing process; Man Ray was also enlisted to document photographically a number of Duchamp's works. In a photograph entitled *Dust Breeding* (1920; see 1988 exh. cat., p. 88) he recorded layers of dust that had accumulated on the surface of the *Large Glass*, and in the same year he took several pictures of an optical construction on which Duchamp was working at the time. Man Ray also took the only known pictures of Duchamp dressed in drag (e.g. see 1973 New York exh. cat., p. 17), in which he posed as Rose Sélavy, his notorious female alter-ego. With Man Ray's support, in 1920 Dreier and Duchamp founded the SOCIÉTÉ ANONYME in New York to display and promote modern art in the USA. In 1921

Duchamp and Man Ray produced the single issue of *New York Dada*, the only such manifestation of the Dada movement in the USA.

(iv) France, 1923–42. Duchamp returned in 1923 to France, where, apart from three brief trips to the USA, he remained for the next 20 years, although he also travelled within Europe to attend various chess tournaments, usually participating as a member of the French team. For ten years after he became chess champion of Haute-Normandie in 1924 his passion for the game intensified as his professional play improved; his particular enthusiasm for endgame situations resulted in the publication of *L'Opposition et les cases conjuguées sont réconciliées* (Paris and Brussels, 1932), written in collaboration with the German chess master Vitaly Halberstadt. While the book shall probably forever be judged an obscure contribution to the literature of chess, it remains of interest for its layout and design, painstakingly prepared by Duchamp.

Duchamp's decision to abandon painting became well known in art circles during the early 1920s, and his professional involvement with chess caused many to conclude that he had ceased artistic activities altogether. While it is true that he preferred to assume a low profile in the art world, steadfastly declining offers to exhibit his work publicly, he continued to develop ideas from his earlier work. When the occasion presented itself, for example, he made amusing plays on words, often with scurrilous implications, as part of a literary game that had been a growing interest from the time of his youth in Paris. But, perhaps in an effort to perpetuate the notion of a private persona, these puns were usually published under his female pseudonym, Rrose Sélavy: the first name was now spelt with a double r, which Duchamp thought created an appropriate and amusing reference to the French *arroser*, meaning 'to wet', or 'to moisten'.

Just as Duchamp had presented an alternative to traditional sculpture in the form of the ready-made, it may have been the reputation he had established for having ceased painting that led him to investigate an alternative mode of artistic expression that still pertained to the concerns of traditional painting. As early as 1918 he began a serious study of the scientific principles of perspective and optics. Through experiments that continued over the course of the following 20 years, Duchamp made repeated efforts to generate effects of depth on a two-dimensional surface, at first through the use of shadows or stereoscopic images and later by means of elaborate motorized devices. In *Rotary Glass Plates (Precision Optics)* (1920; New Haven, CT, Yale U. A.G.), for example, the sensation of a compressed space is created when a series of fragmented circular shapes (painted on the ends of rectangular glass plates) are aligned and spun rapidly. This experiment was followed by *Rotary Demisphere (Precision Optics)* (1925; New York, MOMA), in which a series of concentric circles aligned in the shape of a spiral and painted on to a convex surface are spun in a circular motion, producing the sensation of an ambiguous, undulating space. Similar experiments were conducted throughout the 1920s and 1930s, culminating in an unsuccessful attempt to market them commercially. He designed a series of spirals and objects positioned on spiral patterns, which he had inexpensively printed and mass-produced in an unnumbered edition of 500. When set in motion on the turntable of an ordinary record player, these discs were intended to create a sensation of depth. In 1935, these *Rotoreliefs*, as he called them, were offered for sale at an annual inventor's fair on the Concours Lepine in Paris, but few sales resulted.

Throughout his life Duchamp maintained an aversion to the more commercial aspects of the art system, particularly where his own work was concerned, yet he openly acted as an agent or broker in placing work he admired in various public and private collections; he continued in these years to serve as the principal adviser and European agent for the Arensbergs and Dreier. In partnership with Henri-Pierre Roché (1879–1959) and Mrs Charles Rumsey, Duchamp arranged in 1927 to purchase a group of Constantin Brancusi's sculptures, as well as three of his own paintings, from the estate of John Quinn; he sold these over the years to supplement his income but still lived frugally, inhabiting a small and sparsely decorated studio on the Rue Larrey in Paris.

Although Duchamp had many friends who participated actively in Dada and Surrealism, his work bore little stylistic affinity with either of these movements. Nevertheless, he continued to promote the activities of his friends, supporting the basic ideology of Dada throughout his life, and he participated in various Surrealist exhibitions in Paris and New York. Perhaps recognizing the inappropriateness of his work in a traditional context, in 1935 he began a six-year project of assembling miniature reproductions of his work for inclusion in a one-man portable museum, which, because the first limited editions were packed into a leather suitcase, he called *Boîte-en-valise* (New York, 1941).

(v) Final years in the USA, 1942–68. In 1942, during the Nazi occupation of Paris, Duchamp again left for the USA, taking with him many examples of his newly assembled miniature museum. He renewed contact in New York with his Surrealist friends, many of whom gathered at the home and gallery of Peggy Guggenheim, who exhibited Duchamp's valise in her gallery, Art of This Century, in a special installation designed by Frederick Kiesler. Shortly after his arrival in the USA Duchamp seems to have concluded that, in order for an artist to remain free of outside influences, he needed to keep his activities secret. In 1942 he moved into a studio on West 14th Street, and, with the exception of one or two close friends, he told no-one about a major project on which he worked intermittently for the next 22 years: *Given: 1° The Waterfall; 2° The Illuminating Gas* (1946–66; Philadelphia, PA, Mus. A.; see fig. 4), often referred to by its original title in French, *Etant donnés: 1° La Chute d'eau, 2° Le Gaz d'éclairage.* Essentially, as the complete title implies, this work represents a literal manifestation of those elements that were meant to be invisible or rendered only abstractly in the *Large Glass*. It is a large, three-dimensional tableau, where, through two tiny peepholes in an old Spanish door, we are accorded the view of an unclothed, anonymous woman lying on her back with her legs spread open; in one hand she holds a glowing gas lantern, while in the background a waterfall flows endlessly in silence.

4. Marcel Duchamp: *Given: 1° The Waterfall; 2° The Illuminating Gas (Etant donnés)* (interior view), mixed media, 2.43×1.78 m, 1946–66 (Philadelphia, PA, Museum of Art)

Duchamp began construction of *Etant donnés* in 1946, although he seems to have had the idea for the work some years earlier. Just as for the *Large Glass*, the finished work was preceded by a number of preparatory studies, and several independent works were derived from it. Three small erotic objects are particularly closely related to its production: *Female Fig Leaf* (1950; Paris, priv. col., see Moure, pl. 119), the phallic *Objet-Dard* (galvanized plaster, 1951; Paris, priv. col., see Moure, pl. 120) and *Wedge of Chastity* (plaster version, 1954; New York, MOMA). In accordance with Duchamp's wishes, *Etant donnés* was placed on public display immediately after his death, next to his other works in the Arensberg Collection at the Philadelphia Museum of Art.

2. INFLUENCE. Compared with artists of the magnitude of Picasso and Matisse, Duchamp exerted relatively little influence on the work of his immediate contemporaries. On the other hand, his art and ideas were of singular importance to close friends and associates such as Man Ray, Picabia, Crotti, Joseph Stella and the American painter John Covert (1882–1960), each of whom, in separate ways, incorporated the legacy of Duchamp's work into his own. Only in the last decade of his life, however, did Duchamp's work become known to a larger audience. The opening to the public of the galleries installed with the Arensberg Collection at the Philadelphia Museum of Art in 1954, followed by the publication of the first major monograph on the artist in 1959, established Duchamp as a cult figure among avant-garde artists in both the USA and Europe. A generation of painters and sculptors in the 1950s and

1960s professed their admiration for him. Among the major artists who openly acknowledged the influence of his work were Roberto Matta, Robert Rauschenberg, Arman, Jasper Johns, Allan Kaprow, Richard Hamilton, Robert Morris (ii), Jean Tinguely, Andy Warhol, Joseph Kosuth and the composer John Cage. Duchamp was 76 years old when the first retrospective of his work was held at the Pasadena Museum of Art in 1963. After his death in 1968, major exhibitions were held at the Philadelphia Museum of Art and the Museum of Modern Art, New York (1973), the Musée National d'Art Moderne, Centre Pompidou, Paris (1977), and the Palazzo Grassi, Venice (1993).

Duchamp could be considered the single most important historical figure to affect the formation and direction of Pop art, Minimalism and conceptual art in the 1960s and 1970s. If his contribution is assessed in terms of the general ideological shift that took place in the late 20th century, from a dependence on industrialization to a more intellectually oriented role within an information-gathering society, his importance can be judged not only in terms of his artistic influence but also as a harbinger of changes in society at large.

WRITINGS

Boîte-en-valise (New York, 1941)

From the Green Box, trans. and preface G. H. Hamilton (New Haven, 1957)

M. Sanouillet and E. Peterson, eds: *Marchand de sel* (Paris, 1958); Eng. trans. as *Salt Seller: The Writings of Marcel Duchamp* (New York, 1973) and *The Essential Writings of Marcel Duchamp* (London, 1975)

R. Hamilton, ed.: *The Bride Stripped Bare by her Bachelors, Even*, trans. G. H. Hamilton (London and New York, 1960) [typographic version of notes contained in Duchamp's *Green Box*]

A l'infinitif, with trans. by C. Gray (New York, 1966)

with P. Cabanne: *Entretiens avec Marcel Duchamp* (Paris, 1967); Eng. trans. as *Dialogues with Marcel Duchamp* (New York, 1970, and London, 1971)

A. Schwarz, ed.: *Notes and Projects for the Large Glass* (New York, 1969)

P. Matisse, ed.: *Notes*, preface P. Hulten, trans. P. Matisse (Paris, 1980) [in Fr. and Eng., with reproductions and transcriptions of handwritten notes by Duchamp from 1912 to 1968]

S. Stauffer, ed.: *Die Schriften* (Zurich, 1981)

F. M. Naumann, ed.: '*Affectueusement, Marcel*: The Letters from Marcel Duchamp to Suzanne Duchamp and Jean Crotti', *Archvs Amer. A. J.*, xxii/4 (1982), pp. 2–19

——: 'Marcel Duchamp's Letters to Walter and Louise Arensberg, 1917–1921', *Dada Surrealism*, xvi (1987), pp. 203–27

Briefe an Marcel Jean / Letters to Marcel Jean (Munich, 1987) [parallel Ger., Fr. and Eng. texts]

F. M. Naumann, ed.: '*Amicalement, Marcel*: Fourteen Letters from Marcel Duchamp to Walter Pach', *Archvs Amer. A. J.*, xxix/3–4 (1989), pp. 36–50

BIBLIOGRAPHY

MONOGRAPHS

R. Lebel: *Sur Marcel Duchamp* (Paris, 1959); Eng. trans. as *Marcel Duchamp* (New York, 1959, rev. 1967) [first cat. rais., des. and layout by Duchamp]

C. Tomkins: *The Bride and the Bachelors: The Heretical Courtship in Modern Art* (New York, 1965), pp. 69–144

——: *The World of Marcel Duchamp* (New York, 1966)

A. Schwarz: *The Complete Works of Marcel Duchamp* (New York, 1969, rev. 1970) [most exhaustive cat. rais.]

O. Paz: *Marcel Duchamp or the Castle of Purity* (New York, 1970)

Opus International, 49 (March 1974) [special issue on Duchamp]

P. Cabanne: *Les Trois Duchamp: Jacques Villon, Raymond Duchamp-Villon, Marcel Duchamp* (Neuchâtel, 1975); Eng. trans. as *The Brothers Duchamp* (New York, 1976)

M. Calvesi: *Duchamp invisibile: La costruzione del simbolo* (Rome, 1975)

M. Calvesi and A. Schwarz, eds: *Su Marcel Duchamp* (Naples, 1975)

J. Masheck, ed.: *Marcel Duchamp in Perspective* (Englewood Cliffs, 1975) [reprints of ess. by Guillaume Apollinaire, Clement Greenberg, Jasper Johns and others]

A. Bonito Oliva: *Vita di Marcel Duchamp* (Rome, 1976) [in It. and Eng.]

J.-F. Lyotard: *Les Transformateurs Duchamp* (Paris, 1977)

A. G. Marquis: *Marcel Duchamp: Eros, c'est la vie: A Biography* (Troy, NY, 1981)

H. Molderings: *Marcel Duchamp: Parawissenschaft, das Ephemere und der Skeptizismus* (Frankfurt am Main, 1983)

J.-C. Bailly: *Marcel Duchamp* (Paris, 1984)

T. de Duve: *Nominalisme pictural: Marcel Duchamp, la peinture et la modernité* (Paris, 1984)

R. Lebel: *Marcel Duchamp* (Paris, 1985)

U. Linde: *Marcel Duchamp* (Stockholm, 1986)

G. Moure: *Marcel Duchamp* (Barcelona, 1988; Eng. trans., London, 1988)

R. E. Kuenzli and F. M. Naumann, eds: *Marcel Duchamp: Artist of the Century* (Cambridge, MA, 1989)

T. de Duve, ed.: *The Definitively Unfinished Marcel Duchamp* (Cambridge, MA, 1991)

EXHIBITION CATALOGUES

Marcel Duchamp: A Retrospective Exhibition (exh. cat. by R. Lebel and W. Hopps, Pasadena, CA, A. Mus., 1963)

The Almost Complete Works of Marcel Duchamp at the Tate Gallery (exh. cat., preface G. White, intro. R. Hamilton; London, ACGB, 1966)

La delicata scacchiera: Marcel Duchamp, 1902–68 (exh. cat., ed. A. Bonito Oliva; Naples, Pal. Reale, 1973)

Marcel Duchamp (exh. cat., ed. A. d'Harnoncourt and K. McShine; New York, MOMA; Philadelphia, Mus. A.; 1973; *R* Munich, 1989)

L'Oeuvre de Marcel Duchamp, 4 vols (exh. cat., ed. J. Clair; Paris, Pompidou, 1977)

Übrigens sterben immer die anderen: Marcel Duchamp und die Avantgarde seit 1950 (exh. cat., ed. A. M. Fischer and D. Daniels; Cologne, Mus. Ludwig, 1988)

Marcel Duchamp (exh. cat. by J. Gough-Cooper and J. Caumont, ed. P. Hulten; Venice, Pal. Grassi, 1993)

SPECIALIST STUDIES

W. Hopps, U. Linde and A. Schwarz: *Marcel Duchamp Readymades, etc (1913–1964)* (Paris, 1964)

A. d'Harnoncourt and W. Hopps: '*Etant donnés: 1° La Chute d'eau 2° Le Gaz d'éclairage*: Reflections on a New Work by Marcel Duchamp', *Bull. Philadelphia Mus. A.*, lxiv/299–300 (1969), pp. 6–58; as booklet (Philadelphia, 1973/*R* 1987)

J. Clair: *Duchamp et la photographie: Essai d'analyse d'un primat technique sur le développement d'un oeuvre* (Paris, 1977)

T. Zaunschirm: *Robert Musil und Marcel Duchamp* (Klagenfurt, 1982)

E. Bonk: *Marcel Duchamp: The Portable Box in a Valise, an Inventory of an Edition* (London, 1989) [comprehensive study of Duchamp's *Boîte-en-valise*]

B. Clearwater, ed.: *West Coast Duchamp* (Miami Beach, 1991)

F. Naumann: 'The Bachelor's Quest', *A. America*, lxxi/9 (1993), pp. 67, 69, 72–81

THE 'LARGE GLASS'

A. Schwarz, ed.: *Marcel Duchamp: Notes and Projects for the Large Glass* (New York, 1969) [an ordering and Eng. trans. of notes pertaining to the *Large Glass* contained in Duchamp's *Green Box* and *A l'infinitif*]

J. Golding: *Marcel Duchamp: The Bride Stripped Bare by her Bachelors, Even* (New York, 1972)

J. Clair: *Marcel Duchamp ou le grand fictif: Essai de mythanalyse du Grand Verre* (Paris, 1975)

L. D. Steefel: *The Position of Duchamp's Glass in the Development of his Art* (New York, 1977)

C. E. Adcock: *Marcel Duchamp's Notes from the Large Glass: An N-Dimensional Analysis* (Ann Arbor and Epping, 1983)

FRANCIS M. NAUMANN

Duchamp-Villon [Duchamp], **(Pierre-Maurice-)Raymond** (*b* Damville, Eure, 5 Nov 1876; *d* Cannes, 7 Oct 1918). French sculptor and draughtsman. The second son of a Normandy notary, he played a central role in the development of modern aesthetics, as did his elder brother JACQUES VILLON and his younger brother MARCEL DUCHAMP. He came from an educated family and was an assiduous student at secondary school in Rouen; in 1894 he registered at the Faculté de Médecine in Paris, where he attended classes for several years. Rheumatic fever forced him to break off his studies in 1898 just before completion and left him immobilized for a considerable length of time; this unforeseen event altered the whole course of his life. During this period of enforced leisure (1899–1900), he modelled small statuettes (of subjects such as familiar animals and female figures), discovering his true vocation as a sculptor. He was essentially self-taught and rapidly attained a high level of mastery and maturity. He settled in Paris *c*. 1901 and changed his name to Duchamp-Villon at his father's insistence. As early as 1902 he exhibited a portrait of his future wife (whom he married in 1903) in the Société Nationale, and he exhibited works regularly at the Salon d'Automne from its foundation in 1903. In 1905 he held his first private exhibition with Jacques Villon in the Galerie Legrip, Rouen.

Although the influence of Rodin is noticeable in Duchamp-Villon's decision to detach the face only partly from the block of marble in *Woman Reading* (1905), the verisimilitude of the image reveals his sensitivity and talent for capturing likenesses. His first successful study of the body in movement is the *Football Players* (1906; Rouen, Mus. B.-A.), which groups three figures in a composition ascending towards the ball. He also produced several studies of a woman startled by a cock perching on her shoulder; these resulted in the powerful bronze *Torso of a Woman* (h. *c*. 1.3 m, 1907; Paris, Pompidou), in which the imposing size accentuated the vigorous musculature. The expressive realism of both sculptures is in the tradition of Rodin's work, but in the bust of a sick old man, entitled *Aesop* (plaster, h. *c*. 1.83 m, 1906; untraced; wax study, h. 76.2 mm, Paris, Jacques Bon priv. col., see 1967 exh. cat., p. 31), and in the bronze portraits of his sisters *Yvonne* (1908; Paris, Mme Duvernoy priv. col., see 1967 exh. cat., p. 39) and *Madeleine* (1908/9; priv. col., see 1976 exh. cat., p. 34) Duchamp-Villon explored a wider range of influences.

In 1906 Duchamp-Villon moved to a house in a garden he shared with Jacques Villon and Kupka in Puteaux, on the site now occupied by the Défense district, where he built himself a studio. In 1908 he sculpted *Dream, Seated Girl* (bronze; Los Angeles, Niels Onstad priv. col., see 1967 exh. cat., p. 43) and *Song* (wood version, Chicago, IL, A. Inst.). From this time onwards he sought a harmonious equilibrium of rounded forms in his female nudes, using modelling as a means of smoothly directing the light. During 1910 a transition occurred between Duchamp-Villon's early style—still traditional, yet already showing personal qualities—and his exploration of the new possibilities brought to sculpture by Cubism. His preoccupation with treating the geometrization of forms first appeared in the plaster group entitled *Pastoral* (1910; Paris, Pompidou; also known as *Adam and Eve*) and in the bronze *Torso of a Young Man* (1910; Paris, Pompidou; also known as *The Athlete*), based on the figure of Adam. Duchamp-Villon's admiration for ancient Greek sculpture, together with the lessons of Cubism, led him to accentuate the ridges and unify the planes of this slender and well-muscled frame. A *Decorative Basin* (1911; Williamstown, MA, Williams Coll. Mus. A.), executed in stone, dates from this period. The impressive bronze *Head of Baudelaire* (1911; Paris, Pompidou) was intended for a monument

to the poet; by way of several studies and a large drawing, Duchamp-Villon stripped away all ornament to arrive at an extremely lifelike composition. Jacques Villon recalled that his brother was very familiar with the statues of Chartres Cathedral. Duchamp-Villon went further in *Maggy* (1912; New York, Guggenheim), a portrait of the wife of the poet Georges Ribemont-Dessaignes in which, while remaining faithful to the model, he interpreted her features freely.

Duchamp-Villon took a leading role in the gatherings in his and Jacques Villon's Puteaux studios attended by Gleizes, Metzinger, La Fresnaye, Le Fauconnier and Léger (*see* PUTEAUX GROUP). It was thanks to Duchamp-Villon, since he was in charge of hanging the works in the 1911 Salon d'Automne, that their works were hung together in the same hall. They later took part in the Section d'or (*see* SECTION D'OR (ii)) group exhibition held in October 1912 in the Galerie La Boétie, Paris. At the same time Duchamp-Villon wanted to renovate architectural decoration on similar principles. He designed, constructed and sculpted the façade of the *Maison Cubiste* (untraced, see 1967 exh. cat., pp. 64, 67–8) in plaster for his friend the artist André Mare (*b* 1885). The presentation of this work at the Salon d'Automne in 1912 created a stir that reached as far as the Chamber of Deputies.

Duchamp-Villon began to produce work at a greater rate, sculpting a plaster bas-relief entitled *Lovers* (1913; New York, MOMA; lead version, London, Tate) and participating in André Mare's 'boudoir' (1913 Salon d'Automne) with four large bronze medallions, *The Cat, The Dog, The Doves* and *The Parrot* (all priv. col., see 1976 exh. cat., p. 43), which alternated with paintings by Marie Laurencin and La Fresnaye. Through Walter Pach, the American art critic, Duchamp-Villon took part in the New York Armory Show (1913), where he sold several pieces, to John Quinn in particular. He also exhibited in the Manès Gallery in Prague in February 1914 and in the Der Sturm Gallery in Berlin in July 1914 and held a private exhibition in the Galerie Groult in Paris.

While working on the bronze *Seated Woman* (1914; New Haven, CT, Yale U., A.G.), Duchamp-Villon produced a number of sketches and studies depicting riders, culminating in the plaster maquette *Horse* (h. 440 mm; 1914), which was unfinished when World War I broke out and which Duchamp-Villon completed while on leave. An enlargement was cast in bronze *c*. 1930–31 under the supervision of Jacques Villon as *Grand Cheval* (also called *Horse*, h. 1.02 m; New York, MOMA; see fig.), and a further enlargement was cast in 1966 under the supervision of Marcel Duchamp as *Cheval Majeur* (h. 1.5 m). As an expression of the invasion of modern life by mechanization, it has a plastic energy and dynamic equilibrium that make it one of the masterpieces of 20th-century sculpture.

Duchamp-Villon volunteered as an auxiliary doctor and was sent to the Champagne front in 1915, where he contracted fatal septicaemia. While he was able to, he continued to sculpt and realized the large coloured plaster medallion *French Cockerel* (1916; priv. col., see 1976 exh. cat., p. 52), to decorate an army theatre. He also executed a remarkable portrait head of *Professeur Gosset* (version, 1918; Buffalo, NY, Albright-Knox A.G.), who attended to him at Châlons in 1917, in which the subject is treated

Raymond Duchamp-Villon: *Horse*, bronze, h. 1.02 m, 1914, cast *c.* 1930–31 (New York, Museum of Modern Art)

in terms of almost completely abstract sculptural masses. He envisaged a new version of the *Horse*, of which he executed only the head (*Head of Horse*, bronze, 1914; Paris, Pompidou), modifying its design in numerous small sketches until his death. Despite his early death, his ten years of creativity produced some of the greatest works of Cubist sculpture.

BIBLIOGRAPHY

W. Pach: *Raymond Duchamp-Villon: Sculpteur, 1876–1918* (Paris, 1924)

Sculptures de Duchamp-Villon (exh. cat., intro. A. Salmon; Paris, Gal. Pierre, 1931)

B. Dorival: 'Raymond Duchamp-Villon au Musée d'Art Moderne', *Mus. France*, 3 (1949), pp. 64–8

J. Villon: 'Duchamp-Villon', *Les Sculpteurs célèbres*, ed. P. Francastel (Paris, 1954), pp. 306–7

M. N. Pradel: 'Dessins de Duchamp-Villon', *Rev. des A.*, 4–5 (1960), pp. 221–4

——: 'La Maison Cubiste en 1912', *A. Fr.*, 1 (1960), pp. 176–86

——: *Raymond Duchamp-Villon: La Vie et l'oeuvre* (diss., Paris, Ecole Louvre, 1960)

Le Cheval majeur (exh. cat. by J. Cassou and R. V. Gindertaël, Paris, Gal. Louis Carré & Cie, 1966)

Duchamp-Villon (exh. cat., notes W. C. Agee, intro. G. H. Hamilton; New York, Knoedler's, 1967) [incl. bibliog. and list of writings]

P. Cabanne: *Les Trois Duchamp: Jacques Villon, Raymond Duchamp-Villon, Marcel Duchamp* (Paris, 1975); Eng. trans. as *The Brothers Duchamp* (New York, 1976)

Raymond Duchamp-Villon (exh. cat. by O. Popovitch, Rouen, Mus. B.-A., 1976)

J. Zilczer: 'Raymond Duchamp-Villon: Pioneer of Modern Sculpture', *Bull. Philadelphia Mus. A.*, lxxvi/330 (1980), pp. 2–24

MARIE-NOELLE DE GRANDRY-PRADEL

Duchange, Gaspard (*b* Paris, April 1662; *d* Paris, 6 Jan 1757). French printmaker, print-seller and print publisher. He was a pupil of Guillaume Vallet (1632–1704). He was appointed Graveur du Roi and accepted (*agréé*) by the Académie Royale in 1704; he was received (*reçu*) in 1707 with his portraits, both after Hyacinthe Rigaud, of *Charles de La Fosse* (Roux, no. 10) and *François Girardon* (R 9). He enjoyed a considerable reputation: according to Claude-Henri Watelet he was one of the printmakers who were able to produce the softest effects in engraving and who knew how best to suggest the velvety texture of a woman's skin; in this domain he was often imitated but never equalled. His reproductions of Corregio's *Io* (R 8), *Leda* (R 16) and *Danaë* (R 33) are among the most celebrated of his works, which are not numerous; only 58 have been identified, probably owing to his activities as a print publisher. He distributed works by Laurent Cars and his family, by Jacques-Philippe Lebas and by the Audran family. He also collaborated with Jean-Marc Nattier in executing and publishing reproductions after Peter Paul Rubens for the *Galerie du Luxembourg* (R 11–15), a compilation for which he himself engraved some plates. He also made several plates for *La Galerie du Président Lambert* and for the *Coronation of Louis XV* (1728; R 38–41), after Nicolas Dulin, and studies (1722) of parts of Raphael's cartoons of the *Acts of the Apostles* (London, Hampton Court, Royal Col.).

Besides portraits, which included a notable engraving of a *Self-portrait* by Antoine Coypel (R 3), Duchange made large-scale engravings of sacred subjects. They included *Christ Driving the Money-changers from the Temple* (R 6), *Christ at Supper with Simon the Pharisee* (R 7) and the *Raising of the Widow's Son of Nain* (R 50), all after Jean Jouvenet, and the *Death of Dido* (R 26), *Tobias Restoring his Father's Sight* (R 20), *Jephthah Sacrificing his Daughter* (R 19) and *St Cecilia* (R 22), all after Antoine Coypel. Duchange is said to have still been at work at the age of 91; he was often consulted as an expert when inventories were drawn up on the deaths of his colleagues.

BIBLIOGRAPHY

M. Roux: *Inventaire du fonds français: Graveurs du dix-huitième siècle*, Paris, Bib. N., Cab. Est. cat., vii (Paris, 1951), pp. 375–95 [R]

French Royal Academy of Painting and Sculpture: Engraved Reception Pieces, 1672–1789 (exh. cat. by W. McAllister Johnson, Kingston, Ont., Queen's U., Agnes Etherington A. Cent.; Montreal, Mus. F.A.; London, U. W. Ont., McIntosh A.G.; and elsewhere; 1982–3), cat. nos 24, 25

M. Préaud, P. Casselle, M. Grivel and C. Le Bitouzé: *Dictionnaire des éditeurs d'estampes à Paris sous l'Ancien Régime* (Paris, 1987), pp. 111–12

VÉRONIQUE MEYER

Duché, Andrew (*b* Philadelphia, *c.* 1710; *d* Philadelphia, 1778). American potter and trader. The son of the stoneware potter Anthony Duché (*fl* Philadelphia, 1700–62), he claimed to be the first person in the West to make porcelain, but he produced only a few curiosities in the late 1730s, described by others as being translucent. No pieces have been positively attributed to him. Before 1735 he settled in South Carolina and from 1736 was in Savannah, GA, where he had a small pottery. He tried for several years to obtain financial backing from the colonial trustees in London but failed to provide enough evidence of his success. Between 1744 and 1769 he was principally occupied in trading with the Native Americans in South Carolina and, later, in Virginia. He returned to Philadelphia in 1769.

BIBLIOGRAPHY

G. Hood: 'The Career of Andrew Duché', *A.Q.*, xxxi (1968), pp. 168–84

ELLEN PAUL DENKER

Duchesne, Jean (*b* Versailles, 28/29 Dec 1779; *d* Paris, 4 March 1855). French museum curator and writer. The financial ruin brought upon his family by the Revolution made his appointment as a junior assistant in the Cabinet des Estampes of the Bibliothèque Nationale in 1795 especially welcome. He rose steadily to become Assistant Curator (1832) and Curator in Chief (1839) and was a member of such erudite societies as the Société de l'Histoire de France. At the Cabinet des Estampes he made a number of important innovations, establishing classification by subject-matter, drawing up a new catalogue and, in 1807, organizing a permanent exhibition of prints for educational purposes. During the Revolution and the First Empire the collection was increased tenfold by the acquisition of the prints and illustrated books held in Versailles, the Trianon and the royal palaces and also by selected works from churches and monasteries that had become national property. In 1824 and 1834 he made a study of the private and public print collections in England, and Holland and Germany respectively. This resulted in *Voyages d'un iconophile* (Paris, 1834), a critical description of the prints and of the important architectural sights. Duchesne wrote prolifically, the most monumental of his publications being *Musée de peinture et de sculpture* (1828–33), which consisted of 16 volumes covering all the major art works in Europe, illustrated with engravings and providing well-ordered information on a then largely unexplored subject.

WRITINGS
Musée français, recueil des plus beaux tableaux, statues et bas-reliefs qui existaient au Louvre avant 1815, 4 vols (Paris, 1815)
Musée de peinture et de sculpture, ou recueil des principaux tableaux, statues et bas-reliefs des collections publiques et particulières de l'Europe, 16 vols (Paris, 1828–33)

BIBLIOGRAPHY
DBF
A. Bonnardot: *Lettre au bibliophile Jacob, rédacteur du bulletin des arts sur le Cabinet des Estampes et l'excellente administration de M. Duchesne aîné* (Paris, 1848) [with a description of Duchesne's cataloguing and classification systems]

Duchesne, Nicolas (*d* Paris, 1628). French painter. He enjoyed an extended period of royal patronage during the reigns of Henry IV of France and the regent Marie de' Medici. In 1599 he was 'valet de chambre et peintre du roi', and in 1621, at the baptism of his son, he still retained this title. In 1619 Duchesne received payment for 22 paintings of fountains, grottoes and other decorations he had made for the *Ballet de la Reyne*. His most important work, however, commissioned on 15 April 1621, was the decoration of the Grande Salle and Galerie of the newly built Palais du Luxembourg in Paris for Marie de' Medici. Shortly afterwards he was named 'Premier peintre de la reine'. Under his supervision in 1621–2 two then unknown young artists, Nicolas Poussin and Philippe de Champaigne, worked at the palace. Champaigne later married Duchesne's daughter and, on Duchesne's death early in 1628, succeeded him as painter to Marie de' Medici.

Only a few fragments of the original interior decoration remain at the Palais du Luxembourg. In the Salle du Livre d'Or a series of eight paintings with figures have, despite their Flemish character, been attributed to Duchesne and as such would represent his only known surviving works. The strong influence of 16th-century Flemish painting is evident in the works of other little-known Parisian painters of Duchesne's generation, such as Jean Rabel (*d* 1603) and Nicolas Moillon (*d* 1619). In 1621 Duchesne was in Italy at Cardinal Richelieu's request to copy a painting of

the Virgin by Caravaggio. The copy is now lost but probably formed a link in the introduction of the Italian's revolutionary style into France.

BIBLIOGRAPHY
Le Comte de Laborde: *La Renaissance des arts*, i (Paris, 1850), p. 326
Nouv. Archvs A. Fr., n. s. 2, i (1872), pp. 60, 223; n. s. 3, ii (1885), pp. 113–15; n. s. 3, viii (1892), p. 187

THOMAS NICHOLS

Ducis, (Jean-)Louis (*b* Versailles, 14 July 1775; *d* Paris, 3 March 1847). French painter. Around 1795 he entered the studio of Jacques-Louis David, where he was a member of the group of artists from southern France known as the 'parti aristocratique' (Pierre Révoil, Fleury Richard, Comte Auguste de Forbin and François-Marius Granet), who were among the first to paint small-scale pictures of French history. Ducis remained a friend of Granet throughout his life (e.g. *Portrait of Mme Granet*, Aix-en-Provence, Mus. Granet). He exhibited regularly in the Salon between 1804 and 1838, winning a medal for history painting in 1808. He rapidly acquired a considerable reputation with scenes of sentimental mythology such as *Orpheus and Eurydice* (exh. Salon 1808; untraced), in part due to his links with the poet Jean-François Ducis (his uncle) and with his brother-in-law, the actor François Joseph Talma. (He exhibited *Talma's Débuts* (Paris, Mus. Comédie-Française) at the Salon of 1831.) Josephine and her daughter Hortense were among his patrons; at Malmaison the Empress owned four portraits by Ducis of children, probably the two youngest sons of Hortense and the elder daughters of her son, Eugène Beauharnais (untraced). For Napoleon Ducis executed a stiff composition, halfway between a group portrait and a history painting, *Napoleon and his Family at Saint-Cloud* (exh. Salon 1810; Versailles, Château). In 1811 he stayed in Naples, where he painted portraits of the royal family.

Ducis was still in favour during the Restoration. In 1814, in a letter to the Minister of the Maison du Roi listing the names of artists worthy of the King's attention (Paris, Archv. N., O³ 1389), the Director of Museums cited Ducis as an 'educated man of refined taste'. During the same period Ducis was entrusted with the restoration of the ceiling paintings in the apartments of Louis XIV in the château of Versailles. He received a commission from the Maison du Roi, *Louis XVIII Watching the Return of Troops from Spain from the Balcony of the Tuileries* (exh. Salon 1824; Versailles, Château), a history painting composed like a genre scene, the figures shown from behind and against the light, their costumes and accessories rendered with the detailed precision of a goldsmith. He also executed a portrait of *Charles X* (Cambrai, Mus. Mun.).

Ducis owed his fame to his TROUBADOUR STYLE paintings. These small, technically brilliant paintings were popular with the public and were frequently reproduced on porcelain. Far from being an erudite painter like most of the Troubadour artists, he knew how to please his public with easily read anecdotes, and he did not hesitate to repeat his most successful compositions. This was the case with the *Arts under the Empire of Love*, in which Poetry, Sculpture, Painting and Music were represented allegorically by four pairs of lovers, who evoked the artistic life of former times. In the Salon of 1814 he exhibited

Tasso Reading his Verses to Eleonora d'Este, which was acquired by Queen Hortense, who had already bought *Tasso in the House of his Sister Cornelia in Sorrento* (exh. Salon 1812; both Arenenberg, Napoleonmus.). To this composition symbolizing Poetry he added *Properzia de' Rossi and her Last Bas-relief* (Sculpture), *Van Dyck Painting his First Picture* (Painting) and *Mary Stuart Making Music with David Rizzio* (Music). The series (exh. Salon 1822; Limoges, Mus. Mun.) was bought by the Maison du Roi. Ducis repeated it for the Duchesse de Berry (untraced). This 'poem in four cantos', as it was called by the critics, propounded the idea of 'chivalry' in a mythical era of love, poetry and reverie, when Woman was seen as the protectress of the arts and the instigator of noble actions by men.

Throughout his career Ducis displayed a constant preoccupation with costume and picturesque detail, seen, for example, in *Flight of Bianca Capello* (exh. Salon 1824; Cherbourg, Mus. Henry). His Troubadour paintings lacked the archaeological purpose that was so important to Richard and Révoil but prefigured the sparkling and colourful works of Richard Parkes Bonington and Eugène Devéria. The decline of Troubadour painting began in 1824, and henceforth the critics, while they continued to appreciate the freshness of colouring and the delicacy of Ducis's work, stressed that the public were tiring of his repetition of the same characters and costumes. In 1831, when his career was in decline, Ducis became Director of the Ecole de Dessin in Cambrai. He was made Chevalier of the Légion d'honneur in 1832.

BIBLIOGRAPHY

E. J. Delécluze: *Louis David: Son école et son temps* (Paris, 1855), pp. 49–52

C. de Beaumont: 'Jean-Louis Ducis, peintre (1775–1847)', *Réun. Soc. B.-A. Dépts*, xxiv (1900), pp. 520–47

M.-C. Chaudonneret: *Fleury Richard et Pierre Révoil: La Peinture troubadour* (Paris, 1980), pp. 43–4

MARIE-CLAUDE CHAUDONNERET

Duck [Duyck], Jacob (*b* ?Utrecht, *c.* 1600; *d* Utrecht, *bur* 28 Jan 1667). Dutch painter and etcher. He was long confused with Jan le Ducq (1629/30–76). In 1621 he was listed as an apprentice portrait painter in the records of the Utrecht Guild of St Luke. His teacher was probably Joost Cornelisz. Droochsloot (1586–1666). The St Job's Hospital in Utrecht acquired a *Musical Company* by him in 1629. By 1630–32 he was a master in the guild. Like Pieter Codde, he painted guardroom scenes (*kortegaerdjes*), for example *Soldiers Arming Themselves* (*c.* 1635; New York, H. Shickman Gal., see 1984 exh. cat., no. 36) or the *Hoard of Booty* (Paris, Louvre), in which the figures and their interactions are apparently full of underlying symbolic meaning. He also painted merry companies (e.g. *c.* 1630; Nîmes, Mus. B.-A.) and domestic activities, such as *Woman Ironing* (Utrecht, Cent. Mus.), employing motifs perhaps symbolic of domestic virtue. He placed his figures in high, bare interiors in which the deep local colours of the foreground stand out well against the cool, greyish-brown background. Only a few of his etchings are known (Hollstein, *Dut. & Flem.*, vi, pp. 9–11), depicting figures in contemporary dress, for example *Young Gentleman with Broad Hat and Cloak* (Hollstein, no. 10) or *Virgin and Child with Magi* (nos 1–4). Between 1631 and 1649 Duck's

presence is documented in Utrecht, Haarlem and Wijk bij Duurstede. Afterwards, and probably by 1656, he was living in The Hague. He was buried at the monastery of St Mary Magdalene in Utrecht.

BIBLIOGRAPHY

Hollstein: *Dut. & Flem.*; Thieme–Becker; Wurzbach

F. Würtenberger: *Das holländische Gesellschaftsbild* (Schramberg im Schwarzwald, 1937), p. 65

S. Béguin: 'Pieter Codde et Jacob Duck', *Oud-Holland*, lxvii (1952), pp. 112–16

E. Plietzsch: 'Randbemerkungen zur holländischen Interieurmalerei am Beginn des 17. Jahrhunderts', *Wallraf-Richartz-Jb.*, xviii (1956), pp. 174–86

J. A. Welu: '*Cardplayers and Merrymakers*: A Moral Lesson', *Worcester A. Mus. Bull.*, iv (1975), pp. 8–16

Tot lering en vermaak: Betekenissen van Hollandse genrevorstellingen uit de zeventiende eeuw [To instruct and delight: meanings of Dutch genre painting in the 17th century] (exh. cat., ed. E. de Jongh; Amsterdam, Rijksmus., 1976), nos 18–19

H. Miedema: *De archiefbescheiden van het St Lukasgilde te Haarlem* [Archival documents from the St Lukasgilde in Haarlem], 2 vols (Alphen aan den Rijn, 1980), ii, p. 159

Masters of Seventeenth-century Dutch Genre Painting (exh. cat., ed. P. C. Sutton; Philadelphia, PA, Mus. A.; W. Berlin, Gemäldegal.; London, RA; 1984), nos 36–8

AGNES GROOT

Dücker, Eugen [Dyukker, Yevgeny (Eduardovich)] (*b* Kuresaare, Saaremaa Island, 10 Feb 1841; *d* Düsseldorf, 6 Dec 1916). Estonian painter. His first teacher was Friedrich Stern (1812–89) in Arensburg, and he subsequently studied at the St Petersburg Academy of Arts under Sokrat Vorob'yov (1827–88). In 1862 he was awarded a gold medal for *Oak Trees near Reval* (Moscow, Tret'yakov Gal.), in which the academic tradition of landscape painting initiated by 17th-century Dutch artists is closely interwoven with techniques used by members of the WANDERERS. In 1863–9 Dücker travelled around Europe visiting Germany, Holland, Belgium and France; he continued to work intensively and was influenced by the Düsseldorf school. He was based in Germany from 1864, but he maintained links with both Estonia and Russia. In 1873 he was appointed a professor in St Petersburg and a year later in Düsseldorf, at the Kunstakademie. He completed commissions from Estonia and exhibited in St Petersburg. In paintings such as *Sea Shore* (1875) and *On the Pärnu River* (1879; both Tallinn, A. Mus. Estonia) Dücker created accurate representations using fluid brushstrokes. In *After the Rain* (1886; Tartu, Mus. A.) he became concerned for the first time with the portrayal of light, thus drawing close to the ideas of the BARBIZON SCHOOL. His influence on a whole generation of Estonian artists was considerable.

BIBLIOGRAPHY

E. Dyukker, 1841–1916 (exh. cat., Tallinn, A. Mus., 1954)

Die Düsseldorfer Malerschule (exh. cat., ed. D. Graf; Düsseldorf, Kstmus., 1979)

Düsseldorfi koolkond eesti kunstis [The Düsseldorf school in Estonian art] (exh. cat., Tallinn, A. Mus., 1980)

SERGEY KUZNETSOV

Duclos, Antoine-Jean (*b* Paris, 1742; *d* Paris, 30 Oct 1795). French engraver and etcher. He was a pupil of Augustin de Saint-Aubin, whose drawings he often reproduced. Duclos was a typical practitioner of the small-scale engraving that was in vogue in France in the second half of the 18th century. His dry, precise style was particularly suited to the execution of vignettes, and so most of his work was devoted to illustration. He was a skilled etcher who prepared numerous plates, to be finished by other engravers, after drawings by Charles-Nicolas Cochin, II, Jean-Michel Moreau, Charles Eisen, Gravelot and Clément-Pierre Marillier. He also executed some larger-scale engravings, the best known of which are the *Concert* (Roux, no. 90) and the *Dress Ball* (R 100) after Saint-Aubin; both were made in 1774. His book illustrations include those for the *Almanach iconologique* (Paris, 1774–81; R 13–28), the works of Jean-Jacques Rousseau (Paris, 1774–83; R 116–19) and the *Monument du costume* (Paris, 1777–83; R 150–52).

BIBLIOGRAPHY

H. Cohen: *Guide de l'amateur de livres à gravures du XVIIIe siècle* (Paris, 1912)
L'Oeuvre gravé de A. J. Duclos (Paris, 1939)
M. Roux: *Inventaire du fonds français: Graveurs du dix-huitième siècle*, Paris, Bib. N., Cab. Est. cat., vii (Paris, 1951), pp. 399–489 [R]

MADELEINE BARBIN

Ducreux, Joseph (*b* Nancy, 26 June 1735; *d* Paris, 24 July 1802). French painter, pastellist and engraver. He lived in Paris from 1760 and from 1762 kept a list of his works. Among the portraits he completed in his early years were those in pastel of the well-known connoisseurs *Pierre-Jean Mariette*, the *Comte de Caylus* and *Ange-Laurent de la Live de July* (all untraced), which apparently were copies after Maurice-Quentin de La Tour. Ducreux has traditionally been seen as de La Tour's favourite pupil, while Jean-Baptiste Greuze is supposed to have initiated him into oil painting. From his age, it can be assumed that by the time Ducreux reached Paris he had already acquired a grounding in his art.

In 1769 Ducreux was selected to paint Louis XVI's future wife, Marie-Antoinette, in Vienna. The official portrait he made (untraced) survives only in the engraving (1771) by Charles Eugène Duponchel (1748–80). Two surviving portraits of the future queen (both priv. col.) are conventional and not very expressive. Ducreux spent two years at the Austrian court. While there he also received a commission to paint the portrait of *Emperor Joseph II* (*c.* 1769; untraced; engr. 1793 by Louis-Jacques Cathelin, 1739–1804) and became a member of the Vienna Kunstakademie. Then he returned to Paris, where Marie-Antoinette's patronage ensured him work at the court. He painted portraits of the sisters of Louis XVI (all untraced) and received many commissions from the nobility. Only rarely did Ducreux go beyond conventional patterns in expression and pose. To some degree his pastels, for example the portrait of the poet *Jacques Delille* (priv. col.) or that of *Gen. Pierre Choderlos de Laclos* (Versailles, Château), have the same quality of an unfinished drawing that characterizes those of de La Tour.

Ducreux's portrait of the *Abbesse Louise Claude de Bourbon Busset* (1779; Lignières, Château Ussé) is one of his best works of this period. In 1783 Ducreux, who was never a member of the Académie Royale (and so could not exhibit in the official Salons), exhibited some of his works in a 'counter-exhibition', the Salon de la Correspondance, and presented a portrait of the founder of that institution, *M. Pahin de la Blanchérie* (untraced). He also

Joseph Ducreux: *Self-portrait* (Paris, Musée Jacquemart-André)

exhibited a portrait of the singer *Marie Fel* (untraced), de La Tour's long-time companion, and one of *Benjamin Franklin* (untraced), as well as a *Self-portrait, Smiling* (Paris, Louvre). Like de La Tour, Ducreux regularly painted self-portraits. One of them (Paris, Mus. Jacquemart-André; see fig.) closely follows the pattern of de La Tour's *Self-portrait* now in the Musée de Picardie, Amiens. Ducreux attached special artistic importance to his self-portraits; in 1791 in London, where he fled during the Revolution, he engraved and published three of them.

Not a success in London, Ducreux returned in 1793 to Paris, where he exhibited work at the Salon, then open to all artists. His association with Jacques-Louis David made it easier for him to continue an official career. In the 1790s he produced a portrait drawing of *Louis XVI* (untraced) and the expressive portrait of *Robespierre* (priv. col.). In his last years the former Hôtel d'Angiviller, where Ducreux lived from 1797, became a focal point for lovers of art and music. Works he produced during this period include the sympathetic pastel portrait of the composer *Melhul* (Paris, Louvre).

BIBLIOGRAPHY

Thieme–Becker
P. Dorbec: 'Joseph Ducreux', *Gaz. B.-A.*, n. s. 2, xxxvi (1906), pp. 199–216
R. Crozet: 'Un Pastel inédit de Joseph Ducreux', *Rev. A.* [Paris], vi (1956), pp. 117–18
G. Lyon: *Joseph Ducreux (1735–1802), Premier Peintre de Marie Antoinette: Sa vie et son oeuvre* (Paris, 1958)

CATHRIN KLINGSÖHR-LE ROY

Ducros, (Abraham-)Louis(-Rodolphe) (*b* Moudon, Switzerland, 21 July 1748; *d* Lausanne, 18 Feb 1810). Swiss painter. From 1769 to 1771 he studied in Geneva at the private academy of Nicolas Henri Joseph Fassin. After a journey to Flanders he returned to Geneva, where he sketched and painted in watercolours in the countryside and became fascinated by the analysis and recording of natural phenomena. In 1776 he travelled to Rome and in 1778 found employment as a specialist in topographical landscapes with Nicolas ten Hove, a Dutch antiquary who was embarking on a journey through southern Italy, Sicily and Malta. Among the watercolour drawings that Ducros produced on that expedition are the *Temple of Hercules at Agrigento* (Amsterdam, Rijksmus.) and a *View of the Harbour at Pozzuoli near Naples* (U. Manchester, Whitworth A.G.). On his return to Rome in 1779 he established a business with the engraver Giovanni Battista Volpato, producing large quantities of souvenir views of Rome for tourists. A work of that period is the watercolour *Temple of Peace* (1779; New Haven, CT, Yale Cent. Brit. A.). In the following year Ducros and Volpato published their first series of prints, *Vues de Rome et de ses environs* (Rome, 1780). Their collaboration continued until 1789, but by 1782 Ducros was beginning to take on commissions for his own paintings. His first important commissions were for oil paintings, such as those commemorating the visit to Italy in 1782 of Grand Duke Paul Romanov: the *Grand Duke Paul and the Grand Duchess Maria at Tivoli* and the *Grand Duke Paul and his Suite at the Forum* (both St Petersburg, Peter & Paul Fortress). In 1782 Ducros painted *Pius VI Visiting the Drainage Works at the Pontine Marshes* (St Petersburg, Peter & Paul Fortress) and in 1786 produced another version of the same event (Rome, Pal. Braschi). By 1783 he had probably already begun to paint the large-scale watercolours that made his name. In 1786 he met Sir Richard Colt Hoare, who became his most important patron and bought 13 landscapes between 1786 and 1793. These included *View at Tivoli* and the *Arch of Constantine* (both Stourhead, Wilts, NT). In 1793 Ducros left Rome for Naples and in 1800 travelled to Malta, where he painted a series of large views of Valletta (e.g. *View of Grand Harbour, Valletta*, Lausanne, Pal. Rumine; version, Valletta, N. Mus.). In 1807 he returned to Switzerland.

Ducros belonged to the generation of foreign painters working in Italy who broke with the traditions of the Italian *vedutisti*. His style was developed from that of Giovanni Paolo Panini, Giovanni Battista Piranesi and Hubert Robert. His work influenced the younger generation of British watercolour artists, in particular J. M. W. Turner, who knew Hoare's collection of watercolours.

BIBLIOGRAPHY

Images of the Grand Tour: Louis Ducros, 1748–1810 (exh. cat., ed. P. Chessex; London, Kenwood House; U. Manchester, Whitworth A.G.; Lausanne, Pal. Rumine; 1985–6) [with complete bibliog.]

Reisjournaal in aquarel: De Zwitserse tekenaar Louis Ducros vergezelt Hollandse toeristen in Italie in 1778 [A tour in words and watercolour: the Swiss artist Louis Ducros accompanies Dutch tourists in Italy in 1778] (exh. cat., ed. J. W. Niemeijer; Amsterdam, Rijksmus., 1986)

□

Dudgeon, Philip Maurice (*b* Dublin, 1852; *d* Bath, 13 Jan 1891). Irish architect, active in South Africa. He was articled to the firm of Lanyon, Lynn and Lanyon of Dublin and Belfast at the age of 15, serving an apprenticeship for 5 years. The firm was dissolved in 1872 and Dudgeon joined William Henry Lynn as manager and chief assistant. He left towards the end of 1875, travelled for 12 months and arrived in Durban in January 1877. Only 6 of the 44 buildings designed or altered by him are extant. They encompass a variety of building types and styles. The major source of inspiration for the Standard Bank (1878–83) in Pietermaritzburg was Charles Lanyon's Head Office of the Northern Bank (1851–2) in Belfast. The potential of the salmon-pink Pietermaritzburg brick is fully exploited in a stripped classical building with a central portico *in antis*.

Dudgeon won the competition for Durban Town Hall (1882–5). The building comprises a hexastyle Corinthian portico with flanking wings and a tower rising behind it. Although it was based on British prototypes, Dudgeon made concessions to the climate in the large size and convenience of areas, in the attention paid to ventilation and in the loggia protecting the north façade from the sun. For Maritzburg College (1885–8) Dudgeon chose a Collegiate Gothic vocabulary: the façade consists of a central block flanked by wings, a band of black bricks linking the elements and separating the ground floor from the upper storey. By the prolongation of the wings he formed a finely-proportioned quadrangle with a generous verandah to the rear. In contrast to these symmetrical buildings Dudgeon's domestic architecture reflects a free-flowing asymmetry and an inventive and picturesque use of the characteristic Natal verandah. Despite his sound knowledge of the various styles that he selected for different building types, he remained above all a classicist. He was a skilful planner who showed great interest in materials, ventilation, acoustics and lighting. He produced pioneering work, designing the first major bank buildings, hotels, educational institutions and hospitals in Natal. For many years different aspects of his design for Durban Town Hall were mirrored in town halls throughout South Africa. In 1884 Dudgeon was elected a Fellow of the RIBA, and in 1887 he left Natal for Bath, where he married but did not practise as an architect.

BIBLIOGRAPHY

M. Martin: *Philip Maurice Dudgeon, Architect: His Work in Natal during the Period 1877–1888* (diss., Johannesburg, U. Witwatersrand, 1980)

——: 'Philip Maurice Dudgeon: Some of his Work in Natal', *De arte*, 33 (1985), pp. 34–41

MARILYN MARTIN

Dudley. English family of patrons.

(1) John Dudley, 1st Duke of Northumberland (*b* ?1502; *d* London, 22 Aug 1553). As one of the executors of Henry VIII's will, he was made a member of the council under Edward Seymour, 1st Duke of Somerset, which effectively ruled England during the minority of Edward VI. In 1549 he achieved supreme political power and was elevated to a dukedom two years later, but in 1553 he overreached himself with his proclamation of Lady Jane Grey, his daughter-in-law, as queen. This bold move quickly collapsed and resulted in his execution.

Dudley shared his interest in architecture with the intellectual circle at the centre of events during the minority. He had his principal seat, Dudley Castle, Staffs, remodelled in a manner reminiscent of Sir William Sharington's work at Lacock Abbey, Wilts, and he patronized such craftsmen as John Chapman, who did much of the carving at Lacock and was subsequently to work for Sir John Thynne at Longleat House, Wilts. Dudley's most significant act of patronage was to send John Shute, a member of his household, to Italy in 1550. Shute was to examine surviving monuments but also 'to confer with the doings of ye skilful maisters in architectur'. He returned before Dudley's downfall, and his *The First and Chief Groundes of Architecture* (1563), the first book on the Classical orders written by an Englishman, is of seminal importance and remains a testament to Dudley's architectural sensibility.

BIBLIOGRAPHY

DNB

W. E. Clark-Maxwell: 'Sir William Sharington's Work at Lacock, Sudeley and Dudley', *Archaeol. J.*, lxx (1913), pp. 175–82

MALCOLM AIRS

(2) Robert Dudley, 1st Earl of Leicester (*b* 24 June 1532 or 1533; *d* Cornbury, Oxon, 4 Sept 1588). Son of (1) John Dudley. Despite his father's execution in 1553, the family was fully restored to royal favour at the accession of Elizabeth I in 1558, and he was created Earl of Leicester in 1564. His loyalty to the Queen and his bid to marry her led to the lavish patronage of visual spectacles, from the first tournament he fought before her in 1559 to the entertainment he mounted at Kenilworth Castle, Warwicks, in 1575. His political power culminated in 1586, when he was made Governor-General of the United Provinces of the northern Netherlands; this occasioned the effusive pageant that was subsequently engraved and described as *Leycester's Triumph*.

Leicester commissioned several portraits of himself. These range widely both in scale and characterization, from the earliest known half-length, probably by Steven van der Meulen (*c.* 1560–65; London, Wallace), to the last, painted when Leicester was Governor-General (Parham House, W. Sussex). Italian artists were particularly favoured: in 1565 he sought to employ a painter from Florence, and in 1575 he arranged the visit to England of Federico Zuccaro, who painted a full-length portrait (destr.). Leicester was a patron and supporter of Nicholas Hilliard, who produced a 'booke of portraitures' for him in 1571; at least two miniatures of Leicester by Hilliard survive, one of which was made in 1576 (version, London, N.P.G.). Inventories of Leicester's goods list many portraits and some history paintings based on New Testament subject-matter.

Leicester's role as a patron of architecture ranged from domestic to religious and charitable building. In the 1560s and 1570s he modified the medieval keep at Kenilworth Castle and built a new gatehouse at the northern end as well as new ranges of apartments, including a pillared courtyard. His pleasure garden there (*see* GARDEN, fig. 49) is the earliest instance known in England of the landscaping of the terrain to make a terrace that descended to a garden and may have been influenced by his knowledge of French châteaux, such as Amboise. At Warwick in 1571 he founded the still-surviving Leycester's Hospital, and at Denbigh, Clwyd, in 1578 he initiated construction of a new church known as Leicester's Church (ded. St Asaph; partly built, work abandoned 1584), which is of fundamental importance to the history of building for Anglican worship: a plain, relatively unadorned, rectangular space with no division between nave and chancel. Ten years after the Earl's death, John Stow noted in his *Survey of London* (1598) that Leicester House in the Strand, London (destr.), was 'late new built'.

BIBLIOGRAPHY

J. Nichols: *The Progresses and Public Processions of Queen Elizabeth*, 3 vols (London, 1788–1821; rev. 2/1823) [includes the Kenilworth entertainments]

R. Strong and J. A. van Dorsten: *Leicester's Triumph* (Leiden, 1964)

R. Strong: *Tudor and Jacobean Portraits*, 2 vols (London, 1969)

L. Butler: 'Leicester's Church, Denbigh: An Experiment in Puritan Worship', *J. Brit. Archaeol. Assoc.*, xxxvii (1974), pp. 40–62

M. W. Thompson: *Kenilworth Castle* (London, 1976)

MAURICE HOWARD

Dudok, W(illem) M(arinus) (*b* Amsterdam, 6 July 1884; *d* Hilversum, 6 April 1974). Dutch architect. He studied military engineering at the Koninklijke Militaire Academie in Breda (1902–5). After designing some buildings for the army he left the armed forces and became acting Director of Public Works for the city of Leiden, remaining there for two years (1913–15). He applied for the post of Director of Public Works in Hilversum and began his duties in 1915. In 1928 he became Municipal Architect, a position he retained until 1954. In addition to these 39 years with the city government, he also operated his own architectural office and worked on private commissions. Hilversum was experiencing a period of rapid growth as a commuter town for Amsterdam and a centre of the national broadcasting industry; it provided Dudok with an ideal architectural environment. Of his 239 known projects, dating from 1907 to 1967, most of the built works are in the Netherlands, chiefly in Hilversum; of those that are elsewhere the Pavillon des Pays-Bas (1927) at the Cité Universitaire in Paris is a notable example. He played an important role as an urban planner in his native city and also worked on planning schemes in The Hague and Velsen. On his death he was buried in the northern cemetery in Hilversum, whose severe and enigmatic entrance complex is one of his own designs (1927–9).

Dudok's career can be conveniently divided into seven periods. The first phase (until 1916) shows the influence of H. P. Berlage, which was all-pervasive in the Netherlands at that time; Dudok's design of 1908 for a guard building in a barracks copies Berlage's Beursgebouw almost literally. From 1916 to 1920 his building showed his awareness of the flourishing Amsterdam school in both its earlier decorative phase (the *Leids Dagblad* newspaper offices in Leiden, 1916–17) and in its more developed form (Geraniumschool, Hilversum, 1917–18). In the early 1920s under the influence of De Stijl, Dudok's work underwent a noticeable change into its next phase. Ornament disappeared, to be replaced with overall form compositions achieved by indenting corners, for example the Villa Sevensteyn (1920–21) in The Hague, and by shifting and stacking individual building volumes, for example Dr Bavinck School (1921–2), Hilversum. The influence of Frank Lloyd Wright began to appear in his work, but whether this was immediate or through De Stijl and other Dutch sources remains open to discussion;

W. M. Dudok: Raadhuis, Hilversum, 1927–31

throughout most of his life Dudok denied any direct influence.

Dudok had been preparing designs for the new Raadhuis in Hilversum since his arrival there; his version of 1924 marks the beginning of the peak phase of his career, lasting until the end of the decade, in which he achieved international fame and a truly personal style. The Raadhuis (see fig.) was constructed in 1927–31; the lowest sections, one- and two-storey utility wings, are at the perimeter of the complex, and the composition rises through ceremonial and office components to a high tower with a square top. Clear visual distinctions are made between individual elements and between those parts of the building with monumental public functions, such as the council chamber and reception hall, and those with more repetitive uses, such as offices. In contrast to the verticality of the tower, the horizontality of the rest of the building is emphasized by the overhanging edges of flat roofs and canopies and by the use of thin yellow-buff brick with a deep edge joint. The brick shape and the joint technique were later known by Dudok's name.

The Bijenkorf department store in Rotterdam (1929–30; destr.; see Fanelli, p. 130) marked a distinct change in Dudok's work, beginning another stylistic phase, which also lasted for about ten years and in which he evolved his own version of the rationalism of the 1930s. His buildings gradually became flatter and less assertive; works from the earlier part of this period still show individuality and skill, but by the end of this decade works such as the Erasmus flats (1938–9) in Rotterdam were in a canonical International Style, and the Stadsschouwburg (1939–41) in Utrecht already showed a late modern heaviness that would reappear in Dudok's work after World War II. During the Occupation, however, he built little, preparing projects that tended to the traditional and rustic. The last phase of his career, from 1946 until the late 1960s, is marked by a continuing shift to a more anonymous style in such relatively conventional works as the Hoofdgebouw Hoogovens steel-works office building (1948) in Velsen or the Havengebouw (1952–65) in Amsterdam.

Dudok's work was highly esteemed at an early stage; his first social housing complexes in Hilversum attracted great attention at home and abroad. The designs for the Raadhuis in Hilversum were published widely, including coverage in an entire issue of *Wendingen* magazine, and its construction went forward at the urging of many prominent Dutch architects. This building also confirmed Dudok's international reputation, especially in England. A number of town halls in England derived from its design; Charles Holden's London Underground stations also show the influence of his work of the 1920s. In the USA the attention of designers such as Perkins & Will focused on Dudok's school buildings, particularly those of the early 1930s such as the Snelliusschool (1930–32) in Hilversum. Dudok's name entered the international vocabulary of architectural criticism, and he accumulated many foreign awards, including the RIBA Gold Medal (1935), the American Institute of Architects' Gold Medal (1955) and the Médaille d'Or d'Architecture (1966).

In the Netherlands Dudok received adverse as well as favourable notice. His aesthetic positions, which were seen as praiseworthy in England, had the opposite effect in the Netherlands when conflict between traditionalists and modernists reached its peak during post-war reconstruction. He was also criticized for his naive attitude in allowing German architectural magazines to publish his work during the Occupation, and his strong personality, which tolerated little contradiction, became less and less in step with changing society in the Netherlands.

BIBLIOGRAPHY
Wendingen, 8 (1924) [issue containing des. of the Raadhuis, Hilversum]
G. Friedhof: *W. M. Dudok* (Amsterdam, 1928)
R. M. H. Magnee, ed.: *Willem M. Dudok* (Amsterdam and Bussum, 1954)
G. Fanelli: *Architettura moderna in Olanda, 1900–1940* (Florence, 1968; Dut. trans., The Hague, 1978, 2/1981), pp. 128–30, 178, 257–60
L. Benevolo: *History of Modern Architecture*, ii (Boston, 1978), pp. 462–71
V. M. Cramer, H. van Grieken and H. Pronk: *W. M. Dudok, 1884–1974* (Amsterdam, 1981)
'Willem Marinus Dudok, Townhall Hilversum, 1928–1931', *GA*, lviii (Tokyo, 1981) [Jap. and Eng. text]
Willem Marinus Dudok, 1884–1974: Stadsbouwmeester van wereldallure [Municipal architect of world renown] (Baarn, 1993)
MAX CRAMER

Duesbury, William (*b* ?Longton Hall, Staffs, 7 Sept 1725; *d* Derby, 30 Oct 1786). English porcelain manufacturer. He trained as an enameller, and between 1751 and 1753, in his decorating shop in London, he painted wares from Staffordshire and Derbyshire and porcelain from the factories of Bow and Chelsea. He spent a short time (1754–5) at the Longton Hall Porcelain Factory in Longton Hall before entering into a partnership on 1 January 1756 with John Heath, a Derby banker, and André Planché (*c.* 1727–1809), a French refugee, to manufacture porcelain. The factory, in Nottingham Road, Derby, was managed by Duesbury and traded as W. Duesbury & Co. (*see* DERBY). In 1764 he was able to introduce the technique for successful over- and underglaze transfer-printing (e.g. transfer-printed mug, *c.* 1768; Derby, Mus. & A.G.), the details of which he learnt from Richard Holdship, a former partner of the Worcester Porcelain Co. (est. 1751) whom he had engaged as an employee. On 5 February 1770 Duesbury purchased the Chelsea Porcelain Factory and until 1784 ran both factories, this being known as the

'Chelsea–Derby' period (*see* CHELSEA PORCELAIN FAC-TORY). He also bought the bulk of the undecorated stock from the failed Longton Hall Porcelain Factory in 1770 for decorating at Derby. In 1773 he opened a showroom in Covent Garden, London, and in 1776 purchased the moulds and plant of the Bow Porcelain Factory. The Chelsea Porcelain Factory was closed in 1784, and much of the plant and some of the skilled craftsmen were transferred to Derby. By the time of his death, Duesbury had built up a world-famous porcelain factory, which he described as 'a second Dresden'.

BIBLIOGRAPHY
G. A. Godden: *British Pottery and Porcelain* (London, 1966)
C. Williams-Wood: *English Transfer Printed Pottery* (London, 1983)

JOHN MAWER

Duèse, Jacques. *See* JOHN XXII.

Duetecum, van. *See* DOETECHUM, VAN.

Duez, Ernest-Ange (*b* Paris, 8 March 1843; *d* Forest of Saint-Germain, 5 April 1896). French painter. He studied under Isidore-Alexandre-Augustin Pils and made his début at the Salon in 1868. One of his earliest paintings, *The Honeymoon* (1873), caused a scandal at the Salon owing to its depiction of two lovers in modern dress walking through a sunlit forest. His triptych *St Cuthbert* (1879; Paris, Pompidou) was hailed as a masterpiece of modern art and bought by the State for the Musée du Luxembourg in Paris. The painting depicts the stages of St Cuthbert's life, from child to hermit. Contemporary viewers were struck by the artist's use of a real landscape setting, based on Villerville in Normandy where Duez spent much of his time. In addition to genre, religious and history paintings, in 1876 he began to produce portraits: *Alphonse de Neuville* (1880; Versailles, Château) is a typical example. His brooding, suggestive portrait of *Mme Duez* (1877; see Montrosier, 1896, p. 429) shows the influence of Symbolism. However, he soon returned to painting works that were essentially landscapes, such as the decorative panel *Virgil Seeking Inspiration in the Woods* (1888) for the Sorbonne and a pair of allegorical figures, *Botany* and *Physics* (1892), for the Hôtel de Ville in Paris. He also devoted time to applied art, producing a variety of textile designs. His work was praised for its adept use of colour and for bringing what were seen as modern techniques to traditional subjects.

BIBLIOGRAPHY
E. Montrosier: *Les Artistes modernes*, iii (Paris, 1882), pp. 60–64
——: 'Ernest Duez', *Gaz. B.-A.*, 3rd ser., v (1896), pp. 422–31

Duff, Thomas (J.) (*b* Newry, Co. Down, 1792; *d* Newry, 1848). Irish architect. He is first recorded in 1813 as executant architect of the Church of Ireland St Mary's, Newry, Co. Down. During the 1820s and 1830s he built up a formidable reputation as a designer of churches, country houses and public buildings, and he became one of the most important local architects working in Ulster. For a brief period he had a partnership with Thomas Jackson (1807–90) of Belfast, but this ended in 1834 when the latter commenced his own practice there. Duff's Neoclassical Fisherwick Place Presbyterian Church (1827;

destr. 1899), Belfast, was the first in Ulster where the Presbyterians decided to have a full portico, thereby setting a fashion that lasted until mid-century. His Greek Revival museum (1831; with Jackson) for the Belfast Natural History and Philosophical Society at College Square North was the first scholarly compilation of Athenian sources seen in Belfast. Other public buildings, including Newry Court House (1838–41), were designed in a simpler and less archaeological classical manner, as was his ordinary domestic work, but for large country houses such as Narrow Water Castle (completed 1837), Warrenpoint, Co. Down, and Parkanaur (1839–48), Co. Tyrone, he worked in a picturesque Tudor Revival style. In three large church commissions for the Roman Catholic denomination he created two of the best examples of Perpendicular Gothic Revival in Ireland: the cathedral of SS Patrick and Colman (1825–9), Newry, and St Patrick's (1834–7), Dundalk, Co. Louth, the latter directly inspired by King's College Chapel, Cambridge. He also designed a third, St Patrick's Cathedral (1840), Armagh; his great Perpendicular scheme there was, however, curtailed in 1848 due to the famine in Ireland, and when work was re-started in 1854 Duff was dead and the building was completed in Decorated Gothic style by J. J. McCarthy of Dublin.

BIBLIOGRAPHY
H. Dixon: *Ulster Architecture, 1800–1900* (Belfast, 1973)
H. Dixon and B. M. Walker: *In Belfast Town, 1864–1880* (Belfast, 1984)
F. Hanna Bell: *Newry, Warrenpoint and Rostrevor* (Belfast, 1989)

PAUL LARMOUR

Duffaut, Préfète (*b* Jacmel, 1 Jan 1923). Haitian painter. His imaginative landscapes take as their framework the labyrinth of narrow streets, colourful houses and glimpses of the sea of Jacmel, on Haiti's southern coast. Claiming to have had a vision of the Virgin (or the Vodoun goddess Erzulie) on the Ile de la Gonave, he treated her image repeatedly in his paintings. She appeared, according to him, to exact a promise from him to paint her image on the local church. It was a photograph of this image that brought Duffaut to the attention of the American watercolourist Dewitt Peters (1901–66) and led to his affiliation with the Centre d'Art in Port-au-Prince.

Duffaut remained faithful to the geometricized, even diagrammatic abstraction that he had developed early in his career. His two frescoes in Ste-Trinité Episcopal Cathedral in Port-au-Prince, the *Temptation of Christ* and the *Processional Road* (both 1951), are based upon the same pattern. Using intense, flat colours and clearly delineated shapes, he shunned illusions of volume and depth, rendering the costumes and features of his naive figures as patterns on flat shapes. He showed little concern for relative proportion and also rendered architecture without perspective, in a manner curiously resembling a gouache of the *Palace of Sans Souci* (Port-au-Prince, Bib. Haït. F.I.C.) painted by Numa Desroches (1802–80) in the early 19th century. Duffaut's later work tended to slip into mannerisms that were unfortunately adopted by lesser Haitian painters.

BIBLIOGRAPHY
P. Apraxine: *Haitian Painting: The Naive Tradition* (New York, 1973), p. 32
Haitian Art (exh. cat. by U. Stebich, New York, Brooklyn Mus., 1978)

M. P. Lerrebours: *Haïti et ses peintres*, i (Port-au-Prince, 1989), pp. 295–306
DOLORES M. YONKER

Duflos [Duflaud]. French family of printmakers. Claude Duflos (*b* Coucy-le-Château, 1665; *d* Paris, 18 Sept 1727) was essentially a reproductive engraver and etcher: skilful, but lacking genius. He may have been a pupil of Sébastien Leclerc (i), whose portrait he engraved (Roux, no. 123). He made prints after most contemporary painters. His total oeuvre numbers more than 300 pieces, a third of which are portraits: these include *Louis XV* (1710; R 134) and the *Marquis d'Argenson* (1711; R 75, 76), both after Hyacinthe Rigaud. His son Claude-Augustin Duflos (*b* Paris, 10 May 1700; *d* Paris, 27 Feb 1786) was an etcher and line engraver, who worked mainly after François Boucher and collaborated on the illustration of numerous books. Another of Claude's sons, Simon-Nicolas Duflos (*b* Paris, *c.* 1701; *d* Paris, after 1752), was an engraver, the pupil of Jean-Joseph Baléchou. From 1727 until 1752 he settled in Lyon; he then returned to establish himself in Paris, engraving popular prints and occasional pieces. A third son of Claude, Philothée-François Duflos (*b* Paris, *c.* 1710; *d* Lyon, 1746), was a painter, as well as an etcher. He was a pupil of Jean-François de Troy at the Académie de France in Rome; in 1729 he was awarded the first Prix de Rome. His engraved oeuvre, executed in Rome where he stayed until 1744, is mainly composed of *vedute* (e.g. *Diverse Vedute di Roma*, R 1). His painted *Self-portrait* is in the Galleria degli Uffizi, Florence. Pierre Duflos (*b* Lyon, 19 Aug 1742; *d* Paris, 26 April 1816) was the son of Simon-Nicolas Duflos. His work was largely devoted to book illustration (e.g. the Old and New Testaments; Voltaire's *La Pucelle d'Orléans* (R 48–67); Cervantes's *Don Quixote* (R 315–34)). He also made series of portraits (such as the *Collection complète des poètes françois*) and of costumes, often in colour. Duflos executed about 350 pieces. His wife, Marie-Elisabeth Thibault (*fl* 1780-98), was also an engraver and contributed *c.* 50 pieces to her husband's publications.

BIBLIOGRAPHY
Thieme–Becker
E. Fleury: 'Claude Duflos graveur et sa descendance', *Bull. Soc. Acad. Laon*, xxv (1881–2), pp. 245–330
M. Roux: *Inventaire du fonds français: Graveurs du dix-huitième siècle*, Paris, Bib. N., Cab. Est. cat., viii (Paris, 1955), pp. 1–137 [R]
MAXIME PRÉAUD

Dufour, Joseph, & Cie. French wallpaper manufacturing company founded in 1804 in Mâcon by Joseph Dufour (1757–1827). He was trained in Lyon, where there was a flourishing wallpaper industry at the end of the 18th century, and started working at the Ferrouillat & Cie factory some time before 1789. In 1797 he founded a factory in Mâcon with his brother Pierre Dufour under the name Dufour Frères; they employed Jean-Gabriel Charvet (1750–1829), who had worked in other Lyon wallpaper companies, as designer. In 1801 the factory—now suffering financial difficulties—was renamed Joseph Dufour & Cie, and in 1804 it launched its first panoramic wallpaper, the 'Savages of the Pacific', designed by Charvet. In 1808 the factory moved to the Faubourg Saint-Antoine in Paris and took on a new collaborator, the designer and engraver Xavier Mader (1789–1830), who had almost certainly trained in the calico printing industry in Nantes. Mader worked with the Dufour company until 1823 when Dufour took on his son-in-law, Amable Leroy (1788–1880), as a partner and changed the company name to Joseph Dufour & Leroy. After Dufour's death this name was retained until 1835. The business was taken over by the Desfossé company in 1865.

Although there are various publications about Dufour's panoramic wallpapers, an exceptional example of which is the *Cupid and Psyche* series (1816; U. Manchester, Whitworth A.G.), what little is known of his day-to-day production can only be attributed on the basis of printing and engraving quality. Possibly under Mader's influence, Dufour apparently produced more work in a rigorously Neo-classical style than did other manufacturers. Almost nothing is known of his ornamental or floral designs because, apart from the panoramic wallpapers (*see* WALLPAPER, colour pl. III), little material has survived from what was one of the most important wallpaper factories in France in the early 19th century.

BIBLIOGRAPHY
H. Clouzot: *Tableaux-tentures de Dufour & Leroy* (Paris, n.d.)
S. Lenormand: *Nouveau manuel complet du fabricant d'étoffes imprimées et du fabricant de papier peint* (Paris, 1832)
H. Clouzot and C. Follot: *Histoire du papier peint en France* (Paris, 1935), pp. 163–80
Joseph Dufour (1757–1827) (exh. cat., Mâcon, Mus. Mun. Ursulines, 1982)
O. Nouvel-Kammerer, ed.: *Papiers peints panoramiques* (Paris, 1990), pp. 312–21
BERNARD JACQUÉ

Dufresne, Charles (Georges) (*b* Millemont, Seine-et-Oise, 23 Nov 1876; *d* La Seyne, Var, 8 Aug 1938). French painter. He left school at the age of 11 and worked for an industrial engraver, studying drawing at night classes. He later entered the Ecole des Beaux-Arts in Paris and studied under Hubert Ponscarme. There he met Charles Despiau, and, to support himself financially, he worked in the studio of Alexandre Charpentier. He first exhibited in 1905 at the Salon des Indépendants in Paris with a number of works in pastels. The following year he travelled extensively around Italy with the American engraver Herbert Lespinasse (*b* 1884). In 1910 he won the Prix de l'Afrique Nord with a pastel and therefore spent the years from 1910 to 1912 at the Villa Abd El Tif in Algiers, travelling all over the country and absorbing the local culture. His work up to 1910 had been mainly of Parisian theatres and cafés, executed in pastels or occasionally in tempera on canvas. In Algiers he abandoned pastels and began to work in oils, producing a number of brilliantly coloured works such as *Courtyard in Algiers* (1912–13; Paris, Pompidou).

After Dufresne's return to Paris this contact with North Africa left a sense of nostalgia for exotic lands that affected his later paintings. In 1912 he met the painters André Dunoyer de Segonzac, Jean-Louis Boussingault and Luc-Albert Moreau, with whom he shared a similar approach to painting. At the onset of World War I he was called up, but in 1916 he was seriously gassed. He was then sent to join the camouflage unit commanded by Dunoyer de Segonzac, and he painted a number of watercolours and oils depicting war scenes, which showed the influence of

Cubism, such as *Two Cuirassiers on Horseback during the War of 1914* (1917; Versailles, Mus. Lambinet).

After the war Dufresne returned to his Algerian experiences for many of his paintings. Executed in sombre browns, greens and reds, several works were based on animal hunts, such as *Lion Hunt* (*c.* 1925; Troyes, Mus. A. Mod.). The influence of Cubism on Dufresne's work, though never great, can still be detected in the shallow space of these works. In 1921 the director of the Paris Opéra, Jacques Rouché, commissioned him to produce scenery for the drama *Antar*, and his designs again reflected his taste for the exotic. In 1923 Dufresne was one of the co-founders of the Salon des Tuileries, Paris, and he exhibited there that year. The following year he taught at the Académie Scandinave in Paris and was also commissioned by the firm Süe et Mare to design a series of tapestry cartoons. Based on Bernardin de Saint-Pierre's novel *Paul et Virginie* and woven at Aubusson, these tapestries were exhibited in Paris at the Exposition Internationale des Arts Décoratifs et Industriels Modernes (1925).

In the early 1930s Dufresne's painting was beginning to brighten in colour, as in the *Kidnap of the Sabine Women* (1934; Paris, Mus. A. Déc.). No longer bearing the traces of Cubism, his painting showed the influence of Baroque masters such as Giambattista Tiepolo and of 18th-century French tapestries, with colours close to those of the Fauves. In 1936 he was commissioned by Guillaume Janneau, director of Garde-Meuble National, to provide tapestry cartoons to be used as covers for Rollin furniture, on the theme of 'The Beach and the Pleasures of Summer'. At the exhibition *Les Maîtres de l'art indépendant* at the Petit Palais in Paris in 1937, an entire room was devoted to his work. The same year he was commissioned to produce large decorative panels for the Palais de Chaillot in Paris on the theme 'The Theatre of Molière'. In 1938 he received a similar commission for five mural paintings for the Ecole de Pharmacie, Paris.

BIBLIOGRAPHY
Charles Dufresne (exh. cat. by J. Alazard, London, Leicester Gals, 1954)
Dufresne: Paintings, Watercolours (exh. cat. by C. P. Vallotton, London, Sphinx Gal., 1966)
Charles Dufresne 1876–1938: Rétrospective (exh. cat. by P. Chabert, Troyes, Mus. A. Mod., 1988)
Hommage à Charles Dufresne, 1876–1938 (exh. cat. by P. Chabert, Lausanne, Gal. Paul Vallotton, 1989)

□

Du Fresnoy [Dufresnoy], **Charles-Alphonse** (*b* Paris, 1611; *d* Villiers-le-Bel, Val d'Oise, 16 Jan 1668). French painter and writer. Although he is chiefly known for his Latin poem *De arte graphica*, which made a major contribution to the aesthetic debate in France in the later 17th century, he was also active as a painter, working in the classicizing style of Simon Vouet and Nicolas Poussin.

1. LIFE AND PAINTING. Du Fresnoy was the son of Mathieu Du Fresnoy, a well-to-do apothecary established in the Rue Saint-Honoré in Paris. Because his father intended him to go into medicine he received a good education, learning Greek, geometry, anatomy, perspective and architecture. He showed, however, a pronounced taste and talent for poetry and a passion for painting. Persisting

in the latter inclination against his parents' will, he studied with François Perrier and with Vouet, probably in 1631–3. At the end of 1633 or at the beginning of 1634 Du Fresnoy left for Italy. He arrived in Rome without resources and tried to make a living by painting architectural perspectives and views of buildings. The arrival in Rome two years later of Pierre Mignard I, whom he had known while working under Vouet, marked the beginning of a more prosperous period for Du Fresnoy. The two painters were constant companions, sharing lodgings, studying antique art and the works of Raphael together, executing copies commissioned by Alphonse-Louis du Plessis Richelieu (1582–1653), Cardinal of Lyon, of the Carracci decorations in the Palazzo Farnese and spending their evenings drawing from life. The only certain pictures dating from Du Fresnoy's two decades in Rome were the pendants, the *Arrival of Venus at Cythera* and the *Toilet of Venus* (Potsdam, Neues Pal., destr. 1945), which were signed and dated 1647. These works revealed Du Fresnoy's attraction to the works of Poussin, Raphael and Classical antiquity. Surviving pictures usually attributed to Du Fresnoy's Italian period are *Socrates Drinking the Hemlock* (1650; Florence, Uffizi) and *Rinaldo Abandoning Armida* (Paris, priv. col., see Thuillies, 1983, fig. 19). A painting of *Mars, Venus and Cupid* (Toledo, OH, Mus. A.) is also sometimes attributed to his Italian period. A widely scattered group of weak and perfunctory drawings, formerly attributed to Poussin or his immediate followers, is now recognized to be by Du Fresnoy (e.g. Paris, Louvre; Vienna, Albertina).

In 1653 Du Fresnoy was summoned back to Paris on family business. He left Rome with Mignard around May of that year, travelling through Lombardy to Venice, where he spent 18 months. While he was in Venice the 'particular esteem for the works of Titian' that, according to André Félibien, could be seen in Du Fresnoy's work as early as 1647 grew still further. Félibien also noted that 'he took a singular pleasure in seeing them, and making copies of those that he could have at his disposal'. In direct contact with the works of the great Venetian painters of the 16th century, Du Fresnoy began to consider colour to be the essential element of 'the Beautiful', moderating his former almost exclusive interest in draughtsmanship and perspective, learnt in Roman artistic circles.

In Paris, where he arrived in 1656, Du Fresnoy enjoyed a solid reputation as a painter and as a poet. He received official support and collaborated on several important decorative schemes, including a cabinet at the Paris home of a M. Potel, his host on his arrival, as well as one for Jacques Bordier (*d* 1660), the Intendant of Finance, at his château at Le Raincy (destr.), where he executed the *Burning of Troy* on the ceiling. Du Fresnoy was also responsible for several paintings, presumably landscapes, for the Erwart or Erval mansion, formerly the Hôtel d'Epernon, in Paris. Du Fresnoy also executed religious commissions, among which is a *St Margaret* (Evreux, Mus. Evreux), signed and dated 1656, painted for the high altar of Ste Marguerite in the Faubourg Saint-Antoine, Paris. This is the only securely attributable painting to have survived out of some 60 works mentioned by Félibien and Roger de Piles as painted after Du Fresnoy's return to France. From Mignard's return to Paris in 1658 until the stroke that left Du Fresnoy paralysed and forced him to retire to the home of one of his brothers at Villiers-le-Bel, Du Fresnoy shared lodgings with his friend and with the latter's wife. At around this time he apparently collaborated with Mignard on the work of decorating the dome of the Val-de-Grâce, Paris, as may be deduced from a famous letter addressed by Mignard and Du Fresnoy to Charles Le Brun in February 1663, in which they refused to take any part in the business of the Académie Royale because of commitments at the church.

2. WRITINGS. The relatively small number of pictures produced by Du Fresnoy is explained by his perfectionism in the composition, correcting and polishing of his great Latin poem *De arte graphica*. He apparently devoted himself to this project as soon as he arrived in Rome and worked on this text for 25 years, succeeding in concentrating the academic artistic theory of his day into 549 hexameters of excellent Latin verse. He is said to have submitted his verses 'to all the most skilful painters in the places where he [passed], including to Francesco Albani and Guercino'. Following the example of Horace's *Ars poetica*, Du Fresnoy cast poetry and painting as sister arts and founded his concept of art on the theory, in the opening lines of his poem, that '*Ut pictura poesis erit; similisque poesi/sit pictura . . .*' ('As a painting so a poem will be, and likewise let a painting be as poetry'). He also stated that the manifestation of the Beautiful is an indisputable fact that artists are called upon to interpret each after his own fashion. In doing so they could adopt one of several different aesthetic categories, corresponding to the characters of various famous antique statues—the *Antinous*, the Farnese *Hercules*, the Belvedere *Venus* and the *Dying Gladiator*. The work was published in Latin shortly after Du Fresnoy's death in 1668, and a French edition translated and copiously annotated by Roger de Piles appeared later the same year under the title *L'Art de peinture de Charles-Alphonse Du Fresnoy, traduit en français, avec des remarques nécessaires et très amples*. This was supplemented by *Sentiments de C.-A. Du Fresnoy sur les ouvrages des principaux et meilleurs peintres des derniers siècles*, which Du Fresnoy had compiled since 1649. He also touched on the importance of colour, a subject amplified by de Piles in his notes. Du Fresnoy's treatise, which made him famous, was later translated into English by John Dryden (1695) and into German (1699), Italian (1713) and Dutch (1733). It continued to appear in new editions until the beginning of the 19th century. (*See also* UT PICTURA POESIS, §3.)

WRITINGS

De arte graphica (Paris, 1668); Fr. trans by R. de Piles as *L'Art de peinture de Charles-Alphonse Du Fresnoy, traduit en français, avec des remarques nécessaires et très amples* (Paris, 1668, 2/1673)

Sentiments de C.-A. Du Fresnoy sur les ouvrages des principaux et meilleurs peintres des derniers siècles [appended to de Piles's translation of *De arte graphica*]

BIBLIOGRAPHY

Mariette

A. Félibien: *Entretiens sur les vies et sur les ouvrages des plus excellens peintres anciens et modernes* (Paris, 1688, 2/1705/*R* 1960), ii, pp. 661–8

R. de Piles: *Abrégé de la vie des peintres* (Paris, 1699), pp. 488–92

A.-J. Dézallier D'Argenville: *Abrégé de la vie des plus fameux peintres* (1745–52, 2/1762), ii, 283–6

Abbé de Fontenai: *Dictionnaire des artistes*, i (Paris, 1776), pp. 616–17

P. Vitry: *De C.-A. Dufresnoy pictoris poemata quod 'De arte graphica' inscribitur* (Paris, 1901)

L. Demonts: 'Deux peintres de la première moitié du XVIIe siècle: Charles Blanchard et Charles-Alphonse Dufresnoy', *Gaz. B.-A.*, n. s. 4, xii (1925), pp. 162–78

J. Thuillier: 'Les *Observations sur la peinture* de Charles-Alphonse Dufresnoy', *Walter Friedlaender zum 90. Geburtstag* (Berlin, 1965), pp. 193–210

A. Blunt: *The Drawings of Poussin* (New Haven and London, 1979), pp. 163–74, 198

J. Thuillier: 'Propositions pour Charles-Alphonse Du Fresnoy, peintre', *Rev. A.* [Paris], 61 (1983), pp. 29–52

J. Montagu: 'Le Maître du *Cléobis et Biton* de la collection Corsini, le jeune Thomas Blanchet?', *Bull. Soc. Hist. A. Fr.* (1985), pp. 85–104

ALEXANDRA SKLIAR-PIGUET

Dufy, Raoul (*b* Le Havre, 3 June 1877; *d* Forcalquier, Basses-Alpes, 23 March 1953). French painter, printmaker and decorative artist. From the age of 14 he was employed as a book-keeper, but at the same time he developed his innate gift for drawing at evening classes at the Ecole des Beaux-Arts in Le Havre, given by the Neo-classical painter Charles Lhuillier (?1824–98). He discovered the work of Eugène Boudin, Poussin and Delacroix, whose *Justice of Trajan* (1840; Rouen, Mus. B.-A.) was 'a revelation and certainly one of the most violent impressions' of his life (Lassaigne, Eng. trans., p. 16). In 1900, with a grant from Le Havre, he joined his friend Othon Friesz in Paris and enrolled at the Ecole Nationale Supérieure des Beaux-Arts in the studio of Léon Bonnat. At the Musée du Louvre he studied the art of Claude Lorrain, to whom he painted several *Homages* between 1927 and 1947 (e.g. 1927; Nice, Mus. Masséna). His encounter with works by van Gogh at the Galerie Bernheim-Jeune and with Impressionism at Durand-Ruel is reflected in such early works as *Beach at St Adresse* (1904; Paris, Pompidou).

The revelation of Fauvism at the Salon des Indépendants in 1905 decisively changed the course of Dufy's art. Matisse's *Luxe, calme et volupté* particularly impressed him. Dufy immediately adopted the Fauves' glowing colours and broad sweeping brushstrokes in canvases such as the *Rue pavoisée* and *Posters at Trouville* (both 1906; Paris, Pompidou). Already apparent in these works is a characteristic decorative quality and *joie de vivre*.

The retrospective exhibition of Cézanne's work at the Salon d'Automne of 1907 led Dufy to a more rigorously structured organization of space and forms and an austerity of colour in such paintings as *Trees at L'Estaque* (1908; Paris, Pompidou). Another painting inspired by Cézanne, the *Large Bather* (1914; The Hague, Roell-Jas priv. col.), was the first of a series of variations on the theme of bathers. Dufy's discovery of Expressionism on a visit to Munich in 1909 (just before the formation of the Blaue Reiter) also suggested to him the decorative possibilities of wood-engraving. He made four wood-blocks, *Fishing* (1910; Paris, R. S. Levy priv. col.), *The Hunt* (1910; Paris, Pompidou), *The Dance* and *Love* (both 1910; Nice, Mus. B.-A.), creating motifs to which he later returned in watercolours such as *Fishing* (*c.* 1919) executed for the Maison Bianchini-Férier (*in situ*), an important fabric-designing firm in Lyon.

In 1910 Dufy's expressive woodcuts for Guillaume Apollinaire's *Bestiaire ou cortège d'Orphée* (Paris, 1911) marked the beginning of his work as a decorative artist.

Raoul Dufy: *Henley Regatta*, oil on canvas, 0.94×1.16 m, 1934 (Nice, Musée des Beaux-Arts)

In 1911 he and Paul Poiret established La Petite Usine, a cloth-printing workshop in which Dufy produced water-colour designs for textiles for Bianchini-Férier from 1912 to 1928. In the early 1920s Dufy elaborated the style for which he remains best known. Considering truth to appearances to be an unsubstantiated 'hypothesis', in works such as *Swimmers out at Sea and Shells* (1925–7; Paris, Pompidou) he created a poetic universe of emblems, ideograms and subjective symbols of reality as a kind of 'shorthand of the essential'. A free invention in drawing was coupled with an arbitrary use of colour independent of line, creating an impression of verve and dynamism.

Dufy travelled extensively in the 1920s, in Italy, including Sicily (1922–3), Morocco (1926) and southern France (1927 and 1929). In the 1930s he often stayed in England, where his work (e.g. his portrait of the *Kessler Family*, 1931; Paris, Pompidou) was highly valued. He also painted a series of race-course scenes such as *Races at Ascot* (1931; Paris, Mus. A. Mod. Ville Paris) and *Derby at Epsom* (1939; Boston, MA, C. Narins priv. col.). This favourite subject, which he had first treated in his painting *Deauville* (1924; Jerusalem, C. Bergman priv. col.), allowed him to express his love of crowds and movement and to juxtapose areas of colour to generate a sense of animation. Dufy

also painted several variations on the theme of regattas, both English, for example the *Henley Regatta* (1934; Nice, Mus. B.-A.; see fig.) and the *Cowes Regatta* (1934; Washington, DC, N.G.A.), and French, for example the *Regatta at Deauville* (1935; Jerusalem, C. Bergman priv. col.). The lively brushstrokes and bright, randomly applied colours in these works create a persuasive atmosphere while emphasizing the stylization of the forms.

Dufy's drawings and prints translated the grace and humour of his painting style into a lively, allusive network of commas and arabesques. Among his most admired book illustrations are the 36 lithographs in Apollinaire's *Le Poète assassiné* (Paris, 1926), the etchings commissioned by Ambroise Vollard in 1930 for Eugène de Montfort's *La Belle Enfant ou l'amour à 40 ans* (Paris, 1930) and colour lithographs executed between 1931 and 1937 for Alphonse Daudet's *Aventures de Tartarin de Tarascon* (Paris, 1937). His first stage designs were for *Le Boeuf sur le toit* in 1920 (text by Jean Cocteau with music by Darius Milhaud), and among his best were those for the production in New York in 1950 of Jean Anouilh's *Invitation au château* as *Ring around the Moon*.

Between 1922 and 1930 Dufy worked on ceramics with two Catalan artists, Josep Llorens Artigas and Nicolau

Maria Rubiò i Tuduri (1891–1981). During the same period he produced fourteen tapestry hangings for one of three barges moored on the Seine and extravagantly decorated by Paul Poiret for the Exposition des Arts Décoratifs et Industriels Modernes in 1925. One of the hangings depicted the *Official Reception of the Admiralty*. Besides tapestry cartoons on the theme of Paris begun in 1924 for the Gobelins, he also produced two tapestry cartoons for Mme Marie Cuttoli entitled *Paris* (1934 and 1937; both Paris, Pompidou) and *Amphitrite* (1936; Göteborg, Röhsska Kstslöjdmus.). These reflect both Dufy's amused observation of Parisian society and his interest in seaside subjects, which can be traced back to his childhood in Le Havre. In 1941 he collaborated with Jean Lurçat to produce *Collioure* and the *Beautiful Summer* (Le Havre, Mus. B.-A.), and in 1948–9 he completed seven cartoons for the Galerie Louis Carré, Paris, which possesses both the tapestries and some of the cartoons, including *Amphitrite*, *Pastoral Scenes* and the *Rivers Seine, Oise and Marne*. (For an illustration of his tapestry designs *see* FRANCE, fig. 94.)

Dufy also produced architectural decorations, of which the most famous is the *Electricity Fairy* (Paris, Mus. A. Mod. Ville Paris), produced for the Exposition Internationale des Arts et Techniques dans la Vie Moderne (1937). For this work, covering 600 sq. m, Dufy used a new medium perfected by the chemist Jacques Maroger (an emulsion consisting of fish glue in water with a drying agent, oil and varnish) to achieve the lightness and freshness of watercolour. Dufy's other large-scale decorations include the *Rivers Seine, Oise and Marne* (1936–40; Paris, Pompidou), intended for the bar of the Théâtre du Palais de Chaillot, and the contemporaneous decorations *Scientists* and *Explorers* for the monkey house in the Muséum National d'Histoire Naturelle in Paris.

In 1942 Dufy began a series of orchestra paintings based on preparatory sketches of musicians and instruments. His passion for music is evident in such works as the *Grand Concert* (1949; Nice, Mus. Masséna), *Homage to Claude Debussy* (1952; Le Havre, Mus. B.-A.), *Homage to Bach* (1952; Jerusalem, Israel Mus.) and *Homage to Mozart* (1951; Tokyo, Gal. A. Point). Towards the end of his life Dufy's art once again became more austere. He abandoned colour contrasts in favour of an almost monochrome tonal painting in the *Red Violin* (1948; Geneva, Mus. A. & Hist.) and the *Yellow Console of the Violin* (1949; Toronto, A. G. Ont.). His preoccupation with light culminated in *Black Freighter* (1952; Lyon, Mus. B.-A.) and related works in which black becomes the equivalent of a dazzling luminosity.

BIBLIOGRAPHY

M. Berr de Turique: *Raoul Dufy* (Paris, 1930)
G. Stein: 'Raoul Dufy', *A. Plast.*, 3–4 (1949), pp. 135–45
P. Courthion: *Raoul Dufy* (Geneva, 1951)
B. Dorival: *La Belle Histoire de la Fée Electricité de Raoul Dufy* (Paris, 1953)
A. Werner: *Raoul Dufy* (New York, 1953, 2/1970, rev. 2/1985)
Raoul Dufy (exh. cat. by P. Courthion, Geneva, Mus. A. & Hist., 1953)
Raoul Dufy (exh. cat. by B. Dorival, Paris, Mus. N. A. Mod., 1953)
S. Hunter: *Raoul Dufy* (New York, 1954)
J. Lassaigne: *Raoul Dufy* (Geneva, 1954; Eng. trans., Geneva, 1970)
B. Dorival: 'Raoul Dufy et le portrait', *Rev. des A.*, 3 (1955), pp. 175–80
——: 'Le Thème des baigneuses chez Raoul Dufy', *Rev. des A.*, 4 (1955), pp. 238–42
R. Cogniat: *Dufy décorateur* (Geneva, 1957)
B. Dorival: 'Un Chef d'oeuvre de Dufy entre au Musée d'Art Moderne', *Rev. des A.*, vii/5 (1957), pp. 225–8
R. Cogniat: *Raoul Dufy* (Paris, 1962)
Legs de Mme Dufy au Musée du Havre, cat. of Mme Dufy bequest (Le Havre, Mus. B.-A., 1962)
B. Dorival and M. Hoog: 'Le Legs de Mme Raoul Dufy au Musée d'Art Moderne de Paris', *Rev. Louvre*, 4–5 (1963), pp. 209–36
Donation Dufy (exh. cat., Paris, Louvre, 1963)
Raoul Dufy: Créateur d'étoffes, 1910–1930 (exh. cat., Paris, Mus. A. Mod. Ville Paris, 1977)
Raoul Dufy (exh. cat., Tokyo, Gal. A. Point, 1983)
Raoul Dufy (exh. cat., ed. B. Robertson and S. Wilson; London, Hayward Gal., 1983)
Raoul Dufy (exh. cat., New York, Holly Solomon Gal., 1984)
D. Pérez-Tibi: *Raoul Dufy* (Paris and London, 1989)

DORA PÉREZ-TIBI

Dugahiti. *See under* SANKHU.

Dugdale, Sir William (*b* Shustoke, Warwicks, 6 Sept 1605; *d* Feb 1686). English historian, topographer and herald. Educated at school until he was 15, he studied law and history at home. He was ten when he was being instructed by William Raper in the study of antiquities. On his marriage at 18 he bought Blythe Hall, near Coleshill, Warwicks, which remained his home. After his marriage Dugdale met William Burton (1575–1645), author of the *Description of Leicestershire* (1622), and through him Sir Symon Archer (1581–1662), who had long been collecting material for a history of Warwickshire. A scholarly circle was being formed in the Midlands with Dugdale at the centre, speedily enlarging its connections. Archer introduced Dugdale to Sir Henry Spelman (?1564–1641), who had been working on monastic charters of Norfolk and Suffolk. Spelman put Dugdale in touch with Roger Dodsworth (1585–1654), who had over many years accumulated a vast amount of similar material for the northern counties. Spelman thought that 'this work might be improved into a Monasticum [sic] Anglicanum' and 'should the design miscarry, Mr. Dugdale should be prevailed upon to do this work'.

In 1638, on the revival of the Society of Antiquaries under the title Antiquites Redevivus, Sir Edward Dering (1598–1644), Christopher Hatton, 1st Baron Hatton (?1605–70), Sir Thomas Shirley and Dugdale agreed to share their studies. Hatton, a longtime patron of Dugdale, used his influence to have the latter appointed a Pursuivant herald; he later became Garter King-of-Arms, assured of a career and a place in London at the College of Arms. It was Hatton who in 1640–41 sent Dugdale and William Sedgewick, a draughtsman, to Old St Paul's Cathedral, Westminster Abbey and many other religious houses throughout England to make measured drawings of the monuments he thought would be in danger during those times of civil and religious unrest. Dugdale followed Charles I to Oxford; his estates were sequestrated and his movements restricted. During months of exile in France he investigated monastic establishments with alien foundations in England.

The first volume of the *Monasticon Anglicanum* was published in 1655, at considerable expense to Dodsworth and Dugdale. Owing to Dodsworth's death, Dugdale had to finance alone the second and third volumes (1661 and 1673). The *Monasticon* was the work of many, but it was

Dugdale who edited and brought to fruition the vast amount of material, which became a standard work of reference for every serious student of medieval studies, remarkable not only for its documentation but also for its lavish illustration, which demonstrated as never before the historical and architectural importance of the English monasteries. In 1656 Dugdale had published his *Antiquities of Warwickshire*, illustrated from records, ledger books, manuscripts and the evidence of tombs, beautified by maps, prospects (*see* GARDEN, fig. 49) and portraitures. It has remained a model for subsequent county histories. Dugdale's *History of St Paul's Cathedral* (1658) illustrates prospects, plans and tombs engraved by Wenceslaus Hollar before many were defaced during the Civil War (*see* LONDON, fig. 24). It remains the best description of Old St Paul's and its contents.

UNPUBLISHED SOURCES

London, BL, Loan MS. 38 [*Book of Monuments*]
London, Coll. Arms [Misc. cols]
London, Soc. Antiqua., MS. 839 [*Origines Judiciales*]; MS. 851 [*Book of Drafts*]
Oxford, Bodleian Lib., MSS Bodl. 6491–6536

WRITINGS

ed.: *Monasticon Anglicanum*, 3 vols (London, 1655–73)
The Antiquities of Warwickshire (London, 1656)
The History of St Paul's Cathedral in London (London, 1658)
The History of Imbanking and Drayning (London, 1662)
Baronage of England, 2 vols (London, 1675–6)

BIBLIOGRAPHY

DNB
W. Hamper: *Life, Diary and Correspondence of Sir William Dugdale, Knt* (London, 1827)
D. C. Douglas: *English Scholars* (London, 1943)
Sir William Dugdale: His Life and Works (exh. cat., Warwick, 1953)

JOHN HOPKINS

Dughet [Poussin], Gaspard [Gaspar; Gaspare; Gasper; Gaspero] [le Guaspre] (*b* Rome, 15 June 1615; *d* Rome, 25 May 1675). Italian painter. He was one of the most distinguished landscape painters working in Rome in the 17th century, painting decorative frescoes and many easel paintings for such major Roman patrons as Pope Innocent X and the Colonna family. He is associated with a new genre of landscape, the storm scene, although of some 400 catalogued works little more than 30 treat this theme. His most characteristic works depict the beauty of the scenery around Rome, particularly near Tivoli, and suggest the shifting patterns of light and shade across a rugged terrain. Dughet drew from nature, yet his landscapes are carefully structured, and figures in antique dress suggest the ancient beauty of a landscape celebrated by Virgil. Very few can be securely dated; his development may be inferred from his few dated fresco paintings and from the wider context in which he was working. Most writers, following Pascoli, have divided Dughet's career into three periods. His first landscapes were 'a little dry' (Pascoli); in his second period he developed a more learned style, closer to that of his teacher, Nicolas Poussin; his late works were more intimate and more original.

1. Life and work. 2. Working methods and technique. 3. Critical reputation and influence.

1. LIFE AND WORK.

(i) Training and early works, to c. 1635. Dughet's father was French, his mother Italian. From before Easter 1631 until 1635 he was apprenticed to Poussin, who had married his sister Anne-Marie. Poussin encouraged him to select fine views in the countryside around Rome and insisted that he should master the rudiments of figure drawing. The deep and lasting affection between master and apprentice probably explains why Dughet became known as Gaspard Poussin.

Most scholars now accept John Shearman's suggestion that a group of paintings, gathered together by Anthony Blunt under the name of the Silver Birch Master, are in fact the earliest works of Gaspard Dughet. (For alternative views *see* NICOLAS POUSSIN and MASTERS, ANONYMOUS, AND MONOGRAMMISTS, §I: SILVER BIRCH MASTER.) These works, which include *Nymph Riding a Goat* (Rome, priv. col.; see Boisclair, 1986b, fig. 2), *Satyr Offering Fruits to a Nymph* (Rome, priv. col.; Boisclair, 1986b, fig. 3) and the *Landscape near ?Albano* (London, N.G.; see fig.1), are strikingly naturalistic and often show unassuming sections of rocky and wooded scenery. In all of them a screen of slender trees, which resemble silver birches, stretches before a shallowly receding space, and the skies are veiled by lacy patterns of slender leaves. The lyrical colour and sensitive lighting is reminiscent of Titian, while the asymmetrical, often diagonal composition derives from the landscape tradition established in Rome by such northern European artists as Adam Elsheimer and Paul Bril. In the *Landscape near ?Albano* (which some scholars have redated as late as 1670) the academic figure style reflects the influence of Poussin, but Dughet subsequently developed more supple, graceful figures whose only relationship to the Antique and to Poussin was the tunics they wore. Towards 1635, when Dughet left Poussin's studio, his works show a less decorative, freer style, as in *Hagar and Ishmael* (*c.* 1635; Wilton House, Wilts) and the *Storm* (*c.* 1635; Florence, Fond. Longhi), an early example of a storm landscape.

Dughet never left Italy, but he made two successive journeys outside Rome during this period, probably in 1635: the first, which was very brief, was with Francesco Ariti to Milan, and the second, of some months, was to Castiglione del Lago, where he was taken by the Duca della Cornia. These absences from Rome, while not very productive of paintings, nevertheless provided a period of reflection that bore fruit in the new breadth and drama of the eight landscape etchings that he made on his return (see Boisclair, 1986b, figs 42–9). Around the same period he seems to have rented four houses, two in parts of Rome commanding views, another in Tivoli and one in Frascati.

(ii) Middle period, c. 1635–c. 1660. A frieze of 14 landscape frescoes in the Palazzo Muti–Bussi, Rome, drawing liberally on the influence of the decorative landscapes of Bril and Agostino Tassi and showing a study of Claude Lorrain in their varied effects of light, may be dated to 1635–7. These works marked a turning-point, following which it seems probable that Gaspard moved towards the more classical tradition of Bolognese landscapes. The *Landscape with Travellers* (Cambridge, Fitzwilliam) was directly inspired by Domenichino, while the *Landscape with Hunters* (?*c.* 1639), which retains an asymmetrical composition derived from northern European landscape, is nonetheless

1. Gaspard Dughet: *Landscape near ?Albano*, oil on canvas, 483×660 mm (London, National Gallery)

calmer in rhythm than earlier work and achieves a new subtlety of tone.

After a severe illness, Dughet visited Florence, where Pietro da Cortona obtained him a commission from Grand Duke Ferdinando II de' Medici, and then spent about a year in Naples. These events may have occurred between 1642 and 1644, but more probably between 1644 and 1646, since, according to Pascoli, shortly after his return from Naples Dughet began to paint a series of 16 frescoes of scenes from the *Lives of the Prophets Elijah and Elisha*, commissioned by the Prior Giovanni Antonio Filippini, for the Carmelite church of S Martino ai Monti, Rome (*in situ*). Although the documentation is problematic, it seems that the first seven were completed by the end of 1647, the remainder in 1650 or 1651. With these sparse and majestic frescoes, which created a new sense of the primitive grandeur of the natural world, Dughet established his reputation. Innocent X's visit to the church in 1649 may have inspired him to commission four landscape frescoes (1649–50 or 1651) for the Palazzo Pamphili in the Piazza Navona, Rome, and seven large landscapes with religious scenes (completed June 1653; Rome, Gal. Doria-Pamphili) for his family's other palazzo on the Corso; on these Dughet collaborated with Guglielmo Cortese. *Ponte Lucano and Cascade* (Rome, Gal. Doria-Pamphili), a scene entirely lacking figures, may have been painted for the Corso palazzo *c.* 1651–2; like all these

works, it is austere and monumental, portraying nature with startling boldness and vigour.

The success of Dughet's Carmelite frescoes may have led to a renewed closeness between Poussin and Dughet. The *Ascension of Elijah* at S Martino ai Monti influenced Poussin's landscapes of 1651, and it seems likely that this influence was reciprocal and that a number of works reflecting Poussin's lucid and rational structure, among them the *Landscape with the Disobedient Prophet* (Le Havre, Mus. B.-A.), may be dated to 1653–5. The works of the brothers-in-law at this stage have often been confused. A frescoed frieze of the *Four Seasons* (Bordeaux, Mus. B.-A.), painted for the Palazzo Bernini, Rome, was perhaps executed in 1654 or 1655. Works of the later 1650s such as *Landscape with Pyramus and Thisbe* (*c.* 1656; Liverpool, Walker A.G.), however, suggest that Dughet returned from the horizontal planes of Poussin towards compositions employing intersecting diagonals, at the same time portraying more exuberant and picturesque scenery.

In 1657 Dughet was elected to the Accademia di S Luca. The late 1650s contain two datable fresco decorations: the two delicate landscapes (1657) executed in collaboration with Lazzaro Baldi and Filippo Lauri in the Galleria di Alessandro VII in the Palazzo del Quirinale, Rome, and the stark and unprecedentedly bold landscapes in Don Camillo Pamphili's palazzo at Valmontone (1658). Around these may be grouped other, stylistically diverse landscapes, including the rugged and turbulent *Landscape near Tivoli with a Fire* (Dresden, Gemäldegal. Alte Meister), the classically structured *View of Tivoli* (Oxford, Ashmolean) and the rocky and romantic *Landscape with Diana and Actaeon* (Chatsworth, Derbys).

(iii) Late period, c. *1660 and after.* The *Landscape with Diana and Actaeon* belonged to Don Lorenzo Onofrio Colonna, who in Dughet's later years was his most important patron. In 1660 he paid Gaspard for two canvases, probably identifiable as *Abraham's Sacrifice* and the *Storm with Elijah and the Angel* (London, N.G.; see fig. 2) and, if so, are important in establishing Dughet's chronology. They are vast, panoramic landscapes, a manner that seems to have attracted Dughet around 1659. The *Storm with Elijah and the Angel* is Dughet's most celebrated storm picture. As in other related works, such as the earlier *Storm* (c. 1653–4; London, N.G.) and a slightly later composition (mid-1660s; Holkham Hall, Norfolk), he depicted the wind rushing into foliage, pressing the leaves in clusters against the branches and raising clouds of dust, powerful tree trunks uprooted and lightning piercing leaden skies filled with rain.

Three magnificent decorative cycles may be dated to the late 1660s and early 1670s. In 1667–8 Dughet frescoed a small room on the ground floor of the Palazzo Colonna, Rome, and documentary evidence suggests, albeit inconclusively, that a famous series of landscapes (Rome, Gal. Colonna), with scenes in the Roman Campagna that are exquisitely painted in tempera in unusually light and subtle colours, were carried out between 1671 and 1673. His last

frescoes were commissioned by Prince Giovanni Battista Borghese for the decoration of the Palazzo Borghese, Rome. In 1671 Dughet collaborated with Lauri on four landscapes with scenes from Ovid to decorate a small room in the palace, and in 1672 he worked alone on the decoration of a second small room with four oval landscapes that feature scenes of hunting, fishing, a waterfall etc and are distinguished by their successful combination of a free technique and delicate colouring.

The Colonna temperas display a new simplicity and tranquillity, looking back to the naturalistic works of Dughet's early career. It seems likely that other small works, equally serene and intimate, may also date from between 1660 and 1675. These less ambitious small canvases show the waterfalls of Tivoli (e.g. the *Cascades at Tivoli*, London, Wallace), forests (e.g. *Landscape with the Fountain of Grottaferrata*, Rome, Pal. Barberini) or lakes, villas and Romanesque churches in tightly structured, geometric landscapes, such as *The Lake* (1666–8; Edinburgh, N.G.). Dughet almost ceased to paint for the two years before his death.

2. WORKING METHODS AND TECHNIQUE. In his early years Dughet planned his landscapes without figures, so that occasionally they are awkwardly inserted at the edges (e.g. *Landscape with a Shepherd Feeding his Dog*, London, Colnaghi's). Later, however, he left space for figures, which may have been added at the client's request. Carlo Maratti added a figure to the *Landscape with Mary Magdalene* (Madrid, Prado).

Dughet's early drawings, using pen or brush, ink and wash, do not seem to have been studies for paintings: he seems rather to have wished to build up a repertory of motifs. The beautifully finished drawing of a *Landscape with Two Figures* (Florence, Uffizi, 99389), attributed almost unanimously to Dughet, was apparently conceived as a work in its own right; its handling relates it to the etchings of c. 1635. Other drawings formed the starting-point for paintings: for instance a landscape drawing (Marseille, Mus. Cantini) provided the basis for *Landscape with Hagar and Ishmael* (c. 1635; Wilton House, Wilts). Two sheets from the most important collection of Dughet's drawings, in the Kunstmuseum in Düsseldorf, relate to *Landscape with a Grotto* (Rome, Pal. Muti-Bussi): FP 4691, a study of rocks, elaborates a detail from the landscape and is the only known example of this kind of drawing by Dughet, while FP 8049 is a careful working out of the motif in gouache, black and a little red chalk. It is probably a fragment of the preparatory *modello*.

Two drawings (Paris, Louvre, RF 5892 and RF 29015), mainly in brush and wash, are preparatory studies for the landscapes in the frescoes for S Martino ai Monti, Rome: *Elijah Visited by the Angel* and the *Ascension of Elijah*. These and other drawings and an oil sketch (Hamburg, priv. col.; see Boisclair, 1986b, fig. 127) for the *Elijah Anointing Hazach, King of Syria, and Jehu, King of Israel* indicate the meticulous preparation involved in these fresco compositions.

Dughet seems to have virtually abandoned ink and wash c. 1650–51 in favour of black and, occasionally, red chalk on coloured paper (usually blue, grey or green) and, for example, in the *Landscape with Horseman in the*

2. Gaspard Dughet: *Storm with Elijah and the Angel*, oil on canvas, 2.01×1.53 m, late 1650s (London, National Gallery)

Foreground (Sacramento, CA, Crocker A. Mus.) and the *View of Tivoli* (Raleigh, NC Mus. A.). Most of the drawings that survive from after 1650 are records of paintings rather than preparatory studies, although it is not clear what purpose they served. Some are so highly finished that they may have been intended as presentation sheets or autonomous works.

3. CRITICAL REPUTATION AND INFLUENCE. Crescenzio Onofri and Jacques de Rooster (*fl* late 17th century) were pupils of Dughet, but no works by the latter are known. Crescenzio created a more decorative version of Dughet's style, with more freely structured works, especially after he moved from Rome to Florence (before 1691). His place in Rome was taken by Jan Frans van Bloemen, whose pastiches were so skilful that many of his paintings passed under Dughet's name.

Dughet enjoyed great prestige in Britain, and his paintings were enthusiastically collected there, especially those from his last period. Britain still has, after Rome, the largest number of his works. He became one of the foremost models for British landscape painters, admired above all for his selection of picturesque motifs, his realism and the lucid structure of his works. George Lambert (i) and John Wootton imitated his art. Richard Wilson, Gainsborough and Constable were inspired by him and recommended him as a model. German landscape painters were equally indebted to him, and innumerable artists were inspired by him up to the end of the 19th century. The response in France was generally less enthusiastic, but Dughet nevertheless had his imitators there, including Francisque Millet and Georges Focus (1641–1708), and in the 19th century his work inspired some naturalistic artists.

BIBLIOGRAPHY

F. Baldinucci: *Notizie* (1681–1728); ed. F. Ranalli (1845–7), vi, pp. 473–5
L. Pascoli: *Vite* (1730–36), pp. 57–63
A. Blunt: 'Poussin Studies V: The Silver Birch Master', *Burl. Mag.*, xcii (1950), pp. 69–73
J. Shearman: 'Gaspard not Nicolas', *Burl. Mag.*, cii (1960), pp. 326–7
N. Wibiral: 'Contributi alle ricerche sul cortonismo in Roma: I pittori della Galleria di Alessandro VII nel Palazzo del Quirinale', *Boll. A.*, xiv (1960), pp. 134–6, 163, 165
L'ideale classico in Italia e la pittura di paesaggio (exh. cat., Bologna, Pal. Archiginnasio, 1962), pp. 256–89
D. Sutton: 'Gaspard Dughet: Some Aspects of his Art', *Gaz. B.-A.*, civ (1962), pp. 269–312
J. Shearman: 'Landscape Drawings', *The Drawings of Nicolas Poussin*, ed. A. Blunt and W. Friedländer (London, 1963), iv
M. Waddingham: 'The Dughet Problem', *Paragone*, xiv/161 (1963), pp. 37–54
A. B. Sutherland: 'The Decoration of S Martino ai Monti: I and II', *Burl. Mag.*, cvi (1964), pp. 63–9, 117–20
M. Chiarini: 'Gasper Dughet: Some Drawings Connected with Paintings', *Burl. Mag.*, cxi (1969), pp. 750–54
P. Rosenberg: 'Notes: Twenty French Drawings in Sacramento', *Master Drgs*, viii/1 (1970), pp. 31–3
M.-N. Boisclair: 'Documents inédits relatifs à Gaspar Dughet', *Bull. Soc. A. Fr.* (1973), pp. 75–85
J. Dughet: 'Notizie di Gaspero Pussino', appendix to F. Baldinucci: *Notizie*, ed. P. Barocchi (Florence, 1974–5), vii, pp. 125–8
M. Roethlisberger: *Gaspar Dughet, Rome 1615–75* (New York and London, 1975)
L. Salerno: 'La cronologia di Gaspare Dughet', *Etudes d'art français offertes à Charles Sterling*, ed. A. Châtelet and N. Reynaud (Paris, 1975), pp. 227–36
S. J. Bandes: 'Gaspard Dughet and S Martino ai Monti', *Stor. A.*, 26 (1976), p. 291
C. Whitfield: 'Poussin's Early Landscapes', *Burl. Mag.*, cxxi (1979), pp. 10–18
Gaspard Dughet called Gaspar Poussin: 1615–1675: A French Landscape Painter in Seventeenth-century Rome and his Influence on British Art (exh. cat. by A. French, London, Kenwood House, 1980) [entries on drgs by M.-N. Boisclair]
J. Heidemann: 'The Dating of Gaspard Dughet's Frescoes in S Martino ai Monti in Rome', *Burl. Mag.*, cxxii (1980), pp. 540–46
M. Kitson: 'Gaspard Dughet at Kenwood', *Burl. Mag.*, cxxii (1980), pp. 644–51
S. J. Bandes: 'Gaspard Dughet's Frescoes in Palazzo Colonna', *Burl. Mag.*, cxxiii (1981), pp. 77–88
Gaspard Dughet und die ideale Landschaft (exh. cat. by C. Klemm, Düsseldorf, Goethe-Mus., 1981)
M.-N. Boisclair: 'Gaspard Dughet à Saint-Martin-des-Monts, Rome', *Stor. A.*, 53 (1985), pp. 87–102
——: 'Gaspard Dughet: Sa conception de la nature et les fresques du palais Colonna', *Racar* (1986a)
——: *Gaspard Dughet: Sa vie et son oeuvre (1615–1675)* (Paris, 1986b) [with full bibliog.]

MARIE-NICOLE BOISCLAIR

Dugléré, Adolphe (*b* 1805; *d* June 1884). French cook, restaurant manager and collector. His first job was as a cook to the Rothschild family in Paris, after which he worked at a restaurant (Frères Provencaux) and then at the Café Anglais on the Boulevard des Italiens, where he was also the manager. Several dishes were named after him, including Sole Dugléré. During the 1840s he began to collect paintings, many of them from distinguished collections. He owned works by Watteau (*The Rendezvous*; New York, Wildenstein's), Chardin and Murillo and a group of works by the 17th-century Flemish painter Cornelis Huysmans. When these were sold at auction in Paris on 31 January 1853, the art historian and dealer Otto Mündler was among the buyers. During these years Dugléré bought at least two works by Delacroix: *A Brigand* (1825; Basle, Kstmus.) from the collection of Alexandre du Sommerard and a version of *Hamlet and Horatio* (Switzerland, priv. col.). His collection of contemporary pictures epitomized the taste for the ROCOCO REVIVAL fashionable in the 1840s. He owned two paintings of nude subjects by Jean-François Millet, 13 works by Pierre-Paul Prud'hon and 40 paintings by Narcisse Diaz. He sold this collection in Paris on 1 February 1853, possibly to finance his developing career as a restaurateur. Presumably his talents helped to account for the success of the Café Anglais during the Second Empire (1852–70); in 1863 the Goncourt brothers recorded that his salary was 25,000 francs a year. He continued to buy and sell paintings; for example, he bought Prud'hon's portrait of the painter *Constance Mayer* (untraced) from the sale of the collection of Laurent Laperlier (1805–78) and within two years it had entered the collection of the Marquis Maison. The residue of his collection was sold in June 1884, after his death.

BIBLIOGRAPHY

R. Heron de Villefosse: *Histoire et géographie gourmandes de Paris* (Paris, 1956)

LINDA WHITELEY

Dugourc, Jean-Démosthène (*b* Versailles, 23 Sept 1749; *d* Paris, 30 Apr 1825). French designer. He was the only son of François Dugourc, controller to the household of the Duc d'Orléans. Little precise information has survived regarding his early years and artistic training. He developed his gift for drawing and design as a pupil of Charles-Germain de Saint-Aubin. He is thought to have made a brief trip to Italy (*c.* 1764–5), where he is believed to have met Johann Joachim Winckelmann, events that seem to have inspired his passion for the ancient world and its art. His first known work is an allegory for the opera house at Versailles, executed in honour of the wedding of the Dauphin in May 1770. In November 1776 he married Marie-Anne Adélaïde Bélanger, elder sister of FRANÇOIS-JOSEPH BÉLANGER. Together with Bélanger and Georges Jacob, Dugourc worked on the interiors of the château of Bagatelle, as well as for a glittering private clientele that included the Duc d'Aumont (at the château of Brunoy, *c.* 1780–81) and the Duchesse de Mazarin, creating interiors in the late 18th-century Etruscan style. He also collaborated with such leading craftsmen as Pierre Gouthière, François Rémond and Boulard. He produced numerous designs executed in a rapid, light, energetic style for gilt-bronzes and furniture (e.g. design for chimney-piece with clock, candelabra, vases and fire-dogs, *c.* 1785; Paris, Mus. A. Déc.). His career was closely linked with court circles: in 1780 he was appointed Dessinateur de la Chambre et du Cabinet de Monsieur and in 1784 Surintendant des Bâtiments de Monsieur and Dessinateur du Garde-Meuble de la Couronne. He designed furniture for the Chambre des Bains in the château of Compiègne (firescreen, 1785; Lisbon, Mus. Gulbenkian) and a jewel cabinet for Marie-Antoinette (destr.; model, 1787; Baltimore, MD, Walters A.G.). He also had a number of foreign clients, among them Catherine II of Russia, Grand Duke Paul (later Emperor of Russia), General Lanskoï and Gustav III of Sweden, for whom he provided set designs for the theatre of Drottningholm.

From 1786 Dugourc made numerous designs for the Spanish court, many of which were produced by François-Louis Godon, the Parisian master watchmaker who had become watchmaker to the king of Spain, and in April 1800 he settled in Madrid, where he carried out commissions for Charles IV and members of the Spanish aristocracy. In 1814 he returned to Paris and in 1816 was restored to the position of Dessinateur du Garde-Meuble. He once again collaborated with Bélanger on royal commissions, for example the re-interment of Louis XVI and Marie-Antoinette at St Denis in 1815 and the marriage ceremonies for the Duc de Berry in 1816. From 1774 to 1790 Dugourc had produced designs for the silk manufacturer Camille Pernon of Lyon, and this partnership continued after his return to France (e.g. silk panel, *c.* 1815–25; Chicago, IL, A. Inst.). He also executed designs for the royal manufactories at Beauvais and the Savonnerie. His last project was the Throne Room at the Tuileries, where he was responsible for all aspects of decoration and furniture. Dugourc described himself as an architect, decorative painter, designer, engraver and dealer in antiquities, claiming in his autobiography (1800) to be responsible for 'everything fine and tasteful' produced in Paris during the previous ten years. There are important collections of designs by or attributed to him at the Musée des Arts Décoratifs in Paris and in Lyon.

BIBLIOGRAPHY

P. Verlet: 'Objets d'art français de la collection Calouste Gulbenkian', *Connoisseur*, clxxii (1969), pp. 254–5
C. Gastinel-Coural: *Soieries de Lyon: Commandes royales au XVIII siècle*, Doss. Mus. Tissus (Lyon, 1988)
C. Baulez: 'Les Imaginations de Dugourc', *De Dougourc à Pernon: Nouvelles acquisitions graphiques pour les musées*, Doss. Mus. Tissus (Lyon, 1990), pp. 11–43
Forray-Carlier: 'Dessins de Jean-Démosthène Dugourc pour le Garde-Meuble de la Couronne', *Bull. Soc. Hist. A. Fr.* (1991), pp. 133–48
C. Gastinel-Coural: 'La Salle du Trône du Château des Tuileries', *Un Age d'or des arts décoratifs, 1814–1848* (exh. cat., Paris, Grand Palais, 1991)

CHANTAL GASTINEL-COURAL

Du Guernier. French family of miniature painters. Alexandre du Guernier I (*c.* 1550–*c.* 1628) worked in Paris as a painter on vellum, decorating devotional books. His son Louis du Guernier I (*b* Paris, 14 April 1614; *d* Paris, 16 Jan 1659) was probably his father's pupil but also studied with Simon Vouet. In 1648 he was one of the founders of the Académie Royale de Peinture in Paris. In 1655 he was appointed professor, and he became *conseiller* the following year. His portrait by his brother-in-law Sébastien Bourdon was engraved by his pupil Jacques-Samuel Bernard. Du Guernier's surviving miniatures reveal a delicate and flowing hand and include portraits of *Louise Henriette of Orange* (1643; Dutch Royal Col.), *John Cecil, 4th Earl of Exeter* (Burghley House, Cambs) and *James, Duke of York* (1656; Amsterdam, Rijksmus.), the future James II, King of England (*reg* 1685–8). Also attributed to du Guernier is a portrait miniature of *James II as a Child*. He developed a style of his own: he never used white, and he stippled his images on to enamel or vellum. He was generally admired for the accuracy of his likenesses; mention was made of the Book of Hours (untraced) that he painted for Henri, 5th Duc de Guise (1614–64), in which all the images of saints were said to be portraits of ladies of the court, painted from life. Du Guernier also painted landscapes to which his brother Pierre du Guernier (*b* Paris, *c.* 1624; *d* Paris, 26 Oct 1674) added figures. Pierre, who entered the Académie de Peinture in 1663, earned a considerable reputation among his contemporaries as a painter on enamel; his portrait miniatures, such as that of *Marianne de Châteauneuf*, were distinguished by their brightness of colouring.

Louis du Guernier II (*b* Paris, 1658; *d* London, 19 Sept 1716) was the son of Louis du Guernier I. He trained with Louis de Châtillon (1639–1734), becoming a distinguished draughtsman and engraver. In 1708 he moved to London, where he worked mainly for booksellers and collaborated with Claude Dubosc (*fl* 1711–40) on a suite of prints of the *Battles of the Duke of Marlborough*. He engraved numerous portraits and suites of prints, such as *The Gamesters*, and illustrated, among others, poems by John Gay and the works of Spenser and Shakespeare. He seems to have also worked as a goldsmith.

BIBLIOGRAPHY

Thieme–Becker
A. Félibien: *Entretiens* (1666–8); rev. (1725), iv, pp. 206–13
D. Foskett: *A Dictionary of British Miniature Painters* (London, 1972), i, p. 254; ii, pl. 91

LAURENCE GUILMARD GEDDES

Duhameel, Alart. *See* ALART DU HAMEEL.

Duiker, Johannes. *See under* BIJVOET & DUIKER.

Du Jardin [Dujardin; Du Gardijn], **Karel** [Carel] (*b* Amsterdam, 27 Sept 1626; *d* Venice, before 9 Oct 1678). Dutch painter, etcher and draughtsman. His father was

Chaarles de Jardin (Gardyn; *c.* 1599–before 1650), a fat-renderer, and his mother was Catalyn Borchout (1588–before 1650). They had at least one other child, Herbert, who must have died by 1651 and about whom nothing is known.

Du Jardin's artistic training remains a mystery. From Houbraken on he is described as Nicolaes Berchem's ablest pupil, although there is no evidence for this other than a similarity in subject-matter. Pieter van Laer and Paulus Potter have also been mentioned as teachers, but again this is sheer supposition. Du Jardin may have received early stimulus from his brother-in-law, Johannes Pauwelsz. Schors, a painter from Augsburg and husband of Du Jardin's half-sister Tryntje, about whom nothing is known. More directly relevant is Du Jardin's second cousin, the portrait painter Pieter Nason. There is no evidence confirming that they knew each other, but ties between the Du Jardin and Nason families were strong. If Du Jardin did not study with Nason, he may at least have been exposed by him to the rudiments of the craft.

Du Jardin is best known for the Italianate landscapes he painted throughout his career. It has been presumed on the basis of his subject-matter that he travelled to Italy in the 1640s, yet no proof for such a trip exists. He probably travelled to France as a merchant in 1650, an idea supported both by a document and a drawing signed *Dujardin fecit Paris* (Berlin, Kupferstichkab.). Du Jardin met his wife, Suzanne van Royen, in Lyon. They were living on the Rozengracht in Amsterdam by 1652, when Du Jardin made his will. Still in Amsterdam in 1655, by October 1656 Du Jardin had moved to The Hague, where he became a founder-member of De Pictura, the artist's confraternity. He appears in the confraternity's records of 1657 and 1658, at which time his probable first pupil, Martinus Laeckman, is recorded.

Characteristic paintings by Du Jardin of the 1650s, such as the *Landscape with Waterfall and Resting Animals* (1655; Paris, Louvre) or *Farm Animals in the Shade of a Tree, with a Boy and a Sleeping Herdswoman* (1656; London, N.G.), show a strong debt to Paulus Potter's paintings of animals rendered with great precision and naturalism. Du Jardin's small, simply constructed scenes of herders and cattle resting in meadows or travelling through the landscape and travellers halting at an inn are marked by refined detail and bright colours with a sensitive interpretation of light and shade.

Du Jardin made a number of drawings, mainly studies in chalk of cattle, sheep and other animals, as well as a few red chalk portraits (e.g. *Self-portrait*, 1659; London, BM) and a series of Italianate landscape drawings, mostly in brush and wash. The *View of the Piazza di S Maria Maggiore, Rome* (Paris, Fond. Custodia, Inst. Néer.) is dated 1653, suggesting that it was copied from either a print or another artist's drawing, since Du Jardin was back in Amsterdam by 1651. Du Jardin's activity as an etcher also dates from the 1650s. In 1653 he published a series of prints of resting animals, shepherds and related pastoral motifs. Despite the Italianate settings, his etchings appear to have been made in the Netherlands and are close in conception to Pieter van Laer's innovative series of 1636. About 50 etchings by Du Jardin are known.

By May 1659 Du Jardin was again back in Amsterdam, where he is documented in 1670, 1671 and 1674. During the 1660s he continued to paint Italianate landscapes but also painted portraits of important members of Amsterdam society, such as the *Regents of the Spinhuis and the Nieuwe Werkhuis* (1669; Amsterdam, Rijksmus.), as well as a number of remarkable history paintings. These large, impressive works (e.g. the *Conversion of St Paul*, 1662; London, N.G.) reflect the artist's response to the stylistic innovations of the Amsterdam Town Hall commissions of the 1650s, particularly the introduction of Flemish and classicizing elements. They also bear witness to Du Jardin's awareness of Italian Baroque paintings by such artists as Guido Reni. The spectacular *Hagar and Ishmael* (*c.* 1665–7; Sarasota, FL, Ringling Mus. A.; see fig.) displays Du Jardin's command of large-scale, dynamic yet stable compositional formulae and his ability to render imposing figures convincingly with sensitive physiognomies. He used cool, modulated tonalities to create smooth surfaces and brilliant fabrics.

In 1675 Du Jardin sailed to Italy from Texel Island accompanied by Joan Reynst, whose father, a member of Amsterdam's patriciate, had assembled one of the most important collections of Venetian 16th-century painting in the Netherlands. (Du Jardin probably knew the Reynst collection, for in 1672 he was a witness in a legal proceeding concerning the authenticity and worth of some of the paintings.) Reynst and Du Jardin stopped in Tangiers in October 1675, and, although Reynst returned to the Netherlands, Du Jardin continued his journey to Rome, where he signed and dated his *Landscape with Herders and*

Karel Du Jardin: *Hagar and Ishmael*, oil on canvas, 1.84×1.37 m, *c.* 1665–7 (Sarasota, FL, Ringling Museum of Art)

Animals (1675; Antwerp, Kon. Mus. S. Kst.). A number of late landscapes grouped around this painting reveal a drastic change in style. He abandoned his large figure types, replacing them with small, agitated figures situated in large Italian riverside settings; his brilliant, creamy technique and light, clear tonalities gave way to dark, smoky colours with rougher brushwork, harsher contrasts and fewer highlights. Though definitive proof that Du Jardin joined the SCHILDERSBENT, the Netherlandish artists' society founded in Rome in 1623, is lacking, like other members he was given the nickname 'Bokkebaard' (Dut.: 'goatbeard'). He came into contact with the classicizing Dutch painter Johannes Glauber. Works dated 1675, 1676 and 1678 attest to Du Jardin's productivity in Rome, where he painted his last known work, the *Riding School* (1678; Dublin, N.G).

Du Jardin achieved a measure of fame in his own day: he was praised by Cornelis de Bie, and his small, multi-figured scene of *Calvary* (1662; Paris, Louvre) was lauded in a poem by the leading Dutch poet, Jan Vos. Du Jardin also designed the portrait frontispiece to the collected edition (1662) of Vos's poetry. Besides Laeckman, Du Jardin's only other recorded pupil was Erick Wilke (or Van der Weerelt), an orphan under the care of the Civil Orphanage in Amsterdam. He went to study with Du Jardin in Amsterdam in March 1668 for the fee of 80 guilders a year.

BIBLIOGRAPHY

Hollstein: *Dut. & Flem.*
A. Houbraken: *De groote schouburgh* (1718–21), ii, pp. 85, 112, 214, 277; iii, pp. 43–7, 158, 171, 261, 333
C. Hofstede de Groot: *Verzeichnis* (1907–28), ix, pp. 295–417
E. Brochhagen: 'Dujardins späte Landschaften', *Bull. Mus. Royaux B.-A. Belgique*, vi (1957), pp. 236–55
——: *Karel Dujardin: Ein Beitrag zum Italianismus in Holland im 17. Jahrhundert* (diss., U. Cologne, 1958)
Nederlandse 17e eeuwse Italianiserende landschapschilders [Dutch 17th-century Italianate landscape painters] (exh. cat., ed. A. Blankert; Utrecht, Cent. Mus., 1965/*R* 1978)

JENNIFER M. KILIAN

Du Jin [Tu Chin; *zi* Junan; *hao* Chengju, Gukuang, Chingxia tingzhang] (*b* Jiangsu Province; *fl* 1465–1509). Chinese painter and scholar. Active in Beijing, he was one of the finest figure painters of the Ming period (1368–1644) and was also known for his landscapes, portraits and paintings of birds and animals and plants (none extant). His classical heritage can be seen in his earliest handscroll of Qu Yuan's *Nine Songs* (1473; Beijing Pal. Mus.), in which the elegant figures display a lively ink line with limited use of ink wash, in the *baimiao* ('plain-line') style derived from Li Gonglin. Another handscroll painting in the same collection, *Poems by Ancient Worthies* (see Levenson, no. 294, pp. 440–42, and Xu Bangda, pl. 311), consists of a series of nine (originally twelve) scenes depicting scholars in landscape or garden settings. It was also executed in the *baimiao* manner, with handsome calligraphy of Tang (AD 618–907) and Song (960–1279) poems by Li Bai, Han Yu and Du Fu written by Jin Cong (1447–1501), a poet and, like Du, a literati (*wenren*) painter. Each scene sensitively portrays the central emotions of the accompanying poem: the first scene shows the famous 4th-century calligrapher Wang Xizhi writing the text of the *Daode jing* ('Classic of the Way and Virtue') for a

Daoist priest in exchange for a live goose, which Wang had earlier tried unsuccessfully to buy from him.

Among the paintings that demonstrate Du Jin's mastery of bright colours is a large, unsigned hanging scroll (identified in the 1980s on the basis of comparison with other works by Du) illustrating the story of *Tao Gu and Qin Ruolan* (see fig.). Tao Gu, an emissary of the first Song emperor Taizu (*reg* 960–76), who was seeking the submission of the Southern Tang state (937–75), leans forward in his seat to listen to Qin Ruolan, for whom he had earlier composed a poem. Behind him is a splendid three-panel folding screen and beside him a table with all necessary writing implements.

A similar combination of screen and luxury objects is seen in *Enjoying Antiquities* (Taipei, N. Pal. Mus.), a large painting in ink and colours on silk, perhaps originally mounted as a free-standing screen of a type seen in the painting itself. The crisp and meticulous rendering of the painting may indicate that it is a copy by Qiu Ying, who was much influenced by Du, of a fragment of a painting with the same title that survives in the temple Kongobuji on Mt Koya, Japan (see Little). The painting, which exemplifies the elegant life of Ming scholar-gentlemen, would have served to validate its owner's high cultural status. The placing of the table has been likened to that of tables in the *Night Revels of Han Xizai* (handscroll; Beijing, Pal. Mus.) by Gu Hongzhong (*fl c.* 943–60). Du

Du Jin: *Tao Gu and Qin Ruolan*, hanging scroll, ink and colours on silk, 1715×1040 mm, *c.* late 15th century (London, British Museum)

Jin is known to have made a copy of this painting, as also did Du's younger contemporary Tang Yin.

In Du Jin's painting of the *Thunder Gods*, there were seven or eight figures in a group, each over 300 mm high. Some held huge axes, others flaming torches, still others thunderbolts. The owner of this hanging scroll would display it in his central hall on the day of the Dragon-boat Festival and startle his guests by saying, 'This is Du Jin's *Wangchuan Villa!*' Such vigorous depictions of supernatural forces were, of course, a far cry from the static forms in the archaic landscape of Wang Wei's *Wangchuan Villa*. Du Jin's *Thunder Gods*, however, probably resembled Wu Wei's handscroll *Cleansing Weapons* (Nanjing, Jiangsu Prov. Mus.) of 1496, another painting in the *baimiao* manner explicitly following Li Gonglin, but with extensive use of ink washes.

Du Jin's style lies somewhere between the scholar-painting of the Suzhou literati and the professional artists of the Zhe school, but with a lighter touch than the latter. It is marked by playfulness and an ability to capture the individuality of the human figure. His landscape settings may be more conventional, reminicent of Southern Song prototypes.

BIBLIOGRAPHY

J. Cahill: *Parting at the Shore: Chinese Painting of the Early and Middle Ming Dynasty, 1368–1580* (New York and Tokyo, 1978)

Yu Jianhua, ed.: *Zhongguo meishujia renming cidian* [Biographical dictionary of Chinese artists] (Shanghai, 1981), p. 340

R. Barnhart: 'The "Wild and Heterodox School" of Ming Painting', *Theories of the Arts in China*, ed. S. Bush and C. Murck (Princeton, 1983), p. 384

Xu Bangda, ed.: *Zhongguo huihua shi tulu* [Illustrated catalogue of the history of Chinese painting] (Shanghai, 1984), ii, pl. 311, pp. 506–8 [five sections of *Poems by Famous Worthies*]

S. Little: *Du Jin, Tao Cheng, and Shi Zhong: Three Scholar–Professional Painters of the Early Ming Dynasty* (inaug. diss., New Haven, CT, Yale U., 2 vols; microfilm, Ann Arbor, 1987)

J. A. Levenson, ed.: *Circa 1492: Art in the Age of Exploration* (Washington, DC, 1991), pp. 439–42

Painters of the Great Ming: The Imperial Court and the Zhe School (exh. cat. by R. M. Barnhart, Dallas, TX, Mus. A., 1993), pp. 142–3, nos 87–8

RODERICK WHITFIELD

Du Jon, François. *See* JUNIUS, FRANCISCUS.

Duknovich de Tragurio, Ioannes Stephani [Duknović, Ivan]. *See* GIOVANNI DALMATA.

Dulac, Charles-Marie [Marie-Charles] (*b* Paris, 1865; *d* Paris, 29 Dec 1898). French painter and lithographer. Born into a poor family, he was trained at the Ecole Nationale des Arts Décoratifs and worked as a designer of wallpapers and theatrical sets. In 1887 he studied painting in the studios of Ferdinand Humbert (1842–1934), Henri Gervex, Adrien Karbowsky (*b* 1855) and Alfred Roll, and he made his Salon début in 1889. In the early 1890s he painted around Paris and in northern France. Around 1892 Dulac experienced a spiritual conversion and joined a religious society, the Third Order of St Francis. He changed his name to read Marie-Charles Dulac, and from 1892 he concentrated on colour lithography, choosing pure landscape without figures as the medium for expressing his ardent faith.

From sketches made on his travels through France, Belgium and Italy, Dulac created several lithograph series. In *Series of Landscapes* (1892), simplified forms and dramatic tonal qualities convey mood; transient effects and descriptive details are avoided in the artist's search to convey the essence of divine creation. In 1894 Dulac created a series of nine lithographs, the *Canticle of Creatures*, a visual analogue of the *Canticle of Brother Sun* of St Francis of Assisi. With each plate, Dulac juxtaposed a verse by St Francis and a liturgical text. Dulac's final series, *The Creed*, left incomplete at the artist's death, consists of paradisaical visions inspired by the Catholic mass. Mystical gardens and cosmological visions symbolize an ideal universe and eternal peace. Dulac's sacred landscapes were acclaimed by such writers as Joris-Karl Huysmans and Maurice Denis, who recognized that for 'Dulac, Nature is a book which contains the word of God' (1905). A victim of lead poisoning, Dulac died at 33.

BIBLIOGRAPHY

A. Marguillier: 'Charles Dulac', *Gaz. B.-A.*, n.s. 3, xxi (1899), pp. 325–32

M. Denis: 'Propos, sur les lettres et paysages de Marie-Charles Dulac', *L'Occident* (Dec 1905), p. 305

T. Greenspan: *'Les Nostalgiques' Re-examined: The Idyllic Landscape in France, 1890–1905* (diss., New York City U., 1981), pp. 359–93

——: 'Charles Marie Dulac: The Idyllic and Mystical Landscape of Symbolism', *Gaz. B.-A.*, n.s. 6, xcix (1982), pp. 163–6

——: 'The Sacred Landscape of Symbolism: Charles Dulac's *La Terre* and the *Cantique des créatures*', *Register* [Lawrence, KS], v/10 (1982), pp. 63–79

TAUBE G. GREENSPAN

Dülfer, Martin (*b* Breslau, 1 Jan 1859; *d* Dresden, 21 Dec 1942). German architect and teacher. He first trained at the Gewerbeschule, Schweidnitz, then studied architecture (1877–9) in Hannover with Conrad Wilhelm Hase and at the Technische Hochschule, Stuttgart (1879–80). His practical training was in the largest German architectural practice of the time, Kayser & von Grossheim, Berlin, then with Brost and Grosser in Breslau, and finally with Friedrich von Thiersch in Munich (1885–6). Having set up an independent practice in Munich (1887), Dülfer began designing façades, the first being that of the Bernheimer Haus (1887–9), a Baroque-style façade above a tall ground-floor, which is broken up by windows and iron supports. In 1891 he went to London and worked with Emanuel von Seidl (1856–1919) on the decorations for a German exhibition. Although English elements began to appear in his work, he continued to use a mixture of the neo-Baroque and Louis XVI styles in many later façades, notably that of the Staats- und Stadtbibliothek (1892–3), Augsburg, with its symmetrical design. By contrast, the façades of several residences he built for aristocrats in Munich were inspired by the simpler idiom of mid-18th-century Rococo. Dülfer's first monumental building, the Kaimsaal (1895; destr. 1944), Munich, later known as the Neue Tonhalle, was an opulent neo-Baroque building. His first villa, the Villa Kalb, Wilderoth, near Munich, based closely on South German Baroque, dates from the same year. Twelve further villas in a variety of styles can be documented up to 1908. From *c.* 1900 he designed numerous city buildings of unusual monumentality and splendour, for example the offices (1900–01) of the *Allgemeine Zeitung*, Munich. The façade, enlivened with an unprecedented diversity of decorative structure in stucco and paint, is among the more important *Jugendstil* works in Germany.

At about the same time Dülfer was establishing a reputation as a designer of theatres, such as that in the southern Tyrolese spa town of Meran (1899–1900; destr. 1988). This small neo-classical building was decorated with Louis XVI style elements, but in his designs for the Stadttheater (1903–4; destr. 1944), Dortmund, he reduced historical elements in favour of a new monumentality. Here too he designed interior details, using *Jugendstil* elements. Other executed theatre projects include the Stadttheater (1906–8), Lübeck, and the Stadttheater (1909–12), Duisburg, which is again in a more historicist, neo-classical style.

In 1906 Dülfer moved to Dresden on his appointment to the chair of design at the Technische Hochschule. In Dresden itself, Dülfer received no significant commissions apart from university buildings. Among these the Beyer-Bau (1910–13; formerly the civil engineering department) at the Technical University of Dresden, an irregular structure with clinker brickwork and a reinforced-concrete frame, surmounted by an observatory dome, and the chemical institutes (1917–26) of the Technische Hochschule show few historical influences, being in a vernacular style.

Dülfer's artistic development is characteristic of those architects who broke away from a dogmatic to a freer use of historicism. To these forms Dülfer added personal motifs, the charm of which lay primarily in the texture of material and colour, but which were quite at odds with the mainstream of unadorned Functionalism. His versatility, decorative talent and predilection for picturesque and theatrical solutions are also visible in his designs for tombs and fountains, notably the Luitpold Fountain in the market square in Kulmbach.

BIBLIOGRAPHY
LK; Wasmuth
M. Creutz: *Martin Dülfer* (Berlin, 1910)
D. Klein: *Martin Dülfer: Wegbereiter der deutschen Jugendstil-architektur* (Munich, 1981) [comprehensive bibliog. and list of works]
——: 'Das Gesamtkunstwerk im 19. Jahrhundert unter besonderer Berücksichtigung des Werkes von Martin Dülfer', *A. Bavar.*, 25–6 (1982), pp. 115–30
——: 'Der Übergang von Späthistorismus zum Jugendstil in der Münchner Architektur: Das Werk des Architekten Martin Dülfer', *Oberbayer. Archv*, cix/2 (1984), pp. 155–62

VOLKER HELAS

Dulin, Nicolas (*b* Paris, *c.* 1670; *d* Paris, 9 April 1751). French architect. His first known work was the Hôtel d'Etampes (1704; destr.), Paris. The high, narrow building with a mansard roof, Classical orders ornamenting the *avant-corps* of both the court and garden façades and irrationally low attached side wings differed in its proportions from his later works, lending some credibility to Jacques-François Blondel's suggestion that it was actually designed by the Sicilian Duke Fornari. More typical of Dulin was his best-known work, the Hôtel Dunoyer (1708; destr. 1847), Paris, commissioned by an arms dealer. The central section of this balanced and elegant two-storey building was emphasized by the high, pitched roof that crowned the *avant-corps*, contrasting with the flat, balustraded roof of the rest of the *corps de logis*. The decorative features of this work included two putti shown as lovers, positioned at each end of the roof, and sculpted busts in the wide window piers of the upper storey. This building,

called a *folie* by contemporaries, was the type of small, prettified residence that became very popular during the Régence period. Dulin designed another building of this type for M. Galepin's country house (*c.* 1715; destr.) at Auteuil; here he used a high, pitched roof to crown the whole structure, but some of the decorative features were similar to those at the Hôtel Dunoyer, including wide window piers featuring sculpted busts on the garden façade. Other buildings designed by Dulin were the Hôtel Sonning (1711), the Hôtel Locmaria (1724) and the Hôtel de Pontferrière, all in Paris; the château of Villegenis, near Massay; and numerous renovations to existing buildings, notably the Hôtel de Nevers (1709; now the Bibliothèque Nationale), Paris. His work shows the influence of Jules Hardouin Mansart and his office. Dulin was appointed a member of the Académie d'Architecture in 1718 but resigned in 1734. He was also appointed Contrôleur des Bâtiments du Roi. His best-known pupil was Pierre Contant d'Ivry.

BIBLIOGRAPHY
J. Mariette: *L'Architecture française*, 5 vols (Paris, 1727–38/*R* 1927–9)
G. Brice: *Nouvelle description de la ville de Paris*, i–ii (Paris, 1752/*R* 1971)
J.-F. Blondel: *L'Architecture française*, 8 vols (Paris, 1752–6/*R* 1904–5)
L. Hautecoeur: *Architecture classique*, iii (1950)
G. Pillement: *Paris disparu* (Paris, 1966)
M. Gallet: *Paris Domestic Architecture of the Eighteenth Century* (London, 1972)

KATHLEEN RUSSO

Duli Xingyi. *See* DOKURYŪ SHŌEKI.

Dum. *See* THUMB.

Dumaresq, James (Charles Philip) (*b* Sydney, NS, 18 Dec 1840; *d* Halifax, NS, 20 Dec 1906). Canadian architect. He was educated in Sydney and attended Acadia College (now Acadia University), Wolfville, Nova Scotia. In 1870 he founded the firm of Dumaresq & Stimson in Halifax. After a fire devastated the city of Saint John, New Brunswick (1877), he moved there to participate in its reconstruction. He established successive partnerships with a number of local architects. His commissions during this period include buildings for Acadia College (1878), Wolfville, and the imposing Legislative Assembly building (1880) at Fredericton, New Brunswick, with its high dome. The latter commission was the result of a competition in which he was placed ahead of the firm of McKean & Fairweather. He returned to Halifax in 1887 and undertook several public buildings, including the Forrest Building (1887) at Dalhousie University, St Mary's Girls' School (1888) and Pine Hill Library (1898). In 1899 his son, Sydney Perry Dumaresq (1875–1943), first president of the Nova Scotia Association of Architects, joined him. James Dumaresq undertook commissions throughout eastern North America and the West Indies and was known for his forceful public buildings. His houses, by contrast, revealed his facility with form and deftness with materials.

UNPUBLISHED SOURCES
Halifax, Pub. Archvs NS

BIBLIOGRAPHY
W. Cochrane, ed.: *The Canadian Album: Men of Canada* (Brantford, Ont., 1894)
——: *History of Nova Scotia*, iii (Halifax, 1916)

J. B. Weir: *The Lost Craft of Ornamented Architecture: Canadian Architectural Drawings, 1850–1930* (Halifax, 1983)

GRANT WANZEL, AARON BOURGOIN

Dumas, Marlene (*b* Cape Town, 1953). South African painter, draughtswoman and collagist, active in the Netherlands. She studied the fine arts at the University of Cape Town, South Africa (1972–5), and continued studying art at the Ateliers '63, Haarlem, the Netherlands (1976–8). In 1979–80 she followed a general course in psychology at the Psychological Institute of the University of Amsterdam. Dumas became known for her portraits and figurative works. Her exhibition *The Private Versus the Public* (Amsterdam, Gal. Paul Andriesse) presented a number of group and individual portraits based on Polaroid photographs taken either by herself or from magazines (e.g. the *Turkish Schoolgirls*, 1.60×2.00 m, 1987; Amsterdam, Stedel. Mus.). Her emotional involvement with the subjects coupled with her distortion of the original photographs created unnaturalistic renderings that had characteristically a haunting edge. Other significant works include the *Particularity of Nakedness* (1.40×3.00 m, 1987; Eindhoven, Stedel. Van Abbemus.). In the 1990s she produced such installation works as *Black Drawings* (ink on paper and slate, 1991–2; Tilburg, De Pont Found. Contemp. A.). Based on photographs of friends and newspaper cuttings, and placed in a grid formation covering a wall, the hundreds of washes form a crowd or large group, the individual features of which, together with their manner of depiction, invite non-linear comparison.

BIBLIOGRAPHY

Marlene Dumas: The Question of Human Pink (exh. cat. by U. Loock, Berne, Ksthalle, 1989)
Marlene Dumas: Miss Interpreted (exh. cat., ed. A. Brouwers, M. Dumas and S. Klein Essink; Eindhoven, Stedel. Van Abbemus., 1992) [inc. essay by Dumas]

CECILE JOHNSON

Du Maurier, George (Louis Palmella Busson) (*b* Paris, 6 March 1834; *d* London, 8 Oct 1896). English illustrator and writer. The son of a Frenchman and an Englishwoman, he was educated in both countries. After a brief period as an analytical chemist, he entered the Paris atelier of Charles Gleyre in 1856. Whistler, Edward Poynter and Thomas Armstrong were among his fellow students, and Du Maurier's novel, *Trilby* (1894), draws upon this period. Du Maurier left Paris in 1857 to continue his training at the Academy in Antwerp. He intended to become a painter, but, in 1857, he suddenly lost the use of his left eye.

After briefly resuming his artistic training in Düsseldorf in 1859–60, Du Maurier embarked on a career as an illustrator in London at a time when young draughtsmen were giving a new and expressive originality to the woodblock medium. His first published drawings were sketchy cartoons for *Punch*, but he soon recognized that success depended upon acquiring technical skill and giving an impression of depth and solidity. On the advice of Frederick Sandys, he began to make careful drawings from models and to prepare landscape studies in the open air. The result was a number of fine illustrations, published during the early and mid-1860s in such magazines as the *Cornhill Magazine, Good Words, The Leisure Hour, London Society* and *Once a Week*. His most extended commission was for a new edition of the works of Elizabeth Gaskell (1863–7). Like Sandys and Millais, Du Maurier made masterly use of the white outlines of the crinoline, building up designs in which the female form is an element either of strong dramatic force or of controlled elegance.

On the death of John Leech in 1864, Du Maurier was appointed as social cartoonist for *Punch*. For a few years the fine book illustrations continued, but slowly his drawings became more routine. His most impressive contribution to *Punch* was *A Legend of Camelot* (1866), a parody of the Pre-Raphaelite illustrations to Edward Moxon's edition of Alfred Tennyson's *Poems* (1857). The precise observation that lies behind Du Maurier's *Punch* cartoons is often sharply revealing of social nuance, usually within the upper-class world. Something of an outsider himself, he unerringly captured snobbery and pretension. As a fine amateur musician, he used his drawings *Music at Home* (an irregular series, 1871–88) to mock those who talked through after-dinner performances or who shamelessly patronized talented artists. Occasionally, a more alarming note enters. In a *Little Christmas Dream* (1868) a prehistoric monster pursues a little boy down the street, while in *Old Nick-Otin Stealing Away the Brains of his Devotees* (1869) a self-destructive smoking orgy is in progress. Du Maurier's scornful reactions to the Aesthetic movement produced a burst of outstanding cartoons in the late 1870s and early 1880s, centred on the figure of the aesthetic hostess, Mrs Cimabue Brown, and her acolytes, Postlethwaite, the poet, and Maudle, the painter.

Du Maurier's creative path as an artist led downhill. He grew weary of producing two cartoons a week, as the sight of his remaining eye deteriorated. In his last years, encouraged by the friendship of Henry James, he wrote three novels, *Peter Ibbetson* (1891), *Trilby* and *The Martian* (1896). All three combined autobiographical material with a plot involving the supernatural. The strains of the popular success of *Trilby* were in part responsible for Du Maurier's death from heart disease in 1896.

WRITINGS

'The Illustration of Books from the Serious Artist's Point of View', *Mag. A.*, xiii (1890), pp. 349–53, 371–5
Trilby (London, 1894)
Social Pictorial Satire (London, 1898)
The Young George Du Maurier: A Selection of his Letters, 1860–1867, ed. D. Du Maurier and D. P. Whiteley (London, 1951)

BIBLIOGRAPHY

T. M. Wood: *George Du Maurier; The Satirist of the Victorians: A Review of his Art and Personality* (London, 1913)
D. P. Whiteley: *George Du Maurier* (London, 1948)
L. Ormond: *George Du Maurier* (London, 1969)
R. Kelly: *George Du Maurier* (Boston, MA, 1983)

LEONÉE ORMOND

Dumbrell, Lesley (*b* Melbourne, 14 Oct 1941). Australian painter. She studied at the Royal Melbourne Institute of Technology (1959–62). Her style was formed during the 1960s, when the prevailing taste was for hard-edge, colourfield abstraction. Kandinsky's work influenced her towards an exhilarating use of colour, Bridget Riley's work towards an exploration of optical effects. Vital to Dumbrell's art was her ability to combine and synthesize, bringing to her work a greater personal touch without forsaking its mathematically precise arrangement and introducing elements resonant with the abstract patternings of other cultures. In *Harmattan* (1976; Canberra, N.G.), short vertical lines form a tightly woven grid that unifies the composition; contrasting reds and blues and blues and greens are arranged so that the whole surface seems to vibrate. Dumbrell began to expand the grids into increasingly lighter configurations in such works as *Spangle* (1977; Sydney, A.G. NSW), where the lines abut one another in livelier, less rigid patterns.

Dumbrell's watercolours played an important role in the development of her ideas. They provided inspiration for later works and, while still rigorously disciplined, contain a free and joyful rendering of the original impulse. This exuberance is evident as a thread running from watercolour to canvas in the early 1980s, where the geometric shapes and trimly contoured lines seem to explode like fireworks.

In the mid-1970s Dumbrell was a founder-member of the Women's Art Register, and she was actively involved in feminist arts collectives. At that time critical discussion focused on the notion of a 'feminine sensibility' and emphasized women's traditional arts such as needlework. The more positive climate for women's art, together with the greater public role Dumbrell assumed in the art world, may account for the fuller confidence that emerged in her paintings of the 1970s. Journeys to Italy (in 1985 and 1986) encouraged her to adopt a more sensuous palette of rich reds and browns. At the same time Dumbrell altered the way she defined space in her paintings. It had previously appeared as a shallow ambiguous recess on which webs of colour hung. She now pierced it with jagged shapes, thrusting backwards and forwards across the picture plane. The space in *Still-life* (1985; Melbourne, artist's col.) is tight, even claustrophobic, but there is a majestic solemnity to Dumbrell's work of the late 1980s that reflects an unrelenting search for consonant form.

BIBLIOGRAPHY

J. Burke: 'Deneutralising the Mainstream: Three Women Abstract Painters', *Field of Vision, A Decade of Change: Women's Art in the 70s* (Melbourne, 1990), pp. 50–58

G. Gunn: 'Lesley Dumbrell', *A. & Australia*, xviii/1 (1980), pp. 25–8

Colour and Transparency: The Watercolours of Lesley Dumbrell, Robert Jacks and Victor Majzner (exh. cat. by I. Zdanowicz and P. McCaughey, Melbourne, N.G. Victoria, 1986)

JANINE BURKE

Dumée, Guillaume (*b* ?Fontainebleau, 1570; *d* Paris, 1646). French painter. He was primarily a decorative painter, employed on schemes commissioned by Henry IV at the royal palaces of the Louvre, the Tuileries, Saint-Germain-en-Laye and Fontainebleau. None of these works survives, however, and they are known only through the writings of André Félibien and Henri Sauval and from a handful of drawings that have been associated with the work. At Saint-Germain Dumée worked under Toussaint Dubreuil on the decoration of a gallery with scenes from Pierre de Ronsard's *La Franciade*. It is possible that he was in charge of the work after Dubreuil's death. Two drawings associated with the scheme have been attributed to him: *Hyanthus and Clymenus Sacrificing to Venus* (Paris, Louvre) and the *Companions of Hyanthus* (Besançon, Mus. B.-A. & Archéol.). At the Louvre he worked on the Cabinet de la Reine, which he decorated with scenes from

Torquato Tasso's *Gerusalemme liberata c.* 1610–14, collaborating with Jacob Bunel, Ambroise Dubois and Gabriel Honnet. Dumée was responsible for three scenes known from drawings: *Olindo and Sofronia at the Stake* (Rouen, Bib. Mun.), *Clorinda Interceding with the Sultan on Behalf of Olindo and Sofronia* and *Olindo and Sofronia Freed from the Stake* (both Paris, Ecole N. Sup. B.-A.).

Dumée was also active as a portrait painter, delivering in 1612 a group portrait of the *Magistrates and Aldermen of Paris* (untraced) intended for the Hôtel de Ville, Paris. In 1605 he had been appointed Garde des Peintures at Saint-Germain, a title he gave up in 1626 in favour of his son Toussaint Dumée (1601–after 1656), in order to devote himself to the post of Peintre des Tapisseries, to which he had been appointed in 1610.

BIBLIOGRAPHY

A. Félibien: *Entretien sur les vies et les ouvrages des plus excellens peintres, anciens et modernes* (Paris, 1685–8, 2/1725/*R* London, 1967), i, pp. 713–14

H. Sauval: *Histoire et recherches des antiquités de la ville de Paris* (Paris, 1724/*R*/1733, 2/1750)

S. Béguin: 'Guillaume Dumée, disciple de Dubreuil', *Studies in Renaissance and Baroque Art Presented to Anthony Blunt* (London, 1967), pp. 91–7

THIERRY BAJOU

Dumeel, Alart. *See* ALART DU HAMEEL.

Dumile (Feni) [Zwelidumile Geelboi Mgxaji Mslaba Feni] (*b* Worcester, Cape Province, 21 May 1939; *d* New York, 16 Oct 1991). South African sculptor and printmaker, active in South Africa, London and New York. After his mother's death when he was *c.* eight years old, he lived with relatives in Cape Town until the age of eleven. In the early 1950s he moved to Soweto under the care of his uncle. In 1963 and 1964, while undergoing treatment for tuberculosis, he was given some art materials and began his drawing career in earnest. Like many black South African artists from the late 1950s, Dumile had to negotiate the laws of apartheid that made his presence as a self-employed artist in the white city an offence. Dumile described himself as having never received any 'real' tuition and talked of artists learning from one another. Dumile was 'discovered' by Madame Haenggi, an art dealer who promoted his early work.

Before his departure from South Africa in 1968, Dumile had a number of successful exhibitions of drawings and sculptures comprising portrayals of tormented and anguished people, animals and township scenes. These early works were acquired by some of the major museums in South Africa. On arrival in London (1968), he was represented by the Gainsborough Galleries. An invitation by the University of California, Los Angeles (UCLA), in 1978 led him to settle in the USA, where New York became his home. The work that he produced in exile was marked by greater stylization and lacked the searing social content of his earlier work.

BIBLIOGRAPHY

E. J. De Jager: *Contemporary African Art in South Africa* (Cape Town, 1973)

The Neglected Tradition: Towards a New History of South African Art (1930–1988) (exh. cat. by S. Sack, Johannesburg, A.G., 1988–9), pp. 17–18, 45–7, 103

STEVEN SACK

Dumitrescu, Sorin (*b* Bucharest, 18 March 1946). Romanian painter and printmaker. After graduating from the Institute of Fine Arts in Bucharest in 1970, he had his first one-man exhibition at the Orizont Gallery, Bucharest, in 1972. His early works show the influence of Expressionism; both his graphic works and his paintings of this period explored psychic tensions in a figurative vision influenced by Corneliu Baba, by Spanish Baroque painting and by the prehistoric art of Altamira. His exhibition of 1976 at the Institute of Architecture, Bucharest, revealed a new direction: exploring the abstract symbolic values of elementary signs, painted on canvas, paper or on objects. He won public acclaim for his one-man exhibition of 1980, *Hypersigns*, at the Galeria de Artă Dalles, Bucharest, in which he exhibited several series of large canvases with such titles as *Hypersigns* (e.g. see 1980 exh. cat., pl. 1(a–h)), *Places* and *Man*. These were shown in a large exhibition space, organized as a kind of initiation course and with a spiritual atmosphere imbued with esoteric connotations. In these works he explored the expressive values of Asian spiritual and visual traditions and created abstract pyramidal forms that resembled Indian palaces, Japanese pagodas and Assyrian towers. Later Dumitrescu evolved towards an art inspired by Byzantine painting and the culture of Orthodox Christianity. His works of the 1980s sought to reinterpret traditional Christian teaching, but they retained a contemporary relevance through the artist's attempt to find a modern visual vocabulary for ancient religious themes, as in his *Spiritual Environment*, at the exhibition *Filocalia* in 1990 in Bucharest.

BIBLIOGRAPHY

O. Barbosa: *Dictionarul artistilor români* (Bucharest, 1974), p. 166
D. Haülică: 'Sorin Dumitrescu's Projects and Constructive Archetypes', *Secolul 20*, nos 231–2 (1980)
Sorin Dumitrescu (exh. cat. by D. Haülică, Bucharest, Gal. A. Dalles, 1980)
A. Titu: *13 pictori români contemporani* (Bucharest, 1983), pp. 31–2
A. Plesu: *Ochiul și lucrurile* [Eye and objects] (Bucharest, 1986), pp. 176–86

MAGDA CARNECI

Dumonstier [Du Monstier; Dumontier; Dumoustier; Du Moustier]. French family of artists. At least 11 artists of this name are known, working variously as painters, draughtsmen, designers, goldsmiths and sculptors, and active from the 16th century to the 18th (see fig.). The exact relationships of some family members are difficult to determine; these include Cosme Dumonstier I (*d* Rouen, 1552), a goldsmith known to have worked for Rouen Cathedral; Etienne Dumonstier I (*fl* Rouen, *c.* 1501), an illuminator working at the château of Gaillon for Cardinal Georges d'Amboise; Cardin (or Carentin) Dumonstier, a sculptor mentioned in the accounts of the Bâtiments du Roi from 1540 to 1550; and Charles Dumonstier, active in the mid-18th century as a painter and engraver: his works include portraits of *Louis XV* and *Marie Leczinska* (Paris, Louvre). The main branch of the family began with the painter and illuminator Jean Dumonstier (*d* Rouen, *c.* 1535), whose son (1) Geoffroy Dumonstier followed his profession. Another son, Meston Dumonstier (*fl c.* 1535), was a goldsmith in Rouen. Geoffroy's sons (2) Etienne Dumonstier II, (3) Pierre Dumonstier (i) and Cosme Dumonstier II (*b c.* 1545–50; *d* Rouen, 1605), as well as Cosme and Etienne's respective sons, (4) Daniel Dumonstier and (5) Pierre Dumonstier (ii), are best known as portrait draughtsmen working for the French court. Daniel's sons Etienne III and Nicolas were also artists (*see* (4) below). The last member of this branch

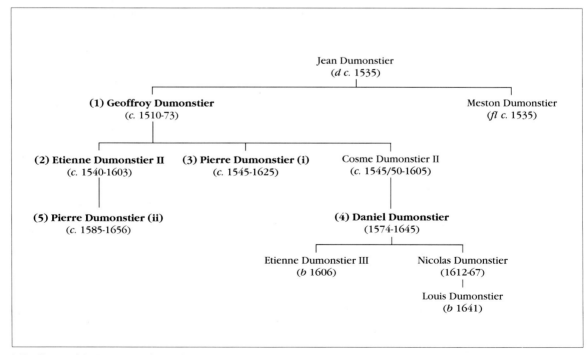

1. Family tree of the Dumonstier family of artists

was Nicolas's son Louis Dumonstier (*b* 25 Nov 1641), a mediocre reproductive engraver.

(1) Geoffroy Dumonstier (*b c.* 1510; *d* Paris, 15 Oct 1573). Illuminator, painter, designer and etcher. He worked for Francis I, Henry II and Catherine de' Medici. Among his most remarkable works is the frontispiece to the *Registre du Chartrier de l'hospice général de Rouen* (Rouen, Bib. Mun.). In 1549 the *Chronologia inclytae urbis Rothonogensis* cited him as the most famous Rouennais painter. He appears to have run the most important illumination studio in the town, and the 60 miniatures of the illuminated manuscript *Chants royaux* (Paris, Bib. N.) were executed under his direction. He is mentioned in the royal accounts from 1537 to 1540 and worked during this period at the château of Fontainebleau under the direction of Rosso Fiorentino. In about 1545 he was in Rouen and executed designs for stained-glass windows; he must also have been the designer of stained-glass windows at the church of St Acceul at Ecouen, near Paris, as well as those of the chapel of the château, and of the ceramic floor by the potter Masséot Abaquene (*fl* 1528; *d* before 1564). A number of his drawings survive (e.g. Paris, Louvre and Ecole N. Sup. B.-A.). Twenty-six etchings, mostly of New Testament subjects, are attributed to Geoffroy; two are dated 1543 and 1547 respectively. Like his other graphic works they are bold in technique and effect; his expressive refinements and the sharp profiles of his characters reveal the influence of Rosso and of Antonio Fantuzzi. In 1570 he is mentioned as a master painter in Paris.

(2) Etienne Dumonstier II (*b c.* 1540; *d* Paris, 23 Oct 1603). Painter and draughtsman, son of (1) Geoffroy Dumonstier. He worked for Henry II, Catherine de' Medici and the last Valois kings, and later for Henry IV. He is mentioned in the royal accounts as 'peintre et valet de chambre' from 1569 to 1599. In 1570 Catherine sent him as a diplomat to Vienna, where he probably drew a portrait of *Elizabeth of Austria*, with a view to her marriage to Charles IX. In 1586 he received an annuity of 1330 livres, greater even than that received by François Clouet. The Bibliothèque Nationale, Paris, possesses about ten portrait drawings by him, which are finely executed, with light modelling and delicate colouring; those of *Charles de Lorraine, Duc de Mayenne* and the *Duchesse de Joyeuse* are the most noteworthy.

(3) Pierre Dumonstier (i) (*b c.* 1545; *d* Paris, 1625). Painter and draughtsman, son of (1) Geoffroy Dumonstier. He was the brother of (2) Etienne Dumonstier II, with whom he collaborated. In 1583 he was appointed Peintre et Valet de Chambre to Henry III and in 1586 to the Queen Mother, Catherine de' Medici. He was the author of more than 40 surviving portrait drawings in red, black and white chalk representing members of the French court (e.g. *Henry IV, Catherine de' Medici* and *Marguerite de Valois*; all Paris, Bib. N.). His minutely detailed drawing technique, relying on a system of hatching, is often uncertain and cumbersome. He made a sketch of himself with his brother Etienne (St Petersburg, Hermitage).

(4) Daniel Dumonstier (*b* Paris, *bapt* 11 May 1574; *d* 22 June 1645). Painter and draughtsman, nephew of (2) Etienne Dumonstier II and (3) Pierre Dumonstier (i). In 1601 he was appointed painter to the Dauphin (later Louis XIII) and in 1603 Peintre et Valet de Chambre to Henry IV. He enjoyed great favour at court; in 1622 he was granted accommodation in the Louvre, and in 1626 he was appointed Peintre et Valet de Chambre to Gaston, Duc d'Orléans, the King's brother. His witty and satirical spirit brought him the friendship of men of letters such as François de Malherbe, Nicolas-Claude Fabri de Peiresc and Gédéon Tallemant des Réaux. His collection of natural history curiosities, medals, objets d'art, books and manuscripts was famous: Jules, Cardinal Mazarin, acquired some of it after his death, while another part of it, judged 'licentious and indecorous', was destroyed on the orders of Anne of Austria.

Daniel Dumonstier was in great demand for his portraits, the fidelity of which was admired. 'They are so stupid', he said of his models, 'that they believe themselves to be like I make them and pay me the better for it.' He would start with a sketch in black and red chalk then add pastel. He was criticized for his choppy, heavy use of the stump in drawing and for his often red-faced figures. His portraits, of uneven quality, are often dated. The earliest bear the date 1600 and the latest 1642; that of the theologian *Jean Duvergier de Hauranne, Abbé St Cyran* (Paris, Louvre) was drawn from memory in 1644. On most of them can be found the inscription *fait par ou pour D. Dumonstier*, but the name of the sitter rarely appears.

Daniel Dumonstier: *Jacqueline Vardes de Bueil, Comtesse de Moret*, black and red chalk with pastels, 500×350 mm, 1623 (Paris, Bibliothèque Nationale)

The considerable number of surviving drawings bears witness to his great productivity. The sitters are presented under life-size, bust-length, turned slightly in three-quarter profile, and they include some of the most famous figures of early 17th-century France. Although there are male portraits in Daniel Dumonstier's oeuvre, such as those of *Brûlart de Sillery* and *François de Béthune*, the majority are of women, including *Jacqueline Vardes de Bueil, Comtesse de Moret* (see fig.) and *Mme de Ballieu* (all Paris, Bib. N.). A large proportion of these drawings are copies of earlier likenesses, with costumes and hairstyles brought up to date. The bulk of his drawings are to be found in Paris (Louvre; Bib. N.) and St Petersburg (Hermitage); several painted portraits have been attributed to him on the basis of his drawings (e.g. *François de l'Aubépine, Marquis de Hauterive*; Chantilly, Mus. Condé). The drawings were widely reproduced by such famous contemporary engravers as Thomas de Leu, Léonard Gaultier, Michel Lasne and Abraham Bosse.

Daniel Dumonstier's sons Etienne Dumonstier III (*b* 1606) and Nicolas Dumonstier (1612–67) were also draughtsmen and painters. The former soon abandoned his career as a draughtsman for that of a lutenist, while the latter was a Peintre et Valet de Chambre du Roi, went to Italy, and in 1665 was elected to the Académie Royale as a painter of pastel portraits.

(5) Pierre Dumonstier (ii) (*b* Paris, *c.* 1585; *d* Paris, 26 April 1656). Draughtsman, son of (2) Etienne Dumonstier II. As a royal equerry and Valet de Chambre he enjoyed a reputation as a man of the world. In 1603 he was in Flanders selling his father's drawings to Archduchess Isabella Clara Eugenia, Regent of the Netherlands. He made several trips to Italy, his presence in Rome in the 1640s being confirmed by a copy (Paris, Louvre, Cab. Dessins) of Raphael's *Disputa* (Rome, Vatican, Stanza della Segnatura) signed *Petrus Du Monstier faciebat 1642 Romae*; he returned to Paris around 1650. Only ten surviving chalk drawings are attributed to him. They include six portraits and a *Head of a Turk* (all Paris, Bib. N.), as well as a drawing of the hand of the painter Artemisia Gentileschi (London, BM). The portraits, the most famous of which is that of *Henri de Lavardin-Baumanoir*, are notable for their modelling and expressiveness; their colouring, which is vigorous but full of nuance and clarity, is of a freshness unequalled by his cousin (4) Daniel Dumonstier.

BIBLIOGRAPHY

DBF; Thieme–Becker

H. Bouchot: *Les Portraits au crayon* (Paris, 1884)
J. Guiffrey: 'Les Dumonstier', *Rev. A.* [Paris], xviii–xix (1905), pp. 5–16, 136–46, 325–42; xx (1906), pp. 47–61
E. Moreau-Nélaton: *Les Frères Dumonstier* (Paris, 1909)
H. Stein: 'L'Origine des Dumonstier', *Rev. A. Anc. & Mod.* (1909), pp. 75–7
J. Guiffrey and P. Marcel: *Inventaire des dessins du Louvre et du musée de Versailles*, iv (Paris, 1910), pp. 52–9
E. Moreau-Nélaton: *Les Clouet et leurs émules*, 3 vols (Paris, 1924)
L. Dimier: *Histoire de la peinture de portraits en France au XVIème siècle*, 3 vols (Paris, 1924–5)
A. Linzeler: *Inventaire du fonds français: Graveurs du seizième siècle*, Paris, Bib. N., Cab. Est. cat. (i) (Paris, 1932), pp. 302–7
T. D. Kamenskewa: *Catalogue des dessins français du musée de l'Ermitage* (Leningrad, 1961), nos 36–45
H. Zerner: *Ecole de Fontainebleau: Gravures* (Paris, 1969)
J. Adhémar: 'Les Dessins de Daniel Dumonstier au Cabinet des Estampes de la Bibliothèque Nationale', *Gaz. B.-A.*, n. s. 5, lxxv (1970), pp. 129–50
——: 'Les Portraits dessinés au XVIème siècle au Cabinet des Estampes', *Gaz. B.-A.*, n. s. 5, lxxxii (1973), pp. 327–50
F. Perrot: 'Les Vitraux d'Ecouen', *Doss. Archéol.*, 26 (1978), pp. 76–85

VÉRONIQUE MEYER

Dumont. French family of sculptors. The first in a long line of sculptors was Pierre Dumont (*d* ?1737), who was a member of the Accademia di S Luca, Rome, and sculptor to Leopold, Duke of Lorraine (*reg* 1697–1729), for whom he provided decorative work in, among other places, Nancy (1719; destr.). The career of his son (1) François Dumont, was cut short by a tragic accident. François's son (2) Edme Dumont, grandson (3) Jacques-Edme Dumont and great-grandson (4) Augustin-Alexandre Dumont were all winners of the Prix de Rome for sculpture.

BIBLIOGRAPHY

G. Vattier: *Une Famille d'artistes: Les Dumont (1660–1884)* (Paris, 1890)

(1) François Dumont (*b* Paris, *c.* 1687–8; *d* Lille, 14 Dec 1726). His earliest independent work was at the chapel of the château of Versailles (1709–11), where he produced ornamental and figurative sculpture in stone and stucco. Although in 1709 he won the Prix de Rome for sculpture, he never went to Italy. In 1710 he modelled the group *Prometheus Bound* (bronze, exh. Salon 1725; Brit. Royal Col.) and in 1712 he was received (*reçu*) as a member of the Académie Royale on presentation of a statuette of a *Titan Struck by Lightning* (marble; Paris, Louvre), a work intensely and emotionally Baroque. The following year he executed decorative relief sculptures (destr.), as well as grandiloquent statues of *St Peter* and *St Paul* (now St Jacques, Compiègne), for the priory of St Pierre-en-Chastres near Compiègne. Among his other works were the marble monument to the *Infant Daughters of Joseph Bonnier de La Mosson* (1719; fragment Montpellier, Mus. Fabre); decorative sculpture at the château of Lunéville, Meurthe-et-Moselle (1721; fragments *in situ*), for Leopold, Duke of Lorraine (*reg* 1697–1729); and dramatic monumental statues of *St Peter*, *St Paul*, *St John the Baptist* and *St Joseph* for the portals of the transept of St Sulpice, Paris (stone, 1725; *in situ*). Dumont was accidentally crushed to death during the installation of his elaborate and theatrical monument to *Louis, Duc de Melun* in the Dominican church at Lille (marble, bronze and lead, 1725–6; destr.; see Souchal, 1977, p. 277).

BIBLIOGRAPHY

Souchal

F. Souchal: 'François Dumont, sculpteur de transition', *Gaz. B.-A.*, n. s. 5, lxxv (1970), pp. 225–50

(2) Edme Dumont (*b* Paris, ?1719; *d* Paris, 10 Nov 1775). Son of (1) François Dumont. He was a pupil of Edme Bouchardon; in 1748 he won the Prix de Rome for sculpture (though he was never in Italy). In 1752, while still a student at the Ecole des Elèves Protégés, he was accepted (*agréé*) by the Académie Royale but was not received (*reçu*) as a full member until 16 years later, on presentation of a statuette of *Milo of Croton* (marble; Paris, Louvre), a weakly classicizing version of a theme popular with Baroque sculptors. Among other works, he executed allegorical pedimental sculptures (stone, 1756; *in situ*) for the Sèvres porcelain manufactory; he also made the sculpture pediment (stone, *in situ*) for the courtyard of the Hôtel des Monnaies in Paris.

(3) Jacques-Edme Dumont (*b* Paris, 10 April 1761; *d* Paris, 21 Feb 1844). Son of (2) Edme Dumont. In 1777 he was admitted to the Ecole des Elèves Protégés. As a student of Augustin Pajou, he won the Prix de Rome in 1788, by which time he had already executed a number of independent works, including the relief of the *Discovery of the Relics of SS Gervase and Protase* (marble, 1783; Sées Cathedral). He was in Italy from 1788 to 1793 and then returned to France in the hope of receiving commissions from the Revolutionary Convention. In this he was disappointed and turned instead to the production of statuettes and medallions (e.g. Lons-le-Saunier, Mus. B.-A.; Semur-en-Auxois, Mus. Mun.). He fared better under the Consulate and the Empire, receiving commissions for, among other works, a monumental statue of *Louis IV* (1801; St Denis Abbey); a statue of *General François-Séverin Marceau* (untraced; sketch models Paris, Louvre); and a seated statue of *Jean-Baptiste Colbert* (stone, 1808; Paris, Pal. Bourbon). He continued in official favour during the Restoration, producing a monument to *Chrétien-Guillaume de Malesherbes* (1819; Paris, Pal. Justice) and a statue of *General Charles Pichegru* (destr. 1830). He was also active as a portrait sculptor. Examples of his work in this genre are the tenderly realistic bust of his mother, *Marie-Françoise Berthault* (plaster; Paris, Louvre) and the severely Neo-classical bust of the *Empress Marie-Louise* (1810; priv. col.).

BIBLIOGRAPHY
Souchal
G. Hubert: 'Deux maquettes de Jacques-Edme Dumont', *Rev. des A.*, 3 (1951), pp. 181–3
J. Pontefract: *Inventaire des collections de sculpture moderne . . . du Musée de Semur-en-Auxois* (1970–71)

(4) Augustin-Alexandre Dumont (*b* Paris, 4 Aug 1801; *d* Paris, 27–28 Jan 1884). Son of (3) Jacques-Edme Dumont. He entered the Ecole des Beaux-Arts, Paris, in 1818, won the Prix de Rome for sculpture in 1823 and spent the next seven years in Italy, producing works such as the *Infant Bacchus Nurtured by the Nymph Leucothea* (1830; Semur-en-Auxois, Mus. Mun.). He returned to France shortly after the July Revolution of 1830; a succession of public commissions followed, including one for the statue of *Nicolas Poussin* for the Salle Ordinaire des Séances in the Palais de l'Institut de France, Paris (1835; *in situ*). The government of the Second Republic commissioned from him a statue of *Maréchal Thomas Bugeaud de la Piconnerie* (*c.* 1850; version, Versailles, Château). As well as the various large public sculptures of historical figures that he produced for provincial centres under the Second Empire, he executed a number of portrait sculptures, such as that of the naturalist *Alexander von Humboldt* (1871; Versailles, Château). Many of the public monuments that Dumont designed were destroyed under the Commune (1871); he was prevented by illness from producing any work after 1875.

BIBLIOGRAPHY
DBE
G. Vattier: *A. Dumont: Notes sur sa famille, sa vie et ses ouvrages* (Paris, 1885)
La Sculpture française au XIXe siècle (exh. cat. by A. Pingeot, Paris, Grand Pal., 1986)

Dumont, Joseph Jonas (*b* Düsseldorf, 1811; *d* Sint Joosten-Node, Brussels, 29 March 1859). Belgian architect. One of the leading personalities in the development of historicism in Belgium in the 1840s and 1850s, he was appointed in 1845 as a draughtsman and architect for the Royal Commission on Monuments. A journey in England in 1846, when he studied recent prison architecture at Pentonville, Reading and Aylesbury, brought him into closer contact with the English Gothic Revival. He mainly designed prisons and also churches, of which he is believed to have built more than 20, most of them in the Gothic Revival style. They include the village churches at Mall (1844–5), Wanfercée-Baulet (1844–8), Ceroux-Mousty (1848) and Erps-Kwerps (1850) and the large church of Bouillon (1848–9), which unusually is in an Italian Renaissance style. His most important ecclesiastical work is the church of St Boniface (1847–9) at Ixelles, a large hall-church with a west front like a screen and stucco detailing typical of the early phase of the Gothic Revival in Belgium.

As an architect of prisons, Dumont established his reputation with his prize-winning design for Leuven (1848), which was followed by the buildings at Brussels (1848), Liège (1850), Charleroi (1851), Dinant (1851) and Antwerp (1854–9). Most are in a castellated Tudor style, severe and military in effect. The Law Courts with prison cells at Verviers (1852) are, however, in a Renaissance style. A complex of three houses (1850; destr.), which Dumont erected in the Rue des Arts in Brussels, attracted attention because of their elaborate French Renaissance detailing. They mark his most important contribution to domestic architecture in Belgium and the transition from Neo-classicism to the Renaissance Revival and Second Empire modes of the second half of the century. As a restorer Dumont devised projects for the Hal Gate and Notre-Dame du Sablon in Brussels and worked on the Cloth Hall and St Martin's Cathedral (destr. 1914) in Ypres and the churches at Aarschot, Tongeren, Sint-Truiden and Nivelles. His approach to medieval architecture was strongly influenced by classical ideas and later attracted severe criticism from Thomas Harper King, W. H. J. WEALE and other protagonists of the archaeological movement.

BIBLIOGRAPHY
BNB
C. Kramm: *De levens en werken der Hollandsche en Vlaamsche kunstschilders, beeldhouwers, graveurs en bouwmeesters* (Amsterdam, 1857–64) [app., p. 41]
Piron: *Algemeene levensbeschrijving der mannen en vrouwen van België* (Mechelen, 1860), p. 102
Exposition nationale d'architecture (exh. cat., Brussels, Pal. B.-A., 1883), p. 77
G. B.: 'Dumont Jozef Jonas', *Winkler Prinz encyclopedie van Vlaanderen*, ii (Brussels, 1973), p. 350
Poelaert en zijn tijd (exh. cat., text V. G. Martiny and others; Brussels, Pal. Justice, 1980), pp. 148–53
J. van Cleven: '19th Century: Architecture', *Flemish Art*, ed. H. Liebaers (Antwerp, 1985), p. 504

JEAN VAN CLEVEN

Dumont, (Gabriel-)Pierre-Martin (*b* Paris, 1720; *d* Paris, 1791). French draughtsman and architect. Having won the Prix de Rome in 1737, he studied at the Académie de France in Rome in 1742–6. In his last year there he was received by the Accademia di S Luca on presentation of his project designs for a *Temple of the Arts* (Rome, Accad.

N. S Luca). During a second stay in Rome in 1750 he accompanied Jacques-Germain Soufflot to Paestum, near Naples, where he collaborated on making measured drawings (Paris, Bib. Ecole Ponts & Chaussées) of the temples; these were engraved for Soufflot's *Suite de plans des trois temples antiques tels qu'ils existaient en 1750 dans le bourg de Paestum* (1764). After his return to Paris, Dumont undertook commissions as an architect (apart from some domestic projects little is known about this aspect of his life), but he mainly specialized in publishing collections of engravings of his own architectural drawings, for example *Les Ruines de Paestum* (1769), and those of such artists as Jean-Laurent Legeay and François de Neufforge. In this way he played an important role in the dissemination of early Neo-classicism in France. His measured drawings of the Roman theatres of Herculaneum and Lyon appeared in the *Parallèle des plans des plus belles salles de spectacles d'Italie et de France* (1764), which appeared in the same year as the first part of his most important work, the *Recueil de plusieurs parties de l'architecture sacrée et profane des différents maîtres* (1764–7), with engravings (many by René Charpentier) after drawings by Legeay, Dumont and others. From 1763 he published reports on the restoration of the dome of St Peter's, Rome; his *Plan général et vue perspective . . . de l'intérieur de Sainte-Geneviève* (1781) was dedicated to the memory of his old friend Soufflot, who had died the previous year.

BIBLIOGRAPHY

M. Gallet: *Demeures parisiennes sous Louis XVI* (Paris, 1964)
Piranèse et les Français (exh. cat., ed. G. Brunel; Rome, Acad. France; Dijon, Mus. B.-A.; Paris, Hôtel de Sully; 1976), pp. 143–5
Actes du colloque 'Piranèse et les Français': Rome, 1976
M. Mosser and D. Rabreau: 'L'Architecture des lumières en France', *Rev. A.* [Paris], lii (1981), pp. 47–52

MARIE-FÉLICIE PÉREZ

Dumouchel, Albert (*b* Salaberry-de-Valleyfield, 15 April 1916; *d* Saint-Antoine-sur-le-Richelieu, 11 Jan 1971). Canadian printmaker and painter. He was born in a working-class village in south-east Quebec and had a musical training from 1926. From 1940 to 1945 he was a designer and printer for the textile firm Montreal Cottons Ltd in Valleyfield. There, with his colleague James Lowe (1889–1975), he took up printmaking and photography. A UNESCO grant enabled him to travel to Europe in 1955 and 1956, extending his knowledge of watercolour and lithography in Paris studios.

Dumouchel also had an active career as a teacher of drawing and painting at Valleyfield College (1942–9) and from 1942 to 1960 taught drawing and printmaking at the Ecole des Arts Graphiques de Montréal (from 1958 the Institut des Arts Graphiques). Here he directed publication of the journal *Les Ateliers d'arts graphiques* in 1947 and 1949. In 1948, he signed the manifesto PRISME D'YEUX, drawn up under the aegis of Alfred Pellan. Dumouchel was head of the printmaking section of the Ecole des Beaux-Arts de Montréal from 1960 until 1969 and was made artist-in-residence at the University of Quebec, Montreal, in 1970.

Dumouchel's mature work is marked by three distinct periods: the first, Surrealist in its inspiration, lasted from the mid-1940s to the beginning of the 1950s; the second, from 1953 to 1963, was in the spirit of lyrical abstraction; and finally, from 1964 to 1971, his work tended towards the new figuration.

BIBLIOGRAPHY

Regard sur l'oeuvre d'Albert Dumouchel (1916–71) (exh. cat., Montreal, Mus. A. Contemp., 1979)

YOLANDE RACINE

Du Mu [Tu Mu; *zi* Muzhi] (*b* Chang'an [modern Xi'an], 803; *d*?852). Chinese poet and calligrapher. He was born into a high-ranking official family, his grandfather, Du You, having been a prime minister under the Tang dynasty (AD 618–907). He was educated by his family and at the early age of 26 received the civil-service degree of *jinshi*. He spent most of his life as an official both in and out of the court. He and the revered poet Du Fu were bracketed together by the respective nicknames Young Du and Old Du. His poetry was diverse: some poems expressed his thoughts on historical events and sites, others, usually thought superior, were lyrical descriptions of rural scenes. Du also wrote critical and prescriptive pieces on social evils, such as the prose–poem *Afang Palace*.

Documents from the Song period (960–1279) claim that his writing could be seen on the doors of the farmer's house in Huzhou, Zhejiang Province, where he worked as a local governor and that his brushstrokes were vigorous and powerful. His only extant authentic work of calligraphy is the *Poem of Zhang Haohao* (Beijing, Pal. Mus.), a poem written to express his sympathy for Zhang Haohao, the destitute former concubine of Du Mu's friend and patron, the minister Shen Chuanshi, with whom Du Mu had become acquainted while he was working for Shen. Writing in the Ming period (1368–1644), the influential art critic, calligrapher and painter Dong Qichang described Du Mu's calligraphy as 'deeply influenced by the style of the Six Dynasties [AD 222–589]'. Du Mu also copied the paintings of GU KAIZHI, and in his *Hua shi* ('History of painting', 1103) Mi Fu considered Du's copies to be 'excellent and charming'.

BIBLIOGRAPHY

W. R. B. Acker: *Some T'ang and Pre-T'ang Texts on Chinese Painting* (Leiden, 1954), pp. 379–80
Miao Yue: *Du Mu zhuan* [Commentary on Du Mu] (Beijing)

HAIYAO ZHENG

Dun Aengus. Fortification on Inishmore, one of the Aran Islands lying off the Atlantic coast of Co. Galway in the west of Ireland. This stone-built multivallate structure is of unproven date between the 6th century BC and the 9th century AD, and it is frequently referred to as one of the finest prehistoric monuments in western Europe. The cashel (fort) stands on the edge of a 100 m-high cliff that drops sheer to the sea. It comprises a series of four defensive walls and a band of *chevaux-de-frise* (see below) enclosing a semicircular area of over 4 ha, each line of defence terminating at the cliff edge. Never excavated (its central area is so devoid of soil cover that investigation might prove fruitless), Dun Aengus fort is of a type conventionally dated in Ireland to the Early Christian period, perhaps between the 5th and 9th centuries AD. However, a stray find of an Iron Age (*c.* 750–*c.* 50 BC) brooch in a wall and dates from the 7th century BC onwards for *chevaux-de-frise* elsewhere in Europe (Scotland, France and Spain) may suggest a rather earlier date for this spectacular site.

The innermost wall, enclosing an area some 50 m in diameter, is constructed in three concentric bands of stone up to 4 m thick, and it still stands 4 m high. The two inner bands of stone form internal terraces or walkways 1.5–2.0 m high, approached by sets of steps; stairways also run vertically or sideways from one level to the next. Access to this central area was via a massively lintelled gateway at the north-east. Unfortunately, much of this inner defence was reconstructed in the early 1880s by the Board of Works, which added buttresses to the outside of the wall and may also have 'enhanced' the internal terraces and steps (no record was kept of the original state of the stonework). The terraced second wall, which survives to a height of 4 m, follows the course of the first wall for half of its circuit and then breaks away to run east for 80 m before turning south to the cliff. The similarly terraced third wall is now fragmentary, although surviving parts measure up to 2.5 m high in places; the outer, fourth, wall is partially destroyed, comprising a low lintelled gateway on the north and remains of wall sections measuring 2.5 m thick and 1.5 m high.

The most impressive aspect of the middle defences is the *cheval-de-frise*, a band of thousands of pointed limestone blocks set immediately outside the third wall in the west and flanking the second wall in the east. Its width varies between 10.0 m and 23.6 m, and the stones, which range from an average of 1.0–1.3 m high to a maximum of 1.7 m high, are set on end and extremely close together, so that walking through them is dangerous, difficult and slow. An avenue leads through the stones to a gateway at the north-east of the second wall.

BIBLIOGRAPHY

E. Estyn Evans: *Prehistoric and Early Christian Ireland: A Guide* (Dublin, 1966)

P. Harbison: 'Wooden and Stone Chevaux-de-frise in Central and Western Europe', *Proc. Prehist. Soc.*, xxxvii/1 (1971), pp. 195–225

SARA CHAMPION

Dunand, Jean [Jules, John] (*b* Lancy, 20 May 1877; *d* Paris, 7 June 1947). French sculptor, metalworker, painter and designer, of Swiss birth. He trained as a sculptor from 1891 to 1896 at the Ecole des Arts Industriels in Geneva and in 1897 was awarded a scholarship by the city of Geneva that enabled him to continue his studies in Paris, where Jean Dampt, a sculptor from Burgundy, introduced him to the idea of producing designs for interior decoration and furnishing. Dunand worked on the winged horses on the bridge of Alexandre III in Paris (*in situ*), while simultaneously continuing his research into the use of metal in the decorative arts. His first pieces of dinanderie (decorative brassware) were exhibited at the Salon de la Société Nationale des Beaux-Arts of 1904 in Paris. In 1906 he gave up sculpture in order to devote his time to making dinanderie and later to lacquering. His first vases (e.g. 'Wisteria' vase, gilt brass with cloisonné enamels, 1912; Alain Lesieure priv. col., see Marcilhac, pl. 138) reflect Art Nouveau forms, but he quickly adopted the geometric forms of Art Deco in his work. In 1912 the Japanese artist Seizo Sugawara asked him to solve a problem concerning

dinanderie, and in exchange he was given instruction in lacquering. From then on he produced vases, folding screens, doors and other furniture (e.g. *Geometric Decor*, black and red lacquered screen, priv. col., see Marcilhac, pl. 46). Around 1925 he started to use egg shell on lacquer. Different effects were produced by varying the size of the pieces and by using the inside or the outside of the shell. He used this technique for both portraits and Cubist compositions (e.g. tray; Geneva, Mus. A. & Hist.). He worked closely with contemporary artists and designers, especially the furniture designer Jacques-Emile Ruhlmann and the couturiers Madeleine Vionnet and Paul Poiret. His jewellery designs demonstrate a preference for pure, geometric forms, with regular black and red lacquer dots on the metal surface.

See also FRANCE, fig. 84.

BIBLIOGRAPHY

Jean Dunand, Jean Goulden (exh. cat., ed. Y. Brunhammer; Paris, Gal. Luxembourg, 1973)

V. Arwas: *Art Déco* (London, 1978)

F. Marcilhac: *Jean Dunand: His Life and Works* (London, 1991)

ANNE WINTER-JENSEN

Dunbar, William Nugent. *See* ANDERSON, JAMES.

Duncanson, Robert S(cott) (*b* Fayette, Seneca County, NY, ?1821; *d* Detroit, MI, 21 Dec 1872). American painter. A self-taught mulatto artist and a landscape painter of the Hudson River school tradition, Duncanson was the first Afro-American artist to receive international recognition. Born into a family of painters and handymen, Duncanson first worked as a house-painter and glazier in Monroe, MI. By 1841 he was in Cincinnati, OH, where he learnt to paint by executing portraits and copying prints. Throughout the 1840s he travelled as an itinerant artist between Cincinnati, Monroe and Detroit. His early work was crude and primitive, betraying his lack of training.

Around 1850 Duncanson was awarded his largest commission, the landscape murals for the Cincinnati estate, Belmont (now Cincinnati, OH, Taft Mus.). These consist of eight landscape panels (2.77×2.21 m each) in *trompe l'oeil* French Rococo frames on the walls of the entrance halls. The painted decorations were inspired by French and English wallpapers. The panels are among the most accomplished domestic mural paintings of pre-Civil War America.

During the 1850s, influenced by the work of Thomas Cole and William Lewis Sonntag, Duncanson began to specialize in landscape painting. His works were either observations of scenery or imaginary compositions that often illustrated literary subjects. A tour of Europe, made in the summer of 1853 with Sonntag, inspired a series of romantic European scenes in the late 1850s. He also produced realistic views of American scenery such as *Landscape with Rainbow* (1859; Washington, DC, N. Mus. Amer. A.). When it was exhibited, this painting was hailed as 'one of the most beautiful pictures painted on this side of the [Allegheny] mountains' (*Cincinnati Enquirer*, 17 Jan 1860). This success prompted Duncanson to create 'a masterwork'—the largest easel painting of his career, *The Land of the Lotus Eaters* (1.34×2.25 m, 1861; Stockholm, Kun. Husgerådskam.). The subject was suggested by

Alfred Tennyson's poem of that title and was also influenced by Frederic Edwin Church's *Heart of the Andes* (1859; New York, Met.). Duncanson's vast tropical landscape earned him the status of 'the best landscape painter in the West' (*Cincinnati Gazette*, 30 May 1862).

In 1863 Duncanson left for Europe again, to exhibit his work. However, the turmoil of the Civil War forced him to travel first to Montreal, where he quickly became recognized as the city's foremost artist. The stark realism of his Canadian paintings, including *Owl's Head Mountain* (1864; Ottawa, N.G.), stimulated a younger generation of artists to establish the first Canadian school of landscape painting. Duncanson's successful entry as a Canadian in the 1865 International Exposition in Dublin took him to Scotland and England in the summer of that year. In England he was patronized by members of the aristocracy and received critical accolades.

On his return to Cincinnati in 1866 Duncanson began 'working up' his European sketches into finished paintings. Among these was *Ellen's Isle, Loch Katrine* (1870; Detroit, MI, Inst. A.), inspired by Sir Walter Scott's poem 'The Lady of the Lake'. The contrast of serene light and the rugged Scottish Highlands makes this Duncanson's most sensitive synthesis of wilderness scenery, pastoral sentiment and literary subject-matter. However at this time he began to experience a dementia marked by schizophrenic behaviour, including the belief that he was possessed by spirits. The paintings of this period reflect his mental condition. While many of his landscapes have the serenity of *Ellen's Isle*, he also painted stormy seascapes like *Sunset on the New England Coast* (1871; Cincinnati, OH, A. Mus.). He was incarcerated at the Michigan State Retreat in 1872 after experiencing a nervous breakdown while hanging an exhibition of his work in Detroit. He died three months later.

BIBLIOGRAPHY

J. Porter: 'Robert S. Duncanson: Midwestern Romantic-Realist', *AIA J.*, xxxix (1951), pp. 99–154

Robert S. Duncanson (exh. cat., ed. G. McElroy; Cincinnati, OH, A. Mus., 1972)

J. Ketner: 'Robert S. Duncanson: The Late Literary Landscape Paintings', *A.J.* [New York], xv (1983), pp. 35–47

Sharing Traditions: Five Black Artists in Nineteenth Century America (exh. cat., ed. L. Hartigan; Washington, DC, N. Mus. Amer. A., 1985)

J. D. Ketner: *The Emergence of the African-American Artist Robert S. Duncanson, 1821–1872* (Columbia and London, 1993)

JOSEPH D. KETNER II

Dundas, Sir Lawrence, 1st Baronet (*b* ?Fingask, Tayside, *c.* 1710; *d* Aske Hall, N. Yorks, 21 Sept 1781). Scottish merchant, MP and collector. Dundas belonged to a cadet branch of an ancient Scottish family and was one of the outstanding merchant contractors of the 18th century. As Commissary-General of the army in Flanders during the Seven Years War he made a fortune of over £600,000. He was created a baronet in 1762 and was MP for Linlithgow (1747–8), Newcastle-under-Lyme (1762–8) and Edinburgh (1768–81).

Dundas was a patron of the arts on an exceptional scale. Among those he commissioned was Robert Adam, who worked at Kerse, Dundas's seat in Stirlingshire, at Moor Park, Herts, and at 19 Arlington Street, London. He also employed Lancelot 'Capability' Brown and John Carr of York at Aske Hall and Sir William Chambers at Dundas House, Edinburgh. He bought furniture from Thomas Chippendale (i), whose work for Arlington Street included an exceptionally expensive (£510 4s.) set of chairs designed by Adam. Richard Wilson was commissioned to paint a set of three large views of Moor Park in 1765 (Aske Hall, N. Yorks). Dundas may well have encouraged his son Thomas, later 1st Baron Dundas, to sit to Batoni in 1764 (Cardiff, N. Mus.) and certainly enabled him to spend lavishly while on the Grand Tour. Sir Lawrence himself was painted with his grandson, later 1st Earl of Zetland, by Zoffany in 1769, in the Pillar Room at Arlington Street (Aske Hall).

Zoffany's portrait was clearly intended to commemorate Dundas's interest in Old Masters. As such contemporaries as Lady Mary Coke recognized, he assembled a remarkable collection of pictures, mainly by Dutch and Flemish painters of the 17th century. Of these Jan van de Cappelle's *A Calm* (1654; Cardiff, N. Mus.) is seen above the chimney in Zoffany's group, flanked by cabinet pictures and by two of Dundas's extensive series of genre scenes by David Teniers II, including *Journeymen Carpenters* (ex-Mrs James Teacher priv. col.). Among the larger works acquired by Dundas was Aelbert Cuyp's *Peasants and Cattle in a Hilly River Landscape* (London, N.G.). The collection was of unusually consistent quality, and of those formed in the third quarter of the 18th century only that of John Stuart, 3rd Earl of Bute, was of greater distinction. Sir Lawrence no doubt bought most of his pictures in London, but he may well have acquired some while in the Low Countries during the Seven Years War and employed agents in Paris, where indeed his taste was paralleled more generally than in Britain. A large part of the collection was sold by Sir Lawrence's heir, Thomas, 1st Baron Dundas, at the auctioneers Greenwood's, London, 29–31 May 1794.

BIBLIOGRAPHY

The Zetland Collection from Aske Hall (exh. cat., Barnard Castle, Bowes Mus., 1962)

L. Namier and J. Brooke: *The House of Commons, 1754–1790*, ii (London, 1964), pp. 357–61

D. Sutton and others: 'The Nasos of the North', *Apollo*, lxxxvi (Sept 1967), pp. 168–225

M. Webster: *Johan Zoffany, 1733–1810* (exh. cat., London, N.P.G., 1976), no. 56

Important Old Master Paintings (sale cat., London, Sotheby's, 21 April 1982)

The Treasure Houses of Britain: Five Hundred Years of Private Patronage and Art Collecting (exh. cat., ed. G. Jackson-Stops; Washington, DC, N.G.A., 1986), pp. 356–7, nos 281–2

FRANCIS RUSSELL

Dunhuang [Tun-huang]. Site of Buddhist cave sanctuaries located 25 km south-east of the county town of Dunhuang, Gansu Province, China. In the wider definition Dunhuang also includes the Yulin caves at Anxi and the Xi qianfo dong (Western Cave of the Thousand Buddhas). From the 4th century to the 14th, Buddhist cave sanctuaries were continuously carved out in four or five tiers on the cliff face of an alluvial hill that faces east over the Dang River. At its height as a Buddhist complex in the 8th century AD, the complex is believed to have comprised more than 1000 caves. A total of 492 caves with wall paintings and sculptures survive, the earliest of which date to the early 5th century AD. A hoard of old and rare manuscripts was also found at Dunhuang, including the world's oldest printed book (*see* CHINA, §XIII, 3).

Dunhuang was first established as a garrison town in the 2nd century BC in the course of the westward expansion of the Han empire (206 BC–AD 220). As the eastern endpoint of the Silk Route that linked China with Central Asia, India and the Mediterranean world, Dunhuang soon gained importance not only as a strategic outpost for military and commercial purposes but also as a meeting point of civilizations (*see* SILK ROUTE, §2). By the 3rd century AD Dunhuang was already well established as a centre of Buddhism. The Buddhist art there fully testifies to the process of artistic transformation that occurred as a result of the interaction between the native tradition of China and those of India and Central Asia.

The caves at Dunhuang fall into three main categories. The first type seems to derive from the Indian *vihāra* (monastery) type: it consists of a rectangular hall with a ceiling in the shape of a truncated pyramid, a recessed niche holding a statue in the west wall, facing the entrance, and small cells along the side walls for monks (e.g. caves 268 and 285). The second type consists of a massive quadrangular pillar dominating the back section, the front face of which is carved with a large niche, with smaller niches at the sides. The pillar resembles those found at the KIZIL and KUMTURA caves in Central Asia but might originally have been derived from the Indian *caitya* cave, which houses a stupa for ritual circumambulation. In the front of this second stage, the ceiling has two sloping sections and is of native Chinese origin (e.g. caves 251, 254 and 259). The third type is the simplest: it is square in plan, with a niche for statues in the west wall and a ceiling in the shape of a truncated pyramid. The first two types are found in caves of the 5th and 6th centuries AD, while the third type predominates from the 7th century onward. In some large caves of the 9th and 10th centuries the niche is replaced by a platform towards the rear to support sculptures.

Because of the softness of the rock, cult images were made of polychrome clay. Larger statues were modelled in clay over an armature of straw or wood, while smaller ones were sculpted directly from clay or sometimes cast from a mould. The cut rock surfaces were smoothed with a layer of plaster that was allowed to dry and was then painted with mineral pigments. Outlining was frequently done free-hand, but templates punched with holes were also used, especially for repeated images of the Buddha (*see* CHINA, §V, 2).

In caves of the Northern Dynasties period (AD 386–581) the most popular images were of Shakyamuni, the historical Buddha, and of the *bodhisattva* Maitreya, the future Buddha, who is represented with legs crossed at the ankles (e.g. caves 275 and 254). Devotion to Shakyamuni was reinforced with the predominant themes in the wall paintings of *jātaka*s, stories of the Buddha's previous lives (caves 257 and 428), and legends of the Buddha's life (caves 254 and 290). Themes based on popular Mahayana *sūtra*s coexisted and became popular towards the end of the 6th century AD, as seen in the representation of Shakyamuni and Prabhutaratna in a scene from the Lotus Sutra (caves 303 and 420), or the debate between Manjushri and Vimalakirti (cave 276). The stucco figures with

Dunhuang, *Buddhist Triad*, detail from a painting of the *Western Pure Land of Amitabha*, colours on silk, Tang period, 8th–9th century AD (London, British Museum)

soft expressions and close-fitting drapery with ringlike folds (caves 259, 248 and 283) are similar to those from other Central Asian sites. Shading, highlighting in white to model the form, and the use of an even, taut line to define contour were methods used in both Indian and Central Asian wall paintings, while the use of fluttering scarves and schematic colouring demonstrates a strong Central Asian influence (caves 272 and 285). By the mid-6th century AD, the native Chinese Wei–Jin (AD 220–420) style, which emphasized flat treatment of form and slender figures outlined in calligraphic lines, was also apparent at Dunhuang (caves 249 and 285).

Under the unified Sui (AD 581–618) and Tang (AD 618–907) dynasties, direct links with the metropolitan centres along the Yellow River brought fresh impetus to Dunhuang. A new wave of Indian influence was integrated into the existing tradition and gave rise to a mature, international Tang style that spread to Dunhuang and further west in the 7th and 8th centuries (e.g. cave 220, which dates to AD 642 and is particularly important in documenting this artistic synthesis). Buddhism was by now well established in China. Pure Land Buddhism became the most successful popular, devotional religion. From the 7th century AD depictions of Pure Lands, most notably Sukhavati, the western Pure Land of Amitabha Buddha, became the most important theme at Dunhuang (caves 220, 217, 320 and 172; see fig.). The Pure Lands, where the faithful will be reborn, were conceived on a grand scale and cover entire wall surfaces; the sensuous images of palatial architecture, lotus ponds, gardens and sumptuous ornaments, as well as heavenly music and dance, are visual metaphors of the attainment of bliss in the Pure Land. The way idealism and realism were used in the portrayal of figures conforms to the Buddhist spiritual hierarchy: the tranquil Buddhas and *bodhisattva*s are portrayed in an idealized manner, whereas the disciples, who are subject to human emotions and the process of aging, are depicted realistically, as are the protective Heavenly Kings and *lokapala*s ('guardians'), with their ferocious demeanour and contorted postures. Integrated with the existing painting techniques are the refined, secular court style (cave 220) and the use of the expressive, modulated, calligraphic line for modelling (cave 103). Architectural diagonals and multiple vanishing points on a central axis were used successfully to represent a deep recession in space, while the symmetry and balance in composition reinforced the iconic nature of the compositions (caves 172 and 148). The narrative content of the *sutra*s was illustrated in great detail against naturalistic landscapes (cave 103). In sculpture and in painting, the figures are fully rounded and well-proportioned, the slender figures of the first half of the 7th century AD (cave 328; *see* CHINA, fig. 68) giving way to an opulent, heavy style in the 8th century (caves 45 and 194).

From AD 781 to 848 Dunhuang was under the control of the Tibetans. From 848 to 1036 the area was governed by local military governors, first the Zhang and then the Cao, who were *de facto* rulers of the region and major patrons of the cave complex. From the 9th century AD a greater range of popular *sutra*s was represented, and large caves were often crowded with many *sutra* panels (caves 159, 98 and 61). These paintings were increasingly conventionalized, although there was also innovation in the conception of the paintings, as in the panorama of Mt Wutai in cave 61. More esoteric images were represented, although devotion to salvation figures such as Avalokiteshvara, Kshitigarbha and Manjushri grew in popularity. The Tangut Xixia and the Mongols, who were in control of Dunhuang from 1036 to 1227 and from 1227 to 1368 respectively, had an impact on the style and iconography of the art of Dunhuang. From the 13th century, however, Dunhuang declined rapidly in importance as a Buddhist site.

In 1900, when thousands of scroll paintings and manuscripts in many languages were recovered from a cave sealed in the early 12th century, the significance of Dunhuang as a medieval Buddhist centre became apparent. Foreign explorers and scholars, most notably AUREL STEIN and PAUL PELLIOT, were the first to investigate the site, and the bulk of portable paintings and manuscripts from the sealed cave are now in the British Museum and British Library, London, the National Museum in New Delhi, the Musée Guimet and the Bibliothèque Nationale in Paris and the Hermitage Museum in St Petersburg, while a collection of the Dunhuang manuscripts are in the National Library, Beijing. Manuscripts from the caves include legal, artistic, religious and medical documents from the 7th century to the 10th and shed light on an otherwise murky period of Tibetan history (*see* TIBET, §VII and CENTRAL ASIA, §II, 5(ii)). A research institute set up by the Chinese government in the 1940s, now known as the Dunhuang Research Academy, continues to undertake conservation and research work on the site.

See also CHINA, §§III, 1(i) and V, 3(i)(a).

BIBLIOGRAPHY

P. Pelliot: *Les Grottes de Dunhuang*, 24 vols (Paris, 1914–24)
A. Stein: *Serindia*, 5 vols (Oxford, 1921)
A. Waley: *A Catalogue of Paintings Recovered from Tun-huang by Sir Aurel Stein* (Delhi and London, 1931)
E. Matsumoto: *Tonkō-ga no kenkyū* [Research on Dunhuang paintings], 2 vols (Tokyo, 1937)
T. Akiyama: *Chūgoku bijutsu* [Arts of China], ii (Tokyo and California, 1969)
Tonkō Bakōkutsu [The Mogao caves at Dunhuang], Chūgoku sekkutsu [Chinese cave temple series], 5 vols (Tokyo, 1980–82)
R. Whitfield: *The Art of Central Asia*, 3 vols (Tokyo, 1982–5)

DOROTHY C. WANG

Dunikowski, Ksawery [Xawery] (*b* Kraków, 24 Nov 1875; *d* Warsaw, 26 Jan 1964). Polish sculptor and painter. He began studying *c.* 1895 at the sculptural studio of Bolesław Syrewicz at the Royal Castle, Warsaw. In 1896–9 he attended the studio of Alfred Daun and then in 1899–1903 the studio of Konstanty Laszczka, both sculptors from the School of Fine Arts, Kraków. From 1904 to 1910 Dunikowski taught sculpture at the School of Fine Arts, Warsaw. In 1914 he went abroad, firstly to England, then France. He returned to Poland in 1922 and took over the chair of sculpture at the Academy of Fine Arts, Kraków (to 1939 and again between 1946 and 1955). During World War II he was interned in Auschwitz concentration camp. From the mid-1950s onwards he lived in Warsaw and commuted to Wrocław where he ran the sculpture studio at the State Higher School of Plastic Arts. He exhibited from 1895 both at home and abroad (e.g. at the Venice Biennali of 1920 and 1954), winning many prizes and distinctions. He held many scholarships and received the highest Polish decorations.

Dunikowski's early sculptures (e.g. the portrait of *H. Szczygliński*, 1898; Warsaw, N. Mus.) are characterized by their realism and impressionistic style and the use of dramatic lighting contrasts. In about 1903 he produced the plaster sculpture *Breath or Waft* (Warsaw, N. Mus.; *see* POLAND, fig. 14), a simple, geometrical work that was strikingly innovative not just by Polish standards. In 1906 Dunikowski produced a series of bronze sculptures without bases, entitled *Pregnant Women* (Warsaw, N. Mus.), the most mature example of Polish Secessionist sculpture. From *c.* 1910 Dunikowski's work (particularly the *Madonna* and the *Adoration of Christ* on the portal of the Jesuit church in Kraków) is distinguished by a schematization of form and the influence of Auguste Rodin. During his Parisian period (1914–22) Dunikowski produced, among others, two large, geometrical and expressive compositions entitled *King Bolesław the Brave* and the polychrome *Self-portrait*, as well as stylized female forms. On returning to Poland he produced in 1925–6 the wood, largely polychrome *Wawel Heads*, an addition to the Renaissance coffered ceiling in Wawel Castle, Kraków. He also attempted sculptural monuments and produced the small but expressive monument to *Józef Dietl* (bronze, 1936). After World War II, due to ill health, he was occupied with painting (e.g. the *Auschwitz* series) and designing monuments, the most outstanding of which is the granite monument to *The Uprising* (1946–52) on St Anna Hill. He had many pupils of diverse artistic tendencies, among them Maria Jarema, Jerzy Bereś and Barbara Zbrożyna (*b* 1923).

BIBLIOGRAPHY

SAP

M. Treter: *Ksawery Dunikowski: Próba estetycznej charakterystki jego rzeźb* [Ksawery Dunikowski: a study of the aesthetic characteristics of his sculptures] (Lwów, 1924)

S. Flukowski and K. Wyka: *Xawery Dunikowski* (Kraków, 1948)

WOJCIECH WŁODARCZYK

Dunker, Balthazar Anton (*b* Saal, nr Stralsund, Sweden [now Germany], 15 Jan 1746; *d* Berne, 2 April 1807). Swiss watercolourist, draughtsman, engraver and illustrator. He received his first drawing lessons in Stralsund from Philipp Hackert in 1762. In 1765 he moved to Paris and became a pupil of Joseph-Marie Vien and Noël Hallé. In Paris Dunker met a number of artists in the circle around the engraver Jean Georges Wille, including Pierre-François Basan, Jacques Gabriel Huquier, Adrian Zingg and Sigmund Freudenberger. At this period he worked as a draughtsman and watercolourist, principally of landscapes. He worked with the engravers and publishers Huquier and Basan, collaborating with other artists on an album of engravings from the collection of Etienne-François, Duc de Choiseul, *Recueil d'estampes gravées d'après les tableaux du cabinet de Monseigneur le duc de Choiseul* (Paris, 1771). In 1772 Dunker was working in Basle and in 1773 in Berne. He produced book illustrations for the *Heptaméron français* (Berne, 1778) as well as vignettes, genre scenes and landscapes, such as *View of Fribourg* (Berne, Kstmus.). He worked on the engravings for Caspar Wolf's Alpine views *Merkwürdige Prospekte aus den Schweizer-Gebürgen* (Berne, 1789) and wrote three small volumes of *Schriften*, containing poems, farces and prose pieces, which were published anonymously between 1782 and 1785. His large family and the worsening political situation in Switzerland brought him into financial difficulty, but from 1798 to 1800 he produced humorous picture sequences and political caricatures, in which he made fun of the representatives of the new order in Switzerland, for example in *Das Jahr MDCCC in Bildern und Versen* (Berne, 1800). His son Philip Heinrich Dunker (*b c.* 1780; *d* 3 May 1836) also became a painter and engraver.

WRITINGS

Schriften (Berne, 1782–5)

BIBLIOGRAPHY

SKL

R. Nicolas: *Balthasar-Antoine Dunker* (Geneva, 1924)

J. Gantner and A. Reinle: *Die Kunst des 19. Jahrhunderts* (1962), iv of *Kunstgeschichte der Schweiz von den Anfängen bis zum Beginn des 20. Jahrhunderts* (Frauenfeld und Leipzig, 1936–62), p. 188

Zeichnungen des 18. Jahrhunderts aus dem Basler Kupferstichkabinett (exh. cat. by Y. Boerlin-Brodbeck, Basle, Kstmus., 1979), pp. 38–40

MATTHIAS FREHNER

Dunkley, John (*b* Savanna-la-Mar, Jamaica, 10 Dec 1891; *d* Kingston, 17 Feb 1947). Jamaican painter and sculptor. Essentially self-taught, he is believed to have been introduced to the rudiments of painting by an amateur painter while living in Panama in the late 1920s. His career, however, began in earnest in Jamaica in the mid-1930s. His painting methods were slow and painstaking, using a variety of unorthodox materials and tools, including housepaint and brushes made from the twigs of trees. His mature work (*c.* 1939–47) reveals an individual approach both to subject-matter and to the formal organization of his paintings. The majority of these are imagined landscapes, although many were probably based on memories of particular places, especially the Rio Cobre Gorge in St Catherine, Jamaica. The landscapes, with their dark tonalities, fantastic overblown foliage and other much-repeated motifs (never-ending roads, trees with phallic truncated branches, ravines) and their unusual creatures (jerboas, spiders, crabs), are truly disquieting works. In many, this unease is heightened by the anticipation of some terror about to strike; a mongoose lies in wait for an unsuspecting bird; a bird is poised to strike a fish; a jerboa approaches a giant spider's web; a woman fishing is perched perilously close to the edge of a cliff.

Dunkley occasionally ventured into social commentary, as in his *President Roosevelt Gazed at Portland Bight* (1940; Kingston, priv. col.) and in *Shepherd* (*c.* 1944; Kingston, priv. col.) where the political activist Alexander Bustamante is cast in the role of the Good Shepherd, to whom a flock of sheep come. His *Parade with Tramcars* (*c.* 1945; Kingston, Bolivar Gal.) lovingly records the Coke Methodist Church and aspects of city life of the 1930s, while *Diamond Wedding* (1939; Kingston, Inst. Jamaica, N.G.), of an old couple, is full of affectionate humour and quiet dignity. Dunkley was a loner. Although in his lifetime he did contribute works to exhibitions, he refused to be drawn into the fervour of activity surrounding the fledgling Jamaican art movement of the late 1930s and the 1940s. When his talent was recognized and he was approached to join the art classes organized by the Institute of Jamaica in the 1940s, he declined, stating: 'I see things a little differently'. Although he produced some 30 stone- and wood-carvings, it is on the basis of his 50 known paintings that his reputation as Jamaica's finest 'primitive' artist rests. He left no true followers, but something of his love of the fantastic existed in younger artists such as Carl Abrahams and Colin Garland.

BIBLIOGRAPHY

John Dunkley (exh. cat. by D. Boxer, Kingston, Inst. Jamaica, N.G., 1976)

Jamaican Art, 1922–1982 (exh. cat. by D. Boxer, Washington, DC, Smithsonian Inst.; Kingston, Inst. Jamaica, N.G.; 1983)

DAVID BOXER

Dunlap, William (*b* Perth Amboy, NJ, 18 Feb 1766; *d* New York, 28 Sept 1839). American painter, historian and playwright. After working in England with Benjamin West between 1784 and 1787, Dunlap concentrated primarily on the theatre for the next 20 years. His two main interests are documented in his large *Portrait of the Artist Showing his Picture of Hamlet to his Parents* (1788; New York, NY Hist. Soc.). He wrote more than 30 plays and was called by some the 'father of American drama'. He was the director and manager of the Park Theatre in New York from 1797 until its bankruptcy in 1805 and again, in its revived form, from 1806 to 1811. He began to paint miniatures to support his family in 1805 and travelled the East Coast of America as an itinerant artist. By 1817 he had become, in his own words, 'permanently a painter'.

Dunlap always lived on the verge of poverty. To increase his income, he produced a large showpiece *Christ Rejected* (1822; Princeton U., NJ, A. Mus.), which was probably inspired by West's painting of the same subject (1814; Philadelphia, PA Acad. F.A.). Though he exhibited it with considerable success, his later religious and historical canvases were not so well received. Dunlap resigned his membership of the American Academy in New York in 1826 to help Samuel F. B. Morse found the rival National Academy of Design, of which he became treasurer and later vice-president. In 1827 he turned again to the theatre, writing three more plays. Casting about for a profitable venture, he began his *History of the American Theater*, published by subscription in 1832.

Dunlap spent his last years writing reviews for the *New York Mirror* and working on his most important publication, the *History of the Rise and Progress of the Arts of Design in the United States*, a comprehensive compilation of biographies of artists working in America. Arranged chronologically according to the date when each artist began his professional work in the USA, the book includes sculptors, engravers and architects but deals most fully with painters. It comprises 287 lives of artists, varying in length from one line to many pages, and an appendix with brief accounts of 176 more. With little source material available to him, Dunlap based his biographies on material solicited directly from the artists, their friends and relatives. In many cases he used the artists' autobiographical contributions without alteration. In other instances he invented dialogue to establish character, making use of his skills as a playwright to create a convincing narrative. He also drew heavily on his own wide experience, recorded in extensive diaries. His expressed goal was to produce a lively account that would both appeal to the general reader and fulfil an educational function. The biographical form, he wrote, 'admits of anecdote and gossip'.

Dunlap's book is full of exhaustive detail and has its heroes (Benjamin West) and villains (John Trumbull). His approach is factual, anecdotal and opinionated, not theoretical. There is very little critical analysis of art, and his judgements are moral rather than aesthetic. Subject-matter was of greater interest to him than style. The work for this book was accomplished in only two years, yet its overall accuracy remains unchallenged, especially in the material relating to the period of Dunlap's own lifetime. The vivid biographies led one critic to call Dunlap 'the American Vasari'. In spite of some shortcomings the book is a remarkably complete record of early American artists and is still the single most valuable source of information on many of the artists, containing much primary source material and preserving important facts not recorded elsewhere.

WRITINGS
History of the Rise and Progress of the Arts of Design in the United States, 2 vols (New York, 1834); ed. A. Wyckoff, intro. N. P. Campbell (New York, 1965)
D. C. Barck, ed.: *Diary of William Dunlap (1766–1839)*, 3 vols (New York, 1930)

BIBLIOGRAPHY
O. S. Coad: *William Dunlap: A Study of his Life and Works and of his Place in Contemporary Culture* (New York, 1917/R 1962)

LEAH LIPTON

Dunoyer de Segonzac, André (Albert Maris) (*b* Boussy-Saint-Antoine, nr Paris, 7 July 1884; *d* Paris, 17 Sept 1974). French painter, draughtsman and printmaker. He began painting in 1903, studying in Paris and frequenting the Académie de la Palette and the studios of Luc Oliver Merson and Jean-Paul Laurens. After doing his military service he shared a studio with Jean-Louis Boussingault in 1907 and befriended Luc-Albert Moreau and Lucien Mainssieux. In 1908 he stayed for the first time in St Tropez, which became the setting for much of his work.

From 1909 Dunoyer de Segonzac exhibited regularly at the Salon des Indépendants, and at the Salon d'Automne in the following year he exhibited *The Drinkers* (1910; Paris, Pompidou), a work indebted in both its subject-matter and handling to the Realist tradition derived from the work of Gustave Courbet. He also took part in the Salon de la Section d'Or in October 1912 (*see* SECTION D'OR (ii)) and in the Armory Show in New York in 1913. His paintings of this period, such as *Le Déjeuner sur l'herbe (Les Pains de fantaisie)* (*c*. 1912–13; Paris, Pompidou), reveal the influence of Cubism and in a few cases that of Expressionism. On being conscripted in August 1914 he left St Tropez to join his army corps in Fontainebleau; during World War I he made a remarkable series of drawings in the trenches. After the War he was introduced by the French printmaker Jean Emile Laboureur (1877–1943) to etching, a medium with which he illustrated the novel *Croix de bois* (1921) by Roland Dorgelès. This marked the beginning of his lifelong involvement with etching: he produced more than 1600 prints, notably a series of 119 etchings for Virgil's *Géorgiques* (Paris, 1947), which celebrated nature and the female body.

In 1925, together with Moreau and the French painter André Villeboeuf (1893–1956), Dunoyer de Segonzac purchased Charles Camoin's villa Val Flor and rechristened it Le Maquis. Henceforth he stayed regularly in St Tropez, often meeting the writer Colette there and taking inspiration from the town and its environs. Unlike many Parisian artists, who on moving to the area were dazzled by the violence of the Mediterranean light, he devoted himself to transcribing the rare moments of dull grey light or cloudy skies, achieving a sense of timelessness and a melancholy mood both in his oil paintings and in drawings combining ink and watercolour, for example *Port de Saint Tropez*, 1933–5, *Saint Tropez vu de la citadelle*, 1950, *Saint Tropez en hiver par temps d'orage*, *c*. 1952 (all St Tropez, Mus. Annonciade). These more apparently conventional works, especially the Cézanne-influenced watercolours to which he increasingly turned at the end of his life, for example *The Marne at Chennevière* (1950; Brit. Royal Col.), ensured his essentially commercial success and earned him official recognition and favour with the establishment. He was made the curator of the Musée de l'Annonciade in St Tropez on its creation in 1955.

BIBLIOGRAPHY
A. Lioré and P. Cailler: *L'Oeuvre gravé de Dunoyer de Segonzac*, 8 vols (Geneva, 1958–70)
C. Roger-Marx: *Dunoyer de Segonzac* (Geneva, 1961)
H. Hugault: *A. D. de Segonzac* (Paris, 1973)
A. Distel: *A. Dunoyer de Segonzac* (Paris, 1980)

ERIC HILD-ZIEM

Dunstan (*b* ?910 or later; *d* Canterbury, 988; *fd* 19 May). Saint, Archbishop of Canterbury and patron. He was educated at Glastonbury Abbey, where he was appointed abbot *c*. 940–46. In 956–7 he was exiled to Ghent. Returning to England he was appointed successively Bishop of

Worcester and London in 958 and Archbishop of Canterbury in 959.

Dunstan's first biographer 'B' (?Byrhthelm) refers to him as adept in the arts of writing, playing the harp and painting and records his providing a design for a stole to be embroidered by a noblewoman. Surviving evidence of his artistic endeavours is sparse. A drawing of a monk prostrate at the feet of Christ (Oxford, Bodleian Lib., MS. Auct. F.4.32, fol. 1*r*) has an inscription probably in Dunstan's own hand identifying the monk with himself, but the drawing is by a different hand. Later writers claimed that Dunstan was an expert metalworker; but this may have been inferred from inscriptions on metalwork presented to churches by Dunstan, such as a water vessel recorded at Malmesbury.

At Glastonbury Dunstan remodelled the abbey church and added a cloister and domestic buildings; but excavation has shown the essentially modest nature of these works. Elsewhere also Dunstan's promotion of the monastic reform movement through his followers led to the erection of new monastic buildings, doubtless influenced by his ideas. But Dunstan's personal artistic contribution to these monasteries seems to have lain mainly in the presentation of pipe organs, bells and other items needed for worship.

See also ANGLO-SAXON ART, §IV, 2(i)(b).

BIBLIOGRAPHY

Vita S. Dunstani, Auctor B, ed. W. Stubbs, Rolls Ser., lxiii (1874), pp. 3–52

J. Higgitt: 'Glastonbury, Dunstan, Monasticism and Manuscripts', *A. Hist.*, ii (1979), pp. 275–90

C. R. Dodwell: *Anglo-Saxon Art: A New Perspective* (Manchester, 1982)

N. L. Ramsay, M. J. Sparkes and T. W. T. Tatton-Brown, eds: *St Dunstan: His Life, Times and Cult* (Woodbridge, 1992)

RICHARD GEM

Dünz, Johannes (*b* Brugg, *bapt* 17 Jan 1645; *d* Berne, 10 Oct 1736). Swiss painter. The son of the painter Hans Jakob Dünz II (*b* 1603; *fl* 1633) and grandson of the glass painter Jakob Dünz I (1580–1649), he settled in Berne in 1661. Dünz produced numerous portraits of the city's patricians and mayors, and his group portraits of the *Berne Library Committee* (1696–7; Berne, Burgerbib.), although harking back to Dutch guild paintings of the early 17th century, are of high quality. In his early years Dünz also produced topographical views for the painter Albrecht Kauw (1621–81) and drawings for the *Bernisches Aemter-, Regiments- und Geschlechterbuch* (Berne, 1701) by Viktor von Erlach. As a hobby he executed flower and fruit paintings, such as those representing the four seasons in his *Still-life* series (1710; Berne, Kstmus.).

BIBLIOGRAPHY

R. von Effinger: 'Leben des Malers Johannes Dünz von Bern', *Neujbl. Kstges. Zürich* (1845), pp. 1–5

M. Huggler: 'Zur Geschichte der barocken Malerei in Bern', *Z. Schweiz. Archäol. & Kstgesch.*, xxii (1962), pp. 123–4

Das Schweizer Stilleben im Barock (exh. cat., ed. P. Vignau-Wilberg; Zurich, Schweizer. Inst. Kstwiss., 1973)

MATTHIAS FREHNER

Dupain, Max(well Spencer) (*b* Sydney, 22 April 1911; *d* 27 July 1992). Australian photographer. By 1929, when he joined the New South Wales Photographic Society, he had been an enthusiastic photographer for five years. In 1930 he began exhibiting and became assistant to Cecil Bostock (1884–1939), a leading commercial photographer and devotee of Pictorial photography. Dupain studied art at the East Sydney Technical College and at Julian Ashton's Art School in Sydney. Within three years he had left Bostock and broken with the Impressionist effects of Pictorialism in favour of European-derived styles emphasizing form, dramatic contrasts and adventurous choice of subject. After a subsequent period of experiment with various modern artistic idioms, by the late 1930s he achieved a distinctive personal style based on perceptive and imaginative attitudes to subject-matter. His work had a growing documentary tendency possessing an affinity with developments in the USA.

During World War II Dupain worked first in a camouflage unit and then for the Department of Information (until 1947). This experience and the influence of British film makers enhanced his interest in the creative potential of documentary photography. Returning to private practice, he concentrated on architecture and industrial work and became Australia's foremost architectural photographer. The historical character of many such assignments and his increasing interest in photographing Australian landscape led to sympathy with campaigns for conservation of the national heritage and the environment. His photographs combine compositional originality and rigour with a sense of spontaneity, almost always with symbolic or metaphorical overtones. In 1975 the Australian Centre for Photography in Sydney organized a retrospective exhibition of his work, and in 1982 he was awarded the OBE.

PHOTOGRAPHIC PUBLICATIONS

Max Dupain's Australia (Melbourne, 1986)

Max Dupain's Australian Landscapes (Melbourne, 1988)

BIBLIOGRAPHY

H. Missingham: *Max Dupain Photographs* (Sydney, 1948)

G. Newton: *Max Dupain* (Sydney, 1980)

ROBERT SMITH

Du Pan, Barthélémy (*b* Geneva, 18 or 19 Aug 1712; *d* Geneva, 4 Jan 1763). Swiss painter. He studied art in Geneva, Paris and, according to Waterhouse, in Rome. He also travelled to The Hague, where he received commissions from the House of Orange. By December 1743 he was in England, where he soon obtained royal patronage, as for example with his large group portrait of the *Children of Frederick, Prince of Wales* (1746; Brit. Royal Col.). In 1746 and 1747 he was producing pictures for Frederick, probably including the full-length portraits of *Frederick, Prince of Wales* and *Augusta, Princess of Wales* (both Belfast, Ulster Mus.). In 1750 Du Pan was in Dublin, where he painted several portraits, including those of *William Stanhope, 1st Earl of Harrington* (known from a mezzotint by Michael Ford (*d* 1765)) and *John Boyle, 5th Earl of Orrery* (ex-Marston House, Somerset). By August 1751 he had returned to Geneva.

Du Pan's soft, decorative style owes much to the work of François Boucher and other French Rococo painters, and the luminous clarity managed in his handling of heads may have been influenced by the work of his compatriot Jean-Etienne Liotard. Du Pan's ability to obtain royal and aristocratic patronage in England lay in the vogue for the contemporary French style of portraiture in which he worked.

BIBLIOGRAPHY

Bénézit; Strickland; Thieme-Becker; Waterhouse: *18th C.*
O. Millar: *The Tudor, Stuart and Early Georgian Pictures in the Collection of Her Majesty The Queen*, 2 vols (London, 1963)

KIMERLY RORSCHACH

Duparc, Françoise(-Marie-Thérèse) (*b* Murcia, *bapt* 15 Oct 1726; *d* Marseille, 11 Oct 1778). French painter. She was the daughter of Antoine Duparc (1680–1755), a sculptor from Marseille, and a Spanish mother. The family returned to Marseille *c.* 1730. She was probably trained by her father but may also have worked in Jean-Baptiste van Loo's studio at Aix-en-Provence. Her sister, Josèphe-Antonia (*b* Murcia, 1728), also became a professional artist and accompanied her to Paris but died young. Françoise then travelled to London and exhibited three figure paintings (untraced) at the Free Society (1763) and three portraits (untraced) at the Society of Artists (1766). She went to Russia and produced some works (untraced) for Catherine the Great. By 1771 she was back in Marseille and became a member of the local Académie de Peinture in 1776. After her death an inventory of her belongings listed 41 canvases in her studio, but only four works are attributed to her now with any certainty. These are the four scenes of everyday life she bequeathed to the city of Marseille (all Marseille, Mus. B.-A.). Among them is the so-called *Knitter*, which depicts a young woman bent over some needlework. The painting is bathed in a softly diffused light that contributes to the subject's tranquil mood. The monumentality of Duparc's treatment of humble figures has led to comparisons with Chardin and Greuze, to whom her works have sometimes been attributed.

BIBLIOGRAPHY

P. Auquier: 'An Eighteenth Century Painter: Françoise Duparc', *Burl. Mag.*, vi (1905), p. 477
J. Billioud: 'Un Peintre de types populaires: Françoise Duparc de Marseille (1726–1778)', *Gaz. B.-A.*, n.s. 6, xx (1938), pp. 173–84
A. M. Alauzen: *La Peinture en Provence du XIVe siècle à nos jours* (Marseille, 1962)

LESLEY STEVENSON

Dupérac, Etienne [Du Perac, Stefano] (*b* Bordeaux, *c.* 1525; *d* Paris, 1601). French painter, engraver and garden designer. He went to Rome in 1550 and stayed there for over 20 years, soon becoming acknowledged as a first-rate engraver and designer. His work provides an invaluable record of later 16th-century Rome, telling much about the state of the ancient ruins, contemporary architecture and urban planning, especially the work of Michelangelo. Many of Dupérac's engravings were published by Antoine Laffréry. Those depicting the work of Michelangelo were published in 1569 after the latter's death (1564); they give a useful insight into Michelangelo's original, unrealized intentions for such projects in Rome as the Capitoline Hill and St Peter's. It has been shown that Dupérac designed and painted part of the decoration of the loggia of Pope Pius IV in the Vatican. His work as a painter continued on his return to France in 1570 when, after the publication of his *Vues perspectives des jardins de Tivoli* dedicated to the Queen, Marie de' Medici, Henry IV engaged Dupérac as court artist. He was also appointed architect to the King

and worked at Fontainebleau, where he executed the painted decoration in the bathroom, consisting of five mythological scenes of sea gods and the loves of Jupiter and Callisto. Dupérac may also have contributed to the garden designs, using his knowledge of Roman examples. Despite these later career developments, Dupérac remains best known for his invaluable contribution to the topographical study of Rome and its ruins in the latter half of the 16th century.

PRINTS

Urbis Roma sciografica (Rome, 1574) [bird's-eye view map of ancient Rome with buildings reconstructed]
Disegni de le ruine di Roma e come anticamente erono (Rome, *c.* 1574–80); ed. T. Ashby (London, 1908); intro. R. Wittkower (Milan, 1963)
I vestigi dell'antichità di Roma (Rome, 1575/*R* London, 1973)
Nova urbis Roma descriptio (Rome, ?1577) [large plan of contemp. Rome]

BIBLIOGRAPHY

T. Ashby: 'Le diverse edizioni dei *Vestigi dell'antichità di Roma* di Stefano du Perac', *La Bibliofilia*, xvi/11–12 (1915), pp. 401–21
E. J. Ciprut: 'Nouveaux documents sur Etienne Dupérac', *Bull. Soc. Hist. A. Fr.* (1960), pp. 161–73
H. Zerner: 'Observations on Dupérac and the *Disegni de le ruine di Roma e come anticamente erono*', *A. Bull.*, xlvii/4 (1965), pp. 507–12
L. H. Heydenreich and W. Lotz: *Architecture in Italy, 1400–1600*, Pelican Hist. A. (Harmondsworth, 1974), pp. 250, 252, 254–7

DANA ARNOLD

Duplessis [Du Plessis; Duplessy]. French family of goldsmiths, bronze founders, sculptors and designers, of Italian descent. Due to the similarity in name, there has been some confusion between father and son and the attribution of their work; they are now generally distinguished as Duplessis père and Duplessis fils. Jean-Claude Chambellan Duplessis [Giovanni Claudio Chiamberlano] (*b* Turin, ?1690–95; *d* Paris, 1774) practised as a goldsmith in Turin before his marriage in 1720 and probably worked for Victor Amadeus II. He moved with his family to Paris *c.* 1740, perhaps encouraged there by Juste-Aurèle Meissonier. In 1742 he was commissioned by Louis XV to design and make two large, bronze braziers, presented to the Turkish ambassador Saïd Mahmet Pasha (e.g. in Istanbul, Topkapi Pal. Mus.). From *c.* 1748 until his death he was employed at the porcelain factories of Vincennes and Sèvres as a designer of porcelain forms and supplier of bronze stands. He also supervised and advised craftsmen. In 1751 he produced eight drawings for the first major dinner-service commissioned by Louis XV. He played an influential role at the factory in the development of new porcelain forms in the Rococo style, and most of the shapes from the 1750s and many from the 1760s are attributed to him or bear his name. These include such vases as the Bras de Cheminée Duplessis (e.g. *c.* 1754; London, V&A), the Vase à têtes d'éléphant, which incorporates candelabra (*c.* 1756; London, Wallace) and such pieces of Rococo fantasy as the Saucière Duplessis in the form of an antique lamp (1756; Paris, Louvre). At least three versions of an écritoire survive (e.g. *c.* 1760; Munich, Residenzmus.), of which the original design by Duplessis is preserved in a collection of his designs at the Musée National de Céramique in Sèvres; another Ecritoire à Globes bears a grisaille head of Louis XV and the monogram of his daughter Madame Adélaïde (1758; London, Wallace). Duplessis showed an interest in Classical forms, and it is thought that either he or his son (who assisted him from 1752) may have influenced the creation of Neo-classical models at Sèvres in the early 1760s. Duplessis continued to maintain his own silversmithing and bronze-founding interests in Paris. Gilt-bronze wall-lights made in Paris and attributed to him include one with acanthus, laurel and reeds (1749; New York, Met.), and he is said to have made an eagle lectern for Notre-Dame, Paris. His customers included the Marquise de Pompadour and Marc-René, Marquis d'Voyer. In the 1750s he executed elaborate chased and gilt-bronze mounts for Chinese porcelain vases, some supplied to the marchand-mercier Lazare Duvaux; he has also been credited with the mounts of a pair of celadon ewers (c. 1745–9; London, Wallace) and a pair of Chinese vases mounted as ewers (c. 1750; Waddesdon Manor, Bucks, NT). In 1758 he was designated Orfèvre du Roi. It is not certain whether he or his son or both in partnership created the models for the rich bronze ornaments, which were cast by Etienne Forestier (c. 1712–68), on Louis XV's Bureau du Roi (1769; Paris, Louvre) made by Jean-François Oeben and Jean-Henri Riesener. The gilt-bronze vases on the bureau correspond to the melon-shaped Vase à Chaîne (c. 1770; London, Wallace). Similarities have also been noted between a Sèvres clock of 1761 and a gilt-bronze clock attributed to Duplessis (1763; London, Wallace).

Duplessis's son Jean-Claude Thomas Chambellan Duplessis (b Turin, c. 1730; d Paris, 1783) was registered as a Maître Fondeur en Terre et Sable in 1765 and in 1766 was a signatory of a bronze founders' model copyright protection resolution. His regular connection with Sèvres came after his father's death, and until 1783 he supplied gilt-bronze mounts and designed such porcelain shapes as the Vase Gobelet Monté (c. 1770–80; London, V&A) and tureens and écuelles; he published some of his vase designs c. 1775 to 1780. About 1775 he made four large Neo-classical, gilt-bronze candelabra for the Paris hôtel of Laurent Grimod de la Reynière, the Fermier Général (e.g. priv. col., see Eriksen, p. 218) and in 1779 designed the mounts for a pair of vases bought by Queen Marie-Antoinette (London, Buckingham Pal., Royal Col.). He mounted pieces from the Comtesse du Nord's Toilet Service in 1782, and other attributions include the figural gilt-bronze mounts on a pair of Sèvres vases (c. 1782–3; London, Wallace). On his death he was succeeded at Sèvres by Pierre-Philippe Thomire.

BIBLIOGRAPHY

G. Levallet: 'Jean-Claude Duplessis, orfèvre du Roi', *La Renaissance de l'art français et des arts de luxe*, v (1922), pp. 60–67
F. J. B. Watson: *Wallace Collection: Catalogue of Furniture* (London, 1956)
G. de Bellaigue: *James A. de Rothschild Collection at Waddesdon Manor*, 2 vols (1974)
S. Eriksen: *Early Neo-Classicism in France* (London, 1974)
M. Brunet and T. Préaud: *Sèvres: Des origines à nos jours* (Fribourg, 1978)
C. C. Dauterman: *Sèvres Porcelain: Makers and Marks of the 18th Century* (New York, 1986)
H. Ottomeyer, P. Proschel and others: *Vergoldete Bronzen: Die Bronzearbeiten des Spätbarock und Klassizismus* (Munich, 1986)
R. Savill: *The Wallace Collection: Catalogue of Sèvres Porcelain*, 3 vols (London, 1988)

☐

Du Plessis, Armand-Jean. *See* RICHELIEU (ii), (1).

Duplessis, Joseph-Siffred (b Carpentras, *bapt* 23 Sept 1725; d Versailles, 1 April 1802). French painter. He trained with his father, an amateur painter, and then with Joseph-Gabriel Imbert (1666–1749), a pupil of Charles Le Brun. In 1744 he went to Rome and worked with Pierre Subleyras. He remained there until at least 1747 and possibly until the death of his master in 1749. He must have learnt portrait painting in Rome, but he also painted landscapes, because Joseph Vernet advised him to specialize in this genre.

The earliest known works of Duplessis are religious subjects. Some, perhaps dating from the period in Rome, are more or less free copies after Subleyras, such as the *Seven Angels Adoring the Holy Lamb* (Carpentras, Mus. Duplessis). Most of his works post-dating his return to Carpentras are commissions from the local clergy, such as the *Invention of the Cross* and the *Last Supper* (both Carpentras Cathedral). They are somewhat banal imitations of Subleyras. Duplessis also continued to paint landscapes, such as the grisaille panels still in the Hôtel Dieu at Carpentras, but he must already have made a reputation for himself locally as a portraitist.

In 1752 Duplessis left Carpentras, but he appears in Paris only from 1764. He is known to have spent some of the intervening years in Lyon. A number of portraits suggest that he remained for some time in the Rhône Valley, where he executed portraits of *Jacques Vincent* (1754; Carpentras, Hôs.) and of *Joseph de Cavet* and his wife *Elisabeth de Florant* (1763; Carpentras, Mus. Duplessis). These portraits, although less refined than the work of Subleyras, demonstrate the great care that Duplessis paid to creating a good likeness, using a technique that he had mastered completely.

In 1764 Duplessis presented five portraits at the exhibition of the Académie de St Luc in Paris, but he passed completely unnoticed. On 29 July 1769, he was approved (*agréé*) by the Académie Royale and exhibited ten portraits at the Salon of that year. They were well received and were commended in Denis Diderot's review of the exhibition. The 1769 Salon thus marked the beginning of his career as a fashionable portrait painter. His portraits of the *Abbé Arnauld* (Carpentras, Mus. Duplessis), *Mme Lenoir* (Paris, Louvre) and *Mme Frévet-Déricourt* (Kansas City, MO, Nelson–Atkins Mus. A.) all demonstrate the artist's preferred portrait format of a half-length figure in a sober style, which was to have a great influence on the portraits of Jacques-Louis David.

None of the paintings that Duplessis showed at the 1771 Salon has been identified. However, as a result of his success he was chosen to paint the Dauphine Marie-Antoinette. Two portraits were planned: the first was to show her on horseback (unexecuted; oil-sketch for the face, Versailles, Château); the other, a bust probably dating from 1773 (untraced), was made into a tapestry at the Gobelins.

Duplessis further extended his reputation with works exhibited at the Salons of 1773 (untraced) and 1775. At the latter he exhibited, among other works, a portrait of the sculptor *Christophe-Gabriel Allegrain* (Paris, Louvre; see fig.), which was one of his *morceaux de réception* as a full member of the Académie the previous year, and another of the composer *Christoph Willibald Gluck* (Vienna, Ksthist. Mus.), a work acclaimed among his contemporaries. He also showed a head-and-shoulders portrait of

Joseph-Siffred Duplessis: *Christophe-Gabriel Allegrain*, oil on canvas, 1.30×0.97 m, 1774 (Paris, Musée du Louvre)

Louis XVI, executed at the same time as his full-length of the King (both Versailles, Château). The latter was exhibited at the Salon of 1777. Duplessis completed his multiple versions of this official representation of the King with his customary slowness, which exasperated the Sur-intendant des Bâtiments du Roi, the Comte d'Angiviller, who was his constant protector and friend. The fame of Duplessis, who from 1775 had lodgings in the Louvre, continued to grow. He exhibited portraits again at the 1777 Salon; they included that of *Mme de Saint-Maurice* (New York, Met.), which shows an exceptional virtuosity in the treatment of the draperies.

The works Duplessis sent to the 1779 Salon display great diversity in their compositions: that of the *Duchesse de Chartres* (Chantilly, Mus. Condé) is one of the artist's most original, showing her abandoned like Ariadne, sitting beside the shore from which her husband's ship sails away. Duplessis here displayed a renewed interest in landscape, although the integration of the model into the setting remained artificial. His portrait of the *Comte d'Angiviller* (Denmark, priv. col.; replica Versailles, Château) is a brilliant homage by the painter to his protector. In a more sober style, the portrait of *Benjamin Franklin* (versions Boston, MA, Mus. F.A.; New York, Met.; Brest, Mus. Mun.) manages to convey the sparkling intelligence of the subject.

In 1780 Duplessis succeeded Chardin as councillor at the Académie. At the Salon the next year he exhibited a *Self-portrait* (Carpentras, Mus. Duplessis), presenting him-self to advantage in a fine silk suit. Nothing can be seen of the torments caused him by his health, in particular his hearing difficulties and the trouble with his eyesight that had bothered him since 1778 and worsened until 1787, when he almost lost his sight. In addition, he was almost ruined by the bankruptcy of the Prince de Rohan-Guéménée.

His contribution to the Salon of 1783 was dominated by the ambitious portraits of *Jacques Necker* and *Mme Necker* (Coppet, Château). At the 1785 Salon he presented the portrait of the painter *Joseph-Marie Vien* (Paris, Louvre), the second work requested by the Académie for his reception as a member but long delayed by the sitter's absence in Rome. This and his other exhibits at the 1785 Salon were his last important group of exhibited works: in 1789 his few portraits met with indifference on the part of the critics.

An assiduous member of the Académie Royale, in 1790 Duplessis opposed the attacks on the institution led by David. Two years later lack of commissions led to his decision to retire to Genoa. In the end he settled in Carpentras, however, where he was asked to make an inventory of the local works of art. His correspondence of the period shows that he was living in great poverty, though he did produce a portrait of *Joseph Peru* (Carpen-tras, Mus. Duplessis) that reveals an astonishing nervous-ness of touch. In 1796, once again back in Paris, he was appointed joint keeper of the museum at Versailles, initially in charge of the paintings and subsequently also of the sculpture. At the 1801 Salon he exhibited a moving *Self-portrait* (Versailles, Château).

BIBLIOGRAPHY
J. Belleudy: *J. S. Duplessis peintre du Roi, 1725–1802* (Chartres, 1913)
Diderot et l'art de Boucher à David (exh. cat., ed. M.-C. Sahut and N. Volle; Paris, Hôtel de la Monnaie, 1984–5), pp. 194–7

THIERRY BAJOU

Du Plessis, Louis-François Armand de Vignerod. *See* RICHELIEU (ii), (2).

Du Plessis-Guénégaud, Henri. *See* GUÉNÉGAUD, HENRI DE.

Du Plessis-Liancourt, Roger, Duc de La Roche-Guyun. *See* LIANCOURT.

Dupont, Gainsborough (*b* Sudbury, Suffolk, 24 Dec 1754; *d* London, 20 Jan 1797). English painter and engraver. He was the nephew of THOMAS GAINSBOR-OUGH. On 14 January 1772 he entered his uncle's studio, where he remained until 1788. The extent of their collab-oration is uncertain, but a contemporary source states that they worked together on the dress in the portrait of *Queen Charlotte* (1781; Windsor Castle, Berks, Royal Col.); yet in this picture there appears to be no diminution of quality, and Dupont may have collaborated similarly in other works. Apart from working as a drapery painter, Dupont made mezzotints from his own reduced copies of Gains-borough's late works and became thoroughly conversant with his master's style. Indeed, such portraits as *J. Phillips* (1789; Southill Park, Beds) are stylistically very close to Gainsborough. Although Dupont's technique was more frenetic, his palette more varied and his draughtsmanship weaker, scholars have only recently been able to separate

Dupont's work from that of his uncle. There is some evidence to suggest that, after Gainsborough's death, patrons approached Dupont as the inheritor of his master's distinctive style. He worked for the royal family and for William Pitt the younger, but his principal portrait works are a series of theatrical portraits (1793–5; many in London, Garrick Club) painted for Thomas Harris (*d* 1820), proprietor of the Covent Garden Theatre, and several full-length portraits commissioned by Trinity House, London, which include the huge canvas of the *Elder Brethren of Trinity House* (1793–5; London, Trinity House). However, his most artistically successful paintings were landscapes; these were also based on his uncle's work (examples in New York, Brooklyn Mus.; Glasgow, A.G. & Mus.; Birmingham, Mus. & A.G.; Sudbury, Gainsborough's House). The increasing agitation of his brushwork reveals his nervous character.

BIBLIOGRAPHY
J. Hayes: 'The Trinity House Group Portrait', *Burl. Mag.*, cvi (1964), pp. 309–16
——: 'Thomas Harris, Gainsborough Dupont and the Theatrical Gallery at Belmont', *Connoisseur*, clxix (1968), pp. 221–7
——: *The Landscape Paintings of Thomas Gainsborough*, 2 vols (London, 1982)
HUGH BELSEY

Du Pont, H(enry) F(rancis) (*b* Winterthur, DE, 27 May 1880; *d* Winterthur, 11 April 1969). American horticulturalist, patron, collector and museum founder. He graduated from Harvard University, Cambridge, MA, in 1903 before returning to the family estate. He served as a director of the family business from 1915. An interest in early Americana led him to collect antiques and architectural ornaments, with an emphasis from 1923 on the works of early American craftsmen. He began to have period rooms installed on the Winterthur estate in 1927. In 1951 the entire house and collection became the H. F. du Pont Winterthur Museum with over 100 rooms representing the styles and living patterns of the settled regions of the country and covering the period 1640 to 1840. Du Pont chaired the White House Fine Arts Committee (from 1961) and acted as a member of the Awards Committee of the National Trust for Historic Preservation. He served on the board of directors of the Archives of American Art and was a founding director of the Cooper–Hewitt Museum in New York; he also served on the boards of many other cultural, charitable and commercial enterprises.

BIBLIOGRAPHY
Obituary, *New York Times* (28 May 1969)
DAVID M. SOKOL

Dupont, Paul. *See* PONTIUS, PAULUS.

Dupont, Pierre (*b* 31 Dec 1908; *d* Bangkok, 17 Oct 1955). French archaeologist and art historian. He studied in Paris at the Sorbonne, the Ecole Pratique des Hautes Etudes, the Institut d'Ethnologie and the Ecole du Louvre, and also at the Institut Français d'Amsterdam and the Institut Français de Berlin. His teachers included Sylvain Lévi, Alfred Foucher, Charles Picard and Philippe Stern. At the age of 25 he wrote on Siamese art in the *Catalogue* for the Musée Guimet, and in 1936 he went as a member of the Ecole Française d'Extrême-Orient to Indochina,

where he studied Khmer archaeology, inscriptions and history. The pre-Angkorian period and the transition to the Angkorian became his main interest. He conducted excavations at Phnom Kulên and wrote a number of articles, sometimes in collaboration with George Coedès, for the *Bulletin* of the Ecole Française. During 1936–7 he studied the Indo-Mon antiquities of Dvaravati at the National Museum, Bangkok, at Nagara Pathama and at other sites. In 1939 he undertook a series of excavations at Nagara Pathama. His studies did much to transform the archaeology of Dvaravati into a coherent system. He next focused his attention on a group of stone statues of Vishnu found in Siam and Cambodia, before turning to the art of Peninsular Siam, bringing order into a category that had formerly been vaguely labelled 'Srivijaya'.

Dupont continued to work in Indochina throughout World War II, being appointed Secretary-General of the Institut Bouddhique in Phnom Penh in 1941, Keeper of the Monuments of Cambodia from 1943 to 1946 and Curator of the Musée Albert Sarraut in Phnom Penh (now N. Mus. Khmer A. & Archeol.). After World War II he became head of the Musée Blanchard de la Brosse in Saigon (now Hô Chi Minh City, N. Mus.) and (in 1948) Keeper of Historic Monuments in Cochinchine. From 1950 he settled in Paris, writing on Khmer lintels, Brahmanic statues, Javanese art and images of Buddha seated on the *nāga* as well as on Chinese influences in Cham art. He taught Far Eastern art at the Université de Paris and was appointed to the professorship of South-east Asian Archaeology at the Sorbonne; he was at the same time administrator of the Institut de Civilisation Indienne. For the dating of art objects he relied much on Philippe Stern's method of detailed comparisons, which he himself helped to develop, and he hoped this method would eventually be applied to the entire field of Indian and South-east Asian art.

WRITINGS
La Version mône du Nārada-jātaka (Saigon, 1954)
La Statuaire préangkorienne (Ascona, 1955)
L'Archéologie mône de Dvāravatī (Paris, 1959)
BIBLIOGRAPHY
J. Auboyer: Obituary, *A. Asiatiques*, ii/4 (1955), pp. 309–12
A. B. Griswold: Obituary, *Artibus Asiae*, xviii/2 (1955), pp. 178–82 [with selected bibliog.]
G. Coedès: Obituary, *Bull. Ecole Fr. Extrême-Orient*, xlix (1959), pp. 637–48 [with bibliog.]

Dupont, Pieter (*b* Amsterdam, 5 July 1870; *d* Hilversum, 7 Feb 1911). Dutch printmaker. He trained at the Rijksnormaalschool voor Teekenonderwijzers and at the Rijksakademie in Amsterdam (1887–93). Having taught in Amsterdam for a short time and having made some trips to Paris and London, he settled in Paris in 1896. He was particularly interested in Parisian daily life and in the region immediately surrounding the city (the loading and unloading of ships on the Seine; horses and carriages in the boulevards; workers busy on the land) and reproduced them in many etchings, a technique that he used almost exclusively at this time. His interest in the purely linear, already apparent in these etchings, led him to experiment with engraving during a short stay in Amsterdam in 1898. Back in Paris he mastered this technique, which as an independent medium had fallen out of use. In 1900 he exhibited for the first time one of his engravings, *Plough-horse near Fontenay-aux-Roses* (1889; see Kersten, p. 18; from the series *Equipment*), in the graphic art section of the Exposition Universelle in Paris, winning a gold medal and achieving instant recognition. His engravings were shown with great success at various exhibitions in the following years.

When the post of professor of graphic art became vacant at the Rijksakademie in Amsterdam in 1902, Dupont was the obvious choice to fill the vacancy. Under his predecessor, the German Rudolf Stang (1831–1927), the subject of printmaking, which originally concentrated on reproductive prints, was completely pushed into the background, so that Dupont had to rebuild it from scratch. There was not even a classroom properly equipped for printmaking. His youthful enthusiasm and his good reputation as an innovative printmaker did, however, bring the students back in droves. The flourishing of the art of the print in the 20th century in the Netherlands was definitely due in part to his efforts. The revival of engraving in particular can be traced back to his teaching. Although his own work suffered under the teaching load, he still made some etchings and engravings during the years of his professorship. Well-known examples include the engraved portrait of *Hector Treub* (1903; see Kersten, p. 24), made for the jubilee of the well-known printing firm Joh. Enschede & Zn of Haarlem, the *Ploughing Horses* (1904; see Kersten, p. 23), a series of etchings of towers in Amsterdam and the equestrian portrait of *Dirk Tulp* (1905–6; see Dupont, pl. 99), after the painting (1653; Amsterdam, Col. Six) by Paulus Potter. Dupont also executed several official commissions for engravings for banknotes and stamps, not only for the Netherlands but also for Brazil and Persia (now Iran). He died suddenly after a short illness.

BIBLIOGRAPHY

R. W. P. de Vries: *Nederlandsche grafische kunstenaars uit het einde der negentiende en begin van de twintigste eeuw* (Amsterdam, 1943), pp. 115–24

W. F. Dupont: *Pieter Dupont, een Nederlandsch graveur—zijn leven en werken* (Oosterwijk, 1947) [incl. cat. of the works, extensive bibliog. and some of Dupont's writings]

A. van der Blom: *Tekenen dat het gedrukt staat—500 jaar grafiek in Nederland* (n.p., 1978), pp. 138–42

A. J. Vervoorn: *Nederlandse prentkunst, 1840–1940* (Lochem, 1983), pp. 39–41

M. Kersten: *De Nederlandse kopergravure, 1900–1975* (The Hague, 1989), pp. 16–26, 88–90

JAN JAAP HEIJ

Dupra, (Giorgio) Domenico (*b* Turin, 1689; *d* Turin, 1770). Italian painter. He was a portrait painter who trained under Francesco Trevisani in Rome but was much influenced by the French school of portraiture. From 1717 he was employed at the court of King John V of Portugal (for illustration *see* BRAGANZA, (7)), though he maintained links with Turin. By 1731 he was in Rome, where he worked for the exiled royal family of Stuart and for many British aristocrats passing through on their Grand Tour. In 1750 he returned to Turin, where, together with his brother Giuseppe Dupra (1703–84), he worked for the royal family. His early portraits are notable for finely painted materials and clothes and often include allegorical embellishments, such as personified virtues and airborne putti: for example his portraits of *Maria Antonia of Spain* and her husband *Victor Amadeus III* (both Turin, Pal. Reale) have the figure of Mars and various allegorical symbols in the background. Dupra's later portraits were influenced by Jacopo Amigoni and Louis-Michel van Loo and are softer and simpler in style, employing pastel colours, as can be seen for example in his portraits of the royal children *Charles Emanuel* and *Maria Caroline* (both Turin, Pal. Reale).

Domenico's brother Giuseppe was also a specialist in portrait painting and worked in a style so similar that it is often difficult to distinguish their works, although Giuseppe's are generally considered inferior. Both brothers exerted considerable influence on the development of portrait painting in Piedmont through their teaching at the royal academy in Turin, of which Giuseppe was elected principal in 1777.

BIBLIOGRAPHY

Mostra del Barocco piemontese (exh. cat., ed. V. Viale; Turin, Pal. Reale, 1963), ii, p. 115

Cultura figurativa e architettonica negli Stati del Re di Sardegna (1773–1861) (exh. cat., ed. E. Castelnuovo and M. Rosci; Turin, Pal. Reale, 1980), i, pp. 2, 6

MARC'ALVISE DE VIERNO

Dupré. French family of medallists.

(1) Augustin Dupré (*b* Saint-Etienne, Loire, 6 Oct 1748; *d* Armentières, 30 Jan 1833). He began his career chasing and engraving the ornament on arms, first in Saint-Etienne and then as an apprentice in Paris. A lucky commission from the Spanish ambassador enabled him to establish his own workshop and to set up as a goldsmith. In 1776 he was asked to execute a jetton for the Corps des Marchands. The exhibition of his design for this medal, which depicts Hercules vainly attempting to break a bundle of sticks, along with others, established his reputation as a medallist and brought him an official commission for the medal representing the *Subterranean Junction of the Escaut and the Somme* (1782). In 1783, through his acquaintance with Benjamin Franklin, he gained the commission for a medal celebrating *American Liberty*. This enormously successful work was followed by further commissions from the government of the United States for medals of *Benjamin Franklin* (1784–6), *Nathaniel Green* (1787), *Daniel Morgan* (1789) and *John Paul Jones* (1789). This celebration of the American Revolution was, in retrospect, a long rehearsal for Dupré's flowering as the medallist who was most in tune with and best expressed the spirit of the French Revolution. His medal for the *Federation of the 14 July* (1790), executed on his own initiative and to his own design, was sold in thousands and, adopted as the type for the Monneron brothers' money medals, it circulated throughout France.

Advised and assisted by Jacques-Louis David, Dupré launched an attack on the system for minting coins in France, alleging a superfluity of incompetent engravers in the provincial mints, deploring the hereditary nature of most of the posts in the monetary administration and demanding an open competition for the post of Graveur-Général. In the spring of 1791 there was a competition for new designs for the coinage, a competition that Dupré, strongly supported by David, won. In July he won a further competition, for the post of Graveur-Général, and for the next few years he was occupied with engraving the dies first for the Revolutionary and then for the Republican coinage. Napoleon Bonaparte's arrival in power spelt the end of Dupré's career, however. His unflattering medallic portrait of *Napoleon as First Consul*, executed to commemorate the erection of a statue to Joan of Arc, reveals his antipathy to the new regime, which ejected him from his post in 1803.

BIBLIOGRAPHY
J. F. Loubat: *The Medallic History of the United States of America* (New York, 1878)
C. Saunier: *Augustin Dupré* (Paris, 1894)

(2) Georges Dupré (*b* Saint-Etienne, Loire, 24 Oct 1869; *d* Paris, June 1909). Like his forebear (1) Augustin Dupré, he began life as a chaser before moving to Paris, where he entered the Ecole des Beaux-Arts, winning the Prix de Rome in 1896. In poetic plaquettes such as *Greetings to the Sun* (1897), *Meditation* (1897) and *Angelus* (1903) he attempted a new fusion between word and image that ensured him wide popular appeal.

BIBLIOGRAPHY
F. Mazerolle: 'Georges Dupré', *Gaz. Numi. Fr.* (1902), pp. 225–33
MARK JONES

Dupré, Giovanni (*b* Siena, 1 March 1817; *d* Florence, 10 Jan 1882). Italian sculptor and writer. He was among the foremost sculptors in Tuscany in the generation after Lorenzo Bartolini. His early experiments in naturalism attracted such hostile criticism that he was forced to abandon this style in favour of a sensual neo-Greek manner. His later works are marked by a richly expressive eclecticism.

1. Training and early work, to 1846. 2. Neo-Greek phase, 1846–57. 3. Eclecticism, 1857–73. 4. Final years, from 1873.

1. TRAINING AND EARLY WORK, TO 1846. He trained with his father, a wood-carver, and briefly attended the Istituto di Belle Arti in Siena. By 1826 or 1827 he was in Florence, where he joined the workshop of the wood-carver Paolo Sani. Dupré alternated this work with practical attempts at teaching himself, particularly drawing, as part of his ambition to become a sculptor. His first proper sculpture, a wooden figure of *St Philomena*, was shown in 1838 at the annual exhibition of the Accademia di Belle Arti, Florence, where it attracted the praise of Lorenzo Bartolini, among others. In 1840 he made a jewel casket, inspired by the interior architecture of the Biblioteca Medicea-Laurenziana, Florence, which was acquired by Gian Giacomo Poldi Pezzoli on the advice of Bartolini.

Dupré's first work in a material other than wood was a plaster bas-relief depicting the *Judgement of Paris* (1840; untraced), which won him joint first prize in the Accademia's triennial competition. Around 1841 he modelled a number of plaster caryatids (destr. World War II) for the Teatro Rossini in Livorno. The work that brought him to public attention, however, was his recumbent statue of the *Dying Abel* (original plaster, Fiesole, Mus. Dupré), shown at the Florentine Accademia in 1842. The naturalistic treatment of the male nude created a scandal, including accusations that Dupré had made it from life casts; other critics considered it to mark a clear break with tradition and a notable advance towards naturalism. A public subscription was begun in Siena to pay for the translation of the *Dying Abel* into marble. Although not completed until 1845, the marble version was bought in 1842 by Maria, Duchesse de Leuchtenberg (1819–76), daughter of Tsar Nicholas I. At the same time she ordered a marble statue of *Cain* (completed 1847). Both figures are now in the Hermitage, St Petersburg, while bronze versions made for the Tuscan grand-ducal collection in 1850 are in the Pitti Palace, Florence. In November 1842 Dupré received a commission for a statue of *Giotto*, for the loggia of the Uffizi, Florence, which was being adorned with figures of famous Tuscans. The marble version was installed in 1845, attracting much praise but also widespread criticism for its 'excessive' naturalism. Dupré responded by adopting a more traditionally conventional style, an impulse that was

1. Giovanni Dupré: *Sleep of Innocence*, marble, 1844–5 (Siena, Museo dell' Opera del Duomo)

reinforced by a journey to Rome in 1844–5, during which he made the acquaintance of Pietro Tenerani, the most important Nazarene-influenced sculptor in Italy. Such works as the marble statues of *Dante* and *Beatrice* (1843; numerous versions), the *Sleep of Innocence* (1844–5; Siena, Mus. Opera Duomo; see fig. 1) and the marble monument to *Pius II* (1843–50; Siena, S Agostino) show a clear abandonment of the naturalism of Dupré's earliest works in favour of a historicist concern with the purity of Antique and Renaissance forms and the expression of religious or moral feelings. This more traditional phase was, however, short-lived.

2. Neo-Greek phase, 1846–57. Dupré then began to introduce into his work a softer style of anatomical modelling, often with strongly sensual overtones. This change of direction is exemplified in his female nude statues *Innocence* (1846–52) and *Purity* (1846–50), as well as a statue of *A Fisherman* (c. 1848); the marble versions are untraced, but the original plasters survive (Florence, priv. col.). Other sculptures executed during this period include works that show traces of Bartolini's influence, such as the great bronze figurated pedestal for the *Table of the Muses* (1850–52; Florence, Pitti) and the more traditional marble bas-relief of the *Temptation of Adam* (1853; Milan, priv. col.). Dupré also completed two works left unfinished by Bartolini at his death in 1850: *Nymph with a Scorpion* (marble; St Petersburg, Hermitage) and *Nymph with a Serpent* (marble; Reggio Emilia, Fond. Magnani-Rocca). In his statue of *St Antonino* (marble; 1847–54), for the loggia of the Uffizi, Dupré aimed at a more complex synthesis of styles, tempering the ascetic, neo-Quattrocento outline of the figure with strongly expressive naturalistic elements. The result, however, brought about a further storm of criticism that aggravated the exhausted state of mind caused in the highly strung sculptor by the political events of 1848.

In October 1853 Dupré travelled to Naples in order to rest. This period is recorded in his memoirs (1879), in which he declared his admiration for the luxuriant forms of the pagan art of Classical antiquity. This concern with the sensual, 'outward' beauty of antique art, as opposed to the spiritual, 'inward' beauty of Christian art, allied him to the *Néo-Grec* movement in France, which found its most explicit expression in the work of Jean-Léon Gérôme, Auguste Clésinger and James Pradier. This trend was soon reflected in a critical debate in Florence between traditionalists and innovators, some of whom favoured an art without subject-matter.

On his return to Florence in 1854, Dupré threw himself into the task of completing the works that had been interrupted by his trip to Naples. He finished a female statue of *Gratitude* (Siena, priv. col.), which, in its pose and in the treatment of the marble, is akin to his *Tired Bacchante* (completed 1857; version, Siena, Ciseri priv. col., see Sapori, 1949, p. 132). The latter contains all Dupré's most important stylistic elements of this period, particularly in its sensual treatment of anatomical form and pose, reminiscent of Greco-Roman statuary. In 1854 Dupré was commissioned to provide a cylindrical base for the porphyry tazza that had been brought from the Baths of Caracalla in Rome to the Palazzo Pitti, Florence;

2. Giovanni Dupré: *Sappho*, marble, 1857–61 (Rome, Galleria Nazionale d'Arte Moderna)

although this did not progress beyond a plaster model (Montecatini Terme, Mus. Accad.), it was widely praised as representing Dupré's new style. Contemporary critics were particularly appreciative of its reminiscences of Pheidias' *Panathenaic Procession* (part of the Parthenon marbles; London, BM), and also of the breadth of its references to a variety of figurative traditions in order to represent allegorically different historical civilizations.

In 1857 Dupré travelled to London to take part in the competition for a monument to Arthur Wellesley, 1st Duke of Wellington, but with scant success. He returned to Florence via Paris, where he was enthralled by the works of the *Néo-Grecs*, as reflected in his statue of *Sappho* (marble, 1857–61; Rome, G.N.A. Mod.; see fig. 2), which marks the climax of his neo-Greek phase.

3. Eclecticism, 1857–73. Shortly after completing *Sappho*, Dupré began the marble funerary monument to *Berta Moltke Ferrari Corbelli* (1857–64; Florence, S Lorenzo), which shows his mastery of a wide range of art-historical sources. While not abandoning the sensual paganism of his neo-Greek works (e.g. *Love Lying in Ambush*, marble, 1858, Siena, Pal. Chigi-Saracini; *Festive Bacchus*, marble, version, 1859, Florence, Pitti), he went on to produce sculptures of considerably greater complexity, alluding to sources ranging from Classical antiquity to the works of Gianlorenzo Bernini.

This exploitation of heterogeneous sources of inspiration (for which he was often taken to task) formed one of the fundamental characteristics of Dupré's new stylistic phase, which lasted into the 1870s and produced a number of important works. In 1863 Dupré finished the lunette for the central door in the new façade of Santa Croce, Florence: an elaborate allegorical relief representing the

Exaltation of the Holy Cross. The most influential work of this period was, however, the marble *Pietà* (1862–8) for Alessandro Bichi Ruspoli destined for his family chapel in the Misericordia Cemetery in Siena. It was shown at the Exposition Universelle (Paris, 1867) to great critical acclaim and achieved international fame, becoming a model for a modern style of religious art; according to Aleardo Aleardi, it combined 'ancient form and modern feeling, Christian spirit holding a Greek chisel' (letter to Dupré, 12 Aug 1864; Fiesole, Mus. Dupré).

By the time of Dupré's second stay in Paris in 1867 he was already involved in work on the marble monument (1865–73) to *Camillo Benso, Conte di Cavour* for the Piazza Carlo Emanuele II in Turin. This lengthy project was a critical failure, largely due to Dupré's decision to represent this modern hero of the Risorgimento in a Roman toga with a semi-nude personification of Italy clinging to him. The artistic quality of the four allegorical groups on the base was virtually ignored. Among other works in which he combined allegory with portrayals of real characters are his funerary monuments to the *Monga Family* (marble and bronze, 1868–71) in the cemetery at Verona and to *Silvestro Camerini* (marble, 1871–7) for the chapel of the Villa Camerini (now Simes) at Piazzola sul Brenta. The neo-Renaissance quality of the *Angel of Prayer* for the funerary stele of *Caterina Corridi* (marble, 1867) in the Porte Sante Cemetery, Florence, gives it a more markedly spiritual character.

4. FINAL YEARS, FROM 1873. During the last decade of his life Dupré's output declined, and he became increasingly religious. This reflective mood informs his widely read *Pensieri sull'arte e ricordi autobiografici* (1879). He made important contributions as an artistic administrator and became deeply involved in the Catholic cultural and political circles of Florence. Among the most memorable of his later works are his marble monument to *Girolamo Savonarola* (1873) for the convent of S Marco, Florence, and the marble funerary monument to *Fiorella Favard de l'Anglade* (1877) for the chapel of the Villa Favard, Rovezzano, in which the angel raising the deceased from the sarcophagus is portrayed in a highly charged and very spiritual neo-Renaissance style. Other notable works are the monument to *Pius IX* (marble, 1878–80) in Piacenza Cathedral and the statue of *St Francis* (marble, 1880–82) in S Ruffino, Assisi.

Most of Dupré's plaster models are in the Museo Dupré, Fiesole, with some smaller groups in the Museo della Contrada dell'Onda, Siena, and in the Museo dell'Accademia, Montecatini Terme.

WRITINGS
Della scultura alla Esposizione universale di Parigi del 1867 (Florence, 1867)
Relazione sulle belle arti quali erano rappresentate all'Esposizione di Vienna nel 1873 (Florence, 1873)
Pensieri sull'arte e ricordi autobiografici (Florence, 1879)
Scritti minori e lettere (Florence, 1885)

BIBLIOGRAPHY
DBI [with full bibliography]
G. La Farina: *Giovanni Dupré* (Florence, 1843)
A. Conti: *Giovanni Dupré o dell'arte* (Pisa, 1865)
P. E. Selvatico: *Una visita allo studio di Giovanni Dupré* (Padua, 1874)
G. Rosadi: *Giovanni Dupré scultore, 1817–1882* (Milan, 1917)
F. Sapori: *Giovanni Dupré scultore* (Milan, 1918)
——: *Scultura italiana moderna* (Rome, 1949), pp. 128–36, 451
G. Marchiori: *Scultura italiana dell'ottocento* (Milan, 1960), pp. 51–60
Disegni italiani del XIX secolo (exh. cat. by C. del Bravo, Florence, Uffizi, 1971), pp. 78–81
C. Del Bravo: 'Il bozzetto dell'Abele di Giovanni Dupré', *Paragone*, xxiii/271 (1972), pp. 69–78
S. Pinto, ed.: *Cultura neoclassica e romantica nella Toscana granducale* (Florence, 1972), pp. 145–7
E. Spalletti: 'Note su alcuni inediti di Giovanni Dupré', *Paragone*, xxiii/271 (1972), pp. 78–88
——: 'Il secondo ventennio di attività di Giovanni Dupré', *An. Scu. Norm. Sup. Pisa*, n. s. 2, iv (1974), pp. 537–612
Da Antonio Canova a Medardo Rosso: Disegni di scultori italiani del XIX secolo (exh. cat., Rome, G.N.A. Mod., 1982), pp. 39–45
Santa Croce nell'ottocento (exh. cat., ed. P. Ruschi; Florence, Santa Croce, 1986)

ETTORE SPALLETTI

Dupré, Guillaume (*b* Sissonne, Aisne, *c.* 1574; *d* Paris, between 19 and 24 Feb 1642). French sculptor and medallist. He was trained in Paris by his co-religionist, the Protestant sculptor BARTHÉLEMY PRIEUR, whose daughter he married in 1600. In 1597 he executed a portrait medal of *Henri IV* with a profile portrait of the royal mistress *Gabrielle d'Estrée* on the reverse (see Mazerolle, no. 623), and it was perhaps this work that launched his official career. In 1603 he was named Sculpteur Ordinaire du Roi and was authorized to cast medals in gold and silver; in 1604 he was made joint Contrôleur Général des Poinçons et Effigies des Monnaies with his rival Jean Pilon (1578–1617). From 1608 he was in charge of the founding of cannon for the French artillery, and in 1611 Prieur obtained for him the reversion of his title as Premier Sculpteur du Roi.

Dupré's reputation rests principally on his work as a medallist. He executed numerous portrait medals of Henri IV, representing him as Hercules (M 628), in contemporary armour (M 626) and *all'antica*. He also produced medallic portraits of *Marie de' Medici* (1601, 1615, 1624; e.g. M 632) and *Louis XIII* (1610, 1623, 1624; e.g. M 663), as well as of royal ministers and noblemen, including *François, Duc de Lesdiguières* (1600, 1623; e.g. M 629), *Maximilien de Béthune, Duc de Sully* (1607; M 657), *Antoine Ruzé, Marquis d'Effiat* (1620, 1629; e.g. M 702) and *Cardinal Richelieu* (1627; M 701).

From 1612 to 1614 Dupré was in Italy where he absorbed the lessons both of antique art and the contemporary Italian Mannerist style. A series of medals of important Italian patrons, including *Francesco I de' Medici, Grand Duke of Tuscany* (1613; M 673), *Cardinal Maffeo Barberini*, the future Urban VIII (M 670), the *Doge Marc-Antonio Memmo* (1612; M 669) and *Francesco Gonzaga, 4th Marchese de Mantua* (1612; M 668), dates from this time.

Dupré also executed more spectacular medals of large dimension, of which the most famous is that of 1603, entitled *Propago Imperii* (diam. 187 mm; M 639). On the obverse are represented Henri IV and Marie de' Medici in antique costume, while between them the Dauphin (later Louis XIII) rests his foot on a dolphin. The reverse represents the King as Mars and the Queen as Pallas Athena. In contrast to this theatrical image of monarchy are Dupré's large, strongly characterized and meticulously chiselled portrait medals in high relief. The profile portrait of the Chancellor *Nicolas Brulart de Sillery* (diam. 330 mm,

1613; M 697), the three-quarter profile portrait of *Nicolas de Verdun* (1622; M 688) and the full-face portrait of *Jean Heroard*, Louis XIII's doctor, reveal the pains he took with realism, expression and volume.

Dupré also sought recognition for his life-size sculpture. In 1610 he was commissioned to model a wax portrait bust of *Henri IV* immediately after his assassination, a work that may possibly be one of the two wax busts of the King preserved at the Musée Condé, Chantilly, and at the Musée Carnavalet, Paris. Around this time Dupré and Prieur jointly received a commission for large marble statues of *Piety* and *Justice* (the latter preserved at Washington, DC, N.G.A.) for the monument for the hearts of Henri IV and Marie de' Medici at the Collège de la Flèche, Sarthe, a project that was never finished. In 1611 Dupré completed Prieur's tomb of *Dominique de Vic, Vicomte d'Ermenonville* (Ermenonville church), providing the confidently modelled but somewhat impersonal marble bust of the deceased (Paris, Louvre). These were presumably not Dupré's only funerary monuments, since documents in the Bibliothèque Inguimbertine, Carpentras, record a tomb for *N.-C. Fabri de Peiresc* decorated with two caryatids and three busts.

Dupré also executed small-scale sculpture. He is said to have made a terracotta statuette of *Louis XIII* aged three, and his name has been associated with the output from the manufactories at Fontainebleau and nearby Avon. The features and the characteristics of the chasing of some of Prieur's bronze busts and statuettes of Henri IV and Marie de' Medici correspond to Dupré's style as a medallist, though the total absence of documentation precludes any definite conclusions about his collaboration in their production.

Dupré's son Abraham (1604–47) was also a sculptor and medallist. He succeeded his father as Contrôleur Général des Poinçons et Effigies at the mint and Commissaire Général des Fontes of the French artillery in 1639. Among his works are bronze portrait medals of *Victor Amadeus I, Duke of Savoy* (1636; M 166) and of his wife *Christine de France* (1637; M 166). He may also have been responsible for the bronze equestrian statuettes of *Henri IV* and *Victor Amadeus*, Duke of Savoy, now in the Wallace Collection, London.

BIBLIOGRAPHY

Forrer; Lami

P. Delaroche, H. Dupont and C. Lenormant: *Trésor de numismatique et de glyptique*, 20 vols (Paris, 1834–58)

J.-J. Guiffrey: 'Guillaume Dupré: Sculpteur et graveur en médailles', *Nouv. Archv A. Fr.*, iv (1876), pp. 172–224

E. Fleury: *Guillaume Dupré de Sissonne* (Laon, 1882)

F. Mazerolle: *Les Médailleurs français du XVème siècle au milieu du XVIIème* (Paris, 1902–4), i, pp. 485–99, ii, pp. 125–43 [M]

J. G. Mann: *The Wallace Collection: Catalogue of Sculpture* (London, 1931), p. 59

M. Lamy: 'Inventaire après décès de Guillaume Dupré', *Archv A. Fr.*, n. s., xxii (1959), pp. 75–8

M. Jones: 'Guillaume Dupré', *Medal*, ix (1986), pp. 22–47

——: *1600–1672*, ii of *A Catalogue of Medals in the British Museum (1982–)* (London, 1988)

GENEVIÈVE BRESC-BAUTIER

Dupré, Jules (*b* Nantes, 5 April 1811; *d* L'Isle-Adam, Val-d'Oise, 6 Oct 1889). French painter. He began his career in Creil, Ile de France, as a decorator of porcelain in the factory of his father, François Dupré (*b* 1781), and later worked at the factory founded by his father in Saint-Yrieix-la-Perche, Limousin. It was in this region of central France that Dupré became enchanted by the beauty of nature. He went to Paris to study under the landscape painter Jean-Michel Diébolt (*b* 1779), who had been a pupil of Jean-Louis Demarne. Dupré began to see nature with a new awareness of its moods, preferring to paint alone and *en plein air*. He was fascinated by bad weather, changes of light and sunsets. Many of his paintings depict quiet woodland glades, often with a pond or stream (e.g. *Plateau of Bellecroix*, 1830; Cincinnati, OH, A. Mus.; for illustration *see* BARBIZON SCHOOL). In 1830–31 he associated with other young landscape painters, including Louis Cabat, Constant Troyon and Théodore Rousseau, and with them sought inspiration for his study of nature in the provinces, exhibiting the finished paintings at the annual Salons. In 1832 he visited the region of Berry with Cabat and Troyon, and in 1834 he was among the first French landscape painters to visit England. He spent time in London, Plymouth and Southampton and painted several views of these cities (e.g. *Environs of Southampton*, exh. Salon 1835; priv. col., see Aubrun, no. 69). While in England he met, and was influenced by, Constable, Turner and Richard Parkes Bonington. He travelled to the Landes and the Pyrenees with Rousseau in 1844, and they also explored the forests of the Ile de France in search of motifs. Dupré also painted in Normandy, Picardy and Sologne. Although he was a member of the Barbizon school, he did not visit the Forest of Fontainebleau as frequently as did others of the group, preferring instead to settle in 1849 in the village of L'Isle-Adam, north of Paris, where he remained for much of his life.

Dupré's approach to nature falls somewhere between realism and Romanticism. For him nature was majestic, and he was fascinated by the alliance of the ephemeral and the eternal. He searched for the mystery of creation by examining the permanence of a natural world dominated by trees, which he saw as a significant element linking heaven and earth. This mystical vision was in part influenced by the paintings of such 17th-century Dutch masters as Meindert Hobbema and Jacob van Ruisdael. One of his most representative works is *The Floodgate* (*c.* 1855–60; Paris, Mus. d'Orsay), with its tormented conception expressed in shifting chiaroscuro and thick, powerful handling of paint, which shape the natural world of light, trees and plants supporting human beings and animals. Despite his independent temperament, his career was successful, and his work was received with enthusiasm during his lifetime. He was made Chevalier de la Légion d'honneur in 1849 and was awarded several medals at the Salons and at the Exposition Universelle in 1867 in Paris, where he showed 13 paintings. In later years he spent summers at Cayeux-sur-Mer and executed paintings inspired by its coastline (e.g. *The Headland*, *c.* 1875; Glasgow, A.G. & Mus.). In these works his feeling for the tragic character of nature is heightened as much by his technique as by his lyrical conception. He also painted watercolours (e.g. the *Duck Pond*, *c.* 1833; Paris, Louvre). He was admired by the Impressionist painters and by their dealer Paul Durand-Ruel for his perception of atmosphere and the rendering of reflections of light, although his popularity declined somewhat in the first half of the 20th century.

BIBLIOGRAPHY

Bellier de La Chavignerie–Auvray

L. Delteil: *J. F. Millet, Th. Rousseau, Jules Dupré, J. Barthold Jongkind,* i of *Le Peintre-graveur illustré (XIXe et XXe siècles)* (Paris, 1906–30/*R* New York, 1969)

M. M. Aubrun: *Jules Dupré, 1811–1889: Catalogue raisonné de l'oeuvre peint, dessiné et gravé,* 2 vols (Paris, 1974–82)

M. Laclotte and J.-P. Cuzin, eds: *Petit Larousse de la peinture,* 2 vols (Paris, 1979)

ANNIE SCOTTEZ-DE WAMBRECHIES

Dupuis, Nicolas-Gabriel (*b* Paris, *c.* 1698; *d* Paris, March 1771). French engraver. He was the younger brother of the engraver Charles Dupuis (1685–1742). He first worked as a dyer and for many years engraved plates of ornaments intended for printing on silk. With his brother he worked in the workshop of Gaspard Duchange, whose daughter he married in 1737; he collaborated with his master in the execution of several large works, including the *Coronation of Louis XV* (Roux, no. 13); parts of Raphael's cartoons of the *Acts of the Apostles* (London, Hampton Court, Royal Col.; R 6–8); and Jean de La Fontaine's *Fables* (R 47–50) after Jean-Baptiste Oudry. Dupuis's interpretations of Jean-Baptiste Massé's drawings for *La Galerie de Versailles* after Charles Le Brun brought him recognition. Massé was so pleased with them that he recommended Dupuis to the Académie Royale de Sculpture et de Peinture. He was approved (*agréé*) in 1751 and received (*reçu*) in 1754 with his portrait of *Charles-François-Paul Le Normand de Tournehem* (R 42) after Louis Tocqué. In 1756 he received a pension for life from Louis XV. At first he worked both at etching and at engraving, but he gradually gave up etching, fearing the effects of the vapours on his health and his sight. His engraving gained in power; his modelling was vigorous, and his backgrounds were sharply defined. He generally signed himself *Dupuis Junior* or *Dupuis le Jeune,* to distinguish himself from his brother. His oeuvre, numbering 86 items, is mainly composed of historical subjects: *Adoration of the Magi* after Veronese; *Concert champêtre* (R 28) after Giorgione for the Recueil Crozat; *Aeneas Rescuing his Father from Burning Troy* (R 17) after Carle Vanloo; genre subjects after Jean-François Colson and Johann Elias Zeissig (1737–1806); and amorous scenes, such as *Sleeping Nymph with Satyrs* (R 1) after Louis Chéron and *Youthful Amusements* (R 63) after François Eisen.

BIBLIOGRAPHY

M. Roux: *Inventaire du fonds français: Graveurs du dix-huitième siècle,* Paris, Bib. N., Cab. Est. cat., viii (Paris, 1955) [R]

French Royal Academy of Painting and Sculpture: Engraved Reception Pieces, 1672–1789 (exh. cat. by W. McAllister Johnson, Kingston, Ont., Queen's U., Agnes Etherington A. Cent.; Montreal, Mus. F.A.; London, U. W. Ont., McIntosh A.G.; and elsewhere; 1982–3), cat. no. 71

M. Préaud, P. Casselle, M. Grivel and C. Le Bitouzé: *Dictionnaire des éditeurs d'estampes à Paris sous l'Ancien Régime* (Paris, 1987), pp. 111–12

VÉRONIQUE MEYER

Duque, Rodrigo. *See* ALEMÁN, RODRIGO.

Duque Cornejo, Pedro (*b* Seville, 14 Aug 1678; *d* Cordoba, 1757). Spanish sculptor. He was the grandson of Pedro Roldán (*see* ROLDÁN, (1)) and the leading Sevillian sculptor in the first half of the 18th century. He learnt the art of sculpture from his grandfather and painting

and polychromy from his mother, Francisca Roldán Villavicencio, Roldán's daughter. Duque Cornejo was active as a draughtsman, designer of altarpieces and engraver of designs for use by goldsmiths as well as a sculptor in both wood and stone. One of his earliest commissions (1706–9) was a retable for the church of the Sagrario, Seville, with the architectural elements by Jerónimo de Balbás (destr. 1824; figure of *St Clement, in situ*). Balbás used Duque Cornejo's design in 1717 for a retable in the Capilla de los Reyes, Mexico Cathedral.

In 1714 Duque Cornejo went to Granada, where he remained until 1719. Here he worked on the over life-size dynamic figures of *Christ,* the *Virgin* and the *Apostles* for the Iglesia de las Angustias, Granada. These, placed along the nave of the church, recall Roman Baroque schemes. In 1718 Duque Cornejo completed the retable of the Virgen de la Antigua, Granada Cathedral, commissioned in 1716 by Archbishop Martín de Azcargorta. This is a rich gilt, polychrome wood structure of swelling curves and scrolls, with vaulted niches containing figures and reliefs by Duque Cornejo surrounding an earlier 15th-century group of the *Virgin and Child.* The overall form may have been influenced by Francisco Hurtado Izquierdo's retable of 1707 for the chapel of Santiago, also in Granada Cathedral. Duque Cornejo's next major project was his part (1723–8) in the decoration of the Cartuja, Granada. Along with José de Mora (ii) and José Risueño he was commissioned to do the sculpture for Hurtado Izquierdo's lavish architectural schemes in the Sagrario of

Pedro Duque Cornejo: tomb of *Archbishop Luis Salcedo y Azcona,* stone, 1734–8 (Seville Cathedral)

the Cartuja. Duque Cornejo's most outstanding contribution is a polychrome wood figure of the *Penitent Magdalene*, whose full draperies and incipient twisting movement echo the swelling forms of the carved illusionistic curtain in wood held aloft by two angels behind. During this period Duque Cornejo was also working on statues of *St Peter, St Paul, John the Baptist* and *Joseph* (1725) for the Sagrario in the Cartuja, El Paular (Madrid), where the architect was again Hurtado Izquierdo. These figures embody a Baroque vivacity typical of Andalusian sculpture of this time.

By the 1730s Duque Cornejo had returned to Seville, where in 1731 he worked on a scheme for S Luis de los Franceses that comprised retables and rich decorative work for the church and its Capilla de los Novicios. The figures by Duque Cornejo, including *St Stanislas Kostka* and *St Aloysius Gonzaga*, recall the work of Pedro de Mena and Alonso Cano.

The court of Philip V was resident in Seville from 1729 to 1733, and the Queen, Isabel Farnese, named Duque Cornejo 'estatuario de su cámara', though this was purely an honorary title. Duque Cornejo followed the court back to Madrid in 1733, where he hoped to be appointed sculptor to the King but was unsuccessful. He returned to Seville, where further commissions included the stone tomb of *Archbishop Luis Salcedo y Azcona* (1734–8; see fig.) and two carved wooden cupboards (1743), both in the cathedral. In 1747 Duque Cornejo was commissioned to design and carve the choir-stalls for Córdoba Cathedral. He moved there with his family, set up his workshop and was occupied with this major project until his death in 1757. The reliefs, of Old and New Testament scenes, are in unpolychromed mahogany and are probably derived from engravings. The work as a whole has a satisfying unity, with a harmonious balance between the delicate carving of the reliefs and the elaborate ornament of the stalls; it stands as one of the last great Baroque works in Spain.

Ceán Bermúdez

BIBLIOGRAPHY
J. J. Martín González: *Escultura barroca en España, 1600–1770* (Madrid, 1983), pp. 409–15 [further bibliog. cited on p. 576]

MARJORIE TRUSTED

Du Quesnoy [De Quesnoy; Duquesnoy; Quesnoi; Quesnoy]. Southern Netherlandish family of sculptors. (1) Jérôme Du Quesnoy (i) was a busy sculptor who played a large part in the artistic revival in the southern Netherlands following the religious and iconoclastic disturbances of the 16th century. His son (2) François Du Quesnoy was one of the most eminent sculptors in Europe in the 17th century. After an early training in his father's studio in Brussels he went to Rome, where he formed a sensitive, classicizing style under the influence of the sculpture of Classical antiquity and the paintings of Titian, as well as of his intimate friend Nicolas Poussin. This style was in marked contrast to the demonstrative Baroque of his foremost contemporary Gianlorenzo Bernini. Such was the appeal of François Du Quesnoy's art that certain of his works—in particular his famous reliefs of children—continued to be influential on sculptors and painters throughout the following century. His brother (3) Jérôme Du Quesnoy (ii) worked in Spain and Portugal and had a

successful career after 1643 in Brussels. He was a competent sculptor but lacked the imagination and sensitivity of his brother.

BIBLIOGRAPHY
L. Hadermann-Misguich: *Les Du Quesnoy* (Gembloux, 1970)

(1) **Jérôme** [Hieronymus] **Du Quesnoy (i)** [*l'ancien*] (*b* ?Quesnoy, southern Netherlands, *c.* 1570; *d* Brussels, 1641–2). He was active mainly in Brussels, and his earliest recorded commission dates from 1597–9, when he was paid for a stone statue of *Christ* (untraced) by the church of Notre-Dame de la Chapelle there. At that time he was a member of the Guilde des Quatre Couronnés. He is known to have sculpted in clay, wood, alabaster, stone and marble and to have worked in Brussels for the palace of the Dukes of Brabant, for churches including St Nicolas, St Géry, St Jacques-sur-Coudenberg, St Michel-St Gudule and St Catherine, as well as for numerous corporate and private patrons. He also worked for the towns of Aalst, Vilvoorde, Halle, Dendermonde and, probably, Ghent. The only certain work of his to survive is the tabernacle of stone, wood and coloured marbles at St Martin, Aalst, executed in 1604. This elaborate but harmonious construction with numerous small figures in an architectural setting was inspired by the formal repertory of Cornelis Floris, in particular the tabernacle at St Catherine, Zuurbemde (1557). Du Quesnoy modified the Renaissance spirit of the earlier work by making his tabernacle more dynamic, simplifying the ornamentation and introducing polychromatic effects. The tabernacle of 1593 at St Jacob, Ghent, has been attributed to him on the basis of stylistic similarities.

In the period 1616–18 two of Du Quesnoy's five children, (2) François Du Quesnoy and (3) Jérôme Du Quesnoy (ii), joined his workshop. In 1616 he made, perhaps with the assistance of François, stone statues of *Justice* and *Truth* (destr.) for the façade of the town hall at Halle. In 1619, the year following the departure of his sons for Italy, he was asked to replace the famous fountain of the *Manneken-pis* in the Rue de l'Etuve, Brussels. Du Quesnoy's statuette of the *putto pisciatore* has been replaced a number of times, and the present décor of the fountain dates from 1770. However, an engraving (Brussels, Mus. Com.) by Jacobus Harrewijn (1660–after 1732) records its original design, while a bronze cast of the statuette (Brussels, Mus. Com.) made in 1630 from Du Quesnoy's mould preserves the well-constructed, finely chiselled appearance of the original. A marble statue of *Mary Magdalene Reading* (Brussels, Mus. A. Anc.) has been attributed to Jérôme Du Quesnoy (i), but its Baroque character makes it more likely to be by Jérôme Du Quesnoy (ii). Despite the paucity of surviving works, which makes an assessment of his style almost impossible, Jérôme Du Quesnoy (i) clearly played a substantial part in the artistic life of Brussels under the Habsburg Archduke and Archduchess Albert and Isabella.

BIBLIOGRAPHY
O. Roelandts: *De beeldhouwers Hieronymus Duquesnoy vader en zoon* (Ghent, n.d.)
G. P. Bellori: *Vite* (1672); ed. E. Borea (1976), pp. 287–8
G. B. Passeri: *Vite* (1679); ed. J. Hess (1934), p. 103

(2) **François** [Francesco; Franz] **Du Quesnoy** [*il Fiammingo*] (*b* Brussels, *bapt* 12 Jan 1597; *d* Livorno, 19

July 1643). Sculptor and draughtsman, son of (1) Jérôme Du Quesnoy (i).

1. Training and early years in Rome. 2. Antique restorations. 3. Reliefs of children and associated works. 4. Monumental works. 5. Small bronzes and other works. 6. Portraits. 7. Last works.

1. TRAINING AND EARLY YEARS IN ROME. François Du Quesnoy was trained by his father, with whom he perhaps collaborated on stone statues of *Justice* and *Truth* (destr.) for the façade of the town hall at Halle. According to early sources he executed a number of independent works, including statues of *St John* and *St Sebastian* and an ivory *Passion* (all untraced), that brought him to the attention of the Archduke Albert. In 1618 he was granted a bursary by the latter to travel to Rome to complete his artistic education, and in August of that year he left for Italy with his brother (3) Jérôme Du Quesnoy (ii); later they separated after a quarrel. The death of the Archduke in 1621 deprived François of funds, and he was obliged to enter the workshop of the carver Claude Poussin (Claudio Lorenese; *d* 1661), where he is said to have made wooden heads of saints for reliquaries. His first patron in Rome was the influential Flemish merchant Pieter Visscher (Pietro Pescatore), who commissioned a life-size marble group of *Venus Suckling Cupid* (untraced) and introduced him to a number of important patrons and collectors, including, probably, Filippo Colonna, for whom he restored an antique marble statue of a *Muse* (Rome, Gal. Colonna). Colonna presented an ivory *Crucifix* (untraced) carved by Du Quesnoy to Urban VIII, and after 1626 the Pope bought a second *Crucifix* (untraced) and an ivory *St Sebastian* (untraced). An extremely sensitively conceived *Crucifix* at S Giovanni in Laterano may be one of the two supplied to the Pope. At this time Du Quesnoy was living with Nicolas Poussin, who had arrived from France in 1624, and they were occupied in studying and copying famous Classical and modern works in Roman collections: Bellori records that they made a cast (untraced) of the *Antinous* and drew and made models (untraced) after the *Laokoon* and the Belvedere *Torso* (all Rome, Vatican, Mus. Pio-Clementino). Du Quesnoy's statuette (untraced) after the former was in the collection of Cardinal Camillo Massimi in 1677. Du Quesnoy and Poussin also studied in the collections of Cassiano dal Pozzo and probably also in that of Vincenzo Giustiniani, as well as admiring the paintings by Titian in the collection of Ludovico Ludovisi—the *Bacchanale* and the *Offering to Venus* (both Madrid, Prado) and *Bacchus and Ariadne* (London, N.G.). These works, ancient and modern, were to have a profound influence on the development of both artists. From 1629 the German painter Joachim von Sandrart, Du Quesnoy's future biographer, became a friend and helped to get commissions for him.

2. ANTIQUE RESTORATIONS. Following Passeri's view that the restoration of the Colonna *Muse* was connected with François Du Quesnoy's need for an income after the death of the Archduke Albert, Du Quesnoy's restorations of antique sculptures have usually been dated to the period around 1620–25. It is difficult to be certain about the bronze and alabaster *Minerva* (Rome, Villa Albani) restored for Ippolito Vitelleschi. However, the three finest works of this class—the *Faun* (marble; London, V&A) restored for Alessandro Rondanini, the *Bacchus* and the Mazarin *Adonis* (both marble; Paris, Louvre)—have affinities with original works produced in the period 1625–30, such as the marble *Bacchus* in the Galleria Doria-Pamphili, Rome, and the *St Susanna* in S Maria di Loreto, Rome, the sketch model of which was prepared in 1627; these three works also have points of similarity with works from the Giustiniani collection and, in the case of the two last, with the Belvedere *Antinous*. Du Quesnoy's skill and sensitivity as a restorer were recognized by his contemporaries: taking his cue from the antique fragments on which he was working, he would produce a composition with a sense of movement akin to that of his original works. The subtle and sensual dance of the Rondanini *Faun* is perhaps the best example of this.

3. RELIEFS OF CHILDREN AND ASSOCIATED WORKS. In the period 1625–30 François Du Quesnoy, under the influence both of Titian's *Offering to Venus* and of antique sarcophagi, produced a series of works in which he explored the motif of the young child, creating in his tender and sensual statuettes and reliefs of cupids, satyrs, bacchantes and other infants some of his most famous and influential sculptures. The *Bacchanale of Children* (or *Children with a Goat*) (1626; Rome, Gal. Doria-Pamphili; associated drawing, Vienna, Albertina) is one of his most pictorial marbles, in which he exploited to the full the possibilities of all gradations of relief to create a scene full of atmosphere and animation. It was highly praised by Bellori, and copies and casts or drawings after it formed part of the studio equipment of numerous painters and sculptors in the following two centuries. Several versions survive of the relief inspired by Virgil's sixth *Eclogue*, *Silenus Asleep with the Stubborn Ass* (1626–30; e.g. red wax, Frankfurt am Main, Liebieghaus; bronze, Antwerp, Rubenshuis; marble, Brussels, Dulière priv. col.), a work of more pronounced and uniform relief than the *Bacchanale of Children* that reinterpreted Virgil by replacing his two shepherds with a faun, a dozen putti and baby satyrs. Cassiano dal Pozzo owned the sketch model (untraced). It is not known if Du Quesnoy himself carved a marble version. The relief *Divine Love Overcoming Profane Love* (*c.* 1630) also exists in a number of versions (stucco, Rome, Gal. Spada; marble, Rome, Gal. Doria-Pamphili; porphyry copy by Tommaso Fedele, *fl* 1630s, Madrid, Prado) and bears witness to an evolution towards classicism in Du Quesnoy's work. The panel, treated with a delicacy that makes it one of the sculptor's masterpieces, is occupied only by two pairs of putti united by an ample sheet of drapery hanging from a tree. Sculpture in the round from this period and deriving from similar themes includes a small bronze *Head of a Satyr* (Vienna, Ksthist. Mus.), an amber group of a *Satyr and Bacchante* (Munich, Bayer. Nmus.), two terracotta pairs of *amorini* (untraced), once in the collection of the French sculptor François Girardon, and a marble *Cupid with Grapes* (Brussels, Mus. A. Anc.) attributed to Du Quesnoy on the basis of its similarity to the life-size *Cupid Carving his Bow* (Berlin, Bodemus.; damaged World War II). The latter work, apparently executed to disprove the accusation that he could do little more than model and carve in ivory, was

bought through the agency of Sandrart by the Dutch merchant, banker and collector settled in Venice, Lucas van Uffele.

4. MONUMENTAL WORKS. Du Quesnoy's principal monumental works, the marble statues of *St Susanna* (Rome, S Maria di Loreto) and *St Andrew* (Rome, St Peter's), were begun at the end of the 1620s. The *St Susanna* (see fig. 1) is perhaps the work in which he combines in the most harmonious and personal fashion the heritage of the Classical tradition, the grace of Mannerism and the sensibility of an artist belonging to that moment of style aptly called High Baroque classicism. The commission from the Guild of Bakers probably dates from early in 1627. By June of that year the model must have been finished, since Bellori, Passeri and Sandrart all agree that Urban VIII awarded the commission for the *St Andrew* in that month because of his admiration for it. Du Quesnoy began carving the marble at the end of 1629 or

1. François Du Quesnoy: *St Susanna*, marble, 1627–33 (Rome, S Maria di Loreto)

the beginning of 1630, and by spring 1633 the figure was in place in a shell-headed niche on the right of the choir. This original setting (it was subsequently transferred to the opposite side) made better sense of the statue's pointing gesture and the gentle torsion of the body, both of which were designed to focus the attention of the viewer towards the altar. Classical sources in the Belvedere *Antinous* (Rome, Vatican, Mus. Pio-Clementino) and the Capitoline *Urania* (Rome, Mus. Capitolino) provided the inspiration respectively for the pose and the calm beauty of the drapery. The dreamy expression of sanctity is shared with the contemporary female saints and martyrs of Domenichino and Andrea Sacchi. Du Quesnoy seems to have developed a number of ideal female heads from the *St Susanna* (e.g. attributed bronze, Vienna, Ksthist. Mus.). In 1627 the *St Andrew* was the first of four colossal statues of saints (h. *c.* 5 m) to be commissioned from different sculptors for niches at the crossing of the transept beneath the dome of St Peter's. The others are *St Longinus* by Gianlorenzo Bernini, *St Veronica* by Francesco Mochi and *St Helena* by Andrea Bolgi. In November 1629 the plaster model of Du Quesnoy's statue was unveiled and was widely praised, but it also seems to have excited a degree of envy, which according to Du Quesnoy's early biographers was the reason why in 1633 the relative positions of the four statues were altered. (In fact, the change reflected a reappraisal by the Congregation of Relics of the relative importance of these saints' relics.) The *St Andrew* was allocated a niche diametrically opposite to the one originally intended, somewhat compromising the figure's composition and gesture when the marble was installed in 1639. It now stands on the south-east corner of the crossing, with Bernini's *St Longinus* on the north-east corner, but the contrast is striking: Bernini's work is tense, with brusque gestures and an ascending rhythm in the drapery; Du Quesnoy's statue, the composition stabilized by the X-shape of the saint's cross, the drapery with an expansive, heavy rhythm, fills its niche with a serene opulence.

5. SMALL BRONZES AND OTHER WORKS. Other works by Du Quesnoy that belong to the period when he was working on the *St Susanna* and the *St Andrew* include terracotta models (untraced) made in 1627–8 for angels for Bernini's baldacchino at St Peter's, Rome, and a number of elegant and gracious male figures. Chief among these is a marble statue of *Bacchus* (1626–7; Rome, Gal. Doria-Pamphili) and a group of three small-scale bronzes made in 1629–35 for Vincenzo Giustiniani, a *Hercules*, a *Mercury* and an *Apollo*, known in a number of casts (e.g. Paris, Louvre; Vienna, Pal. Liechtenstein). The *Mercury*, perhaps an interpretation of the Mazarin *Adonis* that Du Quesnoy had restored (Gaborit), had the rare privilege of being the only modern statue to appear in the *Galleria Giustiniana* (Rome, 1631; i, pl. 84, engraved by Claude Mellan), a sumptuous collection of engravings of works of art in Giustiniani's collection, to which Du Quesnoy contributed as a draughtsman. A taste for the sophisticated reinterpretation of the more elegant antique survivals similar to that shown in the Giustiniani bronzes can be seen in a number of bronze groups depending on originals by Du Quesnoy. Among them are the *Flagellation of Christ*

2. François Du Quesnoy: *Flagellation of Christ*, bronze (Brussels, Musées Royaux d'Art et d'Histoire)

(e.g. Brussels, Musées Royaux A. & Hist.; see fig. 2) and the *Executioner with the Head of John the Baptist* (e.g. Rome, S Giovanni Decollato). Of the marble epitaphs constructed by Du Quesnoy only two survive intact. Both are in S Maria dell'Anima, Rome, and both deploy the same basic design of a pair of winged putti in relief displaying an inscription. In the earlier of the two, that of *Adrien Vrijburgh* (1628–9), there is much use of curves (as in the two frontispieces designed by Du Quesnoy for the *Galleria Giustiniana*), the inscription appearing on an irregular piece of drapery, and the contours of the monument being enveloped by further elaborate drapery; the marble is pictorially worked, and the 'sfumato' of the children's hair is very characteristic of Du Quesnoy's manner. The later monument, to *Ferdinand van den Eynde* (1633–40), is more classicizing both in its structure and in its style: the putti lift a drapery to reveal an inscription on a rectangular slab, and the architectural character of the monument is more clearly defined. The drapery and the putti themselves have a remarkable plasticity, and the working of the marble is extremely subtle.

6. PORTRAITS. During the first half of the 1630s François Du Quesnoy was particularly active as a sculptor of portrait busts, though he produced works in this genre throughout his career. As compared with the portraits of Bernini, with their search for effects of spontaneity of expression, Du Quesnoy's busts have a calmer, timeless quality. The main surviving portraits attributed to Du Quesnoy are the marble busts of *Virginio Cesarini* (disputed; *c.* 1624; Rome, Mus. Conserv.), *Bernardo Guglielmi* (Rome, S Lorenzo al Verano) and the Latin poet *John*

Barclay (Rome, Convent of S Onofrio), commissioned in 1627 by their patron Cardinal Francesco Barberini for their tombs in S Lorenzo al Verano, which were designed by Pietro da Cortona; two small terracotta busts of a man and a woman (*c.* 1630–35; Berlin, Skulpgal.); those in marble of *Nano di Crequi* (before 1634; Rome, Prince Urbano Barberini priv. col., see Lavin) and of *Cardinal Maurice of Savoy* (1635; Turin, Gal. Sabauda; terracotta in Rome, Pal. Braschi); as well as a marble medallion of the priest *Georges Conn* (1640) on his funerary monument in S Lorenzo in Damaso, Rome. Other portraits, now lost, depicted Nicolas Poussin's wife *Anne Marie Dughet* (*c.* 1630), *Prince Giustiniani* (*c.* 1629–35), *Dirk Six* and, most notably, *Cardinal de Richelieu* (before 1641).

7. LAST WORKS. From 1639 Louis XIII and Armand-Jean du Plessis, Cardinal de Richelieu, tried, on the advice of their Surintendant des Bâtiments, François Sublet des Noyers, to tempt François Du Quesnoy and Poussin to Paris. Both were reluctant, having acquired esteem and reputation in Rome. Poussin was in Paris in 1641–2, but Du Quesnoy's visit was postponed until 1643, partly because the Spanish authorities, of whom he was a subject, were unwilling to let him serve the French king. In 1641 he completed a marble relief of a *Concert of Angels* (l. 2 m), which was to serve as a predella to a mosaic of the *Annunciation* by Giovanni Battista Calandra (1586–1644) after Guido Reni. The ensemble was destined for the altar designed by Francesco Borromini in the funerary chapel created by the rich and cultivated Cardinal Ascanio Filomarino in SS Apostoli, Naples. For the relief (*in situ*) Du Quesnoy created a musical composition in which the putti seem to mark the rhythm and melody. All superfluous accessories and background details have been suppressed in this work, which was much admired by contemporaries and which has been widely imitated since. A drawing in the Galleria degli Uffizi, Florence (1420), seems to have provided Du Quesnoy's first inspiration for this subject. Around 1642 he received an invitation to execute the funerary monument of Antoine Triest, Bishop of Ghent, but refused on account of his imminent departure for France. He returned to Triest a design for the tomb, possibly by Peter Paul Rubens, but also sent him terracotta models of two putti (Ghent, Bischops Huis) for inclusion in the project if it was built by another artist. The monument was later constructed by Jérôme Du Quesnoy (ii). The putti are François Du Quesnoy's last known works, and these are the terracottas most certainly from his hand. In June 1643 he left Rome for France in the company of his brother Jérôme but fell gravely ill at Livorno, where he died at the house of the Flemish goldsmith André Ghysels.

François Du Quesnoy was a slow and meticulous worker who paid great attention to the finish of his sculptures in whatever genre or medium. He particularly liked the contrasting effects of polished marble surfaces with areas left relatively rough with chisel or drill marks. His perfectionism—he never regarded a sculpture as completely finished—was part of his search for the work of art to correspond with the ideal vision in his mind. There are further drawings by or attributed to him in the Albertina, Vienna, and the Uffizi, Florence.

BIBLIOGRAPHY

Mariette

C. de Bie: *Het gulden cabinet* (1661), pp. 442–4

G. P. Bellori: *Vite* (1672); ed. E. Borea (1976), pp. 269–84

J. von Sandrart: *Teutsche Academie* (1675–9); ed. A. R. Pelzer (1925), pp. 231–4

G. B. Passeri: *Vite* (1679); ed. J. Hess (1934), pp. 102–16

P. J. Mariette: *Abecedario* (1851–3), ii, p. 137

M. Fransolet: *François du Quesnoy, sculpteur d'Urbain VIII, 1597–1643* (Brussels, 1942)

R. Salvini: 'A Marble Bust by Duquesnoy', *Burl. Mag.*, xc (1948), pp. 92–7

V. Martinelli: 'Un "modello di creta" di Francesco Fiammingo', *Commentari*, xiii (1952), pp. 113–20

I. Faldi: 'Le "virtuose operazioni" di Francesco Duquesnoy scultore incomparabile', *A. Ant. & Mod.*, v (1959), pp. 52–62

E. Dhanens: 'De bozzetti van Frans du Quesnoy: Het probleem van de ontwerpen voor de graftombe van Mgr Triest', *Gent. Bijdr. Kstgesch. & Oudhdknd.*, xix (1961–6), pp. 103–22

K. Noehles: 'Francesco Duquesnoy: Un busto ignoto e la cronologia delle sue opere', *A. Ant. & Mod.*, xxv (1964), pp. 86–96

A. Nava Cellini: 'Duquesnoy e Poussin, nuovi contributi', *Paragone*, xvii/195 (1966), pp. 30–59

——: *Francesco Duquesnoy* (Milan, 1966)

J. Montagu: 'A *Flagellation* Group: Algardi or du Quesnoy', *Bull. Mus. Royaux A. & Hist.* (1966–7), pp. 153–93

S. Rottgen and H. Rottgen: 'An Unknown Portrait by Duquesnoy', *Connoisseur*, clxvii (1968), pp. 94–9

I. Lavin: 'Duquesnoy's *Nano di Crequi* and Two Busts by Francesco Mochi', *A. Bull.*, lii (1970), pp. 132–49

I. Toesca: 'A Group by Duquesnoy?', *Burl. Mag.*, cxvii (1975), pp. 668–71

C. Freytag: 'Neuentdeckte Werke des François du Quesnoy', *Pantheon*, xxxiv (1976), pp. 199–211

U. Schlegel: 'Der Kenotaph des Jakob von Hase von François Duquesnoy', *Jb. Berlin. Mus.* (1976), pp. 134–54

J.-R. Gaborit: 'A propos de l'Hercule de Fontainebleau', *Rev. A.* [Paris], xxxvi (1977), pp. 57–60

A. Nava Cellini: 'Per il Borromini e il Duquesnoy ai SS Apostoli di Napoli', *Paragone*, xxviii/329 (1977), pp. 26–38

La Sculpture au siècle de Rubens dans les Pays-Bas méridionaux et la principauté de Liège (exh. cat., Brussels, Mus. A. Anc., 1977), pp. 70–84

L. Hadermann-Misguich: 'François Du Quesnoy restaurateur d'antiques', *An. Hist. A. & Archéol.*, iv (1982), pp. 27–42

——: 'Deux enfants s'embrassant: Un Motif de François du Quesnoy dans la demeure de Charles Van Poucke,' *An. Hist. A. & Archéol.*, viii (1986), pp. 83–95

A. Sutherland Harris: 'Bernini and Virginio Cesarini', *Burl. Mag.*, cxxxi (1989), pp. 17–23

(3) Jérôme Du Quesnoy (ii) [*le jeune*] (*b* Brussels, *bapt* 8 May 1602; *d* Ghent, 28 Sept 1654). Sculptor and architect, son of (1) Jérôme Du Quesnoy (i). He trained in his father's workshop in Brussels and in 1618 left for Rome with his brother (2) François Du Quesnoy to complete his artistic education. The brothers are said to have separated after a quarrel. The hypothesis that Jérôme was in Rome again with his brother around 1622 is unsubstantiated, and before 1640 he seems to have worked chiefly in Spain and Portugal; no works from this period have been identified. From 1641 to 1643, he was in Rome with his brother before their attempted departure for France; he had previously spent six months in Tuscany. After the death of François Du Quesnoy in 1643 he returned to Brussels, taking with him his brother's effects, including the contents of his studio, among them models and drawings that served him as points of reference for the rest of his life. A high reputation had already preceded him to the Netherlands, and he began a brilliant phase of his career. It is not known when he first came into contact with Antoine Triest, Bishop of Ghent, who had already consulted François Du Quesnoy about his funerary monument, which it ultimately fell to Jérôme (ii) to execute. Jérôme may have made his excellent marble bust of *Triest* (Brussels, Gal. Arenberg, see exh. cat., no. 53) either in Rome or after his arrival in Brussels.

In 1644 the Council of Brabant paid Du Quesnoy for a stone statue of *St Thomas* for the nave of St Michel-St Gudule, Brussels. This is the first and most bombastic of the four statues of apostles that he carved for the church. Those of *St Matthias*, *St Paul* and *St Bartholomew*, completed in 1646, are characterized by a sober and sensitive realism and give a truer picture of the style of his best works. After 1646 he executed stone statues of *St Philip* and *St Matthias* for Notre-Dame de la Chapelle, Brussels. A small marble *Pietà* (Vienna, Ksthist. Mus.), inspired by paintings on the same theme by Anthony van Dyck, has also been attributed to Jérôme Du Quesnoy (ii) in this period. In 1645 he had been named deputy to the court architect Jacob Francart. In this capacity he drew the plans and directed the construction around 1649 of the Chapelle de Notre-Dame in St Michel-St Gudule. After Francart's death in 1651 Du Quesnoy was officially designated 'architecte, statuaire et sculpteur de la Cour'. He made several portraits of *Archduke Leopold William*, the Habsburg Governor of the Netherlands—a medal (untraced), a small ivory bust (London, V&A) and a marble bust (1650; Vienna, Ksthist. Mus.), the latter reproduced in several bronze versions. David Teniers (II)'s set of views of Leopold William's collection shows a table base (untraced) by Du Quesnoy made up of the entwined figures of Ganymede and the eagle. One of his most beautiful works is the kneeling marble statue of *St Ursula* placed after 1651 in the funerary chapel of the Thurn und Taxis family in Notre-Dame du Sablon, Brussels. Affinities in the heavy fall of the draperies have led to the attribution to Jérôme Du Quesnoy (ii) of the marble statue of *Mary Magdalene Reading* (Brussels, Mus. A. Anc.), sometimes also given to his father. The angels in high relief above the cornice of the Thurn und Taxis chapel were possibly executed to Jérôme (ii)'s designs, while two serene, classicizing groups of *St Anne Guiding the Steps of the Virgin* (stone, 1653–4; Brussels, Collégiale; and marble, after 1653; St Jan, Mechelen, Van Leyen-Van den Venne monument) have clear affinities with the *St Ursula* and also with François Du Quesnoy's *St Susanna*.

Jérôme Du Quesnoy (ii)'s last years were devoted to the elaborate funerary monument for *Antoine Triest, Bishop of Ghent* (see fig.) in St Bavo, Ghent. The contract of 1651 makes no mention of the putti designed earlier by François Du Quesnoy for inclusion in the scheme and is ambiguous about the existence of any earlier design. (The one that had been returned to Triest from Rome by François had possibly been conceived by Rubens.) The monument as executed by Jérôme (ii) consists of white marble statues of the Virgin and of Christ looking down upon the recumbent white marble effigy of Triest, which reclines on a sarcophagus decorated with two free-standing putti (based on François Du Quesnoy's terracotta models) and two in relief, supporting a scrolled inscription. The whole is set into a complicated architectural screen in black and white marble, with pilasters and solomonic columns carrying an entablature with a double broken

Jérôme Du Quesnoy (ii): funerary monument of *Antoine Triest, Bishop of Ghent*, marble, 1651–4 (Ghent, St Bavo)

pediment within which two further putti carry the Archbishop's coat of arms. The tomb inaugurated a series of similar constructions, but the obvious derivation of the statuary from works by François Du Quesnoy and from Italian sources underlines the fact that Jérôme Du Quesnoy (ii) was a skilled and sensitive sculptor of the second rank, rather than an original and innovative artist. He was, perhaps, at his best as a sculptor of portraits, that of the aged and meditative Triest on his tomb effigy being particularly fine. His career was abruptly terminated by his arrest and execution on charges of sodomy, while still working at St Bavo.

BIBLIOGRAPHY

Mariette
O. Roelandts: *De beeldhouwers Hieronymus Duquesnoy vader en zoon* (Ghent, n.d.)
M. Fransolet: *François du Quesnoy, sculpteur d'Urbain VIII, 1597–1643* (Brussels, 1942), pp. 137–46
J. Buntinx: 'Jeroom du Quesnoy en het praalgraf van Bisschof Triest in de Sint-Baafskathedraal te Gent', *Hand. Maatsch. Gesch. & Oudhdknd. Gent*, n. s., iv/1 (1949–50), pp. 97–111
La Sculpture au siècle de Rubens dans les Pays-Bas méridionaux et la principauté de Liège (exh. cat., Brussels, Mus. A. Anc., 1977), pp. 85–95
D. Coekelberghs: 'Jérôme Duquesnoy, buste de Monseigneur Antoine Triest, évêque de Gand', *Galerie d'Arenberg, sculptures de maîtres anciens: Des frères Duquesnoy à Dalou* (Brussels, 1991), pp. 6–11

LYDIE HADERMANN-MISGUICH

Dur. *See under* ARABIA, PRE-ISLAMIC, §§II; III; IV, 1.

Dura Europos [now Qal'at as Sāliḥīyah]. Site of a Hellenistic and Roman walled city in eastern Syria, on a plateau between two gorges on the west bank of the middle Euphrates. The name combines elements that are Semitic (Dura) and Macedonian Greek (Europos). Dura Europos was founded by the Seleucids in the late 4th

century BC at the intersection of east–west caravan routes and the trade route along the Euphrates. It was later a frontier fortress of the Parthian empire and after its capture in AD 165 fulfilled the same role for the Roman empire. After the Sasanian siege in AD 256–7 the city was abandoned. The results of excavations by French and American archaeologists in the 1920s and 1930s threw light on the process of synthesis between Classical and indigenous populations and cultures in Syria-Palestine during Hellenistic and Imperial Roman times. The excavated remains include a synagogue (*see* §3 below) with an important cycle of biblical paintings and an Early Christian meeting-house (*domus ecclesiae*) (*see* §4 below). Finds are in the National Museum of Damascus and the Yale University Art Gallery, New Haven, CT.

1. Greek and Parthian. 2. Roman. 3. Jewish. 4. Early Christian.

1. GREEK AND PARTHIAN. Founded *c.* 300 BC under one of Alexander the Great's successors, Seleukos I Nicator of Syria (*reg* 312–281 BC), Dura Europos was built as a Hellenistic Greek town with a rectangular street grid (*see* GREECE, ANCIENT, fig. 37). It had a central agora (market place), an administrative (Parthian) Citadel and Redoubt palace, with a so-called peristyle temple of Artemis with Doric peristyle and altar, and wall with towers and gates, all incorporating mud-brick, timber and ashlar masonry. In *c.* 175–150 BC the palaces were rebuilt, the so-called Zeus Megistos temple with Doric gateway was erected (one of several temples to Zeus), and houses were built. From *c.* 113 BC to AD 165 Dura Europos was incorporated by the PARTHIANs into their empire, and its culture became progressively more Oriental. Inscriptions and (later) written documents in Greek and Aramaic reveal that while a Greco-Macedonian élite was maintained the majority of the population was Semitic (Aramaean), some from Palmyra and Iran; the process of syncretism led to the equation of many of the Greek and Oriental deities. The market place became a crowded bazaar, buildings had flat roofs, and houses now incorporated smaller rooms around inner courts without columns, thus adopting ancient Mesopotamian forms (*see* MESOPOTAMIA, §II, 6(iii)).

Temples were also built on an inward-looking plan from at least 33–32 BC, with walled courtyards enclosing altars, subsidiary chapels and the main sanctuary (*naos*); this sanctuary was generally of the broad room type, often with a vestibule. Temples began to be decorated with modest local religious sculptures, portraying deities, attributes and worshippers, which often functioned as cult objects. In these works of the so-called Parthian style the figures are carved in the unnaturalistic, linear and Oriental style, frequently frontally, as was characteristic of the art of desert Syria, Mesopotamia and Iran. Examples include the relief of the seated, cloaked Zeus Kyrios-Ba'alshamîn before a ram-carrying dedicant (AD 31; New Haven, CT, Yale U. A.G.; see fig. 1), a relief of a standing figure of the god Aphlad in cuirass and trousers (*c.* AD 54; Damascus, N. Mus.) and a fragmentary wall painting of Zeus-Bel wearing Parthian dress in a chariot (*c.* AD 50); later came reliefs of the personified Fortunes (Tyche-Gad) of Dura

1. Dura Europos, cult relief of Zeus Kyrios-Ba'alshamîn, limestone with traces of paint, h. 520 mm, AD 31 (New Haven, CT, Yale University Art Gallery)

Europos and Palmyra (AD 159; both New Haven, CT, Yale U. A.G.).

2. ROMAN. Roman occupation (AD 165–c. 256) brought further commercial and cultural enrichment. The local Parthian culture flourished, and the Parthian influence was predominant in the art of Dura Europos. Large numbers of religious sculptures, particularly statuettes and reliefs (examples in Damascus, N. Mus., and New Haven, CT, Yale U. A.G.), depicted such Greek, Semitic and syncretic deities as Heracles-Nergal and, less frequently, Apollo-Nebu, Aphrodite, Athena-Allat, Nemesis and armed and rider gods; these sculptures are mainly in limestone, gypsum and plaster. Rich wall paintings in temples (see ROME, ANCIENT, §V, 2) depicted divinities and ceremonies such as the sacrifice of Konon, from the Temple of Bel (c. 180; Damascus, N. Mus.), the sacrifice of Otes, also from the Temple of Bel (c. ?230; destr.) and the sacrifice of the tribune Julius Terentius (c. 239; New Haven, CT, Yale U. A.G.), while houses had banquet and hunt scenes. The presence of the Roman garrison brought changes in the architecture, particularly after c. AD 210. Additions included a northern camp area containing the headquarters (211–2), a colonnaded street, baths (applying concrete construction techniques, as imported from Italy, to local materials), a small amphitheatre (216), the palace of the commander (dux ripae) and temples of the soldiers' gods Jupiter Dolichenus (210–11) and Mithras (168); the

Mithraeum contained cult reliefs and, later, Mithraic wall paintings (c. AD 211–16; repainted c. 240). Six wooden parade shields of the early 3rd century AD (New Haven, CT, Yale U. A.G.) are painted with designs, including a map, Amazons and the sack of Troy. During the Roman period moulded plaster cornices were used in the construction of houses.

BIBLIOGRAPHY

F. Cumont: *Fouilles de Doura-Europos* (Paris, 1926)
P. V. C. Baur and others, eds: *The Excavations at Dura-Europos, Preliminary Reports*, 8 vols (New Haven, 1929–52)
M. I. Rostovtzeff: 'Dura and the Problem of Parthian Art', *Yale Class. Stud.*, v (1935), pp. 157–304
A. R. Bellinger and others, eds: *The Excavations at Dura-Europos: Final Report*, i–viii (New Haven, 1943–)
A. Perkins: *The Art of Dura-Europos* (Oxford, 1973)
S. B. Downey: *Mesopotamian Religious Architecture: Alexander through the Parthians* (Princeton, 1988)

MALCOLM A. R. COLLEDGE

3. JEWISH. The discovery in 1932 of the Dura Europos synagogue and its cycle of wall paintings was highly significant for the study of the origins of Christian art and for scholarly ideas about Judaism and imagery. The synagogue was built against the western wall of the city, north of the main gate. It consisted of a prayer-room (13.65×7.68×7.00 m), a pillared forecourt on the east side and a precinct surrounded by houses. Ceiling inscriptions in Aramaic and Greek date the building to AD 244–5. This synagogue was an enlargement of a smaller one built in the late 2nd century AD, from which some painted decoration survives; both were adapted private dwellings with boxlike, high-ceilinged rooms and flat roofs. The prayer-room was of the broad room type familiar from Syro-Palestinian domestic architecture. When the building was partly demolished and filled in to make an embankment that formed part of the city defences against the invading Sasanians in AD 256, the west wall of the prayer-room was left virtually intact, but the side walls were cut down in sloping lines towards the east (entrance) wall, which was reduced to about a third of its original height. The synagogue has been reconstructed in the National Museum of Damascus (see fig. 2).

The inside walls of the prayer-room were completely covered with 5 horizontal bands of secco paintings, comprising 3 large bands depicting 58 biblical episodes with decorative bands above and below. About 29 panels have survived, depicting biblical heroes such as *Jacob*, *Moses* and *David*, and scenes from the books of Genesis, Exodus, Samuel, Kings, Esther and Ezekiel (see JEWISH ART, §IV and fig. 14). Decoration from the earlier synagogue, primarily on the central upper part of the west wall (orientated towards Jerusalem), shows a lioness in a grove, with two lion cubs and a table set with fruit or loaves near by. The later decoration introduced a striking new mode of depiction that originated in 1st-century AD Syria, with human figures in schematic, rigid and hieratic frontality; the scheme may have been modelled on a (lost) synagogue (late 2nd century AD) in Palmyra with a more sophisticated cycle of paintings. The paintings were probably produced by several artists. Their chief interest lies in their narrative skill and in the fact that such paintings exist at all in a 3rd-century synagogue. The same stylistic mixture of western

2. Dura Europos, synagogue; reconstructed north-west corner showing wall paintings and Torah shrine, *c.* AD 244–5 (Damascus, National Museum of Damascus)

Asian and western European elements, and the appearance of the figures occur in other parts of Dura Europos.

There is little agreement on the underlying symbolism or meaning of the paintings, either individually or as a whole. There have been several interpretations of the complete cycle: that there is no unifying concept (see Sukenik, Leveen), that there is a discernible theological theme (Grabar, Sonne, Goodenough) or that the cycle conveys several different religious messages (du Mesnil du Buisson, Kraeling). The seemingly disordered disposition of the narrative scenes and the introduction of legendary stories (e.g. Hiel hiding in the altar of the Baal prophets, the Israelites armed while crossing the Red Sea, the naked princess rescuing the infant Moses and King Ahasuerus on Solomon's throne) may, however, reflect Palestinian liturgical practices and prayers, which took biblical texts out of context to convey meanings never intended by the original stories. The emphasis was now on salvation and resurrection (as in, for example, the scenes of *Moses Saved by the Egyptian Princess, Elijah Triumphing over the Prophets of Baal*, the *Vision of Ezekiel* and *Elijah Restoring the Widow's Son*). The purpose of the cycle was probably to win converts by revealing the superiority of Judaism over the pagan mystery religions and to combat the growing influence of Christianity.

The importance of these provincial synagogue paintings lies in the evidence they provide for an early Jewish tradition of figurative painting (*see* JEWISH ART, §I, 4(i)). The biblical prohibition of graven images had been taken to imply that pre-Christian Jewish art was aniconic and that figurative painting had developed from imitating Christian models. The Dura paintings, however, constitute the earliest continuous narrative cycle of biblical images, pre-dating similar cycles in churches by about 200 years. Although it has been assumed that the paintings were based on a tradition of illustrated Jewish manuscripts in such Hellenistic centres as Alexandria or Antioch, no illustrated Classical manuscript indisputably antedates the 5th century AD, none is mentioned in surviving literary sources, and there are no illustrated Jewish manuscripts from before the late 10th century AD. It seems more likely that the Dura synagogue paintings were based on pictorial guides—pattern, model or motif books—that may have been available in Roman workshops.

BIBLIOGRAPHY

R. du Mesnil du Buisson: *Les Peintures de la synagogue de Dura-Europos, 245–256 après J.-C.* (Rome, 1939)

A. Grabar: 'Le Thème religieux des fresques de la synagogue de Doura', *Rev. Hist. Relig.*, cxxiii (1941), pp. 143–92; cxxiv (1941), pp. 5–35

J. Leveen: 'The Wall Paintings at Dura Europos', *The Hebrew Bible in Art* (London, 1944/*R* New York, 1974)

I. Sonne: 'The Paintings of the Dura Synagogue', *Heb. Un. Coll. Annu.*, xx (1947), pp. 255–362
E. L. Sukenik: *The Synagogue of Dura-Europos and its Paintings* (Jerusalem, 1947) [in Hebrew]
C. H. Kraeling: *The Synagogue* (1956, rev. 1979), viii/1 of *The Excavations at Dura-Europos: Final Report* (New Haven, 1943–)
E. R. Goodenough: *Jewish Symbols in the Greco-Roman Period*, ix–xi (New York, 1964)
K. Weitzmann and H. L. Kessler: *The Frescoes of the Dura Synagogue and Christian Art* (Washington, 1990)
J. Gutmann, ed.: *The Dura Europos Synagogue: A Reevaluation (1932–1992)* (Atlanta, 1992)

JOSEPH GUTMANN

4. EARLY CHRISTIAN. The meeting-house (*domus ecclesiae*) excavated by M. Pillet and C. Hopkins in 1930–32 exemplifies a type of building that must have been common in small towns throughout the empire during the 3rd and 4th centuries AD. It was originally built as an ordinary town dwelling *c*. AD 232–3 and converted to a church *c*. 240 to meet the needs of a growing Christian congregation and an evolving liturgy. Roughly rectangular in plan (20×17 m), it is adjacent to the western city wall, one block south of the main gate. In form and organization it closely resembles other modest Durene houses: the central courtyard, entered from a narrow street through a vestibule, is surrounded on three sides by flat-roofed, box-like rooms and on the fourth (east) side by a portico. The walls of rubble and mud brick coated with mud plaster had no exterior ornament.

Adapting the house to serve Christian ritual involved several structural changes. The courtyard floor was tiled and benches were added. A wall between two rooms south of the courtyard was demolished to create a large assembly hall (5×13 m), with space to seat 60–70 people. A low platform built against the short east wall presumably served as a dais for the bishop. An adjoining room (4×7 m) on the west side of the courtyard was probably used for catechumens since it opens into the baptistery, formerly the north-west corner room of the house. Against the west wall of the baptistery a masonry piscina or font, lined with plaster and set partly into the floor, was surmounted by a vaulted canopy. A ledge or table stood in front of a niche in the south wall, while a bench placed along the east wall provided seating.

The baptistery was the only decorated room in the building. Its walls and ceiling were originally covered with paintings, only a few fragments of which survive (New Haven, CT, Yale U. A.G.). The columns supporting the canopy or ciborium (*see* CIBORIUM, fig. 1) were painted to imitate marble, while the arch above was decorated with a pink ribbon encircling a garland of fruit. Representations of star-studded skies in white and dark blue covered the ceiling and canopy vault. The walls bore Old and New Testament scenes, in a palette primarily of reds, browns, and black with occasional yellow ochre, pink and greens on a white plaster background. The arrangement of scenes comprised the *Good Shepherd* on the west wall, beneath the canopy vault, with *Adam and Eve* added later; *Christ Healing the Paralytic*, *Christ Walking on the Waves* and a garden scene suggesting Paradise in the upper register of the east, south and north walls; and *Christ and the Woman of Samaria*, *David and Goliath* and two scenes from the *Three Marys at the Tomb* in the walls' lower register. They are among the earliest known wall paintings from a building intended specifically for Christian ritual use. Although clumsily executed and combining aspects of both Greco-Roman and Oriental pictorial traditions, the decorative scheme followed a coherent programme centred around the symbolism of baptism: the miracles of Christ, the promise of salvation and resurrection.

Twenty fragments of texts or drawings were found scratched or painted elsewhere in the building, some dating from before its conversion to religious use. Although no other objects of Christian significance have survived, a Greek manuscript fragment of Tatian's *Diatessaron* (*c*. 150–60) was discovered near by. The entire building was destroyed with the neighbouring synagogue and houses in the siege of AD 256–7.

BIBLIOGRAPHY
M. I. Rostovtzeff: *Dura-Europos and its Art* (Oxford, 1938)
J. Villette: 'Que représente la Grande Fresque de la maison chrétienne de Doura?', *Rev. Bibl.*, lx (1953), pp. 398–413
R. Krautheimer: *Early Christian and Byzantine Architecture*, Pelican Hist. A. (Harmondsworth, 1965, rev. 4/1986)
C. H. Kraeling: *The Christian Building* (1967), viii/2 of *The Excavations at Dura-Europos* (New Haven, 1943–)

ANDREW R. SEAGER

Durameau, Louis(-Jean)-Jacques (*b* Paris, 5 Oct 1733; *d* Versailles, 3 Sept 1796). French painter. The son of a copperplate printer, he worked with the sculptor Jean-Baptiste Defernex before entering the Académie Royale in 1754, where he studied under Jean-Baptiste Pierre. After three unsuccessful attempts he won the Grand Prix de Rome in 1757 with *Elijah Raising the Shunammite Woman's Son from the Dead* (Paris, Ecole B.-A.). He studied (1757–60) at the Ecole des Elèves Protégés in Paris under Carle Vanloo, afterwards transferring to the Académie de France in Rome. During his time in Rome (1761–4) Durameau completed his artistic education, while also making copies after the Old Masters for Pierre-Jean Mariette and studying antique art for the Abbé de Saint-Non. In addition, he painted the genre work, the *Saltpetre Factory* (Paris, Louvre), which is one of the first industrial landscapes and in its invention and authority worthy of the finest passages of Jean-Honoré Fragonard.

After his return to Paris Durameau pursued the traditional career of a history painter and was accepted into the Académie Royale in 1766. He exhibited at the Salon from 1767 to 1789 and had a major triumph at the Salon of 1767, when 13 of his works were exhibited, the *Martyrdom of SS Cyr and Juliette* and the *Death of St Francis of Sales* (both Paris, St-Nicolas-du-Chardonnet) being particularly praised. These two works, like those of Joseph-Marie Vien and Gabriel-François Doyen, contributed to the revival of religious painting. However, Durameau's finest works are his large-scale decorations, among them the *Triumph of Justice* for the Rouen Parlement (1767; *in situ*), the *Rising of the Dawn* (1768; Asnières, Banque de France) for Marc-René, Marquis d'Voyer, two ceilings (1769; destr.) for the opera house of the Palais Royal, and the ceiling compartment *Summer* (exh. Salon 1775; Paris, Louvre) for the Galerie d'Apollon of the Louvre. His major work in this genre is the ceiling of the opera house at Versailles, which was inaugurated in 1770 for the Dauphin's wedding. Entitled *Apollo Preparing Crowns for Men of Renown in the Arts* (*in situ*; see fig.), it was greatly admired by the court.

Louis-Jacques Durameau: *Apollo Preparing Crowns for Men of Renown in the Arts*, ceiling painting, 1770 (Versailles, Opéra)

With Nicolas-Guy Brenet and Jacques-Antoine Beaufort, Durameau was also one of the first to bring history painting back into favour. He executed *St Louis Washing the Feet of the Poor* (exh. Salon 1773) for the decorative cycle of the Ecole Militaire (*in situ*). Charles-Claude Flahaut de la Billarderie, Comte d'Angiviller, commissioned him (1773) to paint the *Continence of Bayard* (exh. Salon 1777; Grenoble, Mus. Grenoble), a rather theatrical work. Others in this genre include the *Combat of Entelles and Dares* (exh. Salon 1779; Riom, Mus. Mandet), based on an episode from ancient history and executed in a proto-Romantic manner, and the *Filial Piety of Cleobis and Biton* (exh. Salon 1779; Mont-de-Marsan, Mus. Dubalen Hist. Nat.), which is in the style of Vien's works.

Durameau became a member of the Académie in 1774; he was made an assistant professor in 1776 and professor five years later. In 1778 he was named painter to the Cabinet du Roi. From 1776 to 1784 he also taught as a professor at the Ecole des Elèves Entretenus, where he trained such pupils as Etienne-Barthélemy Garnier, Jean-Charles-Nicaise Perrin and François Watteau. In 1783 Durameau exhibited two royal commissions, *Herminia under the Arms of Clorinda* (untraced) and a pair of religious works from a decorative cycle intended for the chapel of Fontainebleau, *Christ Healing the Cripple* (*in situ*) and *Christ Driving the Money-changers from the Temple* (untraced). Revealing the influence of his master van Loo, these works were not well received by the critics.

Durameau also produced such portrait works as the *Violin Player* (exh. Salon 1775; Besançon, Mus. B.-A. & Archéol.). His drawings were collected by such notable contemporary connoisseurs as Mariette, Louis-François Trouard and Pierre-Adrien Pâris, who bequeathed to Besançon (Bib. Mun.) a fine series for the catafalque of Maria-Theresa of Austria. In 1784 Durameau replaced Etienne Jeaurat (1699–1789) as Garde des Tableaux du Roi at the Surintendance des Bâtiments at the château of Versailles. In this new role he drew up a methodical catalogue of the royal collections. With the Revolution of 1789 he lost the post, but his unique knowledge of Versailles and its collections led to his being recalled by the Commission Temporaire des Arts in July 1795 to act as curator of the Musée Spécial de l'Ecole Française.

Hailed as one of the hopes of the new generation, Durameau quickly disappointed his contemporaries, who attacked the conception of his subjects and the dullness of his palette. Scoffed at by the Parisian critics, he came to paint less and less and instead devoted himself to his administrative tasks. Nevertheless, he did achieve a reputation, established in his lifetime by Claude-Henri Watelet, as a Rembrandtesque painter of light. This characterization was revived by the Goncourt brothers, who in 1854 bought his *Card Game by Candlelight* (1767; Paris, Louvre), an intimate work infused with light. It was Locquin, however, who rediscovered his abilities as a decorator and history painter. Durameau's art perpetuated the tradition of his masters Pierre, van Loo and Charles-Joseph Natoire, but, with his new choice of subjects and his investigation of realism, he combatted the artificiality of the work of such artists as Boucher. He belonged to that transitional generation of the second third of the 18th century that later enabled David to establish the Neo-classical aesthetic.

BIBLIOGRAPHY

J. Locquin: *La Peinture d'histoire en France de 1747 à 1785* (Paris, 1912/R 1978), pls 96, 97, 102, 104, 126

M. Sandoz: *Louis-Jacques Durameau (1733–1796)* (Paris, 1980)

ANNE LECLAIR

Durán. Spanish family of architects, active in Mexico from 1690 to after 1750. It is assumed that José Durán, Miguel Custodio Durán and Diego Durán Berruecos were related, although research to date has not produced any firm evidence. José Durán was responsible for the plan of the basilica of Guadalupe, which was built (1695–1709) by Pedro de Arrieta at the foot of the hill of Tepeyac, north of Mexico City. It is longitudinal in plan, with aisles, but centrally organized with a crossing dome equidistant from the sanctuary and the entrance. This dome presides over each elevation, framed by octagonal bell-towers at the corners. A possible stylistic source is the Basilica del Pilar (begun 1681), Saragossa, Spain.

Miguel Custodio Durán is associated with a series of works carried out in Mexico City. The most important of these is the church of S Juan de Dios (1729) on the north side of the Alameda Gardens. The main elevation is dished inwards in the manner of a *nicchione*. Use is also made of the undulating order of pilasters, invented *c.* 1660 by Fray Juan Andres Ricci (1600–81). The church of S Lazaro and the monastery church of Regina (1731) are also attributed to Miguel Custodio Durán.

The church of SS Sebastian y Prisca in Taxco is attributed to Diego Durán Berruecos. Built between 1748 and 1758 at the expense of the silver magnate José de la Borda (1700–78), it represents an early provincial manifestation of the 'Ultra Baroque' (Kubler). The pink stone church dominates the town, which is itself elevated above the Mexico–Acapulco road. This effect is further emphasized by the verticality of the design, which derives from the use of a double square system of proportions, in which the height of the tower is twice the overall width of the façade and the height of the façade panel is twice its own width. The tower shafts are plain to the height of the nave eaves, save for their circular windows, but above this the belfries are thickly adorned with columns and *estípites*. Paired columns on the main façade are straight at ground-level but twisted at the upper range. The high dome is decorated with polychrome glazed tiles.

BIBLIOGRAPHY

D. A. Iñiguez, E. M. Dorta and M. J. Buschiazzo: *Historia del arte hispanoamericano*, 3 vols (Barcelona, 1945–56)

G. Kubler and M. Soria: *Art and Architecture in Spain and Portugal and their American Dominions, 1500–1800*, Pelican Hist. A. (Harmondsworth, 1959)

M. Toussaint: *Arte colonial en México* (Mexico City, 1962)

E. Vargas Lugo: *La iglesia de Santa Prisca de Taxco* (Mexico City, 1974)

G. Tovar de Teresa: *El barroco en México* (Mexico City, 1981)

R. Gutierrez: *Arquitectura y urbanismo en Iberoamérica* (Madrid, 1983)

MARIA CONCEPCIÓN GARCÍA SÁIZ

Durand, Asher B(rown) (*b* Springfield Township, NJ, 21 Aug 1796; *d* Maplewood, NJ, 17 Sept 1886). American painter and engraver. He played a leading role in formulating both the theory and practice of mid-19th-century American landscape painting and was a central member of the HUDSON RIVER SCHOOL. Five years older than Thomas Cole, he matured considerably later as an artist. After an apprenticeship with Peter Maverick (1812–17), he began his career as an engraver, attaining eminence with plates after John Trumbull's *Declaration of Independence* (1820–23) and John Vanderlyn's *Ariadne* (1835), the latter so accomplished that the chronicler William Dunlap claimed it would win Durand immortality as an engraver. As with many contemporary artists, his training was based on drawing, an experience that influenced his insistence on the importance of outline and precise rendering.

Durand first took up painting in the 1830s, producing portraits of distinguished Americans and occasional history pieces such as the *Capture of Major André* (1834; Worcester, MA, A. Mus.). Perhaps inspired by the success of Thomas Cole, Durand began exhibiting landscape paintings in 1837; Cole's influence is particularly apparent in allegorical landscapes such as the *Morning of Life* and the *Evening of Life* (1840; New York, N. Acad. Des.). This literary or didactic strain was present in Durand's work until the early 1850s; works such as *Thanatopsis* (1850; New York, Met.) embody the 'sister arts' concept that provided American painters with a literary justification for the emergent genre of landscape. At the same time, however, there was a growing interest in precisely observed portraits of American nature.

Durand was credited by his son and biographer, John Durand, with painting the first finished oil landscape studies from nature. *Landscape with a Beech Tree* (1844;

New York, NY Hist. Soc.), a highly finished work, is his first such known study. Increasingly thereafter he advocated direct study from nature, finding a more formal expression of his beliefs in John Ruskin's *Modern Painters* (1843–60). Study from nature, though it carried enormous authority for Hudson River school painters, served for Durand only as the basis for constructing finished compositions that incorporated idealized or composite types distilled out of nature's variety. He distinguished between the imitative and representative, or typical, character of art. His 'Letters on Landscape Painting', written in 1855 for *The Crayon* (a Ruskinian art journal published in New York), constitute a key statement of landscape painting theory in mid-19th-century America, namely that nature served as the arbiter of artistic truth. Such Ruskinian ideas, however, were received by Durand within the context of a native idealism and faith in the intuitive apprehension of nature's inherent beauty and goodness.

By the middle of his career Durand had developed a landscape idiom that allowed him to reconcile the naturalism of direct observation with nationalistic themes. In compositions such as the *Advance of Civilization* (1853; Tuscaloosa, AL, Warner Col., Gulf States Paper Corp.) Durand expressed a progressive vision of national destiny through the organization of the landscape scene itself, beginning with the Indians in the foreground wilderness and moving through the stages of national development defined successively by wagon, steamboat and canal, telegraph system and railway.

In works such as the *View of the Hudson Valley* (1857; Ithaca, NY, Cornell U., Johnson Mus. A.) Durand employed established compositional formulae in landscape painting to imbue American wilderness scenes with a stable harmony reminiscent of the 17th-century classical landscapes of Claude Lorrain. His concern with balanced composition, graduated movement into the distance and refined tonal modulation (through subtle gradation of local colour) also points to the influence of Claude. (As he later wrote, Durand 'visited Europe. . .lured above all by the glory of Claude's famous productions'.) Such an approach gave cultural validation to American nature as a subject for art.

By the second quarter of the 19th century Durand's urban patrons, such as Luman Reed and Jonathan Sturges, were developing important collections of American art. It was Sturges who commissioned *Kindred Spirits* (1849; see fig.), which shows the poet William Cullen Bryant admiring a Catskill gorge with Thomas Cole, who had died the previous year. The painting serves as an artistic testament to the importance of wilderness in the formation of national identity. Durand also produced idyllic scenes of domesticated nature, works that breathed an air of reverence and nostalgia for lost origins that was deeply appealing to Americans in a period of rapid economic and social change.

After the death of Cole in 1848, Durand was generally acknowledged as the foremost landscape painter in America, his work embodying many of the principal aesthetic and moral values ascribed to that genre by his contemporaries. Until his retirement in 1878, Durand's career followed a familiar pattern for many American landscape painters—winter residence in New York, alternating with

Asher B. Durand: *Kindred Spirits*, oil on canvas, 1168×914 mm, 1849 (New York, Public Library)

periodic sketching trips to the Catskills, Adirondacks and other sparsely settled mountainous regions of the northeastern United States. He travelled to Europe only once, from 1840 to 1841. His example for younger artists, his success with wealthy urban patrons and his term as president of the National Academy of Design from 1845 to 1861 all conferred legitimacy on landscape painting.

WRITINGS

'Letters on Landscape Painting', *Crayon*, i/1 (1855), pp. 1–2; i/3 (1855), pp. 34–5; i/5 (1855), pp. 66–7; i/7 (1855), pp. 97–8; i/10 (1855), pp. 145–6; i/14 (1855), pp. 209–11; i/18 (1855), pp. 273–5; i/23 (1855), pp. 354–5; ii/2 (1855), pp. 16–17; portions repr. in J. W. McCoubrey: *American Art, 1700–1960: Sources and Documents* (Englewood Cliffs, 1965)

BIBLIOGRAPHY

W. Dunlap: *History of the Rise and Progress of the Arts of Design in the United States*, iii (New York, 1834/R 1969), pp. 60–65
J. Durand: *The Life and Times of A. B. Durand* (New York, 1894/R 1970)
W. Craven: 'Asher B. Durand's Career as an Engraver', *Amer. A. Q.*, iii (1971), pp. 39–57
A. B. Durand, 1796–1886 (exh. cat. by D. Lawall, Montclair, NJ, A. Mus., 1971)
D. Lawall: *Asher Brown Durand: His Art and Art Theory in Relation to his Times* (New York, 1977)
——: *Asher B. Durand: A Documentary Catalogue of the Narrative and Landscape Paintings* (New York, 1978)
A. Miller: *The Empire of the Eye: Landscape Representation and American Cultural Politics, 1825–1875* (Ithaca, NY, 1993)

ANGELA L. MILLER

Durand, Charles-Emile-Auguste. *See* CAROLUS-DURAN.

Durand, Hippolyte-Louis (*b* Paris, 1809; *d* 1881).
French architect and writer. He studied under Léon
Vaudoyer and Louis-Hippolyte Lebas at the Ecole des
Beaux-Arts, Paris, and subsequently specialized in medieval architecture. He worked on the restoration of the
churches of St Remi (*c.* 1837) at Reims, Notre-Dame de
l'Epine (*c.* 1838) at L'Epine, near Châlons-sur-Marne, and
the church at St Menoux (1841) in the Bourbonnais,
before turning briefly to the Neo-classical style for the
theatre (1842–53) at Moulins. At the Salon of 1845 he
presented studies of sample schemes for religious buildings
in the medieval style, envisaging types of buildings conceived in terms of the size of the municipality they were
to serve, publishing estimates and plans for them in 1849.
By 1848, Durand had a sufficient reputation as a Gothic
Revivalist to be appointed diocesan architect to Bayonne,
but after violent disagreements with the bishop he resigned
in 1852. He was considered arrogant as a man and negligent
as an architect, although Vaudoyer admitted that he did
have ability. In 1846 Durand had made plans for the
church of St André, Bayonne. Work did not begin until
c. 1853, and it was not completed until 1862 (bell-towers
destr. 1898). An important secular commission at this time
was a villa (1854–7; destr. 1903) at Biarritz for the Empress
Eugénie (1826–1920), but Durand was dismissed in 1855
and the villa was finished by Louis Couvrechef (1827–60).
In the early 1860s Durand was appointed diocesan architect to Auch, where he rebuilt the Ursuline priory, and to
Tarbes, where he built the seminary (*c.* 1868). His later
commissions were almost all ecclesiastical, and one of his
last works was the basilica of Notre-Dame at Lourdes
(consecrated 1876), the drawings for which he exhibited
at the Paris Salon in 1872. It is in a 13th-century style with
a tall spire.

UNPUBLISHED SOURCES

Paris, Archvs N., F19 4544–45, 7230, 7805 [reps to the Commission des
 Arts et Monuments]
Paris, Bibliothèque de la Direction du Patrimoine, MS. 8 Doc. 65

WRITINGS

'Quelques considérations sur l'art religieux', *L'Art et l'archéologie en province*,
 xi (1849), pp. 13–16
with A.-T. de Girardot: *La Cathédrale de Bourges: Description historique et
 archéologique* (Moulins, 1849)

BIBLIOGRAPHY

C. E. Godard: *Symbolisme de la nouvelle église St-André à Bayonne au triple
 point de vue de l'architecte, de la perspective et de la musique: Esquisse de
 monographie chrétienne* (Bayonne, 1862)
J. M. Leniaud: 'Les Constructions d'églises sous le Second Empire:
 Architecture et prix de revient', *Rev. Hist. Eglise France* (1979), pp.
 267–78
——: 'Les Restaurations de la cathédrale de Bayonne au XIXe siècle',
 Actes du congrès des sociétés savantes: Bordeaux, 1979, pp. 445–66
The Second Empire, 1852–1870: Art in France under Napoleon III (exh.
 cat., ed G. H. Marcus and J. M. Landola; Philadelphia, PA, Mus. A.,
 1979), pp. 45–6

JEAN-MICHEL LENIAUD

Durand, Jean-Nicolas-Louis (*b* Paris, 18 Sept 1760; *d*
Thiais, 31 Dec 1834). French architect, teacher and writer.
He was one of the most influential teachers of his time,
and his radically rationalist approach, which emphasized
priority of function and economy of means, was expressed
in analytical writings that remained popular into the 20th
century. He studied under Pierre Panseron (*fl* 1736) and
from 1776 in the office of Etienne-Louis Boullée. He also
took courses with Julien-David Le Roy at the Académie
d'Architecture and participated in competitions under the
guidance of Jean-Rodolphe Perronet. He twice came
second in the Prix de Rome: in 1779 for a museum and in
1780 for a school. During the 1780s he worked as a
draughtsman for Boullée and for the engraver Jean-
François Janinet. In 1788 construction began in the Rue
du Faubourg-Poissonnière, Paris, of his Maison Lathuille,
a building with Néo-Grec decoration but with a layout
characterized by its extreme simplicity. About 1790 he
executed a series of drawings entitled *Rudimenta Operis
Magni et Disciplinae*, which are probably a pictorial representation of Boullée's theories, centred on the notion of
expressive forms and 'character' in architecture (*see*
FRANCE, §II, 3).

In 1794 Durand entered into partnership with Louis-
Michel Thibault, another student of Boullée, and the two
architects carried out the decoration for the Fête de Bara
et Viala in the Panthéon, Paris, although for political
reasons the festivity did not take place. They won the
public competitions in 1794, however, when their submitted entries included designs for a column for the Panthéon,
a 'temple décadaire' (a circular structure roofed by a saucer
dome), administrative buildings, a court-house, prison,
public baths and a primary school (all unexecuted). The
first prize was awarded to their Temple to Equality, a
monument intended for the gardens of the Palais de
l'Elysée, Paris.

Durand's competition success secured him an appointment at the new Ecole Polytechnique, from 1795 as a
draughtsman and from 1797 to 1833 as professor of
architecture. During this period the Ecole Polytechnique
provided the basic education for engineers, who then
proceeded to more specialized establishments. Durand's
architectural course was limited to only a few lessons and
took second place to such subjects as Gaspard Monge's
descriptive geometry. Such circumstances required Durand to condense his teaching, which in fact represented
the first systematic course in the history of architecture.
His teachings were published in two volumes as *Précis des
leçons d'architecture données à l'Ecole polytechnique* (1802–5),
of which the first volume focuses on architectural composition, the second on the requirements of public
buildings.

Durand was a radical, being a declared opponent of
Vitruvius and Marc-Antoine Laugier: in his view, economy
and fitness for purpose alone counted in the design of
buildings. His course proposed a standard, simplified
vocabulary of Neo-classical forms and proportions (see
fig.). Around the same time, Durand also published a
somewhat more historical work, the *Recueil et parallèle des
édifices de tout genre* (1799–1801), consisting mainly of
plans from Egyptian architecture to that of the 18th
century. It was distinguished by being organized according
to building types, by the simplification of the historical
models, which Durand redrew and amended to suit his
purpose, and by his comparativist outlook, with all the
buildings drawn to a common scale. Jacques-Guillaume
Legrand wrote the accompanying text, a general history
of architecture. This work was aimed at a wide public. It
was a unique undertaking for its time, and it remained in
use at the Ecole des Beaux-Arts into the 20th century.

Jean-Nicolas-Louis Durand: composition of central areas of buildings; from his *Précis des leçons d'architecture données à l'Ecole polytechnique*, 2 vols (Paris, 1802–5)

Durand's course underwent few modifications. His *Partie graphique des cours d'architecture* (1821) amounts to a simplification of his published teachings of 1802. The *Choix des projets d'édifices publics* (1816) by Durand in collaboration with François-Tranquille Gaucher (1766–1846) contains various projects by students at the Ecole Polytechnique.

Durand took little part in the great projects of the Empire. His few built works include blocks of flats (*c.* 1800), a house (*c.* 1802) at Chessy, near Lagny-en-Brie, for an administrator at the Ecole Polytechnique, his own house (1820) at Thiais and his country house (1825) in the same locality. Durand's buildings illustrate the principles taught on his course; indeed, his importance rests on his teaching and the extent of its influence. His rationalism corresponded to the economic and ideological needs of Napoleonic France, affirmed the pre-eminence of function and opened the way towards a standardization of structural elements that, in his model combinations, are insistently repeated, both horizontally and vertically. Durand cannot be considered one of the fathers of modern architecture and industrialized construction, however, for he did not contest the pre-eminence of antique forms (which he drew from sources as disparate as Early Christian and Renaissance); he also advocated traditional techniques and, despite the radical views expressed in his writings, succeeded in popularizing conventional forms.

The influence of Durand's teaching was nevertheless particularly widespread. For more than 30 years, all students at the Ecole Polytechnique were trained by Durand, whose influence is evident in public architecture in France from the beginning of the 19th century. His influence in Germany, too, was considerable. His writings were translated into German from the beginning of the 19th century and came to occupy an important place in a country where architectural training was still not systematically organized. The lively polemics that Christian Ludwig Stieglitz and Gottfried Semper addressed to Durand confirm the latter's importance.

WRITINGS

Recueil et parallèle des édifices de tout genre, anciens et modernes, remarquables par leur beauté, par leur grandeur, ou par leur singularité, et dessinés sur une meme échelle, 2 vols (Paris, 1799–1801)

Précis des leçons d'architecture données a l'Ecole polytechnique, 2 vols (Paris, 1802–5)

with F.-T. Gaucher: *Choix des projets d'édifices publics et particuliers composés par MM. les élèves de l'Ecole polytechnique* (Paris, 1816)

Partie graphique des cours d'architecture faits à l'Ecole royale polytechnique depuis sa réorganisation; précédée d'un sommaire des leçons relatives à ce nouveau travail (Paris, 1821)

BIBLIOGRAPHY

E. Kaufmann: *Architecture of the Age of Reason* (Cambridge, 1955)
H.-R. Hitchcock: *Architecture: Nineteenth and Twentieth Centuries*, Pelican Hist. A. (Harmondsworth, 1958, 5/1977)
P. Collins: *Changing Ideals in Modern Architecture* (London, 1965)
A. Braham: *The Architecture of the French Enlightenment* (London, 1980, 2/1989)

W. Szambien: *Jean-Nicolas-Louis Durand, 1760–1834: De l'Imitation à la norme* (Paris, 1984)

A. Picon: *Architectes et ingénieurs au siècle des lumières* (Marseille, 1988; Eng. trans., Cambridge, 1992)

WERNER SZAMBIEN

Durand, John (*fl* 1766–82). American painter. A signed portrait (priv. col.) dated 1765 provides the first documentary information on him. He advertised in the *New York Journal* on 26 November 1767 that he had opened a drawing school, and again on 7 April 1768, announcing his availability as a history painter, though no examples of this activity survive. Like other painters in the colonies, he made his living from portrait painting. His most noted work, the *Rapalije Children* (1768; New York, NY Hist. Soc.), demonstrates the strong decorative sense, the delicate use of colour and the attempts at sophisticated value and texture application that characterize all his paintings. His skill as a draughtsman is evident in the carefully described details. Here, as in other works, he used a dark outline to define one plane from another, and he imparted a sense of elegance, particularly in the slightly turned heads and animated arms and hands. The existence of a signed and dated portrait of *Sarah Whitehead Hubbard* (Philadelphia, PA, Mus. A.), painted in Connecticut in 1768, suggests that he left New York at around this time, and indeed no paintings of New York citizens of later date survive.

The issue of the *Virginia Gazette*, Williamsburg, dated 21 June 1770, provides the next indication of Durand's whereabouts, in an advertisement he placed announcing his willingness to travel into the country to do portraits. Stylistic characteristics already demonstrated in the *Rapalije Children* appear in two portraits of Virginians from *c.* 1770: *Thomas Newton Jr* and *Martha Tucker Newton* (both Colonial Williamsburg, VA). In these Durand again stressed textural qualities: the sheen of satin and the stiff folds of fabric of the sitters' expensive garments. By 1772 he had returned to Connecticut, perhaps via New York, where he may have come into contact with John Singleton Copley, who was working there in 1771–2. In that year he signed and dated a portrait of *Benjamin Douglas* (New Haven, CT, Colony Hist. Soc. Mus.). The portraits he painted in Connecticut of *Rufus Lathrop* and *Hannah Choate Lathrop* (*c.* 1772; B. R. Little priv. col., see Kelly, figs 11 and 12) suggest a move away from line towards Copley's manner of representing volume. The treatment of the folds and the painterly handling of silver trim on Rufus Lathrop's brown vest further suggest Copley's influence. Durand was again in Virginia in 1775, from the evidence of two signed and dated portraits showing two wealthy citizens of Dinwiddie County, Mr and Mrs Gray Briggs (1775; both priv. col.). A few years later, after the American War of Independence, the 1782 tax list of this county includes his name. Considering the unsettled circumstances that prevailed, paintings by Durand from between these two dates probably do not exist. The landscapes painted by a John Durand that were shown at the Royal Academy in London in 1777 and 1778 are unlikely to be by him, since landscapes do not feature in his work. There is no evidence either for the Huguenot background that many writers ascribe to him.

BIBLIOGRAPHY

T. Thorne: 'America's Earliest Nude?', *William & Mary Q.*, 3rd ser., iv (1949), pp. 565–8

F. W. Kelly: 'The Portraits of John Durand', *Antiques*, cxxii (1982), pp. 1080–86

DARRYL PATRICK

Durand-Brager, (Jean-Baptiste-)Henri (*b* Château de Belnoe, nr Dol, 21 May 1814; *d* Paris, 25 April 1879). French painter. Originally intended for a naval career, he travelled widely while still a youth. By the time he decided to seek artistic instruction in the atelier of Eugène Isabey, he had already sailed along most of the Atlantic coast of Africa. In 1840 his spirit of adventure and growing artistic ambitions were both served by his appointment as artist on an official mission charged with the return of Napoleon's ashes from St Helena to France. An illustrated album documenting the expedition was published the following year. His subsequent career is a model of the times in its fusion of the wanderer's urge with the artist's commitment to visual record.

Durand-Brager was awarded the Légion d'honneur in 1843 and valuable commissions soon followed, in which his naval experience and artistic skills were called upon. Prominent works of those years were *The Combat between the French Frigate Niémen and the English Frigates Arethusa and Amethyst* (1844; Bordeaux, Mus. B.-A.) and two large canvases showing the bombardment of Mogador and its capture (1845; Versailles, Château). Durand-Brager was a participant in the latter action. Commissions from both the tsar and the Austrian emperor are indicative of his international reputation for creating military panoramas with a conviction based on personal experience.

FRANK TRAPP

Durandelle, Louis-Emile (*b* Verdun, 14 Feb 1838; *d* Bois-Colombes, nr Paris, 12 March 1917). French photographer. He was one of the most accomplished architectural photographers of his time, and much of his work was devoted to constructions and monuments in France. He shared a studio in Paris until 1862 with Hyacinthe-César Delmaet (1828–62), and on the death of Delmaet that same year Durandelle married his widow, Clémence, who kept the surname Delmaet and became his partner. Their prints continued to be signed D & D after the two original partners. He photographed building work and sites in Paris (e.g. *Le Pont d'Arcole*, 1868; see Berger and Levrault, pl. 50), including a series of the Opéra (1865), which was published as two albums of 97 photographs. From 1870 to 1871 he photographed the events of the Paris Commune, and from 1874 to 1876 he worked on a series of Mont-Saint-Michel. From 1877 to 1890 he covered the various stages in the construction of the church of Sacré Coeur in Montmartre, and in 1887–9 he photographed the construction of the Eiffel Tower. His photographs were shown at the Exposition Universelle in Paris in 1878. Other favoured subjects were landscapes, portraits, interiors and reproductions of works of art. He also made a series of photographs of the Prémontré mental hospital in the Aisne region of France. After the death of his wife in 1890 he sold his business and abandoned photography.

PHOTOGRAPHIC PUBLICATIONS
Construction de la Tour Eiffel, 2 vols (Paris, 1889)
Eglise du Sacré Coeur à Montmartre, 2 vols (Paris, 1890)

BIBLIOGRAPHY
Berger and Levrault, eds: *Regards sur la photographie en France au XIXe siècle*, Berger Levrault (Paris, 1980)

PATRICIA STRATHERN

Durandi [Duranti], **Jacques** (*fl* 1454; *d* before 18 April 1469). French painter. He signed an altarpiece of *St Margaret* for Fréjus Cathedral IACOBUM. DURANDI; DE NIC[IA]. He was probably in Marseille in 1450. In 1454 he was commissioned to paint a panel for the chapel of Sainte Croix in the tower of Lérins Monastery and probably painted a portrait of the governor of Nice, Giorgio de Possasco, for the Salle du Conseil. With his brother Christol, mentioned in Aix-en-Provence in 1471, he painted cupboards in the gallery of St Maurice at Nice in 1461. On 18 April 1469 Christol received from the syndics of Cannes an instalment towards finishing within the month the altarpiece of *St Sebastian*, ordered from his late brother for the church of that name. The signed *St Margaret* altarpiece (2.23×2.34 m) is an imposing construction in two registers, executed *c.* 1450. Also attributed to Durandi are the altarpiece of *St John the Baptist* (2.16×1.92 m) of *c.* 1460 from the church of Lucéram and the *Baptism* of *c.* 1465 (1.15×0.52 m; both Nice, Mus. Masséna). These archaizing panels, characterized by precise draughtsmanship and fine modelling together with a slight dryness of execution, show no trace of the influence of 'modern' Provençal painting, such as the work of the Master of the Aix Annunciation or Enguerrand Quarton, but instead show a nostalgia for the more international, Gothic style of the earlier 15th century, especially for the painting of Durandi's predecessor Jean Mirailhet. A relationship with Catalan work seems more evident than the affinities noted by some critics with the painting of the Marches or Tuscany.

BIBLIOGRAPHY
G. Brès: *Questioni d'arte regionale: Studio critico: Altre notizie inedite sui pittori nicesi* (Nice, 1911), pp. 81–4
L. H. Labande: 'Les Primitifs niçois des XVe et XVIe siècles', *Gaz. B.-A.*, liv (1912), pp. 279–97
Abbé H. Requin: 'Les Primitifs niçois chez les notaires d'Aix', *Nice Hist.* (1912), pp. 105–16
Catalogue de l'exposition rétrospective d'art régional (exh. cat., ed. J. Levrot; Nice, Mus. B.-A., 1912), pp. 47–9
Primitifs de Nice et des écoles voisines (exh. cat., ed. J. Thirion; Nice, Mus. Masséna, 1960), pp. 13–14
M. Natale and C. Frulli: *Il quattrocento*, Pitt. Italia (Milan, 1987), i, pp. 15, 19; ii, p. 620

DOMINIQUE THIÉBAUT

Durand-Ruel. French family of dealers. Five generations of the Durand-Ruel family were occupied in the business of exhibiting and dealing in paintings, beginning with (1) Jean-Marie-Fortuné Durand-Ruel, who started the firm in Paris as an artists' supply shop. His son (2) Paul Durand-Ruel went on to become a major figure in the publicizing of Impressionist works, particularly in London. Paul's sons Joseph Durand-Ruel (1862-1928) and Georges Durand-Ruel (1866–1933) managed the firm into the 20th century, succeeded by Joseph's son Charles Durand-Ruel (1905–85). Charles's daughter, Caroline Durand-Ruel Godfroy, maintained the company's archives after the firm closed.

(1) Jean-Marie-Fortuné Durand-Ruel (*b* Auray, 6 Oct 1800; *d* Paris, 19 March 1865). He was born in Brittany of a family originating from Clermont in Picardy. His first recorded employment was as chief assistant in a stationer's shop at 174, Rue St Jacques in Paris. In 1825 he married Marie-Fernande Ruel, who had recently purchased the business, and joining their names, in a form later to be legalized, he began to extend the stock to include artists' materials. This activity led to friendships with a number of artists and eventually to buying watercolours and engravings from them. Gradually Durand-Ruel began to specialize in selling paintings. The gallery began by promoting the fashionable English school and soon afterwards started dealing with a number of young artists, including Alexandre-Gabriel Decamps, Nicolas-Toussaint Charlet, Camille Roqueplan and Camille Flers, often exchanging artists' supplies for paintings.

In 1833 Durand-Ruel opened a second branch at 103, Rue des Petits-Champs. Following a current practice, stock was offered for temporary hire (generally for the purpose of copying) as well as for sale. He left this shop in 1843 for larger premises at no. 83 on the same street. The gallery can be seen in Charles-François Daubigny's lithographed frontispiece to two illustrated volumes that appeared in 1845 under the title *Galerie Durand-Ruel*; it contained works by Delacroix, Narcisse Diaz, Jules Dupré, Pierre-Paul Prud'hon, Prosper Marilhat, Flers, Decamps, Charlet and others. The dealer found himself in difficulty repaying the capital he had borrowed and tried to improve matters by setting off on various foreign expeditions, including spending the whole of one winter in St Petersburg, in search of useful contacts. Finally in 1846, taking his son into the business, he opened a branch nearer the commercial centre, on the Boulevard des Italiens. From then on his affairs began to prosper, until the February Revolution of 1848 put an end to the picture trade.

During the early years of the Second Empire (1852–70) the firm continued a modest trade. In 1856 Durand-Ruel was offered the lease of premises in the Rue de la Paix, where once again his business began to succeed, drawing customers from Germany, Russia and the USA. In 1859, together with the dealers Francis Petit and Louis Martinet, he published an album of photographs illustrating the range of the modern French school, with introductions by Théophile Gautier, Paul de Saint-Victor (1825–81) and Frédéric Henriet. Towards the end of 1862 he transferred the business to his son (2) Paul Durand-Ruel.

(2) Paul(-Marie-Joseph) Durand-Ruel (*b* Paris, 31 Oct 1831; *d* Paris, 5 Feb 1922). Son of (1) Jean-Marie-Fortuné Durand-Ruel. Drawn both to the Church and the army, he decided on the latter as a career, passing the entrance examination for Saint-Cyr in 1851. Illness followed, and with great regret he resigned from the army and agreed to join the family firm. In 1855 he visited the Exposition Universelle in Paris, which he remembered later as the turning-point in the evolution of his artistic tastes and in the determination of his future career. He was strongly drawn to the works of an older generation, especially to Delacroix's paintings. At first he followed his father's practice of buying works from the numerous

landscape artists who had come to prominence during the July Monarchy (1830–48); of these Jules Dupré became a close friend. At the same time he began to visit other artists whose work had impressed him at the Salons; among those of a younger generation he admired Thomas Couture and Henri Regnault, whose work he began to buy after 1855, as well as works by several newly returning Rome prizewinners: William-Adolphe Bouguereau, Alexandre Cabanel, Ernest Hébert and later Emile Lévy, whose immensely popular *Idylle* was copied for the dealer a number of times. He frequently reserved pictures before the Salon and thus gained publicity from the exhibition, particularly if the artists succeeded in winning a medal.

In 1862 Durand-Ruel married Marie-Eva Lafon, niece of the French painter Emil Lafon (1817–86). At about this time, shortly after taking over the family business, he met Hector Brame, who shared his enthusiasm for Delacroix and for the school of 1830. Together they visited the studios of landscape artists, including those of Théodore Rousseau, Charles-François Daubigny, Jean-François Millet, Narcisse Diaz and Courbet. During the 1860s they supplied paintings to a number of prominent figures, sometimes forming whole collections, for instance those of Laurent-Richard and Khalil-Bey (1831–79), thereby publicizing the artists whose works they held and acquiring for their names associations of success. When certain of these collectors auctioned their paintings, sometimes after a comparatively short period, the dealers bid to boost the prices, often buying in paintings they had themselves supplied.

The practice of holding auctions, often used at that date by artists themselves, was a crucial technique in Durand-Ruel's self-imposed task of increasing the monetary value of works by Delacroix and the landscape artists of 1830. He and Brame, often buying pictures jointly, expanded their stock enormously in these years. In 1866, at Rousseau's request, they bought 70 pictures from him and held a special exhibition at the Cercle Artistique in the nearby Rue de Choiseul. They soon afterwards bought the whole of Prince Napoléon-Jérôme Bonaparte's collection of modern paintings. Occasionally they bought works by Old Masters, particularly Goya, El Greco and Rembrandt. Durand-Ruel was buying consistently from Bouguereau during the 1860s, encouraging him to work on genre subjects of maternal affection. These eventually proved highly successful and were probably the direct result of the dealer's influence. Later, when Bouguereau took up a tempting offer from a rival dealer, Adolphe Goupil, he ceased transactions with Durand-Ruel.

Investment on this scale required substantial capital. In 1869, Durand-Ruel took out a loan from Alfred Edwards, an Anglo-Levantine financier, supplying him with pictures to decorate his flat in the Boulevard Haussmann and planning to auction them in due course, thus benefiting from the interest excited by a rich collector's sale. This took place in 1870, directed by Etienne-François Haro. Three prominent critics wrote introductions to the catalogue, and glowing reviews appeared in the press. Critical as well as financial backing was essential to Durand-Ruel's campaign. With his new funds, and with Alfred Sensier as one of his collaborators, he was able to found a review, *La Revue internationale de l'art et de la curiosité*, which first appeared on 15 January 1869. It was short-lived, however, the scheme failing to meet the dealer's expectations.

In October 1869 Durand-Ruel signed a lease on new premises at 11 Rue Le Peletier, hoping to hold large exhibitions there. Six months later he moved into the newly restored building, but the Franco-Prussian War (1870–71) broke out shortly afterwards, and as the Prussians approached Paris, Durand-Ruel sent his family to the country and left for London, where he had numerous business contacts. His first premises were temporary, at Thomas McLean's Gallery in Haymarket, where from 29 October to 1 December 1870 he showed pictures brought from Paris. On 10 December he opened the First Annual Exhibition of the Society of French Artists in his own gallery at 168 New Bond Street. He was to hold ten exhibitions between 1870 and 1875. Although at this period he could not afford to maintain a London branch, he was to return on several occasions to hold exhibitions in temporary premises: in 1882 at 13 King Street; in 1883 at Dowdeswell's, 133 New Bond Street; at the Hanover Gallery in 1901; at an unnamed venue in 1904; and finally an enormous exhibition at the Grafton Galleries in 1905.

In London in 1870 Durand-Ruel met, through Charles-François Daubigny, the exiled Monet and Pissarro, some of whose works he included in his first exhibition, and by 1872 he had shown works by Manet, Degas, Renoir and Alfred Sisley. Pissarro was later to write, 'without him we should have died of hunger in London'. While in Paris in January 1872, Durand-Ruel bought two paintings by Manet that he had seen in the studio of Alfred Stevens (i); the next day he called on the artist and bought a further 23 paintings, the basis for a stock of works by the new young school. At the same time, stimulated by the attention given to his exhibitions in Paris, London and Brussels (where Brame was acting on his behalf), he continued to accumulate paintings by the Barbizon school, buying most of the collection of Emile Gavet (1830–1904) and the whole of that of Alfred Sensier. He rescued Pierre Puvis de Chavannes from neglect as dramatically as he had Manet, by seeking him out, buying several works from him at once and thereafter continuing to buy almost his entire output of paintings. He later wrote in his memoirs that it was not the works of the young Impressionists that had provoked jokes and insults but those of Manet and Puvis de Chavannes, and he attributed a public loss of confidence during the 1870s, both in himself and in his stock, to this hostility. As a result he stopped buying Impressionist paintings for a time, leaving some of his own customers, notably Jean-Baptiste Faure, his London neighbour, to take his place.

Durand-Ruel sold off much of his accumulated stock during these years, and when in 1878 he mounted an exhibition of his favourite artists of the school of 1830, he had to borrow the paintings. Though not particularly successful, this exhibition may have contributed to the increase in prices paid for these artists. Matters were briefly improved in 1880 by loans, and Durand-Ruel began to buy Impressionist works again. However, the collapse of the bank of the Union Générale in 1882 was a disaster for him. He sublet his flat and even part of his galleries. For the next few years his business activities were severely curtailed. At the end of 1885 a representative of the

American Art Association was struck by the interest of his collection and persuaded him to send an exhibition to New York, at the expense of the association. The exhibition, which opened on 10 April 1886, was entitled *Works in Oil and Pastel by the Impressionists of Paris* and included works by Paul Signac and Seurat, notably the *Bathers at Asnières*. Durand-Ruel held another exhibition the following year, this time not exclusively of Impressionist paintings, and shortly afterwards, to avoid increasing difficulty with customs regulations, he opened a gallery in New York. After 1888 he increasingly left the running of the business to his three sons, Joseph Durand-Ruel, Charles Durand-Ruel (1865–92) and Georges Durand-Ruel. His eventual financial success owed everything to the development of the American market, though this was not at first primarily for Impressionist works but for paintings by Delacroix, the Barbizon school and a number of Old Masters, whose works the collector had been buying intermittently since the late 1860s. Some of the artists he had launched were later to exhibit elsewhere; Pissarro and Monet returned to exhibit with him, however, and Monet showed his series at Durand-Ruel's gallery at intervals from 1891 until 1909. His sons held exhibitions of Redon (1894), Bonnard (1896) and Gauguin (1903). In 1911, Joseph and Georges took over the business from him, continuing to specialize in works by Impressionists and those working in similar vein, e.g. Maxime Maufra and Albert-Charles Lebourg. The New York branch of the gallery continued until 1950; the Paris branch, installed since 1924 in the Avenue de Friedland, continued until 1974, directed by Charles Durand-Ruel, the son of Joseph Durand-Ruel. After the closing of the gallery, he continued to maintain and to add to the archives and allowed generous access to his records. The archives were subsequently directed by his daughter, Caroline Durand-Ruel Godfroy, assisted by France Daguet, both of whom worked on research projects based on the records.

BIBLIOGRAPHY

L. Venturi: *Les Archives de l'impressionnisme* (Paris and New York, 1939)
J. Rewald: *The History of Impressionism* (New York and London, 4/1973)
J. House: 'New Material on Monet and Pissarro in London', *Burl. Mag.*, cxx (1978), pp. 636–42
L. M. Whiteley: 'Accounting for Tastes', *Oxford A. J.*, 2 (April 1979), pp. 25–8
L. d'Argencourt: 'Bouguereau et le marché de l'art en France', *William Bouguereau, 1825–1905* (exh. cat., ed. L. d'Argencourt and M. S. Walker; Paris, Petit Pal.; Montreal, Mus. F.A.; Hartford, CT, Wadsworth Atheneum; 1984–5)
J. Rewald: *Studies in Impressionism* (London, 1985)
J. House: *Monet: Nature into Art* (London, 1986)
N. Green: 'Dealing in Temperaments: Transformations of the Artistic Field in France during the Second Half of the Nineteenth Century', *A. Hist.*, x/1 (March 1987)
A. Distel: *Les Collectionneurs des impressionistes: Amateurs et marchands* (Paris, 1989), p. 35

LINDA WHITELEY

Durantino, Francesco (*fl c.* 1543–54). Italian ceramics painter. He was first active in Urbino, where he is recorded as working in the workshop of Guido di Merlino from 1543. His early signed and dated works include a dish painted with a scene showing *Martius Coriolanus and his Mother* (1544; London, BM) and a fragment (1546; Stockholm, Nmus.) illustrating the *Death of Polixena* and bearing the monogram and sign of Urbino. Stylistically very similar to these are plates and dishes illustrating biblical and mythological scenes, dating from 1542 to 1547 (examples in Brunswick, Herzog Anton Ulrich-Mus.; London, V&A; Edinburgh, Royal Mus. Scotland; Pesaro, Mus. Civ.). In 1547 he took over a kiln in Monte Bagnolo, near Perugia. Certain large vessels, decorated both inside and out, have been attributed to this period (examples in Florence, Bargello, and London, V&A), as have albarelli and flasks. His work is characterized by a strong palette of blues, yellows, oranges and greens and lightly marked contours. His compositions were inspired by printed sources including the illustrated version of Livy's *History of Rome* (Venice, 1498).

BIBLIOGRAPHY

J. Lessmann: *Herzog Anton Ulrich–Museum Braunschweig: Italienische Majolika* (Brunswick, 1979)
G. Papagni: *La maiolica del rinascimento in Casteldurante, Urbino e Pesaro: Da Pellipario ed i Fontana ai Patanazzi* (Fano, 1980)
T. Wilson: 'The Origins of the Maiolica Collections of the British Museum, 1851–5', *Faenza*, lxxi (1985), pp. 68–81

LUCIANA ARBACE

Duranty, Louis(-Emile)-Edmond (*b* Paris, 6 June 1833; *d* Paris, 9 April 1880). French writer and art critic. He studied briefly at the Collège Chaptal in Paris. In 1856 he became one of the driving forces behind the literary journal *Réalisme*, together with Jules Assézat (1832–76) and Dr Jean-Baptiste-Henri Thulié (1832–1916). Most of his art criticism dates from the 1860s and 1870s; from the outset it was particularly critical of the established art world. He frequented Parisian cafés such as the Café Guerbois and the Café de la Nouvelle Athènes, where he met the group of intellectuals around Champfleury, among them Gustave Courbet. In 1863 Duranty met Emile Zola, and his lifelong friendship with the writer led to closer personal acquaintance with the leading Impressionists, particularly with Manet and Degas, as well as with other figures in the forefront of the new French painting. Such connections were clearly reflected in his reviews of around 1870 in the *Paris-Journal*, in which he praised such great names of the future as Manet, Degas, Camille Pissarro, Alfred Sisley, Berthe Morisot and Eva Gonzalès. Duranty also wrote about the Barbizon painters, the English painter Richard Parkes Bonington and Delacroix as representing high points in the development of art. In his criticism, especially in *Paris-Journal* from 1869 to 1872 and to some extent in later exhibition reviews in such journals as the *Gazette des beaux-arts*, *Les Beaux-arts illustrés* and *Chronique des arts*, Duranty presented contemporary art, including Impressionism, as a historical consequence of Realism. He launched extraordinarily sharp attacks on established salon painting, particularly in *Paris-Journal*. Ingres was among the victims of the earlier reviews: Duranty's evaluation of him was more ideological than aesthetic, and he later revised it.

In 1870, Duranty reviewed Hippolyte Taine's *De l'intelligence* (Paris, 1870), which examined the newest theories and advances in the study of sensory perception. In this way the new painting was linked with theoretical knowledge about the process of sight, based upon research in progress, particularly in England and Germany. At the time of his death Duranty's library included books by Charles Blanc, founder of the *Gazette des beaux-arts* and a

progressive authority on art, Ernst Wilhelm von Brücke, a doctor and physiologist who propagated German theories of colour perception in France, and Amédée Victor Guillemin, a popularizer of natural science, authors who wrote about visual psychology, especially colour perception. Duranty's relationship with contemporary science and art was, therefore, unusually direct. On the other hand, his conservatism is also apparent in the more muted art reviews he published in the established journals, such as the *Gazette des beaux-arts*, *Les Beaux-arts illustrés* and *Chronique des arts*. In 1876 Duranty wrote a longer work, *La Nouvelle Peinture*, in connection with the second Impressionist exhibition, in which the movement was set with precision in its historical context. He was an astute critic in not simply supporting the most avant-garde work but also in placing the new painting in an objective context, in which stylistic innovation was related to contemporary social and scientific advances.

Although later art history failed to establish any constructive connection between *La Nouvelle Peinture* and Impressionism, this may be the result of an over-narrow definition of the term 'Impressionism'. More recent scholarship seems to endorse Duranty's precise and engaging appreciation of the new and his equally engaging but more detached attitude to established artists. He described, with precision, the work of young artists as an interpretation of the relation between visual perception and knowledge of the physical conditions in the world around them, a relation that he thought could not be criticized from the scientific point of view. Duranty elaborated and refined these observations in 1879 in an article entitled 'La Quatrième Exposition faite par un groupe d'artistes indépendants' in the *Chronique des arts*.

UNPUBLISHED SOURCES

Paris, M. Parturier priv. col. [MS. *Histoire de l'art*]

WRITINGS

La Nouvelle Peinture, à propos du groupe d'artistes qui expose dans la Galerie Durand-Ruel (Paris, 1876)
'La Quatrième Exposition faite par un groupe d'artistes indépendants', *Chron. A.* (1879), pp. 126–8

BIBLIOGRAPHY

'Les Ecoles étrangères de peinture: I—Allemagne–Suède–Norvège–Danemark– Russie–Hollande–Belgique–Angleterre,par M. Duranty', *L'Art moderne à l'Exposition de 1878* (Paris, 1879), pp. 105–73
M. Crouzet: *Un Méconnu du réalisme: Duranty (1833–1880), l'homme, le critique, le romancier* (Paris, 1964) [incl. full bibliog. of Duranty's writings]
M. Marcussen: 'Duranty et les Impressionnistes', *Hafnia*, v (1978), pp. 24–42; vi (1979), pp. 27–49
M. Poprzecka: 'Francuscy pisarze i krytycy o malerstwie, 1820–1876' [French authors and critics write about painting,1820–76], *Pol. A. Stud.*, i (1979), pp. 251–6

MARIANNE MARCUSSEN

Durazzo, Conte Giacomo (*b* Genoa, 27 April 1717; *d* Padua, 15 Oct 1794). Italian diplomat, impresario and collector. Durazzo belonged to a noble Genoese family that from the 16th century produced two cardinals and eight doges, including his brother Marcello. In 1749 he was appointed Genoese ambassador at the court of Vienna, where in 1752 he became assistant to Count Franz Esterházy in the direction of Viennese theatrical affairs and, in 1754, sole *directeur des spectacles*. Though relations with the Empress Maria Theresa (1717–80) and her son, the future Emperor Joseph II (1741–90), were sometimes strained, Durazzo enjoyed the support of the minister Count Anton Wenzel Kaunitz (1711–94) and was able to use his position to reform the character of music and theatre at court. He was responsible for inviting the composer C. W. Gluck (1714–87) to Vienna in 1754 and played a central part in the development of his *Orfeo*, performed in 1762, and the first great Neo-classical *opera seria*. When court intrigues caused Durazzo to resign his post, Kaunitz arranged for him to become, in 1774, the ambassador of the Court of Vienna in Venice, where he embarked upon a new career as a collector of art. Acting from 1774 to 1776 as agent for Duke Albert of Saxe-Teschen and subsequently on his own behalf, Durazzo became one of the most important print collectors of the 18th century. He followed a systematic collecting policy and organized his collection on the principle that prints served the study of the history of painting. Examples were grouped into schools (the Italian, divided into Florentine–Roman, Venetian, Lombard and Bolognese; the northern German; Dutch–Flemish, or *belgica*; French; English), accompanied by biographies of artists and supplemented by three separate indexes for reference and cross-reference. Realizing that the works of early painters would not otherwise be included, Durazzo commissioned some 50 engravings of paintings by artists from Cimabue to Perugino in the Uffizi Gallery in Florence, which he hoped would set an example to other art lovers. Durazzo collected some 30,000 prints and compiled 1400 biographies. His assistants included the Viennese engraver Jakob Schmutzer (1733–1811) and Conte Bartolomeo Benincasa. His work forms the basis of the present Albertina collection in Vienna.

BIBLIOGRAPHY

Grove 5

B. Benincasa: *Descrizione della raccolta di stampe di S.E. Il Sig. Conte Jacopo Durazzo Patrizio Genovese, esposta in una dissertazione sull'arte dell' intaglio a stampa* (Padua, 1784)
Giacomo Conte Durazzo (1717–1794) (exh. cat. by W. Koschatsky, Vienna, Albertina, 1976), pp. 5–37
Maria Theresa und ihre Zeit (exh. cat., Vienna, 1989), pp. 400–01

JANET SOUTHORN

Durban. South African city in Natal, on the Indian Ocean coast. The chief seaport in South Africa, with a population of *c.* 800,000, it is noted for its variety of architectural styles and a subtropical exoticism that has inspired painters. It was founded in 1824 as Port Natal and renamed in 1835 after Sir Benjamin D'Urban, the Governor of Cape Colony. The warm climate, rich vegetation and sloping sites necessitated specific architectural features, including the verandahs typical for houses. Building materials were originally corrugated iron and timber stud walls; later, brick and tiles led to an architecture of large roofs and suspended floors. Durban's civic centre consists of the first Town Hall (1882–5; now Post Office) by PHILIP MAURICE DUDGEON, built in a Neo-classical style, the neo-Baroque City Hall (1909) by Woolacott, Scott & Hudson and the 'free Renaissance' railway station (1895–1904) by WILLIAM STREET-WILSON, who also designed the Gothic Revival Emmanuel Cathedral (1903). In the 1920s and 1930s buildings proliferated in the 'Spanish revival' style, with cool loggias appropriate to the climate. A. A. Ritchie McKinley (1894–1961) was a proponent of

Art Deco variants of this style. A milestone of early 20th-century architecture was the Students' Club House (1938; by Ing, Jackson & Park-Ross; destr. 1992) of the Natal Technical College, while Crofton & Benjamin, influenced by Brazilian Modernism, designed the finest group of Durban's mid-20th-century architecture: the Riviera Hotel, Westpoint and Haven Court (1956–70). The Netherlands Bank building (1961–5) by NORMAN EATON reinterprets the essence of the verandah house in an urban setting.

Of the architects of the 1970s and 1980s HANS HALLEN, who trained at the University of Natal, Durban, was responsible for distinctive residential and institutional projects, and Murphy/Jahn's 88 Field Street building (1984–6; with Stauch Vorster) brought the city an example of High Tech architecture of international stature. Also in the 1980s, with the assistance of REVEL FOX, the beach-front was redeveloped, new uses were found for important buildings, and the city centre was refurbished. Building conservation was also undertaken, including that of the temples and mosques that had been built by indentured labourers brought first from India in 1860. Examples of these include the Narainsamy (Vishnu) Temple (1906–8) by the master builder Kistappa Keddy (1863–1941) and the Juma Masjid Mosque (1941) in Grey Street—the largest mosque in the southern hemisphere.

Among the artists captivated by the lush environment, Clement Sénèque (1896–1930) was the finest painter of the early 20th century; his landscapes, particularly harbour scenes, are historically and artistically significant. Subsequent painters, in particular Nils Andersen ((1897–1972), adopted a quasi-Impressionist style. Patrick O'Connor (b 1940) and Andrew Verster (b 1937), teachers at the Art School of the Natal Technical College in Durban in the 1960s, encouraged new interpretations of the local scene and a greater range of techniques, Verster depicting beach life, buildings and palm trees. The photographers Obie Oberholzer (b 1947) and Omar Badsha (b 1945) studied Durban people at work and at play. AZARIA MBATHA made prints of religious and landscape themes with a strong element of Zulu folklore. The work of Mary Stainbank (b 1899), a local sculptor, combined the influence of Cubism with references to Africa.

BIBLIOGRAPHY
Archit. SA, 13 (1981) [special issue on Durban]
S. Afr. Archit. Rec., i/7 (1985) [special issue on Natal]

W. H. PETERS

Düren, Adam van (b ?Düren; fl 1487; d after 1532). German mason and architect, active in Denmark and Sweden. His name and style, together with the Low German language of many of his inscriptions, indicate his origins in the Rhineland. In 1487 he went to Sweden with the German masons' lodge that was engaged to complete the choir of Linköping Cathedral. His work there included 16 vault bosses with the Instruments of the Passion. In the late 1490s he moved to Denmark and for the following decade worked for John, King of Denmark (reg 1481–1513), and his closest supporters. He carved a monumental image of the King for the castle in Copenhagen, anticipating the Renaissance tendency towards the glorification of rulers. In the Carmelite monastery at Helsingør, Adam

provided a net vault for the chapter house; here also the keystones are decorated with some of the subjects from the Passion reliefs from Linköping. From 1499 he built the castle at Glimmingehus for Jens Ulfstand (d 1523), the Admiral of the Realm. It is a high, rectangular building with Gothic stepped gables, decorated with many reliefs. On one of these the builder is depicted kneeling before the Crucifixion. Adam also carved his name, his mason's mark and the year 1505.

Adam worked for the next two decades on the restoration of the Romanesque cathedral in Lund, Skåne. In the crypt he executed a stone tomb-chest over the grave of Archbishop Birger Gunnarsson (d 1519), depicting him on the lid in high relief. He also carved the basin of a fountain, decorated with satirical reliefs and proverbs and satirizing the king's ambitions, the burghers' acquisitiveness and the monks' hypocrisy. His image of impoverishment as a giant louse biting a sheep was probably aimed at nobles and peasants alike. He strengthened the nave with buttresses and constructed new vaults over the transept, again decorated with Passion bosses. His last inscriptions demonstrate that he had learnt both Runic script and Danish.

Adam was married in Lund, but his wife and children died of plague in 1520 while he was in Stockholm designing fortifications for Christian II (reg 1513–23). From this visit also dates a puzzling inscribed relief in Stockholm Cathedral. He remained active in Lund until c. 1530. As a mason, Adam worked with solid constructions in a German Late Gothic style; as a sculptor he used broad, weighty forms, displaying sharp, occasionally satirical characterization.

BIBLIOGRAPHY
J. Svanberg: 'Adam van Düren: A German Stonemason in Scandinavia in the Early Sixteenth Century', *Hafnia: Copenhagen Papers in the History of Art, 1976* (Copenhagen, 1977), pp. 125–39
——: 'Adam van Dürens valvsköldar i Linköpings domkyrka' [Adam van Düren's vault bosses in Linköping Cathedral], ICO (1984), no. 2, pp. 40–50

JAN SVANBERG

Dürer. German family of artists. Albrecht Dürer the elder (1427–1502), a goldsmith in Nuremberg, was the first teacher of his famous son, (1) Albrecht Dürer, who is renowned for his paintings, drawings, watercolours, prints and theoretical writings. Albrecht the younger trained his brother (2) Hans Dürer, a painter of mostly religious subjects who became court painter in Poland. A third brother, Endres [Andreas] Dürer (1486–1555), became a master goldsmith in Nuremberg in 1514 and carried on their father's business, though no work can be attributed to him with any certainty.

(1) Albrecht Dürer (b Nuremberg, 21 May 1471; d Nuremberg, 6 April 1528). Painter, draughtsman, printmaker and writer. Now considered by many scholars the greatest of all German artists, he not only executed paintings and drawings of the highest quality but also made a major contribution to the development of printmaking, especially engraving, and to the study of anthropometry.

I. Life and work. II. Working methods and technique. III. Theoretical writings. IV. Character and personality. V. Critical reception and posthumous reputation.

I. Life and work.

1. Apprenticeship and early travels, to spring 1494. 2. Nuremberg and first visit to Italy, May 1494 to late spring 1495. 3. Nuremberg, 1495–1500. 4. Expansion of the workshop and first studies of proportion, 1500–05. 5. Second visit to Italy, 1505–7. 6. Years of rational synthesis, 1507–12. 7. The achievement of Classical form, 1512–20. 8. Journey to the Netherlands, 1520–21. 9. The last years, 1521–8.

1. APPRENTICESHIP AND EARLY TRAVELS, TO SPRING 1494. At the age of 13 or 14, while still apprenticed to his father, Dürer captured his own appearance in a silverpoint drawing (1484; Vienna, Albertina; Winkler, 1936–9, no. 1; Strauss, 1974, no. 1484/1), which he carefully preserved and later inscribed. The drawing is the work of a budding genius; it is also one of the earliest autonomous self-portraits. A good-looking boy, careful of his own appearance, with a long, tasselled cap over his long, soft hair (the difference in texture is clearly evident), points earnestly and with great concentration to his own image in the mirror.

In the otherwise laconic text of a family chronicle that Dürer compiled in 1524 from his father's papers (copies: Nuremberg, Stadtbib., Will-Nor. 111 915b, 916 fol. Pap.; Bamberg, Staatsbib., J.H. Msc. Art 50, 111.12), there is a detailed description of the interview in which he told his father, on the completion of his apprenticeship, that he did not want to be a goldsmith but a painter. Albrecht Dürer the elder regretted the time that his son had apparently wasted, but on 30 November 1486 he drew up indentures for him with the painter MICHAEL WOLGEMUT, who worked in the same street in Nuremberg (now Burgstrasse). In Wolgemut's workshop the young Dürer learnt the fundamentals of his art, as handed down through the generations: the 'custom' of painting, as he later called it in his writings. He continued to develop his talent as a draughtsman, exemplified by drawings of horsemen and men-at-arms (1489; ex-Ksthalle, Bremen; London, BM; Berlin, Kupferstichkab.; w 16–18; s 1489/4, 5 and 7) and a contemporaneous *Crucifixion* (1490; Paris, Louvre; w 19; s 1490/1) with an elaborate landscape background.

Among the models that he followed, both for form and for technique, were the engravings by Martin Schongauer that he had seen in Wolgemut's workshop and probably also in his father's. Their powerful impact on him is clear from the pen-and-ink drawing of a *Cavalcade* (1489; ex-Ksthalle, Bremen; w 16; s 1489/4), with its use of line and hatching in imitation of engraving.

The most important influence on Dürer's early career was Wolgemut's work in woodcut book illustration. The designs produced in his workshop transformed the woodcut from a bare indication of outlines, intended to be coloured in by hand, to an independent picture composed according to the laws of painting. The use of hatching in varying degrees of density allowed a gradation of tonal values and a textural representation of solid objects. It was during the period of Dürer's apprenticeship that the woodcut illustrations for the major publications of the Wolgemut workshop were executed or designed, and it is at least probable that he took part in the work.

After completing his apprenticeship in 1489, Dürer painted his father's portrait (1490; Florence, Uffizi), depicting the goldsmith with no indication of his trade, dressed in a simple red gown lined with black fur. In this, his first portrait, also the earliest known painting by him, Dürer showed himself far superior to his German predecessors in his sheer ability to grasp and convey an individual personality. A portrait of his mother, presumably a pendant, seems to have been lost, since a *Portrait of a Woman* (Nuremberg, Ger. Nmus.), listed in the inventories of the Imhoff family of Nuremberg, is not by Dürer. The only certain likeness of his mother is a charcoal drawing (1514; Berlin, Kupferstichkab.; w 559; s 1514/1; see fig. 1) that her son made in the year of her death and later inscribed. Every stroke of the soft charcoal captures the traces of a long, hard, laborious life; but the drawing also expresses great reverence and filial love.

There are signs in Dürer's early work that, on completing his indentures and embarking on his journeyman years (*Wanderjahre*), he followed the example of his father and many other artists of the period and headed north-westward to familiarize himself with the art of the northern Netherlands. According to Christoph Scheurl's *Commentarii de vita et obitu reverendi patris Dn. Anthonii Kressen* (Nuremberg, 1515), 'after travelling all through Germany', Dürer went to Colmar to visit Martin Schongauer. Finding the latter had just died, he was well received by three of Schongauer's surviving brothers and went on to Basle armed with a letter of introduction to a fourth brother

1. Albrecht Dürer: *Portrait of his Mother*, charcoal drawing, 420×300 mm, 1514 (Berlin, Kupferstichkabinett)

who worked there as a goldsmith. The attraction of Basle to Dürer lay no doubt in its reputation as a broadly based centre of academic and literary publishing, in which humanist thought was cultivated and promoted. His knowledge of the artistic and technical advances in the woodcut that had been made in Nuremberg gave him an advantage over local artists, and he was soon in demand.

The existence among the woodcut book illustrations with Basle imprints of some that are Dürer's work is proved by an actual woodblock (1492; Basle, Kstmus.) depicting *St Jerome in his Study* (Passavant, no. 246) with an autograph inscription on the reverse: *Albrecht Dürer von nörmergk*. There is controversy as to whether he only provided the drawing or cut the block himself as a model for local cutters to follow. This woodcut served as the frontispiece for an edition of the saint's letters, *St Hieronymus: Epistolae*, the first part of which appeared in Basle on 8 August 1492 under the imprint of Nikolaus Kessler (*fl* 1478–1510). Dürer's design gives a spatial impression of the room in which the scholar–saint works and sleeps, linking it through an open door with the streets of a town. Further commissions followed. In Basle in 1493 there appeared a volume of the moral tales of Geoffroy de La Tour-Landry, *Der Ritter vom Turn, von den Exempeln der Gotsforcht und Erbarkeit*, with 45 woodcuts by Dürer and assistants that provide an earthy visual counterpart to the tales. *Das Narrenschyff* by Sebastian Brant (1458–1520) followed on 11 February 1494; its extraordinary success was due partly to the 116 illustrations by Dürer and others that are tellingly explicit of the grotesque human follies recounted in the book. Brant went on to produce an edition of the comedies of Terence that was never published, but there remain 126 drawings on the faces of woodblocks, 6 ready-cut blocks and 7 impressions from lost blocks (Basle, Kstmus.). Here again, Dürer shared the work with assistants. The context gave him the opportunity for his first depictions of peasants (in contemporary costume) working on the land.

The Imhoff inventory mentions a painted double portrait on parchment said to be of Dürer's Strasbourg teacher and his wife. His presence in Strasbourg in 1494 is attested by the woodcut frontispiece of an edition of the works of the Paris theologian Jean Gerson (1363–1429), depicting the latter as a pilgrim; it was done in 1494, the year in which the first three volumes of the edition appeared, but was not used until the fourth volume appeared in 1502. It was probably also in Strasbourg that Dürer produced the first of his painted self-portraits (1493; Paris, Louvre), inscribed: *My sach die gat/Als es oben schtat* ('My affairs will go as ordained on high'). This was preceded by a pen drawing (1491; Erlangen, Ubib.; W 26; S 1491/9; see fig. 2.), which shows him with a kerchief round his head, evidently in the midst of some psychological crisis, perhaps precipitated by illness. In the painting—the first autonomous painted self-portrait in Western art—Dürer showed himself as a fashionably dressed young man holding an eryngo (sea-holly), a flower that has several levels of symbolic association.

2. NUREMBERG AND FIRST VISIT TO ITALY, MAY 1494 TO LATE SPRING 1495. Summoned back to Nuremberg by his father, Dürer returned after Whitsun (18 May

1494) to marry Agnes Frey (1475–1539), daughter of a respected coppersmith, Hans Frey (1450–1523). Soon after the wedding (7 July 1494), Dürer captured the childlike appearance of his wife, as if unobserved by her, in a pen drawing (Vienna, Albertina; W 151; S 1494/7), which shows her seated at a table and propping her chin on her hand. The inscription below, *mein angnes*, suggests affection. Before he left Nuremberg for Venice in autumn 1494 he painted two watercolours of local subjects, *St Johanniskirche* (1494; ex-Ksthalle, Bremen; W 62; S 1494/4) and the *Wire Drawing Mill* (1494; Berlin, Kupferstichkab.; W 61; S 1494/3). These are the first known autonomous representations of identifiable localities and served to raise watercolour to the status of an independent medium, the full potential of which Dürer had grasped.

In three drawings dated 1494, probably done in Nuremberg, Dürer for the first time used Italian precedents to depict subjects from Classical antiquity in a classicizing style. The *Bacchanal with a Silenus* and *Tritons Fighting* (both Vienna, Albertina; W 59–60; S 1494/12 and 13) are based on tracings of two engravings by Andrea Mantegna; the *Death of Orpheus* (Hamburg, Ksthalle; W 58; S 1494/11) is derived from a lost original, probably also by Mantegna.

In order to learn more of Italian art and its antique roots, Dürer visited Venice. His route can be traced through his watercolours, in which, with an increasingly virtuoso handling of the medium, combined with a sparing use of gouache, he created landscapes out of light and colour. He passed through Innsbruck (1495; Vienna, Albertina; W 66; S 1495/44), Klausen (used in the engraving *Nemesis* (1501–3; B. 77), the border fortress of Arco (1495; Paris, Louvre; W 94; S 1495/31) and Trento (1495;

2. Albrecht Dürer: *Self-portrait*, pen and brown-black ink, 204×208 mm, 1491 (Erlangen, Universitäts Bibliothek)

Bremen, Ksthalle; w 96; s 1495/33), with its castle (London, BM; w 95; s 1495/32) and its mountain fortress of Dosso di Trento (Bremen, Ksthalle; w 97; s 1495/34). The depiction of the castle of Segonzano in a watercolour of an *Italian Mountain Range* (1495; Oxford, Ashmolean; w 99; s 1495/32) shows that he took a detour into the Cembra Valley, which debouches not far from Trento.

Dürer's first visit to Venice left him with an intense concern with the basic elements of post-medieval painting: the human figure, whether draped or nude, and its relationship to the space in which it moves. While still in his *Wanderjahre*, he had seized an opportunity to draw an unclothed female model frontally and thus create the first nude life drawing by any German artist (1493; Bayonne, Mus. Bonnat; w 28; s 1493/3). In Venice, as is shown by a rear view of a female model in a contrapposto stance (1495; Paris, Louvre; w 85; s 1495/10), he was able to continue his study of the motion of limbs in complex postures. In dealing with draped figures, he took a particular interest in Venetian costume, which he drew both from life (1495; Vienna, Albertina; w 69; s 1495/4) and from Venetian paintings (1495; Cologne, Wallraf-Richartz-Mus.; Berlin, Kupferstichkab.; w 73–4; s 1495/9 and 8). The visual contrast between Venetian dress, which reflected a stable relationship between load and support, and contemporary German dress, which with its combination of gathered skirts and pointed shoes still had a floating, medieval look to it, was captured by Dürer in an elaborate pen drawing (1495; Frankfurt am Main, Städel. Kstinst.; w 75; s 1495/6). His interest in the male nude is attested by a drawing of the *Rape of the Sabine Women* (1495; Bayonne, Mus. Bonnat; w 82; s 1495/2) that shows the abductors, striding along, in both front and rear views. It is based on a painting in the style of Antonio Pollaiuolo.

3. Albrecht Dürer: *House on an Island in a Pond* (or *Small House on a Fish-pond in a Pasture near St Johannis*), brush drawing with watercolour and bodycolour, 213×225 mm, 1496–7 (London, British Museum)

4. Albrecht Dürer: *St John Devouring the Book*, woodcut, 395×284 mm; from the *Apocalypse* series, 1498 (London, British Museum)

Among Dürer's earliest surviving paintings is a panel showing the *Virgin and Child* in front of a stone archway (Reggio Emilia, Fond. Magnami-Rocca). Its discovery in the Capuchin convent at Bagnacavallo, near Bologna (although this was founded after his time), gives some support to the presumption that the painting was done during his first stay in Italy.

3. NUREMBERG, 1495–1500. In 1495 Dürer established himself permanently in Nuremberg. He initially concentrated on drawing and printmaking and was the first Nuremberg artist to take up engraving. He first did a number of unsigned trial prints: the *Great Courier* (B. 81), the *Conversion of St Paul* (B. 110), *The Ravisher* (B. 92) and then, still in 1495, his first large engraving and the only one to bear his early monogram, a large 'A' with a small inscribed 'd', the *Holy Family with a Dragonfly* (B. 44). In style and technique still close to Martin Schongauer's engravings, it incorporates an extensive landscape background, extending to a distant horizon, which makes use of his studies from nature in Nuremberg and South Tyrol.

Alongside traditional religious themes and secular genre scenes, Dürer responded to antique art, as mediated by the influence of Mantegna and other Italian artists, by using his own nude studies to create a sequence of Greek mythological subjects, treated with a freedom that makes iconographical interpretation no easy matter. The constant process of technical refinement reached a peak in the *Hercules at the Crossroads* (c. 1498; B. 73). The nude figures

are created by a network of lines and points that transcends any linear system of outlines and traces the surface of the body. At the same time Dürer concerned himself with an exact rendering of nature, in all its luxuriant profusion, and also of the manmade elements of the landscape. In the engraving *Virgin with a Monkey* (c. 1498; B. 42), accuracy in the depiction of nature is taken to the point of using a topographical watercolour: the *House on an Island in a Pond* (1496–7; London, BM; W 115; S 1496/6; see fig. 3), depicting the Haller family's house west of Nuremberg.

The woodcut, too, emancipated itself from book illustration during this period. Alongside a number of individual prints, including one, the *Men's Bath* (c. 1497; London, BM; B. 128), that is entirely devoted to the male nude, Dürer now produced three series of woodcuts on religious subjects. *The Apocalypse* (1498) comprises 15 woodcuts (B. 61–75) on the Book of Revelation, all with the text printed in letterpress on the back; a new frontispiece was added to them in the 1511 edition. Even in size (picture area 395×284 mm) these went far beyond anything that had been tried in woodcut before (see fig. 4; *see also* APOCALYPSE, fig. 3). They were the making of Dürer's international reputation. He had succeeded in fusing the Late Gothic system of figuration, with its emphasis on intensifying the impact of the events portrayed, with a new treatment of figure and landscape based on first-hand

5. Albrecht Dürer: *Self-portrait with a Landscape*, oil on panel, 520×410 mm, 1498 (Madrid, Museo del Prado)

study. He worked concurrently on a *Large Woodcut Passion* cycle (*c.* 1497–1500; B. 6, 8–13), which initially consisted of seven scenes. Shortly after 1500 he began work on a *Life of the Virgin* (B. 77–92), based on St Luke's Gospel and the apocryphal writings.

In Dürer's work portraiture has a status equivalent to religious subject-matter; his view of its function was that it 'preserves the look of people after their deaths'. His career as an easel painter, which had begun with a portrait of his father, continued with another of the same subject (1497; London, N.G.) and commissioned portraits of two married couples of the Tucher family, executed in 1499 as portable diptychs with the family coat of arms on the reverse of the husband's portrait. Those of *Hans Tucher* and *Felicitas Tucher* (both Weimar, Schlossmus.) and *Elsbeth Tucher* (Kassel, Gemäldegal.), originally corresponding to that of her husband, *Niclas Tucher* (untraced), have in common the division of the background by a curtain and the view deep into a landscape. This combination of portrait and landscape was something that Dürer could have learnt from either Netherlandish or Italian painting. He used it again in his portrait of the Nuremberg representative of the Great Ravensburg Trading Company, *Oswolt Krel* (1499; Munich, Alte Pin.). This work represents an early peak in his career as a portrait painter; in it he deployed all the resources of composition and colour to stress and intensify the individuality of his still youthful sitter.

Two self-portraits date from this period, in which Dürer was establishing himself as the head of a workshop. In the first, *Self-portrait with a Landscape* (1498; Madrid, Prado; see fig. 5), he set out to show what he could do and what he was. The aristocratic costume, worn with pride, marks a new consciousness of his status as an artist. The muted colour values, dominated by light brown, grey and white and accented by the use of black, serve to display his qualities as a painter. He went even deeper in his last painted *Self-portrait* (1500; Munich, Alte Pin.). The painting derives its dignity from a proportional scheme that, like the total frontality of the pose, is an emblem of ultimate sublimity, reserved for images of Christ himself. The explanatory inscription is written in Latin, the language of Church and humanists alike, and its wording emphasizes the imperishability of Dürer's colours.

6. Albrecht Dürer: *Adoration of the Magi*, oil on panel, 0.95×1.14 m, 1504 (Florence, Galleria degli Uffizi)

4. EXPANSION OF THE WORKSHOP AND FIRST STUD-
IES OF PROPORTION, 1500–05. Dürer had employed
assistants in his workshop before 1500, as can be seen
from the quality of execution of an altarpiece or devotional
picture of the *Mater dolorosa* (*c.* 1498; Munich, Alte Pin.),
surrounded by separate panels showing the *Seven Sorrows
of the Virgin* (*c.* 1498; Dresden, Gemäldegal. Alte Meister).
But during the first five years of the 16th century three
young journeymen painters, attracted by Dürer's fame,
entered his workshop. They were Hans Suess von Kulmbach, probably a native of Kulmbach in Upper Franconia,
Hans Baldung, born at Schwäbisch-Gmünd but brought
up and trained in Strasbourg, and Hans Schäufelein (i),
from Swabia. All three worked as designers on woodcuts
for devotional books commissioned from Dürer by Nuremberg publishers and on the books of the humanist
Konrad Celtis. They also drew designs for stained-glass
windows (for illustration *see* HIRSCHVOGEL, (1)). Baldung
added fixed wings (Schwabach, Stadtkirche) to Dürer's
Paumgartner Altarpiece (Munich, Alte Pin.). Schäufelein
painted a *Passion* altarpiece (1505–7; Vienna, Dom- &
Diözmus.) to Dürer's design for Frederick III, Elector of
Saxony. Schäufelein had left Dürer's employment by 1507,
Baldung by 1509; by contrast, Kulmbach settled in Nur-
emberg and remained in close contact with his master.

As the new century opened, Dürer continued with his
graphic work, notably the continuation of the *Life of the
Virgin*, but placed a new emphasis on painting. A *Lamentation* (1500; Munich, Alte Pin.) painted as a commemoration for Margreth Glimm (*d* 1500), wife of the
goldsmith Albrecht Glimm (*fl* 1490; *d* 1533), was followed
by an altar triptych, the Paumgartner Altarpiece, commissioned by the Paumgartner family. The central panel, a
Nativity (*c.* 1502), has a setting of ruined walls and arches
that emphasizes the knowledge of perspective that Dürer
had acquired in Venice. According to an old tradition, the
wings (*c.* 1498) depict the brothers Lukas Paumgartner
(*d* 1515) and Stephan Paumgartner (1462–1525) as *St
George* and *St Eustace*.

In the *Adoration of the Magi* (1504; Florence, Uffizi;
see fig. 6) the three-dimensional structure is completely
manifest. The spatial recession follows the diagonal of the
painting, and figures, architecture and landscape are united
in a synthesis. Concurrently with this, Dürer painted the
wings for another altarpiece, known as the Jabach Altarpiece, probably also commissioned by Frederick III. They
remained until the late 18th century in the private chapel
of the Jabachscher Hof in Cologne. The inner sides of the
wings (Munich, Alte Pin.) show *SS Joseph and Joachim* and
SS Simeon and Lazarus. The outer sides are iconographically unusual: one shows the *Patience of Job*, as he is doused
with water by his wife (Frankfurt am Main, Städel.
Kstinst.); the other shows a *Shawm-player and Drummer*
(Cologne, Wallraf-Richartz-Mus.), the latter bearing the
features of Dürer himself. Originally rounded at the top,
the wings may once have flanked a shrine containing
carved figures.

Around 1504 Dürer was working on a drawn *Passion*
sequence in pen with black wash on green prepared paper;
11 of the sheets have survived (1504; Vienna, Albertina;
W 300, 302, 304, 306–8, 310–14; S 1504/24, 26, 28, 33, 31,
36, 38, 40, 41, 44 and 46). The effect resembles that of

grisaille painting. However, it is by no means universally
agreed that these are autograph works. Several designs for
them are known (Turin, Bib. Reale, W 299, S 1504/22;
Berlin, Kupferstichkab., W 301, S 1504/25; Vienna, Albertina, W 303 and 305, S 1504/27 and 32).

By 1500 at the latest, Dürer was preoccupied with the
construction and proportions of the human figure. A
Venetian painter, Jacopo de' Barbari, who worked in
Nuremberg between 1500 and 1503, showed him 'a man
and woman that he has made by measure' but, as he
refused to reveal to Dürer the constructional formula,
Dürer went straight to the treatise *On Architecture* by
Vitruvius (*see* VITRUVIUS, §3(ii)). Dürer's quest for a
method of constructing the male and female human form
with compasses and ruler on the basis of regular geometrical figures is recorded in a double-sided drawing of a
frontal view of a female nude (1500; London, BM; W 411–
12; S 1500/29 and 30); there are a number of related
drawings. The appended description of the construction
makes great use of the compasses and goes far beyond the
sparse information provided by Vitruvius, although it
follows him in assuming that the head takes up one-eighth
and the face one-tenth of the total height, and also in the
division of the face into three equal parts (*see* HUMAN
PROPORTION). These Vitruvian ratios still appear in the
lateral view of the figure in the engraving *Nemesis* (1501–
3; B. 77).

The ideal figure, derived from canons of proportion
and geometrical construction, finds its total application in
the engraving of *Adam and Eve* (1504; B. 1; for illustration
see STATE). In his preliminary studies for this, Dürer

7. Albrecht Dürer: *Large Piece of Turf*, watercolour, 410×315 mm,
1503 (Vienna, Graphische Sammlung Albertina)

combined separately drawn male and female nudes to make a single drawing (New York, Pierpont Morgan Lib.; W 333; S 1504/17). The final engraving demanded a taller Adam, and this was achieved by lengthening the shin, thus abandoning the Vitruvian canon of eight head-lengths. At the same period Dürer began to concern himself with the proportions of the horse, probably with prior knowledge of the studies of Leonardo da Vinci. The resulting construction, based on squares and segments of circles, bore its first fruits in the horse in the engraving *St Eustace* (*c.* 1500–02; B. 57) and found its final consummation in the later engraving *Knight, Death and the Devil* (1513; B. 98). He also continued his watercolour studies of nature, such as the *Large Piece of Turf* (1503; Vienna, Albertina; see fig. 7).

5. SECOND VISIT TO ITALY, 1505–7. In the late summer of 1505 Dürer set out once more for Venice. His second stay there, which lasted until early in 1507, is documented in a series of ten letters to his humanist friend Willibald Pirckheimer, in which he told of his daily life, how his works progressed, how they were received and also of the hostility of a number of fellow artists. He praised the aged Giovanni Bellini as still the best of the Venetian artists, announced his intention of travelling to Rome with the Holy Roman Emperor Maximilian I for his coronation and reported on his own efforts to carry out Pirckheimer's requests to procure him books and other items. He also asked Pirckheimer to advance money to Agnes Dürer whenever necessary and to find work as a painter for his younger brother Hans.

Dürer's letters to Pirckheimer contain several references to one work that encapsulated all he had learnt from the Italian Renaissance; with it he hoped to vanquish the Italian artists on their own ground, that of colour. German merchants of the Confraternity of the Rosary had commissioned for their church of S Bartolommeo in Venice an altarpiece based on a woodcut in the printed statutes of the first Confraternity of the Rosary, founded in Cologne in 1475 by a Dominican, Jakob Sprenger (*fl* 1436; *d* 1495). The external form of the *Virgin of the Rose Garlands* (1506; Prague, N.G.), an oblong format with no wings, conforms to Italian practice. The scene is dominated by the Virgin seated on a lofty throne; together with the naked Christ Child on her lap and St Dominic, who stands to her right, she distributes rosaries of real roses to the faithful, who kneel before her, led by the Pope and Emperor. On either side of the throne are comparatively narrow glimpses of a mountainous landscape. In the middle ground, at the far right, stands Dürer himself with a *cartolino* in his hand bearing the proud inscription: *Exeqit quinque mestri spatio Albertus/Durer germanus/ MDVI* ('It took five months. Albrecht Dürer the German 1506'). He is accompanied by another man who may be the founder of the Venetian Confraternity of the Rosary, Leonhard Vilt. The faces of those who receive the rose garlands are painted from portrait studies, three of which survive (Berlin, Kupferstichkab., W 380, 382, S 1506/29 and 9; Vienna, Albertina, W 381, S 1506/12).

Concurrently Dürer was working on a painting with half-length figures of *Christ among the Doctors* (1506;

Madrid, Mus. Thyssen-Bornemisza). Writing to Pirckheimer, he called it a painting 'such as I have never done before'. There is no indication of place. Pictorial space exists only in that it is created by the figures clustered around the 12-year-old Jesus who carry the action into the extreme foreground. A bookmark in a folio volume in one of the doctors' hands, intersected by the lower edge of the picture, shows the date, with Dürer's monogram and the explanatory inscription *opus qui[n]que dierum* ('the work of five days'). In Venice, Dürer also received a series of portrait commissions, including one, known only as the *Portrait of a Young Man* (1506; Genoa, Gal. Pal. Rosso), that reveals the influence of the young Giorgione. A man named Burkard, from Speyer, who appears on the left-hand side of the *Virgin of the Rose Garlands*, was also the subject of a separate portrait (1506; Windsor Castle, Berks, Royal Col.). A particularly attractive work, which suggests a close personal relationship, is the unfinished portrait of a *Young Woman in Venetian Costume* (1505; Vienna, Ksthist. Mus.).

In the last letter to Pirckheimer, written on 13 October 1506, Dürer told him that he intended to finish work in Venice in ten days' time and then ride to Bologna 'for the sake of the art in secret perspective' that an unnamed person there had agreed to teach him. From at least his first visit to Venice, Dürer had known that in a correct representation of perspective the receding lines of a building or other object standing parallel to the picture plane must meet at a common vanishing-point. He did not yet know, however, how to determine the correct intervals between straight lines parallel to the picture plane but disposed in depth. He had to gauge the intervals by eye, in accordance with his own feeling for the spatial harmony, and this led, in the perspectival *tour de force* of the colonnaded hall in the woodcut of the *Presentation in the Temple* (*c.* 1505; B. 88) in the *Life of the Virgin*, to an error in the disposition of the piers in depth. The correct construction, supplied by Jean Pélerin in the second edition (Toul, 1509) of his *De artifiziali perspectiva*, reveals that it was only this freedom in the division of space that enabled Dürer to find room for the altar and the people around it. Dürer's unnamed interlocutor for perspectival construction may well have been the mathematician Luca Pacioli, who would have been able to explain to him the plan and elevation technique of division of space in recession, as described first by Leon Battista Alberti and then, in an unpublished treatise, by Piero della Francesca, which Dürer later called 'the shorter way'. Dürer's interest in mathematics, already evinced during his stay in Venice, went beyond the practical concerns of perspective, as is shown by his acquisition of a copy (Wolfenbüttel, Herzog August Bib.) of a Latin edition of the *Elements* of Euclid (*fl c.* 300 BC) in 1507, shortly before leaving for home. No practical application of new discoveries in perspective can be traced in his work before 1510, so it is far from certain that the Bologna interview was in fact his source.

A drawn copy (*c.* 1634; untraced; see Arnolds, 1959) of Dürer's painting *Christ among the Doctors* (Madrid, Mus. Thyssen-Bornemisza) shows the false signature amplified by an inscription: *F[ecit] Romae* ('Done in Rome'). This would suggest that in the late autumn of 1506, Dürer rode on from Bologna to Rome (his originally intended journey there having come to nought with the cancellation of the coronation of Emperor Maximilian I). However, it remains improbable that Dürer took his large and fragile drawings for *Christ among the Doctors* with him to Rome via Bologna, did the painting during a short stay in the city and then took it back to Venice, where it exerted an influence on the late work of Giorgione.

6. YEARS OF RATIONAL SYNTHESIS, 1507–12. The period following Dürer's second stay in Venice has been described (Panofsky) as the years of rational synthesis. He initially concentrated, with renewed energy, on painting, and the theme of Adam and Eve, which was rendered more attractive by the opportunities it offered for the depiction of the nude, was taken up again in 1507, this time without reference to the proportions laid down by Vitruvius. The two panel paintings *Adam* and *Eve* (1507; Madrid, Prado), whose purpose is unknown, have always been regarded as one of his greatest achievements as a painter. The bodies emerge from a neutral, dark ground. The man's body, in shadow, is contrasted with the highlighted flesh tones of the female nude, who is bathed in a silvery light. Both figures have taken on a degree of Gothic weightlessness—although only the *Eve* has undergone any marked change of pose (in the placing of the feet) since the engraving of 1504—and the *Adam* has retained the Classical contrapposto of the *Apollo Belvedere* (4th century BC; Rome, Vatican, Mus. Pio-Clementino). Two other paired panel paintings are the portraits of the *Emperor Charlemagne* and *Emperor Sigismund* (both c. 1510–13; Nuremberg, Ger. Nmus.; *see* NUREMBERG, fig. 2), which Dürer painted for a room in the house on the market place in Nuremberg from which once a year the crown jewels of the Holy Roman Empire, together with the associated relics, were displayed to the people; he sketched the regalia for the sake of adding authenticity to these two paintings. His fee of something over 85 guilders was paid by the city council on 16 February 1513.

Dürer's plan of pursuing the theme of the life-size female nude through a painting of the *Death of Lucretia*, to which a study (1508; Vienna, Albertina; W 436; s 1508/20) testifies, was not carried out until 1518, and then very differently (Munich, Alte Pin.). However, in 1508 he accepted a commission from Frederick III to depict the *Martyrdom of the Ten Thousand* (Vienna, Ksthist. Mus.). Forced to fit a multitude of animated figures on to a small surface, he deployed all his skill in the creation of a pictorial space that serves as a comprehensible setting for figures that pull apart in constantly varying degrees of foreshortening. In the centre stands Dürer himself, accompanied by a man plausibly identified as Konrad Celtis.

Dürer's work for the Church came to an end with two altarpiece commissions. Nine letters written in 1508 and 1509 to his client Jakob Heller (c. 1460–1522) in Frankfurt am Main give an account of the progress of work on an altar triptych that Heller had commissioned for the Dominicans of Frankfurt. Wishing to increase the agreed fee of 130 guilders, Dürer argued that he had painted the central panel, the *Assumption of the Virgin and her Coronation by the Holy Trinity* (ex-Residenz, Munich; destr. 1729), entirely with his own hand. Among the preparatory studies for the Heller Altarpiece are 18 brush

drawings on prepared paper, including the well-known drawing of an apostle's hands upraised in prayer (Vienna, Albertina; W 461; S 1508/9). A copy (1614; Frankfurt am Main, Hist. Mus.) by the Frankfurt painter Jobst Harrich (*b* c.1580) of the lost central panel gives an idea of the distribution of colour and of the composition, which ties the celestial and terrestrial spheres together through the agency of two dominant foreground figures seen from behind. In the centre of the painting the eye penetrates into a distant landscape with a very low horizon line. The hinged wings of the triptych (Frankfurt am Main, Hist. Mus.) were painted by assistants, the later fixed wings (Frankfurt am Main, Städel. Kstinst.; Karlsruhe, Staatl. Ksthalle) by Matthias Grünewald.

The form of Dürer's last altarpiece, a single panel in a frame he designed himself, may have been determined by the location for which it was painted: the chapel of the Zwölfbrüderhaus, a home for 12 needy artisans set up by the Nuremberg merchant Matthias Landauer (*d* 1515). The subject of the Landauer Altarpiece (1511; Vienna, Ksthist. Mus.) is the *Adoration of the Most Holy Trinity by the Communion of Saints*. In a logical progression from the compositional pattern of the Heller Altarpiece, the representatives of living humanity, led by the Pope and Emperor, now float on clouds as they turn their gaze upwards towards God the Father; he, with the dove of the Holy Ghost soaring overhead and surrounded by angels, saints and prophets, stretches out his arms to display his crucified Son. Left behind on earth, represented by a landscape sloping upwards at the sides and stretching away towards a distant sea, Dürer himself stands alone beside a large plaque that names him as a citizen of Nuremberg and the painter of the work.

While Dürer was expanding his repertory as a painter, he was working with equal intensity on his graphic work. In the 15 prints of the *Engraved Passion* series (1508–12; B. 3–15, 17) and *SS Peter and John Healing the Lame Man* (1513; B. 16), the composition of the scenes and the handling of the engraving technique show great virtuosity, which is also evident in individual sheets of the period, such as the *Crucifixion* (1508; Coburg, Veste Coburg; B. 24; *see* DEVOTIONAL PRINTS, fig. 2).

The *Engraved Passion* seems to have been intended for the connoisseur and the collector, whereas the *Small Woodcut Passion* series (1510–11; B. 16–52) is much more popular in its approach. In 37 images, it tells the history of Man's Salvation, from *The Fall* to the *Last Judgement*. This series was published in book form, as the *Passio Christi ab Alberto Dürer . . .* (Nuremberg, 1511), with an explanatory text by a Nuremberg Benedictine, Benedictus Chelidonius (*d* 1521). Dürer thus evolved a new kind of book, the crucial element of which was the pictures. In 1510 the earlier *Large Woodcut Passion* cycle was extended by four scenes (B. 5, 7, 14, 15) for book publication, as the *Passio domini nostri Jesu . . .* (Nuremberg, 1511), and for the same purpose two incidents (B. 93, 94) and a text by Chelidonius were added to the *Life of the Virgin*.

Emperor Maximilian I visited Nuremberg in 1512, and, no doubt on the advice of his literary advisers, Melchior Pfinzing (1481–1535), Johannes Stabius (*fl* 1498; *d* 1522) and Willibald Pirckheimer, Dürer was given overall charge of the various artistic commissions placed by the Emperor with a view to his own greater glory and that of the Habsburg dynasty to which he belonged. In 1515, working with Hans Springinklee (who lived in his house) and Wolf Traut, and within an overall design by the Innsbruck court painter Jörg Kölderer (*fl* 1512; *d* 1540), Dürer completed the *Triumphal Arch* (B. 138), an assemblage of 192 large woodcuts that were printed in 1517–18. Its subject was the exploits of Maximilian I, his ancestors and his imperial predecessors (for illustration of one of the woodcut panels *see* REGALIA, fig. 3). Dürer also contributed one woodcut known as the *Small Triumphal Chariot* (*c.* 1518; B. 229) to the *Triumphal Procession*, which was mainly the work of the Augsburg artist Hans Burgkmair I. The subject of his contribution was the decisive event in the Emperor's life, his marriage to Mary, Duchess of Burgundy. In 1522 Dürer brought out an eight-sheet *Large Triumphal Chariot* (B. 139) of his own, drawn by twelve horses. The programme, based on humanistic conceits, was provided by Pirckheimer, as was the explanatory letterpress. Of the illustrations designed for the Emperor's autobiographical romance, *Freydal* (1515–16), a tale of tourneys, pageants and knight-errantry, only five were printed as woodcuts, in 1516. Only one of these (B. app. 36), representing Freydal's victory over Niclas von Firmian, can be ascribed with certainty to Dürer.

One work of art that was intended to be placed directly in the hands of the Emperor himself was the series of marginal drawings in his own copy of a prayerbook printed in a tiny edition in 1513. The Hours of Emperor Maximilian I (Munich, Bayer. Staatsbib., 2v̇L. impr. membr. 64; see fig. 8) was circulated to the leading artists in southern Germany for illustration, and Dürer was among them. His artistry and fertile invention were such that his contribution has been described as one of the most precious and beautiful works in the entire history of book illustration. The leitmotif of the drawings in red, green and violet ink is an animated swirl of leaf ornament, enfolding a variety of animals, plants and drolleries and verging at times on pure linear arabesque. The figurative subjects are taken from the Judeo–Christian tradition and mix religious subject-matter with secular themes from the Middle Ages and antiquity.

In 1516/17 the Emperor also commissioned a set of silvered armour (untraced), made by the Augsburg armourer Koloman Colman (1470–1532) after designs by Dürer. Drawings for neck and back plates, visors and scabbards (Vienna, Albertina; New York, Pierpont Morgan Lib.; Berlin, Kupferstichkab.; London, BM; W 678–82, 712; S 1517/3–9), dated *1517* in another hand, depict emblems such as cranes, the symbol of vigilance, and pomegranates, the Emperor's personal emblem, which also appear in the Hours of Emperor Maximilian I. During this period Dürer also produced four friezes of religious subjects (perhaps designs for ornamental metalwork for his brother, Endres Dürer, including a frieze of the *Adoration of the Magi* (London, BM; W 724–7; S 1517/33); these would have been used for engraved silverware. Albrecht is also thought to have been closely associated with the workshop of the Krug family of goldsmiths. A naturalistic style of silverware, incorporating tree-trunk or branch stems and apple- or pear-shaped bowls, which

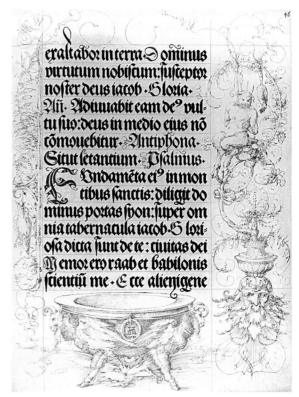

8. Albrecht Dürer: ornamented page from the Hours of Emperor Maximilian I, 280×192 mm, 1515 (Munich, Bayerische Staatsbibliothek, 2v̇l. impr. membr. 64, fol. 46)

were essentially Gothic features, with Renaissance ornament, seems to have been favoured by Dürer: this can be seen in his drawing of six goblets in the Dresden Sketchbook (*c.* 1507; Dresden, Sächs. Landesbib., fol. 1931). A goblet (Nuremberg, Ger. Nmus.), in the form of an apple supported by a stem covered with naturalistic leaf ornament, is similar to Dürer's designs. It does not appear, however, that he was ever actually active as a goldsmith. (For an illustration of a silver and parcel-gilt pendant (*c.* 1510) made from Dürer's design *see* GERMANY, fig. 74.)

On 28 June 1518, Dürer drew *Maximilian I* in Augsburg. After the Emperor's death in January 1519, this drawing (Vienna, Albertina; W 657; S 1518/19) was used as the basis of two paintings (Nuremberg, Ger. Nmus.; Vienna, Ksthist. Mus.) and a woodcut (B. 154), the first printed portrait by Dürer. In recompense for his services, he was paid a stipend of 100 guilders a year, from 1515 onwards, out of the taxes due to the Emperor from Nuremberg.

7. THE ACHIEVEMENT OF CLASSICAL FORM, 1512–20. In 1513–14 Dürer explored his knowledge of Classical form, based on antiquity, and the understanding of perspective that he had developed in Italy in three major works on copper, the so-called *Master Engravings*. In terms of content, too, these are images that operate on a lofty intellectual level. The first, the engraving *Knight, Death and the Devil* (1513; B. 98), was the result of his studies of

the proportions of the horse. In a preparatory study for this engraving (Milan, Bib. Ambrosiana; W 617; S 1513/1) the constructional lines can still be seen: the proportions of the horse's body are based on a network of twice three rectangles, the shorter side of each being equal to the length of the animal's head.

St Jerome, patron saint of the humanists, appears eight times in Dürer's work: after the first attempt, the Basle

9. Albrecht Dürer: *Melencolia I*, engraving, 239×189 mm, 1514 (London, British Museum)

woodblock, there were two paintings (1497–8; Sir Edmund Bacon priv. col., on loan to Cambridge, Fitzwilliam; 1521, Lisbon, Mus. N.A. Ant.), three engravings (1496–7; B. 59–61) and two woodcuts (1512, B. 113; 1511, B. 114). In the *Master Engraving* that Dürer himself entitled *Jerome Indoors*, though it is more commonly known as *St Jerome in his Study* (1514; B. 60; *see* ENGRAVING, fig. 4), the saint is made immediately present through the convincing reality of the things around him. Dürer's enhanced knowledge of perspective means that the room, with all its contents, can clearly be taken in from the step leading up to the entrance. The lines of spatial recession meet at a vanishing-point in some shelving at the right-hand edge. At the same eye-level are the vanishing-points of the 45° diagonals used in the construction of the bench that stands at an angle to the table.

The third of the *Master Engravings* is the scene that Dürer named *Melencolia I* (1514; B. 74; see fig. 9), its title inscribed on a scroll unrolled by a batlike nocturnal creature. A winged genius, with a folio volume on her lap and an opened pair of dividers in her right hand, is surrounded by a number of objects that refer to art as the product of scientific investigation and manual skill. Dürer drew a large polyhedron, which partly blocks the view of the sea in the background, from a real object with the assistance of one of the pieces of equipment shown in his *Vnderweysung der messung* (Nuremberg, 1525; *see* §III below). In detail, *Melencolia I* has been interpreted in a variety of ways—both philosophical, with reference to Florentine Neo-Platonism, and theological— that, however they may differ, are not necessarily mutually exclusive. If the three *Master Engravings* of 1514 are seen as a unity, *Knight, Death and the Devil* shows the moral way to salvation, *St Jerome* the theological way and *Melencolia I* the intellectual way.

In the following years Dürer experimented with the technique of etching, drawing from the medium a number of specific expressive effects. He had already executed several drypoints, including *St Jerome by the Pollard Willow* (1512; Boston, MA, Mus. F. A.; B. 59), the *Holy Family with SS John, Mary Magdalen and Nicodemus* (c. 1512; B. 43) and the *Man of Sorrows* (1512; B. 21). The technique may have come down to him from the work of the Housebook Master, which he had probably seen as early as his *Wanderjahre*.

In his etchings proper, Dürer exploited to the full the linear expressivity and depth of tonal contrast that the medium offers: the *Agony in the Garden* (1515; B. 19), the *Sudarium Spread out by an Angel* (1516; B. 26) and the *Abduction of Proserpine on a Unicorn* (1516; London, BM; B. 72; *see* ETCHING, figs 1 and 2) are treated as dramatic events, tautened by energetic movement and stark tonal contrasts. The most forward-looking of his etchings, the *Big Gun* or *Landscape with a Cannon* (1518; B. 99), is in an oblong format and is the translation of a metalpoint drawing (Rotterdam, Mus. Boymans–van Beuningen; W 479; S 1517/18) made in the mountains of Franconia, with the village of Kirchehrenbach beneath its saddle-backed mountain, the Ehrenburg. The etching extends the foreground of the landscape, which is seen in single receding perspective, to accommodate the gun and its carriage, examined by a group of men, some of whom are clearly Turks. Unlike his earlier landscape drawings and watercolours, this print was intended for public consumption; with it, Dürer launched the new genre of the landscape etching.

Dürer's interest in all forms of the unusual or exotic is clear from his woodcut of a *Rhinoceros* (1515; *see* ANIMAL SUBJECTS, fig. 1) derived from a sketch and description that had come into his hands. His woodcut, accompanied by a long explanatory text, aroused much interest and was used as a model for three-dimensional representations of the animal.

8. JOURNEY TO THE NETHERLANDS, 1520–21. Dürer travelled once more, this time to the Netherlands in 1520–21. The journey was prompted by the prospect of obtaining from Maximilian I's grandson and successor, Charles V, a continuation of the stipend granted in 1515. The request was officially granted in Cologne on 12 November 1520, by which time Dürer had visited Antwerp, Brussels and Mechelen and attended the new Emperor's coronation in Aachen. Returning to Antwerp, he based himself there for visits to Zeeland, Bruges and Ghent. On 2 July 1521 he set out for home, breaking his journey in Brussels. The encounter with past and present Netherlandish art made the journey a significant experience, and the recognition accorded to him by artists in a foreign country was a professional triumph.

A journal, which survives in two copies (Bamberg, Staatsarchv; Nuremberg, Staatsarchv), was no doubt undertaken initially as a record of income and expenditure for Dürer, who was accompanied this time by his wife and a maid. It contains, for almost every day, information on the place in which he stayed, the distance travelled, what was done and the people he met. His expenses were partly covered by gifts of money from portrait sitters and by the sale of the substantial stock of prints he had brought with him, which he also used for exchanges with other artists and as gifts in return for favours. Occasionally the business-like tone of the journal varies, as in Dürer's enthusiastic description of the gifts presented to Hernán Cortés (1485–1547) by the Mexican emperor Motecuhzuma (*reg* 1502–20), which Charles V had brought from Spain; and there is a complete change of manner in the long and eloquent lament written in Antwerp on 17 May 1521, when the rumour spread that Martin Luther had been captured by subterfuge and might already be dead. Dürer's outburst is a panegyric on the reformer, couched in the form of a prayer, and he ends by calling on Erasmus of Rotterdam, as 'the Knight of Christ', to stand up for Truth and win the martyr's crown. Some doubts have been expressed as to the authenticity of this passage, but they do not carry conviction.

Two sketchbooks, now divided, include careful silver-point drawings of *Aachen Cathedral* (London, BM; W 763; S 1520/6) and *Aachen Town Hall* (Chantilly, Mus. Condé; W 764; S 1520/20), as well as buildings in Netherlandish cities and individuals. In the Netherlands, Dürer worked mostly on commissioned portrait drawings, done in charcoal on large sheets of paper and highly finished, which became a substitute for painted portraits. There are, however, two portraits in oil on panel, that of *Bernhard von Reesen* (1521; Dresden, Gemäldegal. Alte Meister) and the *Portrait of an Unknown Man* (1521; Boston, MA, Isabella Stewart Gardner Mus.); the journal mentions a third, of *King Christian II of Denmark* (untraced). An elaborately finished brush drawing on paper with a grey-violet ground, the *Portrait of a 93-year-old Man* (1521; Vienna, Albertina), served as the source for the only non-portrait panel painting done by Dürer in the Netherlands: the *St Jerome* (1521; Lisbon, Mus. N. A. Ant.), which shows the saint working at his desk, with no indication of a spatial setting. He points with his left hand to a skull, which, together with the inkwell and the writing surface, is urgently thrust forward into the viewer's space. Dürer presented the painting to one of his wealthy patrons in Antwerp, the envoy of the King of Portugal, Rodrigo Fernandes d'Almada (*c.* 1465/70–1546/8), who may well be the sitter in the *Portrait of an Unknown Man*. Although the *St Jerome* thus found its way into private hands, it must have become well known, because it was repeated in numerous variants, mostly by Netherlandish artists.

9. THE LAST YEARS, 1521–8. While Dürer was in Antwerp, he was stimulated to embark on drawings for a new *Passion* series, in oblong format, by the example of Netherlandish history painting (a term that in contemporary usage included secular as well as sacred history). This time he included the episode of the *Way to the Tomb* (1521; Florence, Uffizi; Nuremberg, Ger. Nmus.; W 795–6; S 1521/7 and 16), which had been omitted from his other series since it was not customary in German art. Other subjects, all drawn in pen and dated 1520 or 1521, are the *Agony in the Garden* (Karlsruhe, Staatl. Ksthalle; Frankfurt am Main, Städel Kstinst.; W 797–8; S 1520/39 and 20) and *Christ Carrying the Cross* (Florence, Uffizi; W 793–4; S 1520/37–8). A *Last Supper* (1521; Vienna, Albertina), executed in woodcut (B. 53) in 1523, shows a chalice on the table and a jug next to the bread basket on the floor and has therefore been regarded as an expression of Dürer's allegiance to the Reformation. In 1521–3 he also produced large-format studies for an engraved *Crucifixion* showing Christ mourned by putto angels and surrounded by a large number of other figures; there exist impressions of the unfinished plate (Meder, no. 25).

About this time Dürer also embarked on studies (1521; Paris, Louvre; W 838; S 1521/83) for a large painting of the *Virgin and Child*, as a pendant to the *Virgin of the Rose Garlands*. The enthroned Virgin was to be flanked by serried ranks of saints in a wide semicircular formation. The studies of various versions of the overall composition were followed by finished full-size studies of detail, mostly dated 1521. The religious changes that culminated in the official adherence of Nuremberg to the Reformation in 1525 may well explain why the painting was never executed.

Portrait commissions continued to dominate in Dürer's work after his return from the Netherlands, with an increasing tendency towards multiplication through woodcut and engraving. A painted portrait of a mature, energetic man, still unidentified (1524; Madrid, Prado), shows clear signs of the portrait style developed in the Netherlands, though the almost illegible date proves that it was done in Nuremberg. In 1526 he painted portraits of two Nuremberg city councillors, with both of whom he was personally

10. Albrecht Dürer: *Jakob Muffel*, oil on canvas (transferred), 480×360 mm, 1526 (Berlin, Gemäldegalerie)

connected, *Jakob Muffel* and *Hieronymus Holzschuher* (both Berlin, Gemäldegal.; see fig. 10). The portraits show only the sitter's head, shoulders and chest, and the facial features are once more defined by outline drawing: Dürer lived up to his own principle that 'even the smallest wrinkles and veins must not be ignored'. A new departure is represented by the portrait of Pirckheimer's son-in-law, *Johann Kleberger* (1526; Vienna, Ksthist. Mus.), which combines formal elements of widely diverging origins. The antique undraped bust takes on naturalistic flesh tones and becomes the centre of a greenish bronze tondo.

From 1519 onwards, following the example of Lucas Cranach the elder, Dürer explored the application of woodcut and engraving to portraiture. The Imperial Diet in Augsburg in 1518 and the assembly of the caretaker government in Nuremberg in 1521–3 gave him opportunities to draw a number of the territorial princes of the Empire. When he engraved the portrait of *Cardinal Albrecht of Brandenburg* (1519; B. 102) he sent his sitter not only the copperplate but also 200 impressions, and 500 impressions of the profile portrait (1524; B. 103). In the inscription on his portrait engraving of *Frederick III, Elector of Saxony* (1524; B. 104), he followed the style of the epitaphs of antiquity, which were indeed often set up by the subject's friends while he was still alive. Dürer's engravings of outstanding theologians and scholars of the age, such as *Erasmus* (1526; B. 214), *Philipp Melanchthon* (1526; B. 105) and *Willibald Pirckheimer* (1526; B. 106), have served to define their appearance in the eyes of posterity.

In 1526 Dürer presented two panels of the *Four Apostles* (Munich, Alte Pin.; *see* RENAISSANCE, fig. 5), on which he had expended 'more diligence than on others', to the council of Nuremberg, to be kept in the town hall. The monumental foreground figures of *St John* and *St Paul* wear mantles of which the folds seem carved out of stone. Behind them, and with only the upper parts of their bodies visible, stand *St Peter* and *St Mark* respectively. The figures are placed on a surface of which the near edge bears texts from their writings in Martin Luther's translation, prefaced by the injunction not to be led astray by mistaking human words for the voice of God. The *Four Apostles* thus belong to the tradition of the moral admonitions commonly displayed, with appropriate pictorial illustrations, on the walls of town halls.

By 1523 Dürer had largely concluded his studies of human proportion. However, his major theoretical writings demanded considerably more knowledge of geometry and stereometry than his readership could be expected to muster, and so in 1525 he published an introductory manual, *Vnderweysung der Messung, mit dem Zirckel vnd Richtscheyt in Linien Ebenen vnd gantzen Corporen*, and in 1528 the first of his *Vier Bücher menschlicher Proportion*. He died before any more could be published, but Pirckheimer saw the rest of the work through the press. A quickly written treatise, *Etliche Vnderricht, zu Befestigung der Stett, Schlosz vnd Flecken*, had meanwhile been published *c.* 1527.

Dürer's death, on 6 April 1528, came so suddenly, as Pirckheimer noted in his elegy, that the two friends had no time even to take leave of one another. The world of learning acknowledged the importance of the loss: as well as Pirckheimer himself, two other Nuremberg humanists, Helius Eobanus Hessus (1488–1540), professor of rhetoric and poetry since 1526, and Thomas Venatorius (1490–1551), mathematician, theologian and preacher to the Neues Spital since 1522, wrote Latin funerary verses. Mathes Gebel produced a new reverse for the portrait medal he had designed in 1527, giving the day of Dürer's death as *VI [sexto die ante] IDVS*, 8 April, which was probably the day of the funeral. Christoph Scheurl reported to his nephew Albrecht Scheurl (*fl* 1525–42), a godson of Dürer's, that some artists had exhumed the body in order to make a death mask. The epitaph by Pirckheimer proclaims the imperishable quality of Dürer's works: *Quicquid Alberti Dureri mortale fuit, sub hoc conditur tumulo* ('Whatever was mortal in Albrecht Dürer lies beneath this mound').

II. Working methods and technique.

1. WORKSHOP ORGANIZATION. The workshop that Dürer set up in his family home after his return from his first visit to Italy had nothing in common with the kind of large-scale enterprise that he had known during his apprenticeship with Wolgemut. From 1500 onwards the emphasis shifted from the making of altarpieces that combined painting and sculpture to the designing of woodcut book illustration, on which Dürer's pupils Kulmbach, Baldung and Schäufelein were employed. Later it was his younger pupils, Wolf Traut and Hans Springinklee, who drew the designs for the highly labour-intensive commission of the *Triumphal Arch*, working from sketches by their master. The cutting of the blocks was done by outside specialists. In addition, Dürer's altarpieces employed a number of unidentified assistants who are described in a document of 1508 as his 'servants' (Rupprich, i, pp. 246–7). After his return from the Netherlands in 1521, things became quieter in his workshop. The second generation of Nuremberg artists who modelled their style on his work, notably Georg Pencz and the brothers Sebald Beham and Barthel Beham, are unlikely ever to have worked for him.

2. MEDIA. In his work, Dürer more or less exhausted the technical resources of the art of his day. The importance of his drawings, of which nearly a thousand have survived, is unparalleled. He used pen and ink, brush and wash, metalpoint, chalk and charcoal and drew not only on white paper but also on Venetian blue paper and on paper he prepared himself with a wash or coated ground for the demanding medium of silverpoint (for illustration *see* METALPOINT). He was the first artist to recognize and exploit the potential of the autonomous watercolour and the first printmaker to be equally active in the technique of woodcut and engraving. He followed the experimental work of the Augsburg artist Daniel Hopfer I in printing from plates etched with acid and evolved a number of expressive devices specific to the medium of etching.

He chose his media largely in accordance with the subject-matter. Secular subjects, whether from mythology or from contemporary (and especially from peasant) life, were almost always treated in engraving. By contrast, the four great devotional series, the *Apocalypse*, the *Large Woodcut Passion*, the *Small Woodcut Passion* and the *Life of the Virgin*, were done in woodcut; he produced only one *Engraved Passion* cycle. His single images of saints are divided between 'plain' woodcuts and finished engravings, most of which present variations on Marian themes.

In painting, Dürer worked in oil and tempera on a chalk ground applied to a wooden panel that would be made of local softwood or limewood in Nuremberg, of poplar in Italy and of oak in the Netherlands. An unusual support he sometimes employed was fine linen canvas, ungrounded and painted in water-soluble pigments or a dilute tempera.

The most favoured subject in Dürer's paintings is that of the *Virgin and Child*; the *Passion* very rarely appears. The paintings are based on preliminary drawings, which, in the case of the late, unrealized, *Virgin* (W 837–9, 855–6; S 1521/81, 83 and 91), allow the development of the idea and its execution to be followed in detail. From the second stay in Venice onwards he produced large, highly finished studies of detail that are dated and signed as autonomous works of art. Such preliminary studies exist even for the unfinished engraved *Crucifixion* (W 858–69; S 1521/72–9, 1523/2, 3 and 5).

No specialist study of Dürer's painting technique has been published. As was then usual, the painting is built up layer by layer from the ground. A reconstruction by the Dörner Institut in Munich of the left wing panel of the Paumgartner Altarpiece shows that the preparatory drawing was laid down on a white chalk ground coated with a layer of ochre paint. Infra-red photographs of the *Four Apostles* have revealed an underdrawing for the head of *St Paul*, in which volume is already suggested by means of hatching; the photographs also show that the figure of the Apostle had previously been omitted.

In his selection and application of colour, Dürer used the subtlest nuances of brushwork to intensify the depth of the pigment and thus the distinctness and symbolic value of the colour. This reached its apogee in the Landauer Altarpiece, the surface of which has remained intact over the centuries. In several pictures executed under the influence of Venetian and later Netherlandish painting, including the portraits painted in Venice, the *Adam and Eve* and the portrait of *Bernhard von Reesen*, Dürer moderated his colour contrasts and bathed the subject in a soft light. Finally, to conserve the painting, he invented a special varnish (as he wrote to Jakob Heller), which had to be applied after three years, when the wood of the panel had fully dried out.

III. Theoretical writings.

When Dürer returned from Venice in 1507, it was his intention to write a manual of the art of painting. Soon, however, his attention was concentrated on the proportions of the human form. His work on the engraving of *Adam and Eve* (1504; B. 1) taught him that the information given by Vitruvius was insufficient to establish universally valid laws of proportion. If he wanted to progress further towards a systematic description of the external appearance of the ideal human body, his only recourse was to engage in an exact study of nature, through precise measurements of a large number of men, women and children. In doing this, he employed two methods. In the first, distances between clearly defined points on the body were measured and expressed as aliquot parts of the model's total height. By arranging the resulting data and eliminating aberrant values, series of typical values were obtained. Dürer's second method was derived from the 'Exempeda' (six-foot) system described by Alberti in his *De statua* (1434): the total height of the figure is divided into six equal parts to obtain a module that is then used for all subsequent measurements. Dürer called this unit of measurement, which differs from one model to the next, the *Messstab* ('gauge'). As with Alberti, it is expressed in three measurements, calculated decimally.

By 1513 Dürer's research on the basis of the aliquot parts was complete and was incorporated in the first book of his treatise on proportion, the *Vier Bücher von menschlicher Proportion*, of which there exists a manuscript fair copy made in 1523 (Dresden, Sächs. Landesbib., MS. R147f). He immediately embarked on the work with the *Messstab*, which formed the second of the four books; this too is likely to have been substantially completed in 1523. As the human types deduced from anthropometry and defined in these two books were not sufficient for all the practical demands of the working artist, Dürer invented methods and drawing instruments in order to present, in a third book, ways in which the proportions could be varied, still on the basis of the given types. The following sections are devoted to the construction of the head and present a series of transmogrifications of human physiognomy that cross the border into caricature. The third book closes with a reflective passage that considers the nature and essence of art and its relationship to God. This

'aesthetic digression', the first attempt in the language to deal with such a theme, is a superb piece of German prose. Dürer became a linguistic creator, giving every sentence an almost pictorial shape and depth from the riches of his own imagination. In the fourth book, to enhance the practical usefulness of his treatise, Dürer added a theory of movement. Here, however, the concern is only with the external appearance of the body in motion, with no attempt at teaching anatomy, as he expressly emphasized. There is then a special section devoted to twisted and bent postures, which are evolved with the aid of parallel projection from the basic plan.

Dürer's previous work, the *Vnderweysung der Messung* (Nuremberg, 1525), was intended to improve the young artist's basic theoretical equipment. Here too he progressed from practical information to theory and principle. He gave the first account in German of the generation of the ellipse, the parabola and the hyperbola from conic sections. The same determination to base practical application on theoretical speculation also underlies his concern with the geometry of three-dimensional bodies, the five Platonic and seven Archimedean Solids, all of which are figured. He then supplied instructions for folding the pages to make a three-dimensional model 'which is useful for many things'. The third book of the *Vnderweysung* deals with the practical application of geometry in architecture. It includes instructions for making both fixed and movable sundials, including the necessary basic astronomical concepts. The work ends with a comprehensive exposition of scientific perspective.

The practical application of geometrical theory reappears in Dürer's work on fortification, *Etliche Vnderricht, zu Befestigung der Stett, Schlosz vnd Flecken* (Nuremberg, c. 1527). Although he had earlier, mostly Italian, literature to go on, and although most of the designs for fortifications he presented were not of his own devising, the importance of the work transcends the fact that it was the first book in German on the subject. With its plans, elevations, sections and perspectival views (see MILITARY ARCHITECTURE AND FORTIFICATIONS, fig. 23), it was the first printed book in any language to bring together elements of the art of fortification, both speculative and proved in action, from many sources and to present them as a system.

IV. Character and personality.

The best contemporary source for Dürer's personality is contained in his self-portraits, whether from his formative years or his maturity. In the drawings, the reflection of his inner state was intended for his eyes only. This is the case in the youthful *Self-portrait* drawing (1484; Vienna, Albertina; w 1; s 1484/1), which reveals a playful delight in his own good looks. When he executed the next (1491; Erlangen, Ubib.; w 26; s 1491/9), he was 21, an age at which self-examination and self-knowledge can be of the utmost importance in determining the course of the individual's life. Dürer drew himself in a headband, evidently passing through a crisis, caused perhaps by physical pain, which by 1493, to judge from another *Self-portrait* (1493; New York, Met.; w 27; s 1493/6), seems to have been overcome. Apart from a single hasty sketch (1519; Bremen, Ksthalle; w 482; s 1519/2), in which

Dürer points to the part of his body where he feels pain, as the inscription makes clear, only one self-portrait drawing postdates his journeyman years: a drawing (*c.* 1504; Weimar, Schlossmus.) in which, with extraordinary realism, he showed himself from the knees up, naked.

The painted self-portraits lack the intimate quality of the drawings; instead they reveal how Dürer wished to be seen and the social status to which he aspired. In the last of these paintings (1500; Munich, Alte Pin.), with its close approximation to the iconography of Christ, he demonstrated his conviction in the nobility and divine origin of his art. As the inscription makes clear, in this image he sought to take his place before the public and to set up a lasting memorial to himself. The characteristics of Dürer's horoscope are more external: artistic genius, elegant appearance, success with women, financial success, a pleasure in weapons and travel (letter from Lorenz Behaim to Willibald Pirckheimer, 21 May 1507, see Rupprich, i, p. 254).

Dürer enjoyed a special status in his native city of Nuremberg. Nevertheless in 1506, towards the end of his second stay in Venice, Dürer wrote to Pirckheimer: 'Oh, how I shall freeze, there, after the sun. Here I am a gentleman, at home I am a ne'er-do-well.' This is not entirely true, for in 1509, the same year in which he bought his impressive house by the Tiergärtner Tor, he was honoured by being appointed to the city's Greater Council. The city-state took pleasure in adorning its embassies with the reflected glory of its famous artist: in 1518 he went with the Nuremberg delegation to the Imperial Diet of Augsburg; in 1519 he accompanied Pirckheimer on an official mission to Switzerland with Martin Tucher (1460–1528). During his stay in the Netherlands, he was co-opted to the Nuremberg mission that escorted the crown jewels to Aachen for the coronation of Charles V. After Dürer had made representations to the city fathers, to the effect that he had received lucrative offers to stay both in Venice and in Antwerp, they agreed to pay him 50 guilders a year in the form of an enhanced return on a deposit of 1000 guilders. In 1512 the council took action against the fraudulent sale of counterfeit prints bearing his monogram; in 1515, in a case of threatening behaviour and slander, the offender was saved from torture and a heavy prison sentence only by the intercession of Dürer himself; and in 1527, when he was in breach of a municipal building ordinance, the fine was repaid to him in the form of an honorific gift.

The late medieval period was an age of intense religious feeling in Germany, marked by an overriding concern with eternal salvation, and the extraordinary success of Dürer's *Apocalypse* was due not least to the fact that those who saw the prints found in them a reflection of their own fears. He himself shared those same fears, until he was set free by Martin Luther, as he reported in a letter of 1520 to Georg Spalatin (1484–1545), an official in the chancery of Frederick III (Rupprich, i, p. 86). Dürer thought deeply about his faith. He belonged to a circle, of a kind common in Germany, that under the leadership of Johann von Staupitz (*c.* 1465–1524), an Augustinian monk and professor of theology, promoted theological knowledge among the upper echelons of the bourgeoisie and among inmates of religious houses. It is known from a list compiled by

Dürer himself (London, BL, Add. MS. 5231, fol. 115*r*; Rupprich, i, pp. 221–2, 447) that he owned a considerable proportion of the writings published by Luther in 1517–19. In the Netherlands he obtained Luther's *De captivitate Babilonica ecclesiae praeludium* in the German version (Strasbourg, 1520) by Thomas Murner (1475–1537), exchanging it for copies of his own three great books (Rupprich, i, p. 175). His lament over the supposed death of Luther is mingled with passionate protests at the defective, and in some cases the false, understanding of scripture conveyed by the medieval Church.

Dürer's views on the Eucharist were probably close to those of Huldrych Zwingli (1484–1531), whom he probably met in Switzerland. According to Kaspar Peucer (1525–1602), he and Pirckheimer disagreed on this issue, but nothing is known of the grounds for their disagreement (Rupprich, i, p. 306). Dürer cannot be linked in any way with the outbreak of heretical excitement among younger artists in Nuremberg that led in 1524 to the banishment of Pencz and the Beham brothers for atheistic and anarchical utterances; nor can his gift of the *Four Apostles* to the town hall, or the inscriptions on them, be related to the prosecutions of the three painters.

Although the moderation of Luther's own views on the religious use of images prevented an outbreak of iconoclasm in Nuremberg after the city officially embraced the Reformation in 1525, Dürer was filled with anxiety over the future of art works that he found it impossible to imagine as purely secular. In the preface to the *Vnderweysung der Messung*, addressed to Pirckheimer, he expressly defended paintings and sculpture against the charge that they might lead a Christian soul into idolatry. The knowledge of art, he wrote, is easy to lose but hard to recover.

V. Critical reception and posthumous reputation.

Long before Johann Neudorfer, the earliest biographer of the Nuremberg artists, published his brief account of Dürer's life in 1547 (Rupprich, i, pp. 320–21), the artist had been discussed in print by his contemporaries. The first mention was made in 1502 by Jakob Wimpfeling (1450–1528) in his handbook of German history, *Epithoma rerum germanicarum usque ad nostra tempora* (Strasbourg, 1505), referring to Dürer as the outstanding artist of his age, as a pupil of Martin Schongauer and as a native, like Schongauer, of the south-western (Alemannic) part of Germany (Rupprich, i, p. 290). In 1515 this account was corrected by Christoph Scheurl in his biography of Anton Kress, in which he named Dürer as his source and mentioned the Hungarian ancestry of the artist's father (Rupprich, i, pp. 294–5). Johann Cochläus (1479–1552), in his *Cosmographia Ponponii Mele* (Nuremberg, 1512), stated that merchants from all over Europe bought Dürer's engravings and took them home for their own artists to imitate (Rupprich, i, p. 293).

There are few sources that give precise information on the impression Dürer's art made on his contemporaries. Statements about the eye-deceiving realism of his paintings (Konrad Celtis even had an epigram in which the artist's dog barks at a self-portrait) relate more to the tales told of the famous artists of ancient Greece than to what really fascinated people about Dürer's work. Even Erasmus's statement, in *De recta latini graecique sermonis pronuntiatione dialogus* (Venice, 1528; Rupprich, i, pp. 296–7), that Dürer could do with black lines what Apelles would have needed colour to do (namely express shadow, light, radiance, height and depth) is partly lifted from Pliny's *Natural History*. But Erasmus revealed a serious concern with the nature of engravings and woodcuts when he expressed his opposition to the persistent practice of adding colour to the prints. In 1531 Philipp Melanchthon (1497–1560) attempted to characterize Dürer's art by saying that 'Dürer painted everything raised to the sublime and full of variety through closely packed lines' (Rupprich, i, p. 306). Both Erasmus and Pirckheimer had high praise for Dürer's activity as a writer. Sebastian Frank (*c*. 1499–1542), in his *Chronika* (Frankfurt am Main, 1531), emphasized the scientific element in Dürer's work: 'a master of the compasses, he knew true perspective so well that he might without exaggeration be called a master of geometry and arithmetic' (Rupprich, i, pp. 305–6).

After his death, Dürer's name was never quite forgotten; his fame never quite disappeared. This was due primarily to the wide circulation of his engravings and woodcuts, all of which bear his monogram. Copies and imitations appeared in large numbers, especially in northern Germany and the Netherlands, from the mid-16th century onwards. The repetition of his prints and series, above all the *Small Woodcut Passion* and *Engraved Passion*, went on almost without interruption until the 18th century. The engravings and engraved copies were used primarily as illustrations in prayerbooks and devotional works; the copperplates were passed from hand to hand and reprinted over and over again. Some prints were copied in other media: for instance, the *Fall of Man* served as a model for a painting on glass (1686; Zurich, Schweizer. Landesmus.; for illustration *see* GLASS PAINTING) by the Swiss artist Carl Ludwig Thuot (*fl* 1677/8–1687/8).

Vasari, in both the first edition (1550) and the second, expanded edition (1568) of his *Vite*, discussed Dürer at some length in his account of Marcantonio Raimondi. For the Dutch painter and writer van Mander, whose *Schilderboeck* was published in 1604, Dürer was one of the great forerunners whom he constantly cited to bolster a statement of fact or opinion. Apart from a detailed biography, with a long list of works, many of which van Mander knew at first hand, he mentioned Dürer in no fewer than ten of his lives of other painters. Basing his work on Neudorfer and van Mander, Joachim von Sandrart included a life of Dürer in his *Teutsche Academie* (Frankfurt, 1675–9).

As the 16th century progressed, Dürer's work passed out of fashion, but towards the end of the century there was what has been described as a DÜRER RENAISSANCE. The revival of his reputation was largely related, both as cause and as effect, to the interest shown in his works by the Holy Roman Emperor Rudolf II (*reg* 1576–1612) and then by Duke (later Elector) Maximilian I of Bavaria (*reg* 1598–1651). In Prague, Rudolf II collected the Landauer Altarpiece in 1585, the portrait of *Johann Kleberger* in 1588, the *Martyrdom of the Ten Thousand* in 1600, the *Adoration of the Magi* in 1603, the *Adam and Eve* before 1604 and, the crowning glory of the collection, the *Virgin of the Rose Garlands* from Venice in 1606. In 1588 he acquired the drawings that had belonged to Willibald

Imhoff and in 1589 further volumes of drawings from the estate of Cardinal Antoine Perrenot de Granvelle, so that ultimately there were no fewer than 400 drawings in Prague (many now Vienna, Albertina). By financial and also by diplomatic means, Maximilian I also succeeded in acquiring a series of major Dürer paintings, mostly from the imperial city of Nuremberg. In his Residenz in Munich, he had the *Death of Lucretia* by 1598, the Glimm *Lamentation* between 1598 and 1607, the Paumgartner Altarpiece in 1613, the central *Assumption* panel from the Heller Altarpiece in 1614 and from 1627 the most important acquisition of all, the *Four Apostles*.

Nor was Dürer forgotten in the 18th century. In the first half of the century there appeared a series of published assessments of his art. In the second half of the century, long before Romanticism hailed him as its hero, voices were raised that, however much coloured by Neo-classical prejudice, clearly revealed a high opinion of him. In 1764 Johann Joachim Winckelmann named Holbein and Dürer as the fathers of German art, who had lacked only a knowledge of antique art to make them fully equal, and perhaps superior, to the Italians (H. Meyer and J. Schulze, eds: *Werke* (Dresden, 1812), iii, p. 64).

On 6 September 1786, on his way to Italy, Goethe visited the recently opened Hofgartengalerie in Munich, where he saw Dürer's paintings. He recalled them in Bologna on 18 October, noting that he had 'seen a few pieces of his, unbelievably great'; he only regretted that 'good fortune did not bring Albrecht Dürer further into Italy'. There followed, in the *Italienische Reise* (Weimar, 1792), some remarks on Dürer's visits to Venice and the Netherlands that reveal that Goethe had read the excerpts from Dürer's Netherlands journals and letters to Pirckheimer that Christoph Gottlieb Murr had published in the *Journal zur Kunstgeschichte und zur allgemeinen Literatur* (vii, 1779; more appeared in x, 1787). It was, in fact, members of Goethe's circle who produced the first publications addressed to collectors. Heinrich Sebastian Hüsgen (1745–1807), who had known Goethe in his youth in Frankfurt am Main, published the *Raisonierendes Verzeichnis aller Kupfer- und Eisenstiche, so durch die Geschickte Hand Albrecht Dürers selbsten verfertigt Worden* (Leipzig and Frankfurt am Main, 1778), a catalogue raisonné of engravings, based on the author's own collection. A few years later Johann Heinrich Merck (1741–91), who was close to Goethe's circle in Weimar, published a detailed account of a number of copies of Dürer's engravings ('Anmerkungen über einige der betrüglichsten Copien von Kupferstichen Albrecht Dürers', *Der teutsche Merkur vom Jahre 1787*, ii (1787), pp. 158–66). The Dürer biography in Wilhelm Heinrich Wackenroder's *Herzensergiessungen eines kunstliebenden Klosterbrüders* (Berlin, 179[6]), on which Ludwig Tieck (1773–1853) expanded in his novel *Franz Sternbalds Wanderungen* (Berlin, 1798), created the idealized image of Dürer as the archetypal German artist whom the Romantic generation revered as their great ancestor. The first publication of drawings by Dürer came in 1808, with Johann Nepomuk Strixner's lithographs after the marginal drawings in the Hours of Emperor Maximilian I.

The seventh volume of *Le Peintre-graveur* (Vienna, 1808) by Adam von Bartsch and *Das Leben und die Werke*

Albrecht Dürers (Bamberg, 1827) by Joseph Heller (1758–1849) marked the first attempts to work towards an exhaustive catalogue of the works. On the tercentenary of Dürer's death, Friedrich Campe (1777–1846) brought out the first edition of his unpublished writings, *Reliquien von Albrecht Dürer seinen Verehrern geweiht* (Nuremberg, 1828). The stylistic characteristics and changes in Dürer's works were systematically described for the first time in Heinrich Wölfflin's *Die Kunst Albrecht Dürers* (Munich, 1905). Erwin Panofsky, in *Albrecht Dürer* (Princeton, 1942), used iconographic and iconological interpretation of Dürer's imagery to define his position within the religious and secular consciousness of his time.

On the morning of 6 April 1828 some 300 artists and art-lovers, led by Peter Cornelius, gathered at Dürer's tomb to pay tribute. On the same day the foundation stone of the monument designed by Christian Daniel Rauch was laid. The tributes were adulatory, almost religious in tone. Cornelius defined Dürer's character as 'glowing and stern'. There have been more celebrations at each new centenary of his birth or death. The quatercentenary of his birth (1871) occasioned the first commemorative exhibition, held at the Germanisches Nationalmuseum in Nuremberg; it was repeated, on a larger scale, in 1928. The wealth of exhibitions and publications that greeted the 500th anniversary of Dürer's birth in 1971 bore witness to the undiminished fascination of his work and personality.

WRITINGS

Vnderweysung der Messung, mit dem Zirckel vnd Richtscheyt in Linien Ebenen vnd gantzen Corporen... (Nuremberg, 1525); facs. ed. with foreword by A. Wagner (London, 1970); facs. (Unterschneidheim, 1972); Eng. trans. as *The Painter's Manual: A Manual of Measurement of Lines, Areas and Solids by Means of Compass and Ruler, Assembled by Albrecht Dürer*, ed. W. L. Strauss (New York, 1977)

Etliche Vnderricht, zu Befestigung der Stett, Schlosz vnd Flecken (Nuremberg, c. 1527); facs. ed. (Unterschneidheim, 1969); facs. ed. with modern Ger. trans. and critical commentary by A. J. Jaegli (Dietikon and Zurich, 1971)

Hierinn sind begriffen vier Bücher von menschlicher Proportion (Nuremberg, 1528); facs. ed. (Unterschneidheim, 1969; Nördlingen, 1980)

De symmetria partium in rectis formis humanorum corporum, Lat. trans. by J. Camerarius (Nuremberg, 1532)

De varietate figurarum et flexuris partium ac gestibus imaginum libri, duo, Lat. trans. by J. Camerarius (Nuremberg, 1534)

Vnderweisung der Messung, mit dem Zirkel vnd Richtscheyt (Nuremberg, 1538)

H. Rupprich, ed.: *Dürer: Schriftlicher Nachlass*, 3 vols (Berlin, 1956–69), with app., 'Dürer in Urkunde und Schrifttum'

W. M. Conway, trans. and ed.: *The Writings of Albrecht Dürer*, intro. by A. Werner (New York, 1958)

BIBLIOGRAPHY

MONOGRAPHS

J. Heller: *Dürers Bildnisse, Kupferstiche, Holzschnitte und die nach ihm gefertigten Blätter* (Bamberg, 1827), II/ii of *Das Leben und die Werke Albrecht Dürers* [no other parts issued; the only complete listing of copies]

M. Thausing: *Dürer: Geschichte seines Lebens und seiner Kunst*, 2 vols (Leipzig, 1884) [first scholarly treatment of the subject]

H. Wölfflin: *Die Kunst Albrecht Dürers* (Munich, 1905; 9/Munich, 1984, with foreword by P. Strieder, following 5/1926, the last edn rev. by the author) [unsurpassed for formal analysis]

E. Flechsig: *Albrecht Dürer: Sein Leben und seine künstlerische Entwicklung*, 2 vols (Berlin, 1928–31) [deals with attribution and dating, with special ref. to the form of the monogram]

F. Winkler: *Albrecht Dürer: Leben und Werk* (Berlin, 1957) [comprehensive treatment of all works]

M. Levey: *Dürer* (London, 1964)

H. T. Musper: *Albrecht Dürer* (Cologne, 1971)

P. Strieder: *The Hidden Dürer* (Oxford, 1978)

F. Anzelewsky: *Dürer: Werk und Wirkung* (Stuttgart, 1980); English trans. by H. Erlieve as *Dürer: His Art and Life* (London, 1982)

P. Strieder: *Dürer* (Königstein im Taunus, 1981; Eng. trans. New York and London, 1982, rev. New York, 1989) [incl. essays by G. Goldberg: 'Zum technischen Befund von Albrecht Dürers *Vier Aposteln*'; J. Harnest: 'Dürer und die Perspektive'; M. Mende: 'Aus Schriften Dürers: Aus Schriften über Dürer']

CATALOGUES RAISONNÉS

H. Tietze and E. Tietze-Conrat: *Kritisches Verzeichnis der Werke Albrecht Dürers*, 3 vols (Augsburg, 1928; Basle and Leipzig, 1937/8) [highly critical in its attributions]

J. Meder: *Dürer Katalog: Ein Handbuch über Albrecht Dürers Stiche, Radierungen, Holzschnitte, deren Zustände, Ausgaben und Wasserzeichen* (Vienna, 1932) [important for its account of states and listing of copies]

F. Winkler: *Die Zeichnungen Albrecht Dürers*, 4 vols (Berlin, 1936–9) [first compl. crit. edn of all known drgs] [w]

E. Panofsky: *Albrecht Dürer*, 2 vols (Princeton, 1943; 3/1948; 4/rev. as *Life and Art of Albrecht Dürer* (Princeton, 1948), with additions to handlist only; German trans. by L. L. Möller as *Das Leben und die Kunst Albrecht Dürers* (Munich, 1977), with corrections and additions to the handlist as printed in the 3rd edn [ever since its appearance, this work has been regarded as basic to any consideration of Dürer's intellectual achievement]

F. Anzelewsky: *Albrecht Dürer: Das malerische Werk* (Berlin, 1971; rev., 2 vols, 1991) [detailed handling of ptgs; incl. lost works; excl. watercolours]

W. L. Strauss: *The Complete Drawings of Albrecht Dürer*, 6 vols (New York, 1974); suppl. (New York, 1977), suppl. 2 (New York, 1982) [crit. cat. based on Winkler] [s]

——: *Albrecht Dürer: Intaglio Prints, Engravings, Etchings and Drypoints* (New York, 1975) [illus. cat.]

W. L. Strauss, ed.: *Albrecht Dürer: Woodcuts and Woodblocks* (New York, 1980) [comprehensive crit. cat., covering dubious attributions]

F. Anzelewsky and H. Mielke: *Die Zeichnungen Alter Meister im Berliner Kupferstichkabinett: Albrecht Dürer, kritischer Katalog der Zeichnungen* (Berlin, 1984)

GENERAL PRINT CATALOGUES

Hollstein: *Ger.*

A. von Bartsch: *Le Peintre-graveur*, vii (Vienna, 1808) [cat. of woodcuts and engravings arranged according to subject; its numbering is most commonly followed] [B.]

I. D. Passavant: *Le Peintre-graveur*, iii (Leipzig, 1862) [supplements Bartsch]

C. Dodgson: *Catalogue of Early German and Flemish Woodcuts Preserved in the Department of Prints and Drawings in the British Museum*, i (London, 1903), pp. 259–347

M. Geisberg: *The German Single-Leaf Woodcut, 1500–1550*, ed. W. L. Strauss, ii (Washington, DC, 1974) [all woodcuts repr.]

EXHIBITION CATALOGUES

Albrecht Dürer (exh. cat., Nuremberg, Ger. Nmus., 1928) [also covers the preceding generation of Nuremberg artists and members of Dürer's circle]

Dürer und seine Zeit: Zeichnungen und Aquarelle (exh. cat. by B. Degenhard; Milan, Bib. Ambrosiana; Munich, Bayer. Staatsbib.; Munich, Staatl. Graph. Samml., 1968)

Albrecht Dürer: Master Printmaker (exh. cat., Boston, MA, Mus. F.A., 1971) [excellent descrip. of the prts, many of which were exh. in several impressions]

Albrecht Dürer, 1471–1971 (exh. cat., ed. L. von Wilckens; Nuremberg, Ger. Nmus., 1971)

Deutsche Kunst der Dürer-Zeit (exh. cat., Vienna, Albertina, 1971)

Die Dürer-Zeichnungen der Albertina (exh. cat. by W. Koschatzky and A. Strobl, Vienna, Albertina, 1971; Eng. trans., London, 1972) [crit. cat. of all Dürer drgs in the Albertina]

Dürer in America: His Graphic Work (exh. cat., ed. C. Talbot; Washington, DC, N.G.A., 1971) [exhaustive commentary on all drgs in the USA]

The Graphic Work of Albrecht Dürer (exh. cat. by J. Rowlands, London, BM, 1971) [crit. commentary on the BM's drgs by Dürer]

Vorbild Dürer: Kupferstiche und Holzschnitte Albrecht Dürers im Spiegel der europäischen Druckgraphik des 16. Jahrhunderts (exh. cat., ed. L. von Wilckens; Nuremberg, Ger. Nmus., 1978) [with repr. and descrip. of all the copies exh. and of authentic orig.]

Albrecht Dürer und die Tier- und Pflanzenstudien der Renaissance (exh. cat. by F. Koreny, Vienna, Albertina, 1985; Eng. trans., Boston, MA, 1988)

FACSIMILE EDITIONS

F. Lippmann, ed.: *Zeichnungen von Albrecht Dürer*, 7 vols (Berlin, 1883–1929) [text: iii, S. Colom; V. J. Meder; vi, vii, F. Winkler; outstanding repr., some in col., in original size]

H. Bruck: *Das Skizzenbuch von Albrecht Dürer in der königlichen öffentlichen Bibliothek zu Dresden* (Strasbourg, 1905)

G. Leidinger: *Albrecht Dürers und Lucas Cranachs Randzeichnungen zum Gebetbuch Kaiser Maximilians I. in der bayerischen Staatsbibliothek zu München* (Munich, 1922) [compl. pubn of the Munich portion, with col. repr.]

W. Koschatzky: *Albrecht Dürer: Die Landschaftsaquarelle—Örtlichkeit, Datierung, Stilkritik* (Vienna and Munich, 1971)

W. L. Strauss, ed.: *The Human Figure by Albrecht Dürer: The Complete Dresden Sketchbook* (New York, 1972)

——: *The Book of Hours of the Emperor Maximilian the First, Decorated by Albrecht Dürer, Hans Baldung Grien, Hans Burgkmair the Elder, Jörg Breu, Albrecht Altdorfer and Other Artists, Printed in 1513 by Schoensperger at Augsburg* (New York, 1974) [col. repr. of text and drgs; psalms and prayers trans. into Eng.]

Albrecht Dürer: Die drei grossen Bücher, foreword by H. Appuhn (Dortmund, 1979)

REPRODUCTIONS

F. Winkler: *Dürer: Des Meisters Gemälde, Kupferstiche und Holzschnitte*, Klass. Kst (Berlin and Leipzig, 1928)

G. Arnolds: 'Opus quinque dierum', *Festschrift Friedrich Winkler* (Berlin, 1959), pp. 187–90

K. A. Knappe: *Dürer: Das graphische Werk* (Vienna and Munich, 1964)

R. Salvini: *Dürer: Incisioni* (Florence, 1964)

Albrecht Dürer: Sämtliche Holzschnitte, intro. F. Piel (Hamburg, 1968)

G. Zampa and A. Ottino della Chiesa: *L'opera completa di Dürer*, Class. A., xxiii (Milan, 1968) [covers only the easel paintings; details illus. in col.]

M. Bernhard, ed.: *Albrecht Dürer, 1471 bis 1528: Das gesamte graphische Werk*, intro. W. Hütt, 2 vols (Munich, 1970)

L. Grote: *Albrecht Dürer: Die Apokalypse* (Munich, 1970) [woodcuts repr. at original size]

C. White: *Dürer: The Artist and his Drawings* (London, 1971) [biog. intro. and detailed commentaries on 106 drgs repr.]

R. Salvini: *Albrecht Dürer: Disegni* (Florence, 1973)

M. Mende: *Albrecht Dürer: Sämtliche Holzschnitte* (Munich, 1976)

Albrecht Dürer: Sämtliche Holzschnitte, intro. A. Deguer (Ramerding, 1980)

F. Piel: *Albrecht Dürer: Aquarelle und Zeichnungen* (Cologne, 1983) [dating of landscape watercolours; cat. rais. of watercolours; technique]

BIBLIOGRAPHIES

M. Sperlich: 'Perspektive und Proportion bei Dürer: Ein Nachtrag zum Literaturbericht', *Z. Kstgesch.*, xxvi (1963), pp. 179–80

P. Strieder: 'Die Malerei und Graphik der Dürerzeit in Franken: Literatur von 1945–1962', *Z. Kstgesch.*, xxvi (1963), pp. 169–78

M. Mende: *Dürer-Bibliographie*, ed. E. Rücker (Wiesbaden, 1971)

H. J. Berbig: 'Sammelbericht über die Literatur zum Dürer-Jahr 1971', *Archv Kultgesch.*, lv (1973), pp. 35–55

P. Vaisse: 'Albrecht Dürer: Ecrits récents et états des questions', *Rev. A.* [Paris], xix (1973), pp. 116–24

G. Bräutigam and M. Mende: 'Mähen mit Dürer: Literatur und Ereignisse im Umkreis des Dürerjahres 1971', *Mitt. Ver. Gesch. Stadt Nürnberg*, lxi (1974), pp. 204–82

W. Stechow: 'State of Research: Recent Dürer Studies', *A. Bull.*, lvi (1974), pp. 259–70

J. Białostocki: *Dürer and his Critics* (Baden-Baden, 1986)

(2) Hans Dürer (*b* Nuremberg, 21 Feb 1490; *d* ?1538). Painter, brother of (1) Albrecht Dürer. He was first trained in the workshop of his elder brother Albrecht, who wrote to their mother from Venice on 2 April 1506 to ask her to try to get him taken on by Michael Wolgemut or some other painter. In 1509 Hans was again working for his brother, and he was paid a gratuity for the Heller Altarpiece (1508–9; ex-Residenz, Munich; destr. 1729). He was last mentioned in Nuremberg in 1510. Attribution to him of a *Portrait of a Young Man* (1511; Rome, Gal. Spada) painted in the manner of Albrecht Dürer and of an altarpiece of the *Holy Kindred* (1515; s'Heerenberg (Gelderland), Huis Bergh, see Winkler, p. 73, fig. 10) in the style of the school

of Dürer remains uncertain, despite the presence of the monogram HD on both works, as does the attribution of an unmonogrammed altarpiece of the *Calling of St Peter* (Rochlitz, St Kunigunde). An altarpiece of the *Fourteen Auxiliary Saints* (1524; Nysa, Poland, St James) signed HD makes it likely that he spent some time in Silesia. From 1527 he was recorded as receiving payments in Kraków, and from 1529 he was named as court painter to Sigismund I, King of Poland.

In his authenticated late works, the *St Jerome* (1526; Kraków, N. Mus.), the *Rest on the Flight into Egypt* (1526; ex-Wahoske priv. col., Portland, OR) and another *St Jerome* (1533; Venice, Ca' d'Oro), Hans Dürer emancipated himself from Albrecht's style and achieved a distinctive way of looking at nature. A silverpoint drawing (1503; Washington, DC, N.G.A.; w 280; s 1503/38) by Albrecht Dürer, subsequently altered by the addition of a beard, has an autograph inscription that identifies it as a portrait of Hans.

BIBLIOGRAPHY

Thieme–Becker

H. Beenken: 'Beiträge zu Jörg Breu und Hans Dürer', *Jb. Preuss. Kstsamml.*, lvi (1935), 59–73 [crit. survey of earlier lit.; establishes a canon of works with positive attribs]

F. Winkler: 'Hans Dürer: Ein Nachwort', *Jb. Preuss. Kstsamml.*, lvii (1936), pp. 65–74 [addns to the canon]

G. Meinert: 'Hans Dürer in Schlesien', *Jb. Preuss. Kstsamml.*, lviii (1937), pp. 128–36 [attrib. of works in Breslau (Wrocław)]

K. Simon: 'Hans Dürer', *Graph. Kst*, n.s. vii (1942/3), pp. 16–28 [confusion through revival of discredited hypotheses]

W. Hentschel: 'Ein Frühwerk von Hans Dürer', *Festschrift Friedrich Winkler* (Berlin, 1959), pp. 213–20 [attrib. of altarpiece at Rochlitz]

Meister um Albrecht Dürer (exh. cat., ed. L. Grote; Nuremberg, Ger. Nmus., 1961), nos 142–5

Albrecht Dürer, 1471–1971 (exh. cat., ed. L. von Wilckens; Nuremberg, Ger. Nmus., 1971), nos 28, 88

PETER STRIEDER

Dürer Renaissance. Term used since 1971 for the phenomenon of increased interest in Albrecht Dürer (*see* DÜRER, (1)) that occurred in Europe between 1570 and 1630 and resulted in numerous copies and imitations of his work. It was previously thought that such works were created exclusively as forgeries. In practice there are still difficulties in distinguishing some late 16th-century and early 17th-century copies and imitations from 19th-century forgeries, but the Dürer Renaissance and the works it generated are now seen as one of the most striking developments in European Mannerism. Even within the phenomenon there are subtle distinctions: the ingenious variant produced around 1600 is ranked higher than the repetitive copy. The concept most appreciated is 'imitatio', in which the example of the older master is mingled with contemporary taste and trends.

1. LITERARY ORIGINS. Within 40 years of Dürer's death (1528), authors created a literary basis for the retrospective consideration of his achievements. Comments and texts by Lambert Lombard (as recorded by his pupil Domenicus Lampsonius in 1565) and Vasari (1568) were particularly influential, as well as those by Giovanni Paolo Lomazzo (1585) and Karel van Mander I (1604). They saw in Dürer a '*uomo universale*' (Vasari). His gift of visual inventiveness was admired, and his ability as a craftsman (especially as an engraver) was praised, as was his honest character. The Counter-Reformation hailed

Dürer as an artist who remained a Catholic: a decree of the last session (1563) of the Council of Trent on the question of pictures named him a model artist, alongside Cimabue, and in 1582 Cardinal Gabriele Paleotti counted him among the saints and blessed. New editions and translations of his three books on art theory were published, and important sections of his other written work, which was not printed until the end of the 18th century (particularly the so-called diary of the journey to the Netherlands in 1520–21), were copied and circulated. At the same time he was attributed with sculptural work, which even led connoisseurs to consider him a great northern wood-carver. He appeared as an established theoretician and experienced practical man, as in the engraving by Lucas Kilian of *Temple of Honour* after Dürer (1617; Hollstein, no. 177).

2. REGIONAL DEVELOPMENTS. The Dürer Renaissance has been seen incorrectly as a predominantly courtly phenomenon, based on its importance at the imperial court at Prague and the Wittelsbach court in Munich. But this view fails to take account of developments in countries such as Italy, Spain, England and the Netherlands and in towns such as Nuremberg, Augsburg and Antwerp. In the 1570s, Dürer's home town of Nuremberg must have been the centre of the studying and copying of his work. Most of his paintings could then still be found there, and the majority of his surviving drawings were in the collection of Willibald Imhoff the elder (*see* IMHOFF). The late 16th-century and early 17th-century collector PAULUS PRAUN of Nuremberg owned more than 150 drawings, including many imitations by the painter HANS HOFFMANN, who set both the qualitative and the quantitative standard of Dürer imitations. Hoffmann, who was a citizen of Nuremberg in 1576, is now seen as the most important master of the Dürer Renaissance. When he left Nuremberg for Munich in 1584, he made room for other Dürer imitators. In 1613 the Council of Nuremberg enlisted the best of these—Paul Juvenel I, Jobst Harrich (*c.* 1580–1617) and Georg Gärtner II (*c.* 1575/80–1654)—to restore and complete Dürer's frescoes in the assembly room in the town hall.

After Nuremberg, Prague developed as a centre of the Dürer Renaissance. The Holy Roman Emperor Rudolf II brought artists from different countries to Bohemia, among them specialists who copied Dürer's work, including Hoffmann, who arrived in 1585. The Prague court style spread through engravings after drawings by Dürer in the imperial collection, such as those by Aegidius Sadeler II (see fig.). Meanwhile in Munich, Maximilian, Elector of Bavaria, became a serious competitor as a collector of works by Dürer. After the Nuremberg collection was split up, his agents sought Dürer's pictures as far away as Italy and Scandinavia. A peculiarity of the Munich Dürer Renaissance was the tendency to improve and overpaint original Dürer paintings, a practice apparently thought to increase their value. Paraphrases of his work, such as those signed by Georg Vischer, are exceptional: most of the pictures and drawings produced during the Dürer Renaissance are unsigned or bear a false AD monogram. After Dürer's death his prints were also copied, for instance by the Hopfer family in Augsburg, to satisfy the continuing demand for his graphic work.

Dürer Renaissance engraving by Aegidius Sadeler II: *Head of an Apostle* (1597); after a drawing dated 1508 by Albrecht Dürer (Nuremberg, Städtische Graphische Sammlung)

In Italy, interest in Dürer's work persisted throughout the whole of the 16th century and well into the 17th; his prints, in particular, were used by such leading masters as Ludovico Carracci, Caravaggio and Guido Reni. The emphasis placed on Dürer by the Council of Trent was important for artists in the Iberian peninsula: Spanish painters copied his woodcuts, and in the work of El Greco, especially, there are occasional traces of his influence. Dürer's impact on art life in England *c.* 1600 has yet to be clarified, but he was praised by Nicholas Hilliard and Richard Haydocke (*fl* 1598–1640).

The situation is better known in the Netherlands, where deceptive copies of engravings and woodcuts were made, particularly by the Wierix brothers. Antwerp, where Dürer's visit of 1520–21 was never forgotten, became a centre of copying his work. Alongside direct copies of his engravings and others made in reverse, masterful paraphrases of his work were created in which the borders between respectful imitation and deceptive forgery were blurred, as in prints of Hendrick Goltzius.

3. TRANSMUTATIONS. The most speculative products of the Dürer Renaissance include works based on Dürer but transferred to another medium. For example, his engraving *Knight, Death and the Devil* (1513; B. 98) was

transformed into paintings (Karlsruhe, Staatl. Ksthalle; Nuremberg, Ger. Nmus.), as was the engraving of the *Fall of Man* (1504; B. 1; for an illustration of a 17th-century copy painted in reverse on glass *see* GLASS PAINTING). Graphic images of the Virgin became small reliefs (Frankfurt am Main, Liebieghaus). Some painters also developed creative fantasies that isolated details in Dürer's well-known self-portraits and put them together into new 'Dürer' portraits. Similarly, contemporary portrait medals of the artist were enlarged by Hans Schwarz and Mathes Gebel and varied by Hans Petzold.

BIBLIOGRAPHY

Hollstein: *Ger.*
A. von Bartsch: *Le Peintre-graveur* (1803–21) [B.]
M. Mende: *Dürer-Bibliographie* (Wiesbaden, 1971), pp. 544–7
G. Goldberg: 'Zur Ausprägung der Dürer-Renaissance in München', *Münchn. Jb. Bild. Kst*, xxxi (1980), pp. 129–75
Dürers Verwandlung in der Skulptur zwischen Renaissance und Barock (exh. cat., ed. H. Beck and B. Decker; Frankfurt am Main, Liebieghaus, 1981)
H. G. Gmelin: 'Illuminierte Druckgraphik um 1600: Ein Phänomen der Dürerrenaissance?', *Städel-Jb.*, ix (1983), pp. 183–204
Albrecht Dürer und die Tier- und Pflanzenstudien der Renaissance (exh. cat. by F. Koreny, Vienna, Albertina, 1985; Eng. trans., Boston, MA, 1988)
T. DaCosta Kaufmann: *The School of Prague: Painting at the Court of Rudolf II* (Chicago and London, 1988)
B. Decker: 'Im Namen Dürers: Dürer-Renaissance um 1600', *Pirckheimer-Jb.*, vi (1991), pp. 9–49

MATTHIAS MENDE

Duret, François-Joseph [Francisque] (*b* Paris, 19 Oct 1804; *d* Paris, 26 May 1865). French sculptor. Son of a sculptor of the same name (1729–1816) and a pupil of F.-J. Bosio, he entered the Ecole des Beaux-Arts in 1818 and won the Prix de Rome in 1823. Among his works executed at the Académie de France in Rome is *Orestes Mad* (marble, *c.* 1825; Avignon, Mus. Calvet), a colossal head modelled after the Antique that is at the same time a self-portrait, and *Mercury Inventing the Lyre* (marble; destr.), an elegant statue much praised at the 1831 Salon. Journeys from Rome to Naples resulted in *Neapolitan Fisherboy Dancing the Tarantella* (bronze, exh. Salon 1833; Paris, Louvre), which was executed on his return to Paris and was one of the earliest Neapolitan genre subjects in French 19th-century art. In this work Duret reconciled classical form with modern subject-matter and the freedom of modelling allowed by working in bronze. Its popularity led to reduced-scale bronze editions by the founder P.-M. Delafontaine, who also reproduced in this fashion Duret's *Grape-picker Extemporizing* (bronze, 1839; Paris, Louvre).

Duret's interest in genre subjects and the melancholy Romanticism shown in such works as *Chactas Meditating at Atala's Tomb* (bronze, 1836; Lyon, Mus. B.-A.) were abandoned after 1840, as he increasingly devoted himself to working in marble on monumental commissions from the State. He was less at ease working with marble than with his favoured lost-wax method of bronze casting but sought to animate his statues by careful attention to expression and costume, anxiously aspiring after a classical grand manner. He ranged from commemorative statues, such as *Casimir Perier* (1833; Paris, Pal.-Bourbon), *Molière* (1834; Paris, Inst. France) and *Chateaubriand* (1854; Paris, Inst. France), to religious and symbolic works, characterized by ample drapery. This underlines the stances in the low reliefs of the *Stations of the Cross* (1851–2; Paris, Ste

Clothilde) and adds to the severity of *Christ Revealing Himself to the World* (marble, 1840; Paris, La Madeleine). Duret's many other commissions include the statues of *Comedy* and *Tragedy* (marble, 1857) at the Théâtre-Français in Paris and the allegorical stone relief *France Protecting her Children* (stone, 1857; Paris, Louvre, Pavillon Richelieu), a rigorously Neo-classical work whose sole concession to modernity is the inclusion of a steam engine. In his Raphaelesque statue of the *Archangel Michael* (1860) for the Fontaine Saint-Michel, Paris, Duret returned to the use of bronze. He was appointed a professor at the Ecole des Beaux-Arts in 1852. Among his pupils were J.-B. Carpeaux, Henri Chapu and Jules Dalou.

BIBLIOGRAPHY

Lami
C. Blanc: 'Francisque Duret', *Gaz. B.-A.*, xx (1866), pp. 97–118
The Romantics to Rodin: French Nineteenth-century Sculpture from North American Collections (exh. cat., ed. P. Fusco and H. W. Janson; Los Angeles, CA, Co. Mus. A., 1980–81), pp. 247–8
A. Le Normand: *La Tradition classique et l'esprit romantique: Les Sculpteurs à l'Académie de France à Rome de 1824 à 1840* (Rome, 1981)
La Sculpture française au XIXème siècle (exh. cat., ed. A. Pingeot; Paris, Grand Pal., 1986)

ANTOINETTE LE NORMAND-ROMAIN

Duret, (Jules-Emmanuel-)Théodore (*b* Saintes, 19 Jan 1838; *d* Paris, 16 Jan 1927). French writer and collector. He was an heir to the cognac house Duret et De Brie, which gave him the financial freedom to pursue his interest in art. Although he saw Pre-Raphaelite works while staying in London (1855–6), he did not become truly interested in art until 1862, when he saw paintings by Courbet and Jean-Baptiste-Camille Corot that his cousin Etienne Baudry had collected. He also visited the International Exhibition in London in 1862, which he reviewed in *L'Indépendant de Saintes*. In the elections in Saintes in 1863 he made the first of several unsuccessful forays into politics. After this he travelled abroad on behalf of the cognac house, visiting the USA, Egypt, India, China and Japan and collecting various art works.

In 1865 Duret met Manet in Madrid and in his first book *Les Peintres français en 1867* (1867) wrote rather critically of his style, calling it 'too rapid and too hasty'. Nonetheless they became friends, and he soon came to admire Manet's work. Duret founded the Republican newspaper *La Tribune française*, with Emile Zola and others, in 1868, and in the same year Manet painted his portrait (Paris, Petit Pal.). In his first Salon review of 1870, published in *L'Electeur libre*, Duret defended the work of Manet, Camille Pissarro, Degas and others and began to develop an Impressionist aesthetic. He was involved in the Commune of 1871 and narrowly escaped execution, after which he embarked on an extended visit to Asia with his friend Henri Cernuschi. This confirmed his passion for Oriental art, and he was later instrumental in creating public awareness of it in France.

Duret returned to France in 1872 and gave up both politics and business to devote himself to art and literature. He had soon met all the Impressionist artists and supported many of them, either through his own purchases or by his efforts to gain buyers on their behalf. In 1878 he published *Histoire des peintres impressionnistes*, an important work describing the development of Impressionism, with individual chapters devoted to its major exponents. A collection of articles and essays appeared in 1885 as *Critique d'avant-garde*, covering the work of artists as diverse as Manet, Reynolds, Gainsborough, Whistler and Richard Wagner and the philosopher Arthur Schopenhauer as well as Japanese art. On a visit to London in 1883 he met Lucien Pissarro and Whistler.

Financial difficulties at Duret et De Brie in 1894 forced Duret to sell his collection of paintings, which included such works as the *Port of Bordeaux* (1871; Paris, Mus. d'Orsay) by Manet and *The Turkeys* (1876; Zurich, Stift. Samml. Bührle) by Monet, as well as others by Degas, Paul Cézanne, Alfred Sisley and Auguste Renoir. In 1900 he donated a number of Japanese prints to the Bibliothèque Nationale in Paris and also donated works to the Musée de la Ville de Paris, including Manet's portrait of him, and to the Musée Cernuschi. In later life Duret became a renowned expert on Impressionism, while continuing his writings on art.

WRITINGS
Les Peintres français en 1867 (Paris, 1867)
Histoire des peintres impressionnistes (Paris, 1878, rev. 2/1906)
L'Art japonais (Paris, 1882)
Critique d'avant-garde (Paris, 1885) [incl. 1870 Salon review]
Histoire de J. M. N. Whistler (Paris, 1904)

BIBLIOGRAPHY
DBF
J. Rewald: *The History of Impressionism* (London, 1946)
S. Monneret: *Impressionnisme et son époque*, 4 vols (Paris, 1978)

Durfort, Louise-Jeanne de, Duchesse de Mazarin. *See* MAZARIN, (2).

Durham [Lat. Dunelmum]. Cathedral and university city and the county town of Durham, in north-east England. In *c.* AD 995 Bishop Aldhun of Chester-le-Street and his clergy took refuge on a craggy rock almost surrounded by the River Wear, together with their principal treasure, the incorrupt body of their patron saint, Cuthbert. Durham thus became both a bishop's seat and a place of pilgrimage. Traditionally the site had previously been unoccupied, but its natural defences probably already contained a major secular stronghold, and stray finds of Roman pottery hint at earlier occupation. During the 12th and 13th centuries the bishops acquired extensive secular powers over the surrounding region, enhancing the city's administrative importance, while its location near the Scottish border reinforced its strategic significance.

The city's topography and principal stone structures were all essentially created in the century following the Norman Conquest in 1066, obliterating in the process all visible traces of the Anglo-Saxon cathedral and settlement. The famous Romanesque cathedral (*see* §1 below), with its adjacent monastic buildings, forms an enclave within the outer defences of the castle, the bishop's principal residence, which guards the neck of the peninsula to the north. Despite subsequent reconstructions the castle retains unusually complete Romanesque palatial accommodation dating from *c.* 1080 to *c.* 1170, including the early chapel (*see* §2 below). It now houses a college of the university, founded in 1832. The city, always modest in size, centres round the market-place below the castle to the north. Its medieval street plan is largely intact, although the aspect of the town is now predominantly Georgian,

many of the earlier timber-framed houses having been refronted in the 18th and 19th centuries. It is linked to an outer ring of suburbs by two bridges; unusually, one of these, Elvet Bridge, retains much of its original 12th-century fabric.

ERIC CAMBRIDGE

1. Cathedral. 2. Castle chapel.

1. CATHEDRAL. The fortunes of Durham Cathedral were closely tied to the cult of St Cuthbert (*d* 687). By the time the remains of the saint were brought to Durham, the congregation that served his shrine was no longer monastic, and the 11th-century monastic revival did not reach the north of England until after the Norman Conquest (1066). In 1083 a Benedictine community was finally established at Durham, but the cathedral itself was not started until 1093 when Bishop William of St Calais (*reg* 1081–96) returned from exile in Normandy. Progress seems to have been rapid. St Cuthbert's remains were translated into the new choir in 1104, which was presumably vaulted and ready to receive him. The nave vaults were started in 1128 and finished by 1133. By then the church must have been complete apart from the upper parts of the west towers.

Work continued on the monastic apartments until well into the second half of the 12th century. The Galilee Chapel attached to the west front was the contribution of Bishop Hugh of Le Puiset. By 1235 the choir vaults were threatening to collapse on to St Cuthbert's shrine, and they had to be replaced. At the same time a second transept, the chapel of the Nine Altars, was added at the east end. The nature of the site prevented any further extension eastward, so the transept became in effect a retrochoir and reliquary chapel for St Cuthbert as well as a setting for subsidiary altars. These works, which continued until *c.* 1278, were the only major additions to the Norman church. The central tower, which was destroyed during a storm in 1429, was replaced between 1470 and 1476. The belfry stage, the only part of the cathedral that can be seen above the surrounding hills, dates from 1484–94. The internal length of the existing building is 140.5 m, and it is built of sandstone.

(i) Architecture. (ii) Sculpture.

(i) Architecture.

(a) The Anglo-Norman church. In plan Durham was a large monastic church of the so-called Benedictine type, that is, with three parallel apses at the east end but no ambulatory. The choir was four bays long, as opposed to the normal Norman arrangement of two, and can be regarded as the first step towards the use of long eastern limbs as a standard feature of English great churches. The nave comprises three double bays, with an odd single bay at the west end. The elevation is three-storey, but the proportions of the storeys were unusual for their time, the main arcade being almost as high as the gallery and clerestory combined. This emphasis on the arcades is largely responsible for the powerful impression made by the interior.

Durham Cathedral has always been an impressive sight, but when it was built it was on the edge of outer darkness, and it remains a mystery why such an outstanding monument should have been erected there at such a time. Great claims to historical importance have been made on its behalf, largely owing to its reputation as the first church to be rib-vaulted throughout.

In the early 20th century architectural historians began to question the claim, axiomatic since the days of Viollet-le-Duc, that ribbed vaulting began in France. Arthur Kingsley Porter thought it began in Lombardy, German scholars mentioned Speyer Cathedral, and John Bilson argued the case for Durham. The issue was considered important because, while the French claim was disputed, Viollet-le-Duc's main contention that ribbed vaults were different from all other kinds of vault and were the special invention of the Middle Ages was not. It was subsequently recognized that the argument was based on a misconception, and it is no longer a burning issue.

Bilson directed attention to Durham's rib vaults, somewhat at the expense of its other features, but he was right that this is where the historical importance of the building lies. The question of primacy, however, is less significant than what Durham reveals about the origins of medieval vaulting. Bilson made two assumptions, one taken for granted, the other strenuously argued. The former was that the original high vaults of the choir resembled the other Romanesque high vaults, which were later, rather than the contemporary choir aisle vaults. The second was that from the start both the nave and the choir were intended to be vaulted. On this latter point he has been proved wrong. In 1954 Bony showed that the original project was for a vaulted choir only. The decision to vault the nave was taken much later, perhaps not long before the vaults were built. Durham was, therefore, not as precocious a building as Bilson thought. Apart from the novelty of ribs, it was not fundamentally different from other late 11th-century churches with vaulted choirs.

Bilson's supposition concerning the high vaults was not unreasonable; even Bony did not question it, although his interpretation of the building history makes better sense if all the vaults of the first campaign shared a common form. The features that appeared to settle the argument in favour of Bilson, however, the supporting shafts in the middle of each double bay of the choir at triforium level, are compatible with more than one theory. The marks left on the clerestory wall by the first vaults are inconclusive. Outside, there is no buttress on the clerestory wall where one might be expected if Bilson were right. There is also the intriguing fact that of the ten vault compartments in the eastern limb (i.e. the eight aisle bays and the two double bays of the choir), seven are based on recognizable mathematical ratios. (The three exceptions were modified by the transepts and the tower.) There are grounds here for concluding that there was a common plan shape, and from this it can be inferred that the ribs also shared the same shape. On this reading the first high vaults of the choir (those of *c.* 1104) were elongated quadripartites, as in the aisles (see fig. 1), and the shafts at triforium level supported not ribs but an extra diaphragm arch of the kind used later in the nave of La Trinité Abbey at Caen.

The most distinctive aspect of the choir aisle vaults is their shallow segmental curve. They were the last part of the plan to be considered, and they were fitted into spatial

1. Durham Cathedral, north aisle of the choir looking east, before 1104

compartments that made no concessions to their efficient functioning as vaults but were designed in purely abstract geometrical terms, with perhaps an overall aesthetic effect in mind. If this interpretation is correct it goes a long way to explain the unsatisfactory behaviour of the large-scale high vaults, in contrast with those that survived. The only evidence in the choir of insight into the mechanical problems of vaulting is an instinctive, rudimentary sense of buttressing being essentially a matter of weight.

The choir of Durham belongs to the fumbling, experimental stage of medieval vaulting. Progress came swiftly. The segmental arcs of the choir had already disappeared in the transepts. In the nave there are even pointed arches (see fig. 2). These, and the quadrant buttresses under the gallery roofs, which look like flying buttresses, really seem to resemble Early Gothic churches in France, although they do not make Durham Gothic. Perhaps there was a Frenchman at Durham in 1128 to advise on their construction. They exercised singularly little influence in England; even the Romanesque nave vaults (destr.) of Lincoln Cathedral, which are supposed to have been inspired by the example of Durham, may have preceded them.

The static, crowning effect that the original vaults would have imparted to the choir must have been quite different from the receding vista of the nave. Although the nave vaults were an afterthought, there was nothing discordant about them. They filled the spaces between the massive diaphragm arches, which were intended to separate the double bays, and rounded off the already majestic prospect.

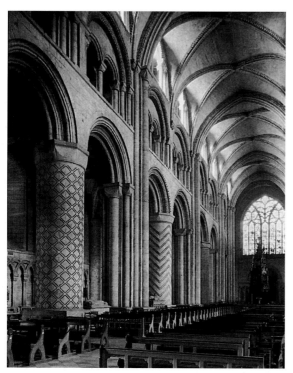

2. Durham Cathedral, interior of the nave looking west, vaulted 1128–33

There is a simple but unanswerable logic about concentrating the strength of the supports where it matters, that is, at the bottom of the walls in the main arcades, and tapering the elevation upward through the diminishing wall of the superimposed storeys, on the principle of the tree trunk or the lighthouse. The distribution of pattern is masterly. The incised spirals, flutes and diamonds on the cylindrical piers cover surfaces that might otherwise be monotonous, while the mouldings, shafts and chevron ornament play off linear delicacy against sheer bulk. It is predominantly an aesthetic of volumes and monumentality; but, despite its apparent success, the design had no future. Durham was exactly contemporary with the second choir of Canterbury Cathedral (see CANTERBURY, §III, 1), which was prepared to relinquish vaults for the sake of light and colour; and it was followed within a few years by Saint-Denis Abbey (see SAINT-DENIS ABBEY, §I, 1), which managed to have vaults without mass, and light and colour as well. These were the buildings that shaped the future of architecture in England and France. If any notice were taken of Durham, it was as an example of what could be done with chevron ornament.

(b) The Galilee Chapel and chapel of the Nine Altars. Le Puiset's Galilee Chapel is the only one of its kind in both form and structure: a single-storey hall with five aisles, entered from the church. If it had been vaulted it would have resembled a displaced retrochoir, and it was intended to serve as the Lady chapel that St Cuthbert allegedly would not tolerate at the east end. Its extreme simplicity is somewhat offset by heavy encrustations of chevron

ornament and the Purbeck marble shafting of the quatrefoil piers (for illustration *see* GALILEE).

The chapel of the Nine Altars stands on a terrace well below the floor level of the rest of the cathedral, and the elevation is therefore higher. Massive elements were unavoidable, but these were turned to advantage, being treated as a giant order. It is a halllike structure, with arcaded dado, tall lancets and a clerestory, all decorated with marble, dogtooth and stiff-leaf foliage. There are two spectacular windows, a French-style rose (completely restored) and a geometrical composition with double tracery that entirely fills the north wall. Grafting the Nine Altars on to the rest of the building produced some lopsided bays. These inspired vault patterns, which are positively breathtaking, both in their eccentricity and their beauty.

It would have been an appropriate compensation if the remoteness and isolation of Durham had protected it from the zeal of restorers and ecclesiologists, but it came in for more than its fair share of attention from both. James Wyatt's restoration at the end of the 18th century was particularly notorious, although it served, as nothing else did, to put Durham firmly where it belongs on the map of architectural history.

BIBLIOGRAPHY
R. Billings: *Architectural Illustrations and Description of the Cathedral at Durham* (London, 1843)
J. Bilson: 'Durham Cathedral: The Chronology of its Vaults', *Archaeol. J.*, lxxix (1922), pp. 101–60
J. Bony: 'Le Projet premier de Durham: Voûtement partiel ou voûtement total?', *Urbanisme et architecture: Etudes écrites et publiées en l'honneur de Pierre Lavedan* (Paris, 1954), pp. 41–9
E. Fernie: 'The Spiral Piers of Durham Cathedral', *British Archaeological Association Conference Transactions*: *Medieval Art and Architecture at Durham Cathedral: Durham, 1977*, pp. 49–58
J. Bony: 'Durham et la tradition saxonne', *Etudes d'art médiéval offertes à Louis Grodecki* (Paris, 1981), pp. 79–92
S. Gardner: 'The Nave Galleries of Durham Cathedral', *A. Bull.*, lxiv/4 (1982), pp. 564–79

PETER KIDSON

(ii) Sculpture. The earliest Romanesque figurative sculptures in the cathedral are the corbel masks (*c.* 1110–25) supporting the high vault ribs on the west wall of the transepts and throughout the nave. They had considerable influence on British Romanesque architecture (e.g. St Cuthbert's, Dalmeny (Lothian), and Lincoln Cathedral), and the motif also occurs in France at, for instance, St-Denis Abbey and Sens Cathedral.

The inner faces of the north and south doorways in the sixth bay of the nave preserve some of the most delicate English sculpture of the 1130s. Chevron and lozenges decorate the shafts on the south, while the inner shafts on the north have figures and beasts in foliage medallions, a motif used in the 1120s at Reading Abbey (Berks). The cushion capitals of both doorways have symmetrical foliage and figurative sculptures, which ultimately derive from Canterbury Cathedral crypt, although the Durham carving is not strictly bound by the geometry of the capital. Rich chevron encrusts the arches of both doorways and also those of the west door of the nave, and in all three the hood-mouldings are dotted with roundels containing figures, beasts and foliage. The same sculptors worked on the chapter house doorway, and similar capitals are used above the caryatids that formerly supported the ribs of the apse vault in the chapter house (1133–40; now set on the north wall). The caryatids suggest a link with north Italian sculpture, perhaps transmitted through an intermediary in Germany or the Netherlands. A weathered, tall rectangular block carved in shallow relief with two bishops probably came from the cloister in the tradition of the cloister reliefs at ST PIERRE, MOISSAC.

Two reliefs, one with the *Transfiguration,* the other with *Noli me tangere* and *Christ's Appearance to Two Marys,* survive from the former choir-screen described in the *Rites of Durham* of 1593 (ed. J. T. Fowler, *Surtees Soc.,* cvii, 1902), which mentions images of 16 kings who were benefactors of Durham and 16 bishops, the last of whom was Hugh of Le Puiset, who probably inaugurated this work shortly after he became bishop in 1153. The panels were executed by two sculptors working in the curvilinear damp-fold tradition derived from Byzantine art, and parallels have been drawn to the Winchester Psalter (London, BL, MS. Cotton Nero D IV); Le Puiset was Archdeacon of Winchester before moving to Durham.

Later sculpture includes the tomb and throne of *Bishop Hatfield (d 1381),* made after 1362, in a northern style of Perpendicular that still relies on abundant use of the ogee arch. The heavy foliage of the lower levels contrasts with the screens and canopies above. The Neville screen, which separates the shrine area from the high altar, was made in London between 1372 and 1376. It is a low wall of Caen stone, surmounted by tiered housings for statues (destr.), and two doors in the wall at either side of the altar give access to the shrine. The attribution to Henry Yevele is uncertain, but the sharp, light effects are generally those of London work.

BIBLIOGRAPHY

F. Saxl: *Early Sculptures of the Twelfth Century,* ed. H. Swarzenski (London, 1954)

C. Wilson: 'The Neville Screen', *British Archaeological Association Conference Transactions: Medieval Art and Architecture at Durham Cathedral: Durham, 1977,* pp. 90–104

English Romanesque Art, 1066–1200 (exh. cat., ed. G. Zarnecki; London, Hayward Gal., 1984), pp. 188–9, cat. 154a and b

2. CASTLE CHAPEL. Durham Castle was founded by King William I in 1072, and the chapel probably dates from this time, although the fact that it abuts an earlier wall may suggest that it was an addition to the original fabric. Unmoulded arches carried on columns with volute capitals divide the chapel into a nave and aisles of seven bays each, groin-vaulted at the same height. The capitals, which have been called the 'richest series of early Anglo-Norman sculpture' (Zarnecki, 1951), are carved with angle volutes and symmetrically placed motifs including masks, chip-carved stars, beasts and stylized leaves. In one case heads of angle-set atlas figures are substitutes for the volutes; in another lions' heads meet at the angle. There is even a historiated capital with a nimbed figure, perhaps representing St Eustace, leading a horse and hounds towards a stag, which is derived from a hunting scene in St Gervais at Falaise, Normandy. The other capitals also depend on Norman prototypes and in turn on Burgundian models at St Benigne, Dijon, and Vignory Priory.

BIBLIOGRAPHY

G. Baldwin Brown: 'Saxon and Norman Sculpture in Durham', *Antiquity,* v (1933), pp. 438–40

G. Zarnecki: *English Romanesque Sculpture, 1066–1140* (London, 1951)

——: '1066 and Architectural Sculpture', *Proc. Brit. Acad.,* lii (1966), pp. 87–104

MALCOLM THURLBY

Durham, Joseph (*b* London, 1814; *d* London, 27 Oct 1877). English sculptor. He was apprenticed to the sculptor John F. Francis and later worked under E. H. Baily. Between 1835 and 1878 he exhibited 128 works at the Royal Academy. He was elected ARA in 1868. Durham first attracted popular attention with his marble bust of *Jenny Lind* (exh. RA 1847; London, Royal Coll. Music), which was widely reproduced in porcelain by the Copeland factory. His most important commission was the *Memorial to the Great Exhibition of 1851* (1863; London, Royal Albert Hall), which consists of a fountain surmounted by a bronze statue of Prince Albert and four figures representing the corners of the world. Durham's other commemorative works include marble statues of *Euclid* and of *George Stephenson* (both 1867; Oxford, U. Mus.) and those of *Jeremy Bentham, William Harvey, John Milton* and *Isaac Newton* (all 1869; London, RA, rear façade). He also produced numerous portrait busts, such as those of *Sir George Pollock* (marble, 1870; London, N.P.G.) and *Hogarth* (stone, 1875; London, Leicester Sq.).

Durham is perhaps best known for genre sculptures such as *At the Spring* [*Early Morn*] (1865; marble version, 1867, Blackburn, Town Hall), *Waiting for his Innings* (marble, 1866; London, Guildhall A.G.) and *The Picture Book* (marble, 1867; Macclesfield, Town Hall). These works are both portraits of sitters, usually the children of patrons, and idealized and timeless sculptures, charming without being sentimental. Durham's use of contour is always sensitive and his finish consistently careful.

BIBLIOGRAPHY

Gunnis; Thieme–Becker

B. Read: *Victorian Sculpture* (London, 1982), pp. 209–10, 212

MARK STOCKER

Dur-Katlimmu. *See* SHEIKH HAMMAD, TELL.

Dur Kurigalzu. *See* AQAR QUF.

Durlacher. English family of art dealers. George L. Durlacher (*b* ?1856; *d* London, 19 Aug 1942) was the son of Henry Durlacher, who in 1843 founded the family firm of art dealers in Bond Street, London. After his father's death, George and his brother Alfred Durlacher took over the running of the firm, which remained in business until a few years before George's death; their clientele included some of the most notable art collectors of the day, among them Richard Seymour-Conway, 4th Marquess of Hertford, the diplomat Henry Bulwer (1801–72) and the American banker J. Pierpont Morgan. One of the Durlachers' most regular clients was Sir Richard Wallace, whose purchases from them included, in 1874, the French wax busts of the *Duc de Guise* and *Duchesse de Guise* and the Italian wax bust of *Lucrezia Borgia* (all London, Wallace).

The Durlachers were associated particularly with *objets d'art* but also dealt in Old Master paintings, especially in the years after World War I, when the Vicomte Bernard d'Hendecourt had become a member of the firm. George Durlacher himself was respected as a connoisseur of fine judgement and a charming and hospitable man; a record of the firm's activities that he compiled in later life was privately published in 1928.

BIBLIOGRAPHY

F. Lugt: *Ventes* (1938–64), ii (1953); iii (1964)
Obituary, *Burl. Mag.*, lxxxi (1942), p. 259

JANET SOUTHORN

Durm, Josef (*b* Karlsruhe, 14 Feb 1837; *d* Karlsruhe, 3 April 1919). German architect and teacher. His preference for the Renaissance Revival style was apparent from his student days at the Karlsruhe Technische Hochschule and was influenced by the writings of Jacob Burckhardt and Gottfried Semper. Graduating in 1860, he was immediately given a post working for the Grand Duchy of Baden. In 1867 he argued in print in favour of a study of the Italian Renaissance as the basis for a proper architectural training, and the following year he was appointed professor at the Technische Hochschule. At about this time he designed the Vierordtbad (opened 1873) in the Italian Renaissance style in KARLSRUHE. As a large, secular, public building, it typified Durm's later commissions, which included about 30 buildings for the Grand Duchy. As the most senior officer in the building administration of Baden (1887–1902), architect of its most important buildings and a university professor (1868–1919), he was a dominant influence on the architecture of Baden. The style of monumental historicism that he originated, drawing on the idioms of the Italian, German, French and Netherlandish Renaissance, typifies late 19th-century German taste for display. His work includes the Städtische Festhalle (1875–7) with its colossal exedra, his most important early work, and the Baroque Revival Erbgrossherzogliches Palais (1892–7), both in Karlsruhe; also the University Library (1901–5) at Heidelberg and his most important late work, the headquarters of the Oberrheinische Versicherungsgesellschaft (1908–11) in Mannheim, which shows an astonishing adaptation to modernist styles. Durm's residential work included some of the grandest villas in Karlsruhe, such as the Prinz-Max-Palais (1881–4; now the Städtische Galerie). He built few churches, although St Johann in der Wiehre (1894–9) in Freiburg is an outstanding example of the late historicist Romanesque Revival. Durm's influence outside Baden and his great versatility are documented by numerous important publications such as the *Handbuch der Architektur*, which he co-founded (1881), and the inventory of Baden's secular monuments directed by him from 1886.

BIBLIOGRAPHY

U. Grammbitter: *Josef Durm, 1837–1919: Eine Einführung in das architektonische Werk* (Munich, 1984)
U. Grammbitter and R. Ostermann: 'Historistische Architektur in Karlsruhe', *Gründerzeit-Adolf Loos* (exh. cat., ed. E. Rödiger-Diruf and S. Bieber; Karlsruhe, Städt. Gal. Prinz-Max-Pal., 1987), pp. 89ff
E. Koch: 'Oberbaudirektor Professor Dr. Josef Durm, 1837–1919', *Baden. Heimat* (June 1987), pp. 288ff

JULIUS FEKETE

Dürner, Hans (*b* Granheim; *fl* Biberach an der Riss, 1583; *d* Ellwangen, nr Biberach, 7 June 1613). German wood-carver. His only securely attributed work is the richly carved ceiling (*c*. 1590) of the chapel of Schloss Heiligenberg, ornamented with figures and heads of angels.

He is also attributed with an altarpiece of a Trinity group with male saints and angels (?1613; Ellwangen, St Vitus). Its carved ornamentation is identified with that of a high altar mentioned in a document of 1613, which states that Dürner was prevented from finishing it by his death. Carvings from the region of Biberach (of which he became a citizen on 12 November 1583), in particular depictions of female saints and the Virgin, are linked with Dürner through their stylistic resemblance to the Ellwangen figures. The rather conventional idiom shown in all these works identifies him as a prime exponent of the traditional tendency of Upper Swabian wood-carving that only hesitantly assimilated contemporary Italian elements.

BIBLIOGRAPHY

A. Schahl: 'Beiträge zur Plastik des Manierismus in Oberschwaben', *Das Münster*, xiv (1961), pp. 361–7
V. Himmelein: 'Skulpturen', *Die Renaissance im deutschen Südwesten*, ii (exh. cat., Heidelberg, Schloss, 1986), p. 565

ELISABETH GUROCK

Dürr. *See* DIRR.

Durra, Muhanna [Durra Muḥanna] (*b* Amman, 1938). Jordanian painter. He was the first Jordanian artist to be sent on a government scholarship to the Accademia di Belle Arti in Rome (1955–8). From 1959 to 1960 he taught history of art at the Teachers Training College in Amman, and from 1960 to 1970 he was press attaché at the Jordanian Embassy in Rome. In 1971 he was appointed director of the Department of Culture and Arts in Amman and, upon his suggestion, the department established the Institute of Music and Arts under his directorship. This was the first institution in Jordan to offer formal training in art. In 1977 Durra received the State Appreciation Award for his contribution to cultural development, and in 1983 he became ambassador in the Arab League and was posted successively to Tunis, Rome, Cairo and Moscow. A prolific artist, he cultivated a distinctive style early in his career. His expressive monochrome portraits and fractured landscapes reveal an ability to manipulate colour, tonality and the distribution of masses (e.g. untitled; 1977; Amman, N.G. F.A.), while his China ink drawings show skill and dexterity (e.g. *Circassian Dancers*, 1982; Amman, N.G. F.A.). Durra trained a number of young artists in his studio and at the Institute, being the only local painter to cultivate his students. He was the first artist to introduce abstraction, Cubism and Expressionism into the mainstream of Jordanian art.

BIBLIOGRAPHY

W. Ali: *A Survey of Modern Painting in the Islamic World and the Development of the Contemporary Calligraphic School* (diss., U. London, SOAS, 1993)

W. ALI

Durrës [Durrazzo]. *See* DYRRHACHION.

Durrie, George Henry (*b* Hartford, CT, 6 June 1820; *d* New Haven, CT, 15 Oct 1863). American painter. Durrie and his older brother John (1818–98) studied sporadically from 1839 to 1841 with the portrait painter Nathaniel Jocelyn. From 1840 to 1842 he was an itinerant painter in Connecticut and New Jersey, finally settling permanently in New Haven. He produced *c*. 300 paintings, of which the earliest were portraits (e.g. *Self-portrait*, 1839; Shelburne, VT, Mus.); by the early 1850s he had begun to paint the rural genre scenes and winter landscapes of New England that are considered his finest achievement. His landscapes, for example *A Christmas Party* (1852; Tulsa, OK, Gilcrease Inst. Amer. Hist. & A.), are characterized by the use of pale though cheerful colours and by the repeated use of certain motifs: an isolated farmhouse, a road placed diagonally leading the eye into the composition, and a hill (usually the West or East Rocks, New Haven) in the distance. By the late 1850s Durrie's reputation had started to grow, and he was exhibiting at prestigious institutions, such as the National Academy of Design. In 1861 the firm of Currier & Ives helped popularize his work by publishing prints of two of his winter landscapes, *New England Winter Scene* (1858; Mr and Mrs Peter Frelinghuysen Carleton priv. col.) and the *Farmyard in Winter* (untraced). Two more were published in 1863 and a further six after his death.

BIBLIOGRAPHY
George Henry Durrie, 1820–1863 (exh. cat. by M. B. Cowdrey, Hartford, CT, Wadsworth Atheneum, 1947)
M. Y. Hutson: *George Henry Durrie (1820–1863): American Winter Landscape: Revived through Currier and Ives* (Santa Barbara, 1977)
ANNE R. MORAND

Durrieu, Paul, Comte (*b* Strasbourg, 2 Oct 1855; *d* Grenade sur l'Adour, 25 Nov 1925). French art historian. At the Ecole des Chartes in Paris Durrieu learnt the methodology of studying history using documents. In 1879, a year after leaving the Ecole des Chartes, he left for the Ecole Française de Rome, where he studied Italian art and had access to the Angevin archives in Naples (Naples, Archv Stato). On his return to Paris he was given responsibility for conservation at the Louvre, which allowed him direct contact with works of art, especially French medieval painting. Thanks to his discriminating taste the Louvre collections were enriched with works by Gerard David, Nicolas Froment, Jean Fouquet and Jan Breughel the elder.

Encouraged by Léopold Delisle, Durrieu began to explore the neglected field of illuminated manuscripts. He helped to promote the *Primitifs français* exhibition at the Louvre and Bibliothèque Nationale in 1904. His published work includes the first serious overview of French Gothic painting, published in André Michel's *Histoire de l'art* (1905–29), a work (1904) on the Très Riches Heures (Chantilly, Mus. Condé, MS. 65) of Jean, Duc de Berry, and several important studies on Jean Fouquet (1907–8). The publication of the Turin Hours (Turin, Bib. N.U., MS. K.IV.29; *see* TURIN–MILAN HOURS) before its destruction in 1904, as well as numerous other works, all remain the foundation of modern research.

Durrieu left the Louvre in 1902 to concentrate on the studies that form the basis of subsequent knowledge of late medieval art. His combination of a historian's scrutiny of documents with a sophisticated analysis of the individual nature of the works and an insistence on studying the original works of art laid the basis for the future study of medieval art. On his death his friend A. de Laborde collected together 640 publications that continue to be influential.

WRITINGS
Les Très Riches Heures de Jean de France, duc de Berry (Paris, 1904)
La Peinture à l'exposition des Primitifs français (Paris, 1904)
'La peinture en France de Jean le Bon à la mort de Charles V', *Histoire de l'art des premiers temps chrétiens jusqu'à nos jours*, ed. A. Michel, iii/1 (Paris, 1907), pp. 101–71
Les Antiquités judaïques et le peintre Jean Fouquet (Paris, 1908)

BIBLIOGRAPHY
A. de Laborde: *Le Comte Paul Durrieu, membre de l'Institut: Sa Vie, ses travaux* (Paris, 1930)
CLAUDE SCHAEFER

Dürrnberg [Dürrnberg bei Hallein]. Site of an Iron Age salt-mining centre *c.* 20 km south of Salzburg in Austria, on the border with Germany (*see also* PREHISTORIC EUROPE, §VI). Set in the foothills of the Alps, the site borders the valley of the Salzach River on what was a major north–south trade route from the Early Iron Age until the Middle Ages. It was occupied without apparent interruption from *c.* 600 BC to Roman times, and it is one of the rare sites where both cemeteries and settlement areas have been found and excavated. Prehistoric corpses were first discovered in the salt mines in 1573. After World War II the pace of scientific excavation increased, noticeably accelerating when a new road necessitated major rescue excavations in 1978–82. Seven uncalibrated radiocarbon dates obtained from the site span the period 720±80 BC to AD 60±90. Dürrnberg is one of the richest sites for finds of CELTIC ART, not so much in terms of precious metals, as is the case in the German sites of the Hunsrück-Eifel, but in the sheer range and quantity of fine artefacts in both metalwork and pottery. To date over 300 graves have been excavated, mostly spanning the late Hallstatt and early La Tène periods, together with settlement and workshop material of local manufacture. The richest finds include a large quantity of Early La Tène-style fibulae (brooches), a fine Early La Tène-style bronze flagon from grave 112 (Salzburg, Mus. Carolino Augusteum), and a bronze pilgrim flask and fittings for a wooden flagon in the chariot burial in grave 44/2; the latter also contained a pointed helmet, an imported Etruscan situla (wine bucket) and an Attic cup dated to *c.* 470 BC. Examples of the Waldalgesheim style and Plastic style of Celtic art found at the site include a gold finger-ring from grave 28/2, flagon mounts from grave 46/2 and an iron sword-scabbard decorated with a dragon-pair from grave 102 (all Hallein, Keltenmus.).

BIBLIOGRAPHY
E. Penninger: *Der Dürrnberg bei Hallein: I*, Münchner Beiträge zur Vor- und Frühgeschichte, xvi (Munich, 1972)
F. Moosleitner, L. Pauli and E. Penninger: *Der Dürrnberg bei Hallein: II*, Münchner Beiträge zur Vor- und Frühgeschichte, xvii (Munich, 1974)
L. Pauli: *Der Dürrnberg bei Hallein: III*, 2 vols, Münchner Beiträge zur Vor- und Frühgeschichte, xviii (Munich, 1978)
F. Moosleitner: *Die Schnabelkanne vom Dürrnberg: Ein Meisterwerk keltischer Handwerkskunst*, Schriftreihe des Salzburger Museums, Carolino Augusteum, vii (Salzburg, 1985)
Arte protoceltica a Salisburgo: Mostra della regione di Salisburgo (exh. cat., ed. F. Moosleitner; Florence, Pitti, 1987)
J. V. S. MEGAW, M. RUTH MEGAW

Dur-Sharrukin. *See* KHORSABAD.

Dur-Untash. *See* CHOGHA ZANBIL.

Du Ry. Franco-German family of architects, of French origin. The founder of the family was (1) Charles Du Ry, who was related to Salomon de Brosse. He worked for de Brosse and also independently on various civic and domestic buildings in Paris. His grandson, (2) Paul Du Ry, moved to Kassel, Germany, in 1685 and was responsible for many town planning and architectural projects in and around the city (*see* KASSEL, §1). His son, (3) Charles Louis Du Ry, was essentially his father's follower, continuing the latter's projects. The most important member of the family was Charles Louis's son, (4) Simon Louis Du Ry, whose work left a deep imprint on Kassel. Although most of his buildings have been destroyed, some as a result of the war damage of 1943, the layout of the area around the now vanished Old Town, with its sequence of squares, streets and prestigious buildings, is based on his ideas.

BIBLIOGRAPHY

Macmillan Enc. Architects; Thieme–Becker; Wasmuth

G. W. C. G. Casparson: 'Die Baumeisterfamilie Du Ry zu Kassel', *Hessische Denkwürdigkeiten*, ii (Kassel, 1800), pp. 255–87

O. Gerland: *Paul, Charles und Simon Louis du Ry: Eine Künstlerfamilie der Barockzeit* (Stuttgart, 1895)

A. Holtmeyer: *Bau- und Kunstdenkmäler im Regierungsbezirk Cassel*, iv (Marburg, 1923)

(1) Charles Du Ry (*b* Argentan, before 1568; *d* after 1638). He was related through his wife, Camille Métivier, to Salomon de Brosse, for whom he carried out work at the château of Blérancourt, Aisne (1612), the château of Coulommiers, near Meaux (1613), and, after de Brosse's death, at the Hôtel de Bullion, Paris (1633; all destr.). He participated in the development of the area of Paris known as the Fossés Jaunes (1611–34) and collaborated in the enlargement of the Porte St-Honoré (1611–12) and the building of the Porte Montmartre (1622). He was in charge of the construction of new walls for Paris and of the Porte Richelieu (1631–4; 1634–7) and was involved on his own account in building new houses in the Rue du Mail. In 1638 he provided plans for garden pavilions at the Palais Cardinal (later Palais Royal) in Paris.

At Coulommiers, Du Ry built the Capuchin church (1617), his only known surviving work. It is an unremarkable building, but it contains a set of plaster reliefs, one showing the château, which may be connected with him. Although he was not the official architect of the château, Du Ry was in charge there from 1613 to 1631 and in de Brosse's continual absence was probably responsible for the rather pedestrian modifications made to the first design before 1630. He is probably the author of all or some of the drawings in an album once owned by de Brosse and several times inscribed as belonging to Du Ry. The album (Paris, Louvre) contains several drawings of Coulommiers, made after de Brosse's death in 1626. If the drawings are by Du Ry, they show him as a skilful but not particularly original designer of decorative features such as doors and chimney-pieces.

BIBLIOGRAPHY

A. Dauvergne: 'Notice sur le château-neuf et l'église des Capucins de Coulommiers (Seine-et-Marne)', *Bull. Mnmtl.*, n. s., ix (1853–4), pp. 597–629

H. Derottleur: *Le Château neuf de Coulommiers, 1613–1738* (diss., U. Paris, 1959)

J.-P. Babelon: *Demeures parisiennes sous Henri IV et Louis XIII* (Paris, 1965)

R. Coope: *Salomon de Brosse* (London, 1972)

ROSALYS COOPE

(2) Paul Du Ry (*b* Paris, 1640; *d* Kassel, 21 June 1714). Grandson of (1) Charles Du Ry. He was the son of the Parisian court architect Mathurin Du Ry and a pupil of François Blondel. Anti-Calvinist persecution under Louis IX caused him to emigrate to the Netherlands, where he built fortifications at Maastricht. In 1685 Charles, Landgrave of Hesse-Kassel, summoned Du Ry to Kassel to organize the settlement of those Huguenots who had arrived in the landgraviate. Du Ry planned the layout of the villages of Carlsdorf (1686), Mariendorf (1687) and Schönberg (1699), north of Kassel, as well as Oberneustadt (from 1688) within Kassel. These towns and villages have a rigidly mathematical street grid; the architecture of the towns is in a simple Classical Baroque style. The layout of Oberneustadt is Paul Du Ry's most important work, and in it stands his most significant building, the Karlskirche (1698–1710), which was the central place of worship for the Huguenots of Hesse-Kassel. Built on an elongated octagonal ground-plan, the church has a simple centralized structure with a polygonal dome and lantern and a sober interior with pews arranged as in an amphitheatre. This outstanding example of Protestant churchbuilding in Germany is more in the tradition of Dutch than of French Classical Baroque. The Karlskirche was rebuilt in heavily modified form after its destruction in 1943. Du Ry built a number of town houses and palaces in Kassel, almost all of which have been destroyed. They were distinguished by their scant use of ornamentation, subtle proportions, solidity and utility. An idea of his work can be gained from the town of Karlshafen (from 1699), which has been preserved intact; although Du Ry's authorship of the architecture is not proven, it is built in his formal style.

BIBLIOGRAPHY

A. Heussner: 'Die französische Kolonie in Cassel', *Geschbl. Dt. Hugenotten-Ver.*, xii/2–3 (1903)

R. Schmidtmann: 'Die Kolonie der Réfugiés in Hessen-Kassel', *Z. Ver. Hess. Gesch. & Landesknd.*, lvii (1929)

H.-Ch. Dittscheid: *Kassel-Wilhelmshöhe und die Krise des Schlossbaues am Ende des Ancien Régime* (Worms, 1987)

(3) Charles Louis Du Ry (*b* Kassel, 26 Feb 1692; *d* Kassel, 28 March 1757). Son of (2) Paul Du Ry. He trained under his father and, following the latter's death, took over his work when only 23. He directed continuing work on the building of Oberneustadt (begun 1688) in Kassel in the idiom of his father. This area has now been totally destroyed, and nothing of his work survives. His own house, 9 Karlstrasse, was situated there, and of his larger works the Palais Hessen-Philippstal in Königstrasse (1730, destr.) was a three-storey structure with symmetrical façade elevation, characteristic of his style. All his buildings were simple and well proportioned, with very sparing rocaille ornamentation and shallow pediments, as in his father's work. Du Ry was not a creative architect. For important commissions other architects were engaged, but he maintained the tradition of French Huguenot architecture founded by his father and passed it to his son (4) Simon Louis Du Ry.

BIBLIOGRAPHY
F. C. Schminke: *Versuch einer genauen und umständlichen Beschreibung der Residenzstadt Cassel* (Kassel, 1767)
P. Heidelbach: *Kassel: Stätten der Kultur* (Kassel, 1920), pp. 148–50

(4) Simon Louis [Ludwig] **Du Ry** (*b* Kassel, 13 Jan 1726; *d* Kassel, 23 Aug 1796). Son of (3) Charles Louis Du Ry. After receiving an education from his father and at the Collegium Carolinum in Kassel, Du Ry, whose talent had been recognized by Landgrave Frederick I (*reg* 1730–51), was sent to continue his studies at Stockholm, as the princely house of Hesse-Kassel had dynastic links with Sweden at the time. In 1746–8 he was a pupil of Carl Hårleman, with limited success by his own account. In Sweden he learnt a restrained classicism and a manner of building in which there is a strong relation to the landscape; both tendencies influenced his later work. During his stay in Sweden he received instruction in drawing and painting from Guillaume Thomas Raphaël Taraval.

In 1752 Du Ry spent an important period at the studio of Jacques-François Blondel in Paris; this and the trip to Holland that followed it encouraged Du Ry's affinity with the strict Classical Baroque style practised in France and Holland. After a short stay in Kassel, where he was appointed architect to Landgrave William VIII, he was sent for further study to Italy (1753–6). There he not only learnt about contemporary and ancient architecture but became an admirer of Palladio. After his previous training it is not surprising that he rejected the Italian architecture of the Late Baroque. He made a thorough study of English Palladianism from models. On his return to Kassel he took over his father's projects after the latter's death.

Soon after, Du Ry was commissioned by Landgrave Frederick II (*see* HESSE-KASSEL, (3)) to lay out prestigious areas of the city, one of the most important court building projects of the day. At the end of the Seven Years War (1756–63), during which hardly anything had been built, the town fortifications were demolished in 1765. It was thus possible to lay out or remodel large squares on their site. These squares included the Parade Ground with a racecourse (planned since 1763) to the south of the medieval Old Town, between the old castle and the Baroque Oberneustadt, with imposing colonnaded architecture (destr. *c.* 1800); the circular Königsplatz north of the Old Town, created in 1764 on the model of the Place des Victoires, Paris (1685), with three-storey buildings of elegant, reserved character mainly designed by Du Ry; and the Friedrichsplatz, constructed from 1768 between the Old Town and the Oberneustadt. The Friedrichsplatz had been created by his grandfather, (2) Paul Du Ry, who first conceived the idea. The large, rectangular square has a view of the open country, which was unimpeded by the light pavilion architecture of the Auetor (1779–82, destr.).

The Friedrichsplatz is dominated by the Museum Fridericianum (1769–79; see fig.), the first purpose-built public museum and library building in Europe (*see* GERMANY, §XIV). It is a programmatically classical building with a temple façade (modelled on such contemporary French pattern books as the *Recueil élémentaire d'architecture*, 1767, by François de Neufforge) typical of the German Enlightenment and one of the first Neo-classical buildings in Germany (the exterior was restored following damage in World War II). On the same square he built the Palais Junken (1767–9) for a government minister, on the same axis and with a similar pediment but modified by the use of pilasters instead of columns, and the Elisabethkirche (1770–74, destr.). The latter was outwardly a secular building, with the same pilastered elevation, but was sumptuous within, showing the influence of the chapel at Versailles (1689–1710) by Jules Hardouin Mansart. Other buildings with a Baroque façade scheme but with very sparing ornamentation were erected on the Königstrasse and the Königsplatz, including the Palais Waitz von Eschen (1770; destr.) and the Roux House (1770; rebuilt).

Du Ry designed the Rathaus in Oberneustadt (1771–5, destr.) and the Charité in Unterneustadt, both simple buildings almost devoid of ornamentation. Outside Kassel he was responsible for the country mansion of Hüffe in Westphalia (1773–84) and the Schloss Fürstenberg near Paderborn (1774–83), both with a three-winged layout and

Simon Louis Du Ry: façade of Museum Fridericianum, Kassel, 1769–79

a Late Baroque character. He made a second journey to Italy, accompanying Landgrave Frederick II, from November 1776 to February 1777. In 1789 he planned the baths at Bad Nenndorf, built from 1797 (altered and built over), and in 1787 he designed the small villa of Mont Cheri (Schönberg) and the Brunnentempel (1792) at Hofgeismar, both in a Neo-classical style.

The main work of Du Ry's later years is the Schloss Wilhelmshöhe near Kassel for Landgrave William IX (*reg* 1785–1821). The first wing to be built (from 1786) was the result of a competition, and this part of the building is in the style of Palladian classicism. The other lateral wing was started in 1787 to match the first, but the centre block that was to replace the old Schloss was executed (1791–8) to designs by HEINRICH CHRISTOPH JUSSOW. In conjunction with the new Schloss the church of Kirchditmold was erected as a *point de vue* in 1790–92, a hall church on a rectangular ground-plan with a west tower. In 1796, at the end of his career and probably against his principles, Du Ry designed a Gothick observation tower in the park at Wilhelmstal.

Du Ry held a number of official posts and in 1766 was appointed to the chair in architecture at the Collegium Carolinum. In 1767 he was appointed Court Architect, in 1785 Director of Works and in 1795 Director of Architecture and Permanent Secretary of the Akademie der Künste in Kassel. His oeuvre was produced in the period of transition between Classical Baroque and Neo-classicism, of which his Museum Fridericianum is a notable precursor. His work as a town planner, with its incorporation of nature into urban squares, is similarly a forerunner, in this case of Romanticism, the paradoxical concomitant of classicism in the field of landscaping.

BIBLIOGRAPHY

P. Heidelbach: *Die Geschichte der Wilhelmshöhe* (Leipzig, 1909)
P. Klopfer: *Von Palladio bis Schinkel* (Esslingen, 1911), p. 227
K. Peatow: *Klassizismus und Romantik auf Wilhelmshöhe* (Kassel, 1929)
F. W. Bätjer: *Das Landschloss Hüffe und Simon Louis Du Ry*, Westfalen, viii (Münster, 1941)
P. du Colombier: *L'Architecture française en Allemagne au XVIIIe siècle* (Paris, 1956), i, pp. 226–43
H.-K. Boehlke: *Simon-Louis du Ry als Stadtbaumeister Landgraf Friedrich II* (Göttingen, 1958)
Aufklärung und Klassizismus in Hessen-Kassel unter Landgraf Friedrich II, 1760–1785 (exh. cat., Kassel, 1979)
H.-K. Boehlke: *Simon-Louis du Ry: Ein Wegbereiter klassizistischer Architektur in Deutschland* (Kassel, 1980)
H.-C. Dittscheid: *Kassel-Wilhelmshöhe und die Krise des Schlossbaues am Ende des Ancien Régime* (Worms, 1987)

VOLKER HELAS

Dusart [du Sart], Cornelis (*b* Haarlem, 24 April 1660; *d* Haarlem, 1 Oct 1704). Dutch painter, draughtsman and printmaker. He was the son of the organist at St Bavo in Haarlem and one of the last pupils of Adriaen van Ostade. He became a member of the Haarlem Guild of St Luke on 10 January 1679 and served as its dean in 1692. Dated pictures by Dusart have survived from almost every year between 1679 and 1702. Two of his earliest pictures of peasants relied heavily on compositions by van Ostade: *Mother and Child* (1679; Dresden, Gemäldegal. Alte Meister) and *Woman Selling Milk* (1679; sold Amsterdam, Muller, 16 Oct 1928, lot 9; the original drawing by van

Cornelis Dusart: *Seated Boy Reading*, black and red chalk and watercolour, 268×187 mm (Amsterdam, Rijksmuseum)

Ostade is in Paris, Fond. Custodia, Inst. Néer., see Schnackenburg, 1981, no. 132).

Over the next few years Dusart remained one of his teacher's closest followers, and in *Peasants outside an Inn* (Vienna, Ksthist. Mus.) and *Farm with a Donkey* (St Petersburg, Hermitage), both dated 1681, the only distinguishing feature is Dusart's more delicate representation of foliage. Shortly after, works such as *Siblings with a Cat* (1682 or 1683; Nijmegen, Esser priv. col., see Trautscholdt, fig. 8) reveal Jan Steen as another source of inspiration. With Steen as his model, Dusart developed figure types whose faces are expressive to the point of grimacing and who make exaggerated movements and wear fantastic clothing (e.g. *Dance outside the Inn*, 1684; Haarlem, Frans Halsmus.). Dusart's figures are often aggressively ugly, as in *St Nicholas's Day* (1685; Basle, Dr T. Christ priv. col., see Trautscholdt, fig. 10). His forte was not so much comedy as broad farce, and it is doubtful that there was any moralizing purpose in his depictions of vice. A graphic scene entitled *Drunken Woman in a Brothel* (1699; sold Göteborg, 9 Nov 1977, lot 1716 with illus.) reveals the influence of Cornelis Bega, examples of whose prints were owned by Dusart. Dusart used lighter and more varied colours, the intense light blue, yellow and red of the costumes predominating over the tonality of the surrounding space (as in the *Pipe Smoker*, 1684; USA, priv. col., see 1984 exh. cat., no. 41), which does not achieve the sensitivity and atmospheric density of van Ostade's work.

After van Ostade's death in 1685, Dusart took over the contents of his studio. Among the works left behind were unfinished paintings by Adriaen van Ostade, some of which Dusart completed (e.g. *Peasant Festivity*; The Hague, Mauritshuis), and paintings by Adriaen's brother Isaack van Ostade, who had died *c.* 1649. The material influenced Dusart profoundly, so that in *Quarrel over a Card-game* (1697; Dresden, Germäldegal. Alte Meister), for instance, the figures resemble those of Steen, but the composition is based on a drawing by Adriaen van Ostade called the *Knife Fight* (Paris, Ecole N. Sup. B.-A.). Dusart also made exact copies of paintings by Adriaen van Ostade (sold Vienna, Dorotheum, 10 Sept 1959, lot 38 with illus.). He also seems to have either completed or adapted some of Steen's oil paintings. Important late paintings include turbulent pictures of fairs with a wealth of figures, such as *Village Kermesse* (1697; sold Amsterdam, Muller, 4–5 Dec 1912, lot 179 with illus.) and the *Quack Doctor* (1702; Bremen, Ksthalle).

Cornelis Dusart was an immensely productive and versatile draughtsman. His most original works are his figure studies drawn from life in black and red chalk, some with watercolour washes (e.g. *Seated Boy Reading*, Amsterdam, Rijksmus.; see fig.) and some on coloured paper and parchment. Not surprisingly, Dusart also adopted the drawing techniques of the van Ostade workshop. Dusart's numerous pen-and-ink drawings, among the best of which were his preparatory studies for prints, often have a distinctive and boldly applied dark brown wash background. Dusart made skilful and systematic use of the stock of drawings the van Ostades left behind, either by copying them or by expanding brief sketches into finished works; in the process he emulated exactly Adriaen's and Isaack's style and stages of development. Dusart frequently copied the preliminary drawings before reworking the pictures. He also used Steen's figure style, leading scholars to attribute certain drawings to Steen himself.

Dusart's extensive graphic oeuvre consists of some 119 etchings and mezzotint engravings. An early group of 12 etchings is dated 1685, the year in which Dusart completed his first mezzotints. There are such series as the *Months*, the *Ages of Man*, the *Five Senses* etc., as well as individual sheets depicting scenes of peasant life. Some of the preparatory drawings were provided by Jacob Gole of Amsterdam, who also acted as publisher. In his prints Dusart vividly expressed the satirical side of his art, reflecting the popular theatre of the Society of Rhetoricians. Dusart's graphic work was his most influential contribution to Dutch art, especially in its impact on caricature.

Dusart remained unmarried and apparently suffered from a weak constitution. The inventory in his will, dated December 1704, included not only his own works and the residue of the van Ostade estate but also a remarkable collection of paintings, drawings and prints by Italian and Dutch artists including Bega, Gerrit Berckheyde and Adriaen van de Velde. His estate was auctioned in Haarlem on 21 August 1708.

BIBLIOGRAPHY

Bénézit; Hollstein: *Dut. & Flem.*; Thieme–Becker
A. Bredius: *Künstler-Inventare*, i (The Hague, 1915), pp. 27–73

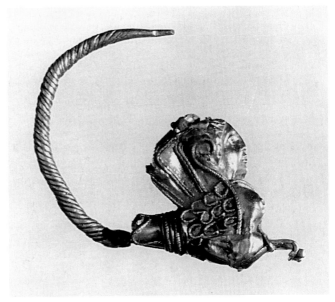

Dushanbe earring with the protome of a sphinx, electrum, 35×22 mm, 2nd century BC (Dushanbe, Republican Historical, Regional and Fine Arts Museum)

J. Q. van Regteren Altena: 'De voorvaderen van Cornelis Dusart', *Oud-Holland*, lxi (1946), pp. 130–33
E. Trautscholdt: 'Beiträge zu Cornelis Dusart', *Ned. Ksthist. Jb.*, xvii (1966), pp. 171–200
O. Naumann: *Netherlandish Artists*, 7 [v/ii] of *The Illustrated Bartsch*, ed. W. Strauss (New York, 1978), pp. 288–325
B. Schnackenburg: *Adriaen van Ostade, Isack van Ostade, Zeichnungen und Aquarelle*, i (Hamburg, 1981), pp. 60–64
Dutch Figure Drawings from the Seventeenth Century (exh. cat. by P. Schatborn; Amsterdam, Rijksmus.; Washington, DC, N.G.A.; 1981–2), pp. 110–12
Dutch Prints of Daily Life: Mirrors of Life or Masks of Moral? (exh. cat. by L. Stone-Ferrier, Lawrence, U. KS, Spencer Mus. A., 1983)
Masters of Seventeenth-century Dutch Genre Painting (exh. cat., ed. P. Sutton; Philadelphia, Mus. A.; London, RA; W. Berlin, Gemäldegal.; 1984), cat. no. 41

B. SCHNACKENBURG

Dusart, François. *See* DIEUSSART, FRANÇOIS.

Dushanbe [Pers. Dūshamba; formerly Dyushambe, Stalinabad]. Capital city of Tajikistan. The area has been exposed to many cultural influences as successive invaders have overrun it. A small, fortified town arose at the end of the 1st millennium BC in the foothills of the Gissar Mountains on the east bank of the Varzob (Dyushambinka) River above its confluence with the Kafirnigan. Chance finds in the area between the present Botanical Gardens and the Radio Station include an electrum earring depicting a sphinx (see fig.), a gilded bronze medallion with an image of Dionysos in high relief, terracotta statuettes etc. (Dushanbe, Tajikistan Acad. Sci., Donish Inst. Hist., Archaeol. & Ethnog.; Dushanbe, Repub. Hist., Reg. & F.A. Mus.). Excavations of a necropolis by B. A. Litvinskiy and E. Gulyamova in the late 1950s and 1960s have uncovered tombs sealed with massive stone blocks, large earthenware storage jars used as ossuaries, carved bone items and jewellery (Dushanbe, Tajikistan Acad. Sci., Donish Inst. Hist., Archaeol. & Ethnog.; Dushanbe, Repub. Hist., Reg. & F.A. Mus.). Dushanbe may have been the site of the early medieval town of

Shuman, the king of which confronted the Arabs under Qutayba in AD 710–11, but others have suggested that Shuman should be identified with Hissar, some 25 km to the west.

The modern city was the site of several villages including Dushanbe, which takes its name from the Persian word for Monday, when the market was held. In 1924 the town of single-storey pisé buildings became the capital of an autonomous republic. After 1929, when (as Stalinabad) it became capital of the Tajik SSR, two- and three-storey buildings were constructed. The city expanded from the east bank, and new European-style buildings, such as the House of Government, the Aini Opera and Ballet Theatre and the Firdousi State Library, were embellished with traditional motifs in carved and painted plaster and wood. The graceful Rokhat Teahouse is a modern structure in a traditional style. The Republican Historical, Regional and Fine Arts Museum provides an overview of art from Tajikistan, and the Donish Institute of History, Archaeology and Ethnography of the Tajikistan Academy of Sciences has a collection of archaeological, numismatic and ethnographic material.

BIBLIOGRAPHY

Ye. M. Linde: 'Greco-baktriyskiy sfinks' [The Greco-Bactrian sphinx], *Soobshcheniya Respub. Istor.-Krayevedcheskogo Muz. Tadzhik. SSR*, i (1952), pp. 5–21

K. V. Trever: 'Baktriyskiy bronzovyy falar s izobrazhniyem Dionisa' [A Bactrian bronze horse-trapping with an image of Dionysos], *Trudy Gosudarstvennogo Ermitazha*, v (1961), pp. 98–109

Drevnosti Tadzhikistana [Antiquities of Tajikistan] (exh. cat., ed. Ye. V. Zeymal'; Leningrad, Hermitage, 1985), pp. 99–100 and colour pls pp. 83, 86

YE. V. ZEYMAL'

Dushkyn, Oleksi (Mykhaylovych) [Dushkin, Aleksey Nikolayevich] (*b* Aleksandrovka, nr Kharkiv, 24 Dec 1903; *d* Moscow, 1 Oct 1977). Ukrainian architect, active also in Russia. He studied in the architectural faculty of the Polytechnical Institute, Khar'kov (Kharkiv), under Aleksey Beketov (1862–1941), completing his studies there in 1930. He developed the general plans (1930) for Gorlovka and Kramatorsk and designed the building (1930–34) for the Institute of Motorized Roads, all in Kharkiv. His design (1932) for the Palace of Soviets, Moscow, won first prize in the second round of the competition. From 1932 to 1939 Dushkin worked in Moscow with Ivan Fomin, who had a profound influence on him. In 1933 he was recruited to design stations for the Moscow metro. His compositions, based on a lively, paradoxical reinterpretation of the classical tradition, set the general character of the architecture of the first phase of the system. Particularly impressive is the 'Palace of Soviets' (later Kropotkinskaya) metro station (1935; with Ya. G. Likhtenberg), in which the piers, with lotus-shaped capitals reminiscent of Egyptian architecture, form part of the lighting system. He also designed the Mayakovskaya metro station (1938), with its domed vaults on stainless-steel parabolic arches, and the Revolution Square (1937), Avtozavodskaya (1943) and Novoslobodskaya (1953) stations.

From 1943 Dushkin directed the reconstruction of the war-damaged railway system. His designs for the railway stations at Dnipropetrovs'k (1947–50), Symferopol' (1951) and Sochi (1952) adapted Neo-classical forms to the asymmetrical layouts suggested by his Rationalist analysis of the practical requirements of the buildings. For the Black Sea resorts of Symferopol' and Sochi the stations were given picturesque associations with local vernacular forms. He was influenced by late 17th-century Moscow Baroque in the multi-storey Ministry of Communications Building (1948–53; with Boris Mezentsev), Lermontov Square, Moscow. The design of the department store Detsky Mir (1954–6; with others), Moscow, is compromised by the vast arcades that were systematically imposed on the façade. After 1959 he worked mainly on monuments, such as that at Vladimir (1960; with the sculptor Ya. B. Ryabichev) in honour of the 850th anniversary of its founding and the monument to the *Victory in Novgorod* (1974) with the sculptor Georgy Neroda (1895–1983).

BIBLIOGRAPHY

Ye. Mel'nikov: 'Aleksey Nikolayevich Dushkin', *Arkhit. SSSR*, 7 (1974), pp. 27–31

A. V. IKONNIKOV

Du Sommerard [Dusommerard], **(Simon-Nicolas-)Alexandre** (*b* Bar-sur-Aube, Aube, 31 Aug 1779; *d* Saint-Cloud, Hauts-de-Seine, 19 Aug 1842). French civil servant, collector and art historian. Descended from a rich family of financial administrators under the Bourbon monarchy, he served in the Revolutionary army after 1789 and then entered the civil service. In 1807 he became a Councillor of the Revenue Court, and he retained this post until he died after returning from a journey to Italy.

Du Sommerard started his career as a collector by acquiring the works of contemporary French masters. In 1825–6, however, he sold these to devote himself entirely to French art from the Middle Ages to the 17th century. His new collection was moved in 1832 to one of the last 15th-century Parisian palaces, the Hôtel des Abbés de Cluny, near the Roman baths of ancient Lutetia. This private museum was managed with purely historical and artistic aims: Du Sommerard intended to reveal the gaps inevitable in any history of France based entirely on written documents, and to make people aware of the progress of history through the history of art.

Each room held numerous pieces of furniture, costumes and weapons, which Du Sommerard tried to arrange according to their functional or symbolic value—reconstructing, for example, the interiors of houses or military harness and equipment. Like ALEXANDRE LENOIR's Musée des Monuments Français, the collection offered visitors not only a rational approach to history but also an emotional one, transporting them through imagination back into the past. To increase the scenographic interest of his museum, Sommerard did not hesitate to construct 'Gothic' furniture out of broken fragments and to attribute prestigious origins to the pieces in his collection. On his death, the Hôtel de Cluny and his collections were acquired by the State. The collection forms the nucleus of the present Musée de Cluny.

In a long, unfinished work entitled *Les Arts du moyen-âge*, Du Sommerard sought to turn his collection to good account. A great admirer of Johann Joachim Winckelmann, he tried to construct his own theoretical model in order to explain the development of French medieval art. He attempted to grasp its organic evolution in time, particularly by retracing the history of his chosen exhibition site itself, the Hôtel de Cluny, from the Roman period to his own day.

WRITINGS

Vues de Provins, dessinées et lithographiées (Paris and Provins, 1822)
Les Arts du moyen-âge en ce qui concerne principalement le Palais Romain de Paris, L'Hôtel de Cluny, issu de ses ruines, et les objets d'art de la collection classée dans cet Hôtel, 5 vols (Paris, 1838–46) [with atlas and album pubd separately]

DBF

BIBLIOGRAPHY

P. Marot: 'Les Origines d'un musée d' *antiquités nationales*: De la protection du "Palais des Thermes" à l'institution du Musée de Cluny', *Mém. Soc. Nat. Antiqua. Fr.*, 9th ser., iv/84 (1968), pp. 259–327
F. Salet and G. Souchal: *The Cluny Museum* (Paris, 1972)
A. Erlande-Brandenburg: 'Evolution du Musée de Cluny: Des collections d'Alexandre du Sommerard à la préservation actuelle', *Mnts Hist.*, 104 (1979), pp. 21–37
F. Joubert: 'Alexandre du Sommerard et les origines du Musée de Cluny', *Le 'Gothique' retrouvé* (exh. cat., Paris, Hôtel de Sully, 1979), pp. 99–104

PASCAL GRIENER

Düsseldorf. German city situated at the confluence of the Rhine and Düssel rivers, capital of North Rhine-Westphalia since 1946. Now an administrative and financial centre and river port with a population of *c.* 560,000, its artistic heyday occurred in the 18th century, when it was the seat of the Electors Palatine. The town was severely damaged in World War II.

1. HISTORY AND URBAN DEVELOPMENT. A settlement at the mouth of the Düssel was first referred to as 'dusseldorp' *c.* 1135, but there had been earlier references to areas that were later incorporated into the town: Kaiserswerth, Gerresheim and Bilk, which boasts the oldest surviving building, the 11th-century Martinskirche. Engelbert I, Count of Berg (*reg* 1166–89), acquired Düsseldorf before 1189; it became an independent parish in 1206, and after the Battle of Worringen in 1288, against the Bishop of Cologne, it was established as a town by Adolf V (*reg* 1259–96). In the same year the 13th-century parish church of St Lambertus was made collegiate. The settlement grew towards a township in the first half of the

14th century, and from 1360 William II (*reg* 1360–1408; Duke from 1380) was an active patron; he extended the castle on the Rhine and founded a new quarter in the town. In 1371 Düsseldorf achieved independence in jurisdiction, becoming a customs post in 1373 and authorized for a mint in 1377. About 1390 St Lambertus was rebuilt as an aisled hall church with an ambulatory; its tower was completed in 1448.

Between 1510 and 1520 a new state emerged with Düsseldorf as the capital, when the Dukes of Cleves had managed to accumulate the duchies and counties of Jülich, Cleves, Berg, Mark and Ravensberg. William V, Duke of Jülich (the Rich; *reg* 1539–92), transformed the medieval town into a Renaissance one; by 1538 he had rebuilt the castle, which had burnt in 1510, as a square Renaissance structure. The division of the state in 1614 left Düsseldorf the capital of the Duchy of Pfalz-Neuburg, the dukes becoming Electors Palatine in 1685 (*see* WITTELSBACH). Wolfgang William von Pfalz-Neuburg, Count Palatine (*reg* 1614–53), built bastioned fortifications that determined the city plan until the late 18th century. The Jesuit church of St Andreas was built from 1622 to 1629, with a theological college attached. The church itself is an aisled hall church with five vaulted bays, strongly influenced by Italian Baroque architecture; a hexagonal, centrally planned building that was added to the choir in 1667 is the mausoleum of seven members of the Pfalz-Neuburg family.

Düsseldorf reached its cultural apogee under Elector John William (known as Jan Wellem; *reg* 1679–1716; Elector from 1690 and married to Anna Luisa de' Medici). He cultivated the visual arts (*see* §2 below), modernized the fortifications, built a new quarter of the town to house the garrison and reorganized the guilds. The court moved to Mannheim in 1720. Under Charles Theodore Pfalz-Sulzbach (Elector from 1742), however, NICOLAS DE PIGAGE built the Rococo Maison de Plaisance Benrath (1755–73) *c.* 10 km from the city, converting the hunting

Düsseldorf, Kunstakademie, by Hermann Riffart, 1875–9

park to a pleasure garden; he also redesigned the older parts of the Hofgarten on the edge of the town itself in 1770. Johann Joseph Couven built the new Jägerhof (1752–63), which served as residence for the Master of the Hunt. Karlstadt, with its central Karlsplatz, was absorbed into the town in 1787. The French, who occupied Düsseldorf from 1795 to 1801, demolished the fortifications, and in 1804 the Königsallee, now the town's main axis, was built, as well as the Heinrich-Heine Allee and the widened Hofgarten east of the old quarter.

In 1815 Düsseldorf was absorbed into Prussia. Development began with the iron industry in the mid-19th century, and three new districts were built to provide for the expanded population. The castle on the Rhine was almost totally destroyed by fire in 1872 (only the tower remains, now a shipping museum). The Kunstakademie (see §2 below), which had occupied part of the castle since 1821, was rehoused in a new Renaissance-style building by Hermann Riffart (1840–1919; see fig.). The 1885 development plan by Josef Stübben (1845–1936) included a railway station and a new ring road. When the new port opened in 1896 the town's economy expanded further, and business corporations moved in. About the turn of the century the administration of companies and organizations emerged alongside the iron and steel industry. Outstanding buildings were constructed in the early 20th century, including the Tietz department store (now Kaufhof AG; 1909), designed by JOSEPH MARIA OLBRICH; the Mannesmann-Haus on the Rhine (1912), by Peter Behrens, Director of the Kunstgewerbeschule, 1903–7; the Stahlhochhaus (Stummhaus, 1923–5), by Paul Bonatz; and the first tower block in Germany, the Wilhelm-Marx Haus (1922–4), built by Wilhelm Kreis (who had also directed the Kunstgewerbeschule, 1909–20). The city airport was opened in 1925, and the new main railway station was built in 1932–6. After recovery from war damage, Düsseldorf has continued to develop as a financial and trading centre.

2. ART LIFE AND ORGANIZATION. Under Elector John William a gallery was built to house his collection of paintings by Rubens (Munich, Alte Pin.); John William also collected plaster casts of antique sculptures. The court sculptor, GABRIEL GRUPELLO, made an equestrian statue (1703–11) of his patron, which stands on the Marktplatz, and Adriaen van der Werff was appointed court painter, together with Jan Douven (1656–1727). In 1762 Charles Theodore founded a drawing school, which between 1765 and 1777 became an academy of painting, sculpture and architecture. The Akademie was refounded in 1819; Wilhelm von Schadow, who took over the directorship in 1826, reorganized it (see SCHADOW, (3)), and under his auspices there flourished the Düsseldorf school of painting practised by, among others, JOHANN PETER HASENCLEVER, JULIUS HÜBNER and LUDWIG KNAUS. In 1829 Schadow founded the Kunstverein for the Rhineland Westphalia, but owing to tension between his pupils and others a group of artists formed their own association in 1844. The picture gallery was re-established in 1846, and two years later, in consequence of the celebrations for German unity, the artists' association 'Malkasten' (Paintbox) was founded.

Among early 20th-century directors of the Akademie was Paul Klee (1931–3). Contemporary artistic life is dominated by the state academy and temporary exhibitions at the Kunsthalle and the Kunstsammlung Nordrhein-Westfalen. The Kunsthalle opened in 1967 and houses the Kunstverein. A Paul Klee collection and other 20th-century art is shown in the Kunstsammlung Nordrhein-Westfalen (opened 1986), with its spectacular curved façade of black marble. The Ehrenhof, a group of Expressionist brick buildings used for exhibitions and concerts, with the domed Tonhalle on one end, runs parallel to the Rhine; it includes the Kunstmuseum (reopened 1985) and the Kunstpalast. The Kunstmuseum has a collection of European art from the Middle Ages to the present (including a collection of drawings with emphasis on the Baroque period), and it has a glass collection, part of which is exhibited in the Grünes Gewölbe in the Tonhalle. Changing exhibitions are shown in the Kunstpalast. The Ehrenhof complex and the alterations to the Kunstpalast (1925–6) are the work of Wilhelm Kreis. The Palais Nesselrode houses the Hetjens Museum of ceramics, dating from prehistoric times to the present. Meissen porcelain of the Ernst Schneider foundation is shown with 18th-century silver in the Jägerhof.

BIBLIOGRAPHY
H. Weidenhaupt: *Kleine Geschichte der Stadt Düsseldorf* (Düsseldorf, 1968) [with earlier bibliog.]
E. Spohr: *Düsseldorf: Stadt und Festung* (Düsseldorf, 1978)
——: *Aus Düsseldorfs Vergangenheit: Aufsätze aus vier Jahrzehnten* (Düsseldorf, 1988)

GUDRUN SCHMIDT

Düsseldorf school [Die Düsseldorfer Malerschule]. Group of painters studying and working from the mid-1820s to the 1860s in Germany at the Düsseldorf Kunstakademie. Among the principal artists were Carl Friedrich Lessing, Ferdinand Theodor Hildebrandt (1804–74), Johann Wilhelm Schirmer, Johann Peter Hasenclever, Karl Wilhelm Hübner, Andreas Achenbach (1815–1910), Ludwig Knaus and Carl Ferdinand Sohn. Several had been pupils of Wilhelm Schadow in Berlin and had followed him to Düsseldorf after he became Director of the Kunstakademie in 1826. Schadow increased the prestige of the school, and his programme of instruction, which involved extreme naturalness of representation, attracted large numbers of students. By 1850 the school had replaced the Dresden Akademie as the favoured place in Germany to study art. Lessing, Hildebrandt and Hübner are best known for their large, carefully staged and somewhat melodramatic paintings of the 1830s and 1840s that often have political content, for example Lessing's *Hussite Sermon* (1836; Düsseldorf, Kstmus.; on loan to Berlin, Alte N.G.). Achenbach and Schirmer were among those who painted landscapes, executing works in which a clear, often brittle, light helps to localize the scene, as in Schirmer's *German Landscape* (1854; Essen, Mus. Folkwang). Group portraits, for example Sohn's the *Bendemann Family and their Friends* (c. 1832; Krefeld, Kaiser-Wilhelm Mus.), are often cramped in composition and have sitters who only occasionally psychologically interact. The artists of the Düsseldorf school admired the subject-matter and the meticulous style of the Lukasbrüder and were also influenced by the Biedermeier painters, particularly Ferdinand Georg Waldmüller. Because of Düsseldorf's proximity to the Netherlands, strong influences of the work of such 17th-century Dutch masters as Gerrit Dou and Gabriel Metsu and such contemporary Dutch and Belgian genre painters as Ferdinand De Braekeleer are also present in their work. By the 1850s much of the work produced by the Düsseldorf school consisted of sentimental and anecdotal genre scenes, for example Knaus's *The Cardsharp* (1851; Düsseldorf, Kstmus.). This type of painting was practised well into the 1880s by some of the original members and their followers. The literal and precise painting taught at the Akademie attracted the Americans Richard Caton Woodville and Eastman Johnson. The Hungarian Mihály Munkácsy, the Swiss Benjamin Vautier and the Norwegian Adolph Tidemand also studied in Düsseldorf and took back to their respective countries the forthright style and approach learnt as students.

BIBLIOGRAPHY

F. Novotny: *Painting and Sculpture in Europe, 1780–1880*, Pelican Hist. A. (Harmondsworth, 1960, 2/1970)
W. Hult: *Die Düsseldorfer Malerschule, 1819–1869* (Leipzig, 1964)
I. Markowitz: *Die Düsseldorfer Malerschule* (Düsseldorf, 1969)
Die Düsseldorfer Malerschule (exh. cat., ed. W. von Kalnein; Düsseldorf, Kstmus.; Darmstadt, Ausstellhallen Mathildenhöhe, 1979)
W. Vaughan: *German Romantic Painting* (New Haven and London, 1980)
Werke der Düsseldorfer Malerschule: Gemälde, Aquarelle (exh. cat., Düsseldorf, Gal. Paffrath, 1986)

□

Dust-cover [dust-jacket]. *See* BOOK JACKET.

Dust Muhammad [Dūst Muḥammad ibn Sulaymān al-Haravī] (*b* Kawashan, nr Herat, *c*. 1490; *d c*. 1565). Persian calligrapher, illustrator and man of letters. A pupil of BIHZAD, Dust Muhammad was in service to the Safavid ruler Tahmasp. The artist's earliest signed works are three calligraphic specimens executed at Herat in 1511–12 and mounted in an album (St Petersburg, Rus. N. Lib., Dorn 147). According to Dickson and Welch, his earliest paintings are six illustrations in a manuscript (St Petersburg, Rus. N. Lib., Dorn 441, fols 8*v*, 10*r*, 31*v*, 32*v*, 36*v*, 53*v*) of 'Arifi's *Gūy u Chawgān* ('Ball and bandy') copied by the shah at Tabriz in 1524–5. They attribute to Dust Muhammad five paintings in the monumental copy (ex-Houghton priv. col., fols 308*v*, 551*v*, 658*v*, 663*v*, 745*v*) of the *Shāhnāma* ('Book of kings') made for Tahmasp. The sparse compositions have awkward, flattened figures with ill-fitting turbans and oddly shaped thumbs and flimsy, planar architecture. A calligraphic specimen (Istanbul, Topkapı Pal. Lib., H. 2156) produced in mid-August 1531 at Herat led Dickson and Welch to surmise that the artist returned to Herat with the shah's brother, Bahram Mirza, governor of the city from 1530 to 1534. Dust Muhammad soon returned to Tabriz, for the earliest surviving manuscript in his hand, a copy (St Petersburg, Rus. N. Lib., Dorn 354) of the Pseudo-'Attar dated 1540–41, is signed 'copyist to the shah'. He continued painting in the Safavid capital, and Dickson and Welch consider the largest painting in the Tahmasp *Shāhnāma*, the complex, mannerist *Haftvad and the Worm* (fol. 521*v*), to exemplify his work of the late 1530s. In 1544 the artist compiled an album of paintings and calligraphy for Bahram Mirza (Istanbul, Topkapı Pal.

Lib., H. 2154); the preface on past and present artists and scribes is one of the main 16th-century sources for the history of the arts of the book.

Dust Muhammad then moved east to join the Mughal court. According to the Mughal chronicler Bayazid, he journeyed uninvited to Kabul to take up service with the emperor Humayun's rebel brother, Kamran, in order to partake of the wine that Tahmasp had forbidden. Bayazid listed the artist as a member of the retinue of painters accompanying Humayun when he left Kabul in November 1554 to reconquer India. Dickson and Welch have attributed a painting of Humayun and his brother Hindal Mirza in the Jahangir Album (Berlin, Staatsbib. Preuss. Kultbes., Libr. Pict. A. 117) to Dust Muhammad *c.* 1550, when the Mughal emperor, prince and artist were together in Kabul. Dust Muhammad remained in India through Akbar's accession in 1556, about the time he painted a portrait identified as Shah Abu'l-Ma'ali, confidant of the late emperor Humayun, and signed by 'Master Dust, the painter' (Geneva, Sadrudin Aga Khan Col.; see 1979–80 exh. cat., no. 75). At the end of his life, Dust Muhammad returned to the Safavid court, now at Qazvin, where he copied four religious manuscripts dated between 1560 and 1564. One is a rare copy of the Koran in *nasta'līq* script (Istanbul, Topkapı Pal. Lib.), perhaps the very one mentioned by the Safavid biographer Qazi Ahmad, for it was as a master of *nasta'līq* script that Mawlana Dust of Herat entered the historical tradition. Adle has proposed, however, that the name Dust Muhammad conceals two, if not three, distinct personalities.

WRITINGS

Preface to the Bahram Mirza Album (1544); Eng. trans., ed. W. M. Thackston, *A Century of Princes: Sources on Timurid History and Art* (Cambridge, MA, 1989), pp. 335–50

BIBLIOGRAPHY

Bāyazīd Bāyāt: *Tazkhira-yi Humāyūn va Akbar* [Memoirs of Humayun and Akbar] (1591), ed. M. Hidayat Hosain (Calcutta, 1941), pp. 65–9
Qāzī Ahmad ibn Mīr Munshī: *Gulistān-i hunar* [Rose-garden of art] (*c.* 1606); Eng. trans. by V. Minorsky as *Calligraphers and Painters* (Washington, DC, 1959), pp. 146–7, 180
Wonders of the Age (exh. cat. by S. C. Welch; London, BM; Washington, DC, Nat. Gal.; Cambridge, MA, Fogg A. Mus.; 1979–80), p. 194
M. B. Dickson and S. C. Welch: *The Houghton Shahnameh* (Cambridge, MA, 1981), pp. 118–28, pls 172, 218, 225, 242, 249, 261, col. pl. 14
M. Bayani: *Ahwāl u āthār-i khushnivīsān* [Accounts and works of calligraphers] (Tehran, 2/Iranian solar 1363/1984), pp. 188–203
C. Adle: 'Autopsia, in absentia: Sur la date de l'introduction et de la constitution de l'album de Bahrâm Mirzâ par Dust-Mohammad en 951/1544', *Stud. Iran.*, xix (1990), pp. 219–56

SHEILA R. CANBY

Dutary, Alberto (*b* Panama City, 3 July 1932). Panamanian painter and printmaker. He studied at the Escuela Nacional de Artes Plásticas in Panama City and at the Real Academia San Fernando and the Escuela Nacional de Artes Gráficas in Madrid, where he held his first one-man show in 1957 before returning to Panama. Although he was always a figurative painter, in paintings such as *Figures at Twilight* (1960; Washington, DC, Mus. Mod. A. Latin America; *see* PANAMA, fig. 3) and in his series of over 50 works, *Saints*, in the early 1960s (e.g. *Mocking Saint*, 1962; Panama City, Mus. A. Contemp.), he combined the rich surface textures of Spanish informal abstraction with mysterious ghost figures expressing an Existentialist point of view. In spite of their apparent simplicity, such pictures as *Objects for a Ceremony* (1973) and the *Consumer as Clay* (1968; both Panama City, Mus. A. Contemp.) are full of symbolic and mythic associations as well as social criticism. In Dutary's later works his iconography became less varied, with a preference for tall, ascetic women and female mannequins as virtually interchangeable figures. Dutary's paintings, drawings, pastels and lithographs were exhibited widely in Panama and abroad. He also helped promote the arts in Panama as one of the founders in 1962 of the Instituto Panameño de Arte and through his teaching in schools and at the Universidad de Panamá.

BIBLIOGRAPHY

M. Molleda: 'Arte de América y España', *A. Int.*, vii/6 (1963), p. 45

X. Zavala Cuadro and others: 'Alberto Dutary: Pintor panameño', *Rev. Pensam. Centamer.*, 155 (1977), pp. 1–9

MONICA E. KUPFER

Dutch Antilles. *See under* ANTILLES, LESSER.

Dutch East Indies. *See* INDONESIA.

Dutch Guiana. *See* SURINAM.

Dutch Italianates. Term conventionally used to refer to the school of Dutch painters and draughtsmen who were active in Rome for more than a hundred years, starting from the early 17th century. These artists produced mainly pastoral subjects bathed in warm southern light, set in an Italian, or specifically Roman, landscape. The term is also often applied, but wrongly, to artists who never left the northern Netherlands but who worked primarily in an Italianate style. The origins of the use of the term date to the early 20th century, when art historians began to distinguish between the native landscapes of Dutch painters such as Jan van Goyen or Jacob van Ruisdael and those of their compatriots, such as Herman van Swanevelt or Jan Both, who travelled to Italy. The Italianates are sometimes confused with the group of artists known as the BAMBOCCIANTI, a name that, although occasionally used as a substitute, correctly refers only to artists in the immediate circle of the Dutch artist Pieter van Laer (called il Bamboccio), who was active in Rome from 1625 to 1639 and painted scenes of popular Roman life. At least some of the Bamboccianti are included in the group of Dutch Italianates.

For northerners arriving for the first time in Rome, its ruins of past splendour excited both interest and admiration, tinged perhaps with a certain nostalgia. Visitors were also inspired by the natural environment, which seemed so varied and lively compared to the flat, uniform landscape of the Low Countries, and the warm, golden glow of Italy had no parallels in the grey light of northern Europe.

The group of artists called Italianate were not the first northern artists to visit Italy. Among the pioneers were the early and mid-16th-century artists Jan van Scorel, Jan Gossart and Maarten van Heemskerck, whose promotion of Italian Renaissance ideals resulted in a style often called ROMANISM. The Flemish artist Paul Bril travelled to Italy *c.* 1580; his earliest landscapes were highly Mannerist, but those painted after *c.* 1605 were far more naturalistic and served as important sources of inspiration for the Dutch Italianates. At the beginning of the 17th century a small group of painters from Utrecht (later known as the UTRECHT CARAVAGGISTI), including Gerrit van Honthorst and Hendrick ter Brugghen, settled in Rome, where they were profoundly influenced by the new ideas introduced by Caravaggio. By the mid-1620s the Utrecht artists were on their way back to the northern Netherlands, just as the first Dutch Italianates were setting out.

The first group of Italianate artists, made up of artists born between 1595 and 1600, including Cornelis van Poelenburch and Bartholomeus Breenbergh (to whom one may add Herman van Swanevelt as a transitional figure), was active in Rome and Florence during the late 1620s and the 1630s. They painted mainly mythological, Arcadian landscapes set in a Roman countryside filled with ruins that were often imaginary (e.g. Poelenburch's *Landscape with the Colosseum, c.* 1620; Toledo, OH, Mus. A.; *see* POELENBURCH, CORNELIS VAN, fig. 1). Besides the late work of Bril, other influences included the small, accurately observed landscape backgrounds in paintings by the German artist Adam Elsheimer, who had died in Rome only a few years earlier, and the light and open landscapes of the Italian Filippo Napoletano. Shortly after 1620 Poelenburch and Breenbergh helped establish the SCHILDERSBENT, a confraternity for northern artists in Rome, the main purpose of which was to oppose the stringent rules of the local Accademia di S Luca.

This first generation was followed by a second group of artists, born *c.* 1615–25, which was active in Rome or the Netherlands between the 1630s and the 1650s: these included Jan Asselijn (see fig.), Thomas Wijck, Jan Both, Jan Baptist Weenix, Nicolaes Berchem, Karel Dujardin and Adam Pynacker. In the work of these artists the repertory based on ancient architecture was tempered by the introduction of contemporary buildings, while mythological subjects were replaced increasingly by pastoral and low-life (*bambocciate*) scenes in either an urban or a country setting.

The third generation was formed of landscape artists born in the mid-17th century, including Johannes Glauber, Aelbert Meyeringh, Jan Frans van Bloemen, Isaac de Moucheron, Jacob de Heusch (1657–1701) and, to a lesser degree, Gaspar van Wittel, all of whom were active at the end of the 17th century or during the early years of the 18th. Apart from van Wittel, who continued the tradition of the naturalistic Italianate landscape, these painters sacrificed the close observation characteristic of the earlier Italianates and produced mainly idealized classical landscapes inspired by Gaspard Dughet and Nicolas Poussin.

Drawing played a prominent part in the work of most of the Dutch Italianate artists. The large number of drawings by Breenbergh, Asselijn, Berchem and Wijck, for example, reflects the intense curiosity and interest they experienced in a natural environment so radically different from that of their homeland. They spent much time and painstaking effort in documenting the views in Rome and in the surrounding Campagna, and the drawings often provided a repertory of motifs that could be used in later paintings, including those executed back in the Netherlands.

The contact with Italy brought about a clear change of direction in the art of those artists who made the journey south. Once back home, many continued to work in an

Dutch Italianate painting by Jan Asselijn: *Landscape with the Ruins of an Aqueduct*, oil on canvas, 550×700 mm, 1646 (Rome, Accademia di S Luca)

Italianate vein. Their work also stimulated stylistic changes in artists who never left the Low Countries, a phenomenon particularly well observed in the effect that Jan Both, who was in Rome from 1636 to *c.* 1641, had on such pupils as Willem de Heusch and Frederick de Moucheron, both of whom painted only Italianate landscapes.

As a genre, Dutch Italianate landscape paintings were highly prized in the northern Netherlands during the 17th and 18th centuries. In the 17th century they fetched higher prices than native Dutch landscapes (see price tables in Chong), and according to Houbraken they were also more popular in the early 18th century. However, during the 19th century these works were dismissed and their authors accused of having given rise to a hybrid style that was neither Dutch nor Italian. Appreciation of their work diminished still further during the Impressionist period, when renewed interest was shown in the local Dutch school and in artists such as Jacob van Ruisdael and Meindert Hobbema, who were seen as precursors of painting *en plein air*. Evidence for renewed interest in the Dutch Italianates dates to the 1920s, when Hoogewerff carried out detailed archival research that established which 17th-century northern artists actually spent time in Italy and for how long, but it was Stechow's critical re-evaluation of 1953 that defined the group and the nature of their art. The use of the stylistic label was codified by the important exhibition *Nederlandse 17e eeuwse Italianiserende landschapschilders* held in Utrecht in 1965.

For further illustrations *see* ASSELIJN, JAN; BERCHEM, NICOLAES; BLOEMEN, JAN FRANS VAN; BOTH, JAN; BREENBERGH, BARTHOLOMEUS; MOUCHERON, ISAAC DE; PYNACKER, ADAM; SWANEVELT, HERMAN VAN; WEENIX, JAN BAPTIST; and WITTEL, GASPAR VAN.

BIBLIOGRAPHY
A. Houbraken: *De groote schouburgh* (1718–21)
G. J. Hoogewerff: *Nederlandsche kunstenaars te Rome, 1600–1725: Uittreksels uit de parocchiale archieven* (The Hague, 1942–3)
W. Stechow: 'Jan Both and the Re-evaluation of Dutch Italianate Painting', *Mag. A.*, xlvi (1953), pp. 131–6; *R* in *Actes du XVIIème congrès international de l'histoire de l'art: The Hague, 1953*, pp. 425–32
Italy through Dutch Eyes: Dutch Seventeenth-century Landscape Artists in Italy (exh. cat. by W. Stechow, Ann Arbor, U. MI, Mus. A., 1964)
Nederlandse 17e eeuwse Italianiserende landschapschilders (exh. cat., ed. A. Blankert; Utrecht, Cent. Mus., 1965); rev. and trans. as *Dutch 17th-century Italianate Painters* (Soest, 1978)
J. Rosenberg, S. Slive and E. H. ter Kuile: *Dutch Art and Architecture, 1600–1800*, Pelican Hist. A. (Harmondsworth, 1966)
W. Stechow: *Dutch Landscape Painting of the Seventeenth Century* (London, 1966/R 1981)
L. Salerno: *Pittori di paesaggio del seicento a Roma*, 3 vols (Rome, 1977–80)
R. Trnek: *Niederländer und Italien: Italienisante Landschafts- und Genremalerei von Niederländern des siebzehnten Jahrhunderts in der Gemäldegalerie der Akademie der bildenden Künste in Wien* (Vienna, 1982)
G. Briganti, L. Trezzani and L. Laureati: *The Bamboccianti: Painters of Everyday Life in 17th-century Rome* (Rome, 1983)

B. Haak: *The Golden Age: Dutch Painters of the Seventeenth Century* (New York, 1984), pp. 143–6

Die Niederländer in Italien: Italienisante Niederländer des 17. Jahrhunderts aus österreichischem Besitz (exh. cat. by R. Trnek; Salzburg, Residenzgal.; Vienna, Gemäldegal. Akad. Bild. Kst.; 1986)

A. Chong: 'The Market for Landscape Painting in Seventeenth-century Holland', *Masters of 17th-century Dutch Landscape Painting* (exh. cat. by P. C. Sutton and others; Amsterdam, Rijksmus.; Boston, MA, Mus. F.A.; Philadelphia, PA, Mus. A.; 1987–8), pp. 104–20

P. C. Sutton: '"The Capital of Pictura's School": The Pre-Rembrandtists Poelenburch and Breenbergh', *ibid.*, pp. 28–32

——: 'Birds of a Feather: The Second Generation of Dutch Italianates', *ibid.*, pp. 41–5

Italian Recollections: Dutch Painters of the Golden Age (exh. cat. by F. J. Duparc and L. L. Graif, Montreal, Mus. F.A., 1990)

LAURA LAUREATI

Du Temple, Raymond. *See* RAYMOND DU TEMPLE.

Duterrau, Benjamin (*b* London, 1767; *d* Hobart, Tasmania, 11 July 1851). English painter, printmaker and sculptor, active in Australia. In London he exhibited six portraits at the Royal Academy (1817–23) and three genre paintings at the British Institution and engraved two colour plates for George Morland, before moving to Hobart, Tasmania, in 1832. At the Hobart Mechanics' Institute in 1833 he delivered the first lecture in Australia on the subject of painting. In 1849 he contributed the paper 'The School of Athens as it Assimilates with the Mechanics Institution' to a series of seven lectures (later published) delivered at the Institute. Duterrau painted landscapes and portraits but is best known for his works depicting the Aborigines of Tasmania and their traditional way of life. He was very interested in the events that led to the exclusion of the Aborigines from Tasmania, and in a series of works begun in 1834 but not executed until the early 1840s he showed George Augustus Robinson under commission from the Governor of Tasmania to restore peace with them. *The Conciliation* (1840; Hobart, Tasman. Mus. & A.G.) depicts Robinson's meeting with the Aborigines, who had been rounded up by the government with the aim of accommodating them on a reserve. This large painting was described by William Moore (1868–1937), the critic and historian, as Australia's first historical picture. When the Aborigines arrived in Hobart, Robinson would take them to the studio where Duterrau used them as models and also made etchings and plaster sculptures of them.

BIBLIOGRAPHY
T. Bonyhady: 'Benjamin Duterrau's Paintings of the Conciliation of the Tasmanian Aborigines', *Bonyang: Work on Changing Australia* (Goodwood, South Australia, 1980), no. 3, pp. 93–5

——: *Australian Colonial Paintings in the Australian National Gallery* (Melbourne, 1986), pp. 76–89

VIDEO RECORDINGS
'The Conciliation' by Benjamin Duterrau, 1840, The Australian Eye: Series 3, 7 [videotape]

Paintings 7 [film, Australian Film Commission, Tasman. Mus. & A.G. and Tasmanian Film Corporation]

CHRISTINE CLARK

Dutert, Charles-Louis-Ferdinand (*b* Douai, 21 Oct 1845; *d* Paris, 13 Feb 1906). French architect. He trained at the Ecole des Beaux-Arts in Paris under Louis-Hippolyte Lebas and Paul-René-Léon Ginain, and in 1869 he won the Grand Prix de Rome with a project for a French embassy building in the capital city of a powerful state. He

was Inspecteur Général des Arts du Dessin from 1869 and became Directeur de l'Enseignement at the Ministère des Arts in 1881. In 1883–9 he built the Ecole Supérieure Nationale des Arts et Industries Textiles at Roubaix, and in 1889 he built the palaeontology gallery in the Muséum National d'Histoire Naturelle in Paris. The Galerie des Machines (*see* IRON AND STEEL, fig. 4) in the Exposition Universelle of 1889 in Paris gave him the opportunity to prove that alongside metal-frame buildings covered with a variety of materials, or even the Eiffel Tower, which had been presented to the public chiefly as a technical performance, a genuine aesthetic of monumental iron architecture could also exist. The Galerie represents an original investigation of proportions—it was composed of a 115 m span of parallel arches, articulated by three ball-and-socket joints, which were probably designed with the help of Victor Contamin (1840–93)—and it can be seen as a repertory of decorative elements, used on a large scale to demonstrate the plastic qualities of industrial iron plates when worked with new equipment.

BIBLIOGRAPHY
Macmillan Enc. Architects

F. Jourdain: 'F. Dutert et le palais des machines', *Rev. Illus.*, viii (1889), pp. 121–3

E. Hénard: *Le Palais des machines à l'exposition universelle de 1889* (Paris, 1891) [with 41 illus.]

JEAN PAUL MIDANT

Duthoit, Edmond-Clément-Marie-Louis (*b* Amiens, 1837; *d* Amiens, 10 June 1889). French architect. After a stint in Eugène-Emmanuel Viollet-le-Duc's short-lived atelier, where his time overlapped with that of Anatole de Baudot and Maurice Ouradou (1822–84), he divided his time between the restoration work at Notre-Dame and Viollet-le-Duc's practice, where he was one of several trusted pupils charged with the growing number of commissions for restorations, or new designs for Gothic Revival châteaux in the style of the restoration under way at Pierrefonds for Napoleon III. The restoration of the Château de Roquetaillade, near Mazères, Gironde (begun 1864), quickly became Duthoit's own, as did that at Chamousset, Rhône (begun by Viollet-le-Duc 1861, completed 1880), and the work at the new château for the explorer Antoine d'Abbadie at Bidassoa, near Hendaye, Basses-Pyrénées (1864–70).

In 1861, on Viollet-le-Duc's recommendation, Duthoit went on an archaeological mission to Cyprus, Sicily and Syria as a draughtsman for Melchior de Vogüé's great *Syrie centrale: Architecture civile et religieuse du Ier au VIIe siècle* (Paris, 1865–77), for which Duthoit drew the plates. (This was one of several publications on which Viollet-le-Duc quickly drew for the arguments evolving in his *Entretiens sur l'architecture.*) During this trip Duthoit also designed the chapel of Lazarists and a church for the Capuchin monastery in Beirut, both in Romano-Byzantine style (both designed 1862, completed 1865). He began integrating Byzantine, Arab and Early Christian motifs into the Gothic repertory inherited from Viollet-le-Duc, a combination, first seen in his restoration of the small chapel at Roquetaillade (1875–7), that saw its fullest expression in his one large-scale work, the great pilgrimage church of Notre-Dame de Brébières at Albert, Somme (1883–96), the last of a series of churches he designed in

Picardy after moving his practice to Amiens in 1870. Duthoit's historicist palette was further enriched by forms culled from his annual trips to North Africa for the Commission des Monuments Historiques, where he made numerous studies of Islamic architecture. The Latin-cross plan served as a framework for a stylistic experiment that was, as he said, 'the synthesis of all I have seen', reconstituting the historical development of the Christian basilican-type church.

BIBLIOGRAPHY

Edmond Duthoit architecte, 1837–1889 (Amiens, 1890)
B. Bergdoll: *The Architecture of Edmond-Clément-Marie-Louis Duthoit* (diss., U. Cambridge, 1979)
J. Gardelles, J.-C. Lasserre and J.-B. Marquette: 'Roquetaillade: La Terre, les hommes, les châteaux', *Cah. Bazadais*, liii–liv (1981) [whole issue]
B. Bergdoll: '"The Synthesis of All I Have Seen": The Architecture of Edmond Duthoit (1837–89)', *The Beaux-Arts and Nineteenth-century Architecture*, ed. R. D. Middleton (London, 1982)
J. Foucart-Borville: 'Une Collaboration exemplaire: Viollet-le-Duc et Edmond Duthoit à Roquetaillade', *Bull. Soc. Hist. A. Fr.* (1987), pp. 269–81

BARRY BERGDOLL

Dutilleul, Roger (*b* 1873; *d* 1956). French collector and industrialist. He was a regular client of the dealer Daniel-Henry Kahnweiler from 1908 to 1914 and the first French collector to buy Cubist paintings by Georges Braque and Pablo Picasso. Both independent and open in his taste, he came from a comfortable bourgeois background and was administrator of a large cement company in Boulogne but did not dispose of a large fortune. In 1907, when he began to collect art seriously, the work of Paul Cézanne was already too expensive for him, but he could afford that of artists influenced by him. Although he continued to admire Picasso after World War I, he could not then afford to buy his work, and the only Cubist-related paintings he acquired after the war were by Fernand Léger. Unlike some other admirers of Cubism, Dutilleul was attracted by expressive, apparently spontaneous styles of painting. He never bought a work by Juan Gris, despite Daniel-Henry Kahnweiler's advocacy, and he criticized Henri Matisse as too contrived.

During the 1920s Dutilleul bought paintings by members of the Ecole de Paris, including Moïse Kisling, Chaïm Soutine, Maurice Utrillo and particularly Amedeo Modigliani, who painted his portrait in 1918 (France, priv. col., see *Amedeo Modigliani*, exh. cat., Paris, Mus. A. Mod. Ville Paris, 1981, p. 148). Between 1928 and 1939 most of Dutilleul's disposable funds went on supporting André Lanskoy, exemplifying his passionate and moral attitude towards patronage. He sold or exchanged numerous works while building up his collection, but he was not interested in the possible financial benefits of his activity. His collection, donated by his nephew Jean Masurel and his wife Geneviève Masurel, forms the core of the Musée d'Art Moderne in Lille.

BIBLIOGRAPHY

'La Parole est aux collectionneurs', *A. & Argent* (1948) [special issue]
'M. Dutilleul, un dénicheur d'artistes', *Plaisirs France* (Feb 1954)
J. Grenier: 'Un Collectionneur pionnier', *L'Oeil*, 15 (March 1956), pp. 40–41
F. Berthier: *Collection Roger Dutilleul* (diss., U. Paris I, 1977)
Donation de Geneviève et Jean Masurel à la communauté urbaine de Lille (exh. cat., ed. M. Peneau, J. Jardez and A. Lefebure; Paris, Luxembourg Pal., 1980)

F. Berthier: 'La Merveilleuse et Grande Aventure de Roger Dutilleul', *Gal. A.*, 220 (Dec 1983–Jan 1984), pp. 46–71

MALCOLM GEE

Düttmann, Werner (*b* Berlin, 6 March 1921; *d* Berlin, 26 Jan 1983). German architect, urban planner and teacher. He studied architecture at the Technische Hochschule, Berlin (1939–42), returning there to the Technische Universität (1947–8) after service in World War II and a period as a prisoner of war in England. He worked in the city building department of West Berlin from 1948 to 1966, with a year of postgraduate study under Thomas Sharp (1901–78) at the Town and Country Planning Institute at the University of Durham in 1950–51. Düttmann's work as an architect belongs to the Neues Bauen tradition of German Modernism, influenced by Hans Scharoun, and his most successful works are marked by intimacy, appropriateness of scale and skilful handling of materials. His early buildings in West Berlin, including a youth hostel (1953), Zehlendorf, and an old people's home (1955), Wedding, were followed by a small library, the Städtische Volksbücherei (1957), Hansaviertel, and the Akademie der Künste (1959–60), an arts complex of three buildings in the Hansaviertel. From 1960 to 1966 he was city architect of West Berlin; notable buildings of this period include the Brücke-Museum (1966–7), Berlin, a museum devoted to the painters of the Expressionist group Die Brücke; and the St Annenkirche (1967), Kreuzberg. The most attractive feature of most of these buildings is the use of carefully scaled, intimate, internal courtyards, designed as places of repose. He fared less well, generally, with his larger buildings in Berlin, such as the high-rise housing in the Märkisches Viertel, a satellite town in the north of Berlin in which he was also involved as a planner, and at Heerstrasse (1971), Spandau. His rebuilding of the war-damaged Mehringplatz, an 18th-century circular Baroque plaza that he turned into a pedestrian precinct, was also much criticized despite his attempt to achieve a new function for the space. A later work, the extension (1975–82) to the Kunsthalle, Bremen, drew on his experience with the Brücke-Museum. Düttmann also taught as a professor (1963–70) at the Technische Universität, West Berlin, and became president of the Akademie der Künste in 1977 until his death in 1983.

WRITINGS

Berlin ist viele Städte (Berlin, 1984)

BIBLIOGRAPHY

E. Schulz: *Das märkische Viertel* (Berlin, 1975)
G. Gress and others: *Werner Düttmann zum Gedenken* (Berlin, 1983)
G. Kühne: 'Werner Düttmann', *Baumeister, Architekten, Stadtplaner*, ed. W. Ribbe and W. Schäche (Berlin, 1987), pp. 595–6

GÜNTHER KÜHNE

Dutuit. French family of collectors. The family fortunes were founded by Pierre-Etienne Dutuit (*b* Rouen, 30 April 1767; *d* Rouen, 20 Sept 1852), who engaged in the import and dyeing of cotton. The eldest of his three sons, (Etienne-Philippe-)Eugène Dutuit (*b* Marseille, 7 April 1807; *d* Paris, 26 June 1886), trained as a lawyer and in 1840 was called to the Bar of Rouen. In the course of a long career in local politics he saved monuments from demolition and paid for the restoration of the churches of

St Vivien and St Maclou. His youngest brother, (Philippe-)
Auguste(-Jean-Baptiste) Dutuit (*b* Paris, 17 June 1812; *d*
Rome, 11 July 1902), saw his vocation as a painter and,
after travelling in Italy in 1836, entered the studio of
Thomas Couture. He exhibited genre paintings at the
Salon in 1868 and 1869 and later decorated his château of
Rouvray with scenes in a Rococo style.

Both brothers, however, devoted most of their energies
to collecting, spending huge sums of money on books,
prints and later paintings. Eugène began with books,
buying heavily at auction, for example at the great Pixéré-
court sale in 1839, and later from booksellers, principally
Damascène-Morgand. He made his first purchases of
prints in 1832 and thereafter amassed astonishing collections. In 1845 he presented a large group of Old Master
prints to the Bibliothèque Municipale at Rouen and was
consequently elected a member of the Académie de Rouen
in the following year. He continued to collect on a vast
scale and conceived his monumental *Manuel de l'amateur
d'estampes*, which was left unfinished at his death. In the
introduction he explained that he wished to make a
synthesis of the works of his predecessors such as Adam
von Bartsch and A. P. F. Robert-Dumesnil, and, in addition, to provide collectors with an enjoyable work to read,
full of 'amusing details'. Of the ambitious scheme to cover
the whole history of engraving, only the general history of
early engraving and nielli (vol. 1) and the Netherlandish
schools (vols 4–6) were published. Material for these works
was drawn not only from Dutuit's own collection but also
from correspondence with a large network of dealers,
collectors and curators. His work was complemented by
the catalogue of etchings by Rembrandt, of which he
owned a nearly complete series.

The Dutuit brothers made their first important purchase
of paintings at Ghent in 1840, when they bought Rembrandt's *Self-portrait in Oriental Dress* (1631) and Metsu's
La Toilette (both Paris, Petit Pal.). Their taste extended to
Dutch cabinet pictures and works by French artists, such
as Poussin's *Massacre of the Innocents* (1625–6; Paris, Petit
Pal.), bought in 1855. Their collection of *objets d'art* was
small but carefully selected; their collection of maiolica,
for example, is comparable only to that of
C. D. E. Fortnum (Oxford, Ashmolean) as an assemblage
of documented and representative pieces. After the death
of Eugène in 1886, Auguste moved to Rome and continued
to expand the family collections. Probably inspired by the
rooms at the Musée du Louvre devoted to the bequest of
Louis La Caze, he bequeathed the entire collection to the
city of Paris. The Dutuit collections are now housed in
the Petit Palais.

WRITINGS
Manuel de l'amateur d'estampes, 6 vols (Paris, 1881)
L'Oeuvre complet de Rembrandt, 3 vols (Paris, 1883–5)

DBF
                                    BIBLIOGRAPHY
H. Lapauze: 'Notice historique sur les frères Dutuit', *Catalogue sommaire
    des collections Dutuit* by H. Lapauze, C. Gronkowski and A. Fauchier-
    Magnan: (Paris, 1925), pp. 11–57
S. de Bussierre: 'Eugène Dutuit (1807–1886) et Rembrandt', *Rembrandt:
    Eaux-fortes* (exh. cat., ed. S. de Bussierre and S.-J. Piver; Paris, Petit
    Pal., 1986), pp. 8–9

Duval, Marc (*b* Le Mans, *c.* 1545; *d* Paris, 13 Sept 1581).
French engraver and painter. He was the son of the painter
and sculptor Bertin Duval (*fl* 1519–62). Although contemporary sources, including the *Bibliothèque . . .* (Paris, 1584)
by François Grudé, Sieur de La Croix du Maine (1552–
92), indicate that Marc Duval was active as a portrait
painter at the courts of Charles IX and Henry of Navarre
(later Henry IV), no authenticated painted work by him is
known to survive. Dimier (1942) suggested that the 13
portraits he initially (1924–6) grouped under the name of
the Master of Luxembourg-Martigues should be attributed
to Duval. These works include *Charlotte de Roye, Comtesse
de La Rochefoucauld* (*c.* 1555; Paris, Louvre). If this identification is correct, it would make Duval one of the most
important French portrait painters in the generation after
François Clouet.

Among Duval's surviving signed engravings are the
small, full-length portrait of the brothers *Odet, Gaspard
and François de Coligny* (1579; preparatory drawing, Paris,
Bib. N.) and portraits of *Catherine de' Medici* and *Jeanne
d'Albret* (both 1579). He also executed a set of engravings
of the *Seasons* with satyrs and grotesques in the style of
the Fontainebleau school. An engraving of 1579 after
Lorenzo Lotto's *Woman Taken in Adultery* (Paris, Louvre)
indicates that Duval was a reproductive engraver, too, and
he may also have been a dealer. According to La Croix du
Maine, at the time of his death he was preparing a collection
of engraved portraits of the kings, queens and nobles of
France. His daughter Elisabeth Duval (*fl* end of 16th
century) was a portrait draughtsman in Paris.

Thieme–Becker
                                    BIBLIOGRAPHY
E. Moreau-Nélaton: *Les Clouet et leurs émules*, 3 vols (Paris, 1924)
L. Dimier: *Histoire de la peinture de portraits en France au XVIe siècle*, 3
    vols (Paris, 1924–6)
A. Linzeler: *Inventaire du fonds français: Graveurs du seizième siècle*, Paris,
    Bib. N., Cab. Est. cat., i (Paris, 1932)
L. Dimier: *La Peinture française au XVIe siècle* (Paris, 1942)
S. Béguin: 'Brèves remarques sur L. Lotto', *A. Ven.*, xxxii (1978), pp. 112–
    16

                                    PHILIPPE ROUILLARD

Duval Le Camus, Pierre (*b* Lisieux, 14 Feb 1790; *d*
Saint-Cloud, 29 July 1854). French painter. A pupil of
Jacques-Louis David, he pursued an uninterruptedly
smooth career, which was almost banal in its lack of
deviation in inspiration or style. He showed regularly in
the Salon between 1819 and 1853, immediately gaining
attention with his first exhibited painting, the *Game of
Piquet between Two Invalids* (exh. Salon 1819; Detroit, MI,
Inst. A.). Far from being an innocent genre scene, it alludes
to the plight of the veterans of Napoleon's armies during
the Restoration. It is one of the few paintings by Duval
Le Camus in which a political meaning is suggested. His
interiors generally depict a familiar and anonymous reality
in the tradition of Martin Drolling, although he was less
skilful than Drolling in the rendering of objects and effects.
Duval Le Camus was a guileless and unaffected narrator.
Throughout his career he executed genre scenes in the
Dutch style, showing a genuine talent as a popular story-
teller (e.g. *Gossiping Porter* and *Little Chimney Sweep*; both
Narbonne, Mus. A. & Hist.). Unlike Louis-Léopold Boilly
he did not seek to amuse but to be sincere. Duval Le
Camus depicted the games and minor dramas of childhood

several times with the simplicity of Chardin (e.g. *The Reprimand*; ex-Duchesse de Berry priv. col.; drawing, Montpellier, Mus. Fabre).

Duval Le Camus's portraits belong to the same tradition as his interiors. The figure is placed in an interior (e.g. *M. Courtin*; Lisieux, Mus. Vieux-Lisieux) or a landscape (e.g. *Artist in a Landscape*; Bordeaux, Mus. A. Déc., and *Returning from the Fields*; exh. Salon 1831; Orléans, Mus. B.-A.) with a naive, poetic simplicity. The integration of the figure into the landscape by means of luminous contrasts recalls the small-scale portraits that were fashionable in Europe around 1790, but Duval Le Camus's sitters, somewhat awkwardly composed in the manner of François Sablet, lack the elegance of 18th-century conversation pieces.

Duval Le Camus was prolific, and his success did not wane despite the repetitiveness of his subjects. He was honoured and respected, obtaining the Légion d'honneur and becoming mayor of Saint-Cloud. In 1844 he was vice-president of the Fondation du Baron Taylor, which brought together artists such as Adrien Dauzats, Hippolyte Sebron (1801–79), Oscar Gué (1809–77), Claude-Marie Dubufe and Edouard Dubufe. The number of prints made after his works testifies to his popularity.

His son, Jules Alexandre Duval Le Camus (*b* Paris, 5 Aug 1814; *d* Paris, 23 June 1878), was also a painter. He was taught by his father, Paul Delaroche and Drolling and won second prize in the Prix de Rome of 1838. He painted mainly religious and historical subjects, including *Jacques Clément* (destr. World War I), which was bought by the State.

BIBLIOGRAPHY

H. Béraldi: *Les Graveurs du XIXe siècle*, ii (Paris, 1889), pp. 81–2
H. Hamel: 'Pierre Duval Le Camus, 1790–1854', *Pays Ange*, ix (1979), pp. 21–7
V. Dunifer: 'Two Veterans Playing "Piquet": A Genre Painting with Disguised Political Content', *Ksthist. Tidskr.*, liv/4 (1985), pp. 170–80

MARIE-CLAUDE CHAUDONNERET

Duvanli. *See* DOUVANLI.

Duvaux, Lazare (*b* ?Paris, ?1703; *d* Paris, 23 Nov 1758). French marchand-mercier. He entered the Parisian guild of marchands-merciers in 1740. He first set up a shop in the Rue de la Monnaie and later in the Rue St Honoré, which had an international reputation for its luxury shops. He specialized in furniture, bronzes and porcelain, and his suppliers included a wide range of French artisans and manufacturers. Like other marchands-merciers, he sold fashionable goods, including objects lacquered with *vernis Martin*, porcelain from East Asia, Meissen and Vincennes, many different types of furniture, mirrors and a range of such bronze items as fireplace furnishings. He specialized in objects that combined different materials, for example porcelain set in gilt-bronze mounts and clocks with porcelain and bronze. Most of his stock was new, but he also sold some furniture by André Charles Boulle, which suggests that he acted as an antique dealer. He is also listed as a buyer at sales of the period (including the collection of Marie-Joseph d'Hostun, Duc de Tallard), either buying for himself or on behalf of his clients. He built up an extremely influential clientele including the French royal family, the aristocracy, financiers and government officials.

After supplying the court regularly for some years he was officially appointed Marchand-Bijoutier du Roi in 1755, a position that carried various privileges. One of his most important customers, both in terms of revenue and prestige, was the Marquise de Pompadour. A day-book (published in 1873) records his daily business transactions between 1748 and 1758 and gives the most comprehensive information about the objects that he sold and his daily business activities.

BIBLIOGRAPHY

L. Courajod, ed.: *Livre journal de Lazare Duvaux, marchand-bijoutier ordinaire du roy, 1748–1758*, 2 vols (Paris, 1873)

CAROLYN SARGENTSON

Duveen, Joseph, 1st Baron Duveen of Millbank (*b* Hull, 14 Oct 1869; *d* London, 25 May 1939). English dealer and patron. His father, Sir Joseph Joel Duveen (1843–1908), a Dutch-Jewish immigrant, was a dealer in Delft ceramics who, with his brother Henry Duveen, built a major international art-dealing firm, Duveen Brothers. Duveen left college at 17 to train in and eventually take over his father's company. His personality was charming but shrewd, avuncular yet forceful. With great confidence and an often flamboyant business style, he was supremely successful—through society contacts and spectacular saleroom bidding—in obtaining exceptional paintings and sculpture, particularly of the Italian Renaissance. He also dealt notably in 18th-century French and English works and the paintings of Albrecht Dürer, Hans Holbein the younger, Rembrandt and Frans Hals. With the aim of suppressing rivals, from 1906 he paid exceptionally high prices for the collections of Oscar Hainauer, Rodolphe Kann and Maurice Kann, R. H. Benson and Gustave Dreyfus.

Duveen channelled major works from an economically pressed European seller's market to an avid buyer's market in America that he created among established American millionaires and the newly rich. His principal clients included Benjamin Altman, Jules S. Bache, Henry Clay Frick, Samuel H. Kress, the Huntington family, Philip Lehman and Robert Lehman, J. Pierpont Morgan, the Rockefeller family, Joseph E. Widener and Andrew W. Mellon. Duveen's virtuosic salesmanship made the acquisition of aesthetically unchallenging and colourful masterpieces into a fashionable pursuit for these often frugal magnates; his advice was followed avidly by powerful but publicly insecure buyers. For some 30 years, too, Bernard Berenson was employed by Duveen as an art expert in a partnership of some notoriety, whereby Duveen was able to sell pictures authenticated by Berenson, who would also discuss them in his books.

Apart from the ultimate enrichment of American art museums through donations from his clients, Duveen envisaged the National Gallery of Art, Washington, DC, founded by Mellon, as a shrine to his own dealing achievements. Duveen donated numerous works to galleries in London, ranging from Correggio's *Christ Taking Leave of His Mother* (before 1514; London, N.G.) to Stanley Spencer's *Resurrection, Cookham* (1923–7; London, Tate). He endowed a chair for art history at the Courtauld Institute, University of London, and donated entire galleries to the National Gallery, the National Portrait Gallery, the Tate Gallery and the British Museum (for the display of the Parthenon marbles), all in London. Among various positions he held, he served as a trustee of the National Gallery, the National Portrait Gallery and the Wallace Collection, London.

BIBLIOGRAPHY

Obituary, *The Times* (26 May 1939)
S. N. Behrman: *Duveen* (London, 1952, rev. 1972)

HARLEY PRESTON

Duveneck, Frank [Decker, Francis] (*b* Covington, KY, 9 Oct 1848; *d* Cincinnati, OH, 3 Jan 1919). American painter, sculptor, etcher and teacher. The eldest son of German immigrants Bernard and Katherine Decker, Duveneck, who assumed his stepfather's name after his father's death and his mother's remarriage in 1850, received his early art training in Cincinnati as an apprentice to Johann Schmitt (1825–98) and Wilhelm Lamprecht (*b* 1838), decorators of Benedictine churches and monasteries. In 1870 he went to Munich to study at the Königliche Akademie, where he was taught by Wilhelm Diez (1839–1907), among others. The school stressed the study of Old Master painters such as Velázquez and Hals and emphasized bravura brushwork. Duveneck was an adept pupil. His realistic portraits of the 1870s, such as *Professor Ludwig Löfftz* (*c.* 1873; Cincinnati, OH, A. Mus.), show the sitter placed against a dark background, the face and hands bathed in an intense light and modelled with thick, broad, fleshy brushstrokes.

Duveneck returned to America in 1873 and in 1874 began teaching at the Ohio Mechanics Institute in Cincinnati, where Robert Frederick Blum and John H. Twachtman were among his students. An exhibition at the Boston Arts Club in 1875 brought him his first major critical attention. Henry James, writing in *The Nation* (3 June 1875), called Duveneck 'an unsuspected man of genius'. Accompanied by Twachtman and Henry Farny (1847–1916), he returned that year to Munich, where William Merritt Chase and Walter Shirlaw were among his close associates. In May 1876 he visited Paris; the following March he, Chase and Twachtman went to Venice for nine months.

When he returned to Munich in 1878, Duveneck started his own painting classes, which, in the summer, he conducted in the Bavarian village of Polling. The American artists John White Alexander, Joseph Rodefer De Camp, Julius Rolshoven (1858–1930) and Theodore Wendel (1857–1932) were among his students and companions. In 1879 some of Duveneck's group left for a two-year stay in Florence and Venice. Known as the 'Duveneck Boys', they provided the model for the 'Inglehart Boys' in *Indian Summer* by William Dean Howells. In Venice, Duveneck met Whistler and with his assistance and that of Otto Bacher (1856–1909) began to experiment with etching. Although Duveneck's prints are more densely detailed than those by Whistler, when they were first shown at the New Society of Painter-Etchers in London, 1881, they were thought to have been done by Whistler under an assumed name. The resulting furore ended the friendship between the two artists.

During this stay in Italy, Duveneck's work began to change. His subject-matter now included more landscapes and genre scenes. His palette became more colourful and his paint surface less dense. In 1886 Duveneck married his pupil Elizabeth Boott (1846–1888), a Bostonian who resided primarily in Florence. The large, elegant portrait of her (1888; Cincinnati, OH, A. Mus.) typifies the change in his portrait work. The face is more carefully delineated, and the background brushwork, while still lively, reveals a lighter, more delicate touch. After his wife's unexpected death in Paris in 1888, Duveneck returned to Cincinnati to teach. While there he modelled a memorial for his wife. A bronze version of this full-length reclining figure marks her grave in the Allori cemetery in Florence. Duveneck remained in Cincinnati except for trips abroad and summers in Gloucester, MA, where he painted brilliantly coloured landscapes in an impressionistic manner, such as *Dock Sheds at Low Tide* (*c.* 1900; Newport News, VA, Mar. Mus.). He was made a member of the National Academy of Design in 1905. In 1915 a major exhibition of his work was presented at the Panama-Pacific Exposition in San Francisco.

BIBLIOGRAPHY

N. Heerman: *Frank Duveneck* (Boston, 1918)
Exhibition of the Work of Frank Duveneck (exh. cat. by W. H. Siple, Cincinnati, OH, A. Mus., 1936)
E. Poole: 'The Etchings of Frank Duveneck', *Print Colr Q.*, xxv (1938), pp. 312–331, 446–463
J. W. Duveneck: *Frank Duveneck: Painter-Teacher* (San Francisco, 1970)
R. Neuhaus: *Unsuspected Genius: The Art and Life of Frank Duveneck* (San Francisco, 1987)
J. Thompson: *Duveneck: Lost Paintings Found* (Santa Clara, 1987)
M. Quick: *An American Painter Abroad: Frank Duveneck's European Years* (Cincinnati, 1988)

CAROLYN KINDER CARR

Duvet, Jean [Drouhot] (*b* ?Dijon, *c.* 1485; *d* ?Langres, after 1561). French goldsmith and engraver. He was the son of Drouhot Duvet, a goldsmith active in Dijon at the end of the 15th century and the beginning of the 16th. He was admitted as a master goldsmith in Dijon in 1509, but most of his career was in Langres. He is known to have participated in the preparation of the decorations for the entry of Francis I into Langres in 1521, and he designed and directed the decorations and floats for the entry of Francis in 1533. Nothing remains of his work as a goldsmith, but he is known to have completed a reliquary bust of *St Mammes* in 1524 for Langres Cathedral, to have sold a damascened basin to Francis I in 1528 when the King visited Dijon and to have made a number of other works.

Duvet is best known as one of the great printmakers of the French Renaissance. His engraved work comprises 72 sheets. The first dated print is an *Annunciation* (Eisler, no. 12) of 1520, an ambitious work that betrays a considerable knowledge of Italian art for a provincial artist at that date. The face of the angel, with its wide features and high, arched brows, is already characteristic of Duvet's peculiar figures, while the body is closely modelled on Marcantonio Raimondi's engraving of *Lucretia* after Raphael. Duvet must have made a number of prints before this, including, in particular, the *Woman of the Apocalypse with Cornucopia* (E 5), another adaptation of the same Raimondi print, in which Duvet followed closely the graphic delicacy of the Italian master. Later, in his mature works, his handling of the burin became much bolder and more personal, made up of long, flowing cuts with short, flickering ones for shading. The result is strikingly unconventional.

Duvet's major work is a series of 23 illustrations of the *Apocalypse* (E 40–61), which he completed in 1555 and which had occupied him over many years. It appeared with printed text in 1561 in Lyon, but the plates were printed separately before that. Although Duvet knew Albrecht Dürer's famous set of woodcuts of the subject made in 1498 and borrowed some motifs and compositional ideas, the general effect is very different. He also added several plates that have no equivalent in the German set. Duvet's plates are entirely, almost wildly, covered with motifs, giving the whole surface an extraordinary ornamental brilliance. He affected a total disregard of perspective. The figures, on the other hand, are always strongly modelled and convey a sense of weight and energy and an incomparable physiognomic vigour. The series is a vehement and impassioned work. The frontispiece (E 65), where the goldsmith-engraver has deliberately projected himself in the image of his patron St John the Evangelist meditating on the *Apocalypse*, is a particularly eloquent and personal piece; there are also two further plates of scenes from the life of St John (E 38–9).

Another set of six prints on the *Unicorn* and its capture (E 32–4, 66–8) has given him the name of Master of the Unicorn. This series demonstrates Duvet's attachment to a vernacular tradition in spite of his careful study and use of Italian prints (Andrea Mantegna's as well as Raimondi's). He left some of his engravings partially incomplete, which may have been voluntary, since one of them, *SS Sebastian, Anthony and Roch* (E 70), was published as a broadsheet against the plague. They have a freedom and immediacy that have no equivalent in Renaissance printmaking.

Another Jean Duvet (called Droz), a French goldsmith who was master of the mint in Geneva from 1540 until 1556 and who has been mistakenly identified with the engraver of the same name, was most probably his nephew, since he is identified as the son of 'Loys Duvey, alias Drot de Dijon', which was the name of the engraver's goldsmith brother (master in 1509). After 1556 Jean Duvet seems to have fallen on hard times, and by 1570 he had died. Yet another goldsmith with the same name, perhaps his son, was active in Geneva and was condemned to death for extortion in 1576.

BIBLIOGRAPHY

E. Julienne de la Boullaye: *Etude sur la vie et sur l'oeuvre de Jean Duvet dit le maître à la licorne* (Paris, 1876)
A. E. Popham: 'Jean Duvet', *Prt Colr Q.*, viii (1921), pp. 122–50
H. Naef: 'Un Artiste français du XVIe siècle, bourgeois de Genève: Jehan Duvet, le maître à la licorne', *Bull. Soc. Hist. & Archit. Genève*, v (1925), p. 39
C. Eisler: *The Master of the Unicorn: The Life and Work of Jean Duvet* (New York, 1979) [E] [with extensive bibliog.]
The French Renaissance in Prints from the Bibliothèque Nationale de France (exh. cat., New York, Met., 1995)

HENRI ZERNER

Duvivier. French family of artists.

(1) Jean Duvivier (*b* Liège, 7 Feb 1687; *d* Paris, 30 April 1761). Medallist, printmaker and painter. He was the son of Gangulphe Duvivier (*fl* 1678–1724), coin engraver to Joseph Clement of Bavaria, Prince Bishop of Liège. He trained as both a die engraver and as a painter before travelling to Paris in 1711. There he studied at the Académie Royale de Peinture and engraved portraits and ornamental prints. In 1714 he was commissioned to execute a medal of *Joseph Clément* (e.g. Paris, Bib. N., Cab. Médailles). During its production he came to the attention of Nicolas De Launay, Director of the Paris mint, who ordered from him a medal of the equestrian statue of Louis XIV at Lyon. From then on he was fully employed revising the series of medals commemorating Louis XIV and, in his capacity as Medal Engraver to the King, producing new medals for Louis XV. In 1717 Duvivier was elected to the Académie Royale de Peinture, and in 1723 he took over what had been Jean Mauger's lodgings in the Louvre. For the next 15 years he was responsible for most of the official medals issued by the Paris mint. In 1737, however, a quarrel with the Académie des Inscriptions over his right to sign medals, followed by Duvivier's refusal to copy Edme Bouchardon's profile portrait of the King, sharply reduced his access to official commissions, and much of his later work was done for provincial estates. There are examples of his medals in the British Museum, London, and of his drawings in the Musée Carnavalet, Paris. None of his paintings has been traced.

(2) (Pierre-Simon-)Benjamin Duvivier (*b* Paris, 5 Nov 1730; *d* Paris, 10 July 1819). Medallist, son of (1) Jean Duvivier. He studied at the Académie, winning prizes in 1744, 1746 and 1756. He succeeded his father as Medal Engraver to the King in 1764 and exhibited at the Salon from 1765 onwards. In 1772 he was appointed Engraver-General of French coinage and in 1776 a member of the Académie. During this period Benjamin engraved a large number of medals, both for the government and for provincial estates, towns and companies. From 1781 to 1789 he was also commissioned to produce a series of medals commemorating the American War of Independence, notably *George Washington before Boston* (1786; e.g. London, BM), which exemplifies his move towards realism, and the *Storming of the Tuileries* (1792; e.g. London, BM), which shows a less successful move towards Neoclassicism. Duvivier did his best to win favour with the Revolutionary authorities in France. His medal celebrating Louis XVI's arrival in Paris (1789) was soon followed by another celebrating the overthrow of the monarchy (1792). However, he lost the post of Engraver-General to Augustin Dupré in 1791, and although he received a certain number of commissions under the Consulate and was elected to the Institut in 1806, his reputation never recovered.

BIBLIOGRAPHY

A. C. Quatremère de Quincy: *Notices historiques*, i (Paris, 1834–7)
L. Gougenot: 'Vie de Jean Duvivier', *Mémoires inédites sur la vie et les ouvrages des membres de l'Académie Royale de Peinture et de Sculpture*, ed. L. Dussieux and others (Paris, 1854), ii, pp. 308–47
H. Nocq: *Les Duvivier* (Paris, 1911)

MARK JONES

Duwe, Harald (*b* Hamburg, 28 Jan 1926; *d* nr Kiel, 15 June 1984). German painter. Towards the end of his apprenticeship as a lithographer (1943), he had a formative experience while viewing Wilhelm Leibl's *Three Women in Church* (Hamburg, Ksthalle; for illustration *see* LEIBL, WILHELM), a picture whose realism exerted a lasting influence on him. After service in World War II he studied from 1946 to 1949 under Willem Grimm (*b* 1904) at the Staatliche Hochschule für Bildende Künste in Hamburg. He spent two terms on a scholarship at the Kungliga Akademi för de Fria Konsterna, Stockholm. In 1951, as an independent artist, he moved to Grossensee in Schleswig-Holstein, where he lived with his family for the rest of his life.

Except for a short phase of painting Impressionistic landscapes, Duwe remained faithful to certain sets of motifs and unswayed by contemporary artistic taste, painting contemporary life—the misery of the post-war years in Germany; scenes of labour and the harbour in Hamburg (e.g. *Changing Shifts at the Harbour*, 1954; priv. col., see 1987 exh. cat., pl. 10); documentation of the political restoration under Chancellor Konrad Adenauer; and many other themes. The pre-eminence of abstract art after World War II did not affect Duwe. In their examination of current political events his works uniquely reflect the history of the Federal Republic of Germany. In his representation of history and his realistic approach he was both a forerunner of and participant in the Berlin Critical Realist group (*see* BERLIN, §II, 5), without being directly connected with it. Since his paintings did not sell well, he was always dependent on his income from teaching. From 1964 to 1967 he taught at the Fachhochschule in Hamburg and from 1975 at the Fachhochschule in Kiel.

BIBLIOGRAPHY

Harald Duwe: Bilder, 1948–1982 (exh. cat., W. Berlin, Gal. Poll, 1983)

In memoriam Harald Duwe, Hamburger Kunsthalle (Gifkendorf, 1984)

Harald Duwe: 1926–1984 (exh. cat. by J. C. Jensen, Kiel, Christian Albrechts-U., Ksthalle, 1987)

DOMINIK BARTMANN

Duweir, Tell ed-. *See* LACHISH.

Duyl-Schwartze, Thérèse van. *See* SCHWARTZE, THÉRÈSE.

Duyster, Willem (Cornelisz.) (*b* Amsterdam, *bapt* 30 Aug 1599; *d* Amsterdam, *bur* 31 Jan 1635). Dutch painter. Duyster was the eldest of four children of Cornelis Dircksz. and his second wife, Hendrikge Jeronimus, from Gramsberge, Norway. His father is recorded as a textile cutter, house carpenter and minor Amsterdam official. In 1620 the family, which also included two children from Cornelis's first marriage, moved into a house in the Koningstraat named 'De Duystere Werelt' ('The Dark World'), which gave Duyster and his half-brother Dirck their adopted surname. The family name first appears in a document dated 1 July 1625 concerning a violent quarrel between Duyster and Pieter Codde, a fellow Amsterdam artist. The argument took place at Meerhuysen, a country house rented by Barent van Someren (*c.* 1572–1632), the painter, dealer and inn-keeper who was a patron of Adriaen Brouwer and a good friend of Frans Hals.

An inventory from 16 October 1631, taken after the death of Duyster's parents, testifies that the family was financially comfortable and lists several anonymous paintings, mainly of popular biblical and mythological subjects.

Although Duyster appears to have been living in the family house at the time the inventory was taken, no mention is made of a studio or any of his works.

In September 1631 he married Margrieta Kick, a cousin of the Haarlem painters Jan and Salomon de Bray. The double wedding ceremony also united Margrieta's younger brother, the Amsterdam genre painter Simon Kick (1603–52), and Duyster's youngest sister, Styntge. Eventually each couple came to live in 'De Duystere Werelt'.

Bredius suggested that Duyster studied under Pieter Codde, but this is unlikely, since the artists were exact contemporaries. It is more probable that either Barent van Someren or the portrait painter and collector Cornelis van der Voort (*c.* 1576–1624) taught them both.

Duyster's limited oeuvre includes genre scenes and portraits. Together with Codde he helped to develop and popularize the interior soldier scene. His *Cortegaerdjes* (guardroom pieces), which are often characterized by an underlying psychological tension, include depictions of soldiers looting, taking hostages or skirmishing among themselves. More frequently, the quieter side of military life is illustrated, with soldiers smoking, gaming, making music, dancing or romancing. These activities are also depicted in his merry company scenes, set in stable, barn or inn interiors. Signed or attributed portraits are rare.

Duyster's paintings are on a small scale with full-length figures and are carefully detailed. Angel (1642) particularly praised his skill at painting silks. In both subject-matter and style his works are similar to those of Pieter Codde. However, Duyster's are more innovative in terms of compositional effects, format and iconography. He experimented successfully with artificial light effects (especially evident in his nocturnal pieces), handling of space and unusual angles of vision. While most of his interiors are quite plain, shadows, angles of walls or openings into subsidiary spaces are often used to create an abstract counterpoint of light and shadow against which the figures are set. The play of tonal values against rich, dark colour accents in his early works, particularly his genre portraits, shows the influence of Amsterdam portrait painters of the 1620s, such as Thomas de Keyser. His later works have quieter tonal harmonies, though they are almost always reinforced with strong colour areas.

Only three extant works ascribed to Duyster are dated: *Portrait of a Man* (1627; Amsterdam, Rijksmus.), *Portrait of a Woman* (1629; Amsterdam, Rijksmus.) and *Officer and Soldiers* (1632; Dublin, N.G.). His *Soldiers beside a Fireplace* (1632; ex-Werner Dahl priv. col., Düsseldorf) is probably a copy after two authentic versions (Philadelphia, PA, Mus. A., John G. Johnson Art Col., see fig.; St Petersburg, Hermitage). A lost portrait, dated 1628, of Joseph del Medico, the noted Jewish physician and writer, is known through an engraving after the original by Willem Delff. No pupils of Duyster are known: his closest direct follower was the little-known painter Daniel Cletcher (*d* 1632), who worked in The Hague. Duyster died of the plague that swept through the Netherlands in early 1635.

BIBLIOGRAPHY

Hollstein: *Dut. & Flem.*; Thieme–Becker; Wurzbach

P. Angel: *Lof der schilderconst* (Leiden, 1642/*R* 1969), p. 55

A. Houbraken: *De groote schouburgh* (1718–21/*R* 1976), ii, p. 145

Willem Duyster: *Soldiers beside a Fireplace*, oil on panel, 426×464 mm, 1632 (Philadelphia, PA, Museum of Art)

A. Bredius: 'Iets over Pieter Codde en Willem Duyster', *Oud-Holland*, vi
  (1888), pp. 187–94
H. F. Wijnman: 'De Amsterdamsche genreschilder Willem Cornelisz.
  Duyster', *Amstelodamum*, xxii (1935), pp. 33–4
C. B. Playter: *Willem Duyster and Pieter Codde: The 'Duystere werelt' of
  Dutch Genre Painting*, c. 1625–35 (diss., Harvard U., 1972)
*Tot lering en vermaak: Betekenissen van Hollandse genrevorstellingen uit de
  17de eeuw* [For instruction and pleasure: meanings of Dutch genre
  paintings of the 17th century] (exh. cat. by E. de Jongh and others,
  Amsterdam, Rijksmus., 1976), pp. 104–11
Masters of 17th-century Dutch Genre Painting (exh. cat. by P. Sutton and
  others; Philadelphia, PA, Mus. A.; W. Berlin, Gemäldegal.; London,
  RA; 1984), pp. 198–9
                                    C. VON BOGENDORF RUPPRATH

Dvin [Gr. Doubios; Arab. Dabil]. Site in Artashat province in the Republic of Armenia, 35 km south of Erevan. The remains of settlements dating to the 3rd millennium BC have been found in its hinterland, including massive structures of cyclopean masonry and the foundations of large temples. Further settlements were established around Dvin in the 2nd and 1st centuries BC, when a temple dedicated to the god Tir was probably built (destr. *c.* AD 314).

Dvin is primarily known for its Armenian architectural remains, which date from its foundation under Khosrov III (*reg* AD 332–9) until the early 13th century. Its ruins were first recorded by Armenian, Russian and European travellers of the 18th and 19th centuries. Excavations were begun in 1899 under N. Mař and resumed in 1907–8 by Khatchik *vardapet* Dadyan. From 1936 to 1939 systematic excavations were undertaken by Smbat Ter-Avetisyan, from 1946 to 1976 by Karo Ghafadaryan and from 1977 by Aram K'alant'aryan. The finds reflect Dvin's important position on the trade route between Anatolia and East Asia.

The centre of the city was occupied by an impressive citadel with high walls built of clay bricks and fortified by over 44 towers. A moat surrounded the citadel, which was connected by bridges to the main part of the fortified city. Among the principal monuments of the 4th to the 7th centuries were the three-aisled episcopal basilica of St

Gregory (early 4th century), which was replaced in the 7th century by a cruciform domed cathedral, an associated palace and extensive monastic buildings, two further palaces and numerous secular monuments, including a caravanserai (6th century), houses and workshops where glass, ceramic and metal wares were produced. The great number and diversity of glass objects indicate that Armenian glassmaking was strongly influenced by Syrian techniques. Ceramic finds include faience, often decorated with blue and green designs and a lustrous finish. The numerous cast and chased metal objects include agricultural tools (e.g. sickles, ploughs), weapons (e.g. arrows, lances; Erevan, Hist. Mus. Armen.; *see* ARMENIA, §VI, 3), and finely crafted gold and silver bracelets, rings and earrings (Erevan, Hist. Mus. Armen.).

After the Arab conquest of AD 640, Dvin became the seat of the Arab viceroyalty of Armenia. Ceramics, metalwork and textiles were brought to Dvin from such major Islamic centres as Damascus, Samarra and Baghdad in exchange for local products. Much of the city was ruined by the earthquake of 894, after which the secular buildings and palaces were reconstructed using locally produced clay bricks and unpolished stone. The emergence of the Bagratid dynasty (885–1045) in Armenia initiated a period of rapid development in Dvin, which became a centre of woollen garment, rug, silk and lace production. It continued to flourish as the seat of several Arab emirates in the 12th century and under the Zak'arian princes in the early 13th. The city was destroyed by the Tatar-Mongols in 1236.

BIBLIOGRAPHY

V. Harut'yunyan: *Dvini 5–7-rd dd. chartarapetakan husharjannerĕ* [The architectural monuments of 5–7th-century Dvin] (Erevan, 1950)

K. G. Ghafadrayan: *Dvin k'aghak'ĕ ev nra peghumnerĕ* [The city of Dvin and its excavations], 2 vols (Erevan, 1950–82)

K. Kafadarian: 'Les Fouilles de la ville de Dvin (Duin)', *Rev. Etud. Armén.*, ii (1965), pp. 283–301

A. Ter Ghévondyan: 'Chronologie de la ville de Dvin (Duin) aux 9e et 11e siècles', *Rev. Etud. Armén.*, ii (1965), pp. 303–18

A. A. K'alant'aryan: *Dvini nyut'akan mshakuyt'ĕ IV–VIdd.* [The material culture of Dvin in the 4th to 6th century] (Erevan, 1970)

H. M. Djanp'oladyan: *Dvini midznadaryan apakin IX–XIIIdd.* [The medieval glasswares of Dvin in the 9th to 13th century] (Erevan, 1974)

A. A. K'alant'aryan: *Dvin* (Erevan, 1976)

F. S. Babayan: *Midznadaryan Hayastani gegharvestakan xec'egheni zardajeverĕ* (The decorative motifs of medieval Armenian pottery) (Erevan, 1981)

N. G. Hakobyan: *Midznadaryan Hayastani gegharvestakan metaghĕ* [The metal treasures of medieval Armenia] (Erevan, 1981)

MANYA GHAZARYAN

Dvořák, Max (*b* Raudnitz [now Roudnice], Bohemia, 24 May 1874; *d* Hrušovany nad Jevišovkou, Moravia [now in Czech Republic], 8 Feb 1921). Austro-Czech art historian. Both his grandfather and father were, in succession, librarian and archivist to Prince Lobkowitz at Schloss Raudnitz on the Elbe, and Max Dvořák was intended to follow them. He therefore began studying history at Prague in 1892 and went to Vienna in 1894 to continue his training at the Institut für Österreichische Geschichtsforschung. He graduated in 1897, but under the influence of Franz Wickhoff and Alois Riegl he then turned to art history. In 1898 he became Wickhoff's assistant and qualified as a lecturer in 1902. After Riegl's death in 1905, Wickhoff secured Dvořák's appointment as Associate Professor despite opposition in German nationalist circles. Dvořák's early studies of medieval art are completely in line with the historical, developmental approach of his teachers. If he was personally closer to Wickhoff, he owed more methodologically to Riegl's purely formal, analytical approach. An outstanding example of this is *Das Rätsel der Kunst der Brüder Van Eyck*, in which Dvořák tried to show that the stylistic change in early Netherlandish painting was part of a continuous development.

As head of conservation of state monuments from 1905, Dvořák took a public stand on numerous issues relating to monuments. He founded his own research institute, published the yearbook of the office for the preservation of monuments and wrote *Katechismus der Denkmalpflege*. When the allies demanded reparations from Germany at the end of World War I, Dvořák fought energetically to preserve Austria's art treasures. Encouraged by Julius Schlosser, Dvořák became professor of art history at the University of Vienna, where he headed a second institute of art history in competition with Josef Strzygowski's individual approach to the subject.

Subject-matter in art had always interested Dvořák and increasingly dominated his work. In his article of 1914 he stressed that to understand any given period it was essential to know something of that period's intellectual history. This emphasis on ideas achieved its full breakthrough after World War I. In a manner analogous to artistic Expressionism, Dvořák devised a method of research that his pupils later characterized by the slogan 'art history as intellectual history'. His study *Idealismus und Naturalismus in der gotischen Skulptur und Malerei* (1917) was a key work in this development. Like Vasily Kandinsky's theory of art, it does not take realistic and abstract art as opposites but as two equal methods of expression. An artist's ability to choose between personal expression and the reflection of the current intellectual climate fascinated Dvořák, and his study of Mannerism revealed an intellectual position related to that of his own time. His article 'On El Greco and Mannerism' (1920) clearly referred also to the work of Oskar Kokoschka.

With his intellectual, history-based approach, Dvořák was, with Wickhoff from the stylistic and Riegl and Schlosser from the linguistic–historical standpoints, one of the great methodological founders of the 'Vienna School'. After Dvořák's death, his work was continued by Hans Tietze and Otto Benesch.

UNPUBLISHED SOURCES

U. Vienna, Inst. Kstgesch. [comprehensive col. of unpubd lectures, essays and reviews]

WRITINGS

'Das Rätsel der Kunst der Brüder Van Eyck', *Jb. Ksthist. Samml. Allhöch. Ksrhaus.*, xxiv (1903), pp. 161–319; as booklet, ed. J. Wilde and K. M. Swoboda (Munich, 1925)

'Über die dringendsten methodischen Erfordernisse der Erziehung zur kunstgeschichtlichen Forschung', *Die Geisteswissenschaften*, i (1913–14), pp. 932–6, 958–61

Katechismus der Denkmalpflege (Vienna, 1916, rev. 2/1918)

Idealismus und Naturalismus in der gotischen Skulptur und Malerei (Munich, 1918; Eng. trans., 1967)

'Ein offener Brief an die italienischen Fachgenossen', *Die Entführung von Wiener Kunstwerken nach Italien*, ed. H. Tietze (Vienna, 1919), pp. 3–9

Oskar Kokoschka: Variationen über ein Thema (Vienna, 1921) [foreword]

'Über Greco und den Manierismus', *Kunstgeschichte als Geistesgeschichte: Studien zur abendländischen Kunstentwicklung*, ed. K. M. Swoboda and

J. Wilde (Munich, 1924, rev. 2/Mittenwald, 1979; Eng. trans. as *The History of Art as the History of Ideas*, 1984)
Geschichte der italienischen Kunst im Zeitalter der Renaissance: Akademische Vorlesungen, 2 vols (Munich, 1927–8)
Gesammelte Aufsätze zur Kunstgeschichte, ed. J. Wilde and K. M. Swoboda (Munich, 1929)

BIBLIOGRAPHY

H. Tietze: 'Max Dvořák', *Kstchron. & Kstmarkt*, xxxii/23 (1921), pp. 441–4
D. Frey: 'Max Dvořáks Stellung in der Kunstgeschichte', *Jb. Kstgesch.*, i(xv) (1923), pp. 1–21
W. Köhler: 'Max Dvořák', *Mitt. Österreich. Inst. Geschforsch.*, xxxix (1923), pp. 314–20
O. Benesch: 'Max Dvořák: Ein Versuch zur Geschichte der historischen Geisteswissenschaften', *Repert. Kstwissen.*, xliv (1924), pp. 159–97
J. Schlosser: 'Die Wiener Schule der Kunstgeschichte: Rückblick auf ein Säkulum deutscher Gelehrtenarbeit in Österreich', *Mitt. Österreich. Inst. Geschforsch.*, xiii/2 (1934), pp. 145–210
G. A. dell'Acqua: *L'arte italiana nella critica di Max Dvořák* (Florence, 1935)
W. Böckelmann: *Die Grundbegriffe der Kunstbetrachtung bei Wölfflin und Dvořák* (Dresden, 1938)
J. Neumann: 'Das Werk Max Dvořáks und die Gegenwart', *Acta Hist. A. Acad. Sci. Hung.*, viii (1962), pp. 177–213
J. Pavel: *Max Dvořák* (Brno, 1971)
'Max Dvořák 1874–1921', *Österreich. Z. Kst & Dkmlpf.*, xxviii/3 (1974) [whole issue]
A. Rosenauer: 'Das Rätsel der Kunst der Brüder Van Eyck—Max Dvořák und seine Stellung zu Wickhoff und Riegl', *Akten des XXV. Internationalen Kongresses für Kunstgeschichte: Wien und die Entwicklung der kunsthistorischen Methode, Wien, 1983*, pp. 45–52
J. Bakoš: 'Die epistemologische Wende eines Kunsthistorikers', *XXVII Congrès international d'histoire de l'art: Révolution et évolution de l'histoire de l'art de Warburg à nos jours, Strasbourg, 1989*
E. Lachnit: 'Ansätze methodischer Evolution in der Wiener Schule der Kunstgeschichte', *XXVII Congrès international d'histoire de l'art: Révolution et évolution de l'histoire de l'art de Warburg à nos jours, Strasbourg, 1989*

EDWIN LACHNIT

Dwight, John (*b c.* 1635; *bur* Fulham [now in London], 13 Oct 1703). English potter. He was employed by the natural philosopher and chemist Robert Boyle in Oxford in the 1650s, which evidently engendered his interest in chemistry. From 1661 he held secretarial and legal appointments under four bishops of Chester, but it was not until 1670–71, when living at Wigan, that after many experiments he concluded that 'he had ye secret of making china ware'. He applied for and was granted a patent on 17 April 1672 for making 'transparent Earthen Ware' and 'stone ware' and moved to London, setting up a pottery in Fulham. By March 1676 the production of stoneware bottles after the Rhenish bellarmines, mugs and similar vessels was sufficiently established for Dwight to negotiate a sales agreement with the Worshipful Company of Glass Sellers of London, who held the London monopoly of the sale of both glassware and stoneware. In June 1684 Dwight obtained a second patent restating his original claims and supplemented with additional 'inventions', including 'opacous redd and darke coloured Porcellane'. Both the extension of the patent on brown stoneware and the 'inventions' led to much inconclusive litigation between Dwight and James Morley of Nottingham, David Elers and John Philip Elers and the Wedgwood family during the period 1693–8. Dwight's production of so-called 'porcellane' appears to have been limited to a number of extremely fine, white, salt-glazed stoneware busts and figures, as in the stoneware bust of *Prince Rupert* (*c.* 1675; London, BM), the result of experimental work *c.* 1673–5.

Production of brown stoneware, however, continued at Fulham Pottery for more than 200 years.

BIBLIOGRAPHY

M. Bimson: 'References to John Dwight in a Seventeenth Century Manuscript', *Trans. Eng. Cer. Circ.*, iv/5 (1959), pp. 10–24
——: 'John Dwight', *Trans. Eng. Cer. Circ.*, v/2 (1961), pp. 95–107
D. Haselgrove and J. Murray, eds: 'John Dwight's Fulham Pottery, 1672–1978: A Collection of Documentary Sources', *J. Cer. Hist.*, 11 (1979), pp. 1–148

DAVID DRAKARD

Dwurnik, Edward (*b* Radzymin, nr Warsaw, 19 April 1943). Polish painter, draughtsman and sculptor. Between 1963 and 1970 he studied painting with Eugeniusz Arct (*b* 1899) and Eugeniusz Eibisch and graphic art with Józef Pakulski at the Academy of Fine Arts, Warsaw. He exhibited at home and abroad from 1971 (e.g. at the Fifth Biennial, Sydney, 1984; the Nouvelle Biennale, Paris, 1985; and *Documenta*, Kassel, 1986).

Dwurnik's work is usually grouped in related cycles over a period of years (e.g. *Hitch-hiking*, 1966; *Workers*, 1975; and *Cross*, 1979), forming an epic record of Polish life from the 1970s and 1980s. Dwurnik, without overstatement, documented specific places and events, producing a faithful, albeit almost gloomy and grotesque picture of Poland. His drawings of workers (1980–81) during the era of the rise of the independent trade union, Solidarnośc (Solidarity), brought him considerable publicity. Although his work belongs to the time of the revival of painting in Poland in the 1970s (two of his student colleagues were Łukasz Korolkiewicz and Tomasz Ciecierski), critics tended to associate his work principally with the 'new' and 'wild' (Pol. *dziki*) painting of the 1980s, in which he was a leading light. Some of his works, particularly from the mid-1980s, have very expressionistic traits (also evident in his sculptures of this period), the former light brushstrokes having given way to more pronounced daubs.

BIBLIOGRAPHY

Edward Dwurnik: Malarstwo [Edward Dwurnik: painting] (exh. cat., Opole, Office A. Exh., 1986)

WOJCIECH WŁODARCZYK

Dyad statue. *See* EGYPT, ANCIENT, §IX, 2(i)(e).

Dyagilev, Sergey (Pavlovich). *See* DIAGHILEV, SERGE.

Dyce, William (*b* Aberdeen, 19 Sept 1806; *d* Streatham, London, 15 Feb 1864). Scottish painter, educationalist, theorist and designer. The son of a lecturer in medicine at Marischal College, Aberdeen, he studied medicine and theology, obtaining his Master's degree in 1823. Episcopalian by upbringing, Dyce was expected, like his cousin, the scholar and bibliophile Alexander Dyce (1798–1869), to proceed to Oxford to take orders. His early interest in art found an outlet in portraiture, his first commission being *Sir James M. D. M'Grigor* (1823; U. Aberdeen). His first attempt at history painting, *The Infant Hercules Strangling the Serpents sent by Juno to Destroy Him* (1824; Edinburgh, N.G.), much influenced by Reynolds, was shown to Sir Thomas Lawrence, who is said to have encouraged Dyce to enter the Royal Academy Schools in 1825. After a few months he set off for Rome in the company of Alexander Day; this somewhat sudden and unconventional departure from academic education was typical of Dyce, who was both conscientious and innovative.

It is uncertain whether he met the NAZARENES while in Rome, but he did make friends with Christian Karl Josias, Freiherr Bunsen, secretary to the Prussian legation in Rome and a keen enthusiast for early church music and 15th-century Italian art. In 1827 Dyce was again in Rome and is said to have painted a *Virgin* in 1828 that aroused the admiration of Johann Friedrich Overbeck and his friends. However, the earliest extant paintings that reveal any departure from *Hercules* and the Poussin-influenced unfinished *Bacchus Nursed by the Nymphs of Nysa* (1826; Aberdeen, A.G.) are the *Dead Christ* of 1835 (Aberdeen, A.G.) and *Virgin and Child* (*c.* 1838; London, Tate). The paintings that caused Dyce to be labelled controversially 'the British Nazarene' date from the mid-1840s: *Joash Shooting the Arrow of Deliverance* (1844; Hamburg, Ksthalle), *Virgin and Child* (1845; Brit. Royal Col.), *Gethsemane* (*c.* 1855; Liverpool, Walker A.G.) and *St John Leading the Blessed Virgin Mary from the Tomb* (1844–60; London, Tate). These works are characterized by a clarity of form, a Neo-classical sharpness of line and a contemporary approach to biblical history (e.g. Gethsemane is located in a Scottish glen).

Although Dyce's output of easel paintings was small, he was very active in other areas; he was a genuine polymath with a strong sense of public duty. In 1830, for example, he was painting portraits for a middle-class Edinburgh clientele, writing a paper on the frescoes of the Baths of Titus at Rome, composing an essay 'On the garments of Jewish priests' and preparing a treatise 'On the relations between the phenomena of electricity and magnetism and the consequences deducible from those relations'. His easel paintings, especially those of his later years, provided relief from his other activities: the *Highland Ferryman* of 1858 (Aberdeen, A.G.) is a loving and detailed record of a timeless occupation, which must have seemed a far remove from Dyce's hectic London responsibilities.

Many of his later works were painted, or at least conceived, on family holidays and were purchased by relatives. In faithfully representing the landscape he followed Pre-Raphaelite handling without using its colour; only *Titian's First Essay in Colour* (1857; Aberdeen, A.G.) approached the brilliance of Pre-Raphaelitism. Paintings such as a *Scene in Arran* (1859; Aberdeen, A.G.), peopled by women and children, also present an intensely nostalgic imagery. In *Pegwell Bay: A Recollection of October 5th 1858* (1859; London, Tate) the nostalgia is explicitly embodied in the specificity of the title. Using a style of cold photographic exactitude, Dyce constructed an iconography of time through a startlingly lucid conjunction of images: Donati's comet visible in the late afternoon sky;

William Dyce: *George Herbert at Bemerton*, oil on canvas, 0.86×1.12 m, 1861 (London, Guildhall Art Gallery)

the geological time-scale of the chalk cliffs; and the human time-scale of the artist and his family as they gather shells.

In 1837 Dyce was appointed Master of the Trustees' Academy in Edinburgh where his first task, in collaboration with Charles Heath Wilson (1809–82), was the preparation of a report on the institution's administration. Published as the *Letter to Lord Meadowbank* in 1837, it came to the attention of the recently established Select Committee on the Arts and their Connections with Manufacture.

Concern about Britain's failure to produce designers adequate to her manufacturing potential resulted in the foundation of the first British government-sponsored School of Design (in London) with Dyce as Superintendent. The dispute between the fine art and the industrial model was fierce; Dyce favoured the Bavarian system where students trained in a workshop to design for specific industries, while Benjamin Robert Haydon argued for fine art training as essential in design education. This dispute has never been fully resolved. In 1843 Dyce resigned in frustration, hoping to devote more time to his art.

Dyce's *Order of Daily Service* was published in 1843 and at the same time he published articles in the *Christian Remembrancer*, planned illustrations for a Society for Promoting Christian Knowledge project and prepared a report on the lighting in the galleries of the Taylorian Institute in Oxford. More ecclesiological projects followed, as well as work with the Motett Society and advice to stained-glass designers (though Dyce's own work in this medium was limited to the window at St Paul's, Alnwick, Northumb., 1853). In *c.* 1849 he executed the fresco reredos *Holy Trinity and Saints* for All Saints, Margaret Street, London. Dyce remained a lifelong member of the Anglican Church, and the pictorial declaration of his faith is encapsulated in his painting of *George Herbert at Bemerton* (1861; London, Guildhall A.G.; see fig.).

Dyce was involved in the fresco revival in England from the start, contributing *Hesperus* to Prince Albert's garden pavilion at Buckingham Palace in 1844 (destr.) and decorating a staircase at Osborne House, Isle of Wight, in 1847 with *Neptune Resigning to Britannia the Empire of the Sea*. When the competition for the decoration of the new Palace of Westminster was held in 1843, Dyce, probably the only man in Britain with a technical knowledge of fresco, was an obvious choice. His most prestigious public commissions were the *Baptism of King Ethelbert* (1846) in the House of Lords Chamber and later a sequence based on Malory's *Morte d'Arthur* (1848–63) in the Robing Room.

These works constitute an important chapter in 19th-century nationalism and, despite the physical deterioration that set in before they were even completed, display an impressive confidence with composition on a monumental scale. The cartoons (Edinburgh, N.G.; U. Manchester, Whitworth A.G.) reveal Dyce as an immensely sensitive draughtsman and an imaginative interpreter of the medieval past. He collapsed at work in the winter of 1863 with the final fresco unfinished. The contents of his studio were auctioned at Christie's on 5 May 1865.

See also HERBERT, J. R.

WRITINGS
Notes on Shepherds and Sheep (London, 1851)
The National Gallery, its Formation and Management, Addressed by Permission to H.R.H. Prince Albert (London, 1853)
Letter on the Connection of the Arts with General Education (London, 1858)

BIBLIOGRAPHY
J. C. Dafforne: 'William Dyce, RA', *A. J.* [London] (1860), pp. 293–6
M. Pointon: *William Dyce, 1806–64; A Critical Biography* (Oxford, 1979) [incl. cat. rais.]
C. Willsdon: 'Dyce "in camera": New Evidence of his Working Methods', *Burl. Mag.* (Nov 1990), pp. 760–65
L. Errington: 'Ascetics and Sensualists: William Dyce's Views on Christian Art', *Burl. Mag.* (Aug 1992), pp. 491–7

MARCIA POINTON

Dyck, Abraham van. *See* DIJCK, ABRAHAM VAN.

Dyck [Dijck], Sir **Anthony** [Anthonie; Antoon] **van** (*b* Antwerp, 22 March 1599; *d* London, 9 Dec 1641). Flemish painter and draughtsman, active also in Italy and England. He was the leading Flemish painter after Rubens in the first half of the 17th century and in the 18th century was often considered no less than his match. A number of van Dyck's studies in oil of characterful heads were included in Rubens's estate inventory in 1640, where they were distinguished neither in quality nor in purpose from those stocked by the older master. Although frustrated as a designer of tapestry and, with an almost solitary exception, as a deviser of palatial decoration, van Dyck succeeded brilliantly as an etcher. He was also skilled at organizing reproductive engravers in Antwerp to publish his works, in particular *The Iconography* (*c.* 1632–44), comprising scores of contemporary etched and engraved portraits, eventually numbering 100, by which election he revived the Renaissance tradition of promoting images of *uomini illustri*. His fame as a portrait painter in the cities of the southern Netherlands, as well as in London, Genoa, Rome and Palermo, has never been outshone; and from at least the early 18th century his full-length portraits were especially prized in Genoese, British and Flemish houses, where they were appreciated as much for their own sake as for the identities and families of the sitters.

Following Rubens, van Dyck responded, not only in the phrasing of his will but also in the fearless manner of his dying, to the Neo-Stoic teaching that was the legacy of the Classical scholar Justus Lipsius at Leuven; not surprisingly a portrait of Lipsius, who was much respected in the Antwerp humanist circle in which both Rubens and van Dyck moved, was included in *The Iconography* (Mauquoy-Hendrickx, no. 22; grisaille model for the engraver, Duke of Buccleuch priv. col.).

Van Dyck's Christian piety expressed itself pictorially with more tender effect in works for private devotion than in larger altarpieces. His profane works, sadly few of which survive, show his quality as northern Europe's most sensitive admirer of Titian's *poesie*. His watercolours have been regarded as the incunables of English landscape.

I. Life and work. II. Sources. III. Studio practice. IV. Character and personality. V. Critical reception and posthumous reputation.

I. Life and work.

1. Background and early work in Antwerp and London, to autumn 1621. 2. Italy and France, autumn 1621–autumn 1627. 3. Antwerp and The Hague, autumn 1627–spring 1632. 4. England, spring 1632–late 1633 or early 1634. 5. Antwerp and Brussels, early 1634–early 1635. 6. England, spring 1635–late 1639. 7. Final years, 1640–41.

1. BACKGROUND AND EARLY WORK IN ANTWERP AND LONDON, TO AUTUMN 1621. Anthony van Dyck was the seventh child of Frans van Dyck and Maria Cuypers [Cuperis], who lived at 'Den Berendans', a substantial house on the Grote Markt in Antwerp. His father was something of a painter as well as a prominent silk and linen merchant. His mother, who died when he was eight, was known for the beauty of her embroidery. In October 1609 the young Anthony was registered with the Antwerp Guild of St Luke as a pupil of the dean that year, Hendrik van Balen I, a competent painter of small figures who often collaborated with the landscapist Jan Breughel I. He himself was registered as a master on 11 February 1618, and four days later, by his father's consent, he was declared of age by the Antwerp Tribunal. He had earlier, while still a minor, been involved in legal proceedings, on 3 December 1616 and 13 September 1617, on behalf of himself, his four sisters and his younger brother (his siblings all followed religious callings), to receive part payment of their grandmother's estate. This was incumbent because his father, formerly well-to-do and respected, the President of the Confraternity of the Holy Sacrament at Antwerp Cathedral, soon after became bankrupt. In order that Anthony's earnings should not be seized to help pay his father's debts, in 1620 he set up on his own, renting a house large enough for a studio with assistants, the 'Dom van Keulen' in the Lange Minderbroederstraat. There he engaged Herman Servaes and Justus van Egmont to make copies of his several sets of *Christ and the Apostles* (dispersed). In this, van Dyck followed the example of Rubens, who had assistants to copy (*c.* 1609–10) the prototype *apostelado* sent to the Duque de Lerma.

Van Dyck's series of larger compositions of the period 1616–21, both sacred and profane, were impressively of his own invention: but financial stress, and perhaps the difficulty of placing his early works except on commission, directed his precocious brilliance rather more than he might have wished to a series of three-quarter-length portraits of burghers and their wives (dated examples, 1618; Vaduz, Samml. Liechtenstein, and Dresden, Gemäldegal. Alte Meister). These were evidently inspired by contemporary work by Rubens of this kind, notably the portrait of *Jan Vermoelen* (1616; Vaduz, Samml. Liechtenstein).

It is not known precisely when or on what terms van Dyck entered the studio of Rubens. The older master, 22 years his senior, must have spotted van Dyck's potential soon after he himself was established in the mansion he had built (1610–17) on the Meer. Van Dyck as a boy—probably while still in van Balen's studio—seems to have

been uniquely privileged in access to the travelling Pocket-Book of Rubens (surviving in part, and through 17th-century copies), which was later celebrated by Bellori. He plundered its contents extensively, methodically and on occasion wittily into the first of his known sketchbooks, the so-called Antwerp Sketchbook (Chatsworth, Derbys), in which he pocketed a wide range of material, from Giacomo della Porta's physiognomic comparisons and Serlio's 4th Book of Architecture to copies of paintings by Titian and recipes for sore eyes and for painters' materials; the sketchbook also records figures or groups by subject categories from all manner of Italian and northern engravings such as were found in abundance in Rubens's house. Significantly, there are neither portraits nor records of portraits. Van Dyck's ambition throughout his working life was to be a history painter.

Writing on 24 April 1618 to Sir Dudley Carleton, English ambassador at The Hague, Rubens offered a painting of *Achilles and the Daughters of Lycomedes* (Madrid, Prado), valued at 600 guilders. This was 'fatto del meglior mio discipolo', then gone over by Rubens himself who was bargaining to part with 'the flower of my stock' in exchange for antiquities that Carleton had brought from his previous post, Venice. On the visual evidence of the picture itself, the 'best pupil' must have been van Dyck. As Bellori recorded, van Dyck had already served Rubens *c.* 1616–18 in the preparation of cartoons for the Decius Mus tapestry cycle, which were sent to Brussels to be woven by May 1618. In this project van Dyck's role was that of chief assistant, transferring the highly complex designs of Rubens's oil sketches on to canvases of heroic dimensions, painted especially to instruct the draughtsmen regularly employed on preparatory cartoons. Van Dyck also, according to Bellori and Mariette, drew *modelletti* for engravings intended to register and advertise afar the prowess of Rubens in design.

By 24 March 1620, in Rubens's contract with the Jesuit Provincial Father Tiry to design 39 ceiling paintings for the aisles and galleries of the Society's new church in Antwerp, the execution was allowed to be by van Dyck and other unnamed studio assistants. This contract also stipulated that van Dyck might make a painting for one of the four side altars at a later time. Van Dyck's early assistance to Rubens in painting figures can already be discerned in such religious works as the *Virgin and Child with Four Great Penitents* (*c.* 1618; Karlsruhe, Staatl. Ksthalle) and *Jesus in the House of Simon the Pharisee* (St Petersburg, Hermitage). His blazing idiosyncracies of morphology and brushwork blended with, but were never wholly absorbed by, the more profoundly creative genius of Rubens, who kept for himself eight of van Dyck's early masterpieces and with whom van Dyck apparently always continued to be on good terms. A letter from Antwerp of 17 July 1620 to Thomas Howard, 2nd Earl of Arundel, written by Francesco Vercellini, his Venetian *gentiluomo* then accompanying Lady Arundel on a continental visit, relates that:

> Van Dyck is still with Signor Rubens, and his works are hardly less esteemed than those of his master. He is a young man of 21 years, with his very wealthy father and mother living in this town, so that it will be difficult to get him to

leave these parts, especially since he sees the good fortune enjoyed by Rubens.

In fact, van Dyck's mother was long dead; and his parents had fallen in fortune. Despite Vercellini's pessimism, 'the father of *virtù* in England' (i.e. Arundel) was anxious to bring this rising star to London.

On 20 October Thomas Locke wrote to William Trumbull from London: 'Van Dyck is newly come to town. . . . I am told my Lo: of Purbeck sent for him hither'. John Villiers, recently created Viscount Purbeck, was half-brother to the royal favourite, the Marquess of Buckingham. On 25 November Tobie Mathew wrote to Carleton at The Hague that King James I had granted van Dyck, Rubens's 'famous *allievo*', an annual pension of £100. On 16 February 1621 van Dyck received £100 'by way of reward for special service performed for his Matie'. What precise service to his Majesty this may have been remains obscure.

Of van Dyck's paintings, Buckingham acquired the *Continence of Scipio* (1620–21; Oxford, Christ Church) from Arundel for York House and the *Venus and Adonis* (1620–21; Harari & Johns, London, 1991, see 1990–91 exh. cat., no. 17), presumably for another of his residences. The latter relates to one of van Dyck's Antwerp mythologies: it is an allegorical portrait painted in haste to celebrate the flamboyant Buckingham's betrothal to Lady Katherine Manners, a match regarded by her father as a *mésalliance*. The first of these two paintings, with full-length figures, evinces van Dyck's youthful admiration for the scenographic taste of Paolo Veronese whose *Esther and Ahasuerus* (1556; Vienna, Ksthist. Mus.) was then at York House; the second his facility in adapting to his purpose both Dürer's engraving of *The Promenade* (B. 94) and Cesare Ripa's emblem into a sensuous combination of the learned and the louche, hardly suitable for the burghers of Antwerp, welcome perhaps only at the Stuart court. Of the noble Arundel, van Dyck painted an appropriately sober portrait seated half-length (1620–21; Malibu, CA, Getty Mus.). It was Arundel who on 28 February 1621 signed a travel pass and permit for him for eight months. No other paintings are known of those van Dyck might have done during this first brief stay in England, unless it were one of the self-portraits (*see* §IV below).

Van Dyck returned to Antwerp in March 1621 for just under eight months to order his family affairs and to prepare for Italy. Usually assigned to this phase of his activity are the portrait of *Susanna Fourment and her Daughter* and that of *Isabella Brant* (both Washington, DC, N.G.A.), wonderful presages of the fashion for full-length portraiture that he later developed to gratify the Genoese families. Also datable to this period are the superb *St Sebastian Bound for Martyrdom* (Edinburgh, N.G.), the *Crowning with Thorns* and the *Betrayal of Christ* (versions of both, Madrid, Prado), masterpieces that manifest his urge to be recognized, like Rubens, principally as a composer of altarpieces and other histories at least on the scale of life.

2. ITALY AND FRANCE, AUTUMN 1621–AUTUMN 1627. In October 1621 van Dyck followed Rubens's example in 1600 by leaving for Italy. It is not clear how long he intended to remain there, nor whether he would

have accepted, as Rubens had, princely service at this stage of his career. He arrived in Genoa, the mercantile equivalent of Antwerp, probably by late November, lodging with his countrymen Cornelis and Lucas de Wael, who were established as art dealers and painters of small-figure genre and battle scenes. Van Dyck came unprepared for the sight in the Spinola, Doria and Grimaldi palaces of the astounding advances in fashionable portraiture made by Rubens during his Mantuan service 15 years before; and there can be little doubt that he conceived his standing portrait of *Marchesa Elena Grimaldi Cattaneo* (see fig. 1) and his equestrian portrait of *Giovanni Paolo Balbi* (*c.* 1625; Parma, Corte Mamiano Found.) to challenge Rubens's portraits of *Brigida Spinola Doria* (1606; Washington, DC, N.G.A.) and *Gian Carlo Doria* (*c.* 1606–7; Florence, Pal. Vecchio). (For van Dyck's portrait of the so-called '*Marchesa Balbi*', *c.* 1621–2, Washington, DC, N.G.A., *see* PORTRAITURE, fig. 17.) Between November 1621 and February 1622 he painted the portrait mentioned by Bellori

1. Anthony van Dyck: *Marchesa Elena Grimaldi Cattaneo*, oil on canvas, 2.46×1.73 m, 1623 (Washington, DC, National Gallery of Art)

of the future Doge *Agostino Pallavicini* (Malibu, CA, Getty Mus.), voluminously robed in crimson brocade as ambassador from Genoa to the Holy See. This was most likely the first of his grand portraits of Genoese notables. From February 1622 he seems to have been in Rome, filling his Italian Sketchbook (London, BM) with observations from life and from the works that took his eye while visiting churches and collections. He sketched (fol. 62*r* and *v*) and then he painted resplendent full-length portraits of *Sir Robert Shirley* and *Teresia, Lady Shirley* (both Petworth House, W. Sussex, NT), gorgeous in Circassian dress during their diplomatic mission to Gregory XV between 22 July and 29 August, and half-length portraits of two northern European sculptors, *François Du Quesnoy* (Brussels, Mus. A. Anc.) and *Georg Petel* (Munich, Alte Pin.). He then moved to Venice to meet Lady Arundel and to accompany her in November/December to Mantua and Milan. They reached Turin late in January 1623. He probably stopped again in Genoa and also visited Florence and Bologna. He painted in fairly quick succession, either in Venice or in Genoa, two portraits of the merchant *Lucas van Uffel* (Brunswick, Herzog Anton Ulrich-Mus.; New York, Met.), the latter (New York) tense with a dazzling depiction of movement arrested on the instant.

News of the death of van Dyck's father on 1 December 1622, leaving him worldly care for his siblings, would have reached him in Rome early in the new year. His immediate reaction to private grief was expressed in his most poignant portrait of himself, the *Self-portrait with the Broken Column* (early 1623; St Petersburg, Hermitage). (The public epitaph would come some six years later with the altarpiece of the *Crucifixion with SS Dominic and Catherine of Siena* (see fig. 2) painted soon after his return to Antwerp, in fulfilment of a promise of his father to the Dominican nuns who had nursed his last illness.)

Between March and October or November 1623 van Dyck was again in Rome. He followed the success of his portraits of van Uffel with two portraits of aristocratic persons just as vivid: the full-length of the former Nuncio in Flanders, *Cardinal Guido Bentivoglio* (1623; Florence, Pitti), seated alert as though giving audience, a state portrait that proved one of the most memorable Baroque achievements of its kind; and, just before that, the three-quarter-length, more intimate revelation of *Principe Virginio Cesarini in Jesuit Garb* (St Petersburg, Hermitage), seated in an armchair as though in private disputation, his gaze and his gesture alerting the viewer to the frailty of his existence. Radiographs have revealed that beneath the surface of the paint in the latter van Dyck had sketched the contrapposto he had wanted for the portrait of *Cardinal Bentivoglio*. He also portrayed another cardinal about this time, the Genoese *Domenico Rivarola* (best-known version in Des Moines, IA State Educ. Assoc.), either in Rome or in Genoa. Certainly it was in Rome that he met Sir Kenelm Digby (1603–65), the English Resident and a future patron. Digby's recollections of van Dyck became the principal source of Bellori's *Vita* of the artist. Significantly, van Dyck was the only Flemish artist, save Rubens and Du Quesnoy, both also active in Rome, who was esteemed enough by Bellori to be included in his publication of 1672.

2. Anthony van Dyck: *Crucifixion with SS Dominic and Catherine of Siena*, oil on canvas, 3.14×2.45 m, 1629 (Antwerp, Koninklijk Museum voor Schone Kunsten)

From autumn 1623 to spring 1624 van Dyck seems to have been in Genoa. In emulation of Titian's portraits of *Clarissa Strozzi* (1542; Berlin, Gemäldegal.) and *Ranuccio Farnese* (1542; Washington, DC, N.G.A.), he revivified a fashion for portraying young children without their parents. The lively charm of this Genoese series, anticipating his work at the Caroline court by eight years, has never been surpassed, from its beginnings with the portraits of *Filippo Cattaneo* and *Clelia Cattaneo* (both late 1623; Washington, DC, N.G.A.) to the *Three Sons of Girolamo de' Franchi* (the '*Balbi Children*', 1625–6; London, N.G.) to the much later portrait of *Mary, Princess Royal* (1637; ex-Governor Fuller priv. col., Boston, MA), which in 1647 was sent clandestinely to Holland by Charles I when he was detained at Hampton Court.

Van Dyck then moved to Palermo in spring 1624 at the invitation of the Viceroy of Sicily, Emanuel-Philibert of Savoy (1588–1624). Towards mid-May the plague struck, and the city was soon in quarantine. With the discovery of St Rosalia's purported remains in a grotto on nearby Monte Pellegrino, her cult expanded; and van Dyck executed at least three commissions to represent her as an intercessor (New York, Met.; London, Apsley House; Ponce, Mus. A.). The plague also claimed the life of the Viceroy himself, on 3 August of that year, shortly after van Dyck painted a scintillating three-quarter-length portrait of him (1624; London, Dulwich Pict. Gal.). On 12 July the 25-year-old van Dyck visited the Italian artist Sofonisba Anguissola, then in her nineties. In his Italian Sketchbook he surrounded a drawing of this relict (fol.

110r) with notes of their conversation about portraiture. He was also commissioned to paint a large altarpiece, the *Madonna of the Rosary*, for the oratory of the Rosario (1624–7; *in situ*). This, his principal religious undertaking in Italy, he began but did not complete before he prudently withdrew to Genoa from a recrudescence of the plague. (After his return to Antwerp, his representative, Antonio della Torre, was paid by the Confraternity of the Rosary on 8 April 1628 for the altarpiece, 'novamente fatto nella città di Genova'.) From van Dyck's pen sketch of the composition (Hilversum, Liberna priv. col., see 1991 exh. cat., no. 45) it is evident that he had in mind Rubens's *Madonna della Vallicella Adored by Saints* (1606–7; Grenoble, Mus. Grenoble), the first version of the altarpiece that Rubens himself had rejected for the Chiesa Nuova in Rome; he knew it as it hung over Rubens's mother's tomb in the abbey of St Michael, Antwerp, where his own younger brother Theodoor held a canonry.

In July 1625 van Dyck reputedly made an excursion to Marseille in order to visit, at Aix-en-Provence or Belgentier, the *savant* who had become the admiring friend and correspondent of Rubens, Nicolas-Claude Fabri de Peiresc. If so, van Dyck is likely to have drawn his portrait. A likeness was eventually engraved in Antwerp for *The Iconography* (M.-H. 89). On his return from Provence, he exulted in painting a dazzling series of portraits, many full-length, of men, women and children of the leading Genoese families (e.g. *Genoese Noblewoman and her Son*, c. 1626; Washington, DC, N.G.A.). His siblings had to declare to the Antwerp magistrate on 12 December 1625, as his brother-in-law had done on 27 November 1624, that he was still abroad.

3. ANTWERP AND THE HAGUE, AUTUMN 1627–SPRING 1632. Van Dyck returned home in evident haste in autumn 1627 for family as well as professional reasons. His parting gift to his hosts in Genoa, the double portrait of *Cornelis and Lucas de Wael* (Rome, Mus. Capitolino), is in parts conspicuously unfinished. His sister Cornelia, a Béguine, died in Antwerp on 18 September. Payment was made on 18 December by Giovanni Francesco di Antonio Brignole to 'Antonio Fiamengo' for the full-length portraits (all Genoa, Gal. Pal. Rosso) of his son *Anton Giulio Brignole-Sale on Horseback*, of *Paola Adorno*, Anton Giulio's wife, and of *Geronima Brignole-Sale with her Daughter Aurelia*, Giovanni Francesco's wife and daughter. Van Dyck's first dated portraits on return to Antwerp were three-quarter-lengths of appropriately rich sobriety but without palatial settings: that of the collector and connoisseur *Peeter Stevens* of 1627 and that of *Anna Wake* of 1628, the year Stevens took her as his wife (both The Hague, Mauritshuis). He painted also in 1628 his first major altarpiece for an Antwerp church, the *St Augustine in Ecstasy*, which was commissioned by Marius Jansenius for the left aisle of the church of St Augustine, flanking a vast *Sacra Conversazione* by Rubens and counterbalancing on the right the altarpiece of similar dimensions to his own, the *Martyrdom of St Apollonia* by Jacob Jordaens (all 1628; Antwerp, St Augustine; on loan to Kon. Mus. S. Kst.). Van Dyck and Jordaens were paid alike, 600 florins, establishing their status as the leading painters after Rubens in their city.

3. Anthony van Dyck: *Rinaldo and Armida*, oil on canvas, 2.37×2.24 m, 1629 (Baltimore, MD, Baltimore Museum of Art)

Van Dyck had made a will in Brussels on 6 March 1628. On 27 May the Earl of Carlisle wrote to Buckingham from Brussels that he had not met Rubens at his home in Antwerp but had met him the following day at 'Monsr Van-digs'. At the Maison Professe in Antwerp, van Dyck was enrolled that same month in the Sodalitedt van de Bejaerde Jongmans, a Jesuit confraternity of bachelors. (He was to paint in 1629 for these devout bachelors the grand altarpiece of the *Virgin and Child with SS Rosalia, Peter and Paul*, redolent of his experience in Venice and Bologna, and in 1630 a smaller, more intimate and more distinctly personal work of devotion, the *Mystic Vision of the Blessed Herman Joseph* (both Vienna, Ksthist. Mus.).) In December 1628 he was presented with a gold chain, valued at 750 guilders, for a portrait of the *Infanta Isabella Clara Eugenia* (version, Turin, Gal. Sabauda), whose court painter, Rubens, was in Madrid on a diplomatic mission to her nephew Philip IV of Spain.

Van Dyck's eye was already on Rubens's eventual return to dominate painting in Antwerp and correspondingly on his own chances of a return to the Stuart court, where Charles I, a truly art-loving prince, had succeeded his father James in 1625. As his spectacular introduction to the new reign, van Dyck painted his most delectable masterpiece hitherto on a profane subject, the gorgeous *Rinaldo and Armida* (see fig. 3; for a later modello on the same theme *see* GRISAILLE, fig. 3), and on 5 December 1629 he wrote to Endymion Porter, whom he had met nine years earlier through Buckingham, that the painting had been passed to his agent for delivery to the King; the following March van Dyck received £72 for it. By then he had more than sufficient financial security; and on 20 March 1630, Antwerp having issued a loan of 100,000 guilders, he subscribed for 4800 guilders. In a proxy dated 27 May, written for Pieter Snayers, who was to figure among the painters whose likeness (Munich, Alte Pin.) was engraved for *The Iconography* (M.-H. 98), van Dyck described himself as 'schilder van Heure Hoocheyd' ('painter to Her Majesty'), the Infanta Isabella. His annual salary was 250 guilders; and, like Rubens before him, he was excused residence at her court in Brussels, continuing to live in the artistic centre Antwerp. In December an Antwerp restorer, J.-B. Bruno, chanced to remark on van Dyck's exquisite collection of paintings (see Wood; Brown and Ramsay).

On 10 May 1631 van Dyck stood godfather for Antonia, daughter of Lucas Vorsterman the elder (who, with his star pupil Paulus Pontius and with Schelte Bolswert, was to be one of the chief engravers of *The Iconography*; for van Dyck's own etched portrait of Vorsterman *see* BELGIUM, fig. 17). During 1631, at the acme of his powers, van Dyck painted the stupendous full-length portrait of *Marie de Raet*, the wife of Philippe Le Roy, whose own full-length portrait dates from the previous year (both London, Wallace). From 4 September to 16 October 1631 Maria de' Medici, exiled from France with her younger son, Gaston, Duc d'Orléans, was in Antwerp, and van Dyck painted their portraits full-length (Bordeaux, Mus. B.-A., and Chantilly, Mus. Condé, respectively). The Queen Mother's secretary, J. P. de La Serre, noted in his travel record his admiration for van Dyck's 'Cabinet de Titien'. Titian, almost from van Dyck's first sightseeing tours south of the Alps, had largely supplanted Veronese in his utmost admiration, as is evident from his altarpiece of the *Crucifixion with SS Francis and Bernardino and a Donor* (*c.* 1620) for the parish church of S Michele di

Pagana, near Rapallo in Liguria (*in situ*). His Italian Sketchbook is crammed with *ricordi* penned from Titian's portraits and compositions. Among the nineteen works of Titian that he owned (he copied four more) were the *Perseus and Andromeda* (*c.* 1555; London, Wallace) and the *Vendramin Family* (*c.* 1543–7; London, N.G.), in which the boys seated on the altar steps with their pet dog surely prompted the purely domestic group of the *Children of Agostino and Vittoria Spinola* (*c.* 1623–5; Genoa, Pal. Durazzo-Pallavicini), itself long acclaimed as a foretaste of the *Children of Charles I and Henrietta Maria* (1635; Windsor Castle, Berks, Royal Col.).

Between 6 and 16 December 1631 Sir Balthazar Gerbier, the British agent in Brussels who had been Buckingham's master of the horse, sent Charles I's treasurer, Lord Weston, van Dyck's *Virgin and Child with St Catherine* (London, Buckingham Pal., Royal Col.) as a New Year's gift to the King. Perhaps out of pique at this high-handed transaction, van Dyck himself wrote to Geldorp that this painting was but a copy. Gerbier wrote to the King on 13 March 1632 that Rubens considered it an original and that the vendor, Salomon Noveliers, confirmed this before a notary; van Dyck himself was in Brussels, planning to travel to London.

Despite any such intention, the painter went for the winter of 1631–2 northward to The Hague, where he painted subject pictures as well as portraits for both the court of Frederick Henry and Amalia von Solms and the court of the deposed 'Winter King and Queen' of Bohemia, Frederick V of the Palatinate and Elizabeth Stuart. For the individual likenesses of the Palatine princelings, he adapted the pattern invented by Titian for his portrait of *Benedetto Varchi* (*c.* 1540–43; Vienna, Ksthist. Mus.). He portrayed in addition the poet and statesman Constantijn Huygens the elder, who entered in his diary for 28 January 1632, 'Pingor a Van Dyckio . . .'. The appearance of the portrait (untraced) is presumably recorded in Pontius's engraving in *The Iconography* (M.-H. 53), the series of engravings for which Huygens himself wrote three mottoes.

4. ENGLAND, SPRING 1632–LATE 1633 OR EARLY 1634. Not until April 1632 was van Dyck in London again. From that time Edward Norgate, an artist and writer in the service of Arundel and brother-in-law of Nicholas Lanier, the court musician who had presented his own portrait by van Dyck (1628; Vienna, Ksthist. Mus.) to the King, had 15 shillings *per diem* 'for dyett and lodging' of van Dyck. The Flemish painter moved soon to Blackfriars, London, beyond the jurisdiction of the jealous Painter-Stainers' Company. He also had lodgings at Eltham in Kent, where the King kept his summer residence. On 5 July 1632 he was knighted and made 'principalle Paynter in ordinary to their Majesties', thus eclipsing Daniel Mijtens who had been portrait painter to the Stuart court since 1625. His 'greate Peece' displaying the royal family settled at home (1632; London, Buckingham Pal., Royal Col.), to be hung at a vantage-point in the Long Gallery at Whitehall, was decorously more staid, it must be said, than the vivid grouping of *The Lomellini Family* (see fig. 4), which he had finished in Genoa. In the still greater, but now so sadly damaged, group portrait of *Philip Herbert, 4th Earl*

4. Anthony van Dyck: *The Lomellini Family*, oil on canvas, 2.69×2.54 m, *c.* 1623–5 (Edinburgh, National Gallery of Scotland)

of *Pembroke, and his Family* (*c.* 1633–4; Wilton House, Wilts), van Dyck, in dealing with so many individual figures, would seem to have overextended his powers of coherent composition in depth. More compact, more coherent and effective in grouping and panoply is the portrait of *Johan Maurits of Nassau-Siegen and his Family* (1634; Firle Place, E. Sussex), in which the count and the countess are shown seated with their four children standing beside them.

Van Dyck was kept busy on portraiture and on the restoration (in one case the replacement) of Titian's series of *Twelve Roman Emperors* (1536–40; destr. 1734), purchased by Charles I from Mantua. Ten commissions from the King were paid at £280 on 8 August 1632, and on 7 May 1633 nine portraits of the King and Queen at £444; in April 1633 he had, in addition, received the gold chain and medal that he is later seen wearing in the enigmatic *Self-portrait with a Sunflower* (*c.* 1635–6; best-known, but doubtfully autograph version, London, Duke of Westminster priv. col.); and on 17 October 1633 he was promised a salary of £200 a year, besides payment for special work. A few days later he had a £40 advance for a portrait of the Queen. During 1632 he had painted the half-length of *Henrietta Maria Handing Charles I a Laurel Wreath* (Kroměříž Castle), an eloquent criticism of Mijtens's effort at the same courtly composition (before 1632, overpainted 1634; London, Buckingham Pal., Royal Col.); also the portrait of *Philip, 4th Lord Wharton* (Washington, DC, N.G.A.). In a census of foreign residents at Blackfriars, he was described as 'Dutch. Sir Anthony Van Dike. Portrait painter. Two years. Six servants'.

5. ANTWERP AND BRUSSELS, EARLY 1634–EARLY 1635. Henrietta Maria in the last week of August 1633 had tried to place Theodoor van Dyck, Anthony's younger brother, as her chaplain. The canon can only have stayed a little while in London; by 14 March 1634 he was back in Antwerp. On private business thither the painter had perhaps even preceded him, for on 28 March he acquired an interest in Het Steen at Elewijt, the estate that Rubens was to buy in May 1635. On 14 April Anthony authorized his sister in Brussels to administer his property. At this point he had little intention of settling to enjoy country life. He was elected on 18 October dean of the Antwerp Guild of St Luke *honoris causa*, an honour previously vouchsafed only to Rubens. He painted a noble version of the *Pietà* (Munich, Alte Pin.). Then on 4 November, the Infanta Isabella having died in Brussels the previous December, Philip IV's brother, the Cardinal-Infante Ferdinand, made his entry into Brussels as the new governor for Spain. The three-quarter-length portrait of him (Madrid, Prado) by van Dyck is noted on 16 December as 'recently painted', the painter being then lodged in Brussels in the house 'In't Paradijs' behind the town hall. During this 12-month stay in Flanders, he painted some of the most impressive male portraits of his career: that of his friend *Jacomo de Cachiopin* (Vienna, Ksthist. Mus.), an inheritor of mercantile wealth who devoted a whole room in the country house he built for himself to portraits by van Dyck, including those of himself and his wife (untraced); a full-length of ineffable elegance, the *Abbé Cesare Alessandro Scaglia* (Hackwood Park, Hants), the worldly

wise, world weary envoy of Savoy, who had returned jobless to Brussels; and two superb equestrian portraits, one of the Spanish general, the *Marqués Francesco de Moncada* (Paris, Louvre), the other of *Prince Thomas-Francis of Savoy-Carignan* (Turin, Gal. Sabauda), who had served as temporary governor for Spain between the death of the Archduchess and the arrival in the Netherlands of the Cardinal-Infante. The portrait of *Cachiopin* is one of the most penetrating studies of a highly civilized melancholic. It contrasts with a more public appearance calculated by van Dyck in his chalk and wash study (see fig. 5) to be etched by Vorsterman for *The Iconography* (M.-H. 75). In the portrait of *Moncada* van Dyck emulated in flattering the rider the revolutionary pattern invented by Rubens for the equestrian portrait of the *Duque de Lerma* in Spain (1603; Madrid, Prado), known to the painter through Rubens's preparatory drawing (Paris, Louvre); a pattern that had guided van Dyck in Genoa for the *Anton Giulio Brignole-Sale on Horseback*, and which he was to elaborate in the stupendous *Charles I with M. de St Antoine* (1633; London, Buckingham Pal., Royal Col.). The magnificent conceit of showing *Prince Thomas-Francis* executing a *levada* on a wild and rocky eminence was to excite Bernini in his equestrian monument in marble, *Constantine the Great* (1654–70; Rome, Vatican, Scala Regia), as well as in his ill-fated equestrian statue of *Louis XIV* (1669–77; subsequently modified into a *Marcus Curtius* by Girardon; Versailles, Château, Gardens). Whence else came to Urban

5. Anthony van Dyck: *Jacomo de Cachiopin*, brush and brown wash over black chalk, 253×176 mm, 1634 (Paris, Musée du Louvre)

VIII's sculptor the crucial idea of a broad cascade of drapery set aslant to show off the Roman Emperor on his rearing horse? Van Dyck in this vision of command was surely matching himself against Rubens's equestrian portrait of *George Villiers, 1st Duke of Buckingham* as Lord High Admiral (1625; ex-Osterley Park House, NT, London; destr. 1949).

It is not only in comparison to these public and private triumphs in male portraiture that the portrait of *Princess Henrietta of Lorraine* (1634; London, Kenwood House), painted in Antwerp with her negro page, seems tame. The relaxation of van Dyck's imaginative creativity over the preceding decade is clear when this picture is compared to the portrait painted 11 years earlier of the *Marchesa Elena Grimaldi Cattaneo* (see fig. 1 above) gliding so regally on to an evocation of a noble terrace at Sampierdarena, her complexion protected by a parasol held over her head by her negro page.

6. ENGLAND, SPRING 1635–LATE 1639. Some sitters, particularly in England, evidently did not fully engage van Dyck's interest. Yet to England he returned in spring 1635 in the fullness of his powers to paint the portrait of *William Laud, Archbishop of Canterbury* (c. 1635–7; Cambridge, Fitzwilliam), the only English prelate who could afford his price for a three-quarter-length. For the Stuarts he had to meet the challenge of depicting the *Head of Charles I in Three Positions* (1635–6; Windsor Castle, Berks, Royal Col.; for illustration *see* STUART, House of, (6)), as a guide for Bernini in Rome to carve a marble bust, and by July the *Three Eldest Children of Charles I and Henrietta Maria* (see fig. 6) for Christina of Savoy in Turin. The triple study of the King's head, inspired in presentation by Lorenzo Lotto's *Portrait of a Jeweller in Three Positions* (c. 1530–35; Vienna, Ksthist. Mus.), then believed to have been painted

by Titian, caused Bernini to remark, it is reported, on 'ce visage funeste'; and the sculptor was understandably reluctant when four years later Henrietta Maria wrote to request a bust of herself in the manner of the portrait van Dyck had essayed of her husband. She promised to send models painted by van Dyck (Memphis, TN, Brooks Mus. A.; London, Buckingham Pal., Royal Col.). The *Three Eldest Children* was commissioned by her for her elder sister in Turin in grateful exchange for portraits of the little Prince and Princess of Savoy. When van Dyck's picture was ready in the autumn, the Savoyard ambassador in London had to write to his Duke that the Queen had told him that: 'The King was angry with the painter Vendec for not having put smocks on them, as is the custom with small children, and that she should ask Madame, her sister, to have them painted in'. The King may have felt shame to have his heir depicted as an infant of five and a half not yet breeched. Nonetheless van Dyck continued as his principal painter, and on 23 February 1637 he was paid £1200 by Charles I 'for Certaine pictures by him delivered for our use'.

It was the year after his return to London that van Dyck completed on Scaglia's commission the last and most deeply moving of his religious works, the *Lamentation* (c. 1636; Antwerp, Kon. Mus. S. Kst.), for a chapel of the Antwerp Recollects. Meanwhile the long-term project to which van Dyck attached particular importance, *The Iconography*, was going ahead; and he wrote on 14 August 1636 to Franciscus Junius, librarian to Lord Arundel, for an appropriately learned tag to inscribe below the portrait of *Kenelm Digby* (M.-H. 71), engraved by Robert van Voerst (1593–1636). At the same time van Dyck, like Rubens, praised highly Junius's new treatise *De pictura veterum* (Amsterdam, 1637).

Highlights of van Dyck's painted production in the later 1630s were the portrait of two brothers-in-law seated, *Thomas Killigrew and William, Lord Crofts* (1638; London, Buckingham Pal., Royal Col.), a painting in which he again used the symbolism of the broken column (of fortitude in mourning) as he had done in the *Self-portrait* of early 1623; and, perhaps a little earlier, the haunting three-quarter-length of a man wracked by anxiety, who has usually and most likely been identified as *Sir Thomas Chaloner* (c. 1637; St Petersburg, Hermitage). Chaloner was to be among the parliamentary judges who condemned the King to death. By contrast to these sensitive portrayals of shared grief or inner tension, he painted in the same phase the portrait of *François Langlois*, the engraver, publisher and fellow art dealer, dressed as a Savoyard, fingering a musette (c. 1637–8; Cowdray Park, W. Sussex). This was not only an instance, rare since van Dyck's Italian years, in which he felt called to convey an instantaneous impression of activity, particularly in the face and hands—indeed for that reason this portrait of 'Ciartes' (Langlois's nickname, derived from his birthplace, Chartres) has sometimes been backdated to those years—but also within its Baroque form it was a startlingly *dégagé* image. Van Dyck also developed in England a pastoral mode of presentation for the pose, dress and setting of select sitters. His successes in this vein were the portraits of *Olivia Porter* (c. 1637; London, Syon House, priv. col.), wife of his friend

6. Anthony van Dyck: *Three Eldest Children of Charles I and Henrietta Maria*, oil on canvas, 1.51×1.54 m, 1635 (Turin, Galleria Sabauda)

Endymion; the earlier *Philip, 4th Lord Wharton* (Washington, DC, N.G.A.) aged about 19; and *Lord George Stuart* (*c.* 1638; London, N.P.G.). For those no longer in the bloom of youth, he enhanced the formal grandeur of rich clothes and hangings. A prime example is another earlier portrait, that of *Robert Rich, 2nd Earl of Warwick* (1634; New York, Met.) standing in court attire on the foreshore, the splendour of his stance and person set off by the rocky cliffs, while the navy that he commanded battles in the distance. This glorification consciously outclasses the more staid full-length of the same personage painted two years earlier by Mijtens (1632; London, N. Mar. Mus.). Another example is the double portrait of the Earl of Arundel and his wife, Aletheia Talbot, known as the *Madagascar Portrait* (1639; London, N.P.G., on dep. Arundel Castle, W. Sussex; for illustration *see* HOWARD (i), (1)). The richly dressed Earl and Countess point to Madagascar on a large globe, alluding to a scheme for colonizing the island in which the Earl was then involved.

A memorandum (?of late 1638) by van Dyck to Charles I lists prices for twenty-five paintings not yet paid for as well as five years' arrears in his £200 salary. He was paid £1603 on 14 December 1638 and £305 on 25 February 1639. The valuation of 14 of the paintings was reduced by the King, who, since van Dyck's return from Flanders, had been short of revenue. Van Dyck had served his prince not only with two beguiling portrait groups of the royal infants, one of which had vexed his employer, and the study of his head in three positions but also with portraits of *Charles I Armoured as a Christian Knight* (see fig. 7) and *Charles I in Garter Robes* (1636; Windsor Castle, Berks, Royal Col.), as well as with numerous portraits of

7. Anthony van Dyck: *Charles I Armoured as a Christian Knight*, oil on canvas, 3.67×2.92 m, *c.* 1635–6 (London, National Gallery)

the Queen, including the enchanting earlier full-length of her in hunting costume with her dwarf Sir Jeffrey Hudson standing at her side (1633; Washington, DC, N.G.A.). But it is perhaps the portrait of the King in hunting costume, *Le Roi à la chasse* (*c.* 1635; Paris, Louvre), that represents van Dyck's supreme tribute to his royal patron.

7. FINAL YEARS, 1640–41. That the King seemed insufficiently grateful and a slow payer was presumably one element in van Dyck's resolve to leave London, reported early in 1640 by the Countess of Sussex to Ralph Verney. His marriage the previous year to Mary Ruthven, one of the Queen's ladies, offered him a position in English society that his long association with Margaret Lemon, a tempestuous enchantress, had not. Yet the dawning prospect in his native city that he might succeed Rubens, who was overburdened with commissions and mortally sick with gout, would have been a major element in his calculation. There was, however, a delay from 30 May, when Rubens died in Antwerp, until 23 September, when, once more from Arundel, a pass was obtained for Sir Anthony and Lady van Dyck to visit the Continent. Ten days later the Cardinal-Infante wrote from Ghent to Philip IV that van Dyck was expected on 18 October at the dinner of the Guild of St Luke in Antwerp. Ferdinand wrote again to his brother on 10 November that van Dyck's pride would not allow him to undertake to complete Rubens's unfinished paintings for the Torre de la Parada, although he would accept a fresh commission. It is not known what work he chose to do in Flanders in 1640. Probably the last commission executed in London was for the widowed Earl of Southampton, the allegorical portrait of his wife, *Rachel de Ruvigny, Countess of Southampton* (*c.* 1638–40; Cambridge, Fitzwilliam), 'la belle et vertueuse Huguenotte', triumphant over death. About that Bellori wrote, not quite accurately on the evidence of Kenelm Digby, that she was portrayed as Fortuna. He also executed a portrait of Inigo Jones (*c.* 1640; *see* ARCHITECT, fig. 2).

Van Dyck, having been frustrated two years earlier in his hopes of realizing through the costliest medium of tapestry a grand design to clad annually on St George's Day the walls of the Banqueting House at Whitehall with four large tapestries of *Charles I and the Garter Knights in Procession* (the project advanced only so far as a swift chiaroscuro oil sketch; Belvoir Castle, Leics), turned his attention to the commission for history paintings to adorn the Grande Galerie of the Louvre. In hopes of that, he went to Paris at the beginning of December 1640. Evidently he visited the Palais du Luxembourg; and there rapidly in pen and wash, mingling with characteristic wit serious purpose, the made a copy (England, priv. col.), so as to stretch his own compositional sense to an unaccustomed scale, of Rubens's *Betrothal of Maria de' Medici and Henry IV* (*c.* 1621–5; Paris, Louvre). Despite this sally, Louis XIII summoned, quite unsuitably, Poussin from Italy to execute that coveted commission.

After this second disappointment, van Dyck returned to London to paint a wedding portrait, presumably his last royal portrait, of *Princess Mary and William II of Orange Nassau* (Amsterdam, Rijksmus.); the children married on 12 May 1641. On 13 August Lady Roxburghe wrote from

Richmond to Count John Wolfert van Brederode at The Hague that van Dyck had recovered from a long illness; in ten to twelve days he would bring the promised painting to Holland on his way to Flanders. In October he was reported again in Antwerp, then on 16 November again in Paris. By then he was so ill that he had to postpone portraying 'Monseigneur le Cardinal' [Richelieu]; and he requested a pass to England. His wife was pregnant; and on 1 December their daughter Justiniana was born in London. Three days later he revised his will, providing not only for his legitimate family but also for his natural daughter, Maria Teresa. On 9 December he died in his house at Blackfriars. It was Jordaens who succeeded to the primacy of Rubens at Antwerp.

II. Sources.

1. ARTISTIC. The enthusiasm of van Dyck for Venetian portraits, especially those by Titian, witnessed in the Italian Sketchbook not only by *ricordi* but by the additional list on the last leaf of those known to van Dyck, can hardly be exaggerated. Titian's double portrait of 'the French ambassador enditing' (*Monsignor Georges d'Armagnac and his Secretary*, late 1530s; Alnwick Castle, Northumb.) was known to him after it had been appropriated by the Earl of Northumberland from the collection of the murdered Buckingham: that picture and knowledge of another then also in England, Sebastiano del Piombo's portrait of *Cardinal Ferry Carondelet and Two Companions* (*c.* 1512; Madrid, Mus. Thyssen-Bornemizza), undoubtedly inspired van Dyck's portrait of *Thomas Wentworth, 1st Earl of Strafford Dictating to Sir Philip Mainwaring* (1640; St Osyth Priory, Essex); and the close recession of columns in the picture by Sebastiano inspired the setting of the portrait of *Albertus Miraeus* (*c.* 1626–32; Woburn Abbey, Beds). The portrait of *Strafford*, depicted on the eve of his departure for Ireland, standing full-length in armour, a bâton in his left hand and an Irish wolfhound under his right, was a patent tribute to Titian's portrait of *Charles V with his Hunting Dog* (?1532; Madrid, Prado) with an imperial hand resting on his faithful white hound. Van Dyck rarely essayed narrative in portraiture: but when he did, as in the *George Gage Being Offered a Marble Statue by a Roman Dealer and his Assistant* (1622–3; London, N.G.), his genius took fire from Titian's portrait of *Pope Paul III with his Grandsons* (1546; Naples, Capodimonte), of which he had penned a *ricordo* in his Italian Sketchbook (fol. 108*r*).

This abounding love for Titian should not allow van Dyck's admiration for Raphael to be overlooked: for the double portraits of *Andrea Navagero and Agostino Beazzano* (before April 1516; Rome, Gal. Doria-Pamphili) and *Raphael and his Fencing-master* (*c.* 1518; Paris, Louvre); for the presumed *Self-portrait* (*c.* 1513–14; ex-Czartoryski Col., Kraków), which he recorded in the Italian Sketchbook (fol. 109*v*); and for the portrait of *Bindo Altoviti* (*c.* 1518; Washington, DC, N.G.A.). Those double portraits were not far from the forefront in van Dyck's mind when he painted the double portrait of *Thomas Killigrew and Lord Crofts* and ten years earlier that of *Cornelis and Lucas de Wael*. A reverberation of Raphael's dandified *Self-portrait* in a furred gown is to be found in van Dyck's

Self-portrait with the Broken Column; and in the oval portrait of *Sir Endymion Porter and Van Dyck* (*c.* 1635; Madrid, Prado), the painter posed himself as Altoviti.

Of contemporary painters, Rubens apart, Guido Reni became the crucially important influence on van Dyck. This developed beyond any actual meeting in Bologna and his years south of the Alps; the pen sketch (Madrid, Real Acad. S Fernando) is not a self-portrait of Reni, but a hasty impression by van Dyck. Before abandoning Genoa, van Dyck had studied Reni's *Assumption of the Virgin* in the Jesuit church of S Ambrogio (1617; *in situ*), and memories of that mighty altarpiece mingled with those of Rubens's treatment of the theme in an oil sketch (Vienna, Akad. Bild. Kst.) painted within a few years of his return to Antwerp. The *Mystic Marriage of St Catherine* (1630; London, Buckingham Pal., Royal Col.) shows not only an addiction to Titian's *gusto* in composition but also a refinement of sentiment, expressed both in silvery tone and in morphology, that evinces a lasting attraction to Reni. Whereas the *Virgin and Child with SS Rosalie, Peter and Paul* (1629; Vienna, Ksthist. Mus.) owes much of its grand conception to a composition by Titian of the *Virgin and Child with a Donor* (untraced), noted by van Dyck in his Italian Sketchbook (fol. 28*v*), the core appears, when reduced in scale and modified to the contemporary *Vision of St Anthony* (1629; Milan, Brera), to be of Reni's mode of refinement of types and sensibility to illumination. That this affinity with Reni was deep rooted is shown nowhere better than in the three-quarter-length portrait of *Nicholas Lanier* (1628; Vienna, Ksthist. Mus.). The Reni-like quality of the finished portrait, the work of a week, emanates from a preparatory drawing in black and white chalk (Edinburgh, N.G.), which in its agitation of rippling light on the ridges and slower movement of shadow in the hollows of drapery so vividly recalls Reni's drawings for the 'gran' Madonna dei Signori Marchesi Tanari' in Bologna (i.e. the *Virgin and Child with St John* or '*Madonna Tanari*', 1627–8; untraced). A paradigm of van Dyck's eclectic progress as a draughtsman in less than 15 years is the comparison of the advancing *Head and Front Quarters of a Grey Horse* (*c.* 1618–21; Chatsworth, Derbys), studied for *St Martin Dividing his Cloak with a Beggar* (versions at Zaventem, St Martin, and Windsor Castle, Berks, Royal Col.) in the boldly plastic manner that he had learnt in Antwerp from Rubens, himself incarnate with the spirit of Annibale Carracci, and the *Studies of a Greyhound* (*c.* 1633; London, BM), seated but quivering with nervous mobility, studied as a companion to the sitter in the portrait of *James Stuart, 4th Duke of Lennox* (*c.* 1633; New York, Met.), with Reni-like vibrancy of surface.

2. LITERARY AND CLASSICAL. Van Dyck retained the Latin of an educated bourgeois. He was able to comment on the *De pictura veterum* of Francis Junius. In the *ex-voto* painted in memory of his father, the *Crucifixion with SS Dominic and Catherine of Siena* (see fig. 2 above), his inscription and funeral device alluded in 'NE PATRIS SVI MANIBUS . . .' to the *manes*, the spirit of the departed. However, as Roger de Piles perceived, he was less minded to be a scholar than Rubens. His interest in antiquity was slighter and evanescent. He drew a fragment of a *Niobid*

frieze (Paris, Fond. Custodia, Inst. Néer.); he included one of the Arundel marbles, a bas-relief from Smyrna (London, Mus. London), in his *Continence of Scipio* for Buckingham; besides his conspicuous placing of a wine ewer with an ithyphallic satyr for a handle in the early *Samson and Delilah* (1619–20; London, Dulwich Pict. Gal.), which was intended to rival Rubens's treatment of that subject for Nicolaas Rockox (*c.* 1609–10; London, N.G.), he also incorporated knowledge of the Belvedere *Torso* (Rome, Vatican, Mus. Pio-Clementino) and the Borghese *Hermaphrodite* (Paris, Louvre); and he drew in his Italian Sketchbook (fol. 33*v*) the statue (Paris, Louvre) believed to be of the ancient Cynic philosopher Diogenes. Moreover, he was sufficiently familiar, doubtless through contact with Rubens, with Otto van Veen's *Amorum emblemata* (Antwerp, 1608), witness his *Time Clipping Cupid's Wings* (1630–32; Paris, Mus. Jacquemart-André); with Virgil's *Aeneid*, witness his *Venus at the Forge of Vulcan* (1630–32; Paris, Louvre); with Tasso's *Gerusalemme liberata* (1580–81), witness his *Rinaldo and Armida* (1629); with Guarini's *Il pastor fido* (1589), witness his *Amaryllis and Myrtillo* (1631–2; Pommersfelden, Schloss Weissenstein); as well as with the common literary stock of painters, Ovid, the Vulgate and the *Lives of the Saints*. To the end of his life he kept up with Jesuit writings, the frontispiece to a recent publication being as essential an ingredient in his conception of the painted memorial to *Rachel de Ruvigny* as was Rubens's *Jupiter* (*c.* 1618; Strasbourg, Mus. B.-A.). In portraits he essayed emblem and allegory rarely. After his contact with Agostino Pallavicini in Genoa, it was not until his association with Sir Kenelm Digby in London that he was fully engaged by learned, posthumous allusions to Rachel de Ruvigny, triumphant over death, and by those contrived by Sir Kenelm for the allegorical portrait of his wife, *Venetia Stanley, Lady Digby as Prudence* (1633; London, N.P.G.), which were based on Juvenal. The pretty fancies of the adolescent *Lady Mary Villiers with Lord Arran as Cupid* (*c.* 1636; Raleigh, NC Mus. A.) and *Mary, Duchess of Lennox as St Agnes* (1637; Windsor Castle, Berks, Royal Col.) strike no deep chords.

III. Studio practice.

Van Dyck, aside from his early involvement in various aspects of Rubens's production in Antwerp, very rarely collaborated with other painters. He furnished ideas, presumably in the form of drawings or grisaille oil sketches, to Jan Boeckhorst; to guide, for example, the *Virgin and Child Adored by St Carlo Borromeo* (Ireland, priv. col.) and the *Martyrdom of St James the Greater* (Valenciennes, Mus. B.-A.). When van Dyck found in Genoa that his countryman Johann Roos, a specialist in painting vegetables, fruit and small animals, was in fashion, he allowed collaboration in at least two instances: in his unidentified *Portrait of a Boy in White* (Genoa, Pal. Durazzo-Pallavicini), later copied by Giovanni Battista Gaulli, and in the foreground of the *Vertumnus and Pomona* (Genoa, Gal. Pal. Bianco).

The participation by van Dyck's own assistants in the studios at Antwerp and Blackfriars—he had none so far as is known south of the Alps—was not apparently graded to the same degree as in the Rubens shop: unalloyed masterpieces; paintings so extensively retouched as to be almost indistinguishable from originals; paintings enlivened by comparatively few masterly retouchings; and paintings not going beyond the capabilities of trained assistants working to a model. Nor from the mid-1630s did van Dyck strive overmuch to correct the productions of his Blackfriars workshop. The eloquent hand hanging down in the prime original of the portrait of *Archbishop Laud* (Cambridge, Fitzwilliam) is allowed to droop with a different splay of fingers in a secondary version in Laud's own college, St John's, Oxford. The right foot of Rachel de Ruvigny is bared on the skull in the prime original (Cambridge, Fitzwilliam), whereas it is covered by her dress in the secondary version (Melbourne, N.G. Victoria; in which only her head passes as autograph); the drapery folds in the secondary version, however, are not adjusted to the new, more decorous situation, and the result jars. The landscape chosen for the portrait of *Anne, Countess of Clanbrassil* (*c.* 1636; New York, Frick) plainly replicates that in the portrait of *James Hamilton, 3rd Marquess and Later 1st Duke of Hamilton* (*c.* 1640; Vaduz, Samml. Liechtenstein), thereby robbing the iconographic use of the chief plant, the burdock ('steadfast loyalty'), of its piquancy. An almost exactly similar pose and setting were used for full-length portraits of *Isabella, Lady Delawarr* (*c.* 1636; Boston, MA, Mus. F.A.) and of *Anne Kirke* (*c.* 1636; San Marino, CA, Huntington Lib. & A.G.). That suggests extensive participation by assistants except for the ladies' heads. It must be said that the Antwerp studio could work to a higher standard. The full-length portrait of *Abbé Scaglia* (*c.* 1639–40; Antwerp, Kon. Mus. S. Kst.) is a creditable replica of the original (Hackwood Park, Hants), although the fluency and allure of van Dyck's own touch is missing. One mark of a primary version, which is found both in that original and in the original (*c.* 1638–40; belonging to a cousin of Sir Ralph Verney, Ballam, Middle Claydon, Bletchley, Bucks) of the portrait of *Sir Edmund Verney* (Claydon House, Bucks, NT), is the penumbra of brushwork with which van Dyck would set off a head painted from life before proceeding with the rest. That accords with Eberhard Jabach's account of van Dyck's working day (for further description *see* PORTRAITURE). Inasmuch as his court appointments relieved him, like Rubens, of the need to register pupils, there is much to learn of their training and qualities. The work of such assistants as can be named—de Reyn, Remi van Leemput and Jan van Belcamp (*c.* 1610–53)—cannot be distinguished with any degree of confidence.

IV. Character and personality.

It is fitting that the earliest known painting of van Dyck should be a bust-length *Self-portrait* (*c.* 1613; Vienna, Ksthist. Mus.) about the age of 14. It is densely painted. The shoulder over which he looks so protectively keeps the beholder at his distance. A few years later he lightly sketched his head, barely more (*c.* 1619–20; Strasbourg, Mus. B.-A.), as it would seem before or just possibly during his first stay in London, rejoicing in his debonair looks. Before he left Antwerp for Italy, he painted, most likely for his family, a more formal three-quarter-length (see fig. 8), displaying himself with conscious elegance, his pose supported on the pedestal of a column. His interest in Titian as a portrait painter may already have been stimulated by the copies Rubens had painted in Italy for his own keeping. The dry, dragged paint, a radical departure from traditional Flemish practice, shows this self-portrait to be close in date to the great pair of portraits of *Frans Snyders* and his wife *Margaretha de Vos* (both *c.* 1620–21; New York, Frick). The poignancy of the column appearing broken in the *Self-portrait* of early 1623 (St Petersburg, Hermitage) is sharpened by the earlier essay in self-scrutiny. The half-length *Self-portrait* (Munich, Alte Pin.), which must follow very closely (radiography has revealed that the right hand was originally posed as the right hand in the St Petersburg version), is probably to be dated 1621 in its original form (it has been expanded on all sides, reworked and embellished with a gold chain reputedly given to van Dyck by the Duke of Mantua). This half-length portrait could be that described as 'Van Dyck with a cape and one hand' which Jan-Baptiste Anthoine came to possess in Antwerp at the end of the 17th century.

The Metropolitan, Alte Pinakothek and Hermitage portraits show van Dyck's head in a virtually identical pose and could have been made from the same sketch model. A substantial ghost of a frontal pose appears by autoradiography beneath the *St Rosalia Interceding for the Plague-stricken of Palermo* (New York, Met.), which is therefore datable 1624. From the post-Italian stay in Antwerp there are two variant versions of the *Artist as the Shepherd Paris* (London, Wallace; New York, priv. col.). Dating from the mid-1630s in England are the friendship portrait of *Sir Endymion Porter with Van Dyck* (Madrid, Prado), in which the oval form, as in the *Abbé Scaglia Adoring the Virgin and Child* (*c.* 1634–5; London, N.G.), follows the elegant fashion instituted by Guido Reni, and the *Self-portrait with a Sunflower*.

This perennial narcissism manifests a neurotic, highly strung personality. Van Dyck's career shows him to have been restive by nature and increasingly so, sometimes difficult to employ because his pride and ambition could be bruised as well as his protective vanity, qualities that his far from robust health, particularly for the last years of his short life, made incandescent. His extraordinary charm and brilliance enabled him to shine not only among the patricians of Genoa, Rome and Savoy but also among those born north of the Alps. The princes and generals, the chosen *savants* and *amateurs* of art and, of extreme significance, the fellow artists whom he regarded—all of those contemporaries whose likenesses were to be engraved from his models painted *en grisaille* for *The Iconography*—must in turn have responded to his charismatic appeal. That he kept himself in Rome as a 'pittore cavalieresco', apart from the rowdy conviviality of the Bentveugels, ostentatiously disdaining them by his style of living, is nothing to the contrary. In England so stiff a courtier as the Earl of Newcastle, writing to van Dyck in February 1637 from Welbeck Abbey, declared how much he enjoyed his company and conversation, signing himself beyond courtly custom, 'passionately your humble servant'. Two of the most powerful noblemen in England, Arundel and Strafford, each sat for him at least three times; the Duke of Lennox and Thomas Killigrew each sat twice.

V. Critical reception and posthumous reputation.

Only once in palatial decoration did van Dyck bring off a baroque triumph of grandeur in action: the *concetto* of *Charles I with M. de St Antoine* (1633; London, Buckingham Pal., Royal Col.) emerging on horseback through a feigned archway, a painting placed at the end of the Gallery at St James's Palace, so that the King appears to review as a modern emperor Titian's series of *Roman Emperors* from Mantua, which van Dyck himself had put in good order for hanging. The sketched composition of *Charles I with the Garter Procession* was never to be woven for the Banqueting House. Of the *profana conversazione* that he completed shortly before his return to England in 1635, the *Seven Echevins of Brussels Ranged beside a Statue of Justice* (destr.), there remains only a grisaille oil sketch (Paris, Ecole B.-A.) and two fine head studies (Oxford, Ashmolean). The painting, which must have been majestic enough, appears to have been rather static in conception. It was burnt in the town hall in Brussels in 1695. Had he had the health and strength to succeed Rubens in the primacy at Antwerp, van Dyck's legacy to art might have been very different and more according to his hopes.

As it was, he is remembered, especially in England, not only for the dazzling array of his portraits in royal and noble collections but also for his sensibility to landscape first manifest in the creative copy he penned in his early maturity of the etching after Titian of *The Flautist* (B. 7)

8. Anthony van Dyck: *Self-portrait*, oil on canvas, 1197×897 mm, *c.* 1619–20 (New York, Metropolitan Museum of Art)

9. Anthony van Dyck: *View of the Ypres Tower, Rye, Sussex*, pen and brown ink, 189×298 mm, 1633 or 1634 (Cambridge, Fitzwilliam Museum)

(Chatsworth, Derbys). What stimulus he could derive from Titian and Campagnola lasted to the late 1630s, as can be discerned in his drawing of a *Landscape with Farm Buildings* (London, priv. col., see 1991 exh. cat., no. 86). It was mingled with the draughtsman's fascination with the intricate hollows of the dying tree, evincing a lingering addiction to the mannerisms of Sebastian Vrancx, who was one of the subjects of *The Iconography* (M.-H. 25). Indeed this sensibility extended to the particulars of vegetation and to the symbolic language of plants (he had no need of the collaboration of Johann Roos in Genoa). Pages of his Italian Sketchbook and his first portrait of *Lucas van Uffel* show his direct interest in the Ligurian coast and shipping. His pen drawings of Rye (1633–4) from seaward (e.g. New York, Pierpont Morgan Lib.) sparkle with attention; and the Ypres Tower in Rye, Sussex, which he recorded in two drawings (Cambridge, Fitzwilliam, see fig. 9; and Rotterdam, Mus. Boymans–van Beuningen), features somewhat unaccountably both in the background of the painted portrait of the banker *Everhard Jabach* (*c.* 1636–7; St Petersburg, Hermitage) and, for *The Iconography*, in Pieter Clouwet's engraving of the goldsmith *Theodoor Rasier* (M.-H. 156). The meticulous observation of trees, berries, brambles, plants and ferns was surely not confined to the rare pen drawings that have survived. Van Dyck's love not only for human figures but also for oak woods, for land and water plants and for the ministration of light by which they grow is evident throughout his career, from the foreground of his tremendous vision of the *Penitent St Jerome* (see fig. 10), to the foreground of the magnificent *Rinaldo and Armida* thirteen years later

(1629; Baltimore, MD, Mus. A.), to the setting of the entrancing idyll of *Cupid and Psyche* ten years after that (1639–40; London, Buckingham Pal., Royal Col.). The distant prospect beyond the grandeur of the equestrian portrait of *Charles I Armoured as a Christian Knight* (see fig. 7 above) reflects the freshness and subtlety of his use of watercolour for recording the radiance of England's wooded hills and vales (*see* WATERCOLOUR, colour pl. VII, fig. 1).

Van Dyck's achievement in portraiture was of clear importance to Peter Lely and Prosper Henry Lankrinck and beloved by Gainsborough, who painted a full-size copy (1789; St Louis, MO, A. Mus.) of the *Lords John and Bernard Stuart* (*c.* 1638–9; London, N.G.; *see* DRESS, fig. 39). It set a new standard for a host of other painters of society in England from Reynolds, who was stimulated to paint his portrait of *Lord Rockingham and his Secretary, Edmund Burke* (*c.* 1766–70; Cambridge, Fitzwilliam) by van Dyck's *Strafford and Mainwaring*, to Thomas Lawrence and John Singer Sargent. The superb presence that van Dyck's portraits created in the palaces of Genoa (before the disturbances and sales consequent on the French Revolutionary Wars) affected Gaulli and, it seems in at least one instance, van Dyck's exact contemporary Veláz-quez, who, in his passages through Genoa, must have visited Casa Invrea and been struck by the lovely effect of the vase of flowers on the table in van Dyck's portrait of *Battina Balbi and Two of her Children* (*c.* 1622; Genoa, Pal. Durazzo-Pallavicini). The Spanish artist's tribute appears in his *Infanta Margarita in Pink* (*c.* 1653; Vienna, Ksthist. Mus.). In France itself the portraits of Sébastien Bourdon

10. Anthony van Dyck: *Penitent St Jerome*, oil on canvas, 1.92×2.15 m, *c.* 1616 (Dresden, Gemäldegalerie Alte Meister)

in the 1650s and 1660s owe much of their elegant poses and play of drapery to what Bourdon had seen of van Dyck's work in Paris and Antwerp; and Watteau was excited to copy in chalks from the portrait prints in *The Iconography* and to bring to his own idiom using red chalk such a powerful study in black chalk as van Dyck had drawn for the man who drags Christ (*c.* 1617–18; U. London, Courtauld Inst. Gals) in the *Carrying of the Cross* for St Paul's, Antwerp (*in situ*).

Van Dyck's rapid and expressive manner of drawing figure compositions in pen and wash was also consequential, especially for his principal follower in Antwerp, Jan Boeckhorst. It was apparently nowhere to be seen to more effect than in Genoa: in Giovanni Battista Merano's studies for the *Adoration of the Shepherds* (*c.* 1659–73; Paris, Louvre, 9449 and 9454); in Bartolomeo Biscaino's *Rest on the Flight* (Genoa, Gal. Pal. Rosso, 2119); and supremely in numerous instances in the works of Giovanni Benedetto Castiglione, conspicuous among them the drawing of a *Group of Figures with a Woman Holding an Inscription* (*c.* 1650; Paris, Louvre, 9459). Indeed van Dyck's importance for Castiglione exceeds that of any would-be imitator of his Genoese achievement, ranging from Vincenzo Malò in mythologies to Giovanni Bernardo Carbone in portraits, let alone Gaulli and Giovanni Andrea della Piane in occasional copies of portraits.

BIBLIOGRAPHY

EARLY SOURCES

C. de Bie: *Het gulden cabinet* (1661)
G. P. Bellori: *Vite* (1672); ed. E. Borea (1976)
R. Soprani: *Vite* (1674); enlarged, ed. C. G. Ratti (1768–9)
J. von Sandrart: *Teutsche Academie* (1675–9); ed. A. R. Peltzer (1925)
R. de Piles: *Abrégé de la vie des peintres* (Paris, 1699), pp. 414–19
A. Houbraken: *De groote schouburgh* (1718–21)
H. Walpole: *Anecdotes of Painting in England* (1762–71); ed. R. N. Wornum (1849)
J. Smith: *Catalogue Raisonné of the Works of the Most Eminent Dutch, Flemish and French Painters*, iii (London, 1831), ix (London, 1842)

W. H. Carpenter: *Pictorial Notices Consisting of a Memoir of Sir Anthony van Dick, with a Descriptive Catalogue of the Etchings* (London, 1844)
G. F. Waagen: *Galleries and Cabinets of Art in Great Britain*, 3 vols (London, 1854; suppl. vol., 1857)

GENERAL

T. Rombouts and T. van Lerius: *De liggeren en andere historische archieven der Antwerpsche St Lucasgilde* (Antwerp, [n.d.])
J. Denucé: *De Antwerpsche konstkamers* (Antwerp, 1932)

MONOGRAPHS

L. Cust: *Anthony van Dyck: An Historical Study of his Life and Work* (London, 1900)
E. Schaeffer: *Van Dyck: Des Meisters Gemälde*, Klass. Kst. Gesamtausgaben, xiii (Stuttgart and Leipzig, 1909) [see also Glück, 1931]
G. Glück: *Van Dyck: Des Meisters Gemälde*, Klass. Kst. Gesamtausgaben, xiii (Stuttgart, 1931) [2nd rev. edn of Schaeffer, 1909]
A. J. J. Delen: *Antoon van Dijck* (Antwerp, 1943)
F. van den Wijngaert: *Antoon van Dyck* (Antwerp, 1943)
L. van Puyvelde: *Van Dyck* (Brussels, 1950)
E. Larsen: *The Paintings of Anthony van Dyck*, 2 vols (Freren, 1988)
S. J. Barnes and A. K. Wheelock, eds: 'Van Dyck 350', *Studies in the History of Art 46, Center for Advanced Studies in the Visual*, Symp. xxvi (Washington, DC, 1994) [Refers to 350th anniversary of van Dyck's death]

EXHIBITION CATALOGUES

Van Dyck tentoonstelling (exh. cat., Antwerp, Kon. Mus. S. Kst., 1949)
100 opere di van Dyck (exh. cat., Genoa, Pal. Accad., 1955)
Antoon van Dyck: Tekeningen en olieverfschetsen (exh. cat. by R. A. d'Hulst and H. Vey, Antwerp, Rubenshuis; Rotterdam, Mus. Boymans–van Beuningen; 1960)
The Age of Charles I: Painting in England, 1620–1649 (exh. cat. by O. Millar, London, Tate, 1972–3)
Van Dyck as a Religious Artist (exh. cat. by J. R. Martin, Princeton U., NJ, A. Mus., 1979)
The Young Van Dyck/Le Jeune van Dyck (exh. cat. by A. McNairn, Ottawa, N.G., 1980)
Van Dyck's 'Iconography'/'L'Iconographie' de van Dyck (exh. cat. by A. McNairn, Ottawa, N.G., 1980)
Antoon van Dyck et son 'Iconographie' (exh. cat., Paris, Fond. Custodia, Inst. Néer., 1981)
Van Dyck in England (exh. cat. by O. Millar, London, N.P.G., 1982–3)
Anthony van Dyck (exh. cat. by A. K. Wheelock jr, S. J. Barnes and others, Washington, DC, N.G.A., 1990–91) [with extensive bibliog.]
Van Dyck Drawings (exh. cat. by C. Brown, New York, Pierpont Morgan Lib.; Fort Worth, TX, Kimbell A. Mus., 1991) [with extensive bibliog.]
Flemish Drawings in the Age of Rubens (exh. cat. by A.-M. Logan, Wellesley Coll., MA, Davis Mus. & Cult. Cent., 1993–4), pp. 145–54
The Age of Rubens (exh. cat., ed. P. C. Sutton; Boston, Mus. F. A.; Toledo, Mus. A.; 1993–4), pp. 321–43

DRAWINGS AND OIL SKETCHES

M. Delâcre: 'Recherches sur le rôle du dessin dans l'iconographie de van Dyck', *Bull. Acad. Royale Belgique*, xiv (1932) [whole issue]
F. Lugt: *Ecole flamande*, 2 vols (1949), v and vi of *Inventaire général des dessins des écoles du nord* (Paris, 1929–88)
H. Vey: *Die Zeichnungen Anton van Dycks*, 2 vols (Brussels, 1962)
G. Adriani, ed.: *Anton van Dyck: Italienisches Skizzenbuch* (Vienna, 1965) [incomplete]
M. Jaffé, ed.: *Van Dyck's Antwerp Sketchbook*, 2 vols (London, 1966)

ETCHINGS

M. Mauquoy-Hendrickx: *L'Iconographie d'Antoine van Dyck: Catalogue raisonné*, 2 vols (Brussels, 1956) [M.-H.]

SPECIALIST STUDIES

Manuscrit inédit sur la vie, les ouvrages et les élèves de van Dyck (MS., [n.d.]; Paris, Archvs Louvre); ed. E. Larsen (Brussels, 1975)
M. Vaes: 'Le Séjour de van Dyck en Italie', *Bull. Inst. Hist. Belge, Rome*, iv (1924), pp. 163–234
——: 'L'Auteur de la biographie d'Antoine van Dyck de la Bibliothèque du Musée du Louvre: Dumont, amateur d'art à Amsterdam', *Bull. Inst. Hist. Belge, Rome*, vii (1927), pp. 139–41
R. R. Wark: 'A Note on Van Dyck's *Self-portrait with a Sunflower*', *Burl. Mag.*, xcviii (1956), pp. 52–4
J. S. Held: '*Le Roi à la ciasse*', *A. Bull.* [Detroit], xl (1958), pp. 139–49
Burl. Mag., cxi (1969) [special issue devoted to van Dyck and Rubens]

C. Brown and N. Ramsay: 'Van Dyck's Collection: Some New Documents', *Burl. Mag.*, cxxxii (1990), pp. 704–6

J. Wood: 'Van Dyck's "Cabinet de Titian"', ibid., pp. 693–5

P. Boccardo: 'I ritratti genovesi di van Dyck: Identificazioni accertate, proposte e respinte', *Van Dyck 350: Symposium at the National Gallery of Art, Washington, DC, 1991*, N.G.A., Rep. & Stud. (Washington, DC, 1994)

D. Freedberg: 'Van Dyck's *Portrait of a Young Cleric Identified*', ibid.

G. Parry: 'Van Dyck and the Caroline Court Poets', ibid.

K. Van der Stighelen: 'Young Anthony: Archival Evidence on his Early Years', ibid.

MICHAEL JAFFÉ

Dyck, Daniel van den (*b* Antwerp, *c.* 1610; *d* Mantua, 1670). Flemish painter and etcher, active in Italy. He was apprenticed to Peter Verhaecht (*d c.* 1652) in the guild year 1631–2 and by 1633 or 1634 was a fully qualified master. Of five portraits in Bergamo (Accad. Carrara B.A.) attributed to him, at least the three dated ones (1633) are unlikely to be by him, since van den Dyck did not leave Antwerp for Italy before late September 1633. In 1634 he settled in Venice, where he married Lucretia, daughter of the painter Nicolas Régnier. With his brother-in-law Pietro Muttoni (della Vecchia) (1605–78), he painted wall decorations in the Palazzo Pesaro in Preganziol. The frescoes (*in situ*) in the Villa Vernier-Contarini-Zen at Mira, near Venice, depicting scenes from the *Legend of Psyche* have also been attributed to him. His style was influenced by Rubens, as can be seen from his *Martyrdom of St Laurence* (Venice, Madonna dell'Orto).

In 1657 van den Dyck moved permanently to Mantua, where he painted theatre sets and became court painter and keeper of the art collection to Carlo Gonzaga II, 9th Duke of Mantua. From this time he became known primarily as a painter of flower-pieces. He made 11 etchings of religious and mythological themes and also etched the title pages of two books by Giovanni Francesco Loredano (1606–61): *Iliade Giocosa* and *Historia Catalana*.

BIBLIOGRAPHY
Hollstein: *Dut. & Flem.*; Thieme–Becker

C. Kramm: *De levens en werken der Hollandsche en Vlaamsche kunstschilders, graveurs en bouwmeesters* (Amsterdam, 1857–64/*R* 1974), i, pp. 406–7

P. Rombouts and T. van Lerius: *De liggeren en andere historische archieven der Antwerpsche Sint Lucasgilde* (Antwerp and The Hague, 1872/*R* Amsterdam, 1961), pp. 19, 26, 47, 57

N. Ivanoff: 'Daniele van den Dyck', *Emporium* (Dec 1953), pp. 242–51

F. Noris: 'Sulla presenza di Daniel van den Dyck a Bergamo', *Not. Pal. Albani*, xi (1982), pp. 72–80

B. W. Meyer: 'Il "caso" Daniele van den Dyck', *Il '600 a Bergamo* (exh. cat., Bergamo, Pal. Ragione, 1987), pp. 246–9

TRUDY VAN ZADELHOFF

Dyck [Dijck], Floris (Claesz.) van (*b* Haarlem, 1575; *d* Haarlem, Nov 1651). Dutch painter. He came from a wealthy patrician family in Haarlem and spent some time in Italy, where he met Cavaliere d'Arpino. In 1610 van Dyck became a member of the Haarlem Guild of St Luke and in 1637 was elected deacon; he presented the Guild with a life-size cast bust of himself by Michelangelo. He enjoyed considerable fame during his lifetime and, with his Haarlem contemporaries Nicolaes Gillis (*fl c.* 1601–32), Floris van Schooten (*fl* 1610–55) and Roelof Koets (1592–1655), was one of the earliest Dutch still-life painters.

There are only four dated works known by van Dyck, three panel paintings and one watercolour. The panel painting *Breakfast-piece* (1613; Haarlem, Frans Halsmus.;

Floris van Dyck: *Breakfast-piece*, oil on panel, 495×775 mm, 1613 (Haarlem, Frans Halsmuseum)

see fig.) is a typical example of the *ontbijtgen* (Dut.: 'small breakfasts') or *bancketgen* ('small banquets') that he produced. It depicts a table covered with a cloth and spread with food and utensils, each item clearly shown owing to the high viewpoint. Despite the number of objects, the composition is well balanced, with strong diagonals leading from the foreground into the distance. In this painting, as in two others, a knife is placed so as to echo the diagonal composition. Van Dyck's use of paint is fluid and the brushwork delicate; the colours are soft, and the lighting is diffused, with an emphasis on texture. His work is very similar to that of Nicolaes Gilles, and the two artists may be seen as the originators of the typically Dutch genre of still-life banquet-pieces.

BIBLIOGRAPHY

A. P. A. Vorenkamp: *Bijdrage tot de geschiedenis van het Hollandsche stilleven in de 17de eeuw* [Concerning the history of Dutch still-life paintings in the 17th century] (Leiden, 1933)

I. Bergström: *Dutch Still-life Painting in the Seventeenth Century* (London, 1956), p. 102

L. J. Bol: *Holländischer Maler des 17. Jahrhunderts nahe den grossen Meistern* (Brunswick, 1969), pp. 15–18

W. Bernt: *The Netherlandish Painters of the 17th Century* (London, 1970), p. 35

N. R. A. Vroom: *A Modest Message as Intimated by the Painters of the 'Monochrome Banketje'*, 2 vols (Schiedam, 1980) [incl. a cat. rais. of van Dyck's oeuvre]

B. Haak: *The Golden Age: Dutch Painting in the Seventeenth Century* (London and New York, 1984), pp. 180–81

H. G. DIJK-KOEKOEK

Dye. Compound that can be applied to textiles (or to such other materials as leather or the gelatine in a photographic emulsion) with the effect of changing their colour more or less permanently (see colour pls III and IV). Not every strongly coloured compound will behave as a dye: the term is used of a substance that can be dissolved and will then migrate from its solution to a fibre, remaining there when the fibre is rinsed free from excess dye. Ideally, it should survive subsequent washing, exposure to light and rubbing without change in colour. If, in addition, it resists the effects of moderately acidic and alkaline liquids, which are common hazards in normal life, it is a good, fast dye. Unfortunately, the dyes used in the past, and most that are used in the late 20th century, are less resistant than the textiles to which they are applied, so care is needed to avoid damaging them.

Dyes have nothing in common with the substances used to impart colours to glass or to the glazes used on the surface of ceramics. The pigments that constitute paints when suspended in a medium, usually oil or water, may relate to dyes (*see* LAKE), may be effectively powdered glass or may be minerals unrelated to either type of colouring matter.

1. Introduction. 2. Natural. 3. Synthetic.

1. INTRODUCTION. Dyes can be divided according to the methods used to fix them to textiles. The simplest to use are the 'direct' dyes, which are absorbed from an aqueous solution, often made weakly acidic or alkaline. They then form saltlike linkages—involving attraction between positive and negative charges—to the basic or acidic groups present in the fibre. This is usually a protein fibre, that is wool or silk. A few direct dyes do exist for the cellulose fibres cotton and linen, but they rely on adsorption forces only for their adhesion to the fibre. Leather and other types of animal skin, horn or feathers may also be coloured by direct dyes. 'Reactive' dyes behave similarly, but they form covalent chemical bonds to the fibre molecules. Whereas direct dyes are sometimes unstable to washing (they may run and migrate to adjacent areas) because the links between the dye molecules and the fibre are not always sufficiently strong, reactive dyes are completely fast to washing. These two types of dye are rare, and neither has played a large part in the history of dyeing.

More important are the 'mordant' and 'vat' dyes, which have probably been known since remote antiquity: what look like representations of dyed kilim wall-hangings have been found on mud-brick walls excavated in Çatal Hüyük, Anatolia, and dated to the pre-ceramic Neolithic, around the 8th millennium BC. Mordant dyes are divided into acid dyes and basic dyes. Acid mordant dyes are applied by first soaking the fibre in the salt of a metal, usually aluminium, iron, chromium or tin. The fibres are dried, then transferred to an acidic dye-bath. The dye combines with the metallic salt, the mordant, to form a lake. (The lakes can be suspended in suitable media and used as paints.) Acid mordant dyes are usually stable to rubbing and washing, but strong acids will break the bond to the mordant. Basic dyes can similarly be fixed with tannins, which again form a chemical bridge from the dye to the fibre.

Vat dyes are converted by means of reduction to a leuco-compound that is soluble in water and usually less coloured. The fibre is soaked in the solution, removed and allowed to come into contact with air, whereupon the leuco-compound oxidizes back to the original dyestuff. The dye is now very intimately associated with the fibre, and the process can be repeated until the desired colour has been built up. Vat dyes are stable to washing and to any acids or bases that the fibre itself will resist, but they can be lost by mechanical creasing or rubbing. They are usually fast to light.

Dyes are coloured because they absorb light of a particular range of wavelengths roughly complementary to their perceived colour. When this happens, the dye molecule acquires a considerable amount of energy. In favourable circumstances the dye can lose this energy by conversion to heat, but in practice it frequently undergoes a chemical reaction that makes it lose its colour. Different types of dye undergo this photochemical bleaching to varying degrees, but the problem is generally most serious for yellow dyes, which absorb in the high-energy, short-wavelength region, and least serious for such blue dyes as indigo. One type of dye, a gallotannin (often derived from oak galls) on an iron mordant, is used for black. On excitation it reacts with the fibre molecule, rendering the fibre mechanically weak, hence the black wool in a tapestry or carpet may have been replaced several times. Other iron-mordanted dyes can show the same effect to some degree.

2. NATURAL. Until 1740 all dyes had an animal or vegetable origin. These early dyes can be investigated in two ways: by finding and examining dyes, dyed materials

and dye by-products or by reading contemporary accounts of the dyeing methods used. The first method suffers from a shortage of examples. Sometimes the actual dyestuff, for example plant material identifiable as madder or weld, has been excavated. Surviving textiles fall into two very different groups: the carefully treasured articles, more or less complete specimens that have always been kept dry and dark, and archaeological fragments from midden heaps, burials and other sources. Undoubtedly more will be learnt as more museum specimens are tested and more excavated scraps recovered, particularly from waterlogged sites. The second method, reading contemporary accounts, suffers more than is sometimes realized from problems of language. Even when the language is as well known as English or Latin, technical terms like 'grain' or *fucus* may be ambiguous, and the problem is of course greater with more obscure languages, those of Mycenean Greece or ancient Egypt, for example.

(i) Indigo. Chemically, this is a mixture of indigotin (blue) and a little indirubin (pink). It is obtainable from many plants, of which woad (*Isatis tinctoria* L.) and indigo (*Indigofera tinctorum* L.) are the most familiar. It is by far the most important vat dye and has probably been used in every culture; it continues to defy predictions that it will give way to modern improvements (the indigo used for colouring denim jeans, however, is synthetic). On textiles indigo is extremely fast to light, and after some loosely fixed dye has been removed by washing, the remainder resists removal well. Mechanical rubbing and creasing, however, give irregular colour effects. Being a highly purified compound, of high value for its weight, indigo has always been traded over long distances.

(ii) Madder. A number of plants of the Rubiacae family contain alizarin (1,2–dihydroxyanthraquinone), purpurin (1,2,4–trihydroxyanthraquinone) and similar compounds, which make excellent mordant dyes. Madder (*Rubia tinctorum* L.) is the best of these. It has been grown for so long and so widely that it no longer occurs in a clearly wild state. These dyes give a range of colours from red, when the mordant is pure aluminium, to violet when it is pure iron. The colour varies with the variety, age and technique of dyeing, and it was controlled with great skill by both home and professional dyers. Turkey red, a bright, fast red associated with cotton, was obtained by impregnating the fibre with oil, then treating it with dung and gall-nuts before the mordanting and dyeing processes. The technique was developed in the Middle East, and it was only in the mid-18th century that Europeans succeeded in emulating it. The attraction of Turkey red lay in the fact that the insect dyes (*see* §vi below) that gave bright reds on the protein fibres (i.e. wool and silk) were not suitable for cellulose fibres.

Madder is reasonably fast to light but dulled by prolonged exposure. Like other acid mordant dyes, it is easily stripped by strong acids, which break the bond to the mordant; if the acid is neutralized with a mild alkali before the mordant is washed out, the dye is refixed, and the yellow area returns to its former shade. Madder has also been traded internationally, but it is much less concentrated than indigo, and the incentive to grow it near a point of use was greater.

(iii) Yellow, black and brown dyes. Yellow dyes are readily available because the majority of plants contain compounds of the flavone and flavonol groups, which are adequate mordant dyes, giving yellow with aluminium. In traditional practice, residues from food crops (vine leaves, onion skins and millet husks) were often used, or common wild plants were gathered. For best results, however, a good source of a flavone such as weld (*Reseda luteola* L.) was grown. Dyes containing flavones (e.g. luteolin, found in weld) are more stable to light than those with flavonols (e.g. quercetin, which is very widely distributed in the plant kingdom), but all these natural yellows are much more easily bleached than madder or indigo. Indeed, it is common to find pale cream areas that are practically devoid of dyestuff but were probably once bright yellow. Weld was traded, but locally produced dyes are the rule for yellows.

A black colour can be obtained from any of a large range of gallotannins applied to an iron mordant, but because of the tendency of iron-black to damage the fibre, its use has often been avoided or proscribed. For wool, the natural brown or black fleece of many sheep could be used, though natural black wool (pigmented with the polymeric compound melanin) is not particularly fast to light and turns a golden brown.

(iv) Mixtures and overdyeing of indigo, madde and yellow, black and brown dyes. Many textiles were made with black and white wool, the latter dyed only with madder or an equivalent, indigo and one of the flavonoid yellows. Mixtures of mordant dyes, such as madder and a yellow to give orange, or madder and a gallotannin with an iron mordant to give brown, are common. It is likely that minor additions were frequently made to a dye-bath to vary the exact shade. Natural dark wool may be dyed with iron-black or with madder. On white wool, double dyeing with indigo, and in a separate process with a yellow to give green, was also common. Since the yellow tends to be fugitive, these once bright greens often fade to blue. Although one might expect indigo and madder to be used similarly to give purple shades, in practice this is rare: the soft purples from iron mordants and madder alone are more often found. Black can be obtained by mixing madder and a yellow, then overdyeing with indigo, but this also was a rare technique. The range of colours available from so simple a palette is remarkable, and in the West it is likely that, until the advent of synthetic dyes, the majority of textiles were dyed with these alone. There are, however, many other natural dyes.

(v) Dyewoods. Brazil-wood, logwood, camwood and others appear frequently in documents and must have been in common use. They do not survive well in archaeological textiles but are found in fabrics that have been cared for all their lives. They are acid mordant dyes, logwood in particular giving a good black with an iron mordant. Brazil-wood from trees of the *Caesalpinia* spp., native to Asia and the Americas, gave various shades of red. It was widely used in Europe but may have become less competitive when cochineal, a faster dye, became available.

(vi) Insect dyes. While the clear reds obtained from madder were most common, the rich wine-red (crimson) colour

from the kermes insect (*Kermes vermilio* Planchon), a parasite found on the kermes oak, was always more valued, and it appears often on the fine cloth of medieval state robes and church vestments. These garments have often survived when those of most of the population have been lost. In eastern Europe its place was taken by an equivalent insect dye, 'Polish cochineal' (*Porphyrophorba polonica* L.), found on a grass; in the Near East another equivalent dye, lac (*Kerria lacca* Kerr), was found as an exudate containing a natural plastic, shellac, from which it was separated. Other similar insects were used in different areas; the entomology is far from simple. All these dyes gave way when the New World insect dye, cochineal, became available after the conquest of Mexico in the early 16th century. Found on the nopal cactus, an arborescent prickly pear, the cochineal insect (*Dactylopius coccus*) had been used for centuries in Mexico and was farmed by the Aztecs. Its advantage was economic, since the insect contains far more colouring matter than, for example, kermes. It steadily replaced kermes and Polish cochineal in Europe during the 16th century. With greater difficulty it replaced lac in Turkey and finally in Iran, but in India it appears that lac held out until synthetic dyes arrived in the 20th century.

Kermes contains kermesic acid, cochineal has carminic acid, Polish cochineal carries a mixture of these two compounds, and lac contains a complex mixture of the laccaic acids. As there are chemical differences (though little or no visible distinctions) between these compounds, it is possible to use analysis (*see* TECHNICAL EXAMINATION, §VIII, 9) to date textiles containing these dyes, with suitable caution: in Iranian carpets, lac suggests a pre–1800 or at least 1850 date, cochineal being used later, but in Britain, cochineal was used in tartans in the 18th century, whereas in the early 19th century a wish to encourage Indian exports led to lac being substituted. Particular care is needed in using written sources dealing with these dyes. The word 'kermes' seems to have been first applied to a little-known Armenian dye (*Porphyrophora hameli* Brand) from Mt Ararat, which is chemically similar to cochineal but contains much less dye. Its normal meaning is the dye of the kermes insect. The word is derived from the same root as 'crimson', and in many languages (e.g. Farsi) it seems to be general for these crimson dyestuffs and applicable to cochineal itself. 'Grain', describing the appearance of the dyestuff, is similarly used in a general sense in English. All these insect dyes have always been valuable and were traded over long distances.

(vii) Lichens and other dyes. A group of dyes less easy to discuss than those listed above derives from lichens. These dyes fall into two classes: one consists of hydroxyaldehydes, which on heating, usually by boiling, with a protein fibre act as reactive dyestuffs and colour the fibre a golden-brown shade, completely unremovable and therefore difficult to study. It may well be that these dyes are also hard to use with precise control and were therefore more important to folk-craft than to any sort of industrial use. The other group of dyes from lichens involves treatment with ammonia, urine being the main traditional source. These are direct dyes. Much the best known is the violet

dye orchil, *Roccella tinctoria*, which gave its name to a prominent Florentine family, the Rucellai. They may be either basic or acidic; they are formed as complex mixtures that can be varied by the choice of species used and by controlling the conditions of the reaction between the lichen constituents. The colours are often very brilliant, but they have two general disadvantages: they are seldom fast to light, and they frequently change colour to a noticeable extent on treatment with mild acids, fruit juice for example, or alkalis. (Litmus, a widely used indicator of acidity, is one of these dyes.) Despite these drawbacks, their use has a long history that may well go back to Classical times: a dye called *fucus* is discussed by Pliny. He associated it with the seashore, and although Fucus is a genus of seaweed, few seaweeds give acceptable dyes, and a lichen may well have been meant. A dye corresponding to Pliny's description (blue–red colour) has been found in 10th-century silks believed to be of Byzantine or Islamic origin and in fragments of excavated wool of late Classical date; this could well be a lichen dye.

Safflower is a sharp pink dye obtained from the flowers of a thistle, *Carthamus tinctorius*, native to India and the Middle East. It is mainly used on silk and is not at all fast to light, fading to a characteristic peach–yellow shade. It is not known how commonly it was used, but it was probably restricted to those textiles that were only seen by candlelight.

A dye much discussed but hardly ever found in surviving textiles is shellfish purple, derived from Murex and other genera. Chemically this is a close relative of indigo and shares its advantages, but it was very expensive and often reserved for élite persons. Late antique Coptic textiles have been found dyed with true purple, but more frequently they contain madder–indigo combinations, rare in most traditions and therefore probably an imitation of Tyrian purple. The commercial production of purple seems to have ceased in Byzantine times. Another rare but much discussed dye is saffron, a yellow of poor light-fastness that must have been expensive as a dye and was mainly used as a food colour. These dyes, and kermes, should never be assumed to be present without chemical analysis, nor should written descriptions be accepted without caution.

This account has focused on the dyes of Europe and the Near East, which progressively converged into a single tradition. In East Asia other dyes have been used; in Japan, for example, *Rubia akane* (which contains purpurin but no alizarin) roughly takes the place of madder; indeed, madder is known by a name equivalent to 'western *akane*'. India is an intermediate case, with some local dyes and some known also in the West. Pre-Columbian America is a distinct dye province, with one or more sources of indigotin, cochineal available from an early date and various little-known dyes, for example *Relbunium hypocarpium*, a madder equivalent. Here, too, traditions have merged, this process having been cut short by the arrival of synthetic dyes.

3. SYNTHETIC. In 1740 the first reference occurs, in French, to what became known as 'essence of indigo', indigodisulphonic acid, which is obtained by treating indigo with concentrated sulphuric acid. It is a blue acid

direct dye. It can be found in, for example, English samplers, sometimes with late 18th-century dates, and it easily runs on washing. It reached Turkey *c.* 1850. The first two fully synthetic dyes came on the market in 1856: picric acid in France (a direct acid yellow) and mauvine (a direct basic mauve) in England. Far more important than either was fuchsine, discovered in 1858, a bright magenta and again a direct basic dye. It was much cheaper than mauvine but less fast to light and mild alkalis. A number of relatives of fuchsine were discovered between 1860 and 1870, extending the colour range into blue and green shades, but these very brilliant 'early anilines' (so-called because oxidation of aniline derivatives was the method of preparation) are all fragile; most faded rapidly, giving synthetic dyes a poor reputation. A second important group of dyes, the direct acid azo-dyes, were introduced from 1875 and provided shades of yellow, orange and red. They did not fade, but many ran easily. Other major and minor groups of synthetic dyes followed, and before long the whole spectrum was covered. The new dyes, essentially pure chemical compounds, were more consistent and often more brilliant and cheaper than the natural dyes previously used. However, the many other qualities needed by the user were not always available, and the synthesis of improved dyes continued to be a main preoccupation of organic chemists. One obvious way of obtaining the advantages of the natural dyestuffs was to synthesize the compounds they contain. Thus alizarin, the main colouring matter of madder, was prepared artificially in 1880, giving dyers in Europe all the advantages of that excellent and versatile dye. Similarly, indigo was made commercially in 1897; the synthetic version is exactly equivalent to and indistinguishable from the natural dyestuff. These achievements dealt a blow to the regions that had grown these once lucrative crops, but they improved both the economics and the technique of dyeing.

By the end of the 19th century thousands of synthetic dyes were available, covering every possible shade, and many (e.g. the chrome dyes, a set of azo-dyes mordanted with chromium salts) had excellent fastness. Around 1920 the last important niche, a green dye of good stability for natural fibres, was filled by Caledon Jade Green, a vat dye. The arrival of synthetic fibres presented new problems, as they proved difficult to dye. New types of dye were produced, the technology becoming progressively more specialized. For example, the advent of photography led to the use of the extremely labile cyanine dyes for the sensitization of silver bromide emulsions to yellow and red light, giving the panchromatic plates and films introduced in the 1920–40 period. Colour photography led to other demands for relatively stable dyes. If the dyes used in the late 20th century have faults, it is usually because low cost has been preferred to high quality; neither impermanence nor unsubtle shades are inevitable. By skilful use of the immense range of modern synthetic dyes, high-value textiles can be produced in any shade imaginable (including the most subtle), with all the desired fastness to washing and good resistance to light.

The use of natural dyes, however, has not entirely disappeared. Since the 1960s craftsmen have been interested in those dyes that can be grown and used in a domestic environment; and in the 1980s natural dyes were seen as an ideal alternative to the cheap synthetic ones that had damaged the reputation of traditional weaving.

See also CHINA, §XII, 1 (iv), INDIA, §VI, 3(i), TEXTILE, §III, 1(ii)(a) and WOOD (i), §III, 5.

BIBLIOGRAPHY
S. Muspratt: *Chemistry: Theoretical, Practical and Analytical* (London, Glasgow and Edinburgh [1860])
A. G. Perkin and A. F. Everest: *The Nature of Organic Colouring Matters* (London, 1918)
The Colour Index, Society of Dyeists and Colourists, 2 vols (Bradford, 1924), rev. in 5 vols (Bradford, 3/1971)
Ciba Z. (1937–70) and *Ciba-Geigy Q.* (1971–5) [articles on various topics relating to dyes]
H. A. Lubs, ed.: *The Chemistry of Synthetic Dyes and Pigments* (New York, 1955)
E. N. Abrahart: *Dyes and their Intermediates* (Oxford, 1968)
F. Brunello: *L'arte della tintura nella storia dell'umanità* (Vicenza, 1968; Eng. trans., Cleveland, 1973)
S. Robinson: *A History of Dyed Textiles* (London, 1969)
R. L. M. Allen: *Colour Chemistry* (London, 1971)
J. H. Hofenk de Graaff and W. G. T. Roelofs: 'On the Occurrence of Red Dyestuffs in Textile Materials from the Period 1450–1600', *ICOM Committee for Conservation: Madrid, 1972*
P. Rys and H. Zollinger: *Fundamentals of the Chemistry and Application of Dyes* (New York, 1972)
J. B. Harbourne, T. J. Mabry and K. Mabry: *The Flavonoids* (London, 1975)
T. W. Goodwin, ed.: *The Chemistry and Biochemistry of Plant Pigments*, ii (London, 1976)
J. Griffiths: *Colour and Constitution of Dyes and Pigments* (London, 1976)
Hali (1977–) [occasional articles on dyes]
K. Venkataraman, ed.: *The Analytical Chemistry of Synthetic Dyes* (New York, 1977)
J. H. Hofenk de Graaff and W. G. T. Roelofs: 'The Analysis of Flavonoids in . . . Textiles', 'Natural Yellow Dyestuffs Occurring in Ancient Textiles', *ICOM Committee for Conservation, 5th Triennial Meeting: Zagreb, 1978*
L. Masschelein-Kleiner and L. Maes: *Ancient Dyeing Techniques in Eastern Mediterranean Regions* (Zagreb, 1978)
M. C. Whiting: 'The Identification of Dyes in Old Oriental Textiles', *ICOM Committee for Conservation, 5th Triennial Meeting: Zagreb, 1978*
M. Grayson, ed.: *Kirk-Othmer Encyclopedia of Chemical Technology*, viii (New York, 1979)
K. Ponting: *A Dictionary of Dyes and Dyeing* (London, 1980)
M. Gittinger: *Master Dyers to the World* (Washington, DC, 1982)
J. B. Harbourne and T. J. Mabry: *The Flavonoids: Advances and Research* (London, 1982)
Dyes Hist. & Archaeol. Textiles (1982–)
K. McLaren: *The Colour Science of Dyes and Pigments* (Bristol, 1986)
R. H. Thompson: *Naturally Occurring Quinones: Recent Advances* (London, 1987)
H. Zollinger: *Colour Chemistry* (New York, 1987)

M. C. WHITING

Dye transfer. Method of producing archival quality, colour photographic prints subject to aesthetic control at every stage. The technique, introduced by Eastman Kodak in the mid-1930s and improved in 1946, can be used for reflection images on paper as well as for transparent ones on a film base; it derives, ultimately, from the 'subtractive' technique of colour photography (*see* PHOTOGRAPHY, §I, 2).

Colour information can be taken from various types of originals: in-camera separation negatives, colour negatives or positive colour transparencies. A colour transparency is translated by means of red, green and blue filters into continuous-tone separation negatives on panchromatic sheet film. Each separation is exposed on to a special paper through an enlarger and then developed, fixed and washed in hot water to remove unexposed gelatin. This

Colour dye transfer by Richard Hamilton: '*I'm Dreaming of a White Christmas*', image size: 360×543 mm, 1969 (artist's collection), retouched and printed in an edition of six at Creative Colour, Hamburg

results in a relief matrix of gelatin selectively hardened according to the amount of light reaching it. Each matrix—a red-, green- or blue-record separation positive—is soaked in the appropriate bath of powerful cyan, magenta or yellow dye, which charges the printing surface with colour in proportion to the thickness and receptivity of the gelatin. A good quality 'receiver paper' is soaked in distilled water and placed, gelatin emulsion side up, on a sheet of glass. After being rinsed to remove surplus dye, the first matrix is rolled or squeegeed, emulsion side down, on to the printing paper, where it is left long enough for dye to transfer; the other matrices, registered by locating pins, follow. The length of contact and colour sequence provide some of the creative variables, while colour balance and density can be adjusted by adding chemicals to rinse baths. Matrices can also be painted with specially mixed colours. Although the method is not suited to mass production, as many as 800 prints can be made from a set of matrices. The maximum size of regularly produced prints is 1.01×1.57 m, and each print takes at least 20 minutes to make. Under magnification, the colour has the soft, slightly unfocused appearance characteristic of photographic enlargements.

Although exquisite monochrome prints can be made, the control possible in dye transfer has proved of particular interest in advertising and illustration and to such creative colour photographers as Eliot Porter (*b* 1901) and William Eggleston. Richard Hamilton, several of whose works have explored focus and its relationship to photographic 'truth', is the best-known painter to have adopted the process, working in 1969 at Creative Colour in Hamburg. In such works as *Bathers (b)* (see Hamilton, no. 72), *Vignette* (see Hamilton, no. 73) and '*I'm Dreaming of a White Christmas*' (1969, see Hamilton, no. 71; see fig.), Hamilton's approach ranged from the straightforwardly commercial to the extensively interventionist. In 1985 he took up the method again for *The Citizen*, producing a seamless collage from fragments of 16 mm film by laser. In the late 1980s he continued to experiment with dye transfer to record images made with the Quantel computer paint-box.

BIBLIOGRAPHY

D. B. P. Hanworth: *Amateur Dye Transfer Colour Prints* (London, 1955)
William Eggleston's Guide (exh. cat., intro. J. Szarkowski; New York, MOMA, 1976)
The Dye Transfer Process, Eastman Kodak Company, Pamphlet E.80 (Rochester, NY, 1978, rev. 1980)
M. Beede: *Dye Transfer Made Easy* (New York, 1981)
A. Gassan: *The Color Print Book*, Extended Photo Media Series, iii (Rochester, NY, 1981), pp. 42–8
D. Doubley: *The Dye Transfer Process* (Detroit, 8/c. 1984)
R. Hamilton: *Richard Hamilton Prints, 1939–83: A Complete Catalogue of Graphic Works* (Stuttgart, 1984)

PAT GILMOUR

Dyk, Philip van. *See* DIJK, PHILIP VAN.

Dymshits-Tolstaya [Pesatti]**, Sof'ya (Isaakovna)** (*b* St Petersburg, 23 April 1889; *d* Leningrad [now St Petersburg], 30 Aug 1963). Russian painter. She first studied painting in 1906–7 in St Petersburg at the studio of Sergey Yegornov (1860–1920) and then from 1908 to 1910 at Yelizaveta Zvantseva's private art school under Mstislav Dobuzhinsky and Léon Bakst. In Paris (1910–11) she studied in the studio of Charles Guérin. On her return to Russia she began to exhibit in Moscow and St Petersburg, participating in the exhibitions of the World of Art group and the more avant-garde shows of the Jack of Diamonds: *1915 god* ('The Year 1915') and *Magazin* ('The Shop'). Her contributions, which showed the influence of Cézanne, Fauvism and Cubism, included still-lifes, portraits and glass reliefs that were painted on both sides. This turn to three-dimensional work presaged Dymshits-Tolstaya's concern with the material itself and the exploration of texture and accompanied her association with Vladimir Tatlin. After the Revolution of 1917 she was active in the organization of IZO Narkompros in Moscow and she subsequently became head of its publications department (late 1920s). Her works of this period include collages using elements such as sand and cord on canvas, as in *Composition of a Compass* (1919; Samara, City A. Mus.), and reliefs made from wood, glass and metal. In addition she designed painted-glass agitprop placards and the cover for the proposed magazine *Internatsional' iskusstva* ('Art international', 1919; Moscow, Cent. Archvs Lit. & A.). She also edited the art sections of the journals *Rabotnitsa* ('Working woman') and *Krest'yanka* ('Peasant woman'; 1925–35). Her unpublished memoirs provide an exceptionally detailed description of the development of Russian avant-garde art in the crucial years 1912–21.

UNPUBLISHED SOURCES

St Petersburg, Rus. Mus., Fond. 100, unit 249 [*Vospominaniya khudozhnitsy S. I. Dymshits-Tolstoy* ('Memoirs of the artist S. I. Dymshits-Tolstaya', 1905–61)]

Moscow Cent. Archvs Lit. & A., Fond. 665, unit 32 [*Intuitsiya kak osnova tvorchestva* ('Intuition as the basis of creative work')]

JEREMY HOWARD

Dyrrhachion [anc. Gr. Epidamnos, Lat. Dyrrachium; It. Durrazzo; now Durrës, Albania]. Site on the Adriatic coast, approximately 30 km west of Tiranë, Albania. It was founded as Epidamnos, as a colony of Corinth and Corfu, in 627 BC, and when the name Dyrrhachion first appeared in the 5th century BC it may have referred only to the port, 5 km north of the walled city. In 437 BC a violent uprising led indirectly, through the involvement of Corfu and Athens, to the Peloponnesian War. In the late 3rd century BC the city became part of the Illyrian kingdom of Glaukias. As Dyrrachium, it remained a free city after the Roman conquests of Macedonia and Epiros (167 BC); as the starting-point for the Via Egnatia (AD 148), the Roman road from the Adriatic to Byzantium, it developed as an important trade and communications centre. The cosmopolitan character of its medieval history reflects its continued strategic significance. It remained a Byzantine stronghold from the 4th century AD, except for a short period when it was taken by the Bulgarian Tsar Samuel (*reg* 989–1005). It was besieged by the Normans of Apulia under Robert Guiscard (1082) and Bohemond (1107) and by the Sicilian Normans in 1185. After the Fourth Crusade (1204) it was controlled successively by the Despots of Epiros, Charles III of Anjou (*reg* 1219–1325), the Albanian

princes of the Thopia dynasty and the Venetians, who named it Durrazzo and from whom the Ottoman Turks captured it in 1501. No longer a significant link between Italy and Constantinople, it had declined to a single-street town by the mid-19th century. Although the whole ancient city is a protected archaeological area, much is covered by modern building as a result of rapid regrowth during the late 20th century.

The principal remains of the Greek and Illyrian city are the tombs of the necropolis on the hills to the east, which have produced 5th- and 4th-century BC Red-figure pottery. A 3rd-century BC pebble mosaic with a female head among floral scrolls was probably the floor of a Hellenistic house. There are terracottas from a Temple of Aphrodite, and inscriptions record Roman temples of Diana and Minerva, a library and a Hadrianic aqueduct (AD 117–38). The chief surviving Roman structure is the 2nd-century AD amphitheatre. Clearance of overlying houses, begun in 1966, uncovered much of its concrete vaulting, faced in stone with courses of tile at intervals; it would have seated about 20,000. The vaults came to be used as a Christian cemetery. A small 10th-century chapel built into the seating has wall mosaics showing *St Stephen* and *Emperor Alexander* (*reg* AD 911–13). Part of the hypocausts and marble-tiled floors of the public baths are displayed, and later excavations near by have uncovered a large circular colonnaded piazza of late Roman date.

The fortification walls (5th–6th century AD) contain inscriptions of Emperor Anastasios I (*reg* 491–518) and have rectangular and triangular towers, as well as circular towers added by the Venetians. Kilns making 13th- and 14th-century maiolica ceramics have been excavated. Other finds include pieces of Greek, Roman, Byzantine and Turkish sculpture, metalwork and pottery (Durrës, Archaeol. Mus.; Tiranë, N. Mus. Archaeol.).

BIBLIOGRAPHY

G. Karaskaij: 'La Forteresse de Durrës au moyen âge', *Monumentet*, xiii (1977)

J. Reynis-Jandot: 'La Mosaïque murale dans la chapelle de l'amphithéâtre de Dyrrachium', *Iliria*, i (1983), pp. 225–32

S. Anamali: 'Illyriens et Hellènes à Dyrrhachion', *Doss. Hist. & Archéol.*, cxi (1986), pp. 34–6

T. F. C. BLAGG

Dysart, François. *See* DIEUSSART, FRANÇOIS.

Dyson, Will(iam Henry) (*b* Alfredtown, Victoria, 3 Sept 1880; *d* London, 21 Jan 1938). Australian draughtsman and printmaker. In his formative years he worked as a caricaturist for several Australian magazines. He moved to London in 1910 where he worked as a cartoonist for the Labour newspapers, the *Daily Herald* and *New Age*, and achieved great success with his biting cartoons (e.g. 'Give Us this Day'; *Cartoons*, 1913), which made him a leading figure among English intellectuals. He worked in the humanist tradition of Honoré Daumier, Théophile-Alexandre Steinlen and Jean-Louis Forain. He was a determined satirist calling for a better world, concerned with political hypocrisy and social injustice, and his cartoons were admired for their apt captions as well as for the hard-hitting images that accompanied them. Dyson visited the Western Front as an Official War Artist during World War I to record the Australian involvement in the war. He worked in the trenches among battle-weary soldiers and was wounded, though not seriously, at Messines and Passchendaele. He made numerous compassionate and frank watercolour-wash drawings of the ordinary soldier (e.g. *Dead Beat, the Tunnels, Hill 60*, 1917; Canberra, Australian War Memorial). After the war he continued to work as a cartoonist in England, Australia and the USA, but in 1919 his wife, Ruby Lind (*b* 1885), herself a talented artist, was a victim of the influenza epidemic. After this much of the enthusiasm went out of his work, though in the 1920s he became interested in etching and drypoint and created a series of satires in this medium.

WRITINGS
Cartoons (London, 1913)
War Cartoons (London, 1916)
Australia at War (London, 1918)

BIBLIOGRAPHY
R. McMullin: *Will Dyson: Cartoonist, Etcher and Australia's Finest War Artist* (Sydney, 1984)
ANNE GRAY

Dyson Perrins, Charles William. *See* PERRINS, CHARLES WILLIAM DYSON.

Dyukker, Yevgeny (Eduardovich). *See* DÜCKER, EUGEN.

Dyushambe. *See* DUSHANBE.

Džamonja, Dušan (*b* Strumica, 31 Jan 1928). Croatian sculptor of Macedonian birth. In 1945 he entered the Zagreb Academy of Fine Arts and studied sculpture under Vanja Radauš (1906–75) and Frano Kršinić, graduating with an MFA under Antun Augustinčić (1900–79) in 1951. Between 1951 and 1953 he worked in the Kršinić workshop but soon started on his own in Zagreb, concentrating on sculpture and drawing. Later on he built a house and a sculpture park at Vrsar and created several major Yugoslav monuments, mostly memorials to the national liberation struggle. In 1977 he was awarded the Rembrandt prize by the Goethe Foundation of Basle.

Until 1957 Džamonja's work largely consisted of stylized human figures, in which the influence of Henry Moore was already perceptible. In 1956 he made his first sculpture of deer, which he saw as symbols of fear and fearfulness. He reduced the volumes of his rounded and bulky figures to accentuated shapes of verticals, horizontals and diagonals that pointed to violence. This became the main theme of his early projects for monuments (Jajinci, Auschwitz, Dachau), most of which were never executed. Unorthodox materials such as concrete, wire netting, iron, glass or their unusual combinations, as well as the newly available techniques of forging, welding or soldering, made his sculptures of this period even more forceful. The most representative example is the 4 m-high *Memorial to the Victims of December* (1959–60) at Dubrava near Zagreb. A special feel for the rough surface of the sculpture led Džamonja to sculptures with characteristic cores, carved segments and voids. A typical example is the *Metal Sculpture* (1956; New York, MOMA), one of the first sculptures he made in this period, in which systematic strings of long nails either covered the wood into which they were hammered, like a welded texture reminiscent of

a hauberk, or formed the inner negative space of the statue with their pointed ends. All the basic qualities of his smaller sculptures of that period were synthesized in his colossal, concrete and aluminium *Monument to the Revolution* (10×20 m), executed at Podgarić in Moslavina between 1965 and 1967.

Džamonja then began to work in a gallery format, producing sculptures whose surface was losing its suggestiveness and becoming more polished and aestheticized. He became interested in generally rounded, organic or geometrical forms, his most frequent theme being the sphere with dissected and newly composed segments. Particularly interesting was a series of tapestries 'woven' from iron chains. He embarked on the problem of dissected forms and rhythmical sequences when he was working on two large commissions for monuments. One was the *Memorial Tomb-Charnel House*, erected in 1968–70 at Barletta near Bari, Italy, and the other the colossal *Memorial to the Revolution* in the memorial park of Mrakovica on Kozara (1970–72). The Barletta monument was noted for its rhythmical strings of elegant and geometrically pure concrete blocks, their meaningful centripetal rhythm creating numerous angles of view. Masterly scattered empty spaces between the blocks direct the spectator's eye to the consecrated site. The Kozara monument achieves unity and harmony between the concrete blocks, the 30 m-high cylindrical pillar with stainless steel and the natural land and forest configuration.

In the 1980s Džamonja executed increasingly pure geometrical forms based on segments of the sphere that were often suggestive of the monumental forms of Roman arches or cupolas. He tested them in drawings, prints and statues of different formats and sizes, many of them demonstrating his sense of real space, his feel for elegant projection of sculptural forms into architectural ones, a perfect sense of proportion and respect for the elements found in a given environment.

BIBLIOGRAPHY
V. Horvat Pintarić: *Dušan Džamonja* (Zagreb, 1960)
Z. Kržišnik: *Dušan Džamonja* (Zagreb, 1969)
Dušan Džamonja (exh. cat. by G. Marchiori, Milan, Rotonda Foppone Osp., 1975)
Dušan Džamonja (exh. cat., ed. Z. Kržišnik; Ljubljana, Gal. Mod. A., 1976)
G. C. Argan: *Džamonja* (Motovun, 1981)
Džamonja (exh. cat. by A. Medved, Piran, Obalne Gal.)
JURE MIKUŽ

Dzhambul. *See* ZHAMBYL.

Dzheytun [Djeitun; Jeitun]. Site of a Neolithic settlement in Turkmenistan, on the southern edge of the Karakum Desert, 25 km north-west of Ashkhabad, which flourished from the late 7th millennium BC to the early 6th. It was excavated from 1956 to 1961 by the Turkmenistan Academy of Sciences, and again in 1989 in conjunction with London University. The houses of the settlement each comprised a small single room, of 15 to 35 m sq., containing a large hearth or stove covered with lime plaster. The floors and walls were painted red or black. Finds included flint implements such as trapezoids and segments, small axes of polished stone, slivers of bone, hide scrapers, stone querns, ceramics painted with simple rows of brackets or vertical wavy lines, stone and bone beads, stone pendants of animal forms and small terracotta human or animal figurines.

The main occupation was farming. Single grain wheat (*einkorn*) was harvested using bone sickles with inserted flint blades. The inhabitants bred cattle, sheep and goats, kept dogs and also hunted antelopes (*gazella subguttorosa* and *saiga*). Judging from the animal remains, livestock was kept primarily for meat, although there was some dairy farming. The site represents a typical early community during the transition from hunter-gathering to farming, with a corresponding development of residential architecture, the appearance of clay vessels, religious utensils and numerous items of jewellery. In southern Turkmenistan some ten sites of this type represent the so-called Dzheytun culture, which has several aspects in common with contemporary sites particularly in north-east Iran. Floors covered with a lime wash and paint are also typical throughout the Near East (e.g. Catal-Hüyük, Jericho), while the Dzheytun flint industry is paralleled at Jarmo, northern Iraq and Mehrgarh I, northern Pakistan.

BIBLIOGRAPHY

V. M. Masson: 'The First Farmers in Turkmenia', *Antiquity*, xxxv (1961), no. 139, pp. 203–13
——: *Poseleniye Dzheytun: Problema stanovleniya proizvodyashchey ekonomiki* [The settlement of Dzheytun: the question of the establishment of a production economy] (Leningrad, 1971)
V. M. Masson and V. I. Sarianidi: *Central Asia: Turkmenia before the Achaemenids* (London, 1972)
D. Harris: 'The Jeitun Project: Soviet–British Collaboration in Turkmenia', *The Brit.–Sov. Archaeol. Newslett.* (Dec 1992), pp. 47–52

V. M. MASSON

Działyński. Polish family of collectors and patrons. In 1817 Count Adam Tytus Działyński (*b* Poznań, 24 Dec 1796; *d* Poznań, 12 April 1861) began adding to his family library at Kórnik Castle, aiming to build up a collection of Polish history, and in 1829 he started publishing early manuscripts. His participation in the Polish insurrection of 1830 resulted in the sequestration of his entire estate by the Prussian authorities until 1838. When his property was restored, Działyński decided to create a historical museum, and he and his wife, Gryzelda Celestyna (née Zamoyska; *b* Zamość, 25 Sept 1804; *d* Poznań, 10 July 1883), rebuilt Kórnik to neo-Gothic designs to incorporate this.

His son Jan Kanty Dzlałyński (*b* Kórnik, 28 Sept 1829; *d* Kórnik, 30 March 1880) inherited Kórnik in 1861, but the property was sequestered and he himself was sentenced to death for having taken part in the 1863 insurrection. However, after the amnesty of 1869 he resumed his father's collecting and publishing work. The library contains a unique collection of historical and literary manuscripts, Polish incunabula and printed books. In accordance with the will of Adam Tytus, it was turned into a public institution on the death of his grandson, Władysław Zamoyski, in 1929, and as the Museum of the Library of the Polish Academy of Sciences it is still open to the public.

In 1857 Jan Kanty married Iza-bela Czartoryska (*b* Warsaw, 14 Dec 1830; *d* Menton, 18 March 1899), a collector of early medieval glass and metalwork, Limoges enamels and antiquities. During an Italian journey with her husband in 1865–7, she acquired an outstanding collection of Greek vases. In the 1870s she rebuilt her castle of Gołuchów as a museum. The castle museum still exists, but the original collection was heavily looted during World War II.

BIBLIOGRAPHY

CVA Poland, Fasc. 1; PSB
J. de Witte: *Description des collections d'antiquités conservées à l'Hôtel Lambert* (Paris, 1886)
W. Froehner: *Collections du Château de Gołuchów: Orfèvrerie* (Paris, 1897)
——: *Collections du Château de Gołuchów: Antiquités* (Paris, 1899)
M. Sokolowski: 'Gołuchów', *Studia i szkice z dziejów sztuki i cywilizacji* [An outline study of the history of art and civilization] (Kraków, 1899)
E. Molinier: *Collections du Château de Gołuchów: Objets d'art du moyen age et de la Renaissance* (Paris, 1903)
J. D. Beazley: *Greek Vases in Poland* (Oxford, 1928)
S. Bodniak: *Tytus Działyński* (Poznań, 1929)

ADAM ZAMOYSKI

Dzibilchaltún. Site of a Mesoamerican Pre-Columbian MAYA city, *c.* 15 km north of Mérida, Yucatán. Excavation and mapping carried out between 1956 and 1965 revealed that the site covers more than 19 sq. km and contains about 8400 ruined structures, most of which are small platforms that formerly supported perishable pole-and-thatch houses. The majority of some 240 stone-faced, vaulted buildings probably served as élite residences, although the largest pyramidal platforms and vaulted structures, located around the central Cenote Xlacah (*cenote*: Maya *tz'onot*, a natural water hole with collapsed limestone sides), probably served for religious and administrative functions. Most of the visible remains lie within this administrative and ceremonial core. North-east of the Cenote Xlacah is the large, open, centralized Main Plaza; another plaza lies to the south-west. Surrounding these are several pyramid-temples and many ranges of vaulted rooms. A central east–west axis is formed by two long *sacbeob* (raised causeways; sing. *sacbé*; *see* CAUSEWAY) that meet at the Main Plaza. *Sacbé* 1 runs east 430 m to the 'Seven Dolls Group', while *sacbé* 2 runs 1280 m to a corresponding western group. Other causeways extend north and south from the Main Plaza at irregular angles and end in plazas or terraces supporting masonry architectural groupings that may have served as kin-related residential compounds. Most of Dzibilchaltún's architecture dates to its locally designated Early period II (see below) and Pure Florescent period, dated between *c.* AD 600 and *c.* 1000. The city reached its greatest size and population during this time: more than 13 sq. km in Early period II (with a population occupying *c.* 90% of the 8400 structures) and a population of *c.* 40,000 by the beginning of the Pure Florescent period.

Dzibilchaltún's occupation has been divided by archaeologists into locally named periods and phases. The site was first occupied during the Middle Pre-Classic period (*c.* 1000–*c.* 300 BC), local Nabanche 1 phase of *c.* 800–*c.* 300 BC, and maintained a substantial occupation during the Late Pre-Classic period (*c.* 300 BC–*c.* AD 250), local Xculul 1 phase of *c.* 300 BC–*c.* AD 150. There were large settlements *c.* 7 km west of Cenote Xlacah at the Mirador Group, comprising masonry-faced platforms surrounding an open plaza, and *c.* 6 km north-west at Komchén, where large masonry pyramid and platform complexes, Structure 450 and Structure 500, were constructed. During the Early period I Piim phase (*c.* AD 250–*c.* 600) the population decreased, and construction was curtailed, although towards the end of this period Structure 612, a small platform with TEOTIHUACÁN-style TALUD-TABLERO terrace profiling, was built. During the Early period II Copo 1 phase (*c.* AD 600–*c.* 830), many important buildings were constructed. Among the best-preserved is the Temple of the Seven Dolls (Structure 1-sub), a radially symmetrical, four-stairwayed pyramid–temple at the east end of *sacbé* 1. The temple's central tower, block wall and slab vault masonry and stucco sculptures have been likened to contemporary architecture at PALENQUE. Coggins identified aquatic and underworld symbolism in the architectural sculpture and suggested that Structure 1-sub and its western counterpart, Structure 66, comprised a planning scheme like that of the twin-pyramid complexes at TIKAL, built to commemorate cyclic completion ceremonies associated with a date in the Maya calendar (*see* MESOAMERICA, PRE-COLUMBIAN, §II) of the *katun* ending 9.13.0.0.0 (AD 692). 'Structure 38-sub' (with a later *talud-tablero* terrace variant) and the Standing Temple (Structure 57) are later examples of Early period II block wall and slab vault architecture.

In the Pure Florescent period Copo 2 phase (*c.* AD 830–*c.* 1000), many buildings were constructed with Puuc-style veneer masonry and geometric stone mosaic sculpture. Three carved stelae featuring Maya rulers holding manikin sceptres were found embedded in the lower terrace of the Pure Florescent pyramid, Structure 36. Stela 9 may be placed in the *katun* 5 *Ahau* ending on 10.1.0.0.0 (AD 849). After a Pure Florescent peak, there seems to have been little activity at Dzibilchaltún until the end of the Modified Florescent period (*c.* AD 1000–*c.* 1200), when Structure 39 was constructed. This corresponds to the 'Toltec–Maya' phase at CHICHÉN ITZÁ, whose political dominance may have prevented development at Dzibilchaltún and other northern Yucatán centres at this time. During the Decadent period (*c.* AD 1200–*c.* 1540) Dzibilchaltún was a minor settlement overpowered by MAYAPÁN, the dominant city in the northern Yucatán plains from *c.* AD 1250 to 1450. Dzibilchaltún's inhabitants reused at least two buried Early period II temples (including the Temple of the Seven Dolls), refurbished several *sacbeob* and vaulted buildings that were still standing and constructed many small, one-roomed houses near Cenote Xlacah, as well as several miniature masonry shrines within the Mirador Group.

BIBLIOGRAPHY
E. W. Andrews IV: *Progress Report on the 1960–1964 Field Seasons, National Geographic–Tulane University Dzibilchaltún Program*, Tulane University Middle American Research Institute Publication xxxi (New Orleans, 1965), pp. 23–67
E. B. Kurjack: *Prehistoric Lowland Maya Community and Social Organization: A Case Study at Dzibilchaltún, Yucatán, Mexico*, Tulane University Middle American Research Institute Publication xxxviii (New Orleans, 1974)
E. W. Andrews IV and E. W. Andrews V: *Excavations at Dzibilchaltún, Yucatán, Mexico*, Tulane University Middle American Research Institute Publication xlviii (New Orleans, 1980)
E. W. Andrews V: 'Dzibilchaltún', *Hb. Mid. Amer. Ind.*, suppl. 1 (1981), pp. 313–41
C. C. Coggins: *The Stucco Decoration and Architectural Assemblage of Structure 1-sub, Dzibilchaltún, Yucatán, Mexico*, Tulane University Middle American Research Institute Publication xlix (New Orleans, 1983)

JEFF KARL KOWALSKI

Dziekoński, Józef Pius (*b* Płock, 5 May 1844; *d* Warsaw, 4 Feb 1927). Polish architect. He studied at the School of Fine Arts in Warsaw (1852–9) and then at the Academy of Arts in St Petersburg in 1866–71. He collaborated with Edward Cichocki (1833–99) on the church of SS Peter and Paul (1883–6; destr. 1944; rebuilt 1946–58), Wspólna Street, Warsaw, and then joined Edward August Karol Lilpop (1844–1911) on the design of the Scheibler family mausoleum in the Evangelist cemetery in Łódź, after which he worked independently.

In the many imposing Warsaw churches he designed, Dziekoński drew on a wide range of past architectural styles: he remodelled St Alexander (1886–94; destr. 1944; rebuilt 1949 to a different design) in Trzech Krzyży Square in a Neo-classical style and designed St Florianus (1888–1901; partly destr. 1944; rebuilt 1947–72) in the Praga district in a style based on Polish Gothic architecture. After 1900 he concentrated on Polish Gothic and Renaissance architecture for his inspiration, in line with the contemporary search for a national Polish style derived from such sources. His church of St Saviour (1901–11) in Marszałkowska Street, Warsaw, uses architectural details and features derived from Polish Renaissance castles, for example Wawel Castle (Kraków).

Dziekoński also designed about 50 churches outside Warsaw (for example the church of the Protection of the Mother of God in Radom, 1894–1911). His secular buildings included the Hospital of the Child Jesus (1897–1901), the largest hospital in Warsaw at that time. He was also an influential teacher, and in 1915 he was among those who established the Architecture Department of Warsaw Technical University, of which he was the first Dean and where he lectured.

BIBLIOGRAPHY
Warszawska szkoła architektury, 1915–1965 [Warsaw school of architecture, 1915–1965] (Warsaw, 1967), p. 239
T. S. Jaroszewski and A. Rottermund: '"Renesans polski" w architekturze XIX i XX w.' [The 'Polish Renaissance' in 19th- and 20th-century architecture], *Renesans: sztuka i ideologia: materiały sympozjum Komitetu Nauk o Sztuce PAN: Kraków, 1972* [Renaissance: art and ideology: proceedings of the symposium of the Art Science Committee of the Polish Academy of Sciences: Kraków, 1972], pp. 613–38
J. A. Chrościcki and A. Rottermund: *Atlas of Warsaw's Architecture* (Warsaw, 1978)

ANDRZEJ ROTTERMUND

E

Eads, James Buchanan (*b* Lawrenceburg, IN, 23 May 1820; *d* Nassau, Bahamas, 8 March 1887). American engineer. His formal education ended when he was 13, and he was self-taught as an engineer. He acquired an early knowledge of river beds and currents from salvaging sunken vessels, and he launched his engineering career in 1842 with a patent for a diving bell. As an authority on the hydrography of the Mississippi, he went to Washington, DC, in 1861 to advise the Lincoln administration on the use of the river for military purposes during the Civil War. During the Mississippi campaign 12 iron-clad boats designed by Eads were used by the Union Army.

In 1865 Eads proposed a three-span arch bridge with two decks, to cross the river at St Louis. The bridge (1867–74) was a pioneer work of unprecedented size: the arches, two spanning 150 m and one 156 m, were of record length for the time; the ribs, bracing and superstructure marked the introduction of chromium steel for structural purposes; and the construction of piers required the deepest pneumatic caissons so far employed, though it was not their first use in the USA, as is widely believed. After the bridge was complete, Eads built a system of jetties along the South Pass of the Mississippi Delta (1875–9), so designed that river currents could sweep sediment out of the pass. In 1880 he proposed a railway to transport ships across the isthmus of Tehuantepec in Mexico to unite the Atlantic and Pacific oceans, but it was never built.

DAB

BIBLIOGRAPHY

C. W. Condit: *American Building Art: The Nineteenth Century* (New York, 1960)
H. S. Miller and Q. Scott: *The Eads Bridge* (Columbia, MO, 1979)
J. A. Kouwenhoven: 'The Designing of Eads Bridge', *Technol. & Cult.*, xxiii (1987), pp. 535–68

CARL W. CONDIT

Eadui (*fl* Canterbury, ?*c*. 1010–30). Scribe and illuminator working in England. He was a monk of Christ Church cathedral priory, Canterbury, and his name (*Eaduuius cognomento Basan*) appears as that of the scribe in the colophon of a Gospel book (Hannover, Kestner-Mus., MS. WM XXI a 36), which has been in Germany since at least the late 11th century. His characteristic English Caroline minuscule script has been identified in a number of liturgical manuscripts and secular documents, including a charter of Canute (*reg* 1016–35) in favour of Canterbury, dated 1018 (London, BL, Stowe Ch. 38). Another, copied into a Gospel book from Canterbury (London, BL, MS. Royal 1 D. IX), is Canute's confirmation of the privileges of Christ Church, delivered in person on a visit between 1016 and 1019. Both apparently show Eadui's hand at its most confident.

Eadui participated in the production of several of the magnificent Gospel books apparently produced at Christ Church in the early 11th century for distribution to other religious houses. These include the Grimbald Gospels, formerly at Winchester (London, BL, Add. MS. 34890), and the York Gospels (York Minster, Chapter Lib., Add. MS. 1). He is usually concerned only with the text, but in the Hannover Gospels and in a Psalter written for his own community (London, BL, MS. Arundel 155) he was probably also the artist. The Gospels include fully illuminated Evangelist portraits and canon tables in which, typically for Canterbury books of the period, gold is lavishly employed. The Psalter includes coloured line drawings and its single miniature is the finest surviving example of a deliberate marriage between the techniques of full illumination and line drawing (*see* BENEDICTINE ORDER, fig. 1).

BIBLIOGRAPHY

T. A. M. Bishop: *English Caroline Minuscule* (Oxford, 1971), nos 24–5
E. Temple: *Anglo-Saxon Manuscripts, 900–1066*, A Survey of Manuscripts Illuminated in the British Isles, iii (London, 1976), nos 61, 64, 66–70
The Golden Age of Anglo-Saxon Art, 966–1066 (exh. cat., ed. J. Backhouse, D. H. Turner and L. Webster; London, BM, 1984), nos 52, 54–7, 59, 169

JANET BACKHOUSE

Eakins, Thomas (Cowperthwaite) (*b* Philadelphia, PA, 25 July 1844; *d* Philadelphia, 25 June 1916). American painter, sculptor and photographer. He was a portrait painter who chose most of his sitters and represented them in powerful but often unflattering physical and psychological terms. Although unsuccessful throughout much of his career, since the 1930s he has been regarded as one of the greatest American painters of his era.

1. Life and work. 2. Working methods and technique.

1. LIFE AND WORK. His father Benjamin Eakins (1818–99), the son of a Scottish–Irish immigrant weaver, was a writing master and amateur artist who encouraged Thomas Eakins's developing talent. Eakins attended the Central High School in Philadelphia, which stressed skills in drawing as well as a democratic respect for disciplined achievement. He developed an interest in human anatomy and began visiting anatomical clinics. After studying at the Pennsylvania Academy of the Fine Arts from 1862, where instruction was minimal, Eakins went to Paris to enrol at

the Ecole des Beaux-Arts, in the studio of Jean-Léon Gérôme. From 1866 to the end of 1869 he worked intensely under Gérôme, supplementing his artistic studies with dissection and also briefly studying under the sculptor Augustin-Alexandre Dumont and the portrait painter Léon Bonnat. He completed his tour of Europe with six months in Spain, the high point of which was his study of Velázquez at the Prado. When he returned to settle in Philadelphia in July 1870, he had determined that he would make portrait painting his life's work, and that, despite his training in the closely detailed style of Gérôme, he would cultivate the broad brushwork and indirect painting techniques of Velázquez. Assured of his father's financial support, he embarked on a career of painting portraits of eminent men and women, mostly from Philadelphia. Although he ultimately painted just under 300 works, he only received commissions for about 25.

Max Schmitt in a Single Scull (see fig. 1), painted at the start of his career, was the first of a number of paintings and watercolours in which Eakins honoured champion rowers. Rowing had recently become popular, celebrated for its demands on physical and mental discipline, and its experts were widely admired. Eakins portrayed his subject—a friend from boyhood—resting on the oars during an afternoon's sculling on Philadelphia's Schuylkill River. Evidence of Schmitt's triumph in the city's first amateur single sculling race is scattered throughout the painting: specific bridges identifying the race-course, rowers in the middle distance wearing Quaker garb, and the name on Schmitt's racing shell. Eakins himself appears in the scene, sculling in the middle distance. Stylistically, the painting combines exactitude in the boats and bridges with sketchy, generalizing forms in the foliage and sky. During the 1870s Eakins also painted hunting scenes, such as *Will Schuster and Blackman Going Shooting for Rail* (1876; New Haven, CT, Yale U. A.G.), as well as portraits of his sisters (*Frances Eakins*, 1870; Kansas City, MO, Nelson–Atkins Mus. A.) and other young women at the piano or in other interior pursuits.

In 1875, inspired by the approaching Centennial exhibition for which artists were urged to paint national subjects, Eakins painted the *Gross Clinic* (see fig. 2). It was the largest and most complex figural composition he had undertaken. Calling the work 'Portrait of Professor Gross', Eakins portrayed the internationally renowned Philadelphia surgeon presiding over an operation in the surgical amphitheatre at Jefferson Medical College. Several other surgeons assist Gross, medical students look on from the tiers of the amphitheatre, and Eakins himself sketches the scene from front left. Gross lectures, holding in his hand a scalpel covered with blood. Painted in a range of dark tones illuminated by brilliant light on Gross's forehead, hand and on the patient, the work shocked the Centennial jury. While it had obvious precedents in Rembrandt's paintings of anatomy lessons and in 19th-century group portraits of French surgeons preparing for dissection, such as Auguste Feyen-Perrin's *Anatomy Lesson of Dr Velpeau* (1864; Tours, Mus. B.-A.), Eakins had

1. Thomas Eakins: *Max Schmitt in a Single Scull*, oil on canvas, 819×1175 mm, 1871 (New York, Metropolitan Museum of Art)

2. Thomas Eakins: *Gross Clinic*, oil on canvas, 2.44×1.99 m, 1875 (Philadelphia, PA, Thomas Jefferson University, Medical Collection)

broken new ground by painting an actual operation in progress, with instruments and blood in full view. With the specific details of his painting he paid tribute to the advances of American surgery and to the particular role that Gross had played in them. The jury rejected the painting, but Gross sponsored its exhibition in one of the medical exhibits. Eakins was to return to such a powerful theme only once. In 1889 the graduating class of the University of Pennsylvania Medical School asked him to paint a portrait of their retiring professor of surgery, Dr D. Hayes Agnew. Instead Eakins insisted on painting a surgical clinic, presided over by Agnew, in which all the advances of surgery since the portrait of Gross are displayed: the use of antiseptic, white operating clothing, sterilization of instruments and a nurse in an operation for breast cancer (the *Agnew Clinic*, 1889; Philadelphia, U. PA).

Despite the critical dismay over the *Gross Clinic*, Eakins gained respect as a teacher at the Pennsylvania Academy of the Fine Arts, becoming its director of instruction in 1882. Drawing on his own experience as a student as well as on his temperament as an artist, he devised a thorough, professional curriculum, at the heart of which was the study of the human figure. Eakins was adamant that the Academy facilities were primarily for professional artists rather than artisans or amateurs. The Board of Directors of the Academy, none of them artists, wanted the programme to be self-sustaining and thus to attract students of all capabilities. In 1886 the Board forced Eakins's resignation, nominally over a dispute about the use of a nude male model in a mixed drawing class: the action deeply hurt him. Although he did teach sporadically at other institutions, he missed the authority the Academy position had given him in Philadelphia's professional community.

The nature of Eakins's portraiture changed after this period. His disappointment at the Academy may have been underlined by the mixed reception that his earlier complex portraits had received and by the personal stress caused by the death of several members of his family. He was sustained emotionally by the artist Susan Hannah Macdowell (1851–1938), a sympathetic companion whom he had married in 1884. After the forced resignation, he travelled to the Dakota territory in late 1886 for a 'rest cure'. Shortly afterwards he met the poet Walt Whitman (1819–92). They developed a friendship, made more intense by their common experience of having their work misunderstood. Eakins's portrait of *Whitman* (1887; Philadelphia, PA Acad. F.A.)—like many of his later works, a bust-length view—shows him tired and aging. Over the next two decades some of his most sensitive portraits in this format were of women. The subjects seem to be isolated and grieving, yet of great emotional strength. One such picture is *Mrs Edith Mahon* (1904; Northampton, MA, Smith Coll. Mus. A.).

Eakins also painted a number of large, full-length portraits in which accessories and background, if present at all, are set apart from the lone figure. As in earlier works, he continued to choose sitters whose achievements impressed him. Physicians, scientists, anthropologists, members of the Catholic hierarchy and musicians came to his studio at his request to be painted. The *Concert Singer* (1892; Philadelphia, PA, Mus. A.) combines many of the methods he used during these years. The singer stands alone on a stage that is only hinted at, giving herself completely to the performance of her music. Both her posture and the fragile colouring of the work convey a deep-seated melancholy.

In the last working decade of his life, between 1900 and 1910, Eakins enjoyed some critical appreciation. He won several prizes, one in Philadelphia (1904) and others at international expositions in Buffalo (1901) and St Louis (1904), and he served on the art jury of the Carnegie International in Pittsburgh. The memorial exhibitions in New York and Philadelphia in 1917 and 1918 led to the enthusiastic appreciation of his art that continues today. Many of the works in those exhibitions came from Eakins's studio, having been rejected by sitters, and now form the core of the major repository of Eakins's work, the Philadelphia Museum of Art.

In comparison to his contemporaries John Singer Sargent and William Merritt Chase, Eakins was technically conservative, resolutely local and non-aristocratic. He had no direct followers among students. It is not clear whether he realized that, especially in his later work, he subverted the traditional role of the portrait as a conveyor of power and grace. He told an admirer that he considered all his sitters 'beautiful' and yet wrote to a student that the mission of the painter was to 'peer deeply into American life'.

2. WORKING METHODS AND TECHNIQUE. Although Eakins is traditionally called a 'scientific realist', the implications of the term must be tempered in understanding

his work. He had an intelligence that demanded precise physical knowledge of his subject, and no other American artist had such a wide range of technical knowledge and skills—several types of perspective, human and equine anatomical dissection, mathematics, the mechanics of stop-motion photography, sculpting and even woodworking. However he made it clear to his students and to interviewers that these skills were subservient to the goal of art, the creation of beauty.

Early in his career Eakins generally made drawings in preparation for paintings. Extraordinarily detailed studies for one of the boat paintings (the *Pair-Oared Shell*, 1872; Philadelphia, PA, Mus. A.) include precise calculations for the movement of the surface of individual waves of water as well as the fall of light. Yet he apparently abandoned drawing as a preparation as early as the mid-1870s, and, except for works of his youth, no independent drawings are known. His normal preparation for a portrait consisted of a very small oil sketch on cardboard, squared up, and then a larger oil study to set tonal and colour relationships. Increasingly over his career, he relied on layering and glazing in the final work to achieve his delicate psychological effects. Often he used a grey ground; on occasions it was warm brown or even orange. He liked costumes with touches of brilliant reds, pinks, blues or greens. His backgrounds are generalized, his bodies built up from dark to light in surfaces that are often richly tactile. He conveyed a strong sense of space kept in control by darkness. Often a single tightly focused detail, such as Gross's scalpel in the *Gross Clinic*, grounded the emotional superstructure of his paintings in a sharply material universe.

While oil painting was the major focus of Eakins's life—though from 1875 to 1886, teaching may have come first—he also worked in other media. In the 1870s and 1880s he painted a number of works in watercolour, like his contemporaries on both sides of the Atlantic exploring the possibilities of the medium with tight work at first and then a gradual loosening of the forms. The subjects of these watercolours are all lighthearted; they include scenes of baseball players, sailing, rowing and, with a historical focus unusual in his work, women spinning.

Eakins used sculpture early in his work as a study, most prominently in his extensive preparations for the paintings *William Rush Carving his Allegorical Figure of the Schuylkill River* (1877; Philadelphia, PA, Mus. A.) and *Fairman Rogers Four-in-Hand* (1879; Philadelphia, PA, Mus. A.), in which he modelled the figures in wax. He made several sculptural reliefs, including *Arcadia* (1883; Philadelphia, PA, Mus. A.) and the horses for two public monuments.

Eakins used the camera from as early as 1875, typically as a vehicle for study, but also to record his family and close friends. He assisted Eadweard Muybridge in his photographic study of men and animals in motion at the University of Pennsylvania in 1884, and later he conducted many photographic motion and anatomical studies, assisted by his students.

For further illustration *see* UNITED STATES OF AMERICA, fig. 15.

UNPUBLISHED SOURCES

Philadelphia, PA, Mus. A., [Eakins archvs]
Philadelphia, PA Acad. F.A. [Eakins archvs]

BIBLIOGRAPHY

L. Goodrich: *Thomas Eakins: His Life and Work* (New York, 1933, rev. 2 vols, Cambridge, MA, 1982)
Thomas Eakins: A Retrospective Exhibition (exh. cat. by L. Goodrich, Washington, DC, N.G.A., 1961)
The Sculpture of Thomas Eakins (exh. cat. by M. M. Domit, Washington, DC, Corcoran Gal. A., 1969)
D. F. Hoopes: *Eakins Watercolours* (New York, 1971)
G. Hendricks: *The Photographs of Thomas Eakins* (New York, 1972)
E. C. Parry and M. Chamberlain-Hellmann: 'Thomas Eakins as an Illustrator', *Amer. A.J.*, v (May 1973), pp. 20–45
G. Hendricks: *The Life and Work of Thomas Eakins* (New York, 1974)
P. Rosenzweig: *The Thomas Eakins Collection of the Hirshhorn Museum and Sculpture Garden* (Washington, 1977)
T. Siegl: *The Thomas Eakins Collection* (Philadelphia, 1978)
Thomas Eakins: Artist of Philadelphia (exh. cat., ed. D. Sewell; Philadelphia, PA, Mus. A., 1982)
E. Johns: *Thomas Eakins: The Heroism of Modern Life* (Princeton, 1983) [with bibliog. essay]
N. Spassky, ed.: *American Painting in the Metropolitan Museum of Art* (Princeton, 1985), ii, pp. 584–619
K. Foster and C. Leibold: *Writing about Eakins: The Manuscripts in Charles Bregler's Thomas Eakins Collection* (Philadelphia, 1989)

ELIZABETH JOHNS

Eames. American architects, designers and film makers. Charles (Orman) Eames (*b* St Louis, MO, 17 June 1907; *d* St Louis, 21 Aug 1978) and his wife, Ray Eames [née Kaiser] (*b* Sacramento, CA, 15 Dec 1916; *d* Los Angeles, CA, 21 Aug 1988), formed a partnership after their marriage in 1941 and shared credit for all design projects. Charles Eames studied architecture at George Washington University, St Louis (1924–6). He then worked part-time as a draughtsman for Wilbur T. Trueblood and Hugo Graf in St Louis. In 1929 he travelled in Europe, looking at both old buildings and the newly emerging work of the International Style. In the early 1930s he associated himself with Charles M. Gray, with whom he had worked in Trueblood's office. The Depression severely limited commissions, and in 1934 he travelled and worked in Mexico. He returned to St Louis in 1935 and established another only marginally successful architectural office with a friend, Robert Walsh. The suburban domestic designs of this partnership were characteristic of the time: a tasteful, slightly modernized interpretation of traditional historic images, particularly 18th-century American Colonial.

In 1936 Charles Eames accepted a fellowship at the Cranbrook Academy in Bloomfield Hills, MI, which was under the direction of Eliel Saarinen. As well as Saarinen's son Eero Saarinen, he met Ray Kaiser, who became his second wife and design partner. Charles Eames and Eero Saarinen collaborated on the design of exhibitions and furniture; they researched techniques of binding and laminating wood and of curving plywood. In 1940 they entered a competition sponsored by MOMA in New York, in which their entries for curved plywood chairs and modular storage units won two awards; they were exhibited in the *Organic Design in Home Furnishings* exhibition at MOMA in 1942. In 1946 their plywood furniture was shown in an exhibition, *Chairs, Eames and Chests*, at MOMA; it included a plywood side chair and dining chair (1946), which quickly became well known and widely used. This exhibition also brought their work to the attention of the Herman Miller furniture company, by whom they were employed as designers and consultants (for illustrations *see* UNITED STATES OF AMERICA, fig. 37 and INDUSTRIAL DESIGN, fig. 6).

Ray Eames studied painting under Hans Hofmann in New York and in Provincetown, MA (1933–9). In 1940 she was a founder-member of American Abstract Artists. Studying at the Cranbrook Academy of Art, Bloomfield Hills, MI, she began to collaborate on designs with Charles Eames. In 1941 they married, shortly afterwards moving to southern California, and thereafter they worked as a partnership. The Eames studio designed not only furniture but also the machinery and production methods needed to manufacture it.

At the same time the Eameses turned their attention to architecture. In 1945 they collaborated with Eero Saarinen and Edgardo Contini on two projected case study houses (nos 8 and 9) for the magazine *Arts and Architecture*. Case Study House no. 9, which was intended for John Entenza, the editor and publisher of the magazine, was a single-level dwelling of steel and stucco and was built (1947–9), essentially as proposed in its first design, at 205 Chautauqua Boulevard, Pacific Palisades, CA. Case Study House no. 8, which was to be the Eames's house, was originally conceived as two steel-framed boxes raised above the site on steel legs. The design was substantially changed, however, and the house was built at ground-level, with two-storey living and studio sections separated by an open atrium (see fig.). It is a typical Eames product, light in appearance and suggesting a tie to the historical (Japanese architecture)

and to the modern. The new siting of the house at 203 Chautauqua Boulevard, Pacific Palisades, set it into the hillside, and through its glass walls the interior could become fully a part of the surrounding eucalyptus grove and take in the view beyond of the Pacific Ocean. The playfulness of the house was reinforced by wall panels of bright colours, panels containing illusionistic photo-murals and by the presence of the Eames's collection of toys and folk art. Charles Eames designed several other houses at this time, including an unbuilt scheme for the film director Billy Wilder in Beverly Hills (1949–51; see Neuhall, Neuhall and Eames, p. 137). His only other realized design on the West Coast was a showroom for the Herman Miller Company, 8806 Beverly Boulevard, Beverly Hills (1949). The street façade of this building is composed of clear and opaque panels set into a thin steel frame and is similar to the wall system used in the Eames's house.

In the 1950s the Eameses, with Harry Bertoia, George Nelson and Eero Saarinen, used the latest technology for furniture. Moulded plastic, foam, artificial leather and supports of a 'cat's cradle' of metal wire and of cast aluminium were employed in a series of designs that became the hallmark of modern interiors of the 1950s and 1960s. These included moulded polyester high and low side chairs (1955), a moulded rosewood plywood lounge chair and ottoman (1956) and polished, die-cast aluminium chairs and ottoman, the 'Indoor–Outdoor' (1958). Concurrent with the Eames's designs for furniture and children's toys was their increased involvement with

Charles Eames and Ray Eames: Case Study House no. 8 for Charles and Ray Eames, Pacific Palisades, California, 1945–9

communication, especially films and exhibitions, and by the 1960s this replaced furniture as their principal work. In 1952 they produced the film *Bread*, followed by *Communication Primer* (1953), *Powers of Ten* (1969) and other films. They also began to experiment with multi-image slide and film presentations, some of which were used in exhibitions designed by the Eameses, including the IBM special exhibition *Mathematica: A World of Numbers and Beyond* (1961), held at the California Museum of Science and Industry, Los Angeles. Other significant exhibitions were *The Scholar's Walk* in the IBM pavilion at the World's Fair, New York, in 1964, and a number of travelling exhibitions, including *Nehru: His Life and India* (1965) and *The World of Franklin and Jefferson* (1973).

WRITINGS

C. Eames: 'Design Today', *CAA. & Archit.*, lviii/9 (1941), pp. 18–19
——: 'Design, Designer and Industry', *Mag. A.*, xliv/12 (1951), pp. 320–21

BIBLIOGRAPHY

A. Drexler: *Charles Eames Furniture from the Design Collection of the Museum of Modern Art, New York* (New York, 1963)
E. McCoy: 'Charles and Ray Eames', *Des. Q.*, xcviii–xcix (1975), pp. 20–29
R. Caplan: *Connections: The Work of Charles and Ray Eames* (Los Angeles, 1977)
G. Holyrod: 'Charles Eames and Eliel Saarinen', *J. RIBA*, lxxxvi/1 (1979), pp. 29–30
D. Spaeth: *An Eames Bibliography* (Monticello, 1979)
J. Neuhall, M. Neuhall and R. Eames: *Eames Design* (New York, 1989)

DAVID GEBHARD

Eardley, Joan (Kathleen Harding) (*b* Warnham, Sussex, 18 May 1921; *d* Glasgow, 16 Aug 1963). Scottish painter. She studied briefly at Goldsmiths' College, London (1938–9), then at the Glasgow School of Art (1940–43). She was influenced by the Scottish Colourists, but also deeply affected by the life and atmosphere of the slums of the city. For her subject-matter she concentrated on street life, young children and the elderly, blending realism and compassion but without sentimentality. Typical is *Street Kids* (*c.* 1949–51; Edinburgh, N.G. Mod. A.). In 1951 she moved to the west coast of Scotland where she often worked outdoors, painting marine and landscape scenes in many different moods, sometimes incorporating real pieces of grass in the paint. Among some of her finest and most powerful works are fierce and bold evocations of the wind and the weather. Notable is *Catterline in Winter* (1963; Edinburgh, N.G. Mod. A.). She was elected an Associate of the Royal Scottish Academy in 1955 and a full Academician in 1963.

BIBLIOGRAPHY

C. Oliver: 'Joan Eardley and Glasgow', *Scot. A. Rev.*, xiv/3 (1974), pp. 16–19
W. Buchanan: *Joan Eardley* (Edinburgh, 1976)
Four Contemporary Scottish Painters: Eardley, Haig, Philipson, Pulsford (exh. cat., Oxford, Ashmolean, 1977)

EMMANUEL COOPER

Earl [Earle]. American and English family of painters. (1) Ralph Earl and his brother James Earl (1761–96) were born in America, but both fled to England in 1778. Ralph Earl returned to New York in 1785. He established the Connecticut style of portraiture and produced some notable landscape works; his son, (2) Ralph E. W. Earl, continued to paint portraits in the same manner as his father. James Earl's son, (3) Augustus Earle, was born in England, but travelled extensively and is best known as a travel artist.

(1) Ralph Earl (*b* Shrewsbury, MA, 11 May 1751; *d* Bolton, CT, 16 Aug 1801). He was born into a prominent family of farmers and craftsmen. Both he and his brother James chose artistic careers at a young age. Ralph had established himself as a portrait painter in New Haven, CT, by 1774. He returned to Leicester, MA, in the autumn of that year to marry his cousin Sarah Gates, who gave birth to a daughter a few months later. But Earl left his wife and child with her parents and returned to New Haven, where he remained until 1777. There he saw the portraits of John Singleton Copley, which had an enduring impact on him. Works such as Earl's notable full-length portrait of *Roger Sherman* (*c.* 1776–7; New Haven, CT, Yale U., A.G.) were painted in the manner of Copley. During this period Earl also produced four sketches of the sites of the Battle of Lexington and Concord, which were engraved in 1776 by his associate Amos Doolittle.

A Loyalist, Earl fled his native country for England in 1778, where he first began painting in Norfolk under the patronage of Colonel John Money. Through the studio of Benjamin West, he absorbed some of the mannerisms of English portraiture and exhibited portraits at the Royal Academy, London, in 1783 and 1784. He also acquired an interest in landscape painting, inspired by English country-house painting and sporting art. Landscape vignettes first appeared in the background of his numerous English portraits.

In 1785, after the American Revolution, Earl settled in New York with his second wife, Anne Whiteside, an Englishwoman. He was imprisoned for debt from 1786 to 1788, but he eventually obtained his freedom by painting portraits of several prominent New Yorkers, including *Mrs Alexander Hamilton* (New York, Mus. City NY). Most of these patrons belonged to a new benevolent organization, the Society for the Relief of Distressed Debtors, and assisted Earl by sitting for their portraits in prison. Upon his release, the court appointed a guardian for Earl, Dr Mason Fitch Cogswell (1761–1830), a native of Connecticut who had a medical practice in New York. When Cogswell moved to Hartford in 1789, he assisted Earl in obtaining portrait commissions of prominent Connecticut families.

Earl established the portrait style that has come to be associated with Connecticut, inspiring a school of local followers including Joseph Steward (1753–1822), John Brewster jr and Captain Simon Fitch (1785–1835). Earl tempered the academic style he had learnt in England to suit the more modest pretensions of his Connecticut patrons, while retaining some of the conventions of English portraiture in the grand manner, including the large scale and the use of red curtains. For the most part, however, Earl's Connecticut portraits departed from these conventions in, for instance, his monumental double portrait of *Chief Justice Oliver Ellsworth and Abigail Wolcott Ellsworth* (1792; Hartford, CT, Wadsworth Atheneum). The subjects were painted in the front parlour of their newly renovated house in Windsor, a view of which appears through the window. In this and his other Connecticut works, Earl tightened his brushwork, painting in a more linear fashion than seen in his earlier portraits. He did not attempt to idealize his subjects but instead created 'true' likenesses of his sitters shown in their own environment. Earl's skill as a landscape painter was encouraged by his later Connecticut patrons, as land ownership had become increasingly important in conveying status in post-Colonial America. In 1796 Earl received three commissions to paint landscapes with the new houses of his patrons in Litchfield County. In 1798 he painted the detailed *View of Old Bennington* (Bennington, VT, Mus.), which includes a self-portrait.

While Earl spent most of his career in Connecticut, he travelled back and forth to Long Island each year from 1791 to 1794, returning to New York City in 1794, where he successfully sought new patrons. That he reverted to a more academic style in these regions to suit his patrons' tastes is demonstrated in such portraits as *Benjamin Judah* (1794; Hartford, CT, Wadsworth Atheneum), a prominent New York City merchant.

From 1799 to 1801, Earl was in Northampton, MA, where he continued to paint portraits and took several students, including his son Ralph E. W. Earl. In 1799 Earl and two business associates from Northampton, one of them the ornamental painter Jacob Wicker, became the first American artists to travel to Niagara Falls. With Wicker's assistance, his sketches of the 'Stupendous Cataract' became the basis for his 'Prospectus' of the Falls (4.25×7.30 m). This panorama was exhibited in the Hall of the Tontine Building in Northampton. From there it was sent on a tour to the major cities in America and was last noted on view in London. Earl died of 'intemperance', according to the local minister in Bolton, CT.

(2) Ralph E(leazer) W(hiteside) Earl

(*b* 1785–8; *d* 1838). Son of (1) Ralph Earl. After his father's death, he continued to paint portraits in the same manner in the Connecticut River Valley as well as in Troy, NY, where his mother had settled. In 1809 he went to London, where he received encouragement from Benjamin West and John Trumbull. He moved to Norwich in 1810, living with his mother's family and receiving support from Colonel John Money, an earlier patron of his father. Four years later, he travelled to Paris, and he returned to America in December 1815.

Influenced by the history paintings of West and Trumbull, Earl planned to produce a painting of the Battle of New Orleans. He travelled throughout the south in order to take likenesses of the heroes of this battle. While on this trip, he met in Tennessee General Andrew Jackson, who became a lifelong friend and whose niece Earl married in 1818. Earl became the leading artist in Nashville from 1817, and he opened the Museum of Natural and Artificial Curiosities there. When Jackson became President in 1828, Earl followed him to the White House, where he became Jackson's 'Court Painter'. At the end of Jackson's term of office in 1836, both he and Earl returned to Tennessee, where the artist spent the rest of his life. He is best remembered for his numerous portraits of Jackson.

BIBLIOGRAPHY
W. Dunlap: *A History of the Rise and Progress of the Arts of Design in the United States*, i (New York, 1834/*R* Boston, 1918, rev. New York, 1969)
W. Sawitsky and S. Sawitsky: 'Two Letters from Ralph Earl with Notes on his English Period', *Worcester A. Mus. Annu.*, viii (1960), pp. 8–41
L. B. Goodrich: *Ralph Earl: Recorder of an Era* (Binghampton, NY, 1967)
The American Earls: Ralph Earl, James Earl and R. E. W. Earl (exh. cat. by H. Spencer, Storrs, U. CT, Benton Mus. A., 1972)
E. M. Kornhauser: 'Regional Landscape Views: A Distinctive Element in Connecticut River Valley Portraits, 1790–1810', *Antiques*, cxxvii/5 (1985), pp. 1012–19
E. M. Kornhauser and C. S. Schloss: 'Painting and other Pictorial Arts', *The Great River: Art and Society of the Connecticut River Valley* (exh. cat., Hartford, Wadsworth Atheneum, 1985), pp. 135–85
G. B. Bumgardner: 'Political Portraiture: Two Prints of Andrew Jackson?' *Amer. A. J.*, xviii/4 (1986), pp. 84–95
E. M. Kornhauser: 'Ralph Earl as an Itinerant Artist: Pattern of Patronage', *Itinerancy in New England and New York*, ed. Peter Benes (Boston, 1986), ix of *Annual Proceedings of the Dublin Seminar for New England Folklife*
——: *Ralph Earl, 1751–1801: Artist–Entrepreneur* (diss., Boston U., 1988)
Ralph Earl: The Face of the Young Republic (exh. cat. by E. M. Kornhauser and others, Harford, CT, Wadsworth Atheneum, 1991)

ELIZABETH MANKIN KORNHAUSER

(3) Augustus Earle

(*b* London, 1 June 1793; *d* London, 10 Dec 1838). Nephew of (1) Ralph Earl. He exhibited at the Royal Academy in London between 1806 and 1815, when he began travelling. He visited the Mediterranean between 1815 and 1817, and lived in North America (1818–20) and South America (1820–24). In February 1824, *en route* to India, he was accidentally abandoned on Tristan da Cunha for eight months. The passing ship that rescued him took him to Australia. Here he lived from 1825 until 1828, a period broken by a seven-month residence in New Zealand. During all of his voyages he made watercolour sketches, particularly of places 'hitherto unvisited by any artist', apparently with the intention of publishing a series of aquatints. These drawings, such as a *Bivouac, Daybreak, on the Illawarra Mountains* (1827; Canberra, N. Lib.), have a robust autobiographical quality. In Sydney he obtained a number of commissions, including a full-length portrait of *Governor Sir Thomas Brisbane* (1825–6; Sydney, Govt House). Earle returned to England in 1829 and produced a series of prints, *Views in New South Wales, and Van Diemen's Land*. In April 1832 he accepted a position as artist to Charles Darwin's expedition in the *Beagle*, but increasing ill-health forced him to give up the position (he was replaced by Conrad Martens) at Rio de Janeiro.

WRITINGS
Sketches Illustrative of the Native Inhabitants and Islands of New Zealand (London, 1838)
E. McCormick, ed.: *Narrative of a Nine Months' Residence in New Zealand and a Journal of Residence in Tristan da Cunha* (Oxford, 1966)

BIBLIOGRAPHY
J. Hackforth-Jones: *Augustus Earle: Travel Artist* (Canberra, 1980)
R. Butler: 'Australia's First Lithographs', *Austral. Connoisseur & Colr*, 3 (1982), pp. 94–9, 130–31
J. Kerr, ed.: *Australian Artists* (Melbourne, 1992), pp. 234–7

ANDREW SAYERS

Earlom, Richard

(*b* London, 1743; *d* London, 9 Oct 1822). English printmaker. Taught by Giovanni Battista Cipriani, he worked in mezzotint, etching and occasionally stipple. His mezzotints of flowers and still-lifes, such as

Roses for the *Temple of Flora* (1805) by Robert John Thornton (?1768–1837) or the *Fruit Piece* (see Wessely, no. 145) after Jan van Huysum, are also found printed in colours or coloured by hand. Earlom's most influential prints were a set of outline etchings combined with mezzotint of the volume, then belonging to the Dukes of Devonshire, of Claude's drawings of his own landscape paintings (now London, BM). The prints were published in 1777 by John Boydell in two volumes as the *Liber Veritatis* (see CLAUDE LORRAIN, §II, 2), a name that subsequently came to be applied to the drawings. A third volume of prints of Claude drawings from other sources was added when the first two were reprinted in 1819 (W 149–448).

As well as working extensively for Boydell, Earlom also made prints for Robert Sayer (1724–94), Robert Laurie (*d* 1836) and John Whittle (*d* 1818). In the 1770s he mezzotinted drawings by Joseph Farington of the collection of Old Master paintings that had been formed at Houghton Hall, Norfolk, by Sir Robert Walpole. In 1795, half a century after Hogarth had published his prints of *Marriage à la Mode*, Earlom mezzotinted the same subjects (W 103–8). He also mezzotinted the *Iron Forge* (W 121) and the *Blacksmith's Shop* (W 122) after Joseph Wright of Derby, and important views of the life class and early exhibitions at the Royal Academy by Charles Brandoin (1733–1807) and Johan Zoffany (W 101–2). Chaloner Smith lists 50 of Earlom's portrait prints. Earlom assisted Robert Laurie with mezzotinting two works after George Stubbs, *Labourers* and *Gamekeepers* (see Lennox-Boyd, Dixon and Clayton, nos 87–8), which appeared under the pseudonym Henry Birche.

BIBLIOGRAPHY

J. Chaloner Smith: *British Mezzotinto Portraits*, i (1883), pp. 242–61
J. E. Wessely: *Richard Earlom: Verzeichnis seiner Radierungen und Schabkunstblätter* (Hamburg, 1886) [w]
C. E. Russell: *English Mezzotint Portraits and their States: Catalogue of Corrections of and Additions to Chaloner Smith's 'British Mezzotinto Portraits'*, ii (London, 1926), pp. 66–72
M. Kitson: *Claude Lorrain: Liber veritatis* (London, 1978)
C. Lennox-Boyd, R. Dixon and T. Clayton: *George Stubbs: The Complete Engraved Works* (London, 1989), pp. 6, 212–15

ELIZABETH MILLER

Early Christian and Byzantine art. The art produced by the peoples of the Roman Empire from the early 4th century AD to *c*. 600—as well as specifically Christian art from *c*. 250—and that produced in the eastern half of the Empire, centred around Constantinople (Byzantium) to 1453. The Byzantine empire (see fig. 1) was the institutional setting for much of the medieval art of the eastern Mediterranean, and from the early 4th century AD for the Orthodox Church and so for Early Christian art. Byzantines regarded their empire as having arisen from the happy coincidence of the foundation of the Roman Empire under Augustus with the incarnation of Jesus Christ; for modern historians the empire has a clear end (1453, when the city fell to the Turks) but no clear beginning. The foundation of Constantinople (324–330) by CONSTANTINE THE GREAT on the site of the small town of Byzantion is the conventional point of departure, when ironically Byzantion both ceased to exist and took on a new existence; it became known later as The City, and under the Turks Istanbul (*see* ISTANBUL, §I). The 'Byzantine empire' was a name never used by its inhabitants, who thought of themselves as Romans, and certainly did not need a term to describe the eastern provinces of the Roman Empire; occasional attempts to administer separately different parts of the Empire (e.g. under the Tetrarchy (293–305) and after the death of Theodosios I) were short-lived; for its inhabitants the Empire (whether expanding or contracting) was a single unit. However, the Empire gradually contracted and the western provinces, which had become barbarian kingdoms, had a divergent history after *c*. 600.

I. Introduction. II. Architecture. III. Monumental painting and mosaic. IV. Sculpture. V. Manuscripts. VI. Icons. VII. Other arts.

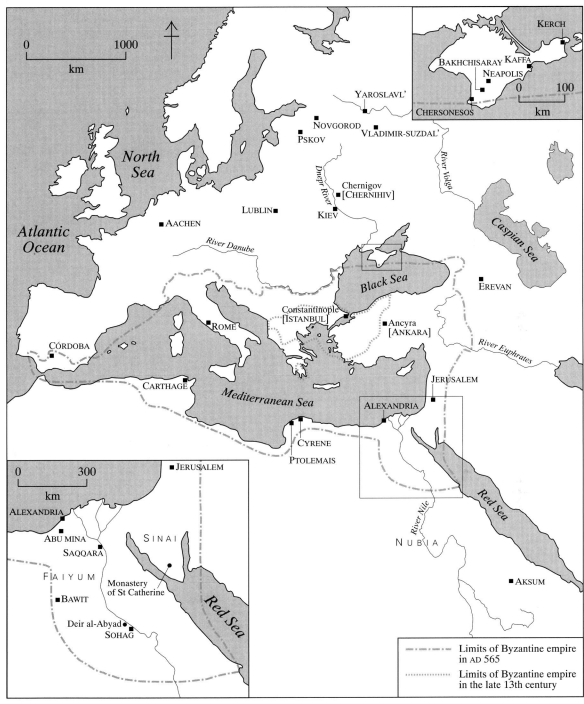

1. Map of the Byzantine empire; those areas with separate entries in this dictionary are distinguished by CROSS-REFERENCE TYPE

I. Introduction.

1. History. 2. Iconography. 3. Patronage.

1. HISTORY. The Byzantine empire's boundaries fluctuated over its 1200 years of history (see figs 2–5), largely shrinking but occasionally winning back territory. Geographically it centred on the city of Constantinople, with its good communications to the east through Asia Minor and to the west along the Via Egnatia. By way of the Bosphoros, the Black Sea was linked with the Sea of Marmara and the Mediterranean; a link to the steppe lands of the north was maintained through the Byzantine hold on the Crimea. In the early centuries the empire was almost synonymous with the cities around the shores of the Mediterranean, but after the climatic changes of the 6th century and general political change, the empire settled around the two major landmasses of the Balkans and Asia Minor, later to shrink to a few possessions around Constantinople. But the variety of geographies—from Egypt to the Crimea and Iberia (Spain) to Iberia (Georgia)—makes generalization about the empire unwise. The occasional loss of territory made the supply of certain raw materials (for example porphyry and papyrus from Egypt) difficult, and, although trade could supply certain minerals, dyes, animal products (e.g. ivory), precious gemstones and the secret of silk, the empire's wealth came mainly from agriculture: it was its landowners who had the surplus (as well as such materials as parchment) necessary for artistic production. It is clear that for much of its history Byzantium was regarded as a wealthy state with envied craftsmen, who were exported to, for example, the first Bulgarian kingdom (681–1018), Norman Sicily (1072–1194) and 14th- to 15th-century Moscow. Byzantine artefacts were desired diplomatic gifts and their export was restricted, though they have been found in western contexts, especially silks (*see* §VII, 8 below; for enamels and ivories, *see* §VII, 5 and 7(ii) below). The famed wealth of Constantinople, especially in relics and small-scale objects, was a contributing cause of the Latin capture of the city in 1204.

(i) Chronological survey. (ii) Byzantine cultural relations.

(i) Chronological survey.

(a) Early Christian, *c.* 250–*c.* 843. (b) Middle Byzantine, *c.* 843–1204. (c) Late Byzantine, 1204–1453.

(a) Early Christian, c. *250–*c. *843.* In the 3rd century, Christianity had spread to many cities of the Roman Empire but was from time to time subject to persecution, hence the dominant pattern of house-church and (for funerary purposes) catacombs, together with prevalent themes of monumental painting and mosaic (*see* §III, 2 below). Communities developed a structure of leadership under the bishop which was clearly in position by the Edict of Milan (313) and led in the 4th century to the confident architectural complexes of basilica and attendant buildings (*see* §II, 2(i) below). The empire, however, faced external threats and internal reassessment; Diocletian's experiment with Tetrarchic government has been associated by some with competing religious faiths and philosophies and a new, less naturalistic, aesthetic, particularly evident in sculpture (*see* ROME, ANCIENT, §IV, 2(ix)). It certainly created a pattern of urban planning (e.g. Trier, Nicomedia, Thessaloniki, Constantinople) and an interpretation of ceremony in art (in triumphal arches, ivories, coins, silver dishes) which looked forward to Byzantine norms. Constantine the Great was responsible for the tentative moves towards the establishment of Christianity which meant an end of persecution, the emperor chairing the first ecclesiastical council at Nicaea (325), and considerable donations to the churches of Rome. The interest of his mother, Helena (*c.* 225–*c.* 330), in the holy places in Palestine led to a major building campaign there. But Constantinople, though it had Christian buildings including the church of the Holy Apostles, was not in the beginning a Christian city, and Constantine maintained many of the trappings of state paganism (*see* ISTANBUL, §I, 1). Throughout the 4th century a major concern was control of the Rhine, Danube and Euphrates frontiers; another was the stabilization of the coinage and the rationalization of administration. The brief reign of the emperor Julian (*reg* 360–63) reinstated paganism in reaction to a period of increased confidence on the part of Christian emperors and intellectuals, when syncretism was visible in art as well as literature, but temples were destroyed and reconstructed as churches.

By the 390s both Christianity and Constantinople had achieved greater status under THEODOSIOS I, who was responsible for major building work in Constantinople and for additions in Palestine. During the 5th century this consolidation of the relationship between the city and Christianity continued with the importation of significant relics such as the Virgin's Robe. As the western provinces met more and more barbarian threats, the government in Constantinople appeared to focus more clearly on the eastern provinces including, from the reign of Zeno (*reg* 474–91), the province of Cilicia in southern Asia Minor. Events in the 5th century also reflect the relationships between the major theological centres of Alexandria, Antioch and Rome with successive ecumenical councils. In 476 the western emperor, who had been established from 395 to control the western provinces from first Rome, then Milan and Ravenna, was succeeded by a barbarian king, Odoacer (*reg* 476–93). Both he and his successor, Theodoric the Great (493–526), ruled in a way that was reminiscent of the emperor in Constantinople, issuing their own coinage and erecting richly decorated churches (e.g. at Ravenna), while practising a form of Christianity (Arianism) no longer in vogue. In 491 Empress Ariadne, widow of Zeno (see fig. 6), chose a Constantinopolitan civil servant, Anastasios, for emperor

2. Map of the Byzantine empire: Latin West; those areas with separate entries in this dictionary are distinguished by CROSS-REFERENCE TYPE

(*reg* 491–518). He attempted to hold together the differing religious viewpoints of the empire and was responsible for two major pieces of building activity, the Long Wall in Thrace and the city of Dara (nr Nusaybin, Turkey) on the eastern frontier to defend the empire against nomadic threats from the west and the Sasanian empire on the east. He was succeeded by a Balkan peasant, Justin (*reg* 518–

27), who imported members of his family including the future emperor JUSTINIAN I. Relations with the papacy, now the main power at Rome, were considerably improved at this time, though heavy-handed imperial treatment was later to make this short-lived.

The 6th century has often been called the age of Justinian in view of the large number of his buildings

3. Map of the Byzantine empire: Greece and Balkans; those areas with separate entries in this dictionary are distinguished by CROSS-REFERENCE TYPE

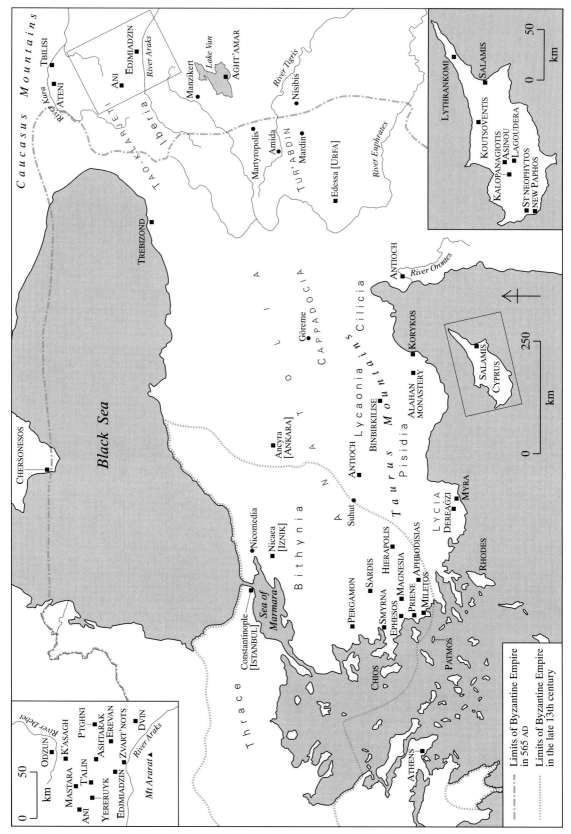

4. Map of the Byzantine empire: Constantinople and Asia Minor; those areas with separate entries in this dictionary are distinguished by CROSS-REFERENCE TYPE

surviving from the period (and a contemporary descriptive work by Prokopios, *Buildings*, purporting to list them), his attempts at reconquering North Africa (533–4), Italy (535–55) and Spain (554), and his efforts in systematizing the law and its teaching. In reality Justinian's achievements glitter rather less when it is seen how transitory were the reconquests (invasions from the Balkans reached Constantinople in the late 550s, Africa was soon lost and the Lombards moved into Italy in 568) and that many of the building activities were merely reconstructions of earlier achievements—a clear pointer to the value placed on renewal rather than originality. The construction of the church of St Polyeuktos (524–7; destr.) in Constantinople by JULIANA ANICIA, a member of the Theodosian house and the old senatorial aristocracy, was matched by Justinian's Hagia Sophia (*see* ISTANBUL, §III, 1(ii)), made possible by the destruction of the Nika riots of 532. This building activity has been seen in terms of dynastic rivalry, as well as of a conflict between an aristocracy that was being constantly eroded, and of Justinian's centralizing policy; this latter also appears to have hit the cities hard, together with such minority groups as Jews and pagans. Nor was the 6th century a period of unrelieved achievement: the highpoint was perhaps the capture of Ravenna in 540, but natural disasters and military reverses devastated Italy, North Africa and along the Euphrates frontier. The effects of the bubonic plague are unknown, but millenarian feeling was high and the period is of great interest as representing a turning away from Roman institutions such as the consulship and an increasingly centralized and autocratic form of government. Under JUSTIN II (*reg* 565–78) there was increased diplomatic activity with the West and a new alliance of church and state, focusing on the cult of icons and the supernatural defenders of Constantinople. The emperor also continued the urban and suburban building programme of his predecessor. In the late 6th century new threats from Persia and the Slav invasions in the Balkans had serious results, despite soldierly leadership from Tiberios (*reg* 578–82) and Maurice (*reg* 582–602).

The last honorific column to be erected in the Forum Romanum, Rome, was that by Phokas (*reg* 602–10). His unpopular rule was brought to an end by Heraklios (*reg* 610–41) who maintained the empire against considerable threats from Slavs, Avars and Persians, by means of eastern campaigns in the 620s and the defence of Constantinople in his absence by Patriarch Sergios and the patrician Bonos in 626. Slav settlement in the Balkans continued, while the Persian empire was defeated and the Holy Cross restored to Jerusalem in 630. In 632, however, after the death of Muhammad, Arab raiding parties (already a threat in the 6th century, as evident from the fortified walls surrounding the monastery of St Catherine on Sinai) began to assault the empire; Egypt, Palestine and Syria were lost to the Arabs following their defeat of Heraklios at the River Yarmuk (Israel) in 636. The rest of the 7th century was a period of considerable difficulty for the empire which some have seen in terms of a general collapse of traditional systems. Both written and visual sources are sparse after the reign of Heraklios, but it is clear that there are important discontinuities with Byzantine society a century earlier. The Roman name system is

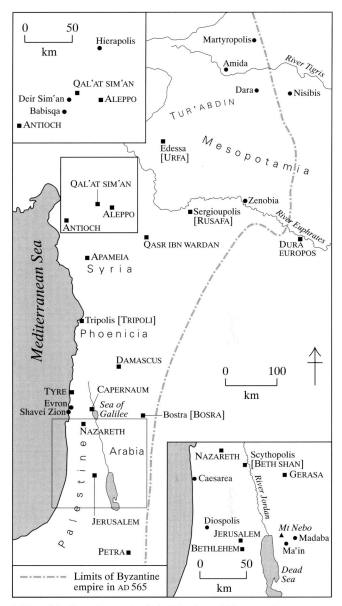

5. Map of the Byzantine empire: Syria, Palestine and Mesopotamia; those areas with separate entries in this dictionary are distinguished by CROSS-REFERENCE TYPE

no longer found, though it is not known whether this means a clear end to the senatorial aristocracy; at any rate family names are not cited. The senate paradoxically took on a new role in this period, as did the army. Bad relations with Rome led to the trial, exile and death of Pope Martin I (*reg* 645–55), inaugurating the much exaggerated Byzantine domination of the papacy. The most significant development of the period is the apparent cessation of urban life in the eastern provinces and considerable lessening in the west, except in such cities as Thessaloniki. The pattern of response to the Arab and Slav invasions is not yet clear; it involved refugee islands, hilltop refuges, a retreat to Constantinople, an increased popularity of

6. *Empress Ariadne*, ivory plaque, 305×136×22 mm, *c.* AD 500 (Florence, Museo Nazionale del Bargello)

village life and possibly the evolution of the characteristic local government system of the Middle Byzantine empire, the theme system. In this system the governor (Gr. *strategos*) and the judge (*krites*) were posted for three years to a military district where the forces were locally recruited and settled; theme castles appear to be the only physical trace, though the efficiency of the system ensured the regular supply of taxes from the provinces for conversion into bricks and mortar in the capital. Little building activity of any kind is known from the 7th century, and increasingly the army held the balance of power. Annual Arab attacks were eventually held off at a siege of Constantinople in 717 under Emperor Leo III (*reg* 717–41).

The iconoclast policy instituted by Leo and Constantine V Kopronymos (*reg* 741–75) opposing the use of images in worship is of considerable interest for the relationship between religion and art in Byzantine society (*see also* §2(i)(c) below). In the preceding centuries the holy man, relics and painted images had become the focus of belief

in supernatural power, thus leading to changes in their use in worship and an ambivalence between explicitness and symbolism that characterized Early Christian art. Military victories and legal activity distinguish the iconoclast emperors as efficient emperors; their ability to impose a religious policy beyond the immediate circle of patriarch and church hierarchy and the capital is less certain. Parts of the empire (e.g. Cyprus, Rome) seem to have escaped the destruction of images; in other parts there is evidence for the concealing of images or of replacement with symbols (e.g. a cross) acceptable to the iconoclasts. Iconoclasts were not opposed to images as such, simply to their use in worship. Coin evidence makes it clear that Umayyad and Byzantine rulers were aware of each other's usage of images in the years running up to the iconoclastic controversy (*see* §VII, 2 below); Byzantine craftsmen contributed to the construction of important mosques and palaces, and Arab buildings and gardens served as an inspiration to Byzantine patronage. The lull in iconoclasm (787–813) and its reinstitution (813–43) are reflected in saints' lives and a succession of images in apse mosaics responsive to the dominant ideology. After 843, psalter illustrations (e.g. CHLUDOV PSALTER; Moscow, Hist. Mus. MS. D.29) suggest a firmness of purpose against the iconoclasts, and iconophile texts show some tendency to exaggerate the danger of iconoclast resurgence.

(b) Middle Byzantine, c. 843–1204. Although a revival in the cultural life of the empire has been detected *c.* 790, with more manuscripts being copied, in particular uncial manuscripts into minuscule, a political recovery that might have supported this was much delayed. The eastern campaigns of Michael III (*reg* 842–67) put the empire once again on the offensive, but his rule was abruptly ended with the coup of Basil I (*see* MACEDONIAN DYNASTY, (1)). An emphasis on renewal combined with a desire to conceal his origins led to an ambitious building programme in Constantinople. The first major decorative programme was unveiled in the apse of Hagia Sophia in 867. Active diplomatic and missionary overtures with the encouragement of Patriarch Photios (858–67; 878–86) showed an expansive foreign policy reaching as far as Bulgaria, Moravia, Baghdad and the Khazars. Less successful relations with Rome and internal divisions resulted from a dispute over the fourth marriage of Leo VI (*see* MACEDONIAN DYNASTY, (2)). In the early and mid-10th century relations with Bulgaria and the Caliphate stabilized, Greece was rehellenized, and cultural phenomena, unhelpfully characterized as a Macedonian renaissance, developed. A general tendency to encyclopedism (collection of saints' lives, medical and agricultural texts, dictionaries) was encouraged by the scholarly and artistic initiatives of Constantine VII (*see* MACEDONIAN DYNASTY, (3)) who was also concerned to whitewash his Macedonian predecessors. A new aristocracy emerged, of big families (e.g. the Doukas and Phokas families), known as 'the powerful' (Gr. *dynatoi*), associated with military commands, and largely based in Asia Minor; monastic foundations also became more numerous in regions other than Constantinople and Bithynia; the foundation of Mt Athos by the 850s established only the most famous of a number of holy mountains that replaced the desert monasteries in

Egypt, Judaea, Syria and Sinai of an earlier age (*see* CHRISTIANITY, §IV, 1). The soldier emperors at the end of the century—Nikephoros II Phokas (*reg* 963–9), John Tsimiskes (*reg* 969–76) and Basil II (*reg* 976–1025)—succeeded in recapturing Crete, creating many new small themes on the eastern frontier and annihilating the first Bulgarian kingdom. A revival of cities in Asia Minor and established campaign routes through Cappadocia provided a setting and market for artistic production. A map of the empire on the death of Basil II indicates the successes of these emperors (the absorption of Bulgaria and Armenia, the presence of Byzantium in Italy), but the cultural assimilation of these former areas was not complete.

The 11th century has been well characterized as a period of peace and prosperity with an expanding economy, increased urbanization and much surplus wealth. Private estates, both lay and monastic, increased in number and size. Power tended to pass through the female line, so Constantine IX (*see* MACEDONIAN DYNASTY, (4)) acceded through his marriage to Zoe (*reg* 1028–50; see fig. 41 below), and Constantinople attracted aristocratic families and intellectuals to found palace complexes and settle. Military difficulties set new priorities, first in Italy with the advance of the Normans (1059–71), and then in Asia Minor with the occupation of the plateau by the Seljuk Turks after their defeat of the Byzantines at Manzikert (nr Lake Van, Turkey, 1071). Mercenary armies and a new fleet replaced the thematic forces; campaigns by the Komnenian (*see* KOMNENOS) dynasty held Albania, reconquered the Aegean islands and began a re-establishment of urban life from the coastlands out. Grants of land in *pronoia* (land granted to a recipient for a defined period, usually until death) established supporters of the emperor on landed estates; administration centred on the imperial family. Lay administration of monasteries gave way to their effective economic management by the community itself, fuelled in some cases (e.g. Hosios Loukas) by pilgrim donations; aristocratic foundations insured the family for the afterlife and articulated the growth of Constantinople in the period.

During the 12th century stable rule by the Komnenoi also encouraged the settlement of Westerners in Constantinople from Pisa, Genoa and Venice, each of these cities having received favourable trading arrangements as the price of support in 1082 against the Normans. Their presence appears to have stimulated trade in the short term, and the period is marked by industrial growth in the cities (e.g. Corinth and Thebes). Despite tax exemptions to aristocrats and monasteries, the workings of the tax machine—more visible at this time than ever before—brought surplus wealth from province to capital. Bishops and officials made the opposite journey and may have spread metropolitan ideas, but, though Byzantium was a centralized state, attempts to prove the imposition of a central culture on outlying parts have failed. The establishment of crusading states in Palestine, Syria and southern Asia Minor changed the diplomatic balance; Byzantium's most dangerous enemy (but also a market for its art) was Norman Sicily, which with Hungary formed the most effective channel of relations with the West. After the death of Manuel I (*reg* 1143–80) ineffectual government and a flagging economy combined to create a power vacuum in which it was possible for the Fourth Crusade to take Constantinople in 1204.

(*c*) *Late Byzantine, 1204–1453.* After the fall of Constantinople, successor states at Nicaea, Trebizond and Arta competed to maintain Byzantine institutions and patronage. Increasingly, however, the market for Byzantine art came from outside the areas of Byzantine control, such as Serbia and Bulgaria. Much of the empire, including the Peloponnese and the Ionian and Aegean islands, was now controlled by Franks. Little survives of the Latin period in Constantinople, and the Latin empire, without the benefit of a functioning tax system, foundered. Constantinople was retaken in 1261 by Michael VII Palaiologos (*reg* 1261–82) and the Byzantine empire restored, although its authority never extended beyond the scattered holdings in the Balkans and Asia Minor. Patronage passed into aristocratic rather than imperial hands as local estates became stronger power bases; civil servants and intellectuals frequently influenced both politics and cultural life. A revival of learning showed a new openness to both Eastern and Western cultures: translations of Latin texts and the adoption of Arab science marked a new mobility of intellectuals; there were Dominicans in Pera and Byzantines lecturing in Italy. Byzantines had frequently also to coexist with the Ottoman Turks as younger sons of emperors served in the Ottoman army. The fragmentation of Byzantine power also highlighted the importance of cities in this period; Thessaloniki had a brief life (1342–9) as a commune and Mystras outlived (until 1461) Constantinople, which fell to the Ottoman Turks on 29 May 1453.

(*ii*) *Byzantine cultural relations.* The Byzantine view of empire was established early: the emperor was God's vice-regent on earth (as expressed in manuscript illustrations and ivories that show Christ crowning the emperor; see fig. 82 below), the defender of Orthodoxy and the 13th Apostle. He represented Classical rhetorical virtues (courage, justice, prudence, piety and, increasingly, philanthropy) and was acclaimed by army and people. His role in the Church was essentially to chair and implement synodal decisions; it was not parallel to that of the pope in the West, nor in practice was that of the patriarch. A series of ecumenical councils, from Nicaea in 325 to Nicaea in 787, arrived at decisions on doctrine, defining the nature of the Trinity (and in so doing losing Arians), the role of the virgin Theotokos ('Mother of God') (so losing Nestorians) and the nature of Christ (so losing in the 5th to the 7th century many Christians in the eastern provinces, known as Monophysites); these losses created the germs of the Coptic, Jacobite, Armenian and Maronite churches. Some of these theological differences are thought to be directly reflected in artistic programmes, as in the 5th-century mosaics of the triumphal arch in S Maria Maggiore. The principle of having five patriarchates and relying on synodal decision-making was to lead to schism with Rome. Byzantine missionary activity in Nubia in the 6th century, in the Balkans in the 9th and Russia in the 10th led to an expansion of the Byzantine ideal carried through Christianity. Demand in neighbouring states for Byzantine artefacts and architects was followed by conversion and incorporation into the Byzantine family of kings, since marriage alliances were an important arm of policy, and the family was central to Byzantine society. Diplomatic relations reflected a firm sense of hierarchy and order (Gr. *taxis*) among these powers as also within the empire, but also enabled the spread of developments in theology, liturgy and spirituality. Even when Byzantine political power was extremely weak, as in the 14th and 15th centuries, there was a market for Byzantine ideas and art; Byzantine ideology in art was taken over wholesale into other states by envious rulers, as in the church of S Maria dell'Ammiraglio (*see* PALERMO, §II, 3).

The empire was always multi-ethnic and multilingual and gained at different times from relations with the East and the Caucasus; the import of foreign women as imperial brides had cultural consequences. Relations with adversaries, such as Persia and the Caliphate, frequently involved cultural exchange as well as military confrontation, and Byzantine policies of exchange of populations (Paulicians, Slavs, Armenians) led to the exchange of local cultures within the empire as well as the dissipation of centres of opposition to central authority. The empire's contribution to the Renaissance, to the Christian Slavonic world and to the new Ottoman world order in the 15th century was striking. Byzantium started as a centralized state and a second-hand empire and maintained both (in image and to a certain extent in reality) for 1200 years. It created not a single style but a diversity of art works which showed constant adaptation to political and ideological change under a cover of external reflection of heavenly splendour.

BIBLIOGRAPHY

GENERAL

G. Ostrogorsky: *Geschichte des byzantinischen Staates* (Munich, 1940); Eng. trans. of 2nd edn by J. Hussey (Oxford, 1968)
C. Mango: *Byzantium: The Empire of New Rome* (London, 1980)
M. F. Hendy: *Studies in the Byzantine Monetary Economy, c. 300–1453* (Cambridge, 1985)
A. Kazhdan and others, eds: *The Oxford Dictionary of Byzantium*, 3 vols (New York and Oxford, 1991)

CHRONOLOGICAL SURVEY

S. Runciman: *The Fall of Constantinople, 1453* (Cambridge, 1965)
A. A. M. Bryer: 'The First Encounter with the West: AD 1050–1204', *Byzantium: An Introduction*, ed. P. Whitting (Oxford, 1971), pp. 83–110
M. Kaplan: *Les Hommes et la terre du VI au XI siècle*, Byzantine Sorbonensia, x (Paris, 1971)
D. M. Nicol: *The Last Centuries of Byzantium, 1261–1453* (London, 1972)
A. A. M. Bryer: 'Cultural Relations between East and West in the Twelfth Century', *Relations between East and West in the Middle Ages*, ed. D. Baker (Edinburgh, 1973), pp. 77–94
P. Lemerle: *Le Premier Humanisme byzantin*, Bibliothèque byzantine, vi (Paris, 1976)
A. A. M. Bryer and J. Herrin: *Iconoclasm* (Birmingham, 1977)
P. Lemerle: *Cinq études sur le XIe siècle byzantin* (Paris, 1977)
R. J. Lilie: *Byzanz und die Kreuzfahrerstaaten* (Berlin, 1981)
P. Brown: *Religion and Society in Late Antiquity* (London, 1982)
M. J. Angold, ed.: *The Byzantine Aristocracy, IX–XIII Centuries*, Brit. Archaeol. Rep., Int. Ser., cxxi (Oxford, 1984)
M. J. Angold: *The Byzantine Empire, 1025–1204: A Political History* (London, 1984)
A. Kazhdan and A. Epstein: *Change in Byzantine Culture in the Eleventh and Twelfth Centuries*, Transformations of the Classical Heritage, vii (Berkeley, 1985)
J. Herrin: *The Formation of Christendom* (Princeton, NJ, and Oxford, 1987)
A. Harvey: *Economic Expansion in the Byzantine Empire, 900–1200* (Cambridge, 1989)
J. C. Cheynet: *Pouvoirs et contestations à Byzance: 963–1210*, Byzantine Sorbonensia, ix (Paris, 1990)

C. Foss: *History and Archaeology of Byzantine Asia Minor* (Aldershot, 1990)
J. F. Haldon: *Byzantium in the Seventh Century* (Cambridge, 1990)
A. Cameron: *Christianity and the Rhetoric of Empire: The Development of Christian Discourse*, Sather Class. Lect., lv (Berkeley, 1991)
S. Curcic and D. Mouriki, eds: *The Twilight of Byzantium: Aspects of Cultural and Religious History in the Late Byzantine Empire* (Princeton, NJ, 1991)
A. Cameron and L. Conrad: *The Byzantine and Early Islamic Near East: Problems in the Literary Source Material*, Stud. Late Ant. & Early Islam, i (Princeton, NJ, 1992)
P. Magdalino: *The Empire of Manuel Komnenos, 1143–1180* (Cambridge, 1993)
M. E. Mullett and D. C. Smythe, eds: *Alexios I Komnenos*, 2 vols (Belfast, 1993)
R. Morris: *Monks and Laymen in the Byzantine Empire in the Tenth and Eleventh Centuries* (Cambridge, 1994)

BYZANTINE CULTURAL RELATIONS

T. Ware: *The Orthodox Church* (Harmondsworth, 1963)
F. Dvornik: *Early Christian and Byzantine Political Philosophy*, 2 vols, Dumbarton Oaks Ser., ix (Washington, DC, 1966)
H. Maguire: *Art and Eloquence in Byzantium* (Princeton, NJ, 1981)
C. Walter: *Art and Ritual of the Byzantine Church*, Birmingham Byz. Ser., i (London, 1982)
R. Cormack: *Writing in Gold* (London, 1985)
R. Loverance: *Byzantium* (London, 1988)
A. Wharton Epstein: *Art of Empire: Painting and Architecture of the Byzantine Periphery: A Comparative Study of Four Provinces* (University Park, PA, and London, 1988)
R. Cormack: *The Byzantine Eye* (Aldershot, 1989)
J. Shepard and S. Franklin: *Byzantine Diplomacy*, Pubns Soc. Promot. Byz. Stud., i (Aldershot, 1992)
P. Magdalino, ed.: *New Constantines: The Rhythm of Imperial Renewal*, Pubns Soc. Promot. Byz. Stud., ii (Aldershot, 1994)

MARGARET MULLETT

2. ICONOGRAPHY. It has sometimes been argued that religion was such an integral part of everyday life in Byzantium that it is impossible to distinguish the religious from the secular in Byzantine culture. Even though some imperial ideology, as reflected in images of the emperor being crowned by divine assistance, stressed their interdependence, there is no evidence that the Byzantines could not perceive the distinction between the religious (*ekklesiastikos*) and the secular (*politikos*). While the innate conservatism of the Orthodox Church, the only institution to survive the collapse of the Byzantine empire in 1453, favoured the preservation of much traditional religious imagery, the disappearance of the secular authority entailed the subsequent suppression by the Ottoman conquerors of much secular art in the form of imperial propaganda. Thus, although through its icons and the painted programmes of the great monastic churches Byzantine art is popularly associated with religion, it was not the exclusive property of the Church. Artists working for a wide variety of patrons developed Christian and secular motifs that ranged from the purely decorative to the narrative in every medium from textiles and ivories to wall painting and mosaic.

(i) Religious. (ii) Secular.

(i) Religious. The earliest Christian images date back only to the beginning of the 3rd century. One factor constraining the development of Christian art was the Old Testament prohibition of graven images. Opposition to images based in large measure on this prohibition eventually culminated in the iconoclastic controversy (726–843). It was argued, however, that Christ and other holy subjects

could be represented, because with the Incarnation Christ had assumed human form, and as incarnate man he could be portrayed. With the victory of the iconophiles and with icons officially acknowledged, at least in the East, as having a status parallel to that of the Gospels (the former expressing in visual form what the latter expressed verbally), religious imagery, which had been eschewed by the earliest Christians, was recognized as an integral and salutary part of religious life.

(a) Before c. 313. The Roman Empire was highly visually orientated and the pull of images was strong, especially for the increasing numbers of Christian converts from the pagan world. Numerous symbols were adapted from the pagan repertory. The peacock, whose flesh was believed to be incorruptible, became a symbol of eternal life; the athlete's palm of victory was adopted as a sign of spiritual triumph; and the fish symbolized both Christianity and Christ. Other images are more allegorical, as in the Good Shepherd, which was originally based on the pagan representation of a man bringing his offering to the altar but, by the 3rd century, had also come to represent the 'ram bearer' with its connotations of philanthropy and loving care. The latter image accorded well with the Christians' understanding of a divine Shepherd who would lay down his life for his flock. In a period of persecution, such images had the advantage of directly addressing the adherents of the Christian faith while not drawing attention to them, since the images were already popular with non-Christians (*see* §III, 2 below).

Judaism, too, offered much that fitted the needs of a developing Christian iconography, although to what extent Christian borrowings were from visual representations is impossible to ascertain. Despite the prohibition of graven images, Jewish representative art is known from the mid-3rd century, by which time the Old Testament had become an important source of inspiration for Christian imagery. Extant examples include paintings of the *Three Hebrews in the Fiery Furnace*, *Jonah and the Whale* and *Noah's Ark* in the catacombs at Rome (*see* ROME, §V, 13). Many of the same themes are depicted on contemporary sarcophagi, with scenes from the *Life of Jonah* being particularly common, as in the marble sarcophagus (*c.* 270; see fig. 7) in S Maria Antiqua. In the centre are a philosopher, an *orans* figure (praying with arms raised) and a *Good Shepherd*;

they are flanked by the *Baptism* and a fisherman on one side, and, on the other, scenes from Jonah's story, including the *Prayer in the Ship*, *Jonah and the Whale* and *Jonah under the Gourd*. From the outset Christian iconography emphasized the mystic harmony between Old and New Testaments. Events in the Old Testament were seen as prefiguring events in the New, the three days Jonah spent in the belly of the whale being viewed as a foreshadowing of Christ in the tomb. Similarly, within the New Testament the *Raising of Lazarus*, with its reference to miraculous healing and resurrection, prefigures Christ's Passion and Easter.

Despite the paring down of many Early Christian images to their essential visual elements (because of which they are referred to as abbreviated images), such images function as an eloquent affirmation of the power and saving grace of God. This message is reinforced by the position of figures such as the *Three Hebrews*, unharmed by the flames which surround them, shown with their arms raised like those of the orant in prayer. Although most extant pre-Constantinian Christian art is funerary, it is impossible to gauge whether this is merely the result of the vicissitudes of time. However, even in the few representations that are not in catacombs or on sarcophagi, such as the wall paintings (*c.* 240) from the baptistery at Dura Europos (*see* DURA EUROPOS, §4), which juxtapose the *Temptation of Adam and Eve* (sin) with the *Good Shepherd* (redemption), the iconographic message of redemption through the power and grace of God remains the same.

(b) c. 313–5th century. The official recognition of Christianity (313) by Constantine the Great coincided with further developments in Christian iconography. There was an increase in the depiction of narrative scenes, with their inclusion of more figures and action, as in the *Crossing of the Red Sea* (e.g. mid-4th-century painting in the catacombs of SS Peter and Marcellinus, Rome), which was a reminder to the Christians of the fate suffered by Constantine's enemies at the Battle of the Milvian Bridge (312). While the representation of Old Testament scenes remained popular, proportionately more scenes were drawn from the New Testament. More striking still, images, particularly those of Christ, began to take on the trappings of imperial grandeur: with the accession of an emperor who favoured Christianity the whole repertory of imperial imagery was

7. Early Christian religious iconography (images of salvation) on a marble sarcophagus, *c.* AD 270 (Rome, S Maria Antiqua)

thrown open to Christian use. At the centre of the upper tier of the sarcophagus of Junius Bassus (*c.* 359; *see* SARCOPHAGUS, fig. 3) Christ is shown royally enthroned, his feet on a personification of the firmament; he is handing on the laws, the promulgation of which was strictly an imperial function, to SS Peter and Paul. The appearance of a young Christ in an august setting is explained by the fact that two types of Christ long coexisted: the young, unbearded Apollo figure and the older, bearded Semitic Christ.

A wider range of subjects was depicted. The earliest extant images of the Nativity date from the 4th century and those of the Crucifixion from the 5th, as in a panel on the wooden doors (432) of S Sabina in Rome and a relief on an ivory casket (*c.* 420–30; Brescia, Mus. Civ. Crist.). Until then symbols such as the *ankh*, the ship's mast and anchor and the chi-rho monogram had all been used to suggest the cross, itself perhaps the oldest of Christian symbols but not because of its association with the instrument of Christ's death. It has been argued that early Christians associated the sign of the cross with the *tau* (written as a 't' or 'x'), which, as the last letter of the Hebrew alphabet, had the same force as the Greek letter 'omega' in signifying God. In addition to Classical, Hellenistic and Judaic influences, iconographic types of Eastern and Egyptian origin contributed to the development of Christian iconography. Examples include the use of the nimbus, which originated in the East, and the zoomorphic symbols of the Evangelists, which may be of Coptic origin (Werner, 1984–6). One of the earliest occurrences of these symbols is in the apse mosaic of S Pudenziana (early 5th century) in Rome.

(c) 6th century–1453. Many of the characteristics associated with later Byzantine religious iconography appear in the mid-6th century under the reign of Justinian I. Representations relating to liturgy and dogma became more popular and fully developed. In S Vitale (*see* RAVENNA, §2(vii)) the high altar is flanked by mosaics of the sacrifices of Abel and Melchisedech and by *Abraham and the Three Angels*, scenes that give visual form to the prayer over the eucharistic offerings when the priest asks God to look upon 'these gifts' with favour, and accept them as he did the gifts of Abel, Melchisedech and Abraham. In the Orthodox tradition *Abraham and the Three Strangers* also symbolizes the *Trinity*, a scene which appeared in the same form more than a century earlier in a mosaic (*c.* 432–40) in S Maria Maggiore, Rome. The *Baptism* is the only other representation of the Trinity to survive beyond the Early Christian period. Although Christian iconography quickly developed an eloquent vocabulary in most areas, the translation of the finer points of dogma into visual terms was more difficult. Byzantine religious art, however, proved to be highly conservative and images such as those of the Trinity, once satisfactorily formulated, continued in use through the centuries. This does not imply that Byzantine iconography was entirely static. Christ in the Crucifixion continues to be depicted as a living, exalted figure who triumphs over his apparent humiliation, as in the late 6th-century Rabbula Gospels. From the 8th century, however, the emphasis shifts to the sacrificial

death of the Redeemer, expressed through the image of the dead Christ on the cross.

The decorative programme of a church as a whole rather than any single image expresses most clearly Byzantine beliefs and spiritual life. While no two churches were the same, artists adhered to a definite canon of appropriateness. Only intensely spiritual images, such as Christ Pantokrator ('all powerful', i.e. holding a Gospel book in his left hand and raising his right in blessing), were considered suitable for the mystical heaven of the dome, with the Evangelists, revealing the Pantokrator to the world, sometimes portrayed in the four squinches. The Virgin is often depicted in the apse, an honoured location but less elevated than the dome; the lower parts of the apse and the side walls are usually decorated with the Feasts of the Church, saints, Church Fathers and more earthly subjects, so that the church becomes a microcosm of the spiritual universe.

An essential factor in the development of Byzantine iconography, and one that played a role in private, liturgical and monastic religious life, was the icon. In the context of Byzantine art the word is used to refer to a holy image worthy of special veneration, the honour paid to it passing on to its prototype (*see* ICON). The icon is seen as a link between the material and spiritual worlds, a window on the divine. So that the icon might fulfil its purpose, a special visual language was developed. For example, in icons executed in the 'true tradition' the painting of shadows is avoided as being indicative of the mundane world of space and time. Even events that presumably took place inside a building, such as the Annunciation, are not constrained by any physical setting. Symbols abound: a mountain suggests the nearness of God; a cave, unredeemed humanity. (For further discussion of icons *see* §VI below; for further discussion of iconography *see* CHRISTIANITY, §III, 1 and 2(i).)

BIBLIOGRAPHY

A. N. Didron: *Iconographie chrétienne: Histoire de Dieu* (Paris, 1843; Eng. trans., New York, 1851/*R* 1963)
H. Leclerq: *Manuel d'archéologie chrétienne*, 2 vols (Paris, 1907)
F. Cabrol, ed.: *Dictionnaire d'archéologie chrétienne et de liturgie*, 15 vols (Paris, 1907–53)
C. R. Morey: *Early Christian Art: An Outline of the Evolution of Style and Iconography in Sculpture and Painting from Antiquity to the Eighth Century* (Princeton, 1942)
K. Weitzmann: *Illustrations in Roll and Codex: A Study of the Origin and Method of Text Illustration* (Princeton, 1947)
O. G. von Simson: *Sacred Fortress: Byzantine Art and Statecraft in Ravenna* (Chicago, 1948)
L. Ouspensky and V. Lossky: *Der Sinn der Ikonen* (Berne, 1952; Eng. trans., Boston, 1952)
K. Weitzmann, ed.: *Late Classical and Mediaeval Studies in Honor of Albert Mathias Friend, Jr* (Princeton, 1955)
L. Réau: *Iconographie de l'art chrétien*, 4 vols (Paris, 1955–9)
G. Bovini: *Ravenna Mosaics* (Greenwich, CN, 1956)
J. Daniélou: *Les Symboles chrétiens primitifs* (Paris, 1961; Eng. trans., Baltimore, 1964)
W. F. Volbach: *Early Christian Art* (London, 1961)
P. du Bourguet: *De vroeg-christelijke schilderkunst* (Amsterdam, 1965); Eng. trans. as *Early Christian Painting* (New York, 1966)
A. Grabar: *L'Age d'or de Justinien* (Paris, 1966; Eng. trans., New York, 1967)
——: *Le Premier Art chrétien* (Paris, 1966; Eng. trans., London, 1967)
G. Schiller: *Ikonographie der christlichen Kunst*, 5 vols (Gütersloh, 1966–; Eng. trans. of vols i and ii, Greenwich, CN, 1971–2)
E. R. Goodenough: *Jewish Symbols in the Greco-Roman Period*, xiii (New York, 1968)
A. Grabar: *Christian Iconography: A Study of its Origins* (Princeton, 1968)

P. du Bourguet: *Art paléochrétien* (Paris, 1971; Eng. trans., New York, 1971)

K. Weitzmann: *Studies in Classical and Byzantine Manuscript Illumination* (Chicago, 1971)

——: '*Loca Sancta* and the Representational Arts of Palestine', *Dumbarton Oaks Pap.*, xxviii (1974), pp. 564–72

A. Cutler: *Transfigurations: Studies in the Dynamics of Byzantine Iconography* (University Park, PA, 1975)

Age of Spirituality: Late Antique and Early Christian Art, Third to Seventh Century (exh. cat., ed. K. Weitzmann; New York, Met., 1977–8)

M. Werner: 'On the Origin of Zoanthropomorphic Evangelist Symbols: The Early Christian Background', *Stud. Iconog.*, x (1984–6), pp. 118–25

D. J. Sahas: *Icon and Logos: Sources in Eighth-century Iconoclasm* (Toronto, 1986)

R. Milburn: *Early Christian Art and Architecture* (Berkeley, 1988)

E. S. Malbon: *The Iconography of the Sarcophagus of Junius Bassus* (Princeton, 1990)

J. Pelikan: *Imago Dei: The Byzantine Apologia for Icons* (Princeton, 1990)

ELIZABETH BRUENING LEWIS

(ii) Secular. Surviving examples of secular art testify to the taste for worldly display indulged in by the Byzantine aristocracy, and considerably more information is available in literary references. In the empire's heyday secular iconography must have offered a lively reflection of everyday life: the sporting activities of the hippodrome, the entertainments of the circus, the imperial hunting parties and tournaments, the gardens of the aristocracy and even the agricultural implements of the peasantry were all recorded by Byzantine artists. Even the fragmentary survivals immensely enrich the picture of their environment painted by the textual sources.

(a) Imperial and chivalric imagery. The greatest patrons were the emperors, who commissioned images vaunting their prowess in battle and in hunting for the edification of the court or the populace. Such iconography was frequently developed on a grand scale, as on the piers of the Arch of Galerius (before 313; *see* THESSALONIKI, §III, 1), the Arch of Constantine (315; *see* ROME, §V, 12), the base of the early 5th-century column (see fig. 53 below) of Arkadios (*reg* 395–408) in the Forum of Arkadios in Constantinople and in the 6th-century mosaics of the Golden Gate at the entrance to the Great Palace (*see* ISTANBUL, §III, 12). Although neither of the last two monuments has survived, the mosaics of the Bronze Gate are described by Prokopios (*Buildings* I.x.15–19) as celebrating Justinian I's victories in Africa and Italy, while the iconography of the base has been preserved in several 16th- and 17th-century drawings (e.g. Cambridge, Trinity Coll.). These show the triumphal imagery divided into three registers: the lower displaying the spoils of war, the middle a labarum flanked by figures, probably captives, who are superintended by two female personifications, and the upper depicting emperors with their troops. Surmounting the whole is a roundel containing a cross, held aloft by angels. This explicitly Christian reference affirms the empire's allegiance to Christianity and the recognition by the secular authority of a higher power. A similar juxtaposition of Christian symbolism with imperial iconography can be seen on the 6th-century Barberini Ivory (Paris, Louvre; *see* §VII, 5 below), on which a mounted emperor, possibly Justinian I, receives tributes while above him a medallion containing a bust of *Christ* is supported by angels. In both cases the iconography remains predominantly secular.

An example of imperial military iconography in which there is no trace of Christian symbolism is the silver presentation dish (388; Madrid, Real Acad. Hist.) celebrating the tenth anniversary of Theodosios I's rule. The Emperor is shown in an architectural setting flanked by his co-emperors and soldiers, and investing an official. Reclining at his feet is the female figure of Abundance accompanied by putti. Another, much later, example is the Gunther Tapestry (Bamberg, Domschatzkam.; *see* §VII, 8 below), on which a mounted emperor is depicted receiving a diadem and a ceremonial helmet from female personifications, possibly of Athens and Constantinople, against a purple background worked with tiny flowers. Although there are no inscriptions to identify the scene, it may refer to the ceremonial triumphs of Basil II (*reg* 976–1025) in Athens and Constantinople after his victory over the Bulgars (1017). It was probably sent to the Western Emperor Henry IV (*reg* 1056–1106) from his Eastern counterpart, Constantine X Dukas (*reg* 1059–67), as a gift and an implicit assertion of Byzantine military strength. Images of imperial ceremonial and the circus also survive on the walls of the stair-tower leading to the galleries in St Sophia in Kiev (1019–54), built with the aid of Byzantine craftsmen, but here they are juxtaposed with scenes of mounted hunters spearing bears and bowmen aiming at squirrels.

In the Middle Byzantine period Manuel I (*reg* 1143–80) is known to have decorated the Blachernai and Great palaces in Constantinople with scenes of his military successes, while his courtiers patronized the arts with expressions of loyalty, such as engraving on the walls of their own homes his triumphs over the sultan in gold and juxtaposing his feats of arms in flattering fashion with those of the Old Testament heroes. According to John Kinnamos (*fl* second half of the 12th century) it was customary to include some reference to the emperor's valour as a slayer of men or wild beasts in the decoration of domestic interiors. On the other hand it was not considered appropriate to extend the range of triumphal iconography to include the successes of the enemy, as one of Manuel's generals, Alexios Axouch, is alleged to have done.

It was in the 12th century, too, that chivalric influences from the West brought jousting and romances to Byzantium. A Greek text (Rome, Vatican, Bib. Apostolica, MS. 1409, fol. 277) describes what was apparently a monumental painting of a tournament in which the emperor took part. A faint echo of this iconography may be seen in a small ivory panel depicting two knights jousting (London, V&A), attributed to 12th-century Constantinople. Although at this time romances were woven around such common themes as the legends of Alexander the Great in both East and West, there is little evidence for any related iconography in contemporary Byzantium. The first illustrated versions of the Greek Alexander Romance may date to the 14th century (e.g. Venice, Inst. Ellenic. Stud. Biz. & Postbiz., no. 5).

(b) Personification, allegory and symbolism. Personifications, whether topographical (e.g. river gods, cities), temporal (e.g. Night, Dawn) or abstract (e.g. Repentance,

8. Secular iconography (figures of Andreia and Phronesis) on a lamp or perfume burner, silver and silver gilt, h. 360 mm, probably from southern Italy, late 12th century (Venice, Tesoro di San Marco); later converted to a reliquary

Boldness), make regular appearances in Byzantine iconography and invariably hark back to Classical models. On the dedication page of a copy of Dioskurides' *De materia medica* (*c.* 512; Vienna, Österreich. Nbib., MS. med. gr. 1, fol. 6*v*), which was presented to Juliana Anicia by her grateful fellow citizens, the virtues of Phronesis (Prudence or Intellect) and Magnanimity appear as stately female figures in Classical garb on either side of the patroness. Abstract and temporal personifications appear in the miniatures of the 10th-century PARIS PSALTER (Paris, Bib. N. MS. grec 139) and in another psalter (the 12th century or 13th; Rome, Vatican, Bib. Apostolica, MS. Pal. gr. 381).

A theme that finds expression in both Eastern and Western literature and in 12th-century Byzantine iconography is that of the complementary virtues of Andreia (Courage) and Phronesis (Intellect). Personifications of the pair appear, in the company of lions, griffins and other fabulous creatures, on an elaborately worked, gilded container (Venice, Tesoro S Marco; see fig. 8). It was probably made in the late 12th century in southern Italy, where Eastern and Western ideas converged, and was originally intended as a lamp or perfume burner before being converted to a reliquary in the 13th century. Andreia, dressed as a soldier carrying spear and shield, and Phronesis, in female attire and pointing significantly to her forehead, stand either side of a central doorway. The same theme recurs on the Bayeux Tapestry (*c.* 1066–*c.* 1097;

Bayeux, Mus. Tap.), in which the inscription *viriliter et sapienter* ('bravely and wisely') is placed above a depiction of the Normans going into battle. Painted personifications of the virtues are also recorded in monumental programmes, as for example at Thessaloniki in the 12th-century house (destr.) of a certain Leo Sikountenos. In the 14th century the poet Manuel Philes (*c.* 1275–*c.* 1345) dedicated some epigrams to the painted virtues of Andreia, Phronesis, Justice and Temperance in the palace of the Blachernai. The iconography of the first two virtues mostly conforms to the figures on the 12th-century perfume burner.

Reminiscences of pagan Greek culture in early Christian and Byzantine art were not, however, confined to these figures. Mythological subjects were depicted in public places (e.g. outside the Golden Gate in Constantinople) and on secular objects. For example, the glass Lycurgus Cup (4th century; London, BM; *see* §VII, 4 below) depicts the story of Lycurgus, a Thracian king who persecuted Dionysos and was destroyed after becoming entangled in a vine. On the silver casket of Projecta (late 4th century; London, BM; for illustration *see* CASKET), found on the Esquiline Hill in Rome, representations of Venus, nereids, tritons and sea-monsters are combined with a Christian inscription and secular scenes. Sometimes objects are decorated with an apparently confused jumble of events, as on the Veroli Casket (late 10th century or early 11th; see fig. 9). This small ivory casket, perhaps originally lined with silk and used as a jewellery box, juxtaposes scenes of the *Rape of Europa*, bacchanalian cherubs and the *Sacrifice of Iphigeneia* in seemingly random order. The choice of motifs may owe more to a prevailing antiquarian aesthetic than to a deep familiarity with Classical mythology. A gilded and painted glass bowl (Venice, Tesoro S Marco; see fig. 79 below), which has been tentatively attributed to the patronage of Constantine VII Porphyrogenitos, displays the same approach to its iconography, with its miscellaneous collection of mythological heroes. The monochrome rendering of the figures, set against dark backgrounds within roundels, is reminiscent of cameo technique, and it has been suggested that Constantine's collection of antique gems provided the inspiration for its design. The pseudo-kufic inscriptions that decorate the bowl underline the cultural eclecticism of Middle Byzantine patrons. These and other Eastern motifs frequently decorate woven and embroidered textiles, perhaps because the techniques were learnt from Oriental masters (*see* §VII, 8 below). Surviving examples include pairs of confronted lions and elephants on Byzantine silks (e.g. Aachen, Domschatzkammer), which were sent to the West as diplomatic gifts.

(*c*) *Naturalism and topographical imagery.* The effect of triumphal imagery on diplomatic gifts, such as the Gunther Tapestry mentioned above, was reinforced by the accounts of returning ambassadors, dazzled by the sumptuous display of the Byzantine court. On a mission to the court of Constantine VII, Liudprand described in the mid-10th century how the contemporary engineers and goldsmiths had combined their skills to create a mechanical menagerie with roaring lions and singing birds in the throne-room of

Secular iconography, *Bellerophon* and the *Sacrifice of Iphigeneia* depicted on the Veroli Casket, ivory and bone on wood, 115×405×155 mm, late 10th
century or early 11th (London, Victoria and Albert Museum)

the Great Palace. Artificial wildlife and associated vegetation were not confined to the decoration of secular buildings in the iconoclast period (726–843). According to the *Life of St Stephen the Younger* (806) the mosaic decoration of the Blachernai Church resembled an aviary set in a mass of foliage and stalked by wild beasts. Despite Manuel Philes's professed admiration of the naturalism of a palace ceiling painted in imitation of a wild garden, it seems unlikely that these Byzantine images had the illusionistic qualities of Roman garden-scapes as at Herculaneum and Pompeii (Naples, Mus. Archeol. N.).

Given the Byzantine preference for allegory and symbolism over illusion and naturalism, it is not surprising that personifications of cities, often depicted standing at the city gate of a sketchily drawn enceinte, are more numerous than topographical paintings. It does not appear that the iconography of an 11th-century liturgical roll (Jerusalem, Mus. Gr. Orthdx Patriarch., Stavrou 109), which presents a schematic depiction of Constantinople, was further developed. Of greater significance, however, is a letter of 1414 or 1415 in which Epifany the Wise described the monumental view of Moscow (*c.* 1400) painted by Theophanes the Greek on a wall in the palace of Prince Vladimir Andreyevich Serpukhovsky (Nekrasov). Since this kind of painting was apparently hitherto unknown in Russia, Theophanes probably learnt it in his formative years in Byzantium.

BIBLIOGRAPHY

Stephen the Deacon: *Life of St Stephen the Younger* (AD 806); ed. in *PG*, c (n.d.), col. 1120
Liudprand: *Antapodosis* (mid-10th century AD); ed. F. A. Wright as *The Works of Liudprand of Cremona* (London, 1930), pp. 207–8
John Kinnamos: *Deeds of John and Manuel Komnenos* (later 12th century); ed. C. M. Brand as *Deeds of John and Manuel Comnenus by John Kinnamos* (New York, 1976), p. 199
Manuel Philes: *Carmina* (early 14th century); ed. E. Miller as *Manuelis Philae Carmina*, 2 vols (Paris, 1855–7), i, pp. 125–6; ii, 127–31
E. H. Freshfield: 'Notes on a Vellum Album Containing Some Original Sketches of Public Buildings and Monuments, Drawn by a German Artist who Visited Constantinople in 1574', *Archaeologia*, lxxii (1921–2), pp. 87–104
A. I. Nekrasov: 'Les Frontispices architecturaux dans les manuscrits russes avant l'époque de l'imprimerie', *L'Art byzantin chez les Slaves*, ed. F. Millet, ii (Paris, 1932), pp. 258–81
J. Beckwith: *The Veroli Casket* (London, 1962)
C. Mango: *Sources and Documents: The Art of the Byzantine Empire, 312–1453* (Englewood Cliffs, NJ, 1972/*R* Toronto, Buffalo and London, 1986)
A. Cutler: 'The Mythological Bowl in the Treasury of San Marco at Venice', *Near Eastern Numismatics: Studies in Honor of George G. Miles* (Beirut, 1974), pp. 235–54

VALERIE NUNN

3. PATRONAGE. Although the patrons of much Early Christian and Byzantine art remain anonymous, surviving evidence of different types of patronage clearly indicates the important role it played in artistic development.

(i) Patronage and style. Much attention has been given to the sociological factor of patronage as a way of explaining the development of Early Christian and Byzantine art. Frequently patronage has been seen in abstract terms, with the groupings often put together as dichotomies: imperial and episcopal, aristocratic and popular, monastic and lay, secular and ecclesiastical, male and female, and so on. For some, these categories of patronage are understood to have triggered distinctive stylistic trends. Such theories are circular, however: too often a stylistic category is identified and then attributed to one of these social groups; this in turn leads to the further attribution of other works of art to such patronage, even when there is no precise information about the patrons or their background. Particularly bedevilled by this kind of reasoning have been the popular notions of 'monastic style' and 'aristocratic style', both formulated on very little evidence, and both being categories unlikely to be socially distinctive: aristocrats often became monks, and monks came from many backgrounds and hardly formed a homogeneous social group. Furthermore, the art found in monasteries is stylistically diverse, depending for its character on many different factors.

Even if general characterizations of patronage in Byzantine art depend on circular or undocumented premises, there nevertheless remains a need for more precise consideration of social factors in Byzantine art: there is a case, for example, for identifying monasteries as the location of new functions and developments in the panel icon in the 11th century. The changes might in part be related to the sources of wealth and patronage at that time. A solution of this issue will depend on a concept more subtle than 'monastic patronage'.

Considerable attention has also been given to the identification of individual patrons and to the role of their personal tastes and interests in the formation of style. In one study (Buchthal and Belting), the method of analysis was to work in reverse by constructing a patron (?a 13th-century princess or Palaiologina) out of a group of stylistically related illuminated manuscripts. Key figures of the period have emerged from such interests: CONSTANTINE THE GREAT, JUSTINIAN I, Constantine VII (see MACEDONIAN DYNASTY, (3)), Constantine IX (see MACEDONIAN DYNASTY, (4)), John II (see KOMNENOS, (1)), the statesman Theodore Metochites (1270–1332) and others. From such names it is clear that historians are mainly interested in the wealthiest patrons, particularly emperors, who had access to immense State funds. Indeed the commonest periodization of Byzantine history marks the intervals of the various imperial dynasties (Constantinian, Theodosian, Justinianic, Macedonian, Komnenian and PALAIOLOGAN). This terminology implies that major changes in Byzantine art depended on the character of succeeding phases of imperial patronage. In future, theological or liturgical factors or other political or cultural circumstances may overrule this traditional identification of styles with dynasties.

Discussions of patronage have therefore either followed general and abstract principles or been reductive and extremely specific. Neither approach has been able to establish any cogent conclusions about the relationship between patronage and style. Nevertheless it is clear that patronage is an essential feature for a complete study of the period.

(ii) Patrons and types of patronage. Perhaps the best way to assess the effect of patronage on Early Christian and Byzantine art is to look chronologically over the whole period and to ask what patrons or what sort of patronage played an important part in the developments (or lack of them) of the period.

A complication in assessing the patronage of Constantine the Great is that he overtly accepted Christianity through baptism only on his deathbed. Yet his importance lies in his promotion of church building throughout the empire (including Rome and Jerusalem) and his foundation of Constantinople (dedicated 330) which, whether planned as such or not, became the Christian capital of the Byzantine empire and the grandest city in medieval Europe. As an individual patron Constantine has a claim to be one of the most influential figures in the transformation of European art; likewise Justinian is a towering figure through his consolidation of the visual culture of Byzantine Christianity. The next crucial stage in imperial patronage is a more negative one; had the iconoclast

emperors (726–843), including perhaps most prominently Theophilos (*reg* 829–42), achieved their aim of eliminating figural art from the Byzantine Church, the visual arts of Eastern Europe might well have followed a course of development similar to that of the Islamic world. The descriptions of the palace architecture and decoration of Theophilos are reminiscent of the court at Baghdad and the contemporary world of 'the thousand and one nights'.

The interlude of iconoclasm was succeeded by a 'renovation' of the Early Christian past and traditional Orthodox art, as interpreted in 9th-century Constantinople. The restoration of Orthodoxy was carried out by the combined patronage of patriarchs and emperors, perhaps most conspicuously by Patriarch Photios (*reg* 858–67; 877–86) and Basil I (see MACEDONIAN DYNASTY, (1)), although much of what is known is derived from carefully prepared texts of the time. On the evidence available, the role in artistic patronage that has been attributed to Constantine VII, 'the greatest patron between Hadrian and Lorenzo the Magnificent', must be regarded as controversial. So, too, is the idea of a Macedonian 'renaissance', as the surviving art does not provide conclusive evidence of it. However, this scholar emperor may have influenced the antiquarian and encyclopedic interests that absorbed the Byzantine aristocracy of the time.

Constantine IX represents the patronage of an emperor whose family belonged to the traditional civil aristocracy. His support of church and monastic building and its decoration was phenomenal. He was recorded as having built the most impressive structure in Constantinople since Hagia Sophia, the monastery of St George at Mangana (1042–54), a few ruins of which may remain. Surviving evidence of his patronage includes the construction of Nea Moni (see CHIOS, §2), his donation of a mosaic panel (1042) in the south gallery of Hagia Sophia (see ISTANBUL, §III, 1(ii)(b)) and his restoration of the church of the Holy Sepulchre (see JERUSALEM, §II, 2(i)); other major works are documented in the sources. Despite all this work, his reign was seen by contemporaries as frivolous and capricious. The obvious emperor to compare with Constantine IX is John II, who donated two mosaic panels to Hagia Sophia in Constantinople. His patronage seems to mark a new piety on the part of the Komnenian dynasty, which was very much a military household: his special commission was the foundation of the monastery of Christ Pantokrator (see ISTANBUL, §III, 2(i)), an extensive complex with churches, an imperial mausoleum and a major public hospital. Another feature of the 12th-century emperors was their intermarriages with Western princesses, who may in their patronage have promoted Western European artistic ideas. Moreover, from this period there was a new factor in the Byzantine world: the presence of crusaders and crusader artists. It is debatable to what extent manuscripts, icons and wall paintings that show a mix of Byzantine and Western style and iconography are evidence of Western patronage of versatile local or immigrant artists.

There is little doubt that monasteries, rather than cathedrals, became increasingly the recipients of patronage in the Byzantine empire. Various archives and charters record the growing wealth of Byzantine monasteries (see CHRISTIANITY, §IV, 1), both in property and in artistic holdings. This trend has been used to explain the decline of the Byzantine economy and manpower. Whether or not this is fair, monastic wealth can be amply documented, not only in the modern holdings of famous monasteries, such as those on MT ATHOS, but in the impressive 11th-century BACHKOVO MONASTERY in Bulgaria, founded by the Byzantine general Grigorios Pakourianos; in the 12th-century wall paintings of the coenobitic complex in ST NEOPHYTOS MONASTERY, which seem to have been donated by a well-wisher, perhaps the local bishop; and in the wall paintings and mosaics of Christ the Saviour in Chora Monastery (*see* ISTANBUL, §III, 3(ii)), restored by Theodore Metochites, who hoped to create for himself a protected place of retirement and a permanent resting-place for his body to await the Last Judgement.

The artistic power gradually invested in the monasteries no doubt influenced the character of Byzantine art. It is not, however, the only type of patronage worthy of investigation. The changing character of the aristocracy over the period needs more consideration. There are also numerous examples of 'middle-class' patronage, as in the proliferation of small churches in 14th-century Thessaloniki, and of communal sponsorship by the village societies of the empire. Rich women, notably widows, were another important source of patronage; ANICIA JULIANA, for example, who built the church of St Polyeuktos (524–7; destr.) in Constantinople, rivalled the ambitions of the emperor.

BIBLIOGRAPHY
C. Mango: *Sources and Documents: The Art of the Byzantine Empire, 312–1453* (Englewood Cliffs, NJ, 1972/*R* Toronto, Buffalo and London, 1986)
H. Buchthal and H. Belting: *Patronage in Thirteenth-century Constantinople: An Atelier of Late Byzantine Book Illumination and Calligraphy* (Washington, DC, 1978)
A. Cutler: 'Art in Byzantine Society', *Jb. Österreich. Byz.*, xxx/2 (1981), pp. 759–87
C. Galatariotou: 'Byzantine Ktetorika Typika: A Comparative Study', *Byzantion*, xlv (1987), pp. 77–138
R. Cormack: *The Byzantine Eye: Studies in Art and Patronage* (London, 1989)
R. M. Harrison: *A Temple for Byzantium: The Discovery and Excavation of Anicia Juliana's Palace Church in Istanbul* (London, 1989)
A. Markopoulos, ed.: *Constantine VII Porphyrogenitos and his Age* (Athens, 1989)

ROBIN CORMACK

II. Architecture.

The evidence for ecclesiastical and secular architecture in the Early Christian and Byzantine period is derived from extant buildings (some in ruins but many still in use as churches), archaeological finds and the occasional, brief references to monuments in the literary sources. Although in the early centuries the debt to antique models is clear, the architecture of the empire and surrounding regions gradually developed a distinctive character that lasted well beyond the fall of Constantinople in 1453.

1. Introduction. 2. Ecclesiastical. 3. Secular.

1. INTRODUCTION. The earliest Christian church buildings developed from domestic architecture, as in the *domus ecclesiae* (*c.* 233; modified *c.* 240) at Dura Europos (*see* DURA EUROPOS, §4); some of the tenement buildings in Rome eventually became public basilican churches. Partly as a response to the Edict of Milan (313), further

new building types and ideas were initiated in Rome and elsewhere in the empire, and these influenced the development of Early Christian and Byzantine architecture both within the empire (*see* ROME, ANCIENT, §II, 2(i)(g)) and beyond its borders. Constantinople, the focal point of Byzantine architecture for over 1000 years, assumed importance as a centre of political power and of architectural achievement only towards the end of the 4th century and during the 5th. After the early 7th century the major developments of Byzantine architecture are largely reflected in the monuments found within an inner core of the empire consisting of western Asia Minor, Greece and parts of the Balkan peninsula. However, Byzantine architecture also includes buildings in many other areas, most of which were at times under Byzantine political control. These monuments may be divided into three groups. The first group is found in regions that had continuous contact with the empire over long periods, for example Bulgaria, Serbia, probably pre-Norman Sicily, and Cyprus. It is difficult to distinguish these monuments from those found in Constantinople or other Byzantine centres. The second group consists of buildings found in Armenia, Georgia, Russia, Romania, Norman Sicily and Coptic Egypt. They exhibit specific features that were strongly influenced by Byzantine models, but not on a continuous basis. Occasionally they may in turn have exerted influence on Byzantine forms. The final group contains individual monuments with distinctive Byzantine characteristics, which are not typical of known local developments. Included are buildings in Venice (e.g. S Marco; *see* VENICE, §IV, 1(i)), southern Italy (*see* STILO), the Crimea (*see* CHERSONESOS), upper Mesopotamia (now Syria/Iraq/Turkey; e.g. *see* TUR 'ABDIN), Syria (*see* RUSAFA) and Palestine (Bethlehem, church of the Nativity; *see* BETHLEHEM, §1). Some examples may be the work of Byzantine builders and craftsmen, while others may have been constructed during relatively brief periods of Byzantine occupation; other buildings may be remnants of local architectural developments that have not been identified.

(i) Building types. (ii) Materials and techniques. (iii) Style. (iv) Influence. (v) Historiography.

(i) Building types. Byzantine patrons and architects focused their major efforts on ecclesiastical buildings, particularly churches, a direct reflection of the pre-eminent role religion played throughout Byzantine history. Churches constitute the majority of published monuments and have been the focus of investigation since interest in Byzantine buildings first developed. Modern stylistic concepts and theories of architectural development are derived almost entirely from forms found in ecclesiastical buildings. Interpretations of the origins, function and development of ecclesiastical architecture are controversial. The ceremony of the mass, baptism, religious processions, the veneration of holy objects, images or martyrs' remains, the provision of ceremonial offerings and the location, within the church, of men and women, catechumens and the clergy, all probably influenced some of the forms of ecclesiastical buildings. These forms cannot, however, be explained simply in terms of function: the same forms were at times used for different functions, and the same

functions were at times fulfilled by different architectural forms.

Equally open to interpretation, but perhaps more significant, is the symbolism that probably played an important part in the creation of many Byzantine architectural forms. The cruciform plan is a case in point, even though it was also used in pre-Christian buildings. The dome was probably understood as a symbolic reflection of heaven, although it is uncertain when that connotation became important. Church buildings may have been thought of as symbols of the heavenly Jerusalem. Hexagons, octagons and other forms based on symbolic numbers were common, and were used, for instance, in the floor-plans of baptisteries (e.g. Ravenna, Orthodox Baptistery). Numerical relationships, such as the harmonic musical scale, traceable to Pythagorean cosmology, were probably used in floor-plans and elevations. By the Middle Byzantine period (c. 843–1204) earlier forms such as the basilica may have acquired symbolic status. The entire church building appears to have been understood as a symbolic reflection of the most important teachings of medieval Christianity, with specific architectural forms standing for specific features of the cosmos, tenets, church festivals and locations sanctified by Christ's earthly life.

Secular architecture has received far less attention, even though numerous examples, some in an excellent state of preservation, have survived. Significant remains of domestic buildings of various periods, ranging from simple structures to extensive complexes, usually including courtyards or peristyles, have been recorded, for instance at Ephesos (see EPHESOS, §I, 3), Pergamon, Sardis (see SARDIS, §1), Corinth, MYSTRAS, MONEMVASIA and several sites in Syria. With some exceptions, their functional, structural, spatial and decorative qualities remain to be investigated, and only occasionally have attempts been made to identify possible socio-economic implications, stylistic developments, regional influences or manifestations of everyday life.

The Great Palace in Constantinople (see ISTANBUL, §III, 12) held a position between secular and ecclesiastical architecture because of the close relationship between Court and Church ceremonials. The palace is known only from fragmentary remains and literary sources, but major churches, including Hagia Sophia and Hagia Eirene, were integral parts of the palace complex. The remains imply that it covered a very large area and that it consisted of many loosely related components, including monumental galleries and richly furnished courtyards and peristyles constructed during different periods. Other notable, somewhat better-preserved remains of much smaller Byzantine palaces exist near the Theodosian wall in Constantinople—the Blachernai Palace and the so-called Tekfur Saray (?late 13th century)—as well as at Nymphaion (first half of the 13th century) near Izmir and at Mystras (see §3 (ii)(b) below). Monasteries, which also combine secular and ecclesiastical characteristics, were of great importance in both Byzantine history and architecture. No single organizational principle may be discerned. Often monks' cells, a refectory and other rooms were loosely grouped around one or more churches, chapels or oratories. Notable remains exist in all parts of the Byzantine world, but particularly well-preserved examples may be seen on Mt Sinai (see SINAI, §2(i)), MT ATHOS and at METEORA.

Public buildings such as baths, praetoria, theatres and stadia are almost unknown after the 6th century. The distinctive shop-lined monumental street arcades found in some Early Christian cities such as Ephesos, Sardis and Caričin Grad provide notable exceptions. Civil construction, including bridges, roads, cisterns and aqueducts, declined drastically after the 6th century. Fortifications, however, were of great importance throughout Byzantine history because defence against ever-present enemies was imperative. Impressive examples (see §3(i) below) are preserved in most parts of the former Byzantine empire, particularly in Istanbul, Thessaloniki, Izmir and Pergamon.

(ii) Materials and techniques. The walls of Byzantine buildings were usually constructed of mortared rubble (i.e. broken bricks and irregular chunks of stone in a coarse mortar bed) encased on both sides by a relatively thin facing of brick (see BRICK, §II, 2), ashlar (cut or roughly trimmed stone), or by a combination of these, which gave form to the amorphous inner mass. Solid brick or stone was used only occasionally, either for structural piers or where other materials were not readily available. Ashlar masonry was particularly common in Syria, Palestine, western Asia Minor, Georgia and Armenia, while brick was preferred in parts of Italy. Brick and ashlar were often used in alternating layers for wall facings, a Late Roman technique used intermittently in Byzantine construction primarily in Constantinople (for example in the church of St John Stoudios, c. 450; see fig. 10), western Asia Minor, Greece and the southern Balkans. In the Middle and Late Byzantine periods, these materials were combined decoratively in chequer-boards, brick herringbone patterns and meander or chevron bands. The cloisonné technique of surrounding each ashlar block with bricks was common in Greece from c. 900 (see §2(iii)(b) below).

In the Early Christian period most buildings, including those with domes, were roofed with tile on wood truss constructions. By the 6th century vaulting was common and significant spans were achieved, as in Hagia Sophia (see ISTANBUL, §III, 1(ii)(a)). In the Middle Byzantine period vaulting on a smaller scale, usually of brick backed with rubbled mortar, became widespread. The most common forms were domes on drums, half domes, cloister vaults, barrel vaults, pendentives, squinches and groin vaults.

Sophisticated methods for assuring structural solidity were developed, such as well-built deep foundations, wooden tie-rod systems in vaults, walls and foundations, and metal chains placed horizontally inside masonry.

Spoils, often taken from ancient buildings, were used throughout the empire, particularly in the medieval period. They included brick, ashlar and marble elements such as columns, capitals and carved ornament. Rich polychrome effects were achieved in building interiors with marble (for instance red porphyry from Egypt, yellow from Tunisia, green from Lakonia and verde-antico from Thessaly) reused for columns and architraves, or sliced into sheets for wall revetment and inlaid floors. Only occasionally were architectural and non-architectural sculptures created anew, as in the marble quarries of the Marmara in

10. St John Stoudios, Istanbul, Turkey, *c.* AD 450; interior view from the south-west

the Early Christian period, and for use as altar screens, capitals, mullions and window- and door-frames in churches.

In the Early Christian period, interiors were frequently decorated with paintings and mosaics, on floors and walls (*see* §III below). In later centuries, wall painting became an inseparable part of church building.

(iii) Style. Although periods defined by political events, for instance the reigns of emperors or dynasties, are useful for placing Byzantine buildings in their historic context, stylistic developments may be discerned that are not directly correlated with Byzantine history (*see* §I, 3(i) above). Byzantine architecture may be described in terms of four major stylistic currents, each of which includes numerous subcurrents and local developments. The first is characterized by simple, clearly defined, self-contained geometric units, usually organized about a dominating axis that is either vertical, as in circular buildings such as S Costanza (*see* ROME, §VI, 18(i)), or horizontal, for instance in basilicas such as S Sabina (422–32), Rome. Spaces linked by column screens predominate, and undifferentiated components are repeated in rhythmic series, for instance windows and colonnades in basilicas (see fig. 10). Light is introduced copiously through large arched windows. Detailing, which usually echoes Classical prototypes, is simple and used sparingly on both interiors and exteriors. Carved marble spolia are used in many buildings. The first style laid the groundwork for all Byzantine architecture and provided the basic forms from which subsequent styles were developed. The aisled basilica was its most prominent building type, but the same stylistic characteristics appear in centralized buildings. Relatively well-preserved examples are S Apollinare in Classe (*see* RAVENNA, §2(v)) and the cathedral of POREČ in Istria. Buildings of the first style

were constructed between the early 4th century and the early 7th.

The second style is characterized by intense experimentation. Many building forms and structural or compositional principles were developed simultaneously, and one building seldom very closely resembled another. Features typical of the first style, for instance the dome, were multiplied, as in the church of St John (probably 6th century) at Philadelphia (now Alaşehir, Turkey), or combined in new ways, as in Hagia Sophia in Constantinople. Complex forms, varied geometric combinations and interlocking spaces predominated. The organization of components about both a vertical and a horizontal axis was common, as in domed basilicas. Such units as windows or arcades were usually grouped, avoiding the repetitive rhythms of the first style. Lighting was often indirect, from windows not readily visible, and served to provide stark contrasts and to display mosaic surfaces to optimum advantage. Inert matter was made to appear weightless, at times with the aid of undercut carved marble details.

Domed basilicas and polygonal ambulatory (double-shell) buildings were frequent in the second style, but they were not standard types because each example was distinctly individual. Hagia Sophia in Constantinople and S Vitale in Ravenna (*see* RAVENNA, §2(vii)) are good examples. Although the highest quality and most daring achievements of the second style appeared under Justinian I (*reg* 527–65), some examples, such as S Lorenzo in Milan, were probably built as early as the second half of the 4th century, and others, such as the church at Dereağzi (Anatolia), as late as the 9th. For about 250 years Byzantine buildings could be constructed in either the first style or the second, for reasons which remain to be determined. The second style may originally have been a court style, and in most areas it was uncommon.

11. Fatih Cami, Zeytinbagi (formerly Tirilye), Turkey, probably 9th century; the minaret, window fillings and white coating are later additions

The third style combines elements that were used earlier: basilica, dome and cruciform plan were amalgamated into harmonious, unified new building types. The third style therefore represents the culmination of earlier efforts. Once new building types had been developed and perfected, experimentation was rare. Most buildings were designed as variations on relatively few standard schemes. Vertical and horizontal components were carefully balanced. Vaulting was almost universal, but its structure was not emphasized. Instead, the curved surfaces of the vaults, covered by wall paintings or mosaics, contributed to the illusion of weightlessness. The unusual colours, distinctive surface textures and reflected highlights, as well as the subtle, flat style of mosaic and wall painting and the minute scale of these churches produced an intense, jewel-like effect. The third style flourished from the 9th century to the 12th. The cross-in-square church represents the most prominent building type. Well-preserved examples exist in Constantinople, such as in the monastery of Christ Pantokrator (see ISTANBUL, §III, 2(i)); in Asia Minor, for instance in the church now known as the Fatih Cami in Zeytinbagi (formerly Tirilye; see fig. 11); and in numerous towns in Greece. A variant with an expanded domed central bay was important from the 10th century to the 12th, as in the katholikon church at HOSIOS LOUKAS in Phokis and at DAFNI near Athens.

The fourth style was characterized by retrospection. Building types were often borrowed from the Byzantine past in their entirety or, more rarely, earlier forms were combined in a new context. Only occasionally were earlier architectural types developed further, as in cross-in-square churches with five domes. Rich polychrome ornament, including brick, tile, ashlar and ceramics, also with antecedents in the Byzantine past, was frequently used to enliven exteriors. The fourth style reached its apex in the 13th century and early 14th, but it is found at least as early as the 12th century and continued in the post-Byzantine period. Examples exist in Constantinople (e.g. 1310, *parekklesion* or funerary chapel of St Mary Pammakaristos), Thessaloniki, Mystras (c. 1310–22, Hodegetria; see fig. 24 below), Meteora, Mt Athos (katholikon of Chilandar Monastery), Nesebăr (St John Aleitourgetos) and in Serbia (church of the Virgin, Matejič Monastery).

(iv) Influence. One of the most significant contributions of Byzantine architecture to architectural history is that it provides a large number of monuments in which architectural forms may be traced in an unbroken chain of development from Late Antiquity onwards. In so doing it also provides a unique insight into the gradual transformation of Classical forms to meet the functional and spiritual needs of medieval Christian civilization. Byzantine architectural forms, however, were never direct imitations of Classical prototypes. When Byzantine architects did revive forms of the past, they chose examples found in earlier Byzantine architecture. This reluctance to imitate

ancient forms demonstrates the independent character of Byzantine architecture, in comparison not only with western Europe, but also with Byzantine literature and the pictorial arts, which were, on the whole, far more dependent upon Classical sources. Another distinctive feature of Byzantine architecture is its nearly total integration with the pictorial arts. After the iconoclast controversy (726–843) all vaulted zones and upper portions of church buildings were designed for the application of sacred images, which were an integral part of the architectural and religious experience.

The Early Christian BASILICA was one of the most flexible and durable forms in the entire history of architecture. Along with its antecedents in the preceding Roman period, it was repeatedly revived and developed in Western Europe as the most prominent church type in Carolingian, Romanesque, Gothic and Renaissance architecture. During the Baroque and Neo-classical periods it survived in several variations, and it was revived in numerous forms during the 19th century. The Christian basilica also had a profound influence on the Great Mosque in Damascus (see DAMASCUS, §3), and perhaps indirectly on the subsequent development of columnar mosques throughout the Islamic world. Centralized and cruciform building types developed by Byzantine architects also influenced Western architecture, particularly in the Carolingian and Romanesque periods, and the design of several buildings in the West was based upon Byzantine models. The Carolingian palatine chapel (now cathedral) in Aachen (see AACHEN, §2(ii)(a)) is a good example.

Specific aspects, details or combinations found in Byzantine churches influenced architecture in western and eastern Europe and in Islamic countries for centuries. Various forms of the transept, for instance, were borrowed and transformed by Carolingian, Romanesque and Renaissance architects. The domed basilica, at times including specific details such as squinches, was used frequently in Romanesque churches, and continued to appear in variations in the Renaissance and Baroque periods. The influence of Hagia Sophia in Constantinople on Turkish architects in the design of major mosques such as the Süleymaniye (see ISTANBUL, §III, 10), and the subsequent use of these mosque types throughout the Ottoman empire, represents the most dramatic impact of Byzantine buildings upon Islamic architecture. In Eastern Europe the Byzantine tradition was even more prominent and survived into the 20th century in variations of the cross-in-square church type, including many Byzantine architectural details. The Byzantine tradition lives on, but with little vigour, in numerous churches constructed for Orthodox congregations in Greece and North America.

(v) Historiography. The powerful visual impact of individual Byzantine monuments, for instance Hagia Sophia in Constantinople, S Vitale in Ravenna and S Marco in Venice, has been recognized for centuries; through their influence on other monuments these buildings have left their mark on architectural history. Some have been of interest to chroniclers, travellers, artists and scholars almost from their inception. Other buildings, such as the Holy Sepulchre in Jerusalem (see JERUSALEM, §II, 2(i)) and the church of the Nativity in Bethlehem, were focal points of religious interest, veneration and pilgrimage throughout the centuries. Byzantine architecture has also been perceived as exotic, obscure and peripheral to the main stream of architectural history. This view is based on an inadequate understanding of the goals of Byzantine architects and of their achievements. It also indicates a lack of familiarity with significant but often remote or poorly preserved monuments. Above all, it is tainted by the strong Classical emphasis of Western civilization since the Renaissance.

Scholarly interest in Byzantine monuments began very late, in comparison with the study of many other periods, with the publication by CHARLES TEXIER of churches in Asia Minor in 1864 and continued with the expedition of MELCHIOR DE VOGÜÉ to Syria in the 1860s, R. Cattaneo's reports on S Marco in Venice in the 1880s, and the work of W. R. LETHABY, H. Swainson and the Fossati brothers (see FOSSATI, (2)) in Constantinople, published in the 1890s. Nineteenth-century accounts of Byzantine architecture tended to emphasize the exotic, unusual character of the buildings. They were often accompanied by drawings that failed to distinguish what actually existed from unreliable reconstructions. Their major contributions lie in the preservation of data, however fragmentary, and in the awakening of interest in the monuments.

After the turn of the 20th century, the publication of more rigorous and more accurate accounts of individual Byzantine monuments flourished. The investigation of Hosios Loukas in Phokis by ROBERT WEIR SCHULTZ and Sidney Barnsley in 1901 was a milestone in this development. Other important early 20th-century accounts were prepared by Hans Rott and GERTRUDE MARGARET LOW-THIAN BELL for Asia Minor, by the Princeton expeditions under HOWARD CROSBY BUTLER for Syria, by A. van Millingen, J. Ebersolt and A. Thiers for Constantinople, by GABRIEL MILLET, G. Lambakis, CHARLES DIEHL, M. Le Tourneau and H. Saladin for Greece. Many comparable accounts appeared in the period after World War I. More reliable results were obtained when masonry and construction sequences could be observed during excavation or restoration; investigations were carried out on a minor scale in the 1920s and 1930s by GEORGE ANGELOS SOTERIOU in Ephesos, G. de Jerphanion in Ankara, A. M. Schneider in Istanbul and RICHARD KRAUTHEIMER in Rome. These techniques bore fruit, particularly in the 1950s and 1960s in work on important churches in Istanbul by the Byzantine Institute of America under PAUL ATKINS UNDERWOOD, R. van Nice and A. H. S. Megaw. The excavation, restoration and recording of Byzantine monuments continues to be an important part of Byzantine architectural scholarship.

Although numerous early references to Byzantine buildings have been published, precisely how the texts relate to specific monuments, construction phases or reconstructions frequently remains unresolved, and for many buildings textual evidence is not available. Moreover, the known monuments probably represent only a small fraction of the buildings that were constructed. The reliable interpretation of Byzantine architecture is therefore difficult and has made less progress than the recording of the monuments. The lack of firm evidence concerning much of

Byzantine architecture permitted broad speculative theories, some of which attempted to identify regional or national architectural developments, traditions and influences. The work of Gabriel Millet and JOSEF STRZYGOWSKI initiated this approach after the turn of the 20th century. Until the 1950s questions concerning architectural character and achievement in the 'East' and 'West', neither of which was clearly defined, and in various provinces, such as Italy, Greece, Bulgaria and Armenia, were subject to heated debates, most of which could not be resolved with the available evidence. At times the debates were exploited to support claims of regional, national or racial superiority.

In a publication of 1914, which in some respects has not been superseded, O. Wulff attempted to define major stylistic currents and problems of architectural development, based on an objective evaluation of the evidence available at the time. In the 1930s A. H. S. Megaw and R. Kautzsch employed methods of analysis that combined the interpretation of textual or stylistic evidence with detailed comparative observations. In the following decades scholarship using comparable methods clarified the history of a number of monuments and architectural developments.

Symbolic connotations in Byzantine architecture received little attention until the 1940s and 1950s, when publications by ANDRÉ GRABAR, KARL LEHMANN, E. B. Smith and G. Bandmann addressed the subject. However, there remain many unanswered questions concerning specific meanings. Questions concerning the use of Byzantine buildings also remain unanswered. Attempts to provide solutions were initiated in the 1940s with research by J. Lassus; they were continued in the following decades by F. W. Deichmann, Cyril Mango, Richard Krautheimer, Gordana Babić and T. F. Mathews. Scholarship concerning structural systems used in Byzantine buildings was largely neglected until the publications of R. M. Mainstone in the 1960s. Other important areas of architectural investigation, such as patronage, social, demographic and economic implications, construction techniques, the role and training of the architect and architectural theory have been addressed only marginally, if at all.

Compendia or collections of material have been prominent in Byzantine architectural scholarship since the 19th century. They were organized geographically (e.g. H. C. Butler on Syria, A. Deroko on Serbia), by building types (e.g. G. Soteriou and ANASTASIOS ORLANDOS on basilicas, A. Khatchatrian on baptisteries, A. Grabar on martyria) or by specific subjects (e.g. L. de Beylie on dwellings and AUGUSTE CHOISY on construction). Early attempts to summarize the known material on Byzantine architecture were provided by Gabriel Millet in 1905, ORMONDE MADDOCK DALTON in 1911 and C. Diehl in 1925. In 1965 Richard Krautheimer compiled a detailed summary that was organized chronologically and geographically. In 1974 Cyril Mango provided a more selective account of Byzantine architecture, written for a wider public, that laid greater emphasis upon topics that are frequently neglected, such as sources of information, building materials and techniques, architectural financing, urban planning and the historical context.

BIBLIOGRAPHY

R. Cattaneo: *L'Architecture en Italie du VI au XI siècle* (Venice, 1895)
O. Wulff: *Altchristliche und byzantinische Kunst* (Berlin, 1914)
C. Diehl, M. Le Tourneau and H. Saladin: *Les Monuments chrétiens de Salonique*, 2 vols (Paris, 1918)
A. H. S. Megaw: 'The Chronology of some Middle Byzantine Churches', *Annu. Brit. Sch. Athens*, xxxii (1931–2), pp. 90–130
R. Kautzsch: *Kapitellstudien: Studien zur spätantiken Kunstgeschichte* (Berlin, 1936)
J. Lassus: *Sanctuaires chrétiens de Syrie* (Paris, 1947)
E. B. Smith: *The Dome: A Study in the History of Ideas* (Princeton, 1950)
A. Orlandos: *I xylostegos palaiochristianiki basiliki tis mesogeiakis lekanis* [The wooden-roofed Early Christian basilicas of the Mediterranean basin], 3 vols (Athens, 1952–7)
A. Deroko: *Monumentalna i dekorativna arhitektura u srednjevekonoj Srbiji* [Monumental and decorative architecture in medieval Serbia] (Belgrade, 1953, rev. 1962)
G. Bandmann: 'Über Pastophorien und verwandte Nebenräume im mittelalterlichen Kirchenbau', *Kunstgeschichtliche Studien für H. Kauffmann*, ed. W. Braunfels (Berlin, 1956), pp. 19–58
A. Khatchatrian: *Les Baptistères paléochrétiens* (Paris, 1962)
R. Krautheimer: *Early Christian and Byzantine Architecture*, Pelican Hist. A. (Harmondsworth, 1965, rev. 4/1986)
K. Mijatev: *Arhitekturata v srednovekovna Bulgarija* [Medieval architecture in Bulgaria] (Sofia, 1965)
G. Babić: *Les Chapelles annexes des églises byzantines: Fonction liturgique et programmes iconographiques* (Paris, 1969)
F. W. Deichmann: *Ravenna: Geschichte und Monumente* (Wiesbaden, 1969)
C. Mango: *Architettura bizantina* (Milan, 1974; Eng. trans., New York, 1976/R London, 1986)
T. F. Mathews: *The Byzantine Churches of Istanbul: A Photographic Survey* (University Park, PA, 1976)

For further bibliography see articles on the individual writers mentioned in text.

HANS BUCHWALD

2. ECCLESIASTICAL. The architectural achievement of the age is revealed above all in the many different types of church, chapel, martyrium and baptistery that emerged between *c.* 313 and 1453.

(i) *c.* 313–*c.* 600. (ii) *c.* 600–*c.* 843. (iii) *c.* 843–*c.* 1204. (iv) *c.* 1204–1453.

(i) c. *313*–c. *600*. During this period the standard church type in the East and West empire was the basilica (see fig. 12). There are numerous variations of this type: it can be a single-aisled structure, or have three, five or more aisles usually separated by colonnades; it can have a transept; it has a clerestory or a gallery; the apse usually projects on the outside but is sometimes contained within a straight wall. Most basilicas originally formed part of a larger complex with appending buildings, such as a baptistery. Other important Early Christian architectural types are the centralized martyria (*see* MARTYRIUM) and churches in the form of octagons (see fig. 17 below), rotundas, cruciforms, trefoils and quatrefoils. The regional differences that developed within these two broad categories of building types reflect the local availability of materials and the continuity of established traditions of construction. (*See also* CHURCH, §I, 1(i)–(ii) and 2(i)–(ii).)

(a) Latin West. (b) Constantinople and Asia Minor. (c) Greece and the Balkans. (d) Syria, Palestine and Mesopotamia.

(a) *Latin West.* After his defeat of Maxentius at the Milvian Bridge in October 312, Constantine the Great entered Rome and was proclaimed Augustus of the western half of the Roman Empire. He undertook a building programme in Rome, which became the centre of Christian architecture until well after his foundation of Constantinople in 324. After his death in 337 the focus of

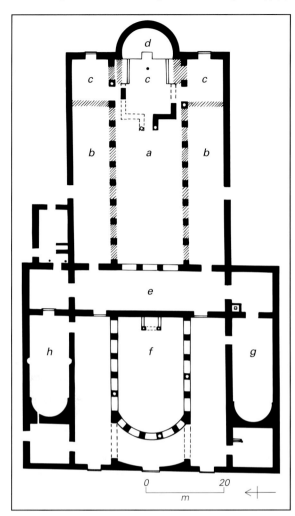

12. Basilica A, Nea Anchialos, c. 470, plan: (a) nave; (b) aisle; (c) transept; (d) apse; (e) narthex; (f) atrium; (g) service room; (h) baptistery

building activity in the Latin West shifted to Milan, and in the 5th and 6th centuries to both Ravenna and Rome. The influence of these innovations is sometimes evident in the numerous Early Christian monuments that have been found in Sicily, Spain, Gaul, England and North Africa. By the early 6th century, however, the most innovative examples of church building were to be found in Constantinople.

Italy, Sicily and Spain, c. 313–late 4th century. As early as November 312 Constantine sponsored the construction of the first securely documented public Christian church, the Basilica Constantiniana (now S Giovanni in Laterano; *see* ROME, §V, 15(ii)). Quite possibly intended as an ex-voto to Christ for his victory over Maxentius, the cathedral is a landmark in the history of Western architecture since it is the first of many churches to have been sponsored by emperors, aristocrats and other persons of substantial means. Large enough to accommodate 2000 worshippers

and a sizeable clergy, the original cathedral was a timber-roofed basilica consisting of a tall nave terminating in a semicircular apse and flanked on either side by a pair of lower aisles. Next to the church was a free-standing octagonal baptistery and an episcopal palace, the earliest recorded examples of their kind. The whole complex was situated just inside the Aurelianic city walls on land controlled by Constantine, in order to avoid conflict with the powerful aristocracy whose important pagan shrines stood in the crowded centre of Rome. Thus the topography of the first Christian cathedral was apparently determined by politics (Krautheimer, 1983).

In plan, Constantine's cathedral derived from the public secular basilica in Roman architecture. Basilicas were suitable for the Christian liturgy and relatively inexpensive to erect because they were timber-roofed rather than vaulted and easily adaptable in layout. As churches, basilicas were adapted to serve various new functions (*see* CHURCH, §I, 1(i)). In using the Roman basilica as the model for his cathedral, Constantine elevated Christian building from the realm of domestic and funerary architecture and placed it in the higher category of public architecture; the basilica remained by far the preferred type of church building in Italy and the rest of western Europe until the end of the Middle Ages. In contrast to the Greek East, centrally planned forms were not often used for churches, although they do appear as baptisteries, mausolea and martyria.

The first cathedral of Rome itself served as the model for several other Early Christian cathedrals, including S Tecla (*see* MILAN, §IV, 4), the basilica (*c.* 324) at Ech Cheliff (formerly el-Asnam) in Algeria, the church of the Holy Sepulchre (*see* JERUSALEM, §II, 2(i)), the original church of the Nativity (*see* BETHLEHEM, §1) and possibly even the first cathedral of Hagia Sophia at Constantinople (*see* ISTANBUL, §III, 1(i)). Aside from these few monuments, however, basilican churches exemplify a wide diversity of form, from single-nave buildings to ones with three, five, seven or nine aisles separated from one another by rows of piers or columns, and with or without an apse or narthexes (vestibules) and atria (courtyards). At AQUILEIA, for example, the cathedral of Bishop Theodore (*reg* 313–19) was formed out of two triple-aisled hall churches connected at their western end by a transverse hall. This complex is the earliest known example in the Latin West and the Balkans of the so-called double cathedral; later examples include those at Pula, Poreč, Nesactium (now Vizače, Croatia), Trieste, Brioni (Friuli-Venezia Giulia), Hemmaberg and Hoischhügel (both Austria).

House churches (*tituli*) continued to function in Rome, although some were redesigned in the 4th century and eventually replaced by basilicas. In the late 4th century, a shrine sheltering the relics of SS John and Paul was installed on a mezzanine landing of the two-storey *titulus Byzantii* on the Caelian Hill in Rome; this house church was replaced in the early 5th century by the basilican church of SS Giovanni e Paolo. Examples of similar conversions include the *titulus Crisogoni* at Rome, which was transformed (*c.* 350) into a large aisleless hall flanked by porticos for Christian use; a hall in the Sessorian Palace, Rome, which was converted into the church of Santa

Croce in Gerusalemme (*c.* 326–8; remodelled 12th century) and the *titulus Clementis*, which was replaced by the lower basilica (*c.* 380–415) of S Clemente (*see* ROME, §V, 17(ii)(a); see also below).

Constantine also founded the basilica of Old St Peter's (*see* ROME, §V, 14(i)(a)), which was intended as a memorial to the saint. It soon became a covered common burial church for the faithful and for the periodic rites of their remembrance. Although Old St Peter's had five aisles, it differed significantly from S Giovanni in Laterano by the addition of an undivided transverse hall or continuous transept at the western end. The church's focal point was the Apostle's shrine, which stood in the centre of the transept directly in front of the main semicircular apse. This transept represents an innovative architectural feature, which was introduced not as an allusion to the cross of Christ but to highlight the shrine of St Peter while at the same time controlling the flow of pilgrim traffic to and from the shrine. The only other Early Christian church in Rome that copied the plan of Old St Peter's was S Paolo fuori le mura (384–5; largely destr. 1823), albeit with significant variations. Although the *basilica orientalis* at Salona and the episcopal basilica at Side may also have been inspired by Old St Peter's, its plan apparently remained otherwise unknown to the east of Italy.

Another type of basilican church is represented by a group of churches erected on cemeteries outside Rome's city walls. Known as 'ambulatory basilicas', they consist of a nave flanked on either side by an aisle that continues around one short end where it is bounded by a semicircular wall. Traces of such a building (66×24 m) exist near the site of the Villa dei Gordiani on the Via Praenestina and may be dated as early as the first decade of the 4th century. It remains to be established whether this ambulatory basilica functioned as a church in which the Eucharist was celebrated or as a martyrium. The ambulatory basilicas of SS Pietro e Marcellino (before 324–6) on the Via Labicana, S Sebastiano (*c.* 312–13; see fig. 13) on the Via Appia and S Lorenzo fuori le mura (*c.* 330) on the Via Tiburtina can all be attributed to Constantine. SS Pietro e Marcellino was built within an enclosed cemetery which the Christians

had begun to use as early as the second half of the 3rd century; the church's interior was paved with graves. A clerestory probably illuminated the nave, which was separated from the side aisles by piers supporting arcades; a narthex stood to the west. Adjoining the narthex was a mausoleum (diam. 20 m; 324–6), the interior wall of which was ringed by alternately curved and rectangular niches. Although this type of mausoleum had precedents, it is the first recorded example of a mausoleum attached to a basilican church. The mausoleum originally housed the porphyry sarcophagus (Rome, Vatican, Mus. Pio-Clementino) of the empress dowager Helena (*c.* 248/9–*c.* 328/9). The church of S Sebastiano is well preserved below a Baroque renovation; it was built near a site where the Christians had venerated the Apostles Peter and Paul in the second half of the 3rd century. A number of small mausolea were erected along its outer perimeter wall. S Lorenzo fuori le mura stands near the catacomb of St Lawrence; its floor is covered with Christian graves.

The last known example of an ambulatory basilica is S Agnese fuori le mura on the Via Nomentana, near the tomb of the martyr saint. It was begun either at the end of Constantine's life or soon after his death. The mausoleum of his daughter, Constantina, now known as S Costanza (*see* ROME, §V, 18), was built alongside the basilica's south flank. The best-preserved Constantinian building in Rome, S Costanza, is a double-shelled edifice consisting of a circular ambulatory encircling a tall cylindrical core capped by a dome. Although novel in Italy, its plan is strikingly reminiscent of the Anastasis Rotunda in the Holy Sepulchre compound (ded. *c.* 350; *see* JERUSALEM, §II, 2(i)), a comparison that may reflect an eastern Mediterranean influence on late Constantinian architecture in the Latin West. The fact that most of these ambulatory basilicas were paved with graves suggests that they served as funerary halls in which banquets commemorating the anniversaries of the departed were held. This type of church is also recorded at Andernos-les-Bains in southwest France.

In the construction of many of these churches, including S Giovanni in Laterano and Old St Peter's, Constantine

13. S Sebastiano, Via Appia, Rome, *c.* 312–13; reconstruction model (Rome, Soprintendenza ai Monumenti del Lazio)

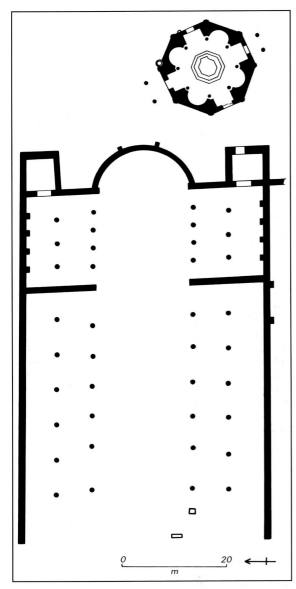

14. Milan Cathedral, before 355, plan; later dedicated to S Tecla

reused architectural elements such as column bases, shafts, capitals, architraves and decorated friezes from earlier Roman monuments. The use of luxurious marble spolia could reflect practical necessity, aesthetic requirements or political considerations (*see also* ROME, §III, 1(ii)). Some monuments, however, were fitted with newly fashioned elements, most of which came from workshops on the island of Prokonnesos near Constantinople and perhaps from Pamphylia in Asia Minor, which mass-produced them for export.

In the 4th century, Milan became the residence of various emperors and acquired several splendid churches. Literary sources record an early cathedral, the 'basilica minor/vetus', which was probably situated somewhere near the present cathedral. By 355 construction had begun on another cathedral (*c.* 80×45 m), referred to as 'basilica

major/nova' and later dedicated to S Tecla (see fig. 14; *see also* MILAN, §IV, 4). In plan it was similar to S Giovanni in Laterano. A more original and dramatic design was adopted for the extramural church of S Lorenzo (*c.* ?352–5, ?370s; *see* MILAN, §IV, 3 and CHURCH, fig. 3). It is a double-shelled quatrefoil punctuated at its four corners by staircase towers built to help buttress the masonry groin vault that presumably once covered the large square central bay. Other original 4th-century elements include a double-apsed narthex and an atrium to the west and the two satellite chapels projecting from the core of the church to the east and south. The plan represents a variant on a design imported from the eastern Mediterranean that continued to be used in Greece, the Balkans, Mesopotamia, Syria, Egypt and Armenia as late as the 11th century.

In the late 4th century at least three martyrium churches were built in the suburbs of Milan: S Ambrogio (see below), the church of the Apostles (now S Nazaro) and S Simpliciano, as well as an intramural single-aisled hall-church, S Giovanni in Conca. The cruciform church of the Apostles was modelled on the earlier 4th-century church of the Holy Apostles at Constantinople (*see* ISTANBUL, §III, 9(i)) with relics of the Apostles Andrew and Thomas and of St John the Evangelist placed under the high altar in the centre bay. The cross-shaped plan of S Simpliciano (see fig. 15 and MILAN, §IV, 5) represents a deliberate variant on the design of S Nazaro, with a shallow forechoir in front of the semicircular apse housing the main altar. Relics of some minor martyrs from the Trentino were housed in a small, separate martyrial chapel near the north transept wing of the church. The church of the Apostles and S Simpliciano influenced a number of churches throughout northern Italy and the Alpine arc, such as SS Pietro e Paolo below the Romanesque church of S Abbondio at Como (first half of 5th century), S Lorenzo at Aosta (end of 4th century), Santa Croce at Ravenna (first half of 5th century; destr.) and S Stefano at Verona (*c.* 450).

Italy, Sicily and Spain, late 4th century–c. 600. Between 380 and 480, but particularly after Alaric's sack of Rome in 410, the papacy assumed political and religious leadership in the Latin West and became a major patron of church building in Rome, which reached a level of activity not matched there until the 17th century. By *c.* 400 church building in the Latin West had begun to differ from that in the Greek East and exemplifies salient characteristics of its own. A standard type of basilica and a standard type of baptistery evolved and spread throughout northern Italy, and from North Africa to southern Spain and Gaul.

The standard type of basilica was meant to hold a congregation of between 800 and 1400. It consists of a nave flanked by aisles and terminating in a semicircular, sometimes rectangular, apse; a narthex and atrium sometimes feature at the west end. A separate martyr's chapel often stands near or adjacent to one of the aisles of the basilica. The high nave is divided from the aisles by columns either specially produced or reused. They usually carry arcades which in turn support the upper walls; these are pierced by large clerestory windows that flood the interior with light and are usually aligned with the intercolumniations of the nave arcades. The interior light was

15. S Simpliciano, Milan, late 4th century; view from the south-west

subdued because the windows were filled with pierced stone plaques or mica, coloured glass or alabaster panes in stucco and wood gratings. Mosaics or wall paintings sometimes adorned the walls between the clerestory and the arcades as well as the semi-dome of the apse. Exteriors were plain. Nave and aisles were covered by timber superstructures, either coffered ceilings or open rafter constructions. Pavements consisted of flagstone or marble (Rome), marble (Milan), or mosaics (north-eastern Italy and North Africa). Chancels projected from the apse into the nave and were marked off by carved parapets separating the clergy from the congregation. As in the 4th century, materials and techniques of construction depended upon local custom.

This standard type of basilica is known as early as the late 4th-century church of S Ambrogio at Milan, which has three aisles and a semicircular eastern apse, a plan that became widespread in northern Italy in the 5th century. After *c.* 380 examples of the type at Rome include S Clemente, S Vitale (401–17), S Stefano on the Via Latina (440–61) and the basilica of Pammachius (end of 4th century) at Portus, the harbour of Ostia. An especially fine example is the parish church of S Sabina (422–32; see fig. 16) on top of the Aventine Hill. The spacious nave (48.0×13.5 m) is separated from the flanking aisles by 24 marble columns and their Corinthian capitals, which are perfectly matched spolia. A large round-headed window is positioned above each intercolumniation of the nave, and three similar windows pierce the apse wall. The spandrels of the nave arcades are covered with their original polychrome marble revetments, but the figural mosaics that decorated the upper nave walls and the semi-dome of the apse are largely lost.

Although S Sabina was founded by the priest Peter of Illyrium, the dedicatory inscription begins with the name of the ruling pope Celestine I (*reg* 422–32). This may reflect an unwritten understanding established in the 4th century that if a newly elected pope lacked the funds to establish a new church building, a prosperous parishioner or clergyman would provide the financial means, but the name of the pope would be conspicuously connected with the foundation.

In addition to the standard basilicas, several major buildings were erected or decorated in Rome in the 5th century that exhibit a classicizing style and have thus been identified as part of a renaissance of Classical Roman architecture launched by Pope Sixtus III (*reg* 432–40): S Maria Maggiore (see ROME, §V, 20), the remodelled Lateran baptistery, S Paolo fuori le mura as decorated under Pope Leo I (*reg* 440–61), the oratory of Santa Croce (destr. 1588) near the Lateran and S Stefano Rotondo (see ROME, §V, 22). This last building was the only large urban sanctuary to be constructed in Rome according to a central plan before the 16th century. The integration of circular and cruciform elements in its planning are reminiscent of imperial villa and garden architecture as well as centralized monuments in Constantinople and the Holy Land. Previously dated to 468–83, this church has been shown to have been erected in the first half of the 5th century (Brandenburg, 1992).

Octagonal baptisteries are common in the Latin West in the 5th century, perhaps inspired directly by Constantine's baptistery (*c.* 315) for S Giovanni in Laterano and the 4th-century baptistery of the cathedral of Milan. Freestanding octagonal baptisteries are known at Fréjus (5th century) in France, Riva St Vitale (*c.* 500) in Switzerland, and in Italy at Albenga (5th century), Aquileia (*c.* 450), Novara (5th century) and Ravenna (the Orthodox and Arian baptisteries *c.* 400 and late 5th century respectively). Although octagonal baptisteries occur in the eastern Mediterranean, as in the cathedral of the Virgin Mary at Ephesos (?4th century) and at ABU MINA, they are rare outside the Latin West. Some octagonal baptisteries are double-shelled structures consisting of a tall centre space separated by a colonnaded shell from an enveloping ambulatory. This variation of the type is recorded as early as *c.* 400 at Marseille, Aix-en-Provence and the baptistery of S Giovanni in Laterano, as transformed *c.* 432–40.

In southern Italy, Sicily and Spain ecclesiastical buildings on a large scale and with Roman and North African characteristics first appeared *c.* 400. Basilicas were the most common church type, but apse walls sometimes have arched openings, as in the single-aisled S Gennaro extra moenia and S Giorgio Maggiore (both *c.* 400) in Naples. The latter church originally had a tripartite transept, possibly under Milanese influence. The influence of North African architecture, however, predominates. S Restituta (*c.* 380–400) at Naples and the cathedral of S Maria di Capua Vetere (?5th century) have a nave and four aisles, as in the early 4th-century basilica at Ech

Cheliff (formerly el-Asnam) in Algeria. The North African counter-apse and arcaded screen in front of an apse (see below) appear in a late 4th-century church at San Pedro de Alcantara (Vega del Mar) between Gibraltar and Málaga. Square baptisteries also occur in southern Italy and may reflect African influence. Triconch chancels (?5th century) at Concordia in the upper Adriatic and at S Pere at Tarrasa in Catalonia are further African characteristics. Only in the late 6th century did Rome exert an impact on church planning in southern Italy and Spain. The planning of S Leucio at Canosa in Apulia, an aisled tetraconch inscribed in a square (?5th–6th century), was inspired not by Roman models but by eastern Mediterranean examples.

In fear of Alaric, the Western emperor Honorius (*reg* 395–423) transferred his residence and the court from Milan to Ravenna *c.* 402–3. During the next 150 years numerous secular and ecclesiastical buildings were founded in Ravenna by members of the court, local bishops and prosperous citizens. The oldest surviving church from this period is S Giovanni Evangelista (*c.* 426/7–34; remodelled) built by GALLA PLACIDIA. Constructed of brick, as were most Roman monuments in the area, it is a well-lit three-aisled basilica terminating in an apse with a polygonal exterior and flanked by sizeable square chambers. The nave was separated from the aisles by colonnaded arcades consisting of reused bases, shafts and capitals, the only known example of spolia in the church architecture of Ravenna. Galla Placidia also founded the cross-shaped church of Santa Croce. Appended to the south end of its long narthex is the

16. S Sabina, Rome, 422–32; apse and nave from the east

mausoleum of Galla Placidia (*see* RAVENNA, §2(ii)). It is a small cruciform structure with a high centre bay surmounted by a pendentive dome and giving access to four low barrel-vaulted arms all sheathed in figural mosaics.

Ravenna became the centre of the Ostrogothic kingdom of Italy, and under Theodoric (*reg* 489–526) several major architectural enterprises were undertaken here and elsewhere in northern Italy. His principal ecclesiastical foundation was his palace church now known as S Apollinare Nuovo (*see* RAVENNA, §2(vi)) which, like S Giovanni Evangelista, is a basilica with a wide nave flanked on either side by an aisle; an atrium originally stood to the west. Theodoric also built an Arian episcopal centre consisting of the cathedral (now Santo Spirito), a free-standing baptistery (*see* RAVENNA, §2(i)) and a bishop's palace (destr.), all presumably intended to rival the older episcopal complex, including the five-aisled Basilica Ursiana (late 4th century; destr.) and octagonal baptistery (*see* RAVENNA, §2(iv)). The Arian cathedral and baptistery, however, incorporate certain intentional differences from their Orthodox predecessors. Santo Spirito is a standard three-aisled basilica, while the mosaic decoration of the Arian baptistery is simpler than that of the Orthodox baptistery. Theodoric's most impressive monument was his two-storey mausoleum (*see* RAVENNA, §2(iii)) which is built entirely of large blocks of ashlar surmounted by a domed single block, a feat of engineering skill that may have been carried out by Isaurian builders who are recorded in 6th-century Thrace, Constantinople, Syria and the Holy Land. Two-storey mausolea had not been built in Italy for over two centuries but were known in 6th-century Syria.

Soon after Theodoric's death the Orthodox bishop Ecclesius (521/2–32) initiated the construction of the church of S Vitale (*see* RAVENNA, §2(vii)) which was financed by a wealthy local banker, Julianus. It is a double-shelled church consisting of an octagonal core surrounded by ambulatories and galleries, and enclosed by an octagonal outer wall. This design was imported from contemporary Constantinople, where the early 6th-century church of SS Sergios and Bakchos (*see* ISTANBUL, §III, 8) represents the same architectural type. Although clearly Byzantine in inspiration, S Vitale reveals local features, such as the greater vertical emphasis and use of earthenware tubes rather than brick in the construction of the dome. Among other churches financed by Julianus, the best preserved is S Apollinare in Classe (*see* RAVENNA, §2(v)). Its plan is rooted in early 5th-century Ravenna and consists of a spacious nave and two aisles preceded by a narthex flanked by two low towers, an apse with a polygonal outside wall and flanked by side chambers, and blind arches framing the wide windows of nave and aisles. Many 6th-century churches survive or are recorded along the northern shore of the Adriatic, for example the cathedral (570s) at GRADO, which replaced a 5th-century church. The planning of these churches is reminiscent of 5th-century models in the Latin West while incorporating certain Eastern elements.

The population of Rome shrank after the 5th century, and the Byzantine occupation of Italy turned the city into a provincial centre. Funds previously available for numerous architectural enterprises dwindled to the point where they were insufficient even to keep older buildings in good repair. Some restoration and even new church construction

were undertaken, however, and the planning of the new churches reveals the infiltration of individual elements from the eastern Mediterranean. Of the two secular public buildings converted to churches, one was the sumptuous hall on the Via Sacra in the Forum, presumably the audience hall of the city prefect, with its domed vestibule, which Pope Felix IV (*reg* 526–30) transformed into the church of SS Cosma e Damiano. The second was the edifice at the foot of the Palatine Hill, which in the second half of the 6th century became the church of S Maria Antiqua (*see* ROME, §V, 19).

Of the five new 6th-century churches, three were built in the centre of Rome: SS Quirico e Giulitta (537), SS Apostoli (*c.* 560) and S Giovanni a Porta Latina (*c.* 550). The two churches outside the Aurelianic walls are the basilica (*c.* 600) over the Domitilla catacomb and the church (579–90) over the tomb of St Lawrence, which forms the chancel of the present 13th-century church of S Lorenzo fuori le mura. These basilicas incorporated some Byzantine elements: a trefoil chancel at SS Quirico e Giulitta and perhaps at SS Apostoli; an apse with a polygonal outside wall, a forechoir and side chambers at S Giovanni a Porta Latina; and galleries over the side aisles and inner narthex at S Lorenzo and possibly in the basilica over the Domitilla catacomb. Aisled basilicas with galleries were previously unknown in Rome and elsewhere in Italy, although they are characteristic of churches in the East and in Algeria from as early as the 4th century. In Rome, it seems, galleries were added to basilicas to provide space for the crowds of pilgrims seeking access to the graves of Roman martyrs.

Transalpine Europe. Trier had been Constantine the Great's residence before he departed for Rome in 312. Possibly as early as 315–21 an aisled basilical hall was begun on the site of the present Liebfraukirche, while later, beginning *c.* 324–6, a second aisled basilica (remains of which survive in the present cathedral) was laid out to the north and parallel to the south basilica. A square bapistery was erected between these parallel basilicas, perhaps between 330 and 340, and was originally accessible from the south basilica. Although these two basilicas were not planned from the outset as a pair and are not known to have functioned in tandem, they have been identified as a double cathedral. For unknown reasons the east end of the north basilica was substantially remodelled between 364 and 383 as a huge block subdivided into nine bays of unequal size, the largest being the centre bay (*c.* 20 m on a side), which rose to a fenestrated square tower and pyramidal roof covered by brick tiles. The towered silhouette of this block closely resembles the slightly earlier church of S Lorenzo in Milan.

The Romanesque church of St Gereon at Cologne (*see* COLOGNE, §IV, 2(i)), preserves the decagon (diam. 24 m) of a late 4th-century martyrium, which rose on the site of a small shrine. A double-apsed narthex gave access to the decagon: while the narthex and atrium resemble the corresponding elements of S Lorenzo at Milan, the decagon is related to the domed decagonal pavilion (diam. 25 m) known as Minerva Medica at Rome (310–20; *see* ROME, ANCIENT, §II, 2(i)(g)). Imperial palace architecture may thus have provided the source for some Early

Christian martyria. In general, however, Early Christian churches in the territories from the Danube and the Rhine to northern Gaul were small aisleless rectangular halls, often lacking an apse. Such box churches remained common in transalpine Europe to the time of Charlemagne; some were constructed of wood.

The earliest evidence of Christian architecture in Britain is found at Lullingstone, Kent, where one wing of the upper floor of a spacious villa or estate home was sealed off from the rest of the complex in the third quarter of the 4th century and converted into a Christian chapel and antechamber provided with figural wall paintings; the rest of the building continued in use as a private residence until the site was destroyed in the 5th century. Research at other sites such as Canterbury, Lincoln, Stoneby-Faversham and Wells suggest that certain Christian buildings continued in use from the 4th to the 7th century.

North Africa. By the early 4th century Christianity had spread throughout the towns and countryside of North Africa, and its growth is reflected in numerous churches and monasteries. This region was also the focal point of many religious disputes, such as Donatism (4th–8th century), Arianism (4th–5th century), the Three Chapters controversy (543–53) and Monotheletism (7th century). The cult of martyrs assumed enormous importance; martyria are usually basilicas rather than centrally planned buildings as in the eastern Mediterranean, although small triconch and tetraconch martyria are known from the 3rd century onwards. Relics were also deposited in churches, often intramural parish churches, in vaults under the altar or in crypts placed below the altar and the apse.

Most Early Christian churches recorded before the Byzantine occupation (534–5) are standard basilicas of the Latin type; they are found in Mauretania (western Algeria), Numidia, Byzacene (Tunisia), Tripolitania, Cyrenaica, Egypt (see COPTIC ART, §II, 3) and the Sudan. They usually incorporate certain local elements, such as a tall timber-roofed nave terminating in a semicircular apse (a building type used by the Romans in the pre-Constantinian era) and separated by arcaded colonnades from the lower side aisles. At least 22 basilicas have more than two side aisles, creating broad rather than elongated buildings, but the number of aisles is unrelated to the overall dimensions of the building. In some instances side aisles supported galleries, as in a 6th-century pilgrimage church at THEVESTIS. More than 15 basilicas with counter-apses are known; the second apse seems related to the cult of martyrs in urban churches, although it was sometimes used as a place of burial, as in the case of Bishop Alexander's nine-aisled basilica (c. 400) at Tipaza, Algeria, which was filled with graves. Nave supports are occasionally arranged in pairs, either as a double column or a column and pier. Triple arcades sometimes screen the front of apses, and the principal altar was often positioned in the middle of the nave. Only a dozen atria are known in North Africa; they characterize the larger churches. Examples of double basilicas include those at Djemila, near Sétif, Algeria, and at Sbeïtla, Tunisia. Baptisteries are usually small rectangular or square rooms, projecting from the rear or flank of a side aisle, but accompanied by subsidiary chambers. Large free-standing baptisteries are rare, although an octagonal example is recorded at Siagu (now Ksar al-Zit, nr Bir bou Rekba), Tunisia.

In contrast to Italy, North African churches sometimes belonged to compounds known as 'Christian quarters', and are reminiscent of pre-Constantinian Christian community centres combining religious and secular structures, but laid out more systematically and on a grand scale. The double basilica at Djemila forms part of such a compound, while another example is at Hippo Regius (both ?early 5th century). In addition to its double basilica, Djemila has a baptistery, baths, two open courtyards, a bishop's palace, dwellings for the clergy and administrative and utilitarian buildings.

The largest church in North Africa is the Damous al-Karita basilica (?4th century) at Carthage. It has a nave and eight aisles (l. c. 65 m) and is accompanied by secondary structures that more than double its length. A corridor or transept runs across the centre with four groups of four piers; each group may have carried a pyramidal roof or a dome. Small mausolea cling to the flanks of the basilica and to the semicircular atrium in front of the church. Halls, basilicas and a subterranean rotunda, as well as other mausolea, are positioned in the vicinity of the basilica. Damous al-Karita was perhaps a pilgrimage centre of a martyr cult or a covered cemetery church.

After the Byzantine capture of North Africa, new elements penetrated church planning, some of which appear in the church of Dar al-Kous (6th century) at Le Kef, Tunisia: paired columns flank the nave, the aisles are covered by groin vaults, and the semi-dome of the apse is scalloped. The 6th-century basilicas in Tripolitania and Tunisia generally had vaulted aisles and timber-roofed naves, although the latter were occasionally vaulted. In the 6th-century 'fortress church' at PTOLEMAIS the nave and aisles were barrel-vaulted, and a pendentive dome covered the side chamber to the north of the apse. Since vaulted naves and aisles are rare in Italy, their appearance in North Africa must have been inspired by Justinianic architecture at Constantinople and in the Aegean coastlands. Apse walls were sometimes hollowed out by a series of niches, as at Leptis Magna and in churches in the Nile Valley.

Basilicas with triconch chancels occur at Deir al-Abyad (c. 440) near SOHAG, at Khirbat Bou Hadef (5th century), Algeria, and at Thevestis (c. 400). These chancels derive from the free-standing trilobed memoriae frequent during the 3rd and 4th centuries in pagan and Christian cemeteries in Tunisia and Algeria. The first recorded example of a triconch apse is in the Basilica Nova (401–3) at CIMITILE-NOLA, which is probably derived from North African examples.

BIBLIOGRAPHY

S. Gsell: *Les Monuments antiques de l'Algérie*, ii (Paris, 1901)
P. Gauckler: *Basiliques chrétiennes de Tunisie* (Paris, 1913)
R. Krautheimer: *Corpus Basilicarum Christianarum Romae: The Early Christian Basilicas of Rome (IV–IX Centuries)*, 5 vols (Vatican City, 1937–77)
P. Verzone: *L'architettura religiosa dell'alto medioevo nell'Italia settentrionale* (Milan, 1942)
A. de' Capitani d'Arzago: *Architetture dei secoli quarto e quinto in alta Italia* (Milan, 1944)
J. B. Ward-Perkins: 'The Italian Element in Late Roman and Early Medieval Architecture', *Proc. Brit. Acad.*, xxxiii (1947), pp. 163–94
——: 'The Christian Antiquities of Tripolitania', *Archaeologia*, xcv (1953), pp. 1–82

R. Krautheimer: 'The Architecture of Sixtus III: A Fifth-century Renascence?', *Essays in Honour of Erwin Panofsky (De Artibus Opuscola XL)*, ed. M. Meiss (New York, 1961), pp. 291–302

L. Voelkl: *Die Kirchenstiftungen des Kaisers Konstantin im Lichte des römischen Sakralrechts* (Cologne, 1964)

R. Krautheimer: 'Constantine's Church Foundations', *Akten des VII. internationalen Kongresses für christliche Archäologie: Trier, 1965*, i, pp. 237–55

Vorromanische Kirchenbauten: Katalog der Denkmäler bis zum Ausgang der Ottonen, 3 vols (exh. cat., ed. F. Oswald, L. Schaefer and H. R. Sennhausen; Munich, Zentinst. Kstgesch, 1966–71)

A. Venditti: *Architettura bizantina nell'Italia meridionale: Campania-Calabria-Lucania*, 2 vols (Naples, 1967)

P.-A. Février and N. Duval: 'Les Monuments chrétiens de la Gaule transalpine', *Actas del VIII Congreso internacional de arqueología cristiana: Barcelona, 1969*, i, pp. 57–106

F. W. Deichmann: *Ravenna, Hauptstadt des spätantiken Abendlandes*, 3 vols (Wiesbaden, 1969–89)

N. Duval: *Sbeitla et les églises africaines à deux absides*, 2 vols (Paris, 1971–3)

B. Brenk: *Spätantike und frühes Christentum* (Frankfurt, 1977)

U. Süssenbach: *Christuskult und kaiserliche Baupolitik bei Konstantin: Die Anfänge der christlichen Verknüpfung kaiserlicher Repräsentation am Beispiel der Kirchenstiftungen Konstantins-Grundlagen* (Bonn, 1977)

R. Krautheimer: 'Success and Failure in Late Antique Church Planning', *Age of Spirituality: A Symposium: New York, 1977–8*, pp. 121–39

H. Brandenburg: *Roms frühchristliche Basiliken des 4. Jahrhunderts* (Munich, 1979)

F. W. Deichmann: *Rom, Ravenna, Konstantinopel, Naher Osten: Gesammelte Studien zur spätantiken Architektur, Kunst und Geschichte* (Wiesbaden, 1982)

Y. Duval: *Loca sanctorum Africae*, 2 vols (Rome, 1982)

F. W. Deichmann: *Einführung in die christliche Archäologie: Die Kunstwissenschaft* (Darmstadt, 1983)

R. Krautheimer: *Three Christian Capitals: Topography and Politics* (Berkeley, 1983)

Actes du XIe Congrès international d'archéologie chrétienne: Lyon, Vienne, Grenoble, Genève et Aoste, 1986 [esp. articles by N. Duval, K. S. Painter and J.-C. Picard]

N. Gauthier and J.-C. Picard, eds: *Topographie chrétienne des cités de la Gaule des origines au milieu du VIIIe siècle* (Paris, 1986–)

G. C. Menis: *Il complesso episcopale teodoriano di Aquileia e il suo battistero* (Udine, 1986)

S. de Blaauw: *Cultus et decor: Liturgie en architectuur in laatantiek en middeleeuws Rome: Basilica Salvatoris Sanctae Mariae, Sancti Petri* (Delft, 1988)

M. J. Johnson: 'Toward a History of Theodoric's Building Program', *Dumbarton Oaks Pap.*, xlii (1988), pp. 73–96

J. Onians: *Bearers of Meaning: The Classical Orders in Antiquity, the Middle Ages, and the Renaissance* (Princeton, 1988)

A. Schwarz: *Architektur und Gesellschaft von Kaiser Konstantin bis zu Karl dem Grossen* (Leipzig, 1989)

Milano: Capitale dell'impero romano, 286–402 d.c. (exh. cat., ed. A. Salvoni; Milan, Pal. Reale, 1990)

H. Brandenburg: 'La chiesa di S Stefano Rotondo a Roma', *Riv. Archaeol. Crist.*, lxvii (1992), pp. 201–22

W. E. Kleinbauer: *Early Christian and Byzantine Architecture: Annotated Bibliography and Historiography* (Boston, 1992)

J. E. James: *Early Christian Cathedral Architecture in Trier* (diss., Bloomington, IN U., 1993)

W. EUGENE KLEINBAUER

(b) Constantinople and Asia Minor. The Christian buildings put up by Constantine the Great in his new imperial centre of Constantinople are known only from literary sources. The most important were the episcopal church of Hagia Eirene (*see* ISTANBUL, §III, 5), which probably replaced a smaller, pre-Constantinian church, and the church of the Holy Apostles (*see* ISTANBUL, §III, 9(i)), which was intended as the Emperor's mausoleum. The initial form of Hagia Eirene is uncertain, since it was completely destroyed by fire in the Nike Riot of 532 and replaced by a domed basilica. That of the Holy Apostles also remains subject to argument. Mango (p. 27) has

suggested that the original church built by Constantine was a round building similar to the mausoleum of Galerius, later converted into the church of Hagios Georgios (*see* THESSALONIKI, §III, 2) and that the present cruciform church was built adjacent to it by Constantine's son Constantius II (*reg* 337–61), who is known to have brought its first relics in 356 and 357. The cruciform plan and the building's use as a self-sufficient MARTYRIUM influenced the construction of numerous churches throughout the empire, including the church of the Holy Apostles (now S Nazaro; 382) in Milan; Santa Croce (*c.* 425) in Ravenna; St Babylas (*c.* 379) at Kaoussie (*see* ANTIOCH (i), §3); the church above the Well of Jacob (*c.* 381–7; destr.) near Shechem (now Tall Balatah), Palestine; the cruciform church (402) founded by Empress Eudokia at Gaza; and the redesigned structure (after 400) over the tomb of St John the Evangelist (*see* EPHESOS, §I, 3).

Constantinople's most famous church, that of Hagia Sophia (*see* ISTANBUL, §III, 1(i)), was first dedicated in 360 and rededicated in 415, after being damaged by fire in 404. In both these phases it was a spacious colonnaded basilica with a portico and grand central propylon that derive from traditional secular building traditions in the Greek cities along the west coast of Asia Minor, such as Ephesos and Miletos. Although the basilica became the standard plan for congregational churches throughout the empire, one of the few 4th-century examples in Asia Minor outside Constantinople is the ruined three-aisled basilica known as Church EA (*c.* 350–60), with a projecting semicircular apse, western narthex and atrium, at Sardis.

Among the 5th-century ecclesiastical foundations in Constantinople, only the monastery church of St John Stoudios (see fig. 10 above and ISTANBUL, §IV, 6) survives: it is a three-aisled basilica with galleries and a semicircular apse encased within a three-sided external shell. The proportions are squat but harmonious. Similar galleried basilicas in and near Constantinople are known from the remains of the Theotokos Chalkoprateia (*c.* 450) near Hagia Sophia, and from contemporary descriptions of the church of Hagia Euphemia (before 450; destr.) at Chalcedon (now Kadiköy) and the church of the Theotokos (*c.* 450; rebuilt 518–27; destr.) in the Blachernai Palace. The influence of this type of basilica with galleries elsewhere in the empire is recognizable in the Old Metropolis (*c.* 6th century; 10th century) at NESEBÅR, and Hagia Sophia (5th or 6th century; rebuilt *c.* 1065) at Iznik (*see* IZNIK, §1).

Despite the continued close contact between Constantinople and Greek settlements in Asia Minor, by the mid-5th century ecclesiastical architecture had begun to reflect the area's division into numerous regions, each with its own traditions. Standard types of the 5th and 6th centuries in Cappadocia (*see* CAPPADOCIA, §2(i)) are domed cross churches and barrel-vaulted basilicas with horseshoe-shaped apses, at times polygonal on the exterior. In Lycaonia (e.g. BINBIRKILISE) basilicas with three aisles and arcades supporting horseshoe-shaped arches prevail. The large-scale basilicas (5th–6th century) of Pisidia and Pamphylia have cross-aisled and continuous transepts (i.e. with and without aisles respectively) in place of simple chancel plans (e.g. Basilica CC, Side; basilicas A and B, Perge; churches E and E1, Sagalassos); the apse is usually flanked by lateral rooms encased within a straight wall. The churches in Lycia usually have a single projecting apse (e.g. Kekova island and Andriake), while in Cilicia the main apse is flanked by rooms that frequently appear as apsed, single-nave chapels, as in the basilica of St Thekla (*c.* 480) at Meriamlık. Another distinctive feature of St Thekla and other Cilician churches is the tribelon or triple arcade linking the nave and aisles with the narthex. Also at Meriamlık are the remains of what may be the earliest known example of a domed basilica (476–94). Its nave was flanked by barrel-vaulted aisles and galleries, and divided by piers into two nearly square bays. Two alternative roofing systems for the central bays have been proposed: the first places a barrel vault over the west bay and a stone dome over the east bay; the second, an ordinary timber roof over the west bay and a pyramidal timber construction over the east bay. Whichever reconstruction is accepted, the building marks a significant stage in the development of domed basilicas. Churches with similar plans are the East Church (late 5th century or early 6th) at ALAHAN MONASTERY, the contemporary basilicas at Dağpazarı and the churches at KORYKOS. A different type of church is the centrally planned octagon within a square (?second half of 5th century) outside the walls of Hierapolis (*see* HIERAPOLIS, §1), which is usually identified as the martyrium of the Apostle Philip.

Although the basilica remained the preferred architectural type for church construction in the 6th century, several domed, centrally planned churches were built with imperial backing in or near Constantinople. The earliest recorded example is the church of St Polyeuktos (524–7; destr.) erected by ANICIA JULIANA. Excavations have revealed that it was a longitudinal building with a narthex and projecting apse and that it stood on an elevated platform to which a staircase led from the ground-level atrium. The church had six curved exedrae and a gallery, and was probably domed. Its unusual and ornate architectural decoration contains many Sasanian motifs that are undoubtedly a reflection of Byzantine building activities on the empire's eastern frontier. Between 527 and 536, Justinian I and Theodora founded the church of SS Sergios and Bakchos; it is a domed octagon within a square and has a vaulted ambulatory and gallery (see fig. 17). According to Prokopios (*Buildings* I.viii.6–16), Justinian built two further churches (*c.* 560; destr.) with domed double-shell octagon plans: St John the Baptist in the Hebdomon (now Macrikeuy) and St Michael in Anaplus (now Arnautkeuy). Another variant of this plan was probably that of the Chrysotriklinos (after 565; destr.), the golden throne room of the Great Palace (*see* ISTANBUL, §III, 12).

The most important and spectacular achievement not only of 6th-century but of all Byzantine architecture is Justinian's rebuilding of Hagia Sophia (*see* ISTANBUL, §III, 1(ii)(a)). Although its plan contains all the elements of a double-shell octagon, it has been divided in half with a dome (diam. 30 m) placed over the centre to create a longitudinal basilica-type structure. The original dome collapsed in 558 and was replaced with what is essentially the present dome. The numerous structural innovations and the failure to respect Classical norms, as in the use of column shafts of uneven height on the ground floor and the non-alignment of ground floor and gallery columns,

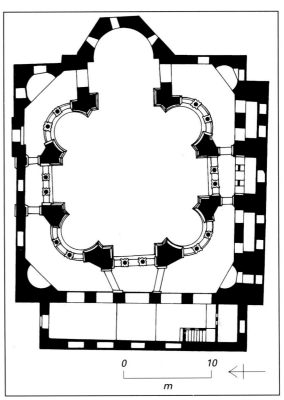

17. SS Sergios and Bakchos, Istanbul, Turkey, 527–36, ground-plan

reflect a conscious rejection of the Classical canon of architecture.

Two further large-scale building projects undertaken by Justinian were the reconstruction of Hagia Eirene as a three-aisled basilica with a central dome (diam. *c.* 16 m), and of the church of the Holy Apostles, which kept its cruciform plan but was surmounted by five domes. The latter design is reflected in the reconstruction of the church of St John the Evangelist (begun before 548) at Ephesos and, much later, in the plan adopted for the church of S Marco (*c.* 1063) in Venice. In general, however, the architectural forms and vaulting techniques found in the 6th-century churches of Constantinople did not gain a foothold in the coastal towns of Asia Minor. Inland, in central Lycia, there are four surviving three-aisled ashlar basilicas with trefoil sanctuaries; one example is the church (530s) at Karabel; the unusual building type seems to reflect Palestinian or Egyptian influences, while the ashlar construction must have had Syrian roots.

BIBLIOGRAPHY

F. W. Deichmann: *Studien zur Architektur Konstantinopels im 5. und 6. Jahrhundert nach Christus* (Baden-Baden, 1956)

R. W. Harrison: 'Churches and Chapels of Central Lycia', *Anatol. Stud.*, xiii (1963), pp. 122–51

T. F. Mathews: *The Early Churches of Constantinople: Architecture and Liturgy* (University Park, PA, and London, 1971)

W. Müller-Wiener: *Bildlexikon zur Topographie Istanbuls* (Tübingen, 1977)

H. Buchwald: 'Western Asia Minor as a Generator of Architectural Forms in the Byzantine Period: Provincial Back-wash or Dynamic Center of Production?', *Jb. Osterreich. Byz.*, xxxiv (1984), pp. 199–234

F. Hild, H. Hellenkemper and G. Hellenkemper-Salies: 'Kommagene, Kilikien, Isaurien', *RBK*, iv (1984) [esp. cols 191–319]

C. Mango: *Le Développement urbain de Constantinople, IVe–VIIe siècles*, Travaux et Mémoires du Centre de Recherche d'Histoire et Civilisation de Byzance, ii (Paris, 1985)

(c) Greece and the Balkans. Although few church remains survive from the 4th century, numerous standing and excavated churches date to the 5th and 6th centuries. The standard building type is the three-aisled basilica with a wooden roof, an atrium and narthex and colonnaded arcades, usually surmounted by galleries, which divide the interior. Distinctive local features are the semicircular shape of the apse both inside and out, and the tribelon, or triple arch, connecting the narthex with the nave. Additional rooms or extensions, such as the diakonikon (service room) and baptistery, are usually found at the west end alongside the narthex. The most frequent variant of the simple basilican type is the transept basilica in which the transverse unit between the nave and the apse is either contained within straight walls, as in Basilica A (*c.* 470; see fig. 12 above) at Nea Anchialos, or, as is more common, projects beyond the north and south walls, as in Basilica A, also known as the Basilica of Dometios (second quarter of the 6th century) at Nikopolis. From the second half of the 5th century numerous large transept basilicas with more complex designs and richer decoration were built. One of the most impressive churches is the ruined three-aisled basilica of St Leonidas (450–60) at Lechaion, the port of Corinth. Its elongated plan (l. *c.* 110 m) includes a narthex, a nave and aisles, a tripartite transept with projecting wings and a half-domed apse. Justin I (*reg* 518–27) added an atrium and semicircular forecourt on the west side, and a separate baptistery to the north of the narthex. Two lavish examples of cross-transept basilicas are the excavated ruins of Basilica A (*c.* 500) at Philippi and the five-aisled basilica of Hagios Demetrios (mid-5th century–early 6th; rebuilt *c.* 620) at Thessaloniki (*see* THESSALONIKI, §III, 3(i)).

A particularly interesting and varied group of church buildings of the 6th century has been recovered at Caričin Grad. Those of basilican plan are drawn from types found in Constantinople and the southern Balkans, and are merged with local elements. Among the smaller churches at Caričin Grad are a vaulted, cross-shaped church and a barrel-vaulted triconch chapel. A similar variety of church plans appeared throughout Greece and the Balkans in the 6th century. Basilicas with cruciform ground-plans were built at THASOS (early 6th century; destr.) and at Salona (*c.* 530; *see* SALONA, §2). At Paramythia, Dodona and Klapsi, all in Epiros, apses project from the ends of tripartite- and continuous-transept basilicas; while the Red Church (*c.* 500) at PERUSHTITSA still preserves its quatrefoil plan. Among the few examples of vaulted transept basilicas with a dome over the crossing are Basilica B (*c.* 540) at Philippi, the church of Katapoliani or Hekatontapyliani (Our Lady of the Hundred Gates; *c.* 550) on Paros, Hagios Titos (late 6th century) at Gortyn, Crete (*see* GORTYN, §2), and St Sophia (6th or 7th century) in SOFIA. A more unusual plan is that of the 6th-century church at Konjuh, south of Caričin Grad. It has a circular nave surrounded by an ambulatory, which creates a rectangular outer shell. Whereas the domed basilicas represent permutations of Justinian's churches at Constantinople, the closest parallel to the church at Konjuh is that of the Archangels (526–7) at Fal'lul in north-west Syria.

BIBLIOGRAPHY
G. Soteriou: 'Ai palaiochristianikai basilikai tis Ellados' [The Early Christian basilicas of Greece], *Archaiol. Ephemeris* (1929), pp. 161–248
R. F. Hoddinott: *Early Byzantine Churches in Macedonia and Southern Serbia* (London, 1963)
D. Pallas: *Les Monuments paléochrétiens de Grèce découverts de 1959 à 1973* (Rome, 1977)
T. Ulbert: 'Die religiöse Architektur im östlichen Illyricum', *Actes du Xe Congrès international d'archéologie chrétienne: Thessalonike, 1980*, i, pp. 161–80

(d) Syria, Palestine and Mesopotamia. The ecclesiastical architecture of these regions includes episcopal and parish constructions as well as important pilgrimage shrines, particularly in the Holy Land. Although this section deals mainly with churches and baptisteries, it is worth noting that non-ecclesiastical types of architecture such as baths, inns, tombs, dormitories and episcopal palaces may also have served a religious function by association with a shrine or monastery (*see* §3(iii) below). In this period, Syria, Palestine and Mesopotamia consisted of the administrative provinces of Syria I and II, two of Euphratensis, Phoenicia Maritima and Libanensis, Arabia, Palestine I–III, Osrhoene, two of Mesopotamia and Armenia IV. Each province was under the jurisdiction of an archbishop who had a cathedral in the capital city (i.e. Antioch, Apameia, Hierapolis, Rusafa, Tyre, Damascus, Bostra (now Bosra), Caesarea, Scythopolis, Petra, Edessa, Amida, Dara and Martyropolis). The bishops of Antioch and Jerusalem had patriarchal churches. Each city in each province had a bishop and a cathedral, as well as numerous parish churches administered by priests. Villages could also have more than one church. Monasteries, which were private institutions in this period, also had a church. Church buildings were funded by the secular State (often ultimately in the name of the emperor), by the church itself and often by private donations. Architectural influences sometimes reflect the administrative links of the church hierarchy, as in the case of the aisled tetraconch church (see below). The principal architectural types used for churches in these provinces, as elsewhere, were of oblong (particularly the basilica) or of centralized plan. Although a few city churches remain standing, most are known through excavation. Their loss is compensated for by the large numbers of village churches that survive to roof height in northern Syria.

Materials, techniques and decoration. The masonry of ecclesiastical architecture in Syria, Palestine and Mesopotamia is principally of well-cut stone assembled with little or no mortar, as in the 6th-century North Church (a basilica; see fig. 18) at Deir Sim'an. Internal supports were provided by either columns or piers. No marble was available locally, but, as elsewhere, Preconnesian and other marbles were imported. In areas where limestone was used, architectural sculpture, including capitals, can be elaborate and inventive: a particularly fine limestone was used at RUSAFA, while the capitals of the monastery church of St Catherine on Sinai (*see* SINAI, §2(i)) were fashioned in a simplified, almost crude style, from basalt. Trussed timber roofs were used for basilicas and other oblong-planned buildings. The roofing of a centralized church or baptistery is often open to speculation (e.g. a wooden or masonry dome, a wooden pyramidal roof), as relatively little direct physical evidence survives. The interiors of buildings were often decorated with wall paintings, tessellated or marble *opus sectile* pavements and glass wall and vault mosaics, examples of which survive in the monastery of St Catherine (*see* SINAI, §2(ii)) and TUR 'ABDIN. In the 4th century and possibly later, the ceilings of oblong buildings were coffered and, perhaps, gilded. There is excavated evidence for windows glazed with colourless and coloured panes. Churches were further adorned with metal: liturgical furniture is known from written sources to have been revetted in silver in some churches, and lighting was provided by bronze polykandela holding glass lamps, which were suspended from the ceiling; some lamps were of silver. Liturgical vessels in precious metals were donated to, and displayed in, churches (*see* §VII, 7(i) below). The building, decoration and furnishing of churches were paid for by a variety of sources, from imperial level down to individual members of village churches. Inscriptions demonstrate that donations paid for entire buildings or individual parts thereof (e.g. particular columns, arches, pavement panels). For example, the pavement (Paris, Louvre) from the church of St Christopher at Qabr Hiram near Tyre was laid in 576/7 at the expense of the directors and farmers of two estates and other donors (see Renan).

Cathedral and parish churches. Twenty cathedral churches have been identified by scholars through texts or archaeological remains in Syria, Palestine and Mesopotamia. The earliest recorded cathedrals were built by their bishops at Edessa (now Urfa; 312/13–23), Nisibis (now Nusaybin; 313–20), Antioch (314–24), Tyre (314–17) and perhaps at Caesarea (314–25). Although none of these churches survive, they were probably large basilicas (*see* CHURCH, §I, 1(i)) similar to the one at Tyre described by Eusebios (see Mango, pp. 5–7) and the large basilicas founded by Constantine the Great at Rome (*see* §(a) above); they were built by local initiative to replace churches destroyed during the persecution of 303–12. As Cyril Mango points out, the five cathedrals were not part of an imperial effort to impose a particular type of church building, because they were constructed while the eastern empire was still under the control of the pagan emperor Licinius (*reg* 307–24). The basilica remained the most common type of church in both city and countryside, except for pilgrimage shrines (see below), which became more elaborate in plan. Following Constantine's victory over the eastern empire (324), the written sources indicate that he built an octagonal patriarchal cathedral (started 327) at Antioch, which influenced cathedral architecture in the late 5th century and the early 6th (see below). In addition to the 20 identified cathedrals, about a further 80 urban churches are known, 20 each at Antioch and Edessa where written records are abundant.

The earliest city church excavated in Syria–Palestine may be that tentatively dated to 345 at Dibsi Faraj (anc. Neocaesarea) on the River Euphrates. This basilica has outer lateral aisles, an international feature, as well as

18. North Church, Deir Sim'an, Syria, west façade, 6th century

indigenous features such as a tripartite sanctuary and south entrance, both inherited from Syrian pagan temples. The three-aisled basilica with tripartite sanctuary continued to be used for cathedrals and parish churches in Syria–Palestine into the 7th century.

In the late 5th century and the early 6th aisled tetraconch churches were built at Seleucia Pieria, ALEPPO and Apameia in Syria, at Bostra (dedicated to SS Sergius, Bacchus and Leontios; 512–13; see fig. 19) and Zorava in Arabia, and at Rusafa and Amida in Mesopotamia. Eugene Kleinbauer has convincingly argued that they were cathedral churches and not martyria, as has long been held, even though the churches at Bostra and Zorava were dedicated to martyr saints. The discovery in 1985 of a larger church of similar plan at Bostra may, however, indicate that this was the city's cathedral. Kleinbauer has also suggested that the prototype of these churches was Constantine's cathedral at Antioch, which was rebuilt with a wooden dome in 526–37/8. A feature well suited to the aisled tetraconch was the U-shaped Syrian bema, which allowed great crowds to hear and view the sermon and readings better (see below).

Pilgrimage churches. Numerous cities were famous for their pilgrimage churches (*see* MARTYRIUM). While some of these Early Christian churches are known only from the literary sources, for example St Leontios at Tripolis (now Trablous, Lebanon), St George at Diospolis (now Lod, Israel) and St Thomas at Edessa, others survive and have been studied. The earliest martyria in the Holy Land were those constructed by Constantine, namely the Holy Sepulchre (*see* JERUSALEM, §II, 2), the Eleona Church (326–35; see fig. 20) on the Mount of Olives, Jerusalem, and the church of the Nativity (before 333; destr. *c.* 529) at Bethlehem. The centralized church of the Ascension was erected on the Mount of Olives *c.* 375 by a lay woman, Pomoenia or Pompeia. From the 4th century onwards, pilgrims flocked to the Holy Land, where they were received and provided for by a well-organized clergy who offered lodging, rituals and souvenirs. Of the pilgrimage shrines that continued to be built in the 5th century and

19. Aisled tetraconch church of SS Sergius, Bacchus and Leontius, Bostra, Syria, 512–13; exterior view from the south-west, from a drawing *c.* 1860

later, some were imperial works such as the church (*c.* 385) at Gethsemane built by Theodosios I, the church founded by Anastasios I (*reg* 491–518) on the River Jordan, the church of the Nativity (*see* BETHLEHEM, §1) apparently rebuilt by Justinian I *c.* 531, and the monastery church of St Catherine on Sinai, also built by Justinian. The shrine of St James the Less (352) at Jerusalem and the Kathisma Church (*c.* 455) south of the city were erected by wealthy laymen.

Outside the Holy Land pilgrimage churches included the cruciform martyrium of St Babylas (*c.* 381) at Kaoussie (*see* ANTIOCH (i), §3). Its plan of four basilicas projecting from a central chamber was later adopted for the shrine of St Simeon the Stylite the Elder (476–91) at QAL'AT SIM'AN. Although the patronage of this impressive church has been ascribed to Emperor Zeno (*reg* 474–91), it was built by a local workforce. The central chamber was octagonal and surrounded Simeon's column; it is still a matter of debate whether this large space was ever roofed. Attached structures included a monastery, a tomb, a baptistery and a hospice; at the foot of the hill were built several inns for pilgrims, four monasteries and the basilical church at Deir Sim'an. The complex of St Simeon the Stylite the Younger (541–91) to the south-west of Qal'at Sim'an on Samandağı ('Wondrous Mountain') was built as a reduced cruciform version of the Elder's shrine with three churches, inns, a forge, a kitchen, a bakery, a granary, cisterns and a monastery. The shrines of SS Cosmas and Damian (*c.* 457) at Cyrrhus and of SS Sergius and Bacchus (Basilica B; early 6th century) at Rusafa are basilicas.

Village churches. Standing churches (e.g. north church, Deir Sim'an) and excavated village churches are particularly numerous in Syria–Palestine; fewer survive and none has been excavated in Mesopotamia where they become more frequent in the 7th and 8th centuries (*see* §(ii)(c) below). Two types of churches prevailed, the three-aisled basilica and the single-aisle hall church; variant types prevailed in rural Mesopotamia (e.g. Tur 'Abdin). The centralized church was rare in the countryside. The village church, particularly in northern Syria, was not necessarily smaller than the city church, some village churches being over 30 m long. Many of these had a side chapel at the east end of the church, flanking the main sanctuary, where large reliquaries modelled on sarcophagi were installed. Relics obtained, possibly on pilgrimage, thus became the subject of a local cult, and many village churches were dedicated to well-known martyrs (e.g. Sergius, George, Cosmas and Damian). Some villages, such as Babisqa, Baqirha, Behyo and Dehes, have at least two churches of about the same size often built in the same century. In other villages, churches were more numerous: Androna had ten, Thantia fourteen and Rihab nine. This proliferation was probably due to the generous gifts of private donors, rather than a multiplicity of religious sects, as has sometimes been argued.

Monastery churches. Most extant Syrian monastic churches date from the 6th century. In his study of the architecture of northern Syria, Tchalenko suggested a diminution in monastery church size from large basilica,

Early Christian & Byz. art, §II, 2(i): Eccles. arch., c. 313–c. 600: Syria, Palestine & Mesopotamia   541

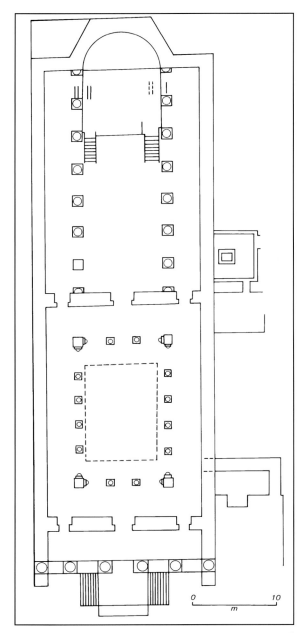

20. Eleona Church, Mount of Olives, Jerusalem, 326–35, ground-plan

to hall church, to chapel, as illustrated by three monasteries at Deir Sim'an. By contrast, the 6th-century monastery churches of Turmanin and Qenneshre were large and magnificent. In the area north of Apameia a new type of monastery church, introduced apparently from Edessa, had its nave in a transverse position to its eastern sanctuary, which in Syria was a single projecting room. In Syria this type of church also had a second storey and a timber roof, rather than a masonry vault.

Baptisteries. The earliest example is the 3rd-century baptistery at Dura Europos (*see* DURA EUROPOS, §4).

According to a Greek dedicatory inscription, the extant baptistery at Nisibis was built by the city's bishop in 359, presumably alongside the cathedral (destr.). The Nisibis baptistery is square in plan with a vestibule and has elaborate sculptural decoration. In 369–70 a baptistery was built at the cathedral of Edessa, also in Mesopotamia. Baptisteries were also built at pilgrimage shrines, as for example the octagonal baptistery at Qal'at Sim'an. Baptisteries were also built in villages, as at Dar Qita, where at least two churches had a baptistery: one church was built in 418 and had a baptistery added in 515; the second church was built in 537 and the baptistery was either built then or added in 567. It is possible that the two baptisteries served two different communities in the village: the Orthodox and the Monophysites.

U-shaped bema. Many churches in northern Syria had in the centre of their naves a rectangular masonry platform with an apse to the west, hence the name U-shaped bema. Although this structure differs in size and shape from a standard Byzantine bema or ambo (*see* CHURCH, §IV, 1 and 2), it has nevertheless been identified variously as a bema, a tribune, an ambo and an exedra. It has rows of seats for up to 12 people along its lateral and its curved side where there was a 'throne' in the centre. The small size of the throne indicates that it was not intended as a seat for a bishop or member of the clergy but to hold a book; a ciborium on four columns stood in the centre of some bemas. Confined mostly to the province of Syria I, the U-shaped bema appears in about 40 churches of both congregational and martyrial function; none occurs in monasteries. Most are in villages; a few appear in the cities of Antioch, Seleucia Pieria and Rusafa. Among the earliest examples are those in the churches at Dibsi Faraj (possibly 345–6), Fafertin (372) and in St Babylas (387) at Antioch; most other bemas are attributed to the 5th or 6th century. They were presumably used for readings and the sermon; the relevant liturgical texts date from the 8th century onwards and are therefore of little use in explaining the bema's precise function.

E. Renan: *Mission de Phénicie* (Paris, 1864), pp. 513–14, 543, 607–26
H. Vincent and F. M. Abel: *Jérusalem nouvelle* (1926), ii of *Jérusalem: Recherches de topographie, d'archéologie et d'histoire* (Paris, 1914–26)
J. W. Crowfoot: *The Churches at Jerash* (London, 1931)
S. J. Saller and B. Bagatti: *The Town of Nebo (Khirbet el-Mekhayyat)* (Jerusalem, 1949)
G. Tchalenko: *Villages antiques de la Syrie du Nord: Le Massif du Bélus à l'époque romaine* (Paris, 1953–80)
A. Ovadiah: *Corpus of Byzantine Churches in the Holy Land* (Bonn, 1970)
C. Mango: *Sources and Documents: The Art of the Byzantine Empire, 312–1453* (Englewood Cliffs, NJ, 1972/R Toronto, Buffalo and London, 1986)
G. Forsyth and K. Weitzmann: *The Monastery of Saint Catherine at Mount Sinai: The Church and Fortress of Justinian* (Ann Arbor, 1973)
W. E. Kleinbauer: 'The Origins and Functions of the Aisled Tetraconch Churches in Syria and Northern Mesopotamia', *Dumbarton Oaks Pap.*, xxvii (1973), pp. 89–114
G. Tchalenko and E. Baccache: *Eglises de village de la Syrie du Nord: Planches et album* (Paris, 1979–80)
A. Ovadiah: 'Supplementum to the Corpus of the Byzantine Churches in the Holy Land', *Levant*, xiii (1981), pp. 200–61; xiv (1982), pp. 122–70
M. Mundell Mango: *Artistic Patronage in the Roman Diocese of 'Oriens', 313–641 AD* (diss., U. Oxford, 1985)
G. Tchalenko: *Eglises syriennes à bêma* (Paris, 1990)
P.-L. Gatier: 'Les Inscriptions grecques d'époque islamique (VIIe–VIIIe siècles) en Syrie du Sud', *La Syrie de Byzance à l'Islam VIIe–VIIIe*

siècles, ed. P. Canivet and J.-P. Rey-Coquais (Damascus, 1992), pp. 145–57

MARLIA MUNDELL MANGO

(ii) c. 600–c. 843. This was a time of great social, political and economic change marked by the permanent settlement of the Slavs in the Balkans; the war with Iran (605–26); the rise of the Arabs under the banner of Islam and their occupation of Syria, Palestine, Egypt, North Africa and Cyprus in the 630s and 640s; the sieges of Constantinople by the Arabs in 674–8 and 717–18; the rise of the Bulgars in the 9th century; and the theological debates that led to the iconoclastic controversy (726–843). Material and documentary evidence for buildings is scant, and the period is often referred to as the Dark Age of Byzantine history. However, the re-examination of existing evidence and the gradual accumulation of new archaeological finds suggest that this rather pessimistic view may have to be tempered.

(a) Constantinople and Asia Minor. One of the few churches that can be dated with some certainty is the rebuilding of Hagia Eirene (*see* ISTANBUL, §IV, 4) after the severe earthquake of 740. Although it retained its basilican plan of a nave, two aisles and a narthex, with galleries over the narthex and aisles, the columnar arcades on the north and south sides are interrupted by heavy piers. These carry the deep transverse barrel vaults and the arches to the east and west over the nave, which in turn support the main dome. This architectural type, sometimes known as the compact-domed basilica, belongs to the cross-domed group of churches built in brick or alternating bands of brick and ashlar. The apse usually has a polygonal outer wall and is flanked by pastophoria (service rooms). Examples of this type include the church (*c.* 750 or late 9th century–early 10th) at DEREAĞZI, Hagios Nikolaos (9th century) at MYRA, and St Clement (?9th century; destr. 1921) at Ankara, which is known only from old photographs and a survey made in 1927. In St Clement, the gallery above the aisles and narthex was supported by two slender marble piers on each side. The

same arrangement of piers was repeated at gallery level. The corner rooms at either end of the aisles were virtually separate from the rest of the structure. The building's pumpkin dome and elegant proportions foreshadow Middle Byzantine ecclesiastical architecture. Among the few genuine cross-domed churches that have survived or are documented is the church of the Dormition (?early 8th century; 1065; destr. 1922) at Nicaea (*see* IZNIK, §1). Its plan originally comprised a cross of four equal barrel vaults flanking a central dome at its core, bordered by aisles and a narthex. Attempts have been made to place all these churches at stages in a process of evolution that linked the domed basilica with the cross-in-square church (*see* §(iii)(a) below), but uncertainty as to the date of most of them and their wide geographical dispersal make the relationship between the different types problematic.

(b) Greece and the Balkans. The two principal churches usually cited for this period are that of Hagia Sophia (now Ayasofya Mosque) at Vize in Thrace and that of Hagia Sophia at Thessaloniki (see fig. 21 and THESSALONIKI, §III, 5(i)). The former is a compact-domed basilica, similar to the churches at Dereagzi, Hagios Nikolaos at Myra and St Clement at Ankara (*see* §(a) above), and probably also dates to the late 8th century or the 9th. Hagia Sophia at Thessaloniki, however, belongs to the true cross-domed type and is often compared with the church of the Dormition at Nicaea. Scholarly opinion favours a mid-8th-century date of construction.

BIBLIOGRAPHY
C. Mango: *Architettura bizantina* (Milan, 1974; Eng. trans., New York, 1976/*R* London, 1986), pp. 90, 96
K. Theocharidou: *The Architecture of Hagia Sophia, Thessaloniki*, Brit. Archaeol. Rep., Int. Ser., 399 (Oxford, 1988)

□

(c) Syria, Palestine and Mesopotamia. In the period *c.* 600–640 these regions were overrun by Persian forces, then by the reconquering armies of the Byzantine emperor Heraklios (*reg* 610–41) and finally by the Umayyad Arabs (*c.* 640). The dominance of Islam for the next 300 years (*see* §(iii)(c) below) ended the favoured status of the Orthodox or Melchite Church, but it did not mean the end of local Christian communities. They continued to build churches, though on a much reduced scale, and to use the numerous and often substantial buildings from earlier centuries. Examples of urban church building and restoration in Syria and Palestine include the construction of churches at Madaba (607–8), Gerasa (611) and perhaps at Areopolis (687), and the paving of another church, possibly in 662, at Madaba. Pilgrimage shrines in Jerusalem, including the Holy Sepulchre, were apparently restored after the reconquest of Heraklios in 628, and it has been suggested, that he, rather than the Umayyad Arabs, initiated construction of the Dome of the Rock (*see* JERUSALEM, §II, 1(iii) and ISLAMIC ART, fig. 17); monasteries were also built in Jerusalem in the 7th century. At another pilgrimage shrine, on Mt Nebo, a chapel was built by private patronage *c.* 604.

More numerous are the churches known to have been built in Mesopotamia, where there are twenty-seven cases recorded in seven cities. At Edessa (now Urfa), a martyrium and bishop's palace were built in 582–602; the 'Old

21. Hagia Sophia, Thessaloniki, Greece, mid-8th century; exterior of east end

Church' was repaired in 679; the Theotokos Church and baptistery were built c. 700; and several other churches were built 793–825. South of Edessa, at Harran, a Jacobite (i.e. Monophysite) church was built in 699 and five other churches were destroyed and then rebuilt c. 813. At Nisibis (now Nusaybin), to the east of Edessa and Harran, a church was built in 600–50; a Nestorian church was built c. 700; five Jacobite churches, monasteries and a hotel (Gr. *xenodochion*) were built or rebuilt in 707–9; and the north church of the cathedral baptistery was apparently built between 713 and 758. North of Nisibis at Dara (now Oğuz) a monastery was built c. 700. Further north, at Amida, Heraklios erected the church of St Thomas (628); it was twice renovated (c. 750 and 770) before its reconstruction in 848. North of Amida at Martyropolis (now Silvan) a Jacobite church was built in 752. On the southern edge of Mesopotamia, at Callinicum (now Raqqa, Syria) on the Euphrates, a monastery was built in 631. The architectural forms of these churches are unknown or uncertain; only the north cathedral church at Nisibis and, possibly, parts of Heraklios' church at Amida have been identified with extant longitudinal or basilical structures. In addition to these documented cases, two centralized urban churches are known: the el-Hadra Church (7th century; destr. after 1911) at Martyropolis and the partially standing 'Octagon' (c. 662) outside the city walls of Constantina (now Viranşehir).

Rural church building in this period is more evenly represented in Mesopotamia, and in the south of Syria–Palestine. Relatively few churches, however, are known to have been built in the central area, namely northern Syria, which was the hinterland of the diocesan capital of Antioch and where there had been much ecclesiastical and secular building between 313 and 600 (*see* §(i)(d) above and §3(iii) below). Some churches from this area include those at Telade (601–2), Deir Solaib (604–5) and Babisqa (609–10). Although new building is apparently lacking, excavations in this area (e.g. at Dehes) have established that the villages here continued to be occupied through the 8th century.

Inscriptions in the southern area of Syria–Palestine record several cases of church building or decorating (e.g. the laying of mosaic pavements), for example at il-Ghariyeh (600), the monastery of Dorotheus, Palestine (c. 600), Nessana (601), Heldua (604–5; 607–8), Muhezzeh and Sobata (605; 607; 639), Shelomi (610), Deir al-Adas (621; 722), Umm el-Halahi (622), Nakhite (624), Sameh (624; 641), Salkhad (633; 665), Kufr (652; 735), Qweisme (717–18), Ma'in (719–20), Nabha (732–3; 746), Umm er-Rassas (?754) and Ramot (762) near Jerusalem. In the village of Rihab in Palestine, as many as five churches were built and decorated between 594 and 623.

In Mesopotamia, rural churches were constructed at Beth Ris'yar (631), Magdal (635), Mar Awgen (643–4), Hah (691; 740), Quluq (c. 700), Habsenas, Tell 'Ubad, Deir Da'il and Mezr'eh (700–34), Büyük Kaşişlik (748), Tell Beshmai (c. 750), Mar Musa (751), Uç Kilise (766), Heshterek (772) and Kefre Be (779).

For bibliography *see* §(i)(d) above.

MARLIA MUNDELL MANGO

(iii) c. 843–c. 1204. The churches that survive in Constantinople and that are scattered throughout Thrace, Anatolia and Greece are but a small portion of what was originally built in this period. Their dates, dedications and functions are often unknown; their fabric has often been distorted by alterations made to convert them to other uses, while paintings and mosaics that might have supplied explanatory inscriptions or images are lost. It is sometimes possible to establish regional traditions of architecture, especially in geographically or socially isolated contexts such as islands or monastic centres, but the isolation of these regions may simply have resulted in the preservation of types that did not survive elsewhere. Some idea of the extent of the losses of Middle Byzantine architecture may be gathered from the hundreds of cave monuments of CAPPADOCIA which, protected from decay and destruction by their nature, exhibit a wide variety of architectural forms. They are a reminder, too, that the greatest area of loss is that of the buildings that were not the products of imperial or aristocratic patronage. The period is dominated by small, domed, centralized churches that take several forms, including the cross-in-square (see fig. 22), the Greek-cross octagon, domed octagon and the atrophied free cross. Construction techniques vary, but generally rely upon traditional combinations of brick and stone coursing for walls, and brick alone for vaulting. Exploitation of the fabric for its decorative possibilities is characteristic of the period, so that niches, brick mouldings and patterned arrangements of brick and stone produce highly textured exterior surfaces. Articulation of the exterior is further enhanced by the fact that internal divisions are usually vaulted at different levels, and so are manifested on the exterior, the domes raised on drums forming the highest points.

(a) Constantinople and Asia Minor. (b) Greece and the Balkans. (c) Syria and Palestine.

(a) Constantinople and Asia Minor. The most common form of domed, centralized church is the cross-in-square, so called because its main vaults form a Greek cross that is inscribed within a square, making a nine-bay core. In the church of Christ Pantepoptes (Turk. Eski Imaret Cami; before 1087; see figs 22 and 23) in Constantinople, for example, the central dome, originally carried on four columns, is flanked by four barrel vaults; the square is completed by four small corner bays, groin-vaulted at a lower level than the barrel vaults. To the east are a large main apse and two small lateral ones, separated from the core by three further bays. The core is preceded by a narthex of three groin-vaulted bays, and an exonarthex that is a later addition.

Exactly where and when the cross-in-square form originated is unclear, and has been the subject of much discussion. It was probably the form used for the Nea Ekklesia (880; destr. 15th century) in Constantinople, and this church may have called on still earlier models. Attempts have been made to place the cross-in-square at the end of an evolution beginning with the domed basilica (*see* §(ii)(a) above), while parallels have also been noted with the domed churches (6th–7th century) of Armenia (*see* ARMENIA, §II). It may, however, be unnecessary to

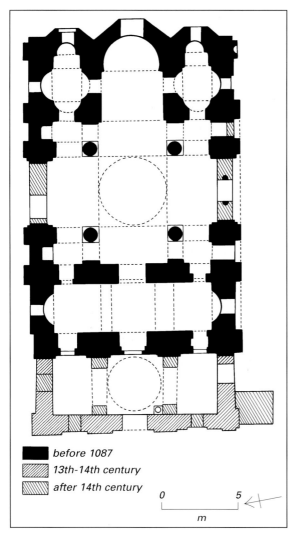

before 1087

13th–14th century

after 14th century

0   5

m

22. Church of Christ Pantepoptes (Turk. Eski Imaret Cami), Istanbul, before 1087, plan showing its first cross-in-square form

funerary chapel (*c.* 1310) attached to St Mary Pammakaristos (*see* ISTANBUL, §III, 7). No central Anatolian example of the type is firmly dated, but it appears in Cappadocia in the cave churches of the early 10th century (e.g. Kılıçlar Kilise) and in built examples such as Çanlı Kilise, near Çeltek, and Karagedik Kilise, Ihlara, which probably date between the 10th century and the mid-11th (*see also* CAPPADOCIA, §2(i)).

There are variations of detail among cross-in-square churches. In Constantinople the four supports below the dome are columns, whereas further east, in Anatolia, piers are more common, even in churches with supposed Constantinopolitan connections (e.g. Çanlı Kilise). The use of columns may have been largely a matter of the availability of spolia from earlier buildings, since many of the columns in churches in the capital appear to be reused. Nor are the four corner bays always groin-vaulted: the corner vaults at Kilise Cami in Constantinople have cupolas, and in the cave churches of Cappadocia groin vaults, domes and barrel vaults may all appear in the same church, as in the Hallaç Monastery church. In Constantinople domes are generally divided into segments, either by ridges, as in the Myrelaion, or by flat ribs, as in Christ Pantepoptes and Kilise Cami.

A significant variation on the cross-in-square plan concerns the arrangements at the east end. The bays fronting the three apses, evident in Christ Pantepoptes, are found in all examples of the cross-in-square church in Constantinople and also at Karagedik Kilise in Ihlara. In general, however, in cross-in-square churches outside the capital the apses open directly off the three easternmost bays of the core. In most cross-in-square churches the naos is preceded by a narthex extending the width of the cross-in-square core. Narthexes generally have three to five bays with groin vaults, as in Christ Pantepoptes, but were sometimes elaborated by the placing of a dome over the central or entrance bay, as in the Myrelaion.

Another type of domed, centralized church is the atrophied free cross, which has a square naos formed by four shallow barrel-vaulted cross arms. The type is not common but is represented in Constantinople by the church (early 12th century, remodelled *c.* 1316–21) of Christ the Saviour in Chora Monastery (*see* ISTANBUL, §III, 3(i); for a plan of the church *see* PAREKKLESION). Several examples do, however, survive among the cave churches of Cappadocia, and it may have been a form used mainly for monuments more modest than most of those that have been preserved. An even more uncommon form is the basilica, which is generally regarded as a relic of the earlier tradition, surviving in contexts removed from the cultural mainstream (*see* §(b) below). Hagia Sophia (*c.* 1065) at Nicaea, however, being so close to the capital, cannot be dismissed as merely a provincial fossil. The basilican form, like the domed cross, which also made intermittent appearances right up to the end of the empire, may have been retained in Byzantine architecture for specific functions.

A characteristic feature of ecclesiastical architecture in this period is the *parekklesion*, which was used for ceremonies or functions supplementary to the main liturgical rites conducted in the naos. It often served as a funerary chapel, with tombs set into the walls or placed below the

search for an evolutionary sequence behind the cross-in-square, except in the most general terms. The importance of the domed basilica and cross-domed developments is that they established the dome as the preferred covering for the naos. Once this step had been taken, the requirements of engineering encouraged the adoption of bilateral symmetry: the cross-in-square may therefore have been a Middle Byzantine invention that drew upon a centuries-old architectural tradition of domed buildings.

Whatever its origins, the cross-in-square plan appeared in Constantinople in much the same form from the 10th to the 14th century; for example in the North Church (907) of the monastery of Constantine Lips (Turk. Fenarı İsa Cami); the Myrelaion (Bodrum Cami; 920–22; for ground-plan *see* CHURCH, fig. 6); St John the Baptist in Trullo (?11th century); the churches (1118–36) of the monastery of Christ Pantokrator (*see* ISTANBUL, §III, 2(i)); Kilise Cami (10th–11th century); and the *parekklesion* or

23. Church of Christ Pantepoptes, Istanbul, before 1087; view from the south-east

floor, or as a chapel dedicated to a saint, perhaps housing relics. The *parekklesion* is usually small, takes several forms and may be attached to various parts of the church: examples include many barrel-vaulted rectangular chapels in the rock-cut architecture of Cappadocia, and in Constantinople the four domed chapels that originally stood on the roof at each corner of the North Church of the monastery of Constantine Lips (907), and the two-domed mausoleum chapel of St Michael (before 1136) built in the irregular space between the two churches of the monastery of Christ Pantokrator.

In Constantinople construction was chiefly of thin tile-like brick. In 10th-century churches, such as the Myrelaion and North Church of the monastery of Constantine Lips, the bricks were laid flush with the wall surface, bonded by mortar, about the same thickness as the brick. From the early 11th century to the late 12th, a 'recessed brick' technique appears, in which alternate layers of brick are placed further back than the wall surface and the resulting space is filled with mortar, giving the impression that the mortar bands between bricks are extremely thick, as in the church of Christ Pantepoptes. Here, too, bricks are arranged in a decorative manner, using meander and other patterns. Examples of more complicated decoration include the tiers of niches on the exterior walls of the churches of the monastery of Christ Pantokrator, the six rounded pilasters applied to each of the long sides of the Myrelaion and the frequent framing of windows by single or double arches.

BIBLIOGRAPHY

A. Van Millingen: *Byzantine Churches in Constantinople: Their History and Architecture* (London, 1912)

A. K. Orlandos: *Monastiriaki architektoniki* [Monastic architecture] (Athens, 1926, 2/1958)

S. Ballance: 'The Byzantine Churches of Trebizond', *Anatol. Stud.*, x (1960), pp. 141–75

T. Macridy, A. H. S. Megaw and C. Mango: 'The Monastery of Lips (Fenarı Isa Camii) at Istanbul', *Dumbarton Oaks Pap.*, xviii (1964), pp. 249–315

C. L. Striker and Y. D. Kuban: 'Work at Kalenderhane Camii in Istanbul: First Preliminary Report', *Dumbarton Oaks Pap.*, xxi (1967), pp. 267–71; 'Second Report', xxii (1968), pp. 185–94; 'Third and Fourth Reports', xxv (1971), pp. 251–8; 'Fifth Report', xxix (1975), pp. 306–18

G. Babić: *Les Chapelles annexes des églises byzantines: Fonction liturgique et programmes iconographiques* (Paris, 1969)

T. F. Mathews: *The Byzantine Churches of Istanbul: A Photographic Survey* (University Park, PA, 1976)

C. Mango: *Byzantine Architecture* (New York, 1976)

C. L. Striker: *The Myrelaion (Bodrum Camii) in Istanbul* (Princeton, 1981)

L. Rodley: *Cave Monasteries of Byzantine Cappadocia* (Cambridge, 1985)

(b) Greece and the Balkans. Among the most renowned examples of the cross-in-square plan (*see* §(a) above) are the churches of the Theotokos (originally St Barbara; mid-10th century) at HOSIOS LOUKAS and the Panagia Chalkeon (1028; see fig. 24 and THESSALONIKI, §III, 6); the form has continued in use in Greece virtually until the present day. Many Greek churches of this type have a combination of piers and columns to support the dome, with piers usually on the east side and columns on the west, as in the 12th-century church dedicated to the Source of Life (Zoodochos Pigi) at Samarina, near Messini. This church also has barrel vaults and cupolas over the eastern

24. Church of Panagia Chalkeon, Thessaloniki, Greece, 1028

and western corner bays respectively, rather than the more common groin vaults. Unlike the domes of cross-in-square churches in Constantinople, those in Greece are not usually divided into segments, except in churches influenced by the architecture of the capital, such as the katholikon (1045) at Nea Moni (*see* CHIOS, §2; and below). In general the apses open directly off the easternmost bays of the core, but in occasional examples, such as the Theotokos Church at Hosios Loukas, a further set of bays is present, as in the churches of Constantinople. This feature has consequently been interpreted as an aspect of metropolitan tradition that appears elsewhere in churches with Constantinopolitan connections (usually via their patrons). It has also been suggested that, in the provinces, these bays were gradually suppressed by fusion with the eastern bays of the core, as in the 11th-century church at Kaisarini on Mt Hymettos, so that churches without them represent the last stage of a provincial modification of a metropolitan type. A difference in form, however, may imply a difference in function, and until there is clearer knowledge of the ways in which churches with and without extra bays were used, no confident distinction between metropolitan and provincial types may be drawn.

A variant of the cross-in-square plan that seems to be distinctive of a particular region is that found on MT ATHOS. Here several monastery churches (late 10th century or early 11th), including those of Vatopedi and Iviron, have the north and south arms of the cross-in-square extending into apses, producing, with the main apse, a triconch outline. This form is thought to have been established by the katholikon (*c.* 961–3) of the Great Lavra, which was built by St Athanasios. As a result of excavations undertaken in 1976, however, it seems that the side apses were not added until 1002 and that they therefore did not form part of the original structure. The adoption of the triconch arrangement was prompted by liturgical requirements and was retained in subsequent cross-in-square buildings into the 20th century, as evidenced by the construction of Simonos Petra (1902).

In addition to the cross-in-square, two other types of domed, centralized church are represented in Greece. The most subtle is the Greek-cross octagon plan, as in the 11th-century church at DAFNI. This has a fairly wide dome set on an octagon formed by squinches spanning the corners of the square central bay (see fig. 25); four groin-vaulted bays form a Greek cross around the domed core, and a near-square plan is completed by three small groin-vaulted bays between each arm of the cross. The main apse opens off the eastern cross-arm and is flanked by side apses; the plan is completed by a three-bay inner

25. Church at Dafni, Greece, *c.* 1080; an example of the Greek-cross octagon plan

narthex and an open-fronted outer narthex. At Dafni the Greek-cross octagon plan is at its simplest; at the katholikon (first half of the 11th century) of Hosios Loukas it is elaborated by the addition of galleries in a U shape above the north, south and west sides of the domed core.

The Greek-cross octagon is found chiefly in southern and central mainland Greece, and includes such churches as Panagia Lykodimou (before 1044) in Athens, Hagios Sotirios (11th century) at Christianou, Hagia Sophia at MONEMVASIA, and Hagios Nikolaos at Kampia near Phokis (both 12th century). The type may not have been confined to this region, however, since the Panagia Kamariotissa (late 11th century) on Heybeli Ada, one of the islands near Constantinople, has a related form. Nor is it confined to the Middle Byzantine period, since there is a Palaiologan example in Hagioi Theodoroi (*c.* 1290–95) at MYSTRAS.

The domed octagon church plan is found on the island of Chios, where it was introduced with the construction of the katholikon of the Nea Moni. This was an imperial foundation built by craftsmen from Constantinople and possibly modelled on the 4th-century mausoleum of Constantine, which was part of the complex of Holy Apostles (*see* ISTANBUL, §III, 9(i)). The square naos is surmounted by an octagonal dome and at the east end has a three-bay chancel with three apses. The church has an inner narthex of three bays, the central one domed, and an outer narthex, also with three bays, all domed and with apsed ends. Several other churches on the island copy Nea Moni, but the form is unknown elsewhere, and its similarity with a few Cypriot monuments, such as the katholikon of

St John Chrysostomos Monastery at Koutsoventis, is only superficial. Nea Moni and its descendants on Chios therefore form a self-contained group.

The basilica, although not a standard church plan after the 6th century, remained in use throughout this period and beyond, particularly in areas of the Balkans that were peripheral to the Byzantine empire, as evidenced by the church of Hagia Sophia (11th century) at OHRID, then part of the new Bulgarian state. In such locations the use of the basilican plan may indicate a desire on the part of new kings to reproduce Early Christian architecture, or it may stem from lack of familiarity with Middle Byzantine architecture. Where the type appears on Byzantine territory, as in the church of the Dormition (Koimisis; 12th century) at Kalambaka and the church (10th–11th century) at Mentzaina, it is usually much smaller than the great Early Christian buildings, with nave arcades of just two or three piers or columns.

Parekklesia also made their appearance in the church architecture of Middle Byzantine Greece. They vary in form from the simplest barrel-vaulted rectangles to more complex types, as in the pair of cross-in-square chapels (11th century) flanking the trefoil katholikon of the Great Lavra and in the atrophied Greek-cross chapel at Iviron and the domed tetraconch at Vatopedi.

Greek churches of the 11th and 12th centuries often exhibit a technique of stone and brick wall construction known as 'cloisonné'. Narrow bricks are placed vertically between the stones of ashlar courses, and brick courses run above and below, so that each stone is enclosed by brick. Examples include the churches of Hosios Loukas, Hagios Sotirios (12th century) at Amphissa, St Sophia at Ohrid and the monastery church of St Panteleimon (1164; rest. 1960s) at Nerezi (*see* NEREZI, ST PANTELEIMON). More complicated arrangements of bricks were used to make ornament resembling kufic script, as in the Theotokos Church at Hosios Loukas and the Panagia Lykodimou (early 11th century) at Athens. This exploitation of the decorative possibilities of brick culminated in the elaborate herringbone, hatching and spiral patterns of the architecture in the 13th and 14th centuries (*see* §(iv) below).

BIBLIOGRAPHY
G. Millet: *Le Monastère de Daphni* (Paris, 1899)
R. W. Schultz and S. H. Barnsley: *The Monastery of St Luke of Stiris in Phocis* (London, 1901)
G. Millet: 'Recherches au Mont Athos', *Bull. Corr. Hell.*, xxix (1905), pp. 55–98, 105–41
C. Diehl, M. Le Tourneau and H. Saladin: *Les Monuments chrétiens de Salonique*, 2 vols (Paris, 1918)
A. K. Orlandos: *Monuments byzantins de Chios* (Athens, 1930)
M. Chatzidakis: *Byzantine Monuments in Attica and Boeotia* (Athens, 1956)
P. M. Mylonas: 'L'Architecture du Mont Athos', *Le Millénaire du Mont Athos*, ii (Chevetogne, 1963), pp. 229–46
C. Bouras: *Nea Moni on Chios: History and Architecture* (Athens, 1982)

LYN RODLEY

(c) *Syria and Palestine.* The fragmentation of power that began to affect the Islamic world in the 9th century left the frontier provinces of Syria and Palestine exposed to the power and influence of a resurgent Byzantine empire. This resurgence allowed Byzantium during the 10th century to carry out a dramatic expansion into eastern Asia Minor and to recapture North Syria in a series of rapid campaigns culminating in the capture of Antioch

26. Monastery of the Holy Cross, Jerusalem, 1038–56

(969; *see* ANTIOCH (i), §3). The re-establishment of Byzantine power, particularly in the ancient sites of Antioch and Edessa (recaptured 1032), meant that Byzantium could exercise not only a direct influence on the areas it had captured but also an indirect influence on those places that lay immediately outside its frontiers.

Literary and other sources confirm that within those frontiers many buildings continued to survive from earlier periods. In Antioch (which became the administrative centre of Byzantine power in North Syria) several Late Antique churches remained standing, while at Edessa it is clear that a large number of churches and shrines survived from the 6th and 7th centuries. Among them was the 6th-century Melchite cathedral of St Sophia, a church famous for the beauty and luxury of its decoration. It was this church that possessed the famous MANDYLION OF EDESSA delivered up to a Byzantine army in 943–4.

Despite the substantial survival of ecclesiastical buildings from earlier centuries, building activity was renewed after the reconquest, both in the restoration of existing structures and in the building of new churches, sometimes employing more contemporary building types. The famous 5th-century monastery of QAL'AT SIM'AN is an example. Its buildings, which were occupied by a monastic community both before and after the 10th-century reconquest, were renewed in 979. As part of that renewal, the east basilica was reconstructed, either as a vaulted basilica or as a domed cross-in-square church, with the addition of four centrally placed masonry piers, and a narthex at the west end; mosaic and *opus sectile* floors were also laid, and incorporated into them was an inscription in Greek and Syriac commemorating the whole work. The opportunity was undoubtedly taken to introduce the cross-in-square type elsewhere into the area. A good example is provided by a church at Nizip in eastern Turkey, where the dome is supported on four slender masonry piers.

Existing buildings were renewed both at Antioch and at two ecclesiastical sites established to the south-west: the monastery of St Simeon the Stylite the Younger on Samandağı ('Wondrous Mountain') and the neighbouring site of St Barlaam, both of which were rebuilt in the 10th and 11th centuries, following, in the case of St Barlaam, a period of abandonment during Muslim rule. It is not apparent at either complex of buildings that the opportunity was taken to adopt contemporary building plans. What is remarkable at both sites is the clear presence of Georgians, as evidenced by the epigraphical survivals. This reflects a more general movement at this period by Georgians to the Syrian borderlands, a movement of some importance in the light of the strong tradition of architecture in Georgia (*see* GEORGIA, §II, 2). This is strikingly attested by an 11th-century church built in Karadağ ('Black Mountains') to the north of St Simeon the Younger. The plan is cross-in-square with the dome supported by four free-standing piers. Somewhat unusually, the apse and side chapels are themselves inscribed within the east wall, which on the exterior is straight; at the west end there was a narthex preceded by a small open central porch. There are five exterior doorways: one on the north side, one on the south and three on the west. Masons' marks and inscriptions confirm the impression given by the rich sculptural decoration (particularly on the porch) that the church was built by Georgian patronage, probably in the mid-11th century. Further afield, Georgian building is evidenced by the church of the monastery of the Holy Cross (1038–56) at Jerusalem, founded by King Bagrat IV of Georgia (*reg* 1027–72) on the site of a 5th-century church (see fig. 26). This represents the appearance of the unusual domed basilica type with four bays and a dome on pendentives. The church is massively built, with large masonry piers supporting the nave and inscribed transepts, and, unusually, it has no narthex or gallery. The architecture is distinguished by the use of pointed arches and groin vaults throughout. Another example of this rare type of building in Palestine is the church of St John at Ain Karim, which probably dates to the same period.

The Byzantine empire was able to promote church building in Palestine during the 11th and 12th centuries. This activity was particularly necessitated by the destruction of Christian churches in Palestine ordered by the Fatimid caliph al-Hakim (*reg* 996–1021); among the devastated churches was the church of the Holy Sepulchre (*see* JERUSALEM, §II, 2(i)). Repair work on the church's Anastasis ('resurrection') rotunda began in the reign of Constantine IX (*reg* 1042–55), who was permitted to send to Jerusalem architects and craftsmen from Constantinople. The need to respect the original circular design and the limited resources available meant that the Byzantine craftsmen produced a building that is not representative of contemporary building styles. The 4th-century basilica that lay east of the Anastasis was abandoned, and the rotunda was rebuilt as a self-contained church by the addition of an eastern apse and a gallery to provide greater accommodation. More interesting is the contemporary chapel of the Holy Trinity built over the ruins of the 4th-century baptistery; its square nave seems originally to have been covered by a dome resting on an octagon formed by closing off the corners by squinches. In the 11th century examples of cross-in-square churches also start to appear in Palestine. The earliest example is probably the church of the Invention of the Head of St John the Baptist at Sebastiya (Israel), where the existing Early Christian columned basilica was rebuilt with a central dome carried on four large granite columns. Other examples of this type continue to appear in Palestine during the 11th and 12th centuries, nearly all of which are Orthodox churches.

Following the Turkish conquest of eastern Asia Minor in the last decades of the 11th century, Byzantine influence in Syria and Palestine declined. Nevertheless, during the 12th century the Byzantine emperor continued to hold himself as the protector of the native Christians of those lands. Rebuilding and restoration appear to have taken place even as late as the reign of Manuel I (*reg* 1143–80), for example at the church of the Nativity (1161–9), Bethlehem, and at the monasteries of St Gerasimus in the Jordan Valley and St George of Choziba. It is reasonable to suppose that at least some of the rebuilding employed current Byzantine designs.

BIBLIOGRAPHY

D. Krencker: *Die Wallfahrtskirche des Simeon Stylites in Kal'at Siman* (Berlin, 1939)

J. B. Segal: *Edessa: The Blessed City* (Oxford, 1970)

D. Pringle: 'Church-building in Palestine before the Crusades', *Crusader Art in the Twelfth Century*, ed. J. Folda, Brit. Archaeol. Rep., clii (Oxford, 1982), pp. 5–46

W. Z. Djobadze: *Archaeological Investigations in the Region West of Antioch-on-the-Orontes* (Stuttgart, 1986)

D. Pringle: *The Churches of the Crusader Kingdom of Jerusalem: A Corpus* (Cambridge, 1993–)

WILLIAM SAUNDERS

(iv) c. 1204–1453.

(a) Introduction. (b) Constantinople and Asia Minor. (c) Greece and the Balkans.

(a) Introduction. The political fragmentation during the last centuries of the Byzantine empire contributed to the creation of an architecture that was eclectic and dominated by regional developments. Although numerous monuments survive from the late 13th century and early 14th, the architectural developments before and after this period are less clear. With the Latin conquest of Constantinople (1204), the city lost its dominant role in the development of Byzantine architecture. In the political configuration that emerged in the wake of the Latin conquest, the architecture of the various minor principalities was subjected to diverse regional influences: the 'empire' of Nicaea in north-west Asia Minor, under the house of Laskaris, was surrounded by Turkish emirates; the Despotate of Epiros, centred on Arta, had to deal with the Franks in Greece and with its Balkan neighbours; the semi-independent empire of Trebizond (1204–1461; *see* TREBIZOND, §1) was flanked by the kingdom of Georgia to the north-east and the Turks to the south. Serbia and Bulgaria prospered in the 13th century. The reconquest of Constantinople by the Palaiologan emperors in 1261 was followed by a flowering of the arts, often referred to as the Palaiologan Renaissance (*see* PALAIOLOGAN). By the late 13th century Constantinople and Thessaloniki had regained their positions as cultural centres. In the 14th century important buildings were constructed in the principality of the Morea (Peloponnese), with its capital at Mystras, and in the Bulgarian city of Nesebăr, while the Ottoman Turks emerged as the dominant patrons in Asia Minor.

Several trends began to emerge in the 13th century that distinguish Late Byzantine architecture from earlier achievements. Planning and spatial articulation were eclectic, with builders borrowing from a variety of sources and combining established building types into new, more complex forms. Subsidiary chapels and ambulatories became important compositional elements, and belfries were introduced into the architectural vocabulary. More emphasis was given to the exterior of buildings, with the use of single- and double-storey portico façades; taller and more numerous domes rising above roof-lines; exterior surfaces were often lavishly decorated with stepped pilasters, niches, patterned brickwork, and other ceramic ornamentation. Façades are usually articulated by arcades, but often the arcading is decorative and bears no relation to the spatial and structural divisions of the interior, thus replacing the 'Classical' logic of Middle Byzantine architecture. In general, churches of this period are small, and the detailing of the parts becomes more important than the larger compositional principles, but construction is frequently of the highest quality; the late architecture should not necessarily be viewed as the result of a decline in standards but rather as evidence of a new aesthetic sensibility.

(b) Constantinople and Asia Minor. In the wake of the Latin conquest, the government in exile, centred on Nicaea (now Iznik), emerged as the heir to the imperial throne. The period was a prosperous one in western Asia Minor, although its architectural achievements have generally been underestimated. The church of Hagios Tryphon at Nicaea, built by Theodoros II Laskaris (*reg* 1254–8), is probably that known as Church C. The small naos has an atrophied Greek-cross plan (i.e. with shallow arms of equal length)

and is enveloped by a U-shaped ambulatory; this latter feature proved popular in subsequent Palaiologan architecture. Although of mediocre construction, the interior of Hagios Tryphon was lavishly decorated. Church E at Sardis may also belong to this period, with a possible date *c*. 1220–45. The excavated remains reveal a church of the cross-in-square type (*see* §(iii)(a) above), with windowless domes rising above the corner compartments. It is not clear whether the interior included galleries, like the later churches at Mystras (*see* §(c) below). The façades included arcades with multiple recessed surrounds and large areas of decorative brick patterning. Latmos church 8 on Kahve Assar Adasi and Latmos church 4 on Ikisada may be slightly later. Both are constructed of reused brick and stone laid in horizontal courses, arcaded façades with banded voussoirs in the arches, and a variety of brick decoration. Church 8 had a cross-in-square plan, but not enough of church 4 remains to determine the plan.

The cross-in-square plan was also used for the church of Hagia Sophia (*c*. 1238–63) at Trebizond (*see* TREBIZOND, §2(i)). Local influence, however, is evident in its elongated form and in the projecting, arcaded porches on the north, south and west sides. The heavy stone construction probably reflects regional developments: stone construction was standard throughout eastern Asia Minor; only the pendentives and drum of the dome are constructed in brick, traditionally used for Byzantine vaulting. Building activity continued at Trebizond into the 15th century.

The reconquest of Constantinople was followed by a period of prosperity (*c*. 1280–*c*. 1330), during which there was considerable building activity. All the major undertakings represent additions to existing buildings. At the monastery of Constantine Lips (Turk. Fenari Isa Cami; 907), Theodora, the widow of Michael VIII (*reg* 1261–82), added the ambulatory-plan church of St John (*c*. 1283–1303) to the existing South Church (*see* CHURCH, fig. 12). During a second construction phase in this period the two churches were linked by an L-shaped ambulatory. Both additions were equipped with numerous arcosolia (niches for tombs), reflecting the funerary function of the building, which served as the mortuary complex of the Palaiologan dynasty, perhaps following the example of the monastery of Christ Pantokrator (*see* ISTANBUL, §III, 2(i)). The walls are of alternating bands of brick and stone, enlivened by arcades and niches, and the east façade is richly decorated with brickwork designs. As is characteristic of architecture in Constantinople, the structural composition of the façade is never overpowered by the decorative aspects.

In imitation of the imperial 'church-cluster' plans of the Pantokrator and Lips monasteries, many existing monastic foundations in the capital were expanded by members of the aristocracy in order to provide funeral chapels and additional space. The Pammakaristos Monastery (*see* ISTANBUL, §III, 7) had several phases of additions, the most important being the construction of a cross-in-square funeral *parekklesion* (*c*. 1310; *see* BRICK, fig. 7) by the widow of the military commander Michael Doukas Glavas Tarchaneiotes. During his restoration of the church of Christ the Saviour in Chora Monastery (*see* ISTANBUL, §III, 3(i)) Theodore Metochites (1270–1332) added a *parekklesion* (*c*. 1316–21), as well as two narthexes, a belfry

and a two-storey northern annexe. In all the examples the end result included an undulating roofline with domes of different shapes, sizes and heights and an irregular row of apses across the east façade. This conscious asymmetry is emphasized by the surface decoration of irregular arcades, niches and ceramic patterning. Formal relationships are small-scale, and there is no clear correspondence between the external articulation and the internal structural system.

The church in Constantinople known as Kilise Cami (10th–11th century) had two phases of additions (*c*. 1320) around its cross-in-square core, including a belfry, a two-storey northern annexe, similar to that of the Chora, and a three-domed, porticoed outer narthex. In the subsequent period of civil wars, both the economy and the building trade declined in Constantinople. The most significant undertaking of the final Byzantine century was the reconstruction of the dome of Hagia Sophia after a third of it had collapsed in the earthquake of 1346. It was repaired in 1354–5 under the direction of an Italian mason; much of the financing came from abroad.

(c) Greece and the Balkans. Among the churches that were probably built shortly after the Latin conquest of Constantinople are several on Chios, including the church of the Panagia Sikelia (?*c*. 1230–45), which has a long plan covered by a barrel vault and a single dome. Walls are constructed of alternating bands of brick and stone, with brick decoration in the lunettes of the façade arcades. The brick arches are outlined with glazed ceramic rosettes. The façades of Hagios Ioannes Prodromos at Chalkios (?13th century) are similar; the small church is barrel-vaulted, without a dome. The Hagioi Apostoloi at Pyrgi (?13th century) is a variation of the domed-octagon plan of the katholikon of Nea Moni (1045). Façade decoration includes glazed ceramic rosettes and bowls. Domes over the naos and narthex have marble colonnettes on the drums.

On the Greek mainland the most important centre of the 13th century was ARTA, capital of the Despotate of Epiros, the chief rival of Nicaea for the throne of Constantinople. Numerous buildings with complex plans and lavishly decorated façades survive from the reign of Despot Michael II (*reg* 1231–67/8). The monastic church at Kato Panagia has a three-aisled plan, with a transverse barrel vault, its central bay raised to form a tetragonal dome. Wall construction is of a brick and stone cloisonné, and the ceramic decoration includes carved bricks. Michael's other foundation, the church of Pantanassa at Philippas, may have been built by a workshop connected with Constantinople, as the recessed brick technique suggests. In a second construction phase, the naos was enveloped by an ambulatory with domed chapels flanking the sanctuary, and a belfry at the south-west corner. The monastic church of the Panagia Vlacherna served as the burial church for members of the ruling family. Although it incorporates the remains of a slightly earlier church, it is largely dated to the mid- or late 13th century. Its three-aisled basilican plan is incongruously surmounted by three domes of varying size, and the external brick decoration is asymmetrical.

The church of the Panagia Parigoritissa (1282–9; see fig. 27) is the most renowned church in Arta, and one of the most original in Byzantine architecture. The naos may have been begun as a cross-in-square church, but it was transformed into a variation of the domed-octagon plan, with the dome raised on a system of corbelled columns. The U-shaped ambulatory is surmounted by a gallery with domes at the four corners, and there is an open lantern on the axis above the western entrance. Two zones of bilobed windows pierce the lateral façades. Construction is of brick and stone cloisonné with some reticulate revetment.

The cross-in-square church of St Clement (formerly dedicated to the Virgin Peribleptos; 1294–5) at Ohrid is similar in its cloisonné walling and decorative detailing to the churches at Arta. The outer narthex (1313–17) added to the church of St Sophia at Ohrid is also of similar construction (see OHRID, fig. 1). It is fronted by two tiers of arcades, which are not aligned vertically, and it is flanked by low, domed towers, thus giving it the appearance of a palace façade.

Although Thessaloniki was recaptured by the Greeks in 1224, the political situation was unstable, and there is no evidence of building activity until the end of the 13th century. Architecture flourished in the 14th century, continuing at least until the first Turkish conquest of the city in 1387. The churches of Thessaloniki are more regular and symmetrical than those of Constantinople. In spite of the complex layering of spaces, most are the result of a single building campaign. The most important undertaking was the cross-in-square church of Hagioi Apostoloi (c. 1310–14; see THESSALONIKI, §III, 7(i)), the katholikon of a monastery of which the name has been lost. It is enveloped on its north, west and south sides by an ambulatory preceded by a narthex. In addition to the vertically attenuated dome and vaulting of the naos, smaller domes surmount the four corner bays of the ambulatory. Porticos originally fronted the western and part of the southern ambulatory. Construction is of brick mixed with mortared rubble, characteristic of Thessaloniki, and the tall apse and eastern façade are decorated with surface patterning in brick. The plan of the slightly earlier church of Hagios Panteleimon is similar. Its tall cross-in-square naos is preceded by a domed narthex and was originally enveloped on three sides by an ambulatory (destr. early 20th century) with chapels at the eastern ends. Domes were positioned above the lateral entrances, on axis with the naos dome, and two additional domes were placed at the western corners of the ambulatory. Despite its elegant design, the church was rather crudely constructed. The church of Hagia Aikaterini also belongs to this group, although it is unclear whether it was constructed just before or just after Hagioi Apostoloi. Its cross-in-square core is also enveloped by an ambulatory with domes over the four corners, and porticos front the western and portions of the north and south façades. The function of these ambulatories remains uncertain, for although in Constantinople a part of them was used for burials, this does not seem to have been the case in Thessaloniki.

The church known as Profitis Elias (c. 1360–70; see THESSALONIKI, §III, 8(i)) was probably the last major construction in the city before the Turkish invasion of 1387. Like the churches on Mt Athos (see §(iii)(b) above), its cross-in-square naos is extended by lateral apses and preceded by a large narthex or lite. These are combined with chapels in the four corners of the trefoil. The walls

27. Church of the Panagia Parigoritissa, Arta, Greece, west façade, 1282–9

are constructed of horizontal courses of brick and stone, with decorative niches and brick patterning on the tall apses. The design is complex and sophisticated, and testifies to the continuation of construction on a grand scale until the Turkish invasion.

The Franks ceded MYSTRAS to the Byzantine emperor in 1262. Among the new buildings recorded after this date are the Metropolis, a three-aisled basilica (1291), and the Brontochion Monastery churches of Hagioi Theodoroi (c. 1290–95) and the Hodegetria (c. 1310–22). The Hagioi Theodoroi combined a cruciform plan with a domed octagon and, like the Metropolis, is built of brick and stone cloisonné characteristic of Greece. The Hodegetria (see fig. 28) is a more complex design, combining a five-domed cross-in-square gallery with a three-aisled, basilican ground floor. Other features include a domed gallery above the narthex, porticos to the north and west and a western belfry. Its banded brick and stone construction and niched apses are closer to Constantinopolitan practices, suggesting that the plan might also have been imported. The design of the Hodegetria is repeated at the monastery church of Pantanassa (1428), although here the walls are of cloisonné with some Gothic-style stone ornament, notably the carved lancets of the east façade. During the first half of the 14th century the Metropolis was remodelled to the same design, with a five-domed cross-in-square gallery level added to the existing basilica.

Numerous buildings survive in Bulgaria from the 13th and 14th centuries, but most are notoriously difficult to date (see BULGARIA, §II, 2). In general the architecture maintains close ties with that of Constantinople. Several churches survive in Tărnovo (see VELIKO TURNOVO), but NESEBĂR gives the best indication of Late Byzantine developments in Bulgaria. Here several buildings may be dated to the period of Tsar Ivan Alexander (reg 1331–71), and perhaps were constructed by artisans from Constantinople. In Bulgarian churches plans remain simple, and ambulatories are rare. On the other hand, façades are

28. Church of the Hodegetria, Brontochion Monastery, Mystras, Greece, *c.* 1310–22

richly decorated and belfries appear frequently above narthexes, following the arrangement that is first known at the Asen Church (late 12th century or early 13th) at Stanimaka (now Asenovgrad). Among the outstanding buildings at Nesebar are the cross-in-square churches of the Pantokrator and St John Aleitourgetos (both 14th century). In the Pantokrator the tall proportions of the dome are balanced by the belfry. Construction is of high quality, of alternating bands of brick and stone, with banded voussoirs in the arches. The lateral façades are articulated by three layers of arcading that do not correspond with the spatial organization of the interior and are not vertically aligned. Glazed ceramic decorations appear in profusion, as well as corbel table friezes on the apses. In St John Aleitourgetos domical vaults rise above the corner compartments, pastophoria and bema. Its façade decoration is even more exuberant than that of the Pantokrator, with arcades and niched pilasters, panels of tile patterning, glazed ceramic ornaments, corbel table friezes and a variety of sculpted stone pieces. The decoration is antitectonic, and links with both Constantinople and Serbia have been suggested.

During the 13th century Serbian architecture was dominated by a local tradition that was influenced by the Romanesque style of the Adriatic coast (*see* SERBIA, §II, 2). Except for its dome, the Holy Trinity (*c.* 1260) at Sopoćani (*see* SOPOĆANI, HOLY TRINITY) may be regarded as a provincial Romanesque product. The church of the Annunciation (late 13th century) at Gradač is similar, but

with Gothic detailing. Under King Stephen Uroš II Milutin (*reg* 1282–1321) Byzantine architecture came to the fore. The katholikon of Chilandar, the Serbian monastery on Mt Athos, was rebuilt in 1303 and is a purely Byzantine product. The domed cross-in-square naos has side apses to the north and south, following the Athonite formula, and domes rise above the corner bays of the deep narthex or *lite*. The construction and decorative detailing have been associated with both Constantinople and Thessaloniki. Located on Byzantine soil, Chilandar may have been Milutin's initial point of contact with Byzantine architecture. Milutin's subsequent building programme included the reconstruction of Bogorodica Ljeviška (1306–7) at Prizren and St George at STARO NAGORIČANO (1313), where five-domed plans were superimposed on to the existing, elongated buildings. Masons for these projects may have come from Epiros. The major achievement of the period is the church of the Dormition at Gračanica (before 1321), which Milutin may have intended as his mausoleum. The head architect may have come from Thessaloniki, as indicated by the bold design and the tall brick domes, although the cloisonné wall construction suggests other influences as well. The plan unifies a cross-in-square core with an enveloping ambulatory and lateral chapels, with domes positioned at the four corners. Forms are attenuated and organized pyramidally, with the central dome rising to a height more than six times its width. The fantastic exterior design is perhaps the finest achievement of Late Byzantine architecture (for illustration *see* GRAČANICA).

A second phase of Byzantine influence is evident under Stephen Uroš Dušan (*reg* 1331–55) and Stephen Uroš (*reg* 1355–71). Wall construction and façade articulation of this period are more strongly influenced by Constantinople. The church of St Demetrius (begun *c.* 1345) at Markov Monastery and the church of the Assumption (after *c.* 1355) at Matejić Monastery were built in traditional Byzantine style, probably by local builders. While numerous decorative elements are maintained, the articulation of the façade is closer to Middle Byzantine Constantinople than to Palaiologan developments.

BIBLIOGRAPHY

A. Rachénov: *Eglises de Mesemvria* (Sofia, 1932)
S. Eyice: *Son devir bizans mimarisi* [The last phase of Byzantine architecture] (Istanbul, 1963, rev. 2/1980)
A. K. Orlandos: *I Parigoritissa tis Artis* [The Parigoritissa of Arta] (Athens, 1963)
H. Hallensleben: 'Untersuchungen zur Baugeschichte der ehemaligen Pammakaristoskirche, der heutigen Fethiye Camii in Istanbul', *Istanbul. Mitt.*, xiii–xiv (1963–4), pp. 128–93
K. Mijatev: *Arhitekturata v srednoveknova Bulgarija* [Medieval architecture in Bulgaria] (Sofia, 1965)
H. Hallensleben: 'Byzantinische Kirchtürme', *Kunstchronik*, x (1966), pp. 309–11
——: 'Untersuchungen zur Genesis und Typologie des "Mystratypus"', *Marburg. Jb. Kstwiss.*, xviii (1969), pp. 105–18
E. Melas, ed.: *Alte Kirchen und Klöster Griechenlands* (Cologne, 1972)
H. Belting, C. Mango and D. Mouriki: *The Mosaics and Frescoes of St Mary Pammakaristos (Fethiye Camii) at Istanbul* (Washington, DC, 1978)
S. Ćurčić: 'Articulation of Church Façades during the First Half of the Fourteenth Century', *L'Art byzantin au début du XIVe siècle* (Belgrade, 1978)
H. Buchwald: 'Lascarid Architecture', *Jb. Österreich. Byz.*, xxviii (1979), pp. 261–96
S. Ćurčić: *Gračanica: King Milutin's Church and its Place in Late Byzantine Architecture* (College Park, 1979)
G. Velenis: 'Oi Hagioi Apostoloi tis Thessalonikis kai i scholi tis Konstantinoupolis' [The Holy Apostles of Thessaloniki and the school of Constantinople], *XVI. internationaler Byzantinistenkongress: Wien, 1981*, ii/4, pp. 457–67
P. L. Vocotopoulos: 'The Role of Constantinopolitan Architecture during the Middle and Late Period', *XVI. internationaler Byzantinistenkongress: Wien, 1981*, xxxi/2, pp. 551–73
S. Eyice: 'Die byzantinische Kirche in der Nähe des Yenişehir-Tores zu Iznik', *Mat. Turcica*, vii–viii (1981–2), pp. 152–67
G. Velenis: *Ermineia tou exoterikou diakosmou sti byzantini architektoniki* [The interpretation of exterior decoration in Byzantine architecture] (Thessaloniki, 1984)
Thessaloniki and its Monuments, Thessaloniki Ephorate of Byzantine Antiquities (Thessaloniki, 1985)
R. G. Ousterhout: *The Architecture of the Kariye Camii in Istanbul* (Washington, DC, 1987)
C. Bouras: 'Byzantine Architecture in the Middle of the 14th Century', *Dečani et l'art byzantin au milieu du XIVe siècle* (Belgrade, 1989), pp. 47–54
S. Ćurčić: 'Architecture in the Byzantine Sphere of Influence around the Middle of the Fourteenth Century', *Dečani et l'art byzantin au milieu du XIVe siècle* (Belgrade, 1989), pp. 55–68
M. Rautman: 'Patrons and Buildings in Late Byzantine Thessaloniki', *Jb. Österreich. Byz.*, xxxix (1989), pp. 295–315
R. G. Ousterhout: 'Constantinople, Bithynia and Regional Developments in Later Palaeologan Architecture', *The Twilight of Byzantium*, ed. S. Ćurčić and D. Mouriki (Princeton, 1991), pp. 75–110
L. Theis: *Die Architektur der Kirche der Panagia Parēgorētissa in Arta/Epirus* (Amsterdam, 1991)

ROBERT OUSTERHOUT

3. SECULAR. Fortifications constitute the largest body of extant secular architecture in the Early Christian and Byzantine period; examples of palaces also survive throughout the period. Other types of secular architecture include the public baths and theatres of the Early Christian period, houses and other domestic and administrative structures.

(i) Fortifications. (ii) Palaces. (iii) Other buildings.

(i) Fortifications. Early Christian and Byzantine fortifications were based on the Greco-Roman tradition of military architecture (*see* MILITARY ARCHITECTURE AND FORTIFICATION, §II, 4 and 5), and the extent to which elements of that tradition were developed to meet changing defensive priorities, resources and political relations has become clearer through systematic examination of their measurements and settings. Although Byzantine fortifications often seem architecturally undistinguished, they nevertheless provide a fertile source of information for Eastern medieval history.

(a) *c.* 313–*c.* 800. (b) *c.* 800–1453.

(a) c. *313*–c. *800.* The developments in military architecture during the 3rd century, from *c.* 240 onwards, and the Tetrarchy (293–311) dominated European fortification systems for a thousand years, above all in the replacement of the traditional fortress by the mortared brick and stone enceinte, with battlemented circuit wall and externally projecting towers. In the 4th and 5th centuries this system was used to refortify cities, legionary and sub-legionary camps, imperial palaces and important villas. It ranged from the simple square or rectangular enclosure with a tower or bastion at each corner (*tetrapyrgion*) found in the Danubian and eastern frontier provinces, to the great double enceintes at Augustae (now Hisar, Bulgaria), Thessaloniki and Constantinople. Their size and strength reflect the military, administrative and political reorganizations of the period, while the lack of broad ceremonial gateways and other Classical features emphasizes their utilitarian purpose. Architectural decoration was usually limited to the orderly combination of bands of brick running through the thickness of the wall, and bands of roughly shaped stone, covering a rubble core (*opus mixtum*). Occasionally the brickwork was articulated over the core in double or triple arcades interspersed with brick prophylactic crosses and separated by brick bands. Sometimes, however, the brick and stone were simply massed to form a stone base and brick superstructure. Both variants are found at Thessaloniki.

The most impressive version of this defensive system was built at Constantinople (413–47; see fig. 29) and comprises a double land wall lined with externally projecting towers. The towers of the inner wall are square and octagonal, and have three or four levels, with lateral and frontal embrasures on the middle levels; the surrounding terraces could be reached by postern gates. In front of the outer wall is a scarp surmounted by breastworks, a moat crossed by bridges and a counterscarp. The distance from inner wall to counterscarp is 55 m, thus exposing the aggressor to fire from several angles and directions at every stage of advance. The system was also designed to thwart sappers and the approach of siege engines.

At Thessaloniki a similar triple line of defence replaced the Hellenistic and Roman walls in the mid-5th century. It lacks polygonal towers, but the inner enceinte is articulated by rectangular and triangular redans; the latter

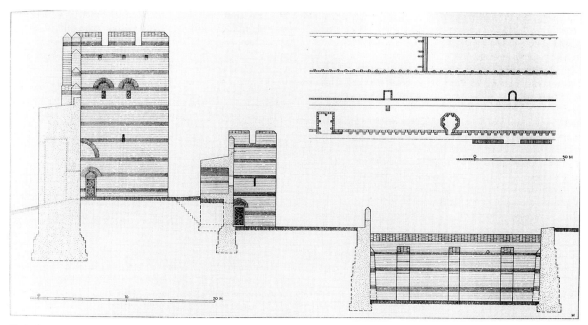

29. Defensive system of land walls and projecting towers, Constantinople (now Istanbul), Turkey, 413–47; from F. Krischen: *Die Landmauer von Konstantinopel*, i (Berlin, 1938), pl. 4

were particularly effective on low ground against catapult-fire and ramming. Another 5th-century refinement is the use of machicolation to defend the gateway at Augustae. Barriers, similar to Hadrian's Wall, were also constructed in the 5th century, such as the one across the Isthmus of Corinth, and the Great Wall (65 km long) in south-eastern Thrace.

Prodigious amounts were spent during the 6th century on fortifying the Balkans, the eastern frontier provinces and North Africa, largely with rectangular forts, simple watch-towers, barriers and irregular polygonal hilltop forts. Roman watch-towers were sometimes surrounded by *tetrapyrgia*, thus resembling small donjons. Justinian I was particularly active in consolidating the empire's frontiers, but he also built or rebuilt barriers across the isthmuses of Gallipoli (now Gelibolu, Turkey), Kassandra and Corinth, and at Thermopylai (Greece), and fortified great roads, such as the Via Egnatia in the Balkans, as well as refortifying some historically important cities, such as Antioch (now Antakya, Turkey) and Nikopolis (nr Préveza, Greece). His reign also marked a reassessment of the role of fortification, for in founding or refounding such cities as Sergioupolis (now RUSAFA, Syria), Justiniana Prima (now CARIČIN GRAD, Serbia) and probably Theologos (now Selçuk, Turkey), he was actually building fortresses. Ranging between 7 and 20 ha, and often including citadels, they protected the main ecclesiastical and administrative buildings. Citadels were also added to existing urban enceintes as at Zenobia (now Halabiyeh, Syria). In Syria and North Africa, Justinian was responsible for the construction of free-standing and engaged residential towers, which covered an area of up to 25 m square. The need for strong defences resulted in the integration of religious and military functions within a single complex or building, as in the fortified monastery of St Catherine

on Mt Sinai (*see* SINAI, §2(i)) and the east-facing, two-storey, 'chapel-shaped' towers found at some smaller fortifications (e.g. Donje Butorke, nr Kladovo, Serbia). Justinian's builders also devised the massed formation of pentagonal towers, as at Salona (now Solin, Croatia) and Vodno, overlooking Scupi (now Skopje, former Yugoslav Republic of Macedonia), which influenced developments in the Dark Ages (e.g. at Ancyra; now Ankara, Turkey).

The permanent settlement of the Slavs in the Balkans as far south as the Peloponnese and the frequent devastation of Asia Minor by the Arabs in the 7th and 8th centuries led to the abandonment of many 3rd- to 5th-century urban fortifications and to the construction of fortresses within or near ancient urban sites and close to important frontiers. Most inner citadels of this period provided the only effective lines of defence and were built by connecting the façades of public buildings and adding a number of small towers, bastions and simple projections, as in Turkey at Ephesos, Miletos and Magnesia on the Maeander. In some instances, however, entire ancient complexes were re-employed with minimal changes, as for example the fortified palace of Diocletian at Split (*see* SPLIT, §2), which became the refuge of the inhabitants of Salona. Some of the new fortresses were built on a large scale, such as that by the ruined city of Ancyra (7th or 8th century; *c.* 350×150 m), reflecting their role as major defensive centres. Others were small hilltop enclosures overlooking roads, rivers and sea-lanes, for example on Mt Lazaros, Samos, with its single bastion, and at Emporio, Chios. Small 'urban' forts are also typical of this period, such as the quadrangular enclosure (*c.* 1000 sq. m) with one tower built over the Asklepieion at Priene (nr Doganbey, Turkey).

Among the changes in military architecture in the 7th to the 8th century was the reintroduction of the barbican (e.g. Ancyra) and the development of the pentagonal tower into the elongated tower *à bec*, examples of which can be seen at Dhidhimotikhon (Greece), Gortyn (Crete) and, above all, Ancyra, which had more than 43 towers. The development of concentric towered enceintes in Anatolia at Korykos (nr Silifke) and Kotyaion (now Kütahya) may also be dated to this period. It remains unclear, however, whether multi-storey watch-towers, such as one (12.5×7.5 m) incorporated within an enceinte near Yahalı (Turkey), belong to this or the following period.

(b) c. 800–1453. Major programmes of refortification were undertaken along the new frontiers in the Balkan peninsula, Syria and eastern Anatolia between the 9th and 11th centuries. Most fortresses were the headquarters of small detachments of peasant soldiers and consist of a restricted enceinte with rectangular and semicircular towers and bastions. Precipitous locations are often their principal protection, as for example at Dereağzi (nr Kaş, Turkey) and Philippi, of the 9th and 10th centuries respectively. Larger fortresses are generally provided with powerful outer baileys, as at Ancyra (9th century) and Attaleia (now Antalya, Turkey; 10th century), both of which sheltered emergent lower towns. Ancyra and the 10th-century fortress of QAL'AT SIM'ĀN (Syria) also acquired citadels and inner and outer baileys, arranged one behind the other rather than concentrically. At Sigon (now Sahyun, Syria) the 10th-century *tetrapyrgion* citadel stands in the centre of the inner bailey. In addition to the *tetrapyrgion*, another example of which (*c.* 36 m square) has been found on Samothrace, such features as the *proteikhisma* (outwork; e.g. Polystylon, nr Abdera, Greece) and the covered gallery with embrasures (e.g. Constantinople and Ancyra) were reintroduced.

Numerous powerful fortresses were built in western Asia Minor in response to the growing Turkish threat during the 12th century. Recalling Early Christian fortifications, they have single circuits and large horseshoe-shaped, circular and semicircular towers, with brick-vaulted embrasured chambers on one or two levels. John II (*reg* 1118–43) is known to have built two such fortresses at Lopadion (nr Bandirma, Turkey) and Akhyraous (nr Balıkesir, Turkey); the extension of the land wall of Constantinople by Manuel I (*reg* 1143–80) to include the Blachernai suburb comprises a similar system of defence. Other features of military architecture from the first half of the 12th century include circular corner towers or bastions, as at Kotyaion (diam. 16–17 m) and horseshoe-shaped catapult platforms, about 60 of which were also built at Kotyaion to replace its towers of the 7th to the 9th century.

In the Late Byzantine period, in order better to defend the growing number of towns that had developed around fortifications built between the 7th and 12th centuries, emperors and local rulers expanded the enceintes of smaller fortresses (e.g. Serres, Greece) and heightened the walls and towers of large ones, as at Nicaea (now Iznik, Turkey), Smyrna, Trebizond, Thessaloniki and Constantinople. At Nicaea, the most powerfully protected city in western Anatolia, Theodore I (*reg* 1204–22) even added a *proteikhisma*, thus emulating the Early Christian systems

at Constantinople and Thessaloniki. Small citadels were sometimes added to the upper parts of cities, as at Smyrna (13th century) and Thessaloniki (probably 14th century). John VI Kantakouzenos (*reg* 1347–54) converted the Golden Gate at Constantinople into a fortified complex, later replaced by the Ottoman Yediküle fortress. Other characteristic features of military architecture from this period are the backless tower, as seen in the 14th- to 15th-century outer and inner baileys surrounding the town of MYSTRAS, and the large residential tower with a raised entrance. The latter was foreshadowed by the tower (*c.* 14 m square) that Isaak II (*reg* 1185–95) inserted into the Blachernai land walls: although scarcely larger than neighbouring towers, it has large well-lit chambers on two levels and a battlemented roof. The large residential tower could either form part of a citadel's enceinte, without access to the connecting walkway, or be free-standing like the Frankish donjon. This second type of tower was used to refortify citadels, such as those in Turkey at Selymbria (now Silivri; 1346) and in Greece at Verroia (1350) and

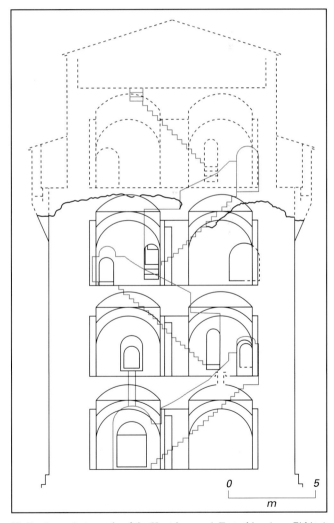

30. Donjon, private castle of the Kantakouzenoi, Empython (now Pithion), Greece, 14th century; restored cutaway view

Serres (1350); in the construction of new fortresses, for example at Kordyle (now Akçakale, Turkey), Rhizaion (now Rize, Turkey) and Gynaikokastron (Greece; *c.* 1330); and in a new class of private fortifications, such as the 14th-century monasteries of Mt Athos. The donjon of the private castle of the Kantakouzenoi at Empythion (now Pithion, Greece; see fig. 30) is unique for its battered sides and machicolation. Most 14th- to 15th-century donjons were constructed as residences, with chimney flues and upper-storey windows in addition to embrasured loopholes. By the mid-14th century, donjons were also being built with slight perimeter walls that served both as watchtowers and as protection for manorial granges. One of the most impressive donjons is the Pyrgos Prosphoriou (Ouranoupolis, Greece) built by the Vatopedi Monastery (Athos) before 1341. It originally had eight floors, unlike most Late Byzantine donjons, which only had four, as for example the tower of the Docheiariou Monastery (8 m square) at Mariana (Greece). Private residential towers based on tall, slender, Italian models became popular for both rural (e.g. Longanikos, Greece) and urban residences. Examples of the latter are shown in the *Panorama of Constantinople* (*c.* 1560; Leiden, Bib. Rijksuniv.) by Melchior Lorck and survive at Mystras, as in the three-storey tower of the Little Palace. Like contemporary churches, these buildings often had highly decorative façades, the finest surviving example being that added to the tower of the outer bailey at Mystras after its incorporation into the refectory of the 14th-century Peribleptos Monastery.

BIBLIOGRAPHY

A. Orlandos: 'Byzantinos pyrgos para ten Olynthon' [A Byzantine tower near Olynthos], *Epeteris Etaireias Byz. Spoudon*, xiii (1937), pp. 393–6
W. Karnapp and E. Schneider: *Die Stadtmauer von Iznik* (Berlin, 1938)
C. Andrews: *Castles of the Morea* (Princeton, 1953/*R* 1978)
W. Müller-Wiener: 'Mittelalterliche Befestigungen im südlichen Jonien', *Istanbul. Mitt.*, xix (1961), pp. 5–122
E. Fischer: *Melchior Lorck* (Copenhagen, 1962), pp. 24–5
A. Bon: *La Morée Franque: Recherches historiques, topographiques et archéologiques sur la principauté d'Achaïe, 1205–1430* (Paris, 1969)
W. Müller-Wiener: *Bildlexikon zur Topographie Istanbuls* (Tübingen, 1977)
B. Tsangadas: *The Fortifications and Defenses of Constantinople* (New York, 1980)
D. Pringle: *The Defense of Byzantine Africa from Justinian to the Arab Conquest*, 2 vols, Brit. Archaeol. Rep., Int. Ser., xcix (Oxford, 1981)
M. Biernacka-Lubańska: *Rzymskie i wczesnobizantyjskie budownictwo obronne w Mezji Dolnej i połnocnej Tracji/The Roman and Early Byzantine Fortifications of Lower Moesia and Northern Thrace* (Wrocław, 1982) [bilingual text]
A. Lawrence: 'A Skeletal History of Byzantine Fortification', *Annu. Brit. Sch. Athens*, lxxviii (1983), pp. 171–227
S. Mitchell, ed.: *Armies and Frontiers in Roman and Byzantine Anatolia*, Brit. Archaeol. Rep., Int. Ser., clvi (Oxford, 1983)
J. Lander: *Roman Stone Fortifications: Variation and Change from the First Century A.D. to the Fourth*, Brit. Archaeol. Rep., Int. Ser., ccvi (Oxford, 1984)
J.-M. Spieser: *Thessalonique et ses monuments du IVe au VIe siècle* (Paris, 1984)
A. Bryer and D. Winfield: *The Byzantine Monuments and Topography of the Pontos*, 2 vols (Washington, DC, 1985)
C. Foss: *Kütahya* (1985), i of *Survey of Medieval Castles of Anatolia*, Brit. Archaeol. Rep., Int. Ser. (Oxford, 1985)
C. Foss and D. Winfield: *Byzantine Fortifications: An Introduction* (Pretoria, 1986)
I. Mikulčić: 'Spätantike Fortifikationen in der S. R. Makedonien', *XXXIII Corso di cultura sull'arte ravennate e bizantina: Ravenna, 1986*, pp. 221–51
M. Ballance and others: *Excavations in Chios, 1952–1955: Byzantine Emporio*, Brit. Sch. Archaeol. Athens, suppl. vol. xx (London, 1989)
M. Korres: 'The Architecture of the Pythion Castle', *Byz. Forsch.*, xiv (1989), pp. 273–8

ARCHIBALD DUNN

(ii) Palaces. During the Early Christian period the term 'palace' was used not only to refer to the official residences of the emperor, but also the residences of high-ranking government and church officials. The distinction between these residences and luxury villas is often blurred. After *c.* 800 fortified palaces became more common.

(a) *c.* 313–*c.* 800. (b) *c.* 800–1453.

(a) c. 313–c. 800. The development of Early Christian palaces can be properly understood only in the context of the proliferation of imperial palaces that began with the establishment of the Tetrarchy, in 285, and the subsequent development of several new imperial capitals, at Trier, Milan, Thessaloniki, Antioch and elsewhere. Until that time the Palatine (*see* ROME, §V, 3) had served as the sole official residence of the Roman emperors, but under the Tetrarchs the seat of imperial power was wherever the emperor happened to be. The builders of the new tetrarchic imperial palaces clearly emulated certain topographical features of the Palatine. Despite the fact that little survives of any of these palaces, it is evident that all the complexes were built next to a circus, within an urban setting. As a stage for great public spectacles sponsored by and presided over by the emperor, the circus served as the main link between the ruler and his subjects, between the palace and the city. The tetrarchic imperial palaces also included other components found in the Palatine, such as triumphal arches fronting the entrance to the palace, public baths near the point of entry, monumental vestibules and huge basilican audience halls.

Another distinctive feature of the tetrarchic imperial palace is its connection with the imperial place of burial. Owing to the fact that Roman law forbade burials within cities, several different solutions were attempted between *c.* 300 and 337. The emperor Maxentius (*reg* 306–12) built a palace with an adjoining circus and a domed mausoleum for his prematurely deceased son, Romulus, on the Via Appia, just outside Rome. In Thessaloniki Emperor Galerius (*reg* 305–11) chose an alternative solution *c.* 300: he added a whole new section to the existing town in order to accommodate his palace with an adjacent circus and, axially opposite the entrance into the palace, a domed rotunda that was probably intended as his mausoleum. It was later converted into the church of Hagios Georgios (*see* THESSALONIKI, §III, 2).

Another alternative to the palace schemes employed by Maxentius in Rome and by Galerius in Thessaloniki is that of the imperial palace–mausoleum complex contained within a miniature fortified city, as in the palace of Diocletian (*c.* 300–*c.* 307) at Split (*see* SPLIT, §1). The architectural finds at Gamzigrad in eastern Serbia show similarities in rural location, form and function with the palace at Split. Excavations have revealed that Gamzigrad was the site of the ancient town of Romuliana, which was built by Galerius in memory of his mother, Romula, and where he himself was buried. Of the two extensive residential complexes that have been discovered, one was almost certainly the palace, to judge from its lavish decoration. Among other finds are two temples, one of which may have been an imperial mausoleum, and a circuit of towered walls with elaborately decorated, multi-storey city gates.

The Great Palace (see ISTANBUL, §III, 12), built by Constantine the Great and subsequently expanded, may be seen as the summation of the different solutions employed in the tetrarchic imperial palaces. The little that is known about the Great Palace is based largely on the literary sources. Its main components and layout match closely those of the tetrarchic palaces: it was approached by a processional avenue (the Regia), at the beginning of which stood a triumphal arch (the Milion), while at its opposite end stood the monumental vestibule of the palace (the Chalke). Close to the palace entrance were the public Baths of Zeuxippos, whereas the long west side of the palace complex was flanked by the hippodrome. It seems that the organizational principles of the interior layout of the palace were similar to those employed in the tetrarchic palatine complexes, with many clusters of 'public' and 'private' structures, loosely linked by open spaces and gardens. Related to the Great Palace, but physically detached from it, was the imperial mausoleum built by Constantine the Great that later became the church of the Holy Apostles (see ISTANBUL, §III, 9(i)).

The lack of physical evidence of Constantinian palace architecture from Constantinople is to some extent counterbalanced by archaeological discoveries made elsewhere. Among the most important is the 'suburban villa' at Mediana, 4 km to the south-east of Constantine's birthplace at Naissus (now Niš, Serbia). The partially excavated remains reveal a large and luxurious residential complex, including a peristyle court (c. 68×40 m) with a large central pool and mosaic floors under the covered porticos. North of the peristyle court was a single-aisled, apsed hall, the dimensions and proportions of which recall audience halls of tetrarchic imperial palaces at Trier and on the Via Appia, Rome. A collection of porphyry and marble statuettes without their heads was found in one of the rooms surrounding three sides of the peristyle. Most of the statuettes may originally have represented pagan divinities, a fact that may prove useful in determining the history of the complex.

The planning formula of a rectangular peristyle court with a basilican audience hall on one side appears to have been in frequent use in luxury residences, both inside and outside cities, at least from the tetrarchic period (the concept may have originated much earlier) to the 6th century. One of the better tetrarchic examples is the villa at Piazza Armerina (see PIAZZA ARMERINA, §1). At the other end of this chronological spectrum is the excavated peristyle court of the Great Palace in Constantinople, which is no earlier than c. 530. A number of impressive examples from the intervening period are known to have existed, as at Löffelbach, Austria; Gorsium (now Tác; early 4th century), Hungary; Abritus (now Razgrad; 4th century), Bulgaria; Ravenna (c. 500); Apollonia (now Marsa Susa; c. 500), Libya; and New Paphos (4th–5th century), Cyprus. Despite the difficulty in identifying the specific patrons of most of these residences, enough is known about them to indicate that they ranged in social rank from emperors to governors and other types of high-ranking government and church officials. Thus it appears

that in the 5th and 6th centuries the number of palaces proliferated and involved a broader spectrum of social ranks, while the meaning of the term 'palace' became even more diffused. The remains of two impressive palaces (first half of the 5th century; see ISTANBUL, fig. 1) excavated to the west of the hippodrome in Constantinople have been positively identified as belonging to high-ranking officials of the imperial administration. The first of these belonged to Antiochos, a eunuch of Iranian extraction who rose to power under Emperor Arkadios (reg 395–408), but fell out of favour under Theodosios II (reg 408–50) c. 421; its hexagonal hall was later converted to the church of Hagia Euphemia (c. 550). The second, adjacent palace, belonged to Lausos, who held the title of the praepositus sacri cubiculi (grand chamberlain). This palace was noted for a relatively collection of ancient Greek sculpture (Istanbul, Archaeol. Mus.). Palaces belonging to bishops and other high-ranking members of the clergy are distinctive by the nature of their location (next to cathedral churches) and function, if not by their architectural layout. Several examples dating from the 5th and 6th centuries are known, such as in Poreč (c. 540), Caričin Grad, Stobi, Miletos and Aphrodisias. Only fragmentary remains of the patriarchal palace, near the southwest corner of Hagia Sophia in Constantinople, have survived.

Fortification walls (see §(i) above) only gradually entered the realm of palace architecture. Although several tetrarchic palaces are known to have been built partially in conjunction with fortification walls (e.g. Antioch, Split), these palaces were not fully walled in, maintaining the old principle of 'openness' towards their urban setting. During the 4th century, probably as a result of the association of imperial palaces with the establishment of 'new cities', the first fully articulated, tower-flanked palace façades made their appearance. This is the case with the sea façade of the palace of Diocletian, and was apparently also the case in the palace at Antioch, according to the 4th-century description by Libanios (see Downey). The most telling example of this phenomenon is the relatively small palace (5th–6th centuries; see fig. 31) at Polače, on the island of Meleda (now Mljet) on the Dalmatian coast. Here two enormous polygonal towers flank the small entrance façade facing the sea, directly behind which is a sizeable single-aisled, apsed audience hall. The various distinctive components of tetrarchic imperial palaces seem to have been juxtaposed in what could be described as a 'compact variant' of an imperial palace. Another comparable example appears to have been the palace of Theodoric in Verona. No longer extant, this palace is known from a description by Anonymous Valesianus (Pars Posterior, ed. T. Mommsen (Berlin, 1892), p. 324) and from a copy of a lost 10th-century drawing, the Iconographia Rateriana (Verona, Bib. Capitolare). The drawing clearly shows the 'Palatium', identifiable by its twin-towered façade, situated within the walled-in 'Castrum' area on the other side of the Adige River from the main part of the city.

One of the crucial developments in palace architecture of the 5th and 6th centuries was the appearance of the fully fortified palace complex. Completely isolated from the city within which it was located, such a fortified palace was conceptually antithetical to earlier ideas of the urban

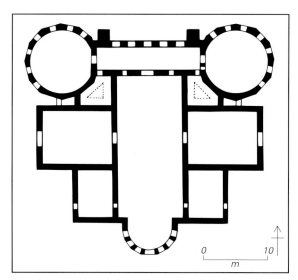

31. Palace, Polače, Meleda (now Mljet), Croatia, 5th–6th centuries AD, plan

palace. Its evolution appears to have been dictated by two factors. The first had to do with the ever-increasing need for improving the security of the palace itself against potential external invaders. More significant is the second factor, which suggests a growing sense of insecurity *vis-à-vis* the surrounding inhabitants. Mounting incidents of urban violence and social uprisings in Early Christian cities must be partly responsible for the gradual emergence of the fortified palace type.

At first relatively scarce, walled-in palaces reflect particular local circumstances rather than any general trends. One of the earliest examples is a large palace referred to as the 'Palace of the Giants' (*c*. 400), built in the southeast corner of the ancient Agora in Athens. Threats from Alaric's Goths in the late 4th century may well have been responsible for the construction of such a walled-in palace at a time when the city's economic situation was improving. Although partly built out of spolia from the ruined buildings in the area, the palace was lavishly embellished. It was enclosed by a continuous wall separating it from the neighbouring urban district that had developed south of the Agora.

Comparable local circumstances must also have influenced the planning of the episcopal palace at Caričin Grad. The palace, together with the cathedral, was located within the heavily fortified acropolis. Here, for the first time, the fortification wall was equipped with massive projecting towers facing the city. The number of such local instances of palace fortification must have gradually increased. According to Theophanes, Justinian II (*reg* 685–95; 705–11) built a circuit wall around the Great Palace during his first reign. Thus, even the character of the once 'open' urban palaces slowly but inevitably gave way to a new, fortified palace type.

(b) c. *800–1453.* A special category of fortified palaces appeared after *c*. 800, apparently under the influence of the Ummayad palaces (*see* ISLAMIC ART, §II, 3(iii)). Palaces belonging to this category are generally found in suburban or country locations; they are self-sufficient and feature rectangular walled enclosures with regularly spaced projecting towers. As such, they recall the small fortified town-palaces such as Romuliana, but they differ from their predecessors in several fundamental ways. Above all, the fortified enclosure of these later palaces does not include any urban quarters; only the palace complex lies within the fortification wall. One of the best-known examples of this type is the palace (829–42) built by Emperor Theophilos at Bryas (now Maltepe), an Asiatic suburb of Constantinople on the Sea of Marmara. The partially excavated remains of this palace reveal a rectangular enclosure, a circular substructure in the middle of the enclosure and an adjoining rectangular substructure on the same axis with rows of columns that originally supported domical vaults of brick. Little is known about the functional layout or the physical appearance of this palace. Some apparent similarities with the early Ummayad palaces have been explained by the fact that an envoy of Emperor Theophilos spent some time on a mission in Baghdad. A palpable impression of a palace of this type is gained from a 10th-century royal palace at Geguti in Georgia. Its rectangular enclosure is protected by a system of massive walls with regularly spaced projecting towers. The interior of the enclosure is entirely given over to the palace building, the centre of which is dominated by a large domed hall.

The most vivid, if fictitious, picture of a 10th- or 11th-century fortified country palace is gleaned from an epic poem, *Digenis Akritas* (vii, pp. 97–103). Located on a canal off the Euphrates, this imaginary palace is said to be enclosed by a wall 'of adequate height'. Within it stands a 'fair-sized', three-storey stone rectangular building constituting the owner's residence. Its interiors are lavishly decorated with marble revetments and gold mosaics. The scenes depict various mythological, biblical and historical battles, victories and heroes. Fronting the palace block is a large open court, in the middle of which stands the church of St Theodore, within which are interred the mortal remains of the owner's parents. The palace is surrounded by a resplendent garden inhabited by exotic birds, which is referred to as 'paradise'. The description of the imaginary palace in *Digenis Akritas*, its decoration and its setting, accords most closely with the 12th-century palace known as La Ziza that was built by the Normans in Palermo and is Islamic in inspiration. Links with the Islamic tradition are also evident in descriptions of the Great Palace in Constantinople, which was substantially remodelled by Theophilos and Basil I (*see* MACEDONIAN DYNASTY, (1)). The appearance of Islamic-looking buildings and decoration in the midst of the Great Palace, as was the case with the 12th-century hall known as Mouchroutas, bespeaks an architectural court style common to the Mediterranean world of the 11th and 12th centuries.

Single block-like palace buildings may also have been introduced from the world of Islam. The main examples in Constantinople are the Mangana and the Blachernai palaces. The former, built by Constantine IX (*see* MACEDONIAN DYNASTY, (4)), is known from the fully excavated remains of its massive substructures. The substructures of the Blachernai palace, built by several Komnenian emperors during the 12th century, have been only partially uncovered, but the form of the main building block seems readily apparent.

The block-palace type continued to be employed during the Late Byzantine period. It has generally been assumed to be of Western derivation, but it differs from Western examples in several ways and it is much more likely that this type evolved from the Middle Byzantine prototypes discussed above. The oldest known Byzantine block-palace from this period is the palace at Nymphaion (formerly Nif, now Kemalpaşa) c. 40 km east of Izmir, Turkey. The palace was probably built during the first half of the 13th century, and served as an important residence of the Laskarid emperors during the Latin occupation of Constantinople. Despite its ruined state, the three-storey building preserves its simple block-like form (25.75×11.50 m). The ground floor was originally vaulted and communicated with the exterior through two large, double-arched openings. The two upper storeys had wooden ceilings and relatively small but numerous arched openings. No trace of any decoration survives, although archaeological exploration, if undertaken, may provide additional information on this and other aspects of the palace, as well as on the nature of its surroundings, apparently an urban quarter.

The most impressive of the Late Byzantine palaces, the Tekfur Saray (late 13th century) in Constantinople, is in many ways closely related to the palace at Nymphaion. Of the main three-storey block (c. 25×13 m), the ground floor was originally vaulted, while the top two storeys had wooden ceilings. Four large arched openings pierce the main north façade of the ground floor, while each of the upper storeys has a row of smaller and more numerous arched windows (see fig. 32). Unlike the palace at Nymphaion, however, the Tekfur Saray has a highly decorative main façade featuring numerous patterns executed in brick, stone, flat tiles and ceramic elements; nothing survives of the building's interior decoration. Again, unlike the Nymphaion, the Tekfur Saray block is not free-standing. It stands between the inner and outer walls of the city and projects a foreboding image towards the city, since its main open façade faces an inner court. Despite the Western appearance of its main façade, the Tekfur Saray differs from contemporary Western palaces on account of its 'anti-urban' exterior. This characteristic of Late Byzantine urban palaces is explained by the deteriorating social conditions in contemporary Byzantine cities. The renaissance of cultural life, of which palaces must have been highly visible symbols, was but a mask of a society consumed by fundamental social, economic and political problems, and the defensive character of the Tekfur Saray reflects the concerns of its owner in regard to a potentially hostile urban environment. The reality of such fears and apprehensions is best illustrated by the recorded incident of the demolition of the private palace of the statesman, scholar and patron Theodore Metochites (1270–1332) by a Constantinopolitan mob during the early 14th century.

This introvert quality of Late Byzantine palace architecture is detectable even in the westernmost of Byzantine outposts, MYSTRAS. Here, the somewhat haphazard growth of the Palace of the Despots (13th century–mid-15th) reveals similar characteristics to those of the Tekfur Saray. Even its Great Hall, a wing of Venetian appearance

32. Tekfur Saray, Istanbul, Turkey, north façade, late 13th century

and Late Gothic detailing, faced a large, irregular inner court. This reveals an attitude diametrically opposite to that evident in the 14th- and 15th-century remodelling of the Doge's Palace (see VENICE, §IV, 6(i)), with its explicit, outward, urban orientation.

BIBLIOGRAPHY

EARLY SOURCES

Theophanes: *Chronographia* (c. AD 760–817); ed. C. de Boor, i (Leipzig, 1883), p. 367
Digenis Akritas (10th–11th century); Eng. trans. by D. B. Hull as *Digenis Akritas: The Two-blood Border Lord* (Athens, OH, 1972), pp. 97–103

GENERAL

K. M. Swoboda: *Römische und romanische Paläste* (Vienna, 1924, rev. 3/1969)
A. Alföldi: 'Die Ausgestaltung des monarchischen Zeremoniels am römischen Kaiserhöfe', *Mitt. Dt. Archäol. Inst.: Röm. Abt.*, xlix (1934), pp. 1–118
I. Lavin: 'The House of the Lord: Aspects of the Role of Palace Triclinia in the Architecture of Late Antiquity and the Early Middle Ages', *A. Bull.*, xliv (1962), pp. 1–27
F. Dirimtekin: 'Les Palais impériaux byzantins', *Corsi Cult. A. Ravenn. & Biz.*, xii (1965), pp. 225–45
S. Runciman: 'The Country and Suburban Palaces of the Emperors', *Charanis Studies: Essays in Honor of Peter Charanis*, ed. A. E. Laiou (New Brunswick, 1980), pp. 219–28
S. G. MacCormick: *Art and Ceremony in Late Antiquity* (Berkeley, 1981)
W. Müller-Wiener: 'Riflessioni sulle caratteristiche dei palazzi episcopali', *Felix Ravenna*, cxxv–cxxvi (1983), pp. 103–45
A. Cameron: 'The Construction of Court Ritual: The Byzantine Book of Ceremonies', *Rituals of Royalty: Power and Ceremonial in Traditional Societies*, ed. D. Cannadine and S. Price (Cambridge, 1987), pp. 106–35

c. 313–c. 800

G. Downey: 'Libanus' Oration in Praise of Antioch (*Oration* XI)', *Proc. Amer. Philos. Soc.*, ciii (1959), pp. 652–86
R. Naumann: 'Vorbericht über die Ausgrabungen zwischen Mese und Antiochos-Palast 1964 in Istanbul', *Istanbul. Mitt.*, xv (1965), pp. 135–48
M. Cagiano de Azevedo: 'Il *Palatium* di Porto Palazzo a Meleda', *Atti del convegno internazionale sul tema: Tardo antico e alto medioevo: La forma artistica nel passaggio dall'antichità al medioevo: Roma, 1967*, pp. 273–83
W. Modrian: *Der römische Landsitz von Löffelbach* (Graz, 1971)
W. A. Daszewski: 'Les Fouilles polonaises à Nea Paphos, 1972–1975: Rapport préliminaire', *Rep. Dept Ant., Cyprus* (1976), pp. 185–225

M. Cagiano de Azevedo: 'Il palazzo imperiale di Salonicco', *Felix Ravenna*, cxvii (1979), pp. 7–28

R. Latković and others: *Medijana* (Niš, 1979), pp. 17–26

L. Cozza and others: *La residenza imperiale di Massenzio: Villa, circo e mausoleo* (Rome, 1980)

D. Srejović and others: *Gamzigrad: Kasnoantički carski dvorac* [Gamzigrad: the Late Antique imperial palace] (Belgrade, 1983) [with Eng. summary]

J. Merten, ed.: *Trier Kaiserresidenz und Bischofssitz* (Mainz, 1984)

S. Ellis: *The 'Palace of the Dux' at Apollonia and Related Houses*, Brit. Archaeol. Rep., Int. Ser., cxxxxvi (Oxford, 1985), pp. 15–25

T. Ivanov and S. Stojanov: *Abritus: Its History and Archaeology* (Razgrad, 1985)

M. Johnson: 'Toward a History of Theodoric's Building Program', *Dumbarton Oaks Pap.*, xlii (1988), pp. 73–96

W. Müller-Wiener: 'Milet 1987, 2. Untersuchungen in Bischofspalast in Milet (1977–79)', *Istanbul. Mitt.*, xxxviii (1988), pp. 279–90

J. Fitz: *Gorsium–Herculia–Tác* (Budapest, 1990)

c. 800–1453

R. Demangel and E. Mamboury: *Le Quartier des Manganes et la première région de Constantinople* (Paris, 1939), pp. 39–47

S. Eyice: 'Quatre Edifices inédits ou mal connus: Les Substructions d'un palais (?) à Küçükyali près d'Istanbul', *Cah. Archéol.*, x (1959), pp. 256–8

C. Mango: 'Constantinopolitana', *Jb. Dt. Archäol. Inst.*, lxxx (1965), pp. 330–36

T. K. Kirova: 'Un palazzo e una casa di età tardo-bizantina in Asia Minore', *Felix Ravenna*, ciii–civ (1972), pp. 276–305

S. Runciman: 'Blacherne Palace and its Decoration', *Studies in Memory of David Talbot Rice*, ed. G. Robertson and G. Henderson (Edinburgh, 1975), pp. 277–83

R. Mepisashvili and V. Tsintsadze: *The Arts of Ancient Georgia* (New York, 1979), pp. 49–50, 58

G. Caronia: *La Zisa di Palermo: Storia e restauro* (Rome, 1982)

S. Sinos: 'Organisation und Form des byzantinischen Palastes von Mystras', *Arch.: Z. Gesch. Archit.*, xvii (1987), pp. 105–28

A. Peribene: 'Il quartiere della Blacherne a Costantinopoli', *Milion: Studi e ricerche d'arte bizantina* (Rome, 1988), pp. 215–24

SLOBODAN ĆURČIĆ

(iii) Other buildings. By *c.* 800 the great public baths, theatres and circuses that had been the centres of urban daily life since Antiquity had ceased to function and largely been replaced by churches. The influence of Christian philanthropy led to an expansion of charitable institutions. Domestic and administrative buildings, however, changed little over the Early Christian and Byzantine period.

(a) c. 313–c. 800. Among the many examples of public secular architecture that continued to form part of Early Christian cities, at least until *c.* 600, are the theatres, public baths, fora and circuses uncovered at such places as Stobi, Thessaloniki, Heraklea Lynkestis, Gerasa (see GERASA, §2), SIRMIUM and Carthage. In Rome, Constantine the Great's victory at the Milvian Bridge (312) and his accession as sole ruler of the Roman Empire in 324 was marked by the construction of baths (now the site of the Palazzo Rospigliosi) on the Quirinal, the Arch of Constantine (see ROME, §V, 12) and the remodelling of the Basilica of Maxentius (see ROME, §V, 11), which was renamed after Constantine. Of even greater significance, however, was his transformation of the ancient town of Byzantion into the new capital of Constantinople (see ISTANBUL, §I, 1). In addition to the existing circus and Baths of Zeuxippos, the city gained various new structures, among them a senate house, an imperial stoa known as the Basilica, and a wide colonnaded street (the Mese) leading to the Forum of Constantine, in the middle of which was a column with a statue of the Emperor. Successive emperors added other honorific columns and fora to Constantinople, as well as major works of public utility including the Aqueduct of Valens (*reg* 364–78), and several enormous uncovered and covered cisterns (4th–6th century; see CISTERN). In the 5th century the city had as many as 9 public baths and 153 private baths.

The adequate supply of water for baths, fountains and public use was a problem for every major city. Aqueducts usually brought water from a source or sources several kilometres outside, as in the case of Constantinople, which drew its supply from a region 15 km to the north-west. At Justiniana Prima (see CARIČIN GRAD), which was founded by Justinian I (*reg* 527–65), water was supplied by an aqueduct over a distance of *c.* 20 km. The vulnerability of aqueducts to the increasing incidence of foreign attack in the 6th century meant that cisterns became the more important sources of water for urban populations. Other utilitarian structures included bridges, an impressive example of which is Justinian's bridge (completed 560; for illustration see JUSTINIAN I) over the River Sangarius (now Sakarya) near Sapanca, Turkey.

There was a gradual change in the types of secular architecture that were built. Under the growing influence of the Church, entertainments that had traditionally taken place in the circus and theatre fell out of favour and were eventually banned. By the late 7th century most of these structures had been abandoned and were being used as quarries of building material or as dumping grounds for rubbish. Large public baths suffered a similar fate, perhaps partly because the Church regarded them as centres of immorality and partly because they became too expensive to maintain. Their building material was often reused, and many were replaced by churches, as at Thessaloniki (see THESSALONIKI, §I). However, baths that formed part of episcopal residences, monasteries and pilgrimage centres continued in use. From as early as the 4th century, charitable institutions that catered for the traveller, the sick and the poor were founded in the cities and on the roads of the empire by the state, ecclesiastical institutions and private citizens. Among the most celebrated foundations of this kind was the Hospice of Sampson (Prokopios: *Buildings* I.ii.14–17) built by Justinian I after 532 for the ill and destitute in Constantinople. Another development was the move away from the agora to the broad street (Gr. *embolos*) as the city's principal commercial centre. The Arkadiane (395–408) at Ephesos (see EPHESOS, §I, 3), for example, served as a main thoroughfare and gave access to rows of shops behind the colonnades on both sides of the street.

In the realm of domestic architecture some of the best-preserved examples have been uncovered at Ephesos. Here, as in other cities of the empire (e.g. Stobi, Athens), the most impressive dwellings, which vary considerably in size, consist of rooms arranged around a peristyle court. Depending on their function, these rooms could be lavishly decorated with mosaic, wall painting and marble revetment. Houses in the countryside were usually modest rectangular structures consisting of small rooms and built of wood, unbaked bricks or reeds. In northern Syria, however, the villages of the Limestone Massif discovered in 1910 by G. Tchalenko are built of ashlar masonry and form rectangular blocks of two or three storeys, each of which is divided into two or more rooms. They usually open out on to a courtyard. Other types of domestic architecture that are often found in association with houses are stables, workshops and storerooms. All these structures form the basis of secular architecture in monasteries. For, in addition to its ecclesiastical buildings, each monastery contains houses for the monks, a refectory, a bakery, a hospital, a guest-house, baths, storage rooms and workshops either randomly grouped or in a quadrangular arrangement and surrounded by a fortified wall (*see* CHRISTIANITY, §IV, 1).

(b) c. 800–1453. The written sources and archaeological finds indicate that baths continued to be built in the Middle and Late Byzantine periods, but not on the scale of their ancient and Early Christian predecessors. One exception, however, was the sumptuously decorated bathhouse (early 10th century) built by Leo VI (*see* MACEDONIAN DYNASTY, (2)) in the Great Palace at Constantinople. Baths came to be associated with healing and are often mentioned in connection with monastic hospitals, as in the hospital of Christ Pantokrator Monastery (1136) in Constantinople, which had room for 50 beds. This monastery also had a hospice for aged men. Numerous hospitals and charitable institutions were established outside monasteries by emperors, church dignitaries and wealthy laymen.

The layout and composition of secular buildings in Middle and Late Byzantine monasteries show little change from that of their Early Christian predecessors. Among the best-preserved examples are the monasteries on Mt Athos (*see* MT ATHOS, §2), while research on the Serbian monasteries of the 12th to the 15th century (e.g. Dečani, Prizren, Studenica, Gradač) has also revealed the usual complement of domestic and administrative structures within a fortified wall.

The earliest evidence for housing in this period has been dated *c.* 1000 and comes from the excavations at Athens, Corinth, Thebes and Pergamon. Most dwellings had two storeys and a rectangular plan centred around a courtyard with stables and storerooms on the ground floor and living quarters above. Simpler houses of two or three small rectangular rooms parallel to each other and erected along narrow alleys have been found at Corinth. There is extensive reuse of architectural elements in many of these structures. Late Byzantine domestic architecture is best preserved at MYSTRAS and MONEMVASIA. Houses are of two or three storeys, of which the ground floor is usually a vaulted room which served as a cellar, storeroom, stables, shop or cistern. Above this was the living space. Although some of the wealthier houses had balconies, arcades, crenellations and protective towers, architectural decoration was usually simple.

BIBLIOGRAPHY
A. K. Orlandos: *Monastiriaki architektoniki* [Monastic architecture] (Athens, 1926, 2/1958)
K. Dalman: *Der Valens-Aquädukt in Konstantinopel* (Bamberg, 1933)
G. Tchalenko: *Villages antiques de la Syrie du nord*, 3 vols (Paris, 1953–8)
D. J. Constantelos: *Byzantine Philanthropy and Social Welfare* (New Brunswick, NJ, 1968)
D. Claude: *Die byzantinische Stadt im 6. Jahrhundert* (Munich, 1969)
C. Mango: 'Daily Life of Byzantium', *Akten des XVI. internationalen byzantinischen Kongresses: Wien, 1981*, 1/ii, pp. 337–53
A. Berger: *Das Bad in der byzantinischen Zeit* (Munich, 1982)
C. Bouras: 'Houses in Byzantium', *Deltion Christ. Archaiol. Etaireias*, xi (1983), pp. 1–26
T. S. Miller: *The Birth of the Hospital in the Byzantine Empire* (Baltimore, MD, 1985)
S. Mojsilovic-Popović: 'Secular Buildings in Medieval Serbian Monasteries', *Zograf*, xvi (1985), pp. 19–25
S. P. Ellis: 'The End of the Roman House', *Amer. J. Archaeol.*, xcii (1988), pp. 565–76
W. Puchner: 'Zum "Theater" in Byzanz: Eine Zwischenbilanz', *Fest und Alltag in Byzanz*, ed. G. Prinzing and D. Simon (Munich, 1990), pp. 11–16

KARA HATTERSLEY-SMITH

III. Monumental painting and mosaic.

A significant part of Byzantine artistic production was the wall, vault and floor decoration of churches, palaces and houses.

1. Introduction. 2. Before *c.* 313. 3. *c.* 313–*c.* 843. 4. *c.* 843–*c.* 1204. 5. *c.* 1204–1453.

1. INTRODUCTION. Most extant material survives in the churches, but the survival rate even of church decoration is uneven. The losses distort our knowledge of Byzantine monumental art; any understanding of the chronological stages and of the precise importance of the geographical location of the material remains incomplete. Little is known, for example, of the monumental art produced in Constantinople in the 10th century; the only documented mosaics of that century seem to be the church of the Tithe (Desyatinnaya) of the Most Holy Mother of God (989–96; destr.) at Kiev and the mihrab (961–6) of the Mezquita of Córdoba (*see* CÓRDOBA (i), §3(i)(a)). Furthermore, the geographical range of Byzantine decorated churches is immense, stretching from Spain to Syria and from the Baltic to Nubia; it is therefore difficult to form an overall picture of the character of Byzantine monumental art.

In trying to compensate for the accidents of survival, art historians usually assume the existence of a model of production linking the extant material. For example, Constantinople, as the capital of an extensive empire, is often portrayed as the source of all change and development, a metropolis with artistically dependent provinces, and Byzantine art history is often the reconstruction of the decimated art of Constantinople itself. There is, of course, some justification in this view: it corresponds with the perception of the 'Queen of Cities' as expressed by contemporary Byzantine writers. The pursuit of this model has, however, left much 'provincial' material (in the main all that survives) too little studied as art in its own right. Another major issue is the perception of Byzantine art as static and conservative. Various explanations are proposed: decline and exhaustion after the dynamic developments of Classical Antiquity; artistic incompetence and lack of skills; economic decline, reflected in shortages of materials, books and patrons; the domination of a suppressive church; or the prevalence of magic and superstition. Such explanations fail to account for the complexity and positive character of Byzantine religious culture. Byzantine art is seldom now regarded as the mere aftermath of Antiquity or as the dormant culture of Europe before the Renaissance. Indeed, the characterization of the period as one of minimal change was always a superficial one. As a culture committed (except during the iconoclast controversy (726–843)) to the visualization of its system and beliefs in figurative art, its range of expression is considerable.

The techniques used in the creation of Byzantine mosaics and wall paintings have been revealed during conservation. The paintings were done on the final of two layers of lime plaster and are a mixture of true fresco and a finishing *al secco* (*see* WALL PAINTING, §I). Mosaics (*see* MOSAIC, §§I and II) were usually set into three layers of plaster, and a full underdrawing was done on the final layer, before the cubes (tesserae) of glass and stone were inserted one by one. The chief evidence was acquired from the careful study at the churches of Hagia Sophia and Christ the Saviour in Chora (Kariye Cami) in Istanbul: the analysis of these monuments disproved earlier theories that mosaics were made in workshops and transferred piecemeal into the buildings. On the contrary, artists on the scaffolding took into account nuances of lighting and visibility as they worked. They also touched up mosaics with paint if they felt the finished product was incomplete: lips and other details of the body were sometimes painted over, and even a whole wash could be put over figures to improve their appearance. The overlaps in technique justify treating these media together. (For a discussion of the decoration and iconographic schemes in the Early Christian and Byzantine church *see* CHURCH, §III, 1 and 2(i)(a); and CHRISTIANITY, §III, 1 and 2(i).)

BIBLIOGRAPHY

E. Diez and O. Demus: *Byzantine Mosaics in Greece: Hosios Lucas and Daphni* (Boston, 1931)
T. Whittemore: *The Mosaics of St Sophia at Istanbul*, 4 vols (Oxford, 1933–52)
O. Demus: *Byzantine Mosaic Decoration: Aspects of Monumental Art in Byzantium* (London, 1948)
——: *The Mosaics of Norman Sicily* (London, 1950)
P. A. Underwood: *The Kariye Djami*, 4 vols (New York, 1966–75)
M. Restle: *Byzantine Wall Painting in Asia Minor* (Recklinghausen, 1967)
R. Cormack: *Writing in Gold* (London, 1985)
D. Mouriki: *The Mosaics of Nea Moni on Chios*, 2 vols (Athens, 1985)
H. Maguire: *Earth and Ocean: The Terrestrial World in Early Byzantine Art* (University Park, PA, 1987)
C. Bertelli and others: *Il mosaico* (Milan, 1988)
A. J. Wharton: *Art of Empire: Painting and Architecture of the Byzantine Periphery: A Comparative Study of Four Provinces* (University Park, PA, 1988)
C. Harding: 'The Production of Medieval Mosaics: The Orvieto Evidence', *Dumbarton Oaks Pap.*, xliii (1989), pp. 73–102
M. Cheremeteff: 'The Transformation of the Russian Sanctuary Barrier and the Role of Theophanes the Greek', *The Millennium: Christianity and Russia, 988–1988*, ed. A. Leong (Crestwood, 1990), pp. 107–24
C. L. Connor: *Art and Miracles in Medieval Byzantium* (Princeton, 1991)

ROBIN CORMACK

2. BEFORE *c*. 313. This period marks the emergence of an identifiable Christian art, when Christian places of worship and burial were decorated with images taken from the Old and New Testaments. With little established iconography of their own, the early Christians had to draw on the existing artistic vocabulary of non-Christian cultures. Early Christian art is therefore very much the product of its Late Antique context (*see* §I, 2(i)(a) above). The remains of this art indicate that by the mid-3rd century Christians had partially overcome their earlier resistance to the presence of images in their religion. The visual evidence, however, does stand opposed to the literary testimony from this time, most of which is apparently openly hostile to the place of images within Christian worship. The baptistery at Dura Europos (*c*. 240; *see* DURA EUROPOS, §4) provides the first unambiguous evidence of a Christian art. New Testament scenes such as the *Three Marys at the Tomb* and *Christ Healing the Paralytic* are included in the programme of decoration. These are set alongside wider allegorical themes from Late Antique art such as the *Good Shepherd*. At Dura Europos the images accompany the initiatory rites of the second birth of baptism. Extensive Christian themes taken from the Old and New Testaments also accompany the burial of the dead in the 3rd-century catacombs of Rome, such as that of St Calixtus on the Via Appia. Christians were thus prepared to have images at key points in their religious experience at this period.

The example from Dura Europos also draws attention to the wider context of Early Christian art. The heavily decorated synagogue in the city indicates that the traditional Judaic prohibition of religious representation had been lifted (*see* DURA EUROPOS, §3), while the Mithraeum and temples dedicated to Bel and Zeus were decorated with pagan imagery. It was clearly a commonplace of this period for religions to use visual representation as a part of their practice. Each faith remained distinct within this culturally diverse city, but the visual representations in the different cult centres reveal a degree of common artistic reference. The problem of identifying the iconographic boundaries between the different religions and their modes of expression is demonstrated by the mosaics in the tomb of the Julii (tomb M; *c*. 250) under St Peter's in Rome. On the vaulted ceiling is a beardless man in a chariot with the rays of a nimbus arranged behind him. The figure could represent the sun god Helios, known as Sol Invictus, a key image of pagan monotheists in the 3rd century, or it could be an image of Christ with the attributes of the sun god (see below). The mosaics on the walls of the tomb show *Jonah and the Whale*, a fisherman and the *Good Shepherd* and are often cited to support the identification of the charioteer with Christ. All these images can, however, be ascribed to non-Christian sources. Jonah is probably based on a character in the Midrash, the fisherman features in pagan funerary contexts, and the Good Shepherd is derived from a pagan figure. Examples of the Good Shepherd image in pagan contexts include the Lion Sarcophagus (260–80) at Tipaza, Algeria, and the Cappella della Velata in the catacomb of Priscilla, Via Salaria, Rome (late 2nd century or early 3rd; see fig. 33).

The image of Helios is also widespread. In addition to its use in the tomb of the Julii, it features on mosaic pavement in the synagogue (*c*. 300) of Hammat Tiberias in Israel and in a house (*c*. 260–80) known as the Maison de Silène at al-Jem, Tunisia, and on a wall painting in the pagan tomb (2nd half of 3rd century) of Fannia Redempta (tomb B) under St Peter's, Rome. Another image employed across religious boundaries is that of Orpheus. David in the guise of Orpheus is found in the synagogue at Dura Europos, as he later appears in a synagogue floor (508–9) at Gaza. Orpheus is depicted in a Christian context in the catacombs of SS Pietro e Marcellino (*c*. 300 and 310–30), Rome, while the baths (*c*. 300) at Oudna, Tunisia, provide a pagan secular example of *Orpheus Charming the Animals with his Music*.

33. Wall painting of the *Good Shepherd*, Capella della Velata, catacomb of Priscilla, Via Salaria, Rome, late 2nd century or early 3rd

The other secular mosaics and wall paintings that survive from this period further testify to the general artistic background from which Early Christian imagery emerged. A characteristic feature of this development is the stylistic similarity between Roman secular art and the paintings in the Christian catacombs. For example, a villa (*c.* 220–50) under S Sebastiano in Rome and chamber 69 of the catacomb of SS Pietro e Marcellino are both painted in an elegant red and green linear style. In the mosaics of the late 3rd century and early 4th at Antioch, AQUILEIA, Piazza Armerina (Sicily) and Trier, to name but a few, a wide variety of secular imagery survives, including scenes of hunting, the circus, drinking and bathing. These scenes often contain personifications adopted by Christian artists. Particularly symbolic of the co-existence of Christian art and pagan secular art are the three scenes (313/14–327/8) from the *Life of Jonah* in the mosaic floors at Aquileia. These were set into earlier mosaics decorated with maritime themes at the time of the Roman hall's conversion into a cathedral.

BIBLIOGRAPHY

J. Kollwitz: 'Die Malerei der konstantinischen Zeit', *Akten des VII. internationalen Kongresses für christliche Archäologie: Trier, 1965*, pp. 29–158

B. Brenk: *Tradition und Neuerung in der christlichen Kunst des ersten Jahrtausends* (Vienna, 1966)

F. Gerke: *Spätantike und frühes Christentum* (Baden-Baden, 1967)

F. Deichmann: 'Zur Frage der Gesamtschau der frühchristlichen und frühbyzantinischen Kunst', *Byz. Z.*, lxiii (1970), pp. 43–68

Age of Spirituality: A Symposium: New York, 1977–8

S. MacCormack: *Art and Ceremony in Late Antiquity* (Berkeley, 1981)

C. Murray: *Rebirth and Afterlife* (Oxford, 1981)

J. Engemann: 'Christianisation of Late Antique Art', *The 17th International Byzantine Congress: Major Papers: Washington, 1986*, pp. 83–115

CHARLES BARBER

3. *c.* 313–*c.* 843.

(i) Floor mosaic. (ii) Wall painting and mosaic.

(i) *Floor mosaic.* Many mosaic floors survive from this period. The methods of laying them remained the same as those described in the 1st century AD by Vitruvius (*On Architecture* VII.i.3–4) and by Pliny (*Natural History*

XXVI.lx–lxi; *see* MOSAIC, §I and ROME, ANCIENT, §VI, 1(i)).

Figural subjects such as hunting, circus and mythological scenes abound in the mosaics found in the immense villas and palaces, private houses and public baths from the 4th and 5th centuries. In the eastern Mediterranean, an adherence to the representation of Classical myths in the form of illusionistic panel mosaics marks Hellenism as a potent cultural force (*see* §§(c) and (d) below). Although the promulgation of the Edict of Milan in 313 meant that Christians were free to construct houses of worship, it was not until the third quarter of the 4th century that church building and decoration were undertaken on a large scale (*see* §II, 2(i) above). Large geometric mosaics were created for this new ecclesiastical context; a fashion for complex and colourful patterns is also evident in contemporary secular buildings. Specifically Christian themes are limited to crosses and christograms; biblical scenes are rare. In the 5th and 6th centuries figural subjects were more frequently employed in churches; they were executed in a two-dimensional style and often borrowed motifs from the secular realm, namely hunts, vintage and pastoral scenes, and representations of nature (e.g. flowering trees, roaming animals). The craft flourished from the 4th to the 6th century, but production declined sharply between the 7th and the 9th century.

(a) Constantinople and Asia Minor. (b) Greece and the Balkans. (c) Cyprus. (d) Syria and Palestine. (e) Latin West. (f) North Africa.

(a) Constantinople and Asia Minor. Most mosaic floors from this region have been found along the north-west and south coasts of Turkey at SARDIS, Ephesos (*see* EPHESOS, §I, 2(i) and 3), Aphrodisias, Anemurium and in a cluster of sites around Adana in Cilicia; mosaics were also produced around Gaziantep near the Euphrates River. While many of these mosaics have geometric designs, there are several significant figural compositions, largely drawn from the world of nature. In contrast to the fashion for mythological compositions in neighbouring Syria (*see* §(d) below), such themes are conspicuously absent among the Early Christian examples in Asia Minor. The few exceptions include the 4th-century mosaic of the *Three Graces* in a building known as the Kızlar Hamami ('bath of the maidens') at Narlı Kuyu, *c.* 17 km north-east of Silifke. Polychromed geometric mosaics predominate in the 4th century, as seen in the variety of patterns set out as framed panels or geometric carpets (mid-4th century with later repairs and additions) along the main hall of the synagogue at Sardis. Mosaic panels with donors' inscriptions are interspersed within the bold designs in the forecourt and main hall, and in the apse with its vine-filled Krater and peacocks. In the bath–gymnasium complex at Sardis a 4th-century *opus sectile* floor of 91 square panels of repeating patterns covers the Marble Court (211; for illustration *see* SARDIS).

At Ephesos the pavements of the terrace houses (1st–7th century) are black-and-white geometric mosaics (*in situ*). Following a series of earthquakes in the mid-4th century, renovations to these houses included the addition of more elaborate mosaics depicting such scenes as *Poseidon and Amphitrite*. The increase in the number of

34. Floor mosaic of two boys riding a camel led by a man (detail), north-east side of the peristyle, Great Palace, Istanbul, Turkey, first half of the 6th century (Istanbul, Mosaic Museum)

pavements from the second half of the 4th century into the 5th along the coast of Asia Minor attests to a period of general prosperity and political stability. Further evidence for the improved economy includes the finds at Aphrodisias, especially the *opus sectile* floor in the episcopal palace, the repairs to the Agora Basilica with the threshold mosaic naming the governor Flavius Constantius, and the animal panels set within a wide swastika meander from the Tetrapylon (or Atrium) House. The Aphrodisias mosaics (*in situ*) illustrate the taste for bold geometric panels surrounded by multiple frames. Close in style and date are the *Eagle* and *Dolphin* mosaics from an early 5th-century villa in Sardis.

During the 5th century, floor mosaics were enriched with pictorial elements, and some of the most unusual compositions were produced in Cilicia. Various versions of the Animal Paradise decorate a group of pavements from ecclesiastical buildings situated around Adana (Ayas, Dagpazari, Korykos, Karlik, Kadirli, Al-Oda) and within the Patriarchate of Antioch, as well as a fragmentary panel from the Necropolis Church at Anemurium. In the late 5th-century mosaic at Karlik a biblical interpretation is made explicit by the inclusion of the verses from Isaiah 11:6–8 describing the Peaceful Kingdom. A rare example of biblical narrative (*in situ*) occurs in one aisle of a basilican church or synagogue at Misis (anc. Mopsuestia), where the cycle of the *Life of Samson* is set out with inscriptions paraphrasing the relevant passages from the Book of Judges; a grand composition featuring *Noah's Ark* was found in the nave of the same building. The mosaic inscriptions from secular and Christian contexts found at Anemurium support the findings at Aphrodisias and Sardis that the late 5th century and first half of the 6th were periods of particular prosperity and building activity. innovative figural motifs were introduced in the early 5th century in Constantinople, where male labourers, identified by inscriptions (e.g. 'piety'), serve as allegorical symbols.

As a rare example of imperial art, the monumental peristyle mosaic (*c.* 1900 sq. m; Istanbul, Mosaic Mus.) from the Great Palace in Constantinople (*see* ISTANBUL, §III, 12) is the most significant pavement. The controversy over its dating, with proposals ranging between the 4th and the 7th century, has been clarified by excavations undertaken as a result of its removal to a special museum; pottery finds below the mosaic indicate a date in the first half of the 6th century. With over 70 scenes extant, the original composition was surely one of the richest figural compositions produced. Heterogeneous episodes drawn from the repertory of the hunt, animal combat, daily life (see fig. 34) and myth are laid out against a neutral white ground. The apparent lack of any thematic unity has led to diverse iconographic interpretations. In the 7th century, the decline of the cities and towns along the coast of Asia Minor, due to the war between the Byzantine and Persian empires, followed by conflicts with the Arabs, led to a halt in mosaic production.

BIBLIOGRAPHY

G. M. A. Hanfmann: 'The Ninth Campaign at Sardis (1966): The Synagogue', *Bull. Amer. Sch. Orient. Res.*, clxxxvii (1967), pp. 21–46
L. Budde: *Antike Mosaiken in Kilikien*, i and ii (Recklinghausen, 1972)
E. Kitzinger: 'Observations on the Samson Floor at Mopsuestia', *Dumbarton Oaks Pap.*, xxvii (1973), pp. 133–44
S. Campbell: 'Roman Mosaic Workshops in Turkey', *Amer. J. Archaeol.*, lxxxiii (1979), pp. 287–92
G. Hellenkemper Salies: 'Die Datierung der Mosaiken im Grossen Palast zu Konstantinopel', *Bonn. Jb. Rhein. Landesmus. Bonn & Ver. Altertfreund. Rheinlande*, clxxxvii (1987), pp. 273–308
J. Russell: *The Mosaic Inscriptions of Anemurium* (Vienna, 1987)
J. Trilling: 'The Soul of the Empire: Style and Meaning in the Mosaic Pavement of the Byzantine Imperial Palace in Constantinople', *Dumbarton Oaks Pap.*, xliii (1989), pp. 27–72
S. Campbell: *The Mosaics of Aphrodisias in Caria* (Toronto, 1991)

CHRISTINE KONDOLEON

(b) Greece and the Balkans. The floor mosaics of this region show eastern and western influences. The Istrian mosaics relate closely to those of northern Italy, while the mosaics from the islands of the Dodekanese are comparable to those of Asia Minor (*see* §(a) above). Mosaic-making flourished particularly in the 5th century and the early 6th, but the craft seems to have died out, except in the islands, after the mid-6th century. Long sequences of mosaics have been found at such sites as Salona (*see* SALONA, §2), STOBI, NEA ANCHIALOS and NIKOPOLIS. Regional variations suggest that the craft was practised in many local centres.

In the early 4th century, monumental complexes built by emperors had elaborate mosaic decoration. Galerius (*reg* 305–11), for example, built an imperial palace at Thessaloniki (*see* THESSALONIKI, §I; and §II, 3(ii)(a) above) with geometric mosaics and a lavish palace at Gamzigrad (*see* SERBIA, §II, 1), identified with Romuliana (his birthplace), decorated with a vast geometric mosaic, hunting mosaics arranged in framed panels and a handsome mosaic of *Dionysos*. Related figural mosaics and large geometric carpets survive from an early 4th-century villa at Niš (anc. Mediana, Serbia).

Some of the earliest ecclesiastical architecture in the Balkans is decorated with floor mosaics featuring a mixture of geometric panels and figural elements. At Poreč in Croatia, a symbolic fish was inlaid into a conventional geometric carpet, evidently when a house was converted into a church. Other Early Christian floors are at Vrsar in Croatia; these are comparable to the mosaics of AQUILEIA, those in the church of St Sophia at Sofia in Bulgaria, in a basilican church (*c.* 360–70) later replaced by the Episcopal Basilica at STOBI, and at Philippi (*see* PHILIPPI, §2), where an elaborate mosaic of a single-aisled basilica beneath the later octagonal church mentions Bishop Porphyrios, presumably the one who attended a church council in 341. The 4th-century mosaic floor of the synagogue at Stobi is geometric, while the synagogue of uncertain date at Plovdiv in Bulgaria has both geometric patterns and an elaborate menorah.

In the later 4th century and first half of the 5th austere geometric pavements with small repeated elements in a restricted number of colours predominated. Such mosaics decorated both residences and churches. Typical examples survive in Crete (*see* CRETE, §4), at Demetrias in Thessaly, Greece, in the later phase of the early basilican church at Stobi, in Basilica A at Dion in Macedonia, Greece, at Athens, Epidauros, and the double basilicas at Poreč, Salona and Ljubljana. Many of these mosaics include prominent donor inscriptions, with Latin being used along the Dalmatian Coast and in Slovenia, and Greek elsewhere.

In the second half of the 5th century and the early 6th a limited selection of figural subjects—the Fountain of Life, peacocks, birds, vines and vessels—were common. They were often integrated into geometric patterns to form figure carpets. The Fountain of Life is extremely popular, with examples at Salona, Zadar in Croatia, Stobi (e.g. the Episcopal Basilica baptistery and House of Psalms), Amphipolis in Macedonia, Greece (e.g. Basilica), and Edessa, also in Macedonia.

Some remarkable mosaics from the first half of the 6th century feature more elaborate figural subjects, often allegories of months, seasons, earth or ocean. The mosaic of the narthex of the Large Basilica at Heraclea Lyncestis near BITOLJ is extraordinary in the quality and complexity of its seasonal imagery. Mosaics from a basilica at Delphi feature elaborate fauna of the earth and ocean. Personified seasons and months decorate mosaics from Thebes in Boiotia, Greece, and in the Villa of the Months at Argos in the Peloponnese, Greece. A mosaic from Arapaj in Albania has shepherds in a pastoral setting. The mosaics from the Doumetios Basilica or Basilica A (*c.* 575) at Nikopolis, with inscriptions explicitly identifying them as depictions of earth and ocean, continue the topographical theme into the age of Justinian. Other complex figural compositions are found at CARIČIN GRAD. Some of these elaborate figural mosaics seem to reflect eastern influences. Mosaic-making continued longest on the Dodecanese islands, where the latest examples on Symi and Kalymnos may date to the late 6th century or even the early 7th.

BIBLIOGRAPHY

J.-P. Sodini: 'Mosaïques paléochrétiennes de Grèce', *Bull. Corr. Hell.*, xciv (1970), pp. 699–755
S. Anamali and S. Adhami: *Mosaïques de l'Albanie* (Tiranë, 1974)
B. Djurić: 'Antični mozaici na ozemlju SR Slovinije' [Ancient mosaics in the territory of the Socialist Republic of Slovenia], *Arheol. Vestnik*, xxvii (1976), pp. 537–625
M. Spiro: *Critical Corpus of the Mosaic Pavements on the Greek Mainland, Fourth/Sixth Centuries with Architectural Surveys* (New York, 1978)
G. Tomašević: *Ranovizantijski podni mozaici: Dardanija, Makedonija, Novi Epir* [Early Byzantine floor mosaics: Dardania, Macedonia, New Epiros] (Belgrade, 1978)
R. Kolarik: 'The Floor Mosaics of Eastern Illyricum: The Northern Regions', *Actes du Xe congrès international d'archéologie chrétienne: Thessalonique, 1980*, i, pp. 445–79
P. Assimakopoulou-Atzaka: *Peloponnesos: Sterea Ellada* [The Peloponnesos: central Greece] (1987), ii of *Syntagma tón palaiochristianikón psiphidoton dapedon tis ellados* [Corpus of the Early Christian mosaic pavements of Greece] Byzantina Mnimeia (Thessaloniki, 1974–87)
R. Kolarik: 'Mosaics of the Early Church at Stobi', *Dumbarton Oaks Pap.*, xli (1987), pp. 295–306
V. Popova-Moroz: *24 Drevni mozaiki ot Bulgarija* [Twenty-four ancient mosaics from Bulgaria] (Sofia, 1987)
P. Assimakopoulou-Atzaka: 'The Mosaic Pavements of the Aegean Islands during the Early Christian Period', *Corsi Cult. A. Ravenn. & Biz.*, xxxviii (1991), pp. 33–65
R. Kolarik: 'Tetrarchic Floor Mosaics in the Balkans', *La Mosaïque gréco-romaine*, iv (Paris, 1994), pp. 171–83

RUTH E. KOLARIK

(c) *Cyprus.* This island is an especially rich source of mosaics from both secular and religious buildings (*see also* CYPRUS, §§II, 5(vi) and III, 3). The compositions, among the most spectacular in the eastern Mediterranean, attest to an independent mosaic production that can be traced back to the Hellenistic period. Similarities with the mosaics from Syria, Palestine (*see* §(d) below), and south-east Asia Minor (*see* §(a) above), reflect the close economic and cultural ties between the eastern provinces of the Byzantine empire. In technique and style, the Cypriot mosaics are closest to those made in Antioch (*see* ANTIOCH (i), §3) which may relate to the fact that Cyprus was under the rule of Antioch.

The official recognition of Christianity in 313 and the concurrent survival of pagan values and Classical iconography (*see* §I, 2(i) above) throughout the 4th century can be charted in the Cypriot mosaics. The unusual interpretation of six mythological scenes (e.g. *Childhood of Dionysos, Apollo and Marsyas, Beauty Contest with Cassiopeia*), replete with personifications and Greek labels, from the House of Aion at NEW PAPHOS attest to a vital pagan culture. Their supposed date in the second quarter of the 4th century has led to the suggestion that these panels were a philosophically inspired challenge to Christianity (see Michaelides). The addition of the *Poseidon and Amphitrite* mosaic and the repairs to the mosaic of *Theseus and the Minotaur* in the adjacent Villa of Theseus emphasize a local interest in mythology throughout the 4th century. From this same period, in what was probably a public reception complex (also known as the House of Achilles) at the entrance to the city of KOURION, visitors were greeted by mosaics of *Achilles and the Daughters of Lykomedes* and the *Rape of Ganymede*.

Geometric decoration predominates in the floor decoration of late 4th-century Christian buildings, such as the three-aisled basilica at Soloi and the seven-aisled basilica of Hagios Epiphanios at Salamis. Notable exceptions are the inscribed panels from the basilica of Hagia Kyriaki or Chrysopolitissa at New Paphos, where verses from the Book of Psalms (Psalm 41) accompany a deer drinking water from a spring, and 'I am the true vine' (John 15:1) is surrounded by vines with grapes and animals.

Classical themes continued to be produced in the 5th century, as evidenced by the mosaic of *Thetis Dipping Achilles in the Styx* in a hall of the Villa of Theseus. A female bust labelled KTICIC ('foundation') from the *frigidarium* of the Bath of Eustolios at Kourion has its closest parallels in Antioch, underlining a common taste for the depiction of personifications. The large early 5th-century peristyle building that adjoins the bathhouse includes a number of floors with significant inscriptions and designs as well as the insertion of bird and fish panels into geometric patterns. It remains uncertain, however, whether these figural motifs can be seen as the new 'symbols of Christ' mentioned in the adjacent inscription: 'In place of big walls and solid iron, bright bronze and even adamant, this house has girt itself with the much venerated symbols of Christ'. The animation of floors in 5th-century Christian basilicas, as for example the flowers, fish and birds in the nave at Soloi, and the jewelled vases flanked by birds in the intercolumniations of the Kourion Basilica, suggest a general development whereby the natural world is brought into the House of the Lord.

The fashion for inhabited compositions seems to have thrived in the 6th century. The animal panels (deer, lions, bear, boar) of the grid design that covered the atrium and nave of Basilica A at Pegia, and the birds, fish, squid and turtles that fill the floret trellis in the altar area are among the boldest examples from after 565. This collection of images may represent Isaiah's vision of a Peaceable

Kingdom and as such may be compared to the group of such mosaics found in Cilicia where inscriptions make their meaning more explicit. As Cyprus came more under the control of Constantinople, there was an increase in the importation of marbles and the decoration of ecclesiastical and secular buildings with *opus sectile* floors. Arab incursions in the mid-7th century brought an end to the luxuries of interior decoration.

BIBLIOGRAPHY
A. H. S. Megaw: 'Interior Decoration in Early Christian Cyprus', *XV Congrès international d'études byzantines: Rapports et co-rapports: Athènes, 1976*, pp. 129–54
D. Michaelides: *Cypriot Mosaics* (Nicosia, 1987)
——: 'Mosaic Pavements from Early Christian Cult Buildings in Cyprus', *Mosaic Floors in Cyprus* (Ravenna, 1988), pp. 81–153

CHRISTINE KONDOLEON

(d) Syria and Palestine. In the 4th century Syria was one of the most prolific centres of mosaic production. Mosaics of the first half of the century exhibit a conservatism in their adherence to the traditions of Hellenistic illusionism and Classical iconography in the use of the central *emblemata* with large mythological compositions, as in the banquet scene (first quarter of the 4th century; Soveida Mus.) from Shahba-Philippopolis. In the second half of the 4th century a new style developed that is characterized by exuberant geometric designs executed in multicoloured bands and known as Rainbow style. This new geometric style was initially combined with panels filled with mythological scenes or other figures, as in the *Ge and the Seasons* mosaic (Brussels, Musées Royaux A. & Hist.) from the Triclinium Building at APAMEIA. By the last quarter of the century, however, purely geometric motifs that could be extended in all directions dominated mosaic decoration. The success of this new decorative style may be related to the official recognition of Christianity and the construction of numerous churches paved with aniconic mosaics, as in the cruciform church (387) at Kaoussie, converted from the pre-existent martyrium of *c.* 379 (*see* ANTIOCH (i), §3), and in the aisles of the church (389–90) at Zahrani in Lebanon. An important innovation in mosaic decoration is evident in the triclinium pavement from the Constantinian Villa at Antioch, where diagonal panels decorated with luxurious full-length figures personifying the Four Seasons divide the square field; a sacrifice scene and hunting episodes that evoke mythological hunts decorate the trapezoidal panels (see fig. 35). The second section of this pavement is decorated in the Rainbow style with mythological figures in circular and square panels.

In Phoenicia and Palestine 4th-century mosaic production was minimal compared to that of Syria. The most important development was the introduction of figural motifs in synagogue decoration in Palestine. Jewish ritual objects such as the torah shrine, menorah (ritual candlestick), *lulav* ('palm branch') and *ethrog* ('citron') are often juxtaposed with personifications of the Four Seasons and the signs of the zodiac in a radiant circle around the figure of Helios (e.g. at Hammath Tiberias). This composition characterized Palestinian synagogue decoration throughout the 6th century, as at Khirbet Susiya, Na'aran, BETH SHAN, BETH ALPHA and Husifa.

The first half of the 5th century was a period of great creativity in both Syria and Palestine; the uniformity of

35. Floor mosaic of a hunting scene, trapezoidal panel from the triclinium pavement of the Constantinian Villa, Antioch, Syria, 4th century (Paris, Musée du Louvre)

stylistic developments from north to south indicates that mosaicists must have travelled. The introduction of plant and animal motifs into the geometric configurations formed by rainbow bands is widespread, both in Palestine (as in the church of the Nativity at Bethlehem, at Evron and at Shavei Zion), and in Syria (as at Qoumhané, Dibsi Faraj and Khirbet Mouqa). A significant development was that of orthogonal and diagonal grid patterns, composed of small four-petal flowers forming a petal trellis. The square intervals formed by the petal trellis are often decorated with rosettes and sometimes with other motifs, such as animals, birds and baskets of fruit (e.g. Khaldé, Lebanon; Dibsi Faraj). The petal trellis becomes extremely popular in the 6th century (e.g. El-Kursi, Israel). The most important development of the second half of the 5th century was the reintroduction of large-scale figural compositions, especially animal carpets and hunt pavements. The camel caravan and animal chase mosaics (*in situ*) of the covered walk of the *cardo maximus* (AD 469) at Apameia may be the earliest of this type. The most dramatic and monumental examples of hunt pavements are the Antioch Hunt pavements *Megalopsychia Hunt* (Antalya, Archaeol. Mus.) and the 'Worcester Hunt' at Antioch. Personifications of abstract ideas and the elements of nature are also prominent in Antiochene pavement decoration, as in the mosaics of *Ananeosis* ('renewal'; Antalya, Archaeol. Mus.), *Ktisis* ('foundation'), *Megalopsychia* ('generosity'), *Ge* ('earth') and the Four Seasons.

In the 6th century, Palestine and Arabia (now divided between Jordan, Egypt and Saudi Arabia) were the centres of mosaic production. Medallions of inhabited vine or acanthus scroll *rinceaux* were often used for border and field compositions. Within the scrolls of church pavements are miniature versions of the hunting themes popular in 5th-century mosaics, along with vintage and pastoral themes at Madaba, Jordan, and Beth Shan). In the synagogue mosaics at Shellal (Canberra, Austral. War Mem.), Maon (*in situ*) and Beth Shan the medallions are filled with animals, inanimate objects and Jewish ritual objects. Biblical scenes were illustrated in the floor mosaics at GERASA, Beth Alpha and Na'aran, while scenes from

Classical mythology appear at Madaba, Jerusalem, Erez and Beth Shan. Elements of the natural world are frequent motifs (e.g. *Ge and the Seasons* at Beth Guvrin (Jerusalem, Israel Mus.) and Madaba), as are illustrations of agricultural labours (Beth Shan, El Hamam, Gerasa). Topographical subjects appear more frequently than in mosaic decoration in other parts of the empire: the Madaba Map (*see* JERUSALEM, fig. 2) represents the principal cities of Palestine and the Nile Delta, and prominent pilgrimage sites. In the mosaic borders of the Acropolis Church (719) at Ma'in and the church of St Stephen (765) at Umm er-Rassas near Mt Nebo, Jordan, the principal cities of the Patriarchates of Jerusalem and Arabia are represented as walled cities or churches. While mosaic production in Syria and Phoenicia had declined by the 7th century, the mosaic in St Stephen reveals that at least some workshops in Palestine/Arabia flourished long after the Arab conquest.

BIBLIOGRAPHY

D. Levi: *Antioch Mosaic Pavements* (Princeton, 1947)
I. Lavin: 'The Hunting Mosaics of Antioch and their Sources', *Dumbarton Oaks Pap.*, xvii (1963), pp. 181–286
E. Kitzinger: 'Stylistic Developments in Pavement Mosaics in the Greek East from the Age of Constantine to the Age of Justinian', *La Mosaïque gréco-romaine*, i (Paris, 1965), pp. 341–51
J. Balty: *Mosaïques antiques de Syrie* (Brussels, 1977)
M. Piccirillo: *I mosaici di Giordania* (Rome, 1986)
A. Ovadiah and R. Ovadiah: *Mosaic Pavements in Israel* (Rome, 1987)
P. Donceel-Voute: *Les Pavements des églises byzantines de Syrie et du Liban*, 2 vols (Louvain-la-Neuve, 1988)
M. Piccirillo: *Chiese e mosaici di Madaba* (Jerusalem, 1989)
The Mosaics of Jordan: Roman, Byzantine, Islamic (exh. cat., London, Sotheby's, 1993)

LUCILLE A. ROUSSIN

(e) Latin West. Floor mosaics in the provinces of the Latin West reached a high level of development between the 4th and 6th centuries. They are characterized by diverse methods of production and a rich use of colour, and were created in special workshops for both Christian and pagan circles. Thus the immense villas of this region all have mosaics that follow Late Roman traditions of rich ornament; examples in Sicily include PIAZZA ARMERINA (second quarter of the 4th century), the villa of Helorus (mid-4th century) near the mouth of Tellaro River, and the villa at Patti (*see* SICILY, §3); in Spain, the Villa de Pedrosa de la Vega, near Palencia; and in France, Montréal-Séviac (early 5th century) in the Bordeaux region. These works display mythological hunting or game scenes, often influenced by African mosaics (*see* §(f) below). At Constanţa in Romania, large-scale, ornate portico pavements with polychrome decorations of the 5th century (*in situ*)

36. Floor mosaic of *Christ* with the chi-rho symbol (detail), from a villa at Hinton St Mary, Dorset, England, 4th century (London, British Museum)

are similar to those in the Palace of Theodoric at Ravenna. Many religious buildings were also decorated with mosaic pavements, for example the 1400 sq. m of mosaic (*in situ*) in the cathedral (313–19) at AQUILEIA, the pavements in the churches (5th–6th century) at PULA, the first cathedral (early 5th century) at Marseille and the beautiful geometric mosaics (*in situ*) in a 5th-century hall adjacent to an Early Christian basilica of St Pierre in Geneva. With the growth of Christianity, pagan images were christianized, as in the 4th-century mosaic of *Bellerophon and Chimaera* and *Christ* with the chi-rho symbol (see fig. 36) from a villa at Hinton St Mary, Dorset, and the effigies of shepherds in the oratories at Aquileia that became evangelical Good Shepherds. In some cases, it is difficult to determine whether the work was executed for Christian or pagan clients, as in the mosaic of *Leda and Agamemnon* (Trier, Rhein. Landesmus.) at Trier. Among the few extant 6th-century mosaics are those in S Vitale at Ravenna and the church (*c.* 534–54) beneath the present 13th-century S Lorenzo in Naples (*see* NAPLES, §IV, 2) with traces of animal and vegetal decoration. From the 7th century onwards the quality of mosaic floors declined: polychromy was replaced by simple black-and-white geometric designs and stylized figures. The 9th-century pavements from S Ilario Abbey in Venice (Venice, Mus. Archeol.), Ste Croix in Poitiers (*in situ*) and St Martial in Limoges (*in situ*) are of a similar simplicity. By the 790s, when Charlemagne was building the palatine chapel at Aachen, the scarcity of mosaicists forced him to use existing mosaics from Ravenna.

BIBLIOGRAPHY

Recueil général des mosaïques de la Gaule, 13 vols (Paris, 1960–95)
W. Oakeshott: *The Mosaics of Rome from the Third to the Fourteenth Century* (London, 1967)
Bulletin de l'association internationale pour l'étude de la mosaïque antique, 11 vols (Paris, 1968–91)
H. Kier: *Der mittelalterliche Schmuckfussboden* (Dusseldorf, 1970)

HENRI LAVAGNE

(f) North Africa. Christian mosaics in this region can be divided into two periods: pre-Vandal invasion (*c.* 313–429) and post-Byzantine conquest (533–*c.* 670). During the first period, which is best represented in Algeria, churches and houses were paved with the same types of polychrome overall geometric schemes. Church nave and aisle pavements are generally subdivided into panels corresponding to one or more bays, each decorated with a different composition. Particularly common are such repetitive units as eight-pointed stars formed of two interlaced squares with heavy borders and floral or geometric filling motifs, and continuous designs such as the meander of swastikas and squares, examples of which survive at Castellum Tingitanum (now Chlef), in the cathedral (4th century) at HIPPO REGIUS (now Annaba) and at the Christian complex at THEVESTIS (now Tebessa; *in situ*). Birds and animals are used as filling motifs in the early

37. Floor mosaic of the *Domain of Julius*, from the villa of Dominus Julius, Carthage, Tunisia, early 5th century (Tunis, Musée National du Bardo)

5th-century North Church at Cuicul (now Djemila; *in situ*). Inscriptions were rare. Occasionally a symbolic representation indicates a sacred area: a vase with vine *rinceaux* in an apse at Caesarea (now Cherchel); an altar amid grapevines (destr.) in the choir at Castellum Tingitanum; deer drinking from the rivers of Paradise in the baptistery at Uppenna, Tunisia. Biblical scenes, such as the story of *Jonah* (destr.) in Basilica I at Furnos Minus, Tunisia, are extremely rare. Most striking are the many tomb mosaics found in cemeteries and churches. In the latter they either formed the pavement, as at Sitifis (now Sétif, Algeria) and in the church of Felix (Tunis, Mus. N. Bardo) at Clupea (now Kelibia, Tunisia), or were inserted into the pavement as in the cathedral at Hippo Regius (*in situ*) and chapel of Martyrs (Tunis, Mus. N. Bardo) at Thabraca (now Tabarka, Tunisia). Most examples comprise an epitaph and appropriate symbols (e.g. monogram, cross, doves, peacocks, vase with grape or rose vines). Several from Thabraca depict orants and, on occasion, the *Sacrifice of Isaac* and the story of *Jonah*. On the pavements in houses there is nothing to distinguish pagan from Christian ownership. Examples include scenes of daily life as in the *Domain of Julius* (early 5th century; see fig. 37) from the villa of Dominus Julius at Carthage, farm scenes at Thabraca, and the depiction of mythological figures such as Venus. Mosaic production continued during the Vandal period (429–533) as evidenced by *Daniel in the Lions' Den* in the mausoleum at Furnos Minus, but dating remains uncertain.

During the second period, mosaics—particularly in Tunisia—were more innovative and more openly Christian in content. They included new complex geometric schemes, as in Basilica Dermech II at Carthage (*in situ*), foliate designs of vine-leaves, as in Basilica Dermech I at Carthage (*in situ*), basilicas I and II at Bulla Regia (*in situ*) and Basilica IV at Sufetula (now Sbeïtla) (*in situ*); acanthus sinusoids at Carthage and El Mouassat (destr.); and vine *rinceaux* issuing from acanthus plants, as in the early 6th-century basilica at Sabratha, Libya. Most are enlivened with fauna. Realistic and mythological figures, even architectural representations, decorate the mosaics from the cathedral (6th century) at Cyrene (*in situ*) and the East Church (6th century) at Qasr-el-Lebia (*in situ*), while hunting, pastoral and marine scenes fill compartments or spread freely over parts of the floors from, for example, Rasguniae (now Matifou, Algeria) and Qasr-el-Lebia. Few houses are known, but one from Carthage contained the only overtly Christian mosaic yet found in a secular context. It represents four figures supporting a cross and is datable to the 7th century. Although mosaics from the different provinces varied stylistically from region to region, they shared compositions and iconography. North African mosaic workshops influenced work elsewhere, particularly in northern Italy and Spain, and remained inventive and vigorous up to the Arab conquest.

BIBLIOGRAPHY

N. Duval and P.-A. Février: 'Le Décor des monuments chrétiens d'Afrique (Algérie, Tunisie)', *Actas del VIII congreso internacional de arqueología cristiana: Barcelona, 1969*, pp. 5–55
P.-A. Février: 'L'Evolution du décor figuré et ornemental en Afrique à la fin de l'antiquité', *Corsi Cult. A. Ravenn. & Biz.*, xix (1972), pp. 159–86
N. Duval: *La Mosaïque funéraire dans l'art paléochrétien* (Ravenna, 1976)
E. Alföldi-Rosenbaum and J. Ward-Perkins: *Justinian Mosaic Pavements in Cyrenaican Churches* (Rome, 1980)
M. A. Alexander: 'Design and Meaning in the Early Christian Mosaics of Tunisia', *Apollo* (Jan 1983), pp. 8–13

MARGARET A. ALEXANDER

(ii) Wall painting and mosaic. Even after the Edict of Milan (313), which decreed that Christians were free to practise their religion openly, Christian wall painting and mosaic continued to follow the Hellenistic stylistic tradition; only their iconography differed from that of pagan art. The Cappadocian fathers, SS Basil the Great (*c.* 330–79), Gregory of Nyssa (*c.* 330–*c.* 395) and Gregory of Nazianzus (329–89), who, thanks to their Classical education, saw art as a medium of instruction, played an important part in developing this difference.

(a) 4th–5th centuries. (b) 6th century. (c) 7th century–mid-9th.

(a) 4th–5th centuries. The earliest mosaics from this period are in S Costanza (*see* ROME, §V, 18(ii)), which was commissioned as the mausoleum of Constantine the Great's daughter, Constantina (*d* 354). The internal decoration is closely linked with ancient tradition. The lower part of the walls are clad in marble revetment, and the curved surfaces are covered in mosaic. The classicizing mosaics in the ambulatory include portraits that may represent the deceased and her husband, foliate scrollwork with bacchanalian scenes and various decorative motifs. The dome mosaics (destr.) portrayed biblical subjects, while the conches of the lateral apses contain the *Delivery of the Law* (*Traditio legis*) to St Peter with St Paul to the left and a rare depiction of the *Delivery of the Keys to St Peter*. Thus, within this programme, Christian scenes symbolizing salvation became part of a secular environment.

Another 4th-century mosaic programme with a similar combination of Christian and purely secular scenes is in the mausoleum at Centcelles (*see* CENTCELLES, MAUSOLEUM) which may have been intended for Emperor Constans (*reg* 337–50). The building's interior preserves part of its decoration, including hunting scenes, Old and New Testament scenes, personifications of the *Four Seasons* and other enthroned figures. Especially interesting is the introduction of the non-naturalistic gold background.

Fourth-century paintings survive only in the catacombs (*see* CATACOMB, §3; ROME, §V, 13), where individual scenes rather than iconographic cycles are depicted, such as *Adam and Eve*, the *Adoration of the Magi*, the *Virgin Orans* (arms outstretched in prayer) between the Apostles, *Christ Teaching* and the story of *Jonah*.

During the reign of THEODOSIOS I (*reg* 379–95) Christianity became appreciably stronger. A return to Hellenistic models, the geometric rendering of form and above all the use of bright colours are the main characteristics of the art of the Theodosian age. Outlines and planes, corporality and volume are represented exclusively with colour. A sense of space is no longer achieved by the use of perspective, but with a multicoloured background, divided into coloured bands. An example of this technique can be seen in the apse of S Pudenziana (probably 401–7) in Rome, although only a few fragments of the original mosaic survived the restoration in the 16th century. A

Christ Enthroned is surrounded by the *Twelve Apostles* and two female figures, probably SS Pudenziana and Prassede, who crown St Peter and St Paul. Originally a dove and a lamb were depicted below the throne; behind the figures stretches a portico and the palaces of the heavenly Jerusalem with the Golgotha Cross rising up in the centre, flanked by symbols of the Evangelists. The composition has a dual symbolism, referring both to the Last Judgement and, by depicting Christ, the lamb and the dove together, the Trinity. The same spirit of Classical revival is evident in the mosaics (*c.* 425) in S Sabina, Rome, which show two female personifications of the *Church of the Jews* and the *Church of the Gentiles*. The figures are statuesque, with a real sense of corporality, and are clothed in elaborate drapery.

The fullest example of a monumental narrative cycle from the Early Christian period is in S Maria Maggiore. The mosaics (432–40) in the nave depict Old Testament scenes, based on models in illustrated manuscripts. One of their hallmarks is the widespread use of gold. In many instances, however, the figures move in a naturalistic environment. The artist was faithful to the painterly tradition, with its sculptural forms, spontaneity of movement, placing of figures in the landscape and illusion of three-dimensionality. On the triumphal arch the decoration is divided into four unframed bands showing the *Hetoimasia* ('preparation of the throne') and scenes from Christ's childhood. The influence of imperial iconography is strong. Christ and the Virgin are depicted like members of the imperial family, surrounded by a heavenly guard of angels. The figures are heavy and stiff, and the narrative unwinds slowly and ceremoniously. Classicizing and abstract styles are combined in a fashion that anticipates new stylistic developments. A complex scheme of decoration is also evident in the mosaics (*c.* 400) of the baptistery of S Giovanni in Fonte, Naples, built by Bishop Severus (362–408). At the centre of the dome is a gold chi-rho set against a starry sky, encircled by a band of foliate ornament. The rest of the dome is divided into eight segments, each containing one or two Christological scenes. The symbols of the Evangelists, depictions of the Good Shepherd and full-length figures, probably Apostles, holding crowns, also appear. In accordance with earlier tradition, all these scenes are set against a blue ground. Colour is used in an impressionistic manner, and the use of gold is restricted. The figures move with relative ease in space, and are distinguished by their large, wide-open eyes.

At this time a local school was taking shape in Milan, characterized by greater freedom in its compositions and the use of bright colours. The earliest surviving mosaics (late 4th century–early 5th) are in the octagonal chapel of S Aquilino, attached to the church of S Lorenzo (*see* MILAN, §IV, 3). They cover the lunettes of two conches and represent Christ as a philosopher with the Apostles and what is probably the *Ascension of Elijah*. The expressive faces, the wealth of colour, the modelling of the figures and the feeling for nature reflect the strong influence of the Hellenistic tradition. Also in Milan are the mosaics in S Vittorio in Ciel d'Oro, a 4th-century chapel in S Ambrogio. The images of St Victor and other saints show a tendency towards insubstantiality, thus placing these mosaics in the artistic milieu of the second half of

the 5th century. Numerous Early Christian mosaics have survived in Ravenna, which as the port linking Italy with Constantinople became a meeting-point for the various artistic trends and influences from both West and East. In the mausoleum of Galla Placidia (*see* RAVENNA, §2(ii)), the mosaics are dominated by the triumphalism that characterizes many works of Imperial Roman art and that the Church adopted once the danger of paganism was past. The iconographic programme relates to the *Last Judgement*, with a gold cross against a starry sky in the dome, and the symbols of the Evangelists represented among cloud formations in the pendentives. The Apostles in the lunettes of the east and west cross-arms turn towards the cross and are shown treading on a verdant ground that gives depth to the composition. Doves, symbolizing the souls of the elect, approach fountains to drink the water. The mosaics are redolent of the Hellenistic tradition, as can be seen in the three-dimensional quality of the landscape and the statuesque figures depicted in the *Good Shepherd* and the *Martyrdom of St Lawrence*.

By contrast, the Hellenistic tradition is on the retreat in the mosaics (449–58) of the Orthodox baptistery (*see* RAVENNA, §2(iv)). The main decoration in the dome is divided into three zones, with the *Baptism* in the centre, the *Apostles* in the middle band and architectural elements in the outer band. Although the faces are expressive, their features are harsh and the heads small in relation to the bodies. The mosaicist created his effects with a rich palette and a marked use of gold. Another mosaic depiction of the *Baptism* (late 5th century) survives in the dome of the Arian baptistery (*see* RAVENNA, §2(i)). This composition is remote from the Hellenistic tradition and is distinguished by geometrical forms, a simplified rendition of figures and a monumental style.

Among the most important Early Christian mosaics are those of Hagios Georgios (*see* THESSALONIKI, §III, 2(ii)). They have been variously dated to the late 4th century, the mid-5th and as late as the early 6th. The central composition in the dome of a triumphant Christ carrying a cross within a large roundel supported by four angels, and a flying phoenix, represents a theophany, probably the *Last Judgement*. The surrounding band of decoration contains 20 male orant figures in front of imposing architectural backdrops, which are both reminiscent of the *scaenae frons* of the Roman theatre and symbolic of the heavenly church. The figures may represent the various categories of saints that make up that church. The strong influence of the Hellenistic tradition is evident in the clearly defined features of the saints' faces and the three-dimensional architectural façades, but new geometric and abstract tendencies are also apparent. This programme may be considered as representative of the best work in Constantinople, with which Thessaloniki always maintained close ties. Mosaics also decorated the three-aisled basilica of the Acheiropoietos (second half of the 5th century) in Thessaloniki. Although only fragments of the original programme survive, showing decorative foliate motifs and such subjects as birds, fish, books and the chi-rho monogram, they successfully merge Hellenistic naturalism with Christian symbolism.

Another important mosaic is the *Vision of Ezekiel* in the conch of the apse at Hosios David (see fig. 38 and

38. Mosaic of the *Vision of Ezekiel* in the conch of the apse of Hosios David, Thessaloniki, Greece, late 5th century or early 6th

THESSALONIKI, §III, 3(ii)). *Christ Emmanuel* is shown in the midst of a heavenly landscape, surrounded by the symbols of the Evangelists with Ezekiel and Habbakuk on the lower left- and right-hand sides. Thus the composition is a theophany in which the revelation of God's majesty is combined with the visions of the two prophets. It shows stylistic similarities with the mosaics in Hagios Georgios. Although the faces preserve many of the characteristics of the Hellenistic tradition, the intense linearity and schematization suggest a date towards the end of the 5th century or in the early 6th.

Relatively few wall paintings survive from the 5th century. Some examples include an early 5th-century roundel with the portrait of Pope Sircius (*reg* 384–99) from the church of S Paolo fuori le Mura in Rome, and several wall paintings (5th–6th century) in the catacomb of S Gennaro (*see* NAPLES, §IV, 1) which depict figures redolent of Hellenistic influence. Fragments of wall paintings have been preserved in the underground baptistery at Carthage (probably early 5th century) and in the ruined tetraconch church, known as the Red Church (*c*. 500–50), at PERUSHTITSA. The iconographic programme in the Red Church seems to have been relatively complex, with scenes from the Old and New Testaments, as well as hagiographic and allegorical subjects. The unframed compositions are arranged in two bands, one above the other, in an uninterrupted sequence, and the agile, slender figures, flowing drapery, colours and echoes of the Hellenistic style can probably be linked with Constantinople.

(b) 6th century. Several monuments survive from this period in the East and West. The stylistic tendencies that emerge in the early years of the 6th century are developed during the reign of JUSTINIAN I, when the empire was strengthened all around the Mediterranean and it seemed that the old imperium was reborn. This idea of the absolute

ruler, as represented by Justinian, also found expression in art. The chief characteristics of monumental painting and mosaic are the attempt to achieve symmetry of composition with figures aligned in a strictly frontal arrangement, a reduction in the brilliance of colours and the predominance of gold backgrounds. The facial expressions become stereotyped with large, accentuated eyes, and an avoidance of individual features.

The hallmarks of the new style emerge in the mosaics of the small chapel dedicated to the Apostle Andrew, built by Bishop Peter II (*reg* 494–519), on the first floor of the Archbishop's Palace in Ravenna. The decoration includes a roundel with the chi-rho symbol supported by four angels on the vault, a representation of a *Triumphant Christ Trampling the Lion and the Dragon*, as well as roundels with figures of Christ, the Apostles and the saints. The palette is restricted and the background is worked in gold.

Some of the largest and most impressive mosaics are in S Apollinare Nuovo (*see* RAVENNA, §2(vi)). They cover the area above the nave arcade and were executed in two phases: each side has two upper bands (*c*. 500) and a third, lower band (*c*. 561). The uppermost bands contain scenes from the *Life of Christ*, the *Passion* and the *Resurrection* that are the earliest of their kind in monumental art. The figures dominate the compositions, while the landscape and buildings take second place. The impression of three-dimensionality is limited. The middle bands are occupied by 32 male figures, who may represent prophets and preachers of the Gospel. The lowest bands contain columns of male and female martyrs, holding crowns: the men on the south side start from the Palace of Theodoric and proceed towards a *Christ Enthroned*; the women on the north side set off from the port of Ravenna at Classe and make their way, behind the three Magi, towards a *Virgin and Child Enthroned*. Both processions of martyrs are inspired by imperial iconography and are marked by a monotonous repetition of figures with no individual features.

The most important monument in Ravenna, and a work of Byzantine imperial propaganda, is S Vitale (consecrated 547; see RAVENNA, §2(vii)) with its complex mosaic decoration in the sanctuary. The roundel with the Agnus Dei supported by four angels in the centre of the vault, immediately above the altar, refers to the mystery of the Holy Eucharist. Most of the other subjects (e.g. *Abraham and the Three Angels*; the *Sacrifice of Isaac*) relate to this. The two panels of *Emperor Justinian* (see MOSAIC, fig. 6) and *Empress Theodora* (see fig. 39) with their retinues are unique in Early Christian art; the luxury of the materials, the immobility of the composition, the lack of depth and volume all give the impression that the figures live and move in a supernatural world. The hallmarks of S Vitale's decoration are the richness of the colours, predominantly linear forms, and the flat, strictly frontal figures. The mosaics in the conch of the apse of S Apollinare in Classe (consecrated 549; see RAVENNA, §2(v)) are even more abstract and schematized. St Apollinarius stands with arms outstretched in prayer and flanked by 12 white sheep,

symbolizing the faithful of his church. Behind the saint is a symbolic depiction of the *Transfiguration* of Christ. The flat figures are represented mainly in outline with no attempt to integrate them in space. The mosaics in the basilica built by Bishop Euphrasius (*reg* 530–60) at POREČ also belong to the artistic tradition of Ravenna. The *Virgin and Child Enthroned* in the apse and other scenes emphasizing the incarnation are also consistent with the church's dedication to the Virgin. Fragments of mosaic also survive on the east façade.

Intense linearity and schematization are combined with such Hellenistic traits as sculptured figures and delicately modelled faces in the mosaics of the first decorative programme (before 620) in the church of Hagios Demetrios (see THESSALONIKI, §III, 3(ii)). They include two votive panels in the form of large-scale icons, one showing a child being dedicated to St Demetrios and the other showing the saint with an angel. A similar combination of styles is evident in the partially preserved mosaic (probably *c.* 526–30) formerly in the basilica of PANAGIA KANIKARIA, LYTHRANKOMI (stolen between 1974 and 1979; untraced). The earliest surviving example of a Virgin in an apse, it showed her enthroned with Christ seated on her knee,

39. Mosaic of *Empress Theodora with her Retinue* in the apse of S Vitale, Ravenna, Italy, consecrated 547

40. Mosaic of the *Transfiguration* in the conch of the apse of the katholikon, monastery of St Catherine, Mt Sinai, 548–65

within a mandorla and flanked by two angels holding sceptres. Although this mosaic has certain similarities with the Ravenna mosaics, the soft modelling of the figures and the strength of expression are derived from the Hellenistic tradition.

The art during the last years of Justinian's reign is best represented by the mosaics in the katholikon of the monastery of St Catherine (*see* SINAI, §2(ii)). Among the scenes depicted are a *Transfiguration* in the conch of the apse (see fig. 40), and an *Agnus Dei* flanked by two archangels and busts of St John the Baptist and the Virgin on the triumphal arch, which constitute the earliest depiction of a Deësis. This subject emphasizes the eschatological nature of the Transfiguration, which is considered a prefiguration of the Second Coming. The mosaics' unique style, the ascetic expressions on the faces, as well as the unclassicizing approach to rendering the figures, all point to a Constantinopolitan workshop, which probably employed local Palestinian artists as assistants.

The apse mosaic in SS Cosma e Damiano (526–30) in Rome is in line with the general trend towards two-dimensional composition. Christ appears in the centre flanked by SS Peter and Paul, who present SS Cosmas and Damian, each holding a crown. On the far right-hand side of the mosaic is St Theodore and on the left Pope Felix, who as the church's founder holds a model of the building. The figures resemble Roman statues and stare fixedly with wide-open eyes into the far distance.

One of the most important wall paintings of the 6th century in Rome is in the catacomb of the matron Turtura

in the cemetery of Commodilla (*c*. 530). It depicts a *Virgin and Child Enthroned* flanked by SS Felix and Adauctus, and Turtura, who is offering votive candles to the Virgin (*see* ROME, fig. 32). The composition resembles an icon in which the figures are flat and somewhat standardized in form and expression. Remains of wall paintings (early 6th century) have also been found in the episcopal basilica and the baptistery at STOBI. They include fragments of the heads of saints and small sections of compositions closely related to ancient art as well as to such 6th-century manuscripts as the Rabbula and Rossano Gospels. An even more rustic, linear and flat style is represented by the Coptic wall paintings (6th century–early 8th; Cairo, Coptic Mus.) originally from the side chapels of the monasteries of St Apollo at BAWIT and St Jeremias at Saqqara (*see* SAQQARA, §5). Scenes include *Christ Enthroned*, the Virgin, alone or with the infant Christ, Apostles, angels and local saints. The figures have huge, staring eyes and are generally arranged frontally.

(c) 7th century–mid-9th. Surviving monuments of the 7th century show the development of the abstract style, with flat, attenuated figures and harsh features. There is also a strong Hellenistic tendency in the art of this period, first seen in such secular works as the mosaic floors (?6th century; Istanbul, Mosaic Mus.) of the Great Palace at Istanbul, and later in religious art.

An example of work produced under Heraklios (*reg* 610–40) may be the apse mosaic in the church of Panagia Angeloklistos at Kiti, Cyprus, in which the bold use of colour and fluid modelling, characteristic of the Hellenistic tradition, is combined with the abstract style (*see* CYPRUS, fig. 24). The date of the mosaic is in dispute, however, the most likely attributions being the late 6th century or early 7th. It depicts a full-length Virgin Hodegetria, holding Christ in her left arm, flanked by archangels Michael and Gabriel; an inscription above her head identifies her as 'I Agia Maria' (St Mary). Two fragmentary mosaics in Constantinople may also belong to the early 7th century: a head of an angel, preserved in the church of St Nicholas (*c.* 1720) in the Fener district of the city, and part of a *Presentation of the Virgin*, uncovered at the east end of the largely 12th-century church of the Kalenderhane Cami. The latter mosaic, in particular, shows the successful combination of the Hellenistic and abstract styles.

In the mosaics of the second decorative programme (after 620) in Hagios Demetrios, Thessaloniki, Hellenistic elements are overshadowed by the abstract style. The flat figures, with their linear features and large, wide-open eyes, are set against sketchy and schematic grounds. Among several representations of St Demetrios is one showing him with two restorers of the church, a bishop and a city governor (*see* THESSALONIKI, fig. 2). In the mosaics in Rome, linearity and a tendency to simplify the rendition of figures predominate, as is evident in the mosaics of S Agnese fuori le Mura (625–38), S Stefano Rotondo (642–9) and the Oratory of S Venanzio (642–9).

The most important wall paintings of the 7th century are those preserved in the church of S Maria Antiqua, Rome. Their impressionistic style is reminiscent of Pompeian wall painting. In the painting of the *Maccabees* with their mother, Solomoni, and their teacher, Eleazar, the figures are well integrated into the landscape, the faces carefully modelled using light and shade and the bodies correctly proportioned. The Greek inscriptions betray the artist's Byzantine origins. Wall paintings of the 7th century also survive in the triconch church of Drosiani, near the village of Moni on Naxos. The two roundels with busts of Christ in the dome probably represent the dual nature of Christ, an issue that was at the heart of contemporary Christological debate. In the central apse is an *Assumption of the Virgin*, while the *Virgin and Child with SS Cosmas and Damian* and a *Deësis* are represented in the north lunette. The paintings are of exceptional quality. The facial characteristics are freely drawn, the eyes large and the figures attenuated and without volume. The warm colours help to create an atmosphere of serenity. The first layer of painting in the church of the Virgin Protothroni at Chalke on Naxos is also dated to the 7th century and includes full-length figures of the Apostles and a bust-length of St Isidore. Another important cycle of paintings from Italy that most probably dates *c.* 700 is that in the triconch church of S Maria Foris Portas at CASTELSEPRIO. The paintings cover themes from before the Nativity and from the infancy of Christ and display great skill in draughtsmanship with correct use of perspective, a sculptural approach to form and elegant drapery. All these features hark back to the Hellenistic tradition.

The iconoclastic controversy (726–843) had a profound effect on artistic development. Many Early Christian monuments featuring pictorial art were destroyed, and many icons disappeared. In the few monuments that survive from the period, the cross decorating the apse is the central motif. Other aniconic motifs are taken from a range of animal and plant subjects. The church of Hagia Eirene (*see* ISTANBUL, §III, 5), for example, preserves a large cross on a three-stepped pedestal in the centre of the apse, surrounded by bands of non-figural ornament and Old Testament inscriptions (741–75). Aniconic decoration is also preserved in Hagia Sophia in Thessaloniki (*see* THESSALONIKI, §III, 5(ii)). A multicoloured cross decorates the sanctuary vault, and traces of a large cross can be seen in the apse lunette. Plant ornament and crosses still exist on the sides of the vault. These mosaics probably date to the joint reign of Constantine VII and his mother Eirene (*reg* 780–97). Non-figural decoration with bands of ornament and interconnected roundels containing rosettes and crosses under arches also survives in the church of St Prokopios in the Mani, Greece. On Naxos aniconic decoration (probably 9th–10th century) survives in Hagia Kyriaki at Apeiranthos, Hagios Artemios and Hagios Ioannis Theologos st'Adisarou near Sankri, and Hagios Ioannis Theologos at Danakos.

BIBLIOGRAPHY

J. Wilpert: *Die römische Mosaiken der kirchlichen Bauten vom IV.–XII. Jahrhundert* (Freiburg im Breisgau, 1916)
A. Frolow: 'L'Eglise rouge de Perustiča', *Bull. Byz. Inst.*, i (1946), pp. 29–42
E. Kitzinger: 'The Cult of Images in the Age before Iconoclasm', *Dumbarton Oaks Pap.*, viii (1954), pp. 83–150
A. Grabar: *Le Premier Art chrétien (200–395)* (Paris, 1956)
——: *L'Iconoclasme byzantin* (Paris, 1957/R 1984)
W. F. Volbach and M. Hirmer: *Frühchristliche Kunst: Die Kunst der Spätantike in West- und Ostrom* (Munich, 1958)
C. Ihm: *Die Programme der christlichen Apsismalerei vom vierten Jahrhundert bis zur Mitte des achten Jahrhunderts* (Wiesbaden, 1960)
J. Beckwith: *The Art of Constantinople: An Introduction to Byzantine Art, 330–1453* (London and New York, 1961)
F. Gerke: *Spätantike und frühes Christentum* (Baden-Baden, 1967)
G. Matthiae: *Mosaici medioevali delle chiese di Roma* (Rome, 1967)
J. Snyder: 'The Meaning of the Majestas Domini in Hosios David', *Byzantion*, xxxvii (1968), pp. 143–52
W. Oakeshott: *Die Mosaiken von Rom* (Munich, 1969)
F. W. Deichmann: *Ravenna, Haupstadt des spätantiken Abendlandes*, 3 vols (Wiesbaden, 1969–76)
S. Pelekanidis: *Paleiochristianika mnimeia Thessalonikis, Acheiropoietos, Moni Latomou* [Early Christian monuments of Thessaloniki, the Acheiropoietos Church and Latomou Monastery] (Thessaloniki, 1973)
M. Sacopoulo: *La Théotokos à la mandorle de Lynthrankomi* (Paris, 1975)
J. D. Deckers: *Der alttestamentliche Zyklus von S. Maria Maggiore in Rom* (Bonn, 1976)
E. Kitzinger: *Byzantine Art in the Making: Main Lines of Stylistic Development in Mediterranean Art, 3rd–7th Century* (London, 1977)
D. Stutzinger, ed.: *Spätantike und frühes Christentum* (Frankfurt am Main, 1984)
A. H. S. Megaw: 'Mosaici parietali paleobizantini di Cipro', *Corsi Cult. A. Ravenn. & Biz.*, xxxii (1985), pp. 137–98
A. Effenberger: *Frühchristliche Kunst und Kultur von den Anfängen bis zum 7. Jahrhundert* (Munich, 1986)
M. Prelog: *Die Euphrasius Basilika von Poreč* (Zagreb, 1986)
N. Drandakis: *Oi palaiochristianikes toichographies sti Drosiani tis Naxou* [Early Christian wall paintings at Drosiani on Naxos] (Athens, 1988)
N. Gioles: *Palaiochristianiki techni, mnimeiaki zographiki (p. 300–726)* [Early Christian art, wall painting and mosaic, *c.* 300–726] (Athens, 1991)

MELITA EMMANUEL

4. *c.* 843–*c.* 1204. The period between the end of iconoclasm in 843 and the sack of Constantinople in 1204 is one of exceptional richness and stylistic diversity in monumental wall paintings and mosaics.

(i) Introduction. (ii) Constantinople. (iii) Greece. (iv) Macedonia and Thrace. (v) Cyprus. (vi) Cappadocia. (vii) Southern Italy and Sicily.

(i) Introduction. The great churches of Hagia Sophia and the Holy Apostles in Constantinople, as well as those of such provincial capitals as Nicaea (now Iznik, Turkey) and Thessaloniki, were redecorated after the triumph of Orthodoxy with prominent images in their apses. The iconophile propaganda inscriptions show that in the latter half of the 9th century the restoration of images was as much a political as a religious issue: for example, an inscription below the apsidal image of the *Virgin and Child* (867) in Hagia Sophia proclaimed, 'The images that the impostors [i.e. the iconoclasts] had formerly cast down here, pious emperors have again set up'.

The desire to restore what had been lost during the iconoclast interlude encouraged a retrospective attitude, frequently drawing upon 6th-century models for the new programmes. Limited economic resources, however, meant generally smaller churches, and the decorations were often carried out in the cheaper medium of fresco rather than mosaic. The increasingly rigid application of certain principles of church decoration led to the emergence of the so-called 'classical system'. The interior of the small, domed, cruciform churches of the Middle Byzantine period could be interpreted as a microcosm of the Christian universe in which images were arranged in a hierarchical order descending from the celestial to the terrestrial levels. Thus a Pantokrator image regularly occupied the cupola, the conch of the apse contained the *Virgin and Child* or occasionally the *Deësis*, while the lower walls of the apse gradually became the usual location for the processions of bishops and by the 11th century frequently took on a liturgical character. The choice of scenes within the festive cycle became increasingly limited to the principal liturgical feasts of the Church, in contrast with the earlier proliferation of narrative scenes. Occasionally, however, scenes from the *Infancy* or *Passion* cycles and the *Life of the Virgin* were also used. Extensive assemblies of saints were often depicted below the festive tier, usually grouped together as Church Fathers, martyrs, holy women, hermit monks and so on. The selection of these saints provided the greatest scope for improvisation.

By the 11th century the Antique and imperial court imagery, as exemplified at S Vitale, Ravenna (6th century; *see* RAVENNA, §2(vii)), had been replaced, and most church decoration conformed to the concept of the Church as a hierarchy of Eucharist celebrations, using imagery derived from liturgical ceremony. Examples of this new decoration can be found in a number of 11th-century churches, including Nea Moni in Chios, the katholikon of Hosios Loukas, Dafni and the column churches at Göreme in Cappadocia.

During this period monasticism was considerably expanded. Many of the traditional monastic centres in Asia Minor and North Africa were lost during the Arab and Saljuq invasions of the 7th to the 10th and the 11th and 12th centuries respectively. As a result the focus of Byzantine monasticism moved west into the Balkans, increasing the diversity of patronage sources and exposing Byzantine art to outside influences. Although the 'classical system' of decoration was frequently used with limited regional variations for the main church of the monastery (the katholikon), distinctive iconographic programmes were devised for the decoration of other monastic buildings, such as refectories and ossuaries. Images of monastic saints, usually shown standing in a frontal attitude and sometimes holding an open didactic scroll, also became particularly popular. More rarely a saint is depicted in a scene from his life.

The geographic expansion of Byzantine monasticism also facilitated a widespread export of Byzantine styles into areas as far afield as Kievan Russia and Norman Sicily. The paucity of extant monuments in Constantinople, however, has made it difficult to differentiate between exported metropolitan models and provincial developments. In a few instances epigraphic or literary evidence links a monument and its decoration with a patron and artists from Constantinople, as at the monastery churches of Nea Moni (*c.* 1049–55), the charnel house at Bachkovo Monastery (1083) and St Panteleimon at Nerezi (1164). Attributions largely based on stylistic analysis of monumental paintings and mosaics are confounded by the persistent survival and revival of Classical elements, which have led scholars to speak of 'a perpetual renaissance or of perennial Hellenism' (Demus). Some have identified the MACEDONIAN DYNASTY (867–1056) and the Komnenian (1057–1185) dynasty (see KOMNENOS) as major periods of classicizing renewal of this kind. In addition, it seems clear that regional styles did emerge from Russia, Cappadocia, southern Italy, Cyprus and Greece during this period.

Although almost all surviving monumental paintings and mosaics belong to ecclesiastical foundations, scraps of evidence in literary sources concern monumental secular art, such as mosaics in the colonnaded hall of the Blachernai Palace portraying the victories of Manuel I Komnenos (*reg* 1143–80) against the barbarians (Niketas Choniates, p. 117). Echoes of this kind of art survive in the wall paintings in the south-west tower of the cathedral of St Sophia in Kiev (1113–25; *see* KIEV, §3(i)) and in the mosaics of the chamber of Roger II (*reg* 1105–54) in the royal palace at Palermo (*see* PALERMO, §II, 2(i)).

(ii) Constantinople. Literary sources document major building activity in Constantinople, especially under Basil I (*reg* 867–86), in the second half of the 11th century and under Manuel I Komnenos. However, no major monumental cycle of decorations is extant in the city from this period; where the buildings themselves have survived, their decorations have largely perished. In the Pantokrator triple church (1118–36; *see* ISTANBUL, §III, 2(ii)), for example, only fragments of the window soffits' mosaic ornament survive. The remnants of wall paintings in the Myrelaion Church (now Bodrum Cami), founded by Romanos I Lekapenos (*reg* 920–44), belong to the period of Palaiologan repairs *c.* 1300. Similarly, the wall paintings in the late 12th-century Kyriotissa Church (now Kalenderhane Cami) date mainly from the period of Latin occupation (1204–61) and from the late 13th century to the early 14th.

The only major Middle Byzantine monumental mosaics to survive belong to a number of different decorative campaigns in Hagia Sophia (*see* ISTANBUL, §III, 1(ii)(b)). The earliest of these campaigns can be dated to *c.* 867

when Patriarch Photios (858–67) had secured sufficient imperial funding to complete the decorations of the apse with a *Virgin and Child* flanked by archangels and then probably decorated much of the church's central interior. All that survive, however, are the *Virgin and Child*, one archangel and three of the original fourteen bishops on the lowest register of the two tympana. In style the bishops relate closely to some of the miniatures in a copy of the *Homilies* of Gregory Nazianzus (880–82; Paris, Bib. N., MS. gr. 510), in which the careful attention to facial expression is largely set against a general awkwardness and stiffness in the poses of individual figures (*see* §V, 2(ii) below). About the same time the main room of the patriarchal palace, which opens on to the south side of Hagia Sophia's west gallery, was also decorated with mosaic. This survives in a ruinous state, the most impressive fragment of which belongs to a lunette *Deësis* and preserves the figures of the Virgin and Christ, which from their style indicate the difficulties that Byzantine mosaicists experienced when working on a monumental scale.

Later in date than the apse mosaic and the tympanum bishops are two lunette mosaics, one of which is set over the imperial doorway leading from the narthex into the nave. It shows a Byzantine emperor prostrating himself before the enthroned Christ, set between medallion images of an angel and the Virgin. The emperor is usually identified as Leo VI (*reg* 886–912), although there is no inscription to support this. In style the work has some similarities with the apsidal mosaic, except that the linear articulation is heavier and the drapery folds more schematic. The second lunette mosaic is over the south-west vestibule door leading into the narthex and depicts Constantine the Great and Justinian offering models of the city and church to an enthroned Virgin and Child. Although this image of the Virgin as the protectress of Constantinople and her Church may relate to any of the numerous occasions when the city was under threat, it is usually attributed to the late 10th century or early 11th. The features of the two emperors are identical and depersonalized, their poses and draperies stiff and unconvincing.

The remaining three panels of this period in Hagia Sophia are all images commemorating specific emperors. The earliest of these is a rather clumsy and cramped full-length portrait of *Alexander* (*reg* 912–13) in the north gallery; it is likely to have been one of numerous imperial portraits. In the south gallery, within what was the royal enclosure, are two imperial offertory panels on the east wall. The first represents Constantine IX Monomachos and Zoe flanking Christ and was probably executed in 1028–34, defaced in 1041 and reset after 1042 when Zoe remarried (see fig. 41). The second represents the Virgin and Child standing between John II and his wife Eirene, and was set up to commemorate their accession in 1118 (*see* ISTANBUL, fig. 9). The portrait of their son Alexios was probably added *c.* 1122. The two panels share similarities in their composition, but whereas the Zoe panel has a certain harshness and sterility, with strong linear articulation and conventional devices used for such features as the highlights on the cheeks, the Komnenian panel shows a greater sophistication in technique, both with the use of shading to create a sense of volume and in the attempt to individualize the portraits.

41. Mosaic of *Christ Enthroned with Empress Zoe and Constantine IX Monomachos* (*c.* 1028–34) south gallery of Hagia Sophia, Istanbul, Turkey; reset after 1042

The scant evidence surviving from Constantinople suggests that the immediate post-iconoclast period was one of rather hurried renovation in which the political aspirations of the patrons generally outstripped the available resources. By the Komnenian period, however, technical excellence was such that Byzantine artists were able to express powerful emotions.

(iii) Greece. There is evidence that artistic activity in Greece was inspired by the events surrounding the triumph of Orthodoxy in Constantinople, and in the second half of the 9th century some of the principal churches in Thessaloniki were redecorated. The apse of Hagios Georgios (*see* THESSALONIKI, §III, 2(ii)) received an impressive wall painting of the *Ascension*, while *c.* 885 the dome of Hagia Sophia was covered with a mosaic of the same subject (*see* THESSALONIKI, §III, 5(ii)). The style of both works has much in common with other contemporary monumental decorations, such as the apsidal archangel in Hagia Sophia in Constantinople and the apsidal decorations in the church of the Dormition in Nicaea (destr. 1922; *see* IZNIK, §1). Most other paintings from Greece in the late 9th century and much of the 10th, such as the wall paintings in St Panteleimon in the Mani (911–12) and the earliest layers of wall paintings in both Hagios Stephanos and Taxiarchis Metropoleos in KASTORIA, are poorly executed provincial works.

The reconquest of Crete in 961 by Nikephoros II Phokas (later emperor, *reg* 963–9) and, more significantly, the defeat of the Bulgarians in 1018 by Basil II (*reg* 976–1025) brought about a period of relative stability and security for Greece that lasted until the Latin occupation of 1204. During this period a number of outstanding wall painting and mosaic cycles were executed in Greece and on its neighbouring islands. The church of Panagia Chalkeon (*see* THESSALONIKI, §III, 6) was commissioned in 1028 by Christophoros, a Byzantine administrator in

42. Wall painting of the *Entry into Jerusalem* (detail; early 11th century), crypt, katholikon of Hosios Loukas, Greece

southern Italy. The wall paintings are of exceptional sophistication, particularly the *Last Judgement* in the narthex and the bishops in the apse, who have long elegant faces and large expressive eyes; draperies are heavily modelled with strong simple vertical folds suggesting the form of a body underneath. The wall paintings in the narthex of Hagia Sophia in Thessaloniki and the rather awkward image of the *Virgin and Child* inserted into the 9th-century non-figural apse mosaic may also be of the same date.

It seems that during the first half of the 11th century the elegant and refined style of the Panagia Chalkeon's paintings co-existed with a more spiritual and abstract style of decoration as represented in the mosaics and wall paintings decorating the katholikon of HOSIOS LOUKAS. The mosaics are stylistically similar to those of St Sophia in Kiev (1043–6). The figures are squat, heavily articulated with dark lines and are generally frontally posed with large heads and wide staring eyes. The monument impresses through its sheer scale and individual elements, rather than through its overall conception. Although the wall paintings of the katholikon's crypt, three upper chapels and west gallery are of a similar date, they seem to be of a higher quality. The crypt has a rare, funerary decorative programme and, while some of the scenes are clearly dependent on the mosaics in the katholikon, the style of the wall paintings is much more expressive and dramatic, probably reflecting the taste of the patron as much as the influence

of metropolitan trends (see fig. 42). This style of decoration is found in a number of churches including the first phase of wall paintings in the Myriokephala Katholikon on Crete, and those in the churches of the Virgin Protothronos at Chalki (1052; *see* NAXOS, §3) and of the Episkopi in Eurytania (Athens, Byz. Mus.).

The classicizing painterly style is most vividly represented in the mosaics at Nea Moni (*see* CHIOS, §2), which are linked with the patronage of Constantine IX and date to between 1045 and 1055. The main artist probably came from Constantinople and his work in the nave has a strong individual character, in which the stressed outlines of the figures and rhythmic arrangement of the scenes are set in a framework of vivid colours against a gold ground. This style was probably similar to that of the narthex mosaics (1065–7; destr.) in the church of the Dormition at Nicaea.

The mosaics in the monastery church of DAFNI (*c*. 1080), although severely disfigured by 19th-century restoration, can probably be dated to the late 11th century. As at Nea Moni the artist displays a strongly individual style rich in Classical references and motifs, as well as in the use of Antique stances, proportions, facial types and drapery conventions for the figures. His work is of exceptional dynamism and includes an awe-inspiring image of the *Pantokrator* on the vault of the dome and a lyrical, gently swaying nude Christ in the *Baptism* on the south-west pendentive. The origins of the Dafni master remain obscure, and his art stands in splendid isolation.

The 12th-century wall paintings in Greece do not match the brilliance of the 11th-century mosaics. The early 12th-century paintings on the apse and west wall of the Old Metropolis at SERRES (i) and those in the church of the Episkopi on Santorini (anc. Thera) are executed in a rather stylized manner with strong linear articulation. The paintings in the dome of Panagia Kyparissiotissa in the monastery of St Ierotheos near Megara and the Evangelistria Church in GERAKI (both late 12th century) present a somewhat dry and mannered ornamental style. Probably of a similar date are the festive cycle mosaics in Hosios David, Thessaloniki (*see* THESSALONIKI, §III, 4(ii)), which, although sombre in style, have a haunting quality, particularly the *Nativity* and *Baptism*.

(iv) Macedonia and Thrace. Between the defeat of the Bulgarians in 1018 and the Latin occupation of 1204 Thrace and Macedonia, which are now divided between Turkey, Greece, Bulgaria and the former Yugoslav republics, were largely under Byzantine control. Consequently they benefited from considerable patronage stemming from Constantinople and retain a number of churches that may reflect changing metropolitan taste. Among the earliest extant wall paintings are those in the cathedral of St Sophia at OHRID (1037–59), which survive mainly in the sanctuary, west wall of the nave and narthex. They are of exceptional iconographic intricacy, and the apse bears very rare liturgical images of SS Basil (*c.* 330–79) and John Chrysostomos (*c.* 347–407). The style is reminiscent of that in the Nea Moni mosaics, except that the folds of the draperies are more sharply defined into segments, as is particularly evident in the *Ascension*, which occupies the vault of the church. A slightly more subdued version of this dynamic and agitated style is encountered in the fragments of wall paintings preserved in the roughly contemporary church of Vodoca and in the more sophisticated paintings of the church at Veljusa (*c.* 1080).

Most of the wall paintings that decorate the two-storey charnel house at BACHKOVO MONASTERY, Bulgaria, probably date to 1083 when the monastery was founded. The iconography of the funerary programme is fairly complex and includes such rare scenes as the *Vision of Ezekiel in the Valley of Dry Bones* and groups of *All Saints* (see fig. 43). The wall paintings are in a classicizing style with beautifully modelled faces and slightly elongated figures.

The wall paintings of the katholikon of the monastery of the Theotokos Kosmosoteira (nr Ferrai, Greece) were commissioned in 1152 by Isaak, the youngest son of Alexios I Komnenos (*reg* 1081–1118). The impressive figures are sophisticated in execution, but they are relatively stiff, with flat and ornamented draperies reminiscent of the mid-12th-century Byzantine mosaics in Norman Sicily, particularly those at Cefalù (*see* §(vii) below). The Kosmosoteira faces are heavily modelled with patches of rouge on the cheeks.

Another Komnenian foundation is the church of ST PANTELEIMON, NEREZI (1164). The figures in the festive cycle and most of the saints have refined classical faces, while the emotional impact of such scenes as the *Presentation in the Temple*, the *Deposition* and the *Lamentation* has been heightened by emphasizing the gestures and

43. Wall painting of *All Saints* (*c.* 1083), charnel house, Bachkovo Monastery, Bulgaria

facial expressions of the participants. This new emotionalism reflects a broader tendency in contemporary Byzantine thought, which favoured iconographic types like the Virgin Eleousa ('merciful') and rhetorical literary conventions that stressed such aspects as lamentation and tenderness.

The subdued emotionalism at Nerezi becomes heightened in the wall paintings of ST GEORGE, KURBINOVO (1191) and those in the Hagioi Anargyroi Church in Kastoria, which were painted at about the same time and possibly by the same workshop. Sometimes this is referred to as the Dynamic style and is characterized by an abstract linearism, an extreme elongation of the bodies with figures having tiny heads and by agitated masses of drapery folds, with curving trains behind the figures. At Kurbinovo the iconographic programme has been rearranged to extract the greatest emotional impact: the *Lamentation*, in which the Virgin mourns her son, is placed opposite the *Nativity*, which shows her rejoicing over his birth, thus achieving a particularly dramatic contrast.

Similar mannered emotionalism is also found in the wall paintings of the church of St Nicholas Kasnitzis at Kastoria, which probably date from the 1180s. When it is handled by a less experienced painter, as here, the style becomes somewhat tired and artificial with arbitrary distortions. The last traces of the classical grace of Nerezi have been lost.

(v) Cyprus. From its reconquest in 965 by Nikephoros II Phokas until its loss to the crusaders in 1192, Cyprus was under continuous Byzantine control. Little has survived from the first 100 years of this period. Byzantine interest in Cyprus apparently increased only with the realization of its strategic importance when threatened by the Saljuq Turks from across the Karamanian Strait. Its art was influenced by both contemporary Byzantine trends and a local stylistic variant that developed from the differing imported strands.

Most Cypriot churches are small and simple in plan. The church of Hagios Nikolaos tis Stegis near Kakopetria was probably first decorated in the earlier 11th century. In the *Entry into Jerusalem*, the *Raising of Lazarus* and some of the individual images of saints there are echoes of the style of the Panagia Chalkeon mosaics (*see* §(iii) above), although the forms are rendered in a more linear manner. The Hagios Nikolaos wall paintings are most notable for the vivid treatment of the individual faces.

The *parekklesion* of the monastery of St John Chrysostomos at Koutsoventis contains the remains of a splendid cycle of wall paintings (*see* CYPRUS, fig. 25). They are linked by inscription to Eumathios Philokales, who was the governor of Cyprus between 1092 and *c.* 1103 and again between 1110 and 1118. The paintings are in a classicizing style with beautifully modelled faces and simple vertically falling drapery folds. In some aspects this style resembles the mosaics at Dafni and the wall paintings at Bachkovo Monastery.

The church of the Panagia Phorbiotissa at ASINOU is dated by inscription to 1105–6 and was commissioned by the Byzantine Magistros, Nikephoros Ischyrios. A substantial number of paintings from this phase survive as 14th-century reproductions and to some extent reflect the work of the painter at Koutsoventis. Apart from the numerous iconographic innovations (Sacopoulo), the wall paintings are drawn in a graceful, linear style and the deliberate actions of the figures are similar to those at Dafni. A monumental architectural backdrop to the large *Death of the Virgin* over the west doorway that leads into the narthex presents a stage-like space into which the mourning figures have been set. The style of the Asinou painter is also evident in the early 12th-century wall paintings of the Panagia Church at Trikomo. The similarities between the Ascension scenes in both churches suggest that they may be the work of the same painter.

An unusual cycle of wall paintings was painted by a certain Theodore Apseudes in 1183 in the Enkleistra of the monastery of St Neophytos near Paphos. The iconographic programme was painted during Neophytos' lifetime and includes an image of the monk addressing a prayer to a Deësis image (*see* CHRISTIANITY, fig. 8) and a unique composition of two archangels carrying him to heaven. The paintings lean towards the mannered Dynamic style, but are without the abstract exaggerations of the wall paintings in St George at Kurbinovo. Although the figures are elongated, they are shown in arrested movement and some attempt is made to mould the flowing draperies to their bodies, thus helping to create uncluttered compositions.

Panagia tou Arakou in Lagoudera was painted in 1192, the year after Richard I of England (*reg* 1189–99) seized Cyprus. In style the agitated drapery is reminiscent of both the wall paintings at Kurbinovo and the *Annunciation* icon of about the same date from Mt Sinai (*see* SINAI, §2(iii)). The Lagoudera painter managed to combine a sense of elegant classicism with the fashionable mannerism of the style. The emotional dynamism of the *Anastasis* and *Ascension* scenes does not detract from their deeply spiritual quality, while the extrovert quality of the prophets, such as *Ezekiel* and *Elias*, is combined with tormented facial expressions to create profoundly moving images.

(vi) Cappadocia. From the early 10th century until the late 11th, when the Saljuqs defeated the Byzantines at Manzikert in 1071 and gradually occupied the territory, Cappadocia was a relatively secure Byzantine province. The nature of the Byzantine settlement is unclear, and the earlier scholarly presumption that it was exclusively a monastic community may not be correct. Nevertheless, almost all the surviving examples of Byzantine painting are found in rock-cut churches and monasteries, and many are rather crudely executed, in a poor state of preservation and difficult to date (*see* CAPPADOCIA, §2(ii) and fig. 4). Under Saljuq domination, however, the style and quality of the wall paintings declined rapidly, although churches were still being cut into the rock and painted well into the 13th century.

The wall paintings of the mid- and later 10th century mark a refinement in style, as can be seen in those of the New Church of Tokalı Kilise in the Göreme Valley. The figures possess a dramatic, psychological power, while the complex iconographic programme presents an extensive Christological cycle and rare hagiographic scenes. The Great Pigeon House at Çavuşin contains an image of Nikephoros II Phokas, Empress Theophano and the royal retinue in the prothesis apse, probably commemorating Nikephoros' victorious compaigns against the Arabs in 964–5. The elongation and disproportionately small heads of the figures, which include monumental *Ascension* and *Pentecost* scenes in the eastern half of the ceiling vault, frieze-like Christological narrative strips in the western half and on the walls, and a row of standing saints, are related in style to the LEO BIBLE and the mid-10th-century Romanos group of ivories from Constantinople (Paris, Bib. N.; *see* §VII, 5(iii) below).

Following on from the classical decoration at Çavuşin are the wall paintings in the church of St Barbara in the Soğanlı Valley, dated by inscription to 1006 or 1021. In this small single-nave barrel-vaulted church, a series of festive scenes within rectangular frames on the vault replaces the earlier arrangement of narrative friezes and frontally posed saints around the walls. Unique to Cappadocia and generally rare within Middle Byzantine painting is a series of eight illusionistically painted medallion portraits, which simulate rectangular icons and are shown as if suspended by rings from the vault. The identity of the figures is unclear as none has a halo or is designated as a saint by inscription. In style, however, their slender, elongated forms, complex drapery folds, which generally end with simple hemlines, and expressive use of broad, white highlights have much in common with wall paintings in the early 11th-century church of Kıçlıçlar Kuşluk in Göreme (Chapel 33).

A more precious style of painting is represented by the wall paintings in the three column churches in Göreme: Çarıklı Kilise, Karanlık Kilise (see fig. 44) and Elmalı Kilise. They can probably be attributed to the second half of the 11th century and are comparable in style to the wall paintings in St Sophia, Ohrid, and to some extent to those in Karabaş Kilise in Soğanlı (1060–61). The three column churches contain a typical Middle Byzantine iconographic arrangement with a *Pantokrator* in the middle dome, festive cycle in the upper vaults and saints below. The ornament in the framing bands is exceptionally rich and illustrates that, although Cappadocia was receptive to current metropolitan trends, its patrons also supported artists working in a local, provincial style.

(vii) Southern Italy and Sicily. The province of southern Italy did not generally attract high-level patronage while under Byzantine rule between 971 and 1071. The founding of S Maria Nea in Bari (*c.* 1030) by a Byzantine governor appears to have been an exception, for high-ranking officials generally preferred to endow churches back home. The peculiarly ascetic form of Byzantine monasticism that developed in southern Italy was also not conducive either to large-scale building activities or to costly decorations.

44. Wall painting of the *Raising of Lazarus* (second half of the 11th century), Karanlık Kilise, Göreme, Turkey

After the Norman capture of Bari in 1071, however, Byzantine art remained supreme, and the new Norman patrons continued to import Byzantine prestige art objects such as the bronze doors manufactured in Constantinople for the cathedral of Monte Sant'Angelo in Amalfi. In some instances they even introduced complete workshops of painters and mosaicists.

The dating of many monasteries in southern Italy is unclear, and their coarse provincial decoration is difficult to relate to metropolitan trends. Although parallels can be drawn with other Byzantine provinces, particularly Cappadocia, certain features point to links with contemporary work at Montecassino and Rome. The case of the wall paintings in the church at Carpignano near Otranto, which can be dated by inscription to 959 and 1020, is rare; elsewhere, especially around Brindisi, wall paintings continued to be produced well into the Norman period.

The Norman conquest of Sicily from the Arabs in 1091 (*see* SICILY, §3) led to the establishment of ties with the Byzantine empire that grew stronger from the mid-12th century. Four major monuments of this period are decorated with mosaic in a style that suggests that Byzantine workshops were specially imported. The apsidal mosaics of Cefalù Cathedral (1148), founded by Roger II, have stylistic features reminiscent of the classical beauty of the Dafni mosaics, although the forms have become stiffer and the drapery more complex and linear (*see also* CEFALÙ CATHEDRAL, §2(ii)). The figures remain elongated and retain their handsome classical features, but the facial highlights have become more formalized rather than being used for soft modelling. This style is repeated at Palermo in some of the mosaics in the Cappella Palatina (*see* PALERMO, §II, 2(ii)), which was also founded by Roger II at about the same time, and in the Martorana (1143).

The extensive mosaic cycle in MONREALE CATHEDRAL was mostly executed under William II (*reg* 1166–89) between 1183 and 1189. The work reflects the influence of the Dynamic style that was then current in Constantinople and is also found to some extent in the churches at Kurbinovo (1191) and Lagoudera (1192) (*see* §(iv) above). It would appear that the Norman despots and later the Venetians regarded Byzantine art as an imperial legitimacy that they wished to simulate. It is ironic that some of the finest late Middle Byzantine mosaics are to be found in the territory of the empire's political rivals.

BIBLIOGRAPHY

GENERAL

Niketas Choniates: *Historia* (*c.* 1207–15); Eng. trans. by H. Magoulias as *O City of Byzantium* (Detroit, 1984)

P. A. Underwood: 'The Evidence of Restorations in the Sanctuary Mosaics of the Church of the Dormition at Nicaea', *Dumbarton Oaks Pap.*, xiii (1959), pp. 235–42

V. N. Lazarev: *Istoriya vizantiyskoy zhivopisi* [History of Byzantine painting], 2 vols (Moscow, 1966); It. trans. as *Storia della pittura bizantina* (Turin, 1967)

D. C. Winfield: 'Middle and Later Byzantine Wallpainting Methods: A Comparative Study', *Dumbarton Oaks Pap.*, xxii (1968), pp. 61–139

O. Demus: *Byzantine Art and the West* (London, 1970)

H. Maguire: *Art and Eloquence in Byzantium* (Princeton, 1981)

C. Walter: *Art and Ritual of the Byzantine Church* (London, 1982)

CONSTANTINOPLE

T. Whittemore: *The Mosaics of St Sophia at Istanbul*, 4 vols (Oxford, 1933–52)

P. Schweinfurth: 'Der Mosaikfussboden der komnenischen Pantokratorkirche in Istanbul', *Jb. Dt. Archäol. Inst.*, lxix (1954), pp. 253–60

P. A. Underwood and E. J. W. Hawkins: 'The Mosaics of Haghia Sophia at Istanbul, 1959–60: The Portrait of the Emperor Alexander', *Dumbarton Oaks Pap.*, xv (1961), pp. 187–217

C. Mango and E. J. W. Hawkins: 'The Apse Mosaics of St Sophia at Istanbul', *Dumbarton Oaks Pap.*, xix (1965), pp. 113–51

C. L. Striker and Y. D. Kuban: 'Work at Kalenderhane Camii in Istanbul: Second Preliminary Report', *Dumbarton Oaks Pap.*, xxii (1968), pp. 185–93

C. Mango and E. J. W. Hawkins: 'The Mosaics of St Sophia at Istanbul: The Church Fathers in the North Tympanum', *Dumbarton Oaks Pap.*, xxvi (1972), pp. 1–41

N. Oikonomides: 'Leo VI and the Narthex Mosaic of St Sophia', *Dumbarton Oaks Pap.*, xxx (1976), pp. 151–72

R. Cormack and E. J. W. Hawkins: 'The Mosaics of St Sophia at Istanbul: The Rooms above the Southwest Vestibule and Ramp', *Dumbarton Oaks Pap.*, xxxi (1977), pp. 175–251

N. Oikonomides: 'The Mosaic Panel of Constantine IX and Zoe in Saint Sophia', *Rev. Etud. Byz.*, xxxvi (1978), pp. 219–32

R. Cormack: 'Interpreting the Mosaics of S. Sophia at Istanbul', *A. Hist.*, iv (1981), pp. 131–49

GREECE

K. Papadopoulos: *Die Wandmalereien des 11. Jahrhunderts in der Kirche Panagia ton Chalkeon* (Graz and Cologne, 1966)

R. Cormack: 'The Apse Mosaics of S Sophia at Thessaloniki', *Deltion Christ. Archaiol. Etaireias* (1980–81), pp. 111–35

K. M. Skawran: *The Development of Middle Byzantine Fresco Painting in Greece* (Pretoria, 1982)

MACEDONIA AND THRACE

A. Grabar: *La Peinture religieuse en Bulgarie* (Paris, 1928)

R. Ljubinković: *La Peinture médiévale à Ohrid* (Ohrid, 1961)

R. Hamann-MacLean and H. Hallensleben: *Die Monumentalmalerei in Serbien und Makedonien vom 11. bis zum frühen 14. Jahrhundert*, 3 vols (Giessen, 1963)

G. Babić: *Les Chapelles annexes des églises byzantines: Fonction liturgique et programme iconographique* (Paris, 1969)

V. J. Djurić: *Vizantijske freske u Jugoslaviji* [Byzantine frescoes in Yugoslavia] (Belgrade, 1974; Ger. trans., Belgrade, 1976)

T. Malmquist: *Byzantine 12th Century Frescoes in Kastoria: Agioi Anargyroi and Agios Nikolaos tou Kasnitzi* (Uppsala, 1979)

S. Grishin: 'Literary Evidence for the Dating of the Bačkovo Ossuary Frescoes', *Byz. Pap.*, i (1981), pp. 90–100

CYPRUS

A. H. S. Megaw and E. J. W. Hawkins: 'The Church of the Holy Apostles at Perachorio, Cyprus, and its Frescoes', *Dumbarton Oaks Pap.*, xvi (1962), pp. 279–348

C. Mango: 'St Chrysostom, Koutsovendi (Cyprus)', *Dumbarton Oaks Pap.*, xviii (1964), pp. 333–9

C. Mango and E. J. W. Hawkins: 'The Hermitage of St Neophytos and its Wallpaintings', *Dumbarton Oaks Pap.*, xx (1966), pp. 119–206

M. Sacopoulo: *Asinou en 1106* (Brussels, 1966)

A. H. S. Megaw: 'Byzantine Architecture and Decoration in Cyrpus: Metropolitan or Provincial?', *Dumbarton Oaks Pap.*, xxviii (1974), pp. 59–88

S. H. Young: *Byzantine Painting in Cyprus during the Early Lusignan Period* (diss., University Park, PA State U., 1983)

A. Stylianou and J. A. Stylianou: *The Painted Churches of Cyprus* (London, 1985)

CAPPADOCIA

L. Giovannini: *Arts of Cappadocia* (Geneva, 1971)

A. W. Epstein: 'The Fresco Decoration of the Column Churches, Göreme Valley, Cappadocia', *Cah. Archéol.*, xxix (1980–81), pp. 27–45

——: *Tokalı Kilise: Tenth-century Metropolitan Art in Byzantine Cappadocia* (Washington, DC, 1986)

SOUTHERN ITALY AND SICILY

H. Belting: 'Byzantine Art among Greeks and Latins in Southern Italy', *Dumbarton Oaks Pap.*, xxviii (1974), pp. 1–29

E. Kitzinger: *The Art of Byzantium and the Medieval West: Selected Studies* (London, 1976)

M. Rotili: *Arte bizantina in Calabria e in Basilicata* (Rome, 1980)

G. Cavallo and others: *I Bizantini in Italia* (Milan, 1987)

ALEXANDER GRISHIN

5. *c.* **1204–1453.** The final phase in the development of Byzantine wall paintings and mosaics began with the Latin conquest of Constantinople and ended with its capture by the Ottoman Turks.

(i) Latin rule, 1204–61. (ii) Palaiologan period, 1261–1453.

(i) Latin rule, 1204–61. After the conquest of Constantinople by the Franks in 1204, decoration of the monuments of the capital with wall paintings or mosaics was apparently curtailed. Beyond the capital, however, the evolution of Byzantine wall painting continued. The loosening of centralized state control and the loss by Constantinople of its dominant role in art favoured the development of a freer style. A sense of monumentality and the simplification of form were emphasized and mark a return to tendencies that were characteristic of the 10th and 11th centuries. This new style was a reaction to the exaggerated linear mannerism of the 12th century.

The most important works of the early 13th century are the wall paintings (1208–9) by a Greek painter in the katholikon dedicated to the Mother of God (Bogorodica; completed 1191) at STUDENICA MONASTERY (*see also* SERBIA, §III, 1(i)). The scenes and the figures are fewer and larger than in the painted decoration of the preceding period. Curving lines articulate the contours of the figures, and are rendered in gradated hues. Although the faces are simply painted, they possess considerable intensity of expression. The wall paintings (*c.* 1230) in the south aisle of the 5th-century church of the Acheiropoietos in Thessaloniki are important examples of the development of wall painting in this phase. The *Forty Martyrs of Sebaste*, for instance, is characterized by its monumentality, calm rhythm, robust forms and free modelling. This monumental style is even more evident in the wall paintings of the monastery church of the Ascension (1234–5) at MILEŠEVA, which was intended as the mausoleum of its founder, King Stephen Vladislav (*reg* 1234–43). Selected scenes from the New Testament, numerous figures of saints and portraits of Stephen and members of his family are preserved. Despite the volume of the figures, they are depicted with dignity and force. The presence of Greek inscriptions suggests that some of the painters were of Greek origin. In many representations the traditional blue ground has been replaced with yellow, imitating the gold tesserae of mosaic. This type of yellow ground is also found in the wall paintings (late 13th century) of the monastery church of the Holy Trinity, Sopoćani (see §(ii) below) and in the monastery church of the Annunciation (1270) at Gradač. It has been suggested that the artists who worked on the Serbian monuments were influenced by the mosaic decoration in the Early Christian churches of Thessaloniki.

The robust and classicizing style of Mileševa is evident in the mid-13th-century wall paintings of the church of the Holy Apostles (*c.* 1230) in PEĆ. The *Deësis* in the apse and the *Ascension* in the dome are probably based on similar representations in the churches of Hagia Sophia (885–6) and of the Panagia Chalkeon (1028) in Thessaloniki. The figures in the Peć paintings have a new, statuesque quality, and a certain realism distinguishes their facial expressions, as in the figure of the Virgin in the *Ascension*.

In Bulgaria the most important decoration of the 13th century is in the small funerary chapel of SS Nicholas and Panteleimon (1259), which was attached to a 12th-century church in Boyana, near Sofia. The founders were the *sebastokrator* Kaloyan and his wife Desislava. The iconographic programme of the chapel contains the traditional subjects: the *Pantokrator* surrounded by angels in the dome; the *Virgin* in the apse; the cycle of the *Twelve Feasts* and saints in the nave. These paintings are stylistically conservative: although the figures are stiff and lack volume, the faces are finely portrayed and are reminiscent of works of the Komnenian period. Of special interest are the representations of Kaloyan (*see* BULGARIA, fig. 5) and Desislava, together with another couple, Constantin Assen and Irene, dressed in court costumes; the faces have individual features and are probably portraits.

(ii) Palaiologan period, 1261–1453. The painting of the Palaiologan period has often been characterized as one of renaissance because of the special emphasis on humanist values and Classical prototypes. During the first phase (*c.* 1261–*c.* 1300), which begins immediately after the occupation of Constantinople by Michael VIII Palaiologos (*reg* 1261–82), the style is notable for its corporeality, the classical harmony of its compositions, its sense of space and its expressive faces. There is also a tendency to exaggerate the volume of the bodies and architectural motifs, so that the style has been described as heavy, cuboid and monumental. After *c.* 1300 it becomes more elegant. Figures are no longer bulky but are well-proportioned and classically modelled, with a particularly natural quality of expression. The increased representation of genre elements gives a sense of familiarity to the scenes. Although there is a deliberate return to Classical models, it is restricted by the repeated use of stylized motifs, while the freshness and vigour of the paintings before *c.* 1300 are absent. After the mid-14th century the painting style becomes even more refined and selectively borrows devices from the previous phases of Palaiologan painting.

During the Palaiologan period the iconographic programme of the churches takes on a more or less narrative character. The *Life of Christ* cycle is enriched with scenes of the *Passion* and the *Miracles of Christ*. New scenes are depicted, such as the Akathistos Hymn, while the narrative character of scenes from the *Life of the Virgin* is emphasized, and episodes from the *Lives of the Saints* are more extensive. During this period the influence of the liturgy on iconography is much greater.

(a) *c.* 1261–*c.* 1300. (b) *c.* 1300–*c.* 1330. (c) *c.* 1330–1453.

(a) c. *1261–c. 1300.* With the return of many artists to Constantinople, the style that had begun to appear in the first half of the 13th century was developed and imbued with a variety of new characteristics. The first monumental painting undertaken in Constantinople after the occupation of the city by Michael VIII was the mosaic *Deësis* in the south gallery of Hagia Sophia (see fig. 45), which shows the art of Palaiologan painting in its early stage. The sensitive modelling of form with fine gradations of colour and tone and the intensely human expression on the faces reveal a deliberate return to the Classical spirit and the rise of a new humanism. The style of this period reaches its peak in the late 13th-century wall paintings of the church of the HOLY TRINITY, SOPOĆANI, works attributed to more than one painter. The iconographic programme of the church includes numerous scenes from the Old and

45. Mosaic from the *Deësis* (*c.* 1261), detail showing head of Christ, south gallery of Hagia Sophia, Istanbul, Turkey

New Testaments, as well as many figures of saints, martyrs, Apostles and Church Fathers. The founder, King Stephen Uroš I (*reg* 1243–76), and members of his family form a group of portraits, a characteristic often seen in Serbian monuments. The statuesque figures with their rhythmically flowing movements are depicted in bright colours, particularly violet and green. The Classical spirit is also reflected in the painted and sculptured ornaments of the church. The classicizing style of Sopoćani appears again in the somewhat provincial wall paintings in the monastery church at Gradać, which was founded around 1270 by Elena, wife of Stephen Uroš I. The nearest equivalent, in terms of quality and style, to the Sopoćani wall paintings are those in the church of Hagia Sophia (1238–63) at Trebizond (*see* TREBIZOND, §2). Their spatial character, and their classicizing and expressive figures are representative of early Palaiologan painting.

The wall paintings of the first phase of decoration (1272–88) of the church of Hagios Demetrios (the Metropolis) at Mystras reveal a different stylistic trend. They include the *Virgin and Child* in the sanctuary, the paintings in the prothesis, the diakonikon and the north aisle (for a scene from the *Life of St Demetrios, see* MYSTRAS, fig. 1) and the *Hetoimasia* in the south aisle. Among their stylistic peculiarities are the heavy or cuboid manner of depicting the figures and some landscape elements, the realism of the facial expressions and the influence of Western art in the rendering of the architectural background. The rest of the decoration belongs to the second phase (1291/2–1315): the *Apostles* and the *Miracles of Christ* in the south

46. Manuel Panselinos (attrib.): wall painting of *SS John the Evangelist and Prochoros* (*c.* 1290 or early 14th century), Protaton Church, Karyes, Mt Athos, Greece

aisle are painted in the mature, heavy style of the late 13th century, while the paintings in the narthex are dated to the early 14th century. Evidence of this style's development towards a cuboid depiction of figures appears in the wall paintings (*c.* 1280–90) in the church of Hagia Euphemia (part of the 5th-century palace of Antiochos at Constantinople, converted into a church *c.* 550) showing scenes from her life.

Among the most important examples of the 'heavy' style are the wall paintings (*c.* 1290 or early 14th century) in the Protaton Church at Karyes on Mt Athos (see fig. 46), which are traditionally attributed to a painter from Thessaloniki, Manuel Panselinos. The church contains scenes of the Church feasts, the *Passion*, the *Life of the Virgin*, visions of the prophets and groups of saints. This iconographic programme corresponds to the annual cycle of services within the Orthodox Church and to the Athonite tradition of spirituality and prayer. It reflects attempts by Andronikos II (*reg* 1282–1328) to consolidate the empire through a stricter adherence to Orthodox principles. The wall paintings are marked by a strong Classical spirit, and, although the 'heavy' style is present, there is an elegance and grace about the figures.

The 'heavy' style acquires its fullest expression in the mosaics in the outer narthex that was added *c.* 1300 to the 11th-century church of Kilise Cami, or more correctly Molla Gürânî Mosque, in Constantinople. In the south dome the Virgin is depicted surrounded by eight kings from the house of David. The figures are voluminous, and the drapery is treated as an entity separate from the body underneath. Other notable examples of the 'heavy' style are to be found in Serbia and Macedonia, including the wall paintings in the church of St Clement (originally dedicated to the Mother of God Peribleptos) at OHRID, which are the earliest known works by the Greek artists Michael, son of ASTRAPAS, and Eutychios, both from Thessaloniki. The classicizing figures are notable for their

vehement gestures and animated expressions. The ample and block-like appearance of the figures is emphasized by the angular folds of the drapery. Buildings are depicted as cubic masses. Examples of the 'heavy' style also survive in Greece, as in the wall paintings in the churches of Olympiotissa (late 1290s) at Elasson and Omorphi Ekklisia (*c.* 1270–80) in Athens, and in churches in Euboea and on Crete (e.g. the churches of Metamorphosis at Pyrgi (1296); of Hagia Thekla and of the Hodegetrea at Spelies on Euboia (1311); and the church of Kera Kritsas (south aisle) in Crete (first half of the 14th century)).

In addition to the 'heavy' style, which represents the most progressive development in painting in the late 13th century, many provincial monuments contain a more conservative decoration, in a style reminiscent of the art of the late Komnenian period (e.g. the churches of the Dormition of the Virgin at Oxylithos (*c.* 1300) and of Hagios Dimitrios at Makrychori on Euboea (1303), the Omorphi Ekklisia on Aigina (*c.* 1284) and the church of Christos at Meskla on Crete (1303)). The dome mosaics in the church of the Panagia Parigoritissa (*c.* 1290) at ARTA are probably by artists from Constantinople. The rendering of the *Pantokrator* and twelve prophets is characterized by features that herald the metropolitan style of the 14th century, with correctly proportioned figures in more restrained positions.

(b) c. 1300–c. 1330. During the reign of Andronikos II there was renewed interest in the arts and the Classical tradition in Constantinople, and several churches were decorated with mosaics. Around 1310 a *parekklesion* was built along the south flank of the 12th-century katholikon of the monastery of St Mary Pammakaristos in memory of Michael Glavas Tarchaneiotes, a distinguished military commander. In the mosaics (1310–15; *see* ISTANBUL, fig. 12) of the chapel the 'heavy' style is less evident and the voluminous figures are depicted in a more restrained manner. The iconographic programme clearly reflects the chapel's funerary role, with the *Pantokrator* and prophets in the dome, the *Deësis* in the apse and bishops, saints and monks on the walls of the sanctuary and nave.

The wall paintings and mosaics (completed 1321) of the katholikon and *parekklesion* of the monastery of Christ the Saviour in Chora are the most important examples of early 14th-century monumental decoration. The church and the outer and inner narthexes (*see* ISTANBUL, fig. 1) are decorated with mosaics, the chapel with wall paintings. In the nave only the figures of *Christ* and of the *Virgin* and the *Dormition of the Virgin* are preserved. The walls of the inner narthex show scenes from the *Infancy of the Virgin* and the *Infancy of Christ*, while the two domes both show *Christ* and the *Virgin* surrounded by biblical patriarchs, prophets and other figures. The mosaics in the outer narthex depict scenes from the *Life of Christ*, particularly the miracles, and are full of picturesque and intimate details. In the mosaic lunette above the central door leading from the inner narthex to the nave, the founder of the monastery, Theodore Metochites, offers a model of the church to the enthroned Christ who is named 'The Land (Gr. *Chora*) of the Living'. The Palaiologan style as expressed in this decoration reflects the refined taste of the aristocracy of Constantinople during this period. The idealized scenes contain freely moving, elegant classicizing figures set against architectural backdrops that are also in the Classical tradition. Among the most original masterpieces of Byzantine art of this period are the wall paintings in the church's *parekklesion*. The iconographic programme is related to the funerary character of the chapel: the *Anastasis* (*see* WALL PAINTING, colour pl. II, fig. 1) occupies the conch of the apse, and on the south and north sides of the sanctuary *Christ Raising the Daughter of Jairus* and *Christ Raising the Widow's Son* are depicted respectively. The *Last Judgement* occupies the domical vault to the west. The choice of subjects depicted in the west part of the chapel, such as the *Souls of the Righteous inside the Hand of God*, indicates that the artist had an extensive knowledge of theological literature. Stylistically, these paintings are similar to the mosaics in the two narthexes of the katholikon.

Other examples of early 14th-century monumental painting and mosaic are in the chapel of the Hagios Euthymios (1303) and the churches of Hagia Aikaterini (*c.* 1315–20), the Hagioi Apostoloi (1310–14; 1328–34; *see* THESSALONIKI, fig. 4) and Hagios Nikolaos Orphanos (*c.* 1320), all in Thessaloniki. They reveal the significant role of the city in the creation of the so-called Macedonian style. The main characteristics of this style are the voluminous figures, quantity of drapery and the expressive realism of the gestures and the faces. The chapel of Hagios Euthymios was built in the south-east corner of the 6th-century basilica of Hagios Demetrios by Michael Glavas Tarchaneiotes and contains scenes from the *Life of Christ* and the *Life of St Euthymios*. Although the ample figures and the almost three-dimensional quality of the buildings in the background are reminiscent of the 'heavy' style, the free use of the brush and the reliance on Classical models differentiate these paintings from earlier ones.

The nave mosaics and the wall paintings (1310–14) in the narthexes of the church of the Holy Apostles in Thessaloniki are closely related to those in the katholikon of the monastery of Christ the Saviour in Chora and have been attributed to artists from Constantinople. The decoration in the nave includes the *Pantokrator* with prophets in the dome, the Evangelists in the pendentives and nine feast scenes (e.g. the *Anastasis*, see fig. 47). Some wall paintings of the *Virgin* and saints are preserved in the two narthexes. The Classical spirit, the elegance and refinement and the exquisite sense of colour are among the most conspicuous characteristics of these works. The paintings (1320s) in the church of Hagios Nikolaos Orphanos include scenes from the Twelve Feasts, the Miracles of Christ, the Passion, the lives of SS Nicholas and Gerasimos, the Akathistos Hymn and the Old Testament. The strongly built figures, the organization of space and the variety of anecdotal details are similar to the painted decoration in other early 14th-century churches in Macedonia and Serbia.

The stylistic trends evident in the paintings in Thessaloniki and Constantinople are also found in several churches built and decorated by King Stephen Uroš II Miliutin (*reg* 1282–1321) in Serbia, including the churches of the Mother of God (Bogorodica) Ljeviška (built 10th century; rebuilt 1306–7; decorated 1308–9) in PRIZREN, the Saviour (*c.* 1311) in Zića, St Nikita (1308) in Ćučer,

47. Mosaic from the *Anastasis* (1310–14), detail showing head of Adam, church of the Hagioi Apostoloi, Thessaloniki, Greece

SS Joachim and Anne (1313–14) in Studenica Monastery, St George (1316–17) in STARO NAGORIČANO and the Dormition (1311–21) in GRAČANICA. Some of these decorations (e.g. the Mother of God Ljeviška, St Nikita, St George) may be attributed to the painters Eutychios and Astrapas, while the influence of Constantinopolitan art is particularly strong in the paintings at Studenica, which recall the elegance of the Christ the Saviour in Chora mosaics rather than the vigour of the Macedonian school. In the paintings at Gračanica, a dramatic effect is created by the lively movements and gestures of the figures; their agitated drapery is depicted in sharply defined colours.

One of the most ambitious painted monuments in Greece, and the one which bears the closest relation to the art of Constantinople, is the church of the Hodegetria or Aphentiko (1311–22) in the Brontochion Monastery at Mystras. Scenes from the liturgy and the *Resurrection* are depicted in the sanctuary; New Testament scenes and figures of the Apostles, patriarchs, prophets (for *Zachariah*, *see* MYSTRAS, fig. 2) and saints appear in the gallery; and scenes from the *Life of Christ* are portrayed in the narthex. The decoration of the chapels is of particular interest. The procession of martyrs, prophets, patriarchs, Apostles and saints addressing a prayer towards Christ underlines the funerary character of the north-west chapel; in the south-west chapel the copies of the four chrysobulls granted by the emperor in 1312–3 and 1322 are among the most original decorations surviving from this period. The paintings are the work of more than one artist. The classicizing figures move freely within the picture space, as they do in the mosaics and paintings of the monastery of Christ the Saviour in Chora. The use of colour is one of the most conspicuous characteristics of the church of the Hodegetria: daring combinations of red, brown, deep blue and green create an impressionistic effect.

(c) c. 1330–1453. The painting of the second half of the 14th century is eclectic, and, although there is a tendency to return to earlier painting styles, these are generally simplified and schematized. The wall paintings in the church of the Peribleptos (*c.* 1370) in Mystras, for example, with their graceful, aristocratic figures and the rhythm and symmetry of their compositions, show a deliberate return to the Classical tendency of the Palaiologan art of the first quarter of the century. The iconographic programme is dominated by scenes from the *Life of the Virgin*, while the prophets in the dome hold symbolic objects and scrolls with texts relating to the Virgin.

The work of THEOPHANES THE GREEK is dated to the second half of the 14th century. After decorating churches in Constantinople and the surrounding areas, he went to Novgorod *c.* 1360 or 1370 and, with the help of his collaborators, painted the church of the Transfiguration (Preobrazhenskaya) in 1378. Although his art is related to the tradition of painting in the monastery of Christ the Saviour in Chora, the distance from the capital freed him from its constraints. He was thus better able to express his passionate and violent nature. He created vigorous figures who are animated by an intense spiritual life, and he used white colour with abrupt brushstrokes in order to accentuate the metaphysical aspect of the faces.

Some elements of this free approach, such as use of fine white lines to create an impression of light, characterize the paintings in the church of the Saviour (1384–96) in Tsalenjikha in Georgia. On the whole, however, the style is more academic. The decoration is the work of the painter Manuel Eugenikos, who was brought from Constantinople and whose use of bright, cold colours is particularly notable. The paintings are also of interest because they represent the monumental art of Constantinople during a period when it is known mainly from icons.

The style of the Morava school (for illustration *see* MORAVA) is related to icon painting, but also reveals a strong Western influence. Its decorative tendency, its anecdotal detail and its refinement are distinctive features, as in the paintings in the churches at Ravanica (*c.* 1375–7), Ljubostinja (early 15th century), Resava (now Manasija; *c.* 1408–18) and Kalenić (*c.* 1413–17).

The last important example of Palaiologan monumental painting is that in the monastery church (*c.* 1430) of the Pantanassa at Mystras (*see* MYSTRAS, fig. 3). The decoration in the sanctuary and the galleries has been attributed to more than one artist and is modelled on the painting in the Peribleptos and the Hodegetria. This classicizing style of the early 14th century is combined with anecdotal and grisaille elements, antiquarian masks and motifs and compositional principles that reflect Western influence. The influence of Palaiologan styles of painting acquired a new dynamism during the post-Byzantine period in the icons painted by the great Cretan masters (*see* POST-BYZANTINE, §II, 1).

BIBLIOGRAPHY

GENERAL

G. Millet: *Recherches sur l'iconographie de l'Evangile aux XIVe, XVe et XVIe siècles* (Paris, 1916/*R* 1960)

O. Demus: 'Die Entstehung des Palaologenstils in der Malerei', *Berichte zum XI. internationalen Byzantinistenkongress: München, 1958*, IV/ii, pp. 1–63

S. Radojčić: 'Die Entstehung der Malerei der paläologischen Renaissance', *Jb. Österreich. Byz. Ges.*, vii (1958), pp. 105–23

Z. Jank: *Ornaments in the Serbian and Macedonian Frescoes from the XII to the Middle of the XV Century* (Belgrade, 1961)

L'Art byzantin du XIIIe siècle: Symposium: Sopoćani, 1965

D. Talbot Rice: *Byzantine Painting: The Last Phase* (London, 1968)

L'Ecole de la Morava et son temps: Symposium: Resava, 1968

M. Chatzidakis: 'Classicisme et tendances populaires au XIVe siècle: Les Recherches sur l'évolution du style', *Actes du XIVe congrès international des études byzantines: Bucarest, 1971*, i, pp. 136–57

L'Art byzantin au début du XIVe siècle: Symposium: Gračanica, 1973

T. Velmans: *La Peinture murale byzantine à la fin du moyen âge* (Paris, 1977)

The Twilight of Byzantium: Aspects of Cultural and Religious History in the Late Byzantine Empire: Colloquium Papers: Princeton, 1989

CONSTANTINOPLE AND TREBIZOND

R. Naumann and H. Belting: *Die Euphemia-Kirche am Hippodrom zu Istanbul und ihre Fresken* (Berlin, 1966)

D. Talbot Rice: *The Church of Hagia Sophia at Trebizond* (Edinburgh, 1968)

W. Grape: 'Zum Stil der Mosaiken in der Kilise Camii in Istanbul', *Pantheon*, xxxii/1 (1974), pp. 3–12

P. A. Underwood, ed.: *The Karive Djami: Studies in the Art of the Karive Djami and its Intellectual Background*, iv (Princeton, 1975)

H. Belting, C. Mango and D. Mouriki: *The Mosaics of St Mary Pammakaristos (Fethive Camii) at Istanbul* (Washington, DC, 1978)

GREECE

G. Millet: *Monuments de l'Athos: La Peinture* (Paris, 1927)

A. Xyngopoulos: *I psiphidoti diakosmisis tou naou ton Agion Apostolon Thessalonikis* [The mosaic decoration in the church of the Holy Apostles at Thessaloniki] (Thessaloniki, 1953)

——: *Thessalonique et la peinture macédonienne* (Athens, 1955)

A. K. Orlandos: *I Parigoritissa tis Artis* [The Parigoritissa at Arta] (Athens, 1963)

A. Vassilaki Karakatsani: *Oi toichographies tis Omorphis Ekklisias stin Athina* [The wall paintings of the 'Beautiful Church' in Athens] (Athens, 1971)

T. Gouma-Peterson: 'The Pareeclesion of St Euthymios in Thessalonica: Art and Monastic Policy under Andronicos II', *A. Bull.*, lviii (1976), pp. 168–84

——: 'Christ as a Ministrant and the Priest as a Ministrant of Christ in a Palaeologan Program of 1303', *Dumbarton Oaks Pap.*, xxxii (1978), pp.199–216

D. Mouriki: *Oi toichographies tou sotira Konta sto Alepochori Megaridos* [The wall paintings of Sotiras near Alepochori Megaridos] (Athens, 1978)

K. Gallas, K. Wessel and M. Borboudakis: *Byzantinisches Kreta* (Munich, 1983)

C. Stephan: *Ein byzantinisches Bildensemble: Die Mosaiken und Fresken der Apostelkirche zu Thessaloniki* (Worms, 1986)

A. Tsitouridou: *O zographikos diakosmos tou Agiou Nikolaou Orphanou sti Thessaloniki* [The painted decoration of Agios Nikolaos Orphanos in Thessaloniki] (Thessaloniki, 1986)

D. Kalomoirakis: 'Ermineutikes paratiriseis sto eikonographiko programma tou Protatou' [Interpretive remarks on the iconographic programme in the Protaton], *Deltion Christ. Archaiol. Etaireias*, xv (1989–90), pp. 197–220

M. Emmanuel: *Oi toichographies tou Hag. Dimitriou sto Makrychori Kai tis Koimiseos tis Theotokou stou Oxylitho tis Euboias* [The wall paintings of Hagios Dimitrios at Makrychori and of the Dormition of the Virgin at Oxylithos in Euboia] (Athens, 1991)

THE BALKANS

G. Millet and A. Frolow: *La Peinture du moyen âge en Yougoslavie*, 3 vols (Paris, 1954–62)

H. Hallensleben: *Die Malerschule des Königs Milutin: Untersuchungen zum Werk einer byzantinischen Malerwerkstatt zu Beginn des 14. Jahrhunderts* (Giessen, 1963)

V. J. Djurić: *Sopoćani* (Leipzig, 1967)

G. Millet and T. Velmans: *La Peinture du moyen âge en Yougoslavie*, iv (Paris, 1969)

D. Panić and G. Babić: *Bogorodica Ljeviska* (Belgrade, 1975)

V. J. Djurić: *Byzantinische Fresken in Jugoslawien* (Munich, 1976)

S. Djurić: *Ljubostina* (Belgrade, 1985)

M. Kasanin and others: *Manastir Studenica* (Belgrade, 1986)

G. Babić: *Krakjeva crkva u Studenici* (Belgrade, 1987)

RUSSIA

G. L. Vzdornov: *Feofan Grek* [Theophanes the Greek] (Moscow, 1983)

L. I. Lifsic: *Monumental'naya zhivopis Novgoroda XIV–XV vekov* [Architectural history of Novgorod, 14th–15th century] (Moscow, 1987)

GEORGIA

H. Belting: 'Le Peintre Manuel Eugenikos de Constantinople, en Géorgie', *Cah. Archéol.*, xxviii (1979), pp. 103–14

D. Mouriki: 'The Formative Role of Byzantine Art on the Artistic Style of the Cultural Neighbors of Byzantium: Reflections of Constantinopolitan Styles in Georgian Monumental Painting', *Akten des XVI. internationalen Byzantinistenkongresses: Wien, 1981*, I/ii, pp. 725–59

T. Velmans: 'Le Décor du sanctuaire de l'église de Calendzikha: Quelques schémas rares: La Vierge entre Pierre et Paul, la procession des anges et le Christ de Pitié', *Cah. Archéol.*, xxxvi (1988), pp. 137–59

MELITA EMMANUEL

IV. Sculpture.

The primary character of Early Christian and Byzantine sculpture is the extensive use of white and coloured marble (e.g. porphyry from Egypt, verde-antico from Thessaly), although fine limestone and wooden sculpture is also attested.

1. Introduction. 2. Stone. 3. Wood.

1. INTRODUCTION. In the most ornate buildings on the coasts of the Aegean and the Black Sea, as well as in several Western cities such as Ravenna, interior surfaces were covered with marble from the floor to the base of the vaults, and most architectural supports (e.g. bases, columns and capitals) were of marble, although some were reused. Sarcophagi, notably those of the emperors but also those of the dignitaries of Constantinople, Rome and Ravenna, were also either of marble or imitated work done in marble, as shown by the fronts of several limestone sarcophagi from Constantinople (*see* §2(ii) below and SARCOPHAGUS, §III, 1). The use of marble demonstrated Byzantine power and symbolized the ideological hold of the empire. Its value in these respects remained constant through the centuries from the foundation of Constantinople (AD 324–30) to the importation of building material from Constantinople by the Ostrogothic king Theodoric (*reg* 493–526) for his churches in Ravenna, to Charlemagne who, anxious to demonstrate his imperial legitimacy, recovered the marble of Ravenna and Rome for his palatine chapel at Aachen (*see* AACHEN, §2, (ii)(b)). Thus it seemed natural that the doges of Venice, after the overthrow of Constantinople in 1204, should strip the city of its marbles to decorate the façades of S Marco, where they served as proof of the antiquity of Venice, as trophies and perhaps, talismans.

Early Christian and Byzantine sculpture in the round was classicizing in character with its roots in Hellenistic and Roman art. However, the Church scarcely employed it, and it was mainly used as a means of personifying the imperial authority. This is reflected in an almost uninterrupted series of imperial statues and busts from Constantine the Great to Marcian (*reg* 450–57) or Leo I (*reg* 457–74), if the bronze colossus (h. 5 m; *see* LATE ANTIQUITY, fig. 2) that stands in the centre of Barletta (Italy) can be identified as one of these two emperors. This series originally lasted until Phokas (*reg* 602–10), whose column (608) was erected in Constantinople and was later found in the Forum Romanum in Rome. Statues of Constantine VI (*reg* 780–97) and his mother Eirene (*reg* 797–802) are also mentioned in the sources. Surviving sculptures of empresses include two beautiful heads, reputedly of *Ariadne* (early 6th century; Paris, Louvre) and *Theodora* (*c*. 500–48; Milan, Castello Sforzesco). Numerous sculptures of governors and praetorian prefects in togas or chlamydes also survive from the end of the 4th century to the 6th in Megara, Athens, Constantinople, Sardis, Aphrodisias and Ephesos, where the remarkable marble head of *Eutropios* (see fig. 48) was found. Charioteers were the other category of person represented, notably in Constantinople. Here, however, only two statue bases of the most famous among them, Porphyrios, have been preserved (*c*. 500; Istanbul, Archaeol. Mus.).

Executed in low relief, the bases of the honorific columns of Theodosios, Arkadios and Marcian and that of Theodosios' obelisk in the Hippodrome at Constantinople express the same imperial ideology, in line with the

48. Head of *Eutropios*, marble, h. 295 mm, from Ephesos, 5th century (Vienna, Kunsthistorisches Museum)

great triumphal arches, such as those of Constantine (*see* ROME, §V, 12) and Galerius (*see* THESSALONIKI, §III, 1).

The uses of marble in architecture, especially in churches, were considerable in the Early Christian period: capitals, bases, columns and specific elements such as the parapets between the aisles and between the sanctuary and nave, the anchoring pillars, the ambos and the ciboria (*see* CIBORIUM (ii), §1). The need for marble persisted after the iconoclastic controversy (726–843), but not sufficiently to revive the quarries. There was a preference for reworking and reusing sculptures, especially those that carried some prestige value. Requirements had changed since before the 8th century; the main thoroughfares in towns were no longer lined with colonnades, and palaces apparently became less sumptuous (*see* §II, 3(ii) and (iii) above), while pieces of sculpture existed that had certainly belonged to secular buildings of the Middle Byzantine period, such as piers decorated with acrobats, two pieces of which were found in Istanbul (Istanbul, Archaeol. Mus., inv. nos 939 and 4282, see Firatli, nos 33–4, p. 18), and a capital with naked dancers (Istanbul, Archaeol. Mus., inv. no. 2291, see Firatli, no. 241, p. 126–7). Marble was mostly employed in churches, but its uses had changed due to modifications of ecclesiastical architecture and the liturgy. Revetments and pavings in *opus sectile* were still much valued. From the 9th century, however, most churches had only four columns as supports for the pendentives of the dome, rather than the long colonnades that flanked the naves of Early Christian basilicas (*see* §II, 2(i) above). Ambos and ciboria declined, but without disappearing entirely. Masonry iconostases, on the other hand, developed (*see* SCREEN (i), §2). Despotic icons (*see* §VI below) were placed on the piers flanking the iconostasis, while the parapet between the chancel and nave was surmounted by an architrave, the decoration of which was firmly uniform throughout the empire and which, if figural, often represented the Deësis (see fig. 51 below). From the 11th century, icons of the Deësis or the Twelve Feasts were often placed above the architrave. The number of extant plaques with the Virgin or saints carved in low relief suggests that iconostases provided frameworks for marble icons as well as for icons painted on wooden panels. Architraves may also have been surmounted by marble icons (e.g. two *Deësis* icons, possibly 10th–11th century; Athens, Byz. Mus.; Christ, 10th–11th century, and two angels, early 14th century; Istanbul, Archaeol. Mus., see Firatli, nos 128–30, pp. 78–9). Tomb arcosolia in the walls of churches and *parekklesia* in Constantinople are surmounted by marble tympana in which the arch is decorated in relief either by a band of acanthus ornament or medallions of the Apostles with Christ in the centre, and the spandrels contain busts of angels (see fig. 52 below). This arrangement of crowning an archivolt was copied in Venice, above the doors of S Marco. In this way new types of sculpture originating in 13th-century Constantinople spread outside the empire.

Marble was also used instead of more expensive or perishable materials, such as wood. In the Early Christian period, openwork slabs from marble parapets are similar to cabinet work. According to Eusebios of Caesarea (*Ecclesiastical History*, pp. 423–7) the church of Tyre (*c*. 317) contained perfectly sculpted wooden parapets,

while the *Miracles of St Artemios* (*d c*. 362) indicates that a wooden chancel surrounded the saint's tomb in the crypt. The marble circular or semicircular tables imitated silver trays. The chancel pillars and the altar tables were covered with silver plate, as can be deduced from contemporary descriptions of Hagia Sophia in Constantinople or the leaves of silver from a 6th-century treasure (e.g. Antalya, Archaeol. Mus.; Washington, DC, Dumbarton Oaks) found near Kumluca in Lycia (Turkey). After the iconoclastic controversy churches became increasingly important as showcases, and marble the substitute for more costly materials. In the North Church (907) of the monastery of Constantine Lips (now Fenarı Isa Cami) in Constantinople, marble icons such as that of *St Eudokia* (Istanbul, Archaeol. Mus.), made up of inlays of stone and coloured pastes inserted into a marble matrix, resembling enamelwork, probably covered the walls. The same technique is evident in an iconostasis architrave (fragments, Uşak Mus.) with deeply carved roundels decorated with molten glass from the 10th-century church at Sebaste (now Selçikler Köyü, Turkey). This type of decoration is known for iconostases and altar tables from the 10th century to the 13th. The large enamels on the Pala d'Oro in S Marco (*see* VENICE, §IV, 1(v)) may originally have been part of an iconostasis in one of the churches of the monastery of Christ Pantokrator (*see* ISTANBUL, §III, 2) which served as the Venetian headquarters during the Latin occupation of Constantinople (1204–61). In general, the style of the marble low reliefs is also close to that of the small medallions of carved hardstones and icons of embossed bronze or ivory also found in the monastery.

Byzantine sculpture also attests to contact with other civilizations. The church of St Polyeuktos (524–7; destr.) at Constantinople, for example, shows the influence of Sasanian art, perhaps through the channels of silverwork and embroidery. These orientalizing trends reappeared in the Middle Byzantine period. In certain cases, as in the North Church of Constantine Lips, they represented the revival of motifs used in the 6th century at St Polyeuktos. In others, these Eastern influences reflected more recent contacts, as in the pseudo-kufic lettering that decorates certain church sculptures in central Greece and the Peloponnese. Despite some Western influences on the sculpture of the 12th century to the 14th in such places as Athens and ARTA, classicizing elements predominated.

BIBLIOGRAPHY

Eusebios of Caesarea: *Ecclesiastical History* (early 4th century); ed. K. Lake, J. E. L. Oulton and H. J. Lawlor as *Eusebius: The History of the Church*, 2 vols (London and New York, 1926–32)

A. Papadopoulos-Keramlus, ed.: 'Miracles of St Artemios, *Varia graeca sacra* (St Petersburg, 1909), pp. 1–79

J. Inan and E. Rosenbaum: *Roman and Early Byzantine Portrait Sculpture in Asia Minor* (London, 1966)

S. Sande: 'Zur Porträtplastik des sechsten nachchristlichen Jahrhunderts', *Acta ad Archaeol. & A. Hist. Pertinentia*, vi (1975), pp. 65–106

J. Inan and E. Alföldi-Rosenbaum: *Römische und frühbyzantinische Porträtplastik aus der Türkei, neue Funde* (Mainz, 1979)

N. Firatli: *La Sculpture figurée au Musée Archéologique d'Istambul*, Bib. Inst. Fr. Etud. Anat. Istambul, xxx (Paris, 1990), nos 33–4, 128–30, 241, pp. 18, 78–9, 126–7

J. Meischner: 'Das Porträt der theodosianische Epoche I (380 bis 405 n. Chr.)', *Jb. Dt. Archäol. Inst.*, cv (1990), pp. 303–24

——:'Das Porträt der theodosianischen Epoche II (400 bis 460 n. Chr.)', *Jb. Dt. Archäol. Inst.*, cvi (1991), pp. 385–407

2. STONE. Although sculpture in the round had virtually ceased to be produced by the Middle Byzantine period, architectural and relief sculpture continued to be made and reused for churches, secular buildings and monuments.

(i) Architectural sculpture. (ii) Non-architectural reliefs.

(i) Architectural sculpture. This section is primarily concerned with the development of architectural sculpture in the Eastern empire. Those carved architectural elements from the Early Christian period that have been found in Spain, Italy, France and North Africa reflect the growth of regional schools and much reuse of spolia (*see* ITALY, §IV, 2; SPAIN, §IV, 1).

(a) 4th–6th centuries. (b) 7th–15th centuries.

(a) 4th–6th centuries. A vigorous expansion in building activity accompanied the prosperity that the Eastern empire maintained between the 4th century and the 6th. The development of Byzantion from a minor provincial city to a capital such as Constantinople required the quarrying of local stone, particularly marble, for public buildings, churches, palaces and the porticos that lined the main thoroughfares, as in the colonnaded streets at Palmyra and Afamea, Syria. Many cities outside Constantinople underwent expansion, notably Jerusalem, or had to be partially reconstructed following war or natural catastrophe. This was particularly so in the 6th century, as for example at Antioch (now Antakya, Turkey) after the earthquakes of 526 and 528. Many small towns in Cyrenaica and Tripolitana (now Libya), which were reconquered by Belisarios in 533–4, were also remodelled in the Byzantine manner, for example Apollonia (now Marsa Susah), Cyrene (now Shaḥḥat) and Latrun. At Ravenna under Theodoric (*reg* 494–526), and then after the Byzantine reconquest in 540, architectural sculpture was imported in impressive quantities from Constantinople and covered all the important buildings, such as S Apollinare Nuovo, S Vitale and S Apollinare in Classe (*see* RAVENNA, §2(v)–(vii)); the brick walls served only to support this display of Constantinopolitan marble. The area around Constantinople produced and distributed its own distinctive architectural sculpture, although the numerous individual quarries are difficult to identify.

Aegean region. Outside Constantinople there are only a few secular monuments with architectural sculpture, such as the tetrastyle of the Arkadiane at Ephesos and the tetrastyle at Ptolemaïs (now Tolmeta, Libya). In the capital the best-known examples are the Arch of Theodosios in the Forum Tauri (officially opened 393) and the honorific columns bearing the statues of emperors; those of Theodosios I (*reg* 379–95) and Arkadios (*reg* 395–408) are imitations of Trajan's Column (AD 112–13; *see* §(ii)(a) below), deliberately recalling the common Spanish origins of Trajan and the Theodosian dynasty. Most extant architectural sculpture was intended for churches, using mass-produced bases, columns and capitals. Many of the varied types of capitals follow Roman models, particularly the Corinthian. Although the soft acanthus decoration derived from the oldest models of this type was still used in the early 5th century, the most widespread form was

49. Corinthian capital with sculptor's mark, Proconnesian marble, h. 627 mm, from Beylerbey, Istanbul, late 5th century AD–early 6th (Istanbul, Archaeological Museum)

the so-called 'Asiatic' acanthus, in which the cutaway outlines of adjacent leaves formed 'acanthus masks'. During the 5th and 6th centuries the number of leaves in each row was reduced from eight to four, and the internal helices disappeared. The form remained lively until the mid-6th century, as shown by examples from Cyrenaica, Ravenna and Constantinople (see fig. 49). Ionic capitals were also produced using the traditional repertory of decorative models, but in a significant development the capital was no longer used on its own, an impost being carved from the same block. Gradually the use of the architrave, although still employed in Constantinople at St John Stoudios (*c.* 450) and at SS Sergios and Bakchos (*c.* 535), was abandoned in favour of the arch. The combination of the Ionic capital and the impost block, which may have originated in Greece, is not found in the West except in regions of strong Byzantine influence, such as Ravenna. The separate impost block was, moreover, used in colonnades with all types of capitals, since it was felt to be an indispensable intermediary between capital and arch. Another older prototype created in the Roman period also returned to favour, the Composite-Ionic. It could have normal acanthus but usually had finely toothed leaves copied from leaf designs of the 3rd century (e.g. in St John Stoudios; the basilica of the Acheiropoietos Thessaloniki; St Leonidas, Lechaion, nr Corinth). The same leaves form the lower zone of a large number of capitals decorated with animal protomes arranged below the abacus: eagles, doves, griffins, rams and, in one instance, Pegasus. These also had prototypes from the 3rd to the 1st century BC or the 2nd century AD, as in the Temple of Mars Ultor at Rome and the Lesser Propylaia at the Sanctuary of Eleusis for Pegasus, and the capitals and consoles at Hierapolis (now Pamukkale, Turkey) for the other motifs. The acanthus leaves were sometimes replaced by palmettes or, from the early 6th century, by sculpted basketwork.

The basket capital seems to have been devised by the architects of Justinian (*reg* 527–65). It was linked to the development of the arch and perfected in Constantinople at the time of the first domed churches (St Polyeuktos;

Hagia Sophia; SS Sergios and Bakchos). The earliest dated examples are found at St Polyeuktos (524–7), accompanied by a wider decorative vocabulary that employed oriental motifs taken from textiles and metalwork. Some motifs were derived from the Sasanian crown (the *pativ*), palmettes were copied from Persian silks, and there are imitations in marble of studded metal rods or beadwork triangles (e.g. chancel plaque from St Polyeuktos, in the Zeyrek Cami, Istanbul; capitals in Istanbul, Archaeol. Mus.; Trabzon, St Sophia Mus.). In the first half of the 6th century a combination of the various elements produced some of the most beautiful sculpture of the period, such as the capitals with cornucopia (Istanbul, Archaeol. Mus.; Damascus, N. Mus.) that were imitated by Phrygian workshops (Afyon, Archaeol. Mus.; Akşehir, Mus. Stone Masonry; Eskişehir, Archaeol. Mus.), or capitals decorated with leaf-masks and gorgoneia, seraphim, personifications or inhabited *rinceaux* (all Istanbul, Archaeol. Mus.). The virtuosity of this sculpture is evident in the architraves and cornices at St John Stoudios, SS Sergios and Bakchos, and especially in the niches of the lower entablature at St Polyeuktos, where the carvings of fantailed peacocks against a background of vines are among the finest examples of Byzantine sculpture.

Plaques from the screen or parapet that separated the sanctuary from the nave and aisles, or the nave from the aisles, and shut off the galleries, usually have simple designs, such as a grid or field of scales with a central motif (usually a cross or chi-rho monogram) inscribed on a disc, or on a lozenge. The chi-rho may be flanked by lateral crosses joined to it by wavy ribbons with heart-shaped, pointed ends. The field may be covered with plant or geometric motifs, sometimes in an openwork design (Ravenna, S Apollinare Nuovo and S Vitale). It may also contain confronted animals (peacocks, deer), often placed either side of a central vase or cross (Istanbul, Archaeol. Mus.; Ravenna, S Apollinare Nuovo; Iznik, Archaeol. Mus.; Thessaloniki, Hagios Demetrios and Hagia Sophia; Nea-Anchialos, Basilica C). Sometimes, especially in the 6th century, these animals overrun the geometric ground (Philippi, Basilica B; Nikopolis, Basilica A). Human figures are rare, exceptions being *Daniel in the Lions' Den* (from Thasos; in Istanbul, Archaeol. Mus.; Ravenna, S Apollinare Nuovo) and *Hercules* (Ravenna, Mus. N.; Venice, S Marco). The piers supporting the plaques are either low or, from the mid-5th century, surmounted by colonnettes, and have little decoration, except for a series from Izmit (Istanbul, Archaeol. Mus.), which have *rinceaux* decorating the uprights, and children's heads or mythological scenes on the top.

The most spectacular of the liturgical fittings are the ambos. Some are large monoliths with a single stairway (e.g. Thessaloniki, Hagios Menas, Hagios Demetrios and Hagia Sophia), while others have two monolithic stairways with a platform between them (e.g. Kos, basilica near Mastichari; Miletos, church built on the Temple of Asklepios; Didyma, Kütahya). The most common type in the Aegean basin is formed of plaques bolted together and supports arranged in two stairways on either side of a relatively high platform (1–2 m) supported by piers or colonnettes. The stringboards and parapets were also decorated with crosses, animals and, in some cases, with

scenes of the *Sacrifice of Isaac* and the *Good Shepherd* (Istanbul, Archaeol. Mus.; Selçuk, Ephesos Archaeol. Mus.). Hollowed shells on the surrounds of the platforms of ambos in Macedonia, northern Greece (e.g. Philippi, Octagon and Basilica A; Amphipolis, basilicas C and E), relate them to others in Turkey (Didyma, Selçikler Köyü, Gediz, Seyitgazı). The finest is the 'fan-shaped' ambo from Hagios Georgios (500–30), Thessaloniki, which has a curved double stairway leading to a platform. The niches in the lower register contain an *Adoration of the Magi* surrounded by a profusion of architectural and plant motifs. Towards the end of the 6th century tower-shaped ambos with walls decorated with compartments containing animals are found at Ravenna.

Altar tables, either with free-standing legs or shaped like a chest (e.g. the magnificent altar frontal in Cleveland, OH, Mus. A.), form another important group, which can be divided into precise categories: rectangular, round or semicircular, with, for example, decorated or smooth edges. These may correspond to the particular styles produced at individual quarries (*see also* ALTAR, §II, 2).

Regional schools. Although it spread over a wide area, this metropolitan sculpture did not stifle the local schools. The copying of works in Proconnesian marble, however, gradually led to the production of replicas that are sometimes barely distinguishable from their prototypes, and it weakened local styles. In Attica around the Pentelic quarries, and throughout the Peloponnese, a regional tradition of sculpture in marble continued. This was characterized by an acanthus with 'ringed voids', which was derived from that on the Arch of Hadrian in Athens (*c.* AD 132), by long water-leaf motifs and by classicizing palmettes. Variations from the Proconnesian repertory were greater in regions that used a material other than marble. The basalt regions east of Aleppo in northern Syria and in Haurân in the south of the country produced poor sculpture, the latter clearly showing a decline from the Roman period; but in northern Syria, Lycia (Turkey) and Egypt the soft limestone was a medium for unrivalled virtuosity. In Lycia, besides imitations in limestone of Corinthian, Composite and double-zone capitals (Muskar Church; Myra, now Demre, St Nicholas; Limyra Church) there developed an extremely involved and brilliant architectural decoration, notably at mountain sites such as Muskar, the triconch church at Alacahisar, the basilical church at Alakilise and the monastery church at Karabel. These buildings were often of dry-stone construction and covered with intricate architectural decoration. Uprights, lintels and cornices are decorated at several levels with various *rinceaux* and meander patterns. Crosses are overloaded with studs, and parapet plaques have the same motifs. Some figures, such as that (perhaps a monk) between two angels on the parapet of an ambo from Elmalı, are strongly reminiscent of Coptic art.

Architectural sculpture in Cilicia (Turkey) also included works in limestone derived from local antecedents. The leaves on the capitals became increasingly undercut during the 6th century, as can be seen in pieces discovered at Tapureli, and in the churches at Erdemli, Akkale and, especially, at Kilise Deresi, where they are very close to the symmetrical openwork found in northern Syria and

Egypt. There are also naive scenes, such as the *Sacrifice of Isaac* depicted on a sanctuary screen pier (Adana, Archaeol. Mus.). The harder limestone used at Anazarbe permitted less elaboration. The decoration on the triumphal arches of the churches built there during Justinian's reign is more Classical (egg-and-dart) and spread out, creating an almost spindly effect. The most successful local example is probably the ALAHAN MONASTERY (6th century), where the anthropomorphic sculptures on the portal of the west basilica, the sculptures on the shrine midway between the two churches, and those on the doors and consoles of the east church are noteworthy: fish, birds and *rinceaux* are evidence of particularly skilful local workshops practising an art unequalled in the region at any other period.

The close links that existed between northern Syria and Cilicia are reflected in the monastery of St Simeon the Stylite the younger near Antioch (541–65), which the Cilician masons modelled on Qal'at Sim'an, the monastery of St Simeon the Stylite of Aleppo (476–91). The decorative repertory of the second half of the 4th century in Syria was poor and provincial (Tuscan style, Ionic and smooth-leaved capitals, undecorated door mouldings, some medallions), but ornament thereafter developed in two main stages. The first stage (*c.* 400) was linked with the work of the 'technites' Markianos Kyris (*fl c.* 390–*c.* 430) in churches at Ba'udeh (390), Kseidjke (414), Dar Qita (418) and Qasr el Banat (*c.* 430) in the Gebel Baris. The mouldings of the door- and window-frames and the cornices are adorned with friezes (e.g. interlace, strips of interwoven leaves, alternating acanthus and palmettes), which are often combined. Kyris revived the use of Corinthian capitals with carved leaves to adorn the east end of the church. The monastery of Qal'at Sim'an was built mainly in the years 476–90 by local masons and others brought from Cilicia and the Euphrates Valley, and its architectural sculpture was to prove influential. Superimposed columns adorn the apse and are placed between the windows of the clerestory. Mouldings run around the exterior walls at the level of the window-sills and frame both the doors and windows. At the ends of the mouldings are highly ornate volutes. Acanthus *rinceaux*, rows of triangles, palmettes and geometric motifs abound. The cornices are hollowed out into niches that are often carved to resemble shells. Various forms of acanthus are used, including 'wind-blown' acanthus (e.g. El Bara, the third and fifth churches), previously used in the 3rd century. Further innovations were introduced during the 6th century, up to the elaborate creations at Kafr Ruma and in the south churches at Bafetin and Banqusa. The bemas in the centre of the naves and other less common pieces, such as the canopies of some baptismal fonts (e.g. Qal'at Sim'an; see fig. 50), are also finely worked with decoration reminiscent of wood-carving.

Early Christian sculpture in Egypt can be divided into two groups: imported works in marble and local limestone imitations, found principally in the coastal regions, and the local works mostly made in central Egypt. Much material in the former group has come from sites such as Abu Mina (now Menas City) and from the Cairo mosques, where Proconnesian marbles have frequently been reused. The limestone imitations are not without character, as for example a double-zone capital with griffin protomes

50. Font canopy from the monastery chapel, Qal'at Sim'an, limestone, 6th century (*in situ*); displayed upside down

(Cairo, Coptic Mus.). There are also numerous local replicas of marble plaques with a central medallion surrounded by a meander border. The most interesting sculptures, however, are the local Corinthian capitals, in which even the exterior volutes are often missing and the leaves are more slender and pointed than in Proconnesian works (e.g. Bahnasa, Bani Suwif), although by the 6th century they are geometric, as in the north church at Bawit (nr Ashmunein). Friezes have finely worked acanthus, containing figures in medallions or animal protomes, interrupted occasionally by angels holding cartouches. Pediments dating from the 4th century to the 6th at Bahnasa (Alexandria, Gr.-Rom. Mus.) and niches with Bacchic themes at Ahnas (Cairo, Coptic Mus.) are closely related to woodworking styles. Crosses or motifs with trailing ribbons often decorate the coronas, imitating an Egyptian feature found in limestone, sandstone and marble.

(b) 7th–15th centuries. The pronounced reduction of building activity and the subsequent closure of quarries must, at least in part, account for the scarcity of sculpture known from the early 7th century to the 9th. Among the few dated pieces are the plaques decorated with crosses from the templon of the church of the Dormition (Koimesis) at Nicaea (now Iznik), which was built before *c.* 730. One of these plaques has the monogram of the founder, Hyakinthos, at the centre of interlacing geometric motifs in shallow relief. This same decoration surrounds the monogram of Constantine V (*reg* 741–75) on a plaque

from Hagia Eirene, Istanbul. The next group of dated sculptures is found in the Greek churches at Skripou (873/4) and of Hagios Georgios in Thebes (872). The lack of newly quarried stone also resulted in the frequent reuse of earlier sculptures, as in the monastery of Constantine Lips of 907, where inscribed tomb slabs from the region of Cyzicus (nr Bandirma, Turkey) were reworked. Perhaps the Phrygian 'sawyers of marble' (*pristai*) mentioned in the late 10th century by Leo of Synnada were engaged in this recycling, of which a common example is the reuse of Early Christian and ancient columns for the architraves of iconostases.

The consolidation of the empire's frontiers in Asia Minor, Greece, the Balkans and parts of Italy in the late 9th century and early 10th marks the beginning of a second great phase in the production of architectural sculpture. The stylistic development of the various carved elements (e.g. iconostases, cornices, the surrounds for monumental icons, tomb niches, doorjambs and lintels) found at the earliest dated churches of the period is, however, unclear. The sculpture at Skripou and Thebes, for example, reveals a concern to decorate every available surface. Peacocks and quadrupeds are rendered schematically, with the emphasis on their decorative aspects, such as plumage, while most floral motifs consist of stems with irregular outlines terminating in pointed, heart-shaped leaves. The abundant decoration of the North Church of the monastery of Constantine Lips marks a return to a more severe style, clearly inspired by the Sasanian ornament of St Polyeuktos (destr.; fragments in Istanbul, Archaeol. Mus.): even the window mullions and bases are covered with minutely carved palmettes. The cornices bearing animal and geometric motifs side by side, the parapet plaques of the same high quality and the sharp edge of the arrises are reminiscent of the silver decoration covering the iconostasis and ciborium of the church of the Virgin of the Pharos in Constantinople (*c.* 864; destr.), as described by Photios at the church's encaenia (*Homily* x:4–6). The walls of the Lips church were decorated with inlaid icons and roundels, including a complete icon of St Eudokia (Istanbul, Archaeol. Mus.) and pictures of animals set into marble matrices.

The Theotokos church and the katholikon of HOSIOS LOUKAS in Phokis (Greece) constitute an equally important ensemble. The drum of the Theotokos dome (*c.* 946–55) has a remarkable exterior entirely covered with marble plaques richly decorated with crosses, and lion-head waterspouts in a classicizing style. The architectural sculpture inside the church is also highly ornate. The capitals have either palmettes or acanthus with miniature lobes, while the zone between the capitals and the abacus contains stud-motifs and cherubim reminiscent of the gorgoneia of some Roman capitals. The iconostasis is decorated with arabesques surrounding palmettes and cruciform motifs, and it is supported on capitals largely copied from Corinthian capitals of the Roman period. Pseudo-kufic lettering and acanthus scrolls imitating Early Christian *rinceaux* decorate the semicircular surrounds above the despotic icons on the piers flanking the iconostasis. The sculpture in the katholikon is more archaic and formal in style than that in the Theotokos. The iconostasis is decorated with archivolts enclosing palmettes, a cross at the centre, and interlacing circles each containing a stud-motif or rosette in high relief. Well-proportioned griffins with supple bodies stand on either side of the architrave's main section, while below the windows on the church's exterior are plaques imitating Early Christian screens.

No complete ensemble of architectural sculpture survives from the Komnenian period (late 11th century–13th). The early 12th-century church of Christ the Saviour in Chora (*see* ISTANBUL, §IV, 7(iii)) is more revealing about later ornamentation, since it was redecorated *c.* 1316–21 by Theodore Metochites. Both its sculpture and mosaics imitate Early Christian models.

A better understanding of the development of architectural decoration may be gained by examining the various sculptural elements in turn. The capitals are less varied in design than those from the Early Christian period. With the exception of the Corinthian capitals in the Theotokos Church at Hosios Loukas, some curious reused Ionic capitals with imposts decorated with niello inlay in S Marco in Venice, and some double-zone capitals from Philomelion (now Akşehir, Turkey), the only type in use was the basket capital. Some examples of this type remained unchanged throughout the Byzantine era, as for example the capitals decorated with pine-cones at the corners and a vine leaf on each face at Hosios Loukas and in the early 10th-century Round Church at Preslav (Bulgaria). The sides of other capitals could be separated by schematized laurel branches, as in the Panagia Chalkeon at Thessaloniki (*c.* 1028), or have monograms inscribed on discs. Of the many capitals with more pronounced medieval decoration, some have busts of saints or angels on their sides, as in four capitals decorated with angels that have been attributed to the early Komnenian phase at Christ the Saviour in Chora (*c.* 1080). Subsequently several capitals, consoles and imposts in the same church were carved with representations of the Evangelists, St John the Baptist and

51. Fragment of architrave with *Deësis*, from St Trophimos, Synnada, Turkey, late 10th century–11th marble (Afyon, Archaeological Museum)

military saints. Similar carved pieces have been found in the church of St Mary Pammakaristos (now Fethiye Cami, Istanbul), or have no known provenance (Istanbul, Archaeol. Mus.; Paris, Mus. Cluny).

Parapet plaques have a rich repertory of motifs characterized by omnipresent interlace. Some are divided into recessed panels linked by interlace and decorated with palmettes, crosses and animal motifs, as in SS Sergios and Bakchos in Constantinople, S Marco in Venice, St Sophia (c. 1037) in Kiev, the church at Nerezi (nr Skopje, Macedonia; c. 1164), the 11th-century church of Hosios Meletios Monastery (nr Megara, Greece), and the *phiale* (wellhead) of the Grand Lavra on Mt Athos (11th century). Crosses, often plaited and raised on a stepped podium, are a frequent feature from the end of the 11th century onwards, as at Hosios Loukas and the example formerly in St John Mangoutis, Athens (destr.). Lozenges or squares set at an angle, usually linked by interlace to the motifs in the corners or on the rims of the frames, are found over a wide area, from Bari in Italy (Bari, Mus. S Nicola) to St Sophia (1037–c. 1140) in Kiev, including Greece and Constantinople.

A wide range of animals is found in the decoration of plaques: confronted or single peacocks (e.g. the North Church of Constantine Lips), an eagle holding a hare in its talons (Athens, Byz. Mus.), an elephant (Istanbul, Archaeol. Mus.), griffins and simurghs, for example two plaques (Istanbul, Archaeol. Mus.) that are similar in technique to those in the North Church of Constantine Lips. S Marco in Venice and the Small Metropolis (Panagia Gorgoepikoös; late 12th century) in Athens have a number of plaques with beautiful representations of animals. Mythological and allegorical subjects were also portrayed, as for example *Hercules and the Nemean Lion* (Thessaloniki, Archaeol. Mus.), the *Prayer of Ixion* and the *Allegory of Kairos* (Torcello, Mus. Torcello), and the *Apotheosis of Alexander* (Istanbul, Archaeol. Mus.).

Iconostasis architraves and pillars, doorjambs, lintels and cornices all share a similar decorative repertory, the most common motifs being floral *rinceaux*, friezes with alternating florets and palmettes, and interlacing circles with repeated rosettes or crosses. The use of arcading to decorate architraves was introduced in the 9th century (e.g. church at Skripou) and became increasingly popular between the 10th century and the 12th over an area extending from Konya (Turkey) to Bari. It is found in the large monasteries of Hosios Loukas and Nea Moni on Chios, as well as in the village churches in the Mani (Greece), where the workshop of the 'marmaras' Niketas flourished in 1075–9. Common motifs are palmettes mounted on stems with their upper ends coiling outwards, or animals, such as griffins, confronted birds with intertwining necks and peacocks.

Perhaps imitating the templon of Hagia Sophia in Constantinople, Phrygian iconostases, such as the one from the church of St Trophimos at Synnada (now Suhut, Turkey) show the *Deësis* with its protagonists Christ, John the Baptist, the Virgin, angels and saints (see fig. 51). The most notable example of this kind of decoration was found in the excavated church at Sebaste (now Selçikler Köyü, Turkey). The face of the architrave was originally

52. Fragment of funerary arch, Proconnesian marble, h. 910 mm, first quarter of the 14th century (Istanbul, Archaeological Museum)

decorated with 21 medallions containing busts of saints, of which 18 are extant and inlaid with coloured materials. In the Palaiologan period (1261–1453) the modelling of figures became more important, as can be seen in the busts of the *Archangel Michael* on an architrave in the church of the Blachernai Monastery near Arta (mid-13th century) and a *Young Apostle* on an early 14th-century fragment of an iconostasis architrave from the church of St Mary Pammakaristos (Istanbul, Hagia Sophia Mus.).

Ciboria became increasingly scarce during this period, although one is mentioned in Photios' description of the church of the Virgin of the Pharos. The carved archivolts once used to decorate them were employed instead as surrounds for mural icons or as arcosolia reliefs (slabs on the arches above tombs). Among the former is the lunette of an arch enclosing a bust of Christ flanked by angels in the corners (Istanbul, Christ the Saviour in Chora). An identical arrangement of angels is found on several arcosolia in the South Church of Constantine Lips (founded before 1282), Christ the Saviour in Chora and elsewhere (see fig. 52).

BIBLIOGRAPHY

EARLY SOURCES

Photios of Constantinople: *Homilies* (mid-9th century); Eng. trans. by C. Mango as *The Homilies of Photios of Constantinople* (Cambridge, MA, 1958), pp. 185–7

Leo of Synnada: *Letters* (late 10th century); ed. J. Darrouzès as *Epistoliers byzantins du Xe siècle* (Paris, 1960), pp. 199–200

GENERAL

A. Grabar: *Sculptures byzantines de Constantinople, 4e–10e siècle* (Paris, 1963)

——: *Sculptures byzantines du moyen âge, 11e–14e siècle* (Paris, 1976)

F. W. Deichmann: *Rom, Ravenna, Konstantinopel, Naher Osten* (Wiesbaden, 1982)

N. Firatli: *La Sculpture figurée au Musée Archéologique d'Istambul*, Bib. Inst. Fr. Etud. Anat. Istambul, xxx (Paris, 1990)

4TH–6TH CENTURIES

R. Kautzsch: *Beiträge zu einer Geschichte des spätantiken Kapitells im Osten vom 4. bis ins 7. Jahrhundert* (Berlin and Leipzig, 1936)

I. Nikolajević-Stojkovic: *Ranovizantiska arhitektonska dekorativna 'plastika' u Makedoniji, Srbjii i Crnoj Gori* [Architectural sculpture decoration of the late Roman period in Macedonia, Serbia and Montenegro] (Belgrade, 1957)

A. L. Jakobson: *Rannesrednevekovyy Khersones: Ocherki istorii material'noy kul'tury* [The town of Chersonesos in the high Middle Ages], Materialy i issledovaniia po arkheologii SSR, lxiii (Moscow, 1959)

O. Feld: 'Bericht über eine Reise durch Kilikien', *Istanbul. Mitt.*, xiii–xiv (1963–4), pp. 88–107

J. Kramer: *Skulpturen mit Adlerfiguren am Bauten des 5. Jahrhunderts n. Chr. in Konstantinopel* (Cologne, 1968)

F. W. Deichmann: *Ravenna: Hauptstadt des spätantiken Abendlandes*, 3 vols (Wiesbaden, 1968–88)

T. Ulbert: *Studien zur dekorativen Reliefplastik des östlichen Mittelmeerraumes* (diss., U. Munich, 1969)

J. B. Ward-Perkins: 'Recent Work and Problems in Libya', *Actas del VIII congreso internacional de arqueología cristiana: Barcelona, 1969*, pp. 219–36

T. Ulbert: 'Untersuchungen zu den byzantinischen Reliefplatten des 6. bis 8. Jahrhunderts', *Istanbul. Mitt.*, xix–xx (1969–70), pp. 339–57

R. M. Harrison: 'A Note on Architectural Sculpture in Central Lycia', *Anatol. Stud.*, xxii (1972), pp. 187–97

N. Asgari: 'Roman and Early Byzantine Marble Quarries of Proconnesus', *Xth International Congress of Classical Archaeology: Ankara, 1973*, pp. 467–80

G. Roux: 'Tables chrétiennes en marbre découvertes à Salamine', *Anthologie salaminienne*, ed. J. Pouilloux (1973), iv of *Salamine de Chypre*, 13 vols (Paris, 1969–87), pp. 133–96

E. W. Betsch: *The History, Production and Distribution of the Late Antique Capital in Constantinople* (diss., Philadelphia, U. PA, 1977)

J.-P. Sodini: 'Remarques sur la sculpture architecturale d'Attique, de Béotie et du Péloponnèse', *Bull. Corr. Hell.*, ci (1977), pp. 423–50

C. Strube: 'Die Formbegung des Apsisdekoration in Qalbloze und Qalat Seman', *Jb. Ant. & Christ.*, xx (1977), pp. 181–91

——: 'Baudekoration in den Kirchen des nordsyrischen Kalksteinmassivs', *Archäol. Anz.* (1978), pp. 577–601

S. Tavano: 'Costantinopoli, Ravenna e l'alto Adriatico: La scultura architettonica dall'antichità al medio evo', *Ant. Altoadriat.*, xiii (1978), pp. 505–36

W. Widrig: 'Two Churches of Latrun in Cyrenaica', *Pap. Brit. Sch. Rome*, xxxiii (1978), pp. 94–131

C. Strube: 'Tempel und Kirche in Me'ez', *Istanbul. Mitt.*, xxix (1979), pp. 355–65

G. Kapitän: 'Elementi architettonici per una basilica dal relitto navale del VI secolo di Marzamemi (Siracusa)', *Corsi Cult. A. Ravennate & Bizantina*, xxvii (1980), pp. 71–136

M. M. Mango: 'The Continuity of the Classical Tradition in the Art and Architecture of Northern Mesopotamia', *East of Byzantium: Syria and Armenia in the Formative Period: Dumbarton Oaks Symposium: Washington, DC, 1980*, pp. 115–34

J.-P. Sodini: 'La Sculpture architecturale à l'époque paléochrétienne en Illyricum', *Praktika tou 10ou diethnous synedriou christianikis archaiologias: Thessaloniki, 1980* [Proceedings of the 10th international congress of Christian archaeology], i, pp. 207–98

A. Bortoli-Kazanski: 'Répartition du marbre de Proconnèse en Crimée', *Geographica Byzantina*, ed. H. Ahrweiler (Paris, 1981), pp. 55–65

H-G. Severin: 'Problemi di scultura tardoantica in Egitto', *Corsi Cult. A. Ravennate & Bizantina*, xxviii (1981), pp. 315–36

N. Harrazi: *Chapiteaux de la Grande Mosquée de Kairouan*, 2 vols (Tunis, 1982)

R. Farioli: 'Ravenna, Costantinopoli: Considerazioni sulla scultura del VI secolo', *Corsi Cult. A. Ravennate & Bizantina*, xxx (1983), pp. 205–53

C. Strube: 'Die Kapitelle von Qasr ibn Wardan', *Jb. Ant. & Christ.*, xxvi (1983), pp. 59–106

W. Djobadze: 'Remains of a Byzantine Ambo and Church Furnishings in Hobi (Georgia)', *Archäol. Anz.* (1984), pp. 627–39

C. Strube: *Polyeuktoskirche und Haghia Sophia* (Munich, 1984)

A. Terry: *The Architecture and Architectural Sculpture of the Sixth-century Euphrasius Cathedral Complex at Poreč* (diss., Urbana- Champaign, U. IL, 1984)

A. Geyer: 'Aspekte der Bauornamentik von Alahan Monastir', *Jb. Ant. & Christ.*, xxvii–xxviii (1984–5), pp. 151–70

R. Fernandez: 'Les Représentations des stylites', *Stud. Orient. Christ.*, xviii (1985), pp. 115–52

N. Duval: 'Mensae funéraires de Sirmium et de Salone', *Bull. Archéol. & Hist. Dalmates*, lxxvii (1986), pp. 186–226

R. M. Harrison: *The Excavations, Structures, Architectural Decoration, Small Finds, Coins, Bones and Molluscs* (1986), i of *Excavations at Saraçhane in Istanbul* (Princeton, 1986–)

V. Deroche: 'L'Acanthe de l'arc d'Hadrien et ses dérivés en Grèce propre', *Bull. Corr. Hell.*, cxi (1987), pp. 425–53

G. Severin and H.-G. Severin: *Marmor vom heiligen Menas*, Liebighaus Monographie, x (Frankfurt am Main, 1987)

J.-P. Sodini: 'Sculpture architecturale, briques, objets métalliques d'époques paléochrétienne et byzantine', *Inscriptions de Cilicie*, ed. G. Dagron and D. Feissel (Paris, 1987), pp. 231–56

A. Terry: 'The Early Christian Sculpture at Grado: A Reconsideration', *Gesta*, xxvi/2 (1987), pp. 93–112

N. Asgari: 'The Stages of Workmanship of the Corinthian Capital in Proconnesus and its Export Form', *Classical Marble: Geochemistry, Technology, Trade*, ed. N. Herz and M. Waelkens (Dordrecht, 1988), pp. 115–25

A. Terry: 'The Sculpture at the Cathedral of Eyphrasius in Poreč', *Dumbarton Oaks Pap.*, xlii (1988), pp. 13–64

C. Barsanti: 'L'esportazione di marmi dal Proconeso nelle regioni pontiche durante il IV–VI Secolo', *Riv. Ist. N. Archeol. & Stor. A.*, n.s. 3, xii, (1989), pp. 91–220

O. Callot: 'A propos de quelques colonnes de stylites syriens', *Architecture et poésie dans le monde grec: Hommage à Georges Roux* (Lyon and Paris, 1989), pp. 107–22

S. Rebenich: 'Zum Theodosiusobelisken in Konstantinopel', *Istanbul. Mitt.*, xli (1991), pp. 447–76

C. Mango, ed.: *Studies on Constantinople* (Aldershot, 1993)

7TH–15TH CENTURIES

T. Macridy: 'The Monastery of Lips (Fenari Isa Cami) at Istanbul', *Dumbarton Oaks Pap.*, xviii (1964), pp. 249–315 [with contributions by A. H. S. Megaw, C. Mango and J. W. Hawkins]

N. Firatli: 'Découverte d'une église byzantine à Sébaste de Phrygie', *Cah. Archéol.*, xix (1969), pp. 151–66

F. Zuliani: *I marmi di San Marco* (Venice, 1970)

H. Belting: 'Eine Gruppe Konstantinopler Reliefs aus dem 11. Jahrhundert', *Pantheon*, xxx (1972), pp. 263–71

——: 'Zur Skulptur aus der Zeit um 1300 in Konstantinopel', *Münch. Jb. Bild. Kst.*, n. s. 3, xxiii (1972), pp. 63–100

N. Drandakis: 'Niketas marmoras (1075)', *Dodone*, i (1972), pp. 21–44

U. Peschlow: 'Neue Beobachtungen zur Architektur und Ausstattung der Koimesiskirche in Iznik', *Istanbul. Mitt.*, xxii (1972), pp. 145–87

O. Hjort: 'A Fragment of Early Paleologan Sculpture in Istanbul', *Acta Archaeol. & Hist. Pertinentia*, vi (1975), pp. 107–13

J.-P. Sodini: 'Une Iconostase byzantine à Xanthos', *Actes du colloque sur la Lycie antique: Istanbul, 1977*, pp. 119–48

O. Hjort: 'The Sculpture of Kariye Camii', *Dumbarton Oaks Pap.*, xxxiii (1979), pp. 201–89

F. W. Deichmann, ed.: *Corpus der Kapitelle der Kirche von San Marco zu Venedig* (Wiesbaden, 1981) [with contributions from J. Kramer and U. Peschlow]

M. Milella Lovecchio: 'La scultura bizantina dell'XI secolo nel Museo di San Nicola di Bari', *Mél. Ecole Fr. Rome*, xciii (1981), pp. 7–87

Z. Swiechowski, A. Rizzi and R. Hamann-Maclean: *Romanische Reliefs von venezianischen Fassaden: Patere e formelle* (Wiesbaden, 1982)

A. Rizzi: *Scultura esterna a Venezia* (Venice, 1988)

J.-P. SODINI

(ii) Non-architectural reliefs. Although the record of discoveries of reliefs on sarcophagi and honorific monuments throughout the Early Christian and Byzantine period is fragmentary, the greater numbers of Christian reliefs provide a more varied overall picture than their fewer secular counterparts.

(a) 4th–6th centuries. (b) 7th–12th centuries. (c) 13th–15th centuries.

(a) 4th–6th centuries. The largest category of Early Christian relief sculpture is the whole or fragmentary sarcophagi (*see also* SARCOPHAGUS, §III, 1), over 1000 of which are in Rome and Ostia alone. Stone relief commissioned by the state had its final resurgence in Rome at the beginning of the 4th century, while in the Eastern empire the three triumphal monuments erected under Theodosios I and his son Arkadios occupy an outstanding position

among the remains of this period. (For the Arch of Galerius *see* THESSALONIKI, §III, 1.)

Secular. The two major examples of state-sponsored sculpture in Rome are the *decennalia* monument in the Forum Romanum (AD 303; *see* ROME, ANCIENT, §IV, 2(ix)) and the Arch of Constantine (*c.* AD 315; *see* ROME, ANCIENT, §IV, 2(x); ROME, §V, 12). The six panels of the arch's historical frieze show events before and after Constantine's triumph over Maxentius at the Milvian Bridge (312). In representing historical events, these reliefs adhere to the tradition of official state art. Stylistically, however, they have moved away from the Classical formal ideal. Two-dimensional sculptures in low relief predominate, with the figures arranged frontally. Ideal figures also occur, such as the Victories in the spandrels of the arch; these are in higher relief, showing some attempt to make the figures stand out from the background. It seems that different styles of sculpture were used for different purposes and that this sensitivity to form was based on a latent trend that was generally overshadowed by recurring classicizing influences. In the 4th century this spirit of classicism culminated in the refined court style of Theodosios I. An example of this style was the Column of Theodosios in the Forum Tauri (officially opened 393; *see* §(i)(a) above and LATE ANTIQUITY, fig. 1), the first of three triumphal monuments erected in Constantinople under Theodosios and Arkadios. The column commemorated the emperor's victory over the Goths in 386 and, in addition to his statue at the top, was decorated with a spiral band of relief depicting battles with the barbarians. The column collapsed *c.* 1500 and fragments of its reliefs were reused a short time later in the construction of baths (1501–6) for Sultan Bayazid II (*reg* 1481–1512).

The second triumphal monument erected in Constantinople is the base of the Obelisk of Tuthmosis III (*reg* 1479–1426 BC), which was brought from Egypt and re-erected in the hippodrome (*c.* AD 390–91; *in situ*). The city prefect Proculus commissioned the base in Emperor Theodosios' honour, and, despite weathering, the iconography of the marble reliefs on its four sides can still be identified. The base is divided into two parts; the lower level shows on opposite sides the erection of the obelisk and a chariot race in the circus, while Greek and Latin inscriptions referring to the emperor's victory over the two usurpers Maximus and Victor cover the other sides. The upper level consists of four large panels showing Theodosios at court, Theodosios receiving an embassy of barbarians, Theodosios in state and Theodosios at the circus. These compositions are an expression of the emperor's claim to universal power and are stylistically significant for showing the participants in each scene in a hierarchic arrangement. Thus the members of the imperial family occupy the centre of the uppermost zone, flanked by the highest state officials and bodyguards; spectators, entertainers and barbarians are depicted on a smaller scale in the zones beneath. Here the dynastic imagery already apparent in the imperial reliefs on the Arch of Constantine and Arch of Galerius has become more sophisticated: typical features include the elongated bodies, the individualized facial features and the rigidly frontal image of the central figure.

The third triumphal monument in Constantinople was the column erected by Arkadios in 400–02. It was demolished in 1715, and the evidence for its relief decoration is based almost exclusively on drawings made in 1574 (Cambridge, Trinity Coll.); some relief remains, presumably depicting the exodus of the Goths from Constantinople (*in situ*), and a small relief fragment survive (Istanbul, Archaeol. Mus.). The theme of the relief spirals on the column shaft was the war against the Goths; each side of the pedestal was divided into four registers depicting groups of figures and other compositions arranged in a strictly hierarchical order. For example, on the west side (see fig. 53) the two lower registers show the submission of the barbarians to imperial rule, with representations of captured weapons and of personages from the provinces bearing gifts. The third register shows the holders of global power, namely emperors Arkadios and Honorius (*reg* 395–423), flanked by soldiers and the highest state officials. The uppermost register, with its Christian Cross in a garland supported by Victories or angels, indicates that the rule of the two emperors was willed by God. It is the earliest known example of Christian symbolism penetrating imperial triumphal iconography, and follows Theodosios' edict of 380 by which Christianity became the state religion.

Although the triumphal columns of Constantinople continued the tradition of Roman historical reliefs, their

53. Reliefs on the west side of the marble base of the Column of Arkadios, Constantinople, 400–02; from a drawing (1574) in the Freshfield Album (Cambridge, Trinity College)

iconography had evolved to represent not so much a single victory over an internal or foreign enemy but rather the virtually timeless, universal rule of the empire. They also served to emphasize the idea of Constantinople as the New Rome, especially since triumphal columns had not been erected at Rome itself for over 200 years.

The subsequent development of secular reliefs in the 5th and 6th centuries cannot be fully understood owing to a lack of finds. The few pieces that have been preserved are largely confined to the more modest Column of Marcian (c. 450–52; in situ) in Constantinople and to chance finds elsewhere in the capital. Among the latter are two bases of statues of the charioteer Porphyrios (c. 500; Istanbul, Archaeol. Mus.), which originally stood in the hippodrome next to the obelisk, and the reliefs of which are similar to those of the older monument. The sole theme is the glorification of the victorious Porphyrios, shown several times in a triumphant frontal pose. Each face of both bases is divided into two or three registers of reliefs and surmounted by one or two panels for inscriptions. All the elements have been borrowed from imperial triumphal iconography. On the side of one base Emperor Anastasios (reg 491–518) is shown in the lower register in his royal box in the hippodrome, flanked by his state officials who acclaim the victorious charioteer; the latter stands in his chariot in the register above. The depiction of the charioteer rather than the emperor in the upper register may be because Porphyrios' victory coincided with an imperial victory.

Two marble slabs with reliefs of mythological scenes also survive from the 6th century, and they are closely linked to the art of Constantinople. One shows Hercules with the Arcadian Stag (Ravenna, Mus. N.); the other, depicting Hercules with the Erymanthian Boar, probably comes from Constantinople and was reused in the west façade of S Marco in Venice. In spite of the depth of the relief, the figures give the impression of being ironed into the surface, since all parts of the bodies are carved to the same foreground level. The two reliefs, together with sarcophagi from Ravenna, bear witness to the tendency towards the flattening out of reliefs in the 6th century.

Christian. Early Christian sculpture on sarcophagi continued the pagan Roman tradition. In the 3rd and 4th centuries the same workshops produced pagan and Christian sarcophagi, which were a luxury only the wealthy could afford. The earliest Christian sarcophagi used elements that were neutral in content, all deriving from the canon of forms used in antique sepulchral symbolism. In this way Christians were able to avoid attention and persecution. A sarcophagus (c. AD 270; see fig. 7 above) in S Maria Antiqua in Rome is the first to show neutral motifs alongside Christian scenes: an orans figure (i.e. with arms outstretched in prayer), a philosopher and a man carrying a ram appear next to such scenes as the Baptism and Jonah under the Gourd. The image of Jonah in ideal nakedness is contrary to biblical tradition and is based on the mythological sleeping figure of Endymion found in pagan sepulchral iconography.

Following the Edict of Milan (313) the use of specifically Christian themes became more widespread, with scenes from the Old and New Testaments predominating. Under Constantine there was a comprehensive biblical iconography based on the canonical and apocryphal books of the Bible as well as on Talmudic texts. The scenes depicted on frieze sarcophagi are generally based on concepts concerning the after-life, in which man's condition after death is perceived as a kind of uncertain interregnum prior to final resurrection. Concern over this intermediate realm resulted in pictures that referred paradigmatically to the story of divine salvation; through these the deceased could ask the Redeemer for safety and security. The individual pictures expressly referred to hope of salvation (e.g. Daniel in the Lions' Den), merciful judgement by God (e.g. the Acquittal of Susanna) or rest after death (e.g. Jonah under the Gourd). From about the mid-4th century onwards hierarchic centralized compositions were more common; these are usually found on columnar, tree and city-gate sarcophagi (e.g. late 4th century; Milan, S Ambrogio). The centre is usually occupied by non-biblical scenes such as an Enthroned Christ, the Delivery of the Creed or the cross, which attest to a more abstract, theological approach. With borrowings from Roman triumphal iconography, Christ appears as the ruler of the kingdom of God. According to these pictures, what was of crucial importance to the believer was no longer the uncertainty in the interregnum after death, but bliss after resurrection.

Many tomb slabs and sarcophagi were exported from Rome to the provincial centres in northern and southern Italy, the Dalmatian coast, southern Gaul, North Africa and the Iberian Peninsula, where they influenced the form and iconography of locally produced sarcophagi. After the collapse of Rome's workshops in the early 5th century, Toulouse and Bordeaux became important centres of sarcophagal production, using marble from the region around St Béat in the Pyrenees. Some sarcophagi were decorated with figural themes, usually Christ and the Apostles (e.g. Toulouse, Mus. Augustins), but most were niche sarcophagi with symbolic plant ornament (e.g. Toulouse, Mus. Augustins; Bordeaux, Mus. Bordeaux). Numerous examples have the chi-rho in the centre, surrounded by vine tendrils, ivy and acanthus leaves stylized as the Tree of Life. Although the figurally decorated sarcophagi are to some extent three-dimensional, sarcophagi with ornamental carvings are in low relief. Production probably ceased as early as the first quarter of the 6th century.

Of the sarcophagi found on the Iberian Peninsula, the earliest examples are a group of c. 40 4th-century sarcophagi imported from Rome (e.g. four frieze sarcophagi, c. early 4th century, Girona, church of S Feliù; frieze sarcophagus, c. 340, Castiliscar, Parish Church; Bethesda-sarcophagus, end of 4th century, Tarragona Cathedral (façade); Constantinian frieze sarcophagus (from the village of Layos), Barcelona, Mus. Marés). The most individual group as regards form and decoration is the Bureba group (c. second half of the 4th century; e.g. sarcophagi found near Briviesca in La Bureba; Burgos, Mus. Arqueol. Prov.), from the eastern part of the province of Burgos, in which each sarcophagus is decorated on all four sides with reliefs. The sarcophagi from Ecija (Ecija, Iglesia de Santa Cruz) in the province of Sevilla, and Alcaudete (Madrid, Mus. Arqueol. N.) in the province of

Jaén form another group distinguished by their provincial manufacture and the use of local limestone. A small group made of local stone in Tarragona (Tarragona, Mus. Paleocrist.) is linked to examples from Rome in form and from Carthage in style (*c.* first quarter of the 5th century).

The earliest Christian reliefs from Constantinople date to the reign of Theodosios I and employ an iconography clearly derived from imperial triumphal scenes. Among the most noteworthy examples are a child's sarcophagus from Sarigüzel (Istanbul, Archaeol. Mus.) showing angels bearing the monogram of Christ in a garland; a standing figure of *Christ* (Berlin, Bodemus.); and two slabs showing *Christ with the Apostles* (Istanbul, Archaeol. Mus.; Barletta, Mus.-Pin. Com.). All these compositions are distinguished by their symmetrical arrangement around a centre point occupied by Christ or the chi-rho symbol. The various methods used to carve them can be attributed to different workshop traditions in Asia Minor.

The scarcity of 5th-century marble sarcophagal sculptures from Constantinople is partly compensated by a whole range of sarcophagi in RAVENNA, which are closely connected with the art of the eastern capital: finished sarcophagi were probably exported from Constantinople, as well as roughed-out marble that was then worked up on site by Constantinopolitan masons. Production on a substantial scale probably began at Ravenna in 402, when the western imperial residence was transferred there from Milan. In the first half of the 5th century the reliefs produced bore mainly representative themes such as the *Delivery of the Creed* between palms (420–30; Ravenna Cathedral) and such scenes as *Daniel in the Lions' Den* (Ravenna, S Apollinare Nuovo). From the second half of the 5th century symbolic motifs such as lambs, peacocks, crosses, palms and vine shoots became more common (Ravenna, S Vitale; Istanbul, Archaeol. Mus.). A number of slabs (Istanbul, Archaeol. Mus.), some from sarcophagi, others of unknown classification, were made of limestone. The stiff and awkward style of their figures looks provincial in comparison with the works from the marble workshops and may indicate the existence of a local Thracian tradition of stone-carving.

The extent to which sacred buildings of the 4th and 5th centuries were decorated with Christian stone reliefs is not clear, since no architectural reliefs have been found *in situ*. Two small groups of reliefs do, however, show signs of use in architectural settings. The first group comprises three *Hetoimasia* reliefs (Berlin, Bodemus.; Venice, north façade of S Marco; Nicosia, Cyprus Mus.), each one consisting of a surrounding frame enclosing symbols of Christ and paradise. They may originally have been part of a more extensive series of reliefs, and the high quality of their carving dates them to the Theodosian period. The second group consists of two severely damaged marble slabs from the church of Damous al-Karita in Carthage (Carthage, Mus. Lavigerie; *see also* CARTHAGE, §3). Like the pieces in the first group, they must have been set into a wall, since the backs of them remain unworked. The Carthaginian reliefs each show two scenes from the Nativity placed one above the other, and they are framed by rows of fine-toothed acanthus leaves. The liveliness of the scenes and the richly animated figures are in sharp contrast to the representative reliefs from Constantinople

and Ravenna. Nevertheless, they probably originated in 5th-century Constantinople and were exported to North Africa.

The technique and content of the few remaining figural reliefs from the Eastern provinces indicate that local traditions were gaining acceptance alongside the dominant range of Constantinopolitan forms. Examples of note include a fragment depicting the *Nativity* (Athens, Byz. Mus.) and a relief of an *Enthroned Mother of God with Angels and Saints* (Cairo, Coptic Mus.).

Although the few surviving examples of architectural sculpture and liturgical furniture confirm that figural sculpture was not completely forgotten in the 6th century, the lack of figural relief, unless attributed to the random nature of archaeological recovery, is striking.

(b) 7th–12th centuries. Not a single securely datable example of relief sculpture is known from the period between the 7th century and the end of the iconoclastic controversy in 843, with the result that the artistic preconditions for the ensuing revival of relief sculpture remain largely unknown. The tradition of depicting historical scenes was not revived; instead, relief art concentrated on the production of icons. In search of a subject, sarcophagal sculpture adopted and developed the existing range of Early Christian symbols; purely ornamental decoration thus predominated. While local masons in Greece and Asia Minor were generally responsible for the reliefs, the marble Yaroslav Sarcophagus (*c.* 1054) in the cathedral of St Sophia at Kiev (*see* KIEV, §3(i)) testifies to the direct influence of Constantinople. The general scarcity of finds from the Middle Byzantine centuries precludes any assessment of the development of relief sculpture in this period. Furthermore, since few pieces have been dated conclusively, the construction of a chronological framework, even for the principal period of relief art in the 11th and 12th centuries, remains problematic.

The term 'relief icon' reflects the trend from painted to relief portraiture, for which marble was the preferred material. In the religious realm depictions were mainly confined to individual portraits of Christ, the Virgin, archangels and saints. The reliefs were painted, with the figure set against a smooth background and surrounded by a frame. Since none of the known examples was found in its original position, their intended function and environment remain unclear: presumably they replaced painted icons in areas that were exposed to the effects of the weather or dampness, such as building façades and fountains. It is also possible that they were fixed to the pillars of church sanctuaries. They may even have been used as devotional pictures on *proskynetaria* (movable stands): possible models from the pre-iconoclastic period for such a use may be the small relief slabs with busts of holy personages from St Polyeuktos (Istanbul, Archaeol. Mus.), which have been dated to the 6th and 7th centuries.

The earliest post-iconoclastic relief icons come from the North Church (907) in the Constantine Lips Monastery and comprise limestone fragments representing two military saints (Istanbul, Archaeol. Mus.), parts of which were inlaid with multicoloured glass paste. The preserved head of one is strongly stylized, and the figures are depicted in frontal poses. Another relief fragment depicting the *Virgin*

Orans decorated the fountain of the church of St George (1042–55) in Constantinople (Istanbul, Archaeol. Mus.). Water originally flowed through the Virgin's drilled hands, and was thus sanctified by the icon. The figure stands in a stiff frontal position on a pedestal, distorted by the smooth background of the icon against which it is set, and fits exactly into the surrounding frame. The statue is characterized by its elongated proportions and clinging, finely pleated robe. A *Virgin Hodegetria* ('pointing the way'; *c.* 1080; Istanbul, Archaeol. Mus.; *see* CHRISTIANITY, fig. 2) already shows a certain simplification of the robe's pleats; the figures of the Virgin and Child remain contained within the surrounding frame and do not project beyond the foreground level it sets. By contrast, two later reliefs from Constantinople, one of the *Virgin Orans* and the other of the *Archangel Michael* (both Berlin, Bodemus.), show the figures' hands, wings and pedestals overlapping the edges of their frames. The fall of the folds has been further simplified, and the bodies are flattened and out of proportion with the heads, which are depicted in high relief.

There is little evidence of reliefs from Asia Minor, while finds in Greece are difficult to assess because the forms of the 12th century cannot be clearly distinguished from those of the 13th. If the two reliefs of a *Virgin Orans* and a *Virgin Hodegetria* (Athens, Byz. Mus.) belong to the 12th century, they indicate the early emergence in the provinces of an abstract and schematic style of relief carving, as suggested by the reduced body volumes and the simple, linear portrayal of the garment folds. Here too, however, the heads have been sculptured in high relief.

As for secular reliefs, the only imperial portraits from either the Middle or Late Byzantine periods come from Venice (Washington, DC, Dumbarton Oaks; Venice, Campiello Argheran, in wall between nos 3717 and 3718). Both pieces are frontal bust portraits set on a circular slab (tondo). They have been tentatively dated to the end of the 12th century by comparisons with coins, but it is difficult to identify the emperor or to determine the origin of the tondo form. The representation of the *Apotheosis of Alexander* (*c.* 1080) on the north façade of S Marco in Venice was probably brought from Constantinople. Stylistically it belongs to a group of works of architectural sculpture and stone reliefs, an important feature of which is the ornamental rows of holes. The group includes the aforementioned *Hodegetria*, the four capitals in the Komnenian church of Christ the Saviour in Chora in Constantinople (*c.* 1080) and another fragment depicting the *Apotheosis of Alexander* (Istanbul, Archaeol. Mus.).

(c) 13th–15th centuries. During the Latin occupation of Constantinople (1204–61) many works of art, including stone reliefs, were looted from the capital by the crusaders and transported to the rich trading cities of Italy, thus becoming known to a wider public. Italian masons, particularly those in Venice, copied these works with great care, with the result that it is often difficult to distinguish between Byzantine and Byzantinizing works. In addition to the diverse traditions of sculpture in the provinces and in the states neighbouring the Byzantine empire, a stylistic trend emerged that reflected a conscious reduction in the use of sculptural techniques, as in the front slab of the tomb of Theodora (*c.* 1270; Arta, Archaeol. Col.). Significant secular reliefs of any note are lacking, and the production of sarcophagal sculpture went into decline in this period.

Arcosolia relief are a particularly important group of monuments in this period (*see* §(i) and fig. 52 above), comprising slabs carved with figures of Christ, the Apostles and angels. The most common type of stone relief, however, is the relief icon. In addition to individual portraits, Christological scenes such as the Baptism, Crucifixion and Deësis were portrayed. Though few in number, the Constantinopolitan examples confirm the existence of two contrasting stylistic trends. The fragment of a gravestone depicting a *Virgin Orans* reflects the revival of antique relief art; both a *Deësis* and a *Virgin Hodegetria with Saints*, on the other hand, are more two-dimensional in conception, building on forms familiar from the 12th century (all items Istanbul, Archaeol. Mus.). The continued use of these forms can be seen more clearly in reliefs from Greece and Asia Minor than in those of the capital city: examples are a *Virgin Orans* (Athens, Byz. Mus.), *St David* (Thessaloniki, Byz. Mus. Rotonda St George), a *Christ in Judgement* (Serres, Old Metropolis; see fig. 54), an *Enthroned Christ* (Mystras, Mus. Mistra) and the *Archangel Michael* from Nicaea (Istanbul, Archaeol. Mus.). The use of sculptural techniques was gradually reduced to a minimum; folds in robes were no longer modelled, but depicted schematically as webs. The *Enthroned Christ* in Mystras shows the final stage of this development: the head and halo have still been given some sculptural emphasis, but the folds of the drapery

54. Relief of *Christ in Judgement*, marble, 1.16×0.93 m, 13th–14th centuries (Serres, Old Metropolis)

have simply been carved into the surface of the body and the robe.

BIBLIOGRAPHY

G. Bruns: *Der Obelisk und seine Basis auf dem Hippodrom zu Konstantinopel* (Istanbul, 1935)

J. B. Ward-Perkins: 'The Sculpture of Visigothic France', *Archaeologia*, lxxxvii (1938), pp. 79–128

H. P. L. Orange and A. von Gerkan: *Der spätantike Bildschmuck des Konstantinsbogens* (Berlin, 1939)

F. Gerke: *Die christlichen Sarkophage der vorkonstantinischen Zeit* (Berlin, 1940)

J. Kollwitz: *Oströmische Plastik der theodosianischen Zeit* (Berlin, 1941)

H. Peirce and R. Tyler: 'A Marble Emperor-roundel of the XIIth Century', *Dumbarton Oaks Pap.*, ii (1941), pp. 1–9

F. Benoit: *Sarcophages paléochrétiens d'Arles et de Marseille* (Paris, 1954)

G. Becatti: *La colonna coclide istoriata: Problemi storici, iconografici, stilistici* (Rome, 1960)

N. Firatli: 'Deux nouveaux reliefs funéraires d'Istambul et les reliefs similaires', *Cah. Archéol.*, xi (1960), pp. 73–92

B. Briesenick: 'Typologie und Chronologie der südwest-gallischen Sarkophage', *Jb. Röm.-Ger. Zentmus.*, ix (1962), pp. 76–182

A. Grabar: *Sculptures byzantines de Constantinople, IVe–Xe s.* (Paris, 1963)

R. Lange: *Die byzantinische Reliefikone* (Recklinghausen, 1964)

T. Macridy and others: 'The Monastery of Lips at Istanbul', *Dumbarton Oaks Pap.*, xviii (1964), pp. 249–315

N. Firatli: 'Encore une façade de faux sarcophage en calcaire', *Cah. Archéol.*, xvi (1966), pp. 1–4

T. Klauser and F. W. Deichmann: *Frühchristliche Sarkophage in Bild und Wort* (Olten, 1966)

K. Wessel: 'Byzantinische Plastik der paläologischen Periode', *Byzantion*, xxxvi (1966), pp. 217–59

H. Wrede: 'Zur Errichtung des Theodosiusobelisken in Istanbul', *Istanbul. Mitt.*, xvi (1966), pp. 178–98

F. W. Deichmann, ed.: *Rom und Ostia* (1967), i of *Repertorium der christlich-antiken Sarkophage* (Wiesbaden, 1967–)

B. Brenk: 'Zwei Reliefs des späten 4. Jahrhunderts', *Acta Archaeol. & A. Hist. Pertinentia*, iv (1969), pp. 51–60

F. W. Deichmann: 'Konstantinopler und ravennatische Sarkophag-Probleme', *Byz. Z.*, xii (1969), pp. 291–307

H.-G. Severin: 'Oströmische Plastik unter Valens und Theodosius I', *Jb. Berlin. Mus.*, xii (1970), pp. 211–52

H. Belting: 'Eine Gruppe Konstantinopler Reliefs aus dem 11. Jahrhundert', *Pantheon*, xxx (1972), pp. 263–71

H. Brandenburg: 'Ein frühchristliches Relief in Berlin', *Röm. Mitt.*, lxxix (1972), pp. 123–54

J. Engemann: *Untersuchungen zur Sepulkralsymbolik der späteren Kaiserzeit* (Münster, 1973)

M. Sotomayor: *Sarcófagos romano-cristianos de España: Estudio iconográfico* (Granada, 1975)

A. Grabar: *Sculptures byzantines du moyen âge* (Paris, 1976)

H. Brandenburg: 'Stilprobleme der frühchristlichen Sarkophagkunst Roms im 4. Jh.', *Röm. Mitt.*, lxxxvi (1979), pp. 439–71

J. Kollwitz and H. Herdejürgen: *Die ravennatischen Sarkophage* (Berlin, 1979)

K. Eichner: 'Die Produktionsmethoden der stadtrömischen Sarkophagfabrik', *Jb. Ant. & Christ.*, xxiv (1981), pp. 85–113

'Les Sarcophages d'Aquitaine', *Ant. Tardive*, i (1993)

T. ZOLLT

3. WOOD. Few examples of Byzantine sculpture in wood have survived from before the 14th century, although its use can be deduced from textual sources and, less equivocally, from areas associated with or formerly part of the empire, including Italy, Egypt (*see* COPTIC ART, §V, 5), Russia and Serbia. Carved wood was used both in architectural contexts and for icons, sculpture, book covers, domestic and liturgical furniture and coffins. The application of dendrochronology and carbon-14 dating to timbers and smaller objects has provided information about the supply and uses of different woods and helped to date particular buildings. The radiocarbon dating of the wooden beams in the west gallery of Hagia Sophia in Istanbul, for example, has shown that, while they are part of the original construction of 532–5, their carved casings of interlacing circles enclosing rosettes, crosses and palmettes were added in the late 8th century or early 9th. Dendrochronological analysis of the tie beam system in the church of Hagia Eirene in Constantinople supports the assumption from archaeological and historical argument that the south nave arcade was a secondary insertion, probably after the earthquake of 740. The early 14th-century church of the Hagioi Apostoloi in Thessaloniki can be dated by analysis of its oak tie beams and assigned to a single construction phase, not several as previously thought.

(i) Architectural. (ii) Other.

(i) Architectural. In architectural contexts wood was used mainly for tie beams, portal doors and sanctuary screens.

(a) Tie beams. Among the most impressive examples of carved woodwork in architectural contexts are the tie-beam roof casings over the nave of the church (548–65) of St Catherine's Monastery at Sinai. Seven are carved with *rinceaux* alone, while the remaining six have a central wreath cross flanked by friezes of animals, birds and plants, divided according to their land or water habitat and banded with ornamental panels. These representations have been interpreted as an allegory of the Messianic paradise of peace on earth (Isaiah 35; Drewer, 1971) or as a literal depiction of the divisions of the Creation (Maguire).

(b) Portal doors. The pair of cypress-wood door-leaves (*c.* 5.5×2.0 m) at the western entrance of S Sabina in Rome (*c.* 430) originally comprised 28 relief panels displaying Old and New Testament scenes, the original arrangement of which remains speculative. Of these 18 survive, out of order, framed by restored carved vine borders. Scenes of Elijah, Habakkuk, Moses, the Hebrews and Israelites are matched by those of the *Life of Christ* and others; they have been compared with carved ivory panels of the late 4th century–early 5th, probably from Rome (e.g. Brescia, Mus Civ. Cristiano; Munich, Bayer. Nmus.). The panels on the inside of the doors are completely aniconic. The cypress-wood narthex doors of the church of St Catherine's Monastery, Sinai, are datable to the 6th century. Alternating rectangular and square panels are carved with animal and foliage designs. Also of the 6th century are the upper and middle panels of the doors from the Coptic church of St Barbara in Old Cairo (Cairo, Coptic Mus.; *see* COPTIC ART, fig. 8).

The two-leaved cedar-wood door of the Jacobite monastery church of Mar Elyan, near Al Qaryatayn, Syria, has been dated to the 7th century by comparison with Umayyad carving in wood and stucco. Measuring 1.77×0.99 m, it originally comprised two leaves of ten panels, alternately square and rectangular, six of which are preserved, one only partially. Framed with carved foliage bands, most of the panels contain a wide variety of vegetal designs. The right central panel, however, is carved with a lion; opposite, on the left leaf, was a hare (Berlin, Schloss Charlottenburg).

Wooden doors dating to the 12th century include those of the *parekklesion* (*c.* 1090) of the monastery of St John

Chrysostomos at Koutsoventis, Cyprus, which display panels of cross and foliage motifs. Two composite figural panels were added to the cypress-wood narthex doors at the church of St Catherine's Monastery, Sinai, which show the *Transfiguration* on the left leaf, as in the church's apse mosaic, and the *Annunciation to Zacharias, Moses Receiving the Tables of the Law* and the *Sacrifice of Isaac* on the right leaf. The surrounding polygonal design of interlocking pieces of wood is similar to both Christian and Islamic wood relief in Egypt of the later 12th century.

The wooden doors from the west portal of the monastery church of the Olympiotissa at Elasson, near Larissa in Greece, comprise a pair of leaves with three main rectangular panels each, framed with geometric and plait design strip-panels. The panels are inlaid with thin strips of bone and darker wood for polychromy; circular and octagonal cartouches contain geometric motifs, stylized foliage and birds. An inscription at the top is legible as either 1296 or 1305. The narthex door (probably 14th century; destr.) of St Nicholas of the Hospital (Bolnički) at Ohrid comprised 23 reliefs arranged into six horizontal registers, the whole with a frame of carved bosses. The central panels of the four main registers displayed affronted equestrian military saints (one at bottom left later replaced by a flute-playing centaur) flanked, in the third register down, by animals and birds, including peacocks. The bottom register was the most diverse, adding other figures and animals, including scenes from the fable of *the Fox and the Cock*. The reliefs compare with stone sculpture on the façades of contemporary Serbian churches (*see* SERBIA, §§II, and IV, 1). The overlap of sacred and profane subjects is given coherence by the protective role shown by the military saints and is paralleled by woodwork in the Eastern Christian world.

(c) Sanctuary screens. The sanctuary screens of the main sanctuary and choir of the church of the Virgin (al-'Adra) at the monastery of the Syrians (es-Suriani) in the Wadi Natrun (Egypt) are closed with doors of ebony with ivory inlay. Dated by Syriac inscriptions to 913–14 and 926–7 respectively, they each comprise two pairs of folding leaves set with rectangular panels. The sanctuary doors depict Christ Emmanuel and the Virgin, flanked by Fathers of the Coptic and Syrian Churches. The choir doors show the *Virgin and Christ Trampling on a Lion and a Dragon* flanked by paradisiac trees. Below are panels with geometric motifs and foliate crosses. The images of the Virgin and saints interceding with Christ are directly related to the iconography of Byzantine sanctuary screens (iconostases), and their content and technique have been compared with the Byzantine bronze doors of Amalfi Cathedral (*c.* 1060; Frazer). Wooden sanctuary screens must have been a common feature of Middle Byzantine churches and, in fully closing off the choir and sanctuary, they warn against the assumption that the 'opaque' sanctuary screen did not develop until the 14th century.

The feasts of the Church are also commonly depicted on 13th-century screens. The *Annunciation, Visitation, Baptism* and *Entry into Jerusalem* were among those shown on the north sanctuary doors (destr.) of the church of the Melkite Monastery of St George in Old Cairo. Comparable feasts are found on wooden panels on the sanctuary screen

doors of the Coptic church of St Sergius in Old Cairo. Here the *Nativity* is accompanied by panels of equestrian saints and angels holding orbs. Paired feast scenes that form a Salvation cycle, spanning the *Baptism* to the *Resurrection*, decorate the cedar panels (probably 1301–2; London, BM) from the baptistery screen of the Hanging Church (al-Mu'allaqa), Old Cairo. The panels may be contemporary with the sanctuary screen of the neighbouring chapel of St Takla Hamanout, dated by a Byzantine imperial refurbishment of 1301–2. This screen comprises polygonal pieces of wood, inlaid with ivory or bone, and its doors bear Arabic inscriptions from the Psalms. The icons of the *Annunciation* and *Nativity* at the top of the screen are of Byzantine workmanship; they complement the screen's aniconic decoration.

Two early 14th-century sanctuary screen doors from Mt Athos survive with ivory or bone inlay. One (see fig. 55) is now in the Protaton Church of Karyes, although its original location is unknown. It comprises two leaves, each of four major sections and rounded at the top. The three upper pairs each housed an ivory relief, but only that

55. Wood and ivory sanctuary screen doors, 1.36×0.75 m, early 14th century, Protaton Church, Karyes, Mt Athos

of St John Chrysostomos is preserved. Frames of rosettes, pine-cones and leaves are also preserved. At the base of the doors, the major panels are square, cut with crosses carved with pine-cones. In one remains part of a bird, perhaps a peacock, bending over a smaller one; in another a stylized wing motif. Framing the whole are thin strands of ivory inlay weaving circles into which pierced diamond shapes are set into fours.

The other sanctuary door is in the altar of the katholikon at Chilandar Monastery (1303), Mt Athos. It is constructed of three pairs of symmetrically placed walnut panels decorated with bone inlay set in geometric patterns, some of which were originally filled with coloured paste. All the panels are framed with a three-stranded strip: the two outer strands contain obliquely placed bone squares, while the central, wider strand has a more complicated decoration of crosses within circles. Technically the doors are superior to 16th- and 17th-century incrustation work, in which the incrustation is thinner and applied to the wood panelling like a veneer.

The architraves of sanctuary screens could also be richly carved, as for example the architrave in the church of the Virgin (1369) at Mali Grad by Great Lake Prespa (Macedonia), which has small balustrades and geometric designs. Another example (destr. 1940), originally in the monastery church of the Virgin at Peć, was carved with animals, geometric motifs and rosettes, and formed the only wooden element of an otherwise marble screen.

Parts of several tall, closed sanctuary screens are preserved from Muscovite and other Russian schools of the 15th and 16th centuries, with rows of icons and painted royal doors. One such example is the screen (1405; 12×10 m) painted by Theophanes the Greek and Andrey Rublyov for the cathedral of the Annunciation in the Moscow Kremlin. Additional rows of icons were added in the 16th and 17th centuries, and silver and bronze casings, colonnettes and doors in the 19th. Elaborately carved sanctuary screens of the 17th and 18th centuries have also survived from several Cypriot churches (e.g Nicosia, Flk A. Mus). (*See also* SCREEN (i), §2.)

(ii) Other. Carved wooden icons served the same purpose as the more conventional painted icons (*see* §VI, 1 below), and were also sometimes revetted, painted or gilded. The two small wooden and silver revetted icons (*c.* 1366) in the monastery treasury at Chilandar, Mt Athos, which were given by Metropolitan Theodore of Ser (now Serres, Greece) to Despot John Uglješa, depict the *Virgin and Child Enthroned with Apostles* in medallions surrounded by vine scrolls, and the *Hospitality of Abraham*. Crude portable icons of the 14th and 15th centuries carved with images of *Christ* and the *Passion* (Belgrade, N. Mus.), excavated at the church of St Nicholas, Novo Brdo, are probably mass-produced versions of higher-quality icons. A 14th-century wooden icon (350×300 mm; Belgrade, N. Mus.), with *SS Nicholas and George* on either side and inscribed in Serbian, was found at Kruševac.

Although Byzantine wooden sculpture has been compared with Byzantine marble reliefs, its development owes as much to Western influences derived during the Crusader period of East–West contact. One such piece is a 13th-century painted sculpture of *St George* from Kastoria (see

56. Wood relief-carving of *St George*, 1.07×0.72 m, from Kastoria, 13th century (Athens, Byzantine Museum)

fig. 56), which shows him at prayer. He wears military uniform, and his shield bears a chequered armorial design in red and blue. The saint's name is inscribed in gold, and the frame around has scenes of his life and martyrdom. The same saint is depicted in a frontally facing two-thirds statue (h. 2.9 m) that occupies a niche in the south wall of the church of Hagios Georgios at Gallista, near Kastoria. This sculpture also retains traces of red and blue paint and was probably made locally when the church was founded in 1286–7. Another 13th-century example is the carved, gessoed and painted icon of the *Life of St George* (1.07×0.82 m; Kiev, Mus. Ukrain. A.), which shows the central full-length figure of the saint, his name inscribed in Greek; it too is framed by scenes of his life and martyrdom.

Wood was also used for crosses, book covers, pulpits, stalls and thrones. The cover of a Psalter (13th century; 130×105 mm; Athos, St Dionysiou Monastery, Cod. 33) depicts scenes of the *Life of Christ* carved in small partitions like ivory-carving. Byzantine wooden furniture included tables, stools, chairs, chests and lecterns, such as an early 15th-century hexagonal lectern of beech-wood at the monastery of Dečani (Serbia), which is decorated with inlay and turned columns of cherry-wood. Similar pieces of furniture are depicted in contemporary Serbian wall paintings; surviving examples include choir benches from Split and a throne at Rila Monastery. Domestic furniture was probably similar in appearance.

The restored late 14th-century sarcophagus of King Stephen Uroš IV Dušan (reg 1331–55) can be found in the monastery church of Dečani. Measuring 1.93× 0.63×0.43 m, it has a cruck-shaped lid, and the lower front and south sides are decorated with carvings of animal and floral motifs. The central motif on the front is a lioness, lion and two panthers, whose tails combine with the interlace. The openwork carving has a leather backing and is painted red, green, gold and white; fragments of the silver repoussé bordering the carved fields also survive.

BIBLIOGRAPHY

G. A. Soteriou: 'La Sculpture sur bois dans l'art byzantin', *Art* (1930), ii of *Mélanges Charles Diehl* (Paris, 1930), pp. 171–80

R. Delbrueck: 'Notes on the Wooden Doors of Sta Sabina', *A. Bull.*, xxxiv (1952), pp. 139–43

H. Stern: 'Quelques oeuvres sculptées en bois, os et ivoire de style omeyyade', *A. Orient.*, i (1954), pp. 119–31

V. Han: [Household furniture on Serbian medieval frescoes], *Recl Trav.: Muz. Primenjene Umětnosti*, i (1955), pp. 7–52

——: 'Dveri iz Hilandara ukrašene intarzijom od kosti' [Doors from Chilandari decorated with bone inlay], *Recl Trav.: Muz. Primenjene Umětnosti*, ii (1956), pp. 5–25

S. Pelekanides: 'Byzantinon bemothuron ex Aghiou Orous' [Byzantine altar throne from Mt Athos], *Archaiol. Ephimeris* (1957), pp. 50–65

S. Tsuji: 'Les Portes de Sainte-Sabine: Particularités de l'iconographie de l'Ascension', *Cah. Archéol.*, xii (1962), pp. 13–28

M. Čorović-Ljubinković: *Srednjevekovni duvorez u istočnim oblastima Jugoslavije* [Wooden sculpture of the Middle Ages in the eastern regions of Yugoslavia] (Belgrade, 1965) [Fr. summary]

C. D. Sheppard: 'A Radiocarbon Date for the Wooden Tie Beams in the West Gallery of St Sophia', *Dumbarton Oaks Pap.*, xix (1965), pp. 237–40

P. Huber: *Athos: Leben, Glaube, Kunst* (Zurich, 1969)

V. Han: 'Sredn'ovekovin primerak nameštaja iz manastira Dečana' [A medieval piece of furniture from Dečani Monastery], *Recl Trav.: Muz. Primenjene Umětnosti*, xiv (1970), pp. 31–41

L. J. Drewer: *The Carved Wooden Beams of the Church of Justinian, Monastery of St Catherine, Mt Sinai* (diss., Ann Arbor, U. Michigan, 1971)

M. E. Frazer: 'Church Doors and the Gates of Paradise: Byzantine Bronze Doors in Italy', *Dumbarton Oaks Pap.*, xxvii (1973), pp. 145–62

P. I. Kuniholm and C. L. Striker: 'The Tie-beam System in the Nave Arcade of St Eirene: Structure and Dendrochronology', *Die Irenenkirche in Istanbul: Untersuchungen zur Architektur*, ed. U. Peschlow (Tübingen, 1977)

B. Radojkovic: *Sitna plastika u staroj srpskoj umetnosti/Les Objets sculptés d'art mineur en Serbie ancienne* (Belgrade, 1977)

D. Kreidl: 'Zur Frage der Bewertbarkeit der Bildträger innerhalb der Ikonenmalerei', *Jb. Österreich. Byz.*, xxviii (1979), pp. 229–40

J. Galey: *Sinai and the Monastery of St Catherine* (New York, 1980), pp. 49–64

L. Drewer: 'Fisherman and Fish Pond: From the Sea of Sin to the Living Waters', *A. Bull.*, lxiii (1981), pp. 533–47

——: 'Leviathan, Behemoth and Ziz: A Christian Adaptation', *J. Warb. & Court. Inst.*, xliv (1981), pp. 148–56

N. Labrèque-Pervouchine: *L'Iconostase: Une Evolution historique en Russie* (Montreal, 1982)

A. Bank: *Byzantine Art in the Collections of Soviet Museums* (Leningrad, 1985)

V. H. Elbern: 'Un gruppo di "Porta Regia" di iconostasi cipriote del settecento', *Corsi Cult. A. Ravenn. & Biz.*, xxxii (1985), pp. 65–72

C. Bouras: 'The Olympiotissa Woodcarved Doors', *The 17th International Byzantine Congress, 1986: Abstracts of Short Papers* (Washington, DC, 1986), p. 41

L.-A. Hunt: 'Iconic and Aniconic: Unknown Thirteenth and Fourteenth Century Byzantine Icons from Cairo in their Woodwork Settings', *Poikilia Byz.*, vi/2 (1987), pp. 33–48

H. Maguire: *Earth and Ocean: The Terrestrial World in Early Byzantine Art* (University Park, PA, and London, 1987), pp. 28–30

L.-A. Hunt: 'The al-Mu'allaqa Doors Reconstructed: An Early Fourteenth-century Sanctuary Screen from Old Cairo', *Gesta*, xxviii (1989), pp. 61–77

LUCY-ANNE HUNT

V. Manuscripts.

This section concentrates on manuscript illustration; for the materials, techniques and conservation of manuscripts *see* MANUSCRIPT, §III, 3 and 4. Although illustrated manuscripts are often treated together, irrespective of the language of the texts they contain (principally Latin, Greek or Syriac), there are sound reasons for considering them within the differing geopolitical and socio-religious contexts for which they were made.

1. Latin. 2. Greek. 3. Syriac.

1. LATIN. The Latin material of the 4th century to the early 7th comprises biblical and Classical texts, with some other material. Three manuscripts provide the prime evidence for the early illustration of the Latin Bible (*see* BIBLE, §I, 1). The earliest (Berlin, Dt. Staatsbib., Cod. theol. lat., fol. 485) is thought to have been produced in Rome in the second quarter of the 5th century, and it can be related in general terms to the Vatican Virgil (see below) and the mosaics (432–40) of S Maria Maggiore. Its six surviving leaves, four with illustrations, were preserved in poor condition when they were used to strengthen the binding of the parish accounts of Quedlinburg in 1618. They contain parts of the four Old Testament books of Kings (1–2 Samuel, 1–2 Kings), and because they were once erroneously thought to preserve the pre-Jerome 'Itala' version of the text (in fact the *Vetus latina*), the manuscript is generally referred to as the Quedlinburg Itala. Each page is filled with illustrations subdivided into rectangular panels and interspersed with the text. Multi-figural narrative scenes are set against backgrounds fully painted in an illusionistic style. An intriguing feature of the manuscript is the presence in each scene of lengthy instructions in a cursive hand, which have become visible beneath the paint surface due to its poor condition. They are formulated as instructions to the artist and imply that a complex and lengthy Kings cycle was specially created for this book.

The illustrations to the ST AUGUSTINE GOSPELS (?late 6th century; Cambridge, Corpus Christi Coll. Lib., MS. 286) are organized in a completely different way. Before St Luke's Gospel (but presumably originally before each of the four Gospels) is a single leaf (fol. 129). On its *recto* are 12 small framed scenes illustrating the *Life of Christ* from the *Entry to Jerusalem* until *Christ Carrying the Cross*. On the *verso*, facing the start of the Gospel, is *St Luke* in the guise of a seated philosopher with his symbol of the calf above (see fig. 57), and on either side a further 12 scenes of the *Life of Christ* from the *Annunciation* until *Zacchaeus in the Fig Tree*, all framed within an architectural setting. The artist worked in a linear style, employing only a small range of pigments, thinly applied. Tradition associates the book with the mission from Rome of St Augustine in 597 to convert the English, and this seems possible. The manuscript remained at Canterbury until the Dissolution of the Monasteries (1535–40) and seems to have been consulted by Insular and Romanesque artists.

The third biblical manuscript, the Ashburnham Pentateuch (? early 7th century; Paris, Bib. N., MS. nuov. acq. lat. 2334), is different again. In addition to a frontispiece, it contains 18 miniatures out of an estimated original total

57. Latin manuscript miniature, *St Luke*, *c.* 210×165 mm, from the St Augustine Gospels, ?late 6th century (Cambridge, Corpus Christi College Library, MS. 286, fol. 129*v*)

of 69, which are distributed irregularly through the first four books of the Old Testament. No part of Deuteronomy has survived, but it was presumably also illustrated. Most of the illustrations occupy a full page and are complex compositions, often subdivided into separate scenes in roughly horizontal registers. There are numerous lengthy inscriptions within the images, and there is a bold use of saturated pigments. The style is thought to be derivative of Italian 6th-century work, and a possible origin in 7th-century North Africa or Spain has been proposed. The manuscript was at Tours in the Middle Ages, and it was consulted for the frontispiece cycles of Carolingian Bibles and in the late 11th century for the decoration of the local church of St Julien.

The principal direct evidence for the illustration of the Latin literary 'classics' is provided by two manuscripts of Virgil. Other texts, such as an illustrated selection of *Comedies* of Terence (*see* TERENCE), or the *Psychomachia* of Prudentius (*d* 410), both well known through Carolingian (e.g. 9th century; Rome, Vatican, Bib. Apostolica, MS. lat. 3868) and later copies, may also be derived from exemplars of this period. The Vatican Virgil and the Roman Virgil (Rome, Vatican, Bib. Apostolica, MSS lat. 3225 and 3867 respectively) provide a fascinating contrast. The former is generally dated, like the Quedlinburg Itala, to the second quarter of the 5th century, the latter to some two or three generations later, and both are thought to have been made in Rome. The Vatican Virgil is painted in a convincing illusionistic style; but in the Roman Virgil proportion, depth, modelling, gesture and colour are all modified or schematized. Even when, as in the *Georgics*, the textual contents of the two manuscripts are precisely comparable, their illustrations are completely unrelated. Both manuscripts were in France in the Middle Ages. The Vatican Virgil was at Tours, where, like the Ashburnham Pentateuch, it was known to the artists of the Carolingian Bibles. The Roman Virgil was at Saint-Denis Abbey until the 15th century, but appears to have been little consulted.

A third category that merits brief consideration comprises a small number of disparate cases which together raise the question of the range of manuscript types that were illustrated in the 4th to the 7th century. The most intriguing is the richly illustrated Calendar or Chronograph of the year 354 (Calendar of Filocalus), known principally through a copy by the 17th-century French antiquarian Nicholas-Claude Fabri de Peiresc (Rome, Vatican, Bib. Apostolica, MS. Barb. lat. 2154; *see* ICONOGRAPHY AND ICONOLOGY, fig. 2) and thought to be based on a Carolingian intermediary. The content of the Roman calendar is pagan, although its dedication is Christian. To some extent, all medieval calendar illustrations with their interest in Labours of the Months, zodiac signs and personifications, can be seen to have developed from such origins (*see* CALENDAR). Less obviously significant for later centuries were such texts as the *Corpus agrimensorum* and *Notitia dignitatum*. The former, a land-surveying treatise, survives in an early 6th-century manuscript from northern Italy (Wolfenbüttel, Herzog August Bib., Cod. Guelf. 36. 23A, 'Codex Arcerianus A'). In addition to geometric diagrams and schematic views of town and countryside it contains a fine full-page drawing of a seated author (fol. 67*v*). The *Notitia dignitatum*, a register of late Roman military and civil officials, with about 100 full-page illustrations of their insignia, is known only through medieval (Codex Spirensis; Speyer Cathedral) and post-medieval (Munich, Bayer. Staatsbib., Clm. 10291; Oxford, Bodleian Lib., Canonici Miscell. 378) copies of a now lost Carolingian intermediary (see the Calendar of 354 above). Its images were remarkably varied in compositional terms, including ships, chariots, town- and landscapes, and figures in medallion, bust or full-length. It is thought to be based on an original made around 400.

In considering all this material, a balance has to be struck between awareness of the strict limitations and sometimes contradictory implications of the evidence that has survived (as in the lack of connection between the two Virgil manuscripts), and the temptation to exploit the paucity and variety of evidence to build wide-ranging hypotheses about the origins, methods and significance of book illustration in the 4th to the 7th century. Geyer's sober arguments for the piecemeal development of illustration (notably in the 5th century) are in stark contrast to the exuberant theories of Weitzmann and provide a sounder base for future investigations.

BIBLIOGRAPHY

O. von Gebhardt: *The Miniatures of the Ashburnham Pentateuch* (London, 1883)

R. Stettiner: *Die illustrierten Prudentiushandschriften*, 2 vols (Berlin, 1895–1905)

H. Woodruff: *The Illustrated Manuscripts of Prudentius* (Cambridge, MA, 1930)

H. Degering and A. Boeckler: *Die Quedlinburger Italafragmente* (Berlin, 1932)

H. Stern: *Le Calendrier de 354* (Paris, 1953)

F. Wormald: *The Miniatures in the Gospels of St Augustine* (Cambridge, 1954)

Corpus Agrimensorum Romanorum: Codex Arcerianus A der Herzog-August-Bibliothek zu Wolfenbüttel (Cod. Guelf. 36.23A), facs. ed. H. Butzmann (Leiden, 1970)

B. Narkiss: 'Reconstruction of Some of the Original Quires of the Ashburnham Pentateuch', *Cah. Archéol.*, xxii (1972), pp. 19–38

E. Rosenthal: *The Illuminations of the Vergilius Romanus* (Zurich, 1972)

K. Weitzmann: *Late Antique and Early Christian Book Illumination* (London, 1977)

Vergilius Vaticanus: Vollständige Faksimile-Ausgabe im Originalformat des Codex Vaticanus Latinus 3225, Codices selecti lxxi; commentary by D. Wright (Graz, 1980–84)

P. Berger: *The Insignia of the Notitia Dignitatum*, Outstanding Dissertations in the Fine Arts (New York, 1981)

T. B. Stevenson: *Miniature Decoration in the Vatican Vergil* (Tübingen, 1983)

I. Levin: *The Quedlinburg Itala* (Leiden, 1985)

C. Bertelli and others, eds: *Vergilius Romanus: Kommentarband zur Faksimileausgabe*, 2 vols (Zurich, 1985–6)

F. Rickert: *Studien zum Ashburnham Pentateuch (Paris, Bibl. Nat. NAL 2334)* (Bonn, 1986)

A. Geyer: *Die Genese narrativer Buchillustration* (Frankfurt am Main, 1989)

D. Wright: *Codicological Notes on the Vergilius Romanus (Vat. lat. 3867)*, Studi e Testi, cccxlv (Rome, 1992)

——: *The Vatican Vergil: A Masterpiece of Late Antique Art* (Berkeley, 1993)

2. GREEK. This subsection considers the historical context for the production of Greek manuscripts (*see* §(i) below) before going on to deal with the material by types as defined by the textual content of the books in question. The principal focus throughout is on illustration, although brief consideration is given to ornamental decoration. Since many other approaches to the material are possible, it may be helpful to explain the chosen method. When a Byzantine ordered or made a new illustrated manuscript, perhaps a Psalter, he or she would have seen that book in terms of a tradition reaching back over many centuries, even to earliest Christian times. Given the sacred content and religious function of the text of such books, strict adherence to precedent is easily understood, but modern scholars must be wary of falling into a trap laid by the Byzantines in presuming the existence of equally long-lived, strictly maintained, pictorial traditions. The surviving evidence suggests a rather different, and much more complex, pattern of production. It is characterized by highly variable amalgam of elements derived from earlier sources, together with iconographic and visual innovation carefully disguised as tradition. This is most readily perceived when similar types of book are considered from across a broad span of time.

(i) Introduction. (ii) Complete Bibles. (iii) New Testament. (iv) Old Testament. (v) Other religious texts. (vi) Classical texts. (vii) Ornamental decoration.

(i) Introduction. The history of Byzantine manuscript illustration may be separated either side of the iconoclastic controversy (726–843; *see* ICONOCLASM), a lengthy religious dispute that coincided with various geopolitical disasters. Material from the pre-iconoclast or Early Christian period is sparse. Whether this is entirely the result of accidents of survival or due in considerable part to a relatively limited production of illustrated manuscripts in those early centuries, as seems more probable, cannot be established empirically. Carefully preserved through the

Middle Ages, these books remain of exceptional significance because of the evidence they provide for the early stages of one of the most remarkable achievements of Western culture, the illustrated book (*see* BOOK ILLUSTRATION, §I).

The main body of Byzantine material, comprising some thousands of manuscripts (more precise figures have not been established), is post-iconoclast. It is usually further subdivided into middle and late (or Palaiologan) periods by the occupation of Constantinople during the Latin empire (1204–61), although manuscript production was not entirely interrupted at that time.

The unifying thread in the study of Byzantine manuscript illustration is provided by the use of Greek for the accompanying text, and the vast majority of the material is broadly religious and specifically biblical. Largely for religious reasons, areas that bordered or at some point fell within the Byzantine empire often owe much in their manuscript illustration to a knowledge of Byzantine style and iconography. This is particularly true of the Slavonic (*see* SERBIA, §III, 1(iii); BULGARIA, §III, 2(iii); UKRAINE, §III, 1(iii); RUSSIA, §IV, 1), Georgian (*see* GEORGIA, §IV, 1(ii)), Armenian (*see* ARMENIA, §III, 1(ii)), Syriac (*see* §3 below), Coptic (*see* COPTIC ART, §IV, 3) and Crusader (*see* JERUSALEM, LATIN KINGDOM OF) worlds. While illustrated Byzantine manuscripts are sometimes also adduced by modern commentators as carriers of the waves of Byzantine influence thought to be highly significant in the history of the art of the Latin West, there is little direct evidence for this, and linguistic as well as religious considerations weaken the hypothesis.

The Byzantine world, even of the 14th and 15th centuries, has not preserved anything resembling the wealth of guild documents, royal account books, tax records and artist's guides that are available in the West. Nor are there many lengthy and informative scribal colophons characteristic of Armenian manuscripts. As a result, questions concerning the producers and users of books, institutional and private libraries, costs of materials and labour, an artist's training and breadth of experience, or almost any issue to which the manuscripts themselves do not provide an answer, can only be addressed haphazardly.

Doubtless there were many changes between the 4th and 15th centuries, but over all this time most of the individuals and institutions involved in the production of Byzantine books remained anonymous. Nevertheless, a pattern of production based on monastic scriptoria, which included artists, and lay professional workshops, probably containing both artists and scribes, can generally be presumed. Two cases exemplify the position.

The St John Stoudios Monastery in Constantinople (*see* ISTANBUL, §III, 6) seems to have been an important centre between the 9th and 11th centuries in the dissemination of minuscule script, notably under the direction of the iconophile theologian and abbot THEODORE OF STOUDIOS, who drew up rules for the operation of the scriptorium. Among the most remarkable achievements of Byzantine manuscripts are the Psalters with marginal illustrations (e.g. the CHLUDOV PSALTER, Moscow, Hist. Mus. MS. D. 29) that may have been a particular phenomenon of the monastery, to which several other important illustrated books of the second half of the 11th century have also been plausibly attributed. These would have been made for internal consumption, on commission or for presentation outside the monastery.

Among the few artists with a distinct personal style is the Kokkinobaphos Master, so-called after two illustrated copies of *Homilies on the Virgin* composed by the 12th-century monk James of Kokkinobaphos (Paris, Bib. N., MS. gr. 1208; Rome, Vatican, Bib. Apostolica, MS. Vat. gr. 1162; see fig. 58). This artist also worked on a number of other manuscripts connected with members of the family of Emperor John II Komnenos, probably in Constantinople. As was commonplace among Byzantine illuminators, whenever possible the Kokkinobaphos Master produced full-page miniatures on separate sheets or gatherings of parchment, unruled by the scribes, and intended to be bound into a book on its completion. On occasions, as in the production of two illustrated Octateuchs (Istanbul, Topkapı Pal. Lib., Cod. gr. 8; İzmir, Gr. Evangel. Sch., A/1 (untraced); *see* §(iv)(b) below), the master can be observed collaborating with assistants, who sought to imitate his style with varying degrees of success. None of the manuscripts with which he was involved seems to have been intended for a monastic setting.

Despite the vast chronological and geographical extent of the Byzantine empire, the precise identification of local or even regional stylistic traits has proved difficult. Only when a scribal colophon specifies where a manuscript was made is it safe to propose a provenance. Southern Italy, Palestine and Cyprus, for example, were at various times distinctive centres of production, as shown by colophons,

but the attribution of books of high quality, without colophons, to these or other areas remains controversial. Scholars often fall back on the simplistic notion that low-quality workmanship probably means provincial manufacture, whereas high quality ought to point to an origin in Constantinople. The true position must have been more complex.

At all times, the producers and patrons of illustrated Byzantine manuscripts put a high premium on the quality of materials and craftsmanship. It is surprising, therefore, that in one vital aspect the artists' technique was often sadly deficient: many failed to use a binding medium capable of holding the pigments permanently to the highly polished (or gilded) parchment surfaces they chose to work on. Although there were exceptions, such as the Kokkinobaphos Master, it is conspicuous that severe flaking of the paint surface has affected many books, from the finest imperial volumes, such as in the PARIS GREGORY, to more modest works. Some manuscripts were restored in Byzantine times, suggesting that the damage is not the result of recent neglect or abuse; nevertheless the conservation problems they present are daunting.

A fortuitous result of the loss of pigment is that it becomes possible to observe the preliminary stages of a miniature. The result is startling: in many cases there is no underdrawing of any sort, or perhaps a few rapid strokes establish the outline of a figure or setting. The usual procedure of the Byzantine illustrator, therefore, must have been to work with pigments directly on to the parchment. How this technique was learnt is a fundamental question that awaits investigation.

58. Manuscript miniatures by the Kokkinobaphos Master: *Adam, Eve, Cain and Abel* and *Paradise*, from James of Kokkinobaphos: *Homilies on the Virgin*, 230×165 mm, 12th century (Paris, Bibliothèque Nationale, MS. gr. 1208, fols 49v–50r)

The identification of styles and their connection with chronological periods have traditionally occupied much space in the study of Byzantine manuscript illustration. The problem is that the stylistic course, far from following a straightforward development, meanders and often turns back upon itself. The volume of surviving material in the early period is so small that an overview is not difficult to achieve, although it must take account of the significant differences to be observed between, for example, the COTTON GENESIS (London, BL, Cotton MS. Otho B. VI), VIENNA GENESIS (Vienna, Österreich. Nbib., Cod. theol. gr. 31), ROSSANO GOSPELS and Vienna Dioskurides (Vienna, Österreich. Nbib., Cod. med. gr. 1), which were probably made within a few decades of one another in the late 5th century and the 6th. The situation after the iconoclastic controversy, however, is more baffling and needs to be considered in a broad historical context.

Until c. 975 the Byzantines made significant efforts to transcribe surviving early books into the new minuscule script, which was introduced c. 800. The desire, seen at many levels, to preserve or recover pre-iconoclast material of all sorts, inevitably affected (without prescribing) the choice of painted images and the style in which artists worked. Weitzmann (e.g. 1971) has popularized the term 'Macedonian Renaissance' for the mid-10th century works in particular, with their interest in personifications and illusionistic landscape settings.

In the period from c. 975, and especially from c. 1050 until after 1200, an ornamental vocabulary of largely standardized composition was used with an emphasis on gold settings, and small-scale floral *rinceaux* of geometrical precision. Gold backgrounds became the norm in images too, and figures were elegant and idealized. Many texts seem to have received lengthy cycles of narrative illustration for the first time in this period.

On the other hand, the late 13th century and the 14th, notably from c. 1275 to c. 1325, was another period of conscious archaism among manuscript illuminators and their patrons. There seems to have been a wish to blot out the memory of the Latin empire by looking back to and imitating works of the 10th century in particular, although this interest was grafted on to the well-established norms of 11th- and 12th-century production, and did not displace them. Finally, from c. 1375 the relative poverty of the empire was such that few illuminated books seem to have been produced.

This pattern has sometimes appeared to modern scholars in terms of a series of renaissances, and has led to a higher value being placed on more classicizing works, notably those of the so-called Justinianic (6th century), Macedonian (10th century) and Palaiologan (late 13th century to 14th) renaissances. There has been a consequent undervaluing of the achievements in the major part of Byzantine illumination, which was produced in an intervening period (c. 975–after c. 1200). The Byzantines themselves had a radically different view: they always proclaimed a cultural continuity reaching back at least to the Church Fathers of the 4th century. Such changes, innovations and developments as occurred in their society often went unremarked, or were masked by contemporary sources in a variety of ways. The resulting situation is often deceptive. The material does not offer up its secrets easily.

BIBLIOGRAPHY

GENERAL WORKS AND COLLECTED STUDIES

N. Kondakov: *Histoire de l'art byzantin considéré principalement dans les miniatures*, 2 vols (Paris, 1886–91)

J. Ebersolt: *La Miniature byzantine* (Paris, 1926)

K. Weitzmann: *Die byzantinische Buchmalerei des 9. und 10. Jahrhunderts* (Berlin, 1935)

——: *Illustrations in Roll and Codex* (Princeton, 1947)

——: *Ancient Book Illumination* (Cambridge, MA, 1959)

N. Eleopoulos: *I bibliothiki kai to bibliographikon ergastirion tis monis ton Stoudiou* [The library and scriptorium of the Stoudios Monastery] (Athens, 1967)

V. Lazarev: *Storia della pittura bizantina* (Turin, 1967)

H. Belting: *Das illuminierte Buch in der spätbyzantinischen Gesellschaft* (Heidelberg, 1970)

Byzantine Books and Bookmen: Dumbarton Oaks Colloquium: Washington, DC, 1971

K. Weitzmann: *Studies in Classical and Byzantine Manuscript Illumination*, ed. H. L. Kessler (Chicago, 1971)

A. Grabar: *Les Manuscrits grecs enluminés de provenance italienne (IXe–XIe siècles)* (Paris, 1972)

K. Weitzmann and others: *The Place of Book Illumination in Byzantine Art* (Princeton, 1973)

I. Spatharakis: *The Portrait in Byzantine Illuminated Manuscripts* (Leiden, 1976)

H. Buchthal and H. Belting: *Patronage in Thirteenth-century Constantinople: An Atelier of Late Byzantine Book Illumination and Calligraphy* (Washington, DC, 1978)

K. Weitzmann: *Byzantine Liturgical Psalters and Gospels* (London, 1980)

I. Spatharakis: *Corpus of Dated Illuminated Greek Manuscripts to the Year 1453*, 2 vols (Leiden, 1981)

H. Buchthal: *Art of the Mediterranean World, A.D. 100–1400* (Washington, DC, 1983)

——: 'Studies in Byzantine Illumination of the Thirteenth Century', *Jb. Berlin. Mus.*, xxv (1983), pp. 27–102

A. Carr: *Byzantine Illumination, 1150–1250* (Chicago, 1987)

G. Galavaris: *Byzantine Illuminated Manuscripts* (1995), x of *Greek Art* (Athens, 1994–6)

COLLECTIONS

H. Bordier: *Description des peintures et autres ornements contenus dans les manuscrits grecs de la Bibliothèque Nationale* (Paris, 1883)

H. Omont: *Miniatures des plus anciens manuscrits grecs de la Bibliothèque Nationale du VIe au XIVe siècle* (Paris, 1929)

W. Hatch: *Greek and Syrian Miniatures in Jerusalem* (Cambridge, MA, 1931)

P. Buberl and H. Gerstinger: *Die byzantinischen Handschriften*, 2 vols (Leipzig, 1937–8)

Oi thisauroi tou Agiou Orous: Eikonographimena xeirographa [The treasures of Mount Athos: illuminated manuscripts], 4 vols (Athens, 1973–91)

V. Likhachova: *Byzantinskaya Miniatura / Byzantine Miniature* (Moscow, 1977)

I. Hutter: *Corpus der byzantinischen Miniaturenhandschriften*, i–iii, *Oxford, Bodleian Library* (Stuttgart, 1977–82); iv, *Oxford, Christ Church* (Stuttgart, 1993)

I. Furlan: *Codici greci illustrati della Biblioteca Marciana*, 4 vols (Padua, 1978–81)

A. Marava-Chatzinicolaou and C. Toufexi-Paschou: *Catalogue of the Illuminated Byzantine Manuscripts of the National Library of Greece*, 2 vols (Athens, 1978–85)

K. Weitzmann and G. Galavaris: *The Monastery of Saint Catherine at Mount Sinai: The Illuminated Greek Manuscripts* (Princeton, 1990–)

EXHIBITION CATALOGUES

Byzance et la France médiévale (exh. cat., Paris, Bib. N., 1958)

Byzantine Art: A European Art (exh. cat., Athens, Zappeion, 1964)

Illuminated Greek Manuscripts from American Collections (exh. cat., ed. G. Vikan; Princeton U., NJ, A. Mus., 1973)

Byzanz und das Abendland (exh. cat., ed. O. Mazal; Vienna, Österreich. Nbib., 1981)

(ii) Complete Bibles. The most important text in the Byzantine world was the Bible, but there is a conspicuous lack of illustrated complete Bibles. Although early Greek Bibles, such as the Codex Sinaiticus (late 4th century;

London, BL, Add. MS. 43725), lack any illustration, a 6th- or 7th-century Bible in Syriac (Paris, Bib. N., MS. syr. 341; *see* §3 below), which has framed miniatures at the beginning of each book, implies that a similar formula may have been followed on occasions in Byzantium before the iconoclastic controversy.

The earliest extant example of an illustrated complete Bible is the LEO BIBLE (Rome, Vatican, Bib. Apostolica, MS. Vat. reg. gr. 1), dated to the first half of the 10th century; only the first of its two volumes survives. Full-page miniatures preface most of the biblical books in a scheme that is significantly more ambitious than that in the Syriac Bible mentioned above. There is still controversy, however, over the extent to which the plan for the Leo Bible's decoration was either a 10th-century development or a reflection of now-lost, pre-iconoclast Byzantine sources.

An intriguing proposal relevant to this discussion has been put forward by Belting and Cavallo, who have reconstructed a 'Bible of Niketas' on the basis of three surviving illustrated Old Testament manuscripts covering the Major Prophets (Florence, Bib. Medicea-Laurenziana, MS. Plut. 5.9), the Minor Prophets (Turin, Bib. N. U., Cod. B.I.2) and Job and the Wisdom Books (Copenhagen, Kon. Bib., Cod. G.K.S. 6). The Florentine manuscript has a single surviving full-page miniature to Jeremiah, while the one in Turin has a prefatory bifolio with medallion busts of the 12 authors (see fig. 59). The manuscript in Copenhagen has lost a full-page miniature before Job, but has a composite image on a full page prefacing the Wisdom Books. All three manuscripts are *catena* books, that is they have an immensely lengthy marginal commentary drawn from a variety of sources. They are all works of exceptional calligraphic, ornamental and painterly quality and can be attributed to late 10th-century Constantinople and the patronage of the courtier Niketas.

A fragmentary colophon in the volume in Turin can perhaps be interpreted as implying that the book was copied from a 6th-century model, precisely dated 535. This may indicate the existence of a pre-iconoclast Bible illustrated with full-page frontispieces, made in the orbit of the court of Justinian I. Yet, while some elements of the three manuscripts' layout and appearance, such as the prefatory texts in three narrow columns, can be seen as a pastiche of early models, other aspects, such as the text itself and the ornament, must have had later sources. The precise significance of the 'Bible of Niketas' thus remains open.

Belting and Cavallo's study has drawn attention to the possibility that other manuscripts containing sections of the Bible, now dispersed, might originally have formed part of 'sets'. As a result, the existence of a late 12th-century illustrated Bible has been proposed on the basis of Old Testament manuscripts (Athens, N. Lib., MS. 44), the Psalms (Istanbul, Topkapı Pal. Lib., Cod. gr. 13), the books of Job and Wisdom (Oxford, Bodleian Lib., MS.

59. Greek manuscript miniatures, *Minor Prophets*, each 293×204 mm, from a Prophet book with *catena*, late 10th century (Turin, Biblioteca Nazionale Universitaria, Cod. B.I.2, fols 11*v*–12*r*)

Auct. E. 2. 16), and the Prophets and Maccabees (Oxford, New Coll., MS. 44). As with the 'Bible of Niketas', however, there is no evidence of a systematic overall plan for the decoration of these manuscripts, which appear rather as ad hoc responses to the particular texts they contain. The scheme varies from a full-page Genesis frontispiece, via smaller miniatures in the text, to no illustrations at all in the Bodleian manuscript. It should also be noted that it has not yet been possible to associate a surviving New Testament manuscript with an illustrated Old Testament volume or volumes.

Always supposing that the manuscripts were indeed intended to form sets, and are not merely related as products of the same workshop, it is difficult to predict the exact appearance of further volumes, since the concept of Bible illustration, in the sense of an overall plan for the entire text, apparently scarcely existed in Byzantium, in sharp contrast to the Latin West (see ROMANESQUE, §IV, 2). The situation is very different, however, when consideration turns from the complete Bible to smaller sections of its text.

(iii) New Testament. For the celebration of the liturgy, every altar in Byzantium required a cross and a copy of the Gospels. While the priest doubtless brought the Gospels with him when officiating in a rarely used chapel, there was still a need for many Gospel manuscripts in the Byzantine world. It is not surprising to discover, therefore, that copies of the Gospels survive in far greater numbers than any other type of Byzantine book, and that illustrated Gospel manuscripts may amount to about half of all surviving illustrated books. Not only are such manuscripts relatively numerous, they are also often particularly costly and magnificent productions, as might be expected in a religious society in which the commissioning of such a work could be seen as earning the donor spiritual rewards.

Only the ROSSANO GOSPELS (Rossano, Mus. Dioc.) and the Sinope fragment (Paris, Bib. N., MS. suppl. gr. 1286; both probably 6th century) survive from before the iconoclastic controversy. To them can be added evidence from the Syriac RABBULA GOSPELS (586; Florence, Bib. Medicea-Laurenziana, MS. Plut.I.56), an illuminated manuscript presumed to reflect to some extent the appearance of a 6th-century Byzantine book. It must be borne in mind that none of these is complete, and each adopts a radically different scheme for its illustration.

The Sinope fragment has small illustrations in the margins of the text pages, but most of the manuscript, including the incipits of all four Gospels, is lost. The Rossano and Rabbula Gospels have their illustrations in the form of full-page frontispieces. In the Rossano much space was given over to Old Testament figures holding scrolls with inscriptions relevant to the scenes from the life of Christ above. The single surviving full-page Evangelist portrait, that of *Mark*, is now thought to be a later addition, but one of the prefatory leaves groups all four Evangelists together in medallion busts within a circular composition. In the Rabbula Gospels particular attention was paid to the Eusebian CANON TABLEs, which constitute diagrams drawn up to assist the reader in cross-referring

between numbered passages in the text. Here they provided the setting for small figures of the prophets, Evangelists and scenes from the life of Christ. There are also full-page illustrations of scenes from the life of Christ, together with two 'devotional' pages showing the *Virgin and Child* and an *Enthroned Christ with Four Monks*. Taken together, the scant evidence from the pre-iconoclast period suggests a range of possible responses to the demands of illustrating the Gospels, without implying an accepted norm.

In the post-iconoclast period, however, the idea of what a Byzantine Gospel manuscript should look like became firmly established. Firstly there was a functional subdivision of the Gospels into two rather different types of book. The Gospel book (Gr. *tetraevangelon* or *tetraevangelion*) contained the full text of the four Gospels in the usual order with a number of more or less standard prefaces. There was also a new type of book known as the Gospel Lectionary (Gr. *evangelion*), containing only selected readings from the Gospels, rearranged and adapted for use in the liturgy. Both types of Gospel manuscript were illustrated, but it is both convenient and necessary to consider each type separately here.

(a) Gospel books. (b) Gospel Lectionaries. (c) Acts and Epistles.

(a) Gospel books. The illuminated Gospel book was usually prefaced by ten pages of canon tables. The setting of these diagrams within a framework of arches or gables resting on marble columns was a formula already adopted in the pre-iconoclast period, to which there were relatively few changes in later centuries. Birds and beasts, naturalistic or fantastic, together with scenes of hunting, for example, were sometimes added to the upper area (e.g. 11th century; Paris, Bib. N., MS. gr. 64). Owing to their privileged position at the front of the book, canon tables were often magnificently decorated, and in some cases they have survived when the more easily detachable (and desirable) Evangelist portraits have not (e.g. 10th century, Athens, N. Lib., MS. 2364; 12th century, Paris, Bib. N., MS. coisl. 197).

Eusebios' letter to Carpianus explaining the use of the tables might be written in a special display script, or enclosed in a decorative frame. Other textual prefaces, such as those of Irenaeus, occasionally received magnificent pictorial treatment, as in the page of the Parma Gospels (*c.* 1100; Parma, Bib. Palatina, MS. gr. 5) depicting *Christ Pantokrator* ('ruler of all things', i.e. holding a Gospel book in his left hand and raising his right in blessing). Sometimes full-page frontispieces were provided without direct connection to a text: images of the pious donor (12th century; Melbourne, N.G. Victoria, MS. 710/5); the Cross (11th century; St Petersburg, Saltykov-Shchedrin Pub. Lib., MS. gr. 67); *Christ Pantokrator* (12th century; Venice, Bib. N. Marciana, MS. gr. Z.540); the *Virgin* (10th century; Princeton U., NJ, Lib., MS. Garrett 6); *Moses* (early 13th century; Mt Athos, St Dionysiou Monastery, Cod. 4); saints (10th century; Mt Athos, Stavronikita Monastery, Cod. 43); or the *Fountain of Life* (10th century; Rome, Vatican, Bib. Apostolica, MS. Vat. gr. 354). It must be borne in mind that these types of frontispiece are all uncommon.

The principal foci for illustration in the Gospel book were the openings of the four Gospels (see fig. 60). The usual pattern comprises an image of each Evangelist in the act of writing, or receiving the inspiration for, his Gospel, in a composition known to modern scholarship as the Evangelist portrait. If allotted a full page, as is often the case, this image would traditionally be placed on the left (*verso*) of an opening, with the incipit of the Gospel, treated in a decorative fashion, facing the Evangelist portrait on the right (*recto*) page. The incipit page commonly has a large headpiece of stylized ornament, generally square or rectangular in plan, and sometimes framing or enclosing an image or title for the book. An enlarged, decorated initial was provided for the start of the Gospel text below.

There are many variations on this formula for the treatment of the Gospel openings. If the pictorial content was reduced, the Evangelist might appear only at small scale within a historiated initial (11th century; Cleveland, OH, Mus. A., MS. acc. 42.152). Alternatively the imagery could be expanded by the addition of further figures or scenes to the Evangelist portrait itself, the headpiece and/or the initial. The Evangelist might be accompanied by the Apostle whose account he is supposed to have recorded (14th century; Athens, N. Lib., MS. 151) or by an unidentified 'inspiring' figure (New York, Pierpont Morgan Lib., MS. M. 748).

Owing to the liturgical use of the incipits of the Gospels on certain feast days, images of those days became associated with the Evangelist portraits: Matthew (Nativity), Mark (Baptism), Luke (Annunciation) and John (Anastasis). This had certainly occurred in the 10th century (cf. Baltimore, MD, Walters A. G., MS. W. 524) but is most commonly found in the 12th (Oxford, Bodleian Lib., MS. Auct. T. inf.1.10) and later. The feast scene may be placed in the upper part of the Evangelist portrait (12th century; Patmos, St John the Divine Monastery, Treasury Lib., Cod. 274) or within the headpiece on the facing page (9th century; Princeton, U., NJ, Lib., Garrett MS.3).

The Evangelist portrait itself, ultimately derived no doubt from Classical philosopher types, represented a firmly established pictorial convention in Byzantium, yet one within which a certain amount of variety was possible. In the Palaiologan period, in particular, a number of 'new' Evangelist types became popular. In earlier centuries alternatives to the usual seated figure may also be found in a variety of more or less standard activities: resting, writing in a book on a lectern or balanced on a knee, and dipping or sharpening a pen. The Evangelist might also be portrayed standing (10th century; Paris, Bib. N., MS. gr. 70). The elderly St John may stand to dictate to his young scribe Prochoros (10th century; Mt Athos, St Dionysiou Monastery, Cod. 588 m). The Evangelist might be isolated against a background of plain gold leaf, incised to suggest a setting (10th century; Rome, Vatican, Bib. Apostolica, MS. Vat. gr. 364), or surrounded by a painted interior with detailed furniture and architecture (11th century; Paris, Bib. N., MS. gr. 64), or an exterior, even an illusionistic landscape (10th century; Mt Athos, Stavronikita Monastery, Cod. 43). In view of the enthusiasm of art historians for the classicizing elements of Byzantine art, it is not surprising that the landscape settings of the Evangelist portraits in the latter manuscript have drawn particular attention, but they are an exception, rather than the norm; most Byzantine Evangelist portraits adopt an 'unclassicizing' approach to questions of recession, depth, illusionism and the natural world.

The most significant variant (to judge by modern scholarship) to the standard type of Gospel book with Evangelist portraits are those manuscripts with a large body of narrative illustrations, either set within the body of the text in some way or supplied as additional frontispieces. The interest these have evoked, however, should not be allowed to disguise the relatively small number of surviving examples. The largest narrative cycles are included within the Gospel text, notably in two well-known manuscripts: one of the late 11th century with 372 illustrations (Paris, Bib. N., MS. gr. 74), the other of the early 12th century with 301 illustrations (Florence, Bib. Medicea-Laurenziana, MS. Plut. 6.23). In both books the miniatures are unframed, small-scale compositions, painted in the area of a few blank lines left by the scribe in the text, often at the break between chapters. These spaces are broad but not high, since the page is laid out in a single column, and accordingly the figures are small, although several scenes or incidents may be included, side by side, in one strip of illustration. Although in some ways closely related, it is notable that these two manuscripts do not simply reproduce a common model. In the 12th-century manuscript the miniatures illustrate the text closely, combining in a single strip, for example, three scenes from Christ's calling of the first Apostles (fol. 9r). In the 11th-century example, on the other hand, there is a greater interest in 'iconic' scenes around a central focus,

60. Greek manuscript miniature, *St Luke*, from a Gospel book, mid-10th century (Mt Athos, Stavronikita Monastery, Cod. 43, fol 12*v*)

as in the consecutive images of Christ addressing the Apostles (fols 8*v*, 9*r*, 11*r* and 13*r*).

It has been proposed that both manuscripts were produced in the St John Stoudios Monastery in Constantinople, although the evidence for this attribution is slight. Since Millet's study on the iconography of the Gospels, they have been held to exemplify a tradition of Gospel illustration with early roots. The manuscripts, however, are much more closely paralleled by the illustrative cycles in other texts probably first developed as late as the mid-11th century (see *Barlaam and Ioasaph* and Climachus' *Heavenly Ladder* below). In 1356 a copy (London, BL, Add. MS. 39627) was made of the 11th-century manuscript for the Bulgarian Tsar John Alexander (*reg* 1331–71).

Of the few Byzantine Gospel books that provide framed miniatures within the text itself, two examples from the late 12th century (Athens, N. Lib., MS. 93) and early 13th (Berlin, Staatsbib. Preus. Kultbes., MS. gr. qu. 66) may be considered. The earlier manuscript distributes 20 small scenes from the life of Christ throughout the four Gospels, with a particular emphasis on scenes of the Passion, which may reflect the influence of the liturgy. The 13th-century example has 33 framed miniatures within the text, but the principle behind their choice remains enigmatic, since they do not follow the life of Christ, or focus on any single obvious theme (Hamann-MacLean).

Two manuscripts from the Palaiologan period (Mt Athos, Iviron Monastery, Cod. 5), and a partially related bilingual manuscript (Paris, Bib. N., MS. gr. 54) have large cycles of framed miniatures within the text, associated with the chapter divisions and their titles. The Mt Athos manuscript has large icon-like images extending the full width of the text. Stylistically it appears to be at the forefront of developments in the second half of the 13th century, and comparisons have been made with roughly contemporary Italian or 'Italo-Byzantine' painting. At the same time, however, the Iviron manuscript appears to owe much to significantly earlier work, and its Gospel cycle may be closely compared with illustrated manuscripts of the late 10th century and early 11th from Ottonian Germany. This comparison may imply that to some extent it reproduces the cycle of a 10th-century Byzantine Gospel book (or Lectionary) of a type also known to artists in Echternach, Reichenau or Trier.

The formula of illustrating the Gospels by including a series of full-page frontispieces was adopted only rarely in Byzantium. In the Parma Gospels there are three full pages of illustration with a total of 16 scenes from the *Life of Christ* set within richly decorated frames before the Gospel of Mark. Since they cover only the events from the Last Supper to Pentecost, they are presumably the surviving parts of a more ambitious scheme originally involving full-page frontispieces to each of the Gospels. In the late 12th-century Patriarchate Gospels (Istanbul, Gr. Orthdx Patriarch., Cod. gr. 3), there are full-page images of the Evangelist symbols, the Evangelists and the *Deësis* (Christ, the Virgin and St John the Baptist), together with depictions of the major Church feasts (e.g. *Nativity* and *Baptism*), each allotted a full page.

(b) Gospel Lectionaries. In the pre-iconoclast period the Gospel readings required during the liturgy would seem to have been taken from the full text contained in a New Testament manuscript, or specifically from a Gospel book. No doubt partly as a result of liturgical developments and standardization in the Byzantine world of the 7th–9th centuries, the special volume known as the Gospel Lectionary was then developed. Nonetheless, the provision or addition of liturgical information in many Gospel books shows that they remained in liturgical use throughout the Byzantine period. For example, an important illuminated manuscript of the mid-12th century (Oxford, Bodleian Lib., MS. Auct. T. inf.1.10) was adapted for liturgical use in 1391 by the scribe Ioasaph of the Constantinopolitan monastery of the Hodegon. It is important, however, to remain aware, as the Byzantines certainly were, of the significant points of textual organization and layout that distinguish the Gospel Lectionary from the straightforward Gospel book.

Lectionaries follow the order of the Church year, invariably commencing with Easter Sunday and a lection taken from the start of St John's Gospel. Lections from all four Gospels are then interspersed but follow the general order John, Matthew, Luke, Mark. In addition to the readings for the principal services (on Saturdays and Sundays), in some examples readings are provided for the rest of the week. The movable calendar is followed by the fixed one (Gr. *synaxarion*), starting with the commencement of the indiction (tax cycle) on 1 September (commemoration of St Symeon the Stylite). A significant proportion of illustrated Lectionaries contain readings for only a selection of the major feasts, and hence were intended for an even more limited use. Most luxury Lectionaries were written in two columns rather than the single-column, or marginal *catena*, layout of most Gospel books. The occasional use in Lectionaries of a mannered late form of uncial script, when minuscule was the prevailing bookhand, was perhaps intended to further differentiate them and add an air of antiquity.

The Lectionary contains no canon tables, and the prime focus of attention for the illustrator is thus the Evangelist portrait of John, facing the incipit of his Gospel. Modern catalogues and descriptions often confuse the Gospel book and Lectionary, but the presence of an image of St John near the first folio is a certain pointer to the type of book in question. Further Evangelist portraits are usually provided, in imitation of the Gospel book, but in the order Matthew, Luke, Mark. As in the Gospel book, these may be isolated full-page miniatures (e.g. 10th century; Rome, Vatican, Bib. Apostolica, MS. Vat. gr. 1522), or smaller images combined with a decorative headpiece in some way (e.g. 12th century; Paris, Bib. N., MS. suppl. gr. 27).

The earliest surviving illustrated Gospel Lectionary (*c*. first half of the 10th century; St Petersburg, Saltykov-Shchedrin Pub. Lib., MSS gr. 21 and 21a) is only a fragment, comprising 16 folios preserved on account of their miniatures. The varying format and placing of the large framed miniatures suggest the lack of a clear overall plan for the book. Some act as a headpiece at the start of the lection (e.g. *Marriage at Cana*, fol. 2*r*), while others are located within the text, close to the particular words they illustrate (*Christ Appearing to the Two Marys*, fol. 10*v*). The *Anastasis* occupies a full page, whereas other images (e.g. *Incredulity of Thomas*) are awkwardly accommodated.

These inconsistencies might be taken as evidence of the novelty of the project to illustrate the Lectionary.

In contrast, a late 11th-century or early 12th-century Lectionary (Mt Athos, St Dionysiou Monastery, Cod. 587) contains a decorative plan of exceptional refinement. In addition to a full-page portrait of *St John and Prochoros*, there are large framed images of the *Anastasis* (fol. 2r), *Agony in the Garden* (fol. 66r, for the lections of the Passion) and *St Symeon the Stylite* (fol. 116r, for the *synaxarion*). Smaller framed images, depicting scenes from the life of Christ or saints, are placed within one of the two text columns before most of the remaining lections. Smaller unframed figures or scenes are fitted into the margins, or combined with historiated initials. The manuscript, which was both planned and executed with great care, remains in superb condition.

Full-page frontispiece images might also be supplied to the Gospel Lectionary, either singly, as in an example (second half of the 12th century; Mt Athos, Grand Lavra Monastery, Treasury) that shows the *Anastasis, Nativity* and *Dormition of the Virgin*, or combined to form short cycles, as in a Lectionary (11th century; Mt Athos, St Panteleimon, Cod. 2) depicting *Christ and John the Baptist* (fol. 221r) and the *Baptism* (fols 221r–v). Frontispieces of more general significance to the book might be collected together at the start, as in the separate images of *Christ*, the *Virgin, St Peter of Monobata*, and the *Four Evangelists* in an 11th-century Lectionary written throughout in gold (Mt Sinai, Monastery of St Catherine, Cod. gr. 204).

Far fewer Lectionaries were illustrated than Gospel books. They were probably only intended for use on special occasions, and their importance in the development of Byzantine illumination is hard to judge but may have been significantly less than is often implied in modern scholarship. Since religious life was focused on the life of Christ, the cycle of images of the great feasts of the Church year would have been familiar to the Byzantine viewer. These images, however, would have been generally known through icons and the monumental decoration of churches rather than through illustrated liturgical manuscripts. It would seem that the Gospel Lectionary's illustration was largely a reflection of trends in other books and media, and not in itself a catalyst for change.

(c) Acts and Epistles. The rest of the New Testament received comparatively little attention from manuscript illuminators in Byzantium. Acts and the Epistles could form a separate volume (sometimes including the Apocalypse), either with the full biblical text, perhaps accompanied by a marginal *catena*, or, more rarely, as a Lectionary. Alternatively the full New Testament (usually without the Apocalypse) could be produced as a single volume or even combined with a Psalter in a characteristic Byzantine book.

The formulae developed for the illustration of Gospel books dominated artistic approaches to the rest of the New Testament. Author portraits, such as those of *SS Luke and James* in a late 13th-century Acts and Epistles (see fig. 61), which imitate those of the Evangelists, could be provided for Acts (Luke; *see* MANUSCRIPT, colour pl. I) and the various Epistles (of Paul, James, Peter, John and Jude). These might be full-page, or smaller, with figures

61. Greek manuscript miniature, *SS Luke and James*, 194×138 mm, from a copy of the Acts and Epistles, late 13th century (Rome, Vatican, Biblioteca Apostolica, MS. gr. 1208, fol. 3v)

standing or seated, alone or accompanied by some inspiring figure. Examples may be cited from the 10th century onward (e.g. Oxford, Bodleian Lib., MS. Canon. gr. 110; Rome, Vatican, Bib. Apostolica, MS. Vat. gr. 1208). A narrative treatment of scenes from these later books is only rarely encountered. Exceptions are the short frontispiece cycles in two 12th-century manuscripts (Paris, Bib. N., MS. gr. 102; the former Phillipps MS. 7681) and the framed scenes within the text of New Testament manuscripts, such as the Rockefeller–McCormick New Testament (12th century; U. Chicago, IL, Lib., MS. 965).

(iv) Old Testament. The Greek text of the Old Testament (the Septuagint) circulated in Byzantium either as a single volume or, more commonly, divided into several volumes. Although a book for liturgical use, containing all the lections from the Septuagint (Gr. *Prophetologion*), was developed probably in the 9th century and then widely circulated, no examples appear to have been illustrated. Nonetheless, liturgical considerations loom large in discussion of the most popular illustrated Septuagint text, the Psalms.

(a) Genesis. (b) Octateuchs. (c) Kings. (d) Job. (e) Prophet books. (f) Psalters.

(a) Genesis. Enormous scholarly attention has been focused on the two surviving illustrated Genesis manuscripts, the COTTON GENESIS (London, BL, Cotton MS.

Otho B. VI) and VIENNA GENESIS (Vienna, Österreich. Nbib., Cod. theol. gr. 31). Both contain the text of Genesis alone and were originally profusely illustrated: the Cotton Genesis with an estimated 339 miniatures, the Vienna Genesis with an estimated 96 (*see* BIBLE, fig. 1). To some extent both manuscripts, which were produced in the late 5th century or more probably the 6th, might be considered picture books. The Vienna Genesis, like the Rossano Gospels, was written throughout in silver on purple-dyed parchment, and the lower half of each page is given over to illustration. In the Cotton Genesis the more numerous illustrations are interspersed with the text. In many further ways the manuscripts differ in their treatment of iconographic subjects and their style.

The interest and controversy generated by these two remarkable books has tended to mask the fact that they are the only known examples of single-volume Genesis manuscripts, with or without illustration, produced at any date in Byzantium. They appear to have satisfied a requirement felt in the pre-iconoclast period but not later, even in the periods of Byzantine 'renaissance'.

(b) Octateuchs. Genesis was also included in a typically Byzantine volume known as the Octateuch, which comprises the Pentateuch together with Joshua, Judges and Ruth. Five closely related illustrated Octateuchs survive: one from the second half of the 11th century (Rome, Vatican, Bib. Apostolica, MS. Vat. gr. 747), three from the first half of the 12th century (formerly İzmir, Gr. Evangel. Sch. A/1 (untraced); Istanbul, Topkapı Pal. Lib., Cod. gr. 8; Rome, Vatican, Bib. Apostolica, MS. Vat. gr. 746) and one from the second half of the 13th century (Mt Athos, Vatopedi Monastery, Cod. 602; *see* BIBLE, fig. 2). There is also a single illustrated Octateuch of unrelated type (Florence, Bib. Medicea-Laurenziana, MS. Plut. 5.38), with a short Genesis cycle, approximately contemporary with the 11th-century Octateuch in Rome. The Topkapı Octateuch has connections with the brother of the Emperor John II Komnenos, and the Kokkinobaphos Master (*see* §(i) above) worked on both it and the Smyrna Octateuch. All were certainly major commissions, presumably produced in Constantinople.

Originally each volume had *c.* 370 framed miniatures scattered through the text, many of them subdivided so that more than 500 scenes were illustrated. These Octateuchs also contain as a similarly illustrated preface the apocryphal Letter of Aristeas, recounting the first translation of the Pentateuch from Hebrew into Greek. An extensive marginal *catena* is a conspicuous element in the planning and layout of almost every page. Although less densely illustrated than the Cotton Genesis, the Octateuchs provide a rich narrative treatment to all eight books, including many rare scenes. Their conspicuous connection to the picture cycle of the JOSHUA ROLL gave them special importance in early studies of Byzantine art. Since Hesseling's publication of all the Smyrna Octateuch miniatures in 1909, the Octateuchs have often been cited as comparative material in studies of Old Testament subjects in the West as well as in Byzantium. It now seems improbable that they are all descended from a lost illustrated Octateuch of the pre-iconoclast period, and more likely that they represent a post-iconoclast development, perhaps of the

1050s, albeit based in part on earlier sources still available at the time.

The observation that the Vatopedi Octateuch is a direct copy of the 12th-century Octateuch in Rome has enabled a close analysis to be made of a Byzantine artist's approach to reproducing a model. This has undermined assumptions about the application of methods derived from textual criticism to the study of narrative illustration, built up in part on evidence from the Octateuchs.

(c) Kings. The book of Ruth is followed in the Septuagint by the four books of Kings or Kingdoms (i.e. 1–2 Samuel, 1–2 Kings). A single illustrated Byzantine manuscript with the text of these books alone has survived: the Vatican Book of Kings (third quarter of the 11th century; Rome, Vatican, Bib. Apostolica, MS. Vat. gr. 333). This contains 104 miniatures scattered through the text as relatively small framed scenes and organized, for the most part, on the scheme of one per chapter division. It is conspicuous that the density of the illustrative cycle decreases markedly as the book progresses: 1 Kings has seventy-five miniatures, 2 Kings has twenty-two, 3 Kings has six, while 4 Kings has just one. The scenes illustrated in 3–4 Kings follow standard iconographic formulae.

The manuscript's significance for an understanding of Byzantine illumination depends to a large extent on hypotheses about its possible sources. If, as has often been proposed, it is a copy of a type of illustrated Kings manuscript originating in the pre-iconoclast period, perhaps as an equivalent of the Latin Quedlinburg Itala fragments (*see* §1 above), its evidence is very valuable. If, however, as seems more plausible, it is an 11th-century Byzantine attempt to extend to other parts of the Bible the type of dense illustrative cycle then in vogue for the Octateuch or Gospels, then its evidence should not be overrated. Despite the fact that 1–4 Kings included the narrative of the life of David, which was of great interest to Byzantines because of his supposed authorship of the Psalms, the isolated survival of Vat. gr. 333 implies little enthusiasm for the illustration of the complete text of these books.

(d) Job. The book of Job, when combined with a lengthy *catena*, became sufficiently bulky to fill an entire volume, and 15 Byzantine manuscripts were provided with lengthy cycles of illustration. Some are frequently referred to incorrectly as 'Olympiodorus in Job', suggesting a different sort of commentary, but all are *catena* books. The Job manuscripts may be divided into two groups, the first comprising four disparate books of the 9th and 10th centuries, and the second books of the 12th to the 14th century.

The first group comprises the closely related Marciana and Vatican Jobs (Venice, Bib. N. Marciana, MS. gr. Z. 548, dated 905; Rome, Vatican, Bib. Apostolica, MS. Vat. gr. 749) and the Patmos and Sinai Jobs (Patmos, St John the Divine Monastery, Treasury Lib., Cod. gr. 171; Mt Sinai, Monastery of St Catherine, Cod. gr. 3). All but the Sinai Job use uncial script for the text, marginal *catena* or both, and have a complex layout with miniatures of varying shapes and sizes fitted into the page at the appropriate point. The painted illusionistic backgrounds of the Sinai Job seem to hark back to books of the pre-iconoclast period.

Whereas the illustrations of the earlier manuscripts are concentrated on the rapidly unfolding events of Job 1–2 and 42, in the much larger later group (e.g. 12th century, Oxford, Bodleian Lib., MS. Barocci 201; 13th century, Mt Athos, Grand Lavra Monastery, B.100) many highly repetitive illustrations are also used for the major part of the text, which consists of a dialogue between Job and his friends. The Barocci Job originally had 237 miniatures, of which six are now missing. The later manuscripts also dispensed with the complex page layout and have passages of text with illustrations followed by the *catena* all in a single column.

(e) Prophet books. The 16 Prophetical books of the Old Testament circulated as a composite volume in Byzantium, rather like the Octateuchs. Seven illustrated copies have survived (Rome, Vatican, Bib. Apostolica, MS. Vat. Chisi. R. VIII. 54, mid-10th century; Florence, Bib. Medicea-Laurenziana, MS. Plut. 5.9, late 10th century; Turin, Bib. N. U., Cod. B.I.2, late 10th century, see fig. 59 above; Rome, Vatican, Bib. Apostolica, MS. Vat. gr. 755, early 11th century; Oxford, New Coll., MS. 44, late 12th century; Oxford, Bodleian Lib., MS. Laud. gr. 30A, late 12th century; Rome, Vatican, Bib. Apostolica, MSS Vat. gr. 1153–4, mid–late 13th century). All are massive books with a marginal *catena*, except for the two volumes in Oxford. Textually, the most recent manuscript reproduces the oldest, but their miniatures have few similarities.

The illustrations to the Prophet books are unambitious, consisting mainly of author portraits and occasional narrative scenes. It is notable that a miniature of *Isaiah with Night and Dawn*, closely related to the image in the PARIS PSALTER, was provided as an illustration to the Canticle of Isaiah in Vat. gr. 755 (fol. 107*r*). The manuscripts in Florence and Turin form part of the nucleus of the reconstructed 'Bible of Niketas', while the New College manuscript has also been grouped with other surviving Old Testament manuscripts (see above). Although a few of the portraits of the prophets maintain recognizable types in these books, notably Isaiah, Daniel and Jonah, for the most part correct identification of the figure seems to have relied upon a conspicuous title within the miniature.

(f) Psalters. Recitation of the Psalms formed an essential part of the monastic offices from the pre-iconoclast period. Presumably in response to the demands of usage, the Byzantines developed a composite volume that often included various prefaces as well as the 150 Psalms and always, as an appendix, the Odes or Canticles, a series of (usually 14) Psalm-like songs excerpted from elsewhere in the Old and New Testaments, such as the *Magnificat* (Luke 1:46–55); further prayers might also be added. This volume, known as the Psalter, seems to have been the second most common book in Byzantium after the Gospels; more than 80 illustrated copies have survived.

Many of the Psalms are difficult, poetic texts, not easily lending themselves to illustration. The Byzantines had a varied and thoughtful approach to the problems presented by the Psalter. Traditionally the material has been divided for the purposes of study into two categories: the Marginal

Psalters (e.g. the CHLUDOV PSALTER; Moscow, Hist. Mus., MS. D. 29), so-called from the restriction of their illustrations to the margins as a sort of visual *catena*, and the Aristocratic Psalters (e.g. the Paris Psalter; Paris, Bib. N., MS. grec. 139), which have full-page, prefatory or other illustrations.

The Aristocratic Psalter category is unsatisfactory, and it has been argued that all Byzantine Psalters should be considered together, with the marginal manuscripts representing a distinctive sub-group. The large volume of material, however, and its disparate nature, has delayed a clear understanding of the range of Byzantine responses to Psalter illustration.

No illustrated Psalters survive from the pre-iconoclast period, although it would be surprising if none had been produced then. The marginal Psalters may have been the first illustrated books produced after the iconoclastic controversy (726–843), perhaps even before 843 as an intellectual reaction in certain areas of the Church against imperial pressure. Books of this type continued to be produced in the 11th century, such as the Theodore and Barberini Psalters (London, BL, Add. MS. 19352; Rome, Vatican, Bib. Apostolica, MS. Barb. gr. 372), and even into the 14th century (e.g. Baltimore, MD, Walters A. G., MS. W. 533).

In the 14th century these marginal Psalters were closely imitated outside the Byzantine world in Serbia, Bulgaria (*see* BULGARIA, fig. 7) and Russia, and in a Greco-Latin manuscript probably made on Cyprus (Berlin, Bodemus., Cod. 78.A.9). The approach to illustration adopted in these books is exceptionally varied (e.g. the Chludov Psalter), and different emphases are found: in the Theodore Psalter (1066), for example, which the monk Theodore made in the St John Stoudios Monastery for its abbot, Michael, new emphasis is placed on the cult of saints, and in particular the 9th-century abbot THEODORE OF STOUDIOS.

What might be termed the cult of the Paris Psalter among modern scholars has tended to distort consideration of the non-marginal tradition in Byzantium. It is notable that no single formula came to be accepted as the 'ideal' approach to Psalter illustration. An image of *David*, such as prefaces the Psalms in the Leo Bible (cf. *c.* 1100; Rome, Vatican, Bib. Apostolica, MS. Barb. gr. 320) or as adapted by the presence of musicians (1088; Mt Athos, Vatopedi Monastery, Cod. 761), was often used as a frontispiece. To this might be added scenes from the life of King David, such as his birth (*c.* 1150–*c.* 1200; Athens, N. Lib., MS. 7), iconic or donor images, such as the *Deësis* (1105; Cambridge, MA, Harvard U., Houghton Lib., MS. gr. 3) or a *Monk before the Virgin and Child* (12th century; Mt Athos, Dionysiou Monastery, Cod. 65). Psalms 50 and 77, and the Odes, might have their own images, perhaps full-page (e.g. 13th century; Jerusalem, Mus. Gr. Orthodx. Patriarch., Cod. Taphou 51) or framed within the text (12th century; Mt Athos, Great Lavra Monastery, B.24). These images were fairly standardized, for example the use of *Moses on Mt Sinai* for the second Ode (Deuteronomy 32:1–43). There might be scenes of *David and Goliath* to illustrate the apocryphal Psalm 151 (1084; Washington, DC, Dumbarton Oaks, Cod. 3).

An impression of the variety of Byzantine approaches may be gained by looking briefly at a few further examples. In a *catena* manuscript (1059; Rome, Vatican, Bib. Apostolica, MS. Vat. gr. 752) the large cycle of miniatures illustrates almost entirely the *catena* text, and not the Psalter itself. For example, at Psalm 32:5 (fol. 97*r*), four bishops are depicted before an altar, accompanied by a quotation from Pseudo-Athanasius. This manuscript is also unusual in containing among its prefaces 13 images of the major feasts commemorating Christ's life (fols 17*v*, 18*r* (full-page) and 18*v*).

In a Psalter of the early 12th century (Rome, Vatican, Bib. Apostolica, MS. Vat. gr. 1927), unique among Byzantine examples, each Psalm is prefaced by an image derived from a literal interpretation of the Psalm title or text. Thus at Psalm 32 a single miniature combines figures of David, musicians, the Lord looking out from heaven and beholding the sons of men, a king on horseback, a giant and a rich man giving money to a poor man.

The Psalter of Basil II (Venice, Bib. N. Marciana, MS. gr. 17), a magnificent *catena* manuscript, contains two full-page frontispieces. The first (fol. III*r*) shows the Emperor Basil II (*reg* 976–1025) as a triumphant warrior, flanked by icons of military saints and assisted by Christ and archangels; his vanquished foes prostrate themselves beneath his feet. The second (fol. IV*v*) has six scenes from the *Life of David*. The images and accompanying verses, however, do not take up the possibilities of comparing Basil and David directly.

It is conspicious that the Byzantines never developed a long frontispiece cycle of Old and New Testament scenes for the PSALTER, such as was widespread in the West from the 12th century, nor did they settle on a 'standard' scheme for its illustration.

(v) Other religious texts. Although a significant number of religious texts other than the Bible were illustrated, the range of books that received narrative or interpretative illustration, as distinct from an author portrait or dedication page of some sort, was limited. The great majority of even the most carefully prepared and written books received no more than non-figural decoration in the form of illuminated headpieces. This lack of illustration was not for reasons of economy; most of the types of book considered here were huge volumes consisting of many hundreds of densely written folios. In terms of time and materials, they must have been very costly.

(a) Gregory. (b) Chrysostomos and Basil. (c) Climachus. (d) Cosmas. (e) Metaphrastian Menologion and other hagiographic manuscripts. (f) 'Barlaam and Ioasaph'. (g) Chronicles. (h) Miscellaneous religious texts.

(a) Gregory. The most important, because most numerous, among the illustrated copies of texts of the Church Fathers are those of Bishop Gregory of Nazianzus (329–89). The surviving material can be divided into two groups. Two late 9th-century uncial manuscripts contain the full text of all Gregory's homilies, but illustrate them in radically different ways. The PARIS GREGORY (Paris, Bib. N., MS. gr. 510) originally had a complex full-page miniature before each homily, which commented, often obscurely, on the subsequent text. Individual scenes or short cycles based on the Old and New Testaments, lives of the saints, Church councils and many other 'sources' were combined in a variety of ways. These large framed miniatures, with fully painted backgrounds, contrast sharply with the marginal illustrations of the Milan Gregory (Milan, Bib. Ambrosiana, MSS E. 49–50 inf.), which mostly comprise single figures, medallions or relatively simple

62. Greek manuscript miniature, *St Gregory*, 227×176 mm, and a decorative title page, 323×254 mm, to his Easter homily, from Gregory of Nazianzus: *Selected Homilies*, mid-12th century (Mt Sinai, Monastery of St Catherine, Cod. gr. 339, fols 4*v*–5*r*)

teaching scenes or narrative compositions, all executed in gold leaf set against the bare parchment. The full-page composition of Gregory beneath a bust of St Basil, now at the end of the book (fol. 814) is a more ambitious work in a painterly technique.

Probably during the 10th century 16 of Gregory's homilies were selected as standard additional lections for the liturgy and arranged to follow the Church year, starting at Easter and combining the fixed and movable calendar. More than 30 illustrated manuscripts of this 'liturgical edition' have survived from the mid-11th century onwards, a relatively large number that is doubtless the result of the decision to produce this special liturgical book.

In addition to author portraits or generalized scenes of Gregory addressing a group of men, many of these texts preface each homily with an appropriate image for the particular feast day. The Sinai Gregory (mid-12th century; Mt Sinai, Monastery of St Catherine, Cod. gr. 339; see fig. 62), for example, contains standard scenes from the *Life of Christ* (the *Anastasis*, *Pentecost*, *Nativity* and *Baptism*), and others specific to the homily, as in the image of Gregory and Julian the tax collector prefacing the text for 21 December (cf. Matthew 18:21–36). Historiated initials (e.g. 1062; Rome, Vatican, Bib. Apostolica, MS. Vat. gr. 463) or marginal figures and scenes (e.g. 12th century; Mt Athos, St Panteleimon, Cod. 6) may add a further level of complexity to the illustration.

Particular attention has been paid to the bucolic scenes provided in some cases to illustrate the homily on New Sunday (the first after Easter), with its idealized depiction of pastoral activities (e.g. 11th century; Jerusalem, Mus. Gr. Orthdx Patriarch., Cod. Taphou 14). This sub-cycle stands somewhat apart, and connections have been found with the illustrated *Cynegetica* of Pseudo-Oppian (*see* §(vi) below).

(b) Chrysostomos and Basil. The treatment of writings by other Church Fathers is very different. SS Basil and John Chrysostomos, for example, were scarcely less important than Gregory of Nazianzus in the life of the Church; indeed, as authors of the two main forms of the liturgy, and of numerous homilies and commentaries, they were probably more important. Their writings, however, were not excerpted by the Byzantines into a convenient single-volume edition in which illustration could be concentrated and, perhaps as a direct result, no formal tradition of illustration was developed. Although some illustrated copies of their works were produced, they are disparate.

Manuscripts of the homilies of John Chrysostomos (*c.* 347–407) are among the most magnificent survivals from the Byzantine world, but their illustration is almost entirely restricted to frontispiece images of the author, donor or subject of the text, or a combination of these (*see* SINAI, fig. 5). In one copy (Paris, Bib. N., MS. Coislin 79, fol. 2*v*) Emperor Nikephoros Botaneiates (*reg* 1078–81) stands with the Archangel Michael on his left, holding a book that he seems to receive from John Chrysostomos on his right (see fig. 63). Other full-page frontispieces in the volume show the Emperor and Empress crowned by Christ; the Emperor, supported by Truth and Justice, and flanked by four senior courtiers; and the enthroned Emperor, attended by a monk, Sabbas, who appears to

63. Greek manuscript miniature, *Emperor Nikephoros Botaneiates with John Chrysostomos and the Archangel Michael*, from John Chrysostomos: *Homilies*, 425×310 mm, 1078–81 (Paris, Bibliothèque Nationale, MS. Coislin 79, fol. 2*v*)

read to him from the works of Chrysostomos with the aid of a long candle.

A rare example of narrative illustration within the text of a Chrysostomos manuscript is a 10th-century book (Athens, N. Lib., MS. 211) with 41 pen-and-ink drawings (unusual as a technique in Byzantium) organized around the titles of the homilies. These show a remarkable inventiveness, as in the drawing (fol. 56*r*) depicting in the upper part a table heavily laden with food for a feast, flanked by two servers, contrasting with the lower part that depicts an altar table with chalice, paten, Gospels and a cross with a dove, flanked by Chrysostomos as a bishop and his congregation, headed by an emperor (cf. Genesis 2:9; Luke 23:43).

In sharp contrast to the Gregory manuscripts, and even those of Chrysostomos, very few copies of the numerous works of St Basil, Bishop of Caesarea (*c.* 330–79) are illustrated. A large volume of Basil's *Homilies on the Psalms* (10th century; Oxford, Bodleian Lib., MS. Canon. gr. 77) has a single frontispiece showing Basil, seated and holding a book, preaching to a group on his right. A copy of Basil's *Ascetics* (12th century; Copenhagen, Kon. Bib., MS. G.K.S. 1343), written by a monk Basil, shows the scribe prostrating himself before the standing figure of the saint, flanked by two groups of monks.

(c) Climachus. The *Heavenly Ladder* of John Climachus (*c.* 570–*c.* 650), abbot of the monastery at Sinai, was an important text of monastic instruction (*see* SINAI, §2(iv)).

It consists of 30 chapters, broadly concerning virtues and vices, envisioned as steps in the perfection of a monk on the rungs of a ladder reaching from earth to heaven. Illustrated copies survive from the 10th century and later. In the mid-11th century a particularly rich and complex cycle of pictures was devised, as exemplified by a copy (Rome, Vatican, Bib. Apostolica, MS. Vat. gr. 394) that contains not only large framed scenes for each rung of the ladder, but also literal illustrations of the text in the margins, such as *Chasing a Shadow* (fol. 18*r*). There are also many personifications, as in the miniatures between chapters 18 and 19 (fol. 94*r*), where the monk is being dragged head first from the ladder by figures identified as Pride, Sleep, False Piety, Anger and Vainglory. At the right, John addresses four other monks, and beyond them a personification of Prayer clubs a prostrate figure of Sleep.

(d) Cosmas. The text known as the *Christian Topography* of 'Cosmas Indicopleustes' (Constantine of Alexandria, *fl* 540–50), although it survives only in post-iconoclast manuscripts, seems to presuppose the presence of illustrations. Cosmas referred to pictures and diagrams of various sorts, and it seems likely that the later manuscripts, in particular a late 9th-century copy (Rome, Vatican, Bib. Apostolica, MS. Vat. gr. 699), imitate to some extent the appearance of a mid-6th-century illustrated book. This makes the study of the Cosmas manuscripts particularly intriguing, given the widespread, but unverifiable, presumption that much post-iconoclast Byzantine art goes back to earlier sources.

The illustrative programme devised by Cosmas mixed cosmological diagrams with single standing figures and full narrative compositions. The core of standard iconographic compositions, such as the *Sacrifice of Isaac* (fol. 59*r*), was adapted by Cosmas with few changes other than the addition of explanatory inscriptions and a rearrangement of the figures. Other images, such as the earth within a cosmos shaped like the tabernacle and surmounted by an image of Christ (fol. 43*r*), were certainly devised for the specific requirements of the text.

(e) Metaphrastian Menologion and other hagiographic manuscripts. An important type of illustrated Byzantine book is represented by the hagiographical collection based on the ecclesiastical calendar. The collection of texts known as the Metaphrastian Menologion provides the most numerous examples. These enormous ten-volume sets of saints' lives were devised in the mid-10th century by Symeon Metaphrastes (Gr. 'the rephraser'). N. Ševčenko has located 43 surviving illustrated manuscripts, all of which were produced between the mid-11th century and the early 12th, and grouped 20 of them into one of seven editions. Their illustrations follow a number of different schemes: full-page frontispieces with the saints of that volume drawn up in ranks in a formula reminiscent of calendar icons; small standing figures within the text before each life; and scenes or even brief cycles of martyrdom. No particular type of hagiographic image became established as the norm for these books.

The variations on the Metaphrastian scheme are probably now more familiar to scholarship, although certainly less familiar to the Byzantines. The key work is perceived to be the confusingly titled MENOLOGION OF BASIL II (late 10th century; Rome, Vatican, Bib. Apostolica, MS. Vat. gr. 1613), which is an illustrated *synaxarion* (calendar) containing brief texts only and 430 large illustrations. It is both the earliest and by far the most ambitious surviving calendar-based manuscript. The study of Byzantine hagiographic illustration constantly returns to its numerous portraits of saints and scenes of martyrdom: for example, the illustrated *synaxarion* of a late 11th-century Gospel Lectionary (Rome, Vatican, Bib. Apostolica, MS. Vat. gr. 1156) has many points of contact with Basil's Menologion, as well as with the Metaphrastian manuscripts.

Other types of special hagiographic volume were also produced, such as a Metaphrastian volume (Mt Athos, Esphigmenou Monastery, no. 14) with selected texts, illustrated by long cycles of frontispiece illustrations, some on purple parchment. Some of the miniatures in Basil's Menologion were closely copied in the so-called Imperial Menologia (e.g. 11th century; Baltimore, MD, Walters A.G., MS. W. 521). In the early 14th century the accompanying text was abandoned completely for the 'picture calendar' (Oxford, Bodleian Lib., MS. theol. gr. f. 1), in which 10 of the original 14 full-page images of the great feasts are followed by 93 pages (of an original 99–100) mostly divided into four parts with saints for the entire year. The cycle culminates with two pages of images of St Demetrios of Thessaloniki. The supplicatory and devotional use of these images is made explicit in the colophon, which records its making for Demetrios Palaiologos, Despot (ruler) of Thessaloniki (*reg* 1322–40).

The type of one-volume illustrated saint's life known in the West (*see* SAINTS' LIVES) is represented by a single Byzantine example (12th century; Turin, Bib. N. U., Cod. B. II. 4), which contains the commemoration of the Five Martyrs of Sebaste (*fd* 13 Dec). Fourteen miniatures from the original cycle have survived, although at least 24 have been cut out. The book was specially laid out with the widely spaced lines of the text in one column and the illustrations placed alongside in the second column, so as to fill an entire volume. It was presumably made for a church or monastery dedicated to the cult of the Five.

(f) 'Barlaam and Ioasaph'. A text occupying an area somewhere between the saint's life and the homily is the illustrated *Barlaam and Ioasaph*. Although sometimes termed a romance, this is in fact a work of spiritual and theological intent. The Barlaam story was only translated into Greek *c.* 1000 and a number of profusely illustrated versions survive from *c.* 1050 onwards. In due course further translations were made into Russian and Arabic, and related illustrated examples were produced in those areas in post-Byzantine times.

One of the illustrated copies (second half of the 11th century; Mt Athos, Iviron Monastery, Cod. 463) contains a full-page portrait of its supposed author, John of Damascus (*c.* 675–*c.* 749), and 80 framed miniatures set within the text. The artist worked with standard Byzantine compositional formulae (e.g. architectural and landscape backgrounds, scenes of conversation, groups of riders) to provide a literal interpretation of the text; only the presence of turbans and some other details of costume suggest the exotic setting for the story. The manuscript has a general similarity to other contemporary works discussed above, such as the Vatican Kings and the Climachus manuscript (Rome, Vatican, Bib. Apostolica, MS. Vat. gr. 394).

(g) Chronicles. Although the Byzantines had a tradition of composing histories and chronicles, the possibilities for illustration offered by such texts, with their strong narrative interest, were rarely taken up. The notable exception is the Madrid Skylitzes (Madrid, Bib. N., MS. 5. 3. N. 2), a copy from the second half of the 12th century of the near contemporary chronicle of John Skylitzes. It is provided with an enormous cycle comprising 574 unframed miniatures within spaces left in the text. Three separate miniatures (fol. 102*r*), for example, recount the journey of the widow Danielis, who travelled to Constantinople in the late 9th century to present her wealth to emperors Basil I and Leo VI.

A Russian translation (Moscow, Rus. Lib.) of the 9th-century *Chronicle* of George the Monk, with narrative illustrations of the 14th century, may be taken to imply the existence of an illustrated Byzantine source. Frontispiece author portraits were also used, as in the copy of Niketas Choniates' *History* (13th century; Vienna, Österreich. Nbib., Cod. hist. gr. 53). In general, however, the readers of Byzantine histories and chronicles do not seem to have required pictures.

(h) Miscellaneous religious texts. The Byzantines could, on occasion, produce an illustrated copy of almost any religious text. Such works often survive in only a single manuscript, but still attract intense scholarly attention. Although such manuscripts are intriguing, and often of high artistic quality, there is a danger of their being studied to the virtual exclusion of the almost unlimited supply of, for example, Gospel books, thus distorting the view of Byzantine illustration.

A case in point is the *Sacra parallela*, an anthology attributed to John of Damascus. This survives in a single magnificent, illustrated uncial copy (Paris, Bib. N., MS. gr. 923), which, if dated to the first half of the 9th century, may originate from Palestine; a more likely dating to the second half of the 9th century might suggest Constantinople. Throughout the manuscript the margins were used to supply small scenes and innumerable busts of the authors of the excerpted texts. All were delineated in black on a ground of gold leaf, with little use of colour. Weitzmann (1979) has argued that the images were excerpted, along with the texts, from now lost illustrated copies of the original works, including, for example, illustrated copies of the writings of Josephus. The hypothesis is far-reaching, but strained, and a shortage of evidence leaves the situation unresolvable. The argument hinges on perceptions of the working methods of Byzantine artists and whether they routinely turned to other books to copy images, or drew on images and formulae retained in their memories.

A striking example of what appears to be the adaptation of standard images and formulae to illustrate a new text is provided by two manuscripts of the second quarter of the 12th century (Paris, Bib. N., MS. gr. 1208; Rome, Vatican, Bib. Apostolica, MS. Vat. gr. 1162). They both contain a collection of six homilies on the Virgin, composed by a contemporary monk, James of Kokkinobaphos, for an aristocratic, probably imperial, lady. There are numerous large-scale framed miniatures, with as many as 76 in the Vatican manuscript. Some repeat well-known scenes, as in the three consecutive versions of the *Annunciation* of the Vatican manuscript (fols 122*r*, 124*r*, 126*r*). In other cases the artist took a standard element, such as the *Virgin and Child* (fol. 50*v*), and placed it in a rich and complex paradisaical setting, to produce an image without close parallels (see fig. 58 above).

In every case a frontispiece of some sort, perhaps an author or donor portrait, was the easiest way to provide pictures in a text for which there was no established tradition of illustration. Even a monastic foundation document, or *typikon*, could be given luxury treatment, as in the example produced for the Convent of Our Lady of Good Hope at Constantinople (1327–42; Oxford, Lincoln Coll., MS. gr. 35), which has 12 full pages of icon-like portraits of the founder, Euphrosyne Komnena Doukaina Palaiologina, her parents, children and grandchildren, together with a group portrait of the nuns of the convent. To a modern viewer used to an impression of Byzantium derived from images of biblical figures in Classical dress, these Palaiologan aristocrats, magnificent in their gold and silk brocades, look strange and exotic; the men have long straight hair hanging down their backs and wear ankle-length kaftan-like robes.

(vi) Classical texts. Comparatively few illustrated Byzantine manuscripts have survived that are not explicitly religious in content, and even most of those were probably produced and intended for use in a broadly religious context. Many only survive as single copies and were probably preserved largely as curiosities. The bias of much modern scholarship in favour of Byzantium as the inheritor and transmitter of the Classical tradition, however, has given these Classical 'survivals', if this is what they are, attention disproportionate to their numbers. A positive result is that they are now more accessible through publication than many other areas of Byzantine production.

Dioskurides' *De materia medica* (the Vienna Dioskurides, *c.* 512; Vienna, Österreich. Nbib., Cod. med. gr. 1), is quite rightly one of the most famous Byzantine books. It is a vast compendium of almost 1000 pages dealing with medicinal plants, drugs of animal origin (e.g. birds, earthworms, fish and jellyfish), paraphrases of treatises on birds (modelled on the *Ornithiaka* of Dionysos) and antidotes to venomous bites and other types of poisoning, attributed to Euteknios after Nicander's *Theriaka* and *Alexipharmaka* of the 2nd century. Its principal illustration consists of 383 full-page miniatures of plants, painted with a remarkable naturalism and botanical accuracy. There are also full-page frontispieces of a peacock (perhaps misbound); a group of doctors around the centaur Cheiron; a second group around Galen; Discovery displaying the mandrake to Dioskurides; Thought holding the mandrake, while an artist paints it on a sheet pinned to an easel and Dioskurides writes about it in a book on his knee; and ANICIA JULIANA enthroned between Magnanimity and Prudence, receiving the book from Gratitude of the Arts. It is recorded that the book was a gift to Juliana from the people of Onoratou, a suburb of Constantinople on the Asiatic shore of the Bosphorus, where she is known to have founded a church of the Virgin in 512/13. She later built the church of St Polyeuktos (*c.* 524–7) in Constantinople, and is reckoned to have been the wealthiest woman in the Byzantine world in the early 6th century.

The Vienna Dioskurides was not only carefully preserved over the centuries, but seems to have been known and consulted. Later Dioskurides manuscripts (e.g. ?7th century, Naples, Bib. N., Cod. suppl. gr. 28; mid-10th century, New York, Pierpont Morgan Lib., MS. M. 652) remain close to its plant illustrations, although dispensing with the frontispieces. Although illustrated examples continued to be produced into the 14th century, it is not clear whether they were treated as picture books, working manuals or both. (*See also* HERBAL, §1.)

Other Classical survivals are more isolated works. Among the most interesting examples are a single illustrated copy of Soranus of Ephesos' treatise on bandaging (mid-10th century; Florence, Bib. Medicea-Laurenziana, MS. Plut. 70.7); the illustrations in a copy of Nicander (11th century; Paris, Bib. N., MS. suppl. gr. 247); Pseudo-Oppian's hunting treatise, the *Cynegetica* (11th century; Venice, Bib. N. Marciana, MS. gr. 479); and a geographical compendium, based on Ptolemy and Strabo, with numerous maps (13th century; mostly Mt Athos, Vatopedi Monastery, Cod. 655). The *Works and Days* of Hesiod, of which 11 or more illustrated copies survive, was provided mainly with diagrams. Numerous medical texts, fables, the *Trojan War* and the works of Aristotle, Sophocles, Appian, Hero of Alexandria and Theocritus received some illustration, albeit sometimes of poor artistic quality, in the Byzantine period.

(vii) Ornamental decoration. Since the pioneering studies of Bordier, Ebersolt and Weitzmann (1935), ornament has played a significant, if minor, role in the study of Byzantine illustration. Increasing knowledge, however, resulting from the overwhelming volume of material, has rendered the subject even more difficult to address. It is now apparent that perhaps as many as 20,000–30,000 Byzantine manuscripts bear some form of decoration. Whereas there are unlikely to be many important illustrated manuscripts as yet unknown, the number of uninvestigated decorated manuscripts is vast.

It must be remembered that the use of ornament in Byzantine manuscripts was profoundly different from Western practice. Starting with Insular manuscripts of the late 7th century (*see* INSULAR ART, §3), it is not possible to separate the study of decoration from that of illustration in the West. By contrast, Byzantine figural painting and illustration, in the broadest sense, remained distinct from ornament and decoration. Historiated initials do occur, but never with the complex intermingling of figures and foliage characteristic of Romanesque initials. Frames of miniatures, which often contain ornament, are not used like Gothic borders to amplify or comment on a scene. Isolated panels forming decorative headpieces are ubiquitous. They may be square or rectangular, pi-shaped or broad bands. They are often combined with display script for a title, but the script does not become absorbed in the

decorative scheme, as, for example, in Insular or Carolingian illumination (*see* CAROLINGIAN ART, §IV, 3).

Accordingly there is some justification for considering the ornament of Byzantine manuscripts a separate field of study from that of their illustration. The main lines of its development are quickly drawn. Up to the 9th and 10th centuries there was a wide diversity of approaches, with many distinct variants, which broadly may be traced back to the ornamental vocabulary of Late Roman art. Around the mid-10th century flower-petal ornament (*Blütenblattstil*) was developed, with its characteristic repetition of small, circular, flower-like forms, distributed often with geometrical precision over the field. The desired effect seems to have been to imitate cloisonné enamelwork and may be seen to perfection in a copy of the *Hippiatrika* (Berlin, Dt. Staatsbib., MS. Phil. 1538), which has hundreds of decorative headbands, all slightly different. The *Hippiatrika* was clearly the work of an artist with an inventive genius for ornament, who may well have played a significant part in establishing the new stylistic canon.

Blütenblattstil retained its prestige as the principal mode for ornament until the end of the Byzantine empire, although classicizing patterns continued to appear on occasion. It was remarkably adaptable and was further developed with a knowledge of Islamic decorative patterns from the late 13th century. Nevertheless it remains characteristically Byzantine and instantly recognizable. A premium was placed on the ornament's regularity and high degree of finish, and the generous use of gold and saturated pigments creates a rich and lustrous effect. Many Byzantine manuscripts containing ornament but no illustration are major works in exceptional condition and deserve systematic study.

BIBLIOGRAPHY

THE BIBLE

K. Weitzmann: *Studies in Classical and Byzantine Manuscript Illumination*, ed. H. L. Kessler (Chicago, 1971), pp. 45–75

H. Belting and G. Cavallo: *Die Bibel des Niketas* (Wiesbaden, 1979)

J. Lowden: 'An Alternative Interpretation of the Manuscripts of Niketas', *Byzantion*, liii (1983), pp. 559–74

NEW TESTAMENT

Codex Purpureus Rossanensis (?6th century; Rossano, Mus. Dioc.); facs. ed. G. Cavallo, J. Gribomont and W. Loerke, Codices selecti, lxxxi (Rome and Graz, 1987)

G. Millet: *Recherches sur l'iconographie de l'évangile aux XIVe–XVe siècles d'après les monuments de Mistra, de la Macédoine, et du Mont Athos* (Paris, 1916)

A. M. Friend: 'Portraits of the Evangelists in Greek and Latin Manuscripts', *A. Stud.*, v (1927), pp. 115–47; vii (1929), pp. 3–33

H. Buchthal: 'Some Representations from the Life of St Paul in Byzantine and Carolingian Art', *Tortulae: Festschrift J. Kollwitz* (Freiburg im Breisgau, 1966), pp. 43–8

R. Hamann-MacLean: 'Der Berliner Codex graecus Quarto 66 und seine nächsten Verwändten als Beispiele des Stilwandels im frühen 13. Jahrhundert', *Studien zur Buchmalerei und Goldschmiedekunst des Mittelalters: Festschrift für K. H. Usener* (Marburg, 1967), pp. 225–50

T. Velmans: *Le Tétraévangile de la Laurentienne, Florence Laur. VI. 23* (Paris, 1971)

H. L. Kessler: 'Paris. Gr. 102: A Rare Illustrated Acts of the Apostles', *Dumbarton Oaks Pap.*, xxvii (1973), pp. 209–16

G. Galavaris: *The Illustrations of the Prefaces in Byzantine Gospels* (Vienna, 1979)

R. Nelson: *The Iconography of Preface and Miniature in the Byzantine Gospel Book* (New York, 1980)

O. Kresten and G. Prato: 'Die Miniatur des Evangelisten Markus im Codex Purpureus Rossanensis: Eine spätere Einfügung', *Röm. Hist. Mitt.*, xxvii (1985), pp. 381–99

J. Anderson: *The New York Cruciform Lectionary* (University Park, 1992)

OLD TESTAMENT

RBA: 'Hiob'

J. J. Tikkanen: *Die Psalterillustration im Mittelalter*, I/i–ii (Helsingfors, 1895–7)

T. Uspenskij: *L'Octateuque de la bibliothèque du Sérail à Constantinople* (Sofia, 1907)

D.-C. Hesseling: *Miniatures de l'Octateuque grec de Smyrne* (Leiden, 1909)

H. Buchthal: *The Miniatures of the Paris Psalter* (London, 1938)

K. Weitzmann: *The Joshua Roll: A Work of the Macedonian Renaissance* (Princeton, 1948)

S. Dufrenne: *Pantocrator 61, Paris grec 20, British Museum 40731* (1966), i of *L'Illustration des psautiers grecs du moyen âge* (Paris, 1966–)

S. Der Nersessian: *Londres Add. 19352* (1970), ii of *L'Illustration des psautiers grecs du moyen âge* (Paris, 1966–)

H. Belting: 'Zum Palatina-Psalter des 13. Jahrhunderts', *Jb. Österreich. Byz.*, xxi (1972), pp. 17–38

J. Lassus: *L'Illustration byzantine du Livre des Rois* (Paris, 1973)

M. B. Shchepkina: *Miniatyri Khludovskoi Psaltiri* [Miniatures of the Chludov Psalter] (Moscow, 1977)

J. Anderson: 'The Seraglio Octateuch and the Kokkinobaphos Master', *Dumbarton Oaks Pap.*, xxxvi (1982), pp. 83–114

A. Cutler: *The Aristocratic Psalters in Byzantium* (Paris, 1984)

C. Havice: 'The Marginal Miniatures in the Hamilton Psalter (Kupferstich-kabinett 78.A.9)', *Jb. Berlin. Mus.*, xxvi (1984), pp. 79–142

K. Weitzmann and H. Kessler: *The Cotton Genesis: British Library Codex Cotton Otho B. VI* (Princeton, 1986)

C. Walter: 'Latter-day Saints and the Image of Christ in the Ninth-century Byzantine Marginal Psalters', *Rev. Etud. Byz.*, xlv (1987), pp. 205–22

J. Lowden: *Illuminated Prophet Books* (University Park, 1988)

——: 'Observations on Illustrated Byzantine Psalters', *A. Bull.*, lxx (1988), pp. 242–60

J. Anderson, P. Canart and C. Walter: *The Barberini Psalter, Codex Vaticanus Barberinianus Graecus 372* (Zurich, 1989)

K. Corrigan: *Visual Polemics in the Ninth-century Byzantine Psalters* (Cambridge, MA, 1992)

J. Lowden: 'The Cotton Genesis and Other Illustrated Manuscripts of Genesis', *Gesta*, xxxi (1992), pp. 40–53

——: *The Octateuchs: A Study in Byzantine Manuscript Illumination* (University Park, 1992)

OTHER RELIGIOUS TEXTS

Cosmas Indicopleustes: *Christianike topographia* (6th century); ed. and Fr. trans. W. Wolska-Conus, 3 vols (Paris, 1968–73)

Menologion of Basil II (late 10th century; Rome, Vatican, Bib. Apostolica, MS. Vat. gr. 1613); facs., Codices e Vaticanis selecti phototypice expressi, vii (Turin, 1907)

C. Stornajolo: *Le miniature della topografia christiana di Cosma Indicopleuste, codice Vaticano greco 699* (Milan, 1908)

——: *Miniature delle omilie di Giacomo Monaco (cod. Vatic. gr. 1162)* (Rome, 1910)

S. Der Nersessian: *L'Illustration du roman de 'Barlaam et Ioasaph'* (Paris, 1937)

A. Grabar: *Les Miniatures du Grégoire de Nazianze de l'Ambrosienne (Ambrosianus E.49–50 inf.)* (Paris, 1943)

J. R. Martin: *The Illustration of the Heavenly Ladder of John Climachus* (Princeton, 1954)

G. Galavaris: *The Illustrations of the Liturgical Homilies of Gregory Nazianzus* (Princeton, 1969)

D. Mouriki-Charalambous: *The Octateuch Miniatures of the Byzantine Manuscripts of Cosmas Indicopleustes* (diss., Princeton U., NJ, 1970)

A. Cutler and P. Magdalino: 'Some Precisions on the Lincoln College Typikon', *Cah. Archéol.*, xxvii (1978), pp. 179–98

A. Grabar and M. Manoussacas: *L'Illustration du manuscrit de Skylitzès de la Bibliothèque nationale de Madrid* (Venice, 1979)

K. Weitzmann: 'Illustrations to the Lives of the Five Martyrs of Sebaste', *Dumbarton Oaks Pap.*, xxxiii (1979), pp. 95–112

——: *The Miniatures of the Sacra Parallela, Parisinus Graecus 923* (Princeton, 1979)

L. Brubaker: 'Politics, Patronage and Art in Ninth-century Byzantium: The *Homilies* of Gregory of Nazianzus in Paris (B.N. gr. 510)', *Dumbarton Oaks Pap.*, xxxix (1985), pp. 1–13

——: 'Byzantine Art of the Ninth Century: Theory, Practice, and Culture', *Byz. & Mod. Gr. Stud.*, xiii (1989), pp. 23–93

N. P. Ševčenko: *Illustrated Manuscripts of the Metaphrastian Menologion* (Chicago, 1990)

J. Anderson: 'The Illustrated Sermons of James the Monk: Their Dates, Order and Place in the History of Byzantine Art', *Viator*, xxii (1991), pp. 69–120

CLASSICAL TEXTS

Vienna Dioskurides (c. 512; Vienna, Österreich. Nbib, Cod. med. gr. 1); facs., Codices selecti, xii (Graz, 1970)

P. Buberl and H. Gerstinger: *Die byzantinischen Handschriften*, ii (Leipzig, 1938), pp. 1–36

K. Weitzmann: *Ancient Book Illumination* (Cambridge, MA, 1959)

Z. Kádár: *Survivals of Greek Zoological Illuminations in Byzantine Manuscripts* (Budapest, 1978)

ORNAMENTAL DECORATION

M. A. Frantz: 'Byzantine Illuminated Ornament', *A. Bull.*, xvi (1934), pp. 43–76

J. Anderson: 'The Illustration of Cod. Sinai. gr. 339', *A. Bull.*, lxi (1979), pp. 167–85

R. Nelson: 'Paleologan Illuminated Ornament and the Arabesque', *Wien. Jb. Kstgesch.*, xli (1988), pp. 7–22

L. Brubaker: 'The Introduction of Painted Initials in Byzantium', *Scriptorium*, xlv (1991), pp. 22–46

For further bibliography see §1 above.

JOHN LOWDEN

3. SYRIAC. Relatively few of the numerous manuscripts written in Syriac are illuminated. They are usually of simple rather than de luxe quality, having well-executed text but little ornamental embellishment. Many Syriac manuscripts are precisely dated by scribal notes (the earliest is of 411), and illuminated examples may be divided into two main chronological groups: those of the 6th to the 10th century (mostly 6th–7th century), and those of the 11th to the 13th century. Syriac manuscripts originated in Syrian Orthodox (Jacobite or Monophysite), Nestorian, Melkite (Chalcedonian) and Maronite milieux. They were produced in scriptoria attached to churches, schools (e.g. at Edessa, now Urfa, and Nisibis, now Nusaybin, Turkey) and monasteries in cities and villages, primarily in northern Mesopotamia and northern Syria, but also in Egypt (e.g. Alexandria and the Wadi Natrun; *see* COPTIC ART, §IV, 3 and Mt Sinai (*see* SINAI, §2(iv)). Many of these manuscripts were preserved until modern times in these monasteries and in Lebanon. Where it survives, illustration takes the form of canon tables, *capitularia lectionum* (tables of contents of liturgical readings), large crosses serving as frontispieces and endpieces, pi-shaped headpieces, author portraits, dedicatory scenes and narrative and Feast cycles. In a few cases the cycles are extensive. Gilding was increasingly used in the 12th and 13th centuries for lettering to emphasize important text in liturgical books. A notable example is a large unillustrated Lectionary (450×300 mm; Homs, Patriarch. Lib.) copied in 1168–9 near Mardin in Turkey with readings in gold and silver Estranghelo (majuscule) letters. An even more elaborate manuscript (destr. 13th century) was made by the historian Michael the Syrian (d 1199) for his monastery of Mar Barsauna, near the River Euphrates: written in gold on silver ground and in silver on gold ground, it was further illuminated with New Testament scenes and was bound in silver. The single Syriac manuscript of tinted (blue) parchment is a small Nestorian liturgical book (190×140 mm; Rome, Vatican, Bib. Apostolica, MS. syr. 662) used for private devotions, written in gold ink in 1298 for a Mongol princess.

(i) 6th–10th centuries. The style of decoration on the few illustrated manuscripts of the 6th and 7th centuries is Byzantine. Ornament is usually restricted to simple motifs flanking a running short title every few folios. Only five

manuscripts have decoration with full-length figures: a Gospel book and a Nestorian Bible (Paris, Bib. N., MSS syr. 33 and 341 respectively), a Book of Kings (Mt Sinai, Monastery of St Catherine, MS. syr. 28), a Gospel book (Diyarbakır, Church of Mar Yakub) and the RABBULA GOSPELS (586). This decoration includes full-page pictures of dedicatory scenes, standing figures and New Testament scenes, such as an *Ascension* (see fig. 64) in the Rabbula Gospels, and a standing *Christ* in the Diyarbakır Gospels (fol. 1*r*). Smaller framed pictures appear at the start of each book of the Nestorian Bible (e.g. Old Testament scenes: fols 8*r*, 25*v*, 46*r*, 118*r*; full-length author portraits: fols 36*v*, 52*v*, 143*v*, 182*r*, 186*r*, 218*v*, 212*r*, 248*r*) and the Mt Sinai Book of Kings (e.g. standing *King David*; New Finds M24). The Paris Bible illustrations had gilded backgrounds. In the Gospel book (Wolfenbüttel, Herzog August Bib., Cod. 31.300) copied at Beth Hala near Damascus in 633–4 a scribal note is decoratively written inside a large full-page cross (fol. 284*v*), which has a central bust of *Christ* of the so-called Syrian type (i.e. with a triangular face and short curly hair). Three manuscripts contain historiated Eusebian canon tables. The Rabbula tables are the most elaborate, featuring prophets, Evangelists, 24 New Testament scenes, fauna and flora. The Paris tables are flanked by five scriptural scenes, various birds and a fountain, and the Diyabakır tables by fauna and flora. Canon tables with simple ornament appear in four other Syriac manuscripts of the 6th to the 7th century (Florence, Bib. Medicea-Laurenziana, MSS Plut. I.40 and I.58; Damascus, Assad. N. Lib. MS. arabe 528; Berlin, Staatsbib. Preuss. Kultbes., MS. Phill. 1388).

In the 8th and 9th centuries bands of plaited and other ornament were used to divide the written text, as in several manuscripts copied at Edessa and, perhaps, Melitene (now Malatya, Turkey): one of Gregory of Nazianzus (790); another of John Climachus (817) in which some dividers resemble horizontal ladders; and a third of collected authors (9th century) in which the dividers appear as horizontal columns and trees festooned with birds (London, BL, Add. MSS 14548, 14593, 14601 respectively). Canon tables continued to precede Gospels (e.g. Birmingham, Selly Oak Coll. Lib.; Rome, Vatican, Bib. Apostolica, MS. syr. 268; Paris, Bib. N., MS. syr. 54; and Dublin, Chester Beatty Lib., MS. syr. 3). The last includes in the second canon table a picturesque figure of a fisherman. *Capitularia lectionum* became more elaborate in the early 8th century and were placed in colourful architectural frames.

(ii) 11th–13th centuries. Scribal notes (often dated) identify the four main areas of illustrated manuscript production in this period as at or near Melitene, near Mosul (Iraq), at Edessa and in the TUR 'ABDIN. The predominant foreign influence on iconography and style is Byzantine, but Armenian, Crusader and Islamic elements are also apparent, thus reflecting the mixed, cosmopolitan society in which these books originated. Most of them date between 1190 and 1250; they include nearly twenty Lectionaries, one Bible, two Qarqaphthian (Masoretic) Bibles, one Psalter, two books of sermons and two liturgical books. The last two, both copied in 1238, one at Edessa (Oxford, Bodleian Lib., MS. Dawkins 58) and the other possibly at Antioch (Paris, Bib. N., MS. syr. 112) are on paper; the others are all on parchment. The Bible (*c.* 1200, Cambridge, U. Lib., MS. 001.002) and 13 of the Lectionaries are of a large format (averaging 400×300 mm) which surpasses that of all Early Christian illustrated manuscripts in both Syriac and Greek. The picture cycles in the Cambridge Bible and five of the Lectionaries (*c.* 1192, Paris, Bib. N., MS. syr. 355; 1219–20, Rome, Vatican, Bib. Apostolica, MS. syr. 599; *c.* 1220, London, BL, Add. MS. 7170; 1226, Midyat, Syr. Orthdx Bishopric; *c.* 1250, Mardin, Church of the Forty Martyrs) number between 20 and nearly 60 mostly framed miniatures, all corresponding to Byzantine Feast or Gospel cycles. They reflect an increased interest in protracted Gospel cycles that characterizes contemporary Levantine manuscripts.

Greek inscriptions appear on the illustrations of seven manuscripts. Some are simply titles that have been copied together with the illustrations from Byzantine originals, as in a Lectionary of 1054 from Melitene (Homs, Patriarch. Lib.), the Cambridge Bible and a collection of sermons from the Tur 'Abdin (12th–13th century; Berlin, Staatsbib. Preuss. Kultbes., MS. Sachau. 220). Others were apparently written by a scribe fluent in Greek, as in a Qarqaphthian Bible (1092) from near Mosul, a collection of homilies (*c.* 1120) of unknown provenance (Rome, Vatican, Bib. Apostolica, MS. Barb. Or. 118 and MS. syr. 118 respectively) and a Lectionary (*c.* 1272; Mardin, Church of the Forty Martyrs) originally from Harput, Turkey. In the Oxford liturgical book produced at Edessa in 1238, the names of the painted subjects are recorded in Greek minuscule and were probably written by the Byzantine artist. Manuscripts painted in the Byzantine style but without any Greek words on their miniatures include a

64. Syriac manuscript miniature, *Ascension*, 336×268 mm, from the Rabbula Gospels, 586 (Florence, Biblioteca Medicea-Laurenziana, MS. Plut. I. 56, fol. 13*v*)

Lectionary (1226; Midyat, Syr. Orthdx Bishopric) with framed miniatures on 32 leaves from Salah in the Tur 'Abdin, which may be by a Byzantine provincial artist, whose work resembles that in contemporary Byzantinizing Armenian manuscripts (*see* ARMENIA, §III, 1(ii)). A single page (Diyarbarkır, Church of Mar Yakub) detached from a Lectionary of the 12th to the 13th century has been described as Byzantine in appearance. Another Lectionary (*c.* 1250; Mardin, Church of the Forty Martyrs) with 20 framed miniatures including scenes from the *Life of Christ* (e.g. the *Baptism*; see fig. 65) combines a strong Byzantine style with local braided ornament.

The influence of Byzantine, Armenian and Latin styles is evident in other manuscripts. These include a Lectionary (Paris, Bib. N., MS. syr. 355) with a long colophon stating that, once written and the necessary funds collected, the manuscript was taken to Melitene (sometime before 1192) where the paintings, the 24 subjects of which are listed, were inserted. The eight surviving scenes, which have symmetrical compositions, each framed by an elaborate arch, have been compared with the miniatures of the MELISENDE PSALTER. A Lectionary with a Byzantine Feast cycle (1221; from Edessa; Jerusalem, ex-St Mark's, MS. 6) has been stylistically compared with an Armenian manuscript of 1193 now in Venice (S Lazzaro degli Armeni, Bib., MS. 1635). The four *Evangelists* combined on a single page of another Lectionary (Paris, Bib. N., MS.

syr. 356) are also considered to be partly of Armenian inspiration.

Other Syriac manuscripts are painted in the Islamic orientalizing style associated with the Mosul school that produced illustrated Arabic manuscripts. Two Syriac Lectionaries (1219–20, Rome, Vatican, Bib. Apostolica, MS. syr. 559; and *c.* 1220, London, BL, Add. MS. 7170), produced respectively at Mar Mattai near Mosul and perhaps in the Tur 'Adbin, are particularly close to each other in iconography, layout and style. The first had about 57 miniatures, the second 50. These are characterized by shallow compositions of geometric precision, a prominent use of flat patterns and arabesque motifs, and frames along fewer than four sides that are often heavily ornamented. The physiognomy of the figures is oriental. The manuscripts are stylistically related to contemporary bronze objects with silver-inlaid Gospel scenes, produced by Christian artisans at Mosul for Islamic patrons.

The complex interaction of scribes and artists working under multiple cultural influences is well illustrated by the following four manuscripts. The same scribe, Bakos, copied at Edessa the parchment Lectionary of 1221 decorated in Armenian style and the paper liturgical book of 1238 illuminated by a Byzantine artist in the metropolitan style. Similarly the scribe Sahda copied at Salah in the Tur 'Abdin the Lectionary of 1226 illustrated in a Byzantine style, and a fragmentary Lectionary (New York, M. Kevorkian priv. col.; Berlin, F. E. Sprigath priv. col.) described as of 'Asiatic' style. This great variety of competently executed painting styles in Syriac manuscripts that date mainly between 1220 and 1240 suggests a high volume of production, although many are now lost.

BIBLIOGRAPHY
W. Stassof: *L'Ornement slave et oriental* (St Petersburg, 1887)
J. Leroy: *Les Manuscrits syriaques à peintures conservés dans les bibliothèques d'Europe et d'Orient* (Paris, 1964)
M. Mundell Mango: 'Patrons and Scribes Indicated in Syriac Manuscripts, 411 to 800 AD', *XVI. internationaler Byzantinistenkongress. Akten: Wien, 1981*, I/iv, pp. 3–12
S. Brock: 'The Syriac Manuscripts', *Sinai: Treasures of the Monastery of Saint Catherine*, ed. K. A. Manafis (Athens, 1990), pp. 358–9, 372–3
MARLIA MUNDELL MANGO

65. Syriac manuscript miniature, *Baptism*, from a Lectionary, *c.* 1250 (Mardin, Church of the Forty Martyrs)

VI. Icons.

Although in its broadest sense an icon may be a representation of a holy person in any medium or size (*see* ICON; *see also* §IV, 2(ii)(b) and (c) above), this article is mainly concerned with the most common type, the painted wooden devotional panel, with some discussion of the fine mosaic icons also produced. The icon played an important role in the religious and secular life of the Byzantines, testifying to artistic trends and to developments in theological and political thought. Indeed, icon painting was so closely connected with the fabric of Byzantine politics as to play a decisive part in one of the empire's greatest crises, the iconoclastic controversy (726–843; *see* ICONOCLASM). As an art form, the icon is derived from the customs and painting styles of Late Antiquity, which took on a new ideological content under the influence of Christianity. New modes of expression gradually evolved and the Byzantine icon acquired a character, distinct from other forms of European art, that it retained for almost 1000 years. During that time, however, it

continued to develop, both following and creating widely influential stylistic trends. Icon painting continued to develop up to the fall of Constantinople in 1453, and Late Byzantine styles remained influential with later peripatetic artists, particularly those who settled in Crete, where a flourishing icon market grew over the centuries (see POST-BYZANTINE, §II, 1). The two most important icon collections to have survived are preserved in the monastery of St Catherine, Sinai, and on Mt Athos. Other notable collections are housed in monasteries and churches at, for example, Meteora, Patmos, Thessaloniki, Jerusalem and Venice, and in many museums (e.g. Athens, Benaki Mus.; Athens, Byz. Mus.; Belgrade, Mus. Serb. Orthdx Ch.; Kiev, Mus. W. & Orient. A.; Moscow, Pushkin Mus. F.A.; Moscow, Tret'yakov Gal.; Ohrid, Gal. Icons; St Petersburg, Hermitage).

1. Introduction. 2. Before c. 843. 3. c. 843–c. 1204. 4. c. 1204–1453.

1. INTRODUCTION.

(i) Development and use. The writings of EUSEBIOS OF CAESAREA, St John Chrysostomos (c. 347–407) and the *Life of St Pankratios* (later 8th century or early 9th) contain accounts of images of the martyrs being painted by their disciples. An even more widespread tradition concerned St Luke painting the Virgin from life, and many icons are traditionally attributed to the Evangelist (see LUKE, §1 and 2). Visual references to the art of icon painting survive in illuminated manuscripts that depict a seated artist painting the portrait of the Virgin (e.g. 11th century; Jerusalem, Mus. Gr. Orthdx Patriarch., Cod. Taphou 14), of St John of Damascus (e.g. 9th century; Paris, Bib. N., MS. gr. 923, fol. 208r) or of another holy person (e.g. 12th century; Mt Athos, Dionysiou Monastery, Cod. 61, fol. 35r).

Until the 6th century some icons were venerated as objects that had come into contact with a holy person, either directly or through the intermediary of a relic. Other icons, such as the image of Christ's face on the MANDYLION OF EDESSA, were venerated as miraculous, that is not made by a human hand. During the late 6th century and the 7th there was a marked growth in the cult of the icon. Images were set up as objects of devotion in private houses and used on public and official occasions. During crises an icon might be invested with the powers of a Palladium, for example the icon of *St Demetrios* that was invoked in Thessaloniki on the occasions that the city was besieged by the Slavs in the late 6th century and the 7th. In addition icons were believed to be a means of bringing the beholder into contact with the divine.

Objections to the use of icons were voiced from as early as the 4th century, although the Christological arguments for and against icons were not really developed until well into the iconoclastic controversy. The result was the establishment of the Orthodox theory of images. According to St John of Damascus (c. 675–749), who was one of the most fervent supporters of the dogma, 'An icon is of like character with its subject, but with a certain difference. It is not like its prototype in every way'. The icon therefore is a portrait that must present the recognizable characteristics of the holy person, while at the same time it must be distinguishable from its subject. If these two conditions are not met, then there is no icon. This point is crucial to an understanding of the transcendent nature of Byzantine icon painting and is expressed in two constant stylistic traits. The first is faithfulness to certain facial characteristics: hairstyle, beard, eyes and even demeanour. Indeed, this is even noticeable in other figure painting, where both the holy figures and scenes in which they appear are easily recognizable. The second trait is the elimination of naturalistic elements: realistic space and light, the position, stance, and even the proportions of figures. These are all subjected to the requirements of a new style at the service of the Christian faith. Thus the icon is situated midway between the world of the senses and that beyond the senses. The figures and scenes represented in icons reflect a mystical world that, while resembling the earthly world, is distinct from it. This similarity and difference create an inherent opposition in the Byzantine icon that gives it its spiritual value. Thus, in the production of icons, the authenticity of the prototype and the faithful reproduction of that model assume great significance, and in creating the painting the artist must work within a framework laid down and sanctioned by the Church. Nevertheless, the artist, depending on the extent and range of his talent, invariably expresses his own personality through the choice of models, their use in his composition and even their interpretation. His work accordingly reflects both contemporary theological trends and the changing tastes of his patrons.

The use of icons in private and public devotion influenced the choice, sanctioning and diffusion of iconographic subjects. Of particular importance was the placing of icons within the church. As well as those positioned on iconostases (see SCREEN (i), §2), an individual devotional icon might have decorated the wall or been placed on a special stand as the church's main icon, often attributed with miraculous powers. From the 10th century onwards iconostases were arranged in tiers according to a definite system. The lowest tier contained the 'despotic' (chief) icons of Christ, the Virgin and St John the Baptist arranged in a *Deësis*, to which was added an icon of the church's patron saint. These icons have an eschatological subject-matter appropriate for images intended to act as a focus for the prayers and entreaties of the faithful for the salvation of their souls. The importance of these icons is often indicated by finely worked silver or gilded mounts, set with gemstones. Sometimes double-sided icons (painted on both sides) were also displayed in this tier on special supports (see §3 below) that enabled the icon to be removed from the iconostasis and carried in procession during special services for which the painting on the reverse was of particular significance. The most common subjects were Christ or the Virgin on the obverse, with the Crucifixion of the reverse, although other combinations might occur according to the liturgical requirements of each church.

Smaller icons were placed in one or two tiers on the architrave above the despotic icons. The theme of the *Deësis* was repeated and expanded on one of these tiers, with the addition of the Twelve Apostles to the assembled company. The other tier usually contained a Christological cycle, most commonly the *Twelve Feasts* or scenes from the *Life of the Virgin* or another saint, depending on the dedication of the church. The formation and prevalence

of this system contributed to the surprising increase in icon production after the 11th century. In addition to the icons on display, every church and monastery had a sizeable collection of icons kept in the sanctuary or treasury, mainly so that the relevant icon might be employed during worship on individual saints' days.

The portability of icons contributed to their widespread diffusion in private devotion; they were found in every home and even taken on journeys. These small-scale icons may depict an enormous range of subject-matter and often appear in the form of diptychs, triptychs or polyptychs (i.e. icons painted on two, three or more folding wings), reproducing the decoration of the iconostasis in miniature.

(ii) Techniques and centres of production. Icons were mostly painted on a wooden panel prepared with a thin layer of plaster, on material stretched over the panel or even directly on to the bare wood. The surface was covered with underpaint and the outline of the composition, usually drawn from a pattern-book, incised with a sharp tool. Successive layers of paint were applied, starting with the background colour, then the areas of drapery and lastly the modelled flesh tones of the face and hands. The paints were made using simple, natural materials, usually earth colours with a binding agent of egg, although the encaustic technique, using hot, melted wax, was employed in some early icons of the 6th and 7th centuries (e.g. Sinai, monastery of St Catherine; *see* §2 below and ENCAUSTIC PAINTING, §1). The most precious material was gold-leaf, which was often used for the background and for haloes, laid over a thin layer of red pigment that helped to bind it to the wooden surface. Yellow ochre was sometimes substituted for gold, or, mainly in Macedonia and Cyprus, silver might be used (e.g. *St John the Baptist*, early 12th century; Asinou, Panagia Phorbiotissa); in these areas, also, the ground and/or haloes might be decorated with low-relief patterns in the plaster (e.g. *St Paul*, 13th century; Nicosia, Panagia Chrysaliniotissa). Vermilion was a costly pigment normally used for drawing in details, although in some 12th-century icons it replaced gold as the ground, for example on various architrave icons from Mt Athos, a *Transfiguration* (St Petersburg, Hermitage) and a *Raising of Lazarus* (Athens, priv. col., see 1987 exh. cat., no. 7). Lapis lazuli, another precious material, was occasionally used for blue draperies in such fine works as a *Crucifixion* on a double-sided icon (14th century; Athens, Byz. Mus.).

As holy objects, icons have generally been treated with great care and restored, when necessary, according to the original lines of the composition, as is evident in a 6th-century *Christ* repainted in the 13th century (Mt Sinai, monastery of St Catherine), a 9th-century *Crucifixion* repainted in the 10th and 13th centuries, and a 12th-century *Virgin* repainted in the 17th century (both Athens, Byz. Mus.). Sometimes the painting was transferred to a new wooden backing: an inscription on the back of the *Five Martyrs of Sebaste* (late 11th century or early 12th; Mt Athos, Great Lavra Monastery), for example, states that it was remounted in 1197.

In addition to the painted icons, many portable and monumental mosaic icons survive, often with mounts in precious metals. Icons made wholly of precious metals include an image of the *Archangel Michael* in silver gilt,

gold, enamels and hardstones (10th century; Venice, Tesoro S Marco), and the silver icons of Georgia (*see* GEORGIA, §V, 1(i)).

Constantinople was the centre of production for painted wooden icons (*see* ISTANBUL, §II, 1), and the emperors, patriarchs, the upper ranks of the clergy, the civil aristocracy and the monasteries were instrumental in the creation, sanction and dissemination of iconographic types, programmes and new styles (*see* §I, 2(i) above). Prestigious icons made there were much sought after in the provinces and in the monasteries on Mt Sinai, Patmos and Mt Athos, spreading Byzantine art beyond the boundaries of the empire to the Orthodox countries of the Balkans, Russia, Georgia and, to some extent, to the West. Icons were also produced in numerous provincial centres.

2. BEFORE *c.* 843. As heir to the Late Antique tradition of portraiture, both in terms of style and iconography, the icon's closest forebears are the funerary portraits found at Faiyum (mid-1st century to mid-4th; e.g. London, BM; *see* ENCAUSTIC PAINTING, fig. 2 and FAIYUM, §2). These remain naturalistic, while emphasizing such characteristics as large staring eyes, and were painted in the encaustic technique.

Few icons survive from the period before the iconoclastic controversy. The earliest (6th century) are found in the monastery of St Catherine (*see* SINAI, §2(iii)), which formerly also housed a *Virgin and Child* (first half of the 6th century), *St John the Baptist* (*c.* 6th century), *SS Sergius and Bakchos* (7th century) and *St Platon and a Female Martyr* (6th–7th century; all Kiev, Mus. W. & Orient. A.). Three of Sinai's 6th-century icons can be ascribed to artists from Constantinople and may have been donated by Justinian I on the occasion of the monastery's foundation (548–65). They are distinguished by a high standard of workmanship, the classicizing figures and the use of encaustic. One depicts the *Virgin and Child Enthroned with SS George and Theodore* (see fig. 66). The saints are in military dress, and two angels standing behind the Virgin look up towards the hand of God, which reaches down from the sky. The figures are set against an architectural background with an exedra, of which only the upper part is visible. The composition is based on imperial iconography, with the ruler flanked by officials, and the iconographic type of the *Virgin and Child Enthroned* was frequently used in the 6th century in monumental mosaics (e.g. Ravenna, S Apollinare Nuovo; Thessaloniki, Hagios Demetrios), textiles (e.g. Cleveland, OH, Mus. A.) and in the decorative arts, for example on an ivory diptych (mid-6th century; Berlin, Skulpgal.). The Classical tradition is evident in the slight turn of the Virgin's head, her youthful, rosy face, the position of the Child and in the two swiftly moving angels, painted in monochrome with diaphanous haloes.

A second icon combines the Classical tradition with an image of *Christ Pantokrator* ('all powerful', i.e. holding a Gospel book in his left hand and raising his right in blessing; *see* SINAI, fig. 3). It is probably a copy of the mosaic icon of *Christ Chalkites* (destr. 726) that decorated the Chalke Gate in the Great Palace at Constantinople (*see* ISTANBUL, §III, 12). An almost imperceptible contrapposto may be discerned in the way the left shoulder and

66. Icon of the *Virgin and Child Enthroned with SS George and Theodore*, encaustic on panel, 685×495 mm, mid-6th century (Mt Sinai, Monastery of St Catherine)

the Gospel book in Christ's right hand seem to push slightly forward. A faint light from the right throws into shadow the left side of Christ's neck, created with olive green brushstrokes. The face is exceptionally fine and reveals an impressionistic modelling of flesh, with thick, free brushstrokes, three-dimensional handling of space and an emphasis on the underlying spirituality of the expression. The features are individualized, with enlarged, slightly asymmetrical eyes, and suggest an idealized inner world, full of beauty and nobility, which surpasses reality. The image corresponds to the ideal type of Christ, for which the great gold halo is well suited. Other classicizing features include the three-dimensional aspect of the exedra behind the figure and the progressively deepening shades of blue in the sky.

In the third icon (*see* LATE ANTIQUITY, fig. 3) St Peter is placed before a similar architectural background. The icon's size (928×533 mm) allows greater projection of the figure into space and the addition of three busts in roundels in the upper part. A bust of Christ occupies the central roundel, with the Virgin on the right and a youthful figure, probably St John, on the left, thus creating a type of *Deësis* that became institutionalized in Byzantine art. The dignified figure of St Peter shares similarities of composition, modelling and a correspondingly impressionistic use of colour with the bust of Christ, although the roundels show

a more linear treatment of drapery. The features of St Peter are also marked by asymmetry, employing a facial type that had become standardized in the 5th and 6th centuries, as is evident from the mosaics of the saint in the Arian baptistery, the Orthodox baptistery and S Vitale, Ravenna.

The other early icons at Sinai include a 6th-century *Ascension* and a 7th-century encaustic *Three Hebrews in the Fiery Furnace*, which bears a Greek inscription (Daniel 3:49–50) in majuscule on the frame. The three Hebrews are depicted in traditional fashion wearing Sasanian costumes, in frontal *orans* poses (with arms outstretched in prayer), while an angel stands to the left in contrapposto, extending his staff to the flames. The figures are marked by an attempt at three-dimensional rendering. Another interesting icon is that of *Christ Enthroned* depicted as the Ancient of Days (*c.* 7th century), set in a mandorla against a starry sky.

Several icons of the 6th to the 8th century were probably made by workshops in Palestine. These include five small, narrative scenes from the *Life of Christ* painted on the lid of a wooden reliquary (Rome, Vatican, Mus. Sacro), the iconography of which is associated with Palestine. The figures are schematic and scaled-down approximations of the human form, and they may be compared with those in the RABBULA GOSPELS (*c.* 586; Florence, Bib. Medicea-Laurenziana). A similar naive style is found on a series of icons depicting individual saints and a *Crucifixion* (7th or 8th century; Sinai, monastery of St Catherine). These were also probably made in Palestine and are characterized by slightly abstract but boldly outlined figures. Several icons of the iconoclastic period are also preserved at Sinai, which remained outside the influence of the central authority. The most interesting of these is a *Crucifixion* (8th century), which is similar iconographically to the wall painting of the same subject (741–52) in S Maria Antiqua, Rome. In the icon Christ is shown wearing a *collobium* (a long, sleeveless tunic). On either side are the two crucified thieves: the figure of the unrepentant thief is marked by curious modelling that gives him the physical attributes of a well-endowed female. The Virgin and St John appear below as witnesses to the scene.

Three large icons to have survived in Rome were also executed in encaustic: the *Virgin and Child* in the Pantheon, the *Virgin* in S Francesca Romana and the *Madonna della Clemenze* (a type of Virgin Eleousa ('merciful')) in S Maria in Trastevere, all dated *c.* 700. These icons are markedly different in character and cannot be attributed with any certainty to Byzantine artists, although they were based on models from Constantinople.

3. *c.* 843–*c.* 1204. The production of icons increased significantly after the official reinstatement of the dogma of their veneration. The influence of Constantinople remained central to the development of new styles, especially the revival of the Classical tradition under the Macedonian and Komnenian dynasties. Local workshops also flourished in this period at Sinai, on Cyprus, in Palestine and Macedonia, often producing work of the highest quality. Icons of the 9th century and the early 10th preserved in the monastery at Sinai are of varying quality. They include a *Crucifixion* (first half of the 9th century)

with some interesting iconographical elements. Some icons that may be attributed to Palestinian workshops, such as a *Nativity* (8th–9th century), an *Ascension* (9th–10th century) and individual saints, such as an equestrian icon of *St Merkurios* (10th century), are distinguished by sharp outlines, two-dimensional figures and simple colouring.

A series of icons of the 10th century or the early 11th at Sinai demonstrates a higher degree of technical perfection and probably originated in Constantinople. One of the most interesting examples (*c*. 945; see fig. 67) is connected with the introduction of new iconographic models by Constantine VII (*see* MACEDONIAN DYNASTY, (3)). Only the two side panels of what was originally a triptych have survived; these were later joined to give the appearance of a single icon. The upper part of the right-hand panel (67a) depicts *King Abgar* as a Byzantine emperor, seated on a throne and holding the Mandylion, which he has just received from Ananias; the lower part (67b) portrays *SS Basil and Ephraim*. The *Apostle Thaddeus* (67d) is seated on a similar throne in the centre of the upper left panel, with *SS Paul the Theban and Anthony* (67c) below. Although two of the saints depicted in the lower parts of the two panels were particularly venerated at St Catherine's, the similarity between the facial features of King Abgar and Constantine VII, and the quality of the workmanship, suggest that the icon was painted in an imperial workshop soon after the Mandylion's translation from Edessa to Constantinople in 944. Two icons at Sinai

67. Composite icon of (clockwise): (a) *King Abgar Holding the Mandylion*; (b) *SS Basil and Ephraim*; (c) *SS Paul the Theban and Anthony*; (d) *Apostle Thaddeus*, tempera on panels, 345×252 mm, *c*. 945 (Mt Sinai, Monastery of St Catherine)

dated to the late 10th century or the early 11th must have been produced in Constantinople and are of outstanding workmanship. The icon of the *Apostle Philip* shows him in a frontal, standing pose against a gold ground. His oval face, with enlarged, symmetrical eyes glancing sideways, is faultlessly drawn, while the linear and slightly modelled treatment of the drapery is reminiscent of 10th-century ivories. The second depicts a bust of *St Nicholas* surrounded by a broad frame containing ten medallions with busts of saints. The gold of the saint's halo and the grounds of the medallions were burnished to give a special gleam.

From the late 10th century onwards the liturgy and the decoration of the iconostasis with several rows of icons had a profound influence on the development of new iconographic types. Inventories, such as the *Typikon* (1081) of Bachkovo Monastery, and wills, such as that drawn up in 1059 by Eustathios Boilas (see Vryonis), indicate than many individual icons from iconostases were kept in monastic treasuries, although only a few have survived. Examples of iconostasis icons include one from an architrave showing *Christ Washing the Feet of the Disciples* in the lower part and the *Communion of the Apostles* above (late 10th century or early 11th; Mt Sinai, Monastery of St Catherine). An icon of the same date and provenance showing the *Apostle Thomas*, which originally formed part of a *Great Deësis*, is painted in the flat, schematic style that characterizes the wall paintings and mosaics in the rock-cut churches in Cappadocia (*see* CAPPADOCIA, §2(ii)) and at HOSIOS LOUKAS. An icon depicting a row of saints under an arcade (11th century; St Petersburg, Hermitage) originally belonged to the upper part of an iconostasis on Mt Athos. The massive icons of *SS Peter and Paul* and the *Cherson Virgin* (*c*. 1050; both Novgorod, Mus. A. Hist. & Archit.) are among the most significant surviving examples, having retained their mounts in precious metal.

The influence of the liturgy on icon painting is most evident in the development of the cycle of the Twelve Feasts and the menologion cycles, as seen in a group of icons at Sinai, including several diptychs, triptychs and polyptychs. The crowded compositions, with a host of tiny figures representing the saints for each month, are clearly related to contemporary manuscript illumination.

Numerous icons made of precious materials in the late 10th century and the early 11th can be attributed with some certainty to workshops in Constantinople. They include two icons of the *Archangel Michael* (Venice, Tesoro S Marco; *see* ICON, colour pl. I) made of repoussé silver gilt with enamelling, which were plundered by the crusaders in 1204. One features a full-length, frontal figure while the other is a bust; the latter's frame has undergone considerable alteration. Examples of mosaic icons include a bust of the *Virgin Hodegetria* ('who points the way', i.e. pointing to the Child as the Way) and a full-length *St John the Baptist* with a small, unidentified donor figure at the bottom left (both 11th century; Istanbul, Mus. Gr. Orthdx Patriarch.); they were probably intended for the iconostasis of the church of St Mary Pammakaristos at Constantinople. Stylistically they reflect the anti-classicizing tendencies evident in the wall mosaics in the katholikon of Hosios Loukas. Also dated to the 11th century are two small, finely crafted mosaic icons of *St Demetrios* (Mt Sinai,

Monastery of St Catherine) and *St Nicholas* (Patmos, St John the Divine Monastery). (For Georgian icons from this period *see* GEORGIA, §IV, 1(iii).)

From the end of the 11th century and throughout the 12th, icon painting attained new heights. Among the most technically proficient works are a classicizing *Crucifixion* (12th century) with saints in medallions on the frame and the *Heavenly Ladder* (second half of the 12th century; both Mt Sinai, Monastery of St Catherine) with its tiny figures led by John Climachus and Archbishop Antonios climbing the ladder; in both, the gold of the haloes has been burnished. Another set of finely painted icons in monumental style that must have come from Constantinople are those of *St Euthemios, Elijah, Moses* and the *Miracle at Chonai* (Mt Sinai, Monastery of St Catherine).

The new interest in expressing emotion through facial expressions is particularly evident in the icon of the *Virgin Eleousa* (Moscow, Tret'yakov Gal.), which was brought to Kiev from Constantinople in 1131; it was later placed in the cathedral of the Dormition (after 1155) at Vladimir, where, as the 'Virgin of Vladimir', it acquired great renown for its miracle-working properties (*see* UKRAINE, §III, 2(ii)). Only the faces and the hands survive from the original icon; the tender expressions of the Virgin and Child are marked by a melancholy associated with a premonition of Christ's Passion.

Numerous double-sided despotic icons, often intended for processional use (*see* §1(i) above), survive from the 12th century, particularly in Cyprus, where they are painted in a style that imitates the wall paintings in their respective churches. The icon of *St John the Baptist* in the Panagia Phorbiotissa (1105–6) at ASINOU is a particularly fine example, showing all the main characteristics of the church's decoration. The saint appears in three-quarter profile in an attitude of supplication, as befits an icon intended to be displayed as part of a *Deësis*. Despotic icons of *Christ Philanthropos* and the *Virgin Eleousa* have been preserved on the wooden iconostasis in the Enkleistra at St Neophytos Monastery, Paphos. Christ carries a closed Gospel book, and the Virgin turns towards him in an attitude of supplication. The same motifs decorate the lower parts and the backs of the icons. Similarities in technique and style between the two icons and the Enkleistra's wall paintings (1183) suggest that they were probably painted by the same artist.

The icons of the *Virgin* and *Christ* (*c.* 1192) in the Panagia tou Arakou at Lagoudera occupied a similar position on the iconostasis. The Christ figure, with faultlessly painted features, bears a striking resemblance to that painted in the church's dome, as does the Virgin to her counterpart in the wall painting of the *Annunciation*, indicating that they are by the same artist. Two other despotic icons can be linked with Cypriot wall paintings of the 12th century: a *St Spyridon* and an *Archangel Gabriel* (USA, priv. col., see 1988 exh. cat., nos 10 and 11).

A double-sided iconostasis icon (second half of the 12th century) in the cathedral at Kastoria is interesting both stylistically and for its innovative iconography. On one side is a *Virgin Hodegetria*, whose face, with its large eyes, is marked by an intense expression of anxiety and whose brow is contracted into deep wrinkles. The reverse shows a new iconographic type of Christ, the *Akra*

tapeinosis ('man of sorrows'). The base of the icon has grooves for attaching it to a support for carrying in processions. Similar depictions of emotional intensity are evident on other faces of the late 12th century, such as an icon of *Moses* on a sanctuary door at Sinai. Two other exceptional examples of late Komnenian art include an imposing icon of *Elijah*, shown in front of the cave, and a large icon of a standing *Virgin and Child* (Kastoria, Archaeol. Col., Chapel of Girls' Orphanage).

Another despotic icon from this period with an interesting iconography is a *Virgin and Child* (late 12th century; Athens, Byz. Mus.) from Thessaloniki, which was discovered under the 17th-century repainting of the same subject. The Virgin holds the Child on her right arm in a new version of the Eleousa type that is characterized by the extreme closeness of their faces, the Child's stiff pose and his elaborate style of dress. He looks at the Virgin with his head thrown back and one arm falling at his side, holding a closed scroll. He wears a short tunic with broad, red shoulder-straps, leaving his arms and legs bare. This image is painted on a silver ground and has a monumental character associated with such fine wall paintings as the *Last Judgement* in the cathedral of St Demetrius (1194–7) at Vladimir (*see* VLADIMIR-SUZDAL').

The number of icons created for the iconostasis increased significantly during the 12th century, above all the type intended for the iconostasis architrave. The largest group of this type is preserved on Mt Sinai, and many were produced by artists trained in the best workshops. One of the most outstanding examples is an *Annunciation*

68. Icon of the *Annunciation*, tempera on panel, 350×260 mm, late 12th century (Mt Sinai, Monastery of St Catherine)

(see fig. 68) from Constantinople, which shows the influence of the linear classicizing style of the late 12th century also found in the contemporary wall paintings of the churches of Hagioi Anargyroi at Kastoria, St George at Kurbinovo, and Panagia tou Arakou at Lagoudera. The slender, tapering figures of the standing angel and the seated Virgin are depicted in graceful, mannered, contrapposto poses and set in a landscape that contains a stream with waterfowl, the Virgin's ornate throne and a building with a roof garden. The drapery is tightly wrapped around the figure of the angel and ends in elaborate, billowing swathes, while a faint image of the infant Christ is sketched on the Virgin's mantle, an allusion to the Incarnation. This mannered, idyllic scene appears against a shining gold ground.

A number of iconostasis architrave icons that have survived at Sinai can be compared with the work produced in Cypriot workshops, including four separate panels each painted with three scenes from the *Twelve Feasts*. The scenes of the *Raising of Lazarus* and the *Transfiguration* are notable for the simplicity of their composition and the Classical appearance of their flattened figures, which bear a striking resemblance to the wall paintings at Asinou. A similar comparison with a Cypriot workshop can be made regarding the scenes from the *Life of St Eustratios* that decorate the iconostasis architrave intended for the chapel dedicated to the saint on Sinai; the scenes appear under an arcade, which is painted to imitate enamelwork. On other architrave icons (late 12th century or early 13th) the figures depicted in the *Twelve Feasts* are more lively, with shorter bodies and fuller faces: they also participate emotionally in the action. The flawless painting technique and the decorative burnishing in circular patterns of the gold ground, as well as of the haloes, indicate that these icons were probably made in Constantinople.

Among the few extant iconostasis architrave icons from Mt Athos are two examples painted on red grounds: a *Transfiguration* (St Petersburg, Hermitage) and a *Raising of Lazarus* (Athens, priv. col., see 1987 exh. cat., no. 7). Their sparse, tranquil compositions and sturdy figures with expressive faces are characteristic of late 12th-century art.

A number of outstanding mosaic icons from this period were probably made in the workshops of Constantinople. They include a *Christ Eleimon* ('merciful'; 1100–50; Berlin, Kstbib. & Mus.; see ICON, colour pl. II, fig. 3), a *Christ* (1150–1200; Florence, Bargello), a *Transfiguration* (c. 1200; Paris, Louvre) and two icons of the *Virgin Hodegetria* (early 13th century; Mt Athos, Chilandar Monastery; Mt Sinai, Monastery of St Catherine; see SINAI, fig. 4).

4. *c.* 1204–1453. With the Latin conquest of Constantinople and other areas of the Byzantine empire in 1204, influences from Western art became increasingly apparent in icon painting; this period was also marked by the definitive development of the iconostasis, which now supported more icons and displayed a greater variety of subject-matter.

(i) Latin rule, 1204–61. (ii) Palaiologan period, 1261–1453.

(i) Latin rule, 1204–61. Two icons of the *Virgin Enthroned* (Moscow, Pushkin Mus. F.A.; Washington, DC, N.G.A.), both probably made in Constantinople, are among the most splendid examples of the successful integration of Italianate elements in a predominantly Byzantine composition. Western artists accompanied the crusaders into Palestine, Jerusalem, Acre and Syria, where it is thought that Frankish artists and painters from Venice and Apulia settled and produced numerous icons of a peculiar hybrid character, often dubbed crusader art (*see* JERUSALEM, LATIN KINGDOM OF). Several icons (Mt Sinai, Monastery of St Catherine) that may be attributed to these workshops contain faultless Greek inscriptions and imitate Byzantine models. Some icons are dominated by bold outlines depicting short, stocky figures with broad faces painted in bright, flat colours against a gold ground; there is also a pronounced taste for elaborate, decorative details, for example in the diptych of the *Virgin and St Prokopios*. The faces are usually marked by a strong sense of anxiety with deeply etched lines on the forehead, as in the *Dormition of the Virgin* and the *Anastasis*. The equestrian *St George with the Boy from Mitylene* (London, BM) is another interesting icon belonging to this group.

A number of icons dating from the period of the Lusignan kingdom of Cyprus (1192–1489) can be related to the crusader icons at Sinai. They are distinguished by their clear lines, the relatively flat modelling of the areas of flesh and the use of decoration on haloes or backgrounds. Of particular interest is a group of icons similar in style and close in date to the wall paintings in the church of the Virgin at Moutoullas (1280); it includes the church's own icons of *Christ* and the *Virgin*, the *St Marina* in the church of the Holy Cross at Pedoulas, the *Apostle Paul* in the church of the Panagia Chrysaliniotissa at Nicosia and a *Virgin Hodegetria* with a silver ground (Athens, Byz. Mus.). In the *Crucifixion* (13th century) in the church of Hagios Loukas in Nicosia, the greater elegance of the figures is combined with more expressive facial features. Several elements that characterize this icon are also evident in the third layer of painting on a *Crucifixion* (Athens, Byz. Mus.) which has been likened to 13th-century Italian treatments of the same subject.

Icons executed in relief on wood panels are also attributed to workshops influenced by Western art. Perhaps the finest example is a double-sided icon of *St George* (13th century; Athens, Byz. Mus.) from Kastoria. The figure of the saint at prayer, depicted full-length in three-quarters profile, is reminiscent of Romanesque art in its facial features, military costume and shield displaying a heraldic device. The scenes from the saint's life that frame the central figure, however, are Byzantine in style and similar to those found in contemporary illuminated manuscripts from Constantinople. In the lower part of the icon there is a tiny female donor figure. On the reverse, two full-length female saints in attitudes of supplication are depicted against a silver ground. Two more large, carved and painted wooden icons of *St George* and *St Demetrios* (13th century) survive in the church of Hagios Georgios (11th century; rest. 1955) at Ormophoklisia, formerly Gallista, near Kastoria. Other 13th-century relief icons include a particularly large example of *St Clement* in a frontal pose (Ohrid, Gal. Icons), the *Virgin Trifotissa* (Alexandroupolis, metropolis of St Nicholas, treasury) and a *St George* from Chersonesos.

Icons unaffected by Western influence continued to be produced. Two large groups of iconostasis architrave icons from Mt Athos were probably produced in Constantinople in the first decades of the 13th century. One of these (Mt Athos, Vatopedi Monastery) consists of four parts with scenes from the *Twelve Feasts*, the *Life of the Virgin* (all under arcading) and figures of Christ and the Apostles from a *Deësis*. The other group (Mt Athos, Great Lavra Monastery; St Petersburg, Hermitage) depicts the *Twelve Feasts*. The scenes and the faces in both groups of icons have more emotional impact than previously; the modelling is painterly, and the soft drapery folds show an affinity with illuminated manuscripts from Constantinople, such as a Gospel book (early 13th century; Mt Athos, Iviron Monastery, Cod. 5).

Another type of large icon from the early 13th century features a saint in the central part and scenes from the saint's life in the border. Examples include a *St Nicholas* and two icons of *St George* (Mt Sinai, Monastery of St Catherine), which were probably made at Sinai by artists from Constantinople, a large icon of *St Gregory the Wonderworker* (St Petersburg, Hermitage) originally from Constantinople, and a full-length *St Nicholas* (13th century), of lesser quality, flanked by scenes from his life in the church of Hagios Nikolaos tis Stegis ('of the Roof') near Kakopetria in Cyprus.

(ii) Palaiologan period, 1261–1453. Art in Constantinople flourished again after the city was reconquered by Emperor Michael VIII Palaiologos in 1261; indeed, production of icons increased still further. Stylistically they tended to reflect the heavy style of monumental painting, especially in the depiction of individual saints. A fine example is the icon of *St James* (Patmos, St John the Divine Monastery; *see* ICON, colour pl. II, fig. 1). His robust, monumental figure, shown half-length, appears all the more imposing against the serene regularity of the drapery folds and the lifelike modelling of the facial features, and shows great similarity with the figures of the Apostles and prophets in the wall paintings (1263–8) in the church of the HOLY TRINITY, SOPOĆANI. The calm nobility of the face and the delicate gradations of colour attest to the classicizing influence of Constantinople. Another important icon is that of *St Matthew* (*c.* 1300; Ohrid, Gal. Icons; see fig. 69), in which he is depicted full-length and moving to the right. Despite his imposing bulk and the intensity of his gaze, he is shown in a state of agitation resembling that in the wall paintings (1294–5) by ASTRAPAS and Eutychios at St Clement in Ohrid. Another contemporary masterpiece is an icon of *St Peter* (Washington, DC, Dumbarton Oaks), in which the Apostle appears as a robust, half-length figure, with a lively expression achieved through a judicious alternation of light and shade. In quality it closely resembles the despotic icons on the iconostasis in the church of the Protaton on Mt Athos, to which it may originally have belonged. The severe expressions and modelling of the figures on icons of *Christ* and the *Virgin* (late 13th century; Mt Athos, Chilandar Monastery) are similar to those in the wall paintings of the churches at PEĆ. A tendency in late 13th-century icons to render the subjects as portraits, giving them individualized features, is evident in a *St Stephen* and a *St George* (Mt Athos, Great Lavra Monastery)

69. Icon of *St Matthew*, tempera on panel, 1060×565 mm, *c.* 1300 (Ohrid, Gallery of Icons)

and a *St Demetrios* and *St George* (Mt Athos, Vatopedi Monastery). Other important examples of this type are a *Christ Pantokrator* (Ohrid, Gal. Icons), which was painted in 1262–3, during the episcopate of Metropolitan Constantine Cabasilas, and a full-length *St George* (1266–7; Struga, St George) by Ioannis the 'illustrator', who may be identified with the Ioannis who painted the wall paintings (1270) in the church of St Nicholas at Manastir (now Bitolj). These dated icons differ in style and quality from those made in Constantinople, being less refined and showing a tendency to improvisation in the choice of materials: yellow ochre, for example, was used for the ground instead of gold, a feature common to numerous icons from western Macedonia.

In 1295 a series of high-quality icons was brought from Constantinople to decorate the church of St Clement at

Ohrid, which was built by Progonos Sgouros. His father-in-law, Emperor Andronikos II (*reg* 1282–1328), donated some of the icons which, as imperial offerings, demonstrate the character of the capital's art in the late 13th century and the early 14th through their splendid mounts, fine technique and elegant style. Among those on display are three double-sided icons: a *Christ Psychosostis* ('saver of souls') and a *Crucifixion*; a *Virgin Psychosostria* and an *Annunciation*; and a *Virgin Hodegetria* and a *Crucifixion*. The melancholic expressions of *Christ* and the *Virgin Psychosostria* are emphasized by dark-toned modelling of their faces. The *Crucifixion* on the reverse of the *Virgin Hodegetria* has a three-dimensional, monumental quality, with an emotional emphasis, while the other *Crucifixion* has a more lyrical character with more delicate shading. The *Annunciation* is characterized by an academic classicism, apparent in the beauty of the faces, the elegant movements and gestures, the symmetrical arrangement of draperies and the attempt at perspective in the depiction of the ornate throne, the upper part of which is supported by tiny caryatids. The fine, early 14th-century icons of the *Twelve Feasts* that have survived in St Clement also came from Constantinople, and they combine originality of composition, for example in the *Anastasis*, with controlled movement in space and a tight construction.

Icons probably produced in Constantinople survive in numerous other places. An exceptional double-sided example from Thessaloniki (earlier 14th century; Athens, Byz. Mus.) has a *Crucifixion* backed by a *Virgin Hodegetria*, in which the delicate figures of the Virgin and Child are clothed in flowing drapery. Another double-sided icon (second quarter of the 14th century) in the church of the Eisodia at Niochori on Rhodes features a *Virgin Hodegetria* and a *St Nicholas*. The double-sided icon of the *Three Hierarchs* (early 14th century; Athens, Byz. Mus.; other side damaged), whose faces are characterized by nobility and spirituality, is similar in style to the wall paintings (1312–15) in the church of the Holy Apostles (1310–14; 1328–34; see THESSALONIKI, §III, 7(ii)) and particularly to those in the church of Christ the Saviour in Chora (1321; see ISTANBUL, §III, 3(ii)). Iconostasis icons of a high quality include two examples of the *Deposition* (Mt Athos, Vatopedi Monastery; ex-Monastery of St John the Baptist, Serres), an *Annunciation* on the Royal Doors in the katholikon of the Great Lavra Monastery on Mt Athos and a *Hospitality of Abraham* (Mt Athos, Vatopedi Monastery). These are all despotic icons for which dogmatic accuracy had to be balanced against the intense emotion and graceful lyricism of the tall, slender figures and the soft evocations of light and shade.

One of the finest icons in the classicizing style from Constantinople is an *Archangel Michael* (second half of the 14th century; Athens, Byz. Mus.). The archangel has a noble appearance and is depicted frontally, holding a glass sphere inscribed with the initial Greek letters of Christos Dikaios Kritis ('Christ Just Judge'). This suggests that the icon once formed part of a set of iconostasis architrave icons depicting the *Great Deësis*. Iconographically the figure of the archangel is similar to that in the wall paintings of Christ the Saviour in Chora.

Few icons of the *Twelve Feasts* have survived from the second half of the 14th century. Those that do, however, reveal a greater freedom of composition, while the often tiny figures are placed against an architectural backdrop, for example in an *Annunciation* (Moscow, Tret'yakov Gal.). The icons of a *Baptism* and a *Miracle at Chonai* (Jerusalem, Mus. Gr. Orthdx Patriarch.) are simpler compositions, distinguished by the fine modelling of the faces. An *Anastasis* (third quarter of the 14th century; Baltimore, MD, Walters A.G.; *see* ICON, colour pl. III) with a strong narrative quality consisting of lively figures and bright colours on a gold ground, may belong to a set of iconostasis architrave icons.

A workshop in Constantinople associated with the production of illuminated manuscripts may have been responsible for a series of icons depicting small-scale scenes from the *Life of Christ*. These include diptychs and polyptychs intended for private devotion (e.g. London, BM; Mt Sinai, Monastery of St Catherine; St Petersburg, Hermitage). An excellent example of this type with scenes from the *Passion* (Thessaloniki, Vlatadon Monastery) features splashes of lapis lazuli on the draperies so that they stand out against the gold ground.

A set of iconostasis architrave icons of the *Apostles* (second half of the 14th century) from the *Great Deësis* in Chilandar Monastery on Mt Athos combines elements of the monumental and classicizing styles. Similar characteristics are also evident in icons of the Apostles in the church of Panagia Chrysaliniotissa at Nicosia: the engraved decoration on the haloes indicates a date towards the end of the 14th century. Another important example is the large-scale *Crucifixion* from Monemvasia (now Athens, Byz. Mus.), in which the crowded composition, reminiscent of the monumental style of the early 14th century, is combined with free and sweeping brushwork in the modelling of the faces, with expressions of intense sadness, which is typical of the last quarter of the 14th century.

A particularly significant work, both stylistically and iconographically, is a double-sided icon from Poganovo (1395; Sofia, N.A.G. Alexander Nevski Cathedral). It was an offering from Empress Eleni in 1395, and it was probably made in Thessaloniki. The *Vision of Ezekiel* on one side was based on the 5th-century mosaic in the apse of Hosios David (*see* THESSALONIKI, §III, 4(ii)). On the reverse are the *Virgin Katafygi* ('Refuge'), with her hands veiled in supplication, and *St John the Evangelist*. Their stance and sad expression are reminiscent of their appearance in the *Crucifixion* from Monemvasia.

Other high-quality icons of the late 14th century include large works depicting the full-length figures of the *Virgin Glykophilousa* ('sweet kiss'), *St John the Baptist* and *Archangel Michael* in Dečani Monastery (for the first *see* SERBIA, fig. 10), which are stylistically related to the monastery's wall paintings (1350). The icon of *Christ Pantokrator* (1363; St Petersburg, Hermitage), which was donated by John the Grand Primikerios and Alexios the Grand Stratopedarch, and a *Christ* (Moscow, Pushkin Mus. F.A.) clearly illustrate the new technique of using dark tones for modelling the flesh and a few, white highlights on curved surfaces. These artistic traits were transferred to Russia from Constantinople during the late 14th century by THEOPHANES THE GREEK, who executed the large icons for the iconostasis (1405) of the cathedral of the Annunciation in Moscow in a style marked by a rare and dramatic intensity.

During the 14th century, anti-Classical painting styles developed alongside the classicizing mode and became widespread, even appearing in Constantinople and Thessaloniki. Several icons from Thessaloniki including a robust-looking *Christ, the Wisdom of God* (a Pantokrator type), two icons of the *Virgin* (Athens, Byz. Mus.), an *Akra tapeinosis* (*c.* 1400; Athens, priv. col., see 1987 exh. cat., no. 27) and a double-sided icon with *Christ* (3rd quarter of the 14th century) and *St John the Evangelist* (2nd quarter of the 15th century; both Mytilene, Byz. Mus.) are characterized by an evident indifference to any sort of idealized, physical beauty or serenity of expression. The figures have a natural vigour and somewhat coarse expressions with accentuated facial features and dark shadows around the eyes. The severe expression and deep frown of the Mytilene *Christ* is similar to another *Christ* (Stockholm, Nmus.) and a *Christ Zoodotis* ('giver of life'; 1393–4; Skopje, A.G.) painted by Metropolitan Jovan from Zrze Monastery, near Prilep. The *Virgin Pelagonitissa* (a type from Pelagonia in Macedonia; 1421–2; Skopje, A.G.) from the same monastery was depicted much more schematically by the monk Makarije in a composite iconographic version of the Glykophilousa type.

Icons from the Thessaloniki region, western Macedonia, Kastoria and Veroia may be identified by the generally poor finish on the panel, which is often thick and in one piece, with a wide carved border around the central scene. Icons from these regions often have silver or yellow ochre grounds. Some icons are characterized by haloes that are carved and decorated with plaster motifs, as in a *Christ* (Athens, Byz. Mus.), or that imitate relief by judicious use of shading, as in a *Christ the Wisdom of God* (*c.* 1360; Athens, Byz. Mus.) and a *Man of Sorrows* (late 14th century; Niš, Archaeol. Mus.) from the monastery of St John at Pogabovo. In many icons from this region the expressionistic element has been so emphasized as to distort all proportions. Among the most interesting examples are two sets of icons on iconostasis architraves, each painted on a single, long, narrow piece of wood, including one (1401; Kastoria, Archaeol. Col., Chapel of Girls' Orphanage) originally from the church of Hagion Treis (Three Saints) and another (late 14th century–early 15th) in the Archaeological Museum at Veroia.

The production of mosaic icons increased significantly in the 14th century. Most surviving examples combine flawless technical skill with a love of extravagance and elegance. Among those that were made in Constantinople are a *St John the Evangelist* (Mt Athos, Great Lavra Monastery; see fig. 70), which shows an outstanding degree of craftsmanship with tesserae as tiny as grains of sand. The depiction of the elderly Evangelist with a heavy, round cranium and high forehead, bulky body and angular drapery is an outstanding example of the monumental style from the early 14th century. Other small mosaic icons belong to the classicizing phase of Palaiologan art and are recognizable by their slender, dainty figures with small faces and dramatic expressions in well-balanced compositions. They include a *Crucifixion* and *St Anne* (late 13th

70. Mosaic icon of *St John the Evangelist*, 170×110 mm, 14th century (Mt Athos, Great Lavra Monastery)

century; Mt Athos, Vatopedi Monastery), a *St John Chrysostomos* (second half of the 14th century; Mt Athos, Vatopedi Monastery; Washington, DC, Dumbarton Oaks), two icons of the *Akra tapeinosis* in the Tatarnas Monastery, in the province of Eurytania, Greece, and in Santa Croce di Gerusalemme, Rome (early 14th century), the *Forty Martyrs* (Washington, DC, Dumbarton Oaks), an *Annunciation* (1350–1400; London, V&A) and a *Twelve Feasts* diptych of rare craftsmanship (second half of the 14th century; Florence, Mus. Opera Duomo). Such large mosaic icons as a *St Nicholas* (Mt Athos, Stavronikita Monastery), a *Virgin Episkepsis* ('visitation'; Athens, Byz. Mus.) from Bithynia and a *Virgin Hodegetria* (Sofia, N. Archaeol. Mus.) from Eregli (anc. Herakleia, Turkey) are characterized by a rugged technique similar to that of monumental mosaics of a more expressionistic nature. Other noteworthy examples, ranging in date up to the mid-15th century, include three icons of a full-length *Christ* (all 14th century; Galatina, Mun.; Mt Athos, Great Lavra Monastery; Mt Athos, Esphigmenou Monastery) and a *St Demetrios* (Sassoferrato, Mus. Civ.), which is reminiscent of the military saints in Christ the Saviour in Chora.

BIBLIOGRAPHY

EARLY SOURCES

St John Chrysostomos: 'Homilia encomiastica in S Patrem nostrum Meletium' (*c.* 400), ed. in *PG*, i (1862)

Life of St Pankratios (MS.; later 8th century or early 9th); ed. F. Halkin in *Bibliotheca hagiographica graeca*, ii (Brussels, 1957), pp. 1410–12

GENERAL

RBK: 'Ikonostas'

O. Wulff and M. Alpatov: *Denkmäler der Ikonenmalerei* (Hellerau bei Dresden, 1925)

W. Felicetti-Liebenfels: *Geschichte der byzantinischen Ikonenmalerei von ihren Anfängen bis zum Ausklange unter Berücksichtigung der Maniera greca und der italo-byzantinischen Schule* (Olten and Lausanne, 1956)

M. Chatzidakis: 'L'Icône byzantine', *Saggi & Mem. Stor. A.*, ii (1959), pp. 11–40; also in *Studies in Byzantine Art and Archaeology*, Variorum Reprints (London, 1972)

O. Demus: 'Two Palaeologan Mosaic Icons in the Dumbarton Oaks Collection', *Dumbarton Oaks Pap.*, xiv (1960), pp. 87–119

R. Lange: *Die byzantinische Reliefikone* (Recklinghausen, 1964)

V. Lazarev: 'Trois fragments d'épistyles peints et le templon byzantin', *Deltion Christ. Archaiol. Etaireias*, iv (1964), pp. 117–43

Byzantine Art: A European Art (exh. cat., Athens, Záppeion, 1964)

K. Weitzmann and others: *Frühe Ikonen: Sinai, Griechenland, Bulgarien, Jugoslavien* (Vienna and Munich, 1965)

K. Weitzmann: 'Byzantine Miniature and Icon Painting in the Eleventh Century', *Thirteenth International Congress of Byzantine Studies: Oxford, 1966*, pp. 207–24; also in *Studies in Classical and Byzantine Manuscript Illuminations*, ed. H. Kessler (Chicago and London, 1971), pp. 271–313

——: 'Icon Painting in the Crusader Kingdom', *Dumbarton Oaks Pap.*, xx (1966), pp. 50–83

D. Talbot-Rice and T. Talbot-Rice: *Icons and their Dating* (London, 1974)

A. Grabar: *Les Revêtements en or et en argent des icônes byzantines du moyen-âge* (Venice, 1975)

M. Chatzidakis: 'L'Evolution de l'icône aux XI–XIIIe siècles et la transformation du templon', *Actes du XVe Congrès international des études byzantines: Athènes, 1976*, iii, pp. 157–92

T. Velmans: 'Rayonnement de l'icône au XIIe et au début du XIIIe siècle', *Actes du XVe Congrès international des études byzantines: Athènes, 1976*, iii, pp. 195–227

I. Furlan: *Le icone bizantine a mosaico* (Milan, 1979)

K. Weitzmann, M. Chatzidakis and S. Radojcic: *Icons* (New York, 1980)

H. Belting: *Das Bild und sein Publikum im Mittelalter: Form und Funktion früher Bildtafeln der Passion* (Berlin, 1981)

G. Galavaris: *The Icon in the Life of the Church*, Iconography of Religions, XXXIV/viii (Leiden, 1981)

K. Weitzmann and others: *The Icon* (New York, 1982)

K. Weitzmann: *The Saint Peter Icon of Dumbarton Oaks* (Washington, DC, 1983)

R. Cormack: *Writing in Gold: Byzantine Society and its Icons* (London, 1985)

H. Belting: *Bild und Kunst: Eine Geschichte des Bildes vor dem Zeitalter der Kunst* (Munich, 1990)

GREECE AND THE BALKANS

S. Radojcic: 'Die serbische Ikonenmalerei vom 12. Jh. bis zum Jahre 1459', *Jb. Österreich. Byz. Ges.*, v (1956), pp. 61–83

S. Vryonis jr: 'The Will of a Provincial Magnate, Eustathius Boilas, 1059', *Dumbarton Oaks Pap.*, xi (1957), pp. 263–77

V. Djuric: *Icônes de Yougoslavie* (Belgrade, 1961)

M. Chatzidakis: 'Eikones epistiliou apo to Agion Oros' [Architrave icons from Mt Athos], *Deltion. Christ. Archaiol. Etaireias*, iv (1964), pp. 377–403 [Fr. summary]; also in *Studies in Byzantine Art and Archaeology*, Variorum Reprints (London, 1972)

A. Xyngopoulos: 'Icônes du XIIIe siècle en Grèce', *L'Art byzantin au XIIIe siècle: Symposium de Sopoćani: Sopoćani, 1965*, pp. 75–82

M. Chatzidakis: *Byzantine Museum, Athens* (Vittoria, 1970)

——: 'Une Icône en mosaïque de Lavra', *Jb. Österreich. Byz.*, xxi (1972), pp. 75–81

A. Grabar: 'Les Images de la Vierge de Tendresse: Type iconographique et thème (à propos de deux icônes de Decani)', *Zograf*, vi (1975), pp. 25–30

Y. Chryssoulakis and T. Chatzidakis: 'The Contribution of Physical and Chemical Methods of Analysis to the Study of Four Double-sided Byzantine Icons in the Byzantine Museum of Athens', *Scientific Methodologies Applied to Works of Art: Proceedings of the Symposium: Florence, 1984*, pp. 124–30

M. Chatzidakis: *Eikones tis Patmou* [The icons of Patmos] (Athens, 1985)

——: 'Chronologimeni byzantini eikona sti Moni Megisti Lauras' [Dated Byzantine icons in the monastery of the Great Lavra], *Byzantium: Tribute to Andreas N. Stratos*, i (Athens, 1986), pp. 225–40

E. Tsigaridas: 'La Peinture à Kastoria et en Macédoine grecque occidentale vers l'année 1200: Fresques et icônes', *Studenica et l'art byzantin autour de l'année 1200: Belgrade, 1986*, pp. 309–20

From Byzantium to El Greco: Greek Frescoes and Icons (exh. cat., London, RA, 1987)

M. Chatzidakis and others: 'The Contribution of Physical and Chemical Methods of Analysis to the Study of 16 Icons Housed in the Byzantine Museum in Athens', *Deltion. Christ. Archaiol. Etaireias*, xiii (1988), pp. 215–45 [Fr. summary]

Holy Image, Holy Space: Icons and Frescoes from Greece (exh. cat., Athens, Byz. Mus.; Baltimore, MD, Walters A.G., 1988)

MT SINAI

G. Sotiriou and M. Sotiriou: *Eikones tis Monis Sina* [Icons of Mt Sinai], 2 vols (Athens, 1956–8)

K. Weitzmann: 'Thirteenth-century Crusader Icons on Mount Sinai', *A. Bull.*, xlv (1963), pp. 179–203

——: 'Eine spätkomnenische Verkündigungsikone des Sinai und die zweite byzantinische Welle des 12. Jahrhunderts', *Festschrift für Herbert von Einem* (Berlin, 1965), pp. 299–312

M. Chatzidakis: 'An Encaustic Icon of Christ at Sinai', *A. Bull.*, xlix (1967), pp. 197–208; also in *Studies in Byzantine Art and Archaeology*, Variorum Reprints (London, 1972)

K. Weitzmann: *The Icons: From the Sixth to the Tenth Century* (1976), i of *The Monastery of Saint Catherine at Mount Sinai* (Princeton, 1976–)

D. Mouriki: 'Four Thirteenth-century Sinai Icons by Painter Peter', *Studenica et l'art byzantin autour de l'année 1200: Belgrade, 1986*, pp. 329–46

G. Galavaris: 'Early Icons at Sinai, from the 6th to the 11th Century', *Sinai: Treasures of the Monastery of Saint Catherine*, ed. K. A. Manafis (Athens, 1990), pp. 91–101

D. Mouriki: 'Icons from the 12th to the 15th century', *Sinai: Treasures of the Monastery of Saint Catherine*, ed. K. A. Manafis (Athens, 1990), pp. 102–25

CYPRUS

A. Papageorgiou: *Icons of Cyprus* (London, 1969)

K. Weitzmann: 'A Group of Early Twelfth-century Icons Attributed to Cyprus', *Studies in Memory of D. Talbot-Rice* (Edinburgh, 1975), pp. 47–65

Byzantine Icons of Cyprus (exh. cat. by A. Papageorgiou, Athens, Benaki Mus., 1976)

D. Mouriki: 'Thirteenth-century Icon Painting in Cyprus', *The Griffon*, i–ii (1985–6), pp. 9–112

RUSSIA

V. Antonova and N. Mneva: *Katalog drevnerusskoy zhivopisi* [Catalogue of old Russian painting], Moscow, Tret'yakov Gal. cat., 2 vols (Moscow, 1963)

A. Bank: *Vizantiyskoe iskusstvo v sobraniyakh Sovetskogo Soyuza/Byzantine Art in the Collections of the USSR* (Leningrad and Moscow, 1966, 2/1977) [Rus. & Eng. texts]

MANOLIS CHATZIDAKIS, NANO CHATZIDAKIS

VII. Other arts.

1. Ceramics. 2. Coins and seals. 3. Dress. 4. Glass. 5. Ivories and steatites. 6. Jewellery. 7. Metalwork and enamelling. 8. Textiles.

1. CERAMICS. The Byzantine world continued to use the pottery of the Roman tradition until the 7th century, when a decisive change in the character and production of ceramics occurred. This section, therefore, begins its treatment of ceramics at that point; for the earlier period *see* ROME, ANCIENT, §X, 8.

(i) Introduction. (ii) 7th–9th centuries. (iii) 10th–12th centuries. (iv) 13th century–1453.

(i) Introduction. Between the 7th century and the 15th an enormous range of ceramics was produced in the east Mediterranean. Byzantine pottery was made—frequently over many centuries—in centres as distant from Constantinople as Chersonesos, Tmutarakan (nr Sennaya, Russia), Dyrrhachion, Nerezi, Preslav, Thessaloniki, Corinth and Mystras, Crete, Cyprus and the southern coast of Asia Minor. Some types were inspired by models developed in the capital and exported to the provinces, but much pottery appears to have been made to supply local needs in styles of local origin. This body of material has long

been neglected, but the application of modern scientific techniques, especially spectrographic and minerological analysis, has enabled the clay sources and glazes of different centres of production to be identified, and kiln excavation has provided more information on firing techniques and decoration.

The vast majority of ceramic objects were unglazed. Huge quantities of uniform amphorae, tiles and pipes were used for cooking and building, and kilns were often established near clay beds and water supplies. Amphorae were also employed in large numbers for the transportation and storage of foodstuffs and liquids. Clay vessels were used for the preparation, cooking and serving of food in all but the wealthiest households, where tableware of silver and other metals was used. Byzantine ceramics frequently imitate metalwork, for example liturgical objects such as censers. Glazed pottery, which constitutes a much smaller proportion of overall production, is normally functional but includes a few pieces created as art objects, such as icons.

(ii) 7th–9th centuries. Until the early 7th century most regions of the Byzantine empire had access to Roman pottery, which continued to be imported from its traditional centres of production in North Africa, Italy and Egypt. The Arab invasions put an end to these supplies, and Late Roman wares and their Byzantine variants, Late Roman C wares, were no longer produced. In their place, a specifically Byzantine pottery was developed to supply local needs across the remaining parts of the Eastern empire. The overlap between both types is evident in the pottery from the Yassı Ada wreck, Turkey, dated by coins to the second quarter of the 7th century (Bodrum Mus.).

The contrast between Late Roman and Early Byzantine tablewares could hardly be more marked. Changes in clay, firing technique and decoration resulted in a startling decline in ceramic production that may be linked to the historic transformation that marked the end of Late Antiquity. In place of the pure, hard-baked, thin-walled, Late Roman red wares, Early Byzantine ceramics are characterized by the use of poorly refined, white, pink and buff clay, which produced generally heavy, thick-walled vessels. The potter's wheel continued in use for the production of various forms of jug, tube-spouted jar, cooking pot, bowl and plate. Decoration was limited to lead oxide glazes in a few colours (yellow, green and brown), with the addition of scratched lines and stamps, which produced images similar to those made by bread and brick stamps. Occasionally a better quality of clay with fewer impurities was baked into a more elegant form of pot, such as the small bowl with a flat rim ornamented with thumb impressions found at Yassı Ada (Bodrum Mus.), although few examples of sophisticated tablewares survive.

Most of the pottery used for transporting and storing foodstuffs shows less dramatic change, inasmuch as amphorae, mortars, cooking pots and storage jars had always been made of coarser clay. Even so, new forms of amphorae have a clumsy, less finished quality, and lack the Late Roman traditions of decorating the handle with a stamp or identifying the potter with a name or monogram. Some of these otherwise undistinguished wares are

partially glazed with a rich, thick translucent glaze, which appears to be unrelated to function or cooking requirements; its use on the rims of mortars, for instance, enhances the gritty clay body with a glossy sheen. Similarly, a white ware produced in Constantinople creates a striking family of everyday objects.

The replacement of Late Roman centres of ceramic production by new ones in Asia Minor, the Aegean islands and the littoral of Greece led to an abrupt change from red to white clay, and good quality red-bodied wares did not re-emerge for many centuries. During the 8th century, however, sources of dark clay were discovered in Byzantium and were exploited for the pleasing contrast of its red tones with the lighter Byzantine clays. Petal ware derives its name from the application of petal or leaf shapes of this dark clay to a white-bodied vessel. The effect becomes more marked under a thick glaze and is highly decorative when used in combination with an impressed design, as on the base of a plate. The same technique is often imitated in red-brown paint, but lacks the contoured effect of the petals.

The drastic reduction in long-distance trade and construction between the 7th and 9th centuries doubtless meant that fewer amphorae and building materials were needed. Local demand was probably met by local production, although when Constantine V Kopronymos (*reg* 741–75) decided to restore the aqueduct of Constantinople, he had to summon craftsmen, including potters, from Greece. Nonetheless, a range of globular amphorae was produced in this period, illustrating the development of new forms to replace Late Roman types previously imported to Byzantium from such centres as Gaza and further afield. At Paphos, Cyprus, ceramic production was associated with glass-blowing, thus revealing a closely related manufacture.

(iii) 10th–12th centuries. The ceramics of this period are marked by innovations both in raw materials and in technical skills. Towards the end of the 9th century, new sources of white clay which could be refined to a much purer quality and baked much thinner became available. Brightly coloured decoration was painted directly on to the bare body in elaborate patterns. This technique seems to have been initiated simultaneously in both Asia Minor and Bulgaria and may be dated by the construction (*c.* 900) of the monastery of Constantine Lips (now Fenarı Isa Cami), Istanbul, and the Golden Church at Preslav. Finds of similar ware have identified Chersonesos in the Crimea as a third centre of production. The novel manufacture and decoration of this Polychrome ware may derive from Islamic models. Previously unused metals such as copper and manganese permitted the stabilization of primary colours: red, blue, yellow, plus white and black. These are employed in extremely delicate patterns and figural representations, particularly on icons (see fig. 71). Polychrome ware extended the use of pottery to the most prominent parts of churches and palaces, such as columns, icon frames and cornices, on to which flat and curved revetment tiles were applied.

In western Asia Minor the first use of such curved revetment tiles may be associated with the redecoration of the church of the Dormition, Nicaea (now Iznik), where a new mosaic programme was established after the restoration of image veneration in 843. Photographs of the mosaics (destr.) reveal a row of polychrome tiles at the lower edge, exactly where they were later used in the Lips Monastery and in the mosaic probably put up by Byzantine craftsmen in the Mezquita at Córdoba (961–6; see CÓRDOBA (i), §3(i)(a)). The clay resembles that used in 14th-century Iznik ware and suggests that local clay beds may have been used for the examples in Nicaea and Constantinople.

Bulgarian production of Polychrome ware was probably stimulated by the construction of the new Bulgarian capital at Preslav. Kilns excavated near by reveal considerable tile and pipe production in coarse fabrics; in addition, craftsmen developed a refined white clay base, which they painted with multicoloured designs. Certain stylistic features point to the cross-fertilization of patterns between Byzantium, Bulgaria and southern Russia. These include decorative foliage on curved tiles; blue floral patterns against a background of tiny red dots; medallions with orange–yellow animals spotted with black dots, on a brilliant blue ground; and highly contrasting black-and-white maze patterns. Small square icons portraying Christ, the Virgin and saints, identified by fine inscriptions, were produced in Bulgaria and Constantinople. The most striking finds are a series of shaped icons from Preslav, associated with a colonnade of columns and arches, which was revetted in painted tiles to form an iconostasis, and the impressive icon of *St Theodore*, composed of 36 tiles.

While Polychrome ware set new standards in ceramic skills and was imported into provincial centres, most 10th-century pottery was made from the coarser Early Byzantine clays and lead oxide glazes. A greater variety of form and decoration is, however, evident in cup-and-saucer style lamps, cooking equipment (e.g. braziers) and serving dishes (e.g. fruit stands), sometimes decorated with external reliefs. Glazes are also used in combination, and over incised line and painted white slip decoration; they are often spattered rather than applied smoothly. Among unglazed wares, new types of amphora are found in construction contexts, such as at the Mangana palace and chapel, Constantinople, as well as in transport, storage and culinary roles.

By the early 11th century, when Byzantine trade and city life were clearly reviving, provincial centres reveal lively traditions of ceramic production. At Corinth, for example, the buff and red clay was used to good effect in large plates with a white slip, through which incised lines are scratched before glazing; animal and floral motifs predominate with only occasional human representation. Pale yellow glazes usually accompany this *sgraffito* (or scratched) style. Other techniques include the use of tiny dots of bright red glaze to produce a spotted 'measles' effect. Using the champlevé technique, a sharp contrast is achieved by removing the white slip from one area to reveal the bare body of the pot under the glaze. These styles of incised, gouged and painted decoration, in a variety of combinations, are common to most glazed Byzantine pottery of the period.

Corinthian ware seems to have been highly prized and was exported throughout the empire, even to distant sites such as Kouklia (Old Paphos) in Cyprus. This export

71. Polychrome ceramic iconic tile depicting *St Nicholas*, enamelled and glazed, 168×164 mm, from Nicomedia (now Izmit, Turkey), *c.* 1000 (Baltimore, MD, Walters Art Gallery)

contributed to an increasing trade in pottery, documented by a shipload of *sgraffito* bowls, similar to those produced in Corinth, which was wrecked off Pelagonnesou–Alonnesou (nr Skopelos, Greece). Quite exceptionally, some fine examples of Imitation Lustreware from Corinth were designed for display rather than use, as is evident from the holes made by the potter to facilitate suspension. Production at Corinth declined after the Norman raid of 1147, when craftsmen and silk weavers were carried off to Sicily. The insecurity generated in this part of central Greece by subsequent piratical activity, Norman attacks and crusader threats is illustrated by the discovery of coin hoards in rough clay vessels, aptly known as treasuries (*thesauraria*).

During the 12th century, tripods were first used to separate pots in the kiln during firing; previously pots had been stacked on top of each other. This development permitted the firing of larger quantities of pots and may have improved their quality. It also appears to coincide with the use in several centres, notably the Crimea and Constantinople, of purer dark clays, which bake hard and thin and approach Late Roman wares in quality. This 'Zeuxippus' ware was first discovered in the Baths of Zeuxippus at Constantinople, and it occurs in two phases separated by the introduction of tripod firing. The earlier phase is closely related to *sgraffito* wares, with bands of decoration often confined to the rims of plates; the later phase presents more ambitious, often figural decoration. Both types are characterized by the combination of incised and red-brown painted decoration under a yellow glaze. The large plates from Chersonesos bear vivid depictions of combat between men and monsters (e.g. St George and the dragon). The discovery of imported Zeuxippus fragments at sites in Asia Minor, Greece, Cyprus and Italy suggests that these high-quality ceramics were much in demand and travelled considerable distances. The flourishing state of ceramic production in Constantinople is well documented from the striking range of glazed and unglazed pottery found at the Kyriotissa Church (late 12th century; now Kalenderhane Cami). Clay was used as a substitute for precious metal in ceramic censers and drinking goblets, while the dramatic use of black and green glazes to depict animals on bowls reveals high artistic standards.

(iv) 13th century–1453. The fall of Constantinople to the Fourth Crusade (1204) and the partition of the empire brought westerners to settle in the Aegean basin. There is little evidence, however, that specifically Western tastes influenced Byzantine ceramic production. The crusaders brought few craftsmen with them and were anxious to retain the services of local potters.

Western warriors depicted on pottery from Cyprus, Athens and Corinth are sometimes armed with Eastern scimitars and wear robes more familiar to Byzantine than European eyes. Protomaiolica wares from southern Italy were distributed throughout the region and were sufficiently prized to be embedded in church walls beside contemporary Byzantine plates. Established Byzantine practices, such as the use of *sgraffito* and champlevé techniques, and of green and brown painted decoration, also continued to develop.

A recognizable buff clay, incised with thickly gouged patterns of circles under a yellow glaze and used for large shallow plates, has been attributed to the Aegean in the 13th century. Bowls with high feet and concave or flaring rims, and goblets on tall stems, are common everywhere, with greater attention paid to their external decoration (see fig. 72). Bowls, plates and cups are often slipped and glazed in a colour contrasting with the internal decoration.

A workshop in Thessaloniki used champlevé decoration to portray different types of birds. Late Zeuxippus wares from Constantinople, Chersonesos and Cyprus include elegant wine jars, with bands of combed and gouged decoration over their bulbous bodies, and bowls with outturned rims embellished with identical patterns under a bright orange glaze. A particularly lively style of figural representation is found on Cypriot bowls commemorating marriages, or depicting dancers with castanets.

Sgraffito wares with brown and green painted decoration under yellow glazes predominate throughout the east Mediterranean, using a common decorative repertory of lozenge shapes, as well as floral, animal, bird and fish images. These features became so widespread that it is often hard to distinguish Byzantine from crusader centres of production, such as 'Atlit, Israel. Entirely novel uses of pottery were developed in formerly Byzantine areas that passed under Western control in the 13th century. The sugar refinery at Kouklia is an exceptionally well documented example of a medieval industry that employed large quantities of rough, unglazed ceramic jars and conical moulds. During this period, which coincided with the empire's final decline, Constantinople continued as a major manufacturer of pottery. Ceramic tableware was even used as a substitute for dishes of precious metal at the imperial court in the 14th century, as contemporary historians noted with some chagrin.

Ceramics form an integral aspect of the spread of Byzantine culture and Orthodox faith in the medieval world and beyond. When Mehmed II (*reg* 1451–81) begged the Byzantine craftsmen to remain after the fall of Constantinople in 1453, he recognized their practical and artistic skills. It is hardly surprising that Late Byzantine cannot be distinguished from Early Ottoman in the brown and green painted *sgraffito* wares produced in the capital in the mid-15th century, for they belong to a 'transitional' phase that reflects the final legacy of Byzantine ceramics.

BIBLIOGRAPHY

GENERAL

J. Ebersolt: *Catalogue des poteries byzantines et anatoliennes du Musée de Constantinople* (Constantinople, 1910)

D. Talbot Rice: *Byzantine Glazed Pottery* (Oxford, 1930)

E. Coche de la Ferté: 'Décoration en céramique byzantine au Musée du Louvre', *Cah. Archéol.*, ix (1957), pp. 187–217

A. H. S. Megaw: 'Glazed Bowls in Byzantine Churches', *Deltion Christ. Archaiol. Etaireias*, iv (1964), pp. 145–62

D. Talbot Rice: 'Late Byzantine Pottery at Dumbarton Oaks', *Dumbarton Oaks Pap.*, xx (1966), pp. 209–19

J. W. Hayes: 'A Seventh Century Pottery Group', *Dumbarton Oaks Pap.*, xxii (1968), pp. 203–16

A. H. S. Megaw: 'Byzantine Pottery, 4th–14th century', *World Ceramics*, ed. R. J. Charleston (London, 1968/*R* 1981)

——: 'Zeuxippus Ware', *Annu. Brit. Sch. Athens*, lxiii (1968), pp. 67–88

A. H. S. Megaw and R. Jones: 'Byzantine and Allied Pottery: A Contribution by Chemical Analysis to Problems of Origin and Distribution', *Annu. Brit. Sch. Athens*, lxxviii (1983), pp. 235–63

V. Zalesskaya: 'Nouvelles découvertes de céramique peinte byzantine du Xe siècle', *Cah. Archéol.*, xxxii (1984), pp. 49–62

N. Déroche, ed.: *Colloque sur la céramique byzantine* (in preparation)

GREECE

R. M. Dawkins and J. P. Droop: 'Byzantine Pottery at Sparta', *Annu. Brit. Sch. Athens*, xvii (1910–11), pp. 23–8

A. Xyngopoulos: *Byzantine Pottery from Olynthus* (1933), v of *Excavations at Olynthus*, ed. D. M. Robinson (Baltimore, 1930–52), pp. 285–92

A. Frantz: 'Middle Byzantine Pottery in Athens', *Hesperia*, vii (1938), pp. 428–67

72. Ceramic goblet, covered with white slip and painted, h. 115 mm, from Cyprus, 13th century (Baltimore, MD, Walters Art Gallery)

C. Morgan: *The Byzantine Pottery* (1942), xi of *Corinth: Results of the Excavations Conducted by the American School of Classical Studies at Athens* (Cambridge, MA, 1929–)

T. Stilwell Mackay: 'More Byzantine and Frankish Pottery from Corinth', *Hesperia*, xxxvi (1967), pp. 249–320

C. Kritzas: 'To Vyzantinon nauagion Pelagonnesou–Alonnesou' [The Byzantine shipwreck at Pelagonnesou–Alonnesou], *Athens An. Archaeol.*, iv (1971), pp. 176–81

H. W. Catling: 'An Early Byzantine Pottery Factory at Dhiorios in Cyprus', *Levant*, iv (1972), pp. 1–82

A. H. S. Megaw: 'An Early Thirteenth Century Aegean Glazed Ware', *Studies in Honour of David Talbot Rice* (Edinburgh, 1975), pp. 34–45

G. Nikolopoulos: 'Céramiques encastrées d'anciennes églises de Grèce', *Faenza*, lxiii (1977), pp. 27–31; lxvii (1981), pp. 166–78

C. Bakirtzis and D. Papanikola-Bakirtzis: 'De la Céramique byzantine en glaçure à Thessalonique', *Byzantino–Bulgarica*, vii (1981), pp. 421–36

C. Bakirtzis: 'Tria thesauraria tou Nomismatikou mouseiou Athenon' [Three 'thesauraria' from the coin museum at Athens], *Athens An. Archaeol.*, xv (1982), pp. 70–76

A. Vavylopoulou-Charitonidou: 'Vyzantine kerameike sten Arta' [Byzantine ceramics from Arta], *Deltion Christ. Archaiol. Etaireias*, xii (1982), pp. 453–72

THE BALKANS AND RUSSIA

T. I. Makarova: *Céramique vernisée de l'ancienne Russie* (Moscow, 1972)

T. Totev: 'Fours à céramique dans le lac … "Vinica"', *Archeol. Bulg.*, xv/4 (1973), pp. 58–68

B. Zwetkow: *Keramische Gebrauchskunst aus Melnik* (Sofia, 1979)

J. Čimbuleva: 'Vases à glaçure en argile blanche de Nessembre (IX–XIIe s.)', *Nessembre*, ii (Sofia, 1980), pp. 202–53

J. Herrin: 'Reflections on Medieval Ceramic Production in Bulgaria and Crimea', *Polata Knigopisnaya*, iii (1980), pp. 35–9

T. Totev: *Le Monastère à 'Tuzlalaka': Centre de céramique peinte à Preslav pendant les IX–Xe siècles* (Sofia, 1982)

——: 'L'Atelier de céramique peinte du monastère royal de Preslav', *Cah. Archéol.*, xxxv (1987), pp. 65–80

TURKEY

R. B. K. Stevenson: *The Pottery, 1936–7* (1947), i of *The Great Palace of the Byzantine Emperors*, ed. G. Brett, W. J. Macauley and R. B. K. Stevenson (Oxford, 1947–58)

E. S. Ettinghausen: 'Byzantine Tiles from the Basilica in Topkapı Sarayi and S John of Studios', *Cah. Archéol.*, vii (1954), pp. 79–88

C. Williams: 'A Byzantine Well-deposit from Anemurium (Rough Cilicia)', *Anatol. Stud.*, xxvii (1977), pp. 175–90

U. Peschlow: 'Byzantinische Keramik aus Istanbul', *Istanbul. Mitt.*, xxvii/xxviii (1977–8), pp. 363–414

G. Bass: 'The Pottery', *Yassi Ada: A Seventh Century Byzantine Shipwreck*, ed. G. Bass and F. van Doorninck jr (College Station, TX, 1982), pp. 155–88

P. Verdier: 'Tiles of Nicomedia', *Okeanos: Essays Presented to I. Ševčenko*, Harvard Ukrainian Studies (Cambridge, MA, 1983), pp. 632–6

J. W. Hayes: 'The Pottery from Saraçhane', *Excavations at Saraçhane*, ii, ed. R. M. Harrison (Princeton, *c.* 1992)

J. Herrin: 'The Significance of Roman and Byzantine Pottery Finds at Kalenderhane Camii', *Excavations at Kalenderhane Camii, Istanbul: Final Report*, ii, ed. C. L. Striker and Y. D. Kuban (in preparation)

A. Sabuncu: 'Catalogue of Byzantine Pottery', *Excavations at Kalenderhane Camii, Istanbul: Final Report*, ii, ed. C. L. Striker and Y. D. Kuban (in preparation)

JUDITH HERRIN

2. COINS AND SEALS. Both coins and seals are the product of the art of engraving. Their blanks of various metals receive the imprint of mobile or hinged dies generally made of iron, while the stamp they bear is normally used for their authentication or identification, enabling most of them to be dated. Although coins were not always minted where the dies were engraved and *boulloteria* (hinged dies in the form of pincers for lead sealing) were sometimes prepared in Constantinople for provincial officials, the provenance of coins and seals can often be determined. They are also of considerable artistic interest and are invaluable as comparative material for Byzantine art history, since they provide useful insights into periods that are not well documented by other works of art and are generally well dated. Numerous catalogues have been published since the mid-1960s. (For wax seals *see* WAX, §II, 3.)

(i) *c.* 313–*c.* 720. (ii) *c.* 720–*c.* 843. (iii) *c.* 843–1453.

(i) c. 313–c. 720. Between the foundation of Constantinople and the edict against images issued by Leo III Isaurikos (*reg* 717–41) in 726, the treatment of themes became increasingly Christian in character. This development is clearer on coins than on lead seals, since 4th- and 5th-century examples of the latter are rare and often badly preserved. By *c.* 400 the naturalistic portraiture in high relief of Roman emperors still evident on the coinage of Constantine the Great had begun to be replaced by a hieratic and characterless image of the ruler, although imperial usurpers such as Magnentius (*reg* 350–53), Decentius (*reg* 350) and Vetranio (*reg* 350) continued to use realistic images of themselves. These portraits contrast with the three-quarter frontal bust introduced by Constantius II (*reg* 337–61) in his issues of 353–61, which became the dominant type from the reign of Arkadios (*reg* 395–408) until 538. This frontal engraving technique and the idealization of the emperor were together responsible for the loss of individuation in imperial portraiture.

These changes to the busts of emperors, which were always imprinted on the obverse, were accompanied by a steadily diminishing number of reverse types. In the 4th century a variety of allegorical representations of cities or political virtues continued to be used on bronze coinage: the successive issues of *Fel temp reparatio* (346–61: Virtus dragging barbarians out of a hut; emperor and captives; a phoenix; Virtus spearing a fallen horseman), *Spes reipublicae* (Virtus standing) and *Securitas reipub* (361–3: Victory and a bull). After 363 legends remained diverse while encompassing a much smaller iconographic range, with the three pagan personifications (Victory, Rome and Constantinople) to have survived the interdiction of the ancient cults appearing on the reverse (otherwise occupied by military representations of the emperor).

The adoption of Christianity is only gradually reflected in the coinage and points to the mixed feelings of public opinion, particularly that of the army, towards the new religion. Its earlier symbol, the chi-rho, was originally a symbol of victory used by Constantine and acquired its meaning of the victory of the Christian faith only after Constantine defeated Licinius (*reg* 307–24) at Chrysopolis in 324. At first it appears as a discreet mark in the background, later becoming more prominent as the central motif of the labarum, which the emperor is frequently shown holding on reverses from 346 to the early 5th century. It even appears with the Greek letters A and ω on the reverse of coins issued by Magnentius, symbolizing his support of Orthodox Gaul against the Arian faith of Constantius II. In the 5th century the chi-rho gives way to the cross, which gradually pervades every monetary representation: it decorates the orb held by rulers and personifies capital cities or victories; surrounded by a wreath, it appears on the main type of Western tremisses (small gold coins) and in the hand of Victory forms the most popular design of Eastern solidi from 420 or 422 onwards.

The monetary reform of 498 has led many numismatists to choose the reign of Anastasios I (*reg* 491–518) as the beginning of Byzantine coinage (see fig. 73, top row). This date, however, has little bearing on the artistic evolution of coin types, and of far greater significance in this respect are two type-changes of the early 6th century: in the first (522–7) the winged Victory on solidi is replaced by the *Archangel Michael* (e.g. gold; Paris, Bib. N., Cab. Médailles, Anc. Fond. 301; see fig. 73, second row); in the second, issued in Nicomedia in 538, Justinian gave up the three-quarter frontal armed bust used by 5th-century Eastern emperors in favour of a full frontal bust in which the spear is replaced by a cross on a globe (e.g. bronze; Paris, Bib. N., Cab. Médailles, Anc. Fond. 19). In both cases, the fully frontal portraits are achieved at the expense of individual expression, and it is at this point that Byzantine art can be seen to have achieved its hieratic character in an original integration of Christian symbolism and Late Roman imperial forms.

The next major development in Byzantine coinage occurred in the late 6th century and the early 7th with the disappearance of allegorical themes: the personification of Constantinople appears for the last time on the solidi of Justin II (*reg* 565–78), while that of Victory is last seen on the semisses of Phokas (*reg* 602–10), although in 629 Heraklios (*reg* 610–41) used a small Victory on a globe to celebrate his victory over the Persians (e.g. Washington, DC, Dumbarton Oaks). Conversely, the cross assumes a primary role on the reverse of all gold denominations under Tiberios II (*reg* 578–82; see fig. 73, third row) and then continuously from 610 onwards. The portrayal of imperial figures on seals follows the monetary pattern, although larger dimensions allow for more detailed designs, as in the seal of Diomedes and Diogenes, *kommerkiarioi* (customs officials) of Tyre (now Sur, Lebanon), with its portraits of *Justin II*, *Empress Sophia* and *Tiberios Caesar* on the obverse (Paris, Bib. N.; see fig. 74, top left and 1992 exh. cat., no. 144). Seals are also more innovative than coins where the cross assumes a primary role; they provide the first examples of religious representations, such as that of the Virgin standing between two crosses on imperial seals from 582 onward (diam. 22 mm; Washington, DC, Dumbarton Oaks). The growth of popular devotion to the Virgin is reflected in most other 6th- and 7th-century seals, on which she is portrayed either as a bust or standing, with the Christ Child in a medallion on her breast or carried on her left arm (see fig. 74, top centre). Those belonging to religious or civilian officials are stamped with a limited range of saints, including Eirene, Anastasia, Michael, Peter, Paul, Theodore, John the Baptist and some local patron saints, as for example St John Chrysostomos for the patriarch of Constantinople and St Titos for the metropolitan of Crete.

The principal innovation of the 7th century, however, was the placing of the Pantokrator ('ruler of all') bust of Christ on gold and silver coins of Justinian II (*reg* 685–95, 705–11). Before then Christ had only appeared on rare ceremonial issues commemorating the imperial marriages of Markianos and Pulcheria (450) and Anastasios I and

73. Byzantine coins, actual size: (top row) gold coin of Anastasios I (obverse) depicting *Victory* (reverse), 491–518; (second row) gold solidus of Justinos I depicting the *Archangel Michael* (reverse), 522–7; (third row) gold solidus depicting *Tiberios II* (obverse) and cross (reverse), Constantinople, 578–82; (fourth row) gold solidus depicting *Justinian II* (obverse) and youthful bust of *Christ* (reverse), 705; (fifth row) gold nomisma of Constantine VII, depicting Romanos I Lekapenos with his son Christopher on the right and Constantine VII on the left (obverse) and Christ on a lyre-back throne (reverse), *c.* 930; (bottom row) gold *hyperpyron* of Michael VIII Palaiologos, depicting the Virgin *orans* within the walls of Constantinople (obverse), after 1261 (Paris, Bibliothèque Nationale)

74. Byzantine seals, actual size: (top left) lead seal of Diomedes and Diogenes, customs officials of Tyre, with portraits of *Justin II, Empress Sophia* and *Tiberios Caesar,* late 6th century (Paris, Bibliothèque Nationale); (top centre and right) imperial seal depicting the *Virgin* (obverse) and *Constantine IV* (reverse), 668–85 (Washington, DC, Dumbarton Oaks Research Library and Collections); (bottom left and centre) imperial seal depicting *Christ* (obverse) and *Romanos I Lekapenos* (reverse), 931–44 (Cambridge, MA, Fogg Art Museum); (bottom right) seal depicting the *Descent into Limbo,* 11th–12th century (Washington, DC, Dumbarton Oaks Research Library and Collections)

Ariadne (491). Justinian's coins reflect contemporary interest in the representation of Christ, for one of the prescriptions of the Council *In Trullo* (692) states that he should be shown in his human form and not as a Paschal Lamb. This new obverse type was beautifully designed and engraved by a die-sinker whose work on solidi can be traced between 685 and 717. Christ was portrayed in two ways: first, as the Pantokrator with a majestic bearded face derived from that of the Pheidian *Zeus* and later, during Justinian's second reign, as a young man with closely curled hair (Paris, Bib. N., Cab. Médailles, Schlumberger 2864; see fig. 73, fourth row), an image of Syrian inspiration and deemed to be a truer portraiture. The reasons why Justinian's successors reverted to the traditional cross type of obverse remain uncertain.

(ii) c. 720–c. 843. Although the effect of the iconoclastic controversy on the iconography of coins and seals is not always obvious, it is undeniable that it interrupted the iconographic tradition. At first Leo III Isaurikos continued to use the cross and Virgin Hodegetria ('who points the way') on gold coin reverses and seals respectively, but with the crowning of his son Constantine as co-emperor in 720, two new reverse types were introduced which dominated the rest of the period. First, the cross on gold coins is replaced by the figure of the young co-emperor shown as a boy and then with a face gradually growing older.

Constantine V Kopronymos (*reg* 741–75) later introduced his deceased father's image as well as his own on the nomisma, a practice that continued until *c.* 867 and led in some cases to overcrowded familial scenes such as on the coins of Constantine VI (*reg* 780–97), where he and his mother, Eirene, appear on the obverse and his three predecessors are accommodated within a diameter of 20 mm on the reverse (Paris, Bib. N., Cab. Médailles, Anc. Fond. 817). Second, the linear, almost abstract, cross combined with epigraphy becomes virtually the only image used on imperial seals and the new silver coin, or *miliaresion,* which was clearly inspired by the aniconic style of the contemporary Arab dirhem. This aniconic trend is also found in common seals, where religious representations are replaced by crosses or, more often, by cruciform monograms invoking the aid of Christ or Theotokos.

With the restoration of images during the first iconophile phase of 787–815 there was only a limited return to iconic devices, and only on seals. Even Empress Eirene kept to iconoclastic practices and, after eliminating her son Constantine VI, went as far as to have herself represented on both faces of the nomisma (Paris, Bib. N., Cab. Médailles, Schlumberger 2946). Nikephoros I (*reg* 802–11) and Leo V (*reg* 813–20), however, adopted the Virgin between two monograms as a reverse type. This revival in the use of religious figures can also be observed in the seals of some iconophile bishops, such as Peter of Thessaloniki (*c.* mid-8th century; diam. 28 mm; Cambridge, MA, Fogg, see Nesbitt and Oikonomides, no. 18.86) and Aimilianos of Cyzicus (*c.* 815; diam. 24 mm; Washington, DC, Dumbarton Oaks, 65.5). The few seals that can be dated securely to the second period of iconoclasm (815–43) revert to earlier aniconic styles which had easily survived in a period during which the restoration of images did not enjoy universal support. The seals belonging to three patriarchs of Constantinople, namely Theodotos Kassiteras (815–21), Antonios I Kassimatas (821–34) and John VII Morocharzanios (834–43), are stamped with the monogrammatic and epigraphic formula of the previous century.

(iii) c. *843–1453.* The restoration of images in 843 resulted in the immediate revival of pre-iconoclastic types, with the use of Christ Pantokrator on nomismata from Michael III onward and on imperial seals (e.g. Romanos I Lekapenos, *reg* 920–44) as well as on patriarchal seals of Ignatios of Constantinople (847–57; diam. 35 mm; Cambridge, MA, Fogg, 862) and of Romanos I (see fig. 74, bottom centre). The decoration of churches and buildings in Constantinople during this period was imitated on both coins and seals, and their precise dating can contribute to the chronology of other works of art. Bellinger and Grierson were thus able to show that the enthroned Christ of Basil I's nomismata (867–86; Paris, Bib. N., Cab. Médailles, Schlumberger 3069), the '*senzata*', was copied from that of the Chrysotriklinos mosaic (856–66) in the Great Palace (*see* ISTANBUL, §III, 12), and that the standing Christ of Romanos I's coronation nomismata (921; diam. 21 mm; Washington, DC, Dumbarton Oaks) can probably be identified with the image of Christ in the vestibule of the Chalke Gate. The similarities between the Christ on an ornate lyre-back throne in the narthex mosaic of Hagia Sophia and his image on the gold coins of Leo VI (*reg* 886–912), Romanos I and Constantine VII (*reg* 912–59; see fig. 73, fifth row) support the dating of the mosaic to 920 proposed by Oikonomides (1976).

The Virgin first appears on patriarchal seals of Methodios (843–7) and then continuously from Photios (858–67, 877–86) onward. Various types of Virgin were used: from 843 to the time of Michael Keroularios (1043–58) she is shown standing and holding the Child; this image was replaced with one of her seated on a throne with the Child on her lap. The throne was shown without a back until 1204, when an elaborately decorated back was added. From 1380, however, the throne was once again backless. This probably reflects changes in the decoration of Hagia Sophia, as is suggested by Photios' homily of 867, in which he celebrated the unveiling of a mosaic of a standing *Virgin*, probably placed in the apse, and by the discovery of a mosaic set up during repair work after the earthquakes of the mid-14th century showing the Virgin seated on a backless throne.

The Virgin rarely appears on coins of the 10th century. From the 1030s, however, her image proliferated with the growth of her cult and the particular devotion of Romanus III Argyros (*reg* 1028–34). His coins show a particular type of Virgin known as the *Nikopoios*, which is probably a replica of an icon found during Romanos' restoration of

the Blachernai Palace chapel, in which the Virgin was depicted holding a medallion of Christ on her bosom. The *Blachernitissa* (diam. 25 mm; e.g. Paris, Bib. N., Anc. Fond. 144), another coin type of the 11th century which shows the Virgin *orans* without a medallion, may also have been derived from an icon in the church. The two types were conflated (Seibt, 1985) into that of a Virgin *orans* with the Christ medallion on her bosom, usually called the *Episkepsis*, as can be seen in the Christ the Saviour in Chora mosaic (*see* ISTANBUL, §III, 3), on some rare gold coins of the joint reign of Zoe and Theodora (1042–50; e.g. Washington, DC, Dumbarton Oaks, 1) and on the *trachea* (diam. 20 mm; e.g. Paris, Bib. N., Cab. Médailles, Anc. Fond. 144) of Andronikos I (*reg* 1183–5). The *Blachernitissa orans* became one of the most frequent monetary types of the Virgin, acquiring a symbolic value in 1261, when Michael VIII Palaiologos (*reg* 1259–82) celebrated the reconquest of Constantinople by showing the Virgin *orans* within the walls of the city (Paris, Bib. N.; see fig. 73, bottom row). This composition lasted until the end of the Byzantine gold *hyperpyron* in the mid-14th century.

From the 11th century, coins and seals are also stamped with a growing variety of religious images, in imitation of the decoration in late 9th-century and later churches. Saints are depicted only occasionally on coins of the 10th and 11th centuries, for example St Michael on the issues of Michael IV (*reg* 1034–41), but become more common, particularly the military saints, in the 12th century. The repertory of images on seals, however, is more innovative and varied, its interest residing partly in the representation of a series of local saints or individual patrons. Bishops tended to use the image of their see's patron, such as St Peter for Antioch, St Demetrios for Thessaloniki, St Euphemia for Chalcedon, St Titos for Crete and St Andrew for Patras, while individuals often, but not systematically, chose their homonymous saint. Dynasties sometimes designed a visual pun on their name, as for example the dynasty of the Angeli (1185–1204) representing the *Annunciation* on its family seals. Various scenes were also stamped on 11th- and 12th-century seals, including the *Crucifixion*, *Dormition of the Virgin* and the *Descent into Limbo* (e.g. Washington, DC, Dumbarton Oaks, 58; see fig. 74, bottom right).

The partition of the empire after 1204, the creation of numerous independent mints and the loosening of ties with Constantinople led to an increase in the variety of numismatic and sigillary types. Coins and seals from Thessaloniki, for example, are remarkably fine and elegant in style, while those from Nicaea and Trebizond bear more rigid and schematic designs respectively.

Although detailed regional studies of Late Byzantine monetary art have not been undertaken, the die-engravers responsible for the best issues from Thessaloniki clearly belong to the Macedonian school (13th–14th centuries), which combined Byzantine and Italian styles. Western and especially Germanic styles also influenced the iconography on Thessaloniki's coinage. Examples include the seated representation of St Demetrios with a sword on his knees, the frequent appearance of a lily and, above all, the inclusion in the 1230s and 1240s of winged figures and objects, such as a winged emperor, a haloed cross between wings, a winged arm holding a sword, and even a single wing. The latter is a particularly unusual motif and is derived from some German coinages (e.g. Brandenburg, Silesia and Bavaria). It does not appear in other forms of Byzantine art and its limitation to monetary art may indicate the presence of Germanic moneyers in Thessaloniki's mint.

During the Palaiologan period (1261–1453) this iconographic repertory was enlarged both in Constantinople and Thessaloniki, which remained the more inventive artistic centre. Western economic dominance is reflected in the adaptation of Italian and French patterns, as for example the Venetian silver *grosso* for the *basilikon* (1294) and the *denier tournois* for the Greek *tornesi*, which often has a circular inscription around a cross. The frequent and probably annual changes of monetary types on token coinage must also have been largely responsible for the extraordinary variety of themes, including every possible combination of the emperor or emperors with Christ, the Virgin and a saint; two emperors holding various symbols of power, or one crowning the other; an emperor presenting or holding a model city; and even a multiple scene of the martyrdom of St Demetrios, which must have been difficult to accommodate within the limited space of a coin. Despite being poorly engraved, slovenly struck and rarely well preserved, Late Byzantine coins clearly influenced the art of the neighbouring states of Serbia and Bulgaria.

BIBLIOGRAPHY

A. Grabar: *L'Empereur dans l'art byzantin* (Paris, 1936)
T. Bertelè: *L'imperatore alato nella numismatica bizantina* (Rome, 1951)
A. Grabar: *L'Iconoclasme byzantin: Dossier archéologique* (Paris, 1957)
J. D. Breckenridge: *The Numismatic Iconography of Justinian II, 685–695, 705–711 AD* (New York, 1959)
G. P. Galavaris: 'The Representation of the Virgin and Child on a "Thokos" on Seals of the Constantinopolitan Patriarchs', *Deltion Christ. Archaiol. Etaireias*, iv/2 (1960–61), pp. 154–81
V. Laurent: *L'Eglise*, 3 vols (1963–72), v of *Le Corpus des sceaux de l'empire byzantin* (Paris, 1963–)
P. M. Bruun: *Constantine and Licinius, A.D. 313–337* (1966), vii of *The Roman Imperial Coinage*, ed. H. B. Mattingly and others (London, 1923–81, 2/1984–)
A. R. Bellinger and P. Grierson: *Catalogue of the Byzantine Coins in the Dumbarton Oaks Collection and in the Whittemore Collection*, 3 vols (Washington, DC, 1966–73)
C. Morrisson: *Catalogue des monnaies byzantines de la Bibliothèque Nationale*, 2 vols (Paris, 1970)
G. Zacos and A. Veglery: *Byzantine Lead Seals*, 2 vols (Basle, 1972–84)
W. Hahn: *Moneta imperii byzantini*, 3 vols (Vienna, 1973–81)
S. Bendall and P. J. Donald: *The Billon Trachea of Michael VIII Paleologos, 1258–1282* (London, 1974)
N. Oikonomides: 'Leo VI and the Narthex Mosaic of Saint Sophia', *Dumbarton Oaks Pap.*, xxx (1976), pp. 153–72
T. Bertelè and C. Morrisson: *Numismatique byzantine* (Wetteren, 1978)
W. Seibt: *Kaiserhof* (1978), i of *Die byzantinischen Bleisiegel in Österreich* (Vienna, 1978)
S. Bendall and P. J. Donald: *The Later Paleologan Coinage, 1282–1453* (London, 1979)
J. P. C. Kent: *The Family of Constantine I, AD 337–364* (1981), viii of *The Roman Imperial Coinage*, ed. H. B. Mattingly and others (London, 1923–81, 2/1984–)
P. Grierson: *Byzantine Coins* (London and Berkeley, 1982)
V. Laurent: *L'Administration* (1982), ii of *Le Corpus des sceaux de l'empire byzantin* (Paris, 1963–)
N. Oikonomides: 'Some Remarks on the Apse Mosaic of Saint Sophia', *Dumbarton Oaks Pap.*, xxxix (1985), pp. 111–15
W. Seibt: 'Der Bildtypus der Theotokos Nikopoios', *Byzantina*, xiii (1985), pp. 549–64
N. Oikonomides: *Dated Byzantine Lead Seals* (Washington, DC, 1986)
W. Seibt: 'Die Darstellung der Theotokos', *Studies in Byzantine Sigillography*, ed. N. Oikonomides (Washington, DC, 1987)
S. Bendall: *A Private Collection of Palaeologan Coins* (Wolverhampton, 1988)
J. Nesbitt and N. Oikonomides: *Catalogues of Byzantine Seals at Dumbarton Oaks and in the Fogg Museum of Art, I: Italy, North of the Balkans, North of the Black Sea* (1991)
J.-C. Cheynet, C. Morrisson and W. Seibt: *Les Sceaux byzantins de la collection Henri Seyrig* (Paris, 1992)
P. Grierson and M. Mays: *Catalogue of Late Roman Coins in the Dumbarton Oaks Collection and in the Whittemore Collection: From Arcadius and Honorius to the Accession of Anastasius III* (Washington, DC, 1992)
C. Morrisson: 'Coins and Seals', *Byzance: L'Art byzantin dans les collections françaises* (exh. cat., Paris, Louvre, 1992)

CÉCILE MORRISSON

3. DRESS. The three major non-literary sources for Early Christian and Byzantine dress are depictions in art, excavated garments (mostly from Coptic cemeteries in Egypt) and silks preserved in west European churches. Each of these has drawbacks, but in particular it should be noted that most surviving art of the period is religious and shows conventionalized costumes, many based on Early Christian models. The evidence for the period between the sack of Constantinople in 1204 and its final loss in 1453 is generally less good than for the earlier centuries. (*See also* DRESS, §II, 2.)

(i) *Secular*. In the Early Christian and Byzantine periods clothing became more elaborate in its decoration and was influenced to a greater extent than before by the costumes of neighbouring peoples, but garment types continued broadly in the tradition of the Roman Empire.

(a) *Types of garment*. Dress in the Mediterranean areas of the Roman Empire consisted of two basic garments: a loose, sleeveless, woollen or linen tunic and a draped wool mantle. In the Greek-speaking East the mantle for both men and women was the rectangular *himation*. In the Latin West women wore a rectangular mantle, but the correct outer garment for men was the semicircular Roman toga. Changes began to occur within the existing repertory of garments in the 3rd and 4th centuries. Tunics with sleeves, not usual before c. 250, were the norm by c. 400. Sleeves were generally tight, meeting the wide body of the garment just above the wearer's elbows, although for a time the dalmatic, a wide-sleeved tunic, was popular for both men and women. By the 4th century most men in the Latin West wore a conical travelling cloak with a hood, the *birrus* or paenula, instead of the toga. The less encumbering Greek mantle fared better than the toga, but the *birrus* was increasingly popular in the East as well.

From the 4th century the expanding ranks of imperial officials wore the chlamys, a long cloak fastened at the shoulder with a brooch and, like the *birrus*, hung from the shoulders in straight, deep folds. In regions where the white or purple-bordered toga was still worn, notably by senators, it was more narrowly draped than in its heyday, with its upper edge folded in a tight band and its loose overfold, the *sinus*, picked up and wrapped around the left forearm. Emperors, empresses, vassal rulers and high-ranking officials also wore a cloth panel, or *tablion*, which hung from chest height across the front right half of the chlamys. The *tablion* could either be of a single colour or decorated with a central image of the emperor or a figural motif, such as a bird, and bordered with gems. The toga most commonly depicted in Early Christian and Byzantine art is the *toga picta*, worn traditionally by generals at their triumphs. It does not, however, appear to have been as full as the plain toga, perhaps owing to the costliness of its gold and purple-dyed wool materials. On ivory diptychs of the 5th century and early 6th, such as that portraying a stag hunt in an amphitheatre (*c.* 400; Liverpool Mus.) and a portrait of the consul Anastasius (517; Paris, Bib. N., Cab. Médailles), it consists of a wide sash passing twice around the body and on top of a sleeveless tunic with similar decoration. A longer tight-sleeved plain tunic was worn underneath. After the 6th century only emperors were allowed to wear the *toga picta* (known as the *loros* by the 9th or 10th century), although a version of it continued to be worn by empresses, the wives of important officials and, in art, by female saints.

Clothing of the 4th and 5th centuries was still mostly made from a single layer of cloth 'woven to shape', with little or no sewn finishing. As the wearing of silk became more widespread, so fine wool clothes associated with complex drapery suffered a corresponding decline (*see* §8(i) below).

(b) Decoration and the application of new weaves. Decoration on clothing became more elaborate during the Early Christian period, with a move away from simple stripes to the use of brighter colours and figural designs. Although most decoration was still in tapestry weave (i.e. woven in one with the rest of the garment) and confined to certain areas, such as around the shoulders, from the 3rd or 4th century some clothing was made from textiles of more advanced weaves with all-over repeating patterns. These

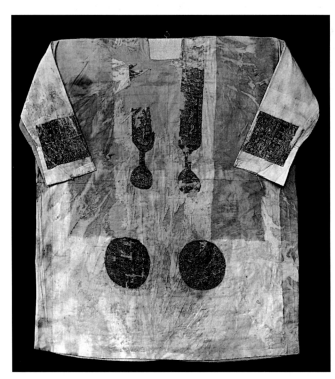

75. Cotton tunic with sewn-on silk panels, from Akhmim, Egypt, *c.* 700–*c.* 750 (London, Victoria and Albert Museum)

changes are evident in the two mosaic panels in S Vitale, Ravenna, showing Justinian I and Theodora (*c.* 500–48) with their respective retinues (*see* MOSAIC, fig. 6). The most traditional garments are the *birrus* and dalmatics worn by Bishop Maximian and the deacons, which had already begun to fossilize into 'vestments'; the chasuble is derived from the *birrus*. A middle category is the chlamys worn by the Emperor and Empress (see fig. 39 above), both in purple, and by their officials. The decoration in stripes and *tablion* panels, although quite complex, was probably still tapestry-woven, while the flower-buds at the hem of Theodora's tunic are similar to those on a number of Coptic tapestry fragments (*see* COPTIC ART, §V, 3). The ladies-in-waiting and the soldiers wear the least traditional clothes, made from textiles with all-over repeating patterns; the designs in strongly contrasting colours and those in a subtler two-toned combination are probably of weft-faced compound twill and twill damask respectively. The repeating leaf pattern on the tunic of the soldier holding the shield is similar in design and colour to a surviving compound twill silk (see fig. 93 below).

The ancient distaste for sewn clothing continued in court circles; the *Book of the Prefect*, which dates from the reign of Leo VI (*reg* 886–912), mentions 'clothing woven in a single piece' as one of the categories of 'forbidden goods' in the gift of the emperors. Although it was still possible, but laborious, to weave areas of tapestry within the more complex weaves, the use of the new textiles generally led to an increase in sewing, as was probably the case with the applied decoration on the soldier's tunic in the S Vitale mosaic. An extant tunic of later date from Akhmim, Egypt (see fig. 75) is made in a similar way. The silk panels were part of a length of compound twill cloth, in this case designed to be cut up and sewn into tunics. The plain cotton base is still partially woven to shape and illustrates the spread of this fibre into the Mediterranean region.

The richness of Byzantine secular clothing is evident from the kaftan found in the tomb of an Alan tribesman in Moshchevaya Balka, northern Caucasus (*c.* 8th–9th centuries; St Petersburg, Hermitage; see fig. 76). Despite the tunic's Central Asian shape and a roundel design of Persian simurghs, the silk used for the facings and probably the main silk are of Byzantine manufacture. When represented in art, such large repeating designs tend to flatten the appearance of the human figure: this effect is well illustrated by the miniatures of the MENOLOGION OF BASIL II (*c.* 985).

(c) Outside influences. Unlike the ancient Greeks and Romans, the Byzantines did not withstand the influence of the costumes of their barbarian neighbours. An example of white fitted trousers with feet (*bracae*) of Germanic origin, such as those recovered from Thorsburg (Schleswig, Schloss Gottorf), is depicted in a late 4th-century wall painting at Silistra, Bulgaria. They became part of official Byzantine dress in the 4th century and may even be identified with the trousers worn under tunics by the Apostles in an *Ascension* wall painting in the New Church of Tokalı (10th century), Cappadocia. The white trousers with feet of Greek folk dress may be a rare Byzantine survival.

a narrow piece of clothing was to be worn on horseback. The tunic underneath, just visible as a gold decorated hem, was probably of a more ordinary type. By this date it is also likely that most gold decoration was embroidered, not woven.

Late portraits of Byzantine emperors sometimes show what is really a Turkish kaftan, a long garment fastened down the front and fitted to the waist. That depicted worn by Constantine Komnenos (*reg* 1399–1400) in the Lincoln College Typicon (1400; Oxford, Bodleian Lib.) may also have been made from Turkish silk. The only traditional part of his costume is the jewelled, red leather belt.

BIBLIOGRAPHY

The Book of the Prefect (*c*. 895); Eng. trans by E. H. Freshfeld in *Roman Law in the Later Roman Empire* (Cambridge, 1938)
J. Ebersolt: *Les Arts somptuaires à Bizance* (Paris, 1923)
N. P. Kondakov: 'Les Costumes orientaux à la cour byzantine', *Byzantion*, i (1924), pp. 7–49
R. Delbrueck: *Die Consulardiptychen und verwandte Denkmäler*, 2 vols (Berlin and Leipzig, 1926–9)
R. Pfister: *Textiles de Halabiyeh* (Paris, 1951)
A. Cameron: 'A Byzantine Imperial Coronation of the 6th Century AD', *Costume*, vii (1973), pp. 4–9
A. Jeroussalimskaja: 'Le Cafetan aux simourghs du tombeau de Mochtchevaja Balka (Caucase Septentrional)', *Stud. Iran.*, vii (1978), pp. 183–211
V. Gervers: 'Medieval Garments in the Mediterranean World', *Cloth and Clothing in Medieval Europe: Essays in Memory of Professor E. M. Carus-Wilson*, ed. N. B. Harte and K. G. Ponting (London, 1983)

HERO GRANGER-TAYLOR

(ii) Religious. This section covers the development of the different types of vestment worn by clerics and monks (*see also* VESTMENTS, ECCLESIASTICAL, §1). The most important liturgical vestments are derived from Late Roman secular dress, especially of the 4th century. Many of these vestments gradually lost their original function and acquired a symbolic significance as the insignia of the functionaries wearing them. Thus in a commentary on the liturgy entitled *Church History*, possibly by Germanos I, Patriarch of Constantinople (715/17–730), and liturgical treatises by Symeon, Archbishop of Thessaloniki (1416/17–29), the origin and meaning of liturgical vestments are explained in an entirely symbolic way. This symbolism is still evident in the vestments of the Eastern Church. A tendency to assign a symbolic meaning to vestments that once had a practical function is also apparent in monastic dress.

(a) Liturgical. (b) Monastic.

(a) Liturgical. At least until the time of Constantine the Great, both clergy and congregation must have worn normal clothes during church services, perhaps reserving a better set for Sundays. The development of a special dress for certain clerics probably started in the 4th century. Over several centuries, certain civil garments gradually became associated with ecclesiastical offices, until their use had become exclusively liturgical in character. In the late 4th century it seems that certain bishops were endowed with the title *illustris*, a rank in the state hierarchy even higher than that of senator. This practice of granting clerics a place in the state hierarchy may have started under Constantine. Certain privileges were connected with the title, such as the use of special garments and insignia including the pallium, *mappa* and *campagi*, the forerunners

76. Silk kaftan, l. 1.4 m, from the tomb of an Alan tribesman, Moshchevaya Balka, northern Caucasus, *c.* 8th–9th centuries (St Petersburg, Hermitage Museum)

By the 11th or 12th century fitted tunics using narrow widths of cloth lengthways, with gores in the side seams, were commonly worn throughout the Mediterranean and Europe. This type of garment may have originated in Central Asia and been brought west via Persia, for five of the ten children's tunics (*c.* 610) found at Zenobia (now Halabiyeh, Syria) on the River Euphrates are of this type, while the rest are woven to shape. Another tunic adopted from the East is the *skaramangion*, a Persian term meaning a riding garment and mentioned in Byzantine texts; it may be the garment worn by Nikephoros III Botaneiates (*reg* 1078–81) in the *Homilies* of John Chrysostomos (1078–81; Paris, Bib. N., MS. Coislin 79, fol. 2*v*; see fig. 62 above). This has a vent in the lower skirt, necessary if such

of later episcopal vestments. The pallium kept its name in the West, while its shape gradually changed from a piece of cloth (*c.* 4×2 m) draped around the body, to a narrow band of white wool, given by the pope to archbishops and certain other bishops as a personal distinction. In the East it became known as the omophorion (see below). The *mappa*, a sort of kerchief held in the hand by high dignitaries such as consuls (see fig. 81 below), was probably the origin of the western maniple and the eastern *enchirion* (see below). The *campagi* were a special type of shoes, the forerunners of the liturgical episcopal shoes. The first prescription concerning a liturgical vestment is in the 41st canon of the Synod of Carthage (*c.* 400), where it is said that the deacon should wear his alb (white tunic) only during the Eucharist and the reading. Not until the canons of several 6th- and 7th-century synods is the use of special garments for the liturgy again attested.

Early Christian liturgical dress can be considered the basis for the vestments of both the Eastern and Western churches. Although regional differences have always existed, from the 9th century the Western Church developed an increasingly complicated system, whereas in the Eastern Church liturgical dress has undergone little change since the 8th century. The vestments of the Early Christian clergy include the alb, a white tunic worn as an undergarment by all ranks. Its name is derived from the *tunica alba* ('white tunic'), a common civil dress. It is also referred to as the *tunica talaris*, the long tunic hanging down to the ankles. When in the 6th century it became the fashion to wear shorter tunics, the clergy kept the habit of wearing the *tunica talaris*, both as a liturgical and as a civil dress. In this way the alb became a distinctive vestment of the clergy.

The dalmatic was a wide-sleeved tunic generally decorated from the shoulders to the lower border with vertical bands (*clavi*) of differently coloured cloth. It was introduced from Dalmatia probably as early as the 2nd century and was worn as an overgarment by men and women. The most famous surviving example are the white silk fragments (Milan, Mus. Sacro S Ambrogio), depicting scenes of lion hunting set in an open landscape, from a dalmatic that probably belonged to St Ambrose (*c.* 334 or 340–97). In the late 5th century the dalmatic went out of fashion as a civil garment but remained in use by the pope of Rome and his deacons. The dalmatic was also used outside Rome, as is evident in the mosaic panel of Justinian with Bishop Maximian, followed by a train of guards and deacons, in S Vitale (*see* RAVENNA, §2 (vii) and MOSAIC, fig. 6). Although the deacons appear with dalmatics over their albs, Maximian wears the chasuble and pallium as his outermost garments (see below). Only in the 9th century was the dalmatic generally accepted as a liturgical vestment for bishops as well as for deacons.

Another Early Christian vestment is the amice, humeral, superhumeral or *anaboladium*, a rectangular piece of linen worn around the neck. It originates from the Roman *amictus*, which was meant to protect the outer vestments from sweat. Originally worn by Christians to keep their Sunday clothes clean and tidy, it became part of the liturgical dress sometime after the 8th century.

In order to facilitate movement a girdle of white or coloured textile, known as a cingulum, was worn around

the tunic. It was of Late Roman origin and must have become part of liturgical dress at an early stage, but because of its humble character it rarely appears in early texts or representations. In the West it is worn by all ranks of the clergy, in the East only by priests and bishops.

From the 4th century onwards one of the most characteristic vestments worn by deacons and priests over the alb was the orarion, which originally may have functioned as a napkin for wiping the mouth. It was worn over the left shoulder by deacons (l. *c.* 4 m), and around the neck with both ends hanging in front by priests (l. *c.* 2.5 m). After the 9th century in the West it is usually referred to as a stole.

The chasuble is an outer garment, generally worn only by priests and bishops. It is probably derived from the Latin *casula* ('little hut'), which was a wide outdoor cloak for men and women, also known as a paenula or *planeta*, and originally an oval or circular piece of textile with a hole in the middle for the head. Some of the earliest evidence for its use as a liturgical vestment are the 6th-century mosaic representations in S Vitale and S Apollinare in Classe, Ravenna, but it may have been used as early as the 4th century.

The pallium was originally reserved for high officials. Although at first worn by bishops to indicate their social status, it gradually became a liturgical vestment. In the West the Roman pope had the right to wear it and to confer it to archbishops and bishops. Early on in the East it became a vestment for all bishops while remaining a sign of imperial distinction for a long time. It was worn around the neck, hanging in a loop over the breast, with one end flung over the left shoulder, the other hanging down in front.

From early on, bishops were conferred with the maniple in the West and the *enchirion* in the East (see above); by the early 6th century it had also become an attribute of priests and deacons in the Western Church.

Until the reign of Justinian, ecclesiastical dress in the East and West had still much in common. In the 8th and 9th centuries, however, there was a gradual divergence, with Byzantine dress tending to be more conservative than the dress of the Roman Church. The most important vestments in the Eastern Church include the sticharion (see fig. 77a), which is the basic undergarment for all ranks, and is comparable in function to the Western alb. In shape it is similar to the dalmatic, with wide sleeves and striped decoration. The *epimanikia* (77b) are separate cuffs worn to prevent the sleeves of the sticharion from hindering the wearer's movements. The earliest evidence for them, a letter from Patriarch Petros of Antochia to Michael Kerullarios, dates to the 11th century (*c.* 1054), and until at least the late 12th century they were reserved for bishops, since when they have also been worn by priests.

Until the 8th century the orarion was worn by both the priests and deacons. Since the 9th century, however, the priest's orarion was called the epitrachelion (77c), and instead of both ends hanging loose over breast and knees they were buttoned, and eventually sewn, together. The epitrachelion also became part of episcopal dress. Byzantine deacons continued to wear the orarion over their left shoulder until the celebration of the Eucharist. For the

77. Byzantine bishop's vestments, *c.* 14th century: (a) sticharion; (b) *epimanikia*; (c) epitrachelion; (d) phelonion; (e) omophorion; (f) *epigonation*

rest of the liturgy they wore it around the waist, with both ends crossing diagonally over the back and flung over the shoulders.

The cingulum worn by priests and bishops, came to be known as the *zonarion* and the chasuble as the phelonion (77d). The latter was plain and undecorated until the 11th century, when the *polystaurion* type with a pattern of crosses was introduced. Although at first reserved for patriarchs, from the 14th century metropolitan bishops have also been entitled to wear the *polystaurion*.

The omophorion (77e) is the Eastern counterpart of the Western pallium. It has always been worn by bishops as a strip of silk (*c.* 3.5×0.25 m), originally in white, but later appearing in several colours and decorated with three crosses. The *epigonation* (77f) is a vestment unique to Eastern bishops and archimandrites (senior monks). It evolved from the *enchirion* and at first was probably held in the hand. Representations from the 10th century onwards show the *enchirion* hanging from the *zonarion*. In the 14th century the shape of the *enchirion* changed from a kerchief into a stiff, lozenge-shaped piece of textile. Probably with the change of shape the name was changed into *epigonation*.

The sakkos is the Byzantine upper-vestment which developed from the dalmatic. It first appears in the 11th century and was worn instead of the phelonion by patriarchs. From the 13th century it was also worn by metropolitan bishops, and after the fall of Constantinople (1453) it has become a vestment for all bishops. This can probably be explained by the fact that the sakkos was primarily an imperial garment and as such only granted to the highest clergy. A surviving example of a Greek patriarchal sakkos is the 'Dalmatic of Charlemagne' (14th century; Rome, Vatican, Mus. Stor. A. Tesoro S Pietro) with a richly embroidered *Calling of the Chosen* on the front and the *Transfiguration* on the reverse (*see* §8 below).

Although occasionally bishops in the Eastern Church may have been granted the privilege to wear a mitre, shaped after the imperial crown (Gr. *Kamelaukion*), it became a rule for bishops to wear this headdress after the collapse of the Byzantine empire. In Russia, the tsar could grant the mitre to priests and archpriests. (For examples of liturgical vestments with byzantinizing decoration *see* SERBIA, §VIII; RUSSIA, §XI.)

(b) Monastic. The origins of monastic dress lie in 4th-century Egypt and Syria. In Egypt two types of monastic dress developed, one according to the prescriptions laid down by St Pachomios (*c.* 290–346) in Upper Egypt and the other under the influence of the followers of St Anthony (*c.* 251–356) in Lower Egypt (*see* CHRISTIANITY, §IV, 1). Important sources for the knowledge of early monastic dress are the rules of Pachomios, the 32nd chapter of the *Lausiac History* by Palladios (*c.* 363–431) and *Institutions of Coenobitic Life* by John Cassian (*c.* 360–435).

The dress worn by the monks of St Pachomios' community included a tunic (Gr. *lebiton*), a leather apron (Copt. *rahtou*), a *zonarion*, either of leather or cloth, a hood (Gr. *koukoullion*), a long linen scarf and a leather travelling-coat (*melote*). Both the Pachomian monastic rule and dress disappeared *c.* 1000. The dress worn by St Anthony's followers (see fig. 78) in Lower Egypt consisted of a tunic called a *thorakeion* ('cuirass'; 78a) because it symbolized protection against evil, a leather *zonarion* (78b), which represented the monk's readiness to serve God and his chastity, and a headscarf (Gr. *phakialion*), which was gradually replaced by a pointed hood known as a *koukoulla* or *kouklion* (78c). Originally this hood was attached to a mantle (Copt. *phork*), which developed into a narrow scapular (78d), sometimes attached to a hood. A system of thin leather straps known as a schema (78e) was worn

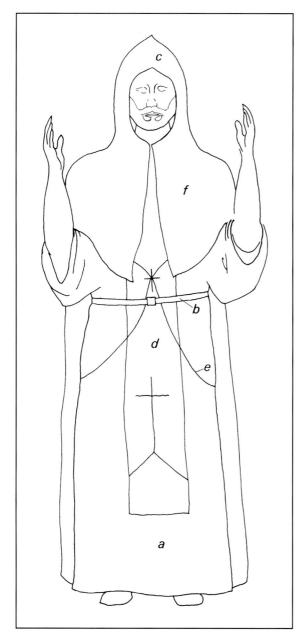

78. Monastic dress of Lower Egypt, 4th century: (a) *thorakeion*; (b) *zonarion*; (c) *koukoulla* or *kouklion*; (d) scapular; (e) schema; (f) *birrus*

The dress worn by St Anthony's followers also provides the basis for later Byzantine monastic dress. In both the Greek and Russian Orthodox tradition the scapular is often embroidered in red or white with images of the cross, the instruments of Christ's torture and different kinds of inscriptions (e.g. a Greek scapular, found on the dried-out body of a monk in an ossuary; see Galey, pl. 190; a Russian monastic hood and a hood with scapular attached, embroidered with instruments of the Passion, crosses and texts; Mt Sinai, monastery of St Catherine; see Innemée, pls 59, 60). Greek monks often wear this scapular underneath instead of over their tunic. The Egyptian hood has been replaced by a cylindrical hat (Gr. *kamelaukion*; Rus. *kamilavka*), over which a veil (Gr. *epirriptarion*; Rus. *klobuk*) is worn.

BIBLIOGRAPHY

J. Galey: *Sinai and the Monastery of St Catherine* (London, n.d.), pl. 190
Pachomios: *Ek ton entolon tou Agiou Pachomiou* [Rules of St Pachomios] (4th century); edn in *PG*, xl (1863), cols 947–52
J. Cassian: *De institutis coenobiorum* [Institutions of coenobitic life] (c. 410–35); ed. J.-C. Guy as *Institutions cénobitiques* (Paris, 1965)
Palladios: *Historia lausiaca* [The Lausiac history] (c. 419); ed. C. Butler as *The Lausiac History of Palladius*, 2 vols (Cambridge, 1898–1904)
Germanos: *Istoria ekklesiastiki* [Church history] (?8th century); edn in *PG*, xcviii (1865), cols 383–454
Symeon of Thessaloniki: *Peri ton ieron teleton* [On the sacraments] and *Peri tis ieras leitourgias* [On the sacred liturgy] (1420s); edn in *PG*, clv (1866), cols 177–238, 253–64
J. Braun: *Die liturgische Gewandung im Occident und Orient* (Freiburg im Breisgau, 1907)
——: *Handbuch der Paramentik* (Freiburg im Breisgau, 1912)
P. Oppenheim: 'Das Mönchskleid im christlichen Altertum', *Röm. Qschr. Christ. Altertknd. & Kirchengesch.*, xxviii, Suppl. (1931)
T. Papas: *Studien zur Geschichte der Messgewänder im byzantinischen Ritus* (Munich, 1965)
E. Piltz: *Trois Sakkoi byzantins: Analyse iconographique* (Stockholm, 1976)
——: *Kamelaukion et mitra* (Uppsala, 1977)
K. C. Innemée: *Ecclesiastical Dress in the Medieval Near East* (Leiden, 1992)

KAREL C. INNEMÉE

4. GLASS.

(i) 4th–8th centuries. (ii) 9th century–1453.

(i) 4th–8th centuries. Glass was in common use in the Byzantine empire between the 4th century and the 7th. It was employed for making vessels and small objects such as beads, pendants and weights, for glazing windows and for making the tesserae and pieces of flat glass from which mosaics and *opus sectile* panels were constructed. In the eastern Mediterranean, large numbers of intact vessels have been found in Syria and Palestine, where they were placed in tombs, and in Egypt. Among the most notable discoveries in Syria or Palestine are the remains of a 4th-century glass workshop at Jalame in Israel. The most common forms from the region are goblets resembling modern wine-glasses, conical lamps that were inserted into metal polykandela, flasks with long necks and unguent containers with elaborate basket-like handles. The best-known objects, however, are jugs and bottles with mould-blown decoration that includes Christian and Jewish motifs, such as crosses, stylite saints and menorahs (Washington, DC, Freer; Toledo, OH, Mus. A.). Although they are often identified as souvenirs from shrines and holy places, including Jerusalem, this interpretation is not confirmed by the literary sources and does not explain the

around the body, forming a diagonal cross on the chest and back. Originally its function was to hold up the tunic during work, but by the 7th century it had acquired the symbolic meaning of the carrying of Christ's cross on the monk's shoulder. An outer mantle or *birrus* (78f) was derived from a 4th-century travelling cloak with a hood (*see* §(i) above).

Syrian monastic dress largely corresponds to that of Lower Egypt, except that in Syria a schema does not occur.

occurrence of both Christian and Jewish ornament. Regardless of their function, it is clear that they were made in quantity in the 6th century and the early 7th. Much of our knowledge of Early Christian glass in Egypt comes from excavations at Karanis in the Faiyum, where large quantities of glassware (Ann Arbor, U. MI, Kelsey Mus.) for everyday use were discovered.

In the central Mediterranean, vessels and window glass of Roman type continued to be made in the Early Christian period. Large quantities of fragments from the 4th century and later have been excavated at Rome (Rome, Mus. N. Romano) and other places in Italy (Ostia Antica, Mus. Ostiense) and at Carthage (Tunis, Mus. N. Bardo). The remains of a workshop, perhaps of the 7th century, have been found at Torcello, near Venice. Among the finest 4th-century objects produced in Italy are vessels with wheel-cut decoration, which includes both Christian (Rome, Antiqua Com.) and pagan scenes (Ostia Antica, Mus. Ostiense), gold glasses and cage cups. Gold glasses are objects decorated with gold leaf cut in elaborate designs, often with figures, and sandwiched between two layers of fused glass (e.g. Toledo, OH, Mus. A.). Cage cups are vessels with elaborate openwork 'cages' made by cutting and grinding, a technique known as *vasa diatreta*. The most elaborate glass object with openwork, the Lykourgos Cup (4th century; London, BM), is made of dichromatic glass, which is green in reflected light but red when light shines through it (*see* ROME, ANCIENT, §VIII, 2(ii)). In addition to vessel and window glass, Early Christian glassmakers produced large numbers of pendants and weights. The pendants are discs, usually *c.* 20 mm across, with a suspension loop and an impressed design (Corning, NY, Mus. Glass). Among the numerous designs are christograms, crosses and scenes of protection, (e.g. the Good Shepherd) or deliverance (e.g. the Sacrifice of Isaac). Glass weights were made in large numbers in the 6th and 7th centuries. These are discs (diam. 17–25 mm) that were issued by the eparch or prefect of Constantinople. Many show the eparch (e.g. Madrid, Roger Percire priv. col.), who is identified by an inscription; others depict the emperor, sometimes with the monogram of the eparch; a third type, without a human figure, simply has a monogram (e.g. London, BM; Washington, DC, Dumbarton Oaks).

The most spectacular use of glass was for the small cuboid tesserae that were used in mosaics. The walls and ceilings of Early Christian churches were decorated with ambitious schemes that required millions of coloured tesserae. In many cases the backgrounds of figural schemes consisted entirely of tesserae in which a layer of gold leaf was sandwiched between two layers of glass. In the Eastern empire, huge mosaics (destr.) are known to have decorated Hagia Sophia (360; rebuilt 532–7) at Constantinople; and, in the West, the most famous mosaics of this period are in the churches of S Vitale (521–47), S Apollinare Nuovo (late 5th century) and S Apollinare in Classe (second quarter of the 6th century) at Ravenna.

There is little evidence of the construction of mural mosaics between the mid-7th century and the mid-9th, and little is known about glass vessels in the empire between the 7th and 10th centuries.

(ii) 9th century–1453. Once the iconoclastic controversy had ended (843), large figured mosaics were again used to decorate churches, as in the apse images of the *Virgin and Child* in Hagia Sophia (867) at Constantinople and in the church of the Dormition (second half of the 9th century; destr.) at Nicaea. Among the greatest achievements of Byzantine mosaicists after the apparent hiatus in the previous centuries are the mosaics in the church of Hagia Sophia (10th–13th century) and in Christ the Saviour in Chora Monastery (Kariye Cami; mosaics completed 1321), both at Constantinople, as well as in the monastery churches of Hosios Loukas (11th century) and Dafni (*c.* 1100). The earliest surviving micro-mosaic was made in the 1060s. Mosaicists from Constantinople were in demand even outside the Byzantine empire. The caliph al-Hakam II (*reg* 961–76) employed Byzantine craftsmen to decorate the mihrab (961–6) of the Mezquita at Córdoba (*see* CÓRDOBA (i), §3(i)(a)); in Kiev, Prince Vladimir I Svyatoslavich (*reg* 978–1015) imported Byzantine craftsmen to build and decorate with mosaics the church of the Tithe (Desyatinnaya) of the Most Holy Mother of God (989–96; destr. 1240); and tesserae, if not mosaic-makers, were probably imported to decorate churches in Sicily such as the cathedral at Monreale (1166–89), the Cappella Palátina and the Martorana (first half of the 12th century) at Palermo and the cathedral (1131–48) at Cefalù, and on the Italian mainland, for example, the cathedral (1080–*c.* 1085) at Salerno.

The treasury of S Marco in Venice contains a number of glass vessels apparently brought as booty after the sack of Constantinople in 1204. They include a bowl of purple glass (10th or 11th century) decorated with gilding and coloured enamels depicting mythological scenes in roundels, and contained in a silver gilt mount (see fig. 79). Similar figures occur on Byzantine ivories of the 10th and 11th centuries (e.g. Veroli Casket; London, V&A; see fig. 9 above) and there is little doubt that the bowl, too, is Byzantine. Among the other glass vessels are hanging lamps of the *lampada pensile* form and a cup. They are made of colourless or greenish glass and have relief-cut ornament consisting of conical bosses and discs, some of which have conical bosses at the centre. One of the lamps has an 11th-century gilt bronze mount. While some scholars maintain that the objects were made in Constantinople, others suggest that they are Sasanian or Islamic.

79. Purple glass bowl with gilding and coloured enamel roundels, silver gilt mount, diam. 170 mm, 10th or 11th century (Venice, Tesoro di San Marco)

It may be significant that, with the possible exception of these objects, the discs on Sasanian or apparently Sasanian vessels do not have conical bosses and that, again with the possible exception of these objects, the Islamic vessels that have discs with conical bosses do not have stand-alone bosses.

More is known about Byzantine glass of the 12th and 13th centuries. In the early 12th century Theophilus recorded that 'Greeks' made gilded and enamelled glass. In all probability Theophilus was referring to a group of bottles and other forms made of dark blue and other coloured glass, with gilded or gilded and enamelled decoration. The most common form is a cylindrical bottle with a short, narrow neck. Regardless of the form, the decoration consists of combinations of friezes, squares and roundels containing vegetal motifs, birds, animals and geometric elements. All these objects are similar, and they were probably made at one place within a relatively short period. Most of the examples were found in the eastern Mediterranean, but single specimens have been discovered at Tarquinia in Italy (Tarquinia, Pal. Vitelleschi), Stanton Harcourt, Oxon, England, and Armenia (Erevan, Hist. Mus. Armenia). Paphos in Cyprus, Corinth in Greece and Novogrudok in Belarus' (St Petersburg, Archaeol. Inst.) have yielded examples of gilded and enamelled vessels as well as evidence of glassworking, and all three have been proposed as places where the objects were made. It is possible, however, that the workshop that produced them was situated at Constantinople.

Byzantine craftsmen may also have produced painted glass windows in the 12th century. The churches of Christ the Saviour in Chora (Kariye Cami; early 12th century; rebuilt c. 1316–21) and of Christ Pantokrator (Zeyrek Cami; 1118–36) contained painted glass windows. It is not clear, however, whether the windows were installed when the churches were built or are additions dating from the Latin occupation (1204–61). The case for regarding them as Byzantine is perhaps strengthened by the existence of 12th-century windows decorated in Byzantine style in the dome of the church of the Mother of God (Bogorodica; completed 1191) at the monastery of Studenica in Serbia. The same technique used for the production of tesserae was employed to make a group of plaques (90 mm square), comprising yellowish glass decorated with triangles of gold leaf arranged in a cruciform pattern and covered with a colourless overlay. These plaques (Damascus, N. Mus.), which are said to have been found at Ma'arrat an Nu'man, 50 km north of Hama, probably decorated the walls of a single building (?church) and are variously dated between the 6th and 12th centuries. The motif they bear has analogies in the 12th-century palace now known as the Tekfur Saray at Constantinople, and in the cathedrals of Monreale and Cefalù in Sicily. It is possible, therefore, that the plaques are Byzantine and closer in date to the 12th than to the 6th century.

Opinions about 12th-century glass vessels have been influenced by the remains of two glassmakers' workshops found at Corinth in 1937. One of the workshops seems to have specialized in making bangles such as occur frequently in Greece and the Balkans. Among the objects made at the other workshop were prunted beakers, beakers with vertical ribs and cups with mould-blown patterns of diamonds, ovals and hexagons (Corinth, Archaeol. Mus.). Coins and other finds from the vicinity of the workshops led to the conclusion that they operated in the 11th and 12th centuries. The prunted beakers and other vessels were assumed to be typical Byzantine products of the period c. 1000 to c. 1150. A third group of discoveries came from Tarquinia (Tarquinia, Pal. Vitelleschi) in Italy, where vessels like the finds from Corinth began to appear in the 1960s. Whenever these objects were found in datable contexts, they belonged to the 13th and 14th centuries. Although many of them are made of transparent yellowish glass, the best are almost colourless—a quality achieved by the careful selection of raw materials and, later, by the addition of manganese to the batch. The conclusion seemed obvious: the Byzantine tradition of glassmaking found at Corinth was introduced to Italy in the 12th or 13th century, flourished there, and was transmitted across the Alps to Switzerland and Germany in the 14th century. Indeed, a connection between Constantinople and Venice already existed in the form of 13th-century mould-pressed medallions and plaques (Washington, DC, Freer; Corning, NY, Mus. Glass) decorated with scenes from the lives of Christ and the Virgin, saints, Apostles and Evangelists. Nearly 200 of these medallions are known. They fall into two groups: those made of translucent glass with images of Orthodox saints and Greek inscriptions, and those made of opaque red glass that have inscriptions in both Greek and Latin. The first group is often said to be from Constantinople; but it is possible that both groups are Venetian.

Research undertaken since 1937, however, appears to suggest that the glass finds from Corinth are untypical of the Byzantine world and are difficult to date. It is not certain that the coins of the 11th and 12th centuries were associated sufficiently closely with the remains of the glassmakers' workshops to provide a date for the glass. Moreover, the finds from Italy, Schaffhausen in Switzerland and Konstanz in Germany form a broadly coherent group that probably came into production in the 13th century and quickly developed distinctive regional characteristics. Thus, while much remains uncertain about European glass in the 13th and 14th centuries, it is reasonable to suppose that it was not inspired by Byzantine glass from southern Greece, that the driving force behind the new developments was not necessarily Venice, and that glassmakers in Germany were every bit as skilful as their Italian counterparts. The prunted beaker, the standard drinking vessel in Italy, Switzerland and Germany in the 13th century, could have been developed in any one of those countries, although Italy may have the strongest claim to its origin.

BIBLIOGRAPHY

Theophilus [Rugerus]: De diversis artibus (?1110–40); Eng. trans. by G. A. Hawthorne and C. S. Smith as On Diverse Art (Chicago and London, 1963), pp. 59–60, 63–4

J. Philippe: Le Monde byzantin dans l'histoire de la verrerie, Ve–XVIe siècle (Bologna, 1970)

H. R. Hahnloser, ed.: Il tesoro e il museo (1971), ii of Il tesoro di San Marco (Florence, 1965–71)

L. Leciejewicz, E. Tabaczyńska and S. Tabaczyński: Torcello: Scavi, 1961–62 (Rome, 1977)

D. B. Harden and others: Glass of the Caesars (Milan, 1987)

G. D. Weinberg, ed.: Excavations at Jalame: Site of a Glass Factory in Late Roman Palestine (Columbia, 1988)

H. Tait: 'Europe from the Middle Ages to the Industrial Revolution', *Five Thousand Years of Glass*, ed. H. Tait (London, 1991), pp. 145–86

DAVID WHITEHOUSE

5. IVORIES AND STEATITES. A fundamental distinction between ivories of the 4th to the 6th centuries, and those of the 9th century to 1453, is justified in terms of chronology, the relative amounts of material available in these two periods and the different ends to which it was put. In Byzantium steatite was carved from the 10th century onwards.

(i) Sources and supply of ivory. (ii) 4th–6th centuries. (iii) 9th century–1453.

(i) Sources and supply of ivory. North and East Africa were probably the main source of dentine (the usable core of the elephant's tusk) from the Roman period until at least the late 6th century. After a hiatus in production that may have lasted as long as 300 years, East Africa appears to have furnished the majority of ivory worked in the Middle Byzantine period (*c.* 843–1204). Asian tusks allow the cutting of plaques no larger than 110 mm across, whereas a CONSULAR DIPTYCH is often as much as a fifth wider. From the 9th century onwards plaques sometimes attained a width of 170 mm, although normal plaques average about 170×130 mm. Smaller pieces carved in both periods could theoretically come from Indian elephants.

The length and width of a plaque provide a rough index to the amount of ivory available, since craftsmen were always concerned to maximize the dimensions of their products. This intention can be inferred from the traces of the 'nerve canal' evident on the reverses of some large plaques, and from the presence of the cement (the natural sheathing of dentine in a tusk) on the outer edges of plaques. These symptoms occur far less often on pieces of the 4th to the 6th century than in the Middle Byzantine period, a fact that suggests that larger quantities of finer quality ivory were available in the earlier centuries. In the early 4th century ivory was a relatively cheap commodity: in Diocletian's Edict on Prices of 301 one (Roman) pound of ivory cost one-fortieth the price of the same weight of bullion silver. Whether this low value continued through to the 6th century is unknown, but certainly the ready availability of the material persisted. There is thus some reason to doubt the applicability to the Early Christian period of the notion, found in both Classical and medieval authors, that ivory was always a rarity. Although, like other natural materials, notably ebony and citrus woods, dentine was prized, its widespread use for statuettes, furniture revetment and ornament, domestic implements and utensils of many kinds, and all sorts of boxes suggests that it was available in ampler quantities at this time than from the 9th century onwards, when it was largely reserved for the production of sacred images.

(ii) 4th–6th centuries. Roman legislation indicates that ivory was worked by craftsmen (Lat. *eborarii*) who also fashioned precious woods. In less regulated areas of the Empire they may also have worked bone. In Egypt and particularly the area around Alexandria, excavation has yielded discarded pieces of both bone and ivory. The latter would have been meant for more affluent clients. The carving of ivory has also been postulated for Gaul, many sites in northern Italy and Asia Minor, and other places where the

80. Ivory reliquary, 240×327×220 mm, *c.* 400 (Brescia, Museo Civico Cristiano)

necessity of importation must have restricted the amount available. There is no physical evidence of the working of dentine in 4th-century Constantinople, but an edict of 337 in the Theodosian Code (XIII.iv.2) included *eborarii* in a list of artisans exempt from civil obligations so that they could improve and disseminate their skills. In the mid-5th century a patriarch of Alexandria sent eight stools and fourteen ivory chairs to Emperor Theodosios II (*reg* 408–50) in Constantinople.

The import of tusks as tribute, depicted on the Barberini Ivory (first half of the 6th century; Paris, Louvre) and attested as late as 573 in historical sources, may have added to the stock of materials available in the various imperial capitals, as would the dentine that survived the slaying of elephants in the circus and in warfare. Most of the supplies, however, would have travelled along established trade routes—above all from Alexandria to Italian ports—and was evidently sufficient to allow widespread fabrication.

Among the earliest objects from this period are a reliquary (*c.* 400; Brescia, Mus. Civ. Crist.; see fig. 80) and the diptych of Probus (Aosta, Tesoro Cattedrale), which depicts Emperor Honorius (*reg* 395–423). The high quality of these artefacts, normally assigned to the end of the 4th century and the beginning of the 5th and often said to be of Milanese origin, is inconceivable without the prior existence of skilled workers: discrimination between Roman and Late Antique or Early Christian production is more a convenience of classification than an expression of palpable differences in the ways of working ivory or the uses to which it was put. Scarcely less arbitrary is the distinction between pagan and Christian work. As in the case of marble sarcophagi (*see* SARCOPHAGUS, §III, 1), there is no reason to suppose that craftsmen accepted commissions along confessional lines, nor that a patron selected his or her workshop on the grounds of belief. The Nicomachorum–Symmachorum Diptych (*c.* 400; Paris, Mus. Cluny and London, V&A), which was perhaps issued to celebrate a marriage between two aristocratic

81. Ivory consular diptych of *Areobindus*, 362×114 mm (left leaf), 362×131 mm (right leaf), 506 (Zurich, Schweizerisches Landesmuseum)

Roman families, is carved in techniques and has ornamental frames identical to those on a plaque depicting the *Three Marys at the Tomb* (Milan, Castello Sforzesco). In another diptych (Florence, Bargello) scenes from the *Life of St Paul* are combined with an ostensibly pagan *Orpheus Charming the Animals with his Music*.

Combs and boxes also suggest that iconographical distinctions along creedal lines are functions not of the way or place in which such objects were produced but of the uses to which they were put. Combs with Christian subjects, such as one with lambs and a wreath (Rome, Vatican, Mus. Sacro), are traditionally described as liturgical objects, while box lids with such scenes as the *Healing of the Blind* (e.g. Rome, Vatican, Mus. Sacro) are sometimes said to have been made to contain the elements of the Eucharist. But the mode of manufacture of these lids, and the fashioning of the troughs that they cover, match those of box lids depicting ancient philosophers, physicians and personifications of cities, and such allegorical figures as Health. This would suggest that the theoretical strictures of the Church Fathers against pagan subject-matter were not specifically directed against the interests of Christian patrons or the products they bought. As in stone-carving

and wall painting, antique iconography was probably co-opted for Christian purposes, even if the equation between ostensible content and matters of function and manufacture is no longer the valid proposition that it was once held to be (*see* §I, 2 above).

Rather than observe a simple distinction between creeds, it seems preferable to suppose that, as on silver and other portable objects, much subject-matter that was not overtly Christian was considered neutral and inoffensive. By the 5th century many persons in a position to buy ivory artefacts were already Christian, yet objects continued to be decorated with hunting scenes, Bacchic revels and other survivals from Late Antiquity. This is particularly true in the case of pyxides, containers manufactured in ivory by being hollowed and cut from sections of a tusk along its vertical axis. Scores of these circular and oval boxes survive; save for their imagery, 'pagan' examples are scarcely distinguishable from many Christian ones (e.g. Cleveland, OH, Mus. A.; Moscow, Pushkin Mus. F.A.). Their quality of carving varies enormously and could reflect the diversity of either their place of fabrication or the markets they served. What is indisputable is the widespread and enduring popularity of such objects, some of which may have contained unguents or wafers for liturgical use.

The chronological and geographical range across which pyxides were made greatly exceeds that of the best-known ivories of this period, the paired slabs (each up to 410×150 mm) known as consular diptychs. Many of these bear not only a portrait of the official in question but also his name and *cursus honorum* (list of offices). The named series starts with Flavius Felix, consul of the West in 428 (one surviving leaf, Paris, Bib. N., Cab. Médailles) and continues until 540 or 541 depending on what identity and thus what date is ascribed to the diptych of a 'Basilius' (Florence, Bargello; Milan, Castello Sforzesco). Some 40 examples are preserved, although a few lack names and therefore exact dates. The fact that all 5th-century examples represent Western consuls and are presumably of Roman manufacture, while, with one exception, all 6th-century examples depict Eastern office-holders and probably originated in Constantinople, may be no more than an accident of survival. Almost all such diptychs lack any positive identification as Christian objects, even though most of the men who issued them must have been members of this faith. Indeed, from the ivories of *Areobindus* (consul of the East in 506; Paris, Louvre; see fig. 81) onwards, they depict the official in the robes of his status, flanked by personifications of Rome and Constantinople and enthroned above scenes depicted in stereotypical, miniature form either of the largesse that the consul scattered on the day of his accession (1 January) or of the games that he offered to the people on this occasion. Some specimens exhibit only the consul's portrait and monogram such as that of *Areobindus*, or else an inscribed dedication, such as that to the Senate on the diptychs of *Justinian* (521; New York, Met.). This diversity of content and degree of elaboration may reflect the varying dignities of those who received these grandiose mementos. The diptychs of *Areobindus* range from one complete with circus scenes (fig. 81) to a much simpler form adorned only with a pair of crossed cornucopias (Lucca, Mus. Opera Duomo).

Consular diptychs were issued in large quantities and bear the marks of production in long series; minor iconographical and epigraphical variants suggest their creation by teams of craftsmen following one or two models. Their visible content is conventional where it is not entirely simple, as befits the production of multiples. They thus differ radically in kind from unique works such as the Brescia Reliquary or the bishop's throne of MAXIMIAN (Ravenna, Mus. Arcivescovile), which necessarily involved designers intent on conveying complex Christian messages. Nonetheless, the ideological programme of the consular diptychs is readily apparent: as an official of the State, the consul appears pompously ensconced beneath portraits of his sovereigns, accompanied by images of the harmonious parts of the empire, and represents the aristocratic, if temporary, exponent of the benefits that the Roman people could expect from his tenure of office. It is scarcely surprising that these objects were imitated by others, as in the diptychs of *Probianus*, 'Vicar of Rome' (*c.* 400; Berlin, Staatsbib. Preuss. Kultbes.) and of several military leaders, such as *Stilicho* (*c.* 400; Monza, Mus. Serpero Tesoro). Although similar ivories, such as the Barberini Ivory, have been labelled 'imperial' diptychs, their origin, nature and purpose is less clear. Originally each leaf consisted of five parts depicting emperors or empresses (unidentified by name), officers and barbarians rendering homage, with personifications of cities between winged genii, or Christ between angels surveying the entire scene. Whether these were presented to or by imperial persons is unsure, as is the belief that they were always diptychs. It is likely, for example, that the Barberini Ivory never possessed a counterpart leaf.

Other diptychs, such as the Nicomachorum–Symmachorum Diptych, depict figures from Greco-Roman rituals or mythology, muses, or military or literary figures. The reverse of each displays the large recess characteristic of Roman writing tablets. Yet it is doubtful that such unwieldy objects functioned in the way that is often supposed of them. Inscriptions written directly on their backs, without an intervening layer of wax, testify to their medieval uses as vehicles for commemorative inscriptions in ecclesiastical settings. Likewise intended for use in church are a number of five-part diptychs with images of *Christ* and the *Virgin Enthroned*, surmounted by a wreathed cross and, below, scenes from the canonical or apocryphal Gospels (e.g. Milan, Tesoro Duomo). Their function, too, may have been to commemorate the deceased, although several were later used as covers for sacred books.

The end of the consular series in the mid-6th century, after which only emperors held the consulship, may only roughly coincide with the evident diminution in the number and quality of carved ivories. The dating of pieces between the late 6th century and the 8th, however, is so lacking in independent evidence that any statement beyond a generalized observation of this decline would be risky. Some ivories have been attributed to Gaul, Syria-Palestine and Coptic Egypt, but Rome and Constantinople most probably ceased to be major centres of production. Arab command of the Mediterranean and piracy are often cited as elements contributing to the reduced access to exotic commodities (silk, gems, spices etc), but internal conditions, notably the marked reduction in the population of large cities and a disappearing money economy, are probably more important as causal factors.

Although the iconoclastic controversy (726–843) must have seriously diminished if not stopped surviving ivory production in Constantinople and its neighbouring provinces, it had no impact on Rome or the Christian communities in Islamic territory. There are no further references to ivories in any Greek document until *c.* 800, when Theodore of Stoudios set down his rules for St John Stoudios Monastery in Constantinople in which he railed against monks who brought ivory buckles and other luxuries into the monastery. Yet ivory-carving, if it did not die out entirely, could hardly have subsisted as other than a marginal effort. The ivory table said to have been owned by the wealthy peasant, St Philaretos (702–92), is more likely to have been a family heirloom than an instance of contemporary production.

(iii) 9th century–1453. Documentation for the production of luxurious artefacts after the end of the iconoclastic controversy is largely confined to the objects themselves. A so-called 'sceptre tip' (Berlin, Bodemus.) was almost certainly produced under Leo VI (*reg* 886–912). It is inscribed with his Christian name, though of course not his regnal number, and shows him being crowned by the Virgin and attended by Christ, an archangel and SS Peter, Paul, Cosmas and Damian. Company of this sort would thereafter often characterize Byzantine ivories and, when the private devotions of the élite are better understood, might lead to identification of the patrons for whom they were made. A casket (Rome, Pal. Venezia) with solid ivory walls depicting the story of David illustrates a commonplace comparison with the emperor in Byzantine ideology. On its lid are a Byzantine ruler and his spouse crowned by Christ. Although this box has been dated to the reigns of Basil I (867–86) and Leo VI, attempts to assign allegedly related objects to successive stages between the 860s and *c.* 900 are based on nothing more substantial than the notion of a linear development in style. Similar intuitive argument underlies efforts to attribute some Middle Byzantine ivories to the provinces, such as the Caucasus or southern Italy, rather than Constantinople.

The existence of datable 9th-century ivories that are firmly connected with members of the imperial family is not evidence enough to postulate a 'Palace school' of ivory-carvers. What such pieces do, however, suggest is a reservation of ivory for sacred ends. In contrast to the plethora of object types between the 4th century and the 8th, ivory in and after the 9th century seems to have been largely confined to the fabrication of icons, sometimes in the form of diptychs or triptychs, and boxes bearing biblical scenes. Apart from religious artefacts, excavations such as that of St Polyeuktos (524–7; destr.) in Constantinople have recovered minimal vestiges of spools, spindles and furniture fittings (Istanbul, Archaeol. Mus.), traces of a body of secular production that was probably never very large in the Middle Byzantine period. While the number of objects from this period is no less than from the 5th and 6th centuries, the restriction of dentine to holy images indicates a deliberate decision regarding its use and one that would not have been necessary had it been available in the quantities enjoyed earlier. In support of this argument is the sometimes poor quality of ivory used even in finely carved works. The number of such pieces is considerably greater than that of objects carved from defective material in the 4th century to the 6th.

Although no ivories can confidently be dated to the first 40 years of the 10th century, it cannot be supposed that the subsequent period of florescence under Constantine VII (*see* MACEDONIAN DYNASTY, (3)) happened *ex nihilo*. According to the traditional view, by the sixth decade of the century there existed five 'groups' of ivories, implicitly the creation of five different workshops. Yet both the absence of evidence for such workshops as historical entities and the broad varieties of technical means and stylistic effects within these groups suggest that the recognition of minimal clusters, carved by identifiable, if unnamed, masters—aided perhaps by an assistant or family member (the means by which technical knowledge was transmitted)—is a more useful model for the classification of Byzantine ivory-carving. Firmly datable to the year 945 is a plaque depicting *Constantine VII Crowned by Christ* and described as 'autokrator' (see fig. 82). Numerous diptychs (e.g. Venice, Mus. Archeol.; Vienna, Ksthist. Mus.; Dresden, Grünes Gewölbe) and triptychs (e.g. Rome, Pal. Venezia) similarly allude to the divine protection of an emperor Constantine or the remission of his sins. The techniques in which these are carved make it almost certain that they are products of the same reign. Beyond directly 'imperial' ivories of this sort, there exist several diptychs (Halberstadt, Dom & Domschatz; Gotha, Schloss Friedenstein; Washington, DC, Dumbarton Oaks) that may have served as documents of appointment for high court officials. The *Kletorologion* of Philotheos (899) describes the issue at court of such diptychs, though without specifying the material of which they were made. It seems reasonable to suppose that, despite their sometimes lower quality, objects of this sort were made by craftsmen accustomed to working for the court.

One object of critical importance for both the chronology and ideology of ivory artefacts is a plaque depicting the coronation by Christ of an emperor named Romanos and his spouse Eudokia (Paris, Bib. N., Cab. Médailles). The emperor has often been identified with Romanos IV (*reg* 1068–71), but the plaque's obvious analogies with that of Constantine VII in Moscow, Romanos' beardless face and the ivory's overall manner of presentation, make it much more likely that the figures depicted are a youthful Romanos II (*reg* 959–63), Constantine VII's junior emperor from 945, and his bride, the daughter of Hugo of Provence. If this is the case, then the plaque in Paris may take its place not only as one ivory among many made for the imperial court in the 940s but also as the exemplar for a version produced in the West for Otto II (*see* SAXONY, (2)) and his Byzantine wife Theophano in 982 or 983 (Paris, Mus. Cluny).

A less direct relationship with an emperor is suggested by the only known Byzantine example of an ivory staurothèque (cross reliquary; Cortona, S Francesco). On the upper part of one side Christ appears between angels in roundels above large images of the Virgin and St John the Baptist, while the lower part depicts SS Stephen and John

82. Ivory plaque of *Constantine VII Crowned by Christ*, 189×93 mm, 945 (Moscow, Pushkin Museum of Fine Arts)

the Theologian above medallions containing images of Constantine the Great, Helena and Longinus, the spear-bearer at the Crucifixion. Although the image of Constantine, a common archetype for Byzantine emperors, does not necessarily refer to a homonymous emperor, the presence of Helena, who is said to have found the 'True Cross' in the 4th century, is appropriate to an object of this type. Even more apt is St Stephen, whose presence matches that of a Stephen named in an inscription on the object reverse as keeper of the treasury at Hagia Sophia in Constantinople. The inscription continues to the effect that, with the aid of this relic, an emperor Nikephoros was able to put the barbarians to flight. The letter forms of the inscription and the well-attested generalship of Nikephoros II (*reg* 963–9) leave little doubt that the ivory must date from his reign. If the second part of the cross reliquary's inscription attests to the militaristic ideology of the Byzantine empire in the 10th century, its first part, which cites the presentation of the object to the monastery in which Stephen was brought up, exemplifies the motivation that underlay such commissions. The combinations of well-known saints named on many ivories may indicate the intended destinations of these precious objects. Yet no Byzantine plaque can be shown to have been commissioned by a monk; surviving inscriptions indicate that the sponsorship of ivories was probably limited to the ruling classes of both Church and State. The most suggestive aspect of such icons is their naturally limited size. They are objects designed for the contemplation and veneration of individuals, best suited to the tiny private chapels retained by the Middle Byzantine élite in both their monastery churches and private houses.

Since the education and culture of this group embraced both Classical and patristic learning, its members must have included the owners of the 100 or so surviving boxes with wooden cores, revetted on the outside with prefabricated strips of rosette ornament and small scenes from mythology or the circus. Of all 10th- and 11th-century objects these most closely reflect the influence of works from the 4th to the 6th century. On a few splendid examples, such as the Veroli Casket (London, V&A; see fig. 9 above) the plaques were carved by the same artists as made ivory icons. The vast majority, however, are of bone, worked no less cunningly but put together in haste by craftsmen who cared little whether the bone pegs with which they attached the plaques intruded on the subject-matter or how long they would hold. A much-restored example (Baltimore, MD, Walters A.G.) shows both how casual was the assembly of such objects and how easily portions of decoration could be lost (see fig. 83). The form and condition of these boxes point to their origin in workshops. They may thus have been addressed to a clientele beyond the restricted circle that commissioned ivory icons, diptychs and triptychs. The less than reverent attitude towards Classical antiquity that some of these artefacts seem to display further suggests their direction towards a broader urban market.

The Latin conquest of Constantinople in 1204 and the subsequent looting of the capital provided the circumstances for the transmission to the West of numerous precious artefacts, such as the cross reliquary now in Cortona (see above). A number of Byzantine ivories had already reached Italy and Germany two centuries before as objects of commerce, thievery or diplomacy. High-quality carvings of this kind include a plaque showing the *Dormition of the Virgin* (Munich, Bayer. Staatsbib., Clm. 4453) and two diptychs depicting *Christ and the Virgin* and *SS Peter and Paul* (Bamberg, Staatsbib.). Shortly after their arrival these ivories were used as the covers of a Gospel book (*c.* 1000; Munich, Bayer. Staatsbib., Clm. 4453; *see* GOSPELS OF OTTO III) and a prayer book for Henry II, Holy Roman Emperor (Bamberg, Staatsbib., MSS Lit. 8 and 7, respectively). These books therefore provide *termini ante quem* for the date of the ivories. While other instances of such exports cannot be accurately dated, the familiarity of Western artists with Byzantine imagery and techniques may be due to an acquaintance with ivories brought from the Orthodox world. The presence in the West of caskets and boxes with the sort of secular iconography found in such pieces as the Veroli Casket is not documented before the 12th century, when they may

83. Bone-clad casket, 124×180×126 mm (with lid), 10th–11th centuries (Baltimore, MD, Walters Art Gallery)

have served as models for the sculptural decoration on the exteriors of Italian churches.

The use of bone on many Byzantine boxes represents the substitution of cheaper, domestic material for expensive, imported ivory. It does not mean that dentine was no longer available, even if, in and after the second half of the 11th century, the evidence for ivory-working in Constantinople ceases. Steatite, a stone that was more readily available and one that was used for jewellery and amulets in the Classical world, was once supposed to be a similar surrogate.

Yet the smaller areas of umblemished stone that steatite offered craftsmen meant that objects fashioned from it were normally of a different order from the larger surfaces presented by ivory. While a few examples, such as one (12th century; Toledo, Mus. Catedralicio) depicting 12 scenes from the *Life of Christ*, could be as large as 310×230 mm, most steatites are much smaller and were turned into pendants or diminutive icons with individual saints or feasts of the Church (e.g. pendant of *St Nicholas*; Paris, Bib. N. Cab. Médailles). Although steatite was carved from the 10th century, most examples date from the 12th century or later. The material continued to be worked after the fall of Constantinople in 1453, and some specimens often regarded as Byzantine may belong to the post-Byzantine period (e.g. Recklinghausen, Ikonenmus.).

By contrast, after the 10th century the only approximately datable ivory is a circular box (Washington, DC, Dumbarton Oaks) depicting members of the imperial family; it has been assigned to either *c.* 1355 or 1403–4. More significant than its proper date is its minute size (diam. 42 mm), which may reflect the amount of ivory available even to august members of Constantinopolitan society. Long before, however, there are signs that the material had generally fallen into disuse. No single piece can be objectively ascribed to the 12th century, an era when one would expect representations in ivory of members of the Komnenian dynasty as, earlier, ivory had been used to depict Macedonian emperors. The disappearance of inscriptions from ivories may indicate less painstaking production in the 11th century, but it also means the loss of an important method of dating such objects. Iconographical innovations of the Komnenian and Palaiologan periods are all but invisible, and many works assigned to these years may have been made in Venice or elsewhere in Italy for Greek-speaking clienteles. Rather than the internal decline that brought about the hiatus in ivory-carving in the 7th and 8th centuries in Constantinople, its virtual cessation in and after the 12th century is more likely to be explained by the domination of Mediterranean trade routes by Italian merchants and the consequent diversion of dentine to centres of production in western Europe. By 1453, in both the quantity and quality of workmanship, Paris had assumed the role that in the 10th century had been played by the Byzantine capital.

BIBLIOGRAPHY

Codex theodosianus (438); Eng. trans. by C. Pharr as The Theodosian Codes and Novels and the Simondian Constitutions (Princeton, 1952/R 1970)
Philotheos: Kletorologion (899); Fr. trans. by N. Oikonomides as Les Listes de préséance byzantines du IXe au Xe siècle (Paris, 1972)
W. F. Volbach: Elfenbeinarbeiten der Spätantike und des frühen Mittelalters (Mainz, 1916, rev. 3/1976)
R. Delbrueck: Die Consulardiptychen und verwandte Denkmäler (Berlin, 1929)
A. Goldschmidt and K. Weitzmann: Die byzantinischen Elfenbeinskulpturen des X.-XIII. Jahrhunderts, 2 vols (Berlin, 1930–34/R 1979)
K. Weitzmann: 'Ivory Sculpture of the Macedonian Renaissance', Kolloquium über spätantike und frühmittelalterliche Skulptur: Mainz, 1970, ii, pp. 1–12
——: Ivories and Steatites (1972), iii of Catalogue of the Byzantine and Early Medieval Antiquities in the Dumbarton Oaks Collection (Washington, DC, 1962–)
I. Kalavrezou-Maxeiner: 'Eudokia Makrembolitissa and the Romanos Ivory', Dumbarton Oaks Pap., xxxi (1977), pp. 307–25
A. Bank: Prikladnoye iskusstvo Vizantii IX.–XII. vv [The applied art of Byzantium in the 9th to the 11th century] (Moscow, 1978)
I. A. Mishakova: 'Rel'yef koronovaniye Konstantina v GMP i vizantiyskaya reznaya kost' gruppy Imperatora Romana' [The relief of the coronation of Constantine in the Pushkin Mus. F. A., Moscow, and the Byzantine ivory of the Romanos group], Iskusstvo zapadnoj Evropy i Vizantij, ed. V. N. Grashchekov, A. I. Komech and M. Libman (Moscow, 1978), pp. 226–36
A. Guillou: 'Deux Ivoires constantinopolitains datés du IXe et Xe siècle', Byzance et les Slaves: Etudes de civilisation: Mélanges Ivan Dujčev (Paris, n. d. [1979]), pp. 207–11
K. Weitzmann: Byzantine Book Illumination and Ivories (London, 1980)
K. J. Shelton: 'The Diptych of the Young Office Holder', Jb. Ant. & Christ., xxv (1982), pp. 132–71
A. Cutler: 'Prolegomena to the Craft of Ivory Carving in Late Antiquity and the Early Middle Ages', Artistes, artisans et production artistique au moyen âge: Colloque international, CNRS: Rennes, 1983, ii, pp. 431–75
——: 'The Making of the Justinian Diptychs', Byzantion, lv (1984), pp. 75–117
——: 'On Byzantine Boxes', J. Walters A.G., xlii–xliii (1984–5), pp. 32–47
J.-P. Caillet: L'Antiquité classique, le haut moyen âge et Byzance au Musée de Cluny (Paris, 1985)
A. Cutler: The Craft of Ivory: Sources, Techniques and Uses in the Mediterranean World (Washington, DC, 1985)
I. Kalavrezou: Byzantine Icons in Steatite, 2 vols (Vienna, 1985)
R. H. Randall jr: Masterpieces of Ivory from the Walters Art Gallery (New York, 1985)
J.-P. Caillet: L'Origine des derniers ivoires antiques', Rev. A. [Paris] (1986), pp. 7–15
J. Engemann: 'Elfenbeinfunde aus Abu Mena/Ägypten', Jb. Ant. & Christ., xxx (1987), pp. 172–86
A. Cutler and N. Oikonomides: 'An Imperial Byzantine Casket and its Fate at a Humanist's Hand', A. Bull., lxx (1988), pp. 77–87
D. Gaborit-Chopin: Avori medievali (Florence, 1988)
I. Kalavrezou: 'A New Type of Icon: Ivories and Steatites', Constantine VII Porphyrogenitus and his Age, ed. A. Markopoulos (Athens, 1989), pp. 377–96
A. St Clair and E. P. McLachlan, eds: The Carver's Art: Medieval Sculpture in Ivory, Bone and Horn (New Brunswick, NJ, 1989)
A. Arnulf: 'Eine Perle für das Haupt Leons VI', Jb. Berlin. Mus., xxxii (1990), pp. 70–84
I. Nikolajević: Gli avori e le steatiti medievali dei musei civici di Bologna (Bologna, 1991)
A. Cutler: The Hand of the Master: Craftsmanship, Ivory and Society in Byzantium (Princeton, 1994)
M. Gibson: The Liverpool Ivories (Liverpool, 1994)

ANTHONY CUTLER

6. JEWELLERY. Constantinople became one of the centres of jewellery-making in the Mediterranean soon after its foundation (AD 330), attracting craftsmen from all over the empire, who continued the Late Roman practice of imitating Hellenistic models. They adopted from such centres as Alexandria and Antioch the technique of embossing, the use of multicoloured gems, Greek motifs such as foliate scrolls, palmettes, dolphins and geometric designs, and such jewellery types as chains with attached jewels, bracelets in the form of bands and pendant earrings. The capital's access to the Indian trade route led to the introduction of further materials and techniques and to a taste for overloaded decoration with dense filigree patterns and the depiction of wild beasts and fantastic plant forms (examples at London, BM). Contact with the migrating tribes of Huns and Goths in the northern steppes and Balkans yielded new jewellery types such as buckles, jewelled straps and massive rings. Finally, the adoption of Christianity brought with it new iconography, symbols and talismans.

Much prestigious jewellery was lost through the pillaging of conquerors, and in times of war the populace offered their most precious possessions to finance the defence of the State. Yet important examples survive in the hoards of coins and silver stamps that have been found throughout the empire and that provide vital dating evidence.

(i) Materials and techniques. Early Christian and Byzantine jewellery was made from sheets of gold and silver, as well as from less precious metals such as copper. Thin gold wire was used for chains, for filigree decoration on metalwork and with enamel, as in two mid- to late 5th-century medallions (Baltimore, MD, Walters A.G.; Paris, Bib. N., Cab. Médailles) and a small pendant cross of the late 6th century or the early 7th (Washington, DC, Dumbarton Oaks; see fig. 88 below). Numerous examples of Early Christian jewellery were worked in *opus interrasile*, a kind of pierced work or metal fretwork (*see* ROME, ANCIENT, fig. 119), which was used from the 3rd century onwards as a means of enlivening the surface of the gold on various sorts of jewellery, such as the early 4th-century medallions that have finely worked, pierced borders of mixed metals (e.g. London, BM; Paris, Louvre; Washington, DC, Dumbarton Oaks). This technique was also used for earrings, necklaces such as the 6th-century one from Egypt (Berlin, Antikenmus.; see fig. 84) and a pair of bracelets (Athens, Benaki Mus., 1835–6). Other popular techniques included engraving and embossing plate, and granulation, whereby minute grains of gold were affixed

to the metal base, as in the pendant of a 6th-century earring (Pforzheim, Schmuckmus.).

Precious stones and pearls predominated in the 5th and 6th centuries, as is evident in the mosaics of *Justinian* and *Theodora* in S Vitale, Ravenna (*see* MOSAIC, fig. 6), and in the ivory plaques of *Empress Ariadne* (*c.* 500; Florence, Bargello; Vienna, Ksthist. Mus.; see fig. 6 above). The jewellery from the Piazza della Consolazione in Rome (Washington, DC, Dumbarton Oaks) and a bracelet from Egypt (New York, Met., 17.190,1670) are among the most characteristic pieces of this kind. Apart from their use in jewellery, precious stones and hardstones in the form of intaglios or cameos with symbols or figural depictions were used as talismans throughout the duration of the Byzantine empire (*see* GEM-ENGRAVING, §I, 8).

After the settlement of the iconoclastic controversy (843), cloisonné enamelling became increasingly widespread and was largely figural. This type of decoration appears on a wide range of rings, necklaces and bracelets including a particularly fine pair of hinged clasp bracelets (*c.* 900; Thessaloniki, Archaeol. Mus.); each bracelet comprises 20 gold cloisonné enamel plaques bearing a bird or plant motif. Other pieces were decorated with more sophisticated scenes such as the *Resurrection* on a late 10th-century quatrefoil pendant (Tbilisi, Mus. A. Georgia). The earliest surviving crown with cloisonné work is a votive item with seven medallions representing saints and the probable donor, Emperor Leo VI (*reg* 886–912; Venice, Tesoro S Marco; see fig. 89 below).

(ii) Types. Early Christian and Byzantine jewellery can be divided into the functional and the purely decorative. An example of the former is the fibula, a type of clasp which fastened the *chiton* or cloak at the shoulder. Worn by officials, it was bow-shaped, with an arm to which the pin was attached, and delicately decorated, as can be seen in examples from the Ténès Treasure (Algiers, Mus. N. Ant.). Many such fibulae appear in depictions of officials, for example the consular diptych of *Stilicho* (early 5th century; Monza, Mus. Serpero Tesoro) or on a Theodosian plate (388; Madrid, Real. Acad. Hist.). Only emperors had the right to wear circular fibulae with pendant chains of multicoloured precious stones, as in the portrait of *Justinian* in S Vitale at Ravenna. Belts too were used as symbols of authority. Made in segments with inset stones, they were worked on strips of leather or fabric and are depicted on ivories, mosaics and statues such as that of the *Tetrarchs* (late 3rd century–early 4th; Venice, Piazza S Marco; *see* ROME, ANCIENT, fig. 82). Gradually belts became narrower and were fastened with long, thin clasps; some were of the chain type, with hooks for fastening and decorative pendants. Two such belts survive from Mytilene (Athens, Byz. Mus.) and one from Syria (Philadelphia, U. PA, Mus.).

Necklaces were among the most common pieces of purely decorative jewellery. They can be divided into two types: chains with pendant elements (mainly talismans and medallions set with stones or precious metals), and items in which the whole fabric has been worked and decorated. *Opus interrasile*, inlaid stones and enamel were the most common methods of enlivening surfaces. Corresponding luxury can be seen in bracelets, which were mostly bands

84. Gold necklace with aquamarines and pearls, diam. 230 mm, from Egypt, 6th century (Berlin, Antikenmuseum)

made up of separate links or torques: often they had floral or geometric decoration or compositions showing Christian influence, for example a bracelet showing a bust of the *Virgin* in a circular medallion surrounded by birds in scrolls (London, BM, AF 351).

All rings were symbolic in character, and originally were the only pieces of jewellery the faithful were permitted to wear. There are the following categories: wedding rings, rings for the head of the family, presents for various occasions and talismans. They were decorated with inscriptions, inset stones and Christian symbols such as birds, fish, olive branches, crosses and depictions of saints; a swivel ring from Syria showing *St Thekla and an Archangel* (6th–7th century; Athens, Benaki Mus.) is a typical example. Earrings were worn by both women and men and are the most common category of jewellery to survive. Popular types included earrings with pendant strings of coloured gemstones or with suspended gold crescents often worked in *opus interrasile* or filigree and depicting crosses, monograms, confronted birds or foliate decoration (examples in Athens, Benaki Mus.).

Crowns were the most prestigious type of jewellery. Only three are extant, but some are depicted in mosaics (e.g. Ravenna, S Vitale), ivories such as those depicting the *Empress Ariadne* (see fig. 6 above) and silverware such as the dish found at Kerch in Ukraine (St Petersburg, Hermitage) with a representation of Constantius II (*reg* 337–61) wearing a jewelled diadem. Apart from the votive crown of Leo VI (*see* §(i) above), the two other surviving crowns belonged to members of the Hungarian royal family (Budapest, N. Mus.). One is an incomplete diadem of six silver-gilt and enamel panels that may have been the gift of Constantine IX to Anastasia of Russia at the time of her marriage to King Andrew I of Hungary (*reg* 1046–61). The panels contain full-length portraits of *Empress Zoe* and *Theodora* (*reg* 1042), *Constantine IX*, personifications of *Sincerity* and *Humility*, and two dancing girls. Their forms are treated as flat, intricate patterns, a style also apparent on the Holy Crown of Hungary (1074–7). The iconography of this piece refers to Byzantine suzerainty over the Hungarian king, showing on one side a cloisonné enamel bust of *Emperor Michael VII Dukas* (*reg* 1071–8; see fig. 90 below) set above busts of his son *Constantine* and *King Geza I of Hungary* (*reg* 1074–7).

BIBLIOGRAPHY

O. M. Dalton: *Catalogue of Early Christian Antiquities and Objects from the Christian East in the Department of British and Mediaeval Antiquities and Ethnography in the British Museum* (London, 1901)
W. Dennison: *A Gold Treasure of the Late Roman Period from Egypt* (New York, 1918)
B. Segall: *Katalog der Goldschmiedearbeiten, Museum Benaki Athen* (Athens, 1938)
Collection Hélène Stathatos, ii, iii (Strasbourg, 1957, 1963), iv (Athens, 1971)
E. Coche de la Ferté: *L'Antiquité chrétienne au Musée du Louvre* (Paris, 1958)
J. Heurgon: *Le Trésor de Ténès* (Paris, 1958)
S. Amiranašvili: *Les Emaux de Géorgie* (Paris, 1962)
M. C. Ross: *Jewelry, Enamels and Art of the Migration Period* (1965), ii of *Catalogue of the Byzantine and Early Mediaeval Antiquities in the Dumbarton Oaks Collection* (Washington, DC, 1962–)
K. Wessel: *Die byzantinische Emailkunst von 5. bis 13. Jahrhundert* (Recklinghausen, 1967)
M. C. Ross: 'Jewels of Byzantium', *A. VA*, ix/1 (1968)
A. Stylianou and J. Stylianou: *Oi thesauroi tis Lambouses* [The treasures of Lambousa] (Nicosia, 1969)
A. Greifenhagen: *Schmuckarbeiten in Edelmetall, Staatliche Museen, Antikenabteilung*, 2 vols (Berlin, 1970–75)
A. Pierides: *Jewellery in the Cyprus Museum* (Nicosia, 1971)
Age of Spirituality: Late Antique and Early Christian Art, Third to Seventh Century (exh. cat., ed. K. Weitzmann; New York, Met., 1977–8)
D. Buckton: 'The Beauty of Holiness: Opus Interrasile from a Late Antique Workshop', *Jewel. Stud.*, i (1983–4)
K. R. Brown: *The Gold Breast Chain from the Early Byzantine Period in the Römisch-Germanischen Zentralmuseum* (Mainz, 1984)

AIMILIA YEROULANOU

7. METALWORK AND ENAMELLING.

(i) Gold and silver. (ii) Enamels.

(i) Gold and silver. Gold was used for coins (*see* §2 above), jewellery (*see* §6 above), embroidery (*see* §8 below), gilding and objects of imperial use, the last being known almost exclusively from written sources. In contrast to gold, silver objects survive in abundance, particularly from the period between the 4th and the 7th century (*see also* ROME, ANCIENT, §IX, 1(iv)).

(a) 4th–7th centuries. (b) 8th century–1453.

(a) 4th–7th centuries.

Gold. Chemical analysis has established that gold used for coin and jewellery was of high purity in this period. Gilding was carried out on a grand scale, particularly in buildings. Based on a postulated 0.1 µm thickness of gold being used for gilding and gold glass mosaic tesserae, one can calculate a total of 150 and 250 lbs of gold used for the wooden coffered ceilings of the church of the Holy Sepulchre (*see* JERUSALEM, §II, 2(i)) and the Lateran basilica (*see* ROME, §V, 15(ii)), both built by CONSTANTINE THE GREAT, and over 500 lbs for the tessellated vaults of Justinian I's Hagia Sophia (*see* ISTANBUL, §III, 1(ii)(b)).

Historical texts citing gold vessels are sometimes ambiguous and may refer to silver gilt. Genuinely gold objects are among the donations made by popes, emperors and others to Italian churches, which are listed by number and weight in the *Liber pontificalis*; these were distinguished from gilded objects (Lat. *deauratus*). Up to 642, 90% of approximately 2300 lbs of recorded gold objects (e.g.

patens, chalices, censers) and furnishings (e.g. lamps) made for the churches of Rome were presented by Constantine the Great. Theodosios II (*reg* 408–50) and Pulcheria (*reg* 414–53) gave a gold gemmed cross to Jerusalem and a gold gemmed altar to Hagia Sophia. Justin I (*reg* 518–27) sent to Rome gold gemmed book covers weighing 15 lbs. Justinian I (*see* MOSAIC, fig. 6) and Theodora (see fig. 39 above) are portrayed with their entourage offering gold ecclesiastical objects on the walls of S Vitale (consecrated 547; *see* RAVENNA, §2(vii)); they also presented a gold gemmed cross to the church of St Sergios (early 6th century) at Rusafa. Maurice (*reg* 582–602) gave gold objects to his newly built church at Arabissos (now Afşin, Turkey). Recorded examples of secular objects of gold are also imperial. Anastasios I (*reg* 491–518) sent the Sasanid king Kavadh I (*reg* 488–96; 498–531) a gold table service, and Justinian I celebrated his victory over the African Vandals (534) with a gold service illustrating triumphal scenes. Imperial prerogative extended to legislated restrictions placed on the use of gold for jewellery in combination with pearls, sapphires and emeralds. Royal objects of gold inlaid with jewels survive only in regions outside the Byzantine empire and include such examples as the book covers (Monza, Mus. Serpero Tesoro) of the Lombard queen Theudelinda (*d* 625; *see* LOMBARD ART) and the votive crown of the Visigothic king Recceswinth (*reg* 649–72; *see* VISIGOTHIC ART, fig. 1). The cross of JUSTIN II (Rome, Vatican, Mus. Stor. A. Tesoro S Pietro; *see* CROSS, fig. 3) is of parcel-gilt silver. The gold vessels found at Pietroassa (Bucharest, Mus. Ant.) and Vrap, Albania (Istanbul, Archaeol. Mus.; New York, Met.) were probably made outside the empire in imitation of Late Antique models.

Silver. In this period, far fewer silver glass tesserae than gold were used in mosaics, and most silver metal was apparently fashioned into vessels and church furniture revetments. Gifts of silver objects and revetments to Italian churches registered in the *Liber pontificalis* are nearly ten times the weight of those of gold, totalling 35,300 lbs. In 537 Justinian I furnished Hagia Sophia in Constantinople with 40,000 lbs of silver (probably vessels and revetments), while in 622 the Persians took 120,000 lbs of silver, much in the form of church furniture revetments, from the Byzantine city of Edessa in Mesopotamia.

About 1500 silver pieces are known from both the western and eastern empires up to the mid-7th century. This number includes at least 30 treasures each composed of four or more large objects in addition to small utensils (e.g. spoons). About half these treasures are domestic and half are identified as ecclesiastical by their dedicatory inscriptions. The high purity (92–98%) of the silver has been established scientifically by the analysis of at least 300 objects.

Nearly 180 silver objects bear State control marks, which were first applied at Nicomedia (now Izmit, Turkey), Antioch and Naissus (now Niš, Serbia) in the early 4th century to some objects made for imperial distribution on the emperor's accession, anniversaries and other occasions. In the second half of the 4th century and in the 5th new types of single stamps were applied to objects with no overt connections with imperial largesse. By the end of the 5th century a complex system of four and, later, five stamps had been introduced to mark a wide variety of domestic and church plate. These stamps, called 'imperial' and incorporating the bust portrait and monogram of the emperor as well as names of officials, are thought to have been applied almost exclusively at Constantinople, although a few stamps name Antioch and, perhaps, Tarsus (near Adana, Turkey); a contemporary but variant stamping system existed at Carthage. The stamps were applied to fashioned objects before they were completely decorated. It is clear from written texts that these stamped objects were sold rather than distributed as largesse. This system, the purpose of which is not entirely clear, lasted until the mid-7th century.

Imperial plate made for distribution as largesse was decorated with the emperor's image or name. Examples include the dishes honouring Licinius I (*reg* 307–24), found at Niš (Belgrade, N. Mus.; Boston, MA, Mus. F.A.; London, BM; Vienna, Ksthist. Mus.), Eni-Eri, Esztergom (Budapest, N. Mus.) and Cervenbreg (Sofia, N. Archaeol. Mus.); the dishes (*c.* 321–2) in the Munich Treasure (Munich, Bayer. Hypo-Bank) for Licinius I, his infant son Licinius, Crispus and Constantine II; the dish for Constantios II (*reg* 337–61; St Petersburg, Hermitage) from Kerch, Ukraine; the plate for Valentinian II (*reg* 375–92; Geneva, Mus. A. & Hist.) found at Arve near Geneva; the large dish of 50 Roman lbs (388; Madrid, Real Acad. Hist.) celebrating the tenth anniversary of Theodosios I's rule and another similar one found at Grossbungen (Halle, Landesmus. Vorgesch.). The distribution of silver by Justin II when he assumed the consulship in 566 is described by Corripus (*d* 567).

Secular and domestic silver objects that continued the Greek and Roman metalware traditions were in production until the mid-7th century. Large treasures of such plate have been found throughout the empire: the 4th-century Esquiline Treasure (London, BM) from Rome; the 4th-century Kaiseraugst Treasure (Augst, Römermus.; *see* AUGST); the 4th- or 5th-century treasure from Carthage (London, BM; Paris, Louvre); the 4th-century Mildenhall Treasure (London, BM; *see* ROME, ANCIENT, fig. 108 and METAL, colour pl. I, fig. 2); the 4th- or 5th-century treasure from near Latakiya, Syria (Cleveland, OH, Mus. A.); the Mytilene Treasure (602–30; Athens, Byz. Mus.); the Lampsacus Treasure (527–630; Istanbul, Archaeol. Mus.; London, BM); the Cyprus Treasure (578–651; Nicosia, Cyprus Mus.; London, BM; New York, Met.; *see* CYPRUS, §III, 4); a set of 6th-century plates from Bubastis, Egypt (Athens, Benaki Mus.); and the Sevso Treasure (4th–5th century), the provenance of which is unknown. Groups of silver objects found outside the empire include those at Traprain Law, Scotland (Edinburgh, N. Mus. Ant.); SUTTON HOO in Anglo-Saxon England; Conçesti, Moldova (St Petersburg, Hermitage); Malaya Pereshchepina (St Petersburg, Hermitage) and Martynovka (Kiev, Archaeol. Mus.; London, BM) in Ukraine; the Kama River valley (e.g. St Petersburg, Hermitage) in northern Russia; and Ballana and Qustul, Nubia (Cairo, Egyp. Mus.).

The contents of the Esquiline, Sevso and Lampsacus treasures are the most varied in function. They comprise objects for dining, eating and washing, lamps, horse

85. Silver dish with relief decoration of *David and Goliath*, diam. 496 mm, from the Cyprus Treasure, *c.* 630 (New York, Metropolitan Museum of Art)

trappings, furniture attachments and revetments, as well as display objects, comparable to the elaborately decorated plates from the Cyprus Treasure with scenes from the *Life of David* including *David and Goliath* (see fig. 85). In general, few silver drinking cups survive from this period, compared with those of earlier periods and with the number of silver Christian liturgical chalices. The size and weights of many types of objects, particularly plates and spoons, increase after the 3rd century. The variety of shapes, decorative styles, subject-matter (mythological and genre scenes and geometric motifs) and metalworking techniques (hammering, casting, repoussé, chasing, gouging, openwork, gilding and niello inlay) are most diverse in the Esquiline, Sevso and Kaiseraugst treasures. Traditionally fashioned vessels with mythological figures such as Aphrodite, Dionysos and Achilles in repoussé or in carved relief exist side by side with newer styles of faceted surfaces and niello-inlaid portraits of the owners and contemporary genre scenes of hunting, the circus and the bath. Some objects were decoratively inscribed on their obverse surfaces with the names or monograms of their owners.

From the 4th century onwards, churches became the repositories of great wealth, much in the form of silverware and revetment, in theory inalienable property but which in crises (e.g. siege, famine) could be used to save the community. In addition to the above-mentioned donations of plate registered in the *Liber pontificalis* and similar documents, about a dozen ecclesiastical treasures have been found, including those from Galgagno, Italy (Siena, Pin. N.), Water Newton, England (London, BM), Luxor (Cairo, Coptic Mus.), several villages in Syria (Baltimore, MD, Walters A.G.; Berne, Kstmus.; Cleveland, OH, Mus. A.; Istanbul, Archaeol. Mus.; London, BM; New York,

86. Silver circular polykandelon with openwork decoration, from the Sion Treasure, diam. 558 mm, c. 565 (Washington, DC, Dumbarton Oaks Research Library and Collections)

Met.; Paris, Louvre; Washington, DC, Dumbarton Oaks) and the Sion Treasure from Kumluca, Turkey (Antalya, Archaeol. Mus.; Washington, DC, Dumbarton Oaks).

All these treasures contain objects with decorative inscriptions explicitly donating them to named churches, many of which stood in villages rather than cities. The Sion Treasure and the reconstructed Kaper Koraon Treasure (mostly Baltimore, MD, Walters A.G.) from Syria each contain over 50 silver objects. The humble destination of many such relatively rich offerings complements the information about imperial, papal and other donations to urban churches in the *Liber pontificalis* and other texts and provides an important index of prosperity in the empire.

Silver belonging to churches took the form both of liturgical and non-liturgical objects and of furniture revetments for altars, ciboria, chancel screens, ambos, synthronons and doors. In the donor lists of the Lateran basilica and St Peter's in Rome, the revetments outweigh the objects by two to one. In these and other Italian churches, altars weighed between 200 and 350 lbs, a ciborium 2000 lbs and shrines came in three ranges: 20–30 lbs, 100 lbs and 300–1000 lbs. The silver furniture revetments of Hagia Sophia are described in a verse EKPHRASIS by Paulos Silentiarios in early 563 (see Mundell Mango, pp. 80–91). The Sion Treasure preserves silver furniture in the form of colonnettes, capital and sheathings for an altar or tomb.

The second weightiest type of silver displayed in churches were the lighting fixtures of standing and suspended lamps or polykandela (pierced discs holding glass lamps). Constantine I gave the Lateran basilica 100 silver lighting fixtures weighing a total of 4000 lbs. Some of the polykandela that hung from long chains within Hagia Sophia as described by Paulos Silentiarios may have resembled the elaborate openwork circular, cruciform and oblong types preserved in the Sion Treasure. The decoration of one of the treasure's circular polykandela (see fig. 86) incorporates dolphins, crosses and the donor's monogram, as well as a niello inlaid dedicatory inscription naming the bishop Eutychianos. The treasure also contains sets of silver openwork and repoussé standing and hanging cup-shaped lamps. The Kaper Koraon Treasure has a pair of inscribed silver columnar pricket lampstands (Baltimore, MD, Walters A.G.) with acanthus leaf capitals.

Other silver objects include liturgical vessels (e.g. patens, chalices and other wine vessels, spoons, strainers, washing sets) as well as fans, censers, crosses and book covers. The paten is a plate with a flat base (sometimes with a foot-ring) and high flairing sides, usually with a large incised cross in its centre surrounded by a dedicatory inscription, but sometimes decorated with a eucharistic scene in relief. The patens in the Sion Treasure are exceptionally large, measuring up to 77 mm across; the heaviest paten listed in inventories weighs 50 Roman lbs. The chalice has a large bowl, either broad or tall, resting on a trumpet-shaped foot with a large knop. A dedicatory inscription usually encircles the top rim of the bowl, the sides of which may be plain or decorated with raised figures. Spoons belonging to church treasures have their bowls decorated with an incised vertical cross. Other vessels used in the eucharistic service included large wine containers, oil flasks, and ewers and basins for hand-washing. The only extant pair of liturgical fans used to keep insects off the sacrament date to 577 (Istanbul, Archaeol. Mus.; Washington, DC, Dumbarton Oaks) and are decorated with images of cherubim and seraphim. Suspended silver censers are without lids and have round or polygonal bodies, often decorated with raised figures, and a foot-ring. Silver processional crosses have a long lower arm terminating in a tang for insertion in a staff; one or both sides of the cross are usually inscribed. Silver book covers are composed of plaques ornamented with raised figures or symbols, as are oblong or cubic silver reliquaries.

(b) 8th century–1453. Although gold and silver continued to be used for similar purposes as in earlier centuries, silver coinage and jewellery are more common in this period.

Gold. Coinage remained of a high purity until the mid-14th century, except between the 1030s and 1092. Gold glass tesserae continued to be used in mosaic decorations, and gold objects and furnishings of imperial use continue to be cited in written sources after the 7th century. The Great Palace (*see* ISTANBUL, §III, 12) was said to contain gold furnishings, such as the great table of the Chrysotriklinos (after 565; the octagonal domed throne room), a throne and other seats. It is not always clear, however, if gold or gilding is intended. A gilded tree on which perched mechanical singing birds is recorded in the palace (see Mundell Mango, pp. 208–10), as is the use of heavy gold plates and washing sets.

Imperial donations of gold or golden objects to churches continued. In the late 8th century, Empress Eirene donated a gold votive crown to the church of the Virgin Pege outside Constantinople. Similar gifts of gold to St Sophia included the vessels of Michael I (*reg* 811–13); the paten, chalice and polykandelon of Michael III (*reg* 842–67); the patens and chalices of Constantine VII, Romanos I (*reg* 919–44) and Constantine IX. On his pilgrimage to Constantinople *c.* 1200 Anthony of Novgorod recorded seeing at least 30 votive crowns of gold suspended over the altar of Hagia Sophia. The church's inventory of 1396 enumerates patens made of jasper and gold. Emperors also sent diplomatic gifts of gold to foreign rulers. Michael III sent to two popes—Benedict III (*reg* 855–8) and Nicholas I (*reg* 858–67)—a book cover, chalices, a paten and a plate. In 946 Constantine VII gave Arab ambassadors from Tarsus plates of gold inlaid with precious stones and presented another to the Russian queen Olga in 957. Alexios I (*reg* 1081–1118) sent Henry IV, Holy Roman Emperor, a gold altar retable, and Manuel I (*reg* 1143–80) presented a gold plate to a Saljuq sultan.

The numerous medieval de luxe objects carried off from Constantinople by the crusaders, particularly to Venice, in 1204 are mostly of gilded silver rather than gold. Whereas before the 7th century gilding had been used on silver to produce a two-colour decoration, after *c.* 700 all-over gilding was used to disguise the silver as gold, perhaps to harmonize with the gold plaques of cloisonné enamel that were frequently mounted on to objects (*see* §(ii) below).

Silver. The metallic purity of silver in this period has not been analysed to any extent. Although silver was coined from 615 onwards, it was alloyed with gold or copper from the 11th century to the 13th, after which high-quality silver coin was revived. Silver jewellery appears, most frequently as reliquary crosses, bracelets and rings. As in the earlier period, historical texts attest to the continued use of silver plate. The inventory of 1200 from the monastery of St John the Theologian on Patmos lists church silver (see Mundell Mango, pp. 238–9), whereas the will of Eustathios Boilas (1059) refers to domestic silver. Other texts refer to various silver objects belonging to imperial and noble families. No treasures of silver plate have been found from this period; most extant silver has been preserved in western, Balkan or Caucasian church or monastic treasuries. The largest collection is in the treasury of San Marco (*see* VENICE, §IV, 1(iv)).

Silver from this period is distinguished by the high number of imperial and aristocratic objects, many identified as such by inscriptions. These include chalices, patens, reliquaries, plaques and book covers, as well as some secular vessels. Many were removed from Constantinople by the crusaders in 1204 and deposited in various European centres (e.g. Halberstadt Cathedral, Treasury; Maastricht, Schatkamer St-Servaasbasiliek; Venice, Tesoro S Marco); those taken to Paris were destroyed in the French Revolution.

Many of the most prestigious vessels are composite, that is made of various materials. Silver was gilded to imitate gold and formed into a support for the main part of the object (perhaps of carved hardstones or glass), and

it could also be encrusted with cloisonné enamel plaques (with figures, motifs, dedicatory or liturgical inscriptions), strings of pearls, gemstones and coloured glass. Silver, often with parcel gilding, was also still decorated in a more traditional manner with figures or crosses in repoussé, particularly for the plaques of reliquaries, book covers, icons and icon frames.

Few silver objects for secular, private use have been identified with any certainty. An outstanding example (Padua, Cathedral Treasury) is a small cylindrical inkpot decorated on its body in traditional repoussé with mythological figures such as Apollo, and on its lid with a Medusa head; a large inscription with decorative lettering of the 9th–11th century reads: 'This is the inkpot of Leo the calligrapher'. The classical style and technique of the receptacle recall the silver objects still stamped in the mid-7th century. Of a more medieval and orientalizing decorative style is a series of bowls (St Petersburg, Hermitage; Kiev, Hist. Mus.), also with repoussé figures of wild and fantastic beasts, the hunt and courtly scenes with musicians. Found in Russia, their origin remains uncertain, but two have Greek inscriptions. The script of one ('Lord help your servant Theodore Tourkeles') resembles that on the inkpot, while its text relates to those on at least two elaborate objects in the treasury at S Marco. The form of these texts, which invoke a holy person to help the lay donor, indicates secular rather than ecclesiastical use. On the first S Marco object, an alabaster plate (10th–11th century) set in a silver gilt mount encrusted with gemstones and pearls, the text refers to 'emperors', and on the second, a hanging glass lamp set in another silver gilt mount (11th century), the legend mentions a 'Zacharias, archbishop of Iberia' (i.e. Georgia); both objects were, therefore, in use in milieux more elevated than those of the inkpot and repoussé bowls.

Examples of church silver include chalices, patens, processional crosses, reliquaries, book and icon covers. Most of the 27 chalices (10th–11th century) in the treasury at S Marco are elaborate composite objects in which silver serves as a setting for more costly materials. Some have inscriptions that mention donors, particularly emperors, or that give liturgical texts. Related to these chalices are alabaster patens banded by silver-gilt and set in the centre with cloisonné enamel medallions (10th–11th century; Venice, Tesoro S Marco; Adolphe Stoclet priv. col.; see Salles and Lion-Goldschmidt, fig. 18a). More reminiscent of silver techniques before the 7th century is a silver paten (Halberstadt Cathedral, Treasury) which is decorated in repoussé with a *Crucifixion* in the centre and busts of saints surrounded by scrolls on its raised border.

Three silver gilt objects of architectural form may have served as reliquaries, censers or lamps. The earliest such reliquary (969–70; Aachen, Domschatzkam.) was made for a Byzantine governor in Syria and was probably modelled on the Holy Sepulchre at Jerusalem. The second (1059–67; Moscow, Kremlin), made for an imperial secretary at Constantinople, is a reproduction of the shrine of St Demetrios at Thessaloniki. The third, of uncertain date and origin (?12th century; see fig. 8 above), has pierced domes, and, in repoussé, fantastic beasts on its walls and personifications of Andreia (Courage) and Phronesis (Intelligence) on its doors.

The most attractive of the several surviving processional crosses is in solid silver (11th century; Mestiya, Mus. Hist. & Ethnog.) with medallions of cloisonné enamel figures on the obverse and medallions inlaid with niello on the reverse; its Greek dedicatory inscription identifies it as monastic in destination. A series of contemporary crosses from Turkey (Cleveland, OH, Mus. A.; Geneva, Mus. A. & Hist.; Paris, Mus. Cluny; Washington, DC, Dumbarton Oaks) is composed of iron cores revetted in silver. Each cross is decorated on one side with figural discs and areas of dense scrollwork, while the other has full-length figures and vignettes executed in niello and gilded; their Greek inscriptions again refer to monasteries. The dedications of other silver crosses refer to named laymen (Athens, Benaki Mus.; Geneva, Mus. A. & Hist.; Genoa, Mus. Tesoro S Lorenzo).

Another large group of silver objects consists of the flat plaques either decorated with figures and motifs in repoussé or encrusted with enamels and gemstones, and used for reliquaries, book covers, icons and icon frames and covers. Silver reliquaries may be divided into two main groups, those of the True Cross and those of popular saints, in particular St Demetrios. The first type is composed of boxes containing recessed panels or triptychs. The best crafted example is the Limburg Reliquary (964–5; see fig. 87) commissioned by Basil the Proedros (President of the Senate, 963–89). The case has a recess for a separate cruciform container (948–59) of a relic of the True Cross that is surrounded by small, secondary recesses for further relics. Each recess is covered with an enamel *Senkschmelz* bust of a member of the celestial hierarchy. Another silver gilt box reliquary (10th century; Venice, Tesoro S Marco) is decorated on the lid with an enamel plaque of the *Crucifixion* surrounded by medallions and gemstones. The bottom of the reliquary is covered by a sheet of silver decorated in repoussé with a large cross, busts of saints and scrolls. Other True Cross reliquaries, such as that from Jaucourt (Paris, Louvre), are decorated with relief figures of SS Constantine and Helena flanking the relic. Among the several reliquaries of St Demetrios of Thessaloniki is one with a full-length portrait of the saint in relief on the lid (11th century; Halberstadt Cathedral, Treasury).

Book covers are composed of decorated plaques often resembling those of the Limburg Reliquary. A 10th-century book cover (Venice, Bib. N. Marciana) has plaques of silver gilt decorated with enamel medallions, mounted gems and pearls framing a central gold cloisonné enamel plaque of the *Crucifixion* on the front, and the *Virgin* enclosed in a cross on the back. The silver cover of a Lectionary presented by Emperor Nikephoros II Phokas (*reg* 963–9) to the Great Lavra Monastery, Mt Athos, shows *Christ* in relief.

The two icons of *St Michael* (Venice, Tesoro S Marco (*see* ICON, colour pl. I)), one a half-length portrait (late 10th century–11th), the other full-length (late 11th century–12th), use the same materials of silver gilt, gold cloisonné enamel, precious stones and coloured glass to different effect. On the earlier of the two angels the flesh is gilded, and his courtly costume is a geometric pattern of roundels and strips of mounted gems, glass and beading; only the sleeves, the wings and halo rim are of cloisonné enamel. The head, halo and military costume as well as the background of the later angel are entirely covered with cloisonné enamel, and the wings, lower arms and legs are gilded. The reverse of the earlier icon is composed of repoussé silver, and silver-gilt sheets and bands displaying a central cross decorated with, and surrounded by, scrollwork and busts in medallions.

Silver frames and revetments were often added to icons painted on wooden panels. Revetments (*c.* 1300; Skopje, Archaeol. Mus. Macedonia) that adorn a pair of icons of the *Annunciation* (h. over 1 m) have stamped patterns of *rinceaux* and roundels with saints and prophets on the borders. Other silver revetments and frames are encrusted with bosses and filigree and contain panels with narrative scenes relating to the subject of the icon. Tales from the history of the MANDYLION OF EDESSA occur on the 14th-century silver repoussé frame surrounding the painted icon of the *Holy Face* in S Bartolomeo degli Armeni, Genoa. Another silver repoussé frame, on a painted icon of the *Virgin and Child* (Moscow, Tret'yakov Gal.), includes portraits of the donors, a Grand Logothete (*d* 1282) and his wife.   Silverware produced in medieval Georgia (*see* GEORGIA, §V, 1(i)) often approximates contemporary Byzantine work and includes repoussé icons, their frames and revetments; one example is a plaque (*c.* 1015; Tbilisi, Mus. A. Georg.) portraying the Syrian saint Symeon the Stylite on his column.

87. Limburg Reliquary, silver gilt, gold, cloisonné enamel and gems, 480×350 mm, 964–5 (Limburg, Domschatzkammer)

BIBLIOGRAPHY

Corippus, Flavius Cresconius: *In laude Iustini Augusti Minoris* (*c.* 566); ed. and Eng. trans. by A. Cameron as *In Praise of Justin II* (London, 1976)

Anthony of Novgorod: *Kniga palomnik* [Pilgrim's book] (*c.* 1200); ed. K. Loparev, *Pravoslavnyy Palest. Sborn.*, li (1899)

L. Duchesne, ed.: *Le Liber pontificalis*, 2 vols (Paris, 1886–92/*R* 1955–7); vol. 3, ed. C. Vogel (1957)

J. Ebersolt: *Les Arts somptuaires de Byzance: Etude sur l'art impérial de Constantinople* (Paris, 1923)

G. A. Salles and D. Lion-Goldschmidt: *Adolphe Stoclet Collection* (Brussels, 1956)

S. Vryonis: 'The Will of a Provincial Magnate, Eustathius Boilas', *Dumbarton Oaks Pap.*, xi (1957), pp. 263–77

C. Dodd: *Byzantine Silver Stamps* (Washington, DC, 1961)

C. Mango: *The Art of the Byzantine Empire, 312–1453: Sources and Documents* (Englewood Cliffs, NJ, 1972/*R* Toronto, Buffalo and London, 1986)

A. Grabar: *Les Revêtements en or et en argent des icônes byzantines du moyen âge* (Venice, 1975)

B. P. Darkevich: *Svetskoye iskusstvo bizantiy* [Byzantine secular art] (Moscow, 1977)

J. P. C. Kent and K. S. Painter, eds: *Wealth of the Roman World, AD 300–700* (London, 1977)

W. Seibt and T. Sanikidze: *Schatzkammer Georgiens: Mittelalterliche Kunst aus dem staatlichen Kunstmuseum Tbilisi* (Vienna, 1981)

M. Mundell Mango: *Silver from Early Byzantium: The Kaper Koraon and Related Treasures* (Baltimore, MD, 1986)

C. Mango: 'La Croix dite de Michel le Cérulaire et la Croix Saint-Michel de Sykeon', *Cah. Archéol.*, xxxvi (1988), pp. 41–9

S. Boyd and M. Mundell Mango, eds: *Ecclesiastical Silver Plate in Sixth-century Byzantium* (Washington, DC, 1993)

MARLIA MUNDELL MANGO

(ii) Enamels. The history of Byzantine enamel can best be understood by recognizing the stages in its development. In the Early Byzantine period, before the onset of the iconoclastic controversy (726–843), Byzantine enamellers worked in the ancient tradition of Hellenistic filigree enamel. Then, in the hundred or so years after 843, they produced cloisonné enamel in the Western style (*see* ENAMEL, §2(i)), with busts, figures and other motifs in enamelled backgrounds, usually of translucent green. Later, from the middle of the 10th century or soon after, the cloisonné enamel subject, instead of having an enamelled background, was set into and silhouetted against the metal of the plaque; this development produced the 'typical' Byzantine enamel. In the 12th and 13th centuries enamelled backgrounds were again the vogue, but this time the enamel was opaque; the 'typical' Byzantine enamel was not supplanted by this new style but co-existed with it. An increasing use of copper, in place of the gold of earlier centuries, led to the adoption and imitation of Western champlevé techniques in the Late Byzantine period (*see* ENAMEL, §2(ii)).

(a) 5th century–mid-9th. (b) Mid-9th century–early 10th. (c) Mid-10th century–11th. (d) 12th century–1453.

(a) 5th century–mid-9th. The gold cloisonné enamel for which Byzantine craftsmen became famous was, at its peak, unrivalled in the medieval world, but the evidence suggests that this particular technique was not practised in Byzantium until the 9th century, when it was introduced from the West: examples of genuine cloisonné enamel formerly regarded as Early Byzantine belong, in reality, to the 9th, 10th and 11th centuries. It has been claimed that the Byzantines inherited their enamel from ancient Greece, but cloisonné enamel had disappeared from the Greek

88. Filigree enamel on a pendent cross, gold and enamel, h. 40 mm, late 6th century or early 7th (Washington, DC, Dumbarton Oaks Research Library and Collections)

world in the 12th century BC. Hellenistic enamel was either *en ronde bosse* (*see* ENAMEL, §2(iv)) or filigree enamel, and it was the latter tradition that was initially taken up by Byzantine goldsmiths.

The central repoussé bust on a medallion (Paris, Bib. N., Cab. Médailles; Rosenberg, fig. 26), surrounded by two concentric enamelled wreaths, has been shown on the evidence of a coin portrait (Cohen, no. 2) to be that of *Empress Licinia Eudoxia* (*reg* 439–*c.* 462). The medallion is in the Hellenistic filigree enamel tradition, with thinly applied glass reaching less than half the height of the gold wire containing it. A comparable medallion (Baltimore, MD, Walters A.G.) is thought to be modern, however (Weisser and Herbert).

A development of the filigree technique can be found on a small pendent cross (Washington, DC, Dumbarton Oaks; see fig. 88) from a late 6th- or early 7th-century hoard, and on a medallion (Mainz, Röm.–Ger. Zentmus.; see Brown), which is part of a necklace datable to *c.* 600. Here the enamel is thicker and reaches almost to the top of the gold strip, but the way in which the strip encloses the enamel and creates isolated shapes proud of the surfaces of the objects is typical of the filigree tradition. The motifs, mostly birds, also make use of round-section wire, which has no place in the cloisonné technique. Crosses similar to the Washington example (Turin, Gal. Sabauda; Florence, Bargello) and a pendant (London, BM) belong to the same group. Where there are inscriptions, these are executed in round-section filigree wire and are not enamelled.

(b) Mid-9th century–early 10th. The course of the development of Byzantine enamel was completely altered by the iconoclastic controversy (726–843), during which images were banned. Post-iconoclast Byzantine enamel was largely figural and almost exclusively cloisonné. The earliest is probably that on the Fieschi-Morgan Reliquary (New York, Met.; Rosenberg, figs 53–7), which has gold cloisonné enamel representations of a *Crucifixion* and 27

89. Gold cloisonné enamel on a votive crown of Leo VI (*reg* 886–912), silver gilt, gems and pearls, diam. 130 mm (Venice, Tesoro di San Marco)

saints on its lid and sides. Engraved and nielloed scenes on the underside of the lid are identical in iconography, style and technique to scenes on other reliquaries, one of which was found at Pliska (Dontcheva; Sofia, N. Archaeol. Mus.) in a 9th- or 10th-century context; post-iconoclast elements in these scenes include busts of David and Solomon in an *Anastasis*, a detail that probably first appeared between 817 and 824. St Nicholas, who was almost never represented before the end of iconoclasm, is portrayed on the Fieschi-Morgan Reliquary. 'Cup-handle' ears, filled with red enamel in the case of saints on the sides of the reliquary, relate to cloisonné enamel busts with red 'cup-handle' ears on the Carolingian altar (824–59; Buckton, 1988, pl. 22) in S Ambrogio, Milan. The lentoid eyes filled with a single colour are found on another Carolingian object, the Altheus Reliquary (780–99; Sion Cathedral, Treasury; Rosenberg, fig. 102), on which cloisonné enamel saints with veiled hands hold undecorated books in front of their chests, a detail that appears on the Fieschi-Morgan Reliquary (apparently misunderstood as patch-pockets on some saints on the lid).

The busts on the Fieschi-Morgan Reliquary, like those on the Altheus Reliquary and the Milan altar, are heavily stylized and virtually indistinguishable from one another, except by full but often misspelt inscriptions of gold strip set in backgrounds of at least three different translucent greens. Their high, smooth hairlines and moustaches defined by a cloison but left flesh-coloured are also found on a *Crucifixion* quatrefoil (*c.* 850; Khuskivadze, no. 1) on the Khakhuli Triptych (Tbilisi, Mus. A. Georgia; *see* GEORGIA, fig. 12).

The Fieschi-Morgan Reliquary was traditionally dated to *c.* 700 and regarded as the precursor of post-iconoclast enamel. With its redating to the early post-iconoclast period, however, it surrenders this role. From this time Byzantine enamellers, with no live tradition of their own to follow, were open to influences from outside the empire, and, as the Fieschi-Morgan Reliquary shows, the true precursor of their work was Carolingian cloisonné enamel, which had a tradition stretching back at least as far as Roman times.

This is endorsed by the cross (now London, V&A; *see* CROSS, fig. 8) that came into the possession of Alexander James Beresford Hope in the 19th century (Rosenberg,

pp. 53–6) and which has often been compared with a Western work, the Cross of Pope Paschal I (*reg* 817–24; Rome, Vatican, Mus. Sacro). The Beresford Hope Cross is less 'primitive' than the Fieschi-Morgan Reliquary and was probably made a decade or so later, together with two medallions (Khuskivadze, nos 3–4) on the Khakhuli Triptych that not only share characteristics with the Beresford Hope Cross but also recall the Carolingian medallions on the Milan altar.

In the Tesoro di S Marco, Venice, is a votive crown on which survive seven cloisonné enamel medallions representing saints and an *Emperor Leo* (see fig. 89). This must be Leo VI (*reg* 886–912), since other emperors of the name either were too early to be associated with this kind of enamel or were iconoclasts and would therefore never have commissioned an object with figural representations. These clearly differentiated portrait busts, identified by abbreviated inscriptions of gold strip set on edge in translucent green backgrounds, are characterized by a simple but effective use of short cloisons. The nose and eyebrows are formed by a single strip, without the addition of colour, and the eyes are simple roundels. The ears, which are attached to the face rather than to the cloison outlining the head, appear to be viewed from the side and not, as they should be, from the front. The saints' haloes are yellow; that of Leo is light blue. Hair and beards are black or, in St Andrew's case, white. A similar medallion, of *St Peter*, is attached to an icon frame (Tbilisi, Mus. A. Georgia; Khuskivadze, no. 2) which should, like the crown, be dated to the late 9th century.

Translucent green backgrounds are also found on a book cover (Venice, Bib. N. Marciana; Frazer, no. 9); on the front is a Crucifix and medallions with busts of angels and saints, and on the back are more medallions and a cross enclosing a figure of the Mother of God (Theotokos) and Greek monograms. These have been deciphered as 'Mother of God, help thy servant Maria Magistrissa', possibly referring to a Maria, the wife of a *magistros* (Byzantine court official), known to have been healed at a shrine of the Mother of God in Constantinople *c.* 900. Certainly the enamel is close in date to that on Leo's crown: the eyes are simple roundels, and the inscriptions and the colours are remarkably similar, although there is a relative lack of precision in the cellwork. However, the cloison forming the eyebrows (except those of the angels) is doubled back and filled with black enamel, anticipating later practice and suggesting that the crown, which does not share this feature, is slightly earlier. Figures on a small triptych of the *Deësis* (Tbilisi, Mus. A. Georgia; Khuskivadze, no. 5) are close in this respect to representations on the book cover and should also be dated *c.* 900.

(c) Mid-10th century–11th. Every example of cloisonné enamel so far mentioned has a background of translucent green enamel, but from *c.* 950 onwards the characteristic form of Byzantine enamel was *Senkschmelz* (Ger.: 'sunk enamel'), where the cloisonné enamel was sunk into a plaque and silhouetted against the metal; this replaced the *Vollschmelz* (Ger.: 'full enamel') of the first century or so of the post-iconoclast period. Inscriptions, instead of being composed of letters of gold strip set on edge in the translucent green background, were now cut into the face

plate of the plaque and filled with enamel—in effect, champlevé.

A large reliquary of the True Cross (Limburg, Dom-schatzkam.; see fig. 87 above; Schnitzler, pls 38–47) has inscriptions showing that it was commissioned by Basil the *Proedros* (President of the Senate, 963–89). Four out of eight *Senkschmelz* busts on the reliquary have almost exact counterparts on two chalices inscribed with the name of an *Emperor Romanos* (Venice, Tesoro S Marco; Hahn-loser, ii, pls 42–5); the closeness of the relationship makes it virtually certain that the emperor was Romanos II (*reg* 959–63) and that the Limburg Reliquary was made early in Basil's term of office as *Proedros*, in 963 or shortly afterwards. The enamel on these three objects is the earliest surviving *Senkschmelz* that can be dated with reasonable certainty.

The chalices, which have carved sardonyx bowls, are decorated around the rim and on the foot with *Senkschmelz* busts. On one chalice, which has carved handles, the rim is shallower, and the busts are arranged two to a plaque; on the other chalice the absence of handles allows a deeper rim, and here the representations are generous half-figures which are particularly elegant. Detailed comparison, however, shows that they are undoubtedly contemporary products of the same workshop, probably of the same enameller. The Limburg Reliquary is decorated with figural and purely decorative enamel. Among the *Senkschmelz* figures are six pairs of saints standing in natural poses, many with subtle contrapposto; although less than 50 mm high, these figures have a rhythm, balance and classicism that place them among the highest achievements of the Macedonian period (867–1056).

The *Senkschmelz* representations on the Romanos chal-ices and on the Limburg Reliquary are powerful and expressive. There is a simple but fluent and economical use of cloisons, producing accurate and easily recognizable iconographic types. Most have long, thin, straight noses broadening into a lozenge shape at the tip; the same cloison outlines strong enamelled eyebrows, often particularly expressive. Eyes are directed sideways and slightly upwards; ears, correctly shown edge-on, are attached to the side of the head to leave strips of hair between ear and face. Folds on the garments have a swirling movement. Considerable use is made of the 'dummy cell', a tiny area of gold, usually round, in the surface of the enamel. Hair and beards are black or, on the elderly saints, light blue. Haloes are generally light blue; saints with blue hair have translucent green haloes. Garments are generally deep blue (often alternating in folds with a light mottled blue) and a translucent maroon; the full-length figures on the reliquary have more shades of blue in their draperies.

A book cover (Munich, Bayer. Staatsbib.; Lasko, frontispiece) is dated by a Latin inscription to the years 1002–14. It incorporates 12 *Senkschmelz* plaques of Christ and Apostles, with Greek inscriptions. It was commissioned by the emperor Henry II (*reg* 1002–24), whose predecessor Otto III (*reg* 983–1002) was half Byzantine, his father having married a Byzantine princess in 972. The plaques, rectangular with rounded tops, could well have come from a Byzantine crown, as the Latin inscription possibly suggests. The *Senkschmelz* half-figures lack the quality and clarity of the enamels on the Romanos chalices, without

having the rhythm and movement of the Limburg figures. The representations on the book cover have eyes that look distinctly upwards as well as sideways, a feature that anticipates 11th-century practice. The colours also lack clarity: an opaque olive has replaced the translucent green in haloes, and garments are mostly blue-black alternating in folds with off-white, the contrast producing a pyjama-stripe effect. Off-white is also used for the hair and beards of elderly saints.

Another 11th-century German object incorporating Byzantine enamel is the Cross of Abbess Theophanu (1039–58; Essen, Münsterschatzmus.; Schnitzler, pl. 155). Gold cloisonné enamel reused on this cross includes eight Byzantine *Senkschmelz* plaques representing two birds, a lion, three fantastic beasts and two plants. These highly decorative enamels, with clean and confident cellwork, dummy cells, bright opaque colours, a semitranslucent blue, and translucent green and crimson, must date from between the invention of *Senkschmelz* (*c.* 960) and their appearance on the cross (before 1058).

A small *Senkschmelz* medallion (Venice, Tesoro S Marco; Hahnloser, ii, pl. 77) shows a bust of *Empress Zoe* (*reg* 1028–50) wearing a tall crown and holding what may be the *anexikakia*, a purple silk purse containing dust as a symbol of mortality, which was part of the imperial regalia. This item may date the medallion to 1042, when Zoe reigned alone, then with her sister Theodora, before marrying Constantine IX Monomachos. The cellwork is clean and confident, and the representation simple and effective.

Zoe also appears with Theodora and Constantine on plaques of a crown (Budapest, N. Mus.; Wessel, no. 32) dated by the combination of figures to 1042–50. Here the figures are full-length, flanked by inscriptions and *Senk-schmelz* birds and vegetal scrolls; four other plaques represent two Virtues and two female dancers. While the representations of the two empresses are comparable with that of Zoe on the S Marco medallion, the overall impression of the plaques is one of fussiness, even confusion. The garments are richly ornamented from high collar to hem; notable among the decoration is a pattern of inverted heart motifs and, where there are draperies, nested V-folds are frequent, with spirals at knee and elbow.

Many details and idiosyncracies are shared by the crown and three oval plaques incorporated in the Khakhuli Triptych, one of which shows the Mother of God crowning or blessing two empresses, who must surely be Zoe and Theodora (Khuskivadze, nos 68–70). One of the empresses appears with John the Baptist on another plaque, and, on the third, an empress bizarrely replaces the Virgin in an *Annunciation* scene.

Among the hundred or so other enamels incorporated in the Khakhuli Triptych is a *Senkschmelz* plaque representing Michael VII Dukas (*reg* 1071–8) and his wife Maria of Alania being crowned by Christ (Khuskivadze, no. 39). The bust of Christ is fluent and confident, but the full-length figures of the imperial couple are wooden and awkward, the cellwork clearly inhibited by the silhouette sawn out of the face plate of the plaque. Like the imperial figures on the 'Monomachos' crown and the oval plaques on the triptych, Michael and Maria are dressed in highly ornate costumes, including garments with the inverted

90. Gold cloisonné enamel portraits of *Emperor Michael VII Dukas* (*reg* 1071–8), his son *Constantine* and *King Geza I of Hungary* (*reg* 1074–7) on the Holy Crown of Hungary, gold, enamel, pearls and gems, diam. 685 mm (Budapest, Hungarian National Museum)

heart pattern. Their noses have squared trefoil tips; their eyes have the white showing under the iris. Christ's draperies are effectively executed, with nested V-folds. The couple's haloes are translucent green with a red border; their complexions are dark, with the cheeks lighter than the forehead and nose.

Michael VII also appears on the Holy Crown of Hungary (Budapest, N. Mus.) together with his son Constantine and King Geza I of Hungary (*reg* 1074–7; see fig. 90). These busts are complemented by a plaque of *Christ Enthroned* and by busts of two archangels, *SS George and Demetrios* and *SS Cosmas and Damian*. The quality of these enamels is far higher than that of the Michael and Maria plaque: the cellwork is crisp and generally well organized, and even where the garments have all-over decoration, the effect is clear and cogent. Inverted heart shapes abound, as do nested V-folds and knee spirals on draperies. Eyes generally look to the side; noses have rounded trefoil tips. Most haloes are translucent green with a red border; dark complexions are darker on the forehead and nose than on the cheeks.

The technical brilliance of the Byzantine enamels on the Hungarian crown is seldom matched in subsequent productions of Byzantine enamellers. On the great enamelled altarpiece known as the Pala d'Oro (see VENICE, §IV, 1(iv)) there is a *Senkschmelz* plaque with a full-length figure of an *Empress Eirene*, almost certainly the wife of Alexios I Komnenos (*reg* 1081–1118). A small head and small hands emphasize the height and bulk of the body; the

silhouette is oversimplified, and the cellwork lacks confidence. On the ornate garments the heart motif has been replaced by a chubby arrow, pointing upwards.

(d) 12th century–1453. All but one of the Greek inscriptions on the Hungarian crown follow the standard *Senkschmelz* practice and are incised into the metal surface of the plaques; the enamelled letters are red on the Michael VII Dukas and Constantine plaques and blue in every other case. Special treatment has been accorded to the inscription of the enthroned Christ, however. Here the characters IC XC (the first and last letters of 'Jesus' and of 'Christ' in Greek) and the marks denoting abbreviation have been outlined in gold strip and filled with blue enamel; the background of each pair of letters is a white disc, outlined with blue.

This special treatment anticipates the practice characteristic of the later 12th and 13th centuries, when letters were outlined in gold strip and filled with an opaque enamel contrasting with a background of a different opaque colour; white characters on a blue ground were particularly popular. In this period, in fact, there was a return to enamelled backgrounds for figures, busts and other motifs, but, in contrast to the translucence of the immediately post-iconoclast examples, the backgrounds of this later *Vollschmelz* were opaque.

A pendent reliquary (London, BM; see fig. 91), which can be dated to the 13th century by stylistic comparison with certain crusader representations, is characteristic of the later *Vollschmelz*. One face is enamelled all over with a half-figure of *St George* against a white background, surrounded by a Greek inscription in white letters on an opaque blue ground. This face and the edge of the discoid reliquary, where there is a technically similar inscription, are enamelled on to the same metal base and must therefore be contemporary.

On a remarkably similar pendent reliquary (Washington, DC, Dumbarton Oaks; Ross, 1965, no. 160), which must be contemporary with the British Museum example, *Senkschmelz* figural subjects and fully enamelled cloisonné inscriptions are juxtaposed, demonstrating that the *Vollschmelz* of the 12th and 13th centuries did not replace *Senkschmelz* but co-existed with it. Other notable examples of the later type of *Vollschmelz* include the Dagmar Cross (Lindahl; Copenhagen, Nmus.), said to have been found in the grave of the Danish queen Dagmar (*d* 1212), and the Sevast'yanov Cross (Washington, DC, Dumbarton Oaks; Ross, 1965, no. 159).

While gold was preferred on technical grounds, it could be regarded as a luxury when it was used as a substrate for opaque enamel and was therefore largely invisible. Whether for this or for another reason, copper was frequently substituted for gold in this type of enamelling, and any metal that was not obscured by the enamel, such as the visible edge of the cloisons, could be mercury-gilded. The relative cheapness of copper removed one of the constraints on size: a St Theodore plaque (190×165 mm; St Petersburg, Hermitage; Bank, pl. 190) provides one instance of this new freedom.

The use of copper did not remain confined to cloisonné enamel, however. The increased contact with the West occasioned by the Crusades led to the introduction of the Western champlevé technique, as seen on a pair of candlesticks (Riggisberg, Abegg-Stift.). An imitation of the same technique is found on a 14th-century censer (Athens, Benaki Mus.) where sheet copper was embossed to produce the visual effect of champlevé. With the constraints on size largely removed, even the typical Byzantine type of enamel achieved remarkable dimensions: a copper *Senkschmelz* standing figure of *Christ Pantokrator* (Rome, Pal. Venezia; Byron, pl. I,*c*) measures no less than 690 mm in height, even though the exposed metal surround has been cut away.

BIBLIOGRAPHY

H. Cohen: *Description historique des monnaies frappées sous l'empire romain* (Paris, 1892)
M. Rosenberg: *Die Frühdenkmäler*, iii of *Zellenschmelz*, 3 vols (1921–2), *Geschichte der Goldschmiedekunst auf technischer Grundlage* (Frankfurt am Main, 1907–22)
O. M. Dalton: 'An Enamelled Gold Reliquary', *Recueil d'études dédiées à la mémoire de N. P. Kondakov* (Prague, 1926), pp. 275–7
R. Byron: 'The Byzantine Exhibition in Paris', *Burl. Mag.*, lix (1931), p. 33
H. Schnitzler: *Rheinische Schatzkammer* (Düsseldorf, 1957)
A. V. Bank: *Iskusstvo vizantii v sobranii Gosudarstvennogo Ermitazha* [Art of Byzantium in the collection of the State Hermitage] (Leningrad, 1960)
M. C. Ross: 'Byzantine Enamels', *Byzantine Art: A European Art* (exh. cat., ed. M. Chatzidakis; Athens, Záppeion, 1964), pp. 391–408
M. C. Ross: *Jewelry, Enamels, and Art of the Migration Period* (1965), ii of *Catalogue of the Byzantine and Early Medieval Antiquities in the Dumbarton Oaks Collection* (Washington, DC, 1962–5)
H. R. Hahnloser, ed.: *Il tesoro di San Marco*, 2 vols (Florence, 1965–71)
K. Wessel: *Die byzantinische Emailkunst vom 5. bis 13. Jahrhundert* (Recklinghausen, 1967)

91. Cloisonné enamel of *St George* on a gold pendent reliquary, diam. 39 mm, 13th century (London, British Museum)

P. Lasko: *Ars sacra, 800–1200*, Pelican Hist. A. (Harmondsworth, 1972)
L. Dontcheva: 'Une Croix pectorale-reliquaire en or récemment trouvée à Pliska', *Cah. Archéol.*, xxv (1976), pp. 59–66
E. Kovács and Z. Lovag: *The Hungarian Crown and Other Regalia* (Budapest, 1980)
F. Lindahl: *Dagmarkorset, Oro-og Roskildekorset* [The Dagmar Cross and the Orø and Roskilde Crosses] (Copenhagen, 1980)
N. P. Ševčenko: *The Life of Saint Nicholas in Byzantine Art* (Turin, 1983)
K. R. Brown: *Three Byzantine Breast Chains: Ornaments of Goddesses and Ladies of Rank* (Mainz, 1984)
L. Z. Khuskivadze: *Medieval Cloisonné Enamels from the Collection of the Georgian State Museum of Fine Arts* (Tbilisi, 1984)
M. E. Frazer: 'Byzantine Enamels and Goldsmith Work', *The Treasury of San Marco, Venice* (exh. cat., ed. D. Buckton; New York, Met., 1985), pp. 109–14
A. D. Kartsonis: *Anastasis: The Making of an Image* (Princeton, 1986)
D. Buckton: 'Byzantine Enamel and the West', *Byz. Forsch.*, xiii (1988), pp. 235–44
T. Weisser and C. Herbert: 'A Filigree Enamel Medallion in the Walters Art Gallery Reconsidered', *Abstracts of Papers from the Sixteenth Annual Byzantine Studies Conference: Baltimore, 1990*, pp. 30–31
D. Buckton: 'All that Glisters...: Byzantine Enamel on Copper', *Thymíami in Memory of Laskarina Bouras*, ed. A. Delivorrias and others (Athens, 1994), pp. 47–9, pls 5, 20–21

DAVID BUCKTON

8. TEXTILES. Early Christian and Byzantine textiles in the form of figured silks are relatively well represented by surviving pieces up until the 12th century. Excavated examples come from sites at the edges of the empire such as Antinoöpolis and Akhmim in Egypt, Halabiyeh in Syria and Moshchevaya Balka and Hassaût (*see* CENTRAL ASIA, fig. 46) in the northern Caucasus. A larger number have been preserved in treasuries and tombs in western European churches, notably at Rome, Ravenna, Sens, Chur,

Sion, Aachen, Cologne, Liège and Maastricht, with important individual pieces in many other churches. The best collections are at Lyon (Mus. Hist. Tissus), Paris (Mus. Cluny), Brussels (Musées Royaux A. & Hist.), London (V&A), Berlin (Tiergarten, Kstgewmus. and Schloss Köpenick) and St Petersburg (Hermitage). Such silks were much in demand outside the Byzantine empire. Understanding them to be adjuncts of political power, the Byzantine emperors strove to maintain a monopoly. According to the *Book of the Prefect* (*c.* 895; IV.i.8), foreign merchants were allowed to export a limited quantity of the second quality only, the products of the private guilds. The best silks, made at Constantinople in the palace workshops by the public guilds (*demosia somata*), were the property of the emperor and belonged to the category of forbidden goods (*kekolymena*). But even some of these got abroad, whether smuggled or as diplomatic gifts and tributes. Wool and linen pieces from Halabiyeh (*c.* 610; Damascus, N. Mus.) and from Coptic Christian cemeteries in upper Egypt give an impression of ordinary Byzantine textiles. Coptic tapestry designs, even dating from after the Arab conquest of Egypt in the 640s, often reflect the influence of the Byzantine silks (*see* COPTIC ART, §V, 3).

(i) Fibres. (ii) Dyes. (iii) Advanced weaves. (iv) Simpler weaves. (v) Identification. (vi) Style. (vii) Subject-matter. (viii) Workshops and distribution. (ix) Embroidery and the use of gold.

(i) Fibres. The Byzantines inherited from the Romans a well-established silk-weaving industry based on imported, mainly Chinese fibre. In the 3rd and 4th centuries silk clothing became accepted wear for men as well as for women, and new weaves were developed which were especially suited to silk. According to the 6th-century historian Prokopios (*History of the Wars* VIII.xvii.2), silkworm eggs were first brought to Constantinople by Christian monks in the 550s from 'a country, Serinda, that lay to the north of . . . India'. The Persian wars at the time may also have encouraged efforts to secure supplies. In addition to worms, however, silk rearing requires mature mulberry trees, mulberry leaves being the sole diet of *Bombyx mori*, the cultivated worm. It is more probable, therefore, that sericulture had spread gradually along the Silk Route from China to Central Asia and Persia; and although a document of about 1050 (Calabria, priv. col.; see Guillou, pp. 92–5) dealing with mulberry planting in Byzantine southern Italy gives a picture of expanding sericulture at that date, a proportion of raw silk was probably imported from the East at all times.

The rise of silk as a textile was probably accompanied by a decline in the status of wool. Up to about 600 very fine wool is sometimes found as the second weft alongside silk in the compound weaves, and even after this wool must have remained the dominant fibre for everyday textiles; many mountainous regions of the empire were well suited to sheep, though there is no sign of the careful sheep farming practised in the Roman period.

In Late Antiquity fine linen had been extensively used for tunics and other garments, and the *Book of the Prefect* (IX) indicates that linen, some of which was bought from the Bulgars, was still important in the economy of late 9th-century Constantinople. But, since plant fibres dye much less readily than animal fibres, linen was not usually dyed and was probably used only for underclothing and domestic textiles such as towels.

By the 8th century cotton was used as an attractive substitute for the cheaper qualities of linen (see fig. 75 above). Knowledge of cotton spinning and weaving was spread by the Arabs, who had long imported raw cotton from the Indian subcontinent, and the rapid expansion in cultivation was made possible by the discovery of an annual variety of the plant. By the mid-14th century northern Syria, Cilicia and Cyprus were exporters of high-quality raw cotton and yarn. Usually undyed (cotton dyed with indigo is the exception), cotton yarn seems often to have been combined with dyed wool or silk yarns; indeed, mixed cotton textiles are still a feature of Greek and Turkish folk textiles.

(ii) Dyes. 'Real purple', an ancient dye giving a range of dark rich purple hues, was made from a gland of common Mediterranean whelks, principally *Murex brandaris* and *Murex trunculus*. New evidence from dye analysis seems to suggest that real purple may have gone out of use as early as the 6th or the 7th century. Considering the continued symbolic importance of purple, this is an unexpected finding. Although purple had long been associated with kingship, legal restrictions on its use had not extended beyond all-purple clothing until the Late Roman and Early Christian periods. Its disappearance from surviving textiles cannot, however, be wholly explained by the existence of an imperial monopoly, since from the mid-7th century the two major centres of production, Tyre and Sidon, were actually in Arab hands. Purple was

92. Durham 'Earth and Ocean' Silk (detail), diam. of roundel *c.* 600 mm, from the tomb of St Cuthbert, first half of the 9th century (Durham, Cathedral Treasury)

first and foremost a wool dye. It may be that it was replaced by less fast dyes, such as fucus, when multicoloured silks not intended for frequent washing rose in favour. Two Byzantine textiles that were almost certainly woven in the palace workshops, the Siegburg 'Lion' Silk (Berlin, Schloss Köpenick) and the Gunther Tapestry (Bamberg, Domschatzkam.), use instead of real purple a cheap imitation, madder red over indigotin. The Siegburg Silk has large gold-coloured lions on a purple-coloured ground; from its woven inscription 'During the reign of Romanos and Christophoros the devout rulers', it can be dated to 921–31. The Gunther Tapestry is multicoloured, with shades of purple and mauve predominating: it shows a mounted emperor between two personifications of cities, and is perhaps a memorial of the victory of Basil II (*reg* 976–1025) over the Bulgars in 1017 (*see also* §I, 2(ii) above).

Second in status after 'real purple' were the insect dyes that gave a dark pink or crimson. These remained in continuous use and are seen in the ground of a number of larger silk designs, such as the Durham 'Earth and Ocean' Silk (Durham, Cathedral Treasury; see fig. 92). The local varieties were kermes, living on Mediterranean dwarf oaks, and Armenian cochineal.

Besides the purple and crimson dyes and the white or cream of undyed fibre, the colours in Byzantine textiles were primaries; red from madder root, yellow from a range of plants, dark blue from woad or imported Indian indigo and green made by overdyeing blue with yellow (the mordant used with the red and yellow dyes was alum).

(iii) Advanced weaves. Classical textiles had been very simple, in plain tabby or twill, with areas of contrasting decoration in weft-faced tabby or tapestry-weave. By the 3rd century two more advanced weaves were becoming popular. The first, applied particularly to silk, was 1:3/3:1 twill damask. The most famous surviving example comprises the group of fragments of a white silk (Milan, Mus. Sacro S Ambrogio) depicting scenes of lion hunting set in an open landscape; they come from a dalmatic that had probably belonged to St Ambrose himself (*c.* 334 or 340–97). Like modern linen damasks, silk twill damask relied on an oblique light to show up the two surface effects.

The second new weave was weft-faced compound tabby. This has two weft lats (for an explanation *see* TEXTILE, §II, 1) and two warps: a binding warp binding the weft and a main warp controlling the pattern. At first applied to furnishings of wool and linen, by the 4th century it was used in silk for clothing. A good example is the 'Huntsman and Acanthus-scroll' Silk from Rimini (probably early 5th century; Ravenna, Mus. N.), in green and white. A feature of the compound weaves is that they allow designs of strongly contrasting colours. The sequence of compound tabbies and twill damasks came to an end in about 600. Both had been ousted by 1:2 weft-faced compound twill, a weave closely related to compound tabby, but which is more lustrous, having a longer weft float. Probably developed in Persia, where a tradition existed of tapestry in 1:2 twill, it became the Byzantine weave *par excellence*; with the exception of the Gunther Tapestry, all the textiles that can be positively identified as Byzantine are compound twill silks. The Byzantine term

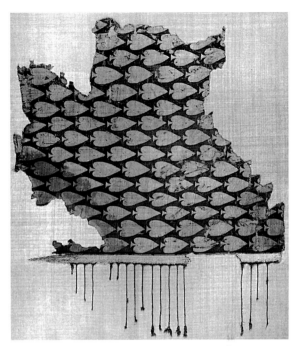

93. Fragments of silk with cotton border, widthways repeat c. 50 mm, from Akhmim, Egypt, 6th century (London, Victoria and Albert Museum)

for this weave was probably *hexamiton* (Gr.: 'woven with six shafts'), from which samite, the modern western European term, is derived.

Technical developments within this weave are illustrated by increasing repeat sizes (up to a maximum in about the 10th century) and the addition of colours. The 6th-century two-colour, two-lat compound twill silk found at Akhmim (London, V&A; see fig. 93) with repeating ace of spades motifs is a relatively early example. This has a widthways repeat of 120 main warp threads which, given a decoupure of 1, represents 120 tail cords on the loom (the decoupure is the unit of threads in the stepping or scaling of the outline of the motifs). With about 57 weft passes per 10 mm and a weft decoupure also of 1, the pattern was achieved with about 570 manipulations of the tail cords, allowing for the two lats.

The Durham 'Earth and Ocean' Silk is a particularly well-woven example of the most complex sort of Byzantine textile, the compound twill silks with large multicoloured roundel designs of the 8th to the 10th century. This has a vertical repeat of 600 mm and a reverse widthways repeat of 300 mm. It has three basic colours or lats, dark pink (for the ground), dark blue and yellow, and an interrupted fourth lat, green. Other colours, including purple and white, replace a main lat as required in the pseudo-brocading method. Here the loom had 258 tail cords requiring about 6500 manipulations per repeat. The Durham Silk may be one of the two lengths of Greek cloth that King Edmund (*reg* 939–46) is said to have placed around the relics of St Cuthbert in 944, though its style suggests that it was woven about 125 years before its final use: the presence in the main warp of paired threads

94. Silk shroud of St Siviard (detail), diam. of roundel *c.* 650 mm, first half of the 11th century (Sens Cathedral)

instead of single ones shows that it is unlikely to date before the late 8th century.

The loom used for the compound twill silks was a sort of draw-loom, but it differed in fundamental ways from the later European model. Although probably horizontal, it seems, like the old vertical looms, to have been very wide, as is suggested by the 'Elephant' Silk (? late 10th century; Aachen, Domschatzkam.), which was at least 2.4 m wide. Uneven spacing of the warp threads in the surviving silks shows that the loom had no reed. Two well-known textiles, the Mozac Silk with paired mounted emperors (Lyon, Mus. Hist. Tissus; *see* DRESS, fig. 8) and the 'Lion-strangler' Silk (Sens Cathedral), were woven without lashes (i.e. the design was not tied into the tail cords and had to be at least partly selected anew for each lengthways repeat). According to tradition the Mozac Silk was given to the shrine of St Austremoine in 761 by Pepin the Short (*reg* 751–68). The 'Lion-strangler' Silk is similar to the Durham Silk in style and technique and therefore almost certainly Byzantine, despite its Near Eastern iconography.

The period 950–1050 was one of further innovation. Incised twill, a variant of compound twill, appeared, with two lats of the same colour; the design showed up in outline where the lats changed place. Many examples are Islamic, but the chasuble of St Ulrich (*d* 973; Augsburg, Maximilianmus.) has a design of Byzantine emperors.

A new type of weave known as lampas is best understood as growing out of the incised compound twills; to begin with it too was generally monochrome. Here the main warp, which was hidden in the weft-faced twills, appears on the surface, creating a matt ground effect contrasting with the more brilliant weft-faced pattern areas. Like compound twill, the lampases probably originated in Persia. The tabby-tabby lampas with a griffin design, which was perhaps placed with St Siviard's relics in 1029 (Sens Cathedral; see fig. 94), is probably Byzantine

because it shares its roundel design with the 'Elephant' Silk at Aachen.

There are apparently no Byzantine examples of later medieval weaves such as velvet, satin and satin damask.

(iv) Simpler weaves. The old method of patterning called tapestry weave was used until at least the 7th century for clothing, mostly to provide the limited areas of decoration within a mainly plain garment that were subsequently supplied by panels cut from compound twill silks (see fig. 75 above). As a furnishing, however, tapestry must have had a continuous history. Surviving examples include an Egyptian wall hanging depicting the *Virgin and Child with Saints* (6th century; Cleveland, OH, Mus. A.) and the Gunther Tapestry which, although made of silk, in technique resembles the Egyptian and later European tapestries of wool. Tapestry is the most naturalistic of the decorative weaves, and of all Byzantine textiles the Gunther Tapestry is stylistically closest to paintings and mosaics.

A class of relatively simple weaves is weft-patterned tabby. Linen and wool examples are common among finds from Egypt. Of the small group found in western Europe, a number are little napkins in white on white silk with semi-abstract designs arranged in bands. The loom employed for weft-patterned tabby, equipped with selection rods rather than tail cords, was similar to that used for self-patterned tabby (a weave without a pattern weft). The weft-patterned weaves were possibly developed from the older weft-pile weaves used from early times for warm clothes and furnishings. There are no identifiable Byzantine pile-weave textiles, but carpets entirely of wool or of wool and linen found in Egypt and Nubia have coloured abstract designs comparable to floor mosaics both at Daphne in Antioch and at Apameia. In technical terms the surviving examples mostly have loops, either unknotted or Sehna, but cut Turkish or Ghiordes knots also occur (e.g. on a carpet from Buhen, *c.* 1.86×1.24 m; London, BM).

(v) Identification. Only a handful of surviving silks are definitely of Byzantine manufacture. The Siegburg 'Lion' Silk has two companions also with inscriptions (one in Cologne, Erzbischöfl. Diöz.-Mus.; the other in fragments in Berlin, Schloss Charlottenburg and Düsseldorf, Kstmus.). The Aachen 'Elephant' Silk, probably placed in the tomb of Charlemagne by Otto III in 1000, gives the names of two officials, one of whom, Peter, was archon of the Zeuxippos, the ancient baths near the Great Palace at Constantinople where dyeing probably took place. The Gunther Tapestry has no inscription, but its history and style leave no doubt about its source. Lastly, there is the Durham Silk, where the quality of the weaving is exceptionally good, and the fragmentary Greek inscription rules out the alternative hypothesis of a Persian origin. A silk (Liège, Mus. A. Relig. A. Mosan) with the monogram of Emperor Heraklios (*reg* 610–41) was believed by Lopez (p. 5) to have been made in Constantinople; but while the monogram is useful for dating, it does not prove place of manufacture. Another monogrammed piece was found at Akhmim (London, V&A).

Byzantine silks are difficult to identify because silks in the same weave were being produced in other areas. From

Persia the weave had also spread eastwards through Central Asia, reaching China in the 7th or 8th century; provinces lost to the Arabs, such as Syria, must have continued to make such textiles. The Turks had their own strong silk-weaving tradition, and by the 12th century compound twill was being woven in western Europe, perhaps as a result of the relocation by Roger II (*reg* 1105–54) of Jews, who may have been silk weavers and dyers, from Athens, Corinth and Thebes, to Sicily. Technical details are of some help. As a rule, silks from Central Asia either have the threads of the main warp grouped in threes or more, or have no twist on the warp threads. There is nothing apart from style to distinguish the Persian silks; it is not surprising that they should be technically so similar to Byzantine silks, since under Justinian I (*reg* 527–65) many weavers left Constantinople to work in Persia (Prokopios: *Secret History* XXV.26), while a century later Heraklios imported Persian weavers. It is not always recognized that Byzantine weavers often borrowed Persian designs and subjects.

(vi) Style. Designs from the 4th century are either simple geometric patterns or naturalistic scenes in open settings. By the end of the 5th century these opposites were merging; motifs were still Classical in feel but were often set into a formal framework such as repeating niches. In the 6th century designs were yet more rhythmical, with the same motif for the first time repeating down as well as across the cloth (see fig. 93 above). Many late 6th- and 7th-century silks have diagonally crossing lines of decoration enclosing stylized vegetal forms or small paired birds. Large roundels with elaborated frames dominated in the 8th and 9th centuries. In many cases the figures inside the roundels are symmetrically paired. In comparison with Late Antique silks, figure types are simplified and scale is distorted (see fig. 92 above). The huge lion and eagle designs of the 10th century and early 11th use fewer colours and are usually set out without roundels. Roundels and their variants came to the fore again in the 11th and 12th centuries, but plant forms now fill the spaces around the main motifs and there is more outlining (compare figs 92 and 94 above). Smaller, abstract designs in Arabic taste also appeared.

The sack of Constantinople in 1204 must have caused a break in workshop traditions. The Paris Hippocrates manuscript (*c.* 1342; Paris, Bib. N., MS. Gr. 2144) shows the High Admiral Apokaukos (*d* 1345) in a kaftan-like garment with large-scale roundels of the old type, but there is no way of knowing where such textiles were made; a silk (Lyon, Mus. Hist. Tissus) with a similar design has a Turkish inscription of the 13th century.

Formalization in Byzantine textile design is probably attributable more to the influence of Oriental art than to textile technology. Although repeats were bound to accompany the more sophisticated looms, there is no technical reason why the widthways reverse repeat should usually be in the form of figures paired within one roundel; but paired animals and horsemen are a regular theme in ancient Persian art. Designs in some cases show a rectilinearity that is similar to silks from Central Asia (*see* CENTRAL ASIA, §I, 6(i)(a)); the parallel strands of hair of the Durham Silk provide an example. Unlike Central Asian textiles, however, Byzantine textiles always had small decoupures (in the warp, of one thread only), thus allowing greater fluidity of design.

(vii) Subject-matter. The early designs ran parallel to the warp and sometimes used their varied repeat for narrative sequences of scenes. Three fragments (all at Sens Cathedral) of this type are the Maenad Silk with the *Death of Orpheus* and the two Joseph Silks, one a compound tabby and the other a compound twill, where the scenes are accompanied by text from the *Life of Joseph*. More commonly, the subject is simply decorative, for example a huntsman pursuing a string of different animals (e.g. the 'Huntsman and Acanthus-scroll' Silk) or nereids riding sea monsters (e.g. a silk of *c.* 500; Sion Cathedral).

After about 200 years of more abstract designs, human figures and large animals reappeared in the 8th century. Many were borrowed from Persian and Near Eastern mythology; lion-stranglers, mounted archers, griffins, simurghs and so on. Classical subjects were now also treated more symbolically: huntsmen are nearly always mounted, their pose deriving from Roman cavalry monuments, though the conquered barbarian has usually been replaced by a symbolic speared animal, as in the St Ursula Silk (Cologne, St Ursula). The 8th-century Munsterbilsen Quadriga Silk (Brussels, Musées Royaux A. & Hist.) can be read on three levels. Superficially, the silk shows chariots with drivers dressed for the circus or hippodrome. The quadriga driver, however, also symbolizes the sun, his crown being in the form of the sun's rays, while the biga driver in the spandrels is the moon. The specific form of the biga driver's crescent-surmounted crown is that of the Sasanian kings, perhaps a reference to Heraklios' short-lived victory of a century earlier over Chosroes II (*reg* 590–628); seen in this context, the quadriga driver is the Byzantine emperor at his triumphal procession. The most obviously pagan silk of this middle period is the Maastricht 'Dioscuri' Silk (Lyon, Mus. Hist. Tissus). Here Castor and Pollux surmount a column while below two bullocks are sacrificed to them. A column surmounted by the Dioscuri was standard iconographic shorthand for the circus at Constantinople; but again there are military overtones, and their figures recall representations of soldiers on Roman coinage. The continuation in Byzantine silks of traditional Roman popular and propagandist art is a reminder of the extent to which the court at Constantinople regarded itself as Roman.

As a rule, subjects are not Christian. A notable exception is the silk with the *Annunciation* and *Nativity* set in roundels on a red ground (Rome, Vatican, Mus. Sacro). Partly because of its date (probably within the period of the iconoclastic controversy, 726–843) and partly because of its relatively naturalistic style, there is a problem in assigning this piece to Constantinople. Falke (p. 7) believed it to have been made in Alexandria. Another possibility is Rome; many Byzantine craftsmen had emigrated to Rome in the 8th century to avoid the restraints of iconoclasm.

(viii) Workshops and distribution. The number of different designs being produced at any one time seems to have been fairly small; but where several silks with the same designs have survived, differences in scale, colour and distribution indicate that they are not all products of the

same workshop. The silk from Egypt (see fig. 93 above) is similar to a fragment of green and beige silk at Beromünster in Switzerland (Beromünster, St Michael), while at Chelles (Mus. Alfred Bonno) in France there is a red fragment with the same design but in silk and wool. There are seven known instances of the design called the *Shot of Bahram Gor*: in the church of S Ambrogio in Milan, lining the doors of the gold altar of 835 (vertical repeat 600 mm); at Cologne (Erzbischöf Diöz.- & Dombib.), from the shrine of St Kunibert (vertical repeat 890 mm); at Saint-Calais, Sarthe, probably used to wrap the bones of St Calais in 837; at Prague (Cathedral, Chapter Lib.), binding a 9th-century manuscript; at St Gall (Stift.-Bib.), binding a manuscript of the first half of the 9th century; at Sion, a tiny scrap (Sion Cathedral); and fragments used as facings on two kaftans found at Moshchevaya Balka (St Petersburg, Hermitage). A small strip of a closely related though perhaps slightly earlier silk was found in the pagan ship burial at Oseberg (*c.* 850; Oslo, Vikingskipshuset). The more complete examples of the *Bahram Gor* design in silk all have a Greek cross at the top and bottom of the roundel frame, showing that, in spite of the Persian style, they were of Christian origin.

Another group of silks (all *c.* 850) seems to show use of a simurgh design moving from Persia to Byzantium. Three examples have crescents in the roundel frame (London, V&A; Reims, Pal. Tau.; Abbadia, San Salvatore). A fourth example, the main silk of one of the kaftans from Moshchevaya Balka, has instead of a crescent a four-petalled rosette, which may in this position be intended as a variant on the cross. The Alans, whose chieftains were buried at Moshchevaya Balka, had probably been able to buy silks from Byzantine trading posts at Trebizond and Chersonesos. The finds from Moshchevaya Balka are a timely reminder that the main use for Byzantine silks would have been as secular clothing (see fig. 76 above).

(ix) Embroidery and the use of gold. Embroidery is really a phenomenon of the Late Byzantine period, when it is principally in gold thread. There are some early examples in a naturalistic multicoloured style from Egypt, notably four panels of the *Seasons* (U. Manchester, Whitworth

A.G.). These are coarser in quality than the best tapestry-woven decoration and were probably used as furnishings. The technique is mainly chain stitch in plied wool yarn on a linen ground.

By tradition gold *filé* thread (metal spun round a silk core) was employed in tapestry weave: it was even possible, though laborious, to interrupt the repeating decoration of the new weaves and to add in integrally woven contrasting tapestry areas. Metal thread was not used as a main weft in the compound twill silks, as this would have been wasteful and impractical. It is, however, sometimes found brocaded in the lampases (see fig. 94 above). Applied decoration (e.g. pearls) sewn to the grandest sorts of textiles, such as the emperor's toga or belt, seems to have had an early history, although for a long time embroidery itself was looked down upon as a second-best to weaving. By the 10th or 11th century, however, even the emperor is likely to have accepted the quicker method, at least as far as decoration in gold thread was concerned. The gold plant design outlined in pearls on the hem of the under-tunic of Nikephoros III Botaneiates (*reg* 1078–81) in an illuminated manuscript of 1078 (Paris, Bib. N., MS. Coislin 79, fol. 2*v*) is reminiscent of the embroidered gold decoration on the 12th-century imperial robes (Vienna, Schatzkam.).

The surviving examples of Byzantine embroidery are all church vestments or liturgical cloths; nearly all have figural designs close in style to contemporary paintings. Worked on a silk ground with a thicker linen backing, most of the embroidery is in couched metal thread, while coloured silks are used for outlining and for the flesh areas of the figures. The subtlety of the overall effect is due especially to the different varieties of gold and silver threads used (by this time including wire as well as *filé*). The oldest surviving pieces are two late 12th-century aers (covers for the chalice and paten) in Halberstadt Cathedral, both showing the *Communion of the Apostles*. Better known is the 'Dalmatic of Charlemagne' (Rome, Vatican, Mus. Stor. A. Tesoro S Pietro): this is a 14th-century *sakkos* with the *Calling of the Chosen* on the front and the *Transfiguration* on the reverse. Most famous of all is the 14th-century *epitaphios* (symbolic cover for Christ's coffin)

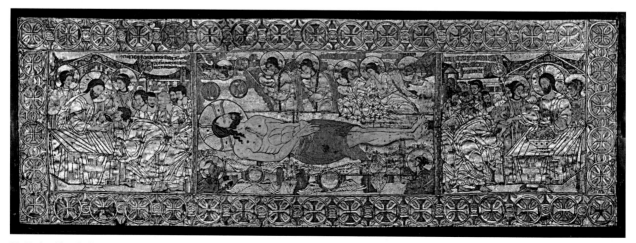

95. Embroidered silk *epitaphios* with the *Dead Christ, c.* 0.70×2.00 mm, from Thessaloniki, 14th century (Athens, Byzantine Museum)

from Thessaloniki (Athens, Byz. Mus.; see fig. 95). The traditions and techniques of Byzantine gold embroidery continued after 1453 in Greece, as well as in Serbia and Romania (*see* ROMANIA, §VII, 1).

BIBLIOGRAPHY

The Book of the Prefect (*c.* 895); Eng. trans. by E. H. Freshfeld in *Roman Law in the Later Roman Empire* (Cambridge, 1938)
O. von Falke: *Kunstgeschichte der Seidenweberei* (Berlin, 1913, abridged 2/1921; Eng. trans., 1922 and 1936)
R. S. Lopez: 'The Silk Industry in the Byzantine Empire', *Speculum*, xx/1 (1945), pp. 1–42
P. Johnstone: *The Byzantine Tradition in Church Embroidery* (London, 1967)
W. F. Volbach: *Early Decorative Textiles* (London, 1969)
M. Reinhold: *History of Purple as a Status Symbol in Antiquity*, Collection Latomus (Brussels, 1970)
J. Beckwith: 'Byzantine Tissues', *Actes du XIVe congrès international des études byzantines: Bucharest, 1971*, i, pp. 343–53
A. Guillou: 'Production and Profits in the Byzantine Province of Italy (Tenth to Eleventh Centuries): An Expanding Society', *Dumbarton Oaks Pap.*, xxviii (1974), pp. 91–109
P. Johnstone: 'The Byzantine "Pallio" in the Palazzo Bianco at Genoa', *Gaz. B.-A.*, n. s., lxxxvii–lxxxviii (1976), pp. 99–108
B. Schmedding: *Mittelalterliche Textilien in Kirchen und Klöstern der Schweiz* (Berne, 1978)
D. K. Burnham: *A Textile Terminology: Warp and Weft* (London, 1981)
Splendeur de Byzance (exh. cat., Brussels, Musées Royaux A. & Hist., 1982)
A. Muthesius: 'A Practical Approach to the History of Byzantine Silk Weaving', *Jb. Österreich. Byz.*, xxxiv (1984), pp. 235–54
M. Martiniani-Reber: *Lyon, Musée historique des tissus: Soieries sassanides, coptes et byzantines, Ve–XIe siècles* (Paris, 1986)
N. Oikonomides: 'Silk Trade and Production in Byzantium from the 6th to the 9th Century', *Dumbarton Oaks Pap.*, xv (1986), pp. 33–53
H. Maguire: 'The Mantle of Earth', *IL. Class. Stud.*, xii (1987), pp. 221–8
H. Granger-Taylor: 'The Earth and Ocean Silk from the Tomb of St Cuthbert at Durham', *Textile Hist.*, xx/2 (1989), pp. 151–66
A. Muthesius: 'From Seed to Samite: Aspects of Byzantine Silk Production', *Textile Hist.*, xx/2 (1989), pp. 135–49
——: *A History of the Byzantine Silk Industry*, 3 vols (Vienna, 1993)

HERO GRANGER-TAYLOR

Early English. Term invented in the early 19th century by Thomas Rickman to denote the style of Early Gothic ecclesiastical architecture that flourished in Britain from *c.* 1190 to *c.* 1250. Like all Rickman's style labels, which were popularized by Nikolaus Pevsner in *The Buildings of England*, the term is still in favour where equivalent labels ('lancet' or 'pointed style') have fallen out of use. The style (see fig.) is characterized by the use of rib vaults, sharply pointed arches, lancet windows, deep mouldings and the use of decorative contrasting marbles and foliage sculpture, especially STIFF-LEAF. It was superseded after the mid-13th century by the window tracery and patterned vaults of the DECORATED STYLE (*see also* GOTHIC, §II, 1).

Early English combined such formal aspects of French Gothic as rib vaults with English pre-Gothic decorative and structural tendencies. It developed from several regional centres of late 12th-century Gothic, the most important of which were the choir of Canterbury Cathedral (1174–84), such northern buildings as Ripon Minster and allied Cistercian abbeys, and the Late Romanesque 'pointed' West Country style (e.g. Wells Cathedral).

The Canterbury work is perhaps the most significant, combining wholly French elements—sexpartite rib vaults, slender supports and flying buttresses—with less 'pure' devices (e.g. polychrome materials, clerestory passages and

Early English style: Salisbury Cathedral, interior of north-west transept, *c.* 1230

curious, half-understood vault-support systems). The resulting hybrid, arising possibly from the unique circumstances of the rebuilding of Canterbury Cathedral (*see* CANTERBURY, §III, 1 and fig. 7), was neither French nor English, and England lost the opportunity to build a coherent essay in contemporary French Gothic, choosing instead a series of highly decorated and individual compromises. Several late 12th-century buildings blithely copied the eccentricities of Canterbury. St Hugh's choir at Lincoln Cathedral (from 1192; *see* LINCOLN, §2(i)), for example, adopted and legitimized such Canterbury oddities as the inherited sprawling plan, the occasional five-part vault and illusionistic devices, while adding architectural diversions of its own. The English preoccupation with patterning is nowhere more evident than the disturbing asymmetry of the Lincoln choir aisles or the famous crazy vaults. Older Romanesque notions of the plastic wall, with endless potential for linear, sculptural and tonal effects, found new expression within the Early English style, quite confounding the minimal, monochrome and shrinking aesthetic of the French Gothic wall.

The survival of English pre-Gothic tendencies extended to the structural engineering. The English, apparently indifferent to the technology of French Gothic, were never able to accommodate its aesthetic, even had they wished to do so. They continued with the Anglo-Norman method of supporting the high vault on a solid, thick-wall structure, which restricted both the interior height and its potential for glazing. The English insistence on using the aisle roof and elevational wall as the principal means of supporting the vault both restricted the internal height of the vault-springing and determined that English elevational walls would remain thick and load-bearing. The dependence upon such outmoded technology was fundamental to the development of the Early English style and dictated that it should be quite divorced from its continental contemporaries.

Such was the English indifference towards the complexities of high-vault construction that many buildings simply omitted them. Yorkshire shows a long tradition of wood-ceilinged, or even false wood-vaulted interiors, perhaps derived from the strong influence of 12th-century Cistercian buildings. Ripon Minster (from *c.* 1185) quickly abandoned any intention to vault in stone, preferring in its transepts a new, rectangular style, with roofs springing from a flat-topped elevation. Such an interior offered more scope for linear effects, with a gridlike system of intersecting shafts and string courses, while the thick-walled clerestory, complete with internal passage and uninterrupted by any vault, could become another horizontal serial pattern the length of the interior.

In true Cistercian style, Ripon, like other northern contemporaries, has no polychromy, but this was not to last. Wells, initially monochrome, was finished by a great screen façade (*see* WELLS, fig. 4) striped with blue lias colonnettes. Lincoln Cathedral employs Purbeck 'marble' against the piers, as dark bands through the triforium and outlining the clerestory passage and windows. The retrochoir of Winchester Cathedral (*c.* 1200) has clustered piers of dark marble and aisle walls delineated with similar materials. Lincoln and Winchester share another decorative feature—a variety of holes fretted through the interior facing and causing dark patterns simply by the play of shadow. Trefoils and quatrefoils predominate, although, predictably, Lincoln turns some at odd angles. By *c.* 1200 the Early English style already displays the English horror of the empty space and the desire to fill it with bizarre detail.

The cathedrals of Lincoln and Salisbury provide the essential examples for the period 1200–25. Lincoln concentrated on decorative and linear features as the work progressed westward. Salisbury Cathedral, begun 1220 on a new site, is the most complete example of the style (*see* SALISBURY, §2(i)). The plan is typically boxlike, and the horizontal predominates both inside and out: the original exterior tolerated no vertical interruption of the lines of walls and roofs, while the interior elevation has the same stratified feeling, emphasized by contrasting coloured zones. The complex tripartite eastern axial chapel is all lancet windows and spindly Purbeck supports, and the presbytery termination shows a casual disregard for adjoining elevations, the lateral walls with large, hard-angled triforium openings conflicting in both height and curvature with the designs of the eastern wall, with which the arcade arches appear to collide. Like Wells Cathedral, from which Salisbury draws its structural technology, the elevation avoids linking verticals. The choir piers are bolder than Wells and, instead of the tight cluster of colonnettes, have groupings of polished Purbeck drums, while the Purbeck capitals are smooth and uniformly moulded. The transepts and nave continue in the same manner, illustrating that

where Early English abandons variety for uniformity it can become tedious.

The interior of the nave of Lincoln Cathedral (*c.* 1230–40; *see* LINCOLN, fig. 2) has a lively spaciousness unique in English medieval buildings. Tall arches rest on a variety of clustered piers, some with alternating coloured shafts but none so different as to stand out. The capitals are mere foliate wreaths. The bay lengths are so generous that the aisle elevations contribute greatly to the overall design, with continuous trefoil-headed wall arcades, twin windows and dark polished responds. The main walls are contained within clustered vault-support shafts rising from corbels set within the arcade spandrels. Twin triforium openings frame triple arches and punched quatrefoil motifs, and while the clerestory is still caught within the low springing-level of the vault, the spaciousness allows a triple passage arcade and answering windows. The vault represents the first in the long line of English conoid tierceron vaults, where linearity spreads from wall to ceiling, and vault construction, within an English context, becomes easier. The additional ribs required extra bosses and, with vaults kept relatively low, highly decorative sculptural cycles became common.

Both Lincoln and Salisbury are reflected in the south transept of York Minster (*c.* 1240), although there the unvaulted, flat-topped elevation maintained the northern tradition. Beverley Minster (Humberside; *c.* 1240) again reflects Lincoln, although the simple quadripartite vault, slighter walls and flying buttresses hint at some dissatisfaction with the native English style.

Sculpture became an essential element of Early English. Bishop Northwold's presbytery at Ely (*c.* 1234–52; *see* ELY, fig. 3) is perhaps the most lavish, with foliate forms sprouting from corbels and bosses and even between the colonnettes of the gallery and clerestory arcades. Great sculpted portals were apparently unknown: free-standing figures were distributed upon empty wall-space or within arcaded bands as on the façades of the cathedrals of Wells and Salisbury.

The two-storey elevation represents a secondary but important strand of Early English. In many smaller Romanesque churches, such as at Melbourne, Derbys, the middle storey was compressed or eliminated, and this tradition continued into Gothic even in vaulted structures. Southwell Minster (Notts; *c.* 1230) demonstrates the considerable potential of a clerestory design enveloping the entire elevation above the arcade. Such diminished middle zones are not 'French', for the glazed area of these English clerestories does not increase: rather, they represent an accommodation between a sense of grandeur and a tight budget.

Early English was transformed into the Decorated style by the arrival of tracery and by the extraordinary development of English vaults. These elements were thrown into the rich mix, while the structural system, the plastic wall, sculptural enrichment and polychromy were all carried over from the Early English style.

BIBLIOGRAPHY

T. Rickman: *An Attempt to Discriminate the Styles of Architecture in England from the Conquest to the Reformation* (Liverpool, 1817)

F. Bond: *Gothic Architecture in England* (London, 1906)

N. Pevsner and others: *The Buildings of England* (Harmondsworth, 1951)

T. S. R. Boase: *English Art, 1100–1216* (Oxford, 1953)

G. Webb: *Architecture in Britain: The Middle Ages*, Pelican Hist. A. (Harmondsworth, 1956, 2/1965)

P. Brieger: *English Art, 1216–1307* (Oxford, 1957/R 1968)

P. Kidson, P. Murray and P. Thompson: *A History of English Architecture* (London, 1962; Harmondsworth, 2/1979)

P. Draper: 'Recherches récentes sur l'architecture dans les Iles Britanniques à la fin de l'époque romane et au début du gothique', *Bull. Mnmtl*, clxiv/4 (1986), pp. 305–28

                                        FRANCIS WOODMAN

Early Gothic [First Gothic; Fr. *premier art gothique*]. The generally accepted term for the first phase of the French Gothic style (*see* GOTHIC, §II, 1), lasting from its beginning at Saint-Denis Abbey (*c.* 1140; *see* SAINT-DENIS ABBEY, §I, 2) until the reconstruction of Chartres Cathedral (begun after 1194; *see* CHARTRES, §I, 1). The Early Gothic style was at first largely confined to the areas in and around Paris and those under royal control, but generally the style spread without respect for political boundaries, having quickly lost its initial Parisian association with the Capetian monarchs. Areas contiguous to the royal domain, such as Normandy and Champagne, were the first to benefit from the structural and spatial changes. The first Gothic buildings in England, Spain and Germany are described as 'Early Gothic', but the practice of adopting stylistic features while rejecting structural innovation indicates that in these countries the main connotations of the term should be chronological. Only with the cathedrals of Wells (*c.* 1185) and Lincoln (from 1192) were new, original and inventive stylistic and structural solutions in the Gothic style created outside French lands.

Recognition and acceptance of the east end of Saint-Denis as the first Gothic structure date from the early 19th century, with the first attempts to establish the sequence of developments following in the second half of the century. Much scholarly effort has been spent in trying to work out chronological and stylistic relationships between buildings, not always with acceptable results. Owing to the lack of documentation and the vagaries of comparative archaeology, attempts to establish sequences and interrelationships continue. Various approaches have been proposed as the means of analysing and grouping Early Gothic churches into a coherent pattern of development based on the organic model of growth; that is, from its beginnings through a period of experiment, growth and progress to the maturity of the classic phase (*see* HIGH GOTHIC). Most of the suggested approaches are conveniently analysed by Frankl; such deterministic models have been almost universally established from a backward perspective that, consciously or unconsciously, could be manipulated to fit the author's approach.

The danger lies, on the one hand, in formulating too strict a sense of the lines of development and, on the other, in fragmenting the material into lists of structural and design features that lose sight of the essential spatial character. Each structure is an entity with its individual problems and solutions. The development of the Gothic style has been analysed in terms of specific elements: round or pointed arches, rib vaults, tribune galleries, wall passages and triforia, flying buttresses, elevations and plans. More important than such constructional features, which can also be traced in Romanesque architecture, was the change in the way builders worked within their architectural vocabularies.

Before Saint-Denis Abbey, builders generally simply borrowed features, more or less unchanged, from other building projects. In the generations that followed Saint-Denis Abbey, when builders borrowed elements, they increasingly integrated them into the total design. More than any individual elements, it is this difference in approach as well as the increasingly comprehensive design sense, together with the unified architectural space in which all the parts are subsumed within the effect of the whole, that set Early Gothic apart from Romanesque. The change occurred, however, not as an absolute solution but as a series of experiments; indeed, designs were often reformulated and modified while construction was in progress.

The most successful attempt at a synthesis of formal analysis (style), structural and historical evidence is that by Bony (1983). In arguing that Early Gothic must be seen not from the present but from the moment of generation—that the creative process must be relived as it happened, as a series of distinct and unforeseeable events—he avoids the organic model but still views and organizes related experiments and achievements as systems. His systems are not mutually exclusive: many buildings show the characteristics of several systems. The most important conclusions to be drawn from Bony's argument are that the period is one of rapid change based on wide-ranging experiment; experiments suggest multiple directions that have nothing to do with 20th-century concepts of progress; builders were not working in isolation but were familiar with the many projects under construction, and information was freely and rapidly exchanged; and experiments were tested by actual construction. Branner (1961) had already described the period as filled with an almost bewildering number of experiments. Work since that time has not only confirmed the validity of his statement but suggested that there was even more experimentation than Branner believed, to the extent that it has called into question the validity of attempts at synthesis. There are as many directions and trends as there are buildings.

The formal sensitivities of Bony should ideally be balanced by Kimpel and Suckale's social-history approach, which stresses the importance of liturgy and of seeing cathedral construction as a social process. But the result should resist the temptation to impose order on the large body of evidence that survives. Here the material will be examined within decades, an obviously imposed system that serves as a constant reminder of its artificial limits, and to elucidate broad changes in thinking and the conceptualization of buildings as it can be understood from them.

In the new two-level chevet at Saint-Denis, dedicated in 1144, medieval architecture became for the first time something other than the additive sum of a series of parts or sequence of units. The second builder faced the challenge of fusing separate but contiguous units into a single spatial entity. The success of the east end lies in the creation and direct expression of a visual logic in the arrangement of every architectural element and a subordination of individual elements to this unified space. In the decade or so following its dedication a number of builders responded to it in a variety of ways, mostly attempting to 'copy' the building as they understood it or borrowing elements in a rather random fashion—as happened even at Sens Cathedral (see SENS, §1(i)), the other important achievement of this period, where the many small changes in design made during construction were all 'responses' to Saint-Denis. Sens differs most from Saint-Denis in the large size and ambitious scale of its volumes and in the absence of Dionysian visual logic in the aisles and ambulatory. That visual logic is explored in varying degrees in other buildings started in the decade 1145–55, such as the cathedrals of Senlis and Noyon and the new chevet of the abbey church of St Germain-des-Prés in Paris.

The second decade of Early Gothic (1155–65) is characterized by experiments in both size and scale, as well as the creation and application of the system of visual logic termed the 'Early Gothic grid' (Bony, 1983). Chief among the surviving buildings are the cathedrals of Paris and Laon, four-storey elevations that achieve both real and apparent height; but equally significant were the massive cathedrals (both destr.) of Cambrai and Arras, in which many novel effects of design were explored. This was also the decade of increasing adaptation of Romanesque structural features to the new vocabulary (Branner). Advanced thinking in the following decade (c. 1165–c. 1175) is characterized by daring experiments in voiding the wall with superposed passages and arcade screens, as in the transept arms of Noyon Cathedral, the transept chapels at Laon and the interior of the façade of St Remi at Reims.

All these experiments were continued in the period c. 1175–c. 1185 but usually on a more modest scale than at Paris or Cambrai, both of which had an internal height of more than 30 m. The first systematic application of the flying buttress, fully realized at the lower level of the nave elevation (c. 1175) at Notre-Dame, Paris, had a profound impact on builders and was quickly incorporated into, for example, the nave of Mantes Cathedral, the chevet of St Remi at Reims and Canterbury Cathedral. The evidence suggests that it was added later to buildings already under construction, such as the nave at Laon Cathedral. So great was the impact of the flying buttress that, to all intents and purposes, other structural experiments ceased. The decade c. 1185–95 was again dominated by the flying buttress; the vocabulary of design solutions was broadened and made ever more complex through the sheer number of buildings, large and small, that were undertaken, but no major new features were introduced.

With the rebuilding of the cathedrals of Chartres, begun after the fire of 1194, and of Bourges (c. 1195), the lines of experiment reached two very different but equally important ends. In 1957 Bony characterized Chartres as 'a radical simplification' and rethinking of the elements of design and construction. Following this line of thought, Bourges becomes the ultimate complication, with its extraordinary pyramidal scheme achieving both a sense of lateral spaciousness and vertical amplitude. Together with such other experiments of the 1190s as Soissons and Lausanne cathedrals, among others, Bourges, Chartres and even Reims Cathedral, begun after the fire of 1208, can all be seen as resulting from the spatial and structural experiments beginning with Saint-Denis and Sens.

BIBLIOGRAPHY

J. Bony: 'The Resistance to Chartres in Early Thirteenth-century Architecture', *J. Brit. Archaeol. Assoc.*, 3rd ser., xx–xxi (1957–8), pp. 35–52

P. Frankl: *The Gothic: Literary Sources and Interpretations through Eight Centuries* (Princeton, 1960)

R. Branner: 'Gothic Architecture, 1160–1180, and its Romanesque Sources', *Studies in Western Art: Acts of the Twentieth International Congress of the History of Art: New York, 1961*, i, pp. 92–104

J. Bony: *French Gothic Architecture of the Twelfth and Thirteenth Centuries* (Berkeley, 1983)

D. Kimpel and R. Suckale: *Die gotische Architektur in Frankreich, 1130–1270* (Munich, 1985)

C. Wilson: *The Gothic Cathedral* (London, 1990)

C. Radding and W. Clark: *Medieval Architecture, Medieval Learning: Builders and Masters in the Age of Romanesque and Gothic* (New Haven, 1992)

WILLIAM W. CLARK

Early Man Shelter. *See under* QUINKAN GALLERIES.

Earth [Serbo-Croat Zemlja] **group.** Croatian group of artists, architects and intellectuals active in Zagreb from 1929 to 1935. The original group included the painters Krsto Hegedušić, Omer Mujadžić (1903–91), Kamilo Ružička (1898–1972), Ivan Tabaković (1898–1977) and Oton Postružnik (1900–78); the sculptors Antun Augustinčić (1900–79) and Frano Kršinić; and the architect Drago Ibler. They aimed to defend their artistic independence against foreign influences such as Impressionism or Neo-classicism and against dilettantism and Art for Art's Sake. They maintained that art should mirror the social milieu from which it springs and should meet contemporary needs, hence their emphasis on the popularization of art, both at home and abroad. In spite of its ideologically heterogeneous membership, the group was Marxist in orientation but never espoused Socialist Realism.

Two additional artists, Vinko Grdan (1900–80) and Leo Junek (b 1899), participated in the first Land group exhibition in November 1929 at Salon Ullrich in Zagreb. The group's manifesto, printed in the catalogue, emphasized the members' belief that the artist cannot evade social developments or remain outside the collective body, for art and life are one. Ideological conflicts arose the following year, however, and some artists left the group. The second exhibition, held in February–March 1931 at Galerie Billiet, Paris, included some guest artists. The exhibition was officially acknowledged, which prompted group members, as enemies of bourgeois art, to object that their revolutionary aims were being compromised.

For the group's third show, in September 1931 at the Art Pavilion in Zagreb, guest architects, designers and the naive painters from Hlebine were invited to exhibit, in the belief that various artistic approaches should be combined in a sort of synthesis. In 1932 more members left the group on ideological grounds while other artists joined: Đuro Tiljak (1895–1955), the architect Lavoslav Horvat (1901–89), Marijan Detoni (1905–81), Edo Kovačević (1906–93), the architect Mladen Kauzlarić, the architect Stjepan Planić, Vanja Radauš (1906–75), Kamilo Tompa (1903–89) and Željko Hegedušić (b 1906). The group came under strong criticism for its Marxist stance when the official political line favoured Fascism, and the eighth exhibition, which opened in 1935 at the Art Pavilion, was closed by the police on the first day.

BIBLIOGRAPHY
J. Depolo: 'Zemlja, 1929–35', *Nadrealizam: Socialna utmetnost* [Surrealism: social art] (exh. cat., Belgrade, Mus. Contemp. A., 1969)
JURE MIKUŽ

Earthworks. *See* LAND ART.

Easel. Stand or rest for a painting during its execution. Some such device is a practical necessity whenever a portable or self-supporting painting is made, hence the term EASEL PAINTING. The most widely used form of easel consists of a rigid frame, made from two front legs, slightly splayed and joined by one or more crossbars; a third hind leg hinges backwards, and the whole forms a stable tripod structure. The front legs are fitted with pegs on which rests the bottom of the painting or a narrow shelf that holds the painting. A series of evenly spaced holes in both front legs allows the pegs to be moved, enabling the easel to accommodate paintings of different sizes.

An object depicted in an ancient Egyptian relief in the tomb of the vizier Mereruka at Saqqara, dating from the Old Kingdom (*c.* 2575–*c.* 2150 BC; *see* EGYPT, ANCIENT, §II) has been interpreted as the earliest form of easel. The *machina* referred to by Pliny in connection with Apelles is also assumed to have been an easel. In the Middle Ages a desk or lectern may have been used to support a painting, but, with the growth of painting on panels and canvases, the easel assumed greater importance from the Renaissance. It was generally a variation on the simple three-legged trestle, as depicted in the late 15th-century illumination *Zeuxis Painting Girls in his Studio* (Ghent, Bib. Rijksuniv.) and in *St Luke Painting the Virgin and Child* (*c.* 1513; London, N.G.) by the school of Quinten Metsys. It was also illustrated by Rembrandt in the *Painter in his Studio* (*c.* 1629; Boston, MA, Mus. F.A.; *see* REMBRANDT, fig. 12), and an 18th-century example appears in William Hogarth's self-portrait *Hogarth Painting the Comic Muse* (*c.* 1757; London, N.P.G.; see fig.). An ornate American easel of this type (*c.* 1805–15; Boston, MA, Mus. F.A.) was possibly intended for the display of finished work. Later examples are shown in Henri Fantin-Latour's *Studio in the Batignolles Quarter* (1870; Paris, Louvre) and in the background of a photograph of *Renoir at Work* (1914; Rewald, p. 584).

During the 18th century portable and collapsible easels, as shown in the aquatint *Artist Travelling in Wales* (1799; London, BM) by Thomas Rowlandson, were developed; these were favoured by itinerant painters and by the increasing number of landscape and amateur painters who worked out of doors. Henry Raeburn also owned an easel of this type (Edinburgh, Royal Scot. Acad.). Studio easels, however, became more complicated and imposing and were intended to impress as well as perform; Joshua Reynolds's oblong framed mahogany easel (London, RA) illustrates this tendency.

By the 19th century the studio easel had evolved a definite form—upright on two legs, rising from heavy feet or a base, often on casters, with the painting resting on a grooved ledge that could be raised or lowered mechanically. Large canvases could be accommodated, even displayed, on such easels, the weighty presence of which,

Easel depicted in *Hogarth Painting the Comic Muse* by William Hogarth, oil on canvas, 451×425 mm, *c.* 1757 (London, National Portrait Gallery)

especially within the increasingly formal, spacious and imposing artists' studios, implied professionalism. A moderately sized example belonging to Eugène Delacroix (Paris, Mus. Delacroix) survives, although a more robust example is depicted in William Powell Frith's *Self-portrait* (1867; Bodelwyddan Castle). A photograph (Paris, Col. H. Roger-Viollet) of Monet's studio in 1920 shows a towering example, and, in comparison, the heavy wheeled easels or cradles carrying his huge paintings of *Waterlilies* shown in photographs *c.* 1924–5 (Paris, Col. Durand-Ruel) look merely workmanlike, though they must surely be the greatest manifestation of the studio easel.

The Impressionists' passion for *plein-air* painting led them to favour lightweight sketching easels. These are illustrated in Renoir's *Monet Working in his Garden at Argenteuil* (1873; Hartford, CT, Wadsworth Atheneum; *see* IMPRESSIONISM, fig. 2) and in *Camille Pissaro at Work* (*c.* 1870; priv. col.; *see* Pissarro, exh. cat., ACGB, 1980, no. 322) by Ludovic Piette. Their versatility is clearly demonstrated by Manet's *Monet Working on his Boat in Argenteuil* (1874; Munich, Neue Pin.).

In the 19th century various combinations of easels with stools or paintboxes (*see* PAINTBOX) were also developed, mostly for the convenience of amateur painters, though the easel-topped workbox used by miniature painters was already an established form. The most practical of these, the paintbox easel with a tray of materials at waist height and a canvas carrier above, possibly features as a backpack carried by Paul Cézanne in a photograph (*c.* 1874; see Rewald, p. 296) of him on his way to work near Pontoise and even earlier in Gustave Courbet's *The Meeting or Bonjour Monsieur Courbet* (1854; Montpellier, Mus. Fabre).

While the traditional form of easel continues to be used, new styles, such as the narrow upright radial easel, are also widely employed; steel and aluminium, as well as wood, are used for the manufacture of easels and drawing boards. The lightweight sketching easel developed to accommodate the watercolourist often tilts from the centre to hold a drawing board horizontally. (Oil paintings are usually held vertically or near vertically during work.) The artist's donkey, a long, narrow stool with a small easel at one end, which has also proved an enduring design, may have originated in the early academies.

BIBLIOGRAPHY
J. Rewald: *History of Impressionism* (New York, 1966, rev. 4/1973/*R* 1980)
J. Ayres: *The Artist's Craft* (Oxford, 1985)
J. Stephenson: *The Materials and Techniques of Painting* (London, 1989)
——: *Paint with the Impressionists* (London, 1995)

Easel painting. Painting executed on an EASEL or other portable support, i.e. the majority of paintings on canvas and panel. Easel painting became pre-eminent in the 16th century and has remained so. The term implies not only physical aspects but also inherent concepts that are very different from those associated with wall paintings or those intended for a fixed position or an architectural scheme. Easel painting is therefore associated with the increased secular use of art from the 16th century and with the identification of paintings as objects of worth in their own right. The rise of easel painting involved a subtle assertion of the independence of the art of painting and the profession of painter. The status afforded to painting in the writings of, for example, Leonardo da Vinci and Giorgio Vasari reflects these developments and anticipates the increased social and intellectual status of the individual artist.

JONATHAN STEPHENSON

Easter Island [Isla de Pascua; indig. Rapanui]. Polynesian island of *c.* 171 sq. km located in the Pacific Ocean 3600 km west of the Chilean coast, 3500 km from Tahiti and over 1500 km from the nearest inhabited island, Pitcairn. The people of Easter Island call themselves, their language and their island, Rapanui. Easter Island has been part of Chile since 1888. The island was settled by people from the Marquesas Islands probably in the early centuries AD. The size of the population is uncertain but stood at about 2200 at the end of the 20th century. Of these about a third are from mainland Chile. The art forms of Easter Island range from huge stone sculptures to portable paperbark figures and wood-carvings. The island is also well known for its petroglyphs and has had a thriving art industry in the 20th century. Traditional body decoration consisted of tattoo and body painting and used some of the same designs found on the petroglyphs. The entire bodies of Easter Island men were covered in tattoos for which a natural blue powder was used. The process could take two years to complete. Women, especially those of high rank, were also tattooed (Loti). Tattooing has had only limited appeal to modern Easter Islanders, but body painting has continued to be used extensively for tourist shows and during competitive exhibitions at the annual Rapanui Week.

1. Monumental stone sculpture. 2. Rock art. 3. Portable art. 4. Modern art.

1. MONUMENTAL STONE SCULPTURE. The huge figures (*moai*) carved from soft volcanic tuff are the best-known works of Easter Island art. They have come to symbolize not only Easter Island itself but also the mystery, exoticism and grandeur that the South Pacific often has for people in the outside world. In general the figures are stereotypical in execution. The largest, known as Te Pito te Kura, would have been *c.* 9.8 m high when mounted on its ceremonial platform (*ahu*) and is estimated to weigh *c.* 82 tonnes. Typically, a *moai* consists of a trunk, carved, inset arms and an angular head, although there are variant forms to which some scholars assign an earlier date of production; these are often carved from a rougher and usually local material with eyes that are typically large in proportion to the rest of the figure. During initial excavations under Thor Heyerdahl, a kneeling *moai* was uncovered on the slopes of the main site of *moai* manufacture; Heyerdahl believes this figure shows signs of being an early production (Heyerdahl and Ferdon, 1961).

The more typical *moai* represented known ancestors, by whose names they were identified. They were carved from the yellowish-grey tuff rock that was found in a single quarry at the site of the extinct volcano Rano Raraku, in the south-eastern part of the island. From there, they were transported up to 20 km to be erected on ceremonial platforms (*ahus*). At some later stage, topknots (*pukaos*) made of red scoria (lava with steam holes) originating from another extinct volcano, Puna Pau, were added. In all, perhaps 800–1000 statues were begun, of which *c.* 150 were never completed or transported. Some platforms had no figures, some carried one or two: Ahu Tongariki (destr. by a tidal wave in 1960) carried some fifteen figures. Most archaeologists believe that the size and number of *moai* reflected the status claimed by the group erecting the monument (Bahn and Flenley). As well as the added topknot, many of the statues have sockets designed to hold eyes and were probably painted with earth pigments. Even the stones in the platforms were chosen for their colour and shape and so arranged. One particularly intricately carved and well-preserved *moai* (see fig. 1), which owes its condition to the fact that, exceptionally, it is carved from very hard basalt, was located originally in one of the drystone houses at Orongo, a village on the south-west of the island that was the centre of the island-wide birdman cult. Orongo's many monuments escaped the destruction of Easter Island's intertribal wars because it was sacred to all the islanders. The *moai* was removed from its cave in 1868, since when it has been on display in London under the name Hoa Haka Nana Ia. The figure is well preserved (the back especially, see Van Tilburg, pl. 4), never having been exposed to the eroding winds and rain that have affected the island's other figures. The techniques used in carving the stones and the methods by which they were erected and raised on to their platforms are now fairly well understood (e.g. Mulloy). It is still unclear, however, how they were moved from the quarry to the sites they occupied.

The megalithic style of Easter Island probably developed slowly over time (Mulloy and Figueroa). While exact

designs. Flat surfaces are crowded with superimposed figures that sometimes extend to the edge of the available surface. Some are realistic portrayals of fish and squid, others are of fantastic figures. One design that seems to have had cultic associations in the late prehistoric period (i.e. before 1722 when Europeans first arrived) is a simple, round face with a mouth and two eyes, thought to represent the god Make-make. At Orongo there are a number of carvings of birdmen (*tangata manu*), which commemorated the annual ceremony to select the king of the island. This ceremony seems to have been part of an attempt to restore order during the period of violence that arose after the 15th century. The figures follow set forms, and more than 150 cover the rocks around the site (Drake).

Rock paintings were executed in caves and overhangs with earth pigments. The most accessible and colourful are in the coastal cave of Ana Kai Tangata. Other smaller caves are decorated with pigmented representations, not unlike the petroglyphs. (*See also* PACIFIC ISLANDS, §II, 5(ii).)

3. PORTABLE ART. The Easter Island art forms best represented in museum collections are paperbark figures and wood-carvings. In the period between 1722 and the coming of slavers from Peru between 1858 and 1870, hundreds of such small artefacts were traded to outsiders, including, later, some models of the *moai*. One type is constructed from the bark of the paper-mulberry tree, often over a frame or stuffed to give the desired shape. The function of these small figures is not clear; larger figures featured in public ceremonies, but none has survived. The carved, wood figures from Easter Island that make up the bulk of the artefacts transported to foreign museums and galleries have been classified into ten groups (Heyerdahl, 1976). The most common type, the gruesome *moai kava-kava*, represents an emaciated figure with protruding ribs (*kava-kava*; see fig. 2). Much rarer is the flatter female figure, *moai papa*, characterized by having hands carved from the figure's trunk pointing to her breast and pudenda. Simple, rounded figures of humans, which seem to demonstrate less advanced carving skills, also exist. Some figures resemble those in the petroglyphs, including the Orongo-inspired birdman or *tangata manu*. The *moko* form represents a lizard, with human ribs and backbone and a sensuous shape. It has continued to be used in the historic period in erotic dances. The other five types of carving were employed for ceremonial purposes. Some, for example the *ao* and *rapa* dance paddles, incorporated human forms, while short-handled (*ua*) and long-handled (*paoa*) clubs were carved with human or animal heads on the butts, as were the orb of office (*tahonga*) and chiefly breast plate (*rei miro*). The earlier wood artefacts were made from the virtually extinct native trees *sophora toromiro* or *thespesia populnea* (*mako'i*). The islanders continue to make fine copies and contemporary interpretations of traditional designs, usually from *melia azederach* (*mirotahiti*), a timber which, as the name suggests, was introduced from Tahiti.

Carvings known as *kohau rongo-rongo* constitute one of the most remarkable features of Easter Island prehistory. There are only *c.* 20 surviving authentic examples. They incorporate a variety of superbly carved, very detailed

1. Easter Island monumental sculpture (*moai*), stone, h. 2.95 m, from Orongo (London, British Museum)

dates for the statues have not been settled, most scholars regard *c.* AD 1000 as a starting-point for production, with *c.* AD 1500 as the time of the last work. This period of production was followed by several centuries of internecine warfare accompanied by the destruction of the statues and some of their platforms. The *moai* were often decapitated by being toppled on to a large stone placed at the point where the neck would hit the ground (Englert).

2. ROCK ART. Petroglyphs can only rarely be found on the *moai* themselves; most are on the flat rock outcrops around the island and, except for those on *moai* and at Orongo, are rarely found in public places. The petroglyphs vary in size and are characterized by individual meandering

in this was a feature of European contact from as early as the 18th century. Certainly by the late 19th century the trade was overt and intentional, and in the 20th century Easter Islanders fulfilled commissions by producing, with varying degrees of skill and artistry, copies of pieces illustrated in photographs and drawings. The Spanish translation of a highly illustrated book on Easter Island (Chauvet) became a reference work for late 20th-century wood-carvers, as did Thor Heyerdahl's *The Art of Easter Island*.

On the whole, Easter Island tourist art is of high quality and expertly done. Traditional motifs have been applied with great inventiveness to models of the stone figures and their platforms as well as to such mundane items as ashtrays (Seaver). Some of these figures, particularly stone ones, have been passed off as genuine antiques. Most male Easter Islanders believe they can carve, but only a few individuals have the necessary expertise. The Atan family are renowned as especially gifted carvers, and many of the Tuki family have also done fine work, including full-scale replicas of *moai* for display overseas. There have been no professional women carvers.

Fine art in the European tradition has not been a major feature of Easter Island culture. One artist, Melchor Huki Tekena (1935–80), produced work in primary colours and with bold motifs that drew on the culture of Easter Island. He was never able to devote his full attention to his painting and did not produce work for sale. Only a dozen or so of his canvases survive, mostly in private collections in Chile. His cousins distinguished themselves as innovative sculptors in the late 20th century. They used the natural grain and shape of wood to produce sensuous, abstract forms: Joel Huki Atan (*b* 1949) worked in the south of France, while his brothers, Carlos Huki Atan (*b* 1945) and Pedro Huki Atan (*b* 1954), were based in Tahiti.

BIBLIOGRAPHY
K. Routledge: *The Mystery of Easter Island* (London, 1919)
Stephen Chauvet: *L'Ile de Pâques et ses mystères* (Paris, 1935; Sp. trans., Santiago, 1946)
A. Metraux: *Ethnology of Easter Island*, Bishop Mus. Bull., clx (Honolulu, 1940/*R* 1971)
T. Barthel: *Grundlagen zur Entzifferung der Osterinselschrift* (Hamburg, 1958)
T. Heyerdahl and E. N. Ferdon, eds: *The Archaeology of Easter Island*, (1961), i of *Reports of the Norwegian Archaeological Expedition to Easter Island and the East Pacific* (Stockholm, 1961–5)
W. Mulloy: 'A Speculative Reconstruction of Techniques of Carving, Transporting and Erecting Easter Island Statues', *Archaeol. & Phys. Anthropol. Oceania*, v/1 (1970), pp. 1–23
S. Englert: *La tierra de Hotu Matu'a* (Santiago, 1974)
T. Heyerdahl: *The Art of Easter Island* (New York, 1975/*R* London, 1976)
W. Mulloy and G. Figueroa: *The A Kivi–Vai Teka Complex and its Relationship to Easter Island Architectural Prehistory*, Asian and Pacific Archaeology Series, viii (Manoa, 1978)
G. McCall: *Rapanui: Tradition and Survival on Easter Island* (Sydney and Honolulu, 1980, rev. 1994)
Rapa Nui J. (1987–)
P. Loti: *L'Ile de Pâques: Journal d'un aspirant de La Flore* (Paris, 1988)
J. Seaver: *An Ethnology of Wood Carving: Continuity in Cultural Transformations on Rapa Nui* (diss., Los Angeles, UCLA, 1988)
T. Heyerdahl: *Easter Island: The Mystery Solved* (London, 1989)
1500 Jahre Kultur der Osterinsel: Schätze aus dem Land des Hotu Matua (exh. cat., ed. A. von Bothmer-Plates, H. M. Esen-Baur and D. F. Sauer; Frankfurt am Main, Natmus. Senckenberg, 1989)
H. M. Esen-Baur, ed.: *State and Perspectives of Scientific Research in Easter Island Culture* (Frankfurt, 1990)

2. Easter Island figure (*moai kava-kava*), wood, h. 470 mm (London, British Museum)

figures on wooden tablets or boards and occasionally staffs that are believed to be part of a writing system. *Rongo-rongo* have been subjected to intense study but have yet to be deciphered (see, for example, Barthel).

4. MODERN ART. By the late 20th century tourism, out-migration, in-migration from Chile and inter-marriage had led to the culture of Easter Island becoming international and diverse. Late 20th-century art has either been intended for the tourist trade or has taken its inspiration from European approaches to painting, drawing and sculpture, sometimes with distinctive local motifs. The volume of portable wood art produced suggests that trade

L'Ile de Pâques: Une Enigme? (exh. cat., ed. A. von Bothmer-Plates and others; Brussels, Musées Royaux A. & Hist., 1990)

F. Forment: *Les Figures moai kavakava de l'île de Pâques*, Working Papers in Ethnic Art, v (Ghent, 1991)

P. Bahn and J. Flenley: *Easter Island, Earth Island: A Message from our Past for the Future of our Planet* (London, 1992)

——: *Easter Island, Earth Island* (London and New York, 1992)

A. Drake: *Easter Island: The Ceremonial Centre of Orongo* (Old Bridge, 1992)

G. Lee: 'Easter Island Rock Art: Symbols of Power, Prayers to the Gods', *Mnmt Archaeol.*, 17 (Los Angeles, 1992)

J. A. Van Tilburg: *HMS Topaze on Easter Island: Hoa Hakananai'a and Five Other Museum Sculptures in Archaeological Context*, BM Occas. Pap., 73 (London, 1992)

S. R. Fischer, ed.: *Easter Island Studies*, Oxbow Monograph, 32 (Oxford, 1993)

GRANT McCALL

Eastern and central Costa Rica, Pre-Columbian. Culture area of the Isthmian region of Latin America, which is more broadly classed by archaeologists as part of the Intermediate area (*see* SOUTH AMERICA, PRE-COLUMBIAN, §II). It comprises the Atlantic watershed and central highlands areas of Costa Rica, from the Caribbean Sea to the Pacific Ocean and from the Nicaraguan to the Panamanian border. Environments include the low coastal wetlands of the Caribbean and the Pacific drylands, numerous river valleys and plateaus, and an almost continuous chain of mountains and volcanoes running north–south. Despite a diversity of ecological niches, the archaeological remains of the region are similar enough to be considered as a single cultural group. The prehistoric archaeological record begins *c.* 1000 BC, with radiocarbon dates up to *c.* AD 1500. Results of excavations in the Reventazon Valley were published in 1893, but the most important late 19th-century works are Carl V. Hartman's excavations of cemeteries in the Cartago Valley and in the Linea Vieja region of the Atlantic watershed, especially at Las Mercedes. More recent work by Michael Snarskis, Oscar Fonseca Zamora and others has concentrated in the same areas. No stone architecture is known from this region, but several sites included earth-filled plazas, paved causeways, house foundations, aqueducts and stairways. Among these are Las Mercedes and GUAYABO DE TURRIALBA, both dated after *c.* AD 1000. Most of Hartman's finds are in the Etnografiska Museet, Stockholm; other major collections of stonework and pottery are in the Museum of the American Indian, Heye Foundation, in the American Museum of Natural History, and in the Brooklyn Museum, all New York; in the Carnegie Museum of Natural History, Pittsburgh; and in the Museo Nacional de Costa Rica, San José.

1. POTTERY. The earliest decorated pottery comprises monochrome and zoned bichrome vessels of brown or buff clay with red slips and engraved, incised or stamped geometric patterns, part of the tradition of 'scarified' wares found from northern Costa Rica to central Panama. Appliquéd and modelled pellets and reptilian, avian and other zoomorphic motifs began to be added before AD 500. Vessel shapes were commonly bowls, plates and jars with flat or rounded bases, some with loop legs and effigy heads. Earlier types included effigy vessels and tripod vessels with solid animal effigy supports. Recognizable animals include birds, turtles, frogs, monkeys, reptiles

and felines. Other clay objects from early tombs include small, hollow human and animal shapes known as Santa Clara figurines. They represent warriors with trophy heads and axes, flute players, bound prisoners and standing male images wearing tiered, feathered headdresses and saurian, avian or feline masks (*see* SOUTH AMERICA, PRE-COLUMBIAN, §II, 5(i)). While they appear in both domestic and ceremonial attitudes, many may have been rattles. There are also clay whistles, ocarinas and flutes; stamps, seals and snuff tubes or pipes. Some tombs held élite burials, and it seems likely that these figurines were intended to serve a ritual purpose.

The cultures of the Atlantic watershed–central highlands zone never produced polychrome ceramics of a quality or quantity to compare to those of the GRAN NICOYA cultures to the north-west. Instead, some of the finest ceramics are tall, graceful tripod vases called Curridabat ware, often elaborately decorated with modelled zoomorphic motifs of reptiles, birds and various mammals similar to Chiriquí imagery to the south-east. Some have combinations of human and animal features, but the most important motif is an alligator or iguana, distinguishable by its scutes. Vessels range from near miniatures to over 300 mm in height. Shapes are most commonly globular jars with long necks, called *floreros*, with plain, slipped or burnished surfaces. Most examples appear to have been 'ritually killed' during the burial ceremonies by punching holes through the base or by breaking the tripod supports.

2. SCULPTURE. Numerous stone sculptures, many of volcanic stone, from this region form two basic categories: figural images; and ceremonial objects, which may also have been functional. Earlier stone objects, such as *mano*s (grinders), mullers and maceheads, were primarily functional. From about the 1st century AD, however, stone objects began to be more elaborately carved, including human images, *metate*s (grinding stones), altars, stools and grave markers. Among the human images are male, female and hermaphroditic figures. Males represent warriors, prisoners, masked men or deities (*see* SOUTH AMERICA, PRE-COLUMBIAN, fig. 11). They stand full-length with their hands at their sides, overhead, on the torso or asymmetrically placed. In addition to such poses female images, possibly fertility figures, sometimes hold their breasts. Another group comprises seated male figures called 'sukias' (medicine men or shamans). These small stone figures sit on their buttocks with knees flexed and drawn toward the chest, arms extended but resting on the knees and holding a thin cylindrical object like a flute or cigar in one or both hands (*see* SOUTH AMERICA, PRE-COLUMBIAN, fig. 12). The hundreds of examples vary little in size (h. *c.* 100–200 mm) and may have been mass-produced. Still another group comprises independent heads, thought to be portrait heads of chiefs and possibly representing the deceased person's spirit or soul, or linked with the trophy-head cult and representing decapitated enemies. The facial and bodily characteristics of these images indicate a developmental sequence. Early figures are small masked males related to the Santa Clara ceramic figurines and to the masked male figures of larger ceremonial altars (see below). Eyes range from rectangular to oval; hips from full shapely, round and fleshy to broad but shapeless;

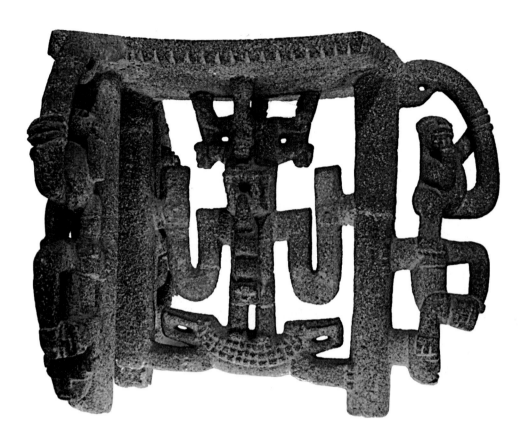

1. Eastern and central Costa Rican sculpture, 'flying panel' *metate* or 'altar', volcanic stone, h. 755 mm, first half of the 1st millennium AD (San José, Museo Nacional de Costa Rica)

legs from heavy and tapered, with clearly delineated knees and ankles, to less naturalistic thick columnar shapes. At a later stage the imagery seems to have changed from primarily zoomorphic or masked figures to truly human representations.

Dating of the images is difficult. Most of the free-standing images are surface finds or objects purchased for museum collections. Only a few have been excavated, including four standing images and one carved head from Chircot and Orosi in the central highlands (for illustrations see Hartman), and several free-standing figures from Las Mercedes and a few other sites in the Atlantic watershed. Ceramics associated with these indicate that most date *c.* AD 1000–1500. Some of the sites where such images were found were still occupied when the Spaniards arrived.

The most common form of functional stone object is the *metate*. Plain three-legged and four-legged varieties are known from throughout the Isthmian region. Crude oval and rectangular examples, with short heavy legs and trough-shaped plates, found at Severo Ledesma along with jade fragments, have been radiocarbon dated *c.* AD 345. Similar examples are known from central highland sites. Another early type is a tripod *metate* with cylindrical or nearly cylindrical legs, usually with a round or oblong plate surrounded by a low raised and notched rim. The grinding

plates are as long as 600 mm, but all known examples are less than 200 mm high. Examples found in archaeological contexts have been dated *c.* AD 144–279, and those from Tibas and La Fabrica de Grecia were found with human burials. This type may be the earliest 'special purpose' *metate*: sculptured bands encircling the plate may be highly stylized human heads, possibly symbolizing the heads of prisoners taken by warriors as trophies of war. From such *metate*s more elaborate types were developed, with notched edges and trophy heads, some supported by atlantean or caryatid-like figures (*see* SOUTH AMERICA, PRE-COLUMBIAN, fig. 13), although such supports are more commonly found at Panamanian sites. Other examples have sculptured motifs in the form of zoomorphic or geometric shapes on the undersides of the plates. A sub-group called 'marimba' *metate*s have lineal appendages centred or radiating from the legs to the centres of their rectangular or circular plates, which range from 310 to 990 mm in diameter or length and from 160 to 260 mm in height.

The most elaborate and complex Isthmian region stone sculptures are called 'flying panel' *metate*s or 'altars' (see fig. 1 and SOUTH AMERICA, PRE-COLUMBIAN, fig. 10). These range from heavy, massive examples to lacy, baroque, intricately carved objects. They vary in size from 340 to 1200 mm in length and from 170 to *c.* 750 mm in height. While most are rectangular, a few have a circular or nearly circular plate. All are tripods, but some have figural or cylindrical legs with figures appended. Regardless of size or shape, the grinding plate of the altar has a low rim forming a continuous series of notches or stylized heads. Beneath the grinding plate there is a 'flying panel', usually an L-shaped support attached on one end to a leg and on the other to the underside of the plate. The most bizarre of these rigidly symmetrical designs have a single large central figure attended by two smaller figures of lesser importance. Central figures include humans wearing enormous masks, long-beaked birds, owls, crocodiles and jaguars; leg adornments include long-beaked birds, owls, monkeys, jaguars, crocodiles and humans, all paralleled on contemporary ceramics. Such iconography is best explained by reference to mythology. Oval tetrapod grinding stones (possibly tables or stools) were also made in the Atlantic watershed–central highlands region. These have slightly curved or concave plates with ornamented rims ranging from fringe-like textile decoration to trophy heads. Legs are cylindrical or conical, human or simian. Some are related to the 'flying panel' *metate*s/altars, as their legs are joined by horizontal bars with small monkey figures.

Another group of stone sculptures comprises circular stands or stools, with drum bases or with atlantean figures standing on an annular base. Drum-base examples range from monolithic cylindrical objects, with solid bases, to those with hollow pedestal bases with vertical slits. On the edge of the lower rim all have trophy heads or feline animals, which vary from highly abstract to extremely realistic. Some appear related to grave slabs with similar jaguar imagery of small feline figures carved in relief and in the round. Atlantean figures on annular-base stands are simian, human or feline. As in drum-base examples, jaguar trophy heads surround the plates. A few such stools are also known from the Gran Chiriquí region. The largest and most unusual volcanic stone objects are oval to rectangular slabs, variously referred to as tables, sacrificial slabs or altars (see fig. 2). These may have functioned as funeral biers and grave markers. Seventeen examples from Las Mercedes (New York, Brooklyn Mus. and New York, Amer. Mus. Nat. Hist.) range from 740 mm to 1100 mm in length. Their carved iconography is clearly related to all the groups previously described and includes relief or free-standing humans, felines and, most commonly, composite anthropomorphic figures with human bodies and feline or crocodilian faces and heads. On several examples, the edges are carved with low-relief, triangular trophy heads with highly stylized, angular features.

The most common ceremonial stone sculptures are jaguar and related effigy *metate*s (for illustration *see* VER-AGUAS), known from Las Mercedes, Orosi, Chircot, Santiago and Anita Grande. All date between *c.* AD 500 and 1500, although the more elaborately decorated examples are probably later than *c.* AD 1000. They have rectangular or oval, flat or curved plates, or bowl-like forms replacing an animal torso, supported on four legs. The earliest appear to be the smallest, most naturalistic and poorly carved. Their rounded, fleshy, realistic legs show anatomical structures. Later examples are larger and less naturalistic, although more carefully carved and finished, and more streamlined and stylized. The head

2. Eastern and central Costa Rican sculpture, carved slab, possibly a grave marker, volcanic stone, h. 740 mm, from Las Mercedes (New York, American Museum of Natural History)

projects from one end of the grinding plate, and most have long curved tails rising from the grinding plate and attached to a hind leg. Many are covered with incised diagonal and diamond interlace, zigzag or guilloche patterns. Some have legs joined by bars supporting monkey images; others have notched rims, trophy heads or small animals attached to the lower edge of the grinding plate.

3. METALWORK AND LAPIDARY ARTS. In general, the jades and gold or gold-alloy objects found in East and central Costa Rica are clearly related to those produced by the other Pre-Columbian cultures of Costa Rica, GRAN CHIRIQUÍ to the south-east and GRAN NICOYA to the

north-west (*see also* SOUTH AMERICA, PRE-COLUMBIAN, §§II, 6(i) and VIII, 5).

BIBLIOGRAPHY
C. V. Hartman: *Archaeological Researches in Costa Rica*, Publications of the Royal Ethnological Museum (Stockholm, 1901)
J. A. Mason: 'Costa Rican Stonework: The Minor C. Keith Collection', *Anthropol. Pap. Amer. Mus. Nat. Hist.*, xxxix/3 (1945) [whole issue]
M. J. Snarskis: *The Archaeology of the Central Atlantic Watershed of Costa Rica* (diss., New York, Columbia U., 1978)
——: 'The Archaeology of Costa Rica', *Between Continents, between Seas: Precolumbian Art of Costa Rica*, ed. E. P. Benson (New York, 1981), pp. 15–84
J. K. Lingen: *Stylistic and Iconographical Study of Lower Central American Stone Sculpture* (diss., Albuquerque, U. NM, 1986)

JOAN K. LINGEN

Easter sepulchre. A temporary structure set up in church to simulate the place of Christ's burial for a symbolic enactment of the Entombment and Resurrection. The Tomb of Christ and the later sacrament house, although also concerned with the bodily presence of Christ, belong to a separate tradition (see below). Special rites for Easter in which some kind of Easter sepulchre played a part are found in some 400 texts from medieval Europe. The earliest description is in the 10th-century English *Regularis Concordia*, according to which a cross wrapped in a linen shroud was placed in the sepulchre on Good Friday and guarded there until Easter Sunday by two or three brethren singing psalms continuously. The cross was removed from the sepulchre by the sacristan before Matins on Easter Sunday. During the service one of the brethren sat quietly by the sepulchre to represent the Angel of the Resurrection, while three others represented the Marys who found the sepulchre empty and announced the Resurrection. In this instance the sepulchre was described as a veil stretched in the form of a circle set beside the vacant part of the altar. This type of Easter sepulchre, a kind of tent, appears in the 12th-century wall paintings in the chancel at St Mary, Kempley (Glos). Both the text and the description in the *Regularis Concordia* remained fairly typical in Europe throughout the Middle Ages. The essential element of the liturgy was the symbolic burial (*Depositio*) and resurrection (*Elevatio*). Sometimes the host took the place of the cross or was 'buried' with it. Despite its early documentation in the *Regularis Concordia*, the dramatic embellishment of impersonation of the Marys and the Angel was relatively rare in England, but common in France and the German states. The sepulchre was normally a temporary structure, perhaps a tabernacle placed on an altar or even just the altar itself. Particularly where drama was involved, a temporary cloth or wooden structure might be placed near by and removed at the end of the Easter period.

A quite separate tradition was the creation of permanent, shrinelike replicas of Christ's tomb in the church of the Holy Sepulchre at Jerusalem. More than 20 examples in the form of tiny buildings have been recorded, dating from the 4th to the 12th centuries (*see* SEPULCHRE CHURCH). Those in St Paul-Serge, Narbonne (4th century), S Petronio, Bologna (5th century), the chapel of St Maurice in Konstanz Cathedral (*c.* 960), the former monastery church at Denkendorf (11th century), the collegiate church of Busdorf at Paderborn (*c.* 1036), Neuvy-Saint-Sépulchre (*c.* 1045), the church of the Holy Cross at Dalby, near Lund (1060; formerly the cathedral), and the Capuchin church at Eichstätt (*c.* 1166) were associated with relics brought from the Holy Land. Their siting was not consistent, some being in crypts or chapels, some outside the church. Some were built explicitly to increase the devotion of the faithful, and indulgences could be granted to pilgrims who visited them. Graves of important ecclesiastics were sited close to a number of the tombs and were believed to derive special spiritual protection and guidance from them. The form of these copies of the Tomb of Christ gradually changed, and by the late 13th century, especially in the upper Rhineland, figured tombs were becoming more common, emphasizing the effigy of Christ rather than the place of his burial, with the three Marys and the Angel of the Resurrection represented around him. A major impetus for this change may have been the growing interest at this period, especially in the Low Countries and Germany, in the feast of Corpus Christi, which finally became established as a major feast in the Church calendar in 1318. New types of monument designed to honour the sacrament, the body of Christ, were devised in response to the new devotions for this feast. These were most common in the Low Countries and Germany and ranged from monstrances and reliquaries to be reserved on altars and carried in processions, to aumbries and tabernacles intended as sacrament shrines, within which the sacrament was continually reserved for masses for the sick and dying and for daily veneration. These sacrament houses were wall-mounted or free-standing and were at the height of their popularity during the 15th century, especially in Westphalia. Some of the free-standing ones, such as those at St Felizitas, Lüdinghausen, SS Peter und Paul, Remagen, and St Lorenz, Nuremberg (for illustration *see* LATE GOTHIC), reached enormous proportions, extending to the roofs of their churches.

The distinctions between the temporary Easter sepulchre, the permanently sited Tomb of Christ and its later development, the sacrament house, are extremely important. While Tombs of Christ could be used as the loci for the *Depositio* and *Elevatio* at Easter, and some, such as those at Aquileia Cathedral in northern Italy, Eichstätt in the Rhineland, the Externsteine at Horn in Westphalia and Strasbourg Cathedral, evidently were, this was not their major function. The Tomb of Christ represented in the church throughout the year the place of burial of his body. It served to recall the Resurrection as a means of extending hope and spiritual guidance to mortals. The Easter sepulchre, on the other hand, was a kind of theatrical effect designed to communicate the events of Easter more clearly and graphically to the faithful. It could be attached to an altar or be free-standing, and from the later 14th century it could even be attached to a tomb, which would thereby gain spiritual enhancement from its proximity. Above all, the Easter sepulchre was a temporary furnishing that was removed at the end of Easter week. Churches could have both a Tomb of Christ and a temporary Easter sepulchre, and a number of instances of this are recorded, for example at Strasbourg Cathedral, Lincoln Cathedral and the parish churches of St Andrew, Horbling (Lincs), and St Gregory, Fledborough (Notts). The Strasbourg Tomb of Christ (mid-14th century; destr.) was a figured tomb, and the effigy of Christ had a cavity in the breast large enough for reception of the Host. The rubrics of the Easter liturgy there, however, call for an Easter sepulchre large enough for five clerics to enter, so presumably it was adapted to its liturgical function at Easter by erecting a screenlike structure around the tomb.   Before the 14th century there was no consistent site in the church for either the copy of the Tomb of Christ or the Easter sepulchre. Sacrament houses, however, were normally situated north of the high altar. They did not necessarily incorporate imagery representing the Resurrection: one of the earliest (late 13th century), at St Martens-Lennik, near Brussels, was carved with a *Calvary*, while the late 14th-century example in St Lorenz, Nuremberg, also had an *Entombment* and numerous images of saints. Some included Christ as the Man of Sorrows, some merely a chalice and Host, but many were without images.

An exceptionally interesting group of monuments surviving in England is related to the tradition of the Tomb of Christ but incorporates elements of the sacrament house. All examples are in eastern England, on the borders between Lincolnshire, Nottinghamshire and Yorkshire, and date from the late 13th century to the mid-14th. The most famous are at Lincoln Cathedral, St Andrew, Heckington, Lincs (*c*. 1330; see fig.), and All Saints, Hawton, Notts. They are situated in the north wall of the chancel near the high altar and usually have a small niche or

Tomb of Christ, St Andrew, Heckington, Lincolnshire, *c.* 1330

aumbry within their structure, surrounded by elaborate sculptures representing events connected with the Resurrection. Like many of the early copies of the Tomb of Christ, all have a founder's tomb in close proximity, often commemorating prominent clerics who had a position in the King's Chancery. They have normally been identified as Easter sepulchres of special importance, owing to their permanence. Their appearance, however, coincides with the increasing importance of the feast of Corpus Christi, when monuments concerned with the body of Christ were undergoing a transformation in the light of their new significance. In their arrangement as elaborate and permanent aumbries to the north of the high altar, and in their association with contemporary sacristies and other liturgical furnishings, they share characteristics with fully fledged sacrament houses. The monument at St Gregory, Fledborough, was not the Easter sepulchre, as a 16th-century will describes that as a temporary structure. It consists of a small wall niche embellished with sculpture representing the three Marys and the Angel of the Resurrection and was referred to in another 16th-century will as 'the Gregorie', recalling the miracle granted St Gregory, whereby the Host was transformed into a bleeding finger to convince one who doubted that it was Christ's body. This significant nomenclature suggests that the Fledborough monument was associated with the Host to the extent that it might have been used as a sacrament house. It is likely that all the monuments in the group shared this function, representing a conflation of the Tomb of Christ and sacrament house traditions at a time of rapid development of sacrament devotion on the Continent. They are very much an exception in Britain, however, as apart from a few 15th-century sacrament houses in the diocese of Aberdeen, Scotland, they never became popular, and celebration of the feast of Corpus Christi took other forms.

During the later 14th century and the 15th, the Easter sepulchre too underwent a transformation in England and assumed properties that had been associated previously with the distinct traditions of the Tomb of Christ and sacrament house. Records indicate that the sepulchre was then invariably sited to the north of the high altar against whatever structure happened to have been placed there. This position became much sought after for mortal, normally secular, burials, and wills frequently stipulated that the tomb should be placed north of the high altar, where the body of Christ was customarily placed on Good Friday. Thus was modified the privileged association that began with the permanent Tomb of Christ and ecclesiastical burials of high status. Easter sepulchres also became highly elaborate, that at St Mary Redcliffe, Bristol, for example, being very large and carved and painted with scenes referring to the Resurrection (destr.). Carvings were common, as were embroidered cloths and other adornments, in some cases transforming the east end of the church at Easter into a scene of splendour. Easter sepulchres suffered the fate of all 'monuments of superstition' in the reign of Edward VI (*reg* 1547–53) and were universally destroyed, being burnt or converted to items of domestic furniture. Only a few have survived, a notable example being at St Michael, Cowthorpe, N. Yorks.

BIBLIOGRAPHY

Regularis Concordia (*c.* 970); ed. in *PL*, cxxxvii (1853), pp. 475–502

A. Heales: 'Easter Sepulchres: Their Object, Nature and History', *Archaeologia*, xli (1869), pp. 263–308

N. C. Brooks: *The Sepulchre of Christ in Art and Liturgy: With Special Reference to the Liturgic Drama* (Urbana, 1921)

G. Bresc-Bautier: 'Les Imitations du Saint-Sépulchre de Jérusalem (IX–XV siècles): Archéologie d'une devotion', *Rev. Hist. Spirit.*, l (1974), pp. 319–42

V. Sekules: 'The Tomb of Christ at Lincoln and the Development of the Sacrament Shrine: Easter Sepulchres Reconsidered', *Medieval Art and Architecture at Lincoln Cathedral: British Archaeological Association Conference Transactions: Lincoln, 1982*, pp. 118–31

P. Sheingorn: *The Easter Sepulchre in England*, Early Drama, Art and Music Reference Series, 5 (Kalamazoo, 1987)

V. Sekules: *The Sculpture and Liturgical Furnishings of Heckington Church and Related Monuments* (diss., U. London, 1990), pp. 69–112

M. Rubin: *Corpus Christi: The Eucharist in Late Medieval Culture* (Cambridge, 1991)

V. SEKULES

Eastlake. English family of artists, museum officials, collectors and writers. (1) Sir Charles Lock Eastlake began his career as a painter before concentrating his interests in connoisseurship and art history. He became first Keeper, then Director of the National Gallery, London, and was President of the Royal Academy. His wife, (2) Lady Eastlake, was a prolific writer on art-historical topics. His nephew, (3) Charles Locke Eastlake, wrote several influential books on design and served as Keeper and Secretary of the National Gallery.

(1) Sir Charles Lock Eastlake (*b* Plymouth, 17 Nov 1793; *d* Pisa, 24 Dec 1865). English painter, museum director, collector and writer. Fourth son of an Admiralty lawyer at Plymouth, he was educated at local grammar schools and then, briefly, at Charterhouse, Surrey. Determined to become a painter, he began work in 1809 as Benjamin Robert Haydon's first pupil and as a student at the Royal Academy Schools in London. In 1815 he exhibited for the first time at the British Institution, visited Paris and studied the pictures in the Musée Napoléon. He achieved his first conspicuous success with a scene from contemporary history that he had himself witnessed, *Napoleon on Board the Bellerophon in Plymouth Sound* (1815; London, N. Mar. Mus.).

Having sold the *Napoleon* for 1000 guineas, Eastlake set out for Italy and arrived in Rome in 1816. He lived there for 14 years, a busy painter and *persona grata* to munificent patrons and *grandes dames* as well as to his fellow artists. He entertained Sir Thomas Lawrence and Turner in his studio; he drew *banditti* of the Apennines for Maria Graham (later Lady Callcott); with other friends he sailed to Naples and journeyed to Athens; he met the Nazarene painters and the mainly German proponents of the new discipline of art history. In 1823 he resumed showing at the British Institution and exhibited for the first time at the Royal Academy. In 1827 he sent the *Spartan Isadas* (1826; Chatsworth, Derbys), commissioned by William Spencer Cavendish, 6th Duke of Devonshire, to the Royal Academy, where its great success prompted his election in absentia to ARA the same year. This grandiose Classical battle scene, heavily influenced by David and Haydon, seems laboured, however. He also produced anecdotal brigand subjects in the manner of Léopold Robert, for example *Sonnino Woman and Brigand Asleep* (1822; untraced, see Robertson, p. 24), and such portraits as the Byronic *Haidee, a Greek Girl* (1827; London, Tate). Perhaps his most successful works were the fresh views of the Italian and Greek landscape painted in the early 1820s. Eastlake returned to London in 1830 as a newly elected RA but continued to paint Mediterranean subjects—scenes from the Bible and Sismondi's *History of the Italian Republics* (e.g. the *Escape of the Carrara Family from the Pursuit of the Duke of Milan, 1389*, 1849; London, Tate), peasants in their villages and pilgrims arriving at Rome, and 'fancy portraits' of English ladies in Italian costume. His treatment tended towards the sweetly sentimental, with warm palette and soft brushwork.

Increasingly, however, having examined the masterpieces in Continental galleries and absorbed the works of European savants, he interested himself in the history of his art: he translated Goethe's *Zur Farbenlehre* (1840), reviewed J. D. Passavant's *Rafael von Urbino* (1840) and edited and annotated a translation of Franz Kugler's *Handbuch der Geschichte der Malerei, von Constantin dem Grossen bis auf die neuere Zeit* (1842). Impressed by his learning and his acquaintance with contemporary German painters in fresco, Sir Robert Peel recommended him in 1841 as Secretary of the Fine Arts Commission, which bore responsibility for decorating the interior walls of the new Palace of Westminster. Eastlake served in this post until 1848. At this time he was chosen by Prince Albert to produce a fresco based on Milton's *Comus, Virtue Ascending* (destr.) for one of the lunettes of the garden pavilion at Buckingham Palace.

At first unofficially, Eastlake was consulted on the acquisition of artistic works for the nation; in 1843 he was appointed Keeper of the National Gallery (the post of Director not yet having been set up). Immediately responsible to the Trustees but hobbled by infelicitous administrative arrangements, particularly vis-à-vis the Treasury, Eastlake also had to cope with rows following the purchase in 1845 of a work incorrectly attributed to Holbein, and the cleaning of four Old Masters in 1846. The controversy, orchestrated principally by Morris Moore, reached a high pitch in January 1847. Though fully supported by Peel and the Trustees, Eastlake resigned in November of that year. His prestige was soon enhanced by the first volume of *Materials for a History of Oil Painting* (1847) and the first volume of *Contributions to the Literature of the Fine Arts* (1848). On 4 April 1849 he married Elizabeth Rigby (*see* (2) below); the couple proved a formidably successful intellectual and social partnership.

The Royal Academy elected Eastlake President on 4 November 1850, and he was knighted shortly afterwards; he retained the post for the rest of his life. Eastlake's presidency was unexciting but satisfied the Academic desire to be presided over by an artist who was also a scholar and a gentleman. The President's discourses in the Schools and the Eastlakes' dinners in Fitzroy Square won admiration and gratitude. Eastlake was appointed to the Commission for the Great Exhibition of 1851 and in 1853 became the first President of the Photographic Society. In December 1853 a Select Committee on the National Gallery, before which Eastlake had testified as a trustee, submitted its report, and in March 1855 a Treasury Minute reconstituted the Gallery, establishing in principle a three-man administrative team and an annual grant for purchases. Treasury Warrants of 2 July 1855 named Eastlake as Director, Ralph Wornum (1812–77) as Keeper, and Otto Mündler as Travelling Agent. At the age of 61 Eastlake moved into a newly created position for which his life had quite extraordinarily prepared him—respected artist, informed connoisseur, conscientious historian, experienced administrator and astute negotiator, usually mild-mannered but capable of firm decision. The National Gallery had purchased nothing on the Continent until 1852; at once, with Lady Eastlake, the Director began his annual Continental tours in quest of eligible pictures.

Between 1855 and 1857 Eastlake and Mündler bought 59 pictures in Italy, 1 at The Hague and 23 in England. Regrettably, the criticisms of Francis, Lord Elcho, led in 1858 to the elimination of Mündler's job. Carrying on alone, Eastlake bought 88 more pictures abroad and 23 in England. Eastlake enriched the National Gallery with a remarkable series of Italian Renaissance masterpieces. Among his acquisitions were Perugino's *Virgin and Child* (in 1856); Pollaiuolo's *Martyrdom of St Sebastian* (in 1857); Veronese's the *Family of Darius before Alexander* (in 1857); the Lombardi-Baldi collection (1857), including Uccello's *Rout of San Romano*; Giovanni Bellini's *Madonna of the Meadow* (in 1858); the Beaucousin collection (1860), including Bronzino's *Allegory*; and Piero della Francesca's *Baptism* (in 1861). In 1861 Eastlake presented to the National Gallery an *Annunciation* by Filippo Lippi. After his death, as he had wished, Lady Eastlake offered other pictures from his own collection at the prices he had paid. His library was also purchased by the National Gallery.

UNPUBLISHED SOURCES
Eastlake's notebooks are in London, N.G.

WRITINGS
trans.: J. W. von Goethe: *Zur Farbenlehre*, 3 vols (Stuttgart, 1810) as *Goethe's Theory of Colours* (London, 1840)
ed.: *A Handbook of the History of Painting from the Age of Constantine the Great to the Present Time: Part 1: The Italian Schools of Painting* (London, 1842); rev. as *Kugler's Handbook of Painting: The Schools of Painting in Italy* (London, 2/1851); rev. as *Handbook of Painting: The Italian Schools* (London, 3/1855); trans. of part of F. T. Kugler: *Handbuch der Geschichte der Malerei, von Constantin dem Grossen bis auf die neuere Zeit* (Berlin, 1837)
Materials for a History of Oil Painting, 2 vols (London, 1847–69)
Contributions to the Literature of the Fine Arts (London, 1848); *Second Series* (London, 1870) [with memoir by Lady Eastlake]

BIBLIOGRAPHY
DNB
O. Mündler: 'Charles Lock Eastlake', *Z. Bild. Kst*, iv (1869), pp. 93–101
Sir Charles Lock Eastlake P.R.A., 1793–1865 (exh. cat., Plymouth, City Mus. & A.G., 1965)
D. Robertson: *Sir Charles Eastlake and the Victorian Art World* (Princeton, 1978) [appendices on his paintings (1812–55) and col. (1816–79), N. G. (1824–65), F. A. Comm. (1841–65) and R A (1850–65)]

DAVID ROBERTSON

(2) Lady Eastlake [née Elizabeth Rigby] (*b* Norwich, 17 Nov 1809; *d* London, 2 Oct 1893). Writer, wife of (1) Sir Charles Lock Eastlake. The niece of Dawson Turner and cousin of Francis Palgrave, she was born into an intellectual provincial family in Norwich. At the age of 18 she travelled to Germany, where she spent two and a half years in Heidelberg. Mainly self-educated, her early publications helped to stimulate interest in German art and art history. Her translation of part of J. D. Passavant's *Kunstreise durch England und Belgien* (1833) was the first text to appear in England that indicated the seriousness with which art was studied in Germany at that time. She later translated other works from the German by Franz Kugler and Gustav Friedrich Waagen. From the 1840s she was closely associated with the publishers John Murray and their periodical the *Quarterly Review*, edited by John Gibson Lockhart (1794–1854). In 1846 she wrote an article on contemporary German painting for the *Quarterly Review*, in which she stated that 'the object of art is, not to imitate a real thing, but to realize an idea' (p. 339). She went on to criticize the Nazarenes for failures of realization in their work while reproaching the landscape painters of the Düsseldorf school for their want of a controlling idea. In 1849 she married (1) Charles Lock Eastlake and became involved in his work as Trustee, and later Director, of the National Gallery in London. They travelled together in Italy and elsewhere, partly in search of works to purchase for the Gallery. After his death in 1865 she was his sole executrix, memoirist and editor.

Elizabeth Eastlake was principally an essayist, and her writings encompass a wide range of topics, among them an article on the 'Art of Dress' (1847), in which she surveyed the history of dress, especially as revealed through paintings. In 1856 she published a penetrating critique of the first three volumes of Ruskin's *Modern Painters* (1843–60). She disagreed with Ruskin's literary characterization of paintings as primarily vehicles for ideas, instead believing painting to be an autonomous art form with its own language. In 1857 she wrote an article on photography that defined limitations of the new medium. After surveying its scientific development she described how photography fails to record nature faithfully because of, for example, its varying sensitivity to different colours. She concluded, 'Photography *is* intended to supersede much that art has hitherto done, but only that which it was both a misappropriation and a deterioration of Art to do.' In the late 1870s and early 1880s she published five essays on Leonardo, Michelangelo, Titian, Dürer and Raphael. These were organized around issues of interpretation, taking account of the latest art historical methods, and all five were reprinted in *Five Great Painters* (1883). She turned more specifically to these new analytical methods in discussions of the research of J. A. Crowe, Giovanni Battista Cavalcaselle and Giovanni Morelli. In her article of 1872 on Crowe and Cavalcaselle she expressed her regret at the lapse of humane writing that the new art history seemed to initiate. She herself enriched that earlier tradition while still applying rigorously critical standards of judgement. More generally, her writings contributed to the late 19th-century view of art as a domain subject to its own laws.

WRITINGS
trans.: *Tour of a German Artist in England*, 2 vols (London, 1836); trans. of part of J. D. Passavant: *Kunstreise durch England und Belgien* (Frankfurt am Main, 1833)
'Modern German Painting', *Q. Rev.*, lxxvii (1846), pp. 323–48
'Art of Dress', *Q. Rev.*, lxxix (1847), pp. 372–99; repr. in *Music and the Art of Dress* (London, 1852), pp. 63–112
trans.: *Kugler's Handbook of Painting: The Schools of Painting in Italy* (London, 2/1851); rev. as *Handbook of Painting: The Italian Schools* (London: 3/1855); trans. of part of F. T. Kugler: *Handbuch der Geschichte der Malerei von Constantin dem Grossen bis auf die neuere Zeit* (Berlin, 1837)

trans.: *Treasures of Art in Great Britain*, 4 vols (London, 1854–7/*R* 1970); trans. of part of G. F. Waagen: *Kunstwerke und Künstler in England und Paris*, 3 vols (Berlin, 1837–9)

'Modern Painters', *Q. Rev.*, xcviii (1856), pp. 384–433

'Photography', *Q. Rev.*, ci (1857), pp. 442–68

'Michael Angelo', *Q. Rev.*, ciii (1858), pp. 436–83

A. B. Jameson: *The History of Our Lord as Exemplified in Works of Art*, 2 vols (London, 1864, rev. 2/1865) [completed by Lady Eastlake]

Life of John Gibson, R.A. Sculptor (London, 1870)

'Crowe and Cavalcaselle on the History of Painting', *Q. Rev.*, cxxxv (1872), pp. 122–49

'Leonardo da Vinci', *Edinburgh Rev.*, cxli (1875), pp. 89–126

'Life and Works of Thorvaldsen', *Edinburgh Rev.*, cxlii (1875), pp. 1–29

'The Letters and Works of Michael Angelo', *Edinburgh Rev.*, cxliv (1876), pp. 104–47

'Titian', *Edinburgh Rev.*, cxlvii (1878), pp. 105–44

'Albert Dürer', *Q. Rev.*, cxlviii (1879), pp. 376–407

'The Life and Works of Raphael', *Edinburgh Rev.*, clvii (1883), pp. 168–204

Five Great Painters, 2 vols (London, 1883)

'Giovanni Morelli: The Patriot and Critic', *Q. Rev.*, clxxiii (1891), pp. 235–52

C. Eastlake Smith, ed.: *Journals and Correspondence*, 2 vols (London, 1895)

BIBLIOGRAPHY

DNB

M. Lochhead: *Elizabeth Rigby, Lady Eastlake* (London, 1961)

C. R. Sherman and A. M. Holcomb, eds: *Women as Interpreters of the Visual Arts, 1820–1979* (Westport and London, 1981), pp. 13–15, 117–18

A. M. Ernstrom: '"Equally Lenders and Borrowers in Turn": The Working and Married Lives of the Eastlakes', *A. Hist.*, xv (1992), pp. 470–85

ADELE M. ERNSTROM

(3) Charles Locke Eastlake (*b* Plymouth, 11 March 1836; *d* London, 20 Nov 1906). Writer, designer and museum official, nephew of (1) Charles Eastlake. He studied architecture under Philip Hardwick and then attended the Royal Academy Schools, London, where he won a silver medal for architectural drawing in 1854. He then travelled for three years in France, Italy and Germany, studying art and architecture. On his return he took up freelance journalism, writing in particular about design. Under the pseudonyms 'Jack Easel' and 'Our Roving Correspondent', he also contributed many pieces to *Punch* (1859–62).

In 1861 Eastlake narrowly missed appointment as curator of Sir John Soane's Museum, London. From 1866 he was assistant secretary at the Royal Institute of British Architects, London, and from 1871 its first permanent, salaried secretary. While at the Institute, Eastlake made his reputation as a writer on design. *Hints on Household Taste in Furniture, Upholstery and Other Details* (1868), a manual of decoration, includes his own designs for furniture, which emphasize function and honesty of construction. Despite its lack of originality (it owes much to such sources as Owen Jones's *Grammar of Ornament* (London, 1856) and Bruce J. Talbert's *Gothic Forms* (London, 1867)), the book made Eastlake a household name, especially in America (*see* EASTLAKE STYLE); it influenced furniture design into the 1890s and was much imitated. *A History of the Gothic Revival* (1872), which traces the origins of the Gothic style, its endurance and resurgence in the 1820s, appeared when the revivalist movement was at its peak. Eastlake's emphasis on facts—although marred by historical vagaries—rather than criticism makes it a work of reference of continuing validity, and his judgement of contemporary architects has proved durable.

In 1878 Eastlake was appointed Keeper and Secretary of the National Gallery, London, a post he held until his retirement in 1898. Eastlake oversaw the extension of the building and rehung the gallery. He classified the works by school and continued the process of cataloguing. He ordered the cleaning of works and controversially placed them under glass as protection from atmospheric pollution. His overall aim to popularize the collection became one of the many causes of friction between Eastlake and the Director, Frederick William Burton. He was deeply disappointed not to succeed Burton, the post going instead to Edward John Poynter. During his tenure, Eastlake published a series of guidebooks to major European galleries and maintained his journalistic output.

WRITINGS

Hints on Household Taste in Furniture, Upholstery and Other Details (London, 1868; Boston, MA, 1872/*R* New York, 1969)

A History of the Gothic Revival (London, 1872); facs., intro. J. M. Crook (Leicester, 1970, 2/1978)

Notes on the Principal Pictures in the Brera Gallery at Milan (London, 1883)

Notes on the Principal Pictures in the Louvre Gallery at Paris (London, 1883)

Notes on the Principal Pictures in the Old Pinakothek at Munich (London, 1884)

'Picture Hanging at the National Gallery', *19th C.* [London], xxii (1887), pp. 817–26

Notes on the Principal Pictures in the Royal Gallery at Venice (London, 1888)

Our Square and Circle (London, 1894) [autobiography]

Pictures in the National Gallery, London (London, 1899)

'The Administration of the National Gallery (A Retrospect)', *19th C. & After*, liv (1903), pp, 926–46

BIBLIOGRAPHY

P. Thornton: *Authentic Decor: The Domestic Interior, 1620–1920* (London, 1984)

C. Gere: *Nineteenth-century Decoration: The Art of the Interior* (London, 1989)

PHILIP MCEVANSONEYA

Eastlake style. Late 19th-century style of American architecture and furniture. It owed its name to the furniture designs of Charles Locke Eastlake (*see* EASTLAKE, (3)), which became widely known because of his book *Hints on Household Taste in Furniture, Upholstery and Other Details*, first published in London in 1868 and in Boston, MA, in 1872. The book was an immediate success in the USA, and six more American editions appeared in the next eleven years. In the preface to the fourth English edition (1878), Eastlake wrote of his dismay at finding 'American tradesmen continually advertising what they are pleased to call "Eastlake" furniture . . . for the taste of which I should be very sorry to be considered responsible'. Eastlake-style furniture of the 1870s by such firms as Mason & Hamlin was decorated profusely with heavily carved Gothic ornament, whereas Eastlake's own furniture had decoration that was simpler and more sparingly applied to emphasize function.

The Eastlake style in architecture was a transformation of the Stick style, or more often the Queen Anne Revival, by the use of forms derived from furniture: columns resembled table legs, and there was a profusion of curved brackets, spindles, knobs of various shapes and ornament consisting of circular perforations. It flourished in the USA from the mid-1870s to *c.* 1890, with a large number of examples in California. Eastlake recorded his amazement and regret in the *California Architect and Building News* in 1882. There was a similar development in England, which has been little noticed. Most Eastlake-style architecture is anonymous street architecture. Three houses in California that show something of the variety of the style are the Baldwin Guest House (1881) in the County Arboretum, Los Angeles, by Albert A. Bennett (1825–90); the Carson house (1884–6), Eureka, by Samuel Newsom and Joseph Cather Newsom; and the Haas-Lilienthal house (1886), San Francisco, by Peter Schmitt.

BIBLIOGRAPHY
C. L. Eastlake: *Hints on Household Taste in Furniture, Upholstery and Other Details* (London, 1868; Boston, MA, 1872/*R* New York, 1969)
H. Kirker: *California's Architectural Frontier: Style and Tradition in the Nineteenth Century* (San Marino, CA, 1960/*R* Salt Lake City, UT, 1986)
Eastlake-influenced American Furniture, 1870–1890 (exh. cat. by W. J. S. Madigan, Yonkers, NY, Hudson River Mus., 1973)

MARCUS WHIFFEN

Eastman, George (*b* Waterville, NY, 12 July 1854; *d* Rochester, NY, 14 March 1932). American inventor and photographer. He took up photography in 1877, and in 1878, dissatisfied with the cumbersome wet collodion process, he started making the new gelatin dry plates (*see* PHOTOGRAPHY, §1). He decided to manufacture them commercially and invented a machine to end the need to hand-coat the glass. In January 1881 he founded the Eastman Dry Plate Company.

Eastman's desire to bring photography to more people, and to satisfy the needs of the growing number of amateur photographers, led him to develop many new products. In 1885 his roll-holder adaptor allowed the heavy and fragile glass plates to be replaced by a roll of sensitive paper; the success of this device inspired him to design a new camera with the roll-holder built in. The result was the Kodak camera (1888), for which Eastman chose the name; it was designed for the general public, who had only to point it in the right direction and release the shutter. When the 100-exposure roll provided with the camera had been exposed the whole apparatus was returned to Eastman's factory, where the paper rollfilm was developed and printed, the camera reloaded and returned to the customer; 'You press the button, we do the rest' was his slogan.

The introduction of the Kodak camera did much to democratize the practice of photography, taking it out of the hands of the experts. Eastman went on to pioneer other major advances in amateur photography, including in 1889 the first commercial celluloid rollfilm (which made motion picture projection possible) and he brought photography within the economic reach of millions with the introduction of the Brownie camera range in 1900. The company he formed (from 1892 Eastman Kodak) grew to be a giant multinational organization responsible for major technical innovations in photography. After his death his home became the International Museum of Photography.

BIBLIOGRAPHY
C. Ackerman: *George Eastman* (London, 1930)
B. Coe: *George Eastman and the Early Photographers* (London, 1973)
C. Ford and K. Steinorth, eds: *You Press the Button and We Do the Rest: The Birth of Snapshot Photography* (London, 1988)

BRIAN COE

Eastman, Seth (*b* Brunswick, ME, 24 Jan 1808; *d* Washington, DC, 31 Aug 1875). American painter and draughtsman. He attended the US Military Academy at West Point, NY, and from 1829 to 1831 he was stationed at Fort Crawford, WI, and Fort Snelling, MN, on topographical duty. He returned to West Point from 1833 to 1840 to teach drawing, and under the guidance of Robert Walter Weir he published *Treatise on Topographical Drawing* (West Point, 1837). From 1841 until 1848 Eastman was stationed again at Fort Snelling. He began painting scenes of the local Indians involved in everyday activities, as in *Chippewa Indians Playing Checkers* (1848; priv. col., see Tyler and others, p. 155). Eastman also created several sketchbooks, such as those depicting scenes of the Mississippi River (1846; some in St Louis, MO, A. Mus.) and of Texas (1848–9; San Antonio, TX, McNay A. Inst.).

In the 1850s Eastman was stationed in Washington, DC, to illustrate Henry R. Schoolcraft's *Information Respecting the History, Condition and Prospects of the Indian Tribes of the United States* (Philadelphia, 1851–7). In 1867 he was commissioned by the US Congress to paint a series of Indian scenes and US forts, a project incomplete at his death (26 in Washington, DC, US Capitol). Eastman provided an invaluable record of the scenery of the American West and life of the American Indian with journalistic directness. As an artist with little formal training, there is a naive aspect to his work.

BIBLIOGRAPHY
J. F. McDermott: *Seth Eastman: Pictorial Historian of the Indian* (Norman, OK, 1961)
——: *Seth Eastman's Mississippi* (Urbana, IL, 1973)
P. H. Hassrick: 'American Frontier Life', *SWA.*, 17 (June 1987), pp. 52–9
R. Tyler and others: *American Frontier Life: Early Western Painting and Prints* (New York, 1987)

CAREY ROTE

Easton & Robertson. English architectural practice formed in 1919 by (John) Murray Easton (*b* Aberdeen, 30 Jan 1889; *d* London, 19 Aug 1975) and Howard (Morley) Robertson (*b* Salt Lake City, UT, 16 Aug 1888; *d* London, 5 May 1963). Easton studied at Aberdeen School of Art and attended design classes at University College, London. Robertson studied at the Architectural Association, London, and the Ecole des Beaux-Arts, Paris. The partnership's outstanding early work, mostly due to Easton's contribution, is the Royal Horticultural Society New Hall, Vincent Square, London (1925), a concrete clerestorey structure with parabolic transverse arches, based on the Congress Hall at the Göteborg Jubilee Exhibition, Sweden (1919–23), by Arvid Bjerke (1880–1952). Robertson was Principal and Director of the Architectural Association School from 1920 to 1935 and one of the first architects in England to write in praise of European Modernist work, including that of Le Corbusier. His own books of architectural theory are more conservative, as are the partnership's buildings, such as the Nurses Home, Great Ormond Street Hospital, London (1932–3), and the Metropolitan Water Board Offices, Rosebery Avenue, London (1938). During the 1930s Robertson designed mainly interiors, such as the Berkeley Hotel, London (1931–9; destr.), but after World War II he had personal charge of the design of Hatfield Technical

College, Herts (1951), and the Shell Centre, London (1961–7), the latter much disparaged for its stripped classicism.

Easton specialized in hospital architecture, bringing Edwin Stanley Hall (1881–1940) into the partnership between 1932 and 1940 to increase this side of the work. Easton also designed Loughton Station, Essex (1940), for London Transport, with a fine barrel-vaulted booking-hall, and the practice designed the Bank of England Printing Works, Debden, Essex (1956), with a striking, curved concrete and glass vault. Robertson was the British member of the Advisory Committee for the United Nations building (1947–8), and President of the RIBA between 1952 and 1954.

WRITINGS
H. Robertson: *The Principles of Architectural Composition* (London, 1924)
——: *Architecture Explained* (London, 1926)
H. Robertson and F. R. Yerbury: *Examples of Modern French Architecture* (London, 1928)
H. Robertson: *Modern Architectural Design* (London, 1932)
——: *Architecture Arising* (London, 1944)
——: 'Obbligato to Architecture', *Builder*, ccii (1962), pp. 700–02, 751–3, 801–3, 854–5, 910–11, 956–7, 1010–12, 1060–61, 1120–21, 1178–80, 1221–3, 1278–80, 1326–7 [autobiography]

BIBLIOGRAPHY
DNB
C. H. Reilly: 'Howard Robertson', *Building* (March 1931), pp. 117–22
R. Banham: 'Howard Robertson', *Archit. Rev.* [London], cxiv (1953), pp. 161–8

ALAN POWERS

Eaton, Norman (*b* Pretoria, Oct 1902; *d* Pretoria, July 1966). South African architect. He studied at the University of the Witwatersrand, Johannesburg, under G. E. Pearse (Dip. Arch., 1928). His training and early experience was formative in leading him to base his work on historical themes and precedents. He was nevertheless versed in the tenets of the emergent International style and the confluence of these influences gave rise to a fusion of the contemporary and the traditional in his work. From the outset, in the mid-1930s, a feature of his architecture was its evocation of locality, deriving from his profound empathy for the landscape, climate, materials and crafts of Africa. He was able to synthesize and bring this to bear within the context of his own time and society, and to capture a regional ethos and a sense of belonging in nonetheless thoroughly modern designs. At a time when concrete, stucco and plate-glass were *de rigueur*, Eaton's creativity focused largely upon traditional materials. His sensitive use of stone, wood, terracotta and above all brick showed that contemporary architecture could achieve richness and warmth without compromising its design principles.

Though evident in all his work, the special qualities of Eaton's buildings were best seen in his houses for private clients in Pretoria and his two buildings for the Netherlands Bank in Pretoria (1946–53) and Durban (1961–5). Virtually all this work was subsequently insensitively altered. Criticized during his lifetime by International style purists, Eaton's unique synthesis of the contemporary, the traditional and the regional acquired fresh significance in the light of Post-modernist thinking and practice.

For an illustration of his House Greenwood, Pretoria, *see* SOUTH AFRICA, fig. 3.

BIBLIOGRAPHY
C. Harrop-Allin: *Norman Eaton: Architect* (Cape Town, 1975)

CLINTON HARROP-ALLIN

Ebauche [Fr.: 'sketch']. Term applied to the first stage of blocking-in the underpainting in an oil painting.

☐

Ebbo [Ebo], Archbishop of Reims (*d* Hildesheim, AD 851). Frankish patron. The son of a royal serf of Saxon stock, Ebbo was raised as a foster brother of the future emperor Louis the Pious (*reg* 813–40) and became Archbishop of Reims in 816. He seems to have invited one or more of Charlemagne's former court artists to Reims, thereby establishing a school of manuscript illumination, which evolved a highly distinctive style by infusing Late Antique illusionism with a new expressive energy. This style is defined in particular by the Ebbo Gospels (Epernay, Bib. Mun. MS. 1) and the Utrecht Psalter (Utrecht, Bib. Rijksuniv., MS. 32; for illustration *see* UTRECHT PSALTER), both made at the abbey of Hautvillers in the diocese of Reims, possibly before Ebbo's mission to the Danes in 822–3 but certainly before 834. Among other manuscripts produced during or shortly after Ebbo's tenure are the *Physiologus* (Berne, Burgerbib., MS. 318) and a Psalter (Troyes, Trésor Cathédrale, MS. 12). Although short-lived at Reims, the style of these manuscripts was to influence medieval art in northern Europe for centuries to come. Ebbo supported the forced abdication of Louis in 833, and therefore had to leave Reims after the Emperor's reinstatement in 834. He was officially deposed at the Synod of Diedenhofen in 835, but was restored to his see by Lothair I (*reg* 840–55) after Louis' death in 840. Expelled once more by Charles the Bald (*reg* 840–77) in 841, Ebbo was then given the bishopric of Hildesheim by King Louis the German (*reg* 817–76).

BIBLIOGRAPHY
J. Hubert, J. Porcher and W. F. Volbach: *L'Empire Carolingian*, A. Mankind (Paris, 1968); Eng. trans. as *Carolingian Art* (London, 1970) and *The Carolingian Renaissance, 750–950* (New York, 1970), pp. 101–21
W. Koehler and F. Mütherich: *Die Karolischen Miniaturen* (Berlin, 1930–), vi: *Die Schule von Reims* (Berlin, 1994)

JOACHIM E. GAEHDE

Ebe & Benda. German architectural partnership formed in 1869 by Gustav Ebe (*b* Halberstadt, 1 Nov 1834; *d* Berlin, 1916) and Julius Benda (*b* Rauden, 1838; *d* Darmstadt, 6 June 1897). Ebe and Benda studied together at the Bauakademie, Berlin, and their practice was founded after they had travelled together to France and Italy. Their main work was concerned with private houses, large residences for the newly rich industrialists of Berlin. During the 1870s and 1880s Ebe & Benda's elegant urban and suburban villas led and defined architectural taste in the new capital. They moved away from the plain classicism of the Schinkel school and introduced a fully developed eclecticism, evident, for example, in the Palais Pringsheim (1872–4) in Wilhelmstrasse, in an Italian Renaissance style, the German Renaissance Palais Tiele-Winkler (1873–6) in Regentenstrasse, and the Baroque Revival Palais Mosse (1882–4; destr.) in Leipzigerplatz, all in Berlin. Apart from private commissions, the firm took part in many major public architectural competitions, such as that for the Reichstag building in 1882. One of Ebe & Benda's main contributions, however, was in the field of domestic planning. For the Berlin art exhibition of 1877 they published the design of an urban middle-class home ('Deutsches Dreifensterhaus mit dem Motiv der alt-deutschen Diele'), arranged around a central space, with detailed descriptions and explanations. Paralleling contemporary English developments, they tried to achieve an individualization of the family home through its architecture and planning. Ebe played the more active role in the partnership, and he wrote extensively about architectural history, particularly in Germany. Benda left the firm in the 1890s to take up a post as lecturer at the Baugewerbeschule in Darmstadt.

WRITINGS

G. Ebe: *Spätrenaissance* (Berlin, 1886)
——: *Architektonische Raumlehre* (Dresden, 1900)
——: *Dekorationsformen des 19. Jahrhunderts* (Leipzig, 1900)

BIBLIOGRAPHY
Thieme–Becker; Wasmuth
V. Hammerschmidt: *Anspruch und Ausdruck in der Architektur des späten Historismus in Deutschland, 1860–1914* (Frankfurt am Main, 1985)

Ebelmann, Hans Jakob (*b* ?Speyer, *c.* 1570; *d* ?Speyer, after 1609). German cabinetmaker and printmaker. Working as a journeyman cabinetmaker at the Zimmerhof in Strasbourg after 1590, he came into contact with Hans Schoch and probably Wendel Dietterlin. In collaboration with Jakob Guckeisen of Cologne, he published a *Seilen Buch* (Cologne, 1598; Hollstein, no. 5) with a two-page engraved title page and 25 plates depicting the orders, with entablatures, string courses and scrollwork. Between 1598 and 1609, again sometimes with Guckeisen, he published four more series of engravings: *Schränke* (6 plates, 1598; Hollstein, no. 1), *Architectura Kunstbuch Darinnen Alerhand Bortalen Reisbetten undt Epitaphien...* (18 plates, 1599; 17 plates and new title page, 1600; Hollstein, no.4), *Schweyf Buch* (25 plates, 1599; Hollstein, no. 2) and an untitled collection of architectural motifs (24 plates, 1609; Hollstein, no. 3), in which the regular and semi-regular forms are in a tradition of geometrical and mathematical proportional figures that goes back to Plato. An engraving depicting the *West Front of Speyer Cathedral* (1609) is Ebelmann's latest extant work. An etched portrait of the Strasbourg clockmaker *Isaak Habrecht* (Hollstein, no. 6) is ascribed to him.

Ebelmann was an important member of the group of cabinetmakers and graphic artists of the Upper Rhineland, including Guckeisen, Veit Eck (*fl c.* 1595) and Wendel Dietterlin, who published pattern books intended for their professional colleagues. Their works, which developed from that of Hans Blum, had a geographically far-reaching influence on the applied arts but scarcely any on early Baroque ornamentation; their ideas of ornamentation came mostly from Hans Vredeman de Vries.

BIBLIOGRAPHY

Hollstein: *Ger.*; Thieme–Becker
H. Graf: 'Kupferstiche eines Speyerer Kunsttischlers', *Pfälz. Heimat*, iii (1952), pp. 57–9

E. Forssman: *Säule und Ornament: Studien zum Problem des Manierismus in den nordischen Säulenbüchern und Vorlageblättern des 16. und 17. Jahrhunderts* (Stockholm, 1956), pp. 29, 171–3

JÜRGEN ZIMMER

Ebenhech [Ebenhecht], **Franz Georg** (*b* ?Lodersleben, *c.* 1710; *d* Berlin, 21 Feb 1757). German sculptor. Before he moved to Berlin in 1746, he is thought to have worked in Italy, Leipzig and Dresden; two signed ivory reliefs in the Museum des Kunsthandwerks, Leipzig, were probably produced during his stay in that city. Ebenhech was particularly admired for his mastery of marble technique. Characteristic of his Rococo sculpture is a delicate treatment of surface with a minute attention to details, especially drapery folds, and a tendency towards a fragile decorativeness. His figures are slender, almost lean. Most of his works produced in Prussia are in the park of Schloss Sanssouci, Potsdam. About 1750 he carved 12 over life-size statues of the *Apostles* (destr.), to drawings by Georg Wenceslaus von Knobelsdorff, for the St Hedwigskirche in Berlin; originally intended for the lantern, they were actually housed in the window niches. There survive only five reliefs, above the three entrances and two niches of the portico, executed in the 19th century to Ebenhech's designs. His 'Corradini' vase (*c.* 1750; Potsdam, Schloss Sanssouci) was especially celebrated. In 1751 Ebenhech was appointed an honorary member of the Berlin Akademie. About the same time he produced four groups portraying women being abducted (e.g. Bacchus and Ariadne) and, to designs by Friedrich Christian Glume (1714–52), two groups with *Flora* and *Pomona*. Two naiads for the Neptune grotto are dated 1752; Ebenhech was commissioned to produce a statue of *Neptune* for this grotto in 1755 but was unable to complete it. The two marble sphinxes at the opening of the main avenue leading to Schloss Sanssouci were produced in 1755.

BIBLIOGRAPHY

F. Nicolai: *Nachricht von den Baumeistern, Bildhauern, Malern, Stukkaturern, und anderen Künstlern welche vom dreyzehnten Jahrhunderte bis jetzt in und um Berlin sich aufgehalten haben* (Berlin and Stettin, 1786)
K. Müller: *Johann Peter Benckert und Johann Gottlieb Heymüller: Bildhauer am Hofe Friedrichs des Grossen* (diss., Friedrich-Wilhelm U., Berlin, 1940)
G. Eckardt: *Verzeichnis der Bauten und Plastik im Park von Sanssouci* (Potsdam, 1962)
C. Theuerkauff: 'Zur Geschichte der Bildhauerkunst in Berlin und Potsdam von der Mitte des 16. bis zum späten 18. Jahrhunderts', *Ethos und Pathos: Die Berliner Bildhauerschule, 1786–1914: Beiträge* (exh. cat. by P. Bloch and others, Berlin, Hamburg. Bahnhof, 1990), pp. 13–36

HELMUT BÖRSCH-SUPAN

Ebéniste. Cabinetmaker specializing in veneered furniture. The term was coined with the reintroduction of ebony, an ideal veneer, early in the 17th century, when a revolution in furniture production took place, particularly in France (*see* FRANCE, §VI, 2).

Eberbach Abbey. Former Cistercian monastery in the Taunus Hills, Hessen, Germany, *c.* 4 km west of Eltville am Rhein. Founded on 13 February 1136 on the site of an Augustinian canons' monastic foundation with the help of Archbishop Adalbert I (*reg* 1109–37) of Mainz, it was the first Cistercian abbey to be built on the right bank of the River Rhine. Heavily endowed by the archbishops of Mainz, the abbey became a large property-owner; in its heyday about 300 monks and lay brothers lived in the monastery and at the granges. Eberbach was the burial place of two archbishops of Mainz and of the Grafs of Katzenelnbogen. The abbey was damaged in 1525 during the Peasants' War and between 1632 and 1635 in the Thirty Years War. In 1803 the monastic complex passed to the Duchy of Nassau; it was used as a prison, a mental asylum and a sanatorium and now belongs to the state of Hessen. The monastery, which has been preserved in its entirety, now houses a state vineyard. The monastic precinct lies in the narrow Kisselbach Valley and is enclosed by a wall dating from the 12th–13th century. The gate-house, originating from the Romanesque period, was altered in the Baroque style (1740–41).

1. ABBEY CHURCH. The abbey church (l. 78 m) was dedicated to SS Mary and John the Baptist; it was constructed in two phases. Building started at the east end during the tenure of the first abbot, Ruthard, but was halted c. 1160 for political reasons. At that stage the choir and transepts, including the piers west of the crossing, had been completed to a height of between 2.5 m and 6.4 m. The ground-plan followed the so-called 'Bernardine' plan, using a proportional system typical of Cistercian churches: a three-aisled cruciform basilica with the choir forming an elongated rectangle and three rectangular side chapels on the east of each transept arm. Quite untypically, the choir is rather narrower than the main body of the church; the crossing is square, and the transepts are rectangles slightly wider than they are long. The building is articulated externally by pilasters and internally by a scheme of half-columns (destr.), which were intended to support wall arches; this pre-established articulation shows that the choir was planned with two bays, each transept with three and the nave with eleven, probably with barrel vaulting in line with the Burgundian tradition (e.g. FONTENAY ABBEY, Noirlac). The first phase was built in light sandstone ashlars.

Work on the church resumed c 1170 under the third abbot, Gerhard; it was probably finished by 1186, when it was consecrated by the Archbishop of Mainz. In keeping with Rhenish Romanesque building traditions (e.g. the abbeys of Steinfeld and Knechtsteden), the nave was vaulted on a double-bay system, with groin vaults supported on heavy, unarticulated pilasters that are corbelled in at the springing of the semicircular arcade (see fig.). Above the arcade is an area of blank wall, with plain, round-headed clerestory windows above. This second phase is characterized by the use of rubble masonry with details articulated in Rhenish limestone; the church is solidly built, completely in the Cistercian architectural tradition, with neither decoration nor ostentatious furnishings, and the extensive wall surfaces are whitewashed. The paradise porch in front of the south door was added shortly after 1200, and the south chapels with their elegant tracery windows and the choir window (destr.) between 1313 and 1335. The door in the south transept, which has a tympanum with blind, trefoiled tracery, was built c. 1250 as the *Totenpforte*. Between 1935 and 1939 the Baroque

Eberbach Abbey, interior of church looking east, founded 1136

alterations were eliminated, and the original windows and doors restored.

2. MONASTIC BUILDINGS. All that remains of the flat-roofed Romanesque cloister (c. 1186) north of the church are fragments in the chapter house and the west wall adjoining the monastery lane. Of the Gothic cloister, begun in the mid-13th century, the east and south walks were demolished down to the springers on the outer walls in the 19th century. The west and north sides have simple buttresses, round-arched tripartite windows with tracery consisting of circles, diamonds and flattened trefoils, and rib vaults resting on foliated consoles. In a round-arched niche inserted into the wall of the north transept is the so-called 'Offenes Grab', a stone sarcophagus dating from the 1190s, which probably served as a *memento mori*. The buildings of the east range are contemporary with the church: the barrel-vaulted sacristy, which used to have a small Gothic choir, and the square chapter house, which was heightened c. 1354 when finely moulded star vaulting was installed, springing from an octagonal central column. The height of the adjacent refectory was raised in 1245 when the dormitory was extended, and in 1260 the building was further extended northwards by five bays and uniformly vaulted. A dormitory (l. 73 m) was created, with two aisles, eleven bays and rib vaults resting on stumpy columns with crocket and foliate capitals. The windows

were altered in 1502 when wooden partitions were built into the dormitory (removed 1930–31).

The north range, which was completed by 1186, was originally single-storey, except for the kitchen, which had the warming house above. Around 1500 a half-timbered storey was added (renovated in a Baroque style in 1720–24). The monks' refectory (built before 1186 and altered in 1501) was entirely rebuilt in 1720–24; its stucco ceiling was executed in 1738 by Daniel Schenk (*fl* 1715–38). Also in 1720–24 the kitchen adjoining it to the west was renovated, but the small, groin-vaulted bakery remained unaltered. Around 1500 a half-timbered upper storey with a projecting octagonal stair-well was built over the west range to house the large library.

On the west side, separated from the other buildings by the monastery lane, is the lay brothers' building (l. 93 m), dating from *c.* 1200 but altered several times: the vaulting was renewed in 1709. North of the central passage (originally the only means of access to the cloister) is the storeroom, and to its south the lay brothers' refectory. On the upper floor is the double-aisled dormitory (l. 83 m; early 13th century) with 13 bays and rib vaulting resting on columns with simple capitals; the spiral staircase dates from 1623.

To the east of the cloister is the former hospital, used since the early 17th century to house the wine-press; this was the last part of the Romanesque monastic complex to be built, erected *c.* 1220 on earlier walls. It is a three-aisled hall with eight bays (16×38 m) and two rows of windows. The interior employs Early Gothic forms still influenced by the Romanesque, and the rib vaulting has steeply pitched pointed arches; the capitals of the slender columns and other forms are reminiscent of Limburg an der Lahn Cathedral (*c.* 1220). The small, square choir with rib vaulting and traceried windows was inserted along the short south side *c.* 1350.

BIBLIOGRAPHY

H. Bär and K. Rossel: *Diplomatische Geschichte der Abtei Eberbach im Rheingau*, 3 vols (Wiesbaden, 1855–86)
F. Luthmer: *Die Bau- und Kunstdenkmäler des Rheingaues* (Frankfurt am Main, 1902, rev. 1907)
H. Hahn: *Die frühe Kirchenbaukunst der Zisterzienser* (Berlin, 1957)
H. Spiess: *Mass und Regel: Eine mittelalterliche Massordnung an romanischen Bauten im Kloster Eberbach* (diss., Aachen, Rhein.–Westfäl. Tech. Hochsch., 1959)
M. Herchenröder: *Der Rheingaukreis* (1965), i of *Die Kunstdenkmäler des Landes Hessen* (Munich, 1965–9), pp. 61–113
F. Arens: 'Das Nischengrab im Kreuzgang der Zisterzienserabtei Eberbach', *Mainz. Z.*, lxii (1967), pp. 110–19
W. Einsingbach: *Das ehemalige Zisterzienserkloster Eberbach im Rheingau* (Wiesbaden, 1973)
W. Krönig: *Altenberg und die Baukunst der Zisterzienser* (Bergisch Gladbach, 1973)
G. Schnorrenberger: *Wirtschaftsverwaltung des Klosters Eberbach im Rheingau, 1423–1631* (Wiesbaden, 1977)
C. Mossig: *Grundbesitz und Güterbewirtschaftung des Klosters Eberbach im Rheingau, 1136–1250* (Darmstadt, 1978)
G. Binding and M. Untermann: *Kleine Kunstgeschichte der mittelalterlichen Ordensbaukunst in Deutschland* (Darmstadt, 1985)

GÜNTHER BINDING

Eberdingen-Hochdorf. Site of an Early Iron Age burial mound near Ludwigsburg in Baden-Württemberg, Germany (*see also* PREHISTORIC EUROPE, §VI, 2(iii)). The excavation in 1978–9 of a flattened and ploughed stony mound 10 km from the high-status Iron Age settlement of Hohenasperg resulted in a spectacular discovery: a 'princely' burial dating to *c.* 550–500 BC. The mound, which had originally measured 60 m in diameter by 6 m high, was found intact and has provided detailed information on a variety of organic objects as well as other, high-quality items, many of which were locally produced.

The mound itself was of elaborate construction and was completed in several stages. A primary mound was built incorporating a stone-lined entrance 6 m wide and flanked by stone walls, while the wooden burial chamber was constructed at a later date. There was time for weeds to grow on the mound before the burial. The remains of workshop debris from the manufacture of special goods for the burial were dug into the primary mound. After the interment the main mound was raised, and a kerb was added at its base. The burial was of a man aged between 40 and 50 years and of exceptional stature for the time: 1.87 m tall with extremely broad shoulders, a large head and well-developed musculature. The body lay on a bronze couch in a chamber lined with rich hangings, surrounded by a large quantity of grave goods of exceptional quality and variety.

The couch measures 2.75 m long with the seat 350 mm off the ground; six large pieces of sheet bronze form the seat, the back and the curved arms. The arms are ornamented with deeply impressed circles. The back, however, is decorated with a frieze: at either end of this is a representation of a four-wheeled wagon drawn by a pair of yoked horses, together with a man bearing a shield and a spear or goad. Between the wagons are shown three pairs of ithyphallic, long-haired dancers, each holding a sword in one hand and an unidentified object in the other; on this side, the lower arm is covered by a glove. The couch is mounted on eight individually cast female figures with small, six-spoked bronze wheels set between their feet to ease its movement. The figures are decorated on the breast, arms, waist and ankles with punched holes inlaid with coral. The ears are pierced for iron earrings, and the eyes are picked out in coral, with the pupils represented by blackened pins.

Eight aurochs-horn drinking horns with gold mouth-pieces and bronze handles and decoration were hung on hooks on the wall. A ninth horn, made of iron, bronze and gold, measured 1.23 m long, with a diameter of 145 mm at the mouth and a capacity of 5.5 litres (see fig.). A bronze cauldron measuring 800 mm high and 1.04 m in diameter with a capacity of 500 litres originally rested on a stand of iron and wood in one corner of the grave. Three figures of lions alternate with three handles on the vessel's shoulder: two of the lions must have been made in a Greek colony in southern Italy, but the third is clearly a locally made replacement. Analysis of the residue in the bottom of the cauldron showed that it had contained mead. A gold bowl, nine large bronze plates and three bronze basins completed the set of drinking equipment.

At least 25 bronze fibulae and 20 iron hooks had been used to hang such items as the drinking horns and to hold together the textiles that lined the chamber. The deceased had been wearing a gold neck-ring measuring 250 mm in diameter, a pair of bronze fibulae and a pair of gold fibulae, an antenna-hilted dagger decorated with gold, a gold arm-band, a gold belt plate and pointed shoes with

Eberdingen-Hochdorf, drinking horn, iron, bronze and gold, l. 1.23 m, diam. 145 mm, late 6th century BC (Stuttgart, Württembergisches Landesmuseum

gold coverings. All the decorated goldwork was very fine and showed no signs of wear and is therefore thought to have been made in an on-site workshop especially for the burial. The man also carried a little leather bag containing a nail-cleaner and three fish-hooks and was accompanied by a skin-covered wooden quiver with 14 arrows, a knife in a wooden sheath and a razor wrapped in a piece of cloth. Other grave goods included the remains of a four-wheeled wagon decorated with bronze, a decorated wooden yoke, horse harness, a large axe and a knife. A cooking spit was associated with items of food. However, it was the organic items in the grave that were of special interest. The rarest find, a conical hat of birchbark, measured 340 mm in diameter by 110 mm high; it was provided with two holes for a cord to hold it in place during wear and was decorated with fine lines and punched decorative patterns. There was also much evidence for the fine textiles that had lined the chamber and been draped over the couch. Much of this material was patterned in bright colours, and most is thought to have been imported from north Italy, though some may have been locally made, as was the hat, the goldwork, the drinking horns and the couch.

BIBLIOGRAPHY

J. Biel: 'The Late Hallstatt Chieftain's Grave at Hochdorf', *Antiquity* (1981), pp. 16–18

Der Keltenfürst von Hochdorf: Methoden und Ergebnisse der Landesarchäologia (exh. cat., ed. D. Planck and others; Stuttgart, Württemberg. Landesmus., 1985)

SARA CHAMPION

Eberhard, Konrad (*b* Hindelang, 25 Nov 1768; *d* Munich, 12 March 1859). German sculptor and painter. He studied sculpture under his father, Johann Richard Eberhard (1739–1813), until 1799, when he moved to Munich and began work with Roman Anton Boos. Seven years of work at the Akademie der Bildenden Künste in Munich earned Eberhard the attention of the future Ludwig I as well as a stipend for two years of study in Rome. Those two years

gradually grew to eight; Eberhard studied with Canova and worked as one of Ludwig's agents, buying antiques for the royal collection. As a sculptor, he developed a crisp and chaste classical idiom that earned his *Cupid and Muse* (1807–9; Munich, Neue Pin.; see fig.) a place in the exhibition of 1809 at the Académie de France in Rome. It was purchased by the Wittelsbachs, who also commissioned *Leda and the Swan* (1810; Munich, Schloss Nymphenburg), *Caritas* (1810–12; ex-Caroline of Bavaria col.), and works for the Ruhmeshalle in Munich (*Wohlgemuth*, 1812–14) as well as Walhalla at Donaustauf, near Regensburg (*Maria Theresa*, 1811–14 and *Herschel*, 1816). Active within classicist circles in Rome, Eberhard developed a close association with the Lukasbrüder without ever being admitted to the Lukasbund itself. He was appointed professor of sculpture at the Munich Akademie in April 1817, but remained in Italy for another two years. The last months of 1817 were spent in Tuscany, where he met Julius Schnorr von Carolsfeld and studied 13th- and 14th-century Italian art. In Rome he continued work for the Wittelsbachs, executing *Diana and Cupid* and *Endymion and Hound* (both 1819–20; Munich, Schloss Nymphenburg). During the spring of 1819, Eberhard displayed a bas-relief *Deposition* (Munich, Sisters of Charity) and over a dozen drawings at the Palazzo Caffarelli in Rome. These works reflected an adaptation of his strong linear propensities to Christian themes.

In September 1819 Eberhard travelled with Peter Cornelius to Munich, where he remained for two years without taking up his duties as professor at the Akademie. Instead he assisted with the Glyptothek decorations, completed several projects for the Wittelsbach and Ringseis families, and set to work on a cycle of Homeric reliefs for the Casino Massimo al Laterano (the Villa Giustiniani) in Rome. It was to complete these, as well as to execute a tomb for the *Princess Carolina*, that he and his brother Franz Eberhard (1767–1836) returned to Italy in 1821.

Konrad Eberhard: *Cupid and Muse*, marble, h. 1.2 m, 1807–9 (Munich, Neue Pinakothek)

The death of the Marchese Carlo Massimo in 1822 cut short Konrad Eberhard's participation in the Casino Massimo decorations. His intentions are revealed, however, in a few drawings (*Judgement of Paris*, 1820; Frankfurt am Main, Städel. Kstinst. & Städt. Gal.) and alabaster bas-reliefs, which were carved in a spare, archaizing manner (*Iliad—Canto XX* and *Zeus and Artemis*, 1820–24; Munich, Busch priv. col.: and *Cantos I & II*, 1820–24; Karlsruhe, Bad. Landesmus.). The tomb of *Princess Carolina*, with its deeply carved yet insistently linear portrayal of maternal grief, was completed by 1824 and was installed in the Munich Theatinerkirche within an architectural setting designed by Leo von Klenze, with whom Eberhard collaborated on numerous occasions.

After his own return to Munich in 1826, Eberhard took up his duties as professor of sculpture and renewed his close contacts with the Ringseis family. In the next decade he came into increasing competition with Ludwig von Schwanthaler but remained in favour for royal commissions with a religious tenor. He produced *Archangel Michael* and *St George* (1835–40; destr.) for the Isartor, five figures for the portal of the Allerheiligenkirche (1829–34; destr.), and tombs for *Johann Michael Sailer, G. Michael Wittmann* and *Franz Xavier Schwäbl* in the cathedral at Regensburg (1830–43). In his later years, he also executed a number of paintings, the best known being *The Triumph of the Church* (1833; Basle, Claraspital), executed for Emilie Linder (1797–1867), and a *Corpus Christi Procession* (1842; Hindelang, Kriegergedächtniskapelle).

In 1836, Eberhard's brother Franz died. He had served as intimate and collaborator since 1819, and his death precipitated Eberhard's retirement from the Akademie at the age of 70 and his withdrawal from the tumultuous art politics of the Bavarian capital. In his last years he concentrated increasingly on devotional commissions for churches in the Allgau.

BIBLIOGRAPHY

J. A. Endres: *Johann Konrad Eberhard, ein Allgäuer-Künstler* (Munich, 1925)

F. Noack: *Das Deutschtum in Rom seit dem Ausgang des Mittelalters* (Berlin and Stuttgart, 1927/*R* Aalen, 1974), ii, pp. 151–2

C. Arnold: *Konrad Eberhard 1768–1859, Bildhauer und Maler: Leben und Werk eines Allgäuer Kunstlergeschlechts* (Augsburg, 1964)

W. Beeh: 'Zu Konrad Eberhards Amor und Musegruppe in München', *Giessen. Beitr. Kstgesch.*, ii (1973), pp. 243–52

M. Bachmayer: 'Die Iliasdarstellungen des Allgäuer Bildhauers Konrad Eberhard', *Jb. Staatl. Kstsamml. Baden-Württemberg*, xii (1975), pp. 179–95

Deutsche Künstler um Ludwig I. in Rom (exh. cat., ed. G. Scheffler; Munich, Staatl. Graph. Samml., 1981), pp. 29–30

G. Finckh: '"Plastisch, das heisst antik, zu denken . . .": Die Bildhauerei an der Münchner Akademie und der Klassizismus von Roman Anton Boos bis Adolf von Hildebrand', *Tradition und Widerspruch: 175 Jahre Kunstakademie München*, ed. T. Zacharias (Munich, 1985), pp. 243–72

ROBERT E. McVAUGH

Eberhard-Ludwig, Duke of Württemberg. *See* WÜRTTEMBERG, (1).

Eberlein, Gustav (Heinrich) (*b* Spiekershausen, 14 July 1847; *d* Berlin, 5 Feb 1926). German sculptor. He attended the Realschule in Hannoversch Münden until 1861. He was apprenticed to a goldsmith in 1861–4 and thus learnt embossing, carving, chasing and engraving. He subsequently travelled as a journeyman, finding employment in Hildesheim, then in Kassel with the court jeweller, Ruhl. From 1867 to 1870, Eberlein trained as a sculptor under August von Kreling (1819–76), director of the Kunstgewerbeschule in Nuremberg, also working as Kreling's assistant to support his studies. On receiving a grant from Elisabeth of Prussia (the widow of Frederick William IV) for three further years of study, he moved to Berlin inspired by the works of Reinhold Begas shown at the first Internationale Kunstausstellung in Munich. Eberlein arrived in Berlin with a letter of recommendation to the sculptor Bernhard Afinger and he soon obtained a post as assistant to the sculptor Gustav Blaeser, who was then engaged on commissions from the Emperor Frederick William III.

In 1872–3, with a supplementary grant, Eberlein spent three winter months in Rome. On his return to Berlin he was at first unsuccessful in obtaining commissions; but he eventually received his first order for architectural sculpture via the architect Martin Gropius, for the Kunstgewerbemuseum (1877–81) building. Gropius gave Eberlein the task of making a frieze in the vestibule and allowed him to set up a studio in the cellar. Gropius also helped Eberlein win the commissions for two statues for the University of Kiel (figures of *Plato* and *Hippocrates*).

Eberlein's first independent work was *Extracting the Thorn*, shown in 1880 at the Akademie in Berlin, and a marble version (1886; Berlin, Alte N.G.; see fig.) followed. Another work in a classical vein was *Psyche* (plaster model,

Gustav Eberlein: *Extracting the Thorn*, marble, 1886 (Berlin, Nationalgalerie)

became more akin to the sculpture of Reinhold Begas—neo-Baroque in both subject and form. In the 1890s Eberlein frequently produced sculptures on religious themes: in 1894, at the Grosse Kunstausstellung in Berlin, he showed a *Pietà*, a subject that had occupied him since the death of his mother in 1888. Between 1895 and 1900 he worked on religious cycles, such as the *First People* (e.g. Hannoversch Münden, Stadt. Mus.), and these were followed by related works such as the group *God Breathing Life into Adam* (marble, 1904; Hannoversch Münden, Schlesierplatz).

In 1897 the Akademie honoured Eberlein at the Grosse Kunstausstellung in Berlin with a retrospective of his work. For a long time Eberlein had also been favoured by Emperor William II who commissioned him, for example, to make the monument to *Goethe* (marble, 1902) in the gardens of the Villa Borghese, Rome. In 1901 Eberlein had won the competition for another large-scale memorial, to *Richard Wagner*, in the Tiergarten, Berlin (unveiled 1903); both works combine an impressive figure of the honoured man with a compelling recreation of characters from his oeuvre. Such works helped Eberlein to achieve fame beyond Germany. He received many commissions in Europe, and in 1912 his *German Fountain* was unveiled in Forestal Park, Santiago, Chile. In 1898 Eberlein opened to the public a museum of his work (now Hannoversch Münden, Städt. Mus.).

BIBLIOGRAPHY

Bénézit; Thieme–Becker
P. Bloch: 'Anmerkungen zu Berliner Skulpturen des 19ten Jahrhunderts', *Jb. Preuss. Kulthes.*, viii (1970), pp. 162–90, E. 179-80
J. Mackay: *The Dictionary of Western Sculptors in Bronze* (Woodbridge, 1977)
P. Bloch and W. Grzimek: *Das klassische Berlin: Die Berliner Bildhauerschule im 19ten Jahrhundert* (Frankfurt am Main, Berlin and Vienna, 1978)
U. Hoffmann: *Christliche Themen im skulpturalen Werk Gustav Eberleins* (MA thesis, U. Göttingen, 1982)
Berliner Kunst von 1770 bis 1930 (exh. cat., W. Berlin, Berlin Mus., 1982)
R. Grimm: *Werkverzeichnis des Bildhauers, Malers und Dichters Prof. Gustav L. H. Eberlein, 1847–1926* (Hemmingen, 1983) [cat. rais.]
G. Kaerger: *Der Bildhauer Gustav H. Eberlein: Das Leben eines grossen Künstlers aus Hannoversch Münden*, Sydekum-Schriften zur Geschichte der Stadt Münden, x (Hannoversch Münden, 1983)
P. Bloch: *Gustav Eberlein: Grösse und Grenzen eines Bildhauers in Wilhelminischer Zeit*, Sydekum-Schriften zur Geschichte der Stadt Münden, xii (Hannoversch Münden, 1984), pp. 41–59
U. Hoffmann: *Gustav H. Eberlein 1847–1926*, Gustav-Eberlein-Forschung (Hannoversch Münden, 1984), pp. 41–59
Rheinland-Westfalen und die Berliner Bildhauerschule des 19ten Jahrhunderts (exh. cat., Cappenberg-Salm, Schloss Cappenberg, 1984)
Von Begas bis Barlach: Bildhauerei im Wilhelminischen Berlin (exh. cat., W. Berlin, Kolbe Mus., 1984)
'O ewich is so lanck': Die historischen Friedhöfe in Berlin–Kreuzberg, Werkstattbericht, Landesarchiv Berlin (Berlin, 1987)

BRIGITTE HÜFLER

1884; Hannoversch Münden, Stadt. Mus.). In 1880 Eberlein was given a post as a teacher of figurative sculpture at the Kunstinstitut of the Berlin Gewerbemuseum; but he refused a professorship at the Akademie in Karlsruhe. In 1882 he took part successfully in the competition for a design for the frieze on the façade of the Ministry of Culture in Berlin. The architect Friedrich Hitzig, who had been a friend of Gropius, engaged Eberlein to make a colossal statue (h. 5.5 m) of *Leonardo da Vinci* (destr.; plaster model, Hannoversch Münden, Stadt. Mus.) for the Technische Hochschule in Berlin. From this time Eberlein began regularly to receive major State commissions for sculpture: in 1889 for the monument to *Emperor William I* for Wuppertal-Elberfeld (unveiled 1893), and in subsequent years for many other works of this type.

From the later 1880s Eberlein's style lost the sober classicism it had inherited from the work of Blaeser and

Eberlein, Johann Friedrich (*b* Dresden, 1695; *d* Meissen, 20 July 1749). German sculptor and modeller. After training as a caster and carver in England, he joined the Meissen Porcelain Factory in 1735 as principal assistant to the Modellmeister Johann Joachim Kändler. Together they collaborated on the conception and creation of the 'Schwanenservice' (1737–41; Meissen Porzellanmus.; see MEISSEN, fig. 2) for Heinrich, Graf von Brühl. He also modelled his own creations, the most successful of which were the series of Classical gods and goddesses on High

Baroque socles, dating from *c*. 1747. Owing to his close working relationship with Kändler, it is difficult to separate their work and obtain a clear picture of Eberlein's artistic powers and achievement.

BIBLIOGRAPHY

W. B. Honey: *German Porcelain* (London, 1947)

R. Ruckert: *Meissener Porzellan* (Munich, 1966)

HUGO MORLEY-FLETCHER

Ebersbach, Hartwig (*b* Zwickau, 17 May 1940). German painter and installation artist. He studied at the Hochschule für Grafik und Buchkunst in Leipzig from 1959 to 1964. At the beginning of his career Ebersbach drew his themes from political events, as in *Dedication to Chile* (1974) or *Anti-imperialist Solidarity* (1977). Although these early works show the influence of Expressionism, he later broke with conventional two-dimensional painting. In 1978 he collaborated on the theatre piece *Missa Nigra* with the composer Friedrich Schenker (*b* 1942) and the experimental Neue Musik Hanns Eisler group. From 1979 to 1983 he was a lecturer at the Hochschule in Leipzig, and between 1981 and 1983 he worked with the experimental Gruppe 37,2, led by H. J. Schulze. In his later works he started to assemble his pictures in labyrinthine arrangements that overlapped and intersected to create a new three-dimensional unity, as in *Kaspar Theatre*, a 17-part installation (1985–6; Grundkreditbank col., Berlin, see 1988 exh. cat., pp. 218–22). While his later work was in part a colourful, aggressive celebration of the cruel destructiveness of human society, at a personal level Ebersbach saw painting as a therapeutic process through which he sought to free himself from childhood traumas and contemporary nightmares. His primary message was the creative frenzy that preceded the publicly performed action of painting. The aggressive rhythm of the application of colour interplaying with acoustic sounds was intended to be experienced by artist and public alike as an act of liberation.

BIBLIOGRAPHY

G. Meissner, ed.: *Leipziger Künstler der Gegenwart* (Leipzig, 1979)

Hartwig Ebersbach: Malerei (exh. cat., Altenburg, Staatl. Lindenau-Mus., 1981)

T. Gierig: *Hans Ebersbach: Malerei* (Frankfurt am Main, 1986)

Zeitvergleich '88: 13 Maler aus der DDR (exh. cat., ed. D. Brusberg; W. Berlin, Neue Kstquartier Tech. & Innovationspark, 1988), pp. 218–22

EUGEN BLUME

Ebla [Tell Mardikh]. Ancient site in northern Syria, some 58 km south-west of Aleppo. It is set in an agricultural region between the last eastern branches of the Jabal al-Zawiya and the swampy lowlands of the Matkh and was occupied from *c*. 3000 BC to *c*. 1600 BC with intermittent later settlement until the Byzantine period. Since 1964 excavations by the University of Rome's Italian Archaeological Mission to Syria have been directed by Paolo Matthiae. Most of the finds, including many of the items mentioned below, are in the Archaeological Museum of Idlib; smaller collections are held in the National Museums of Damascus and Aleppo.

1. EARLY BRONZE AGE (MARDIKH I–II). The earliest evidence for settlement consists of locally produced stamp seals in a naturalistic style, bearing pastoral scenes that include animal and human figures, shepherds and heroic animal-tamers. They may be dated to the late Chalcolithic or Early Bronze I (*c*. 3000 BC). Scattered structures from throughout the first half of the 3rd millennium BC (Early Bronze II–III; Mardikh II A) have been excavated on the south and west sides of the acropolis. By the mid-3rd millennium BC a series of warehouses had been built on the southern part of the acropolis, and the area was subsequently to retain this function.

The city developed from *c*. 2400 BC, when it became the seat of an autonomous dynasty of at least 26 kings that gained control of part of north-central Syria. Its greatest economic and political expansion, lasting about 50 years, coincided with the reigns of the last three kings, Igrish-Khalam, Irkab-Damu and Ishar-Damu, as documented by tablets recovered from the archives. A vast, multi-functional palace, known as Palace G, was created to serve as the royal residence and the focus of administrative and ceremonial activities. It was built in two distinct phases and topographical directions: the original nucleus, located above the older settlement along the edge of the acropolis, comprised various units for the working and storage of agricultural products as well as a recently discovered small ceremonial wing linked to a monumental hypogeum clad in stone and brick. The later ceremonial and administrative areas were set around a vast porticoed open court, below the western edge of the acropolis. The last addition to be built, under the same portico, was the central library, which originally contained around 3000 cuneiform tablets, of which 1757 were nearly intact. The palace's articulated floor-plan was built on different levels, and its wings were not symmetrical; this partly followed the earliest urban layout in a characteristic local fashion. The palace's development also indicates the relatively late increase in the dynasty's economic and political power.

Artefacts found in the palace (it served both for the storage of raw materials and finished goods and for the gathering and distribution of agricultural products) also display local characteristics. The numerous styles have either a Mesopotamian origin (e.g. glyptics, inlay) or a local derivation (e.g. wood-carving, in openwork and in relief, and panels of mixed materials carved in relief) and are executed in a variety of techniques. A series of panels, portraying dignitaries dressed in flounced robes and tufted headdresses, are sometimes carved in as much as three-quarter relief. Local and easily worked raw materials, using wood for the bodies and limestone for the clothing, are combined with ostentatious, imported precious materials, such as lapis lazuli for headdresses, soapstone for beards and hair, marble for clothing and gold for faces, in a manner also found in Mesopotamia. The choice of colours is closely integrated with this technique. A modelled technique was used for high relief and a linear style for bas-relief, often with incised or scratched details; the alternation between these techniques is linked to variations in the use of wood and semi-precious stones. Sometimes this alternation indicates a stylistic evolution resulting from the blending of Mesopotamian influences and local responses that is well documented by the series of inlays. An inlaid panel, bearing several rows of war scenes alternating with heraldic scenes that depict the lion-headed eagle (Imdugud) on human-headed bulls, is related to the

Early Dynastic III A style of Mesopotamia and can be dated to the palace's earliest phase. It was later turned over and reused, perhaps symbolically, as a decorative edge in the floor of one of the service rooms. The warrior groups in the scenes of war are crude but lively. The inlays from the palace's final period possess a naturalism and plasticism that recall the stylistic tendencies of the early AKKADIAN period. The same style is later found in wood-carvings, such as on a panel bearing the heads of dignitaries in profile and in the fragments of a piece of furniture carved in openwork with animals, mythological scenes, warriors, dignitaries and the king himself, all characterized by rounded, plastic forms (Aleppo, N. Mus.). Comparisons with two life-size headdresses in semi-precious stones, which formed part of two composite royal statues (Aleppo, N. Mus.), demonstrate that this is a tendency of the Eblaite school and not only dependent on the use of wood.

There are two types of document relating to seals and two different currents of production. The sealings used by the central administration preserve the impressions of seals produced in a palace workshop: the iconographic repertory is of Mesopotamian derivation with contest scenes prevailing, sometimes incorporating variations inspired by local mythology, such as an animal-taming goddess, a kneeling Atlas figure holding up a four-headed symbol, or friezes of animal heads. A second current of production is documented by the impressions on storage jars brought from nearby villages. These employ a more spontaneous imagery, with a squatting woman alluding to copulation, a serpent coiled around a rosette, simple geometric or floral designs and pastoral scenes. Some are the occasional products of primitive craftsmanship, but more often they belong to a repertory found throughout Syria, based on the theme of human and animal fertility to ward off evil, originating in the late Chalcolithic period.

2. MIDDLE BRONZE AGE (MARDIKH III). The beginning of the 2nd millennium BC, as throughout the Levant, was marked by profound economic, technological, social and political change. The city was radically reorganized on a new plan, and an earth and sandstone rampart was constructed, together with a mud-brick wall along the eastern boundary of the acropolis and a stone retaining wall along its west and north sides. Numerous palaces and temples were built (as well as a large raised stone platform, probably used by a cult), differing in design according to their function and tutelary gods, although they shared a certain symmetry and regularity of floor-plan and the use of massive external walls with high elevations, slabs of basalt and limestone, and monolithic thresholds and doorjambs that emphasize their monumental size. Cisterns, pits and drains were dug or enlarged in the soft limestone rock, and caves were reused as tombs for princes, furnished with rich funerary goods. This new architectural style and other developments are directly linked to technological progress, especially to improvements in metal and stone tools.

The same phenomenon also greatly influenced the other arts of the period. Stone sculpture and statuary, mostly in basalt, limestone, marble and greenstone, replaced the plurality of types and techniques of the preceding period. Carved stelae and basins and statues of functionaries and

gods were mostly found *in situ* in the six temples. The series of statues shows a development from a severe, geometric style in some archaic examples from Gate A (Damascus, Mus. N.) and Temple P 2 that portray dignitaries and princes (Mardikh III A; *c.* 1950–*c.* 1800 BC). The votive inscription of Ibbit-Lim to the goddess Ishtar, on a torso fragment of this group (Damascus, Mus. N.), permitted the identification of Tell Mardikh as Ebla.

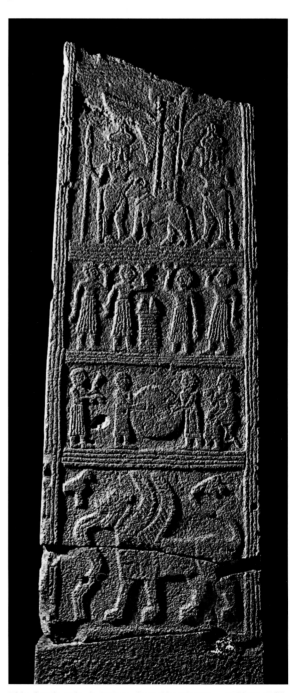

Ebla, basalt stele, h. 1.79 m, from Temple G 3, *c.* 1800 BC (Idlib, Archaeological Museum)

Greater care in modelling is found in a more developed standing statue of a female from Temple P 2, while some seated male figures, one of which, also from Temple P 2, is twice life-size, show a high quality of modelling.

Similar change is found in bas-relief. The basins from the Archaic period are carved with banquet scenes in a linear style and with subject-matter that is well known in Cappadocia and must have had its origins in Syria. In a later basin, with dignitaries embracing on the front and goddesses on the sides, the forms are more plastic. The same evolution appears in the stelae carved on two or four faces with a rich repertory of subjects, often with a complex symbolic background. Musical scenes appear alongside mythological ones, such as in the large stele from Temple G 3 depicting the goddess Ishtar in her winged shrine on a bull above a row of scenes of mythical battles with demons and monsters (see fig.), which recall the different symbolic, earthly and celestial aspects of war and love. A base from Temple N with bull-men carved on the face, and basalt tripods from Palace P with male figures supporting the ritual cups, allude to obscure religious practices. On the other hand the image of a prisoner entangled in a net at the feet of the king, which was carved on the front of a basalt base that probably supported a large statue (perhaps a god) on the prone bodies of two lions, has secular connotations.

Other types are less homogeneous and may be imports. Certainly of local workmanship is an ivory talisman with a banquet scene, perhaps at a funeral, with nude figures, a ram and cynocephaluses or monkeys, derived from the Egyptian repertory. The Egyptian inspiration was stimulated by the circulation both of Egyptian-style objects, such as a panel from Palace P with ivory or bone inlays depicting the figures of a pharaoh, Isis, Osiris, Seth and Anubis, which perhaps came from a coastal centre such as Byblos, and of genuine Egyptian objects, such as the gold sceptre of the pharaoh Hotepibra (13th Dynasty; c. 1756–c. 1630 BC), which was found in the tomb of a certain Immeya, whose name appears on a silver cup decorated with Egyptian motifs, including the palmette and the open hand.

Once again there are various types of seal. Impressions on storage jars show scenes of homage to the gods Adad and Anat by the local kings, among whom appears a son of an Indilimgur; they document the spread during the latter part of the Middle Bronze Age of the modelled style that was adopted for the best dynastic seals of Yamkhad and Alalakh. A class of seal based on the repertory of the 4th and 3rd millennia BC, showing simple sketches of figures and pastoral scenes, was also employed.

3. LATE BRONZE AGE AND LATER (MARDIKH IV–VII). Following its violent destruction at the end of the 17th century BC, perhaps in connection with the Hittite invasions of northern Syria, the city was reduced to a small village on the acropolis between the 16th and 12th centuries BC. Parts of the lower city and acropolis were reoccupied during Iron Age I–III (mid-11th to 6th century BC). The last period of expansion took place under the Achaemenids (550–330 BC), when a small, rustic palace surrounded by private dwellings was constructed in the north-east section of the acropolis. Finally, during the Byzantine period a monastery was built on the ruins of Palace Q, under the western slope of the acropolis. A stylite saint was venerated here, and his image on a column appears on a roughly carved stele.

BIBLIOGRAPHY
P. Matthiae: 'Le sculture in basalto', *Missione Archeologica Italiana in Siria, 1964* (Rome, 1965), pp. 61–80
——: 'Le sculture di Tell Mardikh', *Rendi. Pontificia Accad. Romana Archeol.*, xxxviii (1965–6), pp. 15–59
——: 'I frammenti di sculture in pietra', *Missione Archeologica Italiana in Siria, 1965* (Rome, 1966), pp. 111–38
——: 'Le sculture in pietra', *Missione Archeologica Italiana in Siria, 1966* (Rome, 1967), pp. 103–42
——: 'Empreintes d'un cylindre paléosyrien de Tell Mardikh', *Syria*, xlvi (1969), pp. 1–43
S. Mazzoni: 'Tell Mardikh e una classe di glittica siro-anatolica del periodo di Larsa', *Ist. Orient. Napoli: An.*, xxv (1975), pp. 21–43
P. Matthiae: 'Le Palais royal protosyrien d'Ebla: Nouvelles recherches archéologiques à Tell Mardikh en 1976', *C. R. Séances Acad. Inscr. & B.-Lett.* (1977), pp. 148–72
——: 'Recherches archéologiques à Ebla, 1977: Le Quartier administratif du Palais Royal G', *C. R. Séances Acad. Inscr. & B.-Lett.* (1978), pp. 204–36
——: 'Princely Tombs and Ancestors' Cult at Ebla during Middle Bronze II', *Ugarit-Forsch.*, xi (1979), pp. 563–9
Studi eblaiti, 6 vols (Rome, 1979–83)
P. Matthiae: 'Campagne de fouilles à Tell Mardikh–Ebla en 1979: Les Tombes princières et le palais de la ville basse à l'époque amorrhéenne', *C. R. Séances Acad. Inscr. & B.-Lett.* (1980), pp. 94–118
——: 'Fouilles à Tell Mardikh–Ebla, 1978: Le Bâtiment Q et la nécropole princière du Bronze Moyen', *Akkadica*, xvii (1980), pp. 1–51
——: 'Some Fragments of Early Syrian Sculpture from the Royal Palace G of Tell Mardikh–Ebla', *J. Nr É. Stud.*, xxxix (1980), pp. 249–73
——: 'Fouilles à Tell Mardikh–Ebla, 1980: Le Palais occidental de l'époque amorrhéenne', *Akkadica*, xxviii (1982), pp. 41–87
——: 'Fouilles de 1981 à Tell Mardikh–Ebla et à Tell Touqan: Nouvelles lumières sur l'architecture paléosyrienne du Bronze Moyen I–II', *C. R. Séances Acad. Inscr. & B.-Lett.* (1982), pp. 299–331
——: 'Fouilles de Tell Mardikh–Ebla en 1982: Nouvelles recherches sur l'architecture palatine d'Ebla', *C. R. Séances Acad. Inscr. & B.-Lett.* (1983), pp. 530–54
P. Matthiae, ed.: 'En Syrie: Ebla retrouvée', *Doss. Hist. & Archéol.*, lxxxiii (1984), pp. 1–98
P. Matthiae: 'New Discoveries at Ebla: The Excavation of the Western Palace and the Royal Necropolis of the Amorite Period', *Bibl. Archaeologist*, xlv (1984), pp. 18–32
S. Mazzoni: 'Seal Impressions on Jars from Ebla in Early Bronze IV A–B', *Akkadica*, xxxvii (1984), pp. 18–40
P. Matthiae: *I tesori di Ebla: Ebla e le culture storiche del Vicino Oriente antico* (Rome and Bari, 1985)
——: 'Les Dernières Découvertes d'Ebla en 1983–1986', *C. R. Séances Acad. Inscr. & B.-Lett.* (1986), pp. 135–61
——: 'Una stele paleosiriana arcaica da Ebla e la cultura figurativa della Siria attorno al 1800 a.C.', *Sci. Ant.*, i (1987), pp. 447–95
——: *Ebla: Un impero ritrovato: Dai primi scavi alle ultime scoperte* (Turin, 1989)
S. Mazzoni: *Le impronte su giara eblaite e siriane nel Bronzo Antico* (Rome, 1992)

STEFANIA MAZZONI

Ebner, Louis. *See* DEÁK-ÉBNER, LAJOS.

Ebo. *See* EBBO.

Echagüe, José Ortiz. *See* ORTIZ ECHAGÜE, JOSÉ.

Echave [Chávez]. Mexican family of painters of Spanish origin. Baltasar de Echave Orio the elder (*b* Zumaya, Spain, *c.* 1558; *d* Mexico City, *c.* 1620) arrived in Mexico from Spain *c.* 1580. He worked with his father-in-law, Francisco de Zumaya (also known as Francisco de Ibía and Francisco de Gambo), on the principal retable and the S Miguel retable in Puebla Cathedral in 1590. His most important works date from the first two decades of the 17th century, during which he produced paintings for the retable of the Franciscan church of Santiago de Tlatelolco, Mexico City, of which the *Visitation* (Mexico City, Pin. Virreinal) and *Portiuncula* are certainly by him; the attribution of the *Annunciation* (Mexico City, Pin. Virreinal), *Resurrection* and *Stigmatization of St Francis* (Guadalajara, Mus. Reg. Antropol. & Hist.), originally in the same church, is more cautious. For the church of La Profesa, Mexico City, he executed the *Adoration of the Magi*, *Agony in the Garden*, *Martyrdom of St Aponius* and *Martyrdom of St Pontian* (all Mexico City, Pin. Virreinal). The retables of the churches in Tlalmanalco and Xochimilco are also attributed to him. His mature style, distinguished by its treatment of light and shade, shows evidence of Venetian influence, presumably acquired during his time in Spain. His son Baltasar de Echave Ibía the younger (*b* Mexico City, 1585; *d* Mexico City, 1650) developed a softer style, as is evident in his surviving works: two paintings of the *Immaculate Conception*, the *Conversation of the Hermit Saints Paul and Anthony*, *St John the Baptist*, *Mary Magdalene*, *St John*, *St Luke*, *St Mark*, *St James of Alcalá* and a *Portrait of a Lady* (all Mexico City, Pin. Virreinal); the *Baptism* (Xochimilco, church); and the *Annunciation*, *Visitation* and *St Francis of Paola* (all Guadalupe, Mus. Basílica). Another son, Manuel de Echave Ibía, is known from only one work, the *Virgin Placing the Chasuble on St Ildefonso* (Churubusco, Mus. Hist.). Baltasar de Echave Rioja (1632–82), grandson of Baltasar de Echave Orio, worked in a style closer to the chiaroscuro introduced into Mexico by Sebastián López de Arteaga, and iconographically the influence on him of Rubensian subjects is of great importance. This can be seen in the large canvases depicting the *Triumph of Religion* and the *Triumph of the Church*, painted for Puebla Cathedral (*in situ*). Also by him are the *Martyrdom of St Pedro Arbues* (1667), the *Entombment* (1668; both Mexico City, Pin. Virreinal), the *Last Supper* and *Washing of the Feet* (both 1681; Puebla, S Domingo de Izucar).

BIBLIOGRAPHY

M. Toussaint: 'Baltasar de Echave Orio, llamado "el Viejo"', *El arte en México: Pintura colonial*, iii (Mexico City, 1934)
G. Danes: 'Baltasar de Echave Ibia: Some Critical Notes on the Stylistic Character of his Art', *An. Inst. Invest. Estét.*, iii/9 (1942), pp.15–26
D. Angulo Íñiguez, E. Marco Dorta and J. Buschiazzo: *Historia del arte hispanoamericano* (Barcelona, 1945–56)
M. Toussaint: 'Pinturas coloniales mexicanas en Davenport', *An. Inst. Invest. Estét.*, xiv (1946), pp. 25–32
G. Kubler and M. S. Soria: *Art and Architecture in Spain and Portugal and their American Dominions, 1500–1800* (London, 1969)
G. Tovar de Teresa: *Pintura y escultura del renacimiento en México* (Mexico City, 1979)
N. Sigaut: 'Una pintura desconocida de Manuel de Echave', *An. Inst. Invest. Estét.*, lv (1986), pp. 85–96

MARIA CONCEPCIÓN GARCÍA SÁIZ

Echevarria (y Zuricalday), Juan de (*b* Bilbao, 14 April 1875; *d* Madrid, 8 July 1931). Spanish painter. He came from a family of Basque industrialists and received a cosmopolitan education, studying engineering in Germany, France and Belgium. The death of his mother in 1902 threw him into a profound crisis, and he left his father's factory to start his career as a painter. He attended the studio of the Spanish Basque painter Manuel Losada (1865–1949) and in 1903 left for Paris, where he frequented the Académie Julian and associated with other artists such as Degas, Henri Rousseau and Vuillard, and fellow Spaniards such as Picasso and Ignacio Zuloaga; he also took part in gatherings at the Lapin Agile café in Montmartre. After travelling to London and through Italy, northern Europe and Russia in 1907, he returned in 1908 to Paris, where he had a studio near Montmartre. That year some of his works were exhibited at the Salon d'Automne in Paris, where they were praised by Guillaume Apollinaire. He returned to Spain in 1914, first going to Granada and in 1915 settling in Madrid; in 1916 he exhibited with the Asociación de Artistas Vascos and at the Ateneo in Madrid.

Echevarria executed his most personal work in Spain, combining his abilities as a colourist and draughtsman with contemporary influences from a variety of sources, notably from Vuillard, Gauguin, van Gogh, Cézanne and Fauvism. Rather than evolving stylistically, he fluctuated from one manner to another. His subject-matter was equally varied, ranging from portraits and figure paintings to landscapes and still-lifes. He was fond of dealing with particular figure types such as Basques, Castilians and gypsies (e.g. *Russian Gypsies*, Madrid, Mus. A. Contemp.), and with nudes, as in *Nude Mestiza* (1925; Madrid, Mus. A. Contemp.). As a portraitist he is remembered especially for magnificent paintings of Spanish writers of the 'Generación del '98', such as that of the philosopher *Miguel de Unamuno* (1930; Salamanca, Mus. Salamanca). He was sufficiently wealthy not to have to sell his work, most of which therefore remained with his family. Severely critical of his own paintings, he retouched them heavily and sometimes even destroyed them.

BIBLIOGRAPHY

J. A. Gaya Nuño: *Juan de Echevarria* (Madrid, 1965)
Juan de Echevarria, 1875–1931 (exh. cat. by G. Diego and J. de la Puente, Madrid, Banco de Bilbao, 1974)

PILAR BENITO

Echeverría, Enrique (*b* Mexico City, 1923; *d* 1972). Mexican painter. He studied painting and drawing under the Spanish painter Arturo Souto, who had lived in exile in Mexico since 1940 and whose Post-Impressionist style influenced Echeverría's painting for some time. In 1952 Echeverría became associated with the newly founded Galería Prisse in Mexico City, run by artists opposed to nationalist tendencies in Mexican art, through which he befriended José Luis Cuevas, Alberto Gironella and Vlady. Also in 1952 he was awarded a scholarship by the Instituto de Cultura Hispánica, which enabled him to live in Europe for just over one year.

Echeverría began as a figurative painter but developed a form of abstraction concerned with the interrelationship of form and colour, with imagery still discernible. The play between representation and abstraction was particularly evident in works influenced by Nicolas de Staël, including a series of *Interior Landscapes* characterized by a restrained use of colour. In later years he used bright, contrasting colours and motifs vaguely reminiscent of those employed by Karel Appel, in dynamic, decorative and exuberant pictures dominated by curves. In spite of his premature death from a kidney infection, he became an important figure of the so-called 'generation of rupture' in Mexico.

BIBLIOGRAPHY
T. del Conde: *Un pintor mexicano y su tiempo: Enrique Echeverría* (Mexico City, 1979)

TERESA DEL CONDE

Echinus [Lat.: 'bowl']. Convex projecting moulding of eccentric curve supporting the abacus of a Doric capital. The term is also used for any moulding of similar profile or decoration (*see* GREECE, ANCIENT, fig. 9m; ORDERS, ARCHITECTURAL, fig. 1xi). In the Ionic order it comprises an EGG-AND-DART moulding beneath the cushion of the capital, between the volutes.

☐

Echizen. Centre of ceramics production in Japan, based on some 20 kiln sites 7 km north-west of the city of Takefu (Fukui Prefect.). Echizen is known as one of Japan's 'Six Old Kilns'. It is one of three centres that arose in the area (the others being Kaga and Suzu) in the 12th century in response to increased agricultural production. Ceramics appeared in Fukui Prefecture in the 6th century AD with the manufacture of Sue stoneware, fired in tunnel kilns (*anagama*; *see* JAPAN, §VIII, 2(ii)(a)). In the 12th century, however, increased agricultural production, coupled with the introduction of new technology, encouraged the development of a higher-fired brown stoneware. The use of a tunnel kiln with a dividing pillar, the manufacture of jars with everted rims and incised horizontal bands and the use of the coil-and-paddle technique in the early Echizen wares point to origins in kilns such as TOKONAME and Atsumi (now Aichi Prefect.), which spread these techniques and styles nationwide. Since nearby Tsuruga (Fukui Prefect.) was a port, direct influence on Echizen from continental Asia is also a possibility. The principal shapes were kitchen mortars (*suribachi*), narrow-necked jars (*tsubo*) and wide-necked jars (*kame*). These were made for agricultural use and for human burial.

Early Echizen wares were largely undecorated, but from the early 14th century some vessels display stamped, combed and carved decoration, as well as simple potter's marks. By mid-14th century the potter's marks become quite elaborate. At the same time the Echizen kilns expanded trade throughout the Japan Sea region; excavations demonstrate that products were distributed from Hokkaido in the north to Kyoto in the west. That Echizen wares found favour in the tea ceremony (*see* JAPAN, §XIV, 3) is demonstrated in the excavation of Echizen ware flower containers in the remains of Ichijodani, the Asakura family castle in Fukui. A brown-glazed ware was developed in the 17th century and can be seen on small bowls, spouted bowls, graters and sake bottles. Production at Echizen diminished thereafter, but the kilns survived, making local farm wares into the modern period.

BIBLIOGRAPHY
K. Mizuno and Y. Yoshioka: *Echizen, Kaga, Suzu* (1975), vii of *Nippon tōji zenshū* [Complete collection of Japanese ceramics], ed. M. Satō and others (Tokyo, 1975–7)
Nihon no tōji [Japanese ceramics] (exh. cat., ed. Y. Yabe; Tokyo, N. Mus., 1985)
K. Mizuno: 'Echizen, Wakasa no yakimono' [Ceramics of Echizen, Wakasa], *Nihon yakimono shūsei*, iv (Tokyo, 1981), pp. 98–102

RICHARD L. WILSON

Echoppe. Type of etching needle with a sharp, but rounded end. It was developed by Jacques Callot to make etchings look like engravings, since the line produced can imitate the swelling lines of a burin. It was also extensively used by Abraham Bosse.

☐

Echter (von Mespelbrunn), Julius, Prince-Bishop of Würzburg and Duke of Franconia (*b* Mespelbrunn, 18 March 1545; *d* Würzburg, 13 Sept 1617). German ecclesiastic and patron. He was the second son of Peter Echter, a local magistrate; he was educated in Würzburg, Mainz and the Jesuit college in Cologne. He completed his studies by attendance at several European universities before returning in 1569 to join the cathedral chapter in Würzburg. He became Dean in 1570. In a period of low morale for the Roman Catholic church in Germany, his enthusiasm for the ideas of the Counter-Reformation and his reforming zeal caused him to be elected Prince-Bishop of Würzburg at an early age in 1573. He introduced numerous reforms—of an absolutist tendency—in the administration of the diocese and in education, and he founded the university of Würzburg in 1582 (completed 1591). He promoted the building of hospitals throughout the region, the most famous being the Julius Hospital (1576–80) in Würzburg.

In his efforts to strengthen the Roman Catholic faith Echter initiated the building of numerous churches, as well as other buildings, probably around 300 in all. He had firm ideas on the appearance of churches. Only in very small villages did he allow the naves and choirs to have flat roofs: in the larger villages there had to be a vaulted chancel, often highly ornamented, and the nave had to have at least three aisles and be appropriately high, with a spacious and well ventilated sacristy, usually on the south side of the choir. The church towers had to be visible from a distance. Echter had many new towers built, as well as having existing towers raised by the height of one or two storeys and providing them with very characteristic steeply pointed helm roofs so that they could be seen from far away. He also made sure that the churches were adequately furnished. He insisted on vaulted naves in town churches, pilgrimage churches and monastic churches. Wherever possible he incorporated parts of older buildings in new ones. The church buildings were mostly in a Gothic style (e.g. Wallfahrtskirche, Maria auf dem Sand, Deffelbach), with traceried windows and ribbed vaulting; their ornament was often a mixture of Gothic and Renaissance. The porches, altars, pulpits and fittings often incorporated novel features. Only the university church (1583–97) and the hospital church in Würzburg were deliberately commissioned in a Renaissance style, with some Gothic features, such as traceried windows; this came to be known as the 'Julius' style.

The castles that Echter built show a similar reversion to medieval forms in such elements as towers, gateways, tombstones and drawbridges; he aimed at a style resembling that which prevailed in 15th-century France. Echter's insistence on medieval forms seems to have been not a matter of aesthetic preference but rather a reflection of his conviction that, in order to succeed, the Counter-Reformation had to lead the way back to medieval attitudes of thought.

BIBLIOGRAPHY

R. Pfister: 'Das Würzburger Wohnhaus im XVI. Jahrhundert mit einer Abhandlung über den sogenannten Juliusstil', *Z. Gesch. Archit.*, xiii (1925), pp. 1–19

G. von Pölnitz: 'Julius Echter von Mespelbrunn: Fürstbischof von Würzburg und Herzog von Franken (1573–1617)', *Schrreihe Bayer. Landesgesch.*, xvii (1934) [repr. Aalen, 1973]

W. Engel: 'Eine Finanzstatistik über die Bauten des Fürstbischofs Julius Echter', *Fürstbischof Julius Echter als Bauherr* (Würzburg, 1951), pp. 62–110

M. H. von Freeden: 'Fürstbischof Julius Echter als Bauherr auf dem Schlosse Marienberg zu Würzburg', *Fürstbischof Julius Echter als Bauherr* (Würzburg, 1951), pp. 5–61

Mainfränk. Hft. (1951) [issue devoted to Echter]

C. Schenk: 'Das Würzburger Juliusspital in seiner architekturgeschichtlichen und städtebaulichen Bedeutung', *Das Juliusspital Würzburg: Festschrift aus Anlass der Einweihung der wiederaufgebauten Pfarrkirche des Juliusspitals am 16. Juli 1953* (Würzburg, 1953), pp. 46–79

F. Merzbacher, ed.: *Julius Echter und seine Zeit: Gedenkschrift aus Anlass des 400. Jahrestag der Wahl des Stifters der Alma Julia zum Fürstbischof von Würzburg am 1. Dezember 1573: Auftrag der Bayerischen Julius-Maximilians-Universität Würzburg* (Würzburg, 1973)

B. Schock-Werner: 'Stil als Legitimation: "Historismus" in den Bauten des Würzburger Fürstbischofes Julius Echter von Mespelbrunn', *Pirkheimer-Jb.*, vi (1991), pp. 51–82

BARBARA SCHOCK-WERNER

Echternach. Former monastery in Luxembourg on the Sûre, a tributary of the Moselle. Archaeological finds and excavations have revealed a prehistoric settlement, a Roman villa (*c.* AD 60–70) and a small fortress (*c.* AD 260–75, with subsequent reinforcements) on the hill housing the later parish church of SS Peter and Paul. There are documentary records of the donation in AD 697–8 of part of the Villa Epternacus, together with a *monasteriolum* (small monastery), by St Irmina, Abbess of Oeren near Trier, to the Northumbrian missionary monk St Willibrord (658–739). The remaining part of the villa was donated by St Plektrudis and her husband Pepin II in 706. The first church was replaced *c.* 800 by a three-aisled basilica.

The monastery was run in the 8th century by Anglo-Saxons, and its scriptorium was the most important centre of Anglo-Saxon copyists and illuminators in continental Europe. The so-called Echternach Gospels (Paris, Bib. N., MS. lat. 9389), made in Northumbria in the late 7th century, must have reached Echternach before the Saint's death there in 739. Anglo-Saxon influence can be seen in various manuscripts produced in Echternach in the first half of the 8th century, such as the Gospel book at Trier (Domschatzbib., Cod. 61), the uncial Psalter (Stuttgart, Württemberg. Landesbib., MS. bibl. fol. 12*a*–*c*) and the Gospel book at Augsburg (Ubib., MS. 1.2.4°2).

In the 9th century Echternach was a community of canons. Otto I introduced the Rule of St Benedict in 973, when 40 monks moved to Echternach from the reform abbey of St Maximin, Trier, under Abbot Ravanger (*reg* 973–1007). Under Abbot Humbert (*reg* 1028–51) and the superintendence of St Poppo of Stavelot (1020–48), Cluniac reforms were implemented. The present basilica of St Willibrord essentially dates back to the new structure erected at that time (1031).

The Echternach school of manuscript illumination—alongside those of Reichenau, Cologne and Regensburg—counts as one of the most important of the 11th century.

Written entirely in gold, the Codex Aureus of Echternach (*c.* 1030; Nuremberg, Ger. Nmus., Cod. 2° 156142) is of outstanding quality. Its gold-embossed front cover (440×310 mm) was made earlier, between 985 and 987, probably in Trier. Smaller in format than this lavish manuscript is the Book of Pericopes from between 1039 and 1043 (Bremen, Staats- & Ubib., MS. b. 21; see fig.), which Abbot Humbert presented to Emperor Henry III at the start of his reign (1039–56). Henry in turn commissioned two sumptuous Gospel books from Echternach: the Escorial Codex (Madrid, Escorial, Bib. Monasterio S Lorenzo, MS. Vit. 17; *see* MANUSCRIPT, colour pl. V, fig. 2), executed between 1043 and 1046 for Speyer Cathedral, and the Codex Caesarius Upsaliensis (Uppsala, U. Lib.), produced between 1050 and 1056 for SS Simon and Jude, Goslar. Only a fragment survives of a further luxury Gospel book from Echternach (Paris, Bib. N., MS. nouv. acq. lat. 2196), which is dated earlier than the Escorial Codex on stylistic grounds. It was commissioned by Abbot Gerard II of Luxeuil (*reg* after 1033–*c.* 1050) for his abbey.

The richly illuminated Book of Pericopes (Brussels, Bib. Royale Albert 1er, MS. lat. 9428) of *c.* 1040 was intended for a church dedicated to St Stephen. The Echternach Gospel books from the mid-11th century (Paris, Bib. N., MS. lat. 10438; London, BL, MSS Harley 2821 and Egerton 608) form a related group. Further Echternach manuscripts from the 11th century include the Sacramentary with Gradual from Echternach or Trier (first third of the 11th century; Darmstadt, Hess. Landes- & Hochschbib., MSS 1946), a Lectionary (*c.* 1040; Trier,

Echternach school: *Scribes Working in the Scriptorium*; miniature from the Echternach Book of Pericopes, 1039–43 (Bremen, Staats- und Universitätsbibliothek, MS. b.21, fol. 124*v*)

Bistumsarchiv, MS. 434), the Gospel book from the third quarter of the 11th century (Paris, Bib. N., MSS lat. 11961–2) and the Bible and Homily (Luxembourg, Bib. N., MS. 264), probably executed under Abbot Reginbert (*reg* 1051–81). Echternach went into a gradual decline in the late Middle Ages. Conventual buildings were constructed in the 18th century, but the monastery was dissolved in 1797.

BIBLIOGRAPHY

C. Nordenfalk: *Codex Caesarius Upsaliensis: An Echternach Gospel-book of the Eleventh Century* (Stockholm, 1971)

J. Metzler, J. Zimmer and L. Bakker: *Ausgrabungen in Echternach* (Luxembourg, 1981)

R. Kahsnitz: *Das goldene Evangelienbuch von Echternach: Codex Aureus Epternacensis Hs. 156142 aus dem Germanischen Nationalmuseum Nürnberg* (Frankfurt am Main and Stuttgart, 1982) [incl. an essay by E. Rücker]

D. Ó Cróinín: 'Rath Melsigi, Willibrord and the Earliest Echternach Manuscripts', *Peritia*, iii (1984), pp. 17–49

ULRICH KUDER

Ecija. Spanish city on the River Genil in Seville province, with a population of *c.* 35,000. Originally a Greek settlement named Astigi, it was occupied by the Romans and was an episcopal see by the 3rd century AD. Numerous remains of the Roman city have been found, such as mosaics, pottery and even vestiges of the street layout. The city was captured in the 8th century by the Moors, who named it Estadja ('rich city') or Medina Alcoton ('city of cotton') and under whom it became the capital of an independent kingdom. In 1245, however, the city was retaken by Christian forces, after which Castilian families settled there. In 1402 it was granted the title 'royal' by Henry III (*reg* 1390–1406), and it subsequently became an important agricultural and commercial centre, dominated by its Plaza Mayor but retaining its Moorish street plan until the 18th century. Parts of the Moorish walls, reinforced by Ferdinand III (*reg* 1217–52) have survived, as have some of the towers (Albarrana, Quintata, Picadero and Merino) and some of the city gates, such as the Cerrada or closed gate and the Bridge Gate. Numerous churches and monasteries have also survived from the period after the Reconquest, many of them built in *Mudéjar* style. Some, such as the churches of the Visitation and of S Barbara, retain their original decoration, despite undergoing significant alteration in the Baroque period. One of the most important examples is the church of Santa Cruz (rebuilt in the 18th century by Antonio Matías de Figueroa), which contains a statue of the *Virgin of Mercy* by Jerónimo Hernández Estrada and a monstrance of 1586 by Alfaro. Two churches that have retained their original form are those of S Gil and Santiago (both 15th century). The latter contains paintings by Alejo Fernández and a *Crucifixion* by Pedro Roldán. Notable among convents include that of S Florentina, in *Mudéjar* style but with Baroque alterations, and that of the Teresian nuns, built above a 14th-century *Mudéjar* mansion.

Ecija's most outstanding period, however, came in the 18th century, during which the city was revitalized, particularly in the area of housing. Outstanding palatial mansions to have survived from this period include those of the Peñaflor and Villaseca families. Many such houses, for example that of the Benameji family in the Plaza Mayor, are characterized by their *miradores* or viewing towers, an important symbol of social status. Many new districts also sprang up outside the city in the mid-18th century, and in the second half of the 19th century many of these were brought into alignment with the intramural area.

BIBLIOGRAPHY

J. Hernández Díaz, A. Sancho Corbacho and C. F. Collantes de Terán: *Catálogo arqueológico y artístico de la provincia de Sevilla*, 4 vols (Seville, 1939–55)

A. Bonet Correa: *Andalucía barroca: Arquitectura y urbanismo* (Barcelona, 1978)

A. Morales, M. J. Sanz and E. Valdivieso: *Guía artística de Sevilla y su provincia* (Seville, 1980)

MARÍA DOLORES DÍAZ VAQUERO

Eck, Barthélemy de. *See* EYCK, BARTHÉLEMY D'.

Eckell, Ana (*b* Buenos Aires, 30 Oct 1947). Argentine painter. She studied in Buenos Aires at the Escuela Nacional de Bellas Artes Manuel Belgrano (1961–4) and at the Escuela Nacional de Bellas Artes Prilidiano Pueyrredón (1965–7). Making reference in her paintings to comic strips, to the work of Otto Dix and George Grosz and to the early pictures of Jean Dubuffet, to photograms and to the cinema, she combined a variety of images and styles in a single work without establishing a narrative. Superimposing caricatured human and animal forms on to a surface of animated brushstrokes akin to gestural abstraction, she created from these fragments pictures that were like puzzles for the spectator. By such means she created an art endowed both with the humour and playfulness of childhood and with an exasperation and underlying horror.

BIBLIOGRAPHY

J. Glusberg: *Del Pop-art a la Nueva Imagen* (Buenos Aires, 1985), pp. 518–20

HORACIO SAFONS

Eckel & Mann. American architectural partnership formed in 1880 in St Joseph, MO, by Edmond Jacques Eckel (*b* Strasbourg, France, 22 June 1845; *d* St Joseph, 12 Dec 1934) and George R. Mann (*b* IN, 2 July 1856; *d* Little Rock, AR, 20 March 1939). Eckel graduated (1868) from the Ecole des Beaux-Arts in Paris, and Mann studied at Massachusetts Institute of Technology at a time when few architects in the USA were academically trained. St Joseph, the terminus during the 1860s of the Pony Express, was a fast-growing commercial centre. The firm's early work there, such as the Nodaway County Court House (begun 1881), Maryville, MO, often resembled the eclectic red-brick Gothic Revival style of Richard Morris Hunt's Tribune Building (1873–6) in New York, but little of it survives. In their later work they often used the Romanesque Revival style of H. H. Richardson, as in the five-storey German–American Bank Building (1889) in St Joseph, built of red brick and stone. The partners employed the talented designer Harvey Ellis from about 1889 until 1893 and opened an office in St Louis, MO. Most important was their City Hall (competition entry 1892; built 1894–5) in St Louis, which resembled the Hôtel de Ville (rebuilt 1876–84 by Théodore Ballu) in Paris, but was of pink granite, buff sandstone and pink–orange Roman brick. The partnership was dissolved in 1892. Eckel remained in St Joseph, where he continued to practise with other partners, and Mann went to St Louis and later to Little Rock, where he was the architect for the Arkansas State Capitol.

UNPUBLISHED SOURCES

Kansas City, U. MO ['Edmond J. Eckel: Architectural Records'; Columbia, MO, State Hist. Soc., MS. 355]

St Joseph, MO, Brunner & Brunner Arch. and Engr. [Papers of E. J. Eckel; an extensive col. of drgs and office rec.]

WRITINGS

G. R. Mann: *Sketches from an Architect's Portfolio* (St Louis, 1893)

BIBLIOGRAPHY

'Contemporary Architects and their Works: E. J. Eckel, F. A. I. A.', *W. Architect*, xvii (1911), pp. 79–84

J. A. Bryan, ed.: *Missouri's Contribution to American Architecture* (St Louis, 1928)

[Mann]: Obituary, *Pencil Points*, xx (May 1939), suppl. p. 64

'Edmond Jacques Eckel', *National Cyclopedia of American Biography*, xli (Clifton, NJ, 1956), p. 324

H. R. Hitchcock and W. Seale: *Temples of Democracy* (New York and London, 1976)

L. K. Eaton: *Gateway Cities and Other Essays* (Ames, IA, 1989)

T. M. Prawl: *E. J. Eckel, 1845–1934: A Beaux-Arts Architect at Practice in Missouri* (Columbia, U. MO, 1995)

WESLEY I. SHANK

Eckersberg, C(hristoffer) W(ilhelm) (*b* Blåkrog, southern Jutland, 2 Jan 1783; *d* Copenhagen, 22 July 1853). Danish painter and teacher. He has been called 'the father of Danish painting' because of the influence he exerted on Danish painters in the second quarter of the 19th century. With Christen Købke he was the leading painter of the Danish 'Golden Age' (*c*. 1800–1850). He is best known for his landscapes, portraits and marine paintings, though he also executed some religious themes and subjects from Danish history in Christiansborg Palace.

1. Early training and Paris, to 1813. 2. Rome, 1813–16. 3. Return to Copenhagen and later career, 1816 and after.

1. EARLY TRAINING AND PARIS, TO 1813. Eckersberg learnt the rudiments of painting as a child from his

1. C. W. Eckersberg: *View from the Colosseum*, 1815 (Copenhagen, Statens Museum for Kunst)

father, a carpenter and house painter, and later moved to Åbenrå to serve as a painter's apprentice (1797–1800) to the provincial artist Jes Jessen (1743–1807). This sojourn was cut short by a row with his master and resulted in Eckersberg moving in 1803 to Flensburg (now in Germany but at that time under Danish sovereignty), where he was apprenticed briefly to another minor painter, Johann Jacob Jessen.

In 1803, with money provided by local notables, Eckersberg went to Copenhagen to study at the Kunstakademi. There he came under the tutelage of the great Danish Neo-classical artist and professor, Nicolai Abilgaard, who instilled in him a profound appreciation of Classical form and subject-matter. In 1805 Eckersberg won one gold and two silver medals. However, he became increasingly alienated from his teacher, and it was only after Abilgaard's death in 1809 that he succeeded in winning the great gold medal and the stipend allowing him to travel to Rome.

On 3 July 1810 Eckersberg left Denmark in the company of the courtier T. C. Bruun Neergaard, who supported him financially until the gold medal stipend became available in 1812. Equally importantly, Bruun Neergaard enabled Eckersberg to interrupt his journey to Rome in Paris, where he introduced the artist to Jacques-Louis David. In 1811 Eckersberg became a pupil of David, who exerted considerable influence on his work. Eckersberg's *Three Spartan Youths* (1812; Copenhagen, Hirschsprungske Saml.) is Neo-classical in both subject and composition in the manner of David and may have been produced in the latter's studio. In Paris Eckersberg saw and copied the paintings of Claude Lorrain and Pierre Henry de Valenciennes from whose painterly tradition he derived inspiration. Their influence is apparent in one of the most notable paintings he produced at this time, *View over the Pont Royal from the Quai Voltaire* (1812; Copenhagen, Stat. Mus. Kst). Eckersberg was able to draw from live models in David's studio and to use his acute powers of observation to produce studies after nature, a concept of great importance for Neo-classical artists at that time. *Two Shepherds* (1813; Copenhagen, Stat. Mus. Kst) is an accomplished testament to what he had learnt in Paris, a synthesis of Neo-classical ideal form, careful figure drawing and observation of the natural world. The portrait of *Emelie* (1813; priv. col.), a beautiful young French model, also epitomizes these qualities and demonstrates the importance for Eckersberg of preliminary drawings, the use of which may have been encouraged by his collaboration with the engraver J. F. Clemens, an associate of the Danish portrait painter Jens Juel. Indeed, drawings were always of paramount importance for Eckersberg, and the experience gained in Paris through drawing architecture and people was to be very useful for his work in Rome.

2. ROME, 1813–16. Eckersberg arrived in Rome on 3 July 1813 and remained there until 1816. While there he met Bertel Thorvaldsen and became a resident at the Palazzo Tomati where the sculptor lived. From Thorvaldsen, Eckersberg learnt to appreciate the Classical ruins and archaeological finds in Rome. Perhaps Thorvaldsen's greatest importance for the work of Eckersberg was the personal inspiration he provided while posing for his portrait (1814; Copenhagen, Kon. Kstakad.). In this work

Eckersberg combined a heroic vision of the artist, dressed in the robes of the Accademia di S Luca and seated in front of one of his most Classically inspired works, the *Alexander Frieze* (1812; Rome, Pal. Quirinale), with a naturalistic depiction, strongly indebted to David's portraits.

Eckersberg was as skillful in depicting views of Roman ruins as in portraying people. His *View from the Colosseum* (1815; Copenhagen, Stat. Mus. Kst; see fig. 1) demonstrates his ability to render accurately linear perspective and architectural detail. The three open arches of the Colosseum create a starkly symmetrical frame for the view of the Roman rooftops. The most important feature of Eckersberg's period in Rome was the effect the southern light exerted on his palette and compositional sense. He fused unusual viewpoints and forms of almost hieratic rigidity in the manner of Ingres. In the *Steps and Façade of S Maria in Aracoeli* (1813–16; Copenhagen, Stat. Mus. Kst), the unfinished façade of the church dominates, silhouetted against the sky and placed parallel to the picture plane, while the harsh sunlight picks out each step in front of the church.

3. RETURN TO COPENHAGEN AND LATER CAREER, 1816 AND AFTER. After almost three successful years in Rome and with news of his growing fame reaching Copenhagen, Eckersberg deemed the time ripe to return home. He arrived in Copenhagen in 1816 to find the city still devastated by bombardment and defeat in the Napoleonic Wars, but gradually coming to terms with its reduced political circumstances. Danes were also at this time becoming increasingly aware of their nation's rich culture and inheritance, and Eckersberg benefited from this period of national consolidation. In 1817 he married Jens Juel's daughter, Julie (and after her death married her sister, Susanne). Also in 1817 he was made a member of the Academy; in 1818 he was appointed professor and was allocated a set of rooms in the Academy, within the Charlottenborg Palace.

Eckersberg continued to produce portraits throughout his life. His portrait of the *Nathanson Family* (1818; Copenhagen, Stat. Mus. Kst) is a perfect balance of form and spacing, the evenly lit figures arranged across the canvas as in a Classical frieze. It depicts the family of one of his leading patrons, the businessman and newspaper editor Mendel Levin Nathanson. Eckersberg establishes the wealth and dignity of Nathanson, but also the informal domestic setting, by posing him at the extreme right of the composition. Such works form an important link between the conventionalized formality of portraits by Juel and the intimacy of those painted by Eckersberg's pupil, Vilhelm Marstrand. The smooth modelling and pose of such portraits as *Emilie Henriette Massmann* (1820; Copenhagen, Stat. Mus. Kst) also reflect the influence of Ingres.

Eckersberg produced a number of exquisite small figure paintings in his later years, notably *Study of a Nude in Front of a Mirror* (1830s; Copenhagen, Hirschsprungske Saml.), which matches Vermeer in its delicate control of light and tone. However, it is especially in his maritime paintings that the lessons learnt in Paris and Rome find their fullest expression within a Scandinavian context. In

The Russian Ship of the Line 'Azov' and a Frigate at Anchor off the Coast of Elsinore (1828; Copenhagen, Stat. Mus. Kst; see fig. 2), Eckersberg records with great precision a calm Danish sea and sky, while he applies to the ship, and in particular its rigging, the mastery of perspective and architectural structure that derives from his Roman architectural views. Whether depicting calm seas or turbulent storm-tossed waves, Eckersberg was preoccupied with clarity of detail, both in the structure of the ships and of the sky; thus conditions of poor visibility were eschewed. He made two voyages across the North Sea in 1833 and 1839 to heighten his awareness of extreme weather conditions at sea, producing sketches, noting time and meteorological conditions and often including complicated calculations on perspective. While these sketches are of interest on their own, they were of the greatest importance in producing his finished oils.

Much of Eckersberg's later life was taken up with teaching. He revolutionized the course of study at the Academy to stress life study and perspective theory and, through the example particularly of his landscapes, influenced numerous Scandinavian artists from about 1820 to 1860, including such leading Danish painters as Christen Købke, Constantin Hansen, Vilhelm Marstrand and Martinus Rørbye. Their common inheritance is an emphasis on the bright light of a summer day, keenly observed figurative and architectural detail and intimate domestic interiors that appealed to the rising Danish middle class. Eckersberg succumbed to a cholera epidemic in 1853, having refused to leave his beloved Charlottenborg. His son, Erling Carl Vilhelm Eckersberg (1809–94), was an engraver.

2. C. W. Eckersberg: *The Russian Ship of the Line 'Azov' and a Frigate at Anchor off the Coast of Elsinore*, oil on canvas, 630×510 mm, 1828 (Copenhagen, Statens Museum for Kunst)

BIBLIOGRAPHY

E. Hannover: *Maleren C. W. Eckersberg* [The painter C. W. Eckersberg] (Copenhagen, 1898)

J. Eckersberg: *Optegnelser om C. W. Eckersberg* [Notes on C. W. Eckersberg] (Copenhagen, 1917)

H. Bramsen, ed.: *C. W. Eckersberg i Paris: Dagbog og breve, 1810–13* [C. W. Eckersberg in Paris: diary and letters, 1810–13] (Copenhagen, 1947)

C. W. Eckersberg og hans elever [C. W. Eckersberg and his pupils] (exh. cat., ed. H. Jönsson; Copenhagen, Stat. Mus. Kst, 1983; rev. 1984 with Eng. trans.)

Tegninger af C. W. Eckersberg [Drawings by C. W. Eckersberg] (exh. cat. by E. Fisher and others, Copenhagen, Stat. Mus. Kst, 1983; rev. 1983 with Eng. trans. of intro.)

Danish Painting: The Golden Age (exh. cat. by K. Monrad, London, N.G., 1984), pp. 90–119

K. Monrad: *Hverdagsbilleder. Dansk guldalder: Kunsterne og deres vilkår* [Everyday pictures. The Danish golden age: artists and their milieu] (Copenhagen, 1989)

O. Feldbaek, ed.: *Dansk identitetshistorie*, 4 vols (Copenhagen, 1992)

H. J. Frederiksen and I.-L. Kostrup, eds: *Ny dansk kunsthistorie*, 10 vols (Copenhagen, 1993)

NEIL KENT

Eckersberg, J(ohan) F(redrik) (*b* Drammen, 16 June 1822; *d* Sandvika, 13 July 1870). Norwegian painter. During a stay in the Netherlands as a clerk (1838–41) he became interested in old Dutch art and learnt to copy paintings. Having returned to Oslo he became a pupil of the landscape painter Johannes Flintoe (1787–1870) at the Tegneskolen (1843–6) and made a trip into the Norwegian mountains with Hans Gude in 1846. The same year he went to the Akademie at Düsseldorf with Gude and stayed there until 1848, taking some lessons from the landscape painter J. W. Schirmer.

Eckersberg's artistic point of departure was the romantic and academic landscape style of the Düsseldorf school, although he was by temperament an artist with realist tendencies. He drew well but had a certain lack of imagination and little sense of colour. He composed large mountain landscapes, stressing space and form to great effect in such pictures as *Valle in Setesdal* (1852) and *From Jotunheimen* (1866; both Oslo, N.G.). He visited Madeira (1852–4), depicting exotic views and tropical vegetation. Although there was little development in his style, the works from his last decade are perhaps the most satisfying artistically.

Eckersberg was the first Norwegian painter of any eminence who chose to establish himself in Norway. The elementary school for artists that he ran from 1859 until his death became influential. He modelled it on the Düsseldorf Akademie but encouraged his pupils to travel extensively in Norway in order to draw and to gather impressions.

NBL; NKL

BIBLIOGRAPHY

S. Willoch: *Forleggeren og maleren* [The publisher and the painter] (Oslo, 1948)

VIDAR POULSSON

Eckhardt. German family of artists. Hieronymus Eckhardt the elder (*d* 1572) was master of the Freiberg masons' and sculptors' guild. His son Hieronymus Eckhardt the younger (*d* 5 April 1624) was the municipal mason of Freiberg. The sons of Hieronymus the younger included Uriel Eckhardt (1582–1612), who carved the tomb of *Caspar von Schönberg the younger* (*d* 1605) at St Mary's, Sayda; Gabriel Eckhardt, who carved the font in the town church at Penig; Georg Eckhardt (*c.* 1590–1637), also a sculptor; and Ezechiel Eckhardt (*bapt* Freiberg, Saxony, 24 Feb 1595; traceable until 1664). Ezechiel trained in his father's workshop in Freiberg, where he worked until 1623, when he moved to Dresden, acquiring civic rights in the same year.

Under Elector John-George I of Saxony (*reg* 1611–56) Eckhardt undertook alterations and improvements to various palaces and fortifications in Saxony. In 1623 he was appointed assistant architect in the Elector's office of works. In 1627 Ezechiel is mentioned as the master directing the building at Schloss Hartenfels near Torgau. Before 1628 he was promoted to senior architect for the electorate, and he is referred to that year in the same capacity in connection with the renovation of the Radeberg Palace and again in 1641–2. In 1651 he directed the internal works at Schloss Ortenberg in Bautzen, and in 1654 he was commissioned to undertake some apparently minor alterations to Schloss Hermsdorf. From 1656 to 1664 Eckhardt worked on the building of the Moritzburg. Apart from his alterations to existing buildings, only two original works by Ezechiel can be proved: Hoflössnitz manor house (1650) and the church (1656; nave rebuilt 1884) in neighbouring Kötschenbroda. The house at Hoflössnitz is a plain, two-storey building, the upper floor half-timbered with a hipped roof. An octagonal stair-tower is located on the north side. Inside, the ground-floor is groin-vaulted, with round piers in the central chamber. There is a rectangular hall on the upper floor, with an adjacent room at each end.

Thieme–Becker

BIBLIOGRAPHY

H. Beschorner: 'Die Hoflössnitz bei Dresden', *Dresdn. Geschbl.*, xiii (1904), pp. 209–26, 239–47

M. Lewy: *Schloss Hartenfels bei Torgau* (diss., Dresden, Tech. U., 1908)

H. Beschorner: 'Ezechiel Eckhardt, der Erbauer der Hoflössnitz', *Dresdn. Geschbl.*, xviii (1909), pp. 30–35

J. Hebeda: *Weibergschlösschen Hoflössnitz*, Baudenkmale, 47 (Leipzig, 1980)

S. TRÄGER

Eckhout, Albert (*b* Groningen, *c.* 1610; *d* Groningen, 1666). Dutch painter and draughtsman. Eckhout and Frans Post were the two most important artists who travelled to Brazil in 1637 in the entourage of the newly appointed governor-general, Johan Maurits, Count of Nassau-Siegen (*see* NASSAU, (1)), on whose initiative Eckhout was assigned to paint people, plants and animals as part of a scientific study of the country. Eckhout's studies are characterized by an objectivity that is sober, direct and without artistic embellishment. In 1644 Johan Maurits, nicknamed 'the Brazilian', returned to the Netherlands where he published the collected scientific material as *Historia naturalis Brasíliae* (1648). He also used this material as a diplomatic tool; in 1654 he presented Frederick III of Denmark with a series of room decorations that Eckhout had partially painted in Brazil between 1641 and 1643. This series comprised nine large portraits of aboriginal Indians, twelve still-lifes with Brazilian fruit and three portraits of Congolese envoys (Copenhagen, Stat. Mus. Kst).

The only painting by Eckhout in a Dutch public collection, *Two Brazilian Turtles* (The Hague, Mauritshuis), was probably one of the works of art sold by Johan Maurits in 1652 to Frederick William, the Great Elector.

This group included 800 chalk, oil and watercolour drawings of fish, reptiles, birds, insects, mammals, Indians, mulattos, fruits and plants, most of them presumably by Eckhout. They were collected into seven books, the *Libri picturati*, of which four volumes containing 400 oil sketches were entitled *Theatrum rerum naturalium Brasíliae* (Kraków, Jagiellonian U. Lib.). In 1679 Maurits gave Louis XIV of France a present of eight paintings of Indians and animals in imaginary landscapes with still-lifes of Brazilian and African fruits and plants painted by Eckhout after his return to the Netherlands. In 1668 Maximilian van der Gucht of The Hague made a series of tapestries after these paintings for the Great Elector, and a second series, the 'Tenture des Indes', was woven in 1687 by the French firm later known as Manufacture Royale des Gobelins (Paris, Mobilier N.). The paintings are no longer extant, but the cartoons for the tapestries were used until the 18th century. The many surviving tapestry series woven after 'Les anciennes Indes' (e.g. Amsterdam, Rijksmus.; Valletta, Pal. Grand Masters) testify to the popularity of these representations. At Maurits's recommendation, Eckhout entered the service of John-George I, Prince-Elector of Saxony, in 1653, and he remained in Dresden for the next ten years. His most important commission was for the ceiling decorations in the Hofflössnitz hunting lodge, for which he used his Brazilian studies or drew from memory. During this period he also made a series of large oil paintings of exotic, mainly Asiatic peoples (Schwedt, Schloss). In 1663 he returned to Groningen, where he was awarded citizenship.

BIBLIOGRAPHY
T. Thomsen: *Albert Eckhout* (Copenhagen, 1938)
Soweit der Erdkreis reicht (exh. cat., Cleve, Städt. Mus. Haus Koekkoek, 1979)
Zowijd de wereld strekt (exh. cat., The Hague, Mauritshuis, 1979–80)
B. P. J. BROOS

Eckl, Wilhelm. *See* EGCKL, WILHELM.

Eckmann, Otto (*b* Hamburg, 19 Nov 1865; *d* Badenweiler, 11 June 1902). German designer, illustrator and painter. He trained as a businessman before entering the Kunst- und Gewerbeschule in Hamburg. He studied at the Kunst- und Gewerbeschule in Nuremberg and from 1885 attended the Akademie der Bildenden Künste in Munich. His early paintings are naturalistic landscapes but around 1890 he shifted towards Symbolism (e.g. the *Four Ages of Life*, 1893–4; untraced). In 1894 he decided to devote himself to the decorative arts. Encouraged by Justus Brinckmann, a collector and museum director, and Friedrich Deneken (later Director of the Kaiser Wilhelm Museum, Krefeld), Eckmann studied the Japanese woodcut collection at the Museum für Kunst und Gewerbe, Hamburg. Using traditional Japanese techniques, he began producing his own woodcut designs in 1895. *Three Swans on Dark Water* (1895; Hamburg, Mus. Kst & Gew.) reflects a general preoccupation with late 19th-century music, art and literature with swans as symbolic images, and they were a frequent motif in many of his subsequent works. Eckmann's woodcuts, as well as ornamental borders, vignettes, bookplates and other graphic designs, were illustrated in such periodicals as *Deutsche Kunst und Dekoration, Jugend* and *Pan*. In 1899–1900 he collaborated

with Karl Klingspor at Rudhardsche Schriftgiesserei, Offenbach, to develop a new typeface named Eckmann.

Eckmann's Art Nouveau designs are characterized by strong colours, undulating lines, tense interplay between surface and decoration, and a formal vocabulary abstracted from nature. He worked alongside manufacturers to gain a thorough knowledge of materials, methods and technical processes involved in shaping his designs. Driven by creative frenzy and exacting discipline, he expanded his repertory as a craftsman, designing stained glass, ceramics, furniture and metalwork. He also designed interiors, the most important of which was a study/sitting-room (1897–8) in the Neue Palais (destr.), Darmstadt, for the Grand Duke Ernest Ludwig of Hesse-Darmstadt.

In the 1890s Eckmann was one of several artists, including Hermann Obrist, Richard Riemerschmid and August Endell, who exhibited in two rooms of modern decorative arts at the Munich Glaspalast exhibition of 1897. Eckmann was especially praised for such lighting fixtures as the wrought-iron 'Narcissus' candlestick (1896–7; Hamburg, Mus. Kst & Gew.), manufactured by Josef Zimmermann & Co., Munich. Eckmann designed carpets and tapestries for such firms as H. Engelhard of Mannheim and the Smyrna-Teppich-Fabrik, Berlin. His most famous tapestry, *Five Swans* (1896–7; Hamburg, Mus. Kst & Gew.; *see* TAPESTRY, fig. 13), of which approximately 100 examples were woven, was produced at the Scherrebek tapestry workshops in Schleswig-Holstein (now Skærbaek, Denmark).

In 1897 Eckmann was appointed Professor of Ornamental Painting at the Königliche Kunstgewerbemuseum in Berlin. His designs became more stylized and abstract, and shortly before his death from tuberculosis in 1902 he returned to landscape painting. Eckmann's estate was divided between the Kunstbibliothek Berlin mit Museum für Architektur, Modebild und Grafik-Design, the Kaiser Wilhelm Museum in Krefeld and the Museum für Kunst und Gewerbe in Hamburg. He is also remembered through Lovis Corinth's portrait of him (1897; Hamburg, Ksthalle).

WRITINGS
Neue Formen: Dekorative Entwürfe für die Praxis (Berlin, 1897)

BIBLIOGRAPHY
M. Osborn: 'Otto Eckmanns kunstgewerbliche Tätigkeit', *Dt. Kst & Dek.*, vi (1900), pp. 313–32
E. Zimmermann: 'Professor Otto Eckmann-Berlin-I: Die Jahre künstlerischer Entwicklung', *Dt. Kst & Dek.*, vi (1900), pp. 305–13
H. Loubier: 'Eckmann', *Die Neue Buchkunst: Studien im In- und Ausland*, ed. R. Kautzsch (Weimar, 1902)
Otto Eckmann (1865–1902): Ein Hauptmeister des Jugendstils (exh. cat., ed. G. Fiedler-Bender; Krefeld, Kaiser Wilhelm Mus., 1977–8)
J. Simmon: *Zeichnungen und Druckgraphik von Otto Eckmann: Der Bestand in der Kunstbibliothek Berlin* (Berlin, 1982)
Art Nouveau in Munich: Masters of Jugendstil (exh. cat., ed. K. B. Hiesinger; Philadelphia, PA, Mus. A., 1988)
LAURIE A. STEIN

Eclecticism. Term used to describe the combination in a single work of elements from different historical styles, chiefly in architecture and, by implication, in the fine and decorative arts. It was an important concept in Western architecture during the mid- and late 19th century, and it reappeared in a new guise in the latter part of the 20th century. The term is sometimes also loosely applied to the general stylistic variety of 19th-century architecture after Neo-classicism (i.e. from *c.* 1820), although the revivals of styles in that period have, since the 1970s, generally been referred to as aspects of HISTORICISM. Eclecticism is a term that plays an important role in critical discussions and evaluations but is somehow distant from the actual forms of the artefacts to which it is applied, and its meaning is thus rather indistinct. The simplest definition of the term—that every work of art represents the combination of a variety of influences—is so basic as to be of little use. In some ways Eclecticism is reminiscent of Mannerism in that the term was used pejoratively for much of the period of its currency, although, unlike Mannerism, Eclecticism hardly ever amounted to a movement or constituted a specific style: it is characterized precisely by the fact that it was not a particular style.

The term, which originated in antique philosophy, was revived in the 18th century, notably by Denis Diderot, in connection with Enlightenment attitudes to freedom from prejudice and authoritarianism, leaving each individual to search for truth, guided only by reason. The philosopher Victor Cousin (1792–1867) rejected the continual search for new ideas, advocating instead that philosophers should carefully select from, and combine afresh, all the doctrines that already existed. This seemed highly appropriate to the situation in which architecture found itself in the 1840s. The key issues were style and the prevailing tendency to define architecture in terms of style. While an ever-widening plurality of historical styles had come into general

use, encouraging complete stylistic freedom, academic revivalists, especially A. W. N. Pugin and later adherents of the Gothic Revival, demanded absolute allegiance to one style for all types of buildings. Alongside these opposing views a search began for a style that was not an imitation of the past but an expression of the 'new age'. Eclecticism seemed to offer a solution: its proponents used it to argue away the stigma attached to copyism, at the same time stressing that by skilfully combining the best features of all styles of the past, they could fulfil the demands of modernity for all types of buildings.

Similar trends, in which the term itself was not used, were apparent, for example, in the buildings and writings of JEAN-NICOLAS-LOUIS DURAND, who proposed a solid, arcuated style derived from disparate sources. Out of this arose the RUNDBOGENSTIL (round arch style), which was supported by, among others, HEINRICH HÜBSCH. In England Thomas Hope voiced similar convictions, and there was a rise in popularity of the 'in-between' revival styles—such as Elizabethan and Jacobean—for those who found Neo-classicism old-fashioned but did not want to commit themselves to 'churchy' Gothic Revival. In Munich in the 1850s Maximilian II, King of Bavaria (*reg* 1848–64), fostered a self-consciously mixed 'Maximilian style', which consisted largely of a cross between Venetian Renaissance and polychrome Gothic. In all countries the Greek and Roman classical revivals were enriched with motifs from various versions of the Renaissance style.

Eclectic design (1886; unexecuted) proposed for the Anglican Cathedral, Liverpool, by James M. Hay, showing Neo-classical nave, transepts and west façade, Gothic towers, Byzantine dome and Islamic minaret; from *The Builder*, li (1886), p. 518

In the mid-19th century, however, a theory of 'l'éclectisme' was explicitly formulated by César-Denis Daly, the editor of the first French architectural periodical, *Revue générale de l'architecture et des travaux publics* (1840–90). Daly had reported faithfully all opinions in the heated debate of the 1840s between Raoul Rochette, the classicist, and Jean-Baptiste Lassus, the most ardent of the French Gothic Revivalists, and Daly formulated his conciliating theory of 'l'éclectisme' ('L'éclectisme, c'est à dire l'usage libre de tout le passé') during the years leading up to its main pronouncements in the 1850s (*Rev. Gen. Archit.*, xi, 1853, col. 213; xvi, 1858, col. 5). The English architectural press, especially *The Builder*, followed these efforts closely, and an equally vigorous debate ensued in England. The futility of competing revivalisms seemed finally to be demonstrated in the wrangling from 1856 over the style of the Foreign and India Offices and the Home and Colonial Offices, London, designed by George Gilbert I Scott (ii). Not all of the new mediating solutions were described as eclectic, but one of the most fervent English users of the term was A. J. B. Hope, who preached a 'Liberal' or 'Progressive Eclecticism' in *The Common Sense in Art* (London, 1858).

It is not easy to pinpoint actual designs that fit the new theory precisely. There were, in fact, few proposals that literally combined motifs from a number of diverse sources in such a way that they remained individually recognizable. One of the most extraordinary was the design (1886; unexecuted) for Liverpool Cathedral (see fig.) by James M. Hay (1823–1915). The small-scale combination of recognizably different decorative details in one façade was also rare, although it was apparent in the competition design (1858; unexecuted) for Chelsea Vestry Hall, London, by Sydney Godwin (1828–1916) and Henry Godwin (1831–1917) (see *The Builder*, xvi, 1858, p. 851). A more systematic fusion of motifs, for example of classical 'horizontality' and Gothic 'verticality' and arched forms, was proposed by G. E. Street and George Gilbert I Scott (ii) in the 1850s for secular projects; this represented an eclectic strain within the Gothic Revival, although Street and Scott would not have called themselves 'eclectics'. Similarly, for many French architects the fusion of several different classical styles was seen as part of a generally Rationalist attitude towards construction and form (for discussion and illustration *see* RATIONALISM (i)), rather than primarily an eclectic attitude towards the selection of stylistic motifs (*see* VAUDOYER, (2) and fig. 2). In practice, electicism amounted largely to a continuation of the various 'mixed' styles that had been initiated earlier, for example the Jacobean and French Renaissance, whether of the 'French Château' or Paris Louvre type. The latter was frequently called the SECOND EMPIRE STYLE, a truly eclectic label; one of its most important examples was the extension from 1852 of the Louvre, Paris, under Emperor Napoleon III. Outside France the Second Empire style was practised chiefly in the USA, for example in the State, War and Navy Building (from 1871), Washington, DC, by Alfred B. Mullet and others, as well as for much commercial architecture, especially for hotels in Great Britain (*see* KNOWLES). From the 1870s to the early 1890s most of the more richly decorated commercial façades and many public buildings in Britain and the USA adopted mixed styles.

The emergence of the English QUEEN ANNE REVIVAL movement in the late 1860s at first appeared as a victory for eclecticism over dogmatic Gothic Revivalism, but it also contained a new element of vernacular revivalism. The same applied to the new German 'Deutsch-Renaissance' movement from the 1870s. Indeed, the seriousness of such neo-vernacular styles and of the Arts and Crafts Movement marked the end of mid-19th-century urbane liberalism. Art Nouveau, the Beaux-Arts style of 1900, the European Secession and subsequent advent of Modernism had one major aim in common: to overcome what was then seen as the arbitrariness of all 19th-century stylistic diversity, whereby there seemed no need to distinguish between eclecticism, historicism or revivalism. In the 1960s, however, disillusion with the rigid functionalism of the International Style led to the emergence of new attitudes towards the use of decoration and stylistic elements derived from past sources—or, indeed, any source—and some architects of the 1970s and 1980s, such as Philip Johnson, referred to themselves as 'eclectic'. There was a new stress on 'arbitrariness' and multiform decoration, as in the Portland Public Services Building (1978–82), Portland, OR, by Michael Graves (*see* UNITED STATES OF AMERICA, fig. 11).

See also FRANCE, §II, 4; UNITED STATES OF AMERICA, §II, 4; and POST-MODERNISM, §1.

BIBLIOGRAPHY

Diderot–d'Alembert

H. Hübsch: *In welchem Style sollen wir bauen?* (Karlsruhe, 1828/*R* 1984)

V. Cousin: *Cours de philosophie. . .sur le fondement des idées absolues du vrai, du beau et du bien* (Paris, 1836); Eng. trans. by O. W. Wight as *Lectures on the True, the Beautiful and the Good* (Edinburgh, 1853)

P. Collins: *Changing Ideals in Modern Architecture, 1750–1950* (London, 1965)

J. M. Crook: *The Dilemma of Style: Architectural Ideals from the Picturesque to the Post Modern* (London, 1987)

M. Soboya: *Presse et architecture au XIXe siècle: César Daly et la Revue générale de l'architecture* (Paris, 1991)

W. Herrmann, ed.: *In What Style Should We Build? The German Debate on Architectural Style* (Chicago, 1992)

STEFAN MUTHESIUS

Ecole de Fontainebleau. *See* FONTAINEBLEAU SCHOOL.

Ecole de Paris. Term applied to the loose affiliation of artists working in Paris from the 1920s to the 1950s. It was first used by the critic André Warnod in *Comoedia* in the early 1920s as a way of referring to the non-French artists who had settled and worked in Paris for some years, many of whom lived either in Montmartre or Montparnasse, and who included a number of artists of Eastern European or Jewish origin.

From *c*. 1900 a number of major artists had been attracted to the capital because of its reputation as the most vital international centre for painting and sculpture; these included Picasso, Gris and Miró from Spain, Chagall, Soutine and Lipchitz from Russia or Lithuania, Brancusi from Romania and Modigliani from Italy. The prominence of Jewish artists in Paris and of foreign artistic influences in general began by *c*. 1925 to cause intense resentment and led to the foreigners being labelled as 'Ecole de Paris' in contrast to French-born artists such as André Derain and André Dunoyer de Segonzac, who were said to uphold the purity and continuity of the French tradition. After

World War II, however, these nationalistic and anti-Semitic attitudes were discredited, and the term acquired a more general use to denote both foreign and French artists working in Paris.

See also FRANCE, §III, 6; PARIS, §III, 7.

BIBLIOGRAPHY
Paris—Paris, 1937–1957: Créations en France (exh. cat., ed. K. G. P. Hultén; Paris, Pompidou, 1981)
The Circle of Montparnasse: Jewish Artists in Paris, 1905–1945 (exh. cat. by K. E. Silver and R. Golan, New York, Jew. Mus., 1986)

RONALD ALLEY

Ecole de Rome. *See* SCUOLA ROMANA.

Ecorché [Fr.: 'flayed']. A model of the body with the skin removed and the superficial muscles displayed. Examples survive in a variety of media: plaster, bronze, wax, terracotta, ivory and wood. Like casts after parts of the body kept in artists' studios, the *écorché* served as an example of the structure of the body, obviating the difficulties of studying anatomy by dissection. Artists' and anatomists' shared interest in the structure of the human body is reflected by the frequent inclusion of *écorché* models in their portraits (1991 exh. cat., nos 9 and 77).

The first documented *écorché* models are from 16th-century Italy. Early makers of *écorchés* were Pietro Francavilla, Prospero Scavezzi and Lodovico Cigoli. *Ecorchés* of the 17th century, such as the *Ecorché Archer* (Bayonne, Mus. Bonnat) and the *Dancing Ecorché* (Paris, Ecole B.-A.), formerly attributed to Baccio Bandinelli, exhibit particularly dynamic poses. In the same period large-scale *écorchés* were recorded in Carlo Maratti's design of an academy of art, engraved by Nicolas Dorigny (1728; see Ameisenowa, fig. 37), and in Michiel Sweerts's painting of a *Painter's Studio* (Amsterdam, Rijksmus.). In 1766–7, in preparation for his statue of *St John the Baptist* (Rome, S Maria degli Angeli; destr. 1894), Jean-Antoine Houdon made the *Ecorché au bras tendu* (Paris, Ecole B.-A.). His subsequent large- and small-scale copies of the model met with immediate popularity and were adopted by academies across Europe. A later version, the *Ecorché au bras levé* (Paris, Ecole B.-A.), cast in bronze, was given to the Académie des Beaux–Arts in 1792.

While teaching anatomy at the St Martin's Lane Academy and the Royal Academy in London, the anatomist William Hunter had plaster casts made directly from a flayed, posed cadaver, thus superseding the intermediary of the sculptor (1991 exh. cat., no. 90). Small-scale versions after the life-size *écorchés* of Hunter, Houdon and Ercole Lelli demonstrate that the greater natural truth of the large-scale models did not supplant the convenience of the smaller models. Other *écorchés* cast from 'life' in connection with the Royal Academy were the *Smugglerius* (1776; London, RA), cast by Agostino Carlini, and the *Anatomical Crucifixion* (1801; London, RA), cast by Thomas Banks. Jean-Galbert Salvage (1772–1813) also made life casts in preparation for his *Ecorché Gladiator* (Paris, Ecole B.-A.), on which his book *Anatomie du gladiateur combattant applicable aux beaux arts* (Paris, 1812) was based. The poses of the *Smugglerius* and the *Ecorché Gladiator* were taken from antique sculpture, a method of presenting anatomy seen earlier in the plates of the

Anatomia per uso et intelligenza del disegno (Rome, 1691) by Bernardino Genga (1655–1734).

Ecorché models of animals were also made (1978 exh. cat., no. 169), as were individual human limbs, for example in wax in the late 16th century (London, V&A; Pope-Hennessy, nos 456–60). According to Malvasia, the Carracci made small terracotta *écorché* limbs. The *écorché* leg by Gaspar Becerra owned by Palomino served as a guide for surgeons, thus averting possible amputations. Hunter is also said to have made casts of flayed limbs. The continuing popularity of *écorché* figures and limbs is evidenced by the several examples offered for sale in the late 19th- and early 20th-century catalogues of *mouleurs* (makers and sellers of casts).

BIBLIOGRAPHY
M. Mathias-Duval and E. Cuyer: *Histoire de l'anatomie plastique* (Paris, 1898)
L. Réau and P. Vallery-Radot: 'Les Deux Ecorchés de Houdon', *Aesculape* (1938), pp. 170–84
Z. Ameisenowa: *The Problem of the Ecorché and the Three Anatomical Models in the Jagiellonian Library* (Wrocław, Warsaw and Kraków, 1963)
J. W. Pope-Hennessy with R. Lightbown: *Catalogue of Italian Sculpture in the Victoria & Albert Museum*, ii (London, 1964)
L. P. Amerson, jr: *The Problem of the Ecorché: A Catalogue Raisonné of Models and Statuettes from the Sixteenth Century and Later Periods* (diss., University Park, PA State U., 1975)
Giambologna (1529–1608), Sculptor to the Medici (exh. cat., ed. C. Avery and A. Radcliffe; ACGB, 1978), nos 169, 192–4, 220
The Artist's Model: Its Role in British Art from Lely to Etty (exh. cat., ed. I. Bignamini and M. Postle; Nottingham, A.G.; London, Kenwood House; 1991)

MONIQUE KORNELL

Ecouen, château of. French château in Val d'Oise. The château was built for ANNE MONTMORENCY, Constable of France, between 1531 and 1563, and it is the first example in France of a four-wing plan, with corner pavilions, around a central court. It is sited on a hill, with façades corresponding to the four points of the compass and the entrance wing (destr. 1787) on the east. The steep drop of the north face of the hill is secured by a terrace, beneath which lay a ball-playing pitch (*jeu de paume*) that was demolished in 1793. On all but the north side the château is enclosed by a sizeable moat, from which the core of the building is separated by a narrow terrace. The garden shown to the north-east in a 16th-century engraving (see fig.) was never laid out. The four wings of the château are situated around a court measuring 45×40 m; their façades are articulated with pilaster strips (imposts) and cross-mullioned windows (*croisées*). On several façades porticos were erected, employing antique column orders.

Few documents survive, but the château was almost certainly built by at least two architects in two campaigns. The architect of the first phase (*c.* 1532–50) was probably Pierre Tâcheron; JEAN GOUJON is another likely candidate. Comprising the west (1532–8) and south (1535–41) wings, the north-east pavilion (mid-1540s) and the entrance wing (1547–8), this phase is distinguished by simple pilaster and cornice articulation on the courtyard façades reminiscent of the château of Nantouillet (*c.* 1521) and derived from a Late Gothic Parisian tradition.

The pilasters are continued on the internal façade of the north wing, which belongs to the second phase (1551–*c.* 1563). This was executed by an architect working in a style directly influenced by Roman and Italian Renaissance

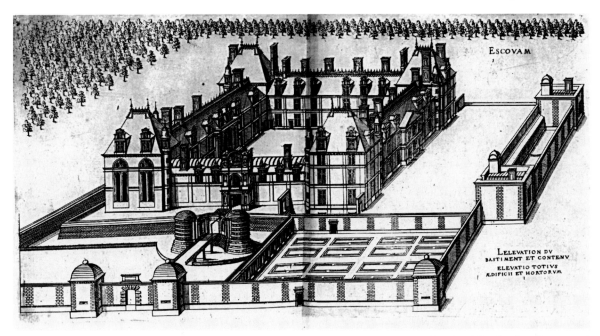

Château of Ecouen, 1531–63, looking south-west; engraving by Jacques Androuet Du Cerceau (i) from *Les Plus Excellents Bastiments de France*, i (Paris, 1576)

architecture, almost certainly JEAN BULLANT, who is recorded at Ecouen in 1553 and probably came to the château two years earlier, when Henry III elevated the barony of Montmorency to a dukedom. Bullant apparently completed the court façade of the north wing to match the other three but added a Classically inspired applied portico (*c.* 1553–6) bearing a dedication to Henry II. Of direct Roman inspiration and using giant order Corinthian columns, this portico has long been admired for the precision of its carving. On the exterior façade, untrammelled by existing work, Bullant raised a two-stage elevation of Tuscan and Doric pilasters with a central three-bay loggia (1551–6). The celebrated triumphal entry pavilion (*c.* 1556; destr. 1787) on the east wing was probably added at the same time. Inspired by Philibert de L'Orme's frontispiece (*c.* 1547–50) at Anet, it carried an equestrian statue of *Anne Montmorency* in a deep arched recess above two stages of triumphal arch motifs.

The interiors retain painted wooden ceilings, grisaille friezes and chimney-pieces and paintings of the Fontaine-bleau school, in particular 12 large oil-on-plaster overmantels depicting scenes from the Old Testament set in broad, figured and grotesque allegorical surrounds, possibly by a Flemish painter working in the style of Nicolò dell'Abate. Windows and furnishings from the chapel in the north-east pavilion are now at the Musée Condé, château of Chantilly. Until *c.* 1793 the chapel contained Rosso Fiorentino's *Pietà* (Paris, Louvre).

After 1632 Ecouen came into the possession of Henri II, 3rd Prince de Condé. Declared state property in 1793, it was a school for the Légion d'honneur until 1962, when it was placed under the management of the Monuments Historiques. Since 1976 it has housed the Musée National de la Renaissance.

BIBLIOGRAPHY

B. Palissy: *Architecture, et ordonnance de la grotte rustique de Monseigneur le duc de Montmorency, Pair & Connestable de France* (La Rochelle, 1563/R Paris, 1919)

J. Androuet Du Cerceau: *Les Plus Excellents Bastiments de France*, 2 vols (Paris, 1576–9)

V. A. Dutocq: 'Château d'Ecouen: Relève et essai de restauration', *Moniteur des Architectes* (1891), pls 20–28

P. du Colombier: 'La Chapelle d'Ecouen', *Gaz. B.-A.*, n. s. 5, xv (1936), 79–94

A. Blunt: *Art and Architecture in France, 1500 to 1700* (Harmondsworth, 1953, 4/1980/R 1988)

E.-J. Ciprut: 'Un Architecte inconnu du Connétable de Montmorency', *Bull. Soc. A. Fr.* (1959), pp. 205–14

V. Hoffmann: *Das Schloss von Ecouen* (Berlin, 1970)

A. Bertrand: *Un Château à Ecouen* (Ecouen, 1974)

W. Prinz and R. Kecks: *Das französische Schloss der Renaissance: Form und Bedeutung der Architektur: Ihre geschichtlichen und gesellschaftlichen Grundlagen* (Berlin, 1985)

V. HOFFMANN

Ecouis, Notre-Dame. Former collegiate church in Normandy, France. It was founded by Enguerran de Marigny, the powerful financial minister of Philip IV. The new church was dedicated on 9 September 1313 in a ceremony that attracted members of the royal court and ecclesiastics from all over France; the ceremony was remarkable enough to be mentioned in the chronicles for the year. Begun in 1308, the building was probably complete at the time of the dedication, because Marigny fell from favour soon after Philip IV's death in 1314 and was hanged the year after. His tomb was not erected until 1375, when the canons succeeded in rehabilitating the memory of their founder and gained possession of his body. Although not large, the building was conceived on a grandiose scale. On the façade, two great towers flank an entrance portal surmounted by a large traceried window. Life-size sculpted figures of *Enguerran de Marigny* and his wife, *Alips de*

Mons, could once be seen placing the new church under the protection of the Virgin, who was represented on the trumeau. The interior was painted and illuminated by stained glass, and the choir was decorated with statues of the *Virgin* and other saints.

The church has a large choir with flanking chapels and projecting transept, which were originally separated from the relatively short nave by a choir-screen containing the parish altar. Its style owes something to local tradition, as seen in parish churches such as Appeville and Marchésiaux, and the two-tower façade seems to be derived from contemporary Norman abbey churches such as Notre-Dame, Lyre (destr.), Saint-Evroul (ruined) and Bec-Hellouin (destr.). A more immediate source for the details, however, especially the original timber barrel vault and the elegant window tracery and mouldings, may be sought in the commissions of Philip IV at St Louis, Poissy (destr.), and at the royal palace being constructed in Paris, where Marigny was the King's overseer. It is likely that Marigny employed the royal architects and sculptors to design and execute architectural details and sculpture for his own church, an accusation that was in fact made against him at his trial. After his death, a chapel was added along the north flank of the nave; it was probably founded by Marigny's brother Jean, Archbishop of Rouen, for his own burial. A tomb effigy of *Jean de Marigny* and a marble *Virgin and Child* appear to have come from this chapel, which was destroyed in the 18th century. The chapel on the south side, erected by the parish before 1528, is an example of local Flamboyant. Between 1765 and 1772 the church was stone vaulted, and strip buttresses were introduced between the windows of the nave and transept. During the Revolution, the canons' cloister, the founder's tomb, the west portal and a portion of the interior sculpture were destroyed. The remaining figures, including those from the original programme, the south chapel sculpture and a 15th-century Annunciation group, are installed in the nave and south chapel.

The 12 surviving figures from Marigny's programme include the *Virgin and Child* from the trumeau of the west portal and a group of saints. Stylistic comparisons with sculpture on the transept portals of Rouen Cathedral suggest that at least some of the Ecouis figures were executed by the same Norman sculptors whom Marigny had employed earlier at his chateaux at Mainneville and Le Plessis. The more important figures (a *St Anne* and the *Virgin* group, *St Veronica*, *St Agnes* clothed in her hair, a figure probably representing *St Mary Magdalene*, *St John the Baptist*, and two abbots, *SS Denis and Nicaise*) were more likely the work of one or possibly two Parisian sculptors. Their similarities to the surviving figures commissioned by Philip IV for St Louis (now in Notre-Dame, Poissy) and a more general resemblance to reliefs at Notre-Dame, Paris, place them among the finest works of the period. The 'Veronica Master' can be followed to Fécamp Abbey, Normandy, where he evidently worked on a tomb programme to commemorate the abbots. The *Virgin and Child* from the trumeau, and by implication the entire west façade programme, should probably be attributed to a third sculptor, possibly Evrard d'Orléans, who was in charge of decoration at Philip IV's palace on the Ile-de-la-Cité. The portal ensemble at Ecouis, with its representation of the living patrons in the presence of the Virgin and Child, established a new type of founder portal that was often repeated; it may have been the model for later portals commissioned by the Valois court, as well as the ultimate source for Sluter's portal at Champmol Charterhouse, Dijon.

UNPUBLISHED SOURCES

Documents concerning the church and community are preserved in the 'Inventaire de titres' (Evreux, Archv), which includes a 16th-century inventory of the reliquaries and liturgical objects.

BIBLIOGRAPHY

L. Régnier: *L'Eglise de Notre-Dame d'Ecouis* (Paris, 1913)
J. Favier: *Un Conseiller de Philippe le Bel, Enguerran de Marigny* (Paris, 1963)
——: *Cartulaire et actes d'Enguerran de Marigny* (Paris, 1965) [includes documents relating to the foundation of Ecouis]
D. Gillerman: *A Contract for Paradise: Enguerran de Marigny and the Church of Notre-Dame at Ecouis* (in preparation)

DOROTHY GILLERMAN

Ecuador, Republic of. South American country. It is in the north-west of the continent and is bordered to the north by Colombia, to the south and east by Peru and to the west by the Pacific Ocean (see fig. 1). It also includes the Galapagos Islands off the Pacific coast. The country occupies an area of 270,690 sq. km and has a population of *c.* 10 million, 40% of which is Indian. The capital is QUITO, but the largest city is the chief port, Guayaquil. The country is tropical, and regional variations in climate are determined by the Andes mountains, running north to south, which divide Ecuador into three regions: the coastal or ante-Andean region; the mountainous Andean region, a volcanic area containing some highly fertile valleys; and the Oriente region to the east, the principal centre for oil production, which led to a period of rapid economic expansion in the 1970s. Throughout its history the country has been beset by earthquakes. The territory that makes up modern Ecuador was under Spanish colonial rule from 1533 until independence was achieved in 1822. This article discusses the art and architecture of Ecuador since colonization. For a discussion of the Pre-Columbian period *see* SOUTH AMERICA, PRE-COLUMBIAN, §II.

I. Introduction. II. Indigenous culture. III. Architecture. IV. Painting, graphic arts and sculpture. V. Patronage, museums and art libraries. VI. Art education.

I. Introduction.

The Spanish conquest of the territory that now constitutes Ecuador began in 1533, when Sebastián de Benalcázar defeated the Incas to conquer Quito, which he burnt down. The following year, with Diego de Almagro, he founded the new city, with a rigidly hierarchical social framework, in which the Spanish ruled over Indian vassals. Subsequently, Quito and its provinces were incorporated into the Viceroyalty of Peru, established in 1542. In 1563 Quito became the seat of government, the Real Audiencia. Architecture in the 16th and 17th centuries was in the Spanish Baroque style, wth churches, monasteries and convents being built extensively by the evangelizing religious orders. Painting, sculpture and wood-carving served to decorate religious buildings, with a distinct regional style that came to be known as the Quito school.

In the early 19th century continuing Spanish oppression of the mixed-race (mestizo) and Indian populations produced a desire for political, social and economic change and led to the development of pro-independence movements. An unsuccessful proclamation of independence in 1809 was followed in 1820 by a proclamation of autonomy in Guayaquil, and independence was achieved in 1822 with the battle of Pichincha. Quito was then incorporated into the Republic of Gran Colombia, and in 1830, when that federation was dissolved, Ecuador became a separate country.

The arts flourished in the new republic, despite the series of dictatorships that dominated the 19th century. In painting, religious themes were gradually supplemented by portraiture and landscapes, and in architecture Neoclassicism prevailed. Political tensions between liberals and conservatives, however, erupted into revolution in 1895, when the liberal Eloy Alfaro introduced anti-clerical reforms and encouraged economic expansion. During the 20th century civilian governments alternated with military regimes; voting was limited to the literate public until 1979. Economic expansion, including increased agriculture in the coastal region and the export of oil, led to increasing urban populations, and housing and commercial building consequently took place.

BIBLIOGRAPHY

J. M. Vargas: *Historia del arte ecuatoriano* (Quito, 1964)

M. Monteforte: *Los signos del hombre: Plástica y sociedad en el Ecuador* (Cuenca, 1985)

D. Bayón and M. Marx: *South American Colonial Art and Architecture* (New York, 1989), pp. 37–41, 136–40

CONSUELO DE PÓVEDA

II. Indigenous culture.

After the colonizing Spaniards arrived in Ecuador in the early 16th century, chroniclers made frequent positive references regarding the artistic capacity of the area's indigenous peoples and their capability in learning how to handle new instruments and tools and easy assimilation of the new techniques of easel painting and polychrome wooden sculpture. The high quality of the work produced by the Quito school of artists brought the city cultural renown (*see* QUITO), and it owes its fame to the work of many indigenous people who learnt the Western techniques of stone masonry to construct churches and civilian buildings and who embellished the surroundings with many works of fine art and craft in a Baroque style. (For further information on indigenous and mestizo artists working in the Western traditions of easel painting and sculpture, *see* §IV below.) A number of indigenous traditions in practice at the time of the Spaniards' arrival persisted into the late 20th century.

There are two specialized centres in Cotopaxi producing ceramics: Pujili and Victoria. The former produces multi-coloured ceramics in a wide variety of popular shapes and nativity scenes of three, five or more pieces. The latter is known for its plates, serving dishes, large earthenware jars and cooking pots, sometimes inscribed at the clients' or patrons' requests. In the provinces of Chimborazo and Cañar early techniques are used to produce male and female *guagtanas* (concave and convex door knockers) and large vessels for storage of corn, water collection or

1. Map of Ecuador; those sites with separate entries in this dictionary are distinguished by CROSS-REFERENCE TYPE

preparation of corn liquor, as well as small containers for domestic use. Jatumpamba, situated between the provinces of Azuay and Cañar, is famous for production of cooking pots and other containers in a red ware, made from clay taken from the public square, and fired in open ovens that make use of the mountain breezes. In the small town of Cera in Loja a highly polished ware is produced; it is named after its centre of production. The ceramics of Sarayacu in the Amazonian region are also outstanding for their very thin sides, varied zoomorphic designs and forms of pictorial decoration dating back to Pre-Columbian times.

Textile production is the most widely practised of the crafts of the indigenous Ecuadorean peoples. Diverse textiles of various materials, including hemp, reed, horse-hair and fibres from local plants, are made, for example for carpets, baskets, mats and sieves, all of which can sometimes be in bright colours. The Otovalan people not only produce and distribute textiles all over Ecuador but also travel to other countries within the Americas and to Europe to sell their baizes, clothing items and other articles in cotton, wool and even synthetic fibres, the designs of which are very old. In the province of Chimborazo the inhabitants of Guano make the best woollen carpets, with beautiful geometric designs that have been traditional from Pre-Columbian times. The people of Cañar specialize in sashes and hatbands decorated with motifs taken from their famed archaeology. In Azuay the ancient technique of ikat still exists, consisting of knotted threads. A special form of weaving using plaited strips of a vegetable fibre known as 'hat straw' (*Carludovica palmata*) has become world famous. The garment produced, the Panama hat, was produced on a large scale from the mid-19th century until the mid-20th. The hat is still produced in the province of Manabi, from which it originates, but most of all in the provinces of Azuay and Cañar.

With regard to metalwork production, the art of working silver or gold by hand for jewellery has remained the trade of craftsmen, although with modification to designs according to fashion and the demands of the upper classes. Indigenous women still favour traditional forms, including the *tupos* (fastenings for clothes) in the shape of suns. Chordeleg, Cuenca and Saraguru produce the most jewellery. The art of the locksmith, using traditional methods similar to those of the colonials, survives in several cities. The simple, decorative crosses intended for the highest part of a house for protection and those hung in the ritual ceremony known as 'Cruz Compadre' or 'Huasipichana' are also renowned.

Work in wood was not favoured traditionally by the indigenous peoples, although its use began to increase after colonization. In San Antonio in Imbabura many artists produce carved frames, furniture, sculpture and iconographic works of Christ and the saints, often depicting them with indigenous features. In Quito, Cuenca and some other cities artisan workshops run in the traditional way with master craftsmen, craftsmen and apprentices produce images of the saints upon commission.

Other indigenous forms of art include the 'bread-dough' sculptures produced in Pichincha and the multi-coloured, highly decorative figures made from *masapán* in the town of Calderon. In Tigua in Cotopaxi naive paintings on animal hide are made and sold in Quito. Production of musical instruments is also traditional, due to their use by peoples in Pre-Columbian times. In the provinces of Bolívar, Cañar and Azuay rondadors, flutes, ocarinas, mouth-organs, quipas, tambourines, drums, guitars, quenas and pinquillos are made, while in the province of Esmeraldas a typical instrument is the marimba drum, made from palm wood and resonant pipes of thick reeds known as *guaduas*.

BIBLIOGRAPHY

H. Crespo Toral, F. Samaniego Salazar and J. M. Vargas: *Arte ecuatoriano*, 2 vols (Quito and Barcelona, 1976)

C. Malo Gonzalez: *Expresiones estéticas populares de Cuenca*, 2 vols (Cuenca, 1983)

M. Naranjo V. and others: *La cultura popular en el Ecuador* (Cuenca, 1986–)

J. E. Hudelson: *La cultura quichua de transición* (Quito, 1987)

C. A. Coba: *Instrumentos musicales populares registrados en el Ecuador* (Quito, 1992)

H. C. Jaramillo: *Inventario de diseños de tejidos indígenas de la provincia de Imbabura* (Quito, 1992)

JUAN CORDERO IÑIGUEZ

III. Architecture.

1. COLONIAL PERIOD, 1534–1822. In the 17th and 18th centuries earthquakes, volcanic action and fires severely damaged and in some cases destroyed such cities as Riobamba, Ambato, Latacunga, Guayaquil and Portoviejo. Most of Ecuador's colonial architectural heritage is therefore concentrated in QUITO. Almost from its foundation in 1534 the city became a centre for the religious orders who embarked on an extensive building programme. The Franciscans, who arrived with the conquistadors, were led by the Flemings Jodoco Ricke de Marsalaer (*d c.* 1574) and Pedro Gosseal ('Pedro el Pintor') and the Castilian Pedro de Rodeñas. They founded an extensive monastery (begun 1530s), more broadly European in character than elsewhere in Latin America and typifying the *quiteño* manner that came to be identified with the city. The fabric of the great MUDÉJAR-panelled, single-naved church of S Francisco, with its octagonal dome on squinches at the crossing, was completed by 1581. The Indian masons Jorge de la Cruz Mitima and his son Francisco Morocho worked on the fabric for 20 years. The late Renaissance façade has Baroque elements in its paired columns, and there is also evidence of the influence of Flemish Mannerism. The decoration of the church is characteristic of the Quito school; richly gilded high-relief panels touched with carmine—by that time part of the *quiteño* tradition—later replaced the *Mudéjar* panelling destroyed in the earthquake of 1755.

Quito Cathedral was built between 1562 and 1565. The three-naved church is divided by stone Gothic arches on square piers and has a *Mudéjar*-panelled roof. The comparatively simple Renaissance lateral elevation on the south side of the Plaza Mayor is in a style still popular in Andalusia at that time, and, although there have been additions, much of the original fabric remains. The Dominicans were allocated land as early as 1541, and the Augustinians arrived in Quito in 1565. After early attempts at building, both orders seem to have commissioned the Spanish architect FRANCISCO BECERRA in 1581. S Domingo was completed in 1623 (cloister 1640); the single-aisled church has a wealth of *Mudéjar* panelling. The adjoining Rosary Chapel, built over an archway across the adjacent street and with two cupolas, dates from the 1730s. The church of S Agustín (completed 1617) has a uniquely patterned rib-vaulted choir derived from the Gothic tradition. Its well-known Sala Capitular dates from the mid-18th century.

The Jesuit church of La Compañía—three-aisled, cruciform, with a dome at the crossing—was begun in 1606 by Ayerdi de Madrigal and Gil de Madrigal and continued after 1634 by the Italian Marco Guerra, who completed the body of the church by 1649. The guild of the Cofradía del Santísimo then commissioned the Franciscan architect Antonio Rodríguez to provide plans for the Sagrario (1669–1706), adjoining the cathedral. Rodríguez also built the Santuaria de Guápulo (1693), near Quito, with an elegant transitional late Renaissance façade rising to a white, three-bell *espadaña* (bell chamber).

Both *Mudéjar* and European Baroque influences are apparent in the few significant provincial buildings remaining from the 17th and 18th centuries. The cathedral of Riobamba (now restored) has a delicately decorated planar façade, divided only by slender pilasters barely raised above the surface; consoles support a simple three-bell *espadaña*. In Cuenca the convent church of Las Monjas has an unbroken rectangular façade with only a balustrade at first-floor level and a two-storey *espadaña*; a lateral portal has bold pilasters with *Mudéjar* surface decoration and an entablature using unusual half-pediments, also found in house portals in Cuenca.

At the beginning of the 18th century José Jaime Ortiz rebuilt the Quito church of La Merced (1701–37), which has been destroyed repeatedly in the previous century, creating a modest but notable domed Baroque church and preserving some earlier elements. The façade of La Compañía, however, is wholly 18th century, in a CHURRIGUE-RESQUE style with free-standing spiralling solomonic columns on the lower range. It was begun (1722) by the German Leonard Deubler and completed (1765) by Venancio Gandolfi. The chapel of the Bethlemite Hospital, completed in 1779, has a remarkable stone portal of archaizing classical design with *Mudéjar* decoration.

BIBLIOGRAPHY
J. G. Navarro: *La iglesia de la Compañía de Jesús en Quito* (Madrid, 1930)
B. Gento Sanz: *Historia de la obra constructiva de San Francisco* (Quito, 1942)
J. G. Navarro: *Religious Architecture in Quito* (New York, 1945)
D. Angulo Iñíguez, E. Marco Dorta and M. J. Buschiazzo: *Historia del arte hispano-americano*, 3 vols (Barcelona, 1945–56), i, pp. 594–620
P. Kelemen: *Baroque and Rococo in Latin America* (New York, 1951), pp. 41–2, 159–64

2. AFTER 1822. After independence there were few developments in architecture before the secession of the Republic of Ecuador from Gran Colombia in 1830. A Neo-classical style was subsequently adopted for the civil building programme in Quito, where new European influences were comparatively quickly absorbed. The work of Thomas Reed (1810–78), a Danish architect of British extraction, is especially notable. Reed designed the Penal Panóptico (penitentiary) in Quito on a cruciform plan and began (*c.* 1850) repairs and modifications to the Palacio de Gobierno (over the original Real Audiencia), work that continued to the end of the 19th century and in which other architects, including Juan Pablo Sanz, were involved. Filling the west side of the Plaza Grande, it was completed as a horizontal three-storey composition with a colonnaded gallery above a sturdy stone ground-floor and pedimented end-pavilions.

Rebuilding and restoration after earthquakes, as well as a number of new commissions, ensured that church building continued in the 19th century. The Recoleta de la Merced at El Tejar, high above Quito, was rebuilt in 1832. A simple stone building, it is notable for the unusual cloisters, the double-rhythm upper floor of which has a scalloped wall between the columns in counterpoint with the arches. The theocratic policy of the dictator Gabriel García Moreno, active between 1860 and 1875, provided a sympathetic environment for church building and restoration in the third quarter of the century. Juan Pablo Sanz, working in a modified Neo-classical manner, was responsible in Quito for the chapel (1860) of the Colegio Jesuita, the south and east cloisters (1866) of S Domingo (where he also rebuilt the church tower after the earthquake of 1868) and the church of S Barbara (1870s). The latter is unusual in Latin America in having a Greek-cross plan and a distinctive timber-lined iron cupola. Sanz showed little inhibition about changing the character of the buildings he was commissioned to restore, a tendency best exemplified perhaps by the conflation of references in his late 19th-century reconstruction of Guayaquil Cathedral (see fig. 2): neo-Byzantine cupolas crown towers that are spectacularly high for such a seismically unstable

2. Juan Pablo Sanz: Guayaquil Cathedral, late 19th century

region. Also notable is the *fin-de-siècle* cathedral of Cuenca (begun 1882; unfinished) by the German architect Juan Stiehle, with its rich array of Carrara marbles.

Developments in the centre of Quito after the turn of the century included the Palacio Arzobispal (1906), completing the north side of the Plaza Grande, one of a number of buildings showing the influence of French academic classicism. Others included the Banco Central de Ecuador and the Círculo Militar (both 1920s). The Teatro Bolívar (1930s) shows continued *Mudéjar* influence in its façade, while in the Casa de la Cultura (1947), of mixed *Mudéjar*, Art Deco and Modernist extraction, José María Vargas and Rodrigo Pallares continued the Latin American tradition of 'plastic integration', or collaboration between architects and fine artists.

Quito experienced rural–urban migration in the 1940s, and a major earthquake in 1949 added to the need to concentrate on housing; nevertheless in the 1950s and 1960s there was a growth also in commercial development in the typical International Style buildings of such architects as Sixto Durán Ballén and Jaime Dávalos, trained in the USA. Among a number of public buildings erected by the municipality of Quito, the work of Diego Banderas Vela (*b* 1936) and Juan Espinosa Páez (*b* 1937) is notable: their Palacio Municipal (completed 1975; for illustration see QUITO), which occupies the east side of the Plaza Grande, is a modest building conscious of its context, although without direct historicist influence. Three storeys of simple rectilinear composition sit comfortably under a flat-pitched tiled roof alongside its distinguished neighbours. The housing effort following fires at Guayaquil was characterized by the rapid construction between 1981 and 1982 of 10,000 basic but carefully sited brick and block dwellings beside the Banco Ecuatoriano de Vivienda. A serious earthquake in 1987, however, again raised the problems of reconstruction and rebuilding.

BIBLIOGRAPHY

J. E. Hardoy and others: *El centro histórico de Quito: Introducción al problema de su preservación y desarrollo* (Quito, 1984)

'Ecuador: Municipalidad de Quito', *Summa*, ccxxxii (1986), pp. 44–9

L. Castedo: *Historia del arte ibero-americano*, ii (Madrid, 1988), pp. 30–31, 205–07

I. del Pino: 'La época republicana en Quito', *Arquit. & Urb.*, ix/2 (1988), pp. 58–61

IV. Painting, graphic arts and sculpture.

1. COLONIAL PERIOD, 1534–1822. As elsewhere in Latin America, the art produced in Ecuador during the colonial period had a predominantly religious function and was principally destined for churches and other religious buildings. It consisted mainly of paintings and sculpture; although European engravings were imported and used by artists as models, the graphic arts were practised little during the colonial period.

An important painter in the early part of the colonial period was Pedro Bedón (1556–1621), a Dominican friar from Quito, also active in Colombia, who founded the Cofradía del Rosario, a guild in which Indian and mestizo painters worked and which played an important part in the development of the distinctive painting style that came to be associated with the Quito school. This was characterized by its lavish treatment of religious themes, the figures displaying dramatic, realistic expressions of either extreme suffering or ecstasy. The same characteristics can be found in the sculpture associated with the school, notable also for the rigid appearance of the usually gilded figures and their vivid, highly coloured decoration. Among Bedón's most important pupils were Tomás del Castillo and Adrian Sánchez Galque, whose *Mulattoes of Esmeraldas* (Madrid, Mus. América) is one of the earliest surviving Spanish colonial paintings. In the 16th century the first collage-type paintings were also created in Quito. These were paintings in which the figures appeared dressed in fabric sewn into the canvas (e.g. the *Death of the Virgin*, Quito, Mus. Franciscano). Notable among wood-carvers in the 16th century were Diego de Robles, whose work included the *Baptism* on the high altar of the church of S Francisco, Quito, and Francisco Benítez, who executed the reliefs on the panels of the choir and balcony in the same church. Perhaps the most important sculptor around this time was Luis de Rivera, who in 1599 executed the catafalque for the death of Philip II, King of Spain.

In the 17th century notable painters included the Panamanian Jesuit Hernando de la Cruz (1591–1646) and his pupil Miguel de Santiago (1626–1706), who was known for the skilled composition of his paintings, his use of colour and the atmosphere of the landscape elements in his work. He decorated the cloister of S Agustín, Quito, with the *Life of St Augustine*; he also executed *The Rule*, a vast painting (8×6 m), also known as 'The Thousand

Faces', in the presbytery. Santiago's relative and follower Javier Gorívar (1665–1740) painted the *Kings of Judah* in the church of S Domingo, Quito. Father Carlos was a significant 17th-century sculptor, producing among other things floats for Holy Week processions. José Olmos, nicknamed 'Pampite', produced dramatic sculptures of Christ as well as paintings (e.g. *Christ in Agony*, Quito, S Roque).

Casimiro Albán, Antonio Albán and Nicolás Albán were among the artists who produced coloured drawings of the *Flora of Bogotá* for the Colombian Expedición Botánica (1784–1817), led by José Celestino Muntis. The illustrations from this nationalistic scientific expedition are held in the Jardín Botánico, Madrid. Leading painters of the 18th century included Bernardo Rodríguez (*fl* 1775–1803) and his relative and pupil MANUEL SAMANIEGO Y JARAMILLO, renowned for his highly developed realism and atmospheric landscapes. His religious works included the *Assumption of the Virgin* (Quito Cathedral). Together with Rodríguez he executed scenes from the *Life of Christ* in Quito Cathedral. During the same period the accomplished wood-carver and painter BERNARDO DE LEGARDA created the finely composed *Virgin of the Apocalypse* or the *Winged Virgin of Quito* (Quito, S Francisco); Legarda's work was held in many Quitan churches. His Indian pupil Manuel Chili, known as CASPICARA, produced outstanding sculptures of religious figures, in which detailed attention to anatomy and expression was coupled with a Baroque treatment of drapery. In such group scenes as *Assumption of the Virgin* (Quito, S Francisco), the figures were arranged in a painterly manner. Towards the end of the 18th century, as pro-independence sentiments began to emerge, Baroque and Rococo styles came to be associated negatively with colonialism, and during the wars of independence (1800–22) a new genre developed in the depiction of patriotic struggle and heroism, as in the anonymous *Execution of the Heroine Rosa Zarate and of Nicolás de la Peña (in Tumaco)* (1812; Quito, Mus. A. Mod.).

BIBLIOGRAPHY

H. Crespo Toral, F. Samaniego Salazar and J. M. Vargas: *Arte ecuatoriano*, 2 vols (Quito and Barcelona, 1976)

J. G. Navarro: *La pintura en el Ecuador del siglo XVI al XIX* (Quito, 1991)

RICARDO DESCALZI

2. AFTER 1822. Ecuador's achievement of independence in 1822 had profound cultural as well as historical and political consequences. In painting the most important of these was the demise of religious art as new models for the development of the arts were set by European Romanticism and Realism. With the formation of the Republic in 1830 the new art began to flourish in the form of portraiture, landscape and *costumbrista* painting, documenting regional customs and people. A significant role in the introduction of these new styles and genres was played by European travellers, scientists and artists, who helped arouse among local artists an interest in nature and in the surrounding social and human environment.

During the 19th century the conservative mentality of the land-owning aristocracy, who retained political power, was gradually obliged to yield to the new ideas of the rising middle class and liberal intellectuals. One of the artists who strove hardest for artistic and social change was JUAN

3. Oswaldo Guayasamín: *Incas and the Conquest*, fresco, 6×9 m, 1948 (Quito, Museo de Arte Moderno)

AGUSTÍN GUERRERO, who advocated seeking inspiration from nature in pursuit of an original, national art. The first major portrait painter was Antonio Salas (1780–1860), founder of a long dynasty of painters and creator of numerous portraits of the heroes of independence. Landscape painters concentrated on local themes, and prominent figures included RAFAEL TROYA, who produced realistic works painted *en plein air*. The *costumbrista* painting of JOAQUÍN PINTO, with its nationalist ideals, contributed to his status as a leading 19th-century artist; he produced scientifically precise illustration work, while continuing to undertake religious commissions. Sculpture during the 19th century showed little development from the colonial period and remained primarily religious in theme and ornate in style. There were no significant sculptors working in bronze or marble, so that the images of liberators and public figures that began to decorate Quito had to be commissioned from Europe.

The incorporation of modern art trends in Ecuador stemmed from the work of several European teachers, who from 1912 rejuvenated teaching at the Escuela de Bellas Artes, Quito, belatedly introducing Impressionism into painting and secular sculpture. The Italian sculptor Luigi Cassadio, for example, influenced such sculptors as Jaime Andrade Moscoso. In the 1930s a period of reflection began on questions of national identity and on the influence of the avant-garde. The social failure of the liberal revolution of 1895, the reception accorded to socialist ideas and the example of the Mexican muralists also helped to reorientate painting towards social criticism, expressed notably in the Indigenism movement, initiated by CAMILO EGAS, which sought to focus on the social situation of the country's Indian population. Its main exponents were Eduardo Kingman, who portrayed the oppression of the indigenous people of Ecuador, and OSWALDO GUAYASAMÍN, who treated similar themes in a style influenced by Expressionism and Cubism. Guayasamín produced both murals and paintings, the former inspired by Mexican muralism (see fig. 3).

In the 1940s and 1950s two painters trained in Europe, MANUEL RENDÓN SEMINARIO and ARECELI GILBERT, introduced abstract art to Ecuador. This was followed in the 1960s by a movement reacting against Indigenism and combining international idioms with a symbolism derived from Pre-Columbian cultures. The outstanding exponents of this style were ENRIQUE TÁBARA, an anti-traditionalist who developed a surrealistic symbolism, Aníbal Villacis (*b* 1927), who used Indian sign systems combined with colonial art motifs, and Estuardo Maldonado (*b* 1930), who used geometric and archaeological symbols in paintings and kinetic sculptures. Another avenue of approach, anthropological in content and anti-traditional in stance and which made use of collage, was pursued by OSWALDO VITERI and Mario Solís (*b* 1940), whose rigorously composed work focused on the use of texture. As in Europe, an anti-establishment mood prevailed at the end of the 1960s. RAMIRO JÁCOME, José Unda (*b* 1948), WASHINGTON IZA and Nelson Román (*b* 1945) founded the group Los Cuatro Mosqueteros, which formed its own 'anti-salon' in Guayaquil in 1968, in opposition to the official salon.

The oil boom of the 1970s and the consequent modernization of the country were reflected in art through the adoption of urban themes and of the latest international contemporary trends. Ramiro Jácome, for example, treated aspects of city life in an ironic neo-figurative style, while MAURICIO BUENO developed post-modern, conceptualist ideas using technological elements in his multi-media work.

Another consequence of the short-lived oil boom was the appearance of a neo-nationalist trend, which took three forms: the first, that of authentic naive art, practised by Quechua Indian painters; the second, a primitivist genre led by GONZALO ENDARA CROW, portraying village scenes with magic realism; and the third, a pseudo-mythical style led by Nelson Román.

Sculpture was less widely practised than painting. The most prolific and stylistically diverse sculptor was JAIME ANDRADE, who created mosaic murals in stone, wood and iron. In the 1980s a revival in sculpture produced two notable 'organicist' sculptors working in marble, Jesús Cobo (*b* 1953) and José Antonio Cauja (*b* 1953), and one 'brutalist' working in wood, stone and ceramics, Gabriel García (*b* 1952).

Graphic art, first introduced through engravings imported from Europe during colonial times, was practised during the 19th century but began to develop in the 20th century, notably in the area of lithography. Significant graphic artists included the wood-engraver and muralist Galo Galecio (*b* 1908) and NICOLÁS SVISTOONOFF, an etcher and painter. Also notable are the drawings of Miguel Varea (*b* 1948).

BIBLIOGRAPHY

D. Bayón, ed.: *Arte moderno en América latina* (Madrid, 1985)

G. Rubiano Caballero: *La escultura en América latina (siglo XX)* (Bogotá, 1986)

D. Bayón: *Historia del arte hispanoamericano, siglos XIX y XX*, iii (Madrid, 1988)

El siglo XX de las artes visuales en Ecuador (exh. cat. by H. Rodríguez Castelo, Guayaquil, Mus. A. Banco Cent., 1988)

L. Oña: *Las artes plásticas del Ecuador en el siglo XX*, xliii of *Ecuador: Historia de la República*, ed. A. Pareja (Quito, 1990)

LENIN OÑA

V. Patronage, museums and art libraries.

The evangelizing missions of the Spanish religious orders led quickly to the construction of churches and other religious buildings in Ecuador. In response to the need to decorate these, numerous workshops appeared throughout Quito, where master craftsmen were aided by skilled artisans and apprentices. Many workshops located near monasteries established regular working relationships with various orders. Such patronage also occurred in other towns: in El Tejar, for example, the order of Nuestra Señora de la Merced patronized José Cortés.

Pedro Bedón (1556–1621), the first significant artist in Quito, grouped mestizo and Indian painters into the Cofradía del Rosario, an artistic guild, and helped them with the creation and sale of their paintings. In some instances paintings were used by artists as payment in kind: Miguel de Santiago (1626–1706), for example, left many paintings in the lower cloister of the monastery of S Agustín, Quito, where he was protected by the monks for a number of years from imprisonment for an act of disrespect to the authorities. Church patronage continued throughout the 18th century, with such artists as Bernardo Rodríguez (*fl* 1775–1803) and Manuel Samaniego y Jaramillo being attached to Quito Cathedral.

In the 19th century commissions for paintings celebrating the achievement of independence were given, among others, to Antonio Salas (1790–1860), to whom a portrait of *Simón Bolívar* (1829; Oswaldo Viteri priv. col.) is attributed. The need for new civil buildings in the early years after independence also led to a number of commissions in the field of architecture, especially in Quito (*see* §III, 2 above). In the 20th century the state was responsible for numerous artistic commissions, including those for the sculptural mural *Quito* (1976–7) at the Municipio de Quito, by Jaime Andrade, and others by Humberto Moré in a number of parks in Quito. Moré was also commissioned to produce a sculptural mural for the company Mutualista Previsión y Seguridad, Quito. Notable private collectors in the 20th century included the poet Alfredo Gangotena, who collected modern realist works.

Few museums in Ecuador pre-date the 20th century, although the Universidad Central del Ecuador, founded in Quito in 1769, had its own museum, and in Guayaquil the Museo Municipal was opened in 1862 with a collection that eventually included colonial and modern painting as well as numismatics. The first major museum founded in the 20th century was the Museo de Arte Colonial (est. 1914) in Quito, with a collection that spanned the colonial period. In 1930 the Museo de Arte e Historia de la Ciudad was founded, also in Quito, with a collection of painting and sculpture and documents relating to the city's past. Religious museums operating in the capital in the late 20th century included those of the Franciscan and Dominican monasteries and the museum of the Jesuits.

Between 1920 and 1940 a number of local museums sprang up in response to important archaeological discoveries. Other important museums outside Quito at the end of the 20th century included the Museo de Artesanías, the Museo Municipal and the Museo del Monasterio de la Concepción, all in Cuenca; the museum of the order of La Concepción in Riobamba, established on the initiative of Ricardo Descalzi and rich in colonial gold- and silverwork; and the Centro Cultural in Guayaquil, which has collections of colonial and modern painting and sculpture. A number of provincial capitals also have regional museums, often with collections of Pre-Columbian pottery. The small town of Cajabamba-Cicalpa has a museum with a collection of exquisitely cut stones from the sites of ruined monasteries at the original city of Riobamba, destroyed by an earthquake in 1797. Another important development in the 20th century was the establishment of museums by private institutions such as banks, either in their local branch offices or as separate entities. The Museo Antropológico y Pinacoteca del Banco Central del Ecuador, founded in 1974 in Guayaquil, for example, houses a collection of archaeological items and contemporary Latin American art.

Art libraries in Ecuador include the Biblioteca de la Casa de la Cultura Ecuatoriana and the Biblioteca de Arte de la Fundación Guayasamín, both in Quito. An important photographic collection is held at the Departmento de Investigaciones Históricas of the Banco Central del Ecuador, also in Quito.

BIBLIOGRAPHY

J. G. Navarro: *Guía artística de Quito* (Quito, 1961)

H. Crespo Toral, F. Samaniego Salazar and J. M. Vargas: *Arte ecuatoriano*, 2 vols (Quito and Barcelona, 1976)

RICARDO DESCALZI

VI. Art education.

Painting, drawing, sculpture and crafts were first taught immediately after the conquest to Indians in the Colegio de S Juan (later the Colegio S Andrés) in Quito, run from 1535 by the Franciscan Pedro Gosseal ('Pedro el Pintor'). Young artists were also trained in the workshops of individual artists and subsequently joined painting and sculpture guilds, such as the Cofradía del Rosario, Quito, run by the Dominican friar Pedro Bedón (1556–1621). A further two monastic schools were established in the 18th century.

Religious teaching institutions continued to exist during the 19th century, and several secular establishments were also founded. The first was initiated by the French artist Ernst Charton and was followed in 1852 by the Escuela Democrática Miguel de Santiago, Quito, where exhibitions were held. The Escuela de Bellas Artes was established by the state in Quito in 1872; the painter Luis Cadena was its first Director. The school closed, however, in 1875 and did not reopen until 1904.

In 1902 the Escuela de Pintura was founded in Cuenca. Increased concern with art education also led to teaching from secondary-school level through to university. There were several university-level institutions dedicated to fine art by the late 20th century, including the Academia de Bellas Artes 'Remigio Crespo Toral' in Cuenca. Faculties of fine arts also existed in a number of universities, such as the Universidad Central de Ecuador, Quito.

Design was first taught at specialist institutions from the early 1970s, and by the late 20th century there were seven design training centres, including the school of design and decoration at the Universidad Laica 'Vicente Rocafuerte' de Guayaquil. By the same period universities throughout the country were offering architectural courses, such as that at the Universidad Técnica Particular de Loja.

BIBLIOGRAPHY

E. Ayala Mora, ed.: *Nueva historia del Ecuador*, ix (Quito, 1988)
A. Kennedy: 'Del taller a la academia: Educación artística en el siglo XIX en Ecuador', *Procesos*, ii (1992)

LENIN OÑA

Ecuelle [Fr.: 'porringer'; 'bowl'; 'basin']. Small, shallow bowl of silver, silver gilt, pewter or ceramic, with vertical sides, a domed cover with a finial, two flat handles and sometimes an en suite stand. It was used for individual portions of soup or gruel that could be drunk without using a spoon. French medieval examples, in pewter, are known; they were very popular in France from the 17th century to the end of the *ancien régime*; they are often engraved with armorials and have decorative handles, rims and finials (e.g. silver écuelle and stand by Louis Landes, 1789; New York, Met.; *see* FRANCE, fig. 78). Some 17th- and 18th-century examples survive in England, Canada and the USA, although in these countries the PORRINGER was more common.   □

Edbrooke. American family of architects of English birth.

(1) Frank E. Edbrooke (*b* England, 1840; *d* Denver, CO, 1918). Following a brief career as a railway architect,

he opened an office in Denver in 1879. Edbrooke brought to the new city his familiarity with the work of H. H. Richardson, Louis Sullivan and other Chicago architects. Working during a period of general prosperity, he was particularly noted for a number of handsome commercial buildings in Second Empire, Romanesque Revival and Renaissance Revival styles. While showing conformity to historic modes, the buildings were nonetheless original and well-proportioned compositions. His crowning achievement is the H. C. Brown Hotel (1890–92), Denver, a nine-storey building with an atrium, covered by a skylight, that extends from ground level to the roof. The exterior recalls Louis Sullivan's Auditorium Building (1887–9) in Chicago.

BIBLIOGRAPHY

R. R. Brettell: *Historic Denver: The Architects and the Architecture, 1858–1893* (Denver, 1973), pp. 32–63

(2) W(illoughby) J. Edbrooke (*b* England, 1843; *d* Chicago, IL, 29 March 1896). Brother of (1) Frank E. Edbrooke. He began practising as an architect in Chicago *c.* 1867. Edbrooke received the commission for the Main Building of Notre Dame University in Indiana (1879) and used Gothic Revival for this and several other buildings that he designed for the university. From 1887 to 1891 he worked with Franklin P. Burnham (*d* 1909): their work included the Georgia State Capitol in Atlanta (1884–91). In 1891 Benjamin Harrison, the President of the USA, appointed Edbrooke to the post of Supervising Architect of the Treasury, a position he held until 1893. He was responsible for federal architecture throughout the country and designed at least 40 federal court-houses and post offices. These buildings were predominantly in the Romanesque Revival style derived from H. H. Richardson and contributed to the spread of the round-arched style. Examples include the Post Office and Customs House (1891–6), Milwaukee, WI, and the Post Office (completed 1899), Washington, DC (now an office building with a gallery of shops). Both are monumental Romanesque Revival buildings. In service with the government, Edbrooke also designed the US Government Pavilion, a huge Renaissance Revival work, for the World's Columbian Exposition (1893) in Chicago.

BIBLIOGRAPHY

Macmillan Enc. Architects; Withey
D. H. Smith: *The Office of the Supervising Architect of the Treasury* (Baltimore, 1923)
T. J. Schlereth: *The University of Notre Dame: A Portrait of its History and Campus* (Notre Dame, 1976)

WILLARD B. ROBINSON

Eddy, Arthur Jerome (*b* Flint, MI, 5 Nov 1859; *d* Chicago, IL, 21 July 1920). American critic, collector and lawyer. He wrote books on legal and economic issues in the 1900s. He first became interested in art, notably that of James Abbott McNeil Whistler and François-Auguste-René Rodin through the World's Fair of Chicago in 1893. He began to lecture on art and aesthetics and published his first art book *Delight, the Soul of Art* (Philadelphia, 1904). In 1912 he became interested in 20th-century art. It was, however, the ARMORY SHOW (1913) that inspired him to become a serious collector of avant-garde art; he acquired 25 works from the exhibition. Subsequently he travelled to London and Germany, where he met Vasily Kandinsky and other artists and added *c.* 100 works to his collection.

In 1914 Eddy published *Cubists and Post-Impressionism* (Chicago). Based on information elicited from the artists themselves, this book is significant as one of the first attempts to explain modern art in the USA, but in its emphasis upon such painters as Kandinsky (it included the first discussion in English of this painter's ideas) it betrays Eddy's enthusiasm for colouristic abstraction. Eddy continued to collect, although the emphasis lay upon American modernism. On his death the collection was dispersed and 23 works went to the Art Institute of Chicago.

BIBLIOGRAPHY

C. J. Bulliet: 'The Eddy Gift to Chicago', *Creative A.* (March 1932), pp. 213–18

P. Kruty: 'Arthur Jerome Eddy and his Collection – Prelude and Postscript to the Armory Show', *Arts Magazine* (Feb 1987), pp. 40–47

A. DEIRDRE ROBSON

Eddy, Don (*b* Long Beach, CA, 4 Nov 1944). American painter and printmaker. He studied at the University of Hawaii in Honolulu (BFA, 1967, MFA, 1969) and came to prominence in the early 1970s as an exponent of PHOTOREALISM, producing airbrushed paintings based on photographs of automobiles (e.g. *Untitled*, 1971; Aachen, Neue Gal.), the displays in shop windows or still-lifes, as in *New Shoes for H* (1973; Cleveland, OH, Mus. A.). He treated similar subjects in screenprints and in colour lithographs such as *Red Mercedes* (1972; see 1973 exh. cat., p. 35). Rather than basing a painting or print on a single photograph, as was the case with other photorealists, Eddy would work from as many as 40 photographs to ensure a consistently sharp focus for his often spatially complex images.

BIBLIOGRAPHY

Amerikanischer Fotorealismus: Grafik (exh. cat., intro. H. Holtmann; Brunswick, Kstver., 1973), pp. 32–5

Don Eddy (exh. cat.; New York, Nancy Hoffman Gal., 1986)

For further bibliography *see* PHOTOREALISM.

MARK W. SULLIVAN

Ede, Jim [James] **(Howard Stanley)** (*b* Cardiff, 7 April 1895; *d* Edinburgh, 15 March 1990). British collector and critic. He studied at Newlyn Art School, Cornwall, shortly before World War I. He then held relatively modest positions, including Assistant to the Director at the Tate Gallery in London from 1920 to 1935, and during this time was able to purchase for his own collection works turned down by his superiors: in 1926 he bought for £100 a large consignment of drawings and sculptures by Henri Gaudier-Brzeska, whose biography he published in 1930 (made into a film by Ken Russell in 1972). In the 1930s Ede lived in Hampstead, north London, close to Henry Moore, Ben Nicholson and Barbara Hepworth (three artists whose work he collected), and also Herbert Read, Paul Nash and Adrian Stokes, all of whom he came to know. From 1936 he lived in north Africa and southern France, moving in 1957 to Cambridge, where he had grown up. He acquired a row of derelict cottages that he converted into his home and an informal museum, Kettle's Yard, which was donated to the University of Cambridge in 1966, with Ede as curator in residence. His collection was open to undergraduates, and works could be loaned to them during term-time. The arrangement of natural and craft objects and vernacular furniture in a sparsely modernist décor reflected the robust aesthetic of the art Ede collected. An affinity with Cornish art dated back to his time as a student at Newlyn, and he had many works by Alfred Wallis. After 1973 he lived in Edinburgh, where on a more modest scale he began to create an art environment comparable to Kettle's Yard.

WRITINGS

A Life of Gaudier-Brzeska (London, 1930); rev. as *Savage Messiah: A Biography of the Sculptor Henri Gaudier-Brzeska* (London, 1931, 2/1971)

A Way of Life (Oxford, 1984) [autobiography]

BIBLIOGRAPHY

D. Robinson: Obituary, *Burl. Mag.*, cxxxii (1990), p. 414

DAVID COHEN

Edelfelt, Albert (Gustaf Aristides) (*b* Kiiala Estate, nr Porvoo [Swed. Borgå], 21 July 1854; *d* Haikko, nr Porvoo, 18 Aug 1905). Finnish painter, illustrator and etcher. He was Finland's leading artist in the late 19th century, introducing French influences into Finnish art but also helping to gain a broader international interest in his country's culture. He was not a great innovator, however, and although his reputation in Finland remained firm, international recognition dwindled after his death until the renewal of interest in realism that took place in the late 20th century.

Edelfelt's father, Carl Albert Edelfelt, was a member of the Swedish aristocracy who had moved to Finland as a young man, eventually rising to the position of General Director in the Department of Housing, while his mother, Alexandra Edelfelt, was an acquaintance of Finland's national poet, J. L. Runeberg. She played an important role in instilling in Edelfelt the romantic idealism that became the guiding principle of his life and art. In 1869, while still at school, Edelfelt began taking classes at the School of Drawing established by the Finnish Arts Association in Helsinki, and from 1871 he continued to study art at the University of Helsinki, where it was hoped that he would become a great historical painter. In 1873 he received a State scholarship to study at the Koninklijke Academie voor Schone Künsten in Antwerp, attracted by the work of Henri Leys and other Belgian artists who treated historical subjects. The following year, however, Edelfelt moved to Paris, where he studied at the Ecole des Beaux-Arts under Jean-Léon Gérôme in 1874–5 and 1876–7. From this time on, he generally spent the winter in Paris and the summer in Finland.

In the late 1870s Edelfelt began to achieve professional success through such works as *Queen Blanka* (1877) and *Duke Charles Insulting the Corpse of Klaus Fleming* (1878; both Helsinki, Athenaeum A. Mus.), both exhibited at the Salon in Paris. In these works Edelfelt's detached realist style and interest in basic human emotions were evident, but he nevertheless began to feel that there was no future for historical painting, and, inspired by his friend Jules Bastien-Lepage, he took up *plein-air* painting, producing depictions of rural scenes. This new approach resulted in 1879 in *Child's Funeral* (Helsinki, Athenaeum A. Mus.), which is similar in its subject-matter to the sentimental tradition of the Düsseldorf school but which is closer stylistically to French naturalism. This brought him international acclaim, winning the first medal ever to be awarded to a Finnish artist at the Paris Salon and leading to numerous offers of commissions. This success was followed by an even greater one in 1882, when Edelfelt's *Church Service in the Southern Archipelago* (Paris, Mus. d'Orsay) won second prize at the Salon. In 1883 Edelfelt built a studio for himself (now a museum) in Haikko, near Porvoo, where he painted during the summer, producing folk scenes such as *At Sea* (1885; Göteborg, Kstmus.) and *Women of Ruokolahti on the Church Hill* (1887; see fig.), in which he experimented with an uninhibited naturalist style.

During the late 1880s Edelfelt began to concentrate on the depiction of light, for example in the *Luxembourg Gardens* (1887; Helsinki, Athenaeum A. Mus.) and *Washerwomen* (St Petersburg, Hermitage), a large-scale interior painted between 1889 and 1893. He was also influenced by the Impressionists, especially in his smaller paintings and studies, but he was never a consistent follower of theirs. A more important influence around the same time was perhaps that of neo-Romanticism, which was becoming noticeable in the religious and nationalist elements that

began to appear in his work. *Christ and Mary Magdalene*, for example, based on a scene described in Finnish folk poetry, is a realistic portrayal set against a Finnish autumn landscape, while *Shepherds' Homage* (1894, Vaasa Parish Church) is his only altarpiece. He also produced some sensitive portraits of the folk singer Larin Paraske (e.g. 1893; Hämeenlinna, A. Mus.), but his most patriotic works of this period are two gouaches depicting scenes from the poetry of J. L. Runeberg: *March of the Men of Pori* (1892; Mänttä, Serlachius A. Mus.) and the *Death of Wilhelm von Schwerin* (1893; Helsinki, Athenaeum A. Mus.). Other important expressions of Edelfelt's patriotism included his illustrations for such books as Runeberg's *Kuningas Fjalar* (King Fjalar, 1895) and *Vänrikki Stoolin tarinat* (The tales of Ensign Stål, 1898–1900). The illustrations for the latter were of tremendous national importance, coming at a time when Russia was attempting to curb Finland's autonomy. Edelfelt also collaborated on the illustration of Zachris Topelius's novel *Välskärin kertomukset* (Tales of an army surgeon's assistant, 1896) and his collection of fairy tales *Lukemisia lapsille* (Stories for children, 1901–3), and from 1899 he also began producing etchings, of which there are 75 known examples.

Albert Edelfelt: *Women of Ruokolahti on the Church Hill*, oil on canvas, 1887 (Helsinki, Athenaeum Art Museum)

Throughout his career portraiture occupied a central place in Edelfelt's work, his talent lying not so much in explicit and faithful representation as in his empathy with his subject and in his psychological insight. In his youth he was happy to paint beautiful young women, and his portraits of older women display skilful gallantry. Particularly important to him was the portrait of his mother (1883; Helsinki, Athenaeum A. Mus.), while his portrait of *Louis Pasteur* (1885; Paris, Mus. d'Orsay), depicting the scientist in his laboratory, engrossed in his experiments, was internationally acclaimed. He eventually executed over 200 portraits, and his subjects included *Tsar Nicholas II of Russia* (1896; Helsinki, U.) and members of several other European royal families (e.g. *Princess Marie of Denmark*, pastel, 1894; Copenhagen, priv. col.). Particularly well known are his portraits of leading cultural figures, such as *Professor Zachris Topelius* (1889; Helsinki, U.), the opera singer *Aino Ackté* (1901; Helsinki, Athenaeum A. Mus.), the actress *Ida Aalberg* (1902; Helsinki, N. Theat.) and the orchestra conductor *Robert Kajanus* (1905; Mänttä, Serlachius A. Mus.).

By 1900 Edelfelt had helped earn international recognition for Finnish art, a fact acknowledged by his presence that year at the Exposition Universelle in Paris, where he was in charge of the Finnish section (he was also asked to take charge of the Russian section but declined for political reasons). His last major work was the mural for the old assembly hall of Helsinki University, which depicts the inauguration of the Turku Academy on 15 July 1640. The earliest designs date from the beginning of the 1880s, and Edelfelt won the commission for the mural by competition at the beginning of the 1890s, but it was not until 1902 that he produced the definitive sketch for the work (Turku, A. Mus.). The final composition, which reflects the influence of Giotto's monumental style, was painted in tempera and oils in 1904–5 but was destroyed in a bomb explosion in 1944.

WRITINGS

T. Söderhjelm, ed.: *Hvad Albert Edelfelt skrifvit: Minnes teckningar, uppsatser och konstbref* [The writings of Albert Edelfelt: memoirs, essays and letters on art] (Helsinki, 1905)

B. Edelfelt, ed.: *Ur Albert Edelfelt's brev* [From the letters of Albert Edelfelt], 5 vols (Helsinki, 1917–30)

BIBLIOGRAPHY

B. Hintze: *Albert Edelfelt*, 3 vols (Helsinki, 1942–4)

——: *Albert Edelfelt* (Porvoo, 1953)

A. Reitala: 'Näkökulmia todellisuuteen' [Viewpoints into reality], *Taide* (1974), no. 4, pp. 10–19

AIMO REITALA

Edelinck, Gérard (*b* Antwerp, *bapt* 20 Oct 1640; *d* Paris, 2 April 1707). French engraver and print publisher of Flemish origin. He was the son of a tailor in Antwerp and trained as an engraver with Gaspar Huybrechts (1619–84) and Cornelis Galle the younger. On arriving in Paris in 1666, he worked with his compatriot Nicolas Pitau the elder, and then with François de Poilly, Robert Nanteuil and Philippe de Champaigne. In 1672 he married the daughter of Nicolas Regnesson, the Parisian engraver and print publisher, thus himself becoming a print publisher. In 1675 he became a naturalized Frenchman and in 1677 was admitted (*reçu*) to the Académie Royale. In 1695 he was made a Chevalier of the Order of St Michel and a

Papal Knight. He became both a councillor at the Académie and Premier Dessinateur du Cabinet du Roi. Among his pupils were his brother Jean Edelinck (*b* Antwerp, *c*. 1643; *d* Paris, 14 May 1680), his godson Nicolas Pitau the younger and Jacques Lubin (*c*. 1659–after 1703). Edelinck specialized in portraits, which make up two-thirds of his work; he was a reproductive engraver, who translated the works of the most important portraitists of his time, such as Hyacinthe Rigaud (e.g. *Charles Colbert, Marquis de Croissy*, 1691; see Weigert, no. 121) and Nicolas de Largillierre (e.g. *Charles Gobinet*, 1691, w 123), and is considered as one of the century's greatest engravers.

Gérard Edelinck's brother Jean Edelinck came to Paris at about the same time as he, and likewise became an engraver, print publisher and print-seller. He made engravings of seven statues from the grotto and gardens of Versailles for the Cabinet du Roi and engraved some portraits, as well as reproducing a good many compositions by Henri Wattelé. Jean Edelinck's early death prevented him from fully exploiting his talent. Another brother, Gaspard-François Edelinck (*b* Antwerp, 18 Nov 1652; *d* Paris, 21 May 1722), was also an engraver. He joined his brothers in Paris, where he seems to have worked mainly in collaboration with Gérard; but *c*. 20 pieces bearing his signature are known. Nicolas-Etienne Edelinck (*b* Paris, 9 April 1681; *d* Paris, 11 May 1767), the eighth son of Gérard Edelinck, also became an engraver; he travelled to Munich, Venice and Rome. His oeuvre, all of it reproductive, numbers only *c*. 30 prints, mostly portraits, such as that of *Gérard Edelinck* (1707; see Roux, no. 2) after François Tortebat (*c*. 1621–90). He also produced some vignettes for books.

Thieme–Becker

BIBLIOGRAPHY

M. Roux: *Inventaire du fonds français: Graveurs du dix-huitième siècle*, Paris, Bib. N., Cab. Est. cat., viii (Paris, 1955), pp. 446–54

R.-A. Weigert: *Inventaire du fonds français: Graveurs du dix-septième siècle*, Paris, Bib. N., Cab. Est. cat., iv (Paris, 1961), pp. 3–81 [w]

M. Grivel: *Le Commerce de l'estampe à Paris au XVIIe siècle* (Paris, 1986)

M. Préaud and others: *Dictionnaire des éditeurs d'estampes à Paris sous l'Ancien Régime* (Paris, 1987)

MAXIME PRÉAUD

Edema, Gerard van (*b* Amsterdam or Friesland, *c*. 1652; *d* Richmond, Surrey, *c*. 1700). Dutch painter, active in England. After training in Amsterdam under Allert van Everdingen, he travelled *c*. 1670 to London, where he found a ready market for his decorative landscapes among English collectors. Competing with many other minor Dutch artists working for the Restoration court, he produced both imaginary and topographical landscapes suitable for installation as overdoors. Van Edema's idealized Italianate views were especially commended by contemporaries such as Buckridge, but many of his characteristically mountainous compositions belong to the northern landscape tradition. He probably followed van Everdingen's example in deriving inspiration from Scandinavian scenery, and his works frequently evoke a wild vision of nature that drew on his experiences travelling to Newfoundland, the West Indies and Dutch Guyana (now Surinam). His affinity for awe-inspiring mountains, steep precipices, rocky gorges, torrential rivers and cascades appealed to aristocratic collectors, such as the Earl of Sunderland, the Duke of Schomberg, the Earl of Radnor and Lord Ranelagh. The artist's versatility ranged from conventional rural or classicizing landscapes, such as those acquired for the British Royal Collection, to monumental canvases, such as those at Chatsworth, Derbys, in which the expansive scale and power of nature overwhelms the diminutive presence of man. His skill at painting waterfalls especially impressed the writer Marshall Smith, and subsequent remarks about his work, as in Walpole's *Anecdotes*, suggest that van Edema collaborated both with the marine painter Willem van de Velde the younger and with the battle-piece and sporting painter Jan Wijck. There is a livelier element of fantasy in his landscapes than in the more topographical works of other fellow Dutchmen in England, for instance Adrien van Diest, Jan Griffier I or Leonard Knyff; and the degree of drama in some of van Edema's more ambitious pictures (e.g. the *Mountainous Landscape with Devastated Fir Trees*; Chatsworth, Derbys) verges on the Sublime. Van Edema's work contributed to the evolution of the Picturesque and to some small extent to the foundation of landscape painting as a genre for further development by the emerging native British school at the end of the 17th century.

BIBLIOGRAPHY

M. Smith: *Art of Painting* (London, 1692, 2/1693), p. 25

B. Buckridge: 'An Essay towards an English School with the Lives and Characters of above 100 Painters', *The Art of Painting and the Lives of the Painters* (London, 1706, 2/1744, 3/1754/R 1969) [Eng. trans. by J. Savage of R. de Piles: *L'Abrégé de la vie des peintres* (Paris, 1699)], pp. 398–480

H. Walpole: *Anecdotes of Painting in England*, 4 vols (1762–71); ed. R. N. Wornum (1849), ii, p. 132

H. and M. Ogden: *English Taste in Landscape in the Seventeenth Century* (Ann Arbor, MI, 1955)

O. Millar: *The Tudor, Stuart and Early Georgian Pictures in the Collection of Her Majesty the Queen* (London, 1963), p. 159, pl. 161

The Age of William III and Mary II: Power, Politics and Patronage, 1688–1702 (exh. cat., ed. R. Maccubbin and M. Hamilton-Phillips; New York, Grolier Club; Washington, DC, Folger Shakespeare Lib., 1988–9), pp. 244–58, ill. 309

MARTHA HAMILTON-PHILLIPS

Edenshaw, Charles [Tahaygen] (*b* Skidegate, Queen Charlotte Islands, BC, *c.* 1839; *d* 1920). Native Canadian Haida sculptor, metalworker and painter. He spent much of his adolescence at Kiusta with his maternal uncle Albert Edward Edenshaw, chief of the Haida Eagle clan, acquiring a considerable knowledge of Haida art and mythology. In 1882 the Eagle clan moved north to Masset, where, on the death of his uncle in 1884, he assumed his titles and privileges, including his chief's name Edenshaw. Edenshaw was an imaginative craftsman who incorporated into his work technical and conceptual ideas from both native and non-native sources. He was a versatile and prolific artist who worked within the Northwest Coast tradition of two-dimensional design (*see* NATIVE NORTH AMERICAN ART, §III, 2). He carved both ritual and commercial objects in wood and argillite, including totem poles, masks, chests, boxes, platters and frontlets; painted designs on spruce root mats and hats, the latter often made by his wife, Isabelle; and produced silver bracelets. His commercial objects included a host of forms for non-native and market use; and his contact with a number of anthropologists and collectors resulted in a large body of well-documented, often commissioned works. The model totem poles and house models, for example, commissioned by the ethnographer and linguist John R. Swanton *c.* 1900 for the American Museum of Natural History, NY, are among Edenshaw's most clearly documented works. Edenshaw is thus the first professional Haida artist whose work can be identified with certainty.

BIBLIOGRAPHY

B. Holm: 'Will the Real Charles Edenshaw Please Stand up', *The World Is As Sharp As a Knife: An Anthology in Honor of Wilson Duff*, ed. D. N. Abbott (Victoria, BC, 1981), pp. 115–200

MARTINE REID

Edessa. *See* URFA.

Edessa, Mandylion of. *See* MANDYLION OF EDESSA.

Edfu [anc. Egyp. Behdet or Djeba; Gr. Apollinopolis; now Idfū]. Site in Upper Egypt. It is dominated by the Temple of Horus, the most completely preserved of all Egyptian temples, dating mainly to the Ptolemaic period (304–30 BC; *see* EGYPT, ANCIENT, fig. 25). To the east of the temple are the ruins of a city (now covered by modern Idfū) dating back at least to the Old Kingdom (*c.* 2575–*c.* 2150 BC). The Temple of Horus was built and decorated by the Ptolemies, although the cult of the god Horus at Edfu is attested since the Middle Kingdom (*c.* 2008–*c.* 1630 BC). The remains at Edfu include part of a pylon of Ramesses III (reg *c.* 1187–*c.* 1156 BC). Blocks from the forecourt, excavated in the 1980s, date back to the New Kingdom (*c.* 1540–*c.* 1075 BC), but they may have been dragged there from another site.

Horus of Behdet was a divine metaphor for the living king who, having vanquished the enemy, ruled as the victorious winged sun-disc. It was therefore especially appropriate and expedient for the Greek rulers of the Ptolemaic period to venerate the victorious Egyptian divine king Horus, perhaps to reinforce their own kingship and to draw the human parallel that they had liberated Egypt from the Persian yoke. Ptolemaic benefactions to Edfu were in the native pharaonic tradition.

The building of the Temple of Horus began in 237 BC, the 10th year of the reign of Ptolemy III Euergetes I (reg 246–221 BC), and its interior was decorated by Ptolemy IV Philopator (reg 221–205 BC) and Ptolemy VI Philometor (reg 180–145 BC). The pronaos (traditionally called the outer hypostyle hall) was built on to the existing temple by Ptolemy VIII Euergetes II (reg 170–163, 145–116 BC) and decorated between 140 and 124 BC. This annexed pronaos emulated the one that his brother Ptolemy VI had built on to the Temple of Isis at Philae. Subsequently, the colonnaded forecourt, pylon and enclosure wall were built (116–71 BC) and decorated by Ptolemy IX Soter II, Ptolemy X Alexander I and Ptolemy XII Neos Dionysos. The MAMMISI (or 'birth-house': an annexe where the annual ritual of divine birth was performed) shows the decoration of Ptolemy VIII Euergetes II, Ptolemy IX Soter II and Ptolemy XII Neos Dionysos. The interior decoration of both monuments is executed in wafer-thin raised relief except on columns, and the exterior decoration, which was addressed late in the Ptolemaic period, is boldly carved within sunken contours.

The Temple of Horus was cleared by Auguste Mariette in 1860, and French Egyptologists have been involved in

Edfu, Temple of Horus, pronaos, built by Ptolemy VIII Euergetes II (*reg* 170–163 and 145–116 BC) and decorated 140–124 BC

its study and publication ever since. Maxence de Chalvet Rochemonteix took squeezes of the reliefs on the temple walls, from which he and Emile Chassinat published 14 volumes under the auspices of the Mission archéologique française. The inadequacies of these early volumes have been rectified by Cauville and Devauchelle in a series of fascicles.

The Ptolemaic hieroglyphic texts at Edfu, which are highly readable, provided a straightforward means for scholars to learn about Egyptian cosmogony, the mythology of Horus, the cult and its practices (which included drama) and the calendar of festivals. The point of departure for the study of the daily rituals that began at dawn was the 'room of purification' (Egyp. *pr dw3t*) and the 'library', both situated in the pronaos, to the west and east of its entrance.

An analysis of the columns of the pronaos (see fig.) has shown that a deity from each major cult site is represented, and thus the pronaos represented a divine receiving hall to maintain the theological union of Egypt. The 'Edfucentric' theologians twisted the qualities of each deity to create an Edfu connection. Such is also the case with many of the deities in the chapels that surround the naos: for example, Hathor of Dendara is connected to Edfu through her marriage to Horus, which was celebrated annually when her cult statue visited Edfu.

The principles of Egyptian temple decoration (the so-called *grammaire du temple*), which first became apparent to scholars at Edfu, reveal certain visual and textual repetitions, alterations and substitutions on one or more architectural members or on coherent groups of surfaces. In the pronaos, for example, the Upper Egyptian deities are represented on the eastern columns sequentially from south to north, whereas the variable position of Lower Egyptian deities on the western columns depends on a geographical and theological analogy with the deity represented in the same position on the east. The remarkable theological cohesion and symmetry of representations are taken to imply premeditation by the theologians and the use of pattern books and cartoons.

LÄ: 'Tell Edfu'

BIBLIOGRAPHY

J. Dümichen: 'Bauurkunde der Tempelanlagen von Edfu', *Z. Ägyp. Spr. & Altertknd.*, viii (1870), pp. 1–13; ix (1871), pp. 25–45; x (1872), pp. 33–42; xi (1873), pp. 109–19

M. de Rochemonteix and E. G. Chassinat: *Le Temple d'Edfou*, 14 vols (Paris, 1892; Cairo, 1918–34); ed. S. Cauville and D. Devauchelle (Cairo, 2/1984–)

H. W. Fairman: 'The Myth of Horus at Edfu, I', *J. Egyp. Archaeol.*, xxi (1935), pp. 26–36

B. Porter and R. L. B. Moss: *Topographical Bibliography*, vi (Oxford, 1939), pp. 119–77

A. M. Blackman and H. W. Fairman: 'The Myth of Horus at Edfu, II', *J. Egyp. Archaeol.*, xxviii (1942), pp. 32–8; xxix (1943), pp. 2–36; xxx (1944), pp. 5–32, 79–80

A. H. Gardiner: 'Horus the Behdetite', *J. Egyp. Archaeol.*, xxx (1944), pp. 23–60

M. Alliot: *Le Culte d'Horus à Edfou au temps des Ptolémées*, 2 vols (Cairo, 1949–54)

H. W. Fairman: 'Worship and Festivals in an Egyptian Temple', *Bull. John Rylands Lib.*, xxxvii (1954), pp. 165–203

C. de Wit: 'Inscriptions dédicatoires du temple d'Edfou', *Chron. Egypte*, xxxvi (1961), pp. 56–97, 277–320

P. Derchain: 'Un Manuel de géographie liturgique à Edfou', *Chron. Egypte*, lxxiii (1962), pp. 31–65

E. A. E. Reymond: *The Mythical Origin of the Egyptian Temple* (Manchester, 1969)

G. Gabra and A. Farid: 'Neue Materialien zu königlichen Baudenkmälern in Edfu', *Mitt. Dt Archäol. Inst.: Abt. Kairo*, xxxvii (1981), pp. 181–6

F. Labrique: 'Observations sur le temple d'Edfou', *Götting. Misz.*, lviii (1982), pp. 31–48

S. Cauville: *La Théologie d'Osiris à Edfou* (Cairo, 1983)

D. Kurth: *Die Dekoration der Säulen im Pronaos des Tempels von Edfu* (Wiesbaden, 1983)

S. Cauville: *Edfou* (Cairo, 1984)

S. Cauville and D. Devauchelle: 'Le Temple d'Edfou: Etapes de la construction, nouvelles données historiques', *Rev. Egyp.*, xxxv (1984), pp. 31–55

D. Kurth: 'Information über ein von der deutschen Forschungsgemeinschaft gefördertes Projekt zur philologischen Gesamtbearbeitung der Inschriften des Tempels von Edfu', *Götting. Misz.*, xcii (1986), pp. 93–4

E. A. E. Reymond: 'The King's Effigy', *Hommage à François Daumas*, ii (Montpellier, 1986), pp. 551–7

S. Cauville: *Essai sur la théologie du temple d'Horus à Edfou*, 2 vols (Cairo, 1987)

A. Egberts: 'A Note on the Building History of the Temple of Edfu', *Rev. Egyp.*, xxxviii (1987), pp. 55–61

ELENI VASSILIKA

Edgerton, Harold E(ugene) (*b* Freemont, NE, 6 April 1903; *d* 10 Jan 1990). American photographer. He learnt photography as a boy and studied electrical engineering at the University of Nebraska. After graduation in 1925, he went to the Massachusetts Institute of Technology, Cambridge, MA, where he received his doctorate and remained as a member of the Electrical Engineering Faculty. From the early 1930s he conducted pioneering research in stroboscopic photography, which permitted him to freeze exceedingly fast movement and make exposures between 1/10,000 and 1/1,000,000 of a second. The famous photographs that resulted revealed to the world for the first time some of the lost mysteries of everyday motion, including a falling drop of milk refracting into a coronet and bullets rupturing such objects as an apple, a balloon, a lightbulb and a tank of water. These exposures, too fast for any camera shutter to capture, were created with an ordinary 35mm camera and Edgerton's electrical control of an absolutely instantaneous flash of light in a dark room, which exposed the film to bright light well within any possible shutter speed.

In his stroboscopic photography Edgerton used a controlled, pulsing strobe light in a dark room and shot the images with a motion picture camera; this permitted successive phases of action to be exposed and superimposed upon each other. He used this method to capture the technique of athletes such as gymnasts, divers and golfers, and these images can be seen as part of a tradition of capturing movement with still photographs dating from the early 1880s with the work of Eadweard Muybridge, Thomas Eakins and Etienne-Jules Marey. While Edgerton's photographs were ostensibly technical breakthroughs, he also intended that this arrest of invisibly fast motion should produce artistic images: he would photograph and rephotograph a phenomenon repeatedly, often over a period of nearly 50 years, in quest of a perfect image of an accident of nature.

WRITINGS

with J. R. Killian: *Flash: Seeing the Unseen by Ultra-high-speed Photography* (Boston, 1939, 2/1954)

Strobe (New York, 1970/*R* 1979) [technical manual]

with J. R. Killian: *Moments of Vision: The Stroboscopic Revolution in Photography* (Cambridge, MA, 1979)

PHOTOGRAPHIC PUBLICATIONS
with E. Jussim and G. Kazafas: *Stopping Time: The Photographs of Harold Edgerton* (New York, 1987)

BIBLIOGRAPHY
J. Darius: *Beyond Vision* (Oxford and New York, 1984), pp. 18, 19, 54, 96–9, 108–9, 116–17

MARY CHRISTIAN

Edhem, Osman Hamdi. *See* OSMAN HAMDI.

Edinburgh. Capital city of Scotland. It is situated to the south of the Firth of Forth and has a population of *c.* 500,000. The city developed in the 12th century beneath Edinburgh Castle, which was begun by Scottish King Malcolm III (*reg* 1058–93) on an extinct volcanic hill that dominates the city. It became the Scottish capital during the 15th century but lost many of its powers after the union of the Scottish and English crowns in 1603, although the Scottish Parliament continued to meet in Edinburgh until 1707. The city's university was founded in 1583, since when Edinburgh has been an important cultural centre, particularly during the 18th century, within the development of Enlightenment thought.

1. History and urban development. 2. Art life and organization. 3. Centre of production. 4. Palace of Holyroodhouse.

1. HISTORY AND URBAN DEVELOPMENT. Edinburgh consists of the Old Town, the New Town and an encircling collection of districts and suburbs built since 1850. The Old Town lies on a ridge that slopes down from the Castle at the west end to the palace and abbey of Holyroodhouse over a mile to the east (see fig. 1). These two places are connected by the High Street and Canongate, forming one continuous street known as the Royal Mile. The New Town lies to the north of the Old Town, across low-lying land that was once a bog or loch and which now consists largely of public gardens.

(i) Before 1707. Castle rock, which has an area of about three hectares, was probably first fortified before AD 1000 and provides an extremely strong defensive position; the castle is accessible only from the east. The oldest surviving building on the rock is St Margaret's Chapel (*c.* 1100), a small fortress-like building with a Romanesque chancel arch. On the south side of the castle yard lies the Great Hall, with a timber roof dating from the early 16th century. The Half-moon battery, a fortification covering the approach to the castle from the Royal Mile, was built in the later 16th century. Another distinctive feature of the Old Town skyline is St Giles' Cathedral in the High Street. Although there has been a church on the site since *c.* 1130, the present building dates principally from the 14th century. The five nave bays, the transepts and four of the five choir bays were all built *c.* 1365–95. Additions including aisles, the distinctive crown spire and the raising of a clerestory over the nave were all made by 1500. The exterior was inappropriately refaced in ashlar in 1829–33. The Abbey of Holyroodhouse was founded in 1128 and was probably used as a royal residence as early as 1329. Edinburgh was a walled city from, at the latest, 1450, and the Palace of Holyroodhouse was begun in 1501 (*see* §4 below).

Of the medieval city almost nothing remains. Edinburgh was sacked by an English army in 1544, and a large number of the houses, many of them with wooden frontages, were

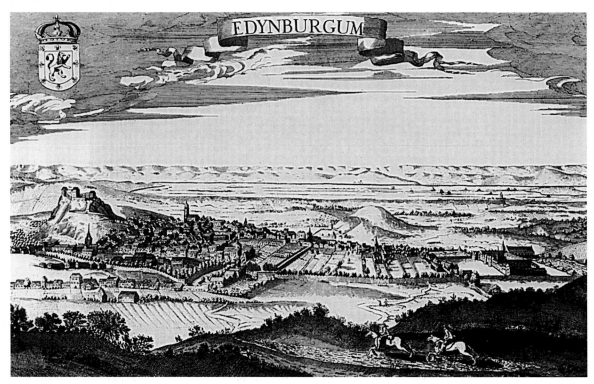

1. Edinburgh, looking north to the Firth of Forth, *c.* 1600

burnt to the ground; the abbey and the palace were also reduced to ruins. Rebuilding was carried out within the city walls, which had been strengthened and extended in 1514 (some fragments remain), helping to produce extreme congestion by the 18th century. Although the court was transferred to London in 1603, taking its artistic patronage with it, one of Scotland's finest early Renaissance buildings dates from the early 17th century. This is George Heriot's Hospital, built from 1628 by WILLIAM WALLACE and William Aytoun (*fl* 1598; *d* ?1643) in the form of a quadrangle facing the southern slopes of the castle rock.

(ii) 1707–c. 1850. Although Edinburgh was never a capital city in the full sense after 1707, it remained the centre of Scotland's political, legal and intellectual life. Enormous strides in the development of Scotland's agriculture and industry were made during the 18th century, and the incomes of landowners, industrialists and merchants rose very quickly. This prosperity financed the building of the New Town, which was further encouraged by cramped living conditions in the Old Town. Buildings six or eight storeys high were packed together in narrow streets or closes running north and south from the Royal Mile, as well as in an almost continuous frontage along it. The proposal to build a New Town was put forward in 1752 and carried out largely through the vision and influence of George Drummond (1687–1766), then the city's Lord Provost. A competition for a plan was held in 1766, and the winning design was submitted by James Craig (1744–95), whose plan provided for three parallel streets, the middle one—George Street—having a square at each end. The remarkable feature of the plan, however, was that the two outer streets were to have houses on one side only, so that Princes Street had a clear view south to the castle and the Old Town, while Queen Street looked across open country and gardens towards the Firth of Forth. Access from the Old Town to the New was via the North Bridge, then being built, and also, later and further west, by a roadway on a rising ramp of earth, known as the Mound. These arrangements proved popular, and houses soon began to be built in Princes Street and in St Andrew's Square, at the east end of George Street. By 1790 building had progressed almost to the west end of Princes Street. The early houses were neither large nor distinguished, unlike those in the splendid Charlotte Square at the west end of George Street. Here Robert Adam (i) (*see* ADAM (i), (3)) was asked to prepare a plan in 1791, although the square was not completed entirely as Adam planned it.

At the beginning of the 19th century the focus of Edinburgh life was still the Old Town, with the Law Courts (begun 1632), the City Chambers (1752–61), St Giles' Cathedral and the university, just south of the High Street. Planned by Robert Adam and begun in 1789 on the site of the 16th-century college buildings, the university has a huge street frontage, behind which were to be two courts, combined when William Henry Playfair (*see* PLAYFAIR, (2)) revised the plan in 1817. In the north range of the quadrangles, the Upper Library (40 m in length, with an arched and coffered ceiling), is possibly the finest Neoclassical interior in Scotland. By the 1790s the population of Craig's New Town was increasing, and in 1802 a plan

2. Edinburgh, looking north, showing the castle and part of the New Town

to extend the city to the north was accepted. In outline this plan was similar to Craig's, except that each street was to be treated as a single architectural composition. Further successive extensions, all in the same regular style, took place during the next 20 years. The last of these, planned in 1822 by JAMES GILLESPIE GRAHAM for Francis Stuart, 10th Earl of Moray, gave Edinburgh its grandest sequence of pedimented and columned mansion façades. Aside from its housing, the rectilinear-planned New Town (see fig. 2) is distinguished by an astonishing display of public buildings and monuments. The Register House, designed by Robert Adam to house the Public Records of Scotland, was begun in 1774 and completed to an altered and extended design 60 years later. The frontage to the east end of Princes Street has a projecting Corinthian portico, pavilions at each end with cupolas, and a rusticated ground floor.

On Calton Hill, beyond the eastern limits of Princes Street, stands the National Monument. Begun in 1824 by William Henry Playfair and C. R. Cockerell (*see* COCKERELL, (2)) as a national memorial of the Napoleonic Wars, this extraordinary construction was to be an exact and complete replica of the Parthenon. Only 12 columns had been erected by 1829, when financial constraints halted work, but it earned Calton Hill the name of Edinburgh's Acropolis, while the wealth of Greek Revival buildings in the city as a whole caused Edinburgh to be dubbed the 'Athens of the North'. Also on Calton Hill are the Nelson Monument (1807–16), the old City Observatory (1818) and Observatory House (1776–92) in castellated Gothic by James Craig, two small circular temples—monuments to *Robert Burns* (1830) and *Dugald Stewart* (1831)—and what was once the Royal High School. Designed by THOMAS HAMILTON and built in 1825–9, this has been described as 'the noblest monument of the Scottish Greek Revival' (Summerson, p. 521). The central feature is a large Doric temple, flanked by low colonnaded wings that terminate in pilastered pavilions. The central temple contains a beautiful oval hall, with shallow coffered ceiling and a balcony supported by cast-iron columns with fine capitals.

Further west on Princes Street is the Scott Monument, begun in 1840 by the young and almost unknown GEORGE M. KEMP, containing a statue of *Sir Walter Scott* (completed 1846) by JOHN STEELL. In a classical city this monument is fantastically Gothic, an intricate pile of arches, buttresses, niches and pinnacles. Still further west on Princes Street stand the Royal Scottish Academy (formerly the Royal Institution) and the National Gallery of Scotland, both by Playfair (for illustration *see* PLAYFAIR, (2)). The Royal Scottish Academy was begun in 1822, and the original Doric temple was extended southward in 1832–5, almost doubling the size of the building and greatly improving its proportions. At the same time the north portico was deepened by an additional row of columns, and the side pavilions were extended; the columns are fluted, and there is a great deal of decorative stonework. The National Gallery of Scotland (1851–7) is an extremely elegant and unfussy building. Each façade has twin projecting Ionic porticos, and on each side there is another portico projecting from blind walls relieved by shallow pilasters.

(iii) After c. 1850. Growing prosperity and population, along with the arrival of the railway in Princes Street Gardens in 1845, caused fairly rapid expansion after 1850. Princes Street, at first purely residential, was increasingly dominated by shops and hotels, and elegant mansions began to be built south of the city. Orderly development throughout the city as a whole came to an end, although street planning after the fashion of the New Town continued in some areas. Population spread north and west, and some of Edinburgh's most notable Victorian buildings are on the western approach roads, including Donaldson's Hospital (1842–54) by William Henry Playfair and Daniel Stewart's College (1846–55) by DAVID RHIND, both with towers and turrets and reminiscent of George Heriot's Hospital, and Fettes College (1864–70) by David Bryce, a notable example of SCOTTISH BARONIAL architecture. More innovative in conception are the Royal Museum of Scotland (begun 1861), a lofty cast-iron Italianate palace by Captain FRANCIS FOWKE beside the original university buildings, and the iron and glass Palm House (1858) by Robert Matheson (1807–82) in the Royal Botanic Gardens north of the New Town.

The proliferation of styles that characterized late 19th-century architecture is well represented in Edinburgh. The horseshoe-shaped Usher Hall (1910–14) is a copper-domed Beaux-Arts construction by J. Stockdale Harrison (*d* 1952). There were also some distinctive local variations on nationally popular styles, such as the rustic cottages (1900) by ROBERT S. LORIMER in Colinton Road, south Edinburgh. Expansion in the 20th century filled in, principally with high-density housing estates, the open country between the north of the New Town and the villages of Granton, Newhaven, the port of Leith and Portobello, all on the Firth of Forth. The arrival of Modernism had little effect on the appearance of the city, although St Andrew's House (1934–9), built by THOMAS TAIT to house the Scottish Office, is an impressive exception. Situated on the southern slopes of Calton Hill, it exploits its site to create a colossal and carefully composed tableau of international Modernism. Striking post-war buildings include the Scottish Widows Assurance Headquarters (1976) by Spence, Glover and Ferguson, an arrangement of dark-brown glass hexagons that reflect, literally and formally, the red stone of Salisbury Crags in the background and contrast with the long horizontal lines of the Royal Commonwealth Pool (1967) by ROBERT MATTHEW, JOHNSON-MARSHALL & PARTNERS across the road. A rare example of Post-modernism is the glass and chrome porticoed shop-front of the Edinburgh Solicitors' Property Centre in George Street, designed by the firm Campbell and Amot.

BIBLIOGRAPHY

E. Topham: *Letters from Edinburgh* (London, 1776)
J. Grant: *Old and New Edinburgh*, 3 vols (London, 1883)
D. Wilson: *Memorials of Edinburgh in the Olden Time* (Edinburgh, 1891)
Old Edinburgh Club, i–xxxiii (1908–69)
W. Mair: *Historic Morningside* (Edinburgh, 1947)
G. Scott-Moncreiff: *Edinburgh* (London, 1947)
I. G. Lindsay: *Georgian Edinburgh* (Edinburgh, 1948)
J. Summerson: *Architecture in Britain, 1530–1830*, Pelican Hist. A. (Harmondsworth, 1953, rev. 7/1983)
A. J. Youngson: *The Making of Classical Edinburgh, 1750–1840* (Edinburgh, 1966)
C. McKean and D. Walker: *Edinburgh: An Illustrated Architectural Guide* (Edinburgh, 1982)
J. Gifford, C. McWilliam and D. Walker: *Edinburgh*, Bldgs Scotland (Harmondsworth, 1984)

A. J. YOUNGSON

2. ART LIFE AND ORGANIZATION. Edinburgh first became an important art centre in the 15th century, after its establishment as the capital city of Scotland. Activities in the fine arts were initially centred around the court, but commissions from the crown for royal portraits and then in the 16th century the decoration of the Palace of Holyroodhouse helped to stimulate a broader interest in tapestry and painting. During the 15th century there were close links between the Netherlands and Scotland—two panels by the Flemish artist HUGO VAN DER GOES for the Trinity College Church are among the few surviving paintings from before the Reformation—and this relationship survived into the late 16th century, when Arnold Brockhorst (*fl* 1580–83) was King's Painter to James VI of Scotland. Gradually, however, such Scottish painters as GEORGE JAMESONE, John Michael Wright, David Scougall (*fl* 1654–77), JOHN MEDINA, JOHN SMIBERT, WILLIAM AIKMAN and Richard Waitt (*fl* 1701–32) established reputations. During the 18th century in Edinburgh painting was nevertheless still considered one of the trades, a fact alluded to in such paintings as Roderick Chalmers's *Edinburgh Trades at Holyrood* (1720; see fig. 3). The NORIE family, for example, founded a firm of decorative painters that gave many artists, including Alexander Runciman and his brother John Runciman, their basic tradesman's training (*see* RUNCIMAN). At an institutional level, in 1760 the Board of Trades and Manufactures (est. 1705) set up one of the earliest publicly funded design schools, the Trustees' Academy, with the aim of improving the standard of design in Scottish manufacturing industries. The French artist William Delacour (*fl* 1740–67) was the Academy's first Master; he was succeeded by Alexander

3. Roderick Chalmers: *Edinburgh Trades at Holyrood*, oil on canvas, 1.04×1.82 m, 1720

Runciman, who taught Alexander Nasmyth (*see* NASMYTH, (1)), who painted landscapes and urban scenes (e.g. *Princes Street, with the Royal Institution Buildings under Construction*, 1825; see fig. 4). Many artists, however, such as Anne Forbes (1745–1834), considered France or Italy more suitable places for serious study. This situation changed dramatically, however, during the Scottish Enlightenment in the late 18th century. Central in this development were the writings and portraits of the philosopher–artist ALLAN RAMSAY, and this interdependence of literature and painting continued in the work of the portrait painter HENRY RAEBURN (e.g. *Sir Walter Scott*; Edinburgh, N.P.G.) and that of the genre painter DAVID WILKIE.

In the 19th century a split developed between students wishing to study drawing as a fine art and teachers of industrial design at the Trustees' Academy. This split was reflected in the subsequent development of the city's educational, organizing and exhibiting institutions, with the Edinburgh College of Art, the fine art department at Edinburgh University and the National Galleries of Scotland all evolving from the Trustees' Academy, while a different strand was embodied in the complicated evolution of the Royal Scottish Academy (est. 1826), in which the history painter WILLIAM ALLAN, Robert Scott Lauder (*see* LAUDER, (1)) and HILL AND ADAMSON, the inventors of the calotype, were all involved (see Errington). The school of the Royal Scottish Academy functioned from 1839 to 1931. Through the 20th century the Academy remained the principal national institution for professional artists, arranging annual exhibitions of contemporary art, providing library facilities for its members and engaging in charitable works. The first Chair of Fine Art in the United Kingdom was established at Edinburgh University in 1881 and was named after the portrait painter JOHN WATSON GORDON; its first incumbent was the classicist Gerald Baldwin Brown (1849–1932), while subsequent professors included HERBERT READ and D. TALBOT RICE. In the 20th century the department became one of the largest in the United Kingdom, and among notable graduates is Elizabeth Blackadder (*b* 1931). The Edinburgh College of Art, founded in 1907, is one of the best-endowed in Britain through the Andrew Grant of Pitcorthie bequest, and many of Scotland's most celebrated artists trained or taught there. For example, the colourist S. J. PEPLOE and the romantic landscape painters Donald Moodie (1892–1963), Penelope Beaton (1886–1963) and Adam Bruce Thomson (1885–1976) all exerted an important internationalist influence through their teaching, visible in the poetic landscapes and rich handling of paint of W. G. Gillies, Robin Philipson (1916–92) and John Houston (*b* 1930). Inspired by the work of the abstract painter ALAN DAVIE, John Bellany (*b* 1942) reacted against the college's traditional values, however, and produced a series of compelling and powerful images during the 1960s.

As the national capital, Edinburgh is also the location of the major Scottish national museums, including the National Gallery of Scotland, the Scottish National Gallery of Modern Art and the Scottish National Portrait Gallery, which comprises the most comprehensive visual record of important figures in Scottish history as well as an important archive of early photographs by Hill and Adamson. The National Portrait Gallery also commissions and displays images of contemporary Scots by such local artists as Victoria Crowe (*b* 1945) and Sandy Moffat (*b* 1943). From the mid-19th century commercial galleries also proliferated in the New Town district of the city, and major auction houses such as Christie's and Sotheby's conducted regular sales; while the annual Edinburgh

4. Alexander Nasmyth: *Princes Street, with the Royal Institution Building under Construction*, oil on canvas, 1.19×1.60 m, 1825 (Edinburgh, National Gallery of Scotland)

International Festival provided a focus for a wide range of artistic activities from the late 1940s.

BIBLIOGRAPHY
R. Brydall: *Art in Scotland: Its Origins and Progress* (Edinburgh and London, 1889)
C. Thomson: *Pictures for Scotland* (Edinburgh, 1972)
E. Gordon: *The Royal Scottish Academy of Painting, Sculpture and Architecture* (Edinburgh, 1976)
D. Thomson: *Scottish National Portrait Gallery Concise Catalogue* (Edinburgh, 1977)
L. Errington: *Master Class: Robert Scott Lauder and his Pupils* (Edinburgh, 1983)
H. A. Smailes: *A Portrait Gallery for Scotland* (Edinburgh, 1985)
I. Gow and T. Clifford: *The National Gallery of Scotland: An Architectural and Decorative History* (Edinburgh, 1988)
J. D. Macmillan: *Scottish Art, 1460–1990* (Edinburgh, 1990)

PATRICIA CAMPBELL

3. CENTRE OF PRODUCTION.

(i) *Metalwork.* By 1483 craftsmen in Edinburgh associated with a variety of metalworking trades had formed the Hammermen's Incorporation, and by 1558 there were 158 hammermen, compared with 178 tailors and 100 bakers. Pewterers, who, until the late 18th century, were permitted to work copper, specialized in the production of measures and drinking vessels. The goldsmiths of Edinburgh formed a separate guild in the mid-16th century, and in 1552 an assay office was established that continues to operate. The town mark consists of a castle with three turrets and is accompanied by the mark of the deacon, replaced by the thistle hallmark in 1759, and a maker's mark. The annual date letter system of marking was introduced in 1681.

BIBLIOGRAPHY
M. Baker: 'The Late 18th Century Edinburgh Silver Trade', *Connoisseur*, clxxxiii (1973), pp. 289–94

PETER HORNSBY

(ii) *Glass.* Edinburgh's geographical position was advantageous for the production of glass, as it was close to sources of coal and the coast, for exporting goods. During the early 17th century Sir Robert Mansell (1573–1656) held the monopoly for glassmaking in England, and in 1627 he took over the factories established in 1610 by Sir George Hay (1572–1634), which resulted in a Scottish monopoly. In 1628 a glasshouse was established in Leith to make green bottle glass, and by 1777 there were seven glass factories in the area around Edinburgh making bottles and drinking vessels. During the 19th century there were many glasshouses in Edinburgh, and the factories of the Ranken family and Alexander Jenkinson and John Ford's Holyrood Flint Glassworks were dominant. Many of the factories copied Bohemian engraving and were influenced by Italian craftsmen, emulating Venetian 'filigree' glass. In the 20th century many of the factories were amalgamated into the Edinburgh Crystal Glass Co., which was taken over by Crown House and operated from Penicuik, outside Edinburgh.

BIBLIOGRAPHY

A. Fleming: *Scottish and Jacobite Glass* (Glasgow, 1938)

K. SOMERVELL

(iii) Furniture. Medieval Edinburgh was an important centre of furniture production. In 1475 the Provost and magistrates granted the right for the existing guild to split into two branches: the masons and the wrights. The latter included those craftsmen who manufactured items from wood. An additional incorporation of wrights existed for the Canongate area, although the superiority of the Edinburgh guild was recognized in 1639. After 1603, when James VI of Scotland also became King of England (as James I), royal and noble patronage declined, as the court moved to London. The Civil War in the mid-17th century further inhibited patronage and innovation, and the rapid advances in furniture design and construction that developed in the London furniture trade after the Restoration in 1660 were slow to be adopted in Edinburgh. In 1676 Jacob Bedford (*fl* 1676–8) was made a burgess of Canongate and allowed by the Incorporation of Wrights of Edinburgh to exercise his claim to be able to produce fine furniture of a type not then made in the city. When Bedford left Edinburgh in 1678 his English journeyman, James Turner (*fl* 1678–1703), attempted to carry on the business, but the Incorporation of Wrights tried to prevent this, and he was obliged to appeal to the Privy Council of Scotland for protection. The conservatism among Edinburgh furniture-makers probably explains why London suppliers were employed to refurbish the Palace of Holyroodhouse in the 1680s. Change was, however, imminent. William Scott (*fl* 1685–1704), Deacon of the Incorporation of Wrights (1692–4), was one of the first Scottish cabinetmakers to practise the art of veneering. In 1697 his former apprentice Robert Moubray opened a business in West Bow that produced fine marquetry. There is also evidence of French craftsmen practising the crafts of clockmaking, japanning and gilding in Edinburgh at this period. The Frenchman Paul Roumieu, a clock- and watchmaker, lived in Edinburgh from 1678. Two of his longcase clocks are contained in fine Anglo-Dutch floral marquetry cases probably made by Moubray. In the 17th century there was a substantial Huguenot population in Edinburgh, which was allowed to use the Yester Church in Canongate. Japanners and gilders with French names were allowed by the Incorporation of Wrights to practise their trades provided that they taught them to the sons of burgesses of the city.

The Act of Union of 1707 reinforced the need for the socially and politically ambitious to live in London, depressing trade in the city until *c.* 1740. From the mid-18th century, however, Edinburgh flourished. The development of the New Town, together with renewed country-house building in Scotland, especially in the Lothians, provided considerable patronage for both London-based and Scottish craftsmen. Although Chippendale & Rannie supplied seat furniture (*in situ*) for the drawing-room of Dumfries House, Strathclyde, in 1757, for example, Alexander Peter (*fl* 1713–72) of Edinburgh provided a set of 24 fine mahogany dining-room chairs and a mahogany sideboard. Associated with Peter was a carver, William

Mathie (*fl c.* 1740–61), who provided frames for looking-glasses. Peter had previously worked for Lord Downe (1734–49) and Lord Glenorchy (1745). Another important craftsman was Francis Brodie (1708–82), who traded at the sign of Palladio's Head off Lawnmarket. He was recommended to the Duke of Hamilton by the architect William Adam and carried out commissions for the Earl of Traquair (12 elm chairs, beech chair and mahogany music desk, 1732; chest-of-drawers in ebonized pear wood, 1748) and Alexander Gordon, 4th Duke of Gordon (1743–1827) (e.g. walnut desk and mahogany clothes press, 1739; mahogany dining table and gilt picture frame, 1741). Francis Brodie's son William Brodie (*d* 1788) was a partner in his father's firm by 1773 and three years later became Deacon of the Incorporation of Wrights. In February 1753 the firm of Young & Trotter advertised its services as 'Merchant-Upholsterers' and ten years later was carrying out work at Hopetoun House, Lothian. In the 1770s the company diversified into cabinetmaking and in 1796 furnished the Palace of Holyroodhouse for the reception of the exiled Comte d'Artois. In 1805 William Trotter ((1772–1833) became sole proprietor, and during his tenure the firm furnished the library and picture gallery at Paxton House, Borders, for George Home. The firm also worked in close association with the architect William Henry Playfair, furnishing the University that he completed between 1818 and 1830. Trotter also provided furniture for the Palace of Holyroodhouse for the visit of George IV in 1822.

Edinburgh remained an important centre of furniture production in the 19th and early 20th centuries, although total production declined relative to that in Glasgow. Some royal patronage continued, and Edinburgh cabinetmakers were involved in the furnishing of Balmoral Castle, Grampian. Trotter's business lost its family connection in 1852 but continued to trade as Cairney, Robb & Ray, receiving a large commission in connection with the Palace of Holyroodhouse, which was fulfilled in 1860, the year in which the firm crashed. By the end of the 19th century the most distinguished firm was Whytock & Reid, which had been established in 1807 as a carpet-making and upholstering business by Richard Whytock (*fl* 1807–45). The firm developed into cabinetmaking and manufactured furniture in medieval and Arts and Crafts styles to the designs of Robert S. Lorimer for Rowallen, Strathclyde (1903), Earlshall, Fife, and Darnaway Castle, Grampian. During the same period Morison & Co. achieved a reputation for high-class cabinetmaking and woodwork, ranging from reproduction furniture to the fitting out of Pullman railway carriages. William Reid (1854–1919), the proprietor of Morison & Co., bought Lauriston Castle in 1902, and many of the items of furniture designed and manufactured for it at this time are *in situ*.

BIBLIOGRAPHY

M. Swain: 'Furniture for the French Princes at Holyroodhouse', *Connoisseur* (Jan 1978), pp. 27–35

F. Bamford: *Dictionary of Edinburgh Wrights and Furniture Makers, 1660–1840* (London, 1983)

D. Jones: 'Scottish Cabinet Makers' Price Books, 1805–1825', *Reg. Furn. Soc. J.*, iii (1989), pp. 27–39

S. Pryke: 'A Study of the Edinburgh Furniture Trade, 1708–1790', *Reg. Furn. Soc. J.*, iii (1989), pp. 52–67

——: 'The Extraordinary Billhead of Francis Brodie', *Reg. Furn. Soc. J.*, iv (1990), pp. 81–100

BRIAN AUSTEN

4. PALACE OF HOLYROODHOUSE. The palace was originally built by James IV of Scotland between 1501 and 1505, as a Gothic palace adjacent to the 12th-century abbey. The oldest part of the present building is the massive north-west tower, built in 1528–32 by William Aytoun (*fl* 1598; *d* ?1643) for James V. Two carved panels have been inserted in the tower, relicas of earlier panels, one with the arms of Mary of Guise, second consort of James V, and the other with a background of thistles and a unicorn in full relief, the Royal Arms of Scotland, and below, the initials IR 5. Except for this tower, the entire 16th-century palace was destroyed by an English army in 1544. Over a century later the building remained semi-derelict, and the decision to re-create a palace on the site was taken by Charles II of England and Scotland (*reg* 1660–85). The contract to rebuild is dated March 1672. Responsibility for the work was shared by Sir WILLIAM BRUCE, His Majesty's Surveyor-General in Scotland, and Robert Mylne (*see* MYLNE, (1)), His Majesty's Master Mason in Scotland. Bruce acted as superintendant and overseer, but his connection with the work seems to have ended in 1678. The original sketch plan seems to have been by Mylne (London, BM, Egerton MSS 2870–1), but several alterations had to be made on the express orders of the King. The proposed 'low vaulted Chappell' was converted into 'a large vaulted cellare', and the number of royal apartments was reduced from three to two. The King also ordered that a passage be made to connect the old royal chambers in the north-west tower to the new royal chambers in the east wing; this passage became the great gallery. These alterations made the internal arrangements of the palace far more orderly and convenient.

The present palace is of a quadrangular form, with an open court in the centre, nearly 30 m square (see fig. 5). It is built entirely of local stone, some of it reused. The west front consists of the original castellated tower, four storeys in height, its windows enlarged to suit 17th-century taste; a second tower very similar to the first; and the two towers joined by a low screen of two storeys, with a platform roof and double balustrade. Both towers have three circular turrets at their exterior angles, rising from the ground to the battlements and topped with conical roofs; the fourth angle of each tower is concealed by the building that surrounds the inner court. In the middle of the connecting screen is the entrance, ornamented by four Doric columns, which support an octagonal cupola surmounted by an imperial crown. Beneath the cupola is a clock, its face bearing the date 1680, and over the gateway are the Royal Arms of Scotland (see fig. 3 above). The elevation to the east has 17 bays, with superimposed pilaster orders. The north and south elevations are almost featureless. The inner court is surrounded by a handsome arcade, faced with Doric pilasters. On the entablature of these are cut the ensigns of Scottish royalty: the thistle and the crown, the sword and the sceptre. Between the windows of the

5. Palace of Holyroodhouse, Edinburgh, begun 1671; aerial view from the north-west, also showing ruins of the abbey church

second floor there is a range of Ionic pilasters, and above these an equal number of the Corinthian. On a pediment on the west-facing façade of the court are the royal arms. At the south-west angle of the court is the large staircase leading to the royal apartments, and on the north side of the building is the great gallery, 45 m long, 7 m broad, and 6 m in height. At one stage a gate with Gothic pillars, arches and towers joined the palace to the abbey, but this was destroyed in 1755.

The series of staterooms in the south range contains some fine late 17th-century work. In the Morning Drawing Room and the King's Bedchamber and Closet there are corniced doorcases with acanthus leaf friezes by Alexander Eizat; elaborate drapery and festoons carved by Jan van Santvoort (*fl* 1685–8); and very fine ceilings by John Houlbert (*fl* 1674–9) and George Dunsterfield (*fl* 1660–75), with deeply moulded plasterwork, drapery, oak leaves and cherubs. The marble mantelpieces are Italian, and there are several French, Flemish and Italian tapestries. In 1740–41 William Adam (*see* ADAM (i), (1)) redecorated and refurnished the apartments of the Duke of Hamilton (Hereditary Keeper of the Palace) in the highest style, but this work was almost completely destroyed in the course of later redecorations. In the north-west tower there are apartments associated with Mary, Queen of Scots. These contain wooden ceilings, probably of the early 16th century, with some painted decoration and friezes in tempera.

BIBLIOGRAPHY

An Inventory of the Ancient and Historical Monuments of the City of Edinburgh (London, 1951)

J. Gifford, C. McWilliam and D. Walker: *Edinburgh*, Bldgs Scotland (Harmondsworth, 1984)

A. J. YOUNGSON

Edingen. *See* ENGHIEN.

Edirne [Adrianople]. City in European Turkey. Situated at the confluence of the Tunca and Maritsa rivers and lying on the main road between Asia Minor and the Balkans, the city was founded on the site of Orestia *c.* AD 125 by the Roman emperor Hadrian (*reg* AD 117–38), after whom it was named. Adrianople covered 36 ha and was fortified with a wall 3 m thick and 6 m high, constructed of alternating courses of stone and brick. Cylindrical towers marked the corners of the square, and three bastions on each side strengthened the walls; only a few segments and one corner tower survive. The scene of battles between the Byzantines and the Goths, Avars, Bulgars, Pecenegs and crusaders, the city fell to the Ottoman sultan Murad I (*reg* 1360–89) in 1361, and in accordance with Islamic custom Hagia Sophia, the largest church in the city, was converted into a mosque (destr.). Built in the 5th century AD but restored extensively in the 12th and 13th centuries, it was a cruciform brick building with a central dome supported on four heavy piers. The building collapsed in the earthquake of 1752, and the site was cleared for new construction. The oldest surviving Ottoman building is the Küpelı Cami (Earring Mosque; 1399), constructed by Bayezid I (*reg* 1389–1402) on the cruciform foundations of a Byzantine building just outside the city walls.

The Ottoman city began to take shape in the 15th century. The nine-domed Eski Cami (Old Mosque) was begun by Bayezid's son Süleyman Çelebi, but it was completed in 1413–14 by his brother Mehmed I (*reg* 1403–21), who also built the 14-domed market (Turk. *bedesten*) next to it. With the exception of a small bath, now a ruin, nothing remains of the Eski Saray (Old Palace) built by Murad I and Bayezid I in the second half of the 14th century. It was abandoned when Murad II (*reg* 1421–51 with interruption) began and Mehmed II (*reg* 1444–81 with interruption) completed the Yeni Saray (New Palace) on an island in the Tunca. The New Palace was kept in good repair while the sultans used it in the hunting season, but in the 19th century it was abandoned and disintegrated rapidly, and only the restored Justice Tower and the ruins of the Cihannüma Pavilion, Kum Pavilion bath, the kitchens and two gateways remain.

Murad II built the Muradiye Mosque (1435–6), famed for its excellent glazed tiles, on the outskirts of the city and the Saatli Madrasa and the Üç Şerefeli (Three Balcony) Mosque (1437–47) close to the centre (*see* MOSQUE, fig. 3). The mosque comprises a nearly square enclosure (66.5×64.5 m) containing an arcaded forecourt with a minaret in each corner and a rectangular prayer-hall. Its central dome (diam. 24 m) sits on a hexagonal base supported by two walls and two huge pillars. On either side are paired smaller (diam. 10.5 m) domes; the interstices are covered with tripartite triangular vaults supporting tiny cupolas. The asymmetrical forecourt of different-sized domes and the minarets of varying height and ornamentation are features that link the building to Anatolian Saljuq architecture, but its design was a milestone in the evolution of the classical Ottoman style, leading to the centrally planned sultan's mosques of 16th-century Ottoman architecture (*see* ISLAMIC ART, §II, 7(i)(b)). The tallest minaret, located on the south-west corner of the forecourt, has three balconies, hence the name of the building. Mehmed II extended the complex with the Peykler Madrasa.

Bayezid II (*reg* 1481–1512) built an important complex (1484–8) outside the city on the banks of the Tunca. Designed by the royal architect HAYREDDIN, it comprises five buildings: a mosque, two service buildings on the east and a hospital and medical college on the west. A spacious forecourt leads to the mosque, a high domed structure (20.25 m sq.) flanked by hospices. Each hospice has nine domed units comprising a central hall surrounded by alternating dervish rooms and vestibules or iwans. Two tall minarets rise at the junction of the hospices and the forecourt. The larger of the service buildings contains a kitchen, dining-hall and staff rooms around an enclosed courtyard; the smaller facility to the north contains a bakery and large store-room. The medical college is typical of the period: student rooms on either side of a class-room line three sides of an arcaded square courtyard. The tripartite hospital extends at right angles to the medical college: a rectangular courtyard has seven rooms and a service area; it leads into a smaller courtyard giving access to the surgery, pharmacy and pairs of patient rooms flanking iwans. This arrangement is repeated around the hexagonal domed hall of the third and innermost section. As in the earlier Ottoman capital at Bursa, these and other foundations, such as the Gazi Mihal (1421–2), of which only the mosque and bath remain, and Beylerbeyi (1428–9) complexes, comprised the nuclei of residential areas and regulated the pattern of the city's expansion.

Edirne lost some of its lustre after Istanbul became the capital of the Ottoman empire in 1453, but it remained the second capital and a commercial centre. Its steady growth is shown by such mosques as the Seljuk Hatun (1455–6), Ayşe Kadin (1468–9), Kasim Pasha (1478–9), Sitti Hatun (1482–3), Lari Çelebi (1514–15) and Kadi Bedreddin (1529–30). The finest is the Selimiye complex (1569–75), the masterpiece by the architect Sinan (*see* SINAN (ii)) for Selim II (*reg* 1566–74). In addition to the mosque (see fig.), in which Sinan achieved his most elegant expression of domical structure, the complex includes a madrasa and school of tradition in the southern corners of the plaza, a barrel-vaulted market (Turk. *arasta*) along the entire western side and a school for Koran reading elevated over a wing of the market. The mosque consists of a rectangular forecourt and prayer-hall covered by a huge dome (diam. 31.28 m; h. 43.30 m) resting on eight massive piers that become contreforts above the roof and buttress the drum. Between the piers, four semi-domes on the diagonals integrate the octagonal baldacchino into the rectangular outer shell created by the walls (*see* ISLAMIC ART, fig. 64). The mihrab, minbar and muezzins' tribune are finely executed in marble. Unusually, the tribune is located above a token fountain in the centre of the prayer-hall and reinforces the centralized plan of the interior. The

Edirne, Selimiye Mosque (1569–75) by Sinan

faience decoration in the mihrab recess and sultan's balcony exemplify the best of the Iznik tile industry. Sinan designed and supervised construction of the mosque and educational buildings; he may also have designed the market and the attached school, but they were constructed by his successor DAVUD AĞA under Murad III (*reg* 1574–95) to provide additional income for the foundation.

Edirne was occupied by the Russians in 1828–9 and again in 1878–9, when several mosques were stripped of their tile decoration. At the end of the 19th century Edirne had 61 mosques, 164 oratories (Turk. *mescid*), 56 Sufi convents, 49 madrasas, 53 schools, 103 tombs, 9 hospices, 4 covered markets, 24 caravanserais and khans, 16 baths, 137 fountains and 8 bridges. Of these Ottoman buildings 84 have survived, including several commercial structures and bridges. In the 1560s Sinan had designed commercial buildings in the centre of Edirne for three grand viziers: a caravanserai for Rüstem Pasha (1560–61; for illustration *see* CARAVANSERAI), a double bath for Sokollu Mehmed Pasha (1568–9) and a covered market 300 metres long for Semiz Ali Pasha, who also built a caravanserai (destr.). The caravanserai of Ekmekçioğlu Ahmed Pasha (1609–10) is intact save for the huge dome over the central hall that connects its two spacious wings. Bridges over the Tunca were built by the vizier Şehabeddin Pasha (1451; also known as the Saraçhane Bridge), sultans Mehmed II (1452), Bayezid II (1487–8) and Süleyman (*c.* 1560; Palace Bridge) and Ekmekçioğlu Ahmed Pasha (1615). The Yeni Köprü (New Bridge) over the Maritsa was completed in 1842–3 under Abdülmecid (*reg* 1839–61).

Edirne reached its cultural heyday in the 14th and 15th centuries when it was the Ottoman capital. A type of decorative wood painting, marked by the brilliance of its dyes and delicacy of its patterns, evolved at this time and was known as Edirne work (Turk. *Edirnekârî*). The term also applied to specially burnished and varnished book bindings, which gave their gilded and painted designs such a luminous quality that they had no equal in the Ottoman world.

BIBLIOGRAPHY

Enc. Islam/2

O. N. Peremecı: *Edirne tarihi* [History of Edirne] (Istanbul, 1939)
O. Aslanapa: *Edirnede Osmanlı devri âbideleri* [Monuments of the Ottoman period at Edirne] (Istanbul, 1949)
M. T. Gökbilgın: *XV–XVI. asırlarda Edirne ve Paşa livası* [Edirne and the Pasha district in the 15th and 16th centuries] (Istanbul, 1952)
R. Osman and A. S. Ünver: *Edirne sarayı* [The palace at Edirne] (Ankara, 1957)
O. N. Peremecı, ed.: *Edirne: Edirne'nin 600. fethi yıldönümü armağan kitabı* [Volume commemorating the 600th anniversary of the conquest of Edirne] (Ankara, 1965)
A. Kuran: *The Mosque in Early Ottoman Architecture* (Chicago and London, 1968)
G. Goodwin: *A History of Ottoman Architecture* (London, 1971)
A. Kuran: *Sinan: The Grand Old Master of Ottoman Architecture* (Washington, DC, and Istanbul, 1987)

APTULLAH KURAN

Edis, Colonel Sir R(obert) W(illiam) (*b* Huntingdon, Cambs, 13 June 1839; *d* Great Ormsby, Norfolk, 23 June 1927). English architect and writer. He probably settled in London in 1859, the year he joined the Architectural Association (President, 1865–7) and, in 1860, the newly formed Artists' Volunteer Rifle Club (Colonel, 1883–1902; knighted for war services, 1919). Although some London warehouses built by Edis in the 1860s and early 1870s (destr.) were designed in a Gothic Revival style, Edis was quick to adopt the Queen Anne Revival style (though not for his country houses). Boscombe Spa Hotel (1873; now the Chine Hotel), Bournemouth, was an early example; others include 94 Bond Street (1878); 10 Fleet Street (1885); 59–61 Brook Street (*c.* 1884); and 114 Mount Street (1892), all in London, all of red brick and terracotta and with Dutch gables. 70 Marine Parade (1879–80), Brighton, is an essay in the Old English style, while 101 Piccadilly (1890–91; formerly the Junior Constitutional Club), London, explores a free Italian style and is entirely faced with marble. For the Great Central Hotel (1897–9), 222 Marylebone Road, he reverted to brick and terracotta and used a variety of elements from a Northern Renaissance Revival style. Edis is probably best known as the author of *Decoration and Furniture of Town Houses* (1881) and *Healthy Furniture and Decoration* (1884). These influential books placed him in the vanguard of those furniture reformers who advocated a greater simplicity and rationality. Edis was also a pioneer of built-in furniture, arguing that it was 'labour saving, cleaner as well as cheaper'.

WRITINGS
Decoration and Furniture of Town Houses (London, 1881)
Healthy Furniture and Decoration (London, 1884)

BIBLIOGRAPHY
S. Neale: 'An Architect Presents Arms', *Country Life*, clxxviii (14 Nov 1985), pp. 1570–72

JILL LEVER

Ēdjmiadzin [formerly Vagharshapat]. Armenian city 15 km west of Erevan in the Ararat plain. ZVART'NOTS, a suburb of the city in the Middle Ages, lies 3 km to the south-east. Ēdjmiadzin, the name adopted by the city in 1945, means descent (Armen. *ēdj*) of the only son (Armen. *miadzin*).

1. HISTORY. The site has been inhabited since prehistoric times and was replanned by the Urartian king Rusa II (*reg c.* 680–*c.* 640 BC). The Armenian king Tigran the Great (*reg c.* 96–56 BC) established a Jewish community here, but it was Vagharsh (*reg* AD 117–40) of the Arsacid dynasty who founded the city and gave it its name. Its occupation by the Romans in the 2nd century AD and its transformation into a provisional capital (AD 163) is attested by two Latin inscriptions. During the 3rd and 4th centuries it was the second royal residence of the Arsacids, after their capital at Artashat.

Vagharshapat was the cradle of Armenian Christianity and the main area of activity for the Armenian evangelist St Grigor the Illuminator (239–325/6). The city became the seat of the Catholicos of the Armenian church and enjoyed an artistic flourishing that lasted until the 7th century. After this period, however, it suffered several invasions and went into decline. The seat of the Catholicos was transferred to various locations before finally returning to Vagharshapat in the 15th century. Ēdjmiadzin was also one of Armenia's intellectual centres of activity during the 18th and 19th centuries especially after Russia's conquest of the eastern part of historical Armenia in 1828.

2. BUILDINGS. The city's cathedral and churches are of great significance in the development of Early Christian architecture.

(i) Cathedral of Ēdjmiadzin. This is the most important church in the city and indeed in the whole of Armenia. Its name refers to the vision of St Grigor, in which a man bathed in light and identified as Christ descended from heaven and showed Grigor where to build a church. Although the church's original name is not known, between the 7th and 10th centuries it was called Shoghakat' ('flood of light'). The term Ēdjmiadzin began to be applied to the cathedral from the 15th century, in the form of Holy Ēdjmiadzin of Vagharshapat.

The history of the building's site predates Christianity, as attested by an Urartian stele found under the apse of the Early Christian cathedral. Sources record the latter's foundation at the beginning of the 4th century and its destruction by the Persians in 364. It was restored under Catholicos Nersēs (353–73) and again under Catholicos Sahak (387–428). Excavations in 1955–9 revealed that it could have had a basilical plan, perhaps with a central dome on four piers. It was damaged in the 5th century and converted for a time into a temple for the Mazdean cult, before being rebuilt as a church *c.* 484–5 by Vahan Mamikonian (*reg c.* 485–505). The surviving foundations and lower walls of this building, which are square in plan with protruding apses and four free-standing piers that presumably supported a central dome, belong to this restoration of the end of the 5th century. This design is the prototype for the centrally planned cruciform churches of the 7th century in Armenia (*see* ARMENIA, §II) and later in the West, as in the 9th-century oratory at Germigny-des-Prés.

The restorations undertaken by Catholicos Komitas (615–28) seem to have been restricted to repairing the

1. Ēdjmiadzin Cathedral, 5th century AD; remodelled 17th century

roof. Repairs carried out in the 17th century were more extensive, and the present appearance of the cathedral owes much to this period (see fig. 1). Features include the central dome (1627) supported by ribbed vaulting as found in contemporary Safavid architecture (see ISLAMIC ART, §II, 7(ii)(a)) and the tall bell-tower (1658) topped by a rotunda on a two-storey baldacchino (1658) in front of the west door; its lavishly carved decoration contrasts sharply with the old part of the cathedral. Lanterns over the conches were added in 1683. In the 18th century the vaults and dome were painted in a Persian style by members of the HOVNAT'ANIAN family. Finally, in 1869 the sacristy was built on the cathedral's east side; it now houses the treasury. The yard of the cathedral contains several *khatchk'ars* (stone slabs with a cross engraved in the centre; see ARMENIA, §IV, 1(ii)), one of which is carved with a rare figural relief showing the *Crucifixion* (1279).

The monastery that grew up around the cathedral still functions as the residence of the Catholicos. Its buildings include a school, winter and summer refectories, visitors' cells and the Trdat Gate, all of which were erected in the 19th and 20th centuries on the sites of earlier structures. In 1939 the monastery's collection of manuscripts was given to the state (now in Erevan, Matenadaran Inst. Anc. Armen. MSS, MS. 2374), the most renowned item being the ĒDJMIADZIN GOSPELS (989). In 1982, the Alex and Marie Manoogian Museum was built near the residence of the Catholicos to house the monastery's many remaining art treasures.

(ii) St Hrip'simē Church. It was founded in 618 by Catholicos Komitas on the site of the martyrium of St Hrip'sime, one of the Christian women executed on the instructions of the King Trdat III (*reg* 298–330). The original martyrium was built by St Grigor and rebuilt at the end of the 4th century; it survives as a crypt beneath the apse of the present church (see fig. 2). Despite later alterations, the church preserves the austere and imposing outline of its 7th-century form. Four cross arms terminating in apses and four cylindrical niches in the diagonals are arranged around a domed core. The dome drum, though relatively low, is pierced by 12 windows and gives an illusion of lightness. Four square rooms lie behind the niches, and the whole structure is enclosed within a massive cube. The severity of the façades is softened by the restrained low relief carvings and the earliest dated example of pairs of deep V-shaped slits flanking the apses.

According to the 17th-century Armenian historian Arak'el of Tabriz, the church had fallen into disrepair when in 1653 Catholicos P'ilippos restored the façades, the steps at the base of the walls and the roofs. He also built four small, western style turrets around the base of the drum and a baldacchino-type porch in front of the west façade.

(iii) St Gayanē Church. Situated to the south of the cathedral commissioned by Catholicos Ezr (630–41), its crypt contains the tomb of St Gayanē, the leader of the group of Christian women who were martyred at the beginning of the 4th century. Most of the church's original structure has survived and comprises a domed cross within a rectangle. Four centrally placed and free-standing piers support the arches and squinches that bear the octagonal drum of the dome, which is pyramidical on the exterior. The domed central bay is buttressed by four cross arms; this cross-plan is visible at roof level.

The walls have a concrete core faced with orange tufa in keeping with traditional building techniques. The carved decoration is limited to simple doorframes and to the arches above the windows. Restoration work undertaken by Catholicos P'ilippos in 1652 is evident in the repairs to the façades and the steepened pitch of the roofs. A porch in the form of a gallery was added to the west side in 1683 and served as a mausoleum for the members of the clergy.

(iv) Shoghakat' Church. Situated to the west of the cathedral, it was built in 1694 and according to tradition marks the spot where a flood of light (Armen. *shoghakat'*) fell upon the group of Early Christian female martyrs. The church's elongated plan is typical of 7th-century churches but unusual for the 17th century. It has a central dome on a 12-sided drum that rests on supports abutting on the lateral walls. The church is preceded to the west by a small porch that was added shortly after the church's construction. The lantern on top of the porch has a pyramidical exterior that is a smaller version of the central dome's one. Although the carved ornament of geometric and interlace motifs, and rosettes and crosses on the arched entrance to the church and the window mounts, are in the 17th-century style, they do not affect the sober appearance of the building, thus perhaps reflecting a concern to conform with tradition.

BIBLIOGRAPHY

A. Khatchatrian: *L'Architecture arménienne du IVe au VIe siècle* (Paris, 1971)
S. Der Nersessian: *L'Art arménien* (Paris, 1977, 2/1989; Eng. trans. London, 1978)
V. M. Harouthiounian: *Ēdjmiadzin* (Erevan, 1978/R 1985)
Treasures of Etchimiadzin (Ēdjmiadzin, 1984)
J. M. Thierry and P. Donabédian: *Les Arts arméniens* (Paris, 1987)

PATRICK DONABÉDIAN

2. Ēdjmiadzin, St Hrip'simē Church, view from the south-east, AD 618

Ēdjmiadzin Gospels. Armenian illuminated Gospel book (350×280 mm; Erevan, Matenadaran Inst. Anc. Armen. MSS, MS. 2374) of 233 folios written in fine uncials. It was kept at the cathedral at ĒDJMIADZIN until 1939 and is one of the earliest dated Armenian manuscripts to have survived. The manuscript was copied in AD 989 at the monastery of Noravank', in the province of Syunik' in eastern Greater Armenia. The colophon gives the name of the owner as Ter Step'annos and of the scribe as Hovhannēs. The book covers consist of two leaves of carved ivory showing scenes from the *Life of Christ* around the two central representations of the *Virgin and Child* and *Child Enthroned with SS Peter and Paul*.

The manuscript includes three different sets of illustrations in sharply contrasting styles: preface miniatures at the beginning of the manuscript, such as the elaborately decorated borders of the Letter of Eusebios to Karpianos (fol. 1*r*) and canon tables (fols 2–5), and the full-page miniatures of *Christ Enthroned with Two Saints* (fol. 6*r*), *Evangelist Portraits* (fols 6*v*, 7*r*), the *Virgin and Child* (fol. 7*v*) and the *Sacrifice of Isaac* (fol. 8*r*); the marginal illustrations within the text; and four narrative miniatures at the end of the book, which are stitched in on a pair of stubs set between the last chapter of the St John's Gospel and the colophon. They come from an older manuscript and represent four subjects: the *Annunciation to Zacharias* (fol. 228*r*), the *Annunciation* (fol. 228*v*), the *Adoration of the Magi* (fol. 229*r*), and the *Baptism* (fol. 229*v*), which includes in its borders portrait busts of the four *Evangelists*.

Josef Strzygowski concluded that the ivory covers and the first and last set of miniatures were of Syriac origin and dated from the 5th century to the 6th, while the marginal miniatures he attributed to Hovhannēs, the Armenian scribe mentioned in the colophon. Sirarpie Der Nersessian has, however, shown (1933, 1961) that the first set of miniatures are consistent in style and content with the colophon's date (989) and place of production (Armenia), while the marginal miniatures are contemporary with the insertion of pericope-divisions into the text, which can be dated on palaeographical grounds to the 11th century or the 12th. The four concluding miniatures belong to a style of Armenian painting before the Arab invasion of Armenia that began in 640; their unifying theme is the *Epiphany*, which in the Armenian Church embraces the birth and baptism of Christ, and it is likely that these fragments from an earlier manuscript represent in compact form the earliest known examples of the 'classic' Armenian system of illustrated Gospel preface pages. It is reasonable to suppose that Palestine, where theophanies were frequently used to decorate shrines in the Holy Places, and with which Armenia maintained close ties, served as a source and model of inspiration for these preface pages.

BIBLIOGRAPHY
J. Strzygowski: *Das Etschmiadzin-Evangeliar: Beiträge zur Geschichte der armenischen, ravennatischen und syro-ägyptischen Kunst* (Vienna, 1891)
S. Der Nersessian: 'The Date of the Initial Miniatures of the Etchmiadzin Gospel', *A. Bull.*, xv (1933), pp. 1–34
——: 'La Peinture arménienne au VIIe siècle et les miniatures de l'évangile d'Etchmiadzin', *Actes du XIIe congrès international des études byzantines: Ohrid, 1961*, iii, pp. 49–57
T. F. Mathews: 'The Early Armenian Iconography Program of the Ejmiacin Gospel', *East of Byzantium: Syria and Armenia in the Formative Period*, ed. N. Garsoian (Washington, DC, 1982), pp. 199–215

A. Mat'evosyan: 'Ēdjmiadzin Avetaranē' [The Ēdjmiadzin Gospels—1000 years], *Ēdjmiadzin*, i–iii (1990), pp. 50–60, 74–8
VREJ NERSESSIAN

Edmond, Maggie. *See under* CORRIGAN, PETER.

Edmonds, Francis W(illiam) (*b* Hudson, NY, 22 Nov 1806; *d* Bronxville, NY, 7 Feb 1863). American painter and banker. He achieved recognition both as a painter and as a banker, juggling careers with consummate skill. In 1826 he enrolled at the National Academy of Design while working in a New York bank. Somewhat insecure, he initially exhibited between 1836 and 1838 under the pseudonym E. F. Williams, but favourable reviews subsequently prompted him to use his own name. In 1840–41 Edmonds spent eight months in Europe where he studied the Old Masters; he particularly admired the 17th-century Dutch painters Pieter de Hooch and Gabriel Metsu. The works of these artists were models for Edmonds's meticulous renderings of everyday scenes and anecdotal literary subjects. There is also a similarity between Edmonds's paintings and those of the Scottish painter David Wilkie who was highly regarded in America at the time.

In his depiction of distinctly American themes, Edmonds paralleled his more famous contemporary, William Sidney Mount. Both were chroniclers of the sense of opportunity and well-being in the young nation. Edmonds's *The Image Pedlar* (1844; New York, Hist. Soc.) mingles the themes of patriotism, family and work ethic, while *The Speculator* (1852; Washington, DC, N. Mus. Amer. A.) warns against unscrupulous financial dealing. Edmonds was an accomplished craftsman, and the exquisitely rendered still-life accessories in his pictures often overshadow the sentimentality of the figures. Despite having two occupations, Edmonds was a productive artist and exhibited in New York, Boston and Philadelphia. He was an officer of the National Academy of Design and a founder-member of the Century Association.

BIBLIOGRAPHY
H. N. B. Clark: 'A Fresh Look at the Art of Francis W. Edmonds: Dutch Sources and American Meanings', *Amer. A. J.*, xiv (1982), pp. 73–94
Francis W. Edmonds (exh. cat., ed. H. N. B. Clark; Fort Worth, TX, Amon Carter Mus., 1988)
H. NICHOLS B. CLARK

Edo. Groups of Edo-speaking peoples living in Nigeria's Bendel state outside Benin City. While their languages are related, they are not all mutually intelligible. The Edo, however, all trace their origins to the Kingdom of Benin. Their ancestors migrated from Benin in a series of waves between the 9th and 18th centuries. These migrants intermixed with indigenous peoples and other settlers from neighbouring areas to form the groups whose art is discussed here. The arts of these peoples reflect a complex history of migration and cultural borrowing.

1. Northern Edo. 2. Southern Edo.

1. NORTHERN EDO. The northern Edo comprise the independent village clusters generally known as the northwest Edo in Akoko-Edo as well as most of the communities in the Owan, Etsako and Ishan areas. The areas of Akoko-Edo, Etsako and Owan were disrupted in the late 19th century by the Islamicized Nupe who scattered some

settlements, conquered others and brought about considerable social and cultural change. Since the turn of the century, the primary artistic forms in these areas have been masks and headdresses worn in masquerades performed at a variety of local festivals, although there are a number of other northern Edo arts.

(i) Mask and masquerade. Northern Edo masks are eclectic in the extreme and may be seen as comprising a stylistic and functional transition between the better documented IGBO traditions to the east and YORUBA traditions to the west. A bell-shaped woven raffia costume, which occurs widely among northern Edo groups in the performance of both age companies and title societies, may represent the earliest extant masking tradition. This type of mask has been documented in the village clusters of Otuo and Ikao in northern Owan, throughout much of Akoko-Edo and in eight of the nine Okpella villages in Etsako. Embellishment of the basic costume varies between groups and according to fashion. The most visually striking masquerades are those in which wooden helmet masks and headdresses with figural superstructures are worn. These are found in Otuo, Ikao, Okpe and Ogbe. A distinctive feature of the caryatid figures on the superstructures is their ringed neck, wrists or ankles (see fig. 1). Both the headdresses and the masks are painted white with details picked out in black or are highly polychromed with enamel paint. Recurrent motifs include the Queen of England, Nigerian soldiers, the colonial officer astride his horse, guns, fans, umbrellas, leopards, pythons, aeroplanes and angels, all symbols of power associated with authority.

Some small wooden figures and headdresses from Sabongida-Ora in southern Owan with single-figure superstructures (Cambridge, Mus. Archaeol. & Anthropol.) stylistically resemble the wood-carvings of the Bini people of the Kingdom of Benin, particularly in the treatment of the head and face. Little, however, is known about their use. A cloth-covered acrobatic masker (Ilo) without a detachable wooden face mask appears to be widespread in this area. Acrobatic masquerades by this name occur in Etsako and Ishan as well.

In contrast to the north-west Edo and Owan groups, Etsako masquerades in general reflect heavy borrowing from the Ebira, Igala and Igbo traditions to the north and east. They present a bewildering variety of forms in a wide range of materials, ranging from wood, plastic, raffia and cloth to such assembled natural materials as resins and animal horns and such assembled manufactured materials as scarves and framed prints. One widespread type is a 'tall ghost', a non-anthropomorphic cloth form used to commemorate individual men of high rank in Okpella and north Ibie, where it may contain relics of the deceased. Among the Weppa-Wano and Ekperi, this type serves a more general role as the senior masker in the masquerade complex.

A female mask of wood, painted white or in bright colours, with an elaborate coiffure and figural superstructure is used by several different groups as well. Typically, these three-quarter helmet masks are carved in a northern Edo style featuring a broadly scalloped hairline, with hair differentiated from the face by colour or chip-carved texture. The browline is stressed, the facial plane is

1. Northern Edo masquerade headdress, wood and paint, h. 1.4 m, from Owo, Nigeria, collected *c.* 1900 (London, British Museum)

recessed, and the face and features are rendered schematically with little or no modelling to suggest natural contours. In Okpella such masks commemorate specific women of rank; in Ekperi and Weppa-Wano they personify a wide range of spirits and perform in concert with maskers wearing a variety of disguises. Appliquéd-cloth versions of these masks, worn with a tight-fitting, embroidered body suit also with appliqué, are used as an alternative to the wooden masks in Etsako. These were introduced *c.* 1920 by Okeleke, an itinerant craftsman from Ibaji, the Igbo–Igala borderland on the east bank of the Niger. They became a feature of northern Edo masking as the Okakagbe dance ensemble, consisting of five or six cloth maskers accompanied by a mythical bush monster clad in fibre and wearing an assemblage of horns.

Masks imported from the Ibibio carving centre of Ikot Ekpene (*see* IBIBIO, §1) have introduced additional variety to the masquerades. Local carvers among the Ekperi, Avianwu, Okpella and Weppa–Wano also began emulating this style. Of particular popularity during the 1970s were images of Mamy Wata, the snake-charming temptress (*see* IBIBIO, §3), and an intentionally grotesque wooden mask with bulging eyes and animal attributes. Anogiri, another intentionally grotesque mask used by the Okpella, derives from an Ebira type. It has a roughly carved wooden face, blackened and decorated with an overall pattern of cowrie shells, orange-coloured seeds (*Abrus precatorius*) and little mirrors.

Spectacle and celebration underlie the use of the many individual masquerades that each Etsako group combines into a distinctive festival form. Weppa–Wano and Avianwu masking have not been well documented. Their festivals are said to occur at the time of the harvesting of new yams. Uzairue communities hire such local masquerade troupes as Ilo or Okakagbe to perform on important occasions. Okpella villages hold an annual masking festival known as Olimi at the end of the dry season to purify the community and honour the ancestors. Ekperi villagers perform a large number of masquerades, in conjunction with the formation of the boys' age-grade, every third year during the annual Otsa festival.

Night masquerades are another widespread Etsako phenomenon. The performers of the night society are cloaked in darkness, and they create their characters through sound, often using voice disguisers. Dancers wear a fringe of dried plantain leaves from a shrine sanctuary. Such night masquerades function as a means of social control through their sanctioning of social behaviour. In some areas the costume has been elaborated so that it consists of layered fringes of plantain, as in Uzairue where single dancers wear the costume, or in Okpella where a group will appear during the day beneath a giant construction referred to as the night society's 'hut'.

Ishan masquerades appear to date from the 1890s and 1900s and are related to the ancestral masking traditions of other northern Edo peoples, including such neighbouring peoples as the Ebira, Igala and Igbo. These masquerades feature an ancestral cloth mask. In Ishan this mask is known as Igbabonelimhin and performs with a companion, Okpodu, who wears a detachable wooden mask. Wooden masks tend to be eclectic in style, reflecting Ebira and Ibibio influences.

(ii) Other arts. Both men and women of title may have a variety of regalia and other paraphernalia. There are, for example, wrought-iron lamp-staffs ranging from complex forms with configurations of chameleon and bird motifs to simple ones with clusters of gong- or bladelike forms. Other forms include cast-brass or carved wooden staffs with finials ranging from simple geometric forms to small figural groups. The palaces of men and women of title may also have large door panels with decoration carved in

relief. Among the numerous small chiefdoms of Ishan, the emphasis of the arts on chiefly authority reflects the culture of the neighbouring Kingdom of Benin more directly than other groups to the north. This is evident in swords of office similar to those used in Benin; in rectangular stools (*agbala*); in verandah posts and doors with figurative ornament reflecting the martial character and hieratic order of the chiefdoms; and in distinctive shrine sculpture in the shape of rams' heads. The palaces at Uromi, Ubiaja, Irua, Ewu, Ogwa and Urogbo have all had over-life-size figured verandah posts at one time or another. That at Uromi, for example, included on one of its ten posts the figure of a swordbearer holding the ruler's sword, a symbol of his right to take a human life (see

2. Northern Edo verandah post, wood and paint, from Uromi, Nigeria, *c.* 1901–18; from a photograph by Carol Ann Lorenz, 1980

fig. 2). Northern Edo women (like their Ebira and Igbo neighbours) weave hand- or machine-spun cotton into cloth panels elaborated with supplementary weft patterns. Specialities of this region, however, are the tufted baby-carrier cloths from Igarra and the distinctive indigo, resist-dyed, handspun cotton cloth used in women's title-taking.

2. SOUTHERN EDO. The southern Edo here include the clans of the Urhobo and Isoko peoples. Like the northern Edo, the southern Edo have a rich masking tradition, though they are also known for their shrine sculptures.

(i) Masks and masquerades. The artistic creativity of the southern Edo finds its fullest expression in elaborate masquerades performed during annual festivals, the most impressive of which are the ancient Oworu ceremonies. Among the Isoko and Urhobo, these celebrations involve huge raffia masks and wooden masks called *okao* or *igbigbi* by the Isoko. Specific steps, danced to the accompaniment of the drum choir's fixed rhythmic patterns, identify individual spirits who visit the community during the celebrations. *Akwakwa* or large wooden slit gongs (*c*. 1.3×0.6 m) with carefully carved and painted decorations are used exclusively for Oworu masquerade performances. The features of these Oworu masks highlight the key stylistic characteristics found in most Isoko and Urhobo carving. They have a high forehead, heavily lidded eyes, a protruding mouth with prominent teeth and a scar extending from the tip of the nose to the hairline. It is difficult to separate stylistically Urhobo and Isoko carving.

Other southern Edo masking traditions are often referred to as social masquerades. These frequently use traditions acquired from other peoples and include stilt dancers, maskers covered in woven cloth and even masks purchased from the Ibibio centre of Ikot-Ekpene (*see* IBIBIO, §1), far to the east.

(ii) Shrine sculpture. The second major form of artistic expression among the southern Edo comprises the over-life-size mud sculptures that are kept in shrines. These represent important clan deities. Although in the 1980s almost every Isoko clan had at least one, the most impressive were to be found in the Isoko villages of Aradhe, Iri, Igbide and Ilue-Ologbo. Significant mud sculptures are found in Urhobo shrines as well, but even more prominent are large wooden ones, often representing ancestors, displayed in groups, especially in the villages of Agbon and Agbarho clans. Other important shrine sculptures include the ubiquitous wooden *ivri* images (see fig. 3), which vary in size from only a few centimetres to over a metre in height. The larger *ivri*, which are housed in their own shrines, are complex carvings with human and animal figures on top of a quadruped whose distinguishing feature is a large mouth with prominent teeth. Smaller *ivri*, and such other carvings as *oma* and *obo* images, are brought to shrines as offerings or kept in private household shrines.

Isoko and Urhobo shrines are repositories not only of carvings but also of such other sacred objects as decorated iron staffs. A few older shrines house unusual bronze and terracotta works. The bronze pieces were probably imported, although bronze and brass bracelets were produced

3. Southern Edo *ivri* shrine sculpture, wood, h. 711 mm, from an Isoko village, Nigeria, 19th–20th centuries (New York, Metropolitan Museum of Art)

locally. Additionally, objects found on farms and in streams, thought to be the work of spirits, are brought to these shrines. Although the terracotta pieces are unique, most of the bronzes are related to other works of bronze industries of the Lower Niger. Not all shrines have a wealth of religious artefacts and devotees' offerings. Some are characterized by stark simplicity. Moreover, large carvings are found not only in shrines. Many meeting halls, especially those of the Isoko clan centre of Okpolo-Enwe, may have a central wooden post decorated by striking carved images.

BIBLIOGRAPHY

R. E. Bradbury: *The Benin Kingdom and the Edo-speaking Peoples of South-western Nigeria*, Ethnographic Survey of Africa, Western Africa, Part xiii (London, 1957)
C. Okojie: *Ishan Native Laws and Customs* (n.p., 1960)
W. P. Foss: 'Festival of Ohworu at Evwreni', *Afr. A.*, vi/4 (1973), pp. 20–27, 94
——: 'Images of Aggression: Ivri Sculpture of the Urhobo', *African Images: Essays in African Iconology*, ed. D. McCall and E. G. Bay (New York, 1975), pp. 133–43
J. M. Borgatti: 'Okpella Masking Traditions', *Afr. A.*, ix/4 (1976), pp. 24–33
W. P. Foss: 'Urhobo Statuary for Spirits and Ancestors', *Afr. A.*, ix/4 (1976), pp. 12–23, 89–90
P. M. Peek: 'Isoko Sacred Mud Sculpture', *Afr. A.*, ix/4 (1976), pp. 34–9, 91
J. M. Borgatti: 'Dead Mothers of Okpella', *Afr. A.*, xii/4 (1979), pp. 48–57
——: *From the Hands of Lawrence Ajanaku*, UCLA Museum of Culture History Pamphlet 6 (Los Angeles, 1979)
P. M. Peek: 'Isoko Bronzes and the Lower Niger Bronze Industries', *Afr. A.*, xiii/4 (1980), pp. 60–66, 87–8
J. M. Borgatti: 'Age Grades, Masquerades and Leadership among the Northern Edo', *Afr. A.*, xv/1 (1982), pp. 36–51
Cloth as Metaphor: Nigerian Textiles from the Museum of Cultural History (exh. cat. by J. Borgatti, Los Angeles, UCLA, Mus. Cult. Hist., 1983)
P. M. Peek: 'The Celebration of Oworu among the Isoko', *Afr. A.*, xvi/2 (1983), pp. 34–41, 98
——: 'Ovia Idah and Eture Egbedi: Traditional Nigerian Artists', *Afr. A.*, xviii/2 (1985), pp. 54–60, 102
——: 'The Isoko Ethos of Ivri', *Afr. A.*, xx/1 (1986), pp. 42–7, 98

JEAN M. BORGATTI, PHILIP M. PEEK

Edom and Moab. Two ancient states that flourished from *c.* 1300 BC to *c.* 600 BC in present-day Jordan. Edom and Moab shared territory east and south of the Dead Sea. Ramesses II (*reg c.* 1279–*c.* 1213 BC) campaigned there *c.* 1274 BC; Israel controlled both states in the 10th century BC, and Moab finally broke free *c.* 840 BC. They were dominated by Assyria in the 7th century BC and then by Babylonia. Excavations at sites such as Buseira, Dibon and Heshbon have uncovered stone buildings and pottery similar to Iron Age Palestinian products. Edomite pottery is distinctive, painted with red and black horizontal bands and chevrons. Monumental sculpture from Moab includes a basalt stele from Balu'a (Amman, Jordan Archaeol. Mus.), north of Kerak, bearing in low relief, in imitation of the Egyptian style, a scene of the gods Amon-Re and Hathor investing a king. Above it, parts of five lines in a barely legible and unidentified script perhaps record a local ruler's accession, under Egypt's aegis, in the 13th century BC. Part of another possibly contemporary stele (Paris, Louvre), from further east near Shihan, exhibits a different style. It depicts a divine warrior, life-size and in quite high relief, which borrows Egyptian conventions and belongs stylistically with other Canaanite pieces. The most famous Moabite monument is the 'Stele of King Mesha' (Paris, Louvre), erected to celebrate the defeat of Israel *c.* 840 BC. An inscription of 34 lines in the Old Phoenician alphabet covers its face; there is no carving. A fragment of an inscribed statue from Kerak (Amman, Jordan Archaeol.

Mus.) shows that sculptures decorated Moabite buildings of the 9th century BC. Neither Edomite nor Moabite seals display artistic features distinguishing them from other Iron Age Levantine types. An impression of the seal of the Edomite king Qos-Gabar (*c.* 670 BC), excavated at Umm al-Biyara (*see* PETRA), shows a poorly engraved winged sphinx.

BIBLIOGRAPHY

C. M. Bennett: 'Fouilles d'Umm al-Biyara', *Rev. Bibl.*, lxxii (1966), pp. 372–403 [pp. 399–401, pl. 22b]
La Voie royale: 9000 ans d'art au royaume de Jordanie (exh. cat., Paris, Luxembourg Pal., 1986), pp. 91–141
P. Bienkowski, ed.: *The Art of Jordan: Treasures from an Ancient Land* (Liverpool, 1991)

A. R. MILLARD

Edo period. Period in Japanese history, 1600–1868 (*see also* JAPAN, §I, 2). The victory of Tokugawa Ieyasu (1543–1616) at the Battle of Sekigahara in 1600 put an end to a century of civil war and brought a reunified Japan under the centralized, feudal rule of the Tokugawa family. In 1603 Ieyasu was confirmed as shogun. In the summer of 1615, the last remnants of opposition were eliminated with the siege and fall of Osaka Castle (*see* OSAKA, §I). Thereafter, Ieyasu's military regime, with its headquarters in the castle town of Edo (now Tokyo), became the undisputed government over all Japan. The next 250 years, under the rule of 15 generations of the Tokugawa, was a time of relative political stability, marked by the growth of cities and the mercantile economy. The feudal state was rigidly divided into four groups: samurai (*shi*), farmers (*nō*), artisans (*kō*) and merchants (*shō*). On the fringes of society were the outcasts (*eta*) and the 'non-people' (*hinin*).

A significant factor governing the nature of growth during this period was Japan's virtual isolation from outside influences. In 1639, in response to the encroachment of Christian missionaries and economic intrusion by the Portuguese, Spanish, English and Dutch, the shogunate enacted a policy of seclusion (*sakoku*) from the West. The Dutch alone were permitted to stay, relegated to Deshima (Dejima) Island in the Bay of NAGASAKI, the only port open to overseas trade. Any knowledge the Japanese had of the outside world for two centuries came indirectly through Dutch books, which, until the early 19th century, had only a limited circulation. By then, aroused by the movements of Western powers in China, a handful of *rangakusha* (scholars of 'Dutch', i.e. Western, learning) began to explore the available texts to understand the West and the potential threat it posed to Japan.

The Chinese, also confined to Nagasaki, likewise played a major role in Edo period culture. The naturalistic style of the Chinese merchant and painter SHEN NANPIN was influential in the development of *Nanga* or *Bunjinga* (literati) painting (*see* JAPAN, §VI, 4(vi)(d)), while the paintings and calligraphy of the Chinese monks of the Ōbaku Zen sect stimulated production of Japanese *Zenga* paintings (*see* JAPAN, §VI, 4(vii)). These elements and the numerous imported Chinese books and paintings also influenced such artists as MARUYAMA ŌKYO and the naturalistic school of painting known as the Maruyama–Shijō school (*see* JAPAN, §VI, 4(viii)).

Internally, economic expansion encouraged the rise of an energetic and educated merchant class, who created their own forms of art, literature and theatre, while increased commerce and improved transport added geographical diversity to Japanese culture by linking urban with provincial areas. Edo and Osaka came to rival the monopoly held for centuries by Kyoto as the national cultural centre. Art in this period differed from the classics of aristocratic and military origin. This was the era of Matsuo Bashō (1644–94), who elevated haiku poetry to a mature art form; of Chikamatsu Monzaemon (1653–1724), playwright for the *bunraku* puppet theatre; of the flamboyant *kabuki* theatre; of exquisitely carved *netsuke* (toggles; *see* JAPAN, §XVI, 17 and figs 238–241) and *inrō* (seal cases). The *ukiyoe* woodblock prints (*see* JAPAN, §IX, 3(ii) and (iii)) depicting the 'floating world' of the courtesans and *kabuki* actors, who frequented the licensed pleasure quarters of the major cities, inspired several schools and generations of printmakers (*see also* WOMEN AND ART HISTORY, §IV, 1). By the early 19th century, KATSUSHIKA HOKUSAI and ANDŌ HIROSHIGE had added the Japanese landscape to the *ukiyoe* genre.

Meanwhile, the aristocracy and the military élite continued to patronize the traditional arts. The KANŌ SCHOOL became the official painters of the Tokugawa shogunate in the 17th century. Kanō Mitsunobu (*see* KANŌ, (7)), for example, tempered and freshened the classical brush and ink painting styles with decorative and lyrical elements from the native Japanese painting tradition (*Yamatoe*). Other artists, such as the Rinpa masters (*see* JAPAN, §VI, 4(v)), including TAWARAYA SŌTATSU, Hon'ami Kōetsu (*see* HON'AMI, (1)) and Ogata Kōrin and Kenzan (*see* OGATA, (1) and (2)), were developing a highly decorative style that drew on classical Japanese tradition. An example is Sōtatsu's *Wind and Thunder Gods* (Kyoto, Keninji; *see* TAWARAYA SŌTATSU, §1(iii)), which uses motifs from 13th-century wood sculpture and painting techniques developed from the Heian (AD 794–1184) to the Momoyama (1568–1600) periods.

BIBLIOGRAPHY
R. Lane: *Masters of the Japanese Print* (New York, 1962)
H. Mizuo: *Sōtatsu to Kōrin* [Sōtatsu and Kōrin], Nihon no bijutsu [Arts of Japan], xviii (Tokyo, 1965); Eng. trans. by J. M. Shields as *Edo Painting: Sōtatsu and Kōrin*, Heibonsha Surv. Jap. A., xviii (New York and Tokyo, 1972)
T. Akiyama: *Japanese Painting* (New York, 1977)
J. Baker: *Japanese Art* (London, 1984)
H. Varley: *Japanese Culture* (Honolulu, 1984)
C. Guth: *Japanese Art of the Edo Period* (London, 1995)

BONNIE ABIKO

Edridge, Henry (*b* Paddington, London, Aug 1769; *d* London, 23 April 1821). English painter. He was apprenticed to the engraver William Pether and then attended the Royal Academy Schools, London, where he was praised by Sir Joshua Reynolds. He began exhibiting at the Royal Academy as a miniaturist in 1786 and was then drawn into the circle of artists around Dr Monro, which included Thomas Girtin. In 1789 he met the watercolourist Thomas Hearne who became his close friend and with whom he went on sketching expeditions; there are two portraits of Hearne by Edridge (1800; London, BM and V&A). The spareness of Hearne's style is probably reflected in Edridge's small-scale portrait drawings of sitters, usually full-length in landscape, for which he is best known

(e.g. *The Hon. Sir Edward Paget*, 1810; London, V&A). It was a successful formula, the figures being drawn in black lead, with careful stippling, with touches of Indian ink and a small amount of coloured wash. He also executed architectural landscape watercolours of Normandy, dating from visits there in 1817 and 1819, that anticipate the work of Samuel Prout. In 1820 he was elected ARA, and he exhibited some 260 works at the Royal Academy. His sketchbooks are in the British Museum, London.

BIBLIOGRAPHY
H. Smith: 'The Landscapes of Henry Edridge, A.R.A.', *Old Wtrcol. Soc. Club*, lii (1977), pp. 9–24

ROBIN SIMON

Education. *See* ART EDUCATION.

Edward, King of Portugal. *See* AVIZ, (2).

Edward I, King of England. *See* PLANTAGENET, (3).

Edward III, King of England. *See* PLANTAGENET, (4).

Edward IV, King of England (*b* Rouen, 28 April 1442; *reg* 1461–70, 1471–83; *d* Westminster, 9 April 1483). English ruler and patron. He was the great-great-grandson of Edward III, King of England, and first king of the House of York. His reign spanned much of the Wars of the Roses (1455–85). According to a Bohemian visitor, Gabriel Tetzel, Edward IV had by February 1466 'the most splendid court. . .in all Christendom'. Lavish expenditure on clothes, jewels, plate and furnishings preceded his coronation in June 1461 and the marriage of his sister, Margaret of York (1446–1503), to Charles the Bold, 4th Duke of Burgundy, in 1468 (*see* BURGUNDY, (5)). Soon after Edward returned from exile in the Netherlands with Louis de Gruuthuse in the winter of 1470–71, such expenditure was to become firmly established as a relatively consistent feature of his reign.

For many luxury goods, including tapestries and illuminated manuscripts, Edward turned to the Netherlands. His most important purchase of tapestries was made in 1467–8, probably from Pasquier Grenier, including sets depicting the *Life of Alexander the Great*, the *Passion* and *Nebuchadnezzar* (all untraced).

In addition to several fortification projects, Edward made significant additions to the residential comforts of Nottingham Castle (destr.), Notts, and Fotheringhay Castle (mostly destr.), Northants, in the 1470s. His most important architectural patronage occurred at Eltham Palace, where he built the Great Hall (*c.* 1475–83; for illustration *see* ELTHAM PALACE), and at Windsor Castle, where the new chapel of St George was begun in 1475 (*see* WINDSOR CASTLE, §2 and fig. 2). Edward and his wife, Elizabeth Woodville (1437–92), are depicted in the stained-glass window (*c.* 1475–85) that they gave to Canterbury Cathedral (*see* CANTERBURY, §III, 3).

Later purchases of Netherlandish tapestry showed *Noah* (1478), *Publius Horatius and Tullius Hostilius* (1480) and the *Story of Thebes* (1482). In addition, about 21 very large illuminated manuscripts of vernacular, non-liturgical texts (now among the Royal Manuscripts; London, BL) bear signs of having been decorated specifically for Edward at Bruges, mostly *c.* 1479–80. The miniatures of two of these manuscripts (London, BL, Royal MSS 18.D.IX, 18.D.X) were the first to be attributed to the Master of Edward IV. Together with several other Netherlandish manuscripts probably also acquired by him, these books formed the core of the first permanent English Royal Library. At least two of Edward's manuscripts (London, BL, Royal MS. 17.F.II; London, Soane Mus., MS. 1) support the idea of the influence of the bibliophile Louis de Gruuthuse.

BIBLIOGRAPHY

C. Ross: *Edward IV* (London, 1974), pp. 257–77
J. Backhouse: 'Founders of the Royal Library: Edward IV and Henry VII as Collectors of Illuminated Manuscripts', *England in the 15th Century: Proceedings of the 1986 Harlaxton Symposium*, pp. 23–41
S. McKendrick: 'Edward IV: An English Royal Collector of Netherlandish Tapestry', *Burl. Mag.*, cxxix (1987), pp. 521–4
——: '*La Grande Histoire César* and the Manuscripts of Edward IV', *Eng. MS. Stud., 1100–1700*, ii (1990), pp. 109–38
——: 'The *Roméleon* and the Manuscripts of Edward IV', *England in the Fifteenth Century: Proceedings of the 1992 Harlaxton Symposium*, ed. N. Rogers (Stamford, Lincs, 1994)

SCOT McKENDRICK

Edwardian Baroque. *See* BAROQUE REVIVAL.

Edwardian style. Term used to describe the architecture produced in Great Britain and its colonies in the period from 1890 to 1914, with the reign of Edward VII (1901–10) at its core, hence its name. It covers a multiplicity of styles, with five main strands: the GOTHIC REVIVAL, which continued to dominate church architecture; a range of approaches for domestic architecture that may usefully be grouped together as 'free style', developed by architects of the ARTS AND CRAFTS MOVEMENT; the NEO-GEORGIAN style, a revival of 18th-century British classical domestic architecture; the BAROQUE REVIVAL, used particularly for public buildings; and a French influence derived from the BEAUX-ARTS STYLE, found mostly in opulent buildings for commerce and entertainment. The question of appropriate style had been a constant preoccupation among Victorian architects. While many agreed on the need for a generally accepted national style for Britain, there was no consensus on what that style should be. From this confused background these five strands emerged.

By the 1890s the older Victorian architects were producing a new type of Gothic Revival church, lighter and airier than before. Around the same time the leaders of the next generation were experimenting with an intensely original adaptation in the Arts and Crafts style. Notable examples include E. S. Prior's Holy Trinity (1887), Bothenhampton, Dorset, and W. R. Lethaby's All Saints' (1901–2), Brockhampton, Hereford & Worcs (for illustration *see* LETHABY, W. R.). The other important development in church architecture of the 1890s was the use of Byzantine or Early Christian forms, for example J. F. Bentley's Roman Catholic cathedral (begun 1895; for illustration *see* BENTLEY, JOHN FRANCIS), Westminster, London; this was part of a BYZANTINE REVIVAL.

In domestic architecture and occasionally in larger buildings, the attempt to create a distinctive national style led several architects to seek freedom from foreign historical precedents and also to adapt local materials and forms, drawing on specifically English styles, such as the Elizabethan work of Robert Smythson and his contemporaries. Leonard Stokes, for example, used an Elizabethan window

grid in the central tower of All Saints' Convent (1899–1903), near London Colney, Herts. The leading designers of this 'free style' were Lethaby, Prior, C. F. A. Voysey, Charles Rennie Mackintosh and, at the beginning of his career, Edwin Lutyens. Mackintosh produced his own masterpiece in designing the Glasgow School of Art (begun 1896; *see* MACKINTOSH, CHARLES RENNIE, fig. 1) and its library (begun 1907), which in essence encapsulate the free style. Important domestic examples include Lutyens's Deanery Garden (1901), Sonning, Berks, and several by Prior, for instance Kelling Place (1903–5; now Home Place), Holt, Norfolk.

The Neo-Georgian style was similarly developed by architects associated with the Arts and Crafts Movement, such as Ernest Newton and Stokes from 1895. The many excellent Neo-Georgian houses include Frithwood House (1900), Northwood, Middx, designed by Mervyn Macartney (1853–1932), and Newton's Luckley (1907), Wokingham, Berks. This style and its associated forms in the decorative arts were much loved by generations of the British middle class. However, its vast spread and popularity over the succeeding decades, often in alternating groups with free style houses in suburban streets, led to its debasement and association with reactionary trends.

Although the fourth style characteristic of Edward VII's reign is usually now called Baroque Revival, it was then typically described as English Renaissance style or the Wren Manner. Surprisingly, this style also had its origins with architects close to the Arts and Crafts Movement. John Belcher and A. Beresford Pite showed in their Institute of Chartered Accountants building (1888–93), London, the artistic possibilities of the Baroque in combining the best contemporary building design, sculpture, painting and craftsmanship. It was, however, J. M. Brydon who planted the idea that the Baroque of Christopher Wren, Nicholas Hawksmoor and John Vanbrugh *c.* 1710, although classical in its origins and therefore foreign, had been transformed into something specifically British. Through its association with buildings such as Vanbrugh's Blenheim Palace and hence with the Duke of Marlborough's military victories, it was deemed an appropriate style for Britain and its Empire at its peak. Thus it was widely used for government and other public buildings, monuments and educational institutions, banks and head offices of large companies. Outstanding works in this style include Belfast City Hall (1898–1906) by Alfred Brumwell Thomas and the War Office (1898–1906), Whitehall, London, by William Young.

The influence of France and of Beaux-Arts style came to bear on some opulent blocks of flats, department stores, theatres and grand hotels. The first major building to reflect it was the Ritz Hotel (1903–6), Piccadilly, London, by Mewès & Davis. It has many Parisian characteristics, and its well-planned interior is reflective of the Beaux-Arts scheme; it was also one of the first large steel-frame buildings in London. Other similar buildings are the Royal Automobile Club (1908–11), Pall Mall, London, also by Mewès & Davis, and the Waldorf Hotel (1906–8), Aldwych, London, by Alexander Marshall MacKenzie and Alexander George Robertson MacKenzie.

British architects were slow to participate in the early 20th-century worldwide movement away from details of style and towards the frank expression of structure. In 1903 J. J. Burnet had dared to abandon elaborate stonework for the simplified rear facade of the steel frame of the Civil Service Stores in Edinburgh. In 1910, with Thomas Tait, he went even further in the front elevations of the Kodak Building, Kingsway, London. The frontage is like a severe elegant temple, stripped of all decoration. The outbreak of World War I in 1914 inevitably brought an abrupt halt to the way of life that had sustained much Edwardian architecture, large country houses, lavish hotels and even municipal display. By the 1920s a simplified, pared-down style had become the predominant one for public building.

BIBLIOGRAPHY
J. M. Brydon: 'The English Renaissance', *AA Notes*, iii (1889), p. 92
W. R. Lethaby: *Architecture, Mysticism and Myth* (London, 1891)
R. N. Shaw and T. G. Jackson, eds: *Architecture: A Profession or an Art?* (London, 1892)
J. A. Gotch: *The Architecture of the Renaissance in England* (London, 1894)
R. Blomfield: *A History of Renaissance Architecture in England, 1500–1800* (London, 1897)
J. Belcher and M. Macartney: *Later Renaissance Architecture in England*, 2 vols (London, 1898–1901)
H. Muthesius: *Das englische Haus* (Berlin, 1904–5)
J. Belcher: *Essentials in Architecture* (London, 1907)
L. Weaver, ed.: *Small Country Houses of Today* (London, 1910)
N. Pevsner: *Pioneers of the Modern Movement* (London, 1936)
H. S. Goodhart-Rendel: *English Architecture since the Regency* (London, 1953)
R. Macleod: *Style and Society* (London, 1971)
G. Naylor: *The Arts and Crafts Movement* (London, 1971)
A. Service, ed.: *Edwardian Architecture and its Origins* (London, 1975)
——: *Edwardian Architecture* (London, 1977)
A. S. Gray: *Edwardian Architecture: A Biographical Dictionary* (London, 1985)

ALASTAIR SERVICE

Edwards, Edward (*b* London, 7 March 1738; *d* London, 10 Dec 1806). English painter and writer. At the age of 15 he was apprenticed to an upholsterer and drew designs for furniture. He became a student at the Duke of Richmond's gallery in 1759 and opened a drawing school in Soho. In 1761 he was a student at the St Martin's Lane Academy. He was one of the first students to enrol in the Royal Academy Schools in 1769. He travelled to Italy in *c*. 1774–6 at the expense of Robert Udney. He exhibited frequently at the Society of Artists, the Free Society and the Royal Academy between 1771 and 1806. His works included biblical and literary subjects such as a scene from the *Two Gentlemen of Verona* (1799; sold London, at Boydell sale, Christie's, 17–20 May 1805) painted for John Boydell's Shakespeare Gallery, portraits, and landscapes such as *Durham Cathedral* (1788; London, V&A).

Edwards was made ARA in 1773, and he was elected Professor of Perspective in 1788, publishing *A Practical Treatise of Perspective* (1803) as a handbook for his students. However, he is best known for his *Anecdotes of Painters* (1808), written to supplement Horace Walpole's *Anecdotes of Painting in England* (1762–71), which Edwards felt was incomplete and did not reflect the superior quality of a growing English school. Edwards's book contains short biographies and assessments of the work of nearly 200 English and foreign painters working in England. Although generally acclaimed, the work was criticized vehemently by John Hoppner in the *Quarterly Review* (Feb 1809) as being too concerned with the trivial productions of coach and sign painters.

WRITINGS
A Practical Treatise of Perspective on the Principles of Dr Brook Taylor (London, 1803, 2/1806)
Anecdotes of Painters who have Resided or been Born in England (London, 1808/*R* 1970) [published posthumously; reprint contains introduction by R. Lightbown]
BIBLIOGRAPHY
DNB; Redgrave; Waterhouse: *18th C.*
R. Edwards: 'Edward Edwards, ARA (1738–1806) and the Furniture of an Earlier Age', *Country Life*, lxvii (June 1930), pp. 840–50

SHEARER WEST

Edwards, Pietro (*b* Loreto, 1744; *d* Venice, 17 March 1821). Italian restorer. He was a pupil of the painter Gaspare Diziani, but is known mainly as a restorer and as the organizer of the restoration workshop set up by the Republic of Venice in 1778 for the conservation of 'public paintings', such as those in the Doge's Palace and in churches under the state's jurisdiction. For this task he called on the services of several restorers, including Giuseppe Bertani (*fl c.* 1717–97) and Diziani's son Giuseppe (*fl* until 1803). Some aspects of Edwards' techniques were unusual. When relining paintings, for example, he would pour warm sand on to the backs in order to paste them to the new canvas, a method that was gradually replaced by the system of hot irons introduced by the French at the end of the 18th century. He always restricted retouching to areas of missing paint and refused to add or remove inscriptions or to make any alterations or 'improvements' to a painting. He also kept careful records of the planning of his restorations, paying attention to the protection of the setting of a work, as well as individual costings. Edwards' extensive restoration of works in the Doge's Palace include the paintings by Veronese on the ceiling of the Sala della Bussola (*in situ* and Paris, Louvre; rest. 1778–9) and Tintoretto's *Presentation of Doge Mocenigo to the Virgin* (rest. 1779; *in situ*). In addition, he worked on most of Bonifazio de Pitati's paintings in the Palazzo dei Camerlenghi on the Rialto (Venice, Accad. and elsewhere), and in 1787 on Titian's *Descent of the Holy Spirit* in S Maria della Salute. Edwards had studied proposals for a gallery to house Venice's finest paintings before the fall of the Republic in 1797, and under the new government he selected the pictures for the recently founded Accademia, ensuring that the greatest works were not sent instead to Milan. After Venice became part of the Regno Italico (1806–15) he once again held posts relating to the conservation of paintings, although his final years were clouded by disputes over restoration techniques with Leopoldo Cicognara, the president of the Accademia.

UNPUBLISHED SOURCES
Venice, Semin. Patriarcale, MS. 787 [restoration records]
BIBLIOGRAPHY
M. P. Merrifield: *Original Treatises on the Arts of Painting* (London, 1849)
A. Conti: *Storia del restauro e della conservazione delle opere d'arte* (Milan, 1973, 2/1988)

ALESSANDRO CONTI

Edwards, (Arthur) Trystan (*b* Merthyr Tydfil, 10 Nov 1884; *d* Merthyr Tydfil, 30 Jan 1973). Welsh writer and amateur cartographer. He studied at the University of Oxford and then as an articled pupil (1907–10) in the office of Sir Reginald Blomfield. He afterwards attended for one year the course in civic design at the University of Liverpool, but he never practised as an architect or urban planner. He became a writer on architecture and its history, and he was an advocate of the Regency style. He published several books including *Good and Bad Manners in Architecture* (1924), *Architectural Style* (1925), *Sir William Chambers* (1924) in the Masters of Architecture series, and various reminiscences of life in the British Navy in which he served as a seaman from 1915–18. In 1933 he founded the Hundred New Towns Association, which was devoted to promoting his idea that the solution to Britain's territorial planning problems was the establishment of 100 new urban settlements to attract population from expanding towns and cities. It was not regarded as realistic in the urban-planning and architectural professions and had no impact on official policies. His other interest was cartography. In 1953 he published *A New Map of the World: The Trystan Edwards Projection*, which was reissued in 1972 under the title *The Science of Cartography: A New Presentation.*

WRITINGS

Good and Bad Manners in Architecture (London, 1924, rev. 1944)
Sir William Chambers (London, 1924)
Architectural Style (London, 1925, rev. 1944)
The Architecture of Shops (London, 1933)

J. M. RICHARDS

Edzná. Site of Pre-Columbian Mesoamerican MAYA urban centre, occupied from *c.* 700 BC to *c.* AD 1000; its ruins lie in the upper part of a shallow basin known as the Edzná Valley, *c.* 50 km north-east of the city of Campeche, Mexico. On the basis of several mapping projects, the site is known to cover at least 17 sq. km and therefore ranks among the largest known archaeological sites in the Lowland Maya area. The importance of Edzná, for both archaeologists and art historians, lies in its strategic location between southern Campeche and the Petén in Guatemala and Yucatán to the north. Some of its sculpted monuments show influences from the 'classic' sculptural style of the Petén, while others show similarities to the Yucatecan style. The same influences can be seen in architecture: the Large Acropolis includes several buildings in the Petén style, while the Cinco Pisos pyramid shows a combination of Chenes and Puuc traits. While much of Edzná's history is still obscure, it seems clear that the western part of central Campeche formed an important regional variant of Lowland Maya culture, with Edzná as its principal centre.

The discovery of Edzná is credited to Nazario Quintana Bello, a state archaeologist who visited the site in 1927. The site was later investigated more thoroughly by other archaeologists, who recorded preliminary data on its largest structure, a huge platform-pyramid complex, the Large Acropolis, which included a five-storey pyramid-temple now known as Cinco Pisos (also called the Palace of Five Floors). Several sculpted stelae were also located; three of these carry decipherable dates ranging from AD 672 to 731. Between 1958 and 1969, the Cinco Pisos pyramid and other structures of the Large Acropolis were excavated and partly restored under the auspices of the Mexican Instituto Nacional de Antropología e Historia, and in 1968

an extensive mapping project and architectural survey was carried out by a group from the University of Oregon. This first drew attention to the ancient hydraulic system, investigated several years later in conjunction with a major ceramic study by a group from the New World Archaeological Foundation. In 1970 further excavations were carried out in the northern part of the Large Acropolis and in several structures to the south-west.

As presently known, Edzná consists of a large central core area, where the principal structures are found, and three 'suburban' residential districts immediately to the east, west and north. Interwoven among the residential areas to the north and east are a series of reservoirs and radial canals, the latter focused on the Cinco Pisos pyramid. Another canal runs southward from the central core to a moated area, now known as the 'fortress', and from its south-west corner an additional canal runs southward for a distance of 15 km, ending in a swamp. More startling than the size and complexity of the canal system—which was devoted to drainage rather than to water storage—is the fact that it appears to have been constructed during the Late Pre-Classic period (*c.* 300 BC–*c.* AD 250). Apart from this hydraulic system, unique among Maya sites, Edzná is best known for its sculpted stelae and for the Large Acropolis, which dominates the central core area. The main platform of this complex, which is *c.* 7 m high, measures *c.* 150 m square along its base. It supports a series of buildings and courtyards, including the Cinco Pisos pyramid, a five-storey structure (*see* MESOAMERICA, PRE-COLUMBIAN, fig. 9) with suites of rooms along the outer edges of the four lower levels and a temple with a high, slotted roof-comb on the upper level. The pyramid itself stands on a low platform reached by a broad stairway with risers covered in hieroglyphic inscriptions; another stairway leads from the top of the platform to the upper temple. The Cinco Pisos pyramid is the only known Maya pyramid with five storeys of rooms, its closest parallel being a four-storey pyramid at Ikil in northern Yucatán.

BIBLIOGRAPHY

F. Mariscal: *Estudio arquitectónico de las ruinas Mayas: Yucatán y Campeche* (Mexico City, 1928)
A. Ruz Lhuillier: 'Campeche en la arqueología Maya', *Acta Antropól.*, i/2–3 (1945) [whole issue]
G. F. Andrews: *Edzna, Campeche, Mexico: Settlement Patterns and Monumental Architecture* (Eugene, 1969/R Culver City, 1984)
D. W. Forsyth: *Investigations at Edzna, Campeche, Mexico*, ii, Papers of the New World Archaeological Foundation, xlvi (Provo, 1983)
R. T. Matheny and others: *Investigations at Edzna, Campeche, Mexico*, i/1–2, Papers of the New World Archaeological Foundation, xlvi (Provo, 1983)

GEORGE F. ANDREWS

Eeckhout, Gerbrand [Gerbrandt] **van den** (*b* Amsterdam, 19 Aug 1621; *d* Amsterdam, *bur* 29 Sept 1674). Dutch painter, draughtsman and etcher. He was the son of the goldsmith Jan Pietersz. van den Eeckhout and 'a great friend' as well as a pupil of Rembrandt, according to Houbraken, who commented that van den Eeckhout painted in the style of his master throughout his career. This is certainly true of van den Eeckhout's (biblical) history paintings, but less so of either his portraits, which gradually displayed more Flemish elegance, or his genre pieces (from 1650), in which he followed various trends; he adapted his style to suit his subject with sensitive versatility. He was also a gifted colourist and an artist of great imagination, superior in both these respects to such better-known Rembrandt pupils as Ferdinand Bol and Nicolaes Maes. Moreover, he was extremely productive, and there is at least one dated painting for virtually every year between 1641 and 1674. In addition, he created a large body of drawings comprising histories, figures, landscapes and genre scenes executed in various media, including watercolour. He also made several etchings, mostly studies of heads, such as the *Self-portrait* (1646; B. 66). He died a bachelor, aged 53.

1. History paintings. 2. Other painted subjects. 3. Drawings.

1. HISTORY PAINTINGS.

(i) 1640–50. It is generally assumed that van den Eeckhout studied with Rembrandt from 1635 to 1640, as his first independently signed piece, the *Presentation in the Temple* (Budapest, Mus. F.A.), is dated 1641. By 1642 he was hard at work, producing four biblical subjects in that year, including *Gideon's Sacrifice* (untraced; see Sumowski, 1983, no. 392), which reveals that Rembrandt's pupils shared their master's unflagging enthusiasm for his teacher Pieter Lastman, whose bright palette is employed in this work alongside a Rembrandtesque chiaroscuro. The *Dismissal*

of Hagar (1642; ex-Edzard priv. col., Munich; see Sumowski, 1983, no. 393) is based on a Rembrandt etching dated 1637 (B. 30). Lastman's palette and Rembrandt's lighting and formal language are again combined in van den Eeckhout's *Jacob's Dream* (1642; Warsaw, N. Mus.) and *Isaac Blessing Jacob* (1642; New York, Met.; see fig. 1). Conspicuous in the latter is the depiction of a famous silver-gilt ewer (1614) by Adam van Vianen, which was owned by the Silversmiths' Guild to which van den Eeckhout's father belonged. (In homage to van Vianen, he drew a variant of this ewer as the first of a series of ornamental designs (e.g. Amsterdam, Hist. Mus.; Schwerin, Staatl. Mus.) that were published as prints *c.* 1651 by Michiel Mosyn and intended as patterns for silversmiths, sculptors and painters.) Van den Eeckhout's interest in his father's craft was occasionally expressed in still-lifes with decorative vases, which appeared as subsidiary motifs in history paintings, for example in two different versions of the *Meeting of Abraham and Melchizedek* (1646, Mänttä, Serlachius A. Mus.; 1664, Budapest, N. Mus.).

In the exceptionally large canvas depicting *The Levite and One of his Wives at Gibeah* (1645; Berlin, Gemäldegal.), van den Eeckhout anticipated similar 'Flemish'-style works of the type that brought acclaim to Bol and Govaert Flinck

1. Gerbrand van den Eeckhout: *Isaac Blessing Jacob*, oil on canvas, 1.02×1.30 m, 1642 (New York, Metropolitan Museum of Art)

in the 1650s. As early as the 1640s a kind of artistic competition seems to have existed between Bol and van den Eeckhout, judging from their choice of rare biblical subjects depicted in related ways, such as *Gideon's Sacrifice* (van den Eeckhout's versions, 1644, Stockholm, Nmus.; 1647, Milan, Brera; Bol's version, 1641, The Hague, Rijksdienst Beeld. Kst). By the end of the 1640s the influence of Lastman's colourful compositions began to wane, as is evident, for example, in *Elisha and the Shunammite Woman* (1649; Warsaw, N. Mus.).

(ii) 1650–74. During the 1650s van den Eeckhout inclined increasingly towards a more detailed style, as in *Boaz and Ruth* (1651; Bremen, Ksthalle), in which he showed himself for the first time to be a proficient landscape painter. Less successful is the landscape in *Granida and Daifilo* (1652; Milan, Mus. A. Ant.; splendid preparatory drawing in Brunswick, Herzog Anton Ulrich-Mus.). The life-size *Rest on the Flight into Egypt* (1653; Milwaukee, WI, A. Bader priv. col., see Sumowski, 1983, no. 415)

recalls Rembrandt's very 'Flemish' *Holy Family* (*c.* 1633; Munich, Alte Pin.), while the motif of Mary showing the Christ Child to Joseph is borrowed from Rembrandt's etching of the same subject (1645; B. 58). Rembrandt's etching of *Medea* (B. 112) may have been the basis for van den Eeckhout's *Idolatry of Solomon* (1654; Brunswick, Herzog Anton Ulrich-Mus.). During this period van den Eeckhout painted in both a broad and a more detailed manner, as can be seen, for example, in the two versions of *Boaz and Ruth* (1655; Rotterdam, Mus. Boymans–van Beuningen; and 1656; Beerse, Bert van Deun priv. col., see Sumowski, 1983, no. 423). In 1658 he even used three different methods: he painted an even larger, 'Flemish'-sized version of *The Levite and One of his Wives at Gibeah* (Moscow, Pushkin Mus. F.A.), the small *Christ and his Disciples* (Dublin, N.G.), painted in Rembrandt's broad manner, and the *Continence of Scipio* (Toledo, OH, Mus. A.), which is executed in a polished, detailed style. He had immediate success with the last subject, for a year later he

2. Gerbrand van den Eeckhout: *SS Peter and John Healing the Cripple*, oil on canvas, 603×687 mm, 1667 (San Francisco, CA, M. H. de Young Memorial Museum)

made a variant of it (Philadelphia, PA, Mus. A.) with the two lovers as portraits of his (probable) patrons.

During the early 1660s van den Eeckhout made an attractive series of small-scale biblical history paintings (comparable to the one in Dublin), executed with a loose brush and in warm red and brown tints. These include *Christ Teaching in the Temple* (1662; Munich, Alte Pin.), the *Widow's Mite* (1663; Turin, Gilberto Zabert priv. col., see Sumowski, 1983, no. 437), *Eliezer and Rebecca* (1663; Leipzig, Mus. Bild. Kst.), *Elisha and the Shunammite Woman* (1664; Budapest, N. Mus.), *Christ and the Woman Taken in Adultery* (probably 1664; Amsterdam, Rijksmus.) and the *Adoration of the Magi* (1665; Moscow, Pushkin Mus. F.A.). A number of large-format works include such *tours de force* as *Sophonisba Receiving the Cup of Poison* (1664; Brunswick, Herzog Anton Ulrich-Mus.) and *Jacob's Dream* (1669; Dresden, Gemäldegal. Alte Meister), painted in a much broader manner. During this period he also reverted to Lastman's palette and manner of composing in such works as the *Dismissal of Hagar* (1666; Raleigh, NC Mus. A.). Painted in variegated colours but with Rembrandt's broad touch are *SS Peter and John Healing the Cripple* (1667; San Francisco, CA, de Young Mem. Mus.; see fig. 2), as well as several undated, rather summarily executed works, including the *Presentation in the Temple* (ex-C. J. K. van Aalst priv. col., Hoevelaken; see Sumowski, 1983, no. 450) and *Vertumnus and Pomona* (Indianapolis, IN, Herron Mus. A.). Van den Eeckhout's later paintings are of variable quality but reach a highpoint with the *Calling of St Matthew* (1674; Munich, Alte Pin.), painted in the year of his death.

2. OTHER PAINTED SUBJECTS. Although history pieces form the great majority of his painted oeuvre, van den Eeckhout also addressed other subjects. During the 1650s he produced interior genre scenes in the vein of Gerard ter Borch (ii) and Pieter de Hooch, though employing a very personal manner of composition. Among these are the *Company on a Terrace* (1652; Worcester, MA, A. Mus.), the *Lute-player and Singers* (1653; The Hague, Gemeentemus.) and the *Music Lesson* (1655; Copenhagen, Stat. Mus. Kst). These glimpses of the leisure time of the affluent reveal a more naturalistic conception of elegance than was held by such predecessors in the genre as Willem Buytewech and anticipate the greater elegance of Dutch genre painting of the 1660s and 1670s. They also demonstrate van den Eeckhout's sensitivity as a narrator. He also painted guardroom scenes, such as the *Soldiers in a Guardroom* (Boston, MA, Mus. F.A.) and *Soldiers in an Inn* (1655; Petworth, priv. col., see Sumowski, 1983, no. 511).

Van den Eeckhout's clear preference for history painting is further demonstrated by the scarcity of his portraits. Contemporary art theory accorded portraiture, which could often be profitable, a very low status, compared with history subjects, and it is interesting to note that a number of his portraits were intended to double as history paintings (e.g. the *Continence of Scipio*). He made several striking portraits of children in arcadian surroundings (e.g. 1667; Hartford, CT, Wadsworth Atheneum; *Portrait of a Family as Shepherds and Shepherdesses*, 1667; Budapest, N. Mus.). Among the more traditional portraits, the most appealing are those of his father, *Jan Pietersz. van den*

Eeckhout (1664; Grenoble, Mus. B.-A.), and his stepmother, *Cornelia Dedel* (1664; the Netherlands, priv. col., see Sumowski, 1983, no. 521). The placing of the figures in a semicircular niche with one arm leaning on a sill is borrowed from Rembrandt's *Self-portrait* (1640; London, N.G.) or the variants that Rembrandt and his pupils painted in the 1640s. In later portraits van den Eeckhout employed international formulae that recall Anthony van Dyck's prototypes, for example the portrait of a *Governor of the Dutch East Indies Company* (1669; Grenoble, Mus. B.-A.). He also painted the group portrait of the *Four Officers of the Amsterdam Coopers' and Wine-rackers' Guild* (versions, 1657; London, N.G., and 1673; Amsterdam, Hist. Mus.), a guild to which his brother Jan van den Eeckhout belonged. In the later version the imaginary marble background with St Matthew, patron saint of the coopers, in a niche is an innovation within the genre.

On a few occasions van den Eeckhout chose landscape as an independent subject: the bright, southern sunlight forms a striking element in the *Mountain Stream with Men Bathing* (Amsterdam, Rijksmus.). He took landscapes by his friend (according to Houbraken) Roelant Roghman as a point of departure for the *Mountain Landscape* (1663; Amsterdam, W. Russell priv. col., see 1987–8 exh. cat., p. 304).

3. DRAWINGS. Landscape was one of van den Eeckhout's favourite subjects for drawings. His earliest sheets are rather Rembrandtesque, but between 1650 and 1655 he produced decorative landscapes intended for sale, in the style of Roghman and Antoni Waterlo, drawn in chalk and heavily washed with the brush (e.g. *Hollow Lane Bordered by Trees, with Ruins on the Left*, 1650; Paris, Fond. Custodia Inst. Néer.). It is unclear whether these are topographically accurate, as are his panoramic landscapes of the early 1660s, such as the *View along the River Rhine in the Vicinity of Arnhem* (1661; Cambridge, Fitzwilliam) and the *View of Haarlem* (Berlin, Kupferstichkab.). Very characteristic of van den Eeckhout is the use of watercolour washes, also evident in the views near Rhenen, Arnhem and Cleves (e.g. Amsterdam, Rijksmus.; Berlin, Kupferstichkab.; Dresden, Kupferstichkab.; Haarlem, Teylers Mus.; London, BM) made during a trip along the River Rhine with Jacob Esselens and Jan Lievens in 1663; all three artists drew at the same locations. Van den Eeckhout also drew biblical scenes, often as studies for his paintings, figure studies in chalk, detailed portraits (some on parchment), ornamental drawings and designs for book illustrations. A distinct group of drawings, executed exclusively with the brush and brown wash, comprises figure studies of boys and women (often after the same models) and a dog (e.g. Amsterdam, Rijksmus.; London, BM; Paris, Fond. Custodia, Inst. Néer.).

BIBLIOGRAPHY
A. Houbraken: *De groote schouburgh* (1718–21), i, p. 174; ii, p. 100
A. von Bartsch: *Le Peintre-graveur* (1803–21) [B.]
W. Sumowski: 'Gerbrand van den Eeckhout als Zeichner', *Oud-Holland*, lxxvii (1962), pp. 11–39
——: *Drawings of the Rembrandt School*, iii (New York, 1980), pp. 601–819
——: *Gemälde der Rembrandtschüler*, ii (Landau/Pfalz, 1983), pp. 719–909
Masters of Dutch 17th-century Landscape Painting (exh. cat., ed. P. C. Sutton; Amsterdam, Rijksmus.; Boston, MA, Mus. F.A.; Philadelphia, PA, Mus. A.; 1987–8)

B. P. J. BROOS

Eeden, Frederik (Willem) van (*b* Haarlem, 3 May 1860; *d* Bussum, 16 June 1932). Dutch physician, psychiatrist, writer and critic. He trained as a doctor of medicine and as a psychiatrist and practised medicine in Bussum. He also played a significant role in the revival of Dutch literature in the late 19th century. His best-known work is the novel *De kleine Johannes* (1887), while his work as a translator included the writings of Rabindranath Tagore. He also had social and political interests and in 1898 established a communal project in Bussum, named Walden after the subject of a book by the American naturalist–poet Henry David Thoreau, and in 1908–9 he founded a commune in North Carolina, USA. Van Eeden was a co-founder and editor (1885–93) of the literary journal *De Nieuwe Gids*. Two of his articles were of particular importance: in the first, he promoted the individual response to art and reported his own physical reaction to good art; in the second (1890), he enthusiastically introduced the Dutch public to the work of Vincent van Gogh, 'a brilliant but virtually unknown Dutch artist who died a few months ago'. He had encountered van Gogh's work in Paris in 1890, when he visited and treated the artist's brother Theo van Gogh shortly after Vincent's death. Van Eeden, in his capacity as a psychiatrist whose literary work Vincent had read, was one of the first critics to link the artist's work to his tragic life. Van Eeden recognized in the article how van Gogh's passionate zeal was expressed in his primitive use of bright colours and his adoption of a Japanese character in his work. In 1934 the Frederik van Eedengenootschap was founded to house his papers and to publish them in *Mededelingen van het Frederik van Eeden-Genootschap*.

WRITINGS
'Over shilderijen-zien', *Nieuwe Gids*, iii/2 (1888), pp. 279ff
'Vincent van Gogh', *Nieuwe Gids*, vi/1 (1890), pp. 263ff
H. W. van Tricht, ed.: *Dagboek, 1878–1923*, 4 vols (Culemborg, 1971–2)
S. A. Stein, ed.: 'Frederik van Eeden *De Nieuwe Gids* "Vincent van Gogh" 1 December 1890', *Van Gogh: A Retrospective* (New York, 1986), pp. 241–6 [Eng. trans.]

BIBLIOGRAPHY
M. I. MacDonald: 'Poet, Novelist, and Practical Communist', *The Craftsman*, xiv (1908), pp. 126–36
G. Kalff: *Frederik van Eeden: Psychologie van een Tachtiger* (Groningen, 1927)
H. W. van Tricht: *Frederik van Eeden: Denker en strijder* (Amsterdam, 1934/R Utrecht, 1978)
A. Verwey: *Frederik van Eeden* (Santpoort, 1939)
H. C. Rümpke: *Over Frederik van Eeden's Van de Koele meren des doods: Een essay* (Amsterdam, 1964)

AMY L. WALSH

Eertvelt [Ertvelt], Andries van (*b* Antwerp, *bapt* 25 March 1590; *d* Antwerp, *bur* 11 Aug 1652). Flemish painter. He enrolled as a member of Antwerp's Guild of St Luke in 1609. In 1615 he married Catherine Vlieger (*d* 1627), after whose death he went to Genoa, where he worked for Cornelis de Wael. By *c.* 1630 he was back in Antwerp, where he had his portrait painted by Anthony van Dyck (1632; Augsburg, Schaezlerpal.). In 1633 Eertvelt married Elisabeth Boots, probably a daughter of the Antwerp painter Jan Boots (*b* before 1620). Eertvelt is regarded as the first Flemish marine painter. Over the years his palette and style changed. His first paintings, mostly of ships in storms (e.g. *Sea Battle in a Storm*; Schwerin, Staatl. Mus.), were painted in greenish-black and brown tones, often using white to highlight the rigging against the dark sea. After his tour of Italy he favoured views of southern harbours, with calm seas painted in soft tones (e.g. *Spanish Ships Leaving a Port*; Vienna, Ksthist. Mus.). In his day Eertvelt was a man of distinction whose artistic qualities were praised by the poet Cornelis de Bie and whose marine paintings were appreciated abroad, some being exported as far as Seville and Lisbon. His pupils included Gaspard van Eyck (1613–73), Hendrik Minderhout (1632–96) and Matthieu van Plattenberg.

BIBLIOGRAPHY
Archibald; Thieme–Becker
C. de Bie: *Het gulden cabinet* (Antwerp, 1661)
R. H. Wilenski: *Flemish Painters, 1430–1830*, i (London, 1960), p. 550
R. Preston: *The Seventeenth-century Marine Painters of the Netherlands* (Leigh-on-Sea, 1974), pp. 19–20, fig. 27

L. J. WASSINK

Eesteren, Cornelis [Cor] van (*b* Kinderdijk, Alblasserdam, 4 July 1897; *d* 21 Feb 1988). Dutch architect, urban planner, writer and teacher. Born into a family of building contractors, he was apprenticed to a firm of builders and carpenters in Dordrecht (1912–14) and then worked for Willem Kromhout in Rotterdam before studying architecture at the Academie van Beeldende Kunsten, Rotterdam (1915–17). He obtained his diploma in 1917 and continued his studies at the Academie van Bouwkunst, Amsterdam (1919–22). In 1922 he won the prestigious Prix de Rome with a design (unexecuted) for the Royal Netherlands Academy of Science building, which was clearly inspired by Frank Lloyd Wright. The scholarship specified a study of traditional North German brick building but van Eesteren spent most of the year visiting the Bauhaus and various architects' offices in Germany and Sweden, including those of Walter Gropius, Adolf Behne (*b* 1885), Hans Richter and László Moholy-Nagy. Behne introduced him to THEO VAN DOESBURG, one of the founders of DE STIJL. Van Eesteren joined De Stijl and began to collaborate with van Doesburg on a number of projects. Together they translated De Stijl's theories of Neo-plasticism into architecture, publicizing them through their manifestos *Tot een beeldende architectuur* [Towards a plastic architecture] (1924) and *Vers une construction collective* (1924), with van Eesteren supplying the necessary architectural expertise. He was also mainly responsible for the axonometric studies of Neo-plasticist houses that were exhibited at De Stijl's exhibition at the Galerie de l'Effort Moderne, Paris, in 1923.

By this time, however, van Eesteren had begun developing his interest in urban planning, which he had studied in Paris. On his return to Amsterdam he became office manager for Jan Wils, where he was involved with the Olympic Stadium and other projects. At the same time, he worked on three urban planning competition designs: for Rokin, Amsterdam, for the centre of Paris and for Unter den Linden, Berlin. For the latter he won first prize in 1925. All three plans (unexecuted) include high-rise buildings and give priority to the uninterrupted flow of traffic, particularly by separating pedestrians and vehicular traffic on different levels. The practical application of his ideas followed when in 1929 van Eesteren joined the City of Amsterdam urban planning department as chief architect. In this capacity he was responsible for the development of the General Extension Plan for Amsterdam (published in 1934). His urban planning schemes were dominated by an ultra-Functionalist and empiricist approach. He broke new ground in basing all plans on detailed demographic studies aimed at precise estimation of population densities and movement, and he favoured the use of open blocks following the example of the German 'Zeilenbauweise'. He also advocated the division of schemes into largely self-sufficient individually planned communities of c. 10,000 inhabitants divided by strips of greenery. His plan for Amsterdam, continually updated, was in operation throughout the remainder of the 20th century and constitutes his most important work. He remained head of the Amsterdam urban planning section until 1959, after which time he continued in an advisory capacity.

Parallel to his work in Amsterdam van Eesteren was active in furthering the cause of urban planning on an international level as President of CIAM between 1930 and 1947. He was charged with the preparatory work in organizing a CIAM IV (1933), planned as the first of a number of congresses centred around the theme of 'The Functional City'. His appointment, championed by Gropius, was largely stimulated by his work in Amsterdam and can be seen as symptomatic of CIAM's shift towards rationalist urban planning policies culminating in the Athens Charter, published in 1934. Van Eesteren was also a member of the Dutch avant-garde groups DE OPBOUW and ARCHITECTENGROEP DE 8, as well as of various committees. He taught briefly (1927–30) at the Staatliche Bauhochschule, Weimar, and in 1947 was appointed Professor of Urban Planning at the Technische Hogeschool, Delft, a post he held until 1967.

WRITINGS
with T. van Doesburg: 'Vers une construction collective', *De Stijl*, 6–7 (1924), pp. 89–96
CIAM: Rationelle Bebauungsweisen (Frankfurt am Main, 1930)
Het algemeen uitbreidingsplan [General extension plan] (Amsterdam, 1934)
Bouw en herbouw van steden, 1945–1957 [The building and rebuilding of cities, 1945–1957] (Delft, 1966)

BIBLIOGRAPHY
H. L. C. Jaffe: 'Cornelius van Eesteren', *Archit. Des.*, xxxvii (1967), p. 541
R. Blijstra: *C. van Eesteren* (Amsterdam, 1968; Eng. trans., 1971)
M. Steinmann, ed.: *CIAM: Dokumente, 1928–1939* (Stuttgart and Basle, 1979)
M. Friedman, ed.: *De Stijl, 1917–1931: Visions of Utopia*, intro. by H. L. C. Jaffe (Oxford, 1982)
Het nieuwe bouwen internationaal: CIAM: Volkshuisvesting, stedebouw (exh. cat., ed. A. van der Woud; Otterlo, Rijksmus. Kröller-Müller, 1983)

Efendi, Necmeddin. *See* OKYAY, NECMEDDIN.

Effettisti. *See under* MACCHIAIOLI.

Effner, Joseph (*bapt* Dachau, 4 Feb 1687; *d* Munich, 23 Feb 1745). German architect. His family had been gardeners in the service of the Electors of Bavaria for several generations, and Effner also trained as a gardener in Paris from 1706. However, with the permission of Elector Maximilian II Emanuel, then living in exile in France, he soon transferred to architecture and became a pupil of Germain Boffrand. Effner collaborated with Boffrand on the decoration (1713) of the château of St Cloud for Maximilian Emanuel II before returning to Munich with the Elector in 1715. As a court architect and, after the death of Enrico Zuccalli, as Chief Court Architect, Effner controlled architectural projects at the court in Munich. At first he altered and extended existing castles in the Munich area, including the Schloss at Dachau, where he also laid out the court garden, the hunting-lodge at Fürstenried and above all Schloss Nymphenburg (*see* MUNICH, §IV, 3), which he enlarged considerably. Effner also worked on the plans for the park at Nymphenburg and created three pavilions there: the Pagodenburg (1716–19) on an octagonal plan with cruciform arms, supposedly in the Chinese taste, the Badenburg (1718–21), famous for its tiled bathroom, and the Magdalenenklause (1725–8), a hermitage built as a ruined cell with mixed classical and Gothic detailing. These early buildings and Effner's staircase at the Schloss in Dachau were influenced by Boffrand, while a journey to Italy undertaken by Effner early in 1718 was the source for such details as the shell motifs in the banqueting hall in the Badenburg or the window surrounds on the façades of Schloss Schleissheim near Munich, which recall the work of Bernini at the Palazzo Barberini in Rome. Zuccalli had begun the Schloss in 1701–4, and Effner finished it, provisionally, in 1719–26, taking over the stuccowork on the façades and, in particular, the interior decoration and furnishing. This project was especially important for Effner's future development as an artist, which from then on lay in the field of interior decoration.

The increasing importance of stuccowork was already evident in the banqueting hall at the Badenburg, but there it remained distinct from the architectural framework. In the south antechamber at Schleissheim, however, the contrast between the structural elements and decoration was dissolved for the first time. The decorative reinterpretation of structural elements on the one hand and the strengthening of the role of decoration on the other, so that it could also take over the task of articulation, were subsequently widely applied to exterior architecture as well. This began to occur at Schleissheim but was especially noticeable at Effner's only noble mansion, the Preysing Palais (1723–9) in Munich (see fig.). For the first time elements of interior decoration were transferred to the exterior, differentiating the Preysing Palais from that phase of town house building in Munich represented by Zuccalli, and it set the trend for secular architecture in the late Baroque period. This change of style also meant that architecture in Munich turned away from its dependence on Italian forms, which subsequently reached Bavaria only indirectly through Austria. As the similarities between the Preysing Palais and the Palais Daun-Kinsky (1713–16) in Vienna show, Effner, and through him Bavarian architecture, owed its main inspiration to Johann Lukas von Hildebrandt. With Johann Baptist Zimmermann (*see* ZIMMERMANN, (1)), the stuccoist responsible at the Preysing Palais, Effner decorated the Reiche Zimmer (from 1726) at the Residenz in Munich (*see* MUNICH, §IV, 2). However, he was replaced there (1729) by François de Cuvilliés I, whom Elector Charles (*reg* 1726–45) regarded as the leading artist of the day. Effner was appointed Director of Gardens in 1738 and continued to be active in the field of arts and crafts, including occasional ecclesiastical work. For the most part, however, he ceased to be prominent after 1730, and his most important urban planning project, for Carlstadt (*see* MUNICH, §IV, 3), which was begun in 1728 and was intended to radiate out from Nymphenburg, with the residential pavilions at the crescent in front of the palace, was barely started.

BIBLIOGRAPHY

M. Hauttmann: *Der kurbayerische Hofbaumeister Joseph Effner* (Strasbourg, 1913)
L. Hager: *Nymphenburg: Schloss, Park und Burgen* (Munich, 1955)
G. Vits: *Joseph Effners Palais Preysing: Ein Beitrag zur Münchner Profanarchitektur des Spätbarocks* (Frankfurt am Main and Berne, 1973)
G. Hojer: *Schleissheim: Neues Schloss und Garten* (Munich, 1976) [official guide]
Kurfürst Max Emanuel: Bayern und Europa um 1700, 2 vols (exh. cat., Munich, Bayer. Nmus., 1976)
G. Hojer and E. D. Schmid: *Nymphenburg: Schloss, Park und Burgen* (Munich, 1979) [official guide]
E. D. Schmid: *Nymphenburg* (Munich, 1979)
D. V. Frank: *Joseph Effners Pagodenburg* (Munich, 1985)
H. Brunner, G. Hojer and L. Seelig: *Residenz München* (Munich, 1986) [official guide]
G. V. Deessen: *Die Badenburg im Park von Nymphenburg* (Munich, 1986)

GISELA VITS

Efrat, Benni (*b* Beirut, 1936). Israeli painter, sculptor, printmaker and film maker of Lebanese birth. He studied from 1959 to 1961 under Yehezkel Streichman at the Avni Art Institute in Tel Aviv. From 1966 to 1976 he lived in London, where he studied at St Martin's School of Art and created sculptures concerned with movement, time and energy, for example *Corners* (1967; Jerusalem, Israel Mus.). He became involved with conceptual art after settling in New York in 1976, producing drawings, prints and photographs that explore energy, space and process of duration, and expanding on problems of perception in sculptural installations. In works such as *August* from *Undercover Blues Series* (1980; New York, Jew. Mus.) he used light to define the relationships between an object and its shadows, while in conceptual films such as *Putney Bridge* (1976) he used the environment to analyse the relationship between reality and illusion. On returning to Europe in 1982, he turned his attention to the human condition in temporary sculptural installations such as *I Heard the Underground Calling my Name, 2030* (exh. 1983; Paris, Pompidou), in which he imagined himself in the year 2030 as a witness to the destruction originating in present-day society.

BIBLIOGRAPHY

Benni Efrat: Matrix 37 (exh. cat., Hartford, CT, Wadsworth Atheneum, 1978)
Benni Efrat (exh. cat. by J. Ober, Knokke-Het-Zoute, Gal. Franck, 1985)

SUSAN T. GOODMAN

Efros, Abram (Markovich) [Rosstsy] (*b* Moscow, 3 May 1888; *d* Moscow, 9 Nov 1954). Russian museum official, art historian, critic and teacher. His interest in art history was formed while he was studying law at Moscow University (1907–11), and on graduation he became art critic for *Russkiye vedomosti*, a position he held until the paper was closed in 1918. There his assessment of contemporary Russian art revealed a sympathy that lay primarily with the lyricism and vibrant colourism of such artists as Nikolay

Joseph Effner: Preysing Palais, Munich, 1723–9

Sapunov, Martiros Saryan and Pavel Kuznetsov. Having been the first to publish his support of Igor' Grabar''s radical reforms of the permanent exhibition in the Tret'yakov Gallery in 1913, Efros was appointed assistant to the curator of the gallery in 1917 and was responsible for the first post-revolutionary rehanging of the exhibits according to the rationalized chronological principles proposed by Grabar'. Efros was head of the department of new painting (1920–29) and simultaneously (1924–9) worked as keeper of the French painting department and deputy director of research at the Pushkin Museum of Fine Arts, where he helped organize the *Revolutionary Art of the West* exhibition in 1926. At the same time he also left his mark on early Soviet stage design, collaborating with Konstantin Stanislavsky and Vladimir Nemirovich-Danchenko in his role as head of the art section of the Moscow Arts Theatre and Music Studio (1920–26), and, in a similar role, inviting such artists as Natan Al'tman, Robert Fal'k and Marc Chagall to create designs for GOSET (State Jewish Theatre). Efros continued to publish many articles dedicated to modern art and literature in numerous Soviet journals, as well as teaching courses on Russian art and theatrical history and museum studies at a variety of institutions (e.g. Svomas, 1919–20, and the State Institute of Theatrical Art, 1940–50). His foremost publications on art included *Profili*, a selection of sketch-like essays on the work of 14 leading Russian painters and graphic artists (from Vasily Surikov to David Shterenberg), *Dva veka russkogo iskusstva*, a skittish survey of Russian painting and sculpture in the 18th and 19th centuries, and a study of Pushkin's drawings (Moscow, 1933).

WRITINGS

'Khudozhestvennyy lik Sapunova' [Sapunov's artistic face], *N. Sapunov: Stikhi, vospominaniya, kharakteristiki* [N. Sapunov: poems, reminiscences, descriptions] (Moscow, 1916), pp. 83–93

'Iskusstvo Pavla Kuznetsova' [The art of Pavel Kuznetsov], *Apollon*, nos 6–7 (1917), pp. 1–16

Profili [Profiles] (Moscow, 1930)

M. Tolmachov, ed.: *Dva veka russkogo iskusstva* [Two centuries of Russian art] (Moscow, 1969)

V. Polikarov and I. Gutt, eds: *Mastera raznykh epokh* [Masters of various epochs] (Moscow, 1979)

JEREMY HOWARD, SERGEY KUZNETSOV

Egas. Netherlandish family of artists active in Spain.

(1) Egas Cueman [Egas de Bruselas] (*fl* 1452; *d* Sept 1495). Sculptor, brother of HANEQUIN DE BRUSELAS. He is referred to as both Egas de Bruselas and Master Egas, but in some documents (e.g. that relating to the Palacio del Infantado, Guadalajara) he signs himself 'Egas Cueman'. The architects (2) Antón Egas and (3) Enrique Egas were his sons; he also had two daughters, Margarita and Isabel. His granddaughter Margarita married the famous Toledan Renaissance architect Alonso de Covarrubias.

Egas Cueman was the principal Toledan sculptor of the second half of the 15th century and the founder of an extremely important workshop. He worked with his brother Hanequin de Bruselas on the latter's architectural projects and contributed with Juan Alemán and Francisco de la Cuevas to the sculpture of the Puerta de los Leones (begun 1452) at Toledo Cathedral, receiving the commission to carve three Apostles and some of the archivolt sculpture. In 1454 he was commissioned to carve the choir-stalls at Cuenca Cathedral (now in the Colegiata, Belmonte). They bear Old Testament and Passion scenes and are a good example of Egas's style, showing his fine decorative sense and the influence of Netherlandish woodcarving. In 1458 he began work on the tomb of *Prior Gonzalo de Illescas* in the monastery of Guadalupe and may have started the wall tomb of *Alonso de Velasco and his Wife* there immediately afterwards. Alonso (*d* 1477) and his wife are represented kneeling in prayer, a novel feature, with pages leaning on swords in the background (see fig.). Drawings and directions for the project survive at Guadalupe and show that a recumbent effigy was originally intended.

Egas Cueman is referred to as Master of the Works at Toledo Cathedral in 1476, which has given rise to his being confused with his brother Hanequin de Bruselas (who held the same office from 1448). The pages on the tombs of the parents of Grand Master Pedro Girón in the Colegiata, Belmonte (Cuenca), are attributed to Egas because he carried out a similar work for the Grand Master in his burial chapel (destr.) at the monastery of Calatrava, Ciudad Real. Egas collaborated with Juan Guas on the sculpture for S Juan de los Reyes, Toledo (began *c*. 1476), for the Palacio del Infantado, Guadalajara (begun 1480), and for the *trascoro* of Toledo Cathedral (1483–93).

(2) Antón Egas (*fl* 1495; *d* by 1532). Architect, son of (1) Egas Cueman. He and his brother (3) Enrique Egas were the last exponents of Late Gothic in Toledo. Antón was assistant architect at Toledo Cathedral in 1495 and was appointed Master of the Works with Enrique the following year. They regularly worked together, collaborating on the design of the Hospital Real (now Hospital de los Reyes Católicos), Santiago de Compostela, in 1499. In 1500 Antón was consulted about the dome of Saragossa Cathedral and in 1503 made plans for the convent of S Fe, Toledo. In 1509 and 1512 he is mentioned in connection with the new cathedral in Salamanca (*see* SALAMANCA, §2(ii)). He was living in Torrijos, Toledo, about this time and must have worked on the Colegiata there. In 1525 he designed the Patio de la Botica at Guadalupe, Cáceres, and prepared designs for the monastery of Valparaiso, near Chinchon, Madrid, with Alonso de Covarrubias. The evidence suggests, however, that he was more of a designer than a supervising architect.

(3) Enrique Egas (*fl* ?1480; *d* Sept 1534). Architect, son of (1) Egas Cueman. He was the most important architect in Toledo in the first quarter of the 16th century and, with his numerous commissions, he spread the ideas of this school throughout Castile. A characteristic feature of his work is his adherence to Gothic values; when

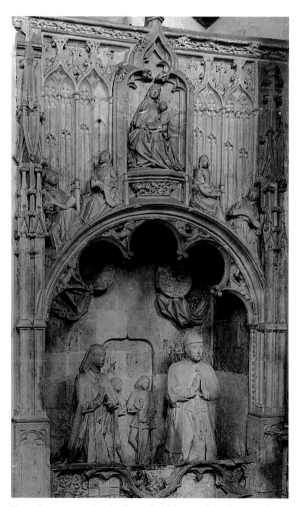

Egas Cueman: tomb of *Alonso de Velasco and his Wife*, mid-15th century (Monastery of Guadalupe)

Renaissance details appear, they are the work of other architects or decorators. He may have contributed to work at the Colegio de Santa Cruz, Valladolid, in 1480, but the reference is unreliable. In 1496 he was appointed Master of the Works of Toledo Cathedral in association with his brother (2) Antón Egas, and designed the cathedral's Capilla Mozárabe (1502–24). He held a similar position at Plasencia Cathedral, Cáceres, the following year and is said to have initiated its rebuilding at this period. He collaborated with his brother at the Hospital de Santa Cruz, Toledo (begun c. 1500), and the Hospital Real (now Hospital de los Reyes Católicos), Santiago de Compostela (1501–11), subsequently taking charge of the work, as he was later to do at the Hospital Real, Granada (begun 1511); this last is of interest because of its Greek cross ground-plan, with patios set between the arms of the cross. From 1505 he supervised the work that he had previously initiated at the Capilla Real, Granada (see GRANADA, fig. 1, and illus. in ARAGON, (6)). Diego Egas the sculptor, Pedro Egas the painter and Enrique Egas, also an architect, were his sons.

BIBLIOGRAPHY

B. Gilman Proske: *Castilian Sculpture: Gothic to Renaissance* (New York, 1951)

J. M. Azcárate: 'Anton Egas', *Bol. Semin. Estud. A. & Arqueol.* (1957)

——: *La arquitectura gótica toledana del siglo XV* (Madrid, 1958), pp. 26–32

——: *Datos histórico-artísticos de fines del siglo XV y principios del XVI*, Colección de Documentos para la Historia del Arte en España, ii (Madrid, 1982), p. 95

——: *Arte gótico en España* (Madrid, 1990), pp. 107, 122–3, 243, 250

JOSÉ MARIA AZCÁRATE RISTORI

Egas, Camilo (*b* Quito, 1889; *d* New York, 18 Sept 1962). Ecuadorean painter and teacher, active in the USA. He studied at the Escuela de Bellas Artes, Quito (*c.* 1908–11), and received a government grant to study at the Regia Scuola di Belle Arti in Rome (1911–14) and at the Academia de San Fernando in Madrid in 1920. His ideology and aesthetic of this period relate him to Spanish *modernismo*. The more monumental style used in *Procession* (1922; Quito, Mus. Camilo Egas Banco Cent.) marks a transition before his years in Paris. In 1923 he attended the Académie Colarrosi, exhibiting between 1924 and 1925 at the Salon des Indépendents and at the Salon d'Automne. He returned to Ecuador between 1925 and 1927, and played a pivotal role in forming the Indigenist movement. The theme of the Indian in his work was related to the rise of Socialism, national indigenous movements and the constitution of Marxist parties in Latin America. He founded Ecuador's first art periodical, *Helice*, in 1926. In 1927 he settled in New York and consecutively assimilated various styles: firstly social realism (e.g. *Street 14*, 1937; Quito, Mus. A. Mod.); then Surrealism, Neo-Cubism and finally Abstract Expressionism. In the 1930s, his work included two murals, *Harvesting Food in Ecuador: No Profit Motif in Any Face or Figure* and *Harvesting Food in North America* (New York, New Sch. Soc. Res). He taught from 1932 and was the first director of art of the New School for Social Research, New York. The Museo Camilo Egas in Quito was inaugurated in 1981 with a permanent exhibition of his work.

BIBLIOGRAPHY

Historia del Arte Ecuatoriano, 4 (1977), pp. 44–52

Camilo Egas (exh. cat., Quito, Mus. Camilo Egas Banco Cent., 1978)

M. Montefiore: *Los Signos del hombre* (1985), pp. 251–2

M. Trinidad Pérez: *The Indian in the 1920s Painting of the Ecuadorian Painter Camilo Egas* (MA thesis, Austin, U. TX, 1987)

ALEXANDRA KENNEDY TROYA

Egbert, Archbishop of Trier (*b c.* AD 950; *reg* 977–93; *d* ?Trier, 8–9 Dec 993). Patron. He was the son of Dirk II, Count of Holland (*reg c.* 940–88), and Hiltigard of Flanders. Educated at Egmond Abbey, he then studied with Bruno, Archbishop of Cologne (*reg* 953–61). He must already have been at the Court of the Holy Roman Emperor, Otto I, and became chancellor in 976 and Archbishop of Trier in 977. In the upheavals during the minority of Otto III, he sided with Henry, Duke of Bavaria, against Empress Theophano (*d* 991). Egbert promoted monastic reforms in Trier and Lotharingia, while scholarship also flourished at Trier and Mettlach; the Archbishop himself corresponded with such Church figures as Gerbert (later Pope Sylvester II, *reg* 999–1003). In Church politics he represented the 'Primatus sedendi in synodis Galliae et Germaniae'. There are two works of art portraying Egbert that support this claim: the splendid Ruodprecht Psalter (Cividale del Friuli, Mus. Archeol. N., Cod. 136), which with its series of miniatures of the bishops of Trier traced back to St Peter served to demonstrate that the apostolic succession belonged to Trier; and the gold sheath for the staff of St Peter (988; Limburg, Domschatzkam.) with representations of bishops of Trier and Roman popes.

The only surviving architectural works associated with Egbert are the octagonal burial chapel at Mettlach (south of Trier) and the piers of the Quadratban at the crossing of Trier Cathedral. Although much has been lost, there survive examples of goldwork from the Trier workshop patronized by Egbert: the portable altar of St Andrew (Trier, Domschatz) and the gold reliquary of the Holy Nail (Trier, Domschatz), the gold covers (985–91) of the Codex Aureus of Echternach (Nuremberg, Ger. Nmus., Cod. 2° 156142), the staff reliquary of St Peter (see above) and a decorative panel (Berlin, Schloss Köpenick). The Servatius Cross (Maastricht) is more probably the work of the successors to the Egbert workshop. These pieces demonstrate a very high standard of goldsmithing and enamelling with the additional use of ivory, pearls and stones (see also OTTONIAN ART, §V, 1). The Trier workshop was influential, even in Egbert's lifetime. The ivory panel of the *Crucifixion* on the Codex Aureus of Echternach book cover is related to a group of reliefs, which include the diptych with *Moses and Christ* or *St Thomas* (Berlin, Staatl. Museen) and the *Christ in Majesty* relief (Berlin, Staatl. Museen). The stylistic inspiration for these pieces derives from Late Antique ivory panels, which were at one time located in and around Trier. A second group of ivories, for example the *Virgin and Child* (Mainz, Landesmus.; see OTTONIAN ART, fig. 11), has been assigned to the Master of the Registrum Gregorii by Nordenfalk and is certainly close to his style, even if it is unlikely to be his work.

Egbert's love of beautiful books was partly the result of his philological interests, as demonstrated by his Psalters:

the Latin–Greek Psalter (in Trier), a tripartite and a glossed Psalter, which he bequeathed along with many other books to his Egmond Abbey. Under his patronage, manuscript production flourished in Trier (*see* TRIER, §2). A book of pericopes, the Codex Egberti (Trier, Stadtbib., MS. 24), is among the finest of Ottonian manuscripts. Although its original place of production is disputed, it was executed under the direction and with the participation of the MASTER OF THE REGISTRUM GREGORII (*see* MASTERS, ANONYMOUS, AND MONOGRAMMISTS, §I and fig.), who worked in Trier; the stylistic roots of its miniatures in Late Antique art are evident. Another manuscript attributed to this master is the *Registrum Gregorii* (two folios, 984; Trier, Stadtbib., MS. 1171/626 and Chantilly, Mus. Condé, MS. 14 *bis*), which was given by Egbert to Trier Cathedral.

BIBLIOGRAPHY

H. V. Sauerland and A. Haseloff: *Der Psalter Erzbischof Egberts von Trier* (Trier, 1901)

H. Westermann-Angerhausen: *Die Goldschmiedarbeiten der Trier Egbertwerkstatt* (Trier, 1973)

F. J. Ronig: *Codex Egberti: Der Perikopenbuch des Erzbischofs Egbert von Trier, 977–993* (Trier, 1977)

——: 'Egbert, Erzbischof von Trier, 977–993: Zum Jahrtausend seines Regierungsantritts', *Festschrift 100 Jahre Rheinisches Landesmuseum Trier* (Mainz, 1979), pp. 347–65

H. Westermann-Angerhausen: 'Spolie und Umfeld in Egberts Trier', *Z. Kstgesch.*, l/3 (1987), pp. 305–36

W. Böhne: 'Erzbischof Egbert von Trier und die Fuldner Schreibs- und Malschule des 10. Jahrhunderts', *Archv Mittelrhein. Kirchgesch.*, xlii (1990), pp. 97–121

FRANZ J. RONIG

Egckl [Eckl; Egkl; Eggl; Ocggl; Öckhel; Oegckhl], **Wilhelm** (*b* ?Augsburg, ?1500–25; *d* Munich, 16 April 1588). German architect-builder. He is first recorded (20 June 1558) in Munich, where he was an official of the ducal armoury (Zeugwart). While still occupying this position he was also put in charge of the construction of a ballroom, the Georgssaal (destr.), in the Neuveste of the Munich Residenz, known only from a miniature painted by Hans Mielich (1565; Munich, Bayer. Staatsbib., MS Cod. mus. A., vol. 1). When the Georgssaal was completed in 1560, Egckl was appointed Master Builder to Duke Albert V of Bavaria (*reg* 1550–79), in control of all building schemes; he evidently held this position until his death, even under Duke William V (*reg* 1579–98). In this capacity he supervised the construction of the Marstall (1563–7) in Munich; it included the ducal stables and also housed the ducal library and art collection (*see* WITTELSBACH, §I(3)). The surviving arcaded courtyard of this monumental building (later the State Mint; now the Bavarian Department of Historic Building Conservation) is considered Egckl's most important achievement. With its three irregular arcade storeys arranged on top of each other in the Italian Renaissance style, it is among the early examples of this type of construction in Germany. It is not known, however, whether Egckl himself, the mason Caspar Weinhart (*d* 1597), who also contributed to the building, or even a third person was responsible for the design.

Egckl probably supervised the construction from 1569 of the Antiquarium of the Munich Residenz, one of the most important structures of the German Renaissance (*see* MUNICH, fig. 5). Egckl worked possibly in collaboration with Simon Zwitzel and followed modified designs by Jacopo Strada, which exploited the use of the Roman style of barrel vaulting. In 1575, in company with Daniel Speckle, Egckl worked for the Duke on fortifications in Ingolstadt and, among other schemes, was probably also in charge of building the Hofkammer (treasurer's office) in the north wing of the Alter Hof in Munich, the earliest residence of the Bavarian dukes, as he is described as Hofbaumeister (court builder) again in documents of 1580. He apparently supervised only briefly, until 1585, the construction of the Jesuit college financed by William V and completed in 1590; the building was probably based on plans by Friedrich Sustris or Wendel Dietrich. Egckl was therefore active as court builder to the two dukes of Bavaria for *c.* 25 years, during which time he oversaw many of this court's most demanding building projects. There is, however, no firm proof of his artistic contribution, and in the light of such evidence as survives, it is probable that the buildings he erected were based on designs by others; it is not even known if he was trained in one of the building trades.

BIBLIOGRAPHY

Thieme–Becker

N. Lieb: *München: Die Geschichte seiner Kunst* (Munich, 1971), pp. 86–9

D. Klein: 'Der Münzhof in München', *Oberbayer. Archv*, cii (1977), pp. 226–334

H. Glaser, ed.: *Wittelsbach und Bayern: Beiträge zur bayerischen Geschichte und Kunst, 1573–1657*, II/i (Munich, 1980), pp. 136–7, 146–7, 152, 154, 164

H. Lietzmann: *Das Neugebäude in Wien* (Munich, 1987), pp. 117, 121, 125–6, 174

JÜRGEN ZIMMER

Egedius [Johnsen], **Halfdan** (*b* Drammen, 5 May 1877; *d* Kristiania [now Oslo], 2 Feb 1899). Norwegian painter and illustrator. His artistic education began at the age of nine, when he enrolled at the school of art of Knud Bergslien (1827–1908) in Kristiania, where he was a pupil from 1886 to 1889. Even from this early period his painted studies and drawings, for instance of his sister *Signe* and brother *Carl* (both 1887; Oslo, N.G.), reveal striking maturity. In 1891 he was a pupil of Erik Werenskiold and from 1891 to 1892 he studied at the Arts and Crafts School in Kristiania. Egedius discovered his strongest impetus and greatest inspiration, however, on his first visit to Telemark in south-west Norway in summer 1892. The artist Torleif Stadskleiv (1865–1946), whom he met there and who became his closest friend, endeared the region to Egedius with stories of its traditions and people. In 1894 Egedius studied for a short period under Harriet Backer, and he made his début at the Kristiania Autumn Exhibition in 1894 with the painting *Saturday Evening* (Oslo, N.G.), painted in Telemark the previous year, which won high praise. In this landscape the atmosphere of the summer night is rendered with a lyrical use of colour and soft brushstrokes. Egedius spent the summer of 1894 in the inspiring and instructive company of a group of artists at Vågå in the Gudbrands Valley in north-west Norway, but for the summer of 1895 he was again in Telemark. Since his previous stay there he had matured artistically and his work now revealed a new confidence and boldness. The most notable paintings from 1895 are *'Juvrestolen' in Telemark*, *The Dreamer*, *Girls Dancing* and the magnificent portrait of *Mari Clasen* (all Oslo, N.G.). He also began work on *Music and Dance* (Oslo, N.G., see fig.), which he continued the following year.

Halfdan Egedius: *Music and Dance*, oil on canvas, 830×955 mm, 1895–6 (Oslo, Nasjonalgalleri)

In the spring of 1896 Egedius spent a few months at Kristian Zahrtmann's school of art in Copenhagen, but he gained relatively little here and in the autumn of that year again returned to Telemark, where he painted the dramatic *Gathering Storm* and the lyrical *Summer* (both Oslo, N.G.). At this time Egedius was beset with brooding uncertainty and his paintings reflect his changing moods.

Egedius painted little during the last two years of his life, and he was largely engaged in designing illustrations. In the autumn and winter of 1896 to 1897 he was commissioned by Fridtjof Nansen, the Norwegian explorer and statesman, to make illustrations for *Fram over Polhavet* ('Across the Polar sea', 1907), for which he produced 25 drawings. He was also involved in the illustrations for the new edition of Snorri Sturlason's *Kongesagaer* ('Sagas of the Norse kings', 1896–9). The 37 drawings he made for this book are regarded as some of his most accomplished works. While Egedius was engaged on the Snorri illustrations he fell ill. He had already accepted another commission for illustrations, for Nordahl Rolfsen's *Norge i det 19 aarhundrede* ('Norway in the 19th century', 1900–02), but he only managed to complete three of these drawings.

BIBLIOGRAPHY

NKL

J. Thiis: *Norske malere og billedhuggere* [Norwegian painters and sculptors], ii (Bergen, 1907), pp. 386–90

A. Aubert: *Die norwegische Malerei im XIX Jahrhundert* (Kristiania, 1910), pp. 86, 87, 90, 93, 94

W. Halvorsen: *Halfdan Egedius* (Kristiania, 1914)

L. Østby: *Fra naturalisme til nyromantikk* [From Naturalism to neo-Romanticism] (Oslo, 1934), pp. 12, 44

——: *Norges kunsthistorie* [History of Norwegian art] (Oslo, 1977), pp. 162, 173–5, 177

Ø. Parmann: *Halfdan Egedius: Liv og verk* [Halfdan Egedius: life and work] (Oslo, 1979)

K. Berg and others, eds: *Nasjonal vekst* [National growth] (Oslo, 1981), v of *Norges kunsthistorie* [History of Norwegian art] (Oslo, 1981–3), pp. 246–51

Dreams of a Summer Night (exh. cat., ACGB, 1986), pp. 76–83

TONE SKEDSMO

Egell, Paul (Johann) (*b* ?9 April 1691; *d* Mannheim, 11 Jan 1752). German sculptor, stuccoist, draughtsman and illustrator. He was the most important sculptor active in Franconia and the Palatinate in the first half of the 18th century; nevertheless, although his very individual late Baroque sculpture, mostly carved in wood, was highly regarded by his contemporaries, he was quickly forgotten after his death. His rich oeuvre was severely depleted, particularly as a result of World War II. It was only after that date that his importance was reassessed. Egell probably served an apprenticeship with the Würzburg sculptor Balthasar Esterbauer (1672–1722) and collaborated on the interior decoration of the Banz monastery. His first documented work is an expressive Crucifix made in 1716 for St Michael's Monastery in Bamberg (now in St Otto, Bamberg). His stylistic development was affected by his work between 1716–17 and 1719 as one of the team directed by Balthasar Permoser, which made all the sculptural decorations at the Zwinger in Dresden for Augustus II (the Strong), Elector of Saxony and King of Poland. Egell made a vital contribution to several works that were formerly attributed to Permoser himself, particularly at the building known as the Wallpavillon. Among those he made, the most beautiful statue is the over life-size sandstone *Nymph at Play*.

At the beginning of the 1720s Egell was in the Palatinate. At first he found work in Oggersheim (now Ludwigshafen-Oggersheim) on the left bank of the Rhine, where Count Palatine Joseph Karl Emanuel von Sulzbach, son-in-law of the Elector Palatine, was building a small castle (destr.). In 1723 Egell moved to Mannheim, capital of the Palatinate, which was then the scene of much building activity. The main project was the decoration of the Schloss being built by Elector Charles Philip; from 1726 to 1731 Egell did an enormous amount of decorative work there. All that is left of the exterior, apart from small-scale sculptures and a statue of *Wisdom* (now Speyer, Hist. Mus. Pfalz), is the stone pedimental relief of the *Trinity* on the Schlosskirche. Inside, Egell's allegorical stucco reliefs of *Morning* and *Evening*, the *Four Continents*, the *Four Elements* and *The Arts* on the walls of the monumental staircase and of the central Rittersaal (restored after bomb damage in 1943) are among the most successful creations of early 18th-century German decorative art.

Egell's first important commission from north Germany was the altar of the *Immaculate Conception* in Hildesheim Cathedral (1729–31). Although the altar was destroyed in World War II, three carved and gilded wood figures, including *St Anne* and the alabaster relief on the antependium, survive *in situ*. The altar was a stepping-stone to Egell's masterpiece, the carved wood high altar of St Sebastian in Mannheim (1739–41; fragments, Berlin, Bodemus.). The altar, which originally filled the choir of the church, was almost 10 m high and consisted of an altarpiece in relief depicting the *Crucifixion*, with freestanding figures of *St Sebastian* and *St Rock* in front of it, and in the foreground an altar in the form of a sarcophagus, with two worshipping angels. The whole was encircled by a radiating nimbus.

Among Egell's surviving works of the 1730s are the portrait bust of *Count Palatine John Christian Joseph of Sulzbach* (sandstone, c. 1730–33; Munich, Residenzmus.), the marble statue of *Apollo Lycius* (1731; Bruchsal, Schwetzingen, Schloss) and, most important, the carved limewood statue of *St John Regis* (1739; Mannheim, Städt. Reiss-Mus.; see fig.).

Paul Egell: *St John Regis*, lime-wood, h. 1.75 m, 1739 (Mannheim, Städtisches Reiss-Museum)

Around 1735 Egell carved two limewood statues of *St Peter* and *St Paul* (Ringingen, nr Ulm, Kath. Pfarrkirche Mariae Himmelfahrt). In 1741–2 he was engaged on unspecified work at the Residenzschloss of the Prince Bishop of Würzburg; he then returned to Mannheim, where Elector Charles Theodore, on coming to power in 1743, confirmed his appointment as court sculptor. Among the few works from this late period that survive are the magnificent lead sarcophagus for Elector Charles Philip (1743; Mannheim, Städt. Reiss-Mus.); five carved wood reliefs of saints (1744; e.g. Frankfurt am Main, Mus. Ksthandwerk); the carved niche with two wooden angels holding candelabra in the Loreto chapel of the Mariae Himmelfahrt church, Oggersheim (1746); three stone statues of *St John of Nepomuk* (c. 1748–51; Mannheim, Städt. Reiss-Mus.); and, most outstanding, the monumental stone pedimental relief of the *Worship of the Holy Name of Jesus* (1749) at the Jesuit church in Mannheim. Also at this time he produced around 100 signed drawings for the compilation *Scriptores historiae romanae* (3 vols, Heidelberg, 1743–8; e.g. Frankfurt am Main, Städel. Kstinst.).

In Egell's work the legacy of German Late Gothic and Mannerist art combines with the influence of Italian Baroque sculpture, French decorative art of the Régence period and the early Rococo, as well as contemporary Venetian painting, to form a most individual style with a high degree of spirituality and expressiveness, though avoiding extreme pathos. Egell's figure types are unmistakable: faces with heavy eyelids and broad-bridged noses are framed by curling hair and beards; the hands are slender and fine. His figures are chiefly organized by their boldly conceived draperies, which give a dominant direction to the pose of the figure, arrested only by a single significant gesture in the opposite direction. The drapery forms flat areas broken by sharp folds with forked edges. His stone sculptures have the same characteristics, derived from his work in wood; and just as in his free-standing figures, a slightly twisting movement starting at the hips conveys spatiality, so the reliefs are composed of counterbalancing diagonals and have surfaces that range from shallow, barely perceptible indentations to areas worked in order to stand out almost completely in the round. The only difference between Egell's late and early works lies in the restraint of the movement, the unity of outline and the spirituality of expression that came with maturity. He did not use the bright polychromy of contemporary south German art, preferring instead to restrict himself to silver or gold leaf, to reinforce the impression of soulfulness and exaltation of his religious work.

Although Egell did not in the strict sense found any 'school', a number of important sculptors emerged from his workshop: Johann Peter Wagner, Joachim Günther, Johann Friedrich Ziesenis (1715–87) and, foremost among them, Ignaz Günther. Paul Egell's son Augustin Egell (1730–86) succeeded him in the office of court sculptor to the Elector Palatine, although he was not his father's equal in talent. His figure sculptures, often worked from his father's designs, are mediocre; his forte was ornamental wood-carvings for the interior decoration of grand houses.

BIBLIOGRAPHY

T. Demmler: 'Der Bildhauer Paul Egell in Mannheim (1691–1751)', *Jb. Preuss. Kstsamml.*, xliii (1922), pp. 137–62
F. Bleibaum: *Bildschnitzerfamilien des hannoverschen und hildesheimischen Barock* (Strasbourg, 1924), pp. 181–94
A. Feulner: *Skulptur und Malerei des 18. Jahrhunderts in Deutschland* (Wildpark-Potsdam, 1929), pp. 95–9
L. Göller: 'Beiträge zur Lebens- und Familiengeschichte kurpfälzischer Künstler im 18. Jahrhundert', *Neues Archv Gesch. Stadt Heidelberg & Kurpfalz*, xiv (1929), pp. 96–164
K. Martin: 'Der Bildhauer Paul Egell als Graphiker', *Oberrhein. Kst*, vi (1933), pp. 179–200
A. Feulner: 'Zum Werk Paul Egells', *Z. Dt. Ver. Kstwiss.*, i (1934), pp. 134–46
G. Jacob: 'Paul Egell (1691–1752): Neue Untersuchungen zur Kunst des Mannheimer Bildhauers', *Mannheim. Geschbl.*, xxxv (1934), columns 5–52
K. Lankheit: *Die Zeichnungen des kurpfälzischen Hofbildhauers Paul Egell* (Karlsruhe, 1954)
Europäisches Rokoko: Kunst und Kultur des 18. Jahrhunderts (exh. cat., Munich, Residenz, 1958), nos 447–9
Ausklang des Barock: Kunst und Künstler des 18. Jahrhunderts in der Pfalz (exh. cat., Heidelberg, Kurpfälz Mus., 1959), nos 138–53, 274–86
P. Volk: 'Unbekannte Zeichnungen von Paul Egell in Köln', *Wallraf-Richartz-Jb.*, xxix (1967), pp. 189–218
K. Lankheit: 'Der kurpfälzische Hofbildhauer Johann Paul Egell (1691–1752)', *Barock in Baden-Württemberg*, 2 vols (exh. cat., Bruchsal, Schloss, 1981), i, pp. 169–85; ii, pp. 35–56
——: 'Überlegungen zur Arbeitsweise des kurpfälzischen Hofbildhauers Paul Egell', *Entwurf und Ausführung in der europäischen Barockplastik*, (Munich, 1986), pp. 177–92
——: *Der kurpfälzische Hofbildhauer Paul Egell, 1691–1752*, 2 vols (Munich, 1988)

KLAUS LANKHEIT

Egenau, Juan (*b* Santiago, 24 Feb 1927; *d* Santiago, 22 April 1987). Chilean sculptor. He studied architecture at the Universidad Católica de Chile in Santiago (1947–8) before transferring to the Escuela de Bellas Artes at the Universidad de Chile, also in Santiago, where he studied painting, drawing and printmaking from 1949 to 1952. In 1959 he obtained a scholarship to study goldwork at the Scuola Porta Romana in Florence. In 1962 he took a course in casting at the Escuela de Artes Aplicadas at the Universidad de Chile, at the same time producing ceramics, enamels and sculptures. While studying casting on a Fulbright scholarship in 1968 at the Rhode Island School of Design in Providence, RI, he developed a technique of modelling for sand-casting in aluminium, which he used exclusively in his later work. From 1956 until his death he was professor of the fine arts faculty at the Universidad de Chile.

Egenau experimented with a spontaneous manner in his early work, first in bronze and later in aluminium, observing natural shapes and their interrelationships as a paradigm of order and harmony. Through these concerns he became interested in transcending history and in tracing human experience back to its mythic origins: in his *Ancestors* series, which he began in *c.* 1966, such as *Monumental Ancestor* (1969; Santiago, Pontificia U. Católica), he externalized his investigation into origins by presenting them, in the manner of genetic coding, as the first models of psychic structures and human behaviour.

In the early 1970s Egenau examined the human reliance on modern technology on the basis of its utility, efficiency and scientific principles. Directing his attention to technical instruments, he sought to analyse their purpose and mode of operation, adopting the schematic language of his source material but suspending or neutralizing its function. In other works he took the human figure as his subject-matter, initially suggesting its presence by means of very simple archaic forms and later in the form of classically structured torsos made of aluminium. The optimistic tone of these works was tempered by intimations of insecurity, aggression and destruction, which he conveyed by protecting them with a hermetic metal armour-plating, as in *My Conquered Love* (1978; Santiago, Mus. N. B.A.). In the mid-1980s he produced his *Black Series* of sculptures, in which he concealed the shiny metal surface in black paint, extending his longstanding interest in mysterious origins and ambiguous meaning.

BIBLIOGRAPHY

Egenau Juan: La alquimia de la materia (exh. cat., essay M. Ivelić; Santiago, Gal. Epoca, 1986)
Egenau Juan: De metal y de fuego (exh. cat., essay M. Ivelić; Santiago, Inst. Cult. Las Condes, 1988)

MILAN IVELIĆ

Eger [formerly Ger. Erlau]. City in northern Hungary on the River Eger. It lies in a valley between the Mátra Mountains and the Bükk Mountains and was for a long time an important military and episcopal see. Even though an 11th-century cathedral and accompanying episcopal canonical buildings stood on the present site of the castle, the hill was fortified only after the Mongol invasion of 1241. King Emeric (*reg* 1196–1204) was buried in the cathedral. Bishop Orbán Dóczy made additions to it, but all that remains are a semicircular sanctuary and several compound columns. In the 15th century the castle enceinte encompassed not only the cathedral but also two provosts' palaces and approximately twenty other church buildings. Following the Turkish victory at Mohács in 1526, Alessandro da Vedano began modernization of the castle under the captaincy of Péter Perényi, incorporating one wall of the newly built sanctuary of the cathedral into the battlements. With renewed Turkish threats, István Dobó, captain from 1549, concentrated on fortifying the castle and its grounds. In 1552 he heroically defended the castle against overwhelming Turkish forces. A direct hit on its sanctuary, used as an arsenal, led to extensive destruction of the cathedral. In 1596 the castle finally fell to the Turks and was held by them until 1687. They made additions to buildings inside the castle walls, the remains of which are notable as the northernmost examples of Turkish architecture in Hungary. The mosque that stood beside the existing minaret became the church of St Joseph (destr. 1841) after the Turks withdrew. The 14-sided minaret, 35 m high, has stairs leading up to a circular iron balcony and is capped by a stone spire added during restoration in 1897. After the retreat of the Turks, the castle lost its military significance, and in 1702 its outer wall was blown up on the orders of the Habsburg emperor Leopold I. Excavation and restoration was carried out between 1925 and 1936 and from 1952. A Gothic Bishop's Palace, built *c.* 1470 by János Bekensloer, was unearthed in its courtyard.

The town acquired its characteristic Baroque appearance in the 18th century under the patronage of Bishop Ferenc Bárkóczy and Bishop Károly Esterházy (*see* ES-TERHÁZY, §II(4)), both of whom invited architects trained in Rome to plan and execute buildings. The Lyceum (1765–85; now the Pedagogical Seminary; *see* HUNGARY, fig. 3), one of the largest buildings in Hungary, was designed by Joseph Gerl, modified by Jakob Fellner and completed by József Grossman (1747–85). It was intended to house a university, but in 1777 this was forbidden by Maria-Theresa. The three-storey building has pedimented central pavilions on three sides; its scale and understated ornamentation recall the style of Louis XVI. The windows have Rococo and *Zopfstil* ornamentation, and there is a three-storey observatory at the top of the tower in the east wing. The interior of the Lyceum is decorated with murals by Franz Sigrist, Franz Anton Maulbertsch, JOHANN LUKAS KRACKER and Joseph Zách (*c.* 1727–80). Several of the original fireplaces designed by the architect are still in place. Numerous houses and churches, among them the Minorite church and the Jesuit (now Cistercian) church, were built in the 18th century by religious orders who settled in Eger. The Minorite church (1758–73; exterior restored 1962–4) was built by János Falk and

János Nietzschmann to plans by Kilian Ignaz Dientzenhofer. Its Italianate façade with twin towers and a bowed central section flanked by coupled columns is a unique feature in Hungary. Its nave bays are roofed by surbased vaults, widened to form transepts at the third bay. The large altarpiece by Kracker depicts the *Virgin and Child with St Anthony of Padua* (1771; *in situ*). The Jesuit church (1731–3) is centrally planned with a barrel-vaulted interior. The Baroque statues on the relatively plain façade and the Rococo narthex are of 1743. The high altar has a number of statues, among them *St Francis Borgia* (1769–70) by Johann Anton Krauss. Bishop Bárkóczy also commissioned the County Hall from Matthäus Gerl in 1750–56. Its most notable feature is a splendid wrought-iron gate (1761), the most accomplished piece of Baroque wrought-iron work in Hungary, by Henrik Fazola (*see* HUNGARY, fig. 24). The cathedral of St Michael and St John Nepomuk (1831–7) is one of the few important examples of Neoclassical architecture in the city and is the second-largest ecclesiastical structure in Hungary. It was built by JÓZSEF HILD to replace a previous Baroque church by Giovanni Battista I Carlone (ii). Its pedimented façade has eight colossal Corinthian columns, above which are allegorical statues of *Faith*, *Hope* and *Charity* by Marco Casagrande (1806–80). Reliefs of the *Life of Christ* above the doors and on either side of the portico are also by Casagrande. Inside are a further 22 reliefs by the artist and a fresco (1770s) by Kracker of *St Ladislaus Kneeling before the Virgin* (actually painted for the earlier church). The city, a well-known spa, remained largely unindustrialized until after World War II. The hilly region surrounding it is noted for the production of red wines.

BIBLIOGRAPHY

V. Bierbauer: *A magyar építészet története* [The history of Hungarian architecture] (Budapest, 1937)
I. Genthon: *Az egri liceum* [The Lyceum at Eger] (Budapest, 1955)
L. Gerő: *Magyarországi várépítészet: Vazlat a magyar varapites fejezeteirol* [Castle architecture in Hungary: an outline of the periods of Hungarian castle construction] (Budapest, 1955)
——: *Történelmi városrészek* [Historic districts] (Budapest, 1971)
I. Genthon: *Magyarország művészeti emlékei* [Recollections of museums in Hungary] (Budapest, 1974)
G. Galavics, ed.: *Magyarországi reneszánsz és barokk* [Renaissance and Baroque in Hungary] (Budapest, 1975)

BARBRA RUCKRIEGEL EGERVARY

Egeri [Aegeri], **Carl** [Carle] **von** (*b c.* 1510; *d* Zurich, 14 June 1562). Swiss glass-painter and designer. In 1536 he settled in Zurich, where he later represented his guild on the Greater Council and held other civic honours. In 1542 and 1555 he was commissioned to make stained-glass windows for the Rathaus. These constructed a powerful new civic iconography for post-Reformation Zurich. Banner-bearing citizens, with finely detailed armour and portrait heads, are set against abstract patterned grounds, the whole framed in elaborate arches. Appropriate biblical scenes of loyalty to the state (e.g. *Judith and Holofernes*) fill the corners. Two impressively drawn lions occupy a roundel (1542) surrounded by the arms of the Zurich domains. In a 1557 window (Zurich, Geshaus Schneggen) of similar design, the lions are instead fully Mannerist, with elongated bodies and twisted mouths. Von Egeri evidently adapted his style to the job; in his Muri Abbey windows (1557) St Martin and St George ride tranquil

Paolo Uccello horses, while the large figures are set against blue skies surmounting perfectly rendered landscapes. Many watercolour designs for windows emanated from von Egeri's prolific workshop in the 1540s; typically, variations on the theme of two figures (usually men) flanking a piece of heraldry (e.g. the *Three Cantons, c.* 1540; Rennes, Mus. B.-A. & Archéol.). These are fine examples of a strand of late Renaissance international decoration; the elaborate costumes show a debt to Lucas Cranach, while the classicized grotesquerie is adapted from Italian engraved models. Some lovely, less formal drawings attributed to von Egeri (e.g. *Standing Woman in Profile, c.* 1530; Basle, Kstmus.) exhibit a Holbeinesque purity of line, worthy of an artist working in one of the great portrait centres of this period. On his death von Egeri was described as 'ein grosser Künstler'.

BIBLIOGRAPHY

B. Anderes: *Glasmalerei im Kreuzgang Muri, Kabinettscheiben der Renaissance* (Berne, 1974), pp. 126–8, 134–6, 140–44, pl. 9
Zürcher Kunst nach der Reformation: Hans Asper und seine Zeit (exh. cat., Zurich, Helmhaus, 1981), pp. 84–91, 100–106, pls 52–64, 77–86

Egerton. English family of collectors and patrons. (1) Francis Egerton, 3rd Duke of Bridgewater, was a wealthy industrialist and jointly acquired with, among others, his nephew GEORGE GRANVILLE LEVESON-GOWER, Earl Gower (later 2nd Marquess of Stafford and 1st Duke of Sutherland), part of the Orléans collection. These paintings, together with a large number of Old Masters he assembled, were added on his death to the collection of his nephew, who was a connoisseur and an active patron and collector. Leveson-Gower's son (2) Francis Egerton, 1st Earl of Ellesmere, inherited the collection built up by his great-uncle and part of his father's collection and added to it, building a new gallery to accommodate it. Francis Henry Egerton, 8th Earl of Bridgewater (1756–1829), assembled a unique collection of manuscripts and autographs, most relating to French and Italian literature and history, which he bequeathed to the British Museum.

(1) Francis Egerton, 3rd Duke of Bridgewater (*b* 1736; *d* London, 3 March 1803). After completing the almost obligatory Grand Tour, in 1759 he concentrated on the development of his coal-mines at Worsley, Lancs, and constructed the first industrially significant canals, linking Worsley and Manchester (1760) and Manchester and Liverpool (1762–72). It is likely that the superb collection of paintings he amassed at considerable expense reflected his shrewd sense of investment as much as, if not more than, his aesthetic sensibilities. In 1798, together with his nephew George Granville Leveson-Gower, Earl Gower (later 2nd Marquess of Stafford and 1st Duke of Sutherland; *see* LEVESON-GOWER, (1)), and Frederick Howard, 5th Earl of Carlisle, he authorized MICHAEL BRYAN to purchase the Italian and French schools of the Orléans collection. Among the paintings that he kept were a large number of works by Annibale and Ludovico Carracci, the Bridgewater *Madonna and Child* by Raphael (Duke of Sutherland, on loan to Edinburgh, N.G.), pictures by Tintoretto and Veronese, Titian's *Diana and Actaeon* and its pendant *Diana and Callista* (Duke of Sutherland, on loan to Edinburgh, N.G.), and Poussin's

series of paintings on the *Seven Sacraments* (1644–8; Duke of Sutherland, on loan to Edinburgh, N.G.). In 1801 he purchased Anthony van Dyck's portrait of *Thomas Howard, Earl of Arundel* (1620–21; Malibu, CA, Getty Mus.). He also commissioned from J. M. W. Turner *Dutch Boats in a Gale; Fishermen Endeavouring to Put their Fish on Board* (exh. RA 1801; Duke of Sutherland, priv. col.). On his death the Bridgewater estates, including Cleveland House and the collection, were left to his nephew George Granville Leveson-Gower.

BIBLIOGRAPHY·

DNB
W. Buchanan: *Memoirs of Painting with a Chronological History of the Importation of Pictures by the Great Masters into England* (London, 1824)
G. F. Waagen: *Treasures of Art in Great Britain*, iii (London, 1854)
F. Lugt: *Marques* (1921)
W. Whitley: *Art in England, 1800–20* (Cambridge, 1921)
F. Lugt: *Marques*, suppl. (1956)

(2) Francis Egerton, 1st Earl of Ellesmere (*b* London, 1 Jan 1800; *d* London, 18 Feb 1857). Great-nephew of (1) Francis Egerton, 3rd Duke of Bridgewater, and second son of George Granville Leveson-Gower, 2nd Marquess of Stafford and 1st Duke of Sutherland. In 1833, on his father's death, he inherited the Bridgewater property, including the collection formed by his great-uncle, the 3rd Duke of Bridgewater, and adopted the name Egerton. After serving as a government minister, he was created Earl of Ellesmere in 1846. He was a trustee of the National Gallery (1835–55) and of the National Portrait Gallery (1856–7) in London and first chairman of the committee for the Manchester Art Treasures exhibition (1856–7). From 1823 he purchased paintings of the Dutch and Bolognese schools, among others, and also by contemporary artists (e.g. *Return of the Hawking Party* by Edwin Landseer, 1838; Duke of Sutherland priv. col.). In 1836 he bought drawings from the collection of Thomas Lawrence that were offered for sale by Samuel Woodburn, including works by the Carracci and Giulio Romano. After inheriting the Bridgewater collection, he continued the tradition of opening the gallery to the public. In 1841 he had the house (then called Cleveland House) and gallery demolished and commissioned Charles Barry (*see* BARRY, (1)) to build a new house (Bridgewater House; *c.* 1841–51) and gallery (1846–51). The pictures remained there in unaltered order until 1898; it was bombed in 1943 and the house sold. Some works that he collected were sold at Christie, Manson & Woods (2 April 1870; 18 Oct 1946), but several others that he was bequeathed or himself purchased, including *Landscape with a View of Bergkerk, Deventer* by Meindert Hobbema and *School for Boys and Girls* by Jan Steen, have been loaned by his descendant, John Sutherland Egerton, 6th Duke of Sutherland, to the National Gallery of Scotland, Edinburgh.

WRITINGS

Catalogue of the Bridgewater Collection of Pictures (London, 1851)
Personal Reminiscences of the Duke of Wellington, with a Memoir of Lord Ellesmere by his Daughter, Alice Countess of Strafford (London, 1903) [pubd posth.]

BIBLIOGRAPHY

A. Jameson: *Companion to the Most Celebrated Private Galleries of Art in London* (London, 1844), pp. 77–163
'Visits to Private Galleries', *Art-Union*, ix (1847), pp. 8–12, 49–52
J. Weale: *London Exhibited in 1851* (London, 1851), pp. 392–7
Obituary, *Gent. Mag.*, n. s. 2, i (1857), pp. 358–9

L. H. Cust: *The Bridgewater Gallery: One Hundred and Twenty of the Most Noted Paintings at Bridgewater House* (London, 1903)

J. Cornforth: 'London's Lost Galleries: Private Collections in the Early 19th Century', *Country Life*, cxliii (13 June 1968), pp. 1566–8

Dutch Art and Scotland: A Reflection of Taste (exh. cat. by J. Lloyd Williams, Edinburgh, N.G., 1992)

SELBY WHITTINGHAM

Egerton, Daniel Thomas (*b* England, 1797; *d* Tacubaya, Mexico City, 27 April 1842). English painter, draughtsman and engraver, active in Mexico. He exhibited with the Royal Society of British Artists, of which he was a founder-member, between 1824 and 1829. Inspired by the writings of Alexander Humboldt, he travelled to Mexico in 1830 and from 1831 made a series of sketches of landscapes including views of mines, ranches and cities. 25 oil paintings and more than 100 watercolours and drawings in red chalk date from this period. On his return to England, his pictures were made into prints to form an album of colour lithographs. As the record of a travelling artist, the album contributed to a fashionable genre of the period. Egerton's work depicted an abundant natural world and prosperous towns, with each urban or rural landscape inhabited by people dressed in traditional costume, who are generally positioned in the foreground and surrounded by typical local vegetation (e.g. *View of the Valley of Mexico* (1837; Mexico City, Dept. Distr. Fed.). In 1841 Egerton returned to Mexico with his wife and settled in the capital. They were both murdered in 1842.

PRINTS
Views of Mexico (London, 1840)

BIBLIOGRAPHY
E. Gutiérrez and T. Gutiérrez: *Daniel Thomas Egerton* (Mexico City, n.d.)

M. Kiek, ed.: *Egerton en México, 1830–1842* (Mexico, 1976)

F. Ramírez: 'La visión europea de la América tropical: Los artistas viajeros', *Hist. A. Mex.*, 67–9 (1982)

Art in Latin America: The Modern Era, 1820–1980 (exh. cat. by D. Ades and others, London, Hayward Gal., 1989), pp. 41–61

ELOÍSA URIBE

Egesta. *See* SEGESTA.

Egg, Augustus (Leopold) (*b* London, 2 May 1816; *d* Algiers, ?26 March 1863). English painter. The son of a prominent London gunsmith, Egg enrolled in Henry Sass's Academy around 1834 and entered the Royal Academy Schools in 1836. In 1837 he and his friends Richard Dadd, William Powell Frith, Henry Nelson O'Neil and John Phillip formed the sketching club THE CLIQUE. Egg's

Augustus Egg: *The Travelling Companions*, oil on canvas, 645×765 mm, 1862 (Birmingham, City of Birmingham Museum and Art Gallery)

earliest pictures included portraits, costume pieces, subjects from Shakespeare, Scott, Cervantes, LeSage and others, as well as historical incidents, taken from accounts of 17th-century diarists such as Pepys. Beginning in the late 1830s Egg exhibited in London, primarily at the Society of British Artists, the British Institution and the Royal Academy, and also in Birmingham, Liverpool and Manchester. His youthful paintings were dependent on his older contemporaries Charles Robert Leslie, Gilbert Stuart Newton and Daniel Maclise. Critics praised a few of his early pictures, including the *Introduction of Sir Piercie Shafton to Halbert Glendinning* (1843; Liverpool, Walker A.G.) from Scott's *The Monastery*, for its robustness of form and firm handling, but in general his early works were criticized for their derivative qualities.

Goaded by this reaction, Egg produced his large, innovative and much acclaimed canvas *Queen Elizabeth Discovers she Is No Longer Young* (1848; priv. col., see R. Strong: *'And when did you last see your father?': The Victorian Painter and British History*, London, 1978, p. 63). It demonstrated his antiquarian knowledge, competent draughtsmanship and dramatic invention and earned him the position of ARA. Equally successful paintings followed, including *Launce's Substitute for Proteus's Dog* from the *Two Gentlemen of Verona* (1849; Leicester, Mus. & A.G.) and *Pepys's Introduction to Nell Gwynne* (1851; Santa Fe, Mus. NM).

Beginning in the early 1850s Egg promoted and patronized younger artists, particularly William Holman Hunt and the Pre-Raphaelites, whose style and subject-matter influenced his own works. From 1853 to 1855 he painted two pendant pictures, the *Life of Buckingham* and the *Death of Buckingham* (both New Haven, CT, Yale Cent. Brit. A.), representing in a manner akin to works by Hogarth the debauched life of George Villiers, 2nd Duke of Buckingham, and his legendary, sordid demise. Egg's famous triptych, exhibited untitled at the Academy in 1858, and now known as *Past and Present* (London, Tate), depicted the downfall of an adulterous wife and demonstrated Egg's concern with moralizing serial narrative and with contemporary social issues. He continued to paint historical and literary subjects and modern themes in the late 1850s, including two pictures based on Thackeray's *History of Henry Esmond* in 1857 and 1858 (Liverpool, Walker A.G., and London, Tate), and *The Night before Naseby* (1859; London, RA), showing Cromwell in his tent on the eve of the battle in 1645. In 1860 Egg was elected RA and married Esther Mary Brown. He frequently travelled to the south of England and to the Mediterranean for his asthma, to which he ultimately succumbed. One of his last paintings, and related to these journeys, *The Travelling Companions* (1862; Birmingham, Mus. & A.G.; see fig.) depicts two sisters in a railway carriage on the outskirts of Menton, and reveals Egg's evolution towards a non-anecdotal art.

Egg's interest in the theatre and literature is evident in the dramatic presentation of his narrative subjects, and his literary friends included Dickens and Wilkie Collins. His concern for the predicament of destitute artists is seen in his *Self-portrait as a Poor Author* (1858; Arbroath, Hospitalfield House), in his support of young artists and in his participation in numerous philanthropic projects, including his performances in Dickens's amateur theatricals. He was an adviser to important collectors of Pre-Raphaelite art, including John Gibbons, Thomas Fairbairn and Thomas Miller, and because of the respect accorded him by many diverse artists he was asked to supervise the installation of modern British paintings at the Manchester Art-Treasures Exhibition, 1857. Egg's studio sale was held at Christie's, London, 18–19 May 1863.

BIBLIOGRAPHY

[W. Holman Hunt]: 'Notes on the Life of Augustus L. Egg', *Reader*, i (1863), pp. 462, 486–7, 557–8; ii (1863), pp. 42–3, 91, 516–17; iii (1864), pp. 56–7

A. Chester: 'The Art of Augustus L. Egg, R. A.', *Windsor Mag.* (1913), pp. 452–66

H. Faberman: *Augustus Leopold Egg, RA (1816–1863)* (diss., New Haven, CT, Yale U., 1983)

HILARIE FABERMAN

Egg and dart [Egg and tongue]. Decorative architectural detailing of Ionic ovolo mouldings, probably originally a leaf pattern (see fig.). Examples can be seen on the Ionic capitals and entablature of the Temple of Artemis at Ephesos (6th century BC) and the Temple of Athena Polias at Priene (4th century BC). It is also occasionally found decorating the echinus of Doric capitals, as on the exterior of the bouleuterion at Miletos (*c.* 170 BC). The pattern is sometimes found on a smaller scale on metalwork, jewellery, sarcophagi and vases.

In Roman architecture the 'eggs' were commonly surrounded by a grooved casing and separated by a shape more like an arrowhead than a tongue. Egg and dart mouldings occur in Rome, for example on the Temple of Concord (ded. AD 10) and on a group of buildings thought to be the work of craftsmen from Asia Minor, among them the Castel Sant' Angelo (completed AD 139; *see* ROME, §V, 9) and the Temple of Venus and Rome. In the late 2nd century AD and the 3rd century the arrowhead became a leaf or some other decorative motif. In this period also the casing around the eggs was commonly replaced by a pair of brackets, as in fragments found at Baalbek and Palmyra.

BIBLIOGRAPHY

W. B. Dinsmore: *The Architecture of Ancient Greece* (New York, 1902, 3/1950/R 1975)

D. S. Robertson: *A Handbook of Greek and Roman Architecture* (Cambridge, 1929, rev. 2/1943); *R* as *Greek and Roman Architecture* (London, 1969)

MARGARET LYTTELTON

Egg and dart moulding from the Erechtheion, Athens, 5th century BC

Eggeling, Viking (*b* Lund, 21 Oct 1880; *d* Berlin, 19 May 1925). Swedish draughtsman, film maker, painter and writer. After a limited education in Sweden he emigrated to Germany in 1897, where he received a commercial training at Flensburg that year. Around 1900 he began work as a bookkeeper at a watch factory in Le Locle in Switzerland, and from *c.* 1901 to *c.* 1907 he worked as a bookkeeper in Milan. There he attended the Accademi di Belle Arti di Brera in the evenings. In 1907 he obtained a post as a bookkeeper at the Lyceum Alpinum in Zuoz, Switzerland, where he was also allowed to teach art. His wife's ill-health forced him to resign the post and, after a visit to Essen in 1910, he moved to Paris (1911) and became acquainted with Arp, Modigliani, Othon Friesz and Moise Kisling; he was particularly impressed by the work of André Derain, but he probably also studied the work of the Cubists.

Eggeling never dated his works and only rarely signed them. This fact coupled with the scant documentary material and the comparatively small number of extant works makes the dating of his work extremely difficult. Such drawings as *In the Trench* (untraced; see O'Konor, p. 187), inspired by the events of World War I, show the influence of Cubism through the simplified, angular treatment of the figures; the painting *Landscape with Church on a Hill* (Basle, Kstmus.) shows the influence of Derain's work through the firmly structured composition and solid forms executed in diagonal brushstrokes. In contrast, the painting *Sacré-Coeur, Paris* (*c.* 1911–15; Lisbon, Mrs Ingeborg Dundas priv. col., see O'Konor, p. 153) is in a looser, more Impressionist style. As these examples show, Eggeling's favoured subject was landscape and he produced a large number of drawings on this theme, often rough or partially finished sketches. Among the more finished examples is *Bare Tree and Gable* (Stockholm, Nmus.), which was a study for the oil painting of the same title (Stockholm, Mod. Mus.).

In 1914 Eggeling spent the summer in Cassis in the south of France. Around 1915 he moved to Switzerland, living first at Ascona in the Ticino and later, among other places, at Saconnex in the canton of Geneva. In 1918 he moved to Zurich where he became involved with the DADA group of artists centred on the Cabaret Voltaire, although he had been in contact with the group since 1916. He did not share the nihilism of many of the Dada artists and events but was sympathetic to the movement's revolutionary fervour, which he thought might help pave the way for a new artistic language. On 9 April 1919 he gave a lecture on abstract art at the eighth large Dada soirée in Zurich. His own work had become abstract by this time and two abstract lithographs appeared in the review *Dada* in 1919 (no. 4–5, pp. 12, 25). These elegant works, using curved and linear geometric elements, are characteristic of Eggeling's late work. He had a one-man show at the Galerie Wolfsberg in Zurich in 1919 and the same year became a member of the group Neue Leben, founded in 1918, and Radikale Künstler. Both had a similar membership, which included Arp, Augusto Giacommetti, Marcel Janco and Hans Richter. The former group was intended to forge links between the Dadaists and other avant-garde artists in Switzerland.

Following the dissolution of the Dada group in Zurich, Eggeling moved to Berlin with Richter in summer 1919 and there he joined the Novembergruppe. Towards the end of the year Eggeling and Richter went to Klein-Kölzig, Nieder-Lausitz, to stay in the house owned by Richter's parents. Around this time Eggeling produced drawings on long scrolls of paper, *Horizontal–Vertical Orchestra* and *Diagonal Symphony* (see fig.), although he had made the first sketches *c.* 1915–17. The former consisted of three parts on two scrolls and the latter of four parts on four scrolls. The original of part I of *Horizontal–Vertical Orchestra* and all those of *Diagonal Symphony* are lost, but posthumous copies (possibly intended as forgeries) are held at the Kunstmuseum, Basle, and in the Moderna Museet, Stockholm; the originals of parts II and III of *Horizontal–Vertical Orchestra* are held at the Yale University Art Gallery, New Haven, CT. The scrolls depict the gradual transformations of abstract designs through a series of separate images laid out across the paper. This essentially cinematic structure prompted Eggeling to try to make a film based on *Horizontal–Vertical Orchestra*. He worked on this with Richter at Klein-Kölzig, but in 1921 the two men argued and the collaboration ceased. Also in 1921 Eggeling had an article published in the Hungarian journal *Ma*, 'Elvi Fejtegések a Mozgóművészetrol', in which he set out the basis of his aesthetic. It included a discussion of *Generalbass*, a crucial concept for Eggeling, which he drew from music, and reflected his desire to forge a 'Generalbass der Malerei' by the use of a universal language.

In 1922 Eggeling moved to Berlin where he continued his film work, and from 1923 he collaborated with Erna Niemeyer. Dissatisfied with the results (of which no copies exist), in summer 1923 he began work with Niemeyer on a film based on *Diagonal Symphony*. Running for under eight minutes this was first shown publicly at the UFA Palast in Berlin on 3 May 1925. Eggeling left a number of

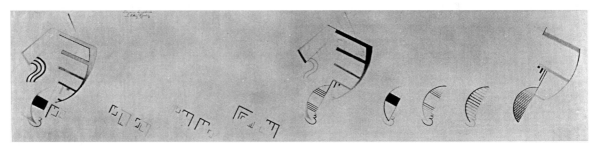

Viking Eggeling: *Diagonal Symphony*, pencil drawing on paper, *c.* 1919 (Stockholm, Moderna Museum); posthumous copy of the lost original

unedited notes (see O'Konor, pp. 92–126), which provide further information on his aesthetic theories.

See also EXPERIMENTAL FILM.

WRITINGS
'Elvi Fejtegések a Mozgóművészetrol' [Theoretical presentations of the art of movement], Ma, vi (1921), pp. 105–6

BIBLIOGRAPHY
Viking Eggeling, 1880–1925: Tecknare och Filmkonstnär [Viking Eggeling, 1880–1925: draughtsman and film artist] (exh. cat., ed. C. Nordenvalk; Stockholm, Nmus., 1950)
Viking Eggeling (exh. cat. by H. Richter and others, Copenhagen, Gal. Tokanten, 1951)
L. O'Konor: Viking Eggeling, 1880–1925: Artist and Film-maker, Stockholm Studies in History of Art, 23 (Stockholm, 1971)

Eggenschwiler, Franz (*b* Solothurn, 9 Dec 1930). Swiss sculptor, painter, printmaker and jewellery designer. From 1946 to 1951 he was apprenticed to a maker of stained glass while at the same time attending the Kunstgewerbeschule in Berne. He then studied at the painting school, also in Berne, run by Max von Mühlenen (1903–71). In 1955 Eggenschwiler, Peter Meier (*b* 1928), Konrad Vetter (*b* 1922) and Robert Wälti (*b* 1937) formed the Berner Arbeitsgemeinschaft, which operated until 1971.

Until the mid-1960s Eggenschwiler's work was essentially Constructivist, although until 1968 he was still regarded as a stained-glass maker. His prints and paintings, as well as his sculptures, were dominated by basic geometric forms, especially the cube, as in the sculpture *Stair Cubes* (iron, 155×155×155 mm, 1968; Westphalia, priv. col., see 1985 exh. cat., p. 41). From the 1960s he worked with *objets trouvés*, collecting discarded objects made of metal, wood or other materials, as well as stones and other natural objects. He either worked on these *objets trouvés* or combined them with objects he had made so as to disorientate the observer and produce unexpected connections. He compiled the resulting works into large thematic groups: *UFOs, Sausage Objects, Breast Objects* and *Pensils* [sic]. In his *Box Reliefs*, such as *Gegen-E-Kasten* (mixed media, 2.5×1.4×0.4 m, 1972–7; Solothurn, Kstmus.), he combined an ever greater number of objects, seeking to elucidate the whole range of their associative possibilities, or to interpret a given theme through combining the most disparate objects. The slight or fundamental alterations to the *objets trouvés*, transforming them into basically humorous art objects, serve to elucidate hidden, non-rational associations and meanings. Photographs of inconspicuous *objets trouvés* were also the inspiration for the prints that he made from 1966 to 1973. The machine-made 'rainbow prints' (*c.* 1970) were again collected into subject groups: *UFOs, Women* and *Folds*. Some of this printed work was produced in collaboration with Vetter (e.g. the plates for *UFO-Mappe* (1970; see 1985 exh. cat., pp. 200–01).

In 1975 Eggenschwiler turned to woodcut printing. In this he used Munch's technique for printing in several colours. In 1977–8 he designed *c.* 200 pieces of jewellery that were made by the jeweller Bernhard Schobinger (*b* 1946), such as *Hängerspiel* (gold, cobalt and steel earrings, 1978; see 1985 exh. cat., p. 116). As with his sculptures, he drew inspiration both from the widest assortment of manufactured and natural *objets trouvés*.

Later he frequently used telephone sketches, produced by doodling during telephone conversations, as a source for his woodcuts and for zinc-plate prints. The resulting virtually unconscious lineations can be compared to the automatic writing of the Surrealists and were worked up into paintings that often had a wooden panel as their support, but the unconscious remained the basis for the secondary creative process. The works often embody both abstract and figurative elements so as to leave plenty of scope for interpretation (e.g. *Adam Katmon*, 1984; Switzerland, priv. col., see 1985 exh. cat., p. 151). Erotic subjects and references can be found in both his sculptural work and his printed and painterly work. He exploited the field of eroticism and unconscious fantasies to arrive at ideas for pictures that were completely original and independent of traditional aesthetics.

WRITINGS
Telefonzeichnungen (London and Stuttgart, 1980)

BIBLIOGRAPHY
Arbeitsgemeinschaft Franz Eggenschwiler, Peter Meier, Konrad Vetter, Robert Wälti (exh. cat. by D. Koepplin and others, Basle, Kstmus., 1971), pp. 24–32
Franz Eggenschwiler: Werke 1950 bis 1985. Objekte, Schmuck, Zeichnungen, Malerei, Druckgraphik (exh. cat. by H. van der Grinten and others, Düsseldorf, Kstver., 1985)
Franz Eggenschwiler: Werkverzeichnis der Holzdrucke (exh. cat. by H. Eggenberger, H. van der Grinten and A. Bardon, Reutlingen, Kstgal. Spendhaus, 1986)
O. Saxer and L. Wirth: Dokumentation zum Kastenrelief von Franz Eggenschwiler (Berne, 1989)

FRANZ MÜLLER

Eggericx, Jean-Jules (*b* Brussels, 21 Aug 1884; *d* Brussels, 21 April 1963). Belgian architect, urban planner and teacher. He graduated from the Université Libre in Brussels and then enrolled at the Académie Royale des Beaux-Arts (1904). Rebelling against teaching he considered atrophied, he left the Académie without completing his studies and worked for a period with Alban Chambon, Jean-Baptiste Dewin (1873–1948) and Victor Horta. During World War I he took refuge in England where he participated in the demonstrations organized in London in 1915 by the International Garden Cities and Town Planning Association. Strongly influenced by English architecture, he became a firm advocate of Raymond Unwin's ideas and was involved in the development of the first garden cities in Belgium. After returning to Brussels he worked with Raphaël Verwilghen at the Office des Régions Dévastées and in 1921 he began a long period of collaboration with Louis Van der Swaelmen on the construction of the garden cities Le Logis and Floréal at Watermael-Boitsfort, Brussels. At the same time he also built the Hainaut children's home (1923–6) at Bredene and some villas (1924–6), including the Marcel Wolfers-Petrucci mansion in Brussels, that were influenced by Dutch architecture. Later works included the theatre for the Exposition Universelle et Internationale (1935), Brussels; participation with Verwilghen and Henry Van de Velde in the design of the Belgian pavilion at the Exposition Internationale des Arts et Techniques dans la Vie Moderne (1937), Paris; blocks of flats in Brussels, such as the Résidence Léopold (1934–37; with Verwilghen); and some industrial buildings. He taught architecture (1929–47) and then urban planning at the Institut Supérieur des

Arts Décoratifs de la Cambre in Brussels, where Van der Swaelmen and Verwilghen had also taught.

BIBLIOGRAPHY

Antoine Pompe et l'effort moderne en Belgique, 1860–1940 (exh. cat., eds M. Culot and F. Terlinden; Brussels, Mus. Ixelles, 1969) [with bibliography]
La Reconstruction en Belgique après 1914 (exh. cat., Brussels, Resurgam, 1985)

ANNE VAN LOO

Egger-Lienz, Albin [Trojer, Ingenuin Albuin] (*b* Stribach bei Lienz, East Tyrol, 29 Jan 1868; *d* St Justina bei Bozen, South Tyrol [now Santa Giustina, Italy], 4 Nov 1926). Austrian painter. He was the illegitimate son of a peasant girl, Maria Trojer, and the Austrian church artist and photographer Georg Egger (1835–1907). Later he adopted the name of his father and home town. He studied at the Akademie der Bildenden Künste in Munich from 1884 to 1893. The main subject-matter of his early works, which were painted in a naturalistic style and influenced by Franz von Defregger, was determined by his background: scenes from peasant life and from the Tyrolean freedom battles of 1809 against the French troops of Napoleon, for example *Ave Maria after the Battle on the Bergisel* (1893–6; Innsbruck, Tirol. Landesmus.). He moved in 1899 to Vienna, where his own style developed: its fresco-like monumentality, as in *The Dance of Death of Year Nine* (1908; Vienna, Belvedere), was a contrast to sophisticated metropolitan culture at the turn of the century. His style was characterized by a concentration on the clearly outlined large form and by a linear rhythm in the picture surface. Bulky figures combine to form voluminous masses that appear against the background as silhouettes. Colours are reduced to mainly monochrome earth-coloured tones of brown.

Though influenced by the work of Ferdinand Hodler, Egger-Lienz expressly distanced himself from it, most notably in a polemic called *Monumentale Kunst*, published under his name though actually written by the art critic Otto Kunz. When it appeared in the daily papers in 1912, it started a public argument about Hodler's work. A year later the article, along with some responses to it, was published by Egger-Lienz as a brochure, also entitled *Monumentale Kunst*. Egger-Lienz was a member of the Vienna Secession from 1909 to 1910, a professor at the Grossherzogliche Kunstschule in Weimar from 1912 to 1913, and then settled in the vicinity of Bozen (now Bolzano, Italy). During World War I he depicted troops in action and after injury in paintings that give a penetrating insight into the power of unleashed force, as in *To the Nameless of 1914* (1916; Vienna, Heeresgesch. Mus.). After the war he painted peasant scenes again, this time in a depersonalized way and often with religious undertones, as in *Christ's Resurrection* (1924; Innsbruck, Tirol. Landesmus.).

BIBLIOGRAPHY

W. Kirschl: *Albin Egger-Lienz: Das Gesamtwerk* (Vienna, 1977)
K. Sotriffer: *Albin Egger-Lienz* (Vienna, 1983)

EDWIN LACHNIT

Eggers, Bartholomeus (*b* Amsterdam, *c.* 1637; *d* Amsterdam, before 23 Feb 1692). Dutch sculptor. In 1646 he was the pupil of Peeter Verbruggen (i) in Antwerp.

Between 1650 and 1654 he moved to Amsterdam, where Artus Quellinus (i), who was Verbruggen's brother-in-law, was working on decoration for the new Stadhuis (now the Koninklijk Paleis). Eggers worked for Quellinus on the extensive sculptural programme of the Stadhuis, but its stylistic uniformity is such that it is impossible to identify Eggers's contribution. He was probably also responsible for part of the sculpture of the tomb of *Feldmarschall Otto von Sparr* (Berlin, Marienkirche, installed 1663), which Quellinus was commissioned to make.

In 1663 Eggers entered Amsterdam's Guild of St Luke, and from then on he worked as an independent master: in that year he had already started to execute sculpture for Frederick William, Elector of Brandenburg, who was to become his most important patron. Eggers also did much work for Johann Maurits, Count of Nassau-Siegen, the Stadholder of Cleve, at his residence in The Hague, the Mauritshuis. In 1664 he made an alabaster bust of *Johann Mauritz* that was first placed in the Mauritshuis gardens and moved in 1669 to its present site, the Fürstengruft (ducal tomb) in Siegen. To accompany the bust, Eggers made three small groups of putti (destr.), as well as four large statues (destr.) for the garden grotto. In 1665 Eggers joined The Hague artists' confraternity. From 1665 to 1667 he worked on the marble funerary monument of *Admiral Jacob van Wassenaar-Obdam* in the Grote Kerk (St Jacobskerk) in The Hague. This monument, his best and most famous work, was designed by the painter Cornelis Moninckx (*c.* 1623–66). Between 1668 and 1689 Eggers made a relief showing the weighing of cheese for the Waag (weigh-house) in Gouda.

Eggers made many statues of children: the few extant specimens include boys representing *Africa* and *Asia* (St Petersburg, Menshikov Pal.), while a marble child representing *Prudence* (*c.* 1670; Amsterdam, Hist. Mus.) has also been ascribed to him. In 1670, being again in Amsterdam, he made a Bentheimer stone *Mercury* (untraced) for Hendrik de Keyser I's Beurs (Exchange). In 1673 he executed a marble bust, signed and dated, of the Amsterdam burgomaster *Johannes Munter* (Amsterdam, Rijksmus.). He also produced a number of pieces for Johann Mauritz's gardens in Cleve, including a *Putto on a Dolphin* (1678; destr. 1794) for one of the lakes. Other pieces there attributed to him include two marble busts representing emperors (Cleve, priv. col.); an *Apollo* (destr.) for the Lustgarten (pleasure garden); as well as two figures, now severely damaged, probably also intended for the Lustgarten, and a female figure, also heavily damaged (all Cleve, Städt. Mus. Haus Koekkoek).

In 1674 Eggers completed for Frederick William 12 marble busts of Roman emperors (Berlin, Schloss Charlottenburg gardens; lead copies, Amsterdam, Rijksmus.). In that same year he was commissioned to make eight small putti in Bentheimer stone. Between 1670 and 1692 he made alterations to the tomb by Rombout Verhulst of *Carl Hieronymus Baron of In- en Kniphuizen and Anna van Ewsum* (Midwolde, Dutch Reformed church), adding the figure of *Georg Wilhelm van In- en Kniphuizen*, Anna's second husband. In 1682 Eggers supplemented the busts of the 12 emperors with another 12 representing the emperors' wives, as well as executing a marble *Minerva* on a vase with four dolphins (all Berlin, Schloss Charlottenburg). The *Minerva* was a copy of Artus Quellinus's *Minerva* (Cleve, Städt. Mus. Haus Koekkoek) made for Johann Mauritz.

In 1685 Frederick William commissioned Eggers to make 11 life-size marble statues of *Electors of Brandenburg*, to which, after Frederick William's death, were added statues of his successor *Frederick II* and of *Julius Caesar*, *Constantine the Great*, *Charlemagne* and *Rudolf I of Habsburg*. Eggers lived to complete most of the 16 statues, of which 14 survive (Potsdam, Schloss Sanssouci). Around 1686 he made a similar life-size statue of *Landgrave Charles of Hesse-Kassel* (Kassel, Schloss Wilhelmshöhe), and he is also credited with the bust of *Admiral Maarten Harpertszoon Tromp* (Amsterdam, Kweeksch. Zeevaart). A marble putto, an allegorical representation of *Prudence* (*c.* 1670; Amsterdam, Hist. Mus.), has also been attributed to him. Eggers was a reputable sculptor, valued by his contemporaries; his talent has, however, been overshadowed by those of Artus Quellinus and Rombout Verhulst.

BIBLIOGRAPHY

E. Neurdenberg: *De zeventiende eeuwsche beeldhouwkunst in de Noordelijke Nederlanden* [17th-century sculpture in the northern Netherlands] (Amsterdam, 1947), pp. 255–62

J. Leeuwenberg and W. Halsema-Kubes: *Beeldhouwwerk in het Rijksmuseum: Catalogus* [Sculpture in the Rijksmuseum: a catalogue] (The Hague and Amsterdam, 1973), pp. 242–3

W. Halsema-Kubes: 'Bartholomeus Eggers keizers- en keizerinnen busten voor keurvorst Friedrich Wilhelm van Brandenburg' [Bartholomeus Eggers's busts of emperors for Frederick William, Elector of Brandenburg], *Bull. Rijksmus.*, xxxvi (1988)

WILHELMINA HALSEMA-KUBES

Eggers, (Hartwig Karl) Friedrich (*b* Rostock, 27 Nov 1819; *d* Berlin, 11 Aug 1872). German art historian, writer and teacher. From 1841 to 1848 he studied history, archaeology and art history in Rostock, Leipzig, Munich and Berlin. He worked as a language teacher and novelist in Berlin from 1844, becoming editor of the *Mecklenburgische Zeitung* in Schwerin for a short time in 1849. He soon returned to Berlin, and in 1850 he co-founded the Verbindung für Historische Kunst. Subsequently supporting himself mainly from lecturing and writing, Eggers undertook an extensive trip in 1862–3 through Germany, France and England. In 1863 he was appointed professor of art history at the Akademie der Künste, Berlin. He also taught art history at the Gewerbe- und Bauakademie, Berlin, and gave lectures on Classical literature. In 1872 he was appointed as an adviser on artistic affairs to the Minister of Culture, resigning shortly after for reasons of health. Eggers's main area of research was German art from the end of the 18th century, and he studied, among others, Adolf von Menzel, Christian Daniel Rauch, Johann Gottfried Schadow, Karl Friedrich Schinkel and Bertel Thorvaldsen. However, he also studied van Dyck and Rembrandt. Eggers adhered to a traditional form of art historical writing, investigating aesthetic and philosophical questions rather than exploring the historicity of objects and techniques, and he remained untouched by the new movement towards specialization in art history that was then taking hold. He nevertheless distinguished himself by his precise and prescient analyses, and he exercised a considerable influence, particularly as a teacher and lecturer. He was also greatly respected among practising artists.

WRITINGS

Von der erziehenden Macht der Kunst für die Jugend (diss., U. Rostock, 1848)

Zweckmässigkeit und Schönheit (Berlin, 1866)

Vier Vorträge aus der neueren Kunstgeschichte (Berlin, 1867)

Blick auf die Kunstrichtung der Gegenwart (Berlin, 1867/R Berlin and Breslau, 1870)

with K. Eggers: *Christian Daniel Rauch*, 5 vols (Berlin, 1873–91)

BIBLIOGRAPHY

ADB

Reden bei der Gedächtnisfeier für Friedrich Eggers (Berlin, 1872)

H. W. Seidel: *Theodor Storms Briefe an Friedrich Eggers, mit einer Lebensskizze von F. E. und Gedichtproben* (Berlin, 1911)

W. von Gossler, ed.: 'Friedrich Eggers und Gustav von Gossler: Ein Briefwechsel', *Z. Ver. Gesch. Berlins*, n.s., lviii (1941), pp. 26–35

W. Gorzny and H. Schmuck, eds: *Gesamtverzeichnis des deutschsprachigen Schrifttums, 1700–1910*, xxxi (Munich, 1981), pp. 277f

WERNER WILHELM SCHNABEL

Eggert, (Georg Peter) Hermann (*b* Burg, nr Magdeburg, 3 Jan 1844; *d* Weimar, 1920). German architect. He studied architecture at the Bauakademie in Berlin with Johann Heinrich Strack. Early in his life he won prizes in competitions, for example with his designs (unexecuted) for Berlin Cathedral (1869) and the Niederwald national monument (1873). From 1875 he worked in Strasbourg, where he won further prizes for his urban planning schemes and his designs (1878; unexecuted) for the Kaiser-Wilhelm Universität. He also built an observatory (1877–82). In 1883 he was awarded the prestigious commission for the Kaiserpalast (1883–9; now the Palais du Rhin). His design followed Palladian principles in its monumental planning, but Eggert stressed the building's national significance through ornamental and decorative details derived from the German Renaissance. During his time in Strasbourg, Eggert won the competition (1880) for the railway station in Frankfurt am Main. This was seen as the most significant and influential of the many competitions for railway stations in the last third of the 19th century. Eggert was commissioned to execute the building (with some alterations) despite criticism from the architectural press. The critics saw the architecture of the façade and the station building as being too plain and taking second place to the engineering design of the train shed. In 1889 he was called to Berlin, to the Ministerium für Öffentliches Arbeiten, where he was mainly responsible for church building. Eggert left the Civil Service in 1898 for Hannover, to oversee the execution of his designs for the new Rathaus (1898–1913), a large building with a central dome in the German Renaissance style. In 1909, however, with only the exterior completed, the town council terminated Eggert's contract because he refused to comply with the council's wishes for interior designs in the new Art Nouveau style. He was replaced by the younger Gustav Halmhuber. Eggert then moved to Weimar, where he lived until his death.

BIBLIOGRAPHY

Thieme–Becker; Wasmuth

C. Kranz-Michaelis: *Rathäuser in deutschen Kaiserreich, 1871–1918*, Stud. Kst 19. Jahrhunderts, xxxiii (Munich, 1976)

U. Krings: *Bahnhofsarchitektur Deutsche Gross-stadtbahnhöfe des Historismus*, Stud. Kst 19. Jahrhunderts, xlvi (Munich, 1985)

Eggl, Wilhelm. *See* EGCKL, WILHELM.

Eggleston, William (*b* Memphis, TN, July 1939). American photographer. Eggleston first became interested in photography in 1962 when he was introduced to the work of Henri Cartier-Bresson. By 1966 he had begun to photograph almost exclusively in colour. Eggleston is regarded as a pioneer among contemporary photographers in the exploration of the artistic potential of colour photography, which had been out of favour because of the impermanence of its tones and its supposed incompatibility with the formal interests of artistic photography. His work came to public attention in the 1970s when it was featured in several exhibitions, notably in 1976 when his one-man show *William Eggleston's Guide* was held at the Museum of Modern Art in New York.

Eggleston's large-format prints of snapshot-like subject-matter create icons out of images from everyday life in the south-east United States. Demonstrating his sensitivity to combinations of highly saturated secondary and tertiary colour, they explore the television-like, surreal intensity normally achieved through dye-transfer prints. These prints monumentalize ordinary scenes of his native south (*see* PHOTOGRAPHY, colour pl. III, fig. 1), such as a wisteria-shrouded pick-up truck, a table set for dinner, or the lavender and aquamarine tiles surrounding a Memphis bathtub, and focus upon the environments of cultural heroes of the south. For his series *Election Eve* (1976) he photographed the barren streets of Plains, GA, on the evening before the election of President Carter. *Graceland* (1984), a portfolio of interiors from Elvis Presley's estate in Memphis, documents the gaudy trappings of the singer's wealth. Eggleston's tight, concentric compositions, which he once remarked to Alfred Barr were based on the Confederate flag, work with the size and colour of his prints to elevate them to the scale and importance of painting.

BIBLIOGRAPHY
M. Kozloff: 'How to Mystify Colour Photography', *Artforum*, xv (1976), pp. 50–52
Mirrors and Windows: American Photography since 1960 (exh. cat., ed. J. Szarkowski; New York, MOMA, 1978)
M. Holborn: 'Colour Codes', *Aperture*, xcvi (1984), pp. 8–15 [on Eggleston's *Graceland*]
P. Schneider: 'The Berlin Series', *Aperture*, xcvi (1984), pp. 60–75
MARY CHRISTIAN

Egg tempera. *See under* TEMPERA.

Egidio da Malines [della Riviera, Egidio Fiammingho]. *See* VLIETE, GILLIS VAN DEN.

Eginhard. *See* EINHARD.

Egkl, Wilhelm. *See* EGCKL, WILHELM.

Egley, William Maw (*b* London, 1826; *d* 20 Feb 1916). English painter. He was the son of the portrait painter and miniaturist William Egley (1798–1870). Under his father's tutelage he began painting around the age of 14. His earliest works were the sort of fashionable literary illustrations of Molière and Shakespeare that Charles Dickens satirized in the first issue of *Household Words* (1850).

Egley was hired by William Powell Frith to paint backgrounds, and under Frith's influence began painting domestic genre scenes, especially of children's play, for example *Coming Events Cast their Shadow before* (1861; U. Bath, Holburne of Menstrie Mus.), in which a boy blows a horn loudly in a girl's ear. He recorded the rural custom of cheering largess in *Hullo Largess! A Harvest Scene in Norfolk* (1860; priv. col., see Reynolds, p. 100). His best-known work is *Omnibus Life in London* (1859; London, Tate), which shows the crowded interior of an omnibus with a mother holding on to her fashionably dressed young son as he squirms on her lap. Egley's efforts were often criticized for harshness of execution and lapses of scale or perspective. He had a special interest, recorded in his account book, in the detailed rendering of costume, especially the elaborately crocheted pantaloons and drawers fashionable for children. These are painted with great care and exactness. He also wrote of such undergarments very extensively in his descriptions of the paintings. He returned to costume and historical pieces in the 1860s, employing a mannered Victorian vision of the 18th century. His accounts list over 1000 paintings, but reviews were disappointing for the greater part of his life.

UNPUBLISHED SOURCES
London, V&A [account books]

BIBLIOGRAPHY
G. Reynolds: *Victorian Painting* (London, 1966)
C. Wood: *Victorian Panorama* (London, 1976, rev. 1990)
LESLIE WILLIAMS

Egmont, Justus van (*b* Leiden, 22 Sept 1601; *d* Antwerp, 8 Jan 1674). Flemish painter and tapestry designer. He was initially a pupil of Caspar van den Hoecke (*d* 1648). After a period in Italy, sometime after 1618, he joined the workshop of Peter Paul Rubens. He is one of the few artists whose collaboration with Rubens is documented. He is mentioned several times between 1625 and 1628, for example in 1625, when he was involved in the installation of some of the 44 decorative panels ('the Medici Cycle') commissioned from Rubens in 1622 by Marie de' Medici for the Palais de Luxembourg in Paris. He may also have collaborated in painting some of the panels. In 1628 he became a Master in the Antwerp Guild of St Luke. Immediately afterwards he left for Paris, where he acquired a considerable reputation, not only as a painter but also as a print publisher. In 1648 he was one of the founders of the Académie Royale de Peinture et de Sculpture. After 1649 various Flemish archives mention him again: first in Brussels (until *c.* 1655) and then in Antwerp, where he settled.

Van Egmont's name as a portrait painter must have been made in Paris. There his sitters included the French royal family as well as such prominent members of the French aristocracy as the Duc de Chevreuse and the Orléans family (portraits mainly known through engraved copies; good examples, Vienna, Ksthist. Mus.). He also executed the decorations in the château of Balleroy for the Orléans family. His portraits show a stylistic refinement that recalls Anthony van Dyck. The same combination of elegance and nonchalant self-assurance in the sitter's pose recurs in the portraits that van Egmont painted in the 1650s after his return to the southern Netherlands, for example the *Archduke Leopold William* (Vienna, Ksthist. Mus.) and *Queen Christina of Sweden* (1654; Stockholm, priv. col., see 1966 exh. cat., pl. 33).

Among van Egmont's most important works after his return from Paris are the tapestry designs for several series based on scenes from Roman history. Only the *History of Zenobia* series (before 1665; examples in Brussels, Musées Royaux A. & Hist., and elsewhere) can be ascribed to him on the basis of documentary evidence, but stylistic parallels suggest that he was also responsible for the *Augustus, Caesar and Cleopatra* cycle (e.g. Vienna, Ksthist. Mus.). Judging from the existence of several copies, these tapestries, executed in Brussels in the workshops of such leading weavers as Geraert van der Strecken (*d* 1677) and Gerard Peemans (*fl* 1665), became well known. The designs for them are among the most interesting examples of Flemish 17th-century secular history painting, possessing the typical intensity of the High Baroque style, in which the drama of the scenes is expressed through the figures' pathetic gestures and exaggerated mimicry.

BIBLIOGRAPHY

'Justus van Egmont, 1601–1674', *Duits Q.*, i (1963), pp. 12–15
Christina, Queen of Sweden (exh. cat., Stockholm, Nmus., 1966)
M. L. Hairs: *Dans le sillage de Rubens: Les Peintres d'histoire anversois au XVIIe siècle* (Liège, 1977), pp. 44–6
Brusselse wandtapijten (fl Rubens' eeuw (exh. cat. by G. Delmarcel, Brussels, Musées Royaux A. & Hist., 1977)
J. Wilhelm: 'Le Décor peint de la grand' salle du château de Balleroy', *Bull. Soc. Hist. A. Fr.* (1985), pp. 61–84
——: 'Portraits peints à Paris par Juste d'Egmont', *Bull. Soc. Hist. A. Fr.* (1987), pp. 25–44

HANS VLIEGHE

Egremont, Earls of. *See* WYNDHAM.

Egry, József (*b* Újlak, Zala, 15 March 1883; *d* Badacsonytomaj, Lake Balaton, 19 June 1951). Hungarian painter and draughtsman. After a difficult childhood he studied first in Munich and Paris with the help of private sponsors, then from 1906 to 1908 he attended the Academy of Fine Arts in Budapest, where he had already exhibited (from 1901). His early works are naturalist in style, but some display a Secessionist tendency in the use of contours and flatly designated space (e.g. *Prehistoric Age*, 1910; priv. col., see 1971 exh. cat., no. 20). In 1912 he went on a study trip to Belgium. The pictures he painted there display a possible leaning towards Constructivism; though the paint is thickly applied, the contours are strongly delineated, as in his *Dock Workers IV* (1912; Budapest, N.G.).

Egry was wounded in World War I and was taken to Keszthely, on Lake Balaton, to convalesce. After his recovery he settled in the nearby village of Badacsonytomaj, where, apart from a few short trips, he remained for the rest of his life. Here he managed to develop his own style. He painted Lake Balaton and its surroundings, with lone figures, mostly fishermen, blending into the landscape. The great expanse of water became a symbol of his yearning for freedom. He gradually attained a lyrical pantheism, though he never fully abandoned the Expressionist forms of his early work. In the Expressionist-influenced paintings of the early 1920s, for example *Lake Balaton Fishermen* (1923; Keszthely, Balaton Mus.), the expressive content is conveyed through shafts of light penetrating a seemingly infinite space, where figures are almost eclipsed by the dramatic power of the water and the exaggerated glow of the sun.

From *c.* 1925 Egry consolidated his style and reduced the dramatic tone. The depiction of landscape becomes more spiritual; the individual details blend into the all pervasive sunlight and become a single cosmic vision. The real subject of the paintings is light, space and infinity, suggesting timelessness and universality and exalting vision. In some of his early paintings Egry had used crayon, and in others oils, but in his later work he employed a technique that mixed both, managing to create soft impasto tonalities and also to highlight the structure and contrasts. In general, because of his thin painting method, his works have a strong graphic quality. These features can be clearly seen in *Self-portrait in Sunshine* (1927), *Clearing Up* (1931) and *Golden Gate* (1943–4; all Budapest, N.G.), among others.

Egry's drawings are closely related to the paintings. Produced in pen and ink, Indian ink, charcoal, watercolour or pastel, they bear witness to his excellent drawing skills. They range from the energetic realist *Self-portrait I* (charcoal, 1920; priv. col., see 1971 exh. cat., no. 196), to the softer and looser *Fishing* (oil pastel on paper, 1941; priv. col., see 1971 exh. cat., no. 173). In the 1930s, whenever he went to Budapest, Egry associated with the GRESHAM GROUP, meeting both friends and patrons. He exhibited in Hungary and abroad (e.g. Berlin, Gal. Gurlitt, 1926 and Vienna, Neumann & Salzer Gal., 1936). A memorial retrospective was held in the Hungarian National Gallery in Budapest in 1971.

BIBLIOGRAPHY

I. Ártinger: *József Egry*, Ars Hungarica, ii (Budapest, 1932)
L. Németh: 'La Peinture de József Egry, 1883–1951', *Acta Hist. A. Acad. Sci. Hung.*, vii (1961), pp. 303–35
József Egry (exh. cat., ed. B. Szij, Budapest, N.G., 1971) [with Fr. summary]
Egry breviárium, intro. by D. Keresztúry (Veszprém, 1973)
S. Láncz: 'Kompozíciós modellek Egry József életművében' [Compositional models in the work of József Egry], *A. Hung.*, ii (1974), pp. 127–42
——: *Egry József* (Budapest, 1980)

MÁRIA SZOBOR-BERNÁTH

Egypt, Arab Republic of [Arab. Jumhūriyya Miṣr al-'Arabiyya]. Country in North Africa extending into Asia at the south-eastern end of the Mediterranean Sea, with its capital at Cairo. It is bounded in the west by Libya, in the south by Sudan and in the east by the Gaza Strip, Israel, the Gulf of Aqaba and the Red Sea. Although its total area is over one million sq. km, this is largely desert; the cultivated and settled part, the Nile Valley and Delta and the oases, is only a quarter of the country's area. (For a description of its geography *see* EGYPT, ANCIENT, §I, 1.) It is the most populous state in the Arab world. Traditionally the majority have been fellahin, peasant farmers; despite massive rural migration to the towns, about half the working population is still engaged on the land. The majority are Sunni Muslim and perhaps 10-15% are Copts, the largest Christian minority. Many Jews emigrated in the 1940s and 1950s. At the beginning of the 20th century there were over 100,000 Europeans, but most left in the 1960s.

Egypt is predominantly an agricultural country, though its industrial programme began in the 1830s, based on textile production from cotton; cotton production dominated agriculture until the 1950s. The construction of the Aswan High Dam (1960–70) produced numerous ecological and environmental problems (e.g. the trapping of silt), and the huge reservoir, Lake Nasser, inundated the ancient land of NUBIA, uprooting its people and its major monuments. With limited natural resources, Egypt has rapid population growth and widespread poverty. In the early 1990s the economy was increasingly dependent on Suez Canal dues, earnings by migrant workers, oil revenues and tourism. This article covers the art produced in the country in the 19th and 20th centuries: for its earlier history *see* EGYPT, ANCIENT; GREECE, ANCIENT; ROME, ANCIENT; EARLY CHRISTIAN AND BYZANTINE ART; COPTIC ART; and ISLAMIC ART.

I. Introduction. II. Architecture. III. Painting and sculpture. IV. Decorative arts. V. Art education. VI. Museums and galleries.

I. Introduction.

Western ideas entered the Ottoman province of Egypt during the French occupation (1798–1801). After the French withdrawal, a new dynasty was established by Muhammad 'Ali (*reg* 1805–48), which lasted until 1953. Modernization began under Muhammad 'Ali and was at its height under his grandson Isma'il (*reg* 1863–79; Khedive from 1867). The opening of the Suez Canal (1869) accelerated the exposure to Western culture, and Isma'il used the occasion to present his country as part of the European world rather than Africa. Cities and towns were transformed, but accumulated debts and an army-led revolt against the European-backed Khedive Tawfiq (*reg* 1879–92) prompted the British invasion of 1882; Egypt was officially a British protectorate from 1914 to 1922. Increased demands for independence, in particular the uprising of 1919, led to the establishment of a constitutional monarchy under Fu'ad I (*reg* 1917–36; King from 1922). In 1936 limited independence was granted under King Faruq (*reg* 1936–52). In 1942 the British forced the King to agree to the Wafd Party forming the government, to ensure Egypt remained an ally in the British war effort. This action sowed the seeds for the 1952 coup, and discontent increased after the defeat of Egyptian troops in Palestine in 1948–9. In 1952 resistance to the British culminated in riots in Cairo, when hundreds of buildings, including the 19th-century Shepheard's Hotel, were burnt down.

The Free Officers' Movement, led by Colonel Gamal Abdul Nasser, forced Faruq to abdicate in July 1952, and Egypt was declared a republic in 1953. A year later Nasser became head of state, and the last British troops left in 1956. Under Nasser's highly personal rule, a programme followed of economic, land and social reforms, industrialization and the building of the Aswan High Dam. Censorship was imposed, and free political debate was restricted, but education was greatly expanded. In July 1956, one month after being elected president (the sole candidate), Nasser nationalized the Suez Canal Company. In response, Egypt was jointly attacked by Israel, Britain and France, but international condemnation forced their withdrawal. In 1958–61 there was a brief union with Syria. Egyptianization and socialist measures in the 1960s caused a major change in the structure of society; numerous Egyptians of foreign origin, particularly Greeks and Italians, were driven out, taking valuable skills with them. In 1967 the Egyptian army was heavily defeated by Israel, who occupied the Gaza Strip and Sinai, and the Suez Canal was closed (reopened 1975).

Nasser was succeeded by Anwar Sadat in 1970. The attempt to end the Israeli occupation in Sinai in 1973 failed but boosted Egyptian morale, and there was a shift in foreign policy towards the USA and away from the USSR. Despite US aid the economic situation worsened, and an austerity package caused riots in 1977. In 1978 Sadat signed the Camp David Accords with Israel and the USA, and a peace treaty was signed in 1979, which returned Sinai to Egypt (1982) but resulted in the severing of ties with other Arab states. In 1981 Sadat was assassinated, and power passed to the vice-president, Husni Mubarak, who strengthened ties with the Arab world.

II. Architecture.

During the reign of Isma'il an urban renewal plan for Cairo was implemented by the engineer and statesman 'Ali Mubarak, and medieval buildings were demolished to create European-style boulevards and plazas. The European architects who were increasingly employed on buildings projects worked in a variety of styles, including the neo-Islamic (or Islamic Revival) style of architecture, in which 'Islamic' elements were applied as a surface veneer to buildings. Such features, for example, were incorporated in the design for the Gazira Palace by Julius Franz (1831–1915), who was engaged for the project by Isma'il in 1863. The neo-Islamic style of architecture remained fashionable until the 1930s. The architects who worked in this style included the Hungarian Max Herz (*b* 1856), who contributed the final design of the mosque of al-Rifa'i in Cairo (completed 1911), and the Italian Antoine Lasciac (1856–1946), who was active in Egypt from 1882 to 1936 and was chief architect of the khedival palaces from 1907 to 1917.

Neo-Islamic structures were also built in the Cairene suburb of Heliopolis, founded by the Belgian developer Edouard Empain in 1906. They included the Heliopolis Palace Hotel, designed by the Belgian architect Ernst Jaspar, which was for a while the largest hotel in the world. Among the Egyptian architects that came to the fore at this time were Mahmud Fahmi al-Mi'mar (1856–1925), who designed the Ministry of Waqfs building (1915) in a neo-Islamic style, and his son Mustafa Fahmi (1886–1972). The latter, who was educated in Paris and returned to Egypt in 1912, worked in the Public Building Service, becoming its Director in 1926. His buildings included the mausoleum of Sa'd Zaghlul (1928–31; see fig. 1) in the 'neo-pharaonic' style, which was adopted by a number of architects in the early 20th century.

In the mid-20th century some Egyptian architects began to challenge the dominance of European styles, both colonial and modern international, and sought to create a contemporary Egyptian style in architecture and urban planning. The most influential was HASSAN FATHY, whose source of inspiration from the late 1930s lay in the indigenous tradition of mud-brick village architecture (*see*

1. Mustafa Fahmi: mausoleum of Sa'd Zaghlul, Cairo, Egypt, 1928–31

VERNACULAR ARCHITECTURE, §II, 7(iii)), though he also used concrete and other materials. Mud-brick is still the commonest building material in rural Egypt. Fathy stimulated the reassessment of Islamic architecture and the use of local materials and local technology. His work and writings inspired ABDEL WAHED EL-WAKIL, whose buildings draw on the indigenous architecture of Egypt and the Middle East to provide a modern traditional style. Mud-brick buildings are labour-intensive and not easily adapted for electricity and piped water, but they are harmonious and well suited to the climate and environment.

Ramses Wissa Wassef (1911–74), architect, potter and weaver, has also been influential. Born in Cairo into a Coptic family, he studied architecture at the Ecole des Beaux-Arts in Paris, and in 1936 he joined the architectural department of the School of Fine Arts in Cairo (retiring in 1969 as head of the department). Wissa Wassef deplored the ugliness of much contemporary architecture in Egypt and sought to develop a style that gave his country's architecture a national character, influenced by the way of life of its people, its cultural inheritance and its climate. On a visit to Upper Egypt with Hassan Fathy and their students in 1940 he was impressed by Nubian village architecture (e.g. around Aswan) with its mud-brick vaults and domes. For his Art Centre at Harrania, near Giza (1951–70), he used mud-brick and Nubian features for the workshops and museums. The buildings are distinctive for their simple beauty and they offer shade and coolness. The first building was erected by bricklayers brought from Upper Egypt, the others by his students. The Centre won the Aga Khan Award for Architecture in 1983. Another of his buildings was the Mahmud Mukhtar Sculpture Museum in Cairo (1962). It is a two-storey building that also contains Mukhtar's mausoleum.

In the early 20th century Cairo had two distinct areas, the old city and the modern city, the latter gradually encircling the former. From the 1930s the pace of urbanization was rapid, and in the 1990s there remained an acute shortage of housing. As the largest city in Africa and the Middle East, Cairo is particularly overcrowded. Urban development schemes were undertaken at various locations.

The New Valley project, begun in the late 1950s, successfully provided new settlements at Kharga and Dakhla oases. The Isma'iliya Development project (begun 1974) was an alternative approach to tackling massive urban growth. Founded in 1863 by the French engineer Ferdinand de Lesseps as a base camp for the construction of the Suez Canal, and laid out with wide avenues and squares, Isma'iliya was badly damaged by shelling in 1967, as were other towns along the Suez Canal. The inhabitants began returning in the 1970s, and a development plan was inaugurated concentrating on Port Said (founded 1859), Isma'iliya and Suez. At Isma'iliya the emphasis was on upgrading existing settlements and on self-help construction by the community rather than government-imposed housing.

At the industrial centre of Helwan (c. 20 km south of Cairo), the New Community project begun in the early 1980s, designed by Egyptian and foreign consultants, involved the government providing the infrastructure and enabling low-income families to buy plots of land, each plot already prepared with foundations and service facilities. After 1976 satellite towns such as Medinet el-Obour and Medinet 15 Mayo were planned to ease the burden on Cairo; others, such as Medinet Ashara Ramadan and Medinet el-Sadat, were intended to be self-sufficient, independent towns. In the early 1980s new settlements were planned for the Sinai Peninsula.

Besides housing schemes there were also commissions for public buildings. After the destruction by fire in 1971 of the Opera House in Opera Square (built 1869) in Cairo, for example, a new opera house was planned, and in 1985 work started on a Cultural and Educational Complex (also known as the National Cultural Centre) in the Gazira exhibition grounds, as a gift from the Japanese government. It was designed by a team of architects and engineers from the Japanese firm Nikken Sekkei, led by the architect Koichiro Shikida. The complex (opened 1988) includes the New Cairo Opera House, with 1200 seats, a theatre-exhibition centre, an open-air theatre, libraries, an art gallery and an opera museum. In 1992 the Aga Khan Award for Architecture was given to the Cultural Park for Children (1982–91) in the Sayyida Zaynab district of Cairo. Designed by Abdel Halim Ibrahim, a professor at Cairo University, it employs domes, arched windows and fountains and uses traditional materials in keeping with the surroundings. The park is laid out according to geometrical patterns that are used by neighbouring schools to teach geometry.

III. Painting and sculpture.

The French invasion by Napoleon's armies abruptly exposed Egypt to European civilization, and during the 19th century European aesthetics were introduced to the urban Egyptian intellectual milieu. Muhammad 'Ali displayed interest in the arts and sciences and sent several study missions to Europe, which included students learning the arts of engraving, painting and sculpture. These individuals taught at technical craft schools on their return. Throughout the 19th century the Egyptian élite showed their desire to emulate the West by commissioning Europeans to decorate their urban and rural palaces, and they imported craftsmen to train local decorators in *trompe l'oeil* decoration. Among the European Orientalist painters who visited the country were David Roberts, Eugène Fromentin, Adrien Dauzats, John Varley, Charles Gleyre, William Holman Hunt and Jean-Léon Gérôme. Some, such as John Frederick Lewis, stayed in Cairo for many years. Yet, despite their numbers, these artists were only popular among a minority of upper-class Egyptians. In 1891 the resident Orientalist painters held Egypt's first exhibition, at the Opera House.

In 1908 Prince Yusuf Kamal opened the School of Fine Arts in Cairo, the first institution in Egypt to teach Western art. For 20 years the School provided free tuition and training for talented Egyptian students, requiring no prerequisite other than the wish to study art. The lack of accomplished Egyptian artists in Western trends forced the School to employ foreigners for tuition. The first students comprised the nucleus of the pioneer generation of modern Egyptian artists. They included the sculptor MAHMUD MUKHTAR and the painters Muhammad Naghi, MAHMUD SAID, Ahmed Sabry (1889–1955) and Raghib Ayyad (1892–1980). Ayyad went on to study in Rome and later became Director of the Museum of Modern Art in Cairo. This group of Egyptian artists laid down the basic concepts of their country's modern art movement. Mukhtar, who is considered the father of modern Arab sculpture, developed the 'neo-pharaonic' style in his work; his monumental pink granite statue *Egyptian Awakening* (1919–28; see fig. 2) dominates the entrance to Cairo University.

Art societies played a crucial role in the advancement of Egyptian modern art. The first art association established in Egypt was the Society of Fine Arts (founded 1918). The Society, which included Mukhtar, Naghi, Said, Sabry, Ayyad and several resident foreign artists, held two exhibitions. In 1920 the art patron Fu'ad Abdul Malik created the House of Arts and Crafts in Cairo to promote the fine arts, with Ayyad as its secretary. The first of their annual exhibitions, Salon du Caire (1922), included work by Egyptian and foreign artists. In 1923 Abdul Malik founded the Society of the Friends of Art, which sought to cultivate, through lectures and exhibitions, artistic taste among the public. In 1925 the government allocated an annual subsidy for the Society as well as a budget to buy works of art. In 1927 a new association called La Chimère was founded by artists from Mukhtar's circle, and in 1928 they held their first exhibition. By 1930, however, most of the group members had dispersed. New avant-garde groups appeared in the 1930s, the most important being ART AND FREEDOM, whose members included the painters Fu'ad Kamil (1919–73) and Ramsis Yunan (1914–66), both of whom were inspired by Surrealism. In 1946 Husayn Yusuf Amin (b 1906) founded the Contemporary Art Group, which derived inspiration from popular and folk images. The painters 'ABD AL-HADI AL-JAZZAR and

2. Mahmud Mukhtar: *Egyptian Awakening*, granite, Cairo University gate, Cairo, 1919–28

Hamid Nada (b 1924) were the most prominent among the members.

At the time of the Revolution of 1952 artists were inspired by political developments, and a number of painters turned to the Egyptian peasantry for their subject-matter. Since then Egyptian painters have explored a range of styles, deriving inspiration from Western art and from ancient Egyptian and Islamic art. Calligraphic art has become important, while other artists have explored aspects of their Egyptian heritage. Among those who reached prominence in the late 20th century were Taha Hussain (b 1929) and members of the Axis Group, who were active in the 1980s to promote modernism: Abd al-Rahman al-Nashar (b 1932), Mustafa al-Razzaz (b 1940), Farghali Abd al-Hafiz (b 1944) and Ahmad Nawar (b 1945). The tradition of sculpture continued in the works of Habib Gorgy (1892–1965), Ahmed Osman (1907–65), Abdel Kader Rizk (1908–70), Ahmed Abdel Wahab (b 1932), Samir Nashid (b 1933), Farouk Ibrahim (b 1937) and Sabry Nashid (b 1938).

IV. Decorative arts.

In the late 19th century the European demand for inlaid metalwares and other items that alluded to the artistic traditions of the Mamluks (reg 1250–1517) encouraged Egyptian craftsmen to produce imitations of Mamluk objects. Such work, known as Mamluk Revival, was produced largely in Cairo and Damascus. The inlay techniques of Mamluk Revival metalwork, however, were distinct from those of the Mamluk period (*see* ISLAMIC ART, §IV, 1(iii) and 3(iii)). The craftsmen gouged projections from the brass or copper surface to secure the silver and copper wires and then hammered flat the projections over the wires and burnished them. Mamluk Revival metalwork remained popular in the early 20th century, although after World War I demand for it declined. Metalworking has, nevertheless, remained an important craft in Egypt, encouraged by the creation of art centres where various techniques were taught and practised. Jewellery is made in a range of designs, from ancient to modern, although gold has replaced silver as the preferred metal. Woodwork has also been important in the late 19th century and 20th, including furniture made in a conservative style. Intricate boxes and game-boards inlaid with ivory, mother-of-pearl or different coloured woods are also made.

In 1894 the Egyptian government invited William De Morgan (*see* DE MORGAN, (1)) to supervise the porcelain industry in Egypt, and a large factory was set up in Old Cairo. Said al-Sadr (1909–86), who trained in Britain and became a pioneer ceramicist in Egypt, was influenced by De Morgan's ceramics and by Bernard Leach, who encouraged him to study his own heritage.

On his return to Egypt, al-Sadr introduced ceramic studies at the School of Applied Arts in Cairo, retiring in 1969. He also established a ceramics centre in Fustat to train the sons of potters, which he supervised for five years, and wrote books on the art of ceramics. Other 20th-century ceramicists include Muhie al-Din Hussein (*b* 1937), Mahrus Abu Bakr (*b* 1940) and Nabil Darwish, who founded a workshop near Harrania with a gallery of ceramics. In 1992 Egypt's first International Ceramics Triennial was held in Cairo.

Among the other crafts revived in the 20th century was glassmaking. Zakaria al-Khonany, for example, who graduated from Cairo University in 1942, experimented with ancient Egyptian techniques and participated in exhibitions in the USA, Europe and Egypt. In factories in Cairo handblown Muski glass, made from recycled bottles, is used for a variety of items, some with painted designs. There has also been a revival of carpet-weaving, and both expensive pile or hand-knotted carpets and cheaper flat-woven carpets are produced. Flat-woven carpets include kilims (Helwan and Asyuti types), rag rugs and Bedouin rugs, which vary in design from tribe to tribe. The crafts of appliqué tent panels and embroidery are also important; the *kiswa*, the embroidered cover for the Ka'ba in Mecca, was traditionally made in Cairo.

Convinced that industrialization made the role of the craftsman more rather than less important, in the 1940s the architect Ramses Wissa Wassef learnt the art of weaving together with the preparation and use of natural dyes, and he began to teach the craft on high-warp looms to children in a poor quarter of Cairo. In 1951 he bought land outside the village of Harrania, near Giza, and began the Wissa Wassef Art Centre with about 12 children from the village. To prevent the deterioration of what he saw as the children's natural sense of colour and rhythm he had three rules: no designs to be made beforehand; no copying of other works of art; and no adult criticism.

3. Karima 'Ali: *Birds and the Old Tree*, wool tapestry, 2.00×1.85 m, 1985 (Harrania, Ramses Wissa Wassef Art Centre)

Tapestries were improvised on the looms and only natural vegetable dyes used for the wool; a part of the garden was devoted to plants for making dyes. The first-generation weavers began with exaggerated images of animals and birds, gradually refining their styles to provide more detail, more background and a wider variety of tones. The primary source of inspiration is the natural world—animals, birds, flowers and trees—and the weavers' everyday lives and immediate surroundings. *Birds and the Old Tree* (see fig. 3) by Karima 'Ali (*b* 1945) was begun, typically, in the bottom right-hand corner, where the weaver first created the bird above her signature; she used neither a pattern nor a sketch.

The first exhibition of tapestries was held in Cairo, Alexandria and Isma'iliya (1956–7); the first international exhibition took place in Switzerland (1958). From 1962 pottery was also taught. In the early 1990s there were about 100 people working at the Centre, both children and adults. After Wissa Wassef's death in 1974, the Art Centre was run by his widow, Sophie Habib Gorgy (*b* 1922)—who introduced cotton-weaving and batik, the only non-Egyptian craft at the Centre—and their two daughters. Suzanne Wissa Wassef (*b* 1950) formed her own group of weavers in 1972, the second generation, aiming to free them from copying the work of their predecessors and to guide them to new forms and the development of personal styles. She was also a ceramicist and was in charge of the production of stoneware ceramics. Yoanna Wissa Wassef (*b* 1952) revived the teaching of low-warp weaving in cotton, which is a more demanding skill; it produces weavings of great clarity and intricacy.

V. Art education.

Egypt was the first Arab country to formalize art education by establishing state-run institutes and schools for both applied and fine arts. During the 19th century several schools were established in Cairo to promote training in architecture and the arts, such as the School of Irrigation and Architecture (founded 1866) and the School of Applied Arts, which opened in 1868. In 1898 the Leonardo da Vinci School of Arts (closed 1976) was founded by the Italian Society of Dante Alighieri to train assistants for architects; at its inception most of the students were foreigners.

In the early 20th century Egyptian painters and sculptors trained largely at the School (later College) of Fine Arts in Cairo, which was opened in 1908 by Prince Yusuf Kamal. The first Director was the French sculptor Guillaume Laplagne, and the instructors were resident foreign artists. In 1909 Yusuf Kamal created a trust fund for a new building and scholarships for outstanding students to study abroad. The first student to be sent abroad on a scholarship, in 1911, was the sculptor Mahmud Mukhtar. From 1917 artists also began to be sent by the Egyptian government to study in the West, and in 1927 an Egyptian Academy was founded in Rome. On their return to Egypt, the graduates were absorbed as teachers into Egypt's various schools and institutes. A further training ground for artists in Cairo from the mid-20th century was the Higher Institute for Art Teachers (College of Art Education).

In 1941 the Atelier of Fine Arts was created by the Ministry of Education for outstanding graduates from the School of Fine Arts. This was the first attempt in Egypt to create postgraduate studies in art. The students at the Atelier pursued their work for two years and then contributed to an exhibition. Through lack of funds the Atelier closed in the 1960s. Some private initiatives in art education have been more successful, notably the Wissa Wassef Art Centre (see §IV above).

In Alexandria a College of Fine Arts was established in 1957 with departments in painting, sculpture, graphics, design and architecture. Its dean, the sculptor Ahmed Osman, employed such prominent local artists as Seif Wanly (1906–79), his brother Adhan Wanly and Hamid Nada as faculty members. In the 1980s the government founded new art-training institutions in areas outside Cairo and Alexandria, and in 1982 an art school was established in El Minya, a provincial city south of the capital.

VI. Museums and galleries.

The French invasion of Egypt in 1798 marked the birth of the new science of Egyptology, which attracted many archaeologists and scholars to the country in the 19th century. In 1835 a department of antiquities was established by decree, and by 1858 a museum had been organized at Bulaq by Auguste Mariette. In 1890 the contents of the museum were transferred to an annexe of the Giza Palace, where they remained until the Egyptian Museum in Cairo was opened in 1902. It now contains over 120,000 items from prehistoric times to the 6th century AD, housing the most important collection of Egyptian antiquities in the world.

There is also a Graeco-Roman Museum in Alexandria, founded in 1892, which contains items from the Greek, Roman and Byzantine eras. Smaller antiquities museums are to be found at various archaeological sites throughout Egypt. At the Coptic Museum in Cairo, founded in 1908, there are sculptures, frescoes, icons, manuscripts, textiles, metalwork, glass, ceramics and woodwork, including items recovered from excavation at monasteries.

The collection of the Museum of Islamic Art in Cairo (before 1952 known as the Museum of Arab Art) has grown since the late 19th century. It includes items recovered from archaeological excavations at Fustat, the old quarter of Cairo, which began in 1912 and have continued sporadically since, providing invaluable information about the material life of medieval Egypt. The Islamic architectural heritage, meanwhile, was protected by the Committee for the Conservation of the Monuments of Arab Art, created in 1881, which had the support in the 20th century of such scholars as the architectural historian K. A. C. CRESWELL. Over 600 buildings in Cairo alone have been recognized as having historical importance. After 1952, when the functions of the Committee were taken over by the Ministry of Culture, there was a demise of its activities.

Since the 1920s the State has played an important role in developing the modern art movement in Egypt and has purchased works of art and sponsored exhibitions. In 1927 approval was given for the creation of the first Museum of Modern Art, which opened in 1931. A committee was formed to acquire a collection of paintings and sculptures by Egyptian and modern European artists, the latter mainly by Impressionist and Post-Impressionist artists, including works by Manet, Monet and Rodin. In 1935 the Museum published its first catalogue, and in 1991 the Egyptian collection moved to a permanent home, the Museum of Modern Egyptian Art at the Gazira exhibition grounds, opposite the new Opera House.

A collection of 19th- and 20th-century French art was also acquired by the politician Muhammad Mahmud Khalil (1878–1955). It was bequeathed with his house to the nation after the death of his French wife, Emilienne Khalil, in 1962. The house was taken over by President Sadat in 1971 and the collection rehoused in the 'Amr Ibrahim Palace in Zamalek, but it has since returned to the original house on Gamal Abdul Nasser Street in Giza. Other museums with permanent displays of modern art include the Muhammad Naghi Museum in Giza, the Mahmud Mukhtar Sculpture Museum in Gazira, and the Wissa Wassef Tapestry Museum and the Habib Gorgy Sculpture Museum at Harrania.

Numerous private and government-owned galleries in Cairo have changing exhibitions of contemporary art. These include the Cairo Atelier and, in Gazira, the Cairo Opera House Art Gallery, the Nile Exhibition Hall and the Hanagir Arts Centre (opened 1992); in Zamalek there is the Centre of Arts (also known as the Akhnaten Halls and Arts Complex) and the Egyptian Centre for International Cultural Cooperation. In Alexandria the Museum of Fine Arts hosts the Alexandria Biennale (inaugurated in 1956). In 1986 the first International Cairo Biennale was held, which took place in several galleries. All the governorates in Egypt have exhibition halls included in the state-built Palaces of People's Culture, where local artists display their work.

BIBLIOGRAPHY

W. Forman, B. Forman and R. Wissa Wassef: *Tapestries from Egypt: Woven by the Children of Harrania* (London, 1961, rev. 1968)

R. Owen: 'The Cairo Building Industry and the Building Boom of 1897–1907', *Coloque international sur l'histoire du Caire: Cairo, 1969*, pp. 337–50

M. Wahba: *Cultural Policy in Egypt* (Paris, 1972)

R. Wissa Wassef: *Woven by Hand* (London and New York, 1972)

N. 'Atiyah: *Al-'Ayn al-'āshiqa* (Cairo, 1976) [on contemporary Egyptian painters and their work]

P. Jullian: *The Orientalists* (Oxford, 1977)

Das Land am Nil: Bildteppiche aus Harrania (exh. cat., ed. A. Eggebrecht; Hildesheim, Roemer-Mus. and Pelizaeus-Mus., 1979)

M. Meinicke, ed.: 'Islamic Cairo: Architectural Conservation and Urban Development of the Historic Centre', *A. & Archaeol. Res. Pap.*, xviii (1980)

E. Naguib: *Themen der ägyptischen Malerei des 20. Jahrhunderts* (Cologne and Vienna, 1980)

R. Ilbert: *Heliopolis: Le Caire, 1905–1922: Genèse d'une ville* (Paris, 1981)

L. Golvin, J. Thiriot and M. Zakariya: *Les Potiers actuels de Fusṭāṭ* (Cairo, 1982)

A. D. C. Hyland, A. G. Tipple and N. Wilkinson, eds: *Housing in Egypt* (Newcastle upon Tyne, 1984)

R. Ilbert and M. Volait: 'Neo-Arabic Renaissance in Egypt, 1870–1930', *Mimar*, xiii (1984), pp. 26–34

E. Rodenbeck and A. J. Ahmed, eds: 'The Arts in Egypt: A Special Supplement', *A. & Islam. World*, ii/2 (1984), pp. 33–78

L. Brown and S. Rachid: *Egyptian Carpets: A Practical Guide* (Cairo, 1985)

J. M. Richards, I. Serageldin and D. Rastorfer: *Hassan Fathy* (Singapore, 1985)

Tunisia, Egypt, Morocco: Contemporary Houses, Traditional Values (exh. cat. by B. B. Taylor, London, Zamana Gal., 1985)

Egyptian Landscapes: Weavings from the Ramses Wissa Wassef School (exh. cat. by Y. Wissa Wassef and H. Weir, London, Barbican Cent.; Newcastle upon Tyne, Poly. Gal.; Edinburgh, City A. Cent.; Swansea, Vivian A.G. & Mus.; and elsewhere, 1985–6)

S. Gharieb: *Surrealism in Egypt and Plastic Arts*, Prism Art Series 3 (Giza, 1986)

M. S. al-Jabakhanji: *Tārīkh al-ḥaraka al-fanniyya fī miṣr ilā 'ām 1945* [A history of modern Egyptian fine art to 1945] (Cairo, 1986)

E. Rodenbeck and A. J. Ahmed, eds: 'Egyptian Art Scene', *A. & Islam. World*, iv/1 (1986), pp. 53–79

L. Karnouk: *Modern Egyptian Art: The Emergence of a National Style* (Cairo, 1988)

J. Steele: *Hassan Fathy* (London, 1988)

M. Volait: *L'Architecture moderne en Egypte et la revue al-'Imara (1939–1959)* (Cairo, 1988)

W. Ali, ed.: *Contemporary Art from the Islamic World* (London, 1989), pp. 33–45

I. Serageldin: *Space for Freedom: The Search for Architectural Excellence in Muslim Societies* (London, 1989)

M. Sharaabi: *Kairo: Stadt und Architektur im Zeitalter des europäischen Kolonialismus* (Tübingen, 1989)

D. Ammoun: *Crafts of Egypt* (Cairo, 1991)

I. Iskander, K. Mallakh and S. Sharouni: *Thamānūna sana min al-fann* [Eighty years of art] (Cairo, 1991)

S. al-Sadr: *Ceramics in Egypt*, Prism Art Series 5 (Giza, 1991)

M. Al-Asad: 'The Re-invention of Tradition: Neo-Islamic Architecture in Cairo', *Akten des XXVIII. internationalen Kongresses für Kunstgeschichte: Berlin, 1992*, pp. 425–36

G. Caselli and A. G. Rossi: *Egypt* (London, 1992) [good pls]

E. A. DeStefano: *Threads of Life: A Journey in Creativity: Ramses Wissa Wassef Art Centre* (Cairo, [1992])

E. El-Din Naguib: *The Dawn of Egyptian Modern Painting*, Prism Art Series 6 (Giza, 1992)

D. M. Reid: 'Cultural Imperialism and Nationalism: The Struggle to Define and Control the Heritage of Arab Art in Egypt', *Int. J. Mid. E. Stud.*, xxiv (1992), pp. 57–76

'Aga Khan Award for Architecture' and 'The Children's Park in Sayyida Zaynab', *Prism*, 34 (1992), pp. 2–6

M. Al-Asad: 'The Mosque of al-Rifa'i in Cairo', *Muqarnas*, x (1993), pp. 108–24

T. M. R. Sakr: *Early Twentieth-century Islamic Architecture in Cairo* (Cairo, 1993)

S. A. H. Engelstad: *Tendencies in Modern Egyptian Painting* (diss., U. Bergen, 1994)

□

Egypt, ancient.

Egypt, ancient. Civilization that flourished in the Nile Valley for three and a half thousand years, from *c.* 3000 BC to AD 395.

I. Introduction. II. Craftsman and artist. III. Religion. IV. Ideology and conventions of representation. V. Iconography. VI. Subject-matter. VII. Materials and techniques. VIII. Architecture. IX. Sculpture. X. Painting and drawing. XI. Writing and books. XII. Funerary equipment. XIII. Ceramics. XIV. Jewellery. XV. Metalwork. XVI. Other arts. XVII. Regional art. XVIII. Rediscovery. XIX. Forgeries. XX. Collectors and dealers. XXI. Museums. XXII. Exhibitions.

I. Introduction.

1. Geography and climate. 2. History. 3. Trade and exchange.

1. GEOGRAPHY AND CLIMATE. The boundaries of ancient Egypt were formed by substantial natural barriers: to the south the 1st Nile cataract, to the north the Mediterranean and to the east and west the deserts (see fig. 1). There are only three basic components of the physical geography of Egypt: the Nile, flowing from south to north between fertile banks, and the two areas of desert on either side. In the north the Nile branches into many streams through the Delta and finally flows out into the Mediterranean.

The fertile plain through which the Nile runs is solely the result of the annual flooding of the Nile and the deposition of silt carried in suspension by the flood waters. The silt deposition is most noticeable in the areas closest to the river, and consequently the land there is slightly higher. The annual inundation of the Nile was a natural phenomenon caused by the large amounts of rain that normally fall in the summer months in the highlands to the south of Egypt and the Sudan, where the Atbara and Blue and White Niles, the three principal sources of the Nile, rise. Before the building of dams at Aswan, the annual flood waters surged through the Nile Valley and out into the Mediterranean. Each year, at the beginning of June, when the waters reached the broad flood plain north of Aswan, they spread out and deposited silt over the land. The Nile flood plain, first laid down c. 22,000 BC, has steadily risen at a rate of approximately 100 mm each century, although the construction of the High Dam at Aswan has ended this process.

The desert regions of Egypt are far more extensive than the flood plain, but Egyptian settlements have naturally tended to be located in the areas bordering the river, that is the Nile Valley and the Delta. The Nile's two principal outflows into the Mediterranean are the Rosetta and Damietta branches, although in the Greco-Roman period the Nile had seven mouths. Throughout Egyptian history the Delta has always been a fertile region and a prime area for animal husbandry. Only in the northernmost parts of the Delta were there areas described by the Greek historian Herodotus (*fl c.* 480 BC) as 'flat, watery and marshy' (*Histories* II.7). In the northern Delta the formation of localized sandy ridges, known as 'turtlebacks', provided ideal locations for settlement and many of the towns that appeared there—such as Tanis, Sais, Tell el-Farain and

Bubastis—are known to have been inhabited in Predynastic times.

The crucial area around the junction between the Delta and the Nile valley, where Memphis (*see* MEMPHIS (i)) and its associated cemeteries of SAQQARA and GIZA are located, has been the site of the capital of Egypt for most of its history. The high-quality limestone of the cliffs flanking the valley at this point has been regularly quarried for building purposes. To the south of Memphis lies Middle Egypt, a region in which the largest areas of agricultural land are located to the west of the river. The principal settlement of Middle Egypt, HERMOPOLIS MAGNA, was therefore also situated on the west bank, whereas the cemeteries, such as BENI HASAN, DEIR EL-BERSHA and DEIR EL-GEBRAWI, were cut into the eastern cliffs that approach close to the bank in this stretch of the Nile.

In northern Middle Egypt, to the west of the Nile Valley proper, is the FAIYUM depression, which is at an average altitude of 53 m below sea-level. The region is dominated by Lake Qarun, the descendant of a larger expanse of water known to the ancient Greeks as Lake Moeris. The Faiyum is occasionally wrongly described as an oasis, but the lake is actually supplied by the Nile, via the Bahr Yusuf. At least twice during Egyptian history the Faiyum was the site of major land reclamation projects whereby the flow of water into the depression was restricted, making more land available for settlement and agriculture.

In the agricultural land of Upper Egypt—at a point where the river deviates in a great bend to flow east–west rather than north–south—were some of the earliest important settlements, such as NAQADA, EL-BADARI, KOPTOS and ABYDOS. A little further to the south the broad flood plain at Thebes encouraged a thriving settlement. Compared with the cliffs in Lower Egypt, the limestone of the Theban cliffs was poor in quality; therefore sandstone (from GEBEL EL-SILSILA) and red and black granite (from ASWAN) provided further building material for the temples of Upper Egypt.

The climate in prehistoric Egypt after the last glacial phase was apparently much moister than in modern times. There is evidence of considerable rainfall in the prehistoric Eastern Desert and the Sahara, sufficient to support savanna-like vegetation. During the 4th millennium BC, however, there was a gradual decrease in rainfall with a sharper decline at about the beginning of the 1st Dynasty (*c.* 2925 BC). Evidence from Lake Moeris in the Faiyum indicates that rainfall continued to decrease gradually until about the end of the 4th Dynasty (*c.* 2465 BC), when there seems to have been a final decline in precipitation. Since then the climate of Egypt has been characterized by hyperaridity. Average annual rainfall now varies slightly according to latitude, from 115 mm in Alexandria to about 5 mm in Upper Egypt (where it may not rain at all for years at a time). Because of this lack of rainfall, the Egyptians have always had to rely on the Nile for irrigation, taking advantage of the annual flood. Only in the 19th and 20th centuries has the flooding of the river been regulated to provide a more even water supply all year round.

The generally arid climate has preserved Egypt's monuments extremely well, particularly those in the desert. In the fertile land on the Nile Valley and the Delta the

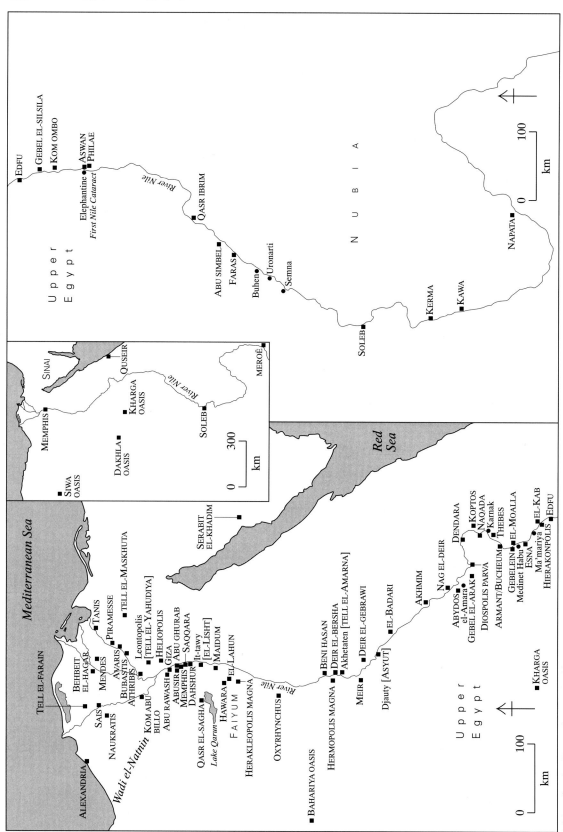

1. Map of ancient Egypt; those areas with separate entries in this dictionary are distinguished by CROSS-REFERENCE TYPE

conditions are moister, owing to the proximity of the river and the practice of irrigation. Consequently, mud-brick and wood, the principal raw materials of Egyptian settlements, have usually deteriorated in these areas. Similarly, most papyri have been found in the desert rather than in the river valley. Changes in climate have occurred during the 20th century as a result of the construction of barrages on the Nile, controlling the river and providing a substantial water supply throughout the year. The resultant dramatic rise in the water table has caused salt to effloresce in the rock and increased the level of humidity throughout the country. These conditions have caused some stone structures to decay and wall paintings to deteriorate. It is possible that droughts in Africa in the late 20th century may have begun to reverse this situation.

BIBLIOGRAPHY

G. Caton-Thompson and F. W. Gardner: *The Desert Fayum*, 2 vols (London, 1934)

P. Montet: *Géographie de l'Egypte ancienne*, 2 vols (Paris, 1957–61)

K. W. Butzer: *Quaternary Stratigraphy and Climate in the Near East* (Bonn, 1958)

H. Kees: *Das alte Ägypten: Eine kleine Landeskunde* (Berlin, 1958); Eng. trans. as *Ancient Egypt: A Cultural Topography* (London, 1961)

K. W. Butzer: *Early Hydraulic Civilization: A Study in Cultural Ecology* (Chicago and London, 1976)

J. Baines and J. Malek: *Atlas of Ancient Egypt* (Oxford, 1980)

V. Seton-Williams and P. Stocks: *Blue Guide: Egypt* (London, 1983, rev. 1988)

HELEN M. STRUDWICK

2. HISTORY. There are close parallels between the art and history of Egypt. The characteristic style of Egyptian art appeared as suddenly as the State itself, as well as its royal and religious institutions and the devices and symbols that defined them. This coherent and close-knit whole, which remained unchanged for over 3000 years, caused Egyptian civilization to appear stagnant, whereas it was simply stable, functioning in a closed system almost impermeable to foreign influence. This system was rapidly destabilized in the Roman period with the disappearance of the institution of the pharaoh—and therefore of the State itself, since in theory only the divine king could perform the rites by which Egypt, and therefore the whole universe, existed and survived. The destruction of the Egyptian royal system was kept in check during the Late Period (*c.* 750–332 BC) by a religious fiction. In the Persian, Ptolemaic and Roman periods the rulers continued to be called pharaohs, despite the fact that they were actually foreign overlords to whom Egypt was no more than a fragment of a vast empire. As far as the Greeks were concerned, Egypt was the provider of financial resources for a political game that no longer directly involved the Egyptians themselves. After the Roman conquest they lost all political autonomy. Soon afterwards Christianity swept away the last followers of the ancient faith as well as the aesthetic style in which Egyptian religion manifested itself. Before long the writing, language and art of millennia had vanished.

The way in which the history of Egypt is organized into different periods (see fig. 2) derives from the ancient Egyptians' own chronologies, based on an almost uninterrupted succession of kings. Manetho, a Greek-speaking Egyptian priest who lived at the time of Ptolemy II Philadelphus (*reg* 285–246 BC), wrote a detailed history of Egypt of which unfortunately only a skeletal summary has

survived. Manetho grouped the kings into 30 dynasties. To these have now been added the Persian 31st Dynasty (343–332 BC) and the Macedonian and Ptolemaic dynasties (332–30 BC), during which the native culture was still robust. The absolute dates assigned to Egypt's kings are established largely by working forwards and backwards from a few fixed astronomical points. For example, the helical rising of the star Sirius in the ninth regnal year of Amenophis I has enabled archaeologists to fix his accession to within a 26-year period, though further precision is not possible. Uncertainty regarding the place from which the rising of Sirius was sited and the precise length of reign for various kings means that there are margins of error in most cases before the middle of the 7th century BC; some dates previously believed to be absolutely accurate are now being reconsidered.

Manetho's dynasties do not always correspond to groups of kings of the same family; sometimes unrelated princes were collected into a dynasty and sometimes a son might belong to a different dynasty from his father. The grouping of the dynasties into long 'kingdoms' and 'periods' tends to correspond to those phases of strength and order or weakness and anarchy that were recognized by the Egyptians themselves (although they did not give these periods specific names). The modern names for the periods of strength are the Old Kingdom (4th–6th dynasties), the Middle Kingdom (11th–13th dynasties) and the New Kingdom (18th–20th dynasties). There were various 'dark ages', including the Early Dynastic period (1st–3rd dynasties), also known as the Archaic or Thinite period, and the three 'intermediate periods' (following the Old, Middle and New kingdoms). After the Third Intermediate Period came a lengthy era known as the Late Period (25th–31st dynasties) and the Greco-Roman period, when Egypt was coveted and eventually encompassed by increasingly numerous and powerful neighbours.

(i) Predynastic and Early Dynastic periods (*c.* 6000–*c.* 2575 BC). (ii) Old Kingdom and First Intermediate Period (*c.* 2575–*c.* 2008 BC). (iii) Middle Kingdom (*c.* 2008–*c.* 1630 BC). (iv) Second Intermediate Period (*c.* 1630–*c.* 1540 BC). (v) Early New Kingdom (*c.* 1540–*c.* 1353 BC). (vi) Amarna period (*c.* 1353–*c.* 1332 BC). (vii) Late New Kingdom (*c.* 1332–*c.* 1075 BC). (viii) Third Intermediate Period (*c.* 1075–*c.* 750 BC). (ix) Late Period (*c.* 750–332 BC). (x) Greco-Roman period (332 BC–AD 395).

*(i) Predynastic and Early Dynastic periods (*c. 6000–*c. 2575 BC).* Before the names and images of the first kings of Egypt appeared, there was a period of prehistory in Africa that stretched back for several million years to the very origins of humanity. Numerous types of worked flints have survived from this vast period of time in the Nile Valley. Egypt did not display its singular character until the Neolithic period (*c.* 6000–2925 BC), which was characterized by the development of agriculture and animal husbandry among increasingly sedentary populations. There was, however, nothing in this so-called Predynastic phase (subdivided into Badarian, Naqada I and Naqada II phases on the basis of a sequence of ceramic vessels' shapes and decoration; see §XIV below) that pointed to the style that was to be the immutable characteristic of Egyptian art.

Both of the basic aspects of Egyptian civilization—its writing and art—were essentially the same (*see* §IV, 1 below) and emerged simultaneously around 3000 BC. The

Palaeolithic	*c.* 250,000-*c.* 10,000 BC
Mesolithic	*c.* 10,000-*c.* 6000 BC
Neolithic (Pre-dynastic period)	*c.* 6000-*c.* 2925 BC
Badarian period	*c.* 6000-*c.* 4000 BC
Naqada I period (Amratian)	*c.* 4000-*c.* 3500 BC
Naqada II (Gerzean)	*c.* 3500-*c.* 2925 BC
Narmer	*c.* 3000 BC
Early Dynastic period	*c.* 2925-*c.* 2575 BC
1st Dynasty	*c.* 2925-*c.* 2775 BC
Menes (?Aha)	
Djer	
Wadj	
Den	*c.* 2850 BC
Anedjib	
Semerkhet	
Qaa	
2nd Dynasty	*c.* 2775-*c.* 2650 BC
Hetepsekhemwy	
Reneb	
Ninetjer	
Peribsen	
Khasekhemwy	
3rd Dynasty	*c.* 2650-*c.* 2575 BC
Sanakht (?Nebka)	*c.* 2650-*c.* 2630 BC
Djoser	*c.* 2630-*c.* 2611 BC
Sekhemkhet	*c.* 2611-*c.* 2604 BC
Khaba	*c.* 2604-*c.* 2600 BC
Huni	*c.* 2600-*c.* 2575 BC
Old Kingdom	*c.* 2575-*c.* 2150 BC
4th Dynasty	*c.* 2575-*c.* 2465 BC
Sneferu	*c.* 2575-*c.* 2551 BC
Cheops (Khufu)	*c.* 2551-*c.* 2528 BC
Radjedef	*c.* 2528-*c.* 2520 BC
Chephren (Kaefre)	*c.* 2520-*c.* 2494 BC
Mycerinus (Menkaure)	*c.* 2490-*c.* 2472 BC
Shepseskaf	*c.* 2472-*c.* 2465 BC

5th Dynasty	*c.* 2465-*c.* 2325 BC
Userkaf	*c.* 2465-*c.* 2458 BC
Sahure	*c.* 2458-*c.* 2446 BC
Neferirkare	*c.* 2446-*c.* 2426 BC
Shepseskare	*c.* 2426-*c.* 2419 BC
Raneferef	*c.* 2419-*c.* 2416 BC
Neuserre	*c.* 2416-*c.* 2392 BC
Menkauhor	*c.* 2396-*c.* 2388 BC
Djedkare	*c.* 2388-*c.* 2356 BC
Unas	*c.* 2356-*c.* 2325 BC
6th Dynasty	*c.* 2325-*c.* 2150 BC
Teti	*c.* 2325-*c.* 2291 BC
Pepy I	*c.* 2289-*c.* 2256 BC
Merenre	*c.* 2256-*c.* 2246 BC
Pepy II	*c.* 2246-*c.* 2150 BC
First Intermediate Period	*c.* 2150-*c.* 2018 BC
7th and 8th dynasties	*c.* 2150-*c.* 2130 BC
Numerous kings of brief reign	
9th and 10th dynasties	*c.* 2130-*c.* 1970 BC
Several kings ruling from Herakleopolis	
11th Dynasty (Thebes)	*c.* 2081-*c.* 1938 BC
Mentuhopte I	
Inyotef I	*c.* 2081-*c.* 2065 BC
Inyotef II	*c.* 2065-*c.* 2016 BC
Inyotef III	*c.* 2016-*c.* 2008 BC
Middle Kingdom	*c.* 2008-*c.* 1630 BC
11th Dynasty (all Egypt)	
Mentuhotpe II (Nebhepetre)	*c.* 2008-*c.* 1957 BC
Mentuhotpe III (Sankhkare)	*c.* 1957-*c.* 1945 BC
Mentuhotpe IV (Nebtawyre)	*c.* 1945-*c.* 1938 BC
12th Dynasty	*c.* 1938-*c.* 1756 BC
Ammenemes I (Amenemhat)	*c.* 1938-*c.* 1908 BC
Sesostris I (Senusert)	*c.* 1918-*c.* 1875 BC
Ammenemes II	*c.* 1876-*c.* 1842 BC
Sesostris II	*c.* 1844-*c.* 1837 BC
Sesostris III	*c.* 1837-*c.* 1818 BC
Ammenemes III	*c.* 1818-*c.* 1770 BC
Ammenemes IV	*c.* 1770-*c.* 1760 BC
Sobekneferu	*c.* 1760-*c.* 1756 BC
13th Dynasty	*c.* 1756-*c.* 1630 BC
Approximately 60 kings, all with brief reigns	

2a. Chronological chart showing the kings of ancient Egypt: Palaeolithic–13th Dynasty; overlapping dates in the 12th Dynasty are the result of assumed co-regencies, the actual existence of which is uncertain

Second Intermediate Period	*c.* 1630-*c.* 1540 BC
14th Dynasty	*c.* 1630-*c.* 1532 BC
Minor kings with capital at Xois (north-central Delta)	
15th Dynasty	*c.* 1630-*c.* 1532 BC
Hyksos kings with capital at Avaris	
16th Dynasty	*c.* 1630-*c.* 1532 BC
Minor Hyskos kings	
17th Dynasty	*c.* 1630-*c.* 1540 BC
Numerous Theban kings who finally repelled the Hyksos invaders	

New Kingdom	*c.* 1540-*c.* 1075 BC
18th Dynasty	*c.* 1540-*c.* 1292 BC
Ahmose	*c.* 1540-*c.* 1514 BC
Amenophis I (Amenhotpe)	*c.* 1514-*c.* 1493 BC
Tuthmosis I (Djehutmose)	*c.* 1493-*c.* 1482 BC
Tuthmosis II	*c.* 1482-*c.* 1479 BC
Tuthmosis III	*c.* 1479-*c.* 1426 BC
Hatshepsut	*c.* 1479-*c.* 1458 BC
Amenophis II	*c.* 1426-*c.* 1400 BC
Tuthmosis IV	*c.* 1400-*c.* 1390 BC
Amenophis III	*c.* 1390-*c.* 1353 BC
Amenophis IV (Akhenaten)	*c.* 1353-*c.* 1336 BC
?Smenkhkare	*c.* 1335-*c.* 1332 BC
Tutankhamun	*c.* 1332-*c.* 1323 BC
Ay	*c.* 1323-*c.* 1319 BC
Horemheb	*c.* 1319-*c.* 1292 BC
19th Dynasty	*c.* 1292-*c.* 1190 BC
Ramesses I	*c.* 1292-*c.* 1290 BC
Sethos I (Seti)	*c.* 1290-*c.* 1279 BC
Ramesses II	*c.* 1279-*c.* 1213 BC
Merneptah	*c.* 1213-*c.* 1204 BC
Sethos II	*c.* 1204-*c.* 1198 BC
Amenmesse (usurper)	*c.* 1203-*c.* 1200 BC
Siptah	*c.* 1198-*c.* 1193 BC
Tausert	*c.* 1193-*c.* 1190 BC
20th Dynasty	*c.* 1190-*c.* 1075 BC
Sethnakht	*c.* 1190-*c.* 1187 BC
Ramesses III	*c.* 1187-*c.* 1156 BC
Ramesses IV	*c.* 1156-*c.* 1150 BC
Ramesses V	*c.* 1150-*c.* 1145 BC
Ramesses VI	*c.* 1145-*c.* 1137 BC
Ramesses VII and VIII	*c.* 1137-*c.* 1126 BC
Ramesses IX	*c.* 1126-*c.* 1108 BC
Ramesses X	*c.* 1108-*c.* 1104 BC
Ramesses XI	*c.* 1104-*c.* 1075 BC

Third Intermediate Period	*c.* 1075-*c.* 750 BC
21st Dynasty (Tanis)	*c.* 1075-*c.* 950 BC
Smendes	*c.* 1075-*c.* 1045 BC
Amenemnisu	*c.* 1045-*c.* 1040 BC
Psusennes I	*c.* 1040-*c.* 997 BC
Amenemope	*c.* 998-*c.* 989 BC
Osorkon I	*c.* 989-*c.* 973 BC
Siamun	*c.* 973-*c.* 964 BC
Psusennes II	*c.* 964-*c.* 950 BC
22nd Dynasty (Libyan)	*c.* 950-*c.* 730 BC
Shoshenq I	*c.* 950-*c.* 929 BC
Osorkon II	*c.* 929-*c.* 914 BC
Takelot I	
Shoshenq II	
Osorkon III	*c.* 888-*c.* 860 BC
Takelot II	
Shoshenq III	
Pami	
Shoshenq V	
Osorkon V	-*c.* 730 BC
23rd Dynasty	*c.* 823-*c.* 732 BC
Various contemporary kings in Thebes, Hermopolis, Herakleopolis, Leontopolis and Tanis	
24th Dynasty (Sais)	*c.* 722-*c.* 715 BC

Late Period	*c.* 750-332 BC
25th Dynasty (Kushite)	*c.* 750-*c.* 656 BC
Piye	*c.* 750-*c.* 719 BC
(Nubia and all Egypt)	
Shabaka	*c.* 719-*c.* 703 BC
Shebitku	*c.* 703-*c.* 690 BC
Taharqa	*c.* 690-664 BC
Tantamani	664-656 BC
26th Dynasty	664-525 BC
Necho I	672-664 BC
Psammetichus I	664-610 BC
Necho II	610-595 BC
Psammetichus II	595-589 BC
Apries	589-570 BC
Amasis	570-526 BC
Psammetichus III	526-525 BC
27th Dynasty (Persian)	525-404 BC
Cambyses II	525-522 BC
Darius I	521-486 BC
Xerxes I	486-466 BC
Artaxerxes I	465-424 BC
Darius II	424-404 BC

2b. Chronological chart showing the kings of ancient Egypt: 14th–27th Dynasties

28th Dynasty	404-399 BC		Ptolemy II Philadelphos	285-246 BC
Amyrtaios	404-399 BC		Ptolemy III Euergetes I	246-221 BC
			Ptolemy IV Philopator	221-205 BC
29th Dynasty	399-380 BC		Harwennefer	205-199 BC
Nepherites I	399-393 BC		(native usurper)	
Psammuthis	393 BC		Ptolemy V Epiphanes	205-180 BC
Hakoris	393-380 BC		Ankhwennefer	199-186 BC
Nepherites II	380 BC		(native usurper)	
			Ptolemy VI Philometor	180-164 BC;
30th Dynasty	380-343 BC			163-145 BC
Nectanebo I	380-362 BC		Ptolemy VIII Euergetes II	170-163 BC;
Teos	365-360 BC			145-116 BC
Nectanebo II	360-343 BC		Ptolemy VII	145 BC
			Neos Philopator	
31st Dynasty	343-332 BC		Harsiese	131 BC
Artaxerxes III Ochus	343-338 BC		(native usurper)	
Arses	338-336 BC		Cleopatra III and	116-107 BC
Darius III Codoman	335-332 BC		Ptolemy IX Soter II	
			Cleopatra III and	107-88 BC
Period interupted by native king			Ptolemy X Alexander I	
Khababash			Ptolemy IX Soter II	88-81 BC
			Cleopatra Berenike	81-80 BC
			Ptolemy XI	80 BC
Greco-Roman period	332 BC-AD 395		Alexander II	
Macedonian dynasty	332-304 BC		Ptolemy XII	80-58 BC;
Alexander III the Great	332-323 BC		Neos Dionysos	55-51 BC
Philip Arrhidaeus	323-316 BC		Berenike IV and	58-55 BC
Alexander IV	316-304 BC		Cleopatra Tryphaena	
			Cleopatra VII	51-30 BC
Ptolemaic dynasty	304-30 BC		Ptolemy XIII	51-47 BC
			Ptolemy XIV	47-44 BC
Ptolemy I Soter I	304-284 BC		Ptolemy XV Caesarion	44-30 BC
			Roman emperors	30 BC-AD 395

2c. Chronological chart showing the kings of ancient Eygpt: 28th Dynasty–Roman period

history of Egypt was precisely documented from the outset; official historical records were preserved in the nation's archives and later largely corroborated by archaeologists' discoveries of contemporary documents. There are no obscure, legendary beginnings to Egypt's history: the break with prehistory is a clean one. To understand fully the sudden birth of Egyptian civilization—a political entity that transcended the family or tribal framework—it is necessary to forget the modern appearance of Egypt and the surrounding geographical and political entities. Both Upper and Lower Egypt figure in the earliest list of the country's enemies, which were symbolized by nine bows from the reign of Djoser (*reg c.* 2630–*c.* 2611 BC) onwards. These enemies included other peoples who were undoubtedly also living close to the Nile Valley, such as the Hau-Nebut in the coastal belt of the Delta and the Libyans to the west of Egypt. Strictly speaking, early Egyptian history and administration involved only the activities of the Nile Valley and the immediate area, apart from expeditions to mines and quarries.

The first kings may have been natives of HIERAKON-POLIS, some distance into Upper Egypt, but the earliest capital city was Thinis, probably in or near the modern town of Girga. The nearby site of Abydos was the royal necropolis. The most important act of Menes, the first king of Egypt (*fl c.* 2920 BC), was the foundation of the administrative centre of MEMPHIS, which was described at length to Herodotus. Menes controlled the course of the Nile at Memphis by means of a dike. The importance of Memphis from the beginning of the 1st Dynasty is apparent in the remarkable dimensions of the tombs that high officials built for themselves at Saqqara (*see* SAQQARA, §1).

Systematic records of past years were already being kept in the form of annals. Starting in the reign of the third king of the 1st Dynasty, the annual height of the Nile was recorded in such venerable inscriptions as the Palermo Stone (Palermo, Mus. Reg.), a fragment of a 5th Dynasty king list carved in stone. Among the most ancient titles of officials, that of 'canal-digger', which eventually signified no more than 'administrator', attests to the first rulers' preoccupation with the control of the Nile.

Dating from the reign of King Narmer (*c.* 3000 BC) is a large shield-shaped slate ceremonial palette (Cairo, Egyp. Mus.; for illustration *see* NARMER) from Hierakonpolis, which is decorated with reliefs including two figures of the King wearing the white crown of Upper Egypt (recto) and the red crown of Lower Egypt (verso). Narmer's name, made up of a few decipherable hieroglyphs, is also found on other documents. Another king's name, Aha, appears on many objects that must date to the beginning of the 1st Dynasty, such as an inscribed ivory plaque from Naqada (Cairo, Egyp. Mus.; for illustration *see* NAQADA). In contrast, the name of Menes is not found on documents of such antiquity. Since each Egyptian king had several names—totalling five after the middle of the Old Kingdom—it is possible that Menes may have simply been the second name of Aha or Narmer. Alternatively, Narmer may have reigned before Menes, at the very end of the Predynastic period.

From the 2nd Dynasty (*c.* 2775–*c.* 2650 BC) onwards royal tombs were set up both at Abydos and Saqqara. Linked with the names of two 2nd Dynasty kings, Khasekhemwy and Ninetjer, are a few surviving statues (Cairo, Egyp. Mus., and Oxford, Ashmolean; see fig. 51 below). In the reign of King Djoser of the 3rd Dynasty the capital was established at Memphis. The 3rd Dynasty was still remembered in the Ptolemaic period (*c.* 304–30 BC) as the time when building with dressed stone began, for the mortuary temple of Djoser (the Step Pyramid at Saqqara) was the first colossal structure in Egypt (and perhaps the world) to be built entirely of stone. Djoser's example was followed by the subsequent kings of the 3rd and 4th dynasties. Djoser's immediate successor, Sekhemkhet (*reg c.* 2611–*c.* 2604 BC), was equally ambitious. He was the first king to have himself portrayed in large-scale rock-cut bas-reliefs in the Sinai Desert (one of which is now in Cairo, Egyp. Mus.), but the funerary complex that he envisaged at Saqqara was never finished. Although his alabaster sarcophagus (Cairo, Egyp. Mus.) was still sealed when discovered, it was found to be empty.

The surviving art and architecture in the Early Dynastic period indicate the high degree of organization and wealth in Egypt, as well as the absolute mastery of Egyptian artists. Already Egyptian thoughts, both in their literature and statuary, were orientated towards the human being and the individual.

(ii) Old Kingdom and First Intermediate Period (c. 2575–c. 2008 BC). Many artistic and architectural monuments have survived from the Old Kingdom, but, as in many other periods of Egyptian history, there are few recorded historical facts. For unknown reasons, the 3rd Dynasty ended in obscurity. The 4th Dynasty, however, began with a demonstration of power and immense resources. King Sneferu (*reg c.* 2575–*c.* 2551 BC), remembered as a good, humane ruler, must have been active in the Sinai region (*see* SINAI, §1), since he became a tutelary deity there. He also built boats and a palace and sent an expedition to Nubia, all firmly in the Egyptian royal tradition. He had no less than three pyramids built for himself (at MAIDUM and DAHSHUR), moving a volume of stone far outstripping the work of his successor Cheops (*reg c.* 2551–*c.* 2528 BC), who is virtually unknown, except as the builder of the 'Great Pyramid' at Giza (for illustration *see* GIZA). The kings Chephren (*reg c.* 2520–*c.* 2494 BC) and MYCERINUS (*reg c.* 2490–*c.* 2472 BC) had their pyramids built next to that of Cheops, but Radjedef (*reg c.* 2528–*c.* 2520 BC) placed his tomb further to the north, at ABU RAWASH. Quarrels apparently occurred within the royal family over

the succession, and sometimes there are indications of religious disputes, as in the case of the last 4th Dynasty king, Shepseskaf (*reg c.* 2472–*c.* 2465 BC), whose tomb at Saqqara—the 'Mastabat Faraoun'—rejected the pyramidal form. In the 5th Dynasty (*c.* 2465–*c.* 2325 BC) the kings Sahure (*reg c.* 2458–*c.* 2446 BC), Neferirkare (*reg c.* 2446–*c.* 2426 BC) and Neuserre (*reg c.* 2416–*c.* 2392 BC) built a new necropolis at Abusir (midway between Giza and Saqqara), incorporating pyramids and sun temples. Unas (*reg c.* 2356–*c.* 2323 BC), the last 5th Dynasty king, is known principally for the first example of the Pyramid Texts, a series of religious and funerary texts carved on the walls of the burial chamber of his pyramid at Saqqara, which were imitated by kings in the following dynasties.

From the 4th Dynasty onwards, numerous private tombs provide glimpses of social organization: in their quality and quantity they bear witness, like the pyramids, to the ready availability of a valuable workforce. The numerous titles borne by important men buried in the MASTABA tombs and hypogea reveal the complex machinery of the civil and religious administration. During the 4th and 5th dynasties these private tombs were grouped together in necropoleis close to Memphis, near the tombs of the pharaohs, but from the 4th Dynasty onwards provincial necropoleis began to appear. During the 6th Dynasty the private necropoleis multiplied near such feudal capitals as Asyut (anc. Djauty), Beni Hasan and Zawyat el-Mayitin (anc. Hebenu), indicating the dispersal of power away from the pharaohs.

Apart from expeditions to the south, with essentially commercial aims, the historical evidence from the 6th Dynasty relates mainly to internal problems in the royal families. Teti (*reg c.* 2325–*c.* 2291 BC) was assassinated by his own bodyguards; Pepy I (*reg c.* 2289–*c.* 2256 BC) was the victim of a conspiracy involving the 'great royal wife' herself, which was later the subject of secret legal investigations; and Pepy II (*reg c.* 2246–*c.* 2150 BC) had one of the longest reigns, from the age of 6 to 100. The 6th dynasty ended with the reign of a woman called Nitocris (*reg c.* 2150 BC)—remembered mainly for her beauty—and was followed by the 7th Dynasty (*c.* 2150–*c.* 2130 BC), a period of obscurity and anarchy described by the historian Manetho as '70 kings ruling for 70 days'. The rulers of the 8th to the 10th Dynasty are equally mysterious, and few private and royal monuments have survived from this phase, known as the First Intermediate Period.

(iii) Middle Kingdom (c. 2008–c. 1630 BC). Literary works such as the *Admonitions of Ipuwer*, the *Song of the Harper* and the *Story of the Eloquent Peasant* contribute some information about the First Intermediate Period. They describe famines, injustice, incursions by nomads, social upheaval and general despondency. This period ended with the war between the king of Herakleopolis and Nebhepetre Mentuhotpe II, Prince of Thebes. Mentuhotpe II (*reg c.* 2008–*c.* 1957 BC) triumphed, the country was reunified and the Middle Kingdom began. The tomb and mortuary temple of Mentuhotpe II are at Deir el-Bahri, in his native Thebes (*see* THEBES (i), §IV). His successors, Mentuhotpe III and IV, are known only for their peaceful activities, mainly consisting of quarrying expeditions—to obtain stone for royal statuary—in the

Wadi Hammamat (a valley running between Koptos and the Red Sea) and trading expeditions to Punt, a poorly defined area to the south of Egypt, from which spices and tropical products were imported. Thebes was the capital throughout the 11th Dynasty.

Ammenemes, a vizier who led an expedition to the Wadi Hammamat on Mentuhotpe IV's behalf, seems to have been the founder of the 12th Dynasty (for dates of 12th Dynasty kings see fig. 2a above). This new dynasty, during which the kings were called Ammenemes or Sesostris, was one of the most powerful and stable periods of Egyptian history. Like the 6th Dynasty, it ended with the reign of a woman, Sobekneferu. Mentuhotpe II had re-established the country's unity, but the local princes—despite acknowledging him as king—had not abandoned their prerogatives in the provinces. It was therefore the task of the 12th Dynasty to dispel this feudalism and to replace these potentates with officials in the service of the central government.

Ammenemes I moved the capital north from Thebes to Itjtawy (EL-LISHT), about 50 km south of Memphis. He established forts designed to control the flow of traffic between Egypt and Asia across the eastern border of the Delta. His son, Sesostris I, ruled for 45 years, pursued grandiose architectural and military projects including the annexation of Nubia (for discussion of Middle Kingdom military architecture in Nubia *see* §VIII, 3 below and NUBIA, §§I and II).

There are few surviving historical details concerning Ammenemes II and Sesostris II. SESOSTRIS III, however, was the most famous king of the dynasty. According to Herodotus, he ventured deep into western Asia and as far north as Thrace, but in reality he merely completed the construction of the forts begun by his predecessors in Nubia and made the southern border absolutely secure in the region of the 2nd Nile cataract. Wiping out the remaining power of the nomarchs in Egypt itself, he consolidated the governmental structure and eradicated the last traces of feudalism. Two viziers oversaw the administration of the country and reported to him directly. The position was by then so stable that his son, AMMENEMES III, simply had to act as steward of the country's prosperity, his only known historical act of any importance being the economic development of the Faiyum region.

The 13th Dynasty (c. 1756–c. 1630 BC) was chaotic; the reigns of some 60 kings, many unrelated, followed one another in quick succession. In contrast, a number of high officials, such as the vizier Ankhu and his family, founded relatively stable dynasties. The country was at this stage already divided. If it is true that the 14th Dynasty was the result of a first wave of Asiatics who had occupied part of the Delta, then the 13th Dynasty is part of the Second Intermediate Period. The 13th Dynasty was, however, so much a cultural and economic continuation of the 12th Dynasty, especially considering the quality and style of both royal and private statuary, that it may also be considered to be part of the Middle Kingdom.

(iv) Second Intermediate Period (c. 1630–c. 1540 BC). The beginning of the Second Intermediate Period coincided with the end of the 13th Dynasty and the seizure of power in the north by the Asiatics, the so-called Hyksos, who made up the 15th Dynasty (c. 1630–c. 1532 BC). Their assumption of power was achieved in several stages by infiltration and peaceful settlement in the eastern Delta, particularly along the east bank of the Pelusiac branch of the Nile. This was the situation described in the Bible on the arrival in Egypt of Joseph, followed by his brothers' settlement in the land of Goshen. Yet, according to Egyptian tradition and archaeological finds, it was a violent and murderous invasion that culminated in the foundation of the 15th Dynasty. The name 'Hyksos' (Egyp.: 'rulers of foreign lands') does not itself indicate their origins or ethnic composition. They were nomads who had blurred the boundary between Egypt and Asia, establishing a common cultural zone, though not a well-defined State. They held the whole of Egypt under a loose feudal regime (rather than an organized autocracy). Egypt thus absorbed numerous elements of Asiatic civilization, such as the horse, the war-chariot, the curved sword and various gods. It was the first time since prehistory that Egypt had submitted to such direct influence.

A second branch of Asiatics (the 16th Dynasty) took possession of another part of the Delta, while at Thebes there appeared a line of princes (the 17th Dynasty) whose descendants eventually reunified the country, founding both the 18th Dynasty and the New Kingdom. After the 13th Dynasty, the capital of which was still at el-Lisht, Egypt withdrew from Nubia, allowing the kingdom of KERMA to expand down the Nile as far as the 1st Nile cataract. Some Egyptians simply remained in Nubia and transferred allegiance to their new masters.

(v) Early New Kingdom (c. 1540–c. 1353 BC). The Egyptian reaction to the Hyksos seems at least in part to have been fuelled by nationalistic and even patriotic feelings, as expressed by the text of the Kamose Stele (Cairo, Egyp. Mus.), in which Kamose, last king of the 17th Dynasty, complains to his apathetic courtiers that he must share his kingdom with a negro and an Asiatic. Hostilities had already begun under Kamose's predecessor Seqenenre Tao, whose mummy (Cairo, Egyp. Mus.) exhibits the gaping holes of mortal wounds inflicted by Hyksos weapons. The reconquest of Lower Egypt finally took place under Ahmose (reg c. 1540–c. 1514 BC), first king of the 18th Dynasty, who recaptured AVARIS, the Hyksos capital in the eastern Delta, and besieged their fortifications at Sharuhen, in southern Palestine, for three years. Ahmose also consolidated the reconquest of Nubia (already effected as far south as Buhen by his predecessor Kamose) and faced internal rebellions, probably as a result of the personal interests of those who had benefited from the Hyksos presence.

Amenophis I (reg c. 1514–c. 1493 BC), the son of Ahmose, waged few wars, whereas Tuthmosis I, TUTHMOSIS III and Amenophis II were great warriors. At the start of its history Egypt had emerged alone from a world without borders or structure. Gradually groups outside Egypt became settled and centres and towns were built, becoming more than just neighbours to be plundered. These states were a threat, even though they remained somewhat indistinct. In Asia the Egyptian armies penetrated as far as northern Syria and in Nubia they passed beyond the 4th Nile cataract. The destruction of the

Kingdom of Kerma allowed the Egyptian occupation of Nubia to remain stable, until the end of the Ramesside period (c. 1075 BC). In the north, on the other hand, the increasing number of Tuthmosis III's campaigns reflects the difficulties encountered in subduing the numerous little groups that constituted the political fabric of Syria-Palestine. Only Mitanni (see MITANNIAN) seems to have been a genuine state. For the first time in Egyptian history the importance of international problems was greater than that of dynastic disputes or internal administration. The kings had events to record and did so with precision, in temple inscriptions such as the annals of Tuthmosis III, and on stelae (including the Tombos Stelae of Tuthmosis I (in situ) and the stelae of Amenophis II). Private individuals were conscious of living through significant events: two soldiers from EL-KAB, Ahmose son of Ebana and Ahmose Pennekhbet, gave succinct accounts of their military careers under the first five kings of the 18th Dynasty.

Another characteristic of the New Kingdom is that many of its kings died young, leaving as heirs youthful princes whose first years of reign were sometimes presided over by a regent–queen. These infant princes included Ahmose, whose rule was secured by his grandmother Tetisheri and his mother Ahhotpe; Amenophis I, who was supported by his mother Ahmose Nefertari; Tuthmosis III, who was aided by his aunt and stepmother HATSHEPSUT; AMENOPHIS III and TUTANKHAMUN. Amenophis II and Tuthmosis IV ascended to the throne as they left adolescence. These kings were perhaps all of a delicate constitution. Amenophis II's extraordinary physical strength in sporting activities (charioteering, archery and rowing) is praised in texts of the period, but even he did not reach the age of 50.

Ahmose's successor, Amenophis I (reg c. 1514–c. 1493 BC), died without a direct heir and the origins of Tuthmosis I (reg c. 1493–c. 1482 BC) are unknown. Tuthmosis I's two children, by different mothers, became the next royal couple: Tuthmosis II and Hatshepsut. Tuthmosis II (reg c. 1482–c. 1479 BC) died after a very brief reign, leaving extremely young children: Nefrure (the daughter of his principal wife, Hatshepsut) and Tuthmosis (the son of a minor wife, Ese). Hatshepsut acted as regent for her stepson, but in the seventh year of his reign she assumed the title and attributes of 'king', a masculine term for which ancient Egyptian had no feminine equivalent. It was probably not purely ambition that led Hatshepsut (reg c. 1479–c. 1458 BC) to seize royal power. Since Tuthmosis III was still young, the probable length of his co-regency with Hatshepsut would perhaps have posed a threat to the nation, deprived of an effective king. Hatshepsut governed the country for about 15 years, until the twenty-second year of the reign of Tuthmosis III. This feminine interlude was an imposing one. Although there were military campaigns in north and south during her reign, it was in her obelisks and her expedition to Punt that Hatshepsut took greatest pride. She also instigated building activities at Thebes (Deir el-Bahri, Medinet Habu and Karnak), Buhen and elsewhere. She gathered around her a team of capable and loyal officials, of whom SENENMUT was the most famous.

The way in which full powers were restored to the adult Tuthmosis, always present on the monuments as co-regent with his aunt and stepmother, is not known. She may simply have stepped to one side without being brutally ousted, but at a certain moment (before or after Hatshepsut's death) Tuthmosis III turned against her memory. He had her statues destroyed everywhere and her name and representations replaced with those of Tuthmosis I and Tuthmosis II, sometimes without deleting the feminine grammatical endings that betray the prior presence of an inscription of Hatshepsut.

After the great warring reigns, the last of which was that of Amenophis II (reg c. 1426–c. 1400 BC), Egyptian civilization underwent profound alterations that finally culminated in the Amarna period (see AMARNA STYLE). This development may principally be seen in the evolution of art, notably the tomb paintings. The reign of Amenophis II marks the transition between an austere artistic style and a more graceful one. From the reign of Tuthmosis IV onwards the new style became more sensual and elegant, but also increasingly generous and bold in its choice of the human form. The reign of Amenophis III is said to have been the most peaceful and opulent of the dynasty. In Asia, however, the state of Mitanni, probably west of the Euphrates, was hostile to Egypt. Tuthmosis IV had already put an end to hostilities with this state by marrying a Mitannian princess, and Amenophis III subsequently married two Mitannian princesses, Giluhepa, in his tenth regnal year, and Taduhepa, at the end of his reign. Matrimonial politics were followed by diplomatic activity with the Syrian principalities. The correspondence associated with this activity, written in the Akkadian language on clay tablets, was discovered at EL-AMARNA, in Egypt. The world known to the Egyptians certainly expanded at this time: on the base of a colossal statue of Amenophis III, still in situ at his mortuary temple at Thebes, are the names of a number of Cretan and Mycenaean towns.

Amenophis III must have come to the throne very young because his father died aged about 28. In his second regnal year he was already married to Tiye, daughter of Yuya and Tuya, natives of Akhmim, of provincial, common parentage. This was a true child-marriage and was commemorated by the 'issue' of large scarabs carrying news of the occasion. Four more such issues of scarabs announced other private events from the early part of the reign. The remaining part of the reign is not well known. Most of the King's activity was in the sphere of art and architecture: the reign is unique for the quality and quantity of its buildings and statues, and as much for the number and delicacy of its colossal works as for its toilet articles.

Queen Tiye's influence must have been considerable. A limestone statue (h. 7 m; Cairo, Egyp. Mus.) portrays her sitting next to the King at the same scale as him. Such equality in a royal couple had not been seen since Mycerinus (reg c. 2490–c. 2472 BC). Royal luxury found a perfect echo in private luxury; this too reached its peak. Great men also came to prominence during this reign, leaving not only remarkable statues and painted or sculpted tombs (as had many others before them during the 18th Dynasty) but sometimes also leaving a renown that persisted throughout Egyptian history—and not merely through a chance resurrection owed to modern archaeology. AMENHOTPE SON OF HAPU, was such a man; like IMHOTEP, Djoser's architect, he was deified in the Late Period (c. 750–332 BC) and worshipped as a saint of healing. Notably it was this Amenhotpe who presided over the erection of two colossal statues at Thebes known as the 'Colossi of Memnon' (see THEBES (i), §V and fig. 5). He took part in the great ceremonies for the renewal of the King's power (the *heb-sed* or royal jubilee festival) and was even accorded the privilege of having a funerary temple constructed among the mortuary temples of the kings.

(vi) Amarna period (c. 1353–c. 1332 BC). During the reign of Amenophis IV (*reg c.* 1353–*c.* 1336 BC), son of Amenophis III and Tiye, foreign policy consisted as usual of reaffirming the Egyptian presence in Nubia and Asia. The diplomatic correspondence found at el-Amarna reveals dangerous tensions among the Syrian potentates—the Hittites became an increasingly great threat and destroyed the state of Mitanni—but Egypt's position in Asia remained stable. In Egypt itself, on the other hand, the new King held beliefs that profoundly changed religion, thought, art, language and literature. Even though Amenophis IV's reign lasted only about 17 years, and the rulers of the 19th and 20th dynasties later destroyed its material remains, Egyptian civilization was long marked by this episode. First, the King replaced the traditional gods with the Aten (see §III below). This term is a common noun generally translated as 'disc', but the convex 18th Dynasty representations of the Aten suggest instead a 'globe'. The word, in fact, designates the sun in its material form as a heavenly body giving light, warmth and life; this is what Amenophis IV deified and honoured. Practically all other gods (including Amun and Osiris) were proscribed. The word 'god' itself was only allowed in the singular form. Later the names and effigies of the gods were destroyed wherever they occurred.

To mark the break with the past, Amenophis IV changed his name and took the name AKHENATEN. After several years spent in Thebes, where the Amarna style was already defined and used, the King decided to build a new capital city, where he could worship his god Aten. The King, 'guided by the god', found an ideal virgin site on a plain on the right bank of the Nile about 400 km north of Thebes. He named it Akhetaten. EL-AMARNA, the name of one of the modern villages near the ruins of Akhetaten, is now used to designate both the site and the whole period covered by the reign of Akhenaten, including that part preceding the choice of the new site. This selection took place in Akhenaten's fourth regnal year; by his sixth year the town was habitable, and the King settled there. In his twelfth regnal year, the zenith of the reign, a great ceremony took place in Akhetaten, in which representatives of subject peoples came to pay homage to the king and his god. The King had married NEFERTITI (who, like Tiye, the Queen-mother, was not of royal birth), and he had six daughters by her. Nefertiti apparently played an important role in his reign. Her name was written in a cartouche, which was not an innovation, though it was a privilege never accorded to the King's minor wives. Nefertiti was treated as the King's equal, being represented on the same scale. She was sometimes shown striking down an enemy, her hand brandishing a weapon in the ancient royal gesture, or sitting on a stool decorated with the symbol of the uniting of the two lands, which was usually reserved strictly for the king. There is a certain romanticism in the sentimental scenes in which the King and Queen may be seen clasped in one another's arms on their chariot or in a family group, playing with their children. Other aspects of this mood are the lyricism of the Hymn to the Aten, composed by the King himself, and the obvious predilection for nature during the Amarna period. Nefertiti was not, however, the only woman in the King's heart; there was also a minor wife, Kiya. The King, overcome by a frenzy of passion, apparently wanted to make Kiya into another Akhenaten, even permitting her to dress as king. Kiya, however, was disgraced, suppressed, or died before the end of the reign and her memory was vilified.

Events between the death of Akhenaten and the accession of TUTANKHAMUN (*reg c.* 1332–*c.* 1323 BC) are unclear. Was the throne occupied for a short time by Merytaten, daughter of Akhenaten, ruling alone? Who was the person bearing the name of Smenkhkare? Who was Tutankhamun himself, and what was his age on accession? The thousands of objects found in his undisturbed tomb at Thebes have thrown little light on his background. The examination of Tutankhamun's mummy has led to a number of hypotheses concerning his age at death, ranging from 16 to over 20. Since he reigned for nearly ten years these variants determine not only his age on accession but also the date of his birth during the reign of Akhenaten. He was a king's son, but he never appears on Akhenaten's numerous monuments, as if Akhenaten had had only daughters, by Nefertiti at least. It is therefore assumed that Tutankhamun was not Akhenaten's son but his brother and thus a son of Amenophis III. Since Akhenaten reigned for 17 years, Amenophis III would have to have been alive for several years of his son's reign in order to have been able to beget another son. A co-regency of this sort would have perhaps lasted 11 years. The problem remains unresolved.

(vii) Late New Kingdom (c. 1332–c. 1075 BC). At his accession, Akhenaten's young successor had the name Tutankhaten, and his wife was Akhenaten's daughter, Ankhesenpaaten. At the outset of his reign Tutankhaten renounced the Aten cult, and from then on the couple were known as Tutankhamun and Ankhesenamun, Akhenaten's city was abandoned, and Memphis, not Thebes, became the capital once again. Ay (*reg c.* 1323–*c.* 1319 BC), an elderly man who had been important under Akhenaten, came to the throne after the premature death of Tutankhamun, who left no heirs. Four years later Ay died, and HOREMHEB (*reg c.* 1319–*c.* 1292 BC) seized power. He had been a general during the preceding three reigns, and his energetic military exploits had sustained Egyptian power in Asia. He had also acted as a sort of regent under Tutankhamun, with an authority second only to that of the King. From the moment he became sole king he devoted himself to restoring order in the country, and he continued Tutankhamun's efforts to re-establish the cult

of Amun. Neither he nor Ay had any family ties with the 18th Dynasty.

The 19th Dynasty (c. 1292–c. 1190 BC) began with the reign of Ramesses I (reg c. 1292–c. 1290 BC), an important man from Horemheb's entourage. During this dynasty, when son once again succeeded father as king, Egypt remained powerful. In contrast, the world around Egypt changed considerably, and certain kings of the 19th Dynasty were forced to go to war frequently, no longer to increase their sphere of influence, as under Tuthmosis I, but to restrain the growth of other nations. Nubia hardly stirred, but in the north the Hittite empire was a major adversary. SETHOS I (reg c. 1290–c. 1279 BC), son of Ramesses I, played a decisive role, often rather forgotten beside the overwhelming reign of his son and successor RAMESSES II (reg c. 1279–c. 1213 BC). After the Amarna period and the troubled times that followed, Sethos I was responsible not only for the strengthening of Egypt's southern and western borders and successful wars in Syria–Palestine (including the first battle of Qadesh), but also for the frequent restoration of monuments necessitated by Akhenaten's erasures and destructions and probably also the defamation of Akhenaten's name. He began huge building projects, including the temple of Abydos and the great hypostyle hall of the Temple of Amun at Karnak (Thebes). He also founded a residential town (later known as PIRAMESSE) in the eastern Delta.

Ramesses II, brought to the throne rather young, had one of the longest reigns in Egyptian history: around 67 years. If measured in terms of the extraordinary quantity and often outstanding quality of the works undertaken on his orders, the country's prosperity must have been great. The publicity given to the second battle of Qadesh, which took place in the fifth year of his reign, adds to the impression that Ramesses II was an even greater warrior than his father. This battle, in which Ramesses II fought the Hittites and their allies from all parts of Asia Minor, was described in text and picture on the principal temples built by the King. Over the next 60 years there were few military operations in Asia, or at least they were less noisily proclaimed. An alliance with the Hittite king, Hattusili III, in Ramesses II's twenty-first regnal year, put a definitive end to hostilities between these peoples. In the treaty, a copy of which was found in each nation, the two heads of state promised each other mutual assistance, and a special clause provided for the extradition of fugitives from each country. The kings negotiated as equals. The motives that led the two monarchs to prefer diplomacy to war are unknown: the Hittites may have felt threatened by Assyria, and Ramesses II may have wanted to be rid of an external menace to deal with trouble inside Egypt. Their alliance was later cemented by marriages; Ramesses II's marriage to a daughter of Hattusili III, in his thirty-fourth regnal year, was proclaimed on stelae as far away as Abu Simbel; and later in his reign he married another daughter of the Hittite king.

The rest of Ramesses II's activities took place mainly in Egypt itself. His longevity allowed him to celebrate at least 11 royal jubilee festivals, and he is said to have had around 100 children (all named in texts of the time) by his principal wives Nefertari, Esenofre and various others. He was succeeded by his thirteenth son, Merneptah (reg c.

1213–c. 1204 BC), whose brothers had died before him (which was not surprising, considering the length of their father's reign).

Under Merneptah Egypt seemed for the first time fragile. The Libyans (their neighbours on the west) had, since prehistoric times, been the object of many Egyptian raids and expeditions. They now, however, became a threat and moved towards Egypt with the intention of settling there. Ramesses II had founded a line of fortresses, along the Mediterranean coast, in order to hold off the Libyans, but this time they were able to penetrate deep into the valley. It is also thought that the Exodus of the people of Israel may have occurred at about this time; the Israel Stele (Cairo, Egyp. Mus.), an inscribed granite stele of Merneptah, carries the only reference to Israel in any Egyptian text. Merneptah did, however, manage to defeat the coalition of Libyans from the west and also various populations often erroneously termed the Sea Peoples who came down from Asia via the Syrian coast, converging on the Delta. This first serious threat arose again, a short time later, under RAMESSES III (reg c. 1187–c. 1156 BC).

The 19th Dynasty ended in confusion. Domestic troubles were not settled until the reign of Sethnakht (reg c. 1190–c. 1187 BC), founder of the 20th Dynasty (c. 1190–c. 1075 BC) and father of Ramesses III. The Libyans to the west and the many peoples to the east (the Tjekker, Sheklesh, Danuna, Weshesh and Philistines) attempted once again to invade Egypt. The King narrowly succeeded in preventing these incursions and gave his victories tremendous publicity on the walls of his mortuary temple at Medinet Habu (Thebes). The Philistines and their allies were held back at the edge of the Delta; there they gave their name to the land of Palestine. The Libyans had been defeated in the military sphere, but they nevertheless filtered into Egypt (settling and becoming mercenaries in pharaoh's armies) and finally assumed supreme power over the native Egyptians with the 22nd Dynasty (c. 950–c. 730 BC).

The successors of Ramesses III, Ramesses IV–XI, brought the New Kingdom to an inglorious close. After Ramesses III royal power decreased and insecurity reigned, while the power of the Amun priesthood grew. Under Ramesses XI (reg c. 1104–c. 1075 BC), Herihor, a high priest of Amun who was also a military commander and viceroy of Kush and thus governor of Nubia, went so far as to write his name in a cartouche, like that of a pharaoh, though he did so discreetly in the interior of the temple of Khons at Karnak. It was Herihor who held real power, despite the existence of Ramesses XI. When this last king was entombed in the Valley of the Kings, the necropolis at Thebes reserved exclusively for monarchs, the New Kingdom came to an end. The schism between royal power and the power of the Amun priesthood gave rise to the Third Intermediate Period.

(viii) Third Intermediate Period (c. 1070–c. 750 BC). The 21st Dynasty, governing only Lower Egypt, was founded in TANIS in the Delta by King Smendes. The southern part of the country, however, was administered by a succession of high priests of Amun beginning with Pinudjem I. It was for the high priests' court in Thebes that the artists' workshops then laboured, with a style both classical and serene. The disorder at the end of the New Kingdom had permitted sacrilegious pillaging even in the Valley of the Kings, and under Pinudjem I work began systematically to recover from the plundered tombs those royal mummies and funerary objects that had escaped the devastation, moving them from one hiding place to another. Eventually most of the royal remains found a safe resting place in a cache near Deir el-Bahri, where they remained forgotten until the end of the 19th century.

After the New Kingdom Egypt once again retreated within her natural boundaries—the edges of the Delta and the 1st Nile cataract. The south of the country was a homogeneous region, but the north was fragmented, with areas under the king's authority and others under the Great Chiefs of the Ma, the leaders of the Libyan groups settled in Egypt. One of these, Shoshenq of BUBASTIS, seized power and founded the 22nd Dynasty (c. 950–c. 730 BC). Shoshenq marked his advent with an expedition into Palestine (in the time of Rehoboam, King of Judah), where he sacked the temple of Jerusalem (1 Kings 14:25–8; 2 Chronicles 12:2–9). To retain control of Thebes he installed his son Iuput as high priest of Amun, taking advantage of a vacancy on the throne. The ill-fated intrigues between the Libyan kings and the Amun priesthood resulted in a full-blown civil war during the following reigns. The tribal structure of the dominant Libyan class also led to the feudalization of the Delta, where rival principalities multiplied. It was also in the Delta that the first royal line of SAIS, in the persons of Tefnakhte and Bocchoris, appeared. This is the picture of the Delta given by texts of the Kushite sovereign Piye (reg c. 750–c. 719 BC) at the time of his unopposed conquest in about 730 BC.

(ix) Late Period (c. 750–332 BC). Nubia had been virtually ignored since the end of the New Kingdom (c. 1075 BC). Egypt's princes had abandoned it, having too many domestic problems and too few resources to maintain their former 'colonization'. This independence allowed a line of dark-skinned rulers, settled in NAPATA at the foot of the 4th Nile cataract, to grow in strength. They decided to conquer the country that had ruled them, and they did so brilliantly. These Kushite kings were not conquerors in the usual sense but rather admirers of Egypt and devout worshippers of Amun, who may well have been a native god of theirs (for further discussion of Kush see NUBIA, §IV).

The Kushite rulers of the 25th Dynasty (c. 750–656 BC) presented themselves as true pharaohs and made their troops respect the country. Piye advanced in one move up to the Delta, conquering both Thebes and Memphis. The Kushite capital remained, however, at Napata and only Upper Egypt, which adjoined their home territory, really belonged to their sphere of influence. By this time the High Priest of Amun had lost his importance, having been replaced as head of this theocratic state by the daughter of a king, the virgin divine adoratrice (or 'God's Wife of Amun'). Each princess adopted another as her successor, but the choice of heiress was more often made under

constraint. Piye was thus able to impose his sister Amenirdis, daughter of Kashta, on the divine adoratrice Shepenwepet, daughter of the Libyan Osorkon IV. Other Kushite princesses, Shepenwepet II and Amenirdis II, followed her. Later, Psammetichus I (reg 664–610 BC), founder of the 26th Dynasty (664–525 BC), imposed his daughter Nitocris on them. Another Saite (26th Dynasty) princess, Ankhnesneferibre, held the position of divine adoratrice until the arrival of the Persians (c. 525 BC), who abolished the institution. In the 25th and 26th dynasties the imposition of a selected princess at the head of the estates of Amun was the most elegant way of controlling the area that continued to be the heart of Upper Egypt. This princess had almost royal status, with a titulary written in two cartouches and the authority to build on her estates, if often under the king's tutelage. The divine adoratrice was attended by a high steward who administered her material possessions: the estates of Amun. These high stewards, such as MENTUEMHET, were men of great note whose tombs and statues constituted a large part of the artistic activity of the time.

The Kushite rulers were securely settled in Upper Egypt; this was the 25th Dynasty of kings Shabaka, Shebitku, TAHARQA and Tantamani. They left behind monuments of high quality, restoring to Egyptian art a monumental quality that had been lost since the beginning of the New Kingdom, though they also built in their own home territory, Nubia and the Sudan. Events in the north were more uncertain as the local potentates had not lost all freedom of action. In addition, Assyria, discovering a prodigious appetite for conquest, seized Palestine, and its king Assurbanipal (reg 668–627 BC) was able to invade Egypt as far as Thebes, which was sacked for the first time in its history. The Kushite king, Tantamani, withdrew southwards and Psammetichus I, Prince of Sais, found in the Assyrian king an unexpected ally to the establishment of his authority throughout the country. This was the 26th Dynasty, known as the Saite dynasty after its capital SAIS; it was an independent and nationalistic period. Greeks were for the first time allowed to settle in the Delta, concentrated in the town of NAUKRATIS. Psammetichus II (reg 595–589 BC) wished to expunge all traces of the Kushite domination; he removed from the foreheads of 25th Dynasty royal figures the uraeus wearing the red crown signifying that they were masters of Lower Egypt. This same Psammetichus led a bitter campaign against Nubia. He captured and sacked the ancient Kushite capital of Napata, though the Kushite princes had by that time already withdrawn further south to MEROË near the 5th Nile cataract. It was during this expedition that Greek and Carian mercenaries carved the most ancient Greek inscription in the whole Nile Valley on the leg of a colossal statue of Ramesses II at Abu Simbel.

The Persians Cambyses II (reg 525–522 BC) and Darius I (reg 521–486 BC) put an end to this last great Egyptian dynasty. For the first time the pharaoh constantly represented on the temple walls was a foreigner living outside Egypt. Egypt itself continued to flourish, and it was at this point that the Greek historian Herodotus made his visit there. The Persian occupation was interrupted c. 404 BC. Three brief native dynasties then followed; the 30th Dynasty (380–343 BC), including Nectanebo I and II, left the most traces. The Persians then regained the advantage (343–332 BC) until the arrival of Alexander the Great (*reg* 332–323 BC) as liberator. Egypt, however, was subsequently no more than a part of Alexander's vast empire. He founded a new town, Alexandria (*see* ALEXANDRIA, §1), on the edge of the Delta overlooking the Mediterranean, although it was never considered truly Egyptian: it was Alexandria 'ad Aegyptum' (Lat.: 'near Egypt').

(x) Greco-Roman period (332 BC–AD 395). Ptolemy I, who inherited Egypt in the division of Alexander's empire, and his successors (all called Ptolemy) pursued the policies of Hellenistic kings. The wealth of Egypt allowed them imperialist designs on the eastern Mediterranean basin: this was a Ptolemaic, rather than an Egyptian, policy. It was the same when Cleopatra VII (*reg* 51–30 BC), the last of the line, attempted by her charms to turn to her own benefit the Roman annexation of Egypt. But whereas the Ptolemaic pharaoh had lived close to Egypt in Alexandria, the Roman pharaoh in Rome was a distant king who lost all the efficacy that for thousands of years had haloed this divine personage. The Christian God supplanted him in the devotions of the Nile Valley's inhabitants and Egypt turned its back on the world of the pharaohs (for further discussion *see* COPTIC ART, §I).

BIBLIOGRAPHY
E. Bevan: *A History of Egypt under the Ptolemaic Dynasty* (London, 1927)
F. K. Kienitz: *Die politische Geschichte Ägyptens vom 7. bis zum 4. Jahrhundert vor der Zeitwende* (Berlin, 1953)
A. H. Gardiner: *Egypt of the Pharaohs* (Oxford, 1961)
W. Helck: *Geschichte des alten Ägypten* (Leiden and Cologne, 1968, 2/1981)
K. A. Kitchen: *The Third Intermediate Period in Egypt (1100–650 BC)* (Warminster, 1973)
E. Hornung: *Grundzüge der ägyptischen Geschichte* (Darmstadt, 1978)
J. Baines and J. Malek: *Atlas of Ancient Egypt* (Oxford, 1980), pp. 30–55
B. G. Trigger and others: *Ancient Egypt: A Social History* (Cambridge, 1985)
N. C. Grimal: *Histoire de l'Egypte ancienne* (Paris, 1988); Eng. trans. by I. Shaw as *A History of Ancient Egypt* (Oxford, 1992)
B. J. Kemp: *Ancient Egypt: Anatomy of Civilization* (London, 1989)
R. Friedman and B. Adams, eds: *The Followers of Horus: Studies Dedicated to Michael Allen Hoffman, 1944–1990* (Oxford, 1992)
T. H. H. James: *Egypt: The Living Past* (London, 1992)
A. J. Spencer: *Early Egypt: The Rise of Civilisation in the Nile Valley* (London, 1992)
J. Vercoutter: *Des origines à la fin de l'Ancien Empire: 12,000–2000 av. J.C.*, i of *L'Egypte et la vallée du Nil*, ed. J. Vercoutter (Paris, 1992)
C. Vandersleyen: *De la fin de l'Ancien Empire à la fin du Nouvel Empire*, ii of *L'Egypte et la vallée du Nil* (Paris, 1994)
CLAUDE VANDERSLEYEN

3. TRADE AND EXCHANGE. In antiquity local and international trade was based on an exchange of surplus raw materials, agricultural produce and manufactured items. Though Egypt lay somewhat south of the focus of international trade (the cities of the Levantine coast), it had strong commercial links, as well as other connections, with the countries of the Mediterranean, Africa and western Asia. Wherever people traded they carried their language, religion, knowledge of art, industrial processes and architectural forms. Trade thus involved an exchange of culture and ideas as well as materials and products.

(i) Trade routes. (ii) Imports and exports. (iii) The mobile middle class. (iv) Artistic exchange. (v) Transition to Hellenism.

(i) Trade routes. The major trade routes out of Egypt went south and north. To the south lay the lands of Nubia,

Sudan and Punt (coastal Eritrea or Somalia), which produced a host of luxury items. Some of these found their way into Egyptian commerce with Europe and western Asia. The routes were via the Nile Valley or along the coast of the Red Sea. To the north lay Syria, rich in woods and wood products greatly desired by Egypt. By sea the routes went up the Syro-Palestinian coast; by land they passed through Sinai and up along the Levantine coastal plains. Both northern routes terminated at such coastal ports as BYBLOS and Beirut.

From the Levant, Egyptian exports and people travelled by ship and caravan to all the corners of the civilized world. One route went east across northern Syria to the upper Euphrates River and down that river valley to the Arabian Gulf. Another went farther north across the Zagros Mountains into Anatolia, connecting with still more land routes to such ports as Miletos and Troy on the western coast of Anatolia. An all-important and heavily travelled sea lane left the Levantine coast, touched on Cyprus and Rhodes, and passed through the Cyclades Islands to reach Crete and mainland Greece. Already in the first half of the 3rd millennium BC, Egyptian objects found their way via this route to the Troad and the Greek islands.

The theory that there was a direct trade route from the Aegean to Africa, with the return voyage along the coast at the eastern end of the Mediterranean, is supported by the apparent evidence of a surviving fresco at Akrotiri on the island of Thera in a house destroyed around 1525 BC by volcanic activity (*see* THERA, §2). It shows scenes of an Aegean fleet moving between towns on seacoasts. The flora and fauna, geographical details, costumes of the inhabitants and other elements in the representation of one of the towns have led some scholars to suggest that it was situated on the North African coast, perhaps even in the Nile Delta.

Ancient trade took place in the face of considerable danger. Egyptian texts frequently referred to *shasu* (Egyp.: 'wanderers') who were brigands and soldiers of fortune. Mariners faced the hazards of pirates and storms attested by the numerous ancient shipwrecks discovered in the late 20th century. The best-known of these are the two small merchantmen that sank near Cape Gelidonya and Kaş off the southern coast of Anatolia around 1200 BC and 1300 BC respectively. Their cargoes consisted mainly of ingots of copper, bronze and tin, broken agricultural tools to be traded for their metal value, raw glass and pottery. The Kaş wreck also included Egyptian ebony and a golden scarab of the Egyptian queen Nefertiti (*c.* 1350 BC). Both ships were heading west, toward the Aegean, and their last port of call had probably been Cyprus. It has been suggested that there was a Syrian merchant on board the Cape Gelidonya wreck who manufactured bronze at various stops *en route* and that there was a Mycenaean merchant aboard the Kaş wreck. These and similar underwater discoveries have added a new dimension to the study of maritime commerce in the Late Bronze Age.

While private trade was carried on in Egypt at the local level, international commerce was a State monopoly. Government expeditions regularly went to southern Sinai for turquoise, the Eastern Desert for minerals, building stones and Nubian gold, and into the Western Desert for amethyst (*see* §VII, 1 and 2 below). Early in the 3rd millennium BC small trading colonies of resident Egyptians were established in southern Palestine and, a few centuries later, there were Egyptian merchants resident at Byblos on the Syrian coast. Egyptian officials travelled north to Byblos and south to Punt to oversee the royal interests at these mercantile outposts. Indirect contacts with the Aegean existed by at least 2000 BC through the Levantine ports. Contacts with Mesopotamia via these same ports had already been under way for a thousand years.

(ii) Imports and exports. These far-flung contacts dealt mainly in luxury items imported for the wealthier classes of society and for temple treasuries. The fertile Nile Valley produced a great variety of foodstuffs so there was no need, as in other societies, to import the daily necessities of life. From the lands to the south came cultivated myrrh and live myrrh trees, a selection of spices, incense, black eye-paint, ebony, ivory, gold, prized animals such as panthers, apes and monkeys, as well as ostrich feathers and eggs. Syria–Palestine supplied wine, vases of precious metal and, above all, the timber, wood oils and resins from the coniferous forests of Lebanon.

Lebanese timber was of particular importance to Egypt, where the native woods did not meet the demands of a society that required ever increasing amounts of cedar, cypress and pine (*see* §VII, 3 below). Sturdy wooden beams were needed for the vast building projects. Wealthy Egyptians preferred household furniture made of cedar, and the oils and resins from Lebanon were ingredients in perfumes and medicinal recipes. It was probably the Egyptian funerary cult, however, that prompted the greatest demand for expensive and more durable woods, since the tomb and its furnishings were meant to last forever. Those who could afford it used imported woods for many of the standard items to be placed in burials, such as coffins, boxes and chests for food and clothing, statuettes and doorways inside the tomb structure. Cedar oil was used in mummification and two of the seven sacred oils usually placed in burials were from lands to the north of Egypt. Doorways in private houses and temples were often made of cedar, and cedar-wood floors were laid down in sacred inner temple areas. The Lebanese woods were used for the masts and rudders of Egyptian ships. These and other uses of Lebanese timber created a unique relationship between Egypt and Byblos, the major supplier of these products. This was an economic bond that lasted throughout pharaonic history.

Trade contacts with the Aegean world were sporadic in the 3rd millennium BC but more regular and continuous in the 2nd millennium. Whether Aegean ships actually sailed to Egypt, or Egyptian ships to the Aegean, is an open question. The rare portrayals of Mediterranean shipping ventures shown in Egyptian reliefs and paintings invariably show the ships and crews as Syrian rather than Aegean. However, representations of foreign peoples in the 'tribute' scenes include many Aegeans in their native costumes; they were therefore presumably well-known to Egyptian artists. It seems likely that the Levantine ports were the meeting-place for ships from both regions and it was there that cargoes were bought and sold. The Mediterranean in the late 2nd millennium BC was probably dominated by the Syrians rather than the Mycenaeans.

Whatever the nature of the contact, Aegean products found their way to Egypt in considerable quantity: vases of silver, gold and bronze, rings and ingots of precious metals, obsidian, herbs, olive oil and sesame oil. The oils were transported in small, finely painted jars, which must have been articles of trade in themselves. Opium was also a prominent Aegean export and was used as a general ingredient in many Egyptian medical prescriptions. Cyprus was an important factor in trade with the Aegean, primarily as a supplier of copper and as an intermediate stage in the tin trade. The copper came from Cyprus, but the origin of the tin used before the 1st millennium BC is debatable. Anatolian texts of the early 2nd millennium BC refer to tin, but they do not mention its source; a few centuries later it was said to come from the east, perhaps Baluchistan. By the early 1st millennium BC, the tin deposits of Iberia were being worked, and this was the major impetus for the westward expansion of the Phoenicians. Until that time, it was mostly through Aegean and Cypriot traders that this valuable metal reached Egypt.

During the New Kingdom (*c.* 1540–*c.* 1075 BC) a great deal of wealth poured into Egypt as booty and taxes from foreign provinces, but trade continued, and this had to be paid for. Egyptian export items consisted of both luxury products and necessities. The latter were primarily foodstuffs, which Egypt produced in great abundance. Wheat and barley were regular exports to Canaan and, eventually, to Anatolia and Greece. Erratic rainfall, growing populations or war conditions created a need for food that could not be met locally. Egypt also exported alabaster vases and bowls and several grades of fine linen cloth (*see* §XVII, 16 and 17 below). The earliest evidence for the export of papyrus is from the 8th century BC, when the alphabet was gaining popularity in Greece and western Asia and literacy was becoming more widespread.

One document, Papyrus Moscow 120 (Moscow, Pushkin Mus. F.A.), records precisely what the Egyptian State paid for timber from Lebanon. Around 1100 BC the envoy Wenamun purchased timber at Byblos with a cargo of gold and silver vases, linen tunics, textiles, rope, ox hides, lentils and fish. In this case, the ruler of Byblos produced court records to show that gold and silver had traditionally been traded for local woods. In addition to Nubian gold, other products from the south such as spices, ebony and ivory found their way through Egypt into the international marketplace. The same is true for the turquoise obtained by the Egyptians from Sinai. Official commercial transactions are not usually recorded in Egyptian documents since they preferred to speak of 'tribute' or 'gifts' from foreign rulers. Such transactions undoubtedly underlie 'gifts' to the Egyptian king recorded in the EL-AMARNA letters, part of the official State archives of *c.* 1360–*c.* 1300 BC that preserve the international correspondence between Egypt and numerous other states. The gilded bedstead and chariot sent from the king of Cyprus were certainly in payment for Egyptian grain or some other commodity (el-Amarna letter 34).

Thousands of small objects from Egypt, such as scarabs, amulets, figurines and beads, have been recovered throughout the east Mediterranean countries, at North African sites and as far away as Italy and Spain. Much of this material probably found its way abroad via normal trade channels, but objects were no doubt also conveyed as souvenirs or trinkets picked up along the way by individuals moving around the ancient world.

(iii) The mobile middle class. The phenomenon of the mobile middle class is important in understanding not only the transfer of objects from one place to another, but also the movement of ideas, artistic motifs, religious beliefs and other elements of culture. Most individuals in ancient societies were engaged in agriculture and therefore more or less tied to one geographical location. A smaller group was involved in government and administration and thus tied to capital cities and bureaucracies. However, a third group, a kind of middle class of artisans, craftsmen, merchants, soldiers and sailors, and even priests, was far freer to move about. These more mobile professions formed much of the creative element in society, transmitting culture as well as objects. Merchants, sailors and others were obviously required to travel, but artists and craftsmen also went abroad. A Syrian artist, who left UGARIT in the 14th century BC to study in Egypt, returned home to produce a striking set of 16 carved ivory panels with strong Egyptianizing influence (*see* ANCIENT NEAR EAST, §II, 3). Phoenician ivory-carvers were hired to decorate palaces in Palestine and Assyria. Canaanite weavers came to ply their trade in Egypt, and it has been suggested that Minoan potters arrived in Egypt after the fall of Knossos around 1360 BC.

The cultural effects of normal commercial relations and of the movement of the mobile middle class are apparent in many ways. For example local imitations of popular foreign products were cheaper and could therefore be made available to more than just the very rich. Such imitations are found everywhere. Craftsmen at Byblos imitated Egyptian jewellery, Canaanite and Aegean stone-workers copied Egyptian stone vases, Egyptian metal-smiths forged Aegean style bowls and so on (*see* MINOAN, §X). Aegean and Cypriot pottery styles with their pleasing decorative patterns were reproduced in Canaan and Egypt. The ubiquitous Egyptian scarab, a highly popular amulet also used as jewellery, was eventually manufactured abroad in Phoenicia, North Africa, Sardinia and elsewhere.

(iv) Artistic exchange. The borrowing of artistic motifs, styles and techniques is more subtle and less easily defined than the movement of objects. Opinions often differ as to the nature of the influences and the way in which they were transmitted. According to Classical sources, DAIDALOS, the mythical sculptor of King Minos of Crete, was inspired by the sense of movement and the form of Egyptian statuary. The same sources note that Egyptian methods of carving were adopted by Greek master sculptors on Samos. Such statements are supported by surviving monuments, particularly the Archaic Greek kouros statues, in which Egyptian influence is readily seen. The artistic canon of proportional representation whereby figures of any size could be given the same proportions (*see* §IV, 3 below) was also borrowed by Greek artists. In this case there are literary statements (Diodorus Siculus I.98.5–9) as well as physical evidence pointing to Egypt as an artistic source.

Prior to the literary evidence of the Classical period, the question of artistic influence is more subjective. For example in 'tribute' scenes painted in several Egyptian private tomb chapels of the 15th century BC, such as those of Rekhmire and Senenmut at Thebes, there are lines of foreigners bringing all manner of valuable objects and raw materials to the Egyptian ruler; the appearance of Aegeans and their products in these scenes has excited many theories on direct trade and influence. But there is some debate over the interpretation of the objects themselves. Some assume that all the vases and other items are Aegean; others suggest that many of the vase forms and some of the decorative patterns on the colourful Aegean costumes are not Aegean at all, but Egyptian. The question is important since decorated textiles are universally thought to be one way in which artistic patterns and motifs moved from one culture to another.

There are, however, a number of definite connections in art, such as the strong Egyptian influences on the art of northern Syria. In the 18th and 17th and again in the 14th and 13th centuries BC, Syrian cylinder seals incorporated Egyptian figures, motifs and hieroglyphs into a characteristic and successful mixture of several artistic traditions, including Egyptian, Hittite, Aegean, Mesopotamian and local (*see* ANCIENT NEAR EAST, §II, 1 (ii)(b)). This pleasing mixture of different traditions appears on carved panels and ivory objects of the same period. In some cases, the Egyptian elements seem to predominate, at least in terms of subject-matter and motifs, including Egyptian royal and divine figures in the appropriate costume and coiffure, numerous symbols, papyrus plants, sphinxes and griffins. Such ivories became famous throughout the ancient world and both objects and craftsmen were a major Syrian export. The ivory craftsmen were clearly not Egyptian, but rather native artists who reproduced Egyptian motifs within the dictates of their own techniques. The proportions of the figures, the position of an arm or leg, the facial features and other details are distinctive; the sphinxes in the ivories are female, whereas the Egyptian sphinx was male; volutes and other frills have been added; and human figures are more rounded and somewhat less rigid than their Egyptian counterparts. The same is true of the shallow metal bowls of Phoenician manufacture common in the earlier 1st millennium BC (*see* PHOENICIAN). The inner surfaces are covered with circular registers of foreign motifs, including many Egyptian figures and symbols that show similar subtle differences. Such vessels were an important export and have been discovered throughout the Mediterranean world.

This 'Egyptianizing' tradition in art was already under way in Canaan in the early 2nd millennium BC. At that time Egyptian jewellery (*see* §XV below) was brought to Byblos, probably as part of royal payments for local timber. Among this jewellery were fine gold pectorals, a common adornment of royalty in Egypt. Such pectorals were imitated for local rulers by the craftsmen of Byblos who maintained the Egyptian subject-matter and general style, but viewed the Egyptian original through their own traditions and techniques. There is always something 'un-Egyptian' about such copies. The use of plant motifs and the particular arrangement or choice of symbols suggests that these were made by Canaanite craftsmen working from Egyptian originals. One pectoral introduces into the overall design a winged sun-disc in its Syrian rather than

Egyptian form. Byblos was the centre for Egyptian commercial ties in Canaan; Egyptian cultural influence was therefore certainly strongest there. In addition to much imitation in art, the local rulers borrowed Egyptian titles and carved their inscriptions in Egyptian hieroglyphs. Ivories from Megiddo and Samaria, the headdress of the goddess Hathor on local female figurines and Egyptian symbols engraved on many kinds of objects are but a few examples.

Reciprocal influences between Egyptian and Aegean art have also been suggested: for instance although early Egyptian mural art is generally characterized by a static quality, in which human and divine figures, animals and plants have a rigid appearance even in compositions intended to portray action (see §IV below), during the 18th Dynasty (c. 1540–c. 1292 BC), when connections with the Aegean were especially close, some wall paintings (such as the hunting scene in the tomb of Rekhmire) have far freer compositions. Swiftness of motion is shown by the 'flying gallop' whereby animals have all four feet off the ground in a leaping movement, and figures are organized in broader spatial relationships instead of along ground lines in horizontal registers. It is generally conceded that such stylistic changes were the result of Aegean influence.

While a great deal of Egyptian influence has been postulated in Aegean art of the 2nd millennium BC, this is far more difficult to support by actual evidence. Representations of the Egyptian hippopotamus-goddess Thoeris are known from Minoan and Mycenaean seals, though it is impossible to state what role, if any, this goddess may have had in Aegean religious beliefs. The sphinx and griffin were old Egyptian motifs that changed their form in the new Aegean context and were then transferred back to the orient in this altered form. Aegean frescoes contain Egyptian elements such as papyrus plants or scenes reminiscent of the Nilotic landscape. Ostrich eggs imported from Egypt were imitated in clay by Aegean potters. It has also been suggested that the convention of portraying male figures in red and female in white came from Egypt. This was an established convention in Egypt, though it may reflect reality since outside work was generally performed by men who were thus more subject to the effects of sunlight.

Two techniques that may have originated in Egypt and spread to the Aegean and elsewhere are the manufacture of glaze and faience. Both terms are often used incorrectly in archaeological publications so that tracing the spread of these techniques is sometimes difficult. Glaze was first used in prehistoric Egypt around 4000 BC (see §XVII, 5 below); soon afterwards Egyptian faience was invented. The manufacture of glazed faience objects had developed on Crete by the end of the 3rd millennium BC. Imported Egyptian faience objects have been found on Crete and the Greek mainland, but the actual techniques of faience production were also borrowed from Egypt or Mesopotamia. There are locally made faience objects on Crete, sometimes mixed with Syrian and Egyptian faience vessels as at Mycenae. The 'Town Mosaic' at Knossos (see MINOAN, §VII), made of faience wall tiles (dating to the early 2nd millennium BC), was a more immediate product of this technological borrowing. The later glazed tile decoration on the walls of Mesopotamian and Persian palaces still preserves a tradition perhaps first known in Egypt.

(v) Transition to Hellenism. During the first half of the 1st millennium BC the ancient world underwent an extraordinary political transformation, which had considerable effects on international commercial and cultural exchanges. In this relatively short period in the east the Assyrian and Babylonian empires came and went to be replaced by the even larger Persian empire. In the west Greece moved toward its Classical age and Rome began its long struggle with Carthage for domination in the western Mediterranean. In this vast arena of newer, more vigorous states, Egypt had only a minor political role, although its commercial and cultural contacts abroad continued. Egyptian surplus food and manufactured goods such as linen cloth and papyrus were exported. Greek soldiers were added to the Egyptian mercenary system and Greek merchants established a mercantile settlement at NAUKRATIS in the Egyptian Delta, implanting for the first time on Egyptian soil a centre of Greek culture. A significant amount of Classical Greek literature, religion, mythology, art and science received its impetus from the older civilizations in the east. How much of this new knowledge came from Egypt is debatable, though Classical writers looked on the ancient culture of the Nile Valley with respect, often with awe. It seems, however, that the extensive cultural borrowing from the orient came mostly from non-Egyptian sources, particularly the Phoenicians.

BIBLIOGRAPHY
H. J. Kantor: *The Aegean and the Orient in the Second Millennium B.C.* (Bloomington, 1947)
——: 'Syro-Palestinian Ivories', *J. Nr E. Stud.*, xv (1956), pp. 153–74
J. Vercoutter: *L'Egypte et le monde égéen préhellénique* (Cairo, 1956)
W. Helck: *Die Beziehungen Ägyptens zu Vorderasien im 3. und 2. Jahrtausend v. Chr.* (Wiesbaden, 1962, rev. 2/1971)
W. A. Ward: 'Egypt and the East Mediterranean from Predynastic Times to the End of the Old Kingdom', *J. Econ. & Soc. Hist. Orient*, vi (1963), pp. 1–57
W. S. Smith: *Interconnections in the Ancient Near East: A Study of the Relationships between the Arts of Egypt, the Aegean, and Western Asia* (New Haven, 1965)
C. H. Gordon: *Ugarit and Minoan Crete: The Bearing of Their Texts on Western Culture* (New York, 1966)
O. Tufnell and W. A. Ward: 'Relations between Byblos, Egypt and Mesopotamia at the End of the Third Millennium B.C.: A Study of the Montet Jar', *Syria*, xliii (1966), pp. 165–241
F. Schachermeyr: *Ägäis und Orient: Die überseeischen Kulturbeziehungen von Kreta und Mykenai mit Ägypten, der Levante und Kleinasien unter besonderer Berücksichtigung des 2. Jahrtausends v. Chr.* (Vienna, 1967)
Trans. Amer. Philos. Soc., lvii/8 (1967) [whole issue dedicated to the Cape Gelidonya wreck]
R. S. Merrillees: *The Cypriote Bronze Age Pottery Found in Egypt* (Lund, 1968)
E. Riefstahl: *Ancient Egyptian Glass and Glazes in the Brooklyn Museum* (Brooklyn, 1968)
W. A. Ward: *Egypt and the East Mediterranean World 2200–1900 B.C.: Studies in Egyptian Foreign Relations during the First Intermediate Period* (Beirut, 1971)
R. S. Merrillees and I. Winter: 'Bronze Age Trade between the Aegean and Egypt: Minoan and Mycenaean Pottery from Egypt in the Brooklyn Museum', *Misc. Wilbouriana*, i (1972), pp. 101–33
Acts of the International Archaeological Symposium 'The Mycenaeans in the Eastern Mediterranean': Nicosia, 1973
R. S. Merrillees: *Trade and Transcendence in the Bronze Age Levant* (Göteborg, 1974)
R. D. Barnett: *A Catalogue of the Nimrud Ivories* (London, 1975)
B. S. Ridgeway: *The Archaic Style in Greek Sculpture* (Princeton, 1977)
W. Helck: *Die Beziehungen Ägyptens und Vorderasiens zur Ägäis bis ins 7. Jahrhundert v. Chr.* (Darmstadt, 1979)

B. J. Kemp and R. S. Merrillees: *Minoan Pottery in Second Millennium Egypt* (Mainz, 1980)

W. M. Davis: 'Egypt, Samos, and the Archaic Style in Greek Sculpture', *J. Egyp. Archaeol.*, lxvii (1981), pp. 61–81

G. F. Bass: 'A Bronze Age Shipwreck at Ulu Burun (Kaş): 1984 Campaign', *Amer. J. Archaeol.*, xc (1986), pp. 269–96

W. A. Ward and S. Joukowsky, eds: *The Crisis Years: The 12th Century BC from Beyond the Danube to the Tigris* (Dubuque, 1992)

WILLIAM A. WARD

II. Craftsman and artist.

In ancient Egypt it is impossible to distinguish between the craftsman and the artist in the sense that these two terms are usually defined in modern times. The modern Western perception of the role of the artist has been conditioned by the history of art from the time of the Renaissance and a distinction is usually made between the 'fine arts' (painting and sculpture) and the 'crafts'. There was no word definable as 'art' in the ancient Egyptian language; the word 'craft' appears to have been considered sufficient.

The primary role of the artist and craftsman was to serve the gods, the State and the king. By extension, and with the implied acquiescence of the ruler, artists were also able to work for society at large. Conformity to canonical strictures was honoured (*see* §IV below) in preference to individuality and innovation, although skill in execution might sometimes be praised. The magical nature of Egyptian symbolic representation conferred on the artist or craftsman an importance beyond individual recognition, for it was his ability that 'gave life' to the paintings and carvings in temples and tombs.

1. Anonymity and status. 2. Training, workshop practice and organization.

1. ANONYMITY AND STATUS. While the names of some ancient Greek artists (e.g. Praxiteles and Apelles) and some biographical facts about them are known, interest in the personality of the artist is a relatively modern idea. There are certainly no Egyptian potters that can be identified in the way that the signatures of Euphronius and Nikosthenes are read on Attic Greek vases (although possible Egyptian artists' signatures appear on some items in the Roman period; *see* §§IX, 3(xiii)(a) and XVII, 14 below). The absence of information concerning specific ancient Egyptian artists is explained by the fact that they were considered to be paid workmen simply plying trades. One further reason for their lack of identification as named artists is that very little work was carried out wholly by a single artist.

In the *Onomasticon of Amenemope*, a literary work composed in the late 20th Dynasty (*c.* 1100 BC), workers are listed and grouped according to affinities or similarities: thus sculptors are listed after carpenters and before copper- and goldsmiths, clearly indicating a place in society shared with artisans rather than high-placed functionaries. There was little recognition of the arts of sculpture and painting or the crafts of metalwork, jewellery, pottery and furniture as anything more than a class of gainful and skilled employment.

Evidence suggests that painters and sculptors were at the higher end of the scale of the 'artistic' trades, but that all workers engaged in the production of arts and crafts were generally considered only on the level of useful servants. Artists and craftsmen singled out by name in inscriptions can almost always be taken as overseers or supervisors of workmen, though they may themselves have risen from the ranks of the trained artisans. In the *Satire of the Trades*, written in the Middle Kingdom (*c.* 2008–*c.* 1630 BC), a father extolling the life and occupation of the scribe says: 'I never saw a sculptor as envoy, nor is a goldsmith ever sent'. This indicates the relatively low social status enjoyed by the artist and craftsman, even allowing for the bias and the motivation of the author. The inference is clear that workers in the visual arts were generally not trusted with matters as complicated as diplomacy.

From the beginning of the Old Kingdom (*c.* 2575–*c.* 2150 BC) there are a number of instances in which artists are named. Names occur on individual works of art, usually embedded in a formula such as 'the sculptor N. was caused to make it'. In some cases unsigned tomb paintings can be associated with named artists by stylistic comparison with drawings on ostraca, limestone chips or pottery fragments that bear the name of the scribe (draughtsman or painter). In other cases named artists are given a title or designation as practitioners of a certain aspect of the work on which they are engaged, such as 'Overseer of Sculptors', 'outline draughtsman' or 'sculptor'. Similar designations are found in tombs in the Theban necropolis.

Often representations of artists are included in sections of the tomb decoration with other craftsmen, suggesting that they are of the same importance or social level. Sometimes named craftsmen are included in groups of offering bearers. Occasionally, as in the Giza tomb of Queen Meresankh III of the 4th Dynasty (*c.* 2575–*c.* 2465 BC), the artist (in this case a painter named Rahay) is depicted in a context and on a scale that suggests honorific intention. In the tomb of Ptahhotpe at Saqqara, Ny-ankhptah, the Overseer of Sculptors enjoys a floating luncheon, oblivious to the standard scene of fighting boatmen beside him. It is usually assumed that the inclusion of an artist in the tomb decoration signifies the approval and satisfaction of the patron. Where artists had achieved enough social status to possess their own tombs, as in the case of the Theban tomb of Nebamun and Ipuky (TT 181, the 'Tomb of the Two Sculptors'), or to create monuments of their own, as did BEK, Overseer of Sculptors (see fig. 3), who claimed to have been personally instructed by Akhenaten, it is because they had risen in the ranks of their trade to high supervisory positions.

The god Ptah of Memphis was the patron deity of all craftsmen, including sculptors. As his chief devotee, the High Priest of Ptah was responsible for all artistic production and architectural works. The office was filled by sons of the king in the 4th Dynasty and became a hereditary position. Titles that accrued to the High Priest of Ptah included 'Chief of Sculptors' and 'Greatest of Craftsmen'; these suggest something of the range of his responsibilities. It has been assumed that such designations implied direct supervisory responsibility for the design and accomplishment of public works and workshop production. The famous IMHOTEP, who was not a High Priest of Ptah but had the title 'Greatest of Seers in Heliopolis', was the Master of the Works for King Djoser (*reg c.* 2630–*c.* 2611

3. The sculptor Bek and his wife, quartzite stele, h. 670 mm, 18th Dynasty, *c.* 1350 BC (Berlin, Ägyptisches Museum)

BC) in the 3rd Dynasty and is usually credited with the design of the Step Pyramid at Saqqara (*see* SAQQARA, fig. 1). The equally famous SENENMUT in the time of Tuthmosis III and Hatshepsut (*c.* 1479–*c.* 1426 BC) has been called the architect of the temple of Deir el-Bahri (*see* THEBES (i), §IV and fig. 4). The ultimate responsibility for temple design and construction as well as the output of the royal and temple workshops rested with men such as Imhotep and Senenmut, but the actual role they played in decisions of design and quality of product is debatable. In a country such as Egypt with its well-developed bureaucracy the designation 'architect' or 'Master of the Works' could well have meant the person who approved the plans, not the one who made them.

2. TRAINING, WORKSHOP PRACTICE AND ORGANIZATION. The available evidence suggests that the education of the artist and craftsman must have been based on a system of apprenticeship. Consistent local and period styles could not have existed had there not been such a system, presumably centred around royal workshops. What is known about artists and their training comes from limited biographical material such as the statement of Bek (mentioned above) or the stele of a sculptor (Paris, Louvre, C 14), who boasts of his abilities as a 'craftsman successful in his craft', able to depict a wide variety of subjects. The inscription also mentions the sculptor's skilled son, which, along with genealogies found in other inscriptions, provides further evidence of the hereditary nature of the occupation.

There are also numerous drawings that can be interpreted as student sketches, trials and practice pieces. In some instances a single object may bear depictions displaying different levels of skill, suggesting the work of a master and a copy by a student, or a trial by a student with a corrected version appended by the master. The basis of practical art education seems to have been rooted in repeated imitation of prescribed forms.

Much of the detailed information concerning the practice of trades is provided by representations in tomb paintings and reliefs. In these, craftsmen are depicted engaged in a rich variety of activities, including virtually all the crafts for which artefacts have survived, such as potterymaking, brickmaking, smelting of metal (see fig. 14 below), carving of stone vessels (see fig. 10 below) and fabrication of furniture, jewellery, leather goods (see fig. 110 below), textiles (see fig. 18 below) and cordage.

Artists are represented at work in the production of three-dimensional sculpture, either carving, polishing or painting, from the Old Kingdom onwards. In the Theban TOMB OF REKHMIRE (TT 100), for example, the activities and products of a sculptor's workshop are shown in detail (see fig. 12 below). The production of several different standard sculptural types is explained with as many as five workmen occupied on the same project, demonstrating the teamwork involved under the direction of a master craftsman. Following standard Egyptian conventions of representation (*see* §IV, 2 below), sequential activities are shown as simultaneous. For instance, the initial drawing of an inscription on the stone, the pecking (hammer-carving) and the polishing probably did not happen at the same time, but for the sake of full explanation they are shown as occurring together. In another example, in the Theban tomb of Ipy (TT 217), 11 craftsmen are shown producing an elaborate shrine or catafalque, simultaneously carving, polishing and painting or gilding (as well as engaging in horseplay and lying down on the job).

There are fewer preserved examples of depictions of artists at work on two-dimensional projects, either wall painting or relief carving, though two exceptions occur in tomb reliefs in tombs of the viziers Mereruka and Khentika at Saqqara. These two compositions suggest that there was a type of portable art form that was similar to the small painted wooden stele, but no examples have survived. In both instances the subject of the portable painting on which the artist is engaged is a depiction of the three seasons (inundation, coming-forth of the land and drought). It has been proposed that the artist shown in both cases is the master of the tomb. There is some debate about the actual identity of the artist in the tomb of Mereruka because the name is now missing, but in the tomb of Khentika the tomb owner is named. In the tomb of Mereruka the panel painting is clearly resting on an easel that supports the work on a serrated rest. In that of Khentika the easel upright is omitted and a small stepped projection at the corner of the painting surface suggests some device for either support or adjustment. Other details show that bivalve shells were used as containers for the paint. However, rather than depicting an actual artist at work, it is more likely that the three seasons expressed the deceased's wish to participate in the ongoing cycle of nature. The position of both of these reliefs (near the door of the tomb) also suggests an importance accorded to the subject beyond mere representation of the deceased engaged as an amateur artist.

The teamwork that typified the process of painted tomb decoration is known from a written source: it was succinctly summarized in the scribal notation on a plan of the tomb of Ramesses IV (*reg c.* 1156–*c.* 1150 BC) preserved on a contemporary papyrus. On those sections of the tomb noted as complete they are described as '... being drawn with outlines, graven with the chisel, filled with colours, and completed'. Examination of unfinished royal tombs of the complexity of those of Horemheb (KV 57) and Sethos I (KV 17) suggest the following stages in their production. After the carving of the corridors and chambers and the smoothing of the walls, the design was laid out with the aid of horizontal and vertical grid lines, presumably by the outline draughtsman. In fact the texts often show evidence of having been transferred to the walls by scribes who may have been literate and familiar with the texts but not skilful designers. The initial layout of the text and the figural decoration was in red. Corrections were made in black over what could sometimes be a shaky beginning. It is conceivable that the outline draughtsman, skilled in linear execution, made the corrections and was responsible for the quality of the overall design. The carvers ('sculptors' and 'chisel wielders') then began their work. In all probability the apprentices or the less skilful craftsmen were assigned the cutting of large areas of background, leaving the details of figural decoration and inscription to the more accomplished journeymen. When the carving was finished, the painters took over and applied the polychrome. The concept of teams of draughtsmen, sculptors and painters, all at work side by side, gives some idea of the complexity involved in the preparation of a large royal tomb in the New Kingdom.

Several sculptors' workshops have been uncovered at the 18th Dynasty (*c.* 1350 BC) city of el-Amarna. One of these, excavated by Ludwig Borchardt in 1912, probably belonged to a sculptor named THUTMOSE. The objects discovered in Thutmose's studio include several unfinished sculptures, a set of plaster masks (Berlin, Bodemus.; *see* §XVII, 14 below) and the famous painted limestone head of Queen Nefertiti (Berlin, Ägyp. Mus.; for illustration *see* NEFERTITI).

For further discussion of craftsmen and artists *see* §§VII, 1(ii)(c), 3(ii) and XI, 1 below.

BIBLIOGRAPHY
LÄ: 'Bauleiter', 'Bildhauer und Bildhauerei', 'Handwerker', 'Hoherpriester von Memphis', 'Kunst', 'Kunstler'
H. Carter and A. H. Gardiner: 'The Tomb of Ramesses IV and the Turin Plan of a Royal Tomb', *J. Egyp. Archaeol.*, iv (1917), pp. 130–58
E. Williams Ware: 'Egyptian Artists' Signatures', *Amer. J. Semit. Lang. & Lit.*, xliii (1926–7), pp. 185–207
W. Stevenson Smith: *A History of Egyptian Sculpture and Painting in the Old Kingdom* (London, 1946, 2/1949), pp. 351–65
A. H. Gardiner: *Ancient Egyptian Onomastica*, 3 vols (Oxford, 1947)
J. A. Wilson: 'The Artist of the Egyptian Old Kingdom', *J. Nr E. Stud.*, vi (1947), pp. 185–207
M. Lichtheim: *Ancient Egyptian Literature*, 3 vols (Berkeley, Los Angeles and London, 1973–80)
R. Drenkhahn: *Die Handwerker und ihre Tätigkeiten in alten Ägypten* (Wiesbaden, 1976)
W. H. Peck and J. G. Ross: *Drawings from Ancient Egypt* (London, 1978)
K. Keller: 'The Draughtsmen of Deir el-Medina: A Preliminary Report', *Newslett. Amer. Res. Cent. Egypt*, cxv (1981), pp. 7–21
P. F. Dorman: *The Monuments of Senenmut* (London and New York, 1989)

WILLIAM H. PECK

III. Religion.

The essential features of Egyptian belief were polytheism and a willingness to assimilate new ideas without rejecting what had gone before. The gods of the early Egyptians were the strong forces in the world around them—sun, storm or wild beast—and it was in the interest of humans to placate, entreat or thank them. The inaccessibility of abstract cosmic powers led to the development of symbolism and anthropomorphism. The Egyptians believed that the same vital force pervaded everything, even inanimate objects, and could be transmitted between deities, enabling them to be identified with each other without losing individuality. This syncretism led to the proliferation of gods in the Egyptian pantheon and to the appearance of one god in many different manifestations.

Religion was omnipresent in Egyptian life, though there was an enormous difference between official cults and private religion. Official cults were concerned with perpetuating cosmic order (*maat*), by which the established world order could survive. God and king were mutually dependent, the gods showing favour to the king in return for ritual observation. Private religion was pragmatic, offering the means for solutions to everyday problems. Individual devotions were centred on localized deities who protected a particular community, and offerings and oracular questions were left at their shrines. A utilitarian rather than a moral basis for good behaviour was advocated: private religion was more concerned with obtaining favours from a god than with spiritual relationships.

DOMINIC MONTSERRAT

1. General. 2. Deities. 3. Gods and worshippers. 4. Cult statues and votive offerings. 5. Death and the underworld.

1. GENERAL. The official manifestations of Egyptian religion centred on the cult of the gods in temples, of which the most important were founded and maintained by the State. The king was the organizational pivot of the cult and, in some senses, of the religion as a whole. Temple reliefs show the gods in exclusive intercourse with the king, who performed actions for them and received benefits from them. In part, the king was the representative of humanity, which is not normally shown. He mediated and interceded on behalf of mankind, but this broader

concern is not always prominent in the material and artistic record. Royal dominance of Egyptian religion was strongest in early periods, when the State's principal monumental undertaking, embodying and displaying fundamental religious values, was the king's mortuary complex, including temples for his cult. The chief focus of non-royal display was also large, decorated tombs; like the king's complex, these had a religious purpose, though this was not always expressed overtly. There is little evidence for artistic production that was not concerned with the cult of the gods or with the next world, though some works of art were certainly more 'religious' than others. Because the less religious and the secular is lost with the disappearance of urban sites, palaces and élite dwellings, the more religious lacks a broader context.

Two aspects of Egyptian art—the assumed 'practical' religious purpose of most works and the lack of an Egyptian global term for 'art'—have led to a claim that Egyptian art was not 'art' in a Western sense and, implicitly, that it should not be studied in terms similar to other artistic traditions. In these respects, however, Egyptian art hardly differs from that of many cultures; the claim uses the standard of Western easel paintings rather than a broader measure. Religion was the chief context for the prestige production of aesthetically and iconographically ordered works whose resonances transcend any simple function. The lack of a term for art goes with a general absence of high-level abstract concepts in the Egyptian language; there is also no word for religion. This relation between religion and art does not imply any evaluation: the function and status of art is affected by religious considerations, but its evaluation by native or other criteria is a separate matter.

Furthermore, religion or magical beliefs did not affect representation as much as has been claimed. Because living beings were represented mutilated or incomplete in some contexts, it has often been proposed that the Egyptians believed representation to substitute for or to recreate reality. This interpretation neglects the symbolic character of religious art, which forms a system with interdependent meaning. Most of the contexts in which mutilation is found are unusual ones, such as coffins, and any animation of the figures would occur as part of a magical enactment in the next world, in a region beyond human verification.

Egyptian culture is sometimes viewed as having a religious origin and being completely permeated by religion in earlier periods (see Morenz; Assmann, 1984). Such a position, however, ignores the profane or secular aspects of Egyptian society, in contrast with which royal and élite ideology defines, protects and celebrates the sacred. Such a unitary model is inappropriate for studying artistic production and for placing it in a social context; it also leaves little room for change, and a looser, more diverse model is preferable. The more neutral term 'ideology' characterizes monumental forms better in many respects than 'religion', since the presentation of ideology embraces a wide range of values and concerns (see §IV, 1 below). In important contexts, such as Old Kingdom (c. 2575– c. 2150 BC) private tombs, ideological restrictions actually prevented the inclusion of explicitly religious material in works that might otherwise be religious and probably incorporated implicit religious meanings. Most preserved

Egyptian art was created for royalty or for a very small élite and conforms to the dominant ideology, which affects its organization at levels from the general to the very detailed; there is no clear division between the religious and the iconographic (see §V below for further discussion of Egyptian iconography).

JOHN BAINES

2. DEITIES. The Egyptian pantheon never consisted of a fixed number of major deities, and the prominence of individual gods fluctuated, partly influenced by political changes. When a particular area became dominant, the local tutelary deity rose in importance. Thus Amun, chief deity of the Theban area, rose to the status of a national god when Thebes was capital of Egypt in the New Kingdom (c. 1540–c. 1075 BC). The process of identifying one god with another began early in Egyptian hisory and led to the bewildering size and variety of the Egyptian pantheon. Points of similarity were found between local gods as regional areas began to forge closer links: since these were often cosmic deities with some particular local association, it was easy to find parallels. Thus Hathor, for example, could be worshipped under different names as a cosmic cow goddess at Dendara, a necropolis goddess at Memphis, a patroness of the mines in the Sinai and a tree-spirit at Deir el-Medina, without any of these local avatars altering the nature of her divinity.

The following gods (see fig. 4) appear most frequently in Egyptian iconography.

Amun. Theban god (4a), nationally important from the 11th Dynasty (c. 2081–c. 1938 BC) onwards, mostly syncretized with Re as a sun god.

Anubis. Jackal or jackal-headed god of necropoleis and embalming (4h).

Bastet. Cat or lioness goddess of Bubastis in the Nile Delta (4k), a popular fertility deity from the Late Period (c. 750–332 BC) onwards (for illustration *see* BUBASTIS).

Bes. Primarily domestic god (4l) shown as a grotesque dwarf, protector of women in childbirth and associated with music and dance.

Buto. See *Wadjet.*

Djehuty. See *Thoth.*

Geb. God of earth and vegetation, very occasionally shown ithyphallic and coloured green, impregnating the sky goddess *Nut* (see fig. 76 below).

Hapy. Personification of the Nile in flood, shown as an obese man, often with a clump of papyrus on his head and holding a laden offering table (see fig. 60 below).

Harpocrates. See *Horus.*

Hathor. Cosmic goddess with fertility associations and numerous other functions, represented most frequently as a cow, as a human mask with cow ears, as a woman wearing a horned head-dress or as a tree-spirit (see also fig. 70 below).

Horus. Hawk- and sky-god (4f) of whom the living ruler was a partial manifestation; avenger of his father Osiris. He had many forms and syncretisms: as Haroeris (a

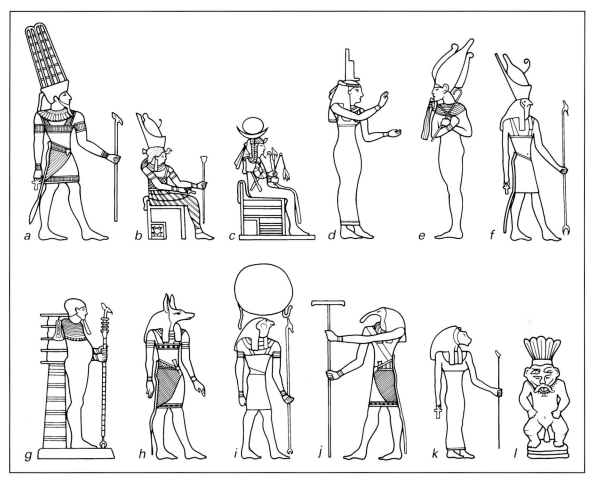

4. The principal ancient Egyptian deities: (a) Amun; (b) Mut; (c) Khonsu; (d) Isis; (e) Osiris; (f) Horus; (g) Ptah; (h) Anubis; (i) Re; (j) Thoth; (k) Bastet; (l) Bes

protector of the Pharaoh), Harpocrates (shown as a naked child with one finger to the mouth; see fig. 70 below), Harsiesis (son of Isis) and Harakhty (the sun god rising on the horizon, personified as a falcon).

Isis. Divine mother goddess, patroness of the dead and of magic, wife of Osiris and mother of Horus. In the Greco-Roman period (332 BC–AD 395) her cult as a saviour goddess spread all over the Roman world, at which time she was shown with her cult emblems of sistrum and fringed shawl; fig. 4d shows her earlier iconography.

Khnum. Creator and fertility god in ram form, worshipped as part of a triad with the goddesses Satet and Anuqet in the First Cataract region, where they presided over the inundation, and elsewhere.

Khonsu. A moon god (4c), represented as a mummiform child with a sidelock and lunar disc on his head: with Mut and Amun, a member of the Theban triad.

Maat. Personification of cosmic order, depicted as a woman with a large feather on her head (*see* GARDEN, fig. 6).

Meretseger. Snake goddess of the Theban mountain, protectress of the Deir el-Medina workmen.

Min. Ithyphallic fertility god, patron of mines and quarries in the Eastern desert, shown mummiform and wearing a plumed cap.

Montu. Warlike god of Armant, patron of the Middle Kingdom kings; shown hawk-headed and wearing a plumed cap.

Mut. Originally a lioness-headed war goddess, she came to be regarded as the consort of Amun (4b) and a member of the Theban triad; also represented as a vulture.

Nefertem. Solar deity, member of the Memphite triad with Ptah and Sekhmet, represented as a man with a lotus headdress or as a child emerging from a lotus.

Neith. Warlike delta goddess, shown as a woman wearing the red crown of Lower Egypt or two crossed arrows on a shield on her head.

Nekhbet. See *Wadjet.*

Nephthys. Protectress of the dead and sister of Isis, often shown as a winged woman with the hieroglyphs of her name on her head.

Nut. Sky goddess whose body formed the vault of heaven; associated with the journey of the sun through the night and shown as a star-spangled woman or cow (see fig. 76 below).

Osiris. God of the next world, fertility and regeneration, with whom the dead king and later all the dead were identified; usually represented as a mummified king (4e), sometimes with green or black skin.

Ptah. Creator god and patron of craftsmen (4g), also (as the syncretistic Ptah-Sokar-Osiris) deity of the Memphite necropolis; shown mummiform with a skull-cap and short, straight beard.

Re. The sun god (4i), closely identified with the king, who held the title 'Son of Re'; often identified with other major deities such as Amun, Harakhty and Sebek.

Sarapis. Fertility and funerary deity of uncertain origin, very popular in the Greco-Roman period, shown as a bearded man with a grain measure on his head.

Sebek. Crocodile deity worshipped under many local forms in the Faiyum and in combination with other major cults at Kom Ombo, Gebelein and elsewhere.

Sekhmet. Vengeful lioness goddess of war and fertility, consort of Ptah in the Memphite triad (*see* ABYDOS, fig. 3).

Seth. God of disorder, storms and violence, murderer of Osiris; represented as a composite beast or as a man with the head of the same animal.

Shu. God of air, shown as a man separating the earth (Geb) from the sky (Nut) (see fig. 76 below); also identified with Onuris and shown with a weapon and a feather crown.

Taueret. Hippopotamus goddess, a protectress of pregnant women.

Thoth. God with ibis and baboon forms with chief cult place at Hermopolis (4j); patron of writing and scribes and god of the moon. Later identified as the Greek god Hermes.

Wadjet. Cobra goddess of Buto in the Delta; along with the vulture goddess Nekhbet she protected and was represented as the uraeus on the crowns of pharaohs and queens.

DOMINIC MONTSERRAT

3. GODS AND WORSHIPPERS. An essential paradox of Egyptian religion was the opposition between the indefinitely large number of deities and the largely unitary role they played in relation to the king and to mankind or, more strongly expressed, their single nature and the single human approach to them (see Hornung, 1971, and Assmann, 1984). In this paradox the central element was the king; he was single and the gods were many. The gods also had many forms, manifestations and modes of action, but their true forms could not be known, and they were not represented in such various guises within sacred contexts except in their lost cult statues. Since representations conformed to decorum (*see* §IV, 1 below) and presented meaning symbolically and metaphorically, they cannot give direct access to the gods' nature. The most significant features on the monuments are general, common elements and architectural symbolism. This generality corresponds with the use of a small number of religious models that apply to most deities. Myth, in the sense of sacred narrative, is surprisingly unimportant in architecture and decoration. Its absence, which is part of its problematic status in Egyptian religion as a whole (see Assmann, 1977, and Baines 1991), is probably influenced by decorum. Some subjects, such as the death of Osiris, were too portentous to be recorded, and in all there are very few narrative myths preserved from Egypt, scarcely any in temples. Religious models and groupings of deities, however, often imply the action and interaction of narrative myth.

The most important of the basic religious models is creation. Major deities could be creators, and this is reflected in general forms of representation, both in the 'cosmographic' sense indicated above and in architecture. A god or gods created the world and provided for the king (and mankind). In return, but also anticipating and soliciting renewed favours, the king created temples for the gods and dedicated to them the fruits of success, including military conquests; monuments were a token of the endless prestations between the royal/human and divine worlds, in which reciprocity and dependence were complementary human strategies and feelings.

This sense that the maintenance of the ordered world was an enterprise shared among divine and human participants was related to its potentially threatened state. Although the existence of the gods is immeasurably greater and longer-lasting than that of mankind, they too were seen as ultimately mortal, as was the entire present cosmos. Texts such as the story of the *Shipwrecked Sailor* evoked 'last things' in a context at the edge of time and space; the same possibilities are evident in magical texts. Disorder and the 'non-existent' surrounded and penetrated order and had constantly to be defeated and kept at bay (Hornung, 1971, pp. 172–85). The massive solidity of Egyptian architecture, from the pyramids to the major temples of the New Kingdom and later, reaffirmed a fragile order and aspired to an ultimately unattainable permanence.

An aspect of the variety of divine manifestations is the ability of gods to fuse with one another, in syncretisms in which divine names are combined in pairs or larger sequences. Syncretism with Re, the sun god, is commonest; after the middle of the Old Kingdom Re was the leading god and the prime creator, so that gods identified with him had an explicit status as creators.

Gods were also organized in numerical groupings, from pairs to enneads. In most major centres of the late New Kingdom and later, triads were worshipped. The normal composition of a triad was a male and a female deity with a youthful third. Although this appears to be a minimal nuclear family, the only case in which kinship is central to its meaning is the Osiris–Isis–Horus triad. Goddesses such as Hathor might have no specific male partner, but rather an important pairing with a child god; as sole creator, the sun god did not need a female partner and often lacked one. Apart from supplying motifs and requiring the development of extended scene types, groupings of deities resulted in the construction of temple complexes for the deities, or, conversely, the temple complexes led to the formation of groups; both occurred. Gods also 'visited' one another during festivals (see §VI, 11 below) and had 'guest' cults in other temples. These possibilities do not exhaust the range of occurrence of deities: any major temple contains scenes of many deities besides those to whom it was dedicated. In order to accommodate many deities and functions, major temples had large numbers of rooms. This larger pantheon can also be seen in votive offerings from single sites, chiefly of the Late Period, which depict many deities and demonstrate the general catholicity of worshippers and their involvement with a broad spectrum of concern.

4. CULT STATUES AND VOTIVE OFFERINGS. Temples were dwellings for the gods who received the principal cults in them. If the god was satisfied with the cult offered to him, he inhabited his cult statue and gave his benefits to the king and mankind or withheld his anger from them. The essential actions of the cult, in which priests played the part of the king, consisted of caring for the cult statue and offering due worship to it (for further discussion of the religious function of statuary, see §IX, 1 below). Unlike the god's image in temple reliefs, the cult statue might be in animal form or in some unusual combination. The statue was clothed, anointed and censed, and received food offerings, which then reverted in turn to lesser deities in the temple, to statues of kings and individuals in the temple precinct, and finally to the priesthood for consumption. The cult statue was kept inside its shrine in the sanctuary (see §VIII, 2(i)(a) below) and was seen only by the officiating priests. The outer doors of the sanctuary were not opened during normal services, and when the cult statue left the temple for festivals, it was enclosed within a portable shrine so that it remained invisible to onlookers.

Participation in the presentation and reversion of offerings was twofold. By dedicating a temple statue of himself, a non-royal individual both honoured the deity and guaranteed offerings for himself in perpetuity; in later times people also made donations of land to temples, perhaps completing the cycle of endowment in this way. Few non-royal individuals could own statues—although some, such as SENENMUT, had a great many—but over the centuries enormous numbers accumulated. In the Late Period, prestige and display shifted away from private tombs, and temple statues became the most widespread élite art form. By that time the original purpose of the statues, to secure offerings, was overlaid with other considerations. Private temple stelae, which were set up from the Middle Kingdom (c. 2008–c. 1630 BC) or New Kingdom onwards, used representations and texts to solicit or record personal interaction with a deity, but they could not receive the reversion of offerings; some were considerable works of art.

Most temples that were the focus of artistic endeavour do not seem to have received many small votive offerings, and the material recovered from them belongs to the principal art forms; this applies even to the local Middle Kingdom shrine of the deified Heqaib at Elephantine (see ASWAN, §4). Exceptions are temples of Hathor, where a wide range of offerings has been found, including female fertility figurines (also found in other contexts) that fall outside normal canons of representation. These problematic figures are important in showing that the normative forms were not always observed, even in as central a context as a temple. Other uncommon types of religious art include magical 'healing statues' completely covered in texts and scenes, which seem to have been set up both inside and outside temples. In the Late Period these, the related Horus on the Crocodile stelae and many other objects acquired a grotesque iconography of pantheistic deities and demons. The statues and stelae display the great diversity of religious intermediaries of the time; a narrower range appears in the mass of votive bronze statuettes, which vary from artistic masterpieces to roughly shaped strips of metal.

5. DEATH AND THE UNDERWORLD. For the successful, death led through various stages into the next world, which might be located in the necropolis, in the mythical 'Fields of Earu' (an agricultural and aquatic paradise) or in the company of the gods, partaking in the solar cycle. The deceased might also return to their old abodes to attend such festivals as that of Osiris at Abydos; if not attended to suitably, they could also afflict the living. This wide range of possibilities for the afterlife relates to the three principal aspects of the person, the *ka*, *ba* and *akh*. The *ka* represented the life force of the individual; it remained with the body throughout his life and subsequently dwelt in the tomb, as well as being passed down through the generations. Offerings were made to the *ka*, often embodied in a statue or in a representation or an offering stele. The *ba*, usually shown as a human-headed bird, left the body at death and could migrate from the tomb and mediate between the living and the dead, though ultimately it had to return to the tomb to dwell in the mummy. The *akh*, also in bird form, existed as a spirit in the next world and did not move between worlds, except perhaps as a 'ghost'.

From an early but unkown date the deceased was subject to an ethical judgement after death. Those condemned died a second death and were tortured eternally: they were cast outside time and the ordered cosmos, into the uncreated sphere (see Hornung, 1971, pp. 172–85). Thus, even the next world was seen as being within the created order and as existing through shared human and divine efforts to reaffirm and ensure its continuity; the rigid ordering of underworld representations is in keeping with these efforts.

Preparation for death absorbed much of the élite's resources, but anxiety over death was not necessarily central to their thinking, and mortuary provision (see §VI, 6 below) was occasionally dismissed as pointless. Kings started to construct their mortuary complexes (see §VIII, 2(i)(b) below) early in their reigns, while non-royal individuals waited until mid-career. The tombs, with their grave goods, offerings (including statue cults) and decoration, guaranteed their owners' positions in the next world, while also testifying to their status in the world of the living. The underlying beliefs are, however, largely unknown. Much in the mortuary texts that accompanied burials from *c.* 2000 BC onwards was magical, concerned with avoiding dangers in the afterlife and bringing about a successful passage to it. Vast deposits of material goods in Early Dynastic (*c.* 2925–*c.* 2575 BC) tombs and large numbers of statues buried with Old Kingdom notables appear to be magical, but they should also be seen as élite display. The apparent egotism of this display is softened by the representation of a social context in which the deceased shows his care for lesser citizens—a feature with textual parallels that is stronger in earlier than in later periods—presenting himself as the focus of a miniature, paternalistic society. A vital part of this presentation is aesthetic, demonstrating the deceased's prestige and wealth as well as his moral worth through the art of the tomb.

Private tombs of the New Kingdom and later include numerous religious scenes. Many of these are from the Book of the Dead (a collection of funerary spells) and other compositions relating to the next world, but others simply show the deceased worshipping the gods; the most widespread decorative theme is that of the solar hymn, in which the deity himself is not depicted (as is also normal in sun temples). From the 21st Dynasty (*c.* 1075–*c.* 950 BC) decorated tombs became relatively rare. They were partly replaced by a rich repertory of decoration on coffins (*see* §XIII, 2(i) below) and 'mythological' papyri (*see* §XII, 3(v) below), some deriving from otherwise unknown sources; many of the most interesting coffins belonged to Theban priests of Amun.

BIBLIOGRAPHY

LÄ: 'Palast', 'Per-nu', 'Per-wer II', 'Sarg', 'Sonnenheiligtum', 'Sonnenschatten', 'Tempelrelief'

E. Naville: *Das ägyptische Todenbuch der XVIII. bis XX. Dynastie*, 3 vols (Berlin, 1886/*R* Graz, 1971)

M. de Rochemonteix: 'Le Temple égyptien', *Rev. Int. Enseign.*, vii/2 (1887), pp. 19–38

A. Bey Kamal: *Steles ptolémaïques et romaines*, Cairo, Egyp. Mus. cat., 2 vols (Cairo, 1904–5)

G. Roeder: *Naos* (Leipzig, 1914)

G. Jéquier: *L'Architecture et la décoration dans l'Egypte ancienne*, 3 vols (Paris, 1923–4)

J. Spiegel: *Die Idee vom Totengericht in der ägyptischen Religion* (Gluckstadt and Hamburg, 1936)

H. Bonnet: 'Zum Verständnis des Synkretismus', *Z. Ägyp. Sprache & Altertknd.*, lxv (1939), pp. 40–52

H. Frankfort: *Ancient Egyptian Religion* (New York, 1948)

H. Bonnet: *Reallexikon der ägyptischen Religionsgeschichte* (Berlin, 1952)

A. Piankoff and N. Rambova: *Mythological Papyri*, 2 vols (New York, 1957)

S. Morenz: *Ägyptische Religion* (Stuttgart, 1960); Eng. trans. by A. E. Keep (London, 1973)

D. Arnold: *Wandrelief und Raumfunktion in ägyptischen Tempeln des Neuen Reiches* (Berlin, 1962)

P. Barguet: *Le Temple d'Amon-Rê à Karnak: Essai d'exégèse* (Cairo, 1962)

E. Winter: *Untersuchungen zu den ägyptischen Tempelreliefs der griechisch-römischen Zeit* (Vienna, 1968)

J. Baines: 'Bnbn: Mythological and Linguistic Notes', *Orientalia*, xxxix (1970), pp. 389–404

E. Hornung: *Der Eine und die Vielen: Altägyptische Gottesvorstellungen* (Darmstadt, 1971); Eng. trans. by J. Baines as *Conceptions of God in Ancient Eygpt: The One and the Many* (Ithaca and London, 1982)

——: *Ägyptische Unterweltsbücher* (Zurich and Munich, 1972, 2/1984)

J. Assmann: 'Die Verborgenheit des Mythos in Ägypten', *Götting. Misz.*, xxv (1977), pp. 7–43

E. Hornung: *Tal der Könige* (Zurich and Munich, 1982), pp. 144–5

E. F. Wente: 'Mysticism in Pharaonic Egypt?', *J. Nr E. Stud.*, xli (1982), pp. 141–62

J. Assmann: 'Schrift, Tod und Identität: Das Grab als Vorschule der Literatur im alten Ägypten', *Schrift und Gedachtnis*, ed. A. Assmann and others (Munich, 1983), pp. 64–93

——: *Sonnenhymnen in thebanischen Gräbern* (Mainz, 1983)

G. Pinch: 'Childbirth and Female Figurines at Deir el-Medina and el-Amarna', *Orientalia*, lii (1983), pp. 405–14

J. Assmann: *Ägypten: Theologie und Frömmigkeit einer frühen Hochkultur* (Stuttgart, 1984)

J. Baines: *Fecundity Figures: Egyptian Personification and the Iconology of a Genre* (Warminster and Chicago, 1985)

A.-A. F. Sadek: *Contribution à l'étude de l'Amdouat* (Fribourg and Göttingen, 1985)

J. Baines: 'Practical Religion and Piety', *J. Egypt. Archaeol.*, lxiii (1987), pp. 79–98

——: 'Egyptian Myth and Discourse: Myth, Gods and the Early Written and Iconographic Record', *J. Nr E. Stud.*, 1 (1991), pp. 81–105

G. Pinch: *Votive Offerings to Hathor* (Oxford, 1993)

IV. Ideology and conventions of representation.

1. Decorum. 2. Methods of representation. 3. Proportion.

1. DECORUM. Rules circumscribing the content and iconography of ancient Egyptian works of art are rules of decorum (Baines, 1985, *Fecundity Figures*, pp. 277–305). Ramifications of the system of decorum, which reach beyond representational art, show that all high culture, including literature and private inscriptions, was subject to similar rules, which probably extended to—and ultimately derived from—formal conduct and associated aspects of material culture. The system of decorum applied to almost any religious situation and deity and thus was rather schematic, with only the most general content. It combined with representational principles to reinforce the uniformity of art. The major context to which it was not well adapted was the solar cult.

(i) Definition. Decorum defines what may be shown in what context, and the forms in which it may be shown. It is thus a more detailed and rigid phenomenon analogous with the theory of DECORUM in European Renaissance art; in Egypt it formed part of the maintenance of the proper order of the world and the cosmos (*see* §III, 1 above). The symbolism of Egyptian decorum was more fundamental to the society itself than Renaissance decorum, which applied principally to art. Its initial premise was the general scarcity of representation and the use of art in prestige contexts, of which the most important was the worship of the gods. There was a hierarchy of representational types, and some features of representation, such as the rarity of full-face images of the human figure, were probably part of the system of decorum. Gods were not shown in their 'true' forms but through the use of conventional imagery based on the human body; they could be freely depicted only in sanctified places, principally the sanctuaries of temples. Elsewhere they might be shown in emblematic form or referred to by their names, which might be written logographically or with phonetic signs. The king was shown in rather more contexts than were the gods; the hierarchy of ways to denote the king ran from direct depiction, through the royal king's Horus name, to various terms by which he could be referred to in texts. Early non-royal monuments do not contain representations of kings or gods; emblematic figures of gods and the King's Horus name are also absent. Apart

from such a definition by context, different areas of a single monument, such as the central and lower areas of a relief or the inner and outer parts of a temple, could be distinguished in terms of decorum.

(ii) Historical development. The earliest evidence for the Egyptian system of decorum is the group of votive monuments (*c.* 3000 BC) of the latest Predynastic kings. These ostensibly show political victories and various rituals. One of them, the NARMER palette (Cairo, Egyp. Mus.), includes a scene of interaction with a god, in which the king is elaborately protected by a sandal-bearer and attendants carrying a set of standards; the god is not shown directly but in the form of a rebus. The palette has a cosmographic organization, in which the main registers represent the ordered world, while the top register, depicting bovine heads (possibly of Hathor), indicates the sky. The lower register is outside the ordered world; the bodies of defeated enemies are formless and spread over the picture surface, while the king is shown not in human guise but as a bull, a manifestation that occurs in other royal monuments and that should be seen as emblematic.

The existence of this palette, which shows the god, the most sacred subject, so indirectly, implies the possibility of reliefs with actual depictions of gods. The earliest preserved examples of these, however, are of the late 2nd Dynasty (*c.* 2775–*c.* 2650 BC) and the 3rd (*c.* 2650–*c.* 2575 BC), and even they are not in the fullest form, in which major gods and the king are shown according to the same conventions, without elaborate emblems, and interact with each other. This full form of interaction is best attested in 5th and 6th Dynasty (*c.* 2465–*c.* 2150 BC) mortuary temples and in later periods. The relationship between these conventions on temple walls with statuary and cult equipment is uncertain, because few statues of deities are known from early times. Cult statues would have been small and probably made of wood and precious materials; one possible example, the golden hawk from Hierakonpolis (Cairo, Egyp. Mus.), is of uncertain date.

(iii) The world of religious art. Egyptian religious art depicts a sanctified, ideal cosmos: an appropriate locus for and a fit subject of worship. It creates, protects and celebrates a world, but that world is abstract, and its elements are hieroglyphic or emblematic, in the form of signs for earth, sky, stars and the sky's supports. Actions depicted within religious art are restricted to generalized forms and to those of the cult, which is itself obliquely presented. An essential organizing principle is direction. There is a royal and a divine side to any scene, and the two main protagonists face each other. The divine side is sanctified, while the royal side is slightly open and may need protection, as the king himself does when he leaves his palace. This is reflected in the formula 'all protection and life around him for ever', commonly inscribed behind figures of the king.

The Egyptian cult temple, of which royal mortuary temples were variants, continued to be governed by comparable rules of decorum through to the Greco-Roman period (332 BC–AD 395). The application of decorum elsewhere changed greatly, and the proportion of religious content increased on royal and non-royal monuments from the Middle Kingdom (*c.* 2008–*c.* 1630 BC)

onwards. In the Old Kingdom (*c.* 2575–*c.* 2150 BC), however, religious material in non-royal tombs was restricted to a few offering formulae, relatively rare depictions of funeral journeys and obscure scenes from burial rituals associated with Buto in the Nile Delta. Gods and the king were absent even from the tombs of queens. The Horus name, the king's most important title, by which he also made his strongest claim to divinity, was absent, although it was used in documents. The decoration of Old Kingdom tombs appears to be purely secular, but this could be an illusion if some scene types, notably hunting in the marshes (see fig. 8 below) and pulling papyrus (for illustration *see* PAPYRUS), refer symbolically to the passage into the next life, as does tomb decoration of later periods. The absence of gods and kings has been explained in various ways apart from decorum; on any understanding it is a religiously motivated 'desacralization'. Decorum deprived the élite of important religious modes of expression but was, nevertheless, accepted for long periods.

The rules of decorum organized works of art into horizontal or vertical hierarchies. Horizontal ordering tends to present separate levels of content in different contexts, the less sacred in the outer parts of temples or tombs and the more sacred within. This principle fits well with architectural symbolism and predominates in New Kingdom (*c.* 1540–*c.* 1075 BC) temples, in which the decoration is often grand in scale and sparsely detailed, and the contrast between outside and inside is reinforced on another level by the use of sunken relief in outside areas and raised relief within. Wall spaces are organized into vertical hierarchies in cosmographic terms and promote the integration of complete statements in single areas. The culmination of this tendency occurs in Greco-Roman temples, which are richly decorated at a relatively small scale, with many walls containing all the elements visible in embryo on the Narmer palette three millennia earlier. The central relief registers (up to four) present the ideal ordered world, while the base area shows marsh and the outside world in its productive aspect, and the frieze and ceiling depict the sky and the stars. Columns, whose forms derive from aquatic plants, provide a colossal framing suited to outer areas of temples; the elaborate design of Greco-Roman columns delicately balances the marginal and aquatic against a more general symbolism, including that of supporting the sky.

An important realm outside the bounds of normal decorum was the underworld, systematic depictions of which occur in New Kingdom royal tombs and may date back to the Middle Kingdom, and more informally in vignettes to the Book of the Dead and related sources (*see* §XI, 4 and fig. 76 below). This material has not been analysed in terms of decorum. Its principles of composition and representation are generally the same as those of the 'secular' world of non-royal tombs and the sanctified world of temples—although the 'depiction' of the unknowable underworld is more symbolic and metaphorical—but the subject-matter is incompatible with that of the 'secular' and religious worlds. In the New Kingdom, the underworld scenes were exclusively royal, but in later periods they became common on non-royal monuments.

The vitality and normative character of Egyptian decorum is visible in the reaction to it during the reign of

Akhenaten (*reg c.* 1353–*c.* 1336 BC; the Amarna period). Akhenaten, whose innovative style and modification of some representational conventions deliberately broke with what had gone before, reversed many decorum-related details. Some of his changes, such as inversion in the ordering of food and hieroglyphic decorative friezes, publicly rejected the past without making a real difference in content. Such departures were the counterpart of more gradual changes that extended the system from within. Thus, when deities were shown on non-royal monuments from the Middle Kingdom onwards, they were initially placed in different registers from figures of the owners and were distinguished iconographically from human beings; such distinctions were reduced over many centuries. Depictions of battles and enemies known from the post-Amarna period (but possibly having antecedents from the early 18th Dynasty) go furthest in dissolving the structure of compositions by registers and in using abnormal bodily forms, especially full-face for defeated figures. Apart from other advantages of the design, these depictions vindicate order and decorum against a visibly immediate threat.

See also §V below.

BIBLIOGRAPHY

E. Naville: *Das ägyptische Todtenbuch der XVIII. bis XX. Dynastie*, 3 vols (Berlin, 1886/*R* Graz, 1971)

J. E. Quibell: *Hierakonpolis*, i (London, 1900), pl. 2

L. Borchardt and others: *Das Grabdenkmal des Königs Śeẕḥu-Reʿ*, ii (Leipzig, 1913)

V. Schmidt: *Sarkofager, mumiekister og mumiehylstre i det gamle Aegypten* [Sarcophagi, coffins and mummies in ancient Egypt] (Copenhagen, 1919)

H. Schäfer and W. Andrae: *Die Kunst des alten Orients*, Propyläen-Kstgesch., ii (Berlin, 1925, rev. 3/1942), p. 179

G. Jéquier: *Le Monument funéraire de Pépi II*, 3 vols (Cairo, 1936–40)

W. S. Smith: *A History of Egyptian Sculpture and Painting in the Old Kingdom* (Oxford, 1946, 2/London and Boston, 1949)

K. Lange and M. Hirmer: *Ägypten: Architektur, Plastik, Malerei* (Munich, 1955, 4/1967), pls 4–5

A. Piankoff: *Mythological Papyri*, 2 vols (New York, 1957)

H. W. Müller: *Ägyptische Kunstwerke, Kleinfunde und Glas in der Sammlung E. und M. Kofler-Truniger, Luzern* (Berlin, 1964), no. A31

E. Winter: *Untersuchungen zu den ägyptischen Tempelreliefs der griechisch-römischen Zeit* (Vienna, 1968)

H. Altenmüller: 'Zur Frage der *Mww*', *Stud. Altägyp. Kult.*, ii (1975), pp. 1–37

Y. M. Harpur: '*Zśś wẕd* Scenes of the Old Kingdom', *Götting. Misz.*, xxxviii (1980), pp. 53–61

M. Eaton-Krauss: 'The Dating of the "Hierakonpolis Falcon"', *Götting. Misz.*, xlii (1981), pp. 15–18

M. Malaise: 'Les Représentations de divinités sur les stèles du Moyen Empire', *Orientalia J. Duchesne-Guillemin oblata* (Leiden, 1984), pp. 393–420

J. Baines: 'Egyptian Twins', *Orientalia*, liv (1985), pp. 461–82

——: *Fecundity Figures: Egyptian Personification and the Iconology of a Genre* (Warminster and Chicago, 1985)

A.-A. F. Sadek: *Contribution à l'étude de l'Amdouat* (Fribourg and Göttingen, 1985)

JOHN BAINES

2. METHODS OF REPRESENTATION. Egyptian art was rooted in objective knowledge and prior experience rather than in specific perception, recording and re-evaluation of ephemeral observed phenomena; it represented the known in an essentially symbolic manner. Such conception has been described by the Egyptologist William Stevenson Smith as 'a kind of diagram of a thing as man knew it to be, not as it appears to the eye under transitory circumstances'. There was no intention of capturing the momentary or the unusual, no particular necessity for innovation and no premium attached to originality. Egyptian art was a method of transmitting knowledge in a highly organized hierarchy of forms intended to convey essential information about the identity of a subject. The criticism of certain elements as primitive or awkward is a result of a misunderstanding of the rules by which Egyptian art functioned.

In an art form that is essentially diagrammatic there is no need to violate the two-dimensionality of the picture plane. In Egyptian art there is seldom any suggestion of depth or recession in space, and the common visual indicators of perspective—converging lines, relative size and colour change or gradation to suggest distance—are almost entirely absent. Only overlap of shape is preserved as an indication that one object or figure is in front of another, but these are arranged in such a way that they seem to occupy the same space and are not significantly 'behind' or 'in front'.

Implications of movement in Egyptian art are also almost entirely absent, because the intention was to convey ideas that were eternal and timeless. Thus, much of what is depicted in the art forms of ancient Egypt can be described as 'static', if that is not taken as a critical term and is used to further define the notion that the purpose of Egyptian art was not to illustrate transitory aspects of life. There are rare attempts to record motion diagrammatically, but the dotted lines that trace the incense pellets from the hand of the king to the bowl of the censer, or the repeated arrows delineating the flight path of a missile from bow to target, are symbolic records of the acts described rather than artistic attempts to create the illusion of motion.

It is clear from the beginnings of Egyptian art that artistic expression and the written language were intertwined, interdependent and often interchangeable. The Egyptian system of writing was pictorial, and the magical importance of pictures was never lost in Egyptian tradition (*see* §XII, 1(i) and (ii) below). It is well known that the image of the deceased in a tomb painting often functions as the determinative for the person's name or that the image of a god can complete the inscription that names him. The signs in the ensemble of 'titles–name–image' tend to share the same orientation, whereas the list of offerings is reversed to face the deceased or the deity. Because of the conservative nature of Egyptian thought and tradition, little change took place in the general form of language, hieroglyphic characters and art (but *see* §1(iii) above for exceptions to the rule).

Egyptian art was codified and the format for certain representations standardized at an early date. Once a method of presentation was accepted, it seems to have been subject to little, if any, change. There are numerous examples of this in the history of Egyptian art (e.g. king with upraised arm smiting conquered enemy, identical in arrangement from Early Dynastic ivory-carvings to Ptolemaic (304–30 BC) reliefs), and it is mentioned here only to emphasize the conservative nature of an art form in which the artist could depend on preordained and canonical solutions to problems of representation.

Linear abstraction was the basis for the visualization of form in all media, whether two- or three-dimensional. From the evidence of unfinished painting, relief and sculpture, it can be seen that line-drawing was the most important single stage in the preparation of a wall or block. The perception of the world and objects in it in terms of linear abstraction is a learnt process; this can be demonstrated in Egyptian art with reference to representations of Nile boats on certain classes of Predynastic pottery. These are not line-drawings but solid images in which human figures and boats are filled in with colour and not simply delineated with an outline. It is only with the first appearance of hieroglyphic inscriptions on hardstone vessels and ivory plaques in the Early Dynastic period (for illustration *see* NAQADA) that the figural images appear to be derived from drawing as a predominant mode of delineation. The design for painting and relief was developed and transferred to the wall in line, while the design for sculpture was applied to the cubic block as three line-drawings for the front and two sides. Colour in all art forms was essentially standardized, and little attention was paid to colouristic effects. Clarity in presentation of subject-matter was important, and there are no indications of the use of colour to obscure or to dramatize the form it serves to define. In an art form concerned with the portrayal of the subject rather than the reaction of the observer to it, there was no need to use colour to create atmosphere.

In the representation of any object—whether images of gods, humans, animals or the inanimate—the most characteristic views of significant parts were combined into one presentation. The most familiar example of this combination of characteristic views is the treatment of the human body, in which various aspects of the different parts are united to make up the symbolic image of man, not the observed representation known to us by experience. This use of conventions and proportions (*see* §3 below) is integral to ancient Egyptian art. Many examples could be cited, but one, the representation of the *senet* gaming board (see fig. 6 below), is most characteristic. The board itself is often shown in plan, whereas the gaming pieces, which are an important part of the set, are shown in section or in profile and appear to be standing on the top of the side of the board (shown as a horizontal rectangle). The sum of the parts describes the whole. The most characteristic views of each part—the plan of the board and the side view of the pieces—combine to recall the 'idea' of the game with its component parts, rather than the look of the board as the pieces are deployed in play.

Nevertheless, in this highly codified system of representation certain rules were violated at will. The standard dictum concerning the use of profile faces could be ignored if a frontal representation would better explain the activity or some inherent trait. In scenes of musicians the female flautists are occasionally shown frontally, the better to describe the action of playing the instrument (see fig. 72 below). The standard hieroglyph phonogram 'm' is a depiction of an owl and is always shown with a frontal head on a profile body. The characteristic look of an owl could only be conveyed in this manner. These apparent exceptions are actually part of the system of symbolic

representation based on the most characteristic views of parts united in a diagrammatic whole.

The symbolic nature of Egyptian art renders specific events in general terms, and the portrayal of narrative rarely exists. Apparent representations of the king performing certain rites or the nobleman overseeing the work of the fields are, in fact, generalized icons, meant to memorialize a type of activity rather than a unique happening. Many details in painting and relief seem to be the result of particular observation but, because they can be duplicated or paralleled in other contexts, prove to be part of the formulaic representation of a generic type. An example in the New Kingdom is the gesture of women depicted at a funerary banquet, who hold a lotus for a companion to smell and enjoy. Once this is understood to be a standard element in the 'funerary banquet' tableau, it takes on a meaning that has moved from the specific to the general and is thus possibly open to a wider and more symbolic meaning.

The rendering of a narrative recounting the successive stages in a specific historical event occurs only rarely and even then is to be understood as more symbolic than particular or representational (*see* NARRATIVE ART, §I, 2). There is no method in Egyptian art by which time of day or season can be conveyed visually; such nuances have to be explained in an accompanying text. The many temple reliefs (e.g. at Karnak and Abu Simbel) that recount the 'victory' of Ramesses II at Qadesh in Syria are not concerned with representing a specific place but with conveying a general sense of actions that could have been described equally well in inscriptions. Reliefs that depict the transport of an obelisk or the movement of a colossal statue may refer to a particular event, but the method of presentation in Egyptian art is still symbolically descriptive.

BIBLIOGRAPHY

LÄ: 'Aspective'
H. Schäfer: *Von ägyptischer Kunst, besonders der Zeichenkunst*, 2 vols (Leipzig, 1919); Eng. trans. by J. Baines as *Principles of Egyptian Art* (Oxford, 1974, rev. 3/1986)
W. S. Smith: *A History of Egyptian Sculpture and Painting in the Old Kingdom* (Oxford, 1946, 2/London and Boston, 1949)
W. S. Smith and W. K. Simpson: *The Art and Architecture of Ancient Egypt*, Pelican Hist. A. (Harmondsworth, 1958, rev. 2/1981)
J. H. Harris: *Egyptian Art* (London, 1966)
C. Aldred: *Egyptian Art* (London, 1980, rev. 2/London and New York, 1984)
H. G. Fischer: *L'Ecriture et l'art de l'Egypte ancienne* (Paris, 1986)
WILLIAM H. PECK

3. PROPORTION. In the Old Kingdom, certain proportions were established for standing figures based on the distance between the soles and hairline. The top of the knee lay at one third of the hairline height, the lower edge of the buttock at half the hairline height, the elbow (when the arm hung vertically by the body) at two thirds of the hairline height and the junction of the neck and shoulders at eight ninths of the hairline height. The proportions were obtained by drawing figures on horizontal guidelines marking these levels; in addition, an axial vertical ran through the ear region.

In the Middle Kingdom, the proportions of figures remained similar, but by the 12th Dynasty the system of guidelines had been replaced by a grid consisting of 18 squares between the base line and hairline of standing figures (see fig. 5). The knee lay on horizontal line 6, the

5. Figure of Sarenput II (left) from his tomb at Aswan, with surviving traces of the original grid completed to run over the whole figure, 12th Dynasty, *c*. 1938–*c*. 1756 BC (approximately half life-size); figure of Sethos I (right) from his temple at Abydos, with a hypothetical 18-square grid added to show proportion, 19th Dynasty, *c*. 1292–*c*. 1190 BC (approximately life-size)

lower edge of the buttock on line 9, the elbow on line 12 and the junction of the neck and shoulders on line 16. Line 17 ran at the bottom of the nose, line 14 on or near the nipple and line 11 on or near the small of the back and the navel. A vertical grid line corresponded to the axial guideline. In male figures, the width across the shoulders along horizontal line 15 was roughly 6 squares; between the armpits about 4 squares; and, at the level of the small of the back, $2\frac{1}{4}$ to $2\frac{1}{2}$ squares. The length of the forearm from elbow to fingertips along its axis was roughly 5 squares.

Similar proportions occur in seated and kneeling figures. The former consisted of 14 squares from soles to hairline: from the hairline to the lower edge of the buttock on which the figure sat was 9 squares and the height of the lower leg to the top of the knee was 6 squares. But since the top of the knee lay one square above the lower edge of the buttocks, only 5 squares of the lower leg contributed

to the figure's total height, which was therefore 14 squares. Some kneeling figures consisted of 11 squares from base line to hairline: 9 squares from the hairline to the lower edge of the buttocks, which rested on the heel of the raised foot 2 squares high; the leg added nothing to the height of the figure. Other kneeling figures comprised only 10 squares because the foot on which the buttocks sat was not raised but placed flat on the floor and occupied only a square in height.

During the New Kingdom, the same grid system continued to be used but some changes in proportions occurred (see fig. 5). The lower border of the buttocks and the small of the back were often raised to horizontal lines 10 and 12 respectively, while line 6 often passed through the lower edge rather than the top of the knee-cap. In some non-royal figures of the 19th and 20th dynasties, the small of the back might lie as high as line 13. In the 20th Dynasty, horizontal line 6 could run below the knee-cap through the patellar ligament. In some cases the width across the shoulder along line 15 is nearer $5\frac{1}{2}$ than 6 squares. By increasing the height of the knee, buttocks and small of the back, the legs were lengthened in relation to the torso, producing an increasingly elegant rendering of the standing figure, which was further enhanced by a tendency to narrow the shoulders.

The proportions of female figures are based on the same system as for males. Women, however, are more slender, being only 5 squares or less across the shoulders and less than 2 squares across the small of the back. The small of the back, and sometimes the maximum convexity of the buttocks, lies at a higher level than in contemporary male figures, and the spread of the buttocks is often greater in female figures.

During the Amarna period, proportions of figures changed (*see* RAMOSE): the king was shown with drooping features, long neck, narrow shoulders, pot belly, heavy buttocks and thighs and short legs. To accommodate these proportions, a grid system was introduced in which standing figures consisted of 20 squares from soles to hairline. The knee lay on horizontal line 6, the lower edge of the buttock on line 9 or 10 and the navel on line 11, as in the traditional system, but two squares were added above the navel. Often one square was inserted between the levels of the navel and nipple, so that the nipple lay on line 15, and one in the neck and face region, so that there were three, instead of two, squares between the junction of the neck and shoulders and the hairline. Differences occur between earlier and later Amarna figures: the levels of the throat, junction of neck and shoulders, nipple region, small of the back and lower edge of the buttock tend to lie up to a square higher in the earlier figures. In all male figures the width across the shoulders is between 4 and 5 squares, that is, between one fifth to one quarter of the hairline height of the figure, compared to one third in a traditional figure; the shoulders of female figures are narrower still.

From the 25th Dynasty, there was a period of archaization in art based on Old and Middle Kingdom models, with a return to the proportions found then. About the same time, a new grid system was introduced. Standing figures consisted of 21 squares between the base line and upper eyelid, with horizontal line 7 running through the tops of the knees, line 11 through or near the lower edge of the buttocks, line 13 through or near the small of the back in male figures and line 14 in female, line 16 through or near the nipple, line 19 through the junction of the neck and shoulder and line 20 through the mouth. The forearm became 6 squares long. This new system did not of itself necessitate major changes in the relative proportions of figures.

See also RAMESSES II and SCHÄFER, HEINRICH. For illustration *see* NARMER.

BIBLIOGRAPHY

R. Lepsius: *Die Längenmasse der Alten* (Berlin, 1884), pp. 99–104
E. Mackay: 'Proportion Squares on Tomb Walls in the Theban Necropolis', *J. Egyp. Archaeol.*, iv (1917), pp. 74–85
H. Schäfer: *Von ägyptischer Kunst, besonders der Zeichenkunst*, 2 vols (Leipzig, 1919); Eng. trans. by J. Baines as *Principles of Egyptian Art* (Oxford, 1974, rev. 3/1986)
G. Robins: 'The Length of the Forearm in Canon and Metrology', *Götting. Misz.*, lix (1982), pp. 61–75
——: 'Amarna Grids: 1', *Götting. Misz.*, lxiv (1983), pp. 67–72
——: 'Amarna Grids: 3. Standing Figures of the King in the Early Style', *Götting. Misz.*, lxxxiv (1985), pp. 51–64
——: 'Standing Figures in the Late Grid System of the 26th Dynasty', *Stud. Altägyp. Kult.*, xii (1985), pp. 101–16
——: *Egyptian Painting and Relief* (Aylesbury, 1986)

GAY ROBINS

V. Iconography.

1. Introduction. 2. Divine and royal. 3. Non-royal

1. INTRODUCTION. In Egyptian art there was no real division between the representational—conveying information by standardized visual resemblance—and the iconographic, in which meaning was conveyed in symbolic form. Features as basic as the equivalence of scale and importance convey meaning in both ways. The idealization that pervades Egyptian art, however, is iconographic rather than representational. Egyptian art integrates the visual, the non-visual and the partly visual through the ubiquity of captions and texts in the hieroglyphic script, the signs of which are themselves pictorial, although not directly representational. There is also an intermediate mode of emblematic representation, in which the pictorial character of hieroglyphs is exploited to make them act out the roles of the words they write. Other entities such as statues may also interact in this mode, which can have additional resonances if the hieroglyph that is 'personified' represents a god. Emblematic representation is more symbolic than representational. Writing and representation are also connected in other ways: statues are in one sense 'determinative' signs in the script for the name and title strings written on them, while cryptographic and 'figurative' writing styles exploit the pictorial associations of signs.

In Egyptian art, textual and pictorial elements may complement each other rather than say the same thing, or they may even point in opposite directions. Whereas religious art from sanctified contexts mostly has a univocal meaning, private, 'secular' art, including such central material as Old Kingdom tombs, is often indirect. As myth plays a subordinate part in Egyptian religion (*see* §§III, 3 and IV, 2 above), so Egyptian iconography is hardly concerned with narrative. The generality of representation and iconography is countered by textual elements: genre scenes may be captioned with the names of individuals but rarely with locations or dates. Much of the purpose of private works of art and monuments is to proclaim the position of their owners in a status hierarchy, and is thus both individual and collective.

The elements of iconography may show things that are possible in actual situations, or they may belong to the system only. An example of 'unreal' iconography is the common form of deities with animal heads and human bodies, which is a convention, not a representation of forms that were believed to exist. In general, what is internal to the system dominates, and the primary reference is not contemporary reality or fashion.

Egyptian iconography centres on figures, especially the human figure, as the form in which royal or non-royal actors and most deities are portrayed. Locations and their appurtenances, such as houses and furniture, are represented sparingly if at all (*see* §VI, 2 and 13 below). Almost any part of the body and what it holds or wears (or the absence of something) can have iconographic significance, from crowns to sandals. Gestures and bodily forms—thin, fat, youthful or old—are conventionalized and carry specific meanings. Groupings of elements, such as specific styles of dress and ornament associated with particular bodily forms, may be iconographic units. Colour, in principle applied to all depicted forms, was both representationally and symbolically significant, being used to give meaning to individual elements and to create patterns over areas of decoration.

Just as representation must be 'read' as a system of signs, so its content must be interpreted according to iconographic conventions. The nature of the audience is problematic. Elite tombs were open and visited for certain festivals, and their architecture and pictorial decoration could be observed and appreciated in detail by people who could read the inscriptions. As prestige enterprises of their owners, the tombs will have been discussed among the living, but the proportion who comprehended the iconography must have been small. In temples and royal tombs, the decoration was seen by few, and much was invisible when the dark interiors it adorned were complete. Its essential audiences were the dedicatees—the gods and the king—and the designers and artists involved in production and transmission. Its complexity was no less great because it was seldom seen.

Egyptian iconography was integral with decorum (see §IV, 1 above). The two together organized buildings and their decoration into cosmographic statements. The most rigid rules of decorum and iconography apply to temple relief, where appearance is secondary to meaning. There is no additional requirement that content in temple relief be coded. This context is so central that it says what it means, but its import and the implications of compositions are difficult to elicit because relevant written records are few and relief captions are terse. What it does not show is the performance of the cult, which would have looked entirely different from what is seen in the reliefs.

Progressively freer contexts than temple relief are royal reliefs, royal and private stelae, non-royal tomb reliefs and secular decoration in palaces and houses and on small objects. There was also a very gradual loosening of conventions outside of temple relief, discernible from the First Intermediate Period onwards. For deities, variation in bodily form is known only among youthful gods or grotesque, liminal beings such as the dwarf Bes (see §III, 2 and fig. 103 below), while for kings it occurs only in statuary. The exaggerated bodily form of the king AKHENATEN—in which attempts to identify a positive symbolism have not so far been successful—seems to react against normal iconography rather than to present a particular meaning or depict a particular physiognomy. At the bottom of the depicted social scale, minor figures in private tombs, especially fine tombs such as that of the TOMB OF TY, may have physical imperfections. The most 'marginal' major iconographic context is non-royal tomb relief. Before the New Kingdom (c. 1540–c. 1075 BC), figures of gods and of the king did not occur there; religious topics and aspirations were not presented directly, and social status was displayed in texts more than representations.

Pattern and composition were iconographically significant. Greco-Roman (332 BC–AD395) temple walls were organized so that the royal 'side' of the scenes formed a colossal proclamation of the king's identity down the four registers. Elaborate thematic and geographical patterns occur in base areas, in wall reliefs and on columns, both in relief scenes and in long texts. More narrowly iconographic patterns are visible in the insignia worn and ritual actions performed in horizontal registers as in the DENDARA temple crypts. These intersecting patterns create complex compositions that are subject to rules of decorum and cosmography; little is left to chance.

2. DIVINE AND ROYAL. In temple relief, essential meanings are conveyed by heads bearing insignia, attributes held in the hand and actions performed with them, and identifying captions. The iconography of deities and kings is similar. In this context their status is comparable, and they interact on a single level. Both share many of the same crowns and items of dress, as well as holding similar attributes, but they can be distinguished because there is always some iconographic difference between any pair of royal and divine figures, and because they face in opposite directions. The major exception to clear distinctions between deities and the king is in figures of youthful gods from the first millennium BC. These are identical with the king in iconography, except that they are normally shown nude and at a small scale; they may face in the same direction as the king or the other gods in a scene. Most royal insignia occur both within and outside temples. Many deities resemble one another, and few items of insignia are exclusive to one god; the combination of iconographic elements and captions guarantees their identities. The range of possible representations is extended by the convention of animal heads which allude to the nature of a god or represent his chief manifestation. There is also an 'attribute-for-head' form, in which something other than a head occurs in its position; this form is found principally in underworld contexts. Major gods, such as Ptah and Osiris, and many underworld figures are in 'mummy form' with white, undifferentiated bodies out of which only the hands emerge. This form may have originated in early sculpture (see §IX, 3(ii) below), later becoming associated with death through Osiris. Its use for youthful deities such as Khons shows that 'mummy form' is not an apt term. A god with a special iconography such as an animal head or mummy form could also have an undistinctive 'general' form.

Several royal headdresses come in pairs. The white and red crowns both originated in Predynastic Upper Egypt. The red crown was associated with the goddess of Lower Egypt, Wadjet, and with the secondary term for 'king', *bity*. Conversely, Upper Egypt, the white crown, and *nisut*, the primary term for 'king', were linked. These two crowns were fused into the 'double crown', first attested in the 1st Dynasty (c. 2900 BC). The *nemes* headcloth (see fig. 59 below), an exclusive royal item, has a pair in the *khat* headcloth. The king also wore a short wig with ringlets (see fig. 63 below), which could form the base for complex feather and horn crowns or for the *atef*-crown. The red and white crowns could be placed on top of wigs or headcloths. Very occasionally the king had no headdress. The repertory was extended c. 1700 BC with the 'blue crown' (see fig. 62 below), which became the premier crown, as well as the yellow 'cap-crown'. In the Late Period (c. 750–332 BC) and especially in Greco-Roman temples, crowns proliferated. From the central Old Kingdom and possibly earlier, the king wore the uraeus, a protective rearing cobra, in combination with the *nemes* and wigs (for illustration *see* AMMENEMES III); later it was used with crowns (see fig. 62 below) and became the most characteristic sign of royalty. It was occasionally combined with a vulture head, referring to the goddesses Nekhbet and Wadjet, as in some objects from the tomb of TU-TANKHAMUN. Kushite rulers wore two uraei, the symbolism of which is glossed as referring to the countries Egypt and Kush. Both crowns and uraei could be deified, and hymns were addressed to them; they had many names, but their symbolism often may not be very specific.

The king often had a short, straight false beard (see fig. 59 below). He wore collars and necklaces, pectorals, armlets, wristlets and anklets (finger-rings were seldom shown), shirts and tunics, cloaks, distinctive kilts and sandals. From the New Kingdom on, he might wear earrings. Except for formal garments such as the cloak worn in the *sed*-festival of renewal (the royal 'jubilee'), dress was subject to fashion, but there was little development after the New Kingdom. Like crowns, dress carried symbolic meanings and might be patterned over large areas. Sandals were both an aggressive symbol of the king trampling on his enemies and an indicator of purity: he did not wear them in sanctified temples, while outside they separated his person from the polluting ground. Dress and insignia gradually became more elaborate.

The king rarely held nothing in his hands. Either he performed ritual actions and held equipment (or had empty hands in prayer), or he held the crook and flail (see fig. 61 below). He might hold special staffs, a mace or a boxlike object called a *mekes*. He often held the *ankh*-sign (Egyp.: 'life'; *see* OBELISK, fig. 1), and one of his principal epithets was 'given life'. Variation in his iconography indicated the degree of his divinity, always problematic because of his position between humanity and the gods. His bodily form could vary. The classic statue of Chephren (Cairo, Egyp. Mus., CG14) has a protecting falcon behind the head and at the same time evoking the Horus Name, the most solemn element in his titulary. In other versions the king could have a falcon's body, while thrones incorporated extensions of this and similar ideas. The most characteristic example of this strategy is the sphinx, in which the ruler's representation in the form of a lion expresses some of his qualities (*see* SPHINX, fig. 1); lions also occur beside and are incorporated into thrones and in life were kept by kings as semi-domestic animals. If a king was deified, he could be shown mummiform.

The distinctive insignia of queens consort was the vulture headdress (*see* THEBES (i), fig. 8). From the Middle Kingdom (c. 2008–c. 1630 BC) onwards, other items were added to wigs, among them a crown of ostrich feathers and cow horns derived from the goddess Hathor. Additional crowns were set on a 'modius' base, often elaborated with uraei. Queens wore a uraeus, a vulture head or, in the New Kingdom, a double uraeus (for illustration *see* SER-ABIT EL-KHADIM), sometimes with vulture head. This mixed royal/divine origin was paralleled in the insignia

they held, which included a flexible whisk apparently derived from the lotus or papyrus.

There was a normal repertory of insignia and attributes for gods, from which any particular deity might depart. Many divine and royal crowns were the same, but gods did not use the blue crown or *nemes* (except youthful gods), and few wore uraei. Deities wore a tripartite wig; some wore a long, outward-curving false beard (*see* ABY-DOS, fig. 3). They held the *ankh*-sign and *was*-sceptre, symbolizing power and well-being. Goddesses increasingly held a shaft of papyrus (*wadj*) in place of the *was*-sceptre. Divine dress changed little. Gods wore a broad collar, armlets, wristlets, a short kilt without elaborate front projection and sometimes a shirt, which might have a scaly feather pattern; goddesses wore a long, plain dress, occasionally coloured green. Late Period sculptures of deities have a more varied iconography, in which features such as the uraeus are common. Pictures of cult images of deities, notably in the temple of Hibis in el-Kharga Oasis (5th century BC), show that these were extremely varied and often bizarre in their iconography, quite unlike the forms shown in almost all temple relief.

3. NON-ROYAL. The dress, insignia and furniture of the élite could convey status through their richness and authority or could be associated with an office or privilege. Examples of the latter are the leopard skin and sidelock associated with priesthoods; from the later New Kingdom onwards, most priests had shaven skulls. Wigs, short beards, necklaces, shirts, kilts and cloaks became more elaborate from the Old Kingdom (c. 2575–c. 2150 BC) onwards. Staffs, sceptres, strips of cloth and short, boxlike objects were also markers of status and distinction. Few had explicit meaning; even a group that has such meaning—the 'gold of honour', a collection of jewellery awarded to officials—was subverted by being worn by the king. Three stages of life are shown: childhood, associated with uncircumcized nudity and a lock of youth; youthful maturity with elaborate garments and wigs (the normal state); and prosperous, often obese middle age, with a plainer iconography. Old people sometimes wear grey or white wigs. Such distinctions are rare on women, most of whom are in an ideal state of slim youth.

At least as important as dress and insignia is comportment. Status, and probably other values, are conveyed by the depiction of élite figures standing or sitting and observing the actions of their inferiors and dependants rather than performing actions; the adoption of this convention allows forms to be similar in relief and in statuary. Dominant scale expresses status and presents tomb owners contemplating a range of activities shown in many registers before them. Overseers and scribes may interact with the owner by presenting him with the products of their activities. Exceptions to élite inactivity include scenes of the deceased sitting before a table of offerings in which he implicitly partakes, and prestige scenes of hunting, especially in the marshes, but even in the latter case he is accompanied by his family and richly dressed (see fig. 8 below). This grouping presents a message of the élite nuclear family's significance, an idea varied to include more extended groups on Middle Kingdom stelae.

There are domestic associations when the deceased, with his wife and sometimes children, is shown with pets and pieces of furniture. Some of these articles, such as cosmetics, are primarily feminine. They may display their owner's prosperity, but they can have erotic overtones, alluding to the woman's sexual role in the next life as well as this one; these overtones are also present in marsh scenes (*see* §VI, 17 below). The importance of kinship and the erotic is suggested by occasional departures from the norm that carry similar meanings relating additionally to passage into the next world and an enjoyable existence there. What is shown is at the same time what was enjoyed and gave prestige in this life. Much of this symbolic meaning in 'secular' scenes has probably been missed; it is also present in more overtly religious material. The iconography of small objects may allude to the Book of the Dead (a set of funerary spells) and to other comparable conceptions, while such motifs as fish have rich symbolic associations.

These possibilities were available to those who could afford them; others were restricted by means, not in principle by being barred from participation. The iconography of those others is sparser than that of the owners, but contains similar distinctions of dress, gesture and position in sequences of figures and, occasionally, scale. The presentation of major figures in ideal form, while imperfections are common among labourers, is ideological or iconographic, expressing values and the artistic quest for variety: in their perfection the owners contemplate pleasurably the shortcomings of others and their unruly actions. Throughout Egyptian art, meaning takes precedence over reportage.

BIBLIOGRAPHY

There is no full study of Egyptian iconography, and the list below concentrates on lexical entries, in which further bibliography may be found.

LÄ: 'Ikonographie', 'Kronen', 'Ornat', 'Sandale', 'Schmuck', 'Tracht'
H. Schäfer: 'Die "Doppelkrone" der Pharaonen, ihr Bild und ihr Sinn', *Orient. Litztg*, xxxv (1932), pp. 697–704
E. Staehelin: *Untersuchungen zur ägyptischen Tracht im Alten Reich* (Berlin, 1966)
E. Feucht-Putz: *Die königlichen Pektorale: Motive, Sinngehalt und Zweck* (Bamberg, 1967)
E. R. Russmann: *The Representation of the King in the XXVth Dynasty* (Brussels and Brooklyn, 1974)
M. Eaton-Krauss: 'The *khat*-headdress to the Amarna Period', *Stud. Altägp. Kult.*, v (1977), pp. 21–39
K. P. Kuhlmann: *Das Thron im alten Ägypten* (Gluckstadt, 1977)
W. V. Davies: 'The Origin of the Blue Crown', *J. Egyp. Archaeol.*, lviii (1982), pp. 69–76
J. Baines: *Fecundity Figures: Egyptian Personification and the Iconology of a Genre* (Warminster and Chicago, 1985)
H. G. Fischer: *L'Ecriture et l'art de l'Egypte ancienne* (Paris, 1986)

JOHN BAINES

VI. Subject-matter.

Certain themes recur repeatedly in Egyptian painting and relief sculpture of all periods: in private tombs and on some stelae there are scenes of daily life, scenes relating to the office of the owner, funerary rites, the bringing of offerings and the hereafter; in royal tombs, scenes from the underworld; and in temples, scenes showing the king performing rites therein. Although good artists used the same basic components to produce the prescribed scenes, their creative ability was such that exact repetition was rare and they were able to produce endlessly various, fresh and successful versions of scenes from within this limited repertory. Scenes of everyday life are assembled and discussed according to subject-matter by Jacques Vandier (1964–78) and, more briefly, by Luise Klebs (1934).

1. Agriculture and famine. 2. Architecture. 3. Astronomy and astrology. 4. Banquet scenes. 5. Caricature and satire. 6. Death and funerary rites. 7. Deities. 8. Demons. 9. Erotica and pornography. 10. Festivals. 11. Flora and fauna. 12. Foreigners. 13. Household activities. 14. Hunting and fishing. 15. Industry and commerce. 16. The king. 17. Landscape. 18. Music and dance. 19. Navigation and travel. 20. Patterns and designs. 21. Sports and games. 22. War. 23. Women.

1. AGRICULTURE AND FAMINE. From the Old Kingdom (*c.* 2575–*c.* 2150 BC) private tombs included scenes relating to the agricultural year, featuring the activities that took place on the owner's estates (for illustration *see* KAB, EL-). These scenes usually show ploughing, breaking the ground with hoes, sowing the seed (which may be trampled on by herds of animals), harvesting the grain with sickles, binding it into sheaves and taking it to the threshing floor. In depictions dating from the Old and Middle kingdoms, and from the late 18th Dynasty and the 19th (*c.* 1400–*c.* 1200 BC), the grain is normally loaded on to donkeys; in 18th Dynasty scenes it is more often packed into a large basket and carried on a pole between two men. Gleaners are often shown following reapers in the field. Threshing is carried out by driving oxen or donkeys across the harvested corn to loosen the grains from the ear. The grain is then piled up and winnowed by tossing it in the air to separate the chaff from the grain. Finally, the corn is measured and stored in granaries. Scribes are usually shown as present during these activities to keep records. In the New Kingdom (*c.* 1540–*c.* 1075 BC), scenes show the measuring of fields with ropes and also depict boundary stones marking the borders of fields. The flax harvest is often shown next to the grain harvest. The flax is pulled up by the roots and not cut, and women sometimes join in the work. In the New Kingdom the process of drawing bundles of flax through a comb to remove the seed capsules was sometimes shown (*see* §VII, 4(ii) below).

Harvest scenes are often accompanied by a figure of the snake-goddess Renenutet to whom offerings were made for a good harvest. In the Book of the Dead (a collection of funerary spells) and in tombs from the end of the 18th Dynasty onwards, for example those at Deir el-Medina (*see* THEBES (i), §XI), agricultural scenes are shown set in the hereafter. In contrast to those of this world, it is the owner and his wife who are shown engaged in the work. Although ancient texts refer to famine in Egypt, it was not considered a suitable subject for depiction. Occasionally famine victims are shown, as in the causeway of the pyramid of King Wenis (*see* SAQQARA, §1) or the tomb chapels at Meir, but they are foreigners not Egyptians (for illustration *see* MEIR).

GAY ROBINS

2. ARCHITECTURE. Since Egyptian artists tended to shy away from representing precise events and locations, they produced few depictions of major buildings. In the Theban tombs of the New Kingdom a few reed shelters appear in scenes of activity in the fields, and private houses

are shown in a number of tombs with some detail of their furnishings and equipment indicating how various rooms were used. A number of Palestinian forts and fortified towns are stylistically illustrated in the reliefs recording the campaigns of Ramesside pharaohs at the Karnak and Luxor temples. There is a uniquely detailed relief depiction of the façade of the Temple of Amun at Luxor in the first court of that same temple, showing the arrangement of statuary, obelisks and flagpoles, some of which can still be seen standing a few yards away from the relief.

A different situation pertains at EL-AMARNA, where the artists working in the nobles' tombs showed actual events in a particular setting; the presentation of awards by the king, for instance, is shown taking place from the 'Window of Appearances' in the royal palace. A number of identifiable buildings are also depicted at el-Amarna in the typical Egyptian combination of cross-section and plan. They include a drawing of the 'Great Temple', in the tomb of Meryre' I, which can be compared with the plan of the actual building revealed by archaeologists. Some architects' drawings have also been preserved (see §XVII, 11 below). Best known is the large fragment of a plan of the tomb of Ramesses IV (at Thebes) on a papyrus in the Museo Egizio, Turin (see fig. 111 below). Others include drawings for a shrine (London, U. Coll., Petrie Mus.) and rough sketches on ostraca. There is even, at el-Amarna, a possible builder's working sketch, scratched out in a wet plaster floor, showing the layout of rooms.

J. RUFFLE

3. ASTRONOMY AND ASTROLOGY. Representations of the night sky appear predominantly in the form of 'astronomical' ceilings, although the earliest appearances are on coffins from the Middle Kingdom. In the 19th and 20th dynasties (c. 1292–c. 1075 BC) astronomical ceilings were set up in the temple and Osireion of Sethos I at ABYDOS, in the mortuary temples of Ramesses II and III at Thebes and in the royal tombs of Sethos I, Merneptah, Tausert, Ramesses IV, Ramesses VI, Ramesses VII and Ramesses IX. They are almost unknown in private tombs, but examples occur at Thebes in the second tomb of Senenmut (TT 353; c. 1460 BC), the Ramesside tomb of Tharwas (TT 232) and the Saite of Petamenopet and Mentuemhet (TT 33 and 34; c. 600 BC). Such ceilings are also found in the Greco-Roman temples of Edfu, Kom Ombo, Dendara and Esna. The following elements may appear: the sky goddess Nut bending over the earth with stars on her body; the 'decan' stars marking the hours of the night; the constellation Orion usually depicted in human form in a bark; the Sothic star (Sirius) usually depicted as a standing woman in a boat; and the five planets shown as gods in boats. The constellations of the northern hemisphere are shown variously as human figures, animal-headed figures and animals, such as hippopotamuses, crocodiles, lions and bulls. The Plough appears as the foreleg of an ox, and from Ptolemaic times (304–30 BC) the 12 figures of the zodiac are found.

4. BANQUET SCENES. These are found in private tombs from the Old Kingdom onwards but occur in their most developed forms in the Theban tombs of the 18th Dynasty (see THEBES (i), §X), when they are associated principally with the 'Beautiful Feast of the Valley' (see also §13 below). Most commonly the tomb owner and his wife or mother, the major figures in the scene, are shown seated facing several registers containing the smaller figures of the guests, who are usually relations. The guests are both male and female. Some are couples and are seated together. Others may be shown individually or as part of a group. The sexes are not rigidly segregated, but there is a tendency towards separation, with maid-servants waiting on the women and men-servants on the men. The guests may be shown sitting on various types of seat, kneeling with their buttocks resting on both legs or on one leg with the other drawn up. Less often they are shown sitting on the ground with both legs drawn up. They commonly hold a flower which they may sniff. They often have small tables of offerings placed in front of them, or are attended by servants who may offer drinks, tie on floral garlands, rub in scented oil or replenish the cone of fat worn on the wig (see fig. 72 below). Entertainment is usually provided by musicians, dancers and singers. Some elements of banquet scenes may have erotic significance (see §9 below).

5. CARICATURE AND SATIRE. Some of the more extreme depictions of foreigners and peasants in subsidiary scenes in Egyptian tombs, showing them deformed by disease or hunger, may possibly have been conscious caricature, and some of the sketches on ostraca may have been drawn in the spirit of caricature. One genre in Egyptian art that may also be partially satirical consists of scenes on papyri and ostraca showing animals performing human activities: making music, dancing, performing religious rituals, fighting, brewing beer and playing board-games (see fig. 6). In some of the scenes predators, often cats, herd birds or wait on mice and in one instance a fortress defended by cats is undergoing a full-scale assault by an army of mice. Some of these scenes no doubt illustrate well-known incidents from orally told animal fables, such as the war of the mice against the cats. A satirical element is also suggested by the fact that many are closely modelled on traditional scenes yet turn the accepted order of things upside down (by having predator subservient to prey).

6. DEATH AND FUNERARY RITES. While foreigners might be shown dying in battle, trampled beneath the pharaoh's feet, crushed by his chariot or slaughtered by victorious Egyptian troops, Egyptians are rarely shown in the act of dying. From the Old Kingdom onwards, scenes in private tombs, on stelae and, later, in vignettes of the Book of the Dead were devoted to the funerary rites of the owner. They usually show the funeral procession in which the coffin is dragged on a sled to the tomb while servants sometimes bring funerary equipment. Priests often carry out rites in the presence of the mummy or a statue of the deceased before the tomb. These rites, including the 'Opening of the Mouth' ceremony (see fig. 75 below), may be depicted in a series of scenes, sometimes in several registers. Another scene might show the funeral procession being received by the Goddess of the West or the Hathor cow coming out of the Theban mountain. Prominent in these processions are groups of professional mourners, sometimes male but mostly female,

6. 'Satirical Papyrus', detail showing an antelope and lion playing a board-game, h. 85 mm, 20th–21st Dynasty, *c.* 1100 BC (London, British Museum)

who often bare their breasts and are sometimes shown with tears on their faces. The different gestures and postures taken up by the figures in their abandonment to grief enabled good artists to compose interesting and rhythmic groups. The widow of the dead man might also be shown mourning by the mummy. A frequent scene in the Ramessid period shows part of the funerary rites when a man presents a foreleg freshly cut from a still-living calf, which stands crying in the presence of its mother.

7. DEITIES. Egyptian deities are extremely widely represented in art (see fig. 4 above). While some are shown in the form of animals, such as the Hathor cow, most appear in human form (for example the national god Amun-Re) or with a human body and the head of an animal (see fig. 97 below), such as Horus with a falcon's head and Thoth with that of an ibis. Osiris, god of the dead, has a body in the form of a mummy with the legs bandaged together and the forearms just emerging from the wrappings. Since the temples were the homes of the gods (*see* §VIII, 2(i) below), deities are present in almost every major temple scene, usually with the king who performs some aspect of ritual before them. By the 18th Dynasty they could also appear with private people in their tombs and on their stelae; Osiris and Anubis, the god concerned with embalming, are frequently depicted, and the Goddess of the West often receives the funeral procession of the owner. Scenes showing the king and deities form part of the decoration in the royal tombs of

the New Kingdom, and some of the vignettes in the Book of the Dead (see fig. 76 above) include deities, one of the most common being the weighing of the deceased's heart by Thoth and Anubis, usually in the presence of Osiris.

For a more detailed discussion of Egyptian deities *see* §III, 2 above.

8. DEMONS. There is no single Egyptian word corresponding to 'demon', but the term may be used to refer to a large group of individually named beings associated with the afterlife who are not gods but are part of the chaos that lies outside the created world. Many guard the various series of gates, portals and caverns through which the dead have to pass to reach the afterlife, threatening them with annihilation if they are not protected by the correct spells. They may be shown as animals (such as snakes, crocodiles or hybrid monsters) or humans. Sometimes they have human bodies with the head of an animal, such as a snake, crocodile, donkey, vulture, lion or baboon, or they may be headless. As guardians, they often carry knives. The serpent Apophis represents the uncreated forces of chaos and unceasingly attacks the bark of the creator god as it passes through the underworld. In the judgement of the dead, the demon Ammut, depicted as a combination of crocodile, lion and hippopotamus, is shown in the scene of weighing the heart, waiting to devour those condemned. The main sources for this material are the vignettes in the various versions of the Book of the Dead and the underworld scenes in royal tombs in the Valley of the Kings and the Valley of the

Queens, and in private tombs from the late 18th Dynasty onwards.

GAY ROBINS

9. EROTICA AND PORNOGRAPHY. The evidence for ancient Egyptian erotica is perhaps not as abundant as in ancient Greece and Rome, but the Egyptians did not lack means of expressing erotic concepts. Tales of gods and men, love poems and books on dreams and magic all refer to their erotic desires. In official representations a coded language was sometimes employed to convey the underlying sexual force essential for a deceased person to be reborn in the hereafter, the idea being visually rendered by including erotic symbols such as lotus flowers, ducks, unguent cones and wigs. For example in banquet scenes in private tombs the concept of the climax of the union was conveyed, through a play on words, by the pouring of wine and beer. The erotic significance of these scenes is emphasized by the semi-transparent garments of the ladies, their jewellery and heavy eye make-up and the way they embrace.

On the walls of temples, gods such as Min are sometimes represented with an erect member. But only unofficial representations contain evidence of the erotic activities of real people in daily life. Flakes of limestone or pottery served as convenient notepads for the draughtsmen. A number of erotic sketches have survived showing different positions of intercourse, sometimes with more than two persons present. The major document celebrating carnal desire is a late New Kingdom erotic papyrus (Turin, Mus. Egizio, 55001) showing 12 scenes of men and women having intercourse or engaged in other sexual acts, with an accompanying text that renders part of their conversation.

As far as sculpture is concerned, there are countless erotic figurines, including many representations of the dwarf Bes (the god of childbirth and the sexual activities of women; see EROTIC ART, fig. 1) and statuettes of musicians copulating with women, sometimes playing a large angular harp resting on the phallus. Greek terracottas from Egypt feature representations of women with their legs open, while amulets were often shaped either like a phallus, with or without testicles, or as persons with disproportionately large members. Painted clay relief figures of Bes, on a monumental scale, decorated the walls of a Greco-Roman sanctuary at Saqqara, but the exact significance of these can only be conjectured. Erotic art was subject to the same conventions as other representations (see §IV above). The intertwining of limbs and members presented certain problems in that, according to the usual conventions of Egyptian art, nothing essential should be concealed. Most surviving erotic drawings, however, are private sketches rather than officially commissioned works of art. Doubtless the surviving material does not give a complete picture of this aspect of Egyptian art, but it does suggest that the genre existed.

LISE MANNICHE

10. FESTIVALS. The ancient Egyptian year was punctuated by a great variety of festivals. Many are indicated by only passing references in Egyptian art but the great religious feasts are well recorded. The *mammisi* (a temple annexe associated with divine birth) at Edfu contains

7. Flora and fauna around the pool of a noble, fragment of wall painting from the so-called tomb of Nebamun, Thebes, h. 640 mm, 18th Dynasty, c. 1375 BC (London, British Museum)

scenes from the 'Feast of the Beautiful Meeting', the annual visit of Hathor, goddess of Dendera, to the Temple of Horus at Edfu. The mystic union of the two gods is conveyed by showing their two sacred boats, while the public welcome of Hathor by Horus and the eventual farewell ceremonies are depicted in the courtyard of the temple. Scenes from the festivals of Min and Sokar, preserved with much of their fine original colour at Medinet Habu (the mortuary temple of Ramesses III at Thebes), show the festival processions clearly with the gods hidden in their shrines carried aloft in a large model boat.

The festival depicted in greatest detail is the Opet Festival, when Amun moved from his state temple at Karnak to the private domain at Luxor. This record, in the colonnade at Luxor temple, is one of the few pieces of temple decoration that can be attributed to the reign of Tutankhamun (reg c. 1332–c. 1323 BC; see THEBES (i), §III).

The great funeral festival, the 'Beautiful Feast of the Valley' in which Amun led the population of Thebes in paying respect to their dead in the western necropolis, is recorded in the temple of Hatshepsut at Deir el-Bahri. The rites surrounding the resurrection of Osiris are depicted in the temple of Sethos I at ABYDOS (c. 1280 BC), which contains some of the finest reliefs in Egypt.

J. RUFFLE

11. FLORA AND FAUNA. Animals and plants are well represented in Egyptian art. In private tombs from the Old Kingdom period onwards, activities in the marshes, including scenes of the owner fishing and fowling (see fig. 8 below), are depicted against a background of marsh plants, particularly papyrus. Artists represented a variety of birds such as the ibis, duck, pigeon and goose (for illustration see MAIDUM), some on their nests with eggs or fledglings, some perched and others flying. Small predators

climb the stems towards the nests. Butterflies fly around and grasshoppers and frogs may land on the plants. In the water different sorts of fish are depicted as well as crocodiles and hippopotamuses, swimming birds and lotus plants. Desert scenes are also common, usually as a setting for hunting by the tomb owner, for which a whole range of wild animals is represented: gazelles, oryxes, ibexes, wild bulls, donkeys, wild sheep, leopards, foxes, lions, hyenas, jerboas, hedgehogs, hares and ostriches. Other scenes show the animals (captured in the marshes and deserts) being brought by servants. In scenes depicting the activities on the owner's estate various aspects of cattle husbandry are shown, and grain and flax are depicted in the fields. Fruit trees such as the sycamore fig, date-palm and *dom*-palm and also the grapevine are frequently represented (see fig. 7). Plants such as the blue and white lotus, the cornflower, mandrake, poppy and pomegranate are widely depicted not only in garden scenes but also with the papyrus as elements in elaborate bouquets and in other decorative motifs (*see* §20 below).

12. FOREIGNERS. Often shown as bound captives (see figs 94 and 120 below), foreigners were depicted in Egyptian art from the earliest times. They usually represent the traditional enemies of Egypt, which are symbolized by nine bows. The figures of foreigners are commonly depicted on the side or base of the king's throne or at the base of the royal kiosk or the 'Window of Appearances' from which the king gave audience to his officials. They are sometimes incorporated into a device symbolizing the union of the Two Lands (i.e. Upper and Lower Egypt). Another common motif shows the king grasping one or more foreign enemies with one hand while raising the other hand to smite them with a mace or scimitar. This scene, already depicted on the Protodynastic (*c.* 3000 BC) Narmer Palette (Cairo, Egyp. Mus.; for illustration *see* NARMER), was still regularly employed in the Ptolemaic period (304–30 BC), especially on the outer faces of temple pylons. The king might also be shown as a sphinx trampling fallen foreigners.

Scenes showing royal campaigns in Syria–Palestine and Nubia naturally portray foreigners as the enemies of Egypt, but there are also scenes (in private Theban tombs of the 18th Dynasty) showing Nubians, Syrians, Cretans and people from Punt bringing produce from their countries (which the Egyptians liked to regard as 'tribute'). Other scenes show Nubian workmen and soldiers (see fig. 98 below); the features and costumes of the foreigners are usually carefully observed and distinguished both from native Egyptians and from each other.

13. HOUSEHOLD ACTIVITIES. Private tombs at Thebes and el-Amarna occasionally include representations of the owner's house. Some are shown in elevation from the outside while others consist of a plan with internal details drawn in elevation. In one depiction of a house, in the tomb of Djehutinefer at Thebes (TT 104), there are living-rooms, grain silos, an area for hanging up meat to dry and rooms for spinning, weaving and baking. In private tombs from the Old Kingdom onwards kitchen scenes including the preparation and cooking of meat, baking and brewing are common (see fig. 55 below). Fish and fowl captured in the marshes are shown being brought in and gutted or plucked and drawn, while cattle are butchered and jointed. The fish, birds and joints of meat are often shown hanging on a line to dry. Scenes also show them being cooked in a cauldron over a fire or roasted on a hand-held spit over a brazier. The bakery is usually depicted next to the brewery, since beer was made from fermented loaves. The scenes show the grinding of grain and the kneading of dough, which is then placed in bread moulds that are stacked over a fire. To make beer the loaves are broken up and soaked in water, the mixture strained into jars and left to ferment. Scenes of spinning and weaving are less common, and some of these belong to temple workshops. Horizontal looms were worked by women, as in the Middle Kingdom tombs at Beni Hasan, and vertical looms, which were introduced in the 18th Dynasty, by men, as in Djehutinefer's house.

GAY ROBINS

14. HUNTING AND FISHING. The environment of Egypt offered a habitat to many wild animals; there were crocodiles and hippopotamuses in the river and swamps, lions in the areas where the wadis ran into the Nile Valley and game in the desert beyond. Scenes in tombs of all periods show that hunting was practised to keep down the numbers of certain animals and to provide food and even adornment such as ostrich plumes. There are dramatic representations of hippopotamus hunts in the Old Kingdom tombs of Mereruka and Ty at Saqqara. Desert hunts are almost a standard feature of the Middle Kingdom nomarchs' tombs at Beni Hasan. The nets set up across the desert to trap the oryx, gazelle and other animals form a frieze in the main chambers. Similar scenes in the New Kingdom tombs of Qenamun and Userhet at Thebes show some particularly sensitive observations of the animals.

Kings hunted to demonstrate their valour: a box (Cairo, Egyp. Mus.) from the tomb of Tutankhamun (*reg c.* 1332–*c.* 1323 BC) shows him alone in his chariot, charging down a pride of lions. A relief at Medinet Habu depicts Ramesses III (*reg c.* 1187–*c.* 1156 BC) killing a wild bull while the prince shoots at oryx, antelopes and wild asses. Wild fowling in the marshes was undertaken to provide food by gangs of hunters with large clap nets and also as a sport by noblemen. These are often shown in a papyrus skiff, accompanied by wife and children, spearing fish on one side of a thicket and throwing weighted sticks or boomerangs at wild birds from the other side (for illustrations see fig. 8 and MOALLA, EL-).

15. INDUSTRY AND COMMERCE. Materials from outside the Nile Valley, such as cedar, gold and precious stones, were made into finished goods in the workshops of the great temples which, in the theocratic society of ancient Egypt, were under the control of the government. Specialist workers were employed on this task, therefore their activities were recorded by the artists in the tombs of the officials who ran the workshops (*see* §II above). The artists show detailed knowledge of the tools and techniques of their fellow-craftsmen.

Many crafts, such as pottery, spinning and weaving and carpentry, were probably carried out by non-specialists but they were sometimes undertaken on a larger scale in workshops attached to the estates of nobles. Such workshops were recorded in the wall paintings of some of the nobles' tombs (see figs 16, 17 and 18 below). Even the very humble trades, such as that of brickmaker and laundryman, were occasionally represented. In the Old and Middle Kingdoms some of them were also represented by figurines, such as the 5th Dynasty painted limestone representation of a female brewer from Giza (Cairo, Egyp. Mus., JE 66624). The products of the temple workshops were intended partly for use within the temples but also for trade (*see* §I, 3 above). Ancient Egypt, was, however, hardly a consumer society and there are only a few depictions of trading. There are six representations of markets or bartering in the tombs of stewards or overseers of granaries at Thebes, and in a relief in the Greco-Roman Temple of Khnum at Esna a shop is depicted.

J. RUFFLE

16. THE KING. The Egyptian ruler occupied a unique position at the head of society, and his depiction is one of the most important themes in Egyptian art and religion. From protodynastic to Roman times, the king is represented performing rituals before the gods, most often offering (see fig. 115 below) or adoring, being purified and crowned by them, smiting his enemies (for illustration *see* NARMER) and conducting victorious campaigns. Scenes showing the king offering to deities also frequently appear on royal stelae. From the 18th Dynasty, kings may be represented in private tombs, most commonly enthroned in a kiosk (a pavilion where the king gave audience) or, from the Amarna period, standing at the 'Window of Appearances', appointing or rewarding the tomb owner, receiving foreign 'tribute' or reviewing the products of royal workshops. In the New Kingdom the king sometimes appears on private stelae and other works offering to a deity on behalf of the owner or receiving offerings from the owner. Also in the New Kingdom kings are shown embracing and offering to deities in their tombs in the Valley of the Kings. A large number of figured ostraca bear practice sketches of the king, testifying to his importance in the artist's repertory.

17. LANDSCAPE. In Egyptian art human activity generally takes precedence over landscape, which acts merely as a setting. However, in private tombs from the Old Kingdom onwards many subsidiary scenes include some landscape elements: desert and marsh plants and animals, trees, flowers and crops. In desert scenes, mostly in private tombs showing the tomb owner hunting, a landscape setting is often quite developed. The base lines frequently undulate to a greater or lesser extent to suggest the rocky desert terrain. In this setting animals fight, copulate, give birth and emerge from their burrows. In marsh scenes (see fig. 8 above), the activities take place against a background of papyrus thickets and water teeming with life: birds, insects, fish, crocodiles and frogs. Many of the details of marsh scenes have erotic overtones. The scenes from the sun temple of Neuserre (*reg c.* 2416–*c.* 2392 BC) of the 5th Dynasty (*see* ABU GHURAB) are particularly important, showing human activities through the seasons of the year set against a background

8. Nebamun hunting birds in the marshes, fragment of wall painting from the so-called tomb of Nebamun, Thebes, h. 820 mm, 18th Dynasty, *c.* 1375 BC (London, British Museum)

of agricultural land, marsh and desert. While much of palace decoration makes use of a formal arrangement of plant motifs, the walls of the 'Green Room', in the North Palace at EL-AMARNA, are decorated with scenes of papyrus thickets, harbouring doves, pigeons, shrikes and kingfishers, above a strip of water filled with lotus leaves, flowers and buds. On the banks on either side of the water are flowering plants; here humans are excluded.

GAY ROBINS

18. MUSIC AND DANCE. Among the arts of ancient civilizations music is the most elusive, but numerous ancient Egyptian representations of musical scenes have survived. The earliest depiction of a musician in action is a scene on a protodynastic ceremonial slate palette (*c.* 3000 BC; Oxford, Ashmolean) portraying a disguised hunter playing an end-blown flute. Musicians playing tambourines were later depicted in similar scenes, while military music was provided by barrel-shaped drums and trumpets. Various reliefs and paintings show that a divine image or bark in procession was usually accompanied by the rhythmic sound of wooden clappers, drums and trumpets. Depictions of scenes inside temples show that tambourines, double oboes and harps were used to entertain the deity. The most important cult instrument was the sistrum, a rattle provided with metal discs.

Secular music, for entertainment at banquets, was depicted in the form of groups of musicians playing harps, oblique flutes and double clarinets (in the Old Kingdom) and harps, lutes, double oboes, lyres and tambourines (in the New Kingdom), frequently accompanied by songs and clapping of hands. The 'blind harpist' and his song was a set character in the tradition of Egyptian music (if not in reality).

Dance was a visual expression of music and ritual. The 'mirror dance' involved Hathor, goddess of music and love, and the reflection of hands in mirrors. In depictions

9. Woman performing an acrobatic dance, limestone ostracon from Deir el-Medina, w. 168 mm, 19th Dynasty, *c.* 1250 BC (Turin, Museo Egizio di Torino)

of public processions girls are shown performing acrobatic dance movements, as in the depicton of a female dancer on an ostracon from Deir el-Medina (*c.* 1250 BC; Turin, Mus. Egizio; see fig. 9). Guests at private functions were apparently entertained by scantily dressed female dancers, such as those portrayed on a fragment of wall painting from the tomb of Nebamun (*c.* 1400 BC; London, BM, 37984; see fig. 72 below).

For further discussion of Egyptian musical instruments *see* §XVII, 12 below.

LISE MANNICHE

19. NAVIGATION AND TRAVEL. The Nile was the main route of travel within Egypt and boats figure widely in Egyptian art from the Old Kingdom onwards. Small skiffs made of papyrus are shown in tomb scenes of fishing and fowling (see fig. 8 above). Other scenes, especially in Old Kingdom tombs, show the owner travelling on a boat propelled by oars going downstream and by sail upstream. In New Kingdom tombs the deceased is often shown making a pilgrimage by boat to Abydos. Flat-bottomed barges were used for transporting building material, statues and obelisks, and famous scenes in the temple of Hatshepsut at Deir el-Bahri show two obelisks being brought from Aswan to Karnak. The same temple shows a voyage down the Red Sea to the land of Punt on the African coast to trade with the inhabitants. During the

Opet Festival at Thebes (*see* §11 above) the divine barks processed by river from Karnak to Luxor and back.

Another mode of travel, often shown in Old Kingdom tombs, was the carrying chair used by officials. The king could also be transported in this way, as shown in scenes at el-Amarna and Medinet Habu. The beast of burden was the donkey, used for transporting loads both within Egypt and in caravans trading abroad. The horse and two-wheel chariot was introduced into Egypt from the Levant during the New Kingdom. They were used for battles, hunting and various official royal appearances. Heavier carriages with four shield-like wheels, pulled by oxen, were probably in use earlier, but they did not play an important role in Egypt, because of the convenient water transport and use of sledges.

20. PATTERNS AND DESIGNS. The main elements in ornamental patterns and designs in Egyptian art are geometric motifs, plants, animals, birds and fish. They occur on ceilings and friezes in private tombs, in the decoration of palaces, on furniture, 18th Dynasty blue-painted pottery (see fig. 86 below), faience bowls and cosmetic objects. Tomb ceilings are often decorated with geometric patterns with combinations of zigzags, squares, spirals, circles, dots and rosettes, sometimes mixed with natural elements such as grapes or bulls' heads. Such patterns are also found on palace ceilings as well as those

composed of natural motifs such as ducks, pigeons and vultures. Rows of vultures with outstretched wings are also common decoration on temple ceilings. One of the most common designs for temple and tomb ceilings is a repeated pattern of staggered rows of yellow stars on a blue background representing the sky (see §3 above).

Among the plants used in ornamental designs are the papyrus, associated with Lower Egypt, the white and blue lotus, associated with rebirth, the poppy, cornflower, mandrake, vine and grape, as well as the 'lily' associated with Upper Egypt but unidentifiable with a real plant. These may be combined in elaborate and formal bouquets and used, for example, to decorate furniture or cosmetic items. Patterns of flowers and fruit formed friezes in tomb and palace decoration. Blue-painted pottery made extensive use of patterns based on lotuses, and designs incorporating lotuses and papyrus, often with fish, are found on blue faience bowls. Some palace floors were decorated with formal designs consisting of various arrangements of the repeated motif of a plant, such as papyrus, poppy or cornflower, combined with a leaping calf or flying birds. Sometimes these were arranged around a depiction of a pool with lotuses, swimming birds and fishes. The plant motif with calves and birds also appears on pottery and cosmetic objects. Sometimes the figure of a naked or almost naked girl appears on these items against a background pattern of papyrus and lotus.

21. SPORTS AND GAMES. In private tombs the owner is often shown hunting on foot with a bow. From the mid-18th Dynasty onwards archery was also practised from chariots as in the scene on the painted box of Tutankhamun (Cairo, Egyp. Mus.), the bull hunt of Ramesses III at Medinet Habu or the scene in the Theban tomb of Userhat. One private tomb (TT 109) shows the future Amenophis II being taught archery as a boy.

Wrestling is depicted fairly frequently from the 1st Dynasty (c. 2925–c. 2775 BC) onwards and is a particularly common theme in Middle Kingdom private tombs, for example at Deir el-Bersha, Meir, Aswan and Beni Hasan. In the latter, it seems to form part of the training for soldiers. In the New Kingdom, examples of wrestling and single-stick contests are found at celebrations associated with the appearance of the king. Swimming is very rarely depicted apart from cosmetic spoons in the form of a swimming girl.

Children apparently playing various types of game, including ball games, are shown in scenes from some Old and Middle Kingdom tombs; some of them seem to involve movements relating to dance and acrobatics. Acrobats, especially as part of processions, feature in private tombs and temples; particularly beautiful and effective examples appear on ostraca (see fig. 9 above). Surviving examples of board games show that they were popular in ancient Egypt, and they are depicted in tombs from the Old Kingdom onwards. The most enduring of them was a game for two called senet (see fig. 6 above). By the 19th Dynasty (c. 1292–c. 1190 BC) it had become associated with the journey of the deceased through the underworld and appears in scenes relating to the afterlife both in tombs and in the Book of the Dead; the deceased usually sits alone at the board without a visible opponent.

The game continued to be played in secular contexts. At Medinet Habu, Ramesses III is shown playing senet in the harem with a princess, and the game appears in archaizing scenes in 26th Dynasty tombs based on Old Kingdom models; a scene in the early Ptolemaic TOMB OF PETOSIRIS at Tuna el-Gebel shows the owner playing senet with a friend.

22. WAR. Scenes of warfare are occasionally depicted in private tombs of the Old and Middle Kingdoms, and fragments of the depictions of a battle survive from the Middle Kingdom temple of Nebhepetre Mentuhotpe II at Deir el-Bahri. It was not until the New Kingdom that war scenes became common, chiefly on the walls of temples as part of the iconography of the king who is depicted as the main protagonist. The best-preserved and most elaborate examples belong to the 19th and 20th dynasties and show, for example, the battles of Sethos I, RAMESSES II and Ramesses III, but earlier fragmentary examples survive from the mortuary temple of Tuthmosis II, the Amarna period and the speos (rock-temple) of Horemheb at Gebel el-Silsila. The 19th and 20th Dynasty scenes are on a large scale and depict actual campaigns in narrative form by showing the course of events in a series of incidents. The topography of the battlefield may be shown and conventional register lines are often abandoned. Typical motifs from these scenes show the king trampling on a fallen soldier, as he shoots or strikes at the enemy, or driving his chariot over chaotic heaps of the defeated. This latter motif also appears on the chariot of Tuthmosis IV and the painted box of Tutankhamun (both Cairo, Egyp. Mus.) but would seem in these cases to be purely symbolic.

23. WOMEN. All classes of women are widely depicted in Egyptian art. They appear more often on private monuments than in temples, where the main protagonists are the king and deities. However, female members of the royal family could be depicted with the king in temple scenes, and this became particularly widespread during the Amarna period, when the queen even appeared alone offering to the Aten. In addition, priestesses, female singers, musicians, dancers and acrobats (see fig. 9 above) may be shown participating in temple ritual, particularly in processions during festivals. In tombs and on private stelae the owner is normally accompanied by his wife or mother (see THEBES (i), fig. 9). Owing to the convention that women should be shown in an ideal form as young and beautiful, the only distinction between the wife and mother often lies in the accompanying text; sometimes the older women are portrayed in a more conservative form of dress. Daughters could be shown as children or young women, accompanying or offering to their parents. Female guests are normally attended by female servants, who in 18th Dynasty scenes are shown virtually naked. Other scenes in private tombs portray female servants spinning, weaving, baking or brewing, often alongside male workers. Women with children are sometimes shown in private tombs, especially foreign women coming to Egypt with their offspring. On ostraca from Deir el-Medina (see THEBES (i), §XI) there are sketches showing seated mothers nursing children in the special building to which women went to give birth. Various sketches, mostly on ostraca, show couples having intercourse (see §9 above).

BIBLIOGRAPHY

E. Naville: *Das aegyptische Todtenbuch der XVIII bis XX Dynastie*, i (Berlin, 1886)

The Book of the Dead: Facsimile of the Papyrus of Ani in the British Museum (London, 1890)

E. Naville: *The Temple of Deir el-Bahari*, 6 vols (London, 1894–1908)

W. M. F. Petrie: *Egyptian Decorative Arts* (London, 1895)

E. A. W. Budge: *The Book of the Dead: Facsimiles of the Papyrus of Hunefer, Anhai, Kerasher and Netchemet* (London, 1899)

F. Guilmant: *Le Tombeau de Ramses IX* (Cairo, 1907)

G. Jequier: *Decoration égyptienne* (Paris, 1911)

L. Klebs: *Die Reliefs des alten Reiches* (Heidelberg, 1915)

H. Schäfer: *Von ägyptischer Kunst, besonders der Zeichenkunst*, 2 vols (Leipzig, 1919, rev. 4/1930); Eng. trans. by J. Baines as *Principles of Egyptian Art* (Oxford, 1974, rev. 3/1986)

L. Klebs: *Die Reliefs und Malereien des mittleren Reiches* (Heidelberg, 1922)

W. Wreszinski: *Atlas zur altägyptischen Kulturgeschichte*, 3 vols (Leipzig, 1923–36) [an invaluable corpus of material]

C. Boreux: *L'Art de la navigation en Egypte jusqu'à la fin de l'ancien empire* (Cairo, 1925)

B. Porter and R. Moss: *Topographical Bibliography* (Oxford, 1927–) [app. to the 2nd rev. edns of vols i–iii list selected scene types]

C. Kuentz: *La Bataille de Qadech* (Cairo, 1928)

H. Frankfort: *The Mural Painting of el-Amarneh* (London, 1929)

J. Wilson: 'Ceremonial Games of the New Kingdom', *J. Egyp. Archaeol.*, xvii (1931), pp. 211–20

P. Bucher: *Les Textes des tombes de Thoutmosis III et d'Amenophis II* (Cairo, 1932)

L. Klebs: *Die Reliefs und Malereien des neuen Reiches* (Heidelberg, 1934)

M. Werbrouck: *Les Pleureuses dans l'Egypte ancienne* (Brussels, 1938)

F. W. von Bissing: *Der Fussboden aus dem Palaste des Königs Amenophis IV. zu el Hawata im Museum zu Kairo* (Munich, 1941)

A. Piankoff: *The Tomb of Ramesses VI* (New York, 1954)

B. Bruyère: *La Tombe de no. 1 de Sen-nedjem à Deir el Medineh* (Cairo, 1959)

T. G. Allen: *The Egyptian Book of the Dead: Documents in the Oriental Institute Museum at the University of Chicago* (Chicago, 1960)

O. Neugebauer and R. Parker: *Egyptian Astronomical Texts*, 3 vols (Providence, 1960–69)

H. Hickmann: *Musikgeschichte in Bildern*, ii/1 (Leipzig, 1961)

P. Fortova-Samalova and M. Vilimkova: *Egyptian Ornament* (London, 1963)

J. Vandier: *Manuel d'archéologie égyptienne* (Paris, 1964–78), iv–vi

A. Radwan: *Die Darstellungen des regierenden Königs und seiner Familienangehörigen in der Privatgräbern der 18. Dynastie* (Berlin, 1969)

A. D. Touny and S. Wenig: *Der Sport im alten Ägypten* (Leipzig, 1969)

B. van de Walle: *L'Humour dans la littérature et dans l'art de l'ancienne Egypte* (Leiden, 1969)

S. Wenig: *The Woman in Egyptian Art* (New York, 1969)

M. Heerma van Voss: *Zwischen Grab und Paradies* (Basle, 1971)

E. Hornung: *Das Grab des Haremhab im Tal der Könige* (Berne, 1971)

J. A. Omlin: *Der Papyrus 55001 und seine satirisch-erotischen Zeichnungen und Inschriften* (Turin, 1973)

E. Russmann: *The Representation of the King in the XXVth Dynasty* (Brussels, 1974)

E.-C. Strauss: *Die Nunschale: Ein Gefässgruppe des Neuen Reiches* (Munich, 1974)

L. Manniche: *Ancient Egyptian Musical Instruments* (Munich, 1975)

G. A. Gaballa: *Narrative in Egyptian Art* (Mainz, 1976)

W. H. Peck: *Drawings from Ancient Egypt* (London, 1978)

E. Brunner-Traut: *Egyptian Artists' Sketches* (Istanbul, 1979)

R. O. Faulkner: *Book of the Dead* (London, 1985)

E. Wilson: *Ancient Egyptian Designs* (London, 1986)

W. Decker: *Sports and Games of Ancient Greece* (New Haven, 1992)

GAY ROBINS

VII. Materials and techniques.

1. Stone. 2. Metal. 3. Wood. 4. Cloth.

1. STONE. Within its varied geological structures Egypt harbours many types of rock that have been extensively used in art and architecture since the beginning of Egyptian history, *c.* 3000 BC.

(i) Types and quarries. (ii) Stoneworking techniques. (iii) Transport.

(i) Types and quarries. Altogether some 40 varieties of stone have been used, many of which were not systematically quarried but were collected as boulders from the wadis in the Eastern Desert. The rocks can be classified into two main groups on the basis of their origins: those from the valley of the Nile (mainly sedimentary limestone and sandstone) and those from more remote desert areas, predominantly the Eastern Desert (crystalline, igneous and metamorphic rocks). The rocks from near the Nile Valley include limestone, lime breccia, chalky sandstone, calcite alabaster, sandstone and silicified sandstone (quartzite). Those from desert areas include greywacke, green breccia, schist, pink granite, granodiorite, quartz diorite, diorite, gabbro, anorthosite, serpentinite, soapstone (steatite), basalt, dolerite and porphyry. Not all these stones are suitable for making objects of any required size—this ability depends mainly on the rock's structure, weathering and the homogeneous formation of lumps of rock. These factors also determine the technologies used to obtain the rock.

(a) Limestone. The number of limestone quarries far exceeds any other type of quarry in Egypt. The Nile Valley from Cairo to south of Esna is flanked for 700 km by Eocene ledges of limestone that vary locally in quality. The way in which most of these limestone ledges are clearly layered must have given the ancient Egyptians the idea of extracting the rock by layers; consequently there are ancient galleried quarries leading into the hillside that follow the strata exactly. There were also opencast quarries where the rock was extracted in blocks from the top surface of the hills, working downwards, but the galleried quarries with their props inside are definitely older.

While building material used for temples and tombs or even for the cores of pyramids was often coarse nummulitic limestone, the use of fine, close-grained limestone was preferred for sculpture in the round, stelae, wall cladding for buildings and free-standing walls where reliefs were to be applied. Its greater resistance to weathering was recognized from an early stage: the Bent Pyramid at DAHSHUR from the 4th Dynasty (*c.* 2575–*c.* 2465 BC) is among the best preserved of those dating from the Old Kingdom (*c.* 2575–*c.* 2150 BC) because its cladding of fine limestone (which has been largely preserved) has protected the less valuable core material from erosion.

Where the cladding stones were removed, the pyramids suffered rapid deterioration from weathering. The quarries that produced this high-quality fine limestone are near modern Tura, south of Cairo, and extend southwards through al-Ma'sara and as far as Helwan. The Muqattam Mountains to the east of Cairo also contain fine limestone, which was already being extracted during the Old Kingdom period.

(b) Calcite alabaster. Especially in the nummulitic limestone areas in Middle Egypt calcite alabaster occurs in cavities and fissures (*see* ALABASTER, §1); from an early stage in Egyptian history it was sought after for use in art and architecture. Calcite alabaster, a translucent and shimmering stone, was mainly used for vessels, but also for sculptures in the round (usually on a small scale) and for

floor surfaces in the pyramid temples of the Old Kingdom. Large objects are rare because of the soft nature of the stone, although the Alabaster Sphinx at Memphis (*in situ*) is an example of its use on a larger scale (for illustration *see* MEMPHIS).

Because of its inscriptions, Hatnub (east of el-Amarna) is the best-known alabaster quarry. However, there are far larger deposits at al-Qawatir south-east of Minya. There are many smaller places where calcite alabaster was demonstrably extracted and used by the pharaohs between Helwan and Asyut in the limestone mountains of the Eastern Desert.

(c) Sandstone. With the transfer of the royal residence from Lower Egypt to Thebes in Upper Egypt at the beginning of the New Kingdom (*c.* 1540–*c.* 1075 BC) there was a marked increase in the use of sandstone as a material for building and sculpture. Extraction was thenceforth concentrated on the sandstone quarries at GEBEL EL-SILSILA north of Kom Ombo. Its most important use was as a building material—virtually all temples in Upper Egypt are constructed from blocks of sandstone—but statues for tombs and temples, stelae and other three-dimensional objects were also made from sandstone.

(d) Silicified sandstone (quartzite). The silicified sandstone found in Egypt is a variant of Nubian sandstone; it is a very hard stone similar to quartzite and was extracted for preference at Gebel Ahmar near Cairo, but also in the Western Desert near Aswan. The two huge seated figures of Amenophis III (*reg c.* 1390–*c.* 1353 BC) at the entrance to his mortuary temple in western Thebes, known as the 'Colossi of Memnon' (*see* THEBES (i), §V and fig. 5), are made from silicified sandstone, probably from the area to the west of Aswan. This stone was much sought after and highly prized. It was the preferred material for royal statues and royal sarcophagi (e.g. Tutankhamun's) as well as building components in temples. It was extracted mainly during the 4th and 5th dynasties (*c.* 2575–*c.* 2325 BC; as at Abu Rawash and Abusir), just before, during and after the Amarna period (*c.* 1360–*c.* 1320 BC) and in the 25th Dynasty (*c.* 750–656 BC). This suggests that silicified sandstone was most popular in periods when worship of the sun-god was at its height.

(e) Granite. The largest quarrying area in the time of the pharaohs is at the 1st cataract near Aswan. This is the source of both the famous pink granite and the grey to grey-black granodiorite. Both types of rock had been used from the beginning of the dynastic period. The first intensive period of its use for sculpture and architecture was during the Old Kingdom (e.g. Chephren's valley temple, cladding on Mycerinus' pyramid). The rock occurs naturally in rounded blocks (known as 'woolsacks'), and in the granite massif at Aswan untreated blocks of any required size are available; these were fashioned into objects of the most varied kinds on the spot: sarcophagi, for both royal and private use, columns, plinths for columns, statues, including the colossal creations of the Ramesside period and later, stelae and, in the Roman period (30 BC–AD 395), ceremonial bathtubs. Incomplete or discarded examples of all these objects can be found in the quarries. Almost all obelisks were made from Aswan granite; only they were cut from the actual rock face, as single blocks of the necessary size were virtually impossible to find. A partly quarried granite obelisk is still *in situ*.

(f) Basalt. This black crystalline rock occurs in an extractable form in several places in Egypt. The largest quarries are near Gebel al-Qatrani, at the northern edge of the Faiyum. There was a marked preference during the Middle Kingdom (*c.* 2008–*c.* 1630 BC) and Late Period for using basalt to make small three-dimensional sculptures and vessels. The natural clefts that occur in the rock make it virtually impossible to extract large homogeneous blocks from the quarries: consequently generally only small objects, such as statues, stelae, vessels and votive platters, are made of this material. Basalt slabs were used as a floor covering in the pyramid complexes of the Old Kingdom (e.g. the mortuary temple of Cheops at Giza). Basalt is often confused by writers with greywacke, since both rocks when polished and worn down have a similar surface.

(g) Anorthosite gneiss. According to inscriptions found in the quarries located about 60 km west of Abu Simbel in the Western Desert where anorthosite gneiss occurred, it was only extracted there until the end of the Middle Kingdom. This rock was wrongly described as 'Chephren diorite', after the famous seated figure of Chephren (*reg c.* 2520–*c.* 2494 BC) with the Horus falcon (Cairo, Egyp. Mus., JE 10062; see fig. 52 below) made from it. Anorthosite gneiss was highly prized and used mainly for three-dimensional sculpture during the Old Kingdom and Middle Kingdom. The few items that can be assigned to a later date—mainly amulets—must have been made from fragments of older statues.

(h) Rocks from the Eastern Desert. The varied rock types found in the Precambrian bedrock between the valley of the Nile and the Red Sea were used to make generally small-sized objects such as mace heads, sculpture in the round and vessels. Suitable boulders from the wadi areas of the Eastern Desert were shaped for these purposes. Surviving stone vessels in particular demonstrate the great richness and variety of these rocks. The main ones are diorite, porphyry, syenite, marble, serpentinite, steatite and schist.

For most of these rocks, there are no properly constructed quarries, except for greywacke, the *bekhen* stone coveted by the Egyptians, which was systematically extracted in an organized quarrying business run at Wadi Hammamat from the 4th Dynasty. This sought-after material was mainly used for sculpture in the round, royal sarcophagi and building components in temple precincts. According to the hundreds of inscriptions in the quarry area dating from every epoch of Egyptian history, the quarries at Wadi Hammamat—situated about halfway between Koptos (Quft) and Quseir—were intensively exploited until the Roman period.

The purple-red porphyry quarries at Mons Porphyrites and the light quartz diorite quarries at Mons Claudianus were not opened up until the early Roman Empire (*c.* 30 BC–*c.* AD 200) and thus had little significance for Egyptian creative art. These rocks were extracted almost exclusively for use as monolithic columns, ceremonial bowls and baths, wall and floor coverings and to a lesser extent also as a medium for sculpture in imperial buildings in Rome. Items were apparently also made in the quarries, judging from the many striking finds of artefacts that have been left at the site, most of them damaged while being made.

(i) Hardstones. A wide range of hardstones (semi-precious stones) were used for jewellery, amulets and art objects in Egypt. Lapis lazuli was presumably imported from Afghanistan, but deposits of the following types of hardstones are known in the Eastern Desert in Egypt: agate, amethyst, beryl, cornelian, chalcedony, feldspar, garnet, haematite, jade, jasper, malachite, azurite, olivine, onyx, rock crystal, amazonite, sardonyx and turquoise. Even obsidian, which was used especially for making amulets, could be found in the Eastern Desert and did not have to be brought in from Asia Minor or Abyssinia, as was previously supposed.

(ii) Stoneworking techniques. From early times, the Egyptians achieved a high degree of skill in the various techniques of working in stone, many of which continued in use long after the end of the dynastic period (*see* STONE (i), §II). Roughly fashioned flint tools were already in use in the late Palaeolithic period (*c.* 15,000–10,000 BC). In the Neolithic period (*c.* 6000–*c.* 2925 BC) various finely wrought tools made from hard rocks from the Eastern Desert were produced. Copper chisels were introduced in the 4th millennium BC; bronze ones were in use from the time of the New Kingdom; and iron chisels came into use only in the 6th century BC.

(a) Extracting the stone. The working methods used by the Egyptians in sandstone and limestone quarries were almost identical. From the beginning of the dynastic period copper chisels and wooden mallets were used to extract the blocks of stone, and this can still be deduced from the marks left on the quarry walls. A comparative study of such chisel marks at the sandstone quarries at Gebel el-Silsila has made it possible to establish a dating schedule for the various periods of exploitation, so that individual sectors can be assigned to particular rulers and it can be shown that the quarries were used extensively until the Roman period (30 BC–AD 395). The successful extraction of a single, precisely defined layer of limestone or sandstone, recognized as being the best in quality, was ultimately dependent on the availability of harder metal alloy working tools. Blocks of limestone were separated and lifted easily out of the subsoil since the various layers were often separated by intervening layers of clay.

The technique employed for working in harder rocks, such as granite, differed fundamentally from that used in the limestone or sandstone quarries. Stone tools made of dolerite, a basalt-like material, were preferred for working in hard rock. This involved striking the rock to be worked with sharp-edged lumps of dolerite. Each lump weighed several kilograms and was held with both hands, so that small chips splintered off from it. The stone hammers used were gradually rounded off in this process, until they turned into useless balls and were discarded. Many such dolerite balls can still be found in the hard rock quarries

in Egypt, and many earlier researchers mistook them for the actual working tools.

A new method of splitting lumps of hard rock, known as wedge cleavage, was developed at the time of the Ptolemies (304–30 BC). In the subsequent Roman period this technique became the normal practice in dealing with many other types of rock. In wedge cleavage a row of regularly spaced wedge holes is bored along a line and metal wedges are inserted. When all the wedges are hammered in equally, the block splits open along the row of wedge holes. This process is still used in quarries. There is no credible evidence to support the long-held theory that the Egyptians used wooden wedges soaked in water until they swelled to split the stone.

(b) Vessels. Stoneworking techniques reached their first peak in the early period with the production of stone vessels (*see also* §XVII, 16 below), for which first basalt and later calcite alabaster were clearly preferred to the various rocks from the Eastern Desert. The stone craftsman began with the outer shape of the vessel, which was created by chipping away and rubbing the stone with specially made stone tools. The inside of the vessel was then hollowed out with a special boring or drilling implement. To do this a sharp-edged piece of rock was securely attached to a cranked wooden drilling bar. The bar was weighted at the sides with two sacks of sand or stones, the weight of which both effected the drilling process and

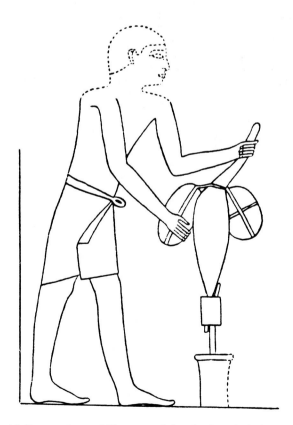

10. Stone craftsman drilling a vessel, line drawing of relief in the temple of Sahure, Abusir, 5th Dynasty, *c.* 2450 BC

centred the drilling bar (see fig. 10). Drilling heads of different sizes allowed the inside of the vessel to be bored out in different diameters according to the outer dimensions of the vessel. The last stage of the work was to smooth the vessel, using quartz sand and polishing stones. Delicate parts on handles, lips or rings were worked with copper tools. From the time of the Old Kingdom the inside of the vessel could also be hollowed out with a trepanning tool in the form of a copper tube.

(c) Statues. There are several visual records representing the making of statues, but in no case is the incomplete statue shown still being worked on; it is always the final version that is portrayed. However, the various steps in the working process can be reconstructed from a large number of unfinished objects in the most varied stages of production (see fig. 11). First the rough shape was hewn out of a suitable block of stone. For small statues this stage took place in the sculptors' workshops (such as that

11. Unfinished stone statue of a standing man, limestone, h. 165 mm, 26th Dynasty, *c.* 663 BC (Detroit, MI, Institute of Arts)

of THUTMOSE), either around the larger quarrying areas or near the royal palaces of the day. Larger objects were rough hewn *in situ* at the quarries. In the granitic area of Aswan it is still possible to see the various stages by which the rough block was transformed into a statue. First a suitable natural block of granite was selected; then the weathered outer crust was chipped away using dolerite hammers until the fresh core of the rock appeared. Even the unfinished obelisk in the Aswan granite quarry clearly shows traces of the impression of dolerite hammers, especially where it was cut out of the rock.

Once the rough shape had been achieved (whether at the quarry or in the workshop), preliminary drawings were made on every side of the cube, giving the outlines of the figure planned in accordance with the proportions then accepted as valid (*see* §IV, 3 above). After the preliminary drawing had been applied, the actual carving began, evidently working from all sides at the same time since none of the statues found unfinished can be seen to be at a different stage on the various faces of the block. Where colossal figures are concerned, this suggests that several sculptors worked simultaneously on one figure (see fig. 12).

While in hard rocks such as granite or quartzite the rough shape was achieved by using stone hammers, as the work progressed they switched to using ever finer metal chisels until they were using chisels with pointed ends. Objects made from limestone or sandstone were produced using only metal chisels and wooden mallets. However metal hammers with wooden handles were definitely not known.

Finally the figure was polished by rubbing powdered quartz sand over it with smoothing stones. The surviving polished stone surfaces on statues, obelisks, sarcophagi and other such stone objects demonstrate a high degree of perfection in the treatment of the surface, on a par with modern machine polishing. After the polishing, the figure was painted in polychromy.

(d) Beads and other small-scale work. Fine metal tools were used for working small-scale rocks, such as hardstones. For example fine saws in the form of copper wires held in tension were used to cut small-sized stones. In some instances these stones have been badly polished, and the serration marks caused by the saws are still visible. For making holes in beads or cylinder seals a fine-pointed drill tensioned with a bow was employed, a method still in use in Egypt for manufacturing beads.

(iii) Transport. The transport of a completed piece of work from the quarries to the Nile was generally effected using wooden sledges; the stone to be transported was placed on the sledge and fixed down with ropes. Ramps were usually installed for the sledge, and rough patches of land were evened out by using wooden planks, stones or tiles made from the mud of the Nile. A moistened coating of Nile mud considerably reduced resistance caused by friction. Some transport ramps can still be identified in the Egyptian countryside. Both wooden transport sledges themselves and the representation of a statue being transported on such a sledge have been preserved. In the tomb of Djehutihotpe (at Deir el-Bersha) there is a picture

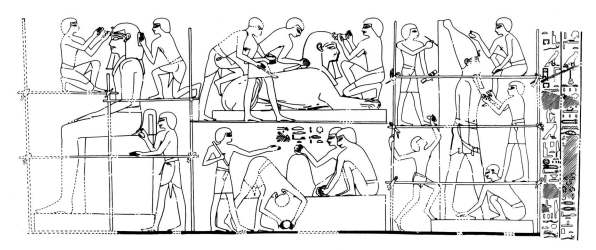

12. Stone craftsmen carving statues, line drawing of wall painting in the tomb of Rekhmire, Thebes, 18th Dynasty, c. 1450 BC

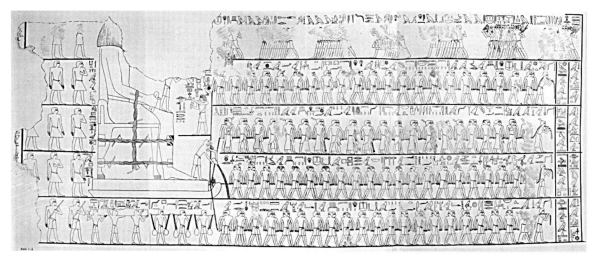

13. Transport of a colossal stone statue, line drawing of wall painting in the tomb of Djehutihotpe, Deir el-Bersha, 12th Dynasty, c. 1900 BC

showing a statue about 8 m high being dragged by 170 people from the calcite alabaster quarries in Hatnub to the place where it was to stand (see fig. 13).

On occasion heavy goods were also drawn by oxen. In the valley of the Nile itself works in stone were loaded on to ships. Even obelisks and monolithic granite columns were transported in this fashion on the waterways.

BIBLIOGRAPHY

LÄ: 'Hatnub', 'Meissel', 'Sarkophag', 'Steinbearbeitung', 'Steinbruch', 'Steingefässe', 'Wadi Hammamat'

A. Lucas: *Ancient Egyptian Materials and Industries* (London, 1926, rev. 4/1962)

S. Clarke and R. Engelbach: *Ancient Egyptian Masonry* (Oxford, 1930)

R. Hartenberg and J. Schmidt jr: 'The Egyptian Drill and the Origin of the Crank', *Technol. & Cult.*, x (1969), pp. 155–65

R. Drenkhahn: *Die Handwerker und ihre Tätigkeiten im alten Ägypten*, Ägyptologische Abhandlungen, xxxi (Wiesbaden, 1976)

A. El-Khouli: *Egyptian Stone Vessels: Predynastic Period to Dynasty III* (Mainz, 1978)

R. Klemm and D. Klemm: *Die Steine der Pharaonen* (Munich, 1981)

——: *Steine und Steinbrüche im alten Ägypten* (Heidelberg, 1992)

ROSEMARIE KLEMM

2. METAL. Metalworking appeared very early in Egypt, at the beginning of the 4th millennium BC, but metal was always scarce and therefore remained a valuable—even a luxurious—commodity. For this reason flint blades were still produced in large quantities as late as the New Kingdom (end of the 2nd millennium BC), alongside tools of copper and bronze. The weights of the metal tools handed out to the tomb workers in the village of Deir el-Medina (in western Thebes) were carefully recorded by scribes to prevent theft. In many bartering transactions the value of goods was estimated in relation to bars of gold, silver or copper, which were too scarce to be used as an actual means of payment.

(i) Types. The main metals exploited in ancient Egypt were copper, bronze, gold, silver, electrum and iron. Cobalt, manganese and lead were used in the production of colourants (in glass) and cosmetics. The use of barium has not yet been attested, and there is no evidence of brass until the 1st century AD, when it appeared as a Roman import.

Copper—and later also bronze—was reserved for making tools and weapons, as well as religious statuettes moulded according to the lost-wax process (see fig. 41 below). All of these objects were usually small in size, since the Egyptians never possessed the technology for heavy metalworking.

The Egyptians' most precious metal was iron, which began to be used in the mid-New Kingdom (14th century BC); a dagger from Tutankhamun's tomb (Cairo, Egyp. Mus.) is of iron, but the use of this metal remained exceptional. The next most important metal was silver, which was fairly scarce but often contained in substantial quantities in the gold worked by goldsmiths. Egyptian smiths did not succeed in separating out gold and silver from naturally occurring electrum—an alloy of gold and silver in which silver makes up 20%—until the Ptolemaic period (304–30 BC). They were also unable to isolate platinum, which was mixed with gold in the ore. Chemical analysis of precious metal objects has revealed the high quality of gold and silver and the extreme rarity of non-precious impurities. Bronze was often formed from empirical alloys, since as much arsenic as tin is found mixed with the copper in extremely variable proportions.

The production of gold, silver and electrum seems to have been under the control of the pharaoh. These metals were used not only for personal jewellery (see §XV below), chiefly among the royal entourage, but also for religious purposes. The points of obelisks and certain engraved images in temples might be covered with gold leaf and the doors of shrines were frequently gilded. The Egyptians exploited the fact that the natural brightness of the metals echoed that of the sun.

(ii) Mines. The supply of metals, traditionally represented as 'tribute' from conquered peoples, was one of the major concerns of the pharaohs, who sent numerous officials to prospect the deserts. Large amounts of cupreous ore were mined in the Sinai Desert and the Red Sea coasts from the Old Kingdom (*c.* 2575–*c.* 2150 BC) onwards, but domestic production was insufficient for demand and copper had to be imported along with tin and arsenic.

Gold and silver came from the eastern deserts and from Nubia. Wells had to be sunk near the mines, since water was essential not only for the survival of the workers but also for washing the gold-bearing ore. Ancient equipment designed for washing gold has been discovered, particularly in Sudan. Egypt was renowned for its gold, but the gold mines were in frontier lands rather than in Egypt itself.

The ores were treated, at least summarily, at the mines themselves. Crucibles for smelting have been discovered in the Sinai, while contemporary paintings and bas-reliefs show metals in the form of ring-shaped ingots or small bags of powder.

(iii) Metalworking techniques. Although crucibles have been excavated at various sites and a bronzesmith's workshop has been found at Kerma in Sudan, no metalworkers' or jewellers' workshops have been definitely identified in Egypt. The various stages of metalworking are well known, thanks to scenes illustrating the activities of daily life found in tombs of all periods, including the mastaba of Mereruka (see fig. 14). The techniques of metalworkers and goldsmiths are portrayed in five basic types of scene: the

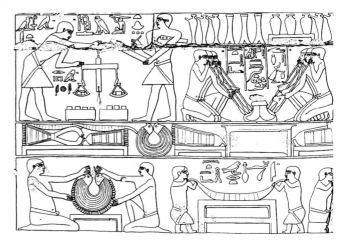

14. Metalworkers weighing and smelting ore, pouring molten metal and displaying the finished products, line drawing of wall painting in the tomb of Mereruka, Saqqara, 6th Dynasty, *c.* 2300 BC

weighing and registering of ingots before they are handed over to the workers; the smelting of metal; the hammering or moulding of the molten metal; the finishing work and the arranging of the finished products. The first three types of scene occur most frequently. It is not always clear which type of metal the workers are processing, but the techniques would have been similar for all metals (*see* METAL, §II): only their melting-points varied.

(a) Weighing, registering and smelting. The ingots were first placed on one of the trays of a pair of scales and their weight scrupulously recorded by a scribe, a practice that certainly ensured good management of the workshop's stocks but also controlled loss and even allowed the detection of theft by the craftsmen. The smelting of the metal, however, was by far the most spectacular stage, requiring the participation of several workers. The ingot—or the ore, if smelting was taking place at the mine—was placed in a crucible (horn-shaped in the Old Kingdom and more open during the New Kingdom) and then in a furnace. The fuel, also scarce, had to be fanned vigorously in order to reach melting-point temperature. From the New Kingdom onwards metalworkers used sets of foot bellows to fan the fire. A Late Period foot bellows consisting of a large circular vessel of clay (London, BM, 22367) was excavated by Flinders Petrie at Tell Dafana. The foot bellows was not an Egyptian invention, for there is evidence of similar bellows far earlier in the Middle East: they seem to have been introduced into Egypt by the Hyksos in the 17th and 16th centuries BC.

It is not known by what methods the Egyptians fanned their furnace fires during the earliest periods; contemporary reliefs and paintings show workers sitting around the furnace blowing into the crucibles through pipes, with the ends pointing towards the fire protected by mud. This method allowed the furnace temperature to be raised to a precise level and the same method was to be used for soldering. However, even with fewer workers than depicted, the process would have produced a low energy output for the effort involved. It must therefore be assumed either that foot bellows were already in use (but not illustrated) or that the furnaces were constructed in such a way that they were naturally subject to a strong draught. The latter would appear more likely and was true of the bronzesmiths' workshops found at Kerma, and also the remains of copper smelting in the Sinai and at Buhen.

The workers who blew into pipes were still present during the New Kingdom, when the furnaces were fanned by foot bellows. Their role was linked to the refining and purification of metals, which facilitated the next stage: hammering. The air produced by the metalworkers was generally directed towards the crucibles. During smelting, the air gave rise to a chemical reaction that oxidized the metal, eliminating any impurities still present. The addition of lead, for example, accelerated this oxidization process and the crucible absorbed all the non-precious elements contained in the ingot or ore. This technique is known as 'cupellation'. Other refining techniques could be used at the same time: poling (molten metal stirred with a stick of green wood, reducing the oxides in the metal) or the use of a charcoal stick, which also produced a reduction in metals. As far as bronze is concerned, arsenic and tin are natural reducers.

(b) Moulding and hammering. To lift the molten metal from the furnace, the workers used flexible sticks of an unknown material, which they grasped at each end, enclosing the crucible. The molten metal was then poured into moulds, which varied according to the intended purpose of the metal. The mould could either be a negative of the object to be made or a specific part of it. The paintings of the tomb of Rekhmire at Thebes, dating from the reign of Tuthmosis III (*reg c.* 1479–*c.* 1426 BC), show the creation of gilded bronze doors for the Temple of Amun (see fig. 15). The metal was introduced into the mould by several apertures. This was an exceptional operation, because of the size of the mould, and the use of closed moulds seems to be more typical during the New Kingdom and subsequent periods. Closed moulds were possibly already in use during the Old Kingdom for very small objects and were placed directly into the furnace. In later periods the use of moulds for making statuettes became common, employing the lost-wax technique. When the object to be made was too large, the metalworkers used a clay core, so that only the exterior of the object

appeared as metal. All the objects were later retouched with chisels to eliminate burrs and imperfections.

During the Old and Middle kingdoms (*c.* 2575–*c.* 1630 BC) the molten metal was poured into open moulds with wide flat surfaces in order to produce sheets of metal. While the metal was still hot workers hammered it with flat pebbles to give it a uniform thickness; it could if required be hammered over a solid shape. For smaller objects the Egyptians used an anvil, after reheating the metal to make if more supple. Precious metals cannot be hammered if they contain impurities, hence the need to refine the metal at an earlier stage of the operation.

(c) Soldering, polishing and decorating. Certain illustrations depict the soldering process, which was allied to smelting. A brazier on a stand served as a furnace and a craftsman, using a pipe which he held in his hand, fanned the fire to a precise temperature. In the other hand he held the object to be soldered in a pair of tongs. It is not known what materials were used for soldering. In many cases the Egyptians heated the two parts to be soldered and joined them just before they reached melting-point; the pieces were thus hard-soldered. Silver was sometimes used to solder copper or silver, probably because of its fairly low melting-point.

At the beginning of the Ptolemaic period craftsmen in the service of Petosiris, portrayed in his tomb at Tuna el-Gebel in Middle Egypt (*see* PETOSIRIS, TOMB OF), used moulding pins, chisels and a hammer to incise the decoration on engraved metal vases. Others are shown polishing these objects with abrasive stones similar to those used by cabinetmakers. Since the depictions are Ptolemaic, it is difficult to know whether these craftsmen were still working according to the Egyptian tradition. However, it is certain that from the earliest times objects made of metal were polished. Many of them incorporate chasing or decorations carried out using a repoussé technique. Inlay was also a widely practised technique. Using a burin the workers prepared the area to be inlaid; this was then replaced with coloured stones or with another metal (often in the form of wire) which was then hammered. There is only one known example of genuine niello from Egypt: the dagger from the tomb of Queen Ahhotpe (*c.* 1550 BC; Cairo, Egyp. Mus., JE 4666).

For a discussion of Egyptian metalworkers' products *see* §XVI below.

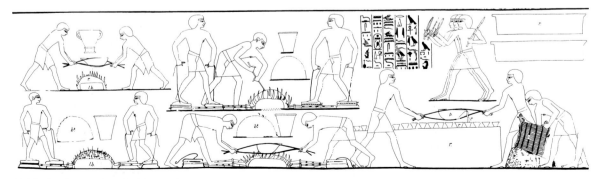

15. Metalworkers casting gilded bronze doors, line drawing of wall painting in the tomb of Rekhmire, Thebes, 18th Dynasty, *c.* 1450 BC

BIBLIOGRAPHY

LÄ: 'Metall', 'Metallarbeiter'

E. Vernier: *La Bijouterie et la joaillerie égyptiennes* (Cairo, 1907)

P. Montet: *Les Scènes de la vie privée dans les tombeaux égyptiens de l'Ancien Empire* (Strasbourg, 1925), pp. 275–88

A. Lucas: *Ancient Egyptian Materials and Industries* (London, 1926, rev. 4/1962), pp. 195–269

J. Vercoutter: 'The Gold of Kush: Two Gold-washing Stations at Faras East', *Kush*, vii (1959), pp. 120–27

J. R. Harris: *Lexicographical Studies in Ancient Egyptian Minerals* (Berlin, 1961)

S. Curto: 'Postille circa la metallurgia antico-egizia', *Mitt. Dt. Archäol. Inst.: Abt. Kairo*, xviii (1962), pp. 59–69

J. Vercoutter: 'Métallurgie, Egypte', *Dictionnaire archéologique des techniques* (Paris, 1964), pp. 657–66

S. Alexander: 'Notes on the Use of Gold Leaf in Egyptian Papyri', *J. Egyp. Archaeol.*, li (1965), pp. 48–52

C. Aldred: *Jewels of the Pharaohs: Egyptian Jewellery of the Dynastic Period* (London, 1971), pp. 46–129

A. Wilkinson: *Ancient Egyptian Jewellery* (London, 1971)

T. G. H. James: 'Gold Technology in Ancient Egypt', *Gold Bull.*, v (1972), pp. 38–42

P. M. Roberts: 'Gold Brazing in Antiquity: Technical Achievements in the Earliest Civilisations', *Gold Bull.*, vi (1973), pp. 112–19

J. H. F. Notton: 'Ancient Egyptian Gold Refining: A Reproduction of Early Techniques', *Gold Bull.*, vii (1974), pp. 50–56

L. B. Hunt: 'The Oldest Metallurgical Handbook', *Gold Bull.*, ix (1979), pp. 24–31

J. L. Chappaz: 'La Purification de l'or', *Bull. Soc. Egyp., Genève*, iv (1980), pp. 19–28

L. B. Hunt: 'The Long History of Lost Wax Casting', *Gold Bull.*, xii (1980), pp. 63–79

W. Vycichl: 'La *Shat*, étalon monétaire de l'Egypte pharaonique', *Bull. Soc. Egyp., Genève*, iii (1980), pp. 27–9

C. A. R. Andrews: *Jewellery from the Earliest Times to the Seventeenth Dynasty* (1981), VI/i of *Catalogue of Egyptian Antiquities in the British Museum* (London, 1975–)

N. H. Gale and Z. A. Stos-Gale: 'Ancient Egyptian Silver', *J. Egyp. Archaeol.*, lxvii (1981), pp. 103–15

S. Aufrère: 'Caractères principaux et origine divine des minéraux', *Rev. Egyp.*, xxxiv (1982), pp. 3–21

H. Jüngst: 'Zur Interpretation einiger Metallarbeiterszenen auf Wandbildern altägyptischer Gräber', *Götting. Misz.*, lix (1982), pp. 15–27

L. Garenne-Marot: 'Le Cuivre en Egypte pharaonique: Sources et métallurgie', *Paléorient*, x/1 (1984), pp. 97–126

R. Maddin and others: 'Old Kingdom Models from the Tomb of Impy: Metallurgical Studies', *J. Egyp. Archaeol.*, lxx (1984), pp. 33–41

C. J. Davey: 'Crucibles in the Petrie Collection and Hieroglyphic Ideograms for Metal', *J. Egyp. Archaeol.*, lxxi (1985), pp. 142–8

N. Gale and Z. Stos-Gale: 'The "Fingerprinting" of Metal by Lead Isotopes and Ancient Iron Production at Timna', *Disc. Egyp.*, i (1985), pp. 7–15

L. Garenne-Marot: 'Le Travail du cuivre dans l'Egypte pharaonique d'après les peintures et les bas-reliefs', *Paléorient*, xi/1 (1985), pp. 85–100

B. Scheel: 'Studien zum Metallhandwerk im alten Aegypten, I: Handlungen und Beischriften in den Bildprogrammen des Gräber des alten Reiches', *Stud. Altägyp. Kult.*, xii (1985), pp. 117–77

A. Nibbi: 'Some Middle Kingdom Oxhide-shaped Objects in the Egyptian Iconography and their Name: *nms* and Ashmolean Ingot, 1892–1919', *Disc. Egyp.*, iv (1986), pp. 41–65

B. Scheel: Studien zum Metallhandwerk im alten Aegypten, II: Handlungen und Beischriften in den Bildprogrammen des Gräber des mittleren Reiches', *Stud. Altägyp. Kult.*, xiii (1986), pp. 181–205

——: 'Studien zum Metallhandwerk im alten Aegypten, III: Handlungen und Beischriften in den Bildprogrammen des Gräber des neuen Reiches und der Spätzeit', *Stud. Altägyp. Kult.*, xiv (1987), pp. 247–64

A. Nibbi: *Ancient Egyptian Pot Bellows and the Oxhide Ingot Shape* (Oxford, 1987)

G. Castel and G. Soukiassian: 'Les Mines de galène pharaoniques du Gebel el-Zeit (Egypte)', *Bull. Soc. Fr. Egyp.*, cxii (June 1988)

B. Scheel: 'Anmerkungen zur Kupferverhüttung und Kupferraffination im alten Ägypten', *Disc. Egyp.*, xi (1988), pp. 87–97

G. Castel and G. Soukiassian: *Gebel el-Zeit I: Les mines de galène* (Cairo, 1989)

El-Sayed El-Gayar and M. P. Jones: 'A Possible Source of Copper Ore Fragments Found at the Old Kingdom Town of Buhen', *J. Egyp. Archaeol.*, lxxiv (1989), pp. 31–40

S. Aufrère: *L'univers minéral dans la pensée égyptienne* (Cairo, 1991)

B. G. Davies: 'O. Berlin 11239 and the Coppersmiths at Deir el-Medina', *Götting. Misz.*, cxxxvii (1993), pp. 39-47

A. Nibbi: 'Pot Bellows and Pot Stands', *Disc. Egypt.*, xxvii (1993), pp. 59-81

JEAN-LUC CHAPPAZ

3. WOOD. Since wood is both strong and easily worked, it was widely used in ancient Egypt from the Predynastic period (*c.* 6000–*c.* 2950 BC) onwards for such items as architectural components, domestic utensils, furniture, boats, funerary equipment, tools, weapons and sculpture. The role of wood as a source of fuel—in the form of charcoal—was also important for the working of other materials. The techniques of Egyptian woodworking can be identified through such sources as the wooden artefacts themselves, funerary reliefs and paintings depicting wood-workers, surviving woodworking tools and models of tools and workshops. From the earliest times, because of the shortage of raw materials, the Egyptians developed various 'patchwork' techniques for joining together small pieces of wood and concealing the numerous joints with coatings or inlays.

(i) Types and uses. (ii) Workshop practice. (iii) Tools. (iv) Woodworking techniques. (v) Decoration.

(i) Types and uses. Since there were only a few indigenous species of trees in Egypt that could have provided proper material for builders and craftsmen, a great deal of timber had to be imported (*see* §I, 3 above). The native Egyptian species were acacia (*Acacia nilotica*), tamarisk (*Tamarix nilotica*), date-palm (*Phoenix dactylifera*), dom-palm (*Hyphoene thebaica*), sycamore fig (*Ficus religiosa*), persea (*Mimusops schimperi*) and sidder (*Zizyphus spina Christi*). Egyptian textual sources as early as the 4th Dynasty (*c.* 2575–*c.* 2465 BC) mention the import of timber, mainly from western Asia and the Syrian coast (modern Lebanon). African countries to the south of Egypt supplied various species of decorative wood, used for such purposes as inlay, veneer and marquetry. The imported species included yew (*Taxus baccata*), pine (*Pinus halepensis*), fir (*Abies cilicica*), elm (*Ulmus campestris*), cypress (*Cupressus sempervirens*), cedar (*Cedrus libani*), ebony (African black-wood: *Dalbergia melanoxylon*), juniper (*Juniperus phoenica*), oak (*Quercus cerris*), willow (*Salix safsaf*), *Dalbergia retusa*, zingana (*Microberlinia bisulcata Brazzavillensis*) and African mahogany (*Sapeli-Meliaceae*; *Entandrophragma candollei Harms*).

The Egyptians' imports of wood were mainly in connection with boat- and shipbuilding, which is attested by the scenes in tombs (e.g. the tomb of Ty), the many models of boats and a few extremely important examples of authentic ships (the funerary boats of Cheops and Sesostris III).

Wood was not an important material in the construction of buildings during the Dynastic period, but certain architectural forms made in stone derive from wooden and reed prototypes, as in the enclosure of Djoser's Step Pyramid at Saqqara. Some tombs of the Predynastic and Early Dynastic periods have wooden linings or ceilings made of logs covered either with branches, mats and a layer of earth or with logs of palm trees side by side. Even in buildings of mud-brick and stone there was great need of wood, for the door frames, doors, ceilings, roofs and columns (as represented in the tombs of Ty and Nefer and Kahay at Saqqara).

(ii) Workshop practice. Egyptian temples and palaces employed woodworkers practising related trades in workshops that were probably grouped into larger units. Reliefs and wall paintings, both in the Old Kingdom (e.g. the tombs of Ty, Nefer and Kahay at Saqqara) and the Middle Kingdom, portray carpenters and joiners working alongside boatbuilders and other craftsmen (see fig. 16). In Old Kingdom tombs, scenes of the felling of trees, work in a joiner's yard, a sculptor's workshop and boatbuilding are usually portrayed side by side. In the Middle Kingdom, a scene in Tomb 3 at Beni Hasan depicts the activity of ropemakers, joiners, lumbermen and shipwrights. In Tomb 2 at Beni Hasan joiners and craftsmen producing bows, arrows and wooden vessels are shown working in close proximity.

A wooden model from the 10th Dynasty (*c.* 2100 BC) tomb of Karenen at Saqqara portrays an independent workshop in which three craftsmen, enclosed by three walls, perform different tasks. One is standing, sawing a vertically positioned beam; the second sits on the ground over a bow-drill; and the third sits carving with an adze. A model (Cairo, Egyp. Mus., JE 46722) from the 11th

Dynasty (*c.* 2000 BC) tomb of Meketre at Thebes shows a much larger workshop—a rectangular area partially covered by a roof—including 12 men and a wooden box containing several sets of miniature tools. The men work in groups at several different tasks: sawing a beam, working with adze and chisel, and polishing products with stone rubbers.

Undoubtedly the system of workshops used in the New Kingdom was analogous to that of earlier periods. However, since it was considered desirable for the wall paintings in New Kingdom tombs to include as many scenes of the decoration of funerary products as possible, different craftsmen are often—perhaps misleadingly—shown as if they were working side by side. The tomb of Nebamun and Ipuky (TT 181) at Thebes contains a fragment of decoration in which the upper register depicts craftsmen working exclusively with wood, producing and assembling the decorative elements of a naos. Some representations show that the workshop usually had an adjoining store for raw materials (e.g. beams, boards and wooden sticks) which were being prepared for further treatment and production. There must also have been a separate room for the storage of completed products.

(iii) Tools. The axe (Egyp. *mainbet*) was one of the most important tools for the felling of trees and the initial preparation of the timber. Axes were first made of copper,

16. Carpenters and joiners at work, relief in the tomb of Ty, Saqqara, 5th Dynasty, *c.* 2465–*c.* 2325 BC

then bronze and finally, much later, iron. The blades were comparatively thin; they had no opening parallel to the cutting edge and no integral shaft. They were usually inserted into a parallel cut in the wooden handle and tied firmly with leather thongs or string. The fixing of the blade in place was facilitated by a set of holes near the end, which fitted over protrusions.

The adze (Egyp. *anet*; *newet*), a much more delicate tool than the axe, was useful to the craftsmen—who had no plane—for many finishing-off processes. Like the axe, it consisted of a copper or bronze blade fixed by leather thongs to a wooden handle. The blade was perpendicular to the handle and always widened towards the lower end. The cutting edge, bow-like in outline, was generally sharpened from one side only.

Metal saws (Egyp. *tefa*; *djasw*), which have their prototypes in prehistoric flint tools, were certainly in use in the Early Dynastic period (*c.* 2925–*c.* 2575 BC). The oldest Egyptian metal saws—seven blades of toughened copper, each 250–400 mm long and 9 mm thick—were excavated in 1st Dynasty tombs at Saqqara. These saws had many closely spaced teeth and were rounded and quite broad at the end. To operate his saw the Egyptian craftsman first attached the beam or trunk intended for cutting to a vertical pole; he could then work from a position that enabled him to move the tool with both hands. The action of a vice (Egyp. *djebet*), keeping the timber in place, was achieved by binding it with string, which could be tightened by a lever or tourniquet weighted with a stone.

Because of the widespread use of mortising, dovetailing and other joints requiring many cavities and notches, the chisel (Egyp. *menekh*) was one of the most important tools of the Egyptian woodworkers. Copper and bronze chisels consisted of two basic elements: the metal part, usually broadening at the cutting edge, and the wooden handle. Much heavier chisels without handles were used by stonemasons. The craftsmen worked by striking the top of a chisel with a wooden mallet, but for more delicate, finishing-off operations, lighter chisels, requiring only hand pressure, were used. Long-bladed chisels were used for making deep holes and 'nests' of dovetails.

The 'carpenter's mallet' (Egyp. *kherpw*) was used mainly in conjunction with the chisel by both joiners and sculptors. There were two types: a heavy hammer of hard wood, bulky at one end and with a clearly formed handle (usually showing intensive signs of wear in the centre of the head), and a hammer in the shape of a long baton, round and of approximately the same thickness all along.

The Egyptians also used a variety of gravers (Egyp. *medjat*) and borers for such purposes as tracing, piercing and marking. A set of 32 gravers was found in a 1st Dynasty tomb at Saqqara. One of the most characteristic Egyptian tools is the bow drill (Egyp. *hetit*), which is attested as early as the Old Kingdom and is still used in modern Egypt. This type of drill, known both from ancient representations and surviving examples, consists of a bow and a wooden shaft, with a metal bit at one end and a revolving cap at the other. The rapid passage of the bowstring sets the drill in motion. Despite the fact that the basic principle of the bow drill is similar to that of the lathe, there seem to be no lathe-produced wooden objects even as late as the New Kingdom. Knowledge of the lathe

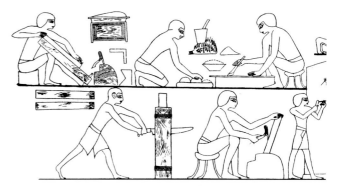

17. Workshop scenes showing carpenters seated on low stumps or stools, line drawing of wall painting in the tomb of Rekhmire (Tomb TT 100), Thebes, 18th Dynasty, *c.* 1450 BC

was probably brought to Egypt by the Greeks, since the earliest lathe-produced objects found in Egypt are associated with a group of 4th-century BC wooden Greek sarcophagi from Abusir. There is a representation of a lathe in the Ptolemaic TOMB OF PETOSIRIS, at Tuna el-Gebel.

Since Egyptian wooden constructions involved many indentations and interlocking parts, they could only have been produced with the use of very precise measuring instruments, such as tri-squares, rules, strings, levels and plumblines, some of which have survived. The smoothing down of finished products was achieved with small stone rubbers, probably of pumice or sandstone, sometimes moistened with olive oil or sprinkled with abrasive material. These rubbers and abrasive materials compensated for the lack of files or planes. There are, however, two 12th Dynasty examples of scrapers or rasps made from shell tied to pieces of reed, as well as one example of a shaping tool consisting of a flat piece of bronze bent in the shape of a cone and pierced with holes, probably originally attached to a handle (London, U. Coll., Petrie Mus.).

Egyptian craftsmen did not work at a bench but sat on the ground. From the New Kingdom onwards they are depicted sitting on low stools or stumps about 300–500 mm above the ground, working on wooden rests at about the same level (see fig. 17). The representations in Theban tombs of the New Kingdom, such as those of Rekhmire (TT 100) and Nebamun and Ipuky (TT 181), suggest that at least four basic types of such rests were used.

(iv) Woodworking techniques.

(a) Preparation. The first stage in the preparation of the wood was the felling of trees. Scenes from tombs of the Old Kingdom (e.g. that of Nefer and Kahay at Saqqara) and the Middle Kingdom (e.g. Tomb 3 at Beni Hasan) show the work of lumbermen alongside other woodworking scenes. By the New Kingdom representations of lumbermen were more sporadic, presumably as a result of deforestation. The growing dependence on imported timber is indicated by the New Kingdom scenes of tree-felling in Punt (at the Deir el-Bahri temple) and Syria–Palestine (at Karnak temple).

The process of preparing the wooden beams—for use as both construction elements and parts of smaller objects—was portrayed with particular care in Old Kingdom representations, such as those in the tombs of Nefer and Kahay, Ibi (at Deir el-Gebrawi) and Shedu (at Dishasha). In a shipyard scene in the tomb of Ty (at Saqqara), three craftsmen are working on a large beam; two are using axes, while the third has an adze. The skill of dividing the beams lengthwise with a saw is attested as early as the Old Kingdom, although at this time timber was also split using wedges, a method that must have preceded the use of the saw. In later periods smaller fragments of wood (suitable for bending and framing without the risk of cracking or distortion) were obtained by splitting beams with wedges. The scenes in the tomb of Shedu include a depiction of a piece of wood, fixed on a low rest, being split by means of a lever inserted into a crack. Above this scene are representations of completed rods produced by this process. A method of bending wood (Egyp. *khened*) is illustrated in Old Kingdom reliefs such as those in the tombs of Ty and Mereruka at Saqqara and the tomb of Serfka at Sheikh Said, as well as a Middle Kingdom relief in a tomb at Beni Hasan.

(b) Types of construction and joints. There were numerous simple methods for connecting the various construction elements, including lashing, pegging and dowelling. Damaged or unsuitable fragments of poorer quality woods were replaced, using lashing and pegging, by specially fitted pieces. Joints were carefully camouflaged by covering marks and cracks with plaster, paint or veneers from woods of higher quality. Wooden elements were connected by tabular joints, to increase length and width, and by angle joints, to obtain corners.

The technique of lashing, using ropes, leather thongs and (rarely) copper bands, was employed from the 1st Dynasty onwards. Original parts preserved from the funerary boat of Cheops (Giza, *in situ*) had a system of grooves and apertures, carved near the edges of boards but not passing all the way through them. These grooves and apertures supported the ropes binding a whole series of overlapping planks. Preserved objects from the Old Kingdom suggest that three basic lashing techniques were used: mortice-lacing, secret mortice-lacing and the holes-and-groove method.

Glue was widely used by Egyptian joiners and carpenters but its application is only definitely attested from the New Kingdom onwards, when such techniques as veneering and marquetry were required in the production of increasingly elaborate furniture. The wall painting in Tomb TT 181 at Thebes includes a scene showing the use of glue to assemble a chapel from wooden openwork sections. Egyptian glues, identified in the analysis of surviving objects, were usually made from animal products, although casein and fish glue were probably also known.

(c) Coopering, wheelwrighting and chariot-making. Coopering is often wrongly considered to be one of the most recently discovered woodworking techniques, first appearing in central Europe and subsequently adopted by the Romans. However, in Egypt there is sparse but unquestionable evidence of coopering as early as the 3rd

millennium BC. Numerous wooden containers were depicted in the 3rd Dynasty TOMB OF HESYRE at Saqqara—the stave technique with which they are constructed is clearly marked, as well as the grain of the wood itself. The staves making up the walls of the vessels are held in place by three hoops of bent wood, which, judging from their colour and grain, are probably ebony. The lower and upper hoops have a rectangular cross-section, while the middle hoop has a semicircular profile. In the 12th Dynasty (c. 1900 BC) Tomb 2 at Beni Hasan, the actual production of wooden containers made of staves is shown, together with work in a joiner's workshop. One of the craftsmen holds in his hand a completed container, which has walls widening towards the top and held in place by two wooden hoops. Three other such containers (without any indication of staves) are shown above the scene, along with a wooden tray made of little planks.

Scenes showing the building of a light two-wheeled chariot (usually consisting of chest, pole, axle and four-spoked wheels) first appear in the New Kingdom, since it was only then that both horse and chariot were introduced into Egypt from the Levant. Chariots were at first imported, but soon afterwards they were being produced by the Egyptians themselves. Many details concerning their production can be reconstructed on the basis of scenes from private Theban tombs (e.g. those of Puyemre and Menkheperreseneb) and surviving chariots, such as those of Tuthmosis IV (Florence, Mus. Archeol.) and Tutankhamun (Cairo, Egyp. Mus.). The wheels consisted of wooden felloes (wheel rims), spokes and a hub. Both hubs and spokes were made of different pieces fitted and glued together; the felloes, linked by mortices and tenons, were usually constructed out of several segments, although there are also a few cases of felloes made from single pieces of bent wood. The felloes were held in place by rawhide tyres that were applied when wet. The tyres contracted as they dried, binding the whole wheel firmly together.

(v) Decoration. Egyptian woodworking also incorporates a range of decorative techniques including carving; application of veneers and inlays; marquetry; lining with semi-precious stones, faience plaques and enamel; and application of metal ferrules. In earlier times inlay was fixed with pegs, but in the New Kingdom the use of glue became more common.

Inlays made from various types of wood and ivory were already in use in the two boxes from the 1st Dynasty tomb of Hemaka at Saqqara (Cairo, Egyp. Mus.). A sedan-chair from the tomb of the 4th Dynasty Queen Hetepheres (Cairo, Egyp. Mus.) is decorated with veneers made from thin ebony strips. A 12th Dynasty set of caskets from el-Lahun (New York, Met.) is decorated with layers of ebony and ivory, and the coffin and canopic box of Senebtisi (also 12th Dynasty) are veneered with thin layers of cedar wood (both Cairo, Egyp. Mus.).

The popularity of inlays and the veneer technique grew during the New Kingdom. A receptacle belonging to Amenophis II (Edinburgh, Royal Mus. Scotland) is decorated with a veneer of thin ebony layers and ornamentation of ivory. The pieces of furniture from the tombs of Yuya and Tuya and of Tutankhamun include veneers and inlays

(Cairo, Egyp. Mus.). A casket from the tomb of Tutankhamun (Cairo, Egyp. Mus.) is decorated with a fine marquetry technique, using thin plates of ebony and ivory to imitate the pattern of woven fabric. The pegs supporting the inlays have heads decorated with gold buttons.

In various periods thin metal plaques of decorative character were occasionally fixed to wooden products. Some of the elements of furniture from the tomb of Hetepheres (Cairo, Egyp. Mus.) were decorated with this technique. The most basic methods of decoration included painting, covering with gesso (see upper register of fig. 17) and gilding. From the tomb of Tutankhamun, some of the chapels and the box bearing battle and hunting scenes are considered among the more perfect examples of these basic techniques.

BIBLIOGRAPHY
LÄ: 'Holz und Holzverarbeitung'
W. M. F. Petrie: *Tools and Weapons* (London, 1917)
A. Lucas: *Ancient Egyptian Materials and Industries* (London, 1926, rev. 4/1962), pp. 429–56
C. Aldred: 'Fine Woodwork', *A History of Technology*, ed. C. Singer, E. J. Holmyard and A. R. Hall, i (Oxford, 1958), pp. 648–703
J. Śliwa: *Studies in Ancient Egyptian Handicraft: Woodworking* (Warsaw, 1975)
R. Drenkhahn: *Die Handwerker und ihre Tätigkeiten im alten Ägypten*, Ägyptologische Abhandlungen, xxxi (Wiesbaden, 1976), pp. 97–132
G. Killen: *Ancient Egyptian Furniture*, i (Warminster, 1980)
D. Grosser, R. Grünewald, B. Kreißl: 'Holz: Ein wichtiger Werkstoff im alten Ägypten', *'Anch' Blumen für das Leben: Pflanzen im alten Ägypten*, ed. S. Schoske, B. Kreißl, R. Germer, Schriften aus der Ägyptischer Sammlung, vi (Munich, 1992), pp. 252–61
G. Killen: *Egyptian Woodworking and Furniture*, Shire Egyptology, xxi (Princes Risborough, 1994)

JOACHIM ŚLIWA

4. CLOTH. The Egyptians, famous for the quality and quantity of their linen cloth, were described by the Roman emperor Caracalla (*reg* AD 198–217) as 'the linen-weavers' (Papyrus Giss, 40). The thousands of textiles that have survived from the pharaonic period can only hint at the importance of cloth as a basic material in Egyptian society (*see* §XVII, 17 below).

(*i*) *Materials.* The earliest known Egyptian cloth, found in the Faiyum region and dating to the Neolithic period (*c.* 6000–*c.* 2925 BC), is a fragment of undyed plain weave (tabby weave) textile (London, U. Coll., Petrie Mus., 2942). It was woven from flax (*Linum usitatissimum*) spun in an anti-clockwise direction (i.e. s-spun). Comparison with later fragments shows that this is the same type of linen cloth as that now regarded as typical of Dynastic Egypt.

Other types of fibre used for cloth during the Dynastic period (such as sheep's wool and goat hair) have been found at Kahun and el-Amarna. The woollen finds discredit a generally held view that the ancient Egyptians refused to use wool. This misconception appears to derive from a statement by Herodotus (*Histories* II.xxxi) that the use of wool was forbidden in temples and for burials. A reference in Papyrus Bologna 1091 (Bologna, Mus. Civ.) has been translated as meaning '50 woollen loincloths'. However, although many flax loincloths have been found in Egypt, no examples in wool appear to have been identified. The earliest cotton in Egypt seems to be that found on a mummy of the 2nd century BC (Philadelphia, PA, U. Mus., PUM II), although there are some doubts about the authenticity of this piece. Cotton was apparently not in widespread use in Egypt until the 1st century AD.

(*ii*) *Manufacture.* The manufacture of linen cloth in Egypt can be reconstructed from a number of tomb paintings and reliefs. The most detailed illustrations are in four tombs of the 11th and 12th dynasties at Beni Hasan (those of Amenemhet, Khnemhotpe, Bakht III and Kheti); the 12th Dynasty tomb of Djehutihotpe at Deir el-Bersha; and four 18th Dynasty tombs at Thebes. Two types of flax were used in Egypt, in the Prehistoric period: *Linum humile*, which has white flowers, and in later periods *Linum usitatissimum*, which has blue flowers. In various depictions of growing flax the plants are probably *Linum usitatissimum*, since they are shown with blue flowers. Once the plants had ripened, the stems were pulled and allowed to dry in the sun. When dry, the seeds were removed by combing the stems on a rippling comb or board (as depicted in the tomb of Pahery, at El Kab). The stems were then submerged in stagnant or gently flowing water and left there for two to three weeks, or until the outer bark of the stems had loosened from the inner part of the plant where the bundles of bast fibres lay. As soon as the bark was loose, the flax stalks were again dried in the sun. They were then ready for the process by which the bark and woody core of the stems were completely removed. The stalks were first broken up into short lengths using a blunt instrument, perhaps a mallet. They were then bent over a narrow object, rolled backwards and forwards by hand and passed through two sticks held in the hand or beaten with a flat wooden blade of some kind. This part

18. Cloth-weavers' workshop, model from the tomb of Meketre at Thebes, painted wood, 430×930 mm, 11th Dynasty, *c.* 2000 BC (Cairo, Egyptian Museum)

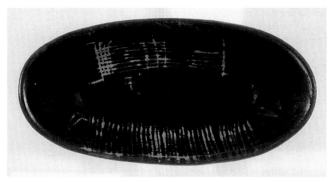

19. Horizontal loom on a painted pottery bowl from Tomb 3802 at el-Badari, h. 57 mm, Predynastic period, c. 4500–c. 4000 BC (London, University of London, University College, Petrie Museum of Egyptian Archaeology)

of the process is shown in the wall paintings of the tomb of Daga, at Thebes, and the tomb of Djehutihotpe, at Deir el-Bersha, as well as in a model from the tomb of Meketre at Thebes (see fig. 18). Subsequently the flax fibres were lightly twisted by hand into long lengths (roves). The fibres were then ready to be spun.

Three basic techniques of spinning are known from Dynastic Egypt. They can be classified according to the different methods of manipulating the spindles: the suspended spindle, whereby the spinner drew thread from a long rove of flax fibres; the supported spindle, whereby the spinner drew the thread from a bowl standing before him and rolled the spindle on his thigh; the grasped spindle, whereby the spinner drew the thread from a bowl, through a forked stick, and then revolved the spindle with both hands. All of these techniques are shown in a wall painting in the tomb of Khety at Beni Hasan. Once the fibres had been spun they were given to the weavers in order to be woven into cloth.

The earliest representation of a loom is on a Predynastic pottery bowl from Tomb 3802 at el-Badari (see fig. 19). It shows a simple horizontal or ground loom, of a type that can also be seen in the Beni Hasan tombs (c. 1900 BC). The vertical loom, a later type, perhaps introduced into Egypt during the Hyksos period (c. 1630–c. 1532 BC), is illustrated in tombs at Thebes. This type of loom was described by Herodotus (Histories II.35): 'Among them [the Egyptians], the women buy and sell, the men abide at home and weave; and whereas in weaving all others push on the woof upwards [on a warp-weighted loom], the Egyptians push it downwards.'

Most Egyptian linen cloth was bleached white in the sun. For a discussion of the few known examples of decorated textiles see §XVII, 17 below.

BIBLIOGRAPHY
H. Ling Roth: Ancient Egyptian and Greek Looms (Halifax, 1913)
G. M. Crowfoot and H. Ling Roth: 'Were the Ancient Egyptians Conversant with Tablet-weaving?', An. Archaeol. & Anthropol., x (1917), pp. 7–20
E. Schiaparelli: La tomba intatta dell'architetto Cha (Turin, 1927)
S. W. Stevenson: 'The Old Kingdom Linen Lists', Z. Ägyp. Spr. & Altertknd., lxxi (1935), pp. 134–49
H. E. Winlock: Models of Daily Life in Ancient Egypt (Cambridge, MA, 1955)
T. Dothan: 'Spinning Bowls', Israel Explor. J., xiii (1963), pp. 97–112
P. Collingwood: The Techniques of Sprang: Plaiting on Stretched Threads (London, 1974)

GILLIAN VOGELSANG-EASTWOOD

VIII. Architecture.

The essential feature of all Egyptian architecture was its blend of functionalism, symbolism and traditionalism, with the result that any building could work on two planes. The primary religious building type, the temple, was practically speaking a home for the god's cult image and a suitable place to carry out daily ritual, but it also functioned symbolically as a microcosm of the universe (see §2(i) below and TEMPLE, §I, 2). Such utilitarian structures as military fortifications (see §3 below) could take on a transcendental meaning by being consecrated to a divinity: Queen Hatshepsut (reg c. 1479–c. 1458 BC) dedicated a fortress at Thebes to the god Amun, 'building it anew as a work for eternity, according to the ancient plan'. Even domestic buildings (see §4 below), such as the humble houses of the Deir el-Medina building workers (see THEBES (i), §XI), could be transformed into temples to the family cult by the addition of a shrine niche.

The largeness of scale and monumentality so characteristic of Egyptian buildings is partly a result of the availability of building stone (see §1(i) below), which led to a preference for cubic forms. However, this monolithic quality has its own symbolism. Egyptian concepts of architecture were inextricably bound up with theories of kingship and the maintenance of cosmic order and the status quo. The king via the gods was seen as the source of architectural inspiration: he is frequently shown preparing the foundations of monumental buildings, and in inscriptions kings are referred to as 'the only one in the possession of [the gods'] architectural designs' and 'the giver of regulations and leader of works on his monuments'.

1. Introduction. 2. Religious. 3. Military. 4. Domestic.

1. INTRODUCTION.

(i) Materials and techniques. (ii) Design. (iii) Architects and builders. (iv) Construction methods.

(i) Materials and techniques. The development of Egyptian architecture was governed by the environment and the availability of basic building material: mud, stone and, to a lesser extent, wood. The first materials were flexible plants such as reeds, rushes, palm fronds and papyrus stalks, which could be woven together easily to form shelters. Later, these were daubed with mud plaster to build more permanent shelters. Wood was always scarce in the Nile Valley, and the types of trees available did not provide the long, straight planks needed for large wooden structures. The rather knotty, small timbers of palm, sycamore and acacia were used mainly for roof beams and doorposts in houses. Wooden architectural components were usually salvaged when houses were abandoned, demonstrating their scarcity and value. Imported woods, such as cedar and fir, were used decoratively, for temple doors and the like.

Sun-dried mud-brick was a natural development from mud plaster, and it is still the most important building material in rural Egypt. Kiln-baked brick was rarely employed, although Egyptian craftsmen certainly had the technology to produce it. Mud-brick was the medium par *excellence* of domestic architecture. However, few mud-brick buildings have survived from town sites, not because of the impermanence of the material but because the same sites have tended to remain settled. The best preserved mud-brick houses in Egypt come from the Roman towns in the Faiyum, and show a strong adherence to what we know of Dynastic house building styles. No tradition developed of using brick for monumental buildings, an exception being the 1st Dynasty funerary complexes (*c.* 2900 BC) such as the Shunet el-Zebib at ABYDOS. Large buildings were sometimes constructed in mud-brick and cased with stone for reasons of economy. Although the Egyptians regarded it as a utilitarian material, this did not prevent them from constructing some pleasing mud-brick buildings, such as the elegantly barrel-vaulted store-rooms of the Ramesseum (*see* THEBES (i), §VI). Modern views of the aesthetic qualities of Egyptian brick architecture would doubtless be different if major mud-brick structures, such as the palaces at Malqata and el-Amarna, had survived in better condition (*see* PALACE, §I, 2).

Buildings that were expected to last, particularly temples and tombs, were built of stone, either rock-cut or constructed from quarried stone blocks. The durability of stone has led to the predominance of sacred buildings among surviving Egyptian architecture. The types of stone used varied according to fashion and political change, but the basic quartet consisted of limestone, sandstone, quartzite and granite (*see* §VII, 1 above). These stones were prized as much for their symbolic associations as for their aesthetic qualities. Certain stones had specific architectural uses; obelisks, for instance, were almost invariably made from pink Aswan granite. Mud-brick buildings also had some stone components, particularly thresholds, window grilles and niches.

Even when comparatively well-preserved, Egyptian buildings convey little of their original appearance because their external decorations have now vanished. The reliefs that adorned the pylons and outside walls of the great temples were covered in polychromy and gilded in parts. Sometimes other decorative elements were used: the south-west wall of the Temple of Hathor at DENDARA was once adorned with a colossal gilded sistrum under a painted wooden canopy. Even the limestone casing of the pyramids at Giza (*see* GIZA, §1) was probably painted in three colours. The portals of royal tombs in the Valley of the Kings were elaborately decorated and had metal-sheathed wooden doors. Private houses were also embellished: the model of Meketre's house (see fig. 38 below) has papyriform columns with painted decoration on the capitals and bases and a painted dado around the courtyard. The outside walls of houses may have had painted decoration, though evidence is sparse. Contemporary representations show houses simply whitewashed, as in the tomb paintings of Mose (TT 254) and Nebamun (TT 90) at Thebes, though both of these have painted window grilles of pierced stone. Other buildings relied for decorative impact on contrasts between the natural colours of the stones, such as the pink granite walls and white calcite floor in the valley temple of Chephren at Giza.

(ii) Design. The theory of the harmonic building in Egyptian architecture—in which the outline of the building was governed by a triangle of geometric definitions (such as a 3:4:5 triangle) and in which rules governed the relationship of the parts to the whole—was first applied in 1904 by Auguste Choisy. In 1965 this theory was elaborated by Alexander Badawy, who observed that even buildings that had apparently grown up by accretion still demonstrated the elements of harmonic design. The Temple of Amun at Karnak (*see* THEBES (i), §II, 1), for instance, had had various structures added to it over several centuries, but still preserved a harmonious plan. This may have been achieved by following detailed plans lodged in the temple archives. The extent to which the Egyptians used detailed plans for constructing buildings is debatable (*see* §XVII, 11 below): no actual plan for a major building is extant, and those sketches that have survived all seem to be ad hoc working drawings used on site. However, dedicatory inscriptions often mention buildings being designed 'according to the ancient plan' or 'according to the accustomed stipulations', implying the existence of standardized plans to be used when designing a new building.

Although there was no concept of architectural orders, the basic elements of Egyptian architectural design are evident from the earliest surviving structures, dating to the late Predynastic period (*c.* 3100 BC). The prototypes of these design motifs were ephemeral building materials—bundles of plant stems for columns, reed mats on wooden supports for walls—which became increasingly stylized as they were transferred to mud-brick and stone. These elements persisted throughout Egyptian building history: the simple papyriform columns of Djoser's *heb sed* court at Saqqara (*see* SAQQARA, §1) are the antecedents of the pillars of the Roman temple at PHILAE with their elaborate plant capitals. Two uniquely Egyptian architectural motifs derived from natural prototypes are the *khekher* frieze and the *serekh* façade. The *khekher* frieze is a stylized plant design, originating in walls constructed from papyrus stalks bundled together with the floral parts at the top forming a natural decorative cornice. A development of this is the leaved cavetto cornice or 'Egyptian gouge', a concave moulding, semicircular in section and carved with vertical leaf-shapes; surmounting a torus moulding, it was generally used as the crowning element of walls, pylons and lintels. The *serekh* or palace façade design, which imitates a wall made of mats lashed to wooden uprights, first appeared transmuted into mud-brick in the Shunet el-Zebib near Abydos and later developed as the stone false door (*see* STELE, §2). Derivatives of the *serekh* façade were used in a wide range of buildings, from the fortifications at Buhen in Nubia (*see* §3 below) to the dais of Ramesses III's throne-room at Medinet Habu (*see* THEBES (i), §VII), where it formed a notional link between the royal apartments and the audience chamber.

This strong continuum in the use of basic architectural elements does not mean that Egyptian architecture became stereotyped early or was unreceptive to external influence. Architectural styles and motifs such as the *serekh* façade could be adapted for all kinds of functional, decorative and symbolic uses. Royal patrons showed their appreciation of earlier buildings by commissioning adaptations of them. The most notable example is the terraced mortuary temple of Hatshepsut at Deir el-Bahri (*see* THEBES (i),

§IV), which is closely modelled on the funerary complex constructed for Nebhepetre Mentuhotpe II over six centuries earlier. The architects of Hatshepsut's building introduced a number of typical 18th Dynasty features, including a decorated colonnade with tapering polygonal or 'proto-Doric' columns. Responsiveness to foreign influence is best exemplified by the eastern gate at Medinet Habu, built in imitation of a Syrian fortified tower or *migdol*, though it does not seem to have had any military purpose. Structures dating to the Second Intermediate Period (*c.* 1630–*c.* 1540 BC) at sites such as AVARIS in the Nile Delta, where there was more contact with foreign cultures, show the influence of Canaanite building styles on secular architecture. In the 26th Dynasty (664–525 BC), a time when Egypt was curious about its past, another form of architectural traditionalism manifested itself as conscious archaization, with Old Kingdom buildings and decorative forms being revived.

(iii) Architects and builders. As with other ancient Egyptian craftsmen, architects seem to have been under the protection of the god Ptah, who is sometimes referred to as 'furnishing the plan for the work of eternity'. Although architects are generally anonymous, the names of some are known, such as AMENHOTPE SON OF HAPU, SENENMUT and Hapuseneb, who was 'appointed to conduct the work on [Queen Hatshepsut's] cliff tomb because of the great excellence of [his] plans'. Little is known about the training of architects and builders, though it was probably based on an apprenticeship in a workshop like that of other craftsmen (*see* §II above). Also like other Egyptian skills and crafts, the architectural profession may have been hereditary. Some architects, for instance Amenhotpe, son of Hapu, seem to have started off by training as scribes. Because of the connection of monumental buildings with religious belief and state ideology, architects may have had a higher status than painters and sculptors, who seem to have been regarded as useful servants.

Even less is known about building workers, who did not apparently form a distinct professional group in ancient Egypt. Labouring on large monuments may have been done by agricultural workers unable to farm during the months of the inundation. On the humblest level, village houses were probably built by their owners, often on top of earlier houses. This system is still in use, a practice that gives many Egyptian villages their characteristic *tell* or mound shape.

(iv) Construction methods. Building sites were chosen by several methods, including oracular consultation, tradition, the local environment and the preference of the individual patron. Queen Hatshepsut, for example, chose a spectacular natural location for her temple at Deir el-Bahri (*see* THEBES (i), §IV). Before building began, the site was levelled and the plan drawn out in the field using a knotted cord, like the one held by SENENMUT in his statue (Paris, Louvre, E 11057). The foundation process was accompanied by elaborate dedicatory ceremonies, in which the king stretched the foundation cord, nominally at least. Some information on the surveying tools used is provided by the 'foundation deposits' (caches of small symbolic items inscribed with royal or divine names and ritually buried during the foundation ceremonies). These include miniature architectural instruments, such as levels, set-squares and plumb-bobs (e.g. Cairo, Egyp. Mus., JE 5640–44). Major Egyptian buildings often have surprisingly insubstantial foundations, consisting of a shallow sand-filled trench covered with a few courses of rough masonry.

The effect of Greek building techniques on Egyptian architecture is evident from the foundations of Greco-Roman period temples, which have extremely solid stone-work foundations, sometimes constructed by recycling material taken from earlier buildings. In spite of their builders' often-expressed desire for permanency, many Egyptian buildings were not well constructed, particularly if there was pressure to complete a funerary complex quickly because of the death of the ruler. The valley temple of Mycerinus at Giza (*see* GIZA, §1) shows signs of being finished off hurriedly using mud-brick instead of stone. Some years later parts of the colonnade collapsed and were repaired rather haphazardly. Even important buildings were sometimes very shoddily constructed: the Hypostyle Hall at Karnak (*see* THEBES (i), §II, 1), one of the glories of Egyptian architecture, had very shallow foundations that were subsequently badly weakened by floodwater, so that the walls began to subside and collapse in the 21st Dynasty. Some restorations were made at that time, but they could not compensate for the poor foundations, and the whole hall remained standing only because it was held together by the roof.

Mortar was rarely employed to join masonry blocks, and its main use was as a lubricant, so that the next course of blocks would slide easily on top of the first. Each block of stone was fitted individually to its neighbour because blocks were rarely perfectly symmetrical. This complex joining technique meant that the largest possible stone blocks could be used.

The Egyptians had little in the way of complex building machinery. Lifting devices seem to have been introduced in the Roman period. The most usual method of moving heavy stone blocks and architectural components was to construct a ramp of rubble or mud-brick behind the wall that was being raised. The ramp was increased as required, and it was normally demolished when the wall had reached its full height: nevertheless, a few ramps can still be seen *in situ*, for example in the first court of the Temple of Amun at Karnak (*see* THEBES (i), §II, 1). Wooden scaffolds were used for completing the stone dressing and for carving and painting the external reliefs. Often, the various stages of work on a building went on simultaneously, so that relief-carvers and painters would be at work on the completed parts of a building before the rest was finished. This is exemplified by the tombs of Meryre' and of 'Ay at el-Amarna (see fig. 29 below), where the walls and columns had been decorated before the transverse hall had even been quarried out of the rock.

For further discussion of quarrying and construction methods, *see* §VII, 1 above and §2(ii) below.

BIBLIOGRAPHY
LÄ : 'Architektur', 'Baumaterial', 'Bauschmuck', 'Holzbauweise', 'Mattenbauweise', 'Musterbücher', 'Steinarchitektur', 'Ziegelbauweise'
A. Choisy: *L'Art de bâtir chez les Egyptiens* (Paris, 1904)
J. H. Breasted: *Ancient Records of Egypt*, 5 vols (Chicago, 1906–7) [useful collection of dedicatory building inscriptions]

E. Baldwin Smith: *Egyptian Architecture as Cultural Expression* (New York, 1938)

J. Capart: 'Sur les cahiers de modèle en usage sous l'ancien Empire', *Chron. Égypte*, xvi (1941), pp. 95–114

A. Badawy: *A History of Egyptian Architecture*, 3 vols (Cairo, 1954; Berkeley and Los Angeles, 1966 and 1968)

W. S. Smith: *The Art and Architecture of Ancient Egypt* (Baltimore, 1958)

A. Badawy: *Ancient Egyptian Architectural Design: A Study of the Harmonic System* (Berkeley, CA, 1965)

——: *Architecture in Ancient Egypt and the Near East* (London, 1966)

S. Lloyd and H. W. Müller: *Ancient Architecture*, History of World Architecture (London, 1980)

D. Arnold: *Building in Egypt: Pharonic Stone Masonry* (Oxford, 1991)

D. Pemberton: *Ancient Egypt*, Travellers' Architectural Guides (London, 1992)

2. RELIGIOUS. The prominence of religion in ancient Egyptian society (*see* §III above) naturally meant that religious concepts heavily influenced much of the architecture. Religious architecture had several manifestations, which can be conveniently classified as temple and funerary. Inevitably, such classifications are not discrete; for example, mortuary temples obviously had close funerary connections, being derived from offering chapels of royal mastabas and pyramids. In as much as they were for ministrations to deified pharaohs, however, they are most suitably dealt with under temples.

(i) Temples. (ii) Tombs. (iii) Sacred animal necropoleis.

(i) Temples. The temple, known as the 'mansion of the god' (*hwt netjer*), and reflecting the Egyptian concepts of the universe and deity, derived its form from the myth of the 'Primeval Mound', symbolized by the sanctuary, in which the essence of the deity inhabited the cult statue. The temple provided the link between the cosmos, or 'Ancestor Gods', and the land of Egypt, the monarch acting as mediator between these two realms (*see* §III, 1 above). Through the king the beneficence of the god could be channelled so as to ensure harmony according to the laws of Maat (divine order and justice), thus guaranteeing the stability and welfare of Egypt and its people. Temple architecture was enhanced by reliefs, paintings, statuary and ritual, all essential to the temple's role in the performance of the cult.

The two main categories of temple were the cult temple, devoted to a deity, and the mortuary temple, which was concerned with the cult of a deceased ruler. During the Old and Middle Kingdoms the sole function of the mortuary temple was to serve the royal mortuary cult but by the New Kingdom it also functioned as a cult temple dedicated to the state god, Amun.

(a) Cult temples. (b) Mortuary temples.

(a) Cult temples. The myth of the Primeval Mound, for example as inscribed on the walls of the Temple of Horus at Edfu, was based on early creation myth traditions. It describes the emergence of a primordial island from the 'waters of chaos' (Nun). In the centre of the island appeared a perch on which a bird—a falcon or heron— alighted, representing the soul of the god. The appearance of the island and the perching bird became known as the 'First Occasion', the time when religion, kingship and an ethical code were first established. The island was the homeland of the 'Ancestors' (or 'Primeval Ones'), and in order to preserve and protect the god and all that he

represented, a rough reed structure was erected around him; from this structure evolved the cult temple.

Predynastic (c. 6000–c. 2925 BC). Predynastic shrines were derived from a domestic context, the dwelling of the tribal chieftain, who acted as priest, assuming the powers of the tribe's totem. The primitive shrines probably emerged as distinct religious features by the Naqada II phase (*c.* 3500–*c.* 2925 BC), but little evidence survives except at HIERAKONPOLIS, where a quadrangular platform with rounded corners and a stepped retaining wall of sandstone blocks, predating the Early Dynastic temple, probably supported an earlier sanctuary; a similar structure, dating to the same period, was discovered at Heliopolis (*see* HELIOPOLIS (i)). Other evidence for this period comes from representations on slate palettes, such as the 'Hunting Palette' (London, BM and Paris, Louvre), Naqada II pottery (*see* §XIII, 4 below), the GEBEL EL-ARAK knife (Paris, Louvre) and the paintings in Tomb 100 at Hierakonpolis. Early shrines took all the forms of the Predynastic private house: first an open shelter, then a circular plan, then oval and finally rectangular. The buildings were lightly framed structures, variously made of reeds, wattle (sometimes with an application of daub), wooden poles, matting, skins or patterned fabrics, all of which continued to be used in the sanctuaries. Papyrus, lotus and palm, all later represented in the stone columns and capitals of religious and funerary structures, were already in use in their original form as posts and wooden columns. Other Predynastic architectural elements that persisted in religious architecture throughout the historic period were the enclosed forecourt, the columnar portico—which may originally have been an addition to the house or part of the tent—and the *kheker* ornament, which was retained in later temples as a frieze.

Some of the representations of boats with cabins found mainly on Naqada II pottery (see fig. 20) may show the transportation of the god and his shrine from one sanctuary to another during special festivals, and it is probably for this reason that the cabin form was adopted as a type of shrine. Two cabins, made of papyrus stalks and matting, stood in the centre of the boat, connected by a shed with a lower roof. These cabins, which later merged into a single structure, were usually square, with corner posts,

20. Design of a prehistoric ship, showing ensign, branch on prow and figures of a woman and a man (probably deities) under a baldachin; from a Naqada II vase, *c.* 3500 BC

the roofs being flat, barrel-vaulted, sloping or a bisected cupola. Flat roofs were enclosed by a projecting wall of reeds, the tops of which were gathered into the *kheker* ornament or were looped, a style that also persisted into Dynastic times. A standard with two streamers bearing an ensign abutted the cabin that served as the shrine.

Early Dynastic (c. 2925–c. 2575 BC). During the Early Dynastic period the primitive Predynastic shrine forms crystallized into various national types that were retained as architectural elements throughout Dynastic Egypt. They are represented on huts, primitive houses or kiosks derived from tents, and on tablets, jar sealings and slate palettes, as hieroglyphs, and in reliefs and paintings.

The Predynastic shrine of Lower Egypt, the *per nu* (Egyp.: 'house of water'; also known as *per neser*, 'house of flame'), represented the royal palace of northern Egypt and the funerary chapel of the kings of Buto. It was a round hut of wattle, often with daub applied, with four posts, set in a square, rising above the roof level. The roof was either vaulted, using concentric circles of reeds, or barrel-vaulted, using reeds as a bed for daub. Next to the shrine was the emblem identifying the deity worshipped. In its rudimentary form, the *per nu* could also appear as a complex comprising a shrine situated at one end of an enclosure. Before the entrance to the enclosure stood two standards surmounted by fans or pennons, a prototype of the flagpoles set before the pylons of later temples; such standards are believed to be an early form of the hieroglyph *netjer* ('god'). Another standard supporting the emblem of the god usually stood within the court in front of the sanctuary; and an aegicranes bucranium or other emblem often surmounted the roof of the shrine, as, for example, at the sanctuaries of the gods Khnum or Herishef. Variations of this occurred, however: the sanctuary of the heron of Buto, in which the deity is shown residing on the roof of his shrine, without a standard in the court; the sanctuary of Neith of Sais, in which only the standard of the goddess with her shield and crossed arrows stood in the court (see fig. 21); or the sanctuary of Sobek, in which the enclosure is divided by parallel walls, one section of which may be a lake, with a skull on the roof of the shrine and a standard supporting an image of the crocodile god set within the enclosure.

The Predynastic national shrine of Upper Egypt at Hierakonpolis, the *per wer* (Egyp.: 'Great House'), was once the royal palace of the south. Some scholars also identify the *per wer* as the shrine of Seth, while others claim that the shrine served the deities of Upper Egypt, especially Hathor, in archaic times. This shrine evolved

out of a tented form, reflecting a more nomadic way of life, and was a less substantial structure than the *per nu*. Its framework, which sometimes appears to be placed on a socle or sledge, consisted of crossed wooden beams forming a rectangular lattice below and a lozenge-shaped vault above. Mats were stretched over the framework. The entrance was at one end of the building and comprised an arched door set between two corner posts rising above the roof-line. Up to four horns, possibly rhinoceros, projected above the door. Another door was set at the end of one side of the shrine. In outline the building resembled the back of an animal, an effect accentuated by the horns above the arched door and by the addition of a tail at the rear.

The shrine of Min, the deity of Akhmim and Coptos, developed from the circular hut. Sometimes placed on a platform, and often set within an enclosure, it rose into a tall conical shape made of reeds and branches, or pisé, and was painted in coloured bands. Surmounting the roof was a long conical projection, probably connected with phallic symbolism, a major attribute of Min, a fertility god. The entrance was crowned with a cavetto cornice. A standard supporting a pair of horns, one tied with a rope, was attached to the shrine; sometimes they were set on top of the entrance cornice. The horns may have been an abbreviated form of the aegicranes bucranium seen in other sanctuaries, perhaps representing part of a sacrifice to the god.

The rare *nesh* shrine, belonging to Seshat, goddess of writing and 'lady of builders', is depicted in the Old Kingdom sun temple of Neuserre at Abu Ghurab (see below): the rectangular and apparently roofless shrine is set upon a sledge and preceded by the ensign of the goddess.

The temple as an architectural form became further defined as the requirements of the cults expanded, and subsidiary chambers were built around the shrines, extending further into the enclosed spaces. Such temples may have first evolved in the north, but the plan appears to have been adopted for various cult places throughout the country. The paradigm for many of the earliest temples is the sanctuary of the goddess Neith, which shows the shrine abutting one of the short ends of the rectangular enclosure. The plan of an early sanctuary at Heliopolis illustrated on a tablet in Turin (Mus. Egizio, 2682) suggests a more developed sanctuary and is similar to one described in the Edfu texts. It comprises a hall or court, around three sides of which were cult chambers.

Monumental forms of temple, built in brick, first appeared in the 1st Dynasty (*c.* 2925–*c.* 2775 BC), although it is possible that there were Predynastic brick temples, since the painted brick tomb at Hierakonpolis appeared at that time. At Elephantine the foundations of the Early Dynastic temple dedicated to the goddess Satis include a sanctuary consisting of a natural formation of huge granite rocks, with an antechamber formed by projecting brick walls enclosing an area of *c.* 1.6×2.2 m. The 1st Dynasty temple at Abydos, dedicated to Khentimentiu ('Foremost of the Westerners'), comprises a more substantial and clearer plan: a large sacrificial court abutted part of one side of the temple, while a forecourt led to an outer hall

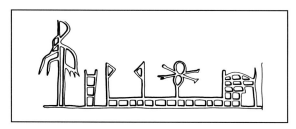

21. Sanctuary of Neith; from an ebony tablet of King Aha, from Abydos, 1st Dynasty, *c.* 2925 BC

giving on to an antechamber leading to a tripartite sanctuary; a narrow side chamber spanned the left side of the outer hall and antechamber.

Old Kingdom (c. 2575–c. 2150 BC). Most surviving Old Kingdom temples are the mortuary and valley temples belonging to the pyramid complexes (*see* PYRAMID, §1). Almost every town or city would have possessed a cult temple to its particular god, the Old Kingdom building replacing a Predynastic or Early Dynastic sanctuary; but many of them were levelled as succeeding buildings were erected, or were quarried for their stone.

The plans of Old Kingdom cult temples indicate that they were not constructed on a standardized plan, but varied according to the dictates of the cult concerned. Surviving funerary architecture suggests that cult temples were either of mud-brick faced with stone or were stone built throughout. The practice of cutting the stone into blocks of unequal height and with oblique faces continued with little modification until the latest times, when true rectangular blocks were introduced. The square pier was the main means of support, but there were also various types of column, including cylindrical forms with panels of text, bundle columns imitating papyrus and lotus plants, and palm columns, reproducing the effect of palm logs decorated with fringes of palm fronds. Monolithic, massive buildings were pre-eminent during the 4th Dynasty, but in the 5th Dynasty vegetal columns introduced a lighter feeling, which was probably employed in smaller religious buildings.

The late Old Kingdom temple of Madamud may have been dedicated to the worship of Osiris or perhaps to the more ancient cult of the *senwt* ('Brothers'), represented by two stelae, each inscribed with a serpent, erected in front of some sanctuaries. Within an irregular whitewashed brick enclosure were two artificial mounds of sand, probably raised within a sacred forest. A court, entered by a pylon gate, lay before two sinuous, vaulted corridors—possibly symbolizing the serpents—leading to sanctuaries within the mounds.

The foundations of a small cult temple called a *hwt ka* ('House of the *ka*' [spirit double]), belonging to Pepy I (*reg c.* 2289–*c.* 2256 BC), survive at Bubastis. This type appears to have served the cult of the royal *ka*, which despite funerary connotations could apparently also be celebrated while the king was still living. The building consisted of a rectangular mud-brick enclosure wall with a gateway leading to the small temple within. Limestone blocks from the roof of the gateway show Pepy with divinities. The entrance to the sanctuary was built of mud-brick with limestone jambs and lay to the right of the enclosure gate. Eight stone piers were set in two rows upon stone foundation blocks and several compartments were set contiguously along the rear wall of the sanctuary.

By the late Old Kingdom the Temple of Satis at Elephantine had developed into a substantial brick structure measuring *c.* 7 m×9 m. The Early Dynastic rock-cut sanctuary was enclosed by a larger outer court, in which a brick altar had been established by the 4th Dynasty. An oven and a fireplace were built along the east wall during the 6th Dynasty. A broad brick bench (*c.* 1 m×3 m), set before the altar against the western wall, may have been used as a depository for cult objects. To the left of the bench, a narrow passage led to the sanctuary (*see* ASWAN).

During the Old Kingdom the Temple of Khentimentiu at Abydos retained its Early Dynastic plan, but additions were built around it: houses in the court of sacrifices, an enclosure to the west of the temple and houses or magazines, separated from the temple by a narrow passage, to the south. Between two 6th Dynasty stone gates were bases of columns arranged in two rows of three. This arrangement may have originally formed a colonnade to serve as a processional entrance to the temple, and it composed part of the thick enclosure wall. Near the north

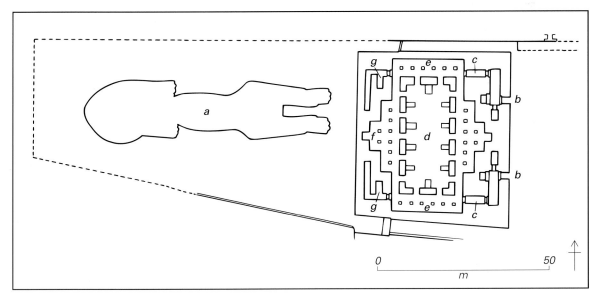

22. Giza, plan of the Temple of the Sphinx, 4th Dynasty: (a) Great Sphinx; (b) entrances to temple; (c) L-shaped passageways leading to court; (d) hypaethral court; (e) colonnade; (f) compound niches; (g) alcoves

gate was a stone with holes for flagpoles, suggesting that the latter were incorporated into pylons well before the Middle Kingdom. Pepy I added, or reconstructed, a reposoir on the rising gradient that led to the temple court's entrance.

The sun cult, with its centre at Heliopolis, had become the Egyptian state religion by the 5th Dynasty. An early form of sun temple may be the Temple of the Sphinx at Giza (see fig. 22), on a lower terrace east of the figure and probably contemporary with it, as it is built of limestone blocks quarried from the same area. Many of the blocks are larger than those used in the Great Pyramid, exceeding 30 tons in weight. Lined with granite, the Sphinx temple is contiguous with and aligned to the valley temple of Chephren: it was built on a symmetrical plan, with two doorways open to the north and south of the eastern face, forming L-shaped passageways leading to an open court. The court is aligned east–west, suggesting a solar connection, and is surrounded by a colonnade of 24 piers, which perhaps represent the 24 hours of day and night. Off the court, two deep compound niches set into the faces of the east and west interior walls were probably used for rites to the rising and setting sun. Before each niche are two pillars believed to symbolize the arms and legs of the sky goddess Nut. L-shaped chambers are set on either side of the western niche.

Of six 5th Dynasty sun temples mentioned in inscriptions, two have been discovered, those of Userkaf (*reg c.* 2465–*c.* 2458 BC) and Neuserre (*reg c.* 2416–*c.* 2392 BC) at ABU GHURAB, north of Abusir. The plan of the temple of Neuserre is in some ways similar to a pyramid complex, with landing stage, valley temple and covered causeway, but there is a sacrificial altar instead of a mortuary temple and a massive coursed masonry obelisk in place of a pyramid. That of the Userkaf temple may be a later addition.

First Intermediate Period, Middle Kingdom and Second Intermediate Period (c. 2150–c. 1540 BC). With the decline of the Old Kingdom, major building ceased until Egypt was reunified under Mentuhotpe II (*reg c.* 2008–*c.* 1957 BC) of the Theban 11th Dynasty. Although the state sun religion lapsed during the First Intermediate Period, local cult sanctuaries undoubtedly still flourished. It was during the Middle Kingdom that the Theban deity Amun began his transformation into a major state god. Other gods, such as Montu, Sobek and Thoth, also became prominent.

Few cult temples survive from these periods, although fragments of Middle Kingdom buildings have been discovered at such Delta sites as Khatana, Bubastis, Leontopolis (now Tell el-Yahudiya) and at numerous sites in the Faiyum, Upper Egypt and Nubia. Many were replaced by a succeeding temple or quarried for later buildings, as was the kiosk (see below) of Sesostris I (*reg c.* 1918–*c.* 1875 BC), which was used as filling for the Pylon III, built by Amenophis III (*reg c.* 1390–*c.* 1353 BC), at Karnak.

The main building materials were limestone, red and black granite and sandstone. Columns were of stone or wood, surmounted by abaci. A common form was the octagonal or 16-sided polygonal column called 'proto-Doric' by the scholar Jean-François Champollion. Created by cutting the angles of a square pillar, their facets were sometimes fluted, or inscribed with panels of text. The monolithic palmiform column was employed in temples, but the lotiform was replaced by the monolithic papyriform column with closed bud capital. An early form of the Hathor capital from Bubastis shows the head of the goddess on opposite sides of the capital with the symbolic plants of Upper and Lower Egypt, the lotus and papyrus, on the remaining faces. The introduction of Osiride figures abutting pillars occurred during this period, at Madamud. A further innovation was the wall, a type of retaining wall between one-half and one brick thick, and set in undulating courses that may symbolize the serpent, but probably also better withstood the pressures of flood water. For the first time the outside corners of the walls were supported by stone pillars, and the internal faces were buttressed.

New forms of cult temple included the kiosk and the rock-cut temple, and in the Second Intermediate Period foreign elements were introduced to temple architecture. In general, forms were now lighter and both the columned portico and the pylon appeared in developed form. The cult temple of simple plan had a portico set before a transverse hall leading to the sanctuary with its shrines set against the rear wall. This layout essentially continued the prehistoric and archaic plan types. Examples include the temples of Medinet Madi and QASR EL-SAGHA in the Faiyum and a building of Ammenemes I (*reg c.* 1938–*c.* 1908 BC) at Ezbet Rushdi in the Delta.

The temple at Medinet Madi built by Ammenemes III (*reg c.* 1818–*c.* 1770 BC) and Ammenemes IV (*reg c.* 1770–*c.* 1760 BC) was dedicated to themselves in company with the deities Renenutet and Sobek. It was partly restored in the 19th Dynasty, with further additions in the Ptolemaic period. The rectangular plan had a portico (possibly an unfinished hypostyle hall) containing two papyrus-bundle columns. The transverse hall, roofed with three monolithic blocks, led to three shrines set on a projecting step, framed with a torus surmounted by a cavetto cornice. The central shrine is the widest and held a statue group of Renenutet between two standing royal figures. The floor before the central shrine was pierced with a square hole for an offering table.

The limestone temple at Qasr el-Sagha, probably unfinished, had a rectangular enclosure, and what may have been a pillared portico preceding a sanctuary of seven shrines abutting the rear wall.

The complex type of cult temple was peripteral and derived from domestic architecture. The layout was rectangular and symmetrical. Beyond a broad pillared hall or portico extending the width of the building lay a deep hall in which stood a shrine surrounded on three sides by small contiguous chambers. The type is exemplified by the temple of Montu at Tod, where Sesostris I renewed an earlier building. A hall with a single row of four pillars preceded the sanctuary, which contained a central shrine open at both ends to accommodate the portable bark on which the divine image was carried in procession. An ambulatory on three sides of the shrine gave access to three chambers on each side of the wall.

Work on the more elaborate temple at Madamud, also dedicated to Montu, was begun by Sesostris III (*reg c.* 1837–*c.* 1818 BC). It had a double enclosure wall pierced by gates on the north and east sides, and the complex included magazines, a royal palace and priests' quarters. The northern gate led to the main body of the temple which had a transverse pillared hall pierced by three doors leading to a central sanctuary flanked by two suites of side chambers. As at Tod, the shrine was open at both ends with a central pedestal for a portable bark or shrine. An unusual feature was a hall beyond the sanctuary with two rows of six columns lining the east and west walls. A single row of engaged Osiris figures anticipated the Osiride colonnades of New Kingdom mortuary temples.

Although possibly adumbrated in the Sun Temple of Neuserre at Abu Ghurab, the pylon gate appeared as a developed form in Middle Kingdom temple architecture. In one example, a small cult temple (possibly a cenotaph) of Mentuhotpe III (*reg c.* 1957–*c.* 1945 BC) in western Thebes, the pylon was surmounted by a limestone crenellation and set in a mud-brick enclosure wall. An intermediate form was found in the Middle Kingdom temple of Ammenmenes II (*reg c.* 1876–*c.* 1842 BC) at Hermopolis Magna. It was built of brick with a portal of white limestone plastered in gypsum and surmounted by a cornice. The north front of the portal was inscribed and reliefs were cut on the jambs. Although the pylon may have had two towers, a horizontal profile is more likely.

The small peripteral chapel or kiosk was introduced at the beginning of the 12th Dynasty. A paradigm is the limestone 'White Chapel' of Sesostris I (see fig. 23), reconstructed from dismantled blocks found among the fill of Pylon III at Karnak. Instead of walls, piers set on four sides of a platform support a stone roof and cavetto cornice. On either side of the building was a stairway with a central ramp leads to a central emplacement for a shrine or sacred bark surrounded by pillars. The kiosk was placed on a large socle or plinth, a new element which symbolized the enclosure wall commonly built around a shrine. This feature became an integral part of peripteral chapels and some temples of the New Kingdom. The kiosk was carved with texts and reliefs some of which were overlain with sheets of beaten gold.

One of the earliest known rock-cut temples is the 12th Dynasty temple of Hathor at SERABIT EL-KHADIM in the Sinai Peninsula, a cave cut into the sandstone and preceded by a court and portico; it was approached by an avenue lined with stelae. Many writers have commented on its similarity to Canaanite 'high places' (*see* SYRIA-PALESTINE, §II).

During the Second Intermediate Period, the Canaanite Hyksos rulers of the eastern Delta established a sacred precinct at their capital, Avaris. This enclosed two major Canaanite temples and a smaller temple—Mortuary Temple I—which is significant in that it incorporates elements from the Egyptian Middle Kingdom temple at Ezbet Rushdi and the Canaanite temple at HAZOR in Palestine. Built of mud-brick, the temple was nearly square in plan, comprising a transverse antechamber or pronaos preceding a sanctuary with three shrines. The eastern wall of the pronaos projected beyond the outer wall of the sanctuary, causing an angle suggesting the presence of a stairway.

New Kingdom (c. 1540–c. 1075 BC). Monumental temple building began in the 18th Dynasty (*c.* 1540–*c.* 1292 BC)

23. 'White Chapel' of Sesostris I, Karnak, 12th Dynasty, *c.* 1918–*c.* 1875; reconstruction

under Amenophis III, and by the 19th Dynasty (*c.* 1292–*c.* 1190 BC) the classic pharaonic cult temple, incorporating adaptations of the traditional temple elements, had been established. Exceptional were the temples of the 18th Dynasty Amarna Period, when the cult of the Aten (sun disc) gave rise to simpler temples that were open to the sky. Peripteral 'chapels' and rock-cut temples were also built in these centuries. Much of the wealth that came to Egypt under the New Kingdom was used to enrich the State and mortuary temples and to glorify the powerful State god, Amun-Re. Wealthy temples were embellished with gold throughout; some had floors lined with silver, doorways covered in electrum and statues encrusted with precious stones.

Building materials included the extensive use of sandstone. The palm column was used only in Nubia (e.g. Soleb, Sesebi) and Middle Kingdom columns were reused at Herakleopolis Magna, Memphis and Bubastis. The predominant form was the papyrus column: campaniform (open papyrus) columns lined the main axes of hypostyle halls, creating the clerestory zones in which windows to light the interior could be set, and were also used to form processional colonnades. By the 19th Dynasty, the papyrus-bud column had developed into a monostyle column, while the uraei surmounting the Hathor capital of the Middle Kingdom were replaced by a naos. The tent pole column of prehistoric derivation was adapted in stone in the Festival Hall of Tuthmosis III (*reg c.* 1479–*c.* 1426 BC) at Karnak.

Orientation was less precise than before: many temples were set at a right angle to the river, probably for easier access by canal, but because the river mostly ran south to north a symbolic east to west direction was maintained. For cult reasons some temples could be oriented to others, as at Thebes, where many mortuary temples seem to have been aligned to the Luxor Temple. Stellar orientation may also have figured in the direction of a cult building. The constellation Ursa Major is mentioned in a text dating to Tuthmosis III, and the Ptolemaic temples of Edfu and Dendara (see below) appear to have been aligned to it.

Although no two New Kingdom temples were identical, in essence their plans were similar, the axial layout reflecting the processional nature of Egyptian cult worship. The temple was set within a pan-bedded mud-brick wall, enclosing a complex of subsidiary temples, service areas, stores, offices and accommodation as well as the main temple building. Most complexes included a SACRED LAKE or ablution tank for ritual purification. The temple was usually approached from a landing stage or quay at the end of a T-shaped canal leading off the Nile, from which a processional way—sometimes a dromos lined with statuary—led to the pylon. Comprising twin towers with battered walls flanking a central gateway, the pylon was an established feature of New Kingdom religious architecture and may have represented the 'mountain horizon' of the sunrise. Niches in the pylon façade held tall flagstaffs, and the temple forecourt may have been further ornamented with royal statuary or pairs of obelisks. Pylons of the pharaonic period were carved with scenes of battle and archaic images of conquered enemies, and they were probably intended to protect the temple against detrimental forces. In the same way, the huge wooden double doors set in the central gateway were sometimes sheathed in metal covered in divine images, while the winged solar disc might be emblazoned on the lintels of doorways throughout the temple.

Beyond the pylon was a peristyle or columned court (see THEBES (i), §II, 1), sometimes with an altar. Scenes portrayed in the reliefs included the pharaoh in battle, or performing in festivals. This area was the threshold between the profane and sacred worlds and no member of the populace was permitted to pass beyond it; public petitions were heard at 'Temples of the Hearing Ear' sited just outside the temple enclosure. Statues of gods and important officials could be set up in the court and also in some of the halls within. From the court to the sanctuary the floor level gradually rose and the light diminished, to evoke the Primeval Mound. The hypostyle hall, or Hall of Appearances, which introduced the sacred area of the temple, was roofed with stone slabs supported by papyrus columns; the stylobates of the central row were often pared to allow unimpeded passage for processions. Scenes carved on the walls illustrated the ritual purpose of each hall. In the hypostyle hall, these scenes included bark processions and royal ceremonies. The hall was lit by a clerestory, and the ceiling was often painted with yellow stars, the central panel of the main axis sometimes emblazoned with vultures in flight toward the sanctuary.

The hypostyle hall was followed by the Hall of Offerings, where the daily offerings to the god were laid out for presentation, and sometimes by an intermediate hall that served as the threshold of the sanctuary, or 'holy of holies'. A sanctuary for the god's bark (which contained a portable image of the deity) was often placed before the permanent naos or shrine of the principal cult statue, but it was the latter that was the focus for the daily ritual illustrated in the reliefs on the sanctuary walls.

Variations in the New Kingdom temple plan occur in some of the temples of Nubia (see NUBIA, §III): Sesebi has three contiguous temples with an interlinking rear hall; the temple at Kumma is asymmetrical and has a rear portico with one column abutting an antechamber and sanctuary. In the small temple at Buhen dedicated to Isis by Amenophis II (reg c. 1426–c. 1400 BC) the forecourt has an unusual arrangement of columns with transverse and parallel colonnades connected by screen walls set on either side of the entrance.

Before Akhenaten (reg c. 1353–c. 1336 BC) removed his court to Akhetaten (see AMARNA, EL-) in Middle Egypt at least five structures dedicated to the Aten had already been built at Thebes. These included the first gem pa Aten (a jubilee temple) which had sandstone walls carved with scenes from the jubilee celebration and was fronted by colossi of the King. The most imposing temple to the Aten at el-Amarna was the Great Temple (see fig. 24), built within a low mud-brick rectangular enclosure c. 760×270 m. Like all the temples at el-Amarna, it was built of the small limestone blocks known as talatat, with additions of quartzite or alabaster from the nearby Hatnub quarries and inlays of highly coloured faience or glass paste. The temple was roofless, and divided into two main areas. The first of these contained the per hai and the gem pa Aten, followed at some distance by a slaughter court, a great stele and the Hall of Foreign Tribute. Aligned west–east, the per hai and gem pa Aten comprised a pylon abutted by pillared porticos, followed by six open courts of decreasing size separated by pylons with broken lintels. Flanking the courts were rows of offering tables numbering at least 365 on each side. The last two courts contained high altars and surrounding chambers. The second area comprised the sanctuary, which stood on a platform, with two small pylons leading to a long, central ramp; a second ramp at a higher level was flanked by rows of stone offering tables. Beyond was a pylon with columned porticos containing statues of Akhenaten and his queen, Nefertiti. A hall beyond, obscured by a screen wall and abutted by narrow chambers, contained more offering tables on either side of a central passage. Two parallel walls projected from the rear wall of the sanctuary, with a square platform slightly beyond them.

A smaller temple to the Aten near the king's estate was divided into three parts, each comprising a pylon—containing an altar, priests' houses and a 'window of appearance'—and a sanctuary built on a plan similar to that of the main temple. The maru Aten, a 'viewing place' for the Aten in the southern sector of el-Amarna, was an enclosure housing a large lake surrounded by a temple, palace, houses, gardens and pavilions. Among the more unusual features of the plan were a water court with T-shaped basins and a kiosk connected by a stairway to an altar set on an island, both of which played a role in the monthly festival celebrating the birth of the Aten. Another Amarnan type was the 'Sunshade Temple' dedicated to the solar deity Re-Horakhty, who was associated with the Aten. The first known examples date from the first quarter of the 18th Dynasty, appearing as altar courts in mortuary

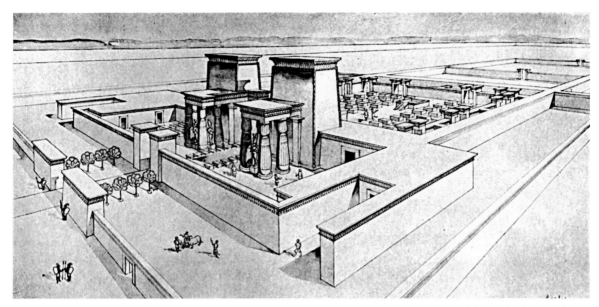

24. Sanctuary of the Great Temple of the Aten, el-Amarna, 18th Dynasty; perspective view from J. D. S. Pendlebury: *The City of Akhenaten III* (London, 1951), pl. IX

temples or on the roof of cult temples, although independent examples also exist. In all cases the central feature was an open court with an elevated altar preceding an enclosed suite of cult rooms.

The peripteral temple (also known as the boat chapel or bark shrine) of the New Kingdom probably developed from the jubilee (*heb sed*) pavilions of Djoser at Saqqara (*see* SAQQARA, §1). Such buildings were often erected for a king's jubilee or as repositories for the divine bark during festival processions, although some were dedicated to a particular cult. One type consists of a shrine set on a platform approached by a flight of stairs and enclosed by a pillared ambulatory and parapet. A variation has flights of stairs at the front and the back, connected by a passage through the main axis of the shrine, as in the Festival Hall of Tuthmosis III at Karnak. A second type is preceded by a stairway and pillared portico open on three sides, followed by rows of columns which can extend to either side or surround a shrine consisting of several chambers, as in an early temple of Hathor at Deir el-Medina.

Although the rock-cut tomb chapel first appeared in the 4th Dynasty at Giza, it was rare until the New Kingdom, occurring mainly in Nubia. Resembling that of the rock-cut funerary chapels at Thebes, the simplest plan is cruciform with a long transverse portico, sometimes pillared, followed by a deep hall with a niche or statue group in the rear wall: examples of this type include the Speos Artemidos at BENI HASAN and the Speos of Horemheb at GEBEL EL-SILSILA. A more complex version, with shrines or asymmetrical chambers leading off a columned hall, is found at Abahuda, Akhmim and Gebel Dosha.

The more elaborate rock temples of Nubia and the Wadi Abbad in the Eastern Desert resemble the grander Theban tombs (*see* §(ii)(d) below). The 19th Dynasty temples usually comprise a pylon and a forecourt with an avenue of sphinxes set within an enclosure wall and preceding a second pylon. This is followed either by a court with a pillared portico or by a court partly cut into the rock and leading into the rock-cut hypostyle hall. The innermost part of the temple comprises a Hall of Offerings joined to a sanctuary with one or three shrines, usually containing carved figures of a divine triad, set against the back wall. Additional deep lateral chambers were often added, as at the Nubian temples of Wadi el-Sebua, ABU SIMBEL, Gerf Hussein, Derr and Beit el-Wali (*see* NUBIA, §III).

Private cult and funerary chapels, many resembling miniature temples, are found in the New Kingdom workers' settlements of el-Amarna and Deir el-Medina. Situated on the escarpments of hills and cliffs surrounding the villages, they date to the 18th Dynasty at el-Amarna and to the 19th and 20th dynasties at Deir el-Medina, where some of the chapels served a 'brotherhood' of servants or workers. Such chapels could accommodate the worship of several deities, including both royal and private ancestor cults, and could also serve for consulting oracles; in some cases they doubled as tomb chapels.

The basic plan consisted of a forecourt, a pylon and one or more halls with inset benches. An outer hall, sometimes containing a pair of pillars or columns, normally led via a flight of stairs to the sanctuary, where the pronaos was often defined by screen walls and a pair of columns. An annexe often found on the building could include a subsidiary shrine and a bench. The roofs were usually flat and lit by skylights, but were occasionally vaulted. Other dependencies could include ovens, storage chambers, garden plots and animal enclosures. The chapels are mostly of mud-brick on stone foundations; the walls were sometimes plastered in mud and gypsum, while the floors were either of packed mud plastered with gypsum, or were laid with limestone slabs. The decoration usually comprises simple banding in the outer hall and more elaborate paintings within, where the images might include deities, deified royalty, officiants, offerings and text; many limestone architraves and door jambs were also inscribed.

Third Intermediate Period and Late Period (c. 1075–332 BC). Because of the disruption caused by invading powers and internal instability, relatively little temple building occurred in these years. When the practice was revived, much of the new building was centred on the oases of the Western Desert. Many of the innovations in religious architecture introduced in the Late Period, especially during the Saite 26th Dynasty (664–525 BC), developed into fully evolved forms during the Greco-Roman period. These include the modification of the heavy Theban temple exterior and the introduction of a stone girdle wall, the replacement of clerestory windows with skylights and the use of varied types of column in the hypostyle hall.

The Temple of Amun at Hibis, north of the KHARGA OASIS, is a typical example. Its foundations date to the Saite Period, but it was reconstructed during the Persian 27th Dynasty (525–404 BC), and work continued until Ptolemaic times. The rectangular temple is set near a lake with a quay and is enclosed by a sandstone girdle wall surmounted by a cavetto cornice and with a torus moulding on each corner. The corridor between the wall and temple was paved with stone slabs. Columned porticos once roofed with wood flank the entrance, connecting the outer and inner walls. The columns featured composite papyrus cluster capitals developed from the campaniform type. The portico leads directly into the hypostyle hall—originally planned as a peristyle court—which has both palm and campaniform papyrus columns. Beyond is a transverse columned hall, lit by skylights, with a screen wall that was once the original temple façade. The sanctuary has a single central shrine surrounded by chambers, one of which accommodated an oracle. Stairs lead to a chapel of Osiris on the roof, while crypts entered by trap doors lie beneath the temple floor; all of these features became standard in later temples.

SIWA OASIS in the Western Desert is the site of two Late Period temples—the 'Oracle Temple' at Aghurmi and the Temple of Amun at Umm el-Ebeida. The former dates from the 26th Dynasty and is a simple, tripartite, rectangular building with a single shrine and a side chamber; only the sanctuary has relief carvings. The Umm el-Ebeida temple, now destroyed, was built in the 30th Dynasty (380–343 BC) and had two girdle walls, but was otherwise built on a conventional plan.

Greco-Roman period (332 BC–AD 395). Monumental building was revived in the more stable conditions of the Greco-Roman period; among the major temples are EDFU (see fig. 25), DENDARA, KOM OMBO, ESNA and PHILAE. Greco-Roman temples were generally on a smaller scale than those of earlier periods, while continuing to conform to Egyptian tradition. Elements that had appeared in the Late Period were now fully established: most temples were enclosed by a stone girdle wall and ambulatory, as at Edfu and Kom Ombo, and the hypostyle hall was normally divided from the peristyle court by a low screen wall. Many varieties of composite capital derived from vegetal

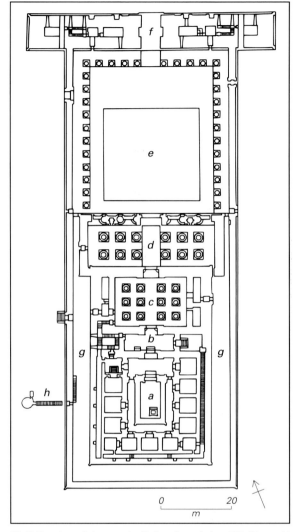

25. Edfu, plan of the temple, Ptolemaic period, *c.* 237–57 BC: (a) sanctuary with naos; (b) offertory; (c) second hypostyle hall; (d) large hypostyle hall; (e) court; (f) pylon; (g) ambulatory; (h) sacred well and Nilometer

forms such as palmettes, papyrus and lotus flowers and vines were created; different types were often used together in one hall, as at Esna. There was increased use of the Hathor column, especially at Dendara, where the face of the goddess appears on all four sides of the capital.

Other common features include suites of small cult or service chambers alongside the columned halls and around three sides of the passage surrounding the free-standing sanctuary. This contained the monolithic naos that housed the cult statue. Crypts, of which Dendara has twelve, symbolized the world of night and served both ritual and storage purposes. Stairs led to roof chapels for the celebration of Osiris rituals and the New Year festival; well-preserved examples survive at Edfu and Dendara. The slaughter court was no longer part of the temple plan.

Ptolemaic temples were concerned mainly with cosmological ideas, and astronomical ceilings play a prominent part in their symbolism. The walls were carved with numerous reliefs of the king and deities arranged in registers of small scenes, while individual chambers were identified with specific symbolic ideas or mysteries. Every part of the building was inscribed with texts related to the cult. Sanctuaries for deities subaltern to the main cult continued to be built within the main enclosure; examples survive at Dendara, Philae, Edfu and Kom Ombo. Also typical of the period, the MAMMISI or 'Birth House' was a small temple dedicated to divine birth rites and related to the 'birth colonnades' found in some New Kingdom temples (*see* THEBES (i), §§III and IV).

(b) Mortuary temples. From the beginning of the New Kingdom (*c.* 1540–*c.* 1075 BC) changes were made in the form and function of the royal mortuary temple, which for the first time was separated from the tomb. Royal tombs were now cut into the limestone cliffs of the Theban west bank, with the temples situated on the edge of the cultivation. Formerly devoted exclusively to the royal mortuary cult, these temples were now dedicated to Amun in addition to providing for the deceased monarch. The plan generally followed that of the New Kingdom cult temple, although there was some variety during the 18th Dynasty; however, by the 19th Dynasty it had become equally standardized.

Strongly influenced by the nearby Middle Kingdom funerary complex of Mentuhotpe II, the temple of Hatshepsut (*reg. c.* 1479–*c.* 1485 BC) at Deir el-Bahri (*see* THEBES (i), §IV) comprised a valley temple connected by a sphinx-lined causeway to the main temple set in the cliffs. This was built on a plan consisting of a forecourt and two rising terraces connected by two ramps; the passage of the queen from the material to the celestial world implicit in the plan is underlined by the reliefs in the colonnades on each level. The upper terrace features a colonnade of engaged Osiride figures of Hatshepsut leading to the three main sanctuaries. These are distributed around a peristyle court, and include an altar court dedicated to Re-Horakhty, a sanctuary of Amun and offering chapels to Hatshepsut and her father Tuthmosis I; the earliest known Window of Appearance is located on the south.

A canal with a quay to facilitate waterborne processions led to a number of 19th and 20th Dynasty temples ranged along the edge of the cultivation. The Ramesseum, the mortuary temple of Ramesses II (*reg. c.* 1279–*c.* 1213 BC; *see* THEBES (i), §VI), and Medinet Habu, the mortuary temple of Ramesses III (*reg. c.* 1187–*c.* 1156 BC; *see* THEBES (i), §VII), both have two peristyle courts with colonnades of engaged Osiride figures. A small royal palace to the south of the temple was connected to the first court by a Window of Appearances. Beyond the courts is the main hypostyle hall, with up to three smaller halls leading to the sanctuary, where the decoration is more elaborate. The smaller halls at the rear of the Ramesseum and Medinet Habu include suites dedicated to Osiris and to the gods of Memphis and Heliopolis; some rooms have astronomical ceilings. The temple complexes also include slaughter courts, vaulted magazines and priests' quarters.

A specially favoured individual, such as Amenhotpe, son of Hapu, the architect to Amenophis III, was allowed an independent mortuary chapel situated among the royal mortuary temples. The general plan of this type included an enclosure with a pylon leading to a garden with a pool, which led in turn to a court with side chapels and a sanctuary. The temple of Amenhotpe had a second pylon with a portico of fluted columns, leading to a pillared court and a series of vaulted chambers with carved scenes. An antechamber preceded three shrines, with interconnecting chambers around the sanctuary.

Some kings built a memorial temple, not strictly a funerary type, in the holy city of Osiris at ABYDOS. One of the most prominent was the temple of Sethos I (*reg. c.* 1290–*c.* 1279 BC), which had a unique L-shaped plan, seven chapels dedicated to the major national deities and a unique underground structure known as the Osireion, which may have been intended as a royal cenotaph. The nearby memorial temple of Ramesses II was built on a more orthodox plan.

BIBLIOGRAPHY

GENERAL WORKS

M. de Rochemonteix: 'Le Temple égyptien', *Rev. Int. Ens.* (July 1887), pp. 3–31

G. Roeder: *Naos*, Cairo, Egyp. Mus. cat., lxxv (Leipzig, 1914)

B. Porter and R. L. B. Moss, eds: *Topographical Bibliography* (Oxford, 1927–)

L. Borchardt: *Ägyptische Tempel mit Umgang*, Beiträge zur ägyptischen Bauforschung und Altertumskunde, ii (Cairo, 1938)

H. Frankfort: 'The Origin of Monumental Architecture in Egypt', *Amer. J. Semit. Lang. & Lit.* [Chicago], lviii/4 (1941), pp. 329–58

H. Nelson: 'The Egyptian Temple with Particular Reference to the Theban Temples of the Empire Period', *Bibl. Archaeologist*, vii (1944), pp. 44–53

Z. Zaba: *L'Orientation astronomique dans l'ancienne Egypte et la précession de l'axe du monde* (Prague, 1953)

H. W. Fairman: 'Worship and Festivals in an Egyptian Temple', *Bull. John Rylands Lib.*, xxxvii (1954), pp. 165–203

J. Vandier: *Les Grandes Epoques: L'Architecture religieuse et civile* (1955), ii of *Manuel d'archéologie égyptienne* (Paris, 1952–78)

E. A. E. Reymond: *The Mythical Origin of the Egyptian Temple* (Cambridge, 1969)

P. Spencer: *The Egyptian Temple: A Lexicographical Study* (London, 1984)

MULTI-PERIOD SITES

E. Chassinat: *Le Temple d'Edfu*, 11 vols (Paris and Cairo, 1892–1934)

W. M. F. Petrie: *Abydos*, ii (London, 1903)

——: *Ehnasya* (London, 1905)

M. Bruyère: *Les Fouilles de Deir el-Médineh*, 15 vols (Cairo, 1924–53)

F. Bisson de la Roque and others: *Rapport sur les fouilles de Medamoud*, 9 vols (Cairo, 1926–33)

G. Legrain: *Les Temples de Karnak* (Paris, 1929)

U. Hölscher: *Excavations at Ancient Thebes, 1930–31* (Chicago, 1932)

U. Hölscher and H. H. Nelson: *Work in Western Thebes, 1931–3* (Chicago, 1934)

E. Chassinat and F. Daumas: *Le Temple de Dendara*, 8 vols (Cairo, 1934–78)

F. Bisson de la Roque: *Tôd, 1934 à 1936* (Cairo, 1937)

A. Varille: *Karnak*, i (Cairo, 1943)

L. Habachi: *Tell Basta* (Cairo, 1957)

P. Barguet: *Le Temple d'Amon-Rê à Karnak* (Cairo, 1962)

Karnak, Centre Franco-égyptien, v–vii (Cairo, 1975–82)

M. Bietak: 'Avaris and Piramesse', *Proc. Brit. Acad.*, lxv (1979); as book (London, 1979, rev. 2/1986), pp. 247–58, 260, 284–5 [entire issue devoted to author's excavations at Tell el-Dab'a]

J. Jacquet: *Karnak Nord*, v (Cairo, 1983)

S. Cauville: *Edfu* (Cairo, 1984)

PREDYNASTIC AND EARLY DYNASTIC PERIODS

LÄ: 'Per-nu', 'Per-wer'

J. E. Quibell: *Hierakonpolis*, i (London, 1900)

G. Jéquier: 'Les Temples primitifs et la persistance des types archaïques dans l'architecture religieuse', *Bull. Inst. Fr. Archéol. Orient.*, vi (1908), pp. 25–41

R. Weill: 'Monuments nouveaux des premières dynasties', *Sphinx*, xv/1 (1911), pp. 1–35

P. Newberry: 'Some Cults of Prehistoric Egypt', *Liverpool An. Archaeol. & Anthropol.*, v (1913), pp. 132–42

W. M. F. Petrie: *Prehistoric Egypt* (London, 1920)

H. Ricke: 'Der Hohe Sand in Heliopolis', *Z. Ägyp. Spr. & Altertknd.*, lxxi (1935), pp. 107–11

G. A. Wainwright: 'Seshat's nš Shrine', *J. Egyp. Archaeol.*, xxv (1939), p. 104

C. Robichon: *Description sommaire du temple primitif de Médamoud* (Cairo, 1940)

H. J. Kantor: 'The Final Phase of Predynastic Cultures', *J. Nr E. Stud.*, iii (1944), pp. 110–36

A. Badawy: 'La Première Architecture en Egypte', *An. Service Ant. Egypte*, li (1951), pp. 1–28

——: 'Philological Evidence about Methods of Construction in Ancient Egypt', *An. Service Ant. Egypte*, liv (1957), pp. 51–74

B. J. Kemp: 'Photographs of the Decorated Tomb at Hierakonpolis', *J. Egyp. Archaeol.*, lix (1973), pp. 36–43

B. Adams: *Ancient Hierakonpolis* (Warminster, 1974)

J. M. Saleh: 'Les Représentations de temples sur plates-formes à pieux de la poterie gerzéene d'Egypte', *Bull. Inst. Fr. Archéol. Orient.*, lxxxiii (1983), pp. 263–96

G. Soukiassian: 'Les Autels à cornes ou "aerotères" en Egypte', *Bull. Inst. Fr. Archéol. Orient.*, lxxxiii (1983), pp. 317–33

F. El Yahky: 'The Concept of the Triad in Prehistoric Egypt', *Abstracts of Papers at the Congress of the International Association of Egyptologists: Munich, 1985*, p. 270

OLD KINGDOM

F. W. von Bissing, ed.: *Das Re-Heiligtum des Königs Ne-Woser-Re (Rathures)* (Berlin, 1905)

S. Schott: 'Le Temple du Sphinx à Giza et les deux axes du monde égyptien', *Bull. Soc. Fr. Egyp.*, liii–liv (1969), pp. 31–41

H. Ricke: *Der Harmachistempel des Chefren in Gizeh*, Beiträge zur ägyptischen Bauforschung und Altertumskunde, x (Wiesbaden, 1970)

M. Lehner: 'Giza', *Archv Orientforsch.*, xxxii (1985), pp. 136–58

G. Dreyer: *Elephantine* (1986), viii of *Der Tempel der Satet* (Mainz, 1980–76)

MIDDLE KINGDOM

A. Vogliano: *Madinet Madi*, 2 vols (Milan, 1936–7)

S. Adam: 'Report on the Excavations of the Department of Antiquities at Ezbet Rushdi', *An. Service Ant. Egypte*, lvi (1959), pp. 207–26

D. Arnold: *Der Tempel Qasr el-Sagha* (Mainz, 1979)

NEW KINGDOM TO LATE PERIOD

E. Naville: *The Temple of Deir el Bahari*, 6 vols (London, 1894–1906)

L. Loat: *Gurob*, Egyptian Research Account (London, 1905) [part volume with M. A. Murray: *Saqqara mastabas*, i]

D. Randall-Maciver and C. L. Woolley: *Buhen*, 2 vols (Philadelphia, 1911)

A. M. Blackman: *The Temple of Derr* (Cairo, 1913)

U. Hölscher and J. A. Wilson: *Medinet Habu Studies, 1928/29* (Chicago, 1930)

Medinet Habu, Epigraphic Survey of the Orient. Inst., 8 vols (Chicago, 1930–70)

H. H. Nelson and U. Hölscher: *Medinet Habu Reports*, Oriental Institute Communications, x (Chicago, 1931)

H. Frankfort: *The Cenotaph of Seti I at Abydos*, 2 vols (London, 1933)

A. M. Calverley, M. F. Broome and A. H. Gardiner: *The Temple of King Sethos I at Abydos*, 4 vols (London, 1933–59)

U. Hölscher: *The Excavation of Medinet Habu*, 5 vols (Chicago, 1934–54)

C. Robichon and A. Varille: *Le Temple d'Amenhotep fils de Hapou* (Cairo, 1936)

H. W. Fairman: 'Preliminary Report on the Excavations at Amarah West, Anglo-Egyptian Sudan, 1938–1939', *J. Egyp. Archaeol.*, xxv (1939), pp. 139–44

J. D. S. Pendlebury: *City of Akhenaten*, iii (London, 1951)

D. Dunham and J. M. A. Janssen: *Semna, Kumma*, i (Boston, MA, 1960)

D. Arnold: *Wandrelief und Raumfunktion in ägyptischen Tempeln des Neues Reiches* (Berlin, 1962)

R. Caminos: 'Surveying Kumma', *Kush*, xiii (1967), pp. 74–7

——: *The New Kingdom Temples of Buhen*, 2 vols (London, 1974)

D. B. Redford: 'The Razed Temple of Akhenaten', *Sci. American*, 239 (December 1978), pp. 100–110

E. P. Uphill: *The Temples of Per Ramesses* (Warminster, 1984)

B. J. Kemp: *Amarna Reports*, i–iv (London, 1984–7)

A. H. Bomann: *The Private Chapel in Ancient Egypt* (MPhil thesis, U. Birmingham, 1987) [a study of the chapels in the workmen's village at el-Amarna, with special reference to Deir el-Medina and other sites]

GRECO-ROMAN PERIOD

G. Benedite: *Le Temple de Philae*, 2 fascs (Paris, 1893–5)

A. E. R. Boak: *Karanis: The Temples, Coin Hoards, Botanical and Zoological Reports, Seasons, 1924–1931* (Ann Arbor, 1933)

S. Sauneron: *Quatre campagnes à Esna* (Cairo, 1959)

——: *Le Temple d'Esna*, ii (Cairo, 1963)

C. M. Zivie: *Le Temple de Deir Chelouit*, i (Paris, 1982)

For further bibliography *see* DENDARA; EDFU; ESNA; KOM OMBO; PHILAE.

THE OASES AND SINAI

W. M. F. Petrie: *Researches in Sinai* (London, 1906)

H. E. Winlock: *The Excavations* (1941), i of *The Temple of Hibis in el-Khargeh Oasis* (New York, 1941–53)

A. Fakhry: *Bahria Oasis*, 2 vols (Cairo, 1942–50)

——: *The Oases of Egypt*, 2 vols (Cairo, 1973–4)

For further bibliography *see* BAHARIYA OASIS; DAKHLA OASIS; KHARGA OASIS; SERABIT EL-KHADIM; SINAI, §1.

ANN BOMANN

(ii) Tombs. The design and development of Egyptian tombs was inextricably linked with religious beliefs. The essential idea was to provide a suitable and enduring setting for eternal life after death. From the earliest periods the tomb was thought of as a 'house of eternity', a burial place where the corpse could be protected, the necessary funerary goods deposited and regular food offerings made for the sustenance of the deceased. The two most characteristic features of Egyptian funerary architecture were the tomb chapel for offerings and the separate (usually subterranean) burial chamber and storeroom.

There were four principal tomb types: pit-graves, mastabas, pyramids and chapel tombs. The simplest, and commonest at all periods, was the pit-grave in the ground at the desert edge, of sufficient size to house the corpse and basic funerary goods. The MASTABA was the natural progression from the pit-grave, adding a superstructure; it was the characteristic tomb of the élite during the Old and Middle Kingdoms (*c.* 2575–*c.* 1630 BC). Pyramid tombs, probably developed from mastabas, were used for royal burials in the Old and Middle Kingdoms; with its associated structures (see fig. 26) the form was revived during the New Kingdom (*c.* 1540–*c.* 1075 BC) and later periods on a much smaller scale in mud-brick for private burials (*see* PYRAMID, §1). A further development from

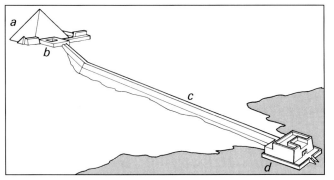

26. Royal tomb of the Old Kingdom: typical pyramid complex of the 4th Dynasty, *c.* 2500 BC: (a) pyramid; (b) mortuary temple; (c) causeway; (d) valley temple

the mastaba was the chapel tomb, which took two forms: tomb chapels with the offering chambers hewn out of the rock and free-standing tomb chapels with the superstructure in the shape of a small shrine. In both cases the chapel has a subterranean room or rooms, reached by a shaft cut through bedrock, to accommodate the burial and grave goods. Some of these tomb types occur contemporaneously in the same cemeteries. Financial factors most influenced the choice of tomb type, but local tradition and topography were also important: rock-cut tombs evolved in areas where there was insufficient level ground to construct mastabas.

(a) Predynastic (*c.* 6000–*c.* 2925 BC). (b) Early Dynastic, Old Kingdom and First Intermediate Period (*c.* 2925–*c.* 2008 BC). (c) Middle Kingdom (*c.* 2008–*c.* 1630 BC). (d) New Kingdom and Third Intermediate Period (*c.* 1540–*c.* 750 BC). (e) Late Period (*c.* 750–332 BC). (f) Greco-Roman period (332 BC–AD 395).

*(a) Predynastic (*c. 6000–*c. 2925 BC). The characteristic Predynastic burial is the shallow pit-grave excavated in the desert gravel. They are usually unlined, rectangular with rounded corners or oval in outline; and range in size from 1.0×0.7×1.0 m deep to 3.0×1.5×2.0 m deep. The deceased was interred in a flexed position, sometimes in a coffin of wood or basketry, or wrapped in a reed mat. By the end of the Naqada II phase (*c.* 3000 BC), square, roofed pits, lined with wood or mud-brick, were made and provided with separate storage chambers for grave goods. There is little evidence for any kind of tumulus or superstructure; these may have been built but have not survived. The simple pit-grave remained the predominant tomb type for poor burials at all periods with little change, and in the absence of grave goods accurate dating can be difficult.

*(b) Early Dynastic, Old Kingdom and First Intermediate Period (*c. 2925–*c. 2008 BC). The earliest pit-tombs with rectangular superstructures were built at the beginning of the 1st Dynasty (*c.* 2925–*c.* 2575 BC). Tombs of this date at Tarkhan had a rubble tumulus over the burial pit and a small brick open-air offering chapel abutting the east wall,

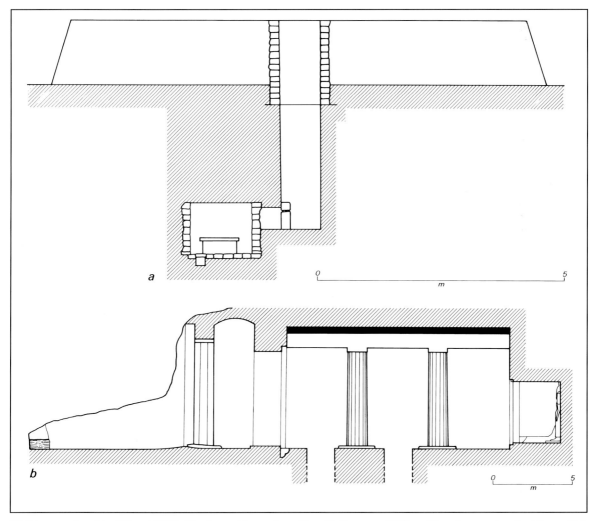

27. Private tombs of the Old and Middle Kingdoms: (a) mastaba at Giza, 4th Dynasty, *c.* 2500 BC; (b) rock-cut tomb at Beni Hasan, 12th Dynasty, *c.* 1900 BC

the whole structure *c.* 3×2 m. At ABYDOS there are much more elaborate 1st Dynasty royal pit-tombs with subdivided chambers: the superstructure of the tomb of Wadj, for example, measured 346×130 m and had 134 subsidiary graves outside its first enclosure wall. It was from such 1st Dynasty monuments that the typical Old Kingdom mastaba developed, with an offering chapel, extensive storerooms within the superstructure and a burial chamber, reached by stairs, and later by a shaft, sunk into the bedrock (see fig. 27a). An unusual variant is found in a 4th Dynasty mastaba at MAIDUM, where the burial chamber and the sloping approach corridor were dug out of the desert gravel and lined with masonry blocks. In the 3rd and 4th dynasties more modest pit-graves proliferated around wealthy mastabas at such necropoleis as Saqqara (*see* SAQQARA). Some had gabled mud-brick vaults over the brick-lined pit, but there is little evidence for any further superstructure.

The first rock-cut tomb chapels appeared in the late 3rd Dynasty (*c.* 2650–*c.* 2575 BC) or the early 4th (*c.* 2575–*c.* 2134 BC), particularly in the desert cliffs of Middle and Lower Egypt, although they were also cut in the poorer quality rock around the Giza and Saqqara necropoleis. Old Kingdom rock-cut tomb chapels at Saqqara developed from mastabas where the offering niche became more elaborate and was withdrawn further into the body of the tomb superstructure to form an enclosed cruciform chapel reached by a passage; the arms of the cross formed two smaller niches flanking the main one. A 'false door' offering stele (*see* STELE, §2) was usually positioned on the east wall, directly over the shaft to the burial chamber, so that the deceased's spirit could have access to the offerings made in the chapel. For reasons of economy, several individuals were often buried in chambers descending from the tomb chapel, as in the 5th Dynasty tomb of Nefer at Saqqara, where the various family members each had his or her own false door stele. At ASWAN during the early 6th Dynasty, larger rock-cut tomb chapels were constructed with pillared halls, created by leaving vertical sections of the sandstone standing as the chapel was hewn out; for example, the tomb of Sabni and Mekhu (A1) has 18 such rough columns. This technique anticipated tomb design in First Intermediate Period and Middle Kingdom provincial cemeteries, such as MEIR and BENI HASAN (see fig. 27b).

Quarrying techniques varied at different times and in different places. The commonest method of hewing out tombs was to excavate the rock face in a series of steps, and to proceed into the mountain by removing marked-out blocks of stone, working downwards from the top of the corridor. Doorways and pillars were outlined on the exposed surfaces and centred on a line running down the ceiling of the main corridor. The rough work of clearing out the rock was carried out with flint chisels and granite pounders; the finer finishing work was achieved by precise diagonal chiselling. The quarrymen were attentive to the exact dimensions of the rock-cut chambers, but the relationships of the individual rooms to each other were partly determined by the quality of the rock: the axes might change if a convenient crack in the rock would assist the quarrying.

The increasing wealth of the tomb deposits led to a proportionate growth in tomb robbery, and the architects of Old Kingdom tombs were responsive to the need for greater security. Placing superstructures over tombs—particularly over shallow pit-graves, which were easy to rob—may have been one early solution; the change in the 3rd Dynasty from sloping corridors to vertical shafts giving access to the burial chamber was another. More drastic measures were taken by the architect of the 3rd Dynasty mastaba K1 at Beit Khalaf, where the sloping shaft was obstructed by five large stone blocks, which had been lowered through vertical shafts from the surface; as a further deterrent, the shaft was then filled with rubble. In other tombs, such as that of Niankhpepi at Saqqara, large boulders were used to plug the shaft. Such portcullis stones and plug-blocks became the standard devices for sealing pyramid corridors and entrances, and they were used in the Great Pyramid at Giza (*see* GIZA, §1) and at DAHSHUR, although none proved effective against tomb robbers.

See also PYRAMID, §1.

(c) Middle Kingdom (c. 2008–c. 1630 BC). The growth in provincial architecture stimulated by the decentralization of authority in the First Intermediate Period (*see* §X below), extended into the early Middle Kingdom, when local magnates commissioned large, rock-cut tomb chapels in such sites as Beni Hasan, Deir el-Bersha, Aswan and Qaw el-Kebir. Although each necropolis has its own variations, the basic pattern for these rock-cut tombs is a façade, sometimes with an exedra supported by polygonal or papyriform columns, a pillared hall and a shrine on the far wall containing a statue of the owner, positioned to face the entrance (see fig. 27b above). The hall of the tomb of Amenemhet at Beni Hasan (BH 2), dating from the reign of Sesostris I (*reg c.* 1918–*c.* 1875 BC), is 12 m square, cut *c.* 25 m into the cliff; it is reached via an antechamber with polygonal 'proto-Doric' columns. The vaulted roof is supported by four columns; two shafts in the floor at the end of the south wall lead to the burial chamber. At Aswan, the tomb of Sarenput II (A3), dating from the reign of Ammenemes II (*reg c.* 1876–*c.* 1842 BC) is longer and narrower, extending 37 m into the rock with the main pillared hall *c.* 8 m wide. A recessed corridor leading to a second hall, with the statue niche, contains twelve engaged Osiride statues of Sarenput. The nomarchs of Qaw el-Kebir constructed even more elaborate tombs on two levels, partly rock-cut and with exterior constructions of stone and mud-brick. The terraced tomb of Wahka I at Qaw el-Kebir, built during the reign of Ammenemes I (*c.* 1938–*c.* 1908 BC) had an outside approach with porticos and twin, covered ambulatories, and on a higher terrace a hypostyle hall leading to the rock-cut tomb chapel. Extensive cemeteries grew up around such large tombs (see BERSHA, DEIR EL-). At Beni Hasan, 39 tomb chapels cluster together in a band of good quality limestone along the cliff face, while in the immediate vicinity are nearly 900 less lavish burials, including pit-graves, simple mastabas and shaft tombs, which probably had mud-brick superstructures.

Rock-cut tombs were also used for royal burials during the Middle Kingdom, although pyramids with satellite tombs for family members remained the dominant form of royal burial, as at EL-LISHT, DAHSHUR and EL-LAHUN. At el-Tarif in the Theban necropolis, the Inyotef kings of the 11th Dynasty were buried in *saff*-tombs (*see* THEBES (i), §IX), which had tomb chapels and burial chambers for courtiers in the side porticos of the courtyard. At Deir el-Bahri (*see* THEBES (i), §IV), the nobles of Mentuhotpe II (*reg c.* 2008–*c.* 1957 BC) were buried in narrow rock tombs ranged alongside the causeway to his monument, just as Old Kingdom nobles had been buried alongside the pyramids at Saqqara and Giza.

Despite the construction of rock-cut tombs all over Egypt in the Middle Kingdom, large mastabas also continued to be built. As before, they were entered by vertical shafts or by sloping corridors, the latter type constructed in the same manner as the open-pit mastabas at Maidum. The construction of wealthy Middle Kingdom mastabas may have been influenced by the designs of the internal chambers of contemporary pyramids, including the use of complex blocking mechanisms and dummy corridors to foil intruders (see HAWARA), and of corbelled ceilings constructed of gabled roofing slabs with brick relieving arches to take the weight of the superstructure. Excavations at Abydos have also uncovered rock-cut burial chambers, which were reached by pits leading from small mud-brick mastabas measuring 4.5 m square.

(d) New Kingdom and Third Intermediate Period (c. 1540–c. 750 BC). The major New Kingdom innovation in tomb design was the free-standing tomb chapel, in which the building containing the offering chapel takes the form of a small shrine; as always, the burial chamber is underground. This type may be regarded as the final form of the mastaba, or as a transfer of the rock-cut chapel to the surface. It is the most graceful and succinct development of Egyptian funerary architecture, reducing the design to the two essential elements of offering place and burial chamber. The burial chambers of such tombs were reached by shafts in the open courtyard; most tombs had only one or two rooms at the bottom of the shaft, but others were more extensive. One of the finest examples of this type is that of HOREMHEB at Saqqara, probably started late in the reign of Amenophis III (*reg c.* 1390–*c.* 1353 BC), some 41 years before Horemheb became pharaoh and constructed his own tomb (KV 57) in the Valley of the Kings. The essential plan of his Memphite tomb—an offering place reached by a series of rooms and open courtyards—is comparable to a temple with its cult room at the end (*see* §(i) above). It has a double entrance pylon, an open court with 24 limestone columns and a

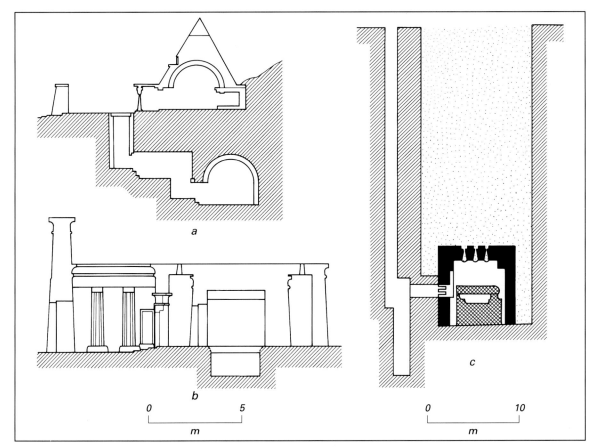

28. Private tombs of the New Kingdom and Late Period: (a) tomb at Deir el-Medina, 19th Dynasty, *c.* 1200 BC; (b) tomb of Amenirdis at Medinet Habu, 25th Dynasty, *c.* 750 BC; (c) shaft tombs at Saqqara, 26th Dynasty, *c.* 600 BC

second courtyard with 16 columns, leading to the statue recess. The inner rooms were lined with limestone reliefs of exceptional quality and had brick vaulted ceilings, parts of which survive.

The most typical New Kingdom tombs are the rock-cut chapels of the Theban necropolis, of which there are more than 450 dotted about in the limestone cliffs of the west bank of the Nile; others probably await discovery. Their basic plan consists of a walled courtyard preceding a rock-cut façade, behind which is a T-shaped chapel comprising a transverse hall or 'broad hall' immediately behind the façade and a corridor, or axial hall, running into the cliff and terminating in a statue niche; a shaft in the courtyard leads down to the burial chamber. There are a number of variations on this basic plan. Sometimes the corridor extends deep into the rock, dwarfing the transverse hall, as in the tomb of Amenemhet (TT 48), measuring 22 m long with 44 pillars; this was also the first known tomb to have a square hall with the statue niche located at the end of the axial corridor. The tomb of Amenemhab (TT 85; *c.* 1450 BC), by contrast, is extremely simple, with a pillared transverse room and a narrow corridor with two rooms running off it forming a cruciform plan. The famous tomb of Menna (TT 69) is similar in plan, but of different proportions, and has no hypostyle hall. Other tomb chapels also vary considerably in size and dimensions. The tomb of Ramose (TT 55), one of the most elaborate of the 18th Dynasty, is unfinished, but has a 25 m-wide hypostyle transverse hall with papyriform columns linked by a short, narrow passage to a second eight-columned hall ending in a statue niche. The tomb of Rekhmire (TT 100) is extremely etiolated in comparison, with a small, narrow anteroom, an unpillared broad hall and a long, high axial corridor penetrating 34 m into the mountain and rising to a height of 8 m. A slightly different type of tomb is exemplified by the chapel of Sennefer (TT 96 and 96B), overseer of granaries of Amun during the reign of Amenophis II (*reg c.* 1426–*c.* 1400 BC): an irregularly cut antechamber curving into the rock, and an uncompromisingly square, subterranean offering chamber,

29. Tomb of Meryre, el-Amarna, hypostyle hall, *c.* 1353–*c.* 1336 BC

reached by a flight of steps, with four crudely-hewn pillars. These rock-cut tombs had a wide range of façades. The tombs of Amenemheb (TT 85) and Neferrenpet (TT 43) had porticos with papyriform columns surmounted by mud-brick pyramids with niches for stelae or stele-like statues (*see* §IX, 2(i)(h) below). Others, such as the tomb of Nebamun and Ipuky (TT 181), have rectangular façades with a central door crowned by a cavetto cornice. Above the entrance there is usually a niche, sometimes studded with rows of earthenware cones inscribed with the names of the deceased; the purpose of these is unclear.

At Deir el-Medina (*see* THEBES (i), §XI) the tombs of the royal necropolis workers differed markedly in design from the 18th and 19th Dynasty tombs of the nobility. The Ramesside tombs of the workmen's village are of two main types: a brick pyramid chapel above ground with a shaft leading to the burial chamber; and a subterranean rock-cut chapel with a pyramidal superstructure. Pyramid chapels, such as those of Ankhorkawy (TT 359) and Sennedjem (TT 1) are raised on a brick or stone socle, plastered on the outside to present a smooth face, and were topped by a pyramidion, probably of black stone (see fig. 28a). The stele is set facing east in a niche or raised in front of the door to the chapel (see fig. 75 below). The interior of the pyramid was corbelled and plastered over to form vaults. The underground rooms have an irregular plan. A vertical shaft descends for 3–4 m to a corridor leading into a vaulted room, which leads to a second room cut at a lower level. All the rooms are brick-lined and vaulted. An example of the second type is the tomb of Ipuy (TT 217). A courtyard surrounds the façade of the chapel, which consists of three brick-lined, plastered rooms running straight into the rock. The façade is ornamented with a portico topped by a pyramid, similar to that of Amenemheb (TT 85).

Rock-cut tombs in provincial cemeteries such as the tombs of Tutu at Deir Rifa and of Nefersekhem at Kom el-Ahmar, conform more or less to the T-shaped Theban plan. At Abydos, mastabas continued to be built, although their brick superstructures are so elaborate and derivative from temple plans that they might be regarded as a transitional form between the mastaba and free-standing tomb-chapel. The tomb of Tutu at Tell el-Amarna (EA 8) was achieved by hollowing out a jutting outcrop of rock, so that the whole chapel resembles a free-standing mastaba. Its internal plan, with hypostyle hall and axial corridor, is, like that of Meryre (see fig. 29), reminiscent of Theban tombs; like most of the funerary buildings at el-Amarna, it was never completed. A unique type of private tomb, dating to the 20th Dynasty (*c.* 1190–*c.* 1075 BC) is found in the necropolis at ESNA. It combines elements of contemporary domestic architecture with the chapel and burial chamber, both above ground. The mud-brick superstructures of such tombs were over 7 m high, each with a staircase leading to a stone-lined burial chamber, which was slightly sunk (*c.* 1 m) into the ground.

There was an enormous difference between private and royal sepulchres of the New Kingdom, a difference that was dictated by factors other than the infinitely greater material resources of the royal family. The tombs of the kings had an immense theological significance: each part of the tomb was connected with a different stage in the spiritual rebirth of the king, analogized with the journey of the sun through the night. The Turin plan (Turin, Mus. Egizio, 1885; see fig. 111 below) of the tomb (KV 2) of Ramesses IV (reg c. 1156–c. 1150 BC) preserves some of the epithets given to the various rooms and corridors: 'the first gods' passage; 'the sanctuary in which the gods of the west repose'; and 'the house of gold in which one lies', the term for the burial chamber itself. The first royal tombs in the Valley of the Kings had a simple plan derived from a structure with four corridors linking two rooms. Such a plan had first been used for late 17th Dynasty royal burials at Dra Abu el-Naga (see THEBES (i), §IX). Later New Kingdom royal tombs, with the exception of Tutankhamun's, repeated this plan. Unlike the rock-cut tombs of nobles New Kingdom tombs constructed for the pharaohs in the c. 175 years between Amenophis I (reg c. 1514–c. 1493 BC) and Amenophis III were not planned axially: the corridors bend from right to left, and the passage descending to the burial chamber is usually at a right angle to the entrance corridor. The tomb (KV 34) of Tuthmosis III (reg c. 1479–c. 1426 BC) has a series of descending galleries, connected by stairs, that lead to a deep rock-sunk pit or well, the purpose of which is unclear; it may have served to collect flash-flood water before it reached the lower-level rooms of the tomb containing the burial chamber, or it may have been intended to confuse tomb robbers. By the Ramesside period, this feature has been reduced to a symbolic hall: the Turin plan calls the vestigial pit the 'Hall of Waiting' or the 'Hall of Hindering'. Beyond this, at a lower level, was the pillared offering chamber, where the king was portrayed offering to the gods, and, at a right-angle to the corridor, the burial chamber with four small subsidiary rooms.

The tomb of Akhenaten at el-Amarna, however, was excavated on a single central axis so that the sun could penetrate the anterooms. There was also a corridor and a second complex of chambers on the right side; one of the rooms was certainly used for the burial of one of Akhenaten's daughters. This plan, in which the main corridor runs in a straight line to the burial chamber, may have been the prototype for the late New Kingdom tombs in the Valley of the Kings, which from the reign of Merneptah (reg c. 1213–c. 1204 BC) comprised a series of rooms and corridors running straight into the rock. A transitional type is represented by the tomb (KV 17) of Sethos I (see fig. 30), the longest tomb in the Valley of the Kings, which extends over 100 m into the mountain. There are five corridors, two consisting of descending flights of steps, leading through the Hall of Waiting into four pillared rooms, and thence to the burial chamber. An unparalleled feature is the passage that runs, for no apparent purpose, from the burial chamber further into the rock. These late New Kingdom tombs have flamboyant façades, usually with portals and a cavetto cornice. For example, the lintel of KV 18, the tomb of Ramesses X (reg c. 1108–c. 1104 BC), had a fine symmetrical relief (destr.) of the King adoring a sun disc; the portals were originally equipped with bronze-sheathed wooden doors.

Ramesses XI (reg c. 1104–c. 1075 BC) was the last pharaoh known to have had a tomb (KV 4) prepared in the Valley of the Kings, but it was never finished and he was

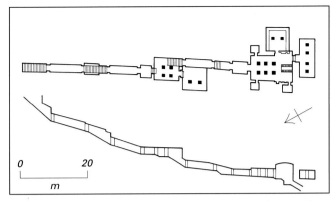

30. Royal tomb of the New Kingdom: tomb of Sethos I at Thebes, c. 1280 BC

buried elsewhere, probably in the Delta. The monarchy effectively bifurcated between Thebes and the Delta during the Third Intermediate Period (c. 1075–c. 750 BC), and no tombs are known for any of the Theban High Priests of Amun, some of whom had secondary burials in the tomb of Queen Inhapy (TT 320; see THEBES (i), §IX). The next royal tombs known are those of the 22nd Dynasty (c. 950–c. 730 BC) pharaohs at TANIS, for which no superstructures have survived, though the probability is that they had some kind of free-standing stone tomb chapel over the stone-lined subterranean chambers, as in the tombs of the Divine Adoratrices at Medinet Habu (see §(e) below).

(e) Late Period (c. 750–332 BC). True rock-cut tombs were less common after the end of the Ramesside period, as the free-standing chapel tomb became the predominant type of élite burial. The 26th Dynasty (664–525 BC) tomb of Bakenrenef at Saqqara demonstrates the final development of the axial corridor plan originated in the Middle Kingdom, though on a much more grandiose scale. Bakenrenef's tomb consists of a hypostyle hall measuring 10×6 m, a second chamber with four satellite rooms and an offering room with an archaizing false door stele typical of the period (see §IX, 3(xi)(a) below). These rooms were surrounded by a passage 1.5 m wide and 45 m long running along three sides of the inner chamber, with entrances on both sides of the hypostyle hall. The descent shaft to the burial chamber also leads from this corridor. The complexity of this structure illustrates the degree of mastery over tunnelling into rock achieved after long practice by Egyptian builders. The contemporary, free-standing tomb chapels of the Divine Adoratrices of Amun (see THEBES (i), §VII) conform to the New Kingdom type found in the Memphite necropolis, with the descent shaft to the substructure located in the external courtyard. Built of limestone blocks, they have an entrance pylon crowned by a cavetto cornice and an enclosed sanctuary (see fig. 28b above). The internal walls and the pylon fronts are decorated with reliefs showing the Adoratrices engaged in various ritual activities.

Monumental free-standing tomb chapels belonging to private individuals dominated the area of the Theban necropolis called Asasif, the best examples being the tomb of MENTUEMHET (TT 34) and Petamenopet (TT 33). Like the tombs of the Adoratrices, they have large pylons leading to their sunken, open courtyards. The exterior walls of the chapels are decorated with the palace façade motif found on earlier dynastic mastabas, another instance of the archaizing tendency of the period. The rock-hewn substructures can be complex, with successive pillared halls linked by passages, and false chambers to protect the burial from plunderers.

No superstructure has survived from the shaft tomb of Amuntefnakht at Saqqara, but the stone-lined, vaulted burial chamber was constructed with the sarcophagus *in situ* in a 30 m deep pit excavated from the rock (see fig. 28c above). Once the pit was filled in over the burial vault, the only access to the chamber was through a narrow vertical shaft with a low connecting passage. Special openings were left in the roof of the burial chamber and plugged with pottery jars, base downwards. When the funeral obsequies were completed, the jars were broken and the chamber was sealed by a deluge of sand from the infill of the pit. This security device was the only really effective one ever developed by the Egyptian tomb architects, and it is unique to the Memphite necropolis.

Humbler people continued to be buried in rock-cut shafts with mud-brick superstructures, and the poorest in pit-graves at the edge of the desert. At Abydos, tombs dating to the 30th Dynasty (380–343 BC) were constructed of brick with a pyramidal superstructure, which, very unusually, contains the burial chamber. An offering chapel was attached to the east wall. The pyramids, like those in the New Kingdom Theban necropolis, were plastered and painted, and like the contemporary pyramids at NAPATA and MEROË had a much steeper angle than pyramids of the Old Kingdom.

(f) Greco-Roman period (332 BC–AD 395). Complex tombs became less popular in the Greco-Roman period, although much attention continued to be lavished on the treatment of the corpse (*see* MUMMY, EGYPTIAN). Early Ptolemaic tombs, such as the TOMB OF PETOSIRIS at Tuna el-Gebel, the necropolis of HERMOPOLIS MAGNA, exemplify the latest style of chapel tomb, which resembles contemporary temple buildings. Less affluent individuals were buried in cyst tombs, each accommodating one or two mummies, cut into the rock of escarpments or sunk into older monuments. The majority of people, however, were interred in communal pit-graves without superstructures, identified only by a label attached to the mummy. Contemporary papyri reveal that these cemeteries were sometimes leased out for cultivation when full. The dominant type of tomb in the necropolis at Terenuthis (*see* KOM ABU BILLO) was reminiscent of the Ramesside tombs at Deir el-Medina, with a mud-brick pyramidal superstructure over a subterranean burial chamber, and showing no influence from Roman tomb types. At Alexandria, however, wealthier citizens were interred in catacombs decorated in a mixture of Greco-Roman and Egyptian styles (*see* ALEXANDRIA, §2(i)).

BIBLIOGRAPHY
LÄ: 'Grab', 'Grabbau', 'Architekturdarstellung' and sites of individual tombs and necropoleis

GENERAL WORKS
S. Clarke and R. Engelbach: *Ancient Egyptian Masonry: The Building Craft* (London, 1930)

G. Reisner: *History of the Giza Necropolis*, 2 vols (Cambridge, MA, 1942)
A. Badawy: *A History of Egyptian Architecture*, 3 vols (Berkeley, 1966–8)
A. J. Spencer: *Death in Ancient Egypt* (London, 1982)
B. J. Kemp: *Ancient Egypt: The Anatomy of a Civilization* (London, 1988)
Mummies and Magic: The Funerary Arts of Ancient Egypt (exh. cat., ed. S. D'Auria, P. Lacovara and C. Roehrig, Boston, MA, Mus. F.A., 1988)
D. Arnold: *Egyptian Stone Architecture* (Oxford, 1992)

PREDYNASTIC AND OLD KINGDOM
N. de G. Davies: *The Rock Tombs of Shiekh Saïd* (London, 1901)
W. M. F. Petrie: *Royal Tombs of the Earliest Dynasties* (London, 1901)
G. Reisner: *The Development of the Egyptian Tomb down to the Accession of Cheops* (Oxford, 1936)
L. Epron and F. Daumas: *Le Tombeau de Ti*, 3 vols (Cairo, 1939–66)
W. B. Emery: *Great Tombs of the First Dynasty* (Cairo and London, 1940–58)
Z. Y. Saad: *Royal Excavations at Saqqara and Helwan* (Cairo, 1948)
W. B. Emery: *Archaic Egypt* (Harmondsworth, 1961)
D. Dunham: *Naq-ed Deir IV: The Predynastic Cemetery* (Los Angeles, 1965)
A. M. Moussa and H. Altenmuller: *Das Grab des Nianchchnum and Chnumhotep* (Mainz, 1977)
W. K. Simpson: *The Mastabas of Kawab and Khafkhufu*, i and ii (Boston, MA, 1978)
B. Adams: *The Fort Cemetery at Hierakonpolis* (London, 1987)
P. Watson: *Egyptian Pyramids and Mastaba Tombs of the Old and Middle Kingdoms* (Princes Risborough, 1987)
A. Dodson: *Egyptian Rock-cut Tombs* (Princes Risborough, 1991)

MIDDLE KINGDOM
N. de G. Davies: *The Rock Tombs of Deir el-Gebrawi*, 2 vols (London, 1902)
H. E. Winlock: *The Tomb of Senebtisi at Lisht* (New York, 1916)
H. Steckewek: *Die Fürstengräber von Qaw* (Leipzig, 1936)
D. Arnold: *Gräber des Alten und Mittleren Reiches in el-Tarif* (Mainz, 1976)
D. O'Connor: 'The "Cenotaphs" of the Middle Kingdom at Abydos', *Mélanges Gamal eddin Mokhtar*, ii (Cairo, 1985), pp. 161–77

NEW KINGDOM
Royal tombs
T. E. Peet: *The Great Tomb Robberies of the 20th Dynasty* (Oxford, 1930)
A. Piankoff: *The Tomb of Ramesses VI* (New York, 1964)
E. Thomas: *The Royal Necropoleis of Thebes* (Princeton, 1966)
G. T. Martin: *The Royal Tombs at Amarna*, 2 vols (London, 1974–89)
J. Romer: *The Valley of the Kings* (London, 1981)
E. Hornung: *Tal der Könige: Die Ruhestätte der Pharaonen* (Zurich, 1985)
C. N. Reeves: *The Valley of the Kings: Decline of a Royal Necropolis* (London, 1990)

Private tombs
N. de G. Davies: *The Tomb of Huy, Viceroy of Nubia in the Reign of Tutankhamun* (London, 1926)
J. Romer: *Tomb Builders of the Pharaohs* (London, 1981)
L. Manniche: *Lost Tombs* (Warminster, 1986)
G. T. Martin: *The Memphite Tomb of Horemheb* (London, 1988)

LATE PERIOD
P. Montet: *Le Nécropole royale de Tanis*, 3 vols (Paris, 1947–60)
D. Eigner: *Grabbauten der Spätzeit* (Vienna, 1985)

PTOLEMAIC AND ROMAN PERIODS
B. P. Grenfell and A. S. Hunt: *Fayum towns and their Papyri* (Oxford, 1900)
C. Parlasca: *Mumienportraits und verwandte Denkmaler* (Wiesbaden, 1966)
R. V. McCleary: *Portals to Eternity* (exh. cat., Ann Arbor, U. MI, Kelsey Mus., 1987)

(iii) Sacred animal necropoleis. The mummified remains of sacred animals associated with the cults of particular Egyptian deities were interred in special burial places. The animals were not themselves objects of worship, but derived sanctity from association with a divinity. Most such cemeteries date from the Late Period (*c.* 750–332 BC) onwards, when animal cults grew in popularity. They are found at major religious centres throughout Egypt.

Egyptian religion encompassed two types of animal cult: those where a single beast at a time was the god's incarnation and those where all members of the species connected with the god were considered worthy of reverence and proper burial. The best example of the first type is the Apis bull of MEMPHIS, identified by a set of distinctive markings as the sole representative of Ptah; the second type is exemplified by the ibises and baboons sacred to Thoth, which were kept in large numbers at his cult centres of HERMOPOLIS MAGNA and SAQQARA. In death, these beasts shared the divinity of Osiris, and pilgrims could pay to deposit a mummified animal in the cemeteries as a votive offering to the god. The production of animal mummies was an important temple industry and source of revenue; at Saqqara alone, there may have been as many as 10,000 ibis burials annually.

The best preserved and most extensive animal necropoleis are at north Saqqara. Apart from the tombs of the Apis bulls and their mothers, there are burials of hawks, baboons, ibises, falcons, cats and jackals. The earliest surviving burials of Apis bulls, dating from the 19th Dynasty (*c.* 1292–*c.* 1190 BC), were in individual, free-standing structures similar to contemporary private tomb chapels. From the reign of Psammetichus I (*reg* 664–610 BC), the bulls were interred in underground galleries in the Serapeum, a practice that continued until the end of the Ptolemaic period. The bulls were buried in massive black granite sarcophagi placed in individual burial chambers linked by a passage extending for nearly 200 m beneath the surface of the Memphis plateau. The sarcophagus emplacements were sunk below the gallery so that the lids of the sarcophagi are at floor level. The galleries themselves were cased with polished limestone, now largely missing, and adorned with stelae detailing the dates of the bulls' births, their installations in the Temple of Ptah and their deaths. Private individuals also sometimes left votive stelae when the galleries were opened for a burial (see fig. 31). The mothers of the Apis bulls were buried in their own sepulchres in a rock-hewn gallery of similar design north of the Serapeum.

Above the gallery of these sacred cows there was a temple built by Nectanebo I (*reg* 380–362 BC), with two underground galleries containing the burials of over 400 baboons and hundreds of thousands of falcons. The baboons were placed in wooden boxes set into niches cut into the walls of the main passage. The falcon necropolis comprises a central gallery (*c.* 3.0×2.5 m) that winds through the rock for over 600 m. Side galleries were stacked with pottery jars containing mummified falcons; as each chamber was filled, it was closed off from the main corridor. The burial of mummified jackals and cats took place in similar subterranean passages near the temples of Anubis and Bastet.

Elsewhere in Egypt, animal necropoleis were of similar catacomb design, with the individual burials placed in wall niches, for example at Tuna el-Gebel (the necropolis of Hermopolis Magna) and at Dendara, where the subterranean passages were lined with mud-brick. At Abydos, mummified ibises were found in large pots buried in the ground with no surrounding substructure. Cat burials at BUBASTIS, however, were above ground in vaulted mud-brick tombs. The Mnevis bulls of Heliopolis and the

31. Sarcophagus of an Apis bull in the burial vaults of the Serapeum at Saqqara

Buchis bulls of ARMANT were buried differently from the Apis bulls. The Mnevis tombs, dating from the late Ramesside period (*c.* 1140 BC), were limestone chambers sunk into the ground and covered by horizontal stone roofing slabs. Some of the Buchis bulls were buried in individual vaulted sepulchres, while others were buried in the BUCHEUM in hypogea linked by axial chambers, as at Saqqara. Occasionally, humans were also buried in animal cemeteries, such as Prince Khaemwese, a son of Ramesses II (*reg c.* 1279–*c.* 1213 BC), whose tomb in the Serapeum was discovered by Auguste Mariette; and Ankhhor, the high priest of Thoth at Hermopolis, whose sarcophagus was guarded by gilded ibis statuettes.

BIBLIOGRAPHY

A. Mariette: *Le Serapeum de Memphis* (Paris, 1857)
J. D. Ray: *The Archive of Hor* (London, 1976)
G. T. Martin: *The Sacred Animal Necropolis at Saqqara: the Southern Dependencies of the Main Temple Complex* (London, 1981)
A. J. Spencer: *Death in Ancient Egypt* (London, 1983)
S. Gabra: *From Tasa to Touna* (Cairo, 1984)
D. J. Thompson: *Memphis under the Ptolemies* (Princeton, 1988)

DOMINIC MONTSERRAT

3. MILITARY. Due to its geographical position, Egypt was difficult for foreign forces to attack. The Nile Valley, protected on the west and east by deserts, was inaccessible to invading armies except through Sinai or the southern frontier, boundaries that were protected by strings of fortresses from the Middle Kingdom (*c.* 2008–*c.* 1630 BC) onwards. Consequently Egyptian towns of the Middle and

New kingdoms had little need of fortification. This contrasted with conditions in the Predynastic and Early Dynastic periods (*c*. 6000–*c*. 2575 BC) and the First Intermediate Period (*c*. 2150–*c*. 2008 BC), when internal upheavals made fortifications necessary. Many of the towns that were planned and built at one time (as opposed to those that grew 'organically' over a longer period) were built with large enclosure walls. A notable exception is el-Amarna, where there are no indications of city walls. Protection was required, however, against the flood waters of the inundation, which could be devastating. The major surviving protective building works are the enclosures of the great temples (*see* §2(i) above), which during the New Kingdom (*c*. 1540–*c*. 1075 BC) were constructed of pan-bedded mud-brick, a technique in which large sections of concave and convex walling were juxtaposed, though not bonded, enabling the wall to rise and settle without harm during flooding.

(i) Predynastic and Early Dynastic (*c*. 6000–*c*. 2575 BC). (ii) Old Kingdom and First Intermediate Period (*c*. 2575–*c*. 2008 BC). (iii) Middle Kingdom (*c*. 2008–*c*. 1630 BC). (iv) New Kingdom (*c*. 1540–*c*. 1075 BC). (v) Later periods (*c*. 1075 BC–AD 395).

*(i) Predynastic and Early Dynastic (*c. 6000–*c*. 2575 BC).* Hieroglyphic writing has a number of different signs for walled enclosures and town sites. The ideogram for 'town' (*niwt*) shows a circular enclosure with a simplified street plan. Such round enclosure walls have been found at HIERAKONPOLIS and at EL-KAB, although neither site has been completely surveyed. A hieroglyph in the form of a rectangular enclosure (*hwt*) designates religious and royal precincts and is represented from the earlier period by the Shunet el-Zebib at ABYDOS and by the enclosure wall of the Step Pyramid of Djoser at Saqqara (*see* SAQQARA, §1).

Slate palettes of the Predynastic period show square enclosures with rounded corners and bastions at regular intervals, or round enclosures with triangular salients. Alexander Badawy has attempted to reconstruct the appearance of these enclosures and tried, on the basis of the buildings shown inside, to indicate their size. The palettes also show the demolition of fortresses by the heraldic signs of conquering kings, as in the NARMER Palette, where a semicircular, walled enclosure with square bastions is battered by the royal bull.

Fortified remains from the reign of Khasekhemwy (*reg c*. 2700 BC) survive at Hierakonpolis and Abydos. At Abydos, the Middle Fort at Shunet el-Zebib is a rectangular enclosure orientated to the cardinal points and closely surrounded by an outer wall that is thinner and lower. The main entrance to such structures was either from a corner gatehouse set between two projecting towers (as at Hierakonpolis) or along a winding approach. At Hierakonpolis, a circular stone wall that probably protected the temple area stood within the town wall, which may itself have originally been circular. The later Early Dynastic walls (probably 3rd Dynasty; *c*. 2600 BC) were rectangular; the presence of Old Kingdom houses within this enclosure suggests that the town itself had been given space to develop. The town of el-Kab was enclosed by a slightly irregular mud-brick circular wall measuring 390 m north–south and 400 m east–west. The walls were, unusually, double, the outer one measuring 2.74 m thick, and the

inner 2.44 m; the two were separated by a space of nearly 5 m. This wall was clearly defensive, the inner section rising higher than the outer in places. The area enclosed would have been *c*. 10 ha, incorporating clearly differentiated religious, palace, town and workshop areas.

*(ii) Old Kingdom and First Intermediate Period (*c. 2575–*c. 2008 BC).* Elephantine, located at the 1st Nile cataract, was an important harbour and the major southern defence during the Old Kingdom. Although naturally defended by its island location, the relatively small (*c*. 1.6 ha) Old Kingdom town site was enclosed by a wavy wall with an elliptical plan measuring *c*. 170×100 m, and containing differentiated areas.

The political situation during the First Intermediate Period doubtless resulted in the construction of fortifications around towns that had previously been open. Khety III of Herakleopolis advised his son to build fortresses as well as towns in Lower Egypt, and the paintings in the tombs of BENI HASAN show attacks on fortified structures in Middle Egypt. The forts or towns in these paintings have vertical walls with a battered base set at an angle of *c*. 55–60°. Badawy estimated their size from the scale of soldiers shown attacking, but, judging from some of the major Syrian fortifications depicted in New Kingdom battle scenes, this is not a reliable method.

*(iii) Middle Kingdom (*c. 2008–*c. 1630 BC).* During the Middle Kingdom, the Egyptian rulers expanded their control into Nubia as far as the 2nd Nile cataract, which they established as their frontier and protected with a string of fortresses. Sesostris I (*reg c*. 1918–*c*. 1875 BC) and Sesostris III (*reg c*. 1837–*c*. 1818 BC) were the principal builders of the Cataract forts, which (until they were submerged by Lake Nasser in the 1960s) provided the major monuments for the study of Egyptian military architecture. Under Sesostris II (*reg c*. 1844–*c*. 1837 BC) the road between the landing places at the head and foot of the 1st Nile cataract was flanked by walls and attempts were made to clear channels through the cataract. The 'Walls of the Prince', mentioned in the story of Sinuhe, which is set at the time of the death of Ammenemes I (*reg c*. 1938–*c*. 1908 BC), and ascribed to the same king's reign in the writings of Neferti, must have comprised a chain of towers and strongholds forming Egypt's eastern border defence on the coastal road to Syria–Palestine. A Middle Kingdom fortress in the Wadi el-Natrun to the west of the Delta is also possibly contemporary with Ammenemes I's reign.

A papyrus discovered in the Ramesseum at Thebes lists 17 fortresses in Nubia, all of which had names indicative of their function: 'Repelling the desert dwellers' (Uronarti), 'Khakaure (Sesostris III) is powerful' (Semna). The largest and most important of the Nubian fortresses were those on the west bank of the river. These were usually rectangular in plan (e.g. Buhen and Semna; see figs 32a and 32c; and Mirgissa). Smaller fortresses were built at significant points in the cataract, on islands, as at Uronarti and Askut, or on the rocky bank, as at Shalfak. The smaller fortresses usually conformed roughly to the shapes of the islands' highest parts, with long spur walls protecting the remainder. Other fortresses were built in Nubia as staging posts,

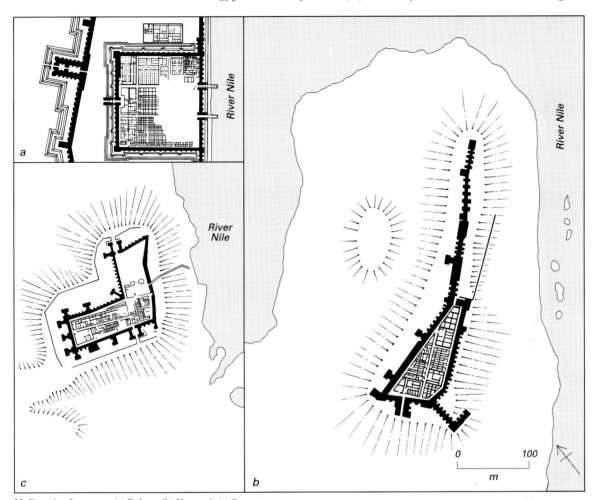

32. Egyptian fortresses: (a) Buhen; (b) Uronarti; (c) Semna

such as Aniba, and to protect the entrance to the gold-mining region of the Wadi el-Allaqi (Quban). Larger fortresses were surrounded on the landward side by a second, lower, wall and a berm beyond a ditch which was occasionally flooded with water, as at Buhen. The approach from the Nile was flanked by massive flange walls, and the entrance was protected by a single-leafed door. Water was brought in through roofed staircases; in island fortresses, such as Uronarti and Askut, these were located opposite the main gateway. Equidistant buttresses were set along the walls, with bastions and towers at the corners. In some fortresses, a second girdle wall enclosed the 'outer fort', with workshops and habitations for Nubian workers located between the two circuit walls. The bases of the high fortress walls usually have the pronounced batter (as at Uronarti; see fig. 33) seen in the paintings at Beni Hasan. There are arrow-slots—particularly elaborate at Buhen—and crenellations are indicated by remains at Buhen, depictions at Beni Hasan and elsewhere.

Internally the layout comprised a main street on the longitudinal axis crossed at right angles by side streets. These were connected to the 'wall street' or *pomoerium* (a Roman term for a road that allows rapid movement of troops around the walls), like that at Medinet Habu (*see* §(iv) below). The commander's mansion near the main gateway was usually two-storey with an outside staircase to the girdle wall. The rooms had painted plaster decoration, and wooden octagonal columns, usually painted red. Larger storage areas (at Askut), barracks (at Semna) or administrative quarters (at Uronarti) occupied the remainder of the area, depending on the significance of the fort.

The twin fortresses of Semna, on the west bank of the Nile, and Kumma, on the east bank, controlled the river at the narrowest part of the 2nd Nile cataract, where the river flows through a rocky channel. They were probably started by Sesostris I but was completed by Sesostris III. Built on an L-shaped rocky eminence on the edge of the river, Semna (see fig. 32c) was surrounded by a wide dry ditch on the north, west and south sides. The enclosure walls of brick on masonry foundations were 6–8 m thick, with massive projecting towers set at intervals. Two strongly fortified gates on the northern and southern sides were connected by a road through the town, which was laid out on the usual grid pattern. The fortress had a small outpost, Semna South, 1 km to the south, which may have been occupied only in times of emergency or perhaps by

33. Uronarti fortress, south-east wing, c. 2008–c. 1630 BC

occasional patrols. It was surrounded by a stone glacis 10 m wide, an outer girdle wall of sun-dried mud-brick 4 m wide, and an inner ditch 7.5 m wide. The main wall, 12 m thick at the base, was built on an artificial terrace cut into the alluvium, and had square bastions to protect the end of each wall. The inner space measured 34×33 m and had no permanent structures. Massive spur walls may have been built in the cataract to make the channels deeper in order to ease the passage of vessels and to ensure that all traffic went through the single, narrow channel between the forts of Semna and Kumma. Considerably smaller than Semna, Kumma fort was roughly rectangular in plan and had brick walls more than 6 m thick built on masonry foundations. Access was by a land entrance on the north-eastern side and by a river gate with a covered way on the north-west.

The small island fortress of Uronarti (see figs 32b and 33) was within signalling distance of Semna and Kumma. It was completed by Sesostris III, although, like Semna, it was possibly begun by Sesostris I. Following the topography of the island, the fortress was triangular in plan, with a spur wall of 230 m running to the northernmost point of the island. Bastions along the northern side of the spur wall, and along the northern side of the fortress proper, indicate that it was from this side, where the ground is flatter, that assault was most feared. A second spur wall, with defensive towers on either side, projected from the southern corner of the fortress. The main gate, in the middle of the west wall, had a projecting, towered gatehouse, and a second gate, in the short, eastern wall, led to a stairway and watergate outside the fortress. A single road bisected the town. This plan remained largely unaltered through the New Kingdom (c. 1540–c. 1075 BC). A large building (possibly a residence) and a temple were built outside the walls. Shalfak, on the west bank of the river, was similar in design to Uronarti. The town site was regularly planned within the towered walls and was entered on the west side through a gateway similar to that at Uronarti. A long spur wall extended to the north-east, with towers on the desert side (see MILITARY ARCHITECTURE AND FORTIFICATION, fig. 4). Mirgissa, also on the

west bank, probably formed a unit with the small island fortress of Dabnarti. Mirgissa was similar in size and design to Buhen.

Buhen, now flooded by Lake Nasser, was the most impressive of the fortresses at the foot of the 2nd Nile cataract. Its importance is clear, for from this point the river was navigable as far as Aswan. Buhen was therefore the major depot, a position it retained in the New Kingdom when many of the cataract fortresses had lost their defensive significance. A settlement had been established at Buhen in the Old Kingdom (4th Dynasty, c. 2500 BC), but there was no fortress until the reign of Sesostris I. The outer fortifications consisted of two enclosure walls; the first, intended for the defence of the site while the inner fort was built, enclosed an area of c. 6 ha. The walls were 4 m thick and had 32 open, rounded bastions set at 22 m intervals; each bastion projected 6.5 m from the outer face of the wall. The bastions were constructed of rubble with brick facing; preserved sockets indicated that they had been fitted with doors on the enclosure side. The main entrance to the whole enclosure was through a gateway in the north-western wall, at the site of the later barbican. This enclosure wall was later elaborated into the outer defence of the whole site by the addition of a wall on the river frontage which connected with two spur walls running from the fortress (see below). The second wall, averaging 5–5.5 m in thickness, had projecting square towers along its outer face, at intervals of 2.75 m. The western wall had five large projecting towers with the barbican gate at the centre, facing the desert. All the towers and the wall had a battered base c. 1.15 m high, and the area between the base of the wall and the berm (dry ditch) was paved in brick. The berm, measuring 6 m wide×3 m deep, followed the lines of the enclosure wall, with salients at intervals where the towers, gates and barbican projected. There was a brick wall on the edge of the counterscarp, from which a glacis descended to ground level. On the western side the ditch was cut into the higher ground of the escarpment; elsewhere it was dug out of the sand and gravel, the scarp and counterscarp being revetted with walls of brick and roughly cut stone. The battered sides of the ditch were faced with thick mud and white-painted gypsum plaster. A drain to the Nile had an outlet near the riverside gate at the northern end of the enclosure.

The barbican, the main entrance from the desert, comprised a massive brick tower 47 m high×30 m wide, with projecting square bastions and a battered base. The approach was over a rock-cut causeway in the centre of the rectangular salient formed by the dry ditch. From a gate in the low defence wall on the edge of the scarp, the road passed through the barbican into the first baffle, an open square flanked by projecting bastions. Brick walls intended to crowd any troops that might breach the entrance preceded the second gate leading into the second baffle, a larger courtyard flanked by four square bastions; a third gateway ran under the walls of the perimeter enclosure.

There were two further gates in the outer perimeter wall, both apparently additions of the later Middle Kingdom. The gates in the salients of the northern and southern walls seem to have been similar in design, although neither was well preserved when excavated. Each gate consisted of a rectangular brick tower on a stone foundation, with a central passage; access may have been via a drawbridge. The riverside gate, also a solid brick tower on a stone foundation, stood at the northern end of the ditch and led directly to the road that ran along the Nile at the foot of the fortress wall.

The inner fort (see fig. 32a) similarly comprised enclosure walls with an outer ditch. The main walls, probably crenellated, were 5 m thick and originally over 11 m high; they enclosed an area of 150×138 m. Bastions or towers set at 5 m intervals and large projecting corner towers were probably higher than the wall. On the river side, two spur walls, each ending in a tower, extended the river frontage to the north-east and to the south-west; at a later date the perimeter wall was extended along the river frontage to connect with these towers. Access to the top of the walls appears to have been by a single staircase in the north-east corner of the enclosure. Built of solid brickwork, and measuring only 1 m wide, this stairway would have permitted only single-file troop movement, but could have been defended easily.

The lower ramparts ran around the three landward sides of the fort within the perimeter wall. Like the outer fortifications, they comprised a brick-paved berm with a fire-step and loop-holed parapets overhanging the scarp of the ditch. Bastions projected into the ditch from the scarp. The defences were elaborate, comprising a system of triple loop-holes, each with a single embrasure. The embrasures were arranged in two rows, the lower row flush with the floor; each bastion had two rows of six embrasures, allowing ten to twelve archers, firing simultaneously, to deliver devastating crossfire. A brick platform two courses high was built at one entrance corner of each of the bastions, perhaps as a deliberate obstacle to prevent anyone turning sharply into the bastions and upsetting the aim of the archers. As in the outer fortifications the dry ditch was cut into the rock of the escarpment on the west side; elsewhere it was excavated and revetted with walls of brick and stone. Measuring 7.3 m wide×3.1 m deep, it was faced with gypsum plaster painted white to show up troops invading at night. The main entrance from the outer enclosure into the fortress was through the west gate (see reconstruction, fig. 34), which had massive double doors of wood and a wooden drawbridge on rollers. If the fort were stormed, access to the lower ramparts would have been easily achieved. The riverside defences, all stone-built, reveal that there was little fear of attack from the river: two quays, 42 m apart, led from the two main streets, which had towered gateways in the fortress wall. These quays had vertical sides for close mooring and extended into the river for at least 21 m. Only the watergate beneath the northern riverside gate was preserved, but there may also have been a second gate on the south. A stairway led from inside the fort to a passage which ran under the corridor of the gate and through the quay. The location of the river entrance has been lost, but it may have been a staircase, or simply a slope, leading down to the water.

The town of Buhen was laid out in rectangular blocks on three terraces sloping toward the river. A small square lay immediately inside the west gate, with the *pomoerium* running north–south. A baffle wall, formed by block 'B', prevented direct penetration of the town by invaders. The

34. Buhen, west gate, *c.* 2008–*c.* 1630 BC; reconstruction drawing

two main streets ran eastward to the riverside gates and were stone-flagged, with stone drains that emptied into the river; there was also a grid of subsidiary streets. Military quarters and a temple occupied the northern sector of the fort.

Aniba, similar in design and size to Buhen, probably dates to the reign of Sesostris I. In the New Kingdom it became one of the chief administrative cities of Nubia and was considerably extended. At the end of the New Kingdom Aniba was abandoned and a fortress established on the opposite bank of the river, on the hill of Qasr Ibrim. Quban was the most important town of Lower Nubia. The walls stood to a height of over 8 m before the raising of the High Dam at Aswan. The fort's significance lay in its key position, controlling access to the Wadi el-Allaqi where the most important gold mines were situated, acting both as a defence and as a depot.

(iv) New Kingdom (c. 1540–c. 1075 BC). Changes in military technology (such as the introduction of chariotry), which took place at the beginning of the New Kingdom necessitated alterations in fortress design. At Buhen, the outer fortifications seem to have been maintained unaltered, but the inner fortifications were reconstructed by the addition of exterior skin walls measuring 1.2 m thick on the landward sides. The river side remained unaltered except for the addition of a new, large temple built by Hatshepsut (*reg c.* 1479–*c.* 1458 BC). The west gate was halved in size by the removal of the first entrance and baffle court. Egyptian military expansion in Upper Nubia led to the building of new fortresses and a number of large

towns, such as Amara West and Sesebi, with massive enclosure walls, perhaps intended to protect them from the sandstorms prevalent in the region.

Although Medinet Habu, the mortuary temple of Ramesses III on the west bank of the Nile at Luxor (*see* THEBES (i), §VII), was essentially a religious complex, it incorporates several elements of military architecture, including a massive brick enclosure wall *c.* 16 m high and 10.5 m thick at the base, with an outer rampart and a wall with a ditch. High gate towers on the east and west resemble the Syrian fortifications shown in battle reliefs and known as *migdol*. The eastern gate contains suites of rooms commonly called the 'harem' from the decoration showing the king with the royal women. Within the outer enclosure wall was a town, built along two streets inside a low girdle wall, the girdle wall forming the back walls of the houses of the outer street. Between the two walls, a raised walkway allowed troops speedy access to the walls. The house entrances in both streets were on the inside. The defensive fortifications of Medinet Habu are unusual for the Theban region, where the enclosure walls of temples were normally more symbolic than practical, and may reflect the disturbances that occurred during the 20th Dynasty (*c.* 1190–*c.* 1075 BC), when increasing numbers of Libyans moved into Egypt; towards the end of the dynasty the workers of the village of Deir el-Medina abandoned their homes for the safety of Medinet Habu. The town remained important until the 8th century AD.

Although the Nubian fortresses are the best preserved and excavated, there were also chains of forts on the other borders of Egypt. Ramesses II (*reg c.* 1279–*c.* 1213 BC) established a series of small forts stretching westwards along the Mediterranean coast. Its defensive line is not yet well known (see Habachi) but certainly consisted of small garrisons spaced one day's march apart. Fragmentary remains indicate that a New Kingdom military post existed at el-Alamein, but of the others in the line only the location of the westernmost is known, at Zawyet Umm el-Rakham, *c.* 25 km west of Mersa Matruh. The area of the fort so far delimited indicates a rectangular structure *c.* 80 m wide× 100 m long. A large gate in the south-eastern corner probably led into an open space, from which a second gate led at right-angles into the inner part of the fort. The temple abuts the north wall. Some stelae dedicated by military officials indicate the role of the fortress in the protection of the region against invasion from Libya. The line of fortresses may have continued 50 km east from el-Alamein to el-Gharbaniyat, Karm Abu Girg and thence along the fringes of the Delta as far as Memphis. Whether it also continued along the coast to Rhakotis (the site of the later city of Alexandria) is, as yet, uncertain.

The eastern border of the Delta and the military road into southern Palestine were protected by fortresses at Sile (Tell Abu Sefa), Pelusium (Tell el-Farama) and Migdol (Tell el-Heir). The border at Sile is depicted in a relief of Sethos I (*reg c.* 1290–*c.* 1279 BC) at Karnak (see fig. 35), along with a number of wells and small fortifications, and the major Syro-Palestinian cities against which the Egyptians campaigned. The border was marked by a canal called 'the dividing canal'—shown bordered with reeds and filled with crocodiles. The fortress has structures on both banks, connected by a bridge; on the Egyptian side

35. Fortifications along the banks of 'the dividing canal' at Sile; from a relief of Sethos I (*reg c.* 1290–*c.* 1279 BC), Karnak temple (Chicago, IL, University of Chicago)

a court is surrounded by buildings and an enclosure wall with two gates—the main gate to the land and an inner gate to the bridge. The Wadi Tumilat, running from the Delta to the region of the Bitter Lakes, also had fortified towns. At Tell el-Rataba a large irregular brick wall 3.12 m thick delimited the first enclosure, with four bastions of 1.27 m each and a gate on the west; William Flinders Petrie thought that this enclosure was of Hyksos date (*c.* 1630–*c.* 1532 BC). Ramesses III built new, larger, walls 9.5 m thick, following a more regular plan.

(v) Later periods (c. 1075 BC–AD 395). There are some indications that the Egyptians built or renewed fortresses to defend the 2nd Nile cataract region during the 26th Dynasty (664–525 BC). This would have followed the invasion of Nubia by Psammetichus II (*reg* 595–589 BC) in 593 BC and its function would have been as a defence against the Kushite kingdom of NAPATA-MEROË. The fortress at QASR IBRIM was established sometime during the 9th or 8th century BC and became one of the major fortresses of the Greco-Roman period. During the 26th Dynasty a number of fortresses were also constructed in the Delta and on the eastern border, all roughly similar in layout and construction. Site 'T.21' at Tell el-Heir (see Oren) covers an area of 4 ha and is enclosed by walls 15–20 m wide and 200 m long on each side. Three of the walls were built with small compartments, each of 3 m sq., set at fixed intervals inside, and with massive buttresses of similar construction. The fourth wall, 20 m wide, had

rectangular compartments and corridors. There were no connecting doors nor any indication that the chambers had been used for storage or dwelling. The contemporary fortress at TELL EL-MASKHUTA in the Wadi Tumilat, 50 km south-west of Tell el-Heir, measuring 200 m sq. and with walls 15 m thick, was of similar construction, as was the fortified palace of Apries (reg 589–570 BC) at Memphis. A fortress may have existed at the Greek trading town of NAUKRATIS in the western Delta, although Petrie identified the massive brick structure there as religious in nature. Daphnae (Tell Dafana), in the eastern Delta, also had a fortress, which had compartmented walls measuring 450×200 m and 17 m thick.

During the Ptolemaic period, a defensive wall was built between el-Riqqa in the Nile Valley and Bubastos in the Faiyum (see Rowe). The wall is about 7.5 km long, with a short spur (at least 0.5 km long) running north-east at el-Riqqa. It averages 1.88 m in width and has rounded buttresses 3.90 m wide and projecting 3.00 m on the northern side, with a corresponding stair on the southern side. As the wall has not been excavated, its original height is unknown, and it is not clear whether it had a ditch on the northern side. The wall is thought to have protected a caravan route, running from el-Riqqa to Bubastos and then north (apparently undefended) for a further kilometre to Philadelphia (Kom el-Hamman). All the pottery sherds identified in the area are Ptolemaic.

The Romans established a number of fortresses conforming to Roman military practice in Egypt. At Babylon (Old Cairo) they rebuilt a fort probably originally dating to the Persian period (27th Dynasty, 525–404 BC). Qasr ibrim in Nubia was important in the early Roman period as a defence against the kingdom of Meroë and remained a major centre into the Christian period. The fortress at Dionysias (Qasr Qarun) at the western end of the Faiyum was built by Diocletian (reg AD 284–305) as a defence against the attacks of the Blemmyes, a Nubian people who were a major threat to Egyptian towns in the 3rd and 4th centuries AD.

BIBLIOGRAPHY
W. M. F. Petrie: *Hyksos and Israelite Cities* (London, 1906)
A. M. Blackman: 'Preliminary Report on the Excavations at Sesebi, Northern Province, Anglo-Egyptian Sudan, 1936–7', *J. Egyp. Archaeol.*, xxiii (1937), pp. 145–50
G. Steindorff: *Aniba*, ii (Glückstadt, 1937)
H. W. Fairman: 'Preliminary Report on the Excavations at Sesebi (Sudla) and Amarah West, Anglo-Egyptian Sudan', *J. Egyp. Archaeol.*, xxiv (1938), pp. 151–6; xxv (1939), pp. 139–44; xxxiv (1948), pp. 3–11
W. M. F. Petrie: *Ceremonial Slate Palettes* (London, 1953)
A. Rowe: 'A Contribution to the Archaeology of the Western Desert: III', *Bull. John Rylands Lib.*, xxxviii (1955), pp. 139–65
D. Dunham and J. M. A. Janssen: *Semna-Kumma*, i of *Second Cataract Forts* (Boston, 1960)
J. Vercoutter: 'Semna South Fort and the Records of Nile Levels at Kumma', *Kush*, xiv (1966), pp. 125–64
A. Badawy: *A History of Egyptian Architecture*, 2 vols (Berkeley, 1968)
W. B. Emery, H. S. Smith and A. Millard: *The Fortress of Buhen: The Archaeological Report* (London, 1979)
L. Habachi: 'The Military Posts of Ramesses II on the Coastal Road and the Western Part of the Delta', *Bull. Inst. Fr. Archéol. Orient.*, lxxx (1980), pp. 13–30
E. D. Oren: 'Migdol: A New Fortress', *Bull. Amer. Sch. Orient. Res.*, ccliii–cclvi (1984), pp. 7–44
The Battle Reliefs of King Sety I, iv of *Reliefs and Inscriptions at Karnak*, Chicago Oriental Institute, The Epigraphic Survey (Chicago, 1986)

R. G. MORKOT

4. DOMESTIC. Despite nearly two centuries of archaeological exploration, relatively little is known of the physical surroundings in which the ancient Egyptians lived. One of the many problems in interpreting ancient Egyptian domestic architecture is that the building materials most often used were highly perishable, in contrast to the stone used for many tombs and temples. Further, only in recent years has the emphasis in Egyptology shifted from the excavation of tomb and temple sites to habitation remains. As a result many gaps exist in the understanding of the development and variety of secular architecture in ancient Egypt. As new information is constantly being amassed, current knowledge, derived chiefly from pictorial representations and early excavations, will undoubtedly be subject to extensive revision.

(i) Predynastic (c. 6000–c. 2925 BC). (ii) Early Dynastic (c. 2925–c. 2575 BC). (iii) Old Kingdom (c. 2575–c. 2150 BC). (iv) First Intermediate Period and Middle Kingdom (c. 2150–c. 1630 BC). (v) Second Intermediate Period and New Kingdom (c. 1630–c. 1075 BC). (vi) Later periods (c. 1075 BC–AD 395).

(i) Predynastic (c. 6000–c. 2925 BC). The earliest dwellings found in the Nile Valley were circular structures, probably constructed of reeds. The floors of these 'hut circles' were sunk below ground level and varied between 1 and 2 m in diameter. Such structures have been excavated at Matmar and el-Hammamiya in Middle Egypt and are dated to the Badarian phase (c. 6000–c. 4000 BC). In Lower Egypt, similar houses with oval foundations ranging between 3 and 4 m in length have been found at contemporary sites in the Faiyum depression, at Merimda and at el-Omari. Many of the Merimda structures were also semi-subterranean, with access by means of steps. Some had interior posts to support the roof while others, less well-preserved, were represented only by a series of post-holes. Granaries of basketwork covered with mud and buried in the ground were also found within the settlement.

During the latter part of the Predynastic period there was a change from these simple, flimsy structures—which may have been seasonal habitations—to more substantial constructions. A clay model (London, BM; see fig. 36) from a grave at el-Amra depicts one such structure. It is

36. Clay model of a house, from el-Amra, Predynastic period, c. 6000–c. 2925 BC (London, British Museum)

37. Giza, plan of the Mycerinus valley temple settlement, Old Kingdom, *c. 2575–c. 2150 BC*; from a drawing by Yvonne Markowitz

rectangular in plan with slightly battered walls and peaked corners in imitation of wattle and daub construction. A doorway is indicated by a rectangular opening surmounted by a lintel and a rolled-up mat which would have functioned as a door; clerestory windows are represented on the end walls. This model is a remarkably faithful replica of the type of wattle and daub vernacular architecture still found in rural Egypt. Traces of such rectangular structures have been found in Naqada II phase (*c. 3500–c. 2925 BC*) settlements at Maadi, Mahasna, Quft and HIERAKONPOLIS. The dwelling excavated at Hierakonpolis also seems to have had a floor below ground level. Little is known of urban design at this early period, but the evidence at Hierakonpolis suggests some rudimentary community organization, with temple and ceremonial structures in the centre of the town and industrial areas on the outskirts.

(ii) Early Dynastic (c. 2925–c. 2575 BC). With the unification of Egypt, established settlement patterns underwent a major shift. A national capital was founded at MEMPHIS, while at Hierakonpolis a vast temple–palace complex became the focus of a new settlement located in the Nile flood-plain. Contact with Mesopotamian civilization had a profound effect on all aspects of pharaonic culture at this formative stage: elaborate mud-brick construction, following the Mesopotamian niched-brick technique, was used for a gateway at Hierakonpolis and appears in representations of temples and palaces on seals and tags. Niched 'palace façade' masonry also appears on many royal and private funerary monuments of the period.

Although few houses of this early period have been found, one of the structures of the Step Pyramid complex at SAQQARA has been tentatively identified as a dummy palace for the king's use in the afterlife. This long, narrow building, known as Temple T, comprises a rectangular,

columned entrance hall, a 'throne room' and a series of smaller rooms to the west. Among the private tombs at Saqqara, one included a latrine and other domestic features in its design, and another had a series of model outbuildings adjacent to it.

(iii) Old Kingdom (c. 2575–c. 2150 BC). Among the better recorded settlements of the Old Kingdom are the 'pyramid towns' associated with some of the pyramid complexes of the 4th and 5th dynasties, such as those of Sneferu (*reg c. 2575–c. 2551 BC*) at DAHSHUR and Queen Khentkawes at Giza. Such settlements were originally built to house the priests and personnel responsible for maintaining the royal mortuary cults but were often rebuilt many times, in many cases encroaching on their founders' monuments. In one such settlement near the valley temple of Mycerinus at Giza (*see* GIZA, §1) the houses were small, rectangular mud-brick structures of one to three rooms each, with associated round grain silos. Although the original plan has been obscured by the multiple periods of rebuilding, the southern wall of the temple and the rectangle of the city enclosure can be traced for *c. 70 m* (see fig. 37).

Clearer evidence exists at ABYDOS, where small, thick-walled buildings with barrel-vaulted roofs were excavated, and walled towns of the period have been excavated at Douch in el-Dakhla Oasis and at Elephantine (*see* ASWAN). The Old Kingdom town at Elephantine originally covered an area of *c. 1.8 ha*, with the town wall along the southern edge, and appears to have been divided into several sectors: a temple at the northern perimeter, a residential zone and an area dedicated to ceramic production.

(iv) First Intermediate Period and Middle Kingdom (c. 2150–c. 1630 BC). Evidence for the appearance of houses in these periods comes from several sources. Ceramic representations of private dwellings were often placed above graves as offering basins. These models, misnamed 'soul-houses', vary in style from simple trays to detailed reproductions of domestic structures. The most elaborate examples show two-storey houses with palm columns and stairways leading to upper floors. Their roofs are surmounted by ventilators and each structure is surrounded by an enclosure wall. More sophisticated wooden models were found in the tomb of Meketre at Thebes (TT 280; see fig. 38). Each model represents an enclosed garden court preceding a house with elaborate doors and windows and a portico supported by two rows of papyrus bud columns. Other models from the same tomb replicate kitchens, granaries, butchers' shops and cattle pens, all presumably part of an upper-class Egyptian estate.

There is also more evidence of the urban planning of this period. For example, a large, planned settlement was associated with the pyramid complex of Sesostris II (*reg c. 1844–c. 1837 BC*) at EL-LAHUN. The town was constructed along an orthogonal plan, subdivided into a number of zones with uniformly planned, contiguous dwellings. The mud-brick house units varied in size from less than 10 m sq. to as large as 40×60 m for the most elaborate mansions, some of which may have had two storeys. The latter had complex floorplans featuring suites of small rooms, magazines and larger, columned rooms, surrounding interior peristyle courts. Entrance from the street was through a series of vestibules and long hallways. A much smaller planned community was connected with the Middle Kingdom temple at Madamud. As at el-Lahun the houses were built on a long rectangular plan, each measuring *c.* 20 m×7.5 m. Each dwelling was preceded by a court; entrance was via a columned portico, and the interior plan comprised a central, columned room with three smaller rooms grouped around it. Other planned communities were associated with the chain of fortifications built along the Nubian frontier at the 2nd Cataract. These massive mud-brick fortresses, such as that at Buhen, served both as defensive garrisons and as trading outposts and thus housed a complement of soldiers and their families within surrounding walled towns. The forts and towns vary widely in plan according to local topography (*see* §3 above).

(v) Second Intermediate Period and New Kingdom (c. 1630–c. 1075 BC). Although it has been suggested that there was a shift in urban design in the New Kingdom, the little available information for the Second Intermediate Period and early 18th Dynasty shows little change from Middle Kingdom styles of architecture.

The late Second Intermediate Period settlement at Deir el-Ballas consisted of a large royal palace situated in the centre of a wide bay in the limestone cliffs of the west bank of the Nile. Grouped around it to the north and south were a number of private houses, ranging from small, two-room huts to large, elaborate structures surrounded by enclosure walls and outbuildings. A group of small contiguously walled houses reminiscent of the pyramid towns of the Old and Middle kingdoms and an administrative quarter have been tentatively identified. A settlement associated with the pyramid of Ahmose at ABYDOS was even closer in plan to the old pyramid towns. Excavations of a small section of the town revealed a series of contiguous blocks *c.* 27 m square, each block comprising a central core of three or four large rooms surrounded by smaller chambers. Of very different design and tradition was the Hyksos' Delta settlement of AVARIS (modern Tell el-Dab'a), where excavations have revealed an unusual mixture of Egyptian and Syro-Palestinian traditions.

The clearest picture of Egyptian urban planning comes from New Kingdom towns. At the workmen's village of Deir el-Medina (*see* THEBES (i), §XI), the town plan was less regular than that of the Ahmose pyramid town at Abydos, but the artisans' houses were similar in style to the workmen's village at Deir el-Ballas. The early 18th Dynasty core of the village comprised a series of rectangular houses flanking a long central corridor bounded by an enclosure wall, but the settlement was expanded during the Ramesside Period (see fig. 39). The plan of the houses is similar to those at el-Lahun, with a front court, a columned hall and three smaller rooms at the rear of the house; each dwelling measured on average *c.* 5×15 m. As space was at a premium, stairs were built to give access to the roof, where such activities as food preparation and sleeping could take place, and subterranean cellars were excavated to provide extra storage space.

Also situated in western Thebes, but closer to the riverbank, was the palace-city of Amenophis III

38. Model of the garden and portico of a house, painted wood, from the tomb of Meketre, Thebes, 11th Dynasty, *c.* 2000 BC (New York, Metropolitan Museum of Art)

(*reg c.* 1390–*c.* 1353) at Malqata (*see* THEBES (i), §XII). Much of the site remains unexcavated, but the palace and temple appear to have been situated in the centre of the settlement, where the kitchens and workshops for servicing the palace were also located. The residential areas are strung out along the desert edge to the north and south, and they probably extend for several kilometres. The contemporary settlement at Kom Medinet Ghurab in the Faiyum had much the same plan: a central palace and temple zone with residential districts to the north and south, and burial grounds on the periphery of these.

Few ancient Egyptian settlements have been as extensively excavated as the Middle Egyptian site of Tell EL-AMARNA, which has long served as the paradigm of an ancient Egyptian city. Established as a new capital by the 18th Dynasty ruler Akhenaten (*reg c.* 1353–*c.* 1336 BC), the city (then called Akhetaten) occupied a narrow plain between the east bank of the Nile and the limestone cliffs of the desert. Extending for 10 km from north to south, Akhetaten was laid out along three main roads running parallel to the river. Its focal point was the great Temple of the Aten, which together with a series of royal palaces and administrative buildings occupied the centre of the city. To the north and south were wealthy residential suburbs, where lavishly appointed villas were set in walled compounds with their own gardens, kitchens, stables, granaries, servants' quarters and votive chapels (see fig. 40).

Many aspects of el-Amarna are unique, such as the peculiar design of the temples, the lavish decoration of some of the houses and the enormous size of the settlement. Although the 'Amarna villa' should not be regarded as the quintessential example of the ancient

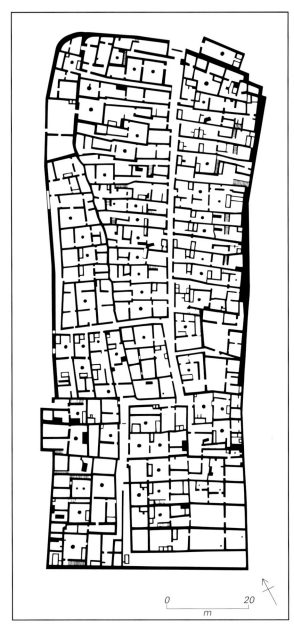

39. Deir el-Medina, plan of the workmen's village, c. 1292–c. 1075 BC

Egyptian home, there is a basic uniformity in the plans of the more elaborate private dwellings. At the centre of the house was a large, square room reached through a rectangular hall and a vestibule. Entrance from the outside was along a non-axial path, from a door at one corner of the compound circuit wall. A variety of storage rooms and private apartments were grouped around the central suite of 'public rooms'. On the other hand, the workmen's village to the east of the central city was similar to those at Deir el-Medina and el-Lahun, and included an associated group of small votive chapels. Tombs for the royal family and administrative officials were built into the cliffs ringing

the city. Cemeteries were also located to the west and north, further out in the desert.

(vi) Later periods (c. 1075 BC–AD 395). Although a number of large settlements from the later periods of Egyptian history have been excavated, particularly in Lower Egypt, few have been adequately published. Many questions remain about the extent to which many of these later sites reflect traditional pharaonic urban design as opposed to Classical town planning. The political instability that continued into the Late Period (c. 750–332 BC) made the security of walled towns essential. Constraints of space within existing city walls led to the adoption of two-storey buildings at such sites as Elephantine and Memphis. Regional building styles evolved, based on the local availability of materials; at Saqqara, for example, roofs were constructed of timber thatched with reeds and mud, while the builders of Elephantine favoured mud-brick barrel vaults. Although brick remained the standard material for domestic building, stone was increasingly employed in royal palaces and wealthy homes, as at the palace of the 26th Dynasty king Apries (*reg* 589–570 BC) at Memphis (*see* PALACE, §I, 2).

Following his conquest of Egypt in 332 BC, Alexander the Great selected the small settlement of Rhakotis on the Mediterranean coast as the site of his future imperial capital. Laid out by the architect Dinokrates, Alexandria was built on the contemporary Hellenistic plan, around a central market and temple area (*see* ALEXANDRIA, §2(i)). The ancient residential areas, along with the remains of the palaces and public buildings, lie beneath the modern city. While wealthy Alexandrians probably lived in opulent villas near the centre, excavations in the Kom el-Dik area of the city have revealed a series of smaller dwellings, of late Roman date, built of local limestone and including two rows of shops with upstairs living quarters.

Older cities, such as the provincial capitals of OXY-RHYNCHUS and HERMOPOLIS MAGNA in Middle Egypt, retained the traditional Egyptian layout. Nonetheless, the new administrators required their treasuries, records offices and council chambers, and along with these came the gymnasia, baths, theatres and hippodromes deemed essential to civilized living. Pressure of population led to the adoption of high-rise building in the cities: at Hermopolis, Roman-style apartment blocks of up to seven storeys have been attested. Wealthier citizens dwelt in large villas such as those excavated at Oxyrhynchus.

In the countryside, mud-brick remained the favoured building material and houses seldom exceeded two storeys. Much current knowledge of rural domestic architecture in the Greco-Roman period is derived from such village sites as Soknopaion Nesos and Karanis in the Faiyum (*see* FAIYUM, §1). Most houses were modest, occupying on average c. 60 sq. m, usually with three rooms. Up to 12 such units were often arranged in apartment blocks. More substantial homes had vaulted underground stores in addition to two or three floors of spacious living accommodation. Walls were plastered and painted, but the use of stone was usually restricted to such features as stair treads. In both rich and poor homes, a large courtyard was the centre of domestic activity, as is indicated by

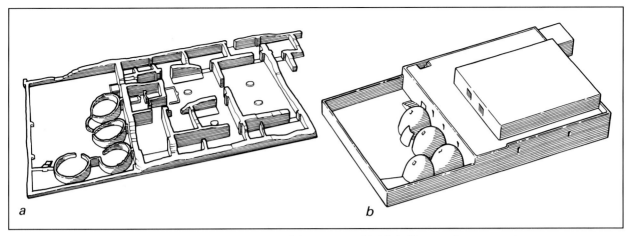

40. El-Amarna, house of the sculptor Thutmose, *c.* 1340 BC: (a) condition as excavated in 1914; (b) perspective reconstruction

numerous finds of millstones, ovens, oil presses, storage jars, animal pens and dovecotes.

BIBLIOGRAPHY

W. M. F. Petrie: *Illahun, Kahun and Gurob* (London, 1889)
R. de P. Tytus: *A Preliminary Report on the Re-excavation of the Palace of Amenhotep III* (New York, 1903)
E. R. Ayrton, T. Currelly and A. E. P. Weigall: *Abydos III* (London, 1904)
N. de G. Davies: 'The Work of the Tytus Memorial Fund', *Bull. Met.*, xv/12, pt 2 (1920), pp. 24–32
G. Brunton and R. Engelbach: *Gurob* (London, 1927)
N. de G. Davies: *The Townhouse in Ancient Egypt* (New York, 1929)
A. E. R. Boak and E. Peterson: *Karanis: Topographical and Architectural Report of Excavations, 1924–8*, U. MI Pubns: Human. Pap., xxv (Ann Arbor, 1931)
A. E. R. Boak: *Socnopaiou Nesos: The University of Michigan Excavation at Dime in 1931–2*, U. MI Pubns: Human. Pap., xxxix (Ann Arbor, 1935)
J. D. S. Pendlebury: *Tell el-Amarna* (London, 1935)
H. Fairman: 'Town Planning in Pharaonic Egypt', *Town Planning Rev.*, xx (1949), pp. 32–51
A. Badawy: *From the Earliest Times to the End of the Old Kingdom* (1954), i of *A History of Egyptian Architecture* (Cairo, Berkeley and Los Angeles, 1954–68)
W. S. Smith and W. K. Simpson: *The Art and Architecture of Ancient Egypt*, Pelican Hist. A. (Harmondsworth, 1958, rev. 2/1981)
G. Roeder: *Hermopolis, 1929–39* (Hildesheim, 1959)
D. Dunham and J. Janssen: *Semna-Kumma*, i of *Second Cataract Forts* (Boston, 1960)
A. Badawy: *The First Intermediate Period, the Middle Kingdom, and the Second Intermediate Period* (1966), ii of *A History of Egyptian Architecture* (Cairo, Berkeley and Los Angeles, 1954–68)
D. Dunham: *Uronarti, Shalafak and Mirgissa*, ii of *Second Cataract Forts* (Boston, 1967)
A. Badawy: *The New Kingdom* (1968), *A History of Egyptian Architecture* (Cairo, Berkeley and Los Angeles, 1954–68)
M. Bietak: 'Vorläufiger Bericht über die erste und zweite Kampagne der österreichischen Ausgrabungen auf Tell ed-Dab'a im Ostdelta Ägyptens', *Mitt. Dt. Archäol. Inst.: Abt. Kairo*, xxiii (1968), pp. 79–114
B. J. Kemp: 'Temple and Town in Ancient Egypt', *Man, Settlement and Urbanism*, P. J. Ucko and others (London, 1972), pp. 657–80
C. Bonnet and D. Valbelle: 'Le Village de Deir el-Medineh: Reprise de l'étude archéologique', *Bull. Inst. Fr. Archéol. Orient.*, lxxv (1975), pp. 429–46
B. J. Kemp: 'The Window of Appearance at el-Amarna and the Basic Structure of this City', *J. Egyp. Archaeol.*, lxii (1976), pp. 81–100
——: 'The City of el-Amarna as a Source for the Study of Urban Archaeology in Ancient Egypt', *World Archaeol.*, ix (1977), pp. 123–39
——: 'The Early Development of Towns in Egypt', *Antiquity*, l (1977), pp. 185–200
M. Bietak: 'Urban Archaeology and the "Town Problem" in Ancient Egypt', *Egyptology and the Social Sciences*, ed. K. R. Weeks (Cairo, 1979), pp. 97–144
L. Borchardt and H. Ricke: *Die Wohnhäuser in Tell el-Amarna* (Berlin, 1980)
B. J. Kemp: 'The Character of the South Suburb at Tell el-'Amarna', *Mitt. Dt. Orient-Ges. Berlin*, cxiii (1981), pp. 81–97
A. J. Spence: *The Topography of the Site* (1983), i of *Excavations at El-Ashmunein* (London, 1983)
M. Rodziewicz: *Les Habitations romaines tartives d'Alexandrie à la lumière des fouilles polonaises à Kôm et Dukka* (1984), iii of *Alexandrie*, ed. K. Muchałowski (Warsaw, 1984)
P. Lacovara: *Deir el-Ballas: Preliminary Report on the Deir el-Ballas Expedition, 1980–1986* (New York, 1990)
D. O'Connor: 'The Royal City of Dynasty 18 and the Urban Process in Egypt', *The Ancient City: An Urban Reader*, ed. R. T. Marchese (in preparation)

PETER LACOVARA, with DELIA PEMBERTON

IX. Sculpture.

Whether miniature or colossal, executed in materials as soft as wood or as hard as granite, Egyptian sculpture incorporates a unique essence that endured throughout 3000 years of Egyptian civilization. Admired and copied for millennia, its styles and conventions have provided models for cultures and movements as diverse as Archaic Greece and 20th-century Cubism. Regardless of their genius, Egyptian artisans were technicians who served the king, the temple or large estates, and in their works they followed formulae set by convention (*see* §IV, 3). Individual creativity was rare and, in general, unwelcome: sculpture was rarely signed by artisans. Thus, although Egyptian sculptures rank among the masterworks of world civilization, the talented hands who created them remain largely anonymous (*see* §II above).

1. Introduction. 2. Forms. 3. Chronological survey.

1. INTRODUCTION. In most examples of Egyptian sculpture the human body is rendered in an idealized form. Males have broad chests, taut waists and an exaggerated muscularity, and females are portrayed with swelling breasts, tiny waists and trim hips. Stoic faces stare straight ahead or gaze downward, betraying no emotion. Representations of old age are few. On the rare occasions when corpulence is shown, it may be interpreted as indicating that the subject had reached maturity. Among kings, only Amenophis III and the pharaohs of the Amarna period

(*see* AMARNA STYLE) display less-than-perfect figures, a reflection of the departure from convention characteristic of that age.

Many sculptural traditions established during Early Dynastic times (*c.* 2925–*c.* 2575 BC) persisted into the Late Period (*c.* 750–332 BC). For example standing males are represented with the left foot advanced, providing a hint of forward movement (see fig. 45 below); this is true for all periods and there are only a few exceptions, notably the god Osiris. Females generally stood with both feet together throughout the Old and Middle kingdoms; from the New Kingdom onwards they also advance their left leg, although the stride tends to be shorter than for men. Size signifies importance. In a statue of a family group, the adult male often towers over his wife and children, who might stand or squat demurely at his feet. Young children are unclothed, gather their hair in a sidelock and suck on an index finger. Most sculpture was at least partially painted. A ruddy skin tone was traditional for men and yellow ochre for women.

Artisans enjoyed the greatest freedom of expression in the depiction of servants and foreigners. In the Old and Middle Kingdoms (*c.* 2575–*c.* 1630 BC) statues of servants were included in tombs in the expectation that they might perform in the afterlife routine chores of the household and estate, ensuring that the tomb owner never lacked food or other provisions. Accordingly, servants are shown engaged in a wide variety of chores (see fig. 82 below). In contrast to stylized reductions intended to symbolize entire activities, a personalized, inessential gesture is sometimes shown, as in the statuette of a servant woman who brushes her hair out of the way as she tends a fire (Boston, MA, Mus. F.A., 21.2600). Representations of foreigners were caricatures of their ethnic type (*see* §VI, 12 above). Syrians are easily recognizable by their exaggerated aquiline noses and full beards, while Nubians are distinguishable by their round faces, wide noses and thick lips.

With rare exceptions, Egyptian sculpture was not intended to be portraiture, but only to reproduce an approximate likeness of the subject represented. Generally, only essential elements are included, and details are kept to a minimum. The same person might be depicted in a number of ways in different statues or even in the same statue. The statue is identified by the name of its owner inscribed on the torso, base or back pillar. The alteration of the name, a common practice of later dynasties, changed the identity of the sculpture, since the faces lacked individualization.

Each statue was ritually animated by means of the 'Opening of the Mouth' ceremony. Magical implements touched to the eyes, ears, nose and mouth enabled those organs to function and opened a channel to permit the *ka*, or soul of the person represented by the statue, to come and go freely. This was especially important for sculpture placed in tombs (as was the case for most sculpture until the Middle Kingdom), since it provided an alternative resting place for the *ka* in the event of the body being lost or destroyed.

Beginning in the Middle Kingdom, sculpture was deposited inside temples as well as in tombs. The owner, by leaving his representation in a temple, signified his perpetual devotion to the gods within. It not only assured him of the gods' favour but also entitled him to partake in food and drink offerings after the gods had consumed their share. Statues of kings placed outside temples or in temple courtyards often portray the monarch in his role as the highest priest in the land. They also acted as intermediaries between the general populace, which was forbidden entry into temples, and the gods at home inside. A villager delivering a petition or prayer to a king's statue outside a temple could count on the king to intercede with the gods on his behalf. Often colossal in scale, these statues provided ever-present reminders of the power of the monarch (*see* §2(i)(j) below).

The royal statues often set the sculptural standard for figures of queens, deities, nobles and servants. Gods might be represented as purely human, purely animal or a combination of the two, but when a god had a human face, his or her features were those of the king. Similarly, representations of private individuals, whose success often depended on the king's favour, largely followed the style established at the royal court. Thus, a nobleman's face might resemble that of the king.

Like many ancient peoples, the Egyptians understood that there were fixed numerical ratios between the parts of the human body, and they used these ratios as guides whenever the body was reproduced. Accordingly, regardless of who was represented or how, the use of a canon of proportion guaranteed a standardized result (*see* §IV, 3 and fig. 5 above).

The enduring nature of stone made it a favoured material for Egyptian sculpture. Egyptian artisans learnt the art of stone-carving in Predynastic times and achieved technical mastery by the 4th Dynasty (*c.* 2575–*c.* 2465 BC). (For further discussion *see* §VII, 1 above.) Although Egyptian artisans created superb works in wood and metal (*see* §XVI below), neither was exploited to the same extent as stone. Bone, ivory, plaster, terracotta, faience and glass also provided raw material for sculpture (*see* §XVII, 5, 8, 9 and 14 below).

In the Old Kingdom most sculpture was produced in or around the capital city, Memphis, which had become the hub of artistic as well as administrative activity. Notwithstanding the break-up of central authority at the end of the Old Kingdom and the rise of politically independent provincial capitals, local artisans strove to continue the artistic conventions of the classical Memphite workshops. Because they had little or no access to Memphite prototypes, ungainly caricatures often resulted from a misapplication of the canon of proportion and other traditional conventions. Tiny heads with wide staring eyes, tubular bodies and spindly limbs only weakly approximated the ideal body form.

One consequence of the reunification of Egypt in the 11th Dynasty (*c.* 2081–*c.* 1938 BC) was the spread of royal building activity. Sculptures created at former outposts, such as Thebes and Aswan, lost their provincial stamp, probably as a result of both Memphite-trained artisans travelling throughout Egypt to work and local artisans visiting Memphis to be trained. By the New Kingdom (*c.* 1540–*c.* 1075 BC) sculptures of high quality were again created throughout the country. Although works from one site became harder to distinguish from those of another, the products of master artisans of Memphis remained unsurpassed in their sensitivity of modelling.

BIBLIOGRAPHY

H. Schäfer: *Von ägyptischer Kunst, besonders der Zeichenkunst*, 2 vols (Leipzig, 1919); Eng. trans. by J. Baines as *Principles of Egyptian Art* (Oxford, 1974, rev. 3/1986)

W. S. Smith and W. K. Simpson: *The Art and Architecture of Ancient Egypt*, Pelican Hist. A. (Harmondsworth, 1958, rev. 2/1981)

C. Vandersleyen, ed.: *Das alte Ägypten*, Propyläen-Kstgesch., xv (Berlin, 1975)

C. Aldred: *Egyptian Art*, World A. (London, New York and Toronto, 1980)

T. G. H. James and W. V. Davies: *Egyptian Sculpture* (London, 1983)

RITA E. FREED

2. FORMS.

(i) Statue types. (ii) Relief types.

(i) Statue types. As well as the familiar standing, seated, squatting and kneeling figures, there were a number of statue types peculiar to ancient Egypt, such as the 'scribe' statue, invariably representing high officials in funerary contexts, and the 'block' statue, usually placed in temples for votive purposes. The 18th Dynasty Theban tombs of Rekhmire (TT 100) and Qenamun (TT 93) contain wall paintings depicting craftsmen at work on the full repertory of types of New Kingdom royal statuary (see fig. 12 above).

GENERAL BIBLIOGRAPHY

LÄ: 'Königsplastik', 'Privatplastik'

W. S. Smith: *A History of Egyptian Sculpture and Painting in the Old Kingdom* (London and Boston, MA, 1946, 2/1949/*R* 1978)

B. Hornemann: *Types of Ancient Egyptian Statuary*, 3 vols (Copenhagen, 1951–7)

J. Vandier: *Les Grandes Epoques: La Statuaire* (1958), iii of *Manuel d'archéologie égyptienne* (Paris, 1952–78)

W. S. Smith and W. K. Simpson: *The Art and Architecture of Ancient Egypt*, Pelican Hist. A. (Harmondsworth, 1958, rev. 2/1981)

T. G. H. James and W. V. Davies: *Egyptian Sculpture* (London, 1983)

E. R. Russmann: *Egyptian Sculpture* (Cairo, 1989)

(a) Standing figure. (b) Seated figure. (c) Block statue. (d) Scribe statue. (e) Dyad and triad. (f) Squatting figure. (g) Kneeling figure. (h) Theophorous, naophorous and stelophorous statues. (i) Prostrate figure. (j) Colossal statue. (k) Reserve head.

(a) Standing figure. Many examples of Egyptian standing figures have been recovered in stone and wood. Copper or bronze must also have been frequently used, although these have not survived in such great numbers. Nearly all stone standing figures have back pillars, often inscribed, to which the backs of the legs are connected for solidity.

The classic male standing pose has both arms hanging naturally by the sides, with hands closed around a short cylindrical object usually considered to be a roll of linen. This attitude was frequent for both royal and private statues from the late Old Kingdom onwards (*see* STONE, colour pl. X, fig. 1), as in the case of the 5th Dynasty limestone statue of Ranefer (Cairo, Egyp. Mus., CG 18; *c.* 2460 BC). Middle and New Kingdom examples often omit the linen roll but it recurs in the Late Period as an archaizing feature. Statues of women, such as the wooden 5th or 6th Dynasty figure of Mitri's wife (New York, Met., 26.2.3), adopt the same pose as the men, but their hands are normally open with palms flat against thighs.

Examples where the left hand is thrust forward holding a long staff and the right hand falls by the side, either empty or holding a sceptre, are frequent in the Old and Middle kingdoms for both royal and private statues, such as the wooden figure of Ka-aper (Cairo, Egyp. Mus., CG 34; *see* SHEIKH EL-BELED), and in the New Kingdom for royal sculptures. This is an exclusively male pose restricted to funerary use and normally executed in wood, although the copper statue of Pepy I (*reg c.* 2289–*c.* 2256 BC; Cairo, Egyp. Mus., JE 33034) is a notable exception. A new pose in which both hands are placed flat against the starched triangular apron of the kilt was introduced by Sesostris III (*reg c.* 1837–*c.* 1818 BC), who is shown in this pose in a black granite statue from Deir el-Bahri (London, BM, 686). This has been interpreted as an attitude of prayer and was popular for both royal and private statues during the Middle Kingdom and early New Kingdom, as in the red granite figure of Tutankhamun (*reg c.* 1332–*c.* 1323 BC; Cairo, Egyp. Mus., CG 42091).

Two forms of votive statue appear among royal sculpture at the end of the 12th Dynasty. These depict the king either presenting a table of offerings or holding a standard. The former pose continues in such 18th Dynasty royal sculptures as the limestone statue of Akhenaten (*reg c.* 1353–*c.* 1336 BC; Cairo, Egyp. Mus., CG 43580) and also lasts into the Late Period (*c.* 750–332 BC). The figure holding a standard (e.g. the wooden statue from the 19th Dynasty, *c.* 1250 BC; Turin, Mus. Egizio, 3049) is particularly common under the Ramesside kings and is not restricted to royal use. The standard is usually held in the left hand and many symbols are found. Private individuals from the New Kingdom onwards are often shown holding a divine statue (*see* §(h) below) or a naos shrine. Standing naophorous statues originated under the Ramesside kings and were particularly popular in the Late Period, with such works as the 26th Dynasty (664–525 BC) steatite figure of Nesptah (Baltimore, MD, Walters A.G., 22.159).

Another genre originating in the Middle Kingdom, but in the private sphere, has the left arm across the stomach and the right hand by the side. This form is most common, in the New Kingdom and later, for figures of women, normally holding something such as a flower, sistrum or *menat* collar in the left hand, as in the 19th Dynasty painted wooden statue of Henutudjebu (Cairo, Egyp. Mus., 801). In a naturalistic variant they occasionally hold a cat or a bird to the chest and push the hair back with the right hand.

(b) Seated figure. The typical Egyptian seated figure is depicted sitting bolt upright on a solid blocklike seat. The seat may be either a backless stool or a chair, in which case the back usually acts as a back pillar and is inscribed. The legs and sides of the chair are often indicated in relief. Most seated statues are made of stone, although wooden ones occasionally appear; bronze is common in the Late Period (see fig. 41), especially for statuettes of seated divinities. Seated statues of private individuals are not common in the Late Period and seated women are considerably less frequent than men in all periods. The feet are placed together in both male and female figures.

The earliest type of seated pose is encountered on the statues of Khasekhemwy (*reg c.* 2700 BC) of the 2nd Dynasty (Cairo, Egyp. Mus., JE 32161, and Oxford, Ashmolean, E 517; see fig. 51 below). In this attitude, one arm (usually the left) is drawn horizontally across the

41. Seated figure of Imhotep, bronze, h. 151 mm, Late Period, *c.* 750–332 BC (London, British Museum)

stomach while the other lies along the length of the thigh. This form persists throughout later periods. Kings in this pose often hold the flagellum in the Old Kingdom, while in the New Kingdom they usually hold the *heka* sceptre. The attitude is not restricted by sex, and women are depicted in this pose in the Old, Middle and New Kingdoms, as in the 12th Dynasty granite statue of Queen Nefert (Cairo, Egyp. Mus., CG 381). In the New Kingdom they often hold a sistrum, *menat* collar or lotus flower.

The classic seated pose is first attested in the mid-4th Dynasty (*c.* 2500 BC). It is found throughout all periods thereafter in both royal and private statuary. The main difference from the Early Dynastic pose described above (in the statues of Khasekhemwy) is that both arms are placed along the thighs with the hands resting on the knees. The hands are sometimes placed flat, palms downwards (see fig. 52 below); sometimes one hand is closed

and holds a short roll of linen (see fig. 53 below). Most of the possible variations are attested, especially in New Kingdom private pieces, but generally women of all periods and New Kingdom royalty tend to keep both hands open and flat. In the Old Kingdom one hand, often the left, is placed flat while the other is closed and holds a short linen roll vertically as in the alabaster statue of Chephren (*reg c.* 2520–*c.* 2494 BC; Cairo, Egyp. Mus., CG 41. Middle Kingdom figures normally hold the linen handkerchief horizontally and it tends to be longer so that one end projects beyond the fist and hangs over the outside of the thigh. The black granite statue of Sesostris III (New York, Brooklyn Mus., 52.1) is a typical example. Occasionally a diminutive standing or kneeling figure of a child is placed to one or both sides of the legs but never higher than knee level. One such piece, dating to the 5th Dynasty, is the painted limestone statue of Akhy and his family (Cairo, Egyp. Mus., CG 44).

An exclusively royal form depicts the king dressed in the *heb-sed* (royal jubilee festival) garment with his arms crossed on his chest and holding the *heka* sceptre and flagellum (or 'crook and flail'). In the Old and Middle kingdoms it is normally the short *heb-sed* garment that is worn; in the New Kingdom both short and long versions are found.

The introduction of a long mantle-like garment in the Middle Kingdom is naturally reflected in the statuary. Seated figures dressed in this garment normally hold the left hand and forearm flat against the chest; the right arm is brought horizontally across the stomach, as in the Early Dynastic pose, and the edge of the garment is grasped with the right hand.

(c) Block statue. Block statues depict men seated on the ground or, later, on a low cushion, with legs drawn up towards the body so that the knees are almost level with the shoulders. Their arms are folded across the knees, usually right over left. The figure is clothed in a long robe which effectively hides all anatomical details except the head, hands and (in some examples) the feet. This reduces the human form to that of a cubic block from which only the head projects. The form is economical in terms of both material and labour, producing large, flat areas for inscriptions. It allows both sculptor and viewer to concentrate on the face by rendering the body in a somewhat amorphous form.

As a genre, the block statue was produced for votive rather than funerary use by private individuals. Many examples have been found at Abydos (e.g. London, BM, 570), and it has been suggested that these were intended to represent the deceased person as a *hesy* (Egyp.: 'sanctified being'). There are no known royal examples and women were only exceptionally depicted. Various hard stones were used, but apparently not other materials; none has survived in wood or bronze. Block statues first appeared during the Middle Kingdom, although their origins are perhaps to be found in the wooden figures found in 6th Dynasty model boats. They became more popular in the New Kingdom and were the most common type of private statue in the Late Period. They remained in fashion until the beginning of the 1st century BC.

In two early Middle Kingdom block statues of the treasurer Hetep, in limestone (Cairo, Egyp. Mus., JE 48857) and granite (JE 48858), no attempt has been made to reduce the angularity of the block and the figure appears to be simply embedded within it, his arms and legs carved in raised relief. All other Middle Kingdom examples show the figure dressed in a long robe either stopping at the ankles, so that the feet are exposed, or enveloping the feet which are then represented simply as a concave extension of the legs.

In the 18th Dynasty the modelling became more subtle; limbs can be clearly discerned beneath the tightly stretched

42. Block statue of Sennefer, black granite, h. 838 mm, 18th Dynasty, c. 1450 BC (London, British Museum)

fabric of the garment, and shoulders and elbows realistically overhang the sides of the block. Later New Kingdom examples increasingly have back pillars. Vertical surfaces were normally covered in texts inscribed in horizontal rows, as in the granite statue of Sennefer (London, BM, 48; see fig. 42). Ramesside pieces remained essentially the same, except that inscriptions were often in vertical columns and some figures were clothed in the finely pleated 19th Dynasty tunic. There were a variety of hand arrangements in the New Kingdom. Sometimes one hand holds a sistrum, flower, ear of corn, scribe's palette or bolt of linen.

During the Late Period block statues depicting figures wrapped entirely in a long robe remained standard. The limestone statue of Iti (London, BM, 24429) is typical of these. Less common examples in which the feet are exposed often consist of figures wearing a long ankle-length kilt belted at the waist and so requiring that the upper body and arms be modelled. The latest examples, such as the 30th Dynasty grey granite statue of Tjanefer (New York, Pierpont Morgan Lib., 10), tend to be rather elongated and appear excessively tall and thin.

Combined block statues are known from the New Kingdom depicting pairs or even larger groups. In the case of SENENMUT (fl c. 1465 BC) the head of princess Neferure also emerges from the block (Cairo, Egyp. Mus., JE 42114). Several block statues have some other element, such as a diminutive figure of the man's wife, sculpted in front of their legs, as in the 12th Dynasty brown quartzite statue of Senusert-Senebefny (New York, Brooklyn Mus., 39.602).

(d) Scribe statue. This pose depicts a scribe seated cross-legged on the ground, wearing a short kilt which is stretched tight across the knees to form a flat, rigid area. The left hand holds a papyrus which is partially unrolled across the lap and the right hand, poised as if holding a reed pen, rests on the right-hand edge of the unrolled papyrus. Some examples depict a reading scribe; in these both hands hold the rolled ends of the papyrus as if the scribe is reading from the middle section. The head usually looks forward with a pensive expression, as though meditating on what to write next, but in some instances the head is bent forward, suggesting concentration on the act of writing or reading itself. There is normally no back pillar, except in a few Late Period examples from Upper Egypt.

Scribe statues were first produced in the Old Kingdom (4th Dynasty) and enjoyed great favour during most periods of Egyptian history. It is unlikely that they were originally merely a subtype of the limestone models of workers common in Old Kingdom tombs. The quality of workmanship is, with few exceptions, consistently high and although examples in limestone are not uncommon, most use harder stones such as granite. There are no examples in wood or bronze. Scribe statues often represent very high officials or even princes, reflecting the envied and noble position of the scribal profession among the Egyptians. The form, however, is restricted to private statuary and no examples of kings depicted in this attitude have been found. Scribe statues were intended only for funerary use.

The pose is represented by some 50 surviving examples from the Old Kingdom, of which the earliest are mid-4th Dynasty. The most celebrated is the 'Unknown Scribe', a 5th Dynasty painted limestone statue from Saqqara (Paris, Louvre, N 2290; see fig. 54 below). In Old Kingdom examples either leg may be in front, usually the left, and the left hand is occasionally shown palm upwards holding a scribe's palette containing two cakes of ink.

In the Middle Kingdom the palette is often shown slung over the shoulder and lying across the chest; the black granite figure of the scribe Mentuhotpe (Luxor Mus., J 37) balances a shell containing a cake of ink on his left knee. Many Middle Kingdom scribe statues are traditionally dressed in Old Kingdom kilts, but some wear a much longer kilt that completely hides the legs and makes the sculpture appear more geometric and solid. The best example is one of Amenhotpe, son of Hapu (c. 1365 BC; Cairo, Egyp. Mus., CG 42127), which dates to the New Kingdom but shows several archaizing features.

In the New Kingdom the classic pose continued, although in works from this period the right leg is invariably in front (for illustration see HOREMHEB). Exceptionally the scribe might be seated on a low cushion. As in the Middle Kingdom the palette is slung over the left shoulder (as in another statue of Amenhotpe; Cairo, Egyp. Mus., JE 44861) or, more rarely, on the left knee. After the New Kingdom the genre went out of fashion until it was revived during the 26th Dynasty. A New Kingdom subtype of the scribe statue, depicting a classic scribe in company with a baboon, sacred animal of Thoth (god of writing), squatting on a plinth, is exemplified by a steatite sculpture from el-Amarna (Cairo, Egyp. Mus., JE 59291).

(e) Dyad and triad. Group statues depicting two people (dyads) or three (triads) are normally made of stone. Individual figures within the group generally adopt one of the appropriate 'classic' poses. They were first made in the 4th Dynasty (c. 2575–c. 2465 BC) and are especially common from the New Kingdom. Late Period examples are rare, except for small amuletic pieces depicting triads of divinities. The five surviving schist triads depicting Mycerinus (reg c. 2490–c. 2472 BC), Hathor and a nome deity (Cairo, Egyp. Mus., and Boston, MA, Mus. F.A.) are among the earliest examples of this type and also the best known. Presumably originally there was one such group for each nome but few have survived. The poses of these Mycerinus triads vary, but examples are known in which the goddess Hathor is seated in the centre, with the other two figures standing to either side (e.g. Boston, MA, Mus. F.A., 09.200). Others (e.g. Cairo, Egyp. Mus., JE 46499) show all three figures standing. In the latter type the king stands in the centre with Hathor to his right and the nome deity to his left. The goddess Hathor unusually adopts the male pose of standing with her left leg advanced.

Royal dyads often depict the king in company with a divinity. The earliest examples, dating to the Old Kingdom, have the king seated next to the deity, but from the Middle Kingdom onwards all of the possible combinations of seated or standing king next to seated or standing divinity occur. The theme was especially popular under the Ramesside kings (for illustration see TANIS). In the New Kingdom seated groups often embrace while standing figures hold hands.

Private dyads invariably depict man and wife, standing or sitting together. Sometimes the husband is seated and the wife is standing. It was a common theme and one of the most endearing poses in all Egyptian sculpture. There are many variations of detail, but often the couple display some gesture of affection, a glimpse of an intimacy usually excluded from Egyptian art. Thus the woman often has one arm around her husband's shoulder or waist or the couple hold hands. In some New Kingdom groups both have their arms around each other, as in the 18th Dynasty painted limestone dyad of Itju and Hentur (London, BM, 375). In the Old Kingdom the position of man and wife to each other varies, whereas in New Kingdom groups the husband is virtually always placed to the woman's right. Old and Middle Kingdom wives are normally shown shorter than their husbands, whereas in the New Kingdom they are the same size. Frequently small-scale figures of one or two children are depicted, never more than knee high, standing or sitting by their parents' feet, as in the 4th Dynasty limestone group of the dwarf Seneb and his family (Cairo, Egyp. Mus., JE 51281; see fig. 43) from Giza. Royal conjugal groups are known, but they are not so frequent as the king with a divinity theme; they originate in the 4th Dynasty with such works as the slate dyad of Mycerinus and his queen (Boston, MA, Mus. F.A., 11.738; for illustration see MYCERINUS) and are common in the early New Kingdom but rare under the Ramesside kings.

43. Dyad of Seneb the dwarf and his family, painted limestone, h. 340 mm, from Seneb's tomb at Giza, 4th Dynasty, c. 2465 BC (Cairo, Egyptian Museum)

A less frequently encountered type of triad depicts three adults, usually husband, wife and adult son, although there are many unique variations. A few examples of 'pseudo-groups' are known from the Old Kingdom, depicting the same person two or even three times, as in the quartzite sculpture of Rawer (Cairo, Egyp. Mus., JE 66615), from Giza. The subject is usually male and he can either sit or stand next to his twin who is identical except occasionally for details of wig or costume.

PHILIP J. WATSON

(f) Squatting figure. The typical Egyptian squatting statue is a male figure, shown seated with the knee of the left leg raised perpendicularly and the right resting parallel to the ground (see fig. 44). The hands are placed on the knees with palms facing downwards. The figure is usually clothed in a kilt or an enveloping cloak. The space between the legs where the garment gapes open is left solid. Most examples are in such stones as limestone or granite: there are no extant examples in wood or bronze.

Squatting statues were commissioned by private individuals for both funerary and votive purposes. The pose is common in reliefs from the 4th Dynasty (*c.* 2575–

44. Squatting statue of a man, yellow limestone, 135×60×95 mm, from Thebes, 11th Dynasty, *c.* 2081–*c.* 1938 BC (New York, Metropolitan Museum of Art)

c. 2465 BC), with an early depiction appearing in the tomb of Kawab at Giza, but it did not appear in sculpture in the round until the 6th Dynasty (*c.* 2325–*c.* 2150 BC). The statue of Niankhra (Cairo, Egyp. Mus.), a court physician assigned to the beginning of this dynasty, is an early and atypical form of the pose with the right leg raised and the right hand adjusting the kilt. In this and other Old Kingdom examples, the figure wears a kilt and a wide, striated wig. Middle Kingdom squatting statues generally represent a middle-aged, corpulent official without a wig. In the New Kingdom the pose was often reserved for male officials who are shown wearing elaborate wigs and costumes, as in the 18th Dynasty limestone statue of an official with the baboon of the god Thoth, patron of scribes (Paris, Louvre, E11153). Later, the type was occasionally employed for a youthful official with a shaven head, as in the 22nd Dynasty (*c.* 950–*c.* 730 BC) statue of the Vizier Hor (Cairo, Egyp. Mus.).

The greatest number of squatting figures date from the 25th and 26th dynasties (*c.* 750–525 BC), with their strong archaizing tendencies. These may be responsible for the marked similarities between the 26th Dynasty statue of Harwa (Cairo, Egyp. Mus.) and the 12th Dynasty type exemplified by the statue of Mentuhotpe. Other examples from the 26th Dynasty revert to the more youthful torsos of the Old Kingdom, as demonstrated by the statues of Bes (Lisbon, Mus. Gulbenkian, 158) and of Nespakashuty (Cairo, Egyp. Mus.), the right foot of which was carved from a separate piece of stone. Most 26th Dynasty examples have an inscribed back pillar.

From the Old Kingdom onwards female figures, generally those of women nursing infants (e.g. New York, Met., 26.7.1405), are represented in this same pose. The 18th Dynasty statue of Senenmut holding the princess Neferure (Cairo, Egyp. Mus., JE 42116) may be regarded as a conscious appropriation of this motif to emphasize his special relationship as the child's tutor. A variation of this attitude may be considered: that of a squatter with both knees raised to the chest, as seen, for example, in the Old Kingdom statue of Pepy II (*reg c.* 2246–*c.* 2150 BC) as a child (Cairo, Egyp. Mus., 50616) and in an exceptional 25th Dynasty statue of Harwa (London, BM) in which he is depicted offering two divine statues.

The squatting statue vanished from the Egyptian sculptural repertory with the end of the 26th Dynasty.

For further illustration *see* TANIS.

BIBLIOGRAPHY
B. V. Bothmer and others: *Egyptian Sculpture of the Late Period* (New York, 1960)

ROBERT S. BIANCHI

(g) Kneeling figure. In Egyptian sculpture the usual pose for kneeling figures depicts them resting on their knees and the balls of their toes, which are bent under the weight, and sitting on their heels. The only exceptions are a few statues from the late New Kingdom showing kings on one knee with the other leg trailing behind, such as the schist statue of Ramesses II (*reg c.* 1279–*c.* 1213 BC; Cairo, Egyp. Mus., CG 42142). Kneeling statues fall into several distinct genres; all except two are votive. The first non-votive type is the Old Kingdom servant statue depicting a man or woman kneeling to grind corn (e.g. the 5th Dynasty

limestone servant statue, Cairo, Egyp. Mus., CG 110) or to carry out another task; such statues were obviously intended for funerary use. The second non-votive type represents a kneeling prisoner with his arms pulled back and tied together at the elbows (see fig. 94 below). These date to the late Old Kingdom (c. 2325–c. 2150 BC) and the New Kingdom, an early example being the 6th Dynasty limestone statue of a Libyan prisoner (New York, Met., 47.2).

The earliest Old Kingdom examples of kneeling figures show priests with hands resting on thighs or in their laps, as in the 3rd Dynasty granite statue of Hetepdief (Cairo, Egyp. Mus., CG 1). This simple, humble gesture, indicating the figure's submissiveness to his god, is occasionally encountered in Middle Kingdom royal statues. It became popular for private individuals during the New Kingdom and later, as exemplified by the quartzite kneeling statue of Nakhterheb (London, BM, 1646), which dates to the 26th Dynasty. Allied to this pose are New Kingdom sculptures depicting the king with arms held before him in a gesture of adoration.

The most celebrated pose for the kneeling king shows him with forearms on thighs and palms upturned, holding two small globular vessels probably symbolizing an offering of wine. The first and only Old Kingdom example of this genre is a green slate statue of Pepy I (reg c. 2289–c. 2256 BC; New York, Brooklyn Mus., 39.121). A similar pose, although with arms held out, is shown earlier on a relief of Neuserre (reg c. 2416–c. 2392 BC). Several 12th Dynasty kings depicted themselves in this attitude and it was especially popular during the New Kingdom and the 26th Dynasty. Earlier examples were carved from stone but in later periods bronze became the favourite medium. The earliest extant bronze piece depicts Tuthmosis IV (reg c. 1400–c. 1390 BC; London, BM, 64564). Few private examples of this genre are known.

A variety of new types was introduced in the New Kingdom, all showing the figure holding a large object on or in front of the knees. From the reign of Hatshepsut onwards pharaohs depicted themselves holding a single large vase. More popular is the king holding a table of offerings (first attested under Amenophis II, reg c. 1426–c. 1400 BC) raised above his knees and sometimes supported on a pedestal. The first example of this type is a granite statue of Amenophis II (Cairo, Egyp. Mus., CG 42073). This form also became very popular for private statues. Other objects can be held, especially a statue of a divinity or a sistrum. Two important types introduced in the New Kingdom are kneeling figures holding either a stele or a naos or small shrine (see §(h) below). It is likely that many kneeling figures, especially the later small bronze examples, had an accompanying, but separate, figurine of a god before which they would be set.

PHILIP J. WATSON

(h) Theophorous, naophorous and stelophorous statues. Related forms of statuary in which a standing or kneeling male figure proffers a divine effigy (theophorous), a small portable shrine containing the image of a deity (naophorous) or an inscribed stele (stelophorous). The majority of these figures were commissioned for display in temples,

although some 18th Dynasty (c. 1540–c. 1292 BC) stelophorous statues (e.g. the statue of Pekhsukher; Edinburgh, Royal Mus. Scotland, 1910.75) were placed in niches on the tomb façade. Royal examples of all three types are known, but the genre was mainly restricted to private use. The most usual material up to the Late Period (c. 750–332 BC) was bronze, after which such stones as schist and basalt prevailed.

These statue types are rarely attested before the 18th Dynasty, but became common in the 19th Dynasty (c. 1292–c. 1190 BC) and remained popular until the end of the Ptolemaic Period (304–30 BC). Naophorous and theophorous statues had antecedents in block statues with a subsidiary figure added in front of the legs as in the 12th Dynasty (c. 1938–c. 1756 BC) quartzite statue of Senusert-Senebefny (New York, Brooklyn Mus., 39.602). The first true instances, however, are the 18th Dynasty images of officials presenting royal or divine insignia, such as the 'rebus' statue of Senenmut offering the symbols of Hatshepsut's name (New York, Brooklyn Mus.). The form of stelophorous statues remained constant from the 18th Dynasty onwards: the subject's hands were either shown gripping the sides of the stele, as in the alabaster statue of Akhenaten (Cairo, Egyp. Mus., JE 42411), or resting on top of it (e.g. the statue of Meryptah; Durham, U. Orient. Mus.).

However, new developments in the theophoric and naophoric forms were introduced during the Third Intermediate Period (c. 1075–c. 750 BC). Most noticeable are the bronze statuettes of officials offering effigies of deities, Osiris being the most common, as seen in the statuette of Khonsumeh (see fig. 45). This practice may represent a usurpation of a royal prerogative: there is a slightly earlier theophoric depiction of Ramesses VII (reg c. 1137–c. 1126 BC) presenting a figure of the god Amun (Cairo, Egyp. Mus., JE 37595). Also from the New Kingdom is a sandstone naophoros of Prince Khaemwese, a son of Ramesses II (reg c. 1279–c. 1213 BC; Cairo, Egyp. Mus., JE 36720). From such figures derive the numerous stone groups of officials offering the image of Osiris (either free-standing or enclosed in a naos) that characterize the sculpture of the 26th and 27th dynasties (664–404 BC). In these, the image may be either held at knee-level, as in the standing theophoros of Ankhpakhered with Osiris (St Louis, MO, A. Mus., 222.24), or rested on the knees, as in the kneeling naophoros of Psamtiksaneith (Cairo, Egyp. Mus., JE 31335). Examples from this period usually have inscribed back pillars, and on naophorous statues the doors may also be inscribed. This formulation also allowed for the substitution of the divine image by other forms, including representations of sacred animals. Such statues testify to the presenter's devotion to the deity represented, which constitutes an eternal plea for the deity's protection in return for the faithful discharge of religious duty. Since most of these images were displayed in temple contexts, such statues also integrate the official depicted into the daily rituals performed for the deity.

Naophorous and theophorous statues were revived and adapted in the 30th Dynasty (380–343 BC). The finest 30th Dynasty piece is a schist statue bearing a small naos-shaped stele engraved with the goddess Neith (San Francisco, CA, de Young Mem. Mus., 54664). The latest

45. Theophorous statuette of Khonsumeh, bronze, h. 320 mm, Third Intermediate Period, *c.* 1075–*c.* 750 BC (Berlin, Ägyptisches Museum)

examples, from the late Ptolemaic Period, display an innovation in which the hands are placed beneath the naos, as if the presenter is actually bearing its weight (e.g. Hannover, Kestner-Mus., 1935.200.773).

BIBLIOGRAPHY
B. V. Bothmer and others: *Egyptian Sculpture of the Late Period* (New York, 1960)
J. van Dijk: 'A Ramesside Naophorous Statue from the Teti Pyramid Cemetery', *Oudhdkund. Meded. Rijksmus. Ouden Leiden*, lxiv (1983), pp. 49–60
M. Saleh and H. Sourouzian: *Official Catalogue: The Egyptian Museum, Cairo* (Mainz, 1987), nos 209, 228
R. A. Fazzini and others: *Ancient Egyptian Art in the Brooklyn Museum*, New York, Brooklyn Mus. cat. (New York and London, 1989), nos 22, 39
R. S. Bianchi: 'Egyptian Metal Statuary of the Third Intermediate Period (*circa* 1070–656 B.C.) from its Egyptian Antecedents to its Samian Examples', *Small Bronze Sculpture from the Ancient World*, ed. B. Gilman (Malibu, 1990)

ROBERT S. BIANCHI

(i) Prostrate figure. Royal prostrate statues are known from the Middle and New kingdoms. A bronze figurine from Deir el-Ballas (Cairo, Egyp. Mus., JE 35687) shows a Middle Kingdom ruler (?Sesostris III) outstretched on the lid of a box that manifestly belonged to a censer. An 18th Dynasty representation of a censer bearing a prostrate figure of the king can be seen in the reliefs of Tuthmosis III, in the Temple of Amun at Karnak. Another figurine (l. 56 mm, *c.* 1400 BC; Philadelphia, U. PA, Mus., 48–16–1), made of steatite and slightly smaller, is identified on the underside as Amenophis III. The rear end is slightly trimmed off to fit into a ritual object of unknown form, possibly a model bark. One such model bark (Cairo, Egyp. Mus., CG 4930), dating to the 19th Dynasty, has a deck with a number of recesses that formerly contained accessories of some kind. In both of these examples of prostrate statues the king's attitude can be explained as an act of humility in the presence of a god, and in the case of Amenophis III the god is identified as Atum, whose name is inscribed between the extended arms of the King. Representations of such statues on a shrine of Nectanebo II (*reg* 360–343 BC; Cairo, Egyp. Mus., CG 70021) show the King's arms bent beneath him rather than extended. In all these cases the head is held erect, unlike some representations in reliefs of Akhenaten, where he literally 'kisses the ground', as phrased in ancient Egyptian.

The king is also represented prostrate on a bier in the cenotaph of Sethos I (the Osireion) at Abydos and the tomb of Ramesses IX (*reg c.* 1126–*c.* 1108 BC; KV 6) at Thebes. There also the King's head is erect, for he is awakening into life. The same idea is evidently conveyed by a diorite statue of Osiris (Cairo, Egyp. Mus., CG 38424), dating to the 26th Dynasty, the head of which bears an electrum feathered emblem of Abydos, while his arms are swathed and not visible.

There are also prostrate statues of foreign foes, such as the figure in a basalt door socket from Hierakonpolis (Philadelphia, U. PA, Mus., E 3959). A statue of Tuthmosis III (*reg c.* 1479–*c.* 1426 BC), as represented in the tomb of Rekhmire at Thebes (TT 100), shows the King enthroned on a base in the form of a prostrate foreigner (or more likely a series of foreigners); the foreigner's arms are bent beneath him and his head is raised. In other cases the prostrate foreigner is surmounted by an outstretched lion, another embodiment of the king. There are two isolated figurines of foreign prisoners with their arms bound behind them, one of which (Paris, priv. col., 1912; see Keimer) is of grey granite, 320 mm long, and appears to be of Ramesside style; it is inscribed for an overseer of priests. The second (Cairo; Lévi de Benzion priv. col., 1949; see Weill) is mounted on the fragmentary top of a small box of stone, the nature of which is unspecified; it is inscribed for Shoshenq III. Both show anomalies in the inscriptions, and the purpose of the sculptural motif is puzzling, casting some doubt as to their authenticity. They do not completely fit the present category because the knees are flexed or drawn forward and they are therefore not completely prostrate, although the chin is pushed down on the base or lid. A third statuette of this kind, made of limestone, is indeed prostrate (Wildung and Schoske).

Another category of figures apparently shows the same attitude as the two royal statuettes described earlier—

namely the nude girls that form the handle of cosmetic spoons dating to the New Kingdom, but the pose is intended to convey the act of swimming.

BIBLIOGRAPHY

J. E. Quibell: *Hierakonpolis*, i (London, 1900), p. 6 and pl. 3
R. Weill: 'Une Boîte en pierre au nom de Sheshonq III', *Recl Trav. Philol. & Archéol. Egyp. & Assyr.*, xxxvi (1914), pp. 93–4
L. Keimer: 'Une Statue de prisonnier remontant au Nouvel Empire', *An. Service Ant. Egypte*, xlix (1949), pp. 37–9
H. G. Fischer: 'Prostrate Figures of Egyptian Kings', *Bull. U. Mus.* [Philadelphia], xx (1956), pp. 26–42
——: 'Further Remarks on the Prostrate Kings', *Bull. U. Mus.* [Philadelphia], xxi (1957), pp. 35–40
D. Wildung and S. Schoske: *Entdeckungen: Ägyptische Kunst in Süddeutschland* (Mainz, 1985), p. 83

HENRY G. FISCHER

(j) Colossal statue. The term 'colossus' is applied to over life-size Egyptian statues regardless of their pose, material or method of manufacture. Most colossi derive from temples and were created as architectural sculptures, forming integral elements of buildings' decorative programmes; few have been found in tomb chapels. They usually represent kings, deities, members of the royal family (particularly queens) or deified individuals.

Limestone and granite were the most popular materials, but alabaster, sandstone and quartzite were also used. Hard material, particularly granite, was common for standing colossi (see fig. 46), although these were sometimes made from limestone. Slightly over life-size statues in private tombs were occasionally made from wood. Usually even the largest colossi were monolithic or, in special circumstances, carved from the living rock. Individual elements may have been made separately or repairs carried out by the insertion of blocks. One type of colossus was made up of blocks (in the same way as pillars) and addorsed to pillars in temple courts (see OBELISK, fig. 1). Although this type is usually referred to as an 'Osirid' statue, since it portrays the king in a form resembling that of the god Osiris, it actually refers to the king's role in the royal jubilee festival.

Sphinxes—mostly human-headed lions—are among the largest colossal statues because of their compact form: the 'Great Sphinx' at Giza, shaped out of the living rock in the reign of Chephren, is 73.5 m long and 20 m high (see SPHINX, fig. 1). The quartzite, seated statues of Amenophis III still *in situ* at Thebes, known as the 'Colossi of Memnon' (see THEBES (i), §V and fig. 5), were originally around 21 m high, while the seated colossi of Ramesses II, carved against the façade of the 'Great Temple' at Abu Simbel, are about 22 m high (for illustration see ABU SIMBEL). The size of colossal sculptures was partly determined by their position. They commanded open spaces, usually outside pylons and gateways or in courts. This made at least some of them publicly accessible and led to their veneration during the New Kingdom.

The earliest colossal statues date to the Predynastic period and represent the god Min (Cairo, Egyp. Mus., JE 30770, and Oxford, Ashmolean, 1894.105). Only a few Old Kingdom colossi have survived, notably a seated alabaster statue of Mycerinus (Boston, MA, Mus. F.A., 09.204) and a red granite head of Userkaf (h. 680 mm; Cairo, Egyp. Mus., JE 52501). A twice life-size seated statue of Chephren's queen Khamerernebty I was found

46. Colossal statue of a king with the names of Ramesses II and Merneptah added, red granite, h. 2.63 m (without restoration of legs from knees downward), probably from Karnak, mid-18th Dynasty, *c.* 1450–*c.* 1350 BC (London, British Museum)

in her tomb at Giza (h. 2.28 m; Cairo, Egyp. Mus., JE 48856).

There are surviving colossi of nearly all of the kings of the 12th Dynasty, as well as several of the 13th Dynasty. Most of them are seated and two to three times life-size (h. 2.0–3.2 m), but there were, at this time, even larger sculptures, judging from two granite heads probably representing Ammenemes III (Cairo, Egyp. Mus., CG 383, and London, BM, 1063).

Many colossal statues were made by the pharaohs of the New Kingdom, especially the two great builders Amenophis III and Ramesses II, whose cult temples at Thebes (the 'Memnonium' and the 'Ramesseum') were adorned with colossi. During the reign of Ramesses II numerous colossi were made for the new capital, Piramesse, as well as for expanded and rebuilt temples (particularly at Memphis and Karnak) and new Nubian temples such as Gerf Hussein and Abu Simbel. A limestone, monolithic colossus of Ramesses II at Memphis (known as Abu al-Hol) is 10.95 m high, without its feet and pedestal, and weighs about 100 tons. Fragments of colossal sculpture found at Tanis (but perhaps originally from Piramesse) may derive from an even larger statue of Ramesses II.

Over life-size statues of the Third Intermediate Period are virtually non-existent, and few have survived from the Late Period, but there was a renewed tendency towards the colossal under the Ptolemies.

BIBLIOGRAPHY

J. Yoyotte: 'Colosses', *Dictionnaire de la civilization égyptienne*, ed. G. Posener, S. Sauneron and J. Yoyotte (Paris, 1959), pp. 64–5

C. Aldred: *Egyptian Art*, World A. (London, New York and Toronto, 1980), pp. 167–8, 193–5

JAROMIR MALEK

(k) Reserve head. Also called 'replacement' or 'portrait' heads, reserve heads were peculiar to the Old Kingdom. They were a rare and short-lived genre; just over 30 examples have survived. Most were found at Giza, principally from the western mastaba field. Single examples have also been discovered at Dahshur, Abusir and Saqqara. They are predominantly of 4th Dynasty date, being especially common during the reigns of Cheops (*reg c.* 2551–*c.* 2528 BC) and Chephren (*reg c.* 2520–*c.* 2494 BC). However, two examples from Abusir and Saqqara are from the 5th and 6th dynasties respectively.

Usually carved from white limestone, reserve heads occasionally still bear traces of paint but some appear to have been unpainted. They were products of the king's sculptors and were bestowed on members of the royal family and higher officials by the king himself. They are approximately life-size and the neck is truncated to form a flat base, usually smoothed, so that the head is free-standing. They were therefore obviously meant to be works in their own right rather than parts of larger composite statues. It is thought that they were intended either as second heads, which could receive offerings should the head of the mummy itself be destroyed, or as substitutes for the entire body in which the essence of the deceased could reside. The tombs containing reserve heads never had any other funerary statues in them and usually had no false door (a type of stele imitating a door). The heads were not placed in a *serdabs* (the room containing a funerary statue, usually completely blocked off except for two spy-holes), nor in statue niches in the chapels. They were normally positioned in the burial chamber itself or in the passage that connected it with the shaft.

The heads appear to be cursorily executed, but closer inspection reveals that non-essential details have been minimized so that the sculptor could concentrate all his attention on the facial features (e.g. Cairo, Egyp. Mus., JE 46216; see fig. 47). The hair is normally indicated

47. Reserve head, limestone, h. 255 mm, from Giza, 4th Dynasty, *c.* 2520 BC (Cairo, Egyptian Museum)

simply by an incised line marking its outer limits, which makes the figure appear to be wearing a smooth, tight-fitting cap. This probably reflects the Egyptian nobles' normal practice of shaving the head, as in the 4th-Dynasty reserve head of a prince (Cairo, Egyp. Mus., JE 46216) from Giza. The ears are nearly always broken and often there are inexplicable gashes, seemingly deliberate, on the back of the head or neck.

No two reserve heads are alike, and the sculptors put such effort into modelling the shape of the face, nose, mouth and eyes that many of them, more than any other Egyptian sculptures, evoke a sense of real personality. The 4th Dynasty head of a princess (Boston, MA, Mus. F.A., 14.719) is particularly evocative. Facial expressions range from smiling (as in the 4th Dynasty head of Sneferu–Seneb; Cairo, Egyp. Mus., JE 46215) through slightly amused and downright impish to solemn, serene and even glum. In this sense the heads must be regarded as portraits. However, they retain a formality and a sense of perfection characteristic of all Egyptian funerary art, fusing the Egyptian funerary ideal with the portrayal of individual characteristics. From an art-historical point of view this sadly short-lived genre is of great importance, since it demonstrates that Egyptian sculptors were as capable of producing sensitive realistic works as they were the more formal and stereotyped pieces that have survived in greater numbers.

PHILIP J. WATSON

(ii) Relief types. The forms of ancient Egyptian relief sculpture gradually evolved during the Predynastic period, when the main examples were rock-carvings and incised

decoration on slate palettes and ivory knife-handles. By the Early Dynastic period, a distinctive set of conventions and proportions and a rigid repertory of subject-matter had emerged. Since Dynastic reliefs mainly took the form of stelae (see STELE, §2) and the decoration on the walls of tombs and temples, subsequent technical developments were primarily dictated by changes in religious and funerary ritual.

The two main types of relief—raised and sunk—were used to varying degrees, depending on such factors as cost, speed and position within a building. There were also subtleties within each basic type, such as 'low relief' (relatively shallow raised relief) and a combination of sunk and raised, in which the background was only partially removed, gradually sloping back up to surface level. All types of reliefs were invariably painted after completion, with reliefs in tombs usually preserving more of the original paint than those in temples.

(a) Raised. The Narmer Palette (*c.* 3000 BC) is one of the earliest examples of Egyptian raised (or bas-)relief, a method of sculpting involving the removal of the material surrounding the figures depicted (see fig. 62 below). This type of relief was used from the late Predynastic period onwards, reaching a peak in the mid-18th Dynasty, particularly in the temples and private tombs of the reign of Amenophis III (*reg c.* 1390–*c.* 1353 BC). Fine raised relief was used in the decoration of the mortuary temple of Sethos I (*reg c.* 1290–*c.* 1279 BC) at Abydos, but the temple was completed in sunk relief by his successor Ramesses II (*reg c.* 1279–*c.* 1213 BC). Raised relief was subsequently rarely used, apart from revivals in the 26th Dynasty (664–525 BC) and the Greco-Roman period (332 BC–AD 395).

(b) Sunk. Egyptian sculptors created sunk relief as a cheaper and faster alternative to raised relief, since its execution required only the carving out of the outlines of the figures, leaving the surrounding material in place (see fig. 64 below). The modelling and details of each figure were then sculpted within the carved outline. It was probably the speed of this technique that led to its use in the ambitious building projects of Akhenaten (*reg c.* 1353–*c.* 1336 BC) and Ramesses II. The lines and modelling of sunk relief are generally cruder and less delicate than those of raised relief, but it was more difficult for successors to re-carve (and therefore usurp). Sunk relief was often used for the external walls of temples, where it created a sharper effect of light and shadow than raised relief, which tends to flatten out in direct sunlight. In terms of material, sunk relief was particularly preferred on harder stones, such as granite or basalt, since less of the surface had to be removed.

3. CHRONOLOGICAL SURVEY. The chronological development of Egyptian sculpture spans five millennia, from the Neolithic period (*c.* 6000–*c.* 2925 BC) to the beginning of the Christian era. Although the naturalistic and stylized works of the Predynastic period are open to various interpretations, most Dynastic sculpture is remarkably consistent in its adherence to a basic set of conventions and proportions, tending constantly towards archaism. Within this canonical framework various new styles and types periodically evolved in response to social, political and religious changes.

(i) Predynastic (*c.* 6000–*c.* 2925 BC). (ii) Early Dynastic (*c.* 2925–*c.* 2575 BC). (iii) Old Kingdom (*c.* 2575–*c.* 2150 BC). (iv) First Intermediate Period (*c.* 2150–*c.* 2008 BC). (v) Middle Kingdom (*c.* 2008–*c.* 1630 BC). (vi) Second Intermediate Period (*c.* 1630–*c.* 1540 BC). (vii) New Kingdom: pre-Amarna (*c.* 1540–*c.* 1353 BC). (viii) New Kingdom: Amarna period (*c.* 1353–*c.* 1332 BC). (ix) New Kingdom: post-Amarna (*c.* 1332–*c.* 1075 BC). (x) Third Intermediate Period (*c.* 1075–*c.* 750 BC). (xi) Late Period (*c.* 750–332 BC). (xii) Ptolemaic period (304–30 BC). (xiii) Roman period (30 BC–AD 395).

*(i) Predynastic (*c. 6000–*c.* 2925 BC).* The Egyptian Predynastic (or Neolithic) period, principally defined by its ceramic types, is usually divided into three phases: Badarian (*c.* 6000–*c.* 4000 BC; characterized by material from EL-BADARI, Deir Tasa and Merimde Beni Salammè), Naqada I (or Amratian, *c.* 4000–*c.* 3500 BC; based on material from el-Amara, Abydos and the lower level at NAQADA) and Naqada II (or Gerzean, *c.* 3500–*c.* 2925 BC; based on material from el-Gerza, Maadi and the upper level at Naqada). Excavations at HIERAKONPOLIS, ABYDOS and KOPTOS have also provided a range of ceramic and sculptural material dating from the late Predynastic period to the Early Dynastic. As the Predynastic craftsmen became more accomplished, they developed the difficult techniques for working the hard stones of Egypt.

BIBLIOGRAPHY
J. Capart: *Primitive Art in Egypt* (London, 1905)
H. Schäfer and W. Andrae: *Die Kunst des alten Orients*, Propyläen Kstgesch., iii (Berlin, 1935)
H. Asselberghs: *Chaos en beheersing: Documenten uit Aeneolithisch Egypte* [Chaos and power: evidence from Neolithic Egypt] (Leiden, 1961)
L'Egypte avant les pharaons: IVe millénaire (exh. cat., Paris, Grand Palais, 1973)
R. T. Ridley: *The Unification of Egypt: A Study of the Major Knife-handles, Palettes and Maceheads* (Deception Bay, 1973)
W. Needler: *Predynastic and Archaic Egypt in the Brooklyn Museum* (New York, 1984)

(a) Statuary. The few crude items of statuary that have survived from the Badarian phase include small anthropomorphic statues and hippopotamus-shaped vessels in ivory, various theriomorphic amulets and a few steatopygous statuettes of women in unfired pottery (e.g. Cairo, Egyp. Mus. and London, BM).

During the Naqada period, especially Naqada II, patrons commissioned luxurious stone and terracotta vessels in the form of animals and steatopygous women (mostly of high quality, e.g. Cairo, Egyp. Mus., JE 31437) and a range of small carved objects, mostly cosmetic items (such as ivory and bone spoons, combs and hairpins incorporating small animal figures) and theriomorphic amulets (see §XVII, 9 and 1 below) in bone or hard stone.

The Predynastic craftsmen also produced slate cosmetic palettes for grinding malachite into eye-paint (see PALETTE (i)). The palettes of the Badarian period were geometrical in form but those of Naqada I and II were animal- or shield-shaped. The shield-shaped palettes were surmounted with the shape of a bird or a small schematic human head (with a conical hat and triangular beard). Similar heads were carved at the tips of engraved ivory horns or tusks used to hold eye-paint (e.g. London, U. Coll., Petrie Mus., 15110).

The third and—for the purposes of this discussion—most important type of sculpture produced in the Naqada

48. Predynastic female figurine, terracotta, h. 293 mm, from Ma'mariya, Naqada II period, c. 3500–c. 2925 BC (New York, The Brooklyn Museum)

period was free-standing statuettes of people and animals. This category included anthropomorphic stone figurines (e.g. Lyon, Mus. B.-A.) similar to the engraved cosmetic horns mentioned above, various animal forms in flint (e.g. London, U. Coll., Petrie Mus., and Berlin, Ägyp. Mus.) and unbaked terracotta statuettes of men and women, some steatopygous and decorated with black tattoos (e.g. Turin, Mus. Egizio, and New York, Brooklyn Mus.). Some of the human statuettes of the Naqada period are modelled roughly and naturalistically, while others are stylized and have beak-like heads (although even the latter may represent a particular human type with an aquiline nose, which was later represented in Dynastic statuary). The arms were either at the figures' sides or raised in the air as if dancing (see fig. 48). More specialized subjects include sailors in their boats (mainly from tombs at Naqada; examples in Oxford, Ashmolean, and Berlin, Ägyp. Mus.), prisoners with their hands tied behind their backs (e.g. Oxford, Ashmolean) and a possible female brewer in a jar (Berlin,

Ägyp. Mus.). The animals most frequently represented are hippopotamuses, crocodiles, tortoises, frogs, flies, bees, gazelles, birds, fish and lions (for illustration *see* KOPTOS). The detailed and accurate style of all these animal figures, especially the representations of particular species of fish and birds, reflects the Egyptians' keen interest in the animals themselves.

The stylized human statuettes and the heads carved on cosmetic horns are thought to be characteristic of hunter-gatherers, whereas the naturalistic human figures are typical of agricultural people. The co-existence of these two sculptural styles in the Naqada period therefore supports the view that the economic base of the Predynastic Egyptians was gradually changing from hunting into settled agriculture. The stylized human figures are remarkable for their formal synthesis, which echoes that of the elegant profiles of several contemporary flint blades, while the naturalistic figures seem less refined and were perhaps produced only for funerary use.

BIBLIOGRAPHY

J. Leclant: 'Compte rendu des fouilles et travaux en Egypte', *Orientalia*, xix (1950), pp. 360–73; xx (1951), pp. 340–51

J. Vandier: *Les Époques de formation: La Préhistoire* (1952), I/i of *Manuel d'archéologie égyptienne* (Paris, 1952–78), pp. 221–30, 409–35

(b) Relief. The first Egyptian reliefs were rock-carvings at various sites in the Western and Eastern deserts (such as Gebel Uweinat and Gilf Kebir) and along the cliffs bordering the Nile in Upper Egypt. The subject-matter and style of the Predynastic rock-carvings were the same as those of Predynastic paintings on walls and ceramics (*see* §XI, 2(i) below) and incised designs on such items as slate cosmetic palettes and ivory combs. The rock-carvings include hunting scenes with wild game and dogs (but only rarely the hunters themselves) and river scenes involving groups of animals or large fleets of boats. The most frequently represented animals are wild cattle, giraffes, various species of gazelle, ostriches, hippopotamuses, crocodiles and tortoises. Lions—often represented in Predynastic statuary—are strangely absent from contemporary rock-carvings. The style of representation is naturalistic: men and animals are generally shown in profile, sometimes foreshortened as they run up the slopes of river banks. The banks themselves are occasionally marked with lines representing the ground-surface and plants, usually as if from a raised perspective. The method of drawing is free and economical. Figures are delineated by means of dots, joined dots or continuous lines; often they are hatched or hammered to produce an almost chromatic effect. Although the rock-carvings have often been described as 'primitive' and 'magical', they are actually sophisticated narrative scenes.

There are several surviving luxury (or votive) ivories from the late Naqada period decorated with animals arranged in registers of very low relief. These luxury ivories—the immediate forerunners of Early Dynastic reliefs—include the Davis Comb, the Carnarvon Knife-handle (both New York, Met.), the Brooklyn Knife-handle (New York, Brooklyn Mus.; see fig. 49) and the Pitt-Rivers Knife-handle (London, BM).

BIBLIOGRAPHY

H. A. Winkler: *Rock-drawings of Southern Upper Egypt*, 2 vols (London, 1938–9)

49. Predynastic knife-handle with carved relief of rows of animals, flint and ivory, l. 234 mm, from Tomb 32, Abu Zaidan, Naqada II period, *c.* 3500–*c.* 2925 BC (New York, The Brooklyn Museum)

J. Vandier: *Les Epoques de formation: La Préhistoire* (1952), I/i of *Manuel d'archéologie égyptienne* (Paris, 1952–78), pp. 373–402, 533–60

W. M. Davis: 'Toward a Dating of the Nile Valley Prehistoric Rock-drawings', *J. Soc. Stud. Egyp. Ant.*, viii/1 (1977), pp. 25–34

——: 'Sources for the Study of Rock-art in the Nile Valley', *Götting. Misz.*, xxxii (1979), pp. 59–74

A. L. Kelley: 'A Review of the Evidence Concerning Early Egyptian Ivory Knife Handles', *Anc. World*, vi (1983), pp. 95–102

S. Curto, V. Maragioglio and C. Rinaldi: *Korosko-Kasr Ibrim/Incisioni rupestri nubiane* (Milan, 1987)

K. H. Otto and G. Buschendorf Otto: *Felsbildern aus dem Sudanesischen Nubien* (Berlin, 1993)

(ii) Early Dynastic (c. 2925–c. 2575 BC). During the Early Dynastic (or Archaic) period many of the characteristic cosmetic and amuletic forms of Predynastic figurative art were abandoned in favour of free-standing statuary and reliefs.

BIBLIOGRAPHY
J. Capart: *Primitive Art in Egypt* (London, 1905)

W. S. Smith: *A History of Egyptian Sculpture and Painting in the Old Kingdom* (London and Boston, MA, 1946, 2/1949)

J. Vandier: *Les Epoques de formation: Les Trois Premières Dynasties* (1952), i/2 of *Manuel d'archéologie égyptienne* (Paris, 1952–78)

W. B. Emery: *Archaic Egypt* (Harmondsworth, 1961)

(a) Statuary. (b) Relief.

(a) Statuary. The style of Early Dynastic statuary still derived primarily from Hierakonpolis, Abydos and Koptos, but a new style emerged combining the two Predynastic styles (naturalistic and stylized) and characterized by a preference for hard stone. Statues of metal and wood were also produced, but only a few wooden fragments from Abydos (Boston, MA, Mus. F.A. and Oxford, Ashmolean) and Saqqara (Cairo, Egyp. Mus.) have survived, along with a reference to a bronze statue of Anubis in the 5th Dynasty text of the Palermo Stone (Palermo, Mus. Reg.).

Because of the practice of carving stone statues without hollowing out the spaces between the arms and the body, between the legs and (in seated figures) between the legs and the seat, Early Dynastic statues preserved the structure of the squared block and the aesthetic character of the stone. This style of statuary was to remain typical throughout the Dynastic period. During the Early Dynastic period various standard types of statue were introduced, including the seated and standing man, the kneeling or praying man

and the chrysaliform (erroneously called 'mummiform') figure.

The gradual process of fusion of naturalistic and stylized schools of statuary is exemplified by a basalt statuette from Naqada, perhaps representing a god (h. 400 mm; Oxford, Ashmolean, 1922.70), which resembles the human figures depicted on Predynastic cosmetic horns but also portrays details in the face and is provided with a penis sheath. Apart from this piece, there are 12 surviving statuettes depicting private individuals, dating from the 1st to the 3rd Dynasty (of which the latest examples have their names and titles engraved on the base or clothing). The heights of these statues, usually around 500 mm (also the most common size in the Dynastic period), tend to reflect the most convenient size of a quarried block of good quality stone. Most of the figures are seated or kneeling. Seated examples include the black granite male statue, erroneously known as the 'Lady of Naples' (h. 440 mm; Naples, Mus. Archaeol. N.), a limestone male figure (h. 420 mm; Berlin, Ägyp. Mus.), a black granite figure of a man called Ankh (h. 620 mm; Leiden, Rijksmus. Oudhd.), two limestone portraits of a man called Nedjemankh (h. 720 mm; Leiden, Rijksmus. Oudhd., and h. 610 mm; Paris, Louvre), the pink granite figure of a chief shipbuilder called Bedjmes (h. 610 mm; London, BM) and the figure of a woman called Redijet (h. 830 mm; Turin, Mus. Egizio). Among the kneeling statues are the pink granite kneeling man (h. 390 mm; Cairo, Egyp. Mus.) and the life-size limestone statue of a Libyan kneeling on one leg with his other leg folded up against his chest (h. 850 mm; Cairo, Egyp. Mus.). There are also four standing figures: a female figure known as the 'Lady of Brussels' (h. 820 mm; Brussels, Mus. Royaux A. & Hist.), two almost identical statues (h. 1.65 m) of a man called Sepa and a figure (h. 1.52 m) of his wife Neset (all Paris, Louvre).

As well as these private statues, there are several surviving statues of kings and gods. Probably the earliest statue of a king is the small ivory statuette of a standing figure wearing the white crown of Upper Egypt (h. 88 mm; London, BM). There are also two statues of King Khasekhemwy (*reg c.* 2700 BC), one in limestone (Oxford, Ashmolean; see fig. 50) and the other in schist (h. 560 mm;

50. Early Dynastic seated statue of King Khasekhemwy, limestone, h. 620 mm, 2nd Dynasty, *c.* 2700 BC (Oxford, Ashmolean Museum)

Cairo, Egyp. Mus.). All three date to the 2nd Dynasty. A limestone, seated, almost life-size statue (h. 1.4 m) of King Djoser of the 3rd Dynasty (*reg c.* 2630–*c.* 2611 BC; Cairo, Egyp. Mus.) was found in the *serdab* (statue chamber) of his Step Pyramid at Saqqara. The missing inlaid eyes of this statue had evidently been made separately in bronze and precious stones, inaugurating a technique that was often used in the Dynastic period. This strongly realistic portrait of Djoser initiated a style that was to become very popular in combination with a more idealizing approach. Also dating to the 3rd Dynasty is a diorite, naked, standing figure of a god wearing a penis sheath (h. 210 mm; New York, Brooklyn Mus.).

There are several surviving Early Dynastic figures of animals, characterized by fine treatment of volumes and the elimination of all non-essential details, such as the seated alabaster figure of a cynocephalous monkey, inscribed with the name of King Narmer (h. 520 mm; Berlin, Bodemus.); hippopotamuses in limestone (e.g. Berlin, Ägyp. Mus.), granite (e.g. Athens, N. Archaeol. Mus.) and terracotta (e.g. Boston, MA, Mus. F.A.); lions in terracotta

(e.g. Oxford, Ashmolean) and granite (e.g. Berlin, Ägyp. Mus.); as well as a slate figure of a jackal (Berkeley, U. CA, Hearst Mus. Anthropol.). These animals, probably totemic in origin, continued to be represented among the funerary and religious equipment of the Dynastic period (with particularly numerous representations of hippopotamuses in Middle Kingdom tombs).

The naturalistic mode, devoted to animals in the Predynastic period, survived in various Early Dynastic sculptures of different human ethnic types, such as a stone door socket from Hierakonpolis, carved in the form of a slaughtered enemy, and a few small ivory heads of foreigners (Oxford, Ashmolean). There are also numerous surviving naturalistic figurines, including women (some holding babies, as in the group at Baltimore, MD, Walters A.G.), dwarfs, servants and animals, many of which were gaming pieces. The stylized Predynastic mode, on the other hand, persisted in the images of the gods Min, Osiris and Ptah, such as the three limestone 3rd Dynasty colossal statues of Min from Koptos (h. originally *c.* 4 m; Oxford, Ashmolean, and Cairo, Egyp. Mus.). There are no Early Dynastic statues of Osiris and Ptah, but the style of Dynastic statues of these gods undoubtedly has the same origin as the statues of Min.

BIBLIOGRAPHY

J. E. Quibell: *Archaic Objects*, 2 vols, Cairo, Egyp. Mus. cat. (Cairo, 1904–5)

W. S. Smith: 'Two Archaic Egyptian Statues', *Bull. Mus. F.A., Boston*, lxv (1967), pp. 70–84

Brief Guide to the Department of Egyptian and Classical Art, New York, Brooklyn Mus. cat. (New York, 1974)

(b) Relief. Some of the relief techniques of the Predynastic period, such as rock-carving and ivory-engraving, survived into the Early Dynastic period, but in general the classical Dynastic sculptural technique of low relief in stone or wood was adopted. Whereas the Predynastic reliefs were primarily narrative in function, the Early Dynastic reliefs were mainly of two basic types: commemorative historical documents and funerary stelae. The Predynastic naturalistic representation of the human figure was superseded by a more precise abstract representation in which the figure was drawn with head in profile, torso in front view and the rest of the body in profile. Figures standing side by side or in groups were arranged in a line or distributed in overlapping registers; buildings were shown in plan, with the façade seen from the front and laid over the plan. The images in Early Dynastic reliefs were supplemented with inscriptions in an early hieroglyphic script that is not yet fully understood. This mode of relief representation was gradually refined during the Early Dynastic period until the classical style of the pharaonic age had emerged.

Commemorative documents. The development of Early Dynastic relief can be traced through a series of objects each of which refers to an important event involving the king (whose presence is often indicated only by his name). The series includes ivory knife-handles, ivory and wooden labels, slate shield-shaped ceremonial palettes, limestone ceremonial maceheads and royal stelae. The most important knife-handles are the Gebel el-Arak and Gebel Tarif handles. The GEBEL EL-ARAK knife-handle (Paris, Louvre)

51. Early Dynastic macehead of King Scorpion, limestone, h. 325 mm, 1st Dynasty, c. 2900 BC (Oxford, Ashmolean Museum)

portrays, on the *recto*, a figure in Sumerian dress between two lions, with wild animals shown below, and on the *verso*, scenes of combat involving the royal ship. The Gebel Tarif knife-handle (Cairo, Egyp. Mus.) is decorated with two long symmetrical serpents embracing a flower-shaped figure symbolizing the king (*recto*) and wild quadrupeds, one with fantastic wings (*verso*). The labels (ivory and wooden tablets of uncertain purpose) include a small ebony tablet (Cairo, Egyp. Mus.; *see* §VIII, 3 and fig. 21 above) bearing a depiction of the foundation of a temple for the goddess Neith of Sais, in the presence of King Aha (*reg c.* 2925 BC); and two wooden tablets from the reign of King Den (*reg c.* 2850 BC), one depicting the ceremony of enthronement, the foundation of a temple and the name and titles of the chief royal architect, and the other showing Den killing a prisoner of war with a mace (both London, BM).

The palettes include the 'Hunting Palette' (London, BM and Paris, Louvre), showing men attacking wild animals with bows and clubs; the Hierakonpolis Palette (Oxford, Ashmolean), showing two dogs and two panthers with very long necks, both symmetrical, enclosing the cosmetic depression, with wild animals below (*recto*), and two symmetrical dogs enclosing wild and fantastic animals (*verso*); the 'Dog Palette' (Paris, Louvre), showing four symmetrical dogs enclosing a panther with a long neck, and other animals (*recto*), and four dogs and two giraffes, symmetrically placed on either side of a palm (*verso*); the 'Battlefield Palette' (London, BM and Oxford, Ashmolean), showing vultures and a lion, symbolizing the king attacking enemies in flight; the 'Libyan Palette' (Cairo,

Egyp. Mus.), showing domesticated animals and cultivated trees with a hieroglyph symbolizing Libya (*recto*), and animals personifying the king dismantling the walls of fortified (?Libyan) cities (*verso*); the 'Bull Palette' (Paris, Louvre), showing a bull (symbolizing the king) goring a foreigner; and the Narmer Palette (Cairo, Egyp. Mus.; for illustration *see* NARMER), which is the most perfect of the series, communicating its information with realistic figures, symbols and inscriptions.

There are two maceheads (both Oxford, Ashmolean) decorated with intricate relief: the macehead of King Scorpion, showing the King taking part in a ritual, with a row of symbols below denoting conquered cities (see fig. 51), and the macehead of King Narmer, portraying the enthronement of the King. There are also two important early royal stelae: the stele of King Wadj (Paris, Louvre), a splendidly composed and proportioned relief from Abydos, consisting of a depiction of the serpent hieroglyph inside the outline of a royal pavilion surmounted by the image of Horus the falcon-god; and the 2nd Dynasty stele of el-Gebelein (Turin, Mus. Egizio), portraying the foundation of a temple and dating to the 2nd Dynasty.

A small number of reliefs have also survived from the walls of temples of the 2nd and 3rd dynasties, including the badly damaged granite raised reliefs of Khasekhemwy from Hierakonpolis and el-Kab (Cairo, Egyp. Mus.) and a few relief fragments from a shrine set up by Djoser at Heliopolis (Turin, Mus. Egizio). A series of 3rd Dynasty raised reliefs worked in the living rock at Wadi Maghara in the Sinai Desert (e.g. London, BM, 691, depicting King Sanakht smiting desert-dwellers; *c.* 2640 BC) continued the Predynastic tradition of rock-carvings.

These Early Dynastic documentary reliefs occasionally incorporate motifs from Sumerian art, as in the symmetrical disposition of figures on the Gebel el-Arak and Gebel Tarif knife-handles, the Hierakonpolis and Dog palettes and the *recto* of the Narmer Palette.

Funerary tablets. During the 1st and 2nd dynasties private tombs began to be supplied with funerary tablets (the forerunners of the tablets placed in the cult rooms of the Old Kingdom mastaba-tombs; *see* STELE, §2) portraying the tomb owner in front of an offering table, as in the case of the 1st Dynasty tablet of Merka (Cairo, Egyp. Mus.; h. 1.73 m). On the left-hand side of each tablet was the name, title and portrait of the tomb owner, who is shown seated with his hand extended over a table loaded with food, ointments and cloth (in the gesture of 'taking possession').

The classical style of Egyptian relief was established in such low-relief tablets as the wooden panels of the 3rd Dynasty noble Hesyre (Cairo, Egyp. Mus.) and the exquisite limestone panels of King Djoser from the subterranean chambers of the Step Pyramid. The reliefs on these funerary tablets and the *verso* of the Narmer Palette indicate a move away from the symmetry of the Protodynastic palettes and knife-handles, adopting instead the harmonic arrangement (with a large figure on one side and smaller counterbalancing figures or objects opposite) that was to characterize Egyptian art of the Dynastic period.

BIBLIOGRAPHY

S. Curto: 'Un rilievo proveniente de el-Gebelen nel Museo Egizio di Torino', *Aegyptus*, xxxiii (1953), pp. 105–24

W. M. F. Petrie: *Ceremonial Slate Palettes, Corpus of Predynastic Pottery* (London, 1953)

S. Curto: 'La funzione delle lapidi funerarie egizie', *Studi Calderini-Paribeni*, ii (Milan, 1957), pp. 1–31

——: 'L'espressione prj-hrw nell'Antico Regno', *Mitt. Dt. Archäol. Inst.: Athen. Abt.*, xvi (1958), p. 47

——: 'Annotazioni su geroglifici arcaici', *Z. Ägyp. Spr. & Altertknd.*, xciv (1967), pp. 15–25

S. CURTO

(iii) Old Kingdom (c. 2575–c. 2150 BC). From the early 4th Dynasty Egyptian sculpture was characterized by firmly established representational conventions, a naturalistic canon of proportions (*see* §IV, 2 and 3 above) and high technical standards. The Old Kingdom was a supremely confident and mature period of sculpture. Most surviving works derive from royal cult temples, sun temples and private tombs, particularly in the Memphite necropoleis (Giza, Abusir and Saqqara). Although royal sculpture of the Old Kingdom seems to have been subjected to severe and systematic destruction, numerous statues and reliefs from private mastabas and rock tombs have survived.

BIBLIOGRAPHY

W. S. Smith: *A History of Egyptian Sculpture and Painting in the Old Kingdom* (London and Boston, 1946, 2/1949/R 1978)

C. Aldred: *Old Kingdom Art in Ancient Egypt* (London, 1949)

W. S. Smith and W. K. Simpson: *The Art and Architecture of Ancient Egypt*, Pelican Hist. A. (Harmondsworth, 1958, rev. 2/1981), pp. 70–149

(a) Statuary. (b) Relief.

(a) Statuary. The heaviness of Early Dynastic statuary gave way to the ordered elegance of the Old Kingdom, characterized by compact, cubic renderings of the human form (with the arms generally close to the body) and dignified static representations. Emotions were not portrayed, except apparently in statues of captives. During the 5th Dynasty (*c.* 2465–*c.* 2325 BC) statues began to be made with back pillars. Most sculptures were painted and the eyes were sometimes inlaid. Most were probably collective efforts (*see* §II above). Attempts have been made to distinguish two 'schools' of sculptors creating royal statues at Memphis during the 4th Dynasty (*c.* 2575–*c.* 2465 BC). These were defined by G. A. Reisner as Sculptors A and B, the former with austere simplified planes, the latter with more detailed softer modelling, which stressed the musculature and bones underneath. Some statues of high officials, often royal relatives, were made in the same workshops. Although realism never entirely disappeared, new developments can be discerned during the 5th and 6th dynasties. They are best observed in private statues. From the mid-5th Dynasty onwards most statues tended to be treated conventionally, with simplified modelling. Much of the variety was, however, due to the training and abilities of the anonymous sculptors. The democratization of the ownership of tomb statues and the appearance of provincial workshops encouraged fresh approaches during the 6th Dynasty (*c.* 2325–*c.* 2150 BC) but also contributed to an overall decline.

Royal. While sculptures of almost all major Old Kingdom rulers have survived, only 4th Dynasty royal statuary

has been preserved in large numbers. Statues were integral parts of the royal cult temples (*see* §VIII, 2(i) above); those of Sneferu (*reg c.* 2575–*c.* 2551 BC), for instance, were in one piece with the back of their shrines. The number of royal statues in a single pyramid complex may have been in excess of 100. A few have also been found in the temples of local gods. Seated royal statues were the most common; a good example—and the most impressive sculpture of the Old Kingdom—is the diorite statue of Chephren (*reg c.* 2520–*c.* 2494 BC), who is protected by the outstretched wings of the hawk-god Horus (Cairo, Egyp. Mus., CG 14; see fig. 52). Standing statues were less frequent. There were also various types of small sculptures, such as the schist statue of Pepy I (*reg c.* 2289–*c.* 2256 BC) kneeling and offering two wine-jars (New York, Brooklyn Mus., 39.121) and the alabaster figures of Pepy II (*reg c.* 2246–*c.* 2150 BC) as a squatting naked child (Cairo, Egyp. Mus., JE 50616) and as a miniature adult on the lap of his mother (New York, Brooklyn Mus., 39.119).

There are several impressive surviving Old Kingdom dyads, such as those depicting Neuserre (*reg c.* 2416–*c.* 2392 BC; Munich, Staatl. Samml. Ägyp. Kst, 6794), Mycerinus and his queen (*c.* 2480 BC; Boston, MA, Mus. F.A., 11.1738; for illustration *see* MYCERINUS), seated Chephren and the goddess Bastet (Cairo, Egyp. Mus., CG

52. Old Kingdom seated statue of King Chephren, diorite, h. 1.68 m, 4th Dynasty, *c.* 2500 BC (Cairo, Egyptian Museum)

11) and seated Sahure (*reg c.* 2458–*c.* 2446 BC) accompanied by a personification of the Koptos nome (New York, Met., 18.2.04). Radjedef (*reg c.* 2528–*c.* 2520 BC) is represented by a quartzite seated statue accompanied, apparently uniquely, by a small figure of a kneeling queen (Paris, Louvre, E.12627). At least one of the triads of Mycerinus, the goddess Hathor and a nome personification combines standing and seated figures. Royal family groups have not been found.

The king usually wears the royal headcloth (*nemes*). The white crown (of Upper Egypt) is less frequent, the red crown (of Lower Egypt) quite exceptional. Unless represented in a *sed*-festival (royal jubilee) cloak, the short royal kilt (*shendyt*) is the king's only garment, and he is barefoot. The hands of seated statues usually rest on their legs, with the left palm down and the right clenched. There is little doubt that each ruler had an 'official' likeness, but it is not known how close this was to reality. Most attention was paid to the face, although sometimes even contemporary monuments display different characteristics. During the 4th Dynasty rapid development took place in the depiction of the eyes. Those of Radjedef still betray a link with the small narrow eyes of Sneferu, but are treated with more sophistication. The rim of the upper eyelid is bordered by a narrow raised band, and the lightly marked impressionistic eyebrows are almost straight. A stylized, sometimes arched, relief band indicating the brow is known from the statues of Chephren, although it may have been introduced earlier. A paint stripe departing from the outer corner of the eye, parallel with the extended eyebrow, appeared at the same time. In the late 5th Dynasty and the 6th the inner canthus acquired a downward slant, but the brows straightened.

Royal sculptures varied in size, from rare colossal statues, exemplified by the granite head of a colossus of Userkaf (Cairo, Egyp. Mus., JE 52501), to small figurines, such as the ivory seated statuette of Cheops (Cairo, Egyp. Mus., JE 36143). Hard stones (granite, greywacke, diorite, quartzite, porphyry and calcite) were generally preferred to limestone (*see* STONE, colour pl. X, fig. 1), and both ivory and copper were also used. The figures of Pepy I and another king, probably Merenre (Cairo, Egyp. Mus., JE 33034–5), were produced by hammering copper sheets over a wooden core.

Sphinxes were made from the reign of Radjedef onwards. The 'Great Sphinx' of Chephren at Giza (*see* SPHINX, fig. 1) consists of a lion's body and a royal head on a huge scale.

Private. Tombs of private individuals usually contained a single statue, but many had two or more. The Giza tomb of Rawer, of the mid-5th Dynasty (*c.* 2400 BC; Cairo, Egyp. Mus.), contained as many as 100 different statues. Most types of private statue were originally introduced as royal types, and most were single figures, although they were sometimes intended to form pairs, as in the case of the painted limestone statues of Rehotpe and Nofret, dating to the early 4th Dynasty (Cairo, Egyp. Mus., CG 3 and CG 4). Dyads and other group statues became widespread from the late 4th Dynasty. These mainly show the tomb owner and his wife, as well as their children or relatives. There are also 'pseudo-groups', showing the

same person two or three times, such as the limestone double statue of Nimaatsed (Cairo, Egyp. Mus., CG 133). Different attitudes—standing, seated and kneeling—were sometimes combined, and the accompanying figures were smaller. There are no statues showing a non-royal figure with a deity.

Scribe statues (e.g. Paris, Louvre, N.2290; see fig. 53) were introduced in the mid-4th Dynasty (*see* §2(i)(d) above) but remained confined to private sculpture, as did nude statues. Partial representations, such as the bust of Ankh-haf (Boston, MA, Mus. F.A., 27.442) and reserve heads (*see* §2(i)(k) above), were made of limestone and mostly date to the mid-4th Dynasty.

Rock-cut tombs contained statues carved into the walls, with little finesse, as if in niches. The appearance of such statues was perhaps subsequently imitated in free-standing sculptures. Rock-cut scribe statues and groups of figures are particularly common in the Giza tomb of Meresankh III, a queen of Chephren, which included a group of ten rock-cut statues of the Queen, her mother and daughters.

The typical Old Kingdom private statue of a man shows him wearing a short curled (or full) wig, often with a parting, but some men are portrayed with closely cropped hair or shaven scalps. Women are shown in short to medium-long wigs, with their natural hair sometimes visible underneath. Some women, particularly queens, have tripartite wigs. During the 4th Dynasty some seated statues of men still show the Early Dynastic position of the arms (one hand held clenched on the chest), but later private sculptures are imitations of contemporary royal statues.

53. Old Kingdom scribe statue, painted limestone, h. 537 mm, from the tomb of Kai, Saqqara, early 5th Dynasty, *c.* 2450 BC (Paris, Musée du Louvre)

Most statues showed the individual in full physical prowess or at the height of his career, and from the 5th Dynasty they tended to be idealized and formalized, conforming to conventional stereotypes. However, even in the earlier naturalistic sculptures it is difficult to recognize portrait statues. Efforts to record reality may be observed in a few rare cases, when individuals are portrayed with similar features both in reliefs and statues, and when representations incorporate physical deformities.

Although the stylistic development of Old Kingdom private statues was largely dependent on their royal contemporaries, the relationship becomes difficult to follow from the mid-5th Dynasty (c. 2400 BC) onwards. Some features of royal sculptures, such as the paint stripe extending the eyes, are never found in private statues. Most private sculptures are smaller than life-size, but larger examples are known, such as the limestone statue of Khamerernebty I, another queen of Chephren (Cairo, Egyp. Mus., JE 48856). Usually they are made of limestone, although more prestigious stone, such as granite or alabaster, was sometimes used. Many statues are made of wood covered with plaster, as in the case of the figure of Ka-aper (Cairo, Egyp. Mus., C634), dating to the late 4th Dynasty or early 5th. These wooden statues, numerous in the 6th Dynasty, were composite, enabling the sculptor to depart from cubic forms, particularly by freeing the arms. There are also a few surviving examples of private statuettes in ivory, such as a naked male figure (Cairo, Egyp. Mus., CG 815).

Servant statuettes are a functionally distinct class of Old Kingdom private statuary, showing the personnel of the tomb owner's estate, commonly engaged in manual tasks such as corn-grinding, baking or brewing (e.g. Cairo, Egyp. Mus., JE 66624). First attested in the mid-4th Dynasty (c. 2500 BC), they were usually anonymous single figures, representing an extension of the scenes in the tomb reliefs. The postures of many of these servant statues are in marked contrast to other types of funerary statue, usually being executed in a summary fashion. Most are made of limestone but wooden statuettes were introduced towards the end of the 5th Dynasty (c. 2350 BC). (For further discussion see §XIII, 3(i) below.)

Pyramid complexes of the 5th and 6th dynasties contained statues of kneeling bound captives of different ethnic types, symbolizing the king's triumph over foreign countries. These statues are about half life-size and have been claimed as attempts at portraying pain and anguish in a realistic fashion.

Animals. In addition to royal dyads and triads with anthropomorphic figures of deities, there are examples with zoomorphic representations of deities. Individual statues of deities are exceptional, probably because little evidence has survived concerning shrines of local gods. There are few monumental animal sculptures in the round, but because of the less rigid conventions they are often depicted with unusual realism. Examples include the granite lions, symbolic of protection, from the reign of Neuserre (Cairo, Egyp. Mus., T.22.11.24.5 and 7.1.15.6), a fragmentary basalt statue of the ram-god Khnum, from the reign of Cheops (Berlin, Bodemus., 22572) and a slate statue of the jackal-god Anubis from the valley temple of

Mycerinus at Giza (Boston, MA, Mus. F.A.). Stone vessels, libation tables and architectural elements, such as gargoyles, were sometimes carved into animal forms.

BIBLIOGRAPHY
G. A. Reisner: *Mycerinus: The Temples of the Third Pyramid at Giza* (Cambridge, MA, 1931), pp. 108–29
A. Scharff: 'On the Statuary of the Old Kingdom', *J. Egyp. Archaeol.*, xxvi (1940), pp. 41–50, pls viii–x
J. H. Breasted jr: *Egyptian Servant Statues* (Washington, DC, 1948)
M. A. Shoukry: 'Die Privatgrabstatue im Alten Reich', *An. Service Ant. Egypte* (1951) [supplement]
J. Vandier: *Les Grandes Epoques: La Statuaire* (1958), iii of *Manuel d'archéologie égyptienne* (Paris, 1952–78), pp. 1–143
J.-Ph. Lauer and J. Leclant: 'Découverte de statues de prisonniers au temple de la pyramide de Pépi I', *Rev. Egyptol.*, xxi (1969), pp. 55–62
C. Aldred: 'Statuaire', *Le Temps des pyramides* (1978), i of *Le Monde égyptien: Les Pharaons*, ed. J. Leclant (Paris, 1978–80), pp. 171–205
B. V. Bothmer: 'On Realism in Egyptian Funerary Sculpture of the Old Kingdom', *Expedition*, xxiv/2 (1982), pp. 27–39

JAROMIR MALEK

(b) Relief. High raised relief was popular in the early Old Kingdom, and the dramatic impact of this style is exemplified by one of the few preserved examples of 4th-Dynasty royal relief, a fragment from the lower cult temple of King Sneferu's 'Bent Pyramid' at Dahshur, which shows the bold profile of a lioness goddess breathing life into the King's nostrils. The same effect is apparent in the raised reliefs of the 4th Dynasty nobles' tombs at Maidum, Dahshur and Saqqara. Raised relief continued to be used throughout the Old Kingdom, varying in thickness from the fine bas-reliefs of the pyramid complex of Sahure (reg c. 2458–c. 2446 BC) at Abusir, to the very high reliefs in the mortuary temple of Pepy II at Saqqara.

During the Old Kingdom, royal sculptors' workshops seem to have been used by private individuals, judging from the fact that certain private reliefs rival royal sculptures in quality, while others bear inscriptions claiming that 'the false door, in limestone from Tura, was made by order of the king'. The sheer size of bas-reliefs from the pyramid complex of Sahure is impressive, but some false-door stelae from private tombs are up to 4 m high, suggesting that certain private tomb chapels may also have been on a large scale.

Royal reliefs probably served as models for those in private tombs, therefore their repertories are often similar, including scenes of hunting in the desert, fishing and fowling in the marshes, the herding of cattle, the slaughtering of oxen, long processions of offering bearers, and the mating and birth of animals. Other scenes are peculiar to royal reliefs: the king massacring his enemies or celebrating the *sed*-festival (royal jubilee), the royal nursling or face-to-face encounters between kings and gods (who were not depicted in private funerary reliefs until the New Kingdom, see §(vii)(b) below).

Scenes in private mastabas include both large-scale stationary figures of the deceased and his family (identified by their names and titles) and smaller-scale anonymous figures attending to the needs of the deceased. Virtually all of these reliefs centre on the production of food, with scenes depicting farmyards, kitchens, fattening and slaughtering of animals (see fig. 54), agricultural labours, fruit harvesting, trap setting, hunting in the desert and marshes, and fishing. The deceased himself participates to a certain extent in food production by chasing water-fowl and

54. Old Kingdom relief of butchers slaughtering an ox, painted limestone, h. 250 mm, in the tomb of Idut, Saqqara, 6th Dynasty, *c. 2325–c. 2150* BC

harpoon-fishing in the papyrus thickets. There are also endless processions of estates (allegorical personifications of the properties of the deceased) carrying the harvest.

The deceased is most often shown seated in front of a table symbolically laden with bread. Sometimes only the funerary 'meal' is portrayed, as in the oldest mastabas, the decoration of which consists only of a single decorated panel (*see* STELE, §2), and in the 4th Dynasty mastabas at Giza, which have the unique feature of a decorated slab concealed in their limestone revetment.

Scenes without any references to food are relatively rare, but they include depictions of markets, craftsmen's workshops (joiners, carpenters, sculptors, goldsmiths and glass-blowers), children's games, nautical competitions between sailors, musical entertainments and dancing displays. There are only a few representations of the deceased's official duties, such as the scenes of male and female textile workers receiving rewards in the 4th Dynasty tomb of Seneb, the chief weaver of the palace, at Giza, and the portrayals of circumcision, pedicure and manicure in the 6th Dynasty tomb of the doctor Ankhmahor, at Saqqara. In other tombs there are scenes of official tours of inspection (in a kind of sedan-chair) and depictions of the deceased listening to the reports of scribes, but they are incomparable with the huge compositions on this theme in New Kingdom private tombs.

The private reliefs vary in such aspects as thickness (1–12 mm), treatment of the surface (ranging from smooth to extremely ornate) and size and number of figures. The reliefs in the mastaba of Uhemka (Hildesheim, Pelizaeus-Mus.) create the impression of entering an ancestral gallery, owing to the large size of the images of the deceased and his family (in relation to the size of the chapel) and the closely packed arrangement of the images, leaving little room for other scenes. There are also variations in facial expressions, the corpulence of the deceased and the artists' interest or lack of interest in anatomy and physiognomy.

It would be premature to trace the history of the repertory and style of Old Kingdom private relief, since the private mastabas are still poorly dated. From the 4th Dynasty onwards, however, certain tombs (such as those of Nefermaat and Khafreankh, at Maidum and Giza respectively) already show a reasonably complete iconographic programme. The mastabas of certain reigns were characterized by distinct ways of representing the deceased (that could reflect the inclinations of an era). Those inscribed with the cartouche of the first 6th Dynasty king Teti (*reg c.* 2325–*c.* 2291 BC), for instance, have depictions of the deceased with large eyes, a radiant expression and an expansive, almost bloated, outline. Such similarity suggests the use of the same teams of sculptors.

BIBLIOGRAPHY

W. S. Smith: *A History of Egyptian Sculpture and Painting in the Old Kingdom* (Oxford, 1946/*R* 1978)
H. Altenmüller: 'Flachbildkunst der Frühzeit und des Alten Reiches', *Das alte Ägypten*, ed. C. Vandersleyen, Propyläen-Kstgesch., xv (Berlin, 1975), pp. 273–92
J. Vercoutter: 'Bas-relief et peinture', *Le Temps des pyramides* (1978), i of *Le Monde égyptien: Les Pharaons*, ed. J. Leclant (Paris, 1978–80), pp. 121–69
Y. Harpur: *Decoration in Egyptian Tombs of the Old Kingdom* (London and New York, 1987)
N. Cherpion: *Mastabas et hypogées de l'Ancien Empire: Le Problème de la datation* (Brussels, 1989)

NADINE CHERPION

(iv) First Intermediate Period (c. 2150–c. 2008 BC). The fall of the Old Kingdom was followed by a chaotic period in which Egypt was divided into two contemporaneous kingdoms: the 9th and 10th dynasties (ruling from Herakleopolis Magna) and the early 11th Dynasty (ruling from Thebes). The output of the royal sculptors' workshops at Memphis was severely curtailed and most surviving First

Intermediate Period sculpture derives from Herakleopolis Magna, Thebes and various provincial centres (e.g. Dendara, Asyut and el-Moalla). Although the sculpture preserved several aspects of the Old Kingdom style—making it difficult to date and often difficult to distinguish from sculpture of the late Old Kingdom or early Middle Kingdom—it was characterized by many iconographic idiosyncracies and local stylistic peculiarities.

(a) Statuary. Only a few royal statues have survived, including two representations of the 11th Dynasty ruler Inyotef II (Horus Wahankh; *reg c.* 2065–*c.* 2016 BC) and an incomplete limestone seated statue of Mentuhotpe-aa, an ancestor of the kings of the 11th Dynasty. These three statues were found at Elephantine.

Most statues of private individuals in this period come from provincial cemeteries in Middle Egypt, particularly Asyut. Other sites, such as Saqqara, have yielded similar sculptures that may be contemporary but have not yet been properly studied. Virtually all private statues were of wood and the most common type was the single standing figure (for illustration *see* ASYUT). Sometimes the figure is quite large (up to two-thirds life-size) with detailed—although simplified—modelling and less strict adherence to the canon of proportions, as in the case of the statue of Wepwawetemhet (Boston, MA, Mus. F.A., 04.1780). Most are slender figures with short, curled wigs, prominent (often inlaid) eyes, horizontal eyebrows, large hands and long fingers. Statues of women are often nude.

During the First Intermediate Period the 'servant statuettes' developed into small-scale wooden models consisting of groups of figures, which are usually quite crude and functionally distinct from statues proper (*see* §XIII, 3(i) below). There are also larger (h. *c.* 600 mm), more carefully made statuettes of women bringing farm produce. The typical statue of a female offering-bearer stands with her left foot advanced, balancing a basket on her head with her left hand and holding a bird in the other (*see* fig. 82).

BIBLIOGRAPHY
E. Chassinat and C. Palanque: *Une Campagne de fouilles dans la nécropole d'Assiout* (Cairo, 1911)
J. H. Breasted jr: *Egyptian Servant Statues* (Washington, DC, 1948)
J. Vandier: *Les Grandes Époques: La Statuaire* (1958), iii of *Manuel d'archéologie égyptienne* (Paris, 1952–78), pp. 147–62
L. Habachi: *Elephantine*, iv (Mainz, 1985), pp. 109–11, pls 187–92

(b) Relief. No royal structures with relief decoration are known from the regions of Memphis and Herakleopolis Magna during this period, but at el-Tarif, in the Theban area, the *saff* tomb (a type of royal rock tomb, *see* THEBES (i), §IX) of Inyotef III (*reg c.* 2016–*c.* 2008 BC) was probably partly decorated in sunk relief.

Some aspects of Old Kingdom relief style were preserved in the private tombs of the region controlled by the Herakleopolitan kings of the 9th and 10th dynasties. The architectural context of the reliefs, however, had changed dramatically. In the small free-standing tomb chapels that were built at Saqqara in the late Old Kingdom and the First Intermediate Period, only the false door stele (*see* STELE, §2) and the two side panels flanking it had relief decoration. The scenes on these are in registers and represent a synopsis of the wall decoration of earlier

chapels, including such themes as the tomb owner at a table laden with offerings, lists or rows of items of funerary equipment, and scenes of butchery and the presentation of offerings. They are usually in low, raised relief with little internal modelling and the outlines of figures showing a pronounced tendency towards straight lines. The accompanying texts are either in raised or sunk relief (sometimes both).

At Herakleopolis Magna free-standing structures, including both burial chambers and cult places, incorporated small chapels decorated with raised reliefs in which most of the traditional Old Kingdom themes were retained (see fig. 55). The quality of line (and occasionally also modelling) is superior to that at Saqqara. Similar raised reliefs

55. First Intermediate Period relief showing servants brewing beer and cooking, Herakleopolis Magna, limestone, 800×350 mm, *c.* 2150–*c.* 2008 BC (Cairo, Egyptian Museum)

have also been found at Dendara (e.g. the early 9th Dynasty free-standing tomb of Mereri).

In the rock-cut tombs of Middle and Upper Egypt figured reliefs were generally replaced by paintings (because of the lack of skilled sculptors and the poor quality of rock). Small scenes in relief (of the tomb owner, his wife, offering bearers and relatives) were often carved on the lintels or jambs of doorways (e.g. at Akhmim and Nag el-Deir). As tomb stelae changed from the 'false-door' type to the Upper Egyptian rectangular slab, their decoration sometimes incorporated additional figures or scenes in relief (see STELE, §2). At Asyut the tomb chapel of Khety II contains scenes executed in shallow sunk relief, portraying Khety and his wife as well as the novel theme of soldiers with battle-axes and shields, arranged in three registers. At Hagarsa the tomb of Meryaa (perhaps dating to the Herakleopolitan period) contains a variety of scenes in shallow sunk relief, including large figures of Mery-aa and his family, preparation of food, fowling and fishing, cattle breeding (including bulls fighting), donkeys and goats. At EL-MOALLA the tomb of Ankhtifi (probably 9th Dynasty) contains flat bas-reliefs depicting large 'formal' figures of the deceased.

BIBLIOGRAPHY

W. M. F. Petrie: *Athribis* (London, 1908), pp. 3–4, pls vi–ix
W. S. Smith: *A History of Egyptian Sculpture and Painting in the Old Kingdom* (London and Boston, MA, 1946, rev. 2/1949/R 1978), pp. 217–43
W. S. Smith and W. K. Simpson: *The Art and Architecture of Ancient Egypt*, Pelican Hist. A. (Harmondsworth, 1958, rev. 2/1981), pp. 151–7
H. G. Fischer: *Dendera in the Third Millennium BC down to the Theban Domination of Upper Egypt* (New York, 1968)
J. Lopez: 'Rapport préliminaire sur les fouilles d'Hérakléopolis (1968)', *Oriens Ant.*, xiv (1975), pp. 57–78
D. Arnold: *Gräber des alten und mittleren Reiches in El-Tarif* (Mainz, 1976)

JAROMIR MALEK

(v) Middle Kingdom (c. *2008*–c. *1630* BC*).* The reunification of Egypt by the Theban Nebhepetre Mentuhotpe II ushered in widespread modifications in the country's political structure, changes in the meaning of kingship and new religious beliefs, all of which are reflected in Middle Kingdom sculpture. The sculptors of the period attempted to accommodate these changes within the existing framework of Old Kingdom artistic conventions and then to go beyond this framework when its parameters no longer fulfilled royal needs.

The reign of Mentuhotpe II was characterized by royal building activity after a period almost devoid of large-scale enterprises. His largest and most important project was his mortuary temple at Deir el-Bahri (see THEBES (i), §IV). The earlier reliefs at Deir el-Bahri were somewhat provincial (see §X, 2 below), but later works were characterized by greater sobriety and a return to the Old Kingdom conventions, perhaps as a result of renewed contact with sculptors at Memphis. By the reign of Sankhkare Mentuhotpe III (*reg c.* 1957–*c.* 1945 BC), a more refined country-wide style of relief had emerged. When Ammenemes I (*reg c.* 1938–*c.* 1908 BC), former vizier of Nebtawyre Mentuhotpe IV (*reg c.* 1945–*c.* 1938 BC) and first king of the 12th Dynasty, moved the capital from Thebes to It-tawy (near EL-LISHT) in the north, he re-established links with the Old Kingdom royal artistic traditions at Memphis.

BIBLIOGRAPHY

D. Wildung: *Sesostris und Amenemhet: Ägypten im mittleren Reich* (Munich, 1984)
Pharaohs and Mortals: Egyptian Art in the Middle Kingdom (exh. cat. by J. Bourriau, Cambridge, Fitzwilliam; Liverpool Mus., 1988)

(a) Statuary. (b) Relief.

(a) Statuary.

11th Dynasty (c. *2081*–c. *1938* BC*).* On a terraced façade of his mortuary temple at Deir el-Bahri, Nebhepetre Mentuhotpe II erected cross-armed statues of himself wearing the knee-length wrapped garment associated with the *sed*-festival (royal jubilee). This was the first time that large numbers of royal sculptures had been set up in an open area visible to the general populace, thereby serving as ever-present reminders of the presence and power of the monarch. This represented a dramatic change from the Old Kingdom ideal of kingship, where the king was the aloof representative of the gods on earth, and royal images were largely restricted to the interior of funerary temples, from which the general public was largely excluded.

The statues of Mentuhotpe II from the Deir el-Bahri temple terraces (e.g. New York, Met., 26.3.29) and another figure of the King, found in an underground cenotaph in the temple's courtyard (Cairo, Egyp. Mus., JE 36195), also depart from the Old Kingdom sculptural style and aesthetic. Stocky proportions successfully convey a strength and energy absent from earlier royal works. In general, Theban-based artisans, who lacked first-hand familiarity with the traditional Old Kingdom schools of the Memphite region, created works with a decided provincial stamp. This is apparent not only in the royal sculpture but also in private pieces (e.g. the statue of Intef; Cairo, Egyp. Mus., JE 89858). Figures have block-like heads, connected to bodies by short, thick necks, and lack delicate surface modelling. Heavy features merely rest on the facial surface rather than being modelled into it.

The greater refinement of the sculpture of Sankhare Mentuhotpe III is especially apparent in the statues of the King in the cross-armed 'Osirid' pose that stood in a temple at Armant dedicated to Montu, its local god (e.g. Boston, MA, Mus. F.A., 38.1395, and Luxor Mus., J. 69). Slender columnar bodies—for the first time entirely enveloped in the cloak of Osiris, god of resurrection—feature subtle torso modelling. The oval shape of the face is emphasized by an elongated Upper Egyptian white crown. Like the torso, the facial surface displays much more modelling than in the previous reign, and the features are more naturalistically rendered.

12th Dynasty (c. *1938*–c. *1756* BC*).* A statue of Ammenemes I found at Tanis (Cairo, Egyp. Mus., JE 37470) shows strong affinities to royal works of the previous dynasty. As far as private statuary is concerned, the block statue (see §(i)(c) above) appeared for the first time at the beginning of the 12th Dynasty (e.g. the limestone statue of the treasurer Hetep, Cairo, Egyp. Mus., JE 48857). It has been suggested that this statue type represents the deceased as a *hesy* (Egyp.: 'sanctified being'), rising from the horizon reborn like the sun each day.

The numerous statues of Sesostris I (*reg c.* 1918–*c.* 1875 BC), son and successor of Ammenemes I, vary in type, style and geographic origin. Since he ruled as co-regent with his father for almost ten years, it is not surprising to find substantial stylistic continuity. The powerful solidity of form and heavy, stylized facial features that characterized 11th Dynasty works continue, especially in sculptures of the King from the Theban area, where, understandably, influence from the 11th Dynasty kings remained strong (e.g. Cairo, Egyp. Mus., CG 42007).

However, other sculptural representations of Sesostris I, such as those from the Faiyum region, display much greater awareness of an organic body structure. For instance, a sweetly idealizing royal face is found on the ten limestone statues of the King (Cairo, Egyp. Mus., CG 411–20) from his funerary precinct at el-Lisht. Timeless and eternally youthful, these statues clearly imitate the Old Kingdom royal image, seen, for example, in representations of Chephren (e.g. Cairo, Egyp. Mus., CG 14; see fig. 52 above) or Mycerinus (e.g. Cairo, Egyp. Mus., JE 40678).

Although Sesostris I's artisans successfully mastered the Old Kingdom physical body type and expanded their repertory to include most Old Kingdom forms, they failed to reproduce the other-worldly aloofness embodied in the Old Kingdom prototypes. By comparison, the Middle Kingdom copies lack emotion and character strength. Statues of private individuals made during the reign of Sesostris I often accentuate some of the idiosyncrasies of the royal works (as in the exaggerated rendering of the rib cage, seen, for example, on the statue of Intef; London, BM, 461).

Comparatively few royal works survive from the reign of Ammenemes II (reg c. 1876–c. 1842 BC), son and successor of Sesostris I. A colossal red granite sphinx found at Tanis (Paris, Louvre, A 23) has the massive face and stylized features common earlier in the dynasty. Here, however, these form a more integral part of the face. Larger than any free-standing sphinx made previously (h. 2.06 m, l. 4.79 m), it heralds a trend toward greater monumentality. Ammenemes II's wives and daughters were also immortalized as sphinxes (as in Paris, Louvre, AO 13075—a small sphinx of Ita found at Qatna in Syria).

From an art-historical point of view, one of the least studied but most innovative kings of the 12th Dynasty was Sesostris II (reg c. 1844–c. 1837 BC), son and successor of Ammenemes II. For the first time statues of an Egyptian monarch began to display signs of age. Sesostris II's eyes are sunk beneath overhanging brows, and diagonal furrows connect the nose to a pursed mouth. In contrast to this expressive facial modelling, his torsos are bland and youthfully idealizing, following the traditional body form of the Old Kingdom. This juxtaposition of age and youth is also seen on contemporary private works.

During the reign of Sesostris III (reg c. 1837–c. 1818 BC), son of Sesostris II, the suggestions of age that appeared on the royal face in sculpture of the previous reign evolved into the unmistakable stamp of rugged maturity evident on all of the King's images (for illustration see SESOSTRIS III). A furrowed brow, pouches under deeply sunk eyes, hollow cheeks, and deep lines running diagonally downward from the corners of the eyes, nose and mouth, turned the countenance of the King, who

attempted to eradicate Egyptian feudalism, into psychological portraits of power and intimidation (such as the granite statue from Thebes; Cairo, Egyp. Mus., RT 18.4.22.4). Many of the statues of Sesostris III are larger than life-size. Stern, self-assured and awesome, they stood outside temples or inside open courtyards where they provided highly visible reminders of the King's temporal power over the destiny of his subjects.

By this time, the increasing prominence of Osiris, god of the netherworld, had altered the focus of worship from this world to the hereafter. Because participation in the rites of Osiris was open to all, vast numbers of small-scale, often mediocre-quality private statues were created so that they might be deposited primarily at Abydos, the god's burial place and cult centre. It was hoped that they would guarantee their owners' eternal presence in the yearly drama of the god's resurrection and a share of his offerings. Many echo the style established by Sesostris III and his successors, but they lack the subtleties and refinements of the royal works. Also beginning around this time there was a tendency to clothe more of the body. Men are portrayed in high-waisted calf-length skirts (e.g. Boston, MA, Mus. F.A., 1973.87) or with their entire torsos enveloped in a cloak (e.g. New York, Brooklyn Mus., 41.83). By the 13th Dynasty a swollen belly was sometimes evident under the increased material (e.g. London, BM, 1842).

The royal physiognomy of Ammenemes III (reg c. 1818–c. 1770 BC), son and successor of Sesostris III, was superficially similar to that of the previous reign, but in execution the signs of age tend to be less pronounced. The face itself is fuller, and shallower furrows render the overall impact somewhat less severe. A number of representations of Ammenemes III focus attention on the mouth, which protrudes slightly as if in a pout. Although the shape of the eye is similar in father and son, Ammenemes III's eyes are often not as severely hooded by an overhanging brow. The image of the king as priest is made explicit in a black granite statue from Mit Faris in the Faiyum (Cairo, Egyp. Mus., CG 395), in which Ammenemes III wears a leopard-skin garment, the first time a king is so shown. Clutched to each side are vertical poles terminating in falcon heads, representing Horus, the god associated with kingship.

This image of the king as priest is the prototype for the standard-bearing statue common in the New Kingdom (see §(vii)(a) below). The brute strength of the King is undoubtedly the emphasis of a black granite statue found at Tanis (Cairo, Egyp. Mus., CG 394), in which a lion's mane encircles the royal face. This differs from earlier sphinxes, which featured only a lion's torso with a human head. The divine king is shown in a head of Amun (Cairo, Egyp. Mus., RT 13.4.22.9), which bears the unmistakable features of Ammenemes III.

Other statues of Ammenemes III bear little of the imagery of advancing years. A seated limestone statue of the King from his funerary temple at Hawara (Cairo, Egyp. Mus., CG 385; for illustration see AMMENEMES III) shows him with a relatively unlined, unemotional face. In its calculated aloofness, it consciously evokes the Old Kingdom ideal of kingship, and in its agelessness it provides an ideal likeness of the King for a funerary context. A representation of King Ammenemes IV offers

56. Middle Kingdom seated statue of Imenj-jatu, grey granite, h. 810 mm, from the sanctuary of Heqaib at Elephantine, late 12th Dynasty, *c.* 1800 BC (Cairo, Egyptian Museum)

only a vague reflection of the vigour of his predecessors. All known statues of the last monarch of the dynasty, Queen Neferusoek, are headless.

13th and 14th dynasties (c. 1756–c. 1532 BC). Kings of the 13th Dynasty incorporated aspects of royal iconography of the late 12th Dynasty in their numerous sculptures. Although usually easy to distinguish from 12th Dynasty works by their somewhat blander faces and oddly proportioned torsos, statues of the many 13th Dynasty kings who ruled in this relatively short period (*c.* 150 years) are often difficult to distinguish from one another unless they are inscribed. The wooden standing figure of King Anibre Hor (*reg c.* 1745 BC; Cairo, Egyp. Mus.) is one of the finest surviving examples.

There are few items of statuary from the Asiatic 14th Dynasty in the western Delta, which may have been contemporary with the 13th Dynasty. The real power of the country may well have rested in the hands of high officials, a number of whom commissioned some of the finest works of the dynasty. There are, for example, the statues of Gebu (Copenhagen, Ny Carlsberg Glyp., AEIN 27), Sobkemsaf (Vienna, Ksthist. Mus., 5801) and Imenj-jatu (Cairo, Egyp. Mus.; see fig. 56). With the invasion of the Hyksos following the 13th Dynasty, the Middle Kingdom sculptural tradition came to a close.

BIBLIOGRAPHY
H. G. Evers: *Staat aus dem Stein*, 2 vols (Munich, 1929)
C. Aldred: 'Some Royal Portraits of the Middle Kingdom in Ancient Egypt', *Met. Mus. J.*, iii (1970), pp. 27–50
W. V. Davies: *A Royal Statue Reattributed*, BM Occas. Pap. 28 (London, 1981).
L. Habachi: *The Sanctuary of Heqaib*, 2 vols (Mainz, 1985)

(b) Relief.

11th Dynasty (c. 2081–c. 1938 BC*).* The raised reliefs on the walls of the tomb chapels dedicated to the minor queens of Nebhepetre Mentuhotpe II at Deir el-Bahri have high, almost three-dimensional, contoured surfaces and there is extensive use of intricate, incised interior detailing. The facial features are attenuated and otherwise oddly shaped, and the figures are awkwardly proportioned due to the lack of technical ability to recreate the Old Kingdom canon of proportion. Sunk reliefs contemporary with the minor queens' chapels feature deep outlining. Many of these characteristics are evident, but to a lesser extent, in reliefs at nearby Gebelein and Dendara, and earlier in Thebes on the stelae of the Inyotef kings and their followers.

A trend towards more naturalistic representation is evident in reliefs from the tomb of Nebhepetre Mentuhotpe II's chief queen, Neferu, built as part of the next phase of the Deir el-Bahri project. They display less exaggerated, more harmoniously integrated facial features, greater selectivity of detail and a less three-dimensional quality (fragments at New York, Met., and New Haven, CT, Yale U. A.G.).

This trend reached its culmination in the last phases of the Deir el-Bahri temple, specifically in the raised reliefs of the colonnades, hall and sanctuary (e.g. Geneva, Mus. A. & Hist., 4583), built after the reunification of Egypt had been completed. Their definite sobriety replaced the playfulness of the pre-reunification works, and the mastery of the more true-to-life canon of the Old Kingdom resulted in less awkwardly proportioned figures. The raised reliefs were decidedly lower and the excessive interior detailing vanished. Outside Thebes at this time, major relief works fell within the broad unifying umbrella of the late Deir el-Bahri style, although there was still regional variation. This represents a decided change from earlier when local tradition supplanted outside influences. Private relief styles largely parallel royal styles.

As with statuary, many of the changes may be attributed to renewed contacts with sculptural schools that served the royal residence at Memphis. There, a multitude of earlier works were available as models, and Old Kingdom traditions were probably maintained, albeit on a much reduced scale, throughout the First Intermediate Period.

During the reign of Sankhkare Mentuhotpe III (*reg c.* 1957–*c.* 1945 BC), regional variations in relief virtually disappeared. Figures, objects and hieroglyphs were executed in an extremely low, flat, raised relief, with meticulously carved interior detail. These details faithfully reproduce nature, unlike the fanciful incised decoration of the reliefs of the tombs of the minor queens of Nebhepetre Mentuhotpe II. Both within the individual figures and in the overall composition, each aspect is coherently integrated into a balanced whole, and the overall effect is one of delicacy and subtlety.

The few surviving private reliefs dated to the reign of Mentuhotpe III display the royal stamp. For instance, reliefs from the tomb of Meketre at Thebes are extremely low and flat, but the fine interior details (the hallmark of Mentuhotpe III's style) were carried out with a paintbrush rather than a chisel.

12th and 13th dynasties (c. *1938*–c.*1630* BC). During the reign of Ammenemes I a deliberate attempt to emulate Old Kingdom works is apparent and understandable given that abundant material of the 5th and 6th dynasties was readily accessible. Royal and private reliefs shared a low, slightly rounded surface, limited use of incised or modelled details, prominent figures with strong, although not exaggerated, facial features, and a pronounced, sometimes forced symmetry in the arrangement of personal effects and offerings. This somewhat austere treatment, a characteristic of many Old Kingdom Memphite works, replaced the Theban preference for more crowded compositions and lavish incised interior detail. Overall, these reliefs display great technical competence, but their studied academicism bears testimony to a deliberate attempt to duplicate rather than to create. Nevertheless, in their subject-matter and purity of design, they successfully reproduce the essence of Old Kingdom Memphite works. Reliefs from Ammenemes I's funerary temple at el-Lisht, for example, display an aloofness befitting the divinity of kingship so strongly expressed during the Old Kingdom. He even incorporated 4th-Dynasty royal reliefs into this temple, perhaps as an expression of reverence for the earlier age.

While artisans executing private commissions at this time uniformly observed the Old Kingdom canon and generally followed the courtly preference for low raised relief, those outside the Memphite area were not bound by the formality of royal works. They began to explore new subjects and new modes of representation, and in the best cases, such as the tomb of Senbi (B1) at MEIR, the

results exhibit an imagination and creativity seen only rarely in Egyptian relief work. In contrast, the tomb of Ihy at Saqqara might easily have been attributed to the Old Kingdom on the basis of the low surface and traditionalism of its reliefs, if the cartouche of Ammenemes I were not present.

Sesostris I's continuation of his father's attempt to reproduce Old Kingdom works is perhaps best exemplified by his funerary temple at el-Lisht, which copied the layout and relief style of the 6th Dynasty funerary temple of Pepy II (*reg c.* 2246–*c.* 2150 BC) at Saqqara. Raised reliefs in this period tended to be markedly higher, more plastically modelled and covered with more incised interior detailing than in the reign of Ammenemes I. Sunk reliefs were correspondingly more deeply outlined and internally decorated.

Overall, the stiff formalism of the previous reign broke down as artists gained confidence and competence. Although the sensitivity and realism manifest in the el-Lisht reliefs make them the finest of their time, other relief projects of Sesostris I, which were more numerous and geographically widespread than under his predecessors, were decidedly similar in style. Thus, the tradition of having a countrywide royal relief style, present already at the end of the 11th Dynasty, was maintained.

During the reigns of Ammenemes II and Sesostris II the geographical extent and amount of royal relief decreased considerably. From the time of Ammenemes II only a poorly preserved pylon at Hermopolis Magna and a few fragments from his pyramid complex at Dahshur have survived. Unfortunately they permit little in the way of stylistic analysis. Private relief is similarly less abundant, but in at least one instance displays a stark realism, perhaps even portraiture, in an age of idealization. The pouting lower lip, upturned nose, sagging chin and wrinkle-filled neck of Ammenemes II's vizier Siese in his tomb reliefs at Dahshur masterfully convey the image of a stern and powerful bureaucrat (see fig. 57).

Reliefs from the funerary temple of Sesostris II at el-Lahun show the beginnings of a trend toward the 'careworn' visage, which reached a high point later in the dynasty. A plastically rendered brow, an incised line above the eye and a slight depression below emphasize the eye area. In contrast, the staid, sterile processions of flat, unmodelled figures are the products of a mechanical formula that is technically competent, but aesthetically uninspired. A similar, generally dry appearance and treatment of the eye may be found in the tomb of the nomarch Ibu at Qaw el-Kebir.

The number of large private tombs declined during the reign of Sesostris III in the wake of his attempt to centralize power. However, at the same time there was a dramatic increase in the number of private stelae, mainly deposited at Abydos and usually featuring the owner and various family members beside tables of offerings. Although earlier in the dynasty (and as early as the 11th Dynasty) they display some variety in their subject-matter and carving method, by the end of the 12th Dynasty they tend to be reduced to sunk-relief figures in repetitive poses accompanied by schematically rendered funerary goods.

The royal building projects of Sesostris III were not as extensive as his military prowess and later heroic reputation

57. Middle Kingdom relief of the vizier Siese, 0.88×1.19 m, from Dahshur, reign of Ammenemes II, *c.* 1876–*c.* 1842 BC (Cairo, Egyptian Museum)

might suggest. His finest reliefs, additions to the Montu temple at Madamud, fully develop the psychological image of the all-powerful ruler. Whether in raised or sunk relief, large eyes protrude from heavy lids and overhanging brows, and furrows delineate the area beneath the eye, span the length of the nose and extend diagonally from nostril to lips. These hallmarks continue to a lesser extent to characterize reliefs of Ammenemes III, but by the 13th Dynasty an attempt by Sobkhotpe I in his temple at Madamud to reproduce both content and style of a lintel of Sesostris III from the same site resulted in an ill-proportioned, vapid echo of the earlier work.

In contrast, private stelae from the end of the 12th Dynasty into the Second Intermediate Period are generally mass-produced and display crudely carved, ill-proportioned figures, and an overall awkwardness. By the Second Intermediate Period, as in the First Intermediate Period, the decline in central authority resulted in the development of regional styles, which in their lack of technical competence strike the modern viewer as humorous, charming and inventive.

BIBLIOGRAPHY

H. Fischer: 'Flachbildkunst der mittleren Reiches', *Das alte Ägypten*, ed. C. Vandersleyen, Propyläen Kstgesch., xv (Berlin, 1975), pp. 292–304

R. Freed: 'A Private Stela from Naga ed-Der and Relief Style of the Reign of Amenemhat I', *Studies in Ancient Egypt, the Aegean and the Sudan: Essays in Honor of Dows Dunham*, ed. W. K. Simpson and W. Davis (Boston, MA, 1981), pp. 68–76

B. Jaros-Deckert: *Grabung im Asasif 1963–1970*, v (Mainz, 1984)

RITA E. FREED

(vi) Second Intermediate Period (c. 1630–c. 1540 BC). This period theoretically comprises the six Hyksos kings (15th Dynasty), a dissident dynasty partly in the Nile Delta (16th Dynasty) and a line of 15 Theban princes (17th Dynasty). There is no surviving original sculpture from the roughly contemporary 15th and 16th dynasties. The strongly Egyptianized Hyksos kings—who bore pharaonic titles and seem to have appreciated Egyptian monuments—preferred to take possession of earlier works by engraving their names on them.

Nevertheless, some Egyptian sculptors must still have been working in the Second Intermediate Period since statues were created for the 17th Dynasty Theban kings, although the rate of production was much reduced compared with the Middle Kingdom. Judging from the reliefs of one of the 17th Dynasty kings, Nubkheperre Inyotef V, at Koptos, the traditional artistic conventions were still being observed, but there were great discrepancies between workshops. All the works have an occasionally sullen seriousness as well as a stiffness inherited from the Middle Kingdom.

(a) Statuary. The statues usurped by 15th Dynasty rulers include an Old Kingdom sphinx (Paris, Louvre, A23), maned sphinxes of Ammenemes III (e.g. Cairo, Egyp. Mus., C. 394) and two colossi of the 13th Dynasty king Mermesha (Cairo, Egyp. Mus., JE 37466–7)—all discovered at Tanis. At Bubastis the Hyksos king Khian took over a statue of a Middle Kingdom ruler.

The 17th Dynasty kings continued to commission Egyptian sculptors. Ten royal statues are known, and six of them were left by a king known as Sebekemsaf, I or II (probably all by the first). Of these statues, two red granite pieces are complete and of exceptional quality: a seated statue (London, BM, 871; see fig. 58), probably from Karnak, and a standing statue (Cairo, Egyp. Mus.) from Abydos. The sculptors who worked this difficult material were master craftsmen. The unpolished standing statue of Sebekemsaf I is muscled, sturdy and vigorous, while the highly polished seated figure has a thin face and abnormally narrow waist. The impressive workmanship of these masterpieces is reminiscent of the 13th Dynasty, and it

58. Second Intermediate Period seated statue of Sebekemsaf I, probably from Karnak, red granite, h. 1.64 m, probably 13th or 17th Dynasty (London, British Museum)

appears that Sebekemsaf I was a king of this dynasty. From the 17th Dynasty, there are four pieces of royal stone statuary: two have survived only in the form of bases; the other two are large, limestone sphinxes (Cairo, Egyp. Mus., JE 48874–5) of Mentuhotpe VII (or Mentuhotepi), the 5th king of the 17th Dynasty, from Edfu, the faces of which are exceedingly barbaric in style. It was only at about the end of the 17th Dynasty that art was revived, as is testified by the four large coffins in gilded wood for the kings Nubkheperre Inyotef (London, BM, 6652), Upmaat Inyotef (Paris, Louvre, E3019), Seqenenre Tao (Cairo, Egyp. Mus., CG61001) and of the queen Ahhotpe I (Cairo, Egyp. Mus., CG28501).

Private 17th Dynasty statuary is rare and difficult to date. The admirable limestone statue of Prince Ahmose, son of one of the last 17th Dynasty rulers (Paris, Louvre, E 15682) and elder brother of King Ahmose (*reg c.* 1540–*c.* 1514 BC), shows great finesse in its details and exceptional expressiveness in the face. There are also various small statues, such as the stiff figure of Princess Ahhotpe (Paris, Louvre, N 446) and the gauche, badly proportioned seated figure of Siamun (New York, Met., 65.115).

(b) Relief. The few remaining fragments of 15th Dynasty reliefs bear little more than the names of kings. The scarab, particularly widespread during this period, carries a distinctive sunk-relief decoration, in which human or animal figures are adapted to a narrow framework and certain parts of the silhouettes are sometimes covered by hatching (*see* §XVI, 15(iii) below).

In the 17th Dynasty, Nubkheperre Inyotef V built at Abydos and Koptos, and excavations at the latter site have revealed the most numerous and significant reliefs of the period. Everything in the Koptos reliefs is correctly drawn and sculpted, including the figures of the King and the gods Min, Horus and Montu, as well as the hieroglyphs, the execution of which is always the best indication of the quality of Egyptian art. In one fragment, the King is depicted in the act of being crowned with the double crown by Horus and another (obliterated) god; he has a very lively physiognomy, strongly resembling that reproduced on his coffin (London, BM). The relief work from Koptos, however, without being negligent, is not particularly scrupulous.

Private stelae of the 17th Dynasty appear to be fewer than in the 13th Dynasty, but this is partly because only those bearing royal names can be reliably dated. The stele of Hornakhte (London, BM, 1645), from Edfu, bears the name of Nubkheperre Inyotef V alongside figures of Horus and Isis, which are represented gauchely but in accordance with the standard conventions. The same style characterizes a number of stelae that are carved with the figure of a king but were probably dedicated by the person depicted following him, such as those of Nakhte (U. Chicago, IL, Orient. Inst. Mus.) and Iahnefer (Philadelphia, U. PA, Mus., E 16021), both from Abydos. A stele of the reign of Kamose, the last king of the dynasty (Paris, Louvre, C 201), on which the text is more copious than the figures, is a mixture of gaucheness, mastery and originality, as are most reliefs from this period of transition.

BIBLIOGRAPHY

W. S. Smith and W. K. Simpson: *The Art and Architecture of Ancient Egypt*, Pelican Hist. A. (Harmondsworth, 1958, rev. 2/1981), pp. 216–23 [relief]

J. Vandier: *Les Grandes Epoques: La Statuaire* (1958), iii of *Manuel d'archéologie égyptienne* (Paris, 1952–78), pp. 216–20, 291–5

W. V. Davies: *A Royal Statue Reattributed*, BM Occas. Pap. 28 (London, 1981) [incl. detailed cat. & bibliog. of Second Intermediate Period royal statuary]

CLAUDE VANDERSLEYEN

(vii) New Kingdom: pre-Amarna (c. 1540–c. 1353 BC). With the expulsion of the Hyksos (*c.* 1540 BC), Egyptian sculptors faced the challenge of reviving an art form that had been largely dormant for over a century. Since few statues were made in the final decades of Hyksos rule, the sculptors working for Ahmose (*reg c.* 1540–*c.* 1514 BC) and Amenophis I (*reg c.* 1514–*c.* 1493 BC) were not obliged to perpetuate a flourishing style; instead they sought inspiration from Egypt's long artistic past. The details of their sculptures recall the style of the Middle Kingdom. Such archaism appeared throughout Egyptian history, particularly at times of political change. The choice of 11th and 12th Dynasty models was part of a general attempt to buoy up the confidence of the nation by paralleling the new rulers' achievements with those of their Middle Kingdom predecessors.

The artistic individuality of the 18th Dynasty was not fully developed until the reigns of Queen Hatshepsut (*reg c.* 1479–*c.* 1458 BC) and Tuthmosis III (*reg c.* 1479–*c.* 1426 BC), reaching a peak during the reigns of Amenophis II (*reg c.* 1426–*c.* 1400 BC) and Tuthmosis IV (*reg c.* 1400–*c.* 1390 BC). The temples of these rulers in Thebes and Nubia depict the evolution of an original style that linked elegance of form with dynamism of expression. The art of this period is infused with the confidence of the New Kingdom monarchy, which had an established power-base thanks to its victories in western Asia and Nubia. This self-confidence is apparent in the smiling faces of the pharaohs' sculptures.

New artistic trends emerged in the time of Tuthmosis IV and reached their full maturity during the long reign of Amenophis III (*reg c.* 1390–*c.* 1353 BC), which acted as a prelude to the revolutionary changes of the Amarna period (*see* §(viii) below).

BIBLIOGRAPHY

C. Aldred: *Egyptian Art*, World A. (London, 1980), pp. 139–202

K. Mysliwiec: *Eighteenth Dynasty Before the Amarna Period*, Iconography of Religions (Leiden, 1985)

(a) Statuary. (b) Relief.

(a) Statuary. A limestone head of King Ahmose (New York, Charles D. Kelekian priv. col.; see Romano) shows the same unnatural treatment of the eyes, eyebrows and mouth as royal sculptures of the 11th Dynasty and early 12th (e.g. the red granite statue of Sesostris I; Cairo, Egyp. Mus., CG 38230), although Ahmose's countenance is far broader than on the Middle Kingdom pieces and the facial details are widely spaced. His sweet, somewhat ingenuous expression is far livelier than typical early Middle Kingdom faces.

During the reign of Amenophis I there were several royal styles, ranging from the idealized image characteristic of Ahmose's reign (e.g. an alabaster statue from Karnak; Cairo, Egyp. Mus., CG 42061) to a group of Osirid statues

(e.g. London, BM, 683) from Deir el-Bahri, showing the King with a sombre cast that is either an innovation or a reflection of the sobering visages of Sesostris III (*reg c.* 1837–*c.* 1818 BC; for illustration *see* SESOSTRIS III). The treatment of certain facial details on Amenophis I's statues and reliefs is so consistent that they may reproduce the physical characteristics of the living King, including his long, straight, aquiline nose and cleft chin. This suggestion of details copied from life continued through the statuary of the next 50 years.

Tuthmosis I (*reg c.* 1493–*c.* 1482 BC) built extensively in the Temple of Amun at Karnak, and the faces of the statues that he erected there show a benign expression with large, widely dispersed features reminiscent of Ahmose and Amenophis I. The face of Tutkmosis I is crisply carved and details are executed sharply and precisely. However, the dramatic tension in the faces of Ahmose and Amenophis I gives way, under Tuthmosis I, to severe, idealizing masks.

After the ephemeral reign of Tuthmosis II (*reg c.* 1482–*c.* 1479 BC), HATSHEPSUT and her nephew TUTHMOSIS III ruled as co-regents for approximately 22 years. The presence of two rulers, one a woman, posed unprecedented problems for the court sculptors. Representations of the Queen (including many at New York, Met.) from her funerary temple at Deir el-Bahri, usually show her with a male body in traditional costume and attitudes, including striding, sitting and offering to the gods. The face, however, often has a decidedly feminine cast. Her artisans gave her a round countenance, and her fleshy cheeks contrasted with the severe angularity of the earlier rulers' faces. The eyebrows, eyelids and mouth feature bold, sweeping curves. The delicate carving of her facial details (particularly her upturned nose) gives Hatshepsut a look of amiability and confidence.

The sculptures of Tuthmosis III convey the same feeling, but his images usually have a wider face, making the King seem more accessible than Hatshepsut, as in the greywacke statue from Karnak (Luxor Mus.; see fig. 59). During the co-regency the faces of both monarchs were dominated by dramatic curves, but statues carved in the later years of Tuthmosis III tend to emphasize the horizontal in the modelling and carving of facial details.

During the first century of the 18th Dynasty private sculpture was fashioned in attitudes and costumes that had been popular in the Middle Kingdom. Examples include a seated statue, cloaked and wearing a wide wig (New York, Brooklyn Mus., 61.196), the sandstone block statue of a high priest (Philadelphia, U. PA, Mus., E.9217) and a basalt scribe statue (Bologna, Mus. Civ. Archeol., 1823). At the same time new poses and attributes appeared: the scribe Seti kneeling with hands raised in prayer (New York, Brooklyn Mus., 37.263 E), SENENMUT standing and holding Princess Neferure (Chicago, IL, Field Mus. Nat. Hist., 173.800) and figures kneeling and proffering a complex religious symbol (Cairo, Egyp. Mus., JE 34582) or architect's rope (Paris, Louvre, E.11057). The appearance of the faces generally reflects the royal style of the time. Sometimes the standard, idealizing faces show hints of individuality, such as the hooked nose on a statue of Senenmut (New York, Brooklyn Mus., 67.68).

59. New Kingdom (pre-Amarna period) standing statue of Tuthmosis III, green greywacke, h. 900 mm, from Karnak, 18th Dynasty, c. 1475 BC (Luxor Museum)

During the last years of Tuthmosis III and the succeeding reigns of Amenophis II and Tuthmosis IV the classic Tuthmosid face grew formulaic, losing much of its earlier charm. Perhaps recognizing this, Tuthmosis IV's court sculptors experimented with a new style featuring highly stylized facial details (as in Cairo, Egyp. Mus., JE 43611). Some new types of statue, such as the 'standard-bearer', were also introduced during these reigns. Much of the evidence derives not from surviving statues but from representations of long-vanished originals painted on the walls of the tombs of Rekhmire (TT 100) and Qenamun (TT 93) at Thebes.

More statues of Amenophis III have survived than of any other 18th Dynasty monarch, suggesting an era of extraordinary artistic innovation. The stylized features first apparent under Tuthmosis IV persist, but they are enhanced by fleshy cheeks and a full sensuous mouth, giving some heads a youthful appearance (e.g. Luxor Mus., JE 16). On several statues fancy, stylized details are applied to highly idealizing, perfect faces (e.g. Cleveland, OH, Mus. A., 52.513). The modelling of statues from the funerary temple at Thebes (e.g. London, BM) was reduced to a minimum, and facial details have more the look of appliqués than sculpted masses. However, naturalistic images, showing the King as a fat man with prominent jowls, as in the case of one wooden standing statue (New York, Brooklyn Mus., 48.28), can also be documented. Private statues continued to follow the royal model throughout Amenophis III's reign. Statues of gods were also frequently carved with the features of the reigning monarch.

BIBLIOGRAPHY
H. W. Müller: 'Ein ägyptischer Königskopf des 15. Jahrhunderts v. Chr.', *Münchn. Jb. Bild. Kst*, iii/4 (1952–3), pp. 67–84
J. Vandier: *Les Grandes Epoques: La Statuaire* (1958), iii of *Manuel d'archéologie égyptienne* (Paris, 1952–78), pp. 295–331, 374–89, 434–518
B. V. Bothmer: 'Private Sculpture of Dynasty XVIII in Brooklyn', *Brooklyn Mus. Annu.*, viii (1966–7), pp. 55–89
J. F. Romano: 'Observations on Early Eighteenth Dynasty Royal Sculpture', *J. Amer. Res. Cent. Egypt*, xiii (1976), pp. 97–111
I. Lindblad: *Royal Sculpture of the Early Eighteenth Dynasty in Egypt* (Stockholm, 1984)
M. Müller: *Die Kunst Amenophis' III und Echnatons* (Basel, 1988)
B. M. Bryan: 'Royal and Divine Statuary' and 'Small-scale Royal Representations', *Egypt's Dazzling Sun: Amenkotep III and his World*, ed. A. P. Kozloff and others (Cleveland, 1992)

JAMES F. ROMANO

(b) Relief. Most New Kingdom relief decoration occurs on the walls of several hundred tombs and dozens of temples in Upper Egypt and Nubia. There are comparatively fewer reliefs from Lower and Middle Egypt, but their specific local features can be clearly distinguished from the general countrywide artistic trends upon which they were based.

There were many stages in the iconographic and stylistic development of relief during the New Kingdom. The most complete illustration of this gradual development from the 16th to the 11th century BC is the decoration in the temples of Karnak and Luxor (*see* THEBES (i), §§II and III) and the tombs of the nobles in the Theban necropolis. The temple reliefs were usually carved in sandstone, limestone and—more rarely—granite, alabaster or other types of stone. As in earlier periods almost all reliefs were originally covered in paint, and the wealth of painted detail which must originally have adorned all New Kingdom temples is exemplified by the surviving decoration of those at Deir el-Bahri, Abydos and Medinet Habu. The hieroglyphic texts that accompany New Kingdom figurative relief scenes may often constitute artistic and sculptural masterpieces in miniature, while their iconography often provides new examples of Egyptian regalia and imagery.

60. New Kingdom relief showing procession of three Nile-gods personifying Egyptian provinces, painted limestone, 423×772 mm, *c.* 1390 BC (Cleveland, OH, Cleveland Museum of Art)

The ritualistic scenes engraved on the limestone stele of King Ahmose (Cairo, Egyp. Mus., JE 36335) from Abydos and the alabaster chapel of Amenophis I (*in situ*) at Karnak are characterized by formal composition, crude modelling, gravity of expression and almost geometric outlines. There was a certain relaxation of this canon during the reign of Tuthmosis I (*reg c.* 1493–*c.* 1482 BC), as in his decoration of the south wall of Amenophis I's alabaster chapel.

The relief decoration on the walls of the temples of the New Kingdom developed alongside the architectonic canon governing these buildings, so that the functions of individual chambers were reflected in the specific types of scenes on their walls, such as episodes from religious feasts, battle scenes, processions (see fig. 60) and depictions of a symbolic nature. These New Kingdom temple reliefs include the earliest known examples of narrative scenes based on historical and mythological themes, which were later revived in the iconographic patterns that were imitated or reproduced by successive rulers. They include, among others, the cycle of scenes representing the divine birth of Hatshepsut from the union of her earthly mother with the god Amun (perhaps a propagandist attempt to prove the right of a woman pharaoh to the throne). A relief of Amenophis III in the Temple of Amun at Luxor uses the same cycle to portray his divine birth.

The decoration of New Kingdom tombs is distinguished by its thematic and structural diversity (*see* THEBES (i), §X). The artists were often successful in making a break with designs that had been the convention for centuries. Rock-cut private tomb chapels usually consisted of two chambers, the first of which (the transverse chamber) was decorated with scenes from the life of the deceased, while the second (the longitudinal chamber) bore scenes of funerary rituals. The decoration of private tombs of the early 18th Dynasty consisted mainly of paintings without a relief base, but during the reign of Amenophis III these were replaced by bas-reliefs with remarkably subtle modelling. During the years leading up to the Amarna period, the reliefs in private tombs were characterized by particularly refined figuration, accompanied by changes in subject-matter, iconography and sculptural technique. This can be seen in the decoration of the tombs of the Theban nobles, particularly those of Ramose (TT 55) and Kheruef (TT 192). The subject-matter reverted from joyful scenes of everyday life to religious subjects full of majesty, and the reliefs frequently depict episodes from various feasts, such as the *sed*-festival (royal jubilee) with its ornate ritual. The faces of mortals and gods began to feature traits that were reminiscent of the king's portrait, with almond-shaped eyes, sometimes placed at a slant between the base of the nose and the temples; sensual modelling of the lips and a new emphasis on the outline of the chin and lower contours of the face, rising in a slanted line towards the ear. This type of portrait evolved towards the extreme realism that characterizes the iconography of Amenophis IV/Akhenaten (*reg c.* 1353–*c.* 1336 BC).

BIBLIOGRAPHY

E. Naville: *The Temple of Deir el Bahari*, 6 vols (London, 1894–1908)
W. Wreszinski: *Atlas zur altägyptischen Kulturgeschichte*, i–ii (Leipzig, 1923–35)
N. de G. Davies: *The Tomb of the Vizier Ramose* (London, 1941)
D. Arnold: *Wandrelief und Raumfunktion in ägyptischen Tempeln des neuen Reiches* (Berlin, 1962)
J. Vandier: *Bas reliefs et peintures* (1964), iv of *Manuel d'archéologie égyptienne* (Paris, 1952–78)
——: *Scènes de la vie quotidienne* (1969), v of *Manuel d'archéologie égyptienne* (Paris, 1952–78)
K. Mysliwiec: *Le Portrait royal dans le bas-relief du nouvel Empire* (Warsaw, 1976)

H. Brunner: *Die südlichen Räume des Tempels von Luxor* (Mainz, 1977)
The Tomb of Kheruef: Theban Tomb 192, U. Chicago, IL, Orient. Inst. (Chicago, 1980)

KAROL MYŚLIWIEC

(viii) New Kingdom: Amarna period (c. 1353–c. 1332 BC).
During the reign of Amenophis IV (*reg c.* 1353–*c.* 1336 BC) an unparalleled breakthrough took place in Egyptian art: the King introduced changes in religious doctrine (the introduction of the cult of the Aten) that led to an abandonment of classic iconographic designs and the introduction of a new canon of proportion based on a 20-unit grid (*see* §IV, 3 above). New subjects were added to the sculptural repertory and elaboration of form, the basic principle of which was the realistic reproduction of nature, developed.

At the beginning of his reign Amenophis IV ordered the construction of at least seven temples and shrines in the precinct of Amun at Karnak, all dedicated to the Aten (*see* §VIII, 2(i) above). Many colossal statues of Amenophis IV and over 40,000 sandstone relief blocks (known as *talatat*) have survived from these temples (Cairo, Egyp. Mus. and Luxor Mus.).

In the fifth year of his reign Amenophis IV changed his name to Akhenaten and transferred the capital from Thebes to a virgin site which he called Akhetaten (Egyp.: 'horizon of the sun-disc'), now known as el-Amarna. The term Amarna is applied to the years of royal residence there and the style of art that characterized the era. Akhenaten himself may well have been the creator of the Amarna style since Bek, the King's chief sculptor, is described as 'the one whom his majesty himself instructed'. A quartzite stele of Bek and his wife (Berlin, Ägyp. Mus., 1/63; see fig. 3 above) shows the couple, nearly in the round, with the same unusual faces and bodies as the royal family.

BIBLIOGRAPHY
C. Aldred: *Akhenaten, Pharaoh of Egypt: A New Study* (London, 1968, rev. 2/1988)
——: *Akhenaten and Nefertiti* (New York, 1973)
D. B. Redford: *Akhenaten: The Heretic King* (Princeton, 1984)

(a) Statuary. The largest structure built by Amenophis IV at Karnak was the Gem Pa-Aten: it featured a central court surrounded by a colonnade with square piers fronted by over life-size statues of the King (e.g. Cairo, Egyp. Mus., 49529; see fig. 61). These figures adopt the attitude and many of the attributes of the god Osiris: the hands are crossed at the chest and hold the ceremonial crook and flail, and the feet are together. They also wear various headdresses, including a double crown (either alone or on top of the *nemes* or *khat* headcloth) and a multiple feather headdress perhaps related to the cult of the god Shu. Most of the figures wear knee-length, pleated kilts bound by an elaborate tie, although one figure, perhaps Queen Nefertiti, is inexplicably naked (Cairo, Egyp. Mus., JE 55938).

In contrast to the style of traditional royal sculptures, showing the king with a handsome, idealizing face, in the Karnak colossi Amenophis IV has an extremely long face capped by a forehead receding at an unnatural angle. His narrow, hooded eyes are surmounted by a deep cavity between the upper lid and eyebrow, giving the eye a three-dimensional quality. The King's sculptors fashioned long, straight noses and incised deep lines running from the

61. New Kingdom (Amarna period) standing statue of Amenophis IV (later called Akhenaten), sandstone, h. 4 m, from Karnak, 18th Dynasty, *c.* 1350 BC (Cairo, Egyptian Museum)

nasal alae past the corners of the mouth. The lips are everted and the mouth tends to be small, with a tiny bump in the centre of the upper lip. The jaw is long, the chin droops, the ears are invariably pierced and the neck always features a pair of horizontal lines. The earlier paradigm of the royal body—athletic and flawless—was also abandoned by Amenophis IV's artisans. The King has spindly arms and legs, swollen (almost feminine) breasts, thick buttocks and a distended abdomen. He may have commissioned such striking and sexually ambiguous images to stress the Aten's role as a primordial and androgynous god (Westendorf); it is also possible that the statues realistically depict

62. New Kingdom relief showing Akhenaten and his wife Nefertiti offering to the Aten, fragment of a stele, red and blue painted limestone, from el-Amarna, 18th Dynasty, *c.* 1353–*c.* 1336 BC (Cairo, Egyptian Museum)

a pathological abnormality, such as Fröhlich's Syndrome (Aldred).

Akhenaten's successors destroyed most of the remains at EL-AMARNA, but enough survives to show that, in the first years there, statues of the King (e.g. New York, Brooklyn Mus., 58.2), his wife Nefertiti (e.g. Hamburg, Mus. Kst & Gew., 1966.96) and their daughters (e.g. ex-Smeets priv. col.) show the same extreme stylization of the face and body devised at Thebes.

The uniformity of style at the beginning of the reign weakened several years after the move to el-Amarna. The workshop of the sculptor THUTMOSE yielded numerous pieces showing little or none of this earlier exaggeration. The painted limestone bust of Nefertiti (Berlin, Ägyp. Mus., 21300; for illustration *see* NEFERTITI) and plaster studies of major court figures (such as Berlin, Ägyp. Mus., 21356) show a new emphasis on grace and naturalism. Echoes of the original Theban style do survive in the unusually elongated skulls of Akhenaten's daughters (such as the sandstone head; Berlin, Ägyp. Mus., 21223) but even these faces reflect a new, exotic elegance. Amarna sculptors also introduced the 'composite statue' to Egyptian art. Heads, arms and feet were carved in colourful stones (such as quartzite) and joined to calcite torsos. New types of statues also appeared in the Amarna period, including the small limestone seated figure of the King kissing one of his daughters (Cairo, Egyp. Mus., JE 44866).

BIBLIOGRAPHY
C. Desroches-Noblecourt: 'La Statue colossale fragmentaire d'Amenophis IV offerte par l'Egypte à la France (Louvre E 27112)', *Mnmts Piot* (1974), pp. 1–44
M. Eaton-Krauss: 'Miscellanea Amarnensia', *Chron. Egypte*, lvi (1981), pp. 245–64
R. Krauss: 'Der Bildhauer Thutmose in Amarna', *Jb. Preuss. Kulthes.*, xx (1983), pp. 119–32
W. Westendorf: 'Amenophis IV in Urgottgestalt', *Pantheon*, xxi/5 (1983), pp. 269–77

JAMES F. ROMANO

(b) Relief. Most items of Amarna relief derive from the Temple of the Aten at Karnak or the temples and tombs at the city of el-Amarna. The sculptors of the Amarna period developed a new method of depicting space on a three-dimensional plane, which is apparent both in the composition of scenes and the modelling of the human form. The Amarna reliefs were more successful than traditional Egyptian art (before and after the Amarna period) in rendering buildings or scenes from nature. An early, middle and late Amarna period can be distinguished, with the portraits of the royal family becoming less 'exaggerated' as the reign of Akhenaten progressed.

During the first years of the reign of Akhenaten the artists relied heavily on the tradition established in the reign of Amenophis III. This is eminently illustrated in the private tombs at Thebes owned by officials (e.g. the TOMB OF RAMOSE) who functioned under both kings. In these tombs one wall might be decorated in excellent traditional reliefs, while another might display the early phases of the Amarna style. This is most apparent in representations of human beings, who were all made to look like the grotesque image of the King mentioned above.

The reliefs from the temples of the Aten at Karnak and el-Amarna celebrate the god, but they also underline the role of the King as the god's representative to whom the people had to turn. Queen Nefertiti plays the part of divine consort, but occasionally she appears without the King. The subject-matter throughout the period concentrates on the royal family (see fig. 62), but this also involves representations of an unprecedented ancillary staff, providing an opportunity for the Amarna sculptors to indulge in pictures of daily activities among the people (almost in spite of the royal occasions taking place in the foreground). Crowds were skilfully arranged in registers, and extra scope for masses of people was created by the use of a 'layering' technique involving the drawing of one or several outlines around the contours of a single person so as to give the impression of several individuals in an identical posture.

The quality of the Amarna reliefs varies a great deal. The sandstone used for the temples at Karnak, and the haste with which the sculptors strove to keep up with the builders, resulted in less accomplished works, as on one fragment bearing a depiction of Nefertiti (Cleveland, OH, Mus. A.). The defects were invariably masked by subsequent thin layers of stucco and paint. The temples at el-Amarna, however, were built of limestone blocks, which provided a much more satisfactory medium.

BIBLIOGRAPHY
N. de G. Davies: *The Rock Tombs of El Amarna*, 6 vols (London, 1903–8)
G. Roeder and R. Hanke: *Amarna-Reliefs aus Hermopolis*, 2 vols (Hildesheim, 1969–78)
J. D. Cooney: *Amarna Reliefs from Hermopolis in American Collections* (Brooklyn, 1975)
R. W. Smith and D. B. Redford: *The Akhenaten Temple Project*, i (Warminster, 1976)

LISE MANNICHE

(ix) New Kingdom: post-Amarna (c. 1332–c. 1075 BC). Despite the collapse of the Amarna period and the return to religious orthodoxy under Tutankhamun (*reg c.* 1332–*c.* 1323 BC), artisans working for the King, in the Memphis area, showed a reluctance to abandon the Amarna style. From the beginning of the Ramesside era (19th and 20th

dynasties), it is possible to trace geographical differentiation in the styles of the sculptural workshops. The artists of Lower Egypt displayed a greater creative freedom and a tendency towards naturalism with a distinctive Amarnastyle base, while the workshops of Upper Egypt, particularly Thebes, generally remained faithful to the traditional canon. However, echoes of Amarna art reappeared in certain Theban portrayals of RAMESSES II (*reg c.* 1279–*c.* 1213 BC) and the rulers of the 20th Dynasty.

(a) Statuary. Statues erected by TUTANKHAMUN, such as the image of Amun and Amunet in the Karnak temple, or a striding figure of the Pharaoh (Cairo, Egyp. Mus., CG

63. New Kingdom (post-Amarna period) statue of Ramesses VI leading a captive, grey granite, h. 720 mm, 20th Dynasty, *c.* 1145–*c.* 1137 BC (Cairo, Egyptian Museum)

42091), show taut faces, full lips and a slickness reminiscent of late Amarna art, along with the same flaccidness as Akhenaten's statuary. These features also occur in the finest private statues, such as a granite scribe statue of Horemheb (New York, Met., 23.10.1; for illustration *see* HOREMHEB), before he became king, and two fragments of limestone group statues (Cairo, Egyp. Mus., CG 779A and B). In the last two reigns of the 18th Dynasty royal sculptors favoured heavier proportions, as in the limestone colossal statue of King Ay (*reg c.* 1323–*c.* 1319 BC; Berlin, Ägyp. Mus., 1479), and they fashioned formal, rigid faces, as in a limestone seated statue of King Horemheb (*reg c.* 1319–*c.* 1292 BC; Vienna, Ksthist. Mus., 8301). Private sculpture, however, still recalls Tutankhamun's fanciness (as in Cairo, Egyp. Mus., JE 44863 from Piramesse).

In the early 19th Dynasty sculpture became eclectic. Some royal statues, for instance a diorite kneeling statue of SETHOS I (*reg c.* 1290–*c.* 1279 BC; New York, Met., 22.2.21), evoke the early Tuthmosid style, while others, such as the statues of Ramesses II, are heavy in appearance (for illustrations *see* ABU SIMBEL and TANIS). The faces of a third group, including a grey granite head of Sethos I (Hildesheim, Pelizaeus-Mus., 1882), show bold modelling reminiscent of works produced during the reign of Tutankhamun. The same three trends continued throughout the later Ramesside period, as in the statue of Ramesses VI (*reg c.* 1145–*c.* 1137 BC; Cairo, Egyp. Mus., CG 42153), which recalls the sculptures of Tuthmosis III. Traditional sculptural types were supplemented by new, complex forms such as the king leading a captive (e.g. Cairo, Egyp. Mus., CG 42152; see fig. 63). Statues commemorating earlier monarchs, particularly Amenophis I, were also produced.

There was great variety in private sculpture, ranging from men and women with elaborate coiffures wearing fussy, pleated garments (e.g. Paris, Louvre, A.73) to figures of the same date wearing traditional simple garb (e.g. Cairo, Egyp. Mus., JE 67878). Block statues proffering divine images, such as the sandstone figure of Ken (Turin, Mus. Egizio, 3016), began to be produced. Both the family group, exemplified by the wooden sculpture of Amenemopet and his wife (Berlin, Ägyp. Mus., 6910), and the scribe statue (e.g. Cairo, Egyp. Mus., 42162) remained popular types.

BIBLIOGRAPHY
H. Brunner: 'Eine Statuette Amenophis I', *Z. Ägyp. Spr & Altertknd.*, lxxxiii (1958), pp. 82–9
H. W. Muller: 'Ein Meisterwerk der ägyptischen Plastik vom Ausgang der XVIII. Dynastie', *Münchn. Jb. Bild. Kst*, xviii (1967), pp. 7–32
H. D. Schneider: 'Maya l'amateur de statues: A propos de trois statues fameuses du Musée de Leyde et d'une sépulture oubliée à Saqqarah', *Bull. Soc. Fr. Egyp.*, lxix (1974), pp. 20–48
M. Eaton-Krauss: 'JE 49536: Horemhab and the Abydene Triad', *Stud. Altägyp. Kult.*, xi (1984), pp. 501–8
C. Vandersleyen: 'L'Iconographie de Toutankhamon et les effigies provenant de sa tombe', *Bull. Soc. Egyp., Genève*, ix–x (1984–5), pp. 309–21
JAMES F. ROMANO

(b) Relief. After the death of Akhenaten, the reliefs in private tombs at Saqqara still show the uninhibited development of the naturalistic style in the area of Memphis, especially in the tomb of Horemheb at Saqqara (built before he became king). Even orthodox Thebes could not escape the influence of Amarna art at the end of the 18th

Dynasty, judging from the reliefs and paintings of Tutankhamun in his tomb and at Luxor temple.

The beginning of the Ramesside era is marked by the academic classicism of the reliefs of Sethos I: their elegant form and painstaking modelling lend a cool tonality to the beautiful reliefs in his temples at Thebes (*see* THEBES (i), §VIII) and ABYDOS. At this time raised relief was dominant, giving clarity of form and a balanced effect of light and shade, but during the reign of Ramesses II it was largely replaced by the sharp chiaroscuro of sunk relief, which was more dramatic and aggressive. Ramesses II expressed his power through military conquests and the building of many temples, the decoration of which provided a considerable challenge to his sculptors. The preference for sunk relief was perhaps dictated by the need to decorate a greater number of buildings at the same time, since raised relief was a more time-consuming technique.

The artistic standard of Ramesses II's reliefs is extremely diverse, including such superb works of art as the reliefs in the temple at Beit el-Wali and the 'Ramesseum' in western Thebes (*see* THEBES (i), §VI), as well as some careless reliefs in which the composition and modelling are schematic and frequently incomplete. However, the presence of many first-rate artists in the Theban region during the reign of Ramesses II and his successors is indicated by the relief decoration of the tombs of the nobles as well as tombs of the kings and their families, which were dominated by combinations of mythological scenes and religious texts forming complete compositions (e.g. 'Amduat', 'The Book of Gates' and 'The Book of the Caves'). Some reliefs in the Valley of the Kings distinguish themselves by their beautiful forms and scrupulous execution (*see* THEBES (i), §IX).

There are three well-preserved royal mortuary temples of the post-Amarna period in western Thebes: those of Sethos I, Ramesses II (the 'Ramesseum') and Ramesses III (Medinet Habu). There are also many post-Amarna reliefs in the temples of eastern Thebes, of which the Temple of Amun at Karnak assumed the most monumental of forms. The walls of these Theban temples are decorated with scenes illustrating the development of the iconographic repertory and the various types of Ramesside relief. The outer walls are chiefly decorated with battle scenes from the pharaohs' victorious campaigns, while the façades of the pylons carry depictions of the capturing and slaying of Egypt's enemies. Despite the growing schematization of the reliefs, many of them (such as the hunting scene on the north-west side of the first pylon at Medinet Habu) are original, dynamic compositions, full of dramatic expression.

BIBLIOGRAPHY

Medinet Habu, U. Chicago, IL, Orient. Inst., 8 vols (Chicago, 1930–70)

A. M. Calverley and others: *The Temple of King Sethos I at Abydos* (London, 1933–)

A. Piankoff: *The Tomb of Ramesses VI* (New York, 1954)

C. Desroches-Noblecourt and C. Kuentz: *Le Petit Temple d'Abou Simbel*, 2 vols (Cairo, 1968)

KAROL MYŚLIWIEC

(x) Third Intermediate Period (*c. 1075–c. 750* BC). The few surviving 21st Dynasty (*c. 1075–c. 950* BC) sculptures are characterized by the decline of the Ramesside style, the beginning of a rise to importance of sculpture in metal and the evolution of a distinctive Third Intermediate Period style influenced by Tuthmosid (mid-18th Dynasty) and 19th Dynasty sculpture. Variants of the style occur at sites throughout the country until the end of the era of Libyan rule, in the late 8th century BC and even survive to a certain extent in some of the reliefs of the 25th Dynasty (*c.* 750–656 BC).

In the 22nd Dynasty (*c. 950–c. 730* BC) there was a dramatic revival of stone sculpture and a blossoming of the metalworking tradition, especially bronzes (*see* §XVI below), some of which were large-scale, their surfaces embellished with precious metal inlays—an aesthetic parallel to the contemporary fondness for adorning numerous surfaces of stone statuary with sunk relief.

(a) Statuary. Little royal stone statuary of the 22nd and 23rd dynasties has survived, although this situation possibly only reflects the limited amount of excavation in Lower Egypt, where at least one of these dynasties was based. The stone statuary of the period is therefore exemplified mainly by private works. Most are simple block statues, but other types known from Ramesside days or earlier also appear: the seated man or woman; the asymmetric squatting figure; the kneeling figure proffering a divine symbol; the kneeling naophorous and stelophorous; the standing theophorous; and the block statue fronted by a deity or naos. These derive especially from the Temple of Amun at Karnak (e.g. Cairo, Egyp. Mus., CG 42188–91, 42193, 42208–32). There are, however, also some pieces from less well explored but important northern sites, such as a small asymmetric squatting figure (Berlin, Ägyp. Mus., E.11637) from the area of Memphis, which is rare evidence for wooden sculpture during the Third Intermediate Period. Many of the statues from Karnak have the wide, striated wigs known in the Middle Kingdom and the first half of the 18th Dynasty, and their facial features continue the 21st Dynasty's inspiration by Tuthmosid sculpture.

These archaizing tendencies were indirect, not inspired by specific earlier objects, and they were not slavishly followed: post-Tuthmosid elements, for instance, are sometimes part of the era's main distinctive stylistic tendency. That tendency remained dominant at Karnak throughout the period, although at least one work of the 23rd Dynasty (Cairo, Egyp. Mus., CG 42229) with its plain double wig, longer, more narrowly opened eyes and straighter eyebrows anticipates later stylistic changes. Furthermore, although some northern private statues preserve a Ramesside tradition, the general Third Intermediate Period style was limited neither to Thebes nor to private statuary. The style is apparent, for instance, in a limestone statue of Osorkon IV proffering a sacred boat (Cairo, Egyp. Mus., CG 42197) from Karnak, and the grey granite head of a stelophorous statue of Osorkon III (*reg c.* 888–*c.* 860 BC; Philadelphia, U. PA, Mus., E.16199) from Tanis. Several bronzes of earlier Third Intermediate Period kings also display similar stylistic traits to contemporary private bronzes.

The most famous private bronze of the period is the elaborately inlaid divine adoratrice, Karamama (Paris, Louvre, N.500; see fig. 95 below). Its elegant elongation and slenderness of form are known in certain other metal works of the era, including some male figures displaying a new tendency towards tripartite rather than bipartite torso modelling. Later bronzes were more varied in style, such as the large figure of the Lady Takushit (Athens, N. Archaeol. Mus., ANE 110), a striking full-figured contrast to the svelte Karamama. Also important are the striding figure of a man called Bepshes (Paris, Louvre, E.7693) and a kneeling figure of Neferkare Peftjau'awybast, a Libyan ruler of Herakleopolis Magna (Boston, MA, Mus. F.A., 1977.16). Bepshes' very broad shoulders and low, narrow waist clearly reflect Old Kingdom sculptures, a new archaizing tendency visible slightly earlier in reliefs. This tendency may explain the massive shoulders and voluminous forms of the figure of Neferkare, paralleled in part by a glassy faience figure of Smendes (*reg c.* 1075–*c.* 1045 BC) kneeling to offer jars of wine, milk or water (New York, Brooklyn Mus., 37.344E), which is another example of a Libyan chieftain usurping Egyptian royal sculptural types and garb.

Works of the 22nd–24th dynasties also include sculptures of deities, harbingers of the later mass production of such figures, especially in bronze. Among these, as befits a period when the cult of child-gods and a theology of birth began to come to the fore, are early statues of the goddess Isis nursing her son Horus, a theme that ultimately became widespread.

(b) Relief. In the few surviving examples of royal and private relief from the 21st Dynasty, the development of a main Third Intermediate Period style can be observed. In the depiction of faces, the Ramesside heavier and more angular forms were replaced by such features as curved eyebrows, relatively small almond-shaped eyes and a break between the lines of the forehead and the nose, which was sometimes aquiline with flaring nostrils. Figural proportions were generally fuller and less elongated than those of the Ramesside period, and carving was generally less bold but with more modulated forms. Elements of this style can be seen on a doorway set up by the high priest of Amun, Masaharta, in the Temple of Amun at Karnak and also in the reliefs decorating the tomb of Psusennes I (*reg c.* 1040–*c.* 997 BC) at Tanis. Both of these monuments mark a revival in the popularity of raised relief, after its virtual eclipse by sunk relief in the late New Kingdom. The Third Intermediate Period's main style appears almost fully evolved in the sunk reliefs of Khons-heb, a courtier at Tanis, and on a lintel of the reign of Siamun (*reg c.* 973–*c.* 964 BC) at Memphis.

In the 22nd Dynasty there was a resurgence of stone architecture, and splendid examples of the evolved main style are found in the reliefs of the Bubastite portal of the Temple of Amun at Karnak (see fig. 64). Based in part on the style of the Tuthmosides and of the 19th Dynasty, it is still distinctive. Variants of it are found in many royal reliefs from sites throughout Egypt until the end of Libyan rule, and it forms a basis for one of the relief styles of the 25th Dynasty. A particularly interesting stylistic development is attested by blocks from Memphis of Shoshenq III and Takelot, the high priest of Ptah (Cairo, Egyp. Mus., JE 46915). These depict male and female figures with very broad shoulders, long arms, tall thin bodies, very narrow waists and—in the case of the man—very muscular knees (later an important aspect of 25th Dynasty art). Such

64. Third Intermediate Period relief showing King Shoshenq I suckled by the goddess Mut, sandstone, h. *c.* 1.25 m, from the Temple of Amun at Karnak, 22nd Dynasty, *c.* 950–*c.* 730 BC

figures, seemingly inspired by Old Kingdom art, became common in the art from northern sites, particularly stelae, by the time of Shoshenq V (*reg c.* 929–*c.* 914 BC). They do not seem to have become common in Upper Egypt until the 25th Dynasty, but related relief figures appear on a statue from Karnak (Cairo, Egyp. Mus., CG 42224) dating from the time of Osorkon IV and Takelot III. Possibly related stylistic developments may also be seen in some bronze statuary of the period, as well as in a relief-decorated faience vase of King Bocchoris (Tarquinia, Pal. Vitellesche) and a faience relief of King Iuput II (New York, Brooklyn Mus., 59.17), the latter possibly influenced by Kushite (25th Dynasty) art.

If Third Intermediate Period art provides a basis for some important elements of 25th Dynasty reliefs, the same is true of iconography. This may be seen in Chapel J of the Precinct of Amun at Karnak, which is dedicated to Isis and datable at least in part to the reign of Osorkon II. Chapel K of the same precinct is dedicated to Osiris and bears reliefs of Osorkon IV and Takelot III. Prominently figured in Chapel K is Shepenwepet I, one of the god's Wives of Amun, important priestesses, familiar from numerous Theban monuments of the 22nd–26th dynasties, and often shown in roles that had formerly been played by the king. Chapels J and K—further examples of the revival of raised relief—also express the rise in popularity of the cults of child-gods and divine family triads, including that of Osiris, Isis and Horus (*see* §III, 2 above). This is graphically demonstrated by the existence of the chapels themselves and by the reliefs in Chapel J depicting Horus in a thicket and the child-Horus = king with a goddess. Reliefs on various objects of the period feature related religious scenes as well as the motif of the child-god born on a lotus. Such objects, showing scenes of daily life, clearly prefigure the revival of that genre in the private tombs of the 25th and 26th dynasties.

BIBLIOGRAPHY

K. Kitchen: *The Third Intermediate Period in Egypt (110–650 BC)* (Warminster, 1973, rev. 2/1986) [for refs to most objects and significant lit.]
R. Fazzini: *Egypt: Dynasty XXII–XXV*, Iconography of Religions, xvi/10 (Leiden, 1987)
C. Ziegler: 'Les Arts du métal a la Troisième Période Intermédiare', *Tanis: L'Or des pharaons* (exh. cat.; Paris, Grand Pal.; Marseille, Cent. Vieille Charité, 1987), pp. 85–101
K. Mysliwiec: *Royal Portraiture of the Dynasties XXI–XXX* (Mainz, 1988), pp. 6–35 [the best photographs of Third Intermediate Period faces]

RICHARD A. FAZZINI

(xi) Late Period (c. *750–332* BC). The final creative phase of Egyptian sculpture began in the 25th Dynasty (*c.* 750–*c.* 656 BC) with an archaizing movement of unprecedented proportions. Archaism had played a role in every period, but never had it been so pervasive, so faithful in its models, or so eclectic in its scope. The 25th Dynasty Kushite kings did not initiate this movement (there is evidence of it in the Delta during the Third Intermediate Period), but it suited them to encourage it. They were foreigners, who had conquered Egypt from the south, but they presented themselves as fully orthodox, legitimate pharaohs (*see* TAHARQA). The antiquarian flavour of the artistic revival over which they presided helps to justify the use of the term 'Kushite Renaissance'. These archaizing tendencies persisted into the 26th Dynasty (664–525 BC) but were soon subsumed in a uniform, idealized style. The Saite style (named after the seat of the 26th Dynasty at Sais in the western Delta)—sometimes called the 'Saite Renaissance'—was one of the strongest and most consistent of all Egyptian sculptural styles. It is characterized by a studied elegance of smooth surfaces and understated details. Archaism was still strong, but borrowed features were modified to produce a harmonious whole.

In the 27th Dynasty (525–404 BC) the Persians conquered Egypt, transforming it into a satrapy (province) of the Achaemenid empire. A statue of Darius I (*reg* 521–486 BC) from Susa (Tehran, Archaeol. Mus.) is Persian in costume, proportions and style, but according to inscriptions in hieroglyphic and cuneiform writing, it was made for an Egyptian temple (*see* ACHAEMENID, §2). This statue may already demonstrate the facility Egyptian sculptors were later to display at making statues in Hellenistic and Roman styles.

The sculpture of the weak dynasties that succeeded the departing Persians is almost unknown, although at least one headless statue of the 29th Dynasty King Hakoris (*reg* 393–380 BC; Boston, MA, Mus. F.A.) seems to anticipate anatomical forms of the following period. The 30th Dynasty (380–343 BC) was sufficiently stable and long to foster a revival in all the arts. Sculpture, often life-size and of high quality, followed Saite precedents. The influence of the Saite style persisted well into the Ptolemaic period (304–30 BC); for the Greeks and Romans it was the definitive Egyptian style, and through them it became one of the major contributors to Western conceptions of Egyptian art.

BIBLIOGRAPHY

W. S. Smith and W. K. Simpson: *The Art and Architecture of Ancient Egypt*, Pelican Hist. A. (Harmondsworth, 1958, rev. 2/1981), pp. 395–427
Egyptian Sculpture of the Late Period: 700 BC to AD 100 (exh. cat. by B. V. Bothmer and others, New York, Brooklyn Mus., 1960/*R* 1973)
J. Leclant: *Montouemhat, quatrième prophète d'Amon, prince de la ville* (Cairo, 1961)
E. R. Russmann: *The Representation of the King in the XXVth Dynasty* (Brussels, 1974)
A. Leahy: 'Saite Royal Sculpture: A Review', *Götting. Misz.*, lxxx (1984), pp. 59–76

(a) Statuary. (b) Relief.

(a) Statuary. Most Late Period statues were made for dedication in temples. Fine sculpture was still made for tombs, but in ever smaller quantities. Surviving examples indicate that an unprecedented proportion of late tomb statues represented deities. One, from the end of the 26th Dynasty, depicts the deceased with the cow-goddess Hathor, in a pose otherwise known only for New Kingdom rulers (Cairo, Egyp. Mus., CG 784). Though perhaps as magically potent as ever, statues of the Late Period are far removed from the original purpose of literally embodying the spirit (*see* §1 above); their role seems to have been largely symbolic or even, in the case of temple sculpture, memorial (in a modern sense).

Simple poses were favoured by Late Period sculptors, and the unadorned standing figure—one of the original Egyptian statue types (*see* §2(i)(a) above)—was among the most important archaizing revivals. The crosslegged pose of a seated scribe maintained its prestige during the 25th and 26th dynasties, though very few were made later. The block statue (*see* §2(i)(c) above) retained and even increased its popularity, as did a New Kingdom type, the theophorous and stelophorous statue (*see* §2(i)(h) above). No new poses were invented, although a new use for sculpture appeared at the end of the Late Period, in the form of the healing statue (or *guérisseur*), which probably developed out of earlier temple statues bearing inscriptions promising supernatural benefits in return for prayers. The healing statue was a block statue or standing stelophorous statue completely covered (except on the face and hands) with magical spells and scenes, designed to infuse healing powers into any water poured over them. Basins might be provided in the statue base, to collect the water thus treated.

Late Period statues—like most Egyptian temple sculpture—were usually carved in hard stones, although limestone and sandstone continued to be used for colossal figures. A small number of surviving wooden statuettes, such as a family triad of the 26th Dynasty (Berlin, Ägyp. Mus., 8812–4) and a 30th Dynasty royal figure (priv. col., New York), demonstrate a continuing tradition of fine work in the more supple manner appropriate to this medium. In hard stone, dark, fine-textured materials were increasingly preferred over coarser or brighter varieties, such as granite or quartzite. Greywacke was especially popular in the Saite period. By the 30th Dynasty a tendency towards more highly polished surfaces encouraged the use of blacker, harder stones, such as diorite and basalt. These dark, gleaming surfaces began to be contrasted with areas of hair or costume that were deliberately left unpolished, to make them look lighter in colour.

As stone regained its traditional pre-eminence, bronze statuary declined rapidly from its peak in the Third Intermediate Period. A number of fine bronze royal statuettes can be dated to the 25th Dynasty and later, and at least one silver figure of a woman, bearing the name of a 26th Dynasty king (New York, Met., 30.8.93), shows that more precious metals were still being used. Even the best of these, however, lack the size and lavish inlaid detail of earlier works. Bronze statuettes of deities were produced in quantity. Though often technically admirable, they are highly conventional in style, and increasingly show the stultifying effects of mass production.

Kushite and Saite dynasties (c. 750–525 BC). A slightly under life-size statue of Mentuemhet, mayor of Thebes at the end of the Kushite period (Cairo, Egyp. Mus., CG 42236; see fig. 65), is typical of Late Period archaism. It vividly evokes Old Kingdom sculpture, not only in its pose, muscular anatomy and kilt style, but also in the latent vigour of its strongly defined planes and firm contours. Yet this is no mechanical copy; the figure is somewhat differently proportioned, the kilt skimpier than on Old Kingdom prototypes. The elaborately curled headdress, a 'double wig' of New Kingdom type, adds an eclectic touch.

Another revival of New Kingdom practice, more frequent in the following dynasty, was the occasional inscription of the name of the reigning king on the arm or chest of a private figure. Middle Kingdom influence is apparent in the renewed popularity of certain statue types, such as the seated cloaked pose, and especially in the resurgence of 'portraiture'. The distinctive face of Mentuemhet's statue is a good example of 'portrait' sculpture in the Kushite period. Not since the Amarna period had statues with individual-looking physiognomies been so frequent or so significant to the mainstream of stylistic development. The extreme harshness of Mentuemhet's expression is typical of the Kushite period; so is an organic quality in the depiction of skin stretched or sagging over flesh and bone, which creates an almost veristic effect. Representations as naturalistic as this were made in Egypt in the 7th century BC, long before the rise of portraiture in Greece or Rome; late Egyptian portraiture was a native development, not the product of foreign influence.

The distinctive, highly idealized Saite style of statuary appeared in the 26th Dynasty. Faces in the Saite style have high-placed eyes, often narrow and slightly slanted, and thin, high brows, shown as artificially straight, horizontal lines. The deep crescent curve of a full lower lip emphasizes the effect of a slight smile. This 'sickle-shaped' smile resembles the 'Archaic smile' of early Greek sculpture and has been suggested as an example of Egyptian influence on the development of Greek sculpture during the 6th century BC.

For all its mannerisms, the Saite style was remarkably flexible. It was even adapted to portraiture when, after an apparent hiatus during the mid-26th Dynasty, individualized likenesses again became important at the end. From this time onwards, portrait sculpture seems to have been continually produced, through the 30th Dynasty and into the Ptolemaic period.

One result of the decline in tomb sculpture in the Late Period is a paucity of late statues of women. Apart from

65. Late Period statue of Mentuemhet, mayor of Thebes, granite, h. 1.37 m, from the 'Cachette Court' of Karnak temple, 25th Dynasty, *c.* 690–*c.* 650 BC (Cairo, Egyptian Museum)

queens and goddesses, women had rarely been represented in statues in Egyptian temples. The Kushite and Saite divine adoratrices (royal princesses who were high priestesses of Amun at Thebes) are virtually the only Late Period women represented in stone sculpture. The Kushite priestesses have rather full hips and thighs, which are often assumed to reflect their ethnic origin but in fact strongly resemble the figure type fashionable in female statuary of the Middle Kingdom. A heavy-bosomed, rather mature type of figure appeared in Saite representations of women. Like other aspects of the style, this innovation persisted, and became the basis for the even fuller figures of Ptolemaic female statuary.

Persian and 30th Dynasty styles. The few Egyptian statues that can be securely dated to the Persian period show that both portraiture and the idealized Saite style continued. Although the Persians were unpopular, a few Egyptian autobiographical inscriptions describe open collaboration with them. Such activities may explain the depiction of Persian jewellery (torques) and shirts on some statues of this time. However, the most important costume innovation, a long, heavy-looking wrapped skirt, often called a 'Persian wrap', is not paralleled in Achaemenid representations and was most likely a native Egyptian garment.

In 30th Dynasty statuary the most distinctive anatomical feature was a small but protruding abdomen, rendered as a circular bulge around a teardrop-shaped navel, which represents a stylized and slightly exaggerated version of the fleshy lower torso of later Saite sculpture. Facial features were even more faithfully imitated, to the point that the later examples can sometimes be distinguished only by their more mannered treatment of details, especially the thin, raised brows. In its most stylized form, this post-Saite face was often combined with a hairless, oversized, egg-shaped cranium. Such 'egg-heads' are characteristic of the 30th Dynasty and later and may have had symbolic connotations. Their bland smiles contrast markedly with the withdrawn or sad expressions of the relatively few 'portrait' faces datable to the 4th century BC.

BIBLIOGRAPHY

P. Lacau: 'Les Statues "guérisseuses" dans l'ancienne Egypte', *Mnmts Piot*, xxv (1921–2), pp. 189–209
D. Dunham: 'Three Inscribed Statues in Boston', *J. Eg-yp. Archaeol.*, xv (1929), pp. 164–6
K. Bosse: *Die menschliche Figur in der Rundplastik der ägyptischen Spätzeit von der XXII. bis zur XXX. Dynastie*, Ägyptologische Forschungen, i (Glückstadt, 1936)
G. Botti and P. Romanelli: *Le sculture del Museo Gregoriano Egizio* (Vatican City, 1951)
J. D. Cooney: 'The Portrait of an Egyptian Collaborator', *Bull. Brooklyn Mus.*, xv (1953), pp. 1–16
H. W. Müller: 'Ein Königsbildnis der 26. Dynastie mit der "Blauen Krone" im Museo Civico zu Bologna', *Z. Ägyp. Spr. & Altertknd.*, lxxx (1955), pp. 46–58
——: 'Der Torso einer Königsstatue im Museo Archeologico zu Florenz: Ein Beitrag zur Plastik der ägyptischen Spätzeit', *Studi in memoria di I. Rosellini*, ii (Pisa, 1955), pp. 181–221
Staatliche Museen Preussicher Kulturbesitz, W. Berlin, Ägyp. Mus. cat. (Berlin, 1967), nos 943–5
H. De Meulenaere and B. V. Bothmer: 'Une Tête d'Osiris au Musée du Louvre', *Kêmi: Rev. Philol. & Archéol. Egyp. & Copt.*, xix (1969), pp. 9–16
H. W. Müller: 'Bildnisse König Nektanebos I. (380–362 v. Chr.)', *Pantheon*, xi (1970), pp. 89–98
——: 'Der "Stadtfurst von Theben", Montemhet', *Münchn. Jb. Bild. Kst*, xxvi (1970), pp. 7–36
E. L. B. Terrace and H. G. Fischer: *Treasures of the Cairo Museum* (London, 1970), pp. 157–72

A. Roullet: *The Egyptian and Egyptianizing Monuments of Imperial Rome* (Leiden, 1972)
E. R. Russmann: 'The Statue of Amenemope-em-hat', *Met. Mus. J.*, viii (1973), pp. 33–46; also in *Ancient Egypt in the Metropolitan Museum Journal* (New York, 1977), pp. 99–112
C. L. Vandersleyen: 'Rundplastik der Spätzeit', *Das alte Ägypten*, Propyläen Kstgesch., xv (Berlin, 1975), pp. 255–73
H. De Meulenaere and P. Mackay: *Mendes*, ii (Warminster, 1976)
Africa in Antiquity: The Arts of Ancient Nubia and the Sudan, ii (exh. cat., ed. S. Wenig; New York, Brooklyn Mus., 1978)
T. Holm-Rasmussen: 'On the Statue Cult of Nektanebos II', *Acta Orient.*, xl (1979), pp. 20–25
C. Traunecker: 'Essai sur l'histoire de la XXIXe dynastie', *Bull. Inst. Fr. Archéol.*, lxxix (1979), pp. 395–436
C. Aldred: 'Statuaire', *L'Egypte du crépuscule* (1980), iii of *Le Monde égyptien: Les pharaons*, ed. J. Leclant (Paris, 1978–80), pp. 121–60
G. Gabra: 'A Lifesize Statue of Nepherites I from Buto', *Z. Ägyp. Sprache & Altertknd.*, ix (1981), pp. 119–23
B. V. Bothmer: 'The Brussels-Brooklyn Statue of Bakenrenef (Membra dispersa VI)', *Mélanges Gamal Eddin Mokhtar* (Cairo, 1985), i, pp. 99–103
T. Holm-Rasmussen: 'Some Monuments of the Last Pharaoh Viewed in the Light of Contemporary Ideology', *Hafnia*, x (1985), pp. 7–23
B. V. Bothmer and H. De Meulenaere: 'The Brooklyn Statuette of Hor, Son of Pawen (with an Excursus on Eggheads)', *Egyptological Studies in Honour of Richard A. Parker* (Hannover, 1986), pp. 1–16
G. Azarpay: 'Proportional Guidelines in Ancient Near Eastern Art', *J. Nr E. Stud.*, xlvi (1987), pp. 183–203
B. V. Bothmer: 'Egyptian Antiquities', *Antiquities from the Collection of Christos G. Bastis* (exh. cat., ed. D. V. Bothmer; New York, Met., 1987), pp. 80–95
M. Saleh and H. Sourouzian: *The Egyptian Museum, Cairo: Official Catalogue*, Cairo, Egyp. Mus. cat. (Mainz, 1987), nos 244–8, 250–55
Antiquités et objets d'art: Collection de Martine, Comtesse de Béhague provenant de la succession du Marquis de Ganay (sale cat., Monaco, Sotheby's, 5 December 1987)
J. A. Josephson: 'An Altered Royal Head of the XXVIth Dynasty', *J. Egyp. Archaeol.*, lxxiv (1988), pp. 232–5
E. R. Russmann: *Egyptian Sculpture: Cairo and Luxor* (Austin, TX, 1989)

(b) Relief. Egyptian relief in the Late Period continued to follow traditional techniques and conventions (*see* §IV, 3 above). However, occasional representations of the near leg passing in front of the far leg, and the increasingly frequent indication of all five toes on the near foot are tenuous evidence of a slightly more naturalistic approach to the two-dimensional form.

This section primarily discusses the surviving remains of architectural reliefs from temples and tombs, but there were also numerous self-contained relief monuments in the form of stelae or plaques. Late Period funerary stelae usually depict the deceased in adoration before solar or chthonic deities. So-called donation stelae, as well as votive stelae for the Apis bulls, dedicated in their catacombs at Saqqara, were made throughout the period. Most Late Period stelae are modest; their iconography and style follow local traditions, which, in the conservative provincial workshops, tended to perpetuate local versions of outmoded styles. Even the great temples, however, could occasionally show crude or provincial work, like that on the late 26th Dynasty fragments discovered at Philae during the 1970s.

Small limestone plaques, decorated on one or both sides with raised relief representations of kings, deities or theriomorphic hieroglyphs, appeared as early as the 26th Dynasty, and were made in quantity during the 30th Dynasty and later. They are traditionally called 'sculptors' models', although many, if not most, seem to have been made as votive objects for dedication in temples.

Kushite and Saite dynasties (c. 750–525 BC). The prime sources of archaizing imitation in 25th Dynasty relief were Old Kingdom monuments of the pyramid zone around Memphis. This concentration of interest contrasts with a much more eclectic taste in statuary, where the models for representing private individuals were drawn from the Old, Middle and New Kingdoms. The difference probably reflects royal influence over the construction and decoration of major temples. Relief representations of Kushite kings revive the muscularity of Old Kingdom figures and the blunt, bunched facial features particularly characteristic of 5th Dynasty kings. Slight exaggerations of these anatomical details, however, create a vaguely foreign appearance that may have had deliberate ethnic reference, for it is often emphasized by jewellery and other regalia unique to the Kushites and probably derived from their indigenous traditions.

Fragments of 25th Dynasty relief found at Memphis raise hopes that further excavation at this site will illuminate the origins of Kushite relief style, in the neighbourhood of its Old Kingdom prototypes. The 25th Dynasty relief blocks found at Edfu and Philae show how uniform and widespread this style was. The only Kushite temple reliefs still in place, however, are in the Theban area, especially in well-preserved chapels at Karnak and Medinet Habu.

In some cases, at least, Late Period archaism consisted of direct copying from the walls of earlier structures. The Kushite king TAHARQA (*reg c.* 690–664 BC) dispatched sculptors from Memphis to his southern homeland to reproduce scenes from Old Kingdom royal funerary temples on his temple walls. Copying also seems the best explanation for an inked grid superimposed on a relief representation of the 3rd Dynasty king Djoser (*reg c.* 2630–*c.* 2611 BC) in a subterranean passage of his Step Pyramid complex at Saqqara. Such grids were primarily draughting devices, to position and proportion the figures in preliminary drawings. In the 25th Dynasty, a grid which divided the height of a standing male figure by 21 squares replaced an earlier version, 18 squares high. This change was formerly assumed to have been associated with a 'late canon' of figural proportions. In 1959, however, the Egyptologist R. Hanke demonstrated that Late Period figures do not, in fact, show new proportions. Whatever the reason for the introduction of the late grid, it represents only a change in the size and number of measuring units.

Theban magnates of the 25th and 26th dynasties, such as Mentuemhet, revived the long obsolete practice of building large tombs, decorated with mural reliefs. These tombs have been the subject of intensive excavation and research. In the earliest of them, the relief style is essentially Kushite, as is the revival of Old Kingdom versions of scenes from daily life. Later, however, the principal sources were royal and private funerary monuments in the immediate vicinity. These models were, of course, convenient; but their choice also reflects a sense of local tradition. An exceptional case is the tomb of a man called Ibi (TT 36), who copied scenes in a late Old Kingdom tomb at the provincial site of Deir el-Gebrawi, well to the north of Thebes (perhaps because the Old Kingdom tomb had also been made for a man named Ibi). The exactitude of copying in the Late Period Theban tomb reliefs varies

66. Limestone raised relief, section of monumental gateway of late Saite king, h. 2.0 m, from 'Palace of Apries', Memphis, 589–526 BC (Copenhagen, Ny Carlsberg Glyptotek)

considerably. Some are so faithful to their originals, in both spirit and detail, that they have often been mislabelled as Memphite Old Kingdom. Others have been so modified that imitation would not be suspected if, as with Ibi, the original sources were not available for comparison.

The kings of the 26th Dynasty (664–525 BC) are known to have built temples and tombs at their Delta capital, Sais, but these monuments and their reliefs have disappeared. Saite remains at Memphis are hardly better preserved. Two very fragmentary monumental gateways dating to the end of the dynasty, one in limestone (largest sections in Cairo, Egyp. Mus., JE 41436; Copenhagen, Ny Carlsberg Glyp., AEIN 1406; see fig. 66; and New York, Met., 09.183.1) and one in quartzite (mostly *in situ*; one block in Memphis, TN, Brooks Mus. A.) show the fully developed Saite relief style. Though still reminiscent of fine Old Kingdom raised relief in their low, delicate plasticity, the elegantly stylized, smiling faces, rather fleshy torsos and unmuscular limbs correspond with those of later Saite statuary. The finesse of this style, particularly its highly developed sense of proportion and placement, is visible even in Saite hieroglyphic inscriptions, which are among the most handsome ever produced.

Mural reliefs in a few early Saite tombs near Memphis, especially that of the vizier Bakenrenef at Saqqara, still show the influence of Kushite style. Most private tomb reliefs from this region are later, however, and consist of limestone blocks, mostly from doorways, which were apparently installed in funerary chapels constructed over the burial shafts. Their small scale enhances the delicacy of these reliefs; the smiling faces, expressive gestures and often elaborate accessories give them at times an almost playful look. The style of these northern tomb reliefs has been termed neo-Memphite. Though the term seems convenient, it is too vaguely defined to be useful, because the chronological and geographical limits of the group are still unclear.

Throughout Egyptian art, individualized or 'portrait' likenesses occur much less frequently in relief than in statuary. Restrictions imposed by the conventions of two-dimensional art (such as the frontal rendering of the eye in a profile face) undoubtedly inhibited such depictions. Since these conventions were still in force, the noteworthy aspect of Egyptian 'portrait' relief in the Late Period is not its rarity, but the fact that it occurs, not just in the Kushite 25th Dynasty, when portrait statuary was important, but also in the more idealized Saite and post-Saite styles.

In their Theban tombs, both Harwa of the late 25th Dynasty (TT 37) and MENTUEMHET, who spanned this dynasty and the next (TT 34), had at least one striking relief representation comparable to their 'portrait' statues; the 'portrait' relief of Mentuemhet is in the Nelson-Atkins Museum of Art, Kansas City, MO (48–28/2). A Memphite relief showing an elderly worshipper, which probably dates to almost the end of the 26th Dynasty (Boston, MA, Mus. F.A., 49.5), and remarkable representations of Psammetichus I and II and Nectanebo I (London, BM, 20 and 22; Vienna, Ksthist. Mus., 213; and Bologna, Mus. Civ. Archeol., 1870) provide sparse but telling evidence of the chronological and social range of relief likenesses in the last centuries before Hellenistic rule.

Persian and 30th Dynasty styles. The transformation of Saite style into the dominant relief style of later dynasties began in a politically troubled period, from which little architectural relief is known. Hibis temple, in el-Kharga Oasis, has been found to contain reliefs bearing the name of Darius I (*reg* 521–486 BC) that were actually originally carved during the 26th Dynasty. There are therefore no temple reliefs attributable to the Achaemenian 27th Dynasty (525–404 BC), although one block (Baltimore, MD, Walters A.G., 22.84), presumably from a tomb, shows a row of men whose costumes and gestures seem typically Persian. Of the following kings, only Hakoris of the 29th Dynasty has left significant reliefs bearing his name. Some of these, however, including the decoration of the bark-station (a shrine for the sacred bark of the god Amun) in front of Pylon I at Karnak, were actually begun by his predecessors.

Nectanebo I and II, of the 30th Dynasty (380–343 BC), resumed temple building on a grand scale. Parts of these monuments still stand, at Dendara, Karnak, Philae and elsewhere. Their relief style is best known, however, in the decoration of numerous, widely distributed blocks from destroyed temples, especially those at Sebennytos and BEHBEIT EL-HAGAR, in the Delta. Among the most mannered and idealized of all Egyptian reliefs, they clearly derive from the soft, fine-drawn forms of Saite style. All modifications are in the direction of an even more mannered exaggeration: thinner, straighter brows; plumper cheeks, more pronounced smiles and double chins; impossibly long fingers; a full circle of flesh round the navel. The modern scholars who first encountered this style attributed its strongly plastic, fleshy modelling to Greek influence, but this persistent misconception has

long since been refuted. The close dependence of 30th-Dynasty style on its Saite parent leaves no doubt that it (like its Ptolemaic descendant) lies in the direct succession of a purely Egyptian style. When Greek influence does appear, it is unmistakable. In the TOMB OF PETOSIRIS at Tuna el-Gebel, built shortly after the death of Alexander the Great (323 BC), the Greek-inspired poses, costumes and accoutrements of mundane figures contrast strikingly with the Egyptian style reserved for cult scenes in the same tomb.

BIBLIOGRAPHY
LÄ: 'Archaismus', 'Hilfslinien', 'Modelle'
G. Maspero: *Le Musée égyptien*, ii (Cairo, 1907), pp. 74–92
A. Erman: 'Saïtische Kopien aus Der el Bahri', *Z. Ägyp. Spr. & Altertknd.*, lii (1914), pp. 90–95
H. Gauthier: 'A Travers la Basse-Egypte III: Quatre bas-reliefs saïtes imités de l'Ancien Empire', *An. Service Ant. Egypte*, xxi (1921), pp. 27–36
C. Kuentz: 'Bas-reliefs saïtes', *Mnmts Piot*, xxxiii (1933), pp. 27–42
F. W. von Bissing: 'Saïtischen Kopien nach Reliefs des Alten Reichs', *Archv Orientforsch.*, ix (1933–4), pp. 35–40
G. Steindorff: 'Reliefs from the Temples of Sebennytos and Iseion in American Collections', *J. Walters A.G.*, vii (1944), pp. 39–59
——: *Catalogue of the Egyptian Sculpture in the Walters Art Gallery*, Baltimore, MD, Walters A.G. cat. (Baltimore, 1946)
J. Leclant: *Recherches sur les monuments thébains de la dynastie dite éthiopienne* (Cairo, 1965)
P. Munro: *Die spätägyptischen Totenstelen*, 2 vols (Glückstadt, 1973)
M. Bietak and E. Reiser-Haslauer: *Das Grab des 'Ankh-Hor*, 2 vols (Vienna, 1978–82)
R. A. Parker, J. Leclant and J.-C. Goyon: *The Edifice of Taharqa by the Sacred Lake of Karnak*, Brown Egyptological Studies, viii (Providence and London, 1979)
F. Daumas: 'Bas-relief et peinture', *L'Egypte du crépuscule* (1980), iii of *Le Monde égyptien: Les Pharaons*, ed. J. Leclant (Paris, 1978–80), pp. 69–119
C. Traunecker, F. Le Saout and O. Masson: *La Chapelle d'Archôris à Karnak*, ii (Paris, 1981)
K. P. Kuhlmann and W. Schenkel: *Das Grab des Ibi, Obergutsverwalters der Gottsgemählin des Amun (Thebanisches Grab Nr. 36)*, 2 vols (Mainz, 1983)
E. R. Russmann: 'Harwa as Precursor of Mentuemhat', *Artibus Aegypti: Studia in Honorem Bernardi V. Bothmer*, ed. H. De Meulenaere and L. Limme (Brussels, 1983), pp. 137–46
W. el-Sadeek: *Twenty-sixth Dynasty Necropolis at Gizeh* (Vienna, 1984)
L. M. Leahy: 'A Saite Lintel Reunited', *J. Egyp. Archaeol.*, lxxi (1985), pp. 122–8
W. Kaiser: 'Die dekorierte Torfassade des spätzeitlichen Palastbezirkes von Memphis', *Mitt. Dt. Archäol. Inst.: Abt. Kairo*, xliii (1987), pp. 123–54
E. Bresciani, M. C. Betrò, A. Giammarusti and C. La Torre: *Tomba di Bakenrenef (L. 24): Attività del Cantiere Scuola 1985–1987 (Saqqara IV)* (Pisa, 1988)
K. Mysliwiec: *Royal Portraiture of the Dynasties XXI–XXX* (Mainz, 1988)
EDNA R. RUSSMANN

(xii) Ptolemaic period (304–30 BC). Ptolemaic sculpture was produced in two idioms: the Hellenistic Greek, essentially using marble and bronze, and the native Egyptian, in limestone and hard stones, rarely bronze. It is debatable whether one culture influenced the other or whether a mixed style existed. From the Late Period (*c.* 750–332 BC) onwards, relief sculpture was generally limited to royal temple reliefs or private stelae, plus some decorative arts such as gems and faience objects; a notable exception is the private funerary temple of Petosiris at Tuna el-Gebel (332–304 BC; *see* PETOSIRIS, TOMB OF), which is decorated with Egyptian-style reliefs incorporating many Hellenistic elements.

(a) Statuary. The Ptolemaic sculptor's style ranged from the idealizing to the non-idealizing, but did not archaize, although all figures ultimately conformed to the traditional proportional grid and were engaged to a backpillar. Forms included block statues, naophorous and stelophorous types, cloaked statues and scribe figures, as well as magic sculptures of individuals inscribed with spells against venomous bites. Striding male figures with fluted drapery, engraved hair and often heavily lined faces also became popular; some highly polished heads have very plastic but unpolished hair. The name of the reigning king disappeared from private statuary, making dating difficult. The Ptolemies, unlike their Persian predecessors, made substantial benefactions to Egyptian temples and commissioned statues in the Egyptian style. A series of limestone heads and body parts, traditionally called 'sculptors' models', date from the late 4th century BC into the early Ptolemaic period.

An Egyptian-style statue of Ptolemy II (*reg* 285–246 BC; see fig. 67) has a blandly idealizing face, pencil-thin cosmetic lines and a gentle smile, a style ultimately derived from images of Nectanebo II (*reg* 360–343 BC). Later royal portraits feature a rectangular face, a low, domed crown, a high headdress band and a thick, long neck; details of the eyes were sometimes applied (e.g. New York, Met., 10.176.44). Subsequent developments included a longer face tapering to the chin, a higher crown of head, a high headband and a thinner neck; these changes resulted in a better integration of the head and torso and a greater prominence for the face and uraeus (e.g. New Haven, CT, Yale U., Peabody Mus. Nat. Hist., 384). Later developments include locks of hair, sometimes tousled, showing below the headband (e.g. New Haven, CT, Yale U., Peabody Mus. Nat. Hist., 388); this may represent a mixed Egyptian and Greek idiom.

Royal portraits in the Hellenistic idiom gracing public buildings and temples varied from reign to reign, but remained idealizing and thus are seldom true likenesses. Formulaic images include the shaved youth (indicating heroism), the upturned head (suggesting a divine association), concerned eyes (pathos) and long (divine) hair in mild disarray bound by a royal diadem (see Smith). An ideal image of the god Serapis, combining Osiris, the Apis bull, Dionysos and the paternal Zeus, was introduced by Ptolemy I (*reg* 304–284 BC). A mature image (Naples, Mus. Archeol. N. N., 5600) probably represents this King, who came to power aged 60, but, as in the case of his son Ptolemy II, no statues in this style have been firmly identified. The bland youthful portraits of Ptolemy IV (*reg* 221–205 BC; e.g. Boston, MA, Mus. F.A., 01.8208) relate to his coins, while long sideburns identify Ptolemy VI (*reg* 180–145 BC; e.g. Alexandria, Gr.-Roman Mus., 24092, 3357) and chubby cheeks Ptolemy VIII (*reg* 170–163, 145–116 BC; e.g. Brussels, Musées Royaux A. & Hist.). More aggressive images characterize their strifing successors.

Surprisingly, women were seldom represented in sculpture from the 26th Dynasty until the Ptolemaic period, when they gained more public freedom. Female statues, both royal and private, reappeared, although Hellenistic queens wearing a diadem or veil can be indistinguishable from goddesses, muses or other personifications; Arsinoe

67. Red granite statue of Ptolemy II, h. 2.66 m, *c.* 285–246 BC (Rome, Vatican, Museo Gregoriano Egizio)

II, the wife of Ptolemy II, was deified as Aphrodite, Isis and Agathe Tyche. In the Egyptian idiom she wore a Lower Egyptian crown with ostrich feathers and ram horns over a vulture headdress, or simply long corkscrew tresses (e.g. Leiden, Rijksmus. Oudhd., F1938/7.20; New York, Met., 20.2.21). In the Greek idiom she wore the same corkscrew hairstyle or a 'melon' coiffure and carried a double cornucopia. However, the popularity of her cult throughout the dynasty renders the dating of such pieces difficult. Numerous uninscribed images of Ptolemaic queens wearing up to three uraei (see Bianchi, 1988) are variously dated but some stronger images are attributed to the powerful Cleopatra III (*reg* 116–88 BC). Cleopatra VII (*reg* 51–30 BC), who (like many late Ptolemaic queens) shared Isis traits, locally enjoyed a beautiful Greek image with the melon coiffure, but a matronly Roman version featured on coins minted abroad. Non-royal women were sculpted with a long or short bobbed wig and often with a lily sceptre (e.g. Cairo, Egyp. Mus., 5/3/25/7).

BIBLIOGRAPHY

B. V. Bothmer and others: *Egyptian Sculpture of the Late Period* (New York, 1960)
H. Kyrieleis: *Bildnisse der Ptolemäer* (Berlin, 1975)
H. Maehler and V. M. Strocka, eds: *Das ptolemäische Ägypten* (Mainz, 1978)
R. S. Bianchi: 'The Egg-heads: One Type of Generic Portrait from the Egyptian Late Period', *Wiss. Z. Humboldt-U.*, ii/3 (1982), pp. 149–51
S. Wood: 'Isis, Eggheads, and Roman Portraiture', *J. Amer. Res. Cent. Egypt*, xxiv (1987), pp. 124–41
R. S. Bianchi: *Cleopatra's Egypt: Age of the Ptolemies* (New York, 1988)
B. V. Bothmer: 'Egyptian Antecedents of Roman Republican Verism', *Quad. Ric. Sci.*, cxvi (1988), pp. 47–65
R. R. R. Smith: *Hellenistic Royal Portraits* (Oxford, 1988)

(b) Relief. There is no evidence for Hellenistic Greek influence on Ptolemaic temple relief carving, and stylistically early Ptolemaic royal reliefs cannot be satisfactorily distinguished from those of the 30th Dynasty (*see* §(xi)(b) above). Comparisons between royal reliefs and Ptolemaic coinage in the Hellenistic idiom are invalid.

Apart from some isolated examples at Luxor and Karnak (*see* THEBES (i), §§II, 1 and III) there is little extant relief decoration dating to the reigns of Alexander the Great (*reg* 332–323 BC) and his successors Philip Arrhidaeus (*reg* 323–316 BC) and Ptolemy I (*reg* 304–284 BC). The Lower Egyptian temple reliefs of Ptolemy II (*reg* 285–246 BC) are almost indistinguishable from those of Nectanebo II (*reg* 360–343 BC), although this is not the case at PHILAE in the south (see fig. 68). Relief scenes of Ptolemy II show much free space around the figures, while the cartouches and the words spoken by the King are equally short. However, with the longer cartouche of Ptolemy III (*reg* 246–221 BC), text length increased, framing devices appeared and distinctions occurred between male and female proportions: there is compression of the female shoulders, thickening of the arms, and narrowing of a high waist. A lower root of the nose compressed the lower face and a fleshier cheek was emphasized by a diagonal throat. Such excesses disappeared in subsequent reigns, although the scenes became more cluttered with text. By the time of Ptolemy XII (*reg* 80–58, 55–51 BC), figures were carved in higher and rounder relief and the legs developed a characteristic 'locked knee' effect anticipating the even more exaggerated reliefs of the Roman period.

Since the end of the New Kingdom (*c.* 1075 BC), temple reliefs had made little attempt at narrative, and the separate rites shown on a register reflected neither the order of ritual performance nor the function of the chamber. However, as the temple architecture reflected the cosmos, so too the position of the scenes and their components could be purposefully deployed and symmetry between the scenes' iconographic content governed their deployment. Iconographic features can provide Ptolemaic benchmarks. For example, the Ptolemaic queen never wore the vulture headdress, unless shown deified and on the divine side of a scene; the nipple on the male was never indicated; and both the repository table and the tail springing out before the knees of the seated god disappeared under

68. Raised relief of Ptolemy II, sandstone, from the Temple of Isis, Philae, 285–246 BC

Ptolemy VI (*reg* 180–145 BC). Columns of inscriptions flanked each scene and rhetorical, stylistic and orthographic rules became firmly fixed from the time of Ptolemy VIII (*reg* 170–163, 145–116 BC).

At Philae, graphic changes in attributes and scenes occurred from reign to reign. Also, although deities wore specific crowns, variants were used to distinguish a special cult site. Royal offerings could be specific to the deity concerned (for example, lettuce was offered to Min and a palette to Thoth) or gender specific (hunting or spearing foes were regarded as appropriate for male deities, mirrors for female deities). Some scenes were architecturally determined: reliefs of the king supporting the heavens are uppermost, the offering of fields lowermost. Despite certain conventions, temples reveal individualized treatments.

The immigrant Greeks accentuated social barriers as a ruling élite, so despite religious syncretism, the architecture and decoration were stylistically mutually exclusive. However, privately dedicated stelae, mostly in limestone, reveal both the strictly Egyptian style (e.g. U. Amsterdam, Pierson Mus., 8549 and 7776) and a style with mixed motifs (e.g. Cairo, Egyp. Mus., JE 44048). Royal relief images in the Hellenistic idiom were disseminated as coinage, engraved gems, clay seal impressions (e.g. Toronto, Royal Ont. Mus.) and faience vessels, some with appliqué relief images of Ptolemaic queens. Faience vessels (Naukratis ware) in low and bichrome relief which show an Egyptian system of friezes but with Greek motifs were also produced.

See also DENDARA, EDFU and KOM OMBO.

BIBLIOGRAPHY
B. V. Bothmer: 'Ptolemaic Reliefs I; II; III; IV', *Bull. Mus. F.A., Boston*,
    l (1952), pp. 19–27, 49–56; li (1953), pp. 2–7, 80–84
P. Derchain: 'Un Manuel de géographie liturgique à Edfu', *Chron. Egypte*,
    lxxiii (1962), pp. 31–65
E. Winter: *Untersuchungen zu den ägyptischen Tempelreliefs der griechisch-
    römischen Zeit* (Vienna, 1968)
S. Cauville: *La Théologie d'Osiris à Edfou*, Bibliothèque d'Etudes, xci
    (Geneva, 1983)
D. Kurth: *Die Dekoration der Säulen im Pronaos des Tempels von Edfu*,
    Götting. Orientforsch., iv/11 (1983), pp. 1178–82
A. Gutbub: 'Remarques sur quelques règles observées dans l'architecture,
    la décoration et les inscriptions des temples de basse époque', *Mélanges
    offerts à J. Vercoutter* (Paris, 1985), pp. 123–36
S. Cauville: *Essai sur la théologie du temple d'Horus à Edfou*, i, Bibliothèque
    d'Etudes, cii/1–2 (1987)
J. Spier: 'A Group of Ptolemaic Engraved Garnets', *J. Walters A.G.*, xlvii
    (1989), pp. 21–38
E. Vassilika: *Ptolemaic Philae*, Orientalia Lovaniensia Analecta, xxxv
    (Leuven, 1989)
A. Abdalla: *Graeco-Roman Funerary Stelae from Upper Egypt* (Liverpool,
    1992)
                                                        ELENI VASSILIKA

(xiii) Roman period (30 BC–AD 395). The Roman emperors followed the example that had been set by the Ptolemies and had themselves portrayed as pharaohs on the monuments erected in their name. This section discusses native Egyptian sculpture produced during the Roman period, rather than Greek or Roman sculpture of the same period found in Egypt.

(a) Statuary. The native Egyptian statuary of the Roman period, usually described as Greco-Egyptian, has various subjects, from emperors to private individuals and deities. The statues combine surviving elements of the traditional pharaonic style with certain features of post-Ptolemaic art (a softer treatment of faces, the style of clothing and headdress, beards, hairstyles), but the products of this process are rarely anything more than an unsuccessful juxtaposition, failing to blend the two styles either artistically or conceptually.

Large-scale imperial statues retained, as a guarantee of the continuity of pharaonic power, the traditional Egyptian model of the advancing pharaoh, clad in the *shendyt* (pleated kilt) and crowned with the traditional regalia (the double crown of Upper and Lower Egypt), but these iconographic elements were invariably sterile 'Egyptianizing' imitations with no inner unity. During the Roman period Egyptian sculptors also sometimes replaced the pharaoh's head on an old statue with that of the emperor. There were attempts to represent a Roman emperor in accordance with the old canons, as in the case of the colossal statue of Septimius Severus (*reg* AD 193–211; Cairo, Egyp. Mus., CG 703), who is shown in the conventional advancing attitude of the pharaoh, with the double crown on his head but with a thick beard and curly hair. Such statues achieved an effect of brutal caricature by their exaggeration of the tendency of Roman portraiture to make the subject recognizable. There is another statue of an emperor (Liverpool Mus.; fig. 69), probably Septimius Severus again or perhaps Caracalla (*reg* AD 198–217), shown triumphing over a hirsute barbarian, which is interesting because of its mixture of Classical and pharaonic elements (particularly the traditional portrayal of the sovereign victorious over his enemy, *see* §VI, 12 above).

69. Roman period statue of an emperor (Septimius Severus or Caracalla) triumphing over a barbarian, marble, h. 555 mm, *c.* AD 200 (Liverpool, Liverpool Museum)

Large numbers of statues of private individuals—especially native priests or magistrates—were produced for dedication in temples. Local stone was used, particularly the hard stones that had been traditionally used for sculpture for thousands of years (such as basalt, diorite and granite). The presence of a back pillar identifies them as belonging to the native tradition; their style, however, is for the most part tired and repetitive, even though it often preserves the traditional values of mass and volume. Certain Hellenistic or Roman-style details of dress (such as crowns made of flowers), as in reliefs, are only adjuncts. Among the most noteworthy statues are those of a certain Petosiris from Memphis (Cairo, Egyp. Mus.), and the 'provincial' series from the village of Dimai (Soknopaiou Nesos) in the Faiyum, which in some cases bear the signature of their Egyptian sculptor in Greek or a demotic text. This series includes the basalt statue of Horpit (Cairo, Egyp. Mus., CG 1191), from the 19th year of the reign of Tiberius (AD 321), which is seated in a hieratic pose and has eyes inset with enamel.

Religious and cult sculpture, depicting the deities of the ancient Egyptian religion (such as Isis, Osiris, Anubis and Sobek), preserves, by virtue of its sacred character, at least the outward signs of the ancient iconography, in contrast to the mixed characteristics of the numerous surviving likenesses of Serapis, a god imposed on Egypt from Ptolemaic times in an attempt to unify Greeks and Egyptians. One of the most successful examples of the mixed Egyptian and Hellenistic style is the large stone statue of Kronos–Suchos (Cairo, Egyp. Mus.) from the time of Septimius Severus; the Greek god Kronos is represented in Greek pose and dress, but at the same time he holds a crocodile in his hand, symbol of the Egyptian god Sobek (Gr. Suchos), with whom he had become syncretistically assimilated. The most widespread forms of sculpture in Egypt during the Roman period were small terracotta figurines of Hellenistic type and bronze statuettes of divinities, mainly of very low quality.

BIBLIOGRAPHY

P. Graindor: *Bustes et statues-portraits d'Egypte romaine* (Cairo, n.d.)
G. Grimm and D. Johannes: *Kunst der Ptolemäer- und Romerzeit im Ägyptischen Museum, Kairo* (Mainz, 1975)
H. D. Schneider: *Beelden van Behnasa: Egyptische kunst uit de Romeinse Keizertijd, 1e–3e eeuw na Chr.* [Images from Behnasa: Egyptian art of the Roman imperial period, 1st–3rd centuries AD] (Zutphen, 1982)
Z. Kiss: *Etudes sur le portrait impérial romain en Egypte* (Warsaw, 1984)

EDDA BRESCIANI

(b) Relief. The Roman conquest of Egypt in 30 BC did not immediately affect the style of Egyptian relief: the characteristics of monumental reliefs in the Roman period are very similar to those of the Ptolemaic period. There are two main categories of relief: those in sanctuaries and cult places and those carved for the funerary monuments of private individuals. Since the decoration of Egyptian temples consisted of very codified and specific images of the pharaoh offering to the gods (and the associated liturgy), the reliefs were rarely susceptible to external influences. Usually only the names in the cartouches change, and concessions to the real world are rare (occasionally the king may be shown wearing the royal Macedonian robe).

During the reign of Augustus (*reg* 30 BC–AD 14) the programmes of decoration of the great temples such as Philae, Dendara and Kom Ombo were continued, but new sites were also established. This activity was maintained throughout Egypt (including Nubia and the oases of the Western Desert), almost without interruption, until the reign of Antoninus Pius (*reg* AD 138–61). Relief decoration diminished during the 3rd century, when work took place only at Esna and Kom Ombo. The last known temple reliefs in the pharaonic style were found at Tahta and dated to the reign of Maximinus II Daia (*reg* AD 305–313; Cairo, Egyp. Mus.). In 394, however, the Gate of Hadrian at Philae was carved with an image of the Nubian god Mandulis, accompanied by a double inscription in hieroglyphics and demotic (the latest such inscription found in Egypt), suggesting that pharaonic influence was still present.

The reliefs in temples of the Roman period were carved by teams of specialists, sometimes itinerant. Several artists' signatures (in demotic script) on the southern face of the 2nd pylon at the Temple of Isis at Philae suggest that a team of sculptors from Dendara (a scribe, draughtsman and sculptor) were working on the forecourt and 2nd pylon at Philae. The 'outline scribes', who drew the designs for reliefs, continued to use the guiding grid of 21 squares, measured from the sole of the foot to the eyebrow (*see*

§IV, 3 above), and in some cases templates or patterns were used. The process of sculpting was the same as in the Ptolemaic period: sunk relief for exterior walls and raised reliefs for the interior (although there are many exceptions to this rule). The reliefs were painted in vivid colours and sometimes certain figures were gilded.

In spite of the great diversity of Roman relief styles, some general trends can be discerned. The most characteristic aspect is the abundance—and occasionally superabundance—of attention to items of dress, such as decorative loincloths and very ornate necklaces and pectorals. Sometimes the relief work is too emphatic and the rules of proportion are not respected. The overall effect is heavy and turgid, particularly in the relief decoration of Hadrian (*reg* AD 117–138) and Antoninus Pius in the Temple of Isis at Deir el-Shelwit (Western Thebes). In the latest scenes at Kom Ombo, the anatomical details (such as the outline of the mouth and the muscles of the knee) are treated with a clumsiness and a stiffness that render them almost caricatures.

The unevenness of the work produced in the Roman period resulted more from a coincidence of local factors—such as the nature of the materials, the size of the representation, the quality of the workmen and the time available—than from a general stylistic development. For instance, two sets of reliefs from the reign of Claudius (*reg* AD 41–54), on two neighbouring sites (Dendara and

70. Roman period relief showing Hathor suckling Ihy, sandstone, h. *c.* 2 m, on the south wall of the Roman *mammisi* at Dendara, *c.* AD 98–117

Koptos), present a huge contrast: at Dendara is the very beautiful workmanship of the hypostyle hall, and at el-Qal'a (north-east of Koptos) is the ugly decoration of the small Temple of Min, Isis and Horus. Claudius' sculptors were handicapped at el-Qal'a by the material—shelly limestone. Even within the same building and under the same reign, sculptures cut with care can stand next to scenes executed in a much more improvised style, as at el-Qal'a.

Sometimes the conjunction of favourable factors gave birth to remarkable works, such as the exterior decoration of the Roman MAMMISI of Trajan (reg 98–117) at Dendara (see fig. 70) or certain scenes dating to the time of Tiberius (reg 14–37) in the temple at Kom Ombo. Some time after the clumsy work of the last sculptors at Kom Ombo (c. 217) the final scenes of the temple of Esna, from the reign of Decius (reg 249–51), are still of creditable workmanship, although a little heavy. Much later, the fragments of decoration of Maximinus Daia (i.e. the block from Tahta, now in Cairo, Egyp. Mus.) distinguish themselves stylistically from the average works of the preceding centuries.

Funerary reliefs and other private monuments attempted to reproduce the ancestral pattern. Their workmanship is often less accomplished than that of temple decoration, but their inspiration is less restrained. Sometimes the deceased is shown dressed in Greek style or even in a frontal view. A stele in the Egyptian Museum, Cairo (CG 22197) combines in one monument the traditional Egyptian stele and full-relief Roman portraiture. In certain circumstances the deities take on the appearance of Roman divinities; thus a stele from Koptos (Oxford, Ashmolean, 1894/106) has the Egyptian deity Geb portrayed frontally and leaning on a lance. In the main, however, the influence of the Classical world remained discreet.

Certain scenes in the chapel of the underground cemetery of Kom el-Shuqafa (at Alexandria) attempt to blend Hellenistic sculpture with pharaonic iconography. In some scenes Egyptian subjects are reproduced in high relief with the effect of perspective; in others Egyptian deities, such as Anubis or Makedon, are clad in Roman breastplates and treated in the Classical style. This rare and scarcely convincing effort dates from the end of the 1st century AD or the beginning of the 2nd.

There is also one instance of an attempt to introduce this hybrid style into temple decoration. The exterior partition wall north of the kiosk of the temple at el-Maharraqa (Hierasykaminos) in Nubia bears a curious bas-relief portraying Isis, dressed in Roman style, viewed frontally and seated under a tree receiving the offering of a figure represented in Hellenistic style. A divine triad, comprising Min, Isis and Serapis, is represented frontally and the clothing is partly in Roman style. On the same wall other divine figures have been carved in traditional style.

These attempts at the fusion of the Alexandrian and pharaonic styles had no future and for a long time the sculptors who were contemporaries of the Caesars did their best to remain faithful to the traditions of pharaonic relief work.

BIBLIOGRAPHY

LÄ: 'Hierasykaminos', 'Kom esch-Schugafa'

A. Kamal: *Stèles hiéroglyphiques d'époque ptolémaïque et romaine*, 2 vols, Cairo, Egyp. Mus. cat. (Cairo, 1904–5)

F. W. von Bissing: *Denkmäler ägyptischer Skulptur* (Munich, 1914), nos 114–21

F. L. Griffith: *Catalogue of the Demotic Graffiti of the Dodecaschoenus*, 2 vols (Cairo, 1937), pls 26, 27/i, 30, 41, 224, 244, 317

J. Capart and H. Gregoire: 'L'Enigme de Tahta', *Chron. Egypte*, xxix (1940), pp. 45–50, 119–23 [relief blocks of Maximinus Daia]

F. Daumas: 'Bas-relief et peinture', *L'Egypte du crépuscule* (1980), iii of *Le Monde égyptien: Les Pharaons*, ed. J. Leclant (Paris, 1978–80), pp. 69–119

CLAUDE TRAUNECKER

X. Painting and drawing.

There was no ancient Egyptian word specifically for the artist who practised what is now defined as painting or drawing. Like the men who produced architecture and sculpture, those responsible for two-dimensional work were anonymous craftsmen (see §II above), who were trained to create products that fulfilled the specific requirements of religious cults, funerary practice or everyday need. The paintings in tombs served as aids whereby the deceased person might be able to attain the kind of afterlife considered necessary for the survival and nourishing of his immortal spirit. Paintings in houses or palaces, by contrast, were essentially decorative, although they frequently incorporated religious elements and even inscriptions with religious content. Drawing in ancient Egypt was almost always preparatory to some further artistic process: it was used for sketching out on a block of stone the outline of a proposed sculpture (see §VII, 1(ii)(c) above) and for outlining the scenes on surfaces that would subsequently be either carved in relief or painted. Although drawing was fundamental—providing the basis for all two-dimensional art—and aesthetically the most fruitful element in Egyptian artistic achievement in this field, most of its finest results were either destroyed by carving or obscured by the addition of paint.

1. Introduction. 2. Wall painting. 3. Drawing. 4. Papyrus illustration.

1. INTRODUCTION. Throughout the pharaonic period, the man who was generally of greatest importance in the team production of two-dimensional works of art was the one who drew the initial design. He was the 'outline scribe', 'scribe' being the word that characterizes his function most precisely. In training the scribe learnt how to write with rush-brush and paint; the outline scribe learnt how to draw with the same materials and also how to apply paint generally. Even if the identity of most individual ancient Egyptian scribe–artists is not known, much information about their methods of creating works of art can be gained through the examination of partly finished work. The execution of a wall painting involved several stages, including the preparation of the surface, the initial drawing, the process of correction and emendation and the application of colour. It is likely that each stage was carried out by a different craftsman, especially in the case of important works, and the last stage may have involved one craftsman applying simple colour and another adding detail. Many incomplete examples have survived, one of the best being the painted decoration in the tomb of King Sethos I (reg 1290–c. 1279 BC) in the Valley of the Kings at Thebes

(which shows successive stages from preparation of the wall to completed painted low reliefs).

Little is known of the ways in which decisions were reached concerning the subject or layout of a particular painted decoration. The standard repertory of scenes used in tomb decoration (*see* §V above) changed from period to period, but while many themes, and even incidental activities, were repeated, there is considerable variation in arrangement and detail in surviving works, suggesting that the Egyptian artist had some opportunities to exercise individuality and initiative. Even so, he followed rigid conventions of representation (*see* §IV, 2 above), supported by a canon of proportions (*see* §IV, 3 above) that was established in its simple form in the early years of the Dynastic period (*c.* 2900 BC). In some unfinished scenes or in scenes where there has been a loss of surface colour, the proportional grids of this system can still be seen and studied. Among the visual conventions that characterize Egyptian two-dimensional art is the linear or processional method of presentation, by which contemporaneous or successive events and activities are placed in sequence on a wall, often arranged in narrow horizontal bands or registers.

Good draughtsmanship, the perfection of line, the use of colour (with its virtuoso exploitation of a limited palette), the introduction of shading, the representation of texture and attention to detail are among the qualities on which the estimation of excellence in two-dimensional Egyptian art is based. The severe standards set during initial scribal training generally ensured that most Egyptian painting and drawing was at least competent. It had to be so if the results were to fulfil the ritual function required of them in tomb and temple decoration.

2. WALL PAINTING. The technique used by the Egyptian wall painter was essentially that of tempera or gouache; it was not fresco as has often inaccurately and misleadingly

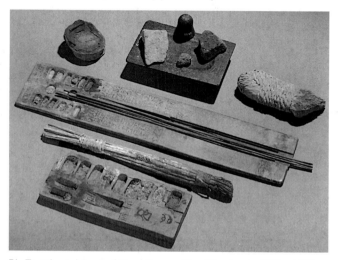

71. Egyptian painter–scribe's equipment, New Kingdom, *c.* 1540–*c.* 1075 BC (top from left to right): potsherd with remains of paint; grinder with raw pigment material; brush; palette of Meryre with twelve pigment depressions; brush; palette with nine pigment depressions (London, British Museum)

been claimed. The pigments employed were mostly prepared from naturally occurring mineral substances that were not subject to fading, even in the brightest of Egyptian sunlight: white was chalk or gypsum; black was carbon obtained from the undersides of cooking pots, from ground-up charcoal or bone-black; for red, iron oxides were used; for yellow, orpiment (an arsenical compound and a less stable colour) or yellow ochre; for green and blue, manufactured frits were most common, although ground malachite and lapis lazuli were occasionally used. For the application of paint, an unidentified medium was employed. Different materials may have been used at different times. Egg was readily available, but it is thought to have been unsuitable for use in the prevailing hot conditions. Alternative possibilities were gum and size, the former obtainable from several native trees, particularly the acacia, while the second could have been prepared from animal waste such as bones and skin. Brushes were made from fibrous materials: beaten palm-ribs, bruised twigs and chewed rushes; surviving examples seem hopelessly crude and inefficient (see fig. 71), but there was nothing inefficient about the way in which the ancient artist used them.

Much of the fine effect achieved by Egyptian painting, particularly the luminous quality, derives from the careful preparation of the ground. Ideally tomb paintings were executed directly on the stone of the tomb walls, whether these were constructed of quarried blocks or cut into the living rock. This occurred only with the finest quality limestones, which were dense and regular in texture, providing a ground to which paint could be applied directly. More often than not, however, the surface (quarried or built) required considerable preparation with the final application of a wash. This was commonly white, though frequently a pale bluish-grey during the Old Kingdom (*c.* 2575–*c.* 2150 BC), and occasionally yellow in the Theban necropolis during the New Kingdom (*c.* 1540–*c.* 1075 BC). If the underlying rock was of poor quality and incapable of taking even a roughly smoothed surface, an artificial surface was applied, consisting of a coarse mud plaster, reinforced with chaff and covered with a thin layer of gypsum plaster (gesso), which provided an excellent surface for painting (*see* §XVII, 14 below).

Painted wall decorations in domestic buildings (houses and palaces) were less carefully applied, although the results, as in the palace of King Amenophis III (*reg c.* 1390–*c.* 1353 BC) at Malqata in Western Thebes (*see* THEBES (i), §XII) and in the houses and palaces at EL-AMARNA, were often highly accomplished and very decorative. Such domestic buildings were built of sun-dried mud bricks, and the interior walls that were to be decorated were simply rendered smooth with mud plaster (ready to receive paint without the intervention of a layer of gesso or even of a light-coloured wash). An unusual feature found in the painting of mud floors at el-Amarna has been interpreted as a kind of primitive fresco technique, since the paint was apparently applied before the mud was fully dry. The purpose seems to have been to bind the colour to the pavement to give it greater resistance to wear. Unfortunately, there has been insufficient investigation of this technique for convincing conclusions to be reached.

(i) Early Dynastic (*c.* 2925–*c.* 2575 BC). (ii) Old Kingdom and First Intermediate Period (*c.* 2575–*c.* 2008 BC). (iii) Middle Kingdom and Second Intermediate Period (*c.* 2008–*c.* 1540 BC). (iv) New Kingdom (*c.* 1540–*c.* 1075 BC). (v) Third Intermediate Period–Ptolemaic period (*c.* 1075–30 BC).

*(i) Early Dynastic (*c. 2925–*c. 2575 *BC).* The painting of formal compositions on prepared surfaces can be traced back to tomb decorations of the earliest Egyptian dynasties (*c.* 2925–*c.* 2575 BC), with one earlier example in a tomb at Hierakonpolis (*c.* 3200 BC) now known only from a copy made at the time of discovery in the 1890s (for illustration *see* HIERAKONPOLIS). This early example, from a place of particular importance during the period of Egyptian unification, shows that a tradition of wall painting had already been established by the time of the 1st Dynasty. The Predynastic Hierakonpolis Painted Tomb contained polychrome decoration on a surface of smoothed mud plaster applied to the mud-brick lining of the tomb chamber. The elements of the decoration—representations of boats and of men and animals involved in activities that have been variously interpreted as hunting and warfare—were freely placed in the available field and not set on base-lines or in registers, as became customary in the Dynastic period. The style and character of the elements may be more readily related to contemporary, late Predynastic decoration on pottery and on the few surviving carved ivories than to the pictorial art that was to evolve as characteristically Egyptian after unification.

The first substantial remains of wall painting of the Dynastic period have been found on the outer walls of the rectangular mud-brick superstructures of great mastaba-tombs of the earliest two dynasties. Geometrical patterns of quite elaborate intricacy (clearly reproducing hangings of matting) were painted on white gesso applied to the walls. Identifiable colours included red, white, black, blue-green and yellow. Of paintings within mastabas, no evidence earlier than the 3rd Dynasty (*c.* 2650–*c.* 2575 BC) has so far been found. In the superstructure of the mastaba of Hesyre (*see* HESYRE, TOMB OF), dated to the reign of Djoser (*c.* 2630–*c.* 2611 BC), the walls of a corridor were not only painted with mat-hangings but also decorated with objects and scenes distinctly related to those found in the later, elaborately decorated tombs of the 5th and 6th dynasties (*c.* 2465–*c.* 2150 BC). The wall paintings in the mastaba of Hesyre include items of tomb furniture (placed in registers), furniture, boxes and vessels, on which details of wood-graining and variegated stone textures were diligently reproduced. There are also painted traces of cattle and a crocodile that must surely have formed part of an early marsh scene, such as later became a popular theme (*see* §VI, 10 above).

*(ii) Old Kingdom and First Intermediate Period (*c. 2575–*c. 2008 *BC).* The best work in royal and private tombs and in temples during the Old Kingdom was carried out in fine low relief from which the colour has to a great extent been lost. Where colour has survived, as in the 6th-Dynasty tomb of Mehu at Saqqara, it appears as a rather crude addition. The highest achievement in the field of pure painting in the Old Kingdom is exemplified by the surviving fragments from the tomb of Neferma'at and his wife Itet at Maidum. This tomb, which was built for a son of Sneferu (*reg c.* 2575–*c.* 2551 BC), first king of the 4th

Dynasty, has a superstructure of mud-brick; its interior seems to have been planned by someone determined to demonstrate the widest possible range of decoration. Some walls and architectural features were faced with limestone, carved with relief and painted; there was also, more unusually, carved sunk relief in limestone filled with coloured pastes; finally, and most successfully, there was straight painting on mud plaster overlaid with fine gypsum plaster. The finest and best known fragment, the 'Maidum Geese' (Cairo, Egyp. Mus.; for illustration *see* MAIDUM), is a true masterpiece: it shows six geese walking in line and cropping vegetation. Egyptian artists excelled in the representation of birds and animals, and in this work the geese are observed with exceptional precision both in their general form and in their individual markings. By the imaginative mixing of primary colours, the artist has produced a range of subtle browns and greys, further heightened by fine detailing, which have allowed him to surpass by far the commonplace results of less accomplished craftsmen. This remarkable work is outstanding for any period of Egyptian painting; it is the more so standing as it does at the beginning of a tradition that lasted 2000 years.

In the later years of the Old Kingdom the focus of painting activity shifted to Upper and Middle Egypt, where the important tombs of nobles and high officials were rock-cut rather than built of brick or stone, as was regularly the case at Memphis (particularly in the necropolis of Saqqara). Even in places where the cliff rock into which the tombs were cut was of sufficient quality for carving, decoration was commonly executed in paint alone. Although in style, execution and colouring the scenes included in these tombs derived directly from the cosmopolitan repertory of Memphis, they exhibited eccentricities that are usually attributed to provincial gaucherie and lack of tradition. In 6th Dynasty tombs at Aswan, for example, where the local stone is sandstone, the walls are not laid out with the care and comprehensiveness found at Saqqara: scenes are placed, with an apparent lack of plan or order, on specially levelled surfaces throughout the tomb chapels; the established proportions of human figures are seemingly ignored; and colours are garish and poorly matched. At places further north, in Middle Egypt, in the necropoleis of Meir and Deir el-Gebrawi, the planning and execution of wall paintings was far more careful, but there remained the tendency to distortion and garishness (for illustrations *see* MEIR and PAPYRUS, §I). Judged against the high standards set by the Memphite artists, most provincial work seems to have been carried out by artists uninstructed in the rigorous conventions that typify the best Egyptian art.

The two-dimensional arts were deeply affected during the shadowy time known as the First Intermediate Period (*c.* 2150–*c.* 2008 BC) when the loss of political control from Memphis was accompanied by the disappearance of the tradition embodied in the Memphite style. An extreme but instructive example of the resulting artistic anarchy is provided by the paintings in the tomb of the provincial noble Ankhtifi at el-Moalla, about 30 km to the south of Thebes (for illustration *see* MOALLA, EL-). There the scenes, conventional enough in terms of subject-matter, are executed with scant regard for the well-established conventions of Memphite style: not only was the canon of proportions apparently abandoned, so too the accepted use of space in the disposition of scenes; colour was also eccentrically employed, particularly in the depiction of animals and birds. In a sense this tomb represents a new, unconventional style that replaced the old. Its manifestations presumably found favour with the distinguished patrons for whom such work was commissioned. A similar departure from convention and an eccentric use of colour can be observed in scenes from the roughly contemporary (First Intermediate Period) tomb of Iti at GEBELEIN, now at the Museo Egizio, Turin. Although in the late 20th century the paintings in the tombs of Ankhtifi and Iti may be appreciated for their 'primitive' qualities, in the context of Egyptian art the naivety of First Intermediate Period art represents a severe deterioration of standards. This disintegration occurred very rapidly in the late 3rd millennium BC. Significantly, the return to convention and the revival of the tradition came equally rapidly. They can best be marked in the region of Thebes where the return to political stability was consolidated in the 11th Dynasty.

(iii) Middle Kingdom and Second Intermediate Period (c. 2008–c. 1540 BC). This return to stability coincided with the start of the new era usually described as the Middle Kingdom (*c. 2008–c.* 1957 BC). In the few surviving private 11th Dynasty tombs at Thebes, such as that of Djar, the painting shows much of the provincial naivety of the preceding period; but already the organization of design and the use of colour is far less eccentric than those in the tomb of Ankhtifi.

In royal work the assertive effect of the old Memphite tradition was rapid and complete; and a similar re-establishment can be seen in the few remains from the tombs of very high officials. The finest work was executed in carved relief, for which the best Theban limestone was well suited. The outstanding exemplar is the work in the Theban mortuary temple of King Nebhepetre Mentuhotpe II (*reg c.* 2008–*c.* 1957 BC), at Deir el-Bahri, of which substantial, brightly painted fragments have survived. In these paintings the brilliant quality of natural colour applied to the stark white of Theban limestone is fully exploited for the first time. The effect is altogether more luminous and striking than that which could be achieved on the honey-coloured, or even greyish, limestone found in the region of Memphis.

Pure painting, as opposed to painted relief, was used to decorate both the great wooden coffins found in private burials of the period and the walls of the tombs of nomarchs in Middle Egypt. The best of the latter are to be found at BENI HASAN, in the necropolis of the nobles of the Oryx nome, and particularly in the tomb chapels of Ammenemes and Khnumhotpe—great vaulted halls, the walls of which are filled with narrow registers containing a huge variety of scenes. They are painted directly on the smoothed rock surface, consisting of a reasonably hard limestone of a pinkish hue, with the intervention of only a thin wash. Much of the interest in the tomb decoration at Beni Hasan lies in the subject-matter of the scenes. Numerous new themes, including trades, industrial processes and daily activities, were introduced into the old

Memphite repertory. Among the most original are representations of wrestling bouts in which the participants are depicted in a wide variety of poses, many of which seem unusually awkward. In attempting to depict the contortions of the contenders and even to suggest the movement of their actions, the artist had to solve many challenging problems of representation. The successive holds and positions, set out sequentially in registers, somewhat resemble the individual frames of a moving picture; taken separately they suggest that the artists did not always succeed in their difficult intention. But it would be wrong to assume that the results would have appeared awkward and unresolved to the ancient Egyptians. Conforming to standard Egyptian practice, each painter showed what he knew had to be seen, not what he could actually see.

The application of colour in the wall paintings of Beni Hasan is generally simple—essentially the areas outlined by the initial artist have been filled in. The use of shading and attempts to indicate texture are limited. Nevertheless, there are vignettes within the overall scheme of decoration which, by their liveliness of design and unconventional content, reveal very good, if not first-class, artists at work. The greater effort needed to tackle an unusual subject seems to have stimulated the painters to produce rather better work. Vignettes such as the scenes in the tomb of Khnemhotpe of birds in an acacia tree, of baboons 'assisting' men in the picking of figs and of the arrival of a party of Asiatics demonstrate an excellent appreciation of the use of space and generally reveal the technical skills of the anonymous artists. The scene of the Asiatics is of special interest because it seems to record an actual event and not some generalized activity; it is dated and specific, referring to the arrival of a consignment of eye-paint. Such 'events' are rare in the decoration of tombs, and when they occur they surely indicate the intention of the tomb owner to incorporate a moment of importance in the timeless activities prepared for his posthumous existence. Conservation of the Beni Hasan tomb paintings began in the 1980s to remove the film of dirt that obscures much of the detail and modifies much of their colour; careful study of the restored works should revolutionize the common assessments of Middle Kingdom wall painting.

(iv) New Kingdom (c. 1540–c. 1075 BC). The painting in the tombs of relatively modest officials at Thebes during the 18th and 19th dynasties (*c.* 1540–*c.* 1190 BC) represents the highpoint of achievement for the ancient Egyptian two-dimensional artist (*see* THEBES (i), §X). There are several reasons for this remarkable flowering during the New Kingdom. Administration was concentrated in the city of Thebes, so there was a substantial body of workmen and artists who were available for work on private tombs, when they were not needed for royal or temple commissions. In the Theban necropolis itself, only a few parts of the natural limestone rock of the western hills were good enough for fine carved relief, and the best places outside the Valley of the Kings and the Valley of the Queens were usually taken for the tombs of the highest officials. Thus the tombs of others, including those of most minor officials, were commonly cut into rock of such poor quality that the walls were simply smoothed level with mud and

chaff plaster, faced with gesso and decorated with straight-forward mural painting. This form of wall preparation and decoration was also quick and cheap, ideally suited to the small chapels found in most of the non-royal Theban tombs. The tally of private Theban tombs so far discovered and considered worthy of numbering (including those that include carved relief) is substantially over 400.

At the outset of the 18th Dynasty (c. 1540 BC), when the Egyptian state was once again unified after a period of political disintegration, the renewal of artistic activity took its inspiration from an earlier settled period. One particularly important influence for the New Kingdom was the two-dimensional art of the Middle Kingdom in Thebes, which had itself looked back to the Memphite style of the Old Kingdom. In both cases the strong thread of tradition and convention provided the connecting link. The best examples of tomb painting from the early 18th Dynasty down to the reigns of Hatshepsut and Tuthmosis III (c. 1479–c. 1426 BC) seem initially to have a formal academicism in which most of the elements in the decoration are conventional, to the point of being stiff. Draughtsmanship is accomplished and restrained; most of the colour is applied in a flat, regular manner, unrelieved by the adventurous employment of painterly skills; there is scarcely any use of shading or indication of texture. Closer acquaintance with the paintings of the New Kingdom reveals that the Theban artist was by no means completely tied to the past; the intellectual excitement generated by a time of expansion and adventure resulted in a degree of artistic experiment and innovation both in the use of space and in the enlargement of the old repertory of subjects. Interest and variety were introduced into well-established scenes by the addition of small, adventitious vignettes of particular charm. For example, in hunting scenes the strict layout of registers was abandoned and figures were allowed to float in space, as it were, in a manner scarcely found in Egyptian art since the decoration of the Predynastic Painted Tomb at Hierakonpolis (see §(i) above), almost 2000 years earlier. Desert landscapes, the characteristic environment of the hunt, were also represented in a much freer manner, with the unusual use of background colours and undulating lines to suggest the contours of hills and valleys.

An early essay in this freer form of representation can be found in the tomb of Ineni (TT 81), where there is an unusual detail of a female hyena attempting to remove an arrow sticking in its jowl, while being harassed by a hunting dog, a novel motif that was repeated in later tombs. In the TOMB OF REKHMIRE (TT 100), a vizier in the reign of Tuthmosis III (reg c. 1479–c. 1426 BC), the animals in the hunt are driven into a kind of stockade in which they can be shot down at leisure by the huntsmen. The trapped animals initially appear to be tangled in the utmost confusion in the stockade (hounds snapping at ostriches, antelopes and wild cattle; here the female hyena is shown worrying the arrow it has succeeded in tearing from its breast). The confusion, however, is cunningly contrived by a master who has used convention in an imaginative way to express unconventionality: the animals individually

72. Wall painting showing a banquet scene, paint on plaster, h. 610 mm, from the so-called tomb of Nebamun, Thebes, 18th Dynasty, c. 1375 BC (London, British Museum)

are shown conventionally, but by their disposition, the changing angles, the crowding and the use of irregular lines, a remarkable vitality is introduced into the scene.

The great tomb of Rekhmire is exceptional in being cut in an area of good limestone but decorated mostly with wall painting. The design of the tomb is also unusual: there is a conventional cross-corridor at right angles to the entrance, and a long corridor running directly from the entrance into the hill, with a ceiling that rises sharply as the corridor penetrates deeply into the limestone. The wall area thus available for decoration was huge and it has been generously exploited. Ritual and non-ritual scenes are shown with a detail and variety unparalleled in other New Kingdom Theban tombs. A wide range of industrial and craft activities is represented, all shown to be taking place in the king's workshops, over which Rekhmire had control (see figs 12, 15 and 17 above). Scenes of the bringing of tribute from the supposed subject countries in Asia, the Aegean, Libya and black Africa provided the artist with excellent opportunities to depict exotic peoples, animals and products. The substantial increase of official contacts with foreign countries at that time is attested by similar scenes in a number of early to mid-18th Dynasty tombs, such as those of Menkheperraseneb (TT 86) and SENEN-MUT (TT 71).

The wall paintings in the later 18th Dynasty private Theban tombs reveal extraordinary technical advances. A century and a half of steady practice and development by a large community of artists working under the highest patronage had stimulated confidence. The immense variety of styles employed at this time is unparalleled in any branch of Egyptian art at any other period. The handling of conventional subjects is bold and innovative. New details are introduced and copied, but rarely in a slavish manner: a sleeping peasant in the harvest field in the TOMB OF MENNA (TT 69) is repeated, but with originality, in the relief of the tomb of Khaemhet (TT 57). The groups of musicians and singers shown entertaining the guests at the funerary banquet are variously and vigorously portrayed. The somewhat stiff musical ensemble of Rekhmire's tomb (TT 100) from the earlier years of the 18th Dynasty is superseded by the lithe and dramatic grouping of musicians in the TOMB OF NAKHT (TT 52). In the corresponding

scene from the so-called tomb of Nebamun (fragments in London, BM; *see* WALL PAINTING, colour pl. I, fig. 1) the artist, with exceptional daring, has portrayed two singers full-face, an experiment that seems to have been only partially successful (see fig. 72). But his palette—rich, but not gaudy—his delicacy of brush, his use of shading, of design and of detail can scarcely be matched elsewhere. One scene, showing the tomb owner, traditionally identified as Nebamun, with his wife and daughter hunting birds in the marshes (see fig. 8 above), although only a part of a composition originally much larger, can still be appreciated as if it were self-contained. Nebamun, with throw-stick raised, dominates the scene; he is surrounded by the multifarious life of the marshes—birds, fish, insects, all represented with a wealth of details executed in a variety of techniques to differentiate the textures of scales, wings, feathers and flesh. The retriever cat, grasping three captured birds, is outstanding for its observation of feline grace and power and the uncanny skill with which its fur is painted.

Painting in a strict, conventional, academic style persisted in some tombs, especially those prepared for the most important people. On one wall in the TOMB OF RAMOSE (TT 55), a vizier, the funeral procession is depicted with accomplished precision, a prime example of the finished style of artists trained in the traditional manner. Even the scene of female mourners, a subject that often provided an opportunity for the interesting grouping of figures, is here somewhat stiffly managed. Far freer treatments of conventional subjects are found in the tombs of less important officials, for instance the much visited tombs of Menna (TT 69) and Nakht (TT 52), with their unusual details, looser draughtsmanship and adventurous colour combinations. The TOMB OF QENAMUN (TT 93) has an innovative deep yellow background instead of the common white ground. In the tomb of Userhet (TT 56) animals are represented with bold and assured draughtsmanship: a few dramatic lines delineate a hare, its tawny coat filled in with sweeping brush strokes and splashes of white; a fox in the chase collapses exhausted in the branches of a bush, its pathetic plight vividly conveyed with great economy.

The exceptionally fluid lines of the painter of the tomb of another Nebamun (TT 90) might have been thought careless, and even slovenly, by contemporary Egyptians; but to modern eyes his work has immediate appeal. The depiction of vines in the vintage scene of the same tomb reflects the free approach to the representation of plants which was developed to such great success in the domestic painting found in the palaces and villas at el-Amarna, the new city founded by Akhenaten (*reg c.* 1353–*c.* 1336 BC). Fragments of mural decorations and floor paintings show a predominance of natural subjects, especially marsh scenes and elaborate, though freely executed, designs of intertwining branches and flowers. On the four walls of the 'Green Room' in the 'North Palace' at el-Amarna a remarkable decorative scheme depicting life in the marshes was carried out with exceptional care, the visual effect of which has been compared with that of certain Chinese wallpapers. Papyrus and lotus flowers bend in all directions; kingfishers flit between the reeds, diving to the waters below; and a background of vertical plant-stems

73. Wall painting fragment showing two daughters of Akhenaten and Nefertiti, paint on plaster, 0.40×1.65 m, from el-Amarna, 18th Dynasty, *c.* 1350 BC (Oxford, Ashmolean Museum)

provides a unifying structure to the whole. The surviving parts (London, BM), preserved with the greatest difficulty, can only suggest the appearance of the original scheme. Fragments of figure scenes, also from palaces at el-Amarna, such as that showing the daughters of Akhenaten and Nefertiti sitting at their parents' feet (Oxford, Ashmolean; see fig. 73) provide tantalizing hints of larger compositions of great charm.

Painted relief during the New Kingdom is best exemplified by the well-preserved scenes in the royal tombs in the Valley of the Kings and in some temples where paint remains in good quantity, such as the temples of Sethos I and Ramesses II at Abydos, the 18th Dynasty shrines at Karnak and Hatshepsut's funerary temple at Deir el-Bahri. In some royal tombs (Tuthmosis III, Amenophis II) much of the decoration is executed directly on the prepared limestone walls in a very simplified manner. The abbreviated treatment of figures for the most part defies aesthetic appreciation, but examples of fine draughtsmanship occasionally occur in small vignettes (such as that showing Tuthmosis III suckled by the tree-goddess) or in fully laid out 'preliminary' drawings (such as the scenes of the King with various deities on the pillars in the burial chamber of Amenophis II). The effect of the striking colour that is applied to the low reliefs in the tombs of Sethos I, Horemheb and Queen Nefertari and in the temple of Sethos I at Abydos, is often overwhelming, and there is little doubt that in scenes where paint has not been applied or has been lost, the appreciation of the plain, uncoloured, very finely carved limestone reliefs is greatly enhanced. The true virtuosity of the ancient Egyptian painter is always more clearly revealed in simple wall painting than in painted relief.

The high level of achievement reached by painters in the 18th Dynasty is not found in the Theban tombs of the 19th and 20th dynasties (c. 1292–c. 1075 BC). The small painted private tomb chapels decorated by the workmen of the royal tombs contain vignettes, even whole scenes, of charm and originality, but the use of colour is generally cruder and the draughtsmanship less accomplished than in the 18th Dynasty. The tradition had become stale; it needed exceptional, and perhaps personal, commitment on the part of the artist to infuse the conventional repertory of tomb scenes with some liveliness of spirit. Such can be found in parts of the tomb of Ipy (TT 217) and the tomb of Sennedjem (TT 1).

(v) Third Intermediate Period–Ptolemaic period (c. 1075–30 BC). In the period from the end of the 20th Dynasty until the Roman conquest of Egypt (30 BC) wall painting languished with the general decline in the form and decoration of Egyptian tombs. Painting skills were still required for many purposes, including the decoration of funerary equipment (such as coffins, chests and stelae), the illumination of papyri, the painting of reliefs and the embellishment of houses (scarcely any of which have survived). But wall painting, even in the general artistic renaissance of the Saite period (664–525 BC), never again achieved the standards reached in earlier times.

3. DRAWING. Fortunately, a large part of planned work, especially in tombs, was never completed; consequently substantial areas of drawing have survived, frequently of large scale. While the care and attention to detail lavished on drawings that were destined to disappear, perhaps under the mason's chisel, may seem remarkable to the modern observer, there were good reasons for this.

74. Preliminary drawing or copy of a scene showing Ramesses IX attended by his crown prince and his vizier, red painted outlines on limestone ostracon, 483×763 mm, from Thebes, 20th Dynasty, *c.* 1125 BC (London, British Museum)

First, good drawing was essential for a good final result, whether painted or carved. Second, the ritual functions of a tomb scene could be carried out as well by an initial drawing (if properly executed) as by a completed carved relief. The time allowed for completing a tomb, especially a huge royal corridor-tomb of the New Kingdom, was sometimes insufficient (especially if the eventual occupier of the tomb died prematurely). Work on decorating the tomb had to be completed by the day of the burial, and what was drawn, but not carved and painted, remained ritually efficient.

In the subterranean burial chambers of some mastaba tombs of the Old Kingdom, particularly at Saqqara, the drawn representations and inscriptions are carried out in black paint, often with signs of haste and occasionally with red corrections and even heightenings. An unfinished series of small scenes in the 5th Dynasty tomb chapel of Neferherenptah at Saqqara present a remarkable and unquestionable example of fine drawing originally destined to be obliterated by the chisel. Some of the scenes are carved, some partly carved, others fortunately untouched. In these scenes, executed for a relatively unimportant person in the official hierarchy (an overseer of hairdressers of the royal palace), the draughtsman, or 'outline scribe', was not simply content with outlining the elements in the scene; he added detail, shading, stippling on the bodies of birds and animals, and a red wash in selected areas. The piled funerary offerings in the early 6th Dynasty TOMB OF MERERUKA (c. 2300 BC), vizier of King Teti (reg c. 2325–c. 2291 BC), also at Saqqara, are drawn with confidence, an exceptional delicacy of line and a fine sense of composition; small errors indicate the speed employed, yet the result has style and movement not unlike that found in the arranged elements of a Dutch still-life. The aesthetic satisfaction to be derived from the drawn, but uncarved, decorations in parts of the tomb of Sethos I in the Valley of the Kings (c. 1279 BC), 1000 years later in date, is noticeably greater than that inspired by the completed carved and painted decorations in the same tomb. To examine the outline of a standing figure, drawn almost at life-size, as on the pillars of the burial chamber in the tomb of Amenophis II (c. 1400 BC), is to observe the mastery of the best 'outline scribe'. The line of the back of the figure, for example, sweeps from shoulder to foot without evident hesitation or pause; elsewhere the line following facial features or bodily contours is thinned or thickened to emphasize detail and fleshy lineaments in a notably sensual manner.

The continuity, confidence and accuracy of the artist's line and the skilful organization of the space, observed in so many of the surviving 'preliminary' drawings in tombs, demonstrate both the discipline of the artist's training and his individual mastery of the available equipment. The simple rush brush and carbon-based paint were the basic items in the draughtsman's kit. In addition, a suitable medium was required to allow the paint (ink) to run freely, so as not to clog the brush and so as to allow the line to be completed before the brush dried. Red paint was also used, often for the preliminary work and frequently in the occasional casual drawings found on ostraca (limestone flakes) such as the sketch of Ramesses IX attended by the crown prince and vizier (London, BM, 5620; see fig. 74).

Ostraca (including fragments of pottery) were extensively used for writing and drawing purposes in ancient Egypt, especially by the scribe and outline scribe of the New Kingdom working in the Theban necropolis. There the excavated stone from tombs provided an almost unlimited supply of suitably sized, smooth flakes of limestone, admirably adaptable for short texts and informal sketches. The artist often used ostraca as a surface on which to practise drawing in his unofficial time. The practice sketches represent tomb scenes drawn freely, often satirical, frequently humorous, occasionally obscene. In such drawings the artist worked without the constraints of commissions, without his teacher or his peers looking over his shoulder; except perhaps to approve of his unbuttoned skill. Frequently, animals and birds provided the inspiration for the drawings; the Egyptian artist had always excelled in such subjects from the beginning of the pharaonic period. Often the creatures parody their human counterparts, as they are commonly depicted taking part in the activities found in tomb scenes. In such drawings the artist is in effect a caricaturist; and like most good caricatures, the Egyptian examples are economical in line, deft in execution, suggesting ideas visually without the need for verbal comment (for a discussion of Egyptian caricature and satire see §VI, 5 above).

4. PAPYRUS ILLUSTRATION. Egyptian funerary texts written on papyrus were often illuminated, sometimes lavishly, with small drawings or paintings appropriate to the subject-matter of the texts (see §XII below). Like medieval illuminators, the papyrus painters occasionally used gold leaf to enrich their work. The repertory of

75. Papyrus illustration or 'vignette' from the papyrus showing last rites performed over the mummy of the royal scribe Hunefer before it is placed in the tomb, paint on papyrus, h. 400 mm, from the Book of the Dead papyrus of Hunefer, early 19th Dynasty, c. 1290 BC (London, British Museum)

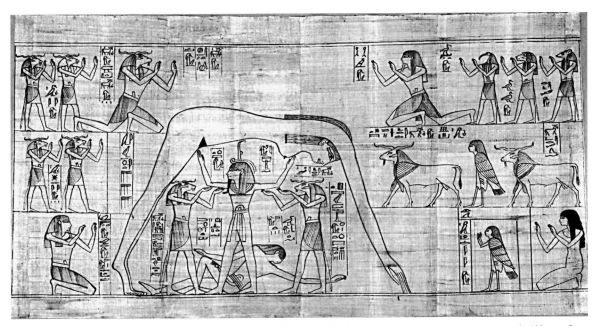

76. Papyrus illustration or 'vignette' showing Nut, the goddess of the sky, and Geb, the god of the earth, paint on papyrus, h. 480 mm, from the Book of the Dead papyrus of Nesitanebtasheru, daughter of the high priest of Amun, Pinedjem I, from Thebes, 21st Dynasty, c. 1050 BC (London, British Museum)

'vignettes', as they are usually called, was determined by the ritual requirements of the texts and were largely established by conventions; they did not admit the small, incidental, episodes of unconventional content and humour that enlivened the decorations in the private New Kingdom tombs. Certain subjects became almost obligatory for all copies of the Book of the Dead, for example the judgement of the deceased in which the subject (the owner of the papyrus) is shown in the Hall of Judgement where he or she is subjected to a series of 42 questions (all requiring the answer 'No!') which establish guilt or justification (innocence). The heart of the deceased is weighed against Truth or Order (Egyp.: Maat) and the ceremony is attended by appropriate deities. The composition can be presented simply or with an elaboration of detail. In such vignettes there is plenty of scope for originality, whether the individual artist is illustrating with simple line or with the full range of colours available on his palette.

The earliest illustrated, or illuminated, papyri date from the mid-18th Dynasty (c. 1450 BC), when funerary compositions of the kind exemplified by the Book of the Dead were first produced regularly in the form of papyrus scrolls. In the earliest surviving examples, the painting style reproduces in miniature the somewhat stiff, formal style of contemporary tomb painting. The Book of the Dead of the architect Kha (Turin, Mus. Egizio, Suppl. 8438) contains a limited range of subjects painted in a precise, correct manner, with flat, simple areas of colour. The copy prepared about the same date for the scribe Nebseny (London, BM, 9900) contains a greater range of subjects, drawn without colour in very fine line by a most accomplished hand. It is remarkable to think that such first-class illustrations were provided for funerary

texts, which, as part of the tomb equipment, were always placed rolled up, sometimes inserted into hollowed wooden figures, and frequently anointed with unguents that eventually hardened. They were not to be seen by anyone other than the deceased, who could consult his copy without being obliged to unroll it.

The finest illustrations in funerary papyri are found in Books of the Dead dated to the late 18th Dynasty and the early 19th, such as those of the royal scribes Hunefer (London, BM, 9901; see fig. 75), Nakhte (London, BM, 10470) and Ani (London, BM, 10471). The painterly skills developed in the fields of tomb decoration and domestic decoration in the course of the 18th Dynasty were adapted to the small scale required for papyrus illustration. The papyrus of Nakhte is distinguished by the precision of its draughtsmanship, the brilliance of its colour and the imaginative additional detail contained in its larger vignettes (such as the representation of Nakhte's home from which he and his wife advance to greet and worship the sun at dawn). The papyrus of Ani is marked by the diversity of techniques employed by the artist (or, more probably, artists), by the rich but muted tones of the colours used and by the scale with which the repertory of vignettes is explored and exploited (such as the judgement scene and the representation of the goddess Hathor as a cow emerging from the Western Mountain).

The tradition of papyrus illumination, well established in the New Kingdom, was continued and expanded in the 21st and 22nd dynasties (c. 1075–c. 730 BC), when funerary texts other than the Book of the Dead were often included as burial equipment. New vignettes, often adapted from those scenes used earlier in royal tombs, enlarged the repertory. The results were often brilliantly executed, as in the papyrus of the priestess Djedmaatiusankh (Cairo,

Egyp. Mus.). The contemporaneous Book of the Dead of Nesitanebtasheru (London, BM; see fig. 76), on the other hand, demonstrates how excellently the tradition of pure drawing was maintained. Drawing in particular, the natural form of expression of the outline scribe, survived actively, and to some extent, inventively, until the end of the pharaonic period. Even during the Macedonian and Ptolemaic dynasties (c. 332–30 BC) fine line drawings were sometimes provided in religious papyri in which all the other elements, including the texts and even the form of hieratic script, were in a sense atrophied. When the strict tradition was abandoned, coloured vignettes became coarse and gaudy, line became slack, proportions became distorted. The control of many centuries of scribal training had disappeared; the outline scribe could scarcely even fill in areas of colour within his poorly drawn outline.

BIBLIOGRAPHY

E. A. W. Budge: *The Greenfield Papyrus in the British Museum* (London, 1912)
N. de G. Davies: *The Tomb of Nakht at Thebes* (New York, 1917)
H. Frankfort, ed.: *The Mural Painting of el-'Amarneh* (London, 1929)
N. de G. Davies: *The Tomb of Kenamun at Thebes* (New York, 1930)
A. M. Calverley and M. Broome: *The Temple of King Sethos I at Abydos*, 4 vols (London, 1933–58)
J. Vandier d'Abbadie: *Catalogue des ostraca figures de Deir el Médineh*, 4 fascs (Cairo, 1935–59)
N. M. Davies: *Ancient Egyptian Paintings*, 3 vols (London, 1936)
——: *The Mastaba of Mereruka*, 2 vols (Chicago, 1938)
N. de G. Davies: *The Tomb of Rekh-mi-Rēʿ at Thebes*, 2 vols (New York, 1943)
W. S. Smith: *A History of Egyptian Sculpture and Painting in the Old Kingdom* (London and Boston, 1946, 2/1949/R 1978)
J. Vandier: *Moʿalla: La Tombe d'Ankhtifi et la tombe de Sébekhotep* (Cairo, 1950)
A. Mekhitarian: *Egyptian Painting* (London, 1954/R 1978)
E. Brunner-Traut: *Die altägyptischen Scherbenbilder (Bildostraka) der deutschen Museen und Sammlungen* (Wiesbaden, 1957)
A. Piankoff: *Mythological Papyri*, 2 vols (New York, 1957)
W. H. Peck and J. G. Ross: *Drawings from Ancient Egypt* (London, 1978)
E. Brunner-Traut: *Egyptian Artists' Sketches* (Istanbul, 1979)
C. Aldred: *Egyptian Art*, World A. (London, 1980)
A. Page: *Ancient Egyptian Figured Ostraca in the Petrie Collection* (Warminster, 1983)
C. K. Wilkinson and M. Hill: *Egyptian Wall Paintings: The Metropolitan Museum of Art's Collection of Facsimiles* (New York, 1983)
T. G. H. James: *Egyptian Painting and Drawing in the British Museum* (London, 1985)
G. Robins: *Egyptian Painting and Relief* (Aylesbury, 1986)

T. G. H. JAMES

The survey of **ancient Egypt** continues in vol.10.

Illustration Acknowledgements

We are grateful to those listed below for permission to reproduce copyright illustrative material and to those contributors who supplied photographs or helped us to obtain them. The word 'Photo:' precedes the names of large commercial or archival sources who have provided us with photographs, as well as the names of individual photographers (where known). It has generally not been used before the names of owners of works of art, such as museums and civic bodies. Every effort has been made to contact copyright holders and to credit them appropriately; we apologize to anyone who may have been omitted from the acknowledgements or cited incorrectly. Any error brought to our attention will be corrected in subsequent editions. Where illustrations have been taken from books, publication details are provided in the acknowledgements below.

Line drawings, maps, plans, chronological tables and family trees commissioned by the *Dictionary of Art* are not included in the list below. All of the maps in the dictionary were produced by Oxford Illustrators Ltd, who were also responsible for some of the line drawings. Most of the line drawings and plans, however, were drawn by the following artists: Diane Fortenberry, Lorraine Hodghton, Chris Miners, Amanda Patton, Mike Pringle, Jo Richards, Miranda Schofield, John Tiernan, John Wilson and Philip Winton. The chronological tables and family trees were prepared initially by Kate Boatfield and finalized by John Johnson.

Diploma work Permanent Collection, Royal Academy of Arts, London

Diptych *1* Museum of the Polish Army, Warsaw; *2* Trustees of the National Gallery, London

Disegno e colore *1* Syndics of Cambridge University Library; *2* Trustees of the British Museum, London

Display of art *1–2, 6* Photo: Conway Library, Courtauld Institute of Art, London; *3* Royal Collection, Windsor Castle/© Her Majesty Queen Elizabeth II; *4* Mauritshuis, The Hague; *5* National Portrait Gallery, London; *7* Statens Konstmuseer, Stockholm; *8* Photo: Country Life Picture Library, London; *9* British Library, London (no. 139.g.6); *10* Board of Trustees of the Victoria and Albert Museum, London

Dissemination *1–2* Trustees of the British Museum, London; *3* Board of Trustees of the Victoria and Albert Museum, London

Dix, Otto Galerie der Stadt Stuttgart/© DACS, 1996

Diyala region *1–2* Oriental Institute of the University of Chicago, IL

Diziani, Gaspare Soprintendenza ai Beni Culturali della Provincia Autonoma, Trent

Dobson, William Tate Gallery, London

Dock Aerofilms of Borehamwood

Doesburg, Theo van Haags Gemeentemuseum, The Hague

Dogon *1* Metropolitan Museum of Art, New York (Gift of Lester Wunderman, 1977; no. 1977.394.15); *2* Metropolitan Museum of Art, New York (Gift of Lester Wunderman, 1979; no. 1979.541.12); *3* National Museum of African Art, Smithsonian Institution, Washington, DC/Photo: Eliot Elisofon, 1959/Eliot Elisofon Photographic Archives (photo no. XII-R7,12); *4* Metropolitan Museum of Art, New York (Gift of Ernst Anspach, 1977; no. 1977.21)

Dolci, Carlo *1* Birmingham Museums and Art Gallery; *2* Photo: A.C. Cooper Ltd, London

Domenichino *1* Vatican Museums, Vatican City, Rome; *2, 4* Photo: Archivi Alinari, Florence; *3* Photo: © RMN, Paris

Domenico di Bartolo Photo: Archivi Alinari, Florence

Domenico di Michelino Photo: Archivi Alinari, Florence

Domenico Veneziano *1* Staatliche Museen zu Berlin, Preussischer Kulturbesitz; *2, 4* Gabinetto Fotografico, Soprintendenza ai Beni Artistici e Storici, Florence; *3* Syndics of the Fitzwilliam Museum, Cambridge

Domínguez, Oscar Museum of Modern Art, New York

Dominican Order *2–3* Photo: Archivi Alinari, Florence; *4* Museo Bellas Artes, Seville

Dominican Republic *2–3, 5–6* Photo: Mariano Hernandez; *4* Photo: Ampliaciones y Reproducciones MAS, Barcelona

Donatello *1, 66* Photo: Overseas Agenzia Fotografica, Milan; *2, 5* Photo: Archivi Alinari, Florence; *3* Board of Trustees of the Victoria and Albert Museum, London; *4* Museo Civico, Padua

Dongen, Kees van Photo: RMN, Paris/© ADAGP, Paris, and DACS, London, 1996

Dong Qichang *1* National Gallery of Victoria, Melbourne; *2* Nelson–Atkins Museum of Art, Kansas City, MO (Purchase: acquired through the generosity of the Hall Family Foundations and the exchange of other trust properties; no. 83-6/7)

Dong Yuan National Palace Museum, Taipei

Donjon Photo: Royal Commission on the Ancient and Historical Monuments of Wales/© Crown Copyright

Donner: (1) Georg Raphael Donner Österreichische Galerie im Belvedere, Vienna

Doomer, Lambert Bildarchiv, Österreichische Nationalbibliothek, Vienna

Door *2* Photo: Bundesdenkmalamt, Vienna; *3* Photo: Hirmer Fotoarchiv, Munich; *4* Photo: Antikvarisk–topografiska Arkivet, Stockholm; *5* Photo: Archivi Alinari, Florence; *6* Photo: Scala, Florence; *7* Photo: W. Denny; *8* Photo: © American Institute of Indian Studies, Varanasi; *9* Photo: © Tettoni, Cassio and Associates Pte Ltd, Singapore; *10* Trustees of the British Museum, London; *11* South American Pictures, Woodbridge, Suffolk/Photo: Tony Morrison

Doré, Gustave Trustees of the British Museum, London

Dorigny: (1) Michel Dorigny Photo: © RMN, Paris

D'Orsi, Achille Photo: Gabinetto Fotografico Nazionale, Istituto Centrale per il Catalogo e la Documentazione, Rome

Doshi, Balkrishna V. Aga Khan Trust for Culture, Geneva/Photo: Joseph St Ann

Dossi: (1) Dosso Dossi *1* Metropolitan Museum of Art, New York (Maria DeWitt Jesup Fund, 1926; no. 26.8.3); *2* J. Paul Getty Museum, Malibu, CA

Dotted print Bibliothèque Nationale de France, Paris

Dotzinger: (2) Jodok Dotzinger Photo: Barbara Schock-Werner

Dou, Gerrit *1* Photo: © RMN, Paris; *2* Nelson–Atkins Museum of Art, Kansas City, MO

Douffet, Gérard Bayerische Staatsgemäldesammlungen, Munich

Doxiadis, Constantinos A. Photo: Doxiadis Associates

Doyen, Gabriel-François Photo: Giraudon, Paris

Drawing *1* Graphische Sammlung Albertina, Vienna/Photo: Bildarchiv, Österreichische Nationalbibliothek, Vienna; *2* Statens Konstmuseer, Stockholm; *3* J. Paul Getty Museum, Malibu, CA; *4–6* Trustees of the British Museum, London; *7* Nelson–Atkins Museum of Art, Kansas City, MO; *8* Staatliche Museen zu Berlin, Preussischer Kulturbesitz/Photo: Jörg P. Anders

Dresden *1–3* Sächsische Landesbibliothek, Dresden; *4* Photo: Friedrich Press, Dresden

Dress *1–2, 5, 9, 46* Trustees of the British Museum, London; *3–4* National Archaeological Museum, Athens (Archaeological Receipts Fund); *6* Parrocchia di San Giovanni Battista, Museo del Duomo, Monza; *7, 11* Antikvarisk–topografiska Arkivet, Stockholm; *8* Musée

Easel National Portrait Gallery, London

Easter Island *1–2* Trustees of the British Museum, London

Eastern and central Costa Rica, Pre-Columbian *1* Museo Nacional de Costa Rica/Photo: D. Donne Bryant, DDB Stock photo, Baton Rouge, LA; *2* Department of Library Services, American Museum of Natural History, New York (neg. no. 125822)

Easter sepulchre Photo: Anthony Kersting, London

Eberbach Abbey Photo: Bildarchiv Foto Marburg

Eberdingen-Hochdorf Württembergisches Landesmuseum, Stuttgart

Eberhard, Konrad Bayerische Staatsgemäldesammlungen, Munich

Eberlein, Gustav Staatliche Museen zu Berlin, Preussischer Kulturbesitz

Ebla Photo: Missione Archeologica Italiana in Siria, Università di Roma la Sapienza, Rome

Echternach Photo: Ludwig Reichert Verlag, Wiesbaden

Eckersberg, C. W. *1–2* Statens Museum for Kunst, Copenhagen

Eclecticism British Library, London

Ecouen Photo: British Architectural Library, RIBA, London

Ecuador *2* South American Pictures, Woodbridge, Suffolk/Photo: Tony Morrison; *3* Casa de la Cultura Ecuadoriana, Quito

Edelfelt, Albert Ateneum, Helsinki/Photo: Central Art Archives, Helsinki

Edfu Photo: Anthony Kersting, London

Edinburgh *1* Photo: David C. Simpson; *2* Cambridge University Collection of Air Photographs; *3* United Incorporation of St Mary's Chapel, Edinburgh; *4* National Gallery of Scotland, Edinburgh; *5* Royal Commission on Ancient Monuments of Scotland/© Crown Copyright

Edirne Photo: Dr Donna Kurtz

Edjmiadzin *1* Photo: NOVOSTI Photo Library, London; *2* Photo: VAAP, Moscow

Edo *1* Trustees of the British Museum, London; *2* Photo: Jean M. Borgatti; *3* Metropolitan Museum of Art, New York (Paul and Ruth Tishman Collection)/Photo: Jerry L. Thompson

Eeckhout, Gerbrand van den *1* Metropolitan Museum of Art, New York (Bequest of Collis P. Huntington, 1925); *2* Fine Arts Museums of San Francisco, CA (Gift of Mr and Mrs George T. Cameron; no. 47.7)

Effner, Joseph Photo: Gisela Vits

Egas: (1) Egas Cueman Photo: Ampliaciones y Reproducciones MAS, Barcelona

Egedius, Halfdan Nasjonalgalleriet, Oslo

Egell, Paul Reiss-Museum der Stadt Mannheim

Egg, Augustus Birmingham Museums and Art Gallery

Eggeling, Viking Statens Konstmuseer, Stockholm

Egypt *1–2* Photo: Bernard O'Kane; *3* Photo: Werner Forman Archive, London

Egypt, ancient *3, 45* Staatliche Museen zu Berlin, Preussischer Kulturbesitz; *6–8, 36, 41–2, 46, 58, 71–2, 74–6* Trustees of the British Museum, London; *9* Museo Egizio di Torino, Turin; *11* Detroit Institute of Arts, Detroit, MI (Founders Society Purchase; Miscellaneous Memorials Fund); *13* British Library, London (no. 7703.p.1/3); *14* British Library, London; *16* British Library, London (no. 7710.t); *18, 57, 61, 63, 65* Egyptian Museum, Cairo; *19* Petrie Museum of Egyptian Archaeology, University College, London; *23, 43, 47, 52, 54, 59* Photo: Hirmer Fotoarchiv, Munich; *24, 34* Committee of the Egypt Exploration Society; *29, 31* Photo: James H. Morris; *33* Museum of Fine Arts, Boston, MA; *35* Oriental Institute of the University of Chicago, Chicago, IL; *38* Metropolitan Museum of Art, New York, Museum Excavation, 1919-20 (Rogers Fund, supplemented by contribution of Edward S. Harkness; no. 20.3.13); *44* Metropolitan Museum of Art, New York (Theodore M. Davis Collection, Bequest of Theodore M. Davis, 1915; no. 30.8.76); *48* Brooklyn Museum, New York; *49* Brooklyn Museum, New York (Museum Collection Fund; no. 09.889.118); *50–51, 73* Ashmolean Museum, Oxford; *53* Photo: © RMN, Paris; *55* Deutsches Archäologisches Institut, Cairo/Photo: Dieter Johannes; *56* Deutsches Archäologisches Institut, Cairo; *60* Cleveland Museum of Art, Cleveland, OH (John L. Severance Fund); *62* Photo: Karol Myśliwiec; *64* Photo: Richard A. Fazzini; *66* Ny Carlsberg Glyptotek, Copenhagen; *67* Photo: Scala, Florence; *68* Photo: Eleni Vassilika; *69* Board of Trustees of the National Museums and Galleries on Merseyside, Liverpool; *70* Photo: Claude Traunecker